Journey Across Time

Features and Benefits

Dynamic Instructional Strategies

. . . present a clear and comprehensive coverage of world history.
- Engaging section introductions include *Get Ready to Read!*, *What's the Connection?*, *Focusing on the Main Ideas*, and *Reading Strategy*.
- *You Decide* allows students the opportunity to compare primary sources.
- *Main ideas* are noted throughout the text to alert students to the "big picture."

A Strong Reading Strand

. . . encourages active reading and learning for students of all reading levels.
- *Foldables*™ help students organize and process key concepts as they read.
- A two-page *Reading Strategy* at the beginning of each chapter reinforces good reading habits.
- *Writing prompts* and writing activities develop writing and retention skills for students.
- *Reading Checks* help students check their reading comprehension.

Differentiated Instruction

. . . makes *Journey Across Time* accessible to students of all learning levels.
- *Differentiated Instruction* activities and strategies are designed for students of differing abilities and learning challenges.
- *Booklink CD-Rom* allows teachers to generate reading lists by topic, reading level, or theme.

Standardized Test Preparation

. . . gives students the opportunity to practice for state and national exams.
- *Section and Chapter assessments* provide a variety of standardized test practice opportunities.
- *Standardized Test Practice* is offered in the Appendix.

A Variety of Interdisciplinary Activities and Features

. . . are essential for student success and get students excited about world history.
- *Geography Handbook* shows students how to use essential geographic tools, such as globes, maps, and graphs.
- The *Tools of the Historian* section gives students background in all the tools historians use in their research.
- *Primary Sources* throughout allow students many opportunities to read the words of people in history.

Teacher Resources

. . . provide convenient strategies to help new and experienced teachers.
- The *Planning Guide* in each unit provides background information to help you prepare for each unit.
- *Fast File*™ unit resources contain important reproducible masters.
- *Chapter Videos* offer high interest previews of each chapter.

Technology

. . . provides time-saving software products to help creatively engage students and reduce your preparation time.
- *Online Homework Helper*™ makes more content, skills practice, and vocabulary development available to students.
- *Glencoe Skillbuilder Interactive Workbook, Level 1* offers individual skills practice.
- *NGS Online* provides lesson plans, atlas updates, cartographic activities with interactive maps, an online map store, and geographic links.
- Web site jat.glencoe.com holds additional, text-specific resources.

Improving Active Reading and Study Skills
Dinah Zike's FOLDABLES™

Foldables are easy-to-make, three-dimensional, interactive graphic organizers that students create out of plain sheets of paper. The Teacher Classroom Resources includes *Dinah Zike's Reading and Study Skills Foldables™*. This booklet provides you with step-by-step instructions for using Foldables in your classroom. Each Foldable is designed to be used as a study guide for the main ideas and key points presented in a chapter. Foldables can also be used for a more in-depth investigation of a concept, idea, opinion, event, or a person or place studied in a chapter. These unique hands-on tools for studying and reviewing were created exclusively for Glencoe by education specialist Dinah Zike.

Why Use Foldables in Social Studies?

Because they:

- organize, display, and arrange information, making it easier for students to grasp social studies concepts, theories, facts, opinions, questions, research, and ideas.
- are student-made study guides that are compiled as students listen for main ideas, read main ideas, or conduct research.
- integrate language arts, the sciences, and mathematics into the study of social studies.
- provide a multitude of creative formats in which students can present projects, research, interviews, and inquiry-based reports.
- replace teacher-generated writing or photocopied sheets with student-generated print.
- incorporate the use of such skills as comparing and contrasting, recognizing cause-and-effect, and finding similarities and differences.
- continue to immerse students in previously learned vocabulary, concepts, information, generalizations, ideas, and theories, providing them with a strong foundation that they can build upon with new observations, concepts, and knowledge.
- can be used by students or teachers to easily communicate data through graphs, tables, charts, models, and diagrams, including Venn diagrams.
- allow students to make their own journals for recording observations, research information, primary and secondary source data, surveys, and so on.
- can be used as alternative assessment tools by teachers to evaluate student progress or by students to evaluate their own progress.
- provide a sense of student ownership or investiture in the social studies curriculum.

▼ *Student Edition, p. 113*

FOLDABLES™ Study Organizer

Summarizing Information *Make this foldable to help you organize and summarize information about the ancient Greeks.*

Step 1 *Mark the midpoint of a side edge of one sheet of paper. Then fold the outside edges in to touch the midpoint.*

Step 2 *Fold the paper in half again from side to side.*

Reading and Writing *As you read the chapter, write information under each appropriate tab. Be sure to summarize the information you find by writing only main ideas and supporting details.*

Step 3 *Open the paper and cut along the inside fold lines to form four tabs.*

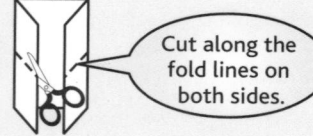

Cut along the fold lines on both sides.

Step 4 *Label as shown.*

The Early Greeks | Sparta and Athens | Persia Attacks the Greeks | The Age of Pericles

Teacher Wraparound Edition

World History
JOURNEY ACROSS TIME

Jackson J. Spielvogel, Ph.D.

NATIONAL GEOGRAPHIC

Mc Graw Hill **Glencoe**

New York, New York   Columbus, Ohio   Chicago, Illinois   Peoria, Illinois   Woodland Hills, California

Authors

Jackson J. Spielvogel is associate professor emeritus of history at the Pennsylvania State University. He received his Ph.D. from The Ohio State University, where he specialized in Reformation history under Harold J. Grimm. His articles and reviews have been published in several scholarly publications. He is co-author (with William Duiker) of *World History,* published in 1994 (3rd edition, 2001). Professor Spielvogel has won five major university-wide awards, and in 1997, he became the first winner of the Schreyer Institute's Student Choice Award for innovative and inspiring teaching.

The National Geographic Society, founded in 1888 for the increase and diffusion of geographic knowledge, is the world's largest nonprofit scientific and educational organization. Since its earliest days, the Society has used sophisticated communication technologies, from color photography to holography, to convey geographic knowledge to a worldwide membership. The Education Products Division supports the Society's mission by developing innovative educational programs—ranging from traditional print materials to multimedia programs including CD-ROMs, videodiscs, and software.

Contributing Authors

Stephen F. Cunha, Ph.D.
Professor of Geography
Director, California Geographic Alliance
Humboldt State University
Arcata, California

Douglas Fisher, Ph.D.
Professor
San Diego State University
San Diego, California

Nancy Frey, Ph.D.
Assistant Professor
San Diego State University
San Diego, California

Robin C. Scarcella, Ph.D.
Professor and Director
Academic English/ESL
University of California, Irvine
Irvine, California

Emily M. Schell, Ed.D.
Visiting Professor, San Diego State University
Social Studies Education Director
SDSU City Heights Educational Collaborative
San Diego, California

David Vigilante
Associate Director
National Center for History in the Schools
San Diego, California

About the Cover: Throughout history, people around the world have channeled, spanned, and sailed upon one of Earth's greatest resources—its water reserves. Top: the great Pont du Gard aqueduct built in France by ancient Romans; middle right: the Tower Bridge, London, spanning the Thames; bottom left: a Chinese junk sailing in Hong Kong Harbor.

 Glencoe

The McGraw-Hill Companies

Send all inquiries to:
Glencoe/McGraw-Hill
8787 Orion Place
Columbus, OH 43240-4027

ISBN: 0-07-869371-3 *(Teacher Wraparound Edition)*
ISBN: 0-07-868873-6 *(Student Edition)*

Printed in the United States of America.

2 3 4 5 6 7 8 9 10 071/055 09 08 07 06 05

Consultants & Reviewers

Academic Consultants

Winthrop Lindsay Adams
Associate Professor of History
University of Utah
Salt Lake City, Utah

Sari J. Bennett
Director, Center for Geographic Education
University of Maryland Baltimore County
Baltimore, Maryland

Richard G. Boehm
Jesse H. Jones Distinguished Chair in
    Geographic Education
Texas State University
San Marcos, Texas

Sheilah Clarke-Ekong
Associate Professor of Anthropology and
    Interim Dean
Evening College
University of Missouri, St. Louis
St. Louis, Missouri

Timothy E. Gregory
Professor of History
The Ohio State University
Columbus, Ohio

Robert E. Herzstein
Department of History
University of South Carolina
Columbia, South Carolina

Kenji Oshiro
Professor of Geography
Wright State University
Dayton, Ohio

Joseph R. Rosenbloom
Adjunct Professor, Jewish and Near
    Eastern Studies
Washington University
St. Louis, Missouri

FOLDABLES **Dinah Zike**
Educational Consultant
Dinah-Might Activities, Inc.
San Antonio, Texas

Reading Consultants

Maureen D. Danner
Project CRISS
National Training Consultant
Kalispell, Montana

ReLeah Cossett Lent
Florida Literacy and Reading Excellence
    Project Coordinator
University of Central Florida
Orlando, Florida

Steve Qunell
Social Studies Instructor
Montana Academy
Kalispell, Montana

Carol M. Santa Ph.D.
CRISS: Project Developer
Director of Education
Montana Academy
Kalispell, Montana

Bonnie Valdes
Master CRISS Trainer
Project CRISS
Largo, Florida

Teacher Reviewers

Destin L. Haas
Social Studies Teacher
Benton Central Junior-Senior High School
Oxford, Indiana

Anna Marie Lawrence
Social Studies Teacher
Snellville Middle School
Snellville, Georgia

Richard Meegan
Social Studies Department Chair
Masconomet Regional School District
Topsfield, Massachusetts

J. Keith Miller
Social Studies Teacher
Bragg Middle School
Gardendale, Alabama

Beth Neighbors
Social Studies Teacher
Pizitz Middle School
Vestavia Hills, Alabama

Virgina Parra
Social Studies Teacher
Osceola Middle School
Ocala, Florida

Susan Pearson
Social Studies Teacher
The Academy for Science and
    Foreign Languages
Huntsville, Alabama

Nancy Perkins
Social Studies Implementer 1–12
Bonny Eagle Middle School
Buxton, Maine

Beverly Prestage
Social Studies Program Supervisor
Cranston High School West
Cranston, Rhode Island

Julie A. Scott
Social Studies Teacher
East Valley Middle School
Spokane, Washington

Larry W. Smith
Heritage Education Teacher
Massie Heritage Interpretation Center
Savannah, Georgia

Jerry A. Taylor
Social Studies Teacher
Towns County Comprehensive School
Hiawassee, Georgia

Contents

▼ Ancient Assyrian soldiers

◀ Ancient Egyptian artwork of a funeral boat

Contents

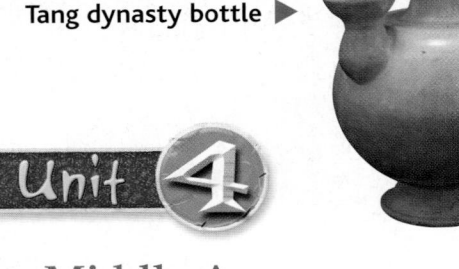

Tang dynasty bottle ▶

Contents

Figure of Mayan ► leader

◄ The Alhambra

Contents

▲ Stalin, Roosevelt, and Churchill at the Tehran Conference

Features

Primary Source

Features

NATIONAL GEOGRAPHIC The Way It Was

Primary Sources Library

WORLD LITERATURE

Biography

◀ Albert Einstein

Queen Elizabeth I ▶

Features

Primary Source Quotes

Ed. = Editor	Tr. = Translator	V = Volume

Primary Source Quotes

Primary Source Quotes

Maps, Charts, Graphs, and Diagrams

National Geographic Maps

NATIONAL GEOGRAPHIC Reference Atlas

NATIONAL GEOGRAPHIC Geography Handbook GH1

Unit 1

Unit 2

Unit 3

Unit 4

Maps, Charts, Graphs, and Diagrams

NATIONAL GEOGRAPHIC

Germany Divided

5°E
0   100 mi.
0   100 km
Chamberlin Trimetric projection

N
W—E
S

DENMARK

0   10 mi.
0   10 km
Lambert Azimuthal Equal-Area projection

EAST GERMANY

FRENCH SECTOR
BRITISH SECTOR
WEST BERLIN
EAST BERLIN
SOVIET SECTOR
AMERICAN SECTOR

EAST GERMANY

55°N

10°E   15°E

Hamburg

British Zone

Berlin   POLAND

Hannover

Braunschweig

WEST GERMANY (FEDERAL REPUBLIC OF GERMANY)

EAST GERMANY (GERMAN DEMOCRATIC REPUBLIC)

Frankfurt   50°N

French Zone

American Zone

FRANCE

KEY

Allied occupation zone

Soviet occupation zone

Routes of the Berlin Airlift, 1948–1949

Division of Allied zone

45°N

Charts and Graphs

Diagrams

Project CRISS
How Can I Teach My Students How to Learn Social Studies?

by Carol M. Santa, Ph.D.

We all know that teaching social studies involves far more than teaching just course content. We understand that students need to become engaged, confident learners. Achieving that goal means helping them to understand, organize, and retain information.

Teaching Both Content and Skills

In other words, we want our students to have the skills and confidence to be lifelong learners. With its rich content, social studies offer an ideal arena for teaching both content and skills.

✔ **A Dual Responsibility** Let's take a moment to consider why the dual responsibility of teaching both content and skills is so important. Think back to your own middle and high school years. What do you remember about the content

you learned? If I recall my experiences, I find I remember remarkably little content. What did I learn in biology or history? What did my textbooks look like? As the years go by, I don't even remember the names of most of my teachers.

✔ **An Inspiring Teacher** Yet I have vivid memories of my eighth-grade social studies teacher, who came out of retirement to fill in for a history teacher who left on maternity leave. I remember how fascinated I became with ancient history; I recall giving oral reports and how she helped me become comfortable speaking before a group. In fact, I remember more from her class than any other I took during high school.

✔ **Teach How to Learn** More important, I now understand that she taught me how to learn to learn. She showed me how to underline, how to organize information using different note-taking formats, and how to write coherent

answers on essay tests. She taught me the need to test myself on what I knew. And during that vulnerable, adolescent year, I went from being a mediocre student to being an excellent one.

This inspirational teacher did something else for me. At some point during that eighth-grade year, I decided to become a teacher. Later I realized that she had launched me on my professional mission—to spread her wisdom to others. Eventually this led to Project CRISS.

What Is CRISS?

CRISS stands for **CR**eating Independence through **S**tudent-owned **S**trategies. It is a staff development program that I created in collaboration with middle and high school teachers in Kalispell, Montana.

✔ **Origin of CRISS** CRISS had its start 20 years ago in a lunchtime conversation in a teacher's lounge. One of the social studies teachers said, "My students aren't doing a good job of answering chapter questions. In fact, I don't think they even read my assignments. My reading assignments are becoming a waste of time!" His words struck a chord. "My students don't have a clue about how to study, and they don't write very well either," another teacher lamented.

✔ **Evolving Strategies** Supported by a state grant, we started working together to find practical ways to help students read, write, and learn content. We met in teams, read professional literature, and designed studies to test classroom strategies. From these efforts, we evolved a project to help students become better readers, writers, and

Tom & DeeAnn McCarthy/CORBIS STOCK MARKET

learners. Once the project took shape, we shared our discoveries with other teachers by offering a two- or three-day CRISS workshop to schools and districts in the state.

✔ **Constant Growth** Over the last two decades, Project CRISS has spread from teacher to teacher across this country, into Canada, and to several European countries. The project seems to sell itself. Teachers who use CRISS principles and strategies find that their students attain a deeper understanding of course content and become better readers, writers, and learners at the same time. In fact, data from numerous quantitative studies shows that using CRISS strategies improves student learning. (For the most recent data and for information on CRISS workshops, see www.projectcriss.com)

CRISS Strategies in the Teacher Edition

When the editors of Glencoe/McGraw-Hill asked me and my colleagues to help them integrate CRISS strategies into their social studies texts, we welcomed the opportunity. In this teacher wraparound edition, we offer many references to CRISS strategies. We have packed the pages with strategies that help students gain a deeper understanding of specific content.

CRISS Training

We have one word of caution, however: the integration of CRISS strategies within this teacher wraparound edition does not take the place of a Project CRISS workshop, which provides an in-depth knowledge of CRISS. So, if you haven't yet participated in a CRISS workshop, we encourage you to do so. During a workshop, CRISS trainers take you step-by-step through the philosophy and instructional strategies. Participants are actively involved in all aspects of the program—practicing, adapting, and applying strategies to meet teaching needs.

Long-lasting change occurs when teachers and administrators work together to share, extend ideas, and problem solve. The most effective implementations occur when the initial workshop is supported by follow-up sessions, including a specific follow-up day. At this session, teachers bring examples of strategies they have used since the initial training. Part of this time may be spent in review and in learning new strategies. The rest of the time is for sharing applications. Additional ongoing support can occur in teacher planning periods.

In any case, for those of you unfamiliar with Project CRISS, let's begin with a little background knowledge. In this way you will have some context for the various activities suggested throughout the teacher wraparound edition.

The CRISS Philosophy

The first thing to know is that Project CRISS is more than a collection of learning strategies. Its underlying power rests not on the individual strategies but on the teaching philosophy behind them. This philosophy integrates work from cognitive psychology, social learning theory, and neurological research about how the brain learns. It includes these overlapping principles:

✔ background knowledge and purposeful reading
✔ author's craft
✔ active involvement
✔ discussion
✔ organization
✔ writing
✔ teacher modeling

Let's look at each of these principles in more detail, along with examples of instructional strategies that illustrate them.

Background knowledge and purposeful reading are powerful determinants of reading comprehension.

Teachers involved in Project CRISS often talk about the importance of background knowledge. Readers are

(Continued on next page)

Using CRISS to Set a Purpose

Advice from Malla S. Kolhoff
Palm Harbor University High School
International Baccalaureate Program
Palm Harbor, Florida

As educators, it is our responsibility to set a purpose for historical reading. Students often must struggle to connect history with their own lives. To compare and contrast, establish cause and effect, and sequence events in chronological order presents a challenge for even the best reader. CRISS strategies allow students to move beyond words to the real significance for their society. With CRISS, my students are able to become engaged in the learning process through:

a. background knowledge
b. active reading, listening, and learning
c. discussion
d. metacognition
e. writing
f. organization
g. understanding

I have found that these strategies help my students attain a higher level of historical thinking and understanding.

Project CRISS

far more likely to learn new information when they have some previous knowledge and have a purpose in mind before they read or listen.

✔ **More Than Simply Reading** We warn students not to simply begin reading. We ask them, *"What might you already know about the topic? What questions do you have about the topic?"* We also remind them to preview the assignment and think about their goals for reading. We often have to be very explicit about the goals. For example, we might tell students, *"After reading this selection, you should be able to . . . ,"* or, *"After viewing the video, you should be able to identify . . ."*

✔ **KWLH** In the teaching strategies included for each chapter in this book, we offer ideas for helping students tap into their background knowledge. For example, we suggest that students preview their reading assignment and consider what they already know about a topic. Or, we might develop a whole class **KWLH** chart (**K**now, **W**ant to learn, **L**earned, **H**ow to learn more), where students work on this task together. They can generate questions about what they want to learn, and then, after completing the assignment, they can list the new information they have learned and how they can learn more.

K	W	L	H
What I **Know**	What I **Want** to Find Out	What I **Learned**	**How** I Can Learn More

✔ **Reading Goals** We also suggest ways to make sure your students have clear goals for their reading. Each section opener lists reading strategies and main ideas that outline reading goals. Most students will skip over this material and simply start reading. Teachers need to help students understand that the reading goals are important tools for understanding. We tell students, *"Don't ignore your purposes for reading. Take time to think about them before delving into your reading."* Project CRISS also provides hints about how to get students to use these purpose statements to evaluate whether they have understood their reading.

Good readers have an intuitive understanding of the author's craft.

When students know how authors craft their writing, they can more readily understand and remember what they read.

✔ **Pay Attention** Good readers and writers know that paying attention to how text is organized—its headings and paragraphs, for example—makes it easier to comprehend its content. Good readers will analyze the author's style of presentation as they read. They might ask themselves, *"What is this author doing to help me learn key concepts? How does the writer lead me from one idea to the next?"* When students become aware of what the author is doing to impart content, they have a clearer idea of what the author is saying.

✔ **The Walk Through** In the sample lesson on pages T24–T25, we offer advice about "walking through" the text to discover the author's style of presentation. Our suggestions go beyond examining the surface structure (headings, bold print, color coding of topical headings, italicized words) to analyzing how the author elaborates on key topics.

Effective learners are actively involved when they listen and read.

We learn best when we act on the information presented. We can do this by using a variety of organizing activities that require us to write, talk, and transform the information we are absorbing. None of us learns much from reading alone—it's far too passive.

CRISS strategies encourage active engagement in learning. We might ask students to read a section and describe what they are learning to a partner, or we might be more elaborate and have students develop concept maps or write summaries.

Students need many opportunities to talk with one another about what they are learning.

Discussion is critical to learning. The discussions we advocate are different from those in which the teacher remains the authority figure, with students simply reciting answers to

(Continued on next page)

Jose L. Pelaez/CORBIS STOCK MARKET

questions. If discussion becomes mere recitation and there is little interaction among students, little learning occurs. Thus we focus on how to get students to lead their own discussions about a topic. We want them to understand that it is their discussing, their oral grappling with meaning—not ours—that leads to deeper understanding.

Competent readers know several ways to organize information for learning.

Learning depends on organization. We show students different ways to organize information. They can take notes, underline selectively, develop concept maps, and summarize ideas in charts. Once we have taught students these techniques, we tell them, "*You have to do more than just read this assignment. How are you going to organize the information from this assignment? You have to change it, to transform it so that it becomes your own.*"

For each chapter of this text, we offer ideas for assisting students in organizing information. Once students have learned a variety of organizing systems, we suggest ways to help them apply these structures independently.

Students deserve opportunities to write about what they are learning.

Writing is an integral part of the CRISS project. Writing lets us figure out what we know and what we still need to know. We cannot write about something we do not understand. While we teach students how to write expository papers and essay exams, we also encourage students to write more informally by questioning, speculating, and writing explanations in learning logs. We make sure that students are writing continually about what they are learning.

For each chapter of this text, we offer ideas for assisting students in organizing information. Once students have learned a variety of organizing systems, we suggest ways to help them apply these structures independently.

Teaching involves explanation and modeling.

Our final principle has to do with our own teaching. Students learn to think strategically when we use these processes as part of our instruction. Our demonstrations are especially critical for struggling readers. Most have never been taught how to learn.

We have to show them how.

✔ **Take Center Stage** When you introduce a new strategy, you should take the center stage: showing, telling, modeling, demonstrating, and explaining not only the content but the process of active reading. As students learn, gradually release responsibility to them. Strategy instruction involves two overlapping steps. First, we explain what the strategy is and why students should use it. If students do not know why they are performing an activity, they will rarely use the activity on their own. Next, we demonstrate and talk about procedures for carrying out the strategy. We discuss, demonstrate, and think aloud while modeling. Then, students practice under our guidance and feedback.

✔ **A Systematic Approach** Project CRISS is a valuable basis for instruction. It provides a systematic approach for using what we now know about teaching and learning. The following chart lists questions we need to continually ask ourselves while we are teaching. Use this chart to monitor your efforts to incorporate CRISS principles into your teaching.

CRISS Principles	The CRISS Philosophy	Yes	No	Somewhat
Background knowledge:	Did I assist students in thinking about what they already knew about the topic before beginning the unit? Did I develop necessary concepts before students read?			
Purpose setting:	Did my students have a clear purpose about what they were going to learn before beginning the lesson?			
Author's craft:	Can my students use the author's style of presentation to facilitate their understanding?			
Active involvement:	Were my students engaged in the topic? Did I help students become actively involved in their learning?			
Discussion:	Did my students have opportunities to talk about what they were learning?			
Organization:	Did my students organize information in a variety of ways?			
Writing:	Did my students write about what they were learning?			
Teacher modeling:	Did I do enough teacher modeling of learning strategies so that students could begin doing them on their own?			

Project CRISS

How Do I Use Project CRISS to Teach Journey Across Time?

When students know how authors structure their writing, they can more readily understand and remember what they read. For the first several chapters of this book, show students how to analyze the author's craft by "walking through" the chapter noting text features. Then demonstrate how to use the author's organization to develop two-column notes.

For demonstrating these strategies, make transparencies of the first several pages of Chapter 1, "Early Civilizations." Divide students into small groups.

Introducing the Chapter

Tell students: *"Before reading a text, I take time to figure out how the author has presented the information. If I understand the author's craft, I can do a better job of reading and learning. The authors of this book have a consistent organizational plan for presenting information. Let's discover what they do."*

Ask students to preview the introductory pages (pp. 1–3) of Unit 1: *"Why do you think the author has included the sections: Why It's Important, the time line, map, Places to Locate, and People to Meet? How might you use these features to gain an overview of what this unit is about?"*

Next ask students to turn to Chapter 1 (page 4). *"Notice the time line and how it is used to identify key topics included in this chapter. Now look at the Chapter Preview on page 5. Read the brief summaries of each of the sections. Why do you think the*

author has told you information about the three civilizations before you read? Notice the foldable activity and the suggestion for using the foldable for taking comparison notes on the three different civilizations. How might you use History Online to expand your understanding of the chapter content?"

(Ask one or more students to explore what is available online for this chapter and report to the class on ways that this information could be used.)

Ask students to turn to the Reading Social Studies skill described on page 6. Use the ideas described here and "walk" the students through the lesson.

Place a transparency of pages 8 and 9 on the overhead and begin modeling.

Introducing the Section

1. Get Ready to Read!

Ask students to turn to page 8. *"Notice how this page is organized."* (It begins with a Get Ready to Read! that includes: What's the Connection?, Focusing on the Main Ideas, Locating Places, Building Your Vocabulary, and Reading Strategy.) *"Let's take a moment and talk about how these features might help you."*

Read aloud and point out the What's the Connection? introduction that states: . . . Read to find out how early humans lived by moving from place to place. . . . *"Keep this purpose in mind as you read."*

✔ **Focusing on the Main Ideas:** *"Why has the author included the main ideas at the beginning of the section?"* (Helps readers know what they are going

to learn; helps readers think about what they might already know about the chapter information; helps set goals for reading)

✔ **Locating Places:** *"How might locating these places on the map (p. 13) before you read help you prepare to read this section?"* (Helps readers build a geographical context for places mentioned in the chapter.)

✔ **Building Your Vocabulary:** *"Now look at the list of vocabulary words (historian, archaeologist, etc.) and skim the first several pages of the chapter. What do you notice about how the vocabulary words are sequenced and highlighted in this chapter?"* (The vocabulary words are highlighted in yellow and presented in the same order in the chapter as listed here.)

✔ **Reading Strategy:** *"Why is it important to organize information you read? How might the strategy suggested here help you?"*

2. Visual Information

"Notice the visuals on pages 9, 10, and 11. Why do you think the author has included these references? Why should you pay attention to them? It's a good idea to read through these references before reading the chapter." (Makes the topics more interesting, provides background knowledge, includes important information for understanding the content, and so on.)

Walking Through the Chapter

As you talk aloud, note features on the transparencies for pages 8–15.

"Now let's see how the authors have helped us figure out the main topics covered in this chapter. Notice the bold print headings. The main topics are printed in larger red print and the subtopics are printed in smaller blue print. Vocabulary terms are noted in yellow. This organization and color coding should help you figure out what is important.

"At the end of each subsection, notice the Reading Check. There are also assessments at the end of each section (page 15). The Reading Check questions will help you know if you have comprehended each subsection. When you come to a Reading Check, you will stop and try to answer the question. If you can't answer the question, you should reread. You should read through these questions before you begin reading. In this way, you would know what you are supposed to get out of this section. The end-of-section assessment questions will also help you know what you are to learn."

Have students read the topical headings and subheadings for the first section of the chapter and make some predictions about what they will learn. "Notice how the author has stated some main points as rhetorical questions." Explain that good readers take time to preview and to make predictions before reading. Talk about how using the topic headings helps with this process.

Reading the Chapter

Assign students to read the introduction to the chapter stopping on page 10 at the heading, "Who Were the Hunter-Gatherers?" Have them turn to a partner and retell what they have just read. Explain: "Good readers are active when they read. They stop and think about what they have just read. If they can't remember the information, they go back and reread."

Continue having students read the rest of Section 1. At the end of each subsection, have them turn to a partner, and, without looking back at the

text, retell what they have just read. Also, model how to turn topical headings into questions as a way to evaluate comprehension.

Main Idea-Detail Notes

Ask students to divide their notebook paper into two columns and record key points in the left column and details explaining the key points in the right column. Main points could be questions or key words. Students then use their notes as a study guide using the key words or questions to quiz themselves.

✔ Demonstrate how to use the author's clues (headings, highlighted vocabulary, Reading Check questions) to develop main idea-detail notes. The authors also might include within this text many rhetorical questions which assist readers in determining main ideas. Talk about how the examples help

clarify content, and show students how to include these rhetorical questions and examples within their notes. On a blank transparency, develop two-column notes over the first section of the chapter while students write down their own notes at their desks. Model how to include main topics, rhetorical questions, and vocabulary essential to understanding the content in the left column. In the right column, record details elaborating the main points. Talk about being brief and using your own words. Explain why making the author's message your own insures better comprehension and retention.

✔ Continue modeling notes over the rest of this section. Then ask students to work in pairs or small groups to develop two-column notes over the rest of the chapter. Ask them to share their notes in a whole class discussion.

SAMPLE ORGANIZER

Main Ideas	Details
Early Humans History Prehistory Archaeologists Anthropologists	Story of human past Time before people developed writing Uncover clues about early human life—artifacts, fossils Study how humans began and developed—bones, artifacts
Paleolithic or Old Stone Age	Earliest part of Stone Age (2.5 million years ago)
Hunter-gatherers How did they adapt to the environment?	Moved from place to place finding food—nomads Lived in groups: Men—hunted, clubs; later spears, bows & arrows Women—close to camp Warm climates—few clothes Cold climates—caves Fire—life-changing discovery
Ice Ages What was this time like?	100,000 B.C. to about 8000 B.C. Extreme cold, ice sheets covered parts of Europe, Asia, North America Threatened human life, people built sturdier shelters, changed diet, used animal furs
Major developments	Fire, language, art, tools (stones, hunting spears—later fishhooks, needles)

Classroom Solutions

Test-Taking Strategies
How Can I Help My Students Succeed on Tests?

It's not enough for students to learn social studies facts and concepts—they must be able to show what they know in a variety of test-taking situations.

How Can I Help My Students Do Well On Objective Tests?

Objective tests may include multiple choice, true/false, and matching questions. Applying the following strategies can help students do their best on objective tests.

Multiple Choice Questions

✔ Students should read the directions carefully to learn what answer the test requires—the best answer or the right answer. This is especially important when answer choices include "all of the above" or "none of the above."

✔ Advise students to watch for negative words in the questions, such as *not, except, unless, never,* and so forth. If the question contains a negative, the correct answer choice is the one that does not fit.

✔ Students should try to mentally answer the question before reading the answer choices.

✔ Students should read all the answer choices and cross out those that are obviously wrong. Then they should choose an answer from those that remain.

True/False Questions

✔ It is important that students read the entire question before answering. For an answer to be true, the entire statement must be true. If

one part of a statement is false, the answer should be marked *False*.

✔ Remind students to watch for words like *all, never, every,* and *always*. Statements containing these words are often false.

Matching Questions

✔ Students should read through both lists before they mark any answers.

✔ Unless an answer can be used more than once, students should cross out each choice as they use it.

✔ Using what they know about grammar can help students find the

right answer. For instance, when matching a word with its definition, the definition is often the same part of speech (noun, verb, adjective, and so forth) as the word.

How Can I Help My Students Do Well On Essay Tests?

Essay tests require students to provide thorough and well-organized written responses, in addition to telling what they know. Help students use the following strategies on essay tests.

Analyze:	To **analyze** means to systematically and critically examine all parts of an issue or event.
Classify or Categorize:	To **classify** or **categorize** means to put people, things, or ideas into groups, based on a common set of characteristics.
Compare and Contrast:	To **compare** is to show how things are similar, or alike. To **contrast** is to show how things are different.
Describe:	To **describe** means to present a sketch or impression. Rich details, especially details that appeal to the senses, flesh out a description.
Discuss:	To **discuss** means to systematically write about all sides of an issue or event.
Evaluate:	To **evaluate** means to make a judgment and support it with evidence.
Explain:	To **explain** means to clarify or make plain.
Illustrate:	To **illustrate** means to provide examples or to show with a picture or other graphic.
Infer:	To **infer** means to read between the lines or to use knowledge and experience to draw conclusions, make a generalization, or form a prediction.
Justify:	To **justify** means to prove or to support a position with specific facts and reasons.
Predict:	To **predict** means to tell what will happen in the future, based on an understanding of prior events and behaviors.
State:	To **state** means to briefly and concisely present information.
Summarize:	To **summarize** means to give a brief overview of the main points of an issue or event.
Trace:	To **trace** means to present the steps or stages in a process or event in sequential or chronological order.

Read the Question

The key to writing successful essay responses lies in reading and interpreting questions correctly. Teach students to identify and underline key words in the questions, and to use these words to guide them in understanding what the question asks. Help students understand the meaning of some of the most common key words, listed in the chart on page T26.

Plan and Write the Essay

After students understand the question, they should follow the writing process to develop their answer. Encourage students to follow the steps below to plan and write their essays.

1. Map out an answer. Make lists, webs, or an outline to plan the response.

2. Decide on an order in which to present the main points.

3. Write an opening statement that directly responds to the essay question.

4. Write the essay. Expand on the opening statement. Support key points with specific facts, details, and reasons.

5. Write a closing statement that brings the main points together.

6. Proofread to check for spelling, grammar, and punctuation.

How Can I Help My Students Prepare for Standardized Tests?

Students can follow the steps below to prepare for a test.

✔ **Read About the Test** Students can familiarize themselves with the format of the test, the types of questions that will be asked, and the amount of time they will have to complete the test.

✔ **Review the Content** Consistent study throughout the school year will help students build social studies knowledge and understanding. If there are specific objectives or standards that are tested on the exam, help students review these facts or skills to be sure they are proficient.

✔ **Practice** Provide practice, ideally with real released tests, to build students' familiarity with the content, format, and timing of the real exam. Students should practice all the types of questions they will encounter on the test—multiple choice, short answer, and extended response.

✔ **Analyze Practice Results** Help students improve test-taking performance by analyzing their test-taking strengths and weaknesses. Spend time discussing students' completed practice tests, explaining why particular answers are right or wrong. Help students identify what kinds of questions they had the most difficulty with. Look for patterns in errors and then tailor instruction to review the appropriate test-taking skills or social studies content.✦

Bill Aron/PhotoEdit

Help Students Learn by Reviewing Graded Tests

Advice from Tara Musslewhite
Humble Independent School District
Humble, Texas

Frequently reviewing graded tests is a great way for students to assess their test-taking skills. It also gives teachers the opportunity to teach test-taking strategies and review content. As the class re-reads each test question, guide students to think logically about their answer choices. Show students how to:

1. Read each question carefully to determine its meaning.
2. Look for key words in the question to support their answers.
3. Recognize synonyms in the answer choices that may match phrases in the question.
4. Narrow down answer choices by eliminating ones that don't make sense.
5. Anticipate the answer before looking at the answer choices.
6. Circle questions of which they are unsure and go back to them later. Sometimes a clue will be found in another question on the test.

Alternative Assessment Strategies

How Can I Go Beyond Tests to Assess Students' Understanding of Social Studies Facts and Concepts?

In response to the growing demand for accountability in the classroom, educators must use multiple assessment measures to accurately gauge student performance. In addition to quizzes, tests, essay exams, and standardized tests, assessment today incorporates a variety of performance-based measures and portfolio opportunities.

What Are Some Typical Performance-Based Assessments?

There are many kinds of performance-based assessments. They all share one common characteristic—they challenge students to create products that demonstrate what they know. One good way to present a performance assessment is in the form of an open-ended question.

Writing

Performance-based writing assessments challenge students to apply their knowledge of social studies concepts and information in a variety of written ways. Writing activities are most often completed by one student, rather than by a group.

✔ **Journals** Students write from the perspective of a historical character or a citizen of a particular historical era.

✔ **Letters** Students write a letter from one historical figure to another or from a historical figure to a family member or other audience.

✔ **Position Paper or Editorial** Students explain a controversial issue and present their own opinion and recommendations, supported with strong evidence and convincing reasons.

✔ **Newspaper** Students write a variety of stories from the perspective of a reporter living in a particular historical time period.

✔ **Biographies and Autobiographies** Students write about historical figures either from the third person point of view (biography) or from the first person (autobiography).

✔ **Creative Stories** Students integrate historical events into a piece of fiction, incorporating the customs, language, and geography of the period.

✔ **Poems and Songs** Students follow the conventions of a particular type of song or poem as they tell about a historical event or person.

✔ **Research Reports** Students synthesize information from a variety of sources into a well-developed research report.

Oral Presentations

Oral presentations allow students to demonstrate their social studies literacy before an audience. Oral presentations are often group efforts, although this need not be the case.

✔ **Simulations** Students hold simulations, or reenactments, of actual events, such as trials, acts of civil disobedience, battles, speeches, and so forth.

✔ **Debates** Students debate two or more sides to a historical policy or issue. Students can debate from a contemporary perspective or in a role play in which they assume a viewpoint held by a historical character.

✔ **Interview** Students conduct a mock interview of a historical character or bystander.

✔ **Oral Reports** Students present the results of research efforts in a lively oral report.

✔ **Skits and Plays** Students use historical events as the basis for a play or skit. Details should accurately reflect customs, language, and the setting of the period.

Visual Presentations

Visual presentations allow students to demonstrate their social studies understandings in a variety of visual formats. Visual presentations can be either group or individual projects.

✔ **Model** Students make a model to demonstrate or represent a process, place, event, battle, artifact, or custom.

✔ **Museum Exhibit** Students create a rich display of materials around a topic. Typical displays might include models, illustrations, photographs, videos, writings, and audiotaped explanations.

✔ **Graph or Chart** Students analyze and represent historical data in a line graph, bar graph, table, or other chart format.

✔ **Drawing** Students represent or interpret a historical event or period through illustration, including political cartoons.

✔ **Posters and Murals** Posters and murals may include maps, time lines, diagrams, illustrations, photographs, and written explanations that reflect students' understandings of historical information.

Jonathan Nourok/PhotoEdit

- ✔ **Quilt** Students sew or draw a design for a patchwork quilt that shows a variety of perspectives, events, or issues related to a key topic.
- ✔ **Videotapes** Students film a video to show historical fiction or to preserve a simulation of a historical event.
- ✔ **Multimedia Presentation or Slide Show** Students create a computer-generated multimedia presentation containing historical information and analysis.

How Are Performance Assessments Scored?

There are a variety of means used to evaluate performance tasks. Some or all of the following methods may be used.

- ✔ **Scoring Rubrics** A scoring rubric is a set of guidelines for assessing the quality of a process and/or product. It sets out criteria used to distinguish acceptable responses from unacceptable ones, generally along a scale from excellent to poor.
- ✔ **Models of Excellent Work** Teacher-selected models of excellent work concretely illustrate expectations and help students set goals for their own projects.
- ✔ **Student Self-Assessment** Common methods of self-assessment include ranking work in relation to the model, using a scoring rubric, and writing their own goals and then evaluating how well they have met the goals they set for themselves. Regardless of which method or methods students use, they should be encouraged to evaluate their behaviors and processes, as well as the finished product.
- ✔ **Peer or Audience Assessment** Many of the performance tasks target an audience other than the classroom teacher. If possible, the audience of peers should give the student feedback. Have the class create rubrics for specific projects together.

- ✔ **Observation** As students carry out their performance tasks, you may want to formally observe students at work. Start by developing a checklist, identifying all the specific behaviors and understandings you expect students to demonstrate. Then observe students as they carry out performance tasks and check off the behaviors as you observe them.
- ✔ **Interviews** As a form of ongoing assessment, you may want to conduct interviews with students, asking them to analyze, explain, and assess their participation in performance tasks. When projects take place over an extended period of time, you can hold periodic interviews as well as exit interviews. In this way the interview process allows you to gauge the status of the project and to guide students' efforts along the way.◆

Targeting Multiple Intelligences

Advice from John Cartaina
Consultant, New Jersey Council of Social Studies

Authentic performance assessment provides students with different learning styles opportunities to demonstrate their successful learning. The table below list types of learning styles.

Learning Style	Characteristics of Students
Linguistic	Read regularly, write clearly, and easily understand the written word
Logical-Mathematical	Use numbers, logic, and critical thinking skills
Visual-Spatial	Think in terms of pictures and images
Auditory-Musical	Remember spoken words and produce rhythms and melodies
Kinesthetic	Learn from touch, movement, and manipulating objects
Interpersonal	Understand and work well with other people
Intrapersonal	Have a realistic understanding of their strengths and weaknesses
Naturalist	Can distinguish among, classify, and use features of the environment

You may want to assign activities to students that accommodate their strongest learning styles, but frequently ask them to use their weakest learning styles.

Primary Source Strategies
How Do I Use Primary Sources in My Classroom?

PhotoDisc

A primary source is direct evidence of an event, idea, period, or development. It is an oral or written account obtained from actual participants in an event. Examples of primary sources include the following:

✔ official documents (records, statistics)
✔ political declarations, laws, and rules for governance
✔ speeches and interviews
✔ diaries, memoirs, and oral histories
✔ autobiographies
✔ recipes and cookbooks
✔ advertisements and posters
✔ letters

Physical objects, such as tools and dishes, can be primary sources; so can visual evidence in the form of fine art, photographs, maps, films, and videotapes. Primary sources can also include songs and audio recordings.

Why Use Primary Sources in Your Classroom?

Using primary sources to teach transforms the study of social studies from a passive process to an active one. Students become investigators—finding clues, formulating hypotheses and drawing inferences, making judgments, and reaching conclusions. Bringing primary sources into the classroom stimulates students to think critically

about events, issues, and concepts rather than just memorizing dates, names, and generalizations reached by others.

Choosing Primary Sources

✔ Provide exposure to a variety of source types, including historic photographs, folk or popular music, financial records or household accounts, as well as letters, journals, and historic documents.
✔ When choosing print sources, consider the interests and reading levels of your students. Many texts contain challenging vocabulary and unfamiliar sentence structure. You may need to create a reader's guide that defines key vocabulary and paraphrases the main points of the reading.
✔ Some documents may be too long. Decide whether using an excerpt will provide enough information for students to draw conclusions.
✔ Depending upon the topic and your instructional objectives, you may need to provide several different primary sources to expose students to a variety of perspectives.
✔ Decide how students will access the primary sources: through the Internet, the library, a museum, or other print resources. Consider the possibility of an

Internet virtual field trip for students. Moving from URL to URL, students can visit museum sites and other Web pages to view artifacts; interpret economic or census data; and read journals, letters, and official documents.

How Do I Introduce Students to Primary Sources?

Carefully explain the nature of primary sources when you introduce them to students. Although primary sources contain valuable clues, be sure to alert students that primary sources contain biases and prejudices, and must be approached with caution. Every primary source reflects the creator's point of view to some degree.

Using Primary Sources in the Classroom

Primary sources provide a rich source of inspiration for a variety of instructional strategies. They can be used to spark interest in a new topic, foster deeper exploration into a historical era, or assess students' understanding of social studies concepts and facts.

✔ **Prereading Activities** Present a primary source for students to study at the beginning of a new chapter or topic. Have students analyze the source, using the questions and guidelines presented on the next page. Then have students make

Anthony Redpath/CORBIS STOCK MARKET

Aaron Haupt

Interpreting a Primary Source

Before students interpret a primary source, they need to know the context into which the source fits. Then they can use questions and guidelines, such as those below, to help them analyze and interpret the primary source.

Print Sources

- Who created the source, and what was the purpose for doing so?
- Did the writer personally experience or witness the event(s)?
- At what point did the writer record the information—as it happened or afterward? How long after?
- Who was the intended audience?
- Was the writer trying to record facts, express an opinion, or persuade others to take action?
- What is the author's main message?
- What values does the document convey?
- What bias does it reflect?
- What information about the topic can you gather from this document?
- Compare this document with what you know about the topic. Does it confirm those ideas or introduce a new perspective?
- How might other accounts about this topic support or modify the message this source delivers?

Visual Sources

- Who created the source, and what was the purpose for doing so?
- What does the image show?
- What mood does the image convey?
- Who or what dominates the image or catches your eye?
- How does the view impact the message?
- What details can you learn from the image?
- What is excluded from view?
- What bias does the visual reflect?
- What information about the topic can you gather from this visual?
- How might other visuals about this topic support or modify the message this one delivers?

Audio Sources

- Who created the source? What was the purpose for creating this source?
- What is the main idea of the audio?
- What mood does the recorder's voice convey?
- What bias does the audio text reflect?
- What information about the topic can you gather from this audio source?
- Compare the information in this source with what you already know about the topic. Does it confirm those ideas or introduce a new perspective?
- How might other sources about this topic support or modify the message that this one delivers?

predictions about what they might learn in the upcoming lessons.

✔ **Exploring Information** Provide a variety of primary sources related to a topic or time period. Have students compare and contrast the items, analyzing the information, making inferences, and drawing conclusions about the period.

✔ **Evaluation Activities** Have students evaluate a primary source and tell how it supports or refutes what they learned in the textbook or have students read a primary source document that provides one perspective on a topic, and have students write their own account, presenting another perspective or opinion.✦

Classroom Activity: Reading and Understanding Primary Sources

Advice from Leslie Espinosa
Humble Independent School District
Humble, Texas

1. Before class make a list of student reading partners. Make sure one of the two is a good reader.
2. Have students read a primary source document (or part of a primary source document), taking turns as they go. They should "mark" any words that they do not understand.
3. After each paragraph, the student pair should stop and paraphrase what it says in their own words.
4. Students should look up unfamiliar words they've marked and create an illustrated dictionary entry for each term (over the course of the year or semester).
5. Ask student pairs to present their paraphrased primary source to the rest of the class.

Reading in the Content Areas

How Can I Use Jamestown Education Products to Help Struggling Readers?

For over 30 years, Jamestown Education has made its primary focus helping older readers become better readers. The Jamestown products shown on this page support the basic elements of reading cited by the National Reading Panel. Each of them can help your struggling readers become better readers.

Timed Readings Plus in Social Studies

✔ **Reading Levels:** 4–13+

✔ **Benefits:**

This ten-book series will help your students increase both reading rate and comprehension. The nonfiction passages cover current social studies topics and are similar to those found on both state and national tests. Each of the two-part lessons focuses on reading rate, factual recall, comprehension strategies, and higher-level critical thinking skills.

Reading in the Content Areas: Social Studies

✔ **Reading Levels:** 4–12+

✔ **Benefits:**

This book concentrates on six essential reading skills that will help your students better comprehend what they read. Seventy-five high-interest nonfiction passages written at increasing levels of difficulty, followed by consistent, targeted skills, teach the techniques needed to organize, understand, and apply information.

Reading Fluency

✔ **Reading Levels:** 1–10

✔ **Benefits:**

This seven-book series will help your students read smoothly, accurately and expressively. Students work in pairs to provide immediate feedback and self-assessment. Author Camille Blachowicz states that "the ability to read fluently is highly correlated with many other measures of reading competence."

Jamestown's Reading Improvement

✔ **Reading Levels** 4–10

✔ **Benefits:**

Authored by renowned reading expert Edward Fry, this eight-book series focuses on helping build your students' comprehension, vocabulary, and skimming and scanning skills. Repeated practice with targeted exercises ensures mastery of valuable reading skills.

Critical Reading Series

✔ **Reading Levels:** 2–8
✔ **Benefits:**

This 24-book high-interest series, written at three reading spans, encourages your reluctant readers to build a love for nonfiction while focusing on critical reading skills. Topics ranging from Fateful Journeys to Weird Science to Heroes draw students in, while giving students ample opportunities to master important skills found on both state and national tests.

To order Jamestown products, call 1-800-334-7344

In addition to the Project CRISS Reading Strategies, you may find it effective to implement some of the following instructional methods. They help *your* struggling students take increasing ownership of the reading process.

Reciprocal Teaching

Reciprocal teaching is characterized by a dialogue between you and your student, and ultimately among students in a group, in which students take the role of dialogue reader. Construction of meaning is built upon four reading strategies:

✔ **Summarizing** Readers identify the most important information in a segment of text and state that information in their own words. Summarizing involves students in recognizing and communicating the significant ideas in a text.

✔ **Questioning** Readers ask themselves questions about the text segment. Self-questioning aids comprehension by helping students identify where their understanding of the text has broken down and what they still need to know in order to understand what they have read.

✔ **Clarifying** Readers try to find answers to the questions they have raised and to make sense of parts of the text that have caused confusion. They seek clarification by rereading, reading ahead, or by seeking outside help, such as through a peer or a reference source.

✔ **Predicting** Readers tell what they think will happen next, basing their predictions on evidence from the text they have already read.

Modeling

An important element of strategic instruction is teacher modeling. As a part of the modeling process, think aloud as you apply a strategy to solve a reading problem, putting words to the inner voice that successful readers have with text, and demonstrating the strategy used for understanding. To construct a "think-aloud," read aloud a passage, stopping at pertinent points to talk about what you are thinking. A think-aloud demonstrates the cognitive process and allows students to observe how a proficient reader approaches a problem with reading.

"Fix-Up" Strategies

Explain that readers perform certain tasks. Guide them through these following steps:

✔ **Stop** Tell students to stop and fix the problem when they do not understand.

✔ **Identify the Problem** Have students ask themselves when they stopped understanding and what they do not understand.

✔ **Apply a Fix-up Strategy** Encourage students to try these strategies:

✔ **Reread**

✔ **Read ahead**

✔ **Alter** the pace or voice

✔ **Ask** for help

CRISS and the Jamestown Reader

Advice from Dr. Sara Wartenberg
Palm Harbor University High School
International Baccalaureate Program
Palm Harbor, Florida

Help your students achieve testing success by combining CRISS strategies with the Jamestown Readers. The stories appeal to students of all reading levels. The stories are interesting and informative for students and teachers alike. Implementing CRISS strategies as students read the selections will help them respond with greater success to the questions that accompany each selection. Students will gain confidence and thus work for greater skill in reading comprehension and critical thinking.

Journey Across Time to the NCSS Thematic Strands

In *Curriculum for Social Studies: Expectations of Excellence,* the National Council for the Social Studies (NCSS) identified 10 themes that serve as organizing strands for the social studies curriculum at every school level. These themes are interrelated and draw from all of the social science disciplines. Each theme provides student performance expectations in the areas of knowledge, processes, and attitudes. The 10 NCSS themes were the basis for the themes used in *Journey Across Time.*

Theme and Performance Expectation	Student Pages
I. Culture The study of culture helps students understand similarities and differences within groups of people. By studying a culture's beliefs, values, and traditions, students begin to gain a perspective that helps them relate to different groups. In the middle grades, students begin to examine aspects of culture and how culture influences human behavior.	
A. Compare similarities and differences in the ways groups, societies, and cultures meet human needs and concerns.	8, 47, 50, 74, 102, 143, 144, 148, 154, 155, 156, 162, 163, 188, 206, 214, 238, 247, 552, 572, 587, 599, 623, 653, 726–727
B. Explain how information and experiences may be interpreted by people from diverse cultural perspectives and frames of reference.	12, 181, 238, 248, 333, 600, 617, 625, 626, 737, 827
C. Explain and give examples of how language, literature, the arts, architecture, other artifacts, traditions, beliefs, values, and behaviors contribute to the development and transmission of culture.	15, 33, 64, 75, 156, 157, 161, 163, 168, 188, 214, 334, 476, 499, 501, 549, 606, 607, 617, 618, 632, 652, 736
D. Explain why individuals and groups respond differently to their physical and social environments and/or changes to them on the basis of shared assumptions, values, and beliefs.	85, 104, 148, 158, 159, 160, 161, 163, 173, 183, 186, 188, 208, 264, 267, 325, 334, 350, 351, 378, 381, 386, 392, 394, 397, 504, 592, 619, 621, 623, 626, 652, 653, 689, 694, 729, 827
E. Articulate the implications of cultural diversity, as well as cohesion, within and across groups.	188, 208, 396, 429, 469, 560, 626, 732
II. Time, Continuity, and Change Understanding time, continuity, and change involves being knowledgeable about what things were like in the past and how things change and develop over time. Knowing how to read and reconstruct the past helps students gain a historical perspective. In the middle grades, students will continue to increase their knowledge of the past and of historical concepts. Students will also begin to learn how individual experiences, social values, and cultural traditions influence interpretations of the past.	
A. Demonstrate an understanding that different scholars may describe the same event or situation in different ways but must provide reasons or evidence for their views.	33, 163, 243, 267, 277, 297, 502, 511, 521, 560, 600, 703, 737
B. Identify and use key concepts such as chronology, causality, change, conflict, and complexity to explain, analyze, and show connections among patterns of historical change and continuity.	21, 32, 33, 61, 74, 80, 85, 248, 326, 340, 408, 429, 433, 490, 519, 521, 543, 553, 555, 558, 560, 609, 610, 611, 615, 652, 658, 660, 687, 700, 715
C. Identify and describe selected historical periods and patterns of change within and across cultures, such as the rise of civilizations, the development of transportation systems, the growth and breakdown of colonial systems, and others.	23, 32, 44, 60, 61, 67, 72, 74, 105, 132, 146, 209, 216, 262, 317, 324, 326, 336, 385, 386, 412, 415, 429, 436, 438, 444, 460, 478, 576, 581, 602, 615, 625, 700, 725
D. Identify and use processes important to reconstructing and reinterpreting the past, such as using a variety of sources, providing, validating, and weighing evidence for claims, checking credibility of sources, and searching for causality.	46, 75, 135, 179, 478, 561, 617, 879
E. Develop critical sensitivities such as empathy and skepticism regarding attitudes, values, and behaviors of people in different historical contexts.	12, 71, 105, 216, 326, 337, 394, 566, 567, 581, 680, 827
F. Use knowledge of facts and concepts drawn from history, along with methods of historical inquiry, to inform decision-making about and action-taking on public issues.	9, 25, 189, 337, 632, 700, 807

III. *People, Places, & Environments*

The study of people, places, and environments will help students as they create their spatial views and geographic perspective of the world. Students begin to make informed and critical decisions about the relationship between humans and their environment. In the middle school years, students can relate their personal experiences to happenings in other environments. These experiences will help students increase their abstract thought when analyzing human behavior in relation to physical and cultural environments.

A.	Elaborate mental maps of locales, regions, and the world that demonstrate understanding of relative location, direction, size, and shape.	33, 174, 197, 334, 429, 478, 752
B.	Create, interpret, use, and distinguish various representations of the earth such as maps, globes, and photographs.	13, 17, 33, 39, 62, 70, 75, 105, 117, 121, 125, 132, 134, 144, 149, 176, 179, 189, 190, 195, 210, 213, 241, 246, 251, 263, 269, 274, 292, 297, 323, 329, 337, 352, 361, 367, 374, 380, 383, 385, 397, 409, 424, 425, 433, 438, 445, 448, 451, 452, 465, 469, 473, 478, 485, 507, 513, 514, 516, 518, 538, 540, 542, 548, 555, 557, 561, 573, 575, 577, 590, 603, 609, 639, 645, 653, 662, 667, 668, 688, 691, 694, 695, 703
C.	Use appropriate resources, data sources, and geographic tools such as aerial photographs, satellite images, geographic information systems (GIS), map projections, and cartography to generate, manipulate, and interpret information such as atlases, databases, grid systems, charts, graphs, and maps.	75, 105, 478
D.	Estimate distance, calculate scale, and distinguish other geographic relationships such as population density and spatial distribution patterns.	39, 132, 411, 431, 433, 448, 752
E.	Locate and describe varying landforms and geographic features, such as mountains, plateaus, islands, rain forests, deserts, and oceans, and explain their relationship within the ecosystem.	39, 250, 376, 445, 446, 583, 585, 591
F.	Describe physical system changes such as seasons, climate and weather, and the water cycle and identify geographic patterns associated with them.	198, 373, 374, 446
G.	Describe how people create places that reflect cultural values and ideals as they build neighborhoods, parks, shopping centers, and the like.	29, 30, 52, 66, 70, 74, 90, 101, 162, 163, 178, 211, 251, 297, 303, 309, 310, 325, 334, 392, 432, 436, 504, 506, 507, 527, 528, 544, 549, 561, 578, 579, 592, 603, 610, 643
H.	Examine, interpret, and analyze physical and cultural patterns and their interactions, such as land use, settlement patterns, cultural transmission of customs and ideas, and ecosystem changes.	15, 17, 32, 44, 80, 117, 148, 226, 235, 265, 267, 396, 478, 485, 490, 506, 513, 514, 573, 578, 581, 583, 590, 591, 592, 602, 692, 725
I.	Describe ways that historical events have been influenced by, and have influenced, physical and human geographic factors in local, regional, national, and global settings.	23, 28, 40, 46, 68, 70, 72, 74, 119, 121, 148, 263, 276, 296, 490, 514, 773
J.	Observe and speculate about social and economic effects of environmental changes and crises resulting from phenomena such as floods, storms, and drought.	41, 75, 119, 123, 225, 390, 497, 576, 579
K.	Propose, compare, and evaluate alternative uses of land and resources in communities, nations, and the world.	189, 603, 861

IV. *Individual Development & Identity*

People and culture influence a person's identity. Examining the different forms of human behavior improves one's understanding of social relationships and the development of personal identity. The study of human behavior helps students become aware of how social processes influence a person's identity. In the middle years, issues of personal identity become important as students begin to view themselves in relation to others.

A.	Relate personal changes to social, cultural, and historical contexts.	49, 69, 115, 157, 169, 175, 182, 205, 229, 233, 241, 274, 282, 300, 316, 322, 329, 377, 388, 420, 424, 451, 476, 488, 519, 541, 557, 619, 637, 640, 656, 659, 661, 671, 691, 695, 715, 893
B.	Describe personal connections to place—as associated with community, nation, and world.	20, 45, 95, 97, 145, 189, 207, 227, 390, 394, 439, 470, 475, 476, 496, 500, 531, 533, 586, 592, 653, 893

Theme and Performance Expectation	Student Pages
C. Describe the ways family, gender, ethnicity, nationality, and institutional affiliations contribute to personal identity.	75, 81, 89, 94, 98, 99, 167, 172, 201, 271, 301, 306, 310, 316, 330, 334, 343, 412, 422, 459, 471, 486, 498, 504, 526, 624, 647, 808–810, 827, 893
D. Relate such factors as physical endowment and capabilities, learning, motivation, personality, perception, and behavior to individual development.	104, 179, 181, 304, 318, 459, 476, 485, 507, 552, 622, 644, 679, 893
E. Identify and describe ways regional, ethnic, and national cultures influence individuals' daily lives.	65, 211, 216, 307, 350, 506, 641, 649, 719–720, 892–893
F. Identify and describe the influence of perception, attitudes, values, and beliefs on personal identity.	58, 203, 270, 279, 297, 305, 350, 367, 374, 382, 384, 386, 459, 474, 510, 546, 558, 689, 893
G. Identify and interpret examples of stereotyping, conformity, and altruism.	65, 211, 216, 344, 348, 489, 561, 638, 809
H. Work independently and cooperatively to accomplish goals.	189, 239, 337, 507, 571, 603, 653, 669, 892–893

V. *Individuals, Groups, & Institutions*

Institutions, such as schools, governments, and churches, influence people and often reflect a society's values. Because of the vital role that institutions play in people's lives, it is important that students know how institutions develop, what controls and influences them, and how humans react to them. Middle school students will gain experience by studying how institutions change over time. They should also be able to use their understanding to suggest ways how institutions can work for the common good.

A.	Demonstrate an understanding of concepts such as role, status, and social class in describing the interactions of individuals and social groups.	45, 52, 74, 93, 102, 123, 229, 239, 250, 273, 276, 283, 286, 296, 302, 316, 336, 375, 378, 390, 413, 439, 465, 468, 471, 478, 490, 491, 492, 493, 494, 495, 497, 506, 512, 522, 526, 531, 558, 560, 582, 587, 615, 652, 686, 715, 717
B.	Analyze group and institutional influences on people, events, and elements of culture.	45, 63, 95, 102, 104, 194, 201, 205, 266, 267, 303, 306, 310, 329, 332, 336, 352, 364, 378, 380, 386, 387, 421, 453, 466, 475, 478, 497, 545, 550, 552, 560, 580, 584, 588, 597, 635, 684, 689, 809
C.	Describe the various forms institutions take and the interactions of people with institutions.	46, 267, 294, 306, 334, 350, 351, 357, 366, 380, 383, 438, 543, 650, 653, 660, 689, 715
D.	Identify and analyze examples of tensions between expressions of individuality and group or institutional efforts to promote social conformity.	97, 201, 202, 347, 349, 354, 414, 521, 547, 633, 636, 641, 648, 649, 652, 675, 679
E.	Identify and describe examples of tensions between belief systems and government policies and laws.	83, 85, 173, 186, 231, 239, 310, 344, 347, 348, 350, 356, 357, 364, 366, 415, 478, 484, 490, 497, 504, 528, 548, 551, 552, 634, 637, 640, 641, 650, 653, 660, 689, 693
F.	Describe the role of institutions in furthering both continuity and change.	67, 102, 104, 189, 353, 357, 361, 364, 415, 497, 504, 519, 533, 541, 560, 642, 643, 650, 810
G.	Apply knowledge of how groups and institutions work to meet individual needs and promote the common good.	92, 244, 248, 294, 322, 328, 342, 355, 360, 366, 506, 517, 520, 521, 524, 545, 603, 642, 650, 684

VI. *Power, Authority, & Governance*

Studying structures of power, authority, and governance and their functions in the United States and around the world is important for developing a notion of civic responsibility. Students will identify the purpose and characteristics of various types of government and how people try to resolve conflicts. Students will also examine the relationship between individual rights and responsibilities. During the middle school years, students apply what they have learned about rights and responsibilities in more complex contexts.

A.	Examine persistent issues involving the rights, roles, and status of the individual in relation to the general welfare.	22, 127, 171, 173, 175, 181, 331, 413, 427, 533, 603, 681, 682, 683, 685, 686, 702
B.	Describe the purpose of government and how its powers are acquired, used, and justified.	46, 130, 148, 173, 231, 281, 396, 467, 478, 487, 488, 506, 523, 531, 538, 540, 588, 592, 600, 602, 615, 639, 646, 650, 652, 681, 808
C.	Analyze and explain ideas and governmental mechanisms to meet needs and wants of citizens, regulate territory, manage conflict, and establish order and security.	48, 92, 95, 130, 133, 148, 149, 210, 230, 239, 242, 265, 267, 283, 285, 286, 288, 289, 320, 326, 327, 366, 378, 428, 429, 431, 438, 461, 462, 472, 483, 561, 614, 646, 702

Theme and Performance Expectation	Student Pages
D. Describe the ways nations and organizations respond to forces of unity and diversity affecting order and security.	28, 32, 44, 67, 69, 87, 188, 212, 296, 318, 336, 343, 386, 396, 438, 467, 497, 589, 682, 697, 698, 700, 715
E. Identify and describe the basic features of the political system in the United States and identify representative leaders from various levels and branches of government.	43, 88, 89, 140, 141, 148, 272, 280, 283, 289, 296, 320, 359, 439, 467, 493, 634
F. Explain conditions, actions, and motivations that contribute to conflict and cooperation within and among nations.	30, 85, 96, 102, 104, 105, 126, 130, 137, 148, 149, 174, 176, 177, 179, 242, 267, 275, 276, 296, 326, 336, 354, 379, 384, 386, 396, 426, 438, 464, 467, 490, 497, 521, 534, 543, 558, 560, 585, 596, 600, 652, 64, 696, 698, 808–810
G. Describe and analyze the role of technology in communications, transportation, information processing, weapons development, or other areas as it contributes to or helps resolve conflicts.	30, 439, 593, 869, 888
H. Explain and apply concepts such as power, role, status, justice, and influence to the examination of persistent issues and social problems.	173, 285, 296, 497, 683
I. Give examples and explain how governments attempt to achieve their stated ideals at home and abroad.	30, 72, 105, 148, 179, 250, 267, 276, 283, 294, 296, 330, 336, 423, 438, 449, 483, 488, 496, 521, 543, 560, 689, 763, 808–810

VII. *Production, Distribution, & Consumption*

Societies try to meet people's needs and wants by trying to answer the basic economic questions: What is to be produced? How should goods be produced? How should goods and services be distributed? How should land, labor, capital, and management be allocated? By studying how needs and wants are met, students learn how trade and government economic policies develop. In the middle grades, students increase their knowledge of economic concepts, principles, and reasoning.

A. Give and explain examples of ways that economic systems structure choices about how goods and services are to be produced and distributed.	247, 336, 478, 669, 702, 861
B. Describe the role that supply and demand, prices, incentives, and profits play in determining what is produced and distributed in a competitive market system.	43, 334, 389, 417, 422, 447, 449, 450, 667, 861
C. Explain the difference between private and public goods and services.	62, 319, 409, 436, 478, 503
D. Describe a range of examples of the various institutions that make up economic systems such as households, business firms, banks, government agencies, labor unions, and corporations.	213, 394, 390, 417, 436, 529, 531, 543, 611, 612, 614, 615, 667
E. Describe the role of specialization and exchange in the economic process.	74, 233, 294, 320, 390, 451, 462, 478, 531, 581, 608, 613, 615, 652
F. Explain and illustrate how values and beliefs influence different economic decisions.	245, 453, 869, 888
G. Differentiate among various forms of exchange and money.	121, 242, 245, 293, 294, 320, 388, 529
H. Compare basic economic systems according to who determines what is produced, distributed, and consumed.	10, 15–16, 17–18, 20, 23, 33, 43–44, 46, 48, 62, 64, 72, 81, 117, 118–119, 120–121, 125–126, 142–143, 178–179, 196–197, 199–201, 211, 213, 230, 233–234, 246–247, 265, 274, 278–279, 292–294, 309, 319, 320, 330, 332–333, 381, 382–383, 388–389, 411, 417–418, 426, 447–448, 449, 450, 451–452, 461–462, 488–489, 492–493, 494, 496–497, 516, 523, 524–525, 526, 528, 529–530, 532–533, 611–612, 613–614, 615, 659–660, 666–667, 668–669, 687, 694–696, 696–697, 698
I. Use economic concepts to help explain historical and current developments and issues in local, national, or global contexts.	434, 436, 451, 595, 613, 666
J. Use economic reasoning to compare different proposals for dealing with a contemporary social issue such as unemployment, acid rain, or high quality education.	The concept of analyzing economic indicators is on page 724. Use this opportunity to address this strand.

Theme and Performance Expectation	Student Pages
VIII. *Science, Technology, & Society* The study of science, technology, and society is ever changing. It raises questions about who will benefit from it and how fundamental values and beliefs can be preserved in a technology–driven society. By the middle grades, students research the complex relationships among technology, human values, and behavior. Students will learn how technology and science have brought about change and how they have often challenged accepted societal beliefs.	
A. Examine and describe the influence of culture on scientific and technological choices and advancement, such as in transportation, medicine, and warfare.	14, 20, 27, 30, 32, 38, 45, 52, 185, 186, 216, 231, 235, 305, 391, 396, 410, 416, 419, 422, 438, 480, 531, 554, 621, 626, 671, 674, 676, 677, 678, 679, 702, 727, 728, 730
B. Show through specific examples how science and technology have changed people's perceptions of the social and natural world, such as in their relationship to the land, animal life, family life, and economic wants, needs, and security.	11, 15, 23, 32, 52, 186, 188, 199, 216, 391, 397, 418, 420, 422, 453, 560, 561, 626, 659, 669, 672, 679, 702, 727, 732
C. Describe examples in which values, beliefs, and attitudes have been influenced by new scientific and technological knowledge, such as the invention of the printing press, conceptions of the universe, applications of atomic energy, and genetic discoveries.	23, 184, 310, 396, 670, 673, 679, 738, 741, 829
D. Explain the need for laws and policies to govern scientific and technological applications, such as the safety and well–being of workers and consumers and the regulation of utilities, radio, and television.	Use the new technologies that led to European exploration and the changes brought on by the Scientific Revolution as discussed in Chapter 18 as an opportunity to address this strand.
E. Seek reasonable and ethical solutions to problems that arise when scientific advancements and social norms or values come into conflict.	Use the strains caused by European exploration and the Scientific Revolution as discussed in Chapter 18 as an opportunity to address this strand.
IX. *Global Connections* As countries grow more interdependent, understanding global connections among world societies becomes important. Students will analyze emerging global issues in many different fields. They will also investigate relationships among the different cultures of the world. In the middle years, students analyze the interactions among states and countries and respond to global events and changes.	
A. Describe instances in which language, art, music, belief systems, and other cultural elements can facilitate global understanding or cause misunderstanding.	102, 310, 358, 364, 594, 650, 661, 737
B. Analyze examples of conflict, cooperation, and interdependence among groups, societies, and nations.	92, 102, 104, 294, 364, 366, 390, 473, 570, 585, 594, 597, 598, 669, 690, 702, 752–754
C. Describe and analyze the effects of changing technologies on the global community.	574, 669, 729, 832–836
D. Explore the causes, consequences, and possible solutions to persistent, contemporary, and emerging global issues, such as health, security, resource allocation, economic development, and environmental quality.	375, 668, 889, 890
E. Describe and explain the relationships and tensions between national sovereignty and global interests in such matters as territory, natural resources, trade, use of technology, and welfare of people.	148, 436, 695, 703, 752–754, 862
F. Demonstrate understanding of concerns, standards, issues, and conflicts related to universal human rights.	102, 558, 603, 872, 886
G. Identify and describe the roles of international and multinational organizations.	362, 367, 865, 889

Theme and Performance Expectation	Student Pages
X. *Civic Ideals & Practices* Understanding civic ideals and practices is crucial to complete participation in society and is the main purpose of social studies. Students will learn about civic participation and the role of the citizen within his or her community, country, and world. By the middle grades, students will broaden their understanding to analyze and evaluate relationships between civic ideals and practices.	
A. Examine the origins and continuing influence of key ideals of the democratic republican form of government, such as individual human dignity, liberty, justice, equality, and the rule of law.	83, 100, 145, 173, 182, 268, 276, 321, 326, 537, 543, 552, 560, 700, 702, 703, 746
B. Identify and interpret sources and examples of the rights and responsibilities of citizens.	32, 46, 175, 237, 269, 282, 337, 535, 536, 556, 700
C. Locate, access, analyze, organize, and apply information about selected public issues—recognizing and explaining multiple points of view.	251, 297, 397
D. Practice forms of civic discussion and participation consistent with the ideals of citizens in a democratic republic.	The rise of democracy in ancient Greece is discussed in Chapter 4. The rise of the Roman Republic is discussed in Chapter 8. Use these opportunities to address this strand.
E. Explain and analyze various forms of citizen action that influence public policy decisions.	52, 102, 699, 882
F. Identify and explain the roles of formal and informal political actors in influencing and shaping public policy and decision-making.	251, 853
G. Analyze the influence of diverse forms of public opinion on the development of public policy and decision-making.	Use the Athenian democratic system discussed in Chapter 4 and the Roman political system discussed in Chapter 8 to address this strand.
H. Analyze the effectiveness of selected public policies and citizen behaviors in realizing the stated ideals of a democratic republican form of government.	276, 868
I. Explain the relationship between policy statements and action plans used to address issues of public concern.	261, 297, 882
J. Examine strategies designed to strengthen the "common good," which consider a range of options for citizen action.	Use the discussions of citizenship in ancient Greece as discussed in Chapter 4 and ancient Rome as discussed in Chapter 8 to address this strand.

Scope and Sequence

Each section of *Journey Across Time* focuses on one central theme, although related themes also appear in each section. The section numbers highlighted here in red indicate the central theme that is key to that section. Related themes are listed in black.

Chapter	1	2	3	4
Politics and History	Sections 2, 3	Sections 1, 2, 3, 4	Sections 2, 3	Sections 1, 2, 3, 4
The Role of Ideas	Sections 1, 2, 3	Sections 1, 2, 4	Sections 1, 3	Sections 1, 2, 4
Economics and History	Sections 1, 2	Sections 3, 4	Section 2	Sections 1, 2, 3, 4
The Importance of Cultural Development	Sections 1, 2	Sections 1, 2, 3, 4	Sections 1, 2, 3	Sections 1, 2, 3, 4
Religion in History	Sections 1, 2	Sections 2, 3	Sections 1, 2, 3	Sections 1, 3
The Role of Individuals	Sections 2, 3	Sections 1, 2, 3	Sections 1, 2, 3	Sections 1, 2, 3, 4
The Impact of Science and Technology	Sections 1, 2, 3	Sections 1, 2, 3, 4	Section 1	Sections 1, 3
The Environment and History	Sections 1, 2	Sections 1, 3	Section 1	Sections 1, 3

5	6	7	8	9	10	11
Sections 2, 3	Sections 1, 2, 3	Sections 1, 2, 3	Sections 1, 2, 3, 4	Sections 2, 3	Sections 1, 2, 3	Sections 1, 2, 3
Sections 1, 2, 4	Sections 1, 2, 3	Sections 1, 2, 3	Sections 1, 2, 3, 4	Sections 1, 2, 3	Sections 1, 2, 3	Section 1, 2, 3
Section 2	Sections 1, 3	Sections 2, 3	Sections 1, 2, 3, 4	Sections 1, 2, 3	Section 1	Sections 1, 2, 3
Sections 1, 3, 4	Sections 1, 2, 3	Sections 1, 2, 3	Sections 1, 2, 3, 4	Sections 1, 2, 3	Sections 1, 2, 3	Sections 1, 2, 3
Section 1	Sections 2, 3	Sections 1, 3	Section 1	Sections 1, 2, 3	Sections 1, 2, 3	Sections 1, 2, 3
Sections 1, 2, 3, 4	Sections 2, 3	Sections 1, 2, 3	Sections 1, 2, 3, 4	Sections 1, 2, 3	Sections 1, 2, 3	Sections 1, 2, 3
Sections 2, 4	Sections 1, 3	Sections 1, 2, 3	Sections 1, 4	Section 1		Section 3
Section 3	Sections 1, 3	Sections 1, 2, 3	Sections 1, 2	Sections 2, 3	Sections 2, 3	Sections 1, 2

Chapter	12	13	14	15	16
Themes and Concepts					
Politics and History	Sections 1, 3, 4	Sections 1, 2, 3	Sections 1, 2, 3	Sections 1, 2, 3, 5	Sections 1, 2
The Role of Ideas	Sections 1, 2, 3, 4	Sections 1, 2, 3	Sections 1, 2, 3	Sections 1, 2, 3, 4	Sections 1, 2, 3
Economics and History	Sections 1, 2, 3, 4	Sections 1, 2, 3	Sections 2, 3	Sections 2, 3, 5	Sections 1, 2, 3
The Importance of Cultural Development	Sections 1, 2, 3, 4	Sections 1, 2, 3	Sections 1, 2, 3	Sections 1, 2, 3, 4, 5	Sections 1, 2, 3
Religion in History	Sections 1, 4	Sections 1, 2, 3	Sections 1, 2, 3	Sections 1, 3, 4, 5	Sections 2, 3
The Role of Individuals	Sections 1, 2, 3, 4	Sections 1, 2, 3	Sections 1, 2, 3	Sections 1, 3, 4, 5	Sections 2, 3
The Impact of Science and Technology	Sections 1, 2, 3	Section 1	Section 3	Section 2	Sections 1, 3
The Environment and History	Sections 1, 3, 4	Sections 1, 3	Sections 1, 2	Sections 1, 2, 3, 5	Sections 1, 2

17	18	19	20	21	22
Sections 1, 2, 3, 4	Section 1, 3, 4	Sections 1, 4	Sections 1, 2, 3	Sections 1, 4, 5	Sections 1, 2
Section 1, 2, 3, 4	Section 1, 2, 3, 4	Section 2	Section 1	Sections 1, 5	Sections 3, 4
Section 1, 3	Section 1, 3, 4	Sections 2, 3	Section 1	Sections 1, 4	Sections 1, 2
Section 1, 2, 3, 4	Section 1, 2, 3, 4	Sections 2, 3	Sections 1, 2, 3	Sections 1, 5	Section 4
Section 1, 2, 3, 4	Sections 3, 4	Section 1	Section 2	Sections 3, 5	Sections 1, 2, 4
Section 1, 2, 3, 4	Sections 1, 2, 3, 4	Sections 2, 3	Sections 2, 4	Sections 1, 2, 4, 5	Section 1
Section 2	Sections 1, 2	Sections 2, 3	Sections 3, 4	Sections 1, 3, 4	Sections 3, 4
Sections 1, 2	Sections 1, 4	Sections 1, 2, 3, 4	Section 4	Section 3	Section 1, 2

Be an Active Reader

Think about your textbook as a tool that helps you learn more about the world around you. It is an example of nonfiction writing—it describes real-life events, people, ideas, and places. Here is a menu of reading strategies that will help you become a better textbook reader. As you come to passages in your textbook that you do not understand, refer to these reading strategies for help.

1 Before You Read

Set a Purpose
- Why are you reading the textbook?
- How does the subject relate to your life?
- How might you be able to use what you learn in your own life?

Preview
- Read the chapter title to find what the topic will be.
- Read the subtitles to see what you will learn about the topic.
- Skim the photos, charts, graphs, or maps. How do they support the topic?
- Look for vocabulary words that are boldfaced. How are they defined?

Draw From Your Own Background
- What have you read or heard concerning new information on the topic?
- How is the new information different from what you already know?
- How will the information that you already know help you understand the new information?

Question

- What is the main idea?
- How do the photos, charts, graphs, and maps support the main idea?

Connect

- Think about people, places, and events in your own life. Are there any similarities with those in your textbook?
- Can you relate the textbook information to other areas of your life?

Predict

- Predict events or outcomes by using clues and information that you already know.
- Change your predictions as you read and gather new information.

Visualize

- Pay careful attention to details and descriptions.
- Create graphic organizers to show relationships that you find in the information.

Look for Clues As You Read

Comparison and Contrast Sentences

- Look for clue words and phrases that signal comparison, such as *similarly, just as, both, in common, also,* and *too.*
- Look for clue words and phrases that signal contrast, such as *on the other hand, in contrast to, however, different, instead of, rather than, but,* and *unlike.*

Cause-and-Effect Sentences

- Look for clue words and phrases such as *because, as a result, therefore, that is why, since, so, for this reason,* and *consequently.*

Chronological Sentences

- Look for clue words and phrases such as *after, before, first, next, last, during, finally, earlier, later, since,* and *then.*

3 After You Read

Summarize

- Describe the main idea and how the details support it.
- Use your own words to explain what you have read.

Assess

- What was the main idea?
- Did the text clearly support the main idea?
- Did you learn anything new from the material?
- Can you use this new information in other school subjects or at home?
- What other sources could you use to find more information about the topic?

Previewing Your Textbook

Follow the reading road map through the next few pages to learn about using your textbook. Knowing how your text is organized will help you discover interesting events, fascinating people, and faraway places.

Units

Your textbook is divided into units. Each unit begins with four pages of information to help you begin your study of the topics.

WHY IT'S IMPORTANT

Each unit begins with a **preview** of important events and *Why It's Important* to read about them.

TIME LINE

A time line shows you **when** the events in this unit happened. It also compares events and people from different places.

MAP

This map shows you where the events in this unit happened.

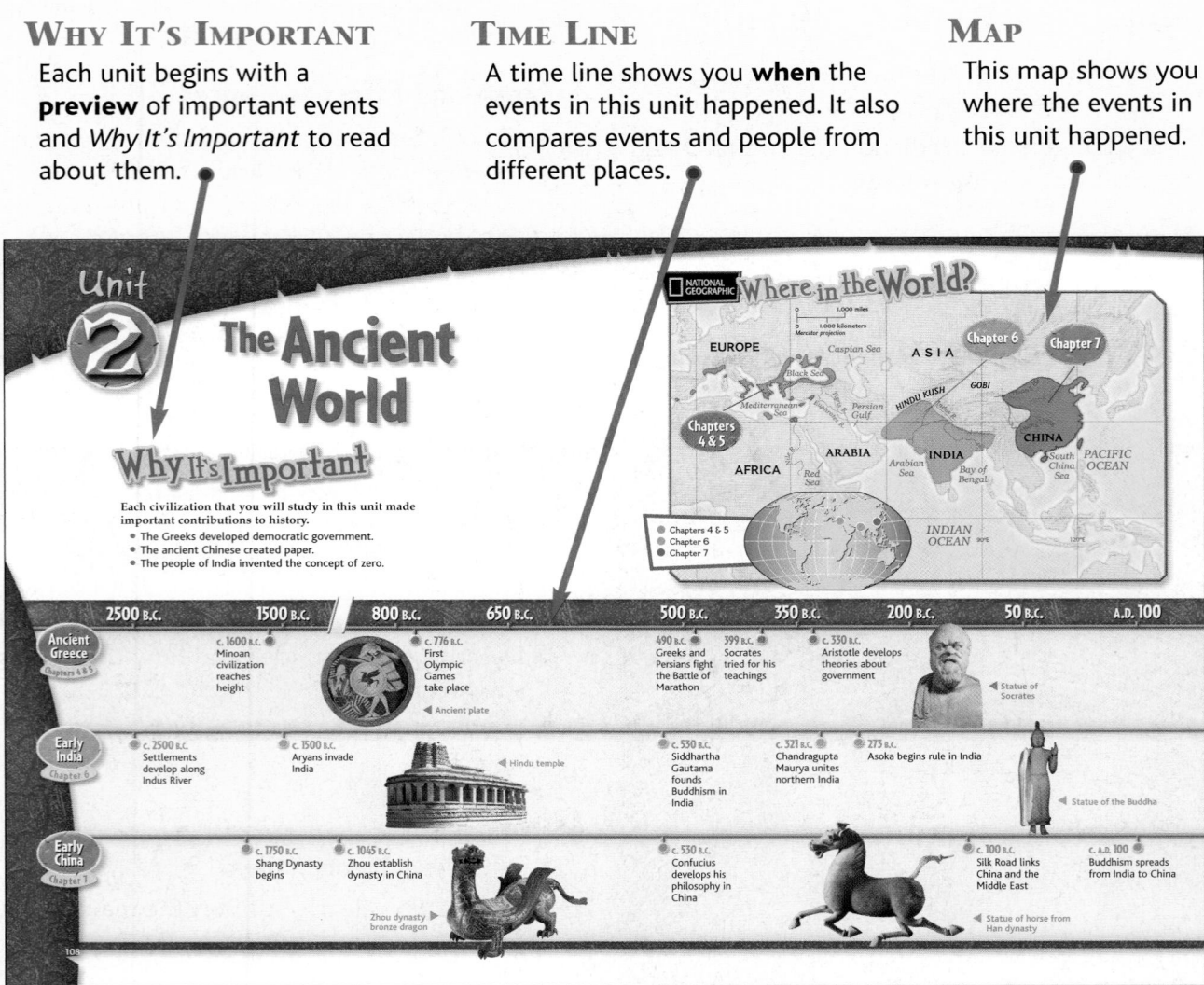

Chapters

Each unit of *Journey Across Time* is divided into chapters. Each chapter starts by giving you some background information about what you will be reading.

CHAPTER TITLE
The chapter title tells you the **main topic** you will be reading about.

CHAPTER PREVIEW
The **preview** describes what you will be reading about in this chapter.

HISTORY ONLINE
This tells you where you can go **online** for more information.

WHEN AND WHERE?
Here you can see **when** and **where** events in this chapter happened.

SUMMARIES
Summary statements give you the **main idea** in each section.

FOLDABLES™
Use the *Foldables* to **take notes** as you read.

Previewing Your Textbook

Chapter Reading Skill

Because reading about Social Studies is different than reading a novel or magazine, every chapter offers help with reading skills.

READING STRATEGY

This shows you what *Reading Skill* you will be learning about—**making connections.**

PRACTICE IT!

Next comes an easy-to-follow **practice** activity.

WRITING

Writing about what you read will help you remember the event.

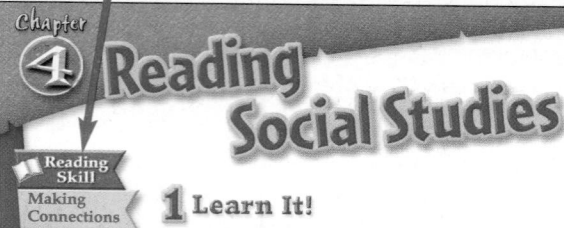

Chapter

4 Reading Social Studies

Reading Skill
Making Connections

1 Learn It!

Use What You Know

Unlock meaning by making a connection between what you read and what you already know. Your own experiences can help you understand words or ideas that are unfamiliar. Read the paragraph below. Make a connection between a Greek **agora** and a place that is familiar to you.

Do you know what an **agora** looks like?

> Below the acropolis was an open area called an agora (A • guh • ruh). This space had two functions: it was both a **market** and a place where people could meet and debate issues.
>
> — *from page 122*

You know what a *market* looks like. Can you also visualize *a place where people could meet*? If so, then you have a good idea of what an agora might look like.

Reading Tip

Try to create a picture in your mind as you read. Imagine a mini-movie as you "see" what the author is describing.

114

2 Practice It!

Making the Connection

Read the following paragraph from Chapter 4. What ideas can you connect to your own experiences? Use the questions below to help you begin a class discussion about things in your life that relate to life in ancient Greece.

Read to Write
Choose one of the connections from your discussion. Write a paragraph to explain why you made such a connection. Use vivid details.

> At age 20, Spartan men entered the regular army. The men remained in military barracks for 10 more years. They ate all their meals in dining halls with other soldiers. A typical meal was a vile-tasting dish called black broth—pork boiled in animal blood, salt, and vinegar.
>
> Spartans returned home at age 30 but stayed in the army until age 60. They continued to train for combat. They expected to either win on the battlefield or die, but never to surrender. One Spartan mother ordered her son to "Come home carrying your shield or being carried on it."
>
> —*from pages 126–127*

- Do you have any family members or friends who are 20 years old? What would they say if they were required to serve in the army for 40 years?
- Have you ever seen or tasted food that looks like "black broth"?

3 Apply It!

As you read the chapter, choose five words or phrases that make a connection to something you already know.

115

READING TIP

This **Reading Tip** tells you more about making connections.

APPLY IT!

Here is an opportunity to **apply** what you have learned.

Previewing Your Textbook

Sections

A Section is a division, or part, of the chapter. The first page of the Section, the Section Opener, helps you set a purpose for reading.

GET READY TO READ!
Read the **connection** between what you already know and what you are about to read.

MAPS
Maps help you learn how **geography** and history are related.

MAIN IDEAS
Preview the **main ideas** in each section.

READING CHECK
This is a **self-check** to see if you understand the main ideas.

SECTION REVIEW
Review the main ideas and answer the questions.

Previewing Your Textbook

Special Features

Look for special features that help history come alive.

YOU DECIDE . . .
Imagine you were there and could give your **opinion.**

You Decide . . .

Alexander the Great: Villain or Hero?

Villain

Was Alexander the Great really great? Or was he an evil conqueror? Those who see him as bloodthirsty and cruel give this as evidence against Alexander. They say he
- destroyed Persepolis
- attacked Tyre, killing 10,000 people and enslaving 30,000
- treated his slaves harshly
- ordered the murder of several close advisers.

Many legends about Alexander been told. One historian found account to support the "villain i

"The following is my favour which is found all the way from Kazakhstan: Iskander [Alexander ally a devil and he had horns. was long and wavy and the never seen. Only his barbers feared they could not keep th he killed them when they di last barber pretended not t kept the secret. Eventually could bear and, as he one, he ran called dow 'Iskander h in the bottc were whis [used in fl echoed th went rou world."

180   ▲ Alexander the Great (at far left)

Biography

PERICLES
c. 495–429 B.C.

Pericles was born just outside Athens, to a wealthy and powerful family. He received his education from philosophers. As a young man, he was known for his skill with words. Later, when he became a political leader, he strongly supported democracy.

Although he was from a wealthy family himself, he believed that citizenship should not be limited to the wealthy and powerful. He made changes to take power from the few and give it to the many. However, in describing Pericles's rule over Athens, Greek historian Thucydides wrote "In name democracy, but in fact the rule of one man."

The "Age of Pericles" was Athens's Golden Age, and the city blossomed under his leadership. Pericles wanted Athens to be a model for the world. He made it a centerpiece of art, philosophy, and democracy.

Pericles' goal was to make Athens a city that Greeks could be proud of. He hired hundreds of workers to construct public buildings in Athens. The most well known is the Parthenon. Based on the value of money today, it cost about $3 billion to build. Workers hauled 20,000 tons of marble from a nearby mountain and spent almost 15 years completing it.

Pericles was a private person. He avoided being in public as much as possible. He spent most of his time alone, with family, or with close friends. He married and had three sons. In 429 B.C. Pericles died from the plague.

Pericles ▶

"Athens...is the school of Greece."
—Pericles, as recorded by Thucydides

Then and Now
Consider what Thucydides wrote about Pericles' rule in Athens. Do research to find out how the U.S. Constitution ensures that our government is not dominated by one leader.

▲ The Parthenon sits at the top of the Acropolis.

141

BIOGRAPHY
Read more about famous **people.**

Greek Drama

Main Idea Greek drama still shapes entertainment today.

Reading Focus Think about your favorite movie. How would you describe it? Is it a tragedy? Is it a comedy? Read to find out how Greek plays still influence our entertainment.

What is drama (DRAH•muh)? Drama is a story told by actors who pretend to be characters in the story. In a drama, actors speak, show emotion, and imitate the actions of the characters they represent.

Today's movies, plays, and television shows are all examples of drama.

Tragedies and Comedies The Greeks performed plays in outdoor theaters as part of their religious festivals. They developed two kinds of dramas—comedies and tragedies.

In a **tragedy** (TRA•juh•dee), a person struggles to overcome difficulties but fails. As a result, the story has an unhappy ending. Early Greek tragedies presented people in a struggle against their fate. Later Greek tragedies showed how a person's character flaws caused him or her to fail.

Linking Past & Present
The Theater

THEN Tragedies and comedies were staged at a theater on the slopes of the Acropolis in Athens. The plays included music and dance. Greek actors wore costumes and held large masks. The masks told the audience who the actor was supposed to be—a king, a soldier, or a god. All the actors were men, even those playing female parts.

▲ A modern-day play

NOW Actors today include both men and women—and even children and animals. Special effects and makeup have replaced handheld masks. Music in modern theater is sometimes just as important as the actors' words. *If you watched a Greek play, what might it tell you about life in ancient Greece?*

▲ Ruins of a Greek theater

160   CHAPTER 5   Greek Civilization

The Way It Was
NATIONAL GEOGRAPHIC

Focus on Everyday Life

Women's Duties In ancient Athens, a woman's place was in the home. Her two main responsibilities were caring for the household and raising children. The Greek writer Xenophon (ZEH•nuh•fuhn) recorded a man's explanation of women's duties.

"Your duty will be to remain indoors and send out those servants whose work is outside, and supervise those who are to work indoors . . . and take care that the sum laid by for a year be not spent in a month. And when wool is brought to you, you must see that cloaks are made for those who want them. You must see that the dry corn is in good condition for making food."

—Xenophon, *Memorabilia and Oeconomicus*

The second of each home was the women's quarters. An Athenian woman lived there with her children. She was expected to keep her children well and happy. She encouraged them to learn sports and play with toys, and taught them how to interact with friends and family members. Although boys left home at age seven to attend school, girls stayed with their mothers, learning how to care for a house and children.

▲ Greek woman and servant

Connecting to the Past
1. Why do you think women and children lived on the second floor of the home?
2. Over what areas of life did an Athenian woman have authority?

CONNECTING PAST & PRESENT
See the connections between the **past** and the **present.**

T50

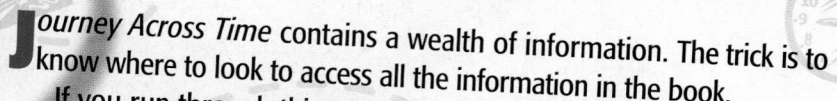

Scavenger Hunt

Journey Across Time contains a wealth of information. The trick is to know where to look to access all the information in the book.

If you run through this scavenger hunt exercise with your teacher or parents, you will see how the textbook is organized, and how to get the most out of your reading and study time. Let's get started!

1 What civilizations are discussed in Unit 3?
Ancient Rome, the Christians, the Islamic civilization

2 What is the topic of Chapter 10?
The Romans

3 Who is the topic of the *Biography* on page 272?
Lucius Quinctius Cincinnatus

4 What *Reading Skill* will you be learning about on pages 340–341?
Sequence Clues

5 What does the *Foldables™ Study Organizer* on page 369 ask you to do?
Take notes on the people and places of the Islamic civilization

6 How are the key terms in Chapter 9, Section 2, *plague* and *inflation*, highlighted in the text?
Highlighted in yellow

7 There are four types of Web site boxes in Chapter 11. One box previews the chapter, one suggests a Web activity, and one provides help with homework. What does the fourth box provide help with?
Preparing for the chapter test

8 What do you find on page 365?
Reading Review

9 What is the topic of *The Way It Was* feature on page 389?
Muslim carpets and weavings

10 What is the topic of the map on page 269?
Growth of the Roman Republic 500–146 B.C.

REFERENCE ATLAS

NATIONAL GEOGRAPHIC

ATLAS KEY

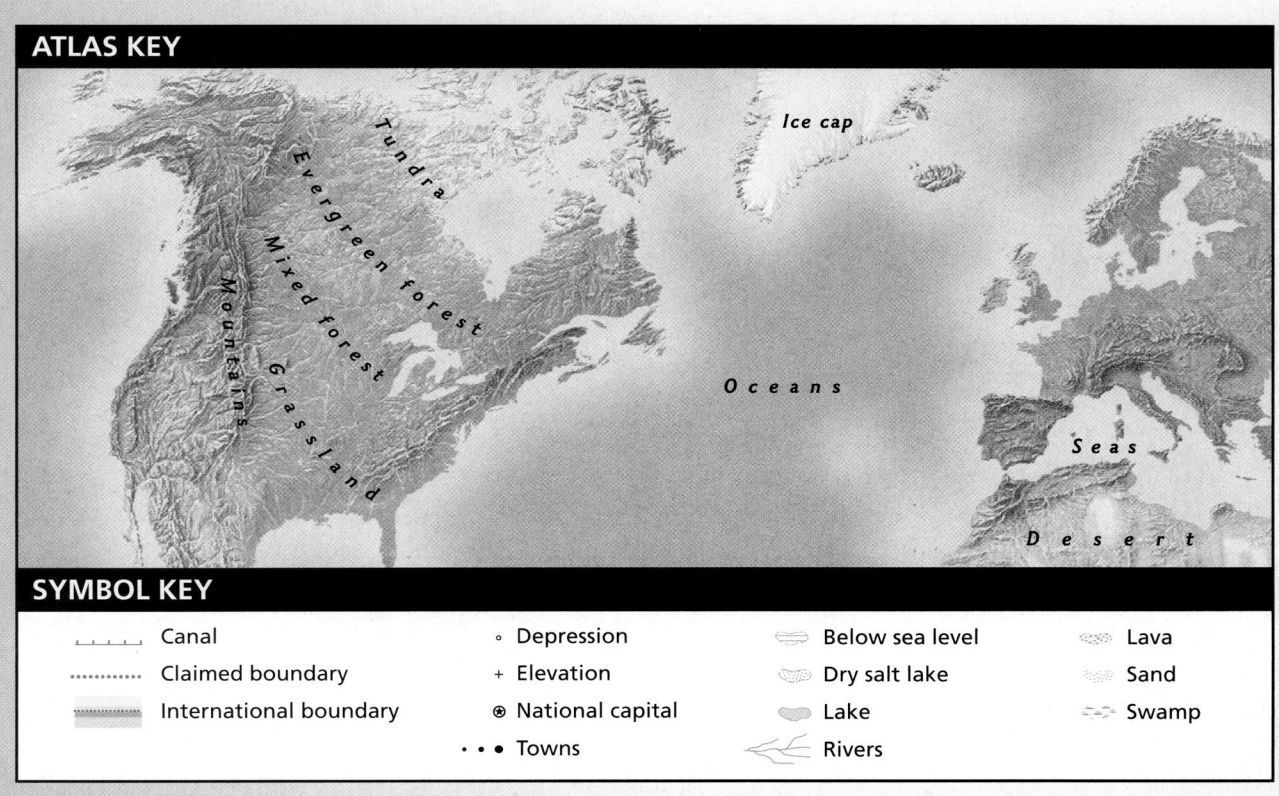

SYMBOL KEY

⊔⊔⊔⊔	Canal	°	Depression	�	Below sea level	≈≈	Lava
....	Claimed boundary	+	Elevation	≈≈	Dry salt lake	≈≈	Sand
▓▓▓▓▓	International boundary	⊛	National capital	≈	Lake	⊃⊃	Swamp
		• • •	Towns	≈≈	Rivers		

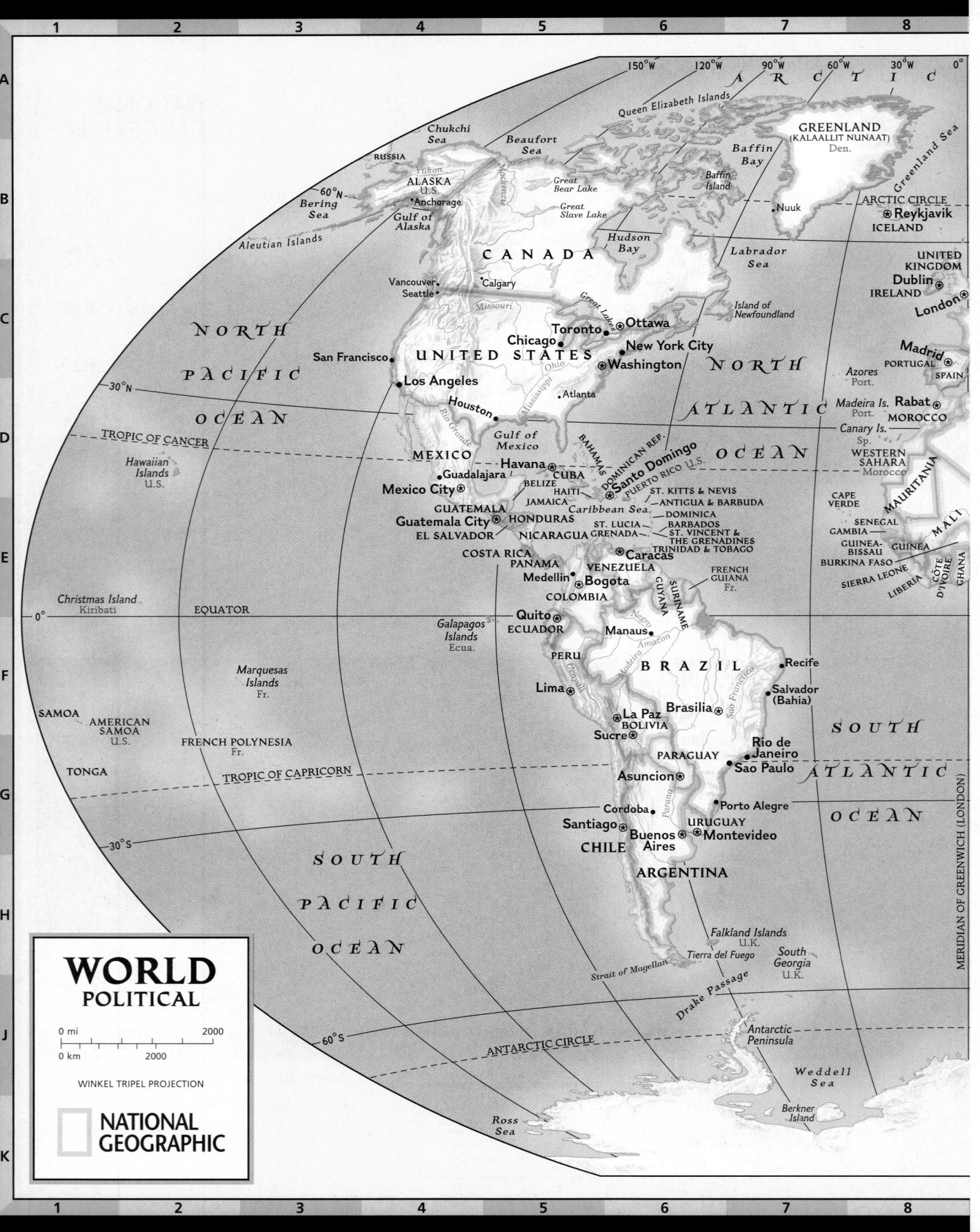

WORLD
POLITICAL

0 mi   2000
0 km   2000

WINKEL TRIPEL PROJECTION

NATIONAL GEOGRAPHIC

A

B

C

D

E

F

G

H

J

K

O C E A N

Franz Josef Land
30°E   60°E   90°E   120°E   150°E
Svalbard
Nor.
Barents Sea
Novaya Zemlya
Kara Sea
Severnaya Zemlya
New Siberian Islands
Laptev Sea
East Siberian Sea

Norwegian Sea
NORWAY
SWEDEN
FINLAND
Oslo ⊛
EST.
LATVIA
LITH.
St. Petersburg
Yekaterinburg
Omsk
Novosibirsk
Yakutsk
60°N
Bering Sea
Kamchatka Peninsula

DENMARK
NETH.
BELG.
GERMANY
POLAND
BELARUS
⊛ Moscow
Samara
Ural
Volga
Astana ⊛
Sea of Okhotsk
Sakhalin

⊛ Kiev
UKRAINE
CZECH REP.
SLOVAKIA MOLD.
AUST. SLOV.
CROAT.
B.&H.
ROMANIA AZERBAIJAN
SERB. AND MONT.
BULGARIA GEORGIA
MACED.
ALBANIA
GREECE
ARMENIA
⊛ Ankara
TURKEY
CYPRUS
LEBANON
ISRAEL
SYRIA
JORDAN
IRAQ
KUWAIT
BAHRAIN
QATAR
U.A.E.
KAZAKHSTAN
Aral Sea
Caspian Sea
Tashkent
⊛ Almaty
⊛ Bishkek
UZBEKISTAN
KYRGYZSTAN
TURKMENISTAN
TAJIKISTAN
Ashgabat ⊛
Dushanbe ⊛
AFGHANISTAN
Tehran ⊛
IRAN
⊛ Baghdad
Islamabad ⊛
Lahore
PAKISTAN
Delhi
New Delhi
Ulaanbaatar ⊛
MONGOLIA
Harbin
Shenyang
Beijing ⊛
Tianjin
CHINA
Chengdu
Yellow
Yangtze
Wuhan
NORTH KOREA
⊛ Pyongyang
⊛ Seoul
SOUTH KOREA
Shanghai
Hokkaido
Sapporo
Honshu
JAPAN
⊛ Tokyo
Osaka
Kyushu
30°N

SWITZ.
FRANCE
⊛ Paris
ITALY
Rome ⊛
Black Sea
Algiers ⊛
TUNISIA
Mediterranean Sea
⊛ Tripoli
Cairo ⊛
EGYPT
Red Sea
Nile
⊛ Riyadh
SAUDI ARABIA
Muscat
OMAN
Karachi
Mumbai
Hyderabad
INDIA
Bangalore
Chennai
NEPAL
Brahmaputra
BHUTAN
BANGLADESH
Dhaka ⊛
Kolkata
Ganges
MYANMAR
(BURMA)
Yangon
LAOS
THAILAND
Bangkok ⊛
Guangzhou
Hong Kong
Hanoi ⊛
VIETNAM
Taipei
TAIWAN
The People's Republic of China claims Taiwan as its 23rd province.
NORTHERN MARIANA ISLANDS
U.S.
Philippine Sea
PHILIPPINES
Manila ⊛
Luzon
MARSHALL ISLANDS
NORTH
PACIFIC
OCEAN

ALGERIA
LIBYA
NIGER
Niamey
CHAD
ERITREA
Khartoum ⊛
SUDAN
N'Djamena ⊛
Sanaa ⊛
YEMEN
DJIBOUTI
Yemen
Socotra
Arabian Sea
Colombo
SRI LANKA
MALDIVES
Bay of Bengal
Phnom Penh ⊛
CAMBODIA
Ho Chi Minh City
South China Sea
Hainan
Mindanao
PALAU
FEDERATED STATES OF MICRONESIA
KIRIBATI

NIGERIA
Lagos
BENIN
TOGO
CENTRAL AFRICAN REPUBLIC
Bangui ⊛
CAMEROON
EQ. GUINEA
SAO TOME & PRINCIPE
GABON
CONGO
CABINDA
Ang.
DEM. REP. OF THE CONGO
Brazzaville ⊛
Kinshasa ⊛
UGANDA
RWANDA
BURUNDI
KENYA
Nairobi ⊛
SEYCHELLES
EQUATOR
BRUNEI
Kuala Lumpur
MALAYSIA
SINGAPORE
Borneo
Celebes
Sumatra
Java
Jakarta ⊛
Surabaya
INDONESIA
New Guinea
PAPUA NEW GUINEA
Port Moresby ⊛
SOLOMON ISLANDS
NAURU
TUVALU

Luanda ⊛
ANGOLA
ZAMBIA
Lusaka
MALAWI
MOZAMBIQUE
Zambezi
TANZANIA
Dodoma ⊛
Dar es Salaam
COMOROS
Antananarivo ⊛
MADAGASCAR
MAURITIUS
Reunion Fr.
INDIAN
OCEAN
TIMOR-LESTE (EAST TIMOR)
Arafura Sea
Darwin
Coral Sea
VANUATU
FIJI ISLANDS

NAMIBIA
Windhoek ⊛
Harare ⊛
ZIMBABWE
BOTSWANA
Gaborone ⊛
Pretoria ⊛
Maputo ⊛
SWAZILAND
Bloemfontein ⊛
SOUTH AFRICA
LESOTHO
Cape Town ⊛
Orange
Kerguelen Islands Fr.
AUSTRALIA
Perth
Darling
Murray
Brisbane
Sydney
Canberra ⊛
Melbourne
Tasmania
Tasman Sea
SOUTH
PACIFIC
OCEAN
New Caledonia Fr.
North Island
Auckland
60°S
NEW ZEALAND
Wellington ⊛
South Island

A N T A R C T I C A
Ross Sea

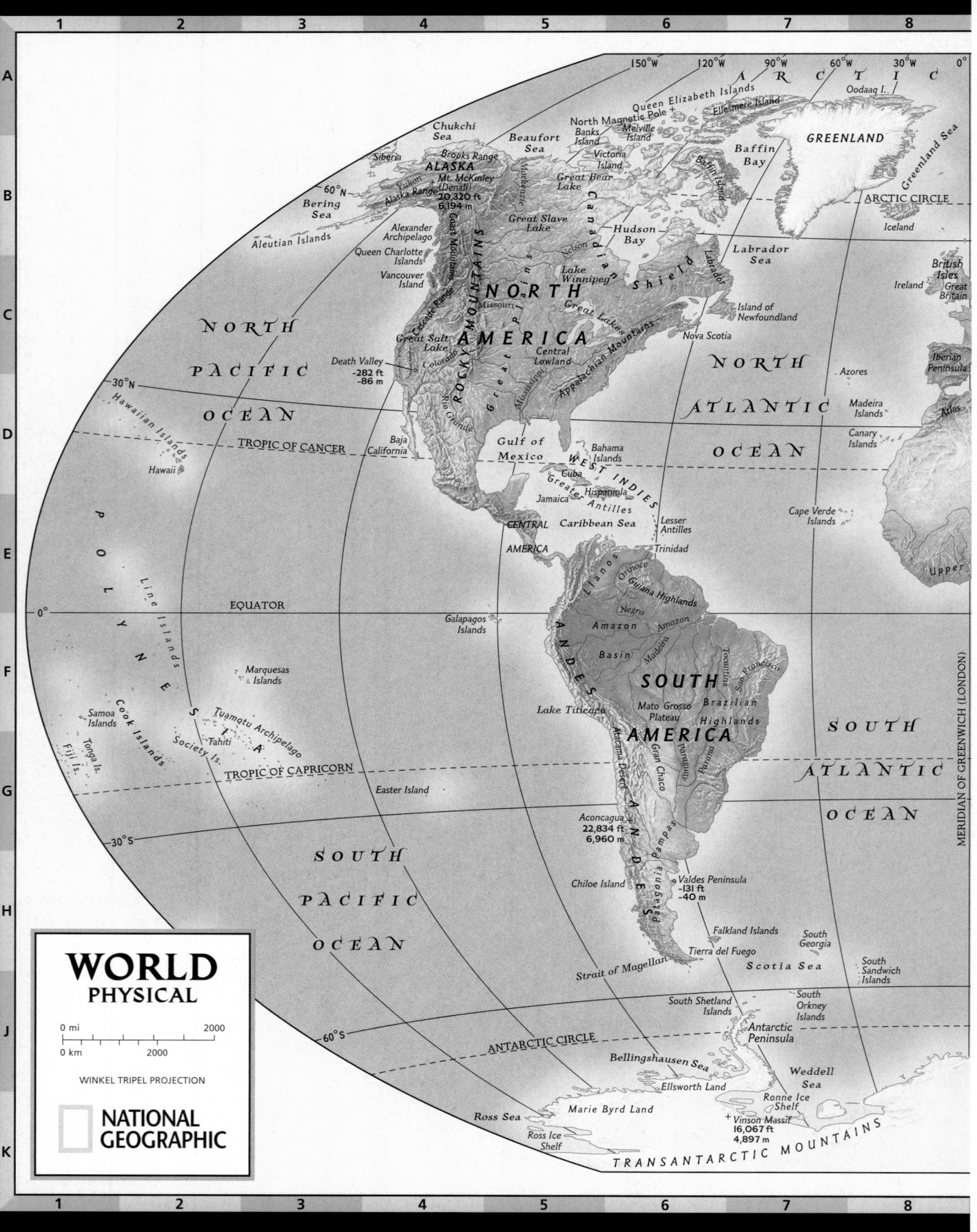

WORLD
PHYSICAL

0 mi — 2000
0 km — 2000

WINKEL TRIPEL PROJECTION

NATIONAL GEOGRAPHIC

O C E A N

30°E 60°E 90°E 120°E 150°E

Svalbard

Barents Sea

Novaya Zemlya

Kara Sea

Laptev Sea

East Siberian Sea

Norwegian Sea

Scandinavia

Northern European Plain

Baltic Sea

Ural Mountains

Ob

West Siberian Plain

Yenisey

Central Siberian Plateau

Lena

Angara

Lena

Amur

60°N

Bering Sea

Kamchatka Peninsula

Aleutian Is.

North Sea

EUROPE

A S I A

Elbrus 18,510 ft 5,642 m

The Steppes

Aral Sea

Ob

Irtysh

Altay Mountains

Tian Shan

GOBI A

Lake Baikal

Hokkaido

Kuril Islands

Sea of Okhotsk

Japan

Sea of Japan (East Sea)

Honshu

NORTH

Corsica Sardinia

Alps

Danube

Caucasus Mts.

Black Sea

Caspian Sea

Taklimakan Desert

Kunlun Shan

Tian Shan

Yellow

North China Plain

Korea

Yellow Sea

PACIFIC

Sicily

Mediterranean Sea

Cyprus

Zagros Mountains

Plateau of Tibet

Indus

HIMALAYA

Brahmaputra

Yangtze

East China Sea

Nampo Shoto

30°N

Mountains

Dead Sea -1,349 ft -411 m

Mt. Everest 29,035 ft 8,850 m

Ganges

Salween

Taiwan

Ryukyu Islands

OCEAN

SAHARA

Libyan Desert

Red Sea

ARABIAN PENINSULA

Arabian Sea

INDIA

Deccan Plateau

Bay of Bengal

Mekong

Hainan

Indochina Peninsula

Luzon

Philippine Islands

South China Sea

Philippine Sea

Mariana Islands

S A H E L

Nile

Blue Nile

Gulf of Aden

Andaman Islands

Andaman Sea

M I C R O N E S I A

AFRICA

Niger

White Nile

Ethiopian Highlands

Somali Peninsula

Sri Lanka

Nicobar Is.

Malay Peninsula

Marshall Islands

Guinea

Maldive Islands

EQUATOR

Sumatra

Borneo

Indonesia

Celebes

Moluccas

New Guinea

Bismarck Archipelago

Gilbert Islands

Gulf of Guinea

Congo

Lake Victoria

Kilimanjaro 19,340 ft 5,895 m

Greater Sunda Islands

Solomon Islands

M E L A N E S I A

Lower Guinea

Congo Basin

Lake Tanganyika

Seychelles

Java

Arafura Sea

New Caledonia

Vanuatu

Fiji Islands

Zambezi

Madagascar

Coral Sea

SOUTH

Namib Desert

Mascarene Islands

INDIAN

Great Sandy Desert

AUSTRALIA

Great Dividing Range

PACIFIC

Kalahari Desert

Drakensberg

OCEAN

Lake Eyre -52 ft, -16 m

Great Victoria Desert

Darling

OCEAN

Murray

Mt. Kosciuszko 7,310 ft 2,228 m

Tasman Sea

North Island

NEW

Kerguelen Islands

Tasmania

ZEALAND

South Island

Auckland Islands

60°S

South Magnetic Pole

Queen Maud Land

ANTARCTICA

Transantarctic Mountains

Victoria Land

Ross Sea

Ross Ice Shelf

NORTH AMERICA
POLITICAL

0 mi — 1000
0 km — 1000

AZIMUTHAL EQUIDISTANT PROJECTION

NATIONAL GEOGRAPHIC

1. BAJA CALIFORNIA
2. BAJA CALIFORNIA SUR
3. SONORA
4. CHIHUAHUA
5. SINALOA
6. DURANGO
7. COAHUILA
8. NUEVO LEON
9. ZACATECAS
10. TAMAULIPAS
11. NAYARIT
12. AGUASCALIENTES
13. SAN LUIS POTOSI
14. JALISCO
15. GUANAJUATO
16. QUERETARO
17. HIDALGO
18. COLIMA
19. MICHOACAN
20. MEXICO
21. DISTRITO FEDERAL
22. TLAXCALA
23. MORELOS
24. PUEBLA
25. VERACRUZ
26. GUERRERO
27. OAXACA
28. TABASCO
29. CHIAPAS
30. CAMPECHE
31. QUINTANA ROO
32. YUCATAN

NORTH AMERICA

PHYSICAL

0 mi   1000

0 km   1000

AZIMUTHAL EQUIDISTANT PROJECTION

NATIONAL GEOGRAPHIC

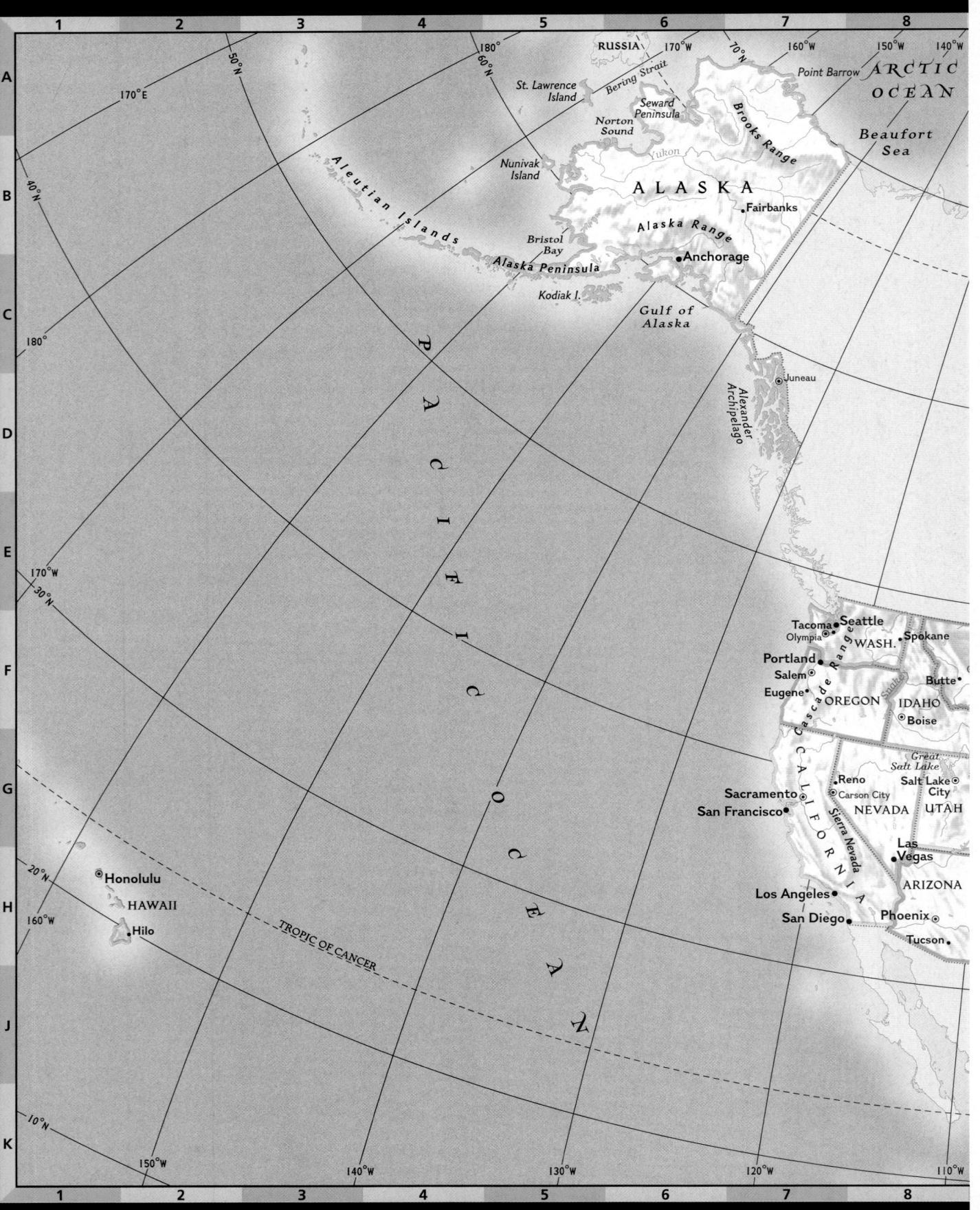

	1	2	3	4	5	6	7	8

A

170°E   50°N   180°   60°N   **RUSSIA**   170°W   70°N   160°W   150°W   140°W

St. Lawrence Island

Bering Strait

Point Barrow   *ARCTIC OCEAN*

Seward Peninsula

Norton Sound

Yukon

Brooks Range

Beaufort Sea

B

40°N

Aleutian Islands

Nunivak Island

A L A S K A

Alaska Range

•Fairbanks

Bristol Bay

Alaska Peninsula

•Anchorage

C

180°

Kodiak I.

Gulf of Alaska

Juneau

Alexander Archipelago

D

P a c i f i c

E

170°W

30°N

F

Tacoma• •Seattle
Olympia◎ •Spokane
WASH.

Portland•
Salem◎   Butte•
Eugene•   *Cascade Range*
OREGON   IDAHO
◎Boise

Great Salt Lake

G

170°W

O c e a n

Sacramento◎   •Reno   Salt Lake◎ City
  ◎Carson City
San Francisco•   NEVADA   UTAH

Sierra Nevada

Las •Vegas

ARIZONA

H

20°N

◎Honolulu

HAWAII

160°W

•Hilo

Los Angeles•

San Diego•   Phoenix◎

- - - TROPIC OF CANCER - - -

Tucson•

J

K

10°N

150°W   140°W   130°W   120°W   110°W

	1	2	3	4	5	6	7	8

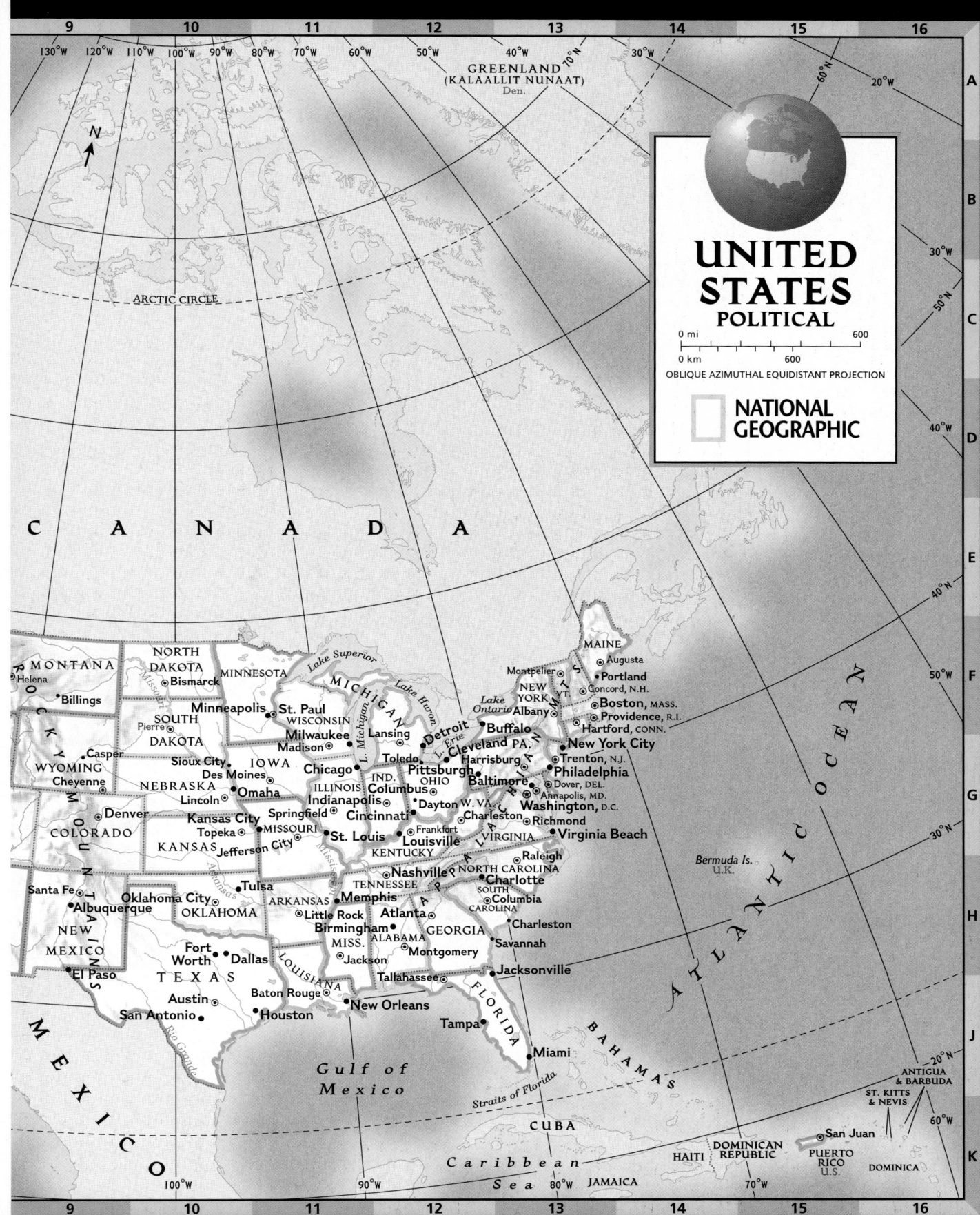

UNITED
STATES
POLITICAL

0 mi   600
0 km   600
OBLIQUE AZIMUTHAL EQUIDISTANT PROJECTION

NATIONAL
GEOGRAPHIC

GREENLAND
(KALAALLIT NUNAAT)
Den.

N

ARCTIC CIRCLE

C A N A D A

MONTANA
Helena
Billings
NORTH DAKOTA
Bismarck
MINNESOTA
SOUTH DAKOTA
Pierre
WYOMING
Casper
Cheyenne
COLORADO
Denver
NEBRASKA
Lincoln
Omaha
Sioux City
Des Moines
IOWA
KANSAS
Topeka
Kansas City
MISSOURI
Jefferson City
St. Louis
Springfield
Minneapolis
St. Paul
WISCONSIN
Milwaukee
Madison
Chicago
Lansing
MICHIGAN
Lake Superior
Lake Huron
L. Michigan
Lake Erie
Lake Ontario
Detroit
Toledo
Cleveland
Buffalo
PA.
Pittsburgh
Harrisburg
Baltimore
ILLINOIS
IND.
Indianapolis
Columbus
OHIO
Cincinnati
Dayton
Frankfort
Louisville
KENTUCKY
Nashville
TENNESSEE
Memphis
ARKANSAS
Little Rock
Tulsa
OKLAHOMA
Oklahoma City
Santa Fe
Albuquerque
NEW MEXICO
El Paso
TEXAS
Fort Worth
Dallas
Austin
San Antonio
Houston
Baton Rouge
New Orleans
LOUISIANA
Jackson
MISS.
ALABAMA
Birmingham
Montgomery
Atlanta
GEORGIA
Tallahassee
FLORIDA
Jacksonville
Savannah
Charleston
SOUTH CAROLINA
Columbia
Charlotte
NORTH CAROLINA
Raleigh
Richmond
Virginia Beach
VIRGINIA
W. VA.
Charleston
Washington, D.C.
Annapolis, MD.
Dover, DEL.
Philadelphia
Trenton, N.J.
New York City
Hartford, CONN.
Providence, R.I.
Boston, MASS.
Albany
NEW YORK
Montpelier
VT.
Concord, N.H.
Portland
Augusta
MAINE
N.H.

Tampa
Miami

Rio Grande

M E X I C O

Gulf of
Mexico

ROCKY MOUNTAINS

APPALACHIAN MOUNTAINS

Straits of Florida

CUBA

Caribbean
Sea

JAMAICA

HAITI
DOMINICAN
REPUBLIC

BAHAMAS

Bermuda Is.
U.K.

ATLANTIC OCEAN

PUERTO
RICO
U.S.
San Juan

DOMINICA

ANTIGUA
& BARBUDA

ST. KITTS
& NEVIS

A

B

C

D

E

F

G

H

J

K

1 2 3 4 5 6 7 8

130°W **125°W** **50°N** **120°W** **115°W** **110°W** **105°W** **100°W**

Cape Flattery
Mt. Olympus
7,965 ft
2,428 m · Seattle

C A N A D A

Columbia

COLUMBIA PLATEAU

Blue Mts.

Clearwater
Mts.

Bitterroot Range

Missouri

Salmon
River
Mts.

Absaroka Range

Bighorn Mts.

Laramie Mts.

Black
Hills

Missouri

G R E A T

Great Sandy
Desert

Snake

Snake River
Plain

Shoshone
Falls

Wind River Range

R O C K Y

N. Platte

Sand Hills

Platte

Cape Mendocino

130°W
40°N

PACIFIC

OCEAN

35°N

SIERRA NEVADA

Central Valley

Lake
Tahoe

San Francisco

Great Salt
Lake

GREAT
BASIN

Wasatch Range

Uinta Mts.

M O U N T A I N S

14,433 ft
4,399 m · Mt. Elbert

· Denver

H i g h   P l a i n s

Colorado

Mt. Whitney
14,494 ft
4,418 m

Death Valley °
-282 ft, -86 m

Lake
Mead

Lake
Powell

Colorado

Grand
Canyon

Colorado
Plateau

San Juan Mts.

Sangre de Cristo Mts.

Arkansas

Point Conception

Channel
Islands

· Los Angeles

Mojave
Desert

Salton
Sea

San Diego ·

Sonoran
Desert

Colorado

Phoenix ·

Sacramento Mts.

Llano
Estacado

Red

Dallas ·

Brazos

125°W
30°N

120°W

115°W

Rio Grande

Edwards
Plateau

C O

ALASKA inset:

ARCTIC OCEAN

Point Barrow

Beaufort
Sea

Chukchi
Sea

180°
68°N

RUSSIA

Bering
Strait

ARCTIC CIRCLE

North Slope
Brooks Range

ALASKA

68°N

CANADA

Seward
Pen.

St. Lawrence
Island

172°W
60°N

Nunivak
Island

Kuskokwim

Yukon

Tanana

Alaska Range

Mt. McKinley (Denali)
20,320 ft, 6,194 m

· Anchorage

110°W

60°N

25°N

Bering
Sea

Bristol
Bay

Alaska Peninsula

Kodiak I.

Gulf of
Alaska

Alexander Archipelago

MEXICO

TROPIC OF CANCER

ALASKA

0 mi   300
0 km   300

PACIFIC

OCEAN

52°N

52°N

164°W **156°W** **148°W** **140°W** **132°W** **105°W** **100°W**

1 2 3 4 5 6 7 8

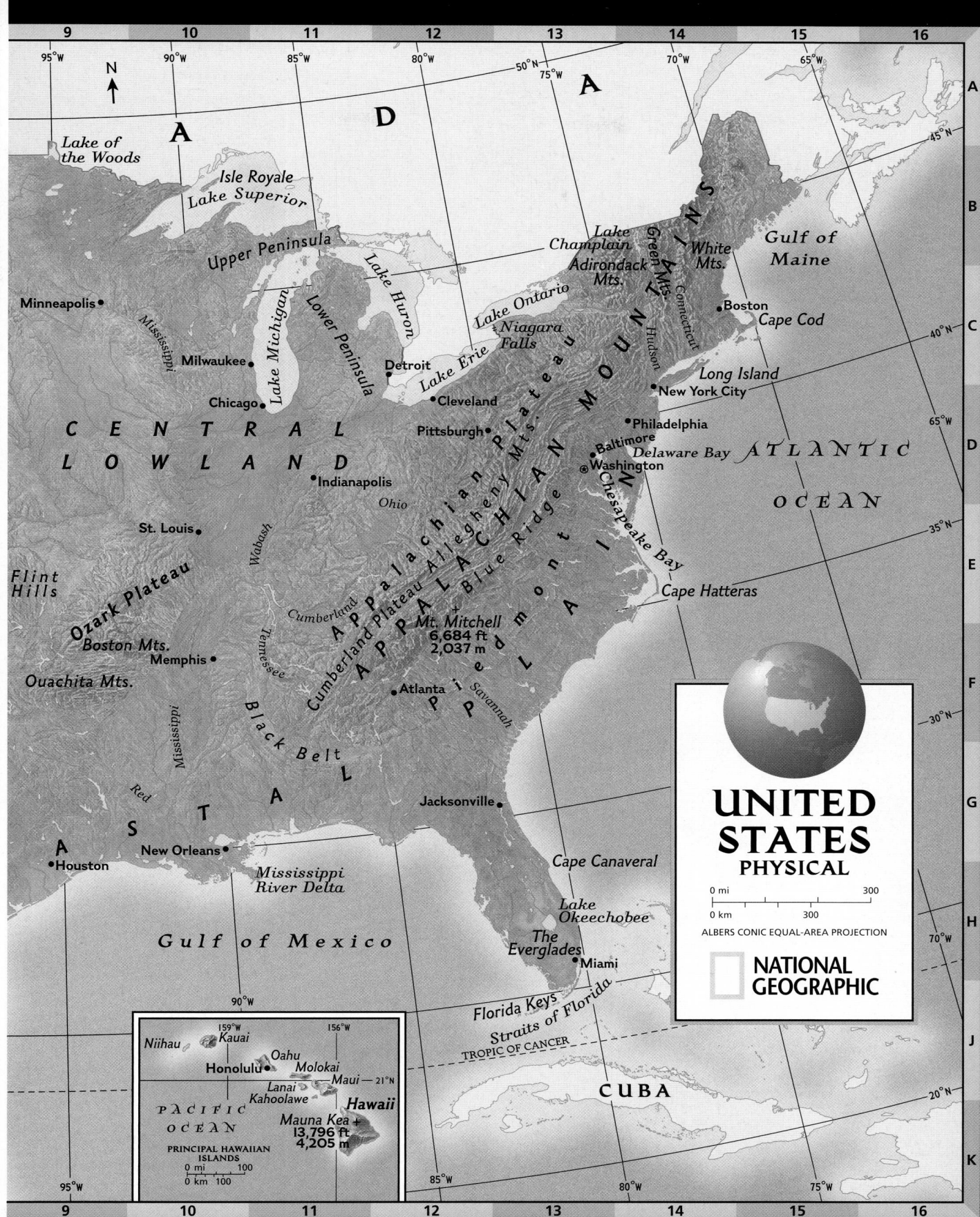

9 10 11 12 13 14 15 16

95°W 90°W 85°W 80°W 50°N 75°N 70°W 65°W

N

C A N A D A

45°N

Lake of
the Woods

Isle Royale
Lake Superior

Gulf of
Maine

B

Upper Peninsula

Lake Huron

Lake
Champlain
Adirondack
Mts.

Green Mts.
White
Mts.

Boston
Cape Cod

Minneapolis

Lower Peninsula

Lake Ontario

40°N

C

Milwaukee

Lake Michigan

Niagara
Falls

Connecticut

Mississippi

Detroit

Lake Erie

Hudson

Long Island
New York City

Chicago

Cleveland

CENTRAL

Pittsburgh

Appalachian Plateau

Philadelphia

65°W

D

Allegheny Mts.

Baltimore
Delaware Bay

ATLANTIC

LOWLAND

Indianapolis

Washington

Ohio

Cumberland Plateau

Blue Ridge

Chesapeake Bay

OCEAN

35°N

E

St. Louis

Wabash

APPALACHIAN MOUNTAINS

Flint
Hills

Ozark Plateau

Cumberland

Mt. Mitchell
6,684 ft
2,037 m

Piedmont

Cape Hatteras

Boston Mts.

Tennessee

Memphis

Ouachita Mts.

Black Belt

Atlanta

Savannah

30°N

F

Mississippi

C O A S T A L

Jacksonville

UNITED
STATES

G

Red

PHYSICAL

Houston

New Orleans

Cape Canaveral

0 mi   300

Mississippi
River Delta

0 km   300

Lake
Okeechobee

ALBERS CONIC EQUAL-AREA PROJECTION

70°W

H

Gulf of Mexico

The
Everglades

Miami

NATIONAL
GEOGRAPHIC

Florida Keys

Straits of Florida

J

90°W

159°W   156°W
Niihau   Kauai
            Oahu
Honolulu   Molokai
           Lanai   Maui — 21°N
           Kahoolawe

PACIFIC
OCEAN

Hawaii

Mauna Kea +
13,796 ft
4,205 m

TROPIC OF CANCER

CUBA

20°N

PRINCIPAL HAWAIIAN
ISLANDS

0 mi   100

0 km   100

85°W   80°W   75°W

K

9 10 11 12 13 14 15 16

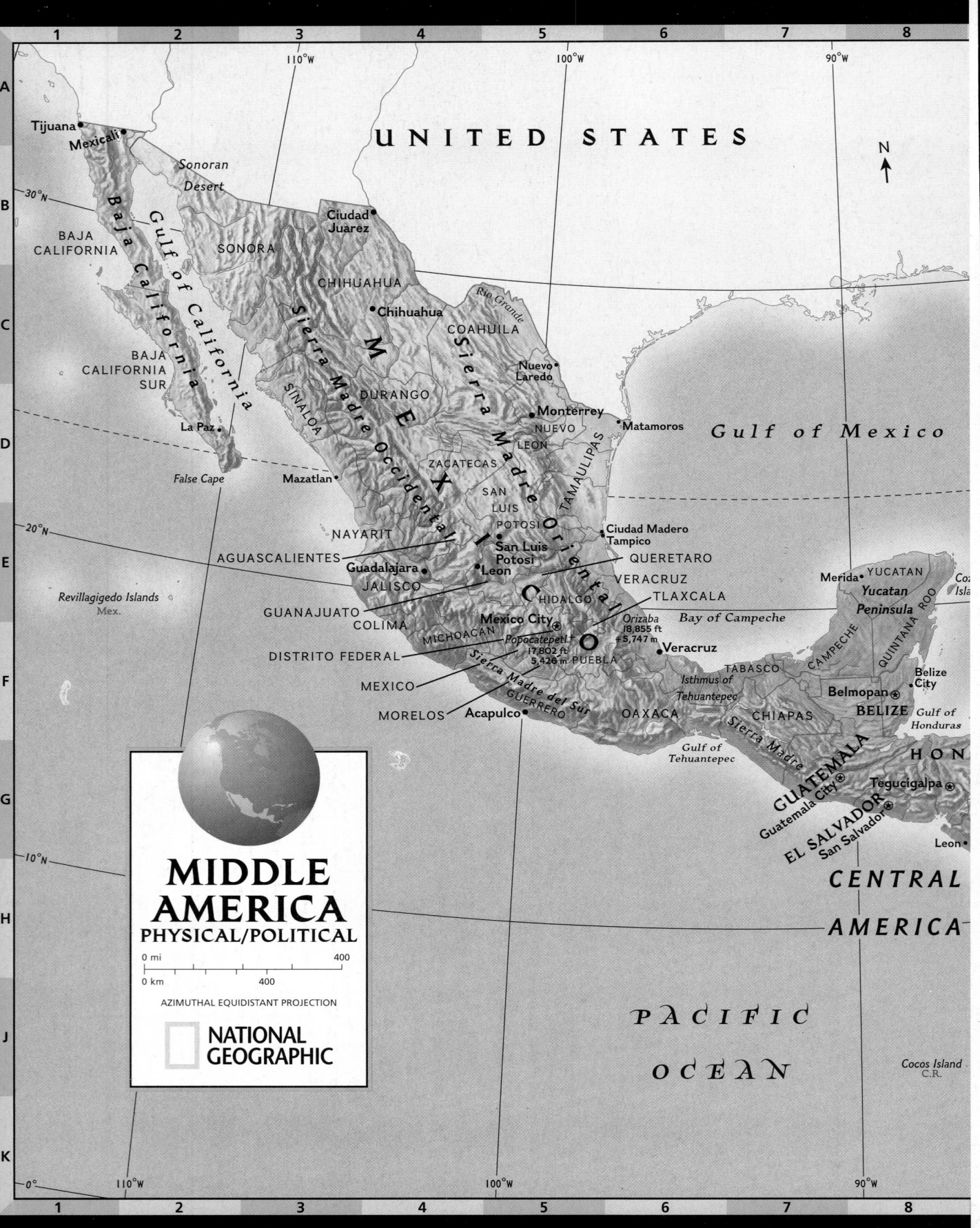

MIDDLE
AMERICA
PHYSICAL/POLITICAL

0 mi   400
0 km   400

AZIMUTHAL EQUIDISTANT PROJECTION

NATIONAL
GEOGRAPHIC

UNITED STATES

Tijuana
Mexicali

Sonoran
Desert

BAJA
CALIFORNIA

Gulf of California

Baja California

BAJA
CALIFORNIA
SUR

La Paz

False Cape

Mazatlan

Revillagigedo Islands
Mex.

SONORA

CHIHUAHUA

Chihuahua

Rio Grande

COAHUILA

Ciudad
Juárez

DURANGO

Sierra Madre Occidental

SINALOA

ZACATECAS

Nuevo
Laredo

Monterrey
NUEVO
LEON

Matamoros

Gulf of Mexico

Sierra Madre Oriental

SAN
LUIS
POTOSI

TAMAULIPAS

NAYARIT

AGUASCALIENTES

Guadalajara

JALISCO

GUANAJUATO

COLIMA

San Luis
Potosi
Leon

MICHOACAN

DISTRITO FEDERAL

MEXICO

MORELOS

Mexico City

Popocatepetl
17,802 ft
5,426 m

Sierra Madre del Sur

Acapulco

GUERRERO

Ciudad Madero
Tampico

QUERETARO

VERACRUZ

TLAXCALA

HIDALGO

Orizaba
18,855 ft
5,747 m

PUEBLA

Veracruz

Bay of Campeche

TABASCO

OAXACA

Gulf of
Tehuantepec

Isthmus of
Tehuantepec

Merida

YUCATAN

Yucatan
Peninsula

Co
Isl

QUINTANA ROO

CAMPECHE

CHIAPAS

Sierra Madre

Belmopan

BELIZE

Belize
City

Gulf of
Honduras

HON

GUATEMALA

Guatemala City

EL SALVADOR

San Salvador

Tegucigalpa

Leon

CENTRAL

AMERICA

PACIFIC

OCEAN

Cocos Island
C.R.

N

30°N

20°N

10°N

0°

110°W

100°W

90°W

ATLANTIC

OCEAN

TROPIC OF CANCER

30°N

20°N

BAHAMAS

• Freeport

⊛ Nassau

Straits of Florida

Andros
Island

Turks &
Caicos Islands
U.K.

W   E   S   T   I   N   D   I   E   S

ST. KITTS & NEVIS

⊛ Havana

CUBA • Camaguey

• Holguin

• Santiago
de Cuba

Isle of Youth

Cozumel
Island

Cayman
Islands
U.K.

Greater

Montego
Bay •

JAMAICA

⊛ Kingston

HAITI

Port-au-
Prince ⊛

Santiago •

Hispaniola

Santo
Domingo

DOMINICAN
REPUBLIC

San Juan
⊛

Puerto
Rico
U.S.

Antilles

Virgin
Islands
U.S. & U.K.

ANTIGUA &
BARBUDA

Guadeloupe
Fr.

DOMINICA

Bird I.
Venez.

Martinique
Fr.

ST. LUCIA

BARBADOS

ST. VINCENT &
THE GRENADINES

GRENADA

Lesser

Antilles

Caribbean   Sea

TRINIDAD & TOBAGO
Port-of-Spain ⊛

Tobago

Neth.

Curacao
Bonaire

10°N

Aruba
Neth.

Lesser Antilles

Trinidad

60°W

DURAS

Coco

Mosquito Coast

NICARAGUA

⊛ Managua

Lake
Nicaragua

COSTA

Puerto
• Limon

Gulf of
Mosquitos

Isthmus of Panama

San Jose ⊛

RICA

⊛ Panama City

PANAMA

• David

Gulf of
Panama

SOUTH

AMERICA

0°

EQUATOR

Caribbean Sea

A

80°W

Barranquilla
Santa Marta
Cartagena
Maracaibo
Lake
Maracaibo
Barquisimeto
Caracas
Valencia
60°W
Ciudad Guayana

10°N

VENEZUELA
Bucaramanga
San
Cristobal
Medellin
GUYANA
Georgetown
SURINAME
Paramaribo
Cayenne
FRENCH
GUIANA
Fr.

50°W

40°W

B

Bogota
COLOMBIA
Malpelo I.
Col.

Boa Vista

Boundary claimed
by Suriname

ATLANTIC
OCEAN

Esmeraldas
Quito
ECUADOR
Guayaquil
0°

A M A Z O N

Negro

Amazon
Marajo
Island
Belem

EQUATOR
0°

C

Iquitos
Amazon (Solimoes)
Manaus
Madeira
Santarem

Teresina
Fortaleza
Natal

Maranon

Ucayali
Purus
B A S I N
Tapajos
Xingu

Campina Grande
Recife

Rio
Branco
Porto Velho
B R A Z I L
Tocantins
Sao Francisco

10°S

D

Callao
Lima
Machu Picchu
Cuzco
Ayacucho
Telles Pires

Salvador
(Bahia)

10°S

Arequipa
Lake Titicaca
Trinidad
BOLIVIA
La Paz
Goiania
Brasilia

Uberandia

E

Arica
Oruro
Sucre
Santa Cruz
Uberaba
Belo Horizonte

E

Iquique
Tarija
PARAGUAY
Campo Grande
Campinas
Nova Iguacu

20°S

San Felix I.
San Ambrosio I.
Chil.

Antofagasta
Salta
Asuncion
Londrina
Sao Paulo
Santos
Rio de Janeiro
Curitiba

20°S

F

TROPIC OF CAPRICORN

Parana

Paraguay

F

La Serena
Coquimbo
A N D E S
Cordoba
Parana
Uruguaiana
Uruguay
Santa Maria
Porto Alegre

G

Juan Fernandez Is.
Chil.
Valparaiso
Santiago
Mendoza
Rosario
Buenos
Aires
URUGUAY
Montevideo
Rio de la Plata

30°S

La Plata

G

Concepcion
A R G E N T I N A
Mar del Plata

H

Puerto Montt
Negro
Bahia Blanca

40°S

H

P A C I F I C

O C E A N

Comodoro Rivadavia

J

Falkland Islands
(Islas Malvinas)
Stanley   Administered by
United Kingdom
(Claimed by Arg.)

J

Rio Gallegos
Punta Arenas
Strait of Magellan
TIERRA DEL FUEGO

**SOUTH
AMERICA**
POLITICAL

0 mi   800
0 km   800

AZIMUTHAL EQUIDISTANT PROJECTION

**NATIONAL
GEOGRAPHIC**

K

Ushuaia
Cape Horn
South Georgia I.
U.K.

50°S

100°W   90°W   80°W   70°W   60°W   50°W   40°W   30°W   20°W

1   2   3   4   5   6   7

Caribbean Sea

●Caracas

Lake Maracaibo

VENEZUELA

Orinoco

Malpelo I.

●Bogota

COLOMBIA

GUIANA HIGHLANDS

Angel Falls
Total drop=
3,212 ft 979 m

GUYANA
Georgetown●

SURINAME
Paramaribo●
●Cayenne
FRENCH
GUIANA

Boundary claimed
by Suriname

ATLANTIC
OCEAN

●Quito

ECUADOR

Negro

Amazon

A M A Z O N

Marajo
Island

EQUATOR

Amazon

A N D E S

Ucayali

P E R U

Purus

Selvas

BASIN

Madeira

Tapajos

Xingu

Teles Pires

Tocantins

São Francisco

B R A Z I L

●Lima

Machu Picchu

Lake Titicaca

BOLIVIA
●La Paz

MATO GROSSO

PLATEAU

BRAZILIAN

●Brasilia

HIGHLANDS

Altiplano

●Sucre

Salar
de Uyuni

GRAN CHACO

PARAGUAY
●Asuncion

Iguazu
Falls

San Felix I.   San Ambrosio I.

TROPIC OF CAPRICORN

Paraguay

Parana

Uruguay

A N D E S

Juan Fernandez Is.

Aconcagua
●Santiago

22,834 ft
6,960 m

A R G E N T I N A

P A M P A S

Buenos
Aires●

URUGUAY
●Montevideo

Rio de la Plata

Negro

Chiloe Island

P A T A G O N I A

-131 ft
-40 m Valdes Peninsula

PACIFIC
OCEAN

Taitao
Peninsula

Gulf of
San Jorge

Wellington I.

Falkland Islands
(Islas Malvinas)
●Stanley

Strait of Magellan
Tierra del Fuego

South Georgia I.

Cape Horn

N

SOUTH
AMERICA
PHYSICAL

0 mi   800
0 km   800

AZIMUTHAL EQUIDISTANT PROJECTION

NATIONAL
GEOGRAPHIC

EUROPE
POLITICAL

0 mi — 400
0 km — 400

AZIMUTHAL EQUIDISTANT PROJECTION

NATIONAL GEOGRAPHIC

1 2 3 4 5 6 7 8

**Row labels:** A B C D E F G H J K

60°N · 40°W · 30°W · 20°W · 10°W · 70°N · 0° · 10°E · 30°W · 50°N · 20°W · 40°N · 10°W · 0° · 10°E · 30°N

ARCTIC CIRCLE
MERIDIAN OF GREENWICH (LONDON)

Akureyri
⊛ Reykjavik
ICELAND

Norwegian Sea

Tromso

NORWAY

Trondheim · Are
Alesund · Sundsvall
Bergen
Stavanger · Oslo ⊛

SWEDEN

Uppsala
Stockholm ⊛
Goteborg
Gotland

Gulf of
Baltic

Faroe Islands
Den. · Torshavn

Shetland Islands
Lerwick

Orkney Islands

Rockall
U.K.

Isle of Lewis

Inverness

UNITED · Aberdeen
SCOTLAND
Glasgow · ⊛ Edinburgh
NORTHERN IRELAND · Belfast
IRELAND · Irish Sea
Dublin ⊛ Liverpool · Manchester
· Cork
KINGDOM
WALES · Birmingham
Cardiff · ENGLAND
London ⊛
Southampton

North Sea

Skagerrak

DENMARK
Copenhagen
Arhus
Malmo

Kiel
Hamburg

Gdansk

Bydgoszcz

Berlin ⊛

POLAND
Lodz
Wroclaw
Oder

GERMANY

NETH.
The Hague · Amsterdam
Brussels ⊛
BELGIUM · Bonn
LUX. · Frankfurt
Rhine

Celtic Sea

Land's End

English Channel

Le Havre

ATLANTIC
OCEAN

Brest

Rennes
· Paris
Nantes
La Rochelle
Bay of Biscay
Limoges
Bordeaux

FRANCE

Strasbourg

⊛ Prague
CZECH REP.

Bratislava ⊛
SLOVAKIA
Vienna ⊛
AUSTRIA
Budapest ⊛

Munich
LIECH.
Zurich
Bern ⊛
SWITZERLAND
Geneva
Lyon
ALPS

SLOVENIA · HUNGARY
Ljubljana ⊛ · Zagreb ⊛
CROATIA

A Coruna ·
Vigo
Porto ·
Coimbra ·
PORTUGAL

Donostia-San Sebastian
Bilbao
Pyrenees
Valladolid
Toulouse
ANDORRA
Zaragoza
MONACO
Marseille
Nice
Turin
Milan
Genoa
SAN MARINO
Venice
ITALY
Adriatic Sea
BOSNIA & HERZEGOVINA
Sarajevo ⊛

Lisbon ⊛
Madrid ⊛
SPAIN
Barcelona
Valencia
Corsica
Fr.
VATICAN CITY · Rome
Naples
Tirana ⊛
ALBANIA

Cape St. Vincent
Cordoba
Seville
Cadiz · Malaga
GIBRALTAR
U.K.
Murcia
Cartagena
Palma
Balearic Islands
Sp.
Sardinia
It.
Cagliari
Tyrrhenian Sea
Ionian Sea

Strait of Gibraltar

Mediterranean

AFRICA

Palermo
Sicily
Messina
Catania

Valletta ⊛
MALTA

9   **10**   **11**   **12**   **13**   **14**   **15**   **16**

30°E   40°E   70°N   50°E   •Tobseda   70°E   60°N

Barents Sea

A

Kola Peninsula   Pechora•   80°E

•Murmansk

•Kirovsk   *Kola Peninsula*

White Sea   •Umba

B

•Kiruna   *LAPLAND*

•Ivalo

Kemi   •Syktyvkar

•Lulea   Kem•   •Archangel   *URAL MOUNTAINS*   A commonly accepted division between Asia and Europe—here marked by a gray line—is formed by the Ural Mountains, Ural River, Caspian Sea, Caucasus Mountains, and the Black Sea with its outlets, the Bosporus and the Dardanelles.

•Oulu   Severodvinsk

•Umea   *Bothnia*

•Vaasa   •Kuopio   *Lake Onega*   **ASIA**

C

•Pori   *Lake Ladoga*   **R U S S I A**   •Perm   Europe–Asia boundary

•Tampere   •Kirov   70°E

•Turku   •Helsinki   •St. Petersburg   •Ufa   50°N

D

⊛Tallinn   Velikiy•   •Yaroslavl

ESTONIA   Novgorod   •Nizhniy   •Kazan

•Riga   Novgorod   •Samara   **K A Z A K H S T A N**

LATVIA   •Tver   Orenburg•

•Daugavpils   •Moscow⊛

LITHUANIA   •Ryazan   •Penza   •Oral   **E**

RUSSIA   •Vitsyebsk   •Smolensk   *Volga*

•Vilnius

•Kaunas   ⊛Minsk   •Saratov

BELARUS   •Bryansk

•Warsaw   Homyel•   •Kursk   •Volgograd   60°E   **F**

•Krakow   Chernihiv•   •Astrakhan   40°N

Carpathian Mts.   Sumy•   **U K R A I N E**   •Kharkiv   *Caspian Sea*

•Lviv   Kiev ⊛   •Poltava

Dniester   •Vinnytsya   •Donetsk   •Stavropol   **G**

MOLDOVA   •Dnipropetrovsk   •Rostov

⊛Chisinau   *Sea of Azov*

ROMANIA   •Odesa   *Crimea*   •Kerch   •Groznyy   **AZERBAIJAN**

⊛Belgrade   •Bucharest   •Simferopol   *Caucasus Mountains*   ⊛Baku   **H**

SERBIA AND   *Danube*   •Yalta   **GEORGIA**

MONTENEGRO   *Balkan Mts.*   Sevastopol   *Black Sea*

•Varna

BULGARIA

KOSOVO   •Sofia   *Bosporus*

⊛Skopje   **J**

MACED.   Istanbul•

•Thessaloniki   **TURKEY**   50°E

Dardanelles   *Sea of Marmara*   **ASIA**

GREECE   *Aegean Sea*

•Athens   *Peloponnesus*

Rhodes   Nicosia⊛   **K**

Crete   •Iraklio   **CYPRUS**   30°N

Sea   30°E   40°E   50°E

9   **10**   **11**   **12**   **13**   **14**   **15**   **16**

A B C D E F G H J K

1 2 3 4 5 6 7 8

10°E 20°E 30°E 40°E

EUROPE

Black Sea

40°N

Sea of Marmara

Istanbul

ANATOLIA

Ankara

TURKEY

Tunis

TUNISIA

Mediterranean Sea

Tripoli

30°N

Taurus Mountains

CYPRUS

SYRIA

Aleppo

LEBANON

Damascus

Beirut

ISRAEL

Syrian Desert

Jerusalem

Alexandria

Amman

Cairo

JORDAN

El Giza

Sinai Pen.

See inset below

LIBYA

EGYPT

Nile R.

Hejaz

SAHARA

Aswan High Dam

Boundary claimed by Sudan

Red Sea

SUDAN

AFRICA

Khartoum

30°E

30°E

Eastern Mediterranean Area

TURKEY

N

CYPRUS

SYRIA

Aleppo

LEBANON

Beirut

Damascus

Mediterranean Sea

Sea of Galilee

Golan Heights

Jordan River

Tel Aviv–Yafo

West Bank

Suez Canal

Jerusalem

Amman

Gaza Strip

Dead Sea

ISRAEL

JORDAN

El Giza

Cairo

EGYPT

Nile River

Gulf of Suez

SAUDI ARABIA

Gulf of Aqaba

30°N

0 mi 100

0 km 100

Red Sea

50°E   60°E   70°E   40°N A

Aral Sea

UZBEKISTAN   ★ **Tashkent**

Caucasus Mountains   **TAJIKISTAN**   B

Caspian Sea

GEORGIA
Tbilisi ★   Baku ★   **TURKMENISTAN**   ★ Dushanbe

Yerevan ★   **A S I A**

ARMENIA   ★ Ashkhabad   Kabul ★   C

▲ *Mt. Ararat*
(16,854 ft.   **Mashhad** •
5,137 m)   **AZERBAIJAN**   **AFGHANISTAN**

Elburz Mountains
Tigris R.   *Plateau*
★ Tehran   *of Iran*   30°N   D

IRAQ   *Zagros Mountains*

★ Baghdad   **IRAN**

Euphrates R.   **PAKISTAN**   E

Al Basrah •

KUWAIT

Kuwait ★   *Persian Gulf*   F

Manama   *Gulf of Oman*   TROPIC OF CANCER
★   Abu
BAHRAIN★ **QATAR** Dhabi   *Arabian*
SAUDI   ★ Doha ★ Muscat ★   *Sea*   G
ARABIA   ★ Riyadh   **UNITED**
                            ARAB
                          EMIRATES **OMAN**   20°N

ARABIAN   H
PENINSULA

A s i r
Rub al Khali   J
(Empty Quarter)

                                          MIDDLE EAST
                                          PHYSICAL / POLITICAL

★ Sanaa **YEMEN**   N   0 mi   500
                          ↑   0 km   500
Aden •   *Gulf of Aden* 50°E   AZIMUTHAL EQUIDISTANT PROJECTION   K

40°E   **NATIONAL
                                              GEOGRAPHIC**

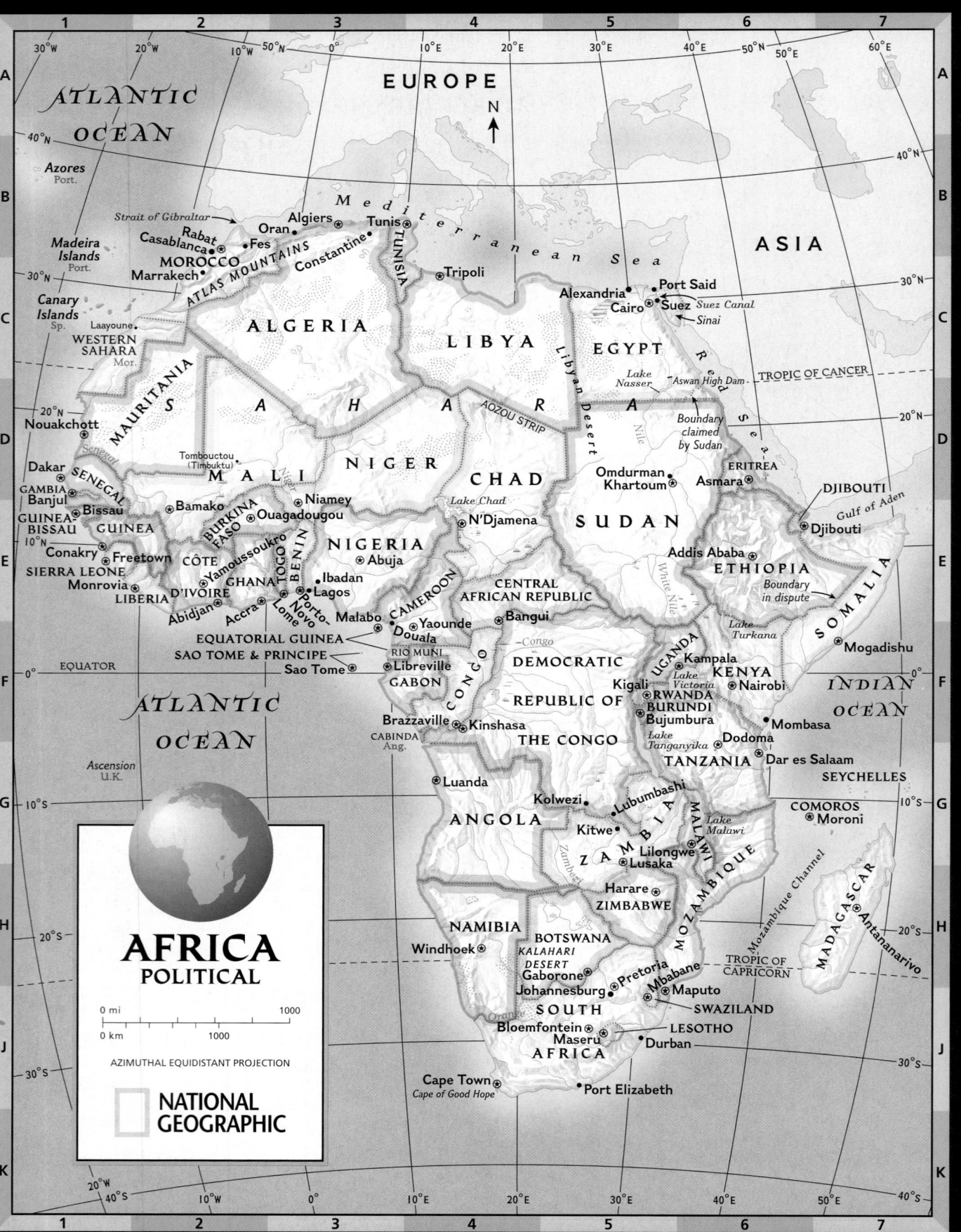

ATLANTIC OCEAN

Azores
Port.

40°N

30°W   20°W   10°W   0°   50°N   10°E   20°E   30°E   40°E   50°E   60°E

EUROPE
N

40°N

Madeira
Islands
Port.

Strait of Gibraltar

ASIA

30°N

Canary
Islands
Sp.

Laayoune

WESTERN
SAHARA
Mor.

Algiers   Tunis
Oran   TUNISIA
Rabat   Fes
Casablanca
MOROCCO   Constantine
Marrakech
ATLAS MOUNTAINS

Mediterranean Sea

Tripoli

Alexandria   Port Said
Cairo   Suez   Suez Canal
Sinai

30°N

ALGERIA

LIBYA   EGYPT

Lake
Nasser   Aswan High Dam   TROPIC OF CANCER

20°N

MAURITANIA   S   A   H   A   R   A
Senegal

Nouakchott

AOZOU STRIP

Libyan Desert   Nile   Boundary
claimed
by Sudan   Red Sea

20°N

Dakar
SENEGAL
GAMBIA
Banjul   Bissau
GUINEA-
BISSAU   GUINEA   Bamako

Tombouctou
(Timbuktu)

MALI   Niger   NIGER   CHAD

Niamey
Ouagadougou
BURKINA
FASO

Lake Chad
N'Djamena

Omdurman   ERITREA
Khartoum   Asmara
DJIBOUTI
Gulf of Aden

Conakry
Freetown
SIERRA LEONE
Monrovia
LIBERIA

CÔTE
D'IVOIRE   GHANA

Yamoussoukro   BENIN
TOGO

Abidjan   Accra   Lome

NIGERIA
Abuja
Ibadan
Lagos
Porto-
Novo   Malabo

CAMEROON   CENTRAL
AFRICAN REPUBLIC
Yaounde   Bangui
Douala

SUDAN   Addis Ababa
ETHIOPIA

White Nile   Boundary
in dispute   SOMALIA

Djibouti

10°N

EQUATOR

ATLANTIC
OCEAN

Ascension
U.K.

0°

10°S

EQUATORIAL GUINEA
SAO TOME & PRINCIPE
Sao Tome

RIO MUNI
Libreville
GABON

CABINDA
Ang.

Luanda

ANGOLA

DEMOCRATIC

REPUBLIC OF

THE CONGO

Brazzaville   Kinshasa

Congo

Congo

Kolwezi
Kitwe

Lubumbashi

ZAMBIA

Lake
Turkana

Lake
Victoria
UGANDA   Kampala
Kigali   KENYA
RWANDA   Nairobi
BURUNDI
Bujumbura
Lake
Tanganyika   Dodoma
TANZANIA

Mombasa

Dar es Salaam

Mogadishu

INDIAN
OCEAN

0°

SEYCHELLES

COMOROS
Moroni

10°S

Harare
ZIMBABWE

Lake
Malawi
Lilongwe
Lusaka   MALAWI

Zambezi

MOZAMBIQUE

Mozambique Channel

MADAGASCAR

Antananarivo

20°S

NAMIBIA   BOTSWANA
KALAHARI
DESERT
Windhoek
Gaborone
Johannesburg
SOUTH

Orange

Pretoria
Mbabane
Maputo
SWAZILAND
LESOTHO
Durban

TROPIC OF
CAPRICORN

20°S

AFRICA
POLITICAL

0 mi   1000
0 km   1000

AZIMUTHAL EQUIDISTANT PROJECTION

NATIONAL
GEOGRAPHIC

Maseru
Bloemfontein   AFRICA
Cape Town
Cape of Good Hope   Port Elizabeth

30°S

20°W   10°W   0°   10°E   20°E   30°E   40°E   50°E
40°S

40°S

1   2   3   4   5   6   7

AFRICA
PHYSICAL

0 mi _____ 1000
0 km _____ 1000

AZIMUTHAL EQUIDISTANT PROJECTION

NATIONAL GEOGRAPHIC

EUROPE

ASIA

ATLANTIC OCEAN

Azores

Madeira Islands

Canary Islands

Strait of Gibraltar

Mediterranean Sea

Algiers ⊛ Tunis ⊛

Rabat ⊛
MOROCCO
ATLAS MOUNTAINS
TUNISIA

⊛ Tripoli

Suez Canal

Cairo ⊛ Sinai

ALGERIA

LIBYA

EGYPT

Red Sea

TROPIC OF CANCER

WESTERN SAHARA

Ahaggar Mts.

Lake Nasser

Boundary claimed by Sudan

MAURITANIA

S   A   H   A   R   A

Air

Tibesti

Libyan Desert

Nouakchott ⊛

MALI

NIGER

CHAD

SUDAN

Khartoum ⊛ Asmara ⊛ ERITREA

Cape Verde ⊛ Dakar ⊛
SENEGAL
Senegal

Niger

Lake Chad

Nile

Lake Tana

Lake Assal -512 ft -156 m

Gulf of Aden

GAMBIA
Banjul ⊛
Bissau ⊛
GUINEA-BISSAU

Bamako ⊛
BURKINA FASO
Niamey ⊛
Ouagadougou ⊛

N'Djamena ⊛

DJIBOUTI
⊛ Djibouti

Conakry ⊛
GUINEA
SIERRA LEONE
Freetown ⊛
Yamoussoukro ⊛
Monrovia ⊛
LIBERIA
CÔTE D'IVOIRE
GHANA
Accra ⊛
Abidjan ⊛
TOGO
BENIN
Porto Novo
Lome ⊛

NIGERIA
Abuja ⊛

UPPER GUINEA

Malabo ⊛
CAMEROON
Yaounde ⊛

CENTRAL AFRICAN REPUBLIC

Bangui ⊛

White Nile
Blue Nile

Addis Ababa ⊛
ETHIOPIA

Boundary in dispute

SOMALIA

⊛ Mogadishu

EQUATORIAL GUINEA
SAO TOME & PRINCIPE
Sao Tome ⊛
Libreville ⊛
GABON
RIO MUNI

CONGO

Congo

CONGO BASIN

Virunga Mts. 14,787 ft 4,507 m

DEM. REP. OF THE CONGO

UGANDA
Kampala ⊛
Lake Victoria
Kigali ⊛
RWANDA
BURUNDI
Bujumbura ⊛

Kilimanjaro + 19,340 ft 5,895 m

KENYA
⊛ Nairobi

Lake Turkana

Great Rift Valley

EQUATOR

ATLANTIC OCEAN

Ascension Island

LOWER GUINEA

CABINDA

Brazzaville ⊛
Kinshasa ⊛

Lake Tanganyika

Dodoma ⊛
TANZANIA
⊛ Dar es Salaam

INDIAN OCEAN

Luanda ⊛

ANGOLA

Katanga Plateau

Great Rift Valley

Lake Malawi

SEYCHELLES

COMOROS
⊛ Moroni

ZAMBIA

MALAWI
Lilongwe ⊛
Lusaka ⊛

Zambezi

Etosha Pan

Victoria Falls

Harare ⊛
ZIMBABWE

MOZAMBIQUE

Mozambique Channel

MADAGASCAR

⊛ Antananarivo

NAMIBIA

Windhoek ⊛

BOTSWANA

KALAHARI DESERT
Gaborone ⊛

Drakensberg

Mbabane ⊛
Maputo ⊛

TROPIC OF CAPRICORN

Kalahari Desert

Orange

SOUTH AFRICA

Bloemfontein ⊛
Maseru ⊛
LESOTHO

SWAZILAND

Pretoria ⊛

Cape Town ⊛
Cape of Good Hope

Cape Agulhas

ASIA
POLITICAL

A commonly accepted division
between Asia and Europe—here
marked by a gray line—is
formed by the Ural Mountains,
Ural River, Caspian Sea, Caucasus
Mountains, and the Black Sea
with its outlets, the Bosporus
and the Dardanelles.

0 mi 1000
0 km 1000

TWO-POINT EQUIDISTANT PROJECTION

NATIONAL GEOGRAPHIC

9   **10**   **11**   **12**   **13**   **14**   **15**   **16**

NORTH AMERICA
Bering Strait

Chukchi Sea

North Pole

O C E A N   180°

Wrangel I.

160°E   *East Siberian Sea*

Gulf of Anadyr   •Anadyr

B e r i n g   S e a

Commander Is.

North Land

New Siberian Islands

120°E
100°E   *Laptev Sea*

Kamchatka Peninsula

Cherskiy Range

Verkhoyansk Range

Kolyma Range

•Magadan

Sea of Okhotsk

S I A

E R I A   Yakutsk•

Lena   *Aldan*

Sakhalin

Kuril Islands

Irkutsk•   *Yenisey*   *Lake Baikal*

Herlen   *Amur*

M A N C H U R I A   Vladivostok•

Hokkaido
Sapporo•

MONGOLIA   Changchun•

Ulaanbaatar ⊛   *GOBI*

ALTAY MTS.

Shenyang•   NORTH KOREA
Pyongyang ⊛

Sea of Japan (East Sea)

JAPAN
⊛Tokyo

Honshu

Beijing ⊛   Seoul ⊛   Kyoto•

Marcus I. Jap.

S H A N   Lanzhou•

Shijiazhuang•   Qingdao•   SOUTH KOREA
Hiroshima•   Osaka•

TROPIC OF CANCER

C H I N A   Xian•   *Yellow*   *Kyushu*

Xuzhou•   *Sea*

Yellow   Nanjing•   *East China Sea*   *Ryukyu Islands*

Bonin Is. Jap.

Chengdu•   Shanghai•   *Yangtze*

Nanchang•   Fuzhou•

Volcano Is. Jap.

Guiyang•   Changsha•

BHUTAN

BANGLADESH   Kunming•   Guangzhou•   ⊛Taipei

Okinawa

Parece Vela Jap.

⊛Dhaka   *Irrawaddy*   Hong Kong•   TAIWAN
Macau•

The People's Republic of China claims Taiwan as its 23rd province.

P h i l i p p i n e

MYANMAR (BURMA)   Hanoi ⊛   •Haiphong

South   *Luzon*
•Quezon City

S e a

Yangon (Rangoon)   Vientiane ⊛   *Hainan*
L A O S   Da Nang•   *China*   •Manila

Samar

THAILAND   VIETNAM   *Sea*   *Mindoro*   PHILIPPINES

Bangkok ⊛   *Mekong*   *Panay*   *Leyte*

Andaman Islands India   CAMBODIA
Phnom Penh•   *Palawan*   *Negros*

Ho Chi Minh City•

Gulf of Thailand   Bandar Seri Begawan ⊛   *Mindanao*

Morotai

Nicobar Islands India   *Andaman Sea*   BRUNEI   SABAH   *Halmahera*   *Biak* Jayapura

Kuala Lumpur ⊛   SARAWAK   *New Guinea*

Medan•   M A L A Y S I A

SINGAPORE ⊛   *Borneo*   *Celebes*   *Buru*   *Ceram*   *Kepi•*
Aru Is.   Merauke•

Sumatra   I N D O N E S I A   *Moluccas*   *Dolak*

Jambi•   G R E A T E R   *Tanimbar Is.*

Mentawai Islands   S U N D A I S L A N D S   Dili ⊛   TIMOR-LESTE (EAST TIMOR)

Java Sea   AUSTRALIA

Jakarta ⊛   **Java**   Kupang•   *Timor Sea*

100°E   110°E   120°E   130°E   140°E   150°E

9   **10**   **11**   **12**   **13**   **14**   **15**   **16**

160°W

170°W

180°

20°N

170°E

10°N

160°E

0°

EQUATOR

10°S

20°S

P A C I F I C   O C E A N

A B C D E F G H J K

A | RUSSIA

Bering Sea

KAMCHATKA PENINSULA

Lake Baikal

Yablonovyy Range

Sea of Okhotsk

ALEUTIAN ISLANDS

B | Ulaanbaatar ⊛

MONGOLIA

ALTAY MOUNTAINS

GOBI

Greater Khingan Range

Manchurian Plain

Amur

Sikhote Alin Range

Sakhalin

KURIL ISLANDS

Hokkaido

C | Beijing ⊛

CHINA

Yellow

Yangtze

Mekong

PYONGYANG ⊛
NORTH KOREA
⊛ Seoul
SOUTH KOREA

Yellow Sea

Sea of Japan (East Sea)

Honshu

JAPAN
⊛ Tokyo

Kyushu

Shikoku

NORTH PACIFI

Hawaiian

D | INDIA

MYANMAR (BURMA)

⊛ Hanoi

LAOS
⊛ Vientiane
VIETNAM

Hainan

East China Sea

⊛ Taipei
TAIWAN

RYUKYU ISLANDS

NAMPO SHŌTŌ

NORTHERN MARIANA ISLANDS
U.S.

MARIANA ISLANDS

E | Yangon (Rangoon) ⊛

THAILAND
⊛ Bangkok

CAMBODIA
Phnom Penh ⊛

Andaman Sea

South China Sea

Luzon

PHILIPPINE ISLANDS

⊛ Manila
PHILIPPINES

Philippine Sea

Sulu Sea

Mindanao

GUAM
U.S.

M
I
C
R
O
N
E
S
I
A

CAROLINE ISLANDS

Ralik Chain

Ratak Chain

MARSHALL ISLANDS

Majuro ⊛

P
O
L

F | Kuala Lumpur ⊛
MALAYSIA

SINGAPORE ⊛

PALAU
Koror ⊛

Bandar Seri Begawan
BRUNEI ⊛

Celebes Sea

Borneo

INDONESIA

GREATER SUNDA ISLANDS

Java Sea

Sumatra

Celebes

MOLUCCAS

FEDERATED STATES OF MICRONESIA

⊛ Palikir

Gilbert Islands

⊛ Tarawa

KIRIBATI

Phoenix Is.

M
E
L
A
N
E
S
I
A

Yaren ⊛
NAURU

TUVALU
Funafuti ⊛

Tokelau N.Z.

Jakarta ⊛

Java

LESSER SUNDA ISLANDS

Dili ⊛
TIMOR-LESTE (EAST TIMOR)

Arafura Sea

NEW GUINEA

PAPUA NEW GUINEA
Port Moresby ⊛

Solomon Is.

SOLOMON ISLANDS

Honiara ⊛

Santa Cruz Islands

WALLIS AND FUTUNA IS.
Fr.

AMERICAN SAMOA
U.S.

SAMOA
Apia ⊛

G | CORAL SEA ISLANDS TERRITORY
Austral.

VANUATU

NEW CALEDONIA
Fr.

Port-Vila ⊛

Suva ⊛

FIJI ISLANDS

TONGA
Nukuʻalofa ⊛

Niue N.Z.

Coral Sea

TROPIC OF CAPRICORN

AUSTRALIA

H | *Great Australian Bight*

Darling

Norfolk Island Austral.

Lord Howe Island Austral.

Kermadec Islands N.Z.

J | INDIAN OCEAN

⊛ Canberra

Tasman Sea

Tasmania

NEW ZEALAND
Wellington ⊛

Chatham Island N.Z.

K |

105°E | 120°E | 135°E | 150°E | 165°E | 180°

1 | 2 | 3 | 4 | 5 | 6 | 7 | 8

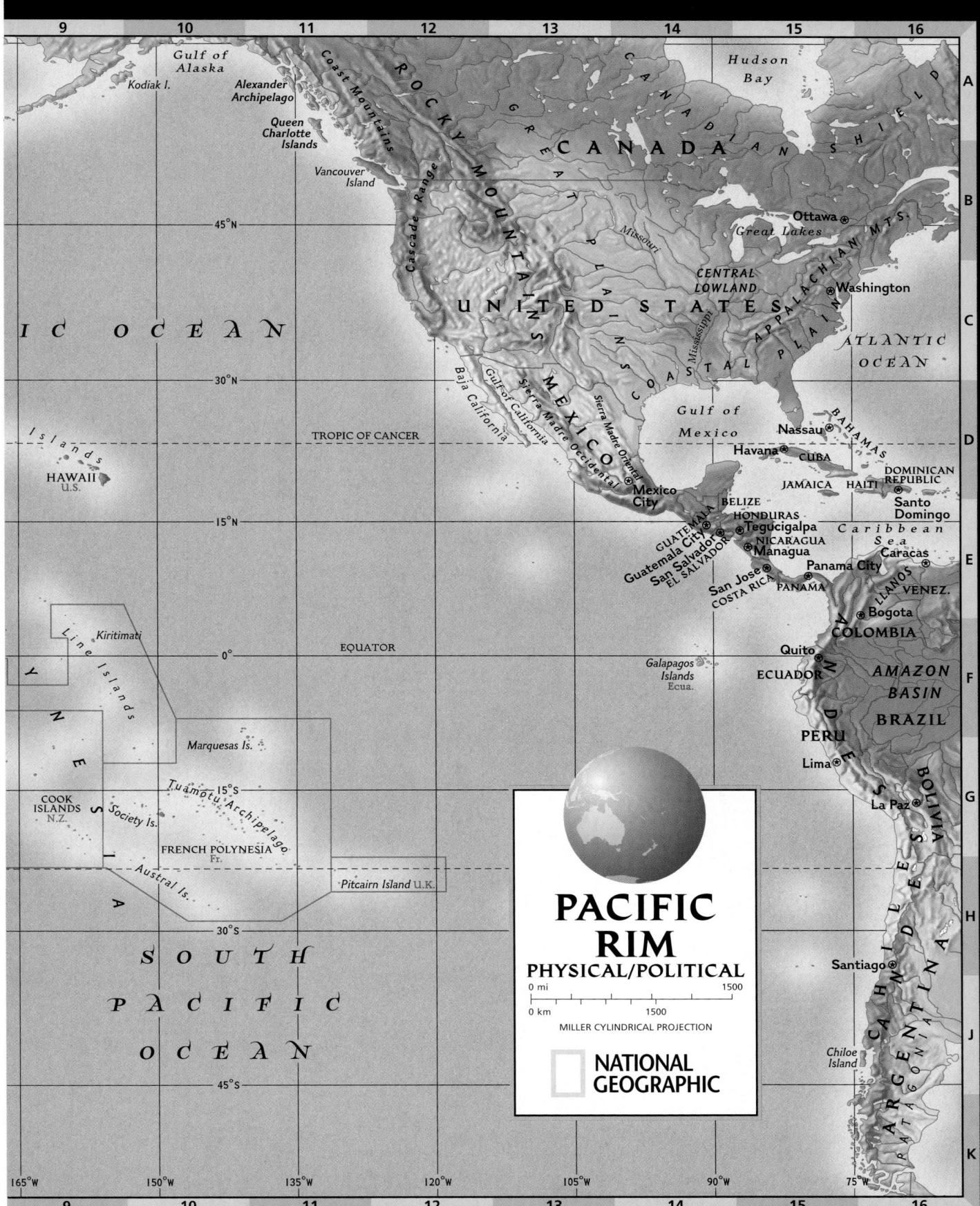

PACIFIC RIM
PHYSICAL/POLITICAL

0 mi 1500
0 km 1500

MILLER CYLINDRICAL PROJECTION

NATIONAL GEOGRAPHIC

ARCTIC OCEAN
PHYSICAL

0 mi 800
0 km 800
AZIMUTHAL EQUIDISTANT PROJECTION

NATIONAL GEOGRAPHIC

RUSSIA

Ob
Yenisey
Gulf of Ob
Taymyr Peninsula
Kara Sea
Novaya Zemlya
Barents Sea
White Sea
FINLAND
SWEDEN
NORWAY
GERMANY
LUX.
DENMARK NETH.
BELGIUM FRANCE
North Sea
UNITED KINGDOM
IRELAND
Norwegian Sea
ARCTIC CIRCLE
Svalbard
Greenland Sea
ICELAND
ATLANTIC OCEAN
Denmark Strait
30°W
Cape Farewell
Lena
Laptev Sea
North Land
Franz Josef Land
90°E
60°E
30°E
0°
70°N
80°N
60°N
50°N
120°E
New Siberian Islands
150°E
ARCTIC OCEAN
North Pole ★
Oodaaq Island
Lincoln Sea
GREENLAND
Baffin Bay
Davis Strait
Sea of Okhotsk
KAMCHATKA PENINSULA
East Siberian Sea
180°
150°W
120°W
90°W
60°W
Queen
Ellesmere Island
Elizabeth
Islands
Hayes Peninsula
Devon I.
Somerset I.
Baffin Island
Wrangel Island
Chukchi Sea
Point Barrow
Melville Island
Prince of Wales I.
Boothia Peninsula
Melville Peninsula
Foxe Basin
Hudson Strait
Chukchi Peninsula
Bering Strait
North Slope
Beaufort Sea
Banks Island
Victoria Island
Southampton Island
Hudson Bay
Aleutian Islands
Bering Sea
St. Lawrence Island
Seward Peninsula
Brooks Range
Yukon
ALASKA
Mackenzie
Great Bear Lake
CANADA
PACIFIC OCEAN
Nunivak Island
Bristol Bay

ANTARCTICA
PHYSICAL

0 mi 600
0 km 600
AZIMUTHAL EQUIDISTANT PROJECTION

NATIONAL GEOGRAPHIC

SOUTH ATLANTIC OCEAN
South Orkney Is.
30°W
15°W
0°
15°E
30°E
45°E
60°E
ANTARCTIC CIRCLE
Fimbul Ice Shelf
Ruser–Larsen Ice Shelf
QUEEN MAUD LAND
ENDERBY LAND
INDIAN OCEAN
South Shetland Islands
ANTARCTIC PENINSULA
Weddell Sea
COATS LAND
Valkyrie Dome
GRAHAM LAND
Larsen Ice Shelf
Mt. Jackson 13,747 ft 4,190 m
PALMER LAND
Filchner Ice Shelf
Berkner Island
Ronne Ice Shelf
Amery Ice Shelf
Alexander I.
Bellingshausen Sea
AMERICAN HIGHLAND
ELLSWORTH LAND
Vinson Massif 16,067 ft 4,897 m
Ellsworth Mts.
ANTARCTICA
TRANSANTARCTIC MOUNTAINS
EAST ANTARCTICA
West Ice Shelf
POLAR PLATEAU
★ South Pole
SOUTH PACIFIC OCEAN
Bentley Subglacial Trench -8,327 ft -2,538 m
WEST ANTARCTICA
Shackleton Ice Shelf
MARIE BYRD LAND
Dome Circe
Ross Ice Shelf
Roosevelt I.
WILKES LAND
Ross Sea
Ross I. Mt. Erebus 12,448 ft 3,794 m
VICTORIA LAND
Talos Dome
INDIAN OCEAN
60°W
75°W
90°W
105°W
120°W
135°W
150°W
165°W
180°
165°E
150°E
135°E
120°E
105°E
90°E
75°E
60°S
70°S

NATIONAL GEOGRAPHIC
Geography Handbook

The story of the world begins with geography—the study of the earth in all of its variety. Geography describes the earth's land, water, and plant and animal life. It is the study of places and the complex relationships between people and their environment.

The resources in this handbook will help you get the most out of your textbook—and provide you with skills you will use for the rest of your life.

▼ The Gui River, Guilin, China

▲ Saharan sand dunes, Morocco

The Amazon, Brazil ▶

GH1

TEACH

HANDBOOK OBJECTIVES

After studying this handbook, students should be able to

1. understand the themes and elements associated with the study of geography;
2. understand the purpose and uses of globes and map projections;
3. describe how to use maps, graphs, and charts;
4. identify the most commonly used geographic terms.

PRETEACHING VOCABULARY

Survey the students' knowledge of geographic terms. Create three columns on the board with these headings: Landforms, Map Elements, and Bodies of Water.

List one term that fits each column, such as "canyon," "meridian," and "bay." Ask students to identify as many other terms for each column as they can. Then have students turn to the **Geographic Dictionary** on pages GH14–GH15 and identify additional terms for each column. Write the terms on the board in the appropriate columns of the chart. **L1**

GEOGRAPHY HANDBOOK RESOURCES

 Reproducible Masters
- Glencoe Social Studies Outline Map Resource Book
- Building Geography Skills for Life Workbook
- Inclusion Strategies for the Middle School Social Studies Classroom

✎ **Transparencies**
- Chapter In-text Map Transparencies
- NGS PicturePack Transparencies: Physical Geography of the World

Multimedia
- NGS Dynamic Earth CD-ROM
- Picture Atlas of the World, Revised Edition CD-ROM

GH1

How Do I Study Geography?

To understand how our world is connected, some geographers have broken down the study of geography into five themes. The **Five Themes of Geography** are (1) location, (2) place, (3) human/environment interaction, (4) movement, and (5) regions. You will see these themes highlighted in the Chapter Assessment Geography Skills of *Journey Across Time.*

Six Essential Elements

Recently, geographers have begun to look at geography in a different way. They break down the study of geography into **Six Essential Elements.** Being aware of these elements will help you sort out what you are learning about geography.

Element 1

The World in Spatial Terms
Geographers first take a look at where a place is located. **Location** serves as a starting point by asking "Where is it?" Knowing the location of places helps you develop an awareness of the world around you.

Element 2

Places and Regions
Place has a special meaning in geography. It means more than where a place is. It also describes what a place is like. It might describe physical characteristics such as landforms, climate, and plant or animal life. Or it might describe human characteristics, including language and way of life.

To help organize their study, geographers often group places into regions. **Regions** are united by one or more common characteristics.

Element 3

Physical Systems
When studying places and regions, geographers analyze how **physical systems**—such as hurricanes, volcanoes, and glaciers—shape the earth's surface. They also look at communities of plants and animals that depend upon one another and their surroundings for survival.

UNDERSTANDING THE SIX ESSENTIAL ELEMENTS

Have students complete the following activities to learn more about the Six Essential Elements of Geography.

Element 1: The World in Spatial Terms Have students create a map that shows the route they traveled from their homes to school. *(Students should identify major roads and human-made landmarks on their maps.)* Display the maps on the class bulletin board. **L2**

Element 2: Places and Regions Explain that physical characteristics play a part in shaping human characteristics in a given place. For example, Native Americans in Alaska and Native Americans in Mexico had widely differing clothing, economic pursuits, architecture, and lifestyles because of the physical characteristics of their regions. Ask students to describe a favorite city, state, or country. Ask them how the physical characteristics of the place might influence characteristics or customs of the inhabitants. **L1/ EL**

Element 3: Physical Systems Ask students to think of ways that physical systems affect their lives and cultures. Have students explain how events such as hurricanes influence a region's population and economy. **L2**

DIFFERENTIATED INSTRUCTION

Less-proficient Readers: Students who have trouble understanding the Six Essential Elements of Geography could use graphic organizers to help them organize the information. Students could create two-column tables with the headings "Element" and "Description." As they read each element, they should complete their tables.

☞ Refer to *Inclusion Strategies for the Middle School Social Studies Classroom* in the TCR.

Element 4

Human Systems

Geographers also examine **human systems,** or how people have shaped our world. They look at how boundary lines are determined and analyze why people settle in certain places and not in others. A key theme in geography is the continual **movement** of people, ideas, and goods.

Element 5

Environment and Society

How does the relationship between people and their natural surroundings influence the way people live? This is one of the questions that the theme of **human/environment interaction** investigates. It also shows how people use the environment and how their actions affect the environment.

Element 6

The Uses of Geography

Knowledge of geography helps us understand the relationships among people, places, and environments over time. Understanding geography and knowing how to use the tools and technology available to study it prepares you for life in our modern society.

Geography Handbook   **GH3**

Element 4: Human Systems Call on volunteers to name places from which their family or ancestors moved. (*Students may describe a move within the United States or a migration from another country.*) Discuss the reasons that people move to different places. **L1/ EL**

Element 5: Environment and Society Give examples of ways that humans use and modify the environment in places they live. For example, people convert fields and forests into towns and irrigate arid land to support farming. Call on students to give examples of the ways people have modified the environment where they live in both positive and negative ways. **L2**

Element 6: The Uses of Geography Have students give examples of ways businesses use geography. Have students explain how geography influences where businesses such as gas stations and shopping malls are built. **L2**

EXTENDING THE CONTENT

Regions Geographers organize regions into three categories. Formal regions are characterized by the presence of a common human property (*for example, language, religion, nationality, and political identity*) or common physical property (*for example, climate, landforms, and vegetation cover*). Functional regions are organized around a node or focal point with surrounding areas linked to that node through transportation or communication systems or economic associations. Perceptual regions reflect human feelings or attitudes and are defined by subjective images of the area (*for example, New England and the Corn Belt*).

How Do I Use Maps and Globes?

TEACH

SYNTHESIZING INFORMATION

Emphasize the difficulty in portraying the curved surface of the earth on a flat map by giving one student an orange. Using a permanent marker, have the student draw outlines of the continents on the orange. Then ask the student to peel the orange and try to place the peel flat on the desk. Point out that the student has to tear the peel to get it to lie flat. **L1/ EL**

Did You Know

There is a place with no latitude and no longitude. The absolute location where the Prime Meridian and the Equator intersect is 0° N–S, 0° E–W.

Hemispheres

To locate a place on the earth, geographers use a system of imaginary lines that crisscross the globe. One of these lines, the **Equator,** circles the middle of the earth like a belt. It divides the earth into "half spheres," or **hemispheres.** Everything north of the Equator is in the Northern Hemisphere. Everything south of the Equator is in the Southern Hemisphere.

Another imaginary line runs from north to south. It helps divide the earth into half spheres in the other direction. Find this line—called the **Prime Meridian** on a globe. Everything east of the Prime Meridian for 180 degrees is in the Eastern Hemisphere. Everything west of the Prime Meridian for 180 degrees is in the Western Hemisphere.

NATIONAL GEOGRAPHIC

Hemispheres

Northern Hemisphere — Asia, Africa, Europe, North Pole, Pacific Ocean, Atlantic Ocean, North America

Southern Hemisphere — Indian Ocean, Australia, Africa, Atlantic Ocean, South Pole, Antarctica, Pacific Ocean, South America

Western Hemisphere — North America, Atlantic Ocean, Pacific Ocean, South America

Eastern Hemisphere — Europe, Asia, Africa, Indian Ocean, Australia

COOPERATIVE LEARNING ACTIVITY

Creating a Presentation Organize the class into two groups. Assign one group to research the National Geographic Society and the other group to research the United States Geological Survey. Have each group prepare a presentation on what the organization does, what research and resources it provides, how it is funded, and career opportunities. Encourage students to contact their assigned organization and, if possible, arrange for a speaker to talk to the class about the organization's purpose and goals. **L2**

Understanding Latitude and Longitude

Lines on globes and maps provide information that can help you easily locate places on the earth. These lines—called **latitude** and **longitude**—cross one another, forming a pattern called a grid system.

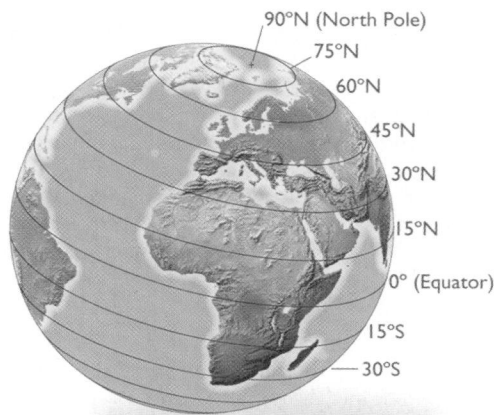

90°N (North Pole)
75°N
60°N
45°N
30°N
15°N
0° (Equator)
15°S
30°S

Latitude

Lines of latitude, or **parallels,** circle the earth parallel to the **Equator** and measure the distance north or south of the Equator in degrees. The Equator is at 0° latitude, while the North Pole lies at latitude 90°N (north).

45°W
30°W
15°W
0° (Prime Meridian)
45°E
30°E
15°E

Longitude

Lines of longitude, or **meridians,** circle the earth from Pole to Pole. These lines measure distances east or west of the starting line, which is at 0° longitude and is called the **Prime Meridian.** The Prime Meridian runs through the Royal Observatory in Greenwich, England.

90°N (North Pole)
75°N
60°N
45°N
30°N
15°N
0° (Equator)
15°S
30°S
60°E
75°E
90°E
105°E
120°E
135°E

Absolute Location

The grid system formed by lines of latitude and longitude makes it possible to find the absolute location of a place. Only one place can be found at the point where a specific line of latitude crosses a specific line of longitude. By using degrees (°) and minutes (') (points between degrees), people can pinpoint the precise spot where one line of latitude crosses one line of longitude—an **absolute location.**

TEACH

MONITORING COMPREHENSION

After students read this page, check their comprehension by asking them the following questions: **What line is at 0° latitude?** (*Equator*) **What is the latitude of the North Pole?** (*90° N*) **Through which continents does the Prime Meridian pass?** (*Africa, Europe*) **L1**

CURRICULUM CONNECTION

Language Arts
The word *longitude* comes from the Latin word for "length," and the word *latitude* comes from the Latin word for "breadth."

EXTENDING THE CONTENT

International Time Zones Present an international time zones map to students. Explain how time changes according to the direction in which you are traveling. Also point out that the division of time zones often follows lines of longitude. Have students use time zones maps to practice calculating time changes based on travel from one time zone to another. **L2**

DIFFERENTIATED INSTRUCTION

Less-proficient Readers: Knowing how to use the grid system is a prerequisite for understanding other aspects of geography, so ensure that all students grasp it at this point. To help students who are having difficulty understanding the grid system, make a simplified grid of three horizontal lines labeled A, B, and C, and three vertical lines labeled 1, 2, and 3. Have students practice naming locations with this simple grid system. When they are comfortable with the basic concept, make a more complex grid of 10 horizontal and three vertical lines labeled with degrees. Finally, have students practice finding a city's absolute location on a globe or map.

Refer to *Inclusion Strategies for the Middle School Social Studies Classroom* in the TCR.

From Globes to Maps

TEACH

UNDERSTANDING MAPS

Give students a copy of a world map and ask them to draw a line connecting San Francisco, California, to Istanbul, Turkey, by the most direct route. Give two students a piece of string and, using a classroom globe, ask them to connect those same two cities by the most direct route. Ask all students to note the location of the string on the globe and trace its course on their maps. Discuss with students how these exercises illustrate the difficulty of projecting the earth's curved surface on a flat map. **L1**

CURRICULUM CONNECTION

Geography
Citizens of all countries speak "grid language," the language of latitude and longitude.

The most accurate way to depict the earth is as a *globe*, a round scale model of the earth. A globe gives a true picture of the relative sizes of continents and the shapes of landmasses and bodies of water. Globes accurately represent distance and direction.

A **map** *is a flat drawing of all or part of the surface of the earth. Unlike globes, maps can show small areas in great detail. Maps can also display political boundaries, population densities, or even voting results.*

From Globes to Maps

Maps, however, do have their limitations. As you can imagine, drawing a round object on a flat surface is very difficult. **Cartographers,** or mapmakers, use mathematical formulas to transfer information from the round globe to a flat map. However, when the curves of a globe become straight lines on a map, the size, shape, distance, or area can change or be distorted.

Great Circle Routes

Mapmakers have solved some problems of going from a globe to a map. A **great circle** is an imaginary line that follows the curve of the earth. Traveling along a great circle is called following a **great circle route.** Airplane pilots use great circle routes because they are the shortest routes.

The idea of a great circle shows one important difference between a globe and a map. Because a globe is round, it accurately shows great circles. On a flat map, however, the great circle route between two points may not appear to be the shortest distance. Compare Maps A and B on the right.

Mapmaking With Technology

Technology has changed the way maps are made. Most cartographers use software programs called **geographic information systems (GIS).** This software layers map data from satellite images, printed text, and statistics. A **Global Positioning System (GPS)** helps consumers and mapmakers locate places based on coordinates broadcast by satellites.

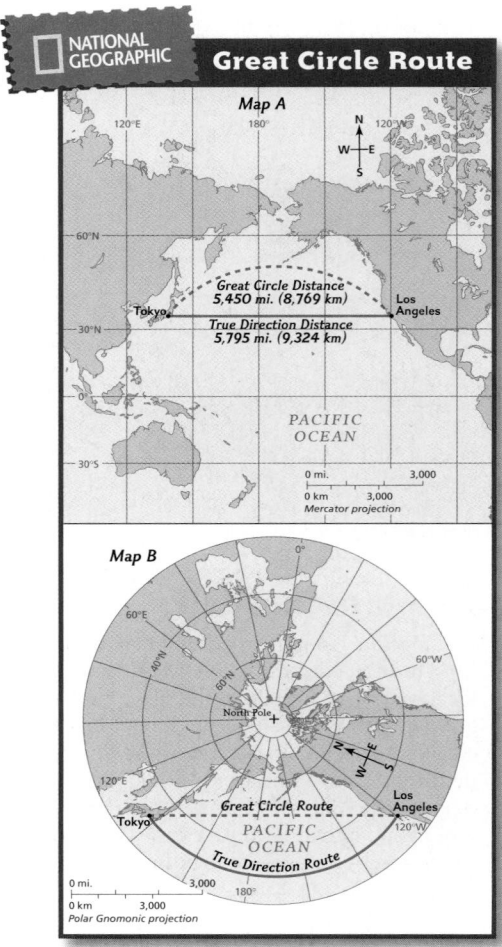

Great Circle Route

EXTENDING THE CONTENT

Geographers Geographers work for the federal government in the Defense Mapping Agency, United States Geological Survey, Central Intelligence Agency, Army Corps of Engineers, National Science Foundation, Smithsonian Institution, and Office of the Geographer in the Department of State. State environmental and transportation agencies hire geographers as analysts, planners, and cartographers. In the private sector, geographers work as professors, researchers, and cartographers for high-tech computer mapmakers. Businesses as varied as fast-food chains and ski resorts consult geographers about such topics as finding optimal locations for new restaurants and understanding the effects of pollution on the ski slopes.

Common Map Projections

Imagine taking the whole peel from an orange and trying to flatten it on a table. You would either have to cut it or stretch parts of it. Mapmakers face a similar problem in showing the surface of the round earth on a flat map. When the surface of the earth is flattened, big gaps open up. To fill in the gaps, mapmakers stretch parts of the earth. They choose to show either the correct shapes of places or their correct sizes. It is impossible to show both. As a result, mapmakers have developed different **projections,** or ways of showing the earth on a flat piece of paper.

Goode's Interrupted Equal-Area Projection

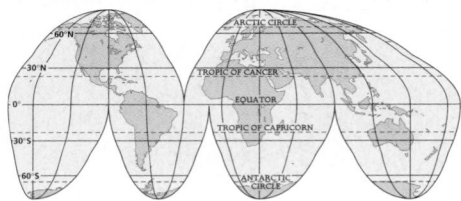

▲ Take a second look at your peeled, flattened orange. You might have something that looks like a map based on **Goode's Interrupted Equal-Area** projection. A map with this projection shows continents close to their true shapes and sizes. This projection is helpful to compare land areas among continents.

Robinson Projection

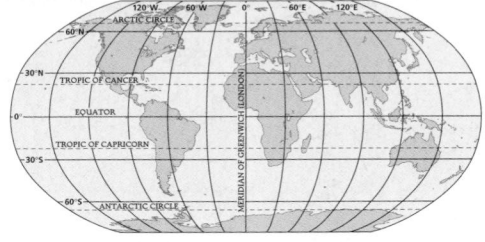

▲ A map using the **Robinson** projection has minor distortions. Land on the western and eastern sides of the Robinson map appears much as it does on a globe. The areas most distorted on this projection are near the North and South Poles.

Winkel Tripel Projection

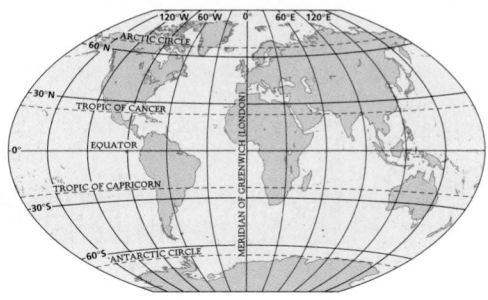

▲ The **Winkel Tripel** projection gives a good overall view of the continents' shapes and sizes. Land areas in a Winkel Tripel projection are not as distorted near the Poles as they are in the Robinson projection.

Mercator Projection

▲ The **Mercator** projection shows true direction and land shapes fairly accurately, but not size or distance. Areas that are located far from the Equator are quite distorted on this projection. Alaska, for example, appears much larger on a Mercator map than it does on a globe.

TEACH

UNDERSTANDING INFORMATION

The National Geographic Society is renowned for the quality and accuracy of its maps. The Society changed from the Robinson projection to the Winkel Tripel projection as its official base map projection in 1998. Ask students to research why the Society made the change. Students should write a brief paper describing the results of their research. **L3**

Did You Know ?

Flemish mathematician, geographer, and cartographer Gerardus Mercator created his well-known projection in 1568. The Mercator projection exaggerates areas as they increase in distance from the Equator. Even so, it has been favored by sailors for more than 400 years.

EXTENDING THE CONTENT

Tactile Maps The Americans with Disabilities Act is opening the door to the production of tactile maps—maps that can be accessed with senses other than sight. Examples include a tactile subway map and a three-dimensional talking map. These maps are, by necessity, much simpler and handle less data since the sense of touch distinguishes less information than the eye. Cartographers are convinced, however, that with increased computer capabilities and innovations in technology, tactile maps will soon be as detailed and informative as any visual maps currently being produced.

Parts of Maps

TEACH

USING SCALE

Write the words *Distance* and *Direction* on the board. **Ask: How do maps show distance and direction?** *(with scale bars and compass roses)* Give students practice in determining distance by showing them how to mark a map scale on the edge of a piece of paper. Have students practice measuring the distance between cities on the map. **L1**

UNDERSTANDING DIRECTION

Have students practice cardinal directions by asking questions such as: **What state is to the west of Indiana?** *(Illinois)* **Is Los Angeles located in northern or southern California?** *(southern)* **Where is Alabama located in relation to Georgia?** *(to the west)* **L1**

Map Key An important first step in reading a map is to note the map key. The **map key** explains the lines, symbols, and colors used on a map. For example, the map on this page shows the various climate regions of the United States and the different colors representing them. Cities are usually symbolized by a solid circle (•) and capitals by a (✪). On this map, you can see the capital of Texas and the cities of Los Angeles, Seattle, New Orleans, and Chicago.

NATIONAL GEOGRAPHIC

Climate Regions of the United States

Key:
- Desert
- Highland
- Humid continental
- Humid subtropical
- Marine
- Mediterranean
- Steppe
- Subarctic
- Tropical
- Tundra

Lambert Equal-Area projection

Scale A measuring line, often called a **scale bar,** helps you figure distance on the map. The map scale tells you what distance on the earth is represented by the measurement on the scale bar.

Compass Rose A map has a symbol that tells you where the **cardinal directions**—north, south, east, and west—are positioned.

GH8   Geography Handbook

COOPERATIVE LEARNING ACTIVITY

Making Maps Organize students into several groups to work as cartographers. Assign each group a particular map—for example, a map of the classroom, the school grounds, or another small area. Different group members should be responsible for the following tasks: measuring and making a scale, using a compass to determine direction and making a compass rose, creating a map key, and creating the map itself. Group members should cooperate to coordinate their work. Display students' maps around the classroom. **L1/ EL**

Types of Maps

General Purpose Maps

Maps are amazingly useful tools. Geographers use many different types of maps. Maps that show a wide range of general information about an area are called **general purpose maps.** Two of the most common general purpose maps are physical and political maps.

Physical Maps

Physical maps call out landforms and water features. The physical map of Sri Lanka (below) shows rivers and mountains. The colors used on physical maps include brown or green for land and blue for water. In addition, physical maps may use colors to show **elevation**—the height of an area above sea level. A key explains what each color and symbol stands for.

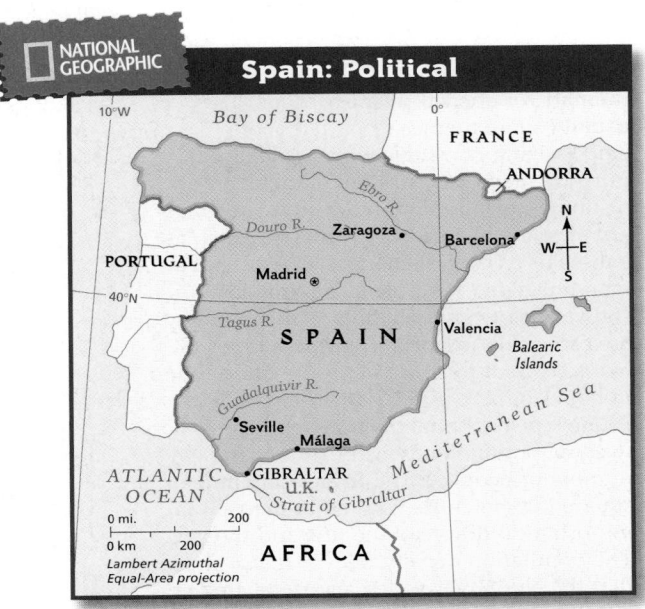

NATIONAL GEOGRAPHIC

Spain: Political

Bay of Biscay
FRANCE
ANDORRA
Ebro R.
Douro R. Zaragoza
Barcelona
PORTUGAL
Madrid
Tagus R.
SPAIN
Valencia
Balearic Islands
Guadalquivir R.
Seville
Málaga
ATLANTIC OCEAN
GIBRALTAR U.K.
Strait of Gibraltar
Mediterranean Sea
AFRICA
0 mi. 200
0 km 200
Lambert Azimuthal Equal-Area projection

Political Maps

Political maps show the names and boundaries of countries, the location of cities and other human-made features of a place, and often identify major physical features. The political map of Spain (above), for example, shows the boundaries between Spain and other countries. It also shows cities and rivers within Spain and bodies of water surrounding Spain.

NATIONAL GEOGRAPHIC

Sri Lanka: Physical

Point Pedro
Jaffna
Gulf of Mannar
Trincomalee
Bay of Bengal
SRI LANKA
Chilaw
Kattankudi
Matale
Pidurutalagala 8,281 ft. (2,524 m)
Colombo
INDIAN OCEAN
Matara 0 mi. 100
0 km 100
80°E

Elevations

Feet	Meters
3,280	1,000
1,640	500
650	200
380	100
0	0

▲ Mountain peak
⊛ National capital
• Major city

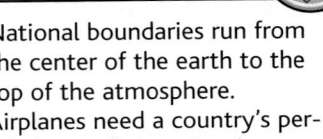

EXTENDING THE CONTENT

Longitude Until the 1700s, sailors seldom knew exactly where they were because they had only lines of latitude to guide them. John Harrison, an English instrument maker, invented a clock that could keep accurate time at sea. A navigator can determine longitude by figuring the difference between Greenwich Mean Time and the time at the ship's location.

TEACH

USING SPECIAL PURPOSE MAPS

Ask volunteers to bring special purpose maps to class to show how they are used in everyday life. Students may bring in maps showing bus routes, weather forecasts, or bike routes. **L1**

ACTIVATING PRIOR KNOWLEDGE

Have students look carefully at the population density map of Egypt. Ask them to think about what they already know about Egypt and speculate as to why certain areas have high density and others have low density. **L2**

READING A MAP

Refer students to the map of China's defenses. Ask them to point out the elements in the map key. Then have students study the map and make a list of the natural and human-made features that provide protection to China. **L1**

Special Purpose Maps

Some maps are made to present specific kinds of information. These are called **thematic** or **special purpose maps.** They usually show themes or patterns, often emphasizing one subject or theme. Special purpose maps may present climate, natural resources, or population density. They may also display historical information, such as battles or territorial changes. The title of a map tells what kind of special information it shows. Colors and symbols in the map key are especially important on these types of maps. Special purpose maps are often found in books of maps called atlases.

One type of special purpose map uses colors to show population density, or the average number of people living in a square mile or square kilometer. As with other maps, it is important to first read the title and the key. The population density map of Egypt shows that the Nile River valley and delta are very densely populated.

Some other special purpose maps such as the one of China's Defenses are not presented in color. They print in black and white. This is an example of a map you might find on a standardized test or in a newspaper.

DIFFERENTIATED INSTRUCTION

Less-proficient Readers: To help students remember the different categories and examples of maps discussed in the **National Geographic Geography Handbook,** guide them in creating a graphic organizer entitled "Types of Maps." Branching from this main head should be three boxes labeled "Political," "Physical," and "Special Purpose." Have students complete the organizer by taking notes on each of the different types of maps.

Refer to *Inclusion Strategies for the Middle School Social Studies Classroom* in the TCR.

Using Graphs, Charts, and Diagrams

Bar, Line, and Circle Graphs

A graph is a way of summarizing and presenting information visually. Each part of a graph gives useful information. First read the title of the graph to find out its subject. Then read the labels along the **axes** of the graph—the vertical line along the left side of the graph and the horizontal line along the bottom. One axis will tell you what is being measured. The other axis tells what units of measurement are being used.

Graphs that use bars or wide lines to compare data visually are called **bar graphs.** Look carefully at the bar graph (right) which compares world languages. The vertical axis lists the languages. The horizontal axis gives speakers of the language in millions. By comparing the lengths of the bars, you can quickly tell which language is spoken by the most people. Bar graphs are especially useful for comparing quantities.

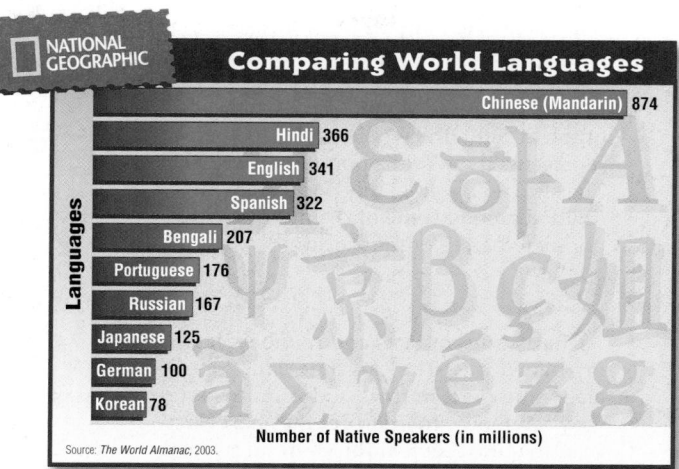

NATIONAL GEOGRAPHIC

Comparing World Languages

Language	Number of Native Speakers (in millions)
Chinese (Mandarin)	874
Hindi	366
English	341
Spanish	322
Bengali	207
Portuguese	176
Russian	167
Japanese	125
German	100
Korean	78

Source: *The World Almanac*, 2003.

Bar graph

A **line graph** is a useful tool for showing changes over a period of time. The amounts being measured are plotted on the grid above each year and then are connected by a line. Line graphs sometimes have two or more lines plotted on them. The line graph (below) shows that the number of farms in the United States has decreased since 1940.

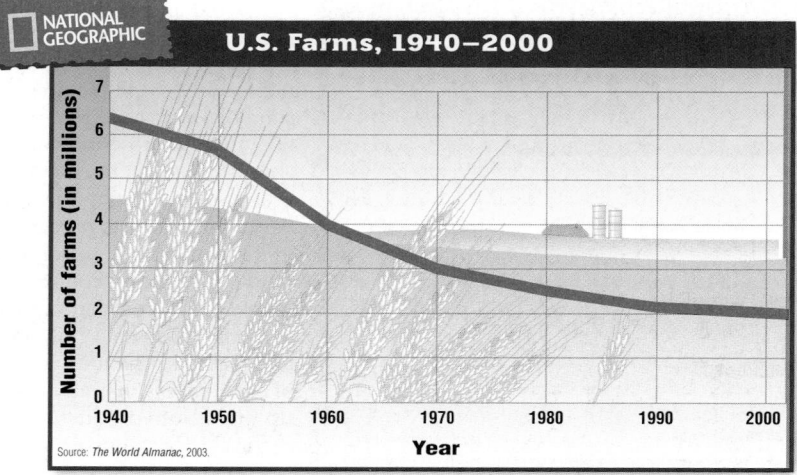

NATIONAL GEOGRAPHIC

U.S. Farms, 1940–2000

Number of farms (in millions) / Year

Source: *The World Almanac*, 2003.

Line graph

Geography Handbook   **GH11**

TEACH

UNDERSTANDING INFORMATION

Bring several newspapers to class, and have students look through them for charts, graphs, and diagrams. Ask students to summarize the information that several of these visuals portray. **L1**

INTERPRETING GRAPHS

Have students look carefully at the line graph showing the number of U.S. farms. Ask students about how many farms existed in 1960. *(about 4 million)* What overall trend do they see on the graph? *(a steady decline in the number of farms)* **L1**

MAKING GRAPHS

Have students use the Internet and other library resources to research the latest population figures of the world's five most populous countries. Then have students make a bar graph comparing the world's most populous countries. Before students begin, ask them to think about and explain what labels should go on the graph's axes. *(vertical: number of people in millions; horizontal: countries)* **L3**

DIFFERENTIATED INSTRUCTION

Kinesthetic: Students who do well with the kinesthetic mode of learning can benefit by translating some two-dimensional models. For example, students can make a line graph using tacks and string, make a bar graph out of blocks, or create a circle graph using clay in a pie tin.

☞ Refer to *Inclusion Strategies for the Middle School Social Studies Classroom* in the TCR.

ANALYZING GRAPHS

Have students look at the pictograph on this page. **Ask:** About how many passenger cars did the United States produce in 2001? *(about 5 million)* Japan? *(8 million)* Have students study the climograph on the next page. **Ask:** What are the two coldest months in Moscow? *(January and February)* **L1**

MAKING CHARTS

Have students use the data in the world population graph on this page to make a chart entitled "World Population." Ask them to decide how the data will be arranged in rows and columns and what labels will be used at the top of each column and on the left side of the chart. **L2**

You can use **circle graphs** when you want to show how the whole of something is divided into its parts. Because of their shape, circle graphs are often called pie graphs. Each "slice" represents a part or percentage of the whole "pie." On the circle graph at right, the whole circle (100 percent) represents the world's population in 2002. The slices show how this population is divided among some of the most heavily populated areas of the world.

Charts

Charts present facts and numbers in an organized way. They arrange data, especially numbers, in rows and columns for easy reference. To interpret the chart, first read the title. Look at the chart on page 91. It tells you what information the chart contains. Next, read the labels at the top of each column and on the left side of the chart. They explain what the numbers or data on the chart are measuring.

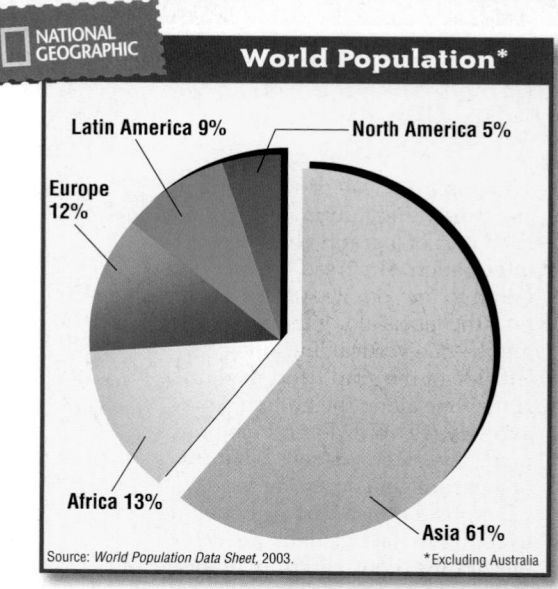

NATIONAL GEOGRAPHIC

World Population*

Latin America 9%
North America 5%
Europe 12%
Africa 13%
Asia 61%

Source: *World Population Data Sheet*, 2003.   *Excluding Australia

Circle graph

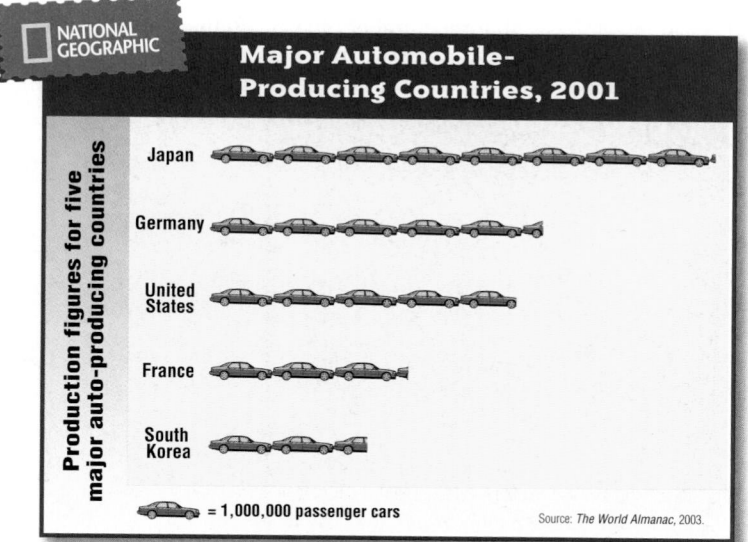

NATIONAL GEOGRAPHIC

Major Automobile-Producing Countries, 2001

Production figures for five major auto-producing countries

Japan
Germany
United States
France
South Korea

= 1,000,000 passenger cars   Source: *The World Almanac*, 2003.

Pictograph

Pictographs

Like bar and circle graphs, pictographs are good for making comparisons. **Pictographs** use rows of small pictures or symbols, with each picture or symbol representing an amount. Look at the pictograph (left) showing the number of automobiles produced in the world's five major automobile-producing countries. The key tells you that one car symbol stands for 1 million automobiles. The total number of car symbols in a row adds up to the auto production in each selected country.

CRITICAL THINKING ACTIVITY

Recognizing Bias Point out the source lines at the bottom of the graphs and charts. Make sure students understand what source lines signify. Then ask students what qualities make an organization a good source of information. Ask them what qualities make a bad source of information. Tell them that some organizations bias their information or delete information in order to support their point of view. Ask them what biases the following sources might have: an industry trade group, a foreign government, and an environmental group. **L3**

Climographs

A **climograph,** or climate graph, combines a line graph and a bar graph. It gives an overall picture of the long-term weather patterns in a specific place. Climographs include several kinds of information. The green vertical bars on the climograph of Moscow (right) show average monthly amounts of precipitation (rain, snow, and sleet). These bars are measured against the axis on the right side of the graph. The red line plotted above the bars represents changes in the average monthly temperature. You measure this line against the axis on the left side.

NATIONAL GEOGRAPHIC
Climograph: Moscow, Russia

Source: World Weather Guide.

Climograph

Diagrams

Diagrams are drawings that show steps in a process, point out the parts of an object, or explain how something works. An **elevation profile** is a type of diagram that can be helpful when comparing the elevations—or height—of an area. It shows an exaggerated side view of the land as if it were sliced and you were viewing it from the side. The elevation profile of Africa (below) clearly shows sea level, low areas, and mountains.

NATIONAL GEOGRAPHIC
Africa: Elevation Profile

Diagram

Geography Handbook   **GH13**

TEACH

WRITING A BROCHURE

Assign students to create a travel brochure for the destination of their choice. The brochure should contain information about its absolute location, place and region, physical and human systems, environment, and society. Encourage students to review the beginning of the **National Geographic Geography Handbook** before they begin writing. **L2**

UNDERSTANDING INFORMATION

The terms that geographers use to describe the earth sometimes originate from different languages. For example, *mesa* is a Spanish word that means "table." Have students check the dictionary definition of *mesa,* and ask them why the Spanish used this word to label a particular natural feature. Ask student volunteers to look up in the dictionary the terms *tsunami* and *fjord.* Have them tell the class the origin and meaning of these geographical terms. **L1**

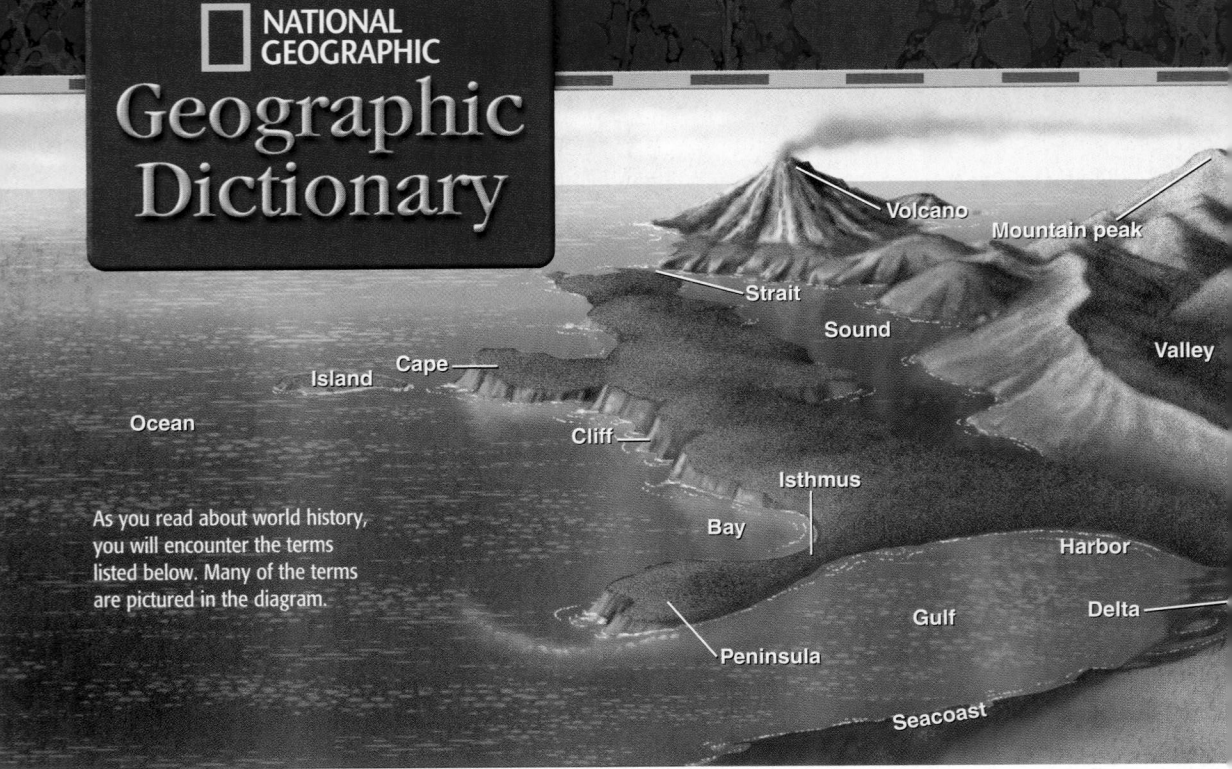

NATIONAL GEOGRAPHIC
Geographic Dictionary

As you read about world history, you will encounter the terms listed below. Many of the terms are pictured in the diagram.

absolute location exact location of a place on the earth described by global coordinates

basin area of land drained by a given river and its branches; area of land surrounded by lands of higher elevation

bay part of a large body of water that extends into a shoreline, generally smaller than a gulf

canyon deep and narrow valley with steep walls

cape point of land that extends into a river, lake, or ocean

channel wide strait or waterway between two landmasses that lie close to each other; deep part of a river or other waterway

cliff steep, high wall of rock, earth, or ice

continent one of the seven large landmasses on the earth

cultural feature characteristic that humans have created in a place, such as language, religion, housing, or settlement pattern

delta flat, low-lying land built up from soil carried downstream by a river and deposited at its mouth

divide stretch of high land that separates river systems

downstream direction in which a river or stream flows from its source to its mouth

elevation height of land above sea level

Equator imaginary line that runs around the earth halfway between the North and South Poles; used as the starting point to measure degrees of north and south latitude

glacier large, thick body of slowly moving ice

gulf part of a large body of water that extends into a shoreline, generally larger and more deeply indented than a bay

harbor a sheltered place along a shoreline where ships can anchor safely

highland elevated land area such as a hill, mountain, or plateau

hill elevated land with sloping sides and rounded summit; generally smaller than a mountain

island land area, smaller than a continent, completely surrounded by water

isthmus narrow stretch of land connecting two larger land areas

lake a sizable inland body of water

latitude distance north or south of the Equator, measured in degrees

longitude distance east or west of the Prime Meridian, measured in degrees

lowland land, usually level, at a low elevation

map drawing of the earth shown on a flat surface

meridian one of many lines on the global grid running from the North Pole to the South Pole; used to measure degrees of longitude

mesa broad, flat-topped landform with steep sides; smaller than a plateau

COOPERATIVE LEARNING ACTIVITY

Map Quiz Organize the class into two teams. Provide one team with a map of their county and the other team with a map of their state. Assign each team the following task: Locate every major body of water in your assigned area. Record your findings, including 1) the name of each major body of water; 2) what type of body of water it is—lake, river, bay, and so on; and 3) its absolute location. When each team has completed its task, have them create a map quiz based on their work. The teams should then trade maps and challenge each other with their quizzes. **L2**

Labels on the illustration:
Mountain range · Glacier · Source of river · Highland · Channel · Plateau · Lake · Hills · Mouth of river · Canyon · Desert · River · Upstream · Downstream · Lowland · Plain · Basin · Tributary

Did You Know ?

One of the most violent volcanic eruptions in history occurred in 1883 on the island of Krakatau in Indonesia. The volcano collapsed from a height of 2,640 feet (800 m) above sea level to 1,000 feet (300 m) below sea level. Its collapse triggered a tidal wave that killed 36,000 people in nearby Java and Sumatra.

CLOSE

MAKING A SHOE MAP

To help give students a sense of appreciation for the complexities of mapmaking, conduct the following activity. Students will need drawing paper and no more than five different colored crayons or markers. Their assignment is to "draw" a map of their shoe, designing a projection or system that will indicate the shoe's three-dimensional, or curved, characteristics.

Allow students to attempt to draw a cross-section, top view, or other perspective that they choose. Remind students that they will need a key and a scale bar on their completed maps. **L3**

---

mountain land with steep sides that rises sharply (1,000 feet [305 m] or more) from surrounding land; generally larger and more rugged than a hill

mountain peak pointed top of a mountain

mountain range a series of connected mountains

mouth (of a river) place where a stream or river flows into a larger body of water

ocean one of the four major bodies of salt water that surround the continents

ocean current stream of either cold or warm water that moves in a definite direction through an ocean

parallel one of many lines on the global grid that circle the earth north or south of the Equator; used to measure degrees of latitude

peninsula body of land jutting into a lake or ocean, surrounded on three sides by water

physical feature characteristic of a place occurring naturally, such as a landform, body of water, climate pattern, or resource

plain area of level land, usually at a low elevation and often covered with grasses

plateau area of flat or rolling land at a high elevation, about 300–3,000 feet (91–914 m) high

Prime Meridian line of the global grid running from the North Pole to the South Pole through Greenwich, England; starting point for measuring degrees of east and west longitude

relief changes in elevation over a given area of land

river large natural stream of water that runs through the land

sea large body of water completely or partly surrounded by land

seacoast land lying next to a sea or ocean

sea level position on land level with surface of nearby ocean or sea

sound body of water between a coastline and one or more islands off the coast

source (of a river) place where a river or stream begins, often in highlands

strait narrow stretch of water joining two larger bodies of water

tributary small river or stream that flows into a larger river or stream; a branch of the river

upstream direction opposite the flow of a river; toward the source of a river or stream

valley area of low land between hills or mountains

volcano mountain created as liquid rock or ash erupts from inside the earth

---

Reading Strategy   READING THE TEXT

Understanding Cause and Effect As students read the textbook, remind them to think about how geography affects a region. Students should create graphic organizers for each chapter that show how geography has shaped the environment, people, culture, and events in a region. As students study the chapters, ask questions that focus on geographical cause-and-effect relationships.

TOOLS OF THE HISTORIAN OBJECTIVES

After studying **Tools of the Historian,** students should be able to

1. demonstrate and apply basic tools of historical research;

2. describe ways of interpreting archaeological evidence;

3. analyze and evaluate historical materials;

4. apply geography to historical research;

5. connect the current world to the ancient world.

① FOCUS

Have students select one item from their lives (CD, baseball card, etc.) and list its characteristics. Ask them what this item will tell future archaeologists and historians about life in the twenty-first century. **L2**

② TEACH

DEFINING TERMS

The term *carbon-14 (C-14)* refers to a radioactive element found in all living things. After plants, animals, and humans die, the C-14 gradually disappears. By measuring how much C-14 a skeleton, for example, contains today, scientists can calculate how old it is as far back as about 50,000 years.

Tools of the Historian

A historian is a person who studies and writes about the people and events of the past. Historians find out how people lived, what happened to them, and what happened around them. Historians look for the reasons behind events. They also study the effects of events.

Have you ever wondered if you could be a historian? To answer that question, you will need to find out how history is researched and written. Historians use a number of tools to research and organize information. You can learn about these tools in the next few pages. As you study this textbook, you will see that these tools will help you understand world history.

Archaeologists are scientists who unearth the remains of the past. Historians depend on their work.

Digging Up the Past

What Do Archaeologists Study?
- Human and animal bones, seeds, trees
- Pottery, tools, weapons
- Mounds, pits, canals

▲ **Prehistoric pottery**

How Do They Gather Data?
- Surveys on foot
- Photographs taken from airplanes or satellites
- Ground-penetrating radar
- Locations plotted on maps
- Evidence gathered with tools from heavy equipment to shovels
- Sonar scanning to find underwater objects

How Do They Interpret Findings?
- Organize artifacts into groups based on similarities
- Compare objects in relation to other objects
- Look for evidence of changes over a period of time
- Date once-living objects by measuring carbon-14 levels
- Use microscopic and biological tests to date objects

Carbon-14 dating ▶

Do Your Own Digging

Research the library and Internet to find information on two archaeological diggings, one past and the other, very recent. Compare and contrast the methods used in each digging. What changes do you notice in tools archaeologists have used over time?

EXTENDING THE CONTENT

A Difference in Terms The abbreviations "B.C." and "A.D." are Western- and Christian-oriented. Some historians believe that terms used to date world events should be neutral with respect to all global regions and religions. They prefer to use the abbreviations "B.C.E." ("before the common era") and "C.E." ("common era"). For example, *1850 B.C.* can be written as "1850 B.C.E.," and *A.D. 1900* as "C.E. 1900."

Measuring Time

Main Idea
Historians rely on calendars and the dating of events to measure time.

Reading Focus Have you ever thought about traveling back in time to a place long ago? Historians do just that. Read to see how historians keep track of past events.

Calendars Historians rely on *calendars,* or dating systems, to measure time. Cultures throughout the world have developed different calendars based on important events in their history. Western nations begin their calendar on the year in which Jesus was thought to have been born. The Jewish calendar begins about 3,760 years before the Christian calendar. This is the time when Jewish tradition says the world was created. Muslims date their calendar from the time their first leader, Muhammad, left the city of Makkah for Madinah. This was a.d. 622 in the Christian calendar.

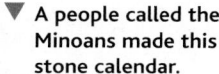

▼ A people called the Minoans made this stone calendar.

▲ About A.D. 500, a Christian monk, or religious person, developed the Western way of dating events.

The dates in this book are based on the Western calendar. In the Western calendar, the years before the birth of Jesus are known as "B.C.," or "before Christ." The years after are called "A.D.," or *anno domini.* This phrase comes from the Latin language and means "in the year of the Lord."

Dating Events To date events *before* the birth of Christ, or "B.C.," historians count backwards from A.D. 1. There is no year "0." The year before A.D. 1 is 1 B.C. (Notice that "A.D." is written before the date, while "B.C." is written following the date.) Therefore, a date in the 100 years before the birth of Christ lies between 100 B.C. and A.D. 1.

To date events after the birth of Christ, or "A.D.," historians count forward, starting at A.D. 1. A date in the first 100 years after the birth of Christ is between A.D. 1 and A.D. 100.

Thinking Like a Historian

1. **Identify** What do "B.C." and "A.D." mean? How are they used?

2. **Dating Events** What year came *after* 184 B.C.?

3. **Comparing and Contrasting** As you read, use the Internet to find out the current year in the calendars mentioned in your text. Why are calendars different from culture to culture?

Tools of the Historian **TOOLS 1**

Thinking Like a Historian Answers

1. B.C.—"before Christ"; A.D.—*anno domini,* "in the year of the Lord"; B.C.—dates events before the birth of Christ; A.D.—dates events after Christ's birth
2. 183 B.C.

3. Students may use the Internet or consult encyclopedias, almanacs, or other library resources to find the current year. Cultures develop different calendars based on key events in their histories.

Tools of the Historian

Ask students how they would explain or define the concept of time to a space alien who comes from a planet where time does not exist.

② TEACH

DEFINING TERMS

Ask a volunteer to define the term *chronology*. (*the order of the dates when different things happened*) Tell them that the word comes from two Greek roots meaning "time" and "word." Ask them to explain in what way chronology incorporates both ideas. (*It arranges events in time order, helping to explain them.*) **L1**

MAKING INFERENCES

Ask students to speculate on why historians refer to the years from A.D. 500 to A.D. 1500 as the Middle Ages. In what way are they "in the middle"? Did these years seem "in the middle" to people living during them? (*From our vantage point, they are between ancient history—which students may recognize as including civilizations such as Greece and Rome—and modern history. The Middle Ages naturally did not seem to be a middle age to those living through them.*) **L2**

Organizing Time

◀ Tools made by prehistoric people

Main Idea ....

Historians organize history by dividing it into blocks of time.

Reading Focus Have you ever thought about the names given to a block of events, such as "summer vacation" or "the baseball season?" Read to see how historians use names to describe different stretches of time in history.

....

Periods of History Historians divide history into blocks of time known as *periods*, or *eras*. For example, a period of 10 years is called a *decade*. A period of 100 years is known as a *century*. Centuries are grouped into even longer time periods, which are given names.

The first of these long periods is called *Prehistory*. Prehistory refers to the time before people developed writing, about 5,500 years ago. This is followed by the period known as *Ancient History*, ending c. A.D. 500. (c., or *circa*, means "about"). Historians call the next thousand years the *Middle Ages*, or the medieval period. From c. 1500, *Modern History* begins

▲ A young couple of ancient Rome

◀ A woman of medieval Japan playing a musical instrument

◀ Educated Europeans of the early modern period discussing new ideas

TOOLS 2   Tools of the Historian

EXTENDING THE CONTENT

Periods in History Historians have delineated many different periods in history. Some periods, such as the Renaissance, the Reformation, and the Enlightenment, are based on dominant religious or intellectual movements of the time. Other periods are based on the reigns of monarchs or the tenures of leaders, such as the Victorian and Edwardian Ages in modern Britain, and the Age of Pericles in ancient Greece. Still others refer to notable scientific or technological developments. These include the first Industrial Revolution (c. 1750 to c. 1850), the Nuclear Age (1945 to c. 1986), and the Information Age (c. 1986 to the present). Have students hypothesize on other names they might use to describe the period in which they live. Students may refer to current events, such as the 9/11 attacks and the war in Iraq, for clues.

Three Ancient Civilizations

	2500 B.C.	1500 B.C.	800 B.C.	650 B.C.

Ancient Greece *Chapters 4 & 5*
- c. 1600 B.C. Minoan civilization reaches height
- c. 776 B.C. First Olympic Games take place

◄ Ancient plate

Early India *Chapter 6*
- c. 2500 B.C. Settlements develop along Indus River
- c. 1500 B.C. Aryans invade India

Hindu temple ►

Early China *Chapter 7*
- c. 1750 B.C. Shang Dynasty begins
- c. 1045 B.C. Zhou establish dynasty in China

Zhou dynasty ► bronze dragon

and continues to the present day. In this book, you will study the history of the world from prehistory to the beginning of the modern period.

What Is a Time Line? Which came first: the American Civil War or World War II? Did the train come before or after the invention of the airplane? In studying the past, historians focus on *chronology*, or the order of dates in which events happened.

You might be wondering how to make sense of the flow of dates and events. An easy way is to use or make a time line. A *time line* is a diagram that shows the order of events within a period of time.

Most time lines are divided into sections in which the years are evenly spaced. In some cases, however, a spread of time may be too long to show all of the years in even spaces. To save space, a period of time may be omitted from the time line. Where this happens, a slanted or jagged line appears on the time line to show a break in the even spacing of events. For example, the time line above shows a break between 1500 B.C. and 800 B.C.

A time line also labels events. Each event on the time line appears beside the date when the event took place. Sometimes events and their dates are shown on a single time line. In other cases, two or more time lines are stacked one on top of the other. These are called multilevel time lines. They help you to compare events in different places at certain periods of time. For example, the multilevel time line above shows events in three ancient civilizations from 2500 B.C. to 650 B.C. The skill "Reading a Time Line" on page 905 will help you learn to work with time lines.

Thinking Like a Historian

1. **Reading a Time Line** Look over the time line above to get an idea of what a time line shows. What is the title? When does it begin and end? What two features make this time line different from many other time lines? Why are they used?

2. **Understanding a Time Line** Why do you think the dates on the time line are marked with a "c."?

3. **Making a Time Line** Create a time line using the terms B.M.B. (before my birth) and A.M.B. (after my birth). Fill in the time line with five key events that happened before and after you were born. Illustrate the time line with copies of photos from your family album.

Tools of the Historian   **TOOLS 3**

Thinking Like a Historian Answers

1. Three Ancient Civilizations; 2500 B.C., 650 B.C.; a break line to symbolize a gap in time, three time lines (one placed on top of the other) are used for comparing events in different places

2. The use of "c." (meaning "about") indicates that the exact dates of these events are not known.

3. Time lines will vary. Students should include significant milestones, such as weddings, birthdays, graduations, and vacations.

Tools of the Historian

1 FOCUS

Tell students that historians and detectives are alike in many ways. Ask them to describe what detectives do. *(search for clues, examine evidence, build cases, and write reports)* Then explain that, in the case of historians, they search for and use evidence to solve problems about the past.

2 TEACH

DEFINING TERMS

Ask volunteers to define "primary" *(first, basic)* and "secondary" *(second, afterward, following)* and use them in sentences that illustrate their different meanings. Then explain that these words have a special significance in history. Ask students to look for these special meanings as they read this lesson. **L2**

COMPARING AND CONTRASTING

Ask students to give examples of a primary source that would tell what your class is doing at this moment *(an account by a class member)* and a secondary source *(a report from a friend of a class member)*. Ask students to explain the difference. **L1**

How Does a Historian Work?

Main Idea
Historians study a variety of sources to learn about the past.

Reading Focus Have you ever searched for clues on a treasure hunt? Read to find out how historians look for clues to create a written record about the past.

Where Is the Evidence? Historians begin by asking questions, such as: Why did two particular countries go to war? What effect did their fighting have on the lives of their people? How does the conflict influence our world today? Such questions help historians identify and focus on historical problems.

Historians generally find evidence in primary sources and secondary sources. *Primary sources* are firsthand pieces of evidence from people who saw or experienced an event. They include written documents, such as letters, diaries, and official records. They also include spoken interviews as well as objects, such as photos, paintings, clothing, and tools. The skill "Analyzing Primary Source Documents" on page 910 will give you a chance to work with written primary sources.

Secondary sources, on the other hand, are created *after* the events by people who played no part in them. Secondary sources can be partially based on primary sources. They include biographies, encyclopedias, and history books—even this textbook.

Historians study secondary sources for background information and for a larger view of an event. However, to get new evidence that advances knowledge, historians must turn to the firsthand information found only in primary sources.

TOOLS 4   Tools of the Historian

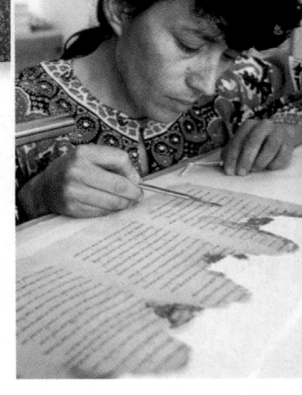

▲ Scientist studying Dead Sea Scrolls from southwest Asia

Examining Sources
Historians *analyze,* or examine, primary and secondary sources. First, they determine *where* and *when* a source was created. Another important question historians consider is *why* a source was created. Was it a letter meant to be kept secret? Was it a government document published for all citizens to read?

Can the Sources Be Trusted? Historians examine sources for *credibility,* or truthfulness. This is because each source reflects a *point of view,* or a general attitude about people and life. The creator of a source uses his or her point of view to decide what events were important, which people were key players, and what details were worth recording. Sometimes point of view is expressed as a *bias,* or an unreasoned, emotional judgment about people and events.

Historians try to be aware of point of view and bias both in their sources and in themselves. Therefore, they check new

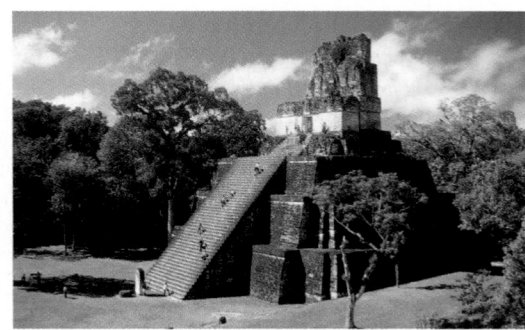

▲ Ruins of Mayan temple in Central America

CRITICAL THINKING ACTIVITY

Types of Primary Sources Recently, spoken words that make up oral histories have gained importance as primary sources. Oral histories provide historical evidence about people who were often historically overlooked or did not leave behind written primary sources. Visual documents and artifacts, such as photographs, films, and different kinds of artwork, are also primary sources. Like other primary sources, a visual document has a creator with a point of view—such as a painter, sculptor, or filmmaker. Using visual documents as primary sources requires careful analysis of the content and point of view of the creator. Have students examine different written and visual primary sources about a twentieth-century historical event (such as the assassination of John F. Kennedy). Ask them to speculate on the differing points of view the sources reflect. **L3**

The Decline of Rome

Weak Roman Government
- Dishonest government officials provide poor leadership.

Social Problems
- Famine and disease spread throughout the empire.

Declining Economy
- Income and wages fall.
- Wealthy fail to pay taxes.

Reform Fails and Rome Divides in Two
- Government fails to keep order.
- Violence and tension increase.
- Diocletian divides the empire.

Eastern Roman Empire
- Constantinople becomes the new capital.
- The empire survives attacks and prospers.

Western Roman Empire
- Numerous attacks threaten the empire.
- Territory is slowly lost to invaders.

Byzantine Empire
- This empire is created from the Eastern Roman Empire and lasts nearly 1,000 years.

Rome Falls
- The city of Rome falls in A.D. 476.
- The Western Roman Empire is divided into Germanic kingdoms by A.D. 550.

sources and their own ideas against sources already known to be trustworthy. They also examine many sources that express different points of view about an event. In this way, historians try to get a clear, well-rounded view of what happened.

Historians piece together the credible evidence and draw conclusions. In drawing conclusions, they use their own thinking and knowledge of the past to *interpret,* or explain, the meaning of the events.

Cause and Effect

Historical events are linked by cause and effect. A *cause* is what makes an event happen. The event that happens as a result of the cause is known as an *effect.* Historians look for cause-and-effect links to explain *why* events happen.

Usually, one event is produced by many causes. Similarly, one event often produces several different effects. These cause-and-

effect links form what is called a *cause-and-effect chain.* Because so many historical events are related, cause-and-effect chains can become very long and can include events that occur over a long period of time. The chart above shows such a chain of events.

Thinking Like a Historian

1. **Understanding Evidence** Suppose a friend wanted to write a history of your life so far. What primary sources might he or she use to find evidence of your daily activities?

2. **Analyzing Sources** Find two written accounts of a recent event in your town. Which of the two accounts do you think is the most credible? Why?

3. **Recognizing Cause and Effect** Study the cause-and-effect chart on this page. What were three major causes of Rome's decline? What were two important effects of Rome's decline upon history?

③ ASSESS

ENRICH

Making a Source Checklist Divide the class into two groups, one to focus on each kind of source. Each group will discuss and prepare a checklist of questions to ask when evaluating a primary or a secondary source.

For example, the group focusing on **primary sources** might include these questions:

- Who created it? How was the creator linked to the events?
- When was it created? How might the creator's culture have affected the writing?
- Why was it created?
- Who was the intended audience?
- How can I find out more about the events or the creator's time and culture?

A group focusing on **secondary sources** might include these questions:

- Who is the creator?
- How did the creator get his or her information?
- Is the creator trustworthy? How can I find out?
- What biases might the creator have?
- What questions does the creator not address? Why?

Conclude the activity with a discussion and post the questions in the classroom. **L3**

Thinking Like a Historian Answers

1. Answers will vary but might include diaries, letters, newspaper articles, oral interviews with friends, artifacts (bicycles, baseball gloves, etc.), and photos.

2. Answers will vary. Students may consult local newspapers and periodicals, including the editorials and letters to the editor.

3. weak Roman government, social problems, declining economy; the creation of the Byzantine Empire, the Western Roman Empire was divided into Germanic kingdoms

Tools of the Historian

① FOCUS

Ask students to brainstorm ways they have interacted with their natural surroundings over the last few days. Tell them that interaction with the environment is one of the major themes of geography and history. **L1**

② TEACH

DEFINING TERMS

Tell students that the words *absolute* and *relative* play an important role in studying the location of a place. Explain the words by saying that one student's *absolute* location is in the first row, first seat of your classroom. His or her *relative* location is defined in relation to other locations. For example, the student is in front of one student and next to another.

DETERMINING CAUSE AND EFFECT

Ask a volunteer to define *migrate* for the class. (*to move from one place to another*) Ask students to list reasons why people migrate. (*war, search for better living conditions, flight from natural disasters or disease*) Then ask students if they have moved recently or know someone who has moved. Ask them to decide which causes and effects are at work. Students might create cause-and-effect charts to illustrate these concepts **L2**

History and Geography

▲ Growing rice in China

◀ The Acropolis, Athens, Greece

Main Idea

Historians try to understand how climate, landforms, and human activities have shaped past events.

Reading Focus Have you ever had a party or sports event cancelled because of bad weather? Read to find out how historians study the effects of the natural world on history.

Geography is the study of the earth's physical and human features. In this text, you will discover how geography has shaped the course of events in world history. Sometimes the study of geography is broken down into five themes. *The Five Themes of Geography* are:

- **location** (Where is it?)
- **place** (What is it like?)
- **human/environment interaction** (What is the relationship between people and their surroundings?)
- **movement** (How do people in one area relate to people in other areas?)
- **region** (What common features bring geographical areas together?)

Location

"Where is it?" In using geography, historians first look at where a place is located. Every place has an absolute location and a relative location. *Absolute location* refers to the exact spot of a place on the earth's surface. For example, the city of Atlanta, Georgia, is located at one place and one place only. No other place on Earth has exactly the same location. *Relative location* tells where a place is, compared with one or more other places. Atlanta is northwest of Miami, Florida, and southwest of New York City.

TOOLS 6   **Tools of the Historian**

Place

"What is it like?" *Place* describes all of the characteristics that give an area its own special quality. These can be physical features, such as mountains, waterways, climate, and plant or animal life. Places can also be described by human characteristics, such as language, religion, and architecture.

Human/Environment Interaction

"What is the relationship between people and their surroundings?" Landforms, waterways, climate, and natural resources all have helped or hindered human activities. People in turn have responded to their environment, or natural surroundings, in different ways. Sometimes they have adjusted to it. At other times, people have changed their environment to meet their needs.

EXTENDING THE CONTENT

Irrigation Bringing water to places where is it scarce has been one of the most important ways people have interacted with the environment through the ages. The practice dates back to at least 5000 B.C., when the Egyptians used water from the Nile River to irrigate their fields. People in ancient Mesopotamia used canals and ditches to move water, and then animal-powered machines made the task easier. Today, irrigation is critical to agriculture in many dry parts of the world. People use reservoirs, ponds, rivers, canal systems, and aluminum pipes, as well as electricity and other power sources, to deliver water. Some irrigation systems even use sewage, rich in nitrogen, to add fertility to the soil in fields.

◄ Settlement in Mongolia

▲ Camel caravan in North Africa

▲ Wall painting showing life in ancient Egypt

Movement

"How do people in one area relate to people in other areas?" Historians answer this question within the theme of *movement*. Throughout history, people, ideas, goods, and information have moved from place to place. Movement has brought the world's people closer together. Transportation—the movement of people and goods—has increased the exchange of ideas and cultures. Communication—the movement of ideas and information—has allowed people to find out what is happening in other parts of the world.

Region

"What common features bring geographical areas together?" To make sense of all the complex things in the world, historians often view places or areas as regions. A *region* is an area that is defined by common features. Regions can be defined by physical features, such mountains and rivers, or by human features, such as religion, language, or livelihood.

Six Essential Elements

Recently the study of geography has been broken down into *Six Essential Elements:*
• The World in Spatial Terms
• Places and Regions
• Physical Systems
• Human Systems
• Environment and Society
• The Uses of Geography
You can learn about the Six Essential Elements in the Geography Handbook on pages GH2–GH3. Knowing these elements will help you in your study of history.

Thinking Like a Historian

1. **Identify** How are absolute location and relative location different?

2. **Analyzing Themes** What characteristics do geographers use to describe a place?

3. **Linking History and Geography** Make a list of the Five Themes of Geography. Under each theme, explain how you think geography has shaped the history of your community.

Tools of the Historian   **TOOLS 7**

Thinking Like a Historian Answers

1. Absolute location: tells the exact spot of a place on the earth's surface; relative location: tells where a place is compared with one or more other places.
2. Characteristics include physical features (mountains, waterways, climates, plants, animals) and human characteristics (language, religion, architecture).
3. Answers will vary, but students should respond to the questions asked for each of the Five Themes as given in the text (location, place, human/environment interaction, movement, region).

TOOLS 7

Ask students if they have ever asked someone "Do I have to draw you a map?" What did they mean by the question? What is it about maps that makes them clearer than some other ways of presenting information? Conclude by telling students that they are about to learn how historians use special kinds of maps to show different types of historical information.

2 TEACH

DEFINING TERMS

Tell students that the word *atlas* comes from a Greek legend by way of a sixteenth-century mapmaker. Gerardus Mercator, who invented a popular kind of map presentation, placed a picture of the Greek mythological character Atlas on the map book's title page. According to legend, Atlas was condemned to carry the earth on his shoulders. To Mercator, Atlas seemed a good symbol for a collection of world maps—and we still use this term today.

What Is a Historical Atlas?

Main Idea

Maps give information about areas of the world at different periods of history.

Reading Focus Have you used a map to go from one place to another? Read to find out how you can rely on maps for clues about the past.

Historical Maps An *atlas* is a book of maps showing different parts of the world. A *historical atlas* has maps showing different parts of the world at different periods of history. Maps that show political events, such as invasions, battles, and boundary changes, are called *historical maps.*

Some historical maps show how territories in a certain part of the world changed over time. Below are two maps. One map shows the areas of Europe, Asia, and Africa that were ruled by Alexander the Great in 323 B.C. The other map shows the same region as it looks today. Placed next to each other, the maps help you compare historical changes in the region from ancient times to today.

In the larger map, Alexander's empire stretches from the Mediterranean Sea in the west to the Indus River in the east. There are no political borders. Instead, other things are shown. For example, the arrows on the map represent the movement of Alexander's armies as they conquered new lands. On the smaller map, lines show modern political boundaries in the region today.

NATIONAL GEOGRAPHIC

Alexander's Empire *323 B.C.*

KEY
Extent of empire
← Alexander's routes of conquest
✳ Major battle

MACEDONIA
Danube R.
Black Sea
Granicus 334 B.C.
Chaeronea 338 B.C.
Aegean Sea
Athens
ASIA MINOR
Issus 333 B.C.
Caspian Sea
Gaugamela 331 B.C.
Tigris R.
Euphrates R.
Mediterranean Sea
Tyre • SYRIA
Babylon
Susa
PERSIA
Alexandria
Persepolis
EGYPT
Persian Gulf
Indus R.
Arabian Sea

0   500 mi.
0   500 km
Lambert Azimuthal Equal-Area projection

The Region Today

BULGARIA
UZBEKISTAN
GREECE
TURKEY
TURKMENISTAN
LEBANON
SYRIA
IRAN
AFGHANISTAN
ISRAEL
IRAQ
KUWAIT
JORDAN
PAKISTAN
LIBYA
EGYPT
SAUDI ARABIA

TOOLS 8

EXTENDING THE CONTENT

Ancient Mapmakers The oldest existing map was made on a clay tablet in Mesopotamia (now part of Iraq) about 2300 B.C. It shows settlements, rivers, and mountains. However, it was the ancient Greeks who first studied the world in an accurate and systematic way. The most famous geographer of ancient times was Ptolemy, a Greek geographer who worked in Egypt about A.D. 150. His map of the world (as known to Europeans) was the best of its kind in Europe until the time of Christopher Columbus. At about the same time as Ptolemy, a Chinese astronomer named Zhang Heng developed one of the first geographic grid systems for maps.

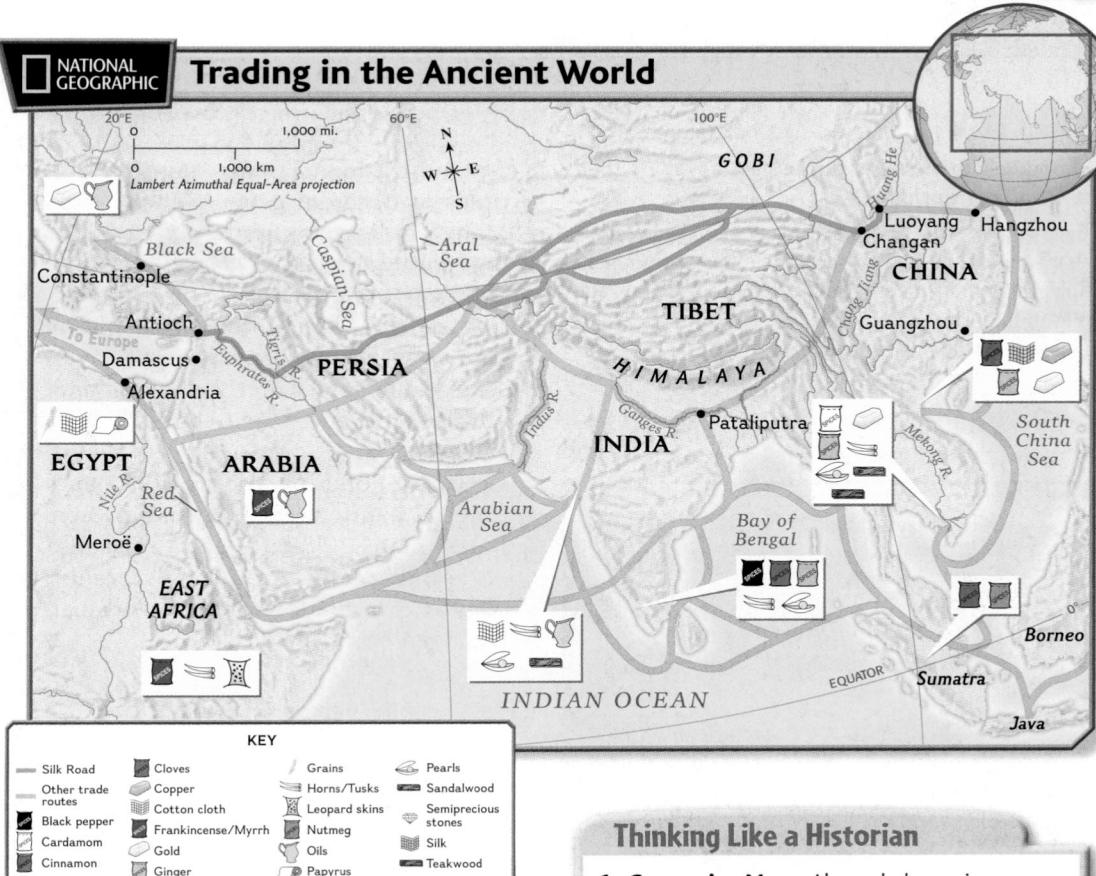

NATIONAL GEOGRAPHIC · Trading in the Ancient World

KEY

Silk Road	Cloves	Grains	Pearls
Other trade routes	Copper	Horns/Tusks	Sandalwood
Black pepper	Cotton cloth	Leopard skins	Semiprecious stones
Cardamom	Frankincense/Myrrh	Nutmeg	Silk
Cinnamon	Gold	Oils	Teakwood
	Ginger	Papyrus	

Historical Routes

On some maps, lines may show *historical routes.* These are roads or courses over which people or goods have traveled all through history. Such routes are often colored. On the map above, the purple line shows the Silk Road, the ancient trading route between Asia and Europe.

On maps of historical routes, the key gives clues to what is shown on the maps. This map key shows the different goods traded throughout the ancient world.

Thinking Like a Historian

1. **Comparing Maps** Alexander's empire included many different territories. In what territory was the city of Persepolis located? What present-day country covers this area today?

2. **Reading a Map Legend** Look at the map of ancient trade routes. What goods came from southern India? How were goods carried from place to place in ancient times?

3. **Analyzing Maps** Select any chapter in your textbook. List the titles of the maps found in that chapter. Beside each map title, state what kind of symbols are used in each map key and what they represent.

Tools of the Historian   **TOOLS 9**

COMPARING AND CONTRASTING

Have student groups select historical maps of areas from the text. Then have them search student atlases for maps of the same areas today. Ask group members to compare and contrast their historical and present-day maps in chart form. One column will list historical map features, and the other column will list those on the present-day map.

After the charts are completed, have each group write one or two paragraphs stating how their area has changed or stayed the same over the course of time, as represented by the two maps. **L3**

③ ASSESS

ENRICH

Imaginary Maps, Real Information
Ask students to draw a map of an imaginary place using the map details they have learned about on these pages. Have them begin by choosing the type of map they want to create. Then have them make up an imaginary landscape appropriate to their choice of map. If possible, students may use computer-generated graphics to enhance the appeal of their maps. Have volunteers share their maps with the class, explaining the different details they have included. **L2**

Thinking Like a Historian Answers

1. Persia; Iran
2. various spices, animal horns and tusks, pearls; overland by human or animal transport, overseas by ship
3. Students' answers will be based on the maps found in the chapter they select.

Tools of the Historian

① FOCUS

Have students think of an event that occurred in their lives that still affects them today. For example, students might mention how they made new friends when they moved from elementary school to middle school or how their family life changed when a younger brother or sister was born. Have students describe whether this event affected them negatively or positively and ask them to speculate about how their lives might be different if this event had not occurred. Tell students that, just as their lives change when something happens to them, so does history when events or developments occur. **L1**

② TEACH

DEFINING TERMS

Point out to students that our form of government—a democratic republic—is partly based on one that existed much earlier (the ancient Roman Republic). Have students look in the dictionary to find a definition of the word *republic*. Then ask if any students can identify the roots of our republican form of government. If not, ask them to look for this information as they read **Links Across Time**. **L3**

ACTIVATING PRIOR KNOWLEDGE

Have students create a photo or pictorial essay of images they associate with Greek and Roman civilizations. **L2**

Links Across Time

Main Idea

The people and events of the past have left their mark on our world today.

Reading Focus How have older family members shaped your life today? In the same way, many things link past to present in world history. Read about examples of past-and-present links for each of the six units you will be studying in your text.

▲ Fighting today between Palestinians and Israelis

Unit 1 Early Civilizations

Civilizations arose at different times in different parts of the world. Many civilizations grew out of farming settlements in river valleys. Southeast Asia was an early center of civilized life. For centuries, people in southwest Asia have fought over scarce land and water. Religious and ethnic differences also have led to wars.

Today, one of the fiercest and longest conflicts has been between Palestinian Arabs and Israelis. Although many Arabs and Israelis support peace efforts, hatred and fear run deep on both sides.

▼ Ancient warriors attack walled city

TOOLS 10   Tools of the Historian

EXTENDING THE CONTENT

Developing Mathematics The ancient Greeks were heir to all the mathematical knowledge of the Mesopotamian and Egyptian civilizations. They built upon that inheritance by using their sense of reason to pursue the "Why?" and "What does it mean?" questions of mathematics. Thales of Miletus began the mathematical revolution. He laid the foundation that is still part of the introductory courses in geometry. The followers of Pythagoras advanced mathematics into a quasi-religion. Euclid simplified and organized the new knowledge. Apollonius explored the aspects of conic sections. Archimedes is the father of scientific notation.

Unit 2 The Ancient World

People in ancient civilizations admired the deeds of their heroes. The ancient Greeks held the first Olympic games about 776 B.C. Athletes came from all over the Greek-speaking world to compete in the games. Today the modern Olympics draw athletes from all over the world.

▼ Ancient Greek athletes

▲ Racers in modern Olympics

▲ Roman Senate

Unit 3 New Empires and New Faiths

After 500 B.C., strong governments and new religions arose in many parts of the world. The Romans created a common culture among the many different peoples living in the Mediterranean world. The Roman system of laws was a lasting achievement. The Romans believed that laws apply equally to all citizens. Today, the U.S. Congress is the part of our national government that makes laws. Its upper body—the U.S. Senate—is named after the Senate of ancient Rome.

◀ U.S. Congress

Tools of the Historian   TOOLS 11

③ ASSESS

ENRICH

Learning History's Lessons Write on the board this famous quotation from the Spanish American philosopher George Santayana: "Those who do not remember the past are condemned to repeat it."

Have students analyze and evaluate the quotation by asking them the following questions:

• What do you think Santayana means?

• Do you agree with him? Why or why not?

• What are some examples that support or oppose his statement?

• Why do you think that some people seem to ignore the lessons of history?

• What are some ways people can better learn the important lessons that history can teach? **L3**

Reading Strategy   **READING THE TEXT**

Using Word Parts A *root* is the part of the word that contains its basic meaning. Unlike a base word, a root is not a word by itself. Many roots come from Greek or Latin. For example, *bio* means "life" (biology, biography); *tele* means "distant" (television, telescope); *dent* means "tooth" (dentist, trident). Have students find root words as they read the textbook and find their meanings using a dictionary. **L1**

Tools of the Historian

① FOCUS

Ask students to describe ways that the Internet has changed the lives of people around the world. (*Students may note that the Internet allows people to communicate and share ideas more easily, along with allowing people to achieve more economic success as a result of increased trade.*) As students read about technological advances in Units 4, 5, and 6, remind them that these advances had similar effects on people then as the Internet does today. **L1**

② TEACH

DEFINING TERMS

Ask students to brainstorm a list of definitions for the word *prosperity*. (*Answers may include wealth, riches, and success.*) **Ask: How do countries achieve economic prosperity?** (*Students may note that countries trade freely with other countries and provide resources or create products that countries need.*) As students read the units, have them identify the circumstances that helped some countries achieve economic prosperity. **L2**

ACTIVATING PRIOR KNOWLEDGE

Have students explain the differences and similarities between the words *reformation* and *revolution*. Ask students to identify revolutions that they have heard of and describe how they brought about change. **L2**

Links Across Time

Unit 4 The Middle Ages

The period from about A.D. 500 to A.D. 1500 is known as the Middle Ages. During this time, trade routes expanded, and ideas and goods spread. Sometimes, these contacts led to wars that lasted for years. In other cases, ideas and practices were peacefully adopted.

In medieval China, the Grand Canal increased trade and prosperity. Today, modern China is building the Three Gorges Dam to provide electric power for its growing cities.

▲ Grand Canal

Three Gorges Dam ▶

▲ Early telescope, A.D. 1600s

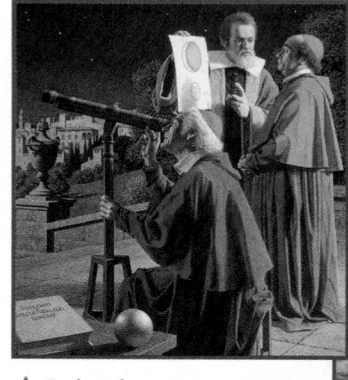

Unit 5 A Changing World

Beginning about A.D. 1500, thinkers developed new ideas about government. An age of exploration led to global trade and the conquest of empires. Meanwhile, people began to use scientific ideas to explore nature. One discovery or invention led to another, creating an explosion of knowledge. Advances in science continue today.

◀ Modern Space Station

CRITICAL THINKING ACTIVITY

Determining Cause and Effect Use this activity to extend what students learned in the *Thinking Like a Historian* activity on the following page. Students should research an article that describes a recent current event that occurred in the region that they are studying. Have students find reasons in the article that the writer cites that explain why the event occurred. Then have them identify the author's predictions about how the event might affect the region. If the author does not provide predictions, have students create their own. Students might want to create a cause-effect diagram to help them as they read the article and evaluate its information. Students should share their articles with the class. Discuss whether the students' predictions are logical and reasonable. **L3**

Unit 6 Modern Times

Modern times refers to the period from the late 1700s to the present. During this era of momentous change, uprisings led to the overthrow of vast empires and the rise of new nations. Dictators ruled in some countries, but democracy and respect for human rights became widely accepted. New inventions and discoveries raised standards of living and brought the world's cultures closer together. However, access to new weapons threatened world peace. Nations began to work together to find answers to common problems.

▼ Students using computers to access the Internet

▼ Building collapses in London during World War II

Thinking Like a Historian

As you read *Journey Across Time*, notice how the past affects the present. When you begin each unit, collect newspaper or magazine articles about a current event from the area you are studying. Then, after completing each unit, write down how you think a past event in that region is related to the current event.

③ ASSESS

ENRICH

Identifying Solutions Help students understand that many challenges faced by the world are interrelated. These challenges include:

- the dangers of nuclear power and the greenhouse effect
- advancements in computer technology and people's right to privacy
- the desire for personal freedom and the need to fight terrorism
- the desire to keep people healthy and the need to bring medical costs under control

Have students research one of the above challenges and write a persuasive essay that addresses a way of resolving it. Students' essays should include information about the challenge and the problems associated with its complexity. Then students should identify a resolution and support it with a well-constructed argument using factual evidence and logical reasoning. Ask for volunteers who picked the same challenge but with different solutions to read their essays aloud. Have the class discuss which argument is more persuasive and why. **L3**

Thinking Like a Historian Answers

Students' examples of links between past and present will vary. To clarify relationships, students might wish to create a graphic organizer or chart that illustrates the linkages. Current events that students might consider include the Arab-Israeli conflict, the war on terrorism, the war in Iraq, the expansion of the European Union, the modernization of China, and any technological breakthrough related to the Information Revolution.

Unit 1 Planning Guide

Unit Resources

Note: The following materials may be used when teaching Unit 1.
Chapter and section level support materials can be found on the chapter and section resource pages.

TEACHING TRANSPARENCIES

- Writing Process Transparencies **L1**

DIFFERENTIATED INSTRUCTION

- Step Into World History Activity 1

ASSESSMENT

- Unit 1 Test Form A **L2**
- Unit 1 Test Form B **L2**

ADDITIONAL RESOURCES

- Glencoe Skillbuilder Interactive Workbook CD-ROM, Level 1
- Glencoe World History Primary Source Document Library CD-ROM
- Focus on World Art Prints
- Outline Map Resource Book
- World Desk Map
- World Art and Architecture Transparencies
- World Music: Cultural Traditions
- World Music: A Cultural Legacy
- Glencoe World Literature Library
- Reading in the Content Area
- Teaching Strategies for the World History Classroom (Including Block Scheduling Pacing Guides)
- Inclusion Strategies for the Middle School Social Studies Classroom

Blackline Master	CD-ROM
Poster	Audio Program
Transparency	DVD
Music Program	Videocassette

READING SUPPORT FROM JAMESTOWN EDUCATION

- *Timed Readings Plus in Social Studies* help students increase their reading rate and fluency while maintaining comprehension. The 400-word passages are similar to those found on state and national assessments.
- *Reading in the Content Area: Social Studies* concentrates on six essential reading skills that help students better comprehend what they read. The book includes 75 high-interest nonfiction passages written at increasing levels of difficulty.
- *Reading Fluency* helps students read smoothly, accurately, and expressively.
- *Jamestown's Reading Improvement,* by renowned reading expert Edward Fry, focuses on helping build your students' comprehension, vocabulary, and skimming and scanning skills.
- *Critical Reading Series* provides high-interest books, each written at three reading levels.

To order these products, call Glencoe at 1-800-334-7344.

Reading List Generator CD-ROM

GLENCOE BOOKLINK

The Glencoe BookLink CD-ROM is a database that allows you to search more than 15,000 titles to create a customized reading list for your students.

- Reading lists can be organized by students' reading level, author, genre, theme, or area of interest.
- The database provides Degrees of Reading Power™ (DRP) and Lexile™ readability scores for all selections.
- A brief summary of each selection is included.

Leveled reading suggestions for this unit:

For students at a Grade 5 reading level:
- ***The Awesome Egyptians,*** by Terry Deary and Peter Hepplewhite

For students at a Grade 6 reading level:
- ***The Death of Enkidu: from The Epic of Gilgamesh***

For students at a Grade 7 reading level:
- ***Genesis 6–9: The Flood: from the Tanakh***

To order this CD-ROM, call Glencoe at 1-800-334-7344.

Unit ① Planning Guide

Unit Reading Strategies

Each chapter in this unit contains special reading strategies. The following preview will help you teach these reading skills to your students.

CHAPTER 1: Get Ready to Read!

"Getting into" a project, task, or hobby can sometimes be the most difficult part of an otherwise enjoyable experience. In the same way, students who are asked to read a chapter without being given a preview can find the content overwhelming. Walking students through the chapter by skimming headings and pointing out illustrations, captions, main ideas, new vocabulary, or topics of interest can make students comfortable with the text and better prepare them for reading. This skills spread will teach students how to skim the basic components of the book.

CHAPTER 2: What Do You Predict?

When students learn to predict what is coming next in a text, they become active participants rather than passive observers in the process of reading. Having students make predictions, as they read silently and as they discuss the content, engages their cognitive processing in ways that will have long-term positive effects on their abilities to comprehend and remember what they have read. Predictions can be in the form of questions, hypotheses, anticipation guides, or small group discussions. This exercise teaches students to make predictions based on the **Main Ideas** found in each section.

CHAPTER 3: Finding the Main Idea

As students develop skimming and previewing skills, they will be prepared to engage the text more actively. The next step in the process of understanding textual content is to determine the purpose for a given paragraph, or finding the main idea. This skills spread will teach students that main ideas are the most important ideas in a paragraph, section, or chapter. Supporting details further develop the main idea by providing facts or examples. The exercise will demonstrate how to visually organize main ideas and supporting details through graphic organizers.

Use the **SkillBuilder Handbook** on pages 902–919 to help students practice important skills.

0:00 **OUT OF TIME?**

If time does not permit teaching each chapter in this unit, you may use the *Reading Essentials and Study Guide* summaries.

UNIT OVERVIEW

Unit 1 starts with early humans and traces how they developed civilizations.

UNIT OBJECTIVES

After studying this unit, students should be able to

1. describe the impact of farming on the development of early civilizations;

2. analyze the development of Egypt's empire;

3. describe important events in the history of Israel.

Why It's Important

Explain to students that all civilizations—both past and present—have certain things in common. For example, all developed governments to help meet the needs of their people. Discuss with students the needs addressed by governments today. Ask whether students think governments would have provided the same services thousands of years ago. **L1**

Unit 1

Early Civilizations

Why It's Important

Each civilization that you will study in this unit made important contributions to history.

- The Mesopotamians developed writing.
- The Egyptians created papyrus.
- The Israelites' scripture influenced the religions of Europe.

8000 B.C.	5000 B.C.	2000 B.C.

First Civilizations
Chapter 1

c. 8000 B.C.
Farming begins in southwest Asia

c. 3200 B.C.
Sumerians in Mesopotamia develop writing

c. 1790 B.C.
Hammurabi introduces code of laws

◄ Hammurabi stands before a god

Ancient Egypt
Chapter 2

c. 5000 B.C.
Hunter-gatherers settle Nile River valley

c. 2540 B.C.
Egyptians complete building of Great Pyramid

c. 1500 B.C.
Queen Hatshepsut becomes pharaoh

◄ Pyramids at Giza, Egypt

Ancient Israelites
Chapter 3

c. 2000 B.C.
Abraham enters Canaan

◄ Abraham leads Israelites to Canaan

TIME LINE ACTIVITY

Direct students to the multiple-tier time line on these pages. Explain that it tells when different empires in different places thrived. Ask volunteers to come to the world map and take turns locating each of the places identified on the time line as other students point out the location on the maps in their texts. Point out that civilizations grew around the same time in different places around the world. **L1**

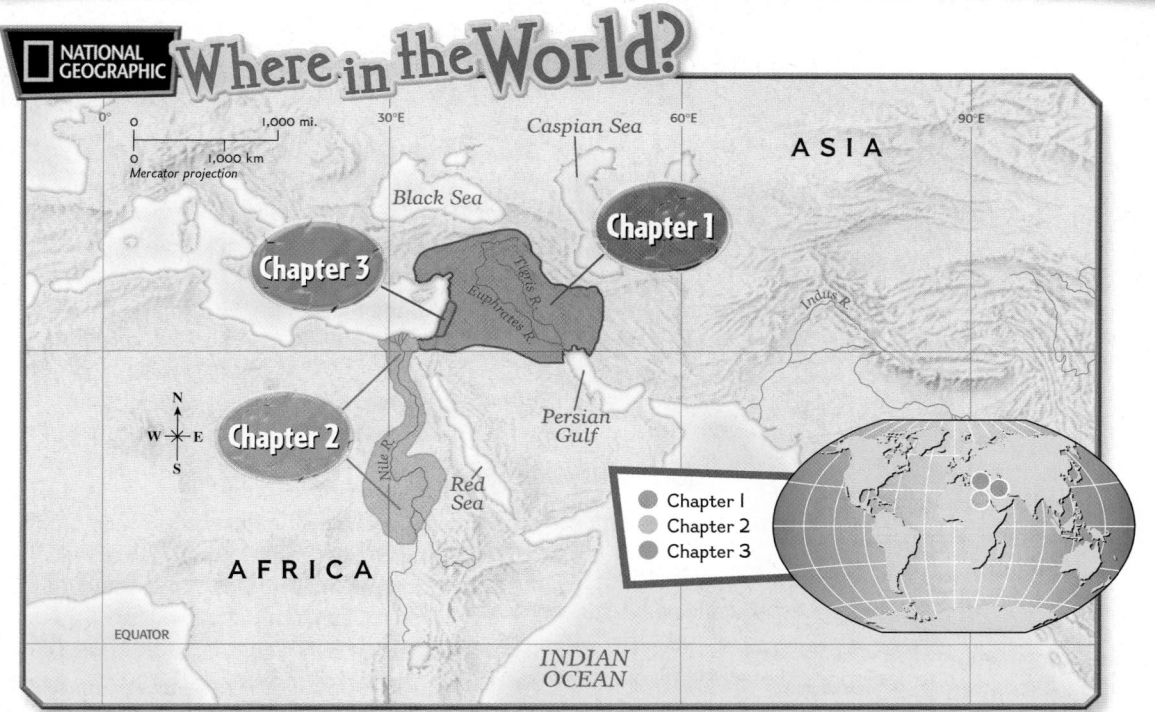

NATIONAL GEOGRAPHIC — Where in the World?

ASIA

Chapter 1

Chapter 3

Caspian Sea

Black Sea

Tigris R.

Euphrates R.

Chapter 2

Nile R.

Persian Gulf

Red Sea

AFRICA

EQUATOR

INDIAN OCEAN

0°   30°E   60°E   90°E

0 ___ 1,000 mi.
0 ___ 1,000 km
Mercator projection

N W E S

● Chapter 1
● Chapter 2
● Chapter 3

GLENCOE TECHNOLOGY

World History Primary Source Document Library CD-ROM

Use the **World History Primary Source Document Library CD-ROM** to access primary source documents related to the world's first civilizations.

NCLB — NO CHILD LEFT BEHIND

Teaching Tip The goals of the NCLB Act include a strong emphasis on reading. Using modeling in your class will help students become better readers. For example, point out to students that there are many vocabulary terms in the first section of this book. Read aloud a sentence containing a vocabulary term. Then demonstrate how to use other words in a sentence as clues to the meaning of a new term. Complete the model by asking volunteers to read aloud other sentences containing vocabulary terms. Ask each volunteer to think aloud as he or she uses the context to determine a possible meaning for the vocabulary term.

1000 B.C.	750 B.C.	500 B.C.	250 B.C.	A.D. 100

● c. 744 B.C. Assyria expands into Babylon

● c. 612 B.C. Chaldeans capture Assyrian capital

► Hanging gardens of Babylon

● c. 1000 B.C. Kush breaks free of Egypt

● 728 B.C. Kush conquers Egypt

◄ Kushite king Taharqa

► Lion statue honoring Kushite king Aspalta

● c. 1000 B.C. King David rules Israel

● 586 B.C. Chaldeans capture Jerusalem

168 B.C. Maccabean revolt

A.D. 70 ● Romans destroy temple in Jerusalem

◄ Jews led into exile

◄ Ancient Jerusalem

1

DIFFERENTIATED INSTRUCTION

English Learners: To help students understand that important events occurred around the world at the same time, have them make a list of all the events on the time line by breaking them into 200-year intervals. Rather than group them by civilization, have students group them by date.

Visual/Spatial: Have students take a simple outline map of the region covered in this unit. Then have them mark the time line events on the map to illustrate where they took place.

Gifted and Talented: Have students research several events on the time line from different cultures. Then have them write a short description of each event and present it to the class.

FOCUS

The unit preview provides a general layout of the regions and significant figures in the unit.

PREVIEWING GEOGRAPHY

Ask students to answer the following questions using the map.

1. **What major bodies of water are shown?** (*Mediterranean Sea, Black Sea, Red Sea, Caspian Sea, Persian Gulf*)

2. **Which continents are labeled?** (*Africa, Asia*)

PREVIEWING
People to Meet

Ask students the following questions using the biographies.

1. **Which of the people pictured ruled Egypt?** (*Hatshepsut, Ramses II*)

2. **Who ruled Babylon?** (*Hammurabi*)

3. **Could Ruth and Naomi have known King David? Why or why not?** (*probably not, because Ruth and Naomi were alive approximately 90 years before David was born*)

☞ Refer to **People to Meet Activities** in the Unit Resources Books.

Unit 1 — Places to Locate

1 Ishtar Gate
See First Civilizations Chapter 1

2 Sumerian figures
See First Civilizations Chapter 1

Mediterranean Sea

AFRICA

Red Sea

③ ⑤ ④

People to Meet

Ötzi
c. 3300 B.C.
Iceman found in the Alps
Chapter 1, page 12

Hammurabi
Ruled c. 1792–1750 B.C.
Babylonian king
Chapter 1, page 22

Hatshepsut
Ruled c. 1473–1458 B.C.
Egyptian pharaoh
Chapter 2, page 63

2

PREVIEWING Places to Locate

Use the following descriptions to explain the images on the map.

 1 The Ishtar Gate of Babylon was built in approximately 575 B.C. One of eight gates, it was the main entrance to the city.

 2 These marble Sumerian votive statues date from c. 2500 B.C. They were probably placed on an altar to stand in for the donor who brought them to honor the gods.

ASIA

Caspian Sea

Persian Gulf

3 Egyptian sphinx

See Ancient Egypt Chapter 2

4 Kushite pyramids

See Ancient Egypt Chapter 2

5 Western Wall

See Ancient Israelites Chapter 3

Ramses II

Ruled 1279–1213 B.C.
Egyptian ruler
Chapter 2, page 66

Ruth and Naomi

c. 1100 B.C.
Israelite women
Chapter 3, page 99

King David

Ruled c. 1000–970 B.C.
King of Israel
Chapter 3, page 88

3

PREVIEWING Places to Locate

 3 The Great Sphinx at Giza, near the Great Pyramid, was carved out of natural rock.

 4 The kingdom of Kush built many pyramids based on the Egyptian style.

 5 The Western Wall in Jerusalem is a remnant of the retaining wall of the Second Temple.

INTRODUCING UNIT 1

TEACH

Organizing Information Have students complete a table like the one below to organize information about the people discussed on these pages. *(Answers are provided.)* **L1/ EL**

Clue	Ruler
Ruled Egypt from 1279–1213 B.C.	Ramses II
Ruled Israel	King David
Two loyal Israelite Women	Ruth and Naomi
Found in the Alps	Ötzi
Began her Rule of Egypt in 1473 B.C.	Hatshepsut
King of Babylon	Hammurabi

Creating a Map Provide students with a copy of a map of the region covered in Unit 1 from the *Outline Map Resource Book.*

- Have students number each of the historical figures shown in the **People to Meet** feature.

- Have students use the table of contents to find maps of the civilizations covered. Then have them label their maps with the number of each figure in the appropriate location.

- For names with little geographic descriptions on this spread, suggest that students look up the page reference to learn more about that figure. **L1**

Chapter 1 Resources

TEACHING TRANSPARENCIES

- Graphic Organizer Transparencies with Teaching Strategy and Student Activity **L2**
- Cause-and-Effect Transparencies with Teaching Strategy and Student Activity **L2**
- Then and Now Transparencies with Teaching Strategy and Student Activity **L2**
- In-text Map Transparency with Teaching Strategy and Student Activity **L1**
- Map Transparencies with Overlay, Teaching Strategy, and Student Activity **L2**

DIFFERENTIATED INSTRUCTION

- Differentiated Instruction Activity 1
- Time Line Activity 1
- Primary Source Reading 1 (with Document-Based Questions)
- Inclusion Strategies for the Middle School Social Studies Classroom
- StudentWorks Plus™ CD-ROM (with Audio Program)

READING SUPPORT

- Take-Home Review Activity 1 **L2**
- World Literature Reading 1 **L2**
- Workbook Activity 1 **L1**
- Reading Strategies for the Social Studies Classroom **L1/ EL**

ASSESSMENT

- Authentic Assessment Activity 1 **L1/ EL**
- Chapter 1 Test Form A **L2**
- Chapter 1 Test Form B **L2**
- ExamView® Pro Testmaker CD-ROM

INTERDISCIPLINARY CONNECTIONS

- Geography and History Activity 1 **L2**
- People to Meet Activity 1 **L2**
- Economics Activity 1 **L2**
- Citizenship and Service Learning Activity 1 **L2**

SPANISH RESOURCES

- Spanish Reading Essentials and Study Guide
- Spanish Guided Reading Activities
- Spanish Quizzes, Tests, and Authentic Assessment (with Rubrics)
- Spanish Take-Home Review Activities

MULTIMEDIA

- ExamView® Pro Testmaker CD-ROM
- Glencoe Skillbuilder Interactive Workbook CD-ROM, Level 1
- Interactive Tutor Self-Assessment CD-ROM
- MindJogger Videoquiz
- Presentation Plus! CD-ROM
- StudentWorks Plus™ CD-ROM (with Audio Program)
- TeacherWorks CD-ROM
- Vocabulary PuzzleMaker CD-ROM
- *World History: Journey Across Time* Video Program
- World History Primary Source Document Library CD-ROM

STANDARDIZED ASSESSMENT SKILLS

- Standardized Test Skills Practice Workbook Activity 1 **L2**
- Critical Thinking Skills Activity 1 **L2**

Teaching strategies have been coded with suggested ability levels. However, most are suitable for all levels.

L1 BASIC activities for all students

L2 AVERAGE activities for average to above-average students

L3 CHALLENGING activities for above-average students

EL ENGLISH LANGUAGE activities

Chapter ① Resources

⏱ TIME MANAGEMENT

Unit Introduction	Chapter Introduction	Section 1	Section 2	Section 3	Chapter Wrap-Up
1 Day	1 Day	2 Days	2 Days	1 Day	1 Day

Block Scheduling Activities that are suited to use within the block scheduling framework are identified by:

0:00 OUT OF TIME? Assign the Chapter 1 *Reading Essentials and Study Guide.* * 🗁

SECTION RESOURCES

DAILY OBJECTIVES	REPRODUCIBLE RESOURCES	MULTIMEDIA RESOURCES
Section 1 **Early Humans** 1. Paleolithic people adapted to their environment and invented many tools to help them survive. 2. In the Neolithic Age, people started farming, building communities, producing goods, and trading.	🗁 Reproducible Lesson Plan 1–1 🗁 Daily Lecture and Discussion Notes 1–1 🗁 Vocabulary Activity 1–1 🗁 Active Reading Note-Taking Guide 1–1 🗁 Guided Reading Activity 1–1* 🗁 Section Quiz 1–1* 🗁 Reading Essentials and Study Guide 1–1*	🖰 Daily Focus Skills Transparency 1–1 ⦿ Interactive Tutor Self-Assessment CD-ROM ⦿ Exam*View*® Pro Testmaker CD-ROM ⦿ Presentation Plus! CD-ROM ⦿ Glencoe BookLink CD-ROM
Section 2 **Mesopotamian Civilization** 1. The people of Sumer, an early Mesopotamian civilization, invented writing and made other important contributions to later peoples. 2. Sumerian city-states gave way to empires, including the Babylonian Empire under Hammurabi.	🗁 Reproducible Lesson Plan 1–2 🗁 Daily Lecture and Discussion Notes 1–2 🗁 Vocabulary Activity 1–2 🗁 Active Reading Note-Taking Guide 1–2 🗁 Guided Reading Activity 1–2* 🗁 Section Quiz 1–2* 🗁 Reading Essentials and Study Guide 1–2*	🖰 Daily Focus Skills Transparency 1–2 ⦿ Interactive Tutor Self-Assessment CD-ROM ⦿ Exam*View*® Pro Testmaker CD-ROM ⦿ Presentation Plus! CD-ROM ⦿ Glencoe BookLink CD-ROM
Section 3 **The First Empires** 1. Assyria's military power and well-organized government built a vast empire in Mesopotamia. 2. The Chaldean Empire built important landmarks in Babylon and developed the first calendar with a seven-day week.	🗁 Reproducible Lesson Plan 1–3 🗁 Daily Lecture and Discussion Notes 1–3 🗁 Vocabulary Activity 1–3 🗁 Active Reading Note-Taking Guide 1–3 🗁 Guided Reading Activity 1–3* 🗁 Section Quiz 1–3* 🗁 Reading Essentials and Study Guide 1–3*	🖰 Daily Focus Skills Transparency 1–3 ⦿ Interactive Tutor Self-Assessment CD-ROM ⦿ Exam*View*® Pro Testmaker CD-ROM ⦿ Presentation Plus! CD-ROM ⦿ Vocabulary PuzzleMaker CD-ROM

*Also available in Spanish

Chapter ① Resources

History Online

Use our Web site for additional resources. All essential content is covered in the Student Edition.

You and your students can visit jat.glencoe.com, the Web site companion to *World History: Journey Across Time*. This innovative integration of electronic and print media offers your students a wealth of opportunities. The student text directs students to the Web site for the following options:

- Chapter Overviews
- Self-Check Quizzes
- Study Central™
- Student Web Activities
- Multi-Language Glossaries

Answers to the student Web activities are provided for you in the **Web Activity Lesson Plans.** Additional Web resources and ePuzzles and games are also available.

Videotape programs are available from Glencoe as supplements to the chapters.

To order, call Glencoe at 1-800-334-7344. To find classroom resources to accompany many of these videos, check the following home pages:

A&E Television: www.aande.com
The History Channel: www.historychannel.com

MEETING SPECIAL NEEDS

In addition to the Differentiated Instruction strategies, the following resources are suitable for students with special needs:

- *ExamView® Pro Testmaker CD-ROM* allows teachers to tailor tests by reducing answer choices.
- *StudentWorks Plus™ CD-ROM (with Audio Program)* includes the entire narrative of the student edition so that less-proficient readers can listen to the words as they read them.
- The *Reading Essentials and Study Guide* provides the same content as the student edition but is written two grade levels below the textbook.
- *Guided Reading Activities* give less-proficient readers point-by-point instructions to increase comprehension as they read each textbook section.
- *Differentiated Instruction Activities* include a stimulating collection of readings and activities for students of all levels.

TEACHER'S CORNER

Index to National Geographic Magazine:
The following articles relate to this chapter:

- "Baghdad Before the Bombs," by Alexandra Boulat, June 2003.
- "The Face," by Rick Gore, August 2002.
- "Dawn of Humans," by André Keyser, May 2000.

National Geographic Society Products:
To order the following, call National Geographic at 1–800–368–2728

- *PicturePack: Ancient Civilizations: The Fertile Crescent* (Transparencies)
- *National Geographic Atlas of the World* (Book)

NGS ONLINE

Access National Geographic's new dynamic MapMachine Web site and other geography resources at:

www.nationalgeographic.com
www.nationalgeographic.com/maps

Meeting NCSS Standards

World History: Journey Across Time
The following standards are highlighted in Chapter 1:

Section 1 **I** Culture: A, B, C, H
II Time, Continuity, and Change: E, F
III People, Places, and Environments: B, H
VIII Science, Technology, and Society: A, B

Section 2 **IV** Individual Development and Identity: B
VI Power, Authority, and Governance: A
VIII Science, Technology, and Society: A, B, C

Section 3 **III** People, Places, and Environments: G, I
VI Power, Authority, and Governance: D, F, G, I
VIII Science, Technology, and Society: A

State and Local Objectives

_____

_____

Timesaving Tools

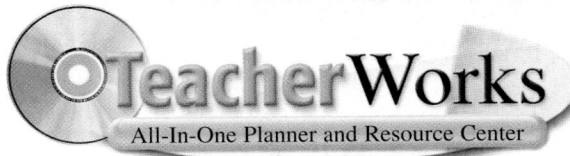

TeacherWorks
All-In-One Planner and Resource Center

● **Interactive Teacher Edition** Access your Teacher Wraparound Edition and your classroom resources with a few easy clicks.

● **Interactive Lesson Planner** Organize your week, month, semester, or year with all the lesson helps you need to make teaching creative and relevant.

Use Glencoe's **Presentation Plus!** multimedia teacher tool to easily present dynamic lessons that visually excite your students. Using Microsoft PowerPoint® you can customize the presentations to create your own personalized lessons.

FOLDABLES™ Study Organizer

Dinah Zike's Foldables

Foldables are three-dimensional, interactive graphic organizers that help students practice basic writing skills, review key vocabulary terms, and identify main ideas. Every chapter contains a foldable activity, with additional chapter activities found in the *Reading and Study Skills Foldables* booklet. You can use the foldables as they are presented, or modify them to suit the needs of your individual class.

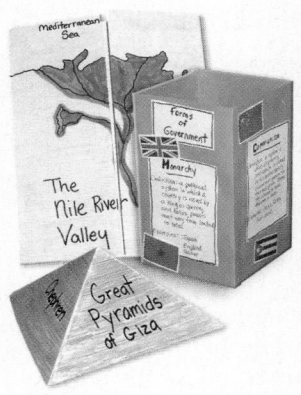

Planning Ahead

CHAPTER CULMINATING ACTIVITY

The Chapter Culminating Activity will help students organize and learn the important information from the chapter. Begin the chapter with this activity, and have students complete it as a culminating activity.

CREATING A PHOTO-ESSAY

Purpose The old adage "A picture is worth a thousand words" can be proven with a photo-essay. Students—especially students with limited verbal skills—have the opportunity to use art to impart a great deal of information in a small amount of space. The photo-essay students create will provide them with a visual summary of the chapter's main ideas.

Introduction to Modeling

1. Direct students' attention to a photograph or other image in their textbooks. Have students spend five minutes identifying information imparted by the photograph. Point out that visual communications can put a lot of information into a small space.

2. Provide each student with three sheets of 8½" × 11" paper and have students use their rulers to draw on each an

8" × 10" square. As students read each section of this chapter, ask them to think of a photograph that would illustrate that section. Have them draw that photograph onto one of their papers. Explain that the border is the picture frame, and students can decorate that, too.

3. When students have completed their three sections and their three photographs, have volunteers share their photo-essays with the class. Ask the volunteers to explain what each photo is meant to say about its section.

Chapter 1

The First Civilizations

Ruins of a ziggurat in Iraq ▶

NATIONAL GEOGRAPHIC **When & Where?**

3000 B.C.	2000 B.C.	1000 B.C.
c. 3000 B.C. Bronze Age begins	c. 1792 B.C. Hammurabi rules Mesopotamia	612 B.C. Nineveh captured; Assyrian Empire crumbles

Reading Strategy   PURPOSE FOR READING

Analyzing Geography As a class, look at each of the maps in this chapter. For each, have students identify any bodies of water present. Then have students work in pairs and skim the chapter, looking for water-related words—such as rivers and other bodies of water, floods and flooding, and irrigation—in the text. Point out that these water-related words appear frequently. **Ask:** Why do you think words related to water appear so often in a chapter about early civilizations? *(Students should indicate that access to water is necessary for a civilization to develop. As a result, settlements of all sizes had to assure a water source and develop ways to use water effectively.)* **L1/ EL**

Chapter Preview

Some of the first civilizations arose in southwest Asia. The people of these civilizations gradually learned how to farm and developed systems of government, writing, and religion.

 View the Chapter 1 video in the *World History: Journey Across Time* Video Program.

Section 1 — Early Humans

The earliest humans hunted animals and gathered plants for food. When farming developed, people settled in towns and cities.

Section 2 — Mesopotamian Civilization

In early Mesopotamian civilizations, religion and government were closely linked. Kings created strict laws to govern the people.

Section 3 — The First Empires

New empires arose in Mesopotamia around 900 B.C. These civilizations included the Assyrians and the Chaldeans. They used powerful armies and iron weapons to conquer the region.

FOLDABLES™ Study Organizer

Compare and Contrast *Make this foldable to help you compare and contrast the ancient civilizations of Mesopotamia.*

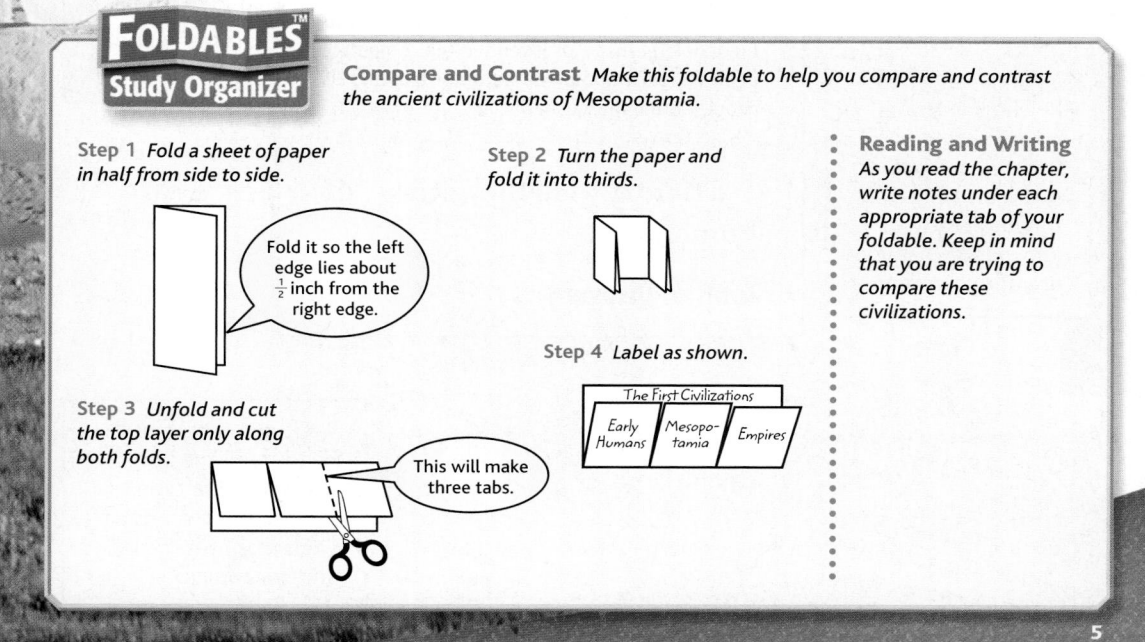

Step 1 *Fold a sheet of paper in half from side to side.*

Fold it so the left edge lies about ½ inch from the right edge.

Step 2 *Turn the paper and fold it into thirds.*

Step 3 *Unfold and cut the top layer only along both folds.*

This will make three tabs.

Step 4 *Label as shown.*

The First Civilizations

| Early Humans | Mesopotamia | Empires |

Reading and Writing *As you read the chapter, write notes under each appropriate tab of your foldable. Keep in mind that you are trying to compare these civilizations.*

History Online

Introduce students to chapter content and key terms by having them access **Chapter Overview 1** at jat.glencoe.com

CHAPTER PREVIEW

After reading Chapter 1, students will be able to

1. explain how learning to farm changed the way early peoples lived;

2. describe the development of the first major civilizations in Mesopotamia's river valleys;

3. describe the rise and fall of the Assyrian and Chaldean Empires.

FOLDABLES™ Study Organizer — Dinah Zike's Foldables

Purpose Students use this foldable to compare and contrast the ancient civilizations of Mesopotamia. As students read each section, they should take notes under the appropriate label on the foldable.

☞ Have students complete *Reading and Study Skills Foldables* Activity 1.

MORE ABOUT THE PHOTO

Ziggurats The ruins of the ziggurat in the photo are from the ancient city of Nippur, which lies about 100 miles south of Baghdad. Because Nippur was a religious center, rather than a capital city, it was spared much of the destruction that occurred in other Mesopotamian cities. Nippur has provided archaeologists with a wealth of artifacts, including tens of thousands of cuneiform clay tablets, along with pottery, jewelry, and bronze artifacts. The clay tablets found here have contained government and business records, textbooks, and literary works. It is believed Nippur was inhabited for almost 6,000 years, finally being abandoned around A.D. 800.

1 Learn It!

Explain that previewing, like watching a preview for a movie, sets expectations and gives readers an idea of what is coming. This mental "hook" on which they can hang new information is an important step in comprehending information in the text. Model for students how to "walk through" a chapter before beginning to read or study it. Point out to them the main head, main idea, reading focus, and subheads as described in **Get Ready to Read!** Then have students flip through the first section of Chapter 1 to see how this structure is carried out throughout the book.

To help students make sense of the structure of the text, have them use colored pencils to write down the major components of the text. Major headings, for example, could be written in blue, subheadings in green, main ideas in red, captions in purple, and titles of graphs in black. **L1**

Chapter 1 Reading Social Studies

Reading Skill
Previewing

1 Learn It!
Get Ready to Read!

Before you read, take time to preview the chapter. This will give you a head start on what you are about to learn. Follow the steps below to help you quickly read, or skim, Section 1 on page 9.

2–The Main Idea under each main head tells you the "big picture." It summarizes the main point of what you are about to read.

3–The **Reading Focus** helps you to make a connection between what you might already know and what you are about to read.

1–Read the main headings in large red type. They show the main topics covered in the section or chapter.

Early Humans

Main Idea Paleolithic people adapted to their environment and invented many tools to help them survive.

Reading Focus What do you view as the greatest human achievement? Sending people to the moon, perhaps, or inventing the computer? Read to learn about the accomplishments of people during the Paleolithic Age.

History is the story of humans . . .

Tools of Disovery

4–Under each main head, read the subheads in blue type. Subheads break down each main topic into smaller topics.

Reading Tip

As you skim, also look at pictures, maps, and charts.

Reading Strategy | **SETTING A PURPOSE**

Readers are much more likely to become engaged in text when a purpose has been clearly set for the reading. Good readers generally set a purpose without consciously thinking about it, but poor readers may need some help. For example, before reading the subsection on Mesopotamian religion entitled "Gods and Rulers," ask students why they think the Sumerians might have built temples. For the subsection "Why Was Writing Important?," ask students how civilization might have been different if people had never developed a writing system. Such questions not only generate interest but also provide a technique for students to get actively engaged in the reading. **L1/ EL**

2 Practice It!

Preview by Skimming

Read to Write ·······
Use each main head, the main ideas, and the subheads in Section 2 of this chapter to create a study outline.

Section

3 The First Empires

Skim all of the main heads and main ideas in Section 3 starting on page 26. Then, in small groups, discuss the answers to these questions.

- Which part of this section do you think will be most interesting to you?
- What do you think will be covered in Section 3 that was not covered in Section 2?
- Are there any words in the Main Ideas that you do not know how to pronounce?
- Choose one of the Reading Focus questions to discuss in your group.

3 Apply It!

Skim Section 2 on your own. Write one thing in your notebook that you want to learn by reading this chapter.

7

---

2 Practice It!

Classifying Use the same colors to "walk through" each chapter before you begin so students practice classifying types of information. Other colors can designate sections used less frequently, such as biographies.

Clarifying As students note the headings, ask if they have questions about words or concepts that they would like explained prior to the reading.

Responding Take time to allow students to respond in groups or pairs to the questions in the **Practice It!** section. This is a valuable way of making personal connections to the text.

3 Apply It!

Interactive Chapter Walls For each section in the chapter, post the headings and subheadings on large posters using the designated colors. This will focus students on ideas they want to investigate. The same technique can be repeated for other chapters. Such chapter walls can be interactive if you leave space under each heading and encourage students to write appropriate comments or create drawings that are relevant to the subject. **L1**

📖 Reading Strategy ⟩ READ TO WRITE

The outlines students create will be useful in learning the major concepts in the chapter. However, there is beneficial information contained in other features too. Time constraints may make it difficult to study important illustrations, drawings, and captions in the chapter. This material may be the key that unlocks difficult concepts for students. After students have created their outlines, encourage them to study the visual aids in the chapter. To encourage careful analysis of nonprint features, have students write captions and display them on the board or have caption contests with awards for most creative, funniest, most descriptive, or "most like a textbook" caption. **L1/ EL**

① FOCUS

SECTION OVERVIEW

This section describes the world's earliest humans and relates their change from nomadic hunters to farmers.

📖 Project **Daily Focus Skills Transparency 1–1** and have students answer questions. Discuss their responses.

Get Ready to Read!

Preteaching Vocabulary:
Historians, or people who study and write about the past, use many tools to learn about the past. For example, they use written records, physical remains such as buildings and roadways, and artifacts, or items left behind by humans.

Answers to Graphic: warm weather: little clothing; cold weather: use of caves as shelter; discovery of fire: protection and ability to cook foods to make them healthier and longer-lasting; Ice Age: change of diet, built sturdier shelters, made warmer clothing

Section ① Early Humans

Get Ready to Read!

What's the Connection?
Today people live in towns and cities of various sizes and make their living in different ways. Read to find out how early humans lived by moving from place to place, forming settlements, and exploring different ways to provide for themselves and their families.

Focusing on the Main Ideas
• Paleolithic people adapted to their environment and invented many tools to help them survive. *(page 9)*

• In the Neolithic Age, people started farming, building communities, producing goods, and trading. *(page 13)*

Locating Places
Jericho (JEHR•ih•KOH)
Çatal Hüyük
(chah•TAHL   hoo•YOOK)

Building Your Vocabulary
historian (hih•STOHR•ee•uhn)
archaeologist
(AHR•kee•AH•luh•jihst)
artifact (AHR•tih•FAKT)
fossil (FAH•suhl)
anthropologist
(AN•thruh•PAH•luh•jihst)
nomad (NOH•MAD)
technology (tehk•NAH•luh•jee)
domesticate (duh•MEHS•tih•KAYT)
specialization
(SPEH•shuh•luh•ZAY•shuhn)

Reading Strategy
Determine Cause and Effect Draw a diagram like the one below. Use it to explain how early humans adapted to their environment.

Cause:	➡	Effect:
Cause:	➡	Effect:
Cause:	➡	Effect:

When & Where?

	8000 B.C.	6000 B.C.	4000 B.C.	2000 B.C.
	c. 8000 B.C. Jericho founded	c. 6700 B.C. Çatal Hüyük settled		c. 3000 B.C. Bronze Age begins

Çatal Hüyük •

• Jericho

SECTION RESOURCES

📁 **Reproducible Masters**
• Reproducible Lesson Plan 1–1
• Daily Lecture and Discussion Notes 1–1
• Vocabulary Activity 1–1
• Active Reading Note-Taking Guide 1–1
• Guided Reading Activity 1–1
• Section Quiz 1–1
• Reading Essentials and Study Guide 1–1

📖 **Transparencies**
• Daily Focus Skills Transparency 1–1

Multimedia
🖲 Interactive Tutor Self-Assessment CD-ROM
🖲 ExamView® Pro Testmaker CD-ROM
🖲 Presentation Plus! CD-ROM
🖲 Glencoe BookLink CD-ROM

Early Humans

Main Idea Paleolithic people adapted to their environment and invented many tools to help them survive.

Reading Focus What do you view as the greatest human achievement? Sending people to the moon, perhaps, or inventing the computer? Read to learn about the accomplishments of people during the Paleolithic Age.

History is the story of humans in the past. It tells what they did and what happened to them. **Historians** (hih•STOHR•ee•uhns) are people who study and write about the human past. They tell us that history began about 5,500 years ago, when people first began to write. But the story of people really begins in prehistory—the time *before* people developed writing.

Tools of Discovery What we know about the earliest people comes from the things they left behind. Scientists have worked to uncover clues about early human life. **Archaeologists** (AHR•kee•AH•luh•jihsts) hunt for evidence buried in the ground where settlements might once have been. They dig up and study **artifacts** (AHR•tih•FAKTS)—weapons, tools, and other things made by humans. They also look for **fossils** (FAH•suhls)—traces of plants or animals that have been preserved in rock. **Anthropologists** (AN•thruh•PAH•luh•jihsts) focus on human society. They study how humans developed and how they related to one another.

Historians call the early period of human history the Stone Age. The name comes from the fact that people during this time used stone to make tools and weapons.

Archaeological Dig

Archaeologists use special techniques and tools when carrying out a dig. Artifacts are photographed or sketched and their locations are mapped and noted. Soil is passed through a mesh screen to collect small fragments of tools or bone. *What types of artifacts do archaeologists look for?*

BELOW THE SURFACE
Layers of soil are deposited one on top of another. In general, the farther the layer is below the surface, the older its soil and artifacts are.

PRESERVING
Archaeologists may use plaster to make a form or an imprint of something they have found.

LOOKING FOR FRAGMENTS
This scientist uses a wire mesh screen to sift the soil to discover small fragments of artifacts.

GRIDS
Grids like these help archaeologists record and map any artifacts found.

CLEANING
Artifacts must be handled and cleaned carefully, often with soft brushes or other instruments.

② TEACH

Language Tell students they are going to play a game of charades. Have small groups each choose one of the activities common to people during Paleolithic times. For example, a group could choose making a fire, gathering berries, or hunting with spears. Then have each group perform its charade, while others in the class speculate on the activity being portrayed. Point out that without language, it is much more difficult to communicate even the simplest ideas. **L1/EL**

Daily Lecture and Discussion Notes 1–1

Use **Daily Lecture and Discussion Notes 1–1** for an outline of key concepts found in the section.

More About the Art

Archaeologists often find some of their most useful information in locations used by earlier people as garbage dumps. These areas provide clues about what people ate, wore, and used for tools.

Caption Answer:
weapons, tools, and other things made by humans

Reading Strategy — READING THE TEXT

Using Word Parts Point out to students that there are other words that begin with *paleo-* or *neo-*. Organize students into small groups and provide each group with a dictionary. Have groups find and make a list of three words that begin with *paleo-* and three words that begin with *neo-*. Have groups also write the definition for each word they choose and share their words and definitions with the class. (*Possible answers: paleoanthropology, paleobiology, paleobotany; neoclassic, neocolonialism, neocortex*) As students read the chapter, have them continue to look up words they do not understand. **L2**

Primary Source

Some of the most famous cave paintings are in the Lascaux Cave in Dordogne, France. They were discovered in 1940 by four teenage boys. About 600 drawings and paintings adorn the cave's walls. In 1948 the cave was opened to the public. However, visitors' lights began to damage the art, fading its colors and exposing it to bacteria. In 1963 the cave was closed to protect it.

Answer:
Paleolithic people hunted animals for food and other necessities. They also began to create art.

Writing Activity

Have students write an article describing the invention of tools by people in Paleolithic times. Tell them to write the article as if they were magazine writers visiting an archaeological site. **L2**

Primary Source — Paleolithic Cave Paintings

The oldest examples of Paleolithic art are cave paintings found in Spain and France. Most of the paintings are of animals. The paintings show that Paleolithic artists often used several colors and techniques. They sometimes used the uneven surface of the rock to create a three-dimensional effect.

▲ Painting of bison in Spanish cave

DBQ Document-Based Question

What does this cave painting tell us about life in the Paleolithic Age?

The earliest part of the period is the Paleolithic or Old Stone Age. *Paleolithic* means "old stone" in the Greek language. Paleolithic times began roughly 2.5 million years ago and lasted until around 8000 B.C.

Who Were the Hunter-Gatherers?
Try to imagine the world during the Stone Age, long before any roadways, farms, or villages existed. Early humans spent most of their time searching for food. They hunted animals, caught fish, ate insects, and gathered nuts, berries, fruits, grains, and plants.

Because they hunted and gathered, Paleolithic people were always on the move. They were **nomads** (NOH•MADS), or people who regularly move from place to place. They traveled in bands of 30 or so members because it was safer and made the search for food easier.

Men and women did different tasks within the group. Women stayed close to the campsite, which was typically near a stream or other water source. They looked after the children and searched nearby woods and meadows for berries, nuts, and grains.

Men hunted animals—an activity that sometimes took them far from camp. They had to learn the habits of animals and make tools for the kill. At first, they used clubs or drove the animals off cliffs. Over time, Paleolithic people invented spears, traps, and bows and arrows.

Adapting to the Environment
The way that Paleolithic people lived depended on where they lived. Those in warm climates needed little clothing or shelter. People in cold climates sought protection from the weather in caves. Over time, Paleolithic people created new kinds of shelter. The most common was probably made of animal hides held up by wooden poles.

Paleolithic people made a life-changing discovery when they learned to tame fire. Fire gave warmth to those gathered around it. It lit the darkness and scared away wild animals. Food cooked over the fire tasted better and was easier to digest. In addition, smoked meat could be kept longer.

Archaeologists believe that early humans started fires by rubbing two pieces of wood together. Paleolithic people later made drill-like wooden tools to start fires.

What Were the Ice Ages?
Fire was a key to the survival of Paleolithic people during the Ice Ages. These were long periods of extreme cold. The last Ice Age began about 100,000 B.C. From then until about 8000 B.C.,

DIFFERENTIATED INSTRUCTION

Verbal/Linguistic: Organize students into small groups, and have each group list on a sheet of paper the vocabulary terms for this section. Ask groups to skim the section for definitions. When the groups have finished, have them compare their definitions for each term.

Auditory/Musical: Point out to students that the vocabulary terms in this section may seem to be long. Read aloud each term, emphasizing its syllables. Then have students repeat the words.

Gifted and Talented: Have students write a paragraph using all the vocabulary words.

📂 Refer to *Inclusion Strategies for the Middle School Social Studies Classroom* in the TCR.

thick ice sheets covered parts of Europe, Asia, and North America.

The Ice Age was a threat to human life. People risked death from the cold and also from hunger. Early humans had to adapt by changing their diet, building sturdier shelters, and using animal furs to make warm clothing. The mastery of fire helped people live in this environment.

Language, Art, and Religion Another advance in Paleolithic times was the development of spoken language. Language made it far easier for people to work together and to pass on knowledge.

Early people expressed themselves not only in words but in art. They crushed yellow, black, and red rocks to make powders for paint. Then they dabbed this on cave walls, creating scenes of lions, oxen, panthers, and other animals.

Historians are not sure why these cave paintings were created. They may have had religious meaning. Early people also might have thought that painting an animal would bring good luck in the hunt.

The Invention of Tools Paleolithic people were the first to use **technology** (tehk•NAH•luh•jee)—tools and methods to help humans perform tasks. People often used a hard stone called flint to make tools. By hitting flint with a hard stone, they could make it flake into pieces with very sharp edges. To make hand axes or hunting spears, they tied wooden poles to pieces of flint that were the right shape for the tool.

Over time, early people grew more skilled at making tools. They crafted smaller and sharper tools, such as fishhooks and needles made from animal bones. They used needles to make nets and baskets and to sew hides together for clothing.

✓ **Reading Check** **Contrast** How are fossils and artifacts different?

Science and Inventions

Tools One of the most important advances of prehistoric people was the creation of stone tools. Tools made hunting, gathering, building shelter, and making clothing much easier.

The first tools were made of stones. Early humans quickly learned that grinding, breaking, and shaping the stones to create sharp edges made them more useful.

As technology advanced, people began making specific tools such as food choppers, meat scrapers, and spear points. In time, people learned that hitting a stone in a particular way would produce a flake—a long, sharp chip. Flakes were similar to knives in the way they were used.

▲ Stone tools

▲ Flaking tools from a larger stone

Connecting to the Past
1. Why do you think early people chose stones to make their first tools?
2. How were flakes created?

HISTORY Mystery

How Do We Know How Old Things Are?
On Earth, all living things contain carbon and radioactive carbon-14. When a living thing dies, carbon-14 starts to decay. Because carbon-14 decays at a measurable rate, scientists can determine how long something has been dead.

NATIONAL GEOGRAPHIC
The Way It Was

Answers:
1. Stones were easy to fashion into tools.
2. by chipping stone pieces until they flaked into the right shape

✓ **Reading Check**

Answer: Fossils are traces of plants and animals. Artifacts are weapons, tools, and other things made by humans.

CRITICAL THINKING ACTIVITY

Comparing and Contrasting Tell each student to compare and contrast Paleolithic and Neolithic times by copying this sentence:

"Paleolithic people ____, while people of Neolithic times ____."

Ask students to create a two-column graphic organizer and fill in the details of each era under the appropriate headings. Students might consider topics such as patterns of migration, influence of geography and agriculture, economic development, and evidence from archaeology. **L2**

Biography

Biography

TEACH

Scientists have determined that Ötzi the iceman was 5'2½" tall. He was probably in his mid-40s, which was very mature for people of that time. Today, Ötzi is kept in a refrigerated room at the South Tyrol Museum of Archaeology in Bolzano, Italy, because the body was found just inside that country's border. Visitors can view him through a little window there.

Have students imagine they are going hiking. Have them make a list of the things they would take with them. How do their lists compare with the items with which Ötzi traveled? *(Answers should include hiking equipment, food, and other items for survival.)* **L1/ EL**

Then and Now

Answers will vary, but students should list things people carry and what clues those items would provide.

ÖTZI THE ICEMAN

c. 3300 B.C.

In A.D. 1991 two hikers near the border between Austria and Italy discovered the frozen body of a man. The man was called "Ötzi" after the Ötztal Alps, the mountains where he was found. Scientists studied Ötzi's body, his clothes, and the items found with him to uncover clues about his life and death. One of the first amazing facts scientists learned was that Ötzi lived 5,300 years ago, during the Neolithic Age.

Ötzi was dressed warmly because of the cold climate. He was wearing a fur hat and a long grass cloak. Under the cloak was a leather jacket that was well-made but had been repaired several times. To keep his feet warm, he had stuffed grass in the bottom of his leather shoes. Scientists studied the tools and supplies Ötzi was carrying and decided that he planned to be away from home for many months. A bow and arrows, copper ax, and backpack were among the supplies found near Ötzi's body. Experts believe Ötzi was a shepherd who traveled with his herd. Ötzi probably returned to his village only twice a year.

From recent tests, scientists have learned more about the last hours of Ötzi's life. Shortly before he died, Ötzi ate a type of flat bread that is similar to a cracker, an herb or other green plant, and meat. Pollen found in Ötzi's stomach showed that he ate his last meal in the valley, south of where he was found. When Ötzi finished eating, he headed up into the mountains. Eight hours later, he died. Scientists believe that Ötzi's last hours were violent ones. When found, he clutched a knife in his right hand. Wounds on his right hand suggest that he tried to fight off an attacker. His left shoulder had been deeply pierced by an arrow. Some scientists think Ötzi may have wandered into another tribe's territory. Ötzi is now displayed at the South Tyrol Museum of Archaeology in Bolzano, Italy.

▲ Scientists created this reproduction to show what Ötzi may have looked like.

▲ This copper ax, along with the bow and arrows that you can see above, were Ötzi's main weapons.

Then and Now

If scientists 5,300 years from now discovered the remains of someone from our time, what might they conclude about our society?

Reading List Generator CD-ROM

GLENCOE BOOKLINK RECOMMENDED READING

Use the **Glencoe BookLink CD-ROM** to create customized reading lists based on your students' interests and reading levels. Below is an example based on content in this chapter. Also, see the Suggested Readings on pages 944–946 of the Appendix.

- Baumann, Hans. *In the Land of Ur: The Discovery of Ancient Mesopotamia.* Discover Mesopotamia through archaeologists' eyes. For thousands of years the region was dotted with temples and palaces, but today it is a desert wasteland.

- Khashoggi, Soheir. *Mirage.* A privileged daughter in a Middle Eastern family attempts to flee to the United States to escape an arranged marriage.

Neolithic Times

Main Idea In the Neolithic Age, people started farming, building communities, producing goods, and trading.

Reading Focus Did you know that, today, more than a third of the world's people work in agriculture? Read to learn how farming began and how it changed the world.

After the last Ice Age ended, people began to change their way of life. They began to **domesticate** (duh•MEHS•tih•KAYT), or tame animals and plants for human use. Animals provided meat, milk, and wool. They also carried goods and pulled carts.

In addition, people also learned how to grow food. For the first time, people could stay in one place to grow grains and vegetables. Gradually, farming replaced hunting and gathering.

This change in the way people lived marked the beginning of the Neolithic Age, or New Stone Age, which began about 8000 B.C. and lasted until about 4000 B.C.

Why Was Farming Important? Historians call the changes in the Neolithic Age the farming revolution. The word *revolution* refers to changes that greatly affect many areas of life. Some historians consider the farming revolution the most important event in human history.

Farming did not begin in one region and spread. People in different parts of the world discovered how to grow crops at about the same time. In Asia, people grew wheat, barley, rice, soybeans, and a grain called millet. In Mexico, farmers grew corn, squash, and potatoes. In Africa, they grew millet and a grain called sorghum.

CHAPTER 1
SECTION 1, 8–15

Connecting Across Time

The well-planned layout of Çatal Hüyük made it possible to keep the city clean even with a rising population. Have students consider how well organized their own community is. What kinds of services are available to keep the area clean? **L1/EL**

CURRICULUM CONNECTION

Architecture
The houses at Çatal Hüyük were built close together. Any space between houses often was used as a garbage dump. The houses did not have doors. Instead, archaeologists believe people used ladders to enter from the roofs. The dead often were buried below the floor of a house. Babies usually were buried wearing jewelry, but the bodies of adults were accompanied by few such goods.

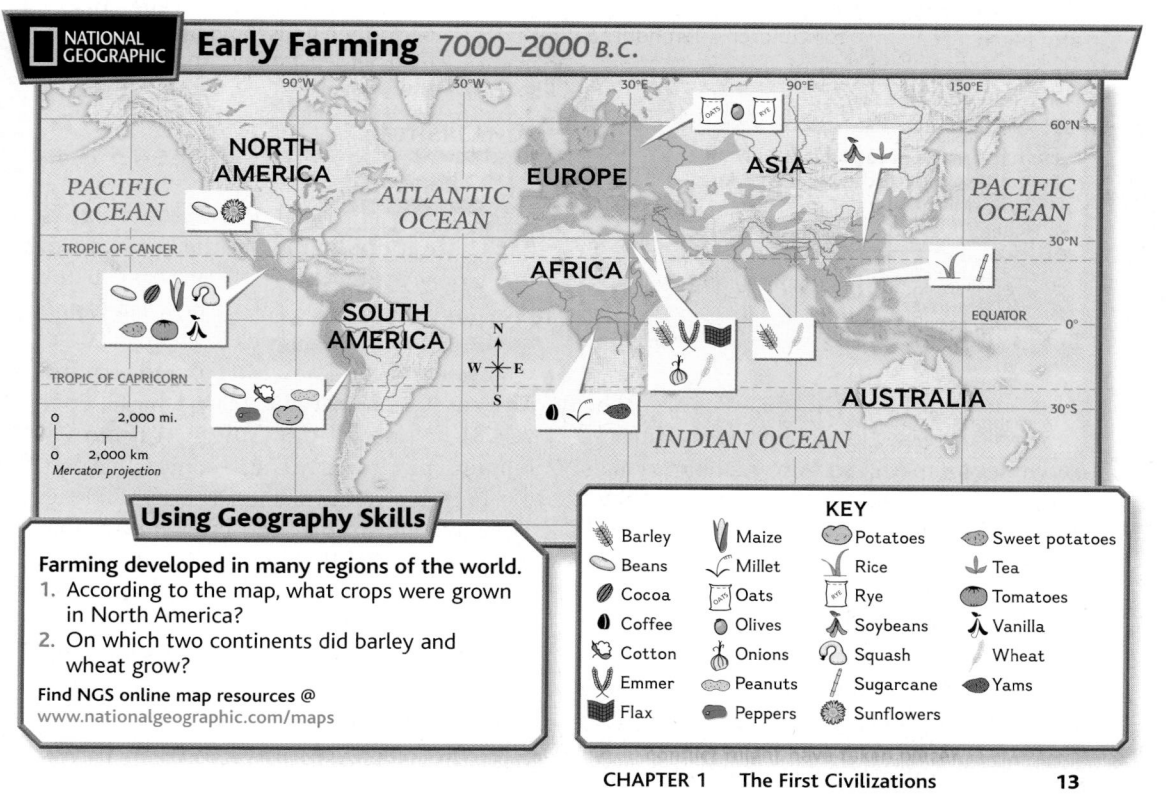

NATIONAL GEOGRAPHIC **Early Farming** *7000–2000 B.C.*

0   2,000 mi.
0   2,000 km
Mercator projection

Using Geography Skills

Farming developed in many regions of the world.
1. According to the map, what crops were grown in North America?
2. On which two continents did barley and wheat grow?

Find NGS online map resources @ www.nationalgeographic.com/maps

KEY

Barley	Maize	Potatoes	Sweet potatoes
Beans	Millet	Rice	Tea
Cocoa	Oats	Rye	Tomatoes
Coffee	Olives	Soybeans	Vanilla
Cotton	Onions	Squash	Wheat
Emmer	Peanuts	Sugarcane	Yams
Flax	Peppers	Sunflowers	

Using Geography Skills

Answers:
1. sunflowers, beans, cocoa, maize, squash, sweet potatoes, tomatoes, vanilla
2. Africa and Asia

CHAPTER 1   The First Civilizations   **13**

INTERDISCIPLINARY CONNECTIONS ACTIVITY

Art Direct students' attention to the cave painting on page 10. Point out that the things drawn on the cave walls had importance in the everyday lives of early peoples. Organize students into small groups. Have each group discuss what kinds of items could be drawn on a wall to tell something about our lives today. Then supply each group with a large square of butcher-block paper, and have group members work together to decorate a "wall" that tells something about our present-day culture. Ask groups to share their completed "walls" with the class. You may wish to mount the "walls" around the classroom. **L2**

Reading Support L1/ EL

Assign **Guided Reading Activity 1–1** to help students organize the information in the section.

③ ASSESS

Assign Section 1 Review as homework or as an in-class activity.

🌐 Have students use the **Interactive Tutor Self-Assessment CD-ROM** to review the section.

Assessment L2

Assign **Section 1 Quiz** to assess mastery of the material found in the section.

Reading Support L1/ EL

Assign **Reading Essentials and Study Guide 1–1** to help students review section material.

Understanding Charts

Answers:
1. from hunting to herding, farming, and protecting the village
2. They developed copper and bronze tools.

Comparing the Neolithic and Paleolithic Ages

	Paleolithic Age	Neolithic Age
Description of Art and Crafts	Paleolithic people painted cave walls. They usually painted animals.	Neolithic people made pottery and carved objects out of wood. They also built shelters and tombs.
How Humans Obtained Food	People hunted animals and gathered nuts, berries, and grains.	People began to farm in permanent villages. They continued to raise and herd animals.
How Humans Adapted	People learned to make fire, created a language, and made simple tools and shelters.	People built mud-brick houses and places of worship. They specialized in certain jobs and used copper and bronze to create more useful tools.
Work of Women and Men	Women gathered food and cared for children. Men hunted.	Women cared for children and performed household tasks. Men herded, farmed, and protected the village.

Understanding Charts

Humans made great advances from the Paleolithic Age to the Neolithic Age.
1. How did the work of men change from the Paleolithic Age to the Neolithic Age?
2. **Describe** What advances were made in toolmaking between the Paleolithic and Neolithic Ages?

The Growth of Villages People who farmed could settle in one place. Herders remained nomadic and drove their animals wherever they could find grazing land. Farmers, however, had to stay close to their fields to water the plants, keep hungry animals away, and harvest their crops. They began to live in villages, where they built permanent homes.

During the Neolithic Age, villages were started in Europe, India, Egypt, China, and Mexico. The earliest known communities have been found in the Middle East. One of the oldest is **Jericho** (JEHR•ih•KOH) in the West Bank between what are now Israel and Jordan. This city dates back to about 8000 B.C.

Another well-known Neolithic community is **Çatal Hüyük** (chah•TAHL hoo•YOOK) in present-day Turkey. Little of it remains, but it was home to some 6,000 people between about 6700 B.C. and 5700 B.C. They lived in simple mud-brick houses that were packed tightly together and decorated inside with wall paintings. They used other buildings as places of worship. Along with farming, the people hunted, raised sheep and goats, and ate fish and bird eggs from nearby marshes.

14   CHAPTER 1   The First Civilizations

EXTENDING THE CONTENT

Science Teaches Us About Ötzi For a long time, scientists thought that Ötzi had remained frozen from the time he died until he was discovered in modern times. Then scientists studying the body realized that layers of fat under the corpse's skin had turned into another substance—a substance sometimes called grave wax. Fat turns to this wax only when a body lies in water. As a result, scientists now believe it possible that at one time the body unfroze and the grave wax formed. Interestingly, grave wax hardly decays. This helps explain why the body was in such good shape after 5,000 years.

The Benefits of a Settled Life The shift to settled life brought Neolithic people greater security than they had ever known. Steady food supplies meant healthy, growing populations. With a bigger population, there were more workers to produce a bigger crop.

Because villagers produced more than enough to eat, they began to trade their extra foodstuffs. They traded with people in their own communities and also with people who lived in other areas.

People began to practice **specialization** (SPEH•shuh•luh•ZAY•shuhn), or the development of different kinds of jobs. Because not everyone was needed for farming, some people had the time to develop other types of skills. They made pottery from clay to store their grain and other foods. They used plant fibers to make mats and to weave

cloth. These craftspeople, like farmers, also took part in trade. They exchanged the things they made for goods they did not have.

In late Neolithic times, people continued to make advances. Toolmakers created better farming tools, such as the sickle for cutting grain. In some places, people began to work with metals. At first they used copper. They heated rocks to melt the copper inside and then poured it into molds for tools and weapons.

After 4000 B.C., craftspeople in western Asia mixed copper and tin to form bronze. Bronze was harder and longer lasting than copper. It became widely used between 3000 B.C. and 1200 B.C., the period known as the Bronze Age.

✓**Reading Check** **Compare** How did the Paleolithic and Neolithic Ages differ?

 Section ① Review

History Online
Study Central™ Need help with the material in this section? Visit jat.glencoe.com

Reading Summary
Review the Main Ideas

- Early humans were nomads who moved around to hunt animals and gather food. They built shelters and used fire to survive. In time, they developed language and art.

- During the farming revolution, people began to grow crops and domesticate animals, which allowed them to settle in villages.

What Did You Learn?
1. Who are archaeologists and what do they study?
2. How did domesticating animals help the Neolithic people?

Critical Thinking
3. **Determine Cause and Effect** Draw a diagram like the one below. List some of the effects that farming had on people's lives.

Cause: Farming begins	→ Effect:
	→ Effect:
	→ Effect:

4. **Explain** Why were Paleolithic people nomads?
5. **Compare** Compare the technology of the Paleolithic Age with that of the Neolithic Age.
6. **Analyze** Why was the ability to make a fire so important?
7. **Reading** **Previewing** Create a three-column chart. In the first column, write what you knew about early humans before you read this section. In the second column, write what you learned after reading. In the third, write what you still would like to know.

CHAPTER 1 The First Civilizations 15

ENRICH
Some scientists consider the Neolithic era the beginning of civilization. Have students write a short paragraph describing what they think a group of people needs to be considered a civilization. **L2**

RETEACH
Remind students that farming made such an important difference in human life that scientists call the beginning of the farming era a "revolution." Ask students to defend this label. **L2**

✓**Reading Check**

Answer: During the Paleolithic Age, people were nomadic hunters and lived in small groups. In the Neolithic Age, people learned to farm, settled in villages, and began to develop other jobs and trade.

History Online
To help students understand section material, have them visit **Study Central**™ at jat.glencoe.com

 CLOSE
Ask students to summarize the impact of farming on the human race. **L1/EL**

SECTION 1 REVIEW ANSWERS

1. Archaeologists are scientists who hunt for, dig up, and study artifacts.
2. Animals supplied meat, milk, and wool. They also carried goods and pulled carts.
3. People had a steady supply of food; people settled in villages and worked at jobs other than farming; people began to trade.
4. They moved around to hunt animals and gather other foods.
5. Paleolithic: stone, bone, and wooden tools and weapons; Neolithic: metal tools and weapons
6. Fire kept humans warm, scared animals away, and was used to cook food.
7. Charts should reflect information from the text.

① FOCUS

SECTION OVERVIEW

This section describes Mesopotamia, one of the regions where the world's earliest civilizations developed.

BELLRINGER
SKILLBUILDER ACTIVITY

✎ Project **Daily Focus Skills Transparency 1–2** and have students answer questions. Discuss their responses.

Get Ready to Read!

Preteaching Vocabulary: Have students find and review the definition of *civilization* in the section. Explain that Mesopotamia is often called the "cradle of civilization." Discuss with students the meaning of that phrase.

Answers to Graphic: City-states formed and began fighting with each other; fighting weakened the city-states; the Akkadians, led by Sargon, took over Mesopotamia and set up an empire.

Section 2 — Mesopotamian Civilization

Get-Ready to Read!

What's the Connection?

In Section 1, you learned about early humans settling in towns. Some settled in Mesopotamia, an area called the "cradle of civilization."

Focusing on the Main Ideas

- Civilization in Mesopotamia began in the valleys of the Tigris and Euphrates Rivers. *(page 17)*
- Sumerians invented writing and made other important contributions to later peoples. *(page 20)*
- Sumerian city-states lost power when they were conquered by outsiders. *(page 23)*

Locating Places

Tigris River (TY•gruhs)
Euphrates River (yu•FRAY•teez)
Mesopotamia (MEH•suh•puh•TAY•mee•uh)
Sumer (SOO•muhr)
Babylon (BA•buh•luhn)

Meeting People

Sargon (SAHR•GAHN)
Hammurabi (HA•muh•RAH•bee)

Building Your Vocabulary

civilization (SIH•vuh•luh•ZAY•shuhn)
irrigation (IHR•uh•GAY•shuhn)
city-state
artisan (AHR•tuh•zuhn)
cuneiform (kyoo•NEE•uh•FAWRM)
scribe (SKRYB)
empire (EHM•PYR)

Reading Strategy

Sequencing Information Use a diagram to show how the first empire in Mesopotamia came about.

city-states formed
↓
↓

NATIONAL GEOGRAPHIC When & Where?

3000 B.C.   **2250 B.C.**   **1500 B.C.**

● **3000 B.C.**
City-states arise in Sumer

● **c. 2340 B.C.**
Sargon conquers Babylon

● **c. 1792 B.C.**
Hammurabi rules Mesopotamia

Babylon • Uruk

16   CHAPTER 1   The First Civilizations

SECTION RESOURCES

📁 **Reproducible Masters**
- Reproducible Lesson Plan 1–2
- Daily Lecture and Discussion Notes 1–2
- Vocabulary Activity 1–2
- Active Reading Note-Taking Guide 1–2
- Guided Reading Activity 1–2
- Section Quiz 1–2
- Reading Essentials and Study Guide 1–2

✎ **Transparencies**
- Daily Focus Skills Transparency 1–2

Multimedia
- Interactive Tutor Self-Assessment CD-ROM
- ExamView® Pro Testmaker CD-ROM
- Presentation Plus! CD-ROM
- Glencoe BookLink CD-ROM

Mesopotamia's Civilization

Main Idea Civilization in Mesopotamia began in the valleys of the Tigris and Euphrates Rivers.

Reading Focus Do you live in a region that receives plenty of rain or in a region that is dry? Think about how that affects you as you read how the Sumerians' environment affected them.

Over thousands of years, some of the early farming villages developed into civilizations. **Civilizations** (SIH•vuh•luh•ZAY•shuhns) are complex societies. They have cities, organized governments, art, religion, class divisions, and a writing system.

Why Were River Valleys Important? The first civilizations arose in river valleys because good farming conditions made it

easy to feed large numbers of people. The rivers also made it easy to get from one place to another and to trade. Trade provided a way for goods and ideas to move from place to place. It was no accident, then, that cities grew up in these valleys and became the centers of civilizations.

As cities took shape, so did the need for organization. Someone had to make plans and decisions about matters of common concern. People formed governments to do just that. Their leaders took charge of food supplies and building projects. They made laws to keep order and assembled armies to fend off enemies.

With fewer worries about meeting their basic needs, people in the river valleys had more time to think about other things. They developed religions and the arts. To pass on

② TEACH

Illustrating Culture Remind students that Sumer's people were divided into three different social classes. Organize students into small groups. Direct the groups to think of a way to illustrate these classes. For example, a group might draw a rough ziggurat and assign to each of its tiers one of Sumer's social classes. Have groups share their illustrations with the class. **L2**

Daily Lecture and Discussion Notes 1–2

Use **Daily Lecture and Discussion Notes 1–2** for an outline of key concepts found in the section.

Reading Support L1/ EL

Use **Vocabulary Activity 1–2** to review important terms in the section.

Using Geography Skills

Answers:

1. the Persian Gulf
2. The rivers provided good farming conditions and easy trade opportunities.

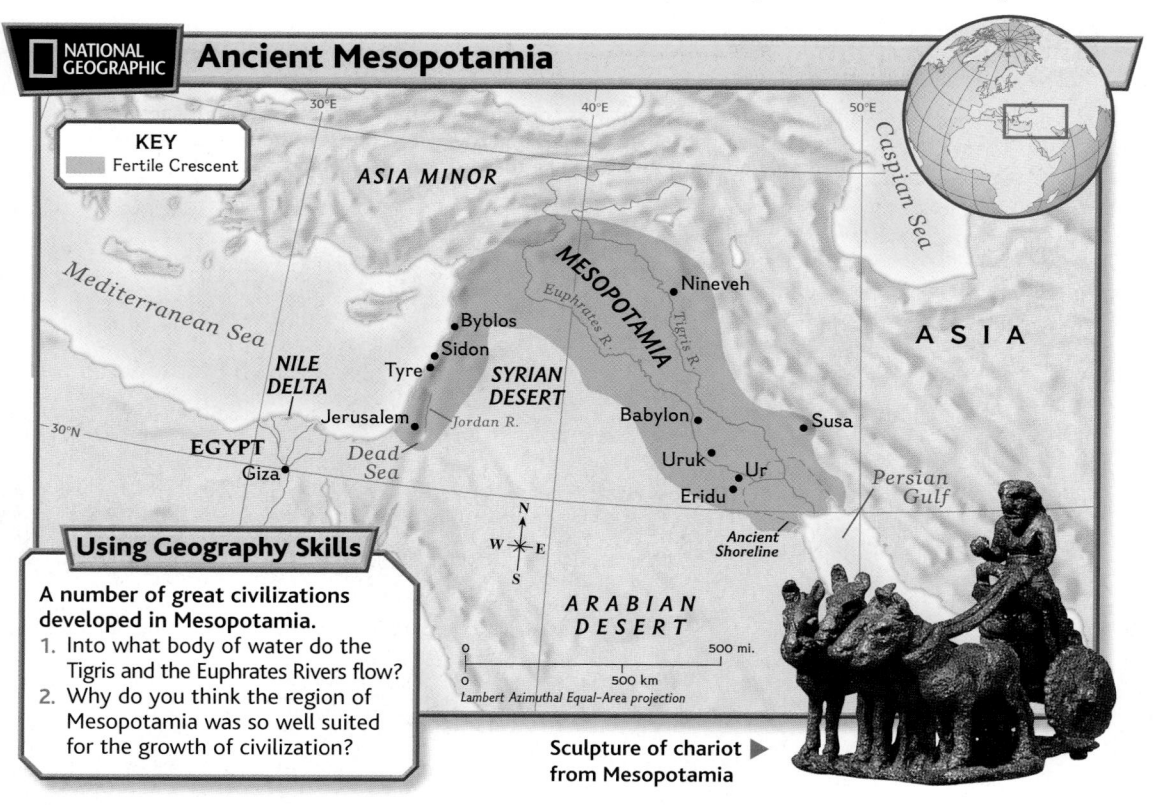

NATIONAL GEOGRAPHIC — Ancient Mesopotamia

KEY
Fertile Crescent

ASIA MINOR

Mediterranean Sea

NILE DELTA

Byblos
Sidon
Tyre

SYRIAN DESERT

Jerusalem
Jordan R.

EGYPT
Giza
Dead Sea

30°N

MESOPOTAMIA

Euphrates R.
Tigris R.

Nineveh

Babylon
Uruk
Ur
Eridu

Susa

Persian Gulf

Ancient Shoreline

Caspian Sea

ASIA

ARABIAN DESERT

N W E S

0   500 mi.
0   500 km
Lambert Azimuthal Equal-Area projection

Using Geography Skills

A number of great civilizations developed in Mesopotamia.

1. Into what body of water do the Tigris and the Euphrates Rivers flow?
2. Why do you think the region of Mesopotamia was so well suited for the growth of civilization?

► Sculpture of chariot from Mesopotamia

CHAPTER 1   The First Civilizations   **17**

Reading Strategy   READING THE TEXT

Outlining With students' help, write on the board a master outline of this section. As students read through the section, have them volunteer one or two key words for each outline entry. The key words should be significant enough to provide clues about the contents of that particular portion of the section. When study of the section is completed, have students use the outline and its key words to review the section's content together. **L1/ EL**

The City of Ur today sits lifeless in the desert, perhaps 10 miles from the Euphrates River. Thousands of years ago, when the city was built, the river ran much closer to the site. Over time, the river's path has changed, moving it farther and farther from Ur.

CONNECTING ACROSS TIME

Discuss with students the importance of natural resources to the civilizations of ancient Mesopotamia. Mention that conflicts often arose over who controlled and used these resources. Ask students to research the present-day nations that are part of the Mesopotamian region. Have them use this information to facilitate a class discussion about recent or ongoing conflicts over natural resources in the region. Also, have them discuss United States's involvement in the region. **L3**

More About the Art

Sumerians believed that cities were the property of the gods. Therefore, a ziggurat would be dedicated to a city's most important god or goddess.

Caption Answer: the main stair to the top, side stairs to the upper levels

information, they invented ways of writing. They also created calendars to tell time.

Early civilizations shared another feature—they had a class structure. That is, people held different places in society depending on what work they did and how much wealth or power they had.

The Rise of Sumer The earliest-known civilization arose in what is now southern Iraq, on a flat plain bounded by the **Tigris River** (TY•gruhs) and the **Euphrates River** (yu•FRAY•teez). This area was called **Mesopotamia** (MEH•suh•puh•TAY•mee•uh), which is Greek for "the land between the rivers." Mesopotamia lay in the eastern part of the Fertile Crescent, a curving strip of land that extends from the Mediterranean Sea to the Persian Gulf.

Mesopotamia had a hot, dry climate. In the spring, the rivers often flooded, leaving behind rich soil for farming. The problem was that the flooding was very unpredictable. It might flood one year, but not the next. Every year, farmers worried about their crops. They came to believe they needed their gods to bless their efforts.

Over time, the farmers learned to build dams and channels to control the seasonal floods. They also built walls, waterways, and ditches to bring water to their fields. This way of watering crops is called **irrigation** (IHR•uh•GAY•shuhn). Irrigation allowed the farmers to grow plenty of food and support a large population. By 3000 B.C., many cities had formed in southern Mesopotamia in a region known as **Sumer** (SOO•muhr).

Sumerian Ziggurat

The top of the ziggurat was considered to be a holy place, and the area around the ziggurat contained palaces and royal storehouses. The surrounding walls had only one entrance because the ziggurat also served as the city's treasury. *How did people reach the upper levels of the ziggurat?*

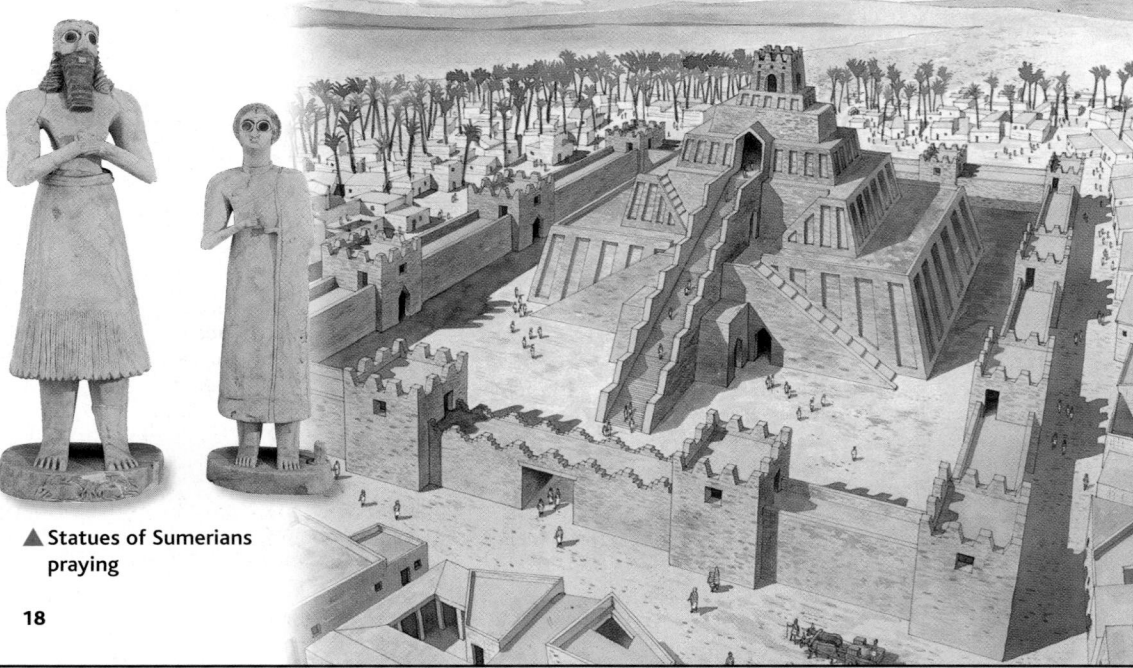

▲ Statues of Sumerians praying

18

DIFFERENTIATED INSTRUCTION

Visual/Spatial: Have students study the images of Sumerian cities in this section. Lead a discussion in which students relate what the pictures illustrate about life during that time.

Auditory/Musical: Ask a volunteer to read aloud the subsection titled "What Was Life Like in Sumer?" After the reader is finished, lead a discussion in which students identify the class distinctions that help distinguish Sumer as a civilization.

English Learners: Review with students the role of irrigation in early Mesopotamian civilizations. Have students write in their own words a definition for the word *irrigation*.

 Refer to *Inclusion Strategies for the Middle School Social Studies Classroom* in the TCR.

What Were City-States? Sumerian cities were isolated from each other by geography. Beyond the areas of settlement lay mudflats and patches of scorching desert. This terrain made travel and communication difficult. Each Sumerian city and the land around it became a separate **city-state.** It had its own government and was not part of any larger unit.

Sumerian city-states often went to war with one another. They fought to gain glory and to control more territory. For protection, each city-state surrounded itself with a wall. Because stone and wood were in short supply, the Sumerians used river mud as their main building material. They mixed the mud with crushed reeds, formed bricks, and left them in the sun to dry. The hard waterproof bricks were used for walls, as well as homes, temples, and other buildings.

Gods and Rulers The Sumerians believed in many gods. Each was thought to have power over a natural force or a human activity—flooding, for example, or basket weaving. The Sumerians tried hard to please the gods. They built a grand temple called a ziggurat (ZIH•guh•RAT) to the chief god. The word *ziggurat* means "mountain of god" or "hill of heaven."

With tiers like a giant square wedding cake, the ziggurat dominated the city. At the top was a shrine, or special place of worship that only priests and priestesses could enter. The priests and priestesses were powerful and controlled much of the land. They may even have ruled at one time.

Reading Strategy

Writing Activity

Have students write a paragraph identifying some of the responsibilities of the governments of early civilizations. **L2**

Geography Over thousands of years, the separate mouths of the Tigris and Euphrates Rivers gradually came together to form a swampy, single stream emptying into the Persian Gulf. Ask students to consider how a river changing its course would affect a civilization.

Also, discuss with students the impact of the rivers on present-day countries. Point out that the Tigris and Euphrates are the only major sources of freshwater in the Mesopotamian region. Ask students to point out difficulties countries might face with limited water supplies. Have students research ways in which the United Nations and United States have tried to help settle the disputes over water resources. **L3**

▲ A portion of the Royal Standard of Ur, a decorated box that shows scenes of Sumerian life

◄ These ruins are from the Sumerian city-state of Uruk. *What was a city-state?*

CHAPTER 1   The First Civilizations   **19**

More About the Art

While many ancient ziggurats have been destroyed or are in ruins, some have been preserved or reconstructed. These include ziggurats at Ur, Choqa Zanbil, and Nanna.

Caption Answer: an independent city with its own government

CRITICAL THINKING ACTIVITY

Analyzing Information Organize students into small groups. Direct the groups to use what they have learned from this section to prove or disprove this statement: With the rise of cities came a need for government. As groups brainstorm, draw on the board a two-column chart, with one column titled "Agree" and the other titled "Disagree." Ask a representative from each group to put a check mark in the appropriate column and explain the thought processes that led the group to that answer. **L3**

CURRICULUM CONNECTION

Literature

The *Epic of Gilgamesh* is about an actual king, the king of Uruk in Babylonia. The stories of his life—both truth and myth—were written in cuneiform onto 12 clay tablets. Unbelievably, these 12 tablets were found, damaged but readable, in the ruins of a library that had been destroyed by Persians. Have students research information about the *Epic of Gilgamesh,* either on the Internet or at the library. Then have them write a short paragraph describing its importance.

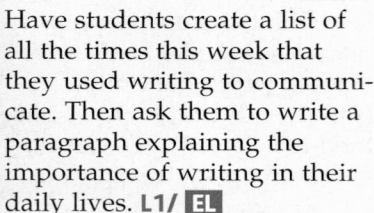

Writing Activity

Have students create a list of all the times this week that they used writing to communicate. Then ask them to write a paragraph explaining the importance of writing in their daily lives. **L1/ EL**

✓ Reading Check

Answer: They built dams and channels to control seasonal floods. They also used irrigation—walls, waterways, and ditches that brought water to their crops.

Later, kings ran the government. They led armies and organized building projects. The first kings were probably war heroes. Their position became hereditary. That is, after a king died, his son took over.

What Was Life Like in Sumer?
While Sumerian kings lived in large palaces, ordinary people lived in small mud-brick houses. Most people in Sumer farmed. Some, however, were **artisans** (AHR•tuh•zuhns), or skilled workers who made metal products, cloth, or pottery. Other people in Sumer worked as merchants or traders. They traveled to other cities and towns and traded tools, wheat, and barley for copper, tin, and timber—things that Sumer did not have.

People in Sumer were divided into three social classes. The upper class included kings, priests, and government officials. In the middle class were artisans, merchants, farmers, and fishers. These people made up the largest group. The lower class were enslaved people who worked on farms or in the temples.

Enslaved people were forced to serve others. Slaveholders thought of them as property. Some slaves were prisoners of war. Others were criminals. Still others were enslaved because they had to pay off their debts.

In Sumer, women and men had separate roles. Men headed the households. Only males could go to school. Women, however, did have rights. They could buy and sell property and run businesses.

▲ Sumerian cuneiform

✓ Reading Check Explain How did Mesopotamians control the flow of the Tigris and Euphrates Rivers?

A Skilled People

Main Idea Sumerians invented writing and made other important contributions to later peoples.

Reading Focus Do you like to read? If so, you owe a debt to the Sumerians, because they were the first to invent writing. Read about this achievement and others.

The Sumerians left a lasting mark on world history. Their ideas and inventions were copied and improved upon by other peoples. As a result, Mesopotamia has been called the "cradle of civilization."

Why Was Writing Important?
The people of Sumer created many things that still affect our lives today. Probably their greatest invention was writing. Writing is important because it helps people keep records and pass on their ideas to others.

People in Sumer developed writing to keep track of business deals and other events. Their writing was called **cuneiform** (kyoo•NEE•uh•FAWRM). It consisted of hundreds of wedge-shaped marks cut into damp clay tablets with a sharp-ended reed. Archaeologists have found thousands of these cuneiform tablets, telling us much about Mesopotamian life.

Only a few people—mostly boys from wealthy families—learned how to write. After years of training, they became **scribes** (SKRYBS), or record keepers. Scribes held honored positions in society, often going on to become judges and political leaders.

Sumerian Literature
The Sumerians also produced works of literature. The world's oldest known story comes from Sumer. It is called the *Epic of Gilgamesh* (GIHL•guh•MEHSH). An epic is a long poem that tells the story of a hero. The hero Gilgamesh is a king who travels around the world with a friend and performs great deeds. When his

---

INTERDISCIPLINARY CONNECTIONS ACTIVITY

Mathematics Have students research the history of mathematics in Sumeria, including why the Sumerians developed mathematical concepts and any important contributions to the math we use today. Besides the number system based on 60, students should find that the Sumerians also used multiplication tables, tables of squares and square roots, and reciprocals. You may wish to have students create arithmetic problems for other students to solve based on their research. For example, students may create problems dealing with time, such as "How many hours is 420 minutes?" Have students share their research and problems with the class. **L2**

friend dies, Gilgamesh searches for a way to live forever. He learns that this is possible only for the gods.

Advances in Science and Math The Mesopotamians' creativity extended to technology too. You read earlier about Sumerian irrigation systems. Sumerians also invented the wagon wheel to help carry people and goods from place to place. Another breakthrough was the plow, which made farming easier. Still another invention was the sailboat, which replaced muscle power with wind power.

Sumerians developed many mathematical ideas. They used geometry to measure fields and put up buildings. They also created a number system based on 60. We have them to thank for our 60-minute hour, 60-second minute, and 360-degree circle.

In addition, Sumerian people watched the skies to learn the best times to plant crops and to hold religious festivals. They recorded the positions of the planets and stars and developed a 12-month calendar based on the cycles of the moon.

Reading Check **Identify** What kind of written language did the Sumerians use?

Linking Past & Present

Education

THEN In ancient Mesopotamia, only boys from wealthy and high-ranking families went to the *edubba*, which means "tablet house." At the *edubba*—the world's first school—boys studied reading, writing, and mathematics and trained to be scribes. For hours every day, they copied the signs of the cuneiform script, trying to master hundreds of words and phrases.

▲ Mesopotamian cuneiform tablet

▼ Students today

NOW Today, both boys and girls go to school. They study reading, writing, and mathematics, but also many other subjects. As students advance in their education, they have a great number of career choices and are able to choose the career that fits their talents. *In what way is education different today than it was in Mesopotamia?*

CHAPTER 1   The First Civilizations   **21**

CITIZENSHIP AND YOU

Exploring Citizens' Rights Remind students that during Sumerian times, only a few Sumerians were allowed to become scribes. In the United States today, we take for granted that everyone has the opportunity to learn to read and write. Ask students to imagine that because there are not enough places in school for every student, not everyone can attend. Now organize students into groups, and have each group brainstorm reasons why its members should be allowed to go to school. Have one member from each group present that group's list of reasons to the class. **L2**

☞ See the **Citizenship and Service Learning Activities** in the Unit Resource Books for more participatory projects.

TEACH

Much of what we know about Hammurabi's acts as king comes from an unusual source. At that time, people in Mesopotamia gave a name to each year, with each name reflecting a recent kingly act. By looking at the names of the years during Hammurabi's reign, we can learn about what he accomplished as ruler of Babylon.

Discuss with students how control of the region's waters helped Hammurabi maintain control of the region. How did it help Hammurabi that Larsa was downriver from Babylon? *(Students may say that Hammurabi could withhold water from Larsa or release dammed water to cause flooding in Larsa.)* **L2**

Then and Now

Answers will vary, but students should give specific examples of current laws and reasons for their opinions.

Biography

HAMMURABI
Reigned c. 1792–1750 B.C.

▲ Hammurabi

Hammurabi was a young man when he succeeded his father, Sinmuballit, as king of Babylon. When Hammurabi became king, Babylon was already a major power in Mesopotamia. During his reign, however, Hammurabi transformed Babylon from a small city-state into a large, powerful state. He also united Mesopotamia under one rule. Hammurabi called himself "Strong King of Babel."

Hammurabi was directly involved in the ruling of his kingdom. He personally directed projects, such as building city walls, restoring temples, and digging and cleaning irrigation canals. A great deal of planning went into his projects. City streets, for example, were arranged in straight lines and intersected at right angles, much like the way our cities are planned today.

One of Hammurabi's goals was to control the Euphrates River because it provided water for Babylon's farms and trade routes for cargo ships. However, other kings also wanted control of the river. One of Hammurabi's rivals in the battle for the Euphrates was Rim-Sin of Larsa. During Hammurabi's last 14 years as king, he and his soldiers fought against Rim-Sin and other enemies. Hammurabi actually used water to defeat Rim-Sin and his people. He sometimes did this by damming the water and releasing a sudden flood, and sometimes by withholding water needed for drinking and for crops.

After defeating his enemies, Hammurabi ruled briefly over a unified Mesopotamia. Hammurabi soon became ill, and his son, Samsuiluna, took over his duties and was crowned king after his death. Because of Hammurabi's great efforts, however, the center of power in Mesopotamia shifted from the south to Babylon in the north, where it remained for the next 1,000 years.

Then and Now

Do any nations currently have law codes that resemble Hammurabi's? Use the Internet and your local library to identify countries with law codes that you think are somewhat fair but somewhat cruel.

Reading List Generator CD-ROM | **GLENCOE BOOKLINK** | **RECOMMENDED READING**

Use the **Glencoe BookLink CD-ROM** to create customized reading lists based on your students' interests and reading levels. Below is an example based on content in this chapter. Also, see the Suggested Readings on pages 944–946 of the Appendix.

- *The Death of Enkidu:* From the *Epic of Gilgamesh.* Excerpt from the epic.
- Hickox, Rebecca. *The Golden Sandal.* Maha, a young Iraqi girl, is rescued from her evil stepmother with the aid of a little red fish.
- Landau, Elaine. *The Babylonians.* One of the great empires of the ancient world arose in Babylon.

Sargon and Hammurabi

Main Idea Sumerian city-states lost power when they were conquered by outsiders.

Reading Focus Have you heard of the Roman Empire, the Aztec Empire, or the British Empire? The rise and fall of empires is an important part of history. Read on to learn about the first empires in the world.

Over time, conflicts weakened Sumer's city-states. They became vulnerable to attacks by outside groups such as the Akkadians (uh•KAY•dee•uhnz) of northern Mesopotamia.

The king of the Akkadians was named **Sargon** (SAHR•GAHN). In about 2340 B.C., Sargon conquered all of Mesopotamia. He set up the world's first empire. An **empire** (EHM•PYR) is a group of many different lands under one ruler. Sargon's empire lasted for more than 200 years before falling to invaders.

In the 1800s B.C., a new group of people became powerful in Mesopotamia. They built the city of **Babylon** (BA•buh•luhn) by the Euphrates River. It quickly became a center of trade. Beginning in 1792 B.C., the Babylonian king, **Hammurabi** (HA•muh•RAH•bee), began conquering cities to the north and south and created the Babylonian Empire.

Hammurabi is best known for his law code, or collection of laws. (See pages 24 and 25.) He took what he believed were the best laws from each city-state and put them in one code. The code covered crimes, farming and business activities, and marriage and the family—almost every area of life. Although many punishments in the Code of Hammurabi were cruel, his laws mark an important step toward a fair system of justice.

✓ Reading Check **Explain** Why was Sargon's empire important?

Study Central™ Need help with the material in this section? Visit jat.glencoe.com

Section 2 Review

Reading Summary

Review the Main Ideas

- In time, farming villages developed into civilizations with governments, art, religion, writing, and social class divisions. The first city-states developed in Mesopotamia.
- Many important ideas and inventions, including writing, the wheel, the plow, and a number system based on 60, were developed in the region of Mesopotamia.
- Several empires, including the Babylonian Empire, took control of Mesopotamia.

What Did You Learn?

1. What is a civilization?
2. What was the Code of Hammurabi?

Critical Thinking

3. **Summarize Information** Draw a chart like the one below. Use it to list the achievements of Mesopotamian civilization.

Achievements of Mesopotamian Civilization

4. **Geography Skills** How was the geography of Mesopotamia suited for the growth of population and creation of a civilization?
5. **Science Link** Why did the Sumerians record the positions of stars and planets and develop a calendar?
6. **Persuasive Writing** Imagine you are living in a city-state in ancient Sumer. Write a letter to a friend describing which Mesopotamian idea or invention you believe will be the most important to humanity.

CHAPTER 1   The First Civilizations   **23**

Reading Support L1/ EL

Assign **Reading Essentials and Study Guide 1–2** to help students review section material.

ENRICH

Have groups look through the local government pages of the telephone book. Ask them to discuss which services they think are most important. **L2**

✓ Reading Check

Answer: It was the world's first empire.

To help students understand section material, have them visit **Study Central™** at jat.glencoe.com

RETEACH

Ask small groups of students to write down five class rules. Then discuss how fairness is encouraged by having a written list of rules. **L1/ EL**

④ CLOSE

Have students review the Sumerian technologies that changed the world. **L2**

SECTION 2 REVIEW ANSWERS

1. a complex society with cities, an organized government, art, religion, a system of writing, and class divisions
2. a set of laws that the Babylonian leader Hammurabi established for his empire
3. irrigation, writing, wheel, plow, sailboat, use of geometry to measure fields and erect buildings, number system based on 60, the 12-month calendar
4. Mesopotamia was located in the valley of the Tigris and Euphrates Rivers. These rivers often flooded, leaving behind rich soil for farming, which made it easier to feed large numbers of people.
5. to learn the best times to plant crops and hold religious festivals
6. Answers will vary. Students' letters should contain valid reasons for their choice.

You Decide...

1 FOCUS

Whether Hammurabi's laws were fair or cruel, the culture benefited from having a written code that applied to everyone. Ask students to think about what it would be like to live in a society with no written rules.

2 TEACH

DEFINING TERMS

Have students working in pairs use dictionaries to find the definitions of the words *fair* and *cruel*. Have pairs determine whether *unfair* and *cruel* mean the same thing. **L2**

COMPARISON

Draw on the board and have students copy this graphic organizer. As they read the passage, direct them to write laws that are either fair or cruel in the appropriate blanks. *(Answers may vary.)* **L2**

Hammurabi's Code	
Fair Laws	Cruel Laws

Hammurabi's Laws: Fair or Cruel?

Fair

Around 1750 B.C., King Hammurabi wrote 282 laws to govern the people of Babylon. Historians and scholars agree that these ancient laws were the first to cover all aspects of society. However, historians and scholars do not agree whether Hammurabi's laws were fair or cruel.

Those who see the laws as just and fair give the following reasons. They say the laws

- stated what all people needed to know about the rules of their society
- brought order and justice to society
- regulated many different activities, from business contracts to crime.

King Hammurabi wrote an introduction to his list of laws. In that introduction, he says that the laws were written to be fair. His intention was "to bring about the rule of righteousness in the land, to destroy the wicked and evil-doers, so that the strong should not harm the weak. . . ."

Some of the laws reflect that fairness.

- Law 5: If a judge makes an error through his own fault when trying a case, he must pay a fine, be removed from the judge's bench, and never judge another case.
- Law 122: If someone gives something to someone else for safe-keeping, the transaction should be witnessed and a contract made between the two parties.
- Law 233: If a contractor builds a house for someone and the walls start to fall, then the builder must use his own money and labor to make the walls secure.

▶ Stone monument showing Hammurabi (standing) and his code

24

Extending the Content

Hammurabi's Code In his code, Hammurabi addressed many everyday concerns. For example, he included laws to help regulate the economy. These laws addressed such money issues as prices and tariffs on certain items, as well as salaries to be paid. Law #257 said, "If any one hire a field laborer, he shall pay him eight gur of [grain] per year." Other laws in the code dealt with family issues. Law #185 prevented a man from taking his son back from someone else who had already adopted him, reared him to adulthood, and given him his name. Still other laws addressed the punishments for criminal behavior. Law #25 was straightforward: "If fire breaks out in a house, and someone . . . take the property of the master of the house, he shall be thrown into that self-same fire."

▲ Cuneiform tablet with the text of the introduction to the Code of Hammurabi

Cruel

Some historians and scholars think Hammurabi's laws were cruel and unjust. They say the laws
- called for violent punishments, often death, for nonviolent crimes
- required different punishments for accused persons of different social classes
- allowed no explanation from an accused person.

Some of the laws reflect this cruelty.
- Law 3: If someone falsely accuses someone else of certain crimes, then he shall be put to death.

- Law 22: If someone is caught in the act of robbery, then he shall be put to death.
- Law 195: If a son strikes his father, the son's hands shall be cut off.
- Law 202: If someone strikes a man of higher rank, then he shall be whipped 60 times in public.

You Be the Historian

Checking for Understanding
1. Why do some people think Hammurabi's laws were fair?
2. Why do others think the laws were cruel?
3. Were the laws fair or cruel? Take the role of a historian. Write a brief essay that explains how you view Hammurabi's laws. Be sure to use facts to support your position. You can compare Hammurabi's laws to our modern laws to support your argument.

25

③ ASSESS

Reading Strategy

DEBATE THE ISSUE

Organize a class debate on this question: Which word—*fair* or *cruel*—better describes Hammurabi's Code of Laws? Assign small groups one of the points of view, making sure to have an equal number of groups supporting each side. Tell them to prepare for the debate by reviewing the laws mentioned in the text. Also, students should research more of Hammurabi's laws either in library resources or on the Internet. The more laws they are able to find, the better able they will be to support their arguments. Remind them to use their graphic organizers to organize their thoughts.

Once students are ready, conduct the debate. At the end, ask students to vote on who had the stronger argument.

When the debate is finished, point out that in the code, crimes against slaves are treated differently—and more lightly—than crimes against free people. Ask whether this changes their opinions. **L3**

You Be the Historian Answers

1. The laws stated what people needed to know about the rules of society. They also brought order to society and regulated activities.

2. The laws often called for violent punishments, frequently death. Punishments for breaking the laws varied according to a person's social class.

3. Responses will vary. Most students probably will see Hammurabi's laws as unjustly cruel and harsh. They may point to examples in our modern laws to show how laws today are more fair in fitting the punishment to the crime.

① FOCUS

SECTION OVERVIEW

This section discusses the Assyrian and Chaldean Empires.

BELLRINGER
SKILLBUILDER ACTIVITY

✎ Project **Daily Focus Skills Transparency 1–3** and have students answer questions. Discuss their responses.

Get Ready to Read!

Preteaching Vocabulary: Discuss with students how governing a large area is often easier when the area is organized into smaller government units, similar to states and counties in the United States. In the ancient Assyrian Empire, these smaller government units were called provinces.

Answers to Graphic: Assyrians: iron weapons; ferocious warriors; large empire; capital was Nineveh; divided empire into provinces; built roads; brutal laws. Chaldeans: capital was Babylon; constructed Hanging Gardens; expanded trade; advanced astronomy. Both: lived in Mesopotamia; large army; built temples and palaces.

Section 3

The First Empires

Get Ready to Read!

What's the Connection?
In Section 2, you learned about the empires of Sargon and Hammurabi. Later empires—those of the Assyrians and the Chaldeans—used their military power in new ways.

Focusing on the Main Ideas
• Assyria's military power and well-organized government helped it build a vast empire in Mesopotamia by 650 B.C. *(page 27)*

• The Chaldean Empire built important landmarks in Babylon and developed the first calendar with a seven-day week. *(page 29)*

Locating Places
Assyria (uh•SIHR•ee•uh)
Persian Gulf (PUHR•zhuhn)
Nineveh (NIH•nuh•vuh)
Hanging Gardens

Meeting People
Nebuchadnezzar
(NEH•byuh•kuhd•NEH•zuhr)

Building Your Vocabulary
province (PRAH•vuhns)
caravan (KAR•uh•VAN)
astronomer
(uh•STRAH•nuh•muhr)

Reading Strategy
Compare and Contrast Complete a Venn diagram like the one below listing the similarities and differences between the Assyrian Empire and the Chaldean Empire.

Assyrians   Chaldeans

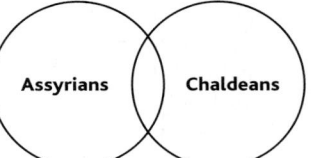

NATIONAL GEOGRAPHIC **When & Where?**

Nineveh
Babylon

900 B.C.   **700 B.C.**   **500 B.C.**

● c. 900 B.C.
Assyrians control
Mesopotamia

612 B.C. ●
Nineveh captured;
Assyrian Empire
crumbles

● 539 B.C.
Persians conquer
Chaldeans

SECTION RESOURCES

📁 **Reproducible Masters**
• Reproducible Lesson Plan 1–3
• Daily Lecture and Discussion Notes 1–3
• Vocabulary Activity 1–3
• Active Reading Note-Taking Guide 1–3
• Guided Reading Activity 1–3
• Section Quiz 1–3
• Reading Essentials and Study Guide 1–3

✎ **Transparencies**
• Daily Focus Skills Transparency 1–3

Multimedia
⊜ Interactive Tutor Self-Assessment CD-ROM
⊜ ExamView® Pro Testmaker CD-ROM
⊜ Presentation Plus! CD-ROM
⊜ Vocabulary PuzzleMaker CD-ROM

The Assyrians

Main Idea Assyria's military power and well-organized government helped it build a vast empire in Mesopotamia by 650 B.C.

Reading Focus Today, many countries have armed forces to protect their interests. Read to find out how the Assyrians built an army strong enough to conquer all of Mesopotamia.

About 1,000 years after Hammurabi, a new empire arose in Mesopotamia. It was founded by a people called the Assyrians (uh•SIHR•ee•uhns), who lived in the north near the Tigris River. **Assyria** (uh•SIHR•ee•uh) had fertile valleys that attracted outside invaders. To defend their land, the Assyrians built a large army. Around 900 B.C., they began taking over the rest of Mesopotamia.

Why Were the Assyrians So Strong? The Assyrian army was well organized. At its core were groups of foot soldiers armed with spears and daggers. Other soldiers were experts at using bows and arrows. The army also had chariot riders and soldiers who fought on horseback.

This fearsome and mighty force was the first large army to use iron weapons. For centuries, iron had been used for tools, but it was too soft to serve as a material for weapons. Then a people called the Hittites (HIH•TYTZ), who lived northwest of Assyria, developed a way of making iron stronger. They heated iron ore, hammered it, and rapidly cooled it. The Assyrians learned this technique from the Hittites. They produced iron weapons that were stronger than those made of copper or tin.

The Assyrians at War

When attacking a walled city, the Assyrians used massive war machines. The wheeled battering ram was powered by soldiers. It was covered to protect the soldiers inside, but it had slits so they could shoot arrows out.
What other methods did Assyrian soldiers use to attack cities?

CONNECTING ACROSS TIME

Discuss with students why the Hanging Gardens of Babylon may have been considered a wonder of the ancient world. Have them research and list the other six ancient wonders. Then have small groups consider what they would include on a list of the Seven Wonders of the United States. **L1/ EL**

Using Geography Skills

Answers:

1. the Tigris, Euphrates, and Nile Rivers

2. mountains to the north, desert to the south

✓ Reading Check

Answer: They punished anyone who resisted their rule, drove people from their lands, and made settlers pay taxes.

Reading Support L1/ EL

Assign **Guided Reading Activity 1–3** to help students organize the information in the section.

---

③ ASSESS

Assign Section 3 Review as homework or as an in-class activity.

⚫ Have students use the **Interactive Tutor Self-Assessment CD-ROM** to review the section.

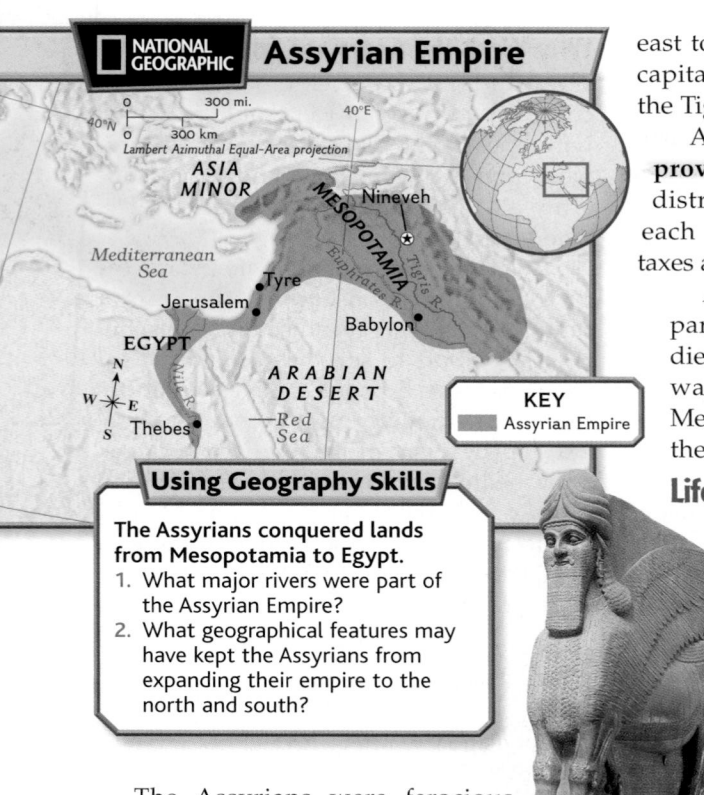

NATIONAL GEOGRAPHIC **Assyrian Empire**

300 mi.
300 km
Lambert Azimuthal Equal-Area projection

ASIA MINOR
Nineveh
Mediterranean Sea
Tyre
Jerusalem
Babylon
EGYPT
ARABIAN DESERT
Thebes
Red Sea

KEY
Assyrian Empire

Using Geography Skills

The Assyrians conquered lands from Mesopotamia to Egypt.

1. What major rivers were part of the Assyrian Empire?

2. What geographical features may have kept the Assyrians from expanding their empire to the north and south?

▲ Assyrian winged bull

The Assyrians were ferocious warriors. To attack cities, they tunneled under walls or climbed over them on ladders. They loaded tree trunks onto movable platforms and used them as battering rams to knock down city gates. Once a city was captured, the Assyrians set fire to its buildings. They also carried away its people and goods.

Anyone who resisted Assyrian rule was punished. The Assyrians drove people from their lands and moved them into foreign territory. Then they brought in new settlers and forced them to pay heavy taxes.

A Well-Organized Government

Assyrian kings had to be strong to rule their large empire. By about 650 B.C., the empire stretched from the **Persian Gulf** (PUHR•zhuhn) in the east to Egypt's Nile River in the west. The capital was at **Nineveh** (NIH•nuh•vuh) on the Tigris River.

Assyrian kings divided the empire into **provinces** (PRAH•vuhn•suhs), or political districts. They chose officials to govern each province. These officials collected taxes and enforced the king's laws.

Assyrian kings built roads to join all parts of their empire. Government soldiers were posted at stations along the way to protect traders from bandits. Messengers on government business used the stations to rest and change horses.

Life in Assyria

The Assyrians lived much like other Mesopotamians. Their writing was based on Babylonian writing, and they worshiped many of the same gods. Their laws were similar, but lawbreakers often faced more brutal and cruel punishments in Assyria.

As builders, the Assyrians showed great skill. They erected large temples and palaces that they filled with wall carvings and statues. The Assyrians also produced and collected literature. One of the world's first libraries was in Nineveh. It held 25,000 tablets of stories and songs to the gods. Modern historians have learned much about ancient civilizations from this library.

Assyria's cruel treatment of people led to many rebellions. About 650 B.C., the Assyrians began fighting each other over who would be their next king. A group of people called the Chaldeans (kahl•DEE•uhns) seized the opportunity to rebel. They captured Nineveh in 612 B.C., and the Assyrian Empire soon crumbled.

✓ Reading Check **Explain** Why were the Assyrian soldiers considered brutal and cruel?

28 CHAPTER 1 The First Civilizations

DIFFERENTIATED INSTRUCTION

Verbal/Linguistic: Have each student research one of the Seven Wonders of the Ancient World and write a paragraph describing it. Tell them to make sure they use descriptive words in their paragraphs. Have volunteers read aloud their paragraphs as others identify the descriptive words used.

Kinesthetic: Have each student use papier-mâché, clay, cardboard, or another medium to create a three-dimensional image of one of the Seven Wonders of the Ancient World.

Gifted and Talented: In addition to creating three-dimensional images, have students prepare a short report to present their project to the class.

📁 Refer to *Inclusion Strategies for the Middle School Social Studies Classroom* in the TCR.

The Chaldeans

Main Idea The Chaldean Empire built important landmarks in Babylon and developed the first calendar with a seven-day week.

Reading Focus What landmarks exist in your town or the nearest city? Read to learn some of the special landmarks that made the Chaldean capital of Babylon famous.

The Chaldeans wanted to build an empire. Led by King **Nebuchadnezzar** (NEH• byuh•kuhd•NEH•zuhr), they controlled all of Mesopotamia from 605 B.C. to 562 B.C.

The City of Babylon Most of the Chaldeans were descendants of the Babylonian people who made up Hammurabi's empire about 1,200 years earlier. They rebuilt the city of Babylon as the glorious center of their empire.

Babylon quickly became the world's largest and richest city. It was surrounded by a brick wall so wide that two chariots could pass on the road on top. Built into the wall at 100-yard (91.4-m) intervals were towers where soldiers kept watch.

Large palaces and temples stood in the city's center. A huge ziggurat reached more than 300 feet (91.4 m) into the sky. Another marvel, visible from any point in Babylon, was an immense staircase of greenery: the **Hanging Gardens** at the king's palace.

These terraced gardens showcased large trees, masses of flowering vines, and other beautiful plants. A pump brought in water from a nearby river. Nebuchadnezzar built the gardens to please his wife, who missed the mountains and plants of her homeland in the northwest.

History Online

Web Activity Visit jat.glencoe.com and click on *Chapter 1—Student Web Activity* to learn more about the first civilizations.

Hanging Gardens

The Hanging Gardens of Babylon were considered one of the Seven Wonders of the Ancient World. A complex irrigation system brought water from the Euphrates River to the top of the gardens. From there, the water flowed down to each of the lower levels of the gardens. *What other sights made Babylon a grand city?*

▲ Ruins of the Hanging Gardens

CHAPTER 1
SECTION 3, 26–30

Assessment L2

Assign **Section 3 Quiz** to assess mastery of the material found in the section.

Reading Support L1/ EL

Assign **Reading Essentials and Study Guide 1–3** to help students review section material.

History Online

Objectives and answers to the student activity can be found in the **Web Activity Lesson Plan** feature at jat.glencoe.com

More About the Art

Some archaeologists believe that the ruins of the Hanging Gardens have been found. Others doubt that the gardens ever existed.

Caption Answer: the massive wall, the tall ziggurat

CRITICAL THINKING ACTIVITY

Applying Information The Hanging Gardens of Babylon were famous for the wonderful plants they contained. King Nebuchadnezzar, who had the gardens made for his wife, put plants there that would remind his wife of her home in the mountains of Media (in northwestern Iran). Have students research the geography of northwestern Iran and make a catalog of the plants that may have existed in the Hanging Gardens. Then have students make a catalog of plants that Nebuchadnezzar might have placed in the Hanging Gardens had his wife come from the students' own region. L3

ENRICH

The Chaldeans named constellations that we still can identify today. Ask students to identify heavenly objects they have read about. **L1/ EL**

> **Caption Answer:** The brick wall was wide enough at the top for two chariots to ride on and had towers every 100 yards.

RETEACH

Have students identify and discuss some of the contributions of the Assyrians. **L2**

 Reading Check

Answer: terraced gardens at the king's palace that could be seen from any point in Babylon

 History Online

To help students understand section material, have them visit **Study Central™** at jat.glencoe.com

④ CLOSE

Ask students to describe two main points about the Assyrians and Chaldeans. **L1**

▲ The Ishtar Gate was at the main entrance to ancient Babylon. *Describe the wall that surrounded Babylon.*

One Greek historian in the 400s B.C. described the beauty of Babylon. He wrote, "In magnificence, there is no other city that approaches it." Outside the center of Babylon stood houses and marketplaces. There, artisans made pottery, cloth, baskets, and jewelry. They sold their wares to passing **caravans** (KAR•uh•VANZ), or groups of traveling merchants. Because Babylon was located on the major trade route between the Persian Gulf and the Mediterranean Sea, it became rich from trade.

Babylon was also a center of science. Like earlier people in Mesopotamia, the Chaldeans believed that changes in the sky revealed the plans of the gods. Their **astronomers** (uh•STRAH•nuh•muhrs)—people who study the heavenly bodies—mapped the stars, the planets, and the phases of the moon. The Chaldeans made one of the first sundials and were the first to have a seven-day week.

Why Did the Empire Fall? As time passed, the Chaldeans began to lose their power. They found it hard to control the peoples they had conquered. In 539 B.C. Persians from the mountains to the northeast captured Babylon. Mesopotamia became part of the new Persian Empire.

✓ **Reading Check** **Identify** What were the Hanging Gardens of Babylon?

Section ③ Review

 History Online

Study Central™ Need help with the material in this section? Visit jat.glencoe.com

Reading Summary
Review the Main Ideas

- Using cavalry and foot soldiers armed with iron weapons, the Assyrians created a large empire that included all of Mesopotamia and extended into Egypt.

- The Chaldeans built a large empire that included Babylon, the largest and richest city in the world at that time.

What Did You Learn?

1. Why was the Assyrian army a powerful fighting force?

2. What were some of the accomplishments of Chaldean astronomers?

Critical Thinking

3. **Summarize Information** Draw a chart like the one below. Use it to describe the city of Babylon under the Chaldeans.

Babylon under Chaldeans

4. **Analyze** How did the Assyrians set up a well-organized government?

5. **Conclude** Why do you think the Assyrians took conquered peoples from their lands and moved them to other places?

6. **Science Link** What different types of knowledge and skills would the Babylonians need to build the Hanging Gardens?

7. **Descriptive Writing** Write a paragraph that might be found in a travel brochure describing the beauty of ancient Babylon.

SECTION 3 REVIEW ANSWERS

1. It had a well-organized army with advanced weapons.

2. mapped stars, planets, phases of the moon; created sundial and seven-day week

3. world's largest and richest city; surrounded by a massive wall; large palaces and temples with a tall ziggurat; Hanging Gardens; on a major trade route

4. divided empire into provinces, chose provincial officials to collect taxes and enforce laws

5. Possible answer: It would make it more difficult for conquered people to rise up against the Assyrians.

6. Students' answers will vary but should utilize information from the text.

7. Answers will vary but should include relevant facts.

Section 1 Early Humans

Vocabulary
historian
archaeologist
artifact
fossil
anthropologist
nomad
technology
domesticate
specialization

Focusing on the Main Ideas
- Paleolithic people adapted to their environment and invented many tools to help them survive. *(page 9)*
- In the Neolithic Age, people started farming, building communities, producing goods, and trading. *(page 13)*

Section 2 Mesopotamian Civilization

Vocabulary
civilization
irrigation
city-state
artisan
cuneiform
scribe
empire

Focusing on the Main Ideas
- Civilization in Mesopotamia began in the valleys of the Tigris and Euphrates Rivers. *(page 17)*
- Sumerians invented writing and made other important contributions to later peoples. *(page 20)*
- Sumerian city-states lost power when they were conquered by outsiders. *(page 23)*

Sumerian figurines ▶

Section 3 The First Empires

Vocabulary
province
caravan
astronomer

Focusing on the Main Ideas
- Assyria's military power and well-organized government helped it build a vast empire in Mesopotamia by 650 B.C. *(page 27)*
- The Chaldean Empire built important landmarks in Babylon and developed the first calendar with a seven-day week. *(page 29)*

PREVIEW/REVIEW

Vocabulary Activity Have students identify the time period and civilization related to each term, if possible.

🌐 **Vocabulary PuzzleMaker CD-ROM**

🌐 **Interactive Tutor Self-Assessment CD-ROM**

CONDENSE

📁 Chapter 1 **Guided Reading Activities**

📁 **StudentWorks Plus™ CD-ROM (with Audio Program)**

RETEACH

📁 **Differentiated Instruction Activity 1**

📁 Chapter 1 *Reading Essentials and Study Guide*

CHAPTER CULMINATING ACTIVITY

Have students finish the Chapter Culminating Activity from page 4D.

Suggestions for rubrics may be found in the *Quizzes, Tests, and Authentic Assessment (with Rubrics)* booklet.

Reading Strategy   READ TO WRITE

Write a Paragraph Have students write a paragraph explaining the connection between early civilizations and Mesopotamia. Direct them to use as many of the vocabulary terms as possible in their paragraphs. Use the following rubric to assess students' work:

- **L1** students should include one or two vocabulary terms and should identify Mesopotamia's early civilizations.
- **L2** students should include additional vocabulary terms and explain why this region was the site of early civilizations.
- **L3** students should also include a detailed description of Mesopotamia.

Chapter ① Assessment and Activities

ASSESSMENT AND ACTIVITIES

GLENCOE TECHNOLOGY

MindJogger Videoquiz

Use the **MindJogger Videoquiz** to review Chapter 1 content.

Available in DVD and VHS

Review Vocabulary

1. Paragraphs will vary but should reflect information in the chapter.

2. scribe

3. true

4. empire

Review Main Ideas

5. They adapted to the environment by making tools and clothes and by using fire.

6. People who lived in the Paleolithic period were hunters and gatherers. Neolithic people were farmers and traders who built communities.

7. in the valleys of the Tigris and Euphrates Rivers

8. Conflicts weakened them and they became vulnerable to attacks by outsiders.

9. its military power and well-organized government

10. mapped the stars, planets, and phases of the moon; created the sundial; used the seven-day week

Critical Thinking

11. Some of the earliest known civilizations arose in Mesopotamia and had a great effect on world history.

Review Vocabulary

1. Write a brief paragraph that describes and compares the following terms.

    historian   archaeologist   artifact

    fossil   anthropologist

Indicate which of the following statements are true. Replace the word in italics to make false statements true.

___ 2. An *artisan* kept records in cuneiform.

___ 3. Assyrian kings divided their empire into political districts called *provinces*.

___ 4. A *civilization* is a group of many different lands under one ruler.

Review Main Ideas

Section 1 • Early Humans

5. How did Paleolithic people adapt to their environment?

6. What were the major differences between people who lived in the Paleolithic period and those who lived in the Neolithic period?

Section 2 • Mesopotamian Civilization

7. Where were the first civilizations in Mesopotamia?

8. How did Sumerian city-states lose power?

Section 3 • The First Empires

9. What helped Assyria build an empire in Mesopotamia?

10. What scientific advancement did the Chaldeans make?

Critical Thinking

11. **Explain** Why do you think Mesopotamia is sometimes called the "cradle of civilization"?

12. **Analyze** Why was the switch from hunting and gathering to farming important enough to be called the farming revolution?

13. **Describe** What rights did women have in the city-states of Sumer?

14. **Predict** How successful do you think the Assyrian army would have been if it had not learned how to strengthen iron?

Review Reading Skill Previewing Get Ready to Read!

Choose the best answer.

15. In this textbook, to make a connection between what you know and what you are about to read, you should look at the ___.

    a. Reading Tip

    b. Reading Focus

    c. main head

    d. subhead

16. What is the purpose of a subhead?

    a. to break down a large topic into smaller topics

    b. to show the main topic covered in a section

    c. to summarize the "big picture"

    d. to help you study for a test

To review this skill, see pages 6–7.

12. Farming allowed early humans to settle into villages, which was a new way of living that led to the rise of civilizations.

13. They could buy and sell property and run businesses.

14. Answers will vary. Students should note that the Assyrians still would have been powerful because of their strategies and ruthlessness.

Reading Skill

15. b

16. a

Geography Skills

17. Africa

18. Australia

Geography Skills

Study the map below and answer the following questions.

17. **Location** On what continent was the earliest fossil evidence of humans found?

18. **Movement** Based on fossil evidence, where did early humans go first, Europe or Australia?

19. **Analyze** Which three continents are not shown on this map? How do you think early humans reached those continents?

NATIONAL GEOGRAPHIC **Spread of Early Humans**

40,000 years ago

25,000 years ago

ASIA

EUROPE

100,000 years ago

AFRICA

150,000–200,000 years ago EQUATOR

50,000 years ago

AUSTRALIA

0   2,000 mi.
0   2,000 km
Mercator projection

N W E S

KEY
Movement of early humans

Read to Write

20. **Persuasive Writing** Suppose you are a merchant in Çatal Hüyük. A new group of people wants to trade with you and the other merchants in the village. You think trading with them is a good idea, but other merchants are not so sure. Write a short speech you could give to convince them.

21. **Using Your** FOLDABLES Use your Chapter 1 foldable to create an illustrated time line. Your time line should extend from the date Jericho was founded to the fall of the Chaldean Empire. Create drawings or photocopy maps, artifacts, or architecture to illustrate your time line. Use your time line as a study tool for the Chapter Test.

Self-Check Quiz To help you prepare for the Chapter Test, visit jat.glencoe.com

Using Technology

22. **Using the Internet** Use the Internet to locate a university archaeology department Web site. Use the information on the site to create a summary that describes current research. Include location of archaeological sites and relevant discoveries.

Linking Past and Present

23. **Analyzing Information** Imagine you are a nomad who travels from place to place to hunt and gather food. What things would you carry with you to help you survive? Make a list of items to share and discuss with your classmates.

Analyze

The following passage is from a poem called "The Mesopotamian View of Death" that was written by an unknown Mesopotamian mother.

Hark the piping!
My heart is piping in the wilderness
  where the young man once went free.
He is a prisoner now in death's kingdom,
  lies bound where once he lived.
The ewe gives up her lamb
  and the nanny-goat her kid.
My heart is piping in the wilderness
  an instrument of grief.

—"The Mesopotamian View of Death,"
Poems of Heaven and Hell from Ancient Mesopotamia, N.K. Sanders, trans.

DBQ **Document-Based Questions**

24. To what does the mother compare death's kingdom?

25. What is the "instrument of grief"?

Have students visit the Web site at jat.glencoe.com to review Chapter 1 and take the **Self-Check Quiz**.

Using Technology

22. Answers should describe current research at archaeological sites.

Linking Past and Present

23. Lists will vary. Students should place only necessities on the list.

Primary Source

24. a prison

25. the mother's heart

Bonus Question

Ask: In your opinion, which civilization discussed in this chapter has had the most impact on civilization today? Why? *(Answers will vary but should be supported by details from the text.)*

---

19. North America, South America, Antarctica; early humans may have traveled from Asia to North America, then down to South America. Students may mention a land bridge connecting Asia and North America, or a boat route. Explorers from different nations sailed to Antarctica many centuries later.

Read to Write

20. Speeches will vary but may include the following advantages: getting rid of extra food and supplies, getting food and supplies you do not already have, and learning advancements from the new group.

21. FOLDABLES Time lines and illustrations should be based on students' foldables.

Chapter 2 Resources

TEACHING TRANSPARENCIES

- Graphic Organizer Transparencies with Teaching Strategy and Student Activity **L2**
- Cause-and-Effect Transparencies with Teaching Strategy and Student Activity **L2**
- Then and Now Transparencies with Teaching Strategy and Student Activity **L2**
- In-text Map Transparency with Teaching Strategy and Student Activity **L1**
- Map Transparencies with Overlay, Teaching Strategy, and Student Activity **L2**

DIFFERENTIATED INSTRUCTION

- Differentiated Instruction Activity 2
- Time Line Activity 2
- Primary Source Reading 2 (with Document-Based Questions)
- Inclusion Strategies for the Middle School Social Studies Classroom
- StudentWorks Plus™ CD-ROM (with Audio Program)

READING SUPPORT

- Take-Home Review Activity 2 **L2**
- World Literature Reading 2 **L2**
- Workbook Activity 2 **L1**
- Reading Strategies for the Social Studies Classroom **L1/ EL**

ASSESSMENT

- Authentic Assessment Activity 2 **L1/ EL**
- Chapter 2 Test Form A **L2**
- Chapter 2 Test Form B **L2**
- ExamView® Pro Testmaker CD-ROM

INTERDISCIPLINARY CONNECTIONS

- Geography and History Activity 2 **L2**
- People to Meet Activity 2 **L2**
- Economics Activity 2 **L2**
- Citizenship and Service Learning Activity 2 **L2**

SPANISH RESOURCES

- Spanish Reading Essentials and Study Guide
- Spanish Guided Reading Activities
- Spanish Quizzes, Tests, and Authentic Assessment (with Rubrics)
- Spanish Take-Home Review Activities

MULTIMEDIA

- ExamView® Pro Testmaker CD-ROM
- Glencoe Skillbuilder Interactive Workbook CD-ROM, Level 1
- Interactive Tutor Self-Assessment CD-ROM
- MindJogger Videoquiz
- Presentation Plus! CD-ROM
- StudentWorks Plus™ CD-ROM (with Audio Program)
- TeacherWorks CD-ROM
- Vocabulary PuzzleMaker CD-ROM
- *World History: Journey Across Time* Video Program
- World History Primary Source Document Library CD-ROM

STANDARDIZED ASSESSMENT SKILLS

- Standardized Test Skills Practice Workbook Activity 2 **L2**
- Critical Thinking Skills Activity 2 **L2**

Teaching strategies have been coded with suggested ability levels. However, most are suitable for all levels.

L1 BASIC activities for all students
L2 AVERAGE activities for average to above-average students
L3 CHALLENGING activities for above-average students
EL ENGLISH LANGUAGE activities

Chapter 2 Resources

⌛ TIME MANAGEMENT

Chapter Introduction	Section 1	Section 2	Section 3	Section 4	Chapter Wrap-Up
1 Day	2 Days	1 Day	2 Days	1 Day	1 Day

Block Scheduling Activities that are suited to use within the block scheduling framework are identified by: 📦

`0:00` **OUT OF TIME?** Assign the Chapter 2 *Reading Essentials and Study Guide.* * 📂

SECTION RESOURCES

DAILY OBJECTIVES	REPRODUCIBLE RESOURCES	MULTIMEDIA RESOURCES
Section 1 **The Nile Valley** 1. Egyptian civilization arose in the fertile Nile River valley, where natural barriers discouraged invasion. 2. Around 3100 B.C., Lower and Upper Egypt united into one kingdom organized into social classes.	📂 Reproducible Lesson Plan 2–1 📂 Vocabulary Activity 2–1 📂 Guided Reading Activity 2–1* 📂 Section Quiz 2–1* 📂 Reading Essentials and Study Guide 2–1*	🖐 Daily Focus Skills Transparency 2–1 💿 Interactive Tutor Self-Assessment CD-ROM 💿 ExamView® Pro Testmaker CD-ROM 💿 Presentation Plus! CD-ROM
Section 2 **Egypt's Old Kingdom** 1. All-powerful pharaohs ruled the Old Kingdom. 2. Egyptians believed in many gods and goddesses and built pyramids for their pharaohs.	📂 Reproducible Lesson Plan 2–2 📂 Vocabulary Activity 2–2 📂 Guided Reading Activity 2–2* 📂 Section Quiz 2–2* 📂 Reading Essentials and Study Guide 2–2*	🖐 Daily Focus Skills Transparency 2–2 💿 Interactive Tutor Self-Assessment CD-ROM 💿 ExamView® Pro Testmaker CD-ROM 💿 Presentation Plus! CD-ROM
Section 3 **The Egyptian Empire** 1. Egypt enjoyed a golden age of culture and peace during the Middle Kingdom. 2. In the New Kingdom, Egypt reached its height of power, with pharaohs building a huge empire and great monuments.	📂 Reproducible Lesson Plan 2–3 📂 Vocabulary Activity 2–3 📂 Guided Reading Activity 2–3* 📂 Section Quiz 2–3* 📂 Reading Essentials and Study Guide 2–3*	🖐 Daily Focus Skills Transparency 2–3 💿 Interactive Tutor Self-Assessment CD-ROM 💿 ExamView® Pro Testmaker CD-ROM 💿 Presentation Plus! CD-ROM 💿 Glencoe BookLink CD-ROM
Section 4 **The Civilization of Kush** 1. The Nubians settled to the south of Egypt and built a civilization based on farming and trade. 2. Kush emerged as a leading power after it learned iron-making skills.	📂 Reproducible Lesson Plan 2–4 📂 Vocabulary Activity 2–4 📂 Guided Reading Activity 2–4* 📂 Section Quiz 2–4* 📂 Reading Essentials and Study Guide 2–4*	🖐 Daily Focus Skills Transparency 2–4 💿 Interactive Tutor Self-Assessment CD-ROM 💿 ExamView® Pro Testmaker CD-ROM 💿 Presentation Plus! CD-ROM 💿 Vocabulary PuzzleMaker CD-ROM

*Also available in Spanish

Use our Web site for additional resources. All essential content is covered in the Student Edition.

You and your students can visit jat.glencoe.com, the Web site companion to *World History: Journey Across Time.* This innovative integration of electronic and print media offers your students a wealth of opportunities. The student text directs students to the Web site for the following options:

- Chapter Overviews
- Self-Check Quizzes
- Study Central™
- Student Web Activities
- Multi-Language Glossaries

Answers to the student Web activities are provided for you in the **Web Activity Lesson Plans.** Additional Web resources and ePuzzles and games are also available.

The following videotape programs are available from Glencoe as supplements to Chapter 2:

Mummies and the Wonders of Ancient Egypt (4-video set)
(ISBN 1-56501-773-0)

Secret Life of King Ramses II
(ISBN 0-7670-0111-7)

Tomb of the Gods: The Great Pyramid
(ISBN 0-7670-0081-1)

To order, call Glencoe at 1-800-334-7344. To find classroom resources to accompany many of these videos, check the following home pages:

A&E Television: www.aande.com
The History Channel: www.historychannel.com

MEETING SPECIAL NEEDS

In addition to the Differentiated Instruction strategies, the following resources are suitable for students with special needs:

- *ExamView® Pro Testmaker CD-ROM* allows teachers to tailor tests by reducing answer choices.
- *StudentWorks Plus™ CD-ROM (with Audio Program)* includes the entire narrative of the student edition so that less-proficient readers can listen to the words as they read them.
- The *Reading Essentials and Study Guide* provides the same content as the student edition but is written two grade levels below the textbook.

Index to National Geographic Magazine:
The following articles relate to this chapter:

- "Egypt's Forgotten Treasures," by Zahi Hawass, January 2003.
- "Mystery of the Sun God's Servant," by Alain Zivie, November 2003.
- "Death on the Nile," by A.R. Williams, October 2002.

National Geographic Society Products:
To order the following, call National Geographic at 1–800–368–2728

- *National Geographic Desk Reference* (Book)
- *National Geographic Atlas of the World* (Book)

NGS ONLINE

Access National Geographic's new dynamic MapMachine Web site and other geography resources at:

www.nationalgeographic.com
www.nationalgeographic.com/maps

 ## Meeting NCSS Standards

World History: Journey Across Time
The following standards are highlighted in Chapter 2:

Section 1 **III** **People, Places, and Environments: B, D, E, H, I, J**

VI **Power, Authority, and Governance: B, D, E**

Section 2 **I** **Culture: A, G**

VIII **Science, Technology, and Society: A, B, E**

X **Civic Ideals and Practices: E**

Section 3 **V** **Individuals, Groups, and Institutions: B, F**

VII **Production, Distribution, and Consumption: C**

Section 4 **II** **Time, Continuity, and Change: C, E**

IV **Individual Development and Identity: A**

State and Local Objectives

_____

_____

_____

Timesaving Tools

TeacherWorks
All-In-One Planner and Resource Center

● **Interactive Teacher Edition** Access your Teacher Wraparound Edition and your classroom resources with a few easy clicks.

● **Interactive Lesson Planner** Organize your week, month, semester, or year with all the lesson helps you need to make teaching creative and relevant.

Use Glencoe's **Presentation Plus!** multimedia teacher tool to easily present dynamic lessons that visually excite your students. Using Microsoft PowerPoint® you can customize the presentations to create your own personalized lessons.

FOLDABLES™
Study Organizer
Dinah Zike's Foldables

Foldables are three-dimensional, interactive graphic organizers that help students practice basic writing skills, review key vocabulary terms, and identify main ideas. Every chapter contains a foldable activity, with additional chapter activities found in the *Reading and Study Skills Foldables* booklet. You can use the foldables as they are presented, or modify them to suit the needs of your individual class.

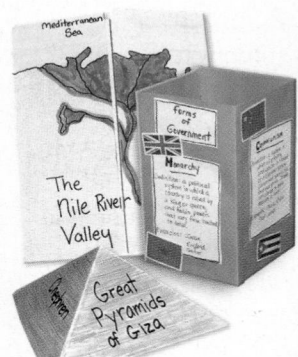

Planning Ahead

CHAPTER CULMINATING ACTIVITY

The Chapter Culminating Activity will help students organize and learn the important information from the chapter. Begin the chapter with this activity, and have students complete it as a culminating activity.

BUILDING STORY PYRAMIDS

Purpose A story pyramid helps students think visually about a topic, much like a scriptwriter does. It leads them to take a creative and selective look at the sequence of events as they read through a chapter.

Introduction to Modeling

1. Begin by determining students' prior knowledge of pyramids—their shape, what they are made of, where they are found, and so on. Then introduce students to one of the pyramids in this chapter by referring them to photos in the chapter.

2. Tell students they are going to get a chance to build some pyramids too. But they will build their pyramids with words instead of stone. Draw a copy of the following pyramid on the board, and have students copy it onto poster-sized paper.

Story Pyramid

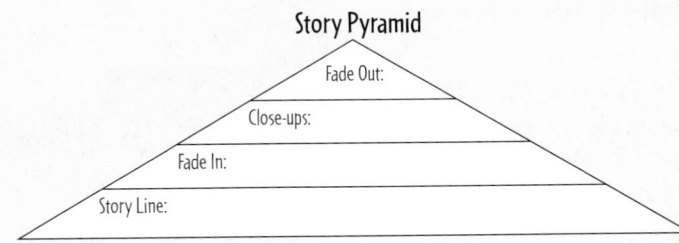

3. Explain to students that they will be creating a story pyramid about ancient Egypt. Advise students that they will need to think visually because this plan could be used to script a movie.

4. Have students begin building the pyramid's base by deciding the theme that will hold the script together.

5. Have students decide where they want the story to begin. As students work their way through the chapter, they should think of the key events they want to highlight. These will vary but should be based on main ideas.

6. Ask students to consider how they want the story to end. If this were a movie, what closing scene would they choose as the movie ends?

7. When completed, the story pyramid can be turned into storyboards or an actual movie script.

Authentic Assessment

Refer to Activity 2 in the Authentic Assessment section of the *Quizzes, Tests, and Authentic Assessment (with Rubrics)* booklet.

When & Where?

Refer students to the time line. Tell them that the story of Egypt is very old and very long. Ask students how the time line proves this. *(Narmer united Egypt more than 5,000 years ago. Events show Egyptian power extending from 3100 B.C. to 728 B.C., a period of more than 2,370 years.)* **L1**

GLENCOE TECHNOLOGY

World History: Journey Across Time Video Program

To learn more about ancient Egypt, students can view the Chapter 2 video in the *World History: Journey Across Time* Video Program.

MindJogger Videoquiz

Use the **MindJogger Videoquiz** to preview Chapter 2 content.

Available in DVD and VHS

Chapter 2
Ancient Egypt

▼ Sphinx and pyramid in Giza, Egypt

NATIONAL GEOGRAPHIC **When & Where?**

3500 B.C.	2500 B.C.	1500 B.C.	500 B.C.
c. 3100 B.C. Narmer unites Egypt	c. 2540 B.C. Great Pyramid at Giza built	c. 1500 B.C. Queen Hatshepsut reigns	728 B.C. Piye of Kush defeats Egyptians

Reading Strategy   PURPOSE FOR READING

Prereading Organizer This activity gets students to consider what they know about the subject of this chapter. Draw a two-column chart on the board and label it "Ancient Egypt." Label the left column "What I Already Know" and the right column "How I Know This." Tell students to copy the chart in their notebooks and fill it out. Then have them read the **Chapter Preview** on page 35. **Ask:** What questions does this information raise? *(Answers will vary, such as "What was the Middle Kingdom?")* Have students save these questions and look for the answers as they read the chapter. **L1**

Chapter Preview

While the people of Mesopotamia fought wars, people along Africa's Nile River formed rich and powerful civilizations. Read this chapter to learn how the people of Egypt and Kush built large monuments that still stand today.

 View the Chapter 2 video in the *World History: Journey Across Time* Video Program.

 Chapter Overview Visit jat.glencoe.com for a preview of Chapter 2.

 Section 1 ## The Nile Valley

The fertile land along the great Nile River supported the Egyptian civilization.

 Section 2 ## Egypt's Old Kingdom

During the Old Kingdom period, Egyptians built cities, great pyramids, and a strong kingdom.

 Section 3 ## The Egyptian Empire

Many changes occurred during Egypt's Middle and New Kingdoms. It expanded into a great empire as art, literature, and architecture blossomed.

 Section 4 ## The Civilization of Kush

South of Egypt a new civilization arose called Kush. Kushites adopted Egyptian ways and eventually conquered Egypt itself.

Organizing Information *Make this foldable to help you organize the key events and ideas from ancient Egypt and Kush.*

Step 1 *Stack two sheets of paper so that the front sheet is one inch higher than the back sheet.*

Step 2 *Fold down the top edges of the paper to form four tabs. Align the edges so that all of the layers or tabs are the same distance apart.*

This makes all the tabs the same size.

Step 3 *Crease the paper to hold the tabs in place, then staple them together. Cut the top three thicknesses to create a layered book.*

Staple together along the fold.

Step 4 *Label the booklet as shown and take notes on the inside.*

Reading and Writing *As you read the chapter, take notes under the appropriate tabs. Write main ideas and key terms under the "what" tab.*

INTRODUCING CHAPTER 2

Introduce students to chapter content and key terms by having them access **Chapter Overview 2** at jat.glencoe.com

CHAPTER PREVIEW

After reading Chapter 2, students will be able to

1. describe how the Nile River influenced Egyptian civilization and the reasons a united government arose along its banks;

2. discuss government and religion during the Old Kingdom;

3. analyze the accomplishments of the Middle and New Kingdoms;

4. describe the Nubian kingdom south of Egypt.

 Dinah Zike's Foldables

Purpose This foldable helps students create a booklet detailing the main ideas and key terms from each section. As students read the chapter, they should list information under the appropriate tabs.

☞ Have students complete *Reading and Study Skills Foldables* Activity 2.

MORE ABOUT THE PHOTO

The Pyramids of Egypt The sphinx and the pyramids of Egypt are some of the most magnificent structures of the ancient world. The Great Pyramid at Giza was designated one of the Seven Wonders of the World. Both symbolize the magnificence of ancient Egypt. There are actually three large pyramids behind the sphinx. Pictured here is the pyramid of King Khafre. Although smaller than the Great Pyramid of his father, Khufu (also known as Cheops), it was set on higher ground so as to appear taller. The pyramids were originally encased with stone, giving them a smooth outer shell. The third pyramid was built by Menkaure, thought to be the grandson of Khafre, and is significantly smaller than the other two.

1 Learn It!

Making predictions about what will come in the text sets a purpose for reading and allows students to become actively engaged in the reading.

Students can make predictions based on section headings, subheadings, or illustrations. Show students how to make predictions by modeling this strategy:

For example, in Section 3, under the subheading "Expanding the Empire" a student could make the prediction that the term *expanding* suggests that under the New Kingdom, Egypt became more powerful. A student could also predict that Egypt attacked and conquered neighboring regions and brought them under Egyptian control. **Ask: What else could the word** *expanding* **mean?**

Have students develop an understanding of this concept by reading the **Get Ready to Read!** feature for Section 2. Have them make a list of predictions they think will be answered in the text. **L1**

Chapter 2 Reading Social Studies

Reading Skill
Predicting

1 Learn It!
What Do You Predict?

A *prediction* is a guess based on what you already know. Making predictions before you read can help you understand and remember what you read.

How do you make predictions? Read the Main Ideas below. They were taken from the opening page of Section 2 on page 47. Use these main ideas to make predictions about what you will read in this chapter.

> Predict what the term "all-powerful" means.

> What does "life after death" mean?

> Can you predict what tools the Egyptians used to build the pyramids?

Main Ideas
- Egypt was ruled by **all-powerful** pharaohs.
- The Egyptians believed in many gods and goddesses and in **life after death** for the pharaohs.
- The Egyptians of the Old Kingdom built huge stone pyramids as tombs for their pharaohs.

—*from page 47*

Reading Tip

As you read, check your predictions to see if they were correct.

36

Reading Strategy — **PREDICTING AND CONFIRMING**

Predicting Pose a general question to the students based on the text, such as "What was life like in Egypt?" Allow students to brainstorm and record their answers on the board. Then provide students with words or concepts from the text that will help them guess what life was like. Revise the statements based on these concepts. Students should check the accuracy of their predictions as they read. When students discover discrepancies, they should come to the board and update the statements.

2 Practice It!

Making Predictions

Read the Main Ideas below from Section 1 of this chapter.

Read to Write
Select one blue sub-head in this chapter. Without reading the text under that subhead, write a paragraph that you think might appear there. Check the facts in your paragraph to see if they are correct.

2 Practice It!

Confirming Encourage the writing of creative or nonsensical predictions to keep interest high. After students make their predictions, have them read carefully to confirm or correct their predictions.

Practicing Predicting Assign the sections of the chapter to different groups of students. Have each group create a prediction guide for its assigned section. Use the statements created in **Practice It!** as a guide. Pass out the prediction guides to students as an aid for the sections they have not read.

Main Ideas
- The Egyptian civilization began in the fertile Nile River valley, where natural barriers discouraged invasions.
- The Egyptians depended on the Nile's floods to grow their crops.
- Around 3100 B.C., Egypt's two major kingdoms, Upper Egypt and Lower Egypt, were combined into one.
- Egyptian society was divided into social groups based on wealth and power.

—*from page 38*

Make at least one prediction about each of the main ideas. Write down each prediction. Then, as you read this section, decide if your predictions were correct.

3 Apply It!

As students read, have them take notes on information related to their predictions. When they have finished a section, have them use their predictions and notes to write summaries of what they have read. **L2**

3 Apply It!

Before you read the chapter, skim the questions on pages 74–75 in the Chapter Assessment and Activities. Choose three questions and predict what the answers will be.

37

Reading Strategy READ TO WRITE

Using Predictions to Interpret After students have made their predictions for a particular subhead, have them write specific details about life in Egypt that they can use in creating a mock journal entry. They should try to understand what it would have been like for a young man or woman to live during that time. To aid their work, students should give themselves a name, a family, and an occupation. Have them make predictions based on the **Get Ready to Read!** portion of each section and update their work as they go. Once students have finished the chapter, they should be able to use their corrected predictions to write their journal entries.

More About the Photo

The Nile River delta silt varies in depth from 50 to 75 feet and comprises the richest soil in Africa. Population density on the floodplain south of the delta stands at more than 3,000 people per square mile.

Caption Answer: They kept invaders away from Egypt's territory.

CURRICULUM CONNECTION

Geography
The Nile is the world's longest river. Assign students to research and prepare a chart of the world's 10 longest rivers. Column heads should include: River Name, Location, Length (in miles and kilometers), Countries Crossed.

✓ Reading Check

Answer: Egypt lay in the fertile Nile River valley surrounded by deserts and the Mediterranean and Red Seas.

▲ Today, the Nile River valley makes up only about 3 percent of Egypt's land, yet most Egyptians live and work in the area. *How did the deserts surrounding the Nile Valley help protect Egypt?*

On both sides of the Nile Valley and its delta, deserts unfold as far as the eye can see. To the west is a vast desert that forms part of the **Sahara** (suh•HAR•uh), the largest desert in the world. To the east, stretching to the Red Sea, is the Eastern Desert. In some places, the change from green land to barren sand is so abrupt that a person can stand with one foot in each.

The ancient Egyptians called the deserts "the Red Land" because of their burning heat. Although these vast expanses could not support farming or human life, they did serve a useful purpose: they kept outside armies away from Egypt's territory.

Other geographic features also protected the Egyptians. To the far south, the Nile's dangerous cataracts blocked enemy boats from reaching Egypt. In the north, the delta marshes offered no harbors for invaders approaching from the sea. In this regard, the Egyptians were luckier than the

people of Mesopotamia. In that region, few natural barriers protected the cities. The Mesopotamians constantly had to fight off attackers, but Egypt rarely faced threats. As a result, Egyptian civilization was able to grow and prosper.

Despite their isolation, the Egyptians were not completely closed to the outside world. The Mediterranean Sea bordered Egypt to the north, and the Red Sea lay beyond the desert to the east. These bodies of water gave the Egyptians a way to trade with people outside Egypt.

Within Egypt, people used the Nile for trade and transportation. Winds from the north pushed sailboats south. The flow of the Nile carried them north. Egyptian villages thus had frequent, friendly contact with one another, unlike the hostile relations between the Mesopotamian city-states.

✓ **Reading Check** **Summarize** What was Egypt's physical setting like?

DIFFERENTIATED INSTRUCTION

Verbal/Linguistic: Assign students to create acrostic poems about the Nile. Tell them to write the letters N-I-L-E R-I-V-E-R in a vertical line on a sheet of paper and to compose a line of verse starting with each letter. *(Sample: **N**o river is longer than the Nile.)*

English Learners: Ask several students to write adjectives describing the Nile. They might give these words to the verbal/linguistic learners to use in their poems.

Auditory/Musical: Call on several students to research songs about the Nile. Have them review these songs for the class, and read the lyrics aloud or play one on a stereo.

◱ Refer to ***Inclusion Strategies for the Middle School Social Studies Classroom*** in the TCR.

The River People

Main Idea The Egyptians depended on the Nile's floods to grow their crops.

Reading Focus When you hear about floods, do you picture terrible damage and loss of life? Read on to learn why the Egyptians welcomed, rather than feared, the flooding of the Nile.

In Chapter 1, you learned that the people of Mesopotamia had to tame the floods of the Tigris and Euphrates Rivers in order to farm. They learned to do so, but the unpredictable rivers loomed as a constant threat.

Regular Flooding Like the Mesopotamians, the Egyptians also had to cope with river floods. However, the Nile floods were much more dependable and gentle than those of the Tigris and the Euphrates. As a result, the Egyptians were able to farm and live securely. They did not worry that sudden, heavy overflows would destroy their homes and crops, or that too little flooding would leave their fields parched.

Every spring, heavy rains from central Africa and melting snows from the highlands of east Africa added to the waters of the Nile as it flowed north. From July to October, the Nile spilled over its banks. When the waters went down, they left behind a layer of dark, fertile mud. Because of these deposits, the Egyptians called their land *Kemet* (KEH•meht), "the Black Land."

How Did the Egyptians Use the Nile? The Egyptians took advantage of the Nile's floods to become successful farmers. They planted wheat, barley, and flax seeds in the wet, rich soil. Over time, they grew more than enough food to feed themselves and the animals they raised.

One reason for their success was the wise use of irrigation. Egyptian farmers first dug basins, or bowl-shaped holes, in the earth to trap the floodwaters. The farmers then dug canals to carry water from the basins to fields beyond the river's reach. The Egyptians also built dikes, or earthen banks, to strengthen the basin walls.

In time, Egyptian farmers developed other technology to help them in their work. For example, they used a shadoof (shuh•DOOF), a bucket attached to a long pole, to lift water from the Nile to the basins. Many Egyptian farmers still use this device today.

Primary Source — Hymn to the Nile

This passage is part of a hymn written around 2100 B.C. It shows how important the Nile River was to the people of ancient Egypt.

"You create the grain, you bring forth the barley, assuring perpetuity [survival] to the temples. If you cease your toil and your work, then all that exists is in anguish."

—author unknown, "Hymn to the Nile"

▲ A shadoof

DBQ Document-Based Question

How does this hymn show that the ancient Egyptians thought of the Nile as a god?

CHAPTER 2   Ancient Egypt   41

CONNECTING ACROSS TIME

In 1929 ten African nations signed the River Nile Treaty to share water rights. Under the treaty, Egypt received the major share of water rights. In recent times, East African nations have demanded greater rights at the Nile's source and have threatened to pull out of the treaty. Call on students to research this topic and prepare a round table discussion with at least one person speaking for each of the 10 nations. **L3**

Primary Source

The earliest Egyptians did not know how or why the Nile flooded each year. They attributed it to a god named Hapi, a well-fed man who dressed like a farmer. They probably called the river Hapi at first, but later settled simply on *iterw,* or "the river." The name *Nile* comes from the Greeks. During the annual floods, Egyptians threw offerings into the rising waters and sang hymns such as this one.

Answer:
It credits the river with causing everything to exist and prosper.

CRITICAL THINKING ACTIVITY

Evaluating Extend the **Primary Source** by reading these lines: "Men offer you the first-fruits of corn; all the gods adore you! . . . It is believed that with your hand of gold you make bricks of silver! But we are not nourished by lapis-lazuli [a precious blue stone]; wheat alone gives vigor." **Ask:** How does the Nile god rank among other gods? *(They adore him.)* Why is this god so powerful? *(provides wheat for life/strength)* Have students research other Egyptian writings about their gods to compare to this view of the Nile. **L3**

HISTORY Mystery

How Did We Decipher the Egyptian Alphabet?
In 1799 soldiers in Napoleon's army found the Rosetta Stone, a large tablet that recorded the coronation of Ptolemy V, king of Egypt, in 196 B.C. Interestingly, *what* was written on the stone was not nearly as significant as *how* it was written. The same passage was repeated in three different scripts: two in Egyptian scripts (hieroglyphic and demotic) and one in Greek. Scholars who knew Greek were able to use this stone to finally decipher the Egyptian alphabet, something that had baffled people for centuries.

✓ Reading Check

Answer: wheat, barley, and flax

Early Egyptians also developed geometry to survey, or measure, land. When floods washed away boundary markers dividing one field from the next, the Egyptians surveyed the fields again to see where one began and the other ended.

Papyrus (puh•PY•ruhs), a reed plant that grew along the shores of the Nile, became a useful resource. At first the Egyptians harvested papyrus to make baskets, sandals, and river rafts. Later, they used papyrus for papermaking. The first step was to cut the stalks of the plant into narrow strips. Then the Egyptians soaked the strips and pounded them flat. Left in the air to dry, the strips became stiff. They could then be joined to form a roll of paper.

What Were Hieroglyphics?

The Egyptians used their papyrus rolls as writing paper. Like the people of Mesopotamia, the Egyptians developed their own system of writing. Called **hieroglyphics** (HY•ruh•GLIH•fihks), it was made up of hundreds of picture symbols. Some symbols stood for objects and ideas. To communicate the idea of a boat, for example, a scribe would draw a boat. Other symbols stood for sounds, just as the letters of our alphabet do.

Scribes painstakingly carved hieroglyphics onto stone walls and monuments. For everyday purposes, scribes invented a simpler script and wrote on papyrus.

In ancient Egypt, few people could read and write. Some Egyptian men, however, went to special schools located at Egyptian temples to study reading and writing and learn to become scribes. Scribes kept records and worked for the rulers, priests, and traders.

✓ **Reading Check** **Identify** What crops did the ancient Egyptians grow?

NATIONAL GEOGRAPHIC The Way It Was

Focus on Everyday Life

From Farming to Food Harvesting wheat and turning it into bread was vital to the ancient Egyptians. Some people were full-time farmers, but many others were drafted by the government to help during busy seasons.

The process began as men cut the wheat with wooden sickles and women gathered it into bundles. Animals trampled the wheat to separate the kernels from the husks. The grain was then thrown into the air so the wind would carry away the lightweight seed coverings. Finally, the grain was stored in silos for later use.

▲ Tomb painting showing wheat being harvested

▲ Tomb painting showing Egyptian man and woman plowing and planting

42

INTERDISCIPLINARY CONNECTIONS ACTIVITY

Economics Have students draw bar graphs showing estimates for the percentage of workers in three labor categories in present-day Egypt: agriculture 29%, industry 22%, and services 49%. Define *services* as "useful labor that does not produce goods." Use lawn mowing as an example. Percentages should be plotted on the vertical axis and categories (bars) on the horizontal axis. Supply graph paper, if necessary. **Ask:** How did most ancient Egyptians earn a living? *(by farming)* How many farm today? *(29%)* What do you think is the biggest change that has taken place? *(probably the rise of service jobs)* Assign groups to research and report on Egypt's most important agricultural products today. **L2**

A United Egypt

Main Idea Around 3100 B.C., Egypt's two major kingdoms, Upper Egypt and Lower Egypt, were combined into one.

Reading Focus What types of services does your local government provide? Read on to find out about the government in ancient Egypt.

In Egypt, as in Mesopotamia, skillful farming led to surpluses—extra amounts—of food. This freed some people to work as artisans instead of farmers. They wove cloth, made pottery, carved statues, or shaped copper into weapons and tools.

As more goods became available, Egyptians traded with each other. Before long, Egyptian traders were carrying goods beyond Egypt's borders to Mesopotamia. There they may have picked up ideas about writing and government.

The Rise of Government The advances in farming, crafts, and trade created a need for government in Egypt. Irrigation systems had to be built and maintained, and surplus grain had to be stored and passed out in times of need. In addition, disputes over land ownership had to be settled. Gradually, government emerged to plan and to direct such activities.

The earliest rulers were village chiefs. Over time, a few strong chiefs united groups of villages into small kingdoms. The strongest of these kingdoms eventually overpowered the weaker ones. By 4000 B.C., Egypt was made up of two large kingdoms. In the Nile delta was Lower Egypt. To the south, upriver, lay Upper Egypt.

Egypt's Ruling Families About 3100 B.C., the two kingdoms became one. Credit for this goes to **Narmer** (NAR•muhr), also known

◀ Wheat being harvested today

Baking bread in pots ▶

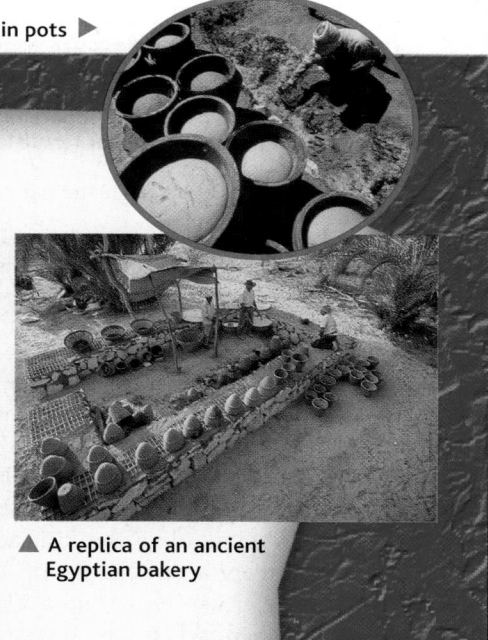

▲ A replica of an ancient Egyptian bakery

Turning grain into bread was a long process. Women ground the grain into flour, then men pounded it until it became very fine. For the wealthy, seeds, honey, fruit, nuts, and herbs were added to the dough for flavor. Unfortunately, it was almost impossible to keep small stones and sand out of the flour. As a result, many Egyptians developed tooth decay as these particles wore down their tooth enamel.

Connecting to the Past

1. How did the government ensure that enough people were available to harvest the wheat?
2. Why do you think seeds, fruit, and other additives were reserved for the wealthy?

TIME TRAVELER

Amulets, or sacred charms, held special power for Egyptians. They believed, for example, that the scarab beetle carried the sun to heaven. Some people wore a kind of amulet designed to look like this beetle. The ankh, a cross with a loop at the top, stood for the breath of life. Many Egyptians—from ordinary people to pharaohs—wore them. Priests tucked them into tombs and mummies.

NATIONAL GEOGRAPHIC The Way It Was

43

EXTENDING THE CONTENT

What Was It Like to Be an Egyptian Farmer? Farmers paid a high price for the security of a strong government. Life was hard, even with a stable ruler in power. As one scribe wrote: "[R]emember the condition of the farmer who is faced with paying his harvest-tax when the snake has carried off half the corn and the hippopotamus has eaten the rest. . . . Then the mice abound, the locusts come, the cattle devour, the sparrows bring disaster, and what remains . . . is taken by thieves. And now the clerk lands on the river bank to collect the tax."

The Importance of Agriculture The agricultural revolution occurred at different times and in different places around the world. In most regions it happened in river valleys, as it did in the Near East. Focus students' attention on this similarity in the locations of Mesopotamia and Egypt. **Ask:** Why did farming peoples, rather than hunters, start the world's earliest civilizations? *(Farmers were able to accumulate surpluses to support large, permanent settlements and people who worked at nonfarming trades.)* **L2**

Understanding Charts

Answers:

1. Egypt: Nile delta, Sahara, Eastern Desert, and cataracts isolated the area.

2. Mesopotamia: city-state led by kings and priests, empires eventually formed; Egypt: villages led by chiefs were united into kingdoms, which were eventually united by pharaohs.

Reading Check

Answer: a line of rulers from one family

Comparing Mesopotamia to Egypt

	Mesopotamia	Egypt
Natural Defenses	Flat mud plains; few natural defenses	Many defenses: Nile delta, Sahara, Eastern Desert, and cataracts
Rivers	Tigris and Euphrates Rivers	Nile River
Floods	Unpredictable, and a constant threat to the people	Dependable and regular; not feared
Economy	Farming and trade	Farming and trade
Government	City-state led by kings and priests; eventually empires formed	Villages led by chiefs, then united into kingdoms; kingdoms later united and ruled by pharaohs
Work of Artisans	Metal products, pottery, cloth	Metal products, pottery, cloth
Advances	• Cuneiform writing • Number system based on 60 • 12-month calendar • Wagon wheel, plow, sailboat	• Hieroglyphic writing • 365-day calendar • Number system based on 10, and fractions • Medicine and first medical books

Understanding Charts

The civilizations of both Mesopotamia and Egypt depended on rivers for fertile lands and irrigation.

1. Which civilization had greater natural defenses? Explain.
2. **Compare** Use the chart to compare the governments of the two civilizations.

as Menes (MEE•neez). As king of Upper Egypt, he led his armies north and took control of Lower Egypt.

Narmer ruled from Memphis, a city he built on the border between the two kingdoms. To symbolize the kingdom's unity, Narmer wore a double crown: the helmet-like white crown represented Upper Egypt, and the open red crown represented Lower Egypt.

Narmer's united kingdom held together long after his death. Members of his family passed the ruling power from father to son to grandson. Such a line of rulers from one family is called a **dynasty** (DY•nuh•stee). When one dynasty died out, another took its place.

Over time, ancient Egypt would be ruled by 31 dynasties, which together lasted about 2,800 years. Historians group Egypt's dynasties into three main time periods called kingdoms. The earliest period, the Old Kingdom, was followed by the Middle Kingdom and then the New Kingdom. Each marked a long period of strong leadership and stability.

Reading Check **Define** What is a dynasty?

CITIZENSHIP AND YOU

Voting for President See if any of your students can name the presidents of the United States who were related. Relationships include father/son, grandfather/grandson, and cousins. *(Father/Son: John Adams, John Quincy Adams; George H.W. Bush, George W. Bush; Grandfather/Grandson: William Henry Harrison, Benjamin Harrison; Cousins: Theodore Roosevelt, Franklin Roosevelt)* Recall the definition of *dynasty*. **Ask:** Would a candidate's family relationship to a past president affect your vote? Why or why not? *(Possible answers: Yes; that relationship might help that person be a better president. No; the best candidate should be chosen regardless of family connections.)* **L2**

Early Egyptian Life

Main Idea Egyptian society was divided into social groups based on wealth and power.

Reading Focus Did you play with dolls or balls when you were young? Egyptian children did too. Keep reading for more details about the Egyptians' daily life.

If you made a diagram of the different social groups in ancient Egypt, you would find that they make a pyramid shape. At the top was the king and his family. Beneath that level was a small upper class of priests, army commanders, and nobles. Next came a larger base of skilled middle-class people, such as traders, artisans, and shopkeepers. At the bottom was the largest group—unskilled workers and farmers.

Egypt's Social Classes Egypt's upper class was made up of nobles, priests, and other wealthy Egyptians who worked as the government officials. They lived in cities and on large estates along the Nile River. They had elegant homes made of wood and mud bricks, with beautiful gardens and pools filled with fish and water lilies. Wealthy families had servants to wait on them and to perform household tasks. The men and women dressed in white linen clothes and wore heavy eye makeup and jewelry.

Egypt's middle class included people who ran businesses or produced goods. They lived in much smaller homes and dressed more simply. Artisans formed an important group within the middle class. They produced linen cloth, jewelry, pottery, and metal goods.

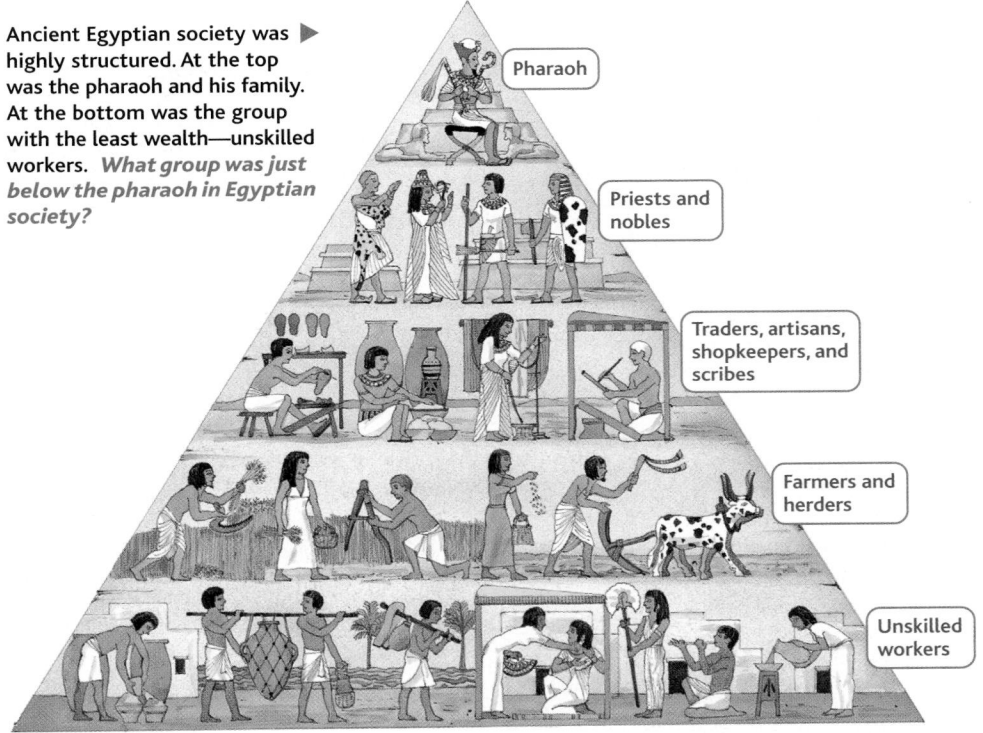

Ancient Egyptian society was ▶ highly structured. At the top was the pharaoh and his family. At the bottom was the group with the least wealth—unskilled workers. *What group was just below the pharaoh in Egyptian society?*

Pharaoh

Priests and nobles

Traders, artisans, shopkeepers, and scribes

Farmers and herders

Unskilled workers

CHAPTER 2   Ancient Egypt   **45**

Reading Support L1/ EL

Assign **Guided Reading Activity 2–1** to help students organize the information in the section.

3 ASSESS

Assign Section 1 Review as homework or as an in-class activity.

Have students use the **Interactive Tutor Self-Assessment CD-ROM** to review the section.

Assessment L2

Assign **Section 1 Quiz** to assess mastery of the material found in the section.

Caption Answer: priests and nobles

Reading Support L1/ EL

Assign **Reading Essentials and Study Guide 2–1** to help students review section material.

COOPERATIVE LEARNING ACTIVITY

Interpreting Proverbs Tell students that proverbs, or wise sayings, formed an important part of ancient Egyptian life. Adults often used them to teach children. Organize the class into small groups and assign each group one of these proverbs to interpret. Have students share their proverbs and interpretations with the class.

(1) Put by for a rainy day. (2) For every joy there is a price to be paid. (3) There grows no wheat where there is no grain. (4) You do all good and destroy all evil. (5) Learn politeness from the impolite. **L1/ EL**

ENRICH

Tell students that scribes worked as record keepers for officials, nobles, and priests. **Ask: Where did scribes fit into the social pyramid?** *(in the third tier, with traders, artisans, and shopkeepers)* **L1**

 Reading Check

Answer: farmers

To help students understand section material, have them visit **Study Central™** at jat.glencoe.com

RETEACH

Organize a round-circle brainstorming session in which each student calls out an important fact learned in the section. Allow for a second round, third round, and so on as necessary. **L1**

 CLOSE

Ask students to explain what the "gift of the Nile" means. **L2**

Farmers made up the largest group of early Egyptians. Some rented their land from their ruler, paying him with a hefty portion of their crops. Most, however, worked the land of wealthy nobles. They lived in villages along the Nile, in one-room huts with roofs made of palm leaves. They had a simple diet of bread, beer, vegetables, and fruit.

Many of Egypt's city dwellers were unskilled workers who did physical labor. Some unloaded cargo from boats and carried it to markets. Others made and stacked mud bricks for buildings. Workers lived in crowded city neighborhoods. They had small mud-brick homes with hard-packed dirt floors and a courtyard for the family's animals. On the flat rooftops, families talked, played games, and slept. Women worked on the rooftops, drying fruit, making bread, and weaving cloth.

Family Life In ancient Egypt, the father headed the family. However, Egyptian women had more rights than females in most other early civilizations. In Egypt, women could own and pass on property. They could buy and sell goods, make wills, and obtain divorces. Upper-class women were in charge of temples and could perform religious ceremonies.

Few Egyptians sent their children to school. Mothers taught their daughters to sew, cook, and run a household. Boys learned farming or skilled trades from their fathers. Egyptian children had time for fun, as well. They played with board games, dolls, spinning tops, and stuffed leather balls.

Reading Check **Identify** Who made up the largest group in Egyptian society?

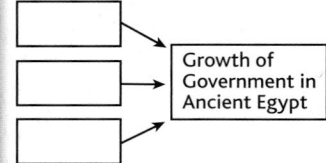
Study Central™ Need help with the material in this section? Visit jat.glencoe.com

Section 1 Review

Reading Summary

Review the Main Ideas

- The deserts on either side of the Nile Valley, along with the Nile cataracts and delta marshes, protected Egypt from invaders.
- The Egyptians became successful farmers using the Nile River's floods and irrigation.
- About 3100 B.C., Narmer united Lower Egypt and Upper Egypt.
- Egypt's society was divided into upper-class priests and nobles, middle-class artisans and merchants, and lower-class workers and farmers.

What Did You Learn?

1. What is papyrus and how did the Egyptians use it?
2. What rights did women have in ancient Egypt?

Critical Thinking

3. **Cause and Effect** Draw a diagram to show three things that led to the growth of government in ancient Egypt.

```
[ ]  →
[ ]  →   Growth of
         Government in
         Ancient Egypt
[ ]  →
```

4. **Geography Skills** How did the geography of the Nile River valley lead to the growth of a civilization there?
5. **Describe** Describe the Egyptian writing system.
6. **Analyze** What was the significance of Narmer's double crown?
7. **Reading** **Predicting** Use what you have learned in this section to write a paragraph predicting what life might have been like on an ancient Egyptian farm.

46   CHAPTER 2   Ancient Egypt

SECTION 1 REVIEW ANSWERS

1. It is a reed plant that was used to make baskets, sandals, river rafts, and paper.
2. Women could own and pass on property, buy and sell goods, make wills, obtain divorces, and take part in religious ceremonies.
3. farming; crafts; trade
4. The Nile River valley had natural barriers for protection, enriched soil for farming, and the river and seas for trade.
5. Picture symbols, called hieroglyphics, stood for objects, ideas, and sounds.
6. It symbolized the unity of Upper and Lower Egypt.
7. Answers will vary but should be drawn from text information describing farmers, as well as features.

Section 2
Egypt's Old Kingdom

Get Ready to Read!

What's the Connection?
In Section 1, you learned that Egyptian dynasties are divided into the Old Kingdom, Middle Kingdom, and New Kingdom. In Section 2, you will learn about the Egyptians' leaders, religion, and way of life in the Old Kingdom.

Focusing on the Main Ideas
- Egypt was ruled by all-powerful pharaohs. *(page 48)*
- The Egyptians believed in many gods and goddesses and in life after death for the pharaohs. *(page 49)*
- The Egyptians of the Old Kingdom built huge stone pyramids as tombs for their pharaohs. *(page 50)*

Locating Places
Giza (GEE•zuh)

Meeting People
King Khufu (KOO•foo)

Building Your Vocabulary
pharaoh (FEHR•oh)
deity (DEE•uh•tee)
embalming (ihm•BAHM•ihng)
mummy (MUH•mee)
pyramid (PIHR•uh•MIHD)

Reading Strategy
Organizing Information Use a graphic organizer like the one below to identify the different beliefs in Egypt's religion.

Egyptian beliefs

When & Where?

NATIONAL GEOGRAPHIC

Memphis · Giza
Nile R.

2600 B.C. 2400 B.C. 2200 B.C.

c. 2600 B.C.
Old Kingdom period begins

c. 2540 B.C.
Great Pyramid at Giza built

c. 2300 B.C.
Old Kingdom declines

CHAPTER 2   Ancient Egypt   47

---

1 FOCUS

SECTION OVERVIEW
This section discusses government, religion, and ways of life during the Old Kingdom.

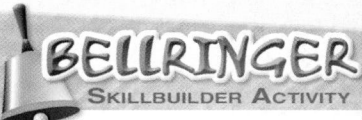
SKILLBUILDER ACTIVITY

Project **Daily Focus Skills Transparency 2–2** and have students answer questions. Discuss their responses.

Get Ready to Read!

Preteaching Vocabulary: Embalming was the process of taking a human corpse and preparing it for its journey into the afterlife. This process created a mummy.

Answers to Graphic: belief in many gods; magic spells needed to gain life after death; hopeful view of life after death; pharaoh needed body for afterlife; for centuries, believed only the elite had afterlife

---

SECTION RESOURCES

Reproducible Masters
- Reproducible Lesson Plan 2–2
- Daily Lecture and Discussion Notes 2–2
- Vocabulary Activity 2–2
- Active Reading Note-Taking Guide 2–2
- Guided Reading Activity 2–2
- Section Quiz 2–2
- Reading Essentials and Study Guide 2–2

Transparencies
- Daily Focus Skills Transparency 2–2

Multimedia
- Interactive Tutor Self-Assessment CD-ROM
- ExamView® Pro Testmaker CD-ROM
- Presentation Plus! CD-ROM

② TEACH

Evaluating Visual Evidence Have students study the pictures of the pyramids in this section then brainstorm ways in which Egyptians could have built them. Compare answers with the text. **L1**

Daily Lecture and Discussion Notes 2–2

Use **Daily Lecture and Discussion Notes 2–2** for an outline of key concepts found in the section.

More About the Photo

According to an ancient Greek myth, a sphinx slew all people who could not answer its riddle: "What walks on four feet in the morning, on two at noon, and three in the evening?" Oedipus answered the riddle: "Man crawls as a baby, walks as an adult, and uses a cane in old age." The sphinx then killed itself.

Caption Answer: "great house"; rulers lived in grand palaces

✓ Reading Check

Answer: Egyptians believed that a strong leader ensured unity and that the pharaoh was the son of the god Re.

Old Kingdom Rulers

Main Idea Egypt was ruled by all-powerful pharaohs.

Reading Focus Would you want your student body president or your sports team captain to have unlimited authority? Think what it would be like to have such a leader as you read about the rulers of ancient Egypt.

Around 2600 B.C., the period known as the Old Kingdom began in Egypt. The Old Kingdom lasted until about 2300 B.C. During those years, Egypt grew and prospered. The Egyptians built cities and expanded trade, and their kings set up a strong government.

The Egyptian kings, or **pharaohs** (FEHR• ohs) as they were called, lived with their families in grand palaces. In fact, the word *pharaoh* originally meant "great house." The pharaoh was an all-powerful ruler who guided Egypt's every activity. His word was law, and it had to be obeyed without question.

Pharaohs appointed many officials to carry out their wishes. These officials saw to it that irrigation canals and grain storehouses were built and repaired. They made sure that crops were planted as the pharaoh directed. They also controlled trade and collected tax payments of grain from farmers.

Why did Egyptians willingly serve the pharaoh? One reason was that they believed the unity of the kingdom depended on a strong leader. Another was that they considered the pharaoh to be the son of Re (RAY), the Egyptian sun god. As a result, his subjects paid him the greatest respect. Whenever he appeared in public, people played music on flutes and cymbals. Bystanders along the road had to bow down and "smell the earth," or touch their heads to the ground.

The Egyptians thought their pharaoh was a god on earth who controlled Egypt's welfare. He carried out certain rituals that were thought to benefit the kingdom. For example, he drove a sacred bull around Memphis, the capital city. The Egyptians believed this ceremony would keep the soil rich and ensure good crops. The pharaoh was also the first to cut ripe grain. Egyptians believed this would bring a good harvest.

✓ **Reading Check** **Analyze** Why did the pharaohs hold so much power?

◀ The Great Sphinx, a huge statue with the head of a man (perhaps a pharaoh) and the body of a lion, stands guard outside the tomb of a pharaoh. *What did the word pharaoh mean, and why was it used for Egypt's rulers?*

Reading Strategy   READING THE TEXT

Monitoring Comprehension Tell students that most readers stop to reexamine something they have read that they do not understand and often look up a word they do not know. Assign students to write down any questions that may come up as they read this section, along with answers found upon a second or further reading. Also, have students look up any unfamiliar words and write them down along with their definitions. Ask students to share their questions with the class. Use questions that cannot be answered by information in the text as a springboard for research assignments. **L1/ EL**

Egypt's Religion

Main Idea The Egyptians believed in many gods and goddesses and in life after death for the pharaohs.

Reading Focus Have you seen mummies in horror movies? Maybe you've even wrapped yourself in strips of cloth to be a mummy for a costume party. Keep reading to find out how the ancient Egyptians made mummies, and why.

Religion was deeply woven into Egyptian culture. Like the people of Mesopotamia, the ancient Egyptians worshiped many **deities** (DEE•uh•teez), or gods and goddesses. The Egyptians believed these deities controlled the forces of nature and human activities.

The main Egyptian god was the sun god Re. This was probably because of Egypt's hot, sunny climate and the importance of the sun for good harvests. Another major god was Hapi (HAH•pee), who ruled the Nile River. The most important goddess was Isis (EYE•suhs). She represented the loyal wife and mother, and she ruled over the dead with her husband Osiris (oh•SY•ruhs).

Life After Death Unlike the Mesopotamians, who imagined a gloomy life after death, the Egyptians took a hopeful view. They believed that life in the next world would be even better than life on Earth. Following a long journey, the dead would reach a place of peace and plenty.

One of the most important manuscripts written in ancient Egypt was the *Book of the Dead*. This was a collection of spells and prayers that Egyptians studied to obtain life after death. They believed that the god Osiris would meet newcomers at the entrance to the next world. If they had led good lives and knew the magic spells, Osiris would grant them life after death.

▲ During the embalming process, the pharaoh's body was placed on a special table. The chief embalmer was dressed as Anubis, the god of mummification. *Why did the Egyptians embalm the pharaoh's body?*

For centuries, Egyptians believed that only the pharaohs and an elite few could enjoy the afterlife. They also believed that the pharaoh's spirit needed a body to make the journey to the afterlife. If the pharaoh's body decayed after death, his spirit would be forced to wander forever. It was vital that a pharaoh's spirit reach the next world. There, the pharaoh would continue to care for Egypt.

To protect the pharaoh's body, the Egyptians developed a process called **embalming** (ihm•BAHM•ihng). First, priests removed the body's organs. A special kind of salt was then applied to the body, and it was stored for a number of days to dry. After this, the body was filled with spices and perfumes, then stitched closed. Next, it was cleaned with oils and tightly wrapped with

CHAPTER 2   Ancient Egypt   **49**

Reading Support L1/ EL

Use **Vocabulary Activity 2–2** to review important terms in the section.

TIME TRAVELER

Mummified animals—especially those associated with gods—got the royal treatment when they died. Embalmers mummified them just like they did humans so that they, too, could continue into the afterlife.

More About the Art

The term *mummy* comes from *mummie,* a word used in medieval times that referred to a medicinal powder made from embalmed corpses.

Caption Answer: to prepare it for the afterlife

CONNECTING ACROSS TIME

Have students write an inscription that they think describes the role of the president of the United States. Explore reasons people in the United States would reject a leader with unlimited power such as the pharaoh had. **L2**

DIFFERENTIATED INSTRUCTION

Visual/Spatial: Remind students about the Seven Wonders of the Ancient World from the activities in Chapter 1. If you skipped those activities, describe to students what the Seven Wonders were: the Hanging Gardens of Babylon, the Temple of Artemis, the Lighthouse of Alexandria, the Mausoleum at Halicarnassus, the Statue of Zeus at Olympia, the Great Pyramid at Giza, and the Colossus of Rhodes. Assign students to find pictures to create their own "Seven Wonders of Ancient Egypt" booklet.

Kinesthetic: Call on students to turn one of these "wonders" into a diorama from the past, including the surrounding landscape and Egyptian figures.

Verbal/Linguistic: Request volunteers to design a brochure explaining the diorama.

☞ Refer to *Inclusion Strategies for the Middle School Social Studies Classroom* in the TCR.

HISTORY Mystery

What Lies Inside an Unexplored Shaft of the Great Pyramid?
Nobody knows exactly what lies inside a blocked shaft of the Great Pyramid. It has three doors barring the way to a queen's 4,000-year-old sarcophagus. In the early 2000s, scientists sent a small robot into the shaft to take a look at the "Queen's Chamber." However, the doors did their work well. Not even the robot could squeeze past.

Reading Check

Answer: Re, Hapi, Isis, Osiris

More About the Art

According to Egyptian legend, Osiris brought to people the knowledge of agriculture and civilization.

Caption Answer: a collection of spells and prayers that Egyptians studied to obtain life after death

Reading Support L1/ EL

Assign **Guided Reading Activity 2–2** to help students organize the information in the section.

---

long strips of linen. The wrapped body was known as a **mummy** (MUH•mee). It was put in several wooden coffins, one fitting inside the other. The pharaoh was then ready for burial in a tomb.

Egyptian Medicine In the course of embalming the dead, the Egyptians learned much about the human body. Egyptian doctors used herbs and drugs to treat many different illnesses. They grew skilled at sewing up cuts and setting broken bones.

Some doctors focused on treating particular parts of the body, becoming the first specialists in medicine. Egyptians also wrote the world's first medical books on scrolls of papyrus.

Reading Check Identify Who were some of the Egyptians' main gods and goddesses?

Egypt's Religion

The Pyramids

Main Idea The Egyptians of the Old Kingdom built huge stone pyramids as tombs for their pharaohs.

Reading Focus Do you think the Statue of Liberty or the White House will still be here in 4,000 years? The giant pyramids of Egypt have stood for about that long. Read to find out how and why they were built.

No ordinary tomb would do for a pharaoh of Egypt. Instead, the Egyptians built mountainlike **pyramids** (PIHR•uh•MIHDS) entirely of stone. These gigantic structures, the size of several city blocks, protected the bodies of dead pharaohs from floods, wild animals, and grave robbers. The pyramids also held supplies that the pharaoh might need in the spirit world, including clothing, furniture, jewelry, and food.

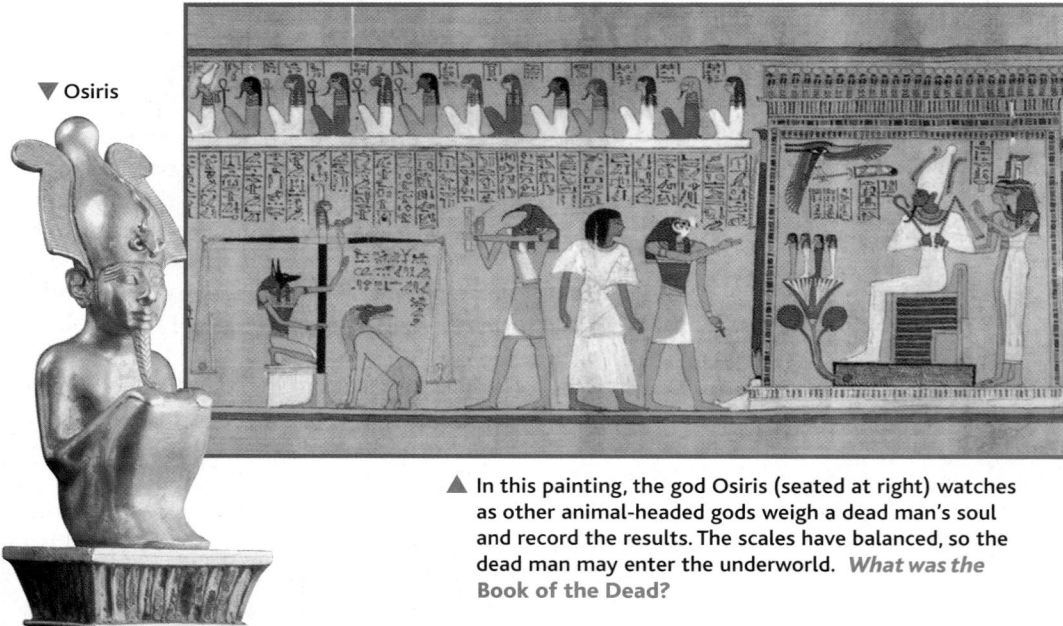

▼ Osiris

▲ In this painting, the god Osiris (seated at right) watches as other animal-headed gods weigh a dead man's soul and record the results. The scales have balanced, so the dead man may enter the underworld. *What was the Book of the Dead?*

50　　CHAPTER 2　Ancient Egypt

CRITICAL THINKING ACTIVITY

Making Generalizations Our concept of modern medical science dates back to ancient Egyptian writings on medicines, treatments, and studies of anatomy. Their embalming techniques were so advanced that Russians used them to preserve the body of Vladimir Lenin, the famous Communist leader. Ask students to discuss why embalming or preserving the body is often a part of our rituals during death and funerals. **Ask:** Why was embalming so important to the Egyptians? *(Possible answer: It prepared the pharaoh's body for the journey to the afterlife.)* L2

How Was a Pyramid Built? It took thousands of people and years of backbreaking labor to build a pyramid. Most of the work was done by farmers during the Nile floods, when they could not tend their fields. In addition, surveyors, engineers, carpenters, and stonecutters lent their skills.

Each pyramid sat on a square base, with the entrance facing north. To determine true north, the Egyptians studied the heavens and developed principles of astronomy. With this knowledge, they invented a 365-day calendar with 12 months grouped into 3 seasons. This calendar became the basis for our modern calendar.

To determine the amount of stone needed for a pyramid, as well as the angles necessary for the walls, the Egyptians made advances in mathematics. They invented a system of written numbers based on 10. They also created fractions, using them with whole numbers to add, subtract, and divide.

After the pyramid site was chosen, workers went wherever they could find stone—sometimes hundreds of miles away. Skilled artisans used copper tools to cut the stone into huge blocks. Other workers tied the blocks to wooden sleds and pulled them to the Nile over a path "paved" with logs. Next, they loaded the stones onto barges that were floated to the building site. There, workers unloaded the blocks and dragged or pushed them up ramps to be set in place.

Writing Activity

Some Egyptians would like to close the pyramids to save them from tourist damage. Have students write their opinion on this issue in a letter to the editor. For examples of such letters, have students examine letters in their local newspaper. **L2**

③ ASSESS

Assign Section 2 Review as homework or as an in-class activity.

⊚ Have students use the **Interactive Tutor Self-Assessment CD-ROM** to review the section.

Assessment L2

Assign **Section 2 Quiz** to assess mastery of the material found in the section.

Reading Support L1/ EL

Assign **Reading Essentials and Study Guide 2–2** to help students review section material.

Inside a Pyramid

Ancient Egyptians buried their kings within large stone buildings called pyramids.

1. **Air Shaft**

2. **King's Burial Chamber** The king's mummified body was placed in a room at the pyramid's center.

3. **Grand Gallery** This tall, sloping hall held large granite blocks that sealed the tomb.

4. **Queen's Burial Chamber** This chamber held a statue of the king, not the queen's body.

5. **Entrance**

6. **Underground Burial Chamber** Sometimes kings were buried here instead.

7. **Queen's Pyramids** These smaller pyramids are believed to be tombs for the king's wives.

8. **Mastaba** These tombs surrounding the pyramids held royal family members and other nobles.

9. **Valley Temple** This temple may have been used for rituals before the king was buried.

INTERDISCIPLINARY CONNECTIONS ACTIVITY

Science Tell students that scientists have used X rays and CT scans to get an inside look at mummies without damaging the bodies. These technologies have revealed a wealth of information, such as the diseases suffered by ancient Egyptians. Have students research how technology helps to reveal the past. Have them report their findings to the class. Be sure to have students give descriptions of how the various technologies they research function. **L2**

ENRICH

Much of the work on the pyramids took place during the months when the Nile overflowed its banks. Ask students to speculate on the timing of these projects. *(Farmers would have been free to work because they could not farm.)* **L2**

> **Caption Answer:** nearly 500 feet tall

✓ Reading Check

Answer: served as tombs for pharaohs

History Online

To help students understand section material, have them visit **Study Central™** at jat.glencoe.com

RETEACH

Read the subheadings of this section. Have students share what they have learned. **L1**

④ CLOSE

Have students name some of the achievements during the Old Kingdom. **L2**

▲ The pyramid shown above is that of King Khafre, son of Khufu. Although smaller than the Great Pyramid, Khafre's pyramid was built on higher ground so as to appear taller. *About how tall is the Great Pyramid?*

The Great Pyramid About 2540 B.C., the Egyptians built the largest and grandest of the pyramids known as the Great Pyramid. It is located about 10 miles from the modern city of Cairo. This pyramid, built for **King Khufu** (KOO•foo), is one of three still standing in **Giza** on the west bank of the Nile. It rises nearly 500 feet (153 m) above the desert, covers an area about the size of nine football fields, and contains more than 2 million stone blocks. Each block weighs an average of 2.5 tons.

The Great Pyramid was the tallest structure in the world for more than 4,000 years. It is equal to the size of a 48-story building and is the largest of about 80 pyramids found in Egypt. The Great Pyramid is truly a marvel because the Egyptians built it without using beasts of burden, special tools, or even the wheel.

✓ Reading Check **Explain** What was the purpose of pyramids?

Section ② Review

History Online

Study Central™ Need help with the material in this section? Visit jat.glencoe.com

Reading Summary
Review the Main Ideas

- The all-powerful rulers of Egypt, called pharaohs, were believed to be related to Egypt's main god.
- The Egyptians believed in many gods and goddesses. They also believed in life after death for the pharaoh, whose body would be mummified before burial.
- The pyramids, built as huge stone tombs for the pharaohs, required many years and thousands of workers to construct.

What Did You Learn?

1. How was stone for a pyramid transported to the building site?

2. What did Egyptians learn from embalming bodies?

Critical Thinking

3. **Organize Information** Draw a diagram like the one below. Fill in details about the pharaohs of the Old Kingdom and their duties.

> **Pharaohs**

4. **Math/Science Link** How did the building of the pyramids lead to advances in science and mathematics?

5. **Compare and Contrast** How did the Egyptians' religious beliefs compare to those of the Mesopotamians?

6. **Persuasive Writing** Suppose you are an Egyptian pharaoh who wants a pyramid built to house your tomb. Write a letter to the farmers and workers in your kingdom explaining why it is their duty to build the pyramid for you.

52   CHAPTER 2   Ancient Egypt

SECTION 2 REVIEW ANSWERS

1. Cut blocks were placed on a sled and dragged over a path of logs to the Nile, then floated on a barge to the building site.

2. use of herbs and drugs to treat illnesses; how to sew up cuts and set broken bones

3. lived in palaces, were all-powerful, were considered gods, carried out religious rituals, appointed officials to handle government matters

4. used astronomy to find true north; 12-month calendar; number system based on 10

5. Both believed in many gods and goddesses. Mesopotamians took a gloomy view of the afterlife; Egyptians took a hopeful view.

6. Answers will vary but should reflect the text.

THE PRINCE WHO KNEW HIS FATE

Translated by Lise Manniche

Before You Read

The Scene: This story takes place in ancient times in Egypt and in an area that is now Iraq.

The Characters: The first characters introduced are the king of Egypt, his son, and the seven Hathor goddesses, who predict the prince's death. When the prince travels, he meets Chief of Naharín and his daughter.

The Plot: For many years, the king of Egypt protects his son from the death that was predicted for him. The prince convinces his father to let him travel. He meets a princess, and together they try to prevent his fate.

Vocabulary Preview

destiny: an already-determined course of events

ferried: carried by boat

enchant: to cast a spell on something

fugitive: a person who runs away or escapes

folly: a foolish action

vessel: a container

exalting: praising

In this story, a prince must avoid three types of animals because it was predicted that one of them would kill him. The people who love him try to prevent him from coming into contact with the animals, but the prince does not want to live in fear.

SUMMARY

Seven goddesses declare that a crocodile, snake, or dog will someday kill the only son of an Egyptian king. To protect his son, the king keeps him in a protected home. Eventually, the prince persuades his father to free him. Then the prince goes north and weds a chief's daughter. Despite his wife's watchfulness, the prince is stalked by a snake, captured by a crocodile, and finally torn to pieces by his own dog. His wife puts together the pieces, and the prince reappears.

Vocabulary Preview Before students begin reading, have them read **Before You Read** and the **Vocabulary Preview.** Point out that difficult words are footnoted throughout the text.

① FOCUS

Mixing Unreality and Reality Fairy tales fall into the category of folktales—stories shared by members of a culture or nation. Tell students that fairy tales include unreal elements, such as giants and talking crocodiles. However, the emotions and conflicts of the characters are often those of real people.

▌ Reading Strategy ⟩ READING REINFORCEMENT

Previewing the Selection Have students look at the title, introduction, illustrations, and footnoted words throughout the story. **Ask:** What do you already know about fairy tales? (*Answers may include that fairy tales often have princes, princesses, and villains.*) What can you tell the rest of the class about Egypt, Iraq, or Syria? (*Answers may include that Egypt is in northern Africa and that Iraq and Syria are in western Asia.*) Next, tell students to formulate questions about the story based on the title, introduction, illustrations, footnoted words, and what they already know. List the students' questions on the board. Then instruct students to look for answers to the questions as they read the story. **L1**

② TEACH

A ACTIVE READING STRATEGIES

QUESTION Ask students what information in this passage will probably be important later in the story. *(A dog, snake, or crocodile will kill the prince.)*

B ACTIVE READING STRATEGIES

VISUALIZE Ask students to visualize the setting here. Ask them what it would be like to grow up in these circumstances.

C CRITICAL THINKING

INFERRING Ask students to explain why the king ordered all sorts of weapons for the prince. *(The king hoped the weapons would protect the prince from his destiny.)*

D ACTIVE READING STRATEGIES

COMPREHEND Have students determine which bank of the Nile the prince came from and who ferried him over the river. *(The prince came from the west bank, and servants ferried him over.)*

As You Read

This is one of the world's oldest known fairy tales. It was written in hieroglyphics more than 3,000 years ago. The places in the tale are real, and the prince and princess may have been based on real people, as well. The ancient Egyptians often made important people the main characters in their stories.

There once was a king of Egypt who had no sons at all. So the king asked the gods of his time for a son and they decided that he should have one. . . .

The seven Hathor goddesses[1] came to decide the boy's fate and they declared, "He is destined to be killed by a crocodile or a snake or a dog."

The people who were at the boy's side heard this. They reported it to the king and his heart grew sad.

The king had a house of stone built for the boy at the edge of the desert, supplied with servants and with all sorts of good things from the palace, for the child was not to go outside. There the boy grew up.

One day he climbed up to the roof of the house and saw a dog following a man, who was walking along the road.

"What is that?" he asked his servant.

[1]**seven Hathor goddesses:** goddesses who visited newborn children to discover their fates

54

▌▌Reading Strategy ▶ VOCABULARY READING TIP

Context Clues Explain that context clues often give the meaning of unfamiliar words. Two kinds of context clues are definitions and synonyms. A definition is a phrase that describes the new word. Commas, dashes, or parentheses often set off the phrase that gives this type of clue. Synonyms are words with similar meanings. A familiar word is often a clue to the meaning of its unfamiliar synonym. Write the following sentences on the board:

1. In hieroglyphics, picture symbols are used to represent ideas.
2. After all, my destiny has been determined. Allow me to do as I wish until I meet my fate.

Ask: What is the definition of *hieroglyphics?* *(picture symbols used to represent ideas)* Which word is a synonym for *destiny? (fate)* **L1**

"It's a dog," the servant replied.

"Let me have a dog like that," the boy said.

The servant reported this to the king and the king said, "His heart is sad. Let him have a bounding little puppy."

So they gave the boy a dog.

In time, the young prince grew restless and he sent a message to his father, saying, "Why should I stay here doing nothing? After all, my destiny has been determined. Allow me to do as I wish until I meet my fate."

The king replied saying "Let a chariot[2] be prepared for him, equipped with all sorts of weapons, and assign a servant to accompany him."

So they did as the king commanded and gave him all that he needed. Then they ferried him across the Nile to the east bank and said to him, "Now go as you wish."

And the dog was with him.

The prince traveled as he pleased northwards across the desert, living on the best of all desert game.

Thus he came to the realm of the Chief of Naharín,[3] who had no children—except one daughter. He had built a house for her with a window seventy cubits[4] from the ground.

The Chief of Naharín then sent for all the sons of all the chiefs of Kharu,[5] saying, "He who can jump up to the window of my daughter shall have her for his wife."

The sons of all the chiefs had been trying to reach the window each day for many days when the prince passed by them.

They took the prince to their house, and they bathed him, they rubbed him with oil, and they bandaged his feet. They gave fodder[6] to his horses and food to his servant. They did everything for the young man.

And to start a conversation, they said, "Where do you come from, you handsome youth?"

"I am the son of a chariot officer from Egypt. My mother died and my father took another wife. My stepmother grew to hate me and I have fled her."

They welcomed him and kissed him.

---

[6]**fodder:** food for cattle, horses, and sheep

---

[2]**chariot:** a two-wheeled, horse-drawn car
[3]**Naharín:** an area east of the Euphrates River in present-day Iraq
[4]**cubits:** units of length based on the length of the arm from the elbow to the fingertips
[5]**Kharu:** an area in present-day Syria

E LITERARY ELEMENTS

FOLKTALES: Point of View Ask students to explain who is telling the story and what he or she reveals about the characters. (*A nameless narrator informs readers about the characters' actions and conversations.*)

F ACTIVE READING STRATEGIES

VISUALIZE Read the passage to the students, and have them sketch a picture that comes to mind as they listen.

G AUTHOR'S CRAFT

INDIRECT CHARACTERIZATION Ask students how the chiefs' sons describe the prince and how the prince's appearance reinforces a cultural value found in many fairy tales. (*He is handsome; heroes are supposed to be good looking.*)

DIFFERENTIATED INSTRUCTION

Verbal/Linguistic: Have students think about how the story might change if it were told from the princess's point of view. **Ask:** What parts of the story might be left out? (*Answers may include the prince's early life, his arrival in Naharín, and his conversation with the chiefs' sons.*) What might the princess's point of view explain that the original story does not? (*Answers may include how the princess thinks and feels.*)

Gifted and Talented: Have interested students rewrite the first two pages from the princess's point of view. Invite them to share the rewritten pages with the class.

H LITERARY ELEMENTS

FANTASY Have students explain what is fantastic about this passage. (*The prince jumped more than 100 feet in the air.*)

I AUTHOR'S CRAFT

INDIRECT CHARACTERIZATION Tell students to find evidence in this passage that suggests that the Chief of Naharín is arrogant. (*Although the chief is willing to have his daughter marry the son of another chief, he is unwilling to have her marry a fugitive from Egypt.*)

J LITERARY ELEMENTS

PLOT: Suspense Ask students why the story might be called a "cliffhanger" if it ended with this passage. (*Readers would not know whether the prince and princess died or lived so, figuratively, the characters would be left hanging from a cliff.*)

GLENCOE
BOOKLINK

Use **Glencoe BookLink** to create customized reading lists for your students' reading levels, interests, and abilities.

Several days later the prince asked the youths, "What are you doing here in Naharín?"

"The past three months we have spent each day jumping, for the Chief of Naharín will give his daughter to the one who reaches her window," they said.

"Oh, if only I could enchant my feet, I would jump with you," said the prince.

H The youths went off to jump, as it was their daily custom, while the prince stood at a distance, watching.

From her window the daughter of the Chief of Naharín gazed at him.

At last, when many days had passed, the prince joined the sons of the chiefs.

He jumped and he reached the window of the daughter of the Chief of Naharín.

She embraced him and she kissed him.

56

A messenger went to inform her father.

"One of the young men has reached the window of your daughter," the messenger said.

"Whose son is it?" the Chief of Naharín inquired.

"He is the son of a chariot officer from Egypt. He has fled from his stepmother."

The Chief of Naharín grew very angry. "Am I to give my daughter to a fugitive from Egypt? Send him home!"

"You must go back where you came from," the messenger said to the prince.

But the princess clung to the prince, and she swore, "As Re lives, if they take him from me, I will not eat, I will not drink, I will die within the hour!"

When the messenger had reported everything she had said to her father, her father sent men to kill the prince then and there.

Again the princess swore, "As Re lives, if they kill him, I shall die before sunset. I will not live an hour more than he!"

They repeated this to her father, and the Chief of Naharín had the prince and his daughter brought before him.

The young man impressed the Chief, who welcomed him and kissed him and said, "Now you are like my own son. Tell me about yourself."

"I am the child of a chariot officer from Egypt," said the young man, "My mother died and father took another wife. She grew to hate me, and I have fled from her."

The Chief of Naharín gave his daughter to the prince, and he gave him a house and fields and herds and everything they needed.

CRITICAL THINKING ACTIVITY

Determining Main Ideas and Supporting Details Tell students to read page 57. **Ask:** What is the main idea of this page? (*The prince's wife is trying to protect the prince from his fate.*) How does the idea fit in with the first part of the story? (*In the first part of the story, the prince's father is trying to protect the prince.*) Organize the class into groups of four. Have each group circulate a sheet of paper. Have each member of each group contribute one sentence from the story on this topic, and continue until each group has recorded the supporting details. Have groups compare their results. **L2**

When they had lived together for some time, the young man told his wife, "I know my fate. I shall be killed by one of three: a crocodile or a snake or a dog."

"Then," she said, "the dog that follows you everywhere must be killed."

"That would be folly," he replied. "I will not have the dog killed for I have had it ever since it was a puppy."

So his wife began to watch over him closely, and she did not allow him to go out alone.

It so happened that on the very day the prince had arrived in Naharín, the crocodile, his fate, began to follow him. It caught up with him in the town where the prince lived with his wife.

But there in the lake was a giant who would not let the crocodile out, and so the crocodile refused to let the giant out. For three whole months they had been fighting all day long, beginning each day at sunrise.

The prince spent many pleasant days in his house, and in the evenings when the breeze died down, he went to bed. One evening when sleep had overcome him, his wife filled a vessel with wine and another with beer. Then she sat down beside him, but she did not sleep.

A snake came out of its hole intending to bite the prince, but the vessels tempted it and the snake drank from them, got drunk and rolled over on its back to sleep.

His wife chopped the snake in three pieces with her axe. Then she roused her husband and said to him, "See, your god has placed one of your fates in your hands. He is protecting you."

The prince made offerings to his god Re, adoring him and exalting his power each day that passed.

After some time, the prince went for a stroll around his estate. His wife stayed at home, but his dog followed him.

Suddenly the dog turned on him and the prince fled from it.

He ran to the edge of the lake and jumped into water to escape the dog, but there the crocodile seized him and dragged him off to find the giant.

K LITERARY ELEMENTS

IRONY Explain that a situation is ironic when what happens is the opposite of what we expect, often with surprising or humorous results. Ask students to explain why the princess might think the prince's answer to her suggestion that he kill the dog is ironic. *(Most likely, the princess thinks that keeping the dog, not killing the dog, is folly.)*

L AUTHOR'S CRAFT

FORESHADOWING Ask students what event the arrival of the crocodile foreshadows. *(the rapidly approaching death of the prince)*

M CRITICAL THINKING

PROBLEM AND SOLUTION Point out that the princess's solution to the problem of a snake killing her husband was to set out wine and beer. Ask students how they would prevent snakes from biting them while they sleep. *(Answers may include that they would shut their bedroom door and windows.)*

EXTENDING THE CONTENT

Isis and Osiris According to another Egyptian story, Osiris, the fourth pharaoh of Egypt, was a god—the great-grandson of Re, the god to whom the prince in this story made an offering. These two stories share another element besides allusions to deities. In the story of Osiris, his brother cut him into pieces and scattered the pieces across Egypt. Isis, the wife of Osiris, put the pieces back together. As in the case of the prince, the newly assembled Osiris came alive. According to Egyptian legend, the process that Isis used to reassemble Osiris's body was embalming.

W★RLD LITERATURE

DIFFERENTIATED INSTRUCTION

EL Students Point out that the characters in the story have no names. Then tell students to name each character for a trait he or she exemplifies in the story. For example, the king might be dubbed "Doting" because he worries about his son.

Average Students Assign students the roles of characters from the story to read aloud. Suggest that they shade the meaning of their lines by emphasizing certain words. Model this technique with the following lines: What are *you* doing here? What are you doing *here*?

Gifted Students Remind students that Egyptians wrote in hieroglyphics. Challenge students to rewrite the story with simple picture symbols.

③ ASSESS

Assign the **Responding to the Reading** questions as an in-class activity or as homework.

④ CLOSE

Have students choose their favorite character and explain their choice. **L2**

"I am pursuing you, for I am your fate," said the crocodile. "Listen, for three whole months I have been fighting with the giant. I will let you go now if you will take my side and kill the giant when he returns to fight."

So the prince waited by the water all that night, and when dawn broke and a second day began, the giant returned.

The giant began to fight the crocodile at once, but the prince stepped forward with his scimitar[7] in his hand. He cut out the heart of the giant and the giant died.

At that very moment the dog sneaked up behind the prince. It attacked him and tore him to bits and spread the pieces all about.

When the prince failed to return, his wife set out to look for him. After seven days and seven nights in search for him, she came upon his remains.

She collected all the pieces of her husband's body and put them back together again—except for his heart. That she placed in a lotus flower which was blooming on the water.

Lo and behold, the prince reappeared as he had been before.

From that day on the prince and princess lived together happily until they crossed over to the fields of the blessed.

❦

---

[7]**scimitar** (SIH • muh • tuhr): a long sword with a curved blade

Responding to the Reading

1. How did the prince's father and wife try to protect him?
2. How would this story be different if it were told from the point of view of the prince?
3. **Evaluating Information** Do you think the prince paid enough attention to the goddesses' warning? Why or why not? Support your opinion with examples.
4. **Drawing Conclusions** Why do you think the prince lied to the Chief of Naharín about his parents?
5. **Reading** Read to Write Suppose you are the prince, captive in the stone house, or the princess, captive in the tower. Write three diary entries about your daily life, your feelings about being kept away from society, and your hopes for the future.

58

Responding to the Reading Answers

1. The prince's father confined the prince to a stone house. The prince's wife wanted to kill his dog, watched the prince closely, and did not allow him to go out alone.
2. The reader would know what the prince felt, how he jumped to the princess's window, and why he lied to the chief.
3. Answers will vary but should be supported with examples from the text.
4. Answers may include that the prince did not want to draw attention to himself or that he feared others would discover his fate.
5. Diary entries will vary. Encourage students to be complete in their entries.

Section 3
The Egyptian Empire

Get Ready to Read!

What's the Connection?
During the Old Kingdom, Egyptians established their civilization. During the Middle Kingdom and the New Kingdom, Egypt's powerful pharaohs expanded the empire by conquering other lands.

Focusing on the Main Ideas
- The Middle Kingdom was a golden age of peace, prosperity, and advances in the arts and architecture. *(page 60)*
- During the New Kingdom, Egypt acquired new territory and reached the height of its power. *(page 61)*
- Akhenaton tried to change Egypt's religion, while Tutankhamen is famous for the treasures found in his tomb. *(page 64)*
- Under Ramses II, Egypt regained territory and built great temples, but the empire fell by 1150 B.C. *(page 65)*

Locating Places
Thebes (THEEBZ)

Meeting People
Ahmose (AHM•OHS)
Hatshepsut (hat•SHEHP•soot)
Thutmose III (thoot•MOH•suh)
Akhenaton (AHK•NAH•tuhn)
Tutankhamen (TOO•TANG•KAH•muhn)
Ramses II (RAM•SEEZ)

Building Your Vocabulary
tribute (TRIH•byoot)
incense (IHN•SEHNS)

Reading Strategy
Categorizing Information Create a diagram to show the major accomplishments of Ramses II.

Ramses

NATIONAL GEOGRAPHIC
When & Where?

Memphis
Thebes
Nile R.

2400 B.C.	1600 B.C.	800 B.C.
c. 2050 B.C. Middle Kingdom begins	c. 1500 B.C. Queen Hatshepsut reigns	c. 1279 B.C. Ramses II takes the throne

---

① FOCUS

SECTION OVERVIEW
This section discusses the cultural advances and territorial expansion that occurred during the Middle and New Kingdoms.

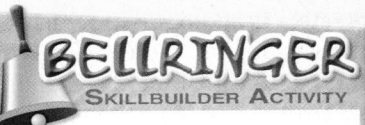
BELLRINGER
SKILLBUILDER ACTIVITY

🖑 Project **Daily Focus Skills Transparency 2–3** and have students answer questions. Discuss their responses.

Get Ready to Read!

Preteaching Vocabulary: Incense is a material that, when burned, produces a fragrant odor. There are many different kinds of incense with many different odors. Incense was highly valued in ancient Egypt, particularly for use in religious ceremonies.

Answers to Graphic: rebuilt the empire, constructed many temples, ruled for a remarkably long reign

---

SECTION RESOURCES

📁 **Reproducible Masters**
- Reproducible Lesson Plan 2–3
- Daily Lecture and Discussion Notes 2–3
- Vocabulary Activity 2–3
- Active Reading Note-Taking Guide 2–3
- Guided Reading Activity 2–3
- Section Quiz 2–3
- Reading Essentials and Study Guide 2–3

🖑 **Transparencies**
- Daily Focus Skills Transparency 2–3

Multimedia
- 💿 Interactive Tutor Self-Assessment CD-ROM
- 💿 ExamView® Pro Testmaker CD-ROM
- 💿 Presentation Plus! CD-ROM
- 💿 Glencoe BookLink CD-ROM

② TEACH

Writing Monologues Organize the class into six groups, and assign each group one of the pharaohs in this section. As they read, groups should take careful notes on their pharaohs. Have them use these notes to create a monologue in which the various pharaohs describe their accomplishments. Call on students to present their monologues to the class. **L2**

Daily Lecture and Discussion Notes 2–3

Use **Daily Lecture and Discussion Notes 2–3** for an outline of key concepts found in the section.

Caption Answer: Instead of pyramids, pharaohs had tombs cut into cliffs.

Objectives and answers to the student activity can be found in the **Web Activity Lesson Plan** feature at jat.glencoe.com

The Middle Kingdom

Main Idea The Middle Kingdom was a golden age of peace, prosperity, and advances in the arts and architecture.

Reading Focus Have you heard older people talk about enjoying their "golden years"? Countries can also experience such happy, productive times. In the following paragraphs, you'll learn why the Middle Kingdom was a golden age for Egypt.

About 2300 B.C., the pharaohs lost control of Egypt as nobles battled one another for power. Almost 200 years of confusion followed. Finally, a new dynasty of pharaohs came to power. They moved their capital south from Memphis to a city called **Thebes** (THEEBZ). There they restored order and stability, ushering in a new period called the Middle Kingdom.

The Middle Kingdom lasted from about 2050 B.C. to 1670 B.C. During this time, Egyptians enjoyed a golden age of stability, prosperity, and achievement.

The Drive for More Land During the Middle Kingdom, Egypt took control of new lands. Soldiers captured Nubia to the south and attacked what is now Syria. The conquered peoples sent **tribute** (TRIH•byoot), or forced payments, to the Egyptian pharaoh, enriching the kingdom. Within Egypt, the pharaohs added more waterways and dams. They increased the amount of land being farmed and built a canal between the Nile River and the Red Sea.

The Arts Blossom During the Middle Kingdom, arts, literature, and architecture thrived. Painters covered the walls of tombs and temples with colorful scenes of the deities and daily life. Sculptors created large wall carvings and statues of the pharaohs, showing them as ordinary people rather

▲ This artwork with gold inlay from the Middle Kingdom period shows a funeral boat. *How did architecture change during the Middle Kingdom?*

than godlike figures. Poets wrote love songs and tributes to the pharaohs.

A new form of architecture was also created. Instead of building pyramids, pharaohs had their tombs cut into cliffs west of the Nile River. This area became known as the Valley of the Kings.

Who Were the Hyksos? The Middle Kingdom came to an end in 1670 B.C. Nobles were again plotting to take power from the pharaohs. This time, however, Egypt also faced a serious threat from outside. A people known as the Hyksos (HIHK•SAHS), from western Asia, attacked Egypt.

Web Activity Visit jat.glencoe.com and click on *Chapter 2—Student Web Activity* to learn more about ancient Egypt.

60   CHAPTER 2   Ancient Egypt

▊ Reading Strategy ❭ READING THE TEXT

Taking Notes Have students create two web diagrams to help them take notes on this section. Label the central oval of the first diagram "Middle Kingdom" and the central oval of the second diagram "New Kingdom." Ovals around each central oval should contain key facts about either the Middle Kingdom or the New Kingdom. Encourage students to work on newsprint or poster board so they have lots of room to write. As an alternative, you can draw the diagrams on the board, and have students take turns adding entries. **L2**

🗁 Refer to the *Quizzes, Tests, and Authentic Assessment (with Rubrics)* booklet for rubrics.

The Hyksos were mighty warriors. They crossed the desert in horse-drawn chariots and used weapons made of bronze and iron. Egyptians had always fought on foot with copper and stone weapons. They were no match for the invaders.

The Hyksos ruled Egypt for about 150 years. Then, around 1550 B.C., an Egyptian prince named **Ahmose** (AHM•OHS) led an uprising that drove the Hyksos out of Egypt.

✓ **Reading Check** **Identify** Who were the Hyksos?

The New Kingdom

Main Idea During the New Kingdom, Egypt acquired new territory and reached the height of its power.

Reading Focus Do you know the names of any women who hold political office? In ancient civilizations, women rarely held positions of power. Read to learn how a woman became ruler of Egypt.

Ahmose's reign in Egypt began a period known as the New Kingdom. During this time, from about 1550 B.C. to 1080 B.C., Egypt became even richer and more powerful.

Reading Support L1/EL

Use **Vocabulary Activity 2–3** to review important terms in the section.

✓ **Reading Check**

Answer: warriors from western Asia who conquered Egypt around 1670 B.C.

TIME TRAVELER

Pharaohs wrote their names or the names of gods on an oblong emblem enclosed by a length of rope known as a cartouche. The cartouche symbolized a pharaoh's rule of all that the sun encircled. Egyptians also believed the cartouche prevented the theft of a name or an identity, especially after death.

Linking Past & Present

Hieroglyphs and Computer Icons

THEN The ancient Egyptian system of writing was made up of hundreds of different characters called hieroglyphs. Each hieroglyph was a picture that represented a word. For example, a large circle with a smaller circle drawn in its center meant "sun." Egyptian scribes carved hieroglyphic symbols on monuments and used them for everyday communication.

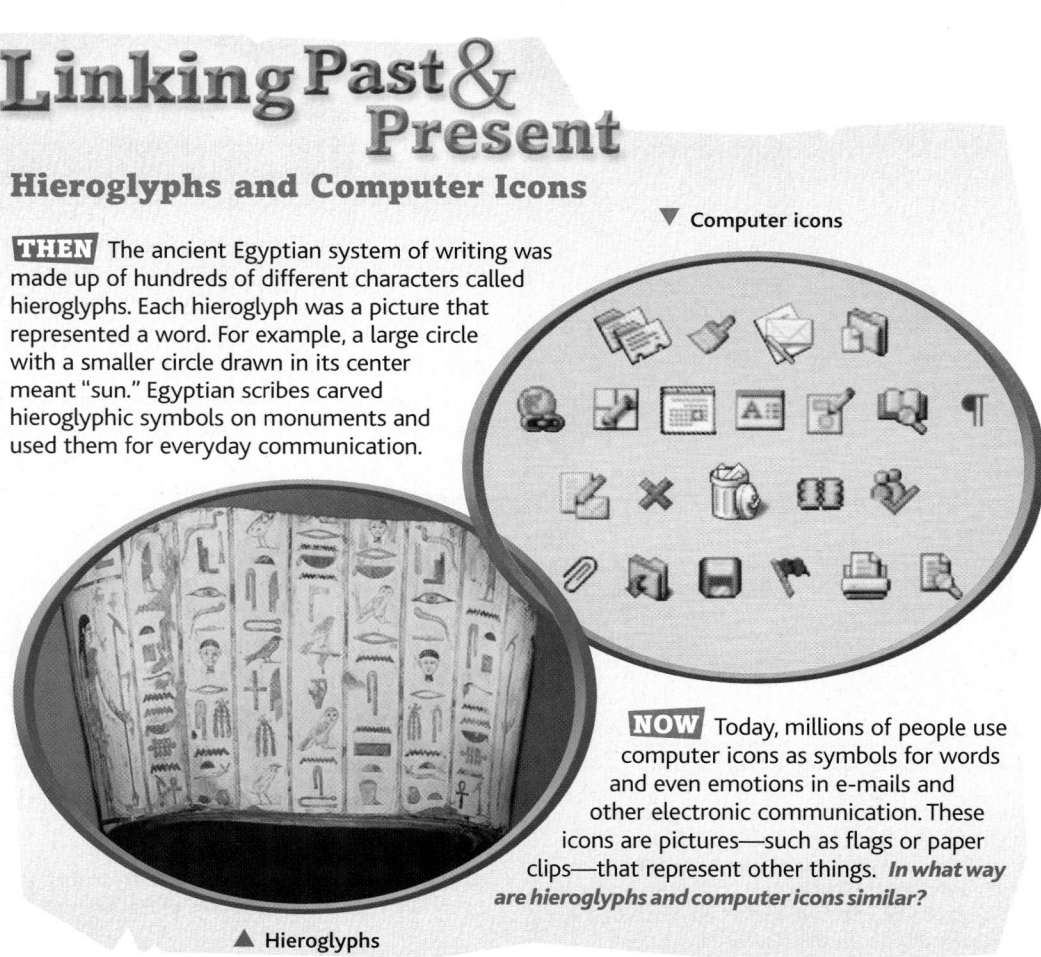

▼ Computer icons

▲ Hieroglyphs

NOW Today, millions of people use computer icons as symbols for words and even emotions in e-mails and other electronic communication. These icons are pictures—such as flags or paper clips—that represent other things. *In what way are hieroglyphs and computer icons similar?*

CHAPTER 2   Ancient Egypt   **61**

Linking Past & Present

Answer: Both use pictures to communicate information. However, hieroglyphs involved hundreds of symbols understood mostly by scribes, while millions of everyday people use and understand computer icons.

DIFFERENTIATED INSTRUCTION

Visual/Spatial: Introduce hieroglyphs by having students design rebuses for their names. A rebus is a representation made up of words and pictures or symbols whose names sound like the syllables in a word. Shuffle the rebuses and hand them out for students to solve.

Kinesthetic: Read the **Time Traveler** on page 61, which discusses cartouches. Have students use pencils or other utensils to "carve" their rebuses onto oblong slabs of clay. Then have them use cord or twine to form a cartouche around the emblem.

Gifted and Talented: Call on students to locate and show photos of cartouches with the hieroglyphic names of Egyptian rulers. 📖

CONNECTING ACROSS TIME

Tell students that in 1972, UNESCO started the World Heritage list—a collection of cultural and natural treasures that the world should try to preserve. Explore reasons that Thebes appears on the list. Ask students to name areas in the United States that might be on the list. **L2**

Using Geography Skills

Answers:

1. the New Kingdom

2. the Red Sea

Skills Practice

Ask: Why do you think none of the kingdoms controlled much of the Arabian Peninsula? *(The Arabian Peninsula is mostly desert, and it is far from the easy access to water that characterizes each kingdom's territories.)*

✓ Reading Check

Answer: Egyptians sailed along the coast of east Africa, trading beads, metal tools, and weapons for ivory, wood, leopard skins, and incense. The increased trade brought great wealth to Egypt.

Most pharaohs made empire building a priority. They marched their armies east into western Asia and fought wars to bring other lands under their control. During the New Kingdom, Egypt reached the height of its glory.

A Woman Ruler About 1473 B.C., a queen named **Hatshepsut** (hat•SHEHP•soot) came to power in Egypt. She ruled first with her husband and then, after his death, on behalf of her young nephew. Finally she made herself pharaoh. Hatshepsut became one of the few women to rule Egypt.

Hatshepsut was more interested in trade than conquest. During her reign, Egyptian traders sailed along the coast of East Africa. They exchanged beads, metal tools, and weapons for gold, ivory, ebony, and **incense** (IHN•SEHNS), a material burned for its pleasant smell. These trade journeys brought even greater wealth to Egypt.

Hatshepsut used some of this wealth to build monuments. One of her greatest projects was a great temple and tomb in the limestone cliffs of the Valley of the Kings.

Expanding the Empire When Hatshepsut died, her nephew, **Thutmose III** (thoot•MOH•suh), became pharaoh. Under Thutmose, Egypt began aggressive wars of conquest. Thutmose's armies expanded Egypt's borders north to the Euphrates River in Mesopotamia. His troops also moved south and regained control of Nubia, which had broken free from Egypt earlier. Under Thutmose, Egypt controlled more territory than it ever had.

Thutmose's empire grew rich from trade and tribute. In addition to claiming gold, copper, ivory, and other valuable goods from conquered peoples, Egypt enslaved many prisoners of war. These unlucky captives were put to work rebuilding Thebes. They filled the city with beautiful palaces, temples, and monuments.

Slavery had not been widespread in Egypt before. During the New Kingdom, however, it became common. Enslaved people did have some rights. They could own land, marry, and eventually be granted their freedom.

✓ Reading Check **Summarize** Describe Egyptian trade during the rule of Hatshepsut.

NATIONAL GEOGRAPHIC

Egyptian Kingdoms

Cyprus
SYRIA
Mediterrranean Sea
NILE DELTA
Giza
Memphis
LOWER EGYPT
ARABIAN PENINSULA
0   300 mi.
0   300 km
Lambert Azimuthal Equal-Area projection
Nile R.
Red Sea
Thebes
TROPIC OF CANCER
UPPER EGYPT
20°N
30°E
30°N

KEY

Old Kingdom
Land added during Middle Kingdom
Land added during New Kingdom
▲ Pyramids

Using Geography Skills

During the Middle Kingdom, the capital of Egypt moved from Memphis to Thebes.
1. Which kingdom included lands across the Mediterranean Sea?
2. What physical feature makes up much of the eastern border of the Middle Kingdom?

62   **CHAPTER 2**   Ancient Egypt

CRITICAL THINKING ACTIVITY

Making Generalizations Tell students to think of generalizations as summaries. These draw together, or summarize, the known facts in a broad statement. Have students study the images of various pharaohs from the chapter, such as Tutankhamen, Hatshepsut, and Ramses II. **Ask: What generalizations can you form about the way these rulers wanted to be remembered?** *(Possible answers: as all-powerful, as eternal, as larger than life, and so on)* Explore details in the art that support each generalization. **L2**

HATSHEPSUT

Reigned 1473–1458 B.C.

Hatshepsut ▶

Hatshepsut was the daughter of King Thutmose I and Queen Aahmes. Even as a young princess, she was confident, describing herself as "exceedingly good to look upon . . . a beautiful maiden" who was "serene [peaceful] of nature." During her marriage to King Thutmose II, Hatshepsut influenced her husband's decisions and hoped to someday have more power. She saw an opportunity when Thutmose died and declared herself pharaoh.

Because the position of pharaoh was usually passed from father to son, Hatshepsut had to prove that she was a good leader. She often wore men's clothing to convince the people that she could handle what had always been a man's job. Unlike other pharaohs, Hatshepsut avoided military conquests. She focused her attention instead on expanding Egypt's economy. She restored Egypt's wealth through trade with Africa and Asia. Returning home from trading expeditions, cargo ships were loaded with ebony, gold, ivory, incense, and myrrh. During her reign, Hatshepsut also rebuilt many of Egypt's great temples, including the temple at Karnak. In her temple at Deir el Bahri, the reliefs on the walls recorded the major events of Hatshepsut's reign.

Hatshepsut's 21-year reign was peaceful, but her stepson, Thutmose III, was plotting against her. He overthrew Hatshepsut and her government. It is unknown how Hatshepsut died, but after her death, Thutmose III ordered that the reliefs and statues in Hatshepsut's temple be destroyed.

> **"A dictator excellent of plans"**
> —Egyptian scribe quoted in
> *Barbarian Tides*

Then and Now

Make a list of Hatshepsut's strengths as a leader. Then choose a present-day female leader and list her leadership strengths. Write a paragraph comparing their similarities and differences.

63

TEACH

Hatshepsut enhanced her status by claiming descent from Amon-Re, who was considered one of the most important Theban gods and the protector of pharaohs. Hatshepsut's power came from the support of an inner circle of influential officials and priests. Unfortunately for her, as Thutmose III grew older, he won the support of the army, which he used to topple his stepmother. **Ask: How do these facts help explain the differing policies of these two rulers?** (*Hatshepsut used building projects and trade to strengthen the power of priests and nobles; Thutmose III used wars to strengthen the army.*) **L2**

Then and Now

Comparisons will vary depending upon the present-day leader chosen. Students should support their answers with concrete examples.

Writing Activity

Have students research encyclopedias or the Internet for additional information on Hatshepsut to investigate how she came to power and how she was perceived by her contemporaries. Have them pay particular attention to how she wrestled with members of the royal family to maintain control of Egypt. Have them write a half-page summary of what they learned. **L2**

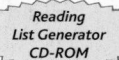

Reading List Generator CD-ROM

GLENCOE BOOKLINK   **RECOMMENDED READING**

Use the **Glencoe BookLink CD-ROM** to create customized reading lists based on your students' interests and reading levels. Below is an example based on content in this chapter. Also, see the Suggested Readings on pages 944–946 of the Appendix.

- Berger, Melvin, and Gilda Berger. *Mummies of the Pharaohs: Exploring the Valley of the Kings.* Journey to the Valley of the Kings, home of the tombs of the pharaohs.
- Carter, Dorothy Sharp. *His Majesty, Queen Hatshepsut.* After her husband's death, young Queen Hatshepsut decides to defy convention and name herself pharaoh.
- Perl, Lila. *Mummies, Tombs, and Treasure: Secrets of Ancient Egypt.* The Egyptians believed a person's spirit would live forever if the body was mummified.

Economics Have groups of students research the following aspects of present-day Egypt: trade, tourism, and involvement in international organizations. Ask each group to share its findings. Then have the class use what they have learned to discuss Egypt's level of interaction with the United States and other nations. **L3**

Writing Activity

Assign groups of students to write a series of news stories about Amenhotep IV for the newspaper the *Daily Papyrus.* Headlines might include the following: "Pharaoh Takes New Name," "Worship of Aton Shocks Priests," "Pharaoh Leaves Thebes for New Capital," "Hittites Threaten Egypt," "Boy King Restores Old Religion." Encourage students to do additional research and to pattern their stories after those in their local newspaper. **L2**

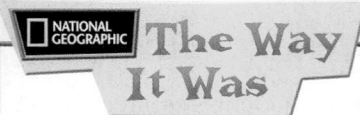
NATIONAL GEOGRAPHIC **The Way It Was**

Answers:
1. Cats protected grain supplies from mice and rats.
2. the goddess Bastet

NATIONAL GEOGRAPHIC The Way It Was

Focus on Everyday Life

Cats in Ancient Egypt In ancient Egypt, cats were loved and even worshiped. Egyptians valued the ability of wild cats to protect villages' grain supplies from mice and rats. Over several hundred years, cats became tame, and their role developed from valued hunter to adored family pet to goddess.

In ancient Egyptian tombs, archaeologists have found many wall paintings, carvings, and statues of cats. Often the statues were adorned with beautiful jewelry, such as silver or gold earrings, nose rings, and collars. When an Egyptian family's cat died, its owners shaved their eyebrows to show their grief and had the cat's body mummified.

▲ **Egyptian goddess depicted as a cat**

Egyptians worshiped cats because they associated them with the goddess Bastet. She represented motherhood, grace, and beauty, and often appears in paintings and statues as a woman with the head of a cat.

Connecting to the Past
1. Why did ancient Egyptians first value cats?
2. With what goddess did the ancient Egyptians associate cats?

The Legacies of Two Pharaohs

Main Idea Akhenaton tried to change Egypt's religion, while Tutankhamen is famous for the treasures found in his tomb.

Reading Focus If you ask people to name an Egyptian pharaoh, the answer you're likely to get is "King Tut." Read on to find out more about him and his predecessor.

About 1370 B.C., Amenhotep IV (AH•muhn•HOH•TEHP) came to the throne. With the help of his wife, Nefertiti (NEHF•uhr•TEET•ee), Amenhotep tried to lead Egypt in a new direction.

A Religious Reformer Amenhotep realized that Egypt's priests were gaining power at the expense of the pharaohs. In an attempt to maintain his own power, Amenhotep introduced a new religion that swept away the old gods and goddesses. Instead, only one god, called Aton (AH•tuhn), was to be worshiped. When Egypt's priests resisted these changes, Amenhotep removed many from their positions, seized their lands, and closed temples. He then changed his name to **Akhenaton** (AHK•NAH•tuhn), which means "Spirit of Aton." He began ruling Egypt from a new city.

To most Egyptians, Akhenaton's attacks on the gods seemed to be an attack on Egypt itself. They refused to accept Aton as the only god. Meanwhile, Akhenaton became so devoted to his new religion that he neglected his duties as pharaoh. The administrators he appointed were not as experienced as the priests they replaced, and Akhenaton took no action when enemies from what is now Turkey, the Hittites, attacked Egypt. As a result, Egypt lost most of its lands in western Asia, greatly shrinking the empire.

INTERDISCIPLINARY CONNECTIONS ACTIVITY

Civics Assign students to read Article II, Section 1 of the United States Constitution to find out the basic qualifications for president. *(native-born citizen, at least 35 years old, has lived in the United States for at least 14 years)* Ask what other unwritten qualifications students might add. Now have them brainstorm a list of qualifications for pharaoh. *(Sample responses: member of ruling dynasty, preferably male, able to handle palace intrigue, and so on)* Have students use their answers to write help-wanted ads for each position. **L2**

◀ Tutankhamen's gold mask

The Boy King When Akhenaton died, his son-in-law inherited the throne. The new pharaoh, **Tutankhamen** (TOO•TANG•KAH•muhn), was a boy about 10 years old. He relied on help from palace officials and priests, who convinced him to restore the old religion. After ruling for only nine years, Tutankhamen died unexpectedly. He may have suffered a fall or been murdered; no one is sure.

What *is* certain is that "King Tut," as he is nicknamed, played only a small role in Egypt's history. Why, then, is he the most famous of all pharaohs? The boy king captured people's imaginations after a British archaeologist, Howard Carter, found his tomb in A.D. 1922.

The tomb contained the king's mummy and incredible treasures, including a brilliant gold mask of the young pharaoh's face. Carter's find was a thrilling discovery, because most royal tombs in Egypt were looted by robbers long ago.

✔ **Reading Check** **Evaluate** Why is Tutankhamen so famous today?

The End of the New Kingdom

Main Idea Under Ramses II, Egypt regained territory and built great temples, but the empire fell by 1150 B.C.

Reading Focus Egypt remained mighty for thousands of years, but it finally fell to outsiders. Read to learn about Egypt's last great pharaoh and the empire's decline.

During the 1200s B.C., pharaohs worked to make Egypt great again. The most effective of these pharaohs was **Ramses II** (RAM•SEEZ). He reigned for a remarkable 66 years, from 1279 B.C. to 1213 B.C. During this time, Egyptian armies regained lands in western Asia and rebuilt the empire. Ramses also launched an ambitious building program, constructing several major new temples.

▲ Temple of Karnak

Reading Support L1/ EL

Assign **Guided Reading Activity 2–3** to help students organize the information in the section.

③ ASSESS

Assign Section 3 Review as homework or as an in-class activity.

⊙ Have students use the **Interactive Tutor Self-Assessment CD-ROM** to review the section.

Assessment L2

Assign **Section 3 Quiz** to assess mastery of the material found in the section.

Reading Support L1/ EL

Assign **Reading Essentials and Study Guide 2–3** to help students review section material.

✔ **Reading Check**

Answer: His tomb was found intact with its ancient treasure.

EXTENDING THE CONTENT

How Was Abu Simbel Saved? Construction of the Aswan High Dam in the mid-1900s offered more irrigated farmland at the cost of flooding the temples at Abu Simbel. More than 50 nations responded to the crisis by funding the relocation of the temples to higher ground. Workers and engineers disassembled and relocated some 16,000 blocks of stone, fulfilling the dream of Ramses II to be remembered forever.

TEACH

Ramses II wanted to be known as a great conqueror. When he fought the Hittites, he took along royal scribes to record events in three styles—prose, poetry, and pictorial carvings. Ask students how Egyptian temple paintings of battles with the Hittites might be slanted. *(They are versions approved by Ramses II, and therefore favorable to him.)* **Ask: What other information would historians need to interpret these battles accurately?** *(accounts in Hittite records, archaeological remains, research by other scholars, and so on)* **What evidence could you use to prove that Ramses II was a great builder?** *(any of the architectural feats mentioned or shown in the text)* **L2**

Then and Now

Answers will vary, but both are monumental stone works. Rushmore honors four people, while Abu Simbel honors one leader—Ramses II.

Writing Activity

Have students write down notes about what they consider the most important events in the life of Ramses II. Then have them compose their own three-verse poem to describe the events for posterity. Remind students that as royal scribes they should portray Ramses II positively. **L3**

Biography

RAMSES II
Reigned 1279–1213 B.C.

Statue of Ramses II ▶ holding an offering table

Ramses II began his military training at a very young age. Ramses' father, Seti I, allowed his 10-year-old son to serve as a captain in his army. Seti also made his son coruler of Egypt. By the time Ramses was crowned pharaoh of Egypt, he was a great warrior and experienced leader. Nine kings who ruled after Ramses II named themselves in his honor. Many centuries later, archaeologists nicknamed the pharaoh "Ramses the Great" because of his fame on the battlefield, his construction and restoration of buildings and monuments, and his popularity among the Egyptian people. His subjects fondly called him "Sese," an abbreviation of Ramses.

Ramses continued in his father's footsteps by trying to restore Egyptian power in Asia. In the early years of his reign, he defeated forces in southern Syria and continuously battled Egypt's longtime enemy, the Hittites. Details about one costly battle with the Hittites were carved on temple walls, showing the Egyptians succeeding against great odds.

During his 66-year reign, Ramses II undertook a large-scale building program. He could afford such an expensive plan because Egypt was very prosperous during his reign. He restored the Sphinx, completed the Temple of Karnak, and built himself a city with four temples as well as beautiful gardens and orchards. He is famous for the temple built at Abu Simbel. It was carved out of a solid rock cliff and featured four huge statues of Ramses II, two on each side of the doorway.

Ramses' first wife, Queen Nefertari, died early in his reign. Like other pharaohs, Ramses had many wives. Ramses II was proud of his large family, which included more than 100 children.

> **"They all came bowing down to him, to his palace of life and satisfaction."**
>
> —hieroglyphic translation by James B. Pritchard, *Ancient Near Eastern Texts*

▲ Coffin of Ramses II

Then and Now

Use the Internet and your local library to learn about Mount Rushmore, a monument in South Dakota. Describe Mount Rushmore, and then compare it to Ramses' temple at Abu Simbel.

Reading List Generator CD-ROM

GLENCOE BOOKLINK   **RECOMMENDED READING**

Use the **Glencoe BookLink CD-ROM** to create customized reading lists based on your students' interests and reading levels. Below is an example based on content in this chapter. Also, see the Suggested Readings on pages 944–946 of the Appendix.

- **Haslam, Andrew, and Alexandra Parsons.** *Ancient Egypt.* Learn about ancient Egypt by making a tunic and a pair of Egyptian-style sandals, preparing fig cakes, and making a water clock.
- **Millard, Anne.** *The Egyptians.* What was life like in ancient Egypt? How did people dress? What were their houses like? What did scribes do? What did Egyptians believe about death?
- **Murdoch, David.** *Tutankhamun: The Life and Death of a Pharaoh.* Learn who discovered King Tut's tomb and what they found inside.

Why Were Temples Built? Under Ramses II and other New Kingdom rulers, scores of new temples rose throughout Egypt. Many were built by enslaved people captured in war. The most magnificent was Karnak at Thebes. Its huge columned hall decorated with colorful paintings still impresses visitors today.

Unlike modern churches, temples, and mosques, Egyptian temples did not hold regular services. Instead, most Egyptians prayed at home. They considered the temples as houses for the gods and goddesses. Priests and priestesses, however, performed daily temple rituals, washing statues of the deities and bringing them food.

The temples also served as banks. Egyptians used them to store valuable items, such as gold jewelry, sweet-smelling oils, and finely woven cloth.

Egypt's Decline and Fall After Ramses II, Egypt's power began to fade. Later pharaohs had trouble keeping neighboring countries under Egyptian control. Groups from the eastern Mediterranean attacked Egypt by sea, using strong iron weapons. The Egyptians had similar arms, but they paid dearly for them because Egypt lacked iron ore.

By 1150 B.C., the Egyptians had lost their empire and controlled only the Nile delta. Beginning in the 900s B.C., Egypt came under the rule of one outside group after another. The first conquerors were the Libyans from the west. Then in 760 B.C., the people of Kush, a land to the south, seized power and ruled Egypt for the next 70 years. Finally, in 670 B.C., Egypt was taken over by the Assyrians.

Reading Check Identify What groups conquered Egypt starting in the 900s B.C.?

ENRICH

When Howard Carter peered into King Tut's tomb, someone asked, "Can you see anything?" He replied, "Yes, wonderful things." Call on students to recall what was so special about this discovery. (*first intact tomb, the amount of gold, and so on*) L1/EL

Reading Check

Answer: Libyans, people of Kush, and Assyrians

To help students understand the section material, have them visit **Study Central™** at jat.glencoe.com

RETEACH

Ask students to skim through this section, noting each time the word *pharaoh* is used. Have them summarize the impact of pharaohs on the development of Egyptian civilization. L1/EL

④ CLOSE

Create a list of Egyptian achievements during the Middle and New Kingdoms. L2

Section 3 Review

Study Central™ Need help with the material in this section? Visit jat.glencoe.com

Reading Summary
Review the Main Ideas
- During the Middle Kingdom, Egypt expanded its borders, and the arts flourished.
- Under New Kingdom rulers, Egypt built a strong empire and expanded trade.
- Akhenaton failed in his attempt to create a new religion. Tutankhamen ruled briefly but gained fame because of treasures found buried with him.
- Ramses II was Egypt's last great pharaoh. In the 900s B.C., Egypt lost power to outside invaders.

What Did You Learn?
1. What improvements did the Middle Kingdom rulers make?
2. What purposes did temples serve in Egypt?

Critical Thinking
3. **Organizing Information** Create a chart like the one below. Fill in details about Egypt's Middle Kingdom and New Kingdom.

Middle Kingdom	New Kingdom

4. **Evaluate** What was unusual about the reign of Hatshepsut?
5. **Analyze** How did Akhenaton upset the traditional order?
6. **Compare and Contrast** Describe the similarities and differences between the rule of Hatshepsut and Ramses II.
7. **Expository Writing** Which of the rulers discussed in this section do you think had the greatest effect upon Egyptian history? Write a short essay to explain your answer.

CHAPTER 2 Ancient Egypt 67

SECTION 3 REVIEW ANSWERS
1. added more waterways and dams for irrigation, increased amount of land used for farming, built a canal between Nile River and Red Sea, improved art and architecture
2. houses for gods and goddesses, places for priests to perform rituals, banks, and warehouses
3. Details should reflect major features and accomplishments of each kingdom.
4. She was the first woman to rule Egypt in her own right.
5. He stopped worship of old gods in favor of one god.
6. Similar: built many temples; Different: Hatshepsut increased Egypt's wealth through trade; Ramses II waged war to expand the empire.
7. Answers will vary but should be supported by the text.

① FOCUS

SECTION OVERVIEW

This section traces how the Nubians built the civilization of Kush, which eventually took control of Egypt.

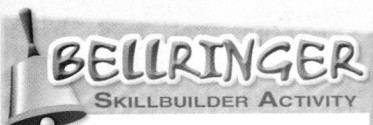

👆 Project **Daily Focus Skills Transparency 2–4** and have students answer questions. Discuss their responses.

Get Ready to Read!

Preteaching Vocabulary: One of the most distinguishing features of central Africa is the savanna. These grassy plains cover much of the region south of the Sahara and provide excellent pastureland for cattle.

Answers to Graphic: Napata: original capital of Kush, white sandstone temples and monuments; Meroë: later capital of Kush, ironmaking center, looked like Egyptian city; Both: used Nile for trade and transportation

Section 4
The Civilization of Kush

Get Ready to Read!

What's the Connection?
In Sections 1, 2, and 3, you learned about the rise and fall of civilizations in ancient Egypt. Another civilization in early Africa was Kush. It was located near Egypt and was very similar.

Focusing on the Main Ideas
- To the south of Egypt, the Nubians settled in farming villages and became strong warriors. *(page 69)*
- The people of Kush devoted themselves to ironworking and grew wealthy from trade. *(page 70)*

Locating Places
Nubia (NOO•bee•uh)
Kush (KUHSH)
Kerma (KAR•muh)
Napata (NA•puh•tuh)
Meroë (MEHR•oh•ee)

Meeting People
Kashta (KAHSH•tuh)
Piye (PY)

Building Your Vocabulary
savanna (suh•VA•nuh)

Reading Strategy
Compare and Contrast Use a Venn diagram like the one below to show the similarities and differences between Napata and Meroë.

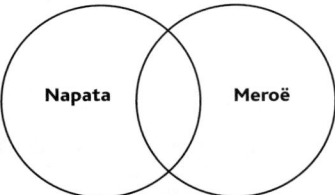

NATIONAL GEOGRAPHIC **When & Where?**

800 B.C.	700 B.C.	600 B.C.	500 B.C.

c. 750 B.C. Kashta of Kush conquers part of Egypt

728 B.C. Piye of Kush defeats Egyptians

c. 540 B.C. Kush moves capital to Meroë

SECTION RESOURCES

📁 **Reproducible Masters**
- Reproducible Lesson Plan 2–4
- Daily Lecture and Discussion Notes 2–4
- Vocabulary Activity 2–4
- Active Reading Note-Taking Guide 2–4
- Guided Reading Activity 2–4
- Section Quiz 2–4
- Reading Essentials and Study Guide 2–4

🖍 **Transparencies**
- Daily Focus Skills Transparency 2–4

Multimedia
- Interactive Tutor Self-Assessment CD-ROM
- ExamView® Pro Testmaker CD-ROM
- Presentation Plus! CD-ROM
- Vocabulary PuzzleMaker CD-ROM

Nubia

Main Idea To the south of Egypt, the Nubians settled in farming villages and became strong warriors.

Reading Focus Are you on good terms with your neighbors? It's not always easy–for individuals or countries. Read on to find out about the Egyptians' neighbors to the south and the ways the two civilizations mixed.

The Egyptians were not alone in settling along the Nile River. Farther south, in present-day Sudan, another strong civilization arose. This was in a region called **Nubia** (NOO•bee•uh), later known as **Kush** (KUHSH).

Historians do not know exactly when people arrived in Nubia. Evidence suggests that cattle herders arrived in about 2000 B.C. They grazed their herds on the **savannas** (suh•VA•nuhs), or grassy plains, that stretch across Africa south of the Sahara. Later, people settled in farming villages in Nubia. They grew crops, but they were also excellent hunters, skilled at using the bow and arrow. Soon the Nubians began forming armies known for their fighting skills.

The Kingdom of Kerma The more powerful Nubian villages gradually took over the weaker ones and created the kingdom of **Kerma** (KAR•muh). Kerma developed close ties with Egypt to the north. The Egyptians were happy to trade for Kerma's cattle, gold, ivory, and enslaved people. They also admired Nubian skills in warfare and hired Nubian warriors to fight in their armies.

Kerma became a wealthy kingdom. Its artisans made fine pottery, jewelry, and metal goods. Like Egyptian pharaohs, the kings of Kerma were buried in tombs that held precious stones, gold, jewelry, and pottery. These items were as splendid as those found in Egypt during the same period.

▲ In this wall painting, four Nubian princes offer rings and gold to an Egyptian ruler.
What kingdom was formed when more powerful Nubian villages took over weaker ones?

CHAPTER 2 Ancient Egypt 69

② TEACH

Making Inferences The Greek historian Herodotus had trouble distinguishing between Egyptian and Kushite culture. **Ask:** What inferences can you draw about their cultures based on this? Have students write down their inferences, then make adjustments as they read the section. **L2**

Daily Lecture and Discussion Notes 2–4

Use **Daily Lecture and Discussion Notes 2–4** for an outline of key concepts found in the section.

Reading Support L1/ EL

Use **Vocabulary Activity 2–4** to review important terms in the section.

CONNECTING ACROSS TIME

Archaeologists have uncovered new evidence of Nubian cultural achievements. Have students research some of their latest finds. **L2**

Caption Answer: Kerma

Reading Strategy **READING THE TEXT**

Understanding Text Structure Tell students that the fist three sections of the chapter cover a very large time span. Have them look at the **When & Where?** feature at the beginning of Section 4 to familiarize themselves with the time frame covered in this section. **Ask:** What period of time will you be looking at now? *(roughly 800 B.C. to 500 B.C.)* Where does most of the action take place? *(Egypt and the area south of Egypt)* Have students look at time line entries. What questions do the events raise in their minds? Write down some of these questions on the board, and have students look for answers as they read the section. **L1/ EL**

Writing Activity

Tell students that King Ezana boasted of his conquest of Meroë in engravings on a stele, or upright stone slab. Have students use the **Primary Source** feature on page 71 to create an inscription that Ezana might have written. **L1**

✓ Reading Check

Answer: south of Egypt along the Nile River, in what is present-day Sudan

Using Geography Skills

Answers:

1. Napata
2. African peoples farther to the south and Egypt

Caption Answer: The temples, avenues, palaces, and colors resembled those of Egypt.

Reading Support L1/ EL

Assign **Guided Reading Activity 2–4** to help students organize the information in the section.

Why Did Egypt Invade Nubia? As you learned earlier, the Egyptian pharaoh Thutmose III sent his armies into Nubia in the 1400s B.C. After a 50-year war, the kingdom of Kerma collapsed, and the Egyptians took control of much of Nubia. They ruled the Nubians for the next 700 years.

During this time, the people of Nubia adopted many Egyptian ways. They began to worship Egyptian gods and goddesses along with their own. They learned how to work copper and bronze and changed Egyptian hieroglyphs to fit their own language. As people and goods continued to pass between Nubia and Egypt, the two cultures mixed.

✓ **Reading Check** **Identify** Where was Kush located?

The Rise of Kush

Main Idea The people of Kush devoted themselves to ironworking and grew wealthy from trade.

Reading Focus Do you and your friends ever trade video games or CDs? Trading may be a casual activity for you, but it was very important to ancient peoples. Read to find how Kush took advantage of its location along an important trade route.

As Egypt declined at the end of the New Kingdom, Nubians saw their chance to break away. By 850 B.C., a Nubian group had formed the independent kingdom of Kush. For the next few centuries, powerful Kushite kings ruled from the city of **Napata** (NA•puh•tuh).

Napata was in a favorable location. It stood along the upper Nile where trade caravans crossed the river. Caravans soon carried gold, ivory, valuable woods, and other goods from Kush to Egypt.

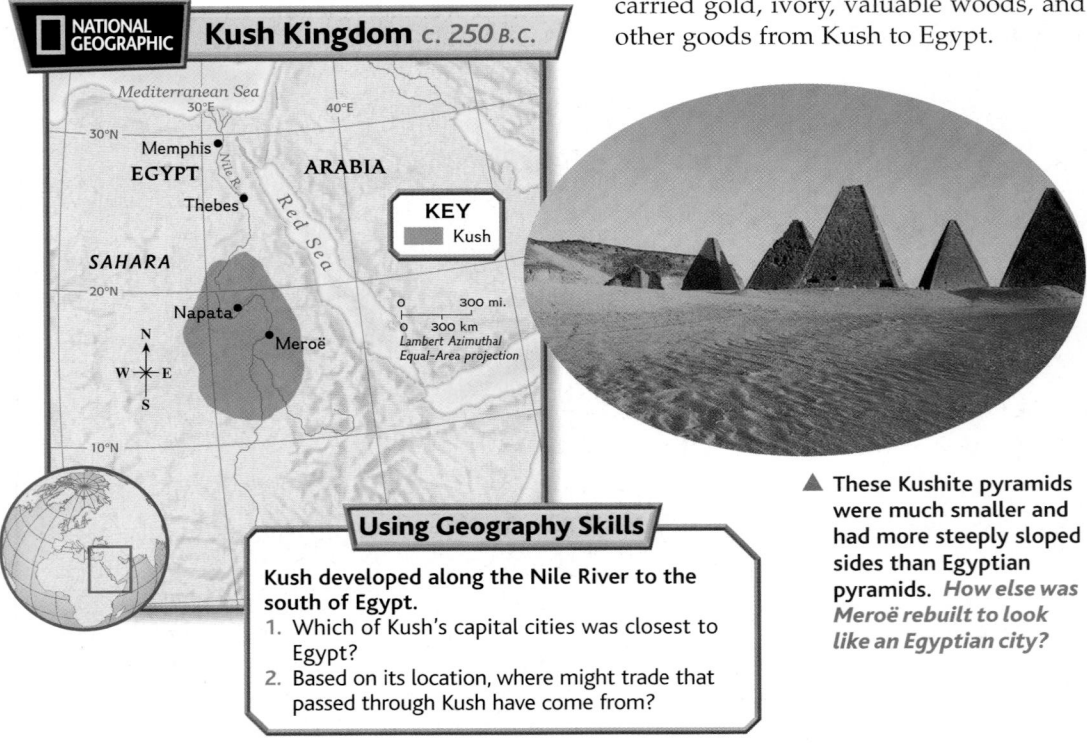

NATIONAL GEOGRAPHIC **Kush Kingdom** c. 250 B.C.

KEY
Kush

▲ These Kushite pyramids were much smaller and had more steeply sloped sides than Egyptian pyramids. *How else was Meroë rebuilt to look like an Egyptian city?*

Using Geography Skills

Kush developed along the Nile River to the south of Egypt.

1. Which of Kush's capital cities was closest to Egypt?
2. Based on its location, where might trade that passed through Kush have come from?

70 CHAPTER 2 Ancient Egypt

DIFFERENTIATED INSTRUCTION

Visual/Spatial: Tell students that in 1997, the Nubia Museum opened in Aswan, Egypt. Have students design a mural celebrating Nubian cultural achievements the museum might have displayed.

English Learners: Explain that in hieroglyphics, the word *Nubia* means "Land of Gold." Ask students to design glyphs illustrating this phrase and copy them below the word "Nubia."

Gifted and Talented: After creating the mural, have students write a short magazine-style article explaining the images.

📁 Refer to *Inclusion Strategies for the Middle School Social Studies Classroom* in the TCR.

In time, Kush became rich enough and strong enough to take control of Egypt. About 750 B.C., a Kushite king named **Kashta** (KAHSH•tuh) headed north with a powerful army. His soldiers began the conquest of Egypt that his son **Piye** (PY) completed in 728 B.C. Piye founded a dynasty that ruled both Egypt and Kush from Napata.

The kings of Kush greatly admired Egyptian culture. In Napata they built white sandstone temples and monuments similar to those of the Egyptians. The Kushites also built small pyramids in which to bury their kings. The ruins of these pyramids can still be seen today.

The Importance of Iron Kush's rule in Egypt did not last long. During the 600s B.C., the Assyrians invaded Egypt. Armed with iron weapons, they drove the Kushites back to their homeland in the south.

Despite their losses, the Kushites gained something from the Assyrians—the secret of making iron. The Kushites became the first Africans to devote themselves to iron-working. Soon, farmers in Kush were using iron for their hoes and plows instead of copper or stone. With these superior tools, they were able to grow large amounts of grain and other crops.

Kush's warriors also began using iron spears and swords, increasing their military power. Meanwhile, traders from Kush carried iron products and enslaved people as far away as Arabia, India, and China. In return, they brought back cotton, textiles, and other goods.

A New Capital About 540 B.C., Kush's rulers left Napata and moved farther south to be out of the Assyrians' reach. In the city of **Meroë** (MEHR•oh•ee), they set up a royal court. Like Napata, the new capital had

Primary Source
Selecting a New King

When their king died, the Kushites asked the god Amon-Re to appoint a new leader.

"[The Kushite officials said] 'We have come to you, O Amon-Re . . . that you might give to us a lord. . . . That beneficent office [helpful task] is in your hands—may you give it to your son whom you love!'

Then they offered the king's brothers before this god, but he did not take one of them. For a second time there was offered the king's brother . . . Aspalta . . .

[Amon-Re said] 'He is your king.'"

—author unknown,
c. 600 B.C.,
"The Selection of Aspalta
as King of Kush"

▲ Lion statue in honor of King Aspalta

DBQ Document-Based Question

Do you think Aspalta was qualified to be king? Why or why not?

access to the Nile River for trade and transportation. The rocky desert east of Meroë, however, contained rich deposits of iron ore. As a result, Meroë became not only a trading city but also a center for making iron.

With their growing wealth, Kush's kings rebuilt Meroë to look like an Egyptian city. Small pyramids stood in the royal graveyard. A huge temple sat at the end of a grand avenue lined with sculptures of rams. Sandstone palaces and red-brick houses had walls decorated with paintings or blue and yellow tiles.

CHAPTER 2   Ancient Egypt   71

Primary Source

Answer:
Answers might include: yes, because the people believed he had the god's blessing; no, because his abilities were not discussed.

③ ASSESS

Assign Section 4 Review as homework or as an in-class activity.

Have students use the **Interactive Tutor Self-Assessment CD-ROM** to review the section.

Assessment L2

Assign **Section 4 Quiz** to assess mastery of the material found in the section.

Reading Support L1/ EL

Assign **Reading Essentials and Study Guide 2–4** to help students review section material.

CRITICAL THINKING ACTIVITY

Making Inferences Read aloud this brief description of Piye's storming of Memphis, the capital of Egypt: *Then his majesty . . . said: "I swear, as Re loves me, as my father Amon (who fashioned me), favors me, . . . according to the command of Amon . . . I will take it like a flood of water."* **Ask:** What can you infer about Egypt's influence on Kush? Explain. (*The Kushites had adopted Egyptian gods.*) Based on the reading in this section, what other things did Kush adopt? (*building styles, pyramids, and so on*) **L2**

ENRICH

Point out that Europeans "rediscovered" Kushite centers in the early 1800s. Have students speculate on why the various pyramids and ruins might have startled them. **L1**

Caption Answer: Axum

Answer: built its wealth through trade, which was greatly expanded when Kushites learned ironworking skills

---

History Online

To help students understand section material, have them visit **Study Central™** at jat.glencoe.com

---

RETEACH

Ask students to summarize the main topic of this section. **L2**

④ CLOSE

Have students discuss how geography linked Kush and Egypt. **L2**

Building a Profitable Trade Meroë became the center of a huge trading network that stretched north to Egypt's border and south into central Africa. Kush's traders received leopard skins and valuable woods from the interior of Africa. They traded these goods, along with enslaved workers and their own iron products, to people throughout the Mediterranean and the Indian Ocean area.

Kush remained a great trading power for some 600 years. By the A.D. 200s, though, the kingdom began to weaken. As Kush declined, another kingdom rose to take its place. The kingdom is called Axum and was located in what is today the country of Ethiopia. Around A.D. 350, the armies of Axum burned Meroë to the ground. You will read more about the kingdom of Axum when you study Africa.

Reading Check **Explain** How did Kush become a wealthy kingdom?

Kushite King

The Kushite king Taharqa was one of the most powerful leaders in Nubian history. During his reign, the kingdom grew and prospered. He built many large temples in and around Egypt and Kush. *What kingdom replaced Kush?*

◀ Kushite king Taharqa

Section ④ Review

History Online

Study Central™ Need help with the material in this section? Visit jat.glencoe.com

Reading Summary

Review the Main Ideas

• In the Nile Valley to the south of Egypt, the Nubians founded the kingdom of Kerma and traded with the Egyptians.

• The Kushites set up a capital at Meroë that became a center for ironmaking and the base of a huge trading network.

What Did You Learn?

1. Who were the Nubians?
2. What were the Kushites' most important economic activities?

Critical Thinking

3. **Sequencing** Draw a diagram to show events that led up to the Kushite conquest of Egypt.

Kush Conquest of Egypt

4. **Geography Skills** Why was Napata's location advantageous?
5. **Analyze** How did the Kushite kings demonstrate their admiration for Egyptian culture?
6. **Compare** Describe the similarities between Kush and Egypt.
7. **Persuasive Writing** Create an advertisement that could have been used in ancient Egypt and Kush to promote the many uses of iron.

72   CHAPTER 2   Ancient Egypt

SECTION 4 REVIEW ANSWERS

1. cattle herders in the savannas and founders of Kerma
2. trade and ironworking
3. New Kingdom declines; Nubians rebel and found Kush; Kush grows rich from trade; Kush conquers Egypt.
4. It was located at a point where trade caravans crossed the Nile.
5. They built similar monuments, temples, and pyramids.
6. Possible answers: Kush modeled architecture on Egypt; both profited from trade along the Nile.
7. Students' advertisements should reflect the versatility and importance of iron, including weapons and tools as well as other uses.

Section 1 The Nile Valley

Vocabulary
cataract
delta
papyrus
hieroglyphics
dynasty

Focusing on the Main Ideas
- The Egyptian civilization began in the fertile Nile River valley, where natural barriers discouraged invasions. *(page 39)*
- The Egyptians depended on the Nile's floods to grow their crops. *(page 41)*
- Around 3100 B.C., Egypt's two major kingdoms, Upper Egypt and Lower Egypt, were combined into one. *(page 43)*
- Egyptian society was divided into social groups based on wealth and power. *(page 45)*

Section 2 Egypt's Old Kingdom

Vocabulary
pharaoh
deity
embalming
mummy
pyramid

Focusing on the Main Ideas
- Egypt was ruled by all-powerful pharaohs. *(page 48)*
- The Egyptians believed in many gods and goddesses and in life after death for the pharaohs. *(page 49)*
- The Egyptians of the Old Kingdom built huge stone pyramids as tombs for their pharaohs. *(page 50)*

Section 3 The Egyptian Empire

Vocabulary
tribute
incense

Focusing on the Main Ideas
- The Middle Kingdom was a golden age of peace, prosperity, and advances in the arts and architecture. *(page 60)*
- During the New Kingdom, Egypt acquired new territory and reached the height of its power. *(page 61)*
- Akhenaton tried to change Egypt's religion, while Tutankhamen is famous for the treasures found in his tomb. *(page 64)*
- Under Ramses II, Egypt regained territory and built great temples, but the empire fell by 1150 B.C. *(page 65)*

▲ Tutankhamen's gold mask

Section 4 The Civilization of Kush

Vocabulary
savanna

Focusing on the Main Ideas
- To the south of Egypt, the Nubians settled in farming villages and became strong warriors. *(page 69)*
- The people of Kush devoted themselves to ironworking and grew wealthy from trade. *(page 70)*

73

CHAPTER 2 REVIEW

PREVIEW/REVIEW

Vocabulary Activity Have students write incomplete sentences in which they omit the definition of each vocabulary term. Tell students to exchange sentences and devise definitions based on context clues.

⊙ **Vocabulary PuzzleMaker CD-ROM**

⊙ **Interactive Tutor Self-Assessment CD-ROM**

CONDENSE

☞ Chapter 2 **Guided Reading Activities**

⊚ **StudentWorks Plus™ CD-ROM (with Audio Program)**

RETEACH

☞ **Differentiated Instruction Activity 2**

☞ Chapter 2 *Reading Essentials and Study Guide*

CHAPTER CULMINATING ACTIVITY

Have students finish the Chapter Culminating Activity from page 34D.

Suggestions for rubrics may be found in the *Quizzes, Tests, and Authentic Assessment (with Rubrics)* booklet.

Reading Strategy ▸ READ TO WRITE

Taking Notes Tell students to design a chart with these two heads—Column 1: "Ways Geography Shaped Egypt," and Column 2: "Ways Egyptians Shaped Geography." Have them record examples that fit under each head. Use the following rubric for assessment.

- **L1** students should have at least two examples in Column 1 and at least one example in Column 2.
- **L2** students should include several examples in each column and exhibit an understanding of how humans interact with the environment.
- **L3** students should think beyond the written text, drawing examples and inferences from information presented in maps and photographs.

Chapter 2 Assessment and Activities

GLENCOE TECHNOLOGY

MindJogger Videoquiz

Use the **MindJogger Videoquiz** to review Chapter 2 content.

  Available in DVD and VHS

Review Vocabulary

1. c	**5.** e
2. f	**6.** g
3. d	**7.** b
4. a	

Review Main Ideas

8. deserts, cataracts in the Nile, delta marshes

9. wealth and power

10. They believed in many gods and goddesses and in an afterlife.

11. in large tombs, often in pyramids

12. It was a time of prosperity, the empire was strong, and advances were made in the arts and architecture.

13. Akhenaton tried to change Egypt's religion. Tutankhamen's tomb was found with many treasures.

14. on the Nile in present-day Sudan

15. Trade and iron gave them superior weapons and better farming tools.

Critical Thinking

16. top: pharaoh and royal family; upper class: priests, army commanders, and nobles; middle class: traders, artisans, shopkeepers, and other skilled workers; lower class: unskilled workers and farmers

Review Vocabulary

Match the definitions in the second column to the terms in the first column. Write the letter of each definition.

___	1. savanna	**a.**	area of fertile soil at the end of a river
___	2. tribute	**b.**	reed plant used to make baskets, rafts, and paper
___	3. cataract	**c.**	grassy plain
___	4. delta	**d.**	rapids
___	5. hieroglyphics	**e.**	Egyptian writing system
___	6. pharaoh	**f.**	forced payments
___	7. papyrus	**g.**	title for Egyptian leaders

Review Main Ideas

Section 1 • The Nile Valley

8. What natural barriers protected Egypt from invasion?

9. What factors divided Egyptians into social groups?

Section 2 • Egypt's Old Kingdom

10. What were the Egyptians' religious beliefs?

11. Where did Egyptians of the Old Kingdom bury their pharaohs?

Section 3 • The Egyptian Empire

12. Why was the Middle Kingdom called a golden age?

13. Why are Akhenaton and Tutankhamen well-known?

Section 4 • The Civilization of Kush

14. Where did the Nubians live?

15. What made the Kushites wealthy?

Critical Thinking

16. **Describe** Identify the four social groups in ancient Egypt, and explain who belonged to each group.

17. **Synthesize** How do you think religious leaders reacted to Akhenaton's changes?

18. **Analyze** Do you agree that Egyptian civilization can be called "the Gift of the Nile"? Explain.

19. **Compare** In what ways did Meroë look like an Egyptian city?

Review Reading Skill Predicting — What Do You Predict?

Read these sentences from page 72.

As Kush declined, another kingdom rose to take its place. The kingdom is called Axum and was located in what is today the country of Ethiopia. Around A.D. 350, the armies of Axum burned Meroë to the ground. You will read more about the kingdom of Axum when you study Africa.

20. Based on what you know about the location of Ethiopia and the culture of Kush and Egypt, predict what the kingdom of Axum might be like. Check your predictions when you read about medieval Africa.

To review this skill, see pages 36–37.

74 CHAPTER 2 Ancient Egypt

17. probably resisted because of a loss of power and challenge to belief systems

18. Answers will vary, but most students will note how much Egyptians relied on the Nile.

19. Meroë had small pyramids, a huge temple at the end of a grand avenue lined with sculpture, and decorated walls.

Reading Skill

20. Answers will vary. Students may suggest that Axum borrowed from Egypt and Kush, that villages and towns were similar to Kush, and that trade and iron-working were important.

Geography Skills

Study the map below and answer the following questions.

21. **Location** The Nile River delta empties into what body of water?
22. **Movement** Why would ancient Egyptians find it easier to travel north and south than to travel east and west?
23. **Human/Environment Interaction** Why is most farming in ancient Egypt and in present-day Egypt done along the Nile?

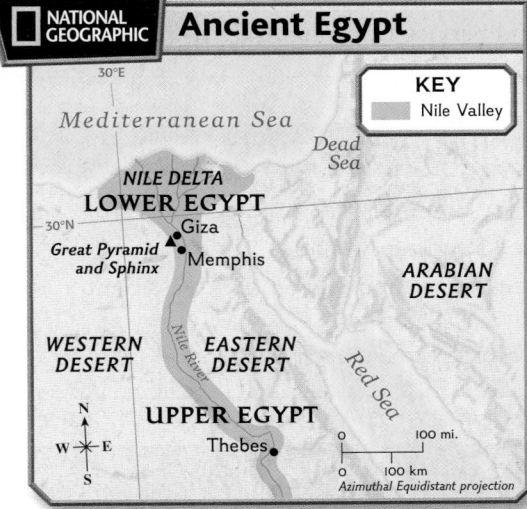

NATIONAL GEOGRAPHIC **Ancient Egypt**

KEY
Nile Valley

Mediterranean Sea

Dead Sea

30°E

NILE DELTA
LOWER EGYPT
30°N
Giza
Great Pyramid and Sphinx Memphis

ARABIAN DESERT

WESTERN DESERT **EASTERN DESERT**

Nile River

Red Sea

UPPER EGYPT
Thebes

0   100 mi.
0   100 km
Azimuthal Equidistant projection

N S W E

Read to Write

24. **Descriptive Writing** Imagine you are an ancient Egyptian pharaoh. You are making plans that your followers will carry out after your death. Describe the types of items you want buried with you in your pyramid. Then explain what people from later centuries will know about you if they find those items.

25. **Using Your** Use your foldable to describe one of the civilizations from the chapter, including such things as religious life, family life, and contributions. A classmate should identify which civilization you are describing. Then your classmate will describe a civilization, and you will identify it. When you are finished, discuss similarities and differences among the civilizations.

History Online

Self-Check Quiz To help prepare for the Chapter Test, visit jat.glencoe.com

Using Technology

26. **Developing Multimedia Presentations** Use the Internet and your local library to find out more about the reign of one of the Egyptian pharaohs. Create a computer slide show presentation that includes details about the pharaoh's reign and life. Include an illustrated time line of significant events.

Linking Past and Present

27. **Organizing Information** Use the Internet and atlases to locate present-day countries that rely heavily on a major river. Make a chart listing the country, the river, the river's length and average depth, and how the people of that country use the river.

Primary Source Analyze

The Greek historian Herodotus noticed that the Nile was different from other rivers.

"The Nile, when it floods, spreads over not only the Delta but parts of what are called Libya and Arabia for two days' journey in either direction, more or less. . . . This that I have mentioned was the subject of my persistent asking why, and also why it is that it is the only river that has no breezes blowing from it."

—Herodotus, *The History*, 2.19

DBQ Document-Based Questions

28. According to Herodotus, how much land does the Nile cover when it floods?
29. What two questions does Herodotus ask about the Nile?

CHAPTER 2   Ancient Egypt   75

CHAPTER 2
ASSESSMENT AND ACTIVITIES

History Online

Have students visit the Web site at jat.glencoe.com to review Chapter 2 and take the **Self-Check Quiz.**

Using Technology

26. Presentations will vary. Students should include significant details about the pharaoh and a detailed time line.

Linking Past and Present

27. Answers will vary but should include all requested details.

Primary Source

28. spreads over the delta and parts of Libya and Arabia for two days' journey in either direction
29. Why does the Nile flood for two days' journey in either direction? Why does it not have breezes blowing from it?

Bonus Question

Ask: Under which of the rulers of Egypt would you have most liked to have lived? Why? *(Answers will vary, but students should cite examples of activities or policies that influenced their choice.)*

Geography Skills

21. Mediterranean Sea
22. The Nile provided easy north/south travel by boat. Deserts lay east and west.
23. The Nile enriches and waters the soil while the rest of the area is desert.

Read to Write

24. Descriptions and explanations should be based on the examples in the text.
25. **FOLDABLES** Students' foldables should have enough data for students to recognize one another's descriptions.

Chapter ③ Resources

Note: The following materials may be used when teaching Chapter 3.
Section level support materials are shown at point of use in the margins of the Teacher Wraparound Edition.

TEACHING TRANSPARENCIES

- Graphic Organizer Transparencies with Teaching Strategy and Student Activity **L2**
- Cause-and-Effect Transparencies with Teaching Strategy and Student Activity **L2**
- Then and Now Transparencies with Teaching Strategy and Student Activity **L2**
- In-text Map Transparency with Teaching Strategy and Student Activity **L1**
- Map Transparencies with Overlay, Teaching Strategy, and Student Activity **L2**

DIFFERENTIATED INSTRUCTION

- Differentiated Instruction Activity 3
- Time Line Activity 3
- Primary Source Reading 3 (with Document-Based Questions)
- Inclusion Strategies for the Middle School Social Studies Classroom
- StudentWorks Plus™ CD-ROM (with Audio Program)

READING SUPPORT

- Take-Home Review Activity 3 **L2**
- World Literature Reading 3 **L2**
- Workbook Activity 3 **L1**
- Reading Strategies for the Social Studies Classroom **L1/ EL**

ASSESSMENT

- Authentic Assessment Activity 3 **L1/ EL**
- Chapter 3 Test Form A **L2**
- Chapter 3 Test Form B **L2**
- ExamView® Pro Testmaker CD-ROM

INTERDISCIPLINARY CONNECTIONS

- Geography and History Activity 3 **L2**
- People to Meet Activity 3 **L2**
- Economics Activity 3 **L2**
- Citizenship and Service Learning Activity 3 **L2**

SPANISH RESOURCES

- Spanish Reading Essentials and Study Guide
- Spanish Guided Reading Activities
- Spanish Quizzes, Tests, and Authentic Assessment (with Rubrics)
- Spanish Take-Home Review Activities

MULTIMEDIA

- ExamView® Pro Testmaker CD-ROM
- Glencoe Skillbuilder Interactive Workbook CD-ROM, Level 1
- Interactive Tutor Self-Assessment CD-ROM
- MindJogger Videoquiz
- Presentation Plus! CD-ROM
- StudentWorks Plus™ CD-ROM (with Audio Program)
- TeacherWorks CD-ROM
- Vocabulary PuzzleMaker CD-ROM
- *World History: Journey Across Time* Video Program
- World History Primary Source Document Library CD-ROM

STANDARDIZED ASSESSMENT SKILLS

- Standardized Test Skills Practice Workbook Activity 3 **L2**
- Critical Thinking Skills Activity 3 **L2**

Teaching strategies have been coded with suggested ability levels. However, most are suitable for all levels.

L1 BASIC activities for all students

L2 AVERAGE activities for average to above-average students

L3 CHALLENGING activities for above-average students

EL ENGLISH LANGUAGE activities

Chapter ③ Resources

TIME MANAGEMENT

Chapter Introduction	Section 1	Section 2	Section 3	Chapter Wrap-Up	Unit Wrap-Up
1 Day	1 Day	1 Day	2 Days	1 Day	1 Day

Block Scheduling Activities that are suited to use within the block scheduling framework are identified by: 📦

`0:00` **OUT OF TIME?** Assign the Chapter 3 *Reading Essentials and Study Guide.** 📁

SECTION RESOURCES

DAILY OBJECTIVES	REPRODUCIBLE RESOURCES	MULTIMEDIA RESOURCES
Section 1 **The First Israelites** 1. The Israelites believed in one God who set down moral laws for his people. They recorded their history in the Bible. 2. The Israelites had to fight the Canaanites to return to their promised land.	📁 Reproducible Lesson Plan 3–1 📁 Daily Lecture and Discussion Notes 3–1 📁 Vocabulary Activity 3–1 📁 Active Reading Note-Taking Guide 3–1 📁 Guided Reading Activity 3–1* 📁 Section Quiz 3–1* 📁 Reading Essentials and Study Guide 3–1*	🔦 Daily Focus Skills Transparency 3–1 💿 Interactive Tutor Self-Assessment CD-ROM 💿 Exam*View*® Pro Testmaker CD-ROM 💿 Presentation Plus! CD-ROM
Section 2 **The Kingdom of Israel** 1. King David built an Israelite empire and made Jerusalem his capital city. Solomon built a great temple in Jerusalem. 2. The Israelites were conquered and forced to leave their country.	📁 Reproducible Lesson Plan 3–2 📁 Daily Lecture and Discussion Notes 3–2 📁 Vocabulary Activity 3–2 📁 Active Reading Note-Taking Guide 3–2 📁 Guided Reading Activity 3–2* 📁 Section Quiz 3–2* 📁 Reading Essentials and Study Guide 3–2*	🔦 Daily Focus Skills Transparency 3–2 💿 Interactive Tutor Self-Assessment CD-ROM 💿 Exam*View*® Pro Testmaker CD-ROM 💿 Presentation Plus! CD-ROM 💿 Glencoe BookLink CD-ROM
Section 3 **The Growth of Judaism** 1. The Jews continued their religion during their exile in Babylon. 2. Jews spread their beliefs to the Greek world and regained control of Judah. 3. Under Roman rule, the Jews were divided and rebellious. In response, the Romans destroyed the temple and exiled the Jews.	📁 Reproducible Lesson Plan 3–3 📁 Daily Lecture and Discussion Notes 3–3 📁 Vocabulary Activity 3–3 📁 Active Reading Note-Taking Guide 3–3 📁 Guided Reading Activity 3–3* 📁 Section Quiz 3–3* 📁 Reading Essentials and Study Guide 3–3*	🔦 Daily Focus Skills Transparency 3–3 💿 Interactive Tutor Self-Assessment CD-ROM 💿 Exam*View*® Pro Testmaker CD-ROM 💿 Presentation Plus! CD-ROM 💿 Vocabulary PuzzleMaker CD-ROM 💿 Glencoe BookLink CD-ROM

*Also available in Spanish

History Online

Use our Web site for additional resources. All essential content is covered in the Student Edition.

You and your students can visit jat.glencoe.com, the Web site companion to *World History: Journey Across Time*. This innovative integration of electronic and print media offers your students a wealth of opportunities. The student text directs students to the Web site for the following options:

- Chapter Overviews
- Self-Check Quizzes
- Study Central™
- Student Web Activities
- Multi-Language Glossaries

Answers to the student Web activities are provided for you in the **Web Activity Lesson Plans.** Additional Web resources and ePuzzles and games are also available.

The following videotape programs are available from Glencoe as supplements to Chapter 3:

Israel: Birth of a Nation
(ISBN 0-7670-1107-4)

King David
(ISBN 1-56501-833-8)

To order, call Glencoe at 1-800-334-7344. To find classroom resources to accompany many of these videos, check the following home pages:

A&E Television: www.aande.com
The History Channel: www.historychannel.com

MEETING SPECIAL NEEDS

In addition to the Differentiated Instruction strategies, the following resources are suitable for students with special needs:

- *ExamView® Pro Testmaker CD-ROM* allows teachers to tailor tests by reducing answer choices.
- *StudentWorks Plus™ CD-ROM (with Audio Program)* includes the entire narrative of the student edition so that less-proficient readers can listen to the words as they read them.
- The *Reading Essentials and Study Guide* provides the same content as the student edition but is written two grade levels below the textbook.
- *Guided Reading Activities* give less-proficient readers point-by-point instructions to increase comprehension as they read each textbook section.

NATIONAL GEOGRAPHIC TEACHER'S CORNER

Index to National Geographic Magazine:
The following articles relate to this chapter:

- "Ashkelon: Ancient City of the Sea," by Rick Gore, January 2001.
- "Israel's Galilee: Living in the Shadow of Peace," by Don Belt, June 1995.
- "Satellite Revelations: New Views of the Holy Land," by Richard Cleave, June 1995.

National Geographic Society Products:
To order the following, call National Geographic at 1–800–368–2728

- *National Geographic Desk Reference* (Book).
- *National Geographic Atlas of the World* (Book).

NGS ONLINE

Access National Geographic's new dynamic MapMachine Web site and other geography resources at:

www.nationalgeographic.com
www.nationalgeographic.com/maps

Meeting NCSS Standards

World History: Journey Across Time
The following standards are highlighted in Chapter 3:

Section 1	I	Culture: D, G
	II	Time, Continuity, and Change: B
	V	Individuals, Groups, and Institutions: E
	X	Civic Ideals and Practices: A
Section 2	III	People, Places, and Environments: G
	VI	Power, Authority, and Governance: C, D, E
	IX	Global Connections: B
Section 3	IV	Individual Development and Identity: B, C
	V	Individuals, Groups, and Institutions: A, B, D, F
	X	Civic Ideals and Practices: A, E

State and Local Objectives

_____

_____

Timesaving Tools

TeacherWorks
All-In-One Planner and Resource Center

- **Interactive Teacher Edition** Access your Teacher Wraparound Edition and your classroom resources with a few easy clicks.
- **Interactive Lesson Planner** Organize your week, month, semester, or year with all the lesson helps you need to make teaching creative and relevant.

Use Glencoe's **Presentation Plus!** multimedia teacher tool to easily present dynamic lessons that visually excite your students. Using Microsoft PowerPoint® you can customize the presentations to create your own personalized lessons.

FOLDABLES™
Study Organizer
Dinah Zike's Foldables

Foldables are three-dimensional, interactive graphic organizers that help students practice basic writing skills, review key vocabulary terms, and identify main ideas. Every chapter contains a foldable activity, with additional chapter activities found in the *Reading and Study Skills Foldables* booklet. You can use the foldables as they are presented, or modify them to suit the needs of your individual class.

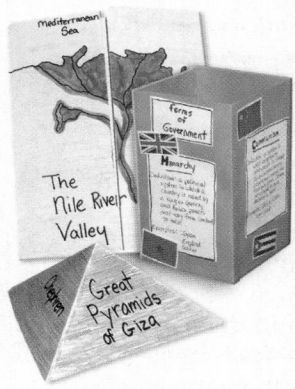

Planning Ahead

CHAPTER CULMINATING ACTIVITY

The Chapter Culminating Activity will help students organize and learn the important information from the chapter. Begin the chapter with this activity, and have students complete it as a culminating activity.

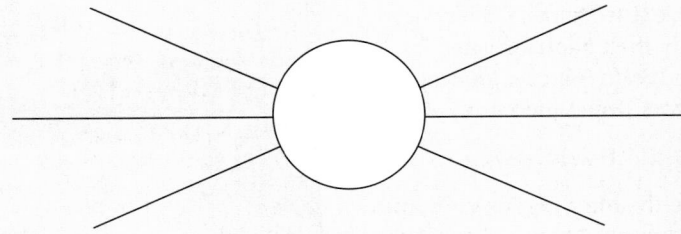

CREATING AN ATTRIBUTE GRAPHIC ORGANIZER

Purpose This type of graphic organizer helps students analyze and understand information by identifying important events, people, places, and ideas. Students can then use the organizer to collect and analyze details about the various topics. It can also be used to organize information for reports and as a study aid.

Introduction to Modeling

1. Begin the discussion with a brainstorming session. Ask students to list what they know or believe they know about the ancient Israelites. Write the information on an overhead transparency.

2. Ask students to copy this graphic organizer into their notebooks:

As students read the chapter, ask them to fill in the central circle with an important event, person, place, or idea connected with the ancient Israelites. Then have them read to find attributes and fill in the rays. For example, if students write "Moses" in the center, they might add as attributes such phrases as *found by pharaoh's daughter, heard God's voice in a burning bush, led the Israelites out of Egypt (the Exodus), received the Ten Commandments on Mount Sinai,* and *died before reaching Canaan.* Have them draw more graphic organizers as necessary.

3. As part of your chapter review, have students share their attribute graphic organizer. Encourage them to complete more organizers during this class wrap-up and use them as study aids.

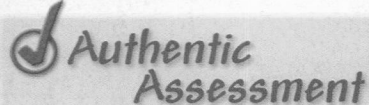

Authentic Assessment

Refer to Activity 3 in the Authentic Assessment section of the *Quizzes, Tests, and Authentic Assessment (with Rubrics)* booklet.

As students read the chapter, have them review the time line on this page. Ask them to make a list of important events related to the Israelites' struggle for unity that they might add to the time line. **L2**

GLENCOE TECHNOLOGY

World History: Journey Across Time Video Program

To learn more about the ancient Israelites, students can view the Chapter 3 video in the *World History: Journey Across Time* Video Program.

MindJogger Videoquiz

Use the **MindJogger Videoquiz** to preview Chapter 3 content.

Available in DVD and VHS

Chapter 3

The Ancient Israelites

The wall surrounding the ▼ old city of Jerusalem

NATIONAL GEOGRAPHIC When & Where?

2000 B.C.	1300 B.C.	600 B.C.	A.D. 100
c. 1800 B.C. Israelites settle in Canaan	c. 1290 B.C. Moses leads Israelites from Egypt	722 B.C. Assyrians conquer Israel	A.D. 66 Jews revolt against Romans

Reading Strategy | PURPOSE FOR READING

Predicting Making an informed guess about the content of what they are going to read is a good way for readers to interact with text. Students who make predictions use prior knowledge as well as information they get from previewing the chapter to create an expectation of what they will read. This expectation provides a purpose for reading and generates enthusiasm for reading the chapter. Have students write a paragraph predicting what Chapter 3 will be about. As you read the chapter, encourage them to revisit their predictions, adjusting them as they encounter new information in the text. **L2**

Chapter Preview

Like the Sumerians, the ancient Israelites developed a society based on ideas of justice and strict laws. The Israelites believed that there was only one God.

 View the Chapter 3 video in the *World History: Journey Across Time* **Video Program.**

 Chapter Overview Visit jat.glencoe.com for a preview of Chapter 3.

 ## The First Israelites

Abraham founded the 12 tribes of Israel in the land of Canaan. The Israelites believed in one God.

 ## The Kingdom of Israel

Under David and Solomon, the people of Israel built a powerful kingdom with a new capital in Jerusalem.

 ## The Growth of Judaism

The Jews continued to keep their religion even though other people ruled them. They settled in many places in Asia and Europe.

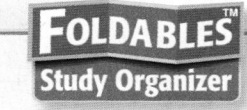

Summarizing Information *Make this foldable and use it to organize note cards with information about the Israelites.*

Step 1 *Fold a horizontal sheet of paper (11"x17") into thirds.*

Step 2 *Fold the bottom edge up two inches and crease well. Glue the outer edges of the tab to create three pockets.*

Glue here.

Glue here.

Step 3 *Label the pockets as shown. Use these pockets to hold notes taken on index cards or quarter sheets of paper.*

First Israelites | Israel's Kingdom | Judaism Spreads

Reading and Writing *As you read the chapter, summarize key facts on note cards or on quarter sheets of paper about Israel and the growth and spread of Judaism. Organize your notes by placing them in your pocket foldable inside the appropriate pockets.*

INTRODUCING CHAPTER 3

Introduce students to chapter content and key terms by having them access **Chapter Overview 3** at jat.glencoe.com

CHAPTER PREVIEW

After reading Chapter 3, students will be able to

1. describe the Israelites' beliefs and their early history;

2. discuss the history of the kingdom of Israel;

3. discuss Judaism during the period when Jews were ruled by other people.

FOLDABLES Study Organizer

Dinah Zike's Foldables

Purpose Students use this foldable to organize information about the development and growth of Israel and Judaism. As students read this chapter, they should make notes about events, people, and ideas that contributed to this development.

Have students complete **Reading and Study Skills Foldables** Activity 3.

77

MORE ABOUT THE PHOTO

Old City The old city is the historic center of the city of Jerusalem. The area is about 220 acres in size and is surrounded by a wall built by the Ottoman Turks around A.D. 1537. The wall is more than 30 feet tall and approximately $2\frac{1}{2}$ miles long. A number of gates allow entrance into the old city, but several ancient gates were sealed over the years. The Golden Gate was closed by the Muslims in the 1500s because, according to Jewish tradition, that is the gate the messiah will use to enter Jerusalem.

1 Learn It!

Often, students are unaware of what is important in a text and what are simply details that support an important concept. The sheer quantity of words in a textbook can be overwhelming, especially if students are unable to distinguish between what is necessary to remember and what is there for interest or informational purposes. Show students how to identify the main idea in a paragraph, section, or chapter as a way of helping them develop reading skills that are necessary for comprehension.

Explain to students that the section heading can often indicate a main idea. For example, in Section 3 under the heading "The Jewish Way of Life," it is clear that the main idea in this section will focus on the everyday life of Jews, with details provided on topics such as education, food, and clothing. Write *Jewish Life* in a box on the board and add connecting ovals that contain the words *Education, Food,* and *Clothing.* Have students copy the diagram and fill in supporting details on lines extending from the ovals. **L1**

Chapter 3 Reading Social Studies

Reading Skill — Main Idea

1 Learn It!

Finding the Main Idea

Main ideas are the most important ideas in a paragraph, section, or chapter. Supporting details are facts or examples that explain the main idea. Read the following paragraph from Section 1 and notice how the author explains the main idea. The main idea is identified for you. The supporting details are highlighted in color.

Main idea →

Through trade, the Phoenicians spread ideas and goods. One of their most important ideas was an alphabet, or a group of letters that stood for sounds. The letters could be used to spell out the words in their language.

—from page 85

← Supporting details

Reading Tip

Often, the first sentence in a paragraph will contain a main idea, and supporting details will come in following sentences. However, main ideas can also appear in the middle or at the end of a paragraph.

Reading Strategy — SCAFFOLDING

The instructional technique known as scaffolding can help students to read independently and comprehend more of what they read. Just as scaffolds are used to construct a building and are removed as the structure is able to support its own weight, students' learning can be scaffolded by teachers as they nudge students toward independence. At first, model finding the main idea and show students how the author supports it with supporting details. Then, ask students to find the main idea by themselves but provide guidance as they look for supporting details. As students become more comfortable with this skill, allow them to work in groups, pairs, or alone in targeting the main idea and identifying supporting details with no assistance from you. **L1**

2 Practice It!

Create a Graphic Organizer

Read the following paragraph. Draw a graphic organizer like the one shown below. Write the main ideas in a box and supporting details in circles around the box.

Read to Write

Choose one of the **Main Ideas** listed on page 93. Use it as a topic sentence, and add supporting details to create a full paragraph.

While in Babylon, small groups of Jews met on the Sabbath. This was their weekly day of worship and rest. The Jews would pray and discuss their religion and history. These meetings took place at synagogues, or Jewish houses of worship. The synagogue meetings gave the people hope.

—*from page 94*

▲ Menorah

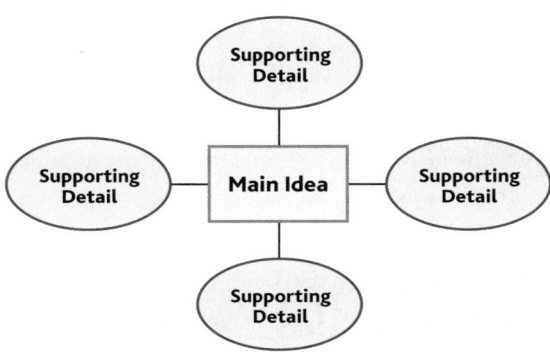

3 Apply It!

As you read Chapter 3, create your own graphic organizer to show the main idea and supporting details from at least one paragraph.

79

2 Practice It!

Categorizing For students who have trouble understanding the concept of main idea and supporting details, demonstrate how to categorize concepts while reading using column headings such as *Main Ideas, Supporting Details,* and *Minor Details.* Using colored highlighters on pages photocopied from the textbook may also aid students in distinguishing between what is most important and what is supporting information.

Have students working in groups read sections and create graphic organizers showing main ideas and supporting details. Have each group explain their organizers to the class and discuss which details are most important to the main idea. **L1**

3 Apply It!

Extending Using section headings as main ideas, have students find at least three supporting details by researching the topics online or in the library. Allow students, in pairs, to choose one main idea from the chapter. They can begin their search by finding supporting details from the text, and then provide other details they discover in their research. By having students provide supporting details to a main topic, they can more easily distinguish main ideas from supporting details. **L2**

Reading Strategy ▷ READ TO WRITE

To help students prepare for writing a paragraph with a main idea and supporting details, have them choose several of the blue subheadings from Section 2, such as "The Rule of King Saul." For each subheading, students should write a topic sentence, much like the **Main Idea** for the larger subsections. Then students should list anywhere from one to three supporting details for the subsection, depending upon its length. Have students work in pairs to compare and discuss their topic sentences and supporting details. Discuss as a class whether students believe they could write short paragraphs based on the work they have done. **L2**

① FOCUS

SECTION OVERVIEW

This section discusses the early history of the ancient Israelites, including their relationship with God, their escape from slavery, and their conflicts with the Canaanites over land.

BELLRINGER
SKILLBUILDER ACTIVITY

🖎 Project **Daily Focus Skills Transparency 3–1** and have students answer questions. Discuss their responses.

Get Ready to Read!

Preteaching Vocabulary: The term *monotheism* means "belief in one god." The two parts of the word are *mono,* meaning "one," and *theism,* meaning "belief in god."

Answers to Graphic: Abraham moves followers to Canaan from Mesopotamia; Israelites leave Canaan for Egypt; Israelites led by Moses escape Egypt and travel in Sinai; Joshua leads Israelites into Canaan; Israelites capture Jericho and central Canaan.

Section ① The First Israelites

Get Ready to Read!

What's the Connection?

You have read how the Egyptians built a great civilization. At about the same time, another nation was forming. The Egyptians called the people of this nation *habiru,* or foreigners. The people called themselves Israelites or the Children of Israel.

Focusing on the Main Ideas

- The Israelites believed in one God who set down moral laws for his people. They recorded their history in the Bible. *(page 81)*
- The Israelites had to fight the Canaanites to return to their promised land. *(page 84)*

Locating Places
Canaan (KAY•nuhn)
Mount Sinai (SY•NY)

Meeting People
Abraham
Jacob
Moses
Deborah
Phoenician (fih•NEE•shuhn)

Building Your Vocabulary
monotheism (MAH•nuh•thee•IH•zuhm)
tribe
Torah (TOHR•UH)
covenant (KUHV•nuhnt)
alphabet

Reading Strategy
Sequencing Information Create a sequence chart to help trace the movement of the Israelites.

NATIONAL GEOGRAPHIC When & Where?

• Jerusalem
• Memphis

1400 B.C.	1200 B.C.	1000 B.C.
c. 1290 B.C. Moses leads Israelites from Egypt	c. 1125 B.C. Deborah defeats Canaanites	c. 1000 B.C. Israelites settle in Canaan

80 CHAPTER 3 The Ancient Israelites

SECTION RESOURCES

📁 **Reproducible Masters**
- Reproducible Lesson Plan 3–1
- Daily Lecture and Discussion Notes 3–1
- Vocabulary Activity 3–1
- Active Reading Note-Taking Guide 3–1
- Guided Reading Activity 3–1
- Section Quiz 3–1
- Reading Essentials and Study Guide 3–1

🖎 **Transparencies**
- Daily Focus Skills Transparency 3–1

Multimedia
- Interactive Tutor Self-Assessment CD-ROM
- ExamView® Pro Testmaker CD-ROM
- Presentation Plus! CD-ROM

The Early Israelites

Main Idea The Israelites believed in one God who set down moral laws for his people. They recorded their history in the Bible.

Reading Focus Where do your ideas about right and wrong come from? Read on to find out how the Israelites developed their ideas about right and wrong.

About 1200 B.C., great changes took place around the Mediterranean Sea. Empires fell and new people entered the region. Many set up small kingdoms. Around 1000 B.C., a people called Israelites (IHZ•ruh•LYTS) built a kingdom in **Canaan** (KAY•nuhn). Canaan lies along the Mediterranean Sea in southwest Asia.

Who Were the Israelites?
Although the Israelite population was small, the religion they practiced would one day affect most of the world. Most people at this time worshiped many gods and goddesses. The Israelite religion focused on only one God. The belief in one god is called **monotheism** (MAH•nuh•thee•IH•zuhm).

The Israelite faith became the religion known today as Judaism (JOO•dee•IH•zuhm). The followers of Judaism were eventually known as Jews. Judaism influenced Christianity and Islam, and also helped shape the beliefs and practices of societies in Europe and America.

The Israelites spoke a language called Hebrew. They wrote down much of their history and many of their religious beliefs in what later became the Hebrew Bible. Through this book, Jewish values and religion later spread to Europe.

The earliest Israelites were herders and traders. According to the Bible, they came from Mesopotamia and settled in Canaan. Today, Lebanon, Israel, and Jordan occupy the land that was once Canaan.

▲ This painting shows Abraham leading the Israelites from Mesopotamia to Canaan. *Why did the Israelites eventually leave Canaan?*

The Israelites believed they were descended from a man named **Abraham.** In the Bible, it says that God told Abraham and his followers to leave Mesopotamia and go to Canaan. There, they were to worship the one true God. In return, God promised that the land of Canaan would belong to Abraham and his descendants. According to the Bible, this is the reason that the Israelites settled in Canaan.

Abraham had a grandson named **Jacob.** Jacob was also called Israel, which means "one who struggles with God." Later this name was given to Jacob's descendants.

According to the Bible, Jacob raised 12 sons in Canaan. His family was divided into **tribes,** or separate family groups. These groups later became known as the 12 tribes of Israel. The Israelites lived in Canaan for about 100 years. Then a long drought began. Crops withered and livestock died. To survive, the Israelites went to Egypt.

From Slavery to Freedom
Life was not good in Egypt. The Egyptian pharaoh needed men to build his pyramids, so he

CHAPTER 3   The Ancient Israelites   **81**

Reading Support L1/ EL

Use **Vocabulary Activity 3–1** to review important terms in the section.

More About the Art

Scholars disagree about where the Israelites might have crossed the Red Sea. Some believe the name for the Red Sea was incorrectly translated long ago, and the correct reference is to the "Sea of Reeds," a marshy, inland lake north of the Red Sea proper.

Caption Answer: the Exodus

HISTORY *Mystery*

How Do We Know About the Exodus?

Historians of the early Israelites and biblical scholars have painstakingly identified the three oldest surviving written sources for the story of the Hebrew Exodus from Egypt. Two of these written sources probably date from the 900s B.C., while the third is from the 500s B.C. All three are believed to retell much older, oral traditions. The biblical book of Exodus relates to all three.

Moses and the Ten Commandments

▲ In this painting, Moses watches as the Red Sea closes in on the Egyptian soldiers who were pursuing the Israelites. *What is the Israelites' escape from Egypt called?*

▲ Jews celebrating Passover today

enslaved the Israelites. To prevent a rebellion he ordered all baby boys born to Israelites thrown into the Nile River.

The Bible says that one desperate mother put her baby in a basket and hid it on the riverbank. The pharaoh's daughter found the baby and named him **Moses.**

When Moses grew up, he tended sheep outside Egypt. Around 1290 B.C., he saw a burning bush and heard a voice. He believed that God was telling him to lead the Israelites out of Egypt to freedom.

To get the pharaoh to let the Israelites go, the Bible says that God sent 10 plagues to trouble Egypt. A plague is sometimes a disease, but it can also mean something that causes problems for a lot of people. The last plague God sent killed all first-born children, except for those of Israelites who marked their doorway with lamb's blood. This plague convinced the pharaoh to let the Israelites leave. Jews today celebrate a holiday called Passover to remember

how God "passed over" their homes with the tenth plague and then delivered them from Egypt.

As Israelites headed east out of Egypt, the pharaoh changed his mind and sent his army after the Israelites. According to the Bible, God parted the Red Sea to let his people pass. When the Egyptians followed, the water flowed back and drowned the soldiers. The Israelite escape from Egypt is known as the Exodus.

What Are the Ten Commandments? On their way back to Canaan, the Israelites had to travel through the Sinai desert. The Bible says that during this journey, Moses went to the top of **Mount Sinai** (SY•NY). There, he received laws from God. These laws were known as the **Torah** (TOHR•uh). They later became the first part of the Hebrew Bible. The Torah described a **covenant** (KUHV•nuhnt), or agreement, with God. In the agreement, God promised to return the Israelites to Canaan if they followed his laws.

82   CHAPTER 3   The Ancient Israelites

DIFFERENTIATED INSTRUCTION

Auditory/Musical: Have students use a tape or video recorder to record questions that they would like to ask a rabbi about Judaism or the early history of the Israelites. If possible, arrange a class visit from a local rabbi. If a visit is not possible, investigate having a rabbi tape-record answers to the students' questions.

English Learners: Ask students to paraphrase the Ten Commandments in English or translate them into their native languages.

Gifted and Talented: Have students research and report to the class about the Haggadah, the book that contains the story of the Exodus and is read at the Seder, or traditional Passover meal.

☞ Refer to *Inclusion Strategies for the Middle School Social Studies Classroom* in the TCR.

▲ The Ark of the Covenant was a box, which, according to Jewish beliefs, held the Ten Commandments. *How did the Ten Commandments help shape the basic moral laws of many European nations?*

The Torah explained what God considered to be right and wrong. The most important part of the Torah is the Ten Commandments. They are summarized in the feature to the right. The Ten Commandments told the Israelites to be loyal only to God, whose name was never to be spoken. They must never worship any other gods or images. The belief that there should be only one god became the foundation for both Christianity and Islam.

The Ten Commandments helped shape the basic moral laws of many nations. The Ten Commandments told people not to steal, murder, or tell lies about others. They told people to avoid jealousy and to honor their parents. The Ten Commandments also helped develop a belief in the "rule of law." This is the idea that laws should apply to everyone equally.

✓ **Reading Check** **Explain** What covenant was described in the Torah?

Primary Source — The Ten Commandments

According to the Bible, Moses received the Ten Commandments and other laws from God on Mount Sinai. Moses and the Israelites promised to follow these laws.

1. Do not worship any god except me.
2. Do not . . . bow down and worship idols.
3. Do not misuse my name.
4. Remember that the Sabbath Day belongs to me.
5. Respect your father and your mother.
6. Do not murder.
7. Be faithful in marriage.
8. Do not steal.
9. Do not tell lies about others.
10. Do not want anything that belongs to someone else.

—Exodus 20:3-17

◀ Moses with the Ten Commandments

▲ Mount Sinai

DBQ Document-Based Questions

1. How many of the commandments tell people how to interact with other people?
2. How many tell them how to worship and show respect for God?

CHAPTER 3   The Ancient Israelites   83

CRITICAL THINKING ACTIVITY

Comparing and Contrasting Spirituals and other songs from the period when African Americans were enslaved in the United States often speak of "getting to the Promised Land." Ask students to discuss the meaning this expression might have had for enslaved Africans. Why was it particularly appropriate? How did their condition compare to that of the Israelites in Egypt? Conclude by reminding students that Harriet Tubman, one of the leaders of the Underground Railroad, was sometimes referred to as "Moses." Why was this name suitable for her? **L2** ▢

The Promised Land

Main Idea The Israelites had to fight the Canaanites to return to their promised land.

Reading Focus What qualities do you think a good leader should have? Read on to find out about the leaders of the Israelites.

It probably took the Israelites about 40 years to reach Canaan. Moses never lived to see the Promised Land. After Moses died, a leader named Joshua took over and brought the Israelites into Canaan. When they arrived, however, they found other people living there. Most were Canaanites (KAY•nuh•NYTS). The Israelites believed it was God's will that they conquer the Canaanites, so Joshua led them into battle.

The story of the campaign is told in the Bible. Joshua led the Israelites to the city of Jericho and told them to march around the city's walls. For six days, they marched while seven priests blew their trumpets. On the seventh day, the trumpets sounded one last time, and Joshua told the Israelites to raise a great shout. According to the story, the walls of Jericho crumbled, and the Israelites overran the city.

Joshua led the Israelites in three more wars. The land they seized was divided among the 12 tribes.

Who Were the Fighting Judges?
After Joshua died, the Israelites looked to judges for leadership. A judge was usually a military leader. Generally, he or she commanded 1 or 2 tribes, but seldom all 12. The Bible tells about Barak, Gideon, Samuel, Eli, Samson, and others, including a woman judge. Her name was **Deborah.**

Deborah told Barak to attack the army of the Canaanite king Jabin. She went along to the battlefield as an adviser. With Deborah's help, Barak and 10,000 Israelites destroyed King Jabin and his army in about 1125 B.C.

Over time, the Israelites won control of the hilly region in central Canaan. The Canaanites kept the flat, coastal areas. To protect themselves, the Israelites built walled towns. They also created an alphabet and a calendar based on Canaanite ideas.

The Phoenician Alphabet
One group of Canaanites, the **Phoenicians** (fih•NEE•shuhns), lived in cities along the Mediterranean

▲ According to the Bible story, the walls of Jericho came down as the trumpets of the Israelites sounded. *Who led the Israelites in their return to Canaan?*

▲ The town of Jericho today

84   CHAPTER 3   The Ancient Israelites

Sea. The Phoenicians were skilled sailors and traders. Their ships carried goods across the Mediterranean to Greece, Spain, and even western Africa.

Through trade, the Phoenicians spread ideas and goods. One of their most important ideas was an **alphabet,** or a group of letters that stood for sounds. The letters could be used to spell out the words in their language.

The alphabet made writing simpler and helped people keep records. The Phoenicians brought the idea of an alphabet to the Greeks. They, in turn, passed it on to the Romans. Most Western alphabets are based on the Roman alphabet.

✓ **Reading Check** **Identify** Who led the Israelites into Canaan, and what city did they conquer under his leadership?

Alphabets

Modern Characters	Ancient Phoenician	Ancient Hebrew	Ancient Greek	Early Roman
A	⼤ ⼤	⼤	◁ A A	⋔ ⋀ A
B	⼄ 9	⼄ 9	9 E	B B
G	�7 �3	⼍ ⼍	⟨ Γ ⼍	C C
D	⼤ ⼤	⼤ ⼤	⼤ ⟨ A	△ D
E	⼅	E	⼅ Ⅎ E	E
F	⼁	⼅	F F Ϛ	F
Z	Z		I	Z
TH	⊗		⊙	
I	⼍ ⼍	⼤	⼤ ⼤	I

▲ The Phoenician idea of an alphabet was passed on to the Greeks and then the Romans. It is the basis for the English alphabet today. *Which modern letter most closely resembles its Phoenician character?*

Study Central™ Need help with the material in this section? Visit jat.glencoe.com

Section 1 Review

Reading Summary
Review the Main Ideas

• Led by Abraham, the Israelites settled in Canaan. They later moved to Egypt and were enslaved, but then escaped. The Israelites used the Ten Commandments as rules to live by.

• Joshua and the judges, including Deborah, won back territory in central Canaan for the Israelites.

What Did You Learn?

1. Why was the religion of Israel unique in the ancient world?

2. What is the Torah, and how did the Israelites obtain it?

Critical Thinking

3. **Summarizing Information** Use a web diagram like the one below to list the parts of Jewish religion that are still important in our society.

Jewish Ideas

4. **Analyze** What was the importance of the Phoenician alphabet?

5. **Summarize** What problems did the Israelites face when they returned to Canaan?

6. **Expository Writing** Which one of the Ten Commandments do you think is most important today? Write a short essay to explain your selection.

7. **Reading** **Main Idea** Write a paragraph by adding supporting details to this main idea: The Phoenician alphabet had an impact on many civilizations.

CHAPTER 3   The Ancient Israelites   **85**

Caption Answer: the letter Z

ENRICH

Ask students to use their artistic skills to respond to one of the events described in this section. They may create a mural or a drawing, or a work of poetry, fiction, music, or dance. Have volunteers share their production with the class and explain its connection to the text. **L3**

✓ **Reading Check**

Answer: Joshua; Jericho

To help students understand section material, have them visit **Study Central**™ at jat.glencoe.com

RETEACH

Have students write a short paragraph about each of the following: Abraham, Jacob, and Moses. **L2**

④ CLOSE

Have students explain the most important contribution of the Israelites. **L2**

SECTION 1 REVIEW ANSWERS

1. Unlike most other religions, it had only one God.

2. The Torah is the collection of laws which God gave to Moses on top of Mount Sinai.

3. Possible answers: belief in one god; Ten Commandments; Hebrew Bible; belief that God gave Canaan to the Jews

4. It made writing simpler and helped in keeping records.

5. The Israelites had to fight a number of wars to get back part of the lands of Canaan from the Canaanites who lived there.

6. Answers will vary but should demonstrate a thoughtful response and a basic understanding of the commandments.

7. Answers will vary. Students should engage in a logical argument that draws on information in the text.

❶ FOCUS

SECTION OVERVIEW

This section focuses on the creation of the kingdom of Israel; its great kings Saul, David, and Solomon; and the challenges Israel faced.

BELLRINGER
SKILLBUILDER ACTIVITY

👆 Project **Daily Focus Skills Transparency 3–2** and have students answer questions. Discuss their responses.

Get Ready to Read!

Preteaching Vocabulary: A proverb is a short, wise saying. One book of the Hebrew Bible is made up entirely of proverbs.

Answers to Graphic: Israel—Location: northern Canaan; Capital City: Samaria; Date Conquered: 722 B.C.; Conquered By: Assyrians; Judah—Location: southern Canaan; Capital City: Jerusalem; Date Conquered: about 620 B.C.; Conquered By: Egyptians

Section 2
The Kingdom of Israel

Get Ready to Read!

What's the Connection?
In Section 1, you read about the constant fighting between the Israelites and the Canaanites. The tribes of Israel longed for peace. Many thought the way to peace was to unite as one nation.

Focusing on the Main Ideas
• The Israelites chose a king to unite them against their enemies. *(page 87)*
• King David built an Israelite empire and made Jerusalem his capital city. *(page 89)*
• The Israelites were conquered and forced to leave Israel and Judah. *(page 90)*

Locating Places
Jerusalem (juh•ROO•suh•luhm)
Judah (JOO•duh)

Meeting People
Philistine (FIH•luh•STEEN)
Saul (SAWL)
David
Solomon (SAHL•uh•muhn)
Nebuchadnezzar (NEH•byuh•kuhd•NEH•zuhr)

Building Your Vocabulary
prophet (PRAH•fuht)
empire (EHM•PYR)
tribute (TRIH•byoot)
proverb (PRAH•VUHRB)

Reading Strategy
Categorizing Information Complete a chart like the one below identifying characteristics of Israel and Judah.

Location		
Capital City		
Date Conquered		
Conquered By		

NATIONAL GEOGRAPHIC **When & Where?**

Samaria • Babylon •
Jerusalem •

1000 B.C. — **750 B.C.** — **500 B.C.**

● c. 1000 B.C. David becomes king

722 B.C. ● Assyrians conquer Israel

597 B.C. ● Nebuchadnezzar captures Jerusalem

SECTION RESOURCES

📁 **Reproducible Masters**
• Reproducible Lesson Plan 3–2
• Daily Lecture and Discussion Notes 3–2
• Vocabulary Activity 3–2
• Active Reading Note-Taking Guide 3–2
• Guided Reading Activity 3–2
• Section Quiz 3–2
• Reading Essentials and Study Guide 3–2

📖 **Transparencies**
• Daily Focus Skills Transparency 3–2

Multimedia
💿 Interactive Tutor Self-Assessment CD-ROM
💿 ExamView® Pro Testmaker CD-ROM
💿 Presentation Plus! CD-ROM
💿 Glencoe BookLink CD-ROM

The Israelites Choose a King

Main Idea The Israelites chose a king to unite them against their enemies.

Reading Focus What does "united we stand, divided we fall" mean to you? Read on to find out what it meant to the 12 tribes of Israel.

Around 1000 B.C., the strongest people living in Canaan were not the Israelites, but the **Philistines** (FIH•luh•STEENS). The Philistines had strong cities, and they knew how to make iron tools and weapons. Fearing the power of the Philistines, many Israelites copied their ways and worshiped their gods.

In the past, the 12 tribes often quarreled. If they were going to save their religion and way of life, they would have to learn how to work together. They needed a king to unite them against the Philistines.

History Online

Web Activity Visit jat.glencoe.com and click on *Chapter 3—Student Web Activity* to learn more about the ancient Israelites.

The Rule of King Saul In 1020 B.C. the Israelites asked Samuel to choose a king. Samuel was a judge and a **prophet** (PRAH•fuht). A prophet is a person who claims to be instructed by God to share God's words. Samuel warned that a king would tax the Israelites and make them slaves. The Israelites still demanded a king, so they chose a warrior-farmer named **Saul** (SAWL).

Samuel anointed Saul as king. In other words, he blessed him with oil to show that God had chosen him. Saul was tall and handsome and had won many battles.

Saul defeated the Israelites' enemies in battle after battle. However, according to the Bible, the king displeased God by disobeying some of his commands. God then chose another king and instructed Samuel to anoint him in secret. The new king was a young shepherd named **David.**

✓ **Reading Check** **Explain** Why did the Israelites want a king?

▼ According to the Bible, David had to be called in from the fields where he was tending his sheep when Samuel arrived to anoint him. *Why did God have Samuel anoint David?*

② TEACH

Daily Lecture and Discussion Notes 3–2

Use **Daily Lecture and Discussion Notes 3–2** for an outline of key concepts found in the section.

Reading Support L1/EL

Use **Vocabulary Activity 3–2** to review important terms in the section.

History Online

Objectives and answers to the student activity can be found in the **Web Activity Lesson Plan** feature at jat.glencoe.com

✓ **Reading Check**

Answer: to unite them against their enemies

Caption Answer: Saul disobeyed some of God's commands.

Reading Strategy **READING THE TEXT**

Connecting Students who connect what they read to personal experiences and beliefs, as well as to other selections they have read, often find it easier to construct meaning in text materials. Making connections between what they read and their own ideas, feelings, and experiences also helps increase the enjoyment of a selection. As students read this section, have them ask themselves such questions as:

• How would I feel if I were forced to leave my home, family, and friends?
• What difference can a good leader make to a team or group?
• What kinds of things do I feel proud about?

Encourage students to make notes, connecting what they read to their own experiences. L1

Biography

One of the reasons David chose Jerusalem as the capital of the new united kingdom was its central location. Neither the Israelites in the north nor the Judeans in the south would object.

Ask students how Jerusalem's central location and acceptance by both countries in David's time is similar to and different from its position today in the Middle East. *(The city is a major source of conflict, claimed by both Israelis and Palestinians.)* **L2**

Making Inferences Ask students why Psalm 23 might have had special meaning to David. *(He worked as a shepherd, and the imagery of the psalm is of a careful shepherd looking after his flock.)* **L2**

Then and Now

Possible answers include George Washington, Andrew Jackson, William Henry Harrison, Zachary Taylor, Ulysses S. Grant, Theodore Roosevelt, and Dwight D. Eisenhower.

Biography

DAVID
Reigned c. 1000–970 B.C.

▲ King David

The story of David's life is told in several books of the Old Testament, including Samuel I and II and Psalms. During his youth, David worked as an aide in King Saul's court. While at court, he formed a close friendship with the king's son, Jonathan. David fought courageously against the Philistines as a soldier in Saul's army. He also killed the Philistine giant, Goliath, with only a slingshot and stones. The first book of Samuel tells how David's harp playing pleased King Saul. But the king grew jealous of David's friendship with Jonathan and of David's growing popularity as a brave soldier.

To save his own life, David fled into the desert. During this time, David led a group of other outlaws. David and his band protected people from raiders and returned possessions that had been stolen. By the time David returned to Jerusalem, he was well-known throughout the land.

After the death of King Saul, David became the second king of Israel. David successfully united all the tribes of Israel. He then conquered Jerusalem and made it the kingdom's capital. During his reign, David built Israel into an empire and dominated neighboring kingdoms.

David was not only a brave warrior and successful leader, he was also a talented poet. Many of the hymns in the Old Testament's book of Psalms have been credited to David, including Psalm 23, which begins "The Lord is my shepherd, I shall not want; he makes me lie down in green pastures. He leads me beside still waters; he restores my soul. He leads me in paths of righteousness for his name's sake."

> "The sweet psalmist of Israel"
> —David, 2 Samuel 23:1

▲ David versus Goliath

Then and Now

In David's time, kings were expected to excel in battle. Conduct research to find at least three U.S. presidents who built their reputations in the military.

Reading List Generator CD-ROM

GLENCOE BOOKLINK   **RECOMMENDED READING**

Use the **Glencoe BookLink CD-ROM** to create customized reading lists based on your students' interests and reading levels. Below is an example based on content in this chapter. Also, see the Suggested Readings on pages 944–946 of the Appendix.

- Schwartz, Howard. *Next Year in Jerusalem: 3,000 Years of Jewish Stories.* Eleven folktales and legends set in the ancient holy city of Jerusalem.
- Thoennes, Kristin. *Israel.* Israel is a small country in the Middle East. It is the only country in the world where most people are Jewish. Find out what life at home is like in Israel.
- Waldman, Neil. *The Golden City: Jerusalem's 3,000 Years.* Discover the history of Jerusalem from the time of King David to the present day.

David and Solomon

Main Idea King David built an Israelite empire and made Jerusalem his capital city.

Reading Focus What person do you think was most important in the history of the United States? Read to learn why King David is so important to the history of the Jewish people.

David's fame as a warrior spread. The Bible shows his fame by telling this story. Just before a battle against the Philistines, a giant Philistine named Goliath called out in a loud voice. He dared any Israelite to fight him one-on-one. David stepped forward with his shepherd's staff, a slingshot, and five smooth stones.

"Am I a dog that you come against me with a staff?" Goliath roared. He rushed forward with a heavy spear, but David was too quick for him. He hurled one stone straight at the giant's forehead, and Goliath dropped dead on the spot.

Saul put David in charge of the army. As his victories grew, Israelite women sang his praises. "Saul has slain his thousands, and David his ten thousands." Saul grew envious and plotted to kill David.

David hid out in enemy territory until Saul and his three sons were killed in battle. The bitter rivalry was over. David was able to take the throne in about 1000 B.C.

Once in power, David drove the Philistines from the area. He conquered other neighboring nations and created an **empire** (EHM•PYR). An empire is a nation that rules several other nations. Conquered peoples in the area had to pay David and the Israelites **tribute** (TRIH•byoot). Tribute is money or slaves given to a stronger ruler.

David made the Israelites pay heavy taxes. He needed money to expand his new capital of **Jerusalem** (juh•ROO•suh•luhm). He wanted a fine temple there so that

Primary Source
Proverbs

Solomon's proverbs are recorded in the Bible. Read these three, then answer the question.

"What you gain by doing evil won't help you at all, but being good can save you from death.

At harvest season it's smart to work hard, but [unwise] to sleep.

You will be safe, if you always do right, but you will get caught, if you are dishonest."

—Proverbs 10: 2, 5, 9

▲ King Solomon

DBQ Document-Based Question
How would the third proverb above convince people to tell the truth?

sacred religious objects cherished by the Israelites would finally have a permanent home. David died before he built the temple, but for centuries, the Israelites remembered him as their greatest king.

The Rule of King Solomon When David died, his son **Solomon** (SAHL•uh•muhn) became king. It was Solomon who built a splendid stone temple in Jerusalem. It became the symbol and center of the Jewish religion.

In the Bible, Solomon was known for his wise sayings, or **proverbs** (PRAH•VUHRBS), but many Israelites hated his rule. Solomon taxed the people to pay for his great buildings.

CHAPTER 3   The Ancient Israelites   **89**

Primary Source

While the proverbs in the Bible are among the best known, they are not the only proverbs. Such short sayings exist in almost every time, culture, and tradition. Probably the most famous American examples are found in Benjamin Franklin's collection, *Poor Richard's Almanack*. Franklin used many proverbs from other cultures, placing them in an American context.

Answer:
It says that anyone who is dishonest will be caught.

☞ See the **Primary Source Readings (with Document-Based Questions)** in the Unit Resource Books.

Writing Activity

Read some of the proverbs in the Bible to students to give them a sense of how they sound and their purpose. Ask students to write some proverbs of their own and share these with the class. Provide additional examples to help them if necessary. **L2**

DIFFERENTIATED INSTRUCTION

Verbal/Linguistic: Have students write a newspaper article describing the battle between David and Goliath. Students may wish to refer to other sources to add more details to the story. Their articles should also describe why the results of the battle help qualify David for the leadership of Israel.

English Learners: Have students draw a poster that shows support for David as the king of Israel, perhaps by showing the story of David and Goliath.

Gifted and Talented: Ask students to use their imagination to update the story of David and Goliath by using present-day examples.

☞ Refer to *Inclusion Strategies for the Middle School Social Studies Classroom* in the TCR.

CONNECTING ACROSS TIME

One reason Israelites became unhappy with Solomon's rule was high taxes. Ask students to list positive and negative aspects of paying taxes. L1/EL

 Reading Check

Answer: to pay for his great buildings

More About the Art

Jews revere the only remaining part of the second temple, which replaced Solomon's temple and was destroyed in A.D. 70. This structure is known as the Wailing Wall.

Caption Answer: They disliked the high taxes and being forced to work in the mines.

Using Geography Skills

Answers:

1. Judah
2. Israel

Skills Practice

Ask: About how many miles was the kingdom of Judah from east to west at its widest? *(about 70 miles)*

The Israelites in the north were especially unhappy with Solomon. To get more money, Solomon had made many of their young men work in the mines of a neighboring country.

When Solomon died, the northerners rebelled and fighting broke out. Ten of the 12 tribes set up their own nation in the north. It was called the kingdom of Israel, and its capital was Samaria. In the south, the other two tribes founded the smaller kingdom of **Judah** (JOO•duh). Its capital was Jerusalem, and its people were called Jews.

✓ **Reading Check** **Explain** Why did Solomon tax the people so heavily?

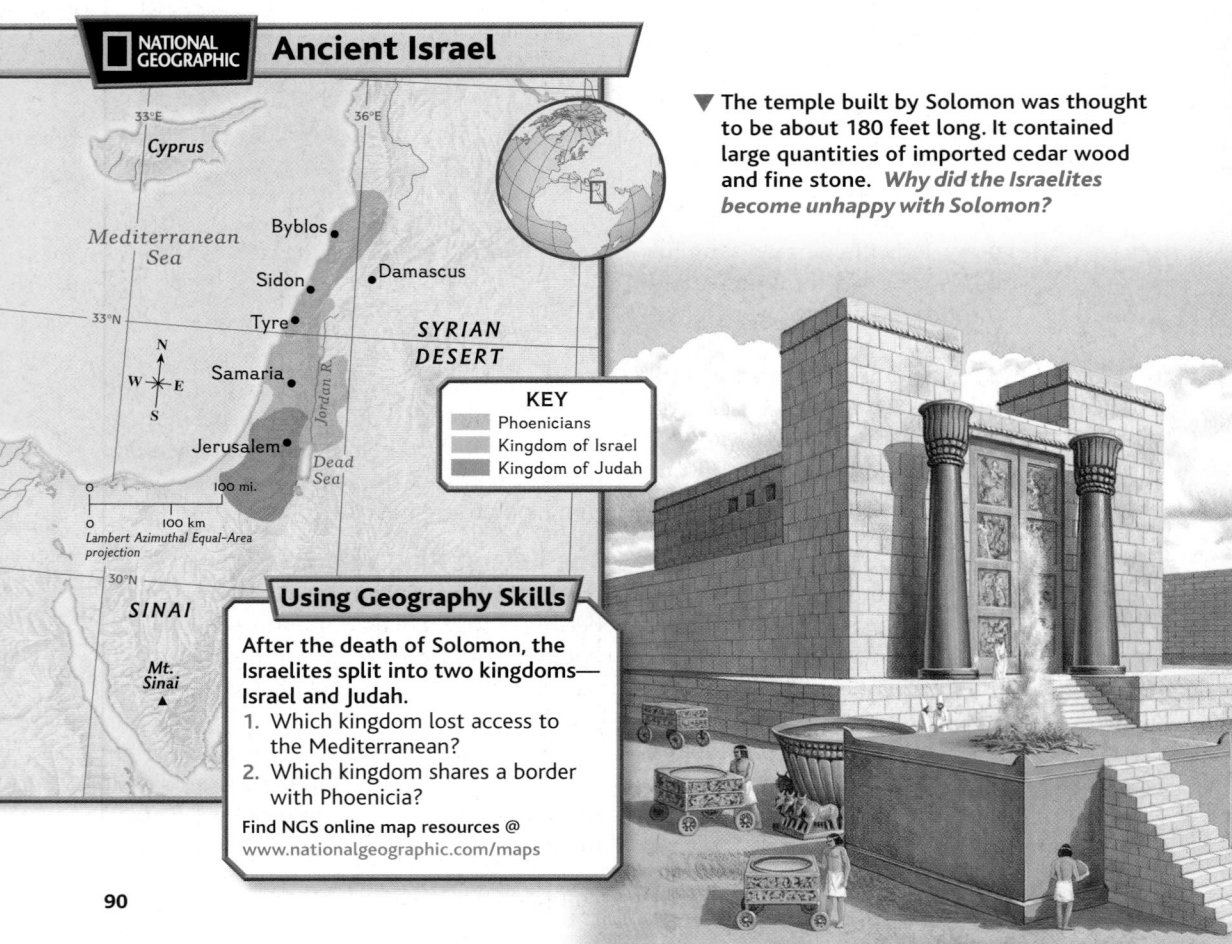

NATIONAL GEOGRAPHIC **Ancient Israel**

KEY
- Phoenicians
- Kingdom of Israel
- Kingdom of Judah

Using Geography Skills

After the death of Solomon, the Israelites split into two kingdoms—Israel and Judah.
1. Which kingdom lost access to the Mediterranean?
2. Which kingdom shares a border with Phoenicia?

Find NGS online map resources @ www.nationalgeographic.com/maps

90

A Troubled Time

Main Idea The Israelites were conquered and forced to leave Israel and Judah.

Reading Focus Have you ever moved and left a home you loved? Read to find out why many Israelites were forced to leave their home.

While the Israelites were dividing their kingdom, the Assyrians and Chaldeans (kal•DEE•uhns) were building empires in southwest Asia. These peoples wanted to control the trade routes that ran through the Israelite kingdoms. Small and weak, the kingdoms of Israel and Judah felt threatened by their powerful neighbors.

▼ The temple built by Solomon was thought to be about 180 feet long. It contained large quantities of imported cedar wood and fine stone. *Why did the Israelites become unhappy with Solomon?*

CRITICAL THINKING ACTIVITY

Synthesizing Information Many of the customs and beliefs people have today have been passed down from earlier civilizations. For example, Judaism, which is based on the concept of monotheism, influenced both Christianity and Islam. Ask students to summarize the historical origins and central ideas of Judaism. Then ask students to research and summarize the spread of Judaism from its beginning through modern times. Also have students identify examples of the ways in which Judaism has influenced the historic and contemporary world. L3

Major Hebrew Prophets

Name	Time Period	Teachings
Elijah	874–840 B.C.	Only God should be worshiped—not idols or false gods.
Amos	780–740 B.C.	The kingdom of King David will be restored and will prosper.
Hosea	750–722 B.C.	God is loving and forgiving.
Isaiah	738–700 B.C.	God wants us to help others and promote justice.
Micah	735–700 B.C.	Both rich and poor have to do what is right and follow God.
Jeremiah	626–586 B.C.	God is just and kind—he rewards as well as punishes.
Ezekiel	597–571 B.C.	Someone who has done wrong can choose to change.

Understanding Charts

The Israelites believed that God shared his word with them through a series of prophets.
1. Which prophet taught that both the rich and the poor needed to obey God's word?
2. **Compare** What do the teachings of Isaiah, Micah, and Ezekiel have in common?

Who Were the Prophets?

During this troubled time, many Israelites forgot their religion. The rich mistreated the poor, and government officials stole money.

The prophets wanted to bring Israelites back to God's laws. Their special message was that being faithful meant more than going to a temple to worship. It meant working for a just society. The prophet Amos said that justice should "roll down like waters and righteousness as a mighty stream." The goal of a just society became an important part of Christianity and Islam.

What Caused the Fall of Israel?

The warlike Assyrians were feared everywhere in the region. When they conquered a nation, the Assyrians destroyed its main buildings and scattered the population. Assyrians then settled in the territory.

In 722 B.C. the Assyrians conquered Israel and scattered the 10 tribes across their empire. Over time, the Israelites who were forced to move lost their religion and way of life. They are often called the "lost tribes of Israel."

The Assyrians settled the area around Samaria and became known as Samaritans. The Assyrian settlers were afraid that Israel's God might punish them for taking the Israelites' land, so they offered sacrifices to Israel's God. They also read the Torah and followed the Israelites' religious laws. After many years, the Samaritans worshiped only the God of Israel.

The people of Judah looked down on the Samaritans. They believed that God accepted only the sacrifices from the temple

Reading Support L1/ EL

Assign **Guided Reading Activity 3–2** to help students organize the information in the section.

Understanding Charts

Answers:
1. Micah
2. All three concern people's behavior.

③ ASSESS

Assign Section 2 Review as homework or as an in-class activity.

⊕ Have students use the **Interactive Tutor Self-Assessment CD-ROM** to review the section.

Assessment L2

Assign **Section 2 Quiz** to assess mastery of the material found in the section.

Reading Support L1/ EL

Assign **Reading Essentials and Study Guide 3–2** to help students review section material.

INTERDISCIPLINARY CONNECTIONS ACTIVITY

Music Ask students to research the use of biblical imagery in African American spirituals. Suggest that they consult the school or community library, the Internet, or local church leaders for information. Have students put together a presentation with musical examples for the class. L3 📖

📂 Refer to **Quizzes, Tests, and Authentic Assessment (with Rubrics)** booklet for rubrics.

Have students create a chart with headings to help them group and compare the teachings of the major Hebrew prophets. **L2**

Answer: They wanted to control the trade routes that ran through the Israelite kingdoms.

To help students understand section material, have them visit **Study Central™** at jat.glencoe.com

RETEACH

Ask students to work in pairs to outline the life and accomplishments of one of the important figures discussed in this section. **L1**

4 CLOSE

Ask students to brainstorm how the events described in this section have influenced our lives today. **L2**

---

at Jerusalem. They did not believe that other people were God's people too.

Why Did Judah Fall? Now, only the small kingdom of Judah was left of the once proud empire of David. It did not last long, because the Egyptians conquered it about 620 B.C. The Jews were able to keep their king but paid tribute to Egypt.

However, Egyptian rule was cut short when the Chaldeans conquered Egypt in 605 B.C. The Chaldeans became the new rulers of Judah. At first, the Chaldeans treated the Israelites like the Egyptians had before. They allowed the Jews to keep their king as long as they paid tribute.

Several years later, the Jews united with the Egyptians to rebel against the Chaldeans. Judah held out against the Chaldean invasion until 597 B.C. That year, King Nebuchadnezzar (NEH•byuh•kuhd•NEH•zuhr) of the Chaldeans captured Jerusalem. He punished the Jews severely. He made 10,000 Jews leave the city and live in Babylon, the Chaldean capital. Then he appointed a new Jewish king.

Soon the new king of Judah was planning a revolt against the Chaldeans. A prophet named Jeremiah warned him that another revolt was dangerous, but the king did not listen. In 586 B.C. he revolted. This time, the Chaldean ruler crushed Jerusalem. He destroyed the temple, bound the king in chains, and took him and thousands of Jews to Babylon. In Jewish history, this time became known as the Babylonian Captivity.

✓ **Reading Check** **Explain** Why did the Assyrians and Chaldeans want to control the land belonging to the Israelites?

Section 2 Review

History Online
Study Central™ Need help with the material in this section? Visit jat.glencoe.com

Reading Summary
Review the Main Ideas
- Saul was the first king of the Israelites. He united the 12 tribes into one kingdom.

- King David built an Israelite empire and made Jerusalem his capital. Solomon built a great temple at Jerusalem, but after he died, the Israelites split into two kingdoms—Israel and Judah.

- The Assyrians and then the Chaldeans conquered Israel and Judah, and forced many Israelites to leave their homeland.

What Did You Learn?
1. Why was David anointed king while Saul was still in charge of the Israelites?

2. Who were the prophets, and why were they important to the Israelites?

Critical Thinking
3. **Compare** Draw a chart like the one below. Use it to compare the accomplishments of King David and King Solomon.

King David	King Solomon

4. **Summarize** What happened to the Israelites after the death of Solomon?

5. **Describe** Who were the Samaritans, and what did the people of Judah think of them?

6. **Infer** Why do you think the Assyrians, and later the Chaldeans, moved Jews away from Israel and Judah after those areas were conquered?

7. **Reading** **Main Idea** Choose one paragraph from the Biography on page 88. Create a graphic organizer to show the main idea and supporting details in that paragraph.

SECTION 2 REVIEW ANSWERS

1. Saul displeased God by disobeying some of God's commands, so God chose another king.

2. messengers who claimed to be instructed by God and who taught the Israelites how to live properly

3. King David—drove the Philistines from Israel and created an empire, built Jerusalem; King Solomon—built a temple in Jerusalem, known for his proverbs

4. Fighting broke out among the Israelites, and they formed two separate kingdoms.

5. Assyrian settlers who settled around Samaria; the people of Judah looked down on them

6. to decrease the chance of revolt

7. Answers will vary.

Section 3

The Growth of Judaism

Get Ready to Read!

What's the Connection?
In Section 2, you learned that the Chaldeans forced thousands of Jews to go to Babylon. Life in Babylon was very difficult. Many of Judah's people looked to their religion for hope and strength.

Focusing on the Main Ideas
- The Jews continued their religion during their exile in Babylon. **(page 94)**
- Jews spread their beliefs to the Greek world and regained control of Judah. **(page 95)**
- Religion shaped the Jewish way of life. **(page 97)**
- Under Roman rule, the Jews were divided and rebellious. In response, the Romans destroyed the temple and exiled the Jews. **(page 100)**

Locating Places
Babylon (BA•buh•luhn)

Meeting People
Judas Maccabeus
  (JOO•duhs   MAK•uh•BEE•uhs)
Herod (HEHR•uhd)
Zealot (ZEH•luht)
Johanan ben Zakkai
  (YOH•kah•nahn   behn•zah•KY)

Building Your Vocabulary
exile (EHG•ZYL)
Sabbath (SA•buhth)
synagogue (SIH•nuh•GAHG)
Diaspora (dy•AS•pruh)
messiah (muh•SY•uh)
rabbi (RA•BY)

Reading Strategy
Summarizing Information Use a diagram like the one below to describe the Maccabees.

Maccabees

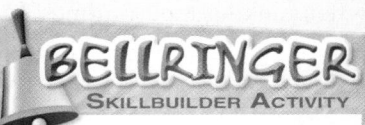

① FOCUS

SECTION OVERVIEW
This section focuses on the growth of Judaism, including the challenges it overcame and the setbacks it suffered.

BELLRINGER
SKILLBUILDER ACTIVITY

✎ Project **Daily Focus Skills Transparency 3–3** and have students answer questions. Discuss their responses.

Get Ready to Read!

Preteaching Vocabulary: The word *rabbi* comes from two Hebrew words meaning "my master." It is used for the leader of a synagogue, or Jewish temple.

Answers to Graphic: led by Judas Maccabeus; formed an army in the hills of Judah to rebel against the Greeks; drove the Greeks out of Judah and cleansed the temple, giving rise to Hanukkah; priests from Judas Maccabeus's family became the new rulers of Judah; reclaimed land that had once been part of Israel

NATIONAL GEOGRAPHIC When & Where?

	600 B.C.	250 B.C.	A.D. 100
	538 B.C. Cyrus allows Jews to return to Judah	**168 B.C.** Judas Maccabeus rebels against Antiochus	**A.D. 66** Jews revolt against Romans

Babylon
Jerusalem

CHAPTER 3   The Ancient Israelites   **93**

SECTION RESOURCES

📁 **Reproducible Masters**
- Reproducible Lesson Plan 3–3
- Daily Lecture and Discussion Notes 3–3
- Vocabulary Activity 3–3
- Active Reading Note-Taking Guide 3–3
- Guided Reading Activity 3–3
- Section Quiz 3–3
- Reading Essentials and Study Guide 3–3

📊 **Transparencies**
- Daily Focus Skills Transparency 3–3

Multimedia
- Interactive Tutor Self-Assessment CD-ROM
- Exam*View*® Pro Testmaker CD-ROM
- Presentation Plus! CD-ROM
- Vocabulary PuzzleMaker CD-ROM
- Glencoe BookLink CD-ROM

② TEACH

Reading Strategy

Outlining Ask students to outline the subsection "The Jewish Way of Life." Remind them to use the headings as guides when making their outlines. **L1**

Daily Lecture and Discussion Notes 3–3

Use **Daily Lecture and Discussion Notes 3–3** for an outline of key concepts found in the section.

Reading Support L1/ EL

Use **Vocabulary Activity 3–3** to review important terms in the section.

More About the Photo

According to Jewish law, the text of the Torah may not be decorated or illustrated. To show reverence to the Torah, however, various forms of ornamentation are used on cases and wrappings for the text.

Caption Answer: the Hebrew Bible

Exile and Return

Main Idea The Jews continued their religion during their exile in Babylon.

Reading Focus Have you ever learned something important by experiencing a hardship? Read on to find out what lessons the Jews learned from hard times.

The Jews called their time in Babylon an **exile** (EHG•ZYL). This means they were forced to live in a foreign land. During their exile, the Israelite religion became what we call Judaism.

While in **Babylon** (BA•buh•luhn), small groups of Jews met on the **Sabbath** (SA•buhth). This was their weekly day of worship and rest. The Jews would pray and discuss their religion and history. These meetings took place at **synagogues** (SIH•nuh•GAHGS), or Jewish houses of worship. The synagogue meetings gave the people hope.

Why Did Jews Return to Judah? During the 500s B.C., a group of people called Persians swept across southwest Asia. The Persians defeated the Chaldeans and took over Babylon. In 538 B.C. the Persian king Cyrus permitted Jews to return to Judah.

Some Jews stayed in Babylon, but many went home. They rebuilt Jerusalem and the temple. Cyrus appointed officials to rule the country and collected taxes from the people. Because Persians controlled their government, the Jews looked to their religion for leadership.

The leaders of the Jews became the temple priests and scribes, or religious scholars and writers. Under a scribe named Ezra, the Jews wrote the five books of the Torah on pieces of parchment. They sewed the pieces together to make long scrolls. The Torah and writings that were added later made up the Hebrew Bible.

◄ Torah scrolls are carried in decorated cases such as this one from the main synagogue in Jerusalem. *What larger text is made up of the Torah and other important writing?*

▼ Torah scrolls

▲ A rabbi reads from the Torah.

94

Reading Strategy   READING THE TEXT

Drawing Conclusions A conclusion is a general statement made by reasoning and by using supporting details. A conclusion can be the end result of the process of inferring. Drawing conclusions helps students see connections between ideas and events as they read. Ask students to notice details about ideas, people, events, and other information as they read the section. Then have them use these details to write general statements about their reading. Caution them against "overgeneralizing," or making generalizations that are not supported by details. **L2**

What Is in the Hebrew Bible? The Hebrew Bible is really a series of books collected together. It includes the five books of the Torah and 34 other books. These books describe events in Jewish history. The Jews believed that God had a special role for them in history and that events had meaning.

For example Genesis, the first book of the Torah, tells how God punished the world for its bad behavior. In Genesis, God tells Noah to build an ark, or large boat. Noah, his family, and two of every animal on Earth boarded the ark. Then a great flood covered the land, and only those on the ark escaped drowning. After the flood, God created a rainbow as a symbol of his promise to never again destroy the world with a flood.

Genesis also explains why the world has languages. It tells how the people of Babel tried to build a tower to heaven. God disapproved and made the people speak in different languages, then scattered them across the earth.

The Jews Look to the Future Parts of the Bible described God's plan for a peaceful future. The book of Daniel addressed this issue. Daniel lived in Babylon and was a trusted adviser of the king. However, he refused to worship Babylonian gods. The Chaldeans threw Daniel into a lion's den, but God protected Daniel from the lions. The story was meant to remind Jews that God would rescue them.

The Jews believed that evil and suffering would eventually be replaced by goodness. Christians and Muslims share this idea of good triumphing over evil.

✓ **Reading Check** **Identify** Who allowed the Jews to return to Judah?

The Jews and the Greeks

Main Idea Jews spread their beliefs to the Greek world and regained control of Judah.

Reading Focus How do you show loyalty to friends and family? In the following paragraphs, you'll learn how Jews showed loyalty to their religion and country.

In 334 B.C. a king named Alexander the Great began taking over kingdoms around the Mediterranean. In 331 B.C. his armies defeated the Persians, so Judah came under his control. Fortunately, Alexander allowed the Jews to stay in Judah. However, Alexander, who loved all things Greek, introduced the Greek language and Greek ways to Judah.

What Was the Diaspora? At the time, Jews were also living in other parts of Alexander's empire. Many still lived in Babylon. Some lived in Egypt and other lands around the Mediterranean Sea. The Jews outside of Judah became known as the

▼ According to the Bible, Daniel is thrown into a lion's den for refusing to worship the Babylonian gods. God, however, kept Daniel safe from the lions. *What lesson did this story present to the Jews?*

CURRICULUM CONNECTION

Music
Psalm 137 is a famous lament of the Jews in Babylon for their homeland. It has been adapted and set to many different types of music, from reggae to folk to hymns. Have students find and play for the class a variety of musical selections based on this text.

✓ **Reading Check**

Answer: the Persian king Cyrus

More About the Art

According to the Bible, King Darius had Daniel removed from the lion's den after one night. The king then had Daniel's accusers thrown to the lions. Daniel continued as a trusted adviser to Darius and other rulers.

Caption Answer: that God would rescue them

DIFFERENTIATED INSTRUCTION

Verbal/Linguistic: Ask students to think about how the exiled Jews must have felt during their forced stay in Babylon. What would they miss about their homeland? How would they react to their hard lives and lack of freedom? Have students write a journal entry about how they would feel if they were one of the Jews in exile.

English Learners: Ask learners to work in pairs to find adjectives in a dictionary that would describe how the exiled Jews felt.

Gifted and Talented: Have students research the Jews' Babylonian exile and write a short paper explaining how this period might have affected Judaism.

📂 Refer to *Inclusion Strategies for the Middle School Social Studies Classroom* in the TCR.

CONNECTING ACROSS TIME

Ask Jewish students to describe how their families celebrate Hanukkah. If there are no Jewish students in your class, have students research how Hanukkah is celebrated around the world. Then have students compare their findings with those of others in the class to see if Jews in different areas have different traditions. **L2**

Jewish Holidays The English translations of some of the Jewish holiday names are: Yom Kippur (day of atonement), Rosh Hoshana (beginning of the year), Purim (lots, as in drawing lots), and Hanukkah (dedication). Have students examine the chart showing the major Jewish holidays. **Ask: Which two holidays fall closest to each other?** (*Rosh Hoshana and Yom Kippur*) **L1/EL**

✓ Reading Check

Answer: He conquered Judah but allowed the Jews to remain in their homeland. He introduced Greek ideas and the Greek language to them.

Diaspora (dy•AS•pruh). *Diaspora* is a Greek word that means "scattered."

Many Jews of the Diaspora learned the Greek language and Greek ways but remained loyal to Judaism. A group of them copied the Hebrew Bible into Greek. This Greek version helped people who were not Jews to read and understand the Hebrew Bible. As a result, Jewish ideas spread throughout the Mediterranean world.

Who Were the Maccabees? In 168 B.C. a Greek ruler named Antiochus (an•TY•uh kuhs) controlled Judah. He decided to make the Jews of Judah worship Greek gods and goddesses. A priest named **Judas Maccabeus** (JOO•duhs MAK•uh•BEE•uhs) and his followers rebelled. They fled to the hills and formed an army known as the Maccabees.

After many battles, the Maccabees drove the Greeks out of Judah. They destroyed all traces of Greek gods and goddesses in their temple and made it a temple for worshiping the God of Israel. Each year Jews recall the cleansing of the temple when they celebrate Hanukkah (HAH•nuh•kuh).

Priests from Judas Maccabeus's family became the new rulers of Judah. Under their leadership, Judah took over land that had been part of the kingdom of Israel.

✓ **Reading Check** **Analyze** How did Alexander the Great affect the Israelites?

Major Jewish Holidays

Name	Time of Year	Length	Reason for the Holiday	Customs
Passover	April	8 days (7 in Israel)	to celebrate God's passing over of the Jews during the final plague in Egypt that enabled the Jews to return to the Promised Land	limited work; some fasts; sell certain foods that cannot be eaten or owned during the holiday; perform rituals
Rosh Hoshana	September or October	2 days	to celebrate the Jewish New Year	plan changes for the new year; no work; synagogue services; a shofar (horn) is blown in synagogues
Yom Kippur	September or October	25 hours	to make amends for sins of the past year	no work; synagogue services; pray; fast; apologize for wrongs during the past year
Hanukkah	December	8 days	to celebrate the Maccabees' victory, and reclaiming of the temple in Jerusalem	light candles each night; eat fried foods; play a game called dreidel; give gifts

◄ Menorah

96

CRITICAL THINKING ACTIVITY

Determining Cause and Effect Have students work in pairs for this activity. Have each student prepare several cause-and-effect charts for two of the subsections. Students should fill in either a cause or an effect for each subsection. Then have students exchange charts and fill in the missing information. For example, a chart might include the cause "Jews sent into exile in Babylon." The other students might fill in an effect like "Jews meet in small groups on the Sabbath." Conclude the activity by having pairs share their charts with the class. Have students offer suggestions on the accuracy of the charts. **L2**

The Jewish Way of Life

Main Idea Religion shaped the Jewish way of life.

Reading Focus What types of things influence the way you live? Read to find out how religion influenced Jewish life.

Jewish law set out many rules for Jews to follow that affected their daily life. These laws influenced their education, the foods they ate, and even the clothes they wore. The laws emphasized self-control and reminded Jews of their religion. This became important when they no longer had their own land and king.

Family Life The Jews placed great importance on family. Sons were especially valued because they carried on the family name. Upon a father's death, the son became head of the family.

Education was also important. Jewish children's first teachers were their mothers. When sons grew old enough, fathers taught them how to earn a living and to worship God. Later, elders took over the religious education of boys and taught them the Torah. Because reading the Torah was central to Jewish life, religious teachers became important community leaders.

Linking Past & Present

Head Coverings

THEN Under Greek rule, Jewish leaders began covering their heads to distinguish themselves from the Greeks and to remind themselves to think about God. Gradually, all Jewish men started wearing turbans or skull caps. Jewish women always kept their heads covered because a woman's hair was considered very private.

▼ Jews in modern-day head coverings

NOW Jews still wear head coverings, but only the most conservative—Orthodox Jews—wear them at all times. Most Jewish men wear skull caps called yarmulkes. Jewish women wear scarves or skull caps. *Why do you think Jews of the Diaspora are more reluctant to wear head coverings than Jews in Israel?*

▲ Ancient Jewish head covering

CHAPTER 3   The Ancient Israelites   **97**

INTERDISCIPLINARY CONNECTIONS ACTIVITY

Health The Jewish religion is not the only one that includes dietary guidelines. For example, Muslims do not eat pork or drink alcohol; Hindus do not eat beef; Mormons do not drink alcohol, coffee, or tea; and many Buddhists, Seventh-Day Adventists, and Quakers are vegetarians. Have students research the dietary practices of a religious group and report to the class about the practices, restrictions, and reasons behind the eating guidelines. **L2**

in a word . . .

"Kosher" food is food prepared according to Jewish dietary laws. One of the most recognizable Jewish foods is the doughnut-shaped bagel. This chewy bread, dropped into simmering water then baked, can be found all over the United States in many different versions. The word *bagel* is Yiddish, the Germanic dialect spoken by Jews in Eastern Europe, and means "ring." Bagels are often eaten with cream cheese and lox, a Yiddish word meaning "salmon."

The Way It Was

Answers:

1. They believed that those who have knowledge have everything, meaning it gave great abilities and wisdom.

2. It was the father's role to begin his son's education, teaching the commandments and about Jewish religious traditions and holy feasts.

✔ Reading Check

Answer: They carried on the family name and, on the father's death, became head of the family.

NATIONAL GEOGRAPHIC The Way It Was

Young People In...
Education in Ancient Israel and Judah

Early Israelites placed a high value on education. Rabbis—Jewish religious teachers—taught their followers, "If you have knowledge, you have everything." Unfortunately, only boys were allowed to go to school.

Fathers taught their young sons the commandments. They also taught them about the meanings of Jewish traditions and holy feasts. At age five, boys went to a school that was connected with the synagogue. There, the hazan, or minister of the synagogue, taught them the Torah. Everything the students learned—from the alphabet to Jewish history—they learned from the Torah.

Jewish laws decided the stages of students' education. Different subjects were introduced at the ages of 5, 10, and 13. Most Jewish boys finished their education at age 13. At that age, boys became adults.

▲ Children studying the Torah today

Connecting to the Past

1. Why was education important to the ancient Israelites?

2. What was a father's role in his son's education?

Mothers educated their daughters at home. The girls learned to be good wives, mothers, and housekeepers. This included learning Jewish laws about food and clothing. They also learned about the courageous women of ancient Israel. One of these women was named Ruth. Her biography appears on the next page. Her courage and devotion to her family provided an example for Jewish girls to follow.

The Jewish Diet Under Jewish law, Jews could eat only certain animals. For example, they could eat beef and lamb but not pork. They could eat scaly fish, like salmon, but not smooth-skinned fish, like eels. Laws about food were known as kashrut, which means "that which is proper."

Today, food that is prepared according to Jewish dietary laws is called kosher. Animals used for kosher meat must be killed in a special way. The meat must be inspected, salted, and soaked. To be kosher, Jews must not cook or eat milk products with meat.

In ancient times, everyday meals were made up of fish, fruit, vegetables, and barley bread. Beverages included mainly milk, water, wine, and beer.

Jewish Clothing Jewish law forbade mixing some fabrics. So women used flax or wool to make cloth but did not combine the two.

Jewish men wore tunics made of linen next to their skin. Some men layered another tunic on top of the first. In cold weather, they added wool or sheepskin cloaks. On their heads, they wore caps or turbans. On their feet, they wore sandals.

Women draped themselves in long, simple dresses. They covered their heads with shawls. Only wealthy women could afford leather shoes. They also wore makeup and jewelry.

✔ **Reading Check** **Analyze** Why were sons especially valued in Jewish society?

EXTENDING THE CONTENT

The Dead Sea The Dead Sea is one of the most intriguing bodies of water in the world, as well as the lowest. It lies an average of 1,312 feet (400 m) below sea level. Its name, which dates from the 300s B.C., comes from its extreme saltiness. Nothing lives in it except certain kinds of bacteria. Fish carried into the sea by the Jordan River die almost instantly. The Dead Sea Scrolls were discovered in caves nearby. Some historians also believe that the ruins of the ancient cities of Sodom and Gomorrah, infamous for their wickedness, may lie beneath the Dead Sea.

RUTH AND NAOMI

To show the importance of family love and devotion, Jewish girls learned about the relationship between Ruth and Naomi. The Book of Ruth in the Hebrew Bible tells about Ruth's life and of her dedication to her mother-in-law, Naomi. Years before, there was so little food in Bethlehem that Naomi, her husband, and their two sons moved to Moab. There, one of their sons married Ruth. Tragically, Naomi's husband and both of her sons died. Naomi wanted to return to Bethlehem, but she urged Ruth to stay in Moab with her parents and friends. Ruth refused to leave Naomi by herself. She insisted on traveling with her to Bethlehem. Ruth said to Naomi, "Wherever you go, I will go; wherever you lodge; I will lodge; your people shall be my people, and your God my God."

Naomi and Ruth arrived in Bethlehem at the beginning of the barley harvest. Because Ruth was from Moab, she was considered an outsider by the Israelites. Furthermore, because Ruth was a widow and did not have children, she did not have any property rights. To survive in Bethlehem, she had to rely upon her mother-in-law's advice and the kindness of a wealthy landowner named Boaz.

During the harvest, Ruth worked in Boaz's fields, gathering grain left behind on the ground by the reapers. It was hard work that began at dawn and ended at dusk, but Ruth never complained. She soon earned the respect and admiration of her new people. In time, Ruth married Boaz. They had a son named Obed. In the Hebrew Bible, at the end of the Book of Ruth, Obed is named as the grandfather of David, the future king of Israel.

Then and Now

To survive in Bethlehem, Ruth had to rely on Naomi and Boaz. If a present-day woman moved to a new city, what resources would she use to help her find work, shelter, and other necessities?

▲ Naomi and Ruth

99

TEACH

Ruth was a Moabite, a member of a group of people who lived east of the Dead Sea. Aside from the Book of Ruth in the Old Testament, most of what we know about ancient Moab comes from an ancient basalt column, called a stela. Words in the Moabite language were carved on the stone, now in the Louvre Museum in Paris. The stela was discovered near the city of Dhiban, Jordan, and tells the story of the conquest of Moab by the Israelite king Omri in the 800s B.C.

Ask students what values the story of Ruth emphasizes. *(loyalty, kindness, love, courage, hard work)* L1/ EL

Then and Now

Answers will vary, but students may mention job placement and other social service agencies, rental and realty companies, chambers of commerce, religious institutions, and so on.

Reading List Generator CD-ROM

GLENCOE **BOOKLINK** **RECOMMENDED READING**

Use the **Glencoe BookLink CD-ROM** to create customized reading lists based on your students' interests and reading levels. Below is an example based on content in this chapter. Also, see the Suggested Readings on pages 944–946 of the Appendix.

- *The Book of Ruth: From the Tanahk.* During a time of famine in Judah, Naomi's daughter-in-law Ruth does not desert her. From Ruth's first son will come the future king David.
- Frank, Anne. *Anne Frank: The Diary of a Young Girl.* Young Anne Frank keeps a diary of events, ideas, and emotions of two Jewish families hiding in an Amsterdam attic during the Nazi occupation.
- Haugaard, Erik C. *The Rider and His Horse.* Roman soldiers have surrounded Masada, a hill-top fortress in ancient Israel. David, 13, is one of the Jewish defenders inside.

Monitoring Comprehension Have students make a time line of the events described in the subsection "The Jews and the Romans." Ask students to discuss with a partner the significance of each event listed. (*Possible events: 63 B.C., Romans conquer Judah; A.D. 66, Zealots revolt; A.D. 132, Jews revolt again; A.D. 135, Romans put down revolt and remove Jews from Jerusalem; A.D. 1948, nation of Israel founded*) **L1**

Reading Support L1/ EL

Assign **Guided Reading Activity 3–3** to help students organize the information in the section.

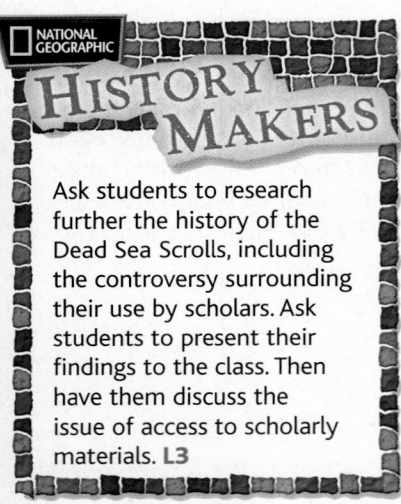

NATIONAL GEOGRAPHIC

HISTORY MAKERS

Ask students to research further the history of the Dead Sea Scrolls, including the controversy surrounding their use by scholars. Ask students to present their findings to the class. Then have them discuss the issue of access to scholarly materials. **L3**

The Jews and the Romans

Main Idea Under Roman rule, the Jews were divided and rebellious. In response, the Romans destroyed the temple and exiled the Jews.

Reading Focus Do you consider freedom worth fighting for? Read to find out what happened to the Jews after they fought for their freedom.

In 63 B.C. a people known as the Romans conquered Judah. Led by powerful generals, the Romans were intent on expanding their empire. The Roman capital was far to the west in what is today the country of Italy. When the Romans conquered Judah, they renamed it Judaea (joo•DEE•uh). At first, the Romans allowed Jewish rulers to run Judaea.

The Rule of King Herod The most famous ruler of Judaea during this time was King **Herod** (HEHR•uhd). He was known for his cruelty and his changes to the Jewish temple in Jerusalem. He made the temple one of the most awe-inspiring buildings in the Roman world. Today he is best known as the king who ruled Judaea when Jesus was born.

Shortly after Herod died, the Romans replaced the Jewish king with Roman officials. The Jews were eager to regain control, but because they had splintered into different groups, they did not have as much power.

One group of Jews was known as the Pharisees (FAR•uh•seez). They taught the Torah and how to apply its laws to daily life. In doing so, they helped make Judaism a religion of the home and family. The Pharisees taught in synagogues and were supported by the common people.

The Sadducees (SA•juh•seez) also accepted the Torah. However, they were more concerned about how it applied to the priests in the Temple. This was because most of them were priests and scribes. They did not agree with many of the Pharisees' teachings.

A third group was called Essenes (ih•SEENZ). They were priests who broke away from the Temple in Jerusalem. Many Essenes lived together in the desert. They spent their lives praying and waiting for God to deliver the Jews from the Romans.

NATIONAL GEOGRAPHIC

HISTORY MAKERS

Dead Sea Scrolls

In A.D. 1947 shepherd boys in the Judaean desert near the Dead Sea found the first of the Dead Sea Scrolls in a cave. The Dead Sea Scrolls are ancient scrolls of leather, papyrus, and copper written between 200 B.C. and A.D. 68. The documents include the oldest complete copy of the book of Isaiah and pieces of many other books of the Hebrew Bible. Most scholars believe that the scrolls were part of a library that belonged to an early Jewish community.

▶ Restoration of the Dead Sea Scrolls

100   CHAPTER 3   The Ancient Israelites

CITIZENSHIP AND YOU

The Impact of Education Education was very important to the Jews of ancient Israel. After being taught by their parents, some children went on to be educated in community schools that were run by religious elders. Many people in the United States also believe that education is not only the key to success, but necessary in order to be actively and effectively involved as a citizen. However, many people have become successful in business and in the arts without a formal education, for example some of the early computer developers and pop musicians. **Ask:** Is a good education necessary for most people to be successful? Is it necessary to be involved in a democratic government? (*Students should support their opinions with evidence and sound reasoning.*) **L3**

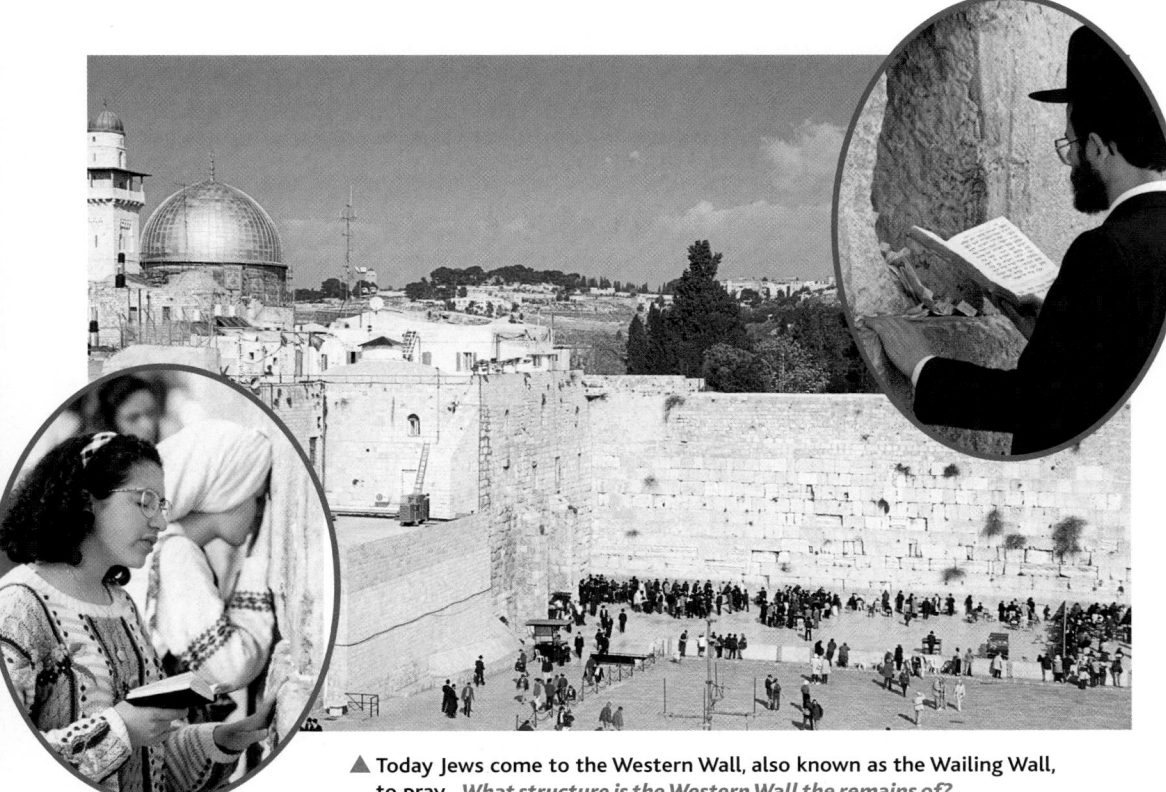

▲ Today Jews come to the Western Wall, also known as the Wailing Wall, to pray. *What structure is the Western Wall the remains of?*

In A.D. 1947 ancient scrolls were found in the desert near the Dead Sea. They were probably written by Essenes and are called the Dead Sea Scrolls. The scrolls have helped historians understand more about Judaism during Roman times.

Jewish Revolts During the A.D. 60s, Jewish hatred of Roman rule was at its peak. Many Jews were waiting for a **messiah** (muh•SY•uh), or deliverer sent by God. Other Jews known as **Zealots** (ZEH•luhts) wanted to fight the Romans for their freedom.

In A.D. 66 the Zealots revolted against the Romans and drove them out of Jerusalem. Four years later, the Romans retook Jerusalem. They killed thousands of Jews and forced many others to leave. The Romans also destroyed the temple in Jerusalem. The Western Wall is all that remains of it today.

The Jews revolted again in A.D. 132. Three years later, the Romans put down the revolt. This time, the Romans forbade Jews to live in or even visit Jerusalem. They gave Judah the name of Palestine. This name refers to the Philistines, whom the Israelites had conquered centuries before.

Jewish Teachers Despite losing their land, the Jews managed to survive. They no longer had priests. Instead, leaders called **rabbis** (RA•BYZ) became important. Rabbis were teachers of the Torah.

One of the most famous rabbis was **Johanan ben Zakkai** (YOH•kah•nahn behn zah•KY). After the revolt of A.D. 70, he made sure the study of the Torah continued.

CHAPTER 3 The Ancient Israelites 101

③ ASSESS

Assign Section 3 Review as homework or as an in-class activity.

Have students use the **Interactive Tutor Self-Assessment CD-ROM** to review the section.

Assessment L2
Assign **Section 3 Quiz** to assess mastery of the material found in the section.

More About the Art
For many years, worshipers at the Western Wall have written prayers and requests to God on small pieces of paper, folded them, and slipped them into cracks in the ancient wall.

Caption Answer: the temple in Jerusalem

Reading Support L1/EL
Assign **Reading Essentials and Study Guide 3–3** to help students review section material.

ENRICH
Ask students to present a news program focused on an event discussed in the section. L3

COOPERATIVE LEARNING ACTIVITY
Service Learning In this chapter, students have learned about the tensions that sometimes arise when groups of different religious, ethnic, and cultural backgrounds try to live together. Most communities have service organizations that attempt to bridge religious, ethnic, or cultural differences and perform services for residents. Have students research organizations in your community. Then have them choose an organization, contact it about volunteer opportunities, and perform volunteer work. Then have them report back to the class on their experiences, paying particular attention to how the group promotes religious, ethnic, and cultural diversity. L3

Primary Source

Talmud is the Hebrew word for "learning or study." The Talmud comments on many topics, including geography, domestic relations, religion, and folklore.

Answer:
Possible answer: so that lives could be saved and certain important business carried out on the Sabbath.

✓ Reading Check

Answer: The Jews were forced from Jerusalem and most moved away from Palestine.

History Online

To help students understand section material, have them visit **Study Central**™ at jat.glencoe.com

RETEACH

Have students work in groups to identify and explain important concepts from the section. **L1**

④ CLOSE

Ask students to identify influences of the civilization of early Israel on life today. **L2**

He founded a school in northern Palestine that became a center of Torah studies for centuries. Other rabbis founded Torah schools in places as far away as Babylon and Egypt.

The rabbis wanted to save and pass on teachings about the Torah. They combined the teachings in a book called the Talmud. To this day, the Talmud remains an important record of Jewish law.

For 2,000 years, most Jews lived outside of Palestine. They often faced hatred and persecution. In A.D. 1948 Palestine was divided, and a new Jewish nation called Israel was created.

✓ Reading Check **Explain** How did the Roman conquest affect the Jews?

▲ Jews reading the Talmud today

Primary Source — The Talmud

Part of the Talmud declares that most types of work and business are not allowed on the Sabbath, or Jewish day of worship. This passage identifies the only times it is okay to break those rules.

"One is permitted to remove debris on the Sabbath in order to save a life or to act for the benefit of the community; and we may assemble in the synagogue on the Sabbath to conduct public business [i.e., matters of community concern]."

—*The Talmud for Today*, Rabbi Alexander Feinsilver, trans. and ed.

DBQ **Document-Based Question**

Why do you think these exceptions were made for the benefit of the community?

History Online

Study Central™ Need help with the material in this section? Visit jat.glencoe.com

Section ③ Review

Reading Summary

Review the Main Ideas

- During their exile in Babylon, the Jews developed their religion, which is based upon the stories in the Hebrew Bible.
- Jews spread their ideas to the Greek world. About 168 B.C., they fought the Greeks for control of Judah.
- Religious laws concerning food and clothing affected everyday Jewish life.
- In 63 B.C. Judah was taken over by the Roman Empire.

What Did You Learn?

1. What was the Diaspora?
2. What was education like within a Jewish family?

Critical Thinking

3. **Organizing Information** Draw a table to describe the differences between these three Jewish groups.

Pharisees	Sadducees	Essenes

4. **Summarize** How did the Jews practice their religion during the exile in Babylon?

5. **Identify** Who were the Zealots, and why were they important?

6. **Draw Conclusions** Do you think that Jewish beliefs and values would have spread so widely if the lands of Israel and Judah had not been conquered by other peoples? Explain.

7. **Persuasive Writing** Imagine you are living in Judaea during the Roman conquest. Write a letter to a friend describing how you might have felt about the Romans and what actions you would like to see taken to make Judaea free again.

SECTION 3 REVIEW ANSWERS

1. Scattered Jews living outside of their homeland in Judah
2. Mothers taught young children. Fathers taught older boys religion and the father's trade. Boys also learned the Torah from religious teachers. Mothers taught girls the basic skills of being good wives, mothers, and housekeepers.
3. Students' tables should match the text.
4. The Jews worshiped on the Sabbath and met in synagogues to pray and discuss their religion and history.
5. Jews who revolted and drove the Romans out of Jerusalem
6. Answers will vary but should express plausible reasons.
7. Letters will vary but should show thoughtful consideration of the Jewish situation.

Chapter 3 Reading Review

Section 1 The First Israelites

Vocabulary
monotheism
tribe
Torah
covenant
alphabet

Focusing on the Main Ideas
- The Israelites believed in one God who set down moral laws for his people. They recorded their history in the Bible. *(page 81)*
- The Israelites had to fight the Canaanites to return to their promised land. *(page 84)*

Moses with the ▶
Ten Commandments

Section 2 The Kingdom of Israel

Vocabulary
prophet
empire
tribute
proverb

Focusing on the Main Ideas
- The Israelites chose a king to unite them against their enemies. *(page 87)*
- King David built an Israelite empire and made Jerusalem his capital city. *(page 89)*
- The Israelites were conquered and forced to leave Israel and Judah. *(page 90)*

Section 3 The Growth of Judaism

Vocabulary
exile
Sabbath
synagogue
Diaspora
messiah
rabbi

Focusing on the Main Ideas
- The Jews continued their religion during their exile in Babylon. *(page 94)*
- Jews spread their beliefs to the Greek world and regained control of Judah. *(page 95)*
- Religion shaped the Jewish way of life. *(page 97)*
- Under Roman rule, the Jews were divided and rebellious. In response, the Romans destroyed the temple and exiled the Jews. *(page 100)*

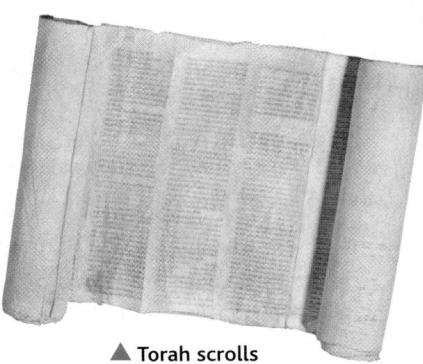

▲ Torah scrolls

CHAPTER 3   The Ancient Israelites   103

PREVIEW/REVIEW

Vocabulary Activity Have students create a crossword puzzle, including clues, using at least 10 vocabulary terms from this chapter. Have students exchange puzzles with a partner and complete the puzzles.

🌐 **Vocabulary PuzzleMaker CD-ROM**

🌐 **Interactive Tutor Self-Assessment CD-ROM**

CONDENSE

📁 Chapter 3 **Guided Reading Activities**

🎧 **StudentWorks Plus™ CD-ROM (with Audio Program)**

RETEACH

📁 **Differentiated Instruction Activity 3**

📁 Chapter 3 *Reading Essentials and Study Guide*

CHAPTER CULMINATING ACTIVITY

Have students finish the Chapter Culminating Activity from page 76D.

Suggestions for rubrics may be found in the *Quizzes, Tests, and Authentic Assessment (with Rubrics)* booklet.

📖 **Reading Strategy** ◀ **READ TO WRITE**

Taking a Position Ask students to take a position on this statement and support it with reasoning and details from the chapter: The Israelites caused as many problems for their civilization as outsiders did by fighting among themselves.

- **L1** students should include one or two reasons and details in their position statement.
- **L2** students should include several appropriate details and reasons and attempt grammar mastery.
- **L3** students should write logical, detailed, well-considered position statements that provide strong support for their opinion.

Chapter 3 Assessment and Activities

CHAPTER 3
ASSESSMENT AND ACTIVITIES

GLENCOE TECHNOLOGY

MindJogger Videoquiz

Use the **MindJogger Videoquiz** to review Chapter 3 content.

 Available in DVD and VHS

Review Vocabulary

1. c	5. g
2. b	6. f
3. a	7. h
4. d	8. e

Review Main Ideas

9. in the Hebrew Bible

10. They believed it was God's will that they conquer the Canaanites and return to their Promised Land.

11. to unite them against their enemies, the Philistines

12. They were forced to leave Israel and Judah.

13. Some Jews of the Diaspora copied the Hebrew Bible into Greek, which helped others learn about Jewish ideas.

14. The Jewish rebellions were forcefully put down, and the Romans destroyed the temple in Jerusalem and exiled the Jews.

Critical Thinking

15. The Jewish religion had one God, while other religions had many gods and goddesses. The Jews could not create images of their God. The Ten Commandments applied to everyone equally.

16. The Jews believed they had received the Promised Land through a covenant with God.

Review Vocabulary

Match the definitions in the second column to the terms in the first column.

1. tribe   a. Jewish house of worship
2. prophet   b. claims to be inspired by God
3. synagogue   c. family group
4. Sabbath   d. holy day of worship and rest
5. messiah   e. forced absence
6. monotheism   f. belief in one god
7. covenant   g. deliverer sent by God
8. exile   h. agreement

Review Main Ideas

Section 1 • The First Israelites

9. Where did the Israelites record their history and religious beliefs?

10. Why did the Israelites fight the Canaanites?

Section 2 • The Kingdom of Israel

11. Why did the Israelites choose a king?

12. What happened when the Israelites were conquered?

Section 3 • The Growth of Judaism

13. How did Jewish ideas spread throughout the Mediterranean world?

14. How did Romans respond to Jewish rebellions?

Critical Thinking

15. **Contrast** How was the Jewish religion different from religions of other ancient cultures?

16. **Analyze** Why do you think the Israelites felt so strongly about a Promised Land?

17. **Compare and Contrast** How were Saul and David similar, and how were they different?

18. **Explain** How did the Jewish religion survive during the exile of the Jews?

19. **Describe** What is celebrated on the Jewish holiday Hanukkah?

Review · **Reading Skill** · Main Idea

Finding the Main Idea

20. Read the paragraph at the right from page 101. Create a graphic organizer that shows the main idea and supporting details.

In A.D. 1947 ancient scrolls were found in the desert near the Dead Sea. They were probably written by Essenes and are called the Dead Sea Scrolls. The scrolls have helped historians understand more about Judaism during Roman times.

To review this skill, see pages 78–79.

17. Both led the Israelites to victory against their enemies. Saul displeased God by disobeying him. He plotted to kill David and was eventually killed in battle. David defeated Goliath, drove the Philistines out of Israel, and built Jerusalem.

18. The Jews worshiped on the Sabbath and met in synagogues.

19. the Maccabees' defeat of the Greeks and the reclaiming and cleansing of the temple in Jerusalem

Reading Skill

20. Main idea: Dead Sea Scrolls; Details: found near the Dead Sea in A.D. 1947, probably written by the Essenes, have helped historians learn more about Judaism during Roman times

Geography Skills

Study the map below and answer the following questions.

21. **Location** Which kingdom—Israel or Judah—had an advantage when it came to trade? Why?

22. **Identify** What advantage did Judah have over Israel?

23. **Analyze** Why did the Phoenicians focus on trade rather than farming?

History Online
Self-Check Quiz To help you prepare for the Chapter Test, visit jat.glencoe.com

Using Technology

27. **Organizing Information** Search the Internet or your local library for information about the early Phoenicians and Philistines. Use the computer to create a chart comparing the two cultures. Include headings such as Location, Time Period, Major Contributions, and Achievements.

Linking Past and Present

28. **Making Comparisons** The Israelites moved from place to place within the same region along the Mediterranean. Trace the route of one of their journeys on a map of ancient times. Then trace the route again on a map showing that region as it is today. Identify the current nations and landmarks in that region.

NATIONAL GEOGRAPHIC
Israelite Kingdoms

Mediterranean Sea
Byblos
Sidon
Damascus
Tyre
SYRIAN DESERT
Jordan R.
Samaria
Jerusalem
Dead Sea

KEY
- Phoenicians
- Kingdom of Israel
- Kingdom of Judah

N W E S

0   100 mi.
0   100 km
Lambert Azimuthal Equal-Area projection

Read to Write

24. **Descriptive Writing** Imagine you are living in Jerusalem during the time of King Solomon. Write a letter to a friend describing the things Solomon is doing as leader. Be sure to mention which of these things the people like and which they do not like.

25. **Summarize** Choose three events in this chapter that you think were the most important to the history of the Israelites. Write a headline for each that might have appeared in a newspaper of that time.

26. **Using Your FOLDABLES** Use the information you wrote in your three-pocket foldable to create a fill-in-the-blank quiz for a classmate. Write a paragraph about one of the sections, leaving blanks for your classmate to fill in. Leave blanks for vocabulary words or significant places and people.

Primary Source
Analyze

The following passage describes the effects of the attack on Judaea. The passage is written by Josephus, a Jewish historian in the Roman era.

"Throughout the city people were dying of hunger in large numbers. . . . In every house the merest hint of food sparked violence, and close relatives fell to blows. . . . No respect was paid even to the dying; the ruffians searched them, in case they were concealing food somewhere in their clothes."

—Josephus, "The Siege of Jerusalem"

DBQ Document-Based Questions

29. What does Josephus mean when he says "No respect was paid even to the dying"?

30. How might this account have been different if it had been written by a Roman soldier?

CHAPTER 3   The Ancient Israelites   **105**

History Online
Have students visit the Web site at jat.glencoe.com to review Chapter 3 and take the **Self-Check Quiz.**

26. **FOLDABLES** Quizzes will vary but should accurately reflect the information in the chapter.

Using Technology

27. Charts will vary but should reflect information in the chapter and from each student's research.

Linking Past and Present

28. Responses will vary depending on which journey students choose.

Primary Source

29. He means that instead of taking care of the dying, people were searching them for pieces of food.

30. The Romans would have been glorified.

Bonus Question

Ask: Do you think religion affected the daily lives of the ancient Israelites more, less, or about the same as people in the United States today? Why? (*Answers should include information from the chapter, knowledge of current events, and sound reasoning to support each opinion.*)

Geography Skills

21. Israel, because it was on the Mediterranean Sea

22. Jerusalem was in Judah.

23. They had three major cities on the Mediterranean Sea, which made trade easy for them.

Read to Write

24. Letters will vary but should contain the following information: popular acts of Solomon—built a temple, wrote proverbs; unpopular acts of Solomon—demanded high taxes, forced people to work in mines

25. Answers will vary but should be based on information in the text.

REVIEWING UNIT OBJECTIVES

Having studied this unit, students should now be able to

1. explain how the first civilizations emerged;
2. describe the cultures of ancient civilizations in Egypt and Mesopotamia;
3. describe the culture of the ancient Israelites and identify their contributions to Western civilization.

UNIT REVIEW ACTIVITY

Comparing Civilizations To help students review the unit objectives, have them consider the **Comparing Civilizations** chart. Have them use the notations in the chart to help them write short answers to these theme-based questions:

- How did individual people in each civilization relate to the greater society?
- What methods did governments use to make decisions affecting the well-being of people and of the civilization as a whole?
- How did culture reflect the concerns and interests of the people?
- How did science and technology change people's lives? **L2**

Unit 1 Review

Comparing Civilizations

Compare the civilizations that you have read about by reviewing the information below. Can you see how the people of these civilizations helped to build the world we live in today?

Where in the World?
- Chapter 1
- Chapter 2
- Chapter 3

NATIONAL GEOGRAPHIC

	First Civilizations Chapter 1	Ancient Egypt Chapter 2	Ancient Israelites Chapter 3
Where did these civilizations develop?	• Between the Tigris and Euphrates Rivers	• Along the banks of the Nile River	• In an area called Canaan
Who are some important people in these civilizations?	• Sargon, c. 2340–2279 B.C. • Hammurabi, c. 1792–1750 B.C. • Nebuchadnezzar, c. 605–562 B.C.	• King Khufu, c. 2540 B.C. • Hatshepsut, c. 1470 B.C. • Ramses II, c. 1279–1213 B.C. • Kashta, c. 750 B.C.	• Abraham, c. 1800 B.C. • Moses, c. 1250 B.C. • David, c. 1000–970 B.C. • The Maccabees, 168 B.C.
Where did most of the people live?	• Most people lived on farms near walled cities • The center of the city was the ziggurat	• Some people lived in large cities • Most people lived in villages along the Nile	• Most people lived in small villages or near the city of Jerusalem

106

END-OF-UNIT RESOURCES

Reproducible Masters
- Unit 1 Test Form A
- Unit 1 Test Form B
- Step Into World History Activity 1

 Transparencies
- Unit 1 Map Overlay Transparencies

Multimedia
- Interactive Tutor Self-Assessment CD-ROM
- ExamView® Pro Testmaker CD-ROM
- Presentation Plus! CD-ROM

	First Civilizations Chapter 1	Ancient Egypt Chapter 2	Ancient Israelites Chapter 3
What were these people's beliefs?	• Worshiped many different gods • The gods appointed the rulers	• Worshiped gods and goddesses • Believed in life after death	• Worshiped one God • Used the Bible as a record of their history
What was their government like?	• Early Mesopotamians were ruled by priests • Later, kings ruled the people; they believed kings had divine approval	• King was a ruler-priest and a god • Pharaoh owned all land in Egypt	• Early Israelites were led by prophets • Later, they were led by judges, then kings
What was their language and writing like?	• Early: cuneiform: wedge-shaped characters • Later: a Semitic language	• Hieroglyphics: images that stood for ideas	• Adapted Phoenician characters to form letters and words
What contributions did they make?	• Developed writing • Created system of mathematics • Studied systems of time and created calendars • Introduced iron weapons	• Built machines to move water to crops • Developed a calendar • Built large temples and pyramids	• Developed ideas of legal system • Passed on ideas of justice, fairness, and compassion in society and government • Believed in one God
How do these contributions affect me? *Can you add any?*	• Similar measurements are still used in building today • Our system of time is based on seconds, minutes, and hours	• Pyramids and other structures still amaze people today	• Many religions today are based on ideas similar to those of the early Israelites

107

UNIT WRAP-UP ACTIVITY

Analyzing Cause and Effect One of the most important relationships to examine when studying history is cause and effect. Events cause other events, which in turn influence still other events. Have students work in pairs to review the **Comparing Civilizations** chart. Ask one student in each pair to make a list of three important events in the history of the civilizations discussed in Unit 1. Have the other student in each pair explain the causes and effects of those three events, then discuss these with his or her partner. Then have students switch roles and do the exercise again.

Conclude the unit wrap-up activity by having each pair share several of their cause-and-effect relationships with the class. **L2**

PROFESSIONAL DEVELOPMENT: TEACHING READING

- Calkins, Lucy McCormick. *The Art of Teaching Reading.* Longman, 2001.
- Robb, Laura, and Judy Lynch. *Teaching Reading in Social Studies, Science, and Math.* Scholastic, 2003.
- Pinnell, Gay Su et al. *Teaching for Comprehension in Reading.* Scholastic, 2003.
- Routman, Regie. *Reading Essentials: The Specifics You Need to Teach Reading Well.* Heinemann, 2003.
- Harvey, Stephanie, and Anne Goudvis. *Strategies That Work: Teaching Comprehension to Enhance Understanding.* Stenhouse, 2000.
- Lewin, Larry. *Paving the Way in Reading and Writing: Strategies and Activities to Support Struggling Students in Grades 6–12.* Jossey-Bass, 2003.

Unit ② Planning Guide

Unit Resources

Note: The following materials may be used when teaching Unit 2.
Chapter and section level support materials can be found on the chapter and section resource pages.

TEACHING TRANSPARENCIES

- Writing Process Transparencies **L1**

DIFFERENTIATED INSTRUCTION

- Step Into World History Activity 2 **L1**

ASSESSMENT

- Unit 2 Test Form A **L2**
- Unit 2 Test Form B **L2**

ADDITIONAL RESOURCES

- Glencoe Skillbuilder Interactive Workbook CD-ROM, Level 1
- Glencoe World History Primary Source Document Library CD-ROM
- Focus on World Art Prints
- Outline Map Resource Book
- World Desk Map
- World Art and Architecture Transparencies
- World Music: Cultural Traditions
- World Music: A Cultural Legacy
- Glencoe World Literature Library
- Reading in the Content Area
- Teaching Strategies for the World History Classroom (Including Block Scheduling Pacing Guides)
- Inclusion Strategies for the Middle School Social Studies Classroom

---

- Blackline Master
- Poster
- Transparency
- Music Program
- CD-ROM
- Audio Program
- DVD
- Videocassette

READING SUPPORT FROM JAMESTOWN EDUCATION

- *Timed Readings Plus in Social Studies* help students increase their reading rate and fluency while maintaining comprehension. The 400-word passages are similar to those found on state and national assessments.
- *Reading in the Content Area: Social Studies* concentrates on six essential reading skills that help students better comprehend what they read. The book includes 75 high-interest nonfiction passages written at increasing levels of difficulty.
- *Reading Fluency* helps students read smoothly, accurately, and expressively.
- *Jamestown's Reading Improvement,* by renowned reading expert Edward Fry, focuses on helping build your students' comprehension, vocabulary, and skimming and scanning skills.
- *Critical Reading Series* provides high-interest books, each written at three reading levels.

To order these products, call Glencoe at 1-800-334-7344.

Reading List Generator CD-ROM

GLENCOE BOOKLINK

The Glencoe BookLink CD-ROM is a database that allows you to search more than 15,000 titles to create a customized reading list for your students.

- Reading lists can be organized by students' reading level, author, genre, theme, or area of interest.
- The database provides Degrees of Reading Power™ (DRP) and Lexile™ readability scores for all selections.
- A brief summary of each selection is included.

Leveled reading suggestions for this unit:

For students at a Grade 5 reading level:
- *Dateline: Troy,* by Paul Fleischman

For students at a Grade 6 reading level:
- *Shower of Gold: Girls and Women in the Stories of India,* by Uma Krishnaswami

For students at a Grade 7 reading level:
- *China: City and Village Life,* by Julia Waterlow

To order this CD-ROM, call Glencoe at 1-800-334-7344.

Unit Reading Strategies

Each chapter in this unit contains special reading strategies. The following preview will help you teach these reading skills to your students.

CHAPTER 4: Making Connections

Making connections from the printed word to what readers have seen, heard, read about, or experienced in their own lives provides a framework on which to build new information. Discovering such connections builds cognitive reading and understanding. While this may seem simple, it is necessary that this become a part of a reader's natural processing in order to effectively comprehend new text. Often, teachers must assist readers in making these vital connections by asking questions that guide students to make such connections.

CHAPTER 5: Using Context Clues

Using context clues involves looking for the meaning of difficult words and passages by using the phrases and words located nearby. Seeing a word, phrase, or concept within its context will provide valuable insights on how the word or concept is intended to be understood. Students who are capable of using context clues, such as synonyms, explanations in the sentence, or nontext features such as graphs and illustrations, will comprehend the text more easily and fully.

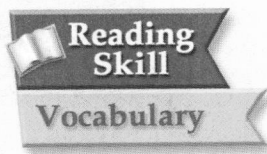

CHAPTER 6: Building Your Vocabulary

This skill uses techniques similar to those found in "Using Context Clues." Both emphasize the importance of developing vocabulary in order to aid comprehension of text materials. When there are terms students do not understand, students can use context to determine meaning. They can also look for clues in prefixes, suffixes, or root words; look the word up in the glossary or dictionary; ask someone for help; or simply guess based on what they have read. Ultimately, a solid and growing vocabulary is essential to good comprehension.

CHAPTER 7: Headings and Punctuation

Many students jump directly into a text, ignoring print signals that make reading easier. Without understanding that text structure and punctuation marks direct student reading much like road signs direct travelers, student navigation of the text can become laborious and limit understanding. In this skill, students learn how proficient readers use headings, subheadings, words in bold, punctuation marks, and other text features as valuable comprehension tools.

Use the **SkillBuilder Handbook** on pages 902–919 to help students practice important skills.

UNIT OVERVIEW

Unit 2 describes the development and contributions of ancient Greece, India, and China.

UNIT OBJECTIVES

After studying this unit, students should be able to

1. trace the rise of Greek city-states with an emphasis on Athens and Sparta, and describe Greek cultural accomplishments and the spread of Greek culture;

2. discuss early Indian civilizations and empires, including the development of Hinduism and Buddhism;

3. explore China's first civilizations and the rise of the Qin and Han dynasties.

Why It's Important

Tell students that our civilization is a product of the accomplishments of earlier civilizations. Ask them how their lives would be different without the accomplishments of early Greece, China, and India. **L2**

Unit 2
The Ancient World

Why It's Important

Each civilization that you will study in this unit made important contributions to history.

- The Greeks developed democratic government.
- The ancient Chinese created paper.
- The people of India invented the concept of zero.

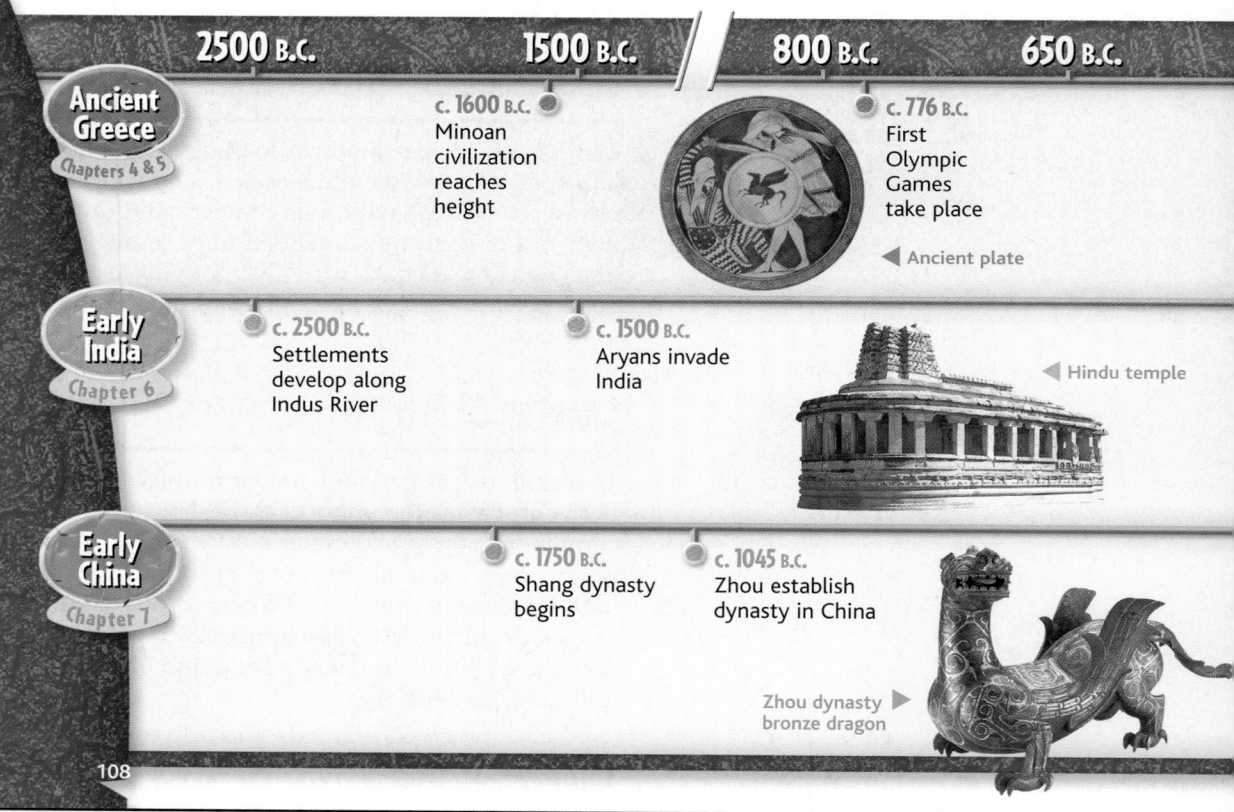

2500 B.C.	1500 B.C.	800 B.C.	650 B.C.

Ancient Greece
Chapters 4 & 5

c. 1600 B.C.
Minoan civilization reaches height

c. 776 B.C.
First Olympic Games take place

◄ Ancient plate

Early India
Chapter 6

c. 2500 B.C.
Settlements develop along Indus River

c. 1500 B.C.
Aryans invade India

◄ Hindu temple

Early China
Chapter 7

c. 1750 B.C.
Shang dynasty begins

c. 1045 B.C.
Zhou establish dynasty in China

Zhou dynasty bronze dragon

108

TIME LINE ACTIVITY

Have students use the multiple-tier time line on these pages to develop a time frame for the period they will be studying in this unit. Assign groups of students ranges of time in the upper time line and then have them describe what was happening in other parts of the world during this period. Then have them create their own copy of the time line with room to add information. As students read the chapters in the unit, have them add significant events to the time line. **L1**

NATIONAL GEOGRAPHIC — Where in the World?

0   1,000 miles
0   1,000 kilometers
Mercator projection

EUROPE

Caspian Sea

ASIA

Chapter 6

Chapter 7

Black Sea

GOBI

HINDU KUSH

Huang He

Mediterranean Sea

Tigris R.

Euphrates R.

Persian Gulf

Indus R.

Chapters 4 & 5

Chang Jiang

CHINA

ARABIA

Nile R.

Arabian Sea

INDIA

Red Sea

Bay of Bengal

South China Sea

PACIFIC OCEAN

AFRICA

INDIAN OCEAN   90°E   120°E

- Chapters 4 & 5
- Chapter 6
- Chapter 7

500 B.C.	350 B.C.	200 B.C.	50 B.C.	A.D. 100

490 B.C. Greeks and Persians fight the Battle of Marathon

399 B.C. Socrates tried for his teachings

c. 330 B.C. Aristotle develops theories about government

◄ Statue of Socrates

c. 530 B.C. Siddhartha Gautama founds Buddhism in India

c. 321 B.C. Chandragupta Maurya unites northern India

273 B.C. Asoka begins rule in India

◄ Statue of the Buddha

c. 530 B.C. Confucius develops his philosophy in China

c. 100 B.C. Silk Road links China and the Middle East

c. A.D. 100 Buddhism spreads from India to China

◄ Statue of horse from Han dynasty

NCLB — NO CHILD LEFT BEHIND

Teaching Tip To help achieve some of the goals of the NCLB Act, you might try a shared writing exercise in which you act as the scribe while students dictate their answers or messages. Have them look over each tier in the time line and the **Where in the World?** map. Ask questions such as: Where is our journey going to take us in this unit? What are some of the important stopping points along the way? Who are some of the people we might meet? What big events can we expect to see? Record student answers on the board. Encourage students to modify the answers/messages that you are recording as they see their words in writing.

DIFFERENTIATED INSTRUCTION

English Learners: Have students write down unfamiliar words from the time line on separate index cards. Then have pairs of students look up these terms in the glossary in the back of the text or in a dictionary.

Verbal/Linguistic: Ask students to organize a geography bee in which they name an accomplishment, event, or person. The rest of the class should call out the civilization to which each is linked—Greece, India, or China.

Gifted and Talented: Have students research and prepare reports called "Milestones in Human Culture." Reports should focus on at least one event in each of the three civilizations.

FOCUS

The unit preview provides a general layout of the regions and significant figures covered in the unit.

PREVIEWING GEOGRAPHY

Ask students to answer the following questions using the map.

1. **Greece lay at a central location near three major continents. Name them.** *(Europe, Africa, Asia)* **L2**

2. **Which civilization was China's closest neighbor?** *(India)* **L1**

3. **What geographic features helped isolate China?** *(mountains)* **L1**

PREVIEWING
People to Meet

Ask students the following questions using the biographies.

1. **Which one of these people founded the religion of Buddhism?** *(Siddhartha Gautama)* **L1**

2. **What were Homer's famous achievements?** *(wrote* Iliad *and* Odyssey*)* **L1**

3. **What were common characteristics of these leaders?** *(Answers will vary, but students may note that they were thinkers and/or soldiers.)* **L2**

👉 Refer to **People to Meet Activities** in the Unit Resources Books.

Unit
2 Places to Locate

① Greek Parthenon

See Ancient Greece Chapters 4 & 5

EUROPE

② Alexandria lighthouse

See Ancient Greece Chapter 5

AFRICA

①

②

People to Meet

Homer
c. 750 B.C.
Greek poet, wrote *Iliad* and *Odyssey*
Chapter 5, page 159

Siddhartha Gautama
c. 563–483 B.C.
Founder of Buddhism
Chapter 6, page 207

Confucius
551–479 B.C.
Chinese philosopher
Chapter 7, page 237

Pericles
c. 495–429 B.C.
Athenian general and leading statesman
Chapter 4, page 141

110

PREVIEWING Places to Locate

Use the following descriptions to explain the images on the map.

1 The Parthenon in Athens represents one of the crowning achievements of Greek architecture.

2 The lighthouse in Alexandria, built around 280 B.C., lasted until the A.D. 1300s. It provided a guiding light for ships miles out to sea.

ASIA

3 Harappan priest-king

See Early India
Chapter 6

4 Statue of god Siva

See Early India
Chapter 6

5 Great Wall of China

See Early China
Chapter 7

5

Pacific
Ocean

4

dian
cean

Aristotle

384–322 B.C.
Greek philosopher
Chapter 5, page 172

**Alexander
the Great**

c. 356–323 B.C.
**Macedonian
general and king**
Chapter 5, page 180

Asoka

Ruled c. 273–232 B.C.
Philosopher-king of India
Chapter 6, page 212

**Qin
Shihuangdi**

c. 259–210 B.C.
**Built the first Great
Wall of China**
Chapter 7, page 243

111

TEACH

Organizing Information Have students create a graphic organizer like the one below to organize information about the figures in the unit preview. *(Answers are provided.)* **L1/ EL**

Historical Figure	Civilization
Asoka	India
Aristotle	Greece
Siddhartha Gautama	India
Pericles	Greece
Homer	Greece
Confucius	China
Shihuangdi	China
Alexander the Great	Macedonia

Creating a Map Provide students with a copy of a map of the region covered in Unit 2 from the *Outline Map Resource Book.*

• Have students number each of the historical figures shown at the bottom of the unit preview.

• Tell students to label their maps with the number of each figure in the correct location.

• Ask students to discuss the prominent features of each civilization. **L2**

PREVIEWING **Places to Locate**

3 This statue of a priest-king shows the high level of civilization of a Harappan city called Mohenjo-Daro. Scholars think it was the capital of a large state near the Indus River.

4 Siva is one of the important Hindu gods. He can create with one hand and destroy with the other.

5 The Great Wall of China was first begun by the Qin. It covered thousands of miles.

Chapter 4 Resources

Note: The following materials may be used when teaching Chapter 4.
Section level support materials are shown at point of use in the margins of the Teacher Wraparound Edition.

TEACHING TRANSPARENCIES

- Graphic Organizer Transparencies with Teaching Strategy and Student Activity **L2**
- Cause-and-Effect Transparencies with Teaching Strategy and Student Activity **L2**
- Then and Now Transparencies with Teaching Strategy and Student Activity **L2**
- In-text Map Transparency with Teaching Strategy and Student Activity **L1**
- Map Transparencies with Overlay, Teaching Strategy, and Student Activity **L2**

DIFFERENTIATED INSTRUCTION

- Differentiated Instruction Activity 4
- Time Line Activity 4
- Primary Source Reading 4 (with Document-Based Questions)
- Inclusion Strategies for the Middle School Social Studies Classroom
- StudentWorks Plus™ CD-ROM (with Audio Program)

READING SUPPORT

- Take-Home Review Activity 4 **L2**
- World Literature Reading 4 **L2**
- Workbook Activity 4 **L1**
- Reading Strategies for the Social Studies Classroom **L1/ EL**

ASSESSMENT

- Authentic Assessment Activity 4 **L1/ EL**
- Chapter 4 Test Form A **L2**
- Chapter 4 Test Form B **L2**
- ExamView® Pro Testmaker CD-ROM

INTERDISCIPLINARY CONNECTIONS

- Geography and History Activity 4 **L2**
- People to Meet Activity 4 **L2**
- Economics Activity 4 **L2**
- Citizenship and Service Learning Activity 4 **L2**

SPANISH RESOURCES

- Spanish Reading Essentials and Study Guide
- Spanish Guided Reading Activities
- Spanish Quizzes, Tests, and Authentic Assessment (with Rubrics)
- Spanish Take-Home Review Activities

MULTIMEDIA

- ExamView® Pro Testmaker CD-ROM
- Glencoe Skillbuilder Interactive Workbook CD-ROM, Level 1
- Interactive Tutor Self-Assessment CD-ROM
- MindJogger Videoquiz
- Presentation Plus! CD-ROM
- StudentWorks Plus™ CD-ROM (with Audio Program)
- TeacherWorks CD-ROM
- Vocabulary PuzzleMaker CD-ROM
- *World History: Journey Across Time* Video Program
- World History Primary Source Document Library CD-ROM

STANDARDIZED ASSESSMENT SKILLS

- Standardized Test Skills Practice Workbook Activity 4 **L2**
- Critical Thinking Skills Activity 4 **L2**

Teaching strategies have been coded with suggested ability levels. However, most are suitable for all levels.

L1 BASIC activities for all students
L2 AVERAGE activities for average to above-average students
L3 CHALLENGING activities for above-average students
EL ENGLISH LANGUAGE activities

TIME MANAGEMENT

Unit Introduction	Chapter Introduction	Section 1	Section 2	Section 3	Section 4	Chapter Wrap-Up
1 Day	1 Day	2 Days	1 Day	1 Day	2 Days	1 Day

Block Scheduling Activities that are suited to use within the block scheduling framework are identified by:

`0:00` **OUT OF TIME?** Assign the Chapter 4 *Reading Essentials and Study Guide.*🗀

SECTION RESOURCES

DAILY OBJECTIVES	REPRODUCIBLE RESOURCES	MULTIMEDIA RESOURCES
Section 1 **The Early Greeks** 1. The geography of Greece influenced Greece's early civilizations—the Minoans and the Mycenaeans. 2. Colonies and trade spread Greek culture, which included the idea of citizenship.	🗀 Reproducible Lesson Plan 4–1 🗀 Vocabulary Activity 4–1 🗀 Guided Reading Activity 4–1* 🗀 Section Quiz 4–1* 🗀 Reading Essentials and Study Guide 4–1*	Daily Focus Skills Transparency 4–1 Interactive Tutor Self-Assessment CD-ROM Exam*View*® Pro Testmaker CD-ROM Presentation Plus! CD-ROM
Section 2 **Sparta and Athens** 1. Tyrants seized control over many city-states. 2. The Spartans focused on military rule, while the Athenians were more interested in democracy.	🗀 Reproducible Lesson Plan 4–2 🗀 Vocabulary Activity 4–2 🗀 Guided Reading Activity 4–2* 🗀 Section Quiz 4–2* 🗀 Reading Essentials and Study Guide 4–2*	Daily Focus Skills Transparency 4–2 Interactive Tutor Self-Assessment CD-ROM Exam*View*® Pro Testmaker CD-ROM Presentation Plus! CD-ROM
Section 3 **Persia Attacks the Greeks** 1. The Persian Empire united a wide area under a single government. 2. Sparta and Athens joined forces to defeat the Persians.	🗀 Reproducible Lesson Plan 4–3 🗀 Vocabulary Activity 4–3 🗀 Guided Reading Activity 4–3* 🗀 Section Quiz 4–3* 🗀 Reading Essentials and Study Guide 4–3*	Daily Focus Skills Transparency 4–3 Interactive Tutor Self-Assessment CD-ROM Exam*View*® Pro Testmaker CD-ROM Presentation Plus! CD-ROM
Section 4 **The Age of Pericles** 1. Athens became very powerful and more democratic. 2. Athens and Sparta went to war over control of Greece.	🗀 Reproducible Lesson Plan 4–4 🗀 Vocabulary Activity 4–4 🗀 Guided Reading Activity 4–4* 🗀 Section Quiz 4–4* 🗀 Reading Essentials and Study Guide 4–4*	Daily Focus Skills Transparency 4–4 Interactive Tutor Self-Assessment CD-ROM Exam*View*® Pro Testmaker CD-ROM Presentation Plus! CD-ROM Vocabulary PuzzleMaker CD-ROM Glencoe BookLink CD-ROM

*Also available in Spanish

History Online

Use our Web site for additional resources. All essential content is covered in the Student Edition.

You and your students can visit jat.glencoe.com, the Web site companion to *World History: Journey Across Time*. This innovative integration of electronic and print media offers your students a wealth of opportunities. The student text directs students to the Web site for the following options:

- Chapter Overviews
- Self-Check Quizzes
- Study Central™
- Student Web Activities
- Multi-Language Glossaries

Answers to the student Web activities are provided for you in the **Web Activity Lesson Plans.** Additional Web resources and ePuzzles and games are also available.

The following videotape programs are available from Glencoe as supplements to Chapter 4:

Lost City of Atlantis
(ISBN 0-7670-0627-5)

Mystical Monuments of Ancient Greece
(ISBN 0-7670-0012-9)

The Trojan City
(ISBN 0-7670-0647-X)

To order, call Glencoe at 1-800-334-7344. To find classroom resources to accompany many of these videos, check the following home pages:

A&E Television: www.aande.com
The History Channel: www.historychannel.com

MEETING SPECIAL NEEDS

In addition to the Differentiated Instruction strategies, the following resources are suitable for students with special needs:

- *ExamView® Pro Testmaker CD-ROM* allows teachers to tailor tests by reducing answer choices.
- *StudentWorks Plus™ CD-ROM (with Audio Program)* includes the entire narrative of the student edition so that less-proficient readers can listen to the words as they read them.
- The *Reading Essentials and Study Guide* provides the same content as the student edition but is written two grade levels below the textbook.

TEACHER'S CORNER

Index to National Geographic Magazine:
The following articles relate to this chapter:

- "Golden Age Treasures," by George Bass, March 2002.
- "Ancient Greece, Part 1," by Caroline Alexander, December 1999.
- "Ancient Greece, Part 2" and "Ancient Greece, Part 3," by Caroline Alexander, February and March 2000.

National Geographic Society Products:
To order the following, call National Geographic at 1–800–368–2728

- *PicturePack: Ancient Civilizations: Ancient Greece* (Transparencies)
- *PictureShow: Ancient Civilizations: Greece and Rome* (CD-ROM)

NGS ONLINE

Access National Geographic's new dynamic MapMachine Web site and other geography resources at:

www.nationalgeographic.com
www.nationalgeographic.com/maps

Meeting NCSS Standards

World History: Journey Across Time
The following standards are highlighted in Chapter 4:

Section 1 III **People, Places, and Environments: B, H, I, J**

V **Individuals, Groups, and Institutions: A**

Section 2 III **People, Places, and Environments: B**

VI **Power, Authority, and Governance: A, B, C, F**

Section 3 II **Time, Continuity, and Change: C, D**

III **People, Places, and Environments: B, D**

VI **Power, Authority, and Governance, C, F**

Section 4 I **Culture: A**

II **Time, Continuity, and Change: C**

X **Civic Ideals and Practices: A**

State and Local Objectives

_____

_____

Timesaving Tools

TeacherWorks
All-In-One Planner and Resource Center

- **Interactive Teacher Edition** Access your Teacher Wraparound Edition and your classroom resources with a few easy clicks.
- **Interactive Lesson Planner** Organize your week, month, semester, or year with all the lesson helps you need to make teaching creative and relevant.

Use Glencoe's **Presentation Plus!** multimedia teacher tool to easily present dynamic lessons that visually excite your students. Using Microsoft PowerPoint® you can customize the presentations to create your own personalized lessons.

FOLDABLES™
Study Organizer
Dinah Zike's Foldables

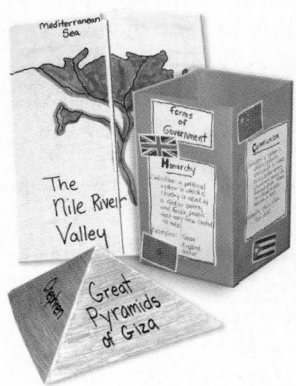

Foldables are three-dimensional, interactive graphic organizers that help students practice basic writing skills, review key vocabulary terms, and identify main ideas. Every chapter contains a foldable activity, with additional chapter activities found in the *Reading and Study Skills Foldables* booklet. You can use the foldables as they are presented, or modify them to suit the needs of your individual class.

Planning Ahead

CHAPTER CULMINATING ACTIVITY

The Chapter Culminating Activity will help students organize and learn the important information from the chapter. Begin the chapter with this activity, and have students complete it as a culminating activity.

CREATING AN ABC ORGANIZER

Purpose An ABC organizer helps students gather information while they read or review a chapter. It encourages them to look for terms, concepts, key ideas, or facts related to each letter of the alphabet. The organizer can be done individually, in small groups, or as a whole-class activity.

Introduction to Modeling

1. Have students read the **Chapter Preview** to gain a grasp of the main ideas in each section.

2. Introduce the concept of an ABC organizer. Copy the following model on the board or distribute copies for students to use in preparing their charts. Have students use large drawing paper or poster board for the complete chart, or index cards for each letter, which would later be pasted onto poster board.

3. Have students find important ideas, names, and terms from the chapter that begin with each letter. Tell them to include a short definition with each entry.

ABCs of Ancient Greece		A	B	C
		D	E	F
G	H	I	J	K
L	M	N	O	P
Q	R	S	T	U
V	W	X	Y	Z

4. Some letters, such as *J* and *U*, may be more difficult and require creativity. Sample entries include: **J**umping—one of the contests at the ancient Olympics; **U**ndersea earthquakes—may have caused waves that destroyed Minoan cities.

5. Finished organizers will be excellent study aids for the chapter test and writing essays.

Use the **SkillBuilder Handbook** on pages 902–919 to help students learn the skill of taking notes.

Authentic Assessment

Refer to Activity 4 in the Authentic Assessment section of the *Quizzes, Tests, and Authentic Assessment (with Rubrics)* booklet.

When & Where?

Refer students to the time line on this page. **Ask:** What was one of the dominant features of political life in ancient Greece? (*Most students will note the armed conflicts.*) Tell students that they will learn about these conflicts and the way in which the Greeks responded. **L2**

GLENCOE TECHNOLOGY

World History: Journey Across Time Video Program

To learn more about ancient Greece, students can view the Chapter 4 video in the *World History: Journey Across Time* Video Program.

MindJogger Videoquiz

Use the **MindJogger Videoquiz** to preview Chapter 4 content.

 Available in DVD and VHS

Chapter 4
The Ancient Greeks

The Parthenon rises above the city of Athens. The people of ancient Greece built this temple to celebrate their goddess Athena. ▶

NATIONAL GEOGRAPHIC When & Where?

700 B.C.	600 B.C.	500 B.C.	400 B.C.
c. 750 B.C. Greece's Dark Age comes to an end	c. 650 B.C. Tyrants overthrow nobles in city-states	480 B.C. Xerxes invades Greece	431 B.C. Peloponnesian War begins

Reading Strategy — PURPOSE FOR READING

Seed Discussion Tell students that democracy got its start in ancient Greece. Ask students to reach a consensus on a definition of *democracy* as they understand it. **Ask:** Do you think democracy meant the same thing to the ancient Greeks as it means to us? Why or why not? (*Activate prior knowledge by recalling how our own definition of democracy has expanded since the U.S. Constitution was written, including such things as voting rights for all adults.*) Record and save responses. Then direct students to focus on the development and meaning of democracy as they read Chapter 4.

Repeat this activity at the end of the chapter. Ask students to identify some of the things they learned about Greek democracy. **L2**

Chapter Preview

Greek civilization began almost 4,000 years ago, but Greek ideas about government, science, and the arts are still important today.

 View the Chapter 4 video in the *World History: Journey Across Time* Video Program.

Chapter Overview Visit jat.glencoe.com for a preview of Chapter 4.

Section 1 — The Early Greeks

The earliest civilizations in Greece were the Minoans and the Mycenaeans. Greece's mountains, climate, and surrounding seas played a large role in their history.

Section 2 — Sparta and Athens

Athens and Sparta became the two most powerful city-states in ancient Greece. Sparta focused on its military force, while Athens focused on trade, culture, and democracy.

Section 3 — Persia Attacks the Greeks

The Persian Empire gained control of most of southwest Asia. However, when the Persians tried to conquer the Greeks, Athens and Sparta united to defeat them.

Section 4 — The Age of Pericles

Under the leadership of Pericles, Athens became a powerful city-state and culture blossomed.

Summarizing Information *Make this foldable to help you organize and summarize information about the ancient Greeks.*

Step 1 *Mark the midpoint of a side edge of one sheet of paper. Then fold the outside edges in to touch the midpoint.*

Step 2 *Fold the paper in half again from side to side.*

Step 3 *Open the paper and cut along the inside fold lines to form four tabs.*

Cut along the fold lines on both sides.

Step 4 *Label as shown.*

  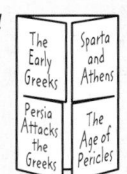

Reading and Writing *As you read the chapter, write information under each appropriate tab. Be sure to summarize the information you find by writing only main ideas and supporting details.*

113

INTRODUCING CHAPTER 4

Introduce students to chapter content and key terms by having them access Chapter Overview 4 at jat.glencoe.com

CHAPTER PREVIEW

After reading Chapter 4, students should be able to

1. describe how geography and the Minoan and Mycenaean civilizations influenced Greek culture;

2. compare the city-states of Sparta and Athens;

3. identify the causes and effects of Greek wars with Persia;

4. describe Athens under the leadership of Pericles and reasons Athens declined.

FOLDABLES
Study Organizer
Dinah Zike's Foldables

Purpose This foldable helps students identify and record the main ideas and supporting details in each section of the chapter. Make sure students understand the difference between the two items.

Have students complete *Reading and Study Skills Foldables* Activity 4.

MORE ABOUT THE PHOTO

The Parthenon The Parthenon was built on the Acropolis, the fortified center of Athens. It was a holy site. Many other temples were built there, including the Erechtheum—a small temple dedicated to Athena and Poseidon; the Temple of Athena Nike—dedicated to the goddess of victory; and the Sanctuary of Zeus—where burnt offerings were made to the chief god. The Parthenon stood as the grandest of all temples on the hill. It was built to honor the goddess Athena with money collected from Athens's empire. High walls surrounding the rocky hill protected the temples there. The Athenians would flee to the Acropolis as a last resort in times of war.

1 Learn It!

Good readers visualize details of the text as they read, making connections between the known and the unknown. Help students visualize by reading aloud a particularly vivid or interesting passage and asking them what they "see" as you are reading. Remind them to think of places they may already be familiar with through movies, books, or other experiences. Read the following passage from page 118 aloud as a way to practice this technique with students:

> The palace at Knossos (NAH•suhs) revealed the riches of an ancient society. Its twisting passageways led to many different rooms: private quarters for the royal family and storerooms packed with oil, wine, and grain. Other spaces were workshops for making jewelry, vases, and small ivory statues. The palace even had bathrooms.

Some students may wish to draw as you read to help them make the visualization more concrete. **L1/ EL**

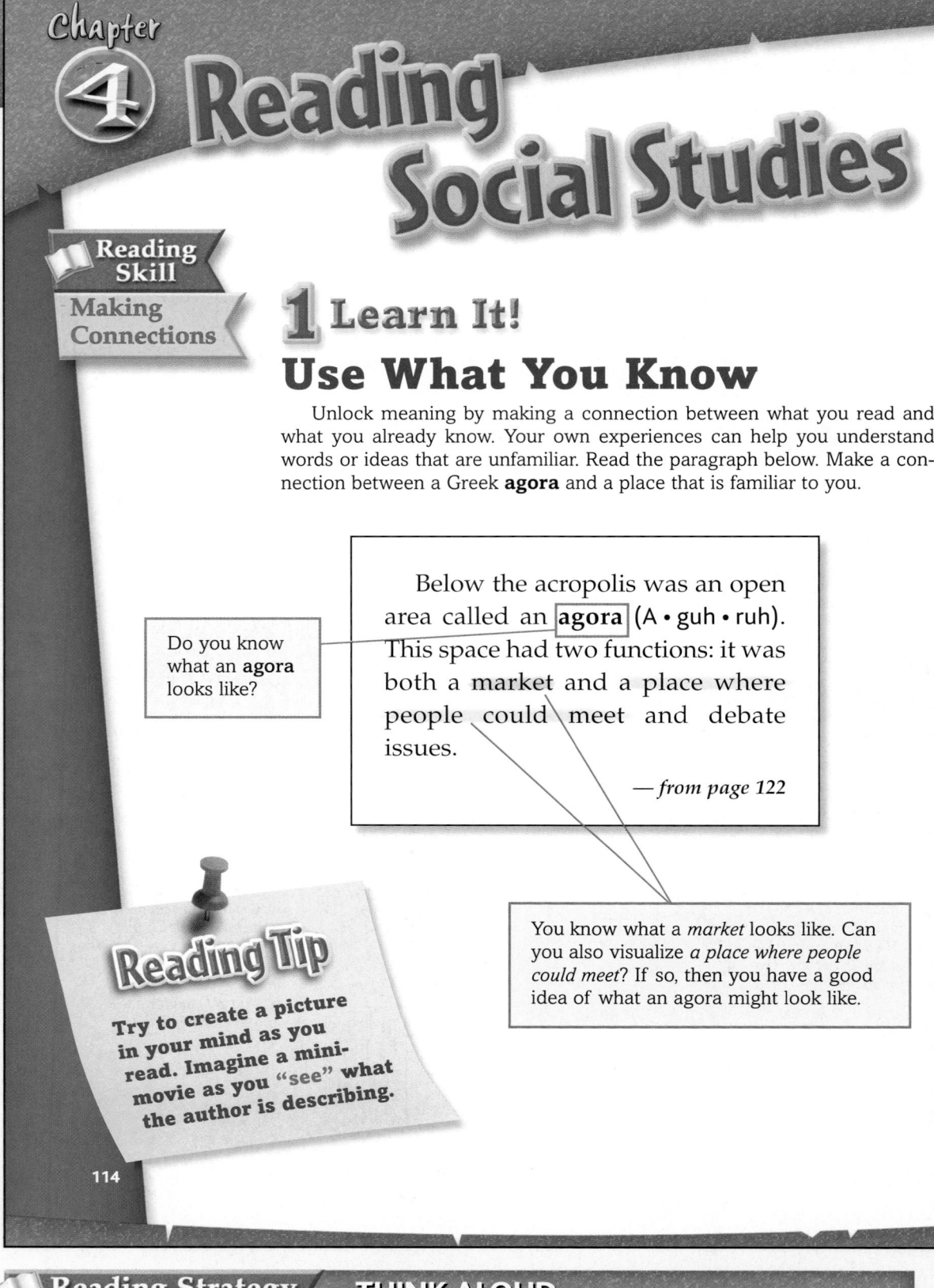

Chapter

4 Reading Social Studies

Reading Skill

Making Connections

1 Learn It!

Use What You Know

Unlock meaning by making a connection between what you read and what you already know. Your own experiences can help you understand words or ideas that are unfamiliar. Read the paragraph below. Make a connection between a Greek **agora** and a place that is familiar to you.

> Below the acropolis was an open area called an **agora** (A • guh • ruh). This space had two functions: it was both a **market** and a place where people could meet and debate issues.
>
> — *from page 122*

Do you know what an **agora** looks like?

You know what a *market* looks like. Can you also visualize *a place where people could meet*? If so, then you have a good idea of what an agora might look like.

Reading Tip

Try to create a picture in your mind as you read. Imagine a mini-movie as you "see" what the author is describing.

114

Reading Strategy   THINK ALOUD

A powerful way to help students internalize the process of comprehension is to read aloud to them and stop frequently to verbalize your own methods of comprehension. For example, you might stop when you come to a difficult word and "talk through" how you come to know its meaning based on the context of the passage. You could share your own visualization or connection as you read to demystify the process of reading. This type of modeling is extremely effective in helping students understand how good readers construct meaning from text.

2 Practice It!

Making the Connection

Read the following paragraph from Chapter 4. What ideas can you connect to your own experiences? Use the questions below to help you begin a class discussion about things in your life that relate to life in ancient Greece.

Read to Write

Choose one of the connections from your discussion. Write a paragraph to explain why you made such a connection. Use vivid details.

At age 20, Spartan men entered the regular army. The men remained in military barracks for 10 more years. They ate all their meals in dining halls with other soldiers. A typical meal was a vile-tasting dish called black broth—pork boiled in animal blood, salt, and vinegar.

Spartans returned home at age 30 but stayed in the army until age 60. They continued to train for combat. They expected to either win on the battlefield or die, but never to surrender. One Spartan mother ordered her son to "Come home carrying your shield or being carried on it."

—*from pages 126–127*

- Do you have any family members or friends who are 20 years old? What would they say if they were required to serve in the army for 40 years?
- Have you ever seen or tasted food that looks like "black broth"?

3 Apply It!

As you read the chapter, choose five words or phrases that make a connection to something you already know.

115

2 Practice It!

Visualizing Group students in pairs. Have students skim through the chapter and choose a passage that interests them, one with which they can easily make a connection. The first student will read his or her chosen passage aloud. The other student will draw, write, or describe orally what he or she visualizes as the passage is read. Students will then exchange roles.

Share the visualizations by displaying the drawings or allowing students to read their pieces to the class as a way of activating background knowledge and enhancing comprehension. **L1**

3 Apply It!

Have students create a connection board of artifacts that connect the chapter of study to their daily lives. Encourage them to use magazine pictures, drawings, stories, Web-based research, and reviews of movies or books that are related to the chapter. Showing clips of movies related to Greek times is another way to demonstrate to students how visualizations are created from printed text. **L2**

Reading Strategy — READ TO WRITE

To help students make connections and visualize as they read, they can turn the text into scenes from movies. After reading about King Minos, for example, have students create a script with Minos as the star. What actor would students choose to play his part in a film? Where would it be filmed? Who would be the voice of the Minotaur? What series of events would happen to create a plot in a movie?

📂 Refer to the *Quizzes, Tests, and Authentic Assessment (with Rubrics)* booklet for rubrics.

① FOCUS

① FOCUS

SECTION OVERVIEW

This section describes the impact of geography on ancient Greece and the rise of the Minoan and Mycenaean civilizations.

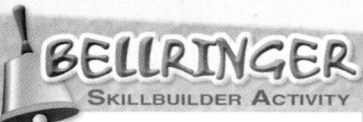

BELLRINGER
SKILLBUILDER ACTIVITY

🖱 Project **Daily Focus Skills Transparency 4–1** and have students answer questions. Discuss their responses.

Get Ready to Read!

Preteaching Vocabulary: Explain the meaning of *peninsula. (body of land with water on three sides)* Point out Greece's location on a peninsula, and have students speculate about ways that location might have influenced how the early Greeks lived.

Answers to Graphic: Possible answers: a tiny country; main gathering place on a hill; a fortified area called an acropolis; agora—marketplace and meeting area; varied in size and population

---

Section 1

The Early Greeks

Get Ready to Read!

What's the Connection?

In Chapters 1 and 2, you learned about Mesopotamia and Egypt. These civilizations grew up in great river valleys with rich soil. Greece had no great river valleys. Instead, it had mountains, rocky soil, and many miles of seacoasts.

Focusing on the Main Ideas

- The geography of Greece influenced where people settled and what they did. *(page 117)*

- The Minoans earned their living by building ships and trading. *(page 118)*

- Mycenaeans built the first Greek kingdoms and spread their power across the Mediterranean region. *(page 119)*

- Colonies and trade spread Greek culture and spurred industry. *(page 121)*

- The idea of citizenship developed in Greek city-states. *(page 122)*

Locating Places

Crete (KREET)
Mycenae (my•SEE•nee)
Peloponnesus (PEH•luh•puh•NEE•suhs)

Meeting People

Agamemnon (A•guh•MEHM•nahn)

Building Your Vocabulary

peninsula (puh•NIHN•suh•luh)
colony (KAH•luh•nee)
polis (PAH•luhs)
agora (A•guh•ruh)

Reading Strategy

Finding Details Draw a diagram like the one below. In each oval write one detail about a polis.

NATIONAL GEOGRAPHIC **When & Where?**

GREECE

Mycenae •

Crete — • Knossos

2000 B.C.

c. 2000 B.C.
Minoans control eastern Mediterranean

1250 B.C.

c. 1200 B.C.
Mycenaean civilization declines

500 B.C.

c. 750 B.C.
Greece's Dark Age comes to an end

116   CHAPTER 4   The Ancient Greeks

SECTION RESOURCES

📁 **Reproducible Masters**
- Reproducible Lesson Plan 4–1
- Daily Lecture and Discussion Notes 4–1
- Vocabulary Activity 4–1
- Active Reading Note-Taking Guide 4–1
- Guided Reading Activity 4–1
- Section Quiz 4–1
- Reading Essentials and Study Guide 4–1

🖱 **Transparencies**
- Daily Focus Skills Transparency 4–1

Multimedia
- Interactive Tutor Self-Assessment CD-ROM
- ExamView® Pro Testmaker CD-ROM
- Presentation Plus! CD-ROM

The Geography of Greece

Main Idea The geography of Greece influenced where people settled and what they did.

Reading Focus Do you rake leaves in the fall? Do you walk uphill to school? Your answers explain how geography shapes your life. Read to learn how geography shaped life in early Greece.

If you fly over Greece today, you will see a mountainous land framed by sparkling blue water. To the west is the Ionian (eye•OH•nee•uhn) Sea, to the south is the Mediterranean Sea, and to the east is the Aegean (ih•JEE•uhn) Sea. Hundreds of islands lie offshore, stretching across to Asia like stepping-stones. Mainland Greece is a

peninsula (puh•NIHN•suh•luh)—a body of land with water on three sides.

Many ancient Greeks made a living from the sea. They became fishers, sailors, and traders. Others settled in farming communities. Greece's mountains and rocky soil were not ideal for growing crops. However, the climate was mild, and in some places people could grow wheat, barley, olives, and grapes. They also raised sheep and goats.

Ancient Greeks felt deep ties to the land, but the mountains and seas divided them from one another. As a result, early Greek communities grew up fiercely independent.

Reading Check **Cause and Effect** How did geography discourage Greek unity?

NATIONAL GEOGRAPHIC

Ancient Greece c. 750 B.C.

MACEDONIA

Mt. Olympus ▲

40°N

BALKAN PENINSULA

GREECE

Ionian Sea

Delphi
Gulf of Corinth
Thebes
Corinth
Mycenae
Athens

Mediterranean Sea

PELOPONNESUS
Sparta

Sea of Marmara

Troy

Aegean Sea

ASIA MINOR

KEY
Ancient Greece

Miletus

0 ___ 100 miles
0 ___ 100 kilometers
Lambert Azimuthal Equal-Area projection

Sea of Crete

Knossos

Crete

Mountains and seas played an important role in Greek history. ▶

Using Geography Skills

All parts of ancient Greece were near water.
1. What body of water lies east of the Balkan Peninsula?
2. What transportation was probably most useful to the early Greeks?

Find NGS online map resources @ www.nationalgeographic.com/maps

② TEACH

Identifying Location Distribute outline maps of the Mediterranean region. Tell students to label places on the map as they read through the section. **Ask: How did the region's geography help the Greeks settle in new areas?** (*The sea connected the seafaring Greeks with lands throughout the region.*) **L2**

Daily Lecture and Discussion Notes 4–1

Use **Daily Lecture and Discussion Notes 4–1** for an outline of key concepts found in the section.

Reading Support L1/ EL

Use **Vocabulary Activity 4–1** to review important terms in the section.

Using Geography Skills

Answers:
1. the Aegean Sea
2. boats

Reading Check

Answer: The mountains and seas kept the Greeks apart, and early Greek communities became fiercely independent.

Reading Strategy **READING THE TEXT**

Setting a Purpose Encourage students to set their own purpose for reading. Write on the board the six question words—*Who, What, When, Where, Why,* and *How*—that reporters use to search for information on a topic. Then organize the class into small groups and have them write questions about the section using these words. Get students started with this example: Who built the early Greek civilizations? **L1/ EL**

CURRICULUM CONNECTION

Science

Tell students that the movement of "plates" causes earthquakes like the one that may have destroyed Minoan cities. Plates are large layers of rock, or crust, that float on the earth's melted inner core. Have students work in groups to research the world's major tectonic plates. **Ask:** Why might this information explain the destruction of Minoan cities? *(The collision of plates near Greece might have produced enough force to create huge waves.)*

✓ Reading Check

Answer: The Minoans used the islands' trees to build ships that carried them all over the eastern Mediterranean.

More About the Art

The palace at Knossos covered about 5 acres (2 ha). Archaeologists believe it had hundreds of rooms, including bathrooms with running water, toilets, and bathtubs.

Caption Answer: Arthur Evans

The Minoans

Main Idea The Minoans earned their living by building ships and trading.

Reading Focus Imagine what it would be like to uncover a building that is more than 5,000 years old. Read to learn how such a discovery unlocked clues to Greece's ancient past.

The island of **Crete** (KREET) lies southeast of the Greek mainland. There, in 1900, an English archaeologist by the name of Arthur Evans made the find of a lifetime. Evans uncovered the ruins of a grand palace that had been the center of Minoan (muh•NOH•uhn) civilization. The Minoans were not Greeks, but their civilization was the first to arise in the region that later became Greece.

The palace at Knossos (NAH•suhs) revealed the riches of an ancient society. Its twisting passageways led to many different rooms: private quarters for the royal family and storerooms packed with oil, wine, and grain. Other spaces were workshops for making jewelry, vases, and small ivory statues. The palace even had bathrooms.

The Minoans made their wealth from trade. They built ships from oak and cedar trees and sailed as far as Egypt and Syria. There they traded pottery and stone vases for ivory and metals. By 2000 B.C., Minoan ships controlled the eastern Mediterranean Sea. They carried goods to foreign ports and kept the sea free of pirates.

About 1450 B.C., the Minoan civilization suddenly collapsed. Some historians think undersea earthquakes caused giant waves that washed away the Minoans' cities. Others think the cities were destroyed by a group of Greeks from the mainland. These invaders were called the Mycenaeans (MY•suh•NEE•uhns).

✓ Reading Check **Explain** How did the Minoans become a trading civilization?

▲ This wall painting from Knossos shows Minoans participating in a dangerous sport called bull leaping. *Who discovered the palace at Knossos?*

◄ Minoan calendar

118   CHAPTER 4   The Ancient Greeks

DIFFERENTIATED INSTRUCTION

Visual/Spatial: Tell students that we learned much of what we know about Minoan culture from its art. Ask them to compile a list describing the most important visual details in the painting from Knossos.

Verbal/Linguistic: Have students form conclusions about Minoan culture from these details.

Gifted and Talented: Ask several students to test these conclusions by researching further information on the Minoans and reporting on it to the class.

📂 Refer to *Inclusion Strategies for the Middle School Social Studies Classroom* in the TCR.

The First Greek Kingdoms

Main Idea Mycenaeans built the first Greek kingdoms and spread their power across the Mediterranean region.

Reading Focus What is the most important building in the area where you live? Is it a government building, a grocery store, or a hospital? Read to find out what building was most important in the Mycenaean civilization.

The Mycenaeans were originally from central Asia. They invaded the Greek mainland around 1900 B.C. and conquered the people living there. The Mycenaean leaders became the first Greek kings. Their warriors became nobles who ruled the people they had conquered. In the late 1800s, a German named Heinrich Schliemann (HYN•rihk SHLEE•MAHN) discovered one of their walled palaces in **Mycenae** (my•SEE•nee). He named the people of this civilization the Mycenaeans.

What Were Mycenaean Kingdoms Like?

The centerpiece of each Mycenaean kingdom was a fortified palace on a hill. The ruler lived there, surrounded by giant stone walls. Beyond the palace walls lay large farms, or estates, that belonged to the nobles. Slaves and farmers lived on the estates and took shelter inside the fortress in times of danger.

Mycenaean palaces hummed with activity. Artisans tanned leather, sewed clothes, and made jars for wine and olive oil. Other workers made bronze swords and ox-hide shields. Government officials kept track of the wealth of every person in the kingdom. Then they collected wheat, livestock, and honey as taxes and stored them in the palace.

Power From Trade and War

Soon after the Mycenaeans set up their kingdoms, Minoan traders began to visit from Crete.

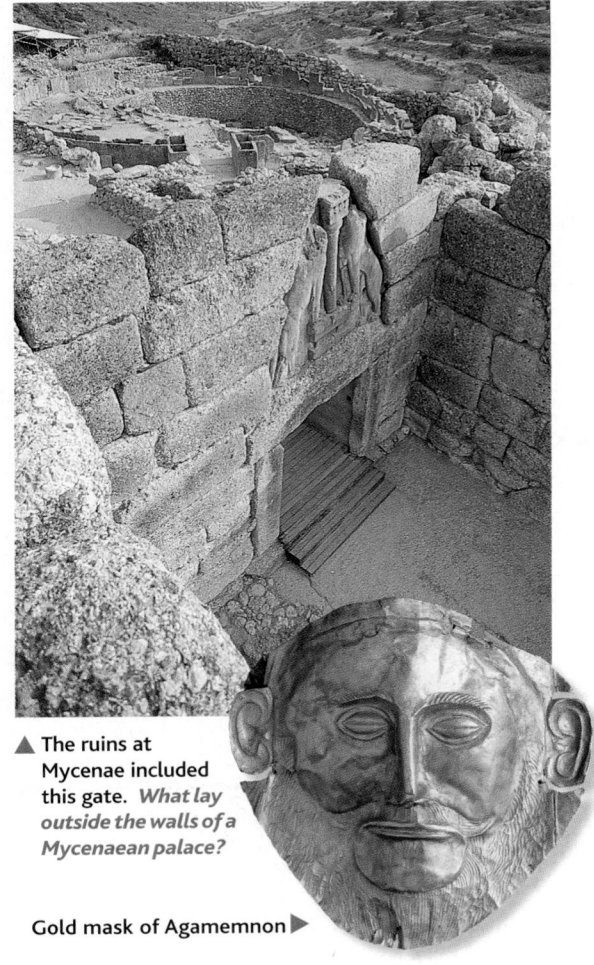

▲ The ruins at Mycenae included this gate. *What lay outside the walls of a Mycenaean palace?*

Gold mask of Agamemnon ▶

As a result, Mycenaeans learned much about Minoan culture. They copied the ways Minoans worked with bronze and built ships. They learned how the Minoans used the sun and stars to find their way at sea. The Mycenaeans even started worshiping the Earth Mother, the Minoans' chief goddess.

Around 1400 B.C., the Mycenaeans replaced the Minoans as the major power on the Mediterranean. They traded widely, sailing to Egypt and southern Italy. Some

CHAPTER 4   The Ancient Greeks   119

CONNECTING ACROSS TIME

We can thank the Greek alphabet for the prefixes *mega* and *micro*. **Ask:** What English words use the prefixes *mega* and *micro*? (*Possible answers: mega—megaphone, megabyte, megalopolis; micro—microphone, microscope, microbe*) **L1/EL**

Understanding Charts

When studying **The Greek Alphabet** chart, students should spot connections to our system of writing. **Ask:** How does the Greek system of writing differ from Egyptian hieroglyphics? (*Greek writing uses phonetic symbols to represent sounds, while hieroglyphics uses pictures to represent ideas.*)

Answer: It was no longer used and eventually forgotten.

✓ Reading Check

Answer: Trade slowed, poverty took hold, farming decreased, many people stopped teaching others how to write or do craftwork, and people settled in new areas, expanding the reach of Greek culture.

The Greek Alphabet

Greek Letter	Written Name	English Sound
A	alpha	a
B	beta	b
Γ	gamma	g
Δ	delta	d
E	epsilon	e
Z	zeta	z
H	eta	e
Θ	theta	th
I	iota	i
K	kappa	c, k
Λ	lambda	l
M	mu	m
N	nu	n
Ξ	xi	x
O	omicron	o
Π	pi	p
P	rho	r
Σ	sigma	s
T	tau	t
Y	upsilon	y, u
Φ	phi	ph
X	chi	ch
Ψ	psi	ps
Ω	omega	o

▲ The Greek alphabet was based on the Phoenician alphabet. *What happened to Greek writing during the Dark Age?*

historians think they conquered Crete and nearby islands.

Although trade made the Mycenaeans wealthy, they were prouder of their deeds in battle. Their most famous victory is probably the Trojan War. In the next chapter, you will learn the legend of how the Mycenaean king **Agamemnon** (A•guh•MEHM•nahn) used trickery to win that war.

What Was the Dark Age? By 1200 B.C., the Mycenaeans were in trouble. Earthquakes and fighting among the kingdoms had destroyed their hilltop forts. By 1100 B.C., Mycenaean civilization had collapsed.

The years between 1100 B.C. and 750 B.C. were difficult for the Greeks. Overseas trade slowed and poverty took hold. Farmers grew only enough food to meet their own family's needs. People also stopped teaching others how to write or do craftwork. Before long, the Greeks had forgotten their written language and how to make many things. As a result, historians call this time the Dark Age.

The changes that took place in the Dark Age were not all bad, however. One positive development was a huge population shift. Thousands of Greeks left the mainland and settled on islands in the Aegean Sea. Other Greeks moved to the western shores of Asia Minor, to what is now the country of Turkey. This wave of movement expanded the reach of Greek culture.

Meanwhile, a Greek-speaking people known as the Dorians (DOHR•ee•uhns), who lived in Greece's northern mountains, began to move south. Many settled in the **Peloponnesus** (PEH•luh•puh•NEE•suhs). The Dorians brought iron weapons with them, giving Greece more advanced technology. Iron weapons and farm tools were stronger and cheaper than those made of bronze.

Gradually, people began to farm again and to produce surplus food. As a result, trade revived. One benefit of the increased trade was a new way of writing. As you read in Chapter 3, the Greeks picked up the idea of an alphabet from the Phoenicians, one of their trading partners who lived on the coast of the eastern Mediterranean.

The Greek alphabet had 24 letters that stood for different sounds. It made reading and writing Greek much simpler than ever before. Soon people were writing down tales that had been passed down by storytellers for generations.

✓ Reading Check **Identify** What changes occurred during Greece's Dark Age?

INTERDISCIPLINARY CONNECTIONS ACTIVITY

Mathematics Tell students that the word *arithmetic* comes from the Greek word *arithmos*. However, Greek math was a lot different from ours. For one thing, the Greeks did not have a symbol for zero. Explain that the Greeks invented different methods to help count. One involved the use of the abacus—an instrument used for addition, subtraction, division, and multiplication. Call on students to research the history and use of the abacus and demonstrate its use in class. In a follow-up discussion, compare this tool to the electronic calculator. **L3**

A Move to Colonize

Main Idea Colonies and trade spread Greek culture and spurred industry.

Reading Focus If you read labels, you know that your food and clothing come from all over the world. Read to find out where the early Greeks got their goods.

As Greece recovered from its Dark Age, its population rose quickly. By 700 B.C., farmers could no longer grow enough grain to feed everyone. As a result, cities began sending people outside Greece to start **colonies** (KAH•luh•nees). A colony is a settlement in a new territory that keeps close ties to its homeland.

Between 750 B.C. and 550 B.C., adventurous Greeks streamed to the coasts of Italy, France, Spain, North Africa, and western Asia. With each new colony, Greek culture spread farther.

Colonists traded regularly with their "parent" cities, shipping them grains, metals, fish, timber, and enslaved people. In return, the colonists received pottery, wine, and olive oil from the mainland. Overseas trade got an extra boost during the 600s B.C., when the Greeks began to mint coins. Merchants were soon exchanging goods for money rather than for more goods.

The growth of trade led to the growth of industry. As the demand for goods grew, producers had to keep pace. People in different areas began specializing in making certain products. For example, pottery making became popular in places with large amounts of clay.

Reading Check Cause and Effect How did new colonies affect industry?

Reading Support L1/ EL

Assign **Guided Reading Activity 4–1** to help students organize the information in the section.

③ ASSESS

Assign Section 1 Review as homework or as an in-class activity.

⊙ Have students use the **Interactive Tutor Self-Assessment CD-ROM** to review the section.

Assessment L2

Assign **Section 1 Quiz** to assess mastery of the material found in the section.

Reading Check

Answer: Colonies increased the demand for goods and specialization, which in turn led to the growth of industry.

Using Geography Skills

Answers:
1. Cyprus, Sicily, Corsica
2. Europe, Asia, Africa

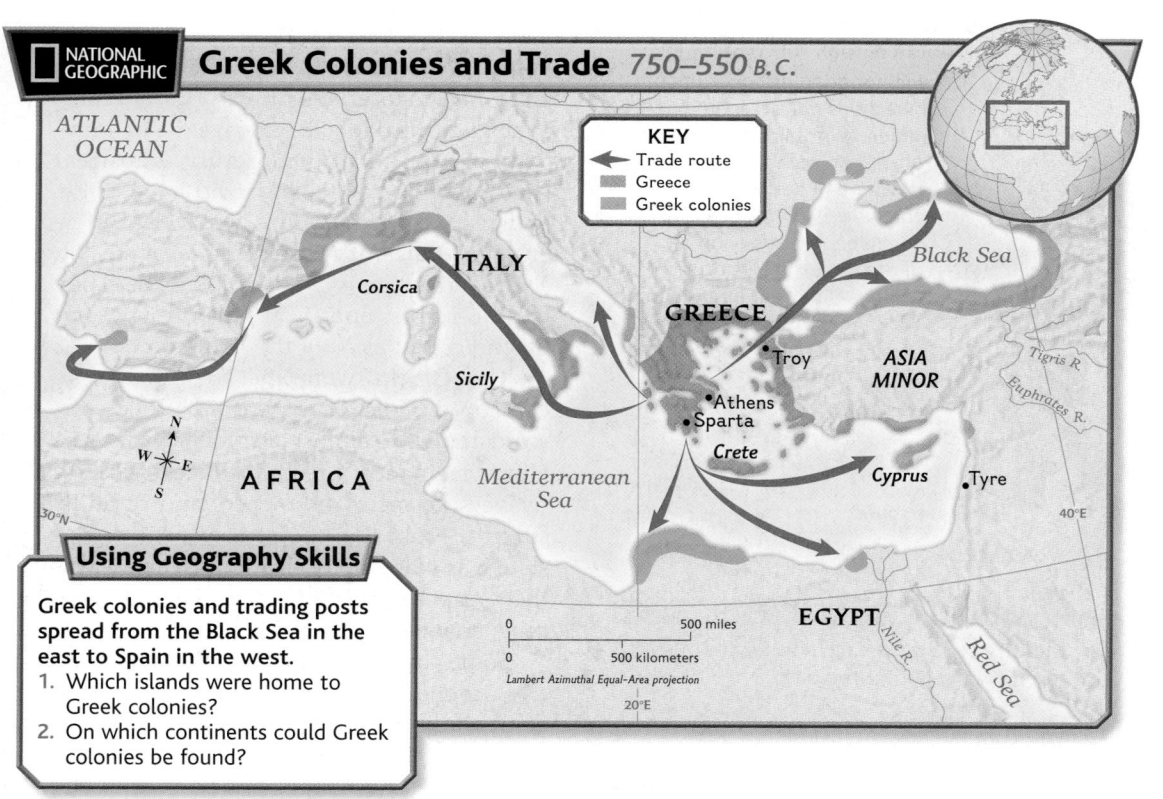

NATIONAL GEOGRAPHIC
Greek Colonies and Trade *750–550 B.C.*

KEY
← Trade route
■ Greece
■ Greek colonies

ATLANTIC OCEAN
ITALY
Corsica
Sicily
AFRICA
Mediterranean Sea
GREECE
Troy
Athens
Sparta
Crete
ASIA MINOR
Black Sea
Tigris R.
Euphrates R.
Cyprus
Tyre
EGYPT
Nile R.
Red Sea

0   500 miles
0   500 kilometers
Lambert Azimuthal Equal-Area projection

Using Geography Skills

Greek colonies and trading posts spread from the Black Sea in the east to Spain in the west.
1. Which islands were home to Greek colonies?
2. On which continents could Greek colonies be found?

EXTENDING THE CONTENT

What English Words Come From Greek? Students might be surprised by how many words they know that come from Greek. Some of these include: *geometry, physics, astronomy, star, galaxy, atom, music, melody, chorus, drama, comedy, poet, character, history, metropolis, athlete,* and *stadium.*

Primary Source

The Athenians gave the name epheboi to a special class of young men between the ages of 18 and 20 who trained for military service. If they completed the first year satisfactorily, the government outfitted them with a spear, a shield, a broad-rimmed helmet, and a cloak.

Answer:
They promise not to dishonor their weapons, not to desert their comrades, to improve the fatherland, to uphold and protect the constitution, to honor the temples, and to honor the religion of their forefathers.

☞ See the **Primary Source Readings (with Document-Based Questions)** in the Unit Resource Books.

The Polis

Main Idea The idea of citizenship developed in Greek city-states.

Reading Focus Did you know that the word "politics" comes from *polis*, the Greek term for a city-state? Read to find how the Greeks also created the idea of citizenship.

By the end of the Dark Age, many nobles who owned large estates had overthrown the Greek kings. They created city-states. Like the Mesopotamian city-states you read about in Chapter 1, those in Greece were made up of a town or city and the surrounding countryside. Each Greek city-state, known as a **polis** (PAH•luhs), was like a tiny independent country.

The main gathering place in the polis was usually a hill. A fortified area, called an acropolis (uh•KRAH•puh•luhs), stood at the top of the hill. It provided a safe refuge in case of attacks. Sometimes the acropolis also served as a religious center. Temples and altars were built there to honor the many Greek gods and goddesses.

Below the acropolis was an open area called an **agora** (A•guh•ruh). This space had two functions: it was both a market and a place where people could meet and debate issues.

City-states varied in size. Some were a few miles square, while others covered hundreds of square miles. They also varied in population. Nearly 300,000 people lived in Athens by 500 B.C. Most city-states were much smaller, however.

What Was Greek Citizenship? Each Greek city-state was run by its citizens. When we speak of citizens, we mean members of a political community who treat each other as equals and who have rights and responsibilities. This was very different from ancient Mesopotamia or Egypt. There, most people were subjects. They had no rights, no say in government, and no choice but to obey their rulers.

The Greeks were the first people to develop the idea of citizenship. Today, the word applies to almost everyone in a society. However, in most Greek city-states, only free native-born men who owned land could be citizens. From their point of view, the city-state was made up of their lands, and it was their responsibility to run it. They did not think anyone else should be a citizen.

Some city-states, such as Athens, eventually dropped the land-owning requirement. Slaves and foreign-born residents, however,

Primary Source
Athenian Soldier's Oath

In the Greek city of Athens, soldiers took this oath:

"I will not bring dishonor upon my weapons nor desert the comrade by my side. I will strive to hand on my fatherland greater and better than I found it. I will not consent to anyone's disobeying or destroying the constitution but will prevent him, whether I am with others or alone. I will honor the temples and the religion my forefathers established."

—oath of enrollment in Epheboi corps, c. 300s B.C.

◀ Greek soldier

DBQ Document-Based Question
Identify six things each soldier promises to protect in taking the oath.

CITIZENSHIP AND YOU

Defining Citizenship As written in 1787, the U.S. Constitution did not offer citizenship to all Americans. In the 1860s, however, the Fourteenth Amendment provided guidelines to protect citizenship status. Distribute Sections 1 and 2 of this amendment and have a student read them aloud.
Ask: How does Section 1 define citizenship? *(People born or naturalized in the United States are U.S. citizens.)* What rights are guaranteed to citizens? *(rights to life, liberty, property, due process, and equal protection under the law and the right to vote)* Ask students to compare the rights associated with citizenship in ancient Greece with those in the United States and decide which are more inclusive. **L1/ EL**

continued to be excluded. As for women and children, they might qualify for citizenship, but they had none of the rights that went with it.

What exactly were the rights of Greek citizens? They could gather in the agora to choose their officials and pass laws. They had the right to vote, hold office, own property, and defend themselves in court. In return, citizens had a duty to serve in government and to fight for their polis as citizen soldiers.

Citizens as Soldiers In early Greece, wars were waged by nobles riding horses and chariots. As the idea of citizenship developed, however, the military system changed. By 700 B.C., the city-states had begun to depend on armies of ordinary citizens called hoplites (HAHP•LYTS).

Unable to afford horses, the hoplites fought on foot and went into battle heavily armed. Each carried a round shield, a

Greek plate ▶ showing soldiers in battle

short sword, and a 9-foot (2.7-m) spear. Row upon row of soldiers marched forward together, shoulder to shoulder. With their shields creating a protective wall, they gave their enemies few openings to defeat them.

Hoplites made good soldiers because, as citizens, they took pride in fighting for their city-state. However, "hometown" loyalties also divided the Greeks and caused them to distrust one another. A lack of unity always existed among the Greek city-states.

 Explain How did citizenship make the Greeks different from other ancient peoples?

Section 1 Review

Reading Summary

Review the Main Ideas

- Geography influenced the way Greek communities developed.

- The Minoan civilization, on the island of Crete, built ships and became wealthy from trade.

- The Mycenaeans created the first Greek kingdoms.

- After the Dark Age, the Greeks set up colonies and trade increased.

- The idea of citizenship developed in Greek city-states.

What Did You Learn?

1. What made the Minoans wealthy?

2. How was a Greek city-state different from a city?

Critical Thinking

3. **Compare** Create a Venn diagram to compare the Minoans and Mycenaeans.

   Minoan (Both) Mycenaean

4. **Summarize** What changes occurred in Greece during the Dark Age?

5. **Citizenship Skills** Name three rights granted to Greek citizens that American citizens have today.

6. **Link to Economics** Why did the use of money help trade to grow?

7. **Reading Making Connections** Choose one passage from this section. Write a paragraph to explain how it connects to something you already know or something you have experienced.

 Study Central™ Need help with the material in this section? Visit jat.glencoe.com

ENRICH

Have students compare the map of the Greek colonies with a modern map of the Mediterranean world. Ask students to name nations where Greek colonies once thrived. *(Possible answers: Spain, France, Italy, Ukraine, Romania, Bulgaria, Syria, Libya, Egypt, Cyprus, Georgia, Turkey)* **L1**

✓ **Reading Check**

Answer: Other ancient peoples were mostly subjects of kings and had little or no say in government.

To help students understand section material, have them visit Study Central™ at jat.glencoe.com

RETEACH

Ask students to compare the Greek view of citizenship with the current view of citizenship in the United States. **L2**

4 CLOSE

Have students discuss the following statement: "The geography of Greece influenced where people settled and what they did." **L2**

SECTION 1 REVIEW ANSWERS

1. trading pottery and stone vases

2. City-states were tiny independent countries, while cities are part of a country.

3. Minoan: lived on Crete, built first civilization in Greece, worked in bronze; Mycenaean: lived on Greek mainland, first Greek kings, built fortified palaces on hills, borrowed ideas from Minoans; Both: earned wealth from trade

4. Trade slowed, poverty took hold, people stopped farming, people stopped teaching writing and craftwork, and many Greeks moved elsewhere.

5. Answers include: voting, holding office, owning property, defending themselves in court.

6. Money is small and easier to trade than bartered goods.

7. Paragraphs will vary but should include concrete examples.

123

Section 2

Sparta and Athens

Get Ready to Read!

① FOCUS

SECTION OVERVIEW

This section traces the development of Greek governments and compares the systems adopted by Sparta and Athens.

BELLRINGER
SKILLBUILDER ACTIVITY

✏ Project **Daily Focus Skills Transparency 4–2** and have students answer questions. Discuss their responses.

Get Ready to Read!

Preteaching Vocabulary: A democracy is a system of government in which all citizens share in running government. It comes from the Greek words *demos,* for "people," and *kratia,* for "rule."

Answers to Graphic: Sparta: harsh, focused on military, women had greater freedoms and could own property; Athens: emphasis on education and arts for males, household duties for females, concern with democracy; Both: spoke Greek and excluded women, slaves, and non-Greeks from government

What's the Connection?

Although Greek city-states developed the idea of citizenship, they had many different types of government. This section describes their different governments and compares the best-known city-states, Athens and Sparta.

Focusing on the **Main Ideas**

• Tyrants were able to seize power from the nobles with the support of Greek farmers, merchants, and artisans. *(page 125)*

• The Spartans focused on military skills to control the people they conquered. *(page 126)*

• Unlike Spartans, Athenians were more interested in building a democracy than building a military force. *(page 128)*

Locating Places
Sparta (SPAHR•tuh)
Athens (A•thuhnz)

Meeting People
Solon (SOH•luhn)
Peisistratus (py•SIHS•truht•uhs)
Cleisthenes (KLYS•thuh•NEEZ)

Building Your Vocabulary
tyrant (TY•ruhnt)
oligarchy (AH•luh•GAHR•kee)
democracy (dih•MAH•kruh•see)
helot (HEH•luht)

Reading Strategy
Compare and Contrast Use a Venn diagram to compare and contrast life in Sparta and Athens.

(Sparta (Both) Athens)

NATIONAL GEOGRAPHIC **When & Where?**

700 B.C.	600 B.C.	500 B.C.

GREECE
Athens
PELOPONNESUS
Sparta

c. 650 B.C.
Tyrants overthrow nobles in city-states

594 B.C.
Solon takes power in Athens

508 B.C.
Cleisthenes reforms Athenian government

124   CHAPTER 4   The Ancient Greeks

SECTION RESOURCES

📁 **Reproducible Masters**
• Reproducible Lesson Plan 4–2
• Daily Lecture and Discussion Notes 4–2
• Vocabulary Activity 4–2
• Active Reading Note-Taking Guide 4–2
• Guided Reading Activity 4–2
• Section Quiz 4–2
• Reading Essentials and Study Guide 4–2

🖇 **Transparencies**
• Daily Focus Skills Transparency 4–2

Multimedia
💿 Interactive Tutor Self-Assessment CD-ROM
💿 ExamView® Pro Testmaker CD-ROM
💿 Presentation Plus! CD-ROM

Tyranny in the City-States

Main Idea Tyrants were able to seize power from the nobles with the support of Greek farmers, merchants, and artisans.

Reading Focus How do you feel when someone makes a decision that affects you without asking for your opinion? Read to find out how ancient Greeks who were shut out of governing made their voices heard.

As you read in the last section, kings ruled the first Greek communities. However, by the end of the Dark Age, the nobles who owned large farms had seized power from the kings.

Rule by the nobles would also be short-lived. The first challenge to their rule came from the owners of small farms. These farmers often needed money to live on until they could harvest and sell their crops. Many borrowed money from the nobles, promising to give up their fields if they could not repay the loans. Time and time again, farmers lost their land. Then they had to work for the nobles or become laborers in the city. In desperate cases, they sold themselves into slavery.

By 650 B.C., small farmers began to demand changes in the power structure. Merchants and artisans also wanted to share in governing. Both groups had become very wealthy from the trade between city-states. Because they did not own land, however, they were not citizens and had no say in running the polis.

The growing unhappiness led to the rise of tyrants. A **tyrant** (TY•ruhnt) is someone who takes power by force and rules with

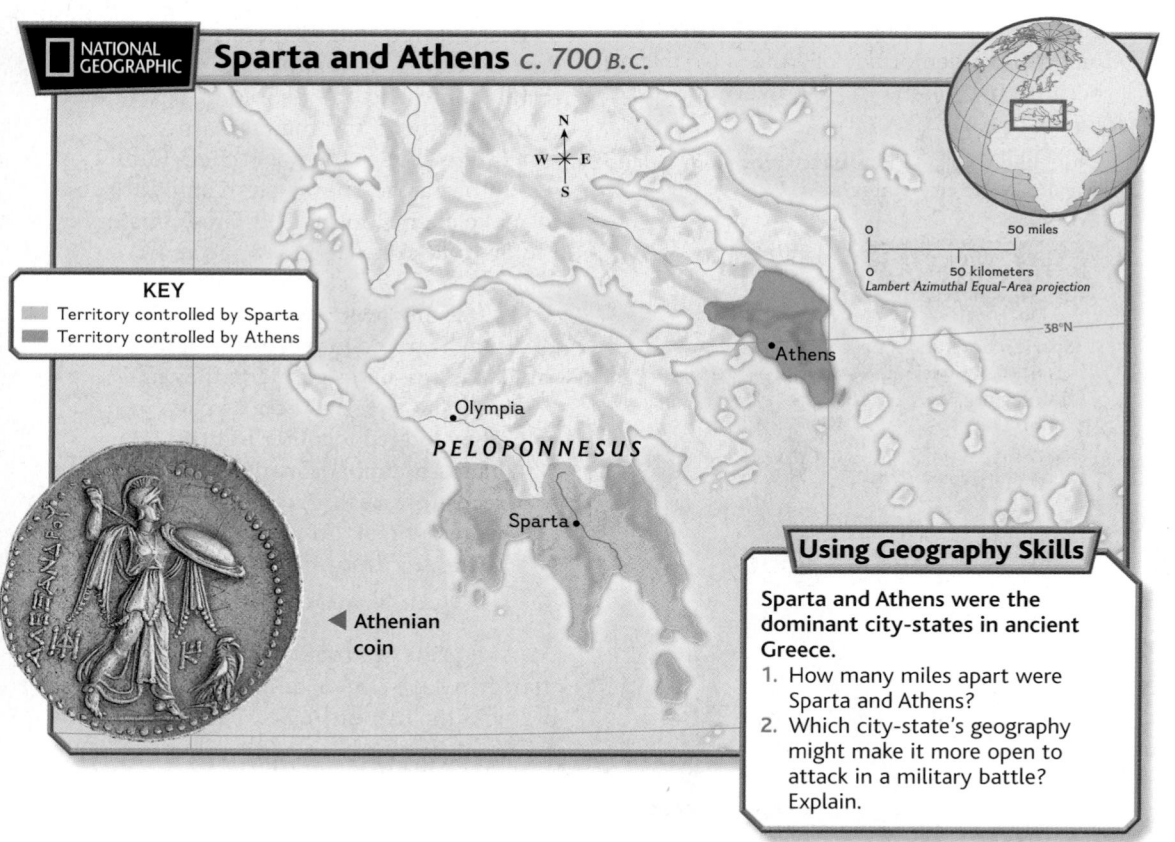

NATIONAL GEOGRAPHIC

Sparta and Athens C. 700 B.C.

KEY
- Territory controlled by Sparta
- Territory controlled by Athens

50 miles
50 kilometers
Lambert Azimuthal Equal-Area projection

38°N

Athens

Olympia

PELOPONNESUS

Sparta

◀ Athenian coin

Using Geography Skills

Sparta and Athens were the dominant city-states in ancient Greece.
1. How many miles apart were Sparta and Athens?
2. Which city-state's geography might make it more open to attack in a military battle? Explain.

2 TEACH

Making Comparisons Have students brainstorm nations that have very different governments than our own. Write these on the board, and have students compile a list of ways life in these nations differs from life in our country. Use this as a springboard to introduce the main topic of this section: the differing governments of Sparta and Athens. **L2**

Daily Lecture and Discussion Notes 4–2

Use **Daily Lecture and Discussion Notes 4–2** for an outline of key concepts found in the section.

Reading Support L1/ EL

Use **Vocabulary Activity 4–2** to review important terms in the section.

Using Geography Skills

Answers:
1. about 100 miles apart
2. Answers will vary, but students should refer to physical barriers, such as mountains and water, in their answers.

Reading Strategy ❮ **READING THE TEXT**

Using Possible Sentences Copy the places, people, and vocabulary terms for this section on an overhead transparency. Then write 10 sentences using some of the words correctly and some of them incorrectly. Ask students to comment on whether each of these sentences is correct. After reading Section 2, show students the sentences again. Ask them to suggest any necessary revisions. **L1/ EL**

Reading Strategy

Writing Activity

Read aloud these lines by Spartan poet Tyraeus: ". . . And he who falls among the champions and loses his own sweet life, So blessing with honor his city, his father, and all his people." **Ask: How does the poet view death in battle?** *(as a glorious honor)* Assign students to compose their own poem about Spartan warriors. Advise them to use information about warriors and life in Sparta from the textbook as a guide. **L2**

Reading Check

Answer: Tyrants built new marketplaces, temples, and walls.

More About the Art

Spartan soldiers took great pains to prepare for battle. Weapons and armor had to be well maintained, and years of training honed them into powerful warriors. Before battle, they carefully dressed their hair before engaging the enemy.

Caption Answer: age 7

total authority. Today the word describes a harsh, oppressive ruler. Most early Greek tyrants, though, acted wisely and fairly.

During the 600s B.C., tyrants managed to overthrow the nobles because they had the backing of the common people. Key support came from the hoplites in the army, many of whom were also farmers.

Tyrants made themselves popular by building new marketplaces, temples, and walls. However, rule by one person was the opposite of what most Greeks wanted. They longed for rule by law with all citizens participating in the government.

By 500 B.C., tyrants had fallen out of favor in Greece. Most city-states became either oligarchies or democracies. In an **oligarchy** (AH•luh•GAHR•kee), a few people hold power. In a **democracy** (dih•MAH•kruh•see), all citizens share in running the government. The oligarchy of **Sparta** (SPAHR•tuh) and the democracy of **Athens** (A•thuhnz) became two of the most powerful governments of early Greece.

Reading Check **Evaluate** Why were tyrants popular in the city-states?

Spartan Warrior

Spartan boys and men spent many years training for war. *At what age did Spartan boys leave their families for the military?*

126

Sparta

Main Idea The Spartans focused on military skills to control the people they conquered.

Reading Focus What would it be like to leave home when you were only seven? Read to learn how Spartan boys faced this challenge.

As you read in the last section, Sparta was founded by the Dorians—Greeks who invaded the Peloponnesus in the Dark Age. Like other city-states, Sparta needed more land as it grew, but its people did not set up colonies. Instead, they conquered and enslaved their neighbors. The Spartans called their captive workers **helots** (HEH•luhts). This name comes from the Greek word for "capture."

Why Was the Military So Important?

Spartans feared that the helots might someday rebel. As a result, the government firmly controlled the people of Sparta and trained the boys and men for war.

At age seven, boys left their family to live in barracks. They were harshly treated to make them tough. The Greek historian Plutarch describes life for Spartan boys:

> "After they were twelve years old, they were no longer allowed to wear any undergarment; they had one coat to serve them a year; . . . They lodged together in little bands upon beds made of the reeds [grasses] . . . which they were to break off with their hands without a knife."
> —Plutarch, "Spartan Discipline"

At age 20, Spartan men entered the regular army. The men remained in military barracks for 10 more years. They ate all their meals in dining halls with other soldiers.

DIFFERENTIATED INSTRUCTION

Verbal/Linguistic: The Greek historian Plutarch said that the author of Sparta's constitution, Lycurgus, "considered children not so much the property of their parents as of the state." Have students write a short paragraph to explain the meaning of this remark in their own words.

English Learners: Assign students to copy on a sheet of paper sentences that show ways Sparta controlled the upbringing of children.

Gifted and Talented: Have students turn these sentences into a military handbook written for seven-year-old boys in the Spartan barracks.

Refer to *Inclusion Strategies for the Middle School Social Studies Classroom* in the TCR.

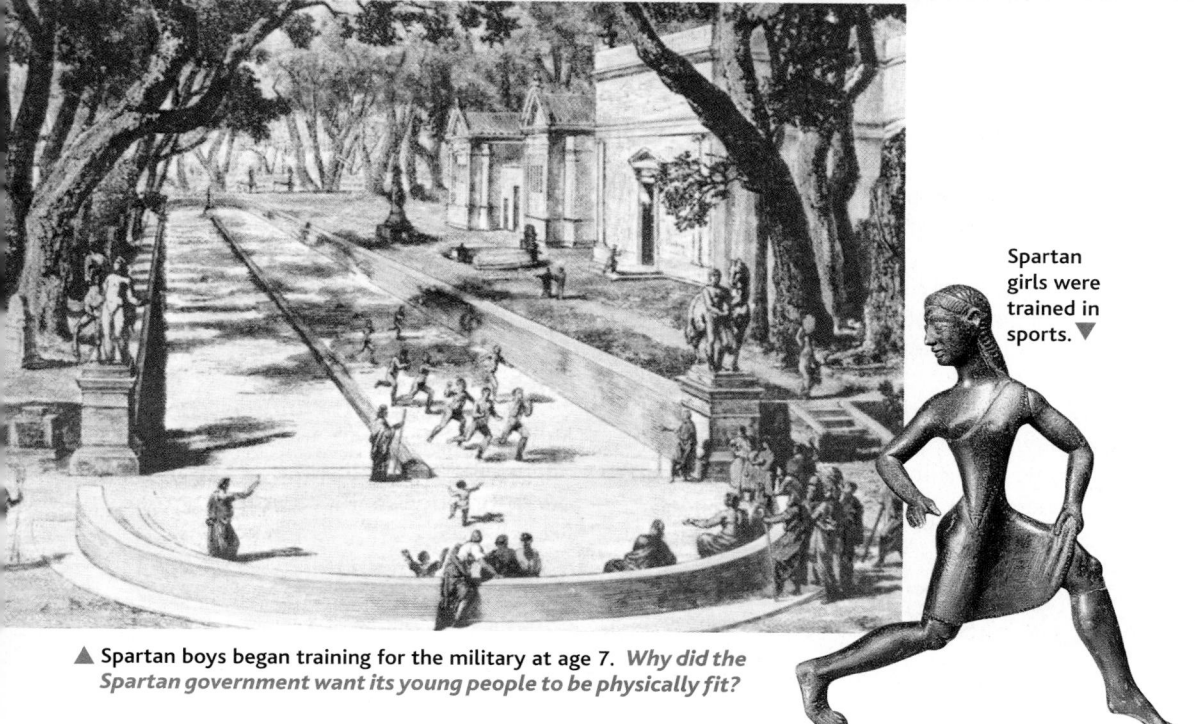

Spartan girls were trained in sports. ▼

▲ Spartan boys began training for the military at age 7. *Why did the Spartan government want its young people to be physically fit?*

A typical meal was a vile-tasting dish called black broth—pork boiled in animal blood, salt, and vinegar.

Spartans returned home at age 30 but stayed in the army until age 60. They continued to train for combat. They expected to either win on the battlefield or die, but never to surrender. One Spartan mother ordered her son to "Come home carrying your shield or being carried on it."

Girls in Sparta were trained in sports—running, wrestling, and throwing the javelin. They kept fit to become healthy mothers. Wives lived at home while their husbands lived in the barracks. As a result, Spartan women were freer than other Greek women. They could own property and go where they wanted.

What Was Sparta's Government Like?

The Spartan government was an oligarchy. Two kings headed a council of elders. The council, which included 28 citizens over age 60, presented laws to an assembly.

All Spartan men over age 30 belonged to the assembly. They voted on the council's laws and chose five people to be ephors (EH•fuhrs) each year. The ephors enforced the laws and managed tax collection.

To keep anyone from questioning the Spartan system, the government discouraged foreign visitors. It also banned travel abroad for any reason but military ones. It even frowned upon citizens who studied literature or the arts.

The Spartans succeeded in keeping control over the helots for nearly 250 years. However, by focusing on military training, the Spartans fell behind other Greeks in trade. They also knew less about science and other subjects. However, their soldiers were especially strong and swift. The Spartans would play a key role in defending Greece.

✔ **Reading Check** **Cause and Effect** Why did the Spartans stress military training?

CHAPTER 4   The Ancient Greeks   **127**

in a word . . .

"School" comes from the Greek word *skolle,* but it meant something different to the Greeks than it does to us. They defined the term simply as "conversation." They thought schooling could happen anyplace—especially in public places.

Linking Past & Present

Answer: Ancient Greek winners received a crown of olive leaves and glory for their cities. Present-day winners receive a medal and glory for themselves, their team, and their nation.

Reading Support L1/ EL

Assign **Guided Reading Activity 4–2** to help students organize the information in the section.

Athens

Main Idea Unlike Spartans, Athenians were more interested in building a democracy than building a military force.

Reading Focus When visiting a new city, does everything feel strange to you? Spartans who visited Athens probably felt the same way. Read to find out why.

Athens lay northeast of Sparta, at least a two-day trip away. The two city-states were also miles apart in their values and systems of government.

What Was Life in Athens Like? Athenian citizens raised their children very differently from Spartans. In Athenian schools, one teacher taught boys to read, write, and do arithmetic. Another teacher taught them

Linking Past & Present

The Olympics

THEN In ancient Greece, only men could participate in and view the Olympic games. Athletes competed by themselves, not as part of a team. Contests included running, jumping, wrestling, and boxing. Each winning athlete won a crown of olive leaves and brought glory to his city.

▼ Modern Olympic athletes

NOW In today's Olympic games, both men and women compete. These athletes come from all over the world. They may compete in either individual or team sporting events. Olympic athletes strive to win gold, silver, or bronze medals. *What did ancient Greek Olympic winners receive? What do present-day Olympic winners receive?*

▲ A warrior's race in the ancient Olympics

INTERDISCIPLINARY CONNECTIONS ACTIVITY

Technology Remind students that Athenians chose the members of the council by lottery. Tell them that Athenians developed a rather sophisticated machine for determining random names. Ask students if they know how votes are cast today. *(by paper ballot, by mechanical machine, by computerized machine)* **Ask:** What might the benefits be of technology in voting, such as online voting? Are there any drawbacks? *(Possible answers: Benefit—it makes it easier for people to vote. Drawback—not everybody can afford computers.)* **L1**

sports. A third teacher taught them to sing and to play a stringed instrument called the lyre. This kind of education created well-rounded Athenians with good minds and bodies. At age 18, boys finished school and became citizens.

Athenian girls stayed at home. Their mothers taught them spinning, weaving, and other household duties. Only in some wealthy families did girls learn to read, write, and play the lyre. When they married, women stayed home to keep house and to teach their own daughters.

A Budding Democracy Early Athens, like other city-states, was ruled by landowning nobles during the 600s B.C. An assembly of all citizens existed, but it had few powers. Actually, the government was an oligarchy, as in Sparta.

Around 600 B.C., the Athenians began to rebel against the nobles. Most farmers owed the nobles money, and many sold themselves into slavery to pay their debts. Over and over, farmers demanded an end to all debts, along with land for the poor.

In 594 B.C. the nobles turned to the one man both sides trusted: a noble named **Solon** (SOH•luhn). Solon canceled all the farmers' debts and freed those who had become slaves. He also allowed all male citizens to participate in the assembly and law courts. A council of 400 wealthy citizens wrote the laws, but the assembly had to pass them.

Solon's reforms were popular among the common people. However, the farmers

◄ The city of Athens was named for the goddess Athena. *What group ruled Athens during the 600s B.C.?*

continued to press Solon to give away the wealthy nobles' land. This he refused to do.

After Solon, there were 30 years of turmoil. Finally, a tyrant named **Peisistratus** (py•SIHS•truht•uhs) seized power in 560 B.C. He won the support of the poor by dividing large estates among landless farmers. He also loaned money to poor people and gave them jobs building temples and other public works.

▲ Token used to select jurors for Athenian courts.

More About the Art

According to legend, Athena competed with Poseidon, god of the sea, to become the protector of Athens. Each had to create something of value for the city-state. Athena won by creating the olive tree.

Caption Answer: landowning nobles

③ ASSESS

Assign Section 2 Review as homework or as an in-class activity.

◉ Have students use the **Interactive Tutor Self-Assessment CD-ROM** to review the section.

Assessment L2

Assign **Section 2 Quiz** to assess mastery of the material found in the section.

Reading Support L1/ EL

Assign **Reading Essentials and Study Guide 4–2** to help students review section material.

EXTENDING THE CONTENT

What Athletic Contest Did Greek Women Start? The Greeks dedicated the Olympic games to Zeus. Although married women could not compete in the games, they could enter their horses and chariots. However, women organized an athletic festival to honor Zeus's wife, Hera. The festival, known as the Heraia, pitted unmarried women against each other in a series of footraces organized by age groups.

129

ENRICH

Ask students to compare Athenian democracy with the governments of Mesopotamia and Egypt. **L2**

 Reading Check

Answer: made the assembly the center of government, gave citizens more powers, created a citizen council to help the assembly

To help students understand section material, have them visit **Study Central™** at jat.glencoe.com

RETEACH

Ask students to explain why they would have preferred to live in Athens or Sparta. **L2**

4 CLOSE

Ask how a citizen of Sparta would complete this sentence: "I'm proud of my city-state because _____." **L1**

The most important leader after Peisistratus died was **Cleisthenes** (KLYS•thuh•NEEZ). When he came to power in 508 B.C., he reorganized the assembly to play the central role in governing. As before, all male citizens could belong to the assembly and vote on laws. However, members had new powers. They could debate matters openly, hear court cases, and appoint army generals.

Most importantly, Cleisthenes created a new council of 500 citizens to help the assembly carry out daily business. The council proposed laws, dealt with foreign countries, and oversaw the treasury.

Athenians chose the members of the council each year in a lottery. They believed this system was fairer than an election, which might favor the rich.

Cleisthenes' reforms did not bring all Athenians into the political process.

Stone carving of ▶ Democracy crowning a figure that symbolizes Athens. *What leader is credited with making Athens a democracy?*

Non-citizens, which included all women, foreign-born men, and slaves, were still excluded. Nonetheless, Cleisthenes is credited with making the government of Athens a democracy.

✓ **Reading Check** **Explain** How did Cleisthenes build a democracy in Athens?

Section 2 Review

Study Central™ Need help with the material in this section? Visit jat.glencoe.com

Reading Summary

Review the Main Ideas

- The support of wealthy merchants and artisans helped tyrants seize power from nobles in the city-states.

- Sparta was a powerful city-state. It created a military state to control the people it conquered and to prevent uprisings.

- Athens was a powerful democratic city-state. Athenians were more involved in government, education, and the arts than the Spartans.

What Did You Learn?

1. Who were the helots?
2. Why did tyrants fall out of favor with the Greeks?

Critical Thinking

3. **Classifying Information** Draw a diagram like the one below. In each oval write a fact about the Spartan oligarchy.

   Oligarchy

4. **Evaluate** Why did Athenians choose officials by lottery? Would there be drawbacks to this method? Explain.

5. **Explain** How did Greek nobles gain power?

6. **Analyze** Why was Solon popular among some Athenian farmers and unpopular among others?

7. **Civics Link** How did Athenian democracy keep one person from gaining too much power?

8. **Descriptive Writing** Imagine that you are a 28-year-old man living in Sparta in 700 B.C. Write a letter to your 6-year-old nephew telling him what to expect when he leaves home on his next birthday.

130 CHAPTER 4 The Ancient Greeks

SECTION 2 REVIEW ANSWERS

1. captive workers in Sparta
2. because most Greeks longed for rule by law with all citizens participating in government
3. Answers will vary but should be based on the text.
4. They thought elections might favor the rich. Possible answer: the most qualified people might not be picked.
5. They seized power from kings during the Dark Age.
6. He canceled farmers' debts and freed those who had become enslaved, but he refused to give away wealthy nobles' land.
7. A large council chosen by lottery kept power distributed among the people.
8. Letters should discuss early military training and the importance of serving Sparta.

Section 3

Persia Attacks the Greeks

Get Ready to Read!

What's the Connection?
Section 2 explained how Greeks built strong but separate city-states. At the same time far to the east, the Persians were building a powerful empire. It was only a matter of time before Persia would try to invade Greece.

Focusing on the Main Ideas
- The Persian Empire united a wide area under a single government. *(page 132)*
- Both Sparta and Athens played roles in defeating the Persians. *(page 134)*

Locating Places
Persia (PUHR•zhuh)
Marathon (MAR•uh•THAHN)
Thermopylae (thuhr•MAH•puh•lee)
Salamis (SA•luh•muhs)
Plataea (pluh•TEE•uh)

Meeting People
Cyrus the Great (SY•ruhs)
Darius (duh•RY•uhs)
Xerxes (ZUHRK•SEEZ)
Themistocles (thuh•MIHS•tuh•KLEEZ)

Building Your Vocabulary
satrapies (SAY•truh•peez)
satrap (SAY•TRAP)
Zoroastrianism (ZOHR•uh•WAS•tree•uh•NIH•zuhm)

Reading Strategy
Organizing Information Create a chart like the one below to list the accomplishments of Cyrus, Darius, and Xerxes.

Ruler	Accomplishments
Cyrus	
Darius	
Xerxes	

NATIONAL GEOGRAPHIC When & Who?

650 B.C. **550 B.C.** **450 B.C.**

660 B.C. Zoroaster born

559 B.C. Cyrus becomes ruler of Persia

480 B.C. Xerxes invades Greece

---

❶ FOCUS

SECTION OVERVIEW

This section traces the rise of the Persian Empire and how the Greeks prevented the Persians from conquering them.

BELLRINGER
SKILLBUILDER ACTIVITY

📽 Project **Daily Focus Skills Transparency 4–3** and have students answer questions. Discuss their responses.

Get Ready to Read!

Preteaching Vocabulary: Two vocabulary words are related—*satrapies* and *satrap*. A satrap was a Persian governor of a local province called a satrapy.

Answers to Graphic: Cyrus: united Persians into a powerful kingdom, started to build empire; Darius: reorganized government into satrapies; Xerxes: built huge army but waged failed war against Greece, held empire together

---

SECTION RESOURCES

📂 **Reproducible Masters**
- Reproducible Lesson Plan 4–3
- Daily Lecture and Discussion Notes 4–3
- Vocabulary Activity 4–3
- Active Reading Note-Taking Guide 4–3
- Guided Reading Activity 4–3
- Section Quiz 4–3
- Reading Essentials and Study Guide 4–3

📽 **Transparencies**
- Daily Focus Skills Transparency 4–3

Multimedia
- 💿 Interactive Tutor Self-Assessment CD-ROM
- 💿 Exam*View*® Pro Testmaker CD-ROM
- 💿 Presentation Plus! CD-ROM

② TEACH

Daily Lecture and Discussion Notes 4–3

Use **Daily Lecture and Discussion Notes 4–3** for an outline of key concepts found in the section.

CONNECTING ACROSS TIME

Both Darius and the founders of the United States found ways to manage the territories of their nations. How were their solutions similar? *(They divided the area into states.)* How were their solutions different? *(Answers will vary, but may include that satraps answered to the king, while governors and other state officials in the United States answer to the people.)* **L2**

Trade and the Persian Empire

Have students research trade in the Persian Empire, examining aspects such as roads and other improvements, the use of coins, and weights and measures. **L2**

Using Geography Skills

Answers:
1. about 1,700–1,800 miles long
2. It had conquered land just to the north and east of the Greek mainland.

The Persian Empire

Main Idea The Persian Empire united a wide area under a single government.

Reading Focus Have you ever seen soldiers marching through city streets on the news? Imagine the same thing happening in Asia in the 500s B.C. Read to learn what happened as Persian armies marched westward from Asia.

The people of **Persia** (PUHR•zhuh) lived in what is today southwestern Iran. Early Persians were warriors and nomads who herded cattle. For a time, they were dominated by others. Then one remarkable leader, **Cyrus the Great** (SY•ruhs), managed to unite the Persians into a powerful kingdom. Under Cyrus, who ruled from 559 B.C. to 530 B.C., Persia began building an empire larger than any yet seen in the world.

The Rise of the Persian Empire In 539 B.C. Cyrus's armies swept into Mesopotamia and captured Babylon. Then they took over northern Mesopotamia, Asia Minor, Syria, Canaan, and the Phoenician cities. Cyrus treated all his new subjects well. As you read in Chapter 3, he allowed the captive Jews in Babylon to return home. Cyrus's merciful rule helped hold his growing empire together.

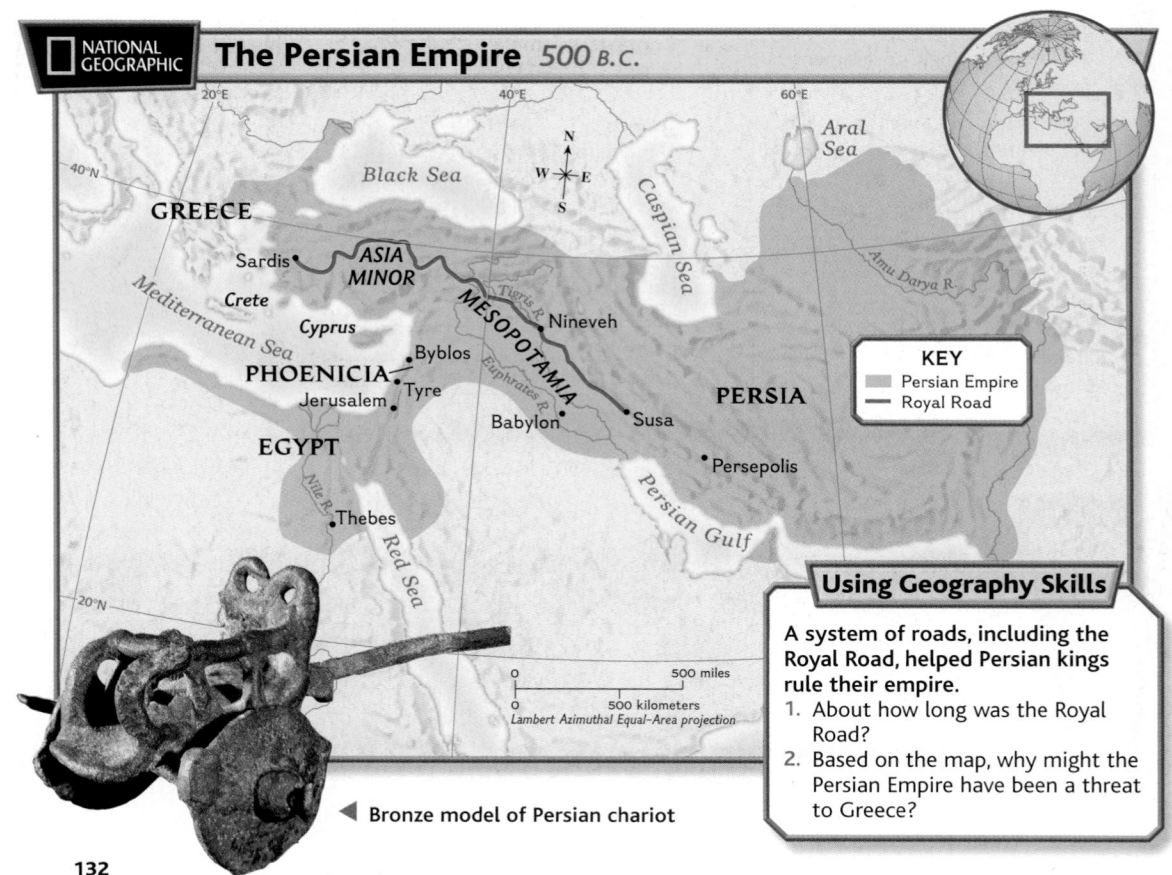

NATIONAL GEOGRAPHIC
The Persian Empire 500 B.C.

KEY
Persian Empire
Royal Road

◀ Bronze model of Persian chariot

Using Geography Skills

A system of roads, including the Royal Road, helped Persian kings rule their empire.
1. About how long was the Royal Road?
2. Based on the map, why might the Persian Empire have been a threat to Greece?

132

Reading Strategy ⟩ READING THE TEXT

Sequencing Information Assign students to draw an expanded version of the section time line. Suggest that they divide it into 10-year intervals and expand it to end with 330 B.C. Tell students to plot events and dates as they read through the section. Suggest that students illustrate their time lines. Once students finish their time lines, have them create a short quiz for their classmates to test their understanding of important events. Then have them quiz each other. **L2**

The leaders who followed Cyrus continued to add to Persian territory. They conquered Egypt, western India, and Thrace, a region northeast of Greece. From one end to the other, the Persian Empire was about the size of the continental United States today.

To connect their vast holdings, the Persians built miles of roads. The Royal Road stretched from Asia Minor to Susa, the Persian capital. Along the way, the Persians set up roadside stations to supply food, shelter, and fresh horses to the king's messengers.

What Was Persian Government Like? As the Persian Empire grew bigger, it became very difficult to manage. When **Darius** (duh•RY•uhs) came to the throne in 521 B.C., he reorganized the government to make it work better.

Darius divided the empire into 20 provinces called **satrapies** (SAY•truh•peez). Each was ruled by an official with the title of **satrap** (SAY•TRAP), meaning "protector of the kingdom." The satrap acted as tax collector, judge, chief of police, and head recruiter for the Persian army. However, all the satraps answered to the Persian king.

The king's power depended upon his troops. By the time of Darius, Persia had a large army of professional soldiers. Unlike the Greek city-states, where the citizens took up arms in times of war, in Persia the government paid people to be full-time soldiers. Among them were 10,000 specially trained soldiers who guarded the king. They were called the Immortals because when a member died, he was immediately replaced.

The Persian Religion The Persian religion was called **Zoroastrianism** (ZOHR•uh•WAS•tree•uh•NIH•zuhm). Its founder, Zoroaster,

King Darius

Darius helped to organize the Persian government. *What methods did he use?*

was born in 660 B.C. He began preaching after seeing visions as a young man.

Like the Jews, Zoroaster believed in one god. He viewed this supreme being as the creator of all things and a force of goodness. However, Zoroaster recognized evil in the world, too. He taught that humans had the freedom to choose between right and wrong, and that goodness would triumph in the end. The Persians practiced Zoroastrianism for centuries, and it still has a small number of followers today.

✓ **Reading Check** **Explain** Why did Darius create satrapies?

Reading Support L1/ EL

Use **Vocabulary Activity 4–3** to review important terms in the section.

More About the Art

This carving decorated the stone facade of the grand staircase at Persepolis, one of the ceremonial capitals built by Darius.

Caption Answer: He divided the empire into satrapies, each ruled by an official called a satrap who reported to him.

TIME TRAVELER

The Royal Road was lined with more than 110 inns. Each was built about 15 miles (24 km) apart, or about one-day's journey by horseback. The king's messengers carried information from inn to inn, keeping travelers and locals informed.

✓ Reading Check

Answer: to make the government work better

DIFFERENTIATED INSTRUCTION

Auditory/Musical: Tell students to take notes on the Royal Road as you read the **Time Traveler** on this page.

Verbal/Linguistic: Have students find more information on the Royal Road and add it to their notes. Assign them to write a letter describing a typical day's journey on the road.

Gifted and Talented: Have students research information on the Pony Express. Have them use a Venn diagram to compare these riders to messengers on the Royal Road.

☛ Refer to *Inclusion Strategies for the Middle School Social Studies Classroom* in the TCR.

Writing Activity

Assign students to write a two-paragraph account of the Battle of Marathon, slanting it in favor of the Greeks. Introduce the idea of "loaded words," or words that have an emotional impact and thus create a biased or opinionated statement. Have students exchange papers, circling loaded words that might influence a reader's opinion of the battle. (*Sample words:* glorious, greatest, smashed, pitiful, *and so on.*)
L1/EL

Suggestions for rubrics may be found in the *Quizzes, Tests, and Authentic Assessment (with Rubrics)* booklet.

Using Geography Skills

Answers:

1. Salamis
2. The Persians were deep in enemy territory and far from supply bases.

Skills Practice

Ask: Which battle between the Greeks and Persians ended the war? *(Plataea)* Was it a land battle or sea battle? *(land battle)*

The Persian Wars

....

Main Idea Both Sparta and Athens played roles in defeating the Persians.

Reading Focus Have you and a rival ever set aside your differences to work for a common cause? This happened in ancient Greece when Sparta and Athens came together to fight the Persians. Read about the outcome.

....

As the Greeks set up colonies in the Mediterranean area, they often clashed with the Persians. By the mid-500s B.C., Persia already controlled the Greek cities in Asia Minor. In 499 B.C. the Athenian army helped the Greeks in Asia Minor rebel against their Persian rulers. The rebellion failed, but King Darius decided the mainland Greeks had to be stopped from interfering in the Persian Empire.

The Battle of Marathon

In 490 B.C. a Persian fleet landed 20,000 soldiers on the plain of **Marathon** (MAR•uh•THAHN), only a short distance from Athens. For several days, the Persians waited there for the Athenians to advance. The Athenians, however, did not take the bait. They had only 10,000 soldiers compared to the Persians' 20,000. They knew that attacking was too dangerous. Instead they held back in the hills overlooking the plain.

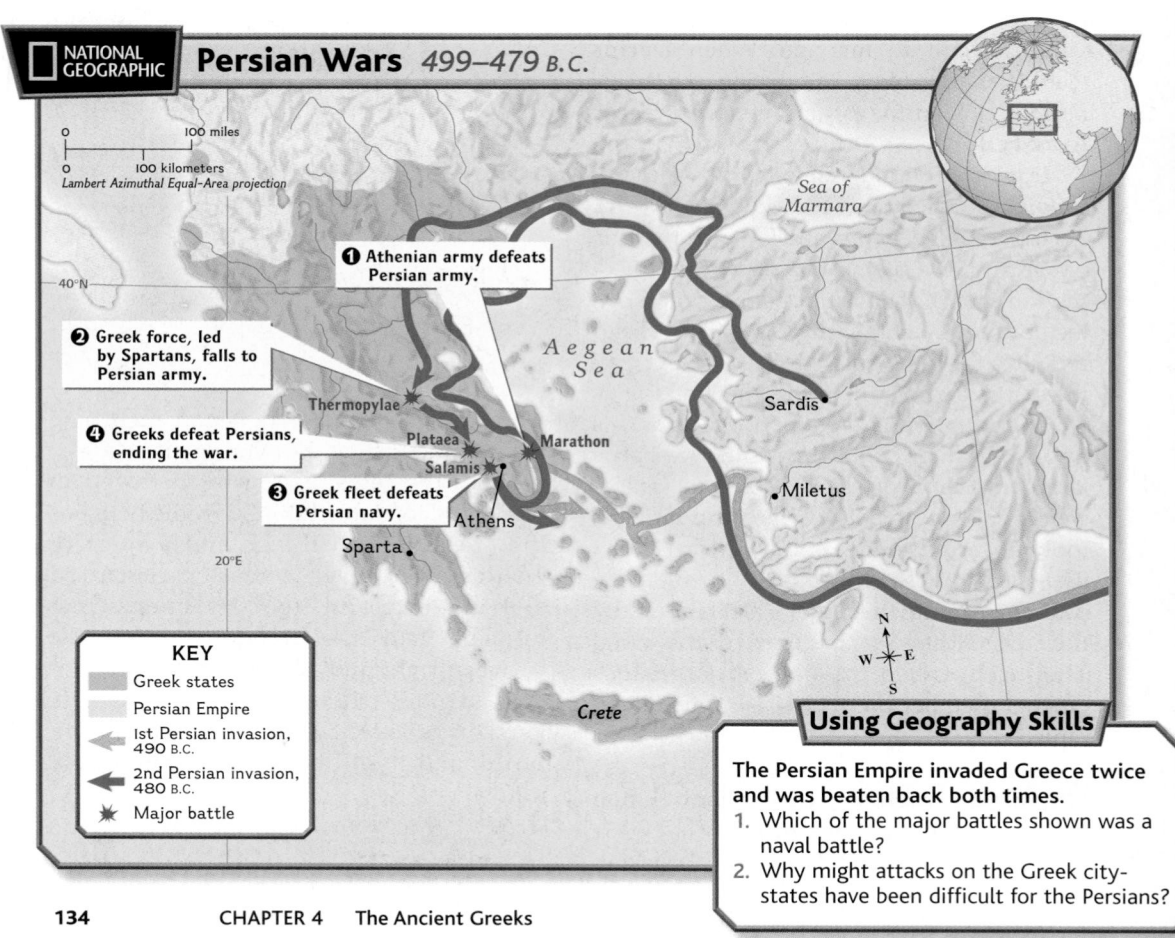

NATIONAL GEOGRAPHIC
Persian Wars *499–479 B.C.*

0 — 100 miles
0 — 100 kilometers
Lambert Azimuthal Equal-Area projection

Sea of Marmara

40°N

❶ Athenian army defeats Persian army.

❷ Greek force, led by Spartans, falls to Persian army.

Aegean Sea

Thermopylae

Sardis

❹ Greeks defeat Persians, ending the war.

Plataea

Marathon

Salamis

❸ Greek fleet defeats Persian navy.

Athens

Miletus

Sparta

20°E

KEY
Greek states
Persian Empire
1st Persian invasion, 490 B.C.
2nd Persian invasion, 480 B.C.
★ Major battle

Crete

N W E S

Using Geography Skills

The Persian Empire invaded Greece twice and was beaten back both times.
1. Which of the major battles shown was a naval battle?
2. Why might attacks on the Greek city-states have been difficult for the Persians?

CRITICAL THINKING ACTIVITY

Predicting Tell students that predictions are based on trends or patterns over time. **Ask:** What patterns have you seen in the relations between Athens and Sparta? *(For much of their histories, they have been rivals.)* What predictions can you make about the partnership they formed during the Persian Wars? *(Answers will vary, but most students will predict a revival of tensions when the war ended.)* Instruct students to write down their predictions and check them when they read Section 4.
L2

Tired of waiting, the Persian commander decided to sail south and attack Athens directly. He ordered his troops back onto the ships, and it was then that he made a big mistake. The first to board, he decided, would be the horsemen in the cavalry, the strongest part of the Persian army.

As soon as the cavalry was out of fighting range, the Greeks charged down from the hills and onto the plain of Marathon. They caught the Persian foot soldiers standing in the water, waiting their turn to board the ships. Unable to defend themselves, the Persians were easily defeated.

According to legend, the Athenians sent a messenger named Pheidippides (fy•DIHP•uh•DEEZ) home with the news. The runner raced nearly 25 miles (40.2 km) from Marathon to Athens. He collapsed from exhaustion and, with his last breath, announced, "Victory." Then he died. Modern marathon races are named for this famous run and are just over 26 miles long.

Another Persian Strike After Darius died in 486 B.C., his son **Xerxes** (ZUHRK•SEEZ) became the Persian king. Xerxes vowed revenge against the Athenians. In 480 B.C. he launched a new invasion of Greece, this time with about 180,000 troops and thousands of warships and supply vessels.

To defend themselves, the Greeks joined forces. Sparta sent the most soldiers, and their king, Leonidas (lee•AH•nuh•duhs), served as commander. Athens provided the navy. An Athenian general, **Themistocles** (thuh•MIHS•tuh•KLEEZ), came up with a plan to fight the Persians.

The Greeks knew that as the huge Persian army marched south, it depended on shipments of food brought in by boat. Themistocles argued that the Greeks' best strategy would be to attack the Persians' ships and cut off food supplies to the army.

Primary Source
Herodotus's History

▲ Herodotus reading to a crowd

The Greek historian Herodotus (hih•RAH•duh•tuhs) wrote *History of the Persian Wars*. This is thought to be the first real history in Western civilization. Herodotus described the conflict between the Greeks and Persians as one between freedom and dictatorship. Here he tells of Xerxes' address to Persian nobles:

"And truly I have pondered upon this, until at last I have found out a way whereby we may at once win glory, and likewise get possession of a land which is as large and as rich as our own . . . while at the same time we obtain satisfaction and revenge . . . My intent is to . . . march an army through Europe against Greece, that thereby I may obtain vengeance from the Athenians for the wrongs committed by them against the Persians and against my father."

—Herodotus,
The Persian Wars, Book VII

DBQ **Document-Based Question**

What reasons besides revenge does Xerxes have for invading Greece?

Creating a Presentation Organize the class into small groups to prepare an oral and visual presentation on the Persian Wars for the other groups. Within each group, assign students specific topics, such as the impact of geography on the battles and the leaders involved. Visual presentations might include drawings of soldiers, weapons, battle formations, fortifications, and ships as well as time lines of events. **L2**

Primary Source

Herodotus traveled to Persia to collect stories about the wars. He read parts of his manuscript to eager crowds in Athens before it was "published," or copied onto papyrus scrolls by scribes. This speech stirred up pride in Athens, which was at the height of its power when he compiled this work.

Answer:
glory and winning a wealthy land

Reading Support L1/ EL

Assign **Guided Reading Activity 4–3** to help students organize the information in the section.

INTERDISCIPLINARY CONNECTIONS ACTIVITY

Mathematics Students may have noticed the use of the metric system in the text in sentences such as this: "The runner raced nearly 25 miles (40.2 km) from Marathon to Athens." They also may have noticed a metric scale on maps. See if students have any prior knowledge of the metric system, which is used in much of the world today. Write this formula on the board: *miles* × *1.609* = *kilometers*. Then call out some easy distances in miles and have students practice converting miles to kilometers. **L2**

3 ASSESS

3 ASSESS

Assign Section 3 Review as homework or as an in-class activity.

Have students use the **Interactive Tutor Self-Assessment CD-ROM** to review the section.

Assessment L2

Assign **Section 3 Quiz** to assess mastery of the material found in the section.

More About the Art

Greek warships—called triremes—had three levels of oarsmen on each side. Shipbuilders armed the boat with a bronze-and-wood ram that weighed hundreds of pounds. They could sink other ships by hitting them with their rams.

Caption Answer: Athens

Reading Support L1/ EL

Assign **Reading Essentials and Study Guide 4–3** to help students review section material.

To ready their fleet for battle, the Greeks needed to stall the Persian army before it reached Athens. The Greeks decided the best place to block the Persians was at **Thermopylae** (thuhr•MAH•puh•lee). Thermopylae was a narrow pass through the mountains that was easy to defend. About 7,000 Greek soldiers held off the Persians there for two days. The Spartans in the Greek army were especially brave. As one story has it, the Greeks heard that Persian arrows would darken the sky. A Spartan warrior responded, "That is good news. We will fight in the shade!"

Unfortunately for the Greeks, a traitor directed the Persians to a mountain path that led them around the Greeks. As the Persians mounted a rear attack, King Leonidas sent most of his troops to safety. He and several hundred others, however, stayed behind and fought to the death. The Greeks lost the battle at Thermopylae, but their valiant stand gave Athens enough time to assemble 200 ships.

The Greek fleet attacked the Persian fleet in the strait of **Salamis** (SA•luh•muhs), not far from Athens. A strait is a narrow strip of water between two pieces of land. The Greeks expected to have the upper hand in the battle because their ships could maneuver well in tight spaces. Greek ships were smaller, faster, and easier to steer than the big Persian ships, which became easy targets.

The Greek plan worked. After a ferocious battle, the Greeks destroyed almost the entire Persian fleet. Still, the Persian army marched on. When their troops reached Athens, the Greeks had already fled.

The Persians burned the city. This only stiffened the resolve of the Greek city-states.

Battle of Salamis

At the Battle of Salamis, smaller, faster Greek ships defeated the Persian fleet. *Near what Greek city-state was the strait of Salamis located?*

EXTENDING THE CONTENT

Who Were the Scythians? The Persians used many different peoples to bolster their army. The Scythians lived in the grasslands north of the Black Sea and used hit-and-run tactics to keep the Persians from seizing their homeland. Darius so admired their skills with bows and arrows and their lightning strikes on horseback that he hired them to help invade Greece. Later kings used Scythian teachers to train Persian archers.

In early 479 B.C., they came together to form the largest Greek army ever assembled. With solid body armor, longer spears, and better training, the Greek army crushed the Persian army at **Plataea** (pluh•TEE•uh), northwest of Athens.

The battle was a turning point for the Greeks, convincing the Persians to retreat to Asia Minor. By working together, the Greek city-states had saved their homeland from invasion.

What Caused the Persian Empire to Fall?

When the Greeks defeated the Persian army, they helped to weaken it. The empire was already facing internal problems. As these problems worsened, the empire would gradually lose its strength.

Persia remained intact for almost 150 more years. However, after Darius and Xerxes, other Persian rulers raised taxes to gain more wealth. They spent the gold and silver that flowed into the treasuries on luxuries for the royal court.

The high taxes angered their subjects and caused many rebellions. At the same time, the Persian royal family fought over who was to be king. Many of the later Persian kings were killed by other family members who wanted the throne.

Persian kings had many wives and children. The sons had little, if any, power so they were constantly plotting to take over the throne. As a result of such plots, six of the nine rulers after Darius were murdered.

All of these problems made Persia vulnerable to attack. By the time a young Greek conqueror named Alexander invaded the empire in 334 B.C., the Persians were no match for his troops.

By 330 B.C., the last Persian king was dead and Alexander ruled over all his lands. You will learn more about Alexander the Great and his many achievements in Chapter 5.

Reading Check **Cause and Effect** What led to the Persian Wars?

History Online

Study Central™ Need help with the material in this section? Visit jat.glencoe.com

Section 3 Review

Reading Summary

Review the Main Ideas

- The Persian Empire united its many lands under a single government.

- The Persian Empire attacked Greece several times. Despite their rivalry, Athens and Sparta joined forces to defeat the Persians.

What Did You Learn?

1. Why was Cyrus considered a fair ruler?

2. What was the Royal Road?

Critical Thinking

3. **Summarize** Draw a table like the one below. Then summarize what happened at each battle in the Persian Wars.

Battle	Action
Marathon	
Thermopylae	
Salamis	
Plataea	

4. **Persuasive Writing** Imagine you are an adviser to Xerxes and are alarmed about his plan for revenge on Greece. Compose a letter to him outlining reasons why he should cancel his invasion of Greece.

5. **Reading** Making Connections The Persians wanted revenge against the Greeks. Describe an event in your own life or on the news where revenge was involved. What was the outcome?

CHAPTER 4   The Ancient Greeks   137

ENRICH

The Greek phalanx carried the day on the battlefield at Plataea. Hoplites attacked the much larger Persian force, refusing to break their tight lines. Ask students to name other factors that helped the Greeks defeat Persia. (*Possible answers: good tactics, powerful navy, citizen-soldiers, fighting on their own territory*) L2

Reading Check

Answer: Persian expansion, Greek rebellions, revenge of Persian defeats

History Online

To help students understand section material, have them visit Study Central™ at jat.glencoe.com

RETEACH

Ask students to review the main ideas in this section, recalling details and facts that support each one. L2

4 CLOSE

Ask students to speculate on reasons historians consider the Greek defeat of the Persians a turning point in history. (*It led to the rise of Athenian power and to a period of great philosophy.*) L2

SECTION 3 REVIEW ANSWERS

1. He treated new subjects well.
2. a vast road that connected Persian cities
3. Marathon: Greeks overwhelmed Persians; Thermopylae: Greeks were betrayed, Persians won; Salamis: Greek ships defeated Persians in the strait; Plataea: Greeks crushed Persians
4. Answers will vary but should demonstrate that students understand how Greek city-states could be formidable opponents if allied.
5. Events will vary but should recognize that revenge usually has bad results. Encourage students to be honest but fair in their answers.

① FOCUS

SECTION OVERVIEW

This section explores how Athens blossomed under Pericles and the reasons Athens and Sparta went to war.

SKILLBUILDER ACTIVITY

🖥 Project **Daily Focus Skills Transparency 4–4** and have students answer questions. Discuss their responses.

Get Ready to Read!

Preteaching Vocabulary:
Democracy as the Greeks knew it was different from democracy in the United States. In Athens, the direct democracy meant that every citizen could vote on every issue, as opposed to having representatives vote for them.

Answers to Graphic: Citizens: 150,000; Foreigners: 35,000; Enslaved people: 100,000

GLENCOE
BOOKLINK

Use **Glencoe BookLink** to create customized reading lists for your students' reading levels, interests, and abilities.

Section 4

The Age of Pericles

Get Ready to Read!

What's the Connection?
In Section 3, you learned how the Greeks defeated the Persians at Plataea. One lesson the Greeks drew from the war was that they needed each other for security. Athens and several other city-states soon banded together in a league for the common defense.

Focusing on the Main Ideas
• Under Pericles, Athens became very powerful and more democratic. *(page 139)*

• Athenian men and women had very different roles. *(page 142)*

• Sparta and Athens went to war for control of Greece. *(page 144)*

Locating Places
Delos (DEE•LAHS)

Meeting People
Pericles (PEHR•uh•KLEEZ)
Aspasia (as•PAY•zhuh)

Building Your Vocabulary
direct democracy (dih•MAH•kruh•see)
representative democracy (REH•prih•ZEHN•tuh•tihv)
philosopher (fuh•LAH•suh•fuhr)

Reading Strategy
Organizing Information Create a circle graph to show how many citizens, foreigners, and enslaved people lived in Athens in the 400s B.C.

NATIONAL GEOGRAPHIC When & Where?

GREECE
• Athens
Sparta •
Delos

| 500 B.C. | | 450 B.C. | | 400 B.C. |

478 B.C.
Delian League forms

461 B.C.
Pericles leads Athens

431 B.C.
Peloponnesian War begins

SECTION RESOURCES

📁 **Reproducible Masters**
• Reproducible Lesson Plan 4–4
• Daily Lecture and Discussion Notes 4–4
• Vocabulary Activity 4–4
• Active Reading Note-Taking Guide 4–4
• Guided Reading Activity 4–4
• Section Quiz 4–4
• Reading Essentials and Study Guide 4–4

🖥 **Transparencies**
• Daily Focus Skills Transparency 4–4

Multimedia
💿 Interactive Tutor Self-Assessment CD-ROM
💿 ExamView® Pro Testmaker CD-ROM
💿 Presentation Plus! CD-ROM
💿 Vocabulary PuzzleMaker CD-ROM
💿 Glencoe BookLink CD-ROM

The Athenian Empire

Main Idea Under Pericles, Athens became very powerful and more democratic.

Reading Focus Do you vote in school elections? Why do you choose one classmate over another? Read to learn why Athenians kept electing Pericles.

As you read in Section 3, the Battle of Plataea in 479 B.C. put an end to the Persians' invasion of Greece. Although the Persians retreated, they still remained a threat. In 478 B.C. Athens joined with other city-states—but not Sparta—to form the Delian League.

The Delian League promised to defend its members against the Persians. It also worked to drive Persia out of Greek territories in Asia Minor. Eventually, the league freed almost all of the Greek cities under Persia's control.

At its start, the Delian League had headquarters on the island of **Delos** (DEE•LAHS). However, its chief officials—the treasurers in charge of its money and the commanders in charge of its fleet—were from Athens, as were most of the troops. Little by little, Athens gained control over the other city-states in the alliance. Soon the league was no longer a partnership to fight Persia but an Athenian empire.

In 454 B.C. the Athenians moved the Delian League's treasury from Delos to Athens. The Athenians also began sending troops to other Greek city-states, to help the common people rebel against the nobles in power.

Democracy in Athens Athenians had a strong faith in their democratic system. We call their system **direct democracy** (dih•MAH•kruh•see). In a direct democracy, people gather at mass meetings to decide on government matters. Every citizen can vote firsthand on laws and policies.

▲ These ruins are of the agora—an ancient marketplace in Athens where the assembly met. *What type of democracy did Athens have?*

Can you imagine such a system in the United States? A mass meeting of our millions of citizens would be impossible! Instead, in the United States we have a **representative democracy** (REH•prih•ZEHN•tuh•tihv). Under this type of democracy, citizens choose a smaller group to make laws and governmental decisions on their behalf. This is a much more practical system when the population is large.

What made direct democracy workable in ancient Athens was the relatively small number of citizens. In the mid-400s B.C., about 43,000 male citizens over 18 years old made up the assembly. Usually fewer than 6,000 attended the meetings, which were held every 10 days. The assembly passed all laws, elected officials, and made decisions on war and foreign affairs. Ten officials known as generals carried out the assembly's laws and policies.

CHAPTER 4   The Ancient Greeks   **139**

②TEACH

Reading Strategy

Forming Questions Focus students' attention on the graphic organizer under **Get Ready to Read!** Assign students to write two questions that they might use to interview a member from each of the three groups shown: citizens, foreigners, and enslaved people. Instruct students to look for possible answers to these questions as they read. **L1/EL**

More About the Art

Public buildings, such as temples, law courts, and government buildings, lined the Athenian marketplace. The site was aptly called the *agora*, meaning "gathering place." Men came to conduct business and find out what was happening in the assembly.

Caption Answer: direct democracy

Daily Lecture and Discussion Notes 4-4

Use **Daily Lecture and Discussion Notes 4-4** for an outline of key concepts found in the section.

Reading Strategy   **READING THE TEXT**

Understanding Pronouns Distribute copies of these personal and possessive pronouns to students.

First Person: I, me, my, mine, we, us, our, ours

Second Person: you, yours

Third Person: he, him, his, she, her, hers, it, its, their, theirs

As students read the section, they should copy down two sentences on each page that use personal or possessive pronouns. Have them rewrite the sentences using the name of the person(s), place(s), or thing(s) to which each pronoun refers. When students find the word *you*, they should use their own names. **L1/EL**

140

Reading Support L1/EL

Use **Vocabulary Activity 4–4** to help students learn important terms in the section.

Understanding Charts

The United States has a representative system based on federalism, or shared powers among national, state, and local governments. **Ask: How is the approval of laws different in the United States than it was in Athens?** *(In Athens, all citizens could vote on any law. In the U.S., elected officials vote on laws.)*

Answers:

1. by a majority vote in the assembly
2. American Democracy

Civics Most states require students to attend school until age 16. **Ask: Why is attending school important in a democracy?** *(because citizens learn skills to make informed decisions on issues)* **L1**

✓ Reading Check

Answer: Direct democracy: all citizens vote on laws. Representative democracy: elected officials vote on laws.

Comparing Governments

	Athenian Democracy	American Democracy
Type of Democracy	Direct	Representative
Right to Vote	Only adult males born in Athens	All citizens, male and female age 18 or over
Laws	Proposed by the council and approved by a majority in the assembly	Approved by both houses of Congress and signed by the president
Citizen Involvement	Citizens with voting rights can vote for or against any law	Citizens with voting rights can vote for or against the officials who make the laws

Understanding Charts

The small number of citizens made a direct democracy possible in Athens.

1. In Athens, how was a law approved?
2. **Compare** Which government granted the right to vote to more of its population?

The Achievements of Pericles Athenians reelected their favorite generals again and again. After the Persian Wars, the leading figure in Athenian politics was a general named **Pericles** (PEHR•uh•KLEEZ). This great statesman guided Athens for more than 30 years, from 461 B.C., when he was first elected, until 429 B.C., shortly before his death.

Pericles helped Athens dominate the Delian League. He treated the other city-states like subjects, demanding strict loyalty and steady payments from them. He even insisted that they use Athenian coins and measures.

At the same time, Pericles made Athens more democratic at home. He believed that people's talents were more important than their social standing. For this reason, Pericles included more Athenians than ever before in government. He allowed lower-class male citizens to run for public office, and he also paid officeholders. As a result, even poor citizens could, for the first time, be part of the inner circle running the government.

Culture also blossomed under the rule of Pericles. The Age of Pericles was a period of tremendous creativity and learning that peaked in the mid-400s B.C. The Persians had destroyed much of the city during the Persian Wars. So Pericles started a major rebuilding program. He had new temples and statues built across the city.

Pericles supported artists, architects, writers, and **philosophers** (fuh•LAH•suh•fuhrs). Philosophers are thinkers who ponder questions about life. In Chapter 5, you will read more about the Greeks' achievements and understand why Pericles called Athens "the school of Greece."

✓ **Reading Check** **Identify** What is the difference between a direct democracy and a representative democracy?

DIFFERENTIATED INSTRUCTION

Kinesthetic: Have a group of students design a floor plan or cutaway drawing of a modern home to compare with the image of a Greek home in this section. Suggest using tracing paper to copy the three-dimensional outline of the Greek home, which they then can modify.

English Learners: Have students use a Venn diagram to compare a modern home with the Greek home.

Gifted and Talented: Have students study the graphic organizers and present oral summaries of how the two homes compare. Ask them to explain the benefits of each.

➤ Refer to *Inclusion Strategies for the Middle School Social Studies Classroom* in the TCR.

PERICLES
c. 495–429 B.C.

Pericles was born just outside Athens, to a wealthy and powerful family. He received his education from philosophers. As a young man, he was known for his skill with words. Later, when he became a political leader, he strongly supported democracy.

Although he was from a wealthy family himself, he believed that citizenship should not be limited to the wealthy and powerful. He made changes to take power from the few and give it to the many. However, in describing Pericles' rule over Athens, Greek historian Thucydides wrote "In name democracy, but in fact the rule of one man."

The "Age of Pericles" was Athens's Golden Age, and the city blossomed under his leadership. Pericles wanted Athens to be a model for the world. He made it a centerpiece of art, philosophy, and democracy.

Pericles' goal was to make Athens a city that Greeks could be proud of. He hired hundreds of workers to construct public buildings in Athens. The most well known is the Parthenon. Based on the value of money today, it cost about $3 billion to build. Workers hauled 20,000 tons of marble from a nearby mountain and spent almost 15 years completing it.

Pericles was a private person. He avoided being in public as much as possible. He spent most of his time alone, with family, or with close friends. He married and had three sons. In 429 B.C. Pericles died from the plague.

◀ Pericles

"Athens...is the school of Greece."
—*Pericles*, as recorded by Thucydides

Then and Now

Consider what Thucydides wrote about Pericles' rule in Athens. Do research to find out how the U.S. Constitution ensures that our government is not dominated by one leader.

▲ The Parthenon sits at the top of the Acropolis.

141

TEACH

Pericles' influence over Athenian politics lasted for more than 30 years. As a statesman, he was responsible for some of the greatest achievements in Athens, including beautifying the city and establishing relative peace in the region. Although he dominated rule in Athens, he did work to increase people's involvement in politics.

Ask students what it takes to be involved in politics in the United States today. Can anyone do it? (*Anyone who wants to and meets the proper citizenship qualifications [age/residency] can run for political office.*) **L1/ EL**

Then and Now

The U.S. Constitution provides for separation of powers into judicial, legislative, and executive branches. The legislative branch passes laws, the executive branch enforces laws, and the judicial branch interprets laws.

Reading List Generator CD-ROM

GLENCOE BOOKLINK   **RECOMMENDED READING**

Use the **Glencoe BookLink CD-ROM** to create customized reading lists based on your students' interests and reading levels. Below is an example based on content in this chapter. Also, see the Suggested Readings on pages 944–946 of the Appendix.

- Coolidge, Olivia. *Men of Athens.* The Golden Age of Athens. The poets, sculptors, architects, historians, and storytellers of Athens's Golden Age.
- Pearson, Anne. *What Do We Know About the Greeks?* Answers questions such as: What did the Greeks wear? Were the Greeks scientists? What was life like in the Greek army?
- Wroble, Lisa. *Kids in Ancient Greece.* The story about a boy who lived in ancient Athens.

Writing Activity

Have students clip, copy, or download from the Internet some classified ads from their local newspaper advertising homes for sale. Assign students either individually or in small groups to write similar ads listing the Greek home shown in the text. Tell them to omit a price, explaining that it will be negotiated at the time of sale. *(Sample opening line: Beautiful home within sight of the Acropolis for sale.)* **L2**

Suggestions for rubrics may be found in the *Quizzes, Tests, and Authentic Assessment (with Rubrics)* booklet.

More About the Art

The warm Mediterranean climate allowed Greeks to spend a lot of time in the courtyard. Compared to homes today, Greek homes had little furniture, except in the dining room where men held dinner parties. Typical meals might include bread dipped in wine, goat cheese, fruit, olives, and perhaps fish.

Caption Answer: altar to favorite family god in the courtyard

Daily Life in Athens

Main Idea Athenian men and women had very different roles.

Reading Focus School may be difficult at times, but how would you feel if you could not go to school? Read on to learn about the limits placed on some Athenians.

In the 400s B.C., more people lived in Athens than in any other Greek city-state. Athens had about 285,000 residents in all. Some 150,000 were citizens, although only 43,000 of these were men with political rights. Foreigners in Athens numbered about 35,000. The population also included about 100,000 enslaved people.

Slavery was common in the ancient world. There was at least one enslaved person in most Athenian homes, and wealthy Athenian households often had many. Some worked as household servants—cooks, maids, or tutors. Others toiled in the fields, in industry, and in artisans' shops. Without their labor, Athens could not have supported its bustling economy.

Athenian Homes

Many wealthy Athenians had large homes made of mud bricks and tiled roofs. They had many small windows to let light and air in the house. *Where are religious influences seen in the house?*

Wool Room Yarn was spun and cloth was woven here.

Altar and Courtyard Greek courtyards usually had an altar to the favorite family god.

Family Room

Bedroom

Kitchen Cooking was often done over an open fire.

Dining Room Men ate their meals alone while served by women.

◀ Athenian urn

142   CHAPTER 4   The Ancient Greeks

CRITICAL THINKING ACTIVITY

Forming Generalizations Remind students that a generalization is a statement that links together or summarizes certain facts. To a form a generalization about Athenian democracy, have students brainstorm a list of facts about it. Record statements, and ask students to identify and eliminate any opinions. Then have them form valid generalizations about the topic. *(Answers will vary, but generalizations should account for all the facts without making claims not supported by them.)* **L3**

What Drove the Athenian Economy?

Many Athenians depended on farming for a living. Herders raised sheep and goats for wool, milk, and cheese. Some farmers grew grains, vegetables, and fruit for local use. Others grew grapes and olives to make wine and olive oil to sell abroad.

Athens did not have enough farmland to grow crops for all its people. As a result, the city had to import grain from other places. During the 400s B.C., Athens became the trading center of the Greek world. Merchants and artisans grew wealthy by making and selling pottery, jewelry, leather goods, and other products.

Roles of Men and Women

Athenian men usually worked in the morning and then exercised or attended meetings of the assembly. In the evenings, upper-class men enjoyed all-male gatherings where they drank, dined, and discussed politics and philosophy.

For Athenian women, life revolved around home and family. Girls married early—at 14 or 15—and were expected to have children and take care of household duties. Poor women might also work with their husbands in the fields or sell goods in the agora. Respectable upper-class women, however, stayed at home. They supervised the household servants and worked wool into cloth—spinning, dyeing, and weaving it. They rarely went out, except to funerals or festivals. Even then, they could leave the house only if a male relative went with them.

Although Athenian women could not attend school, many learned to read and to play music. Still, even educated women were not considered the equals of men. They had no political rights and could not own property. Fathers took charge of unmarried daughters. Husbands looked after their wives. Sons or other male relatives looked after widows.

The Way It Was

Focus on Everyday Life

Women's Duties In ancient Athens, a woman's place was in the home. Her two main responsibilities were caring for the household and raising children. The Greek writer Xenophon (ZEH•nuh•fuhn) recorded a man's explanation of women's duties.

"Thus your duty will be to remain indoors and send out those servants whose work is outside, and superintend those who are to work indoors . . . and take care that the sum laid by for a year be not spent in a month. And when wool is brought to you, you must see that cloaks are made for those that want them. You must see too that the dry corn is in good condition for making food."

—Xenophon, *Memorabilia and Oeconomicus*

The second floor of each home was the women's quarters. An Athenian woman lived there with her children. She was expected to keep her children well and happy. She encouraged them to learn sports and play with toys, and taught them how to interact with friends and family members. Although boys left home at age seven to attend school, girls stayed with their mothers, learning how to care for a house and children.

▲ Greek woman and servant

Connecting to the Past

1. Why do you think women and children lived on the second floor of the home?
2. Over what areas of life did an Athenian woman have authority?

CONNECTING ACROSS TIME

Have students discuss the differences between the rights of women in ancient Athens and the rights of women in the United States today. **Ask: What rights do you have here in the classroom?** *(Possible answers: Girls are permitted to go to school. Boys and girls are allowed to wear similar clothing.)* **L2**

TIME TRAVELER

An Athenian woman's childhood ended when she married. The day before the wedding, she took her toys to the Temple of Artemis (goddess of the hunt, protector of women in childbirth). After the wedding, her husband carried the bride across the threshold—a custom sometimes still practiced today.

The Way It Was

Answers:

1. Possible answer: to keep them separate from men
2. caring for the household, raising children

INTERDISCIPLINARY CONNECTIONS ACTIVITY

Language Arts Tell students that *poetry* originally meant "words set to music." The lyre, an instrument played by women, gave us the word *lyric*. A feisty woman poet named Korinna won Athens's most important poetry competition five times. Assign students to write a poem or song about Athens in the 400s B.C. Encourage them to read or perform their lyrics aloud. **L1/ EL**

📁 Refer to the *Quizzes, Tests, and Authentic Assessment (with Rubrics)* booklet for rubrics.

✓ **Reading Check**

Answer: Men worked and exercised, and some went to all-male gatherings and socialized. Most women read, played music, wove cloth, and took care of children and the home.

Reading Support L1/ EL

Assign **Guided Reading Activity 4–4** to help students organize the information in the section.

Using Geography Skills

Answers:
1. 429 B.C.; Athens's territory
2. Corinth and Thebes; helped Sparta surround Athens and provided soldiers to fight in the war

A few women did move more freely in public life. **Aspasia** (as•PAY•zhuh) is perhaps the most famous example. Aspasia was not a native Athenian. This gave her special status. She was well-educated and taught public speaking to many Athenians. Her writings have not survived, but Plato, the famous Greek philosopher, said her work helped shape his ideas. Pericles often consulted Aspasia, as did many other Athenian leaders. In this way, she became influential in politics even though she was not allowed to vote or hold office.

✓ **Reading Check** **Describe** How did Athenian men and women spend their time?

The Peloponnesian War

Main Idea Sparta and Athens went to war for control of Greece.

Reading Focus Have you ever tried to get people to work together and been frustrated when they will not cooperate? Read to find out how the Greek city-states' refusal to cooperate nearly led to their destruction.

As the Athenian empire became rich and powerful, other city-states grew suspicious of its aims. Led by Sparta, they joined forces against Athens. Sparta and Athens had built two very different kinds of societies, and neither state understood or trusted the other. The two groups clashed several times over

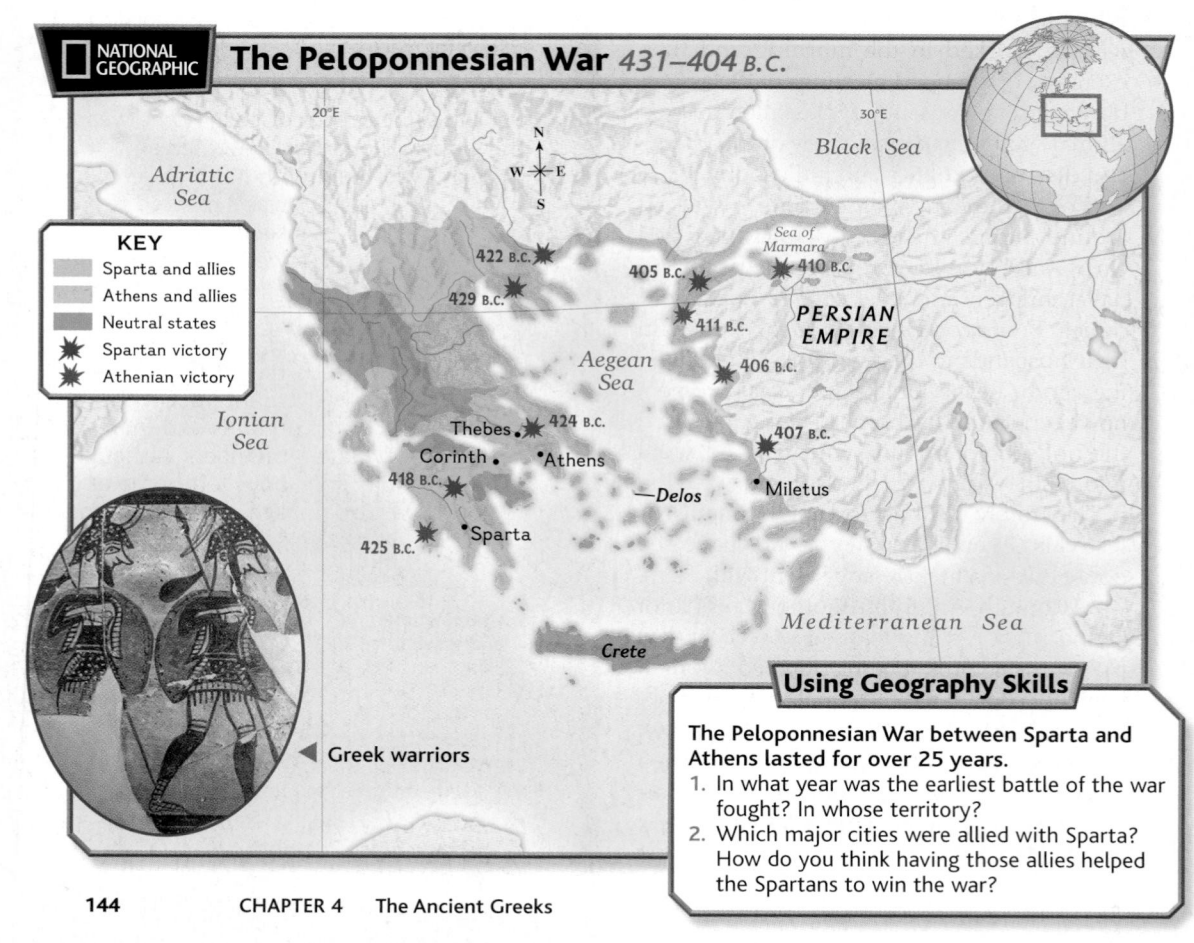

NATIONAL GEOGRAPHIC

The Peloponnesian War 431–404 B.C.

KEY
- Sparta and allies
- Athens and allies
- Neutral states
- ✷ Spartan victory
- ✷ Athenian victory

Adriatic Sea
Ionian Sea
Aegean Sea
Black Sea
Sea of Marmara
PERSIAN EMPIRE
Mediterranean Sea

422 B.C.
429 B.C.
405 B.C.
410 B.C.
411 B.C.
406 B.C.
424 B.C. Thebes
Corinth • Athens
418 B.C.
407 B.C.
425 B.C. • Sparta
• Miletus
—Delos
Crete

20°E   30°E

◄ Greek warriors

Using Geography Skills

The Peloponnesian War between Sparta and Athens lasted for over 25 years.
1. In what year was the earliest battle of the war fought? In whose territory?
2. Which major cities were allied with Sparta? How do you think having those allies helped the Spartans to win the war?

144   CHAPTER 4   The Ancient Greeks

EXTENDING THE CONTENT

Who Was Lysimache? Lysimache, the high priestess of Athena, held her office longer than Pericles—almost 65 years. She performed many religious and public duties, including offering advice from the goddess. She may have served as the model for the antiwar comedy *Lysistrata*, written by Aristophanes during the Peloponnesian War. In the play, the married women of Athens threaten to go on strike unless their husbands end the fighting with Sparta.

what Sparta and its allies saw as Athenian aggression. Finally, war broke out in 431 B.C. It would drag on until 404 B.C. and shatter any possibility of future cooperation among the Greeks. Historians call this conflict the Peloponnesian War because Sparta was located in the Peloponnesus.

Pericles' Funeral Oration
In the first winter of the war, the Athenians held a public funeral. Its purpose was to honor those who had died in battle. The relatives of the dead wept for their loved ones. The rest of the citizens joined in a procession.

As was the custom, a leading Athenian addressed the crowd. On this day, Pericles spoke. He talked about the greatness of Athens and reminded the people that they made their government strong.

In this famous speech, called the Funeral Oration, Pericles pointed out that Athenians were part of a community. As citizens, they agreed to obey the rules in their constitution—their framework of government. They accepted certain duties, such as paying taxes and defending the city. They also gained certain rights, such as the ability to vote and run for office.

Pericles' speech reminded Athenians of the power of democracy and gave them the courage to keep fighting. Its ideas are still important for people living in democratic nations today.

Why Was Athens Defeated?
At the beginning of the Peloponnesian War, both Sparta and Athens thought they knew how to win. The Spartans and their allies surrounded Athens. They hoped that the Athenians would send out an army to fight. However, Pericles knew that Spartan forces could beat the Athenians in open battles. Believing his people would be safe behind the city walls, he urged farmers and others on the outskirts to move inside the city. There

 Pericles' Funeral Oration

Pericles was a dominant figure in Athenian politics between 461 B.C. and 429 B.C., a period historians call the Age of Pericles. In his Funeral Oration, given during the Peloponnesian War, Pericles described democracy, the importance of the individual, and citizenship.

▲ Pericles

"Our constitution is called a democracy because power is in the hands not of a minority but of the whole people. When it is a question of settling private disputes, everyone is equal before the law; when it is a question of putting one person before another in positions of public responsibility, what counts is not membership of a particular class, but the actual ability which the man possesses. No one . . . is kept [out of government] because of poverty. And, just as our political life is free and open, so is our day-to-day life in our relations with each other."

—Pericles, as recorded by Thucydides,
History of the Peloponnesian War

DBQ Document-Based Question
When Pericles said "everyone is equal before the law," what did he mean?

Athenians stayed put and had the navy deliver supplies from their colonies and allies. Because Sparta did not have a navy, it could not attack the Athenian ships.

Athens escaped serious harm for some time. Then, in the second year of the war, a deadly disease spread through the overcrowded city. It killed more than a third of the people, including Pericles himself in 429 B.C. Despite these terrible losses, the

Thucydides, who recorded this speech, served as a general early in the war, but later was banished for 20 years for losing a battle. He explained in his history how he composed the speeches: "I have therefore put into the mouth of each speaker the sentiments . . . as I thought he would be likely to express them."

Answer:
People are chosen for duty based not on class but on ability.

③ ASSESS

Assign Section 4 Review as homework or as an in-class activity.

🔘 Have students use the **Interactive Tutor Self-Assessment CD-ROM** to review the section.

Assessment L2

Assign **Section 4 Quiz** to assess mastery of the material found in the section.

COOPERATIVE LEARNING ACTIVITY

Oral Presentations Organize the class into five groups, and assign each group one of the sentences in Pericles' Funeral Oration. The second sentence, which is very long, should go to a group with verbally gifted readers (or you might divide the sentence). Tell groups to translate the sentences into everyday English, using a dictionary if necessary. Then have one person from each group perform a dramatic reading of the translation. Request volunteers to describe their feelings as they hear the speech. **L1/EL**

📂 Refer to the ***Quizzes, Tests, and Authentic Assessment (with Rubrics)*** booklet for rubrics.

Reading Support L1/ EL

Assign **Reading Essentials and Study Guide 4–4** to help students review section material.

ENRICH

Have students compare the Preamble to the Declaration of Independence to Pericles' Funeral Oration. **L2**

✓ **Reading Check**

Answer: weakened all of Greece and made it open to conquest

To help students understand section material, have them visit **Study Central™** at jat.glencoe.com

RETEACH

Tell students that an *epitaph* is an inscription written on a tombstone or burial place. Ask them to write an epitaph summarizing Pericles' life. **L1/ EL**

CLOSE

Ask students to summarize relations between Sparta and Athens. **L2**

146

Athenians fought on. The standoff continued for another 25 years.

The historian Thucydides recorded what he saw:

❝ This, then, was the calamity which fell upon Athens, and the times were hard indeed, with men dying inside the city and the land outside being laid waste. ❞

—Thucydides,
History of the Peloponnesian War

Finally, desperate to win, the Spartans made a deal with the Persian Empire. In exchange for enough money to build a navy, they gave the Persians some Greek territory in Asia Minor.

In 405 B.C. Sparta's new navy destroyed the Athenian fleet. The next year, after losing more battles on land, Athens surrendered. The Spartans and their allies then tore down the city walls and broke up the Athenian empire. The war was over at last.

The Peloponnesian War weakened all of the major Greek city-states, both the winners and the losers. Many people died in the fighting, and many farms were destroyed. Thousands of people were left without jobs. The war also made it impossible for the Greeks to unite and work together again.

After defeating Athens, Sparta tried to rule all of Greece. Within 30 years, however, the city-states rebelled, and a new war began. While they were fighting amongst themselves, the Greeks failed to notice that to their north, the kingdom of Macedonia was growing in power. This would eventually cost them their freedom.

✓ **Reading Check** **Cause and Effect** What effects did the Peloponnesian War have on Greece?

Section 4 Review

History Online
Study Central™ Need help with the material in this section? Visit jat.glencoe.com

Reading Summary
Review the Main Ideas

- Democracy and culture in Athens flourished under the leadership of Pericles.
- Athenian men worked as farmers, artisans, and merchants, while most women stayed secluded at home.
- Athens and Sparta fought each other in the Peloponnesian War. The fighting led to the defeat of Athens and the weakening of all the Greek states.

What Did You Learn?

1. What caused the Peloponnesian War?

2. According to Pericles, what duties did Athenian citizens have?

Critical Thinking

3. **Summarize** Use a chart like the one below to summarize what Athens was like in the Age of Pericles.

Government	
Economy	
Culture	
Wars	

4. **Analyze** What caused the lack of trust between Sparta and Athens?

5. **Interpreting Visuals** Examine the drawing of the Athenian home on page 142. What does it show about the role of women in Athens?

6. **Civics Link** How did the direct democracy of Athens differ from the democracy we have in the United States?

7. **Expository Writing** Describe the role of the Delian League in the creation of the Athenian empire.

146   **CHAPTER 4**   **The Ancient Greeks**

SECTION 4 REVIEW ANSWERS

1. expansion of Athenian power, Spartan jealousy
2. obey rules, pay taxes, defend the city
3. Government: democracy; Economy: farming and trade; Culture: great creativity,

major rebuilding program; Wars: Peloponnesian War, Athens defeated
4. lack of understanding of their differing societies, perceived Athenian aggression
5. Women performed most

domestic chores and did not eat with men.
6. Answers should reflect information from the text.
7. Athens gradually took over the Delian League and replaced it with its empire.

Section 1 The Early Greeks

Vocabulary
peninsula
colony
polis
agora

Focusing on the Main Ideas
• The geography of Greece influenced where people settled and what they did. *(page 117)*
• The Minoans earned their living by building ships and trading. *(page 118)*
• Mycenaeans built the first Greek kingdoms and spread their power across the Mediterranean region. *(page 119)*
• Colonies and trade spread Greek culture and spurred industry. *(page 121)*
• The idea of citizenship developed in Greek city-states. *(page 122)*

▲ Minoan calendar

Section 2 Sparta and Athens

Vocabulary
tyrant
oligarchy
democracy
helot

Focusing on the Main Ideas
• Tyrants were able to seize power from the nobles with the support of Greek farmers, merchants, and artisans. *(page 125)*
• The Spartans focused on military skills to control the people they conquered. *(page 126)*
• Unlike Spartans, Athenians were more interested in building a democracy than building a military force. *(page 128)*

Section 3 Persia Attacks the Greeks

Vocabulary
satrapies
satrap
Zoroastrianism

Focusing on the Main Ideas
• The Persian Empire united a wide area under a single government. *(page 132)*
• Both Sparta and Athens played roles in defeating the Persians. *(page 134)*

Section 4 The Age of Pericles

Vocabulary
direct democracy
representative democracy
philosopher

Focusing on the Main Ideas
• Under Pericles, Athens became very powerful and more democratic. *(page 139)*
• Athenian men and women had very different roles. *(page 142)*
• Sparta and Athens went to war for control of Greece. *(page 144)*

CHAPTER 4   The Ancient Greeks   147

PREVIEW/REVIEW

Vocabulary Activity Have students determine under which of these heads each term belongs: Government, Geography, Culture, Society.

🔵 **Vocabulary PuzzleMaker CD-ROM**

🔵 **Interactive Tutor Self-Assessment CD-ROM**

CONDENSE

🗂 Chapter 4 **Guided Reading Activities**

🔵 **StudentWorks Plus™ CD-ROM (with Audio Program)**

RETEACH

🗂 **Differentiated Instruction Activity 4**

🗂 Chapter 4 *Reading Essentials and Study Guide*

CHAPTER CULMINATING ACTIVITY

Have students finish the Chapter Culminating Activity from page 112D.

🗂 Suggestions for rubrics may be found in the *Quizzes, Tests, and Authentic Assessment (with Rubrics)* booklet.

📕 Reading Strategy   READ TO WRITE

Organizing Main Ideas Have students design a chart organizing main ideas about the governments created by each of the following: Minoans, Mycenaeans, Greek city-states under the tyrants, Sparta, Athens, and the Persian Empire. Each main idea should be expressed in sentence form. Use the following rubric for assessment:

• **L1** students should have at least one main idea for each group.
• **L2** students should include several main ideas and exhibit sentences that are different from those found in the text.
• **L3** students should be able to offer valid verbal generalizations based upon information in their charts.

Chapter 4 Assessment and Activities

Review Vocabulary

1. e   3. d
2. f   4. a

Sentences should include accurate definitions and use correct grammar.

Review Main Ideas

5. The rocky mountains caused people to settle near the seacoasts and become fishers, sailors, and traders.

6. promoted trade, industry, and specialized goods

7. They had the support of the common people, many of whom were hoplites.

8. Sparta emphasized the military and strict living, while Athens focused on democracy and culture.

9. divisions called satrapies with rulers responsible to him

10. They feared Persian conquest of Greece.

11. Pericles involved more people in government and paid officeholders so poorer citizens could serve.

12. Athens declined. Greece grew weaker, opening it to conquest.

Critical Thinking

13. The Greek peninsula gave the Greeks easy access to sea routes all over the Mediterranean.

Review Vocabulary

Write the vocabulary word that completes each sentence. Write a sentence for each word not used.

a. satrap   d. direct democracy
b. agora   e. oligarchy
c. democracy   f. peninsula

1. In a(n) ___, a few wealthy people hold power.
2. The Greek mainland is a(n) ___, a body of land with water on three sides.
3. In a(n) ___, people at mass meetings make decisions for the government.
4. A(n) ___ acted as tax collector, judge, chief of police, and army recruiter.

Review Main Ideas

Section 1 • The Early Greeks

5. How did the geography of Greece influence where people settled and how they made a living?
6. How did the Greek colonies help industry to grow?

Section 2 • Sparta and Athens

7. Why were tyrants able to seize control from Greek nobles?
8. Describe the differences between Athens and Sparta.

Section 3 • Persia Attacks the Greeks

9. What system did Darius use to unite his large empire under one government?
10. Why did Sparta and Athens unite during the Persian Wars?

Section 4 • The Age of Pericles

11. How was democracy expanded during the Age of Pericles?
12. What was the result of the Peloponnesian War?

Critical Thinking

13. **Cause and Effect** How did the geography of Greece help to encourage trade?
14. **Conclude** Did the people of ancient Athens have a full democracy? Explain.
15. **Explain** Do you think people would enjoy more freedom in an oligarchy or a tyranny? Explain.

Review **Reading Skill** Making Connections

Use What You Know

16. Which of these experiences would help you to better understand the meaning of *democracy*?
   ___ a. running for class president
   ___ b. trading CDs with your friend
   ___ c. picking up litter in your neighborhood
   ___ d. checking out a book at a library

17. The lives of Athenian girls were very different than the lives of girls today. Write a paragraph that explains the differences. As examples, use your own experiences or the experiences of someone you know.

To review this skill, see pages 114–115.

14. Yes; all citizens voted and could take part in lawmaking. No; females, foreigners, and enslaved people were excluded.

15. Possible answers include that it depends on the rulers. A tyrant might be fair and well-liked or harsh and disliked. An oligarchy involves more people in government, but rivalries might weaken it. Oligarchs might be more willing to let people suffer.

Reading Skill

16. a. a democracy is a political system; b–d are not good choices because these activities are not necessary to democracy

17. Paragraphs should show things that girls do today that they were not permitted to do in ancient Athens.

Geography Skills

Study the map below and answer the following questions.

18. **Place** What sea lies along the west coast of Greece?
19. **Location** Where was Knossos?
20. **Movement** If you traveled from Athens to Troy, in what direction would you be going?

NATIONAL GEOGRAPHIC — **Ancient Greece**

Read to Write

21. **Paraphrasing** Select a quotation or primary source from one of the sections in this chapter. Reread it and then paraphrase what you have read. Remember that when you paraphrase, you restate in your own words all of the words in the passage, not just the main ideas.

22. **Descriptive Writing** Work in a small group to create a script for a play about an Athenian citizen who visits Sparta for the first time. Perform your play for the class.

23. **Using Your FOLDABLES** Use the information from your completed chapter opener foldables to create a brief study guide for the chapter. Your study guide should include at least five questions for each section. Questions should focus on the main ideas. Exchange your study guide with a partner and answer each of the questions.

History Online

Self-Check Quiz To help you prepare for the Chapter Test, visit jat.glencoe.com

Linking Past and Present

24. **Making Comparisons** Choose a person mentioned in Chapter 4. Write a description of someone in the news today who has similar ideas or has acted in similar ways. Give examples of their similarities.

Building Citizenship Skills

25. **Analyze** Democracy is not easy to achieve or maintain. Make a chart like the one below to identify things that challenged or threatened democracy in Athens.

Democratic Idea	Challenges

 Analyze

Study the following quote, then answer the questions that follow.

"Our constitution does not copy the laws of neighbouring states; we are rather a pattern to others than imitators ourselves. Its administration favours the many instead of the few; this is why it is called a democracy. . . . The freedom which we enjoy in our government extends also to our ordinary life. . . . Further, we provide plenty of means for the mind to refresh itself from business. We celebrate games and sacrifices all the year round."

—Pericles, as recorded by Thucydides, *The Peloponnesian War*

DBQ Document-Based Questions

26. According to Pericles, why is Athens considered a democracy?
27. What does Pericles mean when he says, "we provide plenty of means for the mind to refresh itself from business"?

Have students visit the Web site at jat.glencoe.com to review Chapter 4 and take the **Self-Check Quiz.**

Linking Past and Present

24. Students' comparisons should show informed knowledge of both people, with pertinent examples to support each similarity.

Building Citizenship Skills

25. Possible answers: Idea—all citizens vote; Challenge—limited idea of citizenship. Idea—good leaders run city; Challenge—lottery system to elect leaders. Idea—a rich, democratic Athens; Challenge—jealousy of other city-states leads to war.

Primary Source

26. Its administration favors the many instead of the few.
27. Athens had games and sacrifices to entertain people.

Bonus Question

Ask: If a candidate similar to Pericles ran for president of the United States, would you vote for him? (*Students should list qualifications or experiences that they would back or reject in such a candidate.*)

Geography Skills

18. the Ionian Sea
19. the island of Crete
20. northeast

Read to Write

21. Paraphrased paragraphs should be in students' words and completely restate the original sources.

22. Students' plays should demonstrate an understanding of both Athenian and Spartan culture.

23. **FOLDABLES** Students' study guides should include relevant questions related to main ideas and concepts in each section.

Chapter ⑤ Resources

Note: The following materials may be used when teaching Chapter 5.
Section level support materials are shown at point of use in the margins of the Teacher Wraparound Edition.

TEACHING TRANSPARENCIES

- Graphic Organizer Transparencies with Teaching Strategy and Student Activity **L2**
- Cause-and-Effect Transparencies with Teaching Strategy and Student Activity **L2**
- Then and Now Transparencies with Teaching Strategy and Student Activity **L2**
- In-text Map Transparency with Teaching Strategy and Student Activity **L1**
- Map Transparencies with Overlay, Teaching Strategy, and Student Activity **L2**

DIFFERENTIATED INSTRUCTION

- Differentiated Instruction Activity 5
- Time Line Activity 5
- Primary Source Reading 5 (with Document-Based Questions)
- Inclusion Strategies for the Middle School Social Studies Classroom
- StudentWorks Plus™ CD-ROM (with Audio Program)

READING SUPPORT

- Take-Home Review Activity 5 **L2**
- World Literature Reading 5 **L2**
- Workbook Activity 5 **L1**
- Reading Strategies for the Social Studies Classroom **L1/ EL**

ASSESSMENT

- Authentic Assessment Activity 5 **L1/ EL**
- Chapter 5 Test Form A **L2**
- Chapter 5 Test Form B **L2**
- ExamView® Pro Testmaker CD-ROM

INTERDISCIPLINARY CONNECTIONS

- Geography and History Activity 5 **L2**
- People to Meet Activity 5 **L2**
- Economics Activity 5 **L2**
- Citizenship and Service Learning Activity 5 **L2**

SPANISH RESOURCES

- Spanish Reading Essentials and Study Guide
- Spanish Guided Reading Activities
- Spanish Quizzes, Tests, and Authentic Assessment (with Rubrics)
- Spanish Take-Home Review Activities

MULTIMEDIA

- ExamView® Pro Testmaker CD-ROM
- Glencoe Skillbuilder Interactive Workbook CD-ROM, Level 1
- Interactive Tutor Self-Assessment CD-ROM
- MindJogger Videoquiz
- Presentation Plus! CD-ROM
- StudentWorks Plus™ CD-ROM (with Audio Program)
- TeacherWorks CD-ROM
- Vocabulary PuzzleMaker CD-ROM
- *World History: Journey Across Time* Video Program
- World History Primary Source Document Library CD-ROM

STANDARDIZED ASSESSMENT SKILLS

- Standardized Test Skills Practice Workbook Activity 5 **L2**
- Critical Thinking Skills Activity 5 **L2**

Teaching strategies have been coded with suggested ability levels. However, most are suitable for all levels.

L1 BASIC activities for all students

L2 AVERAGE activities for average to above-average students

L3 CHALLENGING activities for above-average students

EL ENGLISH LANGUAGE activities

Chapter 5 Resources

TIME MANAGEMENT

Chapter Introduction	Section 1	Section 2	Section 3	Section 4	Chapter Wrap-Up
1 Day	2 Days	1 Day	1 Day	1 Day	1 Day

Block Scheduling Activities that are suited to use within the block scheduling framework are identified by: 🗊

0:00 OUT OF TIME? Assign the Chapter 5 *Reading Essentials and Study Guide.**

SECTION RESOURCES

DAILY OBJECTIVES	REPRODUCIBLE RESOURCES	MULTIMEDIA RESOURCES
Section 1 **The Culture of Ancient Greece** 1. Greek poetry and fables taught Greek values. 2. Greek art and architecture expressed Greek ideas of beauty and harmony.	Reproducible Lesson Plan 5–1 Vocabulary Activity 5–1 Guided Reading Activity 5–1* Section Quiz 5–1* Reading Essentials and Study Guide 5–1*	Daily Focus Skills Transparency 5–1 Interactive Tutor Self-Assessment CD-ROM Exam*View*® Pro Testmaker CD-ROM Presentation Plus! CD-ROM Glencoe BookLink CD-ROM
Section 2 **Greek Philosophy and History** 1. Greek philosophers developed ideas that are still used today. 2. Greeks wrote the first real histories in Western civilization.	Reproducible Lesson Plan 5–2 Vocabulary Activity 5–2 Guided Reading Activity 5–2* Section Quiz 5–2* Reading Essentials and Study Guide 5–2*	Daily Focus Skills Transparency 5–2 Interactive Tutor Self-Assessment CD-ROM Exam*View*® Pro Testmaker CD-ROM Presentation Plus! CD-ROM Glencoe BookLink CD-ROM
Section 3 **Alexander the Great** 1. Philip II of Macedonia united Greek states under Macedonia. 2. Alexander the Great conquered the Persian Empire.	Reproducible Lesson Plan 5–3 Vocabulary Activity 5–3 Guided Reading Activity 5–3* Section Quiz 5–3* Reading Essentials and Study Guide 5–3*	Daily Focus Skills Transparency 5–3 Interactive Tutor Self-Assessment CD-ROM Exam*View*® Pro Testmaker CD-ROM Presentation Plus! CD-ROM
Section 4 **The Spread of Greek Culture** 1. Hellenistic cities became centers of learning and culture. 2. Hellenistic scientists made major discoveries in math and science.	Reproducible Lesson Plan 5–4 Vocabulary Activity 5–4 Guided Reading Activity 5–4* Section Quiz 5–4* Reading Essentials and Study Guide 5–4*	Daily Focus Skills Transparency 5–4 Interactive Tutor Self-Assessment CD-ROM Exam*View*® Pro Testmaker CD-ROM Presentation Plus! CD-ROM Vocabulary PuzzleMaker CD-ROM

*Also available in Spanish

Chapter ⑤ Resources

Use our Web site for additional resources. All essential content is covered in the Student Edition.

You and your students can visit jat.glencoe.com, the Web site companion to *World History: Journey Across Time.* This innovative integration of electronic and print media offers your students a wealth of opportunities. The student text directs students to the Web site for the following options:

- Chapter Overviews
- Self-Check Quizzes
- Study Central™
- Student Web Activities
- Multi-Language Glossaries

Answers to the student Web activities are provided for you in the **Web Activity Lesson Plans.** Additional Web resources and ePuzzles and games are also available.

The following videotape programs are available from Glencoe as supplements to Chapter 5:

Hercules: Power of the Gods
(ISBN 1-56501-659-9)

Mystical Monuments of Ancient Greece
(ISBN 0-7670-0012-9)

Powerful Gods of Mount Olympus
(ISBN 1-56501-927-X)

To order, call Glencoe at 1-800-334-7344. To find classroom resources to accompany many of these videos, check the following home pages:

A&E Television: www.aande.com
The History Channel: www.historychannel.com

MEETING SPECIAL NEEDS

In addition to the Differentiated Instruction strategies, the following resources are suitable for students with special needs:

- *ExamView® Pro Testmaker CD-ROM* allows teachers to tailor tests by reducing answer choices.
- *StudentWorks Plus™ CD-ROM (with Audio Program)* includes the entire narrative of the student edition so that less-proficient readers can listen to the words as they read them.
- The *Reading Essentials and Study Guide* provides the same content as the student edition but is written two grade levels below the textbook.

 TEACHER'S CORNER

Index to National Geographic Magazine:
The following articles relate to this chapter:

- "Deep Black Sea," by Robert Ballard, May 2001.
- "Olive Oil: Elixir of the Gods," by Erla Zwingle, September 1999.
- "Let the Games Begin," by Frank Deford, July 1996.

National Geographic Society Products Available From Glencoe:
To order the following products call Glencoe at 1–800–334–7344

- *PicturePack: Ancient Civilizations: Ancient Greece* (Transparencies)
- *National Geographic Atlas of the World* (Book)

NGS ONLINE

Access National Geographic's new dynamic MapMachine Web site and other geography resources at:

www.nationalgeographic.com
www.nationalgeographic.com/maps

 ## Meeting NCSS Standards

World History: Journey Across Time
The following standards are highlighted in Chapter 5:

Section 1 **I** Culture: A, C, D, F, G
II Time, Continuity, and Change: A
III People, Places, and Environments: G

Section 2 **V** Individuals, Groups, and Institutions: E, H
VI Power, Authority, and Governance: A, B, H
X Civic Ideals and Practices: A

Section 3 **IV** Individual Development and Identity: D
VI Power, Authority, and Governance: F

Section 4 **IV** Individual Development and Identity: A
VIII Science, Technology, and Society: A, B, C

State and Local Objectives

_____

_____

Timesaving Tools

TeacherWorks
All-In-One Planner and Resource Center

- **Interactive Teacher Edition** Access your Teacher Wraparound Edition and your classroom resources with a few easy clicks.

- **Interactive Lesson Planner** Organize your week, month, semester, or year with all the lesson helps you need to make teaching creative and relevant.

Use Glencoe's **Presentation Plus!** multimedia teacher tool to easily present dynamic lessons that visually excite your students. Using Microsoft PowerPoint® you can customize the presentations to create your own personalized lessons.

FOLDABLES™
Study Organizer
Dinah Zike's Foldables

Foldables are three-dimensional, interactive graphic organizers that help students practice basic writing skills, review key vocabulary terms, and identify main ideas. Every chapter contains a foldable activity, with additional chapter activities found in the *Reading and Study Skills Foldables* booklet. You can use the foldables as they are presented, or modify them to suit the needs of your individual class.

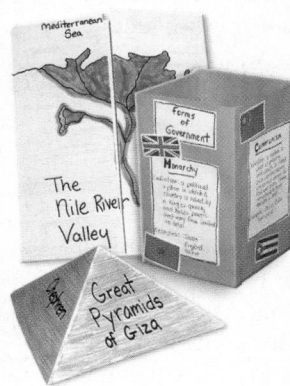

Planning Ahead

CHAPTER CULMINATING ACTIVITY

The Chapter Culminating Activity will help students organize and learn the important information from the chapter. Begin teaching the chapter with this activity, and have students complete it as a culminating activity.

CREATING A MAIN IDEA CHART FOR THE CHAPTER

Purpose This type of organizer helps students analyze and understand information by identifying main ideas and showing how supporting details reinforce this main idea. This chart is useful as students read the chapter. It can also be used to organize information for reports and as a study aid.

Introduction to Modeling

1. Begin the discussion with a brainstorming session about Greek culture. Ask students to list what they know or believe they know about ancient Greek culture. Write the information on an overhead transparency.

2. Ask students to copy this chart into their notebooks:

As students read the chapter, ask them to fill in a main idea about Greek culture, then find supporting details that complete each set of boxes. Have them draw more Main Idea and Supporting Details boxes as they discover them in the chapter.

3. As part of your chapter review, have students share their Main Idea charts. Encourage them to complete more boxes during this class wrap-up and use their completed charts as study aids.

Use the **SkillBuilder Handbook** on pages 902–919 to help students learn the skill of finding the main idea.

When & Where?

As students read the chapter, have them review the time line on page 150. Ask them to find evidence that Greek culture continued to flourish even after Greece itself was no longer a powerful political force. *(The time line shows that cultural advances continued even after Alexander had conquered Greece and Persia.)* **L1**

GLENCOE TECHNOLOGY

World History: Journey Across Time Video Program

To learn more about Greek civilization, students can view the Chapter 5 video in the *World History: Journey Across Time* Video Program.

MindJogger Videoquiz

Use the **MindJogger Videoquiz** to preview Chapter 5 content.

 Available in DVD and VHS

Chapter 5

Greek Civilization

The temple of Delphi was very important to ancient Greeks. Many people believed the priestess here could foretell the future. ▶

NATIONAL GEOGRAPHIC When & Where?

400 B.C.	300 B.C.	200 B.C.
399 B.C. Socrates sentenced to death	**330** B.C. Alexander the Great conquers Persian Empire	**c. 287** B.C. Mathematician and inventor Archimedes is born

---

Reading Strategy — PURPOSE FOR READING

Previewing Ask students to preview the chapter by making a list of the major headings and sub-headings. Then guide the class through a quick discussion of what they expect to learn in each section of the chapter. Previewing will help students gain an understanding of the types of information they will find in the chapter and help them contextualize the information as they come across it. Ask students to write a question they predict will be answered in each section. Use the questions to help students set a purpose for reading. **L2**

Chapter Preview

Many Greeks studied science, philosophy, mathematics, and the arts. When Alexander the Great conquered the Persian Empire, he spread Greek culture and ideas throughout southwest Asia and the Mediterranean world.

Chapter Overview Visit jat.glencoe.com **for a preview of Chapter 5.**

View the Chapter 5 video in the *World History: Journey Across Time* Video Program.

The Culture of Ancient Greece

The Greeks made great strides in the arts. Greek poetry, art, and drama are still part of our world today.

Greek Philosophy and History

The Greeks' love of wisdom led to the study of history, politics, biology, and logic.

Alexander the Great

Alexander the Great was only 25 years old when he conquered the Persian Empire. As a result of his conquests, Greek art, ideas, language, and architecture spread throughout southwest Asia and North Africa.

The Spread of Greek Culture

Greek cities became centers of learning and culture. Greek scientists developed advanced ideas about astronomy and mathematics.

FOLDABLES™
Study Organizer

Organizing Information *Make the following foldable to help you organize information about Greek culture and philosophy.*

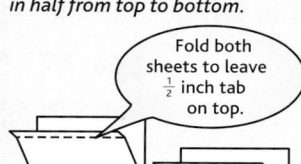

Step 1 *Fold two sheets of paper in half from top to bottom.*

Fold both sheets to leave $\frac{1}{2}$ inch tab on top.

Step 3 *Fit both sheets of paper together to make a cube as shown.*

Step 2 *Place glue or tape along both $\frac{1}{2}$ inch tabs.*

Step 4 *Turn the cube and label the foldable as shown.*

Alexander the Great

The Spread of Greek Culture

The Culture of Ancient Greece

Greek Philosophy

Reading and Writing *As you read the chapter, list the developments that occurred in ancient Greece. Write the developments under the correct foldable category.*

151

INTRODUCING CHAPTER 5

Introduce students to chapter content and key terms by having them access **Chapter Overview 5** at jat.glencoe.com

CHAPTER PREVIEW

After reading Chapter 5, students will be able to

1. describe important Greek developments in the arts;

2. discuss Greek achievements in history, politics, biology, and logic;

3. summarize how Alexander the Great created an empire;

4. describe how Hellenistic kingdoms became centers of learning and culture.

FOLDABLES™
Study Organizer   Dinah Zike's Foldables

Purpose Students use this foldable to organize information about notable developments in ancient Greek civilization. Completed foldables will be a guide to those important developments.

Have students complete *Reading and Study Skills Foldables* Activity 5.

MORE ABOUT THE PHOTO

Temple of Delphi The ancient Greeks considered the site of the Temple of Delphi to be the center of the world. Legend said that Zeus, king of the gods, released two eagles. One flew from the east, the other from the west. They met at Delphi, on the slopes of Mount Parnassus, thus indicating its importance. A stone marking the spot where the eagles met was called the *omphalos*, or navel. Archaeologists have discovered that Delphi has been settled since early Mycenaean times in the 1300s B.C. The influential oracle of Apollo was known all over the Greek world by the 600s B.C. The oracle, a woman who had to be over the age of 50, was consulted frequently on matters of political, military, and even personal importance.

1 Learn It!

Help students learn that everything they see or read in the text can help them derive meaning. If they learn to use words, graphs, or illustrations while tapping into their prior knowledge, comprehension will happen more easily. Read the second and third paragraphs under "What Was a Greek Oracle?" in Section 1, then perform the following exercises:

1. **Ask:** What is an oracle? Point out words from the passage that can serve to deepen understanding, such as *sacred shrine, priest, priestess,* and *Apollo at Delphi.*

2. Have students look at the picture on page 156 of a Greek man consulting the oracle. Ask if the picture in the text is similar to the picture they formed in their minds as they listened to you read about an oracle.

3. Read aloud the paragraph on page 156 that tells how King Croesus of Lydia sent messengers to the oracle at Delphi and was tricked. Ask students how this clarifies what they know of Greek oracles. **L2**

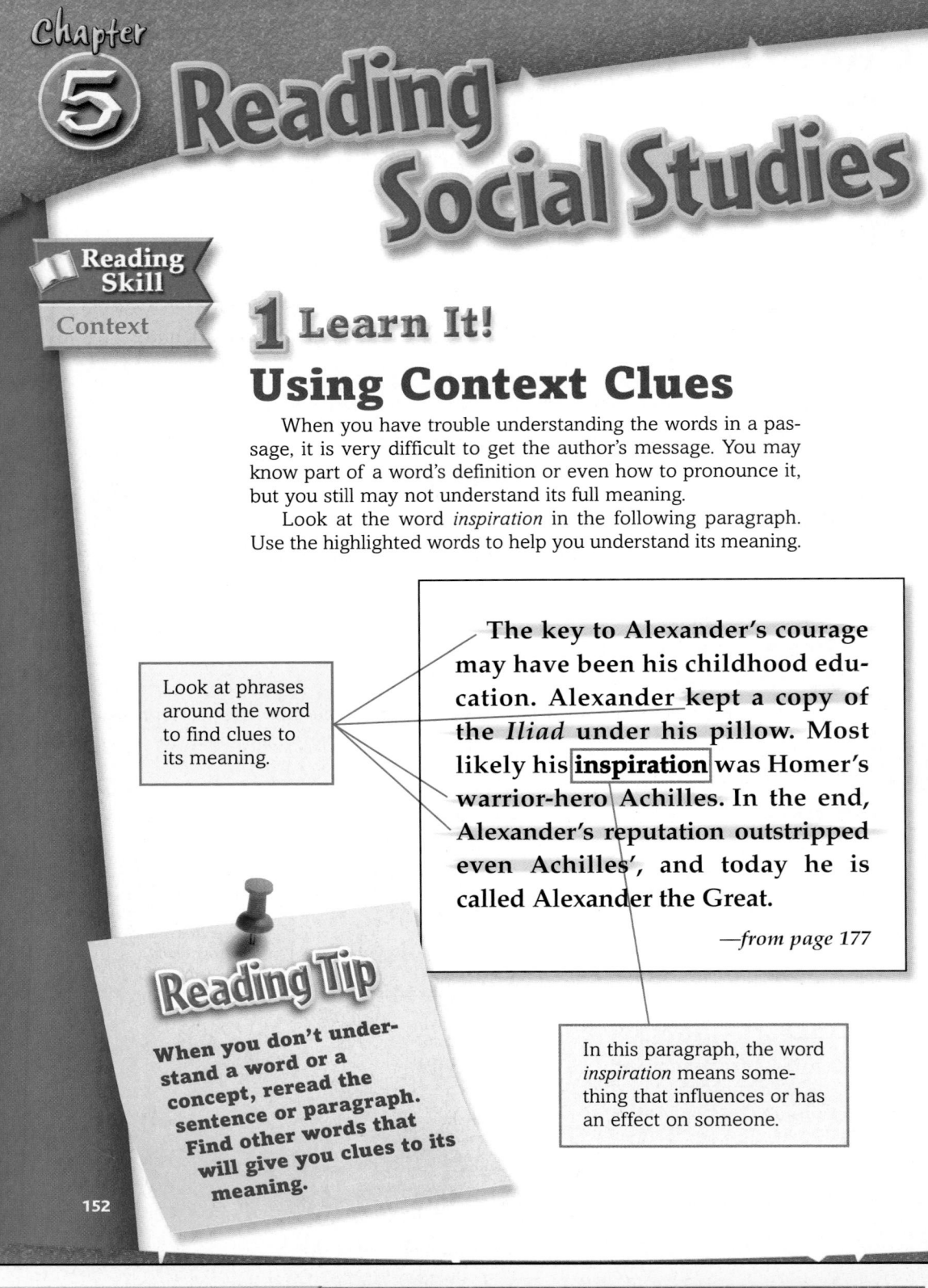

Chapter 5 Reading Social Studies

Reading Skill Context

1 Learn It!

Using Context Clues

When you have trouble understanding the words in a passage, it is very difficult to get the author's message. You may know part of a word's definition or even how to pronounce it, but you still may not understand its full meaning.

Look at the word *inspiration* in the following paragraph. Use the highlighted words to help you understand its meaning.

Look at phrases around the word to find clues to its meaning.

> The key to Alexander's courage may have been his childhood education. Alexander kept a copy of the *Iliad* under his pillow. Most likely his **inspiration** was Homer's warrior-hero Achilles. In the end, Alexander's reputation outstripped even Achilles', and today he is called Alexander the Great.
>
> —*from page 177*

Reading Tip

When you don't understand a word or a concept, reread the sentence or paragraph. Find other words that will give you clues to its meaning.

In this paragraph, the word *inspiration* means something that influences or has an effect on someone.

152

Reading Strategy **QUESTIONING**

One sure way to help students unlock meaning, activate background knowledge, and draw information from context is to create opportunities for relevant discussions. Have students take turns selecting a topic from the text as a subject for discussion. Facilitate the establishment of ground rules, such as speaking respectfully and honoring time limits. In some cases, students can learn to moderate their own discussion topics, practicing such skills as asking thoughtful questions, keeping the discussion moving, and summarizing points made by the class.

2 Practice It!

What Does It Mean?

Read the following paragraph about Aesop. Write down all the words or phrases that help you fully understand the meaning of the word *fable*.

> About 550 B.C., a Greek slave named Aesop (EE·SAHP) made up his now famous fables. A fable (FAY·buhl) is a short tale that teaches a lesson. In most of Aesop's fables, animals talk and act like people. These often funny stories point out human flaws as well as strengths. Each fable ends with a message, or moral.
>
> —*from page 158*

Read to Write

Turn to any page in this chapter. Close your eyes and point to a word. It can be any word, even "a" or "the." Now write a paragraph explaining how the rest of the words in the sentence or paragraph where that word appears helped you to determine its meaning.

Aesop ▶

3 Apply It!

As you read the chapter, create five word webs. Put an important word or idea in a center circle. Surround it with circles containing words from the text that help explain it.

153

---

2 Practice It!

Using Listening Skills Tell students to listen carefully as you read aloud a few paragraphs from the subsection "Greek Poetry and Fables" in Section 1. Ask students to jot down any context clues that help them understand the meaning of the word *epic*. (*long poems, heroic deeds,* Iliad, Odyssey, *Homer, heroes*)

Analyzing Art Have students look at the art piece on the Parthenon on page 162. Ask them to consider what this image suggests about Greek religious practices and culture.

Activate Prior Knowledge Ask students if they have ever heard of the *Iliad* or the *Odyssey*. If so, ask them to share what they know with the class. **L2**

3 Apply It!

Demonstrate how to create a word web with the word *Epicureanism*. Write the word in the center of the board. Then read aloud the paragraph on page 184 that defines Epicureanism and ask students what context clues should go in circles around the word to help them better understand the term. **L1**

Reading Strategy ⟩ **READ TO WRITE**

Having students use context to determine meaning is a skill that can be adapted to different writing styles. For example, in this chapter, students will learn the origin of the word *fable*. After reading about the Tortoise and the Hare, ask students to write their own fables using these animals. Remind them that fables teach moral points. Allow students to brainstorm in groups before beginning their writing. Have them use the word they have found using the **Read to Write** exercise from the student page in their fables. **L2**

① FOCUS

SECTION OVERVIEW

This section discusses the culture of the ancient Greeks as expressed in their religion, literature, and art.

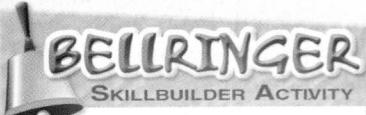
BELLRINGER
SKILLBUILDER ACTIVITY

📖 Project **Daily Focus Skills Transparency 5–1** and have students answer questions. Discuss their responses.

Get Ready to Read!

Preteaching Vocabulary: Explain to students that epics were very important to ancient Greeks. These stories taught important values such as courage and valor. Ask students how values that are important to *our* society are taught.

Answers to Graphic: Epic: long poem, recounts heroic deeds; Fable: short tale, teaches a lesson; Both: Greek literature

---

Section ① The Culture of Ancient Greece

Get Ready to Read!

What's the Connection?

You have read that under Pericles, Athens became a center of beauty and culture. During this Golden Age, Greek thinkers, writers, and artists contributed many new ideas to the world.

Focusing on the Main Ideas

- The Greeks believed that gods and goddesses controlled nature and shaped their lives. *(page 155)*
- Greek poetry and fables taught Greek values. *(page 157)*
- Greek drama still shapes entertainment today. *(page 160)*
- Greek art and architecture expressed Greek ideas of beauty and harmony. *(page 162)*

Locating Places
Mount Olympus (uh•LIHM•puhs)
Delphi (DEHL•FY)

Meeting People
Homer (HOH•muhr)
Aesop (EE•SAHP)
Sophocles (SAH•fuh•KLEEZ)
Euripides (yu•RIH•puh•DEEZ)

Building Your Vocabulary
myth (MIHTH)
oracle (AWR•uh•kuhl)
epic (EH•pihk)
fable (FAY•buhl)
drama (DRAH•muh)
tragedy (TRA•juh•dee)
comedy (KAH•muh•dee)

Reading Strategy
Compare and Contrast Create a Venn diagram showing similarities and differences between an epic and a fable.

Epic | Both | Fable

NATIONAL GEOGRAPHIC When & Where?

GREECE
Olympia
Athens

700 B.C.
c. 700s B.C.
Homer writes the *Iliad* and *Odyssey*

600 B.C.
c. 550 B.C.
Aesop writes a series of fables

500 B.C.
c. 500s B.C.
Greek architects begin using marble columns

SECTION RESOURCES

📁 **Reproducible Masters**
- Reproducible Lesson Plan 5–1
- Daily Lecture and Discussion Notes 5–1
- Vocabulary Activity 5–1
- Active Reading Note-Taking Guide 5–1
- Guided Reading Activity 5–1
- Section Quiz 5–1
- Reading Essentials and Study Guide 5–1

📖 **Transparencies**
- Daily Focus Skills Transparency 5–1

Multimedia
- Interactive Tutor Self-Assessment CD-ROM
- ExamView® Pro Testmaker CD-ROM
- Presentation Plus! CD-ROM
- Glencoe BookLink CD-ROM

Greek Mythology

Main Idea The Greeks believed that gods and goddesses controlled nature and shaped their lives.

Reading Focus Have you ever wondered why crops grow or why the sun rises and sets? To get the answer, you would read a science book. Read to learn how the Greeks used religion to explain nature.

Myths (MIHTHS) are traditional stories about gods and heroes. Greek mythology expressed the Greek people's religious beliefs. The Greeks believed in many gods and goddesses. They believed gods and goddesses affected people's lives and shaped events. That is why the most impressive buildings in Greek cities were religious temples.

Greek Gods and Goddesses The Greeks believed that the gods and goddesses controlled nature. According to Greek myth, the god Zeus ruled the sky and threw lightning bolts, the goddess Demeter made the crops grow, and the god Poseidon caused earthquakes.

The 12 most important gods and goddesses lived on **Mount Olympus** (uh•LIHM•puhs), the highest mountain in Greece. Among the 12 were Zeus, who was the chief god; Athena, the goddess of wisdom and crafts; Apollo, the god of the sun and poetry; Ares, the god of war; Aphrodite, the goddess of love; and Poseidon, the god of the seas and earthquakes.

Greek Gods and Goddesses

KEY
- Brothers and Sisters of Zeus
- Children of Zeus

Zeus King of the gods; god of the sky, rain, and lightning

Hera Goddess of marriage

Hades God of the underworld

Poseidon God of the sea

Hestia Goddess of the home

Artemis Goddess of the hunt and wild animals; twin sister of Apollo

Apollo God of light

Hermes Messenger of the gods; god of the market

Aphrodite Goddess of love and beauty

Athena Goddess of wisdom; protector of cities

Ares God of war

Understanding Charts

The Greeks believed their gods and goddesses were a large family—all related in some way.
1. Who was the twin sister of Apollo?
2. **Explain** How were Ares and Zeus related?

② TEACH

Previewing Ask students to share what they know about Greek gods and goddesses. Ask them to suggest reasons why the Greeks had so many gods and goddesses. (*Answers may include that the deities represented many different natural forces or aspects of human life.*) **L2**

Daily Lecture and Discussion Notes 5–1

Use **Daily Lecture and Discussion Notes 5–1** for an outline of key concepts found in the section.

Reading Support L1/ EL

Use **Vocabulary Activity 5–1** to review important terms in the section.

Understanding Charts

Answers:
1. Artemis
2. Ares was Zeus's son.

📖 Reading Strategy READING THE TEXT

Using Word Maps A word map shows the relationships between words or concepts in a graphic organizer format. Using the central idea of *Greek Values*, as discussed in this section, create a word map on the board. Place "Greek Values" in a circle, and have branches with circles coming off of it. Have students complete the surrounding bubbles to clarify the concept. Possible words and phrases to complete the word map include *gods and goddesses intervened in human life and controlled nature, everyone has a personal destiny, courage, honor, reason, moderation, harmony,* and *balance.* **L2**

CONNECTING ACROSS TIME

Ask students to explain a ritual in their own words. Then have volunteers describe religious rituals in the United States, such as those that take place in churches, mosques, synagogues, or temples. Ask why these rituals are performed. *(Answers may include to honor a god or gods or build community among worshipers.)* L1/ EL

GLENCOE
BOOKLINK

Use **Glencoe BookLink** to create customized reading lists for your students' reading levels, interests, and abilities.

More About the Art

Some scientists believe that the gases seeping into the oracle's chamber included ethylene. Ethylene may have induced the euphoric, trance-like state from which the oracle made her prophecies.

Caption Answer: The oracle's answer was often found in a riddle.

Reading Check

Answer: They hoped the gods would grant good fortune to them.

▲ This painting shows a Greek man at the oracle at Delphi receiving a prophecy. *Why were these prophecies often confusing?*

But Greek gods and goddesses were not thought to be all-powerful. According to Greek myths, even though gods had special powers, they looked like human beings and acted like them. They married, had children, quarreled, played tricks on each other, and fought wars.

Because Greeks sought their gods' favor, they followed many rituals. A ritual is a set of actions carried out in a fixed way. As part of their rituals, the Greeks prayed to their gods and also gave them gifts. In return, they hoped that the gods would grant good fortune to them. Many Greek festivals honored the gods and goddesses. Festivals dedicated to Zeus were held at Olympia.

The Greeks also believed in an afterlife. When people died, the Greeks believed their spirits went to a gloomy world beneath the earth ruled by a god named Hades.

What Was a Greek Oracle? The Greeks believed that each person had a fate or destiny. They believed that certain events were going to happen no matter what they did. They also believed in prophecy. A prophecy is a prediction about the future. The Greeks believed that the gods gave prophecies to people to warn them about the future in time to change it.

To find out about the future, many Greeks visited an **oracle** (AWR•uh•kuhl). This was a sacred shrine where a priest or priestess spoke for a god or goddess. The most famous was the oracle at the Temple of Apollo at **Delphi** (DEHL•FY). The oracle chamber was deep inside the temple. The room had an opening in the floor where volcanic smoke hissed from a crack in the earth.

A priestess sat on a tripod—a three-legged stool—in the oracle chamber and listened to questions. The priests translated her answers. State leaders or their messengers traveled to Delphi to ask advice from the oracle of Apollo.

The priestess in the oracle often gave answers in riddles. When one king, named Croesus (KREE•suhs), sent messengers to the oracle at Delphi, they asked if the king should go to war with the Persians. The oracle replied that if Croesus attacked the Persians, he would destroy a mighty empire. Overjoyed to hear these words, Croesus declared war on the Persians. The Persian army crushed his army. The mighty empire King Croesus had destroyed was his own!

Reading Check **Explain** Why did the Greeks have rituals and festivals for their gods and goddesses?

DIFFERENTIATED INSTRUCTION

Kinesthetic: Ask students to build a model of a Greek theater. Have them use the information in the text, as well as independent research, to build the model. Allow them to choose the materials for the model.

English Learners: Ask students to make a detailed drawing of a Greek theater and explain each part of the drawing to a partner.

Gifted and Talented: Have students build the model and include figure characters, like a doll or puppet theater. Have them present a scene from a Greek play using their model theater.

📂 Refer to *Inclusion Strategies for the Middle School Social Studies Classroom* in the TCR.

Greek Poetry and Fables

Main Idea Greek poetry and fables taught Greek values.

Reading Focus Do you have favorite stories? Are the characters in the stories brave and clever? Read about the characters of the best-loved stories in early Greece.

Greek poems and stories are the oldest in the Western world. For hundreds of years, Europeans and Americans have used these early works as models for their own poems and stories. Shakespeare, for example, borrowed many Greek plots and settings.

The earliest Greek stories were **epics** (EH•pihks). These long poems told about heroic deeds. The first great epics of early Greece were the *Iliad* and the *Odyssey*. The poet **Homer** (HOH•muhr) wrote these epics during the 700s B.C. He based them on stories of a war between Greece and the city of Troy, which once existed in what is today northwestern Turkey.

In the *Iliad*, a prince of Troy kidnaps the wife of the king of Sparta. The kidnapping outrages the Greeks. The king of Mycenae and the brother of the king of Sparta lead the Greeks in an attack on Troy.

The battle for Troy drags on for 10 years. Finally, the Greeks come up with a plan to take the city. They build a huge, hollow, wooden horse. The best Mycenaean warriors hide inside the horse.

The Trojan Horse

After building the Trojan horse, the Greeks returned to their ships and pretended to retreat. Despite warnings, the Trojans brought the horse within their city as a war trophy. The Greeks inside the horse opened the city gates for their fellow soldiers and captured the city. *What epic included the story of the Trojan horse?*

▲ Clay carving of the Trojan horse

The Greek soldiers hid in the belly of the horse.

Troops left the horse through a trapdoor.

The wooden horse was placed on a platform with wheels.

TIME TRAVELER

Odysseus, legendary Greek hero of the *Odyssey,* was famous for his cleverness, resourcefulness, and bravery. He was especially skilled at using trickery to gain success. It was he who thought up the idea of the Trojan horse to finally capture the city of Troy. In his 10-year journey home from the war, he had many opportunities to use his cleverness. He defeated a dreadful one-eyed cyclops, rescued his men from a witch, and saved his men from cannibals.

✓ Reading Check

Answer: short tale, teaches a lesson, often involves funny stories about animals that speak

The Trojans, thinking the horse was a gift from the Greeks, celebrate and roll the giant horse into the city. That night, the Greek warriors quietly climb from the horse and capture the city.

The *Odyssey* tells the story of Odysseus, another Greek hero. It describes his journey home from the Trojan War. Odysseus faces storms, witches, and giants before returning to his wife. Because it took Odysseus 10 years to get home, we use the word *odyssey* today to mean a long journey with many adventures.

Greeks believed the *Iliad* and the *Odyssey* were more than stories. They looked on the epics as real history. These poems gave the Greeks an ideal past with a cast of heroes. Generations of Greeks read Homer's works. One Athenian wrote, "My father was anxious to see me develop into a good man . . . [so] he compelled me to memorize all of Homer."

Homer's stories taught courage and honor. They also taught that it was important to be loyal to your friends and to value the relationship between husband and wife. The stories showed heroes striving to be the best they could be. Heroes fought to protect their own honor and their family's honor. Homer's heroes became role models for Greek boys.

Who Was Aesop? About 550 B.C., a Greek slave named **Aesop** (EE•SAHP) made up his now famous fables. A **fable** (FAY•buhl) is a short tale that teaches a lesson. In most of Aesop's fables, animals talk and act like people. These often funny stories point out human flaws as well as strengths. Each fable ends with a message, or moral.

One of the best-known fables is "The Tortoise and the Hare." In this fable, a tortoise and a hare decide to race. More than

Aesop

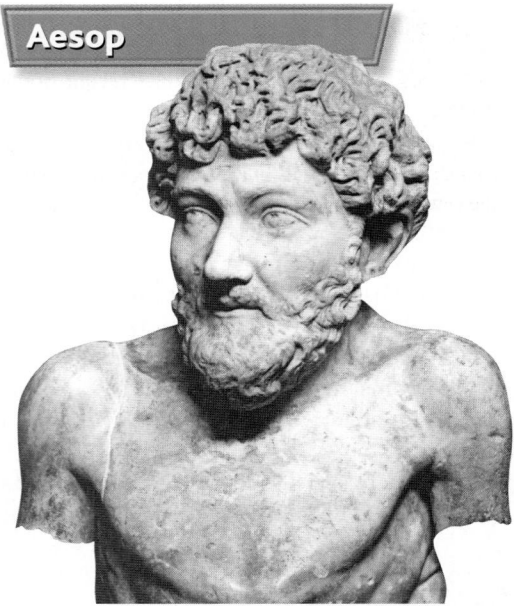

According to legend, Aesop was freed from slavery and became an adviser to Greek rulers. *What is a fable?*

halfway into the race, the hare is way ahead. He stops to rest and falls asleep. Meanwhile, the tortoise keeps going at a slow but steady pace and finally wins the race.

The moral of the story is "slow and steady wins the race." Some of the phrases we hear today came from Aesop's fables. "Sour grapes," "a wolf in sheep's clothing," and "appearances often are deceiving" are examples.

For about 200 years, Aesop's fables were a part of Greece's oral tradition. This means they were passed from person to person by word of mouth long before they were ever written down. Since then, countless writers have retold the stories in many different languages.

✓ Reading Check **Describe** What are the characteristics of a fable?

INTERDISCIPLINARY CONNECTIONS ACTIVITY

Language Arts Ask students to review the example of the Delphic Oracle's cryptic answer to Croesus. Discuss how the answer was true yet difficult to interpret correctly, like a riddle or brainteaser. Have students write a series of questions for the oracle from well-known political, cultural, or other figures of our time. Students should include a cryptic response. Then have them describe a possible result of the question to the oracle. Make sure students understand that the oracle's answer is true, but not in the way the questioner assumed or expected. Have students share their oracle dialogues with the class. **L2**

HOMER

c. 750 B.C.

Homer ▶

Homer's epic poems—the *Iliad* and the *Odyssey*—are famous, but until the 1900s, historians believed that Homer never existed. Historians now know Homer was a real person, but they still debate whether he wrote his poems alone or with the help of other poets.

Many historians have speculated, or made educated guesses, about Homer's personal life. Some say that Homer came from Ionia and seven cities claim to be his birthplace. Some believe that he was blind. Others believe that he wandered from town to town.

Legends tell of Homer's strong influence on his readers. For example, as a young child, Alexander the Great is said to have slept with a copy of the *Iliad* under his pillow.

Homer used the term *aoidos* for a poet. This word means "singer," which tells us that the poetry created during Homer's time was memorized and recited, not written down. Usually, short, simple poems that were easy to remember were told to an audience as entertainment.

Homer created a different style of poetry that influenced all Western literature that followed. His epics are long and involve complex characters, dramatic action, and interesting events. Because each section of the *Iliad* and the *Odyssey* has these characteristics, most historians today think that only one poet could have created both epics. Whoever Homer was, his two epics have influenced readers for more than 3,000 years.

> "I hate as I hate [Hades'] own gate that man who hides one thought within him while he speaks another."
>
> —Homer, the *Iliad*

Then and Now

Review the characteristics of an epic. Then do research to identify a modern epic.

TEACH

How could Homer have memorized his poems? The *Iliad* is more than 16,000 verses long. One technique, used in oral poems even before the time of Homer, was the noun-epithet formula. This technique allows the oral poet to use the same adjectives, in different combinations, to describe things and people. For example, Odysseus is usually described as "wily Odysseus," "many-counseled Odysseus," or "much-enduring divine Odysseus." This repetition allowed Homer to use whichever words and phrases fit the meter of his poem. The repetition also made it easier to recite many verses in an evening's performance.

Ask students to name some words and phrases that recur in some of their favorite songs. *(Answers will vary.)* **L1/ EL**

Then and Now

Answers will vary. Students will likely name a movie or series of movies, such as *Star Wars* or the *Lord of the Rings* trilogy.

159

Reading List Generator CD-ROM

GLENCOE BOOKLINK   **RECOMMENDED READING**

Use the **Glencoe BookLink CD-ROM** to create customized reading lists based on your students' interests and reading levels. Below is an example based on content in this chapter. Also, see the Suggested Readings on pages 944–946 of the Appendix.

- **Bulfinch, Thomas.** *Bulfinch's Mythology: The Age of Fable.* Bulfinch's classic retelling of many ancient Greek myths.

- **Coolidge, Olivia.** *Hercules and Other Tales from Greek Myths.* Many myths, including Hercules and the Nemean lion and Theseus and the minotaur.

- **Homer.** The *Odyssey (Adapted).* Odysseus's adventures returning home after the Trojan War.

Evaluating One of the lessons of early Greek drama was that even though a person failed, attempting to do the right thing was still a worthy goal. **Ask: Is this true today? Why or why not? L2**

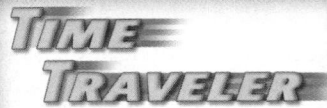

Theaters in Greece were built in naturally occurring amphitheaters. The action took place within a level circle called the orchestra. The audience sat in naturally tiered seats set into the hillside. On the opposite side of the orchestra, a facade was erected that served two purposes: it provided a changing room for the actors and a backdrop for scenery.

Categorizing Information Ask students to name some works of literature, plays, movies, or television shows that are comedies or tragedies and explain why they placed each in its category. **L1**

Linking Past & Present

Answer: Answers will vary but may include Greek values, dress, politics, humor, and so on.

Greek Drama

Main Idea Greek drama still shapes entertainment today.

Reading Focus Think about your favorite movie. How would you describe it? Is it a tragedy? Is it a comedy? Read to find out how Greek plays still influence our entertainment.

What is **drama** (DRAH•muh)? Drama is a story told by actors who pretend to be characters in the story. In a drama, actors speak, show emotion, and imitate the actions of the characters they represent.

Today's movies, plays, and television shows are all examples of drama.

Tragedies and Comedies The Greeks performed plays in outdoor theaters as part of their religious festivals. They developed two kinds of dramas—comedies and tragedies.

In a **tragedy** (TRA•juh•dee), a person struggles to overcome difficulties but fails. As a result, the story has an unhappy ending. Early Greek tragedies presented people in a struggle against their fate. Later Greek tragedies showed how a person's character flaws caused him or her to fail.

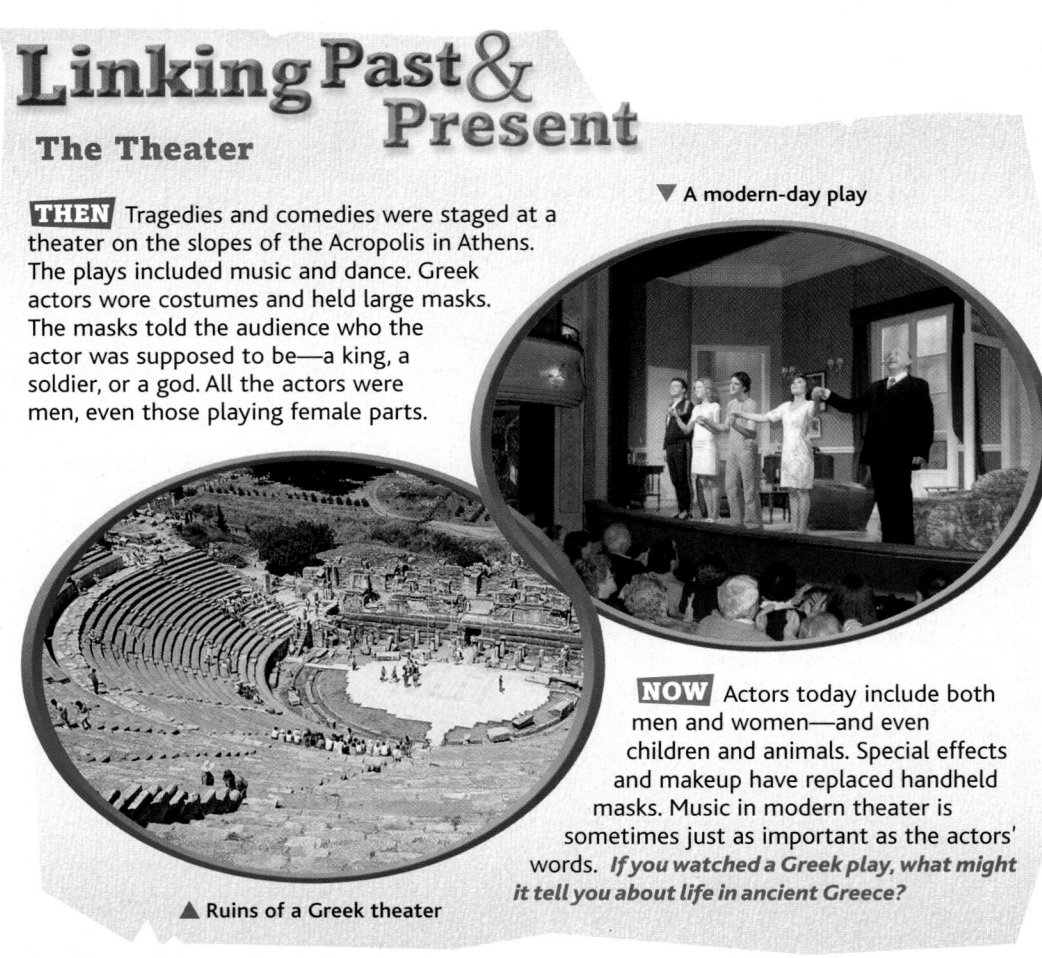

Linking Past & Present

The Theater

THEN Tragedies and comedies were staged at a theater on the slopes of the Acropolis in Athens. The plays included music and dance. Greek actors wore costumes and held large masks. The masks told the audience who the actor was supposed to be—a king, a soldier, or a god. All the actors were men, even those playing female parts.

▼ A modern-day play

NOW Actors today include both men and women—and even children and animals. Special effects and makeup have replaced handheld masks. Music in modern theater is sometimes just as important as the actors' words. *If you watched a Greek play, what might it tell you about life in ancient Greece?*

▲ Ruins of a Greek theater

EXTENDING THE CONTENT

Odysseus Today Homer's original poem has served as a model for modern works of art. One of the best-known twentieth-century novels is *Ulysses* by Irish writer James Joyce. In this novel, Joyce tells about a single day in the life of a typical Dubliner named Leopold Bloom. Joyce follows Bloom's journey, or odyssey, through Dublin, recounting various episodes that correspond to events in Homer's poem. For example, Odysseus's battle with the cyclops Polyphemus is mirrored by Bloom's argument in a bar with a one-eyed Irishman. Another adaptation of Homer's poem is the film *O Brother, Where Art Thou?* In this movie, three escaped prisoners roam throughout the 1930s-era American South, meeting and overcoming various challenges paralleling Odysseus's journey home.

In a **comedy** (KAH•muh•dee), the story ends happily. Today we use the word *comedy* to mean a story filled with humor. The word actually means any drama that has a happy ending.

Greek stories dealt with big questions, such as:

- What is the nature of good and evil?
- What rights should people have?
- What role do gods play in our lives?

The three best-known writers of Greek tragedies were Aeschylus (EHS•kuh•luhs), **Sophocles** (SAH•fuh•KLEEZ), and **Euripides** (yu•RIH•puh•DEEZ). The best-known writer of Greek comedies was Aristophanes (ar•uh•STAH•fuh•NEEZ).

Early Greek tragedies had only one actor who gave speeches and a chorus that sang songs describing the events. Aeschylus was the first to introduce the idea of having two actors. This let the writer tell a story involving conflict between the two people. Aeschylus also introduced costumes, props, and stage decorations—all ideas we still use today.

One of Aeschylus's best-known plays is a group of three plays called the *Oresteia* (ohr•eh•STY•uh). Aeschylus wrote the plays in 458 B.C. They describe what happens when the king of Mycenae returns home from the Trojan War. The *Oresteia* teaches that evil acts cause more evil acts and suffering. In the end, however, reason triumphs over evil. The moral of these plays is that people should not seek revenge.

Sophocles, a general and a writer of plays, developed drama even further. He used three actors in his stories instead of one or two. He also placed painted scenes behind the stage as a backdrop to the action. Two of Sophocles' most famous plays are *Oedipus Rex* (EH•duh•puhs REHKS) and *Antigone* (an•TIH•guh•nee) In *Antigone,* Sophocles

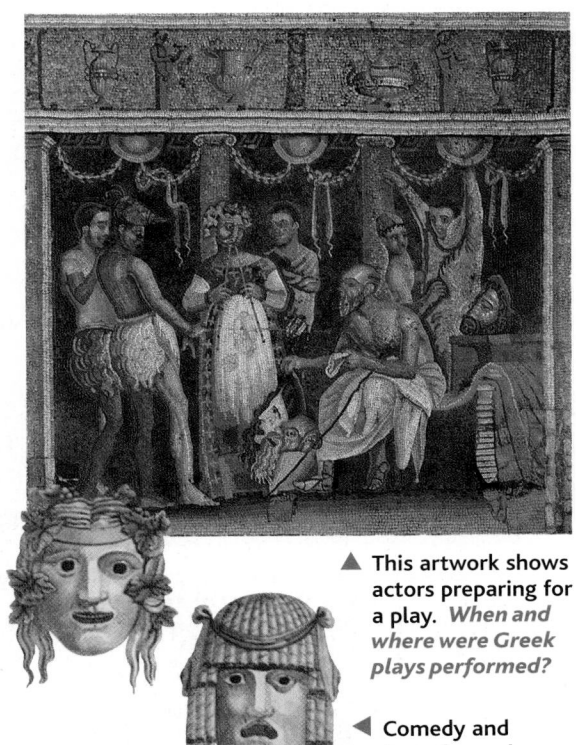

▲ This artwork shows actors preparing for a play. *When and where were Greek plays performed?*

◄ Comedy and tragedy masks

asks the question "Is it better to follow orders or to do what is right?"

Euripides, a later playwright, tried to take Greek drama beyond heroes and gods. His characters were more down-to-earth. Euripides' plots show a great interest in real-life situations. He questioned traditional thinking, especially about war. He showed war as cruel and women and children as its victims.

The works of Aristophanes are good examples of comedies. They make fun of leading politicians and scholars. They encourage the audience to think as well as to laugh. Many of Aristophanes' plays included jokes, just like popular television comedies do today.

✓ Reading Check **Summarize** What two types of drama did the Greeks create?

CHAPTER 5   Greek Civilization   **161**

CURRICULUM CONNECTION

History

The *Oresteia* of Aeschylus describes the cycle of revenge in several generations of a Greek family. The play ends when the goddess Athena decides to end the cycle. Ask students to discuss situations from world history and current events in which a cycle of seeking revenge for past acts of injustice continues to influence people's lives. Ask them how they would try to resolve some of these situations.

✓ Reading Check

Answer: tragedies, comedies

CITIZENSHIP AND YOU

A Higher Calling? Sophocles' play *Antigone* is the story of a difficult choice that falls to the daughter of Oedipus. She must decide which of two laws to follow—obedience to the king or duty to family. The king of Thebes forbids Antigone to bury the body of her brother, whom the king has declared a traitor. However, out of love and respect for her brother, she properly buries his body. For disobeying the king, she is sentenced to death. Readers have seen the story of Antigone as a justification for obeying a higher law, in this case, the requirement of the gods to properly bury a relative. In our own time, some people willingly break laws in order to follow what they consider more important beliefs, such as civil rights issues. Have students discuss civil disobedience and the conflict between laws and higher commands. **L2**

Greek Art and Architecture

Main Idea Greek art and architecture expressed Greek ideas of beauty and harmony.

Reading Focus Do you consider any building in your neighborhood a work of art? Read on to find out about buildings that people have admired as art for centuries.

Artists in ancient Greece believed in certain ideas and tried to show those ideas in their work. These ideas have never gone out of style. Greek artists wanted people to see reason, moderation, balance, and harmony in their work. They hoped their art would inspire people to base their lives on these same ideas.

We know that the Greeks painted murals, but none of them have survived. However, we can still see examples of Greek painting on Greek pottery. The pictures on most Greek pottery are either red on a black background or black on a red background. Large vases often had scenes from Greek myths. Small drinking cups showed scenes from everyday life.

The Parthenon

Standing at almost 230 feet long and 100 feet wide, the Parthenon was the glory of ancient Athens. It was built between 447 and 432 B.C. *What was the purpose of the Parthenon?*

Treasure Room
Held the city's gold

Doric   Ionic   Corinthian

▲ The Greeks used three different styles of columns in their buildings.

Athena
The statue of Athena, covered in ivory and gold, was about 43 feet high.

Festival
Athenians came to honor Athena every four years.

▲ Today the Parthenon still rises above Athens.

COOPERATIVE LEARNING ACTIVITY

Greek Drama Ask students to research the conventions of ancient Greek drama, with special focus on the masks and costumes used in the plays. Have them make masks and costumes and present a scene from a play by one of the dramatists discussed in this section, or write their own play in the style of a Greek drama. After presenting their scene, have students describe the challenges of acting with masks. **L3**

In addition to making pottery, the Greeks were skilled architects. Architecture is the art of designing and building structures. In Greece, the most important architecture was the temple dedicated to a god or goddess. The best-known example is the Parthenon. Temples, such as the Parthenon, had a walled room in their centers. Statues of gods and goddesses and the gifts offered to them were kept in these central rooms.

Large columns supported many Greek buildings. The first Greek columns were carved from wood. Then, in 500 B.C., the Greeks began to use marble. Marble columns were built in sections. Large blocks of marble were chiseled from stone quarries and brought by oxen-drawn wagon to the building site. The sections were stacked on top of each other. To keep them from toppling, the column's sections were joined with wooden pegs. Today, marble columns are common features of churches and government buildings. Some of the best-known buildings in our nation's capital, such as the White House and the Capitol, have columns similar to Greek columns.

Many Greek temples were decorated with sculpture. Greek sculpture, like Greek architecture, was used to express Greek ideas. The favorite subject of Greek artists was the human body. Greek sculptors did not copy their subjects exactly, flaws and all. Instead, they tried to show their ideal version of perfection and beauty.

Reading Check **Identify** What was the most important type of building in ancient Greece?

History Online
Study Central™ Need help with the material in this section? Visit jat.glencoe.com

Section ❶ Review

Reading Summary

Review the Main Ideas

- The Greeks believed gods and goddesses influenced their lives. They believed oracles spoke for the gods and goddesses.

- The Greeks wrote long poems, called epics, and short tales, called fables, to pass on Greek values.

- The Greeks created the ideas of tragedy and comedy that are still used in drama today.

- Greek art forms, such as painting, architecture, and sculpture, expressed Greek ideas of beauty, harmony, and moderation.

What Did You Learn?

1. How and why did the Greeks honor their gods?

2. What values did the epic poems of Homer teach Greeks?

Critical Thinking

3. **Contrast** How do Greek tragedies and comedies differ?

4. **Summarizing Information** Draw a table to describe the characteristics of Greek architecture and pottery.

Greek Architecture	
Greek Pottery	

5. **Evaluate** Do you think the themes of Euripides' plays would be popular today?

6. **Make Generalizations** Why did Greek artists include the ideas of reason, moderation, balance, and harmony in their works?

7. **Expository Writing** Greek literature tells us what the Greeks thought was important. Choose a modern book, movie, or television show. Write a paragraph to explain what it would tell others about our society.

8. **Reading** Context Clues Explain how the words in the following sentence would help you find the meaning of the word *moral*.
"The moral of the story is 'slow and steady wins the race.'"

ENRICH

Ask students to make a list of Greek-inspired architecture in your community. Have them explain how each example incorporates Greek ideas. **L2**

✓ **Reading Check**

Answer: the temple dedicated to a god or goddess, such as the Parthenon

To help students understand section material, have them visit **Study Central™** at jat.glencoe.com

RETEACH

Have students outline the works and contributions of the writers discussed in this section: Homer, Aeschylus, Sophocles, Euripides, and Aristophanes. **L2**

❹ CLOSE

Reading Strategy

Ask students to list the three most important ways the ancient Greeks have influenced our culture. Have them give reasons for their choices. **L1/ EL**

SECTION 1 REVIEW ANSWERS

1. with rituals, festivals, and temples; so the gods would grant good fortune

2. courage, honor, loyalty, and the value of the husband-wife relationship

3. Tragedy: person fails to overcome difficulties because of fate or personal flaws;

Comedy: happy ending

4. Architecture: temple was most important building, decorated with columns and statues; Pottery: showed scenes from myths and everyday life, painted in red on black or reverse

5. Answers will vary but should

demonstrate a thoughtful response.

6. Artists hoped viewers would be inspired by the art.

7. Answers will vary but should demonstrate a thoughtful response.

8. *Moral* is related to the meaning of a story.

SUMMARY

King Minos has imprisoned the master architect Daedalus and his son, Icarus, on an island. Daedalus builds wings that they can use to escape. He warns the boy not to fly too high or too low, but in the joy of flying, Icarus forgets the warning. When he flies too close to the sun, the wax holding his wings together melts, and in terror he falls to his death. Filled with grief, Daedalus vows never to attempt to fly again.

Vocabulary Preview Before students begin reading, have them read **Before You Read** and the **Vocabulary Preview.** Point out that difficult words are footnoted throughout the text.

① FOCUS

Departing From Reality This myth is a retelling of an ancient tale by Josephine Preston Peabody. Tell students that myths often include elements that are impossible or unrealistic. By evoking an unreal world, myths speak to universal truths, letting the reader know that the tale is more than a simple story and has much to teach.

WORLD LITERATURE

ICARUS AND DAEDALUS

Retold by Josephine Preston Peabody

Before You Read

The Scene: This story takes place on the Greek island of Crete in the legendary time when both humans and gods lived in ancient Greece.

The Characters: Daedalus is the master architect for King Minos of Crete. Icarus is the son of Daedalus.

The Plot: King Minos once liked and trusted his servant, the architect Daedalus. The king's favor, though, soon runs out and he locks Daedalus and his son, Icarus, in a high tower. Daedalus secretly plans to escape.

Vocabulary Preview

mortal: human

veer: to shift or change direction

waver: to become unsteady

rash: done without thought or preparation

reel: to turn or seem to turn around and around

quench: to satisfy or put an end to a need or desire

vainly: without success

Have you ever known someone who ignored warnings and did something dangerous? This is the story of a young boy who does not listen to his father and suffers the consequences.

164

Reading Strategy — READING REINFORCEMENT

Identifying Spatial Relationships Words that refer to location or distance help readers visualize the setting, plot, events, and characters' actions in a story. Some words that are clues to location or distance include *between, below, about, left, alongside, here, outside, around, close to, far, right, over, near, in, into, beside, middle, next to, beyond, north, east, on, opposite, there, inside, in front of, under, out, behind, across, above, toward, by,* and *away from.* These words help answer the question "Where?" Have students work in small groups, and have each group choose a scene from the story. Ask each group to develop stage directions and write details for scenery and the location of characters for a play based on the scene they chose from the story. When they have completed their work, have them present their scenes to the class. **L2**

As You Read

Keep in mind that a myth is a special kind of story, usually involving gods or goddesses. Greek myths, like this one, were told and retold over many hundreds of years. Try to figure out why the Greeks told this story. What lesson does it teach?

Among all those mortals who grew so wise that they learned the secrets of the gods, none was more cunning than Daedalus.[1]

He once built, for King Minos of Crete, a wonderful Labyrinth of winding ways so cunningly tangled up and twisted around that, once inside, you could never find your way out again without a magic clue. But the king's favor veered with the wind, and one day he had his master architect imprisoned in a tower. Daedalus managed to escape from his cell; but it seemed impossible to leave the island, since every ship that came or went was well guarded by order of the king.

At length, watching the sea-gulls in the air—the only creatures that were sure of liberty,—he thought of a plan for himself and his young son Icarus,[2] who was captive with him.

Little by little, he gathered a store of feathers great and small. He fastened these together with thread, moulded them in with wax, and so fashioned two great wings like those of a bird. When they were done, Daedalus fitted them to his own shoulders, and after one or two efforts, he found that by waving his arms he could winnow the air and cleave[3] it, as a swimmer does the sea. He held himself aloft, wavered this way and that with the wind, and at last, like a great fledgling,[4] he learned to fly.

---

[1]**Daedalus** (DEH • duhl • uhs): architect for King Minos
[2]**Icarus** (IH • kuh • ruhs): son of Daedalus
[3]**winnow . . . and cleave:** here, both mean "to separate or divide"
[4]**fledgling:** a young bird without feathers that cannot yet fly

165

② TEACH

A ACTIVE READING STRATEGIES

PREDICT Have students read the first page of the story then predict what will happen to Daedalus and Icarus. *(Context clues tell them that Daedalus is an ingenious inventor, so students may predict that he will find a way to escape from the island.)*

B CRITICAL THINKING

Synthesizing Have students explain what seems to be going on here. *(Daedalus made wings to escape his prison and has begun to test them.)*

C ACTIVE READING STRATEGIES

PLOT: Rising Action As Daedalus finishes then tests the wings, he finds that he can fly. However, his emotions are not described. Ask students how this part of the tale helps build suspense. *(By finishing the wings, Daedalus will soon be able to escape. The reader will soon discover if he succeeds.)*

Reading Strategy ❮ **VOCABULARY READING TIP**

Prefixes The prefix *re-* means "again," "once more," or "back," as in *remember* (to be mindful of again), *remain* (to stay back), and *return* (to turn back). Explain that knowing the meaning of *re-* will help students of all English language abilities understand meanings of other words that contain this prefix. Have students write the definitions of the following words that use the prefix *re-*. If necessary, help students look up meanings in the dictionary. **L1**

relearn *(to learn again)*

relight *(to light again)*

recapture *(to capture again)*

D LITERARY ELEMENTS

MYTH: Character Ask students what this passage reveals about Daedalus's relationship with his son. (*He is a caring father.*)

E ACTIVE READING STRATEGIES

CONNECT Ask students if they can relate this passage to instances in their own lives when they have not listened to the advice of an older person. Encourage students to share their experiences.

F AUTHOR'S CRAFT

MYTH: Figurative Language
Discuss the way the author uses figurative language. (*Flying gave Icarus a sense of happiness he had not felt since his mother lifted him in her arms. He longed to be free of captivity.*)

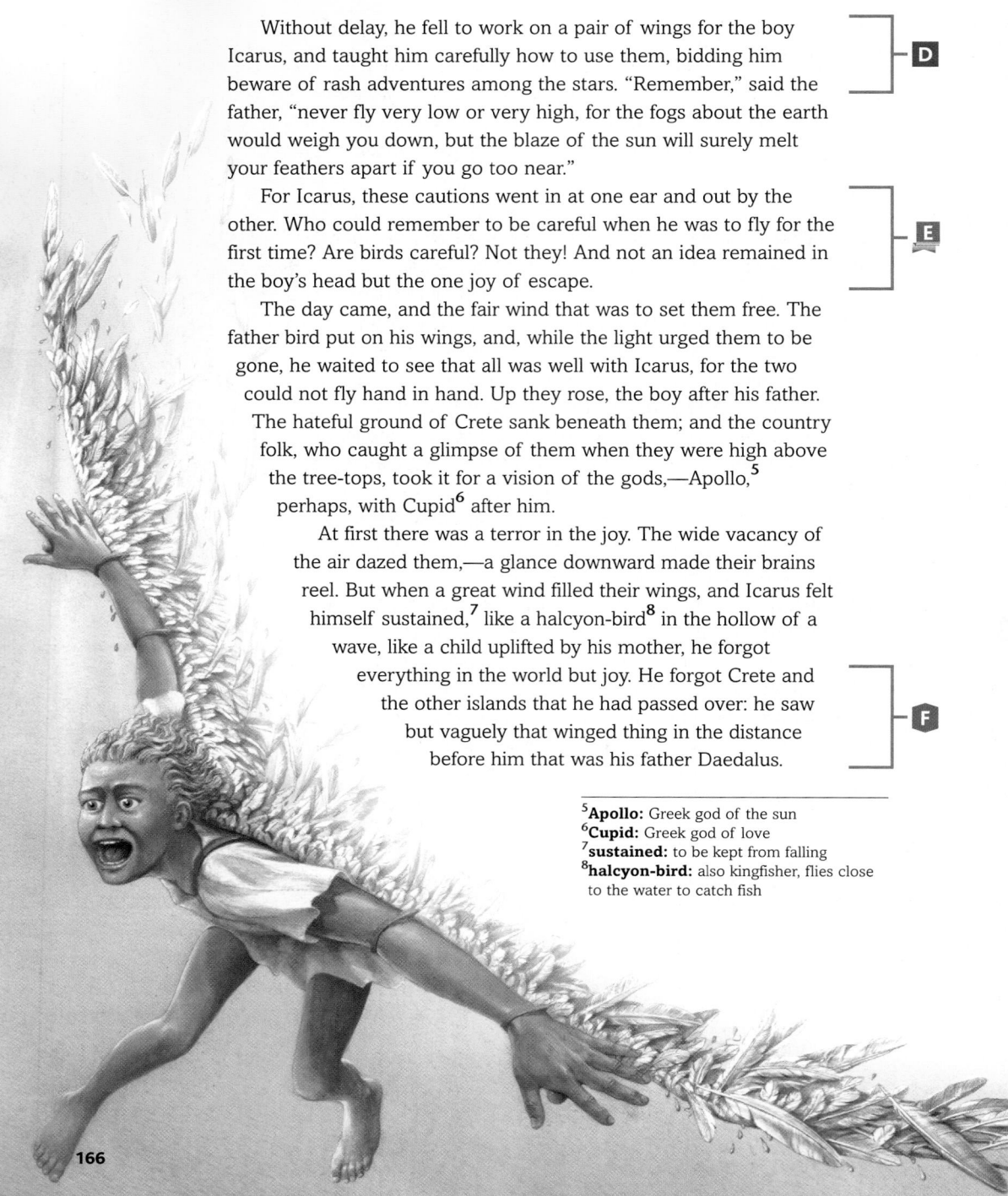

D Without delay, he fell to work on a pair of wings for the boy Icarus, and taught him carefully how to use them, bidding him beware of rash adventures among the stars. "Remember," said the father, "never fly very low or very high, for the fogs about the earth would weigh you down, but the blaze of the sun will surely melt your feathers apart if you go too near."

E For Icarus, these cautions went in at one ear and out by the other. Who could remember to be careful when he was to fly for the first time? Are birds careful? Not they! And not an idea remained in the boy's head but the one joy of escape.

The day came, and the fair wind that was to set them free. The father bird put on his wings, and, while the light urged them to be gone, he waited to see that all was well with Icarus, for the two could not fly hand in hand. Up they rose, the boy after his father. The hateful ground of Crete sank beneath them; and the country folk, who caught a glimpse of them when they were high above the tree-tops, took it for a vision of the gods,—Apollo,[5] perhaps, with Cupid[6] after him.

F At first there was a terror in the joy. The wide vacancy of the air dazed them,—a glance downward made their brains reel. But when a great wind filled their wings, and Icarus felt himself sustained,[7] like a halcyon-bird[8] in the hollow of a wave, like a child uplifted by his mother, he forgot everything in the world but joy. He forgot Crete and the other islands that he had passed over: he saw but vaguely that winged thing in the distance before him that was his father Daedalus.

---

[5] **Apollo:** Greek god of the sun
[6] **Cupid:** Greek god of love
[7] **sustained:** to be kept from falling
[8] **halcyon-bird:** also kingfisher, flies close to the water to catch fish

166

EXTENDING THE CONTENT

Minotaur King Minos had Daedalus build the Labyrinth to house the fearful minotaur, a beast that was half man and half bull. Because the Labyrinth was so complicated, the minotaur could not escape. Every year King Minos demanded that Athens pay a tribute to his kingdom for protection against the minotaur. The hero Theseus, with the help of King Minos's daughter, Ariadne, laid down thread as he entered the maze so that he could find his way out again. Then he defeated the minotaur and escaped the maze.

He longed for one draught[9] of flight to quench the thirst of his captivity: he stretched out his arms to the sky and made toward the highest heavens.

Alas for him! Warmer and warmer grew the air. Those arms, that had seemed to uphold him, relaxed. His wings wavered, drooped. He fluttered his young hands vainly,—he was falling,—and in that terror he remembered. The heat of the sun had melted the wax from his wings; the feathers were falling, one by one, like snowflakes; and there was none to help.

He fell like a leaf tossed down the wind, down, down, with one cry that overtook Daedalus far away. When he returned, and sought high and low for the poor boy, he saw nothing but the bird-like feathers afloat on the water, and he knew that Icarus was drowned.

The nearest island he named Icaria, in memory of the child; but he, in heavy grief, went to the temple of Apollo in Sicily, and there hung up his wings as an offering. Never again did he attempt to fly.

---

[9]**draught:** here, means "a taste"

Responding to the Reading

1. What does King Minos do to keep Daedalus and Icarus from escaping from Crete?

2. How does the setting of the story influence the plot? Support your ideas with details from the story.

3. **Drawing Conclusions** Do you think Daedalus is a concerned father? Why or why not? Support your opinion with examples.

4. **Evaluating Information** Why does Icarus disobey his father's words of caution?

5. **Reading** **Read to Write** Imagine you are Icarus. Would you listen to your father's advice? Write one or two paragraphs explaining what you would have done and why.

167

Responding to the Reading Answers

1. He placed them in a tower.
2. Imprisoned on an island, they could only escape by sea or air. Thus, Daedalus built wings so they could escape by air.
3. Answers may vary but should be logical and attentive to details from the reading.
4. He was so excited about being free and flying that he thought of nothing else.
5. Answers should be thoughtful and explain the students' motivations.

① FOCUS

SECTION OVERVIEW

This section describes Greek contributions to the study of philosophy and the writing of history.

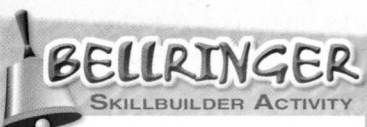
BELLRINGER
SKILLBUILDER ACTIVITY

✎ Project **Daily Focus Skills Transparency 5–2** and have students answer questions. Discuss their responses.

Get Ready to Read!

Preteaching Vocabulary: Explain that the word *philosophy* can mean a system for examining important questions and understanding reality. It comes from the Greek root word for "love of wisdom."

Answers to Graphic: Socrates: all real knowledge is inside each person; learn through questioning; Plato: ideal government has classes—philosopher-kings, warriors, and everyone else; men and women should have equal education and chance for jobs; Aristotle: do nothing in excess; use the senses to make observations; mixed government is best

Section 2
Greek Philosophy and History

Get-Ready to Read!

What's the Connection?
Section 1 discussed early Greek artists and writers. Many of them made the years between 500 and 350 B.C. the Golden Age for Greece. Greek thinkers and historians also produced works that shape people's views of the world today.

Focusing on the Main Ideas
• Greek philosophers developed ideas that are still used today. *(page 169)*

• Greeks wrote the first real histories in Western civilization. *(page 173)*

Meeting People
Pythagoras (puh•THA•guh•ruhs)
Socrates (SAH•kruh•TEEZ)
Plato (PLAY•TOH)
Aristotle (AR•uh•STAH•tuhl)
Herodotus (hih•RAH•duh•tuhs)
Thucydides (thoo•SIH•duh•DEEZ)

Building Your Vocabulary
philosophy (fuh•LAH•suh•fee)
philosopher (fuh•LAH•suh•fuhr)
Sophist (SAH•fihst)
Socratic method (suh•KRA•tihk)

Reading Strategy
Categorizing Information Use diagrams like the one below to show the basic philosophies of Socrates, Plato, and Aristotle.

Socrates

NATIONAL GEOGRAPHIC **When & Who?**

500 B.C.   400 B.C.   300 B.C.

435 B.C. Herodotus writes history of Persian Wars

399 B.C. Socrates sentenced to death

335 B.C. Aristotle opens the Lyceum in Athens

168   CHAPTER 5   Greek Civilization

SECTION RESOURCES

📁 **Reproducible Masters**
• Reproducible Lesson Plan 5–2
• Daily Lecture and Discussion Notes 5–2
• Vocabulary Activity 5–2
• Active Reading Note-Taking Guide 5–2
• Guided Reading Activity 5–2
• Section Quiz 5–2
• Reading Essentials and Study Guide 5–2

✎ **Transparencies**
• Daily Focus Skills Transparency 5–2

Multimedia
💿 Interactive Tutor Self-Assessment CD-ROM
💿 ExamView® Pro Testmaker CD-ROM
💿 Presentation Plus! CD-ROM
💿 Glencoe BookLink CD-ROM

Greek Philosophers

Main Idea Greek philosophers developed ideas that are still used today.

Reading Focus Who are you? Why are you here? Read to learn how the ancient Greeks tried to answer similar "big" questions.

The word **philosophy** (fuh•LAH•suh•fee) comes from the Greek word for "love of wisdom." Greek philosophy led to the study of history, political science, science, and mathematics. Greek thinkers who believed the human mind could understand everything were called **philosophers** (fuh•LAH•suh•fuhrs).

Many philosophers were teachers. One Greek philosopher, **Pythagoras** (puh•THA•guh•ruhs), taught his pupils that the universe followed the same laws that governed music and numbers. He believed that all relationships in the world could be expressed in numbers. As a result, he developed many new ideas about mathematics. Most people know his name because of the Pythagorean theorem that is still used in geometry. It is a way to determine the length of the sides of a triangle.

Who Were the Sophists? The **Sophists** (SAH•fihsts) were professional teachers in ancient Greece. They traveled from city to

▲ This artwork shows Greek philosophers involved in a discussion. *Where does the word* philosophy *come from?*

CHAPTER 5 Greek Civilization **169**

② TEACH

Daily Lecture and Discussion Notes 5–2

Use **Daily Lecture and Discussion Notes 5–2** for an outline of key concepts found in the section.

Reading Support L1/ EL

Use **Vocabulary Activity 5–2** to review important terms in the section.

Writing Activity

Direct students' attention to the Sophist belief that there was no absolute right or wrong. Ask students to agree or disagree with this belief and support their position in a paragraph. **L2**

More About the Art

The mosaic shown here is titled *Plato's School* and dates from the Hellenistic period. Plato's Academy is thought to have been located in a grove of trees that belonged to a man named Academus, a hero of the Trojan War.

Caption Answer: Greek word for "love of wisdom"

Reading Strategy   READING THE TEXT

Know-Want-Learn-How KWLH is a tool to determine students' background knowledge. Students write what they *know* (K) about the topic, generate questions about what they *want* to know (W), record what they *learned* (L), and then ask *how* they can learn more (H).

K—What I Know: Ask students to share what they know about philosophy. Write their comments on large sheets of paper that can be displayed in the classroom.

W—What I Want/Need to Know: What additional information would be necessary to know what philosophy is, what kinds of questions it asks, and how it gives answers to these questions?

L—What I Learned: As the students read, have them add to the list.

H—How I Can Learn More: Ask students how they can learn more. **L1/ EL**

HISTORY Mystery

How Do We Know About Socrates?

No writings by Socrates exist today. All of what we know about his life and thinking comes from works written by others. The most important source is Plato. In a series of mini-plays called the *Dialogues*, Plato shows Socrates meeting and talking with friends about important philosophical issues. The dialogues contain humor and gossip as well as philosophical ideas.

CONNECTING ACROSS TIME

The pictures Greeks painted on their pottery often showed scenes from everyday life: people eating and drinking, playing games, walking, talking, and doing chores. Ask students to choose three scenes that would show future archaeologists what their daily lives are like. **L1/** EL

Reading Support L1/ EL

Assign **Guided Reading Activity 5–2** to help students organize the information in the section.

Greek Philosophers

Thinker Or Group	Sophists	Socrates	Plato	Aristotle
Main Idea	Sophists like Libanius (above) thought that people should use knowledge to improve themselves. They believed that there is no absolute right or wrong.	He was a critic of the Sophists. Socrates believed that there was an absolute right and wrong.	He rejected the idea of democracy as a form of government. Plato believed that philosopher-kings should rule society.	Aristotle taught the idea of the "golden mean." He believed observation and comparison were necessary to gain knowledge.
Important Contribution	They developed the art of public speaking and debate.	He created the Socratic method of teaching.	He described his vision of the ideal government in his work the *Republic*.	He wrote over 200 books on philosophy and science. He divided all governments into three basic types.
Influence on Today	The importance of public speaking can be seen in political debates between candidates.	His methods influenced the way teachers interact with their students.	He introduced the idea that government should be fair and just.	His political ideas still shape political ideas today.

---

city and made a living by teaching others. They believed students should use their time to improve themselves. Many taught their students how to win an argument and make good political speeches.

Sophists did not believe that gods and goddesses influenced people. They also rejected the idea of absolute right or wrong. They believed that what was right for one person might be wrong for another.

The Ideas of Socrates One critic of the Sophists was **Socrates** (SAH•kruh•TEEZ). Socrates was an Athenian sculptor whose true love was philosophy. Socrates left no writings behind. What we know about him we have learned from the writings of his students.

Socrates believed that an absolute truth existed and that all real knowledge was within each person. He invented the **Socratic method** (suh•KRA•tihk) of teaching still used today. He asked pointed questions to force his pupils to use their reason and to see things for themselves.

Some Athenian leaders considered the Socratic method a threat to their power. At one time, Athens had a tradition of questioning leaders and speaking freely. However, their defeat in the Peloponnesian War changed the Athenians. They no longer trusted open debate. In 399 B.C. the leaders accused Socrates of teaching young Athenians to rebel against the state. A jury found Socrates guilty and sentenced him to death. Socrates could have fled the city, but

---

DIFFERENTIATED INSTRUCTION

Visual/Spatial: Have students create a brochure, print advertisement, radio spot, or television commercial storyboard for either Plato's Academy or Aristotle's Lyceum. Have students summarize the important points of each man's thinking and incorporate them into their promotional materials. Have students share their work.

English Learners: Have students target their promotional material to a specific ethnic group.

Gifted and Talented: Have students use video- or audiotaping equipment to produce their television commercial or radio spot.

☞ Refer to *Inclusion Strategies for the Middle School Social Studies Classroom* in the TCR.

he chose to remain. He argued that he had lived under the city's laws, so he had to obey them. He then drank poison to carry out the jury's sentence.

The Ideas of Plato One of Socrates' students was **Plato** (PLAY•toh). Unlike Socrates, we are able to learn a lot about Plato from his writings. One work Plato wrote is called the *Republic*. It explains his ideas about government. Based on life in Athens, Plato decided that democracy was not a good system of government. He did not think that rule by the people produced fair or sensible policies. To him, people could not live good lives unless they had a just and reasonable government.

In the *Republic*, Plato described his ideal government. He divided people into three basic groups. At the top were philosopher-kings, who ruled using logic and wisdom. Warriors made up the second group. They defended the state from attack.

The third group included the rest of the people. They were driven by desire, not by wisdom like the first group or courage like the second. These people produced the state's food, clothing, and shelter. Plato also believed that men and women should have the same education and an equal chance to have the same jobs.

Who Was Aristotle? Plato established a school in Athens known as the Academy. His best student was **Aristotle** (AR•uh•STAH•tuhl). Aristotle wrote more than 200 books on topics ranging from government to the planets and stars.

In 335 B.C. Aristotle opened his own school called the Lyceum. At the Lyceum, Aristotle taught his pupils the "golden mean." This idea holds that a person should do nothing in excess. For example, a person should not eat too little or too much but just enough to stay well.

Aristotle also helped to advance science. He urged people to use their senses to make observations, just as scientists today make observations. Aristotle was the first person to group observations according to their similarities and differences. Then he made generalizations based on the groups of facts.

Like Plato, Aristotle wrote about government. He studied and compared the governments of 158 different places to find the best form of government. In his book *Politics*, Aristotle divided the governments into three types:

- Government by one person, such as a monarch (king or queen) or a tyrant
- Government by a few people, which might be an aristocracy or an oligarchy
- Government by many people, as in a democracy

Aristotle noticed that governments run by a few people were usually run by the rich. He noticed that most democracies were run by the poor. He thought the best government was a mixture of the two.

Aristotle's ideas shaped the way Europeans and Americans thought about government. The founders of the United States Constitution tried to create a mixed government that balanced the different types Aristotle had identified.

✓ **Reading Check** **Contrast** How did Aristotle's idea of government differ from Plato's?

History Online

Web Activity Visit jat.glencoe.com and click on *Chapter 5—Student Web Activity* to learn more about ancient Greece.

CHAPTER 5   Greek Civilization   **171**

3 ASSESS

Assign Section 2 Review as homework or as an in-class activity.

🖱 Have students use the **Interactive Tutor Self-Assessment CD-ROM** to review the section.

Assessment L2

Assign **Section 2 Quiz** to assess mastery of the material found in the section.

Reading Support L1/ EL

Assign **Reading Essentials and Study Guide 5–2** to help students review section material.

✓ **Reading Check**

Answer: Aristotle favored mixed government with rule by the many, while Plato described a state with three distinct classes.

History Online

Objectives and answers to the student activity can be found in the **Web Activity Lesson Plan** feature at jat.glencoe.com

CRITICAL THINKING ACTIVITY

Identifying Central Issues The Greek writer Thucydides considered an understanding of one's place in history important to one's life. Some today do not hold to this idea. Ask students to arrange a debate on the following proposition: Studying politics is a good use of a middle school student's time. Have each side research its case and present its evidence. After the debate, have the audience vote on a winning side. **L2**

Biography

TEACH

Although Plato and Aristotle are often grouped together, they differed in many important ways. One key difference was their understanding of the nature of reality. Plato believed that ideal, spiritual forms existed. What we experience as reality is just a pale imitation of this ideal form. Aristotle disagreed, arguing that this could not be proven by the use of reason or discovered through the senses. Each man's thought has had a great influence at different times and in different subjects.

Ask students to discuss Plato's belief in ideal forms and Aristotle's rejection of it. Are things, such as Plato's forms, necessarily not real because we cannot discover them with our senses? (*Answers will vary. Scientifically inclined students may agree with Aristotle that things not discoverable by reason and the senses could not exist. Spiritually inclined students may recognize the link between Plato's idealism and religion.*) **L2**

Then and Now

Answers will vary. Students may mention that doctors must attend annual seminars to learn about advances or that teachers must take classes about new methods. Others may point out that lifelong learning is necessary in all careers as work requirements change.

PLATO AND ARISTOTLE

Plato c. 428–347 B.C.
Aristotle 384–322 B.C.

Plato was from a noble Greek family and had planned a career in politics. However, he was so horrified by the death of his teacher, Socrates, that he left politics and spent many years traveling and writing. When Plato returned to Athens in 387 B.C., he founded an academy, where he taught using Socrates' method of questioning. His academy drew bright young students from Athens and other Greek city-states. Plato looked for truth beyond the appearances of everyday objects and reflected this philosophy in his writing and teaching. He believed the human soul was the connection between the appearance of things and ideas.

Plato and Aristotle—two of the greatest ancient Greek philosophers—met as teacher and student at Plato's Academy in Athens. Aristotle left his home in Stagira and arrived on the Academy's doorstep when he was eighteen years old. He remained at Plato's Academy for 20 years, until the death of his teacher. Unlike Plato, Aristotle did not come from a noble family. His father was the court physician to the king of Macedonia. At an early age, Aristotle's father introduced him to the topics of medicine and biology, and these became his main interests of study. Aristotle sought truth through a systematic, scientific approach. He liked to jot down notes and details about different topics—from weather to human behavior—and arrange them in categories. He did not trust the senses' ability to understand the universe.

After Plato's death, Aristotle traveled for about 12 years. He also tutored the future Alexander the Great. Later in his life, he returned to Athens and opened his own school, the Lyceum. He made his school the center for research in every area of knowledge known to the Greeks.

Plato ▲

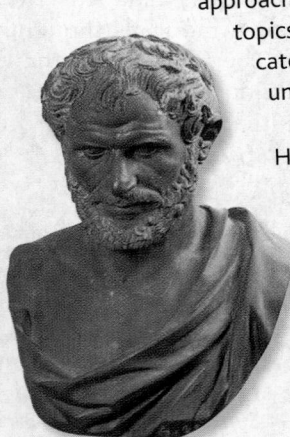

▲ Aristotle

Then and Now

Aristotle spent 20 years at Plato's Academy. What present-day careers or subjects of study require lifelong learning?

Reading List Generator CD-ROM

GLENCOE
BOOKLINK   **RECOMMENDED READING**

Use the **Glencoe BookLink CD-ROM** to create customized reading lists based on your students' interests and reading levels. Below is an example based on content in this chapter. Also, see the Suggested Readings on pages 944–946 of the Appendix.

- **Hamilton, Edith.** *The Greek Way.* An interpretative look at ancient Greek civilization and what it has to offer us today.
- **Plato.** From the *Apology: Dialogues.* Plato's recording of Socrates' speech just before his death.
- **Powell, Anton.** *Ancient Greece.* An introduction to ancient Greece.

Greek Historians

Main Idea Greeks wrote the first real histories in Western civilization.

Reading Focus Why is history important? Read on to find out what Greek historians thought was important.

In most places in the ancient world, people did not write history. Legends and myths explained their past. Some civilizations kept long lists of rulers and the dates they were in power, but no one tried to explain the past by studying events. Then, in 435 B.C., a Greek named **Herodotus** (hih•RAH•duh•tuhs) wrote the history of the Persian Wars.

In his book, Herodotus tried to separate fact from legend. He asked questions, recorded answers, and checked the truthfulness of his sources. Although his history includes some errors and uses gods and goddesses to explain some events, Western historians consider him the "father of history."

Many historians consider **Thucydides** (thoo•SIH•duh•DEEZ) the greatest historian of the ancient world. Thucydides fought in the Peloponnesian War. After he lost a battle, he was sent into exile. There he wrote his *History of the Peloponnesian War.*

Unlike Herodotus, Thucydides saw war and politics as the activities of human beings, not gods. He also stressed the importance of having accurate facts:

> 66 **Either I was present myself at the events which I have described or else I heard of them from eyewitnesses whose reports I have checked with as much thoroughness as possible.** 99

—Thucydides, *History of the Peloponnesian War*

 Reading Check **Identify** How did Thucydides view war and politics?

 History Online
Study Central™ Need help with the material in this section? Visit jat.glencoe.com

Section 2 Review

Reading Summary

Review the Main Ideas

• The ideas of Greek philosophers, including Socrates, Plato, and Aristotle, still affect modern thinking about education, government, and science.

• Herodotus and Thucydides are considered western civilization's first historians. They believed that people could understand the present by studying the past.

What Did You Learn?

1. Who were the Sophists and what were their beliefs?

2. Before Herodotus, how did Greeks explain the past?

Critical Thinking

3. **Organizing Information** Draw a diagram like the one below. Use the diagram to organize Plato's ideas about an ideal government.

4. **Science Link** How are Aristotle's teachings related to the scientific method used by scientists today?

5. **Contrast** What is different about the works of Herodotus and Thucydides?

6. **Summarize** Describe Aristotle's contributions to government.

7. **Persuasive Writing** Do you agree with Plato's vision of the ideal state in the *Republic?* Write an editorial expressing your viewpoint.

CHAPTER 5 Greek Civilization **173**

ENRICH

Ask students to name an institution, element, or other feature of our society that is based on an idea of Plato or Aristotle. Have them explain the connection. **L3**

✔ **Reading Check**

Answer: Thucydides believed that war and politics were the activities of human beings, not gods.

 History Online

To help students understand section material, have them visit **Study Central**™ at jat.glencoe.com

RETEACH

Have students make a series of index cards. On one side, they should write the name of a philosopher or historian. On the other, have them write the person's contributions. **L1/ EL**

4 CLOSE

 Reading Strategy

Ask students to discuss the Athenians' treatment of Socrates. **L2**

SECTION 2 REVIEW ANSWERS

1. The Sophists were traveling teachers. They rejected the idea of absolute right and wrong.

2. through legends and myths

3. Plato's republic: philosopher-kings—ruled using logic and wisdom; warriors—defended; masses—produced food, clothing

4. Both use senses to make observations.

5. Herodotus included gods and goddesses to describe some events. Thucydides examined history as the activities of humans, not gods.

6. He examined different forms of government and concluded mixed was the best.

7. Answers will vary but should demonstrate understanding of the text.

① FOCUS

SECTION OVERVIEW

This section discusses Alexander the Great, his wide-reaching empire, and how his conquest spread Hellenism throughout southwest Asia.

BELLRINGER
SKILLBUILDER ACTIVITY

✍ Project **Daily Focus Skills Transparency 5–3** and have students answer questions. Discuss their responses.

Get Ready to Read!

Preteaching Vocabulary: Explain that a legacy is something transmitted or received from someone in the past. It can be positive or negative.

Answers to Graphic: conquered the Persian Empire; expanded his empire as far as present-day Pakistan and western India; spread Greek culture throughout southwest Asia

Section 3
Alexander the Great

Get Ready to Read!

What's the Connection?

In Section 2, you learned that the Greek philosopher Aristotle was also a teacher. The king of Macedonia admired Greek culture and hired Aristotle to tutor his son, Alexander. Years later, his son would take control of the Greek world.

Focusing on the Main Ideas

• Philip II of Macedonia united the Greek states. *(page 175)*

• Alexander the Great conquered the Persian Empire and spread Greek culture throughout southwest Asia. *(page 176)*

Locating Places
Macedonia (MA•suh•DOH•nee•uh)
Chaeronea (KEHR•uh•NEE•uh)
Syria (SIHR•ee•uh)
Alexandria (A•lihg•ZAN•dree•uh)

Meeting People
Philip II
Alexander the Great

Building Your Vocabulary
legacy (LEH•guh•see)
Hellenistic Era (HEH•luh•NIHS•tihk)

Reading Strategy
Sequencing Create a diagram like the one below to track the achievements of Alexander the Great.

NATIONAL GEOGRAPHIC **When & Where?**

MACEDONIA
Gaugamela •
Babylon •

360 B.C.   **340** B.C.   **320** B.C.

359 B.C.
Philip II becomes king of Macedonia

331 B.C.
Alexander defeats Darius at Gaugamela

323 B.C.
Alexander dies

SECTION RESOURCES

 Reproducible Masters
• Reproducible Lesson Plan 5–3
• Daily Lecture and Discussion Notes 5–3
• Vocabulary Activity 5–3
• Active Reading Note-Taking Guide 5–3
• Guided Reading Activity 5–3
• Section Quiz 5–3
• Reading Essentials and Study Guide 5–3

 Transparencies
• Daily Focus Skills Transparency 5–3

Multimedia
◉ Interactive Tutor Self-Assessment CD-ROM
◉ ExamView® Pro Testmaker CD-ROM
◉ Presentation Plus! CD-ROM

Macedonia Attacks Greece

Main Idea Philip II of Macedonia united the Greek states.

Reading Focus Have you ever wanted something because your neighbor had it? Read to find what the king of Macedonia wanted from his neighbors, the Greeks.

Macedonia (MA•suh•DOH•nee•uh) lay north of Greece. The Macedonians raised sheep and horses and grew crops in their river valleys. They were a warrior people who fought on horseback. The Greeks looked down on them, but by 400 B.C., Macedonia had become a powerful kingdom.

A Plan to Win Greece In 359 B.C. **Philip II** rose to the throne in Macedonia. Philip had lived in Greece as a young man. He admired everything about the Greeks—their art,

their ideas, and their armies. Although Macedonia was influenced by Greek ideas, Philip wanted to make his kingdom strong enough to defeat the mighty Persian Empire. In order to achieve this goal, Philip needed to unite the Greek city-states with his own kingdom.

Philip trained a vast army of foot soldiers to fight like the Greeks. He took over the city-states one by one. He took some city-states by force and bribed the leaders of others to surrender. Some united with his kingdom voluntarily.

Demosthenes (dih•MAHS•thuh•NEEZ) was a lawyer and one of Athens's great public speakers. He gave several powerful speeches warning Athenians that Philip was a threat to Greek freedom. He urged Athens and other city-states to join together to fight the Macedonians.

Primary Source

Demosthenes' Warning

As King Philip II of Macedonia became more powerful, he began to take part in the affairs of Greece. Demosthenes realized that Macedonia's powerful army would eventually be a threat to Greece. He tried to warn the Greeks to take action.

"Remember only that Philip is our enemy, that he has long been robbing and insulting us, that wherever we have expected aid from others we have found hostility, that the future depends on ourselves, and that unless we are willing to fight him there we shall perhaps be forced to fight here.... You need not speculate [guess] about the future except to assure yourselves that it will be disastrous unless you face the facts and are willing to do your duty."

—Demosthenes, *"The First Philippic"* in *Orations of Demosthenes*

▼ **Demosthenes**

DBQ **Document-Based Question**

Which line of Demosthenes' speech tells what he thinks will happen if the Greeks ignore Philip?

CHAPTER 5 Greek Civilization **175**

② TEACH

Activating Prior Knowledge Ask students to recall some of the empires they have already studied. Tell them the empire they are about to study was one of the largest in the history of the world. **L2**

Daily Lecture and Discussion Notes 5–3

Use **Daily Lecture and Discussion Notes 5–3** for an outline of key concepts found in the section.

Primary Source

As a child, Demosthenes was afflicted with poor health and a speech impediment. He overcame the impediment by practicing speaking with pebbles in his mouth.

Answer:
"unless we are willing to fight him there we shall perhaps be forced to fight here"

☞ See the **Primary Source Readings (with Document-Based Questions)** in the Unit Resource Books.

Reading Strategy READING THE TEXT

Carousel Brainstorming This activity motivates students to generate background knowledge on a topic. It also works well as a review. Divide the class into groups of four students. Give each group a large sheet of paper and give each student in each group a different colored marker. Give half the groups this topic: What do you think it means to be a great military leader? Give the rest of the groups this topic: What do you think it means to be an effective ruler? Tell students to write down one thought on the paper and pass it to the next student. Continue this until each student has written at least two items on the paper. Post the lists in the room. As students read, have them decide what they would add or remove from their lists. **L1/ EL**

Reading Support L1/ EL

Use **Vocabulary Activity 5–3** to review important terms in the section.

Mental Mapping The following activity will help students learn relative location skills. **Ask: In what general directions did Alexander's conquests progress?** *(east, then south, then east again)* Have students describe what local landmarks, buildings, parks, etc., they would find if they traveled in these same two basic directions in their community. **L1/ EL**

✓ Reading Check

Answer: He wanted to unite all of Greece under Macedonia in order to defeat Persia.

Using Geography Skills

Answers:
1. Tigris River
2. Afghanistan, Pakistan

Skills Practice

Ask: What geographic feature marks the eastern reach of Alexander's empire? *(the Indus River)* **What geographic features would have made it difficult for Alexander's army to travel from west to east?** *(the many mountain ranges and rivers in Persia)*

However, by the time the Greeks saw the danger, it was too late. The Peloponnesian War had left the Greeks weak and divided. In many Greek city-states, the population had declined after the Peloponnesian War. Fighting had destroyed many farms and left people with no way to earn a living. As a result, thousands of young Greeks left Greece to join the Persian army. Many who stayed behind began fighting among themselves. The city-states grew weaker.

Although the Athenians joined some other Greek states to fight Philip's army, they could not stop the invasion. In 338 B.C. the Macedonians crushed the Greek allies at the Battle of **Chaeronea** (KEHR•uh•NEE•uh) near Thebes. Philip now controlled most of Greece.

✓ Reading Check **Summarize** Why did Philip II invade Greece?

Alexander Builds an Empire

Main Idea Alexander the Great conquered the Persian Empire and spread Greek culture throughout southwest Asia.

Reading Focus What will you be doing at age 20? Read to learn what Philip's son Alexander achieved.

Philip planned to conquer the Persian Empire with the Greeks' help. Before Philip could carry out his plan, however, he was murdered. As a result, the invasion of Asia fell to his son.

Alexander was only 20 when he became king of Macedonia. Philip had carefully trained his son for leadership. While still a boy, Alexander often went with his father to the battlefront. At age 16 he rose to commander in the Macedonian army. After his

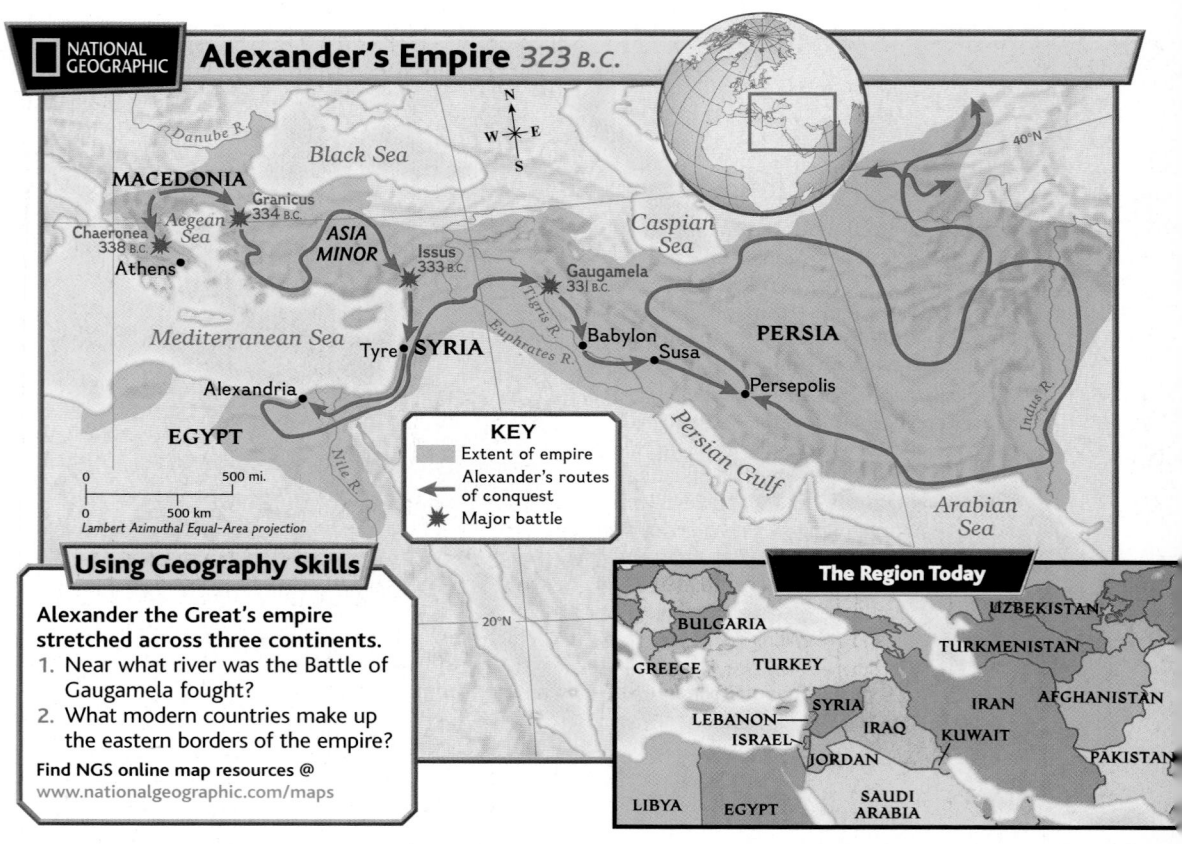

NATIONAL GEOGRAPHIC **Alexander's Empire** 323 B.C.

KEY
- Extent of empire
- Alexander's routes of conquest
- ✴ Major battle

Using Geography Skills

Alexander the Great's empire stretched across three continents.
1. Near what river was the Battle of Gaugamela fought?
2. What modern countries make up the eastern borders of the empire?

Find NGS online map resources @ www.nationalgeographic.com/maps

The Region Today

DIFFERENTIATED INSTRUCTION

Kinesthetic: Have students work in pairs. Have one student read the description of the progress of Alexander's armies across Asia. Have the other student place a finger, pencil tip, or other pointer on Macedonia on the map on page 176. As the first student reads the description, the second student should follow the progress on the map. Have students reverse roles after each paragraph or two.

English Learners: As students do the kinesthetic activity, have the second student describe aloud geographic information based on the map, such as "The Caspian Sea is to the north" or "The Persian Gulf is to the south."

Gifted and Talented: Ask students to research and make a list of all the present-day countries that Alexander's empire encompassed, either fully or partially.

father's death, Alexander was ready to fulfill his father's dream—the invasion of the Persian Empire.

Alexander's Conquests In the spring of 334 B.C., Alexander invaded Asia Minor with about 37,000 Macedonian and Greek foot soldiers. He also took along 5,000 mounted warriors. With Alexander at their head, the cavalry destroyed the forces of the local Persian satraps at the Battle of Granicus.

By the next year, Alexander had freed the Greek cities in Asia Minor from Persian rule and defeated a large Persian army at Issus. He then turned south. By the winter of 332 B.C., he had captured **Syria** (SIHR•ee•uh) and Egypt. Then he built the city of **Alexandria** (A•lihg•ZAN•dree•uh) as a center of business and trade. The city became one of the most important cities in the ancient world.

In 331 B.C. Alexander headed east and defeated the Persians at Gaugamela, near Babylon. After this victory, his army easily overran the rest of the Persian Empire. However, Alexander did not stop at Persia. Over the next three years, he marched east as far as modern Pakistan. In 326 B.C. he crossed the Indus River and entered India. There he fought a number of bloody battles. Weary of continuous war, his soldiers refused to go farther. Alexander agreed to lead them home.

On the return march, the troops crossed a desert in what is now southern Iran. Heat and thirst killed thousands of soldiers. At one point, a group of soldiers found a little water and scooped it up in a helmet. Then they offered the water to Alexander. According to a Greek historian, Alexander, "in full view of his troops, poured the water on the ground. So extraordinary was the effect of this action that the water wasted by

Alexander the Great

▲ This carving of Alexander the Great on his horse decorated the side of a tomb. *Was Alexander able to fulfill his plans of conquest? Explain.*

Alexander was as good as a drink for every man in the army."

In 323 B.C. Alexander returned to Babylon. He wanted to plan an invasion of southern Arabia but was very tired and weak from wounds. He came down with a bad fever. Ten days later he was dead at age 32.

Alexander's Legacy Alexander was a great military leader. He was brave and even reckless. He often rode into battle ahead of his men and risked his own life. He inspired his armies to march into unknown lands and risk their lives in difficult situations.

The key to Alexander's courage may have been his childhood education. Alexander kept a copy of the *Iliad* under his pillow. Most likely his inspiration was Homer's warrior-hero Achilles. In the end, Alexander's reputation outstripped even Achilles', and today he is called **Alexander the Great.**

CHAPTER 5   Greek Civilization   **177**

Writing Activity

Point out that the carving from Alexander's tomb shows him in a characteristic pose, on his horse in battle. Ask students to write a paragraph explaining what scene from their own lives they would want depicted for people to remember them by. Why? **L1/EL**

CURRICULUM CONNECTION

Language Arts
Alexander admired the heroes of the Trojan War so much that he always traveled with a copy of Homer's *Iliad*. Ask students what single book they would choose to carry with them. Why?

CRITICAL THINKING ACTIVITY

Making Inferences Explain to students that, according to legend, in Gordium, capital of the ancient country of Phrygia, stood a great war chariot. The yoke of the chariot was lashed to a pole by an incredibly complicated rope knot. Legend said that the knot could only be undone by the person who would rule Asia. Many ambitious people had tried and failed to undo the knot. When Alexander arrived, he looked at the knot, took out his sword, and sliced it off. Today, "cutting the Gordian knot" means to solve a problem by bold action. **Ask:** What does this legend tell you about Alexander? Why might people have told this legend? *(It shows that Alexander was an impulsive man of action. It may have been told by people who admired Alexander or who wanted to flatter him.)* **L2**

Reading Support L1/ EL

Assign **Guided Reading Activity 5–3** to help students organize the information in the section.

③ ASSESS

Assign Section 3 Review as homework or as an in-class activity.

⊙ Have students use the **Interactive Tutor Self-Assessment CD-ROM** to review the section.

Assessment L2

Assign **Section 3 Quiz** to assess mastery of the material found in the section.

Reading Support L1/ EL

Assign **Reading Essentials and Study Guide 5–3** to help students review section material.

Caption Answer: It was the largest city in the Mediterranean world.

A **legacy** (LEH•guh•see) is what a person leaves behind when he or she dies. Alexander's skill and daring created his legacy. He helped extend Greek and Macedonian rule over a vast area. At the same time, he and his armies spread Greek art, ideas, language, and architecture wherever they went in southwest Asia and northern Africa. Greeks, in turn, brought new ideas back from Asia and Africa.

Alexander's conquests marked the beginning of the **Hellenistic Era** (HEH•luh•NIHS•tihk). The word *Hellenistic* comes from a Greek word meaning "like the Greeks." It refers to a time when the Greek language and Greek ideas spread to the non-Greek people of southwest Asia.

The Empire Breaks Apart Alexander the Great planned to unite Macedonians, Greeks, and Persians in his new empire. He used Persians as officials and encouraged his soldiers to marry Asian women. After Alexander died, however, his generals fought one another for power. As a result, the empire that Alexander had created fell apart. Four kingdoms took its place: Macedonia, Pergamum (PUHR•guh•muhm), Egypt, and the Seleucid Empire (suh•LOO•suhd). Look at the map on page 179 to see where these kingdoms were located.

All government business in the Hellenistic kingdoms was conducted in the Greek language. Only those Asians and Egyptians who spoke Greek could apply

Alexandria, Egypt

▼ Modern Alexandria

Alexandria

◄ The lighthouse of Alexandria was one of the Seven Wonders of the Ancient World. A fire in its tall tower guided ships into harbor. *What was special about Alexandria in 100 B.C.?*

INTERDISCIPLINARY CONNECTIONS ACTIVITY

Geography Alexander's homeland of Macedonia has had a long and complicated history. Its strategic location in the Balkans made it a prize that many empires wanted to control. The Byzantine and Ottoman Empires conquered it in ancient times. More recently, Austria-Hungary and Russia claimed it in the nineteenth century. In the early 1900s, parts of it were controlled by Yugoslavia, Greece, and Bulgaria. Have students use a world almanac, the Internet, or another resource to put together a thumbnail sketch of the new, independent country of Macedonia. **L2**

for government posts. The kings preferred to give the jobs to Greeks and Macedonians. In this way, Greeks managed to stay in control of the governments.

By 100 B.C., the largest city in the Mediterranean world was Alexandria, which Alexander had founded in Egypt. In addition, the Hellenistic kings created many new cities and military settlements.

These new Greek cities needed architects, engineers, philosophers, artisans, and artists. For this reason, Hellenistic rulers encouraged Greeks and Macedonians to settle in southwest Asia. These colonists provided new recruits for the army and a pool of government officials and workers. They helped spread Greek culture into Egypt and as far east as modern-day Afghanistan and India.

Reading Check **Explain** What was Alexander's legacy?

NATIONAL GEOGRAPHIC
Hellenistic World 241 B.C.

Black Sea
Caspian Sea
Pella
ASIA MINOR
Pergamum
Tigris R.
Crete
Cyprus
Euphrates R.
Mediterranean Sea
Seleucia
Alexandria
Nile R.
Red Sea

0 500 mi.
0 500 km
Azimuthal Equal-Area projection

KEY
Egyptian kingdom
Macedonian kingdom
Pergamum kingdom
Seleucid kingdom

Using Geography Skills

Following Alexander's death, his empire separated into four kingdoms.
1. Which kingdom appears to have had the most territory?
2. Which kingdoms were at least partially located in Asia?

History Online
Study Central™ Need help with the material in this section? Visit jat.glencoe.com

Section 3 Review

Reading Summary
Review the Main Ideas
- Following the Battle of Chaeronea in 338 B.C., King Philip of Macedonia ruled all of Greece.
- Alexander the Great, King Philip's son, conquered an empire that stretched to Africa in the south and India in the east. After Alexander's death, his empire split into several kingdoms.

What Did You Learn?
1. How did Philip II of Macedonia feel about the Greeks?
2. What ended Alexander's conquest of India?

Critical Thinking
3. **Analyze** Why was Alexander a good leader?
4. **Summarize** Draw a table to summarize what you know about each topic.

Philip of Macedonia	Alexander the Great	Alexander's Empire After His Death

5. **Predict** How might history have been different if Alexander had lived longer?
6. **Geography Skills** How many continents did Alexander's empire reach?
7. **Reading** Context Clues What do you think the word *assure* means in this passage?

"... assure yourselves that it will be disastrous unless you face the facts and are willing to do your duty."

What words give clues to its meaning?

CHAPTER 5 Greek Civilization **179**

Using Geography Skills
Answers:
1. the Seleucid kingdom
2. the Egyptian, Seleucid, and Pergamum kingdoms

ENRICH
Ask students to research the reasons for the breakup of Alexander's empire into three separate kingdoms. **L2**

Reading Check
Answer: He spread Greek art, ideas, language, and architecture across Asia and brought new ideas from Asia to Greece.

History Online
To help students understand section material, have them visit **Study Central™** at jat.glencoe.com

RETEACH
Have students outline the important information in this section. **L1**

4 CLOSE
Ask students to name current or recent figures who might also merit the title "the Great." Why? **L1/EL**

SECTION 3 REVIEW ANSWERS

1. He admired everything about the Greeks, including their art, ideas, and military.
2. His troops grew tired of fighting and refused to go farther.
3. His bravery inspired his troops.
4. Philip: admired everything about the Greeks, defeated the Greeks in 338 B.C.; Alexander: conquered Persia, built a great empire that stretched to India; Empire: broke up into four kingdoms, spread Greek culture
5. Alexander might have conquered more territory and created a lasting empire.
6. three: Europe, Africa, and Asia
7. "be certain, be sure"; *assure* contains the word *sure*

You Decide . . .

① FOCUS

Whether someone is a villain or hero depends on one's point of view. Ask students to think about what it means to be a villain or hero as they read the assignment.

② TEACH

DEFINING TERMS

Have students work in pairs to look up and write the definitions of *villain* and *hero*. As they read the passage, have them pull out phrases or sentences that would support their definitions of villain and hero. **L2**

COMPARISON

Have students create a graphic organizer like the one below. Then have them read through the passages and summarize the key points for supporting the claim that Alexander was a villain or hero. (*Answers are provided.*) **L2**

Alexander the Great	
Villain	Hero
destroyed Persepolis	*promoted learning*
killed/enslaved thousands	*visited wounded soldiers*
treated slaves harshly	*spared captured queen*
murdered advisers	*built new cities*

Alexander the Great: Villain or Hero?

Villain

Was Alexander the Great really great? Or was he an evil conqueror? Those who see him as bloodthirsty and cruel give this as evidence against Alexander. They say he

- destroyed Persepolis
- attacked Tyre, killing 10,000 people and enslaving 30,000
- treated his slaves harshly
- ordered the murder of several close advisers.

Many legends about Alexander have been told. One historian found this account to support the "villain theory."

"The following is my favourite [story] which is found all the way from Turkey to Kazakhstan: Iskander [Alexander] was actually a devil and he had horns. But his hair was long and wavy and the horns were never seen. Only his barbers knew. But he feared they could not keep the secret. So, he killed them when they discovered. His last barber pretended not to notice and kept the secret. Eventually though he could bear it no longer and, as he could tell no one, he ran to a well and called down the well: 'Iskander has horns!' But in the bottom of the well were whispering reeds [used in flutes] and they echoed the story until it went round the whole world."

—Michael Wood, "In the Footsteps of Alexander the Great"

▲ Alexander the Great (at far left)

180

Extending the Content

Military Might Alexander's army was an extremely effective fighting machine. The infantry lined up in a formation called a *phalanx*. The soldiers carried spears nearly 18 feet long and long shields that, when they stood close together, overlapped to protect each others' flanks. Soldiers stood in rows with their spears passing over the shoulder or between the line of the men in front of them. Because of this, five rows of spear tips stood out in front of the first line of soldiers. The rows of men behind held up their spears to deflect arrows. This created such a formidable mass of spears that even elephants were afraid to charge them!

Arrian, a Greek historian who lived in the A.D. 100s, wrote about Alexander this way:

"For my own part, I think there was at that time no race of men, no city, nor even a single individual to whom Alexander's name and fame had not penetrated. For this reason it seems to me that a hero totally unlike any other human being could not have been born without the agency [help] of the deity [gods]."

—Arrian, *The Anabasis of Alexander*

On two points all historians agree: Alexander was a brilliant general and he was a brave fighter. He once boasted to his men:

"For there is no part of my body, in front at any rate, remaining free from wounds; nor is there any kind of weapon used either for close combat or for hurling at the enemy, the traces of which I do not bear on my person. For I have been wounded with the sword in close fight, I have been shot with arrows, and I have been struck with missiles projected from engines of war; and though oftentimes I have been hit with stones and bolts of wood for the sake of your lives, your glory, and your wealth, I am still leading you as conquerors over all the land and sea, all rivers, mountains, and plains. I have celebrated your weddings with my own, and the children of many of you will be akin to my children."

—Arrian, *The Anabasis of Alexander*

▲ Alexander the Great

Hero

Other historians consider Alexander the Great to be a hero. They claim he brought progress, order, and culture to each new land he conquered. In support of him, they say Alexander
- tried to promote learning
- visited all of his wounded men after each battle
- spared the lives of the queen and princess of Persia
- built new cities where others had been destroyed.

You Be the Historian

Checking for Understanding
1. Why do some people view Alexander the Great as a villain?
2. Why do others view him as a hero?
3. Was Alexander wicked or heroic? Take the role of a historian. Write a brief essay or persuasive speech that explains how you see Alexander the Great. Be sure to use facts to support your position. You can compare him to other famous rulers to strengthen your argument.

181

📖 **Reading Strategy**

DEBATE THE ISSUE

Organize a class debate on whether Alexander the Great was a villain or hero. Form groups supporting each point of view. To support their arguments, have students find additional resources that discuss Alexander and his legacy.

Students may use the library, Internet, or other resources to find additional information about Alexander. Point them to ancient writers such as Plutarch and Arrian, who wrote about Alexander the Great. Once students have compiled their resources, have them present their viewpoints to the class. They should use their graphic organizers to help them in their presentations. Students may want to vote to decide which argument was more persuasive. **L2**

You Be the Historian Answers

1. He destroyed cities, killed and enslaved thousands, and treated slaves harshly. Later, he was so disliked that rumors spread about him being a devil.

2. He built new cities, encouraged his men, promoted learning, and spared the lives of the royalty he conquered. Later, he was remem-bered by many as heroic and more than human.

3. Answers will vary. Students should make a clear argument based on evidence from the text and have opinions that require some thought. Also, they may incorporate their outside research readings.

① FOCUS

SECTION OVERVIEW

This section describes the spread of Hellenistic culture in the wake of Alexander's empire and the achievements of many great philosophers, writers, and scientists.

🔔 Project **Daily Focus Skills Transparency 5–4** and have students answer questions. Discuss their responses.

Get Ready to Read!

Preteaching Vocabulary: Explain that the root of the word *astronomer* is *astro,* the Greek word for "star." The Greeks were very interested in studying the stars in the heavens.

Answers to Graphic: architecture and sculpture, literature, theater, philosophies, advances in astronomy, advances in mathematics

Section 4 — The Spread of Greek Culture

Get Ready to Read!

What's the Connection?

In Section 3, you read that Alexander's conquests helped to spread Greek culture. The kings who came after Alexander also tried to attract the best and brightest Greeks to Asia and Egypt. They hoped to re-create the glory of Greece's Golden Age in their own kingdoms.

Focusing on the Main Ideas

- Hellenistic cities became centers of learning and culture. *(page 183)*
- Epicurus and Zeno showed the world different ways to look at happiness. *(page 184)*
- Hellenistic scientists made major discoveries in math and astronomy. *(page 185)*

Locating Places
Rhodes (ROHDZ)
Syracuse (SIHR•uh•KYOOS)

Meeting People
Theocritus (thee•AH•kruh•tuhs)
Aristarchus (AR•uh•STAHR•kuhs)
Eratosthenes
   (EHR•uh•TAHS•thuh•NEEZ)
Euclid (YOO•kluhd)
Archimedes (AHR•kuh•MEE•deez)

Building Your Vocabulary
Epicureanism
   (EH•pih•kyu•REE•uh•NIH•zuhm)
Stoicism (STOH•uh•SIH•zuhm)
astronomer (uh•STRAH•nuh•muhr)
plane geometry (jee•AH•muh•tree)
solid geometry (jee•AH•muh•tree)

Reading Strategy
Summarizing Information Create a diagram to show the major Greek contributions to Western civilization.

Contributions

When & Where?

350 B.C.		275 B.C.	200 B.C.
	c. 300 B.C. King Ptolemy I invites Euclid to Alexandria	291 B.C. Menander, the playwright, dies	212 B.C. Archimedes killed by Romans

Syracuse • Athens
Alexandria •

SECTION RESOURCES

📁 **Reproducible Masters**
- Reproducible Lesson Plan 5–4
- Daily Lecture and Discussion Notes 5–4
- Vocabulary Activity 5–4
- Active Reading Note-Taking Guide 5–4
- Guided Reading Activity 5–4
- Section Quiz 5–4
- Reading Essentials and Study Guide 5–4

🔦 **Transparencies**
- Daily Focus Skills Transparency 5–4

Multimedia
- 💿 Interactive Tutor Self-Assessment CD-ROM
- 💿 ExamView® Pro Testmaker CD-ROM
- 💿 Presentation Plus! CD-ROM
- 💿 Vocabulary PuzzleMaker CD-ROM

Greek Culture Spreads

Main Idea Hellenistic cities became centers of learning and culture.

Reading Focus Imagine you are a leading citizen in a new city. How would you make it the best city possible? Read to find out how leaders in the Hellenistic Era improved their cities.

During the Hellenistic Era, philosophers, scientists, poets, and writers flocked to the new Greek cities in southwest Asia and Egypt, especially Alexandria. Many came to take advantage of Alexandria's library. Its more than 500,000 scrolls were useful to students of literature and language. Alexandria also had a museum where researchers went to do their work.

Architecture and Sculpture

The Hellenistic kingdoms were lands of opportunity for Greek architects. New cities were being founded, and old ones were being rebuilt. The Hellenistic kings wanted to make these cities like the cultural centers of Greece. They paid handsome fees to line the streets with baths, theaters, and temples.

Hellenistic kings and other wealthy citizens hired Greek sculptors to fill their towns and cities with thousands of statues. These statues showed the same level of workmanship as the statues from Greece's Golden Age.

Literature and Theater

Hellenistic leaders also admired talented writers. Kings and leading citizens spent generous sums of money supporting writers' work. As a result, the Hellenistic Age produced a large body of literature. Sadly, very little of this writing has survived.

One of the works we know about is an epic poem by Appolonius (A•puh•LOH•nee•uhs) of **Rhodes** (ROHDZ). Called *Argonautica*, it tells the legend of Jason and his band of heroes. They sail the seas in search of a ram

---

Primary Source

The Poetry of Theocritus

Theocritus is considered the creator of pastoral poetry. Pastoral poetry deals with rural life, especially the lives of shepherds. It often compares rural and city life. In this selection, he talks about shepherding as a way of life.

"Shepherd, your song is sweeter than the water that tumbles and splashes down from the rocks.

If the Muses get the ewe for their prize,

you'll win the [baby] lamb. But if they choose

the lamb, you'll carry away the ewe."

—Theocritus, "First Idyll"

▲ Sculpture of shepherd

DBQ **Document-Based Question**

How does Theocritus describe the song of the shepherd?

---

with golden fleece. Another poet, **Theocritus** (thee•AH•kruh•tuhs), wrote short poems about the beauty of nature.

Athens remained the center of Greek theater. Playwrights in Athens created a new kind of comedy. The stories had happy endings and still make people laugh. However, unlike the comedies of Greece's Golden Age, they did not poke fun at political leaders. Instead the plays told stories about love and relationships. One of the best known of the new playwrights was Menander (muh•NAN•duhr), who lived from 343 B.C. to 291 B.C.

✓ Reading Check **Explain** How did the Hellenistic kingdoms spread Greek culture?

CHAPTER 5   Greek Civilization   **183**

---

② TEACH

Activating Prior Knowledge Ask students to recall what they read earlier about Greek culture. Ask them how they think Alexander's great empire affected the spread of Greek art and ideas. **L2**

Daily Lecture and Discussion Notes 5–4

Use **Daily Lecture and Discussion Notes 5–4** for an outline of key concepts found in the section.

Reading Support L1/ EL

Use **Vocabulary Activity 5–4** to review important terms in the section.

Primary Source

Answer: sweeter than the splashing of a waterfall among rocks

✓ Reading Check

Answer: They introduced Greek architecture, sculpture, and literature to the new cities in Asia and Egypt.

Reading Strategy **READING THE TEXT**

Predicting After the breakup of Alexander's empire, many people were pessimistic about what would happen to Greek civilization and culture. On the board or an overhead transparency, have students brainstorm: What will happen to Greek culture after the fall of Alexander's empire? After they have established a sufficient list of possible answers, have students select three that they think are the most likely and write them on their papers in complete sentences. As they read the section, have them revisit the sentences and correct any misconceptions. **L2**

CONNECTING ACROSS TIME

Ask students to review the main ideas of Epicureanism and Stoicism. Then ask them to make a list of people they know—relatives, friends, and acquaintances—who fall into one or the other category. **L1/ EL**

Writing Activity

Ask: Does happiness consist of seeking pleasure, or does it lie in doing one's duty? Have students write a paragraph that supports one of these extremes. Have them give reasons to support their choice. **L2**

The Way It Was

Answers:

1. Priests in the temples treated patients with herbs and offered prayers and sacrifice.

2. He separated religion from medicine and stressed examining the body to diagnose illness.

Reading Check

Answer: Epicureanism emphasized emotion and avoiding worry. Stoicism advocated reason and duty.

The Way It Was

Science and Inventions

Greek Medicine The ancient Greeks believed that their gods had the power to cure them of illnesses and injuries. Greek temples were places of healing as well as places of worship. In temples, priests treated patients with herbs, prayed, and made sacrifices to the gods as part of the healing process.

In the 400s B.C., the practice of medicine began to change. Hippocrates (hih • PAH • kruh • TEEZ), a doctor and pioneer of medical science, began to separate medicine from religion. He stressed that it was important to examine the body and look at a patient's symptoms to find out why someone was ill. He also taught that it was important to have a healthy diet.

Hippocrates is well known for the oath, or pledge, that he asked his medical students to recite. His students had to promise never to harm and always to care for their patients. New doctors still take a version of the Hippocratic Oath when they graduate from medical school.

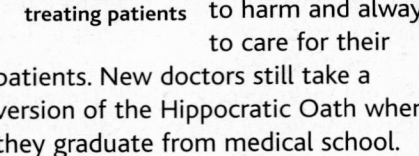
▲ Greek doctor treating patients

Connecting to the Past
1. How were illnesses and injuries treated before Hippocrates?
2. How did Hippocrates change the way medicine was practiced in ancient Greece?

Philosophy

Main Idea Epicurus and Zeno showed the world different ways to look at happiness.

Reading Focus What makes you happy? Read on to learn about different Greek ideas about happiness.

During the Hellenistic Era, Athens continued to attract the most famous philosophers in the Greek world. The two most important philosophers were Epicurus and Zeno.

Epicureans Epicurus founded a philosophy we now know as **Epicureanism** (EH • pih • kyu • REE • uh • NIH • zuhm). He taught his students that happiness was the goal of life. He believed that the way to be happy was to seek out pleasure.

Today the word *epicurean* means the love of physical pleasure, such as good food or comfortable surroundings. However, to Epicurus, pleasure meant spending time with friends and learning not to worry about things. Epicureans avoided worry by staying out of politics and public service.

Who Were the Stoics? A Phoenician named Zeno developed **Stoicism** (STOH • uh • SIH • zuhm). It became a very popular philosophy in the Hellenistic world. When Zeno came to Athens, he could not afford to rent a lecture hall. So he taught at a building known as the "painted porch" near the city market. "Stoicism" comes from *stoa*, the Greek word for "porch."

For Stoics, happiness came from following reason, not emotions, and doing your duty. Today the word *stoic* is used to describe someone who is not affected by joy or grief. Unlike Epicureans, Stoics thought people had a duty to serve their city.

Reading Check **Contrast** What were the differences between Epicureanism and Stoicism?

DIFFERENTIATED INSTRUCTION

Logical/Mathematical: Ask students who are interested in astronomy or math to work with students who may be less interested. Have the more interested students explain to their partners how the discoveries of one of the figures described in this section are important today. Encourage them to use paper and pencil to give mathematical or scientific examples.

English Learners: Ask students to work in pairs to make a list of how the discoveries of three of the scientists discussed in this section have proven useful today.

Gifted and Talented: Ask students to write and present a dialogue between two of the scientists mentioned in the section.

Greek Science and Math

Main Idea Hellenistic scientists made major discoveries in math and astronomy.

Reading Focus Do you know how to find the area of a square? If so, you are doing geometry. Read on to find out about the person who created geometry and other scientists from the Hellenistic Era.

Scientists, especially mathematicians and astronomers, made major contributions during the Hellenistic Era. **Astronomers** (uh•STRAH•nuh•muhrs) study stars, planets, and other heavenly bodies. **Aristarchus** (AR•uh•STAHR•kuhs), an astronomer from Samos, claimed that the sun was at the center of the universe and that Earth circled the sun. At the time, other astronomers rejected Aristarchus's ideas. They thought that Earth was the center of the universe.

Another astronomer, **Eratosthenes** (EHR•uh•TAHS•thuh•NEEZ), was in charge of the library at Alexandria. Eratosthenes concluded that Earth is round. He then used his knowledge of geometry and astronomy to measure Earth's circumference—the distance around Earth.

Eratosthenes put two sticks in the ground far apart from each other. When the sun was directly over one stick, the shadow was shorter than the shadow at the other stick. By measuring the shadows, he was able to calculate the curve of Earth's surface.

Using his measurements, Eratosthenes estimated that the distance around Earth equaled 24,675 miles (39,702 km). Amazingly, his estimate was within 185 miles (298 km) of the actual distance. Using similar methods, he measured the distance to the sun and to the moon. His measurements were quite accurate.

Euclid (YOO•kluhd) is probably the most famous Greek mathematician. His best-known book *Elements* describes plane geometry. **Plane geometry** (jee•AH•muh•tree) is the branch of mathematics that shows

Greek Scientists and Their Contributions

Scientist	Scientific "Firsts"
Archimedes	Established the science of physics Explained the lever and compound pulley
Aristarchus	Established that Earth revolves around the sun
Eratosthenes	Figured out that Earth is round
Euclid	Wrote a book that organized information about geometry
Hipparchus	Created a system to explain how planets and stars move
Hippocrates	Known as the "Father of Medicine" First to write a medical code of good behavior
Hypatia	Expanded knowledge of mathematics and astronomy
Pythagoras	First to establish the principles of geometry

Archimedes ▶

Understanding Charts

The ancient Greeks made advances in science.
1. What were Archimedes' achievements?
2. Identify Who wrote a code of behavior that doctors still follow today?

CRITICAL THINKING ACTIVITY

Comparing and Contrasting The Greek world following the death of Alexander included many different cultural and ethnic groups. Have students discuss how this condition could have been both a strength and a weakness. *(Diversity could have led to many different good ideas, though it also could have led to quarrels and conflict among the different groups.)* Then have them compare the Greek world after the death of Alexander to the United States today. How are they similar and different? **L2**

ENRICH

Ask students to work in small groups to prepare radio documentaries on the achievements of the Hellenistic era in art, science, or politics. Have groups write scripts, record their documentaries, and play them for the class. **L3**

📁 Suggestions for rubrics may be found in the *Quizzes, Tests, and Authentic Assessment (with Rubrics)* booklet.

✓ Reading Check

Answer: Archimedes; solid geometry, value of pi, invention of catapults

To help students understand section material, have them visit **Study Central™** at jat.glencoe.com

RETEACH

Ask students to create a 10-question quiz, with answers, on the content of this section. Have students exchange quizzes and take them. **L1**

④ CLOSE

Ask students to discuss how the world might be different if the Hellenistic era had never occurred. **L2**

186

▲ Euclid

how points, lines, angles, and surfaces relate to one another. Around 300 B.C., King Ptolemy I (TAH•luh•mee) of Egypt asked Euclid if he knew an easier way to learn geometry than by reading *Elements.* Euclid answered that "there is no royal way" to learn geometry.

The most famous scientist of the Hellenistic Era was **Archimedes** (AHR•kuh•MEE•deez) of **Syracuse** (SIHR•uh•KYOOS). He worked on **solid geometry** (jee•AH•muh•tree)—the study of ball-like shapes called spheres and tubelike shapes called cylinders. He also figured out the value of *pi*. This number is used to measure the area of circles and is usually represented by the symbol π.

Archimedes was also an inventor. One story about Archimedes tells how he invented weapons. "Give me a lever and a place to stand on," Archimedes said to the king of Syracuse, "and I will move the earth."

The king of Syracuse was impressed. He asked Archimedes to use his levers to defend the city. So Archimedes designed catapults—machines that hurled arrows, spears, and rocks. When Romans attacked Syracuse in 212 B.C., Archimedes' catapults drove them back. It took the Romans three years to capture Syracuse. During the massacre that followed, Archimedes was killed.

✓ Reading Check **Explain** Who was the most famous scientist of the Hellenistic Era? What did he contribute?

Section ④ Review

History Online
Study Central™ Need help with the material in this section? Visit jat.glencoe.com

Reading Summary

Review the Main Ideas

- Hellenistic cities, such as Alexandria, attracted some of the Greek world's best architects, sculptors, and writers.

- During the Hellenistic Era, new philosophies, such as Stoicism and Epicureanism, developed.

- Hellenistic scientists, including Aristarchus, Eratosthenes, Euclid, and Archimedes, made important advances in the fields of astronomy and mathematics.

What Did You Learn?

1. Why did the city of Alexandria attract scholars?

2. Describe the form of philosophy developed by Zeno.

Critical Thinking

3. **Summarize** Draw a table like the one below. Write several facts about each scientist in the correct column.

Aristarchus	
Eratosthenes	
Euclid	
Archimedes	

4. **Compare and Contrast** How were the comedies of the Hellenistic Era and those of Greece's Golden Age similar and different?

5. **Analyze** How would knowledge of geometry be helpful to the Greeks?

6. **Identify** What did the Epicureans believe about happiness?

7. **📖 Reading** Context Clues Name two words in this sentence that help define the word *playwright.* "Playwrights in Athens created a new kind of comedy."

186   CHAPTER 5   Greek Civilization

SECTION 4 REVIEW ANSWERS

1. had a large library and museum

2. Stoicism: happiness comes from following reason; duty is important.

3. Aristarchus: sun the center of the universe, Earth revolves around sun; Eratosthenes: Earth is round, determined distance from Earth to sun, measured circumference; Euclid: wrote about plane geometry; Archimedes: value of pi, designed catapults

4. Similar: made people laugh; Different: focused on love and relationships, not criticizing people in power

5. It helped them to construct buildings and bridges, determine distances, and design machines.

6. It was the goal of life.

7. created, comedy

Chapter 5 Reading Review

Section 1 The Culture of Ancient Greece

Vocabulary
myth
oracle
epic
fable
drama
tragedy
comedy

Focusing on the Main Ideas
- The Greeks believed that gods and goddesses controlled nature and shaped their lives. *(page 155)*
- Greek poetry and fables taught Greek values. *(page 157)*
- Greek drama still shapes entertainment today. *(page 160)*
- Greek art and architecture expressed Greek ideas of beauty and harmony. *(page 162)*

Section 2 Greek Philosophy and History

Vocabulary
philosophy
philosopher
Sophist
Socratic method

Focusing on the Main Ideas
- Greek philosophers developed ideas that are still used today. *(page 169)*
- Greeks wrote the first real histories in Western civilization. *(page 173)*

Section 3 Alexander the Great

Vocabulary
legacy
Hellenistic Era

Focusing on the Main Ideas
- Philip II of Macedonia united the Greek states. *(page 175)*
- Alexander the Great conquered the Persian Empire and spread Greek culture throughout southwest Asia. *(page 176)*

▲ Alexander the Great

Section 4 The Spread of Greek Culture

Vocabulary
Epicureanism
Stoicism
astronomer
plane geometry
solid geometry

Focusing on the Main Ideas
- Hellenistic cities became centers of learning and culture. *(page 183)*
- Epicurus and Zeno showed the world different ways to look at happiness. *(page 184)*
- Hellenistic scientists made major discoveries in math and astronomy. *(page 185)*

CHAPTER 5   Greek Civilization   **187**

CHAPTER 5 REVIEW

PREVIEW/REVIEW

Vocabulary Activity Have students write a fill-in-the-blank quiz using 10 vocabulary terms from this chapter. Have students exchange and take the quizzes then grade them.

- **Vocabulary PuzzleMaker CD-ROM**
- **Interactive Tutor Self-Assessment CD-ROM**

CONDENSE

- Chapter 5 **Guided Reading Activities**
- **StudentWorks Plus™ CD-ROM (with Audio Program)**

RETEACH

- **Differentiated Instruction Activity 5**
- Chapter 5 *Reading Essentials and Study Guide*

CHAPTER CULMINATING ACTIVITY

Have students finish the Chapter Culminating Activity from page 150D.

Suggestions for rubrics may be found in the *Quizzes, Tests, and Authentic Assessment (with Rubrics)* booklet.

Reading Strategy   READ TO WRITE

Journal Entry Ask students to choose one of the experiences discussed in this chapter, such as visiting the oracle at Delphi, fighting at the battle of Troy, sailing with Odysseus on his way home from the war, watching a play by a great Athenian dramatist, studying in the Academy or Lyceum, flying with Daedalus and Icarus, or marching with Alexander's army. Then have them write a journal entry that describes what it would be like to be undergoing that experience. Have them include details from the chapter about the time and place.

- **L1** students should include one or two details in their description.
- **L2** students should include several appropriate details and attempt grammar mastery.
- **L3** students should write detailed entries that create a vivid picture of the experience.

Chapter 5 Assessment and Activities

Review Vocabulary

1. Paragraphs will vary but should reflect the definitions and characteristics given in the chapter.

2. T

3. T

4. F

5. T

6. T

Review Main Ideas

7. They believed the gods controlled nature and shaped the lives of humans.

8. the Greek ideas of beauty and harmony

9. They are still used today.

10. They wrote the first real histories in Western civilization.

11. Philip II of Macedonia

12. He conquered the Persian Empire and spread Greek culture throughout southwest Asia.

13. They became centers of learning and culture.

14. mathematics and astronomy

Critical Thinking

15. The war divided them and destroyed many farms and lives. Population declined, and many youths went to

---

Review Vocabulary

1. Write a brief paragraph that defines and compares the following terms.

    epic   fable   myth

Decide if each statement is *True* or *False*.

_____ 2. An oracle was a shrine Greeks visited to receive prophecies.

_____ 3. Sophists were professional teachers.

_____ 4. The death of Socrates marks the beginning of the Hellenistic Era.

_____ 5. Astronomers study stars, planets, and other heavenly bodies.

_____ 6. Euclid developed plane geometry.

Review Main Ideas

Section 1 • The Culture of Ancient Greece

7. What did the Greeks believe about their gods and goddesses?

8. What did Greek art and architecture express?

Section 2 • Greek Philosophy and History

9. How long did the ideas of Greek philosophers last?

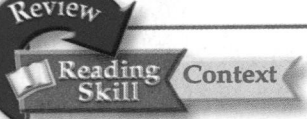

Words in Context

Read this passage from page 158.

"My father was anxious to see me develop into a good man . . . [so] he compelled me to memorize all of Homer."

19. Based on how *compelled* is used in this sentence, what do you think it means?

_____ a. asked

_____ b. taught

_____ c. forced

_____ d. dared

To review this skill, see pages 152–153.

---

10. Why are Greek historians so important?

Section 3 • Alexander the Great

11. Which leader united the Greek states?

12. What are the two main accomplishments of Alexander the Great?

Section 4 • The Spread of Greek Culture

13. Why were Hellenistic cities important?

14. In what fields did Hellenistic scientists make advances?

Critical Thinking

15. **Understanding Cause and Effect** How did the Peloponnesian War weaken the Greek states?

16. **Analyze** Why would knowing the circumference of Earth have been helpful to the Greeks?

17. **Compare** How was religion in ancient Greece similar to religion in ancient Egypt?

18. **Analyze** Why do you think the development of written history is important?

---

fight for Persia. Those who stayed fought among themselves.

16. Possible answers: It would have been helpful in planning land and sea voyages, making maps, and other travel-related tasks.

17. Possible answers: Both groups believed in many gods and goddesses, life after death, and the use of rituals and priests to seek the gods' favor.

18. Answers will vary but should include a thoughtful response.

Reading Skill

19. c

Geography Skills

Study the map below and answer the following questions.

20. Location Analyze the location of the Hellenistic kingdoms. What present-day countries control territory that was controlled by the Seleucid empire?

21. Human/Environment Interaction Which kingdom do you think was the most difficult to govern based on its geography?

NATIONAL GEOGRAPHIC

Hellenistic World

Black Sea
20°E   40°E
Pella
ASIA MINOR   40°N
Pergamum
Crete   Cyprus
Mediterranean Sea   Seleucia
Tigris R.
Euphrates R.
Alexandria
Nile R.

0   500 mi.
0   500 km
Azimuthal Equal-Area projection

KEY
- Egyptian kingdom
- Macedonian kingdom
- Pergamum kingdom
- Seleucid kingdom

Read to Write

22. Descriptive Writing Imagine you are a journalist living in Alexandria, Egypt, during the Hellenistic Era. Write an article describing life in the city.

23. Using Your FOLDABLES Review the developments in early Greece that you listed on your foldable. Using numbers, rank each development from the most valuable to the least valuable. Explain the reason for your highest and lowest ranking.

Linking Past and Present

24. Expository Writing The Nobel prize is awarded yearly to people who have made great achievements. Do research to find out more about the award. Then choose one Greek philosopher, writer, scientist, or leader who you think deserves the Nobel prize. Write a short speech to explain why. Present your speech to the class.

History Online

Self-Check Quiz To help you prepare for the Chapter Test, visit jat.glencoe.com

Using Technology

25. Creating a Multimedia Presentation Use the Internet and print resources, such as newspapers and magazines, to research Greek architecture. Then use the computer or posterboard to design and construct your own building using Greek designs. The Greeks dedicated some of their buildings to gods and goddesses. Dedicate your building to someone in history and design it with that person in mind. Share your research and design with the class.

Primary Source Analyze

In this account, Thucydides describes the masses of people who entered Athens around 430 B.C. seeking relief from the plague.

"There were no houses for them, and, living as they did during the hot season in badly ventilated huts, they died like flies. . . . For the catastrophe was so overwhelming that men, not knowing what would happen next to them, became indifferent to every rule of religion or law. All the funeral ceremonies which used to be observed were now disorganized, and they buried the dead as best they could."

—Thucydides, *History of the Peloponnesian War*

DBQ Document-Based Questions

26. What hardships did newcomers to Athens face during the time of the plague?

27. What does Thucydides mean when he says that men "became indifferent to every rule of religion or law"?

CHAPTER 5   Greek Civilization   **189**

History Online

Have students visit the Web site at jat.glencoe.com to review Chapter 5 and take the **Self-Check Quiz.**

Linking Past and Present

24. Nominees should be appropriate for the prize, such as Archimedes in the field of science, Euclid in mathematics, or Sophocles or Homer in the field of literature. Speeches should show understanding of the person's achievements.

Using Technology

25. Products will vary but should reflect the information in the chapter.

Primary Source

26. lack of housing, bad ventilation, disease

27. People were so overwhelmed by the plague that they did not hold funeral services or rites for the dead, and they did not place bodies in cemeteries.

Bonus Question

Ask: Which of the philosophers discussed in this chapter do you think is the most relevant today? Why? (*Answers should focus on the philosopher's basic beliefs and apply them to the world of today.*)

Geography Skills

20. Turkey, Lebanon, Syria, Jordan, Iraq, and Iran

21. Answers will vary. The Egyptian kingdom held territory in Asia Minor, Cyprus, and Macedonia that was not connected to Egypt by land, thus making it hard to govern. The Seleucid kingdom was the largest in size and therefore hard to control as well.

Read to Write

22. Reports will vary but should accurately reflect the information about Alexandria and the Hellenistic Era in the chapter.

23 FOLDABLES Answers will vary but should accurately reflect the information in the chapter and show evidence of sound critical thinking about the events. You may wish to encourage students to rank separately in each category.

189

Chapter 6 Resources

Note: The following materials may be used when teaching Chapter 6.
Section level support materials are shown at point of use in the margins of the Teacher Wraparound Edition.

TEACHING TRANSPARENCIES

- Graphic Organizer Transparencies with Teaching Strategy and Student Activity **L2**
- Cause-and-Effect Transparencies with Teaching Strategy and Student Activity **L2**
- Then and Now Transparencies with Teaching Strategy and Student Activity **L2**
- In-text Map Transparency with Teaching Strategy and Student Activity **L1**
- Map Transparencies with Overlay, Teaching Strategy, and Student Activity **L2**

DIFFERENTIATED INSTRUCTION

- Differentiated Instruction Activity 6
- Time Line Activity 6
- Primary Source Reading 6 (with Document-Based Questions)
- Inclusion Strategies for the Middle School Social Studies Classroom
- StudentWorks Plus™ CD-ROM (with Audio Program)

READING SUPPORT

- Take-Home Review Activity 6 **L2**
- World Literature Reading 6 **L2**
- Workbook Activity 6 **L1**
- Reading Strategies for the Social Studies Classroom **L1/ EL**

ASSESSMENT

- Authentic Assessment Activity 6 **L1/ EL**
- Chapter 6 Test Form A **L2**
- Chapter 6 Test Form B **L2**
- ExamView® Pro Testmaker CD-ROM

INTERDISCIPLINARY CONNECTIONS

- Geography and History Activity 6 **L2**
- People to Meet Activity 6 **L2**
- Economics Activity 6 **L2**
- Citizenship and Service Learning Activity 6 **L2**

SPANISH RESOURCES

- Spanish Reading Essentials and Study Guide
- Spanish Guided Reading Activities
- Spanish Quizzes, Tests, and Authentic Assessment (with Rubrics)
- Spanish Take-Home Review Activities

MULTIMEDIA

- ExamView® Pro Testmaker CD-ROM
- Glencoe Skillbuilder Interactive Workbook CD-ROM, Level 1
- Interactive Tutor Self-Assessment CD-ROM
- MindJogger Videoquiz
- Presentation Plus! CD-ROM
- StudentWorks Plus™ CD-ROM (with Audio Program)
- TeacherWorks CD-ROM
- Vocabulary PuzzleMaker CD-ROM
- *World History: Journey Across Time* Video Program
- World History Primary Source Document Library CD-ROM

STANDARDIZED ASSESSMENT SKILLS

- Standardized Test Skills Practice Workbook Activity 6 **L2**
- Critical Thinking Skills Activity 6 **L2**

Teaching strategies have been coded with suggested ability levels. However, most are suitable for all levels.

L1 BASIC activities for all students

L2 AVERAGE activities for average to above-average students

L3 CHALLENGING activities for above-average students

EL ENGLISH LANGUAGE activities

Chapter 6 Resources

TIME MANAGEMENT

Chapter Introduction	Section 1	Section 2	Section 3	Chapter Wrap-Up
1 Day	2 Days	1 Day	2 Days	1 Day

Block Scheduling Activities that are suited to use within the block scheduling framework are identified by: 🎲

0:00 OUT OF TIME? Assign the Chapter 6 *Reading Essentials and Study Guide.** 📁

SECTION RESOURCES

DAILY OBJECTIVES	REPRODUCIBLE RESOURCES	MULTIMEDIA RESOURCES
Section 1 **India's First Civilizations** 1. Climate and geography influenced the rise of India's first civilizations. 2. The Aryans conquered India and introduced new ideas and technology. 3. The Aryans introduced the caste system.	📁 Reproducible Lesson Plan 6–1 📁 Daily Lecture and Discussion Notes 6–1 📁 Vocabulary Activity 6–1 📁 Active Reading Note-Taking Guide 6–1 📁 Guided Reading Activity 6–1* 📁 Section Quiz 6–1* 📁 Reading Essentials and Study Guide 6–1*	🔦 Daily Focus Skills Transparency 6–1 💿 Interactive Tutor Self-Assessment CD-ROM 💿 Exam*View*® Pro Testmaker CD-ROM 💿 Presentation Plus! CD-ROM
Section 2 **Hinduism and Buddhism** 1. Hinduism grew out of ancient beliefs of the Aryans. 2. A new religion, Buddhism, appealed to many in India and other parts of Asia.	📁 Reproducible Lesson Plan 6–2 📁 Daily Lecture and Discussion Notes 6–2 📁 Vocabulary Activity 6–2 📁 Active Reading Note-Taking Guide 6–2 📁 Guided Reading Activity 6–2* 📁 Section Quiz 6–2* 📁 Reading Essentials and Study Guide 6–2*	🔦 Daily Focus Skills Transparency 6–2 💿 Interactive Tutor Self-Assessment CD-ROM 💿 Exam*View*® Pro Testmaker CD-ROM 💿 Presentation Plus! CD-ROM 💿 Glencoe BookLink CD-ROM
Section 3 **India's First Empires** 1. The Mauryan dynasty built India's first great empire. 2. The Gupta empire reunited much of northern India. 3. The Mauryan and Gupta empires made important contributions in literature, mathematics, and science.	📁 Reproducible Lesson Plan 6–3 📁 Daily Lecture and Discussion Notes 6–3 📁 Vocabulary Activity 6–3 📁 Active Reading Note-Taking Guide 6–3 📁 Guided Reading Activity 6–3* 📁 Section Quiz 6–3* 📁 Reading Essentials and Study Guide 6–3*	🔦 Daily Focus Skills Transparency 6–3 💿 Interactive Tutor Self-Assessment CD-ROM 💿 Exam*View*® Pro Testmaker CD-ROM 💿 Presentation Plus! CD-ROM 💿 Vocabulary PuzzleMaker CD-ROM 💿 Glencoe BookLink CD-ROM

*Also available in Spanish

Chapter 6 Resources

Use our Web site for additional resources. All essential content is covered in the Student Edition.

You and your students can visit jat.glencoe.com, the Web site companion to *World History: Journey Across Time*. This innovative integration of electronic and print media offers your students a wealth of opportunities. The student text directs students to the Web site for the following options:

- Chapter Overviews
- Self-Check Quizzes
- Study Central™
- Student Web Activities
- Multi-Language Glossaries

Answers to the student Web activities are provided for you in the **Web Activity Lesson Plans.** Additional Web resources and ePuzzles and games are also available.

Videotape programs are available from Glencoe as supplements to the chapters.

To order, call Glencoe at 1-800-334-7344. To find classroom resources to accompany many of these videos, check the following home pages:

A&E Television: www.aande.com
The History Channel: www.historychannel.com

MEETING SPECIAL NEEDS

In addition to the Differentiated Instruction strategies, the following resources are suitable for students with special needs:

- *ExamView® Pro Testmaker CD-ROM* allows teachers to tailor tests by reducing answer choices.
- *StudentWorks Plus™ CD-ROM (with Audio Program)* includes the entire narrative of the student edition so that less-proficient readers can listen to the words as they read them.
- The *Reading Essentials and Study Guide* provides the same content as the student edition but is written two grade levels below the textbook.
- *Guided Reading Activities* give less-proficient readers point-by-point instructions to increase comprehension as they read each textbook section.
- *Differentiated Instruction Activities* include a stimulating collection of readings and activities for students of all levels.

Index to National Geographic Magazine:

The following articles relate to this chapter:

- "In Their Own World: India's Forbidden Hanle Valley," by Karen Lange, January 2004.
- "Untouchable," by Tom O'Neill, June 2003.
- "Indus Civilization," by Mike Edwards, June 2000.

National Geographic Society Products:

To order the following, call National Geographic at 1–800–368–2728

- *NGS PictureShow: Ancient Civilizations: India and China* (CD-ROM)
- *National Geographic Atlas of the World* (Book)

NGS ONLINE

Access National Geographic's new dynamic MapMachine Web site and other geography resources at:

www.nationalgeographic.com
www.nationalgeographic.com/maps

 Meeting NCSS Standards

World History: Journey Across Time

The following standards are highlighted in Chapter 6:

Section 1 — III People, Places, and Environments: A, F
IV Individual Development and Identity: C
VIII Science, Technology, and Society: B

Section 2 — I Culture: A, D, E, F, H
III People, Places, and Environments: D
IV Individual Development and Identity: B, F

Section 3 — II Time, Continuity, and Change: C, E
III People, Places, and Environments: G
VII Production, Distribution, and Consumption: D

State and Local Objectives

_____

_____

_____

Chapter ⑥ Resources

Timesaving Tools

TeacherWorks
All-In-One Planner and Resource Center

- **Interactive Teacher Edition** Access your Teacher Wraparound Edition and your classroom resources with a few easy clicks.
- **Interactive Lesson Planner** Organize your week, month, semester, or year with all the lesson helps you need to make teaching creative and relevant.

Use Glencoe's **Presentation Plus!** multimedia teacher tool to easily present dynamic lessons that visually excite your students. Using Microsoft PowerPoint® you can customize the presentations to create your own personalized lessons.

FOLDABLES™
Study Organizer
Dinah Zike's Foldables

Foldables are three-dimensional, interactive graphic organizers that help students practice basic writing skills, review key vocabulary terms, and identify main ideas. Every chapter contains a foldable activity, with additional chapter activities found in the *Reading and Study Skills Foldables* booklet. You can use the foldables as they are presented, or modify them to suit the needs of your individual class.

Planning Ahead

CHAPTER CULMINATING ACTIVITY

The Chapter Culminating Activity will help students organize and learn the important information from the chapter. Begin teaching the chapter with this activity, and have students complete it as a culminating activity.

IDENTIFYING SUPPORTING DETAILS

Purpose This type of organizer helps students analyze information by identifying the main idea and supporting details. It will focus their attention on the most important points of the chapter as they read. It can also be used to organize information for reports and as a study aid.

Introduction to Modeling

1. Begin by pointing out to students that each section in the chapter begins with the statement of its main idea. The main idea is the same as a summary of the section's contents.

2. Explain that each section contains details, or facts, that help support the main idea. These details answer the who, what, where, when, why, or how questions about the main idea. Indicate that not every paragraph will have details to answer each question.

3. Ask students to draw the following chart in their notebooks:

Main Idea:	
Who?	
What?	
Where?	
When?	
Why?	
How?	

4. Explain that if the most important details are listed under the main idea, that idea and the subsequent details make a summary of that section.

5. As students read the chapter, ask them to fill in a main idea chart for each section.

6. As part of your chapter review, have students share their main idea charts. Ask students to state a summary of each section using these charts.

Use the **SkillBuilder Handbook** on pages 902–919 to help students learn the skill of finding the main idea.

190D

When & Where?

As students read the chapter, have them review the time line on this page. Ask them to consider cause-and-effect relationships, such as how the Aryan migration changed India. *(Aryans improved farming, declared cows sacred, introduced a new language and writing system, developed a caste system, and organized rival kingdoms.)* **L1**

GLENCOE TECHNOLOGY

World History: Journey Across Time Video Program

To learn more about ancient India, students can view the Chapter 6 video in the *World History: Journey Across Time* Video Program.

MindJogger Videoquiz

Use the **MindJogger Videoquiz** to preview Chapter 6 content.

Available in DVD and VHS

Chapter 6

Early India

The Hindu temple of Devi Jagadambi in Khajuraho, India ▼

NATIONAL GEOGRAPHIC When & Where?

2500 B.C.	1500 B.C.	500 B.C.	A.D. 500
c. 3000 B.C. India's first civilization begins	c. 1500 B.C. The Aryans arrive in India	563 B.C. The Buddha is born	A.D. 320 The Gupta empire begins

Reading Strategy ⟩ PURPOSE FOR READING

Analyzing Geography Using a wall map, point out the location of India, the Arabian Sea, the Indian Ocean, the Bay of Bengal, the Hindu Kush, and the Himalaya. Have students follow along on a map in the **Reference Atlas** at the front of their textbooks. **Ask:** How might geography have affected the lives of the ancient Indians? *(Answers may include that mountains protected them from foreign attack but also limited communication with other areas. The long coastline may have encouraged fishing and trading.)* As students read, have them continue to refer to maps to consider the importance of geography on Indian history. **L1**

Chapter Preview

Like ancient Greece, early India was a land of warriors, thinkers, and scientists. Read this chapter to find out how ideas from India affect how you do math today.

 View the Chapter 6 video in the *World History: Journey Across Time* **Video Program.**

Chapter Overview Visit jat.glencoe.com for a preview of Chapter 6.

 India's First Civilizations

The earliest Indian civilization developed on the Indus River. Later, the Aryans arrived in northern India. They changed the government and created a new social system.

 Hinduism and Buddhism

India's two main religions were Hinduism and Buddhism. These two religions affected every aspect of people's lives.

 India's First Empires

India had two great empires: the Maurya and the Gupta. The Mauryans helped spread Buddhism throughout Asia. Art and learning flourished during the Gupta empire.

Identifying *Make this foldable to help you identify and learn key terms.*

Step 1 *Stack four sheets of paper, one on top of the other. On the top sheet of paper, draw a large circle.*

Step 2 *With the papers still stacked, cut out all four circles at the same time.*

Reading and Writing *As you read the chapter, write the terms from Building Your Vocabulary in your foldable. Write a definition for each term. Then turn your foldable over (upside down) to write a short sentence using each term.*

Step 3 *Staple the paper circles together at one point around the edge.*

Staple here.

This makes a circular booklet.

Step 4 *Label the front circle as shown and take notes on the pages that open to the right.*

Chapter 6 Key Terms

191

INTRODUCING CHAPTER 6

History Online

Introduce students to chapter content and key terms by having them access **Chapter Overview 6** at jat.glencoe.com

CHAPTER PREVIEW

After reading Chapter 6, students will be able to

1. describe how climate and geography affected India, and how the Aryans changed India;

2. summarize the main tenets of Hinduism and Buddhism;

3. discuss the effects of the Mauryan and Gupta empires on India.

FOLDABLES™
Study Organizer Dinah Zike's Foldables

Purpose Students use this foldable to define each term and use the term in a sentence. As students read this chapter, they should record each term and its meaning. Then students should write the term in a sentence that shows its meaning.

📁 Have students complete *Reading and Study Skills Foldables* Activity 6.

MORE ABOUT THE PHOTO

Hindu Temples The complex of Hindu temples at Khajuraho was built sometime between the ninth and thirteenth centuries. It is believed that at one time 85 temples existed in the area. Today, remnants of about 25 temples, including Devi Jagadambi, are still standing. The temples, most of which are built of varying shades of sandstone, are decorated with intricate stone carvings of gods, goddesses, musicians, animals, and other figures. Although far removed from major cities and towns, Khajuraho remains a popular tourist destination today.

1 Learn It!

There is a strong relationship between vocabulary knowledge and comprehension. For this reason, it is critical that students develop ways of building vocabulary that go beyond word recognition.

In place of isolated vocabulary lists, teach students concepts to facilitate a deeper understanding of the text.

Have students work in pairs or groups to create a vocabulary graphic using the following activity:

- Have students write a new word or phrase, such as "caste system," in the center of the page.

- Have them draw a circle, triangle, rectangle, and square on the paper.

- In the circle, students should write what they think a caste system is. (Example: status groups)

- In the triangle, they should write types of castes. (Example: warriors, farmers, servants)

- In the rectangle, have students write what caste they would want to belong to and why.

- In the square, have them write what a caste system is *not*. L2

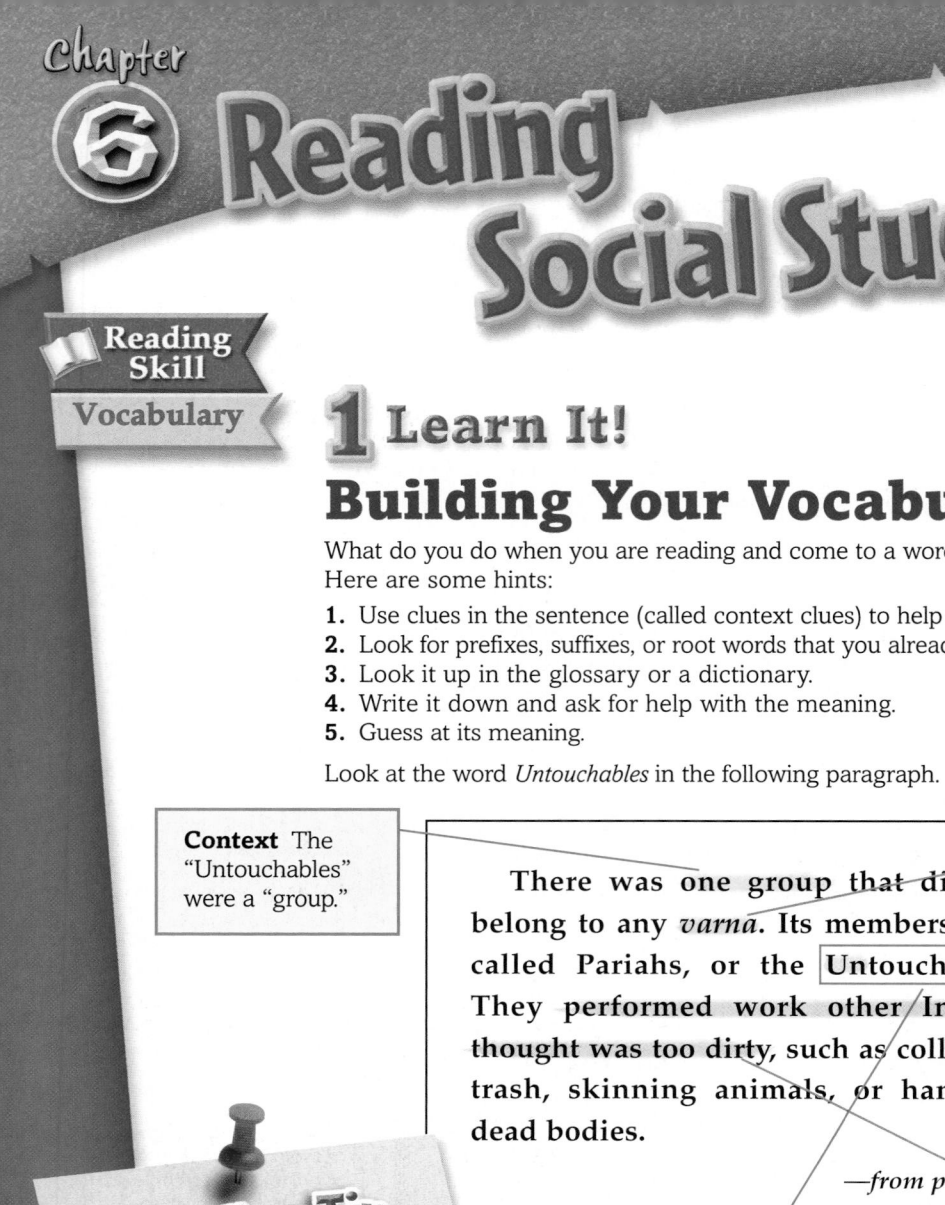

Chapter 6 Reading Social Studies

Reading Skill
Vocabulary

1 Learn It!

Building Your Vocabulary

What do you do when you are reading and come to a word you do not know? Here are some hints:

1. Use clues in the sentence (called context clues) to help you define it.
2. Look for prefixes, suffixes, or root words that you already know.
3. Look it up in the glossary or a dictionary.
4. Write it down and ask for help with the meaning.
5. Guess at its meaning.

Look at the word *Untouchables* in the following paragraph.

Context The "Untouchables" were a "group."

Context If you know what a *varna* is, it will help you figure out the meaning of *Untouchables*.

> There was one group that did not belong to any *varna*. Its members were called Pariahs, or the Untouchables. They performed work other Indians thought was too dirty, such as collecting trash, skinning animals, or handling dead bodies.
>
> —*from page 200*

Reading Tip

Read the paragraphs that appear before and after the word to help you understand its meaning.

192

Prefixes and Suffixes
You might know that the prefix **un-** means "not" and the suffix **-able** means "to be able to." You might guess that the meaning of *Untouchable* is an Indian who was not to be touched by others.

Context The fact that they performed the "dirty" work indicates how they were viewed by others in Indian society.

Reading Strategy **ACTIVATE PRIOR KNOWLEDGE**

Helping students activate their background knowledge enables them to make essential associations for increased vocabulary development. Put students in groups of four and give each student an index card. Call out a vocabulary term, such as "Hinduism" or "karma." For three minutes, have students brainstorm all the words they can that are related to the vocabulary term and record these on the card. When time is called, each student in the group should choose a word from the brainstormed list. One at a time, each student should share the word and explain how the word is related to the vocabulary term. This activity increases understanding of new concepts and activates background knowledge. L1/ EL

2 Practice It!
Defining Words

What are three things you could do to help you understand the meaning of the word *subcontinent* in this paragraph?

Read to Write
Take one word from the vocabulary bookmark that you make in the **Apply It!** activity. Find its definition. Then create a cartoon strip. Have one of the characters in your cartoon strip use the word correctly.

> Look at the map below. India looks like a diamond hanging from the bottom of Asia. India is a **subcontinent** (SUHB • KAHN • tuhn • uhnt) because even though it is part of Asia, huge mountains make a barrier between India and the rest of Asia. These mountains are the **Himalaya** (HIH • muh • LAY • uh), the highest mountains in the world.
>
> —*from page 195*

KARAKORAM RANGE

H I M A L A Y A

Mt. Everest
29,035 ft.
(8,850 m)

30°N

Indus R.

Ganges R.

INDIA

Bay of Bengal

Arabian Sea

3 Apply It!

Make a vocabulary bookmark using a 2-inch-wide strip of paper. As you read the chapter, write down words you do not know or want to find out more about.

193

2 Practice It!

Help students learn to develop a variety of ways to understand words.

Context—Encourage students to look for meaning in surrounding words and sentences.

Textual Aids—Point out that illustrations, maps, or lists might provide valuable clues to vocabulary.

Morphology—Tell students to keep a list of common prefixes, suffixes, and roots, along with their meanings, to help them unlock the meaning of new words.

Definition—Tell students meanings of words, and encourage them to ask parents, other students, or teachers to explain unfamiliar words. **L1/ EL**

3 Apply It!

Periodically collect students' vocabulary bookmarks as a way of monitoring vocabulary development. To help students recognize and understand words, make a game of using the words in a variety of ways. Form a "Vocabulary Team of the Week" that will be responsible for finding ways to incorporate new words into class discussions. The team can also create a weekly class vocabulary bookmark of words and concepts. **L2**

Reading Strategy ❯ READ TO WRITE

Drawing pictures of vocabulary words is an effective way for students to delve deeply into a word's full meaning. Play a game by calling out a new word and asking students to draw pictures of as many synonyms or antonyms as they can within five minutes. As students guess the words depicted in their classmates' drawings, list them on the board. This bank of words may be useful as students create their cartoon strips based on new vocabulary. **L2**

① FOCUS

SECTION OVERVIEW

This section describes how geography and climate affected the Harappans and the changes to India's civilization following the arrival of the Aryans.

BELLRINGER
SKILLBUILDER ACTIVITY

✎ Project **Daily Focus Skills Transparency 6–1** and have students answer questions. Discuss their responses.

Get Ready to Read!

Preteaching Vocabulary: Explain that Sanskrit was the language of the Aryans. These people conquered the Harappans who built the first Indian civilization. Sanskrit is no longer spoken, but three-quarters of Indians speak languages based on Sanskrit.

Answers to Graphic: declared cattle sacred; invented iron plow and improved farming; cleared jungles; built irrigation canals; brought Sanskrit language; introduced tribal organization and caste system

---

Section 1

India's First Civilizations

Get Ready to Read!

What's the Connection?
In India, just as in Egypt and Mesopotamia, the first civilizations developed in fertile river valleys.

Focusing on the Main Ideas
• Climate and geography influenced the rise of India's first civilization. *(page 195)*

• The Aryans introduced new ideas and technology to India. *(page 198)*

• The Aryans created a caste system that separated Indians into groups. *(page 199)*

Locating Places
Himalaya (HIH•muh•LAY•uh)
Ganges River (GAN•JEEZ)
Indus River (IHN•duhs)
Harappa (huh•RA•puh)
Mohenjo-Daro
(moh•HEHN•joh   DAHR•oh)

Meeting People
Aryans (AR•ee•uhnz)
Brahmans (BRAH•muhns)

Building Your Vocabulary
subcontinent
(SUHB•KAHN•tuhn•uhnt)
monsoon (mahn•SOON)
Sanskrit (SAN•SKRIHT)
raja (RAH•juh)
caste (KAST)
guru (GUR•oo)

Reading Strategy
Organizing Information Complete a diagram like the one below showing how the Aryans changed India.

Major Ways Aryans Changed India
⬇ ⬇ ⬇ ⬇

NATIONAL GEOGRAPHIC **When & Where?**

Khyber Pass • Harappa

Ganges R.

3000 B.C. **2000 B.C.** **1000 B.C.**

c. 3000 B.C.
India's first civilization begins

c. 1500 B.C.
Aryans invade India

c. 1000 B.C.
Aryans control northern India

SECTION RESOURCES

📁 **Reproducible Masters**
• Reproducible Lesson Plan 6–1
• Daily Lecture and Discussion Notes 6–1
• Vocabulary Activity 6–1
• Active Reading Note-Taking Guide 6–1
• Guided Reading Activity 6–1
• Section Quiz 6–1
• Reading Essentials and Study Guide 6–1

🖎 **Transparencies**
• Daily Focus Skills Transparency 6–1

Multimedia
◉ Interactive Tutor Self-Assessment CD-ROM
◉ ExamView® Pro Testmaker CD-ROM
◉ Presentation Plus! CD-ROM

The Land of India

Main Idea Climate and geography influenced the rise of India's first civilization.

Reading Focus Do you have tornadoes or hurricanes where you live? Read to find out how geography and weather affected India's first civilization.

Look at the map below. India looks like a diamond hanging from the bottom of Asia. India is a **subcontinent** (SUHB•KAHN•tuhn•uhnt) because even though it is part of Asia, huge mountains make a barrier between India and the rest of Asia. These mountains are the **Himalaya** (HIH•muh•LAY•uh), the highest mountains in the world.

Today, there are five nations that occupy the Indian subcontinent: India, Pakistan in the northwest, Nepal, Bhutan, and Bangladesh in the northeast.

India has two very fertile river valleys. Both are fed by the mountains in the north. When the snow in the Himalaya melts, water flows into the **Ganges River** (GAN•JEEZ) and the **Indus River** (IHN•duhs). If the water is controlled, the land near these rivers can be used for farming.

The Ganges River runs south of the Himalaya and flows into the Indian Ocean. The Indus River empties into the Arabian Sea. The area around the Indus is called the Indus River valley.

South of the river valleys is the dry and hilly Deccan Plateau. The eastern and western coasts of India are lush, fertile plains.

Monsoons (mahn•SOONZ) are an important part of the Indian climate. A monsoon is a strong wind that blows one direction in winter and the opposite direction in summer. The winter monsoon brings the cold, dry air of the mountains. The summer monsoon brings warm, wet air from the Arabian Sea, which produces drenching rains.

When the monsoon rains begin, many farmers celebrate. If the rains come on time and the rainy season lasts long enough, the crop will be good. If the rains are delayed, a drought will occur. This extended period

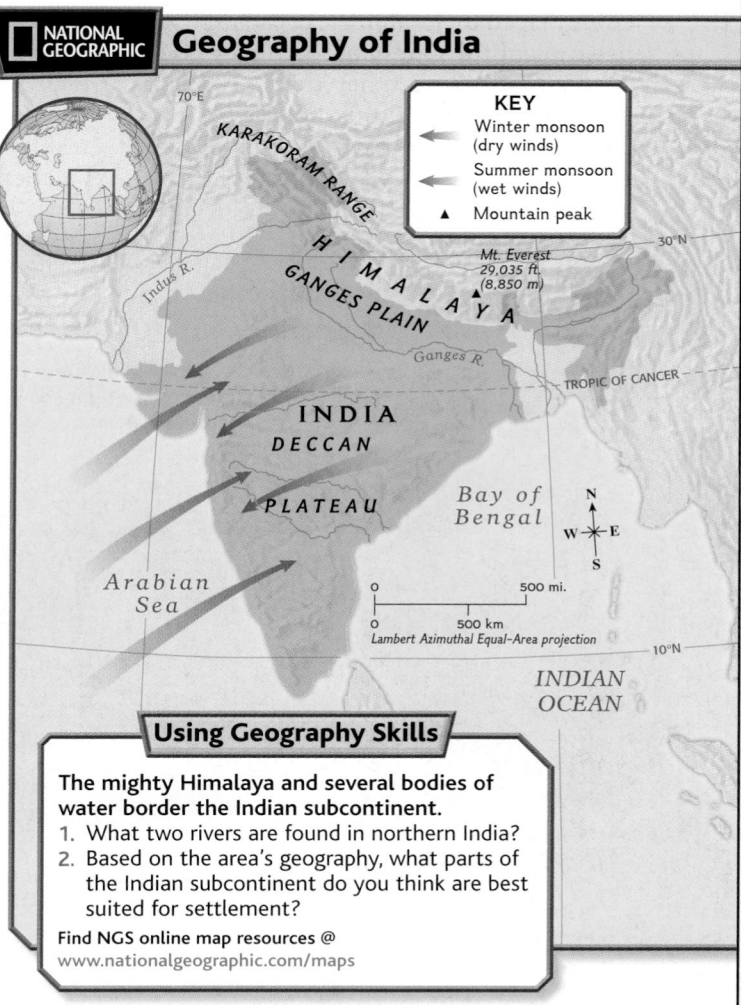

NATIONAL GEOGRAPHIC

Geography of India

KEY
← Winter monsoon (dry winds)
← Summer monsoon (wet winds)
▲ Mountain peak

KARAKORAM RANGE
70°E
Indus R.
HIMALAYA
GANGES PLAIN
Ganges R.
Mt. Everest 29,035 ft. (8,850 m)
30°N
TROPIC OF CANCER
INDIA
DECCAN
PLATEAU
Bay of Bengal
Arabian Sea
N W E S
0 500 mi.
0 500 km
Lambert Azimuthal Equal-Area projection
10°N
INDIAN OCEAN

Using Geography Skills

The mighty Himalaya and several bodies of water border the Indian subcontinent.
1. What two rivers are found in northern India?
2. Based on the area's geography, what parts of the Indian subcontinent do you think are best suited for settlement?

Find NGS online map resources @ www.nationalgeographic.com/maps

---

② TEACH

Making a Map Explain to students that drawing a map from memory is one way to help themselves remember the location of important geographic features. First, give students outline maps of India or let them trace the map on page 195. List on the board several features mentioned in "The Land of India," such as the Himalaya and the Ganges River. Next, allow students time to study the map on page 195. Then ask them to draw the listed features on their maps from memory and compare their maps with the map in the book. Finally, lead a discussion about strategies that helped students accurately remember the features' locations. **L2**

Daily Lecture and Discussion Notes 6–1

Use **Daily Lecture and Discussion Notes 6–1** for an outline of key concepts found in the section.

Using Geography Skills

Answers:
1. Indus and Ganges Rivers
2. the Ganges and Indus River valleys and coastal areas

Reading Strategy · READING THE TEXT

Varying Reading Rate In this section, students will experience using different reading rates. Point out that the geography discussed in "The Land of India" is very detailed. Read aloud the third and fourth paragraphs, stopping as you encounter geographic features, such as the Himalaya, the Ganges, and the Indus. Locate them on the map on this page. Explain that using the map helps readers better understand the text. Then have students read paragraph five using this strategy. Ask them to describe how they employed it. Next, have students read paragraphs two and three in "India's First Civilization." Ask them if they read this material more quickly, at the same speed, or more slowly than the information about India's geography and why. **L1/EL**

Reading Support L1/ EL

Use **Vocabulary Activity 6–1** to review important terms in the section.

Reading Strategy

Writing Activity

In the area where the Harappans lived, there was little stone and not much timber. They built with small, handmade mud bricks that would fire well. The mortar between the bricks was made of mud, which wind, sun, and salt can wear away easily. Have students review Egyptian building techniques discussed in Chapter 2. Then have them write a paragraph to compare the kinds of buildings that the Harappans and the Egyptians built. Students should include how natural resources affected the civilizations' architectural choices. **L3**

More About the Photo

Both Mohenjo-Daro and Harappa were built on a grid pattern. This improved drainage and helped in city-management.

Caption Answer: mud bricks

---

without rain can be disastrous for farmers. Few crops will be harvested and many people will starve.

India's First Civilization

In earlier chapters, you learned about civilizations that began in river valleys. Indian civilization also began in a river valley.

India's first civilization grew up near the Indus River. When the summer monsoon began, the river rose higher and higher. When the river flooded nearby land, it left behind rich, fertile soil.

Farmers used the rich soil to grow crops to feed their families. Because people had a plentiful supply of food, they could spend time doing other things, such as making tools or building houses. As people began to trade their extra food and goods with other people, their wealth grew. This allowed them to build larger and larger cities.

India's first civilization in the Indus River valley began about 3000 B.C. and lasted until 1500 B.C. More than a thousand villages and towns were part of this civilization, which stretched from the Himalaya to the Arabian Sea. We know something about the way these people lived from studying the ruins of two major cities, **Harappa** (huh•RA•puh) and **Mohenjo-Daro** (moh•HEHN•joh DAHR•oh). The civilization of this time is called the Harappan or Indus civilization.

Harappa and Mohenjo-Daro

Harappa and Mohenjo-Daro were large cities for their time. The well-planned cities had as many as 35,000 people. A fortress was built on a brick platform to keep guard over the residents. There were wide main streets and smaller side streets. A wall surrounded each neighborhood, and narrow lanes separated the houses.

Early Indian Civilization

The ruins of Mohenjo-Daro (below) show a carefully planned city. The picture to the right shows a typical house in the city. *From what material were most of the houses in Mohenjo-Daro made?*

▲ Harappan priest-king

Necklace from ▶ Mohenjo-Daro

Model of oxcart from ▶ Mohenjo-Daro

DIFFERENTIATED INSTRUCTION

Visual/Spatial: To help students remember information about the Harappans, have them draw a simple city plan based on material in the section.

English Learners: Help students select 12 characteristics of Harappan history, life, and society. Ask students to draw pictographs for each item and label them in English and in their native language.

Gifted and Talented: Ask students to research information about the geographic extent of the Harappan civilization and share it with the class. Remind them to include dates, when possible, for their findings.

🗀 Refer to *Inclusion Strategies for the Middle School Social Studies Classroom* in the TCR.

Most houses had flat roofs and were built with mud bricks that were baked in ovens. Some houses were larger than others, but they all had a similar layout. There was a courtyard in the middle and smaller rooms around it.

These ancient city dwellers had some surprising conveniences. Wells supplied water, and residents even had indoor bathrooms. Wastewater flowed to drains under the streets, running through pipes to pits outside the city walls. Houses also had garbage chutes connected to a bin in the street. It is likely the city government was well organized to be able to provide so many services.

Harappan Society Because the Harappans left no written records, we do not know much about their society or government. From the ruins, though, we can tell that the royal palace and the temple were both enclosed in the fortress. This reveals that religion and politics were closely connected.

Most Harappans were farmers. They grew rice, wheat, barley, peas, and cotton. City dwellers made copper and bronze tools, clay pottery, and cotton cloth, as well as jewelry from gold, shells, and ivory. Archaeologists have also found many toys among the ruins, such as small monkeys that could be made to climb up a string.

It is likely that the Harappans began trading with the Mesopotamians about 2300 B.C. Some Harappan sailors followed the coastline and crossed the Arabian Sea, and others traveled overland.

One item rarely found in the ruins of Harappan cities was weapons. This suggests that the Harappans were not only prosperous but also peaceful.

✓**Reading Check** **Explain** How is India separated from the rest of Asia?

✓**Reading Check**

Answer: It is a subcontinent protected by seas and vast mountains.

CONNECTING ACROSS TIME

Point out that authorities in a Harappan city provided various services for their inhabitants—wells for water, a sewage system, and garbage collection. Ask students to compare these services with those that local communities provide for their citizens today. **L1/ EL**

Roofs were used to dry crops in the sun. The dried crops were then placed in cool storage rooms in the house.

Outer walls of buildings had no windows. This helped prevent the hot summer sun from heating the insides of the house.

Bathrooms had an advanced drainage system. Drains started from houses and joined the main sewer, which carried the water out of town.

Almost every building had its own well. Cool water was pulled up when needed.

CRITICAL THINKING ACTIVITY

Making Inferences The Aryans brought a new language, Sanskrit, to India. Many languages are spoken in modern India. Have students research what they are. *(They include: Hindi [official], English [official], Bengali, Gujarati, Kashmiri, Malayalam, Marathi, Oriya, Punjabi, Tamil, Telugu, Urdu, Kannada, Assamese, Sanskrit, and Sindhi.)* Have students discuss how having a population that speaks many different languages might affect efforts to unify India. *(Answers may include that speaking several languages might make it difficult for people to think of themselves as part of one nation because they identify with the language group to which they belong.)* **L3**

The Aryans

Main Idea The Aryans introduced new ideas and technology to India.

Reading Focus What would your life be like without cars or computers? Read to find out how new ideas and technology affected the Indians.

The Harappan civilization collapsed about 1500 B.C. Historians think that several earthquakes and floods damaged the cities. Then the Indus River changed its course, killing many people and forcing others to flee the area. In the years that followed, a group of people called the **Aryans** (AR•ee•uhnz) began settling in the region. Soon a new civilization emerged.

Who Were the Aryans? The Aryans lived in central Asia where they raised and herded animals. The Aryans were not a race or ethnic group. They were part of a larger group of people historians refer to as Indo-Europeans. The Indo-Europeans all spoke similar languages. Some migrated south to India and Iran. Others went west to Europe.

Cattle were a prized possession because they provided meat, milk, and butter. Cattle were so important that the Aryans even used them as money. Individual wealth was measured by the number of cattle a person owned.

The Aryans were good warriors. They were expert horse riders and hunters. They had metal-tipped spears and wooden chariots, which they sometimes used to invade nearby villages for food.

After 2000 B.C., the Aryans began leaving their home territory. They moved in waves, and some groups crossed through the mountain passes in the Himalaya. They entered the Indus River valley around 1500 B.C.

Around 1000 B.C., the Aryans began expanding across the Punjab and Ganges Plains and south into the Deccan Plateau. Their civilization spread to all of India except the southern tip.

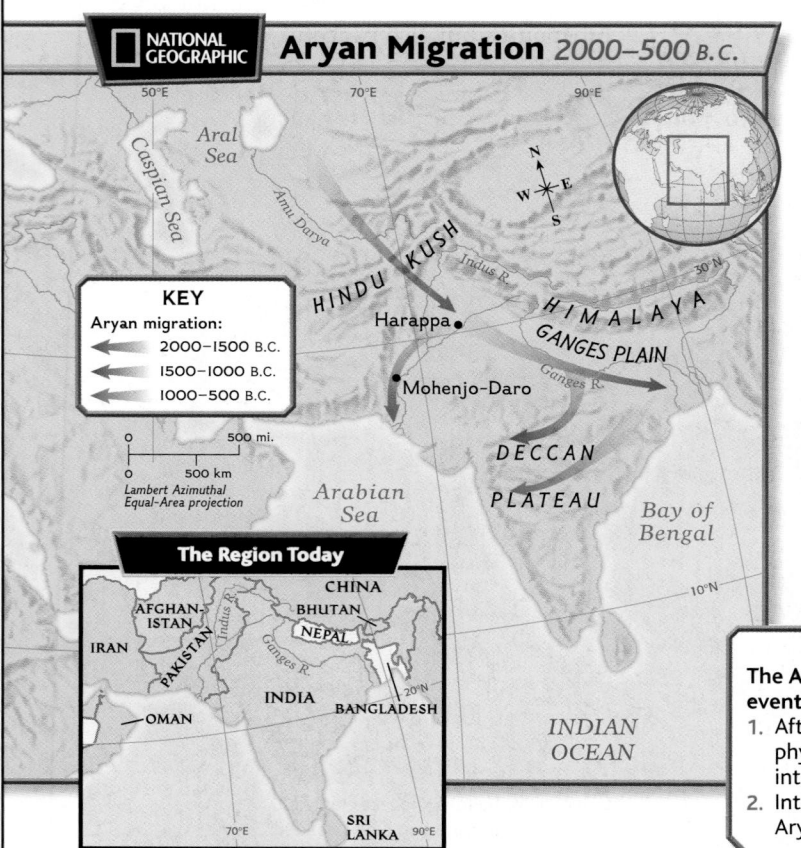

NATIONAL GEOGRAPHIC

Aryan Migration 2000–500 B.C.

KEY
Aryan migration:
2000–1500 B.C.
1500–1000 B.C.
1000–500 B.C.

Lambert Azimuthal Equal-Area projection

The Region Today

198   CHAPTER 6   Early India

INTERDISCIPLINARY CONNECTIONS ACTIVITY

Language Arts According to Hindu tradition, Indian history began with a flood. Read this account to the class: One morning when Manu was washing his hands in a stream, a small fish begged him to protect it from larger fish, saying "Rear me. I will save thee." Manu did. One day the fish warned Manu that a flood was coming. It told him to prepare a ship and to board it when the flood came. Manu did and the fish took the ship to a northern mountain. There the fish told Manu to climb the mountain until the floodwaters went down. Manu did and only he lived. Organize students into small groups and have them compare the Hindu story with the story of "Noah and the Ark" in Chapter 3. **L2**

The Aryans Bring Change When the Aryans arrived in India, they no longer lived as nomads. They became farmers but continued to raise cattle. Eventually, the Aryans would declare that cattle were sacred and forbid them to be used as food.

Because Aryans were skilled ironworkers, they improved farming in India. They invented an iron plow to help clear India's many jungles and built canals to irrigate. They slowly turned the Ganges River valley into good farmland.

India's varied climate supported many types of crops. In the north, farmers grew grains such as wheat, barley, and millet. Rice was grown in the river valleys. In the south, there was a mix of crops, including spices such as pepper, ginger, and cinnamon.

The Aryans also brought a new language to India. As nomads, they had no written language, but in India they developed a written language called **Sanskrit** (SAN•SKRIHT). Now the songs, stories, poems, and prayers that Aryans had known for many centuries could be written down.

The Aryans were organized into tribes. Each tribe was led by a **raja** (RAH•juh), or prince. The rajas ran their own small kingdoms, which often fought among themselves. Rajas fought over cattle and treasure and over women kidnapped from other states. These small rival kingdoms existed in India for about a thousand years, from 1500 B.C. to 400 B.C.

✓**Reading Check** **Analyze** Why do you think nomads like the Aryans were great warriors?

Web Activity Visit jat.glencoe.com and click on *Chapter 6—Student Web Activity* to learn more about India.

Society in Ancient India

Main Idea The Aryans created a caste system that separated Indians into groups.

Reading Focus Have you ever wondered why some people seem to be treated differently than other people? As you read, try to find out why this idea was accepted in India.

One of the results of the Aryan arrival in India was the development of a caste system. A **caste** (KAST) is a social group that someone is born into and cannot change.

HISTORY MAKERS

Development of Sanskrit c. 1500 B.C.

Sanskrit was the language of ancient India. It developed into Hindi—the most widely used language in India today. The earliest example of written Sanskrit appears in the four Vedas—the oldest writings of the Hindu religion. Sanskrit was used until about A.D. 1100.

Sanskrit Influences on English Words			
Sanskrit word	Definition	English word	Definition
Nava	Ship	Naval or navy	A fleet of ships
Dua	Two	Dual	Consisting of two parts
Deva	God	Divine	Divine God; relating to being a god

CHAPTER 6 Early India **199**

HISTORY MAKERS

Although Sanskrit and English seem markedly different, they share a common ancestry. Have students study the chart and write a short paragraph describing the similarities they see.

Reading Support L1/ EL

Assign **Guided Reading Activity 6–1** to help students organize the information in the section.

✓**Reading Check**

Answer: They had horses and were skilled with metal.

Objectives and answers to the student activity can be found in the **Web Activity Lesson Plan** feature at jat.glencoe.com

---

EXTENDING THE CONTENT

Language Origins Ancient Greeks and Romans who studied languages understood that their languages were related. In later years philologists, people who study languages, realized that other European languages, such as French and Spanish, were also related to Latin. In the 1500s, Europeans started learning Sanskrit. In 1786 Sir William Jones stated, "no philologer could examine them [Greek, Latin, and Sanskrit] without believing them to have sprung from a common source." Other languages are also related to Sanskrit—Germanic languages, such as English and Dutch; Celtic languages, such as Irish and Welsh; Iranian languages, plus others. These languages are part of the Indo-European language group spoken in most of Europe and in a large part of southwest and South Asia.

More About the Art

The caste system seems foreign to people in the United States, where the common belief is that anyone can change his or her social class.

Caption Answer: possibly because the Aryans believed they were better than the peoples they conquered and wanted to control them

③ ASSESS

Assign Section 1 Review as homework or as an in-class activity.

⊛ Have students use the **Interactive Tutor Self-Assessment CD-ROM** to review the section.

Assessment L2

Assign **Section 1 Quiz** to assess mastery of the material found in the section.

Reading Support L1/ EL

Assign **Reading Essentials and Study Guide 6–1** to help students review section material.

◀ A Brahman

Today, Untouchables refer to ▶ themselves as *Dalit*, which means "oppressed." *Why did the Aryans create the caste system?*

Early India's Social System

Brahmans Priests
Kshatriyas Warriors, rulers
Vaisyas Common people
Sudras Unskilled laborers, servants
Pariahs Untouchables

Social Classes of Indian Society The thousands of different *jati* in Indian society were grouped together into four classes called *varnas.* The top two varnas were **Brahmans** (BRAH•muhns) and Kshatriyas (KSHA•tree•uhs). Brahmans were the priests—the only people who could perform religious ceremonies. The Kshatriyas were warriors who ran the government and army.

On the next level down were the Vaisyas (VYSH•yuhs), or commoners. Vaisyas were usually farmers and merchants. Below the Vaisyas came the Sudras (SOO•druhs). Sudras were manual laborers and servants and had few rights. Most Indians belonged to the Sudra caste.

There was one group that did not belong to any *varna.* Its members were called Pariahs, or the Untouchables. They performed work other Indians thought was too dirty, such as collecting trash, skinning animals, or handling dead bodies.

Life for an Untouchable was very hard. Most Indians believed that being near an Untouchable was harmful, so they forced them to live apart from others. When Untouchables traveled, they had to tap two

A caste dictates what job you will have, whom you can marry, and with whom you can socialize. In India, the word for caste (a term used by Portuguese merchants) is *jati.* Thousands of *jati* exist in India.

Why was a caste system created? No one is sure, but ideas about skin color were probably part of it. The Aryans were a light-skinned people. They thought they were better than the dark-skinned people they had encountered in India. This idea was wrong, but the Aryans believed it.

Another reason the Aryans might have created the caste system was because the people they encountered in India outnumbered them. The caste system set the rules for everyone's behavior. This helped the Aryans stay in control.

200   CHAPTER 6   Early India

CITIZENSHIP AND YOU

Being a Harappan or an Aryan Citizen Because many Harappans lived in planned cities, they may have had rules or laws for behavior. For example, the location of their garbage chutes suggests that people were supposed to deposit their garbage in a particular place. The arrangement of the streets and the use of oxcarts may indicate that there were traffic rules to follow. Unlike the Harappans, however, the Aryans came from a nomadic society. **Ask:** What might Aryans have believed were characteristics of a good citizen? *(being independent, but loyal to the raja)* What are characteristics of a good citizen in the United States today? *(Possible answers: honesty, obeying the law, voting, paying taxes, serving in the military)* How might you be a good citizen? *(Answers will vary but might focus on community or school activities such as clean-up projects or raising money for a good cause.)* **L2**

sticks together so that everyone would hear them coming and have time to move away.

The Role of Men and Women In ancient India, the family was the center of life. Grandparents, parents, and children all lived together in an extended family. The oldest man in the family was in charge.

Men had many more rights than women. Unless there were no sons in a family, only a man could inherit property. Only men could go to school or become priests.

In families at the top of Indian society, a boy had a **guru** (GUR•oo), or teacher, until he went to the city for more education. Young men from these families could marry only when they had finished 12 years of schooling.

In India, parents arranged marriages for their children. Even today, parents arrange the majority of marriages in India. Boys and girls often married in their teens. Some were as young as 13. Divorce was almost never allowed, but if a couple could not have children, the husband could marry a second wife.

One custom shows how the lives of Indian men were considered more important than the lives of Indian women. In India, people were cremated, or burned, when they died. When a man from a prominent family died, his wife was expected to leap into the flames. This practice was called suttee (suh•TEE). If the wife resisted and did not kill herself, it was a great shame. Everyone would avoid the woman from then on.

 Identify What were the five major groups in Indian society?

Section 1 Review

Reading Summary
Review the Main Ideas
- India's first civilization, including the cities of Harappa and Mohenjo-Daro, developed in the fertile Indus River valley.

- The Aryans, a group of nomadic herders, migrated into the northern part of India by about 1000 B.C. They brought the iron plow and the Sanskrit language to India.

- India's caste system divided people into rigid social and economic classes. Ancient Indian society favored men over women.

What Did You Learn?
1. Describe the cities of Harappa and Mohenjo-Daro.
2. Why are monsoons important to Indian farmers?

Critical Thinking
3. **Cause and Effect** What caused the collapse of Harappan civilization?
4. **Cause and Effect** Draw a diagram to show how the Aryans changed the lifestyle of the Indians.

5. **Contrast** How did the Aryan and Harappan lifestyles differ?
6. **Explain** How did India's social classes, or varnas, shape India's society?
7. **Descriptive Writing** Write a description of the city of Harappa or Mohenjo-Daro that could have been used to attract residents to that city in ancient India.
8. **Reading** **Vocabulary** Explain how the suffix in the word *plentiful* can help you determine its meaning.

CHAPTER 6   Early India   **201**

ENRICH

Issues of caste have remained a problem up until the present time. Discuss why the caste system would help the Aryans stay in control. (*If different groups could not intermingle with each other or rise in station, they could not plan to take control away from the Aryans.*) **L2**

Reading Check

Answer: Brahmans, Kshatriyas, Vaisyas, Sudras, Untouchables

To help students understand section material, have them visit **Study Central**™ at jat.glencoe.com

RETEACH

Have students describe the changes that the Aryans brought to India. **L1**

④ CLOSE

Ask students to discuss the influence of geographic factors on the Harappans and the Aryans. **L1/EL**

SECTION 1 REVIEW ANSWERS

1. Harappa and Mohenjo-Daro were planned cities with wide main streets and a wall around each neighborhood. Each mud brick house had a flat roof and was laid out around a courtyard. Each city had public wells, a sewage system, and garbage disposal.
2. They cause soil-enriching floods.
3. earthquakes, floods, the Indus River changing its course, the Aryan invasions
4. Charts should reflect information in the text.
5. Harappans were city-dwellers; Aryans were warlike nomads.
6. They shaped every aspect of Indian society.
7. Answers should demonstrate understanding of the text.
8. Here, -*ful* means "much"—hence, "much of plenty."

① FOCUS

SECTION OVERVIEW

The religion of Hinduism is based on the beliefs of the Aryans. Buddhism, a new religion, was popular with many people in India and other areas of Asia.

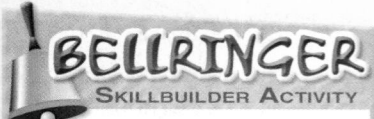

BELLRINGER
SKILLBUILDER ACTIVITY

✎ Project **Daily Focus Skills Transparency 6–2** and have students answer questions. Discuss their responses.

Get Ready to Read!

Preteaching Vocabulary:
According to Hinduism, a soul passes through many lives—both human and animal—on its journey to union with Brahman. As a result, all life is sacred. This belief determines how Hindus treat animals. It is related to the Aryan belief that cows are sacred.

Answers to Graphic: search for universal spirit called Brahman; reincarnation; dharma, or divine law; karma, or consequences of actions

Section 2
Hinduism and Buddhism

Get Ready to Read!

What's the Connection?
Much of Indian civilization is based on Aryan ideas and culture, which you learned about in the last section. One of the most important and long-lasting contributions of the Aryans is the main religion of India, Hinduism.

Focusing on the Main Ideas
• Hinduism grew out of the ancient beliefs of the Aryans. *(page 203)*

• A new religion, Buddhism, appealed to many people in India and other parts of Asia. *(page 205)*

Locating Places
Nepal (nuh•PAWL)
Tibet (tuh•BEHT)

Meeting People
Siddhartha Gautama (sih•DAHR• tuh GOW•tuh•muh)
Dalai Lama (DAH•LY LAH•muh)

Building Your Vocabulary
Hinduism (HIHN•doo•IH•zuhm)
Brahman (BRAH•muhn)
reincarnation
  (REE•ihn•kahr•NAY•shuhn)
dharma (DAHR•muh)
karma (KAHR•muh)
Buddhism (BOO•DIH•zuhm)
nirvana (nihr•VAH•nuh)
theocracy (thee•AH•kruh•see)

Reading Strategy
Summarizing Information Create a web diagram like the one below. In the ovals, identify major beliefs of Hinduism.

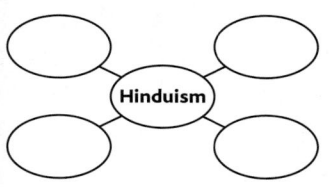

NATIONAL GEOGRAPHIC **When & Where?**

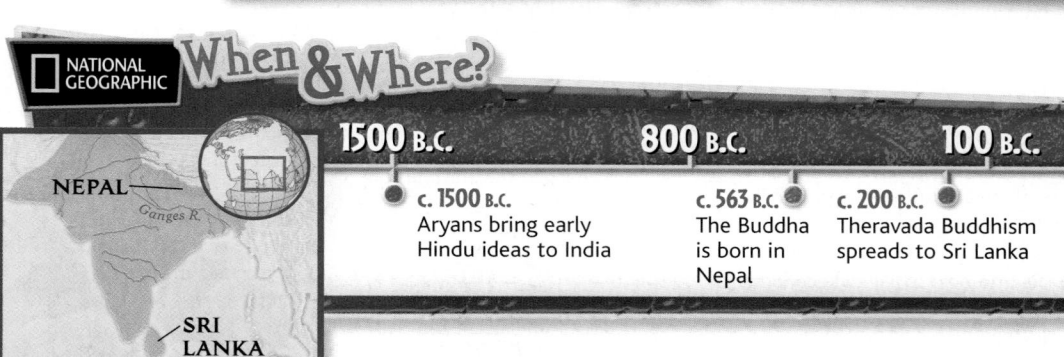

1500 B.C.	800 B.C.	100 B.C.
c. 1500 B.C. Aryans bring early Hindu ideas to India	c. 563 B.C. The Buddha is born in Nepal	c. 200 B.C. Theravada Buddhism spreads to Sri Lanka

NEPAL
Ganges R.
SRI LANKA

SECTION RESOURCES

📁 **Reproducible Masters**
 • Reproducible Lesson Plan 6–2
 • Daily Lecture and Discussion Notes 6–2
 • Vocabulary Activity 6–2
 • Active Reading Note-Taking Guide 6–2
 • Guided Reading Activity 6–2
 • Section Quiz 6–2
 • Reading Essentials and Study Guide 6–2

 Transparencies
 • Daily Focus Skills Transparency 6–2

Multimedia
 🔘 Interactive Tutor Self-Assessment CD-ROM
 🔘 Exam*View*® Pro Testmaker CD-ROM
 🔘 Presentation Plus! CD-ROM
 🔘 Glencoe BookLink CD-ROM

Hinduism

Main Idea Hinduism grew out of the ancient beliefs of the Aryans.

Reading Focus Have you ever wondered why most people try to behave properly or do good deeds? As you read this section, find out how a Hindu would answer this question.

Hinduism (HIHN•doo•IH•zuhm) is one of the oldest religions in the world, and today it is the third largest. It began with the religion of the Aryans, who arrived in India about 1500 B.C. The Aryans believed in many gods and goddesses who controlled the forces of nature. We know about Aryan religion from their ancient hymns and poetry, especially their epics, or long poems.

For centuries, the priests, or Brahmans, recited these works, and much later they were written down in Sanskrit. Over the centuries, Aryan religion changed. It borrowed some religious ideas from the people the Aryans conquered in India. This mix of beliefs eventually became Hinduism.

Early Hinduism Hinduism grew out of the religious customs of many people over thousands of years. This might explain why Hinduism has thousands of gods and goddesses. Hindus tend to think of all gods and goddesses as different parts of one universal spirit. This universal spirit is called **Brahman** (BRAH•muhn).

The search for a universal spirit is described in the ancient religious writings known as the Upanishads (oo•PAH•nih•SHADZ). Those writings say that every living being has a soul that wants to be reunited with Brahman and that this happens when a person dies.

The Upanishads describe how a person unites with Brahman: A soul that becomes one with Brahman is like a lump of salt thrown into water. The lump of salt is gone, but the water tastes salty. The salt has become part of the water.

What Is Karma? Hindus believe that a soul is not joined to the Brahman immediately after a person dies. Instead, a person must pass through many lives to be united

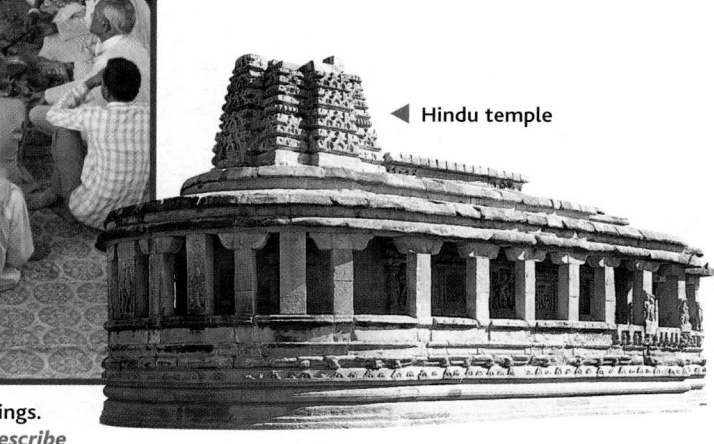

◀ Hindu temple

▲ Hindus meet to discuss holy writings. *What ancient religious writings describe the search for a universal spirit?*

203

Reading Strategy

Comparing Religious Beliefs Have students compare Hinduism to the religions of other ancient peoples they have already studied, such as the Egyptians and the Israelites. List the similarities and differences in a chart on the board. Then have students state generalizations based on this information. Have students copy the chart to compare to Buddhism later. **L2**

Understanding Charts

Answers:
1. Krishna
2. It is an ancient religion that developed from the religious customs of many people.

Reading Check

Answer: The consequences of how you live are called karma. If you live a good life and have good karma, your next life will be closer to Brahman.

Major Hindu Gods and Goddesses

Name	Realm
Brahma	creator of the world
Vishnu	preserver of the world
Siva	destroyer of the world
Ganesha	lord of existing beings; remover of obstacles
Krishna	teacher of the world
Lakshmi	goddess of light, beauty, good fortune, and wealth
Surya	god of the sun
Indra	king of the gods; ruler of the heavens and sky
Saraswati	goddess of knowledge, music, and creative arts
Parvati	universal mother

Ganesha ▶

◀ Siva

Understanding Charts

Brahma, Vishnu, and Siva are considered the three main Hindu gods.
1. Which god is known as the "teacher of the world"?
2. **Conclude** Why does Hinduism have so many gods?

with Brahman. On its journey, a soul might be reborn into a higher *varna* or *jati*. If a person lived a bad life, he or she might be reborn into a lower *varna* or *jati*.

This idea of passing through many lives to reach the Brahman is called **reincarnation** (REE•ihn•kahr•NAY•shuhn). It is very important in Hinduism and it influences how Hindus live their daily lives. It even affects how they treat animals because they consider all life sacred.

To earn the reward of a better life in their next life, Hindus believe they must perform their duty. **Dharma** (DAHR•muh) is the divine law. It requires people to perform the duties of their *jati*. A farmer has different duties than a priest and men have different duties than women.

The consequences of how a person lives are known as **karma** (KAHR•muh). If Hindus do their duty and live a good life, they will have good karma. This will move them closer to the Brahman in their next life.

How did the belief in reincarnation affect Indians? For one thing, it made them more accepting of the *varna* and *jati* system. People believed they had to be happy with their role in life. A dedicated Hindu believes that the people in a higher *varna* are superior and that they are supposed to be on top. The belief in reincarnation gave hope to everyone, even servants. If servants did their duty, they might be reborn into a higher social class in their next life.

✔ **Reading Check** **Explain** How is karma related to reincarnation?

DIFFERENTIATED INSTRUCTION

Auditory/Musical: Pair students and have them take turns reading aloud paragraphs in "Buddhism." After each paragraph, have partners identify the main idea in the paragraph and record it. When a paragraph contains vocabulary words, pairs should also discuss and record their meaning.

English Learners: Record a reading of the subsection "Buddhism." Group an English-speaking student with one or more English learners. Have students play the tape and read along with the text. As English learners encounter unfamiliar words, tell the English-speaking student to stop the tape and explain the meaning of the words.

Gifted and Talented: Ask pairs of students to research the Buddha's teachings. Ask each pair to share with the class one teaching that they found interesting and explain why they chose it.

Buddhism

Main Idea A new religion, Buddhism, appealed to many people in India and other parts of Asia.

Reading Focus What do you think makes a person free and happy? Find out how the Buddha answered this important question as you read this section.

By 600 B.C., many Indians began to question Hindu ideas. The Brahman priests seemed to care only about their temple ceremonies and not about the needs of the people. Ordinary Hindus wanted a simpler, more spiritual religion. Many would find what they needed in **Buddhism** (BOO•DIH•zuhm), a new religion founded by **Siddhartha Gautama** (sih•DAHR•tuh GOW•tuh•muh).

Who Is the Buddha? Prince Siddhartha Gautama was born around 563 B.C. in a small kingdom near the Himalaya. Today, this area is in southern **Nepal** (nuh•PAWL).

Siddhartha seemed to have it all. He was wealthy and handsome, happily married, and had a fine new son. Then one day he decided to explore the kingdom beyond the palace walls. As he traveled, he became very upset. He saw beggars, people who were ill, and people broken down by age with no home and nowhere to go. For the first time, he was truly aware of suffering.

Then and there, Siddhartha decided to seek an answer to this great riddle: Why did people suffer and how could their suffering be cured? He left his family and riches and began his search. At first he lived like a hermit, fasting and sleeping on the hard ground. Siddhartha nearly starved, but he still had no answer to his questions.

Then he decided to meditate for as long as it took to get the answer. Legend tells us that Siddhartha sat under a tree to meditate, and after 49 days, he finally understood. It was as if he had seen a great light.

▲ This shrine in northern India marks the location where it is believed the Buddha delivered his first sermon. *With what groups of Indians did the Buddha's message become popular?*

Siddhartha spent the rest of his life wandering the countryside and telling people what he had discovered. His lessons about life and the nature of suffering became known as Buddhism. To his followers, he became known as the Buddha, or "Enlightened One."

What Is Buddhism? To understand the Buddha's ideas, one first has to see the world as he did. Like any good Hindu, Siddhartha did not think that the normal, everyday world was real. Trees, houses, animals, the sky, and the oceans were just illusions. So were poverty and sickness, pain and sorrow.

Siddhartha believed that the only way to find the truth about the world was to give up all desires. By giving up the desire for fame, the desire for money, and the desire for all worldly things, pain and sorrow would vanish.

If a person gave up all desires, he or she would reach **nirvana** (nihr•VAH•nuh). Nirvana is not a place but a state of wisdom. The word *nirvana* came from the Sanskrit word for blowing out a candle flame.

CHAPTER 6   Early India   **205**

CONNECTING ACROSS TIME

Siddhartha wanted to help the sick, the homeless, and others who suffered. His teachings about life and suffering led to a new religion. Siddhartha hoped his teachings would improve humans' situation in this world and the next. Have students discuss how other religions they have studied and religions they are familiar with today address social problems. **L1/ EL**

Writing Activity ✏

Hindus believe that religion is not one set of particular beliefs, since religious truth is beyond humans' ability to state it. Hindus tend to distinguish themselves from people who belong to other religions by the way they worship. It is possible to be a Hindu and to belong to another religion. Ask students to write a paragraph comparing these attitudes toward religion with those of another religion with which they are familiar. **L3**

> **Caption Answer:** the Untouchables and lower-caste Indians

Reading Support L1/ EL

Assign **Guided Reading Activity 6–2** to help students organize the information in the section.

CRITICAL THINKING ACTIVITY

Comparing and Contrasting Point out to the class that different religions often have some similar teachings even though the religions may be generally very different from one another. Compare Judaism and Buddhism by having small groups locate the Ten Commandments either in a book or on the Internet and then compare them with Buddha's Eightfold Path. Groups should look for similarities and differences. Students should consider whether the intent of a rule in one religion is the same as a similar rule in the other religion. Groups should also look at each set of rules as a whole and decide if there are any differences in emphasis between them. Ask groups to record their findings. As a class, discuss what students found. **L3**

Primary Source

According to one story, a highly respected Brahman named Sonadanda went to debate the Buddha accompanied by hundreds of people. Instead of winning, he and many others became followers of Buddha.

Answer:
wait until it is given

③ ASSESS

Assign Section 2 Review as homework or as an in-class activity.

⊚ Have students use the **Interactive Tutor Self-Assessment CD-ROM** to review the section.

Assessment L2

Assign **Section 2 Quiz** to assess mastery of the material found in the section.

Reading Support L1/ EL

Assign **Reading Essentials and Study Guide 6–2** to help students review section material.

Primary Source — Morality in the Eightfold Path

This passage describes the way a person should act according to the Eightfold Path.

▲ The Buddha

"He avoids the killing of living beings. . . . He avoids stealing, and abstains from [avoids] taking what is not given to him. Only what is given to him he takes, waiting till it is given; and he lives with a heart honest and pure. . . . He avoids lying. . . . He speaks the truth, is devoted to the truth, reliable, worthy of confidence, no deceiver of men."

—*The Word of the Buddha*, Nyanatiloka, trans.

DBQ Document-Based Question

According to the passage, what is the correct way to accept something?

The heart of the Buddha's teachings is contained in the Four Noble Truths. The Four Noble Truths are:

1. *Life is full of suffering.*
2. *People suffer because they desire worldly things and self-satisfaction.*
3. *The way to end suffering is to stop desiring things.*
4. *The only way to stop desiring things is to follow the Eightfold Path.*

The Buddha's fourth truth says people should follow eight steps to eliminate suffering. The Buddha's Eightfold Path was this:

1. *Know and understand the Four Noble Truths.*
2. *Give up worldly things and don't harm others.*
3. *Tell the truth, don't gossip, and don't speak badly of others.*
4. *Don't commit evil acts, like killing, stealing, or living an unclean life.*
5. *Do rewarding work.*
6. *Work for good and oppose evil.*
7. *Make sure your mind keeps your senses under control.*
8. *Practice meditation as a way of understanding reality.*

One reason the Buddha's ideas became popular was that he did not accept the *varna* and *jati* systems. A person's place in life depended on the person, he thought. The Buddha did believe in reincarnation, but with a difference. If people wanted to stop being reborn into new lives, the Buddha said, they would only have to follow his Eightfold Path.

Many people liked the Buddha's message, especially Untouchables and lower-class Indians. For the first time, these groups heard that they, too, could reach enlightenment.

Buddhism in Southeast Asia For more than 40 years, the Buddha preached his ideas. Disciples gathered around him, and after his death, they spread his message all over Asia.

As more and more people practiced Buddhism, disagreements arose about the Buddha's ideas. Finally, Buddhists split into two groups. The first was Theravada Buddhism. *Theravada* means "teachings of the elders." It sees the Buddha as a great teacher, not a god.

Buddhist teachers and merchants spread the ideas of Theravada to the south and east. It was adopted in Ceylon in the 200s B.C. Ceylon, an island located near the southern tip of India, is now called Sri Lanka. Theravada Buddhism also became popular in Myanmar, Thailand, Cambodia, and Laos.

206   CHAPTER 6   Early India

INTERDISCIPLINARY CONNECTIONS ACTIVITY

Art Help students locate appropriate examples of Indian art related to Hinduism and Buddhism. Have them research the imagery that is associated with the depictions of the Buddha and the Hindu gods. To help students understand the term *imagery*, explain that in Hinduism, Shiva usually has a blue neck because he holds in his throat the poison that threatened to destroy humankind at the beginning of the world. He also has three eyes. The third eye lets him see inward, but it causes great damage if he turns it outward. Have groups write brief descriptions to accompany the art they find. Then ask groups to post their art and descriptions. Allow the class time to view these displays. **L2**

Biography

THE BUDDHA
c. 563–483 B.C.

Siddhartha Gautama—the thinker and teacher who would later be called the Buddha—was born in what is now Nepal. According to legend, his mother had a dream shortly before his birth that was interpreted to mean that her son would become a great leader.

The Gautama family belonged to the warrior caste. Siddhartha's father, Suddhodana, ruled a group called the Shakyas. His mother, Maya, died shortly after his birth.

Siddhartha was very intelligent. According to legend, the young man knew 64 languages and mastered all his studies without needing instruction. At age 29, Siddhartha realized that he wanted to search for truth, enlightenment, and a way to rise above suffering. He left his wife, Yasodhara, and son, Rahula, to study with priests.

At age 35, Siddhartha is said to have reached full enlightenment while sitting beneath a tree. The Buddha began traveling to teach others about his discoveries and about the nature of life and suffering.

The Buddha ▶

> "Our life is shaped by our mind; we become what we think."
> —The Buddha

◀ Sculpture of the Buddha sitting on a cobra

Then and Now

What types of present-day occupations often involve traveling to teach others?

207

Biography

TEACH

After the Buddha reached enlightenment, he was reluctant to teach his new ideas because they were so difficult to understand. He finally began to do so because, according to tradition, a Brahman god convinced him that he should. The Buddha traveled through many parts of India spreading his ideas and converting many people to them. He earned a reputation as an excellent teacher. His followers also spread the word.

Ask students if the Buddha's methods would be successful today. What does it take to spread new ideas today? *(Answers as to the Buddha's methods and what it takes may vary.)* **L1/ EL**

Then and Now

Possible answers: visiting teachers and professors, civic leaders, business trainers, writers, and so on

---

Reading List Generator CD-ROM

GLENCOE BOOKLINK **RECOMMENDED READING**

Use the **Glencoe BookLink CD-ROM** to create customized reading lists based on your students' interests and reading levels. Below is an example based on content in this chapter. Also, see the Suggested Readings on pages 944–946 of the Appendix.

- Ganeri, Anita. *Exploration into India.* The story of India—from the mysterious Indus Valley civilization through the adventures of Alexander the Great to the British Raj and its aftermath.
- Krishnaswami, Uma. *Shower of Gold: Girls and Women in the Stories of India.* Stories from India's folklore and Hindu and Buddhist mythology.
- from the *Rig Veda: Creation Hymn.* Portions of the sacred text.

ENRICH

Ask students to research Buddhism in Tibet. They should look for ways in which Buddhism mixed with Bon, Tibet's traditional religion. Have students share their findings. **L2**

Answer: by giving up all desires

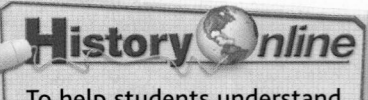

To help students understand section material, have them visit **Study Central**™ at jat.glencoe.com

RETEACH

Remind students that the Buddha did not support the caste system. Have students discuss how Buddhism reflects this position. They should be sure to include the Eightfold Path in their discussion. **L1/ EL**

Point out that Hinduism is more than a religion; it is a whole way of life. Ask students to name facts that support this statement. **L1/ EL**

208

Mahayana Buddhism

The second kind of Buddhism is called Mahayana Buddhism. It teaches that the Buddha is a god who came to save people. Mahayana Buddhists believe that following the Eightfold Path is too hard for most people in this world. They believe that by worshiping the Buddha instead, people will go to a heaven after they die. There, they can follow the Eightfold Path and reach nirvana.

Mahayana Buddhists also have special affection for the bodhisattvas (BOH•dih•SUHT•vuhz). Bodhisattvas are the enlightened people who postpone going to heaven. Instead, bodhisattvas have decided to stay on Earth to help others and do good deeds.

▲ A Tibetan monk today

Mahayana Buddhism spread northward into China and from there to Korea and Japan.

A special kind of Mahayana Buddhism developed in central Asia in the country of **Tibet** (tuh•BEHT). There it mixed with Tibet's traditional religion and with Hinduism.

In Tibet, the Buddhist leaders, called lamas, also led the government. When religious leaders head a government, it is called a **theocracy** (thee•AH•kruh•see). The **Dalai Lama** (DAH•LY LAH•muh) was the lama who headed the government, and the Panchen Lama was the lama who led the religion. Both were considered reincarnations of the Buddha.

Today, many Buddhists live in countries like Thailand, Cambodia, and Sri Lanka, but few live in India where the Buddha first preached.

✓ **Reading Check** **Identify** How could a Buddhist reach nirvana?

Section 2 Review

History Online

Study Central™ Need help with the material in this section? Visit jat.glencoe.com

Reading Summary

Review the Main Ideas

- Hinduism is an old religion with many gods. Hindus believe in reincarnation and that a person's place in life is determined by his or her karma.

- In the 500s B.C., Siddhartha Gautama founded the religion of Buddhism in northern India. According to Buddhism, a person who follows the Four Noble Truths and the Eightfold Path can achieve nirvana.

What Did You Learn?

1. What are the Upanishads?
2. What is reincarnation?

Critical Thinking

3. **Compare and Contrast** Draw a chart like the one below. Then add details to compare the two main branches of Buddhism.

Branches of Buddhism	
Theravada Buddhism	Mahayana Buddhism

4. **Describe** Explain the concept of karma.

5. **Explain** What is the importance of the Four Noble Truths and the Eightfold Path?

6. **Analyze** How did the belief in reincarnation both strengthen the divisions in Indian society and provide hope for the lower classes?

7. **Expository Writing** Write a short essay describing Siddhartha Gautama's journey to enlightenment.

SECTION 2 REVIEW ANSWERS

1. ancient religious writings that describe the search for a universal spirit
2. a religious belief that a soul is reborn many times
3. Theravada: The Buddha is a great teacher. Mahayana: The Buddha is a god; the Eightfold Path is too hard for

most people; if they worship the Buddha, they can get to heaven, where they can seek nirvana.
4. the consequences a soul faces in its next life for its actions in this life
5. The Four Noble Truths explain why people suffer.

The Eightfold Path describes behaviors that will end suffering.
6. One's position in society results from past acts. Lower classes hoped to improve their position in a future life.
7. Answers should be based on the text.

Section 3 — India's First Empires

Get Ready to Read!

What's the Connection?

In the last section, you learned about Hinduism and Buddhism. Both religions developed when India was a land of small kingdoms. These rival kingdoms would be forced to unite, however, when foreigners invaded.

Focusing on the Main Ideas

• The Mauryan dynasty built India's first great empire. *(page 210)*

• The Gupta empire reunited much of northern India and became wealthy through trade. *(page 213)*

• The Mauryan and Gupta empires made important contributions in literature, mathematics, and science. *(page 214)*

Locating Places
Pataliputra
(PAH•tuh•lih•POO•truh)

Meeting People
Chandragupta Maurya (CHUHN•druh•GUP•tuh   MAH•oor•yuh)
Asoka (uh•SOH•kuh)
Kalidasa (KAH•lih•DAH•suh)

Building Your Vocabulary
dynasty (DY•nuh•stee)
stupa (STOO•puh)
pilgrim (PIHL•gruhm)

Reading Strategy
Categorizing Information Complete a chart like the one below, identifying the important dates, capital city, and government of the Mauryan empire.

	Mauryan Empire
Dates	
Capital City	
Government	

When & Where?

350 B.C.

321 B.C. Chandragupta Maurya founds Mauryan dynasty

232 B.C. Mauryan ruler Asoka dies

A.D. 1

A.D. 320 Gupta empire begins

A.D. 350

Pataliputra●

SECTION RESOURCES

Reproducible Masters
• Reproducible Lesson Plan 6–3
• Daily Lecture and Discussion Notes 6–3
• Vocabulary Activity 6–3
• Active Reading Note-Taking Guide 6–3
• Guided Reading Activity 6–3
• Section Quiz 6–3
• Reading Essentials and Study Guide 6–3

Transparencies
• Daily Focus Skills Transparency 6–3

Multimedia
• Interactive Tutor Self-Assessment CD-ROM
• ExamView® Pro Testmaker CD-ROM
• Presentation Plus! CD-ROM
• Vocabulary PuzzleMaker CD-ROM
• Glencoe BookLink CD-ROM

---

① FOCUS

SECTION OVERVIEW

The Mauryan and Gupta dynasties built empires in India, and they contributed greatly to literature, mathematics, and science.

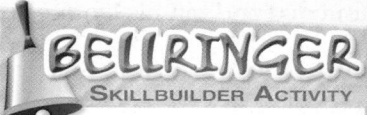
BELLRINGER
SKILLBUILDER ACTIVITY

🔔 Project **Daily Focus Skills Transparency 6–3** and have students answer questions. Discuss their responses.

Get Ready to Read!

Preteaching Vocabulary: Explain that a dynasty is a series of rulers from the same family. The Mauryan and Gupta dynasties were important in India between about 321 B.C. and 183 B.C. and between about A.D. 320 and A.D. 650, respectively.

Answers to Graphic:
Dates: 321 B.C. to 183 B.C.; Capital City: Pataliputra; Government: kings, centralized government

② TEACH

Determining Causes and Effects
Have the class look for causes and effects in "Who Built India's First Empire?" Record the results on the board. Ask how the actions of the Persians and the Greeks may have influenced how Chandragupta founded and ran his empire. **L2**

Daily Lecture and Discussion Notes 6–3

Use **Daily Lecture and Discussion Notes 6–3** for an outline of key concepts found in the section.

▶ **Reading Strategy**

Writing Activity ✎

Ask students to write a paragraph listing problems that Chandragupta may have met in governing this empire. Have students describe how these problems affected his centralized government, strong army, and spy system. **L2**

Using Geography Skills

Answers:
1. along the Ganges River in the northeast
2. the southern tip

The Mauryan Dynasty

Main Idea The Mauryan dynasty built India's first great empire.

Reading Focus Do you think political leaders should promote religion? How might religion help a king hold his country together? Read to learn why one Indian emperor decided to support Buddhism.

....

India's princes fought over their small kingdoms for centuries. Then two big invasions taught the Indians a lesson. First, the Persians invaded the Indus Valley in the

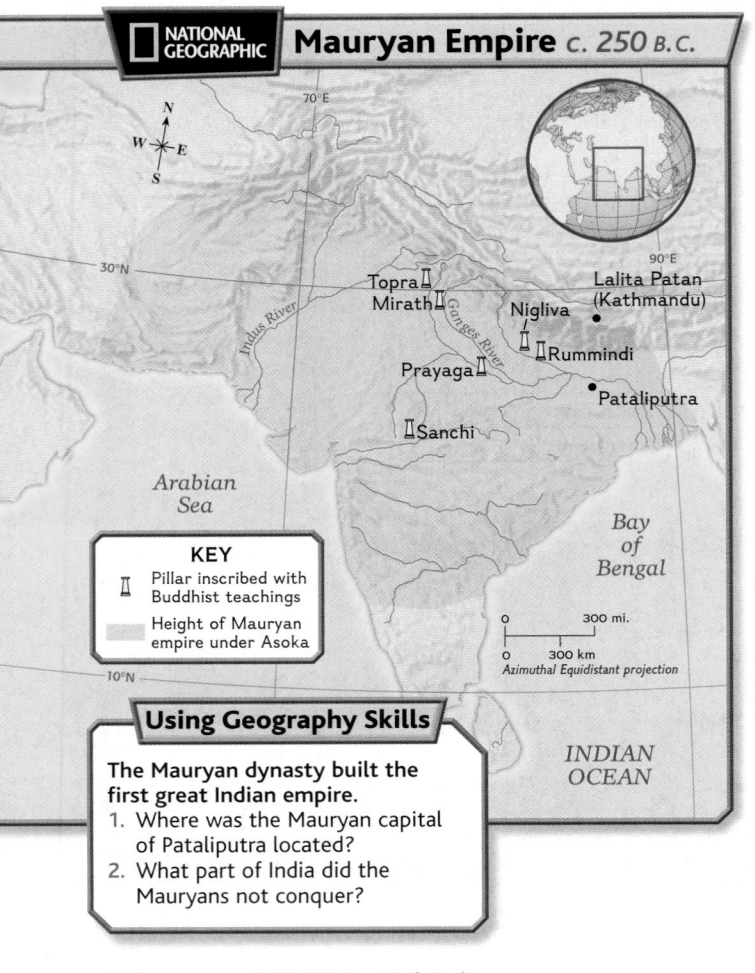

NATIONAL GEOGRAPHIC
Mauryan Empire c. 250 B.C.

KEY
⚏ Pillar inscribed with Buddhist teachings
▨ Height of Mauryan empire under Asoka

0 ___ 300 mi.
0 ___ 300 km
Azimuthal Equidistant projection

Using Geography Skills

The Mauryan dynasty built the first great Indian empire.
1. Where was the Mauryan capital of Pataliputra located?
2. What part of India did the Mauryans not conquer?

210   CHAPTER 6   Early India

500s B.C. and made it part of the great Persian Empire. Then, as you have already read, Alexander the Great invaded India in 327 B.C.

Although Alexander's troops conquered northern India, he did not stay long. His soldiers were homesick and tired and threatened to rebel unless he turned back. The invasion did have one important effect, however. It led to the first great Indian empire.

Who Built India's First Empire? India's first empire was founded by **Chandragupta Maurya** (CHUHN•druh•GUP•tuh MAH•oor•yuh). Chandragupta was an Indian prince who conquered a large area in the Ganges River valley soon after Alexander invaded western India. Alexander's invasion weakened many of India's kingdoms. After Alexander left, Chandragupta seized the opportunity to conquer and unite almost all of northern India.

He founded the Mauryan dynasty in 321 B.C. A **dynasty** (DY•nuh•stee) is a series of rulers from the same family. To run his empire, Chandragupta set up a centralized government. In a centralized government, rulers run everything from a capital city. To control everything from his capital, **Pataliputra** (PAH•tuh•lih•POO•truh), Chandragupta had to have a strong army. He also needed a good spy system to make sure no one was planning to rebel. Communications were also important, so he set up a postal system.

▶ **Reading Strategy**   **READING THE TEXT**

Activate Prior Knowledge Before students read Section 3, explain that both the Persians and Alexander the Great had controlled huge empires and that areas of India had been part of those empires. **Ask:** How did Alexander acquire his empire? *(through military conquests)* How did the Persians maintain control over a huge area? *(satraps; building good roads; establishing a postal system; practicing tolerance toward conquered peoples' customs)* Tell students to keep this information in mind as they are reading "The Mauryan Dynasty." Discuss with students how understanding the history of a people or an area will often help explain later events, beliefs, or attitudes. **L2**

▲ This stupa from central India is one of the best-preserved shrines from the 200s B.C. *What other type of structure did Indians create to honor the Buddha?*

The Buddha ▶

Emperor Asoka's Reign Chandragupta founded the Mauryan dynasty, but many historians think the empire's greatest king was **Asoka** (uh•SOH•kuh). Asoka ruled from about 273 B.C. to 232 B.C.

Asoka was an unusual ruler. Like many kings, he was a strong military leader, but he came to hate bloodshed. After one bloody fight, he walked over the battlefield. When he saw the dead and wounded, he was horrified and made a vow. He would dedicate his life to peace and follow the teachings of the Buddha.

Asoka was history's first great Buddhist king. He built hospitals for people and for animals, too. He built new roads so it was easier to trade and put shelters and shade trees along the roads where travelers could rest.

Asoka sent many Buddhist teachers throughout India and the rest of Asia. They carried the religion to new believers. In India, laborers carved the Buddha's teachings on stone pillars for people to read. Asoka also had laborers build thousands of **stupas** (STOO•puhs). Stupas are Buddhist shrines that have the shape of a dome or mound.

Although he was a Buddhist, Asoka allowed his Hindu subjects to practice their religion. His tolerance was unusual for the time.

With a good road system and a strong ruler, the empire prospered. India became the center of a huge trade network that stretched to the Mediterranean Sea.

The Fall of the Mauryan Empire Asoka died in 232 B.C. Unfortunately, the kings who followed him were not very good leaders, and the empire grew weak.

These kings made bad decisions that turned the people against them. They forced merchants to pay heavy taxes and seized peasants' crops for themselves. Things were so bad that in 183 B.C., the last Mauryan ruler was killed by one of his own generals.

✓ **Reading Check** **Summarize** Why was Asoka an important ruler?

CHAPTER 6   Early India   **211**

Reading Support L1/ EL

Use **Vocabulary Activity 6–3** to review important terms in the section.

CONNECTING ACROSS TIME

Asoka was a Buddhist, but he allowed Hindus to practice their religion. Point out to students that some of the 13 British colonies in North America allowed freedom of religion and some did not. Then ask whether religious toleration exists in the United States today. Help students distinguish between the constitutional right to freedom of religion and violations of that right that are punishable under the law. Discuss why religious freedom is valued in the United States. **L1/ EL**

Caption Answer: stone pillars with his teachings

✓ **Reading Check**

Answer: He built hospitals, roads, rest stops, and stupas; sent Buddhist missionaries throughout India and Asia; practiced religious tolerance; encouraged trade; and caused the empire to prosper.

DIFFERENTIATED INSTRUCTION

Visual/Spatial: Have small groups of students prepare visual summaries for the subsection "Indian Literature and Science." There should be a labeled drawing or cartoon for the *Vedas*, the *Mahabharata*, the Bhagavad Gita, the *Ramayana*, Kalidasa, and for each contribution in math and science. Students should use these visuals to present a summary of each topic for the class.

English Learners: Have students check unknown words in illustrated dictionaries.

Gifted and Talented: Have students research how computers use zeros and ones to write letters of the alphabet. Ask students to share their findings with the class.

📁 Refer to *Inclusion Strategies for the Middle School Social Studies Classroom* in the TCR.

Biography

TEACH

Throughout his empire, Asoka had cliff faces and huge pillars carved with statements related to dharma. Such statements may have dealt with non-violence, right conduct toward fellow humans, and the preservation of all life-forms. These statements appeared in many local languages so that they could be read to people.

Ask students if present-day government leaders talk about and support religious values. If so, what kinds? If not, why not? (*Answers may support either opinion.*) **L1/ EL**

Then and Now

Answers will vary. Encourage students to be thoughtful in their answers.

Biography

EMPEROR ASOKA
Reigned c. 273–232 B.C.

Emperor Asoka vowed to relieve suffering wherever he found it. He discovered that Buddhism reflected his new beliefs, so he became a Buddhist.

Emperor Asoka had a strong, energetic personality. He began preaching the Buddhist ideas that people should be honest, truthful, and nonviolent. He preached that people should live with compassion toward all humans and animals. Asoka taught by example and tried to live his life with "little sin and many good deeds." He ordered his government officials to adopt those virtues for their own lives. He also ordered his officials to keep him informed of the needs of the people in his empire.

Emperor Asoka regularly visited people in the rural areas of his kingdom and found practical ways to improve their lives. He founded hospitals and supplied medicine. He ordered wells to be dug and trees to be planted along the roads.

▼ Asoka

◀ Carving from top of pillar created under Asoka

Then and Now

Asoka combined religion and government. Do you think that the two should be combined or kept separate? Explain, providing examples to support your answer.

Reading List Generator CD-ROM

GLENCOE BOOKLINK   **RECOMMENDED READING**

Use the **Glencoe BookLink CD-ROM** to create customized reading lists based on your students' interests and reading levels. Below is an example based on content in this chapter. Also, see the Suggested Readings on pages 944–946 of the Appendix.

- Ganeri, Anita. *I Remember India.* Renu lives in the United States now, but she was born in India.
- Kalman, Bobbie. *Tibet.* Tibetans lead lives that are harsh but rich in culture and religious devotion.
- Reynolds, Jan. *Himalaya: Vanishing Cultures.* Little Yangshi and her sister live in the Himalaya. They go to the outdoor market and pasture the family's yaks.

The Gupta Empire

Main Idea The Gupta empire reunited much of northern India and became wealthy through trade.

Reading Focus What types of products does the United States trade with other countries? Read to learn how the Gupta empire built its wealth on trade.

For 500 years, India had no strong ruler. Once again, small kingdoms fought with one another and made life miserable for their subjects. Then, in A.D. 320, one prince in the Ganges River valley grew more powerful than the others. Like an earlier ruler, his name was Chandragupta. This Chandragupta chose to rule from the old capital of the Mauryan empire—Pataliputra.

Chandragupta founded the Gupta dynasty. When he died, his son, Samudragupta, took over the throne and expanded the Gupta empire in northern India. Soon, the new kingdom dominated almost all of northern India. The Guptas ruled for about 200 years. Gupta rulers had one advantage over the earlier Mauryan kings. The empire was smaller and that made it easier to manage.

The Gupta empire grew wealthy from trade. Salt, cloth, and iron were common goods traded in India. Indian merchants also traded with China and with kingdoms in southeast Asia and the Mediterranean. The Gupta rulers controlled much of the trade and became very wealthy. They owned silver and gold mines and large estates.

Trade created jobs for people in India and made many people and cities prosperous. Cities grew up along the trade routes, and many people traveled. Some people, called **pilgrims** (PIHL•gruhms), often used the trade routes to travel to a religious shrine or site. Just as cities today make money from tourism, Indian cities that were famous for their temples became wealthy from visiting pilgrims.

NATIONAL GEOGRAPHIC

Gupta Empire C. A.D. 600

Using Geography Skills

The Guptas controlled much of northern India.
1. What river valleys were found within the borders of the Gupta empire?
2. How does the area of the Gupta empire compare to that of the Mauryan empire as shown on the map on page 210?

Asoka had converted to Buddhism, but the Guptas were Hindus like many of their subjects. They made Hinduism the official religion and gave money to support Hindu scholars and Hindu shrines. The shrines they built to Hindu gods and goddesses inspired Hindus. They often had brightly painted sculptures of images from the Upanishads and other sacred writings.

During the Gupta empire, art and science also began to develop. Earlier, you learned that Greece had a golden age of art and learning. India also had a golden age of art and learning during the Gupta empire.

Reading Check **Explain** How did the Gupta empire become wealthy?

CHAPTER 6   Early India   **213**

Comparing Empires Review when the Mauryan and Gupta empires began. Make sure students notice that the date for the Mauryan empire is B.C. and that of the Gupta empire is A.D. Then ask students to compare and contrast the two empires. Write their findings in chart form on the board. **L2**

Monitoring Comprehension Ask students to explain the purpose of the last paragraph in "The Gupta Empire." Then discuss some of the accomplishments of Greece's golden age of art and learning. Ask students why they think the Guptas were also able to have a golden age. **L2**

Using Geography Skills

Answers:

1. the Ganges and Indus River valleys

2. The Mauryan empire was larger and stretched farther to the west and south.

Skills Practice

Ask: What geographic feature seems to have prevented the Gupta empire from expanding beyond the Indus River? *(the Hindu Kush)*

Reading Check

Answer: from trading salt, cloth, and iron, and from silver and gold mines

CRITICAL THINKING ACTIVITY

Drawing Conclusions Explain what constitutional amendments are. Then have students find and read the Twelfth, Twentieth, Twenty-second, and Twenty-fifth Amendments. Make sure that the class understands the meaning of these amendments. Next, have students research on the Internet how Asoka became emperor. *(It took four years for Asoka to become emperor. Like his grandfather, he won the throne through force and cunning. According to tradition, he killed all his rivals, including 99 brothers. Only one brother survived.)* Then discuss how power is won and transferred in the United States. Ask students why power is transferred differently in the United States than it was in the Mauryan empire. **L3**

Summarizing and Comparing List the literary pieces named in "India's Most Famous Poems" on the board. Ask volunteers to summarize orally each one. Record their comments next to the titles. Then have students compare major works of Greek literature that they have learned about in this course, such as the *Iliad* and the *Odyssey*, to the Indian works. **L2**

Primary Source

The battlefield in the story stands for life and poses the question "What should a person do with one's life?" The god Krishna serves as Arjuna's charioteer in the Bhagavad Gita. He reveals that a person has two parts—the soul, which is eternal, and the body, which is caught in the everyday world. The soul is a minute part of god. Arjuna explains that "[the soul] is not slain when the body is slain. The soul . . . abandons old bodies as if they were only old clothes."

Answer:
The soul lives on after death.

☞ See the **Primary Source Readings (with Document-Based Questions)** in the Unit Resource Books.

Indian Literature and Science

Main Idea The Mauryan and Gupta empires made important contributions in literature, mathematics, and science.

Reading Focus What do you think modern movies, books, and television reveal about our values? As you read, try to see if Indian poetry tells a story about values during the Gupta period.

Artists, builders, scientists, and writers produced many works while the Mauryan and Gupta kings ruled.

India's Most Famous Poems

The Vedas of India are ancient hymns and prayers for religious ceremonies. No one is certain how old they are because for a long time they were only recited, not written down. Once Aryan people came to India and developed Sanskrit, then the Vedas could be recorded.

Later, other kinds of literature were also written down. Two epics are very famous in India, and Indians today still love to read them. The first is the *Mahabharata* (muh•HAH•BAH•ruh•tuh), and the second is the *Ramayana* (rah•mah•YAH•nah). Both of these long poems tell about brave warriors and their heroic deeds.

The *Mahabharata* is the longest poem in any written language—about 88,000 verses. Historians think several different authors wrote it and that it was written down around 100 B.C. It describes a great war for control of an Indian kingdom about 1,000 years earlier.

The best-known section is the Bhagavad Gita (BAH•guh•VAHD GEE•tuh), or "Song of the Lord." It is very important in Hindu writings. In it, the god Krishna preaches a sermon before a battle. He tells his listeners how noble it is to do one's duty even when it is difficult and painful.

Primary Source

The Bhagavad Gita

In the Bhagavad Gita, Arjuna prepares to go into battle. He asks the god Krishna questions about war and death. The following passage is part of Krishna's answer.

"Thou grievest where no grief should be! . . .

. . . .

All, that doth live, lives always! . . .

. . . .

The soul that with a strong and constant calm
Takes sorrow and takes joy indifferently,
Lives in the life undying!

—*Bhagavadgita*, Sir Edwin Arnold, trans.

▼ Painting titled *Krishna and Maidens*

DBQ Document-Based Question

What does Krishna believe about life after death?

214   CHAPTER 6   Early India

INTERDISCIPLINARY CONNECTIONS ACTIVITY

Mathematics Demonstrate to students how performing mathematical functions with Indian-Arabic numerals is simpler than with Roman numerals because the former system is a base-ten system that uses place value. Review with students the values of these Roman numerals: I = 1   V = 5   X = 10. Then have students do the calculation below. **L2**

Roman			Indian-Arabic
XXV	XX IIIII	XX IIIII	25
−XIII	− X III	− X III	−13
		X II	12

The *Ramayana* is another long poem. It was written at about the same time as the *Mahabharata*. It tells of the great king Rama and his queen Sita (SEE•tuh). Rama's enemies have him banished from the kingdom. He is forced to live as a hermit in the forest. Later, he fights and defeats the demon Ravana, who had kidnapped Sita. As in many Indian epics, they live happily ever after.

Like the *Mahabharata,* the *Ramayana* contains many religious and moral lessons. Rama is the perfect hero, king, and son. Sita is the perfect, faithful wife. However, people enjoyed the epics for other reasons as well. Like adventure movies of today, these poems told thrilling stories about great heroes.

Other writings from ancient India have also survived. These are quite different from the *Mahabharata* and *Ramayana*. One of India's best-known authors was **Kalidasa** (KAH•lih•DAH•suh). He lived during the Gupta dynasty. Kalidasa wrote plays, poems, love stories, and comedies. His poem *The Cloud Messenger* is one of the most popular Sanskrit poems. It is a love story that also contains beautiful descriptions of the mountains, forests, and rivers of northern India. A completely different work is the *Panchantantra*. It is similar to Aesop's fables. In these tales, talking animal characters present lessons about life. Most Indian literature stresses the importance of dharma. Each person, regardless of social status, must do his or her duty.

Indian Math and Science Indian mathematicians, especially in the Gupta period, made important contributions. Aryabhata (AHR•yuh•BUHT•uh) was the leading mathematician of the Gupta empire. He was

HISTORY MAKERS

The Invention of Zero c. A.D. 500

Early humans understood the idea of nothing, but they did not have a symbol to represent that idea. During the Gupta dynasty, Indian mathematicians invented the symbol "0" and connected it with the idea of nothing. The Indians' invention of zero had a great impact on the study of mathematics and science—then and now. Without the concept of zero, modern technology, such as computers, would not be possible.

▲ The middle dot is the first symbol for zero.

one of the first scientists known to have used algebra. Indian mathematicians developed the idea of zero and a symbol to represent it. They also explained the concept of infinity—something without an end.

Gupta mathematicians created the symbols for the numbers 1 to 9 that we use today. These number symbols, or numerals, were adopted by Arab traders in the A.D. 700s. European traders borrowed them from the Arabs. Use of these numbers

CHAPTER 6   Early India   215

HISTORY MAKERS

The Indians probably used a vocabulary of symbolic words to denote zero, such as "void," "sky," or "space." Ask students what words today can denote the concept of zero.

Reading Support L1/EL

Assign **Guided Reading Activity 6–3** to help students organize the information in the section.

③ ASSESS

Assign Section 3 Review as homework or as an in-class activity.

● Have students use the **Interactive Tutor Self-Assessment CD-ROM** to review the section.

Assessment L2

Assign **Section 3 Quiz** to assess mastery of the material found in the section.

Reading Support L1/EL

Assign **Reading Essentials and Study Guide 6–3** to help students review section material.

EXTENDING THE CONTENT

The *Ramayana* This epic poem is perhaps the most popular Hindu book. There are several versions of the *Ramayana*, which have appeared in different Indian languages. It probably was composed during the 200s B.C. and was originally sung as a ballad. The *Ramayana* describes how Rama and his brothers are born after their mothers and father receive a magical potion. Together, the brothers constitute the seventh avatar (or incarnation) of the god Vishnu. During the story, Rama wins his wife, Sita, because he can bend Shiva's bow, which no one else can even pick up. During his banishment, Rama becomes an ally of the monkey king, Sugriva, and they eventually save the kidnapped Sita. Rama and Sita serve as examples of duty and proper behavior.

ENRICH

Explain that social mobility is the ability of people to move between different social classes and income levels. Discuss with students how social mobility is different in India and the United States. **L1/EL**

 Reading Check

Answer: mathematics, astronomy, and medicine

 History Online

To help students understand section material, have them visit **Study Central**™ at jat.glencoe.com

RETEACH

Discuss with students the various rulers described in this section, the empires they built, and the advancements made during their reigns. **L2**

 CLOSE

Have the class summarize how religion affected the Gupta empire. **L2**

---

spread through Europe in the A.D. 1200s, replacing Roman numerals. Today, this system of number symbols is known as the Hindu-Arabic numerical system.

Early Indians also invented mathematical algorithms. An algorithm (AHL•gohr•ih•thuhm) is a series of steps that solve a problem. If you follow the steps, you get the right answer. Computer programmers today often use algorithms to tell computers what to do.

Ancient Indians made important contributions in other scientific fields, especially astronomy. They followed and mapped movements of planets and stars. They understood that the Earth was round and revolved around the sun. They also seem to have understood gravity.

Indians developed ideas about what the universe was made of. As early as the 500s B.C., Indian thinkers believed that the universe was made up of many very tiny particles. They came up with ideas of atoms before the Greeks in the West did.

In the field of medicine, Gupta doctors were advanced for their time. They could set broken bones and perform operations. They also invented many medical tools.

An Indian doctor named Shushruta (shoosh•ROO•tah) carried out an early form of plastic surgery. He worked to restore damaged noses. Indian doctors used herbs in treating illnesses. They also believed it was important to remove the causes of a disease and not just cure the disease itself.

✓ **Reading Check** **Summarize** In what branches of science did ancient Indians make advances?

Section 3 Review

 History Online

Study Central™ Need help with the material in this section? Visit jat.glencoe.com

Reading Summary

Review the Main Ideas

- The Mauryan empire, under leaders such as Chandragupta Maurya and Asoka, united most of India for over a hundred years.

- The Gupta dynasty reunited northern India and grew wealthy from trade.

- During the Mauryan and Gupta empires, the arts and sciences flourished in India. Several great works of literature, including the *Mahabharata* and the *Ramayana*, came from this period.

What Did You Learn?

1. Describe trade during the Gupta empire.

2. What is the message of the Bhagavad Gita?

Critical Thinking

3. **Organizing Information** Draw a diagram to show the contributions of Indian mathematicians during the Mauryan and Gupta empires.

```
  ⬭       ⬭

      (Contributions)

  ⬭       ⬭
```

4. **Analyze** How were Asoka's Buddhist beliefs reflected in his accomplishments as king?

5. **Expository Writing** Which of the Indian emperors described in this section do you think was the greatest ruler? Write a short essay explaining your choice.

6. **Math Link** Why would the development of a number system be important in a civilization that depended on trade?

7. **Reading Vocabulary** Explain how you could use context to determine the meaning of the word *prospered* in this sentence.

"With a good road system and a strong ruler, the empire prospered."

SECTION 3 REVIEW ANSWERS

1. Indians traded salt, cloth, and iron with China, Southeast Asia, and the Mediterranean.

2. It taught people to do their duty even when it was painful.

3. some of first to use algebra; developed concept of and symbol for zero; explained concept of infinity; invented symbols for 1–9; invented algorithms

4. His improvements were for the overall good. He built hospitals, roads, and rest stops for travelers; sent missionaries throughout India and Asia; carved Buddha's principles on pillars; built stupas; and practiced religious tolerance.

5. Students should provide reasons for their choice of ruler.

6. to keep records of transactions and to monitor the exchange of money

7. Positive word clues: "good," "strong"

Section 1 India's First Civilizations

Vocabulary
subcontinent
monsoon
Sanskrit
raja
caste
guru

Focusing on the Main Ideas
- Climate and geography influenced the rise of India's first civilization. *(page 195)*
- The Aryans conquered India and introduced new ideas and technology. *(page 198)*
- The Aryans created a caste system that separated Indians into groups. *(page 199)*

Section 2 Hinduism and Buddhism

Vocabulary
Hinduism
Brahman
reincarnation
dharma
karma
Buddhism
nirvana
theocracy

Focusing on the Main Ideas
- Hinduism grew out of the ancient beliefs of the Aryans. *(page 203)*
- A new religion, Buddhism, appealed to many people in India and other parts of Asia. *(page 205)*

Ganesha ▶

Section 3 India's First Empires

Vocabulary
dynasty
stupa
pilgrim

Focusing on the Main Ideas
- The Mauryan dynasty built India's first great empire. *(page 210)*
- The Gupta empire reunited much of northern India and became wealthy through trade. *(page 213)*
- The Mauryan and Gupta empires made important contributions in literature, mathematics, and science. *(page 214)*

CHAPTER 6   Early India   217

PREVIEW/REVIEW

Vocabulary Activity For each vocabulary term, have a different volunteer explain how it relates to one of the main ideas for the section in which it belongs.

⊚ **Vocabulary PuzzleMaker CD-ROM**

⊚ **Interactive Tutor Self-Assessment CD-ROM**

CONDENSE

🗀 Chapter 6 **Guided Reading Activities**

⊚ **StudentWorks Plus™ CD-ROM** (with Audio Program)

RETEACH

🗀 **Differentiated Instruction Activity 6**

🗀 Chapter 6 *Reading Essentials and Study Guide*

CHAPTER CULMINATING ACTIVITY

Have students finish the Chapter Culminating Activity from page 190D.

Suggestions for rubrics may be found in the *Quizzes, Tests, and Authentic Assessment (with Rubrics)* booklet.

Reading Strategy READ TO WRITE

Writing Charts Have students consider how religion impacted the development of culture and government in ancient India. Have them create three separate web diagrams. The center oval of each organizer will be labeled, respectively, "Aryan religion," "Hinduism," and "Buddhism," with connecting ovals explaining the impact of each religious movement. Afterward, have students write a one-paragraph summary of the effects they identified for each religion.

- **L1** students should have several ideas per religion.
- **L2** students should include several ideas and attempt grammar mastery.
- **L3** students should have logical, detailed, well-considered paragraphs.

Review Vocabulary

1. Students' paragraphs should use each term correctly.

2. d

3. f

4. h

5. e

Students should use each of the following terms correctly in separate sentences: *stupa, guru, caste, monsoon*.

Review Main Ideas

6. geography and climate

7. no one is sure, but possibly to help Aryans stay in control

8. the ancient beliefs of the Aryans

9. Buddhism

10. the Mauryan

11. It reunited much of India and became wealthy through trade.

Critical Thinking

12. They both describe behaviors that believers must try to follow.

13. It stresses the importance of doing one's duty.

14. The summer monsoon made the Indus River flood, fertilizing the soil and leading to good

---

Review Vocabulary

1. Write a paragraph about the basic beliefs of Buddhism using the following words.

   reincarnation   karma   dharma

   Write the vocabulary word that best completes each sentence. Then write a sentence for each term not chosen.

   a. stupa   e. pilgrim
   b. guru   f. theocracy
   c. *varna*   g. monsoon
   d. raja   h. dynasty

2. Each Aryan tribe was led by a ___.

3. In a ___, government is led by religious leaders.

4. A ___ is a line of rulers who belong to the same family.

5. A ___ travels to religious places.

Review Main Ideas

Section 1 • India's First Civilizations

6. What influenced the rise of India's first civilizations?

7. What was the purpose of the *varna* system?

Section 2 • Hinduism and Buddhism

8. From what did Hinduism form?

9. Which religion appealed to people in India and other parts of Asia?

Section 3 • India's First Empires

10. Which dynasty built India's first great empire?

11. Why was the Gupta empire important?

Critical Thinking

12. **Compare** How do you think the Eightfold Path is similar to the Ten Commandments of Judaism?

13. **Analyze** How does the *Mahabharata* reflect the ideals of ancient India?

14. **Explain** How did the monsoons affect the development of India's first civilizations?

15. **Predict** What do you think might have happened if Asoka had approved of the slaughter on the battlefield during his wars of conquest?

Review

Reading Skill **Vocabulary** **Building Your Vocabulary**

16. Read the following excerpt from page 205. Then explain how context clues can help you determine the meaning of the word *hermit*.

He left his family and riches and began his search. At first he lived like a hermit, fasting and sleeping on the hard ground. Siddhartha nearly starved, but he still had no answer to his questions.

To review this skill, see pages 192–193.

---

farming. Surplus food led to specialization and civilization.

15. Answers may include that wars might have continued during the Mauryan empire; the empire might have been larger; Buddhism may not have spread so quickly.

Reading Skill

16. The phrase "left his family" shows that he was by himself, "fasting and sleeping on the hard ground" shows that he had no money or place of his own, and "nearly starved" shows that he had no food—he did not work or make money.

Geography Skills

Study the map below and answer the following questions.

17. **Human/Environment Interaction** Why did Harappa and Mohenjo-Daro develop so near the Indus River?
18. **Place** The winter monsoon winds come from the northeast. What makes the winds from that monsoon cold?
19. **Location** Name at least two natural features that protected Harappa and Mohenjo-Daro from invaders.

NATIONAL GEOGRAPHIC
Early India

70°E

500 mi.

500 km

Azimuthal Equidistant projection

30°N

HINDU KUSH

HIMALAYA

• Harappa

Indus R.

Ganges R.

• Mohenjo-Daro

THAR DESERT

Arabian Sea

INDIA

KEY
Indus civilization, c. 1500 B.C.

Read to Write

20. **Persuasive Writing** In the *Mahabharata*, the god Krishna advises Arjuna, "Get ready for battle without thought of . . . gain and loss, victory and defeat." Write a paragraph in which you agree or disagree with that advice.
21. **Using Your FOLDABLES** Use the information you recorded in your foldable to create a fill-in-the-blank quiz for a classmate. Write a paragraph about one of the sections, leaving blanks for your classmates to fill in. Also write an answer key.

History Online

Self-Check Quiz To help you prepare for the Chapter Test, visit jat.glencoe.com

Using Technology

22. **Researching** Use the Internet and your local library to find information about the *varnas* and *jati* in India today. You may wish to investigate where the systems are still practiced and how they affect modern society. You may also wish to research attempts at reforming the system and how the system is affected by national law. Prepare a report to share with the class.

Building Citizenship Skills

23. **Analyzing Information** Dharma is the Hindu idea of duty. Is it important for people in a society to do their duty? Make a list of duties Americans have today. Then write a paragraph explaining why those duties are important.

Primary Source — Analyze

Read the excerpt from the Buddha's Farewell Address. Then answer the questions.

"'Hold fast to the truth as a lamp. Seek salvation alone in the truth. Do not look for assistance to anyone besides yourselves. . . .

Those who, either now or after I am dead, shall be lamps unto themselves . . . holding fast to the truth as their lamp, and seeking their salvation in the truth alone . . . it is they . . . who shall reach the very topmost height! But they must be anxious to learn.'"

—*The Teachings of Buddha*, The Buddha's Farewell Address, compiled by Paul Carus

DBQ Document-Based Questions

24. Why does the Buddha compare the truth to a lamp?
25. What quality must people have if they want to reach the topmost height?

CHAPTER 6 Early India **219**

History Online

Have students visit the Web site at jat.glencoe.com to review Chapter 6 and take the **Self-Check Quiz.**

Using Technology

22. Students' reports should contain current information on *varnas* and *jati* today.

Building Citizenship Skills

23. "Yes" answers may include duty to vote, obey the law, and pay taxes. Answers should also include an explanation of why duty helps keep society functioning. Have students who answered "no" defend their answers.

Primary Source

24. A lamp gives physical light. The truth gives spiritual light (enlightenment).
25. be anxious to learn and seek salvation in truth alone

Bonus Question

Ask: Did the Mauryan and Gupta empires follow the Hindu idea of events occurring in cycles? Explain. (*Answers should include this sequence: rule by many rajas; formation of an empire; ineffective rulers, which led to the empire's collapse; and repetition of the cycle.*)

Geography Skills

17. access to clean water and fertile lands
18. the Himalaya
19. Possible answers: Thar Desert, Himalaya, and Hindu Kush

Read to Write

20. Answers will vary but should include reference to Hindu emphasis on doing one's duty.
21. **FOLDABLES** Students' quizzes should contain a sentence for each vocabulary term in the selected section.

Chapter 7 Resources

Note: The following materials may be used when teaching Chapter 7.
Section level support materials are shown at point of use in the margins of the Teacher Wraparound Edition.

TEACHING TRANSPARENCIES

- Graphic Organizer Transparencies with Teaching Strategy and Student Activity **L2**
- Cause-and-Effect Transparencies with Teaching Strategy and Student Activity **L2**
- Then and Now Transparencies with Teaching Strategy and Student Activity **L2**
- In-text Map Transparency with Teaching Strategy and Student Activity **L1**
- Map Transparencies with Overlay, Teaching Strategy, and Student Activity **L2**

DIFFERENTIATED INSTRUCTION

- Differentiated Instruction Activity 7
- Time Line Activity 7
- Primary Source Reading 7 (with Document-Based Questions)
- Inclusion Strategies for the Middle School Social Studies Classroom
- StudentWorks Plus™ CD-ROM (with Audio Program)

READING SUPPORT

- Take-Home Review Activity 7 **L2**
- World Literature Reading 7 **L2**
- Workbook Activity 7 **L1**
- Reading Strategies for the Social Studies Classroom **L1/ EL**

ASSESSMENT

- Authentic Assessment Activity 7 **L1/ EL**
- Chapter 7 Test Form A **L2**
- Chapter 7 Test Form B **L2**
- ExamView® Pro Testmaker CD-ROM

INTERDISCIPLINARY CONNECTIONS

- Geography and History Activity 7 **L2**
- People to Meet Activity 7 **L2**
- Economics Activity 7 **L2**
- Citizenship and Service Learning Activity 7 **L2**

SPANISH RESOURCES

- Spanish Reading Essentials and Study Guide
- Spanish Guided Reading Activities
- Spanish Quizzes, Tests, and Authentic Assessment (with Rubrics)
- Spanish Take-Home Review Activities

MULTIMEDIA

- ExamView® Pro Testmaker CD-ROM
- Glencoe Skillbuilder Interactive Workbook CD-ROM, Level 1
- Interactive Tutor Self-Assessment CD-ROM
- MindJogger Videoquiz
- Presentation Plus! CD-ROM
- StudentWorks Plus™ CD-ROM (with Audio Program)
- TeacherWorks CD-ROM
- Vocabulary PuzzleMaker CD-ROM
- *World History: Journey Across Time* Video Program
- World History Primary Source Document Library CD-ROM

STANDARDIZED ASSESSMENT SKILLS

- Standardized Test Skills Practice Workbook Activity 7 **L2**
- Critical Thinking Skills Activity 7 **L2**

Teaching strategies have been coded with suggested ability levels. However, most are suitable for all levels.

L1 BASIC activities for all students

L2 AVERAGE activities for average to above-average students

L3 CHALLENGING activities for above-average students

EL ENGLISH LANGUAGE activities

Chapter 7 Resources

⏱ TIME MANAGEMENT

Chapter Introduction	Section 1	Section 2	Section 3	Chapter Wrap-Up	Unit Wrap-Up
1 Day	2 Days	1 Day	2 Days	1 Day	1 Day

Block Scheduling Activities that are suited to use within the block scheduling framework are identified by: 🧊

0:00 OUT OF TIME? Assign the Chapter 7 *Reading Essentials and Study Guide.** 📁

SECTION RESOURCES

DAILY OBJECTIVES	REPRODUCIBLE RESOURCES	MULTIMEDIA RESOURCES
Section 1 **China's First Civilizations** 1. Rivers, mountains, and deserts helped shape China's civilization. 2. Rulers known as the Shang became powerful because they controlled land and had strong armies. 3. Chinese rulers claimed that the Mandate of Heaven gave them the right to rule.	📁 Reproducible Lesson Plan 7–1 📁 Daily Lecture and Discussion Notes 7–1 📁 Vocabulary Activity 7–1 📁 Active Reading Note-Taking Guide 7–1 📁 Guided Reading Activity 7–1* 📁 Section Quiz 7–1* 📁 Reading Essentials and Study Guide 7–1*	🔆 Daily Focus Skills Transparency 7–1 ⦿ Interactive Tutor Self-Assessment CD-ROM ⦿ Exam*View*® Pro Testmaker CD-ROM ⦿ Presentation Plus! CD-ROM
Section 2 **Life in Ancient China** 1. Chinese society had three main social classes: landowning aristocrats, farmers, and merchants. 2. Chinese philosophies grew out of a need for order in China.	📁 Reproducible Lesson Plan 7–2 📁 Daily Lecture and Discussion Notes 7–2 📁 Vocabulary Activity 7–2 📁 Active Reading Note-Taking Guide 7–2 📁 Guided Reading Activity 7–2* 📁 Section Quiz 7–2* 📁 Reading Essentials and Study Guide 7–2*	🔆 Daily Focus Skills Transparency 7–2 ⦿ Interactive Tutor Self-Assessment CD-ROM ⦿ Exam*View*® Pro Testmaker CD-ROM ⦿ Presentation Plus! CD-ROM ⦿ Glencoe BookLink CD-ROM
Section 3 **The Qin and Han Dynasties** 1. Qin Shihuangdi used harsh methods to unify and defend China. 2. The Han dynasty tested people for government jobs, and new inventions improved life for all Chinese. 3. The Silk Road carried Chinese goods as far as Greece and Rome.	📁 Reproducible Lesson Plan 7–3 📁 Daily Lecture and Discussion Notes 7–3 📁 Vocabulary Activity 7–3 📁 Active Reading Note-Taking Guide 7–3 📁 Guided Reading Activity 7–3* 📁 Section Quiz 7–3* 📁 Reading Essentials and Study Guide 7–3*	🔆 Daily Focus Skills Transparency 7–3 ⦿ Interactive Tutor Self-Assessment CD-ROM ⦿ Exam*View*® Pro Testmaker CD-ROM ⦿ Presentation Plus! CD-ROM ⦿ Vocabulary PuzzleMaker CD-ROM ⦿ Glencoe BookLink CD-ROM

*Also available in Spanish

Chapter ⑦ Resources

 History Online

Use our Web site for additional resources. All essential content is covered in the Student Edition.

You and your students can visit jat.glencoe.com, the Web site companion to *World History: Journey Across Time*. This innovative integration of electronic and print media offers your students a wealth of opportunities. The student text directs students to the Web site for the following options:

- Chapter Overviews
- Self-Check Quizzes
- Study Central™
- Student Web Activities
- Multi-Language Glossaries

Answers to the student Web activities are provided for you in the **Web Activity Lesson Plans.** Additional Web resources and ePuzzles and games are also available.

  THE HISTORY CHANNEL®

The following videotape programs are available from Glencoe as supplements to Chapter 7:

China's Forbidden City
(ISBN 0-7670-0649-6)

The Great Wall of China
(ISBN 0-7670-0361-6)

Confucius: Words of Wisdom
(ISBN 0-7670-0407-8)

To order, call Glencoe at 1-800-334-7344. To find classroom resources to accompany many of these videos, check the following home pages:

A&E Television: www.aande.com
The History Channel: www.historychannel.com

MEETING SPECIAL NEEDS

In addition to the Differentiated Instruction strategies, the following resources are suitable for students with special needs:

- *ExamView® Pro Testmaker CD-ROM* allows teachers to tailor tests by reducing answer choices.
- *StudentWorks Plus™ CD-ROM (with Audio Program)* includes the entire narrative of the student edition so that less-proficient readers can listen to the words as they read them.
- The *Reading Essentials and Study Guide* provides the same content as the student edition but is written two grade levels below the textbook.

 NATIONAL GEOGRAPHIC **TEACHER'S CORNER**

Index to National Geographic Magazine:

The following articles relate to this chapter:

- "The Han Dynasty," by Mike Edwards, February 2004.
- "The New Story of China's Ancient Past," by Peter Hessler, July 2003.
- "Rising to Life: Treasures of Ancient China," by Peter Hessler, October 2001.

National Geographic Society Products:

To order the following, call National Geographic at 1–800–368–2728

- *PicturePack: Ancient Civilizations: Ancient China* (Transparencies)
- *National Geographic Atlas of the World* (Book)

NGS ONLINE

Access National Geographic's new dynamic MapMachine Web site and other geography resources at:

www.nationalgeographic.com
www.nationalgeographic.com/maps

 ## Meeting NCSS Standards

World History: Journey Across Time

The following standards are highlighted in Chapter 7:

Section 1 **III** **People, Places, and Environments: H, J**
VI **Power, Authority, and Governance: B, C**
VIII **Science, Technology, and Society: A**

Section 2 **I** **Culture: A, B**
IV **Individual Development and Identity: G**
X **Civic Ideals and Practices: B**

Section 3 **I** **Culture: A, B**
II **Time, Continuity, and Change: A, B, C**
V **Individuals, Groups, and Institutions: G**
VII **Production, Distribution, and Consumption: A, F**

State and Local Objectives

_____

_____

_____

Timesaving Tools

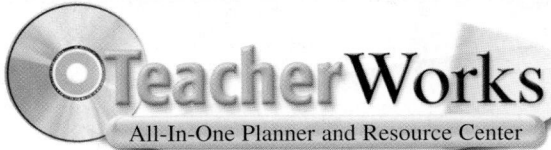

TeacherWorks
All-In-One Planner and Resource Center

- **Interactive Teacher Edition** Access your Teacher Wraparound Edition and your classroom resources with a few easy clicks.
- **Interactive Lesson Planner** Organize your week, month, semester, or year with all the lesson helps you need to make teaching creative and relevant.

Use Glencoe's **Presentation Plus!** multimedia teacher tool to easily present dynamic lessons that visually excite your students. Using Microsoft PowerPoint® you can customize the presentations to create your own personalized lessons.

FOLDABLES™
Study Organizer
Dinah Zike's Foldables

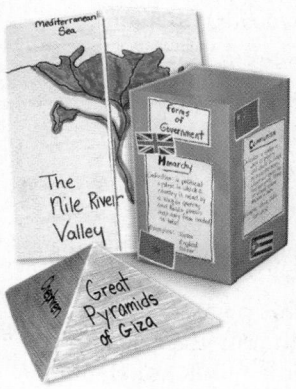

Foldables are three-dimensional, interactive graphic organizers that help students practice basic writing skills, review key vocabulary terms, and identify main ideas. Every chapter contains a foldable activity, with additional chapter activities found in the *Reading and Study Skills Foldables* booklet. You can use the foldables as they are presented, or modify them to suit the needs of your individual class.

Planning Ahead

CHAPTER CULMINATING ACTIVITY

The Chapter Culminating Activity will help students organize and learn the important information from the chapter. Begin the chapter with this activity, and have students complete it as a culminating activity.

CREATING A CAUSE-AND-EFFECT CHART

Purpose This type of organizer helps students analyze information by identifying cause-and-effect relationships. It will focus them on the most important points of the chapter as they read. It can also be used to organize information for reports and as a study aid.

Introduction to Modeling

1. Begin the discussion with a brainstorming session. Ask students to list what they know or believe they know about ancient China. Write the information on an overhead transparency.

2. Ask students to copy this chart into their notebooks:

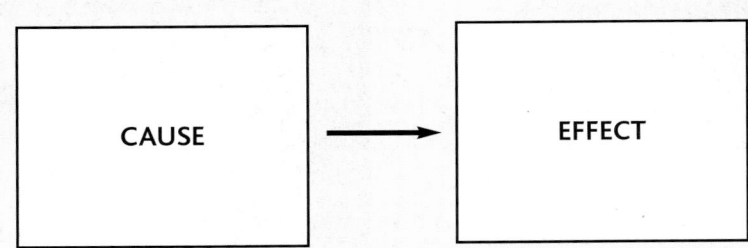

As students read the chapter, ask them to fill in either a cause or an effect, then find the missing cause or effect that completes the set of boxes. Have them draw as many charts as you think necessary to cover the main ideas in the chapter.

3. As part of your chapter review, have students share their cause-and-effect charts. Encourage them to complete more boxes and use their charts as study aids.

Use the **SkillBuilder Handbook** on pages 902–919 to help students learn the skill of understanding cause and effect.

✓ Authentic Assessment

Refer to Activity 7 in the Authentic Assessment section of the *Quizzes, Tests, and Authentic Assessment (with Rubrics)* booklet.

When &Where?

As students read the chapter, have them review the time line on this page. Ask them to explain how the development of the Silk Road changed life in China. (*It greatly increased trade with other countries, brought new ideas and products to China, and expanded China's economy.*) **L1**

GLENCOE TECHNOLOGY

World History: Journey Across Time Video Program

To learn more about ancient China, students can view the Chapter 7 video in the *World History: Journey Across Time* **Video Program.**

MindJogger Videoquiz

Use the **MindJogger Videoquiz** to preview Chapter 7 content.

 Available in DVD and VHS

Chapter 7

Early China

The first Great Wall of China was built more than 2,000 years ago to keep out invaders. The current wall, which is about 4,000 miles long, was built about 500 years ago. ▼

NATIONAL GEOGRAPHIC **When &Where?**

1800 B.C.	1150 B.C.	500 B.C.	A.D. 150
c. 1750 B.C. ● Shang dynasty begins	1045 B.C. ● Wu Wang creates Zhou dynasty	551 B.C. ● Confucius is born	c. A.D. 100 ● Silk Road established

📜 Reading Strategy ⟩ PURPOSE FOR READING

Cause and Effect Point out to students that civilizations generally go through cycles of prosperity and difficult times, of order and disorder. Have students imagine a society in which laws are weakly enforced, crime is common, and the government is unconcerned or ineffective. **Ask:** How might ordinary people cope with these disorderly conditions? What kinds of philosophies might they develop? (*Students may suggest one of several answers, such as that people might become outlaws, developing a philosophy of selfishness and self-protection. People also might withdraw from participation in daily life, developing a philosophy of letting events happen without worrying about how to control them.*) As they read, have students look for ways Chinese people coped with difficult social conditions. **L2**

Chapter Preview

The ancient Chinese, like the Egyptians, established long-ruling dynasties. The Chinese valued three great philosophies: Confucianism, Daoism, and Legalism.

 View the Chapter 7 video in the *World History: Journey Across Time* Video Program.

Chapter Overview Visit jat.glencoe.com for a preview of Chapter 7.

 Section 1

China's First Civilizations

Chinese civilization was shaped by geography such as mountains and large rivers. Long-lasting dynasties gained power through strong armies.

 Section 2

Life in Ancient China

Early Chinese society had three main social classes: aristocrats, farmers, and merchants. During periods of unrest, ideas such as Confucianism and Daoism developed.

 Section 3

The Qin and Han Dynasties

Both the Qin and Han dynasties created strong central governments. New inventions developed during the Han dynasty helped to improve the lives of Chinese people.

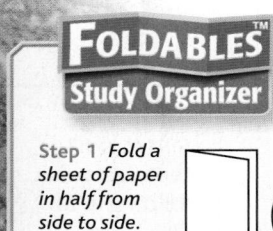 **FOLDABLES™ Study Organizer**

Organizing Information *Make this foldable to help you organize information about the important people in the early history of China.*

Step 1 *Fold a sheet of paper in half from side to side.*

Fold it so the left edge lies about ½ inch from the right edge.

Step 2 *Turn the paper and fold it into thirds.*

Step 4 *Turn the paper and label it as shown.*

Step 3 *Unfold and cut the top layer only along both folds.*

This will make three tabs.

China's First Civilizations
Chinese Philosophers
Qin and Han

Reading and Writing *As you read the chapter, list important people and what they did or taught during these periods in Chinese history.*

221

INTRODUCING CHAPTER 7

Introduce students to chapter content and key terms by having them access **Chapter Overview 7** at jat.glencoe.com

CHAPTER PREVIEW

After reading Chapter 7, students will be able to

1. discuss how river valleys, mountains, and deserts influenced the development of Chinese civilization;

2. discuss how the lack of order encouraged the growth of three important belief systems;

3. summarize the ruling philosophies, accomplishments, and failures of the Qin and Han dynasties.

 FOLDABLES™ Study Organizer — Dinah Zike's Foldables

Purpose Students use this foldable to organize information about notable people in early China by taking notes about them as they read. When students have completed their foldables, they should have a guide to the important figures discussed in this chapter.

📁 Have students complete *Reading and Study Skills Foldables* Activity 7.

MORE ABOUT THE PHOTO

The Great Wall The Great Wall of China is the longest human-built structure in the world. From its start on the shores of the Yellow Sea in northeastern China, the main part of the wall runs about 1,500 miles (2,400 km) along China's northern border. The first emperor of a united China, Qin Shihuangdi, began to connect a number of defensive walls around 214 B.C. The purpose was to keep out nomadic invaders who were attacking China from the north. As many as a half a million workers labored on the wall, and many of them died in the effort. The Great Wall seen today is almost entirely a rebuilt version of the original. It dates mostly from the years of the Ming dynasty (A.D. 1368–1644).

1 Learn It!

Many students are not aware of how punctuation marks, section headings, and other text features help them comprehend what they read. Often, they even skip over these important clues.

Walk through the chapter with students before they read it. Point out textual aids such as illustrations and headings. Then read the first section aloud as students follow silently, pointing out how punctuation helps readers make sense of the text. Explain how phrases or words such as *as a result, however,* or *like* signal comparison or cause-and-effect relationships.

The following example from the second paragraph on page 225 emphasizes a few such contextual clues (in italics):

> *Like* rivers in early Mesopotamia and Egypt, China's Huang He flooded the land. The flooding was good and bad for the Chinese. *When the river overflowed,* many people drowned and many homes were destroyed. *As a result,* the Chinese called the Huang He "China's sorrow."

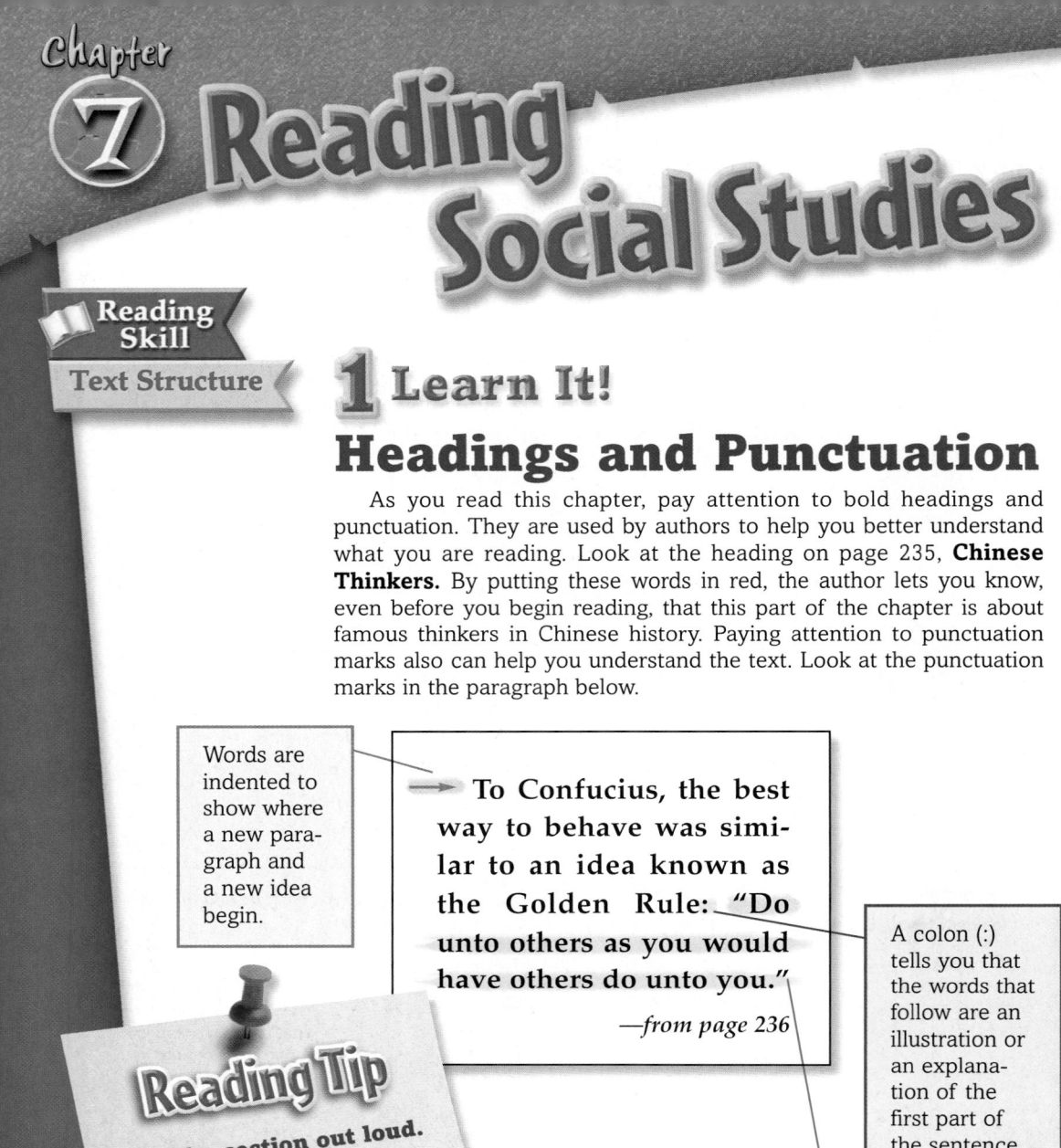

Chapter 7 Reading Social Studies

Reading Skill

Text Structure

1 Learn It!

Headings and Punctuation

As you read this chapter, pay attention to bold headings and punctuation. They are used by authors to help you better understand what you are reading. Look at the heading on page 235, **Chinese Thinkers.** By putting these words in red, the author lets you know, even before you begin reading, that this part of the chapter is about famous thinkers in Chinese history. Paying attention to punctuation marks also can help you understand the text. Look at the punctuation marks in the paragraph below.

Words are indented to show where a new paragraph and a new idea begin.

➡ **To Confucius, the best way to behave was similar to an idea known as the Golden Rule: "Do unto others as you would have others do unto you."**

—from page 236

A colon (:) tells you that the words that follow are an illustration or an explanation of the first part of the sentence.

Reading Tip

Read a section out loud. Say the names of the punctuation marks as you read. This will help you remember why certain punctuation marks are used.

Quotation marks have several uses. Here they are used to set off words taken from another source.

222

Reading Strategy ⟩ PAIRED READING

Just as you, the teacher, model reading as a comprehension strategy, students can practice reading with each other. In pairs or groups, have them take turns reading aloud to each other, stopping to point out the use of punctuation marks, words in bold, or other print conventions that they may not notice as they read silently. Have them make a list of these terms, punctuation marks, or other conventions, including an explanation of how each was used in the text. **L1**

2 Practice It!
Punctuation Clues

Look at the heading and punctuation in the following paragraph and answer the questions that follow.

The Zhou Empire Falls Over time, the local rulers of the Zhou territories became powerful. They stopped obeying the Zhou kings and set up their own states. In 403 B.C. fighting broke out. For almost 200 years, the states battled each other. Historians call this time the "Period of the Warring States."

—from page 231

1. Based on the heading, what do you think this section will be about?

2. Why do you think the phrase "Period of the Warring States" is in quotation marks?

3. How will you know when a new paragraph begins?

Read to Write

Suppose you had a younger brother, sister, or friend who was just learning to read. How could you explain the use of punctuation marks to this person? Write a step-by-step explanation of what he or she would need to know about periods, commas, colons, and quotation marks.

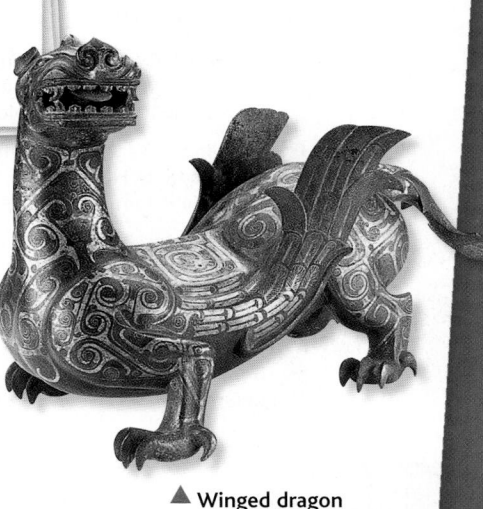

▲ Winged dragon from Zhou dynasty

3 Apply It!

As you read the chapter, jot down punctuation or section headings that you do not understand. Write them in your notebook to discuss later.

223

---

2 Practice It!

- Choose a section heading and ask students to predict what might be in that section based on the title.

- Point out that quotation marks surround the exact words of a speaker or might be used to set off a phrase or word.

- Remind students that authors often define words by placing their meanings in brackets or parentheses.

- Explain that three periods after a word are called *ellipses* and mean that some words have been omitted.

- Point out differences in the text structure of narratives or biographies, poems, or prose.

Answers:

1. how the Zhou empire came to an end

2. title of a period in history

3. indented line or new heading

3 Apply It!

Have students work in groups. Give each group a different passage from the text with the punctuation deleted. Have them insert their own punctuation and read the passage aloud to see if their reading follows the "correct" punctuation. **L2**

Reading Strategy **READ TO WRITE**

Students should take into consideration the level of knowledge of the person for whom they are writing the explanation: someone who has no experience with punctuation. Possible explanations include: A period indicates the end of a sentence. A comma is used to show a pause in a sentence or to join lists together. A colon separates the first part of a sentence from the next part. The second part often gives additional information about the first part. Quotation marks are used to show speech, to set off a quote, or to indicate some other special phrase.

Section
1
China's First Civilizations

① FOCUS

SECTION OVERVIEW

This section describes the first civilizations in China and how the geography of the region, especially its rivers, mountains, and deserts, influenced China's cultural development.

BELLRINGER
SKILLBUILDER ACTIVITY

✎ Project **Daily Focus Skills Transparency 7–1** and have students answer questions. Discuss their responses.

Get Ready to Read!

Preteaching Vocabulary: Explain that a dynasty is a powerful group or family that maintains its ruling power for a considerable time. A long dynasty helps ensure stability.

Answers to Graphic: Shang—Dates: about 1750 B.C. to 1122 B.C.; Leadership: kings; Accomplishments: pictographs and ideographs, silk weaving, bronze; Zhou—Dates: about 1045 B.C. to 221 B.C.; Leadership: kings (with Mandate of Heaven); Accomplishments: irrigation, flood control, iron plows and weapons, trade of silk

Section 1
China's First Civilizations

Get Ready to Read!

What's the Connection?
In earlier chapters, you learned that many civilizations developed in river valleys. The civilizations of China also began in river valleys. However, other features of the land, such as mountains and deserts, affected China's history as well.

Focusing on the Main Ideas
- Rivers, mountains, and deserts helped shape China's civilization. *(page 225)*
- Rulers known as the Shang became powerful because they controlled land and had strong armies. *(page 226)*
- Chinese rulers claimed that the Mandate of Heaven gave them the right to rule. *(page 229)*

Locating Places
Huang He (HWAHNG HUH)
Chang Jiang (CHAHNG JYAHNG)
Anyang (AHN•YAHNG)

Meeting People
Wu Wang (WOO WAHNG)

Building Your Vocabulary
dynasty (DY•nuh•stee)
aristocrat (uh•RIHS•tuh•KRAT)
pictograph (PIHK•tuh•GRAF)
ideograph (IH•dee•uh•GRAF)
bureaucracy (byu•RAH•kruh•see)
mandate (MAN•DAYT)
Dao (DOW)

Reading Strategy
Summarizing Information Complete a chart like the one below describing the characteristics of the Shang and Zhou dynasties.

	Shang Dynasty	Zhou Dynasty
Dates		
Leadership		
Accomplishments		

NATIONAL GEOGRAPHIC When & Where?

Anyang
Luoyang

1750 B.C.	975 B.C.	200 B.C.
c. 1750 B.C. Shang dynasty begins	1045 B.C. Wu Wang creates Zhou dynasty	221 B.C. Qin dynasty begins

224 CHAPTER 7 Early China

SECTION RESOURCES

📁 **Reproducible Masters**
- Reproducible Lesson Plan 7–1
- Daily Lecture and Discussion Notes 7–1
- Vocabulary Activity 7–1
- Active Reading Note-Taking Guide 7–1
- Guided Reading Activity 7–1
- Section Quiz 7–1
- Reading Essentials and Study Guide 7–1

✎ **Transparencies**
- Daily Focus Skills Transparency 7–1

Multimedia
- Interactive Tutor Self-Assessment CD-ROM
- ExamView® Pro Testmaker CD-ROM
- Presentation Plus! CD-ROM

China's Geography

Main Idea Rivers, mountains, and deserts helped shape China's civilization.

Reading Focus Why do you think so many cities and towns were built beside rivers? Read to learn why rivers were important to the development of China.

The **Huang He** (HWAHNG HUH), or Yellow River, flows across China for more than 2,900 miles (4,666 km). It gets its name from the rich yellow soil it carries from Mongolia to the Pacific Ocean.

Like rivers in early Mesopotamia and Egypt, China's Huang He flooded the land. The flooding was good and bad for the Chinese. When the river overflowed, many people drowned and many homes were destroyed. As a result, the Chinese called the Huang He "China's sorrow."

The river, however, also brought a gift. When the river flooded, it left behind rich topsoil in the Huang He valley. As a result, farmers could grow large amounts of food on very small farms.

China also has another great river, called the **Chang Jiang** (CHAHNG JYAHNG), or the Yangtze River. The Chang Jiang is even longer than the Huang He. It flows for about 3,400 miles (5,471 km) east across central China where it empties into the Yellow Sea. Like the Huang He valley, the valley of the Chang Jiang also has rich soil for farming.

② TEACH

Reading Strategy

Comparing and Contrasting Ask students to make a simple chart that includes the positive and negative effects of rivers on Chinese civilizations. (*River flooding caused loss of life and damage; it also left rich soil that improved farming and food production.*) **L1**

Daily Lecture and Discussion Notes 7–1

Use **Daily Lecture and Discussion Notes 7–1** for an outline of key concepts found in the section.

Reading Support L1/ EL

Use **Vocabulary Activity 7–1** to help students learn important terms in the section.

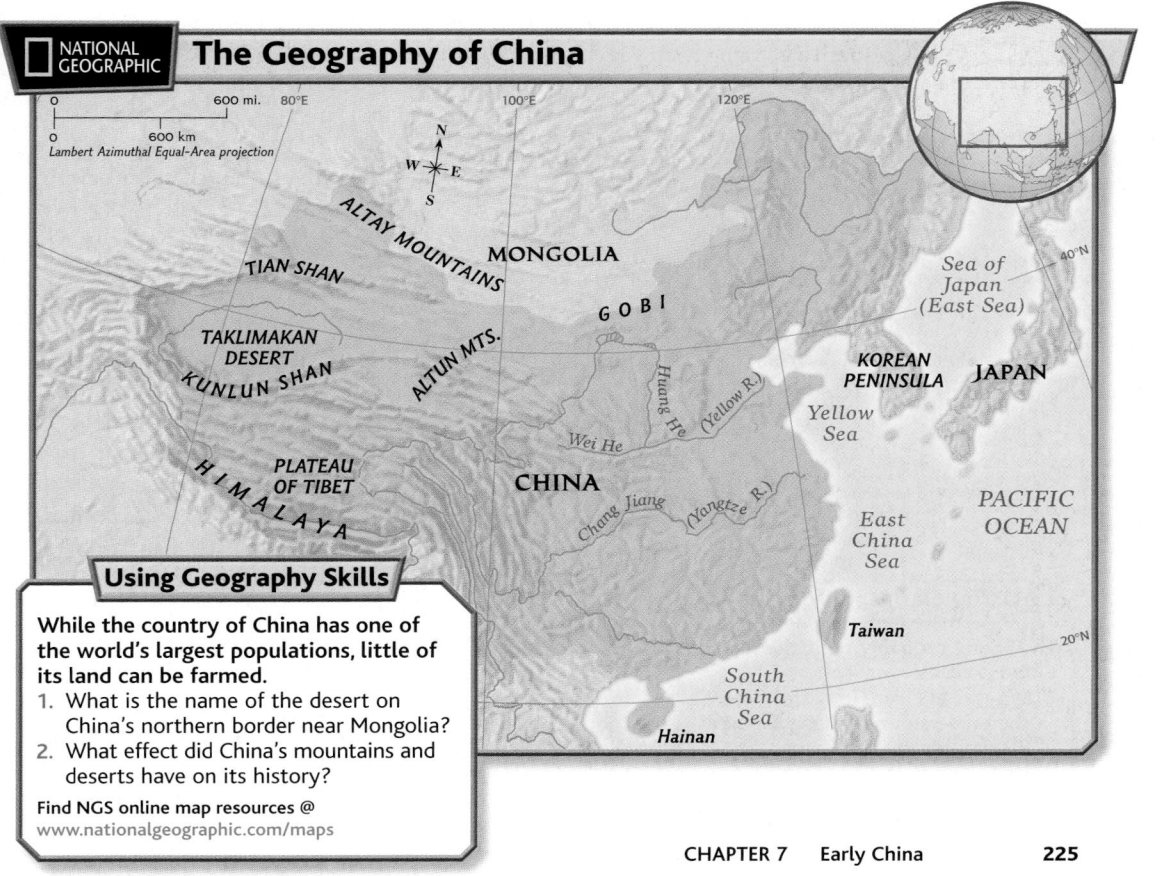

NATIONAL GEOGRAPHIC
The Geography of China

600 mi. 80°E 100°E 120°E
600 km
Lambert Azimuthal Equal-Area projection

ALTAY MOUNTAINS
TIAN SHAN
MONGOLIA
GOBI
TAKLIMAKAN DESERT
ALTUN MTS.
KUNLUN SHAN
Huang He (Yellow R.)
Wei He
PLATEAU OF TIBET
CHINA
HIMALAYA
Chang Jiang (Yangtze R.)
KOREAN PENINSULA
JAPAN
Sea of Japan (East Sea)
40°N
Yellow Sea
East China Sea
PACIFIC OCEAN
Taiwan
20°N
South China Sea
Hainan

Using Geography Skills

While the country of China has one of the world's largest populations, little of its land can be farmed.
1. What is the name of the desert on China's northern border near Mongolia?
2. What effect did China's mountains and deserts have on its history?

Find NGS online map resources @
www.nationalgeographic.com/maps

Using Geography Skills

Answers:
1. Gobi
2. They limited farmland and separated China from the outside world.

CHAPTER 7 Early China **225**

Reading Strategy — **READING THE TEXT**

Activating Prior Knowledge Ask students in what contexts they have heard the term *warlords*. (*Students may refer to regional leaders in countries such as Afghanistan.*) Have students make a class list of the characteristics of modern warlords, how they influence countries, and what U.S. experiences with these people have been. (*Students may argue that warlords promote conflict and hinder nation-building.*) Discuss the social and economic conditions that create warlords and how they can be prevented or resolved. Extend the idea of conflict resolution to students' lives. Ask volunteers to recount a conflict or dispute with which they are familiar. Have them identify the issues involved in the dispute and suggest ways that it could peacefully be settled. **L2**

▶ **Reading Strategy** ◀

Predicting Ask students to read the description of how natural barriers separated China from its neighbors. Then have them write a paragraph predicting what effect this separation would likely have on Chinese civilization and culture. *(Most students will point out that China's isolation would allow it to develop a civilization that is freer from foreign influences than are most other cultures.)* L2

✓ **Reading Check**

Answer: the Huang He and the Chang Jiang

CONNECTING ACROSS TIME

Remind students that archaeologists use artifacts such as pottery to piece together information about the lives of people in early China. Ask students to list items that might help future archaeologists learn about the students' everyday lives. L1/ EL

Using Geography Skills

Answers:

1. Huang He and Chang Jiang

2. northern, near the Huang He

Even though China has rich soil along its rivers, only a little more than one-tenth of its land can be farmed. That is because mountains and deserts cover most of the land. The towering Himalaya close off China to the southwest. The Kunlun Shan and Tian Shan are mountain ranges on China's western border. The Gobi, a vast, cold, rocky desert, spreads east from the mountains. These mountains and deserts shaped much of Chinese history. They were like a wall around the Chinese, separating them from most other peoples.

Over time, the Chinese people united to form one kingdom. They called their homeland "the Middle Kingdom." To them, it was the world's center and its leading civilization. The Chinese developed a way of life that lasted into modern times.

✓ **Reading Check** **Identify** Name two rivers important to early Chinese civilizations.

NATIONAL GEOGRAPHIC **Shang Empire**

0   400 mi.
0   400 km
Lambert Azimuthal Equal-Area projection

120°E

40°N

Huang He (Yellow R.)

Anyang

Wei He   Huang He (Yellow R.)

Chang Jiang (Yangtze R.)

Yellow Sea

East China Sea

KEY
Shang empire, c. 1750-1045 B.C.

Using Geography Skills

The Shang probably built the first Chinese cities.
1. What rivers were found within the borders of the Shang dynasty?
2. In what part of the Shang kingdom was Anyang found?

226   CHAPTER 7   Early China

The Shang Dynasty

Main Idea Rulers known as the Shang became powerful because they controlled land and had strong armies.

Reading Focus Who are the leaders in your community? What gives them their power? Read to learn why some people in early China had more power than others.

Little is known about how Chinese civilization began. Archaeologists, however, have found pottery in the Huang He valley dating back thousands of years. These artifacts show that the Huang He valley was the first center of Chinese civilization. Archaeologists think that people stayed in the valley and farmed the land because of rich soil. As their numbers rose, they began building towns, and soon after, the first Chinese civilization began.

China's first rulers were probably part of the Xia (SYAH) dynasty. A **dynasty** (DY•nuh•stee) is a line of rulers who belong to the same family. Little is known about the Xia. We know more about the next dynasty, the Shang. The Shang kings ruled from about 1750 B.C. to 1045 B.C.

Who Were the Shang? Archaeologists have found huge walls, royal palaces, and royal tombs from the time of the Shang. These remains show that the Shang may have built the first Chinese cities. One of these cities was **Anyang** (AHN•YAHNG) in northern China. Anyang was China's first capital. From there, the Shang kings ruled the early Chinese people.

The people of the Shang dynasty were divided into groups. The most powerful group was the king and his family. The first Shang king ruled over a small area in northern China. His armies used chariots and bronze weapons to take over nearby areas.

DIFFERENTIATED INSTRUCTION

Kinesthetic: Ask students to create a bulletin board, showcase, or other display about the history of early China. Have the students discuss a focus or theme for the display, such as agriculture, cities, daily life, government, or historical artifacts. Students may incorporate photos, drawings, diagrams, dioramas and models, actual objects, or any other appropriate media in their displays. Ask groups to present their display to the class and explain its content.

English Learners: Ask students to paraphrase each caption or informational sheet in the display.

Gifted and Talented: Have students add original artworks to the display.

📁 Refer to *Inclusion Strategies for the Middle School Social Studies Classroom* in the TCR.

In time, the Shang kings ruled over most of the Huang He valley.

Later, Shang kings chose warlords to govern the kingdom's territories. Warlords are military leaders who command their own armies. However, the king controlled even larger armies who defended the kingdom's borders. The king's armies helped him stay in power.

Under the king, the warlords and other royal officials made up the upper class. They were **aristocrats** (uh•RIHS•tuh•KRATS), nobles whose wealth came from the land they owned. Aristocrats passed their land and their power from one generation to the next.

In Shang China, a few people were traders and artisans. Most Chinese, however, were farmers. They worked the land that belonged to the aristocrats. They grew grains, such as millet, wheat, and rice, and raised cattle, sheep, and chickens. A small number of enslaved people captured in war also lived in Shang China.

Spirits and Ancestors People in Shang China worshiped gods and spirits. Spirits were believed to live in mountains, rivers, and seas. The people believed that they had to keep the gods and spirits happy by making offerings of food and other goods. They believed that the gods and spirits would be angry if they were not treated well. Angry gods and spirits might cause farmers to have a poor harvest or armies to lose a battle.

People also honored their ancestors, or departed family members. Offerings were made in the hope that ancestors would help in times of need and bring good luck. To this day, many Chinese still remember their ancestors by going to temples and burning small paper copies of food and clothing.

NATIONAL GEOGRAPHIC The Way It Was

Focus on Everyday Life

The Role of Women Zheng Zhenxiang was China's first female archaeologist. In 1976 she found the tomb of Fu Hao, China's first female general. In the tomb were more than 2,000 artifacts from the Shang dynasty, including weapons, bronze vessels, jade objects, and bones with Chinese characters carved on them.

▲ Bronze vessel

Fu Hao, the wife of King Wu Ding, was given a royal burial. She was famous for her strength, martial arts skills, and military strategies. She often helped her husband defeat their enemies on the battlefield. Fu Hao was the first female in China's history to receive the highest military rank.

Her tomb and its artifacts reveal the grand civilization of China's Shang dynasty. During this period, the Chinese developed writing, a calendar, and musical instruments.

◀ Jade sculpture of a seated human figure

Connecting to the Past
1. What was Fu Hao famous for during her life?
2. Describe what the artifacts found in Fu Hao's tomb might reveal about life during that time.

Reading Strategy

Writing Activity

Religion and government in the Shang dynasty were closely connected. Ask students to review the section of the text that describes this close relationship, then write a paragraph taking a position on the following statement: A close relationship between religion and government may have positive effects on a society. **L3**

CONNECTING ACROSS TIME

Review the discussion of how many early Chinese felt about their ancestors. Ask students what people in the United States do to remember their ancestors. Are there any common practices? **L2**

NATIONAL GEOGRAPHIC The Way It Was

Answers:
1. her strength, martial arts skills, and military strategies
2. The Shang dynasty was a sophisticated civilization, with bronze technology, writing, a calendar, and musical instruments.

CRITICAL THINKING ACTIVITY

Drawing Conclusions Have students review the information about dynasties in ancient China. Then have them discuss whether we have informal ruling dynasties today in the United States. Why do members of certain families appeal to voters? Is the son or daughter of a previous leader also likely to be a good elected leader? Why or why not? Conclude by having students name some American-style political "dynasties" at the city, state, or national level and critique their members' performances as elected leaders. *(Answers will vary, although students will recognize that most political arenas, to some extent, do feature political families. Perceptions of the talents of such family members will vary. Reasons for informal dynasties may include name recognition and admiration for a candidate's relatives.)* **L3**

Needs in the Afterlife Ask students to compare the Shang customs regarding their relatives' needs in the afterlife with those of the ancient Egyptians. **L3**

Shang oracle bones contained as many as 3,000 different characters. In order to write these messages, priests needed to memorize the characters. Because memorizing so many characters was difficult, few people could read and write. Have students discuss other limitations of pictograph-based writing systems and the challenges a present-day pictograph language would need to overcome. **L2**

These copies represent things that their departed relatives need in the afterlife.

Telling the Future Shang kings believed that they received power and wisdom from the gods, the spirits, and their ancestors.

NATIONAL GEOGRAPHIC
HISTORY MAKERS

Chinese Writing

The Chinese writing system was created nearly 3,500 years ago during the Shang dynasty. The earliest examples of Chinese writing have been found on animal bones. The carvings on these bones show that Chinese writing has always used symbols to represent words. Some of the carvings are pictures. For example, the verb *to go* was represented by a picture of a foot. The characters were carved in vertical columns and read from top to bottom, like modern Chinese writing. The writing on the bones recorded the Shang kings' questions about a wide range of topics—from the weather to good fortune. Chinese writing has changed in many ways, but it still reflects its ancient roots in pictures and symbols.

Oracle bone ▶

228   CHAPTER 7   Early China

Shang religion and government were closely linked, just as they were in ancient Mesopotamia and Egypt. An important duty of Shang kings was to contact the gods, the spirits, and ancestors before making important decisions.

The kings asked for the gods' help by using oracle (AWR•uh•kuhl) bones. They had priests scratch questions on the bones, such as "Will I win the battle?" and "Will I recover from my illness?" Then the priests placed hot metal rods inside the bones, causing them to crack. They believed that the pattern of the cracks formed answers from the gods. The priests interpreted the answers and wrote them down for the kings. Scratches on oracle bones are the earliest known examples of Chinese writing.

The Chinese Language The scratches on oracle bones show how today's Chinese writing began. However, the modern Chinese language is much more complex.

Like many other ancient languages, early Chinese writing used pictographs and ideographs. **Pictographs** (PIHK•tuh•GRAFS) are characters that stand for objects. For example, the Chinese characters for a mountain, the sun, and the moon are pictographs. **Ideographs** (IH•dee•uh•GRAFS) are another kind of character used in Chinese writing. They join two or more pictographs to represent an idea. For example, the ideograph for "east" relates to the idea of the sun rising in the east. It is a combination of pictographs that show the sun coming up behind trees.

Unlike Chinese, English and many other languages have writing systems based on an alphabet. An alphabet uses characters that stand for sounds. The Chinese use some characters to stand for sounds, but most characters still represent whole words.

INTERDISCIPLINARY CONNECTIONS ACTIVITY

Religion The Chinese belief in supernatural forces influenced the way the Shang and Zhou leaders governed. Ask students which other civilizations they have studied relied on supernatural forces to govern. *(Sumerians, Egyptians, Israelites)* Have students research and report on the influence of religion on present-day governments. *(Answers will vary but should include a variety of different governments with greater or lesser degrees of religious influence.)* **L3**

Shang Artists The people in Shang China developed many skills. Farmers produced silk, which weavers used to make colorful clothes. Artisans made vases and dishes from fine white clay. They also carved statues from ivory and a green stone called jade.

The Shang are best known for their works of bronze. To make bronze objects, artisans made clay molds in several sections. Next, they carved detailed designs into the clay. Then, they fit the pieces of the mold tightly together and poured in melted bronze. When the bronze cooled, the mold was removed. A beautifully decorated work of art remained.

Shang bronze objects included sculptures, vases, drinking cups, and containers called urns. The Shang used bronze urns to prepare and serve food for rituals honoring ancestors.

✓ **Reading Check** **Explain** What was the role of Shang warlords?

◀ Buffalo-shaped bronze vessel from the Shang dynasty

The Zhou Dynasty

Main Idea Chinese rulers claimed that the Mandate of Heaven gave them the right to rule.

Reading Focus Who gives you permission to do the things you do? Your mother? Your teacher? Read to find out how the rulers of the Zhou dynasty turned to the heavens for permission to rule.

During the rule of the Shang, a great gap existed between the rich and the poor. Shang kings lived in luxury and began to treat people cruelly. As a result, they lost the support of the people in their kingdom. In 1045 B.C. an aristocrat named **Wu Wang** (WOO WAHNG) led a rebellion against the Shang. After defeating the Shang, Wu began a new dynasty called the Zhou (JOH).

The Zhou Government The Zhou dynasty ruled for more than 800 years—longer than any other dynasty in Chinese history.

Zhou kings ruled much like Shang rulers. The Zhou king was at the head of the government. Under him was a large **bureaucracy** (byu•RAH•kruh•see). A bureaucracy is made up of appointed officials who are responsible for different areas of government. Like the Shang rulers, the Zhou king was in charge of defending the kingdom.

▼ Bronze food container from the Shang dynasty

◀ Bronze bowl and ladle from Zhou dynasty

▲ These bronze bells are from the Zhou dynasty. *How long did the Zhou dynasty last?*

CHAPTER 7 Early China **229**

EXTENDING THE CONTENT

Casting Bronze Items Bronze is an alloy, or mixture, of two other metals—copper and tin. Combining different metals in different proportions often creates a metal that has more desirable qualities. Bronze, for example, has several characteristics that make it ideal for casting vessels, cups, and other objects. Bronze melts and pours more easily than copper or tin. The hot liquid metal expands to fill a mold. In addition, when melted bronze cools, it pulls back from the sides of the mold, making it easy to remove. It is also harder than copper or tin. For all these reasons, bronze was perfect for the Shang craftspeople. Today, bronze is used for large statues, coins, bells, and other objects.

③ ASSESS

Assign Section 1 Review as homework or as an in-class activity.

⊙ Have students use the **Interactive Tutor Self-Assessment CD-ROM** to review the section.

Using Geography Skills

Answers:

1. the Yellow Sea
2. to make ruling easier

Assessment L2

Assign **Section 1 Quiz** to assess mastery of the material found in the section.

Reading Support L1/ EL

Assign **Reading Essentials and Study Guide 7–1** to help students review section material.

History Online

Objectives and answers to the student activity can be found in the **Web Activity Lesson Plan** feature at jat.glencoe.com

NATIONAL GEOGRAPHIC Zhou Empire

KEY
Zhou empire, 1045–256 B.C.

400 mi.
400 km
Lambert Azimuthal Equal-Area projection

Using Geography Skills

Zhou rulers maintained the longest-lasting dynasty in Chinese history.
1. What body of water made up the eastern border of Zhou territory?
2. Why did the Zhou divide their kingdom into smaller territories?

The Zhou kings copied the Shang system of dividing the kingdom into smaller territories. The kings put aristocrats they trusted in charge of each territory. The positions the aristocrats held were hereditary. That meant that when an aristocrat died, his son or another relative would take over as ruler of the territory.

The Chinese considered the king their link between heaven and earth. His chief duty was to carry out religious rituals. The Chinese believed these rituals strengthened the link between them and the gods. This belief paved the way for a new idea that the Zhou kings introduced to government. They claimed that kings ruled China because they had the Mandate of Heaven.

What Was the Mandate of Heaven?

According to Zhou rulers, a heavenly law gave the Zhou king the power to rule. This **mandate** (MAN•DAYT), or formal order, was called the Mandate of Heaven. Based on the mandate, the king was chosen by heavenly

order because of his talent and virtue. Therefore, he would rule the people with goodness and wisdom.

The Mandate of Heaven worked in two ways. First, the people expected the king to rule according to the proper "Way," called the **Dao** (DOW). His duty was to keep the gods happy. A natural disaster or a bad harvest was a sign that he had failed in his duty. People then had the right to overthrow and replace the king.

The Mandate of Heaven also worked another way. It gave the people, as well as the king, important rights. For example, people had the right to overthrow a dishonest or evil ruler. It also made clear that the king was not a god himself. Of course, each new dynasty claimed it had the Mandate of Heaven. The only way people could question the claim was by overthrowing the dynasty.

New Tools and Trade For thousands of years, Chinese farmers depended on rain to water their crops. During the Zhou dynasty, the Chinese developed irrigation and flood-control systems. As a result, farmers could grow more crops than ever before.

Improvements in farming tools also helped farmers produce more crops. By 550 B.C., the Chinese were using iron plows. These sturdy plows broke up land that had been too hard to farm with wooden plows. As a result, the Chinese could plow more and produce more crops. Because more food could support more people, the population increased. During the late Zhou dynasty, China had a population of about 50 million people.

History Online

Web Activity Visit jat.glencoe.com and click on *Chapter 7—Student Web Activity* to learn more about ancient China.

230   CHAPTER 7   Early China

COOPERATIVE LEARNING ACTIVITY

Creating Characters Ask students working in small groups to review the discussion of pictographs and ideographs. Then have the groups work together to devise characters for 10 different objects, ideas, places, or events. For example, if the name of your school were East Side Middle School, students might create a pictograph based on the right-hand or east side of a stylized compass. Have groups share and explain their characters. **L2**

Trade and manufacturing grew along with farming. An important trade item during the Zhou dynasty was silk. Pieces of Chinese silk have been found throughout central Asia and as far away as Greece. This suggests that the Chinese traded far and wide.

◄ This statue of a winged dragon is from the Zhou dynasty. *From what metal did the Chinese make plows and weapons during the Zhou dynasty?*

The Zhou Empire Falls Over time, the local rulers of the Zhou territories became powerful. They stopped obeying the Zhou kings and set up their own states. In 403 B.C. fighting broke out. For almost 200 years, the states battled each other. Historians call this time the "Period of the Warring States."

Instead of nobles driving chariots, the warring states used large armies of foot soldiers. To get enough soldiers, they issued laws forcing peasants to serve in the army. The armies fought with swords, spears, and crossbows. A crossbow uses a crank to pull the string and shoots arrows with great force.

As the fighting went on, the Chinese invented the saddle and stirrup. These let soldiers ride horses and use spears and crossbows while riding. In 221 B.C. the ruler of Qin (CHIHN), one of the warring states, used a large cavalry force to defeat the other states and set up a new dynasty.

 Reading Check **Identify** What was the chief duty of Chinese kings?

 History Online
Study Central™ Need help with the material in this section? Visit jat.glencoe.com

Section 1 Review

Reading Summary
Review the Main Ideas
- China's first civilizations formed in river valleys. The Chinese were isolated from other people by mountains and deserts.
- The rulers of the Shang dynasty controlled the area around the Huang He valley.
- The Zhou dynasty replaced the Shang and claimed to rule with the Mandate of Heaven. During the Zhou dynasty, farming methods improved and trade increased.

What Did You Learn?
1. What is a dynasty?
2. What were oracle bones and how were they used?

Critical Thinking
3. **Analyze** How did the Mandate of Heaven allow for the overthrow of kings in ancient China?
4. **Summarizing Information** Draw a diagram like the one below. Add details that describe the members of Shang society.

Shang Society

5. **Evaluate** What were some important technological changes during the Zhou dynasty, and how did they lead to a larger population?
6. **Explain** How did ancient Chinese kings maintain control of their dynasties?
7. **Reading** **Text Structure** Explain why parentheses are used in the following sentence. "The Huang He (HWAHNG HUH), or Yellow River, flows across China for more than 2,900 miles (4,666 km)."

CHAPTER 7   Early China   **231**

ENRICH
Remind students that in Shang and Zhou China, the people who controlled the land had the power. Ask them to discuss whether the same is true today. **L2**

 Reading Check

Answer: to carry out religious rituals

 History Online

To help students understand section material, have them visit **Study Central**™ at jat.glencoe.com

RETEACH
Ask students to describe how rivers, mountains, and deserts helped shape China's civilizations. **L1**

④ CLOSE

Ask students to define the Mandate of Heaven and describe its effect on the rulers and people of ancient China. **L2**

① FOCUS

SECTION OVERVIEW

This section focuses on society in early China, including the great religious and philosophical systems that were created.

BELLRINGER
SKILLBUILDER ACTIVITY

🖋 Project **Daily Focus Skills Transparency 7–2** and have students answer questions. Discuss their responses.

Get Ready to Read!

Preteaching Vocabulary: Explain that the term *social class* has different meanings in different cultures. In our culture, for example, we sometimes speak of middle-class or working-class people. In ancient societies, social classes often corresponded to occupational, or job, classes, such as merchants, farmers, and laborers.

Answers to Graphic: aristocrats, farmers, merchants

Section 2

Life in Ancient China

Get Ready to Read!

What's the Connection?

In Section 1, you learned about the Chinese government under the Zhou dynasty. This section describes what life was like during the Zhou dynasty.

Focusing on the Main Ideas

• Chinese society had three main social classes: landowning aristocrats, farmers, and merchants. *(page 233)*

• Three Chinese philosophies, Confucianism, Daoism, and Legalism, grew out of a need for order. *(page 235)*

Meeting People

Confucius (kuhn•FYOO•shuhs)
Laozi (LOWD•ZOO)
Hanfeizi (HAN•fay•DZOO)

Building Your Vocabulary

social class
filial piety
   (FIH•lee•uhl   PY•uh•tee)
Confucianism
   (kuhn•FYOO•shuh•NIH•zuhm)
Daoism (DOW•IH•zuhm)
Legalism (LEE•guh•LIH•zuhm)

Reading Strategy

Organizing Information Create a pyramid diagram like the one below showing the social classes in ancient China from most important (top) to least important (bottom).

NATIONAL GEOGRAPHIC **When & Who?**

600 B.C.   **400 B.C.**   **200 B.C.**

551 B.C. Confucius is born

c. 300 B.C. Laozi's ideas of Daoism become popular

c. 200 B.C. Hanfeizi develops Legalism

SECTION RESOURCES

📂 **Reproducible Masters**
• Reproducible Lesson Plan 7–2
• Daily Lecture and Discussion Notes 7–2
• Vocabulary Activity 7–2
• Active Reading Note-Taking Guide 7–2
• Guided Reading Activity 7–2
• Section Quiz 7–2
• Reading Essentials and Study Guide 7–2

🖋 **Transparencies**
• Daily Focus Skills Transparency 7–2

Multimedia
 Interactive Tutor Self-Assessment CD-ROM
⊘ Exam*View*® Pro Testmaker CD-ROM
⊘ Presentation Plus! CD-ROM
⊘ Glencoe BookLink CD-ROM

Life in Ancient China

Main Idea Chinese society had three main social classes: landowning aristocrats, farmers, and merchants.

Reading Focus Have you heard the terms *high society* and *working class?* They describe social classes in America. Read on to find out about social classes in early China.

A **social class** includes people who share a similar position in society. Early Chinese society had three main social classes:

- landowning aristocrats
- peasant farmers
- merchants

Classes in Chinese Society China's aristocratic families owned large estates in early China. They lived in large houses with tile roofs, courtyards, and gardens. Fine furniture and silk hangings filled their rooms, and their houses were surrounded by walls to keep out bandits.

The aristocratic families did not own large estates for long. Each aristocrat divided his land among his sons. As a result, sons and grandsons owned much less property than their fathers and grandfathers had owned.

Aristocrats relied on farmers to grow the crops that made them rich. About nine out of ten Chinese were farmers. They lived in simple houses inside village walls. The aristocrats owned the fields outside the village walls. In these fields, farmers in northern China grew wheat and a grain called millet. In the south, where the climate was warmer and wetter, they were able to grow rice.

Chinese Village

Chinese farmers lived in small villages made up of several families. They farmed fields outside the village walls.
How did farmers pay for the use of the land they farmed?

Since horses were more valuable as war animals, farmers used oxen and water buffalo to pull plows and carts.

Villagers built walls that surrounded and protected the town.

Foot-pedaled hammers were used to remove grain and rice from their stalks.

Peasants planted and cultivated rice plants in large flooded fields.

② TEACH

Reading Strategy

Taking Notes Ask students to take notes as they read the subsection titled "Classes in Chinese Society." Then have each student exchange notes with a partner and review them. Have the pairs discuss each set of notes and give each other tips on how to be a more effective note taker. **L1**

Daily Lecture and Discussion Notes 7–2

Use **Daily Lecture and Discussion Notes 7–2** for an outline of key concepts found in the section.

Reading Support L1/ EL

Use **Vocabulary Activity 7–2** to help students learn important terms in the section.

More About the Art

Village homes had thatched or tiled roofs, dirt floors, and no furniture.

Caption Answer: They gave part of their crop to the landowners.

Reading Strategy **READING THE TEXT**

Identifying the Main Idea and Supporting Details Ask students to choose one subsection in Section 2. For their chosen subsection, have them create a main idea and supporting details chart and fill it in. For example, a chart for the subsection titled "What Is Legalism?" might include "People need harsh laws and a firm ruler in order for society to succeed" as the main idea. Supporting details might be "People are naturally evil," "Hanfeizi developed the philosophy," "Aristocrats liked Legalism because it favored power," "Did not require rulers to show kindness or understanding." **L2**

Reading Strategy

CONNECTING ACROSS TIME

Ask students to define in their own words the concept of *filial piety* as practiced in ancient China. Then have students debate whether filial piety exists in the same way in our society today. If it has been weakened, why? Should our society try to strengthen filial piety? How? **L1/EL**

Evaluating Ask students to discuss how the government of early China may have been less effective because merchants were not allowed to have government jobs. *(The input from businesspeople would have helped the government manage its finances and improve its service to the people.)* **L3**

Mental Mapping Few people in ancient China ever traveled more than a few miles from their homes. They often had to walk because other forms of transportation were not always available. **Ask: What is the farthest you have ever walked from your home? Where were you going?** Ask students to explain their reasons for walking, how long it took, and how their lives might be different if they had never been farther from their homes than this distance. **L1/EL**

To pay for the use of the land, the farmers gave part of their crop to the landowners.

Most farmers also owned a small piece of land where they grew food for their family. A typical family ate fish, turnips, beans, wheat or rice, and millet. The farmers had to pay taxes and work one month each year building roads and helping on other big government projects. In wartime, the farmers also served as soldiers.

In Chinese society, farmers ranked above merchants. The merchant social class included shopkeepers, traders, and bankers. The merchants lived in towns and provided goods and services to the landowners.

Many merchants became quite rich, but landowners and farmers still looked down on them. Chinese leaders believed that government officials should not be concerned with money. As a result, merchants were not allowed to have government jobs.

What Was Life Like in a Chinese Family?

The family was the basic building block of Chinese society. Because farming in ancient China required many workers, people had big families to help them produce more and become wealthier. Even the young children of a family worked in the fields. Older sons raised their own crops and provided food for their parents. Chinese families also took care of people in need—the aged, the young, and the sick.

Chinese families practiced **filial piety** (FIH•lee•uhl PY•uh•tee). This meant that children had to respect their parents and older relatives. Family members placed the needs and desires of the head of the family before their own. The head of the family was the oldest male, usually the father. However, a son could take on this role, and then even his mother had to obey him.

NATIONAL GEOGRAPHIC — The Way It Was

Focus on Everyday Life

Chinese Farming Farmers in ancient China had to find ways to grow enough food to feed their large population. It was often difficult because of the dry, mountainous land.

Over centuries, farmers learned to cut terraces—flat areas, like a series of deep steps—into the mountain slopes. Terraces made more land available for farming and kept the soil from eroding, or wearing away. Early farmers also used the terraces as a way to irrigate their crops. As rain fell, it flowed down from one terrace to the

▲ Terrace farming in China

234

DIFFERENTIATED INSTRUCTION

Visual/Spatial: Have students design posters promoting one of the three belief systems described in this section. For example, a poster promoting Confucianism might include a portrait of Confucius, one of his sayings quoted in the text, and some pictorial elements that represent aspects of the philosophy.

English Learners: Have students translate key words from the posters into their native languages.

Gifted and Talented: Ask students to draw a picture, create a collage, or write a poem about one of the subjects represented in the posters.

Refer to *Inclusion Strategies for the Middle School Social Studies Classroom* in the TCR.

Men and women had very different roles in early China. Men were respected because they grew the crops. They went to school, ran the government, and fought wars. The Chinese considered these jobs more important than the work that women did. Most women raised children and managed the household.

Chinese women could not hold government posts. However, women in the royal court could influence government decisions. Wives of rulers or women in the royal family often convinced men in power to see things their way.

▲ Chinese female figurine

✓ **Reading Check** **Explain** Why did the amount of land owned by each aristocrat decrease over time?

Chinese Thinkers

Main Idea Three Chinese philosophies, Confucianism, Daoism, and Legalism, grew out of a need for order.

Reading Focus If people around you were arguing and fighting, what would you do? Read to learn about early Chinese ideas for restoring order.

As the Zhou kingdom weakened in the 500s B.C., violence became common. During the Period of the Warring States, rulers sent armies to destroy enemy states. Whole villages of men, women, and children were beheaded. Many Chinese began looking for ways to restore order to society.

Between 500 B.C. and 200 B.C., Chinese thinkers developed three major theories about how to create a peaceful society. These theories are called Confucianism, Daoism, and Legalism.

▶ Reading Strategy ◀

Categorizing Information Ask students to read the first paragraph of the subsection titled "What Was Life Like in a Chinese Family?" Then have them work with a partner to categorize the information in the text into three categories: information about farms, information about families, and information about both farms and families. *(Farms: required many workers; Families: family was the building block of Chinese society, family took care of the aged, young, and sick; Both: young and older children worked, older sons raised crops for parents)* **L2**

✓ **Reading Check**

Answer: Each aristocrat divided his land among his sons, so each generation owned a smaller fraction of the original land.

The Way It Was

Answers:

1. They built terraces into the mountain slopes.

2. terrace farming, irrigation, and pest control

next, watering the crops. This method of farming, called terrace farming, is still used in China today.

Farmers in ancient China were the first to use insects to protect their crops from damage by other insects. As early as A.D. 304, Chinese farmers used ants to prevent other insects from damaging their citrus fruit trees. They also used frogs and birds for pest control.

The ancient Chinese used bronze and iron tools like those on the right, to farm their land and harvest crops. ▶

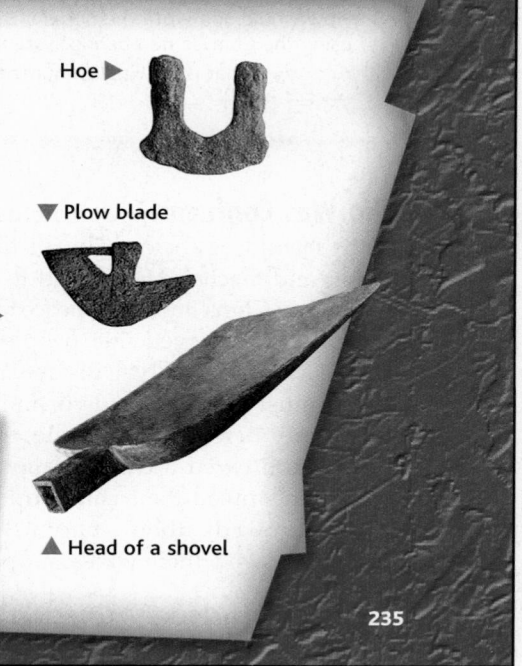
Hoe ▶
▼ Plow blade
▲ Head of a shovel

Connecting to the Past
1. How did farmers in ancient China increase the amount of productive farmland?
2. What three farming methods helped farmers in ancient China grow more food?

235

CRITICAL THINKING ACTIVITY

Drawing Conclusions Ask students to examine each of the three philosophies described in this section with regard to the philosophies' beliefs about government. Ask them to write a paragraph drawing a conclusion about which system of belief would lead to the best government. Have students give reasons for their choice. *(Students' paragraphs should apply the philosophy's beliefs about government in an appropriate way. For example, students may choose Legalism because it endorses strong, even harsh, government control over the population. Others may choose Confucianism because of its emphasis on service. Some may choose Daoism because of its detached view of human interaction and its passivity.)* **L3**

Outlining Have students choose one of the subsections on a thinker and his philosophy, and have them outline the subsection. *(Outlines should include the important points about the founder of the philosophy, its main beliefs and practices, who followed the philosophy, and how it influenced Chinese society.)* **L2**

Understanding Charts

Answers:
1. 三百二十八
2. 641

Writing Activity

Ask students to write a paragraph agreeing or disagreeing with Confucius's belief that a person's family and community should come before one's own needs. Have them include reasons for their position. **L2**

GLENCOE BOOKLINK

Use **Glencoe BookLink** to create customized reading lists for your students' reading levels, interests, and abilities.

Reading Support L1/EL

Assign **Guided Reading Activity 7–2** to help students organize the information in the section.

Chinese Numbering System

Chinese Number	English Number	Chinese Number	English Number
零	0	七	7
一	1	八	8
二	2	九	9
三	3	十	10
四	4	百	100
五	5	千	1,000
六	6	万	10,000

Examples:

二十	(2×10)
二百	(2×100)
三千	$(3 \times 1,000)$
四百五十六	$[(4 \times 100) + (5 \times 10) + (6)]$

Understanding Charts

The Chinese system of numbering is based on units of 10. It uses characters to represent 0 through 9 and the powers of 10 (10, 100, 1,000, and so forth).
1. How would you write the number 328 using the Chinese numbering system?
2. **Analyze** What is the English number for 六百四十一 ?

Who Was Confucius? Confucius (kuhn•FYOO•shuhs) was ancient China's first great thinker and teacher. He wanted to end the problems in China and bring peace to society.

Confucius believed that people needed to have a sense of duty. Duty meant that a person must put the needs of family and community before his or her own needs. Each person owed a duty to another person. Parents owed their children love, and children owed their parents honor. Husbands owed their wives support, and

---

◀ Abacuses, like this one, were used by the Chinese to solve math problems. These ancient calculators held stones on wooden pegs, which would be moved up and down to add, subtract, multiply, and divide.

wives owed their husbands obedience. Above all, rulers had to set good examples. If a king ruled for the common good, his subjects would respect him and society would prosper.

Confucius believed that if each person did his or her duty, society as a whole would do well. He also urged people to be good and to seek knowledge:

> 66 There are those who act without knowing; I will have none of this. To hear a lot, choose the good, and follow it, to see a lot and learn to recognize it: this is next to knowledge. 99
> —Confucius, *Analects*

To Confucius, the best way to behave was similar to an idea known as the Golden Rule: "Do unto others as you would have others do unto you." Confucius urged people to "measure the feelings of others by one's own," for "within the four seas all men are brothers."

Confucius traveled through China trying to persuade government leaders to follow his ideas. **Confucianism** (kuhn•FYOO•shuh•NIH•zuhm) taught that all men with a talent for governing should take part in government. Of course, this idea was not popular with aristocrats, and few leaders listened.

Over time, Confucius won many followers who honored him as a great teacher. They wrote down his sayings and carried his message. After Confucius died in 479 B.C., his sayings spread throughout China.

INTERDISCIPLINARY CONNECTIONS ACTIVITY

Language Arts Several systems exist for spelling Chinese names and words in English. A well-known example is the name of China's famous Communist leader. In the older Wade-Giles system, the leader's name is Mao Tse-tung. In a newer system called Pinyin, his name is spelled Mao Zedong. The latter more accurately reflects the pronunciation in the Mandarin, or official, dialect. The name *Pinyin* comes from two Chinese words meaning "spell sound." It is the official romanized spelling system of the People's Republic of China. Almost all Western newspapers and magazines now use the Pinyin system. Have students research the two systems and report to the class on differences and similarities. **L2**

Biography

CONFUCIUS
551–479 B.C.

Historians believe that the great thinker and teacher Confucius was born in the small state of Lu and named Kong Qui. His parents were poor, although his family had probably been wealthy at one time. One record says that Confucius was only three years old when his father died. His mother may have also died when he was young, because another record describes Confucius as an orphan.

Even as a teenager, Confucius was a talented scholar with strong, fixed beliefs. He devoted himself to learning and mastered literature, history, music, and arithmetic. He served as an apprentice to a bookkeeper and a stable manager but really wanted to obtain a government position. When he was 19, Confucius married and soon had a son and a daughter.

Confucius finally obtained a government job and wanted to use his position to improve society. He wanted everyone to return to the beliefs and rituals of their ancestors, because he felt that would teach them how to live together peacefully. Government officials in Lu were not interested in his ideas, so at age 30 Confucius left politics and began his teaching career. He devoted the rest of his life to improving society through learning and teaching. Confucius did not write down any of his ideas, but his followers put together a book of his sayings called the *Lun Yü* (Analects).

Confucius ▶

"What you do not want done to yourself, do not do to others."

–Confucius

Then and Now

Give an example of how the above quote from Confucius might help society today.

237

Biography

TEACH

The government officials for whom Confucius worked were not interested in his ideas about how to improve government and society. Therefore, Confucius was forced to leave government service in order to spread his ideas.

Ask students to discuss whether government can be changed better by those within it or outside of it. What advantages might each kind of reformer have? *(Within: better knowledge of how government works, more influence with other government officials, more power; Outside: less danger of giving in to financial or other pressure, independence, connections with the people)* **L1/ EL**

Then and Now

Answers will vary. Students may discuss how living Confucius's "golden rule" would keep crime rates down and help society maintain order.

Reading List Generator CD-ROM | **GLENCOE BOOKLINK** | **RECOMMENDED READING**

Use the **Glencoe BookLink CD-ROM** to create customized reading lists based on your students' interests and reading levels. Below is an example based on content in this chapter. Also, see the Suggested Readings on pages 944–946 of the Appendix.

- **Confucius.** From the *Analects*. Excerpts from the text.
- **Lao-tzu.** From the *Tao Te Ching*. Excerpts from the text.
- **Waterlow, Julia.** *China: A Study of an Economically Developing Country.* China today is a country of contrasts: nuclear power and space programs exist side by side with ancient farming techniques, and bustling cities are found alongside rural areas.

③ ASSESS

Assign Section 2 Review as homework or as an in-class activity.

🔵 Have students use the **Interactive Tutor Self-Assessment CD-ROM** to review the section.

Assessment L2

Assign **Section 2 Quiz** to assess mastery of the material found in the section.

Understanding Charts

Answers:
1. Confucianism
2. Answers will vary but should be logical.

Reading Support L1/EL

Assign **Reading Essentials and Study Guide 7–2** to help students review section material.

More About the Photo

According to legend, Laozi traveled to the state of Qin, where he wrote the *Dao De Jing*.

Caption Answer: between 500 B.C. and 300 B.C.

Chinese Philosophers

	Confucianism	Daoism	Legalism
Founder	Confucius	Laozi	Hanfeizi
Main Ideas	People should put the needs of their family and community first.	People should give up worldly desires in favor of nature and the Dao.	Society needs a system of harsh laws and strict punishment.
Influence on Modern Life	Many Chinese today accept his idea of duty to family. His ideas helped open up government jobs to people with talent.	Daoism teaches the importance of nature and encourages people to treat nature with respect and reverence.	Legalists developed laws that became an important part of Chinese history.

Understanding Charts

Three philosophies developed in early China.
1. Which philosophy encourages followers to concentrate on duty and humanity?
2. **Conclude** Which of these philosophies do you think would be most popular in the world today? Explain.

▲ Some legends state that Laozi rode his water buffalo westward into a great desert and disappeared after writing *Dao De Jing*. **When did the ideas of Daoism become popular?**

What Is Daoism? **Daoism** (DOW•IH•zuhm) is another Chinese philosophy that promotes a peaceful society. Daoism (also called Taoism) is based on the teachings of **Laozi** (LOWD•ZOO). Laozi, or the Old Master, lived around the same time as Confucius. Scholars do not know if Laozi was a real person. However, the ideas credited to him became popular between 500 B.C. and 300 B.C.

The ideas of Daoism are written in *Dao De Jing* (The Way of the Dao). Like Confucianism, Daoism tells people how to behave. Daoists believed that people should give up worldly desires. They should turn to nature and the Dao—the

238 CHAPTER 7 Early China

COOPERATIVE LEARNING ACTIVITY

Analyzing Ancient Texts Have students prepare readings from the *Dao De Jing* or the *Analects* of Confucius. Ask the groups to research the backgrounds of and choose representative selections from the works. Suggest that students also prepare artwork, music, costumes, or special props to enhance their readings. Have the groups present their readings to the class. Allow time after the readings for class questions and discussion. **L2**

force that guides all things. To show how to follow the Dao, Daoists used examples from nature:

> ❝Higher good is like water:
> the good in water benefits all,
> and does so without contention.
> It rests where people dislike to be,
> so it is close to the Way.
> Where it dwells becomes
>   good ground;
> profound is the good in its heart,
> Benevolent the good it bestows.❞
>
> —Laozi, *Tao Te Ching*

In some ways, Daoism is the opposite of Confucianism. Followers of Confucius taught that people should work hard to improve the world. Daoism called on people to give up their concerns about the world. It said they should seek inner peace and live in harmony with nature. Many Chinese followed both Confucianism and Daoism.

What Is Legalism? A third group of thinkers disagreed with the idea that honorable men in government could bring peace to society. Instead, they argued for a system of laws. People called their thinking **Legalism** (LEE•guh•LIH•zuhm), or the "School of Law."

A scholar named **Hanfeizi** (HAN•fay•DZOO) developed the teachings of Legalism during the 200s B.C. Unlike Confucius or Laozi, Hanfeizi taught that humans were naturally evil. He believed that they needed harsh laws and stiff punishments to force them to do their duty. His followers believed that a strong ruler was needed to keep order in society.

Many aristocrats liked Legalism because it favored force and power, and did not require rulers to show kindness or understanding. Its ideas led to the cruel laws and punishments often used to control Chinese farmers.

✓ **Reading Check** **Explain** Why did Hanfeizi believe that people needed laws and punishments?

Section 2 Review

Study Central™ Need help with the material in this section? Visit jat.glencoe.com

Reading Summary
Review the Main Ideas

- Early Chinese society had three main social classes: aristocrats, farmers, and merchants. The family was the basis of Chinese society.
- During a time of disorder, three new philosophies developed in China: Confucianism, Daoism, and Legalism.

What Did You Learn?

1. Describe the concept of filial piety.
2. Why did many aristocrats favor the philosophy of Legalism?

Critical Thinking

3. **Compare** Draw a table to compare the three main classes of ancient Chinese society.

Chinese Society		
Aristocrats	Farmers	Merchants

4. **Contrast** How did Daoism differ from Confucianism?
5. **Writing Questions** Suppose you could interview Confucius about his concept of duty. Write five questions you might ask him about the subject. Include possible responses.
6. **Expository Writing** Do you think any of the Chinese philosophies studied in this section are reflected in our society today? Write an essay explaining your answer.

CHAPTER 7   Early China   **239**

ENRICH

Ask students to write a postcard from the point of view of a follower of Confucius, Laozi, or Hanfeizi while visiting the United States today. **L2**

RETEACH

Have students meet in groups of three. Ask one member of each group to explain Confucianism, one to explain Daoism, and the last to explain Legalism. **L1**

✓ **Reading Check**

Answer: to force them to do their duty

History Online

To help students understand section material, have them visit **Study Central™** at jat.glencoe.com

④ CLOSE

Ask students to think about the role of different family members in ancient China. Have them explain which role they would like best and which they would like least. Have them explain their reasons. **L2**

SECTION 2 REVIEW ANSWERS

1. Family members placed the needs of the head of the family above their own.
2. It emphasized force and power and did not require leaders to show kindness or understanding to their subjects.
3. Tables should contain detailed information drawn from a careful reading of the text.
4. Confucianism encouraged people to work hard to improve the world, while Daoism taught that people should give up their concerns about the world and seek inner peace.
5. Answers will vary. Questions and answers should demonstrate thoughtful consideration of Confucius's ideas.
6. Answers will vary but should give reasons to support students' opinions.

① FOCUS

SECTION OVERVIEW

This section looks at the Qin and Han dynasties and the changes they brought to China in the areas of religion, trade, government, and technology.

BELLRINGER
SKILLBUILDER ACTIVITY

✎ Project **Daily Focus Skills Transparency 7–3** and have students answer questions. Discuss their responses.

Get Ready to Read!

Preteaching Vocabulary: Explain that acupuncture is the ancient Chinese medical practice of sticking thin needles into the skin to ease pain and cure disease.

Answers to Graphic: Invention: waterwheels; Effect: millers could grind more grain. Invention: iron drill bits; Effect: miners could mine more salt. Invention: steel; Effect: better tools and weapons. Invention: paper; Effect: recorded documents. Invention: disease prevention, use of herbs, acupuncture; Effect: improved medical care. Invention: rudder and new moving sails; Effect: ships could sail into the wind and travel great distances.

Section 3
The Qin and Han Dynasties

Get Ready to Read!

What's the Connection?
Each of China's early dynasties was led by rulers who were very different. In this section, you will see how the Qin and Han dynasties differed because of their rulers.

Focusing on the Main Ideas
- Qin Shihuangdi used harsh methods to unify and defend China. *(page 241)*
- Developments during the Han dynasty improved life for all Chinese. *(page 244)*
- The Silk Road carried Chinese goods as far as Greece and Rome. *(page 246)*
- Unrest in China helped Buddhism to spread. *(page 248)*

Locating Places
Guangzhou (GWAHNG•JOH)
Silk Road
Luoyang (loo•WOH•YAHNG)

Meeting People
Qin Shihuangdi (CHIHN SHEE•hwahng•dee)
Liu Bang (lee•OO BAHNG)
Han Wudi (HAHN WOO•DEE)

Building Your Vocabulary
acupuncture (A•kyuh•PUHNGK•chuhr)

Reading Strategy
Determining Cause and Effect Complete a diagram like the one below showing the inventions of the Han dynasty and the resulting impact on society.

Invention		Effect
	→	
	→	
	→	

NATIONAL GEOGRAPHIC When & Where?

Changan

200 B.C.

202 B.C. Liu Bang founds Han dynasty

A.D. 1

c. A.D. 100 Silk Road established

A.D. 190 Rebel armies attack Han capital

A.D. 200

SECTION RESOURCES

Reproducible Masters
- Reproducible Lesson Plan 7–3
- Daily Lecture and Discussion Notes 7–3
- Vocabulary Activity 7–3
- Active Reading Note-Taking Guide 7–3
- Guided Reading Activity 7–3
- Section Quiz 7–3
- Reading Essentials and Study Guide 7–3

Transparencies
- Daily Focus Skills Transparency 7–3

Multimedia
- Interactive Tutor Self-Assessment CD-ROM
- ExamView® Pro Testmaker CD-ROM
- Presentation Plus! CD-ROM
- Vocabulary PuzzleMaker CD-ROM
- Glencoe BookLink CD-ROM

Emperor Qin Shihuangdi

Main Idea Qin Shihuangdi used harsh methods to unify and defend China.

Reading Focus Imagine your city or state without any roads. How would people get from one place to another? Read to find out how a Chinese ruler used roads and canals to unite China.

You have read about the problems in China from about 400 B.C. to 200 B.C. The rulers of powerful local states fought one another and ignored the Zhou kings. One of these states was called Qin. Its ruler took over neighboring states one by one. In 221 B.C. the Qin ruler declared himself **Qin Shihuangdi** (CHIHN SHEE•hwahng•dee),

which means "the First Qin Emperor." The Qin ruler made changes in China's government that would last for 2,000 years.

A Powerful Ruler Qin based his rule on the ideas of Legalism. He had everyone who opposed him punished or killed. Books opposing his views were publicly burned. Qin made the central government stronger than ever before. He appointed government officials, called censors, to make sure government officials did their jobs.

Second in power to the central government were provinces and counties. Under Zhou kings, officials who ran these areas passed on their posts to sons or relatives. Under Qin, only he could fill these posts.

② TEACH

Summarizing Information Ask volunteers to summarize the principles of Legalism. Explain that the Qin emperor based his reign on Legalism. L1

Daily Lecture and Discussion Notes 7–3

Use **Daily Lecture and Discussion Notes 7–3** for an outline of key concepts found in the section.

Reading Support L1/ EL

Use **Vocabulary Activity 7–3** to help students learn important terms in the section.

Reading Strategy

Predicting Ask students to write a paragraph predicting the consequences of Qin Shihuangdi's rule. Have volunteers share their predictions with the class. Then have students make corrections as they read the section. L2

Using Geography Skills

Answers:
1. Huang He and Chang Jiang valleys, much of eastern coast and western mountains
2. the Han empire

NATIONAL GEOGRAPHIC

Qin and Han Empires 221 B.C.–A.D. 220

Using Geography Skills

During both the Qin and Han dynasties, China's empire expanded.
1. Which geographical areas did both empires include?
2. Which empire expanded farthest west?

KEY
- Qin empire
- Great Wall in Qin period
- Han empire
- Great Wall in Han period

CHAPTER 7   Early China   **241**

Reading Strategy   READING THE TEXT

Outlining Ask students to work in pairs to outline the section. Have them pay special attention to major headings and subheads, as well as titles of charts, special features, and other special text and graphics sections. When the outlines are completed, have each pair exchange outlines with another pair to compare and discuss them. Conclude the activity by encouraging students to use outlining as a study and review technique. L1

Monitoring Comprehension Have students reread the paragraphs they wrote for the **Predicting** activity on page 241. Have them evaluate their predictions. How accurate were they? Did they base their predictions on textual clues that proved correct? Did they miss any information that might have allowed them to make more accurate predictions? **L2**

CONNECTING ACROSS TIME

Ask students to compare the Great Wall built during the rule of Qin Shihuangdi with walls or fences that people build today. **Ask:** Do they have the same purpose? Are they likely to succeed in their goal? Are they necessary? Why? What other choices exist for fulfilling the same purpose? **L1**

✓ Reading Check

Answer: He killed or punished anyone who opposed him.

More About the Art

Less than 30 percent of the Great Wall remains in good condition, because of the encroaching desert and the use of the wall's bricks for road and house construction.

Caption Answer: the Xiongnu

Qin Shihuangdi unified China. He created one currency, or type of money, to be used throughout the empire. He also ordered the building of roads and a huge canal. The canal connected the Chang Jiang in central China to what is today the city of **Guangzhou** (GWAHNG•JOH) in southern China. He used the canal to ship supplies to his troops in far-off territories.

The Great Wall Northern China was bordered by the vast Gobi. Nomads, people who move from place to place with herds of animals, lived in the Gobi. The Chinese knew them as the Xiongnu (SYEHN•NOO). The Xiongnu were masters at fighting on horseback. They often attacked Chinese farms and villages. Several Chinese rulers in the north built walls to keep out the Xiongnu.

Qin Shihuangdi forced farmers to leave their fields and work on connecting and strengthening the walls. The result was the Great Wall of China, built with stone, sand, and piled rubble. However, Qin did not build the wall that we know today. It was built 1,500 years later.

Why Did People Rebel? Many Chinese viewed Qin Shihuangdi as a cruel leader. Aristocrats were angry because he reduced their power. Scholars hated him for burning their writings. Farmers hated him for forcing them to build roads and the Great Wall. Four years after the emperor died in 210 B.C., the people overthrew his dynasty. Civil war followed, and a new dynasty soon arose.

✓ Reading Check **Explain** Why did Qin face little opposition during most of his reign?

◀ This artwork shows the Great Wall many years after the reign of Qin Shihuangdi. Most of the wall built by Qin was made of stone and rubble, and was located north of the Great Wall we see today. Little remains of Qin's wall. *Who was the wall meant to keep out?*

DIFFERENTIATED INSTRUCTION

Verbal/Linguistic: Ask learners to write a poem, short story, or dramatic scene based on something they learned in this section. Suggest that they consider such elements as how subjects of Qin Shihuangdi felt about his harsh rule, the excitement of setting out on the Silk Road, or the nervousness of an aspiring civil servant before taking the Han examination.

English Learners: Have two students work together to improve spelling, grammar, and expression.

Auditory/Musical: Have students set their literary works to music.

🗁 Refer to *Inclusion Strategies for the Middle School Social Studies Classroom* in the TCR.

Biography

QIN SHIHUANGDI
c. 259–210 B.C.

At the age 13, Ying Zheng became the leader of the Chinese state of Qin. The state was already very powerful because of Zheng's father, the previous ruler. Its government and military were well organized. With the help of his generals, young Zheng defeated Qin's six rival states. By 221 B.C., he had united all of the Chinese states under his rule. To mark a new beginning for China and to show his supremacy, Zheng gave himself the title Qin Shihuangdi—"The First Qin Emperor."

Qin Shihuangdi energetically went to work organizing his country. He divided the land into 36 districts, each with its own governor and a representative who reported directly to him. He made laws and taxes uniform throughout the country. He also standardized weights and measurements. Throughout China, the emperor had his achievements inscribed on stone tablets.

Qin Shihuangdi did strengthen and organize China, but many people disliked him because of his harsh laws and punishments. Many people also disliked how he spent lavish amounts of money to build palaces and a gigantic tomb for himself. He had an entire lifelike army— over 6,000 soldiers and horses—built of clay and placed in the tomb.

Three attempts to kill the emperor were made during the last years of his life. Qin Shihuangdi grew fearful and searched for a magic potion that would give him everlasting life. He died while on a trip in eastern China.

▲ Qin Shihuangdi

"I have brought order to the mass of beings."
—Qin Shihuangdi

▲ Part of the terra-cotta army found in Qin Shihuangdi's tomb

Then and Now

Why do you think modern historians disagree in their evaluation of Qin Shihuangdi's leadership?

243

Reading List Generator CD-ROM

GLENCOE BOOKLINK **RECOMMENDED READING**

Use the **Glencoe BookLink CD-ROM** to create customized reading lists based on your students' interests and reading levels. Below is an example based on content in this chapter. Also, see the Suggested Readings on pages 944–946 of the Appendix.

- **Ganeri, Anita.** *I Remember China.* Sun Dan lives in the United States now, but she was born in China and still misses all her friends and relatives there.
- **Mann, Elizabeth.** *The Great Wall: The Story of Thousands of Miles of Earth and Stone.* How and why the Great Wall was built.
- **Ye, Ting-xing.** *Share the Sky.* Fei-fie lives in China with her grandfather who makes beautiful kites. She worries about leaving China to move to North America.

HISTORY Mystery

How Do We Know About the Ancient Chinese?
In 1974 a group of farmers was digging a well near the city of Xian. They discovered in a huge underground pit the tomb of Qin Shihuangdi. It contained more than 6,000 life-size, hardened clay statues of soldiers and horses. Archaeologists believe this was a re-creation of Qin Shihuangdi's imperial guard and was probably meant to serve him in the afterlife. The soldiers have many different head shapes, and each is individually finished.

More About the Art

During the Han dynasty, Wudi set up a university to train and test future members of the civil service.

Caption Answer: Only the wealthy could afford the education necessary to pass the exams.

The Han Dynasty

Main Idea Developments during the Han dynasty improved life for all Chinese.

Reading Focus How much time do you spend studying for tests? Find out why some Chinese people spent years studying for one special test.

In 202 B.C. **Liu Bang** (lee•OO BAHNG) founded the Han dynasty. Liu Bang, who was once a peasant, became a military leader and defeated his rivals. He declared himself Han Gaozu—"Exalted Emperor of Han." Although Han Gaozu threw out the harsh policies of the Qin dynasty, he continued to use censors and also divided the empire into provinces and counties.

What Was the Civil Service? The Han reached its peak under the leadership of **Han Wudi** (HAHN WOO•DEE), which means "Martial Emperor of Han." He ruled from 141 B.C. to 87 B.C. Because Wudi wanted talented people to fill government posts, job seekers had to take long, difficult tests to qualify for openings in the bureaucracy. Those with the highest scores got the jobs.

In time, Wudi's tests became the civil service examinations. This system for choosing officials remained part of Chinese civilization for 2,000 years. The system was supposed to help anyone with the right skills get a job with the government. However, it actually favored the rich. Only wealthy families could afford to educate their sons for the difficult exams.

Students preparing for these tests learned law, history, and the teachings of Confucius. They began to memorize the works of Confucius at age seven. Students were not allowed to do physical labor or to play most sports. They could go fishing, however, because it was considered the sport of scholars. After many years of schooling, the students took their civil service examinations. Only one in five passed. Those who failed taught school, took jobs as assistants to officials, or were supported by their families.

The Chinese Empire Grows A large bureaucracy was needed to rule the rapidly growing empire. The population had grown from about 20 million under Han Gaozu to more than 60 million under Han Wudi.

Because farmers had to divide their lands among more and more sons, the average farmer owned only about one acre of land. With so little land, farm families could not raise enough to live. As a result, many sold their land to aristocrats and became tenant farmers. Tenant farmers work on land that is owned

▲ This painting shows students taking a civil service examination. *Why did the civil service system favor rich job seekers?*

244 CHAPTER 7 Early China

CRITICAL THINKING ACTIVITY

Determining Cause and Effect Have students discuss the following statement: Increased trade brings benefits to civilization. Ask them to consider causes and effects they have read about in this section, as well as those they can name from current events. Ask students who disagree with the statement to cite evidence of negative effects. *(Those who agree might cite the increased exchange of new ideas, technology, and products; those who disagree might claim that not all new ideas, technology, and products are positive changes and may even be harmful to a civilization.)* **L2**

Linking Past & Present

Papermaking

THEN The Chinese were the first people to make paper. The oldest piece of paper found in China dates from the first century B.C. Papermakers soaked tree bark, hemp, and rags in water and pounded it into pulp. They lowered a bamboo screen into a vat of the pulp and then lifted it out. It held a thin sheet of pulp which dried into a single sheet of paper.

▼ Modern papermaking

▲ A modern artist demonstrates an ancient way of making paper.

NOW Papermaking today is a huge international industry. Most paper is made in paper mills by machines, but the basic process is the same. Instead of tree bark, rags, and hemp, most paper today is made from wood pulp. *Why do you think some modern artists continue to make paper using pulp and a frame?*

Writing Activity

Students have read how, in the Han dynasty, applicants for civil service jobs needed to take a difficult test. Have students write a paragraph discussing what kinds of knowledge a civil servant needs to be an effective administrator today. **L2**

Linking Past & Present

Answer: Students may suggest that those artists want to remember that form of papermaking and that they enjoy creating paper from scratch.

Reading Strategy

Evaluating Ask students to work in groups of three. Have each student review the text about Han-era inventions and decide which one was the most important. Have students justify their choice to other group members. *(Sample answers: Papermaking was the most important because it made possible the vastly greater exchange of information; waterwheels led to increased food production and a larger population.)* **L2**

by someone else and pay rent in crops. The aristocrats now owned thousands of acres. They hired armies to force more farmers into selling their land and working as tenants.

China's empire grew in size as well as in population. Han armies added lands to the south and pushed Chinese borders westward. The Han dynasty also made the country more secure. Wudi's armies drove back the Xiongnu—the nomads to the north. After Wudi's death, the Chinese lived in peace for almost 150 years.

An Era of Inventions New inventions during the Han dynasty helped Chinese workers produce more than ever. Millers used newly invented waterwheels to grind more grain, and miners used new iron drill bits to mine more salt. Ironworkers invented steel. Paper, another Han invention, was used by government officials to record a growing amount of information.

Chinese medicine also improved under the Han. Doctors discovered that certain foods prevented disease. They used herbs to cure illnesses and eased pain by sticking

CHAPTER 7   Early China   **245**

EXTENDING THE CONTENT

Getting the Point Acupuncture is based on the ancient Chinese principles of *yin* and *yang*. Yin is the passive, dark principle. Yang is the active, light principle. A healthy body contains both of these principles in the proper balance. When the balance is upset, the vital life force, or *ch'i*, is obstructed. Acupuncture helps restore the flow of *ch'i* and the proper balance of yin and yang. Needles inserted at specific points in the body can ease pain at other points, often far away from where the needle is inserted. For example, a needle inserted in the proper, specific place in the thumb is said to ease pain in the abdomen. Many Western doctors also believe that acupuncture can ease pain. However, Chinese claims that it can cure diseases have not been proven.

in a word . . .

The Chinese were the first to create "porcelain," what students may know as china. True porcelain was not invented until the A.D. 600s. Chinese skill in forming, glazing, and firing clay allowed them to lead the world in this practical and beautiful art for many centuries. Europeans did not discover the secret to making porcelain until the 1700s.

✓ Reading Check

Answer: Han armies added lands to the south and west.

Reading Support L1/ EL

Assign **Guided Reading Activity 7–3** to help students organize the information in the section.

Using Geography Skills

Answers:

1. silk, cinnamon, ginger, copper, gold
2. China, Tibet, India, Bactria, Persia, Arabia, Egypt

---

thin needles into patients' skin. This treatment is known as **acupuncture** (A•kyuh• PUHNGK•chuhr).

The Chinese also invented the rudder and a new way to move the sails of ships. These changes allowed ships to sail into the wind for the first time. Chinese merchant ships could now travel to the islands of Southeast Asia and into the Indian Ocean. As a result, China established trade as far away as India and the Mediterranean Sea.

✓ **Reading Check** **Explain** How did China's empire increase in size during the Han dynasty?

The Silk Road

Main Idea The Silk Road carried Chinese goods as far as Greece and Rome.

Reading Focus Many of the things we buy today are made in China. How do these goods get to the United States? Read to learn how goods made in China long ago made it all the way to Europe.

Chinese merchants made a lot of money by shipping expensive goods to other countries. Silk was the most valuable trade product. Some of it went by ship to Southeast

NATIONAL GEOGRAPHIC
Trading in the Ancient World

KEY

- Silk Road
- Other trade routes
- Black pepper
- Cardamom
- Cinnamon
- Cloves
- Copper
- Cotton cloth
- Frankincense/Myrrh
- Gold
- Ginger
- Grains
- Horns/Tusks
- Leopard skins
- Nutmeg
- Oils
- Papyrus
- Pearls
- Sandalwood
- Semiprecious stones
- Silk
- Teakwood

Using Geography Skills

The Silk Road allowed the transport of expensive goods all the way from China to the Middle East and beyond.
1. What were some trade goods produced by China?
2. What regions were near or along the route of the Silk Road?

CITIZENSHIP AND YOU

The Highest Calling? Wudi, the great Han emperor, believed that only the most talented people should be employed by the government. Under him, government bureaucrats were held in the highest esteem, and their positions were coveted by many. Have students discuss the role and reputation of government civil service workers today. Ask them to address such questions as why the respect given to some government employees has dropped in our time, why some Americans have a negative opinion of government in general, and why the reputation of the private sector has risen. End by asking students to suggest ways to improve the positive image of government. **L2**

Four Chinese Dynasties

	SHANG	ZHOU	QIN	HAN
When	1750–1045 B.C.	1045–256 B.C.	221–206 B.C.	202 B.C.–A.D. 220
Important Leaders	Numerous kings with large armies and control over the land; ruled from capital city of Anyang	Wu	Qin Shihuangdi	Liu Bang
Main Ideas and Accomplishments	Developed social classes that included farmers, merchants, aristocrats, and royal family	Longest-lasting dynasty in Chinese history; established Mandate of Heaven	Strengthened central government; created single monetary system	Population and landmass grew under Han; opened China to trade and commerce by building Silk Road
Influences on Chinese Culture	Influenced Chinese religion and culture; created Chinese written language	Developed irrigation and flood-control systems to help farmers grow more crops	Introduced use of censors to check on government officials; Qin built the first Great Wall to keep out invaders	Created government's civil service examination; major inventions: steel, paper, acupuncture, advanced sea travel

Understanding Charts

The four dynasties of early China were separated by brief periods of unrest.
1. Under which dynasty was a single monetary system put in place?
2. **Evaluate** Which dynasty do you think contributed the most to Chinese culture? Why?

Asia. However, most went overland on the **Silk Road.** This large network of trade routes stretched 4,000 miles (6,436 km) from western China to southwest Asia.

Merchants began using the Silk Road between 200 B.C. and A.D. 100. Han Wudi sent out a general named Zhang Qian (JAHNG CHYEHN) to explore areas west of China. After 13 years, Zhang returned to China with amazing stories.

He told of a mighty empire to the west with large cities full of people "who cut their hair short, wear embroidered clothes, and ride in very small chariots." Zhang was

describing the Roman Empire. His stories sparked China's interest in the West and trade on the Silk Road increased. Merchants used camels to carry their goods across deserts and mountains to central Asia. From there Arabs carried the goods to the Mediterranean Sea.

The trip over the Silk Road was expensive because it was difficult and dangerous. Merchants had to pay taxes to many kingdoms as they moved the goods east and west. For this reason, they carried only high-priced goods such as silk, spices, tea, and porcelain.

✓ **Reading Check** **Conclude** Why were only expensive goods carried on the Silk Road?

CHAPTER 7   Early China   **247**

3 ASSESS

Assign Section 3 Review as homework or as an in-class activity.

◉ Have students use the **Interactive Tutor Self-Assessment CD-ROM** to review the section.

Assessment L2

Assign **Section 3 Quiz** to assess mastery of the material found in the section.

Reading Support L1/ EL

Assign **Reading Essentials and Study Guide 7–3** to help students review section material.

Understanding Charts

Answers:
1. Qin
2. Answers will vary but should be supported by evidence.

✓ Reading Check

Answer: Only expensive goods could be sold for enough money to make a profit.

COOPERATIVE LEARNING ACTIVITY

Flash Cards Ask small groups of students to prepare a set of a dozen study flash cards for people, places, events, things, and important ideas discussed in this section. For example, the back side of a flash card for the term *Silk Road* might say "important trade route between China and the Mediterranean." Have groups exchange flash cards and quiz each other with them. L1

ENRICH

Ask students to research one of the inventions from the period discussed in this section and prepare a short presentation for the class. **L2**

 Reading Check

Answer: merchants and scholars

To help students understand section material, have them visit **Study Central™** at jat.glencoe.com

RETEACH

Have students describe how Qin Shihuangdi was able to unify China. *(He created a single currency; built canals, roads, and the Great Wall to keep out invaders; and ruled very harshly so that people dared not rebel.)* **L1**

 CLOSE

Reading Strategy

Ask students to work with a partner to make a list of developments they consider positive and developments they consider harmful or negative from the era of the Qin and Han dynasties. **L2**

Major Changes in China

Main Idea Unrest in China helped Buddhism to spread.

Reading Focus What do you do when you feel frightened or unsafe? Read to find out how those feelings triggered the spread of Buddhism from India to China.

As you read in Chapter 6, Buddhism began in India, but it soon spread to other countries as well. Merchants and teachers from India brought Buddhism to China during the A.D. 100s. At first, only a few merchants and scholars were interested in the new religion. In time, however, Buddhism became very popular. One of the most important reasons that the Chinese people began to believe in Buddhism was the fall of the Han dynasty.

The Han emperors after Wudi were weak and foolish. As a result, the central government lost respect and power. At the same time, as you read earlier, the aristocrats began grabbing more land and wealth. Dishonest officials and greedy aristocrats caused unrest among the farmers.

Wars, rebellions, and plots against the emperor put an end to the Han dynasty. In A.D. 190 a rebel army attacked the Han capital, **Luoyang** (loo•WOH•YAHNG). By A.D. 220, China had plunged into civil war. To make the situation worse, the northern nomads invaded the country.

The collapse of the government and the beginning of the civil war frightened many Chinese. They felt unsafe. Buddhist ideas helped people cope with the stress and their fear. Even the followers of other religions found Buddhism attractive. Followers of Confucius and Daoists admired Buddhist ideas. By the 400s, Buddhism had become popular in China.

✓ **Reading Check** **Identify** What groups in China were the first to adopt Buddhism?

Study Central™ Need help with the material in this section? Visit jat.glencoe.com

Section 3 Review

Reading Summary

Review the **Main Ideas**

- The short-lived Qin dynasty helped to unify China.
- During the Han dynasty, people began taking tests for government jobs. New inventions, such as the waterwheel and paper, were created.
- The Silk Road was an important trade route that linked China to the West.
- As the Han dynasty lost power, many Chinese became followers of Buddhism.

What Did You Learn?

1. Why did Qin Shihuangdi have the Great Wall built?
2. What were civil service examinations and why were they created?

Critical Thinking

3. **Cause and Effect** Draw a diagram to show the factors that caused the Han dynasty to fall.

```
┌─────┐  ┌─────┐  ┌─────┐
│     │  │     │  │     │
└─────┘  └─────┘  └─────┘
   │        │        │
   ▼        ▼        ▼
┌────────────────────────┐
│    Han Dynasty Falls   │
└────────────────────────┘
```

4. **Geography Skills** What barriers did merchants who used the Silk Road have to cross?
5. **Explain** How did Qin Shihuangdi make China's central government stronger?
6. **Analyze** Why did the Qin dynasty fall?
7. **Descriptive Writing** Zhang Qian wrote that Romans had short hair, wore embroidered clothes, and rode in chariots. Name three things that he might have written about people in the United States after seeing them for the first time.

SECTION 3 REVIEW ANSWERS

1. to keep out the Xiongnu
2. long, difficult tests used to qualify people for jobs in the government bureaucracy; to find the best and most talented people
3. Weak emperors lost respect and power; officials and aristocrats caused wars and rebellions.
4. mountains, deserts, seas, oceans, harsh terrain
5. He appointed censors who made sure that government officials did their jobs. He also appointed and dismissed aristocrats who ran the provinces rather than allowing their positions to be hereditary.
6. Because Qin Shihuangdi was such a ruthless ruler, his dynasty was overthrown by unhappy subjects soon after his death.
7. Answers will vary but should include three things.

Chapter 7 Reading Review

Section 1 China's First Civilizations

Vocabulary
dynasty
aristocrat
pictograph
ideograph
bureaucracy
mandate
Dao

Focusing on the Main Ideas
- Rivers, mountains, and deserts helped shape China's civilization. *(page 225)*
- Rulers known as the Shang became powerful because they controlled land and had strong armies. *(page 226)*
- Chinese rulers claimed that the Mandate of Heaven gave them the right to rule. *(page 229)*

Bronze bowl and ladle ▶ from Zhou dynasty

Section 2 Life in Ancient China

Vocabulary
social class
filial piety
Confucianism
Daoism
Legalism

Focusing on the Main Ideas
- Chinese society had three main social classes: landowning aristocrats, farmers, and merchants. *(page 233)*
- Three Chinese philosophies, Confucianism, Daoism, and Legalism, grew out of a need for order. *(page 235)*

Laozi ▶

Section 3 The Qin and Han Dynasties

Vocabulary
acupuncture

Focusing on the Main Ideas
- Qin Shihuangdi used harsh methods to unify and defend China. *(page 241)*
- Developments during the Han dynasty improved life for all Chinese. *(page 244)*
- The Silk Road carried Chinese goods as far as Greece and Rome. *(page 246)*
- Unrest in China helped Buddhism to spread. *(page 248)*

CHAPTER 7 REVIEW

PREVIEW/REVIEW

Vocabulary Activity Have students define each term as you read them aloud. Then ask volunteers to use the term in a sentence about early China.

🔵 **Vocabulary PuzzleMaker CD-ROM**

🔵 **Interactive Tutor Self-Assessment CD-ROM**

CONDENSE

📁 Chapter 7 **Guided Reading Activities**

📀 **StudentWorks Plus™ CD-ROM (with Audio Program)**

RETEACH

📁 **Differentiated Instruction Activity 7**

📁 Chapter 7 *Reading Essentials and Study Guide*

CHAPTER CULMINATING ACTIVITY

Have students finish the Chapter Culminating Activity from page 220D.

Suggestions for rubrics may be found in the *Quizzes, Tests, and Authentic Assessment (with Rubrics)* booklet.

Reading Strategy   READ TO WRITE

Letter to the Editor Ask students to consider which of the three philosophies discussed in this chapter is most relevant for the challenges our country faces today. Have students choose and review either Confucianism, Daoism, or Legalism. Then have them write a letter to the editor of your local newspaper discussing how the philosophy they chose could be helpful to people in the United States today. Have them include reasons to support their argument.

- **L1** students should support their choice with one or two reasons.
- **L2** students should include several well-supported reasons and attempt grammar mastery.
- **L3** students should have logical, detailed, well-considered letters that strongly support their arguments.

Chapter 7 Assessment and Activities

GLENCOE TECHNOLOGY

MindJogger Videoquiz

Use the **MindJogger Videoquiz** to review Chapter 7 content.

 Available in DVD and VHS

Review Vocabulary

1. b	6. f
2. c	7. g
3. e	8. i
4. a	9. d
5. h	

Review Main Ideas

10. rivers, mountains, deserts
11. They controlled land and had strong armies.
12. landowning aristocrats, farmers, merchants
13. Confucianism, Daoism, Legalism; grew out of a need for order
14. Their lives were improved.
15. to carry Chinese goods to other areas—as far as Greece and Rome

Critical Thinking

16. The Chinese system used pictographs and ideographs, while cuneiform and hieroglyphics used markings, forms, and some pictures. The Chinese system is still in use, but cuneiform and hieroglyphics were replaced by systems based on speech sounds.

17. They made clay molds in several sections, worked detailed designs into the clay, fit the pieces of the mold together, poured in

Review Vocabulary

Match the words with the definitions below.

___ 1. dynasty
___ 2. aristocrat
___ 3. bureaucracy
___ 4. mandate
___ 5. social class
___ 6. filial piety
___ 7. acupuncture
___ 8. Daoism
___ 9. Confucianism

a. right to command
b. line of rulers in the same family
c. upper class whose wealth is based on land
d. The ideas of ___ included a duty to participate in government.
e. appointed government officials
f. head of family honored by other members
g. medical treatment using thin needles
h. people with a similar position in society
i. The teachings of Laozi are the basis of ___.

Review Main Ideas

Section 1 • China's First Civilizations
10. What geographical features shaped China's civilizations?
11. Why did the Shang rulers become powerful?

Section 2 • Life in Ancient China
12. What were the three main classes in Chinese society?
13. Identify three Chinese philosophies and the reason they emerged.

Section 3 • The Qin and Han Dynasties
14. How did developments during the Han dynasty affect the Chinese people?
15. What was the purpose of the Silk Road?

Critical Thinking

16. **Contrast** How is the ancient Chinese writing system different from cuneiform and hieroglyphic writing?
17. **Describe** How did Shang artisans create bronze urns?
18. **Analyze** How is Daoism the opposite of Confucianism in some ways?

Review — Reading Skill — Text Structure — Headings and Punctuation

19. Read each of the headings below. Three could be subheads in a chapter about ancient China. Which one would most likely be the main head?
    a. The Ideas of Confucius
    b. Daoist Beliefs
    c. Chinese Philosophy
    d. Hanfeizi

20. What would be a good main head for these subheads: Papermaking, Civil Service Examinations, Acupuncture?
    e. The Rise of the Zhou Dynasty
    f. Inventions of the Qin Dynasty
    g. Developments of the Han Dynasty
    h. Life in the Shang Dynasty

To review this skill, see pages 222–223.

molten bronze, and removed the mold after the bronze had cooled.

18. Daoism teaches that people should try to be in harmony with the world; Confucianism teaches that people should work to change and improve the world.

Reading Skill

19. c
20. g

Geography Skills

Study the map below and answer the following questions.

21. **Human/Environment Interaction** Which dynasty controlled the most land?
22. **Location** In what direction did the Qin dynasty expand the most?
23. **Analyze** How do you think the East China Sea affected expansion?

NATIONAL GEOGRAPHIC

Zhou & Qin Empires

Anyang
Luoyang

Anyang
Luoyang

East China Sea

KEY
Zhou empire   Qin empire

Read to Write

24. **Expository Writing** Imagine you are planning a trip on the Silk Road and you need someone to go with you. Write a want ad describing the type of person you need. Explain what will be expected of that person on the trip.

25. **Using Your FOLDABLES** Choose one person that you included in your foldable. Write a list of 10 questions that you would ask that person in an interview. Exchange lists with a partner and play the role of the person being interviewed.

Using Technology

26. **Internet Research** The Chinese built the Great Wall of China to protect themselves. Use the Internet and your local library to research ways other countries have protected themselves from enemies. Describe at least two examples to your classmates.

History Online
Self-Check Quiz To help prepare for the Chapter Test, visit jat.glencoe.com

Building Citizenship Skills

27. **Plan a Debate** With your class, plan and participate in a three-way debate. Divide into three teams. One team will represent the Legalists, one will represent followers of Confucius, and one will represent Daoists. As a team, research each philosophy. Record key points on note cards for easy reference. Begin the debate by asking the question "Which philosophy is best reflected in a democratic society such as that of the United States?"

Primary Source   Analyze

The main ideas of Daoism are explained in a book titled *Dao De Jing* (The Way of the Dao). This passage describes the Daoist position against violence.

"When leading by the way of the Tao [Dao], abominate [hate] the use of force, for it causes resistance, and loss of strength....

Achieve results but not through violence, for it is against the natural way, and damages both others' and one's own true self....

The wise leader achieves results, but does not glory in them ... and does not boast of them.

He knows that boasting is not the natural way, and that he who goes against that way, will fail in his endeavours."

—"A Caveat Against Violence,"
The Tao Te Ching, Stan Rosenthal, trans.

DBQ Document-Based Questions

28. According to Daoist thought, what is the result of using force or violence?
29. What do you think the following statement means?
"The wise leader achieves results, but does not glory in them."

History Online
Have students visit the Web site at jat.glencoe.com to review Chapter 7 and take the **Self-Check Quiz**.

Using Technology

26. Examples will vary. Ensure students use two examples.

Building Citizenship Skills

27. Arguments will vary but should accurately reflect information in the chapter.

Primary Source

28. It causes resistance and loss of strength and damages others' and one's own true self.

29. The wise leader is effective but not proud.

Bonus Question

Ask: How do you think early China's history would be different if the Silk Road had never developed? Why? (*Answers should focus on the lost opportunities for the exchange of ideas and the expansion of trade.*)

Geography Skills

21. Qin
22. south
23. Qin rulers expanded toward the sea, probably to increase trade opportunities.

Read to Write

24. Ads will differ but should accurately reflect information in the chapter.
25. **FOLDABLES** Questions should demonstrate understanding of the person chosen.

REVIEWING UNIT OBJECTIVES

Having studied this unit, students should now be able to

1. trace the rise of Greek city-states with an emphasis on Athens and Sparta, and describe Greek cultural accomplishments and the spread of Greek culture;

2. discuss early Indian civilizations and empires, including the development of Hinduism and Buddhism;

3. explore China's first civilizations and the rise of the Qin and Han dynasties.

UNIT REVIEW ACTIVITY

Comparing Civilizations To help students review the unit objectives, have them read the **Comparing Civilizations** chart and consider the materials they have read in the chapters. Then have them create their own chart that compares the civilizations in areas such as religion, politics, economics, and influence on the world.

After students have created their charts, have them write a sentence or two for each concept that explains why the civilizations had that specific characteristic. Then have them speculate as to why the civilizations were similar and why they were different. **L2**

Unit 2 Review

Comparing Civilizations

Compare the civilizations that you have read about by reviewing the information below. Can you see how the people of these civilizations helped to build the world we live in today?

Where in the World?
● Chapters 4 & 5
● Chapter 6
● Chapter 7

NATIONAL GEOGRAPHIC

	Ancient Greece Chapters 4 & 5	Early India Chapter 6	Early China Chapter 7
Where did these civilizations develop?	• On Mediterranean islands and the Balkan Peninsula	• In the Indus River valley	• In the Huang He valley
Who were some important people in these civilizations?	• Homer, c. 750 B.C. • Pericles, c. 495–429 B.C. • Socrates, c. 470–399 B.C. • Alexander the Great, c. 356–323 B.C.	• Siddhartha Gautama, c. 563–483 B.C. • Chandragupta Maurya, ruled c. 321–298 B.C. • Asoka, ruled c. 273–232 B.C.	• Wu Wang, ruled c. 1045–1043 B.C. • Confucius, 551–479 B.C. • Qin Shihuangdi, ruled 221–210 B.C. • Liu Bang, ruled 202–195 B.C.
Where did most of the people live?	• Early Greeks lived on estates near walled palaces • Later Greeks lived in a polis and in nearby farms and villages	• Many lived in farming villages and towns near major rivers • Some lived in very large cities	• Landowning aristocrats lived in large houses with gardens and courtyards • Most people were farmers living in simple houses in villages or cities

252

END-OF-UNIT RESOURCES

📁 **Reproducible Masters**
- Unit 2 Test Form A
- Unit 2 Test Form B
- Step Into World History Activity 2

🖨 **Transparencies**
- Unit 2 Map Overlay Transparencies

Multimedia
- Interactive Tutor Self-Assessment CD-ROM
- Exam*View*® Pro Testmaker CD-ROM
- Presentation Plus! CD-ROM

	Ancient Greece Chapters 4 & 5	Early India Chapter 6	Early China Chapter 7
What were these people's beliefs?	• Greeks worshiped many gods and goddesses and believed in fate	• Hinduism: complex religion with many gods representing an eternal spirit • Buddhism: enlightenment available to anyone	• Confucianism: duty directs your life • Daoism: people should try to be in harmony with nature • Legalism: people need harsh laws to be good • Worship of ancestors
What was their government like?	• Early Greeks were ruled by kings • Later, some Greeks developed governments run by citizens	• The warrior class ran the government, usually ruled by a king	• A king or emperor ruled the country • Aristocrats ran the provinces
What was their language and writing like?	• Greek: used characters to form letters and words	• Sanskrit: used characters to form letters and words	• Chinese: symbols that represent objects were combined to represent ideas
What contributions did they make?	• Introduced democracy • Architecture was copied by others • Developed the idea of theater and drama	• Made advances in medicine, mathematics, science, and literature • Developed two major religions	• Invented paper and gunpowder • Cultivated silk
How do these contributions affect me? *Can you add any?*	• We have a democratic government in the United States • Modern plays, movies, and television shows have their roots in Greek theater	• "0" is now a part of our number system • Many people still practice Buddhism and Hinduism	• The papermaking process allows us to create books, newspapers, and other paper products • Gunpowder and silk are still in use

253

UNIT WRAP-UP ACTIVITY

Free-Form Mapping With free-form mapping, students create their own text representations. It is a cooperative team effort and occurs as a post-reading activity.

1. Organize students into groups of four. Each group should have markers and a large sheet of paper. Members must decide upon the important ideas in the unit and organize a way of presenting their ideas on paper in words, pictures, and diagrams.

2. Explain to students that there is no correct way to map the unit. The only criterion is to represent main ideas and their interrelationships. Encourage students to use words, pictures, phrases, circles, squares, or whatever creative endeavor they feel best portrays their analysis.

3. Teams then should share their maps with the class and discuss the ideas found on them. Maps can be displayed around the classroom.

Free-form maps can be used for reviewing content for tests. Different topics can be assigned to groups, and they can use their maps to present the information to the entire class. **L1/ EL**

PROFESSIONAL DEVELOPMENT: TEACHING WRITING

• Finney, Susan. *Keep the Rest of the Class Reading & Writing—While You Teach Small Groups.* Scholastic Professional Books, 2000.
• Cary, Stephen. *Working with Second Language Learners: Answers to Teachers' Top Ten Questions.* Heinemann, 2000.
• Meagher, Judy, and Joan Novelli. *Language Arts.* Scholastic Professional Books, 1998.
• Suid, Murray, and Wanda Lincoln. *How to Teach Writing Without Going Crazy.* Monday Morning Books, 1998.

Unit ③ Planning Guide

Unit Resources

Note: The following materials may be used when teaching Unit 3.
Chapter and section level support materials can be found on the chapter and section resource pages.

TEACHING TRANSPARENCIES

📖🗂 Writing Process Transparencies **L1**

DIFFERENTIATED INSTRUCTION

🗂 Step Into World History Activity 3 **L1**

ASSESSMENT

🗂 Unit 3 Test Form A **L2**
🗂 Unit 3 Test Form B **L2**

ADDITIONAL RESOURCES

- 💿 Glencoe Skillbuilder Interactive Workbook, CD-ROM Level 1
- 💿 Glencoe World History Primary Source Document Library CD-ROM
- 🖼 Focus on World Art Prints
- 🗂 Outline Map Resource Book
- 🌐 World Desk Map
- 📖 World Art and Architecture Transparencies
- 🎵 World Music: Cultural Traditions
- 🎵 World Music: A Cultural Legacy
- 📖 Glencoe World Literature Library
- 🗂 Reading in the Content Area
- 🗂 Teaching Strategies for the World History Classroom (Including Block Scheduling Pacing Guides)
- 🗂 Inclusion Strategies for the Middle School Social Studies Classroom

🗂 Blackline Master	💿 CD-ROM
🖼 Poster	🎧 Audio Program
📖 Transparency	💿 DVD
🎵 Music Program	📼 Videocassette

READING SUPPORT FROM JAMESTOWN EDUCATION

- *Timed Readings Plus in Social Studies* help students increase their reading rate and fluency while maintaining comprehension. The 400-word passages are similar to those found on state and national assessments.
- *Reading in the Content Area: Social Studies* concentrates on six essential reading skills that help students better comprehend what they read. The book includes 75 high-interest nonfiction passages written at increasing levels of difficulty.
- *Reading Fluency* helps students read smoothly, accurately, and expressively.
- *Jamestown's Reading Improvement,* by renowned reading expert Edward Fry, focuses on helping build your students' comprehension, vocabulary, and skimming and scanning skills.
- *Critical Reading Series* provides high-interest books, each written at three reading levels.

To order these products, call Glencoe at 1-800-334-7344.

Reading List Generator CD-ROM

GLENCOE BOOKLINK

The Glencoe BookLink CD-ROM is a database that allows you to search more than 15,000 titles to create a customized reading list for your students.

- Reading lists can be organized by students' reading level, author, genre, theme, or area of interest.
- The database provides Degrees of Reading Power™ (DRP) and Lexile™ readability scores for all selections.
- A brief summary of each selection is included.

Leveled reading suggestions for this unit:

For students at a Grade 5 reading level:
- ■ *The Romans and Their Empire,* by Trevor Cairns

For students at a Grade 6 reading level:
- ■ *I Remember Palestine,* by Anita Ganeri

For students at a Grade 7 reading level:
- ■ *The Golden Age of Islam,* by Linda S. George

To order this CD-ROM, call Glencoe at 1-800-334-7344.

Unit Reading Strategies

Each chapter in this unit contains special reading strategies. The following preview will help you teach these reading skills to your students.

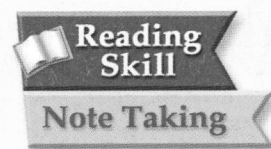

CHAPTER 8: Note Taking

Note taking is a skill that will serve students well for the rest of their lives, whether in preparation for a presentation or in helping them organize information for other courses. Modeling effective note taking and providing students with many opportunities to practice the various forms of note taking will increase their level of comfort and proficiency with this skill. One method practiced in this chapter is a T-shaped outline.

CHAPTER 9: Your Point of View

Young students often need many opportunities to reflect and respond to the text in order to make logical connections. This is a skill that will take time and patience to develop, so a supportive environment in which students can think and write freely is essential. Their responses to activities that encourage them to reflect on the text may be in the form of brainstorming, free writing, discussing, or spending time in silent reflection.

CHAPTER 10: Looking for Sequence Clues

Sequence clues are words or phrases that act as markers, telling students the order in which events occur. They are often called "signal" words because they signal to readers when things happen in reference to other events or concepts. Common sequence clues include dates or words such as *first, next, then, finally, meanwhile, during,* and *later.* Students learn to identify these words first by looking for them in text, then by rewriting paragraphs to include these kinds of words to help them organize events.

CHAPTER 11: Main Ideas and Details

As students read, they often have difficulty separating what is most important to remember from details that may not be essential to the topic. Reading often becomes overwhelming for students when every sentence seems to be equally important. Remind students that the main idea is the focal point of a passage and that supporting details are facts or examples that support that idea. Students will use graphic organizers as a vehicle for helping them to understand this concept.

Use the **SkillBuilder Handbook** on pages 902–919 to help students practice important skills.

0:00 OUT OF TIME?

If time does not permit teaching each chapter in this unit, you may use the *Reading Essentials and Study Guide* summaries.

UNIT OVERVIEW

Unit 3 starts with the history of Rome, then details the beginnings and spread of Christianity and Islam.

UNIT OBJECTIVES

After studying this unit, students should be able to

1. describe the rise and fall of the Roman Republic;

2. relate how the Roman Empire came to be;

3. discuss the beginnings and spread of Christianity;

4. explain the beginnings and spread of the religion of Islam.

Why It's Important

Explain to students that this unit describes how ideas and belief systems spread. To activate prior knowledge, discuss with students how modern-day media, such as television, movies, and newspapers, have influenced how ideas spread. **L2**

Unit 3

New Empires and New Faiths

Why It's Important

Each civilization that you will study in this unit made important contributions to history.

- The Romans invented concrete and used the arch in building.
- The Christians helped shape the West's religious beliefs.
- The Muslims spread the religion of Islam and invented algebra.

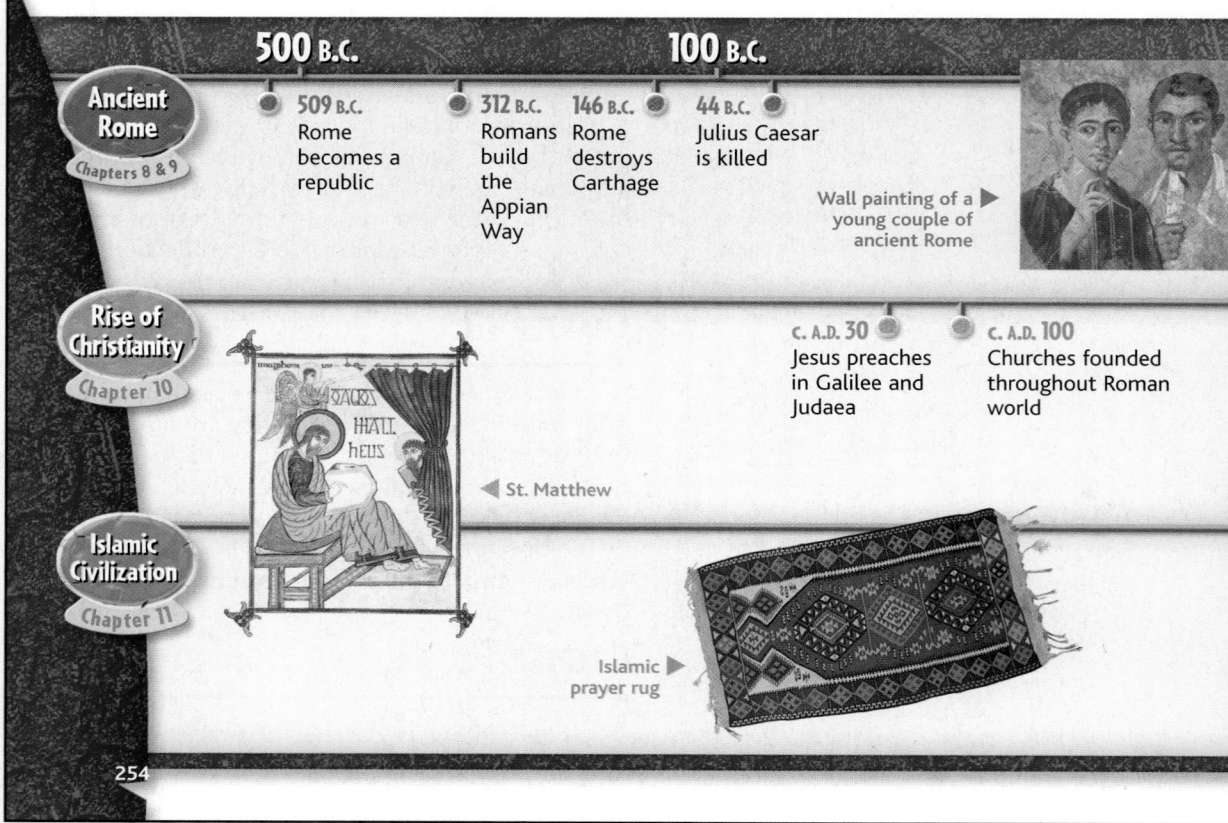

Ancient Rome
Chapters 8 & 9

500 B.C.

509 B.C.
Rome becomes a republic

312 B.C.
Romans build the Appian Way

146 B.C.
Rome destroys Carthage

100 B.C.

44 B.C.
Julius Caesar is killed

▶ Wall painting of a young couple of ancient Rome

Rise of Christianity
Chapter 10

◀ St. Matthew

c. A.D. 30
Jesus preaches in Galilee and Judaea

c. A.D. 100
Churches founded throughout Roman world

Islamic Civilization
Chapter 11

▶ Islamic prayer rug

254

TIME LINE ACTIVITY

Direct students' attention to the multiple-tier time line on these pages. Have student pairs use the information on any of the time lines to create a "When did" question—that is, a question that starts with the words "When did" and whose answer can be found on one of the time lines. When pairs have finished, ask a member from each pair to read that pair's question. Ask the other student pairs to use the time lines to determine the answer to the question. For each question, have the pairs also determine the time line on which the answer was found. For example, for the question *When did Christianity become Rome's official religion?*, students would answer *A.D. 392, from* The Rise of Christianity *time line.* **L1**

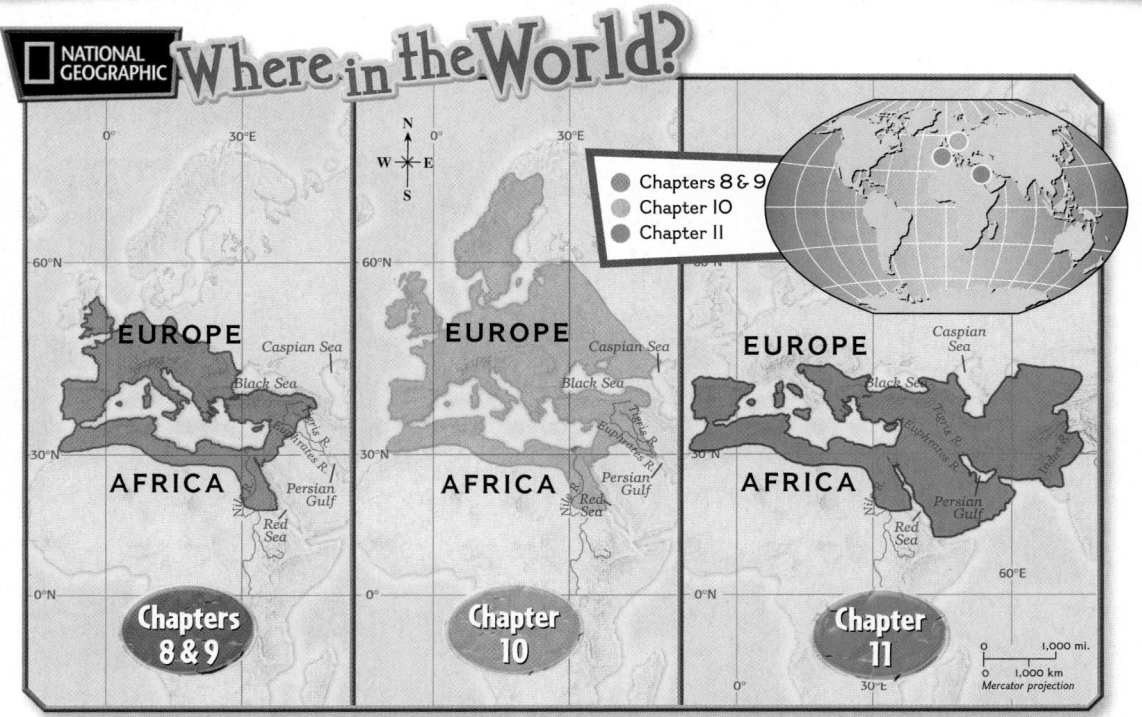

Where in the World?

NATIONAL GEOGRAPHIC

- Chapters 8 & 9
- Chapter 10
- Chapter 11

EUROPE — Caspian Sea, Black Sea, Euphrates R., Persian Gulf, Red Sea, AFRICA

Chapters 8 & 9

EUROPE — Caspian Sea, Black Sea, Euphrates R., Persian Gulf, Red Sea, AFRICA

Chapter 10

EUROPE — Caspian Sea, Black Sea, Tigris R., Euphrates R., Persian Gulf, Red Sea, Indus R., AFRICA

Chapter 11

0   1,000 mi.
0   1,000 km
Mercator projection

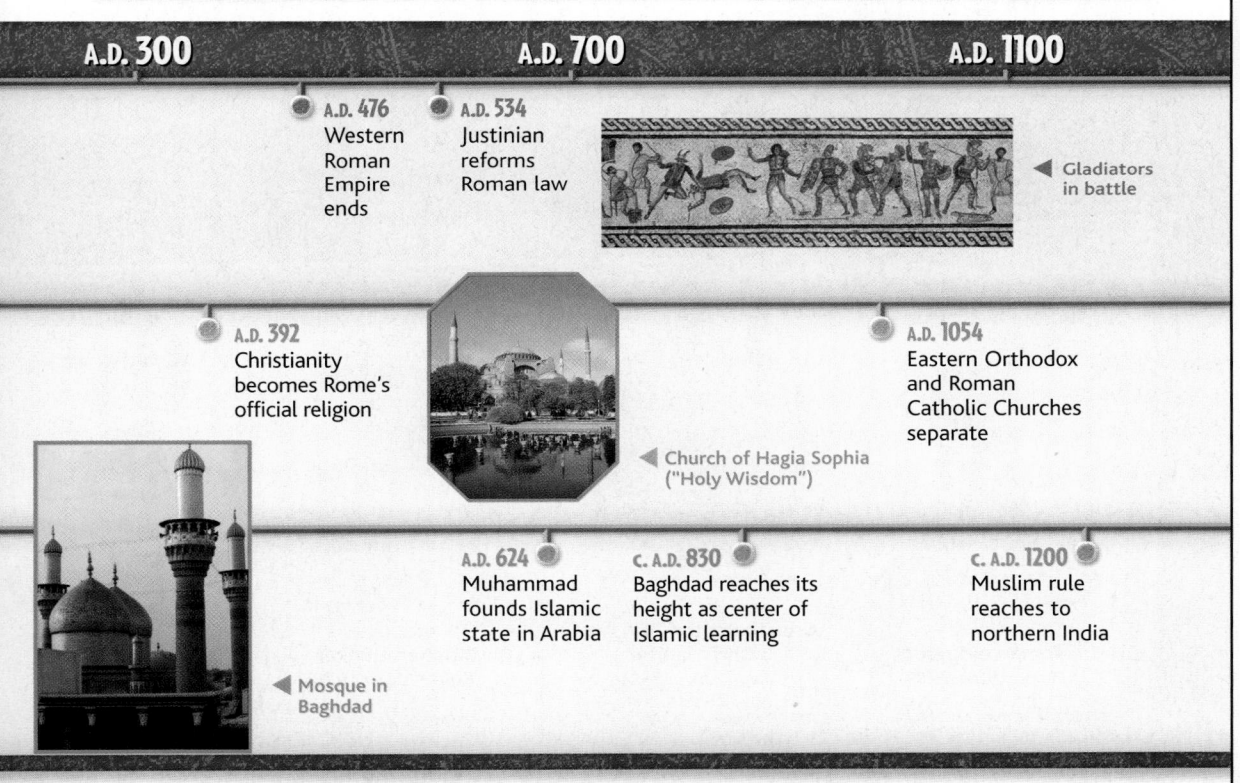

A.D. 300   **A.D. 700**   **A.D. 1100**

A.D. 476 Western Roman Empire ends

A.D. 534 Justinian reforms Roman law

◀ Gladiators in battle

A.D. 392 Christianity becomes Rome's official religion

A.D. 1054 Eastern Orthodox and Roman Catholic Churches separate

◀ Church of Hagia Sophia ("Holy Wisdom")

A.D. 624 Muhammad founds Islamic state in Arabia

C. A.D. 830 Baghdad reaches its height as center of Islamic learning

C. A.D. 1200 Muslim rule reaches to northern India

◀ Mosque in Baghdad

INTRODUCING UNIT 3

GLENCOE TECHNOLOGY

World History Primary Source Document Library CD-ROM

Use the **World History Primary Source Document Library CD-ROM** to access primary source documents related to Rome, Christianity, or Islam.

NCLB NO CHILD LEFT BEHIND

Teaching Tip The goals of the NCLB Act include a stronger emphasis on reading. Using modeling in your class will help students become better readers. For example, ask a question that can be answered by the time lines—Did Christianity outlive the Roman Empire? Then stop and think aloud for the students' benefit. First, verbally identify the time lines that will include information that might help you. Then verbally identify the second page as the page more likely to contain the correct information, since it includes later events. Now verbally identify A.D. 476 as the date the Roman Empire ended. Point out that the Christianity time line continues beyond that point. Therefore, the answer to the question is *yes*.

DIFFERENTIATED INSTRUCTION

Point out to students that the ideas and beliefs about which they will read in this unit continue to influence us today. Direct students' attention to a world map on the board or an overhead transparency, and have students compare the world map to the map in their texts.

English Learners: Have students discuss how the world map might be different if it showed Christianity and Islam today.

Gifted and Talented: Have students create a map using the in-text maps and outside research showing places with strong Christian and Muslim populations today. Have them comment on why they think these religions are strong in these areas, then check their responses as they read the unit.

FOCUS

The unit preview provides a general layout of the regions and significant figures in the unit.

PREVIEWING GEOGRAPHY

Ask students to answer the following questions using the map.

1. **Where does the Pantheon image appear?** (*central Italy*) **L1**

2. **To what civilization does the Kaaba pertain?** (*Islamic*) **L1**

PREVIEWING
People to Meet

Ask students the following questions using the biographies.

1. **Which people's lives spanned from B.C. to A.D.?** (*Augustus and Jesus*) **L1**

2. **Which two people were best known for pondering Christian ideas?** (*Paul and Augustine*) **L2**

3. **Who lived first—Jesus or Muhammad?** (*Jesus*) **L1**

Unit 3

Places to Locate

EUROPE

Mediterranean Sea

AFRICA

1 Roman aqueduct

See Ancient Rome
Chapters 8 & 9

2 Roman Pantheon

See Ancient Rome
Chapters 8 & 9

People to Meet

Augustus

63 B.C.–A.D. 14
Roman emperor
Chapter 8, page 289

Jesus

c. 6 B.C. –A.D. 30
Crucifixion led to rise of Christianity
Chapter 10, page 346

Paul

C. A.D. 10–65
Christian thinker
Chapter 10, page 349

Constantine

C. A.D. 280–337
Roman emperor
Chapter 9, page 321

256

PREVIEWING Places to Locate

Use the following descriptions to explain the images on the map.

 1 This aqueduct, called the Pont du Gard, is located in Nimes, France. It was built in 19 B.C. and is 900 feet long and 160 feet high. The lower tier is still used as a road bridge.

 2 The Pantheon, originally built in 27 B.C, was rebuilt in the A.D. 100s by Agrippa. Although it became a Christian church, it shows the remarkable ability of Roman architects.

ASIA

3 Hagia Sophia
See Ancient Rome
Chapters 8 & 9

4 Mount of the Beatitudes
See Rise of Christianity
Chapter 10

5 Kaaba
See Islamic Civilization
Chapter 11

Arabian Sea

⑤

Augustine
A.D. 354–430
Christian philosopher
Chapter 10, page 357

Theodora
C. A.D. 500–548
Byzantine empress
Chapter 9, page 331

Muhammad
C. A.D. 570–632
Muslims believe Allah dictated the Quran to Muhammad
Chapter 11, page 376

Omar Khayyam
A.D. 1048–1131
Islamic poet and philosopher
Chapter 11, page 392

257

TEACH

Organizing Information Have students complete a table like the one below to organize information about the people discussed on these pages. (*Answers are provided.*) **L1/ EL**

Person	Known For
Augustus	Roman emperor
Jesus	crucifixion led to rise of Christianity
Paul	Christian thinker
Constantine	Roman emperor
Augustine	Christian philosopher
Theodora	Byzantine empress
Muhammad	Received Quran
Omar Khayyam	poet and philosopher

Making a Time Line Have student pairs create a time line illustrating the dates of the births and deaths of the people pictured on these pages. **Ask: Who could have read the writings of Paul?** (*Constantine, Augustine, Theodora, Muhammad, Omar Khayyam*) **Who lived before Muhammad?** (*Augustus, Jesus, Paul, Constantine, Augustine, Theodora*) **L1/ EL**

PREVIEWING Places to Locate

 The Hagia Sophia, built between A.D. 532 and A.D. 537, was a Christian church until the Muslim Turks captured Constantinople in 1453.

 The Mount of the Beatitudes is where Jesus is said to have given the Sermon on the Mount.

 Many Muslims attempt a pilgrimage to see the Kaaba, a great stone structure within the Great Mosque in Makkah.

Chapter 8 Resources

TEACHING TRANSPARENCIES

- Graphic Organizer Transparencies with Teaching Strategy and Student Activity **L2**
- Cause-and-Effect Transparencies with Teaching Strategy and Student Activity **L2**
- Then and Now Transparencies with Teaching Strategy and Student Activity **L2**
- In-text Map Transparency with Teaching Strategy and Student Activity **L1**
- Map Transparencies with Overlay, Teaching Strategy, and Student Activity **L2**

DIFFERENTIATED INSTRUCTION

- Differentiated Instruction Activity 8
- Time Line Activity 8
- Primary Source Reading 8 (with Document-Based Questions)
- Inclusion Strategies for the Middle School Social Studies Classroom
- StudentWorks Plus™ CD-ROM (with Audio Program)

READING SUPPORT

- Take-Home Review Activity 8 **L2**
- World Literature Reading 8 **L2**
- Workbook Activity 8 **L1**
- Reading Strategies for the Social Studies Classroom **L1/ EL**

ASSESSMENT

- Authentic Assessment Activity 8 **L1/ EL**
- Chapter 8 Test Form A **L2**
- Chapter 8 Test Form B **L2**
- ExamView® Pro Testmaker CD-ROM

INTERDISCIPLINARY CONNECTIONS

- Geography and History Activity 8 **L2**
- People to Meet Activity 8 **L2**
- Economics Activity 8 **L2**
- Citizenship and Service Learning Activity 8 **L2**

SPANISH RESOURCES

- Spanish Reading Essentials and Study Guide
- Spanish Guided Reading Activities
- Spanish Quizzes, Tests, and Authentic Assessment (with Rubrics)
- Spanish Take-Home Review Activities

MULTIMEDIA

- ExamView® Pro Testmaker CD-ROM
- Glencoe Skillbuilder Interactive Workbook CD-ROM, Level 1
- Interactive Tutor Self-Assessment CD-ROM
- MindJogger Videoquiz
- Presentation Plus! CD-ROM
- StudentWorks Plus™ CD-ROM (with Audio Program)
- TeacherWorks CD-ROM
- Vocabulary PuzzleMaker CD-ROM
- *World History: Journey Across Time* Video Program
- World History Primary Source Document Library CD-ROM

STANDARDIZED ASSESSMENT SKILLS

- Standardized Test Skills Practice Workbook Activity 8 **L2**
- Critical Thinking Skills Activity 8 **L2**

Chapter 8 Resources

TIME MANAGEMENT

Unit Introduction	Chapter Introduction	Section 1	Section 2	Section 3	Section 4	Chapter Wrap-Up
1 Day	1 Day	1 Day	2 Days	1 Day	2 Days	1 Day

Block Scheduling Activities that are suited to use within the block scheduling framework are identified by:

0:00 OUT OF TIME? Assign the Chapter 8 *Reading Essentials and Study Guide.* ✱ 📂

SECTION RESOURCES

DAILY OBJECTIVES	REPRODUCIBLE RESOURCES	MULTIMEDIA RESOURCES
Section 1 **Rome's Beginnings** 1. Rome's geographic location aided its rise to power. 2. The Romans created a republic and carried out conquests.	📂 Reproducible Lesson Plan 8–1 📂 Vocabulary Activity 8–1 📂 Guided Reading Activity 8–1* 📂 Section Quiz 8–1* 📂 Reading Essentials and Study Guide 8–1*	🖐 Daily Focus Skills Transparency 8–1 💿 Interactive Tutor Self-Assessment CD-ROM 💿 ExamView® Pro Testmaker CD-ROM 💿 Presentation Plus! CD-ROM
Section 2 **The Roman Republic** 1. Rome's republic was shaped by a struggle between wealthy landowners and regular citizens. 2. Rome defeated the Carthaginians and took control of the Mediterranean area.	📂 Reproducible Lesson Plan 8–2 📂 Vocabulary Activity 8–2 📂 Guided Reading Activity 8–2* 📂 Section Quiz 8–2* 📂 Reading Essentials and Study Guide 8–2*	🖐 Daily Focus Skills Transparency 8–2 💿 Interactive Tutor Self-Assessment CD-ROM 💿 ExamView® Pro Testmaker CD-ROM 💿 Presentation Plus! CD-ROM 💿 Glencoe BookLink CD-ROM
Section 3 **The Fall of the Republic** 1. The military hero Julius Caesar seized power, but he was later killed by his rivals. 2. The Roman Republic, weakened by civil wars, became an empire under Augustus.	📂 Reproducible Lesson Plan 8–3 📂 Vocabulary Activity 8–3 📂 Guided Reading Activity 8–3* 📂 Section Quiz 8–3* 📂 Reading Essentials and Study Guide 8–3*	🖐 Daily Focus Skills Transparency 8–3 💿 Interactive Tutor Self-Assessment CD-ROM 💿 ExamView® Pro Testmaker CD-ROM 💿 Presentation Plus! CD-ROM
Section 4 **The Early Empire** 1. Augustus's military and political reforms brought an era of peace and prosperity. 2. Rome's roads, aqueducts, ports, and common currency made the empire prosperous.	📂 Reproducible Lesson Plan 8–4 📂 Vocabulary Activity 8–4 📂 Guided Reading Activity 8–4* 📂 Section Quiz 8–4* 📂 Reading Essentials and Study Guide 8–4*	🖐 Daily Focus Skills Transparency 8–4 💿 Interactive Tutor Self-Assessment CD-ROM 💿 ExamView® Pro Testmaker CD-ROM 💿 Presentation Plus! CD-ROM 💿 Vocabulary PuzzleMaker CD-ROM 💿 Glencoe BookLink CD-ROM

*Also available in Spanish

Use our Web site for additional resources. All essential content is covered in the Student Edition.

You and your students can visit jat.glencoe.com, the Web site companion to *World History: Journey Across Time*. This innovative integration of electronic and print media offers your students a wealth of opportunities. The student text directs students to the Web site for the following options:

- Chapter Overviews
- Self-Check Quizzes
- Study Central™
- Student Web Activities
- Multi-Language Glossaries

Answers to the student Web activities are provided for you in the **Web Activity Lesson Plans.** Additional Web resources and ePuzzles and games are also available.

The following videotape programs are available from Glencoe as supplements to Chapter 8:

Ancient Rome
(ISBN 0-7670-1263-1)

The Lost Legions of Rome
(ISBN 156501-952-0)

Rome's Glorious Cities
(ISBN 0-7670-0611-9)

To order, call Glencoe at 1-800-334-7344. To find classroom resources to accompany many of these videos, check the following home pages:

A&E Television: www.aande.com
The History Channel: www.historychannel.com

MEETING SPECIAL NEEDS

In addition to the Differentiated Instruction strategies, the following resources are suitable for students with special needs:

- *ExamView® Pro Testmaker CD-ROM* allows teachers to tailor tests by reducing answer choices.
- *StudentWorks Plus™ CD-ROM (with Audio Program)* includes the entire narrative of the student edition so that less-proficient readers can listen to the words as they read them.
- The *Reading Essentials and Study Guide* provides the same content as the student edition but is written two grade levels below the textbook.

 TEACHER'S CORNER

Index to National Geographic Magazine:

The following articles relate to this chapter:

- "High-Tech Search for Roman Shipwrecks," by Robert Ballard, April 1998.
- "The Power and the Glory of the Roman Empire, Part 1," by T.R. Reid, July 1997.
- "The Brindisi Bronzes: Classical Castoffs Reclaimed from the Sea," by O. Louis Mazzatenta, August 1995.

National Geographic Society Products:

To order the following, call National Geographic at 1–800–368–2728

- *PicturePack: Ancient Civilizations: Ancient Rome* (Transparencies)
- *National Geographic Atlas of the World* (Book)

NGS ONLINE

Access National Geographic's new dynamic MapMachine Web site and other geography resources at:

www.nationalgeographic.com
www.nationalgeographic.com/maps

 ## Meeting NCSS Standards

World History: Journey Across Time
The following standards are highlighted in Chapter 8:

Section 1 **II** **Time, Continuity, and Change: A, C**
III **People, Places, and Environments: B, H, I**
V **Individuals, Groups, and Institutions: B, C**

Section 2 **IV** **Individual Development and Identity: A, C, F**
X **Civic Ideals and Practices: A, H**

Section 3 **VI** **Power, Authority, and Governance: C, B, E, I, J**

Section 4 **VIII** **Science, Technology, and Society: A**
IX **Global Connections: B**

State and Local Objectives

_____

_____

Timesaving Tools

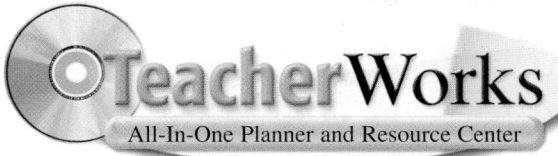

TeacherWorks
All-In-One Planner and Resource Center

● **Interactive Teacher Edition** Access your Teacher Wraparound Edition and your classroom resources with a few easy clicks.

● **Interactive Lesson Planner** Organize your week, month, semester, or year with all the lesson helps you need to make teaching creative and relevant.

Use Glencoe's **Presentation Plus!** multimedia teacher tool to easily present dynamic lessons that visually excite your students. Using Microsoft PowerPoint® you can customize the presentations to create your own personalized lessons.

FOLDABLES™
Study Organizer
Dinah Zike's Foldables

Foldables are three-dimensional, interactive graphic organizers that help students practice basic writing skills, review key vocabulary terms, and identify main ideas. Every chapter contains a foldable activity, with additional chapter activities found in the *Reading and Study Skills Foldables* booklet. You can use the foldables as they are presented, or modify them to suit the needs of your individual class.

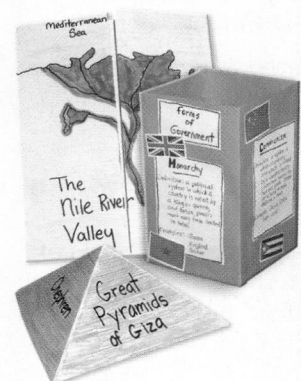

Planning Ahead

CHAPTER CULMINATING ACTIVITY

The Chapter Culminating Activity will help students organize and learn the important information from the chapter. Begin the chapter with this activity, and have students complete it as a culminating activity.

CHARTING CHANGE IN ANCIENT ROME

Purpose One of the difficulties students may have as they read this chapter is that Rome went through many changes. The following chart will use categories to help organize these changes into a visual, cohesive structure.

Introduction to Modeling

1. On a wall map of Europe, point out the present-day city of Rome. Then have students turn to page 292 in their texts. Explain that the maps show the expansion of the Roman Empire. Help students understand how much change must have taken place as Rome conquered these lands.

2. Supply each student with a piece of paper. Have students create a chart like the following:

	Rome's Beginnings	Roman Republic	Early Empire
Land Controlled			
Government			
Economy			
Citizens			
Soldiers			

Explain that these are the categories in which students are going to measure change.

3. Tell students that they should fill in the second column as they read the beginning of the chapter. Explain that students will fill in the third and fourth columns as they progress through the chapter.

4. When students have finished the chapter and their charts are completed, have them use their charts' entries to create a master chart on the board.

Authentic Assessment

Refer to Activity 8 in the Authentic Assessment section of the *Quizzes, Tests, and Authentic Assessment (with Rubrics)* booklet.

When & Where?

Provide students with maps of the Mediterranean region. As students read the chapter, have them keep track of lands that Rome conquered by coloring in the appropriate sections of the map. Ask whether Rome ruled more lands as a republic or as an empire. *(as an empire)* **L1**

GLENCOE TECHNOLOGY

World History: Journey Across Time Video Program

To learn more about the rise of Rome, students can view the Chapter 8 video in the *World History: Journey Across Time* Video Program.

MindJogger Videoquiz

Use the **MindJogger Videoquiz** to preview Chapter 8 content.

 Available in DVD and VHS

Chapter 8

The Rise of Rome

◀ Ruins of the Forum in Rome, Italy

NATIONAL GEOGRAPHIC **When & Where?**

500 B.C.	300 B.C.	100 B.C.	A.D. 100
451 B.C. Romans adopt the Twelve Tables	267 B.C. Rome controls most of Italy	27 B.C. Octavian becomes Rome's first emperor	A.D. 96 Rule of the Good Emperors begins

Reading Strategy ▷ PURPOSE FOR READING

Analyzing Visuals Explain to students that some of the factors that made Rome a great civilization—a common language, a common currency, and vast construction projects—also help advance our civilization. Have student pairs study the pictures in this chapter. **Ask:** What do the pictures tell you about Rome's civilization? *(Answers should come from picture details and may include that Rome had a governing Senate, a great army, a written code of laws, a massive system of roads, great leaders, and so on.)* **L1**

Chapter Preview

While the Chinese civilization arose in East Asia, the Romans created an empire that covered much of the Mediterranean world. Read this chapter to discover how the Romans were able to win control of such a large area.

 View the Chapter 8 video in the *World History: Journey Across Time* Video Program.

Chapter Overview Visit jat.glencoe.com for a preview of Chapter 8.

 Section 1
Rome's Beginnings

The civilization of Rome began in Italy. Rome grew from a small city into an economic and military power.

 Section 2
The Roman Republic

Rome was a republic for almost 500 years. During this time, it gradually expanded the right to vote. After many years of war and following the destruction of the Carthaginian Empire, Rome took control of the Mediterranean region.

 Section 3
The Fall of the Republic

As Rome's territory grew, the army gained political power. The Roman Republic, weakened by civil wars, gave way to the Roman Empire.

 Section 4
The Early Empire

Augustus and many of his successors governed well. Rome's empire grew larger and wealthier.

Study Organizer

Know-Want-Learn *Make this foldable to help you organize what you know, what you want to know, and what you learn about the rise of Rome.*

Step 1 *Fold four sheets of paper in half from top to bottom.*

Step 2 *On each folded paper, make a cut 1 inch from the side on the top flap.*

Cut 1 inch from the edge through the top flap only.

Step 3 *Place the folded papers one on top of the other. Staple the four sections together and label the top four tabs: Rome's Beginnings, The Roman Republic, The Fall of the Republic, and The Early Empire.*

Staple here. → Rome's Beginnings

Reading and Writing *Before reading the chapter, write what you already know about the beginning of Rome, the rise and fall of its republic, and the early Roman Empire under the tabs of your foldable. Also write one question you have on each tab. As you read, summarize what you learn under each tab.*

259

INTRODUCING CHAPTER 8

Introduce students to chapter content and key terms by having them access **Chapter Overview 8** at jat.glencoe.com

CHAPTER PREVIEW

After reading Chapter 8, students will be able to

1. explain how Rome became a republic;

2. describe how Rome gained control of the Mediterranean region;

3. explain how the failure of the republic led to the creation of a Roman Empire;

4. relate how military and political reforms made Rome rich and prosperous.

Study Organizer Dinah Zike's Foldables

Purpose Students use this foldable to illustrate what they learn about the rise of Rome. As students read each section, they should write a summary of what they have learned under the appropriate tab of the foldable.

📂 Have students complete *Reading and Study Skills Foldables* Activity 8.

MORE ABOUT THE PHOTO

Roman Forum The political and economic center of ancient Rome was the Roman Forum. First built during the 600s B.C., the Forum was gradually filled with important political and judicial buildings as well as many temples dedicated to gods and goddesses. Beginning about 498 B.C., a series of temples in honor of Saturn, the Roman god of agriculture, was built. The latest temple (the ruins of which are shown above) was constructed during the reign of Emperor Diocletian in the late A.D. 200s.

1 Learn It!

Taking notes from a text or while listening to a lecture is an important skill that helps learners organize information for future retrieval. It is important for students to find ways of taking notes that fit their learning and studying styles, so encourage students to experiment with a variety of note-taking methods. Following are some examples of note taking that students may find helpful.

Information Notes:
Main Topic
    Important Details

Response Notes
Main Topic
    What I Don't Understand

Category Notes
Important Events, Dates, People
    Memorable detail

Flow Chart

Main Topic → Detail → Detail

Concept Map
Students use boxes, squares, circles or ovals, or any other shape to help them note the information in a visual format.

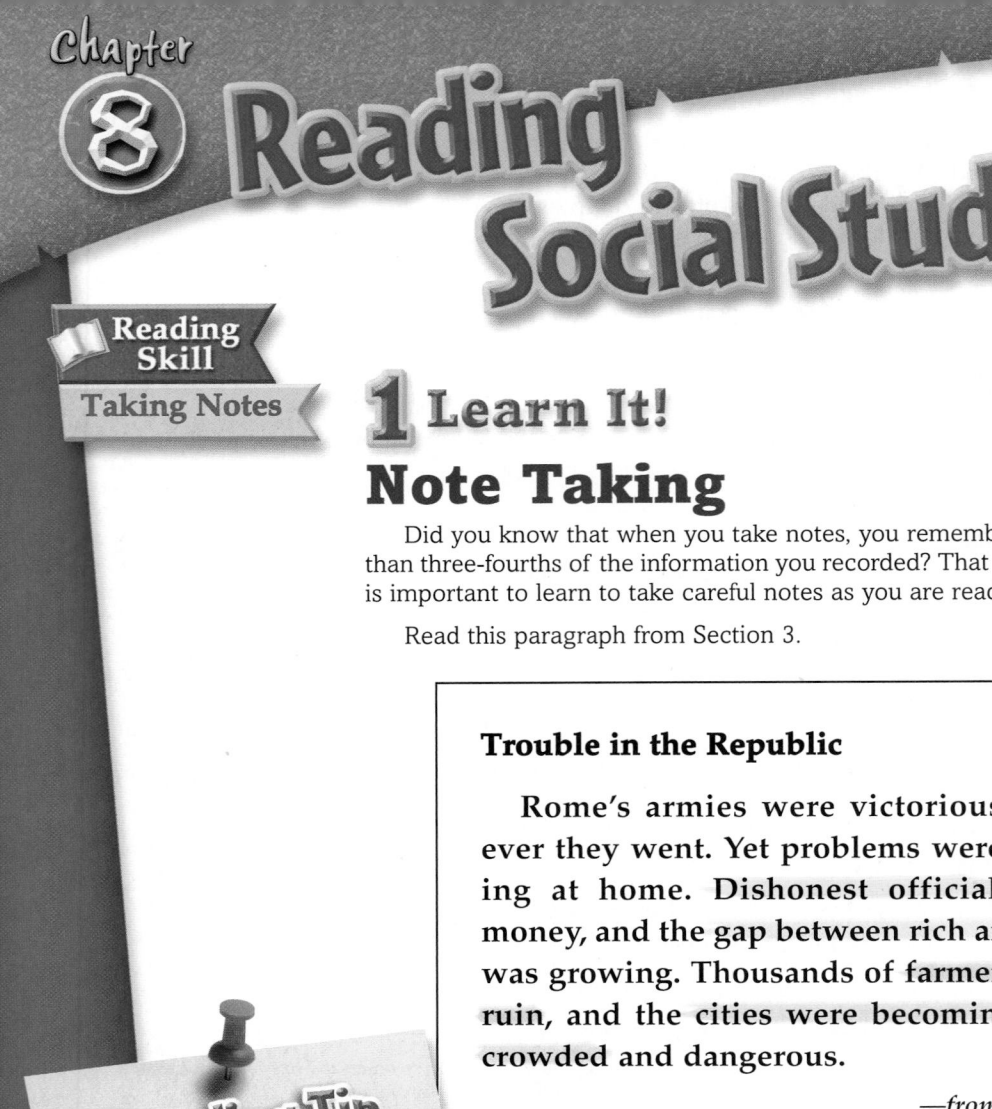

Chapter 8 Reading Social Studies

Reading Skill — Taking Notes

1 Learn It!

Note Taking

Did you know that when you take notes, you remember more than three-fourths of the information you recorded? That is why it is important to learn to take careful notes as you are reading.

Read this paragraph from Section 3.

> **Trouble in the Republic**
>
> Rome's armies were victorious wherever they went. Yet problems were building at home. **Dishonest officials stole money, and the gap between rich and poor was growing.** Thousands of **farmers faced ruin,** and the **cities were becoming overcrowded and dangerous.**
>
> *—from page 278*

Reading Tip

Authors of textbooks help with note taking by giving you headings and subheadings. If you are not sure of the main topic, it is a safe bet that headings in bold are important.

Here is one method of note taking for the above paragraph.

Main Topic	Important Details
Republic's Problems	1. dishonest officials 2. gap between rich and poor 3. farmers faced ruin 4. cities overcrowded

260

Reading Strategy — TAKING NOTES

Students who are slow or reluctant readers may have difficulty reading the entire chapter or even one section of a chapter alone, especially if they are assigned specific tasks based on the reading. One way to help students increase content knowledge and still be responsible for reading a significant part of the text is to have students "split up" the chapter or section. Put students in small groups. Students will divide the section into manageable parts and be given sufficient time to read their assigned portion carefully. Students should take notes as they read so that they can summarize the content for the other students in their group. When they are finished, students should share their notes so that each person has the same completed notes for the section. **L2**

2 Practice It!

Make a T-Chart

Read the first few pages of Section 2 and use this T-chart as a guide to help you practice taking notes.

Main Topic	Important Details
Rome's government	1.
	2.
Social groups in Rome	1.
	2.
Roman law	1.
	2.

Read to Write ·······

On page 273, read about Rome's first code of laws, the Twelve Tables. Come up with your own 12 Tables of School Law, and explain why each one should be used to govern the students in your school.

3 Apply It!

As you read Section 1, write the names of important people or places on the left column of your note-taking paper. On the right side, list details from your reading.

261

2 Practice It!

Cooperative Learning Students often learn best in cooperative settings or with a partner. Show students various methods of taking notes and then have them practice with a partner. One student will orally read a section of the text while the partner takes notes. The student will look at the notes to see if there is anything from the text that he or she would want to add or delete. They will then switch roles. This not only reinforces the content but also allows students to practice the skill of note taking. Display samples of the notes so that students may observe and then attempt different methods of note taking.

3 Apply It!

Read aloud the information about Julius Caesar in Section 3 ("Julius Caesar," "Caesar's Military Campaigns," "Caesar's Rise to Power") to the class. Ask students to take notes using the method that works best for them as you are reading. When you are finished, have students work with partners to compare their methods of note taking, the information they chose to record, and the length of their notes. Ask pairs to share their findings with the class.

Reading Strategy 〈 READ TO WRITE

To complete this assignment, students may need a little more practice. Helping students move from the text to note taking to writing provides a powerful sequence for learning. Ask students to look back with a partner at the section they read and create a piece of writing based on the section. Having them create their own "writing assignment" also encourages critical thinking. An example is the **Read to Write** assignment in the student material. Another example could be the following assignment regarding Julius Caesar: "You are a supporter of Caesar and believe his leadership has vastly improved Rome. Write a letter to those who are plotting to kill him." If students chose the section titled "The 'Good Emperors,'" for example, their assignment could involve writing about the qualities that they believe make good emperors or presidents. **L2**

① FOCUS

SECTION OVERVIEW

This section describes the beginnings of Rome, the founding of the republic, and early conquests.

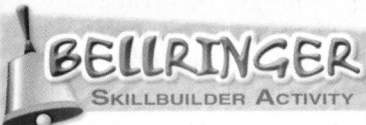
BELLRINGER
SKILLBUILDER ACTIVITY

🔔 Project **Daily Focus Skills Transparency 8–1** and have students answer questions. Discuss their responses.

Get Ready to Read!

Preteaching Vocabulary: Direct students' attention to the two vocabulary terms on this page. Ask them to find both terms in the section so they can determine which of the terms also could be used to describe the United States. *(republic)*

Answers to Graphic: transformed Rome into a city of wood and brick buildings; laid out streets, temples, and public buildings around a central square; taught the Romans to wear short cloaks and togas; Etruscan army served as model for the Romans

---

Section ①

Rome's Beginnings

Get Ready to Read!

What's the Connection?
In previous chapters, you learned about the civilization of ancient Greece. Greek ways did not die with the end of Greece's freedom. They were adopted and spread widely by another civilization, Rome.

Focusing on the Main Ideas
- Geography played an important role in the rise of Roman civilization. *(page 263)*

- The Romans created a republic and conquered Italy. By treating people fairly, they built Rome from a small city into a great power. *(page 265)*

Locating Places
Sicily (SIH•suh•lee)
Apennines (A•puh•NYNZ)
Latium (LAY•shee•uhm)
Tiber River (TY•buhr)
Etruria (ih•TRUR•ee•uh)

Meeting People
Romulus (RAHM•yuh•luhs) **and Remus** (REE•muhs)
Aeneas (ih•NEE•uhs)
Latins (LA•tuhnz)
Etruscans (ih•TRUHS•kuhnz)
Tarquins (TAHR•kwihnz)

Building Your Vocabulary
republic (rih•PUH•blihk)
legion (LEE•juhn)

Reading Strategy
Summarizing Information Use a diagram like the one below to show how the Etruscans affected the development of Rome.

Etruscans	

NATIONAL GEOGRAPHIC **When & Where?**

ITALY
• Rome
Sicily
AFRICA

650 B.C. — 450 B.C. — 250 B.C.

- **c. 650 B.C.** Etruscans rule Rome
- **509 B.C.** Rome becomes a republic
- **267 B.C.** Rome controls most of Italy

262   CHAPTER 8   The Rise of Rome

SECTION RESOURCES

📂 **Reproducible Masters**
- Reproducible Lesson Plan 8–1
- Daily Lecture and Discussion Notes 8–1
- Vocabulary Activity 8–1
- Active Reading Note-Taking Guide 8–1
- Guided Reading Activity 8–1
- Section Quiz 8–1
- Reading Essentials and Study Guide 8–1

🔦 **Transparencies**
- Daily Focus Skills Transparency 8–1

Multimedia
- Interactive Tutor Self-Assessment CD-ROM
- ExamView® Pro Testmaker CD-ROM
- Presentation Plus! CD-ROM

The Origins of Rome

Main Idea Geography played an important role in the rise of Roman civilization.

Reading Focus If you were founding a new city, what natural features would influence your choice of a building site? As you read this section, think about the choices that the early Romans made.

Italy is in an important location in the middle of the Mediterranean region. It is a long, narrow peninsula with a distinctive shape: it looks like a high-heeled boot jutting into the sea. The heel points toward Greece and the toe toward the island of **Sicily** (SIH•suh•lee). Across the top of the boot are the Alps, craggy mountains that separate Italy from European lands to the north. Another mountain range, the **Apennines** (A•puh•NYNZ), runs all the way down the boot from north to south.

The landscape of Italy is similar to that of Greece, but the Apennines are not as rugged as Greece's mountains. They can be crossed much more easily. As a result, the people who settled in Italy were not split up into small, isolated communities as the Greeks were. In addition, Italy had better farmland than Greece. Its mountain slopes level off to large flat plains that are ideal for growing crops. With more capacity to produce food, Italy could support more people than Greece could.

Historians know little about the first people to live in Italy. There is evidence, however, that groups from the north slipped through Italy's mountain passes between about 1500 B.C. and 1000 B.C. Attracted by the mild climate and rich soil, a small but steady stream of newcomers settled in the hills and on the plains. Among these peoples were a Latin-speaking people who built the city of Rome on the plain of **Latium** (LAY•shee•uhm) in central Italy.

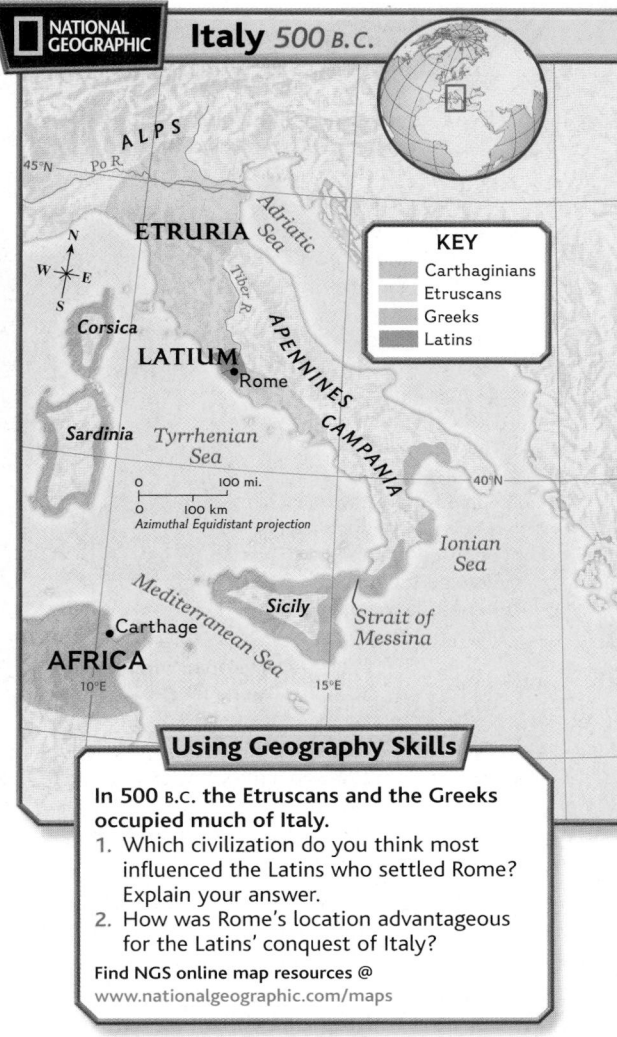

NATIONAL GEOGRAPHIC **Italy** 500 B.C.

KEY
- Carthaginians
- Etruscans
- Greeks
- Latins

Using Geography Skills

In 500 B.C. the Etruscans and the Greeks occupied much of Italy.
1. Which civilization do you think most influenced the Latins who settled Rome? Explain your answer.
2. How was Rome's location advantageous for the Latins' conquest of Italy?

Find NGS online map resources @ www.nationalgeographic.com/maps

Where Was Rome Located? Geography played a major part in the location of Rome. The site chosen for Rome was about 15 miles (24 km) up the **Tiber River** (TY•buhr) from the Mediterranean Sea. The Tiber River gave the Romans a source of water and a way to the rest of the Mediterranean world. At the same time, Rome was far enough from the sea to escape raids by pirates.

CHAPTER 8   The Rise of Rome   263

Publius Vergilius Maro (Virgil's full name) spent more than 10 years working on the *Aeneid*. He was on his way to Greece to spend the next three years finishing the poem when he caught the fever that would kill him. His dying wish, it is said, was for the unfinished *Aeneid* to be burned. The emperor himself saved the poem.

Answer:
persistent, determined, wants to succeed

HISTORY Mystery

How Do We Know About the History of Rome?
Around 200 B.C., the historian Pictor attempted to document Rome's history from its very beginnings. During the next two centuries, a number of other historians wrote about Rome. Because these historians had little factual information about Rome's beginnings, they generally related as history the mythological stories described in this section.

The *Aeneid*

Two legends describe the beginning of Rome. One says that after Troy was destroyed, Aeneas and the other Trojans went in search of another place to live.

"Weeping, I drew away from our old country. . . . I took to the open sea, borne outward into exile with my people, my son, my hearth gods, and the greater gods. . . . Now making landfall under the southwind there, I plotted out on that curved shore the walls of a colony—though fate opposed it—and I devised the name Aeneadae for the people, from my own."

—adapted from Virgil, *Aeneid*

▲ Virgil

DBQ Document-Based Question

What type of person do you think Aeneas was to build a new city after having the first one destroyed?

In addition, Rome was built on seven hills. The Romans did this on purpose. The hills were very steep, making it easy to defend the city against enemy attack. Rome was also located at a place where people could easily cross the Tiber River. As a result, Rome became a stopping place for people traveling north and south in western Italy and for merchant ships sailing in the western Mediterranean.

How Did Rome Begin? Two different legends describe how Rome began. The traditional story is that twin brothers named **Romulus** (RAHM•yuh•luhs) and **Remus** (REE•muhs) founded the city. As babies, the boys were abandoned near the Tiber River. Rescued by a wolf and raised by a shepherd, they decided to build a city in 753 B.C. The twins quarreled, however, and Remus made fun of the wall his brother was building. In a fury, Romulus lashed out at Remus and killed him. Romulus went on to become the first king of Rome, the new city he named after himself.

The seeds of Rome are traced even farther back in the *Aeneid,* a famous epic by the Roman poet Virgil. The *Aeneid* is the story of the Trojan hero **Aeneas** (ih•NEE•uhs). He and a band of followers are said to have sailed the Mediterranean Sea after the Greeks captured Troy. After many adventures, the Trojans landed at the mouth of the Tiber. Through warfare and then marriage to the local king's daughter, Aeneas united the Trojans and some of the **Latins** (LA•tuhnz), the local people. He thus became the "father" of the Romans.

Historians are not sure how Rome began. They think that Latins lived in the area of Rome as early as 1000 B.C. They built huts on Rome's hills, tended herds, and grew crops. Sometime between 800 B.C. and 700 B.C., they decided to band together for protection. It was this community that became known as Rome.

Early Influences After about 800 B.C., other groups joined the Romans in Italy. Two of these groups, the Greeks and the **Etruscans** (ih•TRUHS•kuhnz), played a major role in shaping Roman civilization.

Many Greeks came to southern Italy and Sicily between 750 B.C. and 550 B.C., when Greece was busily building overseas colonies. From the Greeks, Romans learned to grow olives and grapes. They also adopted the Greek alphabet, and they

DIFFERENTIATED INSTRUCTION

Visual/Spatial: Have students prepare a two-column table. Direct them to label the left column "Greek Contributions" and the right column "Etruscan Contributions." As they read about these groups, have students fill in and compare their tables.

Auditory/Musical: Organize students into groups, and have a member of each group read aloud a paragraph from the subsection "Early Influences." Then direct each group to discuss and reach a conclusion about the impact of the Greeks and Etruscans on Rome.

Gifted and Talented: Organize students into two groups: Greeks and Etruscans. Have groups debate this question: Which culture contributed more to Rome's development?

◄ Etruscan jewelry

would eventually model their architecture, sculpture, and literature after the Greeks.

Rome's early growth was influenced most, however, by the Etruscans. The Etruscans lived north of Rome in **Etruria** (ih•TRUR•ee•uh). After 650 B.C., they moved south and took control of Rome and most of Latium.

The Etruscans were skilled metalworkers who became rich from mining and trade. They forced enslaved people to do the heaviest work and made their own lives comfortable. Their tomb paintings show men and women feasting, dancing, and playing music and sports. Some murals also show bloody battle scenes, revealing the Etruscans' pride in their military.

The Etruscans changed Rome from a village of straw-roofed huts into a city of wood and brick buildings. They laid out streets, temples, and public buildings around a central square. Etruscans also taught Romans a new style of dress, featuring short cloaks and togas—loose garments draped over one shoulder. More importantly, the Etruscan army would serve as a model for the mighty army the Romans eventually assembled.

✓ **Reading Check** **Explain** How did geography help the Romans prosper?

The Birth of a Republic

Main Idea The Romans created a republic and conquered Italy. By treating people fairly, they built Rome from a small city into a great power.

Reading Focus Have you heard the phrase "winning hearts and minds"? It means convincing people to support you rather than just forcing them to obey. Read on to learn how the Romans not only conquered other people in Italy but also won their hearts and minds.

The Etruscans ruled Rome for more than 100 years. Under the Etruscans, Rome became wealthy and powerful. However, the ruling family, called the **Tarquins** (TAHR•kwihnz), grew more and more cruel.

Finally, in 509 B.C., the Romans rebelled. They overthrew the Tarquins and set up a **republic** (rih•PUH•blihk). A republic is a form of government in which the leader is not a king or queen but someone put in office by citizens with the right to vote. In a republic, the citizens have the power. The rise of the Roman Republic marked the beginning of a new chapter in Rome's history.

▲ Etruscan murals often showed lively scenes of daily life, such as religious ceremonies or people enjoying music and feasts. *How did the Etruscans become wealthy?*

CHAPTER 8   The Rise of Rome   **265**

CRITICAL THINKING ACTIVITY

Determining Cause and Effect Have students read the material under the heading "The Birth of a Republic" to answer this question: How did Rome's treatment of conquered peoples help it to build the Roman Confederation? *(Rome gave full citizenship to some peoples and the status of allies to others. This gave conquered peoples rights in the Roman Republic.)* **L2** 🗂

③ ASSESS

Assign Section 1 Review as homework or as an in-class activity.

◉ Have students use the **Interactive Tutor Self-Assessment CD-ROM** to review the section.

Assessment L2

Assign **Section 1 Quiz** to assess mastery of the material found in the section.

Reading Support L1/ EL

Assign **Reading Essentials and Study Guide 8–1** to help students review section material.

More About the Art

Warfare in the early republic consisted mostly of raids. The full manpower of legions was rarely used. Later, as Roman warfare became more involved, legions became more sophisticated in their organization.

Caption Answer: Standards—tall poles topped by emblems—helped units stay together.

At the time Rome became a republic, it was still a small city, surrounded by enemies. Over the next 200 years, the Romans fought war after war against their neighbors. In 338 B.C. they finally defeated the other Latins living nearby. Next they attacked the Etruscans and defeated them in 284 B.C. By 267 B.C., the Romans had also conquered the Greeks in southern Italy. With this victory, the Romans became the masters of almost all of Italy.

Roman Legionary

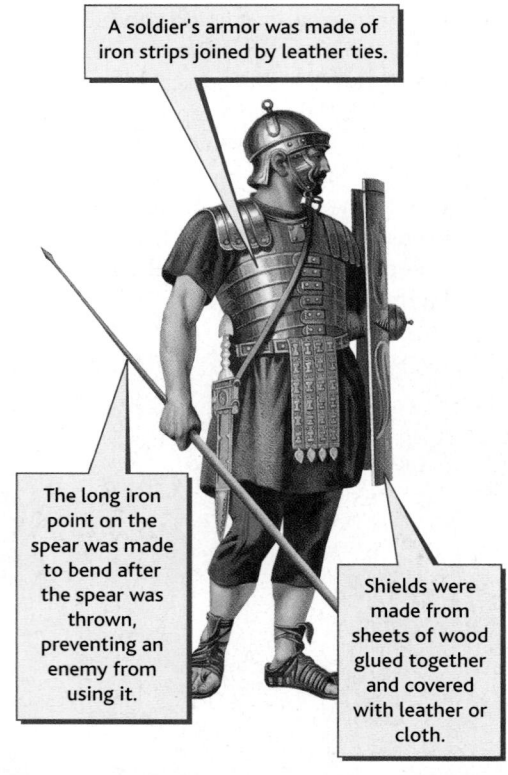

A soldier's armor was made of iron strips joined by leather ties.

The long iron point on the spear was made to bend after the spear was thrown, preventing an enemy from using it.

Shields were made from sheets of wood glued together and covered with leather or cloth.

At first, the Roman army was made up of ordinary citizens. Later the army contained well-trained professional soldiers and was one of the best fighting forces in the world. *What was a standard, and why did the army carry them?*

266   CHAPTER 8   The Rise of Rome

Why Was Rome So Strong? Rome was able to conquer Italy because the Romans were excellent soldiers. In the republic's early days, every male citizen who owned land had to serve in the army. Discipline was harsh, and deserters were punished by death. The tough discipline helped mold Roman soldiers into fighters who did not give up easily. In addition, they were practical problem solvers.

For example, Roman armies at first fought like Greek armies. Row upon row of soldiers marched shoulder to shoulder, keeping their shields together and holding long spears. Roman generals soon realized that this way of fighting was slow and hard to control. They reorganized their soldiers into smaller groups called **legions** (LEE•juhnz). Each legion had about 6,000 men and was further divided into groups of 60 to 120 soldiers. These small groups could quickly cut through enemy lines.

Roman soldiers, or legionaries, were armed with a short sword called a *gladius* and a spear called a *pilum*. Each unit also carried its own standard—a tall pole topped with a symbol. In battle, standards helped keep units together because the soldiers could see them above the action.

Shrewd Rulers The Romans were not only good fighters but also smart planners. As they expanded throughout Italy, they built permanent military settlements in the areas they conquered. Then they built roads between these towns. These roads allowed troops to travel swiftly to any place in their growing territory.

To rule their new conquests, the Romans created the Roman Confederation. Under this system, Romans gave full citizenship to some peoples, especially other Latins. They could vote and serve in the government, and they were treated the

---

INTERDISCIPLINARY CONNECTIONS ACTIVITY

Mathematics Point out to students that Roman legions usually had 6,000 men. In turn, each legion was divided into groups of 60 to 120 soldiers. **Ask:** Into how many 60-soldier groups could a Roman legion be divided? How did you determine the answer? *(100; students probably will say they used their division skills to find the answer.)* **Ask:** Into how many 120-soldier groups could one legion be divided? How did you determine the answer? *(50; students may have used division, or they might have divided the answer of the last question—100—by 2, because 120 is twice as many as 60.)* L1/ EL same as other citizens under the law. The Romans granted other peoples the status of allies.

Allies were free to run their own local affairs, but they had to pay taxes to the republic and provide soldiers for the army. The Romans made it clear that loyal allies could improve their position and even become Roman citizens.

With these policies, the Romans proved themselves clever rulers. They knew that conquered peoples would be more loyal to the government if they were well treated. Rome's generosity paid off. As a result, the republic grew stronger and more unified.

All the same, Rome was not afraid to use force if necessary. If conquered peoples revolted against Roman rule, their resistance was swiftly put down.

✓ Reading Check **Describe** How did Rome rule its new conquests?

▲ This mosaic, or picture made from bits of stone, shows a group of Roman legionaries. *How many soldiers made up a legion?*

Study Central™ Need help with the material in this section? Visit jat.glencoe.com

Section ① Review

Reading Summary
Review the Main Ideas

• The Romans, a Latin-speaking people, settled the region of Rome on the west side of Italy. The region's geography, as well as Etruscan and Greek ideas, helped Rome grow.

• In 509 B.C. the Romans overthrew Etruscan rule and established a republic. By about 275 B.C., Roman legions had conquered most of Italy.

What Did You Learn?

1. Where did the Greeks live in Italy, and how did they influence Roman civilization?

2. Describe the two legends that tell of the founding of Rome. Then describe how and when Rome was actually founded.

Critical Thinking

3. **Geography Skills** Draw a diagram like the one below. List examples of how geography determined Rome's location.

The Location of Rome

4. **Summarize** Describe the Roman conquest of Italy.

5. **Compare and Contrast** How did geography affect the development of civilization in Greece and Italy?

6. **Expository Writing** Write a short essay discussing the reasons Rome was so successful in its conquest of Italy.

7. **Reading Taking Notes** Use the blue subheads in Section 1 to create notes about Rome's beginnings. List each subhead on the left of a T-chart and details on the right.

SECTION 1 REVIEW ANSWERS

1. Greeks colonized southern Italy and Sicily. They passed on farming methods, sculpture, literature, and an alphabet.
2. Romulus and Remus legend; Aeneas story; Rome probably founded by Latins c. 700s B.C.
3. Rome built on Tiber River with access to sea; seven hills good for defense
4. Rome defeated remaining Latins and then Etruscans and Greeks.
5. Italy is less rugged than Greece, so people are not separated from each other; Italy's better farmland supports more people.
6. Essays should note Rome's strong army, settlements and roads, and fair treatment of conquered peoples.
7. Answers will vary. Students may note Greek and Etruscan impact and Rome's favorable location.

① FOCUS

SECTION OVERVIEW

This section describes the Roman Republic's political development and the defeat of Carthage.

BELLRINGER
SKILLBUILDER ACTIVITY

✎ Project **Daily Focus Skills Transparency 8–2** and have students answer questions. Discuss their responses.

Get Ready to Read!

Preteaching Vocabulary: Point out to students that five of the vocabulary terms describe people who lived in Rome. Have small groups use their texts to determine which five terms fit that description. Then ask group members to discuss which position they would like to hold if they were Roman citizens. Have groups verbally defend their choices.

Answers to Graphic: Officials: consuls, praetors, tribunes, dictators; Legislative bodies: Senate, Assembly of Centuries, Council of the Plebs

---

Section 2

The Roman Republic

Get Ready to Read!

What's the Connection?
Romans had suffered under cruel Etruscan kings. When they had the chance to create their own government, they chose something very different.

Focusing on the Main Ideas
• Rome's republic was shaped by a struggle between wealthy landowners and regular citizens as it gradually expanded the right to vote. *(page 269)*

• Rome slowly destroyed the Carthaginian Empire and took control of the entire Mediterranean region. *(page 274)*

Locating Places
Carthage (KAHR•thihj)
Cannae (KA•nee)
Zama (ZAY•muh)

Meeting People
Cincinnatus (SIHN•suh•NA•tuhs)
Hannibal (HA•nuh•buhl)
Scipio (SIH•pee•OH)

Building Your Vocabulary
patrician (puh•TRIH•shuhn)
plebeian (plih•BEE•uhn)
consul (KAHN•suhl)
veto (VEE•toh)
praetor (PREE•tuhr)
dictator (DIHK•TAY•tuhr)

Reading Strategy
Categorizing Information Complete a chart like the one below listing the government officials and legislative bodies of the Roman Republic.

Officials	Legislative Bodies

NATIONAL GEOGRAPHIC When & Where?

450 B.C.	300 B.C.	150 B.C.
451 B.C. Romans adopt the Twelve Tables	**264 B.C.** Punic Wars begin	**146 B.C.** Rome destroys Carthage

SPAIN   ITALY •Rome   Carthage•   GREECE

SECTION RESOURCES

📁 **Reproducible Masters**
• Reproducible Lesson Plan 8–2
• Daily Lecture and Discussion Notes 8–2
• Vocabulary Activity 8–2
• Active Reading Note-Taking Guide 8–2
• Guided Reading Activity 8–2
• Section Quiz 8–2
• Reading Essentials and Study Guide 8–2

📄 **Transparencies**
• Daily Focus Skills Transparency 8–2

Multimedia
🔘 Interactive Tutor Self-Assessment CD-ROM
🔘 ExamView® Pro Testmaker CD-ROM
🔘 Presentation Plus! CD-ROM
🔘 Glencoe BookLink CD-ROM

Rome's Government

Main Idea Rome's republic was shaped by a struggle between wealthy landowners and regular citizens as it gradually expanded the right to vote.

Reading Focus Do you know where our word *republic* comes from? It is made up of two Latin words meaning "thing of the people." Read on to learn about the republican government that early Romans created.

Early Romans were divided into two classes: patricians and plebeians. The **patricians** (puh•TRIH•shuhnz) were wealthy landowners. These nobles made up Rome's ruling class. Most of Rome's people, however, were **plebeians** (plih•BEE•uhnz). This group included artisans, shopkeepers, and owners of small farms.

Both patrician and plebeian men were Roman citizens. They had the right to vote and the responsibility to pay taxes and serve in the army. However, plebeians had less social status. Marriage between members of the two classes was forbidden. Plebeians also lacked an important political right: they could not hold public office. Only patricians could serve in the government.

How Did Rome's Government Work? In the Roman Republic, the top government officials were the **consuls** (KAHN•suhlz). Two consuls—both patricians—were chosen every year. They headed the army and ran the government. Because they served such short terms, there was little risk that they would abuse their power. The consuls also

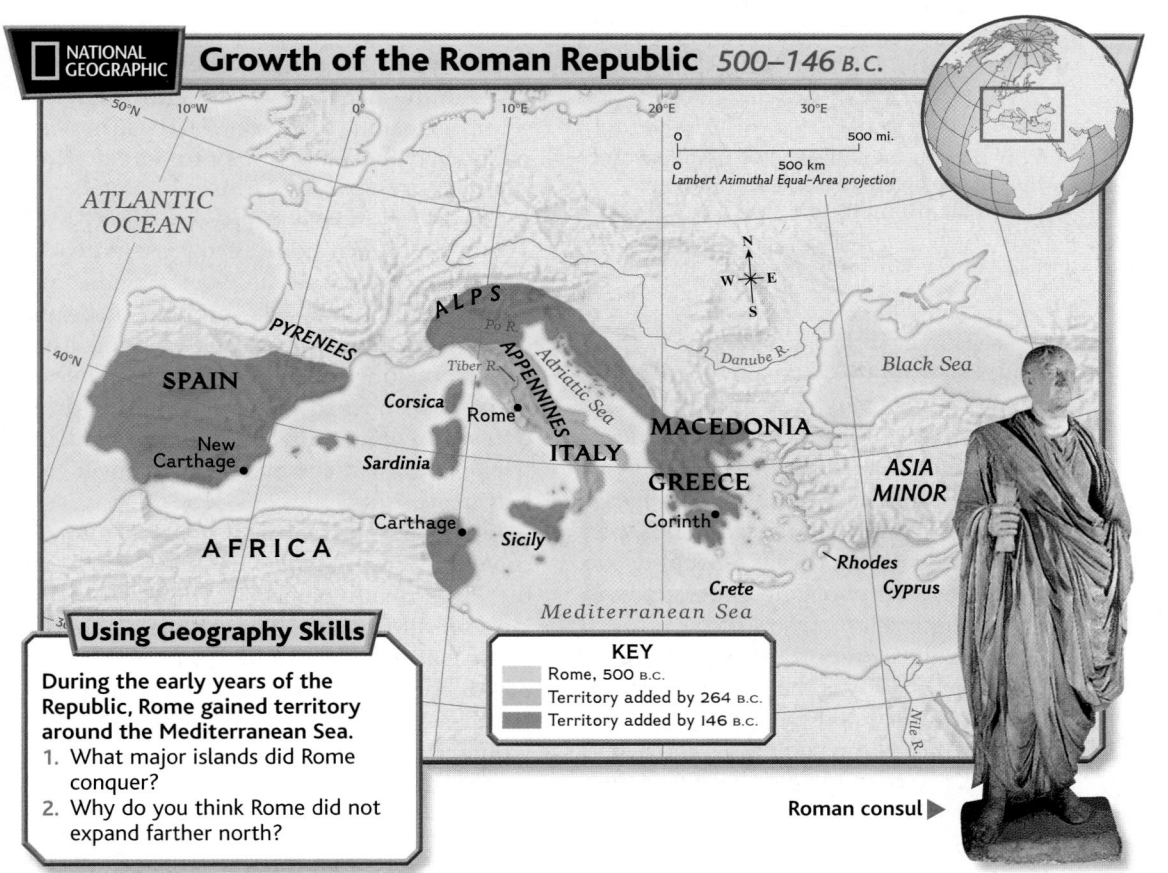

NATIONAL GEOGRAPHIC
Growth of the Roman Republic 500–146 B.C.

500 mi.
500 km
Lambert Azimuthal Equal-Area projection

ATLANTIC OCEAN
SPAIN
PYRENEES
New Carthage
Corsica
Sardinia
Carthage
AFRICA
ALPS
Po R.
Tiber R.
Rome
APPENNINES
ITALY
Sicily
Adriatic Sea
Danube R.
MACEDONIA
GREECE
Corinth
Crete
Mediterranean Sea
Black Sea
ASIA MINOR
Rhodes
Cyprus
Nile R.

KEY
- Rome, 500 B.C.
- Territory added by 264 B.C.
- Territory added by 146 B.C.

Using Geography Skills
During the early years of the Republic, Rome gained territory around the Mediterranean Sea.
1. What major islands did Rome conquer?
2. Why do you think Rome did not expand farther north?

Roman consul ▶

Reading Strategy | READING THE TEXT

Writing a Letter Write the words "Patrician" and "Plebeian" on the board. Have students read the two paragraphs that start this section to determine the difference between these two kinds of Roman citizens. Then have each student write a letter explaining why plebeians should have the right to hold government office. Ask volunteers to read aloud their letters to the class. **L2**

② TEACH

Identifying Similarities Point out that the first heading in this section is "Rome's Government." Explain that the Founders borrowed some of Rome's ideas as they created the U.S. government. Tell students that as they read, they should list any similarities between Rome's government and that of the United States. When the section is complete, have students discuss their lists and use reference books to determine which of the points they cited are correct. **L3**

Daily Lecture and Discussion Notes 8–2

Use **Daily Lecture and Discussion Notes 8–2** for an outline of key concepts found in the section.

Reading Support L1/ EL

Use **Vocabulary Activity 8–2** to review important terms in the section.

Using Geography Skills

Answers:
1. Sicily, Sardinia, and Corsica
2. The Alps and Pyrenees were barriers.

269

Rome celebrated hundreds of triumphs from its beginnings to its fall in the A.D. 400s. The reason for a triumph was to celebrate valiant deeds done in service to the state. A triumph was the highest honor Rome could bestow on a hero.

Answer: to show off their power and might

CONNECTING ACROSS TIME

The Roman Republic has influenced governments for thousands of years. For example, our nation has borrowed from the Romans both the word for and the concept of a *veto*. The president can veto bills even though they have made it through both houses of Congress. Have students research the use of the veto by presidents and discuss why some bills have been vetoed. **L2**

Reading Strategy

Writing Activity

Have students write a summary of what made Cincinnatus a good leader. **L2**

Primary Source

A Roman Triumph

Sometimes military leaders returning to Rome after a victory took part in a great parade called a triumph.

▲ Roman soldiers

"Thus arrayed [decoratively dressed], they entered the city, having at the head of the procession the spoils and trophies and figures representing the captured forts, cities, mountains, rivers, lakes, and seas— everything, in fact, that they had taken.... [When] ... the victorious general arrived at the Roman Forum ... he rode up to the Capitol. There he performed certain rites and made offerings."

—Zonaras, "A Roman Triumph"

DBQ Document-Based Question

Why do you think the military leaders and their troops were dressed decoratively before the triumph?

kept each other in line because each could **veto** (VEE•toh), or reject, the other's decision. The word *veto* is Latin for "I forbid."

Rome had other important officials called **praetors** (PREE•tuhrz). Their main job was to interpret the law and act as judges in court cases. Various other officials performed specialized duties—keeping tax records, handling public finances, supervising public festivals, and so forth.

Rome's most important legislative, or lawmaking, body was the Senate. This was a select group of 300 patrician men who served for life. In the beginning, the Senate only gave advice to the consuls. Over time,

the power of the Senate grew. By the 200s B.C., it could also propose laws, hold debates on important issues, and approve building programs.

Another legislative body was the Assembly of Centuries. It elected important officials, such as consuls and praetors, and passed laws. Like the Senate, the Assembly of Centuries was under the control of the patricians.

Plebeians Against Patricians As you might expect, plebeians complained about having so little power in the Roman Republic. After all, they fought alongside patricians in the army, and their tax payments helped the republic thrive. It seemed reasonable that they should have equal rights.

Eventually, the plebeians took action to bring about change. In 494 B.C. many plebeians went on strike. They refused to serve in the army. They also left the city to set up a republic of their own. These moves frightened the patricians into agreeing to share power.

In 471 B.C. the plebeians were allowed to set up their own body of representatives, called the Council of the Plebs. The assembly elected tribunes who brought plebeian concerns to the government's attention. The tribunes also won the right to veto government decisions. In 455 B.C. plebeians and patricians were allowed to marry, and in the 300s B.C., plebeians were allowed to become consuls.

The most far-reaching political reform came in 287 B.C. In that year, the Council of the Plebs finally gained the power to pass laws for all Romans. Now all male citizens had equal political standing, at least in theory. In practice, a few wealthy patrician families still held most of the power, and women remained without a voice in government. The Roman Republic had

DIFFERENTIATED INSTRUCTION

Visual/Spatial: Draw a two-column table with the title "Rome's Government." Put the heading "Government Arm" in the left column and the heading "Responsibilities" in the right column. Fill in the left column with these entries: consul, praetor, Senate, Assembly of Centuries. Have student pairs copy the table. Then direct the pairs to use the information in the textbook to complete the right column of the table.

Gifted and Talented: Help students identify the two checks that kept consuls from abusing their power. *(one-year term, power of veto)* Have students research the U.S. presidency to determine the checks on presidential power. Direct them to write a paragraph comparing and contrasting Roman consuls with U.S. presidents.

become more representative, but it was far from a full-fledged democracy.

Who Was Cincinnatus? An unusual feature of the Roman Republic was the office of **dictator** (DIHK•tay•tuhr). We define a dictator today as an oppressive ruler with complete control over the state. Roman dictators also had complete control, but they served the people and ruled on a temporary basis during emergencies. The Senate would appoint a dictator in times of great danger. As soon as the danger was past, Roman dictators gave up their power.

The best-known early Roman dictator is **Cincinnatus** (SIHN•suh•NA•tuhs). About 460 B.C., a powerful enemy had surrounded a Roman army. Officials decided that the crisis called for a dictator and that Cincinnatus was the man for the job. The officials found Cincinnatus plowing his fields. A loyal and devoted citizen, Cincinnatus left his farm and gathered an army. He defeated the enemy in short order and returned to Rome in triumph. Although he probably could have continued ruling, Cincinnatus did not want power. Having done his duty, he returned to his farm a mere 15 or 16 days after becoming dictator.

Cincinnatus was widely admired in his own time and in later ages. George Washington, for one, took inspiration from his example. Like Cincinnatus, Washington was a farmer when he was asked to head an army: the Continental Army in the American War for Independence. After leading the Americans to victory, Washington returned to his plantation home. Only later, and with some reluctance, did he agree to become the first president of the United States.

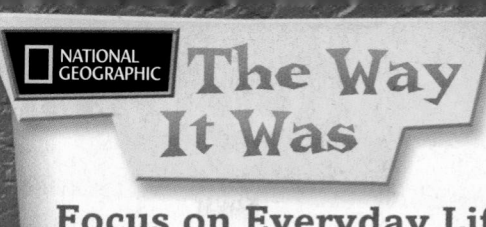

The Way It Was

Focus on Everyday Life

Roman Dinner Parties Before Rome became a powerful empire, Romans ate simple meals of porridge, dried vegetables, and greens. People rarely ate meat or seafood. After Rome's conquests, the dining habits of wealthy Romans changed. Newly rich Romans showed off their wealth with expensive feasts that included exotic foods and lively entertainment for their guests.

At Roman dinner parties, guests reclined on couches. The enslaved servants served the food, which would be carried into the banquet room on great silver platters. Roman dishes might include boiled stingray garnished with hot raisins; boiled crane with turnips; or roast flamingo cooked with dates, onions, honey, and wine.

▼ **A wealthy Roman woman reclining on a couch**

Connecting to the Past
1. Whose eating habits changed after Rome became wealthy and powerful?
2. Describe how their eating habits changed.

Then and Now Have students discuss events in the plebeians' struggle to become equal citizens. Record these on the board on a time line. Ask students what the federal qualifications for voting and holding office in the United States are. If students are unfamiliar with these, have volunteers read them aloud from the U.S. Constitution—Article I, Sections 2 and 3; Article II, Section 5; and Amendments 14 and 19. Elicit from students that these standards allow almost anyone to hold office and vote. Finally, discuss what responsibilities are entailed by having these rights. **L2**

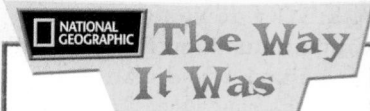

The Way It Was

Answers:
1. the newly rich Romans
2. Wealthy Romans ate costly feasts and entertained guests while reclining on couches.

CRITICAL THINKING ACTIVITY

Comparing and Contrasting Point out that just as Rome had a Senate, so does the United States. Ask a volunteer to read aloud the paragraph that discusses the Roman Senate and its responsibilities. Organize students into small groups. Tell the groups to do research to find out whether the responsibilities of the United States Senate include some of the same responsibilities as the Senate of Rome. When the groups have finished their research, ask them to compare and contrast the two senates in some kind of visual graphic, such as pictures or a chart. Have groups share their completed graphics with the class. **L3**

Biography

TEACH

According to tradition, upon arriving in Rome, newly appointed dictator Cincinnatus ordered all men of military age to muster, bringing with them supplies for five days. He and his quickly-assembled army came upon the enemy camp at night. Cincinnatus's soldiers spread out, each plunging one or two stakes into the earth (an old Roman war trick). When the enemy troops awoke the next morning, they found themselves fenced in and surrounded by Romans. They were forced to surrender, and Rome was saved.

Ask: Why do you think Cincinnatus is so honored for his behavior as dictator? *(Students may suggest that it could be tempting for someone appointed as dictator not to give up the position when the crisis is over.)* **L1/ EL**

Then and Now

Answers will vary. Students should provide valid reasoning for their choice of leader.

LUCIUS QUINCTIUS CINCINNATUS

c. 519–438 B.C.

The loyal devotion of Cincinnatus greatly impressed the Roman historian Livy. In his *History of Rome,* Livy advised his readers to listen to the worthwhile story of Cincinnatus, whose virtue rose high above any rewards that wealth could bring.

According to Livy, Cincinnatus lived in Rome but owned and worked a four-acre field on the other side of the Tiber River. On the day that the officials looked for Cincinnatus, they found him hard at work in his field, covered with dirt and sweat. Cincinnatus was surprised when the officials asked him to put on his toga and listen as they explained the wishes of the Roman Senate. Cincinnatus must not have been aware of the danger the Roman army faced, because he asked the officials if everything was all right before calling to his wife, Racilia, and asking her to bring him his toga quickly.

The officials explained the emergency situation to Cincinnatus. He agreed to the Senate's request that he become a dictator. Cincinnatus and the officials crossed the Tiber River to Rome and were greeted by his three sons, other relatives and friends, and members of the Senate. Later they escorted Cincinnatus safely to his home. The next morning, before daylight, Cincinnatus went to the Forum and gathered his forces to attack the enemy.

▲ Cincinnatus is asked to lead Rome.

> **"The city was in the grip of fear."**
> —Livy, *The Rise of Rome*

Then and Now

Name a modern-day leader that you think historians will write about with great admiration. Explain why.

Reading List Generator CD-ROM

GLENCOE BOOKLINK   **RECOMMENDED READING**

Use the **Glencoe BookLink CD-ROM** to create customized reading lists based on your students' interests and reading levels. Below is an example based on content in this chapter. Also, see the Suggested Readings on pages 944–946 of the Appendix.

- **Chrisp, Peter.** *The Romans.* An introduction to the Roman Republic and the beginnings of the Roman Empire.
- **Kunhardt, Edith.** *Pompeii . . . Buried Alive!* Account of the volcanic destruction of Pompeii.
- **Stanley, Diane, and Peter Vennema.** *Cleopatra.* A biography of the Egyptian queen.

Roman Law One of Rome's chief gifts to the world was its system of law. The legal system of the United States owes much to the Roman system.

Rome's first code of laws was the Twelve Tables, adopted about 451 B.C. Before this time, Rome's laws were not written down. As a result, plebeians claimed that patrician judges often favored their own class. They demanded that the laws be put in writing for everyone to see.

The patricians finally agreed. They had the laws carved on bronze tablets that were placed in Rome's marketplace, or the Forum (FOHR•uhm). The Twelve Tables became the basis for all future Roman laws. They established the principle that all free citizens had the right to be treated equally by the legal system.

▲ These bundles of rods and axes, called fasces, symbolized the legal authority of Roman leaders.

The Twelve Tables, however, applied only to Roman citizens. As the Romans took over more lands, they realized that new rules were needed to solve legal disputes between citizens and noncitizens. They created a collection of laws called the Law of Nations. It stated principles of justice that applied to all people everywhere.

These standards of justice included ideas that we still accept today. A person was seen as innocent until proven guilty. People accused of crimes could defend themselves before a judge. A judge had to look at the evidence carefully before making a decision.

The idea that the law should apply to everyone equally and that all people should be treated the same way by the legal system

HISTORY MAKERS
NATIONAL GEOGRAPHIC

Twelve Tables c. 451 B.C.

The Twelve Tables were laws written on tablets that described the rights of each person in the Roman Republic. The laws were the first set of rules to govern Rome. Writing the laws down and putting them on public display ensured that everyone knew the laws and that judges did not apply the laws differently to different people.

The laws on the Twelve Tables explained a person's rights concerning property, wills, public behavior, family law, and court actions. The Twelve Tables were the first step toward equal rights for citizens of all classes in ancient Rome. They were also a first step toward the idea of the rule of law that we still uphold today.

is called the "rule of law." In the age of Rome, the rule of law was still a new idea. In many lands, people at the top of society often had special privileges and did not have to obey the same laws or use the same courts as people lower down. In some places, people at the bottom of society did not have any legal rights at all. The rule of law is one of the key ideas that the Romans gave to the world. It is still the basis of our legal system today.

✓ **Reading Check** **Contrast** Before 471 B.C., what right did patricians have that plebeians did not?

CHAPTER 8   The Rise of Rome   **273**

GLENCOE
BookLink

Use **Glencoe BookLink** to create customized reading lists for your students' reading levels, interests, and abilities.

HISTORY MAKERS
NATIONAL GEOGRAPHIC

While the Twelve Tables represented a codification of law that benefitted the plebeians, this group still had many rights to be gained. The fasces, as shown in the image, were carried by lictors who walked in front of consuls and praetors as they traveled about Rome. The use of lictors carrying the fasces was a holdover from the days of Etruscan kings.

The Development of Laws Discuss with students why it was necessary for Rome to create the Law of Nations when it already had the Twelve Tables. (Students may recognize that the Tables were drawn up for a smaller territory and population while the Law of Nations applied to the peoples in a vast empire.) **L2**

✓ **Reading Check**

Answer: Only patricians could hold public office.

INTERDISCIPLINARY CONNECTIONS ACTIVITY

Civics Assign each student to take on the responsibilities and powers of different positions in the Roman government. Divide the class into consuls, praetors, and members of the Senate. Create a situation in which the students must work together to solve a crisis or problem in Rome (such as an invasion or attack on the city). Have the students work together to solve the problem in a way that represents the methods of government, law, and leadership that were prevalent during the Roman Republic. **Ask:** How would the United States's government handle a similar situation today? How do you think the Roman leaders worked together to solve similar problems in ancient Rome? **L2**

HISTORY Mystery

Why Did Both Rome and Carthage Want Control of Sicily?
Sicily's geography made it attractive for several reasons. A warm climate, fertile land, and plentiful fresh water made Sicily a center of agriculture. Even today, it is sometimes referred to as Italy's "breadbasket." Sicily was also strategically located in the Mediterranean.

Examining Maps Direct students' attention to the map on this page. Point out that battles between the Romans and Carthaginians are shown on the map with a marker. Ask students to identify the battles on the map and then find information in the text describing each battle's outcome.
L1/ **EL**

Using Geography Skills

Answers:
1. the northwest
2. Hannibal wanted to surprise the Romans.

Rome Expands

Main Idea Rome slowly destroyed the Carthaginian Empire and took control of the entire Mediterranean region.

Reading Focus When you achieve a victory—whether it is in academics, sports, or some other field—do you then strive for more success? That may have been how the Romans felt once they had taken over Italy. Read on to learn how they continued to expand their power.

While Rome developed its government, it also faced challenges abroad. The Romans had completed their conquest of Italy. However, they now faced a powerful rival in the Mediterranean area. This enemy was the state of **Carthage** (KAHR•thihj) on the coast of North Africa. It had been founded around 800 B.C. by the Phoenicians. As you learned earlier, the Phoenicians were sea traders from the Middle East.

Carthage ruled a great trading empire that included parts of northern Africa and southern Europe. By controlling the movement of goods in this region, Carthage made itself the largest and richest city in the western Mediterranean.

The First Punic War Both Carthage and Rome wanted to control the island of Sicily. In 264 B.C. the dispute brought the two powers to blows. The war that began in 264 B.C. is called the First Punic War. *Punicus* is the Latin word for "Phoenician." The war started when the Romans sent an army to Sicily to prevent a Carthaginian

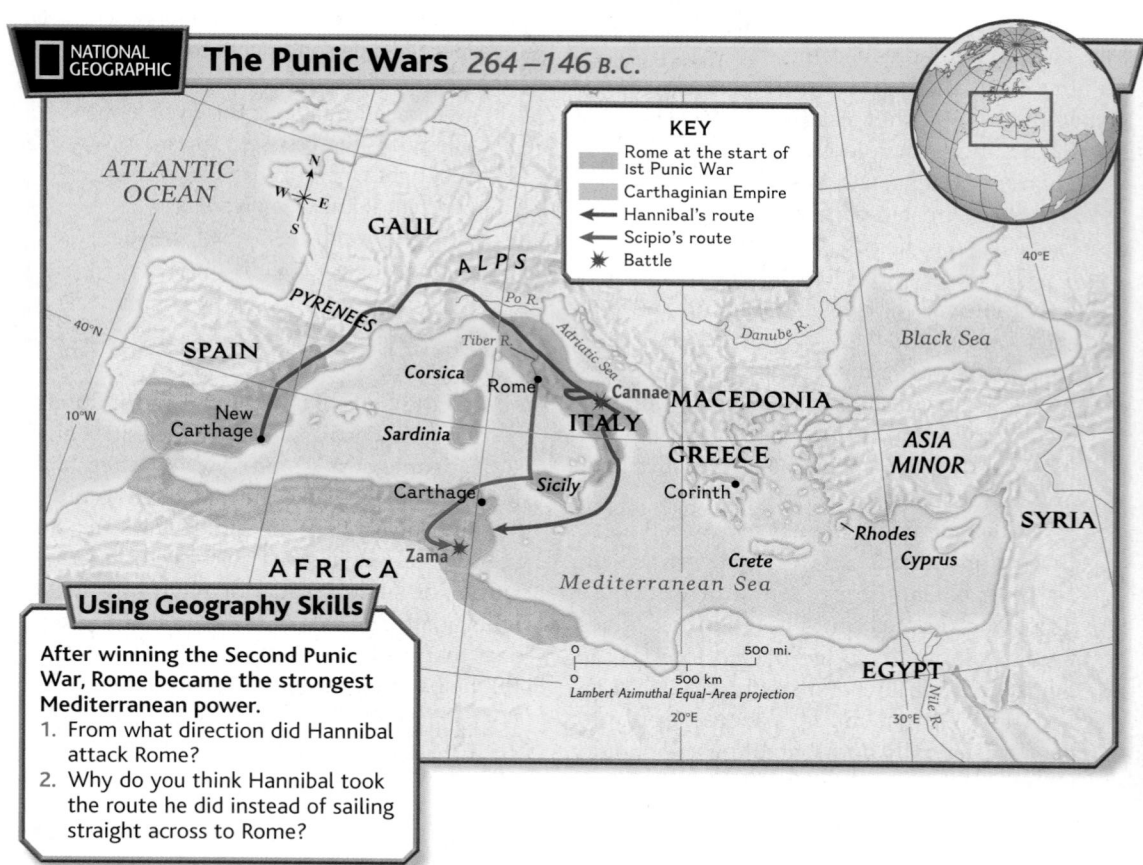

NATIONAL GEOGRAPHIC
The Punic Wars 264–146 B.C.

KEY
- Rome at the start of 1st Punic War
- Carthaginian Empire
- ← Hannibal's route
- ← Scipio's route
- ✷ Battle

Using Geography Skills

After winning the Second Punic War, Rome became the strongest Mediterranean power.
1. From what direction did Hannibal attack Rome?
2. Why do you think Hannibal took the route he did instead of sailing straight across to Rome?

EXTENDING THE CONTENT

How Was Carthage Founded? According to legend, Carthage was founded by Queen Dido, who escaped from the Phoenician city of Tyre after her brother killed her husband. When Dido and her followers came to the place on Africa's north coast where Carthage would stand, she asked the people there if she could claim any land she could enclose with a bull's hide. They agreed. The queen then had a bull hide cut into thin strips, and she used those strips to encircle a large piece of land. On this land, Dido built a fort around which grew the city of Carthage.

takeover. The Carthaginians, who already had colonies on the island, were determined to stop this invasion.

Up until then, the Romans had fought their wars on land. However, they soon realized they could not defeat a sea power like Carthage without a navy. They quickly built a large fleet of ships and confronted their enemy at sea. The war dragged on for more than 20 years. Finally, in 241 B.C., Rome crushed Carthage's navy off the coast of Sicily. Carthage was forced to leave Sicily and pay a huge fine to the Romans. The island then came under Roman rule.

The Second Punic War To make up for its loss of Sicily, Carthage expanded its empire into southern Spain. Roman leaders were not happy about Carthage gaining land near Rome's northern border. They helped the people living in Spain rebel against Carthage. Of course, Carthaginians were angry. To punish Rome, Carthage sent its greatest general, **Hannibal** (HA•nuh•buhl), to attack Rome in 218 B.C. This started the Second Punic War.

Hannibal's strategy was to take the fighting into Italy itself. To do this, Hannibal gathered an army of about 46,000 men, many horses, and 37 elephants. He landed his forces in Spain and then marched east to attack Italy.

Even before reaching Italy, Hannibal's forces suffered severe losses crossing the steep, snowy Alps into Italy. The brutal cold, gnawing hunger, and attacks by

▼ In December 218 B.C., Hannibal's forces and the Roman army met in battle near the Trebbia River in northern Italy. In a well-planned attack, the Carthaginian forces badly defeated the Romans. Hannibal made good use of his elephants in the attack, but most died following the battle. *At what other battle in Italy were the Romans defeated by Hannibal?*

275

CITIZENSHIP AND YOU

Completing a Cause-and-Effect Table Draw on the board a two-column table with the headings "Cause" and "Effect." Now make three rows, and in the "Effect" column for each row, write the words "Rome goes to war." Ask volunteers to take turns reading aloud the material about the three Punic Wars. As the text is read, ask students to identify the cause of each of the wars and write that cause in the appropriate space on the table. When the table is complete, have students imagine they are members of Rome's Senate. For each of the three wars, have students debate that war's merits. In other words, should Rome go to war over this issue? **L3**

ENRICH

At the end of the Second Punic War, Carthage gave up Spain to Rome. It also gave up all but 20 of its navy ships, paid a large fine of 5,000 talents, and agreed to keep Rome's army supplied. Discuss with students why the later destruction of Carthage in the Third Punic War made it possible for Romans to call the Mediterranean "our sea." **L2**

Answer: Rome burned Carthage, enslaved its people, and made it a Roman province.

To help students understand section material, have them visit **Study Central™** at jat.glencoe.com

RETEACH

Have students recall how Rome treated conquered peoples when it first began to expand. Ask them if they think Rome continued to treat its new territories in the same manner after its conquests during the Punic Wars. **L2**

④ CLOSE

Ask students to briefly summarize the expansion of the Roman Empire. **L2**

---

mountain tribes killed almost half of the soldiers and most of the elephants. The remaining army, however, was still a powerful fighting force when it reached Italy.

The Romans suffered a severe loss in 216 B.C. at the Battle of **Cannae** (KA•nee) in southern Italy. Even though Hannibal's army was outnumbered, it overpowered the Roman force and began raiding much of Italy.

The Romans, however, raised another army. In 202 B.C. a Roman force led by a general named **Scipio** (SIH•pee•OH) invaded Carthage. Hannibal, who was waging a war in Italy, had no choice but to return home to defend his people.

At the Battle of **Zama** (ZAY•muh), Scipio's troops defeated the Carthaginians. Carthage gave up Spain to Rome. It also had to give up its navy and pay a large fine. Rome now ruled the western Mediterranean.

More Conquests While Carthage was no longer a military power, it remained a trading center. In 146 B.C. Rome finally destroyed its great rival in the Third Punic War. Roman soldiers burned Carthage and enslaved 50,000 men, women, and children. Legend says that the Romans even spread salt on the earth so no crops would grow. Carthage became a Roman province, or regional district.

During the Punic Wars, Rome successfully battled states in the eastern Mediterranean. In 148 B.C. Macedonia came under Roman rule. Two years later, the rest of Greece became Roman. In 129 B.C. Rome gained its first province in Asia. It was no wonder that the Romans began to call the Mediterranean *mare nostrum*—"our sea."

✓ **Reading Check** **Describe** How did Rome punish Carthage at the end of the Third Punic War?

Study Central™ Need help with the material in this section? Visit jat.glencoe.com

Section ② Review

Reading Summary
Review the Main Ideas

• During the Roman Republic, the government changed as the plebeians, or lower classes, and the patricians, or ruling class, struggled for power.

• Beginning in 264 B.C., Rome fought and won a series of wars with Carthage and other powers and gained control of the Mediterranean region.

What Did You Learn?

1. Who were the top government officials in the Roman Republic, and what were their duties?

2. What does *mare nostrum* mean, and why did the Romans use the term?

Critical Thinking

3. **Sequencing Information** Draw a diagram to describe the sequence of events from the start of the First Punic War to the start of the Second Punic War.

Rome Invades Sicily	→		→	

4. **Geography Skills** Where was Carthage located, and why did it compete with Rome?

5. **Summarize** What other conquests did Rome carry out during the period of the Punic Wars?

6. **Evaluate** Why do you think the legacy of Roman law is considered so important?

7. **Persuasive Writing** Write a speech demanding equal rights for plebeians in the early republic.

276   CHAPTER 8   The Rise of Rome

SECTION 2 REVIEW ANSWERS

1. consuls: headed army and ran the state; praetors: served as judges; tribunes: represented plebeians
2. It means "our sea." The Romans controlled the Mediterranean Sea.
3. Rome builds a large fleet; Rome defeats Carthage at sea; war ends in 241 B.C.; Rome encourages the Spanish to rebel.
4. on the coast of North Africa; was a trading rival
5. Rome conquered Macedonia, Greece, and Asia Minor.
6. Roman law led to the principles that law protects citizens' rights, that a person is innocent until proven guilty, and that a judge must look at evidence carefully before making a decision.
7. Answers will vary but should be based on the text.

Section 3

The Fall of the Republic

Get Ready to Read!

What's the Connection?
By the end of the Third Punic War, Rome ruled the Mediterranean world. All was not well, however. Closer to home, the republic faced increasing dangers that would soon lead to its end.

Focusing on the Main Ideas
- The use of enslaved labor hurt farmers, increased poverty and corruption, and brought the army into politics. *(page 278)*
- Military hero Julius Caesar seized power and made reforms. *(page 280)*
- The Roman Republic, weakened by civil wars, became an empire under Augustus. *(page 282)*

Locating Places
Rubicon (ROO•bih•KAHN)
Actium (AK•shee•uhm)

Meeting People
Julius Caesar
　(jool•yuhs　SEE•zuhr)
Octavian (ahk•TAY•vee•uhn)
Antony (AN•tuh•nee)
Cicero (SIH•suh•ROH)
Augustus (aw•GUHS•tuhs)

Building Your Vocabulary
latifundia (LA•tuh•FUHN•dee•uh)
triumvirate (try•UHM•vuh•ruht)

Reading Strategy
Finding the Main Idea Use a chart like the one below to identify the main ideas of Section 3 and supporting details.

Main Idea		
Supporting Detail	Supporting Detail	Supporting Detail
Supporting Detail	Supporting Detail	Supporting Detail

NATIONAL GEOGRAPHIC When & Where?

100 B.C.   60 B.C.   20 B.C.

82 B.C. Sulla becomes dictator of Rome

44 B.C. Group of senators murder Julius Caesar

27 B.C. Octavian becomes Rome's first emperor

GAUL
SPAIN
ITALY
Rome
GREECE
ASIA MINOR

① FOCUS

SECTION OVERVIEW
This section describes the events that led to the end of the Roman Republic.

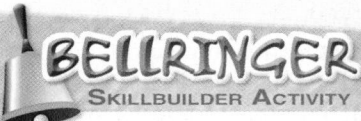

BELLRINGER
SKILLBUILDER ACTIVITY

🖐 Project **Daily Focus Skills Transparency 8–3** and have students answer questions. Discuss their responses.

Get Ready to Read!

Preteaching Vocabulary: Ask students to find the vocabulary term *triumvirate* in the section. Ask if they can tell from the context what *tri* means. *("three")* Now have students take turns writing other words that begin with *tri* on the board as the rest of the class uses dictionaries to determine each word's meaning.

Answers to Graphic: Main Idea: Rome survived political unrest to become the Roman Empire. The first row of supporting details should list the three main ideas of the section. The second row of supporting details should list additional information from the section.

SECTION RESOURCES

Reproducible Masters
- Reproducible Lesson Plan 8–3
- Daily Lecture and Discussion Notes 8–3
- Vocabulary Activity 8–3
- Active Reading Note-Taking Guide 8–3
- Guided Reading Activity 8–3
- Section Quiz 8–3
- Reading Essentials and Study Guide 8–3

Transparencies
- Daily Focus Skills Transparency 8–3

Multimedia
- Interactive Tutor Self-Assessment CD-ROM
- ExamView® Pro Testmaker CD-ROM
- Presentation Plus! CD-ROM

277

② TEACH

Evaluating Leaders Have students write down the names of Roman leaders as they read the section. Then have them rate the leaders, using a "1" for the leader they thought was best for Rome, a "2" for the second-best leader, and so on. Finally, lead a discussion in which they defend their choices using facts from the text. **L1/ EL**

Daily Lecture and Discussion Notes 8–3

Use **Daily Lecture and Discussion Notes 8–3** for an outline of key concepts found in the section.

Reading Support L1/ EL

Use **Vocabulary Activity 8–3** to review important terms in the section.

> ◄ **Reading Strategy** ►

Economics Review with students the meaning of the word *latifundia*. Discuss with students the impact of slavery on crop prices. **L2**

Caption Answer: wealthy landowners were forcing small farmers out of business.

Trouble in the Republic

Main Idea The use of enslaved labor hurt farmers, increased poverty and corruption, and brought the army into politics.

Reading Focus Poverty, corruption, unemployment, crime, and violence are problems we hear about today. Read on to learn how the Romans struggled with these same issues 2,000 years ago.

Rome's armies were victorious wherever they went. Yet problems were building at home. Dishonest officials stole money, and the gap between rich and poor was growing. Thousands of farmers faced ruin, and the cities were becoming overcrowded and dangerous.

Rich Versus Poor As you read in Section 2, most of the people who ruled Rome were patricians—rich people who owned large farms. These rich landowners ran the Senate and held the most powerful government jobs. They handled Rome's finances and directed its wars. Despite some gains for the plebeians, many people became very unhappy about this situation.

Rome had few privileged citizens compared with the many Romans who farmed small plots of land. In the 100s B.C., however, these farmers were sinking into poverty and debt. Why? Many of them had been unable to farm because they were fighting in Rome's wars. Others had suffered damage to their farms during Hannibal's invasion of Italy.

Moreover, small farmers could not compete with wealthy Romans who were buying up land to create **latifundia** (LA•tuh•FUHN•dee•uh), or large farming estates. These rich landowners used a new source of labor—the thousands of prisoners brought to Italy during the wars. By using these enslaved people to tend their crops, wealthy Romans could force owners of small farms out of business.

Faced with debts they could not pay off, many farmers sold their land and headed to the cities, desperate for work. However, jobs were hard to find. Enslaved people did most of the work. If free men were lucky enough to be hired, they earned low wages. These conditions created widespread anger.

▲ This image shows Romans farming their land. *Why were Roman farmers becoming poor in the 100s B.C.?*

278   CHAPTER 8   The Rise of Rome

> ■ **Reading Strategy** ◄   **READING THE TEXT**

Reading to Discover Point out to students that this section mentions many important individuals from this period of Roman history, and that some of them, such as Pompey and Crassus, are not identified in the list on page 277. Have student pairs choose one of the people discussed in this section. Have the pair do research to find out about the person it has chosen. Then have each pair write the answer to this question: How did this person influence Roman history? **L2**

Roman politicians were worried about riots breaking out, but they quickly turned the situation to their advantage. To win the votes of the poor, they began providing cheap food and entertainment. This policy of "bread and circuses" helped many dishonest rulers come to power.

Why Did Reform Fail?
Not all wealthy people ignored the problems facing the Roman Republic. Two prominent officials who worked for reforms were Tiberius and Gaius Gracchus (GRA•kuhs). These brothers thought that many of Rome's problems were caused by the loss of small farms. They asked the Senate to take back public land from the rich and divide it among landless Romans.

Many senators, however, were among those who had claimed parcels of public land. Putting their own interests above the general welfare, they fought the Gracchus brothers' proposals. A band of senators even went so far as to kill Tiberius in 133 B.C. Twelve years later, Gaius met the same fate. These were dark days for the Roman Republic, when the people charged with making and upholding the laws could so shockingly violate them.

The Army Enters Politics
Matters only worsened as the Roman army took on a new role. Until now, the army had mostly stayed out of government affairs. Things changed when a military leader named Marius became consul in 107 B.C. Previously, most soldiers were owners of small farms. Now because this type of farmer was disappearing, Marius began to recruit soldiers from the

History Online
Web Activity Visit jat.glencoe.com and click on *Chapter 8—Student Web Activity* to learn more about the rise of Rome.

◀ Tiberius Gracchus (left) and his brother Gaius believed that moving poor Romans from the city to farms would help solve the republic's problems. *What happened to the Gracchus brothers?*

poor. In return for their service, he paid them wages and promised them the one thing they desperately wanted—land.

Marius changed the Roman army from citizen volunteers to paid professional soldiers. The new troops, however, were motivated by material rewards rather than a sense of duty. They felt loyal to their general, not to the Roman Republic. This gave individual generals a great deal of influence and good reason to become involved in politics. They needed to get laws passed that would provide the land they had promised their soldiers.

Marius's new military system led to new power struggles. It was not long before Marius faced a challenge from a rival general with his own army, a man named Sulla. In 82 B.C. Sulla drove his enemies out of Rome and made himself dictator.

Over the next three years, Sulla changed the government. He weakened the Council of the Plebs and strengthened the Senate. Then he stepped down from office. He hoped that the Roman Republic could heal its wounds and recapture its glory. Instead, Rome plunged into an era of civil wars for the next 50 years. Ambitious men saw how Sulla used an army to seize power. They decided to follow the same path.

Reading Check **Explain** What change did Marius make to the Roman army?

CHAPTER 8   The Rise of Rome   279

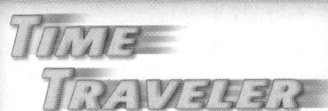

TIME TRAVELER

The Roman "circus" referred to in the policy of "bread and circuses" was not like the circus of today. Instead, it was a great arena that held spectators who came to see chariot races, footraces, and fights to the death between gladiators.

History Online

Objectives and answers to the student activity can be found in the **Web Activity Lesson Plan** feature at jat.glencoe.com

Answer: Marius changed Rome's army from citizen volunteers to paid professionals. They were loyal to their generals, not to the republic.

DIFFERENTIATED INSTRUCTION

Visual/Spatial: Have students create a "recruiting" poster for the army of Marius, Sulla, or Julius Caesar. Posters might explain the rewards for enlisting or the merits of the leader.

Auditory/Musical: Ask students to write several verses to a folk song describing the plight of Rome's small farmers.

Gifted and Talented: Have students debate which group made the best Roman soldiers—paid professionals or citizen volunteers.

☞ Refer to *Inclusion Strategies for the Middle School Social Studies Classroom* in the TCR.

Reading Strategy

Writing Activity

Have students write a sentence or two giving their opinion about whether a triumvirate would make an effective government. **L2**

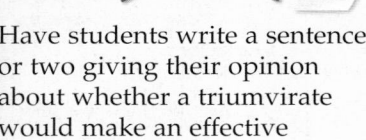

TIME TRAVELER

Julius Caesar created the **Julian calendar,** in order to correct problems that had crept into the old calendar under the Roman Republic. The old calendar had been abused by leaders who shortened it in order to affect the length of an opposing official's term. The new Julian calendar used the same month names as the old calendar. However, the names of two months were changed later to honor Julius Caesar (July), and Caesar Augustus (August). This calendar was used in Russia until 1917 and is still used by the Russian Orthodox Church.

Using Visuals For each of the pictures on these pages, have student pairs find corresponding text. Ask volunteers to read aloud the text they have found that relates to each of the pictures. **L1/ EL**

Julius Caesar

Main Idea Military hero Julius Caesar seized power and made reforms.

Reading Focus Did you know that George Washington, Andrew Jackson, William H. Harrison, Zachary Taylor, Ulysses S. Grant, and Dwight D. Eisenhower all commanded armies before becoming president? Read to learn about a famous Roman who made a similar jump from military leader to political leader.

After Sulla left office, different Roman leaders battled for power, supported by their loyal armies. In 60 B.C. three men were on top: Crassus, Pompey, and **Julius Caesar** (jool•yuhs SEE•zuhr). Crassus was a military leader and one of the richest men in Rome. Pompey and Caesar were not as rich, but both were successful military men. Drawing on their wealth and power, they formed the First Triumvirate to rule Rome. A **triumvirate** (try•UHM•vuh•ruht) is a political alliance of three people.

Caesar's Rise to Power

Caesar was part of the First Triumvirate, whose members are shown below.

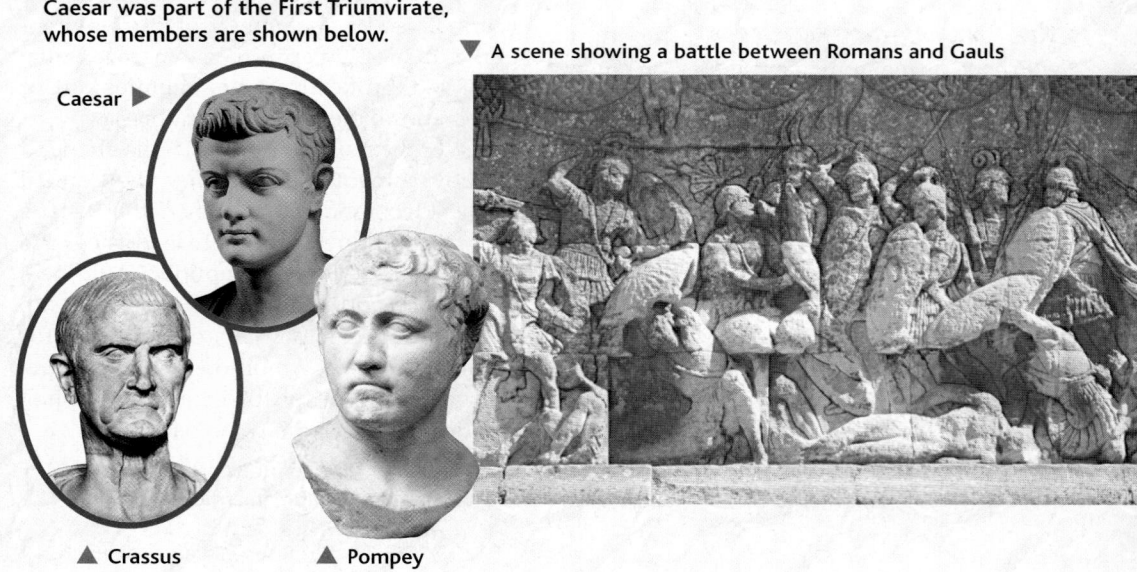

▼ A scene showing a battle between Romans and Gauls

Caesar ▶

▲ Crassus   ▲ Pompey

Caesar's Military Campaigns The members of the Triumvirate each had a military command in a remote area of the republic. Pompey was in Spain, Crassus in Syria, and Caesar in Gaul (modern France). While in Gaul, Caesar battled foreign tribes and invaded Britain. He became a hero to Rome's lower classes. Senators and others back home in Rome feared that Caesar was becoming too popular and might seize power like Sulla.

After Crassus was killed in battle in 53 B.C., the Senate decided that Pompey should return to Italy and rule alone. In 49 B.C. the Senate ordered Caesar to give up his army and come home. Caesar faced a difficult choice. He could obey the Senate and perhaps face prison or death at the hands of his rivals, or he could march on Rome with his army and risk a civil war.

Caesar decided to hold on to his 5,000 loyal soldiers. He marched into Italy by crossing the **Rubicon** (ROO•bih•KAHN), a

CRITICAL THINKING ACTIVITY

Analyzing Explain that Quintilis, the month in which Julius Caesar was born, was renamed "July" in his honor while Caesar was still alive. Discuss with students what problems might occur when such a great honor is bestowed on someone who is still living. *(Students may indicate that it is difficult to look objectively at people and events and judge their importance and meaning until some time has passed.)* How much time do students think should pass following a person's accomplishments before such a great honor is awarded? Students should explain their answers. **L2**

small river at the southern boundary of his command area. By doing so, Caesar knew that he was starting a civil war and that there was no turning back. The phrase "crossing the Rubicon" is used today to mean making a decision that you cannot take back.

Pompey tried to stop Caesar, but Caesar was the better general. He drove Pompey's forces from Italy and then destroyed Pompey's army in Greece in 48 B.C.

Caesar's Rise to Power In 44 B.C. Caesar had himself declared dictator of Rome for life. This broke with the Roman tradition that allowed dictators to hold power for only short periods of time. To strengthen his hold on power, Caesar filled the Senate with new members who were loyal to him.

At the same time, Caesar knew that reforms were needed. He granted citizenship to people living in Rome's territories outside the Italian peninsula. He started new colonies to provide land for the landless and created work for Rome's jobless people. He ordered landowners using slave labor to hire more free workers. These measures made Caesar popular with Rome's poor.

Caesar also created a new calendar with 12 months, 365 days, and a leap year. The Julian calendar, as it was called, was used throughout Europe until A.D. 1582. That year it was modified slightly to become the Gregorian calendar. This calendar, based on the birth of Christ, has been used in the United States since its beginning and is used by most countries in the world today.

While many Romans supported Caesar, others did not. His supporters believed he was a strong leader who brought peace and order to Rome. His enemies, however, feared that Caesar wanted to be king. These opponents, led by the senators Brutus and Cassius, plotted to kill him. Caesar ignored a famous warning to "beware the Ides of March" (March 15). On that date in 44 B.C., Caesar's enemies surrounded him and stabbed him to death.

✓**Reading Check** **Explain** Why did Brutus, Cassius, and others kill Caesar?

HISTORY Mystery

How Did Caesar Help Cause His Own Death?
Julius Caesar's death was caused, in part, by his policy of showing clemency toward his opponents. Caesar had pardoned Gaius Cassius Longinus and Marcus Junius Brutus, two men who later helped plot his murder.

✓**Reading Check**

Answer: They feared that Caesar wanted to be king.

Reading Support L1/ EL

Assign **Guided Reading Activity 8–3** to help students organize the information in the section.

▼ **Caesar crossing the Rubicon**

Brutus (left) was one of the senators who killed Caesar. Antony (above) supported Caesar and his nephew Octavian and fought against Caesar's assassins.

CHAPTER 8   The Rise of Rome   **281**

INTERDISCIPLINARY CONNECTIONS ACTIVITY

Art Ask volunteers to find pictures and descriptions of the entertainments that occurred at the Roman circuses. Have the volunteers share their findings with the class. Then direct each student to draw a scene (without being extremely graphic) that might have been witnessed by spectators attending the circus. Have volunteers use the completed pictures to create a wall display under the heading "Bread and Circuses." L1/ EL

Primary Source

Although Cicero did not approve of Julius Caesar's dictatorship, he did not help plan or participate in Caesar's assassination.

Answer:
Cicero states that Antony has attacked a Roman general and that the only way to stop him is by war.

❸ ASSESS

Assign Section 3 Review as homework or as an in-class activity.

🖲 Have students use the **Interactive Tutor Self-Assessment CD-ROM** to review the section.

Assessment L2

Assign **Section 3 Quiz** to assess mastery of section material.

Reading Support L1/ EL

Assign **Reading Essentials and Study Guide 8–3** to help students review section material.

Rome Becomes an Empire

Main Idea The Roman Republic, weakened by civil wars, became an empire under Augustus.

Reading Focus Have you ever been in a traffic jam and wished that a police officer would show up to get things moving? Read on to learn how Romans welcomed the arrival of a strong new ruler.

Caesar's death plunged Rome into another civil war. On one side were forces led by the men who had killed Caesar. On the other side was Caesar's grandnephew **Octavian** (ahk•TAY•vee•uhn), who had inherited Caesar's wealth, and two of Caesar's top generals, **Antony** (AN•tuh•nee) and Lepidus. After defeating Caesar's assassins, these three men created the Second Triumvirate in 43 B.C.

The Second Triumvirate The members of the Second Triumvirate began quarreling almost at once. Octavian soon forced Lepidus to retire from politics. Then the two remaining leaders divided the Roman world between themselves. Octavian took the west; Antony took the east.

In short order, though, Octavian and Antony came into conflict. Antony fell in love with the Egyptian queen Cleopatra VII and formed an alliance with her. Octavian told the Romans that Antony, with Cleopatra's help, planned to make himself the sole ruler of the republic. This alarmed many Romans and enabled Octavian to declare war on Antony.

In 31 B.C., at the Battle of **Actium** (AK•shee•uhm) off the west coast of Greece, Octavian crushed the army and navy of Antony and Cleopatra. The couple then fled to Egypt. A year later, as Octavian closed in, they killed themselves. Octavian, at the age of 32, now stood alone at the top of the Roman world. The period of civil wars was

Primary Source Cicero Calls for War

This excerpt is from Cicero's sixth speech about the struggle between Octavian and Antony (Marcus Antonius):

"Therefore, when I saw that a nefarious [evil] war was waged against the republic, I thought that no delay ought to be interposed to our pursuit of Marcus Antonius; and I gave my vote that we ought to pursue with war that most audacious [bold] man, who . . . was at this moment attacking a general of the Roman people. . . . I said further, that . . . the garb of war should be assumed by the citizens, in order that all men might apply themselves with more activity and energy to avenging the injuries of the republic."

▲ Cicero

—Cicero, "The Sixth Oration of M.T. Cicero Against Marcus Antonius"

DBQ Document-Based Question
Why did Cicero want Rome to fight Antony?

over, but so was the republic. Octavian would lay the foundation for a new system of government—the Roman Empire.

Who Was Augustus? Octavian could have made himself dictator for life, like Julius Caesar did. He knew, though, that many people favored a republican form of government. One such person was

EXTENDING THE CONTENT

Cleopatra Another important figure in Rome's history during the time of Julius Caesar and Augustus was Egypt's queen, Cleopatra. The year 48 B.C. brought Caesar to Egypt as he pursued Pompey. To prevent a Roman conquest of Egypt, Cleopatra decided to use her feminine wiles to captivate Caesar. She started with their first meeting, when she had a rug delivered to Caesar as a gift. When the rug was unrolled, inside was Cleopatra herself! After Caesar's assassination, Cleopatra also won Antony's affection.

Cicero (SIH•suh•ROH), a political leader, writer, and Rome's greatest public speaker. Cicero had argued against dictators and called for a representative government with limited powers.

Cicero's speeches and books swayed many Romans. Centuries later, his ideas would also influence the writers of the United States Constitution.

Although Cicero did not live to see Octavian rule, he had supported him, hoping he would restore the republic. In 27 B.C. Octavian announced that he was doing just that.

He knew the Senate wanted this form of government. However, Octavian also knew that the republic had been too weak to solve Rome's problems. Although he gave some power to the Senate, he really put himself in charge. His title, *imperator,* translates to "commander in chief," but it came to mean

▲ At the Battle of Actium, Octavian's forces defeated those of Antony after Cleopatra's ships retreated. *How did the Battle of Actium affect the history of Rome?*

"emperor." Octavian also took the title of **Augustus** (aw•GUHS•tuhs)—"the revered or majestic one." From this point on, he was known by this name.

 Explain How did Octavian's government reflect the ideas of Cicero?

Study Central™ Need help with the material in this section? Visit jat.glencoe.com

Section 3 Review

Reading Summary

Review the Main Ideas

- As the gap between the ruling class and the poor in Rome increased, a number of reforms failed, and generals began to gather power.
- Julius Caesar became dictator and carried out reforms to aid Rome's poor. Later he was assassinated by members of the Senate.
- Caesar's grandnephew Octavian defeated Antony and Cleopatra and became Augustus, the first Roman emperor.

What Did You Learn?

1. What is a triumvirate?
2. Who was Cicero, and how did he influence the writers of the United States Constitution?

Critical Thinking

3. **Understanding Cause and Effect** Draw a diagram like the one below. Fill in the chain of effects that was caused by the thousands of enslaved prisoners that were brought to Italy from Rome's many wars.

4. **Summarize** What reforms did the Gracchus brothers suggest?

5. **Analyze** What was the "bread and circuses" policy, and how did Roman politicians benefit from it?
6. **Analyze** What reforms did Julius Caesar put in place that increased his popularity with poor and working-class Romans?
7. **Persuasive Writing** Imagine you are a Roman citizen. Decide whether you would have been for or against Julius Caesar's rise to power and his reforms. Then write a newspaper editorial explaining your views. Be sure to include facts to support your opinions.

CHAPTER 8   The Rise of Rome   283

CHAPTER 8
SECTION 3, 277–283

ENRICH

Ask students to research the life of Cicero. Have them share facts about his life and excerpts from some of his famous speeches with the class. **L3**

Caption Answer: put Octavian in power and ended the republic

Reading Check

Answer: Octavian restored the republic, which Cicero favored.

To help students understand section material, have them visit **Study Central**™ at jat.glencoe.com

RETEACH

Discuss with students how leaders with selfish interests helped bring down the Roman Republic. **L1**

4 CLOSE

Have students discuss the transition from the Roman Republic to the Roman Empire. **L2**

SECTION 3 REVIEW ANSWERS

1. a political alliance of three people
2. Cicero was a political leader whose ideas on a representative government with limited powers influenced the U.S. Constitution.
3. Many enslaved prisoners worked Rome's large farms; farmers lost farms and moved to cities; farmers could not find jobs.
4. The Gracchus brothers wanted the government to take back public land and give it to landless farmers. Landholding senators opposed their proposals.
5. the use of cheap food and free entertainment to win support from the poor
6. Caesar provided land for the poor and created new jobs. He also ordered landholders to hire more free workers.
7. Editorials should include facts to support opinions.

283

① FOCUS

A person who is a powerful political or military figure, like Julius Caesar, is likely to make both friends and enemies. Ask students why some people did not like Caesar's actions, even when those actions helped many people.

② TEACH

DEFINING TERMS

Have student pairs use a dictionary to find the definitions of the terms *reformer* and *dictator*. Discuss with students whether someone could be both a reformer and a dictator at the same time. **L2**

COMPARISON

Have students create a two-column graphic organizer under the heading "Julius Caesar." Ask them to use the table to compare and contrast Caesar's actions. **L2**
(Answers are provided.)

Julius Caesar	
Reformer	**Dictator**
brought order	*disobeyed Senate*
helped poor	*started civil war*
extended citizenship	*sought glory for himself*

You Decide . . .

Was Caesar a Reformer or a Dictator?

Great Reformer

During his life, Julius Caesar was greatly admired by many people. He was also hated and feared by many others. Some believed he was too ambitious—exceptionally eager for fame and power—and that his ambition would keep him from acting in Rome's best interest.

Was Caesar a great reformer or an ambitious dictator? Those who saw him as a great leader and reformer said that he

- won the support of his soldiers through his military leadership and strategy
- treated many of his defeated enemies generously and appointed some of them—including Brutus—to government positions
- ended the rule of corrupt Roman nobles
- brought order and peace to Rome
- restored cities that had been destroyed by the republic
- strengthened and expanded the state of Rome
- started public jobs programs to aid the poor
- granted Roman citizenship to people from foreign countries or states.

▲ The assassination of Julius Caesar

284

Extending the Content

Rome's Civil War Around January 10 in the year 49 B.C., Caesar crossed the Rubicon River, thus committing the first act of civil war. This act is one reason why people feared Caesar's ambitions. However, Caesar believed he had no choice, because if he had not taken control of Rome, he might have been killed by his enemies. The civil war continued from 49 B.C. to 45 B.C. During those years, Caesar and his army crushed opponents as far away as Spain and Egypt. Finally, in March of 45 B.C., Caesar returned home to begin his reforms. A year later, on March 15 of 44 B.C., he was killed.

Ambitious Dictator

Caesar also had many enemies, including some who had been his friends. They saw Caesar as a dangerous dictator and thought he was taking advantage of his growing power.

They said that he

- became an enemy when he refused to follow the Senate's order to return to Rome
- started a civil war that led to the destruction of the republic
- increased the number of senators to add to his number of supporters
- treated his defeated enemies with cruelty
- punished those who wanted to uphold the traditions and laws of the republic
- weakened the Senate to gain absolute power over Rome
- kept hidden any facts that did not make him look brave and intelligent
- sought glory for himself at the expense of the republic.

▲ Julius Caesar

You Be the Historian

Checking for Understanding
1. Define *ambition*. Identify some ways ambition can be a positive characteristic and some ways it can be a negative characteristic.
2. What could Caesar have done to show his enemies that he was not abusing his power?
3. Do you think Caesar was a great leader and reformer or an ambitious dictator? Write a brief essay that explains how you view Caesar. Use facts to support your position.

285

❸ ASSESS

Reading Strategy

DEBATE THE ISSUE

Organize students into two teams and explain that the teams are going to prepare for and present a debate. One team should take the position that Julius Caesar should be remembered as a great reformer. The other team should take the point of view that Julius Caesar should be remembered as an ambitious dictator. Tell teams to practice defending their positions by using the points made in the feature. Explain that they also may use the library or the Internet to find more information to support their position. When they are ready, have them carry out the debate. When the debate is finished, ask students which side seemed to have the stronger argument. **L2**

You Be the Historian Answers

1. Ambition is being exceptionally eager for fame and power. Ambition can be a positive characteristic when an ambitious person works hard and sets goals. It can be a negative characteristic when an ambitious person acts only in his or her self interest, not caring what is right or good for others.

2. Answers will vary. Students may mention giving more power to the Senate, holding town hall meetings to hear concerns, and so on.

3. Responses will vary but should reflect the facts and express clear opinions.

① FOCUS

SECTION OVERVIEW

This section describes the expansion and contributions of the Roman Empire.

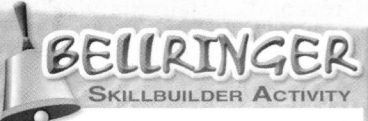
BELLRINGER
SKILLBUILDER ACTIVITY

✍ Project **Daily Focus Skills Transparency 8–4** and have students answer questions. Discuss their responses.

Get Ready to Read!

Preteaching Vocabulary: Ask students which of the terms in the vocabulary list appears to be foreign. *(Pax Romana)* Ask them how they knew. Point out that foreign words are often printed in italics in the text. Ask students what language they think the term is. *(Latin)*

Answers to Graphic: Cause: professional army built; Effect: added conquered territories to the empire; Cause: imported grain; Effect: reduced hunger; Cause: new professional governors; Effect: improved local government; Cause: tax collectors were made government workers; Effect: increased amount of money controlled by government

---

Section 4

The Early Empire

Get Ready to Read!

What's the Connection?
You learned in Section 3 that when Octavian became Augustus, the Roman world began to change. The republic gave way to an empire, and peace and prosperity spread throughout the Mediterranean.

Focusing on the Main Ideas
• By expanding the empire and reorganizing the military and government, Augustus created a new era of prosperity. *(page 287)*

• Rome's system of roads, aqueducts, ports, and common currency made the empire rich and prosperous. *(page 290)*

Locating Places
Rhine River (RYN)
Danube River (DAN•YOOB)
Puteoli (pyu•TEE•uh•LY)
Ostia (AHS•tee•uh)

Meeting People
Caligula (kuh•LIH•gyuh•luh)
Nero (NEE•roh)
Hadrian (HAY•dree•uhn)

Building Your Vocabulary
Pax Romana (pahks roh•MAH•nah)
aqueduct (A•kwuh•DUHKT)
currency (KUHR•uhn•see)

Reading Strategy
Cause and Effect Use a chart like the one below to show the changes Augustus made in the Roman Empire and the effect of each change.

Causes		Effects
	→	
	→	
	→	
	→	

NATIONAL GEOGRAPHIC When & Where?

BRITAIN
GAUL
SPAIN ITALY GREECE
Rome
PALESTINE
EGYPT

A.D. 10
A.D. 14
Augustus dies

A.D. 110
A.D. 96
Rule of the Good Emperors begins

A.D. 210
A.D. 180
Pax Romana ends

SECTION RESOURCES

📁 **Reproducible Masters**
• Reproducible Lesson Plan 8–4
• Daily Lecture and Discussion Notes 8–4
• Vocabulary Activity 8–4
• Active Reading Note-Taking Guide 8–4
• Guided Reading Activity 8–4
• Section Quiz 8–4
• Reading Essentials and Study Guide 8–4

✍ **Transparencies**
• Daily Focus Skills Transparency 8–4

Multimedia
💿 Interactive Tutor Self-Assessment CD-ROM
💿 ExamView® Pro Testmaker CD-ROM
💿 Presentation Plus! CD-ROM
💿 Vocabulary PuzzleMaker CD-ROM
💿 Glencoe BookLink CD-ROM

The Emperor Augustus

Main Idea By expanding the empire and reorganizing the military and government, Augustus created a new era of prosperity.

Reading Focus What makes a good or bad leader? Think about this question as you read about Augustus and other Roman emperors.

Augustus paved the way for 200 years of peace and prosperity in Rome. The emperors who followed him were not all good rulers, but they helped the Roman Empire reach its peak. For centuries, the Mediterranean region had been filled with conflict. Under Augustus and his successors, the region was under the control of one empire. A long era of peace began with Augustus and lasted until A.D. 180. It was called the *Pax Romana* (pahks roh•MAH•nah), or "Roman Peace."

What Did Augustus Achieve?
Upon becoming emperor in 27 B.C., Augustus set out to make the empire strong and safe. To provide security, he built a permanent, professional army of about 150,000 men—all Roman citizens. Augustus also created a special unit called the Praetorian Guard.

This force consisted of about 9,000 men in charge of guarding the emperor. The Praetorian Guard later became very influential in Roman politics.

Augustus's legions conquered new territories and added vast stretches of northern Europe to the empire. All of Spain and Gaul came under Roman rule, as did land in what is today Austria, Hungary, Romania, and Bulgaria.

Meanwhile, Augustus rebuilt Rome with stately palaces, fountains, and splendid public buildings. "I found Rome a city of brick," he boasted, "and left it a city of marble." The arts flourished as never before, and Augustus also imported grain from Africa to feed the poor. He knew that a well-fed population would be less likely to cause trouble.

Augustus devoted much of his energy to improving Rome's government. During his reign, more than 50 million people lived in the Roman Empire. To rule this huge population, Augustus appointed a proconsul, or governor, for each of Rome's provinces. These new officials replaced the politicians who had been chosen by the Senate. Augustus often traveled to the provinces to see how the governors were doing.

▲ The city of Rome at the height of the Roman Empire

CHAPTER 8   The Rise of Rome   **287**

② TEACH

Comparing and Contrasting
Explain that the 200 years of the *Pax Romana* was a long time to maintain peace. Point out that the United States is a little more than 200 years old. **Ask: Has the 200-year history of the United States been a period of peace for its people?** *(Students should cite some of the many conflicts and wars during our 200-year history: World War I, World War II, Korea, Vietnam, and so on.)* **L1/ EL**

Reviewing Prior Knowledge Point out to students that the first topic covered in this section is the emperor Augustus. Remind students that they studied about Augustus in Section 3. Review Augustus' life with students. **L1/ EL**

Daily Lecture and Discussion Notes 8–4

Use **Daily Lecture and Discussion Notes 8–4** for an outline of key concepts found in the section.

Reading Support L1/ EL

Use **Vocabulary Activity 8–4** to review important terms in the section.

Reading Strategy — READING THE TEXT

Reading to Evaluate Organize students into small groups and direct each group to read the material about Augustus at the beginning of this section. Then tell the groups to imagine that they are Roman citizens and they have been asked to speak at Augustus's funeral. Direct each group to write a two-minute speech in which Augustus's most important accomplishments are recognized. Ask a volunteer from each group to present the group's speech to the class. After all groups have presented, discuss with students how evaluations of Augustus and his reign differed and how they were the same. **L1/ EL** 🗂

Evaluating Have volunteers read "What Did Augustus Achieve?" Then direct students to the time line on page 286. Point out the first entry, "Augustus dies." Discuss with students what entry might precede that and indicate Augustus's major effect on the empire. **L2**

Understanding Charts

Under the Julio-Claudian emperors, the Roman Empire prospered and expanded.

Answers:
1. Claudius
2. stable bureaucracy and economy

✓ Reading Check

Answer: created professional army, reformed tax system, and gave rights to noncitizens

The Julio-Claudian Emperors

Emperor	Accomplishments
Tiberius	14–37 A.D. Great military leader; regulated business to prevent fraud; kept Rome's economy stable
Caligula	37–41 A.D. Abolished sales tax; allowed people in exile to return; increased court system's power
Claudius	41–54 A.D. Built new harbor at Ostia and new aqueduct for Rome; conquered most of Britain
Nero	54–68 A.D. Constructed many new buildings; gave slaves the right to file complaints; assisted cities suffering from disasters

Understanding Charts

The four emperors who followed Augustus were all relatives of Augustus.
1. Under which emperor was Britain conquered?
2. **Conclude** Why do you think the Roman Empire remained at peace even with weak emperors such as Caligula and Nero?

Augustus also reformed the Roman tax system. Previously, individual tax collectors paid the government for the right to do the job. To make their investment worthwhile, tax collectors were allowed to keep some of the money they gathered. Many of them, however, were dishonest and took too much. Augustus solved this problem by making tax collectors permanent government workers. This change made the tax system fairer.

Augustus also reformed the legal system. He created a set of laws for people in the provinces who were not citizens. As time passed, however, most of these people gained citizenship. The laws of Rome then applied to everyone, although the legal system generally stressed the authority of the government over the rights of the individual.

Who Came After Augustus?

After ruling for almost 40 years, Augustus died in A.D. 14. No law stated how the next emperor was to be chosen. Augustus, however, had trained a relative, Tiberius, to follow him. The next three emperors—**Caligula** (kuh•LIH•gyuh•luh), Claudius, and **Nero** (NEE•roh)—also came from Augustus's family. They are called the Julio-Claudian emperors. Unfortunately, they were not all fit to lead. Tiberius and Claudius ruled capably. Caligula and Nero, however, proved to be cruel leaders.

Mental illness caused Caligula to act strangely and to treat people cruelly. He had many people murdered, wasted a lot of money, and even gave his favorite horse the position of consul. Eventually, the Praetorian Guard killed him and put Claudius on the throne.

Nero was also a vicious man. Among those he had killed were his mother and two wives. He is best remembered for having "fiddled while Rome burned." According to legend, he was playing music miles from Rome when a fire destroyed much of the city in A.D. 64. Eventually, he committed suicide.

✓ **Reading Check** **Explain** What did Augustus do to make the empire safer and stronger?

DIFFERENTIATED INSTRUCTION

Visual/Spatial: Have students turn to the maps of the Roman Empire on page 292 and then to the map of present-day Europe in the **Reference Atlas**. Ask them to compare the maps and then read the second paragraph under the heading "What Did Augustus Achieve?" As each place is named, have students find that place on the maps.

English Learners: Ask a volunteer to read aloud the second paragraph under the heading "What Did Augustus Achieve?" As each place is named, ask another volunteer to list it on the board. When the list is complete, ask English learners to tell how each name is said in their native languages.

📁 Refer to *Inclusion Strategies for the Middle School Social Studies Classroom* in the TCR.

Biography

AUGUSTUS
63 B.C.–A.D. 14

Octavian was born to a wealthy family in a small Italian town southeast of Rome. During his youth, Octavian suffered a number of illnesses. He refused to let his illnesses interfere with his life, however, showing the determination that would later make him Rome's first emperor.

Octavian's father was a Roman senator, but it was Octavian's great-uncle—Julius Caesar—who first introduced Octavian to public life in Rome. In his late teens, Octavian joined Caesar in Africa and then the following year in Spain. At the age of 18, while Octavian was studying at school, he learned that his great-uncle had been murdered. In his will, Caesar had adopted Octavian as his son. Caesar had also made Octavian his heir—a position that Antony had assumed would be his. Against his family's advice, Octavian went to Rome to claim his inheritance. By the time he reached Rome, however, Antony had seized Caesar's papers and money and refused to give them to Octavian. With remarkable political savvy for someone so young, Octavian turned the situation around in his favor. He won the hearts of Caesar's soldiers and the people of Rome by celebrating the public games that Caesar had started.

In his rise to power and during his reign as Emperor Augustus, Octavian pushed himself and his loyal followers with relentless energy. In his private life, however, he lived simply and quietly and shunned personal luxury. He was devoted to his wife, Livia Drusilla, and spent his spare time with her at their home on the outskirts of Rome.

Augustus ▶

"I extended the frontiers of all the provinces of the Roman people."

–Augustus, "Res Gestae: The Accomplishments of Augustus"

Then and Now

Augustus overcame the obstacles of illness and political enemies to become a great emperor. Can you think of any present-day individuals who overcame obstacles to excel at something?

289

Reading List Generator CD-ROM

GLENCOE BOOKLINK   **RECOMMENDED READING**

Use the **Glencoe BookLink CD-ROM** to create customized reading lists based on your students' interests and reading levels. Below is an example based on content in this chapter. Also, see the Suggested Readings on pages 944–946 of the Appendix.

- Cairns, Trevor. *The Romans and Their Empire.* Introduces students to daily life in the Roman Empire.
- Macdonald, Fiona. *First Facts About the Ancient Romans.* Presents facts about daily life during the time of the empire.
- Williams, John. *Augustus.* Describes Augustus's rise to power.

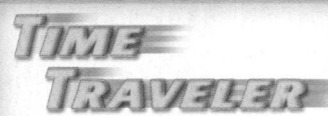

TIME TRAVELER

Mount Vesuvius's eruption immediately coated Pompeii in nine feet of ash. Many people were crushed as this great weight of ash crashed on their roofs. Others died as the ash cocooned and suffocated them. Here is how one historian described the event: "Day was turned into night, and light into darkness; an inexpressible quantity of dust and ashes was poured out, deluging land, sea, and air, and burying two entire cities, Herculaneum and Pompeii. . . ." By the time Vesuvius quieted again, Pompeii had almost disappeared, buried under 20 feet of ash, stone, and debris.

Linking Past & Present

Answer: Answers will vary. Students may suggest that the region is a beautiful place, but the risk of another eruption might outweigh the beauty.

Unity and Prosperity

Main Idea Rome's system of roads, aqueducts, ports, and common currency made the empire rich and prosperous.

Reading Focus Do you find that you are more productive when you are not worried about conflicts at home or school? Read to learn how the Roman Empire prospered during its time of peace.

After Nero committed suicide, Rome passed through a period of disorder until Vespasian, a general and one of Nero's proconsuls, took the throne. Vespasian restored peace and order. He put down several rebellions in the empire, including the Jewish rebellion in Palestine. Troops commanded by his son Titus defeated the Jews and destroyed the Jewish temple in Jerusalem in A.D. 70.

During his reign, Vespasian began construction of the Colosseum—a huge amphitheatre—in central Rome. His son Titus, then his other son Domitian, ruled Rome after he died. Both sons oversaw an era of growth and prosperity in Rome. During Titus's reign, two disasters struck the empire. The volcano Mount Vesuvius erupted, destroying the city of Pompeii, and a great fire badly damaged Rome.

Linking Past & Present
Living in the Shadow of Mt. Vesuvius

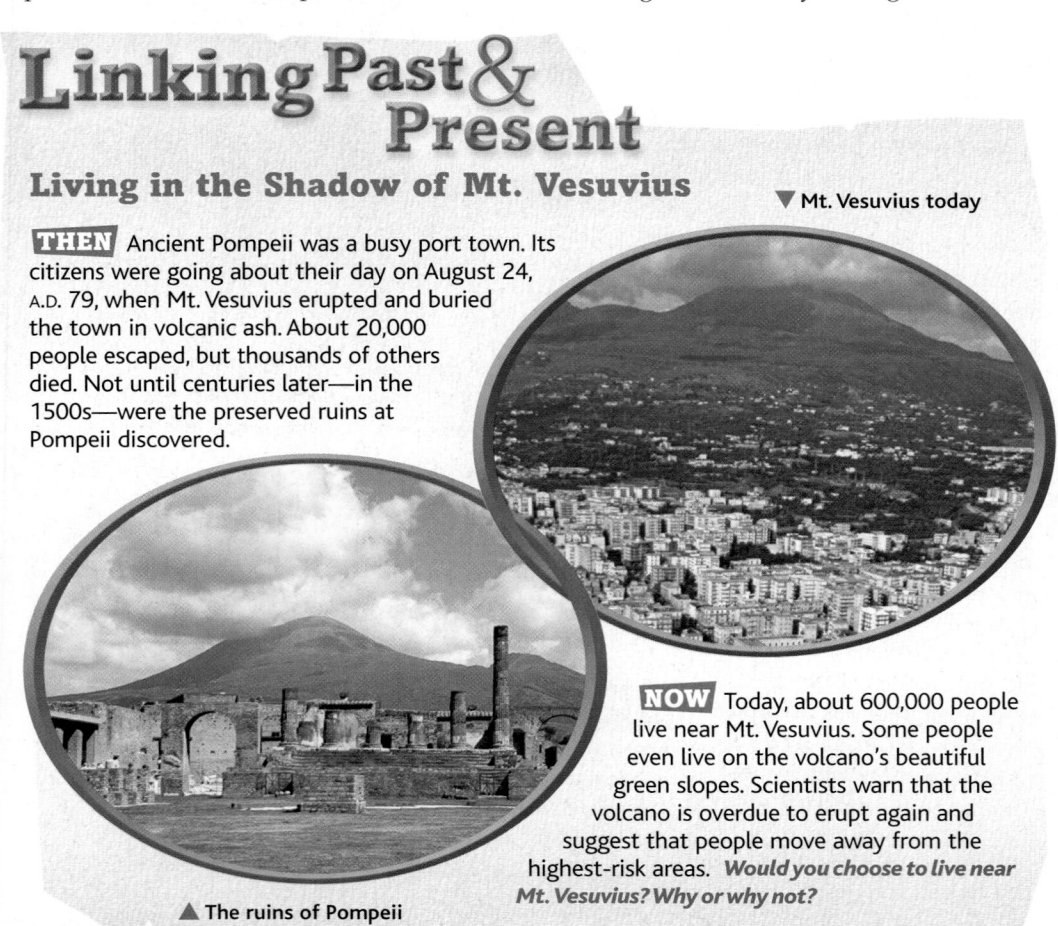

THEN Ancient Pompeii was a busy port town. Its citizens were going about their day on August 24, A.D. 79, when Mt. Vesuvius erupted and buried the town in volcanic ash. About 20,000 people escaped, but thousands of others died. Not until centuries later—in the 1500s—were the preserved ruins at Pompeii discovered.

▼ Mt. Vesuvius today

NOW Today, about 600,000 people live near Mt. Vesuvius. Some people even live on the volcano's beautiful green slopes. Scientists warn that the volcano is overdue to erupt again and suggest that people move away from the highest-risk areas. *Would you choose to live near Mt. Vesuvius? Why or why not?*

▲ The ruins of Pompeii

290

CRITICAL THINKING ACTIVITY

Analyzing Point out to students that like the rulers before him, Vespasian also was succeeded by relatives—in this case, his two sons. Titus served only two years before dying and being succeeded by Domitian, who eventually was killed for his cruelty and his extravagance. Also remind students that some of Augustus's successor-relatives—Caligula and Nero—were mentally unstable. Organize students into small groups, and give each group five minutes to debate this issue: Should the emperor be succeeded by a relative or by someone who earns the position? When time is up, have groups share the results of their debates with the class. **L2**

The "Good Emperors" At the beginning of the A.D. 100s, a series of rulers who were not related to Augustus or Vespasian came to power. These five emperors—Nerva, Trajan, **Hadrian** (HAY•dree•uhn), Antoninus Pius, and Marcus Aurelius—are known as the "good emperors." They presided over nearly a century of prosperity, from A.D. 96 to A.D. 180. Agriculture flourished, trade increased, and the standard of living rose.

During this time, the emperor came to overshadow the Senate more than ever before. The five "good emperors" did not abuse their power, however. They were among the most devoted and capable rulers in Rome's history. They improved Roman life in many ways, naming trained officials to carry out their orders.

Among the achievements of these emperors were programs to help ordinary people. Trajan gave money to help poor parents raise and educate their children. Hadrian made Roman law easier to understand and apply. Antoninus Pius passed laws to help orphans. All the emperors supported public building projects. They built arches and monuments, bridges and roads, and harbors and aqueducts. An **aqueduct** (A•kwuh•DUHKT) is a human-made channel for carrying water long distances.

A Unified Empire Later emperors continued to conquer new territory for Rome. The empire reached its largest size under Trajan. It spread well beyond the Mediterranean, including Britain in the north and part of Mesopotamia in the east.

Trajan's successors, however, realized that the empire had grown too big to rule effectively. Hadrian began to pull back. He removed troops from most of Mesopotamia.

The Way It Was

Science and Inventions

Roman Aqueducts Transporting water is a complex problem. Roman engineers solved it by building aqueducts. Roman aqueducts carried water across a valley or hillside using gravity, aboveground stone arches, and underground pipes made of stone or clay. Between 312 B.C. and A.D. 226, 11 aqueducts were built to bring water to Rome from as far away as 57 miles. Once the water made it to Rome, it was held in collecting tanks. Most people gathered water from these public tanks. Only the rich and high-ranking officials had private water tanks in their homes.

Many Roman aqueducts still stand and are used today. Engineers in ancient Persia, India, and Egypt built similar water systems hundreds of years before the Romans. However, historians agree that the Romans were the greatest aqueduct builders of the ancient world.

◀ **Roman aqueduct**

Connecting to the Past
1. How did the Romans transport water to the city of Rome?
2. Why do you think that only the rich and powerful had private water supplies?

Reading Strategy

Writing Activity

Point out to students that the five emperors who dominated the A.D. 100s became known as the "Good Emperors." Have students leaf through the material they have already read about Rome's emperors and choose another emperor they think qualifies as "good." Ask them to write a short paragraph explaining their reasoning. **L2**

CONNECTING ACROSS TIME

"The 'Good Emperors'" would be an excellent theme for a class discussion. Have students identify ways in which the "Good Emperors" helped the people of Rome. Then ask students to identify ways in which the national government helps people in the United States. **L3**

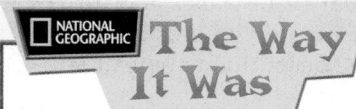

The Way It Was

Answers:
1. gravity, arches, and underground pipes
2. It was very expensive and complicated to pipe water to individual homes, so only a few could afford it.

INTERDISCIPLINARY CONNECTIONS ACTIVITY

Daily Life Point out that the five "Good Emperors" improved Roman life in many ways. Building projects—everything from arches and monuments to bridges and roads to harbors and aqueducts—were one way they initiated these changes. Organize students into small groups. Have them use the material under "The 'Good Emperors'" to identify the kind of building project that, in each group's opinion, would have had the greatest impact on daily life. Have the groups share their choices with the class, as well as the reasoning behind those choices. **L1/ EL**

Exploring Hadrian's Wall Read to students the following description of Hadrian's Wall: "It took soldier-builders six years to build Hadrian's Wall. When it was finished, the Wall extended from ocean to ocean, like a stone belt across the land. A milecastle was built at every Roman mile of wall [a Roman mile is a little longer than our mile]. Between each set of milecastles stood two turrets, set at every one-third Roman mile. Soldiers manned both turrets and milecastles. In front of most of the wall, a deep ditch was dug for added protection."

Have students research to find out more about the wall. You may wish to have them draw the path of the wall on a blank map of Great Britain or draw a depiction of the wall and its battlements. Tell students that Hadrian's Wall measured about 80 Roman miles long. Ask students to determine how many milecastles and turrets stood along the wall based on the description above. **L2**

Reading Support L1/ EL

Assign **Guided Reading Activity 8–4** to help students organize the information in the section.

The Roman Empire: Trade and Expansion

NATIONAL GEOGRAPHIC

Extent of Roman Empire, 146 B.C.

Extent of Roman Empire, 44 B.C.

Extent of Roman Empire, A.D. 14

SPAIN · ITALY · Rome · Carthage · Mediterranean Sea · Black Sea · ASIA MINOR · GREECE

500 mi. / 500 km / Lambert Azimuthal Equal-Area projection

The "Good Emperors" of the *Pax Romana*

Nerva
A.D. 96–98
Reformed land laws in favor of the poor; revised taxes

Trajan
A.D. 98–117
Expanded the empire to its largest size; built many new public works

Hadrian
A.D. 117–138
Built Hadrian's Wall in Britain; made Roman laws easier to understand

Antoninus Pius
A.D. 138–161
Promoted art and science; built new public works; passed laws to aid orphans

Marcus Aurelius
A.D. 161–180
Helped unite the empire economically; reformed Roman law

In Europe, he set the empire's northern boundaries at the **Rhine River** (RYN) and **Danube River** (DAN•YOOB). He also built Hadrian's Wall across northern Britain to keep out the Picts and Scots—two warlike people who lived in northern Britain.

In the A.D. 100s, the Roman Empire was one of the greatest empires in history. It included about 3.5 million square miles (9.1 million square km). Its people spoke different languages—mostly Latin in the west and Greek in the east. They also practiced different local customs. What unified the empire, though, were Roman law, Roman rule, and a shared identity as Romans.

Roman culture had been carried into every province by the soldiers who protected the empire and by the officials sent to govern. The Romans were generous in granting citizenship. In A.D. 212 every free person was made a Roman citizen.

A Booming Economy Most people in the Roman Empire made a living from the land. Small farms dotted northern Italy. In

292   CHAPTER 8   The Rise of Rome

EXTENDING THE CONTENT

The Roman Empire's Influence Continues Many people think that Romance languages got their name because the languages themselves sound romantic. That is not the case. Instead, the word *Romance* actually refers to the fact that those languages derive from Latin, the language of the Romans. The major Romance languages are Portuguese, Spanish, French, Italian, and Romanian. Worldwide, more than 900 million people speak Romance languages.

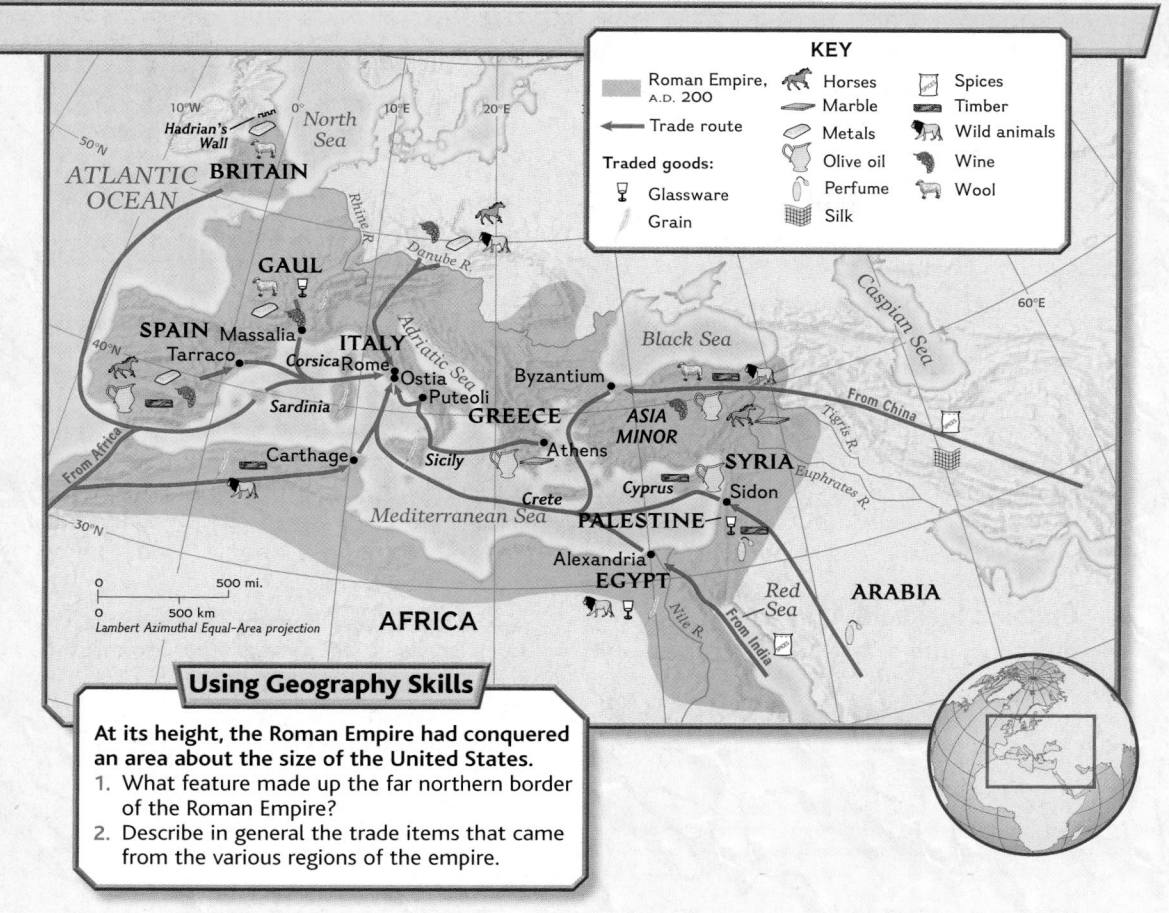

KEY

Roman Empire, A.D. 200

→ Trade route

Traded goods:

Glassware

Grain

Horses

Marble

Metals

Olive oil

Perfume

Silk

Spices

Timber

Wild animals

Wine

Wool

Using Geography Skills

At its height, the Roman Empire had conquered an area about the size of the United States.
1. What feature made up the far northern border of the Roman Empire?
2. Describe in general the trade items that came from the various regions of the empire.

Using Geography Skills

Answers:

1. Hadrian's Wall and the Rhine and Danube Rivers
2. grains, animals, olive oil, timber, and spices

3 ASSESS

Assign Section 4 Review as homework or as an in-class activity.

● Have students use the **Interactive Tutor Self-Assessment CD-ROM** to review the section.

Assessment L2

Assign **Section 4 Quiz** to assess mastery of section material.

Reading Support L1/ EL

Assign **Reading Essentials and Study Guide 8–4** to help students review section material.

southern and central Italy, latifundia, or large estates worked by enslaved people, were common. On these estates and in the provinces of Gaul and Spain, farmers produced grapes and olives. The making of wine and olive oil became big business. In Britain and Egypt, the chief crops were grains. Bountiful harvests from these regions kept Rome's people well fed.

Agriculture was the most important part of the economy, but industry was important too. Potters, weavers, and jewelers produced goods and cities became centers for making glass, bronze, and brass.

Traders came from all over the empire—and beyond—to ports in Italy. Two of the largest port cities were **Puteoli** (pyu•TEE•uh•LY) on the Bay of Naples and **Ostia** (AHS•tee•uh) at the mouth of the Tiber. The docks were lively places. Luxury items, including silk goods from China and spices from India, poured in to satisfy the rich. Raw materials, such as British tin, Spanish lead, and iron from Gaul, went to the workshops of Roman cities.

CHAPTER 8   The Rise of Rome   293

COOPERATIVE LEARNING ACTIVITY

Evaluating Contributions Organize students into five groups, and assign each group one of Rome's "Good Emperors"—Nerva, Trajan, Hadrian, Antoninus Pius, and Marcus Aurelius. Tell the groups to do research on their assigned emperor, then write a short report answering this question: Why was [emperor's name] considered a "good emperor"? When the groups have finished, have a volunteer from each group read aloud that group's report. After each report is read, lead a discussion in which students debate that emperor's greatest contribution to Rome. **L3**

ENRICH

Ask students to research and report on the adoption of the euro in Europe in 2002. Do students think such a system would encourage trade as the common currency of the Roman Empire did? **L3**

✓ **Reading Check**

Answer: Nerva, Trajan, Hadrian, Antoninus Pius, and Marcus Aurelius; they expanded the empire, maintained peace and prosperity, and increased trade.

History Online

To help students understand section material, have them visit **Study Central**™ at **jat.glencoe.com**

RETEACH

Remind students that Augustus once said, "I found Rome a city of brick and left it a city of marble." Discuss the meaning of that sentence. **L2**

④ **CLOSE**

Ask students to discuss the influence of geography and the sea on Roman trade. **L2**

294

Roads and Money A good transportation network was vital to the empire's trade. During the *Pax Romana,* Rome's system of roads reached a total length of 50,000 miles (80,000 km). On the seas, the Roman navy helped to rid the Mediterranean of pirates. Goods could be shipped more safely to and from Rome's ports.

Rome's trade was helped by a common **currency** (KUHR•uhn•see), or system of money. Roman coins were accepted throughout the Mediterranean region by A.D. 100. Merchants could use the same money in Gaul or Greece as they did in Italy. The Romans also created a standard system of weights and measures. This made it easier for people to price goods, trade, and ship products.

Ongoing Inequality The Roman Empire's prosperity did not reach all of its people.

▲ Roman coins could be used throughout most of the empire, making trade much easier. *How else did Rome improve trade during the empire?*

Shopkeepers, merchants, and skilled workers benefited from the empire's trade. Rich Romans built great fortunes and lived in luxury. However, most city dwellers and farmers remained poor, and many remained enslaved.

✓ **Reading Check** **Identify** Who were the "Good Emperors," and what did they accomplish?

History Online

Study Central™ Need help with the material in this section? Visit jat.glencoe.com

Section ④ Review

Reading Summary

Review the Main Ideas

• Augustus conquered new lands and created a professional military and a system of proconsuls. He improved the tax system and the legal system, ushering in the *Pax Romana.*

• Under Vespasian, his sons, and the five good emperors, Romans continued to be prosperous. They built an elaborate system of roads and developed a common currency that promoted trade and economic growth.

What Did You Learn?

1. What was the *Pax Romana?*
2. What products came from the farms of Italy, Gaul, and Spain?

Critical Thinking

3. **Organizing Information** Draw a diagram like the one below. Add details about the improvements and changes Augustus made to the Roman Empire during his reign.

Changes Under Augustus

4. **Sequencing Information** Describe the sequence of emperors who ruled Rome, from Augustus through the "Good Emperors."
5. **Analyze** Why was Rome's creation of a common currency important?
6. **Evaluate** Who do you think was a more important leader, Julius Caesar or Augustus? Explain.
7. **Creative Writing** Write a short play in which several Roman citizens discuss one of the emperors mentioned in this section and his accomplishments.

SECTION 4 REVIEW ANSWERS

1. a period of peace and prosperity lasting 200 years
2. grapes and olives
3. appointed proconsuls; made tax collectors government workers; built new roads and buildings; created laws for noncitizens
4. Augustus, Tiberius, Caligula, Claudius, Nero, Vespasian, Titus, Domitian, Nerva, Trajan, Hadrian, Antoninus Pius, Marcus Aurelius
5. A common Roman currency advanced trade throughout the empire.
6. Answers will vary. Students may note that Julius Caesar conquered new territories. Augustus became the first emperor and carried out many improvements.
7. Plays should note accomplishments based on the text.

Chapter 8 Reading Review

Section 1 Rome's Beginnings

Vocabulary
republic
legion

Focusing on the Main Ideas
- Geography played an important role in the rise of Roman civilization. *(page 263)*
- The Romans created a republic and conquered Italy. By treating people fairly, they built Rome from a small city into a great power. *(page 265)*

Section 2 The Roman Republic

Vocabulary
patrician
plebeian
consul
veto
praetor
dictator

Focusing on the Main Ideas
- Rome's republic was shaped by a struggle between wealthy landowners and regular citizens as it gradually expanded the right to vote. *(page 269)*
- Rome slowly destroyed the Carthaginian Empire and took control of the entire Mediterranean region. *(page 274)*

Roman consul ▶

Section 3 The Fall of the Republic

Vocabulary
latifundia
triumvirate

Focusing on the Main Ideas
- The use of enslaved labor hurt farmers, increased poverty and corruption, and brought the army into politics. *(page 278)*
- Military hero Julius Caesar seized power and made reforms. *(page 280)*
- The Roman Republic, weakened by civil wars, became an empire under Augustus. *(page 282)*

Section 4 The Early Empire

Vocabulary
Pax Romana
aqueduct
currency

Focusing on the Main Ideas
- By expanding the empire and reorganizing the military and government, Augustus created a new era of prosperity. *(page 287)*
- Rome's system of roads, aqueducts, ports, and common currency made the empire rich and prosperous. *(page 290)*

CHAPTER 8 REVIEW

PREVIEW/REVIEW

Vocabulary Activity Ask volunteers to use each of the vocabulary terms in a sentence about ancient Rome. Challenge students to use two terms in the same sentence.

- **Vocabulary PuzzleMaker CD-ROM**
- **Interactive Tutor Self-Assessment CD-ROM**

CONDENSE

- Chapter 8 **Guided Reading Activities**
- **StudentWorks Plus™ CD-ROM (with Audio Program)**

RETEACH

- **Differentiated Instruction Activity 8**
- Chapter 8 *Reading Essentials and Study Guide*

CHAPTER CULMINATING ACTIVITY

Have students finish the Chapter Culminating Activity from page 258D.

Suggestions for rubrics may be found in the *Quizzes, Tests, and Authentic Assessment (with Rubrics)* booklet.

Reading Strategy   READ TO WRITE

Writing a Riddle Have students use section time lines to verbally review Roman leaders and their accomplishments. Direct each student to choose a leader discussed in this chapter about whom they will write a "Who am I?" riddle. Explain that the riddle should start with clues about the leader's identity. These clues can come from the text or other resources. Each riddle must end with the words "Who am I?" When students have finished writing, ask them to read their riddles to the class and have other students guess each riddle's answer.

- **L1** student riddles should offer at least one clue about the leader's identity.
- **L2** student riddles should offer several clues about the leader's identity.
- **L3** student riddles should include clues from outside sources.

Chapter 8 Assessment and Activities

GLENCOE TECHNOLOGY

MindJogger Videoquiz

Use the **MindJogger Videoquiz** to review Chapter 8 content.

 Available in DVD and VHS

Review Vocabulary

1. republic
2. plebeians
3. praetor
4. dictator
5. latifundia
6. aqueduct

Review Main Ideas

7. Rome grew because it was centrally located on the Italian peninsula, near the Mediterranean Sea.

8. made conquered peoples feel themselves to be part of the empire

9. patricians: upper class; plebeians: lower class

10. Rome developed a navy and eventually attacked Carthage.

11. Slaves began to work the farms and forced farmers out of business.

12. replaced it with an empire

13. Yes; students should list Augustus's accomplishments.

14. It grew larger and wealthier.

Critical Thinking

15. Comparisons will vary but should demonstrate students' knowledge of persons and critical judgment.

Review Vocabulary

Each of the following statements is false. Replace each word in italics with a word that makes the statement true. Write the correct words on a separate sheet of paper.

___ 1. A *legion* is a form of government in which the citizens choose their leader.

___ 2. *Patricians* included artisans and shopkeepers.

___ 3. The judge in a Roman court case was a *consul*.

___ 4. In early Rome, the role of *praetor* lasted only until a crisis had passed.

___ 5. Large farming estates that used enslaved people to tend crops were called *aqueducts*.

___ 6. A *veto* was a human-made channel for carrying water.

Review Main Ideas

Section 1 • Rome's Beginnings

7. Describe the role geography played in the rise of Roman civilization.

8. How did treating people fairly help Rome to increase its power?

Section 2 • The Roman Republic

9. How did the roles of patricians and plebeians differ in Roman society?

10. Explain how Rome gradually defeated the Carthaginians.

Section 3 • The Fall of the Republic

11. How did slavery weaken the Roman Republic?

12. How did Augustus change the Roman Republic?

Section 4 • The Early Empire

13. Was Augustus a successful ruler? Explain your answer.

14. How did the Roman Empire change during the *Pax Romana*?

Critical Thinking

15. **Compare** In the chapter, Cincinnatus is compared to George Washington. Think of another person or character who is similar to Cincinnatus. Explain how they are similar.

16. **Explain** Why did Caesar fight Pompey?

17. **Predict** What do you think would have happened if Hadrian had tried to further expand the Roman Empire?

Review Reading Skill — Taking Notes — **Note Taking**

18. Read the following paragraph from page 269. Take notes on the information by making a T-chart.

> Early Romans were divided into two classes: patricians and plebeians. The patricians were wealthy landowners. These nobles made up Rome's ruling class. Most of Rome's people, however, were plebeians. This group included artisans, shopkeepers, and owners of small farms.

To review this skill, see pages 260–261.

16. Students' answers will vary but should describe Caesar's reaction to being ordered to give up his command and face prison or death while Pompey was given sole command.

17. Answers will vary but should reflect the fact that the empire had become so large that it was hard to defend.

Reading Skill

18. T-charts should accurately list the main idea and supporting details.

Geography Skills

Study the map below and answer the following questions.

19. **Place** Which areas did Rome control after the Punic Wars?
20. **Human/Environment Interaction** What does the building of Hadrian's Wall say about the Picts and Scots?
21. **Region** Why was it important to the Romans to control Mediterranean lands?

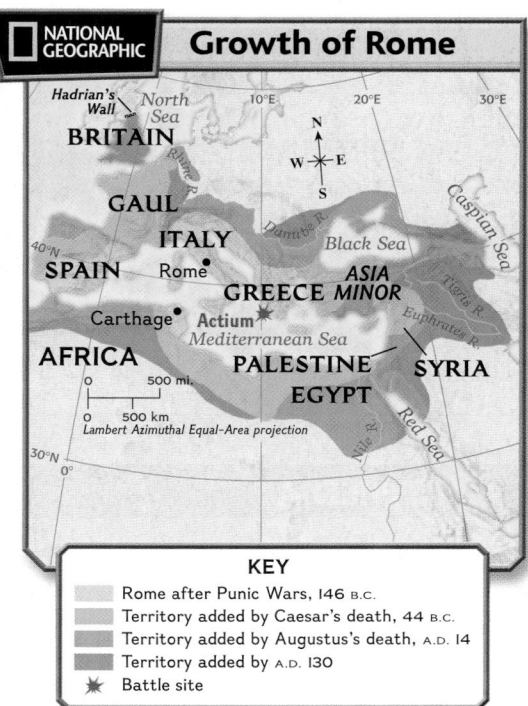

NATIONAL GEOGRAPHIC Growth of Rome

KEY
- Rome after Punic Wars, 146 B.C.
- Territory added by Caesar's death, 44 B.C.
- Territory added by Augustus's death, A.D. 14
- Territory added by A.D. 130
- ✴ Battle site

Read to Write

22. **Persuasive Writing** Suppose you were working with Tiberius and Gaius to reform Rome. Write a letter or speech that explains why reform is needed and what types of reforms should occur.
23. **Using Your FOLDABLES** Use your foldable to write a series of questions about the chapter. With a partner, take turns asking and answering questions until you have reviewed the entire chapter.

Building Citizenship

24. **Making Connections** Use the Internet and your local library to research the Twelve Tables. Work with your classmates to design a similar series of laws, and record them, using modern language. How is your law code similar to and different from the Twelve Tables?

Using Technology

25. **Creating Promotional Materials** Use the Internet to find at least five places related to ancient Rome that can be visited by tourists. Create a guidebook or brochure on the computer advertising these links to the past and persuading people to visit that area. Share your final product in a report to the class.

Primary Source Analyze

Augustus wrote a historical document describing his accomplishments. This passage is about his military leadership.

"About 500,000 Roman citizens were under military oath to me. Of these, when their terms of service were ended, I settled in colonies or sent back to their own municipalities a little more than 300,000, and to all these I allotted lands or granted money as rewards for military service."

—Augustus, "Res Gestae: The Accomplishments of Augustus"

DBQ Document-Based Questions

26. Why did Augustus give money to his retired soldiers?
27. Why do you think Augustus did not explain the reasons for his actions?

CHAPTER 8   The Rise of Rome   297

Building Citizenship

24. Laws, comparisons, and contrasts will vary.

Using Technology

25. Guidebooks and brochures will vary but should include five aspects of ancient Rome that would attract tourists.

Primary Source

26. to reward them for military service
27. Answers will vary. He may have thought that only the actions were important.

Bonus Question

Ask: Who do you think was Rome's greatest leader? Why? (*Answers will vary but should include facts supporting the student's choice.*)

Geography Skills

19. most of Spain, Carthage, Italy, and Greece
20. The Picts and Scots were warlike and not easy to defeat.
21. They could trade more freely and would not have to fear an attack by sea.

Read to Write

22. Suggestions for reform will vary but should mention the plan of Tiberius and Gaius to provide for farmers.
23. **FOLDABLES** Questions will vary but should present a summary of the chapter.

Chapter ⑨ Resources

Note: The following materials may be used when teaching Chapter 9.
Section level support materials are shown at point of use in the margins of the Teacher Wraparound Edition.

TEACHING TRANSPARENCIES

- Graphic Organizer Transparencies with Teaching Strategy and Student Activity **L2**
- Cause-and-Effect Transparencies with Teaching Strategy and Student Activity **L2**
- Then and Now Transparencies with Teaching Strategy and Student Activity **L2**
- In-text Map Transparency with Teaching Strategy and Student Activity **L1**
- Map Transparencies with Overlay, Teaching Strategy, and Student Activity **L2**

DIFFERENTIATED INSTRUCTION

- Differentiated Instruction Activity 9
- Time Line Activity 9
- Primary Source Reading 9 (with Document-Based Questions)
- Inclusion Strategies for the Middle School Social Studies Classroom
- StudentWorks Plus™ CD-ROM (with Audio Program)

READING SUPPORT

- Take-Home Review Activity 9 **L2**
- World Literature Reading 9 **L2**
- Workbook Activity 9 **L1**
- Reading Strategies for the Social Studies Classroom **L1/ EL**

ASSESSMENT

- Authentic Assessment Activity 9 **L1/ EL**
- Chapter 9 Test Form A **L2**
- Chapter 9 Test Form B **L2**
- ExamView® Pro Testmaker CD-ROM

INTERDISCIPLINARY CONNECTIONS

- Geography and History Activity 9 **L2**
- People to Meet Activity 9 **L2**
- Economics Activity 9 **L2**
- Citizenship and Service Learning Activity 9 **L2**

SPANISH RESOURCES

- Spanish Reading Essentials and Study Guide
- Spanish Guided Reading Activities
- Spanish Quizzes, Tests, and Authentic Assessment (with Rubrics)
- Spanish Take-Home Review Activities

MULTIMEDIA

- ExamView® Pro Testmaker CD-ROM
- Glencoe Skillbuilder Interactive Workbook CD-ROM, Level 1
- Interactive Tutor Self-Assessment CD-ROM
- MindJogger Videoquiz
- Presentation Plus! CD-ROM
- StudentWorks Plus™ CD-ROM (with Audio Program)
- TeacherWorks CD-ROM
- Vocabulary PuzzleMaker CD-ROM
- *World History: Journey Across Time* Video Program
- World History Primary Source Document Library CD-ROM

STANDARDIZED ASSESSMENT SKILLS

- Standardized Test Skills Practice Workbook Activity 9 **L2**
- Critical Thinking Skills Activity 9 **L2**

Teaching strategies have been coded with suggested ability levels. However, most are suitable for all levels.

L1 BASIC activities for all students

L2 AVERAGE activities for average to above-average students

L3 CHALLENGING activities for above-average students

EL ENGLISH LANGUAGE activities

TIME MANAGEMENT

Chapter Introduction	Section 1	Section 2	Section 3	Chapter Wrap-Up
1 Day	2 Days	2 Days	1 Day	1 Day

Block Scheduling Activities that are suited to use within the block scheduling framework are identified by: 🔳

`0:00` **OUT OF TIME?** Assign the Chapter 9 *Reading Essentials and Study Guide.* *📁

SECTION RESOURCES

DAILY OBJECTIVES	REPRODUCIBLE RESOURCES	MULTIMEDIA RESOURCES
Section 1 **Life in Ancient Rome** 1. Roman artists and writers borrowed many ideas from the Greeks, while Roman engineers invented new structures, including domes and aqueducts. 2. The rich and poor had very different lives in the Roman Empire, as did men and women.	📁 Reproducible Lesson Plan 9–1 📁 Daily Lecture and Discussion Notes 9–1 📁 Vocabulary Activity 9–1 📁 Active Reading Note-Taking Guide 9–1 📁 Guided Reading Activity 9–1* 📁 Section Quiz 9–1* 📁 Reading Essentials and Study Guide 9–1*	📜 Daily Focus Skills Transparency 9–1 💿 Interactive Tutor Self-Assessment CD-ROM 💿 ExamView® Pro Testmaker CD-ROM 💿 Presentation Plus! CD-ROM
Section 2 **The Fall of Rome** 1. Poor leadership, a declining economy, and attacks by Germanic tribes weakened the Roman Empire during the A.D. 400s. 2. Rome passed on many achievements in government, law, language, and the arts.	📁 Reproducible Lesson Plan 9–2 📁 Daily Lecture and Discussion Notes 9–2 📁 Vocabulary Activity 9–2 📁 Active Reading Note-Taking Guide 9–2 📁 Guided Reading Activity 9–2* 📁 Section Quiz 9–2* 📁 Reading Essentials and Study Guide 9–2*	📜 Daily Focus Skills Transparency 9–2 💿 Interactive Tutor Self-Assessment CD-ROM 💿 ExamView® Pro Testmaker CD-ROM 💿 Presentation Plus! CD-ROM 💿 Glencoe BookLink CD-ROM
Section 3 **The Byzantine Empire** 1. The Eastern Roman, or Byzantine, Empire, which was based on Roman, Greek, and Christian ideas, grew rich and powerful as the Western Roman Empire fell apart. 2. The policies of Justinian and Theodora enabled the Byzantine Empire to survive for centuries.	📁 Reproducible Lesson Plan 9–3 📁 Daily Lecture and Discussion Notes 9–3 📁 Vocabulary Activity 9–3 📁 Active Reading Note-Taking Guide 9–3 📁 Guided Reading Activity 9–3* 📁 Section Quiz 9–3* 📁 Reading Essentials and Study Guide 9–3*	📜 Daily Focus Skills Transparency 9–3 💿 Interactive Tutor Self-Assessment CD-ROM 💿 ExamView® Pro Testmaker CD-ROM 💿 Presentation Plus! CD-ROM 💿 Vocabulary PuzzleMaker CD-ROM 💿 Glencoe BookLink CD-ROM

*Also available in Spanish

History Online

Use our Web site for additional resources. All essential content is covered in the Student Edition.

You and your students can visit jat.glencoe.com, the Web site companion to *World History: Journey Across Time*. This innovative integration of electronic and print media offers your students a wealth of opportunities. The student text directs students to the Web site for the following options:

- Chapter Overviews
- Self-Check Quizzes
- Study Central™
- Student Web Activities
- Multi-Language Glossaries

Answers to the student Web activities are provided for you in the **Web Activity Lesson Plans.** Additional Web resources and ePuzzles and games are also available.

The following videotape programs are available from Glencoe as supplements to Chapter 9:

Rome's Glorious Cities
(ISBN 0-7670-0611-9)

Constantine: The Christian Emperor
(ISBN 0-7670-0577-5)

Justinian: The Last of the Romans
(ISBN 0-7670-0579-1)

To order, call Glencoe at 1-800-334-7344. To find classroom resources to accompany many of these videos, check the following home pages:

A&E Television: www.aande.com
The History Channel: www.historychannel.com

MEETING SPECIAL NEEDS

In addition to the Differentiated Instruction strategies, the following resources are suitable for students with special needs:

- *ExamView® Pro Testmaker CD-ROM* allows teachers to tailor tests by reducing answer choices.
- *StudentWorks Plus™ CD-ROM (with Audio Program)* includes the entire narrative of the student edition so that less-proficient readers can listen to the words as they read them.
- The *Reading Essentials and Study Guide* provides the same content as the student edition but is written two grade levels below the textbook.

NATIONAL GEOGRAPHIC — TEACHER'S CORNER

Index to National Geographic Magazine:
The following articles relate to this chapter:

- "Crucible of the Gods: Black Sea Culture," by Erla Zwingle, September 2002.
- "Istanbul on Edge," by Rick Gore, October 2002.
- "The World According to Rome, Part 2," by T.R. Reid, August 1997.

National Geographic Society Products:
To order the following, call National Geographic at 1–800–368–2728

- *NGS PictureShow: Ancient Civilizations: Greece and Rome* (CD-ROM)
- *National Geographic Atlas of the World* (Book)

NGS ONLINE

Access National Geographic's new dynamic MapMachine Web site and other geography resources at:

www.nationalgeographic.com
www.nationalgeographic.com/maps

Meeting NCSS Standards

World History: Journey Across Time
The following standards are highlighted in Chapter 9:

Section 1
- **IV** Individual Development and Identity: C, D, E
- **V** Individuals, Groups, and Institutions: A, B, C, E
- **IX** Global Connections: A

Section 2
- **II** Time, Continuity, and Change: B, C, E
- **VI** Power, Authority, and Governance: C, E, F
- **VII** Production, Distribution, and Consumption: C, E, H
- **X** Civic Ideals and Practices: A

Section 3
- **I** Culture: B, C, D
- **III** People, Places, and Environments: A, B, G

State and Local Objectives

_____

_____

Timesaving Tools

TeacherWorks
All-In-One Planner and Resource Center

- **Interactive Teacher Edition** Access your Teacher Wraparound Edition and your classroom resources with a few easy clicks.
- **Interactive Lesson Planner** Organize your week, month, semester, or year with all the lesson helps you need to make teaching creative and relevant.

Use Glencoe's **Presentation Plus!** multimedia teacher tool to easily present dynamic lessons that visually excite your students. Using Microsoft PowerPoint® you can customize the presentations to create your own personalized lessons.

FOLDABLES™
Study Organizer
Dinah Zike's Foldables

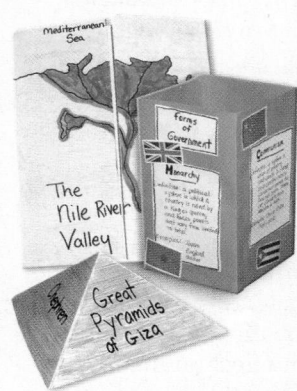

Foldables are three-dimensional, interactive graphic organizers that help students practice basic writing skills, review key vocabulary terms, and identify main ideas. Every chapter contains a foldable activity, with additional chapter activities found in the *Reading and Study Skills Foldables* booklet. You can use the foldables as they are presented, or modify them to suit the needs of your individual class.

Planning Ahead

CHAPTER CULMINATING ACTIVITY

The Chapter Culminating Activity will help students organize and learn the important information from the chapter. Begin the chapter with this activity, and have students complete it as a culminating activity.

CREATING A PROBLEM AND SOLUTION CHART

Purpose This type of organizer helps students organize and analyze information by identifying particular problems and their possible solutions. Because this chapter focuses on the serious challenges faced by both the eastern and western halves of the Roman Empire, a problem and solution chart is especially useful. Identifying and analyzing the problems discussed in the chapter will help students see the complexity of the issues. Suggesting possible solutions, whether they were tried or not, gives students practice in logical and systematic thinking. In addition, this type of chart can be used to organize information for reports and as a study aid.

Introduction to Modeling

1. Begin the discussion with a brainstorming session. Ask students to list what they know or believe they know about the decline and fall of the Roman Empire. Write the information on the board or an overhead transparency.

2. Ask students to copy this chart into their notebooks:

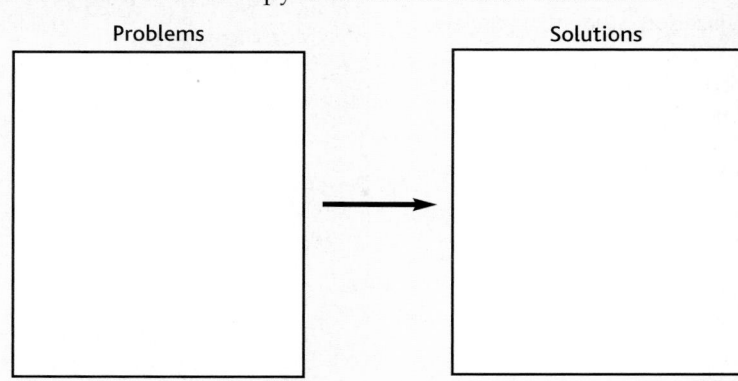

As students read the chapter, ask them to complete the boxes with appropriate problems and solutions. For example, one problem might be "Attacks by Germanic tribes on the borders of the empire." A solution might be "Shrink the empire so that its new borders are defensible."

3. As part of your chapter review, have students share their problem and solution charts. Encourage them to use their charts as study aids.

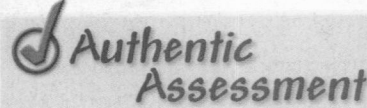
Refer to Activity 9 in the Authentic Assessment section of the *Quizzes, Tests, and Authentic Assessment (with Rubrics)* booklet.

When & Where?

As students read the chapter, have them review the time line on this page. Ask them which event probably had the most important effect on life in the Roman Empire. *(the division of the empire into eastern and western parts)* **L1**

GLENCOE TECHNOLOGY

World History: Journey Across Time Video Program

To learn more about Roman civilization, students can view the Chapter 9 video in the *World History: Journey Across Time* Video Program.

MindJogger Videoquiz

Use the **MindJogger Videoquiz** to preview Chapter 9 content.

Available in DVD and VHS

Chapter 9

Roman Civilization

▼ The Colosseum in Rome, Italy

NATIONAL GEOGRAPHIC When & Where?

100 B.C.	A.D. 100	A.D. 300	A.D. 500
	c. 10 B.C. Livy writes his *History of Rome*	A.D. 395 Roman Empire divided into eastern and western parts	A.D. 527 Emperor Justinian begins rule

---

Reading Strategy — PURPOSE FOR READING

Analyzing Remind students about the rise and fall of several civilizations they may have already studied: Egypt, Mesopotamia, Israel, Greece, India, and China. **Ask:** What are some of the factors that contributed to the downfall or weakening of these earlier civilizations? *(war and military threats from neighbors, natural disasters, bad rulers, social disorder, poverty and inequality, economic pressures)* As they read, have students watch for the role these factors played, or did not play, in the decline and fall of the Roman Empire. **L2**

Chapter Preview

The Romans developed a civilization as well as an empire. Read this chapter to find out about Roman achievements that still influence your life today.

 View the Chapter 9 video in the *World History: Journey Across Time* Video Program.

Chapter Overview Visit jat.glencoe.com for a preview of Chapter 9.

 Section 1 Life in Ancient Rome

The Romans learned from the Greeks but changed what they borrowed to suit their own needs. The lives of rich and poor Romans were very different.

 Section 2 The Fall of Rome

Rome finally fell when Germanic invaders swept through the empire in the A.D. 400s. Roman achievements in government, law, language, and the arts are still important today.

 Section 3 The Byzantine Empire

As the Western Roman Empire fell, the Eastern Roman, or Byzantine, Empire grew rich and powerful. The Byzantines developed a culture based on Roman, Greek, and Christian ideas.

 FOLDABLES™ Study Organizer

Organizing Information *Make this foldable to help you organize and analyze information by asking yourself questions about Roman civilization.*

Step 1 *Fold a sheet of paper into thirds from top to bottom.*

Step 2 *Turn the paper horizontally, unfold, and label the three columns as shown.*

Life in Ancient Rome | The Fall of Rome | The Byzantine Empire

Reading and Writing *As you read the chapter, write the main ideas for each section in the appropriate columns of your foldable. Then write one statement that summarizes the main ideas in each column.*

299

INTRODUCING CHAPTER 9

History Online

Introduce students to chapter content and key terms by having them access **Chapter Overview 9** at jat.glencoe.com

CHAPTER PREVIEW

After reading Chapter 9, students will be able to

1. discuss the cultural achievements of the Romans and describe the daily lives of people in Rome;

2. explain why the Roman Empire fell and summarize its legacy in law, government, language, and the arts;

3. describe the rise and cultural accomplishments of the Byzantine Empire.

FOLDABLES™ Study Organizer
Dinah Zike's Foldables

Purpose Students use this foldable to organize the main ideas in each section. Students then summarize the main ideas for each section in one sentence.

☞ Have students complete *Reading and Study Skills Foldables* Activity 9.

MORE ABOUT THE PHOTO

The Colosseum In the ancient world, the Colosseum was the largest elliptical shaped building. It stood 160 feet (49 m) high with four stories of windows, arches, and columns. Thousands of spectators came in through entrances on the ground level. Upon entering the Colosseum, spectators climbed sloping ramps to their seats. People were seated according to their social group and gender. As a result, the poor and women were assigned to the fourth level. Gladiators and animals waited in underground areas until it was time for them to enter the arena.

1 Learn It!

Explain to students that they can read and understand new material by drawing on their own thoughts and experiences. Ask them to respond to the passage below by discussing their reflections about the text. Point out that there are no right or wrong answers to an assignment of this type.

Example Passage: Roman authors influenced later writers in Europe and America, but the language of the Romans, Latin, had an even bigger impact on future generations. Latin became Europe's language for government, trade, and learning until about A.D. 1500. Latin became the basis of many modern European languages, such as Italian, French, and Spanish, and shaped many others. Many of the English words we use today come from Latin.

If students have trouble responding freely, use the following question and activity to encourage discussion:

Is there a language today that has the same impact on government, trade, and learning as Latin did? If so, what is it?

Have students create a list of vocabulary words they have learned in this course. Then have them look up some of the words in a dictionary or with an Internet source to figure out if they have a Latin origin. **L1**

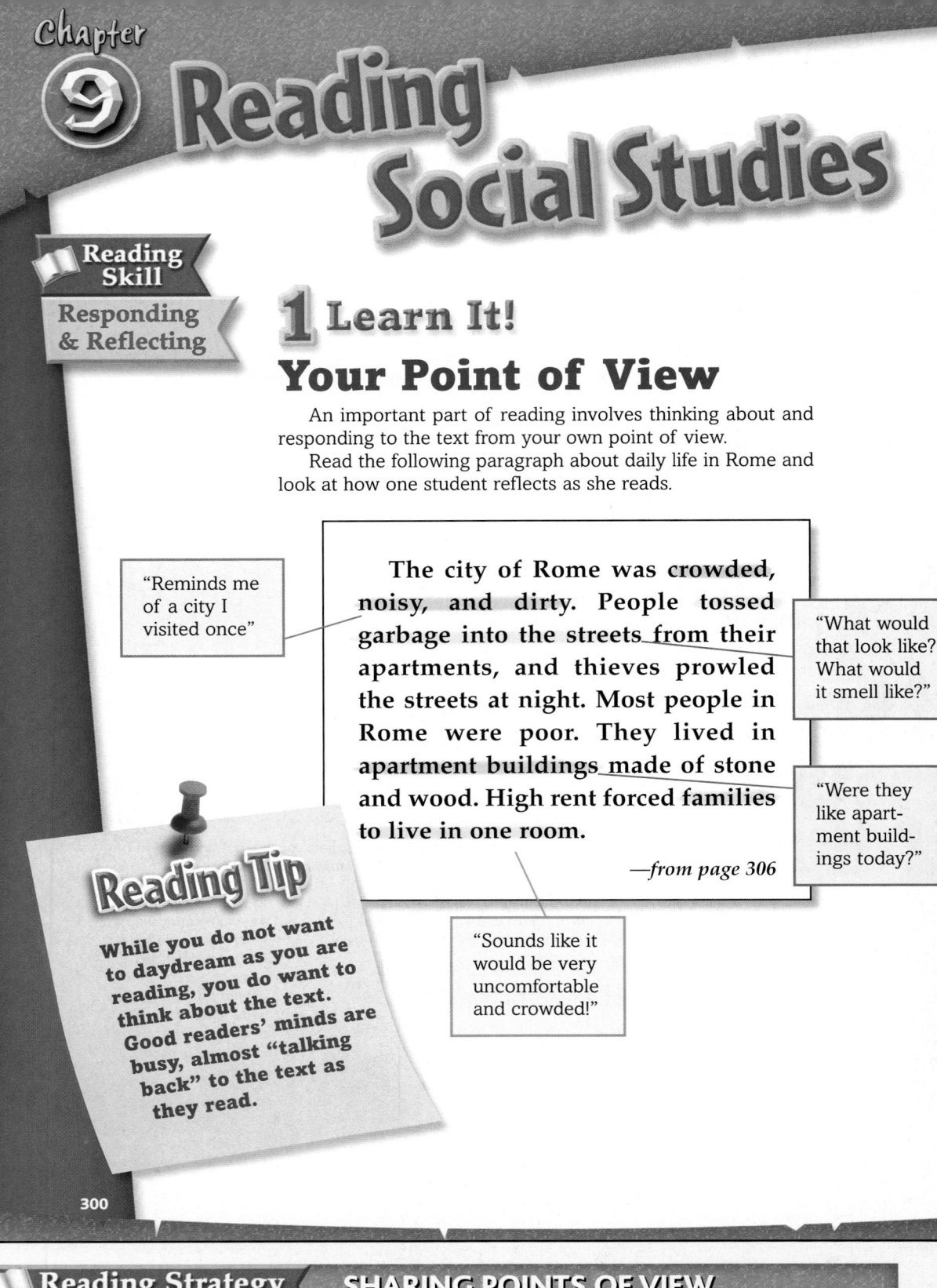

Chapter 9 Reading Social Studies

Reading Skill
Responding & Reflecting

1 Learn It!
Your Point of View

An important part of reading involves thinking about and responding to the text from your own point of view.

Read the following paragraph about daily life in Rome and look at how one student reflects as she reads.

"Reminds me of a city I visited once"

The city of Rome was **crowded, noisy, and dirty.** People tossed garbage into the streets from their apartments, and thieves prowled the streets at night. Most people in Rome were poor. They lived in **apartment buildings made of stone and wood.** High rent forced **families** to live in one room.

—*from page 306*

"What would that look like? What would it smell like?"

"Were they like apartment buildings today?"

"Sounds like it would be very uncomfortable and crowded!"

Reading Tip

While you do not want to daydream as you are reading, you do want to think about the text. Good readers' minds are busy, almost "talking back" to the text as they read.

Reading Strategy **SHARING POINTS OF VIEW**

An effective means of engaging all students in the learning process is to have them share their points of view. After students read a section, either individually or in pairs, ask them a question about the content—one that cannot be answered by yes or no. Then allow a few minutes for each student to ponder the question or prompt silently. Next, give partners two minutes apiece to relay their thoughts on the topic to one another. Finally, call on various pairs to share with the entire class. This strategy ensures that all students are participating, reflecting, and engaging in cooperative learning.

2 Practice It!

Reflect and Respond

Read the following paragraph. Take a few minutes to reflect on what you have read and then respond by exchanging thoughts with a partner. Some suggested topics are listed below.

Read to Write ....

In Section 2, you will read why historians believe the Roman Empire fell. Choose one of the reasons and respond to it, explaining why you think this is the most likely reason for the decline of the Roman Empire.

> Between the ages of 14 and 16, a Roman boy celebrated becoming a man. He would burn his toys as offerings to the household gods. Then he would put on a toga, a loose-fitting robe that Roman men wore. Once he came of age, a man might join his family's business, become a soldier, or begin a career in the government. Roman women did not become adults until they married. A woman usually wore a long flowing robe with a cloak called a *palla*.
>
> —*from pages 307–308*

- Do boys do anything today to show that they have become men?
- What does a toga look like? What does a *palla* look like?
- Why did a woman have to wait until she married to become an adult?
- Why were boys and girls treated so differently?

3 Apply It!

As you read, keep a reader's notebook. Record responses to facts or ideas that you find interesting.

301

2 Practice It!

Use part of the text to model a reflect-and-respond activity. Encourage students to "talk" to themselves as they are reading the first paragraph under the heading "Roman Culture" in Section 1. Have them record any responses on a sheet of paper. Then read the first two sentences aloud. Ask volunteers to share how they responded to any of that text. If no one did, assure students that is all right, but share some possible responses: "Why did the Romans copy the Greeks?" and "That's surprising. The Romans defeated the Greeks." Repeat the process with the next sentence. A possible response might be "That sounds more like the Romans." Last, do the same with the final sentences in the paragraph. A possible response might be "So the Romans were practical and thought the Greeks weren't." **L1**

3 Apply It!

Point out that notebooks state personal reactions to the text. There are no right or wrong facts and ideas to respond to. After students have read each section, ask volunteers to share their responses. **L1/ EL**

Reading Strategy   READ TO WRITE

Have students write their responses as an editorial for a Roman newspaper. In their editorials, students should focus on one problem that led to Rome's fall. They should state what the problem was, what effects it had on Rome and its people, and why they think it was the most likely reason for Rome's fall. **L2**

① FOCUS

SECTION OVERVIEW

This section discusses the cultural achievements and daily life of the Roman people during the height of the empire.

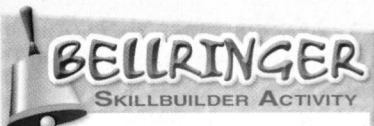
BELLRINGER
SKILLBUILDER ACTIVITY

✋ Project **Daily Focus Skills Transparency 9–1** and have students answer questions. Discuss their responses.

Get Ready to Read!

Preteaching Vocabulary: Tell students that the Latin word *forum* described the public center of a Roman town.

Answers to Graphic: Roman Rich: lived in large, comfortable houses; hired tutors to teach younger children; older boys went to school; had villas on estates; used slave labor; Roman Poor: lived in cramped conditions in poorly built buildings; their children received no education; enjoyed "bread and circuses"; Both: attended chariot races and gladiator contests

Section ① Life in Ancient Rome

Get Ready to Read!

What's the Connection?
You have already learned about Rome's rise to power. Life in Rome was not easy, but as the empire grew, its people accomplished many things in art, science, and engineering.

Focusing on the Main Ideas
• In addition to their own developments in science and engineering, Roman artists and writers borrowed many ideas from the Greeks. *(page 303)*

• The rich and poor had very different lives in the Roman Empire, as did men and women. *(page 306)*

Meeting People
Virgil (VUHR•juhl)
Horace (HAWR•uhs)
Galen (GAY•luhn)
Ptolemy (TAH•luh•mee)
Spartacus (SPAHR•tuh•kuhs)

Building Your Vocabulary
vault (VAWLT)
satire (SA•TYR)
ode (OHD)
anatomy (uh•NA•tuh•mee)
Forum (FOHR•uhm)
gladiator (GLA•dee•AY•tuhr)
paterfamilias (PA•tuhr•fuh•MIH•lee•uhs)
rhetoric (REH•tuh•rihk)

Reading Strategy
Compare and Contrast Use a Venn diagram like the one below to show similarities and differences between the rich and the poor in Rome.

Roman Rich — Roman Poor

NATIONAL GEOGRAPHIC **When & Where?**

BRITAIN
GAUL GREECE
SPAIN ITALY
Rome•
•Constantinople
PALESTINE—
EGYPT

100 B.C.	A.D. 1	A.D. 100
73 B.C. Spartacus leads revolt of enslaved people	c. 10 B.C. Livy writes his *History of Rome*	c. A.D. 80 Colosseum completed

SECTION RESOURCES

📁 **Reproducible Masters**
• Reproducible Lesson Plan 9–1
• Daily Lecture and Discussion Notes 9–1
• Vocabulary Activity 9–1
• Active Reading Note-Taking Guide 9–1
• Guided Reading Activity 9–1
• Section Quiz 9–1
• Reading Essentials and Study Guide 9–1

📊 **Transparencies**
• Daily Focus Skills Transparency 9–1

Multimedia
🖥 Interactive Tutor Self-Assessment CD-ROM
🖥 ExamView® Pro Testmaker CD-ROM
🖥 Presentation Plus! CD-ROM

Roman Culture

Main Idea In addition to their own developments in science and engineering, Roman artists and writers borrowed many ideas from the Greeks.

Reading Focus Are there people in your life that you admire? What have you learned from them? Read to find out what the Romans learned from the Greeks.

The Romans admired and studied Greek statues, buildings, and ideas. They copied the Greeks in many ways. However, they changed what they borrowed to suit their own needs. In one important way, the Romans were very different from the Greeks. The Greeks loved to talk about ideas. To the Romans, ideas were only important if they could solve everyday problems.

What Was Roman Art Like? The Romans admired Greek art and architecture. They placed Greek-style statues in their homes and public buildings. Roman artists, however, carved statues that looked different from those of the Greeks. Greek statues were made to look perfect. People were shown young, healthy, and with beautiful bodies. Roman statues were more realistic and included wrinkles, warts, and other less attractive features.

In building, the Romans also turned to the Greeks for ideas. They used Greek-style porches and rows of columns called colonnades. But they also added their own features, such as arches and domes. Roman builders were the first to make full use of the arch. Arches supported bridges, aqueducts, and buildings. Rows of arches were often built against one another to form a **vault** (VAWLT), or curved ceiling. Using this technique, the Romans were able to build domes from many rings of shaped stone.

The Romans were the first people to invent and use concrete, a mixture of volcanic ash, lime, and water. When it dried, this mix was as hard as rock. Concrete made buildings sturdier and allowed them to be built taller.

Rome's concrete buildings were so well built that many still stand today. One of the most famous is the Colosseum, completed about A.D. 80. It was a huge arena that could seat about 60,000 people. Another famous building is the Pantheon, a temple built to honor Rome's gods. The Pantheon's domed roof was the largest of its time.

▼ **This Roman bridge still stands in Spain.** *In what other structures were arches used?*

② TEACH

Reading Strategy

Solving Everyday Problems Ask students to read the material under the heading "What Was Roman Art Like?" in Section 1 and list Roman contributions to building and architecture. Then elicit that these are examples of the Roman interest in ideas that solve problems. Have students look for more examples of this characteristic as the class studies this section. **L2**

Daily Lecture and Discussion Notes 9–1

Use **Daily Lecture and Discussion Notes 9–1** for an outline of key concepts found in the section.

More About the Photo

This bridge in Córdoba, Spain, shows little of its Roman origins because of frequent rebuilding over the centuries. However, the bridge's arches and cobbled paving still give a sense of what the original structure looked like.

Caption Answer: aqueducts and buildings

Reading Strategy ⟩ **READING THE TEXT**

Activating Prior Knowledge Have students make a four-column chart with the following headings: What I Know, What I Want to Know, What I Learned, and How I Can Learn More. Next, tell students to skim the headings in the section to find the main topics. List them on the board as volunteers name them. Give students time to complete the first two columns. Then ask volunteers to share portions of what they wrote in those columns. Have students complete their charts as they find answers to their questions. After students have finished the first section, ask volunteers to share what they learned and how they learned it. Then have the class brainstorm ideas for how they can learn more about these topics. Repeat the process after each section. **L2**

Use **Vocabulary Activity 9–1** to review important terms in the section.

Primary Source

Horace praises rural life in this poem. However, though he was born on a farm, Horace himself moved at a young age to Rome. There, he eventually became involved in the city's hectic business and political life. Fortunately for Horace, he was able to spend much of the year at his own farm outside of Rome.

Answer:
dangerous and frustrating things; his examples are war, sailing, and dealing with officials

GLENCOE
BOOKLINK

Use **Glencoe BookLink** to create customized reading lists for your students' reading levels, interests, and abilities.

Primary Source — The Book of Epodes

In this poem excerpt, Horace praises the lifestyle of those who farm their family's land.

"Happy the man who, far from business and affairs

Like mortals of the early times,

May work his father's fields with oxen of his own,

Exempt [free] from profit, loss, and fee,

Not like the soldier roused by savage trumpet's blare,

Not terrified by seas in rage,

Avoiding busy forums and the haughty doors

Of influencial citizens."

—Horace, *The Book of Epodes*

▲ Horace

DBQ Document-Based Question

According to Horace, what kinds of things does the farmer avoid?

Roman Literature Roman authors based much of their writing on Greek works. For example, the Roman writer **Virgil** (VUHR•juhl) drew some of his ideas from Homer's *Odyssey.* Virgil's epic poem, the *Aeneid* (uh•NEE•uhd), describes the adventures of the Trojan prince Aeneas and how he came to Italy. Virgil presents Aeneas as the ideal Roman—brave, self-controlled, and loyal to the gods.

Rome's other famous writers also looked to the Greeks for inspiration. Using Greek models, the poet **Horace** (HAWR•uhs) wrote **satires** (SA•TYRZ). These works poked fun at human weaknesses. Horace also composed **odes** (OHDZ), or poems that express strong emotions about life. The

Roman writer Ovid wrote works that were based on the Greek myths. The poet Catullus also admired Greek writings. He wrote short poems about love, sadness, and envy.

Like the Greeks, Rome's historians recorded the events of their civilization. One of Rome's most famous historians was Livy. He wrote his *History of Rome* about 10 B.C. In this book, Livy describes Rome's rise to power. Livy greatly admired the deeds of the early Romans, and he believed that history had important moral lessons to teach people.

Livy celebrated Rome's greatness, but the Roman historian Tacitus took a darker view. He believed that Rome's emperors had taken people's freedom. Tacitus also thought Romans were losing the values that made them strong. He accused them of wasting time on sports and other pleasures.

Also like the Greeks, the Romans enjoyed plays. Roman plays were often based on Greek tragedies and comedies. Playwrights such as the tragedy writer Seneca and the comedy writers Plautus and Terence wrote plays for religious festivals. Romans especially liked plays with humor.

Roman authors influenced later writers in Europe and America, but the language of the Romans, Latin, had an even bigger impact on future generations. Latin became Europe's language for government, trade, and learning until about A.D. 1500. Latin became the basis of many modern European languages, such as Italian, French, and Spanish, and shaped many others. Many of the English words we use today come from Latin as well.

Roman Science and Engineering The Romans also learned from Greek science. A Greek doctor named **Galen** (GAY•luhn)

DIFFERENTIATED INSTRUCTION

Visual/Spatial: List the following topics on the board: Literature, Art and Architecture, Science and Engineering, Families, Women, Slavery, and Religion. Have students choose one and create a poster that helps clarify Roman achievements or practices related to the topic. Display the posters as the class studies the Roman Empire.

English Learners: Ask students to write two or three sentences describing the content in their classmates' posters.

Gifted and Talented: Have students use computer graphics software to create the posters.

Refer to *Inclusion Strategies for the Middle School Social Studies Classroom* in the TCR.

brought many medical ideas to Rome. For example, he emphasized the importance of **anatomy** (uh•NA•tuh•mee), the study of body structure. To learn about inner organs, Galen cut open dead animals and recorded his findings. Doctors in the West studied Galen's books and drawings for more than 1,500 years.

Another important scientist of the Roman Empire was **Ptolemy** (TAH•luh•mee). Ptolemy lived in Alexandria, in Egypt. He studied the sky and carefully mapped over 1,000 different stars. He also studied the motion of planets and stars and created rules explaining their movements. Even though Ptolemy incorrectly placed Earth at the center of the universe, educated people in Europe accepted his ideas for centuries.

While Roman scientists tried to understand how the world worked, Roman engineers built an astonishing system of roads and bridges to connect the empire. Have you ever heard the saying "All roads lead to Rome"? Roman engineers built roads from Rome to every part of the empire. These roads were well built, and some have survived to this day.

The Romans also used advanced engineering to supply their cities with freshwater. Engineers built aqueducts to bring water from the hills into the cities. Aqueducts were long troughs supported by rows of arches. They carried water over long distances. At one time, 11 great aqueducts fed Rome's homes, bathhouses, fountains, and public bathrooms. Roman cities also had sewers to remove waste.

Reading Check **Explain** How was the character Aeneas an ideal Roman?

The Roman Colosseum

The Colosseum in Rome could hold some 60,000 people. The arena even had a removable canvas awning to protect spectators from the hot Roman sun.
What was concrete made from?

A system of cages, ropes, and pulleys brought wild animals up to the Colosseum floor from rooms underground. ▼

305

TIME TRAVELER

The Appian Way was one of the most important Roman roads. It was begun in 312 B.C. At its height, the Appian Way ran south from Rome to key ports on the "heel" of Italy. Surfaced with hard lava blocks, some of the Appian Way can still be walked on today.

Reading Check

Answer: Virgil gave him the characteristics of an ideal Roman—brave, self-controlled, and loyal to the gods.

More About the Art

Unlike almost all other classical amphitheaters, the Colosseum was free-standing, not built into a hillside. This mammoth structure was even the site of mock naval battles! Although largely intact, it is missing much of the marble and part of the exterior wall because it was quarried for building churches during the Middle Ages.

Caption Answer: volcanic ash, lime, and water

CRITICAL THINKING ACTIVITY

Summarizing Have students review the information on Roman architecture and engineering. Then have them state the ways in which Roman contributions in building and engineering have influenced the appearance of your community. For example, are there buildings with domes or arches, or structures made of concrete? Conclude the activity by having students write a paragraph that summarizes the architectural legacy of Rome as it relates to your community. **L2**

in a word ...

The English word **"circus"** comes from the Latin word *circus,* related to the English word for "circle." The Circus Maximus, or "greatest circle," was a large oval track for races. Ask students how a modern circus relates to this root word.

Writing Activity

The ancient Romans admired champion gladiators, just as people today admire sports heroes. Have students write a letter to the editor of a local newspaper discussing the pros and cons of holding sports figures up as heroes and the responsibilities that major sports figures have to the public. **L3**

NATIONAL GEOGRAPHIC — The Way It Was

Answers:

1. Paintings on vases, frescoes, and stone show Romans participating in sports.

2. Today sports do not feature fights between animals, battles between ships, or contests to the death between gladiators. Similarities may include comparisons between chariot racing and horse racing.

NATIONAL GEOGRAPHIC — The Way It Was

Sports & Contests

Ancient Roman Sports Sports were important to the Romans. Paintings on vases, frescoes [moist plaster], and stone show Romans playing ball, including a version of soccer. Roman girls are shown exercising with handheld weights and throwing an egg-shaped ball. Balls were made of different materials such as wool, hair, linen, sponges, and pig bladders wrapped in string.

Some Roman sporting events took place in the Colosseum, amphitheaters, and the Circus Maximus. Wild beast fights, battles between ships, and gladiator contests attracted Roman spectators by the thousands. Chariot racing was held in the Circus Maximus, and the drivers wore team colors of red, white, green, and blue.

▲ Scene showing gladiators in battle

Connecting to the Past
1. How do we know sports were important to the Romans?
2. How are today's sports different from Roman sports? How are they similar?

Daily Life in Rome

Main Idea The rich and poor had very different lives in Rome, as did men and women.

Reading Focus Do you think there is a big difference in the lives of boys and girls you know today? Why or why not? Read to learn how the lives of Roman boys and girls were very different from each other.

What was it like to live in Rome over 2,000 years ago? Rome was one of the largest cities in the ancient world. By the time of Augustus, over a million people lived there. Rome was carefully planned, as were many Roman cities. It was laid out in a square with the main roads crossing at right angles. At its center was the **Forum** (FOHR•um). This was an open space that served as a marketplace and public square. Temples and public buildings were built around it.

Wealthy Romans lived in large, comfortable houses. Each home had large rooms, fine furniture, and beautiful gardens. In the center was an inner court called an atrium. Wealthy Romans also had homes called villas on their country estates.

The city of Rome was crowded, noisy, and dirty. People tossed garbage into the streets from their apartments, and thieves prowled the streets at night. Most people in Rome were poor. They lived in apartment buildings made of stone and wood. High rent forced families to live in one room.

Roman apartments were up to six stories high. They often collapsed because they were so poorly built. Fire was a constant danger because people used torches and lamps for lighting and cooked with oil. Once started, a fire could destroy entire blocks of apartments.

To keep the people from rioting, the Roman government provided "bread and circuses," or free grain and shows. Romans of all classes flocked to the chariot races and gladiator contests. **Gladiators** (GLA•dee•AY•tuhrz)

INTERDISCIPLINARY CONNECTIONS ACTIVITY

Daily Life To give students an idea of what a chariot race was like, show them the chariot race in the movie *Ben Hur.* First, begin by explaining the background of the story. The featured charioteers in the race are Judah Ben-Hur, a Jew, who is racing to defeat Messala, a Roman who had been a friend but betrayed him. Tell students to notice the following: what the Circus Maximus looked like *(U-shaped; low decorated wall in the center, running almost the entire length; spectators along the length and at both ends),* and what a race was like *(chariots pulled by horses; were several competitors; lasted for seven laps; some charioteers were killed).* Ask students if they would or would not like to see a chariot race as the Romans conducted them and to explain the reasons for their opinions. **L2**

▲ Chariot races were held in an arena called the Circus Maximus, one of the largest arenas ever made. *Besides chariot races, what other types of shows attracted Romans?*

fought animals and each other. Most gladiators were enslaved people, criminals, or poor people. Gladiators were admired, much like sports heroes are today.

What Was Family Life Like? Family life was important to the Romans. Their families were large. They included not only parents and young children but also married children and their families, other relatives, and enslaved servants. The father was the head of the household. Called the **paterfamilias** (PA•tuhr•fuh•MIH•lee•uhs), or "father of the family," he had complete control over family members. For example, he punished children severely if they disobeyed. He also arranged their marriages.

In some cases, the paterfamilias made sure his children were educated. Poor Romans could not afford to send their children to school. Wealthy Romans, however, hired tutors to teach their young children at home. Some older boys did go to schools, where they learned reading, writing, and **rhetoric** (REH•tuh•rihk), or public speaking.

Older girls did not go to school. Instead, they studied reading and writing at home. They also learned household duties.

Between the ages of 14 and 16, a Roman boy celebrated becoming a man. He would burn his toys as offerings to the household gods. Then he would put on a toga, a loose-fitting robe that Roman men wore. Once he came of age, a man might join his family's business, become a soldier, or begin a career

▼ A Roman teacher and student

307

HISTORY Mystery

How Do We Know About Daily Life in Ancient Rome?
In August of the year A.D. 79, Mount Vesuvius in southern Italy erupted. The town of Pompeii was covered in volcanic ash and debris in a single day. Nearby Herculaneum was buried in mud and lava. Because the volcanic material covered everything so completely, historians can study everyday Roman life frozen as it was at the time of the eruption. These towns are among the most famous archaeological sites in the world.

More About the Art

The two main parts of the Roman *domus,* or single-family house, were the *atrium* and the *peristyle.* The atrium was a large central courtyard with an opening in the roof. Public functions, such as greeting guests, took place in the atrium. The peristyle included the dining room and bedrooms.

Caption Answer:
similar—made of bricks; different—no windows; central courtyard

---

in the government. Roman women did not become adults until they married. A woman usually wore a long flowing robe with a cloak called a *palla.*

Women in Rome Women in early Rome had some rights, but they were not full citizens. The paterfamilias looked after his wife and controlled her affairs. However, he often sought her advice in private. Women had a strong influence on their families, and some wives of famous men, including emperors, became well-known themselves. For example, the empress Livia (LIHV•ee•uh), wife of Augustus, had a say in Rome's politics. She was later honored as a goddess.

The freedoms a Roman woman enjoyed depended on her husband's wealth and standing. Wealthy women had a great deal of independence. They could own land, run businesses, and sell property. They managed the household and had enslaved people do the housework. This left the women free to study literature, art, and fashion. Outside the home, they could go to the theater or the amphitheater, but in both places they had to sit in areas separate from men.

Women with less money had less freedom. They spent most of their time working in their houses or helping their husbands in family-run shops. They were allowed to leave home to shop, visit friends, worship at temples, or go to the baths. A few women did work independently outside the home. Some served as priestesses, while others worked as hairdressers and even doctors.

A Roman House

▼ Wealthy Romans often lived in spacious houses with central courtyards. The houses had high brick walls without windows. Many of the rooms opened into the courtyard to allow in light and fresh air. *How is a Roman home similar to homes in your neighborhood? How is it different?*

A Roman ▶ couple

Rainwater from the gutters collected in the pool below.

Guests and business associates were entertained in the living room/study.

Some homes had shops or workshops that opened onto the street.

Courtyard

Kitchen

Library

In the dining room, family members ate while reclining on couches.

Bedrooms

CITIZENSHIP AND YOU

The Role of Women Have students review the text discussion about the role of women in ancient Rome. Then ask small groups to stage a short debate about this statement: Women in the United States today are better off than women in ancient Rome. Groups should support their arguments with evidence from the text, research, previous knowledge, and sound reasoning. Encourage students supporting the opposing view to consider ways in which ancient Roman women may have had some material or social advantages over women today. **L3**

📂 Refer to the *Quizzes, Tests, and Authentic Assessment (with Rubrics)* booklet for rubrics.

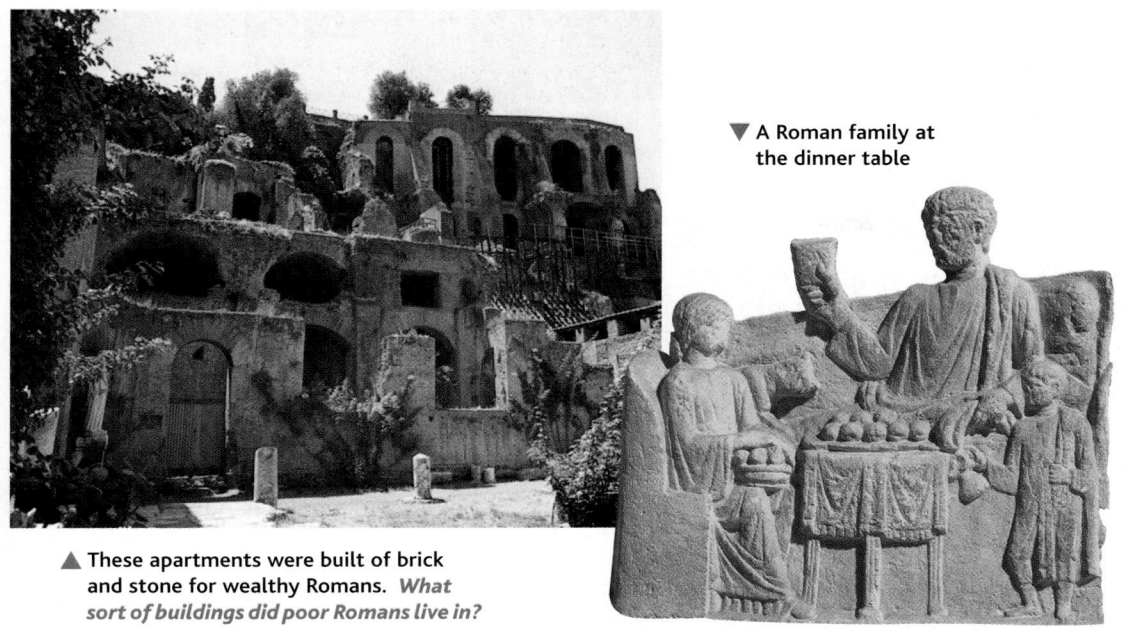

▼ A Roman family at the dinner table

▲ These apartments were built of brick and stone for wealthy Romans. *What sort of buildings did poor Romans live in?*

How Did Romans Treat Enslaved People?

Slavery was a part of Roman life from early times. But the use of slave labor grew as Rome took over more territory. Thousands of prisoners from conquered lands were brought to Italy. Most spent their lives performing slave labor. By 100 B.C., about 40 percent of the people in Italy were enslaved.

Enslaved people did many different jobs. They worked in homes, fields, mines, and workshops. They helped build roads, bridges, and aqueducts. Many enslaved Greeks were well educated. They served as teachers, doctors, and artisans. Enslaved people who earned wages usually were able to buy their freedom.

For most enslaved people, life was miserable. They were punished severely for poor work or for running away. To escape their hardships, enslaved people often rebelled.

In 73 B.C. a slave revolt broke out in Italy. It was led by a gladiator named **Spartacus** (SPAHR•tuh•kuhs). Under Spartacus, a force of 70,000 enslaved people defeated several Roman armies. The revolt was finally crushed two years later. Spartacus and 6,000 of his followers were crucified, or put to death by nailing on a cross.

Roman Religion The ancient Romans worshiped many gods and goddesses. They also believed that spirits lived in natural things, such as trees and rivers. Greek gods and goddesses were popular in Rome, although they were given Roman names. For example, Zeus became Jupiter, the sky god, and Aphrodite became Venus, the goddess of love and beauty. Roman emperors also were worshiped. This practice strengthened support for the government.

Romans honored their gods and goddesses by praying and offering food. Every Roman home had an altar for their household gods. At these altars, the head of the family carried out rituals. Government officials made offerings in temples. There the important gods and goddesses of Rome were honored. Some Roman priests looked for messages from the gods. They studied

CHAPTER 9   Roman Civilization   309

ENRICH

Ask students to research the rebellion led by Spartacus in 73 B.C. Have them share their findings with the class. **L3**

Reading Check

Answer: Only upper-class women could own land, run businesses, sell property, and go to the theater and amphitheater.

History Online

To help students understand section material, have them visit **Study Central™** at jat.glencoe.com

RETEACH

Elicit from students how the lives of Roman boys were different from those of girls. **L1**

④ CLOSE

Reading Strategy

List the following headings on the board and have students list several facts under each one: The Arts, Science and Engineering, Family Life, Slavery, and Religion. Use the information to have students briefly summarize the chapter. **L2**

◄ Minerva, goddess of wisdom ▶

Greek and Roman Gods

Greek God	Roman God	Role
Ares	Mars	god of war
Zeus	Jupiter	chief god
Hera	Juno	wife of chief god
Aphrodite	Venus	goddess of love
Artemis	Diana	goddess of the hunt
Athena	Minerva	goddess of wisdom
Hermes	Mercury	messenger god
Hades	Pluto	god of the underworld
Poseidon	Neptune	god of the sea
Hephaestus	Vulcan	god of fire

the insides of dead animals or watched the flight of birds, looking for meaning.

As the empire grew larger, Romans came into contact with other religions. These religions were allowed, as long as they did not threaten the government.

Those that did faced severe hardships. You will read about one of these religions—Christianity—in the next chapter.

Reading Check **Contrast** Describe the freedoms of upper-class women that were not available to women of other classes.

History Online

Study Central™ Need help with the material in this section? Visit jat.glencoe.com

Section ① Review

Reading Summary
Review the Main Ideas

• Roman art, literature, and science borrowed much from the Greeks. Roman engineers made advances, including the development of cement, the arch, aqueducts, and domes.

• Religion and family were important parts of Roman life. Enslaved people carried out many different tasks in Roman society.

What Did You Learn?

1. What were some of Ptolemy's scientific achievements?

2. How were the Roman and Greek religions similar?

Critical Thinking

3. **Compare and Contrast** Draw a chart like the one below. Fill in details to compare and contrast Roman and Greek art and architecture.

Greek Art	Roman Art
Greek Architecture	Roman Architecture

4. **Analyze** Explain the importance of the language of the Romans.

5. **Describe** Describe the education of Roman children.

6. **Conclude** The Romans borrowed ideas from other peoples. Do you think our culture today borrows ideas from other peoples? Explain your answer.

7. **Reading** Responding and Reflecting Look at the art showing the Roman house on page 308. Write five things that come to mind as you view this picture.

310 CHAPTER 9 Roman Civilization

SECTION 1 REVIEW ANSWERS

1. mapped more than 1,000 stars; studied the motions of the planets
2. The Romans adopted Greek gods and gave them Roman names.
3. Greek Art: sculptors tried to show an ideal image; Roman Art: sculptors made realistic statues; Greek Architecture: used porches, colonnades, and rectangular buildings; Roman Architecture: borrowed Greek styles; used the arch, vault, dome, and concrete
4. Answers should be based on the text.
5. Boys in rich families learned reading, writing, and rhetoric. Girls stayed at home to learn reading, writing, and how to manage households.
6. Answers will vary but should demonstrate a thoughtful response.
7. Answers will vary but should be based on the text.

A WILD-GOOSE CHASE
THE STORY OF PHILEMON AND BAUCIS

Retold by Geraldine McCaughrean

Before You Read

The Scene: This story takes place in ancient Rome in the legendary time when gods visited Earth to interact with humans in person.

The Characters: Philemon and Baucis are the man and woman who welcome guests to their home. Clio is their goose. Jupiter and Mercury are two ancient Roman gods.

The Plot: A husband and wife welcome two guests into their cottage. They have no food for the guests, but they do have a pet goose. As the pair try to provide their guests with food, the guests reveal their identities and reward the host and hostess for their generosity.

Vocabulary Preview

fowl: bird

wielding: controlling

gaped: hung open

quills: feathers

hospitality: friendliness and generosity toward guests

ramshackle: falling apart

disintegrated: broke into small pieces

gilded: decorated with gold

preening: grooming and making pretty

Do you know a person who is always friendly and generous, no matter what the circumstances? In this story, a good-natured husband and wife are rewarded when they receive special guests into their home.

SUMMARY

Jupiter and Mercury go in disguise to visit Philemon and his wife, Baucis. The couple invite the strangers for supper and plan to serve their pet goose, Clio. After Clio seeks refuge in Jupiter's lap, the gods reveal themselves and offer to reward Philemon and Baucis for their hospitality. Philemon asks that they be allowed to go on worshiping at Jupiter's altar. Jupiter makes them keepers of a marble temple until their death at the temple door.

Vocabulary Preview Before students begin reading, have them read **Before You Read** and the **Vocabulary Preview.** Point out that difficult words are footnoted throughout the text.

➊ FOCUS

Emphasizing Cultural Values
Explain that myths usually reflect a culture's deeply held beliefs and values. Tell students that this myth focuses on Roman hospitality, which later became an important value in Western cultures.

Reading Strategy ⟩ READING REINFORCEMENT

Monitoring Comprehension Tell students that they should always ask questions about what they read and evaluate the characters, actions, and events to make sure they understand what is happening. Remind them to question and evaluate while they are reading, not just after they have finished. List the following questions on the board: Does this event make sense? What is really going on here? Would this character really say or do this? What is the writer describing? Why? Suggest that students use them while reading this selection. **L1/ EL**

② TEACH

A ACTIVE READING STRATEGIES

INTERPRET Ask students if they think Philemon and Baucis offered hospitality because they suspected their visitors were gods. Have students explain their answer. *(No, because "Philemon and Baucis did not know the two men on their doorstep" and "they had never yet failed to offer a warm welcome to anyone.")*

B CRITICAL THINKING

Drawing Conclusions Tell students to draw a conclusion about Philemon and Baucis's financial state. *(Philemon and Baucis are probably poor because they have no food in the house.)*

C ACTIVE READING STRATEGIES

RESPOND Ask students how they would feel if they were in Baucis and Philemon's situation. *(Answers will vary. Students may say that they would feel sad or angry to be put in that situation but realize that killing their pet is necessary.)*

As You Read

Keep in mind that this story is a myth. Like the Greeks, Romans passed myths from one generation to the next to explain some aspect of the world. Often, the stories involved gods and goddesses as well as humans.

A knock at the door. A pair of passing strangers. Philemon and Baucis did not know the two men on their doorstep, but they had never yet failed to offer a warm welcome to anyone who called at their little cottage. **A**

"Come in! Sit down! My wife will cook you supper!" said Philemon.

His wife tugged at his sleeve. She did not need to say more. Both of them knew there was no food in the house. Not a bite. Baucis and Philemon themselves had been living on eggs and olives for days. There was not even any bread. **B**

Philemon smiled sadly at Baucis, and she smiled sadly back. "It's the goose, is it?" he said.

"The goose it is," she replied.

Clio was all they had left. She was more like a pet than a farmyard fowl. And yet, guests are a blessing sent by the gods, and guests must be fed. So Philemon fetched his sharp ax and Baucis began to chase the goose, trying to drive it into the cottage. **C**

Jupiter sat back in his chair and waited patiently for dinner. "Do you think we should help?" he said to Mercury, hearing the commotion in the yard.

"I know we shall have a wait," replied Mercury.

"Here—you try," said Baucis, passing the ax to Philemon.

The goose was squawking, Baucis was yelping, and Philemon was coughing as he ran **D**

📖 Reading Strategy 〉 VOCABULARY READING TIP

Suffixes The suffix *-ly* can mean "in a certain manner" as in *sadly*, "at a certain time" as in *instantly*, "to a certain degree" as in *probably*, or "like or suited to" as in *priestly*. Have students fold a sheet of paper in half twice to form four columns. Ask them to write a different definition of *-ly* at the top of each column. Then tell students to list *-ly* words that they find in this selection under the correct headings. Have them determine in which column each word fits. For example, when they come across the word *patiently*, they should ask themselves, "Does this word tell me in what manner the character is waiting?" and so on through all four definitions of *-ly*. Explain that knowing the meanings of *-ly* will help students better understand the author's message. **L1**

about wielding the ax. He struck at Clio, but the goose moved, and he demolished a bush. He swung again and hit the wooden pail. The goose shrieked with outrage, then with terror, and slapped about on her big, triangular feet—plat, plat, plat—skidding into their homemade altar piled high with flowers, into the fish-drying rack,[1] into the washing on the tree.[2] Olives rained down on the roof of the shack.

"Do you think we should go?" said Jupiter, as he and Mercury listened to the wild-goose chase and their hungry stomachs growled quietly.

At last Philemon and Baucis cornered the goose against the cottage door. Her orange beak gaped. Philemon raised the ax . . . and Clio bolted backward into the shack, running around the room like a black-footed pillow fight until she caught sight of Jupiter.

Now, animals are not so easily fooled by disguises, and although Jupiter and Mercury were dressed as peasants, in woolen tunics and straw hats, she instantly recognized the King of the gods and threw herself on his mercy. Neck outstretched, eyes bulging, she ran straight between his knees and into his lap. He was overrun with goose.

"A thousand pardons, friend," gasped Baucis, crawling in at the door, her hair stuck with goose quills. "Won't you take an olive while you wait?"

Jupiter stroked the goose, which stood paddling[3] on his thighs, and spat out a few feathers. "Shield me! Save me! Protect me!" said the goose, in the language of geese.

---

[1]**fish-drying rack:** large wooden structure on which fish are hung to dry
[2]**washing on the tree:** laundry hung on the tree branches to dry
[3]**paddling:** moving its feet

313

D LITERARY ELEMENTS

ONOMATOPOEIA Ask students to search the passage for an example of onomatopoeia, or words that imitate a sound. (*squawking, yelping, coughing, shrieked, slapped, and plat*)

E AUTHOR'S CRAFT

MYTH: Figurative Language
Explain that a simile is a comparison of two unlike things, using the words *like* or *as*. Have students find the simile that the author uses to describe Clio in flight. (*like a black-footed pillow fight*)

F ACTIVE READING STRATEGIES

RESPOND Ask students how they might react if they were in the same room with Baucis, Clio, and Jupiter. (*Answers may include that they would laugh at Baucis and Clio.*)

GLENCOE BOOKLINK

Use **Glencoe BookLink** to create customized reading lists for your students' reading levels, interests, and abilities.

DIFFERENTIATED INSTRUCTION

Gifted and Talented: Tell a small group of students to write the myth of Philemon and Baucis in play format—a character's name followed by a colon. Remind them that plays rely on dialogue, so they will have to add dialogue to the basic story. There should be a narrator to introduce the play.

Verbal/Linguistic: Help students rehearse the play and then present it to students in one or more of the lower grades.

Kinesthetic: Have students prepare "costumes" and a few props that could be used in the dramatic production of this myth. Costumes could be as simple as a set of wings made from construction paper for Clio.

WORLD LITERATURE

G AUTHOR'S CRAFT

INDIRECT CHARACTERIZATION Ask students to explain how the author shows that Philemon and Baucis are unusually generous. *(Jupiter himself declares that their "generosity surpasses that of the gods themselves!")*

H ACTIVE READING STRATEGIES

QUESTION Encourage students to ask themselves why Baucis and Philemon think the gods have been good to them. *(Answers may include that Baucis and Philemon are grateful to have each other.)*

I ACTIVE READING STRATEGIES

PREDICT Have students use what they know already about Philemon and Baucis to predict the reward that the couple will ask for. *(Answers may include that Philemon and Baucis will ask for money or food because they are poor and have little to eat.)*

Jupiter tickled it under the beak. "Your hospitality is a marvel, dear Philemon, gentle Baucis. In all my long travels over the face of the world, I have never met such unselfish hosts. Here is your only goose, and you were ready to cook it for us! Your generosity surpasses that of the gods themselves!" — **G**

"Now, sir," said Baucis sternly. "You may be a guest, but I'll have no ill spoken of the gods in this house. Though we have little to offer, the gods have been good to us, have they not, my love?" — **H**

"They have, they have," said Philemon. Mercury concealed a grin.

"And they shall be good to you ever after!" declared Jupiter, rising to his feet. He rose and rose, 'til his head touched the rafters, and his face brightened 'til the room was light as day. His disguise fell away and Mercury folded it small and smaller 'til it fit inside one fist and was gone.

"As you see, I am Jupiter, King of the gods, and this is my messenger, Mercury. We like to travel the world and visit the people whose sacrificial smoke perfumes the halls of Heaven. But travel where we may and stay where we might, we never met with such hospitality as yours! Name any favor and it shall be your reward. A small kingdom, perhaps? A palace? A chest of sea treasure from the vaults of Poseidon?[4] Wings to fly or the gift of prophecy? Name it!" — **I**

Mercury looked uneasy. He had seen the greed and ambition of mortals all too often. This mild-looking couple would probably demand to be gods and to dine at the table of the gods; would ask for immortality or a banner of stars wide as the Milky Way, spelling out "Philemon the Philanthropist,"[5] "Baucis the Beautiful."

Baucis looked at Philemon, and Philemon smiled back and wrung his hat shyly between his hands.

"Almighty Jupiter, you have done our little house such an honor today that we have — **J**

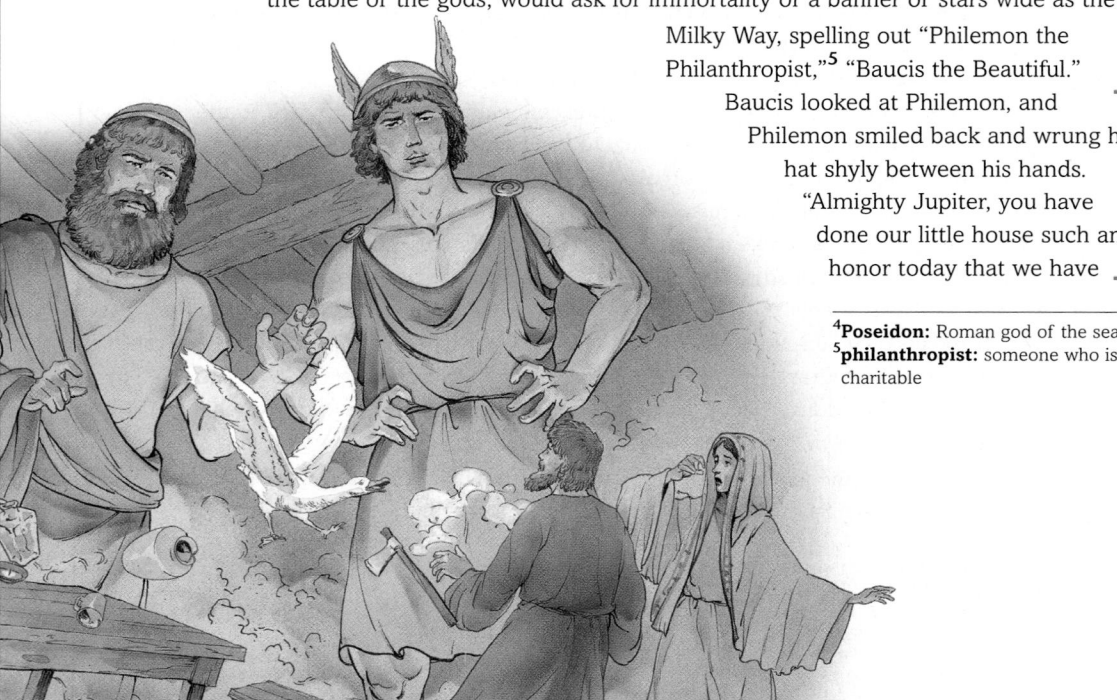

---

[4]**Poseidon:** Roman god of the sea
[5]**philanthropist:** someone who is charitable

CRITICAL THINKING ACTIVITY

Comparing and Contrasting Tell students to fold a sheet of paper in half to form two columns. Have them write "Jupiter" at the top of the first column and "Mercury" at the top of the second. Ask them to list personality traits that each god displays in the story. Suggest that students infer traits from what the gods think, say, and do. For example, they might infer that Mercury is distrustful of humans because he feels uneasy when Jupiter offers to reward Philemon and Baucis. Next, ask volunteers to share their lists of virtues. Then tell students to compare their lists of traits. **Ask:** Based on your comparison, which god would you prefer as a friend? Explain. *(Answers will vary but should include examples from the myth.)*

J LITERARY ELEMENTS

CHARACTERIZATION Explain that an author can convey feeling by having a character act in a certain way. Then ask how the author shows that Philemon feels nervous talking to Jupiter. *(Philemon wrings his hat between his hands as he speaks.)*

K CRITICAL THINKING

CAUSE AND EFFECT Ask students why Jupiter blows his nose loudly and has red-rimmed eyes. *(He is crying because he is touched by the couple's humility and love.)*

L LITERARY ELEMENTS

SETTING Have students describe how the story's setting changes in this passage. *(The ramshackle cottage becomes a richly furnished marble and gold temple.)*

J hardly breath enough to speak our thanks. Our greatest joy in life has always been to worship at our humble little altar—out there in the yard. What more could we ask than to go on doing that—oh, and both to die at the same hour, so that we may never be parted. My Baucis and I."

K Jupiter complained of a speck of dust in his eye and went outside. He could be heard blowing his nose loudly. When he ducked back through the door, his eyes were quite red-rimmed. "Come, priest and priestess of my shrine! Your temple awaits you!"

L All of a sudden, the drafty, ramshackle little hut disintegrated, like a raft of leaves on a river. Around and above it rose the pillars of a mighty temple. The simple cairn[6] of stones that had served for an altar still stood there, piled with firewood and swagged with flowers, but now it stood on a marble floor, and from that floor rose forty marble pillars cloaked with beaten gold, supporting a roof gilded with stars. The living quarters for priest and priestess were piled with feather mattresses and silken pillows, and priestly robes of soft cotton hung waiting about the shoulders of Carrara[7] statues.

---

[6]**cairn:** mound
[7]**Carrara:** an Italian city known for its white marble quarries and statues

315

EXTENDING THE CONTENT

Planets The planets were named for Roman deities because the heavenly bodies shared some trait attributed to their namesake. Jupiter is the largest planet, just as the god Jupiter was king of the gods. Mercury moves across the sky more quickly than the other planets, just as the god Mercury was renowned for his swift flight. The red color of Mars reminds people of Mars, the bloody god of war. The blue color of Neptune recalls the ruler of the deep blue sea—the god Neptune. The starlike brightness of Venus has inspired as many lovers and love stories as Venus, the goddess of love. Finally, the cold, faraway Pluto is as distant from the other planets as the underworld of Pluto was from the heavenly home of the other Roman gods.

DIFFERENTIATED INSTRUCTION

EL Students Ask small groups of students to share stories about geese, ducks, turkeys, and chickens that they might have heard growing up. Then have each group create a comic strip that tells a selected story about a farmyard fowl. Display their comics for the rest of the class to read.

Average Students Ask students to imagine that the couple is selfish and to rewrite the first page to reflect their changed characters.

Gifted Students Ask students to think about what they would have asked Jupiter for if they had been in Baucis and Philemon's place. Then tell students to rewrite the ending of the myth. It should be based on the fact that the writer received his or her requested gift. The story may end well or badly, but the ending should fit the story.

③ ASSESS

Assign the **Responding to the Reading** questions as an in-class activity or as homework.

④ CLOSE

Ask students to change the end of the story by rewriting the last sentence. **L2**

Already, from all corners of the landscape, pilgrims were setting out at a run to visit the marvelous new temple of Jupiter, whose red roof signaled to them across miles of open countryside. Philemon and Baucis would be kept busy receiving their sacrifices, tending the sacrificial flame, sweeping up the ashes.

But they thrived on the hard work, just as they had always done. The worshipers brought not only flowers for the altar but baskets of delicious food for the priest and priestess whose fame spread far and wide. Tirelessly they worked until, being mortal, even Baucis and Philemon became exhausted. Watching from the terraces of Heaven, Jupiter saw them pause now, each time they passed one another, and lean one against the other for a moment's rest, Baucis laying her head on Philemon's shoulder.

"They are weary," said Mercury.

"You are right," said Jupiter. "It is time for them to rest."

So instead of breathing in the fragrance from the altar below, he breathed out—a breath that wafted away the white robes of priest and priestess and left behind two noble trees at the very door of the temple. One was an oak, the other a linden tree, and they leaned one toward another, their branches intertwined, casting welcome shade over the threshold.

Clio the goose liked to rest there at noon, preening her . . . feathers and singing.

Responding to the Reading

1. Why do Philemon and Baucis fail to recognize their guests? Which character does recognize them?

2. Jupiter said that he and Mercury like to "visit the people whose sacrificial smoke perfumes the halls of Heaven." Who does he mean?

3. **Cause and Effect** What is the result of Jupiter's gift to Philemon and Baucis?

4. **Analyze** Why do Philemon and Baucis not ask the gods for fame and power?

5. **Reading** **Read to Write** Imagine that friends who live in another town visit you. What would you provide for them? Would it be different from the things you provide for yourself? Imagine you are Philemon or Baucis, and write one or two paragraphs explaining how you would have treated their guests.

Responding to the Reading Answers

1. The guests are in disguise. Clio, the goose, recognizes them.

2. people who make sacrifices to the gods

3. The couple work at the temple; they have plenty of food, nice clothes, and a comfortable place in which to live.

4. They are content and happy with their lives.

5. Answers should be thoughtful and explain the students' motivations.

Section 2

The Fall of Rome

Get Ready to Read!

What's the Connection?

In Section 1, you learned about Roman life and achievements when the empire was at its height. Over time, however, the Roman Empire began to have problems, and it gradually grew weaker. Eventually, Rome fell to outside invaders.

Focusing on the Main Ideas

- Poor leadership, a declining economy, and attacks by Germanic tribes weakened the Roman Empire. *(page 318)*

- Rome finally fell when invaders swept through the empire during the A.D. 400s. *(page 322)*

- Rome passed on many achievements in government, law, language, and the arts. *(page 325)*

Locating Places

Constantinople
(KAHN•STAN•tuhn•OH•puhl)

Meeting People

Diocletian (DY•uh•KLEE•shuhn)
Constantine (KAHN•stuhn•TEEN)
Theodosius
   (THEE•uh•DOH•shuhs)
Alaric (A•luh•rihk)
Odoacer (OH•duh•WAY•suhr)

Building Your Vocabulary

plague (PLAYG)
inflation (ihn•FLAY•shuhn)
barter (BAHR•tuhr)
reform (rih•FAWRM)

Reading Strategy

Sequencing Information Create a diagram to show the events that led up to the fall of the Western Roman Empire.

```
┌────┐   ┌────┐   ┌──────────┐
│    │ → │    │ → │ Fall of the│
└────┘   └────┘   │   Roman    │
                  │  Empire    │
                  └──────────┘
```

NATIONAL GEOGRAPHIC When & Where?

BRITAIN
GAUL
SPAIN ITALY
   Rome•
      •Constantinople
   GREECE
      EGYPT

A.D. 250	A.D. 350	A.D. 450

A.D. 284
Diocletian tries to reform empire

A.D. 395
Roman Empire divided into eastern and western parts

A.D. 476
Rome's last emperor overthrown

---

1 FOCUS

SECTION OVERVIEW

This section chronicles the decline and fall of the Roman Empire and discusses the empire's important legacy.

BELLRINGER
SKILLBUILDER ACTIVITY

Project **Daily Focus Skills Transparency 9–2** and have students answer questions. Discuss their responses.

Get Ready to Read!

Preteaching Vocabulary: Explain that the word *barter* means "to exchange goods without using money." Have students describe a time when they bartered to obtain goods or services. Tell students that in this section they will read how hard economic times forced Romans to barter.

Answers to Graphic: Visigoths defeat Rome at Battle of Adrianople in A.D. 378; Visigoths capture Rome in A.D. 410; Vandals loot Rome in A.D. 455; Odoacer removes Romulus Augustulus from power in A.D. 476; Theodoric sets up Visigoth kingdom in Italy

---

SECTION RESOURCES

Reproducible Masters
- Reproducible Lesson Plan 9–2
- Daily Lecture and Discussion Notes 9–2
- Vocabulary Activity 9–2
- Active Reading Note-Taking Guide 9–2
- Guided Reading Activity 9–2
- Section Quiz 9–2
- Reading Essentials and Study Guide 9–2

Transparencies
- Daily Focus Skills Transparency 9–2

Multimedia
- Interactive Tutor Self-Assessment CD-ROM
- ExamView® Pro Testmaker CD-ROM
- Presentation Plus! CD-ROM
- Glencoe BookLink CD-ROM

② TEACH

Reading Strategy

Problems in Rome On the board, draw a four-column chart with these headings: Political, Social, Cultural, and Economic. As students read the chapter, have them volunteer examples of Rome's problems to place in each category. List these examples on the chart as a running summary. **L2**

Daily Lecture and Discussion Notes 9–2

Use **Daily Lecture and Discussion Notes 9–2** for an outline of key concepts found in the section.

Reading Support L1/ EL

Use **Vocabulary Activity 9–2** to review important terms in the section.

Understanding Charts

Answers:
1. Rome divides in two.
2. Byzantine Empire lasts almost 1,000 years; Rome falls.

The Decline of Rome

Main Idea Poor leadership, a declining economy, and attacks by Germanic tribes weakened the Roman Empire.

Reading Focus What do you do when you face a difficult problem? Do you try to solve it yourself? Do you ask other people for help? Read to learn about the problems the Roman Empire faced and how its leaders responded.

In A.D. 180 Marcus Aurelius died. His son, Commodus (KAH•muh•duhs), became emperor. Commodus was cruel and wasted money. Instead of ruling Rome, Commodus spent much of his time fighting as a gladiator. In A.D. 192 the emperor's bodyguard killed him. Nearly a century of confusion and fighting followed.

After Commodus, emperors called the Severans ruled Rome. Much of their time was spent putting down revolts and protecting Rome's borders. The Severans stayed in power by paying the army well, but they ignored the growing problems of crime and poverty.

Political and Social Problems When the last Severan ruler died in A.D. 235, Rome's government became very weak. For almost 50 years, army leaders fought each other for the throne. During this time, Rome had 22 different emperors.

Poor leadership was not Rome's only difficulty. Fewer Romans honored the old ideals of duty, courage, and honesty. Many government officials took bribes. As problems

The Decline of Rome

Weak Roman Government
• Dishonest government officials provide poor leadership.

Social Problems
• Famine and disease spread throughout the empire.

Declining Economy
• Income and wages fall.
• Wealthy fail to pay taxes.

Reform Fails and Rome Divides in Two
• Government fails to keep order.
• Violence and tension increase.
• Diocletian divides the empire.

Eastern Roman Empire
• Constantinople becomes the new capital.
• The empire survives attacks and prospers.

Western Roman Empire
• Numerous attacks threaten the empire.
• Territory is slowly lost to invaders.

Byzantine Empire
• This empire is created from the Eastern Roman Empire and lasts nearly 1,000 years.

Rome Falls
• The city of Rome falls in A.D. 476.
• The Western Roman Empire is divided into Germanic kingdoms by A.D. 550.

Understanding Charts

Many issues, including a weak government, lack of food, and fewer jobs, led to Rome's decline.
1. According to the flow chart, what occurs after reform fails?
2. **Cause and Effect** What were the final effects of the Roman Empire being split in two?

318

Reading Strategy ❯ READING THE TEXT

Connecting Students who connect what they read to events in their own lives are often better able to construct meaning in texts. They are also able to increase their enjoyment, comprehension, and recall of the text when they connect it to events, emotions, and ideas in their own lives. Encourage students to connect what they are reading about ancient Rome to what they know about our present-day civilization. Ask them to keep a list of things they think have a connection to something in our society. Have students share their lists and discuss them as part of your section wrap-up. **L2**

increased, talented people often refused to serve in government. Many wealthy citizens even stopped paying taxes. Fewer people attended schools, and a large number of the empire's people were now enslaved. Wealthy Romans supported slavery because it was a cheap way to get work done.

Economic and Military Problems During the A.D. 200s, Rome's economy began to fall apart. As government weakened, law and order broke down. Roman soldiers and invaders seized crops and destroyed fields. Farmers grew less food, and hunger began to spread.

As the economy worsened, people bought fewer goods. Artisans produced less, and shopkeepers lost money. Many businesses closed, and the number of workers dropped sharply. Many workers had to leave jobs and serve in the army. A **plague** (PLAYG), or a disease that spreads widely, also took its toll. It killed one out of every ten people in the empire.

Rome also began to suffer from **inflation** (ihn•FLAY•shuhn), or rapidly increasing prices. Inflation happens when money loses its value. How did this happen? The weak economy meant fewer taxes were paid. With less money coming in, the Roman government could not afford to defend its territories and had to find a way to pay its soldiers and officials. One way for the government to get the money it needed was to put less gold in its coins.

By putting less gold in each coin, the government could make extra coins and pay for more things. People soon learned that the coins did not have as much gold in them, and the coins began losing value. Prices went up, and many people stopped using money altogether. They began to **barter** (BAHR•tuhr), or exchange goods without using money.

NATIONAL GEOGRAPHIC — The Way It Was

Focus on Everyday Life

Slavery in the Roman Empire Public and private slavery were common in Roman society. Public slaves were owned by the state. They took care of important buildings and served government officials. Educated public slaves were used to help organize the governments of conquered areas.

Private slaves were owned by individuals. They were often forced to work long hours and could be sold at any time. Wealthy Romans had hundreds or even thousands of enslaved people. Most enslaved people worked on farms.

Most enslaved people were men. This was probably because their work required great strength. Some enslaved men also became gladiators. Enslaved women made clothing and cooked for their owner's family.

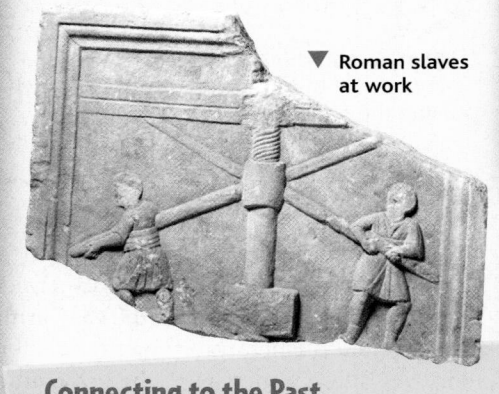

▼ Roman slaves at work

Connecting to the Past
1. What was the main difference between public and private enslavement?
2. Which jobs were probably considered the most desirable by enslaved people?

Reading Strategy

Writing Activity

Ask students to write a journal entry describing life in a Roman city during the A.D. 200s. They should react to at least one of the political, social, economic, and military problems that led to disorder and decline. **L2**

CONNECTING ACROSS TIME

Inflation was a serious problem in Rome during the A.D. 200s. Officials were unable to permanently solve the problem of rising prices. Have students research news and current events sources to find out about inflation in the United States today. Is it a serious problem? If so, how is the government dealing with it? **L3**

NATIONAL GEOGRAPHIC — The Way It Was

Answers:
1. Public slaves were owned by the state. Private slaves were owned by an individual.
2. Answers may include jobs as groundskeepers or personal assistants at country villas.

DIFFERENTIATED INSTRUCTION

Less-proficient Readers: Ask students to copy the time line at the beginning of the section, leaving extra space before A.D. 250 and between each of the existing events. Tell them to add other important events from the section to their time line.

Visual/Spatial: Ask students to draw a chart titled "Emperor's Reforms." The columns should be labeled *Political, Social, Economic,* and *Military,* and the rows should be labeled *Diocletian* and *Constantine.* Tell them to add each emperor's reforms to the chart, showing what kind of problem each reform was intended to solve.

Gifted and Talented: Ask students to research Diocletian and Constantine. Students should look for additional information about their impact on the Roman Empire and share it with the class.

Primary Source

After Julius Caesar, Roman coins usually showed a portrait of the emperor on one side, although under Augustus and Tiberius small denominations did not. Emperors tried to use their coin portraits to present themselves in a favorable way. The other sides of coins usually celebrated important events or featured mottoes and sayings. One coin even carried the message "Happy days are here again" to celebrate Rome's 1,100th birthday.

Answer:
Answers should include that without a currency that people trusted, it would become more and more difficult for businesses to operate and the economy would grow weaker.

Reading Check

Answer: divided the empire into four parts and supervised their officials; tried to control wages and prices; ordered workers to remain at the same jobs until they died

Primary Source — Distrust of Money

As the Roman Empire declined, people refused to trust the value of money issued by each emperor.

"Whereas [because] the public officials have assembled and have accused the bankers of the exchange banks of having closed them because of their unwillingness to accept the divine coin of the emperors, it has become necessary to issue an order to all owners of the banks to open them and to accept and exchange all coin except the absolutely spurious [false] and counterfeit—and not alone to them but to those who engage in business transactions of any kind."

—"Distrust of Imperial Coinage," *Oxyrhynchus Papyrus*, no. 1411, Vol. 2, A.S. Hunt, trans.

▲ Roman coins

DBQ Document-Based Question

What do you think was happening to the economy of the empire as people stopped using the official money?

Meanwhile, invaders swept into the empire. In the west, Germanic tribes raided Roman farms and towns. In the east, armies from Persia pushed into the empire's territory. As fighting increased, the government could no longer enlist and pay Romans as soldiers. It began using Germanic warriors in the army. However, these Germanic soldiers were not loyal to Rome.

What Were Diocletian's Reforms? In A.D. 284 a general named **Diocletian** (DY•uh•KLEE•shuhn) became emperor. To stop the empire's decline, he introduced **reforms** (rih•FAWRMZ), or political changes to make things better. Because the empire was too large for one person to rule, Diocletian divided it into four parts. He named officials to rule these areas but kept authority over all.

Diocletian also worked to boost the economy. To slow inflation, he issued rules that set the prices of goods and the wages to be paid to workers. To make sure more goods were produced, he ordered workers to remain at the same jobs until they died. Diocletian's reforms failed. The people ignored the new rules, and Diocletian did not have enough power to make them obey.

Who Was Constantine? In A.D. 305 Diocletian retired from office. After a period of conflict, another general named **Constantine** (KAHN•stuhn•TEEN) became emperor in A.D. 312. To aid the economy, Constantine issued several orders. The sons of workers had to follow their fathers' trades, the sons of farmers had to work the land their fathers worked, and the sons of soldiers had to serve in the army.

Constantine's changes did not halt the empire's decline in the west. As a result, Constantine moved the capital from dying Rome to a new city in the east. He chose the site of the Greek city of Byzantium (buh•ZAN•tee•uhm). There he built a forum, an amphitheater called the Hippodrome, and many palaces. The city became known as **Constantinople** (KAHN•STAN•tuhn•OH•puhl). Today, Constantinople is called Istanbul.

Reading Check **Explain** How did Diocletian try to reverse the decline of Rome?

CRITICAL THINKING ACTIVITY

Analyzing Information Before students read about the reforms of Diocletian and Constantine, have them brainstorm what could have been done to reverse the decline of the Roman Empire. Have students begin by outlining the problems the empire faced—incompetent rulers, too many different rulers, growing corruption, decreased tax income, crime, decay of traditional Roman values, decline in number of educated population, increase in slavery, currency losing its value, inflation, plague, and threats from Germanic tribes. Then have students suggest policies and actions that might have solved these problems and reversed the decline. **L3**

Biography

CONSTANTINE THE GREAT

c. A.D. 280–337

First Christian Roman Emperor

Constantine was the first Roman Emperor to become a Christian, although he was not baptized until near his death in A.D. 337. He first came to believe in Christianity many years earlier, when he was a military leader. Constantine believed he had seen a flaming cross in the sky that said, "By this sign thou shall conquer." The next day his army was victorious in an important battle. He believed that the cross was a call to the Christian God.

During his reign, Constantine granted new opportunities to Christians and helped advance the power of the early Catholic Church. At the Council of Nicea in A.D. 325, he encouraged discussion about the acceptance of the Trinity (Father, Son, and Holy Spirit). He also boosted the political positions and power of bishops within the Roman government.

Even though Constantine had many political and religious successes, his life was filled with controversy and tragedy. Constantine married a woman named Fausta. His eldest son from a previous marriage was named Crispus. Fausta accused Crispus of crimes and claimed that he was planning to seize the throne. Constantine was so shocked that he had his son killed. Constantine later discovered that Fausta had lied because she wanted her own son to be in line for the throne. He then had Fausta killed.

▲ Constantine

▲ Modern-day Constantinople

Then and Now

Constantine believed freedom of religion was important for the success of his empire and made sure that Christians could no longer be persecuted. What part of the U.S. Constitution protects freedom of religion?

321

Reading List Generator CD-ROM

GLENCOE **BOOKLINK** **RECOMMENDED READING**

Use the **Glencoe Booklink CD-ROM** to create customized reading lists based on your students' interests and reading levels. Below is an example based on content in this chapter. Also, see the Suggested Readings on pages 944–946 of the Appendix.

- Brandt, Keith. *Ancient Rome.* Describes buildings and sites of ancient Rome.
- Corbishley, Mike. *What Do We Know About the Romans?* An introduction to the Romans and their ways of life.
- Mann, Elizabeth. *The Roman Colosseum.* A look at the Colosseum, its games, and the participants and spectators.

Primary Source

Jerome was born in A.D. 347 in present-day Slovenia. He was a famous scholar and the founder of a monastery in Jerusalem. He is best known today for his translation of the Bible into Latin, known as the Vulgate. He translated the Old Testament from Hebrew and the four gospels from Greek.

Answer:
Maybe; he is torn between his desire for peace so that he and the monks can perform their duties of prayer and study, and their obligation to help those in need as the Bible commands.

Rome Falls

Main Idea Rome finally fell when invaders swept through the empire during the A.D. 400s.

Reading Focus How would you feel if a favorite place—a shop, park, or recreation center—was closed after being open for many years? Read to learn how the Romans had to face an even greater loss when their city and empire fell.

Both Diocletian and Constantine failed to save the Roman Empire. When Constantine died in A.D. 337, fighting broke out again. A new emperor called

Primary Source — Rome Is Attacked

In this excerpt from one of his letters, the Christian leader Jerome describes attacks on the Roman provinces.

"Who would believe that Rome, victor over all the world, would fall, that she would be to her people both the womb and the tomb. . . . Where we cannot help we mourn and mingle with theirs our tears. . . . There is not an hour, not even a moment, when we are not occupied with crowds of refugees, when the peace of the monastery is not invaded by a horde of guests so that we shall either have to shut the gates or neglect the Scriptures for which the gates were opened."

▲ Saint Jerome

—Jerome, "News of the Attacks"

DBQ Document-Based Question

Does Jerome think the gates of the monastery should be shut? Explain.

Theodosius (THEE•uh•DOH•shuhs) finally gained control and ended the fighting.

Ruling the empire proved to be difficult. Theodosius decided to divide the empire after his death. In A.D. 395, the Roman Empire split into two separate empires. One was the Western Roman Empire, with its capital at Rome. The other was the Eastern Roman Empire, with its capital at Constantinople.

Rome Is Invaded As Rome declined, it was no longer able to hold back the Germanic tribes on its borders. Many different Germanic groups existed—Ostrogoths, Visigoths, Franks, Vandals, Angles, and Saxons. They came from the forests and marshes of northern Europe.

These Germanic groups were in search of warmer climates and better grazing land for their cattle. They also were drawn by Rome's wealth and culture. In addition, many were fleeing the Huns, fierce warriors from Mongolia in Asia.

In the late A.D. 300s, the Huns entered Eastern Europe and defeated the Ostrogoths (AHS•truh•GAHTHS). The Visigoths, fearing they would be next, asked the Eastern Roman emperor for protection. He let them settle just inside the empire's border. In return they promised to be loyal to Rome.

Before long, trouble broke out between the Visigoths and Romans. The empire forced the Visigoths to buy food at very high prices. The Romans also kidnapped and enslaved many Visigoths.

INTERDISCIPLINARY CONNECTIONS ACTIVITY

Architecture Ask a group of interested students to research and prepare a presentation on the legacy of Roman architecture and building techniques. Students may focus on any of the following:

- Constructions that the Romans built outside Italy (Examples include the Roman baths and Hadrian's Wall in Great Britain and the Pont du Gard aqueduct outside Nîmes, France.)
- Influences on buildings and other constructions built after the fall of the Roman Empire (Examples include the Capitol Building in Washington, D.C.)
- A combination of the two categories **L3**
- Refer to the *Quizzes, Tests, and Authentic Assessment (with Rubrics)* booklet for rubrics.

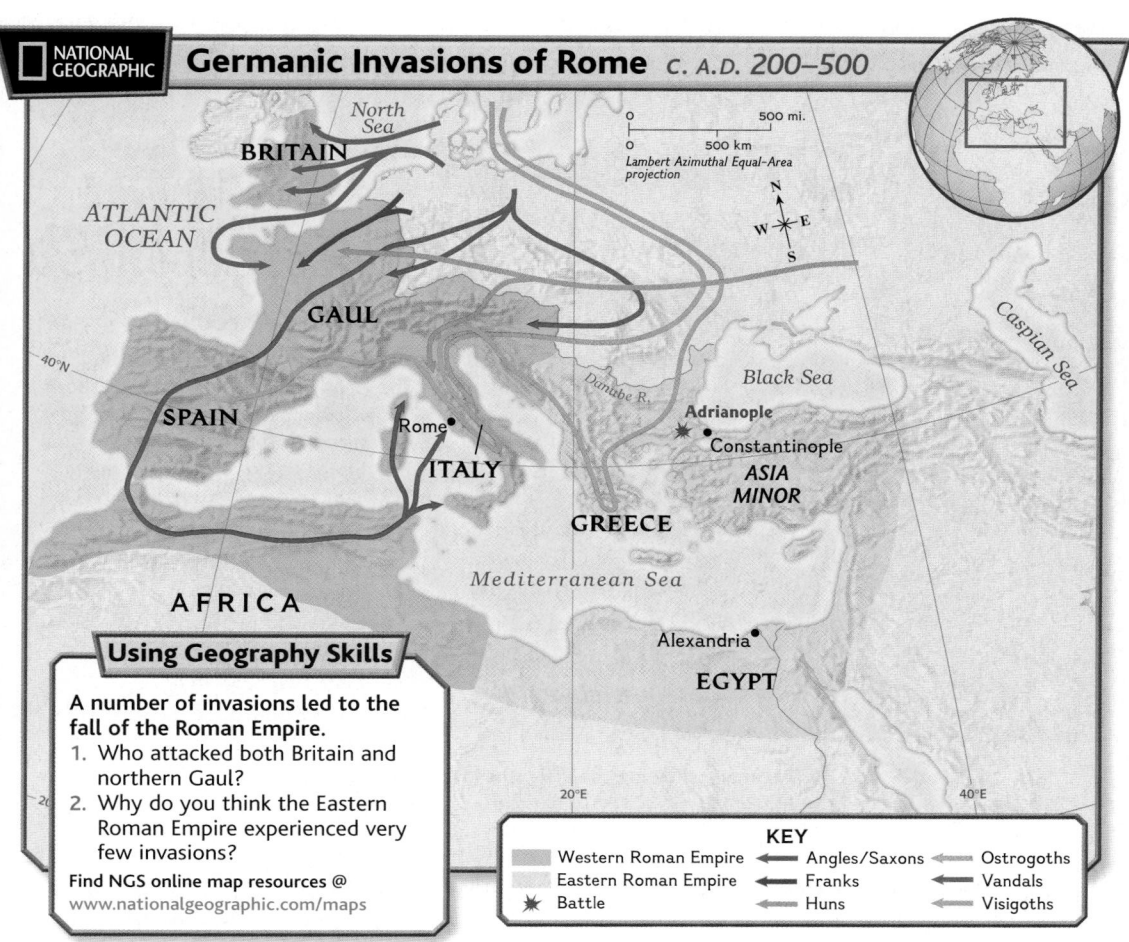

NATIONAL GEOGRAPHIC

Germanic Invasions of Rome C. A.D. 200–500

North Sea

BRITAIN

ATLANTIC OCEAN

GAUL

SPAIN

Rome•
ITALY

AFRICA

Danube R.

Black Sea

Adrianople
✦ •Constantinople

ASIA MINOR

GREECE

Mediterranean Sea

Caspian Sea

Alexandria•
EGYPT

40°N

20°E

40°E

0   500 mi.
0   500 km
Lambert Azimuthal Equal-Area projection

N W E S

Using Geography Skills

A number of invasions led to the fall of the Roman Empire.
1. Who attacked both Britain and northern Gaul?
2. Why do you think the Eastern Roman Empire experienced very few invasions?

Find NGS online map resources @ www.nationalgeographic.com/maps

KEY

▨ Western Roman Empire	← Angles/Saxons	← Ostrogoths
▨ Eastern Roman Empire	← Franks	← Vandals
✦ Battle	← Huns	← Visigoths

Finally, the Visigoths rebelled against the Romans. In A.D. 378 they defeated Roman legions at the Battle of Adrianople (AY•dree•uh•NOH•puhl). After that defeat, Rome was forced to surrender land to the Visigoths.

The Germanic tribes now knew that Rome could no longer defend itself. More and more Germanic warriors crossed the borders in search of land. In the winter of A.D. 406, the Rhine River in Western Europe froze. Germanic groups crossed the frozen river and entered Gaul, which is today

France. The Romans were too weak to force them back across the border.

In A.D. 410 the Visigoth leader **Alaric** (A•luh•rihk) and his soldiers captured Rome itself. They burned records and looted the treasury. Rome's capture by Alaric was a great shock to the empire's people. It was the first time Rome had been conquered in 800 years.

Another Germanic group known as the Vandals overran Spain and northern Africa. They enslaved some Roman landowners and drove others away. Then the Vandals

CHAPTER 9   Roman Civilization   323

in a word . . .

The adjective **"gothic"** comes from *goth*, as in *Ostrogoth* and *Visigoth*. It describes the artistic style in art and architecture that grew in the Middle Ages out of the Greek- and Roman-based Romanesque style. Italian Renaissance writers first applied the term gothic to cathedrals. These writers thought the new style was ugly and named it after the "barbarian" tribes that they felt had destroyed Roman civilization.

EXTENDING THE CONTENT

Why Did Rome Fall? Historians have debated for centuries the reasons for Rome's decline and fall. Among the theories most often suggested are:

• Traditional Roman values may have declined as more non-Italians gained positions of power.
• Christianity's emphasis on spirituality may have weakened Rome's military commitment.
• Plague killed enough of the population to hinder society.
• The empire never developed a stable system for the transfer of power from one emperor to the next.
• Constant Germanic invasions broke down the military and economic systems.

More About the Art

When the emperor refused to give him land and supplies, Alaric besieged Rome in A.D. 408 and again in A.D. 409. Finally, in A.D. 410, Alaric's troops captured the city. Although his troops did plunder Rome, they left after three days. Even so, the Roman Empire was shaken by this occurrence.

Caption Answer: Odoacer

TIME TRAVELER

Romulus was a legendary founder of Rome. It is ironic that the name of the last emperor of Rome bore the same name as one of its founders.

▲ An image showing the Visigoths invading Rome. *What leader did the Visigoths overthrow to take control of Rome?*

✓ **Reading Check**

Answer: the removal of Romulus Augustulus by Odoacer in A.D. 476

Reading Support L1/ EL

Assign **Guided Reading Activity 9–2** to help students organize the information in the section.

sailed to Italy. In A.D. 455 they entered Rome. They spent 12 days stripping buildings of everything valuable and burning them. From these attacks came the English word *vandalism,* which means "the willful destruction of property."

Rome Falls By the mid-A.D. 400s, several Germanic leaders held high posts in Rome's government and army. In A.D. 476 a Germanic general named **Odoacer** (OH•duh•WAY•suhr) took control, overthrowing the western emperor, a 14-year-old boy named Romulus Augustulus (RAHM•yuh•luhs aw•GUHS•chah•luhs). After Romulus Augustulus, no emperor ever again ruled from Rome. Historians often use this event to mark the end of the Western Roman Empire.

Odoacer controlled Rome for almost 15 years. Then a group of Visigoths seized the city and killed Odoacer. They set up a kingdom in Italy under their leader, Theodoric (thee•AH•duh•rihk). Elsewhere in Europe, other Germanic kingdoms arose.

By A.D. 550, the Western Roman Empire had faded away. Many Roman beliefs and practices remained in use, however. For example, Europe's new Germanic rulers adopted the Latin language, Roman laws, and Christianity. Although the Western Roman Empire fell to Germanic invaders, the Eastern Roman Empire prospered. It became known as the Byzantine Empire and lasted nearly 1,000 more years.

✓ **Reading Check** **Identify** Which event usually marks the fall of the Western Roman Empire?

COOPERATIVE LEARNING ACTIVITY

Creating a Talk Show Have students create a daytime talk show featuring guests from ancient Rome that they have read about in this section. For example, students might portray Commodus, Diocletian, Constantine, Alaric, Odoacer, Jerome, Theodoric, and Romulus Augustulus. One student should also play the talk show host, while the remaining students should be the audience. Suggest that students base their show on a real talk show with which they are familiar. Have students representing Roman figures read about these people so they can answer questions in character. Encourage audience members to ask questions and respond to guests' answers, as on real talk shows. **L2**

The Legacy of Rome

Main Idea Rome passed on many achievements in government, law, language, and the arts.

Reading Focus Do you know where the words "doctor," "animal," "circus," and "family" come from? These words come from the Latin language spoken by the Romans. Read to discover other things we have borrowed from the Romans.

Our world would be very different if the Roman Empire had never existed. Many words in the English language and many of our ideas about government come from the Romans. The same is true for our system of laws and our knowledge about building. As you will read in the next chapter, the peace and order brought by Roman rule also allowed the Christian religion to spread.

Roman Ideas and Government Today

Roman ideas about law, as first written in the Twelve Tables, are with us today. We, like the Romans, believe that all people are equal under the law. We expect our judges to decide cases fairly, and we consider a person innocent until proven guilty.

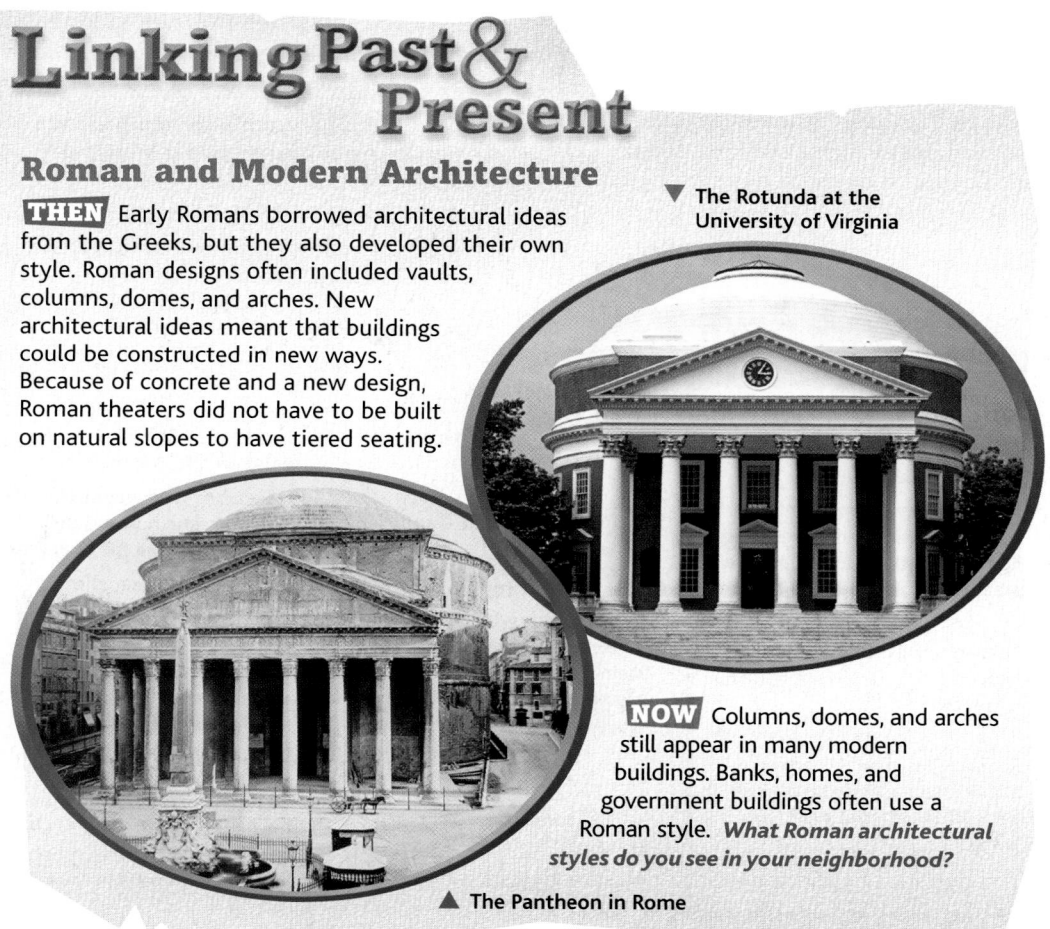

Linking Past & Present

Roman and Modern Architecture

THEN Early Romans borrowed architectural ideas from the Greeks, but they also developed their own style. Roman designs often included vaults, columns, domes, and arches. New architectural ideas meant that buildings could be constructed in new ways. Because of concrete and a new design, Roman theaters did not have to be built on natural slopes to have tiered seating.

▼ **The Rotunda at the University of Virginia**

NOW Columns, domes, and arches still appear in many modern buildings. Banks, homes, and government buildings often use a Roman style. *What Roman architectural styles do you see in your neighborhood?*

▲ **The Pantheon in Rome**

CHAPTER 9 Roman Civilization **325**

③ ASSESS

Assign Section 2 Review as homework or as an in-class activity.

◉ Have students use the **Interactive Tutor Self-Assessment CD-ROM** to review the section.

Assessment L2

Assign **Section 2 Quiz** to assess mastery of the material found in the section.

Reading Support L1/ EL

Assign **Reading Essentials and Study Guide 9–2** to help students review section material.

Linking Past & Present

Answer: Answers will vary but should reflect an understanding of Roman architectural elements.

CRITICAL THINKING ACTIVITY

Understanding Cause and Effect Ask students to discuss to what extent the lack of an orderly succession process contributed to the weakening and fall of the Roman Empire. Have them find examples in the text of problems caused by struggles over succession, the effects of these problems, and possible alternatives the Romans might have used. **L3**

CHAPTER 9
SECTION 2, 317–326

ENRICH

Ask students to write a paragraph in which they agree or disagree with this statement: The United States owes more to Roman culture than to any other civilization that has ever existed. Have them support their answer with reasons and evidence from the text and from other sources. **L3**

✓ **Reading Check**

Answer: government, law, citizenship, language, architecture, Christianity

To help students understand section material, have them visit **Study Central™** at jat.glencoe.com

RETEACH

Discuss the chart "The Decline of Rome" on page 318 with students. Help them connect details in the section with information in the boxes labeled "Western Roman Empire" and "Rome Falls." **L2**

④ CLOSE

Have students discuss how—and if—the Western Roman Empire could have solved its problems and continued to exist. **L2**

Roman ideas about government and citizenship are also important today. Like the early Romans, Americans believe that a republic made up of equal citizens is the best form of government. We also believe that a republic works best if citizens do their duty, participate in government, and work to make their society better.

Roman Influence on Culture Today the alphabet of the Latin language, which expanded from 22 to 26 letters, is used throughout the Western world. Latin shaped the languages of Italy, France, Spain, Portugal, and Romania. Many English words also come from Latin. Scientists, doctors, and lawyers still use Latin phrases. Every known species of plant and animal has a Latin name. Today, we also still admire the works of great Roman writers such as Virgil, Horace, Livy, and Tacitus.

Ancient Rome also left a lasting mark on building in the Western world. We still use concrete today for much of our construction, and Roman architectural styles are still seen in public buildings today. When you visit Washington, D.C., or the capital city of any state, you will see capitol buildings with domes and arches inspired by Roman architecture.

Christianity As you probably know, Christianity is one of the major religions in the world today. Christianity began in the Roman Empire. When Rome's government adopted Christianity in the A.D. 300s, it helped the new religion to grow and spread. After Rome's fall, many Roman ideas blended with those of Christianity.

✓ **Reading Check** **Compare** Which aspects of the Roman Empire are reflected in present-day cultures?

Study Central™ Need help with the material in this section? Visit jat.glencoe.com

Section ② Review

Reading Summary
Review the Main Ideas

- A series of weak emperors, invasions by outsiders, disease, and a number of other factors led to a greatly weakened Roman Empire.

- Numerous invasions by Germanic peoples led to the fall of Rome in A.D. 476.

- Roman ideas about government and Roman architecture are just some of the legacies of ancient Rome.

What Did You Learn?
1. What social problems helped cause the empire's decline?
2. Why did the Roman government use Germanic warriors in its army?

Critical Thinking
3. **Summarizing Information** Draw a diagram like the one below. Fill in details about Rome's legacies in the areas of government, law, and citizenship.

Roman Legacies

4. **Cause and Effect** How did inflation affect Rome?
5. **Describe** Who were the Visigoths, and how did they contribute to the fall of Rome?
6. **Identify** Give examples of Roman ideas in language and architecture that exist today.
7. **Persuasive Writing** Imagine you are living in Rome around the time of the fall of the empire. Write an editorial for a newspaper identifying what you think is the main reason for the decline and fall of the empire, and what might have been done to prevent it.

326   CHAPTER 9   Roman Civilization

SECTION 2 REVIEW ANSWERS

1. dishonest officials; decline in respect for Roman values; widespread slavery; people stopped serving in government and paying taxes; fewer educated people
2. to help defend its borders
3. rule of law, languages derived from Latin, Roman architectural styles, Christianity
4. Prices rose sharply; weak economy meant fewer taxes paid; government could not pay its soldiers and officials; debased currency; people stopped using it.
5. a Germanic people who moved into Roman territory to escape the Huns; they defeated the Romans at Adrianople and sacked Rome
6. English and other modern languages shaped by Latin; Roman architecture reflected in many buildings today
7. Answers will vary.

Section 3

The Byzantine Empire

Get Ready to Read!

What's the Connection?
In the last section, you learned that even though the Roman Empire in the West fell, the Eastern Roman Empire survived and prospered. It became known as the Byzantine Empire. The Byzantines developed a new civilization based on Greek, Roman, and Christian ideas.

Focusing on the Main Ideas

• The Eastern Roman Empire grew rich and powerful as the Western Roman Empire fell. *(page 328)*

• The policies and reforms of Emperor Justinian and Empress Theodora helped make the Byzantine Empire strong. *(page 329)*

• The Byzantines developed a rich culture based on Roman, Greek, and Christian ideas. *(page 332)*

Locating Places
Black Sea
Aegean Sea (ih•JEE•uhn)

Meeting People
Justinian (juh•STIH•nee•uhn)
Theodora (THEE•uh•DOHR•uh)
Belisarius (BEH•luh•SAR•ee•uhs)
Tribonian (truh•BOH•nee•uhn)

Building Your Vocabulary
mosaic (moh•ZAY•ihk)
saint (SAYNT)
regent (REE•juhnt)

Reading Strategy
Cause and Effect Complete a chart to show the causes and effects of Justinian's new law code.

```
┌──────────┐
│  Causes  │
└──────────┘
      │
┌────────────────┐
│ New Code of Laws │
└────────────────┘
      │
┌──────────┐
│ Effects  │
└──────────┘
```

NATIONAL GEOGRAPHIC When & Where?

BALKAN PENINSULA
SPAIN ITALY Rome Constantinople
ASIA MINOR
PALESTINE
EGYPT

A.D. 525	A.D. 550	A.D. 575
A.D. 527 Emperor Justinian begins rule	A.D. 537 Hagia Sophia completed	A.D. 565 Justinian dies

---

SECTION RESOURCES

Reproducible Masters
• Reproducible Lesson Plan 9–3
• Daily Lecture and Discussion Notes 9–3
• Vocabulary Activity 9–3
• Active Reading Note-Taking Guide 9–3
• Guided Reading Activity 9–3
• Section Quiz 9–3
• Reading Essentials and Study Guide 9–3

Transparencies
• Daily Focus Skills Transparency 9–3

Multimedia
• Interactive Tutor Self-Assessment CD-ROM
• ExamView® Pro Testmaker CD-ROM
• Presentation Plus! CD-ROM
• Vocabulary PuzzleMaker CD-ROM
• Glencoe BookLink CD-ROM

---

① FOCUS

SECTION OVERVIEW
This section discusses the rise and accomplishments of the Eastern Roman, or Byzantine, Empire, which carried on the legacies of both Greece and Rome.

BELLRINGER
SKILLBUILDER ACTIVITY

Project **Daily Focus Skills Transparency 9–3** and have students answer questions. Discuss their responses.

Get Ready to Read!

Preteaching Vocabulary: Explain that a saint is a Christian holy person who has contributed in an extraordinary way.

Answers to Graphic: Cause: laws were disorganized and difficult to understand; Effects: the empire's laws were more understandable to officials, businesspeople, and individuals; influenced laws of other countries

327

② TEACH

Comparing and Contrasting Draw a two-column chart on the board. The headings should be "Byzantine Empire in the Beginning" and "How the Empire Changed." Ask students to complete the chart using information from the subsection "Influence of Greek Culture." **L2**

Daily Lecture and Discussion Notes 9–3

Use **Daily Lecture and Discussion Notes 9–3** for an outline of key concepts found in the section.

Reading Support L1/ EL

Use **Vocabulary Activity 9–3** to review important terms in the section.

Geography After students have discussed the advantages of Constantinople's location, have them examine your own community in the same light. What advantages/disadvantages does its location offer? **L1**

The Rise of the Byzantines

Main Idea The Eastern Roman Empire grew rich and powerful as the Western Roman Empire fell.

Reading Focus Think of your own community. How have groups of people from different backgrounds contributed to its character? What would your town or city be like without these contributions from all the different groups? Read to learn about the different groups that made up the Byzantine Empire.

The Eastern Roman, or Byzantine, Empire reached a high point in the A.D. 500s. At this time, the empire stretched west to Italy, south to Egypt, and east to the border with Arabia. Greeks made up the empire's largest group, but many other peoples were found within the empire. They included Egyptians, Syrians, Arabs, Armenians, Jews, Persians, Slavs, and Turks.

▲ The ancient walled city of Constantinople

Why Is Constantinople Important? In the last section, you learned that Emperor Constantine moved the capital of the Roman Empire from Rome to a new city called Constantinople. Constantine's city became the capital of the Byzantine Empire. By the A.D. 500s, Constantinople was thriving and had become one of the world's great cities.

One reason for Constantinople's success was its location. It lay on the waterways between the **Black Sea** and the **Aegean Sea** (ih•JEE•uhn). Its harbors offered a safe shelter for fishing boats, trading ships, and warships. Constantinople also sat at the crossroads of trade routes between Europe and Asia. The trade that passed through made the city extremely wealthy.

Constantinople had a secure land location. Lying on a peninsula, Constantinople was easily defended. Seas protected it on three sides, and on the fourth side, a huge wall guarded the city. Later a huge chain was even strung across the city's north harbor for greater protection. Invaders could not easily take Constantinople.

Influence of Greek Culture The Byzantines at first followed Roman ways. Constantinople was known as the "New Rome." Its public buildings and palaces were built in the Roman style. The city even had an oval arena called the Hippodrome, where chariot races and other events were held.

Byzantine political and social life also were based on that of Rome. Emperors spoke Latin and enforced Roman laws. The empire's poor people received free bread and shows. Wealthy people lived in town or on large farming estates. In fact, many of them had once lived in Rome.

Visualizing Use the second paragraph under the heading "Why Is Constantinople Important?" to help students employ visualizing as a technique. Begin by reading the first two sentences in the paragraph aloud to the class. Have students use the description to help them locate the city on the map on page 329 while you indicate it on a wall map. Then read the next two sentences and tell students to study the map. Next, have students close their books. Read the same portions of the text aloud, but tell students to draw the Mediterranean region on a piece of paper and to label Constantinople's location. Allow them time to compare their maps with the one in the book. Ask volunteers to explain what helped them draw the city's location and to summarize what made this location so useful. **L2**

As time passed, the Byzantine Empire became less Roman and more Greek. Most Byzantines spoke Greek and honored their Greek past. Byzantine emperors and officials began to speak Greek too. The ideas of non-Greek peoples, like the Egyptians and the Slavs, also shaped Byzantine life. Still other customs came from Persia to the east. All of these cultures blended together to form the Byzantine civilization. Between A.D. 500 and A.D. 1200, the Byzantines had one of the world's richest and most-advanced empires.

✓ Reading Check **Explain** Why did the Byzantine Empire have such a blending of cultures?

Emperor Justinian

Main Idea The policies and reforms of Emperor Justinian and Empress Theodora helped make the Byzantine Empire strong.

Reading Focus Do you sometimes rewrite reports to make them easier to understand? Read to learn how Justinian rewrote and reorganized the Byzantine law code.

Justinian (juh•STIH•nee•uhn) became emperor of the Byzantine Empire in A.D. 527 and ruled until A.D. 565. Justinian was a strong leader. He controlled the military, made laws, and was supreme judge. His order could not be questioned.

CONNECTING ACROSS TIME

The Justinian Code had four parts—a collection of past laws (based on custom, legislative laws, and laws decreed by previous emperors), opinions of important Roman jurists (jurists whom the emperor had given the right of declaring law), an outline of the law, and laws that Justinian made. U.S. law is composed of statutory laws (laws passed by a legislature) and common law (laws that have resulted from custom and the decisions made in court cases). Discuss with students if only the legislature should have the right to make law or if traditions should also be a source of law. **L3**

✓ Reading Check

Answer: The empire was located at the crossroads of Europe and Asia.

NATIONAL GEOGRAPHIC
The Byzantine Empire A.D. 527–565

KEY
- Byzantine Empire before Justinian, A.D. 527
- Area added to Byzantine Empire during Justinian's conquests, A.D. 565

Using Geography Skills

Justinian attempted to restore the Roman Empire in the Mediterranean.
1. Describe the area of the Byzantine Empire before Justinian's conquests.
2. How far west did the empire extend after Justinian's conquests?

Using Geography Skills

Answers:
1. located in eastern Mediterranean only
2. Spain, North Africa

Skills Practice

Ask: What conquests of Justinian gave the Byzantines control of the Mediterranean? *(the western mouth of the Mediterranean, Carthage, and Sicily)*

CHAPTER 9   Roman Civilization   **329**

DIFFERENTIATED INSTRUCTION

English Learners: Ask students to make a web diagram. The center circle should be labeled "Justinian." Two other circles connected by lines to the center circle should be labeled "Conquests" and "Law Code." Help students add the most important facts from the subsections "Justinian's Conquests" and "Justinian's Law Code" to the graphic.

Visual/Spatial: Have students use the letters in Justinian's name to remember important details about his reign. Examples: *J:* Justinian took advice from Theodora; *U:* used cavalry; *I:* Italy and North Africa were conquered.

Gifted and Talented: Have students prepare a computer presentation demonstrating the conquests and advances Justinian made.

Primary Source   Theodora Refuses to Flee

Justinian's court historian recorded Theodora's opinion about whether to escape or fight during the A.D. 532 revolt.

"My opinion then is that the present time . . . is inopportune [not a good time] for flight, even though it brings safety. . . . For one who has been an emperor, it is unendurable to be a fugitive. . . . May I not live that day on which those who meet me shall not address me as empress. If, now, it is your wish to save yourself, O Emperor, there is no difficulty."
—Procopius, "The Nika Riot"

Theodora ▶

DBQ Document-Based Question

Why did the empress not wish to escape?

Justinian's wife, the empress **Theodora** (THEE•uh•DOHR•uh), helped him run the empire. Theodora, a former actress, was intelligent and strong-willed, and she helped Justinian choose government officials. Theodora also convinced him to give women more rights. For the first time, a Byzantine wife could own land. If she became a widow, she now had the income to take care of her children.

In A.D. 532 Theodora helped save Justinian's throne. Angry taxpayers threatened to overthrow Justinian and stormed the palace. Justinian's advisers urged him to leave Constantinople. Theodora, however, told him to stay and fight. Justinian took Theodora's advice. He stayed in the city and crushed the uprising.

Justinian's Conquests Justinian wanted to reunite the Roman Empire and bring back Rome's glory. To do this, he had to conquer Western Europe and northern Africa. He ordered a general named **Belisarius** (BEH•luh•SAR•ee•uhs) to strengthen and lead the Byzantine army.

When Belisarius took command, he reorganized the Byzantine army. Instead of foot soldiers, the Byzantine army came to rely on cavalry—soldiers mounted on horses. Byzantine cavalry wore armor and carried bows and lances, which were long spears.

During Justinian's reign, the Byzantine military conquered most of Italy and northern Africa and defeated the Persians in the east. However, Justinian conquered too much too quickly. After he died, the empire did not have the money to maintain an army large enough to hold the territory in the west.

Justinian's Law Code Justinian decided that the empire's laws were disorganized and too difficult to understand. He ordered a group of legal scholars headed by **Tribonian** (truh•BOH•nee•uhn) to reform the law code.

The group's new simplified code became known as the Justinian Code. Officials, businesspeople, and individuals could now more easily understand the empire's laws. Over the years, the Justinian Code has had a great influence on the laws of almost every country in Europe.

✓ Reading Check **Explain** What did Justinian accomplish during his reign?

CRITICAL THINKING ACTIVITY

Predicting Ask students to speculate on the future of the Byzantine Empire. Have them begin by discussing factors that are likely to have an influence on the empire's future. *(geographic location, quality of leadership, strength of enemies)* To help students get started, you may want to point out that Italy, Spain, and Africa are far from Constantinople and that powerful enemies, such as the Arabs, Turks, and Persians, are closer to the city. After students have discussed these factors and their potential influences, conclude by explaining that the Byzantine Empire began to shrink after the death of Justinian. It eventually was conquered by Turkish armies in 1453. **L3**

Biography

EMPRESS THEODORA

c A.D. 500–548

Theodora began life in the lower class of Byzantine society but rose to the rank of empress. The historian Procopius recorded the events of her early life. According to Procopius, Theodora's father worked as a bear keeper at the Hippodrome. After his death, Theodora followed her mother's advice and became an actress. A career in acting was not as glamorous then as it is now. It was a job of the lower class, like wool spinning, which was Theodora's other job.

Even though Theodora was of the lower class, she began dating Justinian. Justinian was attracted to Theodora's beauty and intelligence. Because Justinian wanted to marry Theodora, his uncle, the emperor, changed the law that prevented upper-class nobles from marrying actresses. The two were married in A.D. 525.

Justinian considered Theodora his intellectual equal. In his writings, Justinian said he asked for Theodora's advice on laws and policies. At Theodora's urging, he granted more rights to women. Some historians believe Theodora had great power within the royal court, perhaps more than Justinian. For example, nearly all the laws passed during Theodora's reign as empress mention her name. Theodora and Justinian had no children together. When Theodora died from cancer in A.D. 548, Justinian was overcome with grief. He had her portrait incorporated into many works of art, including numerous Byzantine mosaics.

▲ Empress Theodora advises Emperor Justinian.

> "She was extremely clever and had a biting wit."
> —Procopius, *The Secret History*

Then and Now

Name a modern-day female political leader that you think has great influence in making and changing laws. Explain your choice.

331

Reading List Generator CD-ROM

GLENCOE BOOKLINK

RECOMMENDED READING

Use the **Glencoe BookLink CD-ROM** to create customized reading lists based on your students' interests and reading levels. Below is an example based on content in this chapter. Also, see the Suggested Readings on pages 944–946 of the Appendix.

- Cairns, Trevor. *The Romans and Their Empire.* Traces Rome's growth from a small city to a mighty empire.
- Chubb, Thomas C. *The Byzantines.* Describes the wonders of Constantinople.
- Suter, Joanne. *World Myths and Legends: Greek and Roman.* A survey of characters and tales from Greek and Roman mythology.

Byzantine Civilization

Main Idea The Byzantines developed a rich culture based on Roman, Greek, and Christian ideas.

Reading Focus Do you think a multicultural population adds to a country's interest and success? Read to learn how the diverse groups of the Byzantine Empire contributed to its culture.

The Byzantine Empire lasted approximately 1,000 years. For much of that time, Constantinople was the largest and richest city in Europe. The Byzantines were highly educated and creative. They preserved and passed on Greek culture and Roman law to other peoples. They gave the world new methods in the arts. As you will learn, they also spread Christianity to people in Eastern Europe.

The Importance of Trade From the A.D. 500s to the A.D. 1100s, the Byzantine Empire was the center of trade between Europe and Asia. Trade goods from present-day Russia in the north, Mediterranean lands in the south, Latin Europe in the west, and Persia and China in the east passed through the empire. From Asia, ships and caravans brought luxury goods—spices, gems, metals, and cloth—to Constantinople. For these items, Byzantine merchants traded farm goods as well as furs, honey, and enslaved people from northern Europe.

This enormous trade made the Byzantine Empire very rich. However, most Byzantines were not merchants. Instead they were farmers, herders, laborers, and artisans. One of the major Byzantine industries was weaving silk. It developed around

◀ Sculpture showing chariot racing at the Hippodrome

▲ Byzantine jewelry

▲ The style of the Hagia Sophia, shown here, and other Byzantine churches influenced the architecture of churches throughout Russia and Eastern Europe.
What does the name "Hagia Sophia" mean?

INTERDISCIPLINARY CONNECTIONS ACTIVITY

Language Arts Ask students if they have ever heard the word *icon*, as in the sentence "___ is a pop music icon." *Icon* comes from the Greek word for "to be like/seem," and the Byzantines used it to refer to religious images. In English, an icon is a symbol or an outstanding example of something. An iconoclast, on the other hand, is someone who speaks against traditions or popular ideas. It comes from the Byzantine religious controversy. Iconoclasts objected to the use of icons and destroyed them. Ask students to name some present-day icons and some iconoclasts. **L2**

A.D. 550. At that time, Byzantine travelers smuggled silkworm eggs out of China. Brought to Constantinople, the silkworms fed on mulberry leaves and produced silk threads. Weavers then used the threads to make the silk cloth that brought wealth to the empire.

Byzantine Art and Architecture

Justinian and other Byzantine emperors supported artists and architects. They ordered the building of churches, forts, and public buildings throughout the empire. Constantinople was known for its hundreds of churches and palaces. One of Justinian's greatest achievements was building the huge church called Hagia Sophia (HAH•jee•uh soh•FEE•uh), or "Holy Wisdom." It was completed in A.D. 537 and became the religious center of the Byzantine Empire. It still stands today in Istanbul.

Inside Hagia Sophia, worshipers could see walls of beautiful marble and mosaics. **Mosaics** (moh•ZAY•ihks) are pictures made from many bits of colored glass or stone. They were an important type of art in the Byzantine Empire. Mosaics mainly showed figures of **saints** (SAYNTS), or Christian holy people.

Byzantine Women

The family was the center of social life for most Byzantines. Religion and the government stressed the importance of marriage and family life. Divorces were rare and difficult to get.

Byzantine women were not encouraged to lead independent lives. They were expected to stay home and take care of their families. However, women did gain some important rights, thanks to Empress Theodora. Like Theodora herself, some Byzantine women became well educated and involved in politics. Several

---

NATIONAL GEOGRAPHIC

The Way It Was

Focus on Everyday Life

Byzantine Mosaics Imagine taking bits of glass and turning them into beautiful masterpieces. Byzantine artists did just that starting around A.D. 330. Roman mosaics were made of natural-colored marble pieces and decorated villas and buildings. Byzantine mosaics were different. They were made of richly colored, irregular pieces of glass and decorated the ceilings, domes, and floors of Byzantine churches.

Byzantine mosaics were created to honor religious or political leaders. The centers of domes—because they were the highest points of the churches—were commonly reserved for images of Jesus.

Mosaics were expensive. They were ordered and paid for by emperors, state officials, or church leaders. Many mosaics are still intact and can be seen today inside churches, monasteries, and museums.

◀ **Mosaic from the Byzantine Empire**

Connecting to the Past

1. Why do you think the name of the person who paid for the mosaic—rather than the name of the person who made the mosaic—was often recorded in the inscription?
2. What types of art do present-day artists make with glass?

---

3 ASSESS

Assign Section 3 Review as homework or as an in-class activity.

🔘 Have students use the **Interactive Tutor Self-Assessment CD-ROM** to review the section.

Assessment L2

Assign **Section 3 Quiz** to assess mastery of the material found in the section.

Reading Support L1/ EL

Assign **Reading Essentials and Study Guide 9–3** to help students review section material.

NATIONAL GEOGRAPHIC

The Way It Was

Answers:
1. The person who paid for the mosaic wanted to be remembered for the art.
2. Students may name vases, sculptures, dinnerware, stained glass windows, and so on.

EXTENDING THE CONTENT

Hagia Sophia For almost 1,500 years, Hagia Sophia has stood both as a remarkable architectural site and as a record of historical and political changes. The church has been damaged by earthquakes and fires and even sacked by crusading Christians from Western Europe. The most important changes to the church occurred after Constantinople was conquered by the Turks in 1453. It became a mosque in the 1500s, and the magnificent mosaics and frescoes were plastered over. Muslim rulers added items, such as a pulpit, a preacher's pew, an altar, fountains, and the tall, slender minarets outside the structure. In spite of these changes, however, visitors can still see the building that caused Justinian, remembering the Jewish temple in Jerusalem, to cry out: "Oh, Solomon, I have surpassed thee."

ENRICH

Explain that Justinian agreed to the Nika rioters' first demands. Instead of disbanding, they chose a new emperor. The revolt ended when Belisarius attacked the rebels in the Hippodrome and killed 30,000 people. Ask students what alternatives Justinian could have used to solve this problem. **L2**

Reading Check

Answer: Hagia Sophia

History Online

To help students understand section material, have them visit **Study Central**™ at jat.glencoe.com

RETEACH

Ask students to make a list of Justinian's achievements. **L1**

4 CLOSE

Have students list the contributions of the Byzantine Empire. **L2**

---

royal women served as regents. A **regent** (REE•juhnt) is a person who stands in for a ruler who is too young or too ill to govern. A few ruled the empire in their own right.

Byzantine Education Learning was highly respected in Byzantine culture. The government supported the training of scholars and government officials. In Byzantine schools, boys studied religion, medicine, law, arithmetic, grammar, and other subjects. Wealthy Byzantines sometimes hired tutors to teach their children. Girls usually did not attend schools and were taught at home.

Most Byzantine authors wrote about religion. They stressed the need to obey God and save one's soul. To strengthen faith, they wrote about the lives of saints. Byzantine writers gave an important gift to the world. They copied and passed on the

▲ This Byzantine religious text is beautifully illustrated. *What did Byzantine boys study at school?*

writings of the ancient Greeks and Romans. Without Byzantine copies, many important works from the ancient world would have disappeared forever.

✓**Reading Check** **Identify** What church is one of Justinian's greatest achievements?

History Online

Study Central™ Need help with the material in this section? Visit jat.glencoe.com

Section 3 Review

Reading Summary
Review the Main Ideas
- With its capital at Constantinople and strong Greek influences, the Byzantine Empire grew powerful and wealthy.

- The Byzantine emperor, Justinian, reconquered much of the land that had been held by the old Roman Empire in the Mediterranean. It also issued a new law code known as the Justinian Code.

- As the Byzantine Empire grew wealthy from trade, art, architecture, and education flourished.

What Did You Learn?
1. What is a mosaic, and where were mosaics found in the Byzantine Empire?
2. How did silk weaving develop in the Byzantine Empire?

Critical Thinking
3. **Organizing Information** Draw a diagram like the one below. Fill in details about Constantinople's location.

```
(  )        (  )
    \      /
  Location of
  Constantinople
    /      \
(  )        (  )
```

4. **Describe** What were some of the trade items that were exchanged between merchants in Constantinople?
5. **Explain** Why were divorces difficult to get in the Byzantine Empire?
6. **Analyze** What important service did Byzantine writers provide to the rest of the world? Explain its significance.
7. **Persuasive Writing** Which civilization do you think was the most advanced—that of the Greeks, the Romans, or the Byzantines? Write a speech explaining your answer.

SECTION 3 REVIEW ANSWERS

1. a picture made of tiny pieces of colored glass or stone; in churches and monasteries
2. Byzantine travelers smuggled silkworm eggs from China to the empire.
3. It lay on waterways between the Black and Aegean Seas; at the crossroads between Asia and Europe; located on a peninsula
4. From Asia: spices, gems, metals, and cloth; From Byzantines: farm goods, furs, honey, and enslaved people
5. Religion and the government stressed the importance of marriage.
6. Byzantine writers copied and preserved the writings of the ancient Greeks and Romans; otherwise these works would have been lost.
7. Answers will vary but should demonstrate a thoughtful response.

Chapter 9 Reading Review

Section 1 Life in Ancient Rome

Vocabulary
vault
satire
ode
anatomy
Forum
gladiator
paterfamilias
rhetoric

Focusing on the Main Ideas
• In addition to their own developments in science and engineering, Roman artists and writers borrowed many ideas from the Greeks. *(page 303)*
• The rich and poor had very different lives in the Roman Empire, as did men and women. *(page 306)*

A Roman family at the dinner table ▶

Section 2 The Fall of Rome

Vocabulary
plague
inflation
barter
reform

Focusing on the Main Ideas
• Poor leadership, a declining economy, and attacks by Germanic tribes weakened the Roman Empire. *(page 318)*
• Rome finally fell when invaders swept through the empire during the A.D. 400s. *(page 322)*
• Rome passed on many achievements in government, law, language, and the arts. *(page 325)*

Section 3 The Byzantine Empire

Vocabulary
mosaic
saint
regent

Focusing on the Main Ideas
• The Eastern Roman Empire grew rich and powerful as the Western Roman Empire fell. *(page 328)*
• The policies and reforms of Emperor Justinian and Empress Theodora helped make the Byzantine Empire strong. *(page 329)*
• The Byzantines developed a rich culture based on Roman, Greek, and Christian ideas. *(page 332)*

CHAPTER 9   Roman Civilization   **335**

PREVIEW/REVIEW

Vocabulary Activity Have students write a postcard about a trip to Rome or Constantinople, using at least eight vocabulary words from the chapter.

⊚ **Vocabulary PuzzleMaker CD-ROM**

⊚ **Interactive Tutor Self-Assessment CD-ROM**

CONDENSE

▱ Chapter 9 **Guided Reading Activities**

⊚ **StudentWorks Plus™ CD-ROM** (with Audio Program)

RETEACH

▱ **Differentiated Instruction Activity 9**

▱ Chapter 9 *Reading Essentials and Study Guide*

CHAPTER CULMINATING ACTIVITY

Have students finish the Chapter Culminating Activity from page 298D.

Suggestions for rubrics may be found in the *Quizzes, Tests, and Authentic Assessment (with Rubrics)* booklet.

⫸ Reading Strategy ◁ READ TO WRITE

Writing a Policy Memo As they read the chapter, have students take notes about the challenges facing the later Roman Empire. Then have them use this information to write a policy memo to a Roman emperor. In the memo, they should suggest policies the emperor could follow to improve conditions and stave off decline. Students should support their recommendations with reasoning and details from the chapter and from other information sources they may have already researched.

• **L1** students should include one or two reasons and details in their memo.
• **L2** students should include several appropriate details and reasons and attempt grammar mastery.
• **L3** students should write logical, detailed, well-considered memos that provide strong and persuasive support for their recommendations.

Chapter ⑨ Assessment and Activities

GLENCOE TECHNOLOGY

MindJogger Videoquiz

Use the **MindJogger Videoquiz** to review Chapter 9 content.

 Available in DVD and VHS

Review Vocabulary

1. f
2. e
3. b
4. h
5. g
6. a
7. c
8. d

Review Main Ideas

9. ideas in sculpture, architecture (porches, colonnades), and literature; architecture (vault, dome, concrete), roads, aqueducts; law and government

10. Rich: lived in large, comfortable houses; educated their children; Poor: lived in crowded conditions in unsafe apartment buildings; no education for their children

11. poor leadership, a declining economy, and attacks by Germanic tribes

12. Germanic invasions

13. Justinian's law code; rights for women; reconquered Italy and North Africa; added cavalry to army

14. Greeks, Egyptians, Slavs, Persians, and others

Critical Thinking

15. Rome had not been conquered in 800 years.

16. Answers will vary but should reflect the information in the chapter.

Review Vocabulary

Match the definitions in the second column to the terms in the first column.

___ 1. plague   **a.** pictures made of many bits of colored glass or stone

___ 2. anatomy   **b.** rapidly increasing prices

___ 3. inflation   **c.** father of a family

___ 4. gladiator   **d.** emotional poem about life's ups and downs

___ 5. regent   **e.** study of the body's structure

___ 6. mosaic   **f.** a disease that spreads widely

___ 7. paterfamilias   **g.** a person who stands in for a ruler who cannot govern

___ 8. ode   **h.** a warrior who fought animals and people in public arenas

---

Review Main Ideas

Section 1 • Life in Ancient Rome

9. What did the Romans borrow from the Greeks? What did they develop on their own?

10. What were the lives of the rich and poor like in Rome?

Section 2 • The Fall of Rome

11. What weakened the Roman Empire?

12. What caused the fall of Rome in the A.D. 400s?

Section 3 • The Byzantine Empire

13. What policies and reforms helped make the Byzantine Empire strong?

14. What different groups of people contributed to the Byzantine culture?

Critical Thinking

15. **Cause and Effect** Why did Alaric's capture of Rome shock the Roman people?

16. **Predict** What do you think would have happened if Theodosius had not divided the Roman Empire?

Review Reading Skill — Responding and Reflecting — Your Point of View

17. Read the following paragraph from page 330. Write at least five things you might reflect on as you read this information.

> In A.D. 532 Theodora helped save Justinian's throne. Angry taxpayers threatened to overthrow Justinian and stormed the palace. Justinian's advisers urged him to leave Constantinople. Theodora, however, told him to stay and fight. Justinian took Theodora's advice. He stayed in the city and crushed the uprising.

To review this skill, see pages 300–301.

Reading Skill

17. Answers will vary but may include Theodora's role, angry citizens, pressure on Justinian from advisers, Theodora's influence on Justinian, Justinian's new resolve to crush uprising.

Geography Skills

18. Italy, part of northern Africa, southern and southeastern Spain

19. He wanted to restore the Roman Empire.

20. The empire did not have enough money to pay an army that was large enough to defend its borders.

Geography Skills

Study the map below and answer the following questions.

18. **Place** Which areas were conquered by Justinian's military?

19. **Human/Environment Interaction** Why do you think Justinian decided to conquer lands to the west of his empire?

20. **Movement** What made it difficult for the Byzantine Empire to hold on to Justinian's conquests?

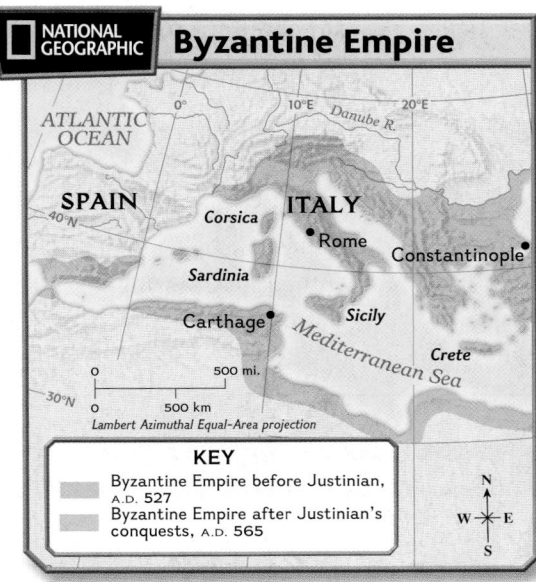

NATIONAL GEOGRAPHIC

Byzantine Empire

ATLANTIC OCEAN

SPAIN

ITALY

Corsica

Rome

Constantinople

Sardinia

Sicily

Carthage

Mediterranean Sea

Crete

Lambert Azimuthal Equal-Area projection

KEY

Byzantine Empire before Justinian, A.D. 527

Byzantine Empire after Justinian's conquests, A.D. 565

Read to Write

21. **Descriptive Writing** Suppose you are a newspaper reporter living in the time of the Roman Empire. Write a front-page article about the slave revolt in 73 B.C., the content of Theodosius's will, or the removal of Romulus Augustulus. Remember to include a headline.

22. **Using Your** Use the information you wrote in your foldable to create a brief study guide for the chapter. For each section, your study guide should include at least five questions that focus on the main ideas.

History Online
Self-Check Quiz To help you prepare for the Chapter Test, visit jat.glencoe.com

Linking Past and Present

23. **Analyzing** In the chapter, you learned that the culture of the Byzantine Empire was greatly influenced by the Romans and Greeks, as well as the Egyptian, Slavic, and Persian cultures. Think about the culture of the United States, in which many cultures have blended. Work with a classmate to identify aspects of the U.S. culture that were originally part of other cultures.

Building Citizenship Skills

24. **Analyzing** Growing political and social problems helped set the stage for Rome's final fall. Traditional Roman ideas of duty, courage, and honesty lost their importance. Why do you think duty, courage, and honesty are important in keeping a society and political system strong?

Primary Source Analyze

The Roman Empire did have some laws to prevent the extreme abuse of slaves.

"At the present time neither Roman citizens nor any other persons who are under the rule of the Roman people are permitted to treat their slaves with excessive and baseless [reasonless] cruelty.... A man who kills his own slave without cause is ordered to be held just as liable as one who kills another's slave."

—Gaius, "Legislation Against the Abuse of Slaves"

DBQ Document-Based Questions

25. How does this law pertain to people passing through the empire?

26. How does this statement leave a loophole in the regulation of abuse against slaves?

CHAPTER 9   Roman Civiliziation   **337**

History Online

Have students visit the Web site at jat.glencoe.com to review Chapter 9 and take the Self-Check Quiz.

Building Citizenship Skills

24. Answers will vary but should demonstrate a thoughtful response. Students may use examples from society today.

Primary Source

25. Travelers are treated the same as Roman citizens.

26. Individuals may kill slaves if they have cause.

Bonus Question

Ask: What is one reason why both the Roman Empire and another civilization that you have studied fell? Name the civilization and the cause. *(Students should use chapter information and a knowledge of world history to support their answers.)*

Read to Write

21. Articles will vary but should reflect chapter content.

22. **FOLDABLES** The questions for the study guides should be appropriate for the main ideas and should accurately reflect information in the chapter.

Linking Past and Present

23. Answers will vary but should include dress, language, customs, music, food, and holidays.

Chapter 10 Resources

Note: The following materials may be used when teaching Chapter 10.
Section level support materials are shown at point of use in the margins of the Teacher Wraparound Edition.

TEACHING TRANSPARENCIES

- Graphic Organizer Transparencies with Teaching Strategy and Student Activity **L2**
- Cause-and-Effect Transparencies with Teaching Strategy and Student Activity **L2**
- Then and Now Transparencies with Teaching Strategy and Student Activity **L2**
- In-text Map Transparency with Teaching Strategy and Student Activity **L1**
- Map Transparencies with Overlay, Teaching Strategy, and Student Activity **L2**

DIFFERENTIATED INSTRUCTION

- Differentiated Instruction Activity 10
- Time Line Activity 10
- Primary Source Reading 10 (with Document-Based Questions)
- Inclusion Strategies for the Middle School Social Studies Classroom
- StudentWorks Plus™ CD-ROM (with Audio Program)

READING SUPPORT

- Take-Home Review Activity 10 **L2**
- World Literature Reading 10 **L2**
- Workbook Activity 10 **L1**
- Reading Strategies for the Social Studies Classroom **L1/ EL**

ASSESSMENT

- Authentic Assessment Activity 10 **L1/ EL**
- Chapter 10 Test Form A **L2**
- Chapter 10 Test Form B **L2**
- ExamView® Pro Testmaker CD-ROM

INTERDISCIPLINARY CONNECTIONS

- Geography and History Activity 10 **L2**
- People to Meet Activity 10 **L2**
- Economics Activity 10 **L2**
- Citizenship and Service Learning Activity 10 **L2**

SPANISH RESOURCES

- Spanish Reading Essentials and Study Guide
- Spanish Guided Reading Activities
- Spanish Quizzes, Tests, and Authentic Assessment (with Rubrics)
- Spanish Take-Home Review Activities

MULTIMEDIA

- ExamView® Pro Testmaker CD-ROM
- Glencoe Skillbuilder Interactive Workbook CD-ROM, Level 1
- Interactive Tutor Self-Assessment CD-ROM
- MindJogger Videoquiz
- Presentation Plus! CD-ROM
- StudentWorks Plus™ CD-ROM (with Audio Program)
- TeacherWorks CD-ROM
- Vocabulary PuzzleMaker CD-ROM
- *World History: Journey Across Time* Video Program
- World History Primary Source Document Library CD-ROM

STANDARDIZED ASSESSMENT SKILLS

- Standardized Test Skills Practice Workbook Activity 10 **L2**
- Critical Thinking Skills Activity 10 **L2**

Teaching strategies have been coded with suggested ability levels. However, most are suitable for all levels.

L1 BASIC activities for all students

L2 AVERAGE activities for average to above-average students

L3 CHALLENGING activities for above-average students

EL ENGLISH LANGUAGE activities

Chapter ⑩ Resources

TIME MANAGEMENT

Chapter Introduction	Section 1	Section 2	Section 3	Chapter Wrap-Up
1 Day	2 Days	1 Day	1 Day	1 Day

Block Scheduling Activities that are suited to use within the block scheduling framework are identified by:

0:00 OUT OF TIME? Assign the Chapter 10 *Reading Essentials and Study Guide.**

SECTION RESOURCES

DAILY OBJECTIVES	REPRODUCIBLE RESOURCES	MULTIMEDIA RESOURCES
Section 1 **The First Christians** 1. While Judaea was under Roman rule, Jesus of Nazareth preached of God's love and forgiveness. Though he won followers, he eventually was crucified. 2. Christianity, based on Jesus' teachings, became a separate religion from Judaism.	Reproducible Lesson Plan 10–1 Daily Lecture and Discussion Notes 10–1 Vocabulary Activity 10–1 Active Reading Note-Taking Guide 10–1 Guided Reading Activity 10–1* Section Quiz 10–1* Reading Essentials and Study Guide 10–1*	Daily Focus Skills Transparency 10–1 Interactive Tutor Self-Assessment CD-ROM ExamView® Pro Testmaker CD-ROM Presentation Plus! CD-ROM Glencoe BookLink CD-ROM
Section 2 **The Christian Church** 1. Christianity won many followers and eventually became the official religion of the Roman Empire. 2. Early Christians set up a church organization and explained their beliefs.	Reproducible Lesson Plan 10–2 Daily Lecture and Discussion Notes 10–2 Vocabulary Activity 10–2 Active Reading Note-Taking Guide 10–2 Guided Reading Activity 10–2* Section Quiz 10–2* Reading Essentials and Study Guide 10–2*	Daily Focus Skills Transparency 10–2 Interactive Tutor Self-Assessment CD-ROM ExamView® Pro Testmaker CD-ROM Presentation Plus! CD-ROM Glencoe BookLink CD-ROM
Section 3 **The Spread of Christian Ideas** 1. Church and government worked closely together in the Byzantine Empire. 2. Christians founded new communities and spread their faith in various parts of Europe.	Reproducible Lesson Plan 10–3 Daily Lecture and Discussion Notes 10–3 Vocabulary Activity 10–3 Active Reading Note-Taking Guide 10–3 Guided Reading Activity 10–3* Section Quiz 10–3* Reading Essentials and Study Guide 10–3*	Daily Focus Skills Transparency 10–3 Interactive Tutor Self-Assessment CD-ROM ExamView® Pro Testmaker CD-ROM Presentation Plus! CD-ROM Vocabulary PuzzleMaker CD-ROM

*Also available in Spanish

History Online

Use our Web site for additional resources. All essential content is covered in the Student Edition.

You and your students can visit jat.glencoe.com, the Web site companion to *World History: Journey Across Time*. This innovative integration of electronic and print media offers your students a wealth of opportunities. The student text directs students to the Web site for the following options:

- Chapter Overviews
- Self-Check Quizzes
- Study Central™
- Student Web Activities
- Multi-Language Glossaries

Answers to the student Web activities are provided for you in the **Web Activity Lesson Plans.** Additional Web resources and ePuzzles and games are also available.

Videotape programs are available from Glencoe as supplements to the chapters.

To order, call Glencoe at 1-800-334-7344. To find classroom resources to accompany many of these videos, check the following home pages:

A&E Television: www.aande.com
The History Channel: www.historychannel.com

MEETING SPECIAL NEEDS

In addition to the Differentiated Instruction strategies, the following resources are suitable for students with special needs:

- *ExamView® Pro Testmaker CD-ROM* allows teachers to tailor tests by reducing answer choices.
- *StudentWorks Plus™ CD-ROM (with Audio Program)* includes the entire narrative of the student edition so that less-proficient readers can listen to the words as they read them.
- The *Reading Essentials and Study Guide* provides the same content as the student edition but is written two grade levels below the textbook.
- *Guided Reading Activities* give less-proficient readers point-by-point instructions to increase comprehension as they read each textbook section.
- *Differentiated Instruction Activities* include a stimulating collection of readings and activities for students of all levels.

TEACHER'S CORNER

Index to National Geographic Magazine:

The following articles relate to this chapter:

- "The Three Faces of Jerusalem," by Alan Mairson, April 1996.
- "Out of the Darkness: Michelangelo's Last Judgment," by Meg Walsh, May 1994.
- "Who Are the Palestinians?," by Tad Szulc, June 1992.

National Geographic Society Products:

To order the following, call National Geographic at 1–800–368–2728

- *Jerusalem: Within These Walls* (DVD)
- *PictureShow: Ancient Civilizations: Greece and Rome* (CD-ROM)

NGS ONLINE

Access National Geographic's new dynamic MapMachine Web site and other geography resources at:

www.nationalgeographic.com
www.nationalgeographic.com/maps

Meeting NCSS Standards

World History: Journey Across Time

The following standards are highlighted in Chapter 10:

Section 1 **I** Culture: D, F
IV Individual Development and Identity: C, E, G
V Individuals, Groups, and Institutions: C, D, E, F, G

Section 2 **III** People, Places, and Environments: B
V Individuals, Groups, and Institutions: B, C, D, E, F, G, H
VI Power, Authority, and Governance: F

Section 3 **V** Individuals, Groups, and Institutions: B, E, F, G
IX Global Connections: A, B, G, H

State and Local Objectives

_____

_____

_____

Timesaving Tools

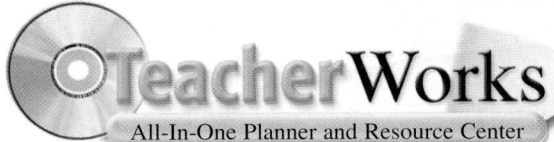

TeacherWorks
All-In-One Planner and Resource Center

- **Interactive Teacher Edition** Access your Teacher Wraparound Edition and your classroom resources with a few easy clicks.
- **Interactive Lesson Planner** Organize your week, month, semester, or year with all the lesson helps you need to make teaching creative and relevant.

Use Glencoe's **Presentation Plus!** multimedia teacher tool to easily present dynamic lessons that visually excite your students. Using Microsoft PowerPoint® you can customize the presentations to create your own personalized lessons.

FOLDABLES™
Study Organizer

Dinah Zike's Foldables

Foldables are three-dimensional, interactive graphic organizers that help students practice basic writing skills, review key vocabulary terms, and identify main ideas. Every chapter contains a foldable activity, with additional chapter activities found in the *Reading and Study Skills Foldables* booklet. You can use the foldables as they are presented, or modify them to suit the needs of your individual class.

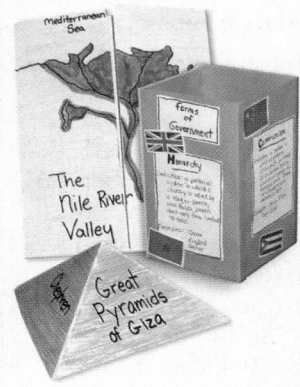

Planning Ahead

CHAPTER CULMINATING ACTIVITY

The Chapter Culminating Activity will help students organize and learn the important information from the chapter. Begin teaching the chapter with this activity, and have students complete it as a culminating activity.

COMPLETING A FLOW CHART

Purpose A flow chart provides students with a visual way to understand the chronological order of events that occurred during a certain time period. Sometimes, cause-and-effect relationships also are illustrated by a flow chart.

Introduction to Modeling

1. Draw on the board three flow charts, one for each section of this chapter. For each, fill in the first box with the information provided. Direct students to complete each flow chart as they read the corresponding section of the chapter. (Answers are provided.)

Section 1 Flow Chart

Jesus of Nazareth is born.
↓
Jesus' teachings make people think in a different, more caring way.
↓
Jesus is crucified and, according to Christian belief, rose from the dead.
↓
Christianity is born.

Section 2 Flow Chart

The Romans persecuted early Christians.
↓
Emperor Constantine grants all Romans, including Christians, religious freedom.
↓
Christian leaders put together the New Testament.

Section 3 Flow Chart

Although religious arguments broke the church into two, Christianity continued to attract more followers.
↓
In both Orthodox and Catholic Churches, the church worked closely with the government.
↓
Christianity continued to spread, reaching north and west as far as Britain and Spain.

2. When students have finished Chapter 10, have them review the chapter content by comparing the flow charts they have created.

Use the **SkillBuilder Handbook** on pages 902–919 to help students learn the skill of sequencing and categorizing information.

338D

Authentic Assessment

Refer to Activity 10 in the Authentic Assessment section of the *Quizzes, Tests, and Authentic Assessment (with Rubrics)* booklet.

When & Where?

As students read the chapter, have them keep track of interactions between Romans and Christians. Ask students to explain how the Roman Empire affected Christianity. *(At first, the Romans persecuted Christians. After Constantine accepted Christianity, the empire supported it.)* **L1**

GLENCOE TECHNOLOGY

World History: Journey Across Time Video Program

To learn more about the rise of Christianity, students can view the Chapter 10 video in the *World History: Journey Across Time* Video Program.

MindJogger Videoquiz

Use the **MindJogger Videoquiz** to preview Chapter 10 content.

 Available in DVD and VHS

Chapter 10

The Rise of Christianity

▼ Mount of the Beatitudes on the Sea of Galilee in Israel

NATIONAL GEOGRAPHIC When & Where?

A.D. 50	A.D. 400	A.D. 750	A.D. 1100
A.D. 30 Jesus preaches in Galilee and Judaea	A.D. 312 Constantine accepts Christianity	A.D. 726 Emperor Leo III removes icons from churches	A.D. 1054 Orthodox and Catholic Churches separate

---

Reading Strategy — PURPOSE FOR READING

Growth of Christianity Direct students' attention to the map on page 352. Explain that the map shows the spread of Christianity from about A.D. 30 to A.D. 325. Help students locate Judaea and Galilee. Point out that Christianity started in this region. Next, have student pairs use rulers and the map key to figure out how far west Christian ideas spread during this time. *(about 1,800 miles/2,897 km)* **Ask:** How do you think a new religion like Christianity could spread so far so fast? *(Answers may include that ship travel on the Mediterranean Sea may have helped the spread of Christianity.)* As students read the chapter, have them take notes on events or circumstances that helped Christianity to spread. **L1**

Chapter Preview

While the Romans built their empire, a group called the Christians spread a new religion called Christianity. Read this chapter to find out how Christianity grew to become one of the major influences on European civilization.

 View the Chapter 10 video in the *World History: Journey Across Time* Video Program.

Chapter Overview Visit jat.glencoe.com for a preview of Chapter 10.

 ## The First Christians

After the Romans conquered Judah, some Jews opposed Rome peacefully, while others rebelled. During that period, Jesus of Nazareth began preaching a message of love and forgiveness. His life and teachings led to the rise of Christianity.

 ## The Christian Church

In time, Christianity became the Roman Empire's official religion. Early Christians organized the church and collected the New Testament of the Bible.

 ## The Spread of Christian Ideas

Church and government worked closely together in the Byzantine Empire. Christians founded new communities and spread their faith through Europe.

Sequencing Information *Make this foldable to help you sequence information about the rise of Christianity.*

Step 1 *Fold a piece of paper from top to bottom.*

Step 2 *Then fold back each half to make quarter folds.*

This makes an accordian shape.

Step 3 *Unfold and label the time line as shown.*

The Rise of Christianity

Step 4 *Fill in important dates as you read like those shown.*

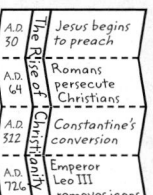

Reading and Writing *As you read the chapter, write the important events that occurred in the rise of Christianity.*

339

History Online

Introduce students to chapter content and key terms by having them access **Chapter Overview 10** at jat.glencoe.com

CHAPTER PREVIEW

After reading Chapter 10, students will be able to

1. describe how Jesus' life, teachings, and death led to the birth of a new religion—Christianity;

2. explain how Christianity became the official religion of the Roman Empire;

3. evaluate the connections between religion and government during Christianity's early years.

FOLDABLES Study Organizer

Dinah Zike's Foldables

Purpose Students use this foldable to organize information about the birth and spread of Christianity. As students read each section, they should add the important events and dates to their foldable time lines.

☞ Have students complete *Reading and Study Skills Foldables* Activity 10.

MORE ABOUT THE PHOTO

Mount of the Beatitudes Perhaps Jesus' most famous teaching took place on this mount. According to biblical tradition, a large group of people from Galilee, Decapolis, Jerusalem, Judaea, and from beyond Jordan had gathered to hear Jesus speak near the Sea of Galilee. Jesus took his position on the hill where his voice would travel well to those attending below. The teaching he gave there is often called the "Sermon on the Mount" because of this location. In this sermon, Jesus delivered a set of guidelines on how to be good and spiritually minded. He also described the beatitudes, or a series of blessings that would be granted to the faithful.

1 Learn It!

Point out that sequence clues, such as *next*, *then*, and *consequently*, help explain when events took place or the order in which they happened. Noticing when sequence words are being used helps the reader understand the order of events, which makes comprehension easier.

Write *Time*, *When*, and *Order* on the board as column headings. Then have students brainstorm sequence words and write them under the headings. Next, begin reading aloud "How Did the Romans Treat Christians?" in Section 2. Ask students to identify the sequence words and phrases as they hear them. Possible responses include *over time*, *as a result*, *in A.D. 64*, *at this time*, *during*, *after A.D. 250*, and *at the same time*. Encourage students to think of other sequence words that were not in the text, such as *next*, *then*, *soon*, and *meanwhile*.

Chapter 10

Reading Social Studies

Reading Skill
Sequence Clues

1 Learn It!
Looking for Sequence Clues

When we speak, read, or write, we automatically use clues to tell us what happened when. These clues are called sequence words, and they show us the order in which events occur.

Read the following passage about the spread of Christianity. Notice the highlighted sequence words or phrases.

> **After the fall of Rome, the people of Western Europe faced confusion and conflict. As a result, people were looking for order and unity. Christianity helped to meet this need. It spread rapidly into lands that had once been part of the Roman Empire.**
>
> —*from page 361*

Reading Tip

When you have trouble understanding the order in which things occur, create a rough time line to help you keep track of events as you read.

Now read the paragraph again and leave out the highlighted sequence words. Do you see how important they are in helping you understand what you are reading?

340

Reading Strategy — SEQUENCE INFORMATION

Draw a horizontal flow chart like the following on the board:

```
[        ] → [        ] → [        ] → [        ]
```

Explain that a flow chart shows the sequence of events or the order in which they happened. Then model how to use the flow chart. As you read aloud "Rome Adopts Christianity" in Section 2, have students raise their hands when an event is mentioned that should be placed in the flow chart. Add it to the flow chart. **L2**

2 Practice It!

Finding Clue Words

Read this passage and write down any word or phrase that helps you recognize the sequence of events.

Read to Write ......

Look at the time line that appears at the bottom of page 342. Write a paragraph that uses sequence clues to describe when these events occurred.

> Even with all of the hardships, Christianity spread. Over time it even began to draw people from all classes. After A.D. 250, many Romans grew tired of war and feared the end of the empire. They began to admire the faith and courage of the Christians. At the same time, many Christians started to accept the empire.
>
> —*from pages 353–354*

The apostle Peter preaching ▼

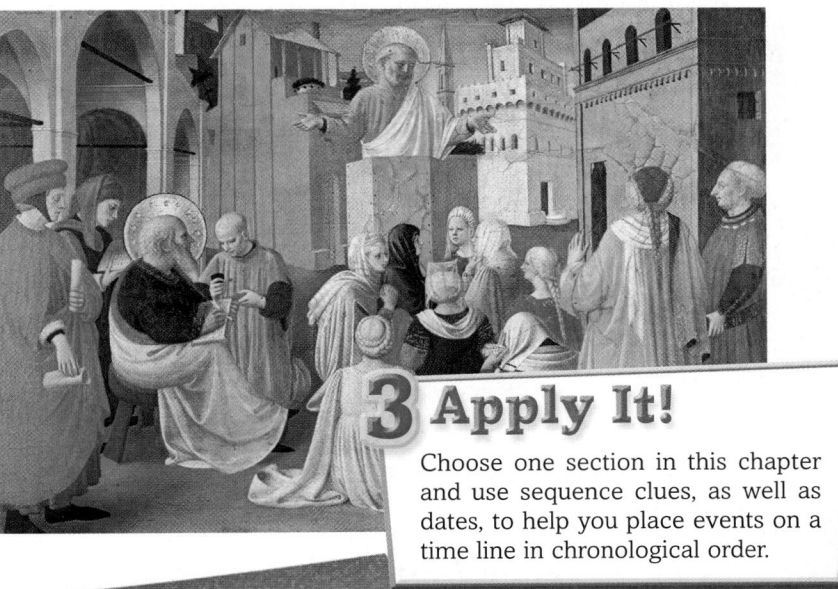

3 Apply It!

Choose one section in this chapter and use sequence clues, as well as dates, to help you place events on a time line in chronological order.

341

2 Practice It!

Explain that different text structures require somewhat different types of sequence clues.

Narratives Explain that a narrative tells a story. Sequence words that tell when events happened in a narrative might include *next, then,* and *after* to indicate time.

Expository Text Point out that text that explains what happened in history may also use these words, but it also uses dates to show order. This type of expository text can easily be placed on a time line to show the chronological order of events. Ask student pairs to read "The Early Church" in Section 2. Tell them to identify the text as narrative or expository and to list all the sequence words and dates in the order in which they appear. Then discuss why selections about history use dates.

3 Apply It!

After students have chosen their sections, have them begin by drawing the time line at the beginning of the selected section. Tell students to leave room so that they can get the events in order. **L1**

Reading Strategy ◀ READ TO WRITE

Before students write their paragraphs, give them practice using sequence words with the time line. Have volunteers describe in several ways the events shown on the time line. For example, the event "Jesus preaches in Galilee and Judaea" might be stated in the following ways:

- Jesus preached in Galilee and Judaea around A.D. 30.
- Jesus preached in Galilee and Judaea before the Jewish uprising against Rome.
- The Jewish uprising against Rome occurred about 30 years after Jesus preached in Galilee and Judaea.

① FOCUS

SECTION OVERVIEW

This section describes the history of Roman-Jewish interaction, as well as the birth of Christianity.

BELLRINGER
SKILLBUILDER ACTIVITY

✎ Project **Daily Focus Skills Transparency 10–1** and have students answer questions. Discuss their responses.

Get Ready to Read!

Preteaching Vocabulary: Explain that parables helped simplify ideas that might otherwise have seemed very complicated. For example, many of the people Jesus spoke to were shepherds. They would, therefore, understand the story of the good shepherd. Parables also showed how people could apply Jesus' teachings to their everyday lives. You may want to compare Jesus' parables to Aesop's tales, which teach moral lessons through simple stories.

Answers to Graphic: pray, study the Hebrew Bible, share in a ritual meal like the Last Supper

---

Section ①

The First Christians

Get-Ready to Read!

What's the Connection?
You learned that the Romans ruled many areas of the Mediterranean. In one of these areas, Judaea, a new religion, Christianity, began.

Focusing on the Main Ideas
- Roman rule of Judaea led some Jews to oppose Rome peacefully, while others rebelled. *(page 343)*
- Jesus of Nazareth preached of God's love and forgiveness. He was eventually crucified and then reported to have risen from the dead. *(page 344)*
- Jesus' life and a belief in his resurrection led to a new religion called Christianity. *(page 348)*

Locating Places
Jerusalem (juh•ROO•suh•luhm)
Judaea (ju•DEE•uh)
Nazareth (NA•zuh•ruhth)
Galilee (GA•luh•LEE)

Meeting People
Jesus (JEE•zuhs)
Peter
Paul

Building Your Vocabulary
messiah (muh•SY•uh)
disciple (dih•SY•puhl)
parable (PAR•uh•buhl)
resurrection (REH•zuh•REHK•shuhn)
apostle (uh•PAH•suhl)
salvation (sal•VAY•shuhn)

Reading Strategy
Summarizing Information Complete a diagram like the one below showing the purposes of early Christian churches.

Purposes of Churches

NATIONAL GEOGRAPHIC When & Where?

ITALY
Rome

ASIA MINOR

JUDAEA
Jerusalem

A.D. 1 — A.D. 50 — A.D. 100 — A.D. 150

A.D. 30 Jesus preaches in Galilee and Judaea

A.D. 66 Jews in Judaea rise up against Rome

A.D. 132 Romans force Jews out of Jerusalem

SECTION RESOURCES

📁 **Reproducible Masters**
- Reproducible Lesson Plan 10–1
- Daily Lecture and Discussion Notes 10–1
- Vocabulary Activity 10–1
- Active Reading Note-Taking Guide 10–1
- Guided Reading Activity 10–1
- Section Quiz 10–1
- Reading Essentials and Study Guide 10–1

✎ **Transparencies**
- Daily Focus Skills Transparency 10–1

Multimedia
- Interactive Tutor Self-Assessment CD-ROM
- *ExamView®* Pro Testmaker CD-ROM
- Presentation Plus! CD-ROM
- Glencoe BookLink CD-ROM

The Jews and the Romans

Main Idea Roman rule of Judaea led some Jews to oppose Rome peacefully, while others rebelled.

Reading Focus Suppose you were separated from your home and could not easily return to it. What effect might this have on you? Read to learn how the Jews were forced to leave their capital city.

As you learned earlier, during the 900s B.C., two great kings, David and Solomon, united the Israelites and created the kingdom of Israel. Its capital was **Jerusalem** (juh•ROO•suh•luhm). This unity did not last long, however. Israel divided into two kingdoms: Israel and Judah. These small kingdoms were later taken over by more powerful neighbors. Israel was destroyed, and its people scattered. But the Jews, the people of Judah, survived.

Roman Rule In 63 B.C. the Romans took over Judah. At first, they ruled through Jewish kings. Then, in A.D. 6, Emperor Augustus turned Judah into a Roman province called **Judaea** (ju•DEE•uh). Instead of a king, a Roman governor called a procurator (PRAH•kyuh•RAY•tuhr) ruled the new province.

The Jews argued among themselves over what to do about the Romans. Some favored working with the Romans. Others opposed Roman rule by closely following Jewish traditions. Still others turned their backs on the Romans. They settled in isolated areas and shared their belongings.

The Jews Rebel Some Jews believed that they should fight the Romans and take back control of their kingdom. These people, called Zealots, convinced many Jews to take up arms against the Romans in A.D. 66. The rebellion was brutally crushed. The Romans destroyed the temple and killed thousands of Jews. A Jewish general named Josephus (joh•SEE•fuhs) fought in the war but later sided with the Romans. He wrote about the horrors of Jerusalem's fall in his work *History of the Jewish War*.

The Jews rebelled again in A.D. 132 and were again defeated. This time the Romans forced all Jews to leave Jerusalem and banned them from ever returning to the city. Saddened by the loss of Jerusalem, many Jews found new homes elsewhere.

By A.D. 700, the Jews had set up communities as far west as Spain and as far east as central Asia. In later centuries, they settled throughout Europe and the Americas. In their scattered communities, the Jews kept their faith alive by studying and following their religious laws.

Reading Check **Explain** Why did many Jews leave Judaea after the A.D. 132 revolt?

These ruins are of the mountaintop Jewish fortress at Masada in Israel. Jewish rebels were defeated by Roman troops here in A.D. 73. *What were the Jewish rebels called?*

CURRICULUM CONNECTION

Religion
Remind students that when Jesus was teaching, the Jews had been a defeated people under Roman rule for almost 100 years. Point out that Jesus taught "Love your neighbor as yourself" in the middle of this tense situation. Have students discuss whom Jews and Romans might have considered their neighbors and what they might have thought about Jesus' message.

More About the Art

Jesus' message was especially popular among social outcasts and the poor.

Caption Answer:
Following Jewish religious laws was not as important as having a relationship with God.

The Life of Jesus

Main Idea Jesus of Nazareth preached of God's love and forgiveness. He was eventually crucified and then reported to have risen from the dead.

Reading Focus If you could give someone advice on how to behave, what would you tell them? Why? Read to learn how Jesus thought people should behave.

During Roman times, many Jews hoped that God would send a **messiah** (muh•SY•uh), or deliverer. This leader would help them win back their freedom. The Israelite prophets had long ago predicted that a messiah would come. Many Jews expected the messiah to be a great king, like David. They thought the messiah would restore the past glories of the Israelite kingdom.

A few decades before the first Jewish revolt against Rome, a Jew named **Jesus** (JEE•zuhs) left his home in **Nazareth** (NA•zuh•ruhth) and began preaching. From about A.D. 30 to A.D. 33, Jesus traveled throughout Judaea and **Galilee** (GA•luh•LEE), the region just north of Judaea, preaching his ideas. Crowds gathered to hear him preach. He soon assembled a small band of 12 close followers called **disciples** (dih•SY•puhlz).

What Did Jesus Teach? According to the Christian Bible, Jesus preached that God was coming soon to rule the world. He urged people to turn from their sins. He also told them that following Jewish religious laws was not as important as having a relationship with God, whom Jesus referred to as his Father.

The main points of Jesus' message are given in a group of sayings known as the Sermon on the Mount. In them, Jesus made it clear that a person had to love and forgive

The Teachings of Jesus

▼ Jesus traveled throughout the regions of Judaea and Galilee, preaching to all who would listen to his religious message. In the Sermon on the Mount, illustrated below, Jesus described God's love and how to be a good person. At right, Jesus is shown as the Good Shepherd, a popular image in early Christian art. *What did Jesus teach about Jewish religious laws?*

DIFFERENTIATED INSTRUCTION

Verbal/Linguistic: Tell students to paraphrase the following beatitudes to make them easier to understand: "Blessed are the merciful, for they will obtain mercy"; "Blessed are the peacemakers, for they will be called the children of God." Have volunteers share their sentences with the class.

Visual/Spatial: Ask students to choose a parable or teaching of Jesus that is in the text or a different parable and to make a piece of art that expresses its meaning. Encourage students to share their art with the class and explain how it relates to Jesus' teachings.

Gifted and Talented: Have students discuss why peacemakers might be considered "the children of God." Then tell students to research what the Nobel Peace Prize is and why some people have received it. Ask students to consider whether such peacemakers are important.

from the heart and not just go through the motions of following religious laws. Among Jesus' sayings were "Blessed are the merciful, for they will obtain mercy" and "Blessed are the peacemakers, for they will be called the children of God."

Jesus told his listeners to love and forgive each other because God loves and forgives people. According to Jesus, God's command was simple. He repeated the age-old Jewish teaching: "Love the Lord your God with all your heart and with all your soul and with all your mind and with all your strength." Jesus also stressed another teaching: "Love your neighbor as yourself." Jesus' message of love and forgiveness helped shape the values many people in Europe and America hold today.

To present his message, Jesus often used **parables** (PAR•uh•buhlz). These were stories that used events from everyday life to express spiritual ideas. In the story of the Prodigal (wasteful) Son, Jesus told how a father welcomed back his reckless son with open arms. He forgave his son's mistakes. In another parable, he told of a shepherd who left his flock unguarded to go after one lost sheep. Both stories taught that God forgives mistakes and wants all people to turn away from bad deeds and be saved.

The parable of the Good Samaritan is one of the best known. In this story, a man is beaten by robbers. A priest and another religious leader refuse to help the injured man. However, a Samaritan, a member of a group looked down upon by Jesus' listeners, stops to help the victim. He treats the man's wounds and pays for his stay at an inn. Jesus asked his followers, "Which man do you think truly showed love to his neighbor?"

▼ Jesus used stories, called parables, to describe correct behaviors to his followers. The parables of the Prodigal Son (below) and the Good Samaritan (right) are shown here. *What lesson was taught by the parable of the Prodigal Son?*

CHAPTER 10   The Rise of Christianity   345

CRITICAL THINKING ACTIVITY

Making Inferences Point out to students that like Jesus' parables, many stories have a message. As an example, elicit the story of George Washington cutting down the cherry tree, or tell the story yourself. **Ask:** What is the message of this story? *(Answers may include that one should tell the truth, even if it means trouble; leaders should be truthful.)* Then organize students into small groups, and ask each group to think of a story that has a message or a point. As a helpful hint, tell students that fables and fairy tales often have a message for the reader. When groups are ready, have each one share its story and its message with the class. **L2**

Writing Activity ✏️

Ask students to write this heading on a piece of paper: What Did Jesus Teach? Tell students that they should list the main points Jesus made when he preached as they read this section. **L1/ EL**

More About the Art

In his parables, Jesus used images from nature, such as the tiny mustard seed, the barren fig tree, and the pearl of great price.

Caption Answer: that God forgives mistakes and wants all people to turn away from bad deeds and be saved

CONNECTING ACROSS TIME

Point out that after Jesus' death, the religion of Christianity emerged. Explain that, despite a common faith in Jesus as savior, Christianity broke into many different branches over the centuries. Have small groups of students identify and list some of them, suggesting that they use a phone book if they have trouble locating names of different branches or churches. When students have finished, ask groups to share their lists with the class. **L1**

Biography

TEACH

Some thought that Jesus' ability to attract large crowds made him politically dangerous. The Romans had executed other people whom they feared could cause an uprising. As Passover neared, Jesus traveled to Jerusalem. Many Jews were there to celebrate the holiday. According to the gospels, Jesus entered the city on a donkey to show that he was a humble servant, not a warrior-king. However, his visit to Jerusalem did not go without incident. That week, Jesus drove traders from the temple's outer court and disputed with religious leaders who questioned his authority. Fearing that Jesus would bring disorder, Roman officials had him crucified.

Ask students what actions officials today might take if a person was seen as a threat to public order. (*Answers will vary but might mention police arrests of suspects.*) **L1/** **EL**

Then and Now

Jesus' birth; answers may include elaborate meals and decorated trees.

Biography

JESUS OF NAZARETH
c. 6 B.C.–A.D. 30

Much of what we know about Jesus, whose life and teachings established the Christian religion, is based on accounts found in the Bible. According to the Bible, Jesus' birth was guided by God. An angel visited Mary, Jesus' mother, to tell her she was going to have a baby. The angel told Mary her baby would be the Son of God. An angel also visited Joseph, Mary's fiancé, and instructed him to marry her.

Jesus was humbly born in a stable, beside barn animals, in the town of Bethlehem. Mary and Joseph had traveled there to take part in a census ordered by the Romans. Shepherds and wise men, possibly princes from neighboring kingdoms, followed a brightly shining star to honor Jesus in the stable. Christmas is a celebration of Jesus' birth.

The Bible tells very little about the middle years of Jesus' life. He grew up in Nazareth, a small town in Galilee, where he learned the carpenter's trade from Joseph. Later in life, Jesus set out to share his religious teachings. At this point, the Bible provides many stories of Jesus' travels and the miracles he performed. The accounts of Jesus' miracles, such as giving a blind man sight, raising a man from the dead, and calming a storm at sea, brought many followers to his teachings. When Jesus entered Jerusalem the week before his death, he was greeted by cheering crowds. One of Jesus' closest followers, however, betrayed him and turned him over to Roman authorities. Jesus was questioned by Jewish and Roman officials and sentenced to death. Soon afterwards, reports that he had risen from the dead would lead to a new religion—Christianity.

▲ Jesus entering Jerusalem

> "I am the light that has come into the world."
> —Jesus of Nazareth, John 12:46

◄ An early depiction of Jesus on his throne

Then and Now

What event does Christmas celebrate? What aspects of Christmas today are not related to its traditional meaning?

Reading List Generator CD-ROM

GLENCOE BOOKLINK   **RECOMMENDED READING**

Use the **Glencoe BookLink CD-ROM** to create customized reading lists based on your students' interests and reading levels. Below is an example based on content in this chapter. Also, see the Suggested Readings on pages 944–946 of the Appendix.

- **Eban, Abba.** *Heritage: Civilization and the Jews.* Tells the history of the Jews and their contributions to other cultures.

- **Green, Robert.** *Herod the Great.* A biography of the ruthless Judaean ruler and builder.

What Is the Crucifixion? Jesus and his message drew strong responses from people. His followers called attention to instances in which they believed he healed the sick and performed other miracles. They said he was the long-awaited messiah. Other Jews disagreed and said he was a deceiver. Above all, Judaea's Roman rulers feared the effects of Jesus' preaching. A person who could spark such strong reactions might threaten law and order.

About A.D. 33, Jesus went to Jerusalem to celebrate Passover, an important Jewish holiday. There he was greeted by large, cheering crowds. In an event known as the Last Supper, Jesus celebrated the holiday with his 12 disciples. Fearing trouble, leaders in Jerusalem arrested Jesus. Jesus was charged with treason, or disloyalty to the government. As punishment, Jesus was crucified, or hung from a cross until dead. This was Rome's way of punishing political rebels and lower-class criminals.

After Jesus' death, his followers made a startling claim. They announced that Jesus had risen from the dead. Christian tradition states that Mary Magdalene, one of Jesus' followers, was the first to see Jesus alive again. Others, including Jesus' disciples, reported seeing him as well. The disciples also pointed to his empty tomb as proof that Jesus was the messiah. These reports of Jesus' **resurrection** (REH•zuh•REHK•shuhn), or rising from the dead, led to a new religion called Christianity.

Reading Check **Describing** What were the main ideas Jesus taught during his life?

▲ According to the Bible, just before his death, Jesus gathered his disciples together for a meal known as the Last Supper. *Why did the Romans fear Jesus?*

TIME TRAVELER

Crucifixion was a common form of capital punishment among peoples such as the Persians, Carthaginians, and Romans. Usually the name and crime of the person being crucified were written above the accused's head. In Jesus' case, his supposed crime was claiming to be King of the Jews.

✓ Reading Check

Answer: to love God and to love one's neighbor

More About the Art

Today most Christian churches commemorate the Last Supper with a ritual meal.

Caption Answer: He could spark strong emotions that might threaten law and order.

Reading Support L1/ EL

Assign **Guided Reading Activity 10–1** to help students organize the information in the section.

INTERDISCIPLINARY CONNECTIONS ACTIVITY

Art Remind students that parables were stories that had special meaning, and were often quite vivid. Tell them that the same can be true of pictures. Organize students into small groups and provide each group with art paper and picture sources, such as magazines, newspapers, and the Internet. Explain that the assignment is to create a collage about a topic currently important in your community. Collages should reflect visually the message. **L1**

③ ASSESS

Assign Section 1 Review as homework or as an in-class activity.

⊙ Have students use the **Interactive Tutor Self-Assessment CD-ROM** to review the section.

Assessment L2

Assign **Section 1 Quiz** to assess mastery of the material found in the section.

Reading Support L1/EL

Assign **Reading Essentials and Study Guide 10–1** to help students review section material.

Primary Source

The Lord's Prayer also was part of the Sermon on the Mount. Read aloud the Lord's Prayer in Matthew 6:9–13. Discuss with students what people are asking when they say this prayer.

Answer:
because they will be rewarded in heaven

The First Christians

Main Idea Jesus' life and a belief in his resurrection led to a new religion called Christianity.

Reading Focus Have you ever read news stories about people sacrificing their lives to help others? Read to learn about the sacrifice Christians believe Jesus made for everyone.

Jesus' disciples began to spread the message of Jesus and his resurrection. Small groups in the Greek-speaking cities of the eastern Mediterranean accepted this message. Some were Jews, but others were not.

Primary Source — Sermon on the Mount

Jesus encouraged his disciples with the Sermon on the Mount.

"Happy are you when men insult you and persecute you and tell all kinds of evil lies against you because you are my followers. Be happy and glad, for a great reward is kept for you in heaven. This is how the prophets who lived before you were persecuted."

—Matthew 5:11–12

▲ Jesus and his followers

DBQ Document-Based Question

Why does Jesus tell his followers to ignore—even rejoice in—persecution?

Those who accepted Jesus Christ and his teachings became known as Christians. The word *Christ* comes from *Christos*, the Greek word for "messiah."

The early Christians formed churches, or communities for worship and teaching. They met in people's houses, many of which were owned by women. At these gatherings, Christians prayed and studied the Hebrew Bible. They also shared in a ritual meal like the Last Supper to remember Jesus' death and resurrection.

Who Were Peter and Paul?
Apostles (uh•PAH•suhlz), or early Christian leaders who helped set up churches and spread the message of Jesus, played an important role in the growth of Christianity. Perhaps the two most important were **Peter** and **Paul.**

Simon Peter was a Jewish fisher. He had known Jesus while he was alive and had been one of the original 12 people Jesus had called to preach his message. Christian tradition states that he went to Rome after the death of Jesus and helped set up a church there. Today, the leader of Catholic Christians resides in Rome.

Paul of Tarsus was another important Christian leader. He was a well-educated Jew and a Roman citizen. Paul at first hated Christianity and persecuted Christians in Jerusalem. The chief Jewish priest in Jerusalem then sent him to Damascus (duh•MAS•kuhs), a city in Syria, to stop Christians in the city from spreading their ideas.

While on the road to Damascus, Paul had an unusual experience. According to Christian belief, he saw a great light and heard Jesus' voice. Paul became a Christian on the spot. He spent the rest of his life spreading Jesus' message. Paul traveled widely. He founded churches throughout the eastern Mediterranean.

EXTENDING THE CONTENT

The Names of Jesus Until his death, Jesus usually went by just one name, as did other Jews of the time. If more information was necessary to identify someone, the place of birth or the father's name might be added to the name. For example, Jesus also was known as Jesus, son of Joseph; Jesus the Nazarene; and Jesus of Nazareth. The title "Christ" was used mostly after his death.

Biography

PAUL OF TARSUS
c. A.D. 10–65

Without the apostle Paul, Christianity might not have become one of the world's most widely accepted religions. It was Paul who spread the word about Jesus to the Gentiles, or non-Jews, and helped Jesus gain acceptance as the messiah.

Paul was a Jew from Tarsus, a major city in Asia Minor. His father was a Roman citizen, and his family followed the laws and rules of the Pharisees—a Jewish group that stressed the need to follow Jewish laws. His parents named their son Saul after the first king of the Jews. The first trade Saul learned was tent making. Around age 10, he was sent to Jerusalem to attend a school under the direction of the famed Pharisee teacher Gamaliel. Saul received a well-rounded education. He learned the language and history of the Romans, Jews, and Greeks.

When Saul was in his twenties, he opposed and persecuted Christians and their newly formed church in Jerusalem. He was on his way to Damascus in Syria to find and arrest Christians there when a vision of Jesus led him to accept Christianity.

Saul began using the Latin name Paul after his conversion to Christianity. He traveled extensively, preaching and writing to Gentiles. He also wrote many important letters, known as epistles, to churches in Rome, Greece, and Asia Minor. These letters are included in the Christian Bible.

Paul convinced many people that if they died as Christians, they would have eternal life. Even though Paul's only meeting with Jesus was supposedly in his vision, Paul visited more places and preached to more people than most of the apostles who had known Jesus in person. Paul worked as a missionary for around 35 years. He was probably killed when the Roman emperor Nero ordered that Christians in Rome be arrested and put to death.

▲ Paul of Tarsus

> "I showed how you should work to help everyone."
> —Paul, Acts 20:35

▲ A book containing the teachings of Paul

Then and Now

Can you think of any groups of people in today's world who are persecuted for their beliefs?

349

TEACH

Paul believed that Jesus' teachings were for everyone, not just for the Jews. Some converted Jews believed that Gentiles had to first convert to Judaism before they could become Christians. Both Peter, one of Jesus' close followers and one of the original 12 disciples, and Paul disagreed. This issue was disputed in the early Christian communities for years, but Paul consistently supported the spread of Christianity to all people.

Ask students how religions spread their teachings today. *(Answers may include that they still use missionaries who personally try to convert people or that some preachers use television to spread their teachings.)* **L1/** **EL**

Then and Now

Answers may include the continuing conflict between Hindus and Muslims in India and Pakistan.

Reading List Generator CD-ROM

GLENCOE BOOKLINK **RECOMMENDED READING**

Use the **Glencoe BookLink CD-ROM** to create customized reading lists based on your students' interests and reading levels. Below is an example based on content in this chapter. Also, see the Suggested Readings on pages 944–946 of the Appendix.

- Brandt, Keith. *Ancient Rome.* The history of the vast Roman Empire at its height.
- Waldman, Neil. *The Golden City: Jerusalem's 3,000 Years.* Presents the history of Jerusalem from the time of King David to the present day.

- Vocabulary Activity 10–2
- Active Reading Note-Taking Guide 10–2
- Guided Reading Activity 10–2
- Section Quiz 10–2
- Reading Essentials and Study Guide 10–2

- Interactive Tutor Self-Assessment CD-ROM
- ExamView® Pro Testmaker CD-ROM
- Presentation Plus! CD-ROM
- Glencoe BookLink CD-ROM

② TEACH

What Do Christians Believe? From the beginning, Christians taught that Jesus was

A Growing Faith

Main Idea Christianity won many followers and eventually became the official religion of the Roman Empire.

Reading Focus Why do you think people like to belong to a community? Read to learn about early Christian communities.

During the 100 years after Jesus' death, Christianity won followers throughout the Roman world. The empire itself helped spread Christian ideas. The peace and order established by **Rome** allowed people to travel in safety. Christians used well-paved Roman roads to carry their message from place to place. Since most of the empire's people spoke either Latin or Greek, Christians could talk with them directly.

Why did Christianity attract followers? First, the Christian message gave meaning to people's lives. Rome's official religion urged people to honor the state and the emperor. Christianity instead reached out to the poor and the powerless who led very hard lives. It offered hope and comfort.

Second, the ideas of Christianity were familiar to many Romans. They already knew about other eastern Mediterranean religions. Like these faiths, Christianity

NATIONAL GEOGRAPHIC

Spread of Christianity A.D. 325

Lambert Azimuthal Equal-Area projection

Using Geography Skills

Even while facing Roman persecution, the Christian religion continued to grow within the Roman Empire.
1. To what areas did Paul's journeys take him?
2. Why do you think Christianity spread as it did by A.D. 325?
Find NGS online map resources @ www.nationalgeographic.com/maps

KEY

Main areas of Christian growth to A.D. 325
Paul's first journey
Paul's second journey

352   CHAPTER 10   The Rise of Christianity

appealed to the emotions and promised happiness after death.

Finally, Christianity gave people the chance to be part of a caring group. Within their churches, Christians not only worshiped together but helped each other. They took care of the sick, the elderly, widows, and orphans. Many women found that Christianity offered them new roles. They ran churches from their homes, spread Jesus' message, and helped care for those in need.

How Did the Romans Treat Christians?

Over time, Roman officials began to see the Christians as a threat to the government. All people in the empire were usually allowed to worship freely, but the Romans expected everyone to honor the emperor as a god. Christians, like the Jews, refused to do this. They claimed that only God could be worshiped. Christians also refused to serve in the army or hold public office. They criticized Roman festivals and games. As a result, the Romans saw the Christians as traitors who should be punished.

In A.D. 64 the Roman government began to **persecute** (PURH•sih•KYOOT), or mistreat, Christians. At this time, the emperor Nero accused Christians of starting a terrible fire that burned much of Rome. Christianity was made illegal, and many Christians were killed.

Other persecutions followed. During these difficult times, many Christians became **martyrs** (MAHR•tuhrz), people willing to die rather than give up their beliefs. In Rome, because of their beliefs, Christians were forced to bury their dead in catacombs, or underground burial places.

Even with all of the hardships, Christianity spread. Over time it even began to draw people from all classes. After A.D. 250, many Romans grew tired of war

Focus on Everyday Life

Christian Catacombs
Christians believed in resurrection, the idea that the body would one day reunite with the soul. For this reason, they would not allow their dead bodies to be burned, which was the Roman custom. Also, Roman law did not allow bodies to be buried aboveground. Therefore, starting in the A.D. 100s, Christians buried their dead beneath the city of Rome in a series of dark, cold, stench-filled tunnels called catacombs.

Each tunnel was about 8 feet (2.4 m) high and less than 3 feet (1 m) wide. Bodies were stacked in slots along the sides of the tunnels. The catacomb walls were painted with images from the Bible or from Greek or Roman mythology.

More than five million bodies were buried under Roman streets and buildings. Many of the Christians buried there were martyrs who had been killed for their beliefs.

◄ Christian catacombs in Rome

Connecting to the Past
1. Why did Christians bury their dead in catacombs?
2. What skills do you think would be necessary to dig and plan catacombs?

Religion The Council of Nicaea, held in A.D. 325, was the first ecumenical, or world, council convened to discuss Christian doctrine. Somewhere between 200 and over 300 bishops gathered to examine issues such as the divinity of Christ and a common date for the holy day of Easter. Have students research and report on the Council of Nicaea.

CONNECTING ACROSS TIME

Explain that the Romans built an extensive road system connecting major cities. In the 1990s, the U.S. highway system included over 45,000 miles (72,405 km) of roads. The Roman system had more than 50,000 miles (80,460 km). Ask students to calculate the difference (about 5,000 miles or 8,045 km). L1/EL

NATIONAL GEOGRAPHIC

The Way It Was

Answers:
1. They did not believe in cremation and it was against the law to be buried aboveground.
2. mathematics, engineering, physics; physical strength

DIFFERENTIATED INSTRUCTION

Verbal/Linguistic: Have students verbally compare the information about the spread of Christianity on the map on page 352 with the information in the text in this section. Have students point out how the map adds to the information.

Visual/Spatial: Have students find on a globe the areas to which Christianity had spread according to the map on page 352. **Ask:** To what continents had Christianity spread? (Europe, Asia, and Africa)

Logical/Mathematical: Have students use a ruler and the map scale on page 352 to determine the place farthest away from Galilee to which Christianity had spread by A.D. 325.

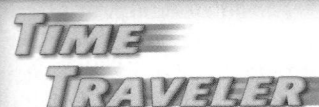

The persecution of Christians was pursued by Nero after the burning of Rome. Many Romans, however, thought that Nero had set the fire himself. Blaming the fire on the Christians was easy, because Romans thought the Christians held to strange beliefs and practices.

Writing Activity

Ask students to imagine that they have just witnessed Constantine's conversion to Christianity. Tell them to write a letter to a cousin describing the event. **L2**

✓ Reading Check

Answer: Christians refused to honor the emperor as a god, refused to serve in the army or hold public office, and criticized Roman festivals and games.

More About the Art

The Milvian Bridge was built in 109 B.C. over the Tiber River near Rome.

Caption Answer: made Christianity legal

---

and feared the end of the empire. They began to admire the faith and courage of the Christians. At the same time, many Christians started to accept the empire.

Rome Adopts Christianity In the early A.D. 300s the emperor Diocletian carried out the last great persecution of Christians. Diocletian failed, and Roman officials began to realize that Christianity had grown too strong to be destroyed by force.

Then, in A.D. 312, the Roman emperor **Constantine** (KAHN•stuhn•TEEN) accepted Christianity. According to tradition, Constantine saw a flaming cross in the sky as he was about to go into battle. Written beneath the cross were the Latin words that meant "In this sign you will conquer."

Constantine won the battle and believed that the Christian God had helped him.

In A.D. 313 Constantine issued an order called the Edict of Milan. It gave religious freedom to all people and made Christianity legal. Constantine began giving government support to Christianity. With the help of his mother, **Helena** (HEHL•uh•nuh), he built churches in Rome and Jerusalem. He also let church officials serve in government and excused them from paying taxes.

Constantine's successor, the emperor **Theodosius** (THEE•uh•DOH•shuhs), made Christianity Rome's official religion in A.D. 392. At the same time, he outlawed other religions.

✓ **Reading Check** **Explain** Why did the Romans see the Christians as traitors?

Constantine's Conversion

▼ Constantine led his troops to victory at the Battle of the Milvian Bridge after his conversion to Christianity. Constantine's enemies were defeated as a bridge made of boats collapsed under their weight. The *X* and *P* symbols on the shields represented the first two letters of the Greek word for *Christ*. *How did Constantine's Edict of Milan support Christianity?*

CRITICAL THINKING ACTIVITY

Evaluating Cause and Effect Point out that because of Constantine's conversion to Christianity, Rome went from persecuting Christians to accepting the religion. Discuss with students how Constantine's conversion affected his position as emperor. Have students suggest ways these changes may have affected Romans who were used to practicing a different kind of religion and who had considered Christians a danger to the empire. **L2**

The Early Church

Main Idea Early Christians set up a church organization and explained their beliefs.

Reading Focus How can good organization make the difference between whether a plan or project fails or succeeds? Read how early Christians organized their churches and chose what to include in the Bible.

In its early years, Christianity was loosely organized. Leaders like Paul traveled from one Christian community to another. They tried to unify the scattered groups. In their teaching, they emphasized that all the individual groups of Christians were part of one body called the church. Early Christians, however, faced a challenge. How were they to unite?

Organizing the Church The early Christians turned to a surprising model to organize the church—the Roman Empire itself. Like the Roman Empire, the church came to be ruled by a **hierarchy** (HY•uhr•AHR•kee). A hierarchy is an organization with different levels of authority.

The **clergy** (KLUHR•jee) were the leaders of the church. They had different roles from the **laity** (LAY•uh•tee), or regular church members. As the church's organization grew, women were not permitted to serve in the clergy. However, as members of the laity, they continued to care for the sick and needy.

By around A.D. 300, local churches were led by clergy called priests. Several churches formed a diocese (DY•uh•suhs), led by a bishop. A bishop in charge of a city diocese was sometimes also put in charge of an entire region. This made him an archbishop. The five leading archbishops became known as patriarchs (PAY•tree•AHRKS). They led churches in large cities and were in charge of large areas of territory.

Early Church Hierarchy

Patriarchs → Archbishops → Bishops → Priests → Laity

The bishops explained Christian beliefs. They also took care of church business. From time to time, bishops met to discuss questions about Christian faith. Decisions they reached at these meetings came to be accepted as **doctrine** (DAHK•truhn), or official church teaching.

What Is the New Testament? Along with explaining Christian ideas, church leaders preserved a written record of the life of Jesus and put together a group of writings to help guide Christians. Jesus himself left no writings. His followers, however, passed on what they knew about him. By A.D. 300, four accounts of Jesus' life, teachings, and resurrection had become well-known. Christians believed these accounts were written by early followers of Jesus named Matthew, Mark, Luke, and John.

Each work was called a **gospel** (GAHS•puhl), which means "good news." Christians later combined the four gospels with the writings of Paul and other early Christian leaders. Together, these works form the New Testament of the Bible.

CHAPTER 10   The Rise of Christianity   **355**

CHAPTER 10
SECTION 2, 351–357

Reading Support L1/ EL

Assign **Guided Reading Activity 10–2** to help students organize the information in the section.

③ ASSESS

Assign Section 2 Review as homework or as an in-class activity.

⊙ Have students use the **Interactive Tutor Self-Assessment CD-ROM** to review the section.

Assessment L2

Assign **Section 2 Quiz** to assess mastery of the material found in the section.

Reading Support L1/ EL

Assign **Reading Essentials and Study Guide 10–2** to help students review section material.

INTERDISCIPLINARY CONNECTIONS ACTIVITY

Geography Using the map on page 352, have students research and analyze the geography of the area Paul traveled on his journeys. Have students discuss the areas where they live that resemble the places which Paul traveled through on his voyages. **Ask:** What forms of transportation could Paul have used on his journeys? *(boats, horses and carts, walking)* What types of terrain did Paul have to cross? *(oceans, seas, mountains, desert, forests)* What forms of transportation would make it easier to travel in the same area today? *(planes, cars, powerboats, trains)* Have students research to find what would be difficult about traveling in that region today. *(cost, area is unstable due to war and fighting, passports and visas needed to travel from one country to another, different languages)* **L2**

Caption Answer: Jesus' life, teachings, and resurrection

ENRICH

According to Catholic tradition, there have been more than 260 popes. Discuss with students how the Christian church changed when the bishop of Rome claimed power over the other bishops. **L2**

Reading Check

Answer: the writings of early Christian leaders describing Jesus' ministry; preserved his teachings

History Online

To help students understand section material, have them visit **Study Central™** at jat.glencoe.com

RETEACH

Have students use the section time line to organize data about the changing relationship between Christians and Romans. **L2**

4 CLOSE

Point out that few people knew how to read at this time. Discuss why missionaries were, therefore, important for the spread of Christianity. **L2**

356

◀ **Saint Matthew wrote one of the four gospels in the New Testament of the Bible.** *What is the subject of the gospels of Matthew, Mark, Luke, and John?*

Other important writings also influenced early Christians. Scholars known as the Church Fathers wrote books to explain church teachings. One leading Church Father was a bishop in North Africa named Augustine. In his writings, Augustine defended Christianity against its opponents. He wrote *The City of God*—one of the first history books written from a Christian viewpoint. He also wrote a work called *Confessions*. It was an account of his personal journey to the Christian faith.

Who Is the Pope? As the church grew, the bishop of Rome, who was also the patriarch of the West, began to claim power over the other bishops. He believed that he had the authority of Peter, Jesus' leading disciple. Also, his diocese was in Rome, the capital of the empire.

By A.D. 600, the bishop of Rome had gained a special title—**pope**. The title comes from a Latin word meaning "father." Latin-speaking Christians accepted the pope as head of the church. Their churches became known as the Roman Catholic Church. Greek-speaking Christians would not accept the pope's authority over them. You will read in the next section about Christians in the Eastern Roman Empire and their form of Christianity.

Reading Check **Identify** What are the gospels, and why are they significant?

History Online
Study Central™ Need help with the material in this section? Visit jat.glencoe.com

Section 2 Review

Reading Summary
Review the Main Ideas

- After its followers suffered Roman persecution for several hundred years, Christianity became the official religion of the Roman Empire under Emperor Theodosius.

- As Christianity grew, the church became more united under a hierarchy of leaders. Christian writings were gathered into the New Testament of the Bible.

What Did You Learn?

1. What is a martyr?
2. What writings are included in the New Testament of the Bible?

Critical Thinking

3. **Organizing Information** Draw a chart like the one below. Fill in details on the effects each of the emperors listed had on the acceptance and growth of Christianity.

Roman Emperors		
Diocletian	Constantine	Theodosius

4. **Analyze** Following Jesus' death, why was Christianity able to attract followers?
5. **Analyze** Why do you think the Christian church came to be ruled by a hierarchy?
6. **Conclude** Do you think the Christian religion would have spread so quickly if it had developed in a time other than that of the Roman Empire?
7. **Writing Questions** Write five questions that a reporter who lived at the same time as Constantine might have asked him about Christianity.

356 CHAPTER 10 The Rise of Christianity

SECTION 2 REVIEW ANSWERS

1. a person willing to die rather than give up his or her beliefs
2. the gospels of Matthew, Mark, Luke, and John, plus the writings of Paul and other early Christian leaders
3. Diocletian: his persecution failed to destroy Christianity; Constantine: made it legal, gave it government support; Theodosius: made Christianity Rome's official religion
4. offered hope and comfort; appealed to the emotions and promised life after death; gave people the chance to be part of a caring group
5. Possible answer: The Roman Empire showed a successful way to unite different peoples in many places.
6. Answers will vary but should show a thoughtful response.
7. Answers will vary but should be based on information available in the text.

Biography

SAINT AUGUSTINE

A.D. 354–430

Augustine was born in North Africa, in what is today the country of Algeria, to upper-class parents. His mother was Christian, but his father was not. His father sent him to the North African city of Carthage to attend good schools. Although he appeared to be an outstanding student, Augustine later said that he made many poor choices during his time at school.

When Augustine finished his education, he returned home to teach grammar. His mother again tried to convince him of the truth of Christianity, but he had joined a group of people who were critical of Christians. According to Augustine's writings, his mother was saddened until a vision promised her that her son would eventually accept Christianity.

Augustine moved to several cities, often teaching rhetoric (the art of speaking). He ended up in Milan, Italy. There he listened to Milan's bishop Ambrose preaching, not because he liked his messages but because he admired the way Ambrose spoke. Slowly, Augustine began to think about the messages of Ambrose's sermons. One day in A.D. 386, Augustine heard a child's voice say to him, "Take up and read." Nearby was a friend's copy of Paul's letters. He began to read the letters and decided that he believed the messages of Christianity. Augustine was soon baptized and founded a monastery—probably the first monastery in his area of North Africa. Later Augustine became a bishop. He recorded his life in A.D. 401 in the book *Confessions*.

▲ St. Augustine being blessed by the pope

▲ St. Augustine

"Even when sad, I remember my times of joy."
—Saint Augustine, *Confessions*

Then and Now

Do research to find out how Christianity has influenced the development of the United States. Provide examples of how it has affected government, society, and the economy.

357

Biography

TEACH

Augustine spent 15 years writing *The City of God*, a 22-volume work. In most of the first half, he explained why the traditional Roman gods were powerless to save Rome from the barbarian attack in A.D. 410. In the remaining books, he described the history of humankind from its beginnings until the Last Judgment. Augustine believed that Christians were most importantly citizens of the City of God, which was the heavenly Jerusalem. Although life in the City of Man (here on Earth) was filled with disasters and disappointment, Augustine held out hope for a better life in the hereafter. His teaching that life in this world should be focused on reaching the City of God and peace in the next life was important for almost 1,000 years.

Ask students why Thucydides would or would not have agreed with Augustine's explanation for the barbarians' victory and his history of humankind. *(Thucydides would have disagreed because he looked for the causal relation between events and human actions.)* **L3**

Then and Now

Answers will vary but should be based on research and demonstrate a thoughtful response.

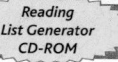
Reading List Generator CD-ROM

GLENCOE BOOKLINK   **RECOMMENDED READING**

Use the **Glencoe BookLink CD-ROM** to create customized reading lists based on your students' interests and reading levels. Below is an example based on content in this chapter. Also, see the Suggested Readings on pages 944–946 of the Appendix.

- Augustine. *The Confessions of St. Augustine.* Augustine's own account of his journey to Christian faith.
- Liversidge, Joan. *Everyday Life in the Roman Empire.* Describes how people lived and worked in the Roman Empire.

① FOCUS

SECTION OVERVIEW

This section describes the relationship between church and government in the Byzantine Empire, as well as the spread of Christianity.

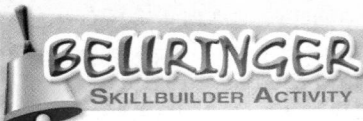

BELLRINGER
SKILLBUILDER ACTIVITY

🖋 Project **Daily Focus Skills Transparency 10–3** and have students answer questions. Discuss their responses.

Get Ready to Read!

Preteaching Vocabulary: Have students look at the icon of the archangel Gabriel in this section. Explain that icons can be simple or very elaborate—perhaps even decorated in gold and precious gems. Point out that the words *icon* (religious picture or image) and *iconoclast* (one who destroys religious images or attacks settled beliefs) are related in meaning and that the word *icon* is part of the word *iconoclast*.

Answers to Graphic: Cyril and Methodius; Patrick and 40 monks

Section 3
The Spread of Christian Ideas

Get Ready to Read!

What's the Connection?
In the last section, you read about the growth of the Christian church. In this section, you will learn how the church underwent a great division and how Christians spread their faith to new lands.

Focusing on the Main Ideas
- Church and government worked closely together in the Byzantine Empire. **(page 359)**
- Christians founded new communities and spread their faith to various parts of Europe. **(page 361)**

Locating Places
Byzantine Empire (BIH•zuhn•TEEN EHM•PYR)
Britain (BRIH•tuhn)
Ireland (EYER•luhnd)

Meeting People
Charlemagne (SHAHR•luh•MAYN)
Basil (BAY•zuhl)
Benedict (BEH•nuh•DIHKT)
Cyril (SIHR•uhl)
Patrick

Building Your Vocabulary
icon (EYE•KAHN)
iconoclast (eye•KAH•nuh•KLAST)
excommunicate (EHK•skuh•MYOO•nuh•KAYT)
schism (SIH•zuhm)
monastery (MAH•nuh•STEHR•ee)
missionary (MIH•shuh•NEHR•ee)

Reading Strategy
Organizing Information Create a diagram to show the reach of Christian missionaries.

```
              Missionaries
             ↙         ↘
Eastern                    Britain/
Europe  ←  [   ]   [   ]  → Ireland
```

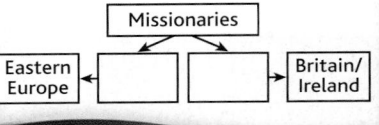

NATIONAL GEOGRAPHIC When & Where?

A.D. 400	**A.D. 800**	**A.D. 1200**
c. A.D. 450 Patrick preaches Christianity in Ireland	A.D. 726 Emperor Leo III removes icons from churches	A.D. 1054 Eastern Orthodox and Roman Catholic Churches separate

Map labels: IRELAND, BRITAIN, GAUL, SPAIN, ITALY, Rome, Constantinople, ASIA MINOR, GREECE, Jerusalem, AFRICA

SECTION RESOURCES

📁 **Reproducible Masters**
- Reproducible Lesson Plan 10–3
- Daily Lecture and Discussion Notes 10–3
- Vocabulary Activity 10–3
- Active Reading Note-Taking Guide 10–3
- Guided Reading Activity 10–3
- Section Quiz 10–3
- Reading Essentials and Study Guide 10–3

🖋 **Transparencies**
- Daily Focus Skills Transparency 10–3

Multimedia
- Interactive Tutor Self-Assessment CD-ROM
- *ExamView®* Pro Testmaker CD-ROM
- Presentation Plus! CD-ROM
- Vocabulary PuzzleMaker CD-ROM

The Byzantine Church

Main Idea Church and government worked closely together in the Byzantine Empire.

Reading Focus In our country, religion and government are separated. Read to learn about the relationship between religion and government in the Byzantine Empire.

As you learned earlier, the church of Rome survived the fall of the Western Roman Empire. Its head, the pope, became the strongest leader in Western Europe. Under the pope, the Latin churches of the region became known as the Roman Catholic Church. In the East, however, the Roman Empire continued. It developed into the **Byzantine Empire** (BIH•zuhn•TEEN EHM•PYR). Like Roman Catholics in the West, the Byzantines developed their own form of Christianity. It was based on their Greek heritage and was known as the Eastern Orthodox Church.

Church and State Church and government worked closely together in the Byzantine Empire. The Byzantines believed their emperor represented Jesus Christ on Earth. The emperor was crowned in a religious ceremony.

The emperor also chose the patriarch of Constantinople, the leading Church official in the Byzantine Empire. In this way, the emperor controlled the Church as well as the government. Byzantines believed that God wanted them to preserve and spread Christianity. All Church and government officials were united in this goal.

History Online
Web Activity Visit jat.glencoe.com and click on *Chapter 10—Student Web Activity* to learn more about the rise of Christianity.

Religious Arguments Byzantines, from the emperor down to the poorest farmer, were very interested in religious matters. In homes and shops, they argued about religious questions. For example, Byzantines loved to discuss the exact relationship between Jesus and God.

In the A.D. 700s, a major dispute divided the Church in the Byzantine Empire. The argument was over the use of **icons** (EYE• KAHNZ). Icons are pictures or images of Jesus, Mary (the mother of Jesus), and the saints, or Christian holy people. Many Byzantines honored icons. They covered the walls of their churches with them. A few important icons were even believed to work miracles.

Some Byzantines, however, wanted an end to the use of icons. They thought that honoring them was a form of idol worship forbidden by God. Supporters of icons,

▼ This gold Byzantine incense burner is in the shape of a church. *What was the Christian church that developed in the Byzantine Empire called?*

CHAPTER 10   The Rise of Christianity   **359**

2 TEACH

Dividing the Christian Church On the board, draw a Venn diagram titled the *Christian Church*. Use this graphic to help students discuss the division of the Christian church into two branches—the Roman Catholic Church and the Eastern Orthodox Church—and to show how the two churches were alike and different. **L1**

Daily Lecture and Discussion Notes 10–3

Use **Daily Lecture and Discussion Notes 10–3** for an outline of key concepts found in the section.

Reading Support L1/EL

Use **Vocabulary Activity 10–3** to review important terms in the section.

Caption Answer: Eastern Orthodox Church

History Online
Objectives and answers to the student activity can be found in the **Web Activity Lesson Plan** feature at jat.glencoe.com

Reading Strategy **READING THE TEXT**

Taking Notes Tell students that as they read this section, they should write down the three things they think will be most difficult to remember. Have students share their notes with the class. Point out to students that taking notes helps people better remember difficult or complex information. **L1**

More About the Art

More About the Art

According to the Gospel of Luke, Gabriel foretold the birth of Jesus to Mary, Jesus' mother.

Caption Answer: They were symbols of God's presence in daily life. They helped explain Christianity to people.

Reading Strategy

Writing Activity

Have students use the information in the text to write a description of the issues that divided the Western and Eastern churches. **L2**

CONNECTING ACROSS TIME

Constantinople has existed for more than 2,500 years. It was Constantine the Great who made the city a capital. He originally named it New Rome, but later ordered it changed to Constantinople. Have students locate Constantinople on the map on page 361. Discuss why its location would be good for trade. Then explain that the city still exists today. Have students look at a world map in the **Reference Atlas** to find its present-day name. **L1/ EL**

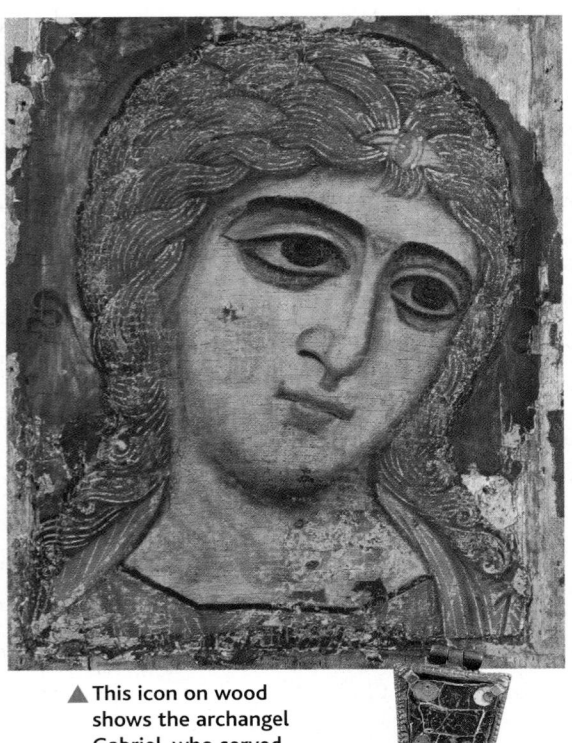

▲ This icon on wood shows the archangel Gabriel, who served as a messenger for God according to the Bible. *What reasons were given to support the use of icons?*

Byzantine cross ▶

however, claimed that icons were symbols of God's presence in daily life. These images, they also said, helped explain Christianity to people.

Emperor Leo III did not approve of icons. In A.D. 726 he ordered all icons removed from the churches. Government officials who carried out his orders were known as **iconoclasts** (eye•KAH•nuh•KLASTS), or image breakers. We use this word today to mean someone who attacks traditional beliefs or institutions.

Most Byzantines, many church leaders, and even the pope in Rome opposed the emperor's order. In fact, the dispute over icons damaged ties between the churches of Rome and Constantinople. Over the next 100 years, the argument cooled, and the use of icons became accepted once again. They are still an important part of Eastern Orthodox religious practice.

Conflicts Between Churches Icons were not the only issue that caused bitterness between the churches of Constantinople and Rome. The most serious argument was about how churches were to be run. The pope claimed that he was the head of all Christian churches. The Byzantines did not accept the pope's claim. They believed the patriarch of Constantinople and other bishops were equal to the pope.

Making matters worse was the fact that each church sometimes refused to help the other when outsiders attacked. In the late A.D. 700s, the Byzantine emperor refused to help the pope when Italy was invaded. The pope turned instead to a Germanic people called the Franks for help. The Franks were Roman Catholics and loyal to the pope.

The pope was grateful to the Franks for stopping the invasion. In A.D. 800 he gave the Frankish king, **Charlemagne** (SHAHR•luh•MAYN), the title of emperor. This angered the Byzantines. They believed the leader of the Byzantines was the only true emperor.

This conflict pointed out the differences in how each church felt about relations with the government. In the Byzantine Empire, the emperor was in control, with church leaders respecting his wishes. In the West, however, the pope claimed both spiritual and political power. He often quarreled with kings over church and government affairs.

360　　　CHAPTER 10　The Rise of Christianity

DIFFERENTIATED INSTRUCTION

Less-proficient Readers: Ask students to define the term *icon*. Then have students look at the illustrations in this section and identify any icons they see.

Visual/Spatial: Have student groups create an illustrated time line for the events that led to the schism in the Christian church. Tell groups to provide illustrations for each item.

Gifted and Talented: Have students research the conflict that arose over the use of icons. Then organize students into two groups. Ask groups to prepare to debate the issue—one in favor of keeping the icons and one against keeping them. After the debate, discuss with students which side presented the stronger case.

Finally, after centuries of tension, the pope and the patriarch of Constantinople took a drastic step in their ongoing feud. In A.D. 1054 they **excommunicated** (EHK•skuh•MYOO•nuh•KAY•tuhd) each other. Excommunication means to declare that a person or group no longer belongs to the church. This began a **schism** (SIH•zuhm), or separation, of the two most important branches of Christianity. The split between the Roman Catholic and Eastern Orthodox Churches has lasted to this day.

✓**Reading Check** **Describe** How did church and government work together in the Byzantine Empire?

Christian Ideas Spread

Main Idea Christians founded new communities and spread their faith to various parts of Europe.

Reading Focus Have you ever tried to get someone to believe something you believe? Read to learn how Christians spread their faith across Europe.

After the fall of Rome, the people of Western Europe faced confusion and conflict. As a result, people were looking for order and unity. Christianity helped to meet this need. It spread rapidly into lands that had once been part of the Roman Empire. It

The Byzantine Empire changed continuously during the millennium in which the empire existed. Its boundaries were redrawn again and again through wars and diplomacy. At different times, the Byzantine Empire encompassed all or part of the present-day nations of Greece, Italy, Egypt, and Syria, in addition to parts of North Africa.

✓**Reading Check**

Answer: The Byzantines believed their emperor represented Jesus Christ on Earth. The emperor was crowned in a religious ceremony, and he chose the patriarch of Constantinople.

Using Geography Skills

Answers:
1. between A.D. 325 and A.D. 600
2. Scandinavia and parts of Russia and Eastern Europe

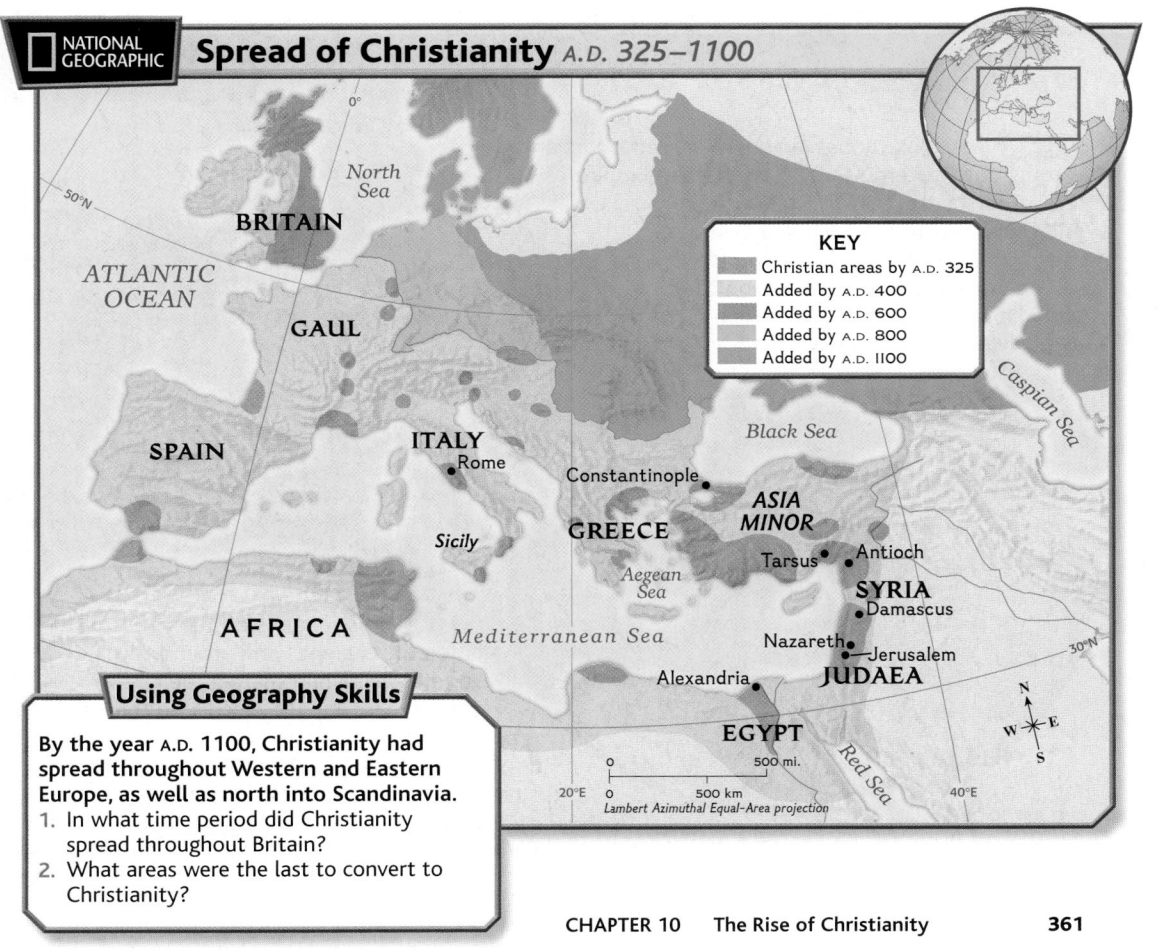

NATIONAL GEOGRAPHIC
Spread of Christianity A.D. 325–1100

KEY
Christian areas by A.D. 325
Added by A.D. 400
Added by A.D. 600
Added by A.D. 800
Added by A.D. 1100

North Sea
BRITAIN
ATLANTIC OCEAN
GAUL
SPAIN
ITALY
Rome
Sicily
AFRICA
Mediterranean Sea
Constantinople
GREECE
Aegean Sea
Black Sea
Caspian Sea
ASIA MINOR
Tarsus
Antioch
SYRIA
Damascus
Nazareth
Jerusalem
JUDAEA
Alexandria
EGYPT
Red Sea

500 mi.
500 km
Lambert Azimuthal Equal-Area projection

Using Geography Skills

By the year A.D. 1100, Christianity had spread throughout Western and Eastern Europe, as well as north into Scandinavia.
1. In what time period did Christianity spread throughout Britain?
2. What areas were the last to convert to Christianity?

CHAPTER 10 The Rise of Christianity **361**

CRITICAL THINKING ACTIVITY

Interpreting Direct students' attention to the map on this page. Point out that it includes the information from the map "Spread of Christianity *A.D. 325*" in Section 2. **Ask:** How is the information on the map in Section 2 and the map on this page different? *(In the map on this page, Christianity had spread to a far greater degree than the time period covered on the map in Section 2.)* As a class, compare the growth of Christianity during the two periods. Then have students write a paragraph summarizing how Christianity grew between A.D. 325 and A.D. 1100. Have volunteers read their paragraphs to the class. **L3**

Designing Letters Point out that the Cyrillic alphabet has 33 letters, which is 7 more than the English alphabet. These extra letters include sounds that are not represented in the English alphabet. The following are some examples: Ц for the "ts" sound, as in *its*; я for the "ya" sound, as in *yard*; and Ш for the "sh" sound, as in *shut*. Tell students to pretend they are entering a contest to design three new letters for these sounds for the English alphabet. After students have designed their letters, ask volunteers to share and explain their letter designs. **L1**

Linking Past & Present

Answer: Answers will vary. Be sure to treat students' responses delicately.

Reading Support L1/ EL

Assign **Guided Reading Activity 10–3** to help students organize the information in the section.

---

also brought new ways of thinking and living to these areas.

What Are Monasteries? During the A.D. 300s, a new kind of religious group was born in the Eastern Roman Empire. Men called monks banded together in religious communities called **monasteries** (MAH•nuh•STEHR•eez). Some monasteries were built near cities, while others arose in isolated areas.

One of the earliest monks was Anthony, who founded a monastery in the deserts of Egypt. Monks tried to live a spiritual life apart from the temptations of the world. Many also tried to do good deeds and be examples of Christian living. Women soon followed the monks' example and formed communities of their own. These women were called nuns, and they lived in convents.

In the early A.D. 400s, Paula, a Roman widow, gave up her wealth and went to Palestine. There she built churches, a hospital, and a convent. Well-educated, Paula helped a scholar named Jerome translate the Bible from Hebrew and Greek into Latin.

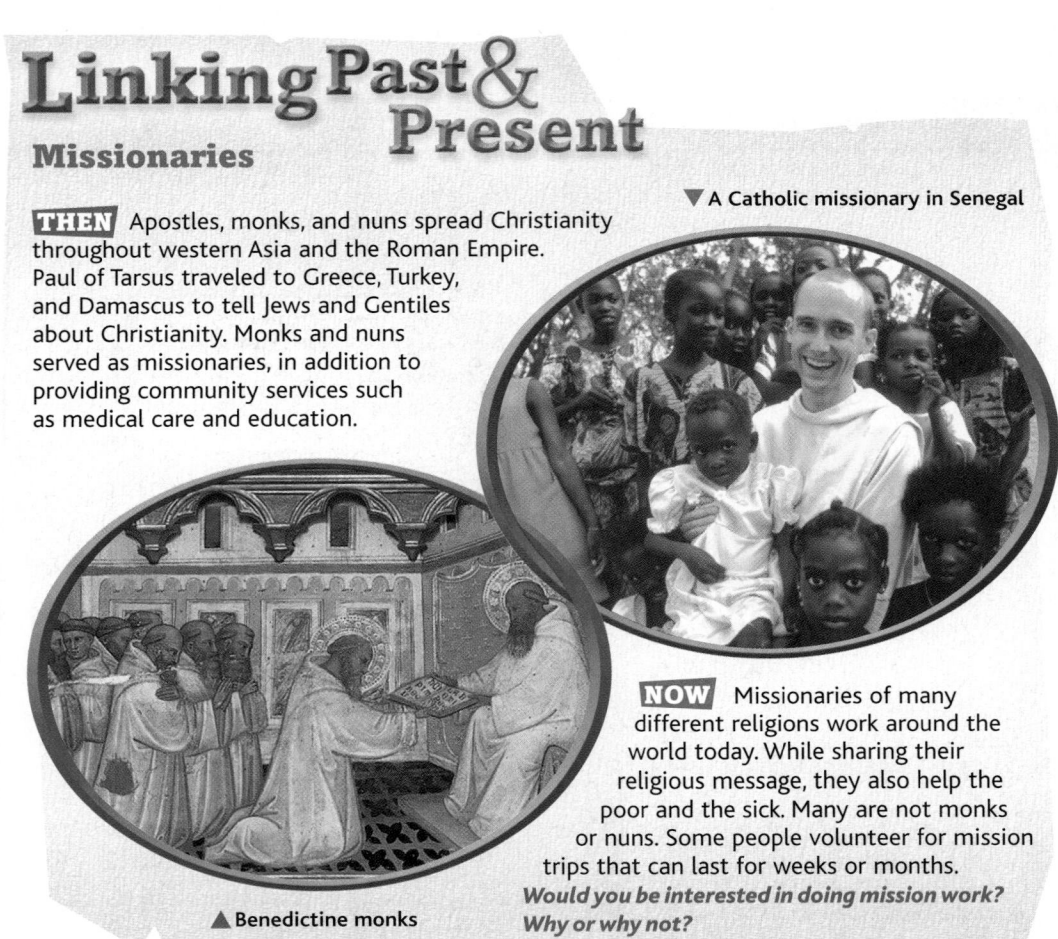

Linking Past & Present

Missionaries

THEN Apostles, monks, and nuns spread Christianity throughout western Asia and the Roman Empire. Paul of Tarsus traveled to Greece, Turkey, and Damascus to tell Jews and Gentiles about Christianity. Monks and nuns served as missionaries, in addition to providing community services such as medical care and education.

▼ A Catholic missionary in Senegal

NOW Missionaries of many different religions work around the world today. While sharing their religious message, they also help the poor and the sick. Many are not monks or nuns. Some people volunteer for mission trips that can last for weeks or months. *Would you be interested in doing mission work? Why or why not?*

▲ Benedictine monks

362 CHAPTER 10 The Rise of Christianity

INTERDISCIPLINARY CONNECTIONS ACTIVITY

Daily Life Have students research different national and international aid programs such as the Peace Corps, AmeriCorp, World Health Organization, Red Cross, etc. Have them discuss the ways in which these programs help people in the United States and abroad. **Ask:** How do modern-day programs and organizations differ from the missionaries discussed on pages 362 and 363? *(They are not always associated with religious groups; they are often supported by governments; they offer more specific services.)* How are modern-day programs and organizations similar to the missionaries? *(They work to help as many people as they can and provide medicine and education to those less fortunate.)* Have students research ways in which they can help those in and around their communities. **L1**

A bishop called **Basil** (BAY•zuhl) drew up a list of rules for monks and nuns to follow. This list, called the Basilian (buh•ZIH•lee•uhn) Rule, became the model for Eastern Orthodox religious life.

In the West, another set of rules was followed. It was written by an Italian monk named **Benedict** (BEH•nuh•DIHKT). Monks who followed the Benedictine Rule gave up their belongings, lived simply, and spent their time in work and prayer. Like Basil's rule in the East, Benedict's rule became the model for monasteries and convents in the West. Basilian and Benedictine communities still exist today.

Monks and nuns began to play important roles in Roman Catholic and Eastern Orthodox life. They ran hospitals and schools and aided the poor. They also helped preserve Greek and Roman writings. One important duty was to serve as **missionaries** (MIH•shuh•NEHR•eez). Missionaries teach their religion to those who do not believe.

Christianity Spreads North

Among the most successful Byzantine missionaries were two brothers, **Cyril** (SIHR•uhl) and Methodius. They carried the Christian message to the Slavs, a people of Eastern Europe.

About A.D. 863, Cyril invented a new alphabet. He wanted to present the Christian message in the Slavic languages. He believed that people would be more interested in Christianity if they could worship and read the Bible in their own languages. The Cyrillic (suh•RIH•lihk) alphabet was based on Greek letters. It is still used today by Russians, Ukrainians, Serbs, and Bulgarians.

Eastern Orthodox missionaries traveled in northern lands that bordered the Byzantine Empire. At the same time, other missionaries from Rome were also busy.

The Cyrillic Alphabet

Cyrillic Letter	Written Name	English Sound
Б	beh	B
Г	gey	G
Ж	zheh	ZH
М	em	M
П	pey	P
С	ess	S
Ф	ef	F
Ч	cheh	CH

Cyril, a Byzantine missionary, developed the Cyrillic alphabet, part of which is shown above. *What peoples still use the Cyrillic alphabet today?*

Christianity Spreads West

In the West, Christian missionaries looked to the islands of **Britain** (BRIH•tuhn) and **Ireland** (EYER•luhnd). In the A.D. 300s, Roman soldiers in Britain were called home to defend the empire against Germanic invaders. When the Romans left, Britain was opened to attack by others.

Starting in the A.D. 400s, tribes from what are today Germany and Denmark invaded Britain. These people were the Angles and the Saxons. These groups united to become the Anglo-Saxons. They built settlements and set up several small kingdoms. The southern part of Britain soon became known as Angleland, or England.

While invading Britain, the Angles and Saxons pushed aside the people already living there. These people were called the Celts (KEHLTS). Some Celts fled to the mountainous regions of Britain. Others went to Ireland.

In the A.D. 400s, a priest named **Patrick** brought Christianity to Ireland. He set up a number of monasteries and churches. Over

CHAPTER 10   The Rise of Christianity   363

CITIZENSHIP AND YOU

The Purpose of Rules Point out to students that as members of society, they must follow certain rules. Remind them that as citizens of their school, they also follow certain rules. Explain that, in the same way, monks and nuns had to follow certain rules. Have students research the Basilian and Benedictine Rules. Then lead a discussion about the kinds of rules monks and nuns had to follow to be good religious citizens. **L2**

ENRICH

Discuss with students their thoughts about the lifestyle of a monk. **L1**

✓ Reading Check

Answer: Both wrote rules for monks and nuns. Basil's rule was the model for the East; Benedict's for the West.

History Online

To help students understand section material, have them visit **Study Central™** at **jat.glencoe.com**

RETEACH

Have students use the section headings to summarize the rise of Christianity. **L1**

④ CLOSE

Have students make generalizations about how one person can have an impact on millions of people. **L2**

---

the next centuries, Irish monks played an important role in preserving Christian and Roman learning.

The Anglo-Saxon kingdoms of Britain were slower than Ireland to accept the new religion. In A.D. 597 Pope Gregory I sent about 40 monks from Rome to take Christianity to England.

The missionaries converted Ethelbert, the ruler of the English kingdom of Kent. Ethelbert allowed the missionaries to build a church in his capital city of Canterbury. In about 100 years, most of England was Christian. Today, Canterbury is still an important center of Christianity in England.

✓ Reading Check Analyze Why were Basil and Benedict important?

◀ Gregory was a monk before he became Pope Gregory I in the late 500s. *How did Gregory impact Christianity in England?*

History Online
Study Central™ Need help with the material in this section? Visit jat.glencoe.com

Section ③ Review

Reading Summary
Review the Main Ideas
- In the Byzantine Empire, Christianity developed into the Eastern Orthodox Church, which in time split with the Roman Catholic Church in the West.

- Eastern Orthodox and Catholic missionaries helped spread Christianity to areas such as Eastern Europe, Ireland, and Britain.

What Did You Learn?
1. What are icons, and why was their use controversial?

2. What roles did monks and nuns play in Roman Catholic and Eastern Orthodox life?

Critical Thinking
3. **Cause and Effect** Draw a diagram to show the causes that led to the schism between the Roman Catholic and Eastern Orthodox Churches.

Cause:	→	Effect:
Cause:	→	Roman Catholic and Eastern Orthodox
Cause:	→	Churches split

4. **Describe** How did Cyril make the Christian message available to the Slavs?

5. **Explain** What role did the Frankish king Charlemagne play in the schism between the Roman Catholic and Eastern Orthodox Churches?

6. **Analyze** Why do you think the Basilian and Benedictine Rules were put in place for monks?

7. **Expository Writing** Write a newspaper article that describes the spread of Christianity to Ireland and Britain.

364   CHAPTER 10   The Rise of Christianity

SECTION 3 REVIEW ANSWERS

1. images of Jesus, Mary, the saints; some Byzantines believed they were idols
2. ran hospitals and schools, aided the poor, preserved Greek and Roman writings, acted as missionaries
3. Byzantines did not accept the pope's claims; each

church sometimes refused to help the other when one was attacked; they excommunicated each other.
4. He invented a new alphabet so the Slavs could read the Bible in their own languages.
5. The pope gave Charlemagne the title of emperor. The

Byzantines refused to recognize an emperor other than their own.
6. Answers will vary but should demonstrate a thoughtful response.
7. Articles will vary but should demonstrate a thoughtful response.

Section ① The First Christians

Vocabulary
messiah
disciple
parable
resurrection
apostle
salvation

Focusing on the Main Ideas
- Roman rule of Judaea led some Jews to oppose Rome peacefully, while others rebelled. *(page 343)*
- Jesus of Nazareth preached of God's love and forgiveness. He was eventually crucified and then reported to have risen from the dead. *(page 344)*
- Jesus' life and a belief in his resurrection led to a new religion called Christianity. *(page 348)*

Section ② The Christian Church

Vocabulary
persecute
martyr
hierarchy
clergy
laity
doctrine
gospel
pope

Focusing on the Main Ideas
- Christianity won many followers and eventually became the official religion of the Roman Empire. *(page 352)*
- Early Christians set up a church organization and explained their beliefs. *(page 355)*

Saint Matthew ▶

Section ③ The Spread of Christian Ideas

Vocabulary
icon
iconoclast
excommunicate
schism
monastery
missionary

Focusing on the Main Ideas
- Church and government worked closely together in the Byzantine Empire. *(page 359)*
- Christians founded new communities and spread their faith to various parts of Europe. *(page 361)*

CHAPTER 10 REVIEW

PREVIEW/REVIEW

Vocabulary Activity Ask volunteers to use each vocabulary term in a sentence about Jesus or Christianity. Students may use two or more terms in the same sentence.

- **Vocabulary PuzzleMaker CD-ROM**
- **Interactive Tutor Self-Assessment CD-ROM**

CONDENSE

- Chapter 10 **Guided Reading Activities**
- **StudentWorks Plus™ CD-ROM (with Audio Program)**

RETEACH

- **Differentiated Instruction Activity 10**
- Chapter 10 *Reading Essentials and Study Guide*

CHAPTER CULMINATING ACTIVITY

Have students finish the Chapter Culminating Activity from page 338D.

Suggestions for rubrics may be found in the *Quizzes, Tests, and Authentic Assessment (with Rubrics)* booklet.

Reading Strategy — READ TO WRITE

Writing a Biography Explain that a biography is the story of someone's life. Ask students to write a biography of Jesus based on what they have learned in this chapter. When students have finished, ask volunteers to read their biographies to the class.

- **L1** students should identify at least one main event in Jesus' life.
- **L2** students should focus on the last three years of Jesus' life.
- **L3** students should include not only the facts of Jesus' life but also the impact he had on the world.

365

Chapter 10 Assessment and Activities

Review Vocabulary

1. Paragraphs will vary but should reflect the information in the chapter.
2. parables
3. pope
4. schism
5. martyrs

Students should write sentences for *laity, missionaries, iconoclasts,* and *apostle.*

Review Main Ideas

6. Some Jews opposed Rome peacefully, while others rebelled.
7. Jesus' life and teachings and belief in his resurrection
8. through Constantine's conversion and passing of the Edict of Milan
9. They set up a hierarchy to rule the church.
10. They worked together closely.
11. through missionaries; Eastern Europe, Britain, Ireland

Critical Thinking

12. because parables used events from everyday life that people knew about and experienced

Review Vocabulary

1. Write a paragraph about the basic beliefs of Christianity using the following words.

   messiah　　**salvation**

   resurrection　　**gospel**

   Write the vocabulary word that completes each sentence. Then write a sentence for each word not chosen.

   a. laity　　　e. parables
   b. missionaries　f. schism
   c. martyrs　　g. apostle
   d. iconoclasts　h. pope

2. Jesus told symbolic stories called ___.
3. The bishop of Rome was called the ___.
4. The ___ in the Christian churches happened in A.D. 1054.
5. Christians who died for their faith were ___.

Review Main Ideas

Section 1 • The First Christians

6. How did Jews react to the Roman rule of Judaea?

7. On what is Christianity based?

Section 2 • The Christian Church

8. How did the Roman Empire eventually recognize Christianity?
9. What did early Christians do to organize their religion?

Section 3 • The Spread of Christian Ideas

10. What was the relationship between the church and the government in the Byzantine Empire?
11. How and where did the Christian religion spread?

Critical Thinking

12. **Analyze** Why do you think Jesus' followers remembered his teachings more when he used parables?
13. **Contrast** How did Jews and Christians differ in their belief about Jesus and his message?
14. **Predict** How would the growth of Christianity have been affected if the emperor Constantine had not become a Christian?

Review — Reading Skill — Sequence Clues — Looking for Sequence Clues

Find the words in each of these sentences that help you identify the order in which events occur.

15. At the same time, many Christians started to accept the empire.
16. While on the road to Damascus, Paul had an unusual experience.
17. It is still used today by Russians, Ukrainians, Serbs, and Bulgarians.
18. The southern part of Britain soon became known as Angleland, or England.
19. After Jesus' death, his followers made a startling claim.
20. At first, they ruled through Jewish kings.

To review this skill, see pages 340–341.

13. Christians believed Jesus was the messiah and had risen from the dead. Jews did not.
14. The Edict of Milan would not have been issued, so the persecution of Christians might have continued. Christianity might not have grown as rapidly.

Reading Skill

15. At the same time
16. While
17. still, today
18. soon
19. After
20. At first

Geography Skills

Study the map below and answer the following questions.

21. **Human/Environment Interaction** What geographical feature do you think most helped the spread of Christianity?

22. **Location** By A.D. 325, Christianity had spread to which continents?

23. **Region** Why do you think the cities of Judaea were all important centers of Christianity?

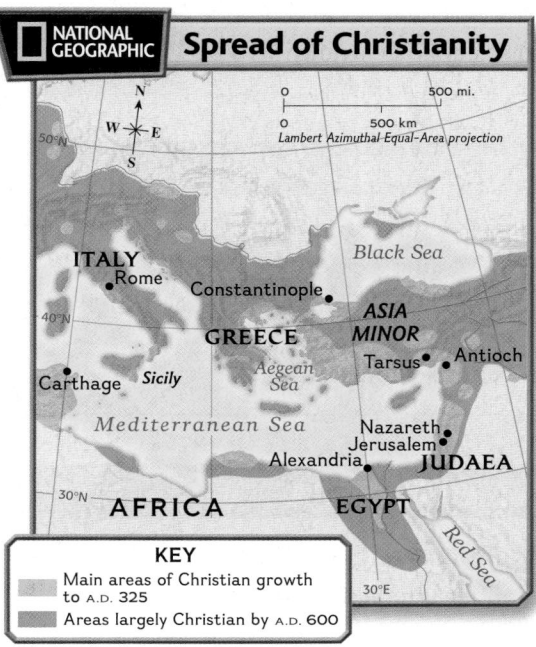

NATIONAL GEOGRAPHIC

Spread of Christianity

0   500 mi.

0   500 km
Lambert Azimuthal Equal-Area projection

ITALY
• Rome
Constantinople •
Black Sea
ASIA MINOR
GREECE
Tarsus • • Antioch
Carthage   *Sicily*   *Aegean Sea*
Mediterranean Sea
Nazareth •
Jerusalem •
Alexandria •   JUDAEA
AFRICA   EGYPT
Red Sea

KEY
- Main areas of Christian growth to A.D. 325
- Areas largely Christian by A.D. 600

Read to Write

24. **Creative Writing** Rewrite the parable of the Good Samaritan as if the events took place in the present day. Read your parable to your classmates, and explain any changes in the meaning that occurred as you modernized it.

25. **Using Your FOLDABLES** Use your foldable to write three sentences that summarize the main ideas of this chapter. Share your sentences with the class, and listen to their sentences. Then vote for the one you think best summarizes the chapter.

History Online

Self-Check Quiz To help you prepare for the Chapter Test, visit jat.glencoe.com

Using Technology

26. **Reviewing Media** Use a video or DVD player to view one of the many films made about the life of Jesus or the impact of Christianity on the people of the Roman Empire. Some examples are *Ben Hur, The Robe, The Silver Chalice,* and *The Greatest Story Ever Told.* After you watch the movie, write a review of it. Based on what you have learned about the Roman Empire and Christianity, how accurate is the movie? How does it present Jesus, his early followers, the different Jewish groups in Judaea, and the Romans? Share your review with your classmates.

Linking Past and Present

27. **Recognizing Patterns** Conduct research to find out the number of people worldwide who are Christian, Jewish, Buddhist, Hindu, and Muslim. Also record the countries where people of each religion live. What do you notice about religions in different regions of the world?

Primary Source

Analyze

Benedict wrote of the importance of keeping busy.

"Idleness [inactivity] is the enemy of the soul. Therefore should the brethren be occupied at stated times in manual labour, and at other fixed hours in sacred reading."

—Benedict, *The Rule*,
"Of the Daily Manual Labour"

DBQ **Document-Based Questions**

28. What does Benedict mean when he says inactivity is "the enemy of the soul"?

29. What do you think probably follows these lines?

History Online

Have students visit the Web site at jat.glencoe.com to review Chapter 10 and take the **Self-Check Quiz.**

Using Technology

26. Reviews should utilize the information in the chapter.

Linking Past and Present

27. Students' conclusions should be based on research. Conclusions should describe concentrations of members of specific religions in particular geographic areas.

Primary Source

28. Inactivity keeps people from growing spiritually.

29. Answers may include clear instructions for prayer, work, and study.

Bonus Question

Ask: What do you think most influenced the spread of Christianity? Why? (*Answers will vary but should include supporting details from the text.*)

Geography Skills

21. Answers may include the Mediterranean Sea.

22. from Asia to Europe and Africa

23. Jesus and his disciples were from this area, and they had success among many Jews.

Read to Write

24. Students' parables should reflect the facts as related in the text.

25. **FOLDABLES** Sentences will vary.

Chapter 11 Resources

TEACHING TRANSPARENCIES

- Graphic Organizer Transparencies with Teaching Strategy and Student Activity **L2**
- Cause-and-Effect Transparencies with Teaching Strategy and Student Activity **L2**
- Then and Now Transparencies with Teaching Strategy and Student Activity **L2**
- In-text Map Transparency with Teaching Strategy and Student Activity **L1**
- Map Transparencies with Overlay, Teaching Strategy, and Student Activity **L2**

DIFFERENTIATED INSTRUCTION

- Differentiated Instruction Activity 11
- Time Line Activity 11
- Primary Source Reading 11 (with Document-Based Questions)
- Inclusion Strategies for the Middle School Social Studies Classroom
- StudentWorks Plus™ CD-ROM (with Audio Program)

READING SUPPORT

- Take-Home Review Activity 11 **L2**
- World Literature Reading 11 **L2**
- Workbook Activity 11 **L1**
- Reading Strategies for the Social Studies Classroom **L1/ EL**

ASSESSMENT

- Authentic Assessment Activity 11 **L1/ EL**
- Chapter 11 Test Form A **L2**
- Chapter 11 Test Form B **L2**
- ExamView® Pro Testmaker CD-ROM

INTERDISCIPLINARY CONNECTIONS

- Geography and History Activity 11 **L2**
- People to Meet Activity 11 **L2**
- Economics Activity 11 **L2**
- Citizenship and Service Learning Activity 11 **L2**

SPANISH RESOURCES

- Spanish Reading Essentials and Study Guide
- Spanish Guided Reading Activities
- Spanish Quizzes, Tests, and Authentic Assessment (with Rubrics)
- Spanish Take-Home Review Activities

MULTIMEDIA

- ExamView® Pro Testmaker CD-ROM
- Glencoe Skillbuilder Interactive Workbook CD-ROM, Level 1
- Interactive Tutor Self-Assessment CD-ROM
- MindJogger Videoquiz
- Presentation Plus! CD-ROM
- StudentWorks Plus™ CD-ROM (with Audio Program)
- TeacherWorks CD-ROM
- Vocabulary PuzzleMaker CD-ROM
- *World History: Journey Across Time* Video Program
- World History Primary Source Document Library CD-ROM

STANDARDIZED ASSESSMENT SKILLS

- Standardized Test Skills Practice Workbook Activity 11 **L2**
- Critical Thinking Skills Activity 11 **L2**

Teaching strategies have been coded with suggested ability levels. However, most are suitable for all levels.

L1 BASIC activities for all students

L2 AVERAGE activities for average to above-average students

L3 CHALLENGING activities for above-average students

EL ENGLISH LANGUAGE activities

TIME MANAGEMENT

Chapter Introduction	Section 1	Section 2	Section 3	Chapter Wrap-Up	Unit Wrap-Up
1 Day	1 Day	2 Days	1 Day	1 Day	1 Day

Block Scheduling Activities that are suited to use within the block scheduling framework are identified by: 🗀

0:00 OUT OF TIME? Assign the Chapter 11 *Reading Essentials and Study Guide.* * 🗀

SECTION RESOURCES

DAILY OBJECTIVES	REPRODUCIBLE RESOURCES	MULTIMEDIA RESOURCES
Section 1 **The Rise of Islam** 1. The deserts, coastline, and oases of Arabia helped shape the Arab way of life. 2. The prophet Muhammad brought the message of Islam to the people of Arabia. 3. The Quran provides guidelines for Muslims' lives and the governments of Muslim states.	🗀 Reproducible Lesson Plan 11–1 🗀 Daily Lecture and Discussion Notes 11–1 🗀 Vocabulary Activity 11–1 🗀 Active Reading Note-Taking Guide 11–1 🗀 Guided Reading Activity 11–1* 🗀 Section Quiz 11–1* 🗀 Reading Essentials and Study Guide 11–1*	📥 Daily Focus Skills Transparency 11–1 💿 Interactive Tutor Self-Assessment CD-ROM 💿 Exam*View*® Pro Testmaker CD-ROM 💿 Presentation Plus! CD-ROM 💿 Glencoe BookLink CD-ROM
Section 2 **Islamic Empires** 1. Arabs spread Islam through conquest, preaching, and trade. 2. While Muslims split into two groups with different beliefs, the Arab Empire reached new heights. 3. Turks and Moguls built Muslim empires in Asia, Africa, and Europe.	🗀 Reproducible Lesson Plan 11–2 🗀 Daily Lecture and Discussion Notes 11–2 🗀 Vocabulary Activity 11–2 🗀 Active Reading Note-Taking Guide 11–2 🗀 Guided Reading Activity 11–2* 🗀 Section Quiz 11–2* 🗀 Reading Essentials and Study Guide 11–2*	📥 Daily Focus Skills Transparency 11–2 💿 Interactive Tutor Self-Assessment CD-ROM 💿 Exam*View*® Pro Testmaker CD-ROM 💿 Presentation Plus! CD-ROM
Section 3 **Muslim Ways of Life** 1. While Muslim traders enjoyed great success and cities grew, most Muslims lived in villages in the country. 2. Muslims made valuable contributions in the sciences and arts.	🗀 Reproducible Lesson Plan 11–3 🗀 Daily Lecture and Discussion Notes 11–3 🗀 Vocabulary Activity 11–3 🗀 Active Reading Note-Taking Guide 11–3 🗀 Guided Reading Activity 11–3* 🗀 Section Quiz 11–3* 🗀 Reading Essentials and Study Guide 11–3*	📥 Daily Focus Skills Transparency 11–3 💿 Interactive Tutor Self-Assessment CD-ROM 💿 Exam*View*® Pro Testmaker CD-ROM 💿 Presentation Plus! CD-ROM 💿 Vocabulary PuzzleMaker CD-ROM 💿 Glencoe BookLink CD-ROM

*Also available in Spanish

Chapter 11 Resources

Use our Web site for additional resources. All essential content is covered in the Student Edition.

You and your students can visit jat.glencoe.com, the Web site companion to *World History: Journey Across Time*. This innovative integration of electronic and print media offers your students a wealth of opportunities. The student text directs students to the Web site for the following options:

- Chapter Overviews
- Student Web Activities
- Self-Check Quizzes
- Multi-Language Glossaries
- Study Central™

Answers to the student Web activities are provided for you in the **Web Activity Lesson Plans.** Additional Web resources and ePuzzles and games are also available.

 Biography THE HISTORY CHANNEL.

The following videotape program is available from Glencoe as a supplement to Chapter 11:

Legends of the Arabian Nights
(ISBN 0-7670-0232-6)

To order, call Glencoe at 1-800-334-7344. To find classroom resources to accompany this video, check the following home pages:

A&E Television: www.aande.com
The History Channel: www.historychannel.com

MEETING SPECIAL NEEDS

In addition to the Differentiated Instruction strategies, the following resources are suitable for students with special needs:

- *ExamView® Pro Testmaker CD-ROM* allows teachers to tailor tests by reducing answer choices.
- *StudentWorks Plus™ CD-ROM (with Audio Program)* includes the entire narrative of the student edition so that less-proficient readers can listen to the words as they read them.
- The *Reading Essentials and Study Guide* provides the same content as the student edition but is written two grade levels below the textbook.
- *Guided Reading Activities* give less-proficient readers point-by-point instructions to increase comprehension as they read each textbook section.
- *Differentiated Instruction Activities* include a stimulating collection of readings and activities for students of all levels.

 TEACHER'S CORNER

Index to National Geographic Magazine:
The following articles relate to this chapter:

- "Kingdom on Edge: Saudi Arabia," by Frank Viviano, October 2003.
- "The World of Islam," by Don Belt, January 2002.
- "Swahili Coast: East Africa's Ancient Crossroads," by Robert Caputo, November 2001.

National Geographic Society Products:
To order the following, call National Geographic at 1–800–368–2728

- *National Geographic Desk Reference* (Book)
- *National Geographic Atlas of the World* (Book)

NGS ONLINE

Access National Geographic's new dynamic MapMachine Web site and other geography resources at:

www.nationalgeographic.com
www.nationalgeographic.com/maps

 ## Meeting NCSS Standards

World History: Journey Across Time

The following standards are highlighted in Chapter 11:

Section 1
- **I** Culture: D
- **III** People, Places, and Environments: E, F
- **IV** Individual Development and Identity: A, F
- **V** Individuals, Groups, and Institutions: A, B
- **IX** Global Connections: D

Section 2
- **II** Time, Continuity, and Change: C
- **VI** Power, Authority, and Governance: D, F

Section 3
- **IV** Individual Development and Identity: B
- **VII** Production, Distribution, and Consumption: B, D, E
- **VIII** Science, Technology, and Society: B, E

State and Local Objectives

_____

_____

Timesaving Tools

TeacherWorks
All-In-One Planner and Resource Center

● **Interactive Teacher Edition** Access your Teacher Wraparound Edition and your classroom resources with a few easy clicks.

● **Interactive Lesson Planner** Organize your week, month, semester, or year with all the lesson helps you need to make teaching creative and relevant.

Use Glencoe's **Presentation Plus!** multimedia teacher tool to easily present dynamic lessons that visually excite your students. Using Microsoft PowerPoint® you can customize the presentations to create your own personalized lessons.

FOLDABLES™
Study Organizer
Dinah Zike's Foldables

Foldables are three-dimensional, interactive graphic organizers that help students practice basic writing skills, review key vocabulary terms, and identify main ideas. Every chapter contains a foldable activity, with additional chapter activities found in the *Reading and Study Skills Foldables* booklet. You can use the foldables as they are presented, or modify them to suit the needs of your individual class.

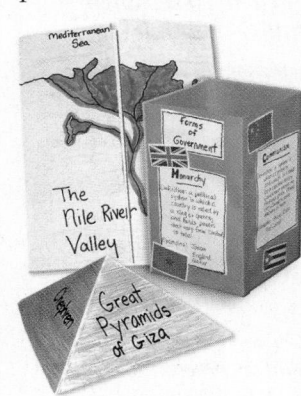

Planning Ahead

CHAPTER CULMINATING ACTIVITY

The Chapter Culminating Activity will help students organize and learn the important information from the chapter. Begin teaching the chapter with this activity, and have students complete it as a culminating activity.

CREATING A SEQUENCE CHART

Purpose This type of organizer helps students organize and analyze information by identifying important events and placing them in appropriate sequential order. It will focus them on the most important events of the chapter as they read, as well as help them see the events in chronological relationship to each other. It can also be used to organize information for reports and as a study aid.

Introduction to Modeling

1. Begin the discussion with a brainstorming session. Ask students to list what they know or believe they know about Islam, Muslims, Arabs, and the civilization of the Middle East. Write the information on an overhead transparency.

2. Ask students to copy this chart into their notebooks:

Rise and Spread of Islam

As students read the chapter, ask them to fill in the boxes with important events related to the rise and spread of Islam. Encourage them to add notes to the boxes to help them recall the events' significance. Have them add more boxes as necessary. You may also wish to assign different sets of sequence charts for different themes from the chapter.

3. As part of your chapter review, have students share their sequence charts. Encourage them to complete more boxes and use their charts as study aids.

Use the **SkillBuilder Handbook** on pages 902–919 to help students learn the skill of sequencing and categorizing information.

When & Who?

As students read the chapter, have them review the time line on this page. Ask them what happened in A.D. 610. (*Muhammad received his call.*) Then have them share what they know about Muhammad. **L1**

GLENCOE TECHNOLOGY

World History: Journey Across Time Video Program

To learn more about Islamic civilization, students can view the Chapter 11 video in the *World History: Journey Across Time* Video Program.

MindJogger Videoquiz

Use the **MindJogger Videoquiz** to preview Chapter 11 content.

Available in DVD and VHS

Chapter 11

Islamic Civilization

Muslims gather around the Kaaba ▼ at the Great Mosque in Makkah.

NATIONAL GEOGRAPHIC When & Who?

A.D. 600	A.D. 900	1200	1500
c. A.D. 610 Muhammad receives prophetic call	**A.D. 750** Abbasids overthrow Umayyads	**c. 1100** Omar Khayyam writes the *Rubaiyat*	**1258** Mongols burn Baghdad **c. 1375** Ibn Khaldun writes histories

Reading Strategy PURPOSE FOR READING

Analyzing Point out to students that they have read about the rise of many different religions. Some survived and spread, while others disappeared. **Ask:** Why might one religion succeed and spread throughout the world, while other religions disappear? (*Students may suggest that those that succeed have messages that appeal to many people, that they become ingrained, that the wealthy or ruling classes adopt them and others follow their lead, or that certain religions become associated with national or other ideals. Answers may be heartfelt or personal. Treat students' feelings carefully.*) As they read, have students look for reasons why the religion of Islam was so successful over the centuries. **L2**

Chapter Preview

A few hundred years after the beginnings of Christianity, another important religion arose in the Middle East: Islam. Followers of Islam conquered much of the Middle East, northern Africa, and part of Europe. They also made great cultural contributions to the world.

 View the Chapter 11 video in the *World History: Journey Across Time* Video Program.

 Section 1 The Rise of Islam

The religion of Islam originated in Arabia. It was based on the teachings of Muhammad.

 Section 2 Islamic Empires

Followers of Islam, called Muslims, conquered or converted people as they spread their faith throughout the Middle East and the Mediterranean.

 Section 3 Muslim Ways of Life

Muslims were skilled traders and builders. They established large cities and made many advances in mathematics, science, and the arts.

History Online
Chapter Overview Visit jat.glencoe.com for a preview of Chapter 11.

FOLDABLES Study Organizer

Categorizing Information *Make the following foldable to organize information about the people and places of Islamic civilization.*

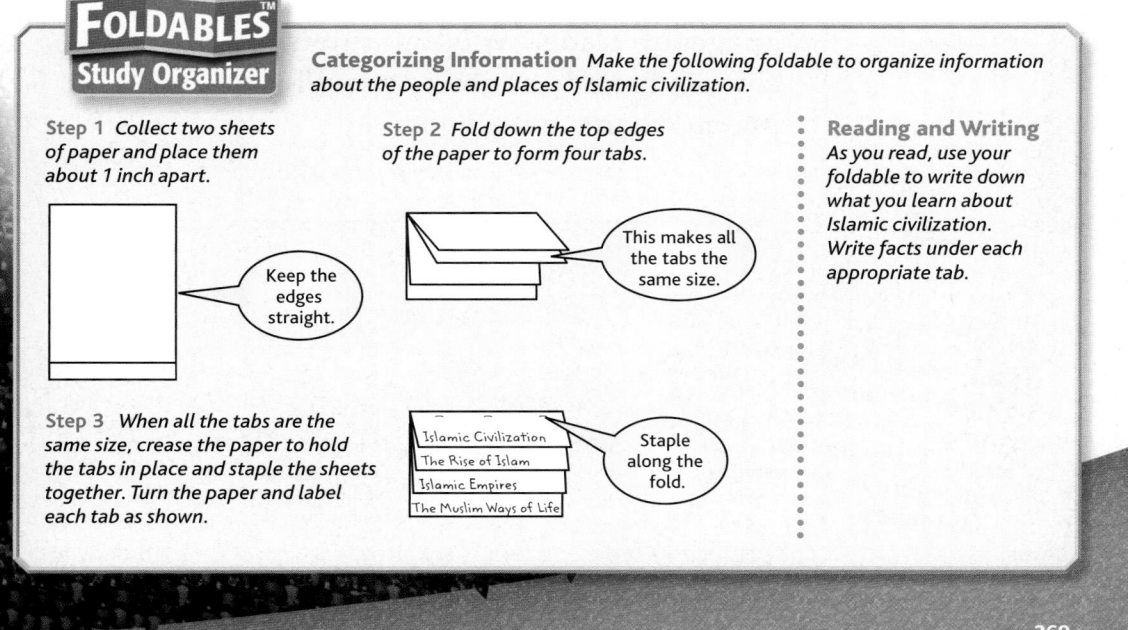

Step 1 *Collect two sheets of paper and place them about 1 inch apart.*

Keep the edges straight.

Step 2 *Fold down the top edges of the paper to form four tabs.*

This makes all the tabs the same size.

Step 3 *When all the tabs are the same size, crease the paper to hold the tabs in place and staple the sheets together. Turn the paper and label each tab as shown.*

Islamic Civilization
The Rise of Islam
Islamic Empires
The Muslim Ways of Life

Staple along the fold.

Reading and Writing *As you read, use your foldable to write down what you learn about Islamic civilization. Write facts under each appropriate tab.*

369

INTRODUCING CHAPTER 11

History Online

Introduce students to chapter content and key terms by having them access **Chapter Overview 11** at jat.glencoe.com

CHAPTER PREVIEW

After reading Chapter 11, students will be able to

1. explain how the religion of Islam began and grew;

2. discuss how Muslims spread their faith throughout the Middle East and the Mediterranean;

3. summarize the achievements of the Muslim empires.

FOLDABLES Study Organizer

Dinah Zike's Foldables

Purpose Students use this foldable to organize information about notable people and places in Islamic civilization. As students read this chapter, they should make notes about these topics. When students have completed their foldables, they should have a guide to the important figures and places discussed in this chapter.

☞ Have students complete *Reading and Study Skills Foldables* Activity 11.

1 Learn It!

Explain to students that, as they read, they should always be attempting to identify the main idea at every level of the text—paragraph, section, and chapter. Students should practice looking for the focus of a section, along with the details that support that focus, by using a variety of reading strategies.

Remind students that a main idea can often be found in the first sentence of a paragraph or in a section heading. For example, in Section 3 under the heading "What Were Muslim Cities Like?" students can conclude that a main idea in this section might be life in Muslim cities. Point out that a heading in the form of a question provides an easy way to find supporting details by looking for answers to the question. Have students create a graphic organizer with the main idea at center surrounded by supporting details using the theme "Life in Muslim Cities."

Muslim Cities — bazaars, government, schools, trade, learning, the arts, mosques

---

Chapter **11**

Reading Social Studies

Reading Skill

Main Idea

1 Learn It!

Main Ideas and Details

Main ideas are the most important ideas in a paragraph, section, or chapter. Supporting details are facts or examples that explain the main idea. Read the following paragraph from Section 3 and notice how the author explains the main idea.

> **Several things explain the success of Muslim trade. When Muslim empires expanded, they spread the Arabic language. As a result, Arabic became the language of trade. Muslim rulers also made trade easier by providing merchants with coins.**
>
> —*from page 388*

Reading Tip

Often, the first sentence in a paragraph will contain a main idea. Supporting details will come in following sentences.

Main Idea — Supporting Detail, Supporting Detail, Supporting Detail, Supporting Detail

---

Reading Strategy — **READING THE TEXT**

Previewing what is going to be read can help students focus on the main ideas in the chapter or section. Have students skim a section of the chapter. They should read each of the blue subsection heads and write a short statement for each heading describing what they believe will be the main idea of that subsection. Students may use illustrations or other clues on the page to help them write their main idea statements. After they have finished a section, briefly discuss with students their thoughts about the main ideas in their reading. Have students reassess and rewrite their statements as they read the chapter in greater detail. **L1/EL**

2 Practice It!

Using a Graphic Organizer

Read the following paragraph, and find the main idea and supporting details. Create a graphic organizer like the one that appears at the bottom of page 370.

Read to Write

"The famous Mogul ruler Akbar could not read, yet he set up a large library because he valued education, books, and art." Write a letter to Akbar telling him about your favorite book and why it should be included in his library.

Times were good in India under Akbar. Farmers and artisans produced more food and goods than the Indians needed. As a result, trade increased. Muslim merchants brought paper, gunpowder, and fine porcelain from China to India. In addition, Muslim architects introduced new building styles, such as the arch and dome, to India.

—from page 386

3 Apply It!

As you read Chapter 11, create your own graphic organizer to show the main idea and supporting details from at least one paragraph.

371

2 Practice It!

Using Graphic Organizers Explain to students that graphic organizers can be helpful aids as they learn to recognize main ideas and supporting details. In addition to the web diagram shown on student page 370, introduce students to other graphic organizers that work well when finding the main idea and supporting details. An example is a main idea chart that places the main idea in a top box with supporting details listed in connected boxes below. A variation has students write a simple topic statement followed by details, with a final box containing a main idea in sentence format. A fishbone diagram has a main idea statement written on a single line to the left. Supporting facts and details are written on lines branching off to the right.

Have students choose several paragraphs from the chapter and create graphic organizers showing the main ideas and details.

3 Apply It!

Extending After students have made several graphic organizers, have them choose one main idea and find at least three additional supporting details.

Reading Strategy ⟩ **READ TO WRITE**

To help students better understand the concept of main idea and supporting details, have them consider a main idea to be supported with facts, examples, or persuasive opinion. In discussing how the Mogul empire prospered under Akbar, students will discover various reasons for his success. Have them create a graphic organizer for this information. Then have them create another graphic organizer with the main idea concerning the decline of the Mogul empire. Once students have finished both organizers, discuss the details they have used and how these details reinforce the main ideas and demonstrate historical relationships.

① FOCUS

SECTION OVERVIEW

This section discusses the life of the prophet Muhammad and the rise of the religion he founded, Islam, in the Arabian desert.

BELLRINGER
SKILLBUILDER ACTIVITY

👆 Project **Daily Focus Skills Transparency 11–1** and have students answer questions. Discuss their responses.

Get Ready to Read!

Preteaching Vocabulary: An oasis is a green area in a desert fed by underground water. In the deserts of Arabia, they were extremely important to traders and travelers alike.

Answers to Graphic: Five Pillars of Faith: declare belief in Allah, pray five times a day facing Makkah, give to the poor, fast during Ramadan, make a pilgrimage to Makkah

---

Section ①

The Rise of Islam

Get Ready to Read!

What's the Connection?
Previously, you learned about early empires in southwest Asia. During the A.D. 600s, people called Arabs began a new empire in the region. The driving force behind their empire building was the religion of Islam.

Focus on the Main Ideas
• The deserts, coastline, and oases of Arabia helped shape the Arab way of life. *(page 373)*

• The prophet Muhammad brought the message of Islam to the people of Arabia. *(page 374)*

• The Quran provided guidelines for Muslims' lives and the governments of Muslim states. *(page 377)*

Locating Places
Makkah (MAH•kuh)
Kaaba (KAH•buh)
Madinah (mah•DEE•nah)

Meeting People
Bedouin (BEH•duh•wuhn)
Muhammad (moh•HAH•muhd)

Building Your Vocabulary
oasis (oh•AY•suhs)
sheikh (SHAYK)
caravan (KAR•uh•VAN)
Quran (koh•RAHN)

Reading Strategy
Organizing Information Use a diagram like the one below to identify the Five Pillars of faith.

Five Pillars				

When & Where?

NATIONAL GEOGRAPHIC

• Madinah
• Makkah (Mecca)

A.D. 550	A.D. 600	A.D. 650

A.D. 570 Muhammad is born

C. A.D. 610 Muhammad receives prophetic call

A.D. 630 Makkah surrenders to Muhammad

SECTION RESOURCES

📁 **Reproducible Masters**
• Reproducible Lesson Plan 11–1
• Daily Lecture and Discussion Notes 11–1
• Vocabulary Activity 11–1
• Active Reading Note-Taking Guide 11–1
• Guided Reading Activity 11–1
• Section Quiz 11–1
• Reading Essentials and Study Guide 11–1

👆 **Transparencies**
• Daily Focus Skills Transparency 11–1

Multimedia
💿 Interactive Tutor Self-Assessment CD-ROM
💿 ExamView® Pro Testmaker CD-ROM
💿 Presentation Plus! CD-ROM
💿 Glencoe BookLink CD-ROM

Daily Life in Early Arabia

Main Idea The deserts, coastline, and oases of Arabia helped shape the Arab way of life.

Reading Focus Do you ever think about how rainfall shapes your life? Read on to find out how lack of rain helped shape the Arabs' way of life.

Desert stretches over most of the Arabian peninsula. The heat is intense, and a sandstorm can blind any traveler. Water is found only at **oases** (oh AY seez), green areas fed by underground water. Not all of Arabia is dry, however. In the mountains of the southwest, enough rain falls to support plants such as juniper and olive trees.

To survive, early Arabs organized into tribes who were very loyal to one another. The head of the tribe was called a **sheikh** (SHAYK).

Who Are the Bedouins?
Some Arabs were desert herders. To water and graze their camels, goats, and sheep, they went from oasis to oasis. They were called **Bedouins** (BEH•duh•wuhnz).

▼ Today, many Bedouins still roam the desert and live in tents. *Where did Bedouins graze their animals in the desert?*

Bedouins lived in tents and ate dried fruits and nuts. They drank the milk of their animals. Only rarely would they eat meat. Their animals were much too valuable to be used as food.

Trade and Towns
Many Arabs lived in villages where they farmed or raised animals. These villages were near oases or in the mountain valleys.

Some of the villagers were merchants who transported goods across the desert. To fend off attacks by Bedouins, many traveled in a **caravan** (KAR•uh•VAN), or group of traveling merchants and animals.

By about A.D. 500, Arabian merchants handled most trade between India and the Mediterranean Sea. As their trade grew, Arab merchants founded towns along the trade routes in Arabia. **Makkah** (MAH•kuh), also known as Mecca, became the largest and richest of them all. It was a crossroads for merchants, and it was also an important religious site. The holiest place in Arabia was in this city.

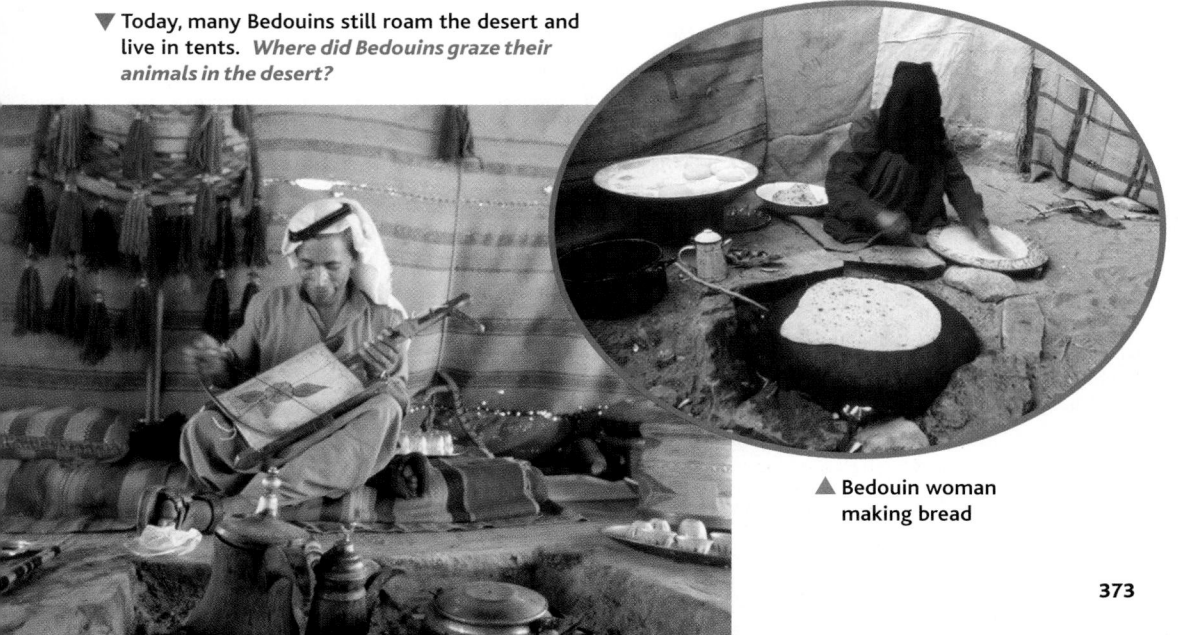

▲ Bedouin woman making bread

373

② TEACH

Daily Lecture and Discussion Notes 11–1

Use **Daily Lecture and Discussion Notes 11–1** for an outline of key concepts found in the section.

CONNECTING ACROSS TIME

The term *sheikh* is still used widely in Arabic and Muslim countries. It generally refers to a respected man over 50 years of age, although it is also applied to heads of religious orders and colleges, village and neighborhood leaders, and learned theologians. It has even been used for anyone of any age who has memorized the entire Quran. Ask students to find references to the term used in current events. **L1/ EL**

More About the Photo

Bedouins are traditionally classified by the animals they raise. Camel nomads are highest in social status, followed by sheep and goat Bedouins. Lowest in prestige are the cattle nomads.

Caption Answer: at oases

Reading Strategy READING THE TEXT

Activating Prior Knowledge Have students take notes on a short class discussion about class members' prior knowledge about Islam. Then have them use their notes to write a list of five things they hope to confirm or learn more about. You may want to carefully evaluate with students any unwarranted assumptions about Islam. **L2**

Reading Support L1/ EL

Use **Vocabulary Activity 11–1** to review important terms in the section.

in a word . . .

The word **"pilgrim"** comes from the same Latin root as *peregrine*, a type of falcon. In the Middle Ages, the peregrine falcon was named because it was captured in passage (while flying), rather than while sitting in its nest.

Using Geography Skills

Answers:

1. the Byzantine Empire
2. about 200 miles

Skills Practice

Ask: What three bodies of water surround the Arabian Peninsula? (*Red Sea, Arabian Sea, Persian Gulf*)

✓ Reading Check

Answer: To survive in the desert, early Arabs organized into loyal tribes. They traveled from oasis to oasis and ate dried fruit and nuts.

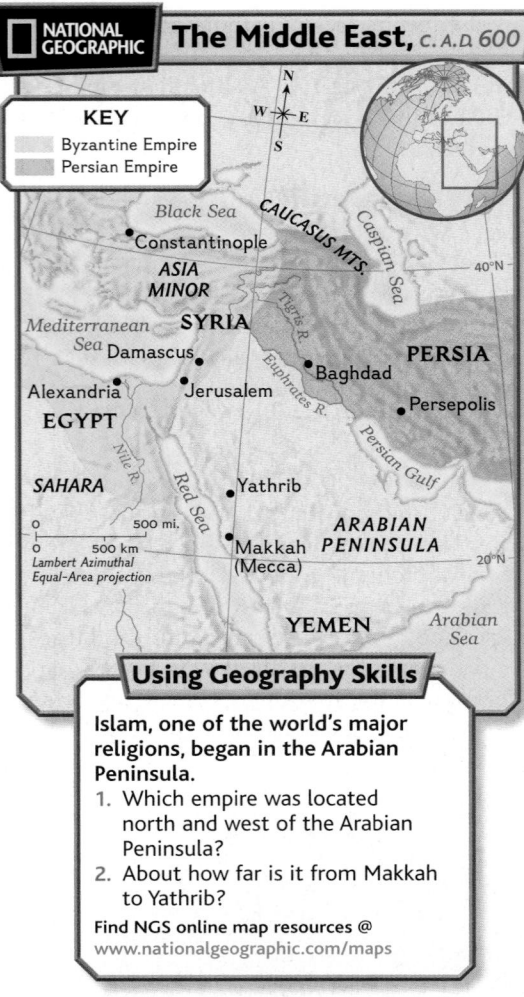

NATIONAL GEOGRAPHIC

The Middle East, C. A.D. 600

KEY
- Byzantine Empire
- Persian Empire

Using Geography Skills

Islam, one of the world's major religions, began in the Arabian Peninsula.
1. Which empire was located north and west of the Arabian Peninsula?
2. About how far is it from Makkah to Yathrib?

Find NGS online map resources @ www.nationalgeographic.com/maps

In the middle of Makkah was the **Kaaba** (KAH buh), a low square building surrounded by statues of gods and goddesses. Arabs believed that the great stone inside the Kaaba was from heaven. Pilgrims, people who travel to a holy place, flocked to Makkah. Arabians worshiped many gods, but the most important was Allah. Allah was considered to be the creator.

✓ Reading Check **Analyze** How did geography shape life in Arabia?

Muhammad: Islam's Prophet

Main Idea) The prophet Muhammad brought the message of Islam to the people of Arabia.

Reading Focus Have you ever heard someone speak and been moved to tears? The following paragraphs tell about a prophet who moved the Arab people with his words.

Muhammad's Message In A.D. 570 a man named **Muhammad** (moh•HAH•muhd) was born in Makkah. An orphan, he was raised by an uncle. As a teenager, he worked in the trusted job of caravan leader and eventually became a successful merchant. He married and had children.

Despite his success, Muhammad was dissatisfied. He felt that the wealthy town leaders should return to the old ways. He thought they should honor their families, be fair in business, and help the poor.

Muhammad went into the hills to pray. In about A.D. 610, he said he was visited by an angel and told to preach Islam. *Islam* means "surrendering to the will of Allah." *Allah* is the Arabic word for "God."

Inspired, Muhammad returned to Makkah. Everywhere he went, he told people to destroy statues of false gods and to worship only Allah, the one true God.

Muhammad also preached that all people were equal and that the rich should share their goods. In Makkah, where most people lived humbly, this vision of a just society was very powerful. Muhammad was saying that wealth was not as important as leading a good life. When the Day of Judgment arrived, he said God would reward the good people and punish the evildoers.

Opposition to Islam Slowly Muhammad convinced people that his message was true. At first, only his family became

---

DIFFERENTIATED INSTRUCTION

Interpersonal: Have students work in small groups to compare the beliefs of Islam with those of two other religions they have read about (Christianity; Judaism; Mesopotamian, Egyptian, Greek, or Roman religion; Hinduism; Daoism; or Buddhism). Have each group share with the class its findings about how the two religions compare and contrast.

English Learners: Ask students to use a dictionary, encyclopedia, or other resource to paraphrase key beliefs of the two religions.

Gifted and Talented: Have students create a display, bulletin board, or other multimedia presentation about the religions they are comparing.

 Refer to *Inclusion Strategies for the Middle School Social Studies Classroom* in the TCR.

Muslims, or followers of Islam. Soon, however, many of the poor were attracted to his message that goods should be shared.

Wealthy merchants and religious leaders did not like Muhammad's message. They thought he was trying to take away their power. They made his life difficult and beat and tortured his followers.

In A.D. 622 Muhammad and his followers left Makkah. They moved north to a town called Yathrib (YA•thruhb). The journey of Muhammad and his followers to Yathrib became known as the Hijrah (HIH•jruh). The word comes from Arabic and means "breaking off relationships." Later Muslims made the year A.D. 622 the first year of a new Muslim calendar. Yathrib welcomed Muhammad and his followers. Their city was renamed **Madinah** (mah•DEE•nah), which means "the city of the prophet."

Muhammad's Government The people of Madinah accepted Muhammad as God's prophet and their ruler. Muhammad proved to be an able leader. He applied the laws he believed God had given him to all areas of life. He used these laws to settle disputes among the people. Muhammad created an Islamic state—a government that uses its political power to uphold Islam. He required all Muslims to place loyalty to the Islamic state above loyalty to their tribe.

To defend his new government, Muhammad built an army. His soldiers conquered Makkah in A.D. 630, and Muhammad then made it a holy city of Islam. Two years later, Muhammad died. By this time, Islam was spreading to all of Arabia.

✓ **Reading Check** **Explain** Why did Muhammad's message appeal to the poor?

A pilgrimage to Makkah ▶

A Holy Journey

A pilgrimage to the holy city of Makkah often involved a long, difficult journey across deserts and other rough country. Muslim travelers carried palm leaves to show that they were on a pilgrimage. *Where was Muhammad born?*

375

Biography

TEACH

One of Muhammad's most controversial teachings was that people should be held responsible for their actions. He preached that those who did good and evil in life would receive a fitting reward or punishment in paradise. This idea frightened the traditional rulers of Makkah. They felt it would undermine their control over society and hinder the growth of their wealth.

Ask students to contrast a society in which people are held responsible for their actions with one in which they are not. In what ways are people in our society held responsible? Are there some ways in which they are not? *(For a society in which people are not held responsible, students will probably describe a lawless society in which the strong mistreat the weak. In our society, the justice system and punishments such as prison are used to hold people responsible for their actions. Examples of how people are not held accountable for their actions will vary.)* L1/ **EL**

Then and Now

Answers will vary but may include that a small number of people have great wealth, while a large number of people in the world live in poverty.

MUHAMMAD

A.D. 570–632

Muhammad experienced great poverty and many hardships early in his life. His father, Abd Allah, died before he was born. His grandfather, Abd al-Muttalib, took care of Muhammad in Makkah for a short time. Abd al-Muttalib felt that Makkah was an unhealthy place to raise a baby, but he could not leave because he was a political leader in the city. So he entrusted Muhammad to a tribe of nomads. They took the baby Muhammad to their home, the desert. When Muhammad was six years old, his mother died. Two years later, when Muhammad was eight, his grandfather also died. Arab custom did not allow minors to inherit anything, so the property and money from Muhammad's father and grandfather could not be passed down to him. To survive, Muhammad needed the protection of Abu Talib, his uncle who now headed the family.

Under the care of Abu Talib, Muhammad traveled by camel on trading journeys to Syria. On one of these trips, when he was about twenty-five years old, Muhammad met a wealthy woman named Khadijah. She and Muhammad married and had four daughters. They also had at least two sons who did not live past childhood. Muhammad's marriage to Khadijah made him a wealthy man and a member of Makkah's prosperous merchant class.

▲ The Mosque of the Prophet in Madinah contains Muhammad's tomb.

However, Muhammad could not forget his early experiences. His childhood had deeply influenced Muhammad and made him a thoughtful person. He often would go up into the hills near Makkah and spend nights in a cave. Alone there, he would reflect on the problems he saw in Makkah and the growing tension between the few people with great wealth and the many people with nothing. It was in these hills that Muhammad claimed an angel told him, "You are the Messenger of God."

▲ The Dome of the Rock in Jerusalem marks the place where Muhammad is believed to have ascended to heaven.

Then and Now

Are any of the problems Muhammad saw in Makkah similar to problems in society we see today? Explain.

Reading List Generator CD-ROM

GLENCOE BOOKLINK **RECOMMENDED READING**

Use the **Glencoe BookLink CD-ROM** to create customized reading lists based on your students' interests and reading levels. Below is an example based on content in this chapter. Also, see the Suggested Readings on pages 944–946 of the Appendix.

- **King, John.** *Bedouin.* In the deserts of northern Africa and the Middle East, the Bedouin travel from place to place with the camels and sheep that provide them with their livelihood.

- From the *Qur'an: The Exordium and Daylight.* Passages from the sacred book of Islam.

- **Warren, Ruth.** *The First Book of the Arab World.* The Arab world, which stretches from northern Africa through the Middle East, is united by a common language—Arabic—and a proud history.

Islam's Teachings

Main Idea The Quran provided guidelines for Muslims' lives and the governments of Muslim states.

Reading Focus Do you ever wonder how you should act in certain situations? In the following paragraphs, you will learn where Muslims looked for guidance.

Islam, Judaism, and Christianity have some beliefs in common. Like Jews and Christians, Muslims believe in one God. Muslims believe this one God holds all power and created the universe. They also believe that God determines right and wrong. People are expected to obey God's laws if they want to be blessed in the afterlife.

Jews, Christians, and Muslims also believe that God spoke to people through prophets. For Muslims, early prophets were Abraham, Moses, Jesus, and finally Muhammad. For Christians, Jesus was more than a prophet. He was the son of God and therefore divine. In Islam, Muhammad is seen as a prophet and a very good person but not as divine.

What Is the Quran? Muslims wrote down the messages that Muhammad said he received from Allah. These writings became the **Quran** (koh•RAHN), or holy book of Islam. For Muslims, the Quran is God's written word. For this reason, Muslims strive to follow the Quran.

The Quran instructs Muslims about how they should live. Many of its moral teachings are like those of the Bible. For example, Muslims are told to be honest and to treat others fairly. They are to honor their parents, show kindness to their neighbors, and give generously to the poor. Murder, lying, and stealing are forbidden.

▲ Muslim pilgrims surround the Kaaba in Makkah. *When did Muhammad's soldiers capture the city of Makkah?*

▲ A child studies the Quran

CHAPTER 11   Islamic Civilization   **377**

CHAPTER 11
SECTION 1, 372–378

Reading Support L1/EL

Assign **Guided Reading Activity 11–1** to help students organize the information in the section.

③ ASSESS

Assign Section 1 Review as homework or as an in-class activity.

🖱 Have students use the **Interactive Tutor Self-Assessment CD-ROM** to review the section.

Assessment L2

Assign **Section 1 Quiz** to assess mastery of the material found in the section.

Reading Support L1/EL

Assign **Reading Essentials and Study Guide 11–1** to help students review section material.

More About the Photo

The black cloth that covers the Kaaba is called the *kiswah*. It contains verses from the Quran embroidered in gold.

Caption Answer: A.D. 630

INTERDISCIPLINARY CONNECTIONS ACTIVITY

Daily Life Ask students to research and prepare a report on a Muslim holiday for the class. Direct them to describe how Muslim families celebrate major holidays. They should pay attention to objects and family items used in the celebrations. **L2**

Caption Answer:
Muslims must pray five times daily facing Makkah.

 Reading Check

Answer: The Quran and Sunna together tell Muslims how to live and worship.

ENRICH

Ask students to write an essay comparing the history and teachings presented in the Quran to those found in another book of sacred writings, such as the Bible. **L3**

 History Online

To help students understand section material, have them visit **Study Central™** at jat.glencoe.com

RETEACH

Have students explain to a partner why Muhammad was an important figure. **L1**

④ CLOSE

Ask students to compare Islam's origins to the beginnings of another religion they have studied. **L2**

The Five Pillars of Islam

Belief	Muslims must declare that there is no god but Allah and that Muhammad is his prophet.
Prayer	Muslims must pray five times per day facing toward Makkah.
Charity	Muslims must give to the poor.
Fasting	Muslims must not eat from dawn to dusk during the sacred holiday of Ramadan.
Pilgrimage	Muslims must visit Makkah once in their life.

▲ The Five Pillars are acts of worship that all Muslims must carry out. *How many times should Muslims pray each day?*

Many rules in the Quran apply to Muslims' daily life. According to these rules, Muslims should not eat pork, drink liquor, or gamble. The Quran also has rules about marriage, divorce, family life, property rights, and business practices.

Muslims are expected to fulfill the Five Pillars of Islam, or acts of worship. These are shown in the chart at the left.

Scholars of Islam also created a law code that explains how society should be run. This code is taken from the Quran and the Sunna (SUH•nuh). The Sunna is the name given to customs based on Muhammad's words and deeds. Islam's law code covers all areas of daily life. It applies the teachings of the Quran to family life, business, and government.

✓ **Reading Check** **Evaluate** What role do the Quran and Sunna play in Muslim daily life?

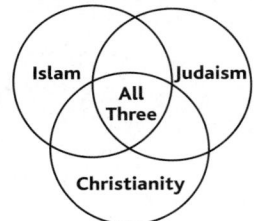 **History Online**
Study Central™ Need help with the material in this section? Visit jat.glencoe.com

Section ① Review

Reading Summary
Review the Main Ideas
• In the desert of the Arabian Peninsula, the Arab people were mostly herders and traders.
• In the town of Makkah, Muhammad began to preach a new religion, Islam, which soon spread to all of Arabia.
• Muslims believe that Muhammad was Allah's final prophet and that their holy book, the Quran, is Allah's written word.

What Did You Learn?
1. What are oases, and why were they important to Arabs?
2. Name some activities the Quran prohibits.

Critical Thinking
3. **Compare and Contrast** Draw a Venn diagram to compare and contrast Islam, Judaism, and Christianity.

Islam — Judaism — All Three — Christianity

4. **Conclude** Why do you think Muhammad's teachings were popular with poorer people?
5. **Analyze** How did Muhammad link religion and government?
6. **Expository Writing** Suppose you are living in Makkah at the time Muhammad began preaching. Write a short newspaper article that describes Muhammad's teachings and the reactions of people in the city to those teachings.
7. **Reading** **Main Idea** Draw a graphic organizer to show the supporting details for this main idea: *Geography shaped the way that the early Arabs lived.*

378 CHAPTER 11 Islamic Civilization

SECTION 1 REVIEW ANSWERS

1. green areas in the desert fed by underground water; supplied water for Arab herders
2. murder, lying, gambling, stealing, eating pork, and drinking liquor
3. Answers should reflect information in the text.
4. Because he said goods should be shared, the poorer people realized the possibility of benefiting through charity.
5. Muhammad applied God's laws to all areas of life and used these laws to settle disputes among the people.
6. Answers will vary but should include his teachings and people's reactions.
7. Answers will vary but should discuss the desert and the importance of oases.

Section 2 — Islamic Empires

Get Ready to Read!

What's the Connection?

In Section 1, you learned how Islam spread from Madinah to Makkah. In time, Islam's followers brought their beliefs to all of Southwest Asia and parts of Southeast Asia, Africa, and Europe.

Focus on the Main Ideas

- Arabs spread Islam through preaching, conquest, and trade. **(page 380)**

- While Muslims split into two groups, the Arab Empire reached new heights. **(page 382)**

- Turks and Moguls built Muslim empires in Asia, Africa, and Europe. **(page 384)**

Locating Places

Damascus (duh•MAS•kuhs)
Indonesia (IHN•duh•NEE•zhuh)
Timbuktu (TIHM•BUHK•TOO)
Baghdad (BAG•dad)
Delhi (DEH•lee)

Meeting People

Umayyad (oo•MY•uhd)
Sufi (SOO•fee)
Abbasid (uh•BA•suhd)
Suleiman I (SOO•lay•MAHN)
Mogul (MOH•guhl)
Akbar (AK•buhr)

Building Your Vocabulary

caliph (KAY•luhf)
Shiite (SHEE•eyet)
Sunni (SU•nee)
sultan (SUHL•tuhn)

Reading Strategy

Cause and Effect Create a diagram to show why the Arabs were successful conquerors.

```
[   ]    [   ]    [   ]
  |        |        |
  v        v        v
[ Arabs were successful conquerors. ]
```

NATIONAL GEOGRAPHIC **When & Where?**

Córdoba • Constantinople • Baghdad • Delhi

A.D. **500** — **1100** — **1700**

A.D. **750** Abbasids overthrow Umayyads

1258 Mongols burn Baghdad

1526 Moguls rule India from Delhi

CHAPTER 11

1 FOCUS

SECTION OVERVIEW

This section highlights the spread of Islamic empires into areas of Asia, Africa, and Europe.

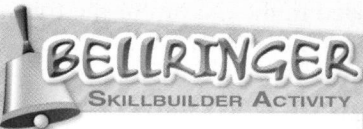

BELLRINGER
SKILLBUILDER ACTIVITY

Project **Daily Focus Skills Transparency 11–2** and have students answer questions. Discuss their responses.

Get Ready to Read!

Preteaching Vocabulary: Sunnis and Shiites form the two main branches of Islam. Sunnis and Shiites originally split over the question of who should rule the Islamic empire.

Answers to Graphic: were skilled horsemen and sword fighters; believed they would go to paradise if they died in battle for Islam; let conquered peoples follow their own religion

---

SECTION RESOURCES

Reproducible Masters
- Reproducible Lesson Plan 11–2
- Daily Lecture and Discussion Notes 11–2
- Vocabulary Activity 11–2
- Active Reading Note-Taking Guide 11–2
- Guided Reading Activity 11–2
- Section Quiz 11–2
- Reading Essentials and Study Guide 11–2

Transparencies
- Daily Focus Skills Transparency 11–2

Multimedia
- Interactive Tutor Self-Assessment CD-ROM
- ExamView® Pro Testmaker CD-ROM
- Presentation Plus! CD-ROM

② TEACH

📖 Reading Strategy

Understanding Terms The Arabic word *caliph*, used for the religious and governmental head of the Muslim state, is also used in the Quran for the roles of Adam and David. **Ask: In what ways was King David of ancient Israel similar to the Rightly Guided Caliphs?** (*All were military leaders, all were heads of the government, and all were closely involved in religious matters.*) **L2**

Daily Lecture and Discussion Notes 11-2

Use **Daily Lecture and Discussion Notes 11-2** for an outline of key concepts found in the section.

Reading Support L1/ EL

Use **Vocabulary Activity 11-2** to review important terms in the section.

Using Geography Skills

Answers:

1. Spain
2. Persia, most of Mesopotamia, Arabia, Egypt, part of North Africa

The Spread of Islam

$\boxed{\text{Main Idea}}$ **Arabs spread Islam through preaching, conquest, and trade.**

Reading Focus When you come up with a new idea, how do you let others know about it? Read on to find out how Arabs spread Islam.

When Muhammad died, his followers chose his successor. He was called a **caliph** (KAY•luhf), which meant successor to the Messenger of God.

The first caliph was Muhammad's father-in-law, Abu Bakr. The first four caliphs ruled from Madinah and were called the Rightly Guided Caliphs. That is because they tried to follow in Muhammad's footsteps. They lived simply, treated others fairly, and also fought hard for Islam. They wanted to spread Allah's message to everyone. Under their rule, the empire expanded to include all of southwest Asia.

Expansion continued under the **Umayyad** (oo•MY•uhd) caliphs, who ruled from A.D. 661 to A.D. 750. They made their capital the city of **Damascus** (duh•MAS•kuhs) in Syria. Now the Arab Empire included North Africa, Spain, and some of India.

The Muslims Build an Empire Just 100 years after Muhammad's death, the Islamic state became a great empire. Why were the Arabs so successful?

Arabs had always been good on horseback and good with the sword, but as Muslims, they also were inspired by their religion. They were fighting to spread

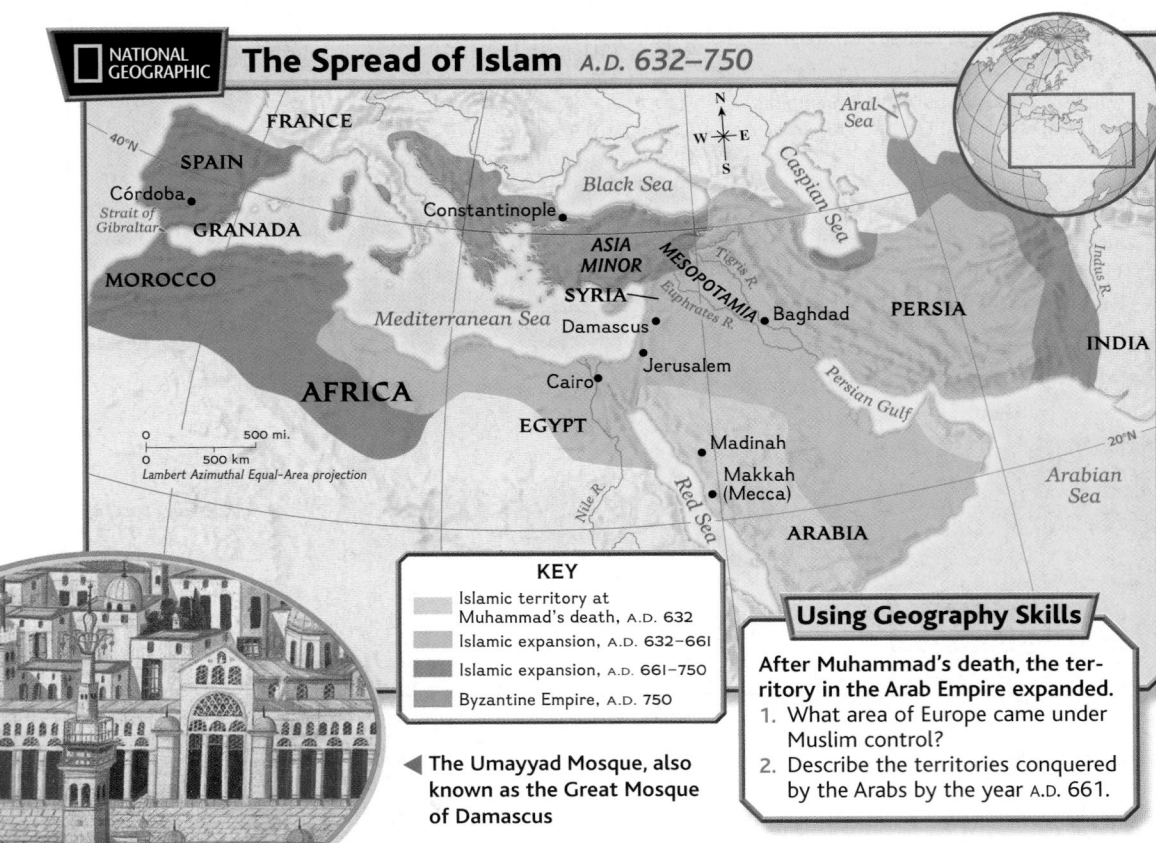

NATIONAL GEOGRAPHIC
The Spread of Islam A.D. 632-750

KEY
- Islamic territory at Muhammad's death, A.D. 632
- Islamic expansion, A.D. 632-661
- Islamic expansion, A.D. 661-750
- Byzantine Empire, A.D. 750

◀ The Umayyad Mosque, also known as the Great Mosque of Damascus

Using Geography Skills

After Muhammad's death, the territory in the Arab Empire expanded.
1. What area of Europe came under Muslim control?
2. Describe the territories conquered by the Arabs by the year A.D. 661.

📖 Reading Strategy READING THE TEXT

Using a Concept-Definition Map A concept-definition map helps students, either individually or in a group, define a word or concept visually. Use a concept-definition map of any design to help students analyze and understand the concept of an empire they will read about in this section. Each map should begin with a word or phrase that serves as a theme. Parts of the map should allow room for answering the questions *What is it? What is it like?* and *What are some examples?* Answers can branch off the question. Have students begin a concept-definition map for one of the empires covered in the section and complete it as they read the section. **L2**

The Rightly Guided Caliphs

	Abu Bakr	Umar	Uthman	Ali
Relationship to Muhammad	father-in-law	friend	son-in-law, member of the Umayyad family	first cousin, son-in-law
Career	merchant	merchant	merchant	soldier, writer
Caliphate	A.D. 632–634	A.D. 634–644	A.D. 644–656	A.D. 656–661
Achievements as Caliph	spread Islam to all of Arabia; restored peace after death of Muhammad; created code of conduct in war; compiled Quran verses	spread Islam to Syria, Egypt, and Persia; redesigned government; paid soldiers; held a census; made taxes more fair; built roads and canals; aided poor	spread Islam into Afghanistan and eastern Mediterranean; organized a navy; improved the government; built more roads, bridges, and canals; distributed text of the Quran	reformed tax collection and other government systems; spent most of caliphate battling Muawiya, the governor of Syria

◀ Islamic glass horse

Understanding Charts

Under the caliphs, Islam spread through the Middle East and into North Africa.
1. Which caliph organized a navy?
2. **Compare** What achievements did Umar and Ali have in common?

Islam. Muslims believed anyone who died in battle for Islam would go to paradise.

The Arabs were also successful because they let conquered peoples practice their own religion. They called Christians and Jews "People of the Book," meaning that these people, too, believed in one God and had holy writings. Muslims did not treat everyone equally, though. Non-Muslims had to pay a special tax.

When a people are conquered, they tend to adopt the religion and customs of their new rulers. In the Arab Empire, many people became Muslims and learned Arabic. The customs of the conquered countries also influenced the Arabic rulers. Eventually, the term *Arab* meant only that a person spoke Arabic, not that he or she was from Arabia.

Preaching and Trading Muslims also spread Islam by preaching. A group called **Sufis** (SOO•feez) spent their time praying and teaching Islam. They won many followers throughout the Arab Empire.

Arab merchants also helped to spread Islam. They set up trading posts throughout southeast Asia and taught Islam to the people there. Today, the country of **Indonesia** (IHN•duh•NEE•zhuh) includes more Muslims than any other nation in the world.

Some Arab merchants crossed the Sahara to trade with kingdoms in West Africa. In the 1300s, the west African city of **Timbuktu** (TIHM•BUHK•TOO) became a leading center of Muslim learning.

✓ **Reading Check** **Explain** How did Arabs spread the religion of Islam through trade?

CHAPTER 11   Islamic Civilization   381

Islam Around the World Ask students to research the Islamic populations of countries around the world today. For a number of major countries, and also those countries with large Muslim populations, they should determine what percentage of the population is Islamic. Provide students with a blank map of the world, preferably with national borders. Have students create a key to show varying percentages of Muslim population and color the map of the world accordingly. Then have students make several generalizations about Islamic empires and the spread of Islam based on the information they found. L3

Understanding Charts

Answers:
1. Uthman
2. Both worked on the tax system and interacted with Syria.

✓ Reading Check

Answer: Merchants set up trading posts along the mainland coasts, on the islands of Southeast Asia, and in West Africa, and taught people there.

DIFFERENTIATED INSTRUCTION

Interpersonal: Arabs spread Islam in several different ways. One way, trading, required extensive interpersonal communication. Ask students to discuss in small groups how the religion of Islam might have been spread from Arab traders to non-Muslims in Southeast Asia or Africa. What did they talk about? How might others have felt about Islamic beliefs? Why might non-Muslims have converted? Why did Muslims want to convert others? Have each group report on its discussion.

English Learners: Ask students to use a dictionary or other resource to make a list of words related to trade or religion.

Gifted and Talented: Have students research ancient Arab trade routes and write a short report on the civilizations with which the Arabs interacted.

📖 **Reading Strategy**

Writing Activity ✍️

Ask students to list reasons for the division of Islam into two main branches, Sunnis and Shiites. Then have them write a paragraph explaining how this might have aided in the rise of the Abbasids. *(Answers will vary. Students may suggest that religious differences contributed to frustration with Umayyad rule.)*
L2

Primary Source

Ibn Khaldun was born in Tunis and held various offices under rulers in northern Africa. In 1382 he moved to Cairo and served as a judge there. He is generally considered one of the greatest Muslim historical thinkers.

Answer:
God made the caliph his substitute.

GLENCOE
BOOKLINK

Use **Glencoe BookLink** to create customized reading lists for your students' reading levels, interests, and abilities.

Struggles Within Islam

Main Idea While Muslims split into two groups, the Arab Empire reached new heights.

Reading Focus Have you ever belonged to a club whose members could not agree on a leader? Read to find out what happened when Muslims disagreed about who should lead them.

From the moment Muhammad died, Muslims began arguing about who had the right to be caliph. The quarrel over who should succeed Muhammad split the Muslim world into two groups, the Sunnis and the Shiites. This division has remained to the present day. Today most Muslims are Sunnis. Iran and Iraq have the largest populations of Shiites.

Primary Source

Royal Caliphs

Ibn Khaldun recorded historical events and his interpretation of them.

"When one considers what God meant the caliphate to be, nothing more needs [to be said] about it. God made the caliph his substitute to handle the affairs of His servants. He is to make them do the things that are good for them and forbid them to do those that are harmful. He has been directly told so. A person who lacks the power to do a thing is never told to do it."

—Ibn Khaldun, *"The Muqaddimah"*

▲ The Great Mosque of Damascus built by the Umayyad caliphs.

Document-Based Question

According to Khaldun, what is the relationship between God and the caliph?

How Did Islam Split? **Shiites** (SHEE•eyets) believed that Ali, Muhammad's son-in-law, should succeed him and that all future caliphs should be Ali's descendants. According to the Shiites, the Umayyad caliphs in Damascus had no right to rule.

Sunnis (SU•nees), who outnumbered Shiites, accepted the Umayyad dynasty as rightful caliphs, though they did not always agree with their policies. Over time, the Shiites and Sunnis developed different religious practices and customs.

Who Were the Abbasids? The **Abbasids** (uh•BA•suhds) were the dynasty that came after the Umayyads. The Umayyads lost power in A.D. 750 because they angered many Muslims, especially in Persia. Persian Muslims felt that Arab Muslims got special treatment. They got the best jobs and paid fewer taxes.

When these Muslims rebelled, people all over the empire joined them. They overthrew the Umayyads, and a new dynasty began. The new caliph was a descendant of Muhammad's uncle. His name was Abu al-Abbas. The new Abbasid dynasty lasted until 1258.

The Abbasids devoted their energies to trade, scholarship, and the arts. They also built a new capital, **Baghdad** (BAG•dad).

Baghdad prospered because it was beside the Tigris River and near the Euphrates River. It was a good location to trade since many people used the rivers to ship goods north and south. As a result, the Arab Empire grew even wealthier.

The Abbasid dynasty is also known for bringing Persian influence into the empire.

CRITICAL THINKING ACTIVITY

Drawing Conclusions Ask students to write a short essay discussing how they think the growth of Islamic empires might have enriched the Islamic state. Students might discuss topics such as added revenue through new taxes; new trading opportunities; natural resources; and the skills, traditions, and cultures of the conquered peoples. **L2**

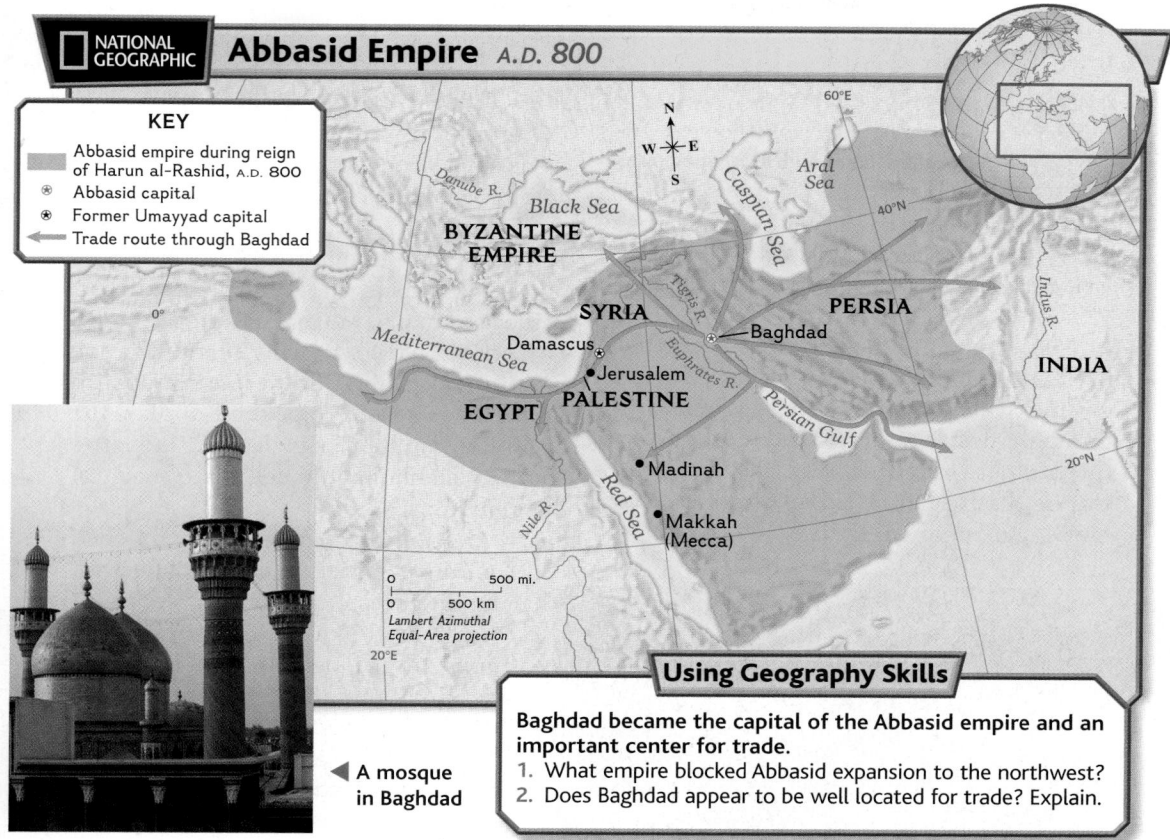

Abbasid Empire A.D. 800

KEY
- Abbasid empire during reign of Harun al-Rashid, A.D. 800
- ⊛ Abbasid capital
- ⊛ Former Umayyad capital
- ← Trade route through Baghdad

500 mi.
500 km
Lambert Azimuthal Equal-Area projection

◀ A mosque in Baghdad

Using Geography Skills

Baghdad became the capital of the Abbasid empire and an important center for trade.
1. What empire blocked Abbasid expansion to the northwest?
2. Does Baghdad appear to be well located for trade? Explain.

CONNECTING ACROSS TIME

Ask students to list the regions added to the Arab Empire under the Rightly Guided Caliphs. (*Arabia, Palestine, Syria, Mesopotamia, Persia, and Egypt*) Then have students find each on a map of the Middle East today. Discuss how they might find the present-day names of the places listed in the text. Have them do the same activity for regions under the Abbasids and Ottomans. **L3**

Using Geography Skills

Answers:
1. the Byzantine Empire
2. Yes; Baghdad is centrally located and well positioned for the trade between Asia and the Mediterranean.

Skills Practice

Ask: In which directions do you think the Abbasid empire could have tried to expand? (*northwest, into Byzantine territory; along the shores of the Mediterranean; east to the Indus River*)

Baghdad was very close to Persia, and the Abbasid rulers came to know and love the art and literature of Persia.

The Seljuk Turks Time brought many changes in the 500 years of Abbasid rule. In Egypt and Spain, the Muslims wanted their own caliphs. About the same time, a new people, the Seljuk Turks of central Asia, began moving south into the Arab Empire. The Abbasids were losing control.

The Seljuk Turks were nomads and great warriors. When they first moved into the empire, the Abbasids hired them as soldiers. Soon, however, the Seljuk Turks saw how weak the Abbasids were. They decided to take power for themselves.

First, the Seljuks took over much of what is now Iran and Turkey. Then, in 1055, they boldly took Baghdad itself. The Seljuks were satisfied to rule only the government and army. They let the Abbasid caliph remain as the religious leader. The Seljuk ruler called himself **sultan** (SUHL•tuhn), or "holder of power."

For 200 more years, the empire continued in this way. The Seljuks ruled, but it was still the Abbasid dynasty. Then, in the 1200s, another people swept into the empire. These were the fierce Mongols of central Asia. The Mongols were building their own empire and destroying many of the civilizations they conquered. In 1258 they stormed into Baghdad and burned it to the ground. The Arab Empire had ended.

✓ **Reading Check** **Contrast** What is the difference between Shiite and Sunni Muslims?

CHAPTER 11   Islamic Civilization   **383**

✓ **Reading Check**

Answer: Shiites believe the caliph should be descended from Ali (Muhammad's cousin and son-in-law). Sunnis believe the caliph does not need to be one of Ali's descendants.

INTERDISCIPLINARY CONNECTIONS ACTIVITY

Geography Ask students to work in small groups to prepare multimedia reports on the great cities of the Arab and Muslim worlds. Suggest "Great Cities: Past, Present, and Future" as a theme for the reports. Possible cities to include are Baghdad, Damascus, Delhi, Alexandria, Constantinople (Istanbul), Makkah, Madinah, Cairo, Córdoba, and Jerusalem. Have students report on the history of the city, its present status in the Muslim and Arab worlds, and what its future may hold. Encourage them to include photos, maps, artifacts, and other multimedia elements in their presentations. **L2**

🗁 Refer to the *Quizzes, Tests, and Authentic Assessment (with Rubrics)* booklet for rubrics.

CURRICULUM CONNECTION

Geography

An important turning point in history occurred in A.D. 732. In this year, the Muslims invaded France. Somewhere near the towns of Tours and Poitiers, they met a French army commanded by a local leader named Charles Martel. The French turned back the Muslim invasion, which marked the farthest Muslim penetration into Western Europe.

More About the Photo

Selim II came to rule the Ottoman empire after a bloody struggle. Once he chose Selim to succeed him, Suleiman killed several of his own sons and grandsons. The empire began its decline under Selim, who was known as "the Drunkard."

Caption Answer: He built many schools and mosques. He was also a brilliant general who brought Ottoman armies north into Europe.

Later Muslim Empires

Main Idea Turks and Moguls built Muslim empires in Asia, Africa, and Europe.

Reading Focus How do you react when someone treats you unfairly? Read on to find out how Muslims in Turkey and India treated the people they conquered.

The Arabs built—and lost—the first Muslim empire. Later on, other Muslim groups created empires in Asia, Africa, and Europe. One of the largest and most powerful of these empires was the Ottoman empire that began in Turkey. Another was the Mogul empire in India.

◄ Muslims pray beneath the large decorated dome of Selimiye Mosque in Edirne, Turkey. Suleiman built this beautiful mosque for his son Selim II. *What were some of the reasons that Suleiman was called "the Magnificent"?*

Who Were the Ottomans? In the late 1200s, a group of Turks in the northwest corner of Asia Minor began to build a new empire. The ruler of these Turks was named Osman, and as a result, these Turks became known as the Ottoman Turks.

The Ottomans quickly conquered most of the land that today makes up the country of Turkey. They attacked the Byzantine Empire and pushed north into Europe. In 1453 they seized Constantinople, the Byzantine capital. They changed the city's name to Istanbul and made it the center of their empire.

Ottoman armies also marched south, conquering Syria, Palestine, Egypt, Mesopotamia, and parts of Arabia and North Africa. They used guns and cannons to fight their battles and built a large navy to control the Mediterranean Sea.

Like the Seljuks, the Ottomans called their leader a sultan. The most famous sultan was **Suleiman I** (SOO•lay•MAHN), who ruled in the 1500s. Suleiman was a man of many talents. He was enthusiastic about architecture and built many schools and mosques.

Suleiman was also a brilliant general, who brought Ottoman armies north into Europe. He even threatened the great European capital of Vienna. For all these reasons, Ottomans called him Suleiman the Magnificent.

After his rule, the Ottoman empire began to weaken. Little by little, they lost territory. The empire finally collapsed at the end of World War I.

EXTENDING THE CONTENT

Islamic Capitals Through the Centuries Unlike the city of Babylon, both Damascus and Baghdad have remained centers of Arab culture and capitals of Arab countries. Damascus may be the world's oldest continuously inhabited city. Its roots stretch back into prehistoric times. Today it is the capital and leading city of Syria, and its population exceeds 2 million. The area around Baghdad, the capital of Iraq, was the center of ancient Mesopotamia. In A.D. 762 it was rebuilt and became the capital city of the Abbasid caliphs. At the beginning of the twenty-first century, it was home to almost 5 million people.

The Expansion of the Ottoman Empire

NATIONAL GEOGRAPHIC

KEY

Ottoman lands, c. 1300
New Territory Gained:
c. 1300–1326 (Osman)
1326–1451
1451–1481
1481–1520
1520–1566 (Suleiman I)
1566–1699

▲ The Ottomans used elite soldiers called janissaries.

Using Geography Skills

The Ottoman empire continued to expand for almost 400 years.
1. How far west into Europe did the Ottoman empire expand?
2. During what time period did the Ottoman empire expand to the Persian Gulf?

How Were Non-Muslims Treated?

The Ottoman empire had many different people, including Turks, Arabs, Greeks, Albanians, Armenians, and Slavs. These groups practiced several religions. While many were Muslims, others were Christians or Jews.

The government made different laws for non-Muslims. They had to pay a special tax, and in return, they were free to practice their religion. They also could run their own affairs. These groups chose leaders to present their views to the sultan.

However, the sultan made some demands on the conquered people. For example, Christian families in Eastern Europe had to send their sons to Istanbul. There the boys became Muslims and trained as soldiers for the sultan.

Who Were the Moguls?

During the 1500s, the **Moguls** (MOH•guhlz) created another Muslim empire in India. These Muslim warriors came from the mountains north of India. The Moguls used guns, cannons, elephants, and horses to conquer territory. In 1526 they made the city of **Delhi** (DEH•lee) the center of their empire.

The greatest Mogul ruler was **Akbar** (AK•buhr). He brought peace and order to the part of India he ruled by treating all his subjects fairly. Most of India's people were Hindu. He allowed them to practice their religion. Both Hindus and Muslims served in Akbar's government.

CHAPTER 11   Islamic Civilization   **385**

Using Geography Skills

Answers:
1. the borders of Austria
2. 1520–1566

Reading Support L1/ EL

Assign **Guided Reading Activity 11–2** to help students organize the information in the section.

③ ASSESS

Assign Section 2 Review as homework or as an in-class activity.

🖳 Have students use the **Interactive Tutor Self-Assessment CD-ROM** to review the section.

Assessment L2

Assign **Section 2 Quiz** to assess mastery of the material found in the section.

Reading Support L1/ EL

Assign **Reading Essentials and Study Guide 11–2** to help students review section material.

CITIZENSHIP AND YOU

Getting Along In this section, students have read about tensions within Arab society between Sunnis and Shiites. This tension continues in Muslim countries today. Have students discuss how groups with important differences in beliefs, practices, and even values coexist in American society. **Ask:** How would you compare the level of tension in our country to that in many other countries? What is there about American society that generally allows different groups to "get along"? How might this characteristic be adopted by countries where tensions are high and can sometimes lead to violence? **L2**

ENRICH

Have students research the battle for Constantinople in 1453. Students should then write and present a TV newscast reporting on the battle. **L3**

Reading Check

Answer: It was taken over by the Ottomans, and its name was changed to Istanbul.

History Online

To help students understand section material, have them visit **Study Central™** at jat.glencoe.com

RETEACH

Ask students to identify and explain the importance of each of the following groups: Umayyads, Abbasids, Ottomans, and Moguls. **L2**

4 CLOSE

Ask students why they think the Muslim empires were successful. **L2**

▲ Mogul emperor Akbar passing the crown to his grandson Shah Jahan

Times were good in India under Akbar. Farmers and artisans produced more food and goods than the Indians needed. As a result, trade increased. Muslim merchants brought paper, gunpowder, and fine porcelain from China to India. In addition, Muslim architects introduced new building styles, such as the arch and dome, to India.

After Akbar, the Mogul empire began to decline. Later rulers spent too much money trying to expand the empire and imposed heavy taxes on the people. Others tried to force the Hindus to convert to Islam and banned the building of Hindu temples. These policies led to many rebellions, and parts of the empire broke away.

At the same time the Moguls began losing power over their subjects, they had to deal with European merchants. The merchants came to India to trade but used their military power to take over Mogul territory. Eventually, the Mogul empire collapsed, and Great Britain took control of most of India.

Reading Check **Describe** How did Constantinople change in 1453?

Section 2 Review

History Online
Study Central™ Need help with the material in this section? Visit jat.glencoe.com

Reading Summary
Review the Main Ideas

- Arab armies spread Islam as far west as Spain and as far east as India. Muslim traders helped spread the religion to southeast Asia and west Africa.
- Despite splitting into two groups, the Sunni and the Shiite, Muslim power reached its greatest height under the Abbasids.
- In the 1400s and 1500s, two great Muslim empires, the Ottoman and the Mogul, arose.

What Did You Learn?

1. How did the Muslims treat conquered peoples?

2. How far did the Arab Empire spread under the Umayyads?

Critical Thinking

3. **Organizing Information** Draw a chart to organize information about the Ottoman and Mogul empires.

Ottoman Empire	Mogul Empire

4. **Contrast** Describe the differences between the Shiite and Sunni Muslims.

5. **Summarize** Besides conquests by Arab armies, how was Islam spread?

6. **Evaluate** Why was Akbar considered a great ruler?

7. **Persuasive Writing** Which Muslim empire—the Umayyads, the Ottomans, or the Moguls—treated its non-Muslim subjects the most fairly? The least fairly? Write a paragraph to defend your answer.

SECTION 2 REVIEW ANSWERS

1. They allowed them to practice their own religion, but they had to pay a tax.

2. to India, North Africa, and Spain

3. Charts should be based on the text.

4. Shiites: caliph should be descended from Ali, rejected the Umayyads; Sunnis: accepted the Umayyad rule, adopted different customs and religious practices

5. Sufis taught Islam, and Arab traders spread Islam.

6. Under Akbar, India was peaceful and orderly. Trade increased and new architecture came to India.

7. Answers will vary but should demonstrate sound evaluation using evidence from the text.

Section 3
Muslim Ways of Life

Get Ready to Read!

What's the Connection?
In Section 2, you learned that many Muslim rulers brought peace and order to their empires. Peace and order helped trade to increase. Trade, in turn, brought great wealth to the Muslim empires.

Focus on the Main Ideas
• While Muslim traders enjoyed great success and cities grew, most Muslims lived in villages in the country. *(page 388)*

• Muslims made valuable contributions in math, science, and the arts. *(page 390)*

Locating Places
Granada (gruh•NAH•duh)
Agra (AH•gruh)

Meeting People
Mamun (mah•MOON)
al-Razi (ahl•RAH•zee)
Ibn Sina (IH•buhn SEE•nuh)
Omar Khayyam (OH•MAHR KY•YAHM)
Ibn Khaldun (IH•buhn KAL•DOON)

Building Your Vocabulary
mosque (MAHSK)
bazaar (buh•ZAHR)
minaret (MIH•nuh•REHT]
crier (KRY•uhr)

Reading Strategy
Organizing Information Create a pyramid to show the social classes in the early Muslim world.

When & Who?

A.D. 800	1100	1400

c. A.D. 900
Al-Razi writes medical texts

c. 1100
Omar Khayyam writes the *Rubaiyat*

c. 1375
Ibn Khaldun writes histories

CHAPTER 11   Islamic Civilization   **387**

1 FOCUS

SECTION OVERVIEW

In this section, students will learn about the cultural and scientific achievements of Muslim civilization, as well as about the daily life of the peoples of the Muslim empires.

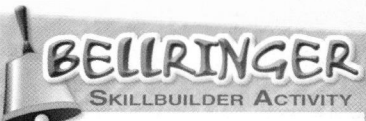

SKILLBUILDER ACTIVITY

Project **Daily Focus Skills Transparency 11–3** and have students answer questions. Discuss their responses.

Get Ready to Read!

Preteaching Vocabulary: A minaret is a special part of a Muslim mosque, or place of worship. It is usually a tall, slender tower from which the call to prayer is issued.

Answers to Graphic: Top: government leaders, landowners, and traders; Middle: artisans, farmers, and workers; Bottom: enslaved people

---

SECTION RESOURCES

 Reproducible Masters
• Reproducible Lesson Plan 11–3
• Daily Lecture and Discussion Notes 11–3
• Vocabulary Activity 11–3
• Active Reading Note-Taking Guide 11–3
• Guided Reading Activity 11–3
• Section Quiz 11–3
• Reading Essentials and Study Guide 11–3

Transparencies
• Daily Focus Skills Transparency 11–3

Multimedia
• Interactive Tutor Self-Assessment CD-ROM
• ExamView® Pro Testmaker CD-ROM
• Presentation Plus! CD-ROM
• Vocabulary PuzzleMaker CD-ROM
• Glencoe BookLink CD-ROM

② TEACH

Trade and Everyday Life

Main Idea While Muslim traders enjoyed great success and cities grew, most Muslims lived in villages in the country.

Reading Focus Have you ever visited a mall or a farm market? These are both places where people gather to sell goods. Read to learn about Muslim traders and their marketplaces.

Muslims were the leading merchants in the Middle East and northern Africa until the 1400s. Their caravans traveled overland from Baghdad to China. Their ships crossed the Indian Ocean to India and Southeast Asia. They carried spices, cloth, glass, and carpets. On their return, they brought rubies, silk, ivory, gold, and slaves.

The Success of Muslim Traders Several things explain the success of Muslim trade. When Muslim empires expanded, they

spread the Arabic language. As a result, Arabic became the language of trade. Muslim rulers also made trade easier by providing merchants with coins.

Muslim merchants kept detailed records of their business deals and the money they made. In time, these practices developed into a new business—banking. Muslims respected traders for their skills and the wealth they created.

What Were Muslim Cities Like? Trade helped the leading Muslim cities grow. Baghdad, Cairo, and Damascus were located on trade routes that ran from the Mediterranean Sea to central Asia. However, Muslim cities were not only places of trade.

▼ **Muslims shop at a textile market.**
What was a bazaar in a Muslim city?

388 CHAPTER 11 Islamic Civilization

They also became important centers of government, learning, and the arts.

Muslim cities looked very similar. The major buildings were palaces and mosques. **Mosques** (mahsks) are Muslim houses of worship. They also serve as schools, courts, and centers of learning.

Another important part of every Muslim city was the **bazaar** (buh•ZAHR), or marketplace. Stalls and shops made up the bazaars. Sellers in the stalls and shops sold goods from Asia. Buyers from all over, including Europe, went from stall to stall to find goods to take home and sell.

Although cities were important, most Muslims lived in villages and farmed the land. Because water was scarce, Muslim farmers used irrigation to bring water to their crops. They grew wheat, rice, beans, and melons in the fields. They raised almonds, blackberries, apricots, figs, and olives in their orchards. Some farmers also raised flowers for use in perfume.

At first, Muslim villagers owned small farms. Later, wealthy landowners took over some of these farms and formed large estates. Farmers and enslaved people worked for the landowners.

Muslim Society The Muslim people fell into social groups based on power and wealth. At the top were government leaders, landowners, and traders. Below them were artisans, farmers, and workers. The lowest group was made up of enslaved people.

As in other civilizations, slavery was widespread. Because Muslims could not be enslaved, traders brought enslaved people

The Way It Was

NATIONAL GEOGRAPHIC

Focus on Everyday Life

Muslim Carpets and Weavings

Carpets were woven in the Middle East long before the coming of Islam. They became popular in the Islamic world because Muslims used them in their daily worship.

▲ A Muslim woman weaving a rug

Carpets were often made of sheep's wool or goat hair. Shepherds might knot them by hand, or the carpets might be made on portable looms. Flowers and geometric shapes were popular designs.

The carpets used for the Muslim's daily prayers are called prayer rugs. No matter where Muslims live, they pray five times daily. They kneel down on their prayer rug and pray facing toward Makkah. Prayer rugs are small and can be folded and carried from place to place.

Fine carpets of silk and wool are often hung on the walls of mosques and public buildings. They are considered fine art.

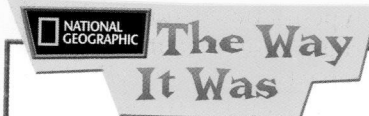

Muslim carpet ▶

Connecting to the Past

1. What animals were needed to make carpets?
2. What is the main reason Muslim carpets have continually been in demand?

CONNECTING ACROSS TIME

Ask students to compare ancient Muslim attitudes toward slavery with those of people in other time periods and places, including our own. Then have them make the same comparisons regarding women in Islamic and other societies. L1/ EL

in a word . . .

"Bazaar" is a Persian word. It originally referred to a public market district of a town. From there, the word spread to Arab countries, India, and Western countries. The word is used in English to mean both a store selling a variety of goods and a fair or market.

The Way It Was

NATIONAL GEOGRAPHIC

Answers:
1. sheep and goats
2. Muslims use them in their daily worship.

DIFFERENTIATED INSTRUCTION

Naturalist: Carpets made by Muslim craftspeople throughout the centuries are famous for their intricate designs and natural motifs, such as plants, flowers, animals, and vines. Ask students to design a carpet using natural motifs from your area. Suggest that students begin by brainstorming indigenous natural elements such as flowers, trees, shrubs, seashells, or local wildlife to include in the rug designs. Have students share their designs with the class.

English Learners: Ask students to write a paragraph describing which local natural elements they have chosen and why they feel they are appropriate.

Kinesthetic: Have students paint, weave, or use computer drawing software to create their rug designs.

Chapter 11 Assessment and Activities

CHAPTER 11
ASSESSMENT AND ACTIVITIES

GLENCOE TECHNOLOGY

MindJogger Videoquiz

Use the **MindJogger Videoquiz** to review Chapter 11 content.

 Available in DVD and VHS

Review Vocabulary

1. minaret
2. caliph
3. sultan
4. bazaar
5. caravan
6. Quran
7. sheikh
8. mosque
9. Shiites
10. Sunnis

Review Main Ideas

11. Early Arabs organized into tribes to survive in the desert and traveled from oasis to oasis.
12. Its ideas were used in government.
13. through preaching, conquest, and trade
14. They disagreed over who should be caliph.
15. perfected the astrolabe, measured the earth, realized the earth was round, experimented with metals, founded chemistry, discovered that blood circulates and how diseases spread
16. He studied the effects of geography and climate on people.

Review Vocabulary

Write the key term that completes each sentence.

a. caravan   f. minaret
b. caliph   g. sheikh
c. sultan   h. bazaar
d. mosque   i. Sunnis
e. Quran   j. Shiites

1. A crier called Muslims to prayer from the ___ of a mosque.
2. After Muhammad died, his followers chose a ___ to lead them.
3. The most famous ___ was Suleiman.
4. In each Muslim city, a ___ sold goods to local and out-of-town merchants.
5. Arab merchants traveling in a ___ used camels to carry goods across the desert.
6. The Muslim holy book is called the ___.
7. Each tribe of early Arabs was led by a ___.
8. Each ___ was a house of worship and a school.
9. The ___ believed that Muhammad's son-in-law should succeed him.
10. According to the ___, the Umayyad dynasty were rightful caliphs.

Review Main Ideas

Section 1 • The Rise of Islam

11. How did geography affect the early Arabs' way of life?
12. What guidelines did the Quran provide for the governments of Muslim states?

Section 2 • Islamic Empires

13. How did the Arabs spread Islam?
14. Why did the Muslims split into two groups?

Section 3 • Muslim Ways of Life

15. What scientific advances were made by early Muslims?
16. What is significant about Ibn Khaldun's recording of history?

Critical Thinking

17. **Compare** How are Islam, Judaism, and Christianity similar?
18. **Evaluate** Do you think a government that allows people to practice any religion they choose will be stronger than one that does not? Explain.

Review — Reading Skill — Main Idea — Main Ideas and Details

19. Read the paragraph below. Create a graphic organizer to show the main idea and supporting details.

> The Muslim people fell into social groups based on power and wealth. At the top were government leaders, landowners, and traders. Below them were artisans, farmers, and workers. The lowest group was made up of enslaved people.

To review this skill, see pages 370–371.

Critical Thinking

17. They are monotheistic, have laws, and believe in an afterlife.
18. Answers will vary. Students should provide details supporting their claims.

Reading Skill

19. Main idea: Muslim social groups were based on wealth and power; Supporting details: top were government leaders, landowners, traders; middle were artisans, farmers, workers; lowest were enslaved people

Geography Skills

Study the map below and answer the following questions.

20. **Movement** Why was the Abbasid empire unable to expand to the Black Sea?

21. **Region** What bodies of water could Abbasid merchants use to trade with the outside world?

22. **Place** You learned that the Abbasids changed the capital city from Damascus to Baghdad. Look at the locations of those cities. Which do you think would have been the best location for a capital city? Why?

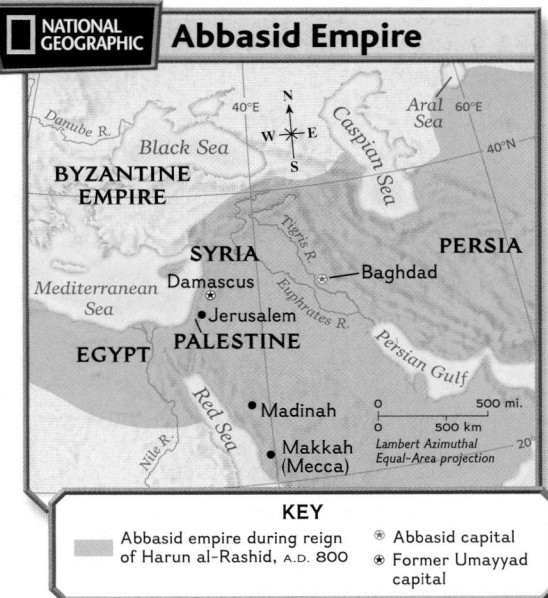

Abbasid Empire

KEY

Abbasid empire during reign of Harun al-Rashid, A.D. 800

⊛ Abbasid capital
⊛ Former Umayyad capital

Read to Write

23. **Descriptive Writing** Suppose you are an Arab merchant traveling in the desert with a caravan. Write three diary entries, each describing the events of your day. Each day you choose to describe should focus on a different aspect of the life of a merchant. Share your entries with the class.

24. **Using Your** Write a poem or short story using the facts from your completed foldable.

History Online
Self-Check Quiz To help you prepare for the Chapter Test, visit jat.glencoe.com

Using Technology

25. **Exploring Language** Use the Internet and your local library to find English words that have their origins in the Arabic language. Create a chart using your computer showing English words and their Arabic roots.

Linking Past and Present

26. **Evaluating Impact** Which Islamic invention or development do you think has the greatest effect on the world today? Explain your choice.

Building Citizenship Skills

27. **Analyzing Documents** Do research to find out how the United States Constitution protects religious freedoms. Do you think the way Muslim empires treated religion would be allowed under the U.S. Constitution? Explain.

Primary Source — Analyze

In the first stanza of the *Rubaiyat,* Omar Khayyam welcomes the morning.

"Wake! for the sun, the shepherd of the sky,
Has penned [confined] the stars within their fold on high,
And, shaking darkness from his mighty limbs,
Scatters the daylight from his burning eye."

—*Rubáiyát of Omar Khayyám: A Paraphrase From Several Literal Translations,* by Richard Le Gallienne

DBQ Document-Based Questions

28. What has been penned up by the sun?
29. *Personification* is when a writer gives human qualities to something that is not human. How does Khayyam personify the sun in this stanza?

History Online

Have students visit the Web site at jat.glencoe.com to review Chapter 11 and take the **Self-Check Quiz**.

Using Technology

25. Answers will vary depending on the words students choose.

Linking Past and Present

26. Choices and explanations will vary. Choices should reflect information in the chapter.

Building Citizenship Skills

27. Answers will vary but should include supporting details from the Constitution.

Primary Source

28. the stars

29. He calls the sun a shepherd who pens the stars as a shepherd does his sheep. The sun has limbs and an eye.

Bonus Question

Ask: Of the three ways that Arabs spread Islam (conquest, preaching, and trade), which one do you think was the most effective? Why? (*Answers should use information from the chapter, knowledge of current events, and sound reasoning to support the opinion.*)

Geography Skills

20. The Byzantine Empire stood in the way.

21. Persian Gulf, Red Sea, Mediterranean Sea, Caspian Sea, Aral Sea

22. Answers will vary. Some students may state that Damascus is near the Mediterranean, or that Baghdad is in a more central location on the Tigris.

Read to Write

23. Diary entries will differ but could describe the caravan, oases, towns along the trade route, or the goods they are transporting.

24. **FOLDABLES** Poems or stories will vary but should contain facts dealing with Islamic civilization.

REVIEWING UNIT OBJECTIVES

Having studied this unit, students should now be able to

1. describe the rise and fall of the Roman Republic;

2. relate how the Roman Empire came to be;

3. discuss the beginnings and spread of the Christian religion;

4. explain the beginning and spread of the religion of Islam.

UNIT REVIEW ACTIVITY

Comparing Civilizations To help students review the unit objectives, have them consider the **Comparing New Empires and Faiths** chart. Have them use the notations in the chart, as well as information from the chapters, to write short answers to these theme-based questions:

• How did geography influence where these empires appeared and developed?

• In what ways did the important people in these societies reflect the values of their civilizations?

• What methods did governments use to make decisions affecting the well-being of people and of the civilization as a whole?

• How did the religious beliefs of these faiths impact the world? **L2**

Comparing New Empires and Faiths

Compare ancient Rome, early Christianity, and early Islam by reviewing the information below. Can you see how the peoples of these civilizations had lives that were very much like yours?

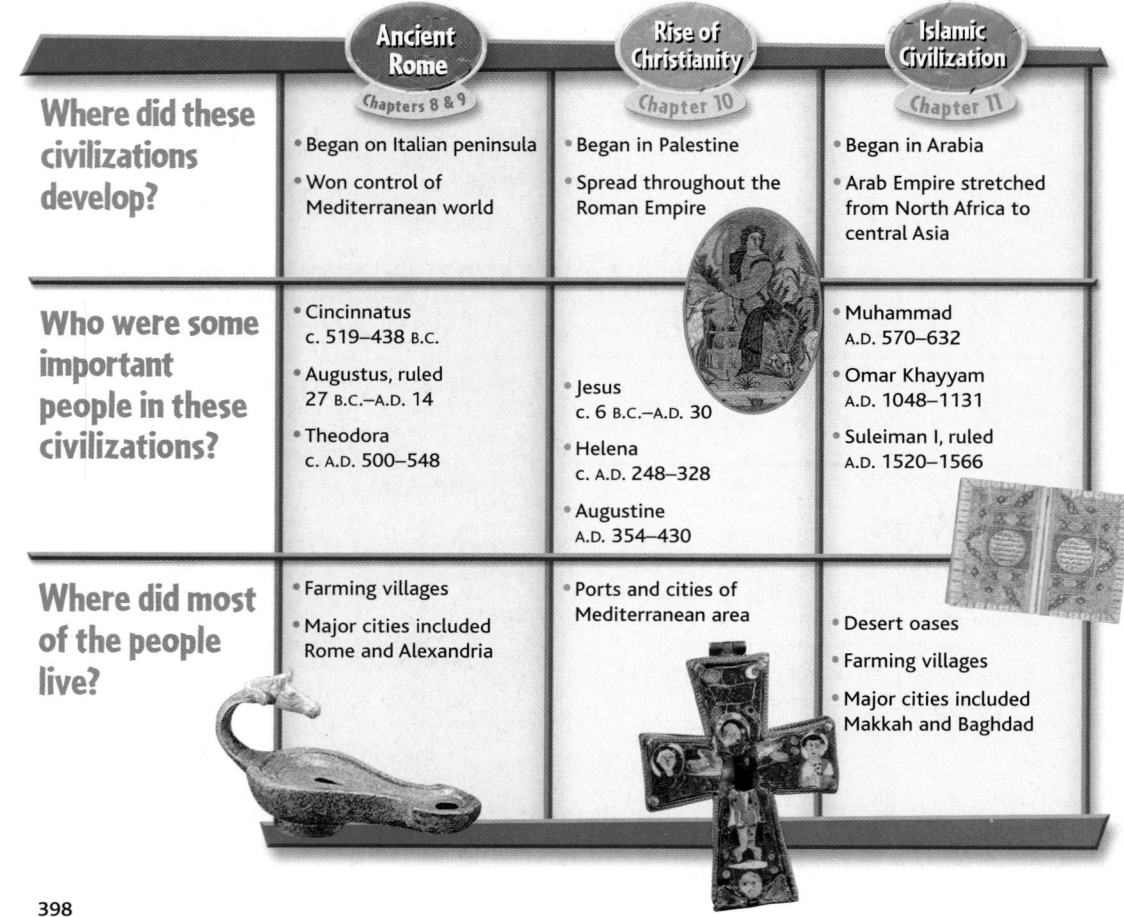

	Ancient Rome Chapters 8 & 9	Rise of Christianity Chapter 10	Islamic Civilization Chapter 11
Where did these civilizations develop?	• Began on Italian peninsula • Won control of Mediterranean world	• Began in Palestine • Spread throughout the Roman Empire	• Began in Arabia • Arab Empire stretched from North Africa to central Asia
Who were some important people in these civilizations?	• Cincinnatus c. 519–438 B.C. • Augustus, ruled 27 B.C.–A.D. 14 • Theodora c. A.D. 500–548	• Jesus c. 6 B.C.–A.D. 30 • Helena c. A.D. 248–328 • Augustine A.D. 354–430	• Muhammad A.D. 570–632 • Omar Khayyam A.D. 1048–1131 • Suleiman I, ruled A.D. 1520–1566
Where did most of the people live?	• Farming villages • Major cities included Rome and Alexandria	• Ports and cities of Mediterranean area	• Desert oases • Farming villages • Major cities included Makkah and Baghdad

398

 END-OF-UNIT RESOURCES

Reproducible Masters
- Unit 3 Test Form A
- Unit 3 Test Form B
- Step Into World History Activity 3

Transparencies
- Unit 3 Map Overlay Transparencies

Multimedia
- Interactive Tutor Self-Assessment CD-ROM
- Exam*View*® Pro Testmaker CD-ROM
- Presentation Plus! CD-ROM

	Ancient Rome Chapters 8 & 9	Rise of Christianity Chapter 10	Islamic Civilization Chapter 11
What were these people's beliefs?	• Belief in many gods and goddesses • Emperors honored as gods • Many local religions	• Belief in one God and Jesus as Son of God and the Savior • Major groups: Eastern Orthodox and Roman Catholic	• Belief in one God (Allah) • Muhammad is final prophet • Major groups: Sunni and Shiite
What was their government like?	• Rome developed from a republic into an empire • An emperor was the chief leader • Army played role in government	• Ranked order of priests, bishops, and archbishops • Bishop of Rome became head of the Roman Catholic Church	• Muhammad founds Islamic state • After Muhammad, leaders called caliphs held religious and political power
What was their language and writing like?	• Latin was official language; Greek spoken in empire's eastern part • Many local languages	• New Testament of Bible written in Greek • Latin became language of Roman Catholic Church	• Quran written in Arabic • Arabic was Arab Empire's official language • Persian and Turkish also spoken
What contributions did they make?	• Introduced ideas about law and government • Developed new styles of building	• Christianity became a world religion • Shaped beliefs and values of Western civilization	• Islam became a world religion • Developed ideas in medicine and mathematics
How do these changes affect me? *Can you add any?*	• Latin contributed many words to English language • Rome's idea of a republic followed by governments today	• Christianity is major religion of the West today • Birth date of Jesus is starting date for Western calendar	• Islam is a major religion today • Developed algebra • Developed game of chess

UNIT WRAP-UP ACTIVITY

Comparing and Contrasting Have students use a three-circle Venn diagram to compare an important thematic concept across the three civilizations discussed in this unit. Some appropriate choices are religion, government, culture, and approach to problems/solutions.

Have students draw and label the three circles, allowing space for the overlap areas. For example, under the "Rome" section of a diagram focusing on religion, students might write the following: *believed in many gods and goddesses, emperors honored as gods, many local religions adopted Greek deities.*

After students have finished their own charts, create class charts for the concepts. Discuss students' suggestions. **L2**

399

PROFESSIONAL DEVELOPMENT: ENGLISH LEARNERS

• Cary, Stephen. *Working with Second Language Learners: Answers to Teachers' Top Ten Questions.* Heinemann, 2000.
• Folse, Keith. *Discussion Starters: Speaking Fluency Activities for Advanced ESL/EFL Students.* University of Michigan, 1996.
• Jesness, Jerry. *Teaching English Language Learners K through 12.* Corwin Press, 2004.
• Peregoy, Suzanne, and Owen Boyle. *Reading, Writing and Learning in ESL: A Resource Book for K-12 Teachers (3rd Edition).* Longman, 2001.

Unit 4 Planning Guide

Unit Resources

Note: The following materials may be used when teaching Unit 4.
Chapter and section level support materials can be found on the chapter and section resource pages.

TEACHING TRANSPARENCIES

- Writing Process Transparencies **L1**

DIFFERENTIATED INSTRUCTION

- Step Into World History Activity 4

ASSESSMENT

- Unit 4 Test Form A **L2**
- Unit 4 Test Form B **L2**

ADDITIONAL RESOURCES

- Glencoe Skillbuilder Interactive Workbook CD-ROM, Level 1
- Glencoe World History Primary Source Document Library CD-ROM
- Focus on World Art Prints
- Outline Map Resource Book
- World Desk Map
- World Art and Architecture Transparencies
- World Music: Cultural Traditions
- World Music: A Cultural Legacy
- Glencoe World Literature Library
- Reading in the Content Area
- Teaching Strategies for the World History Classroom (Including Block Scheduling Pacing Guides)
- Inclusion Strategies for the Middle School Social Studies Classroom

---

- Blackline Master
- Poster
- Transparency
- Music Program
- CD-ROM
- Audio Program
- DVD
- Videocassette

READING SUPPORT FROM JAMESTOWN EDUCATION

- *Timed Readings Plus in Social Studies* help students increase their reading rate and fluency while maintaining comprehension. The 400-word passages are similar to those found on state and national assessments.
- *Reading in the Content Area: Social Studies* concentrates on six essential reading skills that help students better comprehend what they read. The book includes 75 high-interest nonfiction passages written at increasing levels of difficulty.
- *Reading Fluency* helps students read smoothly, accurately, and expressively.
- *Jamestown's Reading Improvement,* by renowned reading expert Edward Fry, focuses on helping build your students' comprehension, vocabulary, and skimming and scanning skills.
- *Critical Reading Series* provides high-interest books, each written at three reading levels.

To order these products, call Glencoe at 1-800-334-7344.

Reading List Generator CD-ROM

GLENCOE BOOKLINK

The Glencoe BookLink CD-ROM is a database that allows you to search more than 15,000 titles to create a customized reading list for your students.

- Reading lists can be organized by students' reading level, author, genre, theme, or area of interest.
- The database provides Degrees of Reading Power™ (DRP) and Lexile™ readability scores for all selections.
- A brief summary of each selection is included.

Leveled reading suggestions for this unit:

For students at a Grade 5 reading level:
- *I Rode a Horse of Milk White Jade,* by Diane Lee Wilson

For students at a Grade 6 reading level:
- *The Market Lady and the Mango Tree,* by Pete Watson

For students at a Grade 7 reading level:
- *The Viking Ships,* by Ian Atkinson

To order this CD-ROM, call Glencoe at 1-800-334-7344.

Unit Reading Strategies

Each chapter in this unit contains special reading strategies. The following preview will help you teach these reading skills to your students.

CHAPTER 12: Making Inferences

Inferring is a process of creating meaning from text beyond what is explicitly stated. This is a critical skill because when students begin to draw inferences, they are then able to remember and apply what they have read, moving into deeper understanding of the text. This strategy involves making logical assumptions based on clues provided by the author. Students practice this by reading passages and asking themselves questions about what they have read. The answers they then generate constitute the inferences they are making.

CHAPTER 13: Making Comparisons

Comparing and contrasting is an organizational structure that often is found in expository writing. When students develop an ability to understand and use the comparison/contrast model, their comprehension of the text improves. Comparing is finding the similarities between people, places, things, events, or ideas; contrasting is finding the differences. Helping students create different kinds of graphic organizers, such as charts and Venn diagrams, will teach them this skill.

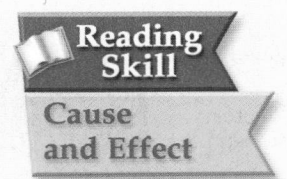

CHAPTER 14: Identifying Cause and Effect

Cause and effect is a pattern of understanding events and their results or consequences. A cause is a reason that something happens, and an effect is the result for the cause or condition. In some instances, the cause and effect may be clearly labeled with words such as *because* or *therefore* to help the reader make the connection. In other cases, the cause and effect may not be as obvious. Graphic organizers can be used to help students practice this strategy. As students recognize cause-and-effect patterns, they will be more successful at engaging more difficult text.

CHAPTER 15: Just Ask

When readers generate and answer questions about their reading, there is little doubt that they have found meaning in the text. The cognitive processes required for such tasks reinforce the skills necessary for proficient reading. Questions created by students can also be extremely effective tools for teachers in targeting problem areas. As students discuss and answer questions posed by their classmates, the engagement becomes authentic and relevant, a key condition to deep learning.

Use the **SkillBuilder Handbook** on pages 902–919 to help students practice important skills.

0:00 OUT OF TIME?

If time does not permit teaching each chapter in this unit, you may use the *Reading Essentials and Study Guide* summaries.

UNIT OVERVIEW

Unit 4 explains how, during the Middle Ages, societies in different parts of the world developed the ideas and institutions that shaped our modern world.

UNIT OBJECTIVES

After studying this unit, students should be able to

1. describe how new technologies, ideas, and political systems influenced China;

2. identify the cultures that grew up in Africa;

3. describe the cultural, economic, and political advances in Japan;

4. explain how, through great turmoil, medieval Europe made cultural and political advances.

Why It's Important

Great historical, cultural, and technological events occurred during this period. Have students discuss which advances mentioned on this spread still impact them today. **L1**

Unit 4 The Middle Ages

Why It's Important

Each civilization that you will study in this unit made important contributions to history.

- The Chinese first produced gunpowder, the compass, and printed books.
- Africans south of the Sahara developed new forms of music and dance.
- The Japanese developed martial arts, such as judo and karate.
- The Europeans took the first steps toward representative government.

	A.D. 300	A.D. 450	A.D. 600	A.D. 750	A.D. 900
China in the Middle Ages Chapter 12	Chinese figurines		c. A.D. 590 Grand Canal links northern and southern China	A.D. 683 Empress Wu begins rule	
Medieval Africa Chapter 13	A.D. 330 Axum's king Ezana accepts Christianity			c. A.D. 700 The Shona establish the Zimbabwe kingdom	c. A.D. 900s Islam spreads in Africa
Medieval Japan Chapter 14	c. A.D. 400 Yamato clan controls Japan		A.D. 631 Prince Shotoku writes constitution		Horyuji temple
Medieval Europe Chapter 15	Medieval manuscript	A.D. 496 King Clovis becomes a Catholic		A.D. 800 Pope crowns Charlemagne emperor — Statue of Charlemagne on horseback	

400

TIME LINE ACTIVITY

Ask students to examine the events on the multiple-tier time line from the four different regions. Then have them list those events that they believe encouraged or are evidence of the spread of ideas from place to place. *(Possible suggestions include the Grand Canal, movable type, and Zheng He in China; Islam spreading in Africa; and Vikings in Europe.)* **L1**

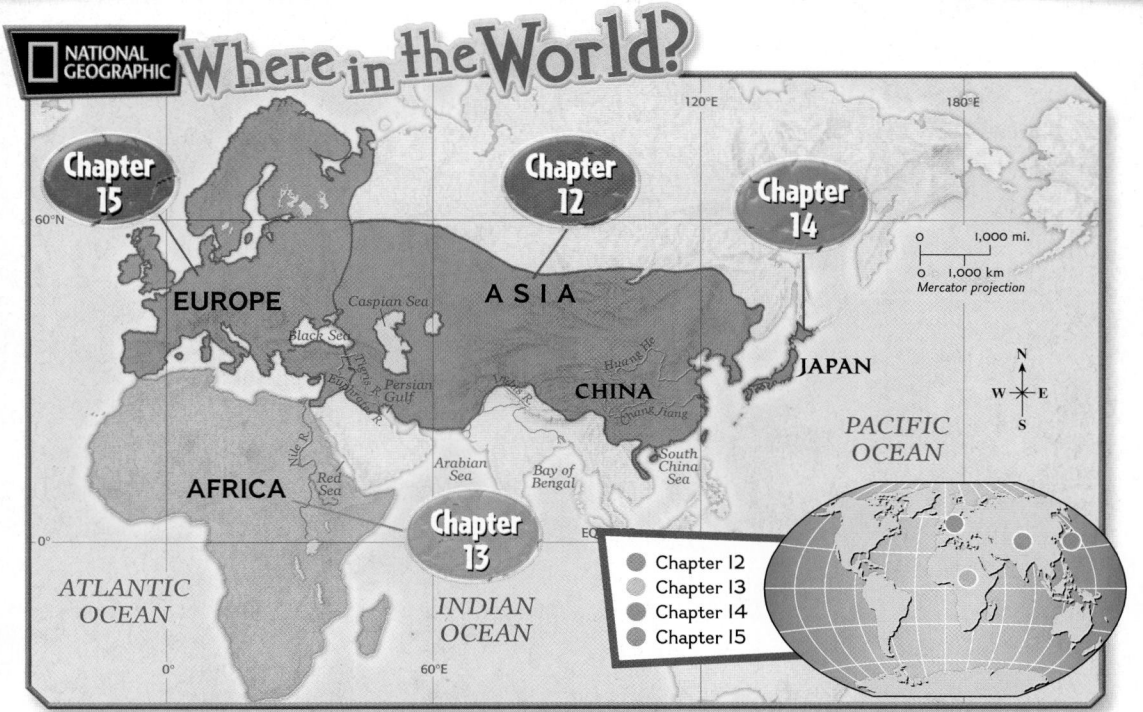

NATIONAL GEOGRAPHIC

Where in the World?

Chapter 15 — EUROPE
Chapter 12 — ASIA
Chapter 14 — JAPAN
Chapter 13 — INDIAN OCEAN

Caspian Sea
Black Sea
Persian Gulf
CHINA
Huang He
Chang Jiang
Arabian Sea
Bay of Bengal
South China Sea
PACIFIC OCEAN
AFRICA
Red Sea
ATLANTIC OCEAN
INDIAN OCEAN

0   1,000 mi.
0   1,000 km
Mercator projection

N W—E S

- Chapter 12
- Chapter 13
- Chapter 14
- Chapter 15

A.D 1050

c. A.D. 1000s
Chinese invent movable type

c. A.D. 1000
Lady Murasaki Shikibu composes *The Tale of Genji*

c. A.D. 1000
Vikings reach North America

◄ Mosque in Mali

▼ Japanese temple in Kyoto

A.D 1200

A.D. 1206
Genghis Khan becomes Mongol leader

A.D. 1312
Mansa Musa becomes Mali's king

A.D. 1281
Mongols attempt second invasion of Japan

A.D. 1215
England's King John signs Magna Carta

◄ Mongol warrior

A.D 1350

A.D 1500

A.D. 1405
Zheng He begins first of seven overseas voyages

Bronze head of queen, West Africa ►

c. A.D. 1450
Civil war divides Japan

◄ Suit of armor worn by samurai warrior

A.D. 1492
Ferdinand and Isabella of Spain defeat Moors

◄ Medieval woman spinning wool

NCLB NO CHILD LEFT BEHIND

Teaching Tip The goals of the NCLB Act include mastering computer technologies by the eighth grade. To help students become proficient users of technology, include assignments that use different technologies to expand students' awareness of history concepts as well as sharpen technology skills. Here are some examples of tasks that do both:

- Ask students to search the Internet for topics using search engines.

- Have students use graphing, note-taking, or outlining software as they read the chapters.

- Encourage students to use computer-presentation programs to make classroom presentations.

DIFFERENTIATED INSTRUCTION

Wars and invasions are often instruments of social, political, and economic change in societies. In this unit, students will read about many wars and invasions and their effects on countries and civilizations.
English Learners: Have students pick one of the civilizations and read an encyclopedia article on it to find out about significant wars that took place at this time. Have them report their findings.
Verbal/Linguistic: Have students write a short essay comparing the results of wars in two of the civilizations.

FOCUS

The unit preview provides a general layout of the regions and significant figures in the unit.

PREVIEWING GEOGRAPHY

Have students compare this map with the **Reference Atlas,** then answer the following questions.

1. In what modern-day country is the Djenne mosque located? *(Mali)* **L1**

2. In what country is the Todaiji temple? *(Japan)* **L1**

PREVIEWING People to Meet

Ask students the following questions using the biographies.

1. Which person was a Mongol conqueror? *(Genghis Khan)* **L1**

2. What was Zheng He's claim to fame? *(Chinese admiral)* **L1**

3. Consider the descriptions of the People to Meet. What characteristics suggest that they had an important impact on people? *(There are kings, rulers, leaders, admirals, and conquerors who had political or military influence. Writers, thinkers, and heroines would have impacted people in a cultural way, although Joan of Arc also had a military impact.)* **L2**

Unit 4 — Places to Locate

1 Buddha statue
See China in the Middle Ages
Chapter 12

2 Djenne mosque
See Medieval Africa
Chapter 13

EUROPE

AFRICA

Atlantic Ocean

People to Meet

Prince Shotoku
A.D. 573–621
Japanese leader
Chapter 14, p. 489

Charlemagne
A.D. 742–814
Frankish ruler
Chapter 15, p. 517

Murasaki Shikibu
C. A.D. 973–1025
Japanese writer
Chapter 14, p. 502

Genghis Khan
C. A.D. 1167–1227
Mongol conqueror
Chapter 12, p. 427

402

PREVIEWING Places to Locate

Use the following descriptions to explain the images on the map.

 1 This giant statue of Buddha in China represents the great impact that Indian religion had on other regions.

 2 The Djenne mosque, made with mud bricks, is one of the prominent symbols of Mali.

ASIA

③ **Todaiji temple**

See Medieval Japan
Chapter 14

④ **Caerphilly Castle**

See Medieval Europe
Chapter 15

⑤ **Mont St. Michel**

See Medieval Europe
Chapter 15

*Pacific
Ocean*

① ③

**Thomas
Aquinas**

A.D. 1225–1274
Christian thinker
Chapter 15, p. 551

Mansa Musa

Ruled A.D. 1312–1337
King of Mali
Chapter 13, p. 466

Zheng He

A.D. 1371–1433
Chinese admiral
Chapter 12, p. 434

Joan Of Arc

A.D. 1412–1431
French heroine
Chapter 15, p. 556

403

TEACH

Organizing Information Have students create a graphic organizer like the one below to organize data about the historical figures in the **People to Meet** feature. *(Answers are provided.)* **L1**

Historical Figure	Contribution
Prince Shotoku	Japanese leader
Charlemagne	Holy Roman Emperor
Murasaki Shikibu	Japanese writer
Genghis Khan	Mongol conqueror
Thomas Aquinas	Christian thinker
Mansa Musa	King of Mali
Zheng He	Chinese admiral
Joan of Arc	French heroine

Students Quizzing Students Have students make an index card for each person on the **People to Meet** feature. Ask them to write the name of the figure on one side of the card and the relevant information about that person on the other side of the card. Once they have made their cards, have students work in pairs to quiz each other by calling out a name on a card and asking the other student to identify it. **L2**

PREVIEWING Places to Locate

③ The Todaiji temple in Nara, Japan, is one of the largest wooden structures ever built.

④ Caerphilly Castle in southern Wales, built between c. 1270 and 1280, has moats, drawbridges, gatehouses, and towers defending the inner ward.

⑤ Mont St. Michel stands as one of the great medieval monasteries. Surrounded by cliffs and walls, it is as impressive today as it was centuries ago.

Chapter 12 Resources

Note: The following materials may be used when teaching Chapter 12.
Section level support materials are shown at point of use in the margins of the Teacher Wraparound Edition.

TEACHING TRANSPARENCIES

- Graphic Organizer Transparencies with Teaching Strategy and Student Activity **L2**
- Cause-and-Effect Transparencies with Teaching Strategy and Student Activity **L2**
- Then and Now Transparencies with Teaching Strategy and Student Activity **L2**
- In-text Map Transparency with Teaching Strategy and Student Activity **L1**
- Map Transparencies with Overlay, Teaching Strategy, and Student Activity **L2**

DIFFERENTIATED INSTRUCTION

- Differentiated Instruction Activity 12
- Time Line Activity 12
- Primary Source Reading 12 (with Document-Based Questions)
- Inclusion Strategies for the Middle School Social Studies Classroom
- StudentWorks Plus™ CD-ROM (with Audio Program)

READING SUPPORT

- Take-Home Review Activity 12 **L2**
- World Literature Reading 12 **L2**
- Workbook Activity 12 **L1**
- Reading Strategies for the Social Studies Classroom **L1/ EL**

ASSESSMENT

- Authentic Assessment Activity 12 **L1/ EL**
- Chapter 12 Test Form A **L2**
- Chapter 12 Test Form B **L2**
- ExamView® Pro Testmaker CD-ROM

INTERDISCIPLINARY CONNECTIONS

- Geography and History Activity 12 **L2**
- People to Meet Activity 12 **L2**
- Economics Activity 12 **L2**
- Citizenship and Service Learning Activity 12 **L2**

SPANISH RESOURCES

- Spanish Reading Essentials and Study Guide
- Spanish Guided Reading Activities
- Spanish Quizzes, Tests, and Authentic Assessment (with Rubrics)
- Spanish Take-Home Review Activities

MULTIMEDIA

- ExamView® Pro Testmaker CD-ROM
- Glencoe Skillbuilder Interactive Workbook CD-ROM, Level 1
- Interactive Tutor Self-Assessment CD-ROM
- MindJogger Videoquiz
- Presentation Plus! CD-ROM
- StudentWorks Plus™ CD-ROM (with Audio Program)
- TeacherWorks CD-ROM
- Vocabulary PuzzleMaker CD-ROM
- *World History: Journey Across Time* Video Program
- World History Primary Source Document Library CD-ROM

STANDARDIZED ASSESSMENT SKILLS

- Standardized Test Skills Practice Workbook Activity 12 **L2**
- Critical Thinking Skills Activity 12 **L2**

Teaching strategies have been coded with suggested ability levels. However, most are suitable for all levels.

L1 BASIC activities for all students
L2 AVERAGE activities for average to above-average students
L3 CHALLENGING activities for above-average students
EL ENGLISH LANGUAGE activities

Chapter 12 Resources

⏱ TIME MANAGEMENT

Unit Introduction	Chapter Introduction	Section 1	Section 2	Section 3	Section 4	Chapter Wrap-Up
1 Day	1 Day	2 Days	1 Day	1 Day	1 Day	1 Day

Block Scheduling Activities that are suited to use within the block scheduling framework are identified by: 🧊

0:00 OUT OF TIME? Assign the Chapter 12 *Reading Essentials and Study Guide.* * 📁

SECTION RESOURCES

DAILY OBJECTIVES	REPRODUCIBLE RESOURCES	MULTIMEDIA RESOURCES
Section 1 **China Reunites** 1. The Sui and Tang dynasties reunited and rebuilt China after years of war. 2. The Tang dynasty returned to the ideas of Confucius and created a new class of scholar-officials.	📁 Reproducible Lesson Plan 12–1 📁 Vocabulary Activity 12–1 📁 Guided Reading Activity 12–1* 📁 Section Quiz 12–1* 📁 Reading Essentials and Study Guide 12–1*	🔖 Daily Focus Skills Transparency 12–1 💿 Interactive Tutor Self-Assessment CD-ROM 💿 ExamView® Pro Testmaker CD-ROM 💿 Presentation Plus! CD-ROM
Section 2 **Chinese Society** 1. The Tang dynasty strengthened China's economy by supporting farming and trade. 2. During the Tang and the Song dynasties, China enjoyed a golden age of art and literature.	📁 Reproducible Lesson Plan 12–2 📁 Vocabulary Activity 12–2 📁 Guided Reading Activity 12–2* 📁 Section Quiz 12–2* 📁 Reading Essentials and Study Guide 12–2*	🔖 Daily Focus Skills Transparency 12–2 💿 Interactive Tutor Self-Assessment CD-ROM 💿 ExamView® Pro Testmaker CD-ROM 💿 Presentation Plus! CD-ROM
Section 3 **The Mongols in China** 1. Genghis Khan built the Mongol Empire, which stretched from the Pacific Ocean to the Caspian Sea. 2. The Mongols conquered China and created a new dynasty that traded with the rest of Asia.	📁 Reproducible Lesson Plan 12–3 📁 Vocabulary Activity 12–3 📁 Guided Reading Activity 12–3* 📁 Section Quiz 12–3* 📁 Reading Essentials and Study Guide 12–3*	🔖 Daily Focus Skills Transparency 12–3 💿 Interactive Tutor Self-Assessment CD-ROM 💿 ExamView® Pro Testmaker CD-ROM 💿 Presentation Plus! CD-ROM 💿 Glencoe BookLink CD-ROM
Section 4 **The Ming Dynasty** 1. Ming rulers strengthened China's government and established peace. 2. China sent fleets of ships to explore other parts of Asia as well as to East Africa.	📁 Reproducible Lesson Plan 12–4 📁 Vocabulary Activity 12–4 📁 Guided Reading Activity 12–4* 📁 Section Quiz 12–4* 📁 Reading Essentials and Study Guide 12–4*	🔖 Daily Focus Skills Transparency 12–4 💿 Interactive Tutor Self-Assessment CD-ROM 💿 ExamView® Pro Testmaker CD-ROM 💿 Presentation Plus! CD-ROM 💿 Vocabulary PuzzleMaker CD-ROM 💿 Glencoe BookLink CD-ROM

*Also available in Spanish

Use our Web site for additional resources. All essential content is covered in the Student Edition.

You and your students can visit jat.glencoe.com, the Web site companion to *World History: Journey Across Time*. This innovative integration of electronic and print media offers your students a wealth of opportunities. The student text directs students to the Web site for the following options:

- Chapter Overviews
- Self-Check Quizzes
- Study Central™
- Student Web Activities
- Multi-Language Glossaries

Answers to the student Web activities are provided for you in the **Web Activity Lesson Plans.** Additional Web resources and ePuzzles and games are also available.

The following videotape programs are available from Glencoe as supplements to Chapter 12:

China's Forbidden City
(ISBN 0-7670-0649-6)

Genghis Khan: Terror and Conquest
(ISBN 1-56501-578-9)

Marco Polo: Journey to the East
(ISBN 1-56501-668-8)

To order, call Glencoe at 1-800-334-7344. To find classroom resources to accompany many of these videos, check the following home pages:

A&E Television: www.aande.com
The History Channel: www.historychannel.com

MEETING SPECIAL NEEDS

In addition to the Differentiated Instruction strategies, the following resources are suitable for students with special needs:

- *Exam*View® *Pro Testmaker CD-ROM* allows teachers to tailor tests by reducing answer choices.
- *StudentWorks Plus*™ *CD-ROM (with Audio Program)* includes the entire narrative of the student edition so that less-proficient readers can listen to the words as they read them.
- The *Reading Essentials and Study Guide* provides the same content as the student edition but is written two grade levels below the textbook.

Index to National Geographic Magazine:

The following articles relate to this chapter:

- "Chasing the Great Wall," by Peter Hessler, January 2003.
- "Mongolian Crossing," by Glenn Hodges, October 2003.
- "Central Asia Unveiled," by Mike Edwards, February 2002.

National Geographic Society Products:

To order the following, call National Geographic at 1–800–368–2728

- *PicturePack: Geography of Asia* (Transparency)
- *National Geographic Atlas of the World* (Book)

NGS ONLINE

Access National Geographic's new dynamic MapMachine Web site and other geography resources at:

www.nationalgeographic.com
www.nationalgeographic.com/maps

Meeting NCSS Standards

World History: Journey Across Time

The following standards are highlighted in Chapter 12:

Section 1 **III** **People, Places, and Environments: B, D**

IV **Individual Development and Identity: C**

V **Individuals, Groups, and Institutions: A, D, E, F, H**

Section 2 **I** **Culture: G**

VII **Production, Distribution, and Consumption: B, D**

VIII **Science, Technology, and Society: A, B**

Section 3 **II** **Time, Continuity, and Change: B, C**

VI **Power, Authority, and Governance: A, C, I, F**

Section 4 **VII** **Production, Distribution, and Consumption: C, D, H, I**

IX **Global Connections: E, H**

State and Local Objectives

_____

_____

Timesaving Tools

TeacherWorks
All-In-One Planner and Resource Center

- **Interactive Teacher Edition** Access your Teacher Wraparound Edition and your classroom resources with a few easy clicks.
- **Interactive Lesson Planner** Organize your week, month, semester, or year with all the lesson helps you need to make teaching creative and relevant.

Use Glencoe's **Presentation Plus!** multimedia teacher tool to easily present dynamic lessons that visually excite your students. Using Microsoft PowerPoint® you can customize the presentations to create your own personalized lessons.

FOLDABLES™
Study Organizer
Dinah Zike's Foldables

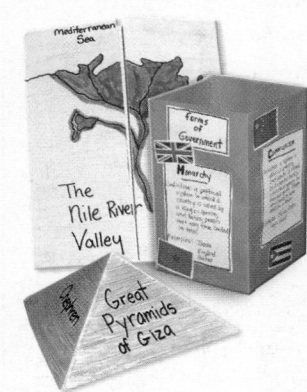

Foldables are three-dimensional, interactive graphic organizers that help students practice basic writing skills, review key vocabulary terms, and identify main ideas. Every chapter contains a foldable activity, with additional chapter activities found in the *Reading and Study Skills Foldables* booklet. You can use the foldables as they are presented, or modify them to suit the needs of your individual class.

Planning Ahead

CHAPTER CULMINATING ACTIVITY

The Chapter Culminating Activity will help students organize and learn the important information from the chapter. Begin the chapter with this activity, and have students complete it as a culminating activity.

CREATING A WHO-WHAT-WHEN-WHERE-WHY CHART

Purpose This type of organizer helps students organize and analyze information by identifying important historical figures and organizing information about them. It will focus students' attention on the most important people of the chapter, as well as help them understand these people's achievements, their role in history, and their place in the chapter chronology. It can also be used to organize information for reports and as a study aid.

Introduction to Modeling

1. Begin the discussion with a brainstorming session. Ask students to list what they know or believe they know about Genghis Khan and Marco Polo. Write the information on an overhead transparency.

2. Ask students to copy this chart into their notebooks:

Who	What	When	Where	Why
Li Bo				
Kublai Khan				
Genghis Khan				
Marco Polo				
Zheng He				

As students read the chapter, ask them to complete the boxes with the appropriate information about each important person. In the "Why" column, have them write notes that help explain why the person is significant.

3. As part of your chapter review, have students share their Who-What-When-Where-Why charts. Encourage them to use their charts as study aids.

Use the **SkillBuilder Handbook** on pages 902–919 to help students learn the skill of summarizing.

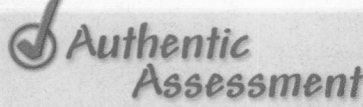

Authentic Assessment

Refer to Activity 12 in the Authentic Assessment section of the *Quizzes, Tests, and Authentic Assessment (with Rubrics)* booklet.

When &Who?

As students read the chapter, have them review the time line on this page. Ask them which events showed that China was advancing technologically. *(the printing of the first book and the voyage of Zheng He)* **L1**

GLENCOE TECHNOLOGY

World History: Journey Across Time Video Program

To learn more about China in the Middle Ages, students can view the Chapter 12 video in the *World History: Journey Across Time* Video Program.

MindJogger Videoquiz

Use the **MindJogger Videoquiz** to preview Chapter 12 content.

 Available in DVD and VHS

Chapter 12
China in the Middle Ages

▼ Imperial Palace at the Forbidden City

NATIONAL GEOGRAPHIC **When &Who?**

A.D. 600	A.D. 900	1200	1500
A.D. 581 Wendi founds Sui dynasty	A.D. 868 Chinese print world's first book	1206 Genghis Khan unites the Mongols	1405 Zheng He begins overseas voyage

---

Reading Strategy PURPOSE FOR READING

Analyzing Point out to students that they have read about periods of peace and order, as well as those of chaos and disorder, in many different civilizations. **Ask:** What forces seem to push societies toward disorder? What forces tend to help them regain peace and order? *(Students may cite as forces for disorder war and threats from outsiders, weak or evil rulers, conflicts among different parts of society, poverty, hunger, natural disasters, and others; forces for order might include rising wealth and prosperity, successful wars, good rulers, and others.)* As they read, have students look for forces that led China toward disorder and compare them to those that led to order. **L2**

Chapter Preview

Like the Arabs, the Chinese were interested in science and technology. Read this chapter to learn about Chinese inventions and how they influence your life today.

 View the Chapter 12 video in the *World History: Journey Across Time* Video Program.

Chapter Overview Visit jat.glencoe.com for a preview of Chapter 12.

 Section 1
China Reunites

During the Middle Ages, Chinese rulers brought peace, order, and growth to China. Buddhism became a major religion in China, but the Chinese government supported Confucian ideas.

 Section 2
Chinese Society

Farming and trade brought wealth to China. The Chinese developed new technology and enjoyed a golden age of art and writing.

 Section 3
The Mongols in China

Led by Genghis Khan, the Mongols built a vast empire. Under his son, Kublai Khan, they went on to conquer China as well.

 Section 4
The Ming Dynasty

China's Ming rulers strengthened government and brought peace and prosperity. They supported trading voyages to other parts of Asia and to East Africa.

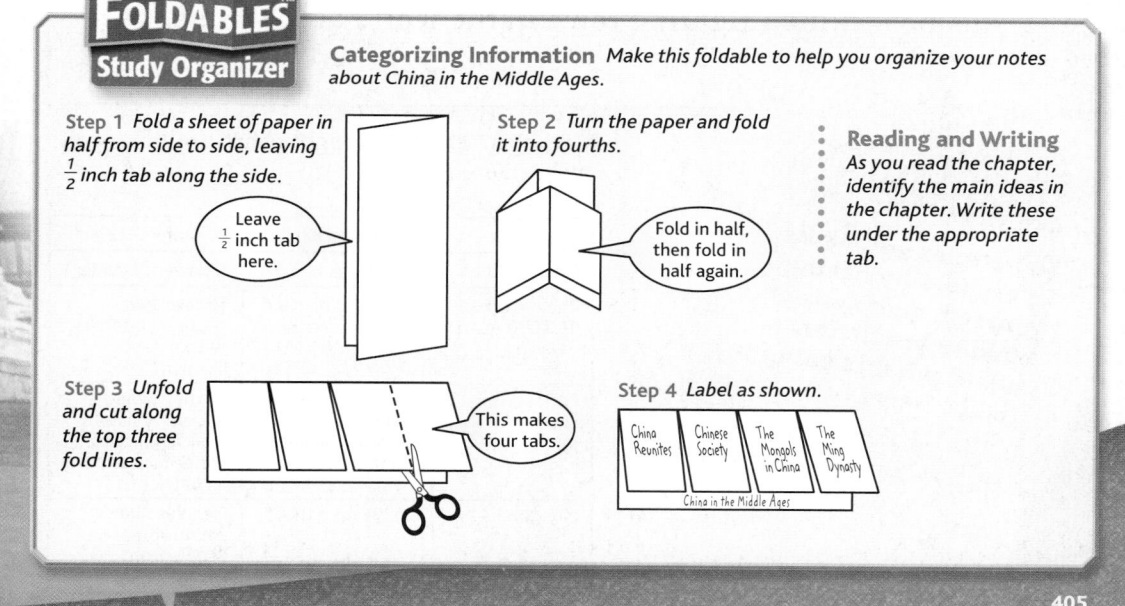

FOLDABLES™
Study Organizer

Categorizing Information *Make this foldable to help you organize your notes about China in the Middle Ages.*

Step 1 *Fold a sheet of paper in half from side to side, leaving ½ inch tab along the side.*

Leave ½ inch tab here.

Step 2 *Turn the paper and fold it into fourths.*

Fold in half, then fold in half again.

Reading and Writing *As you read the chapter, identify the main ideas in the chapter. Write these under the appropriate tab.*

Step 3 *Unfold and cut along the top three fold lines.*

This makes four tabs.

Step 4 *Label as shown.*

| China Reunites | Chinese Society | The Mongols in China | The Ming Dynasty |

China in the Middle Ages

405

INTRODUCING CHAPTER 12

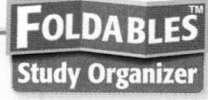
Introduce students to chapter content and key terms by having them access **Chapter Overview 12** at jat.glencoe.com

CHAPTER PREVIEW

After reading Chapter 12, students will be able to

1. discuss how Chinese rulers brought peace, order, and growth to China;

2. describe advances in farming, trade, technology, and culture;

3. summarize how the Mongols created the world's largest land empire;

4. explain how Ming rulers strengthened government and backed trading voyages.

FOLDABLES™
Study Organizer
Dinah Zike's Foldables

Purpose Students use this foldable to organize information about notable people, ideas, and events in medieval China. As students read this chapter, they should make notes in the appropriate locations.

📁 Have students complete *Reading and Study Skills Foldables* Activity 12.

MORE ABOUT THE PHOTO

The Forbidden City The Forbidden City is surrounded by a wall. The city and especially the most important buildings in it are laid out along a north-south line. They face south in honor of the sun. The open areas and the buildings in the Forbidden City, except for the Imperial Garden, are designed to impress the observer. For example, the Golden Water River flows in an arc through a large courtyard on the south side of the city. Five marble bridges cross this river. North of the Golden Water River, there is a seven-acre (three-ha) open space that can hold tens of thousands of people. The Hall of Supreme Harmony, which sits at the top of three levels of marble terraces, dominates this plaza. From the hall, the emperor could sit on his throne and receive the homage of his subjects below.

1 Learn It!

Making inferences, the ability to make logical assumptions, is directly tied to students' background knowledge. Without prior knowledge about a topic, it is very difficult to infer beyond the text.

Predicting also requires students to become actively involved in the text as they connect what they are reading to what might be. For example, in reading about porcelain figurines and vases, students might wonder how many are still in existence or what their value would be today.

Help students internalize the process of making inferences by using the inquiry method of learning so they will get accustomed to asking *who, what, when, where, why,* or *how* as they read. Having students generate their own questions requires higher level thinking processes and substantially increases comprehension. **L1/ EL**

Chapter 12 Reading Social Studies

1 Learn It!

Reading Between the Lines

To infer means to evaluate information and arrive at a conclusion. When you make inferences, you "read between the lines," or draw conclusions that are not stated directly in the text. We naturally make inferences about things we read, see, and hear every day.

Read this paragraph from Section 3.

> Genghis Khan gathered an army of more than 100,000 warriors. He placed his soldiers into well-trained groups. Commanding them were officers chosen for their abilities, not for their family ties. These changes made the Mongols the most skilled fighting force in the world at that time.
>
> —*from page 425*

Reading Tip

Sometimes you make inferences by asking yourself questions or making predictions about what is going to come next.

Use this Think-Through chart to help you make inferences.

Text	Question	Inference
Genghis Khan	Who was he?	A powerful leader?
The army had 100,000 warriors	Why did he need so many warriors?	To take over another country or to defend his own?
Officers not chosen for family ties	Why did Genghis Khan want officers without strong family ties?	So they would not worry about their families to better concentrate on battle?
Mongols	Who were they?	Genghis Khan's countrymen? People from Mongolia?

406

Reading Strategy ⟩ TEXT-BASED INFERENCES

Making inferences is a complex skill that involves drawing conclusions based on information that may not be explicitly stated in the text. While students may struggle to make inferences, it is important that they have the opportunity to respond freely to foster their confidence. As they become more comfortable with the skill, you will want to begin asking them to demonstrate how the text justifies their inferences. Pick several passages from the text and have students practice making Think-Through charts. After students have filled in their charts, have them explain how the information they included helps clarify the topic. **L2**

2 Practice It!

Making Inferences

Read the next paragraph, also about Genghis Khan's warriors, and pay attention to highlighted words as you make inferences.

> Genghis Khan began building his empire by conquering other people on the steppes. These victories brought him wealth and new soldiers to fill the army. Soon the Mongols were strong enough to attack major civilizations. In 1211 Mongol forces turned east and invaded China. Within three years, they had taken all of northern China. They then moved west and struck at the cities and kingdoms that controlled parts of the Silk Road.
>
> —*from pages 425–426*

Read to Write

Read the text under the heading **Scholar-Officials** in Section 1, page 414. Pay attention to the paragraph about how important it was for students to pass tests. Write about any experiences with tests you have had to help you understand the fears and hopes of Chinese students during the Middle Ages.

Create your own Think-Through Chart to help you make further inferences about Genghis Khan's army. You might want to use the highlighted words in your first column and label it **Text.** Your second and third columns can be labeled **Questions** and **Inference.** Read the rest of page 426 to see if your inferences were correct.

3 Apply It!

We also make inferences about other types of text, such as poetry. Read the poems on pages 420–421, and create a Think-Through chart to help understand the poems.

2 Practice It!

Organize students into groups of four. Explain that the Chinese made advances in the following areas: Metalworking, Printing, Weapons, Ship-building. Then assign the following roles to complete a Think-Through chart based on this information:

Facilitator: leads the group in finding words or phrases in the text about which the group may have a question.

Recorder: fills in Think-Though chart.

Background Provider: supplies additional background information from a Web site, other text, or the teacher.

Reporter: shares the group's findings with the class. **L2**

3 Apply It!

Using the principle of making inferences not only helps students understand definitions of words but also different connotations of vocabulary words. As students create their Think-Through charts on the poems, encourage them to consider vocabulary terms they may not understand. Have them use the charts to create possible definitions, then check them against a dictionary. **L2**

Reading Strategy READ TO WRITE

Showing students how to make connections to their own experiences can provide valuable background for future writing assignments. Ask students to jot in their notebooks any words, phrases, or concepts that make a personal connection for them, such as calligraphy, schoolchildren memorizing poetry, or the concept of an Imperial City. Have them compose a paragraph that makes a connection from these concepts to their experiences today. Doing this on a regular basis will increase their fluency with writing. **L1**

① FOCUS

SECTION OVERVIEW

This section looks at how China was reunited under the Sui, Tang, and Song dynasties and how Buddhism spread to China and other parts of Asia.

BELLRINGER
SKILLBUILDER ACTIVITY

👆 Project **Daily Focus Skills Transparency 12–1** and have students answer questions. Discuss their responses.

Get Ready to Read!

Preteaching Vocabulary: Ask a volunteer to define the word *reform. (change intended to bring improvements)* As they read the section, have students look for reforms that Chinese rulers made.

Answers to Graphic: Sui—Time Period: A.D. 581–618; Rulers: Wendi, Yangdi; Decline: Yangdi forced farmers to build Grand Canal and pay high taxes, peasants revolted and killed Yangdi; Tang—Time Period: A.D. 618–907; Rulers: Taizong, Wu; Decline: Turks drove Tang out of central Asia and cut off the Silk Road, revolts in Tibet and among farmers

---

Section ① China Reunites

Get Ready to Read!

What's the Connection?
Earlier you read that the Han dynasty of China collapsed and China plunged into civil war. As you will read, China eventually reunited. The new dynasties took Chinese civilization to even higher levels.

Focusing on the Main Ideas
• The Sui and Tang dynasties reunited and rebuilt China after years of war. *(page 409)*

• Buddhism became popular in China and spread to Korea and Japan. *(page 412)*

• The Tang dynasty returned to the ideas of Confucius and created a new class of scholar-officials. *(page 413)*

Locating Places
Korea (kuh•REE•uh)
Japan (juh•PAN)

Meeting People
Wendi (WHEHN•DEE)
Empress Wu (WOO)

Building Your Vocabulary
warlord
economy (ih•KAH•nuh•mee)
reform
monastery (MAH•nuh•STEHR•ee)

Reading Strategy
Categorizing Information Complete a table like the one below to show the time periods, the most important rulers, and the reasons for the decline of the Sui and Tang dynasties.

	Sui	Tang
Time Period		
Important Rulers		
Reasons for Decline		

When & Where?

NATIONAL GEOGRAPHIC

A.D. 500	A.D. 900	1300
A.D. 581 Wendi founds Sui dynasty	A.D. 907 Tang dynasty falls	1279 Mongols end Song rule

Changan

Hangzhou

SECTION RESOURCES

📁 Reproducible Masters
• Reproducible Lesson Plan 12–1
• Daily Lecture and Discussion Notes 12–1
• Vocabulary Activity 12–1
• Active Reading Note-Taking Guide 12–1
• Guided Reading Activity 12–1
• Section Quiz 12–1
• Reading Essentials and Study Guide 12–1

Transparencies
• Daily Focus Skills Transparency 12–1

Multimedia
💿 Interactive Tutor Self-Assessment CD-ROM
💿 Exam*View*® Pro Testmaker CD-ROM
💿 Presentation Plus! CD-ROM

Rebuilding China's Empire

Main Idea The Sui and Tang dynasties reunited and rebuilt China after years of war.

Reading Focus Have you ever thought about how the economy in your town or city works? How do goods get to your local stores? Who makes sure roads are paved? Read to learn how China dealt with these issues.

Earlier you read that China's Han empire ended in A.D. 220. For the next 300 years, China had no central government. It broke into 17 kingdoms. War and poverty were everywhere. Chinese **warlords**—military leaders who run a government—fought with each other while nomads conquered parts of northern China.

While China was absorbed in its own problems, it lost control of some of the groups it had conquered. One of these groups was the people of **Korea** (kuh•REE•uh). They lived on the Korean Peninsula to the northeast of China. The Koreans decided to end Chinese rule of their country. They broke away and built their own separate civilization.

The Sui Dynasty Reunites China China finally reunited in A.D. 581. In that year, a general who called himself **Wendi** (WHEHN•DEE) declared himself emperor. Wendi won battle after battle and finally reunited China. He then founded a new dynasty called the Sui (SWEE).

NATIONAL GEOGRAPHIC
Tang Dynasty China c. A.D. 700

KEY
Tang dynasty
— Grand Canal

Dynasties of China

500 600 700 800 900 1000 1100 1200 1300

Sui
A.D. 581–618

Civil War
A.D. 907–960

Tang
A.D. 618–907

Song
A.D. 960–1279

Using Geography Skills

The Tang dynasty lasted almost 300 years.
1. What two cities were connected by the Grand Canal?
2. What physical feature made up much of the northern border of the Tang dynasty?

Find NGS online map resources @
www.nationalgeographic.com/maps

CHAPTER 12 China in the Middle Ages **409**

Objectives and answers to the student activity can be found in the **Web Activity Lesson Plan** feature at jat.glencoe.com

Reading Strategy

Economics Improvements in transportation often bring about economic changes. Ask students to describe how the Grand Canal brought economic changes to China. (*China was united into one economy because goods could be shipped between different parts of the country.*) **L2**

Writing Activity

Yangdi's public works programs angered the Chinese people so much that they revolted. Ask students to write a speech from one of two viewpoints: that of Yangdi, justifying the work he required, or that of leaders of the revolt, justifying their actions. **L2**

Linking Past & Present

Answer: Answers will vary based on your state and students' knowledge of issues.

After Wendi died, his son Yangdi (YAHNG•DEE) took the Chinese throne. Yangdi wanted to expand China's territory. He sent an army to fight the neighboring Koreans, but the Chinese were badly defeated. At home, Yangdi took on many ambitious building projects. For example, the Great Wall had fallen into ruins, and Yangdi had it rebuilt.

Yangdi's greatest effort went into building the Grand Canal. This system of waterways linked the Chang Jiang (Yangtze River) and Huang He (Yellow River). The Grand Canal became an important route for shipping products between northern and southern China. It helped unite China's economy. An **economy** (ih•KAH•nuh•mee) is an organized way in which people produce, sell, and buy things.

History Online
Web Activity Visit jat.glencoe.com and click on **Chapter 12—Student Web Activity** to learn more about China.

Linking Past & Present

Grand Canal and Three Gorges Dam Project

The Three Gorges Dam under construction ▼

THEN Opening the Grand Canal boosted Imperial China's economy and made it much cheaper and faster to ship food and goods north and south. It also cost many laborers their lives. In addition, the canal system often flooded, drowning many people and animals and destroying crops.

NOW In 1994 China began building the Three Gorges Dam on the Chang Jiang. The dam will control flooding and produce electricity. Building it, however, requires many areas to be flooded. Millions of people have had to move, and much farmland will be lost. *What have construction projects changed in your state?*

▲ The Grand Canal

410   CHAPTER 12   China in the Middle Ages

DIFFERENTIATED INSTRUCTION

Logical/Mathematical: Have students research how a large canal like China's Grand Canal works. Ask them to find out how a canal's water level is raised so that boats can sail "uphill"; the function of locks and the role of gears, levers, and other machines; and how canals are dug and maintained.

English Learners: Ask students to explain to a partner the simple functions and operations of a canal.

Kinesthetic: Have students create a model or detailed drawing of a canal. Ask them to share their model or drawing with the class.

☞ Refer to **Inclusion Strategies for the Middle School Social Studies Classroom** in the TCR.

Yangdi rebuilt China, but he did it by placing hardships on the Chinese people. Farmers were forced to work on the Great Wall and the Grand Canal. They also had to pay high taxes to the government for these projects. Finally, the farmers became so angry that they revolted. The army took control and killed Yangdi. With Yangdi gone, the Sui dynasty came to an end.

The Tang Dynasty

In A.D. 618 one of Yangdi's generals took over China. He made himself emperor and set up a new dynasty called the Tang (TAHNG). Unlike the short-lived Sui, the Tang dynasty was in power for about 300 years—from A.D. 618 to A.D. 907. The Tang capital at Changan became a magnificent city, with about one million people living there.

Tang rulers worked to strengthen China's government. They carried out a number of **reforms,** or changes that brought improvements. The most powerful Tang emperor was named Taizong (TY•ZAWNG). He restored the civil service exam system. Government officials were once again hired based on how well they did on exams rather than on their family connections. Taizong also gave land to farmers and brought order to the countryside.

During the late A.D. 600s, a woman named Wu ruled China as empress. She was the only woman in Chinese history to rule the country on her own. A forceful leader, **Empress Wu** (WOO) added more officials to the government. She also strengthened China's military forces.

Under the Tang, China regained much of its power in Asia and expanded the areas under its control. Tang armies pushed west into central Asia, invaded Tibet, and took control of the Silk Road. They marched into Korea and forced the Korean kingdoms to pay tribute, a special kind of tax that one country pays to another to be left alone. The Tang also moved south and took control of northern Vietnam.

By the mid-A.D. 700s, however, the Tang dynasty began to have problems. A new group of nomads—the Turks that you read about earlier—drove the Tang armies out of central Asia and took control of the Silk Road. This damaged China's economy. Revolts in Tibet and among Chinese farmers at home further weakened the Tang. In A.D. 907 all of this disorder brought down the Tang dynasty.

The Song Dynasty

For about 50 years after the fall of the Tang, military leaders ruled China. Then, in A.D. 960, one of the generals declared himself emperor and set up the Song (SOONG) dynasty.

Song China c. A.D. 1200

KEY
Song empire
Grand Canal

Using Geography Skills

The Song dynasty moved the capital city to Hangzhou.
1. Use the map of the Tang dynasty on page 409 to compare the areas of the Tang and Song dynasties.
2. About how far is Hangzhou from the northern border of the empire?

Reading Strategy

Writing Activity

Have students review the text about the reinstitution of civil service exams during the Tang dynasty. Have them write a memo to Emperor Taizong with their recommendations about reinstituting the examinations. Have them take a position for or against the exams and try to persuade the emperor to adopt it. **L2**

Using Geography Skills

Answers:
1. The Tang dynasty held much more land, especially in the west.
2. about 600–700 miles

Skills Practice

Ask: Why did the Song borders not extend very far into the southwest? *(Song rulers did not have enough soldiers to control the large empire, and Tibet broke away.)* What northern peninsula did Tang rulers control that Song rulers lost? *(the Korean Peninsula)*

CHAPTER 12   China in the Middle Ages   **411**

CRITICAL THINKING ACTIVITY

Making Inferences Beginning with the Tang rulers, Chinese officials came to fear and distrust Buddhism. Ask students why this fear might have grown among the ruling classes. *(Possible answers: They did not agree with temples and monasteries accumulating wealth, feared that monks and nuns would undermine family life, and worried that people would withdraw from public life.)* Then have them discuss whether governments fear specific religions in the world today. Where? Why? **L2**

Religion Ask students to compare the role of Buddhist temples and monasteries in Tang China to religious institutions today. **L1/ EL**

✓ Reading Check

Answer: He declared himself emperor and won battle after battle until he had reunified China.

More About the Art

Under the Tang, the Chinese welcomed new ideas. Passers-by might have seen Arabian and Persian sailors as they wandered through port cities. Sold in stalls were perhaps the newest developments in pottery—stoneware with a black glaze, white porcelain, and figurines in foreign shapes. There even might have been one of the new huge sculptures of Buddha at the local temple.

Caption Answer: from A.D. 618 to A.D. 907

GLENCOE BOOKLINK

Use **Glencoe BookLink** to create customized reading lists for your students' reading levels, interests, and abilities.

The Song dynasty ruled from A.D. 960 to 1279. This period was a time of prosperity and cultural achievement for China. From the start, however, the Song faced problems that threatened their hold on China. Song rulers did not have enough soldiers to control their large empire. Tibet broke away, and nomads took over much of northern China. For safety, the Song moved their capital farther south to the city of Hangzhou (HAHNG•JOH). Hangzhou was on the coast near the Chang Jiang delta.

▲ Statue of the Buddha, carved about A.D. 460 in the Yun-Kang caves in China.

✓ Reading Check **Explain** How did Wendi unite China?

City Life in Tang China

Under the Tang, China grew and was prosperous. Tang cities could be large, with many activities occurring within the city's walls. A city contained many shops and temples. The homes of rich families often had two or three floors. *When did the Tang rule China?*

Musicians and dancers

Civil service examinations

Farmers selling goods

Print shop

Making pottery

Buddhism Spreads to China

Main Idea Buddhism became popular in China and spread to Korea and Japan.

Reading Focus Where do you turn when you are having problems? Read to learn why many Chinese turned to Buddhism when China was in trouble.

Earlier you learned that traders and missionaries from India brought Buddhism to China in about A.D. 150. At the time, the Han dynasty was already weak. Soon afterward, China collapsed into civil war. People everywhere were dying from war and a lack of food and shelter. It was a time of great suffering. Because Buddhism taught that people could escape their suffering, many Chinese seeking peace and comfort became Buddhists.

Chinese Buddhism Early Tang rulers were not Buddhists, but they allowed Buddhism to be practiced in China. They even

---

INTERDISCIPLINARY CONNECTIONS ACTIVITY

Civics Have a group of students review the reforms that various Chinese rulers instituted, along with the demands they placed on their subjects. Then have students choose one dynasty and present a "town meeting" discussion. To do this, students should write a script for roles for citizens and government officials. Have each side present information, including problems and solutions. **L2**

☞ Refer to the *Quizzes, Tests, and Authentic Assessment (with Rubrics)* booklet for rubrics.

supported the building of Buddhist temples. Many Chinese Buddhists became monks and nuns. They lived in places called **monasteries** (MAH•nuh•STEHR•eez), where they meditated and worshiped.

Buddhist temples and monasteries provided services for people. They ran schools and provided rooms and food for travelers. Buddhist monks served as bankers and provided medical care.

Not all Chinese people liked Buddhism, however. Many thought that it was wrong for the Buddhist temples and monasteries to accept donations. Others believed that monks and nuns weakened respect for family life because they were not allowed to marry.

In the early A.D. 800s, Tang officials feared Buddhism's growing power. They saw Buddhism as an enemy of China's traditions. In A.D. 845 the Tang had many Buddhist monasteries and temples destroyed. Buddhism in China never fully recovered.

Chinese Buddhism Spreads East As you read earlier, Korea broke free of China when the Han dynasty fell in A.D. 220. For several hundred years after, Korea was divided into three independent kingdoms.

In the A.D. 300s, Chinese Buddhists brought their religion to Korea. About A.D. 660, the Koreans united to form one country. After that, with government support, Buddhism grew even stronger in Korea.

Buddhism later spread to the nearby islands of **Japan** (juh•PAN). According to legend, one of Korea's kings wrote to Japan's emperor. The letter contained a statue of the Buddha and Buddhist writings. "This religion is the most excellent of all teachings," the king wrote. As time passed, Buddhism won many followers in Japan as well.

✓ **Reading Check** **Explain** Why did some Chinese people dislike Buddhism?

New Confucian Ideas

Main Idea The Tang dynasty returned to the ideas of Confucius and created a new class of scholar-officials.

Reading Focus Have you ever seen someone get a reward that he or she did not earn? Read to learn how China's rulers tried to avoid this problem when hiring government officials.

You have already read about Confucius and his teachings. Confucius and his followers believed that a good government depended on having wise leaders. The civil service examinations introduced by Han

Primary Source: Defending Confucianism

Han Yü (A.D. 768 to A.D. 824) encouraged the Chinese people to remain faithful to Confucianism.

"What were the teachings of our ancient kings? Universal love is called humanity. To practice this in the proper manner is called righteousness. To proceed according to these is called the Way.... They offered sacrifices to Heaven and the gods came to receive them.... What Way is this? I say: This is what I call the Way, and not what the Taoists [Daoists] and the Buddhists called the Way...."

—Han Yü, "An Inquiry on The Way" (Tao)

▲ Han Yü

DBQ **Document-Based Question**

Why does Han Yü think Confucianism should be followed?

CHAPTER 12   China in the Middle Ages   **413**

✓ **Reading Check**

Answer: Many thought it was wrong for temples and monasteries to receive donations. Others thought it weakened respect for family life because monks and nuns could not marry.

Primary Source

Han Yü became the father of neo-Confucianism, but he is also well known as a great writer. He rejected the ornate and flowery style of his time in favor of a simpler, more direct one. His style was so unusual that he initially failed his civil service examinations because the graders hated his simplicity.

Answer:
He thinks that the gods accepted Chinese people's ancestors who believed in the teachings of Confucius.

EXTENDING THE CONTENT

Ruthless but Efficient The empress Wu gained power in large part because of her willingness to remove her rivals. Eventually, all of them were either dismissed from office, sent into exile, or killed. Her list of enemies included even her relatives. After she claimed power, she ruled effectively, choosing as helpers only those men who were completely loyal to her. Historians agree that her forceful personality, administrative skills, and willingness to use harsh methods inspired loyalty and fear, if not affection. Wu's greatest achievements include helping unify the empire and placing selection of government officials firmly on a merit system.

③ ASSESS

Assign Section 1 Review as homework or as an in-class activity.

🌐 Have students use the **Interactive Tutor Self-Assessment CD-ROM** to review the section.

Assessment L2

Assign **Section 1 Quiz** to assess mastery of the material found in the section.

Reading Support L1/[EL]

Assign **Reading Essentials and Study Guide 12–1** to help students review section material.

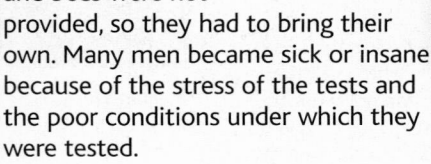
NATIONAL GEOGRAPHIC The Way It Was

Answers:

1. twenties or early thirties
2. Possible answer: They knew their future career, wealth, and status depended on it.

NATIONAL GEOGRAPHIC The Way It Was

Focus on Everyday Life

Civil Service Exams Proficiency tests and final exams today take a lot of preparation, but they are not as difficult as China's civil service examinations given during the Tang dynasty. Men of almost all ranks tried to pass the exams so they could hold government jobs and become wealthy. Thousands attempted the tests, but only a few hundred people qualified for the important positions.

Chinese boys began preparing for the exams in primary school. After many years of learning to read and write more than 400,000 words and sayings, the boys—now men in their twenties or early thirties—would take the first of three levels of exams. Students traveled to huge testing sites to take the tests. Food and beds were not provided, so they had to bring their own. Many men became sick or insane because of the stress of the tests and the poor conditions under which they were tested.

▲ Students taking civil service exams

Connecting to the Past
1. How old were the Chinese when they took the tests?
2. Why do you think taking the tests was so stressful for these men?

rulers were a product of Confucian ideas. They were supposed to recruit talented government officials.

After the fall of the Han dynasty, no national government existed to give civil service examinations. Confucianism lost much support, and Buddhism with its spiritual message won many followers. Tang and Song rulers, however, brought Confucianism back into favor.

What Is Neo-Confucianism? The Tang dynasty gave its support to a new kind of Confucianism called neo-Confucianism. This new Confucianism was created, in part, to reduce Buddhism's popularity. It taught that life in this world was just as important as the afterlife. Followers were expected to take part in life and help others.

Although it criticized Buddhist ideas, this new form of Confucianism also picked up some Buddhist and Daoist beliefs. For many Chinese, Confucianism became more than a system of rules for being good. It became a religion with beliefs about the spiritual world. Confucian thinkers taught that if people followed Confucius's teachings, they would find peace of mind and live in harmony with nature.

The Song dynasty, which followed the Tang, also supported neo-Confucianism. The Song even adopted it as their official philosophy, or belief system.

Scholar-Officials Neo-Confucianism also became a way to strengthen the government. Both Tang and Song rulers used civil service examinations to hire officials. In doing so, they based the bureaucracy on a merit system. Under a merit system, people are accepted for what they can do and not on their riches or personal contacts.

CITIZENSHIP AND YOU

Civil Service The reforms of the Tang rulers, including the important changes in the civil service system, were proposed and carried out by the rulers. In our society, some reforms originate this way, while many others come from the people. Ask students to research some reforms in U.S. history they believe came about as a result of popular demands. Examples include the institution of term limits, the abolition of conscription, the end to slavery, and the crackdown on drunk drivers. Have students discuss how ordinary citizens can make their desire for specific reforms known and how they can get them enacted. **L3**

The examinations tested job seekers on their knowledge of Confucian writings. To pass, it was necessary to write with style as well as understanding. The tests were supposed to be fair, but only men were allowed to take the tests. Also, only rich people had the money that was needed to help their sons study for the tests.

Passing the tests was very difficult. However, parents did all they could to prepare their sons. At the age of four, boys started learning to write the characters of the Chinese language. Later, students had to memorize all of Confucius's writings. If a student recited the passages poorly, he could expect to be hit by his teacher.

After many years of study, the boys took their examinations. Despite all the preparation, only one in five passed. Those who failed usually found jobs helping officials or teaching others. However, they would never be given a government job.

▲ Chinese scholar-officials on horseback

Over the years, the examination system created a new wealthy class in China. This group was made up of scholar-officials. Strict rules set the scholar-officials apart from society. One rule was that they could not do physical work. Students preparing for the tests were taught never to use their hands except for painting or writing.

 Reading Check **Describe** How did Confucianism change in China?

Study Central™ Need help with the material in this section? Visit jat.glencoe.com

Section 1 Review

Reading Summary

Review the **Main Ideas**

- While the Sui dynasty was short-lived, the Tang and Song dynasties lasted for hundreds of years and returned power and prosperity to China.

- Buddhism became popular in China and also spread to Korea and Japan.

- A new kind of Confucianism developed in China during the Tang and Song dynasties, and the government used civil service tests to improve itself.

What Did You Learn?

1. What made Buddhism so popular in China?

2. How was neo-Confucianism a response to Buddhism's popularity, and what did it teach?

Critical Thinking

3. **Compare and Contrast** Create a diagram to show how the reigns of Wendi and Yangdi were similar and how they were different.

(Wendi) (Yangdi)

4. **Cause and Effect** What events led to the fall of the Tang dynasty?

5. **Sequencing Information** Describe the history of Buddhism during the Tang dynasty.

6. **Analyze** Why had Confucianism fallen out of favor in China before the Tang and Song dynasties?

7. **Drawing Conclusions** Do you think China's civil service system truly brought the most talented individuals into the government? How would you make the system fairer?

Ask students if they think job-seekers today are evaluated under a merit system such as the one used in ancient China. Why or why not? **L2**

Reading Check

Answer: became neo-Confucianism; changed from a moral code into a religion

ENRICH

Ask students to research and report on the role of Confucianism in today's China. **L3**

To help students understand section material, have them visit **Study Central**™ at jat.glencoe.com

RETEACH

Ask students to list a contribution of each of the dynasties discussed in this section. **L1**

④ CLOSE

Have students share their questions from the **Reading the Text** activity on page 409. Have the class answer as many of the questions as time permits. **L2**

SECTION 1 REVIEW ANSWERS

1. It allowed people to escape suffering and seek peace and comfort.

2. offset Buddhism's popularity; life in this world and afterlife equally important

3. Wendi: won many battles; founded Sui dynasty; Yangdi: invasion of Korea failed; supported many building projects; high taxes and forced labor; Both: expanded territory

4. Turks taking control of the Silk Road; the loss of trade; revolts in Tibet and China

5. Answers should include initial support then growing fear and attack on temples.

6. no national government to give civil service examinations; Buddhism won many followers

7. Answers will vary but should be thoughtful.

Section 2

Chinese Society

① FOCUS

SECTION OVERVIEW

In this section, students will read about the rise of new agricultural methods, trade activities, and technologies, as well as the blossoming of art and literature.

BELLRINGER
SKILLBUILDER ACTIVITY

✎ Project **Daily Focus Skills Transparency 12–2** and have students answer questions. Discuss their responses.

Get Ready to Read!

Preteaching Vocabulary: The word *calligraphy* comes from two Greek words: *kalli,* meaning "beautiful," and *graphia,* meaning "to write." Calligraphy, then, is the art of beautiful writing.

Answers to Graphic: mixed iron and carbon in a hot furnace to produce steel; block printing allowed faster production of books; produced gunpowder and used it to make explosives; developed the fire lance; built large ships; used compasses

Get Ready to Read!

What's the Connection?
In the last section, you learned about the rise and fall of the Sui, Tang, and Song dynasties. During those dynasties, China's economy began to grow again. Chinese inventors developed many new technologies, and Chinese artists and writers produced new works that are still admired today.

Focusing on the **Main Ideas**
- The Tang dynasty strengthened China's economy by supporting farming and trade. **(page 417)**
- The Chinese developed new technologies, such as steelmaking and printing. **(page 418)**
- During the Tang and the Song dynasties, China enjoyed a golden age of art and literature. **(page 420)**

Locating Places
Changan (CHAHNG•AHN)

Meeting People
Li Bo (LEE BOH)
Duo Fu (DWAW FOO)

Building Your Vocabulary
porcelain (POHR•suh•luhn)
calligraphy (kuh•LIH•gruh•fee)

Reading Strategy
Organizing Information Complete a chart like the one below describing the new technologies developed in China during the Middle Ages.

New Technologies

NATIONAL GEOGRAPHIC When&Where?

| A.D. 600 | A.D. 900 | 1200 |

A.D. 618 Tang dynasty takes power

A.D. 868 Chinese print world's first complete book

c. 1150 Chinese sailors are the first to use compass

Changan

Hangzhou

416   CHAPTER 12   China in the Middle Ages

A Growing Economy

Main Idea The Tang dynasty strengthened China's economy by supporting farming and trade.

Reading Focus Do you know anyone who drinks tea or wears silk clothing? Both of these goods were first produced in China. Read to learn how farming changed under the Tang dynasty.

When the Han dynasty in China collapsed in the A.D. 200s, it was a disaster for China's economy. As fighting began, cities were damaged and farms were burned. Artisans made fewer goods, farmers grew fewer crops, and merchants had less to trade. Under the Tang dynasty, these problems were solved.

Why Did Farming Improve?
When the Tang rulers took power in A.D. 618, they brought peace to the countryside and gave more land to farmers. As a result, farmers were able to make many advances. They improved irrigation and introduced new ways of growing their crops. Farmers also developed new kinds of rice, which grew well in poor soil, produced more per acre, grew faster, and were resistant to disease.

These changes helped farmers grow more and more rice. China's farmers also began to grow tea, which became a popular drink. They made improvements in other crops as well. With more food available, the number of people in China greatly increased. At the same time, more people moved southward, where rice grew abundantly in the Chang Jiang valley.

China's Trade Grows
Tang rulers also had roads and waterways built. These changes made travel within and outside of China much easier. Chinese merchants were able to increase trade with people in other parts of Asia. The Silk Road, now under Tang control, once again bustled with activity.

▲ A worker holds a tray of silkworms eating mulberry leaves. Eventually the worms will spin cocoons. Workers then collect and unravel the cocoons to make silk thread. *Why do you think silk is still expensive today?*

▼ Silk, shown here being harvested, remained an important trade item for the Chinese. *How did Tang rulers help increase trade?*

CHAPTER 12   China in the Middle Ages   **417**

② TEACH

Religious Art In this section, students will learn how religious beliefs influenced Chinese art. Ask students to give other examples of art, books, or films that reflect other religious beliefs. **L2**

Daily Lecture and Discussion Notes 12–2

Use **Daily Lecture and Discussion Notes 12–2** for an outline of key concepts found in the section.

Reading Support L1/ EL

Use **Vocabulary Activity 12–2** to review important terms in the section.

More About the Art

American colonists hoped to introduce the cultivation of silk into the American colonies. The leading advocate of a silk industry was Benjamin Franklin. He considered silk "the happiest of all inventions for clothing."

Caption Answers: Tang rulers built roads and waterways. Silk today is difficult to produce.

Reading Strategy   READING THE TEXT

Visualizing Visualizing is a valuable technique in developing active reading skills and increasing comprehension. Forming a mental picture can also aid recall. As students read this section, ask them to visualize a mental picture of what they read. For example, have them visualize the processes or products of the new technologies, the interactions among people necessary for the resulting increase in trade, or the descriptions of nature in the poems of Li Bo and Duo Fu and the paintings shown in this section. **L2**

Writing Activity

Have students write a "You Are There" report about how life in the Tang dynasty began to change. Have them incorporate details from the text in their report. **L2**

Reading Check

Answer: Because the new kinds of rice grew well in poor soil, produced more per acre, grew faster, and were resistant to disease, farmers grew more and more rice. More food led to increased population.

More About the Art

During the Tang dynasty, Changan was perhaps the largest city in the world. However, it was located on China's northwest frontier, which made it a target for nomadic raiders. In addition, it depended on an extensive irrigation system. As this system wore out in the A.D. 800s, food had to be brought in from many miles away. As a result, the city declined in importance.

Caption Answer: improved irrigation and new kinds of rice

One of the items traded by the Chinese was silk fabric. This product gave the road its name and was popular in markets to the west of China. In addition, China traded tea, steel, paper, and porcelain. **Porcelain** (POHR•suh•luhn) is made of fine clay and baked at high temperatures. In return, other countries sent China products such as gold, silver, precious stones, and fine woods.

Other trade routes were also established. Roads linked China to central Asia, India, and southwest Asia. In addition, the Tang opened new ports along China's coast to boost trade.

✓ Reading Check
Cause and Effect How did the new kinds of rice developed in China help its population grow?

New Technology

Main Idea The Chinese developed new technologies, such as steelmaking and printing.

Reading Focus This book is made of paper with letters printed on the paper by a machine. Read to learn how printing was first invented in China during the Tang dynasty.

During the Tang and Song dynasties, new inventions changed China's society. In time, these discoveries spread to other parts of the world.

China Discovers Coal and Steel For most of China's history, people burned wood to heat their homes and cook their food. By

Changan's Royal Palace

The Tang capital city of Changan may have had a population of one million people at its peak. The city had large blocks that included houses, businesses, and temples set along straight streets. Its layout inspired the design of many later cities. The area containing the royal palace, shown below, was bordered by parklands. *What improvements to agriculture allowed China's population to grow during the Tang dynasty?*

418

DIFFERENTIATED INSTRUCTION

Kinesthetic: Have students present a demonstration on how to prepare a Chinese dish. If possible, have them cook the dish in the classroom using a hot plate or an electric wok. Alternatively, have students bring premade Chinese food to class and discuss how the food was made.

English Learners: Ask students to make a list of all the ingredients in a particular Chinese dish. Have them explain to a partner how the ingredients taste.

Gifted and Talented: In addition to cooking, have students research the origin of the descriptive names of several Chinese dishes, such as Happy Family, Ants Climbing a Tree, Kung Pao Chicken, Dragon Flying and Phoenix Dancing, and Bananas Pulling Golden Threads.

Refer to *Inclusion Strategies for the Middle School Social Studies Classroom* in the TCR.

the time of the Tang dynasty, wood was becoming scarce in China. However, the Chinese had discovered that coal could be used to heat things, and soon a coal-mining industry developed.

The Chinese used coal to heat furnaces to high temperatures, which led to another discovery. When iron was produced in hot furnaces heated by coal, the molten iron mixed with carbon from the coal. This created a new, stronger metal known today as steel.

The Chinese used steel to make many things. They made armor, swords, and helmets for their army, but they also made stoves, farm tools, drills, steel chain, and even steel nails and sewing needles.

The Printing Process Another Chinese invention was a method for printing books. Before printing, books had to be copied by hand. As a result, few books were made, and they were very expensive. The Chinese began printing in the A.D. 600s. They used blocks of wood on which they cut the characters of an entire page. Ink was placed over the wooden block. Then paper was laid on the block to make a print. Cutting the block took a long time. When they were completed, however, the woodblocks could be used again and again to make many copies.

The Chinese soon began printing books. The earliest known printed book dates from about A.D. 868. It is a Buddhist book called the *Diamond Sutra*. The invention of printing was very important. It helped to spread ideas more rapidly.

In the A.D. 1000s, a Chinese printer named Pi Sheng (BEE SHUHNG) invented movable type for printing. With movable type, each character is a separate piece. The pieces can be moved around to make sentences and used again and again. Pi Sheng made his pieces from clay and put them together to produce book pages. However,

Science and Inventions

Printing When the Chinese invented movable type, they improved the art of printing. A Chinese author described the work of Pi Sheng:

"He took sticky clay and cut in it characters as thin as the edge of a copper coin. Each character formed as it were a single type. He baked them in the fire to make them hard. He had previously prepared an iron plate and he had covered this plate with a mixture of pine resin, wax, and paper ashes. When he wished to print, he took an iron frame and set it on the iron plate. In this he placed the type, set close together. When the frame was full, the whole made one solid block of type."

—Shên Kua, *Dream Pool Jottings*

◀ The *Diamond Sutra* is the earliest known printed book.

▲ Composing stick

▲ Movable type block

Connecting to the Past
1. Why do you think Pi Sheng used clay to make his characters?
2. In what instance would woodblock printing have been a better method to use than movable type?

CONNECTING ACROSS TIME

Coal has been used as an energy source for centuries. However, the pollution it causes has become a major problem. Ask students to research and report on the use of coal today in the United States and China. Have them discuss different approaches to pollution abatement. **L3**

Reading Strategy

Evaluating Ask students to write a paragraph explaining which of the inventions and technological advances of the Chinese was the most important. Have them support their choice with reasons. **L2**

The Way It Was

Answers:
1. It was easy to manipulate.
2. to make just a few copies of something

CRITICAL THINKING ACTIVITY

Drawing Conclusions Have students review the text information about the invention and development of printing. Then ask them to discuss the changing role of the printed word in our society.
Ask: Do print materials still have the same importance today as they did in medieval China? How has the importance and use of printing changed? What other sources of information have influenced printing's role in our society? Have students write a short report comparing the use of printing in Tang China to printing today. **L3**

Mental Mapping The ancient Chinese learned to use a compass to find north. With this information, they were able to sail great distances away from land. Ask students to describe what landmarks they would pass if they walked north from their homes. What about south? East? West? **L1/EL**

✔ **Reading Check**

Answer: Printing allowed many copies of a book to be produced, which allowed ideas to spread more quickly.

Primary Source

By the end of his life, Li Bo was the most famous poet in China, as well as a serious student of Daoism. He became a mentor for a younger, unknown poet. This poet, Duo Fu, would soon rival Li Bo in fame.

Answer:
The traveler's thoughts drift from one thing to another.

Reading Support L1/EL

Assign **Guided Reading Activity 12–2** to help students organize the information in the section.

---

because written Chinese has so many characters, woodblock printing was easier and quicker than using movable type.

Other Chinese Inventions The Chinese made gunpowder for use in explosives. One weapon was the fire lance, an ancestor of the gun. It used gunpowder and helped make the Chinese army a strong force. The Chinese also used gunpowder to make fireworks.

The Chinese also built large ships with rudders and sails. About 1150, Chinese sailors began using the compass to help them find their way. This let ships sail farther from land.

✔ **Reading Check** **Analyze** Why was the invention of printing so important?

Primary Source

Li Bo

In the following poem, Li Bo writes about parting from a friend.

"Green hills sloping from the northern wall, white water rounding the eastern city: once parted from this place the lone weed tumbles ten thousand miles. Drifting clouds—a traveler's thoughts; setting sun—an old friend's heart. Wave hands and let us take leave now, *hsiao-hsiao* our hesitant horses neighing."

—Li Bo, "Seeing a Friend Off"

▲ Li Bo

DBQ **Document-Based Question**

How are drifting clouds like a traveler's thoughts?

Art and Literature

Main Idea During the Tang and the Song dynasties, China enjoyed a golden age of art and literature.

Reading Focus If you were to choose one poem to read to the class, which poem would it be? Below, you will read a poem that is a Chinese favorite.

The Tang and Song eras were a golden age for Chinese culture. The invention of printing helped to spread Chinese ideas and artwork. Chinese rulers actively supported art and literature, and invited artists and poets to live and work in the capital city of **Changan** (CHAHNG•AHN).

What Was Tang Poetry Like? Chinese writers best expressed themselves in poems. In fact, the Tang dynasty is viewed as the great age of poetry in China. Some Tang poems celebrated the beauty of nature, the thrill of seasons changing, and the joy of having a good friend. Other Tang poems expressed sadness for the shortness of life and mourned the cruelty of friends parting.

Li Bo (LEE BOH) was one of the most popular poets of the Tang era. His poems often centered on nature. The poem below by Li Bo is probably the best-known poem in China. For centuries, Chinese schoolchildren have had to memorize it. Its title is "Still Night Thoughts."

> **66** Moonlight in front of my bed—
> I took it for frost on the ground!
> I lift my eyes to watch the
> mountain moon,
> lower them and dream of home. **99**
>
> —Li Bo,
> "Still Night Thoughts"

Another favorite poet of that time was **Duo Fu** (DWAW FOO). He was a poor civil servant who had a hard life. Civil war swept

---

INTERDISCIPLINARY CONNECTIONS ACTIVITY

Science Organize the class into four groups. Ask each group to choose one of the following technological advances of the Tang and Song dynasties: block printing, steelmaking, shipbuilding, or gunpowder. Have each group research its topic to learn more about when and how the advance came about, how it was used, and how knowledge of it spread. If possible, each group should find illustrations of its subject. Then have the groups present their findings to the class. **L3**

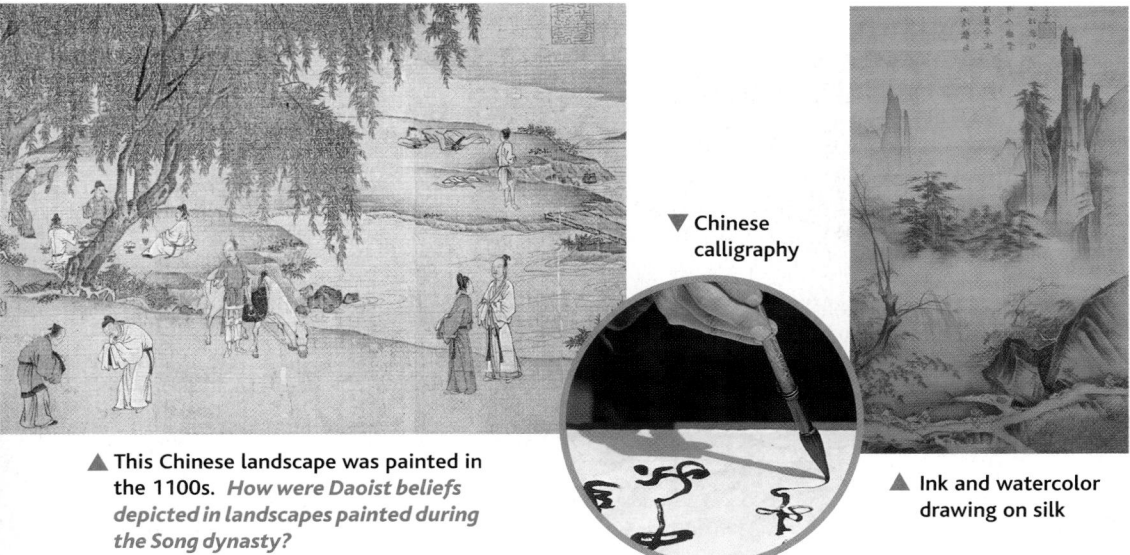

▲ This Chinese landscape was painted in the 1100s. *How were Daoist beliefs depicted in landscapes painted during the Song dynasty?*

▼ Chinese calligraphy

▲ Ink and watercolor drawing on silk

More About the Art

Most traditional Chinese paintings are done on paper or silk with ink or watercolors.

Caption Answer: Empty spaces reflect that a person cannot know the whole truth; people are small to show that they live in but are not part of nature.

China, and food was hard to find. Duo Fu nearly died of starvation. His problems opened his eyes to the sufferings of the common people.

As a result, Duo Fu's poems often were very serious. They frequently dealt with issues such as social injustice and the problems of the poor. Duo Fu wrote the poem below after a rebellion left the capital city in ruins. It is called "Spring Landscape."

> ❝ Rivers and mountains survive
>   broken countries.
> Spring returns. The city grows
>   lush again.
> Blossoms scatter tears thinking of
>   us, and this
> Separation in a bird's cry startles
>   the heart.
>
> Beacon-fires have burned
>   through three months.
> By now, letters are worth ten
>   thousand in gold.
>
> · · · · · · · · · · · ❞
>
> —Duo Fu,
>   "Spring Landscape"

Painting in Song China The painting of landscapes became widespread during the Song dynasty. However, Chinese artists did not try to make exact pictures of the landscapes they were painting. Instead, they wished to portray the "idea" of the mountains, lakes, and other features of their landscapes. Also, empty spaces were left in the paintings on purpose. This is because of the Daoist belief that a person cannot know the whole truth about something.

Daoist beliefs also can be seen in the way people are portrayed. They are tiny figures, fishing in small boats or wandering up a hillside trail. In other words, the people are living in, but not controlling, nature. They are only a part of the harmony of the natural setting.

Chinese painters often wrote poetry on their works. They used a brush and ink to write beautiful characters called **calligraphy** (kuh•LIH•gruh•fee).

Chinese Porcelain During the Tang period, Chinese artisans perfected the making of porcelain. Because porcelain later came from

 ASSESS

Assign Section 2 Review as homework or as an in-class activity.

⊕ Have students use the **Interactive Tutor Self-Assessment CD-ROM** to review the section.

Assessment L2

Assign **Section 2 Quiz** to assess mastery of the material found in the section.

Reading Support L1/ EL

Assign **Reading Essentials and Study Guide 12–2** to help students review section material.

CHAPTER 12   China in the Middle Ages   **421**

EXTENDING THE CONTENT

Black Powder The first kind of gunpowder made is what we now call black powder. It is still popular with fans of antique firearms. This mixture burns rapidly and produces both gas and solid waste products, mostly smoke. In an enclosed space, such as the breech of a gun, the gases can propel a bullet at great speed. Most modern guns use a different kind of gunpowder, known as smokeless powder, that is more powerful and produces less smoke than black powder.

Caption Answer: china

ENRICH

Ask students to research and prepare a class presentation on one aspect of Chinese art or technology. **L3**

✓ Reading Check

Answer: social injustice and the problems of the poor

History Online

To help students understand section material, have them visit **Study Central**™ at **jat.glencoe.com**

RETEACH

Have students make flash cards listing important achievements of the Tang and Song dynasties and use them in pairs to review the section. **L1**

④ CLOSE

Ask students to explain which advance they think was most important. **L2**

◀ Ceramic figures from Tang dynasty tomb

These porcelain figures from the ▶ Tang dynasty show travelers on horseback. *What is porcelain sometimes called today?*

▲ Tang dynasty bottle

China to the West, people today sometimes call porcelain by the name "china."

Porcelain can be made into plates, cups, figurines, and vases. In A.D. 851 an Arab traveler described the quality of Tang porcelain: "There is in China a very fine clay from which are made vases. . . . Water in these vases is visible through them, and yet they are made of clay."

The technology for making porcelain spread to other parts of the world. It finally reached Europe in the 1700s.

✓ Reading Check **Identify** What did Duo Fu often write about?

Section ② Review

History Online

Study Central™ Need help with the material in this section? Visit jat.glencoe.com

Reading Summary
Review the Main Ideas

- During the Tang dynasty, both farming and trade flourished, and the empire grew much larger than ever before.
- Many important inventions were developed in China during the Tang and Song dynasties, including steel, printing, and gunpowder.
- Chinese literature and arts, including poetry, landscape painting, and porcelain making, reached new heights during the Tang and Song dynasties.

What Did You Learn?

1. What products were traded by China along the Silk Road?
2. What were some of the subjects of Tang poetry?

Critical Thinking

3. **Organizing Information** Draw a chart to describe the new technologies developed in China.

Metalworking	
Printing	
Weapons	
Sailing	

4. **Summarize** Describe the changes to Chinese agriculture during the Tang dynasty.
5. **Contrast** How do the two forms of printing invented by the Chinese differ?
6. **Evaluate** Which invention of the Tang and Song dynasties do you think has been most important? Explain.
7. **Creative Writing** Read the poem "Still Night Thoughts" by Li Bo again. Then write a short, four-stanza poem similar to Li Bo's about the view from your bedroom or kitchen window.

422   CHAPTER 12   China in the Middle Ages

SECTION 2 REVIEW ANSWERS

1. silk fabric, tea, steel, paper, and porcelain
2. beauty of nature, changing seasons, good friends, sadness of friends parting, social injustice, problems of the poor
3. steel; woodblock printing, movable type printing; gunpowder; compass
4. Improved irrigation, new ways of growing crops, and new kinds of rice produced more food.
5. Woodblock: entire page cut into a block of wood; Movable type: separate characters made of clay joined to form words
6. Answers will vary. Students should use examples from the text and provide reasons for their answers.
7. Poems will vary.

Section 3 — The Mongols in China

Get Ready to Read!

What's the Connection?
As a complex culture developed in China, a northern enemy waited to attack.

Focusing on the Main Ideas
- Genghis Khan and his sons built the Mongol Empire, which stretched from the Pacific Ocean to Eastern Europe. **(page 424)**

- The Mongols conquered China and created a new dynasty that tried to conquer Japan and began trading with the rest of Asia. **(page 428)**

Locating Places
Mongolia (mahn•GOH•lee•uh)
Gobi (GOH•bee)
Karakorum (KAHR•uh•KOHR•uhm)
Khanbaliq (KAHN•buh•LEEK)
Beijing (BAY•JIHNG)

Meeting People
Genghis Khan
 (GEHNG•guhs KAHN)
Kublai Khan (KOO•BLUH KAHN)
Marco Polo
 (MAHR•koh POH•loh)

Building Your Vocabulary
tribe
steppe (STEHP)
terror (TEHR•uhr)

Reading Strategy
Organizing Information Use a diagram like the one below to show the accomplishments of Genghis Khan's reign.

Accomplishments

When & Where?

NATIONAL GEOGRAPHIC

1200

1206 Genghis Khan unites Mongols

1300

1271 Kublai Khan becomes China's emperor

1400

1368 Yuan (Mongol) dynasty falls

Karakorum
Baghdad
Khanbaliq (Beijing)

CHAPTER 12   China in the Middle Ages   **423**

---

1 FOCUS

SECTION OVERVIEW
This section describes the rise and accomplishments of the Mongol Empire.

BELLRINGER
SKILLBUILDER ACTIVITY

 Project **Daily Focus Skills Transparency 12–3** and have students answer questions. Discuss their responses.

Get Ready to Read!

Preteaching Vocabulary: Ask a volunteer to define the word *tribe. (a group of related families)* Then ask students to discuss why the institution of tribes is no longer such a powerful one in our society. What kind of groupings have taken its place?

Answers to Graphic: Mongol laws brought together in a new code; group of tribal chiefs created to help plan military campaigns; created most skilled fighting force in world at the time; conquered people on the steppes, in northern China, and in areas along the Silk Road

---

SECTION RESOURCES

Reproducible Masters
- Reproducible Lesson Plan 12–3
- Daily Lecture and Discussion Notes 12–3
- Vocabulary Activity 12–3
- Active Reading Note-Taking Guide 12–3
- Guided Reading Activity 12–3
- Section Quiz 12–3
- Reading Essentials and Study Guide 12–3

Transparencies
- Daily Focus Skills Transparency 12–3

Multimedia
- Interactive Tutor Self-Assessment CD-ROM
- ExamView® Pro Testmaker CD-ROM
- Presentation Plus! CD-ROM
- Glencoe BookLink CD-ROM

② TEACH

Literature Read aloud the poem "Kubla Khan" by English poet Samuel Taylor Coleridge. This famous work of the Romantic period describes the splendor of Kublai Khan's court. Ask students what Coleridge seems to admire about the court *(its fantastic beauty)* and to give examples. *(the caves of ice, the river, the incense tree)* **L1/ EL**

Daily Lecture and Discussion Notes 12–3

Use **Daily Lecture and Discussion Notes 12–3** for an outline of key concepts found in the section.

Reading Support L1/ EL

Use **Vocabulary Activity 12–3** to review important terms in the section.

Using Geography Skills

Answers:
1. south; 1209
2. the Himalaya, the Huang He, the Chang Jiang

The Mongols

Main Idea **Genghis Khan and his sons built the Mongol Empire, which stretched from the Pacific Ocean to Eastern Europe.**

Reading Focus Have you ever had the chance to ride a horse? For thousands of years, the horse was the most important form of transportation in the world. Read to learn how one people used their skills as horse riders to build a vast empire.

The Mongols lived in an area north of China called **Mongolia** (mahn•GOH•lee•uh). They were made up of **tribes,** or groups of related families, loosely joined together. The Mongols raised cattle, goats, sheep, and horses. They followed their herds as the animals grazed Mongolia's great **steppes** (STEHPS). Steppes are wide rolling grassy plains that stretch from the Black Sea to northern China.

From an early period in their history, the Mongols were known for two things. One was their ability to ride horses well. Mongols practically lived on horseback, learning to ride at age four or five.

The other skill for which the Mongols were known was the ability to wage war. They could fire arrows at enemies from a distance while charging at them. Then they would attack with spears and swords.

NATIONAL GEOGRAPHIC **Mongol Empire Under Genghis Khan** *1227*

KEY
Genghis Khan's empire, 1227
Mongol homeland
Campaign under Genghis Khan

Two-Point Equidistant projection

Mongol warrior ▼

Using Geography Skills

Under the reign of Genghis Khan, the Mongols conquered kingdoms across central Asia.
1. In what direction from Mongolia did Genghis Khan first strike? In what year?
2. What physical features may have prevented Genghis Khan from capturing more territory to the south?

Mongolian nomads today ▶

Reading Strategy READING THE TEXT

Evaluating One aspect of evaluating is assessing the value of the text being read. Evaluating includes making a judgment or forming an opinion about a text. As students read this section, ask them to evaluate the text by asking and recording answers to such questions as:

• How does the author support the statements that were made?
• Which statements are facts and which are opinions?
• Is there another point of view that is not expressed?
• Does the author show bias?

In your review of the section, have students share their evaluations of the text. **L2**

Who Was Genghis Khan? The man who would unite the Mongols was born in the 1160s. He was named Temujin (teh•MOO•juhn), which means "blacksmith." Temujin showed his leadership skills early. He was still a young man when he began to unite the Mongol tribes.

In 1206 a meeting of Mongol leaders took place somewhere in the **Gobi** (GOH•bee), a vast desert that covers parts of Mongolia and China. At that meeting, Temujin was elected **Genghis Khan** (GEHNG•guhs KAHN), which means "strong ruler." Genghis Khan brought together Mongol laws in a new code. He also created a group of tribal chiefs to help him plan military campaigns. From the time of his election until the end of his life, Genghis Khan fought to conquer the lands beyond Mongolia.

Genghis Khan gathered an army of more than 100,000 warriors. He placed his soldiers into well-trained groups. Commanding them were officers chosen for their abilities, not for their family ties. These changes made the Mongols the most skilled fighting force in the world at that time.

Genghis Khan began building his empire by conquering other people on the steppes. These victories brought him wealth and new soldiers to fill the army.

Mongol Empire 1294

KEY
- The Mongol Empire at its height
- Campaign of the Yuan dynasty (under Kublai Khan)
- Great Wall

0   1,000 mi.
0   1,000 km
Two-Point Equidistant projection

Using Geography Skills

The Mongols created the largest land empire in the history of the world.
1. What physical feature helped prevent the Mongols from capturing India?
2. What is the present-day name for the Mongols' capital at Khanbaliq?

Bronze plaque showing Genghis Khan ▶

CHAPTER 12   China in the Middle Ages   **425**

▲ In the battle scene shown here, Mongol troops storm across the Chang Jiang on a bridge made of boats. *After conquering northern China, what areas did the Mongols attack?*

Soon the Mongols were strong enough to attack major civilizations. In 1211 Mongol forces turned east and invaded China. Within three years, they had taken all of northern China. They then moved west and struck at the cities and kingdoms that controlled parts of the Silk Road.

Genghis Khan and his Mongol warriors became known for their cruelty and use of **terror** (TEHR•uhr). Terror refers to violent actions that are meant to scare people into surrendering, or giving up. Mongol warriors attacked, robbed, and burned cities. Within a short time, the Mongols became known for their fierce ways, and many people surrendered to them without fighting.

The Mongol Empire Genghis Khan died in 1227. His large empire was divided among his four sons. Under their leadership, the empire continued to expand. The Mongols swept into parts of eastern and central Europe. They also conquered much of southwest Asia. In 1258 the famous Muslim city of Baghdad fell to the Mongols. Mongol armies then pushed through Syria and Palestine to Egypt. They were finally stopped by the Muslim rulers of Egypt in 1260.

The Mongols united all of these different territories under their rule. Their empire reached from the Pacific Ocean in the east to Eastern Europe in the west and from Siberia in the north to the Himalaya in the south. It was the largest land empire the world had ever known.

Despite widespread destruction, the Mongols eventually brought peace to the lands they ruled. Peace encouraged trade, which helped the Mongols. Many of Asia's trade routes now lay in Mongol hands. The Mongols taxed the products traded over these roads and, as a result, grew wealthy.

The Mongols felt great respect for the advanced cultures they conquered. Sometimes they even adopted some of the beliefs and customs they encountered. For example, the Mongols in southwest Asia accepted Islam and adopted Arab, Persian, and Turkish ways.

The Mongols also learned many things from the Chinese. As they battled Chinese troops, they learned about gunpowder and its use as an explosive. They also saw the Chinese use the fire lance, a weapon that used gunpowder. Quickly, the Mongols adopted both gunpowder and the fire lance for use in battle. These new weapons made Mongol armies even more frightening to their enemies.

Reading Check **Analyze** What military and economic reasons explain why the Mongols were able to build an empire so quickly?

CRITICAL THINKING ACTIVITY

Making Generalizations Ask students to make a series of generalizations for each subsection. For example, a generalization for the subsection "Who Was Genghis Khan?" might be "Conquerors can create empires by using both superior fighting techniques and cruelty." Have students share their generalizations and the supporting details they used to arrive at them. If necessary, remind students that a generalization is a broad statement based on supporting details. **L2**

Biography

GENGHIS KHAN
c. A.D. 1167–1227

Mongol Leader

Was Genghis Khan a ruthless warrior who enjoyed causing death and destruction, or was he a skilled leader who improved the lives of those in his empire, or both? Genghis Khan built a huge empire across Asia using loyal, strong, and well-trained warriors. His men killed hundreds of thousands on the quest. Although the wars he and his sons fought were brutal and bloody, they eventually brought peace and prosperity to most of Asia.

Genghis Khan was named Temujin by his father, the Mongol chief Yisugei. Folklore says Temujin had a large blood clot in his right hand, which meant he was destined to become a great warrior. Temujin grew up in his father's camp along the Onon River in Mongolia.

Temujin's father arranged a marriage for his nine-year-old son. His wife came from another tribe, and the marriage helped bring wealth to his family. Borte, his wife at age ten, was beautiful. Temujin and Borte, had four sons when they both became older.

Years later, when his father was killed by the Tartars and his loyal warriors left the tribe, Temujin lost his wealth. His poverty and the disloyalty of his father's soldiers angered him so much that he decided to become a great warrior. Over time, Temujin became Ghengis Khan. When he died after falling from a horse, his son Ogodei was picked to succeed him.

▲ Genghis Khan

> "Life is short, I could not conquer the world."
> —attributed to Genghis Khan

▲ Genghis Khan's camp

Then and Now

In Mongolia today, Genghis Khan is considered a national hero. What do you think? Was Genghis Khan a villain or a hero?

Biography

TEACH

Although Genghis Khan has a reputation in the West as a cruel conqueror, in Mongolia today he is a national hero. Newspapers, schools, and other buildings are named after him.

Ask students which of our national heroes might have a different reputation in other countries. As examples, ask them how Sam Houston or Zachary Taylor might be viewed in Mexico. If necessary, remind students that these two men were American heroes of the war with Mexico that resulted in California, Texas, and much of the Southwest becoming part of the United States. **L1/ EL**

Then and Now

Answers will vary. Those who think he was a hero may cite his role in creating a great empire and spreading Mongol culture, while those who say he was a villain may claim that his cruelty and terrorist tactics prove this.

Reading List Generator CD-ROM

GLENCOE BOOKLINK   **RECOMMENDED READING**

Use the **Glencoe BookLink CD-ROM** to create customized reading lists based on your students' interests and reading levels. Below is an example based on content in this chapter. Also, see the Suggested Readings on pages 944–946 of the Appendix.

- **Dramer, Kim.** *Kublai Khan.* The great Mongol warrior ruled China and led the world's fiercest mounted army. Marco Polo marveled at the wealth of his court.
- **Reynolds, Jan.** *Mongolia: Vanishing Cultures.* Dawa and his cousin Olana live in Mongolia in a round tent called a *ger.* They help their fathers round up the family sheep, goats, and horses.
- **Ye, Ting-xing.** *Three Monks, No Water.* Three monks go thirsty as they each stubbornly wait for each other to fetch a bucket of water.

3 ASSESS

Assign Section 3 Review as homework or as an in-class activity.

⊚ Have students use the **Interactive Tutor Self-Assessment CD-ROM** to review the section.

Assessment L2

Assign **Section 3 Quiz** to assess mastery of the material found in the section.

Reading Support L1/ EL

Assign **Reading Essentials and Study Guide 12–3** to help students review section material.

Primary Source

The Mongols mistrusted Chinese people, so they often used other foreigners as aides. Marco Polo served in this capacity for some time.

Answer:
They were food for the gerfalcons and falcons that he kept there.

Mongol Rule in China

Main Idea The Mongols conquered China and created a new dynasty that tried to conquer Japan and began trading with the rest of Asia.

Reading Focus What does it mean to be tolerant? Read to find out how the Mongols used tolerance to rule the Chinese.

In 1260 the Mongols named Genghis Khan's grandson, Kublai, to be the new khan, or ruler. **Kublai Khan** (KOO•BLUH KAHN) continued the Mongol conquest of China that his father had begun. In 1264 Kublai moved his capital from **Karakorum**

Primary Source 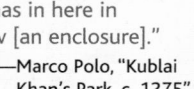 Kublai Khan's Park

Marco Polo recorded a description of the luxury in which Kublai Khan lived.

"[The palace wall] encloses and encircles fully sixteen miles of parkland well watered with springs and streams . . . Into this park there is no entry except by way of the palace. Here the Great Khan keeps game animals of all sorts . . . to provide food for the gerfalcons [large, arctic falcons] and other falcons which he has in here in mew [an enclosure]."

—Marco Polo, "Kublai Khan's Park, c. 1275"

▲ Kublai Khan presents golden tablets to Marco Polo

DBQ Document-Based Question

Why did Kublai Khan keep game animals—ones hunted for sport or food—in his park?

in Mongolia to **Khanbaliq** in northern China. Today the modern city of **Beijing** (BAY•JIHNG) stands on the site of the Mongols' Chinese capital.

What Did the Mongols Do in China?
In 1271 Kublai Khan decided to become China's next emperor. Within 10 years, the Mongols had conquered southern China and put an end to the Song dynasty. Kublai Khan started the Yuan (YOO•AHN) dynasty. *Yuan* means "beginning," and its name showed that the Mongols wanted to rule China for a long time. But the Yuan dynasty would last only about 100 years. Kublai would rule for 30 of those years.

Kublai Khan gave Mongol leaders the top jobs in China's government, but he knew he needed Chinese scholar-officials to run the government. So he let many of the Chinese keep their government jobs.

The Mongols were different from the Chinese in many ways. They had their own language, laws, and customs. This kept them separate from Chinese society. The Mongols were rulers at the top of Chinese society, but they did not mix with the Chinese people.

Like many Chinese, the Mongols were Buddhists. They were tolerant, however, of other religions. For example, Kublai Khan invited Christians, Muslims, and Hindus from outside China to practice their faiths and to win converts.

Under Mongol rule, China reached the height of its wealth and power. Its splendor drew foreigners who came to China over the Silk Road. Khanbaliq, the capital, became known for its wide streets, beautiful palaces, and fine homes.

One of the most famous European travelers to reach China was **Marco Polo** (MAHR•koh POH•loh). He came from the city of Venice in Italy. Kublai Khan was

---

INTERDISCIPLINARY CONNECTIONS ACTIVITY

Language Arts Marco Polo's book describes the wonders he saw in his travels in the empire of the Mongols and beyond. Ask students to consider this scenario: A traveler from a distant land has arrived in their community. The students have been chosen to show the visitor around. Have students write a chapter from a book this traveler would write about the students' community. Remind them that the traveler comes from a place that is as different from their home as China was from Marco Polo's Venice. Have volunteers read their accounts. **L2**

fascinated by Marco Polo's stories about his travels. For about 16 years, Kublai sent Polo on many fact-finding trips. When Polo finally returned to Europe, he wrote a book about his adventures. His accounts of the wonders of China amazed Europeans.

Trade and Conquest The Mongols ruled a large empire that stretched from China to eastern Europe. As a result, China prospered from increased trade with other areas. Goods such as silver, spices, carpets, and cotton flowed in from Europe and other parts of Asia. In return, China shipped out tea, silk, and porcelain. Europeans and Muslims also brought Chinese discoveries, such as steel, gunpowder, and the compass, back to their homelands.

The Mongols enlarged China's empire and conquered Vietnam and northern Korea. The rulers of Korea, called the Koryo, remained in power because they accepted

▲ This drawing from a historic map shows Marco Polo's journey along the Silk Road. *From what European city did Marco Polo travel?*

Mongol control. The Mongols forced thousands of Koreans to build warships. These ships were used by the Mongols to invade Japan. You will read about the Mongol invasions of Japan in a later chapter.

 Identify Who founded the Yuan dynasty?

Study Central™ Need help with the material in this section? Visit jat.glencoe.com

Section 3 Review

Reading Summary

Review the Main Ideas

- Under leaders such as Genghis Khan and his sons, the Mongol Empire expanded until it stretched from the Pacific Ocean to Eastern Europe, and from Siberia south to the Himalaya.

- Kublai Khan conquered China, which led to increased trade between China and other parts of the world.

What Did You Learn?

1. Who was Marco Polo?

2. What areas did the Mongols conquer?

Critical Thinking

3. **Sequencing Information** Draw a time line like the one below. Fill in details to show the Mongols' rise to power in China.

```
|----+----+----+----|
1160s              1281
Temujin            Mongols
born               conquer
                   China
```

4. **Analyze** How did the Mongols use terror in their conquests?

5. **Summarize** How did the Mongols benefit from their contact with the Chinese?

6. **Descriptive Writing** Imagine you are Marco Polo visiting Kublai Khan in Khanbaliq. Write a journal entry describing some of the things you are learning about the Mongol Empire under Kublai Khan.

CHAPTER 12   China in the Middle Ages   **429**

ENRICH

Ask students to research and write a short play about Kublai Khan and Marco Polo. Have them present their play to the class. **L2**

Answer: Kublai Khan

To help students understand section material, have them visit **Study Central™** at jat.glencoe.com

RETEACH

Have students create a word web for the concept "Mongol Empire." Ask them to exchange webs with a partner and discuss the information they have added to their webs. **L2**

④ CLOSE

Ask students if they would have liked to live in the Mongol Empire. Why or why not? Have them support their answers. **L2**

SECTION 3 REVIEW ANSWERS

1. Marco Polo was a European traveler who visited China in the 1200s.

2. China, the steppes of Asia, eastern and central Europe, southwest Asia, Vietnam, and northern Korea

3. 1206: Temujin elected Genghis Khan; 1211: Mongols invade China; 1227: Genghis Khan died; 1260: Kublai Khan ruler; 1264: Kublai Khan moves capital to Khanbaliq; 1271: Kublai Khan begins conquest of southern China

4. Mongol warriors used terror to make their enemies surrender without fighting.

5. The Mongols learned about gunpowder from fighting the Chinese, and they quickly used it in battle.

6. Answers will vary but should include relevant facts about the Mongols in China and Kublai Khan.

① FOCUS

SECTION OVERVIEW

This section focuses on the successors to the Mongols, the Ming dynasty, and how the Ming emperors began to reach out to other parts of the world.

BELLRINGER
SKILLBUILDER ACTIVITY

Project **Daily Focus Skills Transparency 12–4** and have students answer questions. Discuss their responses.

Get Ready to Read!

Preteaching Vocabulary: The word *novel* comes from a Latin word meaning "new." The novel was a new and different literary form in Europe in the 1600s. Ask students how a novel is different from other literary forms, such as poetry, drama, or essays.

Answers to Graphic: Chinese merchants settled in Southeast Asia and India. Trade made China wealthy. Officials grew worried and convinced the emperor to halt foreign trade.

Section 4
The Ming Dynasty

Get Ready to Read!

What's the Connection?

In Section 3, you read about the Mongol conquest. Eventually, the Chinese drove the Mongols out, and a new dynasty arose.

Focusing on the Main Ideas

• Ming rulers strengthened China's government and brought back peace and prosperity. *(page 431)*

• During the Ming dynasty, China sent a fleet to explore Asia and East Africa. *(page 433)*

Locating Places
Nanjing (NAHN•JIHNG)
Portugal (POHR•chih•guhl)

Meeting People
Zhu Yuanzhang
　(JOO　YOO•AHN•JAHNG)
Yong Le (YUNG　LEE)
Zheng He (JUNG　HUH)

Building Your Vocabulary
treason (TREE•zuhn)
census (SEHN•suhs)
novel (NAH•vuhl)
barbarian (bahr•BEHR•ee•uhn)

Reading Strategy
Cause and Effect Use a chart like the one below to show cause-and-effect links in China's early trade voyages.

Cause
Zheng He traveled to parts of Asia and Africa.

NATIONAL GEOGRAPHIC When & Where?

Beijing
Nanjing
Macao

1400 — **1500** — **1600**

1405 Zheng He begins first overseas voyage

1514 Portuguese ships arrive in China

1644 Ming dynasty falls

430 CHAPTER 12 China in the Middle Ages

SECTION RESOURCES

📂 **Reproducible Masters**
• Reproducible Lesson Plan 12–4
• Daily Lecture and Discussion Notes 12–4
• Vocabulary Activity 12–4
• Active Reading Note-Taking Guide 12–4
• Guided Reading Activity 12–4
• Section Quiz 12–4
• Reading Essentials and Study Guide 12–4

🖋 **Transparencies**
• Daily Focus Skills Transparency 12–4

Multimedia
🔘 Interactive Tutor Self-Assessment CD-ROM
🔘 ExamView® Pro Testmaker CD-ROM
🔘 Presentation Plus! CD-ROM
🔘 Vocabulary PuzzleMaker CD-ROM
🔘 Glencoe BookLink CD-ROM

The Rise of the Ming

Main Idea Ming rulers strengthened China's government and brought back peace and prosperity.

Reading Focus Think about all the different things the government does for people. Imagine if you were running the government and had to rebuild the country after a war. What would you do? Read to learn how the Ming rulers in China rebuilt their country after the Mongols left.

Kublai Khan died in 1294. A series of weak rulers followed him, and Mongol power began to decline. During the 1300s, problems mounted for the Yuan dynasty. Mongol groups in Mongolia to the north broke away. At the same time, many Chinese resented Mongol controls and wanted their own dynasty.

How Did the Ming Dynasty Begin? A series of rebellions finally drove out the Mongols. In 1368 a rebel leader named **Zhu Yuanzhang** (JOO YOO•AHN•JAHNG) became emperor. Zhu reunited the country and set up his capital at **Nanjing** (NAHN•JIHNG) in southern China. There, he founded the Ming, or "Brilliant," dynasty.

As emperor, Zhu took the name Hong Wu, or the "Military Emperor." He brought back order, but he also proved to be a cruel leader. Hong Wu trusted no one and killed officials he suspected of **treason** (TREE•zuhn), or disloyalty to the government. Hong Wu ruled China for 30 years. When he died in 1398, his son became emperor and took the name of **Yong Le** (YUNG LEE).

TEACH

The Importance of Titles Zhu Yuanzhang took a new name that meant "Military Emperor." Ask students to think of new titles for important political figures of our time. Have them explain why their suggestions are suitable. **L2**

Daily Lecture and Discussion Notes 12–4

Use **Daily Lecture and Discussion Notes 12–4** for an outline of key concepts found in the section.

Using Geography Skills

Answers:
1. the Great Wall
2. over 2,000 miles (about 3,220 km)

Skills Practice

Ask: What major region lay to the northwest of Ming China? *(Mongolia)* Which body of water is near Beijing? *(Yellow Sea)*

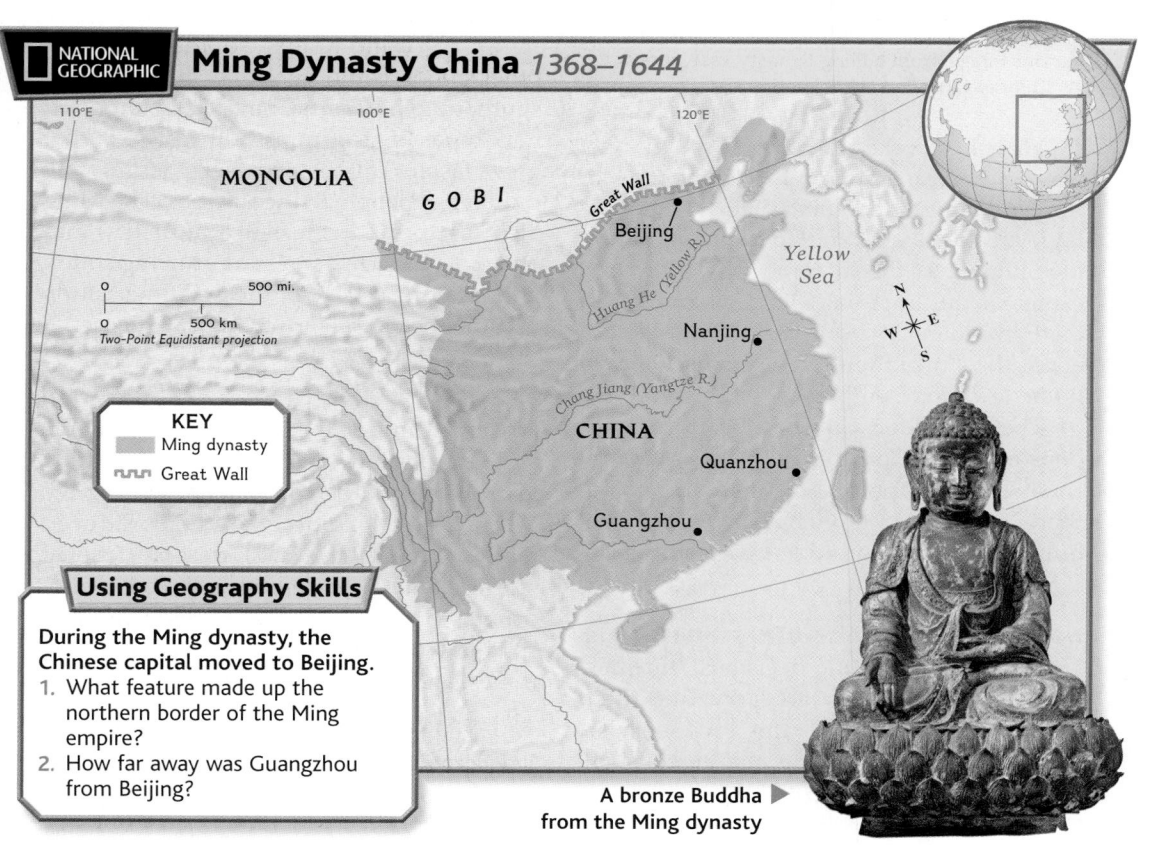

Ming Dynasty China *1368–1644*

Using Geography Skills

During the Ming dynasty, the Chinese capital moved to Beijing.
1. What feature made up the northern border of the Ming empire?
2. How far away was Guangzhou from Beijing?

A bronze Buddha ▶ from the Ming dynasty

Reading Support L1/ EL

Use **Vocabulary Activity 12-4** to review important terms in the section.

TIME TRAVELER

Today the Forbidden City is open to the public as a palace museum. There, visitors can see traditional palace architecture, enjoy the treasures displayed in the palace, and learn about the history and legends of the imperial family and its court.

✓ **Reading Check**

Answer: the home to China's emperors

Writing Activity

Have students write a short newspaper article about Zheng He's arrival in one of the places he visited. **L2**

▲ This image, from a Ming dynasty vase, shows Chinese farmworkers collecting tea.

Yong Le worked hard to show that he was a powerful emperor. In 1421 he moved the capital north to Beijing. There, he built a large area of palaces and government buildings known as the Imperial City. The very center of the Imperial City was known as the Forbidden City. Only top officials could enter the Forbidden City because it was home to China's emperors.

The Forbidden City had beautiful gardens and many palaces with thousands of rooms. The emperor and his court lived there in luxury for more than 500 years. The buildings of the Forbidden City still exist. You can visit them if you travel to China.

How Did the Ming Reform China?
Ming emperors made all the decisions, but they still needed officials to carry out their orders. They restored the civil service examinations and made the tests even harder. From time to time, Ming officials carried out a **census** (SEHN•suhs), or a count of the number of people. This helped them collect taxes more accurately.

With the strong government of the early Ming emperors providing peace and security, China's economy began to grow. Hong Wu ordered many of the canals and farms destroyed by the Mongols to be rebuilt and ordered people to move to the new farms. He also ordered new forests to be planted and new roads to be paved.

Agriculture thrived as farmers worked on the new lands and grew more crops. Ming rulers repaired and expanded the Grand Canal so that rice and other goods could again be shipped from southern to northern China. They imported new types of rice from southeast Asia that grew faster. This helped feed the growing number of people living in cities. The Ming also supported the silk industry and encouraged farmers to start growing cotton and weaving cloth. For the first time, cotton became the cloth worn by most Chinese.

Chinese Culture Chinese culture also advanced under the Ming. As merchants and artisans grew wealthier, they wanted to learn more and be entertained. During the Ming period, Chinese writers produced many **novels** (NAH•vuhls), or long fictional stories. The Chinese also enjoyed seeing dramas on stage. These works combined spoken words and songs with dances, costumes, and symbolic gestures.

✓ **Reading Check** **Identify** What was the Forbidden City?

DIFFERENTIATED INSTRUCTION

Verbal/Linguistic: Ask students to prepare and present "live" TV news interviews with explorer Zheng He. They will portray a Chinese reporter meeting the explorer at the dock on his return from his travels. Have students playing reporters prepare a list of questions for the explorer. Ask the student playing Zheng He to be prepared to answer the questions.

English Learners: Have students write a short script with directions for a "live" television interview.

Gifted and Talented: Have students write an official proclamation in celebration of Zheng He as a part of their TV interview.

📂 Refer to *Inclusion Strategies for the Middle School Social Studies Classroom* in the TCR.

China Explores the World

Main Idea During the Ming dynasty, China sent a fleet to explore Asia and East Africa.

Reading Focus You probably have heard of Christopher Columbus and his trip to America. Imagine if China had sent ships to America first. Read to learn about Chinese explorations of Asia and East Africa.

Early Ming emperors were curious about the world outside of China. They also wanted to increase China's influence abroad. To reach these goals, Ming emperors built a large fleet of ships. The new ships usually traveled along China's coast. However, they could also sail in the open sea.

Who Was Zheng He? From 1405 to 1431, Emperor Yong Le sent the fleet on seven overseas voyages. The emperor wanted to trade with other kingdoms, show off China's power, and demand that weaker kingdoms pay tribute to China.

The leader of these journeys was a Chinese Muslim and court official named **Zheng He** (JUNG HUH). Zheng He's voyages were quite impressive. His first fleet had 62 large ships, 250 smaller ships, and almost 28,000 men. The largest ship was over 440 feet (134 m) long. That made it more than *five times* as long as the *Santa María* that Christopher Columbus sailed almost 90 years later!

Religion Ask students to write a paragraph explaining how the fact that Zheng He was a Muslim might have helped him explore the lands he visited and make contact with the people who lived there. (*Students should recognize that Muslims lived in many of the places Zheng He visited, including Arabia, Persia, India, and Africa.*) **L1/ EL**

CONNECTING ACROSS TIME

Following the end of Zheng He's voyages, China remained isolated for many years. Have students briefly research China's isolationism and its later effects, such as the Opium War or Boxer Rebellion. Ask students to discuss whether a country would want to pursue such a policy of isolationism today. **L2**

NATIONAL GEOGRAPHIC
Zheng He's Voyages 1405–1433

KEY
Exploration routes of Zheng He's fleet

Mercator projection

Zheng He ▶

Using Geography Skills

Zheng He's voyages took him to faraway lands from which he brought back many exotic items.
1. What cities in Africa did Zheng He visit?
2. About how far did Zheng He travel?

Using Geography Skills

Answers:
1. Mogadishu, Malindi, Mombasa
2. Using the scale, students may approximate up to 20,000 miles (32,187 km) based on the indicated routes. Then he came home.

Skills Practice

Ask: What was the farthest south Zheng He sailed? (*Java*) The farthest west? (*Mombasa*)

CHAPTER 12   China in the Middle Ages   433

CRITICAL THINKING ACTIVITY

Analyzing Information Even though Zheng He's voyages increased trade and spread Chinese culture, Chinese officials decided to stop further exploration. Ask students what they might have said to the emperor to convince him to allow the voyages to continue. Then have another group come up with rebuttals to these reasons. (*Possible reasons to encourage exploration include increased trade and greater wealth for China and the importation of beneficial technologies and new, possibly better, ideas about government, science, and other fields. Rebuttals might include that the money could be spent better in China and that the ideas from abroad would be disruptive and possibly dangerous to the rulers.*) **L2**

Biography

TEACH

One of the most important results of Zheng He's voyages was the creation of Chinese colonies throughout Southeast Asia. Large Chinese communities still exist today in such countries as Malaysia, Thailand, Vietnam, and Cambodia.

Ask students how the young Zheng He's desire to learn influenced his later career. (*His knowledge of foreign languages, especially Arabic, made him a good choice to lead the voyages of exploration to the Middle East, and his knowledge of geography helped him navigate on trips.*)
L1/ EL

Then and Now

Students' answers will vary based on their personal experiences. Student research should be based on credible sources.

ZHENG HE
1371–1433
Zheng He ▶

Chinese Navigator

The famous Chinese navigator Zheng He was born in Kunyang in southwest China in 1371. His birth name was Ma He, and he was from a poor Chinese Muslim family. Scholars say that his father and grandfather were honored hajjis—people who successfully made the pilgrimage to Makkah in Arabia. Little did Ma He know that his life would also involve travel. His seven missions across the oceans earned him heroic honors.

His father died when Ma He was little. As a child, Ma He was taken prisoner by the Chinese army. To overcome his sad life, Ma He turned to education. He learned different languages, including Arabic, and studied philosophy and geography. With his language skills and knowledge of the outside world, 10-year-old Ma He became a valuable imperial aide to Chinese officials.

By age 12, he was an assistant to a young prince named Zhu Di. Ma He accompanied the prince on several military missions. The prince, who later became the Emperor Yong Le, became a friend of Ma He. The emperor changed Ma He's name to the honored surname Zheng. Soon after, Zheng He was assigned to lead a fleet of Chinese ships across the Indian Ocean, beginning the career that would make him famous. He's voyages to new lands opened the door for trade among China, India, and Africa. Many of the Chinese moved abroad to sell Chinese goods. Those who learned and spoke more than one language, like Zheng He, prospered.

"We have set eyes on barbarian regions far away."

–Zheng He, as quoted in *Chinese Portraits*

Then and Now

What "Made in China" products do you use on a daily basis? Do research to find out what percentage of goods imported to the United States are from China.

Reading List Generator CD-ROM

GLENCOE BOOKLINK

RECOMMENDED READING

Use the **Glencoe BookLink CD-ROM** to create customized reading lists based on your students' interests and reading levels. Below is an example based on content in this chapter. Also, see the Suggested Readings on pages 944–946 of the Appendix.

- **Andersen, Hans Christian.** *The Nightingale.* The Emperor of China loves to listen to the nightingale's song. Then he is given an artificial bird made of gold. The real nightingale is sent away.
- **Bosse, Malcolm.** *The Examination.* In sixteenth-century China, two brothers make a dangerous journey to take the difficult government examination.
  Louie, Ai-Ling. *Yeh-Shen: A Cinderella Story from China.* Long ago in China, there lived a beautiful girl named Yeh-Shen. But her stepmother and stepsister treated her badly.

Where Did Zheng He Travel? Zheng He took his first fleet to southeast Asia. In later voyages, he reached India, sailed up the Persian Gulf to Arabia, and even landed in East Africa. In these areas, Zheng He traded Chinese goods, such as silk, paper, and porcelain. He brought back silver, spices, wood, and other goods. From Africa, Zheng He returned home with giraffes and other animals for the emperor's zoo.

As a result of Zheng He's voyages, Chinese merchants settled in Southeast Asia and India. There, they not only traded goods but also spread Chinese culture. Chinese merchants at home and abroad grew rich from the trade of the voyages and added to China's wealth.

Despite these benefits, Chinese officials complained that the trips cost too much. They also said that trips were bad for China's way of life because they brought in new ideas from the outside world and helped merchants become rich.

Confucius had taught that people should place loyalty to society ahead of their own desires. To the officials, China's merchants were disobeying this teaching by working to gain money for themselves.

After Zheng He's death, the Confucian officials persuaded the emperor to stop the voyages. The boats were dismantled, and no more ships capable of long distance ocean travel were allowed to be built. As a result, China's trade with other countries sharply declined. Within 50 years, the shipbuilding technology was forgotten.

The Europeans Arrive in China Chinese officials were not able to cut off all of China's contacts with the outside world. In 1514 a fleet from the European country of **Portugal** (POHR•chih•guhl) arrived off the coast of China. It was the first time Europeans had ever sailed to China and the first direct

▲ Italian missionary Matteo Ricci (left) was one of the most famous Europeans to visit China. He helped in the development of math and science in China during the late 1500s.

contact between China and Europe since the journeys of Marco Polo.

The Portuguese wanted China to trade with their country. They also wanted to convince the Chinese to become Christians. At the time, the Ming government was not impressed by the Portuguese. China was at the height of its power and did not feel threatened by outsiders. The Chinese thought the Europeans were **barbarians** (bahr•BEHR•ee•uhns), or uncivilized people.

At first, the Chinese refused to trade with the Portuguese, but by 1600, they had allowed Portugal to set up a trading post at the port of Macao (muh•KOW) in southern China. Goods were carried on European ships between Macao and Japan. Still, trade between China and Europe remained limited.

Despite restrictions, ideas from Europe did reach China. Christian missionaries traveled to China on European ships. Many of these missionaries were Jesuits, a special group of Roman Catholic priests. They

CHAPTER 12   China in the Middle Ages   **435**

③ ASSESS

Assign Section 4 Review as homework or as an in-class activity.

🔘 Have students use the **Interactive Tutor Self-Assessment CD-ROM** to review the section.

Assessment L2

Assign **Section 4 Quiz** to assess mastery of the material found in the section.

Reading Support L1/ EL

Assign **Reading Essentials and Study Guide 12–4** to help students review section material.

Reading Charts Have students create a chart or other visual organizer that shows the influence of Confucian philosophy on Chinese trade and voyages of exploration. (*Graphics should show that Confucian philosophy eventually ended the voyages, because the voyages placed individual needs above society and made merchants wealthy.*) **L2**

INTERDISCIPLINARY CONNECTIONS ACTIVITY

Art Ask a group of students to learn more about the arts of the Ming period. While pottery is probably the best-known Ming art form, suggest that students also investigate architecture (such as seen in the Forbidden City), novels and dramatic works, textiles and costumes, and other media. Have them share their findings with the class in a multimedia presentation. **L2**

Caption Answer: Macao

ENRICH

Ask students to research the history of the Forbidden City and present their findings to the class. **L3**

Answer: Ming emperors became too powerful, then weak. High taxes led to peasant revolts.

History Online

To help students understand section material, have them visit **Study Central™** at jat.glencoe.com

RETEACH

Have students review and explain reasons why the Mongol and Ming dynasties fell. **L1**

4 CLOSE

Reading Strategy

Ask students to summarize Chinese attitudes toward people who are not Chinese. **L2**

▲ This porcelain bowl is from the Ming dynasty.
Where in China did the Portuguese set up a trading post?

were highly educated, and their scientific knowledge impressed the Chinese. To get China to accept European ideas, the Jesuits brought with them clocks, eyeglasses, and scientific instruments. Although they tried, the Jesuits did not convince many Chinese to become Christians.

Why Did the Ming Dynasty Fall? After a long era of prosperity and growth, the Ming dynasty began to decline. Ming emperors had gathered too much power into their own hands. With the emperor having so much control, officials had little desire to make improvements. As time passed, Ming rulers themselves became weak. Greedy officials who lived in luxury took over the country. They placed heavy taxes on the peasants, who began to revolt.

As law and order disappeared, a people called the Manchus attacked China's northern border. The Manchus lived to the northeast of the Great Wall in an area known today as Manchuria. The Manchus defeated Chinese armies and captured Beijing. In 1644 they set up a new dynasty.

✓ **Reading Check** **Cause and Effect** What caused the Ming dynasty to decline and fall?

Section 4 Review

History Online

Study Central™ Need help with the material in this section? Visit jat.glencoe.com

Reading Summary

Review the Main Ideas

• The Ming dynasty rebuilt and reformed China after the Mongols were driven out. Their dynasty restored peace and prosperity to China.

• During the Ming dynasty, China's contacts with the outside world increased as Zheng He led fleets to faraway lands and European ships began arriving in China.

What Did You Learn?

1. What was the purpose of the Forbidden City and where was it located?

2. How did the Chinese react to the arrival of Portuguese traders in 1514?

Critical Thinking

3. **Organizing Information** Draw a diagram like the one below. Fill in details about the achievements of the Ming dynasty.

Ming Dynasty Achievements

4. **Cause and Effect** Why did Ming rulers repair and expand the Grand Canal?

5. **Summarize** Why did the Emperor Yong Le send Zheng He on his voyages? How did Zheng He's voyages benefit China?

6. **Persuasive Writing** Imagine you are living in China at the time of Zheng He's voyages. Write a newspaper editorial either for or against the voyages. Describe why you think the voyages are aiding or hurting the country as a whole.

7. **Predict** What do you think happened after China tried to limit trade?

436   CHAPTER 12   China in the Middle Ages

SECTION 4 REVIEW ANSWERS

1. home to China's emperors; in Beijing

2. The Chinese thought they were barbarians and at first refused to trade with them.

3. Answers should include details from the text.

4. so that rice and other goods could be shipped to northern China

5. to show off China's power and open trade between China and other countries; Chinese traders settled in Southeast Asia and India, where they traded goods and spread Chinese culture; China's wealth grew

6. Answers will vary.

7. Answers will vary. Students may recognize that limiting contact and friendly relations may lead to conflict.

Section 1 China Reunites

Vocabulary
warlord
economy
reform
monastery

Focusing on the Main Ideas
• The Sui and Tang dynasties reunited and rebuilt China after years of war. *(page 409)*
• Buddhism became popular in China and spread to Korea and Japan. *(page 412)*
• The Tang dynasty returned to the ideas of Confucius and created a new class of scholar-officials. *(page 413)*

Section 2 Chinese Society

Vocabulary
porcelain
calligraphy

Focusing on the Main Ideas
• The Tang dynasty strengthened China's economy by supporting farming and trade. *(page 417)*
• The Chinese developed new technologies, such as steelmaking and printing. *(page 418)*
• During the Tang and the Song dynasties, China enjoyed a golden age of art and literature. *(page 420)*

▲ Porcelain figures from the Tang dynasty

Section 3 The Mongols in China

Vocabulary
tribe
steppe
terror

Focusing on the Main Ideas
• Genghis Khan and his sons built the Mongol Empire, which stretched from the Pacific Ocean to Eastern Europe. *(page 424)*
• The Mongols conquered China and created a new dynasty that tried to conquer Japan and began trading with the rest of Asia. *(page 428)*

Section 4 The Ming Dynasty

Vocabulary
treason
census
novel
barbarian

Focusing on the Main Ideas
• Ming rulers strengthened China's government and brought back peace and prosperity. *(page 431)*
• During the Ming dynasty, China sent a fleet to explore Asia and East Africa. *(page 433)*

CHAPTER 12   China in the Middle Ages   **437**

PREVIEW/REVIEW

Vocabulary Activity Have students create a crossword puzzle, with clues, using at least 10 key terms from this chapter. Have students exchange puzzles with a partner and complete the puzzles.

⊙ **Vocabulary PuzzleMaker CD-ROM**

⊙ **Interactive Tutor Self-Assessment CD-ROM**

CONDENSE

🗁 Chapter 12 **Guided Reading Activities**

⊚ **StudentWorks Plus™ CD-ROM (with Audio Program)**

RETEACH

🗁 **Differentiated Instruction Activity 12**

🗁 Chapter 12 *Reading Essentials and Study Guide*

> ### CHAPTER CULMINATING ACTIVITY
>
> Have students finish the Chapter Culminating Activity from page 404D.
>
> 🗁 Suggestions for rubrics may be found in the *Quizzes, Tests, and Authentic Assessment (with Rubrics)* booklet.

Reading Strategy READ TO WRITE

Writing a Memo As they read the chapter, have students take notes about the changing attitudes of China's rulers toward other nations and peoples. Have them use this information to write a memo to an emperor of China. In the memo, they should persuade the emperor to adopt either an open or closed attitude toward people who are not Chinese. Students should support their recommendation with reasoning and details from the chapter.

• **L1** students should include one or two reasons and details in their memo.
• **L2** students should include several appropriate details and reasons and attempt grammar mastery.
• **L3** students should provide strong and persuasive support for their opinion.

Review Vocabulary

1. c
2. d
3. f
4. g
5. b
6. h
7. a
8. e

Review Main Ideas

9. They reunited and rebuilt China after years of war.

10. They returned to ideas of Confucius and created a new class of scholar-officials.

11. by supporting and improving farming and trade

12. steelmaking, printing, gunpowder, compass

13. The Mongols had a powerful army and used terror to get people to surrender.

14. became a ruling class at the top, but kept bureaucracy in place; were tolerant of differences in religion, language, laws, and customs

15. strengthened government, brought peace and prosperity

16. They wanted to trade with China and to teach the Chinese about Christianity.

Review Vocabulary

Match the word in the first column with its definition in the second column.

___ 1. treason   **a.** groups of related families loosely joined together

___ 2. warlord   **b.** change that brings improvement

___ 3. terror   **c.** disloyalty to the government

___ 4. economy   **d.** military leader who also runs a government

___ 5. reform   **e.** a count of the number of people

___ 6. steppe   **f.** violent actions meant to scare others

___ 7. tribe   **g.** organized way to buy, sell, and produce

___ 8. census   **h.** wide grassy plain

Review Main Ideas

Section 1 • China Reunites

9. What did the Sui and Tang dynasties do to improve China?

10. How did the Tang rulers change China?

Section 2 • Chinese Society

11. How did Tang rulers strengthen China's economy?

12. What kind of technologies did the Chinese develop?

Section 3 • The Mongols in China

13. Why were the Mongols able to build a huge empire?

14. How did the Mongols rule China?

Section 4 • The Ming Dynasty

15. How did the Ming rulers affect China?

16. Why did the Portuguese want to explore Africa and Asia?

Critical Thinking

17. **Analyze** How did civil service exams help China develop a strong government?

18. **Explain** How did Confucianism change during the Tang dynasty?

19. **Predict** How do you think China would be different today if Tang rulers had not cracked down on Buddhism in A.D. 845?

20. **Hypothesize** The Mongols conquered a vast amount of land, but their Yuan dynasty lasted only about 100 years. Create a hypothesis that might explain this situation.

Review — Reading Skill — Inferences

Reading Between the Lines

21. Poet Duo Fu's poem "Spring Landscape," on page 421, described what it was like in the capital after a rebellion left the city in ruins. One of the lines from his poem appears here. What can you infer from this line of poetry?

"By now, letters are worth ten thousand in gold."

To review this skill, see pages 406–407.

Critical Thinking

17. Because the examinations made positions based on ability, they made sure that government officials were highly qualified.

18. It absorbed some Buddhist and Daoist beliefs and changed from a system of moral principles to a religion.

19. Predictions will vary but should include speculation that more Chinese might believe in Buddhism and that some of the medieval monasteries and temples might still remain.

20. Hypotheses will vary but should include that fighting and organizing the government require different skills.

Geography Skills

Study the map below and answer the following questions.

22. **Location** What was the length of the Grand Canal?

23. **Human/Environment Interaction** What part of Asia did the Tang control that helped China's trade?

24. **Region** What geographic features do you think helped the Tang dynasty expand?

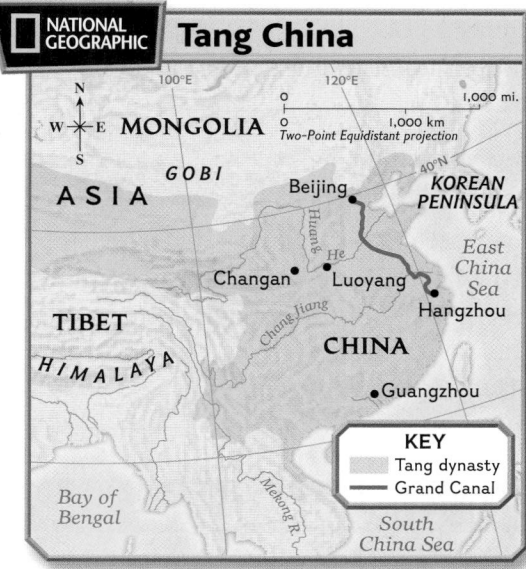

NATIONAL GEOGRAPHIC Tang China

KEY
Tang dynasty
Grand Canal

Read to Write

25. **Persuasive Writing** Imagine you are a Portuguese merchant. You have just traveled to China to persuade the Chinese people to trade with your country. Work with a small group to create a script detailing the dialogue that would take place between the Portuguese merchant and a representative of the Chinese government. (Suppose someone is acting as a translator, but do not incorporate the translator into your dialogue.)

26. **Using Your** [FOLDABLES] On your foldable, add details to the main headings in Section 2. Think about how the changes and arts described there might have had an impact on people's lives. Then write three journal

History Online
Self-Check Quiz To help you prepare for the Chapter Test, visit jat.glencoe.com

entries that tell how these things have affected your family's life in China in the Middle Ages. Illustrate your entries.

Using Technology

27. **Building a Database** Use the Internet to gather more information about Genghis Khan. Use the information to create a database for your classmates. Include text, images, and perhaps a time line. Your database should contain information about Genghis Khan as a person and as a ruler.

Linking Past and Present

28. **Expository Writing** Write a short report that describes similarities and differences between the Imperial City of the Ming dynasty and the United States capital, Washington, D.C.

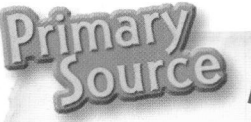

Primary Source Analyze

John of Plano Carpini, a friar, explained why the Mongols were such skilled warriors.

"Their children begin as soon as they are two or three years old to ride and manage horses and to gallop on them, and they are given bows to suit their stature [size] and are taught to shoot; they are extremely agile [move quickly and easily] and also intrepid [fearless]."

—John of Plano Carpini, *History of the Mongols*

DBQ Document-Based Questions

29. Why did each Mongol warrior shoot so well with a bow and arrows?

30. What other qualities made the Mongols excellent warriors?

History Online
Have students visit the Web site at jat.glencoe.com to review Chapter 12 and take the **Self-Check Quiz.**

Using Technology

27. Databases will vary but should reflect solid research and include details about the life of Genghis Khan.

Linking Past and Present

28. Similarities: important government buildings; an area that is off-limits to visitors; Differences: Washington, D.C., does not have palaces; most government buildings in Washington, D.C., can be toured by visitors

Primary Source

29. They begin training at two or three years of age.

30. They are agile and intrepid.

Bonus Question

Ask: Do civilizations, such as China in the Middle Ages, advance more in periods of peace or in periods of war? Why? (*Answers should use information from the chapter, knowledge of world history and current events, and sound reasoning to support the opinion.*)

Reading Skill

21. Since a letter would come from a relative, proving that he or she is alive, it would be very valuable.

Geography Skills

22. about 700 miles (1,126 km)

23. central Asia where the Silk Road was located and the eastern coastline

24. rivers and seas

Read to Write

25. Scripts will vary but should be persuasive and reflect information in the chapter.

26. [FOLDABLES] Entries will vary but should accurately use details from the text to describe everyday life.

Chapter 13 Resources

Note: The following materials may be used when teaching Chapter 13.
Section level support materials are shown at point of use in the margins of the Teacher Wraparound Edition.

TEACHING TRANSPARENCIES

- Graphic Organizer Transparencies with Teaching Strategy and Student Activity **L2**
- Cause-and-Effect Transparencies with Teaching Strategy and Student Activity **L2**
- Then and Now Transparencies with Teaching Strategy and Student Activity **L2**
- In-text Map Transparency with Teaching Strategy and Student Activity **L1**
- Map Transparencies with Overlay, Teaching Strategy, and Student Activity **L2**

DIFFERENTIATED INSTRUCTION

- Differentiated Instruction Activity 13
- Time Line Activity 13
- Primary Source Reading 13 (with Document-Based Questions)
- Inclusion Strategies for the Middle School Social Studies Classroom
- StudentWorks Plus™ CD-ROM (with Audio Program)

READING SUPPORT

- Take-Home Review Activity 13 **L2**
- World Literature Reading 13 **L2**
- Workbook Activity 13 **L1**
- Reading Strategies for the Social Studies Classroom **L1/ EL**

ASSESSMENT

- Authentic Assessment Activity 13 **L1/ EL**
- Chapter 13 Test Form A **L2**
- Chapter 13 Test Form B **L2**
- ExamView® Pro Testmaker CD-ROM

INTERDISCIPLINARY CONNECTIONS

- Geography and History Activity 13 **L2**
- People to Meet Activity 13 **L2**
- Economics Activity 13 **L2**
- Citizenship and Service Learning Activity 13 **L2**

SPANISH RESOURCES

- Spanish Reading Essentials and Study Guide
- Spanish Guided Reading Activities
- Spanish Quizzes, Tests, and Authentic Assessment (with Rubrics)
- Spanish Take-Home Review Activities

MULTIMEDIA

- ExamView® Pro Testmaker CD-ROM
- Glencoe Skillbuilder Interactive Workbook CD-ROM, Level 1
- Interactive Tutor Self-Assessment CD-ROM
- MindJogger Videoquiz
- Presentation Plus! CD-ROM
- StudentWorks Plus™ CD-ROM (with Audio Program)
- TeacherWorks CD-ROM
- Vocabulary PuzzleMaker CD-ROM
- *World History: Journey Across Time* Video Program
- World History Primary Source Document Library CD-ROM

STANDARDIZED ASSESSMENT SKILLS

- Standardized Test Skills Practice Workbook Activity 13 **L2**
- Critical Thinking Skills Activity 13 **L2**

Teaching strategies have been coded with suggested ability levels. However, most are suitable for all levels.

L1 BASIC activities for all students

L2 AVERAGE activities for average to above-average students

L3 CHALLENGING activities for above-average students

EL ENGLISH LANGUAGE activities

Chapter 13 Resources

TIME MANAGEMENT

Chapter Introduction	Section 1	Section 2	Section 3	Chapter Wrap-Up
1 Day	2 Days	2 Days	2 Days	1 Day

Block Scheduling Activities that are suited to use within the block scheduling framework are identified by:

0:00 **OUT OF TIME?** Assign the Chapter 13 *Reading Essentials and Study Guide.** 📁

SECTION RESOURCES

DAILY OBJECTIVES	REPRODUCIBLE RESOURCES	MULTIMEDIA RESOURCES
Section 1 **The Rise of African Civilizations** 1. The African continent has a varied landscape that gave rise to many diverse cultures. 2. Kingdoms in West Africa and East Africa developed centers of trade, where people exchanged a variety of goods and ideas.	📁 Reproducible Lesson Plan 13–1 📁 Daily Lecture and Discussion Notes 13–1 📁 Vocabulary Activity 13–1 📁 Active Reading Note-Taking Guide 13–1 📁 Guided Reading Activity 13–1* 📁 Section Quiz 13–1* 📁 Reading Essentials and Study Guide 13–1*	🖎 Daily Focus Skills Transparency 13–1 ◉ Interactive Tutor Self-Assessment CD-ROM ◉ ExamView® Pro Testmaker CD-ROM ◉ Presentation Plus! CD-ROM
Section 2 **Africa's Government and Religion** 1. The growth of empires led to centralized governments ruled by kings. 2. Traditional religions and Islam shaped African cultures.	📁 Reproducible Lesson Plan 13–2 📁 Daily Lecture and Discussion Notes 13–2 📁 Vocabulary Activity 13–2 📁 Active Reading Note-Taking Guide 13–2 📁 Guided Reading Activity 13–2* 📁 Section Quiz 13–2* 📁 Reading Essentials and Study Guide 13–2*	🖎 Daily Focus Skills Transparency 13–2 ◉ Interactive Tutor Self-Assessment CD-ROM ◉ ExamView® Pro Testmaker CD-ROM ◉ Presentation Plus! CD-ROM ◉ Glencoe BookLink CD-ROM
Section 3 **African Society and Culture** 1. The Bantu migrations spread common ideas to much of Africa. 2. The African slave trade disrupted African society and carried African peoples and cultures around the world.	📁 Reproducible Lesson Plan 13–3 📁 Daily Lecture and Discussion Notes 13–3 📁 Vocabulary Activity 13–3 📁 Active Reading Note-Taking Guide 13–3 📁 Guided Reading Activity 13–3* 📁 Section Quiz 13–3* 📁 Reading Essentials and Study Guide 13–3*	🖎 Daily Focus Skills Transparency 13–3 ◉ Interactive Tutor Self-Assessment CD-ROM ◉ ExamView® Pro Testmaker CD-ROM ◉ Presentation Plus! CD-ROM ◉ Vocabulary PuzzleMaker CD-ROM ◉ Glencoe BookLink CD-ROM

*Also available in Spanish

Use our Web site for additional resources. All essential content is covered in the Student Edition.

You and your students can visit jat.glencoe.com, the Web site companion to *World History: Journey Across Time*. This innovative integration of electronic and print media offers your students a wealth of opportunities. The student text directs students to the Web site for the following options:

- Chapter Overviews
- Self-Check Quizzes
- Study Central™
- Student Web Activities
- Multi-Language Glossaries

Answers to the student Web activities are provided for you in the **Web Activity Lesson Plans.** Additional Web resources and ePuzzles and games are also available.

Videotape programs are available from Glencoe as supplements to the chapters.

To order, call Glencoe at 1-800-334-7344. To find classroom resources to accompany many of these videos, check the following home pages:

A&E Television: www.aande.com
The History Channel: www.historychannel.com

MEETING SPECIAL NEEDS

In addition to the Differentiated Instruction strategies, the following resources are suitable for students with special needs:

- *ExamView® Pro Testmaker CD-ROM* allows teachers to tailor tests by reducing answer choices.
- *StudentWorks Plus™ CD-ROM (with Audio Program)* includes the entire narrative of the student edition so that less-proficient readers can listen to the words as they read them.
- The *Reading Essentials and Study Guide* provides the same content as the student edition but is written two grade levels below the textbook.
- *Guided Reading Activities* give less-proficient readers point-by-point instructions to increase comprehension as they read each textbook section.
- *Differentiated Instruction Activities* include a stimulating collection of readings and activities for students of all levels.

NATIONAL GEOGRAPHIC TEACHER'S CORNER

Index to National Geographic Magazine:
The following articles relate to this chapter:

- "Surviving the Sahara," by John Hare, December 2002.
- "Djénné: West Africa's Eternal City," by Karen Lange, June 2001.
- "Keepers of the Faith: The Living Legacy of Aksum," by Candice Millard, July 2001.

National Geographic Society Products:
To order the following, call National Geographic at 1–800–368–2728

- *Ancient Africa* (GeoKit)
- *PicturePack: Ancient Civilizations: Ancient Africa* (Transparencies)

NGS ONLINE

Access National Geographic's new dynamic MapMachine Web site and other geography resources at:

www.nationalgeographic.com
www.nationalgeographic.com/maps

Meeting NCSS Standards

World History: Journey Across Time

The following standards are highlighted in Chapter 13:

Section 1 III **People, Places, and Environments:** B, D, E, F

VII **Production, Distribution, and Consumption:** B, E, I, F

VIII **Science, Technology, and Society:** B

Section 2 I **Culture:** D, F

V **Individuals, Groups, and Institutions:** A, B, G

VI **Power, Authority, and Governance:** B, C, D, E, F

Section 3 IV **Individual Development and Identity:** A, B, C, D, F

V **Individuals, Groups, and Institutions:** A, B

IX **Global Connections:** B

State and Local Objectives

_____

_____

Timesaving Tools

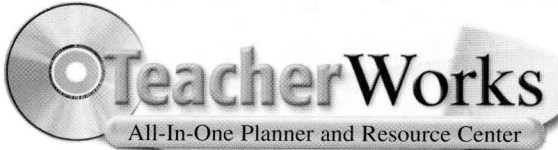

TeacherWorks
All-In-One Planner and Resource Center

● **Interactive Teacher Edition** Access your Teacher Wraparound Edition and your classroom resources with a few easy clicks.

● **Interactive Lesson Planner** Organize your week, month, semester, or year with all the lesson helps you need to make teaching creative and relevant.

Use Glencoe's **Presentation Plus!** multimedia teacher tool to easily present dynamic lessons that visually excite your students. Using Microsoft PowerPoint® you can customize the presentations to create your own personalized lessons.

FOLDABLES™
Study Organizer
Dinah Zike's Foldables

Foldables are three-dimensional, interactive graphic organizers that help students practice basic writing skills, review key vocabulary terms, and identify main ideas. Every chapter contains a foldable activity, with additional chapter activities found in the *Reading and Study Skills Foldables* booklet. You can use the foldables as they are presented, or modify them to suit the needs of your individual class.

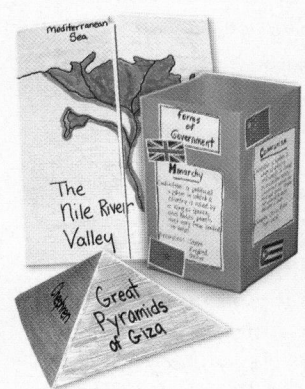

Planning Ahead

CHAPTER CULMINATING ACTIVITY

The Chapter Culminating Activity will help students organize and learn the important information from the chapter. Begin the chapter with this activity, and have students complete it as a culminating activity.

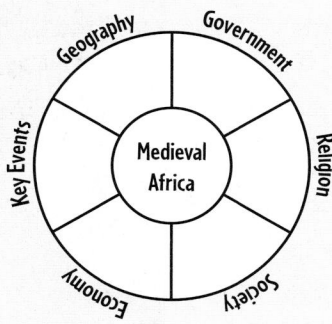

CREATING A DATA DISK

Purpose A data disk helps students organize information about a central topic or idea. It is a circular chart that puts a new spin on note taking. If the disk is large enough, several students can work on it at the same time.

Introduction to Modeling

1. Begin by determining student knowledge of African geography. **Ask: Is Africa bigger or smaller than the United States? What ocean links Africa and the United States? What kinds of landscapes does Africa have?** Have students write down responses.

2. Explain to students that they are going to create data disks to help them organize information about Africa, such as geographic features and information about African society. Tell them that a data disk is a kind of graphic organizer. Draw the following disk on the board or an overhead transparency:

3. Have students make their own data disks. For a group project, you may wish to have students create a large disk on a poster board or butcher paper.

4. Ask students to write a question, such as What is Africa's geography like?, under each head on the disk. Tell them to collect information that answers their questions as they read the chapter and add that information to their data disks. If space becomes an issue, they should write their questions on separate pieces of paper or outside the disk to provide room for the answers.

5. Post finished data disks on the classroom wall.

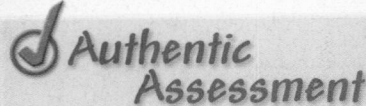 **Authentic Assessment**

Refer to Activity 13 in the Authentic Assessment section of the *Quizzes, Tests, and Authentic Assessment (with Rubrics)* booklet.

 When & Where?

Refer students to the locator map and time line on this page. **Ask:** What generalizations can you form about Africa's size? (*It appears bigger than several other continents shown.*) What events show that Africans interacted with other peoples? (*Arab Muslim traders settle in East Africa; enslaved Africans arrive in Europe*) **L2**

GLENCOE TECHNOLOGY

World History: Journey Across Time Video Program

To learn more about medieval Africa, students can view the Chapter 13 video in the *World History: Journey Across Time* Video Program.

MindJogger Videoquiz

Use the **MindJogger Videoquiz** to preview Chapter 13 content.

 Available in DVD and VHS

Chapter 13

Medieval Africa

Islamic mosque and marketplace in Djenne, Mali ▼

NATIONAL GEOGRAPHIC **When & Where?**

A.D. 300	A.D. 700	1100	1500
c. A.D. 300 ● Axum conquers Kush	c. A.D. 750 ● Arab Muslim traders settle in East Africa	1324 ● Mansa Musa travels to Makkah	c. 1441 ● First enslaved Africans arrive in Europe

Reading Strategy **PURPOSE FOR READING**

Activating Prior Knowledge Organize the class into small groups. Present students with a map of modern Africa and point out its vast size and varied geographic features. Then write the following sentence on the board: "Africa is a continent, not a country." Direct groups to hold a carousel discussion about the meaning of this statement. Ask each student in each group to provide one idea that affirms or disproves the statement, and have them record their group ideas. They should come to suspect that there are different cultures in Africa. Wrap up the activity by telling students to look for evidence of Africa's great cultural and physical diversity as they read the chapter. **L1**

Chapter Preview

While China enjoyed an artistic golden age, kingdoms in Africa grew rich from trading salt and gold. This chapter will tell you about an African ruler who led a great caravan on a long journey from North Africa to the Arabian Peninsula.

 View the Chapter 13 video in the *World History: Journey Across Time* Video Program.

History Online
Chapter Overview Visit jat.glencoe.com for a preview of Chapter 13.

 ## The Rise of African Civilizations

Africa's geography influenced the rise of its civilizations. The growth of trade led to the exchange of goods and ideas.

 ## Africa's Government and Religion

African rulers developed different forms of government. Traditional religions, Christianity, and Islam shaped early African culture.

 ## African Society and Culture

The family was the foundation of African society. A growing slave trade, however, would disrupt African society.

 Study Organizer

Categorizing Information *Make this foldable to help you organize your notes about medieval Africa.*

Step 1 *Draw a map of Africa on one side of a sheet of paper.*

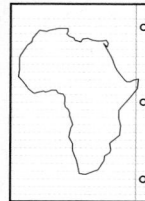

Step 2 *Fold the sheet of paper into thirds from top to bottom.*

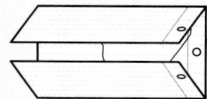

Step 3 *Unfold, turn the paper over (to the clean side), and label as shown.*

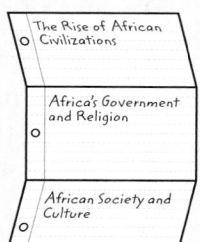

The Rise of African Civilizations

Africa's Government and Religion

African Society and Culture

Reading and Writing *As you read about the civilizations of Africa, write down three main questions under each heading. Then write an answer to each question.*

441

History Online

Introduce students to chapter content and key terms by having them access **Chapter Overview 13** at jat.glencoe.com

CHAPTER PREVIEW

After reading Chapter 13, students should be able to

1. explain how geography and trade shaped the growth of African civilizations in Africa south of the Sahara;

2. describe the governments and religions that influenced life in medieval Africa;

3. discuss how the Bantu migrations shaped African cultures and how the African slave trade disrupted those cultures.

FOLDABLES
Study Organizer Dinah Zike's Foldables

Purpose This foldable helps students focus their reading on key topics by writing questions about them as they read this chapter. Suggest that students use these question words: Who? What? Where? When? Why? How?

📁 Have students complete *Reading and Study Skills Foldables* Activity 13.

MORE ABOUT THE PHOTO

The Mosque in Djenne Great Friday Mosque stands in the marketplace of Djenne, Mali. In the 1200s, Djenne had its first Islamic ruler, Koy Konboro. A convert to Islam, Konboro demolished his palace and built the first Great Mosque, which was as large as the one in the picture. It was elaborately decorated. The mosque lasted until the 1800s, when Muslim rulers erected a smaller and simpler mosque. The current mosque was built in 1906–1907 in the same style and on the same site as the first. It has nine rows of columns, which support a roof made from palm logs. The wooden beams jutting out from the walls support the scaffolding that is erected annually so that a new layer of mud can be plastered on the walls to replace what the rain erodes away.

1 Learn It!

Making comparisons is little more than understanding the organizational pattern of similarities and differences. What may be difficult for students, however, is to determine such patterns when they are not explicitly labeled as such in the text. Help students identify this concept by comparing or contrasting what they are learning in the text with what they already know.

For example, in Section 3, education and community in African society can be compared to family life in the United States today.

Use the following graphic organizer to walk students through the process:

Education and Community in Medieval Africa and the United States

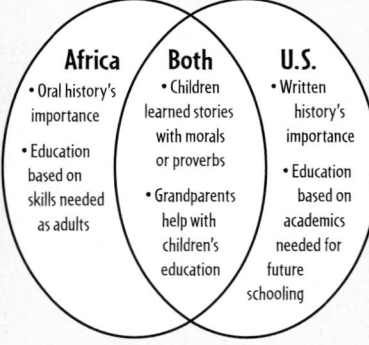

Africa	Both	U.S.
• Oral history's importance	• Children learned stories with morals or proverbs	• Written history's importance
• Education based on skills needed as adults	• Grandparents help with children's education	• Education based on academics needed for future schooling

If students need more concrete examples, have them compare or contrast elementary school with middle school or urban life with rural life. **L2**

Reading Skill
Compare and Contrast

1 Learn It!
Making Comparisons

One way authors help you to understand information is by organizing material so that you can see how people, places, things, or events compare (are alike) or contrast (are different). Read the following passage:

> The contrasts (differences) are highlighted in blue.

> First, look at what is being compared or contrasted. In this case, it is the religions of two groups of people from Africa, highlighted in pink.

Some groups, like **the Nanti in East Africa**, thought people could talk directly with their god. Others, like **the Igbo, thought their creator could only be spoken to through less powerful gods and goddesses who worked for him.**

Even though Africans practiced their religion differently in different places, their beliefs served similar purposes. They provided rules for living and helped people stay in touch with their history.

—*from page 463*

Reading Tip

As you read, look for words that signal the use of comparisons, such as *like*, *similar*, or *different*.

> The comparisons (similarities) are highlighted in green.

Reading Strategy **SIGNAL WORDS**

As students struggle with understanding organizational patterns, such as cause and effect or comparing and contrasting, show them how signal words can indicate that such a structure is being used. Point out that transition words such as *like*, *same as*, *similar to*, *also*, *in addition*, and *related to* can indicate that the author is making a comparison. The use of words such as *however*, *but*, *although*, *despite*, *on the other hand*, *different from*, *as opposed to*, and *instead* can signal a contrast. Ask students to look in the chapter for such words and to read the sentences in which the words occur to see if they can find a comparison or contrast. **L1**

2 Practice It!

Create a Venn Diagram

A Venn diagram can help you to compare and contrast information. Differences are listed in the outside parts of each circle. Similarities are listed in the portion of the two circles that overlap. Read the paragraphs below. Then create a Venn diagram to compare and contrast the roles of European and African women as stated in the paragraphs.

Differences Similarities Differences

Read to Write ⋯⋯⋯⋯

You will read about the rise and fall of many wealthy kingdoms in Africa during the Middle Ages. Choose one of the kingdoms and do research to find out what modern African nation occupies that same area today. Write a report to compare and contrast the modern nation and the early African kingdom.

As in most medieval societies, women in Africa acted mostly as wives and mothers. Men had more rights and controlled much of what women did. Visitors to Africa, however, saw exceptions. European explorers were amazed to learn that women served as soldiers in some African kingdoms.

African women also won fame as rulers. In the A.D. 600s, Queen Dahia al-Kahina led the fight against the Muslim invasion of her kingdom, which was located about where Mauritania is today. Another woman ruler was Queen Nzinga, who ruled lands in what are now Angola and Congo. She spent almost 40 years battling Portuguese slave traders.

—from page 470

3 Apply It!

As you read each section, make Venn diagrams to help you compare and contrast important details.

443

READING SOCIAL STUDIES

2 Practice It!

Classifying An underlying skill that will help students compare and contrast is classifying information into understandable parts. It is for this reason that graphic organizers are so effective in helping students see the relationships among ideas and then linking those ideas together in categories. Have students list the kingdoms that they read about in the chapter and then organize them by listing them based on similar and different characteristics. For example, students could list kingdoms whose wealth depended on trade in one column and kingdoms whose wealth depended on agriculture in a separate column. **L2**

3 Apply It!

Ask students to create a Venn diagram to compare and contrast the similarities and differences in two African kingdoms described in the chapter, such as Ghana and Mali. **L2**

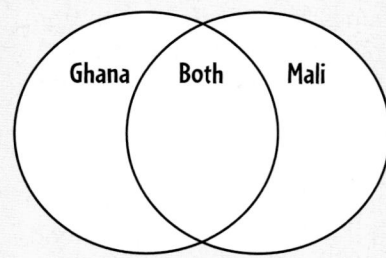

Ghana Both Mali

Reading Strategy ⟩ READ TO WRITE

The report students write will be similar to a newspaper article. An essential skill for journalists is the ability to write in ways that will create a visual experience for their readers. Describing similarities and differences in people, places, and things helps readers form mental images as they are reading. Encourage students to use their imagination, as well as vivid and figurative language, as they write an article describing kingdoms mentioned in the chapter. For example, they could compare how gold dust was a valuable commodity in Ghana, and wearing large trousers was a symbol of status in Mali. Encourage them to use vivid sensory words in all of their descriptions. **L2**

1 FOCUS

SECTION OVERVIEW

This section explores how geography and trade influenced the development of kingdoms in western and eastern Africa.

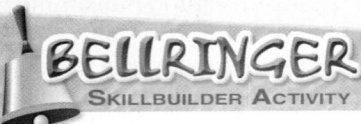

BELLRINGER
SKILLBUILDER ACTIVITY

✍ Project **Daily Focus Skills Transparency 13–1** and have students answer questions. Discuss their responses.

Get Ready to Read!

Preteaching Vocabulary: Explain to students that griots are musician-entertainers in western Africa. Historically, they have been important for preserving genealogies and tribal histories.

Answers to Graphic: Ghana: iron weapons, control of gold mines, huge army, wealth from trade and taxes; Mali: conquests of land, control of gold mines, rebuilt gold-salt trade; Songhai: control of Niger River, control of salt mines, conquests of land in West Africa; Benin and Kongo: grew surplus foods to trade for needed supplies; Axum: controlled trade routes, defeated Kush; Zimbabwe: wealth from trade, huge stone capital, inland empire

Section 1

The Rise of African Civilizations

Get Ready to Read!

What's the Connection?
Egypt and Kush were Africa's first great civilizations. In this section, you will learn about African civilizations that developed later.

Focusing on the Main Ideas
- Africa has a vast and varied landscape. *(page 445)*
- West African empires grew rich from trade. *(page 447)*
- Africa's rain forests blocked invaders and provided resources. *(page 450)*
- East African kingdoms and states became centers for trade and new ideas. *(page 451)*

Locating Places
Ghana (GAH•nuh)
Mali (MAH•lee)
Timbuktu (TIHM•BUHK•TOO)
Songhai (SAWNG•HY)
Axum (AHK•SOOM)

Meeting People
Sundiata Keita (sun•dee•AH•tuh KY•tuh)
Mansa Musa (MAHN•sah moo•SAH)
Sunni Ali (sun•EE ah•LEE)

Building Your Vocabulary
plateau (pla•TOH)
griot (GREE•OH)
dhow (DOW)

Reading Strategy
Summarizing Information Create diagrams describing the accomplishments of each medieval African civilization.

Civilization

NATIONAL GEOGRAPHIC **When & Where?**

Timbuktu
Kilwa
Great Zimbabwe

A.D. 300	A.D. 900	1500
c. A.D. 300 Axum conquers Kush	c. A.D. 750 Arab Muslim traders settle in East Africa	1468 Sunni Ali captures Timbuktu

444 CHAPTER 13 Medieval Africa

 SECTION RESOURCES

Reproducible Masters
- Reproducible Lesson Plan 13–1
- Daily Lecture and Discussion Notes 13–1
- Vocabulary Activity 13–1
- Active Reading Note-Taking Guide 13–1
- Guided Reading Activity 13–1
- Section Quiz 13–1
- Reading Essentials and Study Guide 13–1

Transparencies
- Daily Focus Skills Transparency 13–1

Multimedia
- Interactive Tutor Self-Assessment CD-ROM
- ExamView® Pro Testmaker CD-ROM
- Presentation Plus! CD-ROM

Africa's Geography

Main Idea Africa has a vast and varied landscape.

Reading Focus How can geography discourage people from exploring another place? Read to learn about the geographic features that made it difficult for people to travel across parts of Africa.

In 1906 a teacher named Hans Vischer explored what he called the "death road," a trade route connecting western Africa to the coast of the Mediterranean Sea. No European or American had ever risked the journey before. The "death road" crossed more than 1,500 miles (2,414 km) of the Sahara, the world's largest desert. To get lost meant certain death.

Only nomads living in the region knew the way, but Vischer hoped to map the route. Like the desert nomads, his life depended upon finding oases. Upon his return, Vischer amazed people with stories of the Sahara. He told of swirling winds and shifting sand dunes.

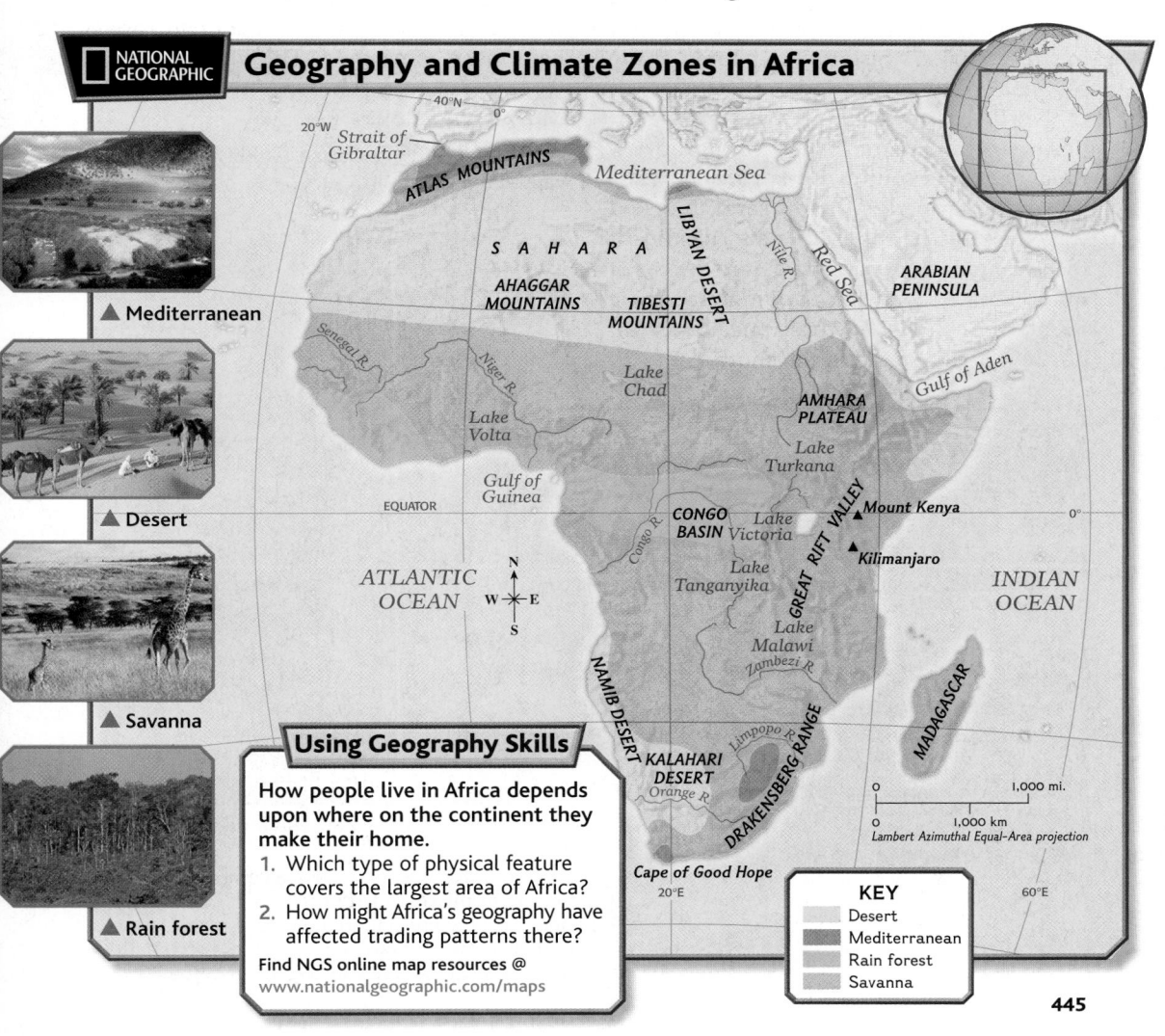

NATIONAL GEOGRAPHIC

Geography and Climate Zones in Africa

▲ Mediterranean

▲ Desert

▲ Savanna

▲ Rain forest

Using Geography Skills

How people live in Africa depends upon where on the continent they make their home.
1. Which type of physical feature covers the largest area of Africa?
2. How might Africa's geography have affected trading patterns there?

Find NGS online map resources @ www.nationalgeographic.com/maps

KEY
- Desert
- Mediterranean
- Rain forest
- Savanna

445

2 TEACH

Drawing Conclusions From a Map
Refer students to the map on page 445. Have them identify the types of information shown. *(climate zones and other geographic features)* **Ask:** What conclusions can you draw about these topics? *(Possible answer: Africa has a varied climate suitable to many different kinds of agriculture.)* **L2**

Daily Lecture and Discussion Notes 13–1

Use **Daily Lecture and Discussion Notes 13–1** for an outline of key concepts found in the section.

Reading Support L1/ EL

Use **Vocabulary Activity 13–1** to review important terms in the section.

Using Geography Skills

Answers:
1. savanna
2. Deserts and jungle would have limited trade, which would be easier on the coast and in river valleys.

Reading Strategy ◁ READING THE TEXT

Visualizing Word Descriptions Distribute outline maps of Africa to the class. Tell students that an important reading and listening skill is the ability to visualize word descriptions. Ask students to make "picture notes" on their maps as you read aloud the subsection "A Vast and Diverse Continent." Have students continue to make picture notes as they progress through this section. If time permits, have them take turns reading aloud paragraphs or subsections as others create their picture notes. Have them keep their notes as a study guide. **L2**

in a word . . .

"Sahara" comes from the Arab word *sahra*, meaning "desert." In terms of precipitation, only one place in the world receives less rain: the polar desert of Antarctica.

✓ Reading Check

Answer: movements of the earth's crust that cracked the continent's surface

Understanding Charts

Africa is a complex land made up of more than 50 countries and peoples who speak hundreds of languages and dialects. Have students do some mathematical calculations to see other differences between Africa and the United States. **Ask:** How much longer than the Missouri River is the Nile River? *(1,595 miles, 2,563 km)* How much bigger in square miles is the Sahara than the Mojave? *(about 3,485,000 square miles)*

Answers:

1. The United States is slightly larger.
2. Africa's population is roughly three times larger.

A Vast and Diverse Continent Africa is the world's second-largest continent. The United States fits into Africa three times, with room to spare. The Equator slices through the middle of the continent. Hot, steamy rain forests stretch along each side of it. Yet the rain forests cover only 10 percent of the land.

Most of Africa lies in the tropics. Here dry, sweeping grasslands reach for thousands of miles. Most of the tropical grasslands, known as savannas, have high temperatures and uneven rains. These wide-open grasslands are perfect for raising herds of animals. For much of Africa's history, the people of the savanna were hunters and herders.

North and south of the savannas are the deserts—the Sahara to the north and the Kalahari to the southwest. For many years, these unmapped seas of sand blocked travel. People had to follow the coastline if they wanted to get past the deserts. Areas of mild climate, good for growing crops, are found along the Mediterranean Sea in northwest Africa and in the south.

The African Plateau Almost all of Africa, except the coastal plains, rests on a **plateau** (pla•TOH)—an area of high flat land. Rivers spill off the plateau in crashing waterfalls and rapids, cutting off inland water routes. Although the Nile River is Africa's longest river, the Congo River winds 2,700 miles (4,345 km) through Africa, near the Equator.

In the east, movements of the earth's crust millions of years ago cracked the continent, and parts of the plateau's surface dropped. This formed the Great Rift Valley, where some of the earliest human fossils have been unearthed. The valley extends through eastern Africa from present-day Mozambique to the Red Sea.

✓ Reading Check **Cause and Effect** What caused the Great Rift Valley?

Comparing Africa to the U.S.

	Africa	United States
Size	11,667,159 square miles (30,217,894 sq. km)	3,794,085 square miles (9,826,680 sq. km)
Population Today	about 891 million people	about 291 million people
Longest River	Nile River 4,160 miles (6,693 km)	Missouri River 2,565 miles (4,130 km)
Largest Desert	Sahara 3,500,000 square miles (9,065,000 sq. km)	Mojave 15,000 square miles (38,850 sq. km)

Sources: *The World Almanac and Book of Facts*, 2004; *World Population Data Sheet*, 2003; *The New Encyclopaedia Britannica*, 1990

Understanding Charts

Africa has a land area roughly three times that of the United States.
1. How does the size of the Sahara compare to the size of the United States?
2. How does the population of Africa compare to that of the United States?

DIFFERENTIATED INSTRUCTION

Verbal/Linguistic: Have students use information from the text to create a detailed chart on Africa's geography, including geographic facts such as biggest valley, highest mountain, largest lake, and so on.

Kinesthetic: Assign students to make a papier-mâché, clay, or salt-and-flour relief map showing as many of the geographic facts from the chart as possible.

English Learners: Ask students to create labels using toothpicks and paper that might be glued to the map or added before the materials dry. *(For example: Nile River—4,160 miles)*

📁 Refer to *Inclusion Strategies for the Middle School Social Studies Classroom* in the TCR.

West African Empires

Main Idea West African empires grew rich from trade.

Reading Focus What would you rather have—a pound of gold or a pound of salt? Both of these goods were important to West Africans and helped them build large trading empires.

Stories of golden lands south of the Sahara seemed hard to believe. There's a country, claimed one story, "where gold grows like plants in the same way as carrots do, and is plucked at sunset."

The Berbers who told the tales had seen the gold with their own eyes. The Berbers, the first known people to settle in North Africa, crossed the Sahara to trade with people in western Africa. They began making the trip about 400 B.C.

For hundreds of years, Berber traders carried goods on horses and donkeys, which often died in the hot Sahara. When the Romans conquered North Africa, they introduced camels from central Asia. Camels, nicknamed "ships of the desert," revolutionized trade. Their broad feet did not sink in the sand, and their humps stored fat for food. In addition, they could travel many days without water.

Traders grouped hundreds, maybe even thousands, of camels together to form caravans. They traded salt and cloth from North Africa and the Sahara for gold and ivory from western Africa. The trade led to the growth of cities in western Africa. Eventually, rulers of these cities began to build a series of empires. During the Middle Ages, these African empires were bigger than most European kingdoms in wealth and size. The first empire to develop was Ghana.

▲ While many of the caravans that crossed the desert going to and from West Africa included about 1,000 camels, some caravans may have had as many as 12,000 camels. *What were some of the items traded by caravans?*

CONNECTING ACROSS TIME

While camel caravans were important to medieval Africa, there are many examples of the modern caravan. For example, the many cars in a train are like the many camels in the caravan. Oftentimes truckers will drive together in clumps to help with wind resistance and make travel easier. Similarly, cyclists often race in clumps. **Ask: What technological advances have allowed people to overcome geographic barriers to trade such as the Sahara?** (*Possible answers: airplanes, Internet, trucks, and so on.*) **L1**

More About the Art

Camel caravans remained the choice of trans-Saharan transportation for hundreds of years. Even in the early 1900s, salt caravans numbered as high as 20,000 camels. Expansion of sea routes and the building of roads and railroads caused the decline of the caravans.

Caption Answer: salt, cloth, gold, ivory

CRITICAL THINKING ACTIVITY

Identifying Cause and Effect Draw a simple graphic organizer on the board to help students identify reasons for the rise of Ghana (or any of the other kingdoms or empires in this section). To do this, write "The Rise of Ghana" and circle the phrase. Then have students state reasons for Ghana's power. Record the answer in a circle and connect it to the central circle with an arrow. Have students continue this process until they have exhausted the materials in the text. (*Answers should include: located at crossroads of trade, had iron weapons, had large army, demand for trade items.*) **L2**

Science Repeat this comment by a Roman politician: "Some seek not gold, but there lives not a man who does not need salt." Point out that our bodies are made up of 70 to 80 percent salty fluids. These fluids help keep our hearts beating and muscles moving. **Ask: How does this information help explain the high value West Africans placed on salt?** *(They needed salt to stay alive.)* **L1/ EL**

Using Geography Skills

Answers:

1. approximately 2,500 miles
2. near the coast of the Atlantic Ocean

Skills Practice

Ask: By taking the most direct trade route, what cities would you pass through traveling from Taghaza to Benin? *(Timbuktu, Gao)* **Which kingdom controlled Taghaza?** *(Songhai)*

Africa Today Have students use an atlas to identify the present-day nations that exist in the areas of the former African empires of Ghana, Mali, Songhai, and Benin. **L1/ EL**

Rise of Ghana Ghana (GAH•nuh) rose to power in the A.D. 400s. It was a "crossroads of trade," a place where trade routes come together. Trade routes reached across the Sahara into North Africa and down the Niger River (NY•juhr) to kingdoms in the rain forest. Some extended all the way to Africa's northeastern coast.

For traders to meet, they had to pass through Ghana. Passage came at a price—a tax paid to Ghana's rulers. These taxes made Ghana rich. Why did traders pay the taxes? First, Ghana knew how to make iron weapons. Like ancient Kush, it used these weapons to conquer its neighbors. Although Ghana owned no gold mines, it controlled the people who did. Second, Ghana built a huge army. "When the king of Ghana calls up his army," said one trader, "he can put 200,000 men in the field."

Third, people wanted the trade items, especially salt and gold, at almost any price. West Africans needed salt to flavor and preserve food, and their bodies needed salt to stay healthy. They paid taxes to get salt from Berber mines in the Sahara. In turn, the Berbers paid taxes to get gold to sell at a huge profit in Europe.

Rise of Mali Ghana did not last forever, however. The discovery of new gold mines outside Ghana's control reduced the taxes it collected. In addition, heavy farming robbed the soil of minerals and made it harder to grow enough crops to feed people. Constant fighting also hurt Ghana. Ghana's rulers had accepted the religion of Islam, but they fought with North African Muslims who wanted to build empires of their own.

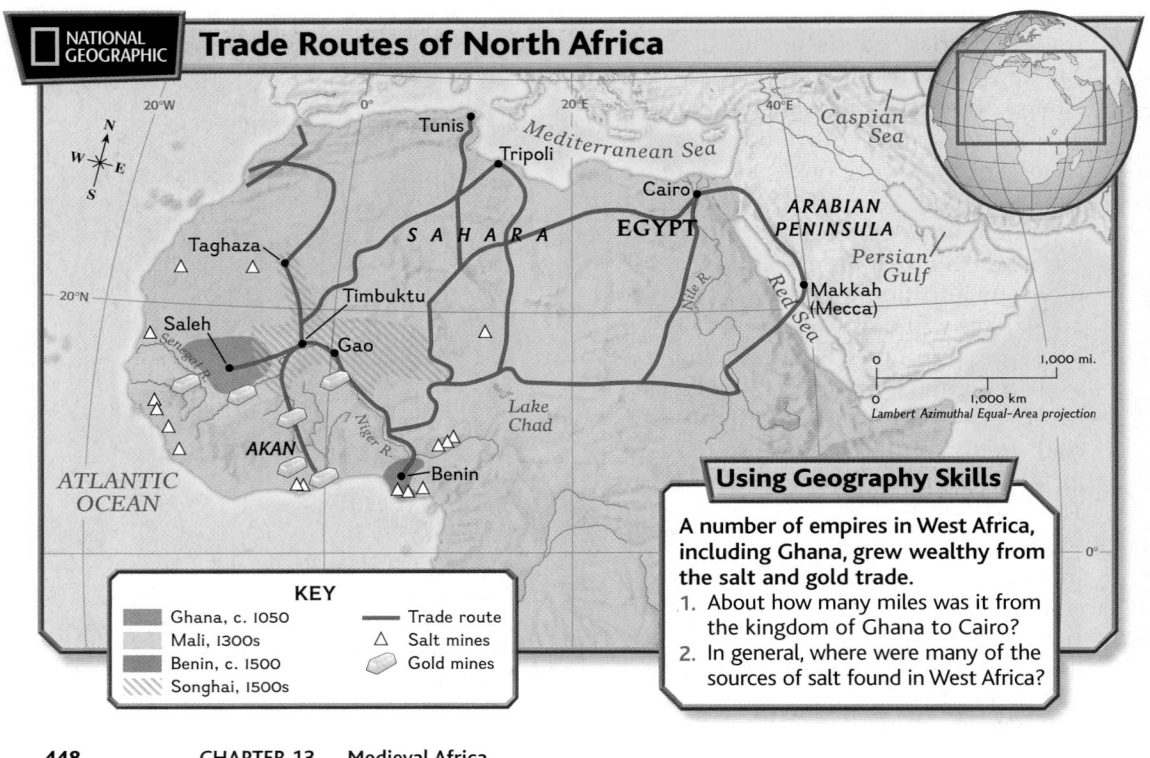

NATIONAL GEOGRAPHIC

Trade Routes of North Africa

KEY

- Ghana, c. 1050
- Mali, 1300s
- Benin, c. 1500
- Songhai, 1500s
- —— Trade route
- △ Salt mines
- ▱ Gold mines

Lambert Azimuthal Equal-Area projection

Using Geography Skills

A number of empires in West Africa, including Ghana, grew wealthy from the salt and gold trade.

1. About how many miles was it from the kingdom of Ghana to Cairo?
2. In general, where were many of the sources of salt found in West Africa?

448 CHAPTER 13 Medieval Africa

INTERDISCIPLINARY CONNECTIONS ACTIVITY

Geography Point out that the territory of medieval Ghana does not coincide with the borders of the modern republic of Ghana. The kingdom took its name from the most powerful leader—*ghana*, or "king." Have students compare the boundaries of the kingdom of Ghana with a political map of Africa. **Ask: What present-day nations did Ghana include?** *(parts of Mauritania and Mali)* Repeat this activity for other civilizations in the section. **L1/ EL**

After Ghana fell in the 1200s, the kingdom of **Mali** (MAH•lee) replaced it. West African **griots** (GREE•ohz), or storytellers, give credit to a great warrior-king named **Sundiata Keita** (sun•dee•AH•tuh KY•tuh)—the "Lion Prince." Sundiata, who ruled from 1230 to 1255, seized the capital of Ghana in 1240. He then won control of lands from the Atlantic coast to the trading city of **Timbuktu** (TIHM•BUHK•TOO) and beyond. His conquests put Mali in control of the gold-mining areas, allowing him to rebuild the gold and salt trade.

Rise of Songhai Mali began a slow decline after the death of its last strong king, **Mansa Musa** (MAHN•sah moo•SAH), in 1337. The kings who followed failed to stop Berber conquerors, who for a time even ruled Timbuktu.

In 1468 **Sunni Ali** (sun•EE ah•LEE), the leader of **Songhai** (SAWNG•HY), stormed into Timbuktu and drove out the Berbers. He then began a campaign of conquest. Sunni Ali used Songhai's location along the Niger River to his advantage. He ordered a fleet of war canoes to seize control of the river trade. His armies then swept westward into the Sahara, where they took over Berber salt mines. By the time of his death in 1492, Sunni Ali had built the largest empire in West Africa.

The empire lasted almost 100 more years. In 1591, however, a small army from the Arab kingdom of Morocco crossed the Sahara. Soldiers with cannons, guns, and gunpowder easily cut down Songhai soldiers armed with swords, spears, and bows and arrows. Within months, Songhai's empire was gone.

Reading Check **Analyze** Why did West Africa become the center of three large trade empires?

The Way It Was

Focus on Everyday Life

Africa's Salt Mines Salt mining began in the Sahara in the Middle Ages. Ancient miners worked underground and in sand dunes to extract solid blocks of salt. The salt trade became a successful business for the African people. In ancient times, salt was so desirable that it was traded ounce for ounce for gold.

There are many salt deposits in western Africa because part of the desert was once a shallow sea made up of salt water. When the sea dried up, salt was left behind.

People need a small amount of salt to stay healthy. It is lost when people and animals sweat, so people need some in their food. In ancient times, before refrigerators or canned foods were invented, salt was used to keep foods from going bad. It also was used to add flavor to food.

ATLANTIC OCEAN · MOROCCO · SAHARA · Taghaza · AFRICA · Niger R.

◀ African salt mine today

Connecting to the Past
1. How do salt deposits form?
2. Why do you think salt was so valuable that it was traded ounce for ounce for gold?

The Way It Was

Answers:
1. As salty water dries, it leaves behind the salt in salt deposits.
2. It was needed to keep people healthy and to preserve and flavor food.

Reading Check

Answer: because of the presence of highly valuable mines, particularly salt and gold

EXTENDING THE CONTENT

What Was It Like to Work at Taghaza? Arab traveler Ibn Battuta found little to admire about Taghaza. He said that "The construction of its houses is of rock salt with camel skin roofing and there are no trees." He also said that workers lived off a diet of dates, camel meat, and bitter water. He complained of lice and dust. The real value of the place, he pointed out, was the huge slabs of salt that Africans traded "as one would exchange gold and silver."

Writing Activity

Tell students that the Kongo ruler King Alfonso protested enslavement of his people in a 1526 letter to King John III of Portugal. The letter said, in part, "Merchants daily seize our subjects. . . . They grab and cause them to be sold." Ask students to write a similar letter, offering reasons the Portuguese should stop the trade in enslaved humans. **L2**

More About the Art

According to oral history, the fourth king of Benin decided to start having lifelike memorial sculptures of royal ancestors made. All of these heads have necklaces made of coral beads because they are part of the royal clothing. At the end of the 1400s the *obas*, or kings, organized craftspeople into guilds. Benin became famous for its brass and bronze sculptures and ivory and wood carvings.

Caption Answer: around 1440

GLENCOE BookLink

Use **Glencoe BookLink** to create customized reading lists for your students' reading levels, interests, and abilities.

Kingdoms of the Rain Forest

Main Idea Africa's rain forests blocked invaders and provided resources.

Reading Focus What does your state make that people in other places want to buy? Africa's rain forest kingdoms had something the savanna kingdoms wanted. It was not gold or salt, but something just as valuable—food.

Ghana, Mali, and Songhai ruled the wide-open savannas. However, the dense rain forests along the Equator kept them from expanding to the southern coast. People living in the rain forests built their own kingdoms and empires. They included Benin, which arose in the Niger delta, and Kongo, which formed in the Congo River basin.

Griots who live in the Niger delta still tell stories about King Ewuare (eh•WOO•ah•ray), who founded the empire of Benin around 1440. In describing his ancestor's accomplishments, one storyteller boasted:

> ❝ He fought against and captured 201 towns and villages. . . . He took their . . . rulers captive and caused the people to pay tribute to him. ❞
>
> —J.V. Egharevba,
> *A Short History of Benin*

Farmers in the rain forest kingdoms enjoyed many natural advantages, including farmable soil and a warm, wet climate. In cleared-out areas of the forest, they often produced a surplus, or extra supply, of foods like bananas, yams, or rice.

The Kingdom of Benin

◀ Bronze statue of queen from Benin

Statue of horn player ▶ from Benin

▲ This bronze casting honored the king of Benin. *Around when was the kingdom of Benin founded?*

450

CITIZENSHIP AND YOU

Preserving History Read aloud this quote by a West African griot: "I teach kings the history of their ancestors so that the lives of the ancients might serve them as an example." **Ask:** What does the griot say is the value of history? *(allows leaders to learn from the examples of their ancestors)* Explore with students reasons citizens should study the histories of their nation's founders. **Ask:** What lessons can be learned from their lives? *(Possible answers: important values and beliefs; good methods of leading)* **L2**

Food surpluses supported rulers and a class of artisans. Kongo weavers, for example, wove fabrics from bark and plant fibers that looked to Europeans like velvet. In Benin, artists excelled at sculpting and carving metal, wood, and ivory.

Rain forest kingdoms that bordered on the dry savannas traded surplus food and crafts for copper, salt, and leather goods from the savannas. Later, when the Europeans arrived, traders from Benin and Kongo met ships along the coast. They traded, among other things, captives taken in war.

✔ **Reading Check** **Describe** What advantages did farmers in the rain forests have over farmers in other parts of Africa?

East Africa

Main Idea East African kingdoms and states became centers for trade and new ideas.

Reading Focus Have you ever met someone who used to live somewhere far away? Did their ideas help you to think about the world differently? Read to learn how new ideas arrived along the coast of East Africa.

People today in the East African country of Ethiopia trace their history back to 1005 B.C. In that year, Queen Makeda rose to the throne of a great empire called Saba or Sheba. According to the *Glory of Kings*, Ethiopia's oldest written history, Makeda traveled to meet with King Solomon, ruler

✔ **Reading Check**

Answer: Rain forests offered rich soil and a warm, wet climate that was good for farming.

Understanding Charts

Answers:

1. Axum
2. salt, gold, and ivory

Skills Practice

Long before the arrival of the Europeans, Africans set up trading networks that linked much of the continent. African empires compared favorably in size and wealth to other empires in the world at that time.
Ask: What data in the chart support the idea that the medieval period was a "golden age" in the history of Africa? *(Answers will vary but might point to the gold traded, the size of empires, the length of time these kingdoms ruled, key accomplishments, and so on.)*

African Trading Empires A.D. 100–1600

	Axum	Ghana	Mali	Songhai	Zimbabwe
Location	East Africa	West Africa	West Africa	West Africa	SE Africa
	AXUM Adulis	GHANA Saleh	MALI Timbuktu	SONGHAI Gao	ZIMBABWE Great Zimbabwe
Time Period	c. 100–1400	c. 400–1200	c. 1200–1450	c. 1000–1600	c. 700–1450
Goods Traded	ivory, frankincense, myrrh, slaves	iron products, animal products, salt, gold	salt, gold	salt, gold	gold, copper, ivory
Key Facts	King Ezana converted to Christianity; made it the official religion.	Taxes from traders passing through made Ghana rich.	King Mansa Musa built mosques and libraries.	Songhai gained control of West African trade by conquering Timbuktu and mastering trade by river.	Kings Mutota and Matope built the region's biggest empire.

Understanding Charts

Large trading kingdoms developed in several areas of Africa.
1. Which kingdom developed earliest?
2. **Generalize** What were some of the common trade items of the West African empires?

COOPERATIVE LEARNING ACTIVITY

Storytelling Organize students into groups. Assign each group one of the African empires. Tell groups to focus on the accomplishments of their empire and to prepare a story that a griot might tell children about the greatness of their ancestors. Allow each group to prepare a monologue. Call on a volunteer from each group to present the monologue to the class. **L3**

📂 Refer to the ***Quizzes, Tests, and Authentic Assessment (with Rubrics)*** booklet for rubrics.

451

Reading Support L1/ EL

Assign **Guided Reading Activity 13–1** to help students organize the information in the section.

③ ASSESS

Assign Section 1 Review as homework or as an in-class activity.

⊕ Have students use the **Interactive Tutor Self-Assessment CD-ROM** to review the section.

Assessment L2

Assign **Section 1 Quiz** to assess mastery of the material found in the section.

Reading Support L1/ EL

Assign **Reading Essentials and Study Guide 13–1** to help students review section material.

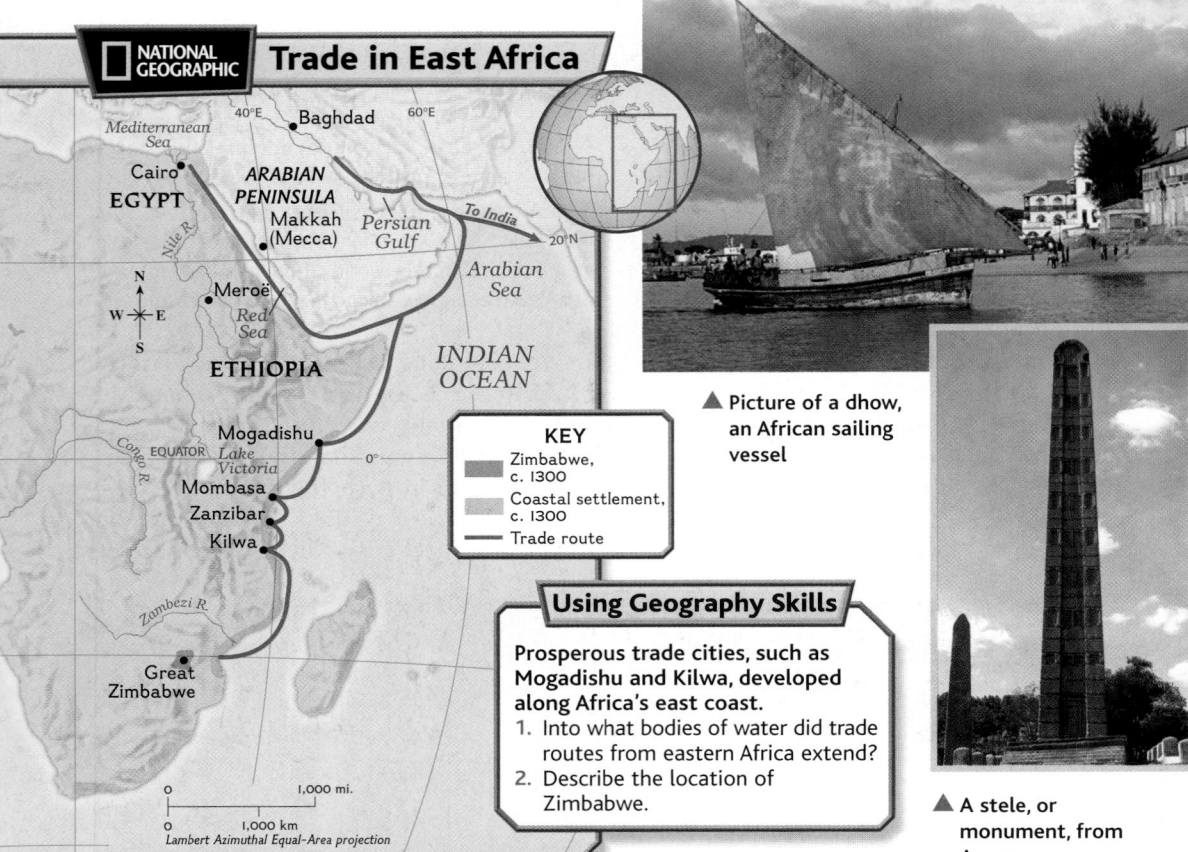

NATIONAL GEOGRAPHIC **Trade in East Africa**

KEY
- Zimbabwe, c. 1300
- Coastal settlement, c. 1300
- Trade route

0   1,000 mi.
0   1,000 km
Lambert Azimuthal Equal-Area projection

▲ Picture of a dhow, an African sailing vessel

▲ A stele, or monument, from Axum

Using Geography Skills

Prosperous trade cities, such as Mogadishu and Kilwa, developed along Africa's east coast.

1. Into what bodies of water did trade routes from eastern Africa extend?
2. Describe the location of Zimbabwe.

---

of the Israelites. On her return, Makeda introduced ancient Israel's religion to her empire. Over time, eastern Africa would feel the impact of two other religions—Christianity and Islam.

The Rise of Axum Like other empires, Saba declined. However, Ethiopia, known in ancient times as Abyssinia, did not. Its power was centered in a city-state called **Axum** (AHK•SOOM). Axum owed its strength to its location on the Red Sea. Goods from Africa flowed into Axum, which served as a trading center for the ancient Mediterranean and East Asian worlds.

Axum fought neighboring Kush for control of trade routes to inland Africa. Around A.D. 300, King Ezana of Axum sent his armies against Kush and defeated it. A few years later, Ezana helped to bring a new religion to Africa when he converted to Christianity. In A.D. 334 he made it the official religion of Axum. Within a few hundred years, another religion—Islam—brought many changes to Axum and other trading states along Africa's eastern coast.

Coastal City-States Arab traders from the Arabian Peninsula had been coming to eastern Africa long before the rise of Islam in the early A.D. 600s. They invented a wind-catching, triangular sail that let them sail to Africa. The sails powered sailboats called **dhows** (DOWZ).

452   CHAPTER 13   Medieval Africa

EXTENDING THE CONTENT

How Sculpture in Benin Changed When the British first entered the palace of the Benin leader in the late 1800s, they found shrines to the leader's ancestors. These were filled with brass heads, figures, and bells. The heads differed in style based on the time period in which they were created. The earliest ones dated from 1400 to 1550 and were small and lifelike. The heads made between 1550 and 1700 became more stylized, and included coral beads around the neck. Later heads were even heavier and more stylized.

In the A.D. 700s, many Arab Muslim traders settled in East African city-states. Here Africans and Arab Muslims shared goods and ideas. By the 1300s, a string of trading ports extended down the East African coast. They included Mogadishu (MAH•guh•DIH•shoo), Kilwa, Mombasa, and Zanzibar. These ports became major links in an Indian Ocean trading network. They traded with places as far away as China.

▲ Some of the walls of Great Zimbabwe still exist. *What trade goods from the interior of Africa passed through Zimbabwe?*

Great Zimbabwe Another great trading center known as Zimbabwe (zihm•BAH•bway) arose inland in southeastern Africa. Founded around A.D. 700 by the Shona people, Zimbabwe supplied gold, copper, and ivory to the East African coast. From there, African goods were shipped to Arabia, Persia, India, and China.

During the 1400s, two kings—Mutota and his son Matope—made Zimbabwe into a large empire. It stretched from south of the Zambezi River to the Indian Ocean. Evidence of Zimbabwe's power can still be seen at Great Zimbabwe, the empire's capital. Here more than 300 huge stone buildings stand—silent reminders of Zimbabwe's past greatness.

✓ **Reading Check** **Explain** How did new technology help East Africa's trade?

History Online
Study Central™ Need help with the material in this section? Visit jat.glencoe.com

Section 1 Review

Reading Summary

Review the Main Ideas

- The continent of Africa has varied landscapes, including rain forests, grasslands, and deserts.

- Beginning in about A.D. 300, a succession of kingdoms, including Ghana, Mali, and Songhai, arose in West Africa.

- Rain forest kingdoms, including Benin and Kongo, traded with the surrounding savanna kingdoms.

- In East Africa, trade with the Arab world helped kingdoms and port cities grow.

What Did You Learn?

1. What items were traded in the kingdoms of West Africa?

Critical Thinking

2. **Organizing Information** Draw a chart like the one below. For each region, write names of the kingdoms and/or city-states that developed there.

West Africa	African Rain Forests	East Africa

3. **Analyze** What city-states grew as trading ports in East Africa, and why were they successful?

4. **Compare and Contrast** Which African kingdoms developed away from the coast? How did their economies compare to other African kingdoms?

5. **Reading** **Compare and Contrast** Create a Venn diagram that shows the similarities and differences of two African kingdoms.

CHAPTER 13   Medieval Africa   **453**

Caption Answer: gold, copper, and ivory

ENRICH

Have students give examples of economic interdependence among the kingdoms or empires studied in this section. **L2**

✓ **Reading Check**

Answer: The dhow, with its wind-catching triangular sail, increased East Africa's ocean trade with areas as far away as China.

History Online
To help students understand section material, have them visit **Study Central™** at jat.glencoe.com

RETEACH

Ask students to explain how geographic location helps explain the rise of empires in West and East Africa. **L1/ EL**

④ CLOSE

Ask students to explain how the Sahara was both a barrier to and a highway for trade. **L1**

SECTION 1 REVIEW ANSWERS

1. Salt and cloth from North Africa/Sahara were traded for gold and ivory from West Africa.

2. West Africa: Ghana, Mali, Songhai; African Rain Forests: Benin, Kongo; East Africa: Saba, Axum, Kush, Mogadishu, Mombasa, Zanzibar, Kilwa, Great Zimbabwe

3. Mogadishu, Mombasa, Zanzibar, Kilwa; part of Indian Ocean trading network

4. Ghana, Songhai, Benin, Kongo, Kush, Great Zimbabwe; economies based on control of land trade routes, food surpluses, and goods from the interior of Africa

5. Answers will vary but should be based on similarities and differences in the text.

WORLD LITERATURE

SUMMARY

A griot tells how the ruler of Mali marries Sogolon, who gives birth to Sundiata. For seven years, Sundiata does not walk or speak. He speaks for the first time when accepting his father's gift: the griot Balla Fasseke. After the king dies, the son of his first wife, Sassouma, takes the throne. Sundiata starts to walk, and he and Sogolon flee to Mema. When the evil Sumanguru invades Mali, Sundiata leads an army from Mema to defeat the invaders. After dispatching Sumanguru, Sundiata returns to Mali, is greeted by twelve kings who swear allegiance, and becomes emperor of the great kingdom of Mali.

Vocabulary Preview Before students begin reading, have them read **Before You Read** and the **Vocabulary Preview.** Point out that difficult words are footnoted throughout the text.

FOCUS

Reality Times Ten The human heroes in many legends are often based on real people. However, over the years, storytellers have embellished their feats until the heroes have become larger than life.

SUNDIATA
THE HUNGERING LION

Retold by Kenny Mann

Before You Read

The Scene: This story takes place in Mali on the continent of Africa in the 1100s.

The Characters: Balla Fasseke is the griot who tells the story of Sundiata. Sundiata is the Lion King of Mali. Sogolon and Maghan Kon Fatta are Sundiata's parents. Sassouma is the first wife of Maghan Kon Fatta. Sumanguru is a rival king.

The Plot: The Lion King of Mali, Sundiata, is denied the throne. Sundiata has to prove that he is the rightful king.

Vocabulary Preview

guardian: one who takes care of another person

infirmity: weakness

brewed: prepared by boiling

smiths: metalworkers

multitude: a great number of people

exile: period of time away from one's country

lance: a steel-tipped spear

Have you ever known someone who overcame obstacles to achieve great things? In this story, a young leader must learn to speak and walk in order to take control of his kingdom.

Reading Strategy ⟨ READING REINFORCEMENT

Activating Prior Knowledge On the board, draw a three-column chart with *K*, *W*, and *L* at the top of the columns. Explain that *K* stands for what students already know, *W* for what they want to find out, and *L* for what they will learn from the story. Have a student locate Mali on a map of Africa and then describe its relative location (such as east of Mauritania or south and southwest of Algeria) and its absolute location (in terms of longitude and latitude) in the column below *K*. Encourage other students to write what they know, such as the location of Africa, in the first column. After students complete **Before You Read,** have them list questions, such as "Why is Sundiata the Lion King?," in the column below *W*. Then tell students to look for answers to the questions and to write them under *L* as they read the story. **L1**

As You Read

Keep in mind that this story is a mixture of fact and legend. However, a king named Sundiata did conquer new lands and expand trade while he ruled the kingdom of Mali.

A

O people, hear my story! I am Balla Fasseke (bah•lah fah•SEE•kay) of Mali. I am a *griot.*[1] I am the guardian of the word. In my mind rest the stories of my people and the history of our land. O hear me and remember, for I speak the truth.

Long, long ago, the last king of Ghana fell to the sword of Sumanguru, the Sosso king; Sumanguru, the cruel warrior and mighty sorcerer; Sumanguru, who was to meet his fate at the hands of Sundiata, the Lion King of Mali.

I am Sundiata's *griot.* O hear me, for I speak the truth!

B

Sundiata was born of Sogolon, who married Maghan Kon Fatta, the ruler of Mali, whose totem[2] was the lion. Sogolon was brought to the king as a maiden, disfigured by a hunchback and ill looks. But she was said to possess the mighty spirit of a buffalo, strong and courageous. Her coming had been foretold to the king, and he took Sogolon as his wife and came to love her.

C

When Sundiata was born, the king rejoiced. The great royal drums carried the news all over the kingdom. But his first wife, Sassouma, was jealous. Her son should inherit the throne! What need had her husband of another son? She vowed that Sundiata would never become king.

---

[1] **griot:** storyteller
[2] **totem:** animal or plant serving as the symbol of a family or clan

455

2 TEACH

A ACTIVE READING STRATEGIES

PREDICT Ask students to use this passage to predict what the story will be about. *(Answers may include that the story will be about how Sundiata became king and defeated Sumanguru.)*

B CRITICAL THINKING

EVALUATING Ask students to form an opinion about Maghan Kon Fatta based on his choice of Sogolon for a wife. *(Answers may include that the king is a good judge of character because he recognizes Sogolon's worth despite her physical appearance.)*

C LITERARY ELEMENTS

PLOT: Rising Action Ask students to describe the conflict established in this passage. *(The king's first wife becomes jealous and vows that Sundiata will never become king.)*

GLENCOE BOOKLINK

Use **Glencoe BookLink** to create customized reading lists for your students' reading levels, interests, and abilities.

Reading Strategy   VOCABULARY TIP

Categorizing Proper Nouns On the board, list these proper nouns from the story: *Balla Fasseke, Mali, Ghana, Sumanguru, Sundiata, Lion King, Sogolon, Maghan Kon Fatta, Sassouma Mema, Kirina,* and *Mount Koulikoro.* Have students fold sheets of paper to form three columns. Challenge them to come up with three categories for classifying all the nouns. Instruct them to write the name of each category at the head of a column and the nouns that fall into the category below the heading. Suggest that they look for clues to a noun's category if it is not immediately clear. *(Answers may include: Males—Balla Fasseke, Sumanguru, Sundiata, Lion King, Maghan Kon Fatta; Females—Sogolon, Sassouma; Places—Mali, Ghana, Mema, Kirina, Mount Koulikoro.)* **L2**

WORLD LITERATURE

D LITERARY ELEMENTS

FIGURES OF SPEECH: Metaphor
Explain that a metaphor compares two seemingly different things by saying one thing is another. Then ask what metaphor the king's griot uses to reassure the king that Sundiata will be strong someday. (*"[F]rom this small seed shall spring a great tree." Sundiata is the seed. Though small and weak, he will grow strong just as a seed becomes a great tree.*)

E ACTIVE READING STRATEGIES

CONNECT Have students identify modern griots, such as people who tell stories about presidents, sports heroes, and other famous people. (*Answers may include public relations people or biographers.*)

F AUTHOR'S CRAFT

DESCRIPTION Ask for words and phrases that describe life for Sogolon and Sundiata under the new king. (*persecuted, evil hatred, banished, dark corner of the palace, tears flowed, unhappiness, despair*)

In time, Sassouma saw that she had nothing to fear, for Sundiata was stricken by a strange infirmity. He could neither speak nor walk! How great was Sogolon's sorrow! For seven long years, she tried to cure her son. She consulted with all the wise men of the kingdom and brewed herbs and potions, but to no avail.[3] And Sundiata's father, King Maghan Kon Fatta, despaired. But his *griot,* who was my father, advised the king. "The young seed must endure the storm," he said. "And from this small seed shall spring a great tree."

One day, when the king felt death approach, he called the child to him. "I shall give you the gift each king gives to his heir," he said. And on that day, my people, the king gave me—Balla Fasseke—to Sundiata to be his *griot,* as my father had been the king's *griot,* and his father before that. And on that day, for the first time in his life, Sundiata spoke. "Balla, you shall be my *griot,*" he said. And the king knew that his son—the son of the lion and the buffalo—was worthy to be king.

But when Maghan Kon Fatta died, the councilors ignored his wishes. It was the son of Sassouma who ascended the throne, and not Sundiata, the rightful heir. And Sassouma persecuted Sogolon and her son with evil hatred and banished them to a dark corner of the palace. Oh, how Sogolon's tears flowed in her unhappiness! When Sundiata saw his mother's despair, he looked at her calmly and said, "Today I will walk." Then he sent me, Balla Fasseke, to the royal forges.[4] "Tell the smiths to make me the sturdiest iron rod possible," he ordered.

---

[3]**avail:** benefit
[4]**forges:** furnaces where metal is heated and shaped

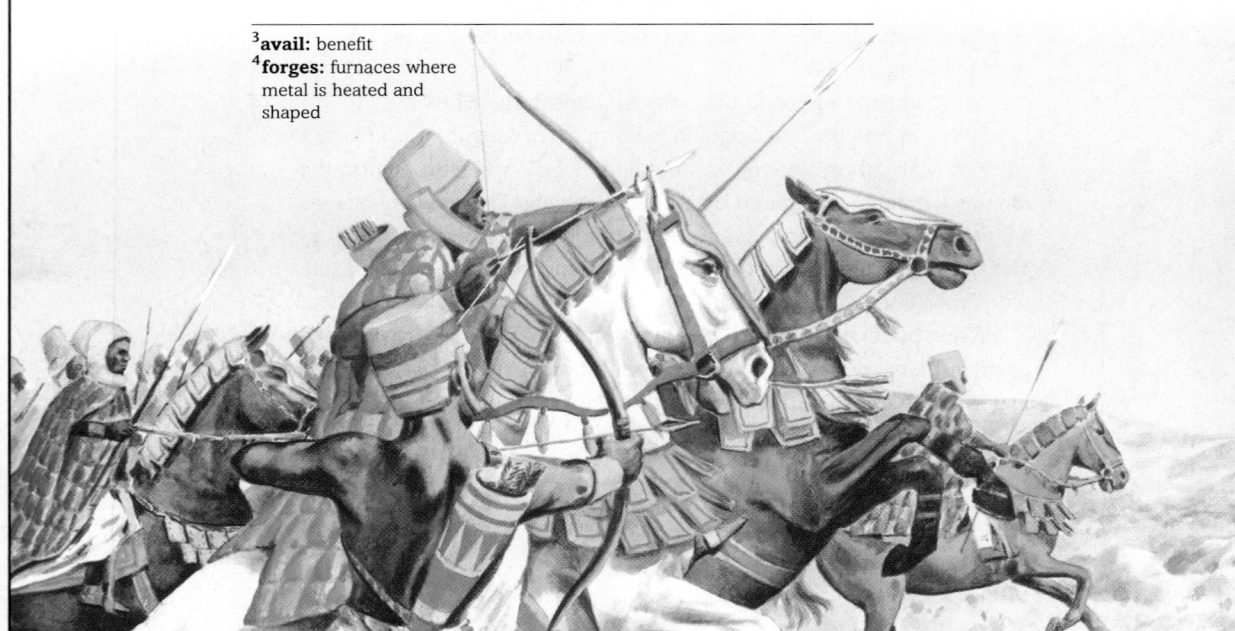

DIFFERENTIATED INSTRUCTION

English Learners: Explain that almost every culture has legends about leaders or warriors. Examples are stories about King Arthur from England, Joan of Arc from France, Hiawatha of the Iroquois, El Cid from Spain, Emilio Zapata from Mexico, and Mulan from China. Have students break into small groups to share legends about leaders and warriors from other cultures. Then have each group select one story and act it out for the rest of the class. Allow students ample time to practice.

Interpersonal: As each group performs, have the class look for values that are stressed in the story.

Kinesthetic: Have students make costumes or backdrops for their stories.

Six men were needed to carry the iron rod to Sogolon's house. They threw it on the ground before Sundiata. A huge multitude of people had gathered to see if Sundiata would walk. "Arise, young lion!" I commanded. "Roar, and may the land know that from henceforth, it has a master!"

Sundiata gripped the rod with his two hands and held it upright in the ground. Beads of sweat poured from his face. A deathly silence gripped the people. All at once, with a mighty thrust, Sundiata stood upright. The crowd gasped. The iron rod was bent like a bow. And Sogolon, who had been dumb with amazement, suddenly burst into song:

> *Oh day, oh beautiful day,*
> *Oh day, day of joy,*
> *Allah Almighty, this is the finest*
> *day you have created,*
> *My son is going to walk!*
> *Hear me, people, for I speak the truth!*

Sundiata threw away the rod, and his first steps were those of a giant.

From that day on, Sundiata grew in strength. He became a fine hunter and was much loved by all the people. But Sassouma, whose son was now king, feared Sundiata's growing power. Her plots to kill him failed. And she knew that I would perform any deed to bring Sundiata to the throne. So, to separate us, Sassouma sent me far away to the court of the demon king, Sumanguru. And there I remained for several years. I pretended allegiance to Sumanguru, but always I waited for the day when I would sing the praises of Sundiata once more.

457

G LITERARY ELEMENTS

TONE Tell students that tone is the author's attitude toward his or her subject. Then have them choose from the following list the best description of the tone in the passage: witty, sad, thankful, sarcastic, scholarly, angry. *(thankful)*

H CRITICAL THINKING

PROBLEM AND SOLUTION Have students define Sassouma's problem. *(She fears Sundiata will gain enough support to take the throne.)* Ask them what they think of her solution. *(Answers may include that trying to have him killed was not wise but that removing Sundiata's biggest supporter was smart.)*

Glencoe Literature Library

As students study the unit, have them read *Catherine, Called Birdy* by Karen Cushman. Written in diary form, this book tells the story of independent, free-spirited young Catherine and life in thirteenth-century England. This and other books from the **Glencoe Literature Library** can be used as students learn about the Middle Ages.

CRITICAL THINKING ACTIVITY

Analyzing Have students imagine that Sogolon and Sassouma have a conversation in which each gives arguments for making her son king. Tell them to write "Should Sundiata Be King?" at the top of a sheet of paper and to fold the sheet in half. Next, have students write "For" at the top of the first half and "Against" at the top of the second. Instruct them to write reasons from the story that Sogolon might give under "For." *(Answers may include the prediction of the king's griot, the king's gift of a griot, the boy's calm in the face of despair, and so on.)* Finish by having students write reasons that Sassouma might give under "Against." *(Answers may include the son of the king's first wife should be king, Sundiata was not fit to rule because he could not speak or walk, the counselors supported Sassouma's son, and so on.)* **L3**

A ACTIVE READING STRATEGIES

VISUALIZE Ask students which kind of line graph best describes Sundiata's life: a straight line up, peaks and valleys, or a straight line across. *(peaks and valleys because his fortunes rose and fell several times, ending high)*

J ACTIVE READING STRATEGIES

QUESTION Point out that Balla is telling the story, yet he is at Sumanguru's court while Sundiata is in Mema. Have students speculate about how Balla knows of the relationship between Sundiata and the king of Mema. *(Answers may include that either the king, Sundiata, or Sogolon told the griot.)*

K AUTHOR'S CRAFT

INDIRECT CHARACTERIZATION Ask students what the passage reveals about the characters of Sassouma and her son. *(Both are cowardly.)*

L CRITICAL THINKING

COMPARING AND CONTRASTING Have students contrast Balla's view of himself with the way Sumanguru probably views him after the events in this passage. *(Balla considers himself loyal to Sundiata, but Sumanguru probably considers Balla a traitor.)*

I / **J** Sogolon fled the palace and took Sundiata far from Sassouma's hatred. For seven years they lived in exile, finding food and shelter wherever they could. At last, they came to the city of Mema. Here they met with good luck, for the king of Mema took a liking to Sundiata and treated him like a son. He admired Sundiata's courage and leadership. This king decided to make the young boy his heir and teach him the arts of government and war. And thus, Sundiata grew to manhood.

K One day, messengers came running to Sundiata. "Sumanguru has invaded Mali!" they cried. "The king and his mother, Sassouma, have fled. Only you can save our people. Return, young lion, and reclaim your throne!"

This, O people, was the moment of Sundiata's destiny. The king of Mema gave him half his forces. And as Sundiata rode at their head, more and more men joined him until a great army thundered across the plains. And from far-distant Mali, Sumanguru, too, raced to meet his destiny. And I, O my people, I followed, for I knew that soon I would be reunited with Sundiata, my Lion King.

L And so it was. Sundiata led his army from Mema, and Sumanguru came from Mali. The two great armies met in battle on the plains of Kirina. I took my chance and escaped at last from Sumanguru. Through the thick clouds of dust and the battle cries of the warriors, I galloped to Sundiata's side. Oh, how great was our joy!

My years with Sumanguru had not been in vain, O my people, for I had learned that Sumanguru feared the magic power of a white rooster. He believed that one touch of the rooster's spur[5] would defeat him forever. And this very spur I had fastened to an arrow, which I gave to my lord, Sundiata.

---
[5]**spur:** a sharp spine on the leg of some birds, especially roosters

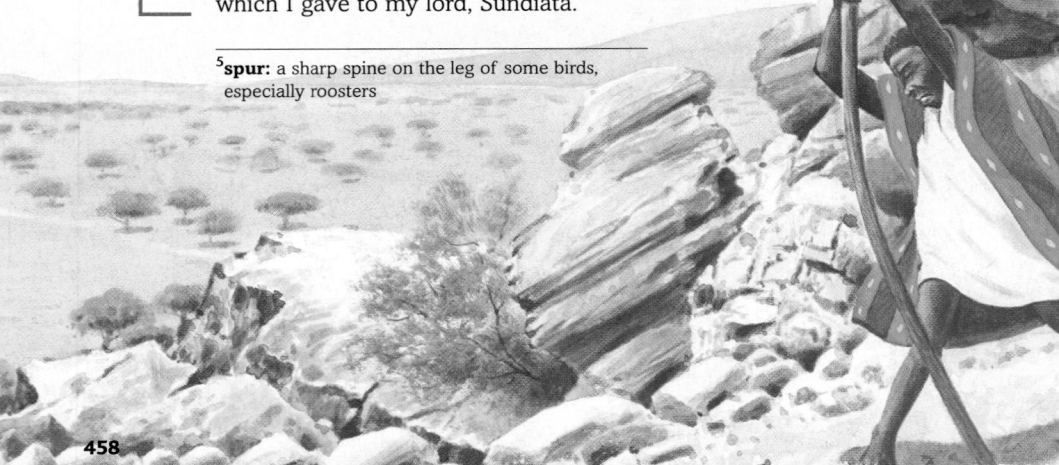

458

EXTENDING THE CONTENT

Mali For many centuries, West Africa lay along the trade routes between the Niger River and North Africa. Caravans carried precious cargoes of gold, ivory, civet, and gum arabic along these routes. Civet was an oily secretion from catlike animals, also called civets, that was used in making perfume. Gum arabic was collected from acacia trees and used to make cosmetics, drugs, and food.

With deadly aim, Sundiata sent the arrow speeding across the battlefield toward Sumanguru. True as a hawk in flight, it met its mark, grazing the sorcerer's shoulder. With a great scream of fear, Sumanguru turned on his horse and fled.

Far away he rode, to the caves of Mount Koulikoro. There we saw Sumanguru, the demon king, fall to his knees and turn to stone. His soldiers, discouraged by his flight, ceased to fight and were defeated.

And so Sundiata returned to Mali to reclaim his throne, and I, Balla Fasseke, went with him to sing of his glory. There waited the twelve kings who had helped Sundiata in exile. Each thrust his lance into the earth before Sundiata. "We shall be united!" they proclaimed. "You have restored peace to our lands. We give you our kingdoms to rule in your great wisdom!" The drums beat out the news. The warriors danced in a joyous frenzy. And the crowd sent a mighty cry to the heavens: "Wassa, Wassa, Ayé!"

And thus did I bear witness to the birth of the great kingdom of Mali. And thus did I see Sundiata become its first emperor.

So listen, O my people, and remember, for I speak the truth. May you live to tell this story to your children, that the name of Sundiata—the Lion King—shall live forever.

Responding to the Reading

1. Why did the king give Sundiata a griot?

2. Foreshadowing is when a storyteller gives you hints of something to come later. This story contains many suggestions that foreshadow Sundiata's successful reign as king. Identify three such hints in the first six paragraphs.

3. **Predict** How might the story be different if Balla Fasseke had not been sent to the court of Sumanguru?

4. **Analyze** Why do you think Sundiata did not walk after receiving his mother's treatments but *did* walk when his half-brother was made king?

5. **Reading** **Read to Write** Suppose you are Sundiata's father. Write a brief speech stating your reasons for choosing Sundiata to be the next king.

459

DIFFERENTIATED INSTRUCTION

EL Students Organize students into pairs. Tell each student to create an acrostic poem using vocabulary words, characters' names, and place names from the story. Then have students exchange papers with their partner and read them.

Average Students Organize students into groups. Tell each group to turn the battle between Sumanguru and Sundiata into a television news report. Have them include eyewitness interviews with Balla and members of the opposing armies.

Gifted Students Remind students that Sundiata knows what can happen if a king uses his power unwisely. Ask them to write a speech that Sundiata might give to his people on the day he is crowned.

ASSESS

Assign the **Responding to the Reading** questions as an in-class activity or as homework.

CLOSE

Have students write appropriate mottoes for Emperor Sundiata's coat of arms. **L1**

Responding to the Reading Answers

1. By giving Sundiata a griot, the king was appointing Sundiata his heir.

2. The griot states that Sumanguru would meet his fate at the hands of Sundiata, that Sundiata is the Lion King of Mali, and that the king's griot said "from this small seed shall spring a great tree."

3. Answers may include that Sundiata would not have defeated Sumanguru as easily.

4. Answers may include that his motivation to help his people was much stronger than anything else.

5. Speeches may discuss how Sundiata's mother was strong and how her coming had been foretold. The king loved her, so he loved her son.

① FOCUS

SECTION OVERVIEW

This section explores the rise of centralized governments in African kingdoms and the variety of religions that influenced peoples throughout the continent.

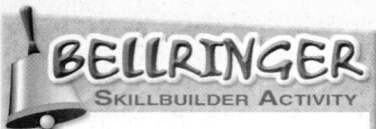

BELLRINGER
SKILLBUILDER ACTIVITY

✎ Project **Daily Focus Skills Transparency 13–2** and have students answer questions. Discuss their responses.

Get Ready to Read!

Preteaching Vocabulary: Explain that Swahili was originally a Bantu language of trade and government in East Africa and in the Congo region.

Answers to Graphic: African influences from interior Africa; Muslim influences from Arab and Persian settlers

---

Section 2 Africa's Government and Religion

Get Ready to Read!

What's the Connection?

In Section 1, you read about some of the kingdoms and empires that developed in Africa. To hold their kingdoms and empires together, Africans had to create their own governments. One unifying force was the religion of Islam, but many Africans continued to practice their traditional religious beliefs as well.

Focusing on the Main Ideas

• The growth of West African empires led to the growth of centralized governments ruled by kings. *(page 461)*

• Traditional African religions shared certain beliefs and provided a guide for living together. *(page 463)*

• Islam played an important role in medieval Africa, but long-held African beliefs and customs still remained strong. *(page 464)*

Locating Places
Makkah (MAH•kuh)

Meeting People
Olaudah Equiano (oh•LOW•duh EHK•wee•AHN•oh)
Ibn Battuta (IH•buhn bat•TOO•tah)
Askia Muhammad (ahs•KEE•uh moh•HAH•muhd)

Building Your Vocabulary
clan (KLAN)
sultan (SUHL•tuhn)
Swahili (swah•HEE•lee)

Reading Strategy
Organizing Information Use a diagram to show the components of Swahili culture and language.

NATIONAL GEOGRAPHIC When & Where?

1300	1400	1500
1324 Mansa Musa travels to Makkah	1352 Ibn Battuta arrives in West Africa	1492 Sunni Ali dies

Timbuktu
Mogadishu

SECTION RESOURCES

📁 **Reproducible Masters**
• Reproducible Lesson Plan 13–2
• Daily Lecture and Discussion Notes 13–2
• Vocabulary Activity 13–2
• Active Reading Note-Taking Guide 13–2
• Guided Reading Activity 13–2
• Section Quiz 13–2
• Reading Essentials and Study Guide 13–2

✎ **Transparencies**
• Daily Focus Skills Transparency 13–2

Multimedia
💿 Interactive Tutor Self-Assessment CD-ROM
💿 ExamView® Pro Testmaker CD-ROM
💿 Presentation Plus! CD-ROM
💿 Glencoe BookLink CD-ROM

Government and Society

Main Idea The growth of West African empires led to the growth of centralized governments ruled by kings.

Reading Focus What makes a system of government effective? Read to learn how African rulers governed their empires.

The loud thumping of drums called the citizens of Ghana to a meeting with the king. Anybody with a complaint could speak. In the royal courtyard, the king sat in an open silk tent. He wore a cap of gold and a jewel-covered robe. Royal officials surrounded him. Guard dogs with gold and silver collars stood watch. Before talking to the king, subjects poured dust over their heads or fell to the ground. Bowing, they stated their business and waited for the king's reply.

Ruler and Subject This, said Arab travelers, was how government worked in West Africa. Kings settled arguments, managed trade, and protected the empire. But they expected complete obedience in return.

With the growth of empires, Africans invented new ways to govern themselves. The most successful states, like Ghana, formed some type of central authority. Power usually rested with a king—or, in a few cases, a queen.

Both rulers and people benefited. Merchants received favors from the kings, and the kings received taxes from the merchants. Local rulers kept some power, and the kings in turn received their loyalty. This allowed kingdoms to grow richer and to extend their control over a larger area. The system also helped keep the peace.

Ghana's Government The kings of Ghana relied on help from a council of ministers, or group of close advisers. As the empire

▼ The carving below shows a king of Benin on his throne. The ivory armband (lower left) was worn by the king during ceremonies. *Why did African kings allow local rulers to keep some power?*

grew, rulers divided it into provinces. Lesser kings, often conquered leaders, governed each of these areas. Beneath them, district chiefs oversaw smaller districts. Each district usually included a chief's **clan** (KLAN)—a group of people descended from the same ancestor.

Kings held tightly to their power. They insisted that local rulers send their sons to the royal court. They rode through the countryside seeking reports of injustice or rebellion. Most important, they controlled trade.

Nobody could trade without the king's permission. Also, nobody could own gold nuggets except the king. People traded only in gold dust. "If kings did otherwise," said one Arab traveler, "gold would become so abundant as practically to lose its value."

CHAPTER 13 Medieval Africa   **461**

② TEACH

Forming Hypotheses Ask students how new ideas spread around the world today. Record their answers on the board. Have students identify methods that were not available to people in medieval Africa. **Ask: How do you think new ideas might have spread at that time?** *(by trade, conquest, travel)* Have students check and modify their theories as they read the section. **L2**

Daily Lecture and Discussion Notes 13–2

Use **Daily Lecture and Discussion Notes 13–2** for an outline of key concepts found in the section.

More About the Photo

The larger image depicts a Benin *oba*, or king, surrounded by his pages and guards. The plaque decorated the palace of the Benin king during the early 1600s.

Caption Answer: They gave kings their loyalty in return. This allowed kingdoms to grow larger and richer and helped keep peace.

📖 Reading Strategy ▶ READING THE TEXT

Setting a Purpose Have students read the **Main Ideas** for this section, and then put away their textbooks. Then have them make a list of questions they anticipate will be answered by reading this section. There should be a minimum of three questions per Main Idea. By putting away their textbooks, students will be required to create questions without peeking at assessments in the text for help. Ask for volunteers to share their questions. Then have students write what they think the answers will be. As they read through the section, have them correct their answers. **L1/ EL**

Primary Source

Reading Support L1/ EL

Use **Vocabulary Activity 13–2** to review important terms in the section.

Primary Source

Answer:
Students may suggest that the dinar was worth more because salt was very expensive—worth its weight in gold.

TIME TRAVELER

Kingly processions in Mali were filled with pomp and circumstance. According to Ibn Battuta, musicians with gold-and-silver stringed instruments preceded the king's entry into the royal court and some 300 armed enslaved guards followed him.

✓ Reading Check

Answer: Mali: generals governed provinces, royal officials had more responsibility; Ghana: lesser kings (often conquered rulers) governed provinces, kings kept gold nuggets for themselves

Primary Source
Ghana Profits From Trade

Al Bekri described the way Ghana taxed merchants to increase its own wealth.
"The king [of Ghana] exacts the right of one *dinar* of gold on each donkey-load of salt that enters his country, and two *dinars* of gold on each load of salt that goes out. A load of copper carries a duty of five *mitqals* and a load of merchandise ten *mitqals*. The best gold in the country comes from Ghiaru, a town situated eighteen days' journey from the capital [Kumbi]."

— Abdullah Abu-Ubayd al Bekri, "Ghana in 1067"

▲ Ghana's wealth came from trade caravans.

DBQ Document-Based Question

Which do you think has more worth, a dinar or a mitqal? Why?

One thing about Ghana's government, however, confused outsiders. "It is their custom," exclaimed an Arab writer, "that the kingdom is inherited only by the son of the king's sister." In Arab states, property passed through a man's sons, not the sons of his sister. In Ghana, the throne went to the king's nephew.

Mali's Government Mali followed the example of Ghana, but on a larger scale. It had more territory, more people, and more trade, so royal officials had more responsibilites. One supervised fishing on the Niger. Another looked after the empire's forests. A third oversaw farming, and a fourth managed money.

Kings divided the empire into provinces, like Ghana. However, Sundiata, the founder of Mali, put his generals in charge of them. People accepted it because the generals protected them from invaders. Also, the generals often came from the provinces they ruled.

Mali's other great king, Mansa Musa, rewarded citizens with gold, land, and horses to keep them loyal. He granted military heroes the "National Honor of the Trousers." As one Arab said:

❝ Whenever a hero adds to the lists of his exploits, the king gives him a pair of wide trousers. . . . [T]he greater the number of the knight's [soldier's] exploits, the bigger the size of his trousers. ❞

—Al-Dukhari, as quoted in *Topics in West African History*

Because only the king and royal family could wear sewn clothes, this was a big honor indeed. Most people wore only wrapped clothes.

Songhai's Government Songhai built on the traditions of Ghana and Mali. Its founder, Sunni Ali, divided his empire into provinces. However, he never finished setting up his empire. Sunni continually moved, fighting one battle or another.

In 1492 Sunni Ali died mysteriously on a return trip home. Some say he drowned while crossing a stream. Others say his enemies killed him. The next year, a Songhai general named Muhammad Ture seized control of the government. Unlike Sunni Ali, Muhammad Ture was a loyal Muslim. His religious ideas affected Songhai's government.

✓ Reading Check Contrast How was Mali ruled differently from Ghana?

DIFFERENTIATED INSTRUCTION

Visual/Spatial: Assign students to draw poster-sized organizational charts showing the arrangement of Ghana's government, from kings to clans. Post the charts at the front of the classroom.

Verbal/Linguistic: Call on a group of students to prepare an oral report pointing out how the rulers of Mali modified or changed Ghana's plan of government.

English Learners: Have students write one or two descriptive sentences for each empire in the section defining its plan of government.

📁 Refer to *Inclusion Strategies for the Middle School Social Studies Classroom* in the TCR.

Traditional African Religions

Main Idea Traditional African religions shared certain beliefs and provided a guide for living together.

Reading Focus What questions do most religions try to answer? As you read this section, look for questions answered by traditional African religions.

For centuries, Europeans believed Africans did not have a religion. **Olaudah Equiano** (oh•LOW•duh EHK•wee•AHN•oh), a member of the Igbo, disagreed. The Igbo, he wrote, "believe that there is one Creator of all things, and that he . . . governs events, especially our deaths and captivity."

Most African groups shared the Igbo belief in one supreme god. They understood the Christian and Muslim idea of a single god, but many wanted to continue their own religious practices.

These practices varied from place to place. Some groups, like the Nanti in East Africa, thought people could talk directly with their god. Others, like the Igbo, thought their creator could only be spoken to through less powerful gods and goddesses who worked for him.

Even though Africans practiced their religion differently in different places, their beliefs served similar purposes. They provided rules for living and helped people stay in touch with their history.

When relatives died, many Africans believed their spirits stayed with the community. They believed these spirits could talk to the supreme god or help solve problems. As a result, many Africans honored their ancestors.

✓ Reading Check **Explain** What was the role of ancestors in African religion?

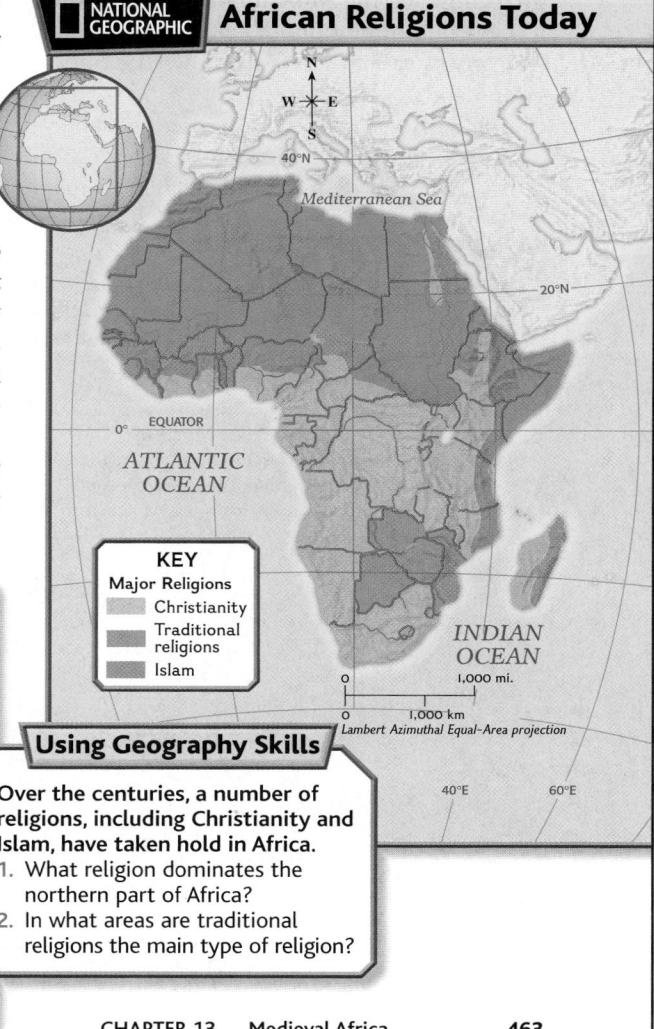

NATIONAL GEOGRAPHIC

African Religions Today

Mediterranean Sea

ATLANTIC OCEAN

EQUATOR

INDIAN OCEAN

KEY
Major Religions
- Christianity
- Traditional religions
- Islam

0 1,000 mi.
0 1,000 km
Lambert Azimuthal Equal-Area projection

Religion in Africa

Traditional African Religions 12.3%

Muslim 40.7%

Christian 46.4%

Other Religions .6%

Source: *The World Almanac and Book of Facts,* 2003

Using Geography Skills

Over the centuries, a number of religions, including Christianity and Islam, have taken hold in Africa.
1. What religion dominates the northern part of Africa?
2. In what areas are traditional religions the main type of religion?

CHAPTER 13   Medieval Africa   **463**

Writing Activity

Assign pairs of students to write a dialogue in which Ibn Battuta interviews Mansa Musa about his accomplishments as king and his recent trip to Makkah. The dialogue should consist of questions and answers. Use these lines to get students started:

Q: How was your trip to Makkah, Your Highness?

A. Spectacular! We stopped in Cairo and several other places along the way. L2

More About the Art

In the 1200s, Djenne became an important marketing center. In addition to gold and salt, slaves were traded there. At its height, Djenne rivaled Timbuktu in terms of prosperity and Muslim culture.

Caption Answer: No; many people in the countryside still followed traditional African religions.

Reading Support L1/ EL

Assign **Guided Reading Activity 13–2** to help students organize the information in the section.

Islam in Africa

Main Idea Islam played an important role in medieval Africa, but long-held African beliefs and customs still remained strong.

Reading Focus Have you ever changed your ideas because someone you respect has different ideas than you do? Learn how African rulers helped spread Islam and how Arabs and Africans influenced each other.

Ibn Battuta (IH•buhn bat•TOO•tah), a young Arab lawyer from Morocco, set out in 1325 to see the Muslim world. Since the A.D. 600s, the religion of Islam had spread from the Arabian Peninsula to Africa and elsewhere.

Ibn Battuta traveled throughout the lands of Islam for almost 30 years. He covered a distance of more than 73,000 miles (117,482 km). When Ibn Battuta arrived in West Africa in 1352, Islam had been practiced there for hundreds of years. Yet he soon realized that not all people in West Africa accepted Islam. Many people in the countryside still followed traditional African religions. Islam was popular in the cities where rulers and traders accepted it by choice or because it helped them trade with Muslim Arabs.

Some Muslims complained that Sundiata Keita and Sunni Ali—western Africa's two great empire builders—did not do enough to win people over to Islam. The two leaders were more concerned about stopping rebellions than spreading religion.

Ibn Battuta found things in West Africa that surprised him. He was amazed that women did not cover their faces with a veil,

The City of Djenne

Like Timbuktu, the city of Djenne became a center for both trade and Islam. Traders from the deserts to the north and the rain forests to the south met at Djenne, located on the Bani River. The first Great Mosque at Djenne was probably built in the 1200s. *Did all of the people in West Africa accept Islam? Explain.*

The Great Mosque
Djenne's Great Mosque was made from baked bricks, and the walls were then covered with mud. The Great Mosque is one of the largest buildings made from mud in western Africa.

Marketplace
Djenne's wealth was based on trade which included items such as gold, salt, and ivory.

Homes
Homes were built from bricks made from clay out of the nearby river. The flat roofs had drains made from palm tree trunks.

Modern-day marketplace in Djenne ▶

INTERDISCIPLINARY CONNECTIONS ACTIVITY

Geography Tell students that today Timbuktu faces invasion by the Sahara. Dry desert winds and shifting sands are destroying plants, drying up water resources, and damaging many of the city's monuments, such as the mosques built by Mansa Musa. Have students research this issue and report their findings in a three-minute news bulletin called "Timbuktu at Risk." L3

Refer to the **Quizzes, Tests, and Authentic Assessment (with Rubrics)** booklet for rubrics.

as was the Muslim custom. However, he did find that West Africans studied the Quran, the Muslim holy book. "They zealously [eagerly] learn the Quran by heart," he wrote.

Mali and Mansa Musa Much of what pleased Ibn Battuta was the work of Mansa Musa. Mansa Musa had allowed different religions but had worked to make Islam stronger. He used the wealth of Mali to build more mosques, or Muslim places of worship. He also set up libraries at Timbuktu, which collected books from all over the Muslim world.

In 1324 Mansa Musa made Mali known to other parts of the world when he set out on a long journey to the city of **Makkah** (MAH•kuh), also known as Mecca. As you read in the chapter on Islam, all Muslims are supposed to make a pilgrimage to the Muslim holy city of Makkah. When Mansa Musa set out on his trip, however, he made sure everybody knew he was the leader of a great empire.

Mansa Musa's caravan had thousands of people, including enslaved people, and 100 pack camels. Each camel carried gold. While in Makkah, Mansa Musa convinced some of Islam's finest architects, teachers, and writers to return with him to Mali. There they helped spread Islam in West Africa.

Songhai and Askia Muhammad Sunni Ali practiced the traditional religion of the Songhai people. However, he declared himself a Muslim to keep the support of townspeople. After Sunni Ali died, his son refused to follow his father's example.

As you read earlier, Muhammad Ture, one of Sunni Ali's generals, saw a chance to take over the government. With the support of Muslim townspeople, he declared himself king. In a bloody war, he drove Sunni Ali's family from Songhai. He then took the name Askia, a rank in the Songhai army.

Primary Source
The Sultan of Mali

The sultan in this passage is Mansa Musa. He is described by an Arab scholar named Ibn Fadl Allah al Omari.

▲ Mansa Musa

"The sultan of this kingdom presides in his palace on a great balcony called *bembe* where he has a great seat of ebony that is like a throne fit for a large and tall person: on either side it is flanked by elephant tusks turned towards each other. His arms [weapons] stand near him, being all of gold, saber, lance, quiver, bow and arrows. He wears wide trousers made of about twenty pieces [of stuff] of a kind which he alone may wear."

—Ibn Fadl Allah al Omari, "Mali in the Fourteenth Century"

DBQ Document-Based Questions

What impression did Mansa Musa want to make on newcomers to his kingdom? How do you know?

Under **Askia Muhammad** (ahs•KEE•uh moh•HAH•muhd), Songhai built the largest empire in medieval West Africa. He kept local courts in place but told them to honor Muslim laws. He also made Timbuktu an important center of Islamic culture and set up some 150 schools to teach the Quran.

History Online

Web Activity Visit jat.glencoe.com and click on *Chapter 13—Student Web Activity* to learn more about medieval Africa.

CHAPTER 13   Medieval Africa   **465**

Primary Source

Answer: He intended to awe visitors; everything was very expensive.

3 ASSESS

Assign Section 2 Review as homework or as an in-class activity.

🖱 Have students use the **Interactive Tutor Self-Assessment CD-ROM** to review the section.

Assessment L2

Assign **Section 2 Quiz** to assess mastery of the material found in the section.

Reading Support L1/ EL

Assign **Reading Essentials and Study Guide 13–2** to help students review section material.

History Online

Objectives and answers to the student activity can be found in the **Web Activity Lesson Plan** feature at jat.glencoe.com

EXTENDING THE CONTENT

How Has Swahili Borrowed From Other Languages? As a language of trade, Swahili has borrowed words from more languages than Bantu, Arabic, and Persian. It has also picked up words from Portuguese, German, and English. Students may recognize some of these Swahili terms: *motokaa, baiskeli, mashini, roketi, kampuni, daktari, chaki,* and *tai. (motorcar, bicycle, machine, rocket, company, doctor, chalk,* and *tie)*

Biography

TEACH

Tell students that when Mansa Musa arrived in Egypt, officials beseeched him to meet with the Egyptian sultan. Protocol obligated the emperor of Mali to kiss the ground before the sultan. Mansa Musa—an imperial power in his own right—at first refused to do this. However, by the advice of a counselor, Mansa Musa then declared, "Very well, I will prostrate [flatten] myself before Allah who created me and brought me into the world." The sultan then rose and asked Mansa Musa to sit beside him. **Ask: Why did this conflict between the two Muslim rulers arise?** *(because both saw themselves as supreme powers with no human above them)* **How was it resolved?** *(Mansa Musa declared he was prostrating himself before Allah, not the sultan.)*

Discuss with students some of the protocols observed with the president of the United States. *(Examples might include: use of a red carpet, members of Congress standing when the president enters the House or Senate, and so on.)* **L2**

Then and Now

Answers will vary. Many students will say that modern technology makes this impossible. Other students may mention that small countries with little economic base may be ignored by other countries.

Biography

MANSA MUSA
Ruled 1312–1337

Mansa Musa ruled the West African empire of Mali with great skill and organization. Under Mansa Musa's guidance, Mali became a great center of education, commerce, and the arts. Mali was one of the largest empires in the world at the time. In fact, the kingdom was so vast that Mansa Musa once bragged it would take a year to travel from the northern border to the southern border.

Despite Mali's enormous size and wealth, the kingdom was not well-known outside the continent of Africa. Mansa Musa's pilgrimage to Makkah in 1324, however, announced Mali's riches and achievements to the world. Traveling on horseback, Mansa Musa was joined by many people, including 8,000 enslaved people, 100 camels to carry baggage, and 24,000 pounds of gold. Each person carried a staff of gold. According to Egyptian historians and the accounts of observers, Mansa Musa spent so much gold in Cairo, Egypt, that the value of gold dropped in Cairo and did not recover for more than 12 years.

Mansa Musa's famous pilgrimage to Makkah brought attention to his kingdom. Mali was included on world maps as early as 1339. Many European nations and kingdoms in North Africa and the Middle East wished to establish trade connections with Mali and gain some of its wealth. Mali's territory and trade connections expanded even further with the capture of the cities Gao and Timbuktu, which also flourished under Mansa Musa's rule.

▲ Mansa Musa

▲ A village in Mali today

Then and Now

Mali was unnoticed by the rest of the world until Mansa Musa's pilgrimage. Is it possible for a present-day country to go unnoticed? Why or why not?

Reading List Generator CD-ROM

GLENCOE BOOKLINK   **RECOMMENDED READING**

Use the **Glencoe BookLink CD-ROM** to create customized reading lists based on your students' interests and reading levels. Below is an example based on content in this chapter. Also, see the Suggested Readings on pages 944–946 of the Appendix.

- **Bleeker, Sonia.** *The Tuareg: Nomads and Warriors of the Sahara.* The Tuareg are a nomadic people who drive their camel caravans across the Sahara.
- **Chu, Daniel, and Elliott Skinner.** *A Glorious Age in Africa: The Story of Three Great African Empires.* Stories of Ghana, Mali, and Songhai.
- **Nwanunobi, C.O.** *Soninke.* The Soninke of West Africa founded the empire of Ghana. Today, many Soninke live in Mali.

The empire survived family disputes. But, as you have read, it did not survive the guns of Moroccan invaders. The invasion in 1591 shattered the empire.

Islam in East Africa In 1331 Ibn Battuta visited Mogadishu, a trading port on the East African coast. Its **sultan** (SUHL•tuhn), or leader, said in perfect Arabic, "You have honored our country by coming." A moment later, Ibn Battuta heard the sultan speak in **Swahili** (swah•HEE•lee).

The word *Swahili* comes from an Arabic word meaning "people of the coast." By 1331, however, it had come to mean two things: the unique culture of East Africa's coast and the language spoken there.

The Swahili culture and language, which exist in East Africa today, are a blend of African and Muslim influences. African influences came from the cultures of Africa's interior. Muslim influences came from Arab and Persian settlers.

When Europeans from Portugal arrived on the coast in the early 1500s, they tried to destroy the Swahili culture. The Swahili responded by halting inland trade. In the end, the Swahili culture outlived European rule.

Islam's Impact on Africa Islam had a far-reaching impact on northern and eastern Africa. Africans who accepted Islam also adopted Islamic laws and ideas about right and wrong. Sometimes these changes were opposed by people who favored traditional African ways.

Islam also advanced learning. Muslim schools drew students from many parts of Africa and introduced the Arabic language to many Africans. Islam also influenced African art and buildings. Muslim architects built beautiful mosques and palaces in Timbuktu and other cities.

✓ **Reading Check** **Explain** How did Askia Muhammad gain control of Songhai?

Study Central™ Need help with the material in this section? Visit jat.glencoe.com

Section 2 Review

Reading Summary
Review the Main Ideas

• The empires of West Africa were ruled by kings, who closely controlled trade and divided their lands among lesser chiefs to aid in governing.

• Many African religions believed in a single creator and honored the spirits of ancestors.

• Islam became the dominant religion in the kingdoms of West and East Africa.

What Did You Learn?

1. How did the kings of Ghana hold tightly to their power?

2. How did Mansa Musa attempt to strengthen Islam in Mali?

Critical Thinking

3. **Cause and Effect** Draw a diagram to show the effects of Islam on West and East Africa.

4. **Analyze** How did having the central authority rest with a single person benefit the king, individuals, and the kingdom? How is this model of a government reflected in modern government?

5. **Expository Writing** Imagine you were a witness to Mansa Musa's pilgrimage to Makkah. Write a newspaper article describing the pilgrimage.

6. **Reading** **Compare and Contrast** Draw a Venn diagram to compare the leadership of Mansa Musa and Askia Muhammad.

ENRICH

Tell students that in Timbuktu, manuscripts were highly valued, perhaps more than any other merchandise. Ask students what that fact indicates about Timbuktu. **L1/EL**

✓ **Reading Check**

Answer: With support from the townspeople, he declared himself king and drove Sunni Ali's family from Songhai.

To help students understand section material, have them visit Study Central™ **at jat.glencoe.com**

RETEACH

Ask students to name some of the places discussed in this section. Record these on the board, and have students cite at least one fact about each. **L2**

④ CLOSE

Have students review causes for the spread of Islam in Africa. **L1**

SECTION 2 REVIEW ANSWERS

1. insisted local rulers send their sons to royal court, traveled through kingdom, controlled trade

2. built mosques, set up Muslim libraries, invited Muslim scholars to Mali

3. Islam influenced laws, art, and architecture and advanced learning.

4. A king granted favors to his subjects, who paid taxes and were loyal to him. Answers may vary.

5. Articles will vary but should give details of the trip.

6. Mansa Musa: rewarded loyal citizens and military heroes; allowed different religions; made Islam stronger; Askia Muhammad: built largest empire in medieval West Africa; combined provinces into five kingdoms; honored Muslim laws; Both: made Timbuktu center of learning

① FOCUS

SECTION OVERVIEW

This section explores the effects of the Bantu migrations and the start of the African slave trade, which carried Africans and their varied cultures around the world.

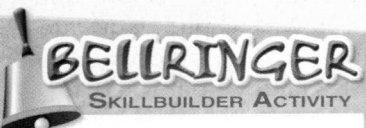

🔔 Project **Daily Focus Skills Transparency 13–3** and have students answer questions. Discuss their responses.

Get Ready to Read!

Preteaching Vocabulary: For many cultures, oral history was their method of preserving history. Storytellers would memorize historical accounts and pass them down by word of mouth rather than in written form. Today, oral history occurs in our society in the form of recorded interviews.

Answers to Graphic: Africa: enslaved persons could gain freedom by buying or earning it, marrying a free person, or escaping; became slaves as criminals or captives of war; Europe: enslaved persons carried to distant lands with little hope of escape; rarely able to buy or earn freedom; Both: had to work in servitude to others

---

Section 3

African Society and Culture

Get Ready to Read!

What's the Connection?
By the time Europeans came to Africa, people all over the continent had developed complex cultures. For most Africans, life centered on farming villages, like the ones you will read about in this section. Here the family formed the basis of society.

Focusing on the Main Ideas
- The Bantu migrations helped shape many cultures in Africa south of the Sahara. *(page 469)*
- The African slave trade changed greatly when Muslims and Europeans began taking captives from the continent. *(page 472)*
- Enslaved Africans developed rich cultures that influenced many other cultures, including our own. *(page 474)*

Locating Places
Benue River (BAYN•way)

Meeting People
Dahia al-Kahina (dah•HEE•ah ahl•kah•HEE•nah)
Nzinga (ehn•ZIHN•gah)

Building Your Vocabulary
extended family
matrilineal (MA•truh•LIH•nee•uhl)
oral history

Reading Strategy
Compare and Contrast Create a Venn diagram like the one below showing the similarities and differences between the enslavement of Africans in Africa and the enslavement of Africans in Europe.

Enslavement in Africa ⬭⬭ Enslavement in Europe

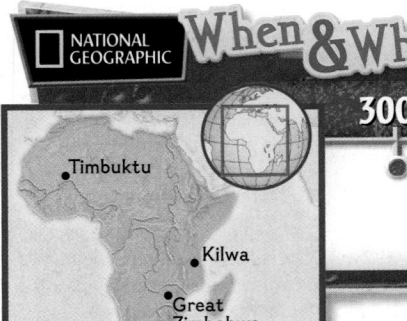

NATIONAL GEOGRAPHIC **When & Where?**

Timbuktu
Kilwa
Great Zimbabwe

3000 B.C.

A.D. 1000

1500

c. 3000 B.C. Bantu begin migration across Africa

c. A.D. 650 Queen Dahia al-Kahina fights Muslims

c. 1441 First enslaved Africans arrive in Europe

SECTION RESOURCES

📁 **Reproducible Masters**
- Reproducible Lesson Plan 13–3
- Daily Lecture and Discussion Notes 13–3
- Vocabulary Activity 13–3
- Active Reading Note-Taking Guide 13–3
- Guided Reading Activity 13–3
- Section Quiz 13–3
- Reading Essentials and Study Guide 13–3

🔦 **Transparencies**
- Daily Focus Skills Transparency 13–3

Multimedia
- 🔘 Interactive Tutor Self-Assessment CD-ROM
- 🔘 ExamView® Pro Testmaker CD-ROM
- 🔘 Presentation Plus! CD-ROM
- 🔘 Vocabulary PuzzleMaker CD-ROM
- 🔘 Glencoe BookLink CD-ROM

Life in Medieval Africa

Main Idea The Bantu migrations helped shape many cultures in Africa south of the Sahara.

Reading Focus Have you ever noticed that even though people are different, they all have some things in common? Read to learn why people in different regions of Africa have similar traditions and cultures.

Around 3000 B.C., fishing groups along the **Benue River** (BAYN•way) in present day eastern Nigeria packed belongings in their canoes and moved south and west. The wanderers called themselves *Bantu,* meaning "the people."

The Bantu traveled slowly and by different routes. At least some paddled up the Congo River—a waterway twisting 2,700 miles (4,345 km) through the rain forests. Many settled, for a time, in the grasslands of central Africa. From there, they fanned out over much of the land south of the Sahara. By A.D. 400, Bantu peoples had settled much of Africa.

Historians are not sure why the Bantu left their homeland. Perhaps the land became too crowded. Maybe farmers wore out the soil. Or the Bantu may have just drifted, the way pioneers sometimes do.

Wherever they went, the Bantu took their culture with them. They spread skills such as pottery making, mining, and ironworking. They also spread their language. Today more than 120 million Africans speak hundreds of Bantu languages, including Swahili.

The Bantu migrations, or movements of a large number of people, are the reason people all across Africa share some common ideas and traditions. The Bantu, for example, believed in one supreme creator and a spirit world where ancestors live. As you read in the last section, this was a common belief in many places in Africa.

Importance of Family The family formed the basis of African society. People often lived in **extended families,** or families made up of several generations. They included anywhere from ten to hundreds of members.

Many villages, especially Bantu villages, were **matrilineal** (MA•truh•LIH•nee•uhl). They traced their descent through mothers rather than fathers. When a woman married, however, she joined her husband's family. To make up for the loss, her family received gifts—cloth, metal tools, cattle, or goats—from the husband's family.

All families valued children greatly. They saw them as a link between the past and the future. Some people, like the Yoruba of what is today Nigeria, believed

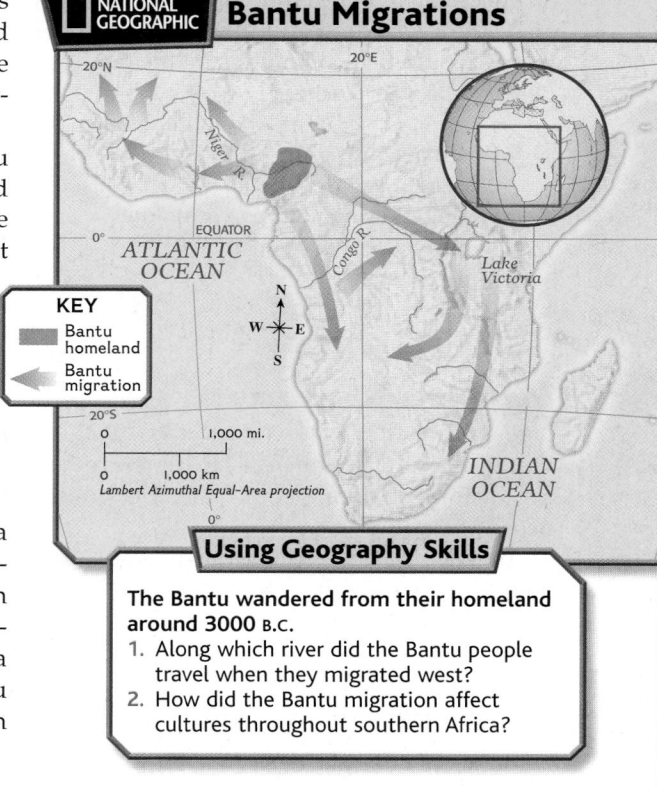

NATIONAL GEOGRAPHIC **Bantu Migrations**

KEY
- Bantu homeland
- Bantu migration

Using Geography Skills

The Bantu wandered from their homeland around 3000 B.C.
1. Along which river did the Bantu people travel when they migrated west?
2. How did the Bantu migration affect cultures throughout southern Africa?

CHAPTER 13   Medieval Africa   469

Reading Strategy

Comparing Cultures Read aloud the **Reading Focus** under the head "Life in Medieval Africa." Ask students to brainstorm a list of some of the things different communities in the United States have in common. To get students started, write "Government Under the Constitution" on the board. As they read this section, have students create a list of things Africans share. **L2**

Daily Lecture and Discussion Notes 13-3

Use **Daily Lecture and Discussion Notes 13–3** for an outline of key concepts found in the section.

Reading Support L1/EL

Use **Vocabulary Activity 13–3** to review important terms in the section.

Using Geography Skills

Answers:
1. the Niger
2. They spread common ideas and traditions across Africa.

Reading Strategy   **READING THE TEXT**

Skimming One reading technique that always benefits from practice is skimming. Remind students that this involves glancing quickly at the pages to peek at what is ahead. The text provides many tools to help a reader skim, such as boldface titles, statements of main ideas, and so on. One technique that is useful in skimming is to look first at opening paragraphs, which often reveal a writer's purpose. Have students skim this section. When they have finished, ask students to state some of the things they have learned and expect to learn after a thorough read. **L1/EL**

More About the Art

Art, such as the piece shown, provides significant information about life in the Congo. Homes, for example, are round with thatched roofs. In addition, some people are farmers, and children help with the work. The role of women as mothers is depicted by the mother holding the child.

Caption Answer: a family made up of several generations

CURRICULUM CONNECTION

Science

When the Bantu reached the island of Madagascar, they learned to grow two crops that were well suited to the rain forests—yams and bananas. These foods became staples in African diets and traveled across the Atlantic with enslaved Africans. Yams added another food to a diet filled with a variety of potatoes native to the Americas.

Reading Check

Answer: as extended families with many generations in one home

▲ This panel shows a family from the Congo at work.
What was an extended family in Bantu society?

an ancestor might be reborn in a child. They also knew children guaranteed that the family would live on. In praising the family, one Yoruba poet wrote:

> 66 When a group of boys, girls,
>   men, or wives,
>   Go together in a happy company,
>   Dignity attends them in
>   every step.
> 99
>
> —Yoruba, "Dignity"

Education and Community In Africa's villages, education was carried out by the family and other villagers. Children learned the history of their people and the skills needed as adults.

In West Africa, griots, or storytellers, helped in schooling. They kept alive an **oral history**—the stories passed down from generation to generation. Many stories included a lesson about living. Lessons also were given through short proverbs.

One Bantu proverb stated: "A good deed will make a good neighbor." Grandparents and other older people also kept oral histories alive.

Role of Women As in most medieval societies, women in Africa acted mostly as wives and mothers. Men had more rights and controlled much of what women did. Visitors to Africa, however, saw exceptions. European explorers were amazed to learn that women served as soldiers in some African kingdoms.

African women also won fame as rulers. In the A.D. 600s, Queen **Dahia al-Kahina** (dah•HEE•uh ahl•kah•HEE•nah) led the fight against the Muslim invasion of her kingdom, which was located about where Mauritania is today. Another woman ruler was Queen **Nzinga** (ehn•ZIHN•gah), who ruled lands in what are now Angola and Congo. She spent almost 40 years battling Portuguese slave traders.

Reading Check **Explain** How were Bantu families organized?

470   CHAPTER 13   Medieval Africa

DIFFERENTIATED INSTRUCTION

Verbal/Linguistic: Have students explain the meaning of each of these Bantu proverbs in their own words: (1) "Every beast roars in his own den." (2) "No man can paddle two canoes at the same time." (3) "The earth is a beehive; we all enter by the same door but live in different cells."

Visual/Spatial: Assign students to design posters illustrating each proverb.

Gifted and Talented: Assign students to research some Swahili proverbs. Then have them compose several of their own. Ask them to display their proverbs on drawings of Kanga cloth, such as is worn all along the Swahili coast, or on poster board.

Biography

QUEEN NZINGA
c. 1582–1663

Angolan Warrior-Leader

It was rare in the 1600s for women to take active roles in politics and war, but one African woman—Queen Nzinga of Matamba—was known for her military leadership and political skills. Nzinga was the daughter of the king of the Ndongo people. The Ndongo lived in southwest Africa in what is today called Angola. Nzinga quickly learned archery and hunting. She was intelligent and a natural athlete. Nzinga's father failed to notice his daughter. He was too busy defending the kingdom from the Portuguese, who wanted to buy enslaved Africans and ship them overseas.

Even though she was female, Nzinga knew she could be a strong leader. She did not want to learn the enemy's language, but she soon realized that it could benefit her. She asked a captured priest to teach her Portuguese.

In 1623 Nzinga became queen. She declared all of her territory to be free territory and promised that all enslaved Africans who made it to the kingdom would be free. For nearly 30 years, she led her people in battles against the Portuguese. She allied with other African kingdoms to seal the trade routes used to ship enslaved Africans out of the country. In 1662 she negotiated a peace agreement with the Portuguese. She died the next year at age 81.

▲ Enslaved Africans in a ship's hold being taken to America.

◄ The Portuguese built Elmire Castle on the coast of Ghana to hold enslaved Africans before shipping them overseas.

Then and Now

Do research to find the name of a modern female leader. Compare her leadership skills to those of Queen Nzinga.

471

TEACH

Nzinga's talents as a ruler-diplomat were exceptional. After becoming queen, she made various alliances to try to protect her people from the slave trade. For example, she allied first with the Portuguese. Later, when the Portuguese betrayed her, she was forced to flee to the west, where she founded a new state at Matamba. She built a small army and allied her country with the Netherlands. Though she never had the forces to reclaim her old kingdom, Nzinga was able to develop Matamba as a trading power and through the years became recognized for her abilities and successes.

Have students consider the personal traits of leaders. Elicit from students what made Nzinga an effective leader. **Ask: What traits do you think help make an effective leader today?** (*Answers will vary but may include the ability to communicate and make difficult decisions.*) **L2**

Then and Now

Students' answers will vary depending on the person they choose. Qualities of an effective leader will also vary depending on students' opinions. Common threads may be the ability to motivate people, athletic skills, and the ability to adapt.

Reading List Generator CD-ROM

GLENCOE BOOKLINK **RECOMMENDED READING**

Use the **Glencoe BookLink CD-ROM** to create customized reading lists based on your students' interests and reading levels. Below is an example based on content in this chapter. Also, see the Suggested Readings on pages 944–946 of the Appendix.

- McKissack, Patricia. *Nzingha: Warrior Queen of Matamba.* Nzingha is a 13-year-old princess who fought against the slave trade.
- Raskin, Lawrie, and Debora Pearson. *52 Days by Camel: My Sahara Adventure.* Lawrie Raskin takes a real-life trek with a camel caravan across the Sahara.
- Watson, Pete. *The Market Lady and the Mango Tree.* A crafty merchant in a West African village comes up with a plan to get rich by keeping all the mangoes from the village trees for herself.

More About the Art

It is estimated that the number of enslaved Africans loaded onto ships may have topped 11 million. It was one of the biggest forced migrations of people in world history.

Caption Answer: because harvesting sugarcane was hard labor and planters could not afford to pay high wages to get workers

TIME TRAVELER

Naming ceremonies were—and still are—an important part of traditional African life. Ceremonies varied from place to place, but a child might receive several names, including the day of birth, the birth order among children, a father's or mother's family name, and a special name, such as "reborn one." The "reborn one" keeps alive the memory of an ancestor.

Slavery

Main Idea The African slave trade changed greatly when Muslims and Europeans began taking captives from the continent.

Reading Focus You know that there was a time in American history when people of African ancestry were enslaved. Read to learn about slavery in African society and the beginning of the European slave trade.

In 1441 a Portuguese sea captain sailed down Africa's western coast. His goal was to bring the first African captives back to Portugal. During the voyage, the captain and his nine sailors seized 12 Africans—men, women, and boys. The ship then sailed back to Portugal. These captives represented only a small portion of a slave trade that would grow into the millions.

Slavery Within Africa Europeans did not invent slavery. For a long time, it had existed throughout the world. In Africa, Bantu chiefs raided nearby villages for captives. These captives became laborers or were freed for a payment.

Africans also enslaved criminals or enemies taken in war. These enslaved Africans became part of the Saharan trade. However, as long as Africans stayed in Africa, hope of escape still existed. Enslaved Africans might also win their freedom through hard work or by marrying a free person.

The trade in humans also grew as the trade with Muslim merchants increased. The Quran forbade enslavement of Muslims. Muslims, however, could enslave non-Muslims. Arab traders, therefore, began to trade horses, cotton, and other goods for enslaved, non-Muslim Africans.

When Europeans arrived in West Africa, a new market for enslaved Africans opened. Africans armed with European guns began raiding villages to seize captives to sell.

▲ On a slave ship, enslaved people were transported in the dark, crowded spaces of the ship's cargo deck. *Why were enslaved Africans used on Portuguese plantations?*

The European Slave Trade In 1444 a Portuguese ship docked at a port in Portugal. Sailors unloaded the cargo—235 enslaved Africans. Tears ran down the faces of some. Others cried for help. A Portuguese official described the scene:

❝ **But to increase their sufferings still more, . . . was it needful to part fathers from sons, husbands from wives, brothers from brothers.** ❞

—Gomes Eannes de Zurara, as quoted in *The Slave Trade*

Barely three years had passed since the arrival of the first African captives in Portugal. Some merchants who had hoped

472 CHAPTER 13 Medieval Africa

CRITICAL THINKING ACTIVITY

Forming Inferences Tell students that the Lamba, a Bantu people, have passed down a story called "A Slave May Work for Freedom." In this story, an enslaved worker discovers how to grow more gourds. When the chief learns the news, he tells the worker, "My servant, you are doing well, now, leave my service and go home." **Ask:** What did the chief mean when he told the servant to leave his service and go home? *(The servant was free and no longer a slave.)* What can you infer about African slavery from this story? *(Answers will vary, but students should see that the hope of freedom existed—a contrast to the European slave trade.)* **L2**

to sell gold brought from Africa now sold humans instead. At first, most enslaved Africans stayed in Portugal, working as laborers. This changed when the Portuguese settled the Atlantic islands of Madeira, the Azores, and Cape Verde. There the climate was perfect for growing cotton, grapes, and sugarcane on plantations, or huge farms.

Harvesting sugarcane was hard labor. Planters could not pay high wages to get workers, so they used enslaved Africans instead. Many Africans had farming skills and the ability to make tools. Enslaved people were not paid and could be fed and kept cheaply. By 1500, Portugal was the world's leading supplier of sugar.

The rest of Europe followed Portugal's example. In the late 1400s, Europeans arrived in the Americas. They set up sugar plantations and brought enslaved Africans across the Atlantic Ocean to work the fields. They also used enslaved people to grow tobacco, rice, and cotton.

✓ Reading Check **Analyze** How did exploration change the African slave trade?

✓ **Reading Check**

Answer: New European colonies used enslaved Africans for hard labor. As more colonies were set up, more people were enslaved.

Using Geography Skills

Answers:
1. the western coast and the interior
2. the east coast of North and South America, the West Indies

Writing Activity

Have students write a list of evidence that supports the argument to end the slave trade. Have students use this information to draw up a petition that a Portuguese citizen might present to the king. The petition should begin: "Resolved: That the trade in enslaved Africans should end immediately. Reasons being:" *(Have students fill in here.)* In a follow-up discussion, explore what the king might say in response and why. **L2**

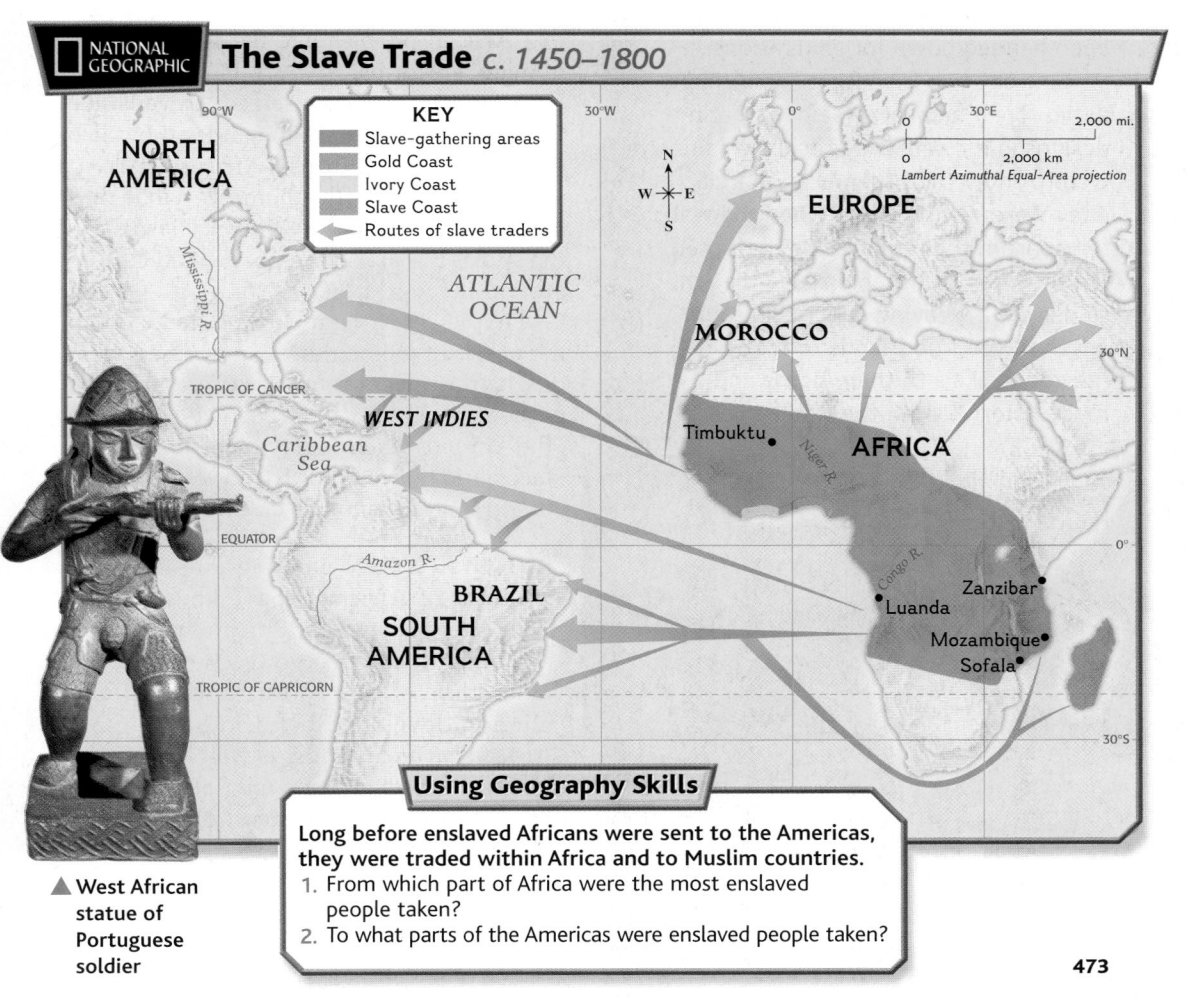

NATIONAL GEOGRAPHIC — The Slave Trade *c. 1450–1800*

KEY
- Slave-gathering areas
- Gold Coast
- Ivory Coast
- Slave Coast
- → Routes of slave traders

Lambert Azimuthal Equal-Area projection

▲ West African statue of Portuguese soldier

Using Geography Skills

Long before enslaved Africans were sent to the Americas, they were traded within Africa and to Muslim countries.
1. From which part of Africa were the most enslaved people taken?
2. To what parts of the Americas were enslaved people taken?

473

INTERDISCIPLINARY CONNECTIONS ACTIVITY

Language Arts Tell students that the slave trade had an impact on American literature. Antislavery poet John Greenleaf Whittier took the lyrics from a song sung by enslaved African women as they trudged across the Sahara and turned them into a poem. Read the poem's opening lines:

Where are we going? Where are we going? . . .
Strange and large the world is growing!

Ask: What do these lines show about the feelings of enslaved Africans? *(Possible answer: They felt fear and confusion as they were led farther and farther from their homes.)* Have students write their own poem describing what a newly enslaved person might feel. **L2**

CONNECTING ACROSS TIME

Mention to students that many African Americans renew their ancestral ties with Africa during Kwanza, a seven-day festival that begins on December 26. Have students find out more about Kwanza through research on the Internet or at the library. **L2**

Drums played an important part in African music. However, when slaveholders in the Americas figured out that drums could be used for secret communications, they banned them. Enslaved Africans turned to other rhythmic sounds—hand clapping, feet tapping, the use of bells and gourds, and vocal sounds.

Answers:

1. because it requires elaborate weaving like spider webs

2. Answers will vary. Students may suggest that men wanted to do this important job or that it was part of their culture to have men weave.

NATIONAL GEOGRAPHIC — The Way It Was

Focus on Everyday Life

Kente Cloth *Kente* is the name of a colorful woven cloth. Its name comes from a word that means "basket." The first weavers were mostly men. They used fibers to make cloth that looked like the patterns in baskets. Strips were sewn together to make colorful patterns. *Kente* was worn by tribal chiefs and is still popular today. This African folktale about *kente* cloth has been handed down for generations:

One day two friends walked through a rain forest and saw a spider creating designs in its web. They took the spider web to show their friends and family. They were greatly upset when the web fell apart in their hands. They returned the next day to watch and learn as the spider did a weaving dance and spun another web. The friends took their newfound skills to their looms and made colorful cloth they called *kente*.

◄ African women wearing *kente* cloth

Connecting to the Past

1. Why does the legend suggest that Africans learned to weave *kente* cloth from a spider?

2. Why do you think the first *kente* cloth weavers were mostly men?

African Culture

Main Idea Enslaved Africans developed rich cultures that influenced many other cultures, including our own.

Reading Focus Do you have any traditions that have been in your family for a long time? Read to learn how Africans took their culture with them when they were enslaved and sent overseas.

"We are almost a nation of dancers, musicians, and poets," declared Olaudah Equiano in describing the Igbo people of West Africa. He might have added artists, weavers, woodcarvers, and metalworkers too. African peoples like the Igbo excelled in many art forms.

When slave traders seized Africans like Equiano from their homelands, they also uprooted their cultures. Africans carried these cultures with them in what has become known as the African Diaspora—the spreading of African people and culture around the world.

People of African descent held on to memories of their cultures and passed them down from generation to generation. The heritage of Africa can be seen and heard in the United States today—not just in the faces and voices of African descendants but in their gifts to our culture.

African Art Cave paintings are the earliest form of African art we know about. They show people hunting animals, dancing, and doing everyday chores. As in other parts of the world, African art and religion developed hand in hand. Early African cave paintings, as well as later art, almost always had some religious meaning or use. Woodcarvers made masks and statues, for example, to celebrate African religious beliefs. Each carved piece of wood captured some part of the spiritual world.

EXTENDING THE CONTENT

Why Were Cowrie Shells Valuable? The slave trade changed the economic system of Africa by spreading the use of cowrie shells—a shell widely found in the shallow waters of the Indian Ocean—as a form of money. The shells were rare in much of Africa and became a kind of international currency. By the late 1700s, the price of an enslaved African might be valued at 160,000 cowries. Africans would then use the cowries to trade for other goods or to decorate jewelry and clothing. Cowries are still valued in Africa for their beauty.

African works of art also told stories and served practical purposes. Artists working in wood, ivory, or bronze showed the faces of important leaders, everyday people, and, later, European explorers and traders. Weavers designed cloth similar to cloth still worn today. You may have seen the brightly colored kente cloth of West Africa. Many people wear it today.

Music and Dance Music played a part in almost all aspects of African life. People used it to express their religious feelings or to get through an everyday task, like planting a field.

In many African songs, a singer calls out a line, then other singers repeat it back. Musical instruments, such as drums, whistles, horns, flutes, or banjos, were used to keep the beat.

Africans believed dance allowed the spirits to express themselves. So they used it to celebrate important events such as birth and death. Nearly everybody danced. Lines of men and women swayed and clapped their hands. Individual dancers

Linking Past & Present

African Music

THEN Traditional African music comes from many different sounds and rhythms. Every culture in Africa contributed to its development. Some used drums. Others used wind and string instruments. Many imitated nature through voice and dance. African music was handed down from one generation to another.

▼ Modern-day musicians

NOW Traditional African music influences rap, hip-hop, pop, and rock music. The use of drums and a steady beat comes from African tribal music. *Can you name current groups or artists who have been impacted by the African musical style?*

▲ Traditional African musicians

CHAPTER 13 Medieval Africa **475**

COOPERATIVE LEARNING ACTIVITY

Creating a Radio Broadcast Break the class into groups, and assign each group one of the forms of popular music that shows the influence of Africa and the African American experience. Choices might include blues, gospel, ragtime, jazz, rock and roll, and rap. Appoint one student to serve as a deejay. This person should meet with each group to plan a program that includes a short introduction from a group member. With rehearsal, the program might be offered as a special school presentation. L1/EL

ENRICH

Encourage students to think about the global effects of the African slave trade. **Ask: What worlds were brought together by the slave trade?** *(Europe, Africa, and the Americas)* **L1**

Answer: They believed dancing allowed the spirits to express themselves.

To help students understand section material, have them visit **Study Central™** at jat.glencoe.com

RETEACH

Quiz students by asking them to define the terms listed in the **Get Ready to Read!** feature. **L1/ EL**

④ CLOSE

Hold a two-minute brainstorming session in which students name some of the things Africans shared despite their great diversity. **L2**

◀ Griots still share the stories and lessons of their ancestors. *What were traditional African stories often about?*

leaped and twirled. In the background, drummers sounded out the rhythm.

Enslaved Africans sometimes relied on music to remind them of their homeland. Songs of hardship eventually developed into a type of music that we know today as the blues. Songs of religious faith and hopes for freedom grew into spirituals or gospel songs. Over time, other forms of African-based music developed, such as ragtime, jazz, rock and roll, and, more recently, rap.

Storytelling Africans also kept alive their storytelling tradition. A few enslaved Africans escaped and were able to record their stories. Others retold their stories aloud. Those who heard the stories repeated them. They also retold tales taught by griots in the African homeland. Popular stories often told how small animals, such as turtles and rabbits, outsmarted larger ones.

In more recent times, some African Americans have renewed ties with their past by taking African names or giving them to their children. This also helps keep alive African history and culture.

✓ **Reading Check** **Explain** Why did Africans use dance to celebrate important events?

Study Central™ Need help with the material in this section? Visit jat.glencoe.com

Section ③ Review

Reading Summary
Review the Main Ideas

- Many Africans south of the Sahara lived in small villages. Family was very important, and women had fewer rights than men.

- Africans had kept slaves long before they began to trade enslaved persons to Muslims and Europeans.

- As enslaved Africans were taken to new areas, African culture, including art, music, and storytelling, spread around the world.

What Did You Learn?
1. What was the African Diaspora?

2. What is the earliest form of African art known? Describe some of the subjects portrayed in the art.

Critical Thinking
3. **Organizing Information** Draw a diagram like the one below. Fill in details about African music and dance.

```
        ○   ○
     ○           ○
   ○  African Music  ○
      and Dance
     ○           ○
        ○   ○
```

4. **Compare** How were African art and religion related?

5. **Identify** What was Queen Dahia al-Kahina's greatest accomplishment?

6. **Infer** Why do you think some Africans liked tales in which small animals outsmarted larger animals?

7. **Persuasive Writing** Portuguese plantation owners relied on slave labor to help them grow sugarcane. Suppose you had a family member who was enslaved on a plantation. Write a letter to the plantation owner explaining why this practice is unacceptable.

SECTION 3 REVIEW ANSWERS

1. the spreading of African peoples and cultures around the world

2. cave paintings; people hunting, doing chores, dancing

3. Web diagrams should reflect traits of African music and dance mentioned in the text.

4. Most artwork had some religious meaning or use or tried to capture some part of the spiritual world.

5. She led the fight against the Muslim invasion of her country.

6. Possible answer: because they saw parallels to their own lives and hoped to outwit those who held them in bondage

7. Answers may include how hard this was on the family and how unjust it was to the enslaved person.

Section 1 The Rise of African Civilizations

Vocabulary
plateau
griot
dhow

Focusing on the Main Ideas
- Africa has a vast and varied landscape. *(page 445)*
- West African empires grew rich from trade. *(page 447)*
- Africa's rain forests blocked invaders and provided resources. *(page 450)*
- East African kingdoms and states became centers for trade and new ideas. *(page 451)*

Section 2 Africa's Government and Religion

Vocabulary
clan
sultan
Swahili

Focusing on the Main Ideas
- The growth of West African empires led to the growth of centralized governments ruled by kings. *(page 461)*
- Traditional African religions shared certain beliefs and provided a guide for living together. *(page 463)*
- Islam played an important role in medieval Africa, but long-held African beliefs and customs still remained strong. *(page 464)*

Section 3 African Society and Culture

Vocabulary
extended family
matrilineal
oral history

Focusing on the Main Ideas
- The Bantu migrations helped shape many cultures in Africa south of the Sahara. *(page 469)*
- The African slave trade changed greatly when Muslims and Europeans began taking captives from the continent. *(page 472)*
- Enslaved Africans developed rich cultures that influenced many other cultures, including our own. *(page 474)*

▲ Family life in the Congo

PREVIEW/REVIEW

Vocabulary Activity Have students organize the vocabulary terms into these categories: Geographic, Political, Social, Economic. Some terms may appear in more than one category.

💿 **Vocabulary PuzzleMaker CD-ROM**

💿 **Interactive Tutor Self-Assessment CD-ROM**

CONDENSE

🗂 Chapter 13 **Guided Reading Activities**

💿 **StudentWorks Plus™ CD-ROM** (with Audio Program)

RETEACH

🗂 **Differentiated Instruction Activity 13**

🗂 Chapter 13 *Reading Essentials and Study Guide*

CHAPTER CULMINATING ACTIVITY

Have students finish the Chapter Culminating Activity from page 440D.

Suggestions for rubrics may be found in the *Quizzes, Tests, and Authentic Assessment (with Rubrics)* booklet.

Reading Strategy   READ TO WRITE

Organizing Ideas Remind students that Arab travelers provided a valuable source of information about West African empires and kingdoms along the East African coast. Have students write journal entries that an Arab traveler might have kept while visiting the following places: Axum, Mombasa, Taghaza, Timbuktu, Songhai, Mali, Ghana. Use the following rubric for assessment:

- **L1** students should include at least one entry about each place.
- **L2** students should include several entries and show a knowledge of travel routes.
- **L3** students should capture the culture of each place and attempt to include "rumors" of other places, such as Great Zimbabwe.

Review Vocabulary

1. dhows
2. True
3. True
4. griots
5. True
6. True

Review Main Ideas

7. Rain forests blocked invaders and provided resources.

8. They were part of the trade network that spanned the Indian Ocean.

9. They were governed by a king who had a strong army.

10. Some people believed in traditional African religions and their gods. Others were followers of Christianity or Islam.

11. They spread their skills, beliefs, and ideas across Africa.

12. Instead of being enslaved to other tribes from whom they could gain freedom, Africans were enslaved to Europeans and sent across the ocean where there was no escape and their culture could be lost.

Critical Thinking

13. The value of gold might have decreased.

Review Vocabulary

Write *True* for each true statement. Replace the word in italics to make false statements true.

___ 1. Wooden boats known as *griots* were powered by triangular sails.

___ 2. An area of high, flat land is a *plateau*.

___ 3. Each district in Ghana usually included a chief's *clan*.

___ 4. African *dhows* are storytellers.

___ 5. *Matrilineal* societies trace their descent through mothers.

___ 6. *Swahili* culture and language exist in Africa today.

Review Main Ideas

Section 1 • The Rise of African Civilizations

7. What were the advantages of living in Africa's rain forests?

8. Why were East African kingdoms and states important?

Section 2 • Africa's Government and Religion

9. How were West African empires governed?

10. Describe the religious beliefs of medieval Africans.

Section 3 • African Society and Culture

11. What was the result of the Bantu migrations?

12. How did slavery in medieval Africa change?

Critical Thinking

13. **Predict** What do you think would have happened in Ghana if the people had been allowed to trade with gold nuggets instead of gold dust?

14. **Explain** What caused the decline of Ghana and Songhai?

15. **Analyze** Why do you think the Bantu language changed as people moved into different parts of Africa?

Review

Reading Skill | Compare and Contrast

Making Comparisons

16. Read the paragraph below, then create a Venn diagram that shows similarities and differences between the continents of Africa and North America.

> Africa is the world's second-largest continent. The United States fits into Africa three times, with room to spare. The Equator slices through the middle of the continent. Hot, steamy rain forests stretch along each side of it. Yet the rain forests cover only 10 percent of the land.

To review this skill, see pages 442–443.

---

14. Ghana: discovery of new gold mines, overfarming, constant fighting; Songhai: advanced weapons of Moroccans

15. The vastness of the land and different geography led the Bantu to divide into different groups that changed over time.

Reading Skill

16. Africa: second-largest continent; hot, steamy rain forests cover 10 percent of the land; United States: fits into Africa three times; Both: large land area

Geography Skills

Study the map below and answer the following questions.

17. **Human/Environment Interaction** What obstacle did the empires in western Africa have to overcome in order to trade with cities in northern Africa?

18. **Location** In which parts of Africa do you think people had the best opportunities to trade by sea?

19. **Movement** How do you think more inland water routes would have changed the cultures of Africa?

NATIONAL GEOGRAPHIC — Kingdoms of Africa

KEY
- Benin
- Ghana
- Mali
- Songhai
- Zimbabwe

0   1,000 mi.
0   1,000 km
Lambert Azimuthal Equal-Area projection

Read to Write

20. **Descriptive Writing** Write an essay describing evidence of the African Diaspora in your community, city, or state. Make note of music, dance, literature, art, and other aspects of culture.

21. **Using Your FOLDABLES** Use the answers in your foldable to create a poster that shows what Africa was like in the past. Draw sketches, create maps, find pictures of artifacts, and so on to visually describe the cultures.

History Online

Self-Check Quiz To help you prepare for the Chapter Test, visit jat.glencoe.com

Using Technology

22. **Multimedia Presentation** Choose a present-day African country to research. Use the Internet to find information on that country from its early history to the present. Then create a multimedia presentation about that country, including images and a time line of important events in the country's history. Be sure to include aspects of culture, natural resources, and government.

Linking Past and Present

23. **Narrative Writing** Even though people record many things on paper or on a computer, they often tell stories about their lives as oral histories. Ask a family member, neighbor, teacher, or other adult to tell a story that has been passed down in his or her family. Record that oral history in narrative form.

Analyze

This report was written by the first engineer ever to see the ruins of Great Zimbabwe.

"The ruins are . . . terraces, which rise up continually from the base to the apex [highest point] of all the hills. . . . The way that the ancients seem to have levelled off the contours of the various hills . . . is very astonishing, as they seem to have been levelled with as much exactitude as we can accomplish with our best mathematical instruments."

—Telford Edwards, as quoted in *The Mystery of the Great Zimbabwe*

DBQ Document-Based Questions

24. What in particular amazes the engineer about Great Zimbabwe?

25. How do you think the people of Great Zimbabwe accomplished such precision?

History Online

Have students visit the Web site at jat.glencoe.com to review Chapter 13 and take the **Self-Check Quiz.**

Using Technology

22. Presentations will vary but should include important events and images.

Linking Past and Present

23. Oral histories may be tape-recorded and then turned into transcripts. Students should also ask permission to share the story with other members of the class.

Primary Source

24. the accuracy and exactness of its buildings
25. Answers will vary.

Bonus Question

Ask: Which of the medieval African empires or kingdoms do you think would have most astonished Europeans? Give reasons for your answers. (*Answers will vary.*)

Geography Skills

17. the Sahara

18. Answers may vary, but most students will probably name East African trading states.

19. Answers may include that cultures may have had more interaction with each other and the world.

Read to Write

20. Essays will vary but should have concrete examples based on your area.

21. **FOLDABLES** Students' posters should accurately reflect each culture on the foldable.

Chapter 14 Resources

Note: The following materials may be used when teaching Chapter 14.
Section level support materials are shown at point of use in the margins of the Teacher Wraparound Edition.

TEACHING TRANSPARENCIES

- Graphic Organizer Transparencies with Teaching Strategy and Student Activity **L2**
- Cause-and-Effect Transparencies with Teaching Strategy and Student Activity **L2**
- Then and Now Transparencies with Teaching Strategy and Student Activity **L2**
- In-text Map Transparency with Teaching Strategy and Student Activity **L1**
- Map Transparencies with Overlay, Teaching Strategy, and Student Activity **L2**

DIFFERENTIATED INSTRUCTION

- Differentiated Instruction Activity 14
- Time Line Activity 14
- Primary Source Reading 14 (with Document-Based Questions)
- Inclusion Strategies for the Middle School Social Studies Classroom
- StudentWorks Plus™ CD-ROM (with Audio Program)

READING SUPPORT

- Take-Home Review Activity 14 **L2**
- World Literature Reading 14 **L2**
- Workbook Activity 14 **L1**
- Reading Strategies for the Social Studies Classroom **L1/ EL**

ASSESSMENT

- Authentic Assessment Activity 14 **L1/ EL**
- Chapter 14 Test Form A **L2**
- Chapter 14 Test Form B **L2**
- ExamView® Pro Testmaker CD-ROM

INTERDISCIPLINARY CONNECTIONS

- Geography and History Activity 14 **L2**
- People to Meet Activity 14 **L2**
- Economics Activity 14 **L2**
- Citizenship and Service Learning Activity 14 **L2**

SPANISH RESOURCES

- Spanish Reading Essentials and Study Guide
- Spanish Guided Reading Activities
- Spanish Quizzes, Tests, and Authentic Assessment (with Rubrics)
- Spanish Take-Home Review Activities

MULTIMEDIA

- ExamView® Pro Testmaker CD-ROM
- Glencoe Skillbuilder Interactive Workbook CD-ROM, Level 1
- Interactive Tutor Self-Assessment CD-ROM
- MindJogger Videoquiz
- Presentation Plus! CD-ROM
- StudentWorks Plus™ CD-ROM (with Audio Program)
- TeacherWorks CD-ROM
- Vocabulary PuzzleMaker CD-ROM
- *World History: Journey Across Time* Video Program
- World History Primary Source Document Library CD-ROM

STANDARDIZED ASSESSMENT SKILLS

- Standardized Test Skills Practice Workbook Activity 14 **L2**
- Critical Thinking Skills Activity 14 **L2**

Teaching strategies have been coded with suggested ability levels. However, most are suitable for all levels.

L1 BASIC activities for all students

L2 AVERAGE activities for average to above-average students

L3 CHALLENGING activities for above-average students

EL ENGLISH LANGUAGE activities

Chapter ⑭ Resources

TIME MANAGEMENT

Chapter Introduction	Section 1	Section 2	Section 3	Chapter Wrap-Up
1 Day	1 Day	1 Day	1 Day	1 Day

Block Scheduling Activities that are suited to use within the block scheduling framework are identified by:

0:00 OUT OF TIME? Assign the Chapter 14 *Reading Essentials and Study Guide.**

SECTION RESOURCES

DAILY OBJECTIVES	REPRODUCIBLE RESOURCES	MULTIMEDIA RESOURCES
Section 1 **Early Japan** 1. Geography isolated Japan and shaped its people, who originally came from northeast Asia. 2. Prince Shotoku created Japan's first constitution and Shinto became an important religion in Japan.	Reproducible Lesson Plan 14–1 Daily Lecture and Discussion Notes 14–1 Vocabulary Activity 14–1 Active Reading Note-Taking Guide 14–1 Guided Reading Activity 14–1* Section Quiz 14–1* Reading Essentials and Study Guide 14–1*	Daily Focus Skills Transparency 14–1 Interactive Tutor Self-Assessment CD-ROM ExamView® Pro Testmaker CD-ROM Presentation Plus! CD-ROM Glencoe BookLink CD-ROM
Section 2 **Shoguns and Samurai** 1. During the A.D. 700s, Japan built a strong national government, but by 1200 the emperor was dominated by shoguns. 2. The power of the shogun weakened, and Japan broke into warring kingdoms run by rulers known as daimyo.	Reproducible Lesson Plan 14–2 Daily Lecture and Discussion Notes 14–2 Vocabulary Activity 14–2 Active Reading Note-Taking Guide 14–2 Guided Reading Activity 14–2* Section Quiz 14–2* Reading Essentials and Study Guide 14–2*	Daily Focus Skills Transparency 14–2 Interactive Tutor Self-Assessment CD-ROM ExamView® Pro Testmaker CD-ROM Presentation Plus! CD-ROM
Section 3 **Life in Medieval Japan** 1. Buddhism and Shinto shaped much of Japan's culture. These religions affected Japanese art, architecture, novels, and plays. 2. Some nobles, merchants, and artisans became wealthy at the time of the shoguns, but the lives of women stayed restricted.	Reproducible Lesson Plan 14–3 Daily Lecture and Discussion Notes 14–3 Vocabulary Activity 14–3 Active Reading Note-Taking Guide 14–3 Guided Reading Activity 14–3* Section Quiz 14–3* Reading Essentials and Study Guide 14–3*	Daily Focus Skills Transparency 14–3 Interactive Tutor Self-Assessment CD-ROM ExamView® Pro Testmaker CD-ROM Presentation Plus! CD-ROM Vocabulary PuzzleMaker CD-ROM Glencoe BookLink CD-ROM

*Also available in Spanish

History Online

Use our Web site for additional resources. All essential content is covered in the Student Edition.

You and your students can visit jat.glencoe.com, the Web site companion to *World History: Journey Across Time*. This innovative integration of electronic and print media offers your students a wealth of opportunities. The student text directs students to the Web site for the following options:

- Chapter Overviews
- Self-Check Quizzes
- Study Central™
- Student Web Activities
- Multi-Language Glossaries

Answers to the student Web activities are provided for you in the **Web Activity Lesson Plans.** Additional Web resources and ePuzzles and games are also available.

The following videotape program is available from Glencoe as a supplement to Chapter 14:

Iwo Jima: Hell's Volcano
(ISBN 0-7670-0462-0)

To order, call Glencoe at 1-800-334-7344. To find classroom resources to accompany the video, check the following home pages:

A&E Television: www.aande.com
The History Channel: www.historychannel.com

MEETING SPECIAL NEEDS

In addition to the Differentiated Instruction strategies, the following resources are suitable for students with special needs:

- *ExamView® Pro Testmaker CD-ROM* allows teachers to tailor tests by reducing answer choices.
- *StudentWorks Plus™ CD-ROM (with Audio Program)* includes the entire narrative of the student edition so that less-proficient readers can listen to the words as they read them.
- The *Reading Essentials and Study Guide* provides the same content as the student edition but is written two grade levels below the textbook.
- *Guided Reading Activities* give less-proficient readers point-by-point instructions to increase comprehension as they read each textbook section.

NATIONAL GEOGRAPHIC TEACHER'S CORNER

Index to National Geographic Magazine:

The following articles relate to this chapter:

- "Samurai: Japan's Way of the Warrior," by Tom O'Neill, December 2003.
- "Fuji: Japan's Sacred Summit," by Tracy Dahlby, August 2002.
- "Japan's Imperial Palace: Beyond the Moat," by Robert Poole, January 2001.

National Geographic Society Products:

To order the following, call National Geographic at 1–800–368–2728

- *Nations of the World Series: Japan* (Video)
- *PicturePack: Geography of Asia* (Transparencies)

NGS ONLINE

Access National Geographic's new dynamic MapMachine Web site and other geography resources at:

www.nationalgeographic.com
www.nationalgeographic.com/maps

Meeting NCSS Standards

World History: Journey Across Time

The following standards are highlighted in Chapter 14:

Section 1   **II**   Time, Continuity, and Change: B

             VI   Power, Authority, and Governance: B, F, I

Section 2   **III**   People, Places, and Environments: J

             V   Individuals, Groups, and Institutions: A, B, E, F

             VI   Power, Authority, and Governance: E, D, H, I

Section 3   **I**   Culture: C, D

             IV   Individual Development and Identity: B, C, D

             VII   Production, Distribution, and Consumption: C

State and Local Objectives

_____

_____

Timesaving Tools

TeacherWorks
All-In-One Planner and Resource Center

● **Interactive Teacher Edition** Access your Teacher Wraparound Edition and your classroom resources with a few easy clicks.

● **Interactive Lesson Planner** Organize your week, month, semester, or year with all the lesson helps you need to make teaching creative and relevant.

Use Glencoe's **Presentation Plus!** multimedia teacher tool to easily present dynamic lessons that visually excite your students. Using Microsoft PowerPoint® you can customize the presentations to create your own personalized lessons.

FOLDABLES™
Study Organizer

Dinah Zike's Foldables

Foldables are three-dimensional, interactive graphic organizers that help students practice basic writing skills, review key vocabulary terms, and identify main ideas. Every chapter contains a foldable activity, with additional chapter activities found in the *Reading and Study Skills Foldables* booklet. You can use the foldables as they are presented, or modify them to suit the needs of your individual class.

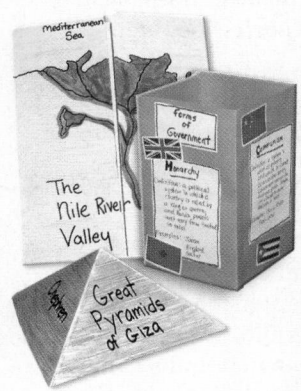

Planning Ahead

CHAPTER CULMINATING ACTIVITY

The Chapter Culminating Activity will help students organize and learn the important information from the chapter. Begin teaching the chapter with this activity, and have students complete it as a culminating activity.

MAKING A MAIN IDEA MINI-WEB SITE

Purpose Students will create visual displays on paper that look like Web sites. While this activity emphasizes writing text and placing images on paper, with simple modifications it could be used to create actual Web pages.

Introduction to Modeling

1. Use an overhead projector to project on the wall images of Web pages you find particularly effective. If computers are available, your students could choose the pages you will use as examples. Discuss with students the ways in which information is expressed on the sample Web pages. Also discuss what the pages have in common. For example, Web pages usually will have an *http* address in the top or bottom margin, the search terms used to arrive at the Web page remain at the top of the page, words and images may be linked to other sites or information, and so on.

2. Distribute to each student four sheets of paper. Explain to students that for each of the sections in the chapter, they are to create a "Web page" reflecting that section's main ideas. Remind them to include the keywords that people might have used to get to that Internet page, as well as links to other sites that might appear on the page.

3. When students have completed their three Web pages, have them use the fourth page to create a home page titled "Ancient Japan." Then direct students to draw three "buttons" on the page and label each one with the name of a different section. Staple together the finished "Web sites."

4. Once students have completed their Web sites, they will have useful study guides to the main ideas in the chapter. These pages can also be used as design boards for creating real Web sites online.

Use the **SkillBuilder Handbook** on pages 902–919 to help students learn the skill of evaluating a Web site.

When & Where?

As students read the chapter, have them keep track of where in the chapter the time line entries would fit. Ask them to explain how shoguns came to power in early Japan. *(The emperor created the position when he made Minamoto Yoritomo the shogun of Japan.)* L1

Chapter 14

Medieval Japan

Kingaku Temple in Kyoto, Japan ▼

NATIONAL GEOGRAPHIC — When & Where?

A.D. 300	A.D. 700	1100	1500
c. A.D. 300 Yayoi people organize into clans	**A.D. 646** Taika reforms strengthen emperor's powers	**1192** Rule by shoguns begins	**c. 1300s** Noh plays first performed

Reading Strategy ‹ PURPOSE FOR READING

Analyzing Geographic Influences Ask a volunteer to locate on a globe the country of Japan as other students find the country in the textbook's **Reference Atlas.** Also have the volunteer and the students locate the bodies of water that separate Japan from other lands. These will include the Pacific Ocean, the East China Sea, and the Sea of Japan. **Ask:** How do you think being surrounded by water might have impacted Japan? *(Students may say that isolation might have encouraged Japan to develop differently from other lands. Students may indicate that fishing would be important to an island country.)* Have students take notes about the impact of geography on Japan's history. L1

Chapter Preview

Warriors in Japan, like those in Africa, were known for their fighting skills. Japanese warriors trained their minds and bodies for battle. Read this chapter to find out about their training methods and how they are used today.

 View the Chapter 14 video in the *World History: Journey Across Time* Video Program.

History Online

Chapter Overview Visit jat.glencoe.com for a preview of Chapter 14.

 ## Early Japan

Japan's islands and mountains have shaped its history. The Japanese developed their own unique culture but looked to China as a model.

 ## Shoguns and Samurai

Japan's emperors lost power to military leaders. Warrior families and their followers fought each other for control of Japan.

 ## Life in Medieval Japan

The religions of Shinto and Buddhism shaped Japan's culture. Farmers, artisans, and merchants brought wealth to Japan.

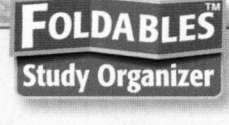

Categorizing Information *Make this foldable to help you organize information about the history and culture of medieval Japan.*

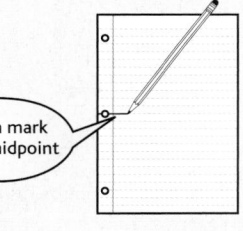

Step 1 *Mark the midpoint of the side edge of a sheet of paper.*

Draw a mark at the midpoint

Step 2 *Turn the paper and fold in each outside edge to touch at the midpoint. Label as shown.*

Japan

Step 3 *Open and label your foldable as shown.*

Early Japan | Shoguns and Samurai | Life in Medieval Japan

Reading and Writing *As you read the chapter, organize your notes by writing the main ideas with supporting details under the appropriate tab.*

481

INTRODUCING CHAPTER 14

History Online

Introduce students to chapter content and key terms by having them access **Chapter Overview 14** at jat.glencoe.com

CHAPTER PREVIEW

After reading Chapter 14, students will be able to

1. describe the role of geography in the development of Japan;

2. discuss the rise and influence of shoguns and samurai in medieval Japan;

3. relate the impact of religion on Japan's culture.

FOLDABLES
Study Organizer Dinah Zike's Foldables

Purpose Students use this foldable to organize information about different eras in Japan's history. As students read each section, they should make entries in the corresponding column. Completed foldables should have three columns, each filled with the main ideas and appropriate supporting details.

📁 Have students complete *Reading and Study Skills Foldables* Activity 14.

MORE ABOUT THE PHOTO

Kingaku Temple The historic Kingaku temple was originally built around 1397 during the Kamakura Period. Ashikaga Yoshimitsu, a retired shogun, was the first owner of the building. He used it as an elegant country villa, living there for most of his later life. After Yoshimitsu died in the early 1400s, the building was converted into a Zen Buddhist temple. It was used by monks for more than fifty years before being partially destroyed during a civil war in the late 1400s. The temple was rebuilt soon after, only to be destroyed again in 1567. After a terrible fire raged through the building in 1950, reducing the temple to ash, the Japanese government rebuilt Kingaku as it was originally created. Tourists from around the world visit the elaborate, beautiful temple each year.

Chapter 14 Reading Social Studies

1 Learn It!

Information is often organized in patterns, and when students learn to make sense of these patterns, their comprehension will increase. One of the most common patterns for expository text is cause and effect. When students understand the relationship between cause and effect, they will better understand many of history's events. To begin teaching this principle, explain that cause-and-effect relationships occur all the time in students' lives. Ask them to brainstorm a topic with which they are familiar and record their responses on the board, using the following graphic organizer. A topic, such as having school year-round instead of only for 9 or 10 months, is an example that utilizes their background knowledge.

Cause	Effect
Year-Round School	No summer vacation
	Fewer gaps in learning
	More vacation days during the school year

Have students think of other concepts in their lives that might have similar relationships and practice creating graphic organizers until they understand how to identify these concepts on their own. **L2**

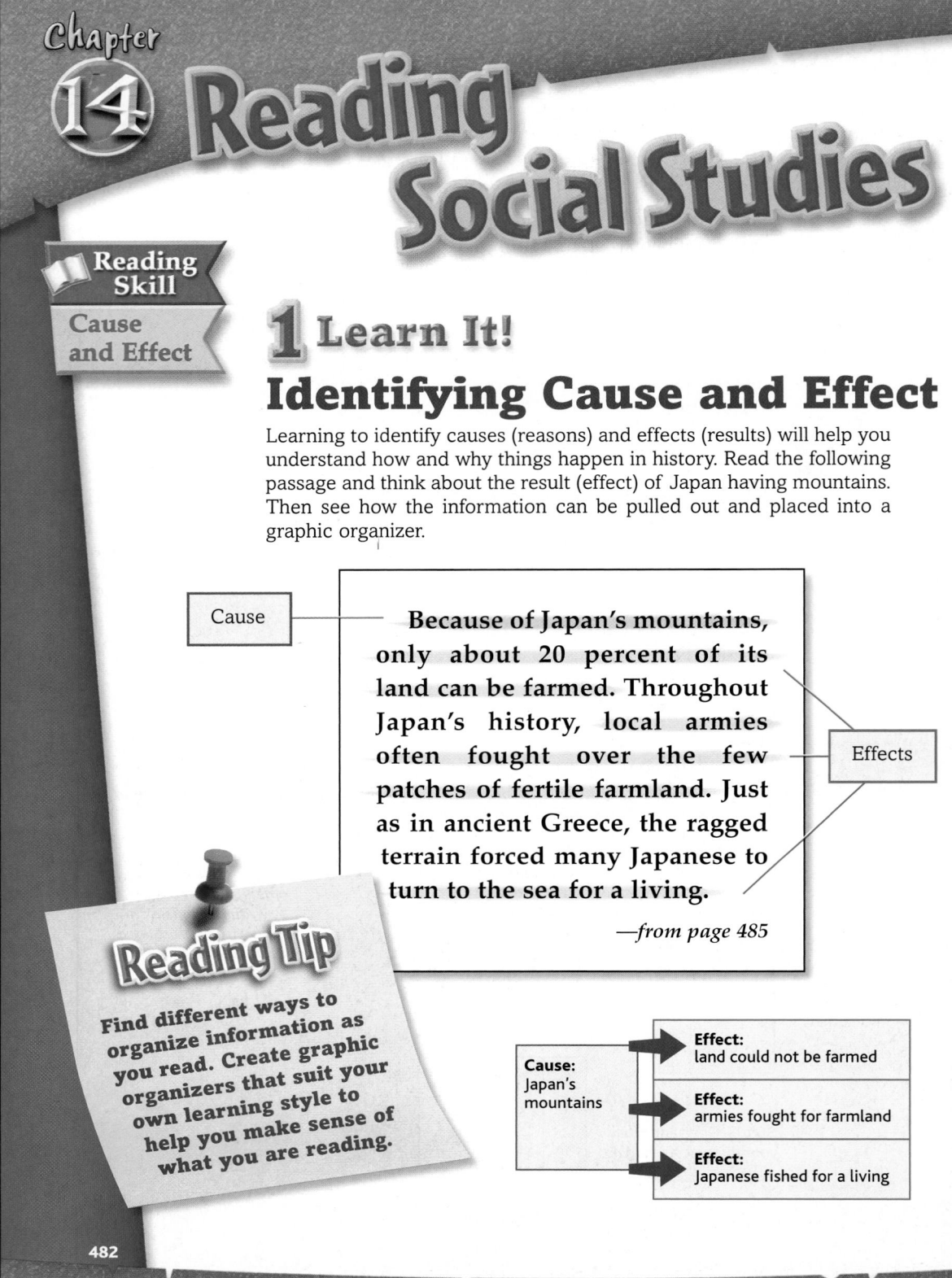

Reading Skill

Cause and Effect

1 Learn It!

Identifying Cause and Effect

Learning to identify causes (reasons) and effects (results) will help you understand how and why things happen in history. Read the following passage and think about the result (effect) of Japan having mountains. Then see how the information can be pulled out and placed into a graphic organizer.

Cause

Because of Japan's mountains, only about 20 percent of its land can be farmed. Throughout Japan's history, local armies often fought over the few patches of fertile farmland. Just as in ancient Greece, the ragged terrain forced many Japanese to turn to the sea for a living.

—from page 485

Effects

Reading Tip

Find different ways to organize information as you read. Create graphic organizers that suit your own learning style to help you make sense of what you are reading.

| Cause:
Japan's mountains | → | Effect:
land could not be farmed |
| | → | Effect:
armies fought for farmland |
| | → | Effect:
Japanese fished for a living |

482

Reading Strategy — INFERENTIAL THINKING

As students seek to understand the pattern of cause and effect, it is an ideal time to teach them the important skill of inferring. Some causes and effects may be explicitly stated in the text, such as this passage from the end of Section 2: "The violence finally brought down the Ashikaga shogunate in 1567. By that time, only a handful of powerful daimyo remained." The next sentence, however, begs inferential thinking: "Each of these daimyo was eager to defeat his rivals and rule all of Japan." More advanced students will infer that because the daimyo wanted to rule all of Japan, the violence must have continued. To assist other students in thinking beyond the text to make cause-and-effect connections, ask questions such as "Do you think the daimyo eventually managed to rule all of Japan?" **L3**

2 Practice It!

Using Graphic Organizers

Read the following paragraph and either use the graphic organizer below or create your own to show the effects of Yoritomo's ruthless rule.

Read to Write

After reading Section 2, write a paragraph that summarizes the reasons why the power of Japan's emperor declined during the A.D. 800s.

> Yoritomo proved to be a ruthless ruler. He killed most of his relatives, fearing that they would try to take power from him. Yoritomo and the shoguns after him appointed high-ranking samurai to serve as advisers and to run the provinces. Bound by an oath of loyalty, these samurai lords ruled Japan's villages, kept the peace, and gathered taxes. They became the leading group in Japanese society.
>
> —from page 495

Cause:

→ **Effect:**

→ **Effect:**

→ **Effect:**

3 Apply It!

As you read Chapter 14, be aware of causes and effects in Japanese history. Find at least five causes and their effects, and create graphic organizers to record them.

READING SOCIAL STUDIES

2 Practice It!

Thinking in Patterns Have students practice organizing events in terms of cause and effect by creating their own cause-and-effect graphic organizers. Organize students into small groups, and have them read the first two pages of Section 1. Have them choose several scenarios that seem to have cause-and-effect relationships. Once groups have decided, ask them to portray the effects graphically.

3 Apply It!

Have students read the text in Section 3 under the heading "The Role of Women." Ask students to find examples of cause-and-effect patterns. For example, the effect of wealthy families wanting to further their fortunes was that daughters were subject to arranged marriages. **L2**

Reading Strategy ⟩ READ TO WRITE

Understanding Cause and Effect Ask students to read the text under the heading "The Emperor's Government" in Section 2. Discuss it, making sure that students understand the source of the emperor's power—control of land and crops. Then tell students to read the text under the heading "The Government Weakens." Point out that the first paragraph starts with an effect; have students identify the causes. Then show students how the last paragraph demonstrates that an effect (the nobles are in charge of governing the lands under their control) can become a cause of *another* effect (nobles began collecting taxes from peasants). Tell students to state the sources of the emperor's power and explain how events affected or changed that power in their summary.

① FOCUS

SECTION OVERVIEW

This section describes the geography of Japan, its early peoples, China's early influences on the country, and the origin of the religion of Shinto.

SKILLBUILDER ACTIVITY

🖐 Project **Daily Focus Skills Transparency 14–1** and have students answer questions. Discuss their responses.

Get Ready to Read!

Preteaching Vocabulary: While many modern governments have a list of rules and laws in a document called a constitution, many ancient cultures did not. One of the earliest constitutions was created in Japan by a prince named Shotoku in the early A.D. 600s.

Answers to Graphic: means "way of the spirits"; spirits called *kami* will help only if a person is pure; many things, such as illness, can bring spiritual stains that must be cleansed before prayer can be offered

Section ① Early Japan

Get Ready to Read!

What's the Connection?
During the Middle Ages, another civilization developed in East Asia. It arose on the islands of Japan off the coast of the Korean Peninsula.

Focusing on the Main Ideas
- Japan's mountains and islands isolated Japan and shaped its society. *(page 485)*
- Japan was settled by people who came from northeast Asia. They were organized into clans and ruled by warriors. *(page 486)*
- Prince Shotoku created Japan's first constitution and borrowed many ideas from China. *(page 488)*
- The Japanese religion called Shinto was based on nature spirits. *(page 490)*

Locating Places
Japan (juh•PAN)
Hokkaido (hah•KY•doh)
Honshu (HAHN•shoo)
Shikoku (shih•KOH•koo)
Kyushu (kee•OO•shoo)

Meeting People
Jomon (JOH•mohn)
Yayoi (YAH•yoy)
Jimmu (jeem•mu)
Shotoku (shoh•TOH•koo)

Building Your Vocabulary
clan (KLAN)
constitution (KAHN•stuh•TOO•shuhn)
animism (A•nuh•MIH•zuhm)
shrine (SHRYN)

Reading Strategy
Organizing Information Create a diagram to show the basics of the Shinto religion.

Shinto Religion

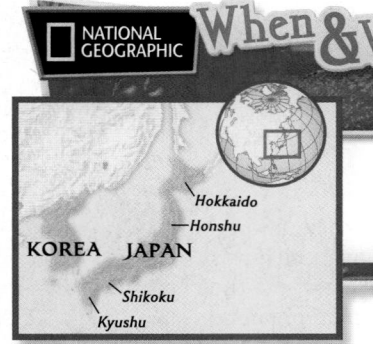

Hokkaido
Honshu
KOREA JAPAN
Shikoku
Kyushu

A.D. 300	**A.D. 500**	**A.D. 700**
c. A.D. 300 Yayoi people organize into clans	c. A.D. 550 Yamoto clan rules most of Japan	A.D. 646 Taika reforms strengthen emperor's powers

SECTION RESOURCES

Reproducible Masters
- Reproducible Lesson Plan 14–1
- Daily Lecture and Discussion Notes 14–1
- Vocabulary Activity 14–1
- Active Reading Note-Taking Guide 14–1
- Guided Reading Activity 14–1
- Section Quiz 14–1
- Reading Essentials and Study Guide 14–1

🖐 **Transparencies**
- Daily Focus Skills Transparency 14–1

Multimedia
- Interactive Tutor Self-Assessment CD-ROM
- ExamView® Pro Testmaker CD-ROM
- Presentation Plus! CD-ROM
- Glencoe BookLink CD-ROM

Japan's Geography

Main Idea Japan's mountains and islands isolated Japan and shaped its society.

Reading Focus Have you ever been in a place with no television, radio, or telephone? How would you feel if you did not know what was going on outside your home? Read to learn how Japan's geography isolated the Japanese and shaped their society.

Japan (juh•PAN) is a chain of islands that stretches north to south in the northern Pacific Ocean. Japan's islands number more than 3,000, and many of them are tiny. For centuries, most Japanese have lived on the four largest islands: **Hokkaido** (hah•KY•doh), **Honshu** (HAHN•shoo), **Shikoku** (shih•KOH•koo), and **Kyushu** (kee•OO•shoo).

Like China, much of Japan is covered by mountains. In fact, the islands of Japan are actually the tops of mountains that rise from the floor of the ocean. About 188 of Japan's mountains are volcanoes. Many earthquakes occur in Japan because the islands lie in an area where parts of the earth's surface often shift.

Because of Japan's mountains, only about 20 percent of its land can be farmed. Throughout Japan's history, local armies often fought over the few patches of fertile

▼ **Mount Fuji is an important national symbol.** *How did the region's mountains affect early settlement in Japan?*

farmland. Just as in ancient Greece, the rugged terrain forced many Japanese to turn to the sea for a living. Early on, they settled in villages along the coast and fished for food. Fish and seafood are still important in the Japanese diet.

The sea surrounding Japan's islands made it easy for people in ships to travel along the coast and from island to island. It encouraged people to become merchants, traveling from village to village with goods to trade. The vast ocean around Japan's islands, however, kept the Japanese people isolated, or separate, from the rest of Asia. As a result, Japan developed its own fiercely independent society with its own religion, art, literature, and government.

Reading Check **Describe** How did Japan's geography shape its society?

NATIONAL GEOGRAPHIC **Geography of Japan**

130°E 140°E
Hokkaido
40°N
Sea of Japan (East Sea)
Honshu
PACIFIC OCEAN
Yellow Sea
Heian (Kyoto)
Mt. Fuji
Edo (Tokyo)
Kamakura
Nara
Shikoku
Kyushu
0 400 mi.
0 400 km
30°N
Lambert Conformal Conic projection

Using Geography Skills

Japan's geography isolated the country and helped form a unique culture.
1. List, from north to south, the four major islands that make up Japan.
2. What body of water separates Japan from mainland Asia?

Find NGS online map resources @ www.nationalgeographic.com/maps

CHAPTER 14   Medieval Japan   **485**

② TEACH

Researching Volcanoes Inform students that volcanoes helped create Japan. Have students research how volcanoes work. Ask volunteers to share what they discover with the class. **L1**

Daily Lecture and Discussion Notes 14–1

Use **Daily Lecture and Discussion Notes 14–1** for an outline of key concepts found in the section.

Reading Check

Answer: The many mountains, small amount of farmland, and many islands led to sea trade and fishing and a fiercely independent society.

Caption Answer: Because of mountains, only 20 percent of the land could be farmed. People fought over this land.

Using Geography Skills

Answers:
1. Hokkaido, Honshu, Shikoku, Kyushu
2. Sea of Japan (East Sea)

Reading Strategy **READING THE TEXT**

Understanding Text Structure This strategy will guide students to find answers to questions. By doing so, they will better understand the section. Write the following questions on the board: During what century did the Yamato clan become leaders of all Japan? Why does Japan experience a lot of earthquakes? Why did Prince Shotoku send people to China? How did the Yayoi people get their name?

Tell students they have two assignments. First, they should write the questions down in the correct order, according to the content of Section 1. Then, as they read the section, they should write answers to the questions. Help students conclude that they can use the headings in the section to order the questions. **L2**

Reading Support L1/ EL

Use **Vocabulary Activity 14–1** to review important terms in the section.

CONNECTING ACROSS TIME

Mount Fuji has long been a sacred place in Japan. In fact, some Japanese believe the mountain has a soul. Every year, tens of thousands climb the mountain to reach the shrine at the top. Ask students to identify places that are important to the people of the United States. Discuss with students which places they would like to visit. **L1/ EL**

GLENCOE
BOOKLINK

Use **Glencoe BookLink** to create customized reading lists for your students' reading levels, interests, and abilities.

Reading Strategy

Writing Activity

Much of what we know about the Yayoi comes from the archaeological evidence they left behind. Have students use information in the text to write a paragraph describing how historians use this evidence to interpret the Yayoi culture. **L2**

The First Settlers

Main Idea Japan was settled by people who came from northeast Asia. They were organized into clans and ruled by warriors.

Reading Focus Do you have many relatives? Do your relatives all come together to do things? Read to learn how the early Japanese people were organized into groups made up of people who were all related to each other.

Japan's earliest people probably came from northeast Asia between 30,000 and 10,000 B.C. At that time, Japan was joined to the Asian continent by land. These early people hunted animals and gathered wild plants. They used fire and stone tools, and they lived in pits dug into the ground.

Who Were the Jomon? In about 5000 B.C., these wandering groups began to develop a culture. They made clay pottery, using knotted cords to make designs on the clay's surface. Today, this culture is called **Jomon** (JOH•mohn), which means "cord marks" in the Japanese language. Modern archaeologists have found many pieces of Jomon pottery throughout Japan. Over time, the Jomon people settled in fishing villages along the coast. Fishing became their way of life.

Why Are the Yayoi Important? The Jomon culture lasted until about 300 B.C. At that time, a new group of people appeared in Japan. Modern archaeologists have named this culture **Yayoi** (YAH•yoy), after the place in Japan where they first dug up its artifacts.

The Yayoi were the ancestors of the Japanese people. They introduced farming to Japan and practiced a number of skills that they may have learned from the Chinese and Koreans. They made pottery on a potter's wheel and grew rice in paddies. A paddy is a rice field that is flooded when rice is planted and drained for the harvest.

The Yayoi also were skilled in metalworking. They made axes, knives, and hoes from iron, and swords, spears, and bells from bronze. Bells were used in religious rituals—a practice that is still common in Japan today.

◀ Female figurine from the Jomon culture (left); Jomon vase (below)

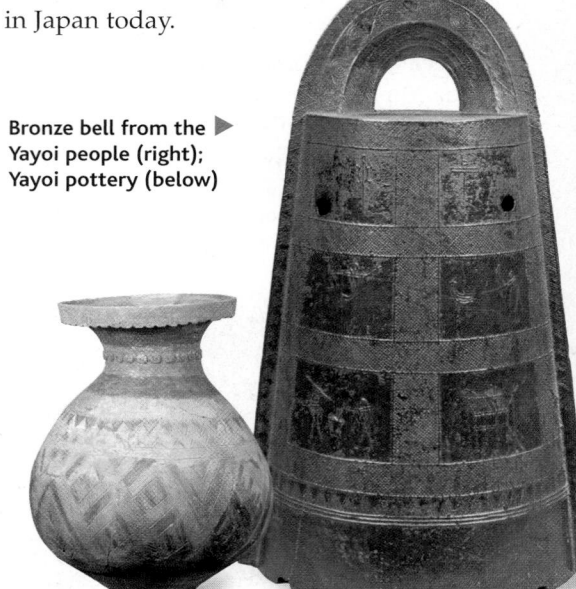

Bronze bell from the ▶ Yayoi people (right); Yayoi pottery (below)

486   CHAPTER 14   Medieval Japan

DIFFERENTIATED INSTRUCTION

Verbal/Linguistic: Explain that before writing came into use, myths, histories, and beliefs were passed from generation to generation verbally, often as stories. Ask students to present parts of the section as oral history.

Less-proficient Readers: Read aloud Japan's creation myth. Organize students into small groups and tell each group to use the text to write down the sequence of events related by the myth. Tell the groups that if they wish, every sentence but the first can start with the word *Then*.

Gifted and Talented: Tell students that most cultures have myths that help explain their creation. Have students research other cultures to find creation myths. Have them share the myths they uncover with the class. Discuss how those myths compare to the story told by the Japanese.

By A.D. 300, the Yayoi, or the early Japanese, had organized themselves into **clans** (KLANZ). A clan is a group of families related by blood or marriage. Yayoi clans were headed by a small group of warriors. Under the warriors were the rest of the people—farmers, artisans, and servants of the warriors. The clan's warrior chiefs protected the people in return for a share of the rice harvest each year.

The Yayoi buried their chiefs in large mounds known as *kofun.* Made of dirt, these tombs were carefully shaped and surrounded by ditches. They were filled with personal belongings, such as pottery, tools, weapons, and armor. Many of the tombs were as big as Egypt's pyramids. The largest tomb still stands today. It is longer than five football fields and at least eight stories high.

Who Are the Yamato? Like many other people whose society began in ancient times, the Japanese have myths, or stories that tell how things began. The most important myth explained the creation of Japan. It says that centuries ago, two gods dipped a spear into the sea. When they pulled it out, drops of salty water fell on the water's surface and formed the islands of Japan. The two gods then created the sun goddess, Amaterasu, to rule over Earth. They also created the storm god, Susanowo, as her companion.

Susanowo was sent to Earth. There, his children became the first people of Japan. Amaterasu, however, sent her grandson Ninigi to rule over them. To make sure that everyone would accept his power, she gave Ninigi her mirror, her jewel, and a great sword. These objects became the sacred symbols of leadership in early Japan.

Historians today are not sure of the actual events on which this myth is based. However, they do know that during the

▲ The sun goddess, Amaterasu, emerges from her cave, bringing light into the world. *Which group claimed that they came from Amaterasu?*

A.D. 500s, a clan called the Yamato became strong enough to bring most of Japan under its rule. The other clans still held their lands, but they had to give their loyalty to the Yamato chief.

Yamato chiefs claimed that they came from the sun goddess and, therefore, had a right to rule Japan. Japanese legend states that a Yamato leader named **Jimmu** (jeem•mu) took the title "emperor of heaven." He founded a line of rulers in Japan that has never been broken. Akihito (AH•kee•HEE•toh), who is Japan's emperor today, is one of his descendants.

✓**Reading Check** **Identify** What do historians know for sure about the rise of the Yamato?

The sword of Ninigi had a name—*Kusanagi,* which means "grass mower." This name came from an event in the myth in which the sword saved a Japanese hero, who used its sharp blade to cut down the grass that had been set ablaze around him.

More About the Art

As in other societies where rulers claimed descent from gods, such as in Egypt, this claim brought an aura of power and wonder to the emperor of Japan.

Caption Answer: the Yamato

✓Reading Check

Answer: During the A.D. 500s, a clan called the Yamato became strong enough to bring most of Japan under its rule. Other clans had to give loyalty to the Yamato chief.

Reading Support L1/ EL

Assign **Guided Reading Activity 14–1** to help students organize the information in the section.

CRITICAL THINKING ACTIVITY

Predicting Consequences Discuss with students why they think two gods were created in the Japanese creation myth. Ask them to consider how the lives of people in the myth would have been different if there had been no god of storms. *(In a world with constant sunlight, every living thing would shortly die for lack of rainwater.)* Have students write an alternative myth for the Japanese culture in which there is no storm god. **L3**

3 ASSESS

Assign Section 1 Review as homework or as an in-class activity.

Have students use the **Interactive Tutor Self-Assessment CD-ROM** to review the section.

Assessment L2

Assign **Section 1 Quiz** to assess mastery of the material found in the section.

Reading Support L1/ EL

Assign **Reading Essentials and Study Guide 14–1** to help students review section material.

Primary Source

Answer:
The emperor is compared to heaven, and his subjects are compared to earth.

✓ Reading Check

Answer: Japan was divided into provinces that were run by officials who reported to the emperor. All land in Japan came under the emperor's control.

Prince Shotoku's Reforms

Main Idea Prince Shotoku created Japan's first constitution and borrowed many ideas from China.

Reading Focus When you try something new, are you tempted to use what someone else has done as a model? Read to find out how Shotoku used China as a model for his reforms in Japan.

About A.D. 600, a Yamato prince named **Shotoku** (shoh•TOH•koo) took charge of Japan on behalf of his aunt, the empress Suiko (swee•koh). He wanted to create a strong government, and he looked to China

Primary Source — Japan's New Constitution

This is part of the constitution created by Shotoku.

"Harmony is to be cherished, and opposition for opposition's sake must be avoided as a matter of principle. . . .

When an imperial command is given, obey it with reverence. The sovereign is likened to heaven, and his subjects are likened to earth. With heaven providing the cover and earth supporting it, the four seasons proceed in orderly fashion, giving sustenance to all that which is in nature. If earth attempts to overtake the functions of heaven, it destroys everything.

Cast away your ravenous desire for food and abandon your covetousness [envy] for material possessions. If a suit is brought before you, render a clear-cut judgement. . . .

Punish that which is evil and encourage that which is good."

—Prince Shotoku,
"The Seventeen Article Constitution"

DBQ Document-Based Question

To what are the emperor and his subjects compared?

as an example of what to do. You remember that in China, a powerful emperor ruled with the help of trained officials chosen for their abilities.

To reach this goal for Japan, Shotoku created a **constitution** (KAHN•stuh•TOO•shuhn), or a plan of government. Shotoku's constitution gave all power to the emperor, who had to be obeyed by the Japanese people. He also created a bureaucracy and gave the emperor the power to appoint all the officials. The constitution listed rules for working in the government. The rules were taken from the ideas of Confucius.

Shotoku also wanted Japan to learn from China's brilliant civilization. He sent officials and students to China to study. The Japanese not only learned about Buddhist teachings but also absorbed a great deal about Chinese art, medicine, and philosophy.

Shotoku ordered Buddhist temples and monasteries to be built throughout Japan. One of them, called Horyuji (HOHR•yoo•JEE), still stands. It is Japan's oldest temple and the world's oldest surviving wooden building.

After Shotoku, other officials continued to make Japan's government look like China's. In A.D. 646 the Yamato began the Taika, or Great Change. They divided Japan into provinces, or regional districts, all run by officials who reported to the emperor. In addition, all land in Japan came under the emperor's control.

Clan leaders could direct the farmers working the land, but they could not collect taxes anymore. Instead, government officials were to gather part of the farmers' harvest in taxes for the emperor. Together with Shotoku's reforms, this plan created Japan's first strong central government.

✓ **Reading Check** **Identify** What happened during the Great Change?

INTERDISCIPLINARY CONNECTIONS ACTIVITY

Language Arts Tell students that a *simile* is a comparison between two different things using the words *like* or *as*. Have students offer examples of some similes. **Ask:** In Japan's constitution discussed in the Primary Source feature, what two similes are used to strengthen the emperor's position? *("The sovereign is likened to heaven" and "his subjects are likened to earth.")* How do these similes reinforce the relationship between emperor and subject? *(Earth supports heaven, which is above it. Therefore, the subjects must support the emperor.)* **L2**

PRINCE SHOTOKU

A.D. 573–621

Prince Shotoku was born into the powerful Soga family, as the second son of Emperor Yomei. Shotoku's real name is Umayado, which means "the prince of the stable door." According to legend, Shotoku's mother gave birth to him while she was inspecting the emperor's stables. During Shotoku's childhood, Japan was a society of clans, or large extended families. There was fighting between Shotoku's own Soga family and their rival, the Mononobe family. The Soga and Mononobe clans were Japan's two most powerful families, and each wanted to rule Japan.

Shotoku was a very bright, articulate child. He learned about Buddhism from one of his great uncles. He then studied with two Buddhist priests and became devoted to Buddhism.

At the age of 20, Shotoku became Japan's crown prince. The early teachings of Buddhism strongly influenced his leadership. He introduced political and religious reforms that helped build a strong central government in Japan modeled after China. At the request of his aunt, the empress, Shotoku often spoke about Buddhism and the process of enlightenment. He also wrote the first book of Japanese history.

▲ Statue believed to be of Prince Shotoku

When Prince Shotoku died, the elderly people of the empire mourned as if they had lost a dear child of their own. A written account describes their words of grief: "The sun and moon have lost their brightness; heaven and earth have crumbled to ruin: henceforward, in whom shall we put our trust?"

▲ The Horyuji temple, built by Prince Shotoku

Then and Now

Think of a recent leader or other public figure whose death caused people to mourn as if they knew that person well. Who is it? Why do you think people identified with that person? Why did the Japanese identify so closely with Shotoku?

TEACH

One of Shotoku's first official acts as crown prince was to reopen diplomatic relations with China. He then brought to Japan many Chinese artists, religious leaders, and builders, so he and his culture could learn from China's ways. For example, Shotoku used China's bureaucracy as a model for his own government. He also began to award government positions based on merit, as the Chinese did, rather than on family name, as did old Japan.

Review with students how Buddhist beliefs spread from one country to another. **Ask: What features in our own lives have come to us from another culture?** (*Answers will vary but may include different foods, different types and makes of clothing, furniture styles, religious beliefs, governmental systems, and so on.*) **L1/ EL**

Then and Now

Answers will vary. Students should note that people felt some connection to the selected person's actions, beliefs, or policies. The Japanese identified with Shotoku because they trusted his reforms, beliefs, and actions.

Reading List Generator CD-ROM

GLENCOE BOOKLINK

RECOMMENDED READING

Use the **Glencoe BookLink CD-ROM** to create customized reading lists based on your students' interests and reading levels. Below is an example based on content in this chapter. Also, see the Suggested Readings on pages 944–946 of the Appendix.

- **Namioka, Lensey.** *The Coming of the Bear.* Two shipwrecked samurai have to defend their primitive rescuers from settlers.
- **Paterson, Katherine.** *The Sign of the Chrysanthemum.* In twelfth-century Japan, Muna searches for the father he has never met. His mother told him only that his father was a samurai and that he would know him by the sign of the chrysanthemum.
- **Sasaki, R. A.** *A Dictionary of Japanese-American Terms.*

ENRICH

Three-quarters of all the land in Japan has a slope of 15° or greater. Discuss the problems farmers would face trying to farm land at such an angle. **L1/ EL**

Answer: They worshiped at shrines and performed rituals.

To help students understand section material, have them visit **Study Central™** at jat.glencoe.com

Reading Strategy

RETEACH

Have students write a summary of the main ideas. **L1**

④ CLOSE

Using a map, discuss how China's relative location and size might have led to its influence on Japan. **L1/ EL**

What Is Shinto?

Main Idea The Japanese religion, called Shinto, was based on nature spirits.

Reading Focus Today we know the importance of protecting the environment. Why is nature important to us? Read to learn why the early Japanese thought nature was important.

Like many ancient peoples, the early Japanese believed that all natural things are alive, even the winds, the mountains, and the rivers. They believed that all of these things have their own spirits. This idea is called **animism** (A•nuh•MIH•zuhm). When people needed help, they asked the nature spirits, whom they called *kami*, to help them.

To honor the *kami*, the Japanese worshiped at **shrines** (SHRYNZ), or holy places. There, priests, musicians, and dancers performed rituals for people who asked the gods for a good harvest, a wife or a child, or some other favor.

These early Japanese beliefs developed into the religion of Shinto. The word *Shinto* means "way of the spirits," and many Japanese still follow Shinto today. Followers believe the *kami* will help only if a person is pure. Many things, such as illness, cause spiritual stains that must be cleansed by bathing and other rituals before praying.

Reading Check **Explain** How did the Japanese honor the *kami*?

◄ Shinto priests

Section ① Review

Study Central™ Need help with the material in this section? Visit jat.glencoe.com

Reading Summary

Review the Main Ideas

- Japan's mountainous islands contain little land for farming, leading many people to turn to the sea for a living.
- Japan was settled by people from northeast Asia, organized into clans and ruled by warriors.
- While ruling Japan, Prince Shotoku made the emperor a strong ruler and set up a government similar to China's.
- Japan's first religion, Shinto, was based on the idea of nature spirits called *kami*.

What Did You Learn?

1. What skills did the Yayoi practice that they may have learned from the Chinese and Koreans?

2. In the Shinto religion, what do people worship? How are they worshiped?

Critical Thinking

3. **Sequencing Information** Draw a time line like the one below. Fill in dates and information related to events in Japanese history from the Jomon to Shotoku.

|———|———|———|———|———|———|
5000 B.C.   **A.D. 646**

4. **Summarize** Describe Japanese society under the Yayoi around A.D. 300.

5. **Analyze** In what ways did Shotoku look to China to improve Japan?

6. **Expository Writing** Imagine you are visiting Japan sometime in the A.D. 300s. Write a letter to a friend describing what you have observed and learned about the Shinto religion.

7. **Reading** Cause and Effect Create a cause-and-effect graphic organizer that shows how geography affected the early development of Japan.

SECTION 1 REVIEW ANSWERS

1. using a potter's wheel and growing rice in paddies
2. spirits called *kami*, which reside in all natural things; through rituals at shrines
3. 5000 B.C.: Jomon culture develops; 300 B.C.: Yayoi appear; A.D. 300: the Yayoi had organized into clans;

A.D. 500s: the Yamato control most of Japan; A.D. 600: Shotoku takes power; A.D. 646: the Great Change begins

4. clans headed by a small group of warriors who protected the farmers, artisans, and servants

5. in government (centralized, with powerful emperor, trained officials), and in learning (Buddhist teachings, art, medicine, philosophy)
6. Letters should describe the *kami* and religious practices.
7. Graphic organizers should draw upon the text.

Section 2 Shoguns and Samurai

Get Ready to Read!

What's the Connection?

In the last section, you learned how Japan's leaders looked to China as a model of government. As you have learned, warlords sometimes took over parts of China. As you will read, Japan had similar problems.

Focusing on the (Main Ideas)

- During the A.D. 700s, Japan built a strong national government at Nara, and Buddhism became a popular religion. *(page 492)*

- Japan's civilian government and the emperor came to be dominated by military rulers known as shoguns. *(page 493)*

- As the shogun's power weakened, Japan broke into warring kingdoms run by rulers known as daimyo. *(page 496)*

Locating Places

Heian (HAY•ahn)
Kamakura (kah•MAH•kuh•RAH)

Meeting People

Minamoto Yoritomo (mee•nah• moh•toh   yoh•ree•toh•moh)
Ashikaga Takauji (ah•shee•kah• gah   tah•kow•jee)

Building Your Vocabulary

samurai (SA•muh•RY)
shogun (SHOH•guhn)
daimyo (DY•mee•OH)
vassal (VA•suhl)
feudalism (FYOO•duhl•IH•zuhm)

Reading Strategy

Showing Relationships Create a diagram to show the relationship between daimyo and samurai.

When & Where?

NATIONAL GEOGRAPHIC

A.D. 700	1100	1500
A.D. 794 Japan's capital moved to Heian	1192 Rule by shoguns begins	1477 Civil war ends in Japan

Heian (Kyoto)   JAPAN
KOREA   Kamakura
Nara

CHAPTER 14   Medieval Japan   491

---

① FOCUS

SECTION OVERVIEW

This section describes the rise of the samurai and the shogunate in Japan.

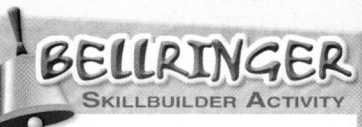

SKILLBUILDER ACTIVITY

✎ Project **Daily Focus Skills Transparency 14–2** and have students answer questions. Discuss their responses.

Get Ready to Read!

Preteaching Vocabulary: Point out to students that the vocabulary terms in this section all relate to political issues in some fashion.

Answers to Graphic: Daimyo: granted land to samurai; Samurai: gave oath of loyalty to serve daimyo in times of war

---

SECTION RESOURCES

📁 **Reproducible Masters**
- Reproducible Lesson Plan 14–2
- Daily Lecture and Discussion Notes 14–2
- Vocabulary Activity 14–2
- Active Reading Note-Taking Guide 14–2
- Guided Reading Activity 14–2
- Section Quiz 14–2
- Reading Essentials and Study Guide 14–2

📇 **Transparencies**
- Daily Focus Skills Transparency 14–2

Multimedia
- Interactive Tutor Self-Assessment CD-ROM
- ExamView® Pro Testmaker CD-ROM
- Presentation Plus! CD-ROM

② TEACH

Analyzing Pictures Direct students' attention to the **Main Idea** listed for "Nara Japan." Have them skim this part of the section looking for pictures that illustrate or support the idea. **L1/ EL**

Daily Lecture and Discussion Notes 14–2

Use **Daily Lecture and Discussion Notes 14–2** for an outline of key concepts found in the section.

TIME TRAVELER

The ancient city of Nara has become a tourist attraction because many ancient buildings and artifacts survive there. For example, the Grand Shrine of Kasuga is one of the country's oldest Shinto shrines. The culture preserved by Nara is so valued that the Japanese have a saying: "See Nara and die."

Reading Support L1/ EL

Use **Vocabulary Activity 14–2** to review important terms in the section.

Nara Japan

Main Idea During the A.D. 700s, Japan built a strong national government at Nara, and Buddhism became a popular religion.

Reading Focus Do you know anyone who was hired for a job because they were friends with the boss or because the boss knew their family? Read to learn how Japan's emperor chose people for government jobs.

In the early A.D. 700s, Japan's emperors built a new capital city called Nara. For the next 100 years, Nara was the center of government and religion in Japan. Because of Nara's importance, the history of Japan during the A.D. 700s is called the Nara Period.

The city of Nara looked much like China's capital of Changan, only smaller. It had broad streets, large public squares, government offices, Buddhist temples, and Shinto shrines. Nobles and their families lived in large, Chinese-style homes. The typical home of a noble had wooden walls,

▲ Built in the early A.D. 600s, the Horyuji temple in Nara, Japan, is the oldest wooden building in the world.

a heavy tile roof, and polished wooden floors. It also included an inner garden.

The Emperor's Government At Nara, Japanese emperors added to the changes begun by Prince Shotoku. They organized government officials into ranks, or levels of importance from top to bottom. However, unlike China, Japan did not use examinations to hire officials. Instead, the emperor gave the jobs to nobles from powerful families. Once a person was appointed to a job, he could pass on his office to his son or other relatives. For their services, top government officials received estates, or large farms. They also were given farmers to work the land.

The emperor's power came from his control of the land and its crops. To measure Japan's wealth, the government carried out a census. It counted all the people in the country. The census also listed the lands on which people lived and worked. Based on the census results, all people who held land from the emperor had to pay taxes in rice or silk cloth. The men counted in the census had to serve in the army.

Buddhism Spreads in Japan At the same time that the emperor's government was growing strong, Buddhism became popular in Japan. Buddhism came to Japan from Korea in the A.D. 500s. Japanese government officials and nobles were the first to accept the new religion. Then, during the A.D. 600s and A.D. 700s, Buddhism spread rapidly among the common people. It soon became a major religion in Japan and had an important role in government and society.

As Buddhism became more powerful, nobles who were not Buddhists began to oppose the religion. Soon, those who backed Buddhism and those who opposed it were fighting for control of the government.

Reading Strategy   READING THE TEXT

Outlining Explain that an outline will help students organize the information presented under the numerous headings. Organize students into small groups. Have each group create a headings-based outline. Tell groups to leave a blank space after each entry. As students read the material under each heading, have them write a summary sentence in the appropriate place. Have the groups review their outlines as they study for the chapter test. **L1/ EL**

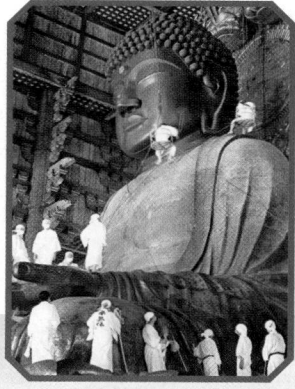

Inside the ▶ Todaji temple is Japan's largest statue of the Buddha. It is made of copper and gold, weighs 250 tons, and is nearly 50 feet tall.

▲ The Todaji temple was first built in A.D. 752 to serve as the head temple for Buddhism in Japan. It is the world's largest wooden structure. This reconstruction was built in 1692.

In A.D. 770 a Buddhist monk who served in the government tried to seize the throne and become emperor. He was stopped by the emperor's family and leading nobles.

Frightened by this event, the emperor and his family briefly turned away from Buddhism. Remember how the government in China attacked Buddhist monasteries when they became strong? In Japan, instead of attacking the Buddhists, the emperor simply decided to leave Nara and its many Buddhist monks.

✔ **Reading Check** **Contrast** How was the Japanese system of hiring officials different from the Chinese system?

The Rise of the Shogun

Main Idea Japan's civilian government and the emperor came to be dominated by military rulers known as shoguns.

Reading Focus Every leader promises certain things to the people in return for their support. In the United States, what promises do politicians make to win votes? Read to learn how Japan's nobles increased their power by giving land in return for people's support.

In A.D. 794, Emperor Kammu of Japan began building a new capital city called **Heian** (HAY•ahn). This city later became known as Kyoto (kee•OH•toh). Like Nara, Heian was modeled on the Chinese city of Changan. It remained the official capital of Japan for more than 1,000 years.

The Government Weakens During the A.D. 800s, the emperor's power declined. Why did this happen? After a time of strong emperors, a number of weak emperors came to the throne. Many of these emperors were still only children, and court officials known as regents had to govern for them. A regent is a person who rules for an emperor who is too young or too sick to rule. When the emperors grew up, however, the regents refused to give up their power.

Most regents came from a clan called the Fujiwara. Under the Fujiwara, Japan's emperors were honored, but they no longer had real power. Instead of ruling, these emperors spent time studying Buddhism or writing poetry in their palace at Heian.

History Online

Web Activity Visit jat.glencoe.com and click on *Chapter 14—Student Web Activity* to learn more about medieval Japan.

CHAPTER 14   Medieval Japan   **493**

Comparing and Contrasting Have volunteers read aloud the subsection titled "The Government Weakens." Discuss with students the advantages and disadvantages of having hereditary emperors or their regents rule. **L2**

CONNECTING ACROSS TIME

Remind students that Heian remained the capital of Japan for more than 1,000 years. During those years, it had several names. These included *Miyako* ("The Capital") and *Saikyo* ("Western Capital"). The name *Kyoto* means "Capital City" and remains the name of the modern-day city. Have students use a map of Japan to analyze what might have been the advantages and disadvantages of having Heian as the capital. **L3**

✔ **Reading Check**

Answer: Unlike the Chinese, Japan did not use examinations to hire officials. Instead, the emperor appointed officials from powerful families and let people inherit jobs from their fathers.

History Online

Objectives and answers to the student activity can be found in the **Web Activity Lesson Plan** feature at jat.glencoe.com

DIFFERENTIATED INSTRUCTION

Verbal/Linguistic: Have students look up the term *Buddhism* in the index. Ask volunteers to find each of the references and read aloud the material pertaining to Buddhism. After each selection, ask a different student to verbally summarize what was read.

Visual/Spatial: Have students define the word *reincarnation*. Then elicit what reincarnation has to do with Buddhism. Have students use this information to create a flow chart illustrating the Buddhist belief in reincarnation.

Gifted and Talented: Have students do research to trace the spread of Buddhism from its beginnings in India to its arrival in Japan.

◤ Refer to *Inclusion Strategies for the Middle School Social Studies Classroom* in the TCR.

CURRICULUM CONNECTION

Language Arts

Haiku is a form of poetry that started in Japan. It has three lines. The first line has five syllables, the second line has seven syllables, and the third line has five syllables. Write on the board the following example of a haiku for students to read and examine:

Ancient Mount Fuji
With your cap of snow-like hair
On an old man's head.

Writing Activity

Organize small groups of students and tell them to analyze the subsections "Who Were the Samurai?" and "What Is a Shogun?" to find out what led to the rise of the samurai. Have students write a paragraph explaining how a decline in the emperor's power led to the rise of the samurai. **L2**

More About the Art

To avoid dishonor, the samurai developed a ritual suicide known as *seppuku* as an accepted way to respond to capture or some other failure.

Caption Answer: Bushido

As the Fujiwara grew wealthy and powerful in Heian, other powerful nobles gained control of much of the land in the provinces of Japan. This happened because the government gave the nobles lands as a way to pay them for their work. At the same time, new lands were settled as Japan's empire expanded. The nobles who settled farmers on these lands were allowed to keep the lands.

To keep the nobles happy, the government let them stop paying taxes, but it put them in charge of governing the lands under their control. In order to govern their lands, the nobles began collecting more taxes from the peasants working the land.

A samurai's helmet was often individually decorated.

A samurai usually carried two swords. The longer one was called the *katana*, the shorter one was the *wakizashi*.

The *naginata* was a blade mounted on a long handle. It was used against cavalry.

A samurai's armor was made from scales of metal or leather, brightly painted, and laced together with silk or leather.

▲ At first, most samurai fought on horseback. Later samurai were foot soldiers who fought with a variety of weapons. *What was the samurai code of conduct called?*

494   CHAPTER 14   Medieval Japan

Who Were the Samurai? To protect their lands and enforce the law, nobles formed private armies. To create their armies, they gave land to warriors who agreed to fight for them. These warriors became known as **samurai** (SA•muh•RY).

In battle, samurai fought on horseback with swords, daggers, and bows and arrows. They wore armor made of leather or steel scales laced together with silk cords. Their helmets had horns or crests, and they wore masks designed to be terrifying.

The word *samurai* means "one who serves." The samurai lived by a strict code of conduct. It was called Bushido, or "the way of the warrior." This code demanded that a samurai be loyal to his master as well as courageous, brave, and honorable. Samurai were not supposed to care for wealth. They regarded merchants as lacking in honor.

Pledged to these principles, a samurai would rather die in battle than betray his lord. He also did not want to suffer the disgrace of being captured in battle. The sense of loyalty that set apart the samurai continued into modern times. During World War II, many Japanese soldiers fought to the death rather than accept defeat or capture. Since that conflict, the Japanese have turned away from the military beliefs of the samurai.

What Is a Shogun? By the early 1100s, the most powerful Japanese families had begun fighting each other using their samurai armies. They fought over land and to gain control over the emperor and his government. In 1180 the Gempei War began. The Gempei War was a civil war between the two most powerful clans: the Taira family

CRITICAL THINKING ACTIVITY

Analyzing Information Organize students into small groups, and have each group consider this question: Should the samurai have pledged loyalty to the emperor or to the shogun? Have each group write a sentence in favor of each viewpoint. Then have groups read aloud their sentences to the class. Once all groups have shared their thoughts, have the class debate the issue. **L2**

and the Minamoto family. In 1185 the Minamoto forces defeated the Taira in a sea battle near the island of Shikoku.

The leader of the Minamoto was a man named **Minamoto Yoritomo** (mee•nah•moh•toh yoh•ree•toh•moh). (In Japanese a person's family name comes first, followed by the personal name.) Yoritomo was the commander of the Minamoto armies. After Yoritomo won the Gempei War, the emperor worried that the Minamoto family would try to replace the Yamato family as the rulers of Japan. He decided it would be better to reward Yoritomo to keep him loyal.

In 1192 the emperor gave Yoritomo the title of **shogun** (SHOH•guhn)—commander of all of the emperor's military forces. This decision created two governments in Japan. The emperor stayed in his palace at Heian with his bureaucracy. He was still officially the head of the country, but he had no power. Meanwhile the shogun set up his own government at his headquarters in **Kamakura** (kah•MAH•kuh•RAH), a small seaside town. This military government was known as a shogunate. Japan's government was run by a series of shoguns for the next 700 years.

Yoritomo proved to be a ruthless ruler. He killed most of his relatives, fearing that they would try to take power from him. Yoritomo and the shoguns after him appointed high-ranking samurai to serve as advisers and to run the provinces. Bound by an oath of loyalty, these samurai lords ruled Japan's villages, kept the peace, and gathered taxes. They became the leading group in Japanese society.

The Mongols Attack In the late 1200s, the Kamakura shogunate faced its greatest test. In 1274 and again in 1281, China's Mongol emperor Kublai Khan sent out ships and

Primary Source

Bushido Code

This passage describes the samurai's Bushido.

"It is further good fortune if . . . [a servant] had wisdom and talent and can use them appropriately. But even a person who is good for nothing . . . will be a reliable retainer [servant] if only he has the determination to think earnestly of [respect and admire] his master. Having only wisdom and talent is the lowest tier [level] of usefulness."

—Yamamoto Tsunetomo, *Hagakure: The Book of the Samurai*

◀ Samurai armor

DBQ Document-Based Question

How powerful is a samurai's determination to respect and admire his master?

warriors to invade Japan. Both times, the Mongols were defeated because violent Pacific storms smashed many of their ships. The Mongol troops who made it ashore were defeated by the Japanese.

The victorious Japanese named the typhoons *kamikaze* (KAH•mih•KAH•zee), or "divine wind," in honor of the spirits they believed had saved their islands. Much later, during World War II, Japanese pilots deliberately crashed their planes into enemy ships. They were named kamikaze pilots after the typhoons of the 1200s.

✓ Reading Check **Identify** Who was the shogun, and why was he important?

Have a volunteer read aloud the excerpt of the Bushido code. Explain that the code does not mean that wisdom and talent are not useful. Instead, it means that for the samurai, those two qualities are not enough. Even the lowliest of people can be reliable if they show their master respect.

Answer:
It is so powerful that it can turn a samurai who is good for nothing into a reliable servant.

Reading Support L1/ EL

Assign **Guided Reading Activity 14–2** to help students organize the information in the section.

✓ Reading Check

Answer: The shogun was the commander of all the emperor's military forces and became the head of a military government.

INTERDISCIPLINARY CONNECTIONS ACTIVITY

Language Arts Samurai valued honor, loyalty, and bravery. They looked favorably to heroes who upheld these ideals. Have small groups identify people they consider heroes—either from literature or from real life. Have each group select one real person and research his or her life. Ask students to write a paragraph, identifying some of the character traits exhibited by the person their group selected. Ask groups to compare those traits with traits valued by the samurai. **L2**

③ ASSESS

Assign Section 2 Review as homework or as an in-class activity.

◉ Have students use the **Interactive Tutor Self-Assessment CD-ROM** to review the section.

Assessment L2

Assign **Section 2 Quiz** to assess mastery of the material found in the section.

Reading Support L1/EL

Assign **Reading Essentials and Study Guide 14–2** to help students review section material.

NATIONAL GEOGRAPHIC — The Way It Was

Answers:
1. Bushido, and to place loyalty, honor, and bravery above all else
2. Answers will vary but should demonstrate a thoughtful response.

NATIONAL GEOGRAPHIC — The Way It Was

Focus on Everyday Life

Samurai The path to becoming a samurai was difficult and dangerous. Mothers in samurai families began teaching their sons Bushido at a young age. They taught their sons to place bravery, honor, and loyalty above all else. Each young warrior knew and could recite from memory the brave feats of his samurai ancestors.

For centuries, young samurai lived apart from their families in the castle of their lord or in the barracks of their lord's town. Beginning in the 1800s, samurai schools were built, and boys lived there to continue the educations their mothers had started. From the age of 10, they trained in the martial arts and studied other subjects, such as math and astronomy. By the age of 16, some young men were already promising warriors who distinguished themselves in battle.

Painting of a ▶ samurai hero

Connecting to the Past
1. What lessons was the mother of a samurai responsible for teaching her young son?
2. Do you think soldiers today have a code of conduct similar to Bushido? Explain.

The Daimyo Divide Japan

Main Idea As the shogun's power weakened, Japan broke into warring kingdoms run by rulers known as daimyo.

Reading Focus Have you ever been promised something and then been upset when the promise was broken? Read to learn how Japan's shogun lost power because the samurai felt he had broken his promises.

The Kamakura shogunate ruled Japan until 1333. By that time, many samurai had become resentful. Over the years, as samurai divided their lands among their sons, the piece of land each samurai owned became smaller and smaller. By the 1300s, many samurai felt they no longer owed the shogun loyalty because he had not given them enough land.

In 1331 the emperor rebelled, and many samurai came to his aid. The revolt succeeded, but the emperor was not able to gain control of Japan because he too refused to give more land to the samurai. Instead, a general named **Ashikaga Takauji** (ah•shee•kah•gah   tah•kow•jee) turned against the emperor and made himself shogun in 1333. A new government known as the Ashikaga shogunate began.

The Ashikaga shoguns proved to be weak rulers, and revolts broke out across Japan. The country soon divided into a number of small territories. These areas were headed by powerful military lords known as **daimyo** (DY•mee•OH).

The daimyo pledged loyalty to the emperor and the shogun. However, they ruled their lands as if they were independent kingdoms. To protect their lands, the daimyo created their own local armies made up of samurai warriors, just as other nobles had done in the past.

Many samurai became **vassals** (VA•suhlz) of a daimyo. That is, a samurai gave an oath

CITIZENSHIP AND YOU

Loyalty Remind students that the daimyo pledged loyalty to the emperor and the shogun, while the samurai pledged loyalty to his daimyo. Point out that Americans, too, pledge loyalty to something. Write on the board, "I pledge allegiance . . ." and explain that *allegiance* is another word for *loyalty*. Discuss with students what promises are made every time someone says the Pledge of Allegiance. **Ask:** How is our pledge different from the pledges made by the samurai? *(Students should indicate that in historic Japan, people made pledges to other people, while in the United States, we make a pledge to our nation.)* **L2**

of loyalty to his daimyo and promised to serve him in times of war. In return, each daimyo gave land to his samurai warriors—more land than they had been given by the shogun. This bond of loyalty between a lord and a vassal is known as **feudalism** (FYOO•duhl•IH•zuhm). In the next chapter, you will learn about a similar form of feudalism that arose in Europe during the Middle Ages.

With the breakdown of central government, Japan's warriors fought each other. From 1467 to 1477, the country suffered through the disastrous Onin War. During this conflict, the city of Kyoto (Heian) was almost completely destroyed. Armies passed back and forth through the city, burning temples and palaces.

For 100 years after the Onin War, a series of weak shoguns tried to reunite Japan. Powerful daimyo, however, resisted their

▲ The Takamatsu castle was built in 1590. It sits on the edge of a sea and was once surrounded by moats, gates, and towers for protection.

control. Fighting spread throughout the country. The violence finally brought down the Ashikaga shogunate in 1567. By that time, only a handful of powerful daimyo remained. Each of these daimyo was eager to defeat his rivals and rule all of Japan.

Reading Check **Analyze** Why were shoguns unable to regain control of Japan after the Onin War?

Section 2 Review

Study Central™ Need help with the material in this section? Visit jat.glencoe.com

Reading Summary
Review the (Main Ideas)
- During the Nara Period, the emperor's power grew, and Buddhism spread among Japan's common people.
- Over time, the Japanese emperors lost power to nobles and their armies of samurai. Eventually a military ruler, called a shogun, ruled the country.
- In the 1400s and 1500s, the shoguns lost power, and military lords, called daimyo, divided Japan into a number of small territories.

What Did You Learn?
1. What was a shogun? Who was the first shogun, and how did he gain his position of power?
2. What prevented the Mongol conquest of Japan?

Critical Thinking
3. **Organizing Information** Draw a diagram like the one below. Add details about the samurai, such as their weapons, dress, and beliefs.

Samurai

4. **Describe** Describe events related to the growth of Buddhism in Japan.
5. **Explain** Why did the power of the Japanese emperors decline during the A.D. 800s?
6. **Analyze** How did the beliefs of the samurai affect Japanese soldiers in World War II?
7. **Expository Writing** Create a constitution, or plan for government, that describes the relationship between the emperor and shogun, the daimyo, and the samurai.

CHAPTER 14   Medieval Japan   **497**

SECTION 2 REVIEW ANSWERS

1. a military ruler of Japan; the emperor appointed Minamoto Yoritomo as first shogun to keep him loyal
2. Violent storms, called typhoons, smashed most of the Mongol ships.
3. fought on horseback, later on foot; used swords, daggers, bows and arrows; wore armor and helmets; lived code of Bushido; were loyal, brave, and courageous
4. Answers should match information in the text.
5. Regents refused to give up their power, while nobles gained power and formed personal armies.
6. They refused to surrender and fought to the death.
7. Constitutions should explain relative relationships.

ENRICH
One definition of the vocabulary term *feudalism* is "an economic, political, or social system in which vassals held land from lords in exchange for military service." Read aloud this definition. Then discuss with students whether Japan's version of feudalism was economic, political, social, or a combination. **L2**

Reading Check
Answer: The powerful daimyo successfully resisted their control.

To help students understand section material, have them visit **Study Central™** at jat.glencoe.com

RETEACH
Remind students of the emperor's decision to create the shogunate. Review the events surrounding this decision, and discuss with students if they think this was a wise course of action given the events. **L1/EL**

④ CLOSE
Ask students to discuss how the power of Japan's emperor changed over time. Allow students to skim the section for clues. **L2**

497

① FOCUS

SECTION OVERVIEW

This section describes the influence of religion on Japan's cultural development and the roles of various social groups.

BELLRINGER
SKILLBUILDER ACTIVITY

✎ Project **Daily Focus Skills Transparency 14–3** and have students answer questions. Discuss their responses.

Get Ready to Read!

Preteaching Vocabulary: Among the many sports included in martial arts are karate, tae kwon do, judo, and kendo.

Answers to Graphic: expected to obey their fathers, husbands, sons; marriages were arranged in wealthy families, had some say in whom they married in farming families; worked long hours in the fields planting or harvesting rice; cooked; spun and wove cloth; cared for the children; helped with family business; some gained fame as artists, writers, and warriors

---

Section 3
Life in Medieval Japan

Get-Ready to Read!

What's the Connection?

In the last section, you learned how warriors known as shoguns and samurai came to rule Japan. During that time, the Japanese suffered from many wars. However, Japan's economy continued to grow, and its people produced beautiful art, architecture, and literature.

Focusing on the Main Ideas

• Buddhism and Shinto shaped much of Japan's culture. These religions affected Japanese art, architecture, novels, and plays. *(page 499)*

• Some Japanese nobles, merchants, and artisans grew wealthy during the shogun period, but the lives of women remained restricted in many areas of life. *(page 503)*

Locating Places
Kyoto (kee•OH•toh)

Meeting People
Murasaki Shikibu (MUR•uh•SAH•kee shee•kee•boo)

Building Your Vocabulary
sect (SEHKT)
martial arts (MAHR•shuhl)
meditation (MEH•duh•TAY•shuhn)
calligraphy (kuh•LIH•gruh•fee)
tanka (TAHNG•kuh)
guild (GIHLD)

Reading Strategy
Summarizing Information Complete a diagram like the one below describing the role of women in the families of medieval Japan.

Role of Women

NATIONAL GEOGRAPHIC **When & Where?**

JAPAN
KOREA
• Heian (Kyoto)

1000
1200
1400

c. 1000
Lady Murasaki Shikibu writes *The Tale of Genji*

c. 1100s
Zen Buddhism spreads in Japan

c. 1300s
Noh plays first performed

SECTION RESOURCES

📁 **Reproducible Masters**
• Reproducible Lesson Plan 14–3
• Daily Lecture and Discussion Notes 14–3
• Vocabulary Activity 14–3
• Active Reading Note-Taking Guide 14–3
• Guided Reading Activity 14–3
• Section Quiz 14–3
• Reading Essentials and Study Guide 14–3

✎ **Transparencies**
• Daily Focus Skills Transparency 14–3

Multimedia
⊙ Interactive Tutor Self-Assessment CD-ROM
⊙ ExamView® Pro Testmaker CD-ROM
⊙ Presentation Plus! CD-ROM
⊙ Vocabulary PuzzleMaker CD-ROM
⊙ Glencoe BookLink CD-ROM

Japanese Religion and Culture

Main Idea Buddhism and Shinto shaped much of Japan's culture. These religions affected Japanese art, architecture, novels, and plays.

Reading Focus Have you ever seen paintings, sculptures, and works of literature that have religious subjects or messages? In medieval Japan, the religions of Shinto and Buddhism greatly influenced the arts.

During the Middle Ages, religion was a part of everyday life for the Japanese. Most Japanese came to believe in both Buddhism and Shinto, and worshiped at Shinto shrines and Buddhist temples. To them, each religion met different needs. Shinto was concerned with daily life, while Buddhism prepared people for the life to come. During the Middle Ages, Buddhist ideas inspired many Japanese to build temples, produce paintings, and write poems and plays.

Pure Land Buddhism

As you have already learned, Mahayana Buddhism began in India and spread to China and Korea. By the time Buddhism reached Japan, it had developed into many different **sects** (SEHKTS), or smaller religious groups.

One of the most important sects in Japan was Pure Land Buddhism. Pure Land Buddhism was a type of Mahayana Buddhism. It won many followers in Japan because of its message about a happy life after death. Pure Land Buddhists looked to Lord Amida, a buddha of love and mercy. They believed Amida had founded a paradise above the clouds. To get there, all they had to do was have faith in Amida and chant his name.

What Is Zen Buddhism?

Another important Buddhist sect in Japan was Zen. Buddhist monks brought Zen to Japan from China during the 1100s. Zen taught that

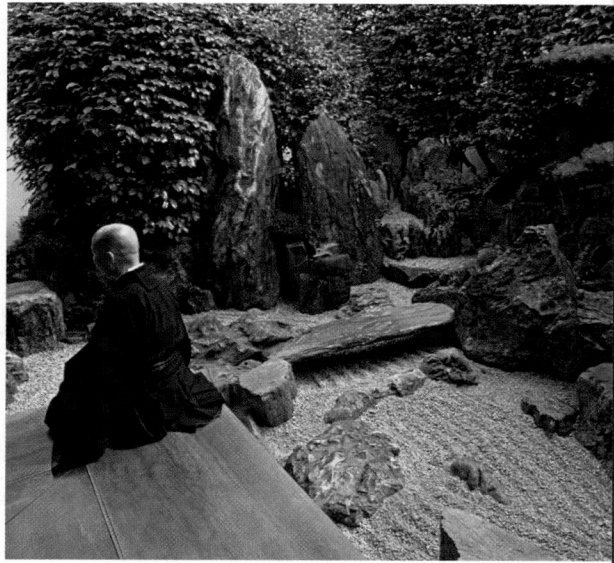

▲ A Zen monk sits beside a Japanese rock garden while meditating. *What is the purpose of meditation?*

people could find inner peace through self-control and a simple way of life.

Followers of Zen learned to control their bodies through **martial arts** (MAHR•shuhl), or sports that involved combat and self-defense. This appealed to the samurai, who trained to fight bravely and fearlessly.

Followers of Zen Buddhism also practiced **meditation** (MEH•duh•TAY•shuhn). In meditation, a person sat cross-legged and motionless for hours, with the mind cleared of all thoughts and desires. Meditation helped people to relax and find inner peace.

Art and Architecture

During the Middle Ages, the Japanese borrowed artistic ideas from China and Korea. Then, they went on to develop their own styles. The arts of Japan revealed the Japanese love of beauty and simplicity.

During the Middle Ages, artisans in Japan made wooden statues, furniture, and

CHAPTER 14 Medieval Japan **499**

② TEACH

Activate Prior Knowledge Point out that this section talks about the impact of religion on Japan's cultural development. Have students review what they have learned about Buddhism in general. Have them compare what they know about Buddhism with Pure Land Buddhism and Zen Buddhism. **L3**

Daily Lecture and Discussion Notes 14–3

Use **Daily Lecture and Discussion Notes 14–3** for an outline of key concepts found in the section.

Caption Answer: to help a person relax and find inner peace

TIME TRAVELER

Pure Land Buddhism was spread through Japan by a man named Honen who believed that the only way to salvation lay in repeating Amida's name. Reciting the name of Amida Buddha was called *nembutsu*.

Reading Support L1/EL

Use **Vocabulary Activity 14–3** to review important terms in the section.

Reading Strategy

Writing Activity

Have students read the subsection on art and architecture, then write a paragraph comparing the impact of Shinto and Buddhism on Japanese architecture. **L2**

Linking Past & Present

Answer: Answers will vary depending on students' interests and activities.

CONNECTING ACROSS TIME

Remind students that there are several kinds of martial arts. Have students research two forms of martial arts and write a short report describing their similarities and differences. **L2**

Linking Past & Present

Martial Arts

▼Modern-day martial artist

THEN According to legend, the Chinese monks who brought martial arts to Japan in the 1100s learned them from an Indian monk named Bodhidharma. In the sixth century, he traveled to China and found monks at a temple who were weak and sleepy from meditation, so he taught them martial arts to strengthen their bodies. Over time, many forms of martial arts developed.

NOW Martial arts remain popular and respected. Current forms include karate, jujitsu, and aikido from Japan; kung fu from China; and tae kwon do from Korea. *What sports or activities do you participate in that help strengthen your mind and body?*

▲Figurine of Bodhidharma

household items. On many of their works, they used a shiny black and red coating called lacquer. From the Chinese, Japanese artists learned to do landscape painting. Using ink or watercolors, they painted scenes of nature or battles on paper scrolls or on silk. Japanese nobles at the emperor's court learned to fold paper to make decorative objects. This art of folding paper is called origami. They also arranged flowers. Buddhist monks and the samurai turned tea drinking into a beautiful ceremony.

Builders in Japan used Chinese or Japanese styles. Shinto shrines were built in the Japanese style near a sacred rock, tree, or other natural feature that they considered beautiful. Usually a shrine was a wooden building, with a single room and a roof made of rice straw. People entered the shrine through a sacred gate called a torii.

Unlike Shinto shrines, Buddhist temples were built in the Chinese style. They had massive tiled roofs held up by thick, wooden pillars. The temples were richly decorated. They had many statues, paintings, and altars.

Around their buildings, the Japanese created gardens designed to imitate nature

500 CHAPTER 14 Medieval Japan

DIFFERENTIATED INSTRUCTION

Visual/Spatial: Explain that many Buddhists meditate by crossing their legs and trying to clear their minds of all thoughts. Have students imitate this practice. After two minutes, discuss whether students were successful. Remind them that many Zen Buddhists meditate like this for hours at a time.

Verbal/Linguistic: Have students verbally compare a Shinto shrine with a Buddhist temple.

Naturalist: Have students research the kinds of places that people make into shrines and the reasons for those choices.

☞ Refer to *Inclusion Strategies for the Middle School Social Studies Classroom* in the TCR.

in a miniature form. Some of these gardens had carefully placed rocks, raked sand, and a few plants. They were built this way to create a feeling of peace and calmness.

Poems and Plays During the A.D. 500s, the Japanese borrowed China's writing system. They wrote their language in Chinese picture characters that stood for whole words. Because the Japanese and Chinese languages were so different, the Japanese found it difficult to use these characters. Then, in the A.D. 800s, they added symbols that stood for sounds, much like the letters of an alphabet. This addition made reading and writing much easier.

Calligraphy (kuh•LIH•gruh•fee), the art of writing beautifully, was much admired in Japan. Every well-educated person was expected to practice it. A person's handwriting was considered to reveal much about his or her education, social standing, and character.

During the Middle Ages, the Japanese wrote poems, stories, and plays. Japan's oldest form of poetry was the **tanka** (TAHNG•kuh). It was an unrhymed poem of five lines. Tanka poems capture nature's beauty and the joys and sorrows of life. The following tanka was written by an anonymous poet:

“ On autumn nights
the dew is
colder than ever—
in every clump of grasses
the insects weep ”
—author unknown,
tanka from the *Kokinshū*

Women living in Heian wrote Japan's first great stories around 1000. One woman,

Lady **Murasaki Shikibu** (MUR•uh•SAH•kee shee•kee•boo), wrote *The Tale of Genji.* This work describes the adventures of a Japanese prince. Some people believe the work is the world's first novel, or long fictional story.

About 200 years later, Japan's writers turned out stirring tales about warriors in battle. The greatest collection was *The Tale of Heike.* It describes the fight between the Taira and the Minamoto clans.

The Japanese also created plays. The oldest type of play is called Noh. Created during the 1300s, Noh plays were used to teach Buddhist ideas. Noh plays were performed on a simple, bare stage. The actors wore masks and elaborate robes. They danced, gestured, and chanted poetry to the music of drums and flutes.

Reading Check **Analyze** How are martial arts and meditation connected to Zen Buddhism's principle of self-control?

▲ Noh masks like these were often carved from a single piece of wood and were lightweight, so an actor could wear it for several hours. *Why were Noh plays performed?*

CHAPTER 14 Medieval Japan 501

CRITICAL THINKING ACTIVITY

Analyzing Statements Explain to students that some Zen Buddhists meditate by thinking about paradoxical statements—that is, statements that seem inconsistent or even absurd. In Japan, these are known as *koan.* Read aloud this example of a koan: "A man was being chased by a tiger. When he came to a cliff, he grabbed hold of a vine and swung down the cliff's side. As he hung there, the man looked up and saw the tiger waiting for him to climb back up. Then he looked down and saw a second tiger waiting for him to fall down the cliff. Now two mice started gnawing through the vine above the man. The man saw a strawberry growing near him on the cliff. He plucked it and ate it. How sweet it was!" Discuss with students what they might learn from meditating on that koan. **L2**

Biography

Biography

TEACH

According to legend, *The Tale of Genji* was inspired when Murasaki Shikibu visited a temple at Lake Biwa. There, during the full moon of the eighth lunar month, Murasaki had a vision of a man she admired—a man who had been unjustly exiled. Quickly, she wrote down the vision, so she would not forget it. Eventually, that first writing would become Chapters 11 and 12 in *The Tale of Genji.*

Tell students that some experts think that over the years, the chapters in *The Tale of Genji* got mixed up. Ask students to describe how their favorite stories would change if the pages somehow got out of order. (*Answers will vary but should indicate how order can affect meaning.*) **L1/ EL**

Then and Now

Answers will vary depending on students' individual interests and considerations of what is important. These may include personal activities, discussions of relationships, ideas on personal beliefs, and so on.

MURASAKI SHIKIBU

c. A.D. 973–1025

Murasaki Shikibu was a great novelist and poet of the Japanese Heian period. She was one of the first modern novelists. Murasaki became famous from writing *The Tale of Genji*, but her work also included a diary and over 120 poems.

Murasaki was born into the Fujiwara clan, a noble family but not a rich family. Her father was a scholar and a governor. In fact, the name Shikibu refers to her father's position at court. Murasaki's mother and older sister died when she was a child. Traditionally, children were raised by the mother and her family, but Murasaki's father decided to raise his daughter himself. He broke another custom by educating his daughter in Chinese language and literature, subjects reserved for boys.

Murasaki married and had a daughter, but her husband died after only a few years of marriage. Around that time, Murasaki began writing *The Tale of Genji* and working as an attendant to Empress Akiko. She based the novel on life at court, which she knew about through her father's job and her own. The last reference to her is in 1014, but many scholars believe that she lived for about a decade after that.

Much about Murasaki's life—and life at the emperor's palace—is revealed in her diary. This excerpt describes the preparations for a celebration honoring the birth of a new prince:

> **"Even the sight of the lowest menials [servants], chattering to each other as they walked round lighting the fire baskets under the trees by the lake and arranging the food in the garden, seemed to add to the sense of occasion. Torchbearers stood everywhere at attention and the scene was as bright as day."**
>
> —Murasaki Shikibu,
> *The Diary of Lady Murasaki*

▲ Murasaki Shikibu

▲ Scene from
The Tale of Genji

Then and Now

Do you keep a diary? What might you and your classmates record in a diary that would be useful to people a few centuries from now?

Reading List Generator CD-ROM

GLENCOE BOOKLINK   **RECOMMENDED READING**

Use the **Glencoe BookLink CD-ROM** to create customized reading lists based on your students' interests and reading levels. Below is an example based on content in this chapter. Also, see the Suggested Readings on pages 944–946 of the Appendix.

- Basho. *Haiku for Four Seasons.*
- Cobb, Vicki. *This Place Is Crowded: Japan.* Imagine living in a place where people do not eat with forks and spoons or sleep in beds, where an express train goes 130 miles an hour, and where a favorite food is raw fish.
- Schroeder, Alan. *Lily and the Wooden Bowl.* Japanese folktale about a lovely girl who wears a wooden bowl over her head to hide her beauty.

Economy and Society

Main Idea Some Japanese nobles, merchants, and artisans grew wealthy during the shogun period, but the lives of women remained restricted in many areas of life.

Reading Focus What determines whether a person is wealthy or poor? Read to find what contributed to the growing wealth of Japan.

Under the shoguns, Japan not only developed its arts but also produced more goods and grew richer. However, only a small number of Japanese benefited from this wealth. This group included the emperor, the nobles at his court, and leading military officials. A small but growing class of merchants and traders also began to prosper. Most Japanese, however, were farmers who remained poor.

Farmers and Artisans Much of Japan's wealth came from the hard work of its farmers. Japanese farmers grew rice, wheat, millet, and barley. Some had their own land, but most lived and worked on the daimyo estates. Despite hardships, life did improve for Japan's farmers during the 1100s. They used better irrigation and planted more crops. As a result, they could send more food to the markets that were developing in the towns.

At the same time, the Japanese were producing more goods. Artisans on the daimyo estates began making weapons, armor, and tools. Merchants sold these items in town markets throughout Japan. New roads made travel and trade much easier. As trade increased, each region focused on making goods that it could best produce. These goods included pottery, paper, textiles, and lacquered ware. All of these new products helped Japan's economy grow.

As the capital, **Kyoto** (kee•OH•toh) became a major center of production and trade. Many artisans and merchants settled there. They formed groups called **guilds** (GIHLDZ) (or *za* in Japanese) to protect and increase their profits. The members of these guilds relied on a wealthy daimyo to protect them from rival artisans. They sold the daimyo goods that he could not get from his country estates.

Japan's wealth also came from increased trade with Korea, China, and Southeast Asia. Japanese merchants exchanged lacquered goods, sword blades, and copper for silk, dyes, pepper, books, and porcelain.

◄ This painting shows Japanese farmers working the land. *What were some crops grown by medieval Japanese farmers?*

503

Using New Technology Improvements in technology almost always lead to benefits for people at some level. Ask students to describe how better irrigation techniques led to economic opportunities for Japan's farmers. **L2**

Japanese Trade Eventually, Japan, like China, isolated itself from much of the rest of the world. Have students research and report on how the end to Japan's isolation differed from that of China. **L2**

❸ ASSESS

Assign Section 3 Review as homework or as an in-class activity.

◉ Have students use the **Interactive Tutor Self-Assessment CD-ROM** to review the section.

Assessment L2

Assign **Section 3 Quiz** to assess mastery of the material found in the section.

Reading Support L1/ EL

Assign **Reading Essentials and Study Guide 14–3** to help students review section material.

Caption Answer: rice, wheat, millet, and barley

INTERDISCIPLINARY CONNECTIONS ACTIVITY

Art Explain that a Noh play is not like a play in this country. There is very little talking or action. Instead, much of the story is told through the masks and costumes the actors wear and the movements they make. Tell students that every Noh play tells one of five kinds of stories: (1) a sacred story of a Shinto shrine; (2) a story with a warrior in the leading role; (3) a story with a woman in the leading role; (4) a story about present-day issues or events; (5) a story with strange or supernatural creatures in the leading role. Distribute a square of cardboard to each student. Have students use the cardboard to design a mask that reflects one of the five kinds of stories listed above. When students have finished, ask volunteers to display their masks and encourage other students to speculate about the kind of story that would be told with that mask. **L1**

ENRICH

Explain that the Japanese use a brush, not a pen, when they are doing calligraphy. **Ask: When is calligraphy used in the United States today?** *(Possible answers: for invitations, to add lettering to pictures)* **L1/ EL**

✓ Reading Check

Answer: The emperor, the nobles at his court, and leading military officials benefited the most. Merchants and traders also began to prosper.

To help students understand section material, have them visit **Study Central™** at jat.glencoe.com

RETEACH

Point out that Japan traded not only goods with its Chinese and Korean neighbors, it also traded ideas. Have students identify ideas Japan borrowed from other cultures. **L2**

 CLOSE

Discuss with students what they have learned about the samurai in medieval Japan. **L1/ EL**

The Role of Women During the Middle Ages, a Japanese family included grandparents, parents, and children in the same household. A man headed the family and had total control over family members. A woman was expected to obey her father, husband, and son. In wealthy families, parents arranged the marriages of their children to increase the family's wealth.

In early Japan, about the time of Prince Shotoku, wealthy women enjoyed a high position in society. There were several women rulers, and women could own property. When Japan became a warrior society with samurai and daimyo, upper-class women lost these freedoms.

In farming families, women had a greater say in whom they married. However, they worked long hours in the fields planting or harvesting rice. In addition, they cooked, spun and wove cloth, and cared for their children. In the towns, the wives of artisans and merchants helped with family businesses and ran their homes. The wives of merchants were perhaps the best off.

Despite the lack of freedom, some women managed to contribute to Japan's culture. These talented women gained fame as artists, writers, and even warriors. In *The Tale of the Heike*, one female samurai named Tomoe is described this way:

> ❝ Tomoe was indescribably beautiful; the fairness of her face and the richness of her hair were startling to behold. Even so, she was a fearless rider and a woman skilled with the bow. Once her sword was drawn, even the gods . . . feared to fight against her. Indeed, she was a match for a thousand. ❞
>
> —Heike Monogatori,
> *The Tale of the Heike*

✓ Reading Check **Identify** Which groups in Japan benefited from the country's wealth?

Section 3 Review

Study Central™ Need help with the material in this section? Visit jat.glencoe.com

Reading Summary
Review the Main Ideas

- In medieval Japan, several forms of Buddhism, along with Shinto, were practiced, and the arts, architecture, and literature flourished.

- During the time of the shoguns, Japan's economy grew stronger. In the family, women lost some of their freedoms as Japan became a warrior society.

What Did You Learn?

1. How did the Shinto and Buddhist religions meet different needs in Japan?

2. What were Noh plays, and how were they performed?

Critical Thinking

3. **Organizing Information** Draw a table like the one shown. Add details to show the characteristics of Pure Land Buddhism and Zen Buddhism.

Pure Land Buddhism	Zen Buddhism

4. **Describe** How did guilds benefit artisans and daimyos?

5. **Analyze** Why do you think women lost some of their freedoms when Japan became a warrior society?

6. **Descriptive Writing** Write a brief article for a travel magazine describing the architecture of Shinto shrines and Buddhist temples in Japan during the Middle Ages.

SECTION 3 REVIEW ANSWERS

1. Shinto: concerned with daily life; Buddhism: prepared people for the life to come

2. Japan's oldest form of play; performed on a simple, bare stage; actors wore masks and danced, gestured, and chanted poetry to music

3. Answers should include details based on the text.

4. Guilds offered protection from rival artisans, and sold daimyo goods they could not get themselves.

5. Answers will vary but should be based on logical cause-and-effect relationships.

6. Articles should note that Shinto shrines were Japanese in style, while Buddhist temples were built in a Chinese style.

Chapter 14 Reading Review

Section 1 Early Japan

Vocabulary
clan
constitution
animism
shrine

Focusing on the Main Ideas

- Japan's mountains and islands isolated Japan and shaped its society. *(page 485)*
- Japan was settled by people who came from northeast Asia. They were organized into clans and ruled by warriors. *(page 486)*
- Prince Shotoku created Japan's first constitution and borrowed many ideas from China. *(page 488)*
- The Japanese religion, called Shinto, was based on nature spirits. *(page 490)*

Section 2 Shoguns and Samurai

Vocabulary
samurai
shogun
daimyo
vassal
feudalism

Focusing on the Main Ideas

- During the A.D. 700s, Japan built a strong national government at Nara, and Buddhism became a popular religion. *(page 492)*
- Japan's civilian government and the emperor came to be dominated by military rulers known as shoguns. *(page 493)*
- As the shogun's power weakened, Japan broke into warring kingdoms run by rulers known as daimyo. *(page 496)*

Section 3 Life in Medieval Japan

Vocabulary
sect
martial arts
meditation
calligraphy
tanka
guild

Focusing on the Main Ideas

- Buddhism and Shinto shaped much of Japan's culture. These religions affected Japanese art, architecture, novels, and plays. *(page 499)*
- Some Japanese nobles, merchants, and artisans grew wealthy during the shogun period, but the lives of women remained restricted in many areas of life. *(page 503)*

Murasaki Shikibu ▶

CHAPTER 14   Medieval Japan   505

CHAPTER 14 REVIEW

PREVIEW/REVIEW

Vocabulary Activity Have students explain each term's connection to Japan by writing a short sentence for each one.

⊙ **Vocabulary PuzzleMaker CD-ROM**

⊙ **Interactive Tutor Self-Assessment CD-ROM**

CONDENSE

📁 Chapter 14 **Guided Reading Activities**

🖥 **StudentWorks Plus™ CD-ROM (with Audio Program)**

RETEACH

📁 **Differentiated Instruction Activity 14**

📁 Chapter 14 *Reading Essentials and Study Guide*

CHAPTER CULMINATING ACTIVITY

Have students finish the Chapter Culminating Activity from page 480D.

Suggestions for rubrics may be found in the *Quizzes, Tests, and Authentic Assessment (with Rubrics)* booklet.

Reading Strategy   READ TO WRITE

Sequencing Information Ask students to consider the rise of the various political powers in Japan, from early warrior rulers to the emperor, shoguns, daimyo, and samurai. Have them make a short list of the influences each had on Japanese history. Then have them create a summary paragraph that ties this information together to demonstrate that they understand the sequence of events.

- **L1** students should include one or two ideas per political power.
- **L2** students should have several ideas per political power and attempt grammar mastery.
- **L3** students should have well-thought paragraphs that make many strong connections.

GLENCOE TECHNOLOGY

MindJogger Videoquiz

Use the **MindJogger Videoquiz** to review Chapter 14 content.

Available in DVD and VHS

Review Vocabulary

1. shogun
2. guilds
3. clans
4. meditation
5. tanka
6. daimyo
7. samurai
8. sects

Review Main Ideas

9. The many mountains limited the amount of farmland. Armies often fought over farmland, and people turned to fishing and trading among the islands.

10. He created a constitution that gave all power to the emperor. He also set up a bureaucracy. He sent officials and students to China to study religion, art, medicine, and philosophy. He also built Buddhist temples and monasteries.

11. Shoguns were military leaders appointed by the emperor to govern. They controlled military forces and ruled provinces through samurai.

12. Japan broke into warring kingdoms ruled by daimyo.

13. Shinto and Buddhism

14. Some nobles, merchants, and artisans grew wealthy, but women's lives remained restricted.

Review Vocabulary

Write the key term that completes each sentence.

a. tanka
b. daimyo
c. clans
d. sects
e. shogun
f. guilds
g. samurai
h. meditation

1. The ___ was the military leader of Japan.
2. Many artisans and merchants formed ___ for protection and profit.
3. The Yayoi formed ___ that were headed by a small group of warriors.
4. In ___, a person clears the mind of all thoughts and desires.
5. The ___ is an unrhymed poem of five lines.
6. Each vassal gave an oath of loyalty to his ___.
7. The private armies of Japanese nobles were made up of ___.
8. Buddhism was divided into many different ___.

Review Reading Skill — Cause and Effect

Identifying Cause and Effect

17. Read the paragraph below. Create a graphic organizer that shows the cause and effects described in the passage.

The sea surrounding Japan's islands made it easy for people in ships to travel along the coast and from island to island. It encouraged people to become merchants, traveling from village to village with goods to trade. The vast ocean around Japan's islands, however, kept the Japanese people isolated, or separate, from the rest of Asia. As a result, Japan developed its own fiercely independent society with its own religion, art, literature, and government.

To review this skill, see pages 482–483.

Review Main Ideas

Section 1 • Early Japan
9. How did geography shape Japanese society?
10. How did Shotoku use Chinese government and culture as a model?

Section 2 • Shoguns and Samurai
11. Describe the roles of shoguns.
12. What happened when the shogun's power weakened?

Section 3 • Life in Medieval Japan
13. Which religions shaped much of Japan's culture?
14. How did the shogun period affect different groups of Japanese people?

Critical Thinking

15. **Analyze** Why do you think the early Japanese people were so independent?
16. **Contrast** How were the Yayoi more advanced than the Jomon?

Critical Thinking

15. Islands and mountains limited contact with the rest of Asia.
16. The Jomon were nomadic, fished, and made pottery. In contrast, the Yayoi farmed and made pottery on a wheel, metal tools, weapons, and bells.

Reading Skill

17. Cause: sea; Effects: led to easy travel and trade; isolated Japan and led to an independent society with its own religion, art, literature, and government

Geography Skills

Study the map below and answer the following questions.

18. **Place** Which of the four major Japanese islands has been home to the country's major cities?

19. **Human/Environment Interaction** How do you think Japan's geography and location have helped it become a center of production and trade?

20. **Location** Identify present-day countries, states, or provinces that are made up largely of islands. How are they similar to and different from the Japanese islands?

NATIONAL GEOGRAPHIC · Geography of Japan

Lambert Conformal Conic projection

Hokkaido

Honshu

Heian (Kyoto)
Mt. Fuji
Osaka
Nara
Edo (Tokyo)

Shikoku
Kyushu

Read to Write

21. **Creative Writing** Review this chapter and conduct research to gather information about the Mongols' attack on the Kamakura shogunate. Work with a group to write a script for a short play about the events before, during, and after the invasion. Use historical figures as well as fictional characters. Create a mask for each character, similar to the style of early Japanese masks. Present your play to the class.

22. **Using Your FOLDABLES** Write a poem, series of journal entries, or short story using the main ideas and supporting details from your completed foldable.

Using Technology

23. **Designing a City** When Emperor Kammu built Heian, he modeled it on Changan. If you were to design a city, what current cities and towns would inspire you? Use the Internet and your local library to research different features and layouts of cities. Combine the components you like best into a plan for a new city. Use a computer to make a scale drawing of your city. Then list the borrowed components and the current cities from which you borrowed them.

Linking Past and Present

24. **Analyzing Art** Medieval Japanese art, architecture, and literature reflected the Japanese love of beauty and simplicity. What values are reflected in present-day art?

Primary Source — Analyze

Seami, a great actor in Noh plays, explained how acting is mastered.

"As long as an actor is trying to imitate his teacher, he is still without mastery.... An actor may be said to be a master when, by means of his artistic powers, he quickly perfects the skills he has won through study and practice, and thus becomes one with the art itself."

—Seami Jūokubushū Hyōshaku, "The Book of the Way of the Highest Flower (*Shikadō-Sho*)"

DBQ Document-Based Questions

25. What is the first step in learning acting?
26. How does an actor "become one with the art itself"?

History Online
Have students visit the Web site at jat.glencoe.com to review Chapter 14 and take the Self-Check Quiz.

Read to Write

21. Scripts will differ but should accurately portray the events.
22. **FOLDABLES** Responses will vary but should be based on the main ideas and supporting details in the foldables.

Using Technology

23. City plans and borrowed components will vary.

Linking Past and Present

24. Answers will vary but should be supported by examples and explanations.

Primary Source

25. imitation
26. by using his artistic powers to perfect the skills he has won through study and practice

Bonus Question

Ask students to write a short paragraph describing China's influence on Japan.

Geography Skills

18. Honshu
19. Answers will vary, but students may mention that because Japan is made up of islands, its cities—where production would usually occur—are close to water, which encourages trade.

20. Answers will vary. Students may give examples, such as Indonesia, the Philippines, and Hawaii, that are entirely comprised of islands—like Japan.

Chapter ⑮ Resources

Note: The following materials may be used when teaching Chapter 15.
Section level support materials are shown at point of use in the margins of the Teacher Wraparound Edition.

TEACHING TRANSPARENCIES

- Graphic Organizer Transparencies with Teaching Strategy and Student Activity **L2**
- Cause-and-Effect Transparencies with Teaching Strategy and Student Activity **L2**
- Then and Now Transparencies with Teaching Strategy and Student Activity **L2**
- In-text Map Transparency with Teaching Strategy and Student Activity **L1**
- Map Transparencies with Overlay, Teaching Strategy, and Student Activity **L2**

DIFFERENTIATED INSTRUCTION

- Differentiated Instruction Activity 15
- Time Line Activity 15
- Primary Source Reading 15 (with Document-Based Questions)
- Inclusion Strategies for the Middle School Social Studies Classroom
- StudentWorks Plus™ CD-ROM (with Audio Program)

READING SUPPORT

- Take-Home Review Activity 15 **L2**
- World Literature Reading 15 **L2**
- Workbook Activity 15 **L1**
- Reading Strategies for the Social Studies Classroom **L1/ EL**

ASSESSMENT

- Authentic Assessment Activity 15 **L1/ EL**
- Chapter 15 Test Form A **L2**
- Chapter 15 Test Form B **L2**
- ExamView® Pro Testmaker CD-ROM

INTERDISCIPLINARY CONNECTIONS

- Geography and History Activity 15 **L2**
- People to Meet Activity 15 **L2**
- Economics Activity 15 **L2**
- Citizenship and Service Learning Activity 15 **L2**

SPANISH RESOURCES

- Spanish Reading Essentials and Study Guide
- Spanish Guided Reading Activities
- Spanish Quizzes, Tests, and Authentic Assessment (with Rubrics)
- Spanish Take-Home Review Activities

MULTIMEDIA

- Exam*View*® Pro Testmaker CD-ROM
- Glencoe Skillbuilder Interactive Workbook CD-ROM, Level 1
- Interactive Tutor Self-Assessment CD-ROM
- MindJogger Videoquiz
- Presentation Plus! CD-ROM
- StudentWorks Plus™ CD-ROM (with Audio Program)
- TeacherWorks CD-ROM
- Vocabulary PuzzleMaker CD-ROM
- *World History: Journey Across Time* Video Program
- World History Primary Source Document Library CD-ROM

STANDARDIZED ASSESSMENT SKILLS

- Standardized Test Skills Practice Workbook Activity 15 **L2**
- Critical Thinking Skills Activity 15 **L2**

Teaching strategies have been coded with suggested ability levels. However, most are suitable for all levels.

L1 BASIC activities for all students

L2 AVERAGE activities for average to above-average students

L3 CHALLENGING activities for above-average students

EL ENGLISH LANGUAGE activities

Chapter 15 Resources

TIME MANAGEMENT

Chapter Introduction	Section 1	Section 2	Section 3	Section 4	Section 5	Chapter Wrap-Up	Unit Wrap-Up
1 Day	2 Days	2 Days	2 Days	2 Days	2 Days	1 Day	1 Day

Block Scheduling Activities that are suited to use within the block scheduling framework are identified by:

`0:00` **OUT OF TIME?** Assign the Chapter 15 *Reading Essentials and Study Guide.* *

SECTION RESOURCES

DAILY OBJECTIVES	REPRODUCIBLE RESOURCES	MULTIMEDIA RESOURCES
Section 1 **The Early Middle Ages** 1. The Franks, Angles, and Saxons built new societies. 2. The Catholic Church helped unite Western Europe.	Reproducible Lesson Plan 15–1 Vocabulary Activity 15–1 Guided Reading Activity 15–1* Section Quiz 15–1* Reading Essentials and Study Guide 15–1*	Daily Focus Skills Transparency 15–1 Interactive Tutor Self-Assessment CD-ROM ExamView® Pro Testmaker CD-ROM Presentation Plus! CD-ROM Glencoe BookLink CD-ROM
Section 2 **Feudalism** 1. A new political system called feudalism developed. 2. Increased trade led to the growth of towns.	Reproducible Lesson Plan 15–2 Vocabulary Activity 15–2 Guided Reading Activity 15–2* Section Quiz 15–2* Reading Essentials and Study Guide 15–2*	Daily Focus Skills Transparency 15–2 Interactive Tutor Self-Assessment CD-ROM ExamView® Pro Testmaker CD-ROM Presentation Plus! CD-ROM
Section 3 **Kingdoms and Crusades** 1. The kings of Europe increased their power. 2. European crusaders captured Jerusalem.	Reproducible Lesson Plan 15–3 Vocabulary Activity 15–3 Guided Reading Activity 15–3* Section Quiz 15–3* Reading Essentials and Study Guide 15–3*	Daily Focus Skills Transparency 15–3 Interactive Tutor Self-Assessment CD-ROM ExamView® Pro Testmaker CD-ROM Presentation Plus! CD-ROM
Section 4 **The Church and Society** 1. The Catholic Church played a major role in medieval Europe. 2. Church and government leaders supported learning and the arts.	Reproducible Lesson Plan 15–4 Vocabulary Activity 15–4 Guided Reading Activity 15–4* Section Quiz 15–4* Reading Essentials and Study Guide 15–4*	Daily Focus Skills Transparency 15–4 Interactive Tutor Self-Assessment CD-ROM ExamView® Pro Testmaker CD-ROM Presentation Plus! CD-ROM Glencoe BookLink CD-ROM
Section 5 **The Late Middle Ages** 1. The Black Death swept through Europe in the 1300s. 2. Western Europe was devastated by war in the 1300s and 1400s.	Reproducible Lesson Plan 15–5 Vocabulary Activity 15–5 Guided Reading Activity 15–5* Section Quiz 15–5* Reading Essentials and Study Guide 15–5*	Daily Focus Skills Transparency 15–5 Interactive Tutor Self-Assessment CD-ROM ExamView® Pro Testmaker CD-ROM Presentation Plus! CD-ROM Vocabulary PuzzleMaker CD-ROM Glencoe BookLink CD-ROM

*Also available in Spanish

History Online

Use our Web site for additional resources. All essential content is covered in the Student Edition.

You and your students can visit jat.glencoe.com, the Web site companion to *World History: Journey Across Time.* This innovative integration of electronic and print media offers your students a wealth of opportunities. The student text directs students to the Web site for the following options:

- Chapter Overviews
- Self-Check Quizzes
- Study Central™
- Student Web Activities
- Multi-Language Glossaries

Answers to the student Web activities are provided for you in the **Web Activity Lesson Plans.** Additional Web resources and ePuzzles and games are also available.

The following videotape programs are available from Glencoe as supplements to Chapter 15:

The Crusades
(ISBN 1-56501-505-3)

Scourge of the Black Death
(ISBN 0-7670-0534-1)

Richard the Lionheart
(ISBN 1-56501-916-4)

To order, call Glencoe at 1-800-334-7344. To find classroom resources to accompany many of these videos, check the following home pages:

A&E Television: www.aande.com
The History Channel: www.historychannel.com

MEETING SPECIAL NEEDS

In addition to the Differentiated Instruction strategies, the following resources are suitable for students with special needs:

- *ExamView® Pro Testmaker CD-ROM* allows teachers to tailor tests by reducing answer choices.
- *StudentWorks Plus™ CD-ROM (with Audio Program)* includes the entire narrative of the student edition so that less-proficient readers can listen to the words as they read them.
- The *Reading Essentials and Study Guide* provides the same content as the student edition but is written two grade levels below the textbook.

NATIONAL GEOGRAPHIC TEACHER'S CORNER

Index to National Geographic Magazine:
The following articles relate to this chapter:

- "Marco Polo, Part 1," by Mike Edwards, May 2001.
- "Marco Polo, Part 2," by Mike Edwards, June 2001.
- "In Search of Vikings," by Priit Vesilind, May 2000.

National Geographic Society Products:
To order the following, call National Geographic at 1–800–368–2728

- *NGS PictureShow: Middle Ages* (CD-ROM)
- *National Geographic Atlas of the World* (Book)

NGS ONLINE

Access National Geographic's new dynamic MapMachine Web site and other geography resources at:

www.nationalgeographic.com
www.nationalgeographic.com/maps

Meeting NCSS Standards

World History: Journey Across Time
The following standards are highlighted in Chapter 15:

Section 1   **II**   **Time, Continuity, and Change: A, B**
          III   **People, Places, and Environments: B, H, I**
          V   **Individuals, Groups, and Institutions: A, D, F, G**

Section 2   **VII**   **Production, Distribution, and Consumption: D, E, H**
          VIII   **Science, Technology, and Society: A**

Section 3   **X**   **Civic Ideals and Practices: A, B**

Section 4   **I**   **Culture: A, C**
          IV   **Individual Development and Identity: D, G**

Section 5   **IX**   **Global Connections: F**

State and Local Objectives

_____

_____

_____

Timesaving Tools

TeacherWorks
All-In-One Planner and Resource Center

- **Interactive Teacher Edition** Access your Teacher Wraparound Edition and your classroom resources with a few easy clicks.
- **Interactive Lesson Planner** Organize your week, month, semester, or year with all the lesson helps you need to make teaching creative and relevant.

Use Glencoe's **Presentation Plus!** multimedia teacher tool to easily present dynamic lessons that visually excite your students. Using Microsoft PowerPoint® you can customize the presentations to create your own personalized lessons.

FOLDABLES™
Study Organizer
Dinah Zike's Foldables

Foldables are three-dimensional, interactive graphic organizers that help students practice basic writing skills, review key vocabulary terms, and identify main ideas. Every chapter contains a foldable activity, with additional chapter activities found in the *Reading and Study Skills Foldables* booklet. You can use the foldables as they are presented, or modify them to suit the needs of your individual class.

Planning Ahead

CHAPTER CULMINATING ACTIVITY

The Chapter Culminating Activity will help students organize and learn the important information from the chapter. Begin teaching the chapter with this activity, and have students complete it as a culminating activity.

CREATING A MAIN IDEA AND SUPPORTING DETAILS CHART

Purpose Reviewing how to locate main ideas throughout the chapter will help students continue to refine their reading skills. This type of organizer aids students in identifying main ideas of sections and the supporting details. It helps them develop the skill of knowing what is important and what is supportive of the main ideas. Students will need to use information about how the text is structured and combine it with what they know about the topic. Identifying main ideas and details can give students practice in logical and systematic thinking.

Introduction to Modeling

1. Begin the discussion with a brainstorming session. Ask students to list what they know or believe they know about the Middle Ages. Write the information on an overhead transparency. Guide them to identify some key main ideas about the Middle Ages that emerge in their com-

ments. You may also want to model how certain comments are, in fact, details that support a main idea.

2. Ask students to copy this chart into their notebooks:

Supporting Details

Main Idea

As students read each section, ask them to search for a main idea and details that support it. Have them fill in the chart with as many supporting details as necessary. Encourage them to create more charts as they encounter important concepts during their reading.

3. As part of your chapter review, have students share their main idea and supporting details charts. Consider asking them to do a final chart with a single main idea for the entire chapter. Encourage them to use their charts as study aids.

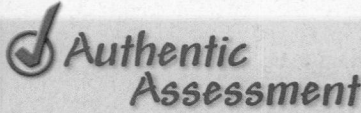

Authentic Assessment

Refer to Activity 15 in the Authentic Assessment section of the *Quizzes, Tests, and Authentic Assessment (with Rubrics)* booklet.

When & Where?

As students read the chapter, have them review the time line on this page. Ask them which events probably had a great influence on religion throughout Europe. *(Clovis's conversion and the First Crusade)* L1

GLENCOE TECHNOLOGY

World History: Journey Across Time Video Program

To learn more about medieval Europe, students can view the Chapter 15 video in the *World History: Journey Across Time* Video Program.

MindJogger Videoquiz

Use the **MindJogger Videoquiz** to preview Chapter 15 content.

 Available in DVD and VHS

Chapter 15

Medieval Europe

Caerphilly Castle in South Wales, United Kingdom ▼

NATIONAL GEOGRAPHIC When & Where?

A.D. 500	A.D. 825	1150	1475
A.D. 496 King Clovis becomes a Catholic	C. A.D. 800 Feudalism begins in Europe	1095 First Crusade begins	1346 Black Death arrives in Europe

Reading Strategy ⟩ PURPOSE FOR READING

Regional Influences Tell students that the culture and civilization of Europe have probably had a greater influence on the United States than those of any other region in the world. **Ask:** What are some people, ideas, and events in this chapter that you think have had a strong effect on how we live today in the United States? In what way? As they read, have students watch for people, ideas, and events that have contributed to the development of our civilization today. **L2**

Chapter Preview

Between A.D. 500 and 1500, Europe was ruled by warriors much like those in early Japan. Despite constant fighting, Europeans made advances in their culture. European ideas about government and religion still shape our lives today.

 View the Chapter 15 video in the *World History: Journey Across Time* Video Program.

Chapter Overview Visit jat.glencoe.com for a preview of Chapter 15.

 ## The Early Middle Ages

During the Middle Ages, Western Europe built a new civilization based on Christian, Roman, and Germanic ways.

 ## Feudalism

Government weakness and the need for safety led to the rise of feudalism.

 ## Kingdoms and Crusades

As the kingdoms of England and France established parliaments, Russia's rulers laid the foundations for its government.

 ## The Church and Society

Religion in medieval Europe helped to shape European culture.

 ## The Late Middle Ages

Disease and war took the lives of millions of people in the late Middle Ages.

Sequencing Information *Make this foldable to help you sequence important events that occurred in medieval Europe.*

Step 1 *Fold two sheets of paper in half from top to bottom. Cut each in half.*

 Cut along the fold lines.

Step 2 *Turn and fold the four pieces in half from top to bottom.*

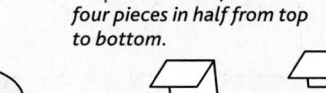

Reading and Writing *As you read the chapter, write the important events and dates that occurred in medieval Europe on each section of your time line.*

Step 3 *Tape the ends of the pieces together (overlapping the edges slightly) to make an accordion time line.*

 Pieces of tape

509

INTRODUCING CHAPTER 15

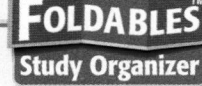

Introduce students to chapter content and key terms by having them access **Chapter Overview 15** at jat.glencoe.com

CHAPTER PREVIEW

After reading Chapter 15, students will be able to

1. summarize the changes in Europe after Rome's fall;
2. describe feudalism and the rise of towns;
3. describe the growth of kingdoms and the effects of the Crusades;
4. discuss the role of the medieval Catholic Church;
5. explain the effects of wars and the Black Death.

FOLDABLES Study Organizer
Dinah Zike's Foldables

Purpose Students use this foldable to organize data about events in medieval Europe. As students read this chapter, they should make notes about events and dates.

📁 Have students complete *Reading and Study Skills Foldables* Activity 15.

MORE ABOUT THE PHOTO

Caerphilly Castle One of the great medieval castles of Western Europe and the second-largest castle in Britain is Caerphilly Castle in Wales. It was built in the late 1200s by Gilbert de Clare, a noble allied with England's King Henry III. The castle's purpose was to secure southern Wales under English rule and to keep the area from falling into the hands of the Welsh leader Llywelyn the Last, who controlled most of central and northern Wales. Llywelyn's forces attacked the castle in 1270 but failed to capture it. The lakes around the castle formed an almost insuperable barrier to attackers.

1 Learn It!

Formulating questions requires students to synthesize several skills, such as predicting, sequencing, and analyzing the main idea and supporting details.

Show students how to create questions by reading the following practice passage aloud:

> Between 1000 and 1200, many women became nuns and entered convents. Convents were ideal places for study and writing. Most learned women of the Middle Ages were nuns. An example was Hildegard of Bingen. She was head of a convent in western Germany. Hildegard also composed church music. Her work is remarkable because at that time, men were primarily the ones writing music for the church.

Brainstorm with students:

- Questions beginning with "who" (*Example: Who was Hildegard of Bingen?*)
- Questions beginning with "what" (*Example: What was remarkable about Hildegard?*)
- Questions beginning with "how" (*Example: How were women able to enter convents?*)
- Questions beginning with "when" (*Example: When did Hildegard live?*)
- Questions not answered in the passage (*Example: What became of Hildegard?*) L1/ EL

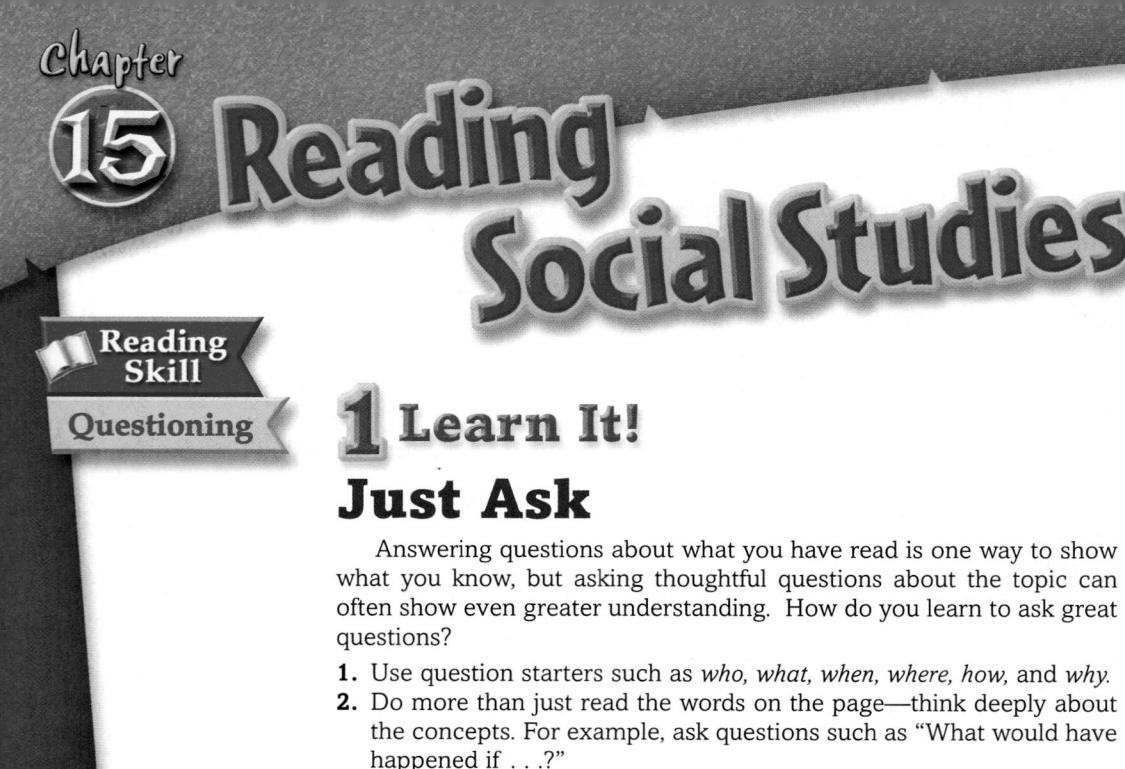

Chapter 15 Reading Social Studies

Reading Skill

Questioning

1 Learn It!
Just Ask

Answering questions about what you have read is one way to show what you know, but asking thoughtful questions about the topic can often show even greater understanding. How do you learn to ask great questions?

1. Use question starters such as *who, what, when, where, how,* and *why.*
2. Do more than just read the words on the page—think deeply about the concepts. For example, ask questions such as "What would have happened if . . .?"

Read the following passage from Section 5, and look at the questions that follow.

> Charles, the prince who ruled southern France, wanted to take back the north. In 1429 a French peasant girl named Joan was brought to him. She told him that her favorite saints had urged her to free France. Joan's honesty persuaded Charles to let her go with a French army to Orléans. Joan's faith stirred the soldiers, and they took the city.
>
> —*from page 557*

Reading Tip

Make studying like a game. Create questions and then read to find answers to your own questions.

510

Here are some questions you might ask about the above paragraph:

- What did Joan say to persuade Charles to let her ride with the army?
- How did Joan's faith stir the soldiers?
- Why did Joan believe saints wanted her to free France?
- What happened to Joan after the French took the city?

Reading Strategy   **PAIRED QUESTIONING**

Just as students read together in pairs to foster comprehension, partners can read silently for a specified amount of time and ask each other questions as a tool for deeper understanding. Creating thoughtful questions requires careful reading, as does answering meaningful questions. Have each student create questions that probe beyond the immediately obvious, and remind them to practice strategic listening as they work with their partners. The goal is for students to incorporate questioning and listening into their own learning experience to form lifelong strategies for active comprehension. L1/ EL

2 Practice It!

Ask and Answer

Read this passage about the Black Death.

> A terrible plague, known as the Black Death, swept across Europe and Asia. A plague is a disease that spreads quickly and kills many people. Most scientists think the Black Death was bubonic plague—a disease caused by a type of bacteria carried by fleas. These fleas infested black rats, and in the Middle Ages, these rats were everywhere.
>
> —*from page 554*

Read to Write

Write a *What If* paragraph based on your reading. For example, *what if* Joan had become Queen of France, or *what if* fleas carried the Black Death today? Add lots of details as if you were answering questions others might ask about your *What If* ideas.

Create three questions based on the above paragraph. Remember that not all questions have answers.

3 Apply It!

As you read the chapter, look for answers to section headings that are in the form of questions. For the other sections, turn the headings into questions that you can answer as you read.

2 Practice It!

Have students use the following categories to create questions based on the Crusades.

What Is Your Prediction? Form a question based on a prediction about the topic. *(Example: How did the Crusades change history?)*

What Is the Purpose? Form a question that shows what you are hoping to learn from the text. *(Example: What were the Crusades?)*

What Does the Text Say? Form a question that can be answered directly from the text. *(Example: When did the Crusades occur?)*

What Is Your Response? Form a question that requires a personal response. *(Example: Why did people support the Crusades?)*

3 Apply It!

Organize students into five groups. Have each group take a different section of the chapter and write four questions about the section, one from each of the categories listed above *(Prediction, Purpose, Text, Response)*. After each group writes their questions, cut the written questions into strips and have students answer questions generated from other groups. **L2**

Reading Strategy   READ TO WRITE

Because writing and reading are parallel processes, students who are able to create meaning through writing are practicing the same skills that are necessary to become proficient readers. Having students generate and answer thoughtful questions reinforces these important skills. Have students exchange their *What If* paragraphs. Each student should write three or more questions based on the paragraph he or she received. Those questions should go back to the paragraph's original writer, who may wish to revise the original paragraph based on the questions. **L2**

① FOCUS

SECTION OVERVIEW

This section focuses on the creation of new kingdoms and the influence of the Catholic Church in medieval Europe.

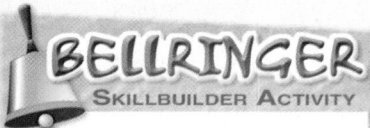

BELLRINGER
SKILLBUILDER ACTIVITY

✍ Project **Daily Focus Skills Transparency 15–1** and have students answer questions. Discuss their responses.

Get Ready to Read!

Preteaching Vocabulary: To *excommunicate* someone means to remove that person from his or her church. It comes from a Latin word based on the Latin prefix *ex-*, meaning "out of" or "not," and the Latin word *communicare*, meaning "to communicate." Hence, it suggests not being able to communicate with God. Discuss with students how a highly religious person might feel about being excommunicated.

Answers to Graphic: Clovis: strengthened kingdom by becoming Catholic; Charles Martel: victory at Battle of Tours; Charlemagne: built large empire; Otto I: first ruler of the Holy Roman Empire

---

Section ①

The Early Middle Ages

Get Ready to Read!

What's the Connection?
After the fall of Rome came a period called the Middle Ages, or medieval times. It is a fitting name for the period that lies between ancient and modern times.

Focusing on the (Main Ideas)
- Geography influenced where medieval Europeans settled and what they did. *(page 513)*
- The Franks, Angles, and Saxons of Western Europe built new societies and defended them against Muslims, Magyars, and Vikings. *(page 514)*
- The Catholic Church spread Christianity through Western Europe. *(page 519)*

Locating Places
Aachen (AH•kuhn)
Scandinavia (SKAN•duh•NAY•vee•uh)
Holy Roman Empire

Meeting People
Clovis (KLOH•vuhs)
Charles Martel (mahr•TEHL)
Charlemagne (SHAHR•luh•MAYN)
Otto I (AH•toh)
Gregory the Great

Building Your Vocabulary
fjord (fee•AWRD)
missionary (MIH•shuh•NEHR•ee)
excommunicate (EHK•skuh•MYOO•nuh•KAYT)
concordat (kuhn•KAWR•DAT)

Reading Strategy
Organizing Information Create a table to show the major accomplishments of medieval leaders.

Leader	Major Accomplishments

NATIONAL GEOGRAPHIC **When & Where?**

SCANDINAVIA
BRITAIN
Aachen • HOLY ROMAN EMPIRE
SPAIN • Rome

A.D. 500   **A.D. 800**   **1100**

A.D. 496 King Clovis becomes Catholic

A.D. 800 Charlemagne is crowned by pope

c. 1050 Most people in Western Europe are Catholic

512   CHAPTER 15   Medieval Europe

SECTION RESOURCES

📁 **Reproducible Masters**
- Reproducible Lesson Plan 15–1
- Daily Lecture and Discussion Notes 15–1
- Vocabulary Activity 15–1
- Active Reading Note-Taking Guide 15–1
- Guided Reading Activity 15–1
- Section Quiz 15–1
- Reading Essentials and Study Guide 15–1

✍ **Transparencies**
- Daily Focus Skills Transparency 15–1

Multimedia
- 💿 Interactive Tutor Self-Assessment CD-ROM
- 💿 ExamView® Pro Testmaker CD-ROM
- 💿 Presentation Plus! CD-ROM
- 💿 Glencoe BookLink CD-ROM

The Geography of Europe

Main Idea Geography influenced where medieval Europeans settled and what they did.

Reading Focus If you wanted to go sledding or swimming, where would you go? Your answer will be based partly on geography. Read to learn how geography shaped life in Europe during the Middle Ages.

The Roman Empire had united all the land surrounding the Mediterranean Sea. When the last Roman emperor in the West fell from power in A.D. 476, that unity was lost. Western Europe was divided into many kingdoms as wave after wave of Germanic invaders swept south and west, conquering large areas of Europe.

Now that Rome no longer united people, Europe's geography began to play a more important role in shaping events. Europe is a continent, but it is also a very large peninsula made up of many smaller peninsulas. As a result, most of Europe lies within 300 miles (483 km) of an ocean or sea. This encouraged trade and fishing and helped Europe's economy to grow.

Rivers also played an important role in Europe. The Rhine, Danube, Vistula, Volga, Seine, and Po Rivers made it easy to travel into the interior of Europe and encouraged people to trade.

The seas and rivers provided safety as well as opportunities for trade. The English Channel, for instance, separated Britain and Ireland from the rest of Europe. As a result,

② TEACH

Reading Maps Have students look at the map of Europe on this page. Ask them to discuss with a partner where they would locate cities and why. Among the factors to consider are transportation, protection, and natural features (seas, rivers, and mountains). **L1**

Using Geography Skills

Answers:
1. Angles, Saxons, Celts (including Scots and Britons)
2. Western Europe, near the Rhine and Seine Rivers

Skills Practice

Ask: Which people settled along the Baltic Sea? *(the Slavs)*

Daily Lecture and Discussion Notes 15–1

Use **Daily Lecture and Discussion Notes 15–1** for an outline of key concepts found in the section.

Reading Support L1/ EL

Use **Vocabulary Activity 15–1** to review important terms in the section.

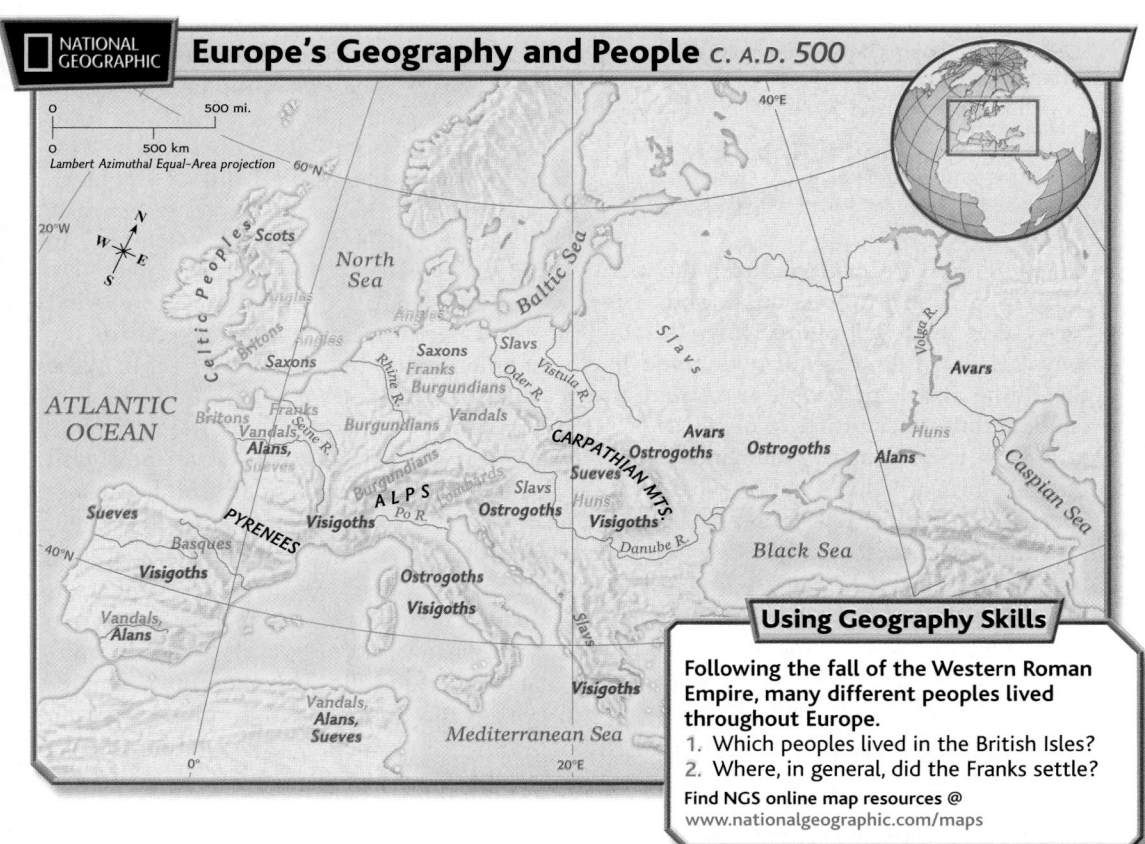

NATIONAL GEOGRAPHIC

Europe's Geography and People *c. A.D. 500*

Using Geography Skills

Following the fall of the Western Roman Empire, many different peoples lived throughout Europe.
1. Which peoples lived in the British Isles?
2. Where, in general, did the Franks settle?

Find NGS online map resources @ www.nationalgeographic.com/maps

Reading Strategy ► READING THE TEXT

Reviewing As students read the section, take time to review what they have learned. Frequent review is especially important when the text is dense with information, dates, names, and so on. Encourage students to make their own review aids, such as charts, graphic organizers, and outlines. These aids will help them organize information as they read and are also useful for reviewing section information after they have read the text. **L1/ EL**

Understanding Cause and Effect

Ask students to make a diagram that shows cause-and-effect relationships related to the history of the Romans, Angles, Saxons, and Celts in Britain. *(Diagrams should reflect that the Roman influence on Britain was small; the Angles and Saxons invaded after the Romans left and pushed aside the Celts; the Celts fled to isolated regions.)* **L2**

✔ Reading Check

Answer: safety, opportunities for trade, encouraged rise of separate societies

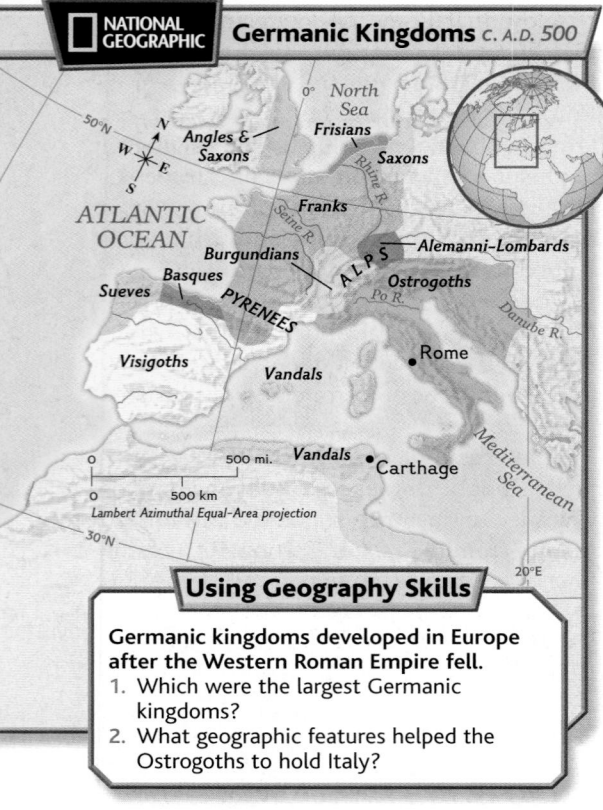

NATIONAL GEOGRAPHIC

Germanic Kingdoms *C. A.D. 500*

Using Geography Skills

Germanic kingdoms developed in Europe after the Western Roman Empire fell.
1. Which were the largest Germanic kingdoms?
2. What geographic features helped the Ostrogoths to hold Italy?

people there were sheltered from the many wars fought on Europe's mainland. They were able to develop their own distinct ways of life. Within Europe, wide rivers like the Rhine also kept people separated and enabled different cultures to develop.

Europe also has many mountain ranges. In the east, the Carpathians cut off what is now Ukraine and Russia from southeast Europe. In the middle, the Alps separated Italy from central Europe. To the southwest, the Pyrenees isolated Spain and Portugal. The mountains, like the rivers, made it difficult for one group to rule all of Europe and encouraged the development of independent kingdoms.

✔ Reading Check **Identify** What did Europe's seas and rivers provide for its people?

The Germanic Kingdoms

Main Idea The Franks, Angles, and Saxons of Western Europe built new societies and defended them against Muslims, Magyars, and Vikings.

Reading Focus Have you ever moved to a new place? What adjustments did you have to make? Read to learn how the Germanic peoples who invaded Europe had to adjust to the lands they occupied.

After Rome fell, Western Europe was divided into many kingdoms. These kingdoms developed different societies based on their locations. The Visigoths in Spain and the Ostrogoths in Italy were close to the center of the old Roman Empire. As a result, they adopted many Roman ways. People farther from Rome held on to more of their Germanic traditions.

In Britain as the empire began to weaken, Roman culture declined quickly. In the A.D. 300s, the Roman legions in Britain began heading home to fight Germanic invaders. By the early A.D 400s, the Romans had pulled out of England. Soon the Angles and Saxons invaded Britain from Denmark and Germany. In time, they became the Anglo-Saxons.

When the Angles and Saxons conquered southeastern Britain, they pushed aside the people living there. These people were called the Celts (KEHLTS). Some Celts fled north and west to the mountains. Others went to Ireland. Scottish, Welsh, and Irish people today are descendants of the Celts.

Who Were the Franks? During the A.D. 400s, a Germanic people called the Franks settled the area that is now France. In A.D. 496 King **Clovis** (KLOH•vuhs) of the Franks became a Catholic. This won him the support of the Romans living in his kingdom. Before long, nearly all of the Franks became Catholic.

DIFFERENTIATED INSTRUCTION

Interpersonal: Have students review the section's information about the Viking raids. Then have them work in groups to write a radio or television public-service announcement (PSA) informing citizens how to be prepared for the raids. Encourage them to include information about where to flee, what to take, how to prepare homes to withstand raids, and other helpful civil defense information.

English Learners: Ask students to research and make a list of words that express danger. Then have them use the words in an announcement about the Viking raids.

Gifted and Talented: Have students record or film their PSAs and present them to the class.

▷ Refer to *Inclusion Strategies for the Middle School Social Studies Classroom* in the TCR.

After Clovis died, his sons divided the kingdom among themselves. Later, their sons divided these kingdoms even further. These kings often fought over land. While they fought, the nobles under them took over many royal duties. The most important of these nobles was called the "mayor of the palace." By A.D. 700, the mayors were giving out land, settling disputes, and fighting their own wars.

Of all the mayors, the most powerful was **Charles Martel** (mahr•TEHL). He wanted to unite all the Frankish nobles under his rule. The Catholic Church wanted to restore order in the lands of the Western Roman Empire and was willing to support strong Catholic rulers. The pope—the head of the Catholic Church—offered his support to Charles Martel.

First, however, Europe had to be kept Christian. In A.D. 711 a Muslim army from North Africa conquered Spain. Later, Muslim forces invaded France. In A.D. 732 Charles Martel led the Franks against the Muslims. He defeated them at the Battle of Tours. This stopped the Muslim advance into Europe, and Christianity remained Western Europe's major religion.

When Charles Martel died, his son Pepin (PEH•puhn) became mayor of the palace. With the help of the pope and most Frankish nobles, Pepin became the new king of the Franks. When a Germanic group called the Lombards threatened the pope, Pepin took his army into Italy and defeated them. He donated the land he had conquered to the pope. The pope ruled these lands as if he were a king, and they became known as the Papal States.

Who Was Charlemagne? After Pepin died, his son Charles became king. Like his father, Charles went to the aid of the pope when the Lombards tried to regain their territory. He also invaded eastern Germany and defeated the Saxons living there. He ordered them to convert to Christianity. He then invaded Spain and gained control of the northeastern corner from the Muslims.

By A.D. 800, Charles's kingdom had grown into an empire. It covered much of western and central Europe. Charles's

The Crowning of Charlemagne

◄ In A.D. 800 the pope crowned Charlemagne "Emperor of the Romans," officially creating a new Roman Empire. *How large was Charlemagne's empire in A.D. 800?*

515

Using Geography Skills

Answers:

1. Charlemagne

2. Muslims

Skills Practice

Ask: In which directions did the conquests of Martel and Pepin extend the Franks' kingdom? *(south and east)*

TIME TRAVELER

The Donation of Pepin is the name for the land that Pepin gave to the pope. It included land around Rome and Ravenna and in east-central Italy. In return for his donation, Pepin—and his sons—were recognized as the protectors of the Church and the pope.

Writing Activity

Ask students to write a memo to Charlemagne advising him on whether he should accept the pope's offer to become emperor of the Romans. Have students consider advantages and disadvantages of the honor and make a recommendation to Charlemagne. **L3**

NATIONAL GEOGRAPHIC

The Frankish Kingdom C. A.D. 500–800

KEY
- Clovis's kingdom
- Added by Martel and Pepin
- Added by Charlemagne
- ★ Battle

0 500 mi.
0 500 km
Lambert Azimuthal Equal-Area projection

Using Geography Skills

The Frankish kingdom expanded greatly under Charlemagne's rule.
1. Under whose reign did the Franks conquer part of Italy?
2. Who controlled Spain while the Franks ruled much of Western Europe?

A bronze statue of Charlemagne ▶

conquests earned him the name of **Charlemagne** (SHAHR•luh•MAYNE), or Charles the Great.

The pope was impressed with Charlemagne. On Christmas day in A.D. 800, Charlemagne was worshiping at the church of St. Peter in Rome. After the service, the pope placed a crown on Charlemagne's head and declared him the new Roman emperor. Charlemagne was pleased but also concerned. He did not want people to think the pope had the power to choose who was emperor.

Charlemagne made **Aachen** (AH•kuhn) the capital of his empire. To uphold his laws, he set up courts throughout the empire. Nobles called counts ran the courts. To keep the counts under control, Charlemagne sent out inspectors called "the lord's messengers" to make sure the counts were obeying orders.

Unlike other earlier Frankish rulers, Charlemagne believed in education. He had tried late in life to learn to write and wanted his people to be educated too. He asked a scholar named Alcuin (AL•kwuhn) to start a school in one of the royal palaces. Alcuin trained the children of government officials. His students studied religion, Latin, music, literature, and arithmetic.

516 **CHAPTER 15** **Medieval Europe**

INTERDISCIPLINARY CONNECTIONS ACTIVITY

Language Arts The French national epic, a long poem called the *Song of Roland*, is about a battle during the eighth-century war with the Muslims. In the poem, Roland is a brave, but headstrong, French knight who commands a part of Charlemagne's army. He is trapped by Muslim forces at a mountain pass in the Pyrenees. Although he could have sounded his horn to alert the rest of the army to come to his rescue, Roland does not and bravely dies a heroic death. Loosely based on real events, the poem was written in the 1100s and shows Roland as a model of knightly honor. Ask students to read and research the *Song of Roland* and write a paragraph describing Roland's sacrifice. **L2**

Biography

CHARLEMAGNE
A.D. 742–814

Charles the Great (Charlemagne) became king of the Franks at age 29. He married and divorced many different women and had at least 18 children.

Charlemagne was an intelligent person. He studied many subjects and especially enjoyed astronomy. He could speak many languages, including German and Latin. He also could read but had trouble writing. Einhard, the king's historian and scribe, wrote that Charlemagne "used to keep tablets under his pillow in order that at leisure hours he might accustom his hand to form the letters; but as he began these efforts so late in life, they met with ill success."

Charlemagne was disappointed to learn that the Franks were not as educated as the people of Britain and Ireland. In A.D. 782 he arranged for several famous scholars to come to his capital in Aachen and create a school in the royal palace. During his reign, schools opened throughout his empire, and many people were educated.

▲ Charlemagne

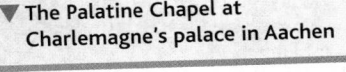
▼ The Palatine Chapel at Charlemagne's palace in Aachen

> "No one shall . . . be kept back from the right path of justice by . . . fear of the powerful."
>
> —Charlemagne, as quoted in "The World of Charlemagne"

Then and Now

Charlemagne realized the importance of education. He arranged reading and writing lessons for his people. What types of school programs does our government fund?

517

Biography

TEACH

A long historical debate has been waged over this question: Are the French or the Germans the true heirs of Charlemagne? His capital, Aachen, also known as Aix-la-Chapelle in French, sits just inside the German border near France, and German kings were crowned in the city's cathedral. On the other hand, Napoleon called himself the successor of Charlemagne.

Ask students if they think Europe could be unified under a single leader like Charlemagne today. Have students describe why they believe such a unification would or would not work in modern Europe. *(Students may recognize that such a unification would be difficult to accomplish because Europe's national identities have become much stronger today.)* **L2**

Then and Now

Possible answers include teacher grants, preschool programs like Head Start, after-school programs, scholarships, awards programs, books and equipment, and so on.

Reading List Generator CD-ROM

GLENCOE BOOKLINK **RECOMMENDED READING**

Use the **Glencoe BookLink CD-ROM** to create customized reading lists based on your students' interests and reading levels. Below is an example based on content in this chapter. Also, see the Suggested Readings on pages 944–946 of the Appendix.

- *Beowulf.* Translation of the Anglo-Saxon epic.
- Hodges, C. Walter. *The Norman Conquests.* Account of William the Conqueror and his conquest of England in 1066.
- Pearson, Anne. *The Vikings.* Visual presentation of Viking ways of life.

in a word...

To **"go berserk"** means to become frenzied or crazed. This word, often used for unruly, out-of-control behavior, comes from Old Norse, the language of the Vikings. It referred to especially fierce warriors who often served as guards for Norse kings. The *berserkers* may have dressed in bearskins, the word's meaning in Norse, and their frightfulness helped shape the myth of the werewolf in northern Europe.

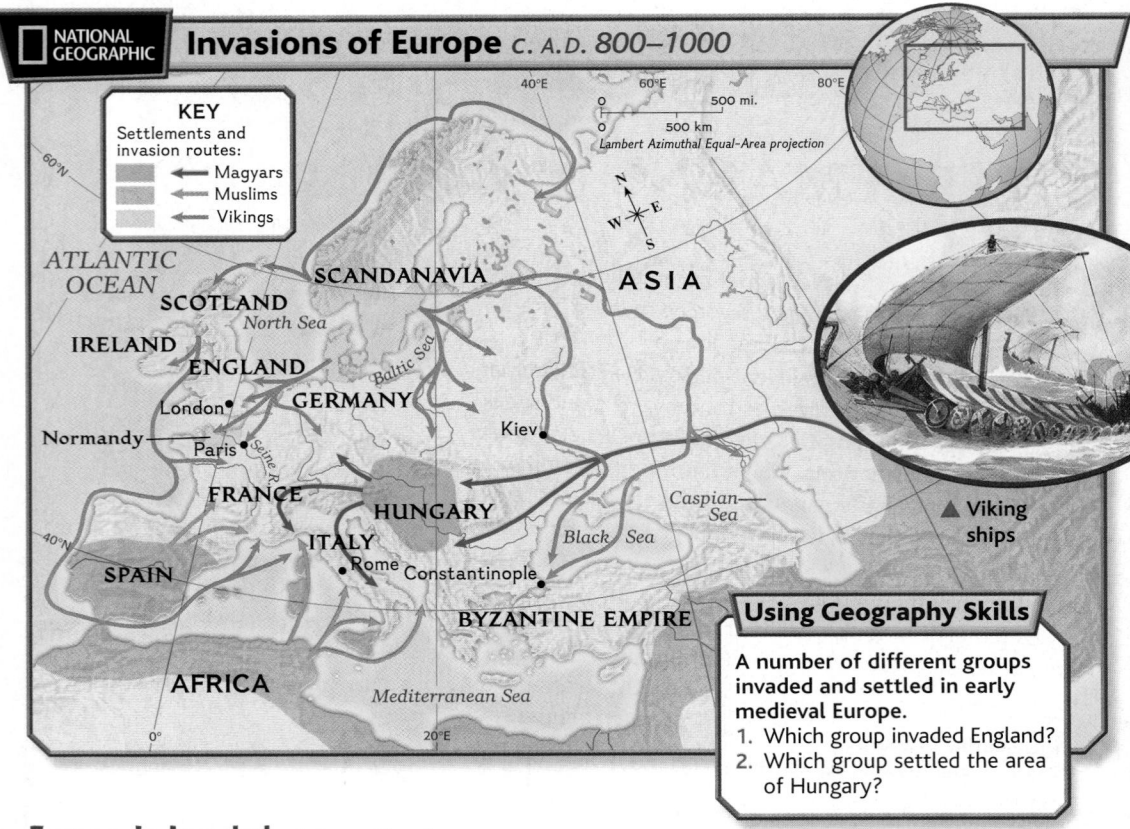

NATIONAL GEOGRAPHIC

Invasions of Europe C. A.D. 800–1000

KEY
Settlements and invasion routes:
← Magyars
← Muslims
← Vikings

Lambert Azimuthal Equal-Area projection

▲ Viking ships

Using Geography Skills

A number of different groups invaded and settled in early medieval Europe.
1. Which group invaded England?
2. Which group settled the area of Hungary?

Europe Is Invaded After Charlemagne died in A.D. 814, his empire did not last long. His son Louis was not a strong leader, and after Louis died, Louis's sons divided the empire into three kingdoms.

These three kingdoms were weakened further by a wave of invaders who swept across Europe in the A.D. 800s and A.D. 900s. From the south came Muslims, who raided France and Italy from Spain and North Africa. From the east came the Magyars, a nomadic people who had settled in Hungary. From **Scandinavia** (SKAN•duh•NAY•vee•uh) came the Vikings, whose raids terrified all of Europe.

Scandinavia is in northern Europe. Norway, Sweden, and Denmark are all part of Scandinavia today. Much of Scandinavia has a long, jagged coastline. It has many **fjords** (fee•AWRDS), or steep-sided valleys that are inlets of the sea. The Viking people lived in villages in the fjords. They were known as the Norsemen, or "north men."

Scandinavia has little farmland. This forced the Vikings to rely on the sea for food and trade. They became skilled sailors and built sturdy boats called longboats. These boats could survive the rough Atlantic and also navigate shallow rivers.

In the A.D. 700s and A.D. 800s, the Vikings began raiding Europe, probably because their population had grown too big to support itself at home. The word *viking* comes from their word for raiding. They robbed villages and churches, carrying off

518   CHAPTER 15   Medieval Europe

EXTENDING THE CONTENT

An Ancient Race Chances are that more than a few students are descendants of the Celtic peoples who were pushed into isolated areas of Great Britain by invading Angles and Saxons. Millions of Americans trace their roots to Ireland, Scotland, Wales, and parts of England where Celtic peoples lived. Celtic tribes also lived on the fringes of the Roman Empire in Spain, France, Asia Minor, Switzerland, and other regions. Even older Celtic settlements have been discovered in Austria and Germany.

grain, animals, and anything else of value. They even conquered part of western France. This area was named Normandy, after the Norsemen who ruled it.

The Holy Roman Empire

The raids by Muslims, Magyars, and Vikings helped to destroy the Frankish kingdoms. In the A.D. 900s, the eastern Frankish kingdom, which became known as Germany, was divided into many tiny states ruled by counts, dukes, and other nobles. In A.D. 911 a group of these nobles tried to unite Germany by electing a king. The king did not have much power, however, because the nobles wanted to remain independent.

One of the stronger kings of Germany was **Otto I** (AH•toh). He fought the Magyars and sent troops into Italy to protect the pope. To reward Otto for his help, the pope declared him emperor of the Romans in A.D. 962. Otto's territory, which included most of Germany and northern Italy, became known as the **Holy Roman Empire.**

Most of the emperors of the Holy Roman Empire were not very powerful. Two of the strongest ones, Frederick I and Frederick II, tried to unite northern Italy and Germany under a single ruler with a strong central government in the 1100s and 1200s. The popes fought against these plans because they did not want the emperor to control them. They banded together with Italy's cities to resist the emperors' forces. As a result, both Germany and Italy remained divided into small kingdoms until the 1800s.

☑ Reading Check Explain Who were the Vikings, and why did they raid Europe?

The Rise of the Catholic Church

Main Idea The Catholic Church spread Christianity through Western Europe.

Reading Focus Do you have a goal you would devote your life to reaching? Read to learn the goals of the Catholic Church in the early Middle Ages.

Both religion and geography played an important role in shaping life in Europe. By the time the Western Roman Empire collapsed, Christianity had become the official religion of Rome. After the Roman government fell apart, the Roman Catholic Church began to play an important role in the growth of a new civilization in Western Europe.

Why Were Monks Important?

At the time Rome fell, much of northwest Europe was not yet Christian. One exception was Ireland. In the A.D. 400s, a priest named Patrick traveled to Ireland, where he spread the Christian message and set up churches and monasteries. For several hundred years,

▲ Pope Gregory I helped spread Christianity in a number of ways. Here he is shown teaching boys the songs that became known as Gregorian chants. *Which area of northwest Europe had accepted Christianity before the fall of the Western Roman Empire?*

CHAPTER 15   Medieval Europe   **519**

▶ Reading Strategy ◀

Understanding Cause and Effect Have students explain how geographical factors led the Vikings to become sailors and sea raiders. *(There is little farmland in Scandinavia, so they turned to the sea. Their long coastlines made it easy to travel to other countries by sea.)* **L1**

Writing Activity

Ask students to write a paragraph examining why people in the Middle Ages believed that a strong king like Otto should lead a kingdom called the Holy Roman Empire. Why did people feel the need to associate a ruler with both the Christian church and the Roman Empire? **L3**

☑ Reading Check

Answer: sailors and travelers from Scandinavia; their population grew too large to support itself at home

Caption Answer: Ireland

EXTENDING THE CONTENT

The Founding Father The man most responsible for the creation of Christian monasteries in the West was Saint Benedict of Nursia (A.D. 480–547). Benedict was an Italian famous for his piety. With a few followers, he founded a monastery south of Rome on a hilltop called Monte Cassino. This monastery became the source for the Benedictine Rule, a form of monastic life that has been the model for many Catholic institutions for 1,500 years. Benedict stressed simplicity, learning, the importance of community, and the goal of helping others. Because his influence was so widespread, in 1964 Pope Paul VI named Benedict one of Europe's patron saints.

Reading Support L1/ EL

Assign **Guided Reading Activity 15–1** to help students organize the information in the section.

③ ASSESS

Assign Section 1 Review as homework or as an in-class activity.

⊙ Have students use the **Interactive Tutor Self-Assessment CD-ROM** to review the section.

Assessment L2

Assign **Section 1 Quiz** to assess mastery of the material found in the section.

Reading Support L1/ EL

Assign **Reading Essentials and Study Guide 15–1** to help students review section material.

▲ Monks eating together in a monastery

▲ The monastery at Mont St. Michel in France is a beautiful work of architecture that took several hundred years to complete. *How did monasteries help local people in Europe?*

▲ Illustrated page created by monks

Irish monks played an important role in preserving Roman learning and passing it on to the people of Europe.

Patrick's success inspired others, including Pope Gregory I, or **Gregory the Great.** Gregory I was pope from A.D. 590 to A.D. 604. He wanted all of Europe to become Christian, and he asked monks to become **missionaries** (MIH•shuh•NEHR•eez)—people who are sent out to teach their religion.

In A.D. 597 Gregory sent 40 monks to southern Britain to teach Christianity. The monks converted Ethelbert, ruler of the kingdom of Kent. Ethelbert allowed the missionaries to build a church in his capital city of Canterbury. Meanwhile, Irish monks brought Christianity to northern Britain. By A.D. 800, monks were spreading Christianity throughout Europe. As a result, most people in Western Europe had become Catholics by 1050.

Monasteries played an important role in medieval Europe. Monks schooled people, provided food and rest to travelers, and offered hospital care for the sick. They taught carpentry and weaving and developed better methods of farming. They also helped to preserve knowledge.

Many monasteries had scriptoria, or writing rooms, where monks made copies of important works. The monks copied Christian writings, including the Bible, as well as works of Roman and Greek writers.

Over time, monasteries began to play a role in Europe's politics. Monks took a vow of poverty, wore simple clothes, and ate simple food, but their monasteries could make money. Each monastery produced goods and owned land, and over time many of them became wealthy. The leader of a monastery is called an abbot (A•buht), and many abbots became involved in politics. They served as advisers to kings and acted as rulers of the lands near their monasteries.

Why Is Gregory VII Important? The growing role of abbots and other Church leaders in Europe's politics caused many arguments over who was in charge. Kings wanted Church leaders to obey them, while the pope claimed he could crown kings.

In 1073 Gregory VII was elected pope. He wanted to stop nobles and kings from interfering in Church affairs. He issued a decree, or order, forbidding kings from appointing high-ranking Church officials.

The pope's decree angered Henry IV, the Holy Roman emperor. For many years, the Holy Roman emperor had appointed bishops in Germany. Without them, Henry IV risked losing power to the nobles.

520   CHAPTER 15   Medieval Europe

COOPERATIVE LEARNING ACTIVITY

Newsmakers Have students arrange a news interview show in the style of "Meet the Press" featuring important figures from this section. For example, students might "invite" Henry IV and Gregory VII to be interviewed by reporters, Clovis and Charles Martel might be invited to discuss their plans for the Frankish kingdom, or Charlemagne or Otto I could be interviewed about important issues facing their governments. Have students assign roles, including a moderator and reporters as well as distinguished guests. Then have the groups present their programs for the class. **L2**

Henry refused to obey Gregory. He declared that Gregory was no longer pope. Gregory then stated that Henry was no longer emperor. He **excommunicated** (EHK•skuh•MYOO•nuh•KAY•tuhd) Henry. This means to exclude a person from church membership. Catholics believed that if they were excommunicated, they could not go to heaven.

When the German nobles defended the pope, Henry backed down. He traveled to Italy and stood barefoot in the snow outside the pope's castle asking to be forgiven. Gregory forgave Henry, but the German nobles still chose a new king. When Gregory accepted the new king as emperor, Henry went to war. He captured Rome and named a new pope. Gregory's allies drove out Henry's forces, but the dispute was not resolved.

In 1122 a new pope and the German king finally agreed that only the pope could choose bishops, but only the emperor could give them jobs in the government. This deal, called the Concordat of Worms, was signed in the city of Worms. A **concordat** (kuhn•KAWR•DAT) is an agreement between the pope and the ruler of a country.

By the time Innocent III became pope in 1198, the Catholic Church was at the height of its power. Innocent was able to control kings. If a ruler did not obey, Innocent would excommunicate him or issue an interdict (IHN•tuhr•DIHKT) against the ruler's people. An interdict forbids priests from providing Christian rituals to a group of people. The pope hoped that by using an interdict, local people would pressure their ruler to obey.

 Contrast How did Gregory VII and Henry IV disagree?

Section 1 Review

 Study Central™ Need help with the material in this section? Visit jat.glencoe.com

Reading Summary
Review the Main Ideas

- During the Middle Ages, Europe's geography affected where people lived, their ways of life, and their relations with other people.
- The Angles and Saxons invaded Britain, the Franks created an empire in Western Europe, and the Saxons created a German kingdom that became the Holy Roman Empire.
- Monks helped spread Christianity throughout Europe, and the Catholic Church became strong in the early Middle Ages.

What Did You Learn?
1. What happened at the Battle of Tours, and why is the battle significant?
2. Why were monasteries important to medieval Europe?

Critical Thinking
3. **Summarizing Information** Draw a diagram like the one below. Use it to describe the role of monks in medieval Europe.

   Monks

4. **Analyze** How did Charlemagne demonstrate his support for education?
5. **Describe** Imagine you live in central Europe in medieval times. Prepare a poster that describes the Vikings and the dangers they pose to your town.
6. **Reading** Asking Questions Henry IV "stood barefoot in the snow" to gain the pope's forgiveness. If you were asked to interview Henry IV about this experience, what three questions would you ask?

CHAPTER 15   Medieval Europe   **521**

Have volunteers prepare a class presentation on the medieval monastery. Have them find information on how and where monks lived, their daily activities, and how they influenced medieval society. **L3**

✓ **Reading Check**

Answer: Gregory VII decreed that kings could not appoint church officials. Henry IV refused to obey the decree because, by appointing bishops, he maintained power over his nobles.

To help students understand section material, have them visit Study Central™ at jat.glencoe.com

RETEACH

Ask students to summarize the contributions of one of the peoples discussed in this section. **L1**

④ CLOSE

Tell students that the early Middle Ages is sometimes called the Dark Ages. Ask them to discuss why this name is inappropriate. **L2**

SECTION 1 REVIEW ANSWERS

1. Charles Martel led the Franks against the Muslim army and stopped the Muslim advance into Europe.

2. Monasteries helped to teach people, provided food and rest, preserved knowledge, spread Christianity, and played a role in politics.

3. provided schools, rest stops, hospitals; spread Christianity

4. He opened a palace school for children of officials. The scholar Alcuin taught classes.

5. Posters should describe the Vikings' lifestyle, including their destruction of European villages and towns.

6. Answers will vary but should focus on papal/royal disagreements.

① FOCUS

SECTION OVERVIEW

In this section, students will learn about the development of feudalism as well as the rise of towns and cities.

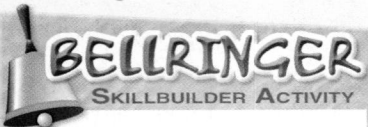
BELLRINGER
SKILLBUILDER ACTIVITY

👆 Project **Daily Focus Skills Transparency 15–2** and have students answer questions. Discuss their responses.

Get Ready to Read!

Preteaching Vocabulary: The word *vassal* refers to a person of lower rank who pledges loyalty to someone of a higher rank. It comes from a Celtic word meaning "one who stands under."

Answers to Graphic: Serfs: given land to support themselves; could not be sold away; protected by lords. Slaves: did not have land at all; anything given could be taken away; not protected by masters. Both: could not move to another area, own property, or marry without approval.

Section 2 — Feudalism

Get Ready to Read!

What's the Connection?
In the last section, you read how the Vikings spread fear and destruction throughout Europe. During the Middle Ages, villagers and townspeople looked to nobles to protect them.

Focusing on the Main Ideas
- Feudalism developed in Europe in the Middle Ages. It was based on landowning, loyalty, and the power of armored knights on horseback. *(page 523)*
- Knights followed a code of chivalry and lived in castles, while peasants lived in simple houses and worked hard all year long. *(page 526)*
- Increased trade led to the growth of towns and cities and the rise of guilds and city governments. *(page 528)*

Locating Places
Venice (VEH•nuhs)
Flanders (FLAN•duhrz)

Building Your Vocabulary
feudalism (FYOO•duhl•IH•zuhm)
vassal (VA•suhl)
fief (FEEF)
knight (NYT)
serf (SUHRF)
guild (GIHLD)

Reading Strategy
Compare and Contrast Complete a Venn diagram like the one below showing the similarities and differences between serfs and slaves.

Serfs — Slaves

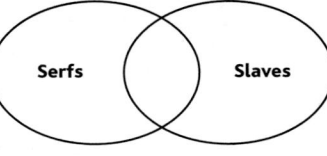
NATIONAL GEOGRAPHIC **When & Where?**

SCANDINAVIA
ENGLAND
Bruges • HOLY ROMAN
FRANCE EMPIRE
SPAIN • Venice • Rome
ITALY

A.D. **800** — **1000** — **1200**

c. A.D. 800s
Feudalism begins in Europe

c. 1100
Flanders and Italy trade goods regularly

c. 1200
Guilds are widespread in Europe

SECTION RESOURCES

📁 **Reproducible Masters**
- Reproducible Lesson Plan 15–2
- Daily Lecture and Discussion Notes 15–2
- Vocabulary Activity 15–2
- Active Reading Note-Taking Guide 15–2
- Guided Reading Activity 15–2
- Section Quiz 15–2
- Reading Essentials and Study Guide 15–2

🖏 **Transparencies**
- Daily Focus Skills Transparency 15–2

Multimedia
- Interactive Tutor Self-Assessment CD-ROM
- *ExamView®* Pro Testmaker CD-ROM
- Presentation Plus! CD-ROM

What Is Feudalism?

Main Idea Feudalism developed in Europe in the Middle Ages. It was based on landowning, loyalty, and the power of armored knights on horseback.

Reading Focus What would it be like to live in a country where the government has fallen apart? Read to learn how the fall of Charlemagne's government changed life for people in the Middle Ages.

When Charlemagne's grandfather, Charles Martel, needed an army to fight the Muslims invading France, he began giving estates—large farms—to nobles willing to fight for him. The nobles used the resources from the estates to obtain horses and weapons. Although Charles Martel did not realize it, he was using a new way of organizing society that would eventually spread across most of Europe.

When Charlemagne's empire collapsed, Western Europe lost its last strong central government. Landowning nobles became more and more powerful. They gained the right to collect taxes and to enforce laws on their estates. When invaders spread ruin throughout Europe, the peasants, or farmers, could not rely on kings. Instead, they looked to nobles for protection.

During the A.D. 800s, this shift of power from kings to nobles led to a new social order known as **feudalism** (FYOO•duhl•IH•zuhm). Under feudalism, landowning nobles governed and protected the people in return for services, such as fighting in a noble's army or farming the land. By A.D. 1000, the kingdoms of Europe were divided into thousands of feudal territories. Some of these territories were large, but most were very small, smaller even than the city-states of Greece and Sumeria. At the center of each, however, was not a city but a noble's castle, or fortress.

Kings and queens

Lords and ladies

Knights

Peasants and serfs

▲ Under feudalism each level of society had duties to the groups above and below it. *Which group in the diagram served as vassals to the lords and ladies?*

The Role of Vassals and Knights

Feudalism was based on ties of loyalty and duty among nobles. Nobles were both lords and vassals. A **vassal** (VA•suhl) was a noble who served a lord of higher rank. In return, the lord protected the vassal.

The tie between a lord and his vassal was made known in a public ceremony. The vassal put his hands together and placed them between the hands of his lord. Then the vassal swore "to keep faith and loyalty to you against all others."

② TEACH

Reading Strategy

Writing About Cause and Effect
Have students write a paragraph describing the rise of feudalism. Have them include a cause-and-effect statement about how the decline of central governments, such as Charlemagne's, led to the growth of feudalism. **L3**

Daily Lecture and Discussion Notes 15–2

Use **Daily Lecture and Discussion Notes 15–2** for an outline of key concepts found in the section.

Reading Support L1/ EL

Use **Vocabulary Activity 15–2** to review important terms in the section.

More About the Art

In theory, feudalism was a simple system. In practice, however, vassals could in turn be lords to other vassals, and a person could be a vassal to more than one person at the same time.

Caption Answer: knights

Reading Strategy ❬ **READING THE TEXT**

Interpreting Ask students what benefits feudalism provided for people at each of its levels. Have them offer suggestions regarding why those on the lower rungs generally accepted their roles. Then ask them to name analogous situations in which all parties benefit from an arrangement, even though it may not be ideal for all participants. **L3**

A vassal showed his loyalty by serving in his lord's army. In return for the vassal's military service, a lord granted his vassal land and permission to rule the people who lived on it. This grant to a vassal was known as a **fief** (FEEF).

These vassals were **knights** (NYTS), or warriors in armor who fought on horseback. Up until the A.D. 700s, nobles in Western Europe mostly fought on foot. They wore coats of mail—armor made from metal links—and carried swords and shields. In the A.D. 700s, a new invention, the stirrup, made it possible for an armored man to sit on a horse and charge while holding a lance, a long heavy spear. Knights would charge enemies, spearing them with their lances. From the A.D. 700s to the 1200s, armored knights on horseback were the most powerful soldiers in Europe.

Europe was not the only place with a feudal society. As you remember from an earlier chapter, Japan had a similar system between A.D. 800 and 1500. Powerful nobles owed only a loose loyalty to the Japanese emperor. The nobles in turn relied on samurai. Like knights, the samurai owed loyalty to their lords and provided military service for them. Also like knights in Europe, the samurai wore armor and fought on horseback.

What Was the Manorial System? The lands of the fiefs of the Middle Ages were called manors. The lords ruled the manor, and peasants worked the land. Some peasants were freemen, who paid the noble for the right to farm the land. They had rights under the law and could move whenever and wherever they wished.

Most peasants, however, were **serfs** (SUHRFS). Serfs could not leave the manor, own property, or marry without the lord's approval. Lords even had the right to try

A Medieval Manor

A medieval manor usually consisted of the lord's manor house or castle, the surrounding fields, and a peasant village. While minor knights or nobles would own only one manor, more powerful lords might own several. A powerful lord would spend time at each of his manors during the year. *What duty did lords have to their serfs?*

Fields
In the spring, serfs planted crops such as summer wheat, barley, oats, peas, and beans. Crops planted in the fall included winter wheat and rye. Women often helped in the fields.

524

serfs in their own court. Serfs were not enslaved, however. Lords could not sell the serfs or take away the land given to serfs to support themselves. Lords also had a duty to protect their serfs, providing them the safety they needed to grow crops.

Serfs worked long hours on the lord's land and performed services for the lord. They spent three days working for the lord and the rest of the week growing food for themselves. They also had to give a portion of their own crops to the lord and pay him for the use of the village's mill, bread oven, and winepress.

It was not easy for serfs to gain their freedom. One way was to run away to the towns. If a serf remained in a town for more than a year, he or she was considered free. By the end of the Middle Ages, serfs in many kingdoms were also allowed to buy their freedom.

How Did Farming Improve? During the Middle Ages, Europeans invented new technology that helped increase the amount of crops they could grow. Perhaps the most important was a heavy wheeled plow with an iron blade. It easily turned over Western Europe's dense clay soils.

Another important invention was the horse collar. The horse collar made it possible for a horse to pull a plow. Horses could pull plows much faster than oxen, allowing peasants to plant more crops and produce more food.

Monitoring Comprehension Ask students to make word webs for the important developments described in this section. *(Sample answer: heavy wheeled plow: could turn clay soils, led to increase in amount of crops grown)* **L1/ EL**

Making Judgments Ask students if they think feudalism was an effective form of government, and have them explain their answers. Have students make a list of recommended changes for improving feudalism. **L2**

CONNECTING ACROSS TIME

Ask students to compare the life of a serf on a medieval manor with that of an enslaved African American on a cotton plantation in the United States before the Civil War. **L3**

Castle
Castles were built in a variety of forms and were usually designed to fit the landscape.

Church
Village churches often had no benches. Villagers sat on the floor or brought stools from home.

Serf's Home
Serfs had little furniture. Tables were made from boards stretched across benches, and most peasants slept on straw mattresses on the floor.

CRITICAL THINKING ACTIVITY

Making Generalizations Remind students that generalizations are broad statements of universal application based on supporting details for a specific situation. Ask students to review one of the three subsections and write generalizations about the content of a subsubsection. For example, a generalization about the first subsubsection, "The Role of Vassals and Knights," might be: *People are usually loyal to those who give them what they need.* Have students share their generalizations with the class. Have them discuss each statement and how it is supported by details. **L2**

Science Techniques for reclaiming land from the sea became another important method for increasing farmland and still play a significant role in agriculture today. Ask students to research and report on the land reclamation around the IJsselmeer in present-day Netherlands. **L3**

✓ **Reading Check**

Answer: A noble could be the lord of a group of vassals, but also could be the vassal of a lord of higher rank.

Caption Answer: They ran the manors.

in a word . . .

Today **"chivalry"** still refers to characteristics such as bravery, courtesy, and honesty, even though we no longer exhibit these traits on horseback. The word's root is the Latin word for "horse," demonstrating the importance of horses to medieval life, especially knights. The same root gives us words like *cavalry*, *cavalier*, and *cavalcade*.

Europeans also found new ways to harness water and wind power. Europe's many rivers powered water mills that ground grain into flour. Where rivers were not available, windmills were used for grinding grains, pumping water, and cutting wood.

Peasants also learned to grow more food by rotating crops on three fields instead of two. The rotation kept soil fertile. One field was planted in fall and another in spring. The third field was left unplanted. The three-field system meant that only one-third, rather than one-half, of the land was unused at any time. As a result, more crops could be grown.

✓ **Reading Check** **Explain** How could a noble be both a lord and a vassal?

▲ Nobles celebrated special occasions with large feasts, which included many courses of meats, fruits, and vegetables. *What were the wife's duties when a nobleman went off to war?*

Life in Feudal Europe

Main Idea Knights followed a code of chivalry and lived in castles, while peasants lived in simple houses and worked hard all year long.

Reading Focus Have you heard the phrase "knight in shining armor"? Read to learn why these words apply to how a knight acts as well as how he dresses.

During the Middle Ages, nobles were the most powerful people in Europe. Great lords had much more wealth and land than ordinary knights. However, their belief in the feudal system united lords and knights in defending their society.

How Did Nobles Live? Knights followed certain rules called the code of chivalry (SHIH•vuhl•ree). A knight was expected to obey his lord, to be brave, to show respect to women of noble birth, to honor the church, and to help people. A knight was also expected to be honest and to fight fairly against his enemies. The code of chivalry became the guide to good behavior. Many of today's ideas about manners come from the code of chivalry.

When noblemen went to war, their wives or daughters ran the manors. This was no small job because manors had many officials and servants. Keeping track of the household's accounts took considerable skill. The lady of a manor also had to oversee the storing of food and other supplies needed to run the household.

The center of the manor was a castle. At first, castles were built of wood. Later, they were built of stone. A castle had two basic parts. One was a human-made or

INTERDISCIPLINARY CONNECTIONS ACTIVITY

Daily Life Have students research, write, and present a play about life on a medieval manor or in a medieval town. Have them review the section for information for their plays. Encourage them to do additional research using other sources. Suggest that they use props, scenery, and other stagecraft to make their plays lively and enjoyable. Have groups present their plays, leaving time for discussion afterward. **L3**

A Medieval Castle

Castles were built to withstand attack during times of war. They were often constructed on high ground or surrounded by moats to make attacks more difficult. *What was the central building of the castle called?*

Drawbridge

Bedrooms

Castle school

Dungeon

Great Hall

Servants' quarters

Storeroom

Chapel

Toilet

More About the Art

Many keeps had a massive inner tower called a donjon (DAHN•juhn), from which we get our word *dungeon*. While both words reference places where prisoners were kept under lock and key, dungeon also came to mean a dark, damp cellar.

Caption Answer: the keep

TIME TRAVELER

Many family names came into use during the Middle Ages. For example, a man who thatched cottage roofs for a living came to be known as "Thatcher." Other common English last names that represent occupations are Miller, Smith, Baker, Mason, Cooper, Barber, Carter, and Cook. A number of English family names come from the important wool and cloth trade: Shepherd, Fuller, Shearer, Weaver, and Dyer.

naturally steep-sided hill called a motte (MAHT). The bailey was an open space next to the motte. High stone walls encircled the motte and bailey. The keep, or central building of the castle, was built on the motte.

The keep had a number of stories. The basement housed storerooms for tools and food. On the ground floor were kitchens and stables, and above the ground floor was a great hall. Here the people of the household ate and sometimes slept, and the lord of the castle held court and received visitors. Smaller rooms opened off the great hall. They included chapels, toilets, and bedrooms with huge curtained beds.

In the later Middle Ages, nobles owned more jewelry, better clothes, and exotic spices. They also built more elaborate castles with thicker walls, more towers, finer furniture, and richer decoration.

What Was Peasant Life Like? The homes of peasants were much simpler. They lived in wood-frame cottages plastered with clay. Their roofs were thatched with straw. The houses of poorer peasants had a single room. Better cottages had a main room for cooking and eating and another room for sleeping.

Peasants worked year-round. They harvested grain in August and September. In October they prepared the ground for winter crops. In November they slaughtered livestock and salted the meat to keep it for winter. In February and March, they plowed the land for planting oats, barley, peas, and beans. In early summer they

CHAPTER 15 Medieval Europe 527

EXTENDING THE CONTENT

Knights in Shining Armor One of the most famous activities of medieval knights was the tournament, a series of mock combats designed to showcase war skills. The earliest tournaments, probably held in France in the 1000s, featured a mock battle called a *melee* between two groups of knights. The familiar joust, in which two riders charged each other and tried to knock their opponent off his horse with a long lance, came later. By around 1300, steps were taken to prevent injury to the contestants, although serious injuries, and even death, sometimes occurred. In the 1500s, fighting on foot became popular, with knights striking each other across a barricade with swords and battle-axes.

HISTORY Mystery

How Do We Know About Peasant Life in the Middle Ages?

Some works of art provide amazing insights into daily life at the time the art was created. One of the best visual sources of information about medieval life is the famous illuminated manuscript, the *Très Riches Heures* (Book of Hours), of the French noble the Duke de Berry. The Book of Hours was a prayer book that was meant to help Christians say the proper prayers at the proper time. The Duke de Berry's book was made by a family of brothers named Limbourg in northern France in the early 1400s. It shows highly detailed scenes of everyday life on a manor, as well as scenes from the lives of saints.

✓ **Reading Check**

Answer: rules stating that a knight had to obey his lord, show bravery, respect women of noble birth, honor the church, and help people

Caption Answer:
Flanders

weeded the fields, sheared the sheep, and tended small vegetable gardens.

Peasants took a break from work and went to church on Catholic feast days. They celebrated more than 50 feast days each year. The most important were Christmas and Easter. On feast days and at Sunday worship, the village priest taught them the basic beliefs of Christianity.

Peasant women worked in the fields and raised children at the same time. They also gathered and prepared their family's food. Each day they mixed bread dough and baked it in community ovens. Bread was a basic staple of the medieval diet. Peasant bread was dark and heavy. Peasants ate it with vegetables, milk, nuts, and fruits. Sometimes they added eggs or meat, and they often had ale to drink.

✓ **Reading Check** **Identify** What was the code of chivalry?

Medieval City Life

528 CHAPTER 15 Medieval Europe

Trade and Cities

Main Idea Increased trade led to the growth of towns and cities and the rise of guilds and city governments.

Reading Focus What effect would a new shopping mall have on your community? Read to learn how the growth of trade and the rise of cities changed the way people lived and worked in medieval Europe.

When the Roman Empire collapsed, almost all trade in Western Europe came to an end. Bridges and roads fell into disrepair. Law and order vanished. Money was no longer used. Most people spent their entire lives in the tiny villages where they were born and knew almost nothing about the rest of the world.

By 1100, feudalism had made Europe safer, and new technology enabled people to produce more food and goods. Nobles

◄ This scene shows a market in a medieval town. *Which area became the center of trade for northern Europe?*

A mayor of London from the early 1200s ▶

CITIZENSHIP AND YOU

Loyalty In the Middle Ages, people felt loyalty to their local lord or town. Countries and states as we know them did not really exist. Ask students to discuss their sense of loyalty and belonging to their community, state, and nation. How are these different loyalties related? Does one always outweigh the others? In what circumstances might a local loyalty outweigh a broader one? If appropriate, remind students that during the American Civil War, most people felt a greater loyalty to their state or region than to the United States. Conclude by asking students to decide if local loyalties are a hindrance or a benefit to our sense of nationhood. **L2**

repaired bridges and roads, arrested bandits, and enforced the law. As a result, trade resumed.

As trade increased, towns grew larger, and several cities became wealthy from trade. For example, the city of **Venice** (VEH•nuhs) in Italy built a fleet of trading ships. It became a major trading center by A.D. 1000. Venice and other Italian cities began trading with the Byzantine Empire and soon became the center of trade in the Mediterranean.

Meanwhile, towns in **Flanders** (FLAN•duhrz)—which today is part of Belgium—became the center of trade for northern Europe. This area was known for its woolen cloth. Merchants from England, Scandinavia, France, and the Holy Roman Empire met there to trade their goods for wool. Flemish towns such as Bruges and Ghent became centers for making and trading cloth.

By 1100, Flanders and Italy were exchanging goods regularly. To encourage

History Online
Web Activity Visit jat.glencoe.com and click on *Chapter 15—Student Web Activity* to learn more about the Middle Ages.

this trade, the counts of Champagne in northern France began holding trade fairs. Northern European merchants exchanged furs, tin, honey, and wool for cloth and swords from northern Italy and silks, sugar, and spices from Asia.

During the early Middle Ages, people bartered, or traded goods for other goods. As trade increased, demand for gold and silver coins rose. Slowly, people began using money again to pay for goods. Merchants set up trading companies and banks to manage the sale of goods and the use of money.

History Online
Objectives and answers to the student activity can be found in the **Web Activity Lesson Plan** feature at jat.glencoe.com

CURRICULUM CONNECTION

Geography
Flanders is today part of Belgium, a country of about 10 million people in northern Europe. The people of Flanders, called Flemings, speak a Dutch dialect. The other, French-speaking part of Belgium is called Wallonia. Its people are known as Walloons.

Reading Maps Have students trace the trade route between Venice and Flanders on a map. Have them find obstacles that would make the trip difficult. *(the Alps and several rivers to cross)* **L1/ EL**

Caption Answer: furs, tin, honey, cloth, swords, silks, sugar, and spices

▲ This illustration from a medieval book shows glassblowers at work. *What were some of the items exchanged at trade fairs?*

▼ A stained glass window showing the arms, or symbol, of a blacksmiths' group

COOPERATIVE LEARNING ACTIVITY

All Aboard for the Middle Ages! Ask groups of students to use the Internet and other resources to make a travelogue of medieval cityscapes. Have the groups use search engines to find photographs of European cities, towns, and villages that retain a medieval character. Have them look for preserved buildings, such as shops, castles, and churches, and unchanged rural and agricultural landscapes. Suggest that they begin by looking at the Cotswold region and the city of York in England; Assisi, Italy; and the towns of the German Romantic Road. Have the groups print out information and photos of preserved places and prepare a bulletin board. **L2**

📁 Refer to the *Quizzes, Tests, and Authentic Assessment (with Rubrics)* booklet for rubrics.

③ ASSESS

How Were Cities Governed? Towns were often located on land owned by lords. This meant the towns were under their control. However, townspeople needed freedom to trade. They wanted to make their own laws and were willing to pay for the right to make them. In exchange for paying taxes, people in towns were granted certain basic rights by their lords. These included the right to buy and sell property and the freedom from having to serve in the army.

Over time, medieval towns set up their own governments. Only males who had been born in the city or who had lived there for a certain length of time were citizens. In many cities, these citizens elected the members of a city council. The council served as judges, city officials, and lawmakers. Candidates from the wealthiest and most powerful families were usually able to control the elections so that only they were elected.

Crafts and Guilds Trade encouraged manufacturing. People produced cloth, metalwork, shoes, and other goods right in their houses. Over time, these craftspeople organized **guilds** (GIHLDZ), or business groups. By 1200, tanners, carpenters, bakers, and almost every other type of craftspeople had guilds. The rise of towns and guilds created a new middle class in medieval Europe. People in the middle class were not lords, vassals, or serfs. They did not own land, but they did have some wealth and freedom.

Craft guilds set standards for quality in products. They decided how goods were to be made and set the prices at which the finished goods were sold. Guilds also decided who could join a trade and the steps they had to follow to do so.

A person could become an apprentice around the age of 10. An apprentice learned a trade from a master craftsperson who provided room and board but no wages. After five to seven years of service, the apprentice became a journeyman and worked for wages. To become a master, a journeyman had to produce a masterpiece—an outstanding example of the craft.

What Was City Life Like? Medieval cities had narrow, winding streets. Houses were crowded against one another, and the

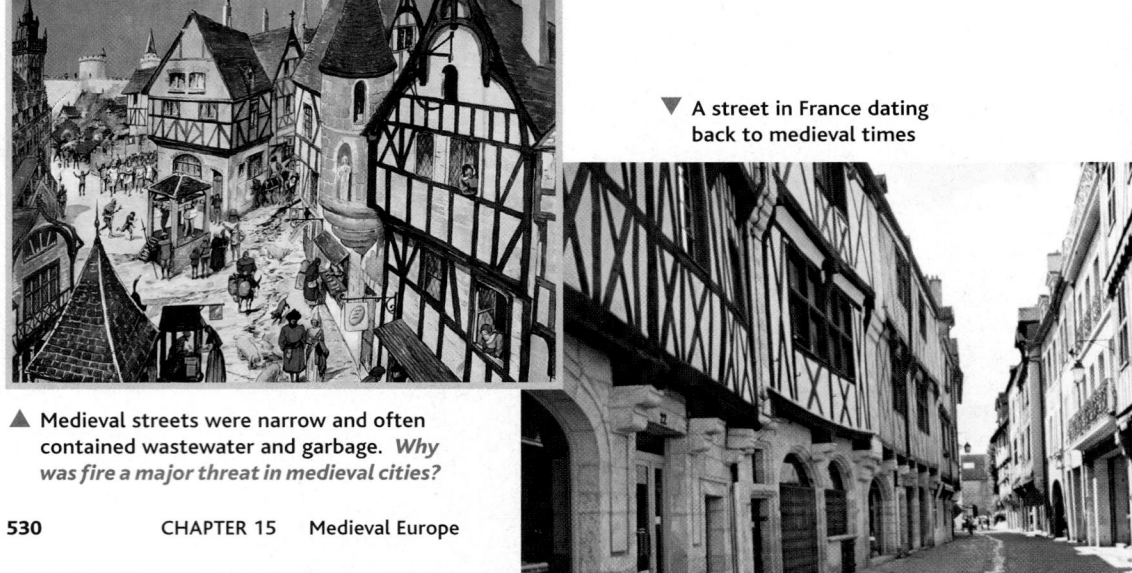

▼ A street in France dating back to medieval times

▲ Medieval streets were narrow and often contained wastewater and garbage. *Why was fire a major threat in medieval cities?*

530   **CHAPTER 15** **Medieval Europe**

EXTENDING THE CONTENT

More About Guilds Guilds in the Middle Ages were of two basic types: merchant guilds and craft guilds. Merchant guilds arose first. They were associations of most or all merchants in a town, including retailers, wholesalers, and importers/exporters. Historians believe they may have begun as a means of protecting traveling peddlers from bandits. They gradually evolved into broader associations as trade became centralized in towns. Craft guilds developed in response to the gradual division of labor. Individuals or family workshops that did similar work joined together to improve distribution, working conditions, and profits.

second and third stories were built out over the streets. Candles and fireplaces were used for light and heat, and the houses were built mostly of wood. As a result, medieval cities could be destroyed rapidly once a fire started.

The cities were often dirty and smelly. Wood fires in people's homes and shops filled the air with ashes and smoke. Brewers, dyers, and poor people who could not afford wood burned cheap coal, polluting the air even more. Butchers and tanners dumped blood and other animal wastes into the rivers. Because of the pollution, cities did not use the rivers for drinking water but used wells instead.

City women ran their households, prepared meals, raised their children, and managed the family's money. Often they

▲ This painting shows a medieval woman spinning wool as her husband warms himself by the fire. *What were some responsibilities of women in medieval cities?*

helped their husbands in their trades. Some women developed their own trades to earn extra money. Sometimes when a master craftsperson died, his widow carried on his trade. As a result, women in medieval towns could lead independent lives. In fact, many women became brewers, weavers, and hatmakers.

 Reading Check **Analyze** In what ways do you think the shift from a barter system to a money system changed medieval Europe?

Study Central™ Need help with the material in this section? Visit jat.glencoe.com

Section 2 Review

Reading Summary

Review the Main Ideas

- Under feudalism, Europe was divided into thousands of territories owned by nobles with the lands worked by serfs.

- During the Middle Ages, nobles lived in large castles, while serfs lived in small wood cottages.

- As medieval trade increased, towns grew and craftspeople organized guilds.

What Did You Learn?

1. What was a vassal?
2. Describe the system of crop rotation used in the later Middle Ages, and explain how it increased the amount of food being grown.

Critical Thinking

3. **Compare and Contrast** Draw a chart to compare the duties and obligations of lords, knights, and serfs.

Lords	Knights	Serfs

4. **Summarize** Explain the shift of power from kings to nobles during the Middle Ages.

5. **Cause and Effect** How did an increase in trade lead to the growth of towns and cities?

6. **Conclude** What were guilds, and why were they important?

7. **Creative Writing** Write a For Sale advertisement for a medieval castle. Describe the castle's rooms and surroundings, including the manor and its residents.

ENRICH

Have students research and prepare short reports on similarities and differences between medieval guilds and today's labor unions. **L3**

 Reading Check

Answer: Trade, banks, and coinage became important, making economies more efficient and helping countries grow.

History Online

To help students understand section material, have them visit **Study Central™** at jat.glencoe.com

RETEACH

Have students create a word web about the concept of feudalism in the Middle Ages. **L1/ EL**

④ CLOSE

Ask students to prepare a class chart that compares life in a medieval town with life on a manor. **L2**

SECTION 2 REVIEW ANSWERS

1. a noble who served a lord of higher rank
2. Peasants rotated crops among three fields. Since only one-third of the land was unused, more crops were grown.
3. Lords: granted a vassal land, offered vassals protection; Knights: served in lord's army, managed small landholdings; Serfs: worked lord's lands, gave part of their crop to lord
4. Europe had no central government. Nobles began to collect taxes and enforce laws.
5. Trade brought more people and prosperity to cities.
6. Guilds were business groups organized by craftspeople. They set standards for quality, decided how goods were made, and set prices.
7. Entries should include relevant details about life in and around a castle.

❶ FOCUS

Whether a social order is good or bad depends on one's point of view. Ask students to think about what makes a system positive or negative as they read the assignment.

❷ TEACH

DEFINING TERMS

Have students work in pairs to look up and write the definitions of *feudal, lord,* and *vassal.* As they read the passage, have them pull out phrases or sentences that support their definitions of these terms. **L2**

COMPARISON

Have students create a graphic organizer like the one below. Then have them read through the passages and summarize the key points for both sides of the argument. **L2**

Feudalism	
Good	Bad

You Decide . . .

Feudalism: Good or Bad?

Feudalism was the major social and political order in medieval Europe. It developed as power passed from kings to local lords.

Good?

Feudalism brought together two powerful groups: lords and vassals. The lords gave vassals land in return for military and other services. Feudalism was a help to Western Europeans for the following reasons:

- Feudalism helped protect communities from the violence and warfare that broke out after the fall of Rome and the collapse of strong central government in Western Europe. Feudalism secured Western Europe's society and kept out powerful invaders.

- Feudalism helped restore trade. Lords repaired bridges and roads. Their knights arrested bandits, enforced the law, and made it safe to travel on roads.

- Feudalism benefited lords, vassals, and peasants. Lords gained a dependable fighting force in their vassals. Vassals received land for their military service. Peasants were protected by their lords. The lord also built mills to grind grain and blacksmith shops and woodworking shops to make tools.

- Feudal ceremonies, oaths, and contracts required lords and vassals to be faithful and to carry out their duties to each other. These kinds of agreements and rituals later helped shape the development of Western governments.

- Feudalism did not allow one person or organization to become too powerful. Power was shared among

◀ Serfs working the land

532

Extending the Content

Serfdom The institution of serfdom was not limited to Europe or to the past. Serfs in China, like those in Europe, were attached to plots of land. They could be traded or punished at the whim of the master. Serfdom was not eliminated in China until the Communist revolution of 1949. In medieval Korea, many people chose to become serfs. This way, they could avoid the forced military service required of tenant farmers. Serfs also existed in parts of southern Africa, Southeast Asia, and South America. Some experts believe it still exists today. One example is the Haratin people of Morocco and Mauritania in northwestern Africa. These serfs work in palm groves and as herders.

◀ Landowning nobles often served as knights.

to many wars among lords. Feudalism protected Western Europe from outside invaders, but it did not bring peace to a region.

- Lords or vassals often placed their personal interests over the interests of the areas they ruled. Feudal lords had complete power in their local areas and could make harsh demands on their vassals and peasants.

- Feudalism did not treat people equally or let them move up in society. A person born a serf was supposed to remain a serf, just as a person born a lord received special treatment without earning it.

- Most peasants were serfs. They were not allowed to leave their lord's lands. Serfs had to work three or four days each week as a payment to the lords or vassals for allowing them to farm for themselves on other days. The serfs were restricted in movement and even daily activities because they could not leave the land without permission.

many people and groups. This was the first step to European ideas about limited government, constitutions, and civil rights.

Bad?

Feudalism did not always work as well in real life as it it did in theory, and it caused many problems for society.

- Feudalism provided some unity and security in local areas, but it often did not have the strength to unite larger regions or countries. Small feudal governments could not afford big projects, such as building aqueducts, sewers, or fleets of ships, that might benefit society.

- Because there was no strong central government to enforce laws fairly, it was easy to use force, violence, and lies to get one's way. This led

You Be the Historian

Checking for Understanding
1. Do you think feudalism helped or hurt Western Europe's development?
2. Is there any way feudal lords could have worked their lands without using serfs?
3. Imagine what your life would have been if you were born into a feudal society. Write at least three brief diary entries. Describe your daily life as a lord, vassal, or serf and your relationship with the other two groups. Your entries should show feudalism as either good or bad.

③ ASSESS

DEBATE THE ISSUE

Organize a class debate on whether the medieval institution of feudalism was good or bad. Form groups supporting each point of view. To support their arguments, have students find additional resources that discuss feudalism and its role in medieval society.

Students may use the library, Internet, or other resources to find additional information about feudalism and serfdom. After students have compiled their resources, have them present their viewpoints to the class. They should use their graphic organizers to help them in their presentations. Students may want to vote to decide which argument was more persuasive. **L2**

533

You Be the Historian Answers

1. Students should mention some of the key points from the feature and explain their choice.

2. Students should see that lords would have to make payments in cash or goods in order to have people work their land.

3. Answers will vary but should reflect information in the chapter and this feature.

① FOCUS

SECTION OVERVIEW

This section discusses the rise of new kingdoms in Europe and the causes and effects of the Crusades.

BELLRINGER
SKILLBUILDER ACTIVITY

✍ Project **Daily Focus Skills Transparency 15–3** and have students answer questions. Discuss their responses.

Get Ready to Read!

Preteaching Vocabulary: Our English word *jury* comes from an old French word meaning "to swear." Today's jury members swear to do their best to reach a responsible and un-biased verdict.

Answers to Graphic: Causes: Byzantine emperor needed help against the Turks; desire to unite Christians against common enemy; Muslim control of Palestine; Effects: trade between Europe and Middle East increased; feudalism broke down; monarchies strengthened

Section 3

Kingdoms and Crusades

Get Ready to Read!

What's the Connection?
In the last section, you read about how Western Europeans lived during the Middle Ages. This section describes the political changes that took place while people went about their daily lives.

Focusing on the Main Ideas
- England developed a system in which the king's power was shared with Parliament. *(page 535)*
- French kings called the Capetians conquered lands held by the English in western France and set up France's first parliament. *(page 538)*
- After the Mongols destroyed the Kievan state, the rulers of Moscow built a new Russian state headed by a czar. *(page 539)*
- European crusaders captured Jerusalem but were later driven out by the Muslims. *(page 541)*

Locating Places
Normandy (NAWR•muhn•dee)
Kiev (KEE•EHF)
Moscow (MAHS•koh)

Meeting People
William the Conqueror
King John
Philip II (FIH•luhp)
Saladin (SA•luh•DEEN)

Building Your Vocabulary
grand jury
trial jury
clergy (KLUHR•jee)

Reading Strategy
Cause and Effect Complete a diagram to show the causes and effects of the Crusades.

Causes		Effects
	⇒	
	⇒	

A.D. 900	1150	1400
c. A.D. 871 Alfred becomes England's king	1095 Pope Urban II calls the First Crusade	1480 Ivan the Great ends Mongol rule

534   CHAPTER 15   Medieval Europe

SECTION RESOURCES

📁 **Reproducible Masters**
- Reproducible Lesson Plan 15–3
- Daily Lecture and Discussion Notes 15–3
- Vocabulary Activity 15–3
- Active Reading Note-Taking Guide 15–3
- Guided Reading Activity 15–3
- Section Quiz 15–3
- Reading Essentials and Study Guide 15–3

✍ **Transparencies**
- Daily Focus Skills Transparency 15–3

Multimedia
- Interactive Tutor Self-Assessment CD-ROM
- ExamView® Pro Testmaker CD-ROM
- Presentation Plus! CD-ROM

England in the Middle Ages

Main Idea England developed a system in which the king's power was shared with Parliament.

Reading Focus Do you know anyone who has had to go to court or has served on a jury? Read to learn how these institutions began in medieval England.

In section one, you learned that Germanic peoples called the Angles and Saxons invaded Britain in the early A.D. 400s. They took over much of the country from the Celts and set up many small kingdoms. In the late A.D. 800s, Vikings attacked Britain. King Alfred of Wessex, later known as Alfred the Great, united the Anglo-Saxon kingdoms and drove away the Vikings. Alfred's united kingdom became known as "Angleland," or England.

Alfred ruled England from A.D. 871 to A.D. 899. He founded schools and hired scholars to rewrite Latin books in the Anglo-Saxon language. However, the Anglo-Saxon kings who came after him were weak rulers.

Who Was William the Conqueror?

In the A.D. 900s, the Vikings conquered part of western France across the English Channel from England. This region came to be called **Normandy** (NAWR•muhn•dee), after the Vikings, or Norsemen, who ruled it. By the middle of the A.D. 1000s, Normandy was ruled by William, a descendant of the Viking ruler who had conquered Normandy. William was also a cousin of King Edward of England.

When Edward died, a noble named Harold Godwinson claimed England's throne. However, William believed that he, not Harold, should be king of England. In 1066, William and his army of knights landed in England. They defeated Harold and his foot soldiers at the Battle of Hastings. William was then crowned king of England and became known as **William the Conqueror.**

▼ This painting of the Battle of Hastings shows Norman knights on horseback led by William the Conqueror attacking the English foot soldiers. *What area did William rule before he attacked England?*

② TEACH

Explaining Ask students to explain the connection between the Vikings and William's rule of Normandy. *(The region was conquered by Vikings in the A.D. 900s, and William was a descendant of the Viking conqueror of Normandy.)* **L1**

Daily Lecture and Discussion Notes 15–3

Use **Daily Lecture and Discussion Notes 15–3** for an outline of key concepts found in the section.

Reading Support L1/ EL

Use **Vocabulary Activity 15–3** to review important terms in the section.

More About the Art

At the Battle of Hastings, the Normans had cavalry and trained infantry, while Harold's army included many untrained peasants. After Harold was killed, the English army slowly fell apart.

Caption Answer: Normandy

Reading Strategy — READING THE TEXT

Analyzing The reading support strategy of analyzing involves looking critically at the different parts of a text. In this way, the reader is able to understand the entire selection. In this section, much of the text serves to explain the factors and events that led to the rise of new kingdoms and strong leaders. As students read this section, they might analyze the different factors by identifying them and making notes. Then have them review their notes on the separate factors and combine them into a comprehensive explanation. **L2**

At first the Anglo-Saxons resisted William's rule. He had to find a way to stop Anglo-Saxon revolts and to control his own soldiers. He did so by giving land to his Norman knights. Then he made them swear loyalty to him as ruler of England.

William wanted to know all about his new kingdom. So he took the first census in Europe since Roman times. This census was known as the Domesday Book. It counted people, manors, and farm animals.

The Normans who ruled England brought Europe's customs to England.

Under William's rule, officials and nobles spoke French. Ordinary Anglo-Saxons still spoke their own language, which later became English. They also learned new skills from Norman weavers and other artisans. The Normans, in turn, kept many of the Anglo-Saxons' government practices. For example, they depended on local officials, called sheriffs, to keep order. As more and more Normans and Anglo-Saxons married, their ways of doing things merged into a new English culture.

Linking Past & Present
The Jury System

THEN The right to a jury trial in England was granted in the Magna Carta, but jury trials began in Europe about 50 years earlier. For each case, 12 jurors were chosen. In some villages, the same jurors were chosen again and again because of their wisdom or status. Jurors were always men. The jury decided whether the accused was guilty or innocent.

▼ A modern jury

NOW In the United States, citizens are chosen at random for possible jury duty. Some states have reduced the number of jurors from 12 to 10, 8, or 6. Juries usually decide a verdict and sometimes decide a sentence. *What is the disadvantage of choosing the same people to serve on juries again and again?*

▲ A medieval court

DIFFERENTIATED INSTRUCTION

Visual/Spatial: Have students watch the 1968 film *The Lion in Winter*, which tells the story of King Henry II, played by Peter O'Toole, and his dynamic queen, Eleanor of Aquitaine, played by Katharine Hepburn. Ask them to report to the class on such elements as settings, costumes, and other visual aspects of the film. If time permits, have a second group do the same for the 1964 film *Becket*, the story of the murder of Henry's friend and rival Thomas à Becket.

English Learners: Ask students to watch the film. Have them take notes on words they find difficult and look them up in a dictionary.

Gifted and Talented: Have students present a scene from the film's screenplay for the class.

Henry II and the Common Law

The power of the English king increased under Henry II. Henry ruled England from 1154 to 1189. Henry used the law courts to increase his power. He set up a central court with trained lawyers and judges. Then he appointed circuit judges, who traveled across the country hearing cases. He also established a body of common law, or law that was the same throughout the whole kingdom.

Henry set up juries to handle arguments over land. In time, two kinds of juries developed. The **grand jury** decided whether people should be accused of a crime. The **trial jury** decided whether an accused person was innocent or guilty.

What Was the Magna Carta?

Henry's son John became king of England in 1199. **King John** raised taxes in England and punished his enemies without trials. Many English nobles resented the king's power. They refused to obey him unless he agreed to guarantee certain rights.

The nobles met with King John at a meadow called Runnymede in 1215. There they forced John to sign a document of rights called the Magna Carta, or the Great Charter. The Magna Carta took away some of the king's powers. He could no longer collect taxes unless a group called the Great Council agreed. Freemen accused of crimes had the right to fair trials by their peers, or equals. The Magna Carta also stated that the king and vassals both had certain rights and duties. The Magna Carta was important because it helped to establish the idea that people have rights and that the power of the government should be limited.

In the 1200s, another English king, Edward I, called for a meeting of people from different parts of England. Their job was to advise him and help him make laws. This gathering, called the Parliament, was an important step toward representative government. At first, Parliaments were made up of two knights from every county, two people from every town, and all high-ranking nobles and church officials. Later, Parliament divided into two houses. High-ranking nobles and church officials met as the House of Lords. Knights and townspeople met as the House of Commons.

Reading Check **Explain** How did the Magna Carta affect the king's power?

Magna Carta

This excerpt from the Magna Carta describes the right to a trial by jury:

"No free man shall be taken, imprisoned, disseised [seized], outlawed, banished, or in any way destroyed, nor will We proceed against or prosecute him, except by the lawful judgment of his peers and by the law of the land."

—Magna Carta

King John signing the Magna Carta ▲

DBQ Document-Based Question

Why do you think this part of the Magna Carta is important?

The text of the Magna Carta was the work of many people, but the guiding force behind it was Stephen Langton, the archbishop of Canterbury.

Answer:
It guarantees the right of law to all people as well as the right to a trial by jury. Our legal system today guarantees the same rights.

Reading Check

Answer: It limited some of the king's powers, such as the power to tax.

Establishing Rights and Responsibilities Help students analyze the Magna Carta.
Ask: What two important principles did the Magna Carta establish? *(that people have rights and that the power of the government should be limited)* Who negotiated the Magna Carta with King John? *(the nobles)* According to this document, who had rights and duties? *(the king and the vassals, or nobles)* Who passes laws in the United States? *(officials elected by citizens)* Point out that democracies need active citizens, and that citizens often form groups to protect their communities and their rights. **L2**

CRITICAL THINKING ACTIVITY

What's a King to Do? Remind students that they have read about many strong and effective monarchs who were followed by weak and incompetent rulers. Have students name some monarchs who fit this description. *(Alfred, Charlemagne, Justinian, Constantine, Akbar [the Mogul ruler of India], Solomon, Qin Shihuangdi, Wudi, Alexander)* Separate students into groups and ask them to write a "Top Ten" list of advice these kings could have given to their successors in order to avoid the weakening or loss of the kingdom. Have groups share their lists with the class. **L2**

Reading Strategy

Comparing and Contrasting Ask students to compare the make-up of the English Parliament and the French Estates-General. *(Parliament: two houses, Lords and Commons; Estates-General: three houses, nobles, clergy, and townspeople and peasants)* **L1**

Reading Check

Answer: He reclaimed the territories of Normandy, Maine, Anjou, and Aquitane from the English. This gave French kings more land and wealth.

Using Geography Skills

Answers:

1. Kingdoms of England and France
2. Kingdoms of Navarre, Aragon, Castile, Leon, and the Muslims

Skills Practice

Ask: What river formed part of the northern border of the Byzantine Empire? *(Danube River)*

The Kingdom of France

Main Idea French kings called the Capetians conquered lands held by the English in western France and set up France's first parliament.

Reading Focus Has a poll ever been taken in your class? Read to find out how one French king found out what his people were thinking.

In A.D. 843 Charlemagne's empire was divided into three parts. The western part eventually became the kingdom of France. In A.D. 987 Frankish nobles chose Hugh Capet to be their king. Hugh was the first of the Capetian (kuh•PEE•shuhn) kings of France. The Capetians controlled the area around Paris (PAR•uhs), the capital. Many French nobles had more power than the kings did. This began to change when **Philip II** (FIH•luhp) became king of France.

Philip ruled from 1180 to 1223. When he took the throne, England's king ruled parts of western France. Philip went to war against England and conquered most of these territories. As a result, French kings gained more land and became more powerful.

Philip IV, called Philip the Fair, ruled from 1285 to 1314. In 1302 he met with representatives from the three estates, or classes, of French society. The first estate was the **clergy** (KLUHR•jee), or people who had been ordained as priests. Nobles made up the second estate, and townspeople and peasants were the third estate. This meeting began the Estates-General, France's first parliament. It was the first step in France toward representative government.

Reading Check **Describe** How did King Philip II bring power back to French kings?

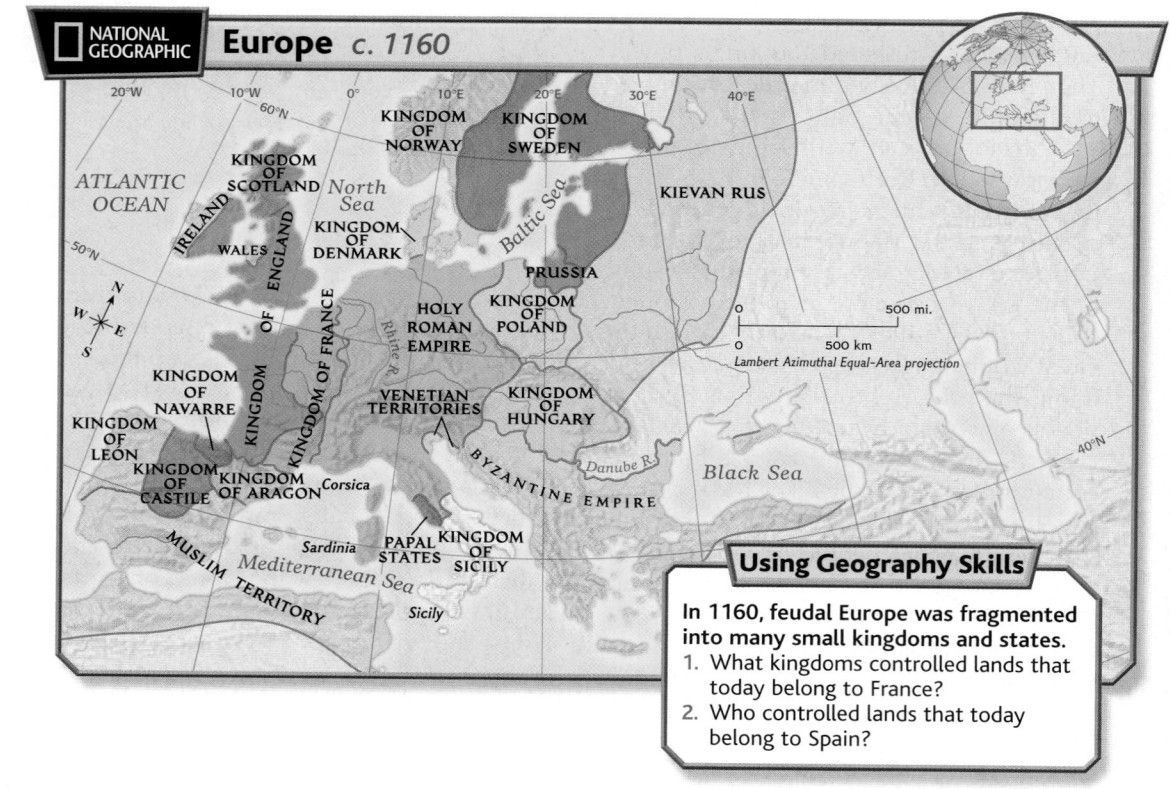

NATIONAL GEOGRAPHIC Europe c. 1160

Using Geography Skills

In 1160, feudal Europe was fragmented into many small kingdoms and states.
1. What kingdoms controlled lands that today belong to France?
2. Who controlled lands that today belong to Spain?

INTERDISCIPLINARY CONNECTIONS ACTIVITY

Art Have students investigate the famous Bayeux Tapestry, which tells the story of the Norman conquest of England. The 231-foot (70-m) long linen cloth is actually an embroidery, not a woven tapestry. It contains eight colors and more than 70 different scenes, ending with the retreat of Harold's army from the battlefield at Hastings. Have students use the Internet or other resources to find photographs of the tapestry, information about the controversies surrounding its origin, and its history. Have them share their research with the class. **L3**

Eastern Europe and Russia

Main Idea After the Mongols destroyed the Kievan state, the rulers of Moscow built a new Russian state headed by a czar.

Reading Focus Why do you think some of the cities in your state grew large while others stayed small? Read to learn how the cities of Kiev and Moscow grew to become the centers of large Slavic states.

About A.D. 500, a people called the Slavs organized villages in Eastern Europe. Each village was made up of families related to each other. The villagers shared their land, animals, tools, and seeds. Each family built its house partly underground. This kept the family warm during the cold winters.

In time, the Slavs divided into three major groups: the southern, western, and eastern Slavs. The southern Slavs became the Croats, Serbs, and Bulgarians. The western Slavs became the Poles, Czechs, and Slovaks. The eastern Slavs became the Ukrainians (yoo•KRAY•nee•uhnz), Belorussians (BEH•loh•RUH•shuhnz), and Russians (RUH•shuhnz).

By A.D. 600, the eastern Slavs controlled the land between the Carpathian Mountains and the Volga River. In the early Middle Ages, the eastern Slavs created farmland by chopping down the forests and then burning the trees to fertilize the soil. They planted barley, rye, and flax.

What Was the Kievan Rus?

In the late A.D. 700s, Vikings began moving into the Slavs' territory from the north. Over time, the Vikings became rulers of the Slavs. The Slavs called their Viking rulers the Rus. Over time, the Vikings and Slavs intermarried and blended into one people.

Around A.D. 900, a Viking leader named Oleg created a Rus state around the city of **Kiev** (KEE•EHF). Called the Kievan Rus, this state was really a group of small territories.

Ibn Fadlan Describes the Rus

In A.D. 921, the Muslim official Ibn Fadlan encountered the Rus while visiting a settlement on the Volga River.

"I have seen the Rūs as they came on their merchant journeys and encamped by the [Volga River]. I have never seen more perfect physical specimens, tall as date palms, blonde and ruddy; they wear neither [coats] nor caftans [long shirts], but the men wear a garment which covers one side of the body and leaves a hand free. . . . They build big houses of wood on the [Volga] shore, each holding ten to twenty persons more or less."

—Ibn Fadlān, *Risāla*

▲ Statue of a Rus leader

DBQ Document-Based Question

Of what occupation are the Rus that Ibn Fadlan describes?

The main ruler was the Grand Duke of Kiev. Local princes, rich merchants, and landowning nobles called boyars (boh•YAHRZ) helped him govern.

The rulers who came after Oleg increased the size of the Kievan Rus. In time, it reached from the Baltic Sea in the north to the Black Sea in the south. It stretched from the Danube River in the west to the Volga River in the east.

The growth of the Kievan Rus attracted missionaries from the Byzantine Empire. One Rus ruler, Vladimir, married the Byzantine emperor's sister. He became an Eastern Orthodox Christian and declared his people Eastern Orthodox.

CHAPTER 15 Medieval Europe   **539**

Primary Source

Although Ibn Fadlān found the Rus admirable physical specimens, the fastidious Muslim traveler was not impressed by their hygiene. "They are the filthiest of God's creatures," he wrote. "They wash their hands and faces every day in incredibly filthy water."

Answer:
They are merchants who travel on the river to trade.

CONNECTING ACROSS TIME

Today the ancient city of Kiev is the capital of the nation of Ukraine. This country of almost 50 million people gained its independence in 1991 with the breakup of the old Soviet Union. Have students look in an encyclopedia, in a world almanac, or on the Internet for basic information about Ukraine and share their findings with the class. **L2**

EXTENDING THE CONTENT

Orthodox Christianity in Kievan Rus There is a famous legend about Vladimir and his decision to bring Orthodox Christianity to Kievan Rus. The source of the story is an eleventh-century monk named Jacob. Jacob wrote that when Vladamir decided to renounce pagan gods, he sent messengers to investigate Roman Catholicism, Judaism, Islam, and Eastern Orthodox Christianity to find the most suitable new religion for him and his people. Vladamir chose Eastern Orthodoxy because of the incredible beauty of its worship service, which the messengers witnessed in Constantinople's Hagia Sophia. Whether or not the story is true, Vladamir's momentous decision prevented Roman Catholicism from spreading eastward and fixed his descendants in the orbit of Eastern Orthodoxy.

540

Using Geography Skills

Answers:

1. Moscow had grown mostly to the north and west, with some growth to the south and west.

2. 1505

Skills Practice

Ask: By what year had Moscow first acquired part of the Volga River? *(1389)*

CONNECTING ACROSS TIME

The Russian czar was not the only ruler who took his title from Caesar. Ask students if they know of others. *(The German emperor of the nineteenth and early twentieth centuries was called the kaiser, as were earlier German, Austrian, and Holy Roman emperors.)* **L1/ EL**

Reading Strategy

Summarizing Information Ask student pairs to summarize the achievements of the following early Russian rulers: Oleg, Vladimir, Alexander Nevsky, and Ivan the Great. **L2**

Reading Check

Answer: He defeated attacks from the west by Germans and Swedes. His son and his descendants became grand dukes of Moscow.

NATIONAL GEOGRAPHIC **Growth of Moscow**

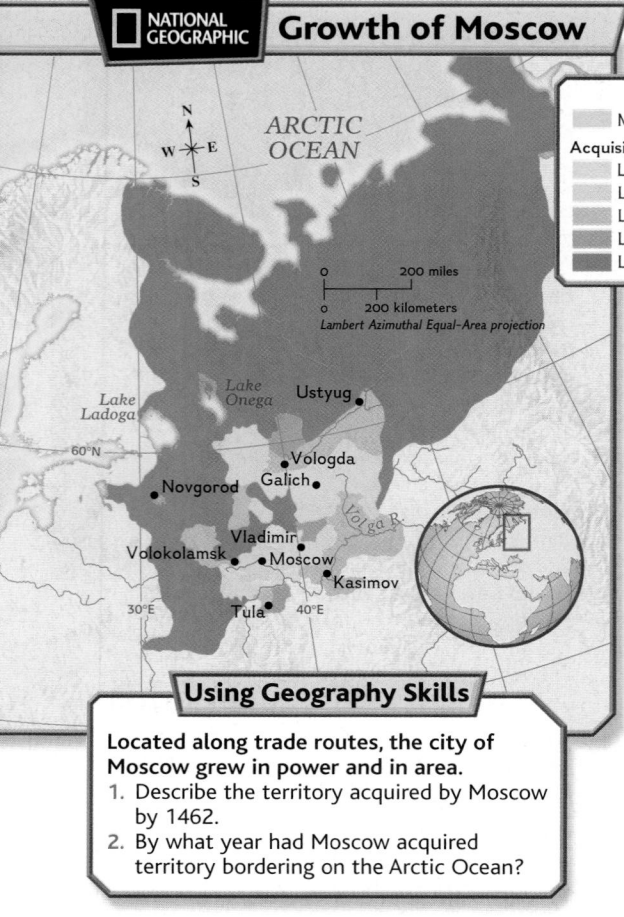

KEY
- Moscow, 1300
- **Acquisitions:**
- Land added by 1340
- Land added by 1389
- Land added by 1425
- Land added by 1462
- Land added by 1505

0   200 miles
0   200 kilometers
Lambert Azimuthal Equal-Area projection

Using Geography Skills

Located along trade routes, the city of Moscow grew in power and in area.

1. Describe the territory acquired by Moscow by 1462.
2. By what year had Moscow acquired territory bordering on the Arctic Ocean?

Kiev Falls to the Mongols About 1240, the Mongols swept into the Kievan Rus. The Slavs called the Mongols "Tatars" because one of the Mongol tribes was the Tata people. The Mongols destroyed nearly all the major cities and killed many people.

The only major city of the Kievan Rus that was spared was the northern city of Novgorod. Nonetheless, Novgorod's rulers as well as other Russian rulers, had to pay tribute to the khan, the Mongol leader, and accept the Mongols as their rulers.

Although Novgorod had been spared by the Mongols, it faced attacks from the west by Germans and Swedes. Led by

Alexander Nevsky, the Slavs of Novgorod defeated the Swedes and Germans. For his help in defending lands controlled by the Mongols, the Mongol khan rewarded Nevsky with the title of grand duke.

The Rise of Moscow As the Slavs recovered from the damage caused by the Mongols, the city of **Moscow** (MAHS•koh) began to grow. Moscow was located at the crossroads of several important trade routes. Alexander Nevsky's son Daniel and his descendants became grand dukes of Moscow.

The dukes of Moscow married women from the ruling families in other Slavic towns. They also fought wars to expand Moscow's territory. Moscow became even more important when it became the headquarters for the Russian branch of the Eastern Orthodox Church. When Ivan I, the Grand Duke of Moscow from 1328 to 1341, was given permission to collect taxes for the Mongols, Moscow grew even greater.

In 1462 Ivan III, known as Ivan the Great, became the grand duke. He married Sophia, the niece of the last Byzantine emperor. Afterward, Ivan began living in the style of an emperor. He had architects build fine palaces and large cathedrals in the Kremlin—the fortress at the center of Moscow. He even began calling himself czar. Czar was a shortened version of Caesar. In Russian, czar means emperor.

Ivan IV lived up to his title. In 1480 he finally ended Mongol rule over Moscow's territory. Then he expanded his territory to the north and west. When Ivan IV died in 1505, the Russians were well on the way toward building a vast empire.

Reading Check **Cause and Effect** Why was Alexander Nevsky important?

EXTENDING THE CONTENT

Hospitallers and Templars The Crusades gave rise to several orders of military monks. The Knights of Malta, also known as the Knights of St. John or the Hospitallers, were formed to care for sick pilgrims and crusaders in Jerusalem. Another group was the Knights Templar, which was founded in the Christian Kingdom of Jerusalem as a kind of private army to protect pilgrims. This group grew very powerful as it became involved in banking, transportation, and land ownership. Others grew jealous of its widespread influence. In the early 1300s, enemies of the Templars succeeded in imprisoning them, seizing their lands, and burning the head of the order at the stake.

The Crusades

Main Idea European crusaders captured Jerusalem but were later driven out by the Muslims.

Reading Focus Have you ever put all your energy into making something important happen? Read to learn why Europeans thought capturing the city of Jerusalem was important.

During the Middle Ages, the Byzantine Empire in the East came under attack. In 1071 an army of Muslim Turks defeated the Byzantines and seized control of most of the Byzantine lands in Asia Minor.

The Byzantine emperor did not have enough money or troops to drive out the Turks. In desperation, he asked the pope to help him defend his Christian empire against the Muslim invaders.

In 1095 Pope Urban II spoke before a large crowd in eastern France. He asked Europe's lords to launch a crusade, or holy war, against the Muslim Turks. He urged them to capture Jerusalem and free the Holy Land where Jesus had lived from the Muslims. The pope explained why the crusade was needed:

> 66 Jerusalem is the navel [center] of the world. . . . This is the land which the Redeemer [Jesus] of mankind illuminated by his coming. . . . This royal city, situated in the middle of the world, is now held captive by his enemies. . . . It looks and hopes for freedom; it begs unceasingly that you will come to its aid. 99
>
> —Pope Urban II,
> as quoted in *The Discoverers*

As the pope spoke, the excited crowd cried out, "It is the will of God, it is the will of God." The Crusades had begun.

Early Victories Several thousand soldiers on horseback and as many as ten thousand on foot headed east. Many of them wore a red cross on their clothes as a sign of their obedience to the pope's call.

In 1098 the First Crusade captured Antioch in Syria. From there, the crusaders entered Palestine, reaching Jerusalem in 1099. After a bloody fight, they stormed the city, killing Muslims, Jews, and Christians alike.

In the painting above, Pope Urban II calls for a crusade against the Muslims. At right, the crusaders attack Jerusalem with siege towers and catapults. *What was the pope's goal for the crusade?*

CHAPTER 15   Medieval Europe   **541**

Using Word Parts Tell students that the word *crusade* comes from the Latin word meaning "cross." Ask them to speculate on the connection between the battles to conquer Jerusalem and the cross. *(Crusaders wanted to undergo hardship, or "carry the cross," to regain the Holy Land for Christianity.)* **L2**

Reading Support L1/ EL

Assign **Guided Reading Activity 15–3** to help students organize the information in the section.

More About the Art

The catapults shown in the illustration to the right threw heavy stones against fortress walls. The arm was pulled back tightly, using ropes made of horsehair or another material, and then suddenly released. The arm shot forward, catapulting the rock at the target.

Caption Answer: to return Jerusalem to Christian rule

COOPERATIVE LEARNING ACTIVITY

Service Learning The Crusades led to centuries of conflict between Christians and Muslims. Today, current events have also led to increased tensions between these two religious groups. Ask students to find in your community a group or organization that is working to increase understanding and lessen conflict between people of different religions or ethnic backgrounds. Have them find out about volunteer opportunities with such a group and work on a project sponsored by the organization. Ask students who are doing a service learning project to make a report to the class. **L2**

Using Geography Skills

Answers:

1. Marseille, Genoa, Venice, and Constantinople

2. from England, France, and the Holy Roman Empire over land and sea to the Holy Land

Skills Practice

Ask: About how far did the soldiers of the First Crusade travel to reach Jerusalem from Clermont? *(about 2,000 miles, or 3,200 km)*

❸ ASSESS

Assign Section 3 Review as homework or as an in-class activity.

⊛ Have students use the **Interactive Tutor Self-Assessment CD-ROM** to review the section.

Assessment L2

Assign **Section 3 Quiz** to assess mastery of the material found in the section.

Reading Support L1/ EL

Assign **Reading Essentials and Study Guide 15–3** to help students review section material.

NATIONAL GEOGRAPHIC

The Crusades 1096–1204

KEY
- ▢ Christian lands, c. 1100
- ▢ Muslim lands, c. 1100
- ← First Crusade, 1096–1099
- ← Second Crusade, 1147–1149
- ← Third Crusade, 1189–1192

500 mi.
500 km
Lambert Azimuthal Equal-Area projection

Using Geography Skills

Crusaders from all across Europe traveled overland and by sea to fight in the Holy Land.
1. From what port cities did warriors on the First Crusade leave to travel to the Holy Land?
2. Describe the route of the Third Crusade.

◀ Medieval painting of a battle during the Crusades

Having driven the Muslims from the region, the crusaders created four states: the Kingdom of Jerusalem in Palestine, the county of Edessa and the principality of Antioch in Asia Minor, and the county of Tripoli where Lebanon is located today. These four states were surrounded by Muslims and depended on the Italian cities of Genoa, Pisa, and Venice for supplies.

The Muslims fought back, however, and in 1144 they captured Edessa. In response, European rulers sent another crusade to regain the lost lands. This Second Crusade, however, was a total failure.

In 1174 a Muslim named **Saladin** (SA•luh•DEEN) became ruler of Egypt. He united Muslims and declared war against the Christian states the crusaders had built. Saladin proved to be a brilliant commander. He defeated the Christians and captured Jerusalem in 1187.

The fall of Jerusalem led to the Third Crusade. Emperor Frederick of the Holy Roman Empire, King Richard I of England,

542   **CHAPTER 15**   **Medieval Europe**

CRITICAL THINKING ACTIVITY

Drawing Conclusions Ask students to discuss this question: Could the crusaders ever have achieved their goal of permanently driving the Muslims from the Holy Land and establishing a strong Christian kingdom there? Why or why not? Ask students to give reasons for their conclusions. *(Students will probably mention some of the following challenges: the Holy Land was too far from Europe; the Turks and other Muslims were too powerful; the unity of the crusaders was too fragile; and Europeans would not want to live in the Middle East and would return home.)* **L2**

(known as Richard the Lion-Hearted), and King Philip II of France gathered their armies and headed east to fight Saladin.

The Third Crusade had many problems. Frederick drowned crossing a river. The English and French arrived by sea and captured a coastal city but were unable to push inland. After Philip went home, Richard secured a small territory along the coast. He then agreed to a truce after Saladin promised that Christian pilgrims could travel to Jerusalem in safety.

Around 1200, Pope Innocent III called for a Fourth Crusade. Merchants from Venice used the crusade to weaken their trading rival, the Byzantine Empire. They convinced the crusaders to attack Constantinople, the Byzantine capital. For three days, the crusaders burned and looted the city. The attack shocked Western Europeans and weakened the Byzantines.

Six more crusades were launched over the next 60 years, but they achieved very little. Gradually, the Muslims conquered all of the territory they had lost to the First Crusade. In 1291, a bit more than 200 years after the First Crusade had set out, the last Christian city fell to Muslim forces.

The Crusades affected Europe in two ways. They increased trade between Europe and the Middle East, and they helped break down feudalism. Nobles who joined the Crusades sold their lands and freed their serfs. This reduced their power and helped kings build stronger central governments. Kings also began taxing the new trade with the Middle East. These taxes helped them build stronger kingdoms in Western Europe.

Reading Check **Compare and Contrast**
What did the First Crusade accomplish? What did the Third Crusade accomplish?

Section 3 Review

Reading Summary

Review the Main Ideas

- The English king granted rights to his people in the Magna Carta and established a parliament.
- French kings regained French territories from the English and, like the English, created a parliament.
- Russia had its beginnings in the territories of the Kievan Rus and Moscow.
- West Europeans launched crusades to capture Jerusalem and Palestine from the Muslims.

What Did You Learn?

1. What is the significance of the Battle of Hastings?
2. What groups developed from the three major divisions of Slavs in Eastern Europe?

Critical Thinking

3. **Organizing Information** Draw a chart to list the kings of England and France and their achievements.

King/Country	Achievements

4. **Evaluate** What was the importance of the Magna Carta?

5. **Summarize** Describe the development of England's Parliament, and discuss its role in changing government.

6. **Explain** Why did cities such as Venice flourish as a result of the Crusades?

7. **Expository Writing** Write an essay describing how the Crusades affected feudalism.

Ask students to research the life of one of the leaders of the Third Crusade, or of Saladin. Have them share their findings with the class. **L3**

Answer: The First Crusade led to the capture of Jerusalem and the rise of four Christian states in the Middle East. The Third Crusade secured only a small strip of land in the Holy Land.

History Online

To help students understand section material, have them visit **Study Central™** at jat.glencoe.com

RETEACH

Have students list three important facts about each nation described in this section. **L1**

4 CLOSE

Ask students to evaluate the positive and negative aspects of the Crusades. **L2**

SECTION 3 REVIEW ANSWERS

1. William the Conqueror defeated Harold Godwinson for control of England.
2. southern Slavs (Croats, Serbs, and Bulgarians); western Slavs: (Poles, Czechs, and Slovaks); eastern Slavs (Ukrainians, Belorussians, and Russians)
3. Alfred: united the Anglo-Saxon kingdoms; William: took census in England; John: signed Magna Carta; Philip II: regained territory from the English; Philip IV: met with the Estates-General
4. It limited the king's powers.
5. Parliament included the House of Lords and the House of Commons. Parliament was a major step toward representative government.
6. Crusaders depended on those cities for supplies.
7. Essays should include details about the Crusades and the decline of feudalism.

① FOCUS

SECTION OVERVIEW

This section focuses on the medieval Catholic Church, the new universities, and developments in art and architecture.

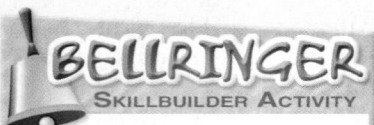

BELLRINGER
SKILLBUILDER ACTIVITY

✍ Project **Daily Focus Skills Transparency 15–4** and have students answer questions. Discuss their responses.

Get Ready to Read!

Preteaching Vocabulary: Tell students that *Semite* is an old word referring to the Jewish people. It comes from the belief that the Jews (and Arabs) are descended from Shem, the oldest son of Noah, who built the ark mentioned in the Bible. Based on that knowledge, ask students what they think *anti-Semitism* might mean.

Answers to Graphic: Romanesque: barrel vaults, huge pillars, thick walls, windows let in little light; Gothic: ribbed vaults and pointed arches, flying buttresses, thinner walls, stained-glass windows; Both: large churches, built of stone

Section 4

The Church and Society

Get Ready to Read!

What's the Connection?
Kings and popes had a powerful effect on the lives of medieval people, as did religion. In this section, you will learn how religion in medieval Europe shaped its culture.

Focusing on the Main Ideas
- The Catholic Church played an important role in medieval Europe and used its power to uphold its teachings. *(page 545)*
- Church and government leaders supported learning and the arts in medieval Europe. *(page 549)*

Locating Places
Bologna (buh•LOH•nyuh)

Meeting People
Francis of Assisi
  (FRAN•suhs uhv uh•SIHS•ee)
Thomas Aquinas
  (TAH•muhs uh•KWY•nuhs)

Building Your Vocabulary
mass
heresy (HEHR•uh•see)
anti-Semitism
  (AN•tih•SEH•muh•TIH•zuhm)
theology (thee•AH•luh•jee)
scholasticism
  (skuh•LAS•tuh•SIH•zuhm)
vernacular (vuhr•NA•kyuh•luhr)

Reading Strategy
Organizing Information Complete a Venn diagram to show the similarities and differences between Romanesque and Gothic cathedrals.

Romanesque Cathedrals   Gothic Cathedrals

NATIONAL GEOGRAPHIC When & Where?

SCANDINAVIA
ENGLAND
HOLY ROMAN EMPIRE
FRANCE
Clermont•
SPAIN
•Rome
ITALY
Jerusalem•

1200 — 1250 — 1300

1209
Francis of Assisi founds Franciscan order

1233
Catholic Church sets up the Inquisition

c. 1267
Thomas Aquinas begins writing *Summa Theologica*

SECTION RESOURCES

📁 **Reproducible Masters**
- Reproducible Lesson Plan 15–4
- Daily Lecture and Discussion Notes 15–4
- Vocabulary Activity 15–4
- Active Reading Note-Taking Guide 15–4
- Guided Reading Activity 15–4
- Section Quiz 15–4
- Reading Essentials and Study Guide 15–4

✍ **Transparencies**
- Daily Focus Skills Transparency 15–4

Multimedia
- Interactive Tutor Self-Assessment CD-ROM
- ExamView® Pro Testmaker CD-ROM
- Presentation Plus! CD-ROM
- Glencoe BookLink CD-ROM

Religion and Society

Main Idea The Catholic Church played an important role in medieval Europe and used its power to uphold its teachings.

Reading Focus Have you ever noticed how many things in society have been influenced by religion? What examples can you give? Read to learn about the important role religion played in the lives of people living in the Middle Ages.

Between 1050 and 1150, a strong wave of religious feeling swept across Western Europe. As a result, more monasteries were built, and new religious orders, or groups of priests, monks, and nuns, were started.

New Religious Orders The Cistercian (sihs•TUHR•shuhn) order was founded in 1098. Cistercian monks farmed the land as well as worshiped and prayed. They developed many new farming techniques that helped Europeans grow more crops.

The most famous Cistercian monk was Bernard of Clairvaux (klar•VOH). Bernard helped promote the Second Crusade. He also advised the pope and defended the poor against the rich.

Many women entered convents between A.D. 1000 and 1200. Most of them were from noble families. They included widows and women unable or unwilling to marry. Women who were scholars found convents ideal places for study and writing.

Most educated women in medieval Europe were nuns. One famous woman was Hildegard of Bingen (HIHL•duh•GAHRD uhv BIHNG•uhn). She headed a convent in Germany and composed music for the Church. Her work is remarkable because at that time, men wrote most church music.

▲ This religious painting from the wall of a church in Italy depicts the pope and other Christian leaders, a number of saints, and Jesus ruling over all.
How did Cistercian monks aid European society?

545

② TEACH

Activating Prior Knowledge Have students use their prior knowledge about medieval women to write a recruitment brochure for a convent. Have them include reasons why convent life might appeal to women. **L2**

Daily Lecture and Discussion Notes 15–4

Use **Daily Lecture and Discussion Notes 15–4** for an outline of key concepts found in the section.

More About the Art

The painting contains a visual pun. Santa Maria Novella was founded by Dominican priests. In Latin, however, the words *Domini canes* mean "dogs of God." The artist included the dogs in the painting because the Dominicans were known for hunting heresy like hunting dogs chase their prey.

Caption Answer: developed new farming techniques

Reading Strategy · READING THE TEXT

Predicting A good way for readers to interact with the text is to make informed guesses about what they are going to read. They should use previous knowledge and the information they get from previewing to create expectations about what the remaining text will include. This expectation creates a purpose for reading and generates interest. Have students preview the section, then make three informed guesses regarding what they will be reading. Have them keep their predictions and return to them as they read the section, adjusting them if necessary as they encounter new information. **L2**

- Howarth, Sarah. *The Middle Ages.* An introduction to medieval daily life.

② TEACH

Oral Reports Have students research and report to the class on more recent outbreaks of plague and other epidemic diseases, for example, the influenza epidemic of 1919 or the Ebola outbreak in Africa in the late twentieth century. **L2**

Daily Lecture and Discussion Notes 15-5

Use **Daily Lecture and Discussion Notes 15-5** for an outline of key concepts found in the section.

Reading Support L1/ EL

Use **Vocabulary Activity 15-5** to review important terms in the section.

Using Geography Skills

Answers:
1. 1349
2. by land and sea trade

Skills Practice

Ask: What major cities in China were affected by the plague? (*Xian, Beijing, and Hangzhou*)

The Black Death

Main Idea A terrible plague, known as the Black Death, swept through Europe in the 1300s, killing millions.

Reading Focus Have you ever been given a shot to prevent the flu or to protect you from another disease? Read to learn what happened in Europe before modern medicine could control contagious diseases.

The Middle Ages in Europe reached a high point during the 1200s. In the 1300s, however, disaster struck. A terrible **plague** (PLAYG), known as the Black Death, swept across Europe and Asia. A plague is a disease that spreads quickly and kills many people. Most scientists think the Black Death was bubonic plague—a disease caused by a type of bacteria carried by fleas. These fleas infested black rats, and in the Middle Ages, these rats were everywhere.

The Black Death probably began somewhere in the Gobi, a desert in central Asia. It had been around for centuries, but in the 1300s, it began to spread farther and more quickly than ever before. Scientists are still not sure why this happened.

Historians believe the Mongol Empire was partly responsible for the plague spreading so fast. The empire covered all the land from Eastern Europe through central Asia to China. The Mongols opened up trade between China, India, the Middle East, and Europe. They encouraged the use of the Silk Road and other trade routes.

By the early 1300s, more goods were being shipped across central Asia than ever before. This made it possible for the Black Death to spread rapidly, as caravans infested with rats carried it from city to city.

The first outbreak took place in China in 1331. It erupted there again in 1353. The

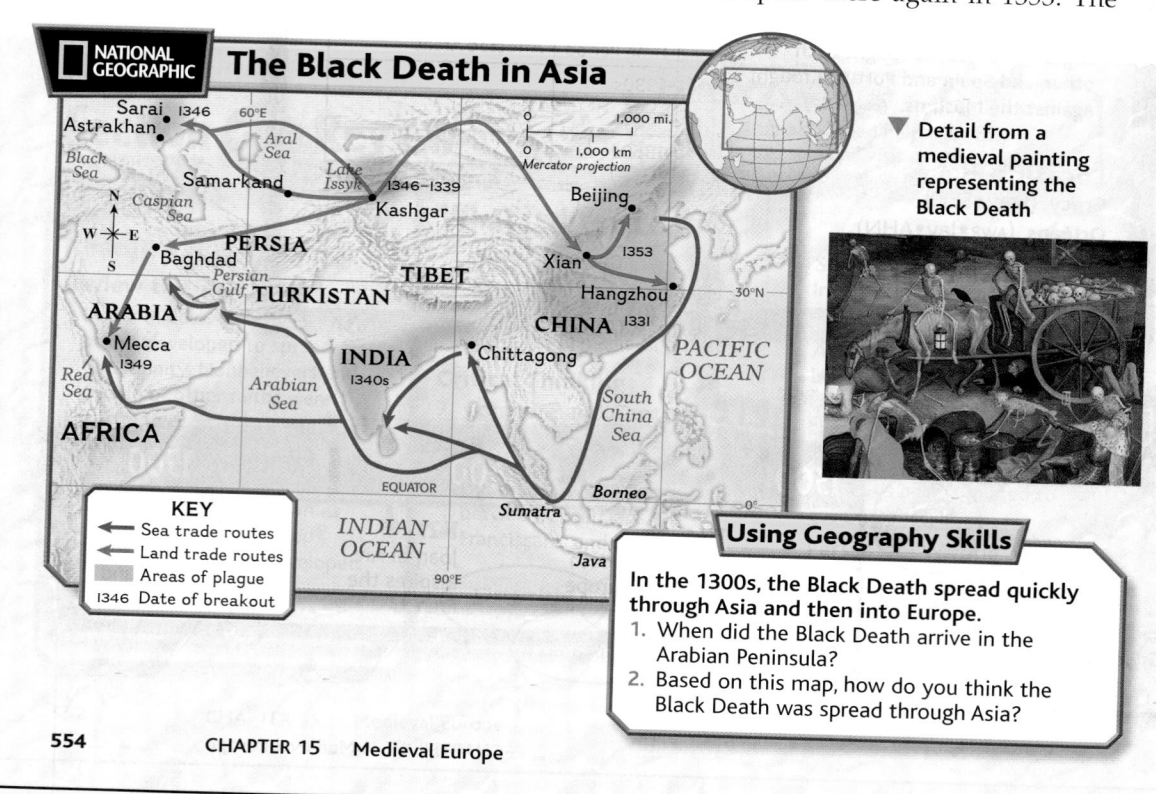

NATIONAL GEOGRAPHIC

The Black Death in Asia

Detail from a medieval painting representing the Black Death

KEY
← Sea trade routes
← Land trade routes
▨ Areas of plague
1346 Date of breakout

Using Geography Skills

In the 1300s, the Black Death spread quickly through Asia and then into Europe.
1. When did the Black Death arrive in the Arabian Peninsula?
2. Based on this map, how do you think the Black Death was spread through Asia?

554   CHAPTER 15   Medieval Europe

Reading Strategy ▷ **READING THE TEXT**

Connecting Ask students to connect the information they read in this section to events in their daily lives and to current events they read about in other sources like magazines, newspapers, and the Internet. Making such connections increases their reading enjoyment and their understanding of the ideas in the text. For example, ask students what current events might affect people the way the Black Death did, or what kind of events similar to the *Reconquista* are taking place today. You might also ask them to describe situations from their own lives that have affected them the way the events in this section affected medieval Europeans. **L2**

disease killed between 40 and 60 million people, cutting China's population nearly in half. The disease appeared in India in the 1340s and reached Makkah, deep inside Muslim lands, in 1349. In the meantime, it also spread to Europe.

The Black Death appeared in Europe in 1346 at the city of Caffa on the Black Sea. The city had been under attack by Mongols when the plague erupted. The Mongols, with their troops dying, called off the attack. In anger they also threw bodies of infected soldiers into the city.

Caffa was a trade colony controlled by Italian merchants from the city of Genoa. Their ships carried the plague to Sicily in October 1347. From there it spread into Europe. By the end of 1349, it had spread through France and Germany and had arrived in England. By 1351, it had reached Scandinavia, Eastern Europe, and Russia.

As many as 38 million Europeans—nearly one out of every two people—died of the Black Death between 1347 and 1351.

The death of so many people in the 1300s turned Europe's economy upside down. Trade declined and wages rose sharply because workers were few and in demand. At the same time, fewer people meant less demand for food, and food prices fell.

Landlords found they had to pay workers more and charge lower rents. Some peasants bargained with their lords to pay rent instead of owing services. This meant that they were no longer serfs. In this way, the plague, like the Crusades, helped to weaken the feudal system and change European society.

Reading Check **Identify** How many Europeans died of the plague between 1347 and 1351?

CURRICULUM CONNECTION

Literature
Many folklorists believe that the popular nursery rhyme "Ring Around the Rosie" is about the plague. The first line refers to the round pink rash that is an early sign of the disease. Posies, or bouquets of flowers, were worn to disguise the terrible smell of the infection. The third line refers to the burning of infected corpses. Finally, almost everyone infected with the plague eventually died, or fell down.

Writing Activity

Have students write a newspaper article describing the arrival or effects of the plague in a medieval city.

Reading Check

Answer: about 38 million people

Using Geography Skills

Answers:
1. Greece, Italy, Mediterranean islands
2. 1351

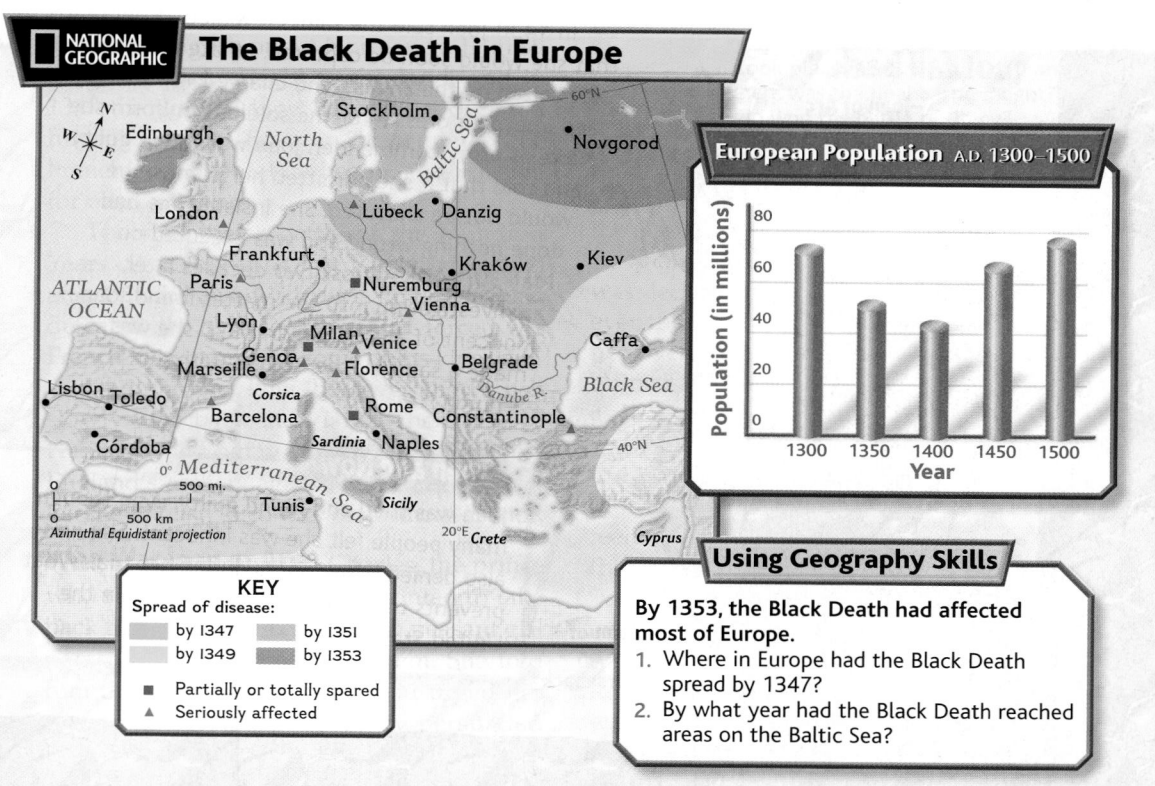
The Black Death in Europe

European Population A.D. 1300–1500

KEY
Spread of disease:
by 1347
by 1349
by 1351
by 1353
■ Partially or totally spared
▲ Seriously affected

Using Geography Skills
By 1353, the Black Death had affected most of Europe.
1. Where in Europe had the Black Death spread by 1347?
2. By what year had the Black Death reached areas on the Baltic Sea?

DIFFERENTIATED INSTRUCTION

Logical/Mathematical: Have students use their math skills to clarify the devastating impact of the Black Death on the population of Europe. Ask them to use the figure one-third (the estimated percentage of Europeans who died during the plague) and apply it to your class, school, community, state, and country to determine the number of people who would die at each level to equal the devastation of the plague.

English Learners: Ask students to read and summarize an encyclopedia article about the Black Death.

Gifted and Talented: Have students create a visual representation, such as a chart or graph, of the numbers of people who died from the Black Death.

ENRICH

Ask students to research the art and culture of Islamic Spain. **L3**

Answer: The French wanted to drive the English from their holdings in France, especially after England's King Edward III declared himself France's rightful ruler.

To help students understand section material, have them visit **Study Central™** at jat.glencoe.com

RETEACH

Ask students to work with a partner to review the important people and vocabulary words for this section. **L1/ EL**

④ CLOSE

Ask students to summarize the ways that the Black Death, the Hundred Years' War, and the *Reconquista* affected Europe. **L2**

558

Spain and Portugal Fight the Muslims

During the Middle Ages, Muslims ruled most of Spain and Portugal. These two lands make up the Iberian Peninsula. Most of the peninsula's people, however, were Christians. Some were also Jews.

The Muslims developed a rich culture in Spain and Portugal. They built beautiful mosques and palaces, such as the Alhambra in the southern kingdom of Granada. They also founded schools where Muslims, Jews, and Christians studied together. Most Christians, however, opposed Muslim rule. Their struggle to take back the Iberian Peninsula was called the *Reconquista* (RAY•kohn•KEES•tuh), or "reconquest."

By the 1200s, the Christians had set up three kingdoms: Portugal in the west, Castile in the center, and Aragon on the Mediterranean coast. Over the next 200 years, the Muslims slowly lost ground, until all that remained was Granada in the south.

In 1469 Princess **Isabella of Castile** married Prince **Ferdinand of Aragon.** Within 10 years, they became king and queen and joined their lands into one country called Spain. Ferdinand and Isabella wanted all of Spain to be Catholic. They turned first to the Jews. To escape persecution, some Jews became Christians. Ferdinand and Isabella, however, believed many still secretly practiced Judaism. So they set up the Spanish Inquisition.

The Spanish Inquisition tried and tortured thousands of people charged with heresy. In 1492 Ferdinand and Isabella told Jews to convert or leave Spain. Most left the country.

Next the king and queen turned to the Muslims. In 1492 Spain's armies conquered Granada. Ten years later, Muslims had to convert or leave. Most left Spain for North Africa.

✓ **Reading Check** **Cause and Effect** What caused the Hundred Years' War?

History Online

Study Central™ Need help with the material in this section? Visit jat.glencoe.com

Section ⑤ Review

Reading Summary
Review the (Main Ideas)

- A plague, known as the Black Death, killed millions of people in Europe and Asia and greatly changed Europe's economy and society.

- Wars between England and France weakened those countries' economies, and Spain became a united Catholic country.

What Did You Learn?

1. How was the Black Death spread?
2. Who was Joan of Arc, and what role did she play in the Hundred Years' War?

Critical Thinking

3. **Understanding Cause and Effect** Draw a diagram like the one below. Fill in some of the effects of the Black Death on Europe.

```
┌─────────┐     ┌──────────┐
│   The   │────▶│          │
│  Black  │────▶│          │
│  Death  │────▶│          │
└─────────┘     └──────────┘
```

4. **Analyze** How did the Hundred Years' War affect the countries involved?
5. **Summarize** Describe the history of Spain and Portugal during the Middle Ages.
6. **Conclude** Do you think the removal of the Jews and Muslims from Spain was a wise policy? Explain your answer.
7. **Reading** **Asking Questions** Write three question that Charles might have asked Joan of Arc to determine if he would support her efforts.

558   CHAPTER 15   Medieval Europe

SECTION 5 REVIEW ANSWERS

1. bacteria carried by fleas on rats, which then carried disease on caravans and ships
2. a peasant girl whose faith and leadership led French soldiers to victories
3. 38 million deaths; decrease of trade; feudalism weakened
4. France united under strong central government; England affected by economic weakness and civil war
5. Muslim rule; Christian *Reconquista* to gain back lands; three kingdoms—Portugal, Castile, and Aragon;
   Spain united under Ferdinand and Isabella
6. Answers will vary. Students may note that diversity would have led to a rich culture.
7. Answers will vary but should focus on motives of Charles and Joan.

Chapter 15 Reading Review

Section 1 — The Early Middle Ages

Vocabulary
- fjord
- missionary
- excommunicate
- concordat

Focusing on the Main Ideas
- Geography influenced where medieval Europeans settled and what they did. *(page 513)*
- The Franks, Angles, and Saxons of Western Europe built new societies and defended them against Muslims, Magyars, and Vikings. *(page 514)*
- The Catholic Church spread Christianity through Western Europe. *(page 519)*

Section 2 — Feudalism

Vocabulary
- feudalism
- vassal
- fief
- knight
- serf
- guild

Focusing on the Main Ideas
- Feudalism developed in Europe in the Middle Ages. It was based on landowning, loyalty, and the power of armored knights on horseback. *(page 523)*
- Knights followed a code of chivalry and lived in castles, while peasants lived in simple houses and worked hard all year long. *(page 526)*
- Increased trade led to the growth of towns and cities and the rise of guilds and city governments. *(page 528)*

Section 3 — Kingdoms and Crusades

Vocabulary
- grand jury
- trial jury
- clergy

Focusing on the Main Ideas
- England developed a system in which the king's power was limited by Parliament. *(page 535)*
- French kings called the Capetians conquered lands held by the English in western France and set up France's first parliament. *(page 538)*
- After the Mongols destroyed the Kievan state, the rulers of Moscow built a new Russian state headed by a czar. *(page 539)*
- European crusaders captured Jerusalem but were later driven out by the Muslims. *(page 541)*

Section 4 — The Church and Society

Vocabulary
- mass
- heresy
- anti-Semitism
- theology
- scholasticism
- vernacular

Focusing on the Main Ideas
- The Catholic Church played an important role in medieval Europe and used its power to uphold its teachings. *(page 545)*
- Church and government leaders supported learning and the arts in medieval Europe. *(page 549)*

Section 5 — The Late Middle Ages

Vocabulary
- plague
- *Reconquista*

Focusing on the Main Ideas
- A terrible plague, known as the Black Death, swept through Europe in the 1300s, killing millions. *(page 554)*
- Western Europe was devastated by war in the 1300s and 1400s as England and France fought each other, and Spain and Portugal fought against the Muslims. *(page 557)*

559

CHAPTER 15 REVIEW

PREVIEW/REVIEW

Vocabulary Activity Have students create a quiz using 10 of the terms and then exchange quizzes with a partner. Have them review their quizzes together.

- **Vocabulary PuzzleMaker CD-ROM**
- **Interactive Tutor Self-Assessment CD-ROM**

CONDENSE

- Chapter 15 **Guided Reading Activities**
- **StudentWorks Plus™ CD-ROM (with Audio Program)**

RETEACH

- **Differentiated Instruction Activity 15**
- Chapter 15 *Reading Essentials and Study Guide*

CHAPTER CULMINATING ACTIVITY

Have students finish the Chapter Culminating Activity from page 508D.

Suggestions for rubrics may be found in the *Quizzes, Tests, and Authentic Assessment (with Rubrics)* booklet.

Reading Strategy — READ TO WRITE

Short Story Ask students to write a short story based on an event in this chapter, such as the Viking raids, Crusades, Black Death, or another event that captures their imagination. Have them include details to make their works lively and accurate.

- **L1** students should include one or two details in their stories, which should be adequately organized and reasonably creative.
- **L2** students should include several appropriate details in their stories, which should be adequately organized and reasonably creative; productions should attempt grammar mastery.
- **L3** students should include many appropriate details in their stories, which should be well-organized, creative, and grammatically correct.

Chapter
15 Assessment and Activities

Review Vocabulary

1. d	**4.** c
2. a	**5.** f
3. e	**6.** b

Review Main Ideas

7. Vikings, Magyars, Muslims
8. helped in the growth of a new civilization
9. owning land
10. growth of towns and cities and rise of guilds and city governments
11. Magna Carta, Parliament; Estates-General
12. Christians and Muslims; control of Jerusalem
13. preaching, Inquisition, expelled Jews and Muslims
14. more wealth; support by church and government
15. plague that killed nearly one of every two Europeans; it changed Europe's economy and weakened feudalism.
16. England and France; Spain and Portugal against Muslims

Critical Thinking

17. heavy wheeled plow with iron plowshare; horse collar for horses plowing; watermills and windmills to grind more grain; increased farmland by drainage and three-field crop rotation

560

Review Vocabulary

Match the word in the first column with its definition in the second column.

___ 1. fief   **a.** worked their own land and a lord's land

___ 2. serf   **b.** the study of religion and God

___ 3. concordat   **c.** people ordained as priests

___ 4. clergy   **d.** land granted to a vassal

___ 5. heresy   **e.** agreement between the pope and the ruler of a country

___ 6. theology   **f.** a belief different from Church teachings

Review Main Ideas

Section 1 • The Early Middle Ages
7. Which peoples invaded Europe in the Middle Ages?
8. How did the Catholic Church affect medieval Europe?

Section 2 • Feudalism
9. What was the basis for wealth and power in medieval Europe?

Review
Reading Skill — Questioning
Just Ask

19. Read the passage from page 525. Write six questions that you might ask about it. Use a different question starter for each question: *who, what, when, where, how,* and *why.*

> During the Middle Ages, Europeans invented new technology that helped increase the amount of crops they could grow. Perhaps the most important was a heavy wheeled plow with an iron blade. It easily turned over Western Europe's dense clay soils.

To review this skill, see pages 510–511.

---

10. What was the result of increased trade?

Section 3 • Kingdoms and Crusades
11. What changes in England and France were steps toward representative government?
12. Which groups were at war with each other in the Crusades? For what were they fighting?

Section 4 • The Church and Society
13. How did the Catholic Church use its power to uphold its teachings?
14. Why did learning and the arts flourish in medieval Europe?

Section 5 • The Late Middle Ages
15. What was the Black Death, and how did it change Europe?
16. Which European nations were at war during the 1300s and 1400s?

Critical Thinking

17. **Cause and Effect** What improvements in farming led to an increase in the production of food?
18. **Compare** What did Alfred the Great and William the Conqueror succeed in doing?

---

18. Both united England. Albert drove out the Vikings, and William united his Norman culture with that of the English.

Reading Skill

19. Each of the six student questions should open with a different question starter: *who, what, when, where, how,* and *why.*

Geography Skills

20. the Loire River
21. Answers will vary. Students should note that the English held more land, the French had won more battles, and the English had a geographical advantage because of the English Channel.
22. The French attacked those areas to regain lost land.

Geography Skills

Study the map below and answer the following questions.

20. **Place** On which river was the battle of Orléans fought?

21. **Interaction** Which rival do you think had an advantage at the point shown on the map? Consider the battles, amount of land held, natural advantages, and so on.

22. **Location** Why were most battle sites near the English Channel?

NATIONAL GEOGRAPHIC **Hundred Years' War**

KEY
- English lands c. 1400
- French lands c. 1400
- ✴ English victory
- ✴ French victory

London

English Channel
Formigny 1450
Crécy 1346
Paris
Seine R.
Agincourt 1415
Orléans 1429
Loire R.

0   200 mi.
0   200 km
Lambert Azimuthal Equal-Area projection

ATLANTIC OCEAN

Bordeaux 1453

Rhône R.

50°N   0°

Read to Write

23. **Script Writing** Suppose you are living in a small medieval town. Suddenly, the people of your town begin dying from the plague. You and your family have to decide whether to stay in the town or leave. Write a dialogue between you, family members, and perhaps some neighbors. The dialogue should give the advantages and disadvantages of both actions and should show the family reaching a decision about what to do.

24. **Using Your FOLDABLES** Discuss as a class why the events of medieval Europe occurred. Then choose one major event from your foldable, and write a paragraph that predicts how history would have been different if that event had not occurred.

Using Technology

25. **Modeling** Do research to find out more about the parts of a manor and its general layout. (For example, you know that the castle of the lord and lady was at the center of the manor.) Then work with your classmates to create a computer drawing or model of a manor.

Linking Past and Present

26. **Comparing** Describe how present-day universities compare to medieval ones, such as those in Bologna, Paris, and Oxford. In your description, explain what it would be like to have to learn without the use of books.

Primary Source Analyze

King Louis IX asked the following of his vassals.

"All vassals of the king are bound to appear before him when he shall summon them, and to serve him at their own expense for forty days and forty nights, with as many knights as each one owes."

—King Louis IX, "Legal Rules for Military Service"

DBQ Document-Based Questions

27. Did knights directly serve the king and appear when he called them?

28. What do you think happened if the king needed the vassals and knights for more than 40 days and nights?

Have students visit the Web site at jat.glencoe.com to review Chapter 15 and take the **Self-Check Quiz.**

Linking Past and Present

26. Student answers will vary. Universities today: books plentiful; computers and other new technologies available; people of all backgrounds can attend; financial help provided.

Primary Source

27. No; they served their lords, who were the king's vassals. When the king summoned his vassals, each vassal summoned his knights.

28. Answers will vary. The king could ask them to remain, but they were not bound to do so unless the king took over the expenses.

Bonus Question

Ask: Do you think the unity that the Catholic Church brought to most of Europe in the Middle Ages was a positive or a negative development? Why? (*Answers should demonstrate an understanding of the Church's role in medieval Europe.*)

Read to Write

23. Scripts will vary but should reflect facts about the plague.

24. **FOLDABLES** Entries should accurately reflect the information in the chapter.

Using Technology

25. Maps and models should reflect chapter information and research.

REVIEWING UNIT OBJECTIVES

Having studied this unit, students should now be able to

1. describe how new technologies, ideas, and political systems influenced China in the Middle Ages;

2. identify the cultures that grew up in different parts of Africa between A.D. 300 and 1500;

3. describe the cultural, economic, and political advances made by the medieval Japanese;

4. explain how medieval Europe began to develop ideas of representative government.

UNIT REVIEW ACTIVITY

Comparing Past to Present While the people who lived in the civilizations and regions covered in this unit lived lives in some ways similar to ours, in other ways their lives differed greatly.

Ask students to use the chart, as well as the textbook chapters, to make a list of the ways the lives of the people of the times and places discussed in the unit were different from ours. *(For example, the chart points out that many people lived on farms and in villages; today the great majority of Americans lives in cities or suburbs, and very few people make a living from farming.)* **L2**

Unit 4 Review

Comparing Medieval Civilizations

Compare civilizations of the Middle Ages by reviewing the information below. Can you see how the peoples of these civilizations had lives that were very much like yours?

Where in the World?
- Chapter 12
- Chapter 13
- Chapter 14
- Chapter 15

NATIONAL GEOGRAPHIC

	China in the Middle Ages Chapter 12	Medieval Africa Chapter 13	Medieval Japan Chapter 14	Medieval Europe Chapter 15
Where did these civilizations develop?	• Mainland of East Asia	• West Africa; Southern Africa; East Africa	• Islands off coast of East Asia	• Northwestern Europe and Mediterranean area
Who were some important people in these civilizations?	• Taizong, ruled A.D. 627–649 • Empress Wu, ruled A.D. 684–705 • Kublai Khan, ruled A.D. 1271–1294 • Zheng He, A.D. 1371–1433	• Ibn Battuta, A.D. 1307–1377 • Mansa Musa, ruled A.D. 1312–1337 • Sunni Ali, ruled A.D. 1464–1492 • Queen Nzinga, ruled c. A.D. 1623–1663	• Prince Shotoku, A.D. 573–621 • Murasaki Shikibu, c. A.D. 973–1025 • Minamoto Yoritomo, A.D. 1147–1199 • Ashikaga Takauji, A.D. 1305–1358	• Charlemagne, ruled A.D. 768–814 • William the Conqueror, ruled A.D. 1066–1087 • Thomas Aquinas, A.D. 1225–1274 • Joan of Arc, A.D. 1412–1431
Where did most of the people live?	• Farming villages and towns along major rivers	• Farming villages; trading centers, such as Timbuktu and Kilwa	• Fishing and farming villages in coastal plains area	• Farming villages on estates located on plains; trading centers in Italy and Flanders

562

END-OF-UNIT RESOURCES

Reproducible Masters
- Unit 4 Test Form A
- Unit 4 Test Form B
- Step Into World History Activity 4

Transparencies
- Unit 4 Map Overlay Transparencies

Multimedia
- Interactive Tutor Self-Assessment CD-ROM
- ExamView® Pro Testmaker CD-ROM
- Presentation Plus! CD-ROM

	China in the Middle Ages Chapter 12	Medieval Africa Chapter 13	Medieval Japan Chapter 14	Medieval Europe Chapter 15
What were these people's beliefs?	• Confucianism, Daoism, Buddhism	• Traditional African religions, Christianity, Islam	• Shintoism, Buddhism	• Roman Catholic with small numbers of Jews and Muslims
What was their government like?	• Emperors ruled with the help of scholar-officials selected by exams	• Ruled by kings, close advisers, and local officials	• Emperors ruled in name but power held by military leaders	• Feudal territories united into kingdoms
What was their language and writing like?	• Chinese: symbols standing for objects are combined to represent ideas	• Many languages and different writing systems, but much knowledge passed on by oral history	• Japanese: Chinese characters standing for ideas as well as symbols representing sounds	• Many languages derived from Latin and Germanic
What contributions did they make?	• Civil service based on merit; invented moveable type, gunpowder, and the compass	• Produced tradition of storytelling, dance, music, and sculpture	• Developed ideas based on harmony with nature; produced martial arts	• Developed universities and representative government
How do these changes affect me? *Can you add any?*	• The Chinese invented fireworks, the compass, and printed books	• Early Africans passed on musical traditions that led to jazz, rap, gospel, reggae	• Japanese warriors developed martial arts, such as judo and karate	• Medieval Europeans passed on Christian ideas and a system of banking

UNIT WRAP-UP ACTIVITY

Comparing Civilizations In each of the regions covered in this unit, the relationship of the rulers to those they ruled had a major influence on daily life, culture, the economy, religion, and politics.

Organize students into groups of four, one for each chapter of the unit. Each group member should write a paragraph about how the political, religious, and economic relationship of the rulers to those they ruled influenced the quality of life in the region. Ask each group member to read his or her paragraph, then have the groups discuss similarities and differences across cultures.

Have groups conclude their discussion by evaluating each region and deciding which one created the most successful society. Remind them that they will also have to decide what makes a successful society. **L2**

563

PROFESSIONAL DEVELOPMENT: DIFFERENTIATED INSTRUCTION

• Forsten, Char. *Differentiated Instruction: Different Strategies for Different Learners.* Crystal Springs Books, 2002.
• Gregory, Gayle, and Carolyn Chapman. *Differentiated Instructional Strategies: One Size Doesn't Fit All.* Corwin Press, 2002.
• Heacox, Diane. *Differentiating Instruction in the Regular Classroom: How to Reach and Teach All Learners Grades 3–12.* Free Spirit Publishing, 2002.
• Witherell, Nancy, and Mary McMackin. *Graphic Organizers and Activities for Differentiated Instruction in Reading.* Scholastic, 2002.

Unit ⑤ Planning Guide

Unit Resources

Note: The following materials may be used when teaching Unit 5.
Chapter and section level support materials can be found on the chapter and section resource pages.

TEACHING TRANSPARENCIES

✋📂 Writing Process Transparencies **L1**

DIFFERENTIATED INSTRUCTION

📂 Step Into World History Activity 5

ASSESSMENT

📂 Unit 5 Test Form A **L2**
📂 Unit 5 Test Form B **L2**

ADDITIONAL RESOURCES

💿 Glencoe Skillbuilder Interactive Workbook CD-ROM, Level 1
💿 Glencoe World History Primary Source Document Library CD-ROM
🖼 Focus on World Art Prints
📂 Outline Map Resource Book
🌐 World Desk Map
✋ World Art and Architecture Transparencies
🎵 World Music: Cultural Traditions
🎵 World Music: A Cultural Legacy
📖 Glencoe World Literature Library
📂 Reading in the Content Area
📂 Teaching Strategies for the World History Classroom (Including Block Scheduling Pacing Guides)
📂 Inclusion Strategies for the Middle School Social Studies Classroom

📂 Blackline Master
🖼 Poster
✋ Transparency
🎵 Music Program

💿 CD-ROM
🔊 Audio Program
💿 DVD
📼 Videocassette

READING SUPPORT FROM JAMESTOWN EDUCATION

- *Timed Readings Plus in Social Studies* help students increase their reading rate and fluency while maintaining comprehension. The 400-word passages are similar to those found on state and national assessments.
- *Reading in the Content Area: Social Studies* concentrates on six essential reading skills that help students better comprehend what they read. The book includes 75 high-interest nonfiction passages written at increasing levels of difficulty.
- *Reading Fluency* helps students read smoothly, accurately, and expressively.
- *Jamestown's Reading Improvement,* by renowned reading expert Edward Fry, focuses on helping build your students' comprehension, vocabulary, and skimming and scanning skills.
- *Critical Reading Series* provides high-interest books, each written at three reading levels.

To order these products, call Glencoe at 1-800-334-7344.

Reading List Generator CD-ROM / GLENCOE BOOKLINK

The Glencoe BookLink CD-ROM is a database that allows you to search more than 15,000 titles to create a customized reading list for your students.

- Reading lists can be organized by students' reading level, author, genre, theme, or area of interest.
- The database provides Degrees of Reading Power™ (DRP) and Lexile™ readability scores for all selections.
- A brief summary of each selection is included.

Leveled reading suggestions for this unit:

For students at a Grade 5 reading level:
■ *Kids During the Renaissance,* by Lisa A. Wroble

For students at a Grade 6 reading level:
■ *Step Into the Aztec and Maya Worlds,* by Fiona Macdonald

For students at a Grade 7 reading level:
■ *Isaac Newton and the Scientific Revolution,* by Gale E. Christianson

To order this CD-ROM, call Glencoe at 1-800-334-7344.

Unit Reading Strategies

Each chapter in this unit contains special reading strategies. The following preview will help you teach these reading skills to your students.

CHAPTER 16: Summarizing Information

As students seek to make sense of facts, the skill of summarizing will help them understand, remember, and manipulate this information. Summarizing reinforces what is to be learned while helping students synthesize the information into their own framework for easier comprehension. Students practice this skill by making outlines of passages they have read. They also develop the skill of retelling what they have just read to help them internalize the information.

CHAPTER 17: Go Beyond the Words

Analyzing and clarifying are ways that students look more deeply into text to foster comprehension. These strategies can be honed in a variety of ways, from a simple rereading of the text to a more in-depth examination of the content. Questioning, reading ahead, discussing, researching, and bringing in additional related information are all ways that students can clarify and deepen their understanding of complex material. Students will practice going beyond the words by reading about new Renaissance painting techniques and comparing what they read to images that demonstrate these techniques.

CHAPTER 18: Your Reading Strengths

Monitoring comprehension means that students check their understanding of the text before, during, and after reading. They strive to be aware of when they begin to experience problems with comprehension, and then they adjust the strategies that they have learned to address the problem. For proficient readers, this process is ongoing and inherent, but less-proficient readers must be taught how to monitor and adjust. Questioning, rereading, predicting, or simply asking for help are all ways students can monitor and adjust their reading. Students will learn to analyze how they read and where they struggle in order to adjust.

Use the **SkillBuilder Handbook** on pages 902–919 to help students practice important skills.

`0:00` **OUT OF TIME?**

If time does not permit teaching each chapter in this unit, you may use the *Reading Essentials and Study Guide* summaries.

UNIT OVERVIEW

Unit 5 discusses how a new age of scientific, political, and cultural advances and religious conflict brought great change to Europe and the Americas.

UNIT OBJECTIVES

After studying this unit, students should be able to

1. describe the major native civilizations of the Americas and the impact of European exploration on them;
2. identify the major events of the Renaissance and Reformation;
3. describe the influence of the Enlightenment and Scientific Revolution on the world.

Why It's Important

Tell students that the time period they are about to study contains the seeds of our own time and that many important developments took shape.

Unit 5
A Changing World

Why It's Important

Each civilization that you will study in this unit made important contributions to history.

- Native Americans built a network of trade routes.
- Renaissance and Reformation Europeans affirmed the importance of the human individual.
- People in early modern Europe and America developed ideas about freedom and democracy.

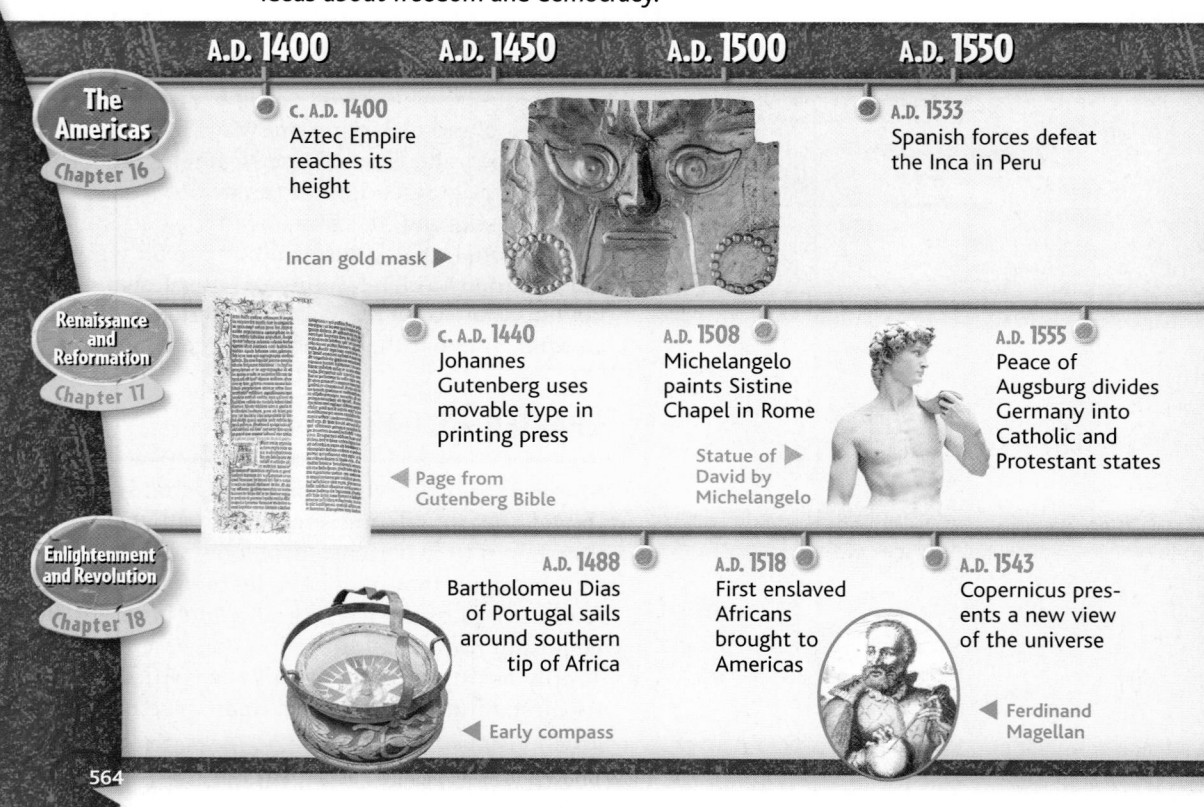

| A.D. 1400 | A.D. 1450 | A.D. 1500 | A.D. 1550 |

The Americas
Chapter 16

c. A.D. 1400
Aztec Empire reaches its height

Incan gold mask ▶

A.D. 1533
Spanish forces defeat the Inca in Peru

Renaissance and Reformation
Chapter 17

c. A.D. 1440
Johannes Gutenberg uses movable type in printing press

◀ Page from Gutenberg Bible

A.D. 1508
Michelangelo paints Sistine Chapel in Rome

Statue of ▶ David by Michelangelo

A.D. 1555
Peace of Augsburg divides Germany into Catholic and Protestant states

Enlightenment and Revolution
Chapter 18

A.D. 1488
Bartholomeu Dias of Portugal sails around southern tip of Africa

◀ Early compass

A.D. 1518
First enslaved Africans brought to Americas

A.D. 1543
Copernicus presents a new view of the universe

◀ Ferdinand Magellan

564

TIME LINE ACTIVITY

Ask students to find events on the multiple-tier time line that are evidence of an increase in the search for knowledge. Have students explain their suggestions and discuss how and why they are indicative of expanding knowledge. *(For example, Dias's voyage around the southern tip of Africa shows how European explorers were becoming more curious about the rest of the world and had developed the technology to actually find out about other places and peoples.)* **L1**

NATIONAL GEOGRAPHIC Where in the World?

Chapter 16

Chapter 17

Chapter 18

ASIA

EUROPE

Caspian Sea

Black Sea

AFRICA

NORTH AMERICA

● Chapter 16
● Chapter 17
● Chapter 18

1,000 mi.
1,000 km
Mercator projection

180°

SOUTH AMERICA

PACIFIC OCEAN

Hudson Bay

Gulf of Mexico

Caribbean Sea

Amazon R.

EQUATOR

0°

1,000 mi.
1,000 km
Mercator projection

60°N

NORTH AMERICA

ATLANTIC OCEAN

EUROPE

Caspian Sea
Black Sea

ASIA

Persian Gulf

Huang He

Chang Jiang

AFRICA

Arabian Sea

Bay of Bengal

South China Sea

PACIFIC OCEAN

SOUTH AMERICA

EQUATOR

0°

INDIAN OCEAN

120°W

60°W

0°

60°E

1,000 mi.
1,000 km
Mercator projection

GLENCOE TECHNOLOGY

World History Primary Source Document Library CD-ROM

Use the **World History Primary Source Document Library CD-ROM** to access primary source documents related to events in Europe and the Americas.

NCLB NO CHILD LEFT BEHIND

The goals of the NCLB Act include an emphasis on science and mathematics, in the hope of building better science and math skills among Americans. To help students sharpen science and math skills, try to focus on scientific advances. This unit is especially useful for applying these skills. For example, have students do special research projects on scientists, their discoveries and inventions, and how they have influenced civilization. To sharpen math skills, take every opportunity to have students use math as a tool for historical analysis. For example, ask students to find out what percentage of residents of colonial America were enslaved Africans.

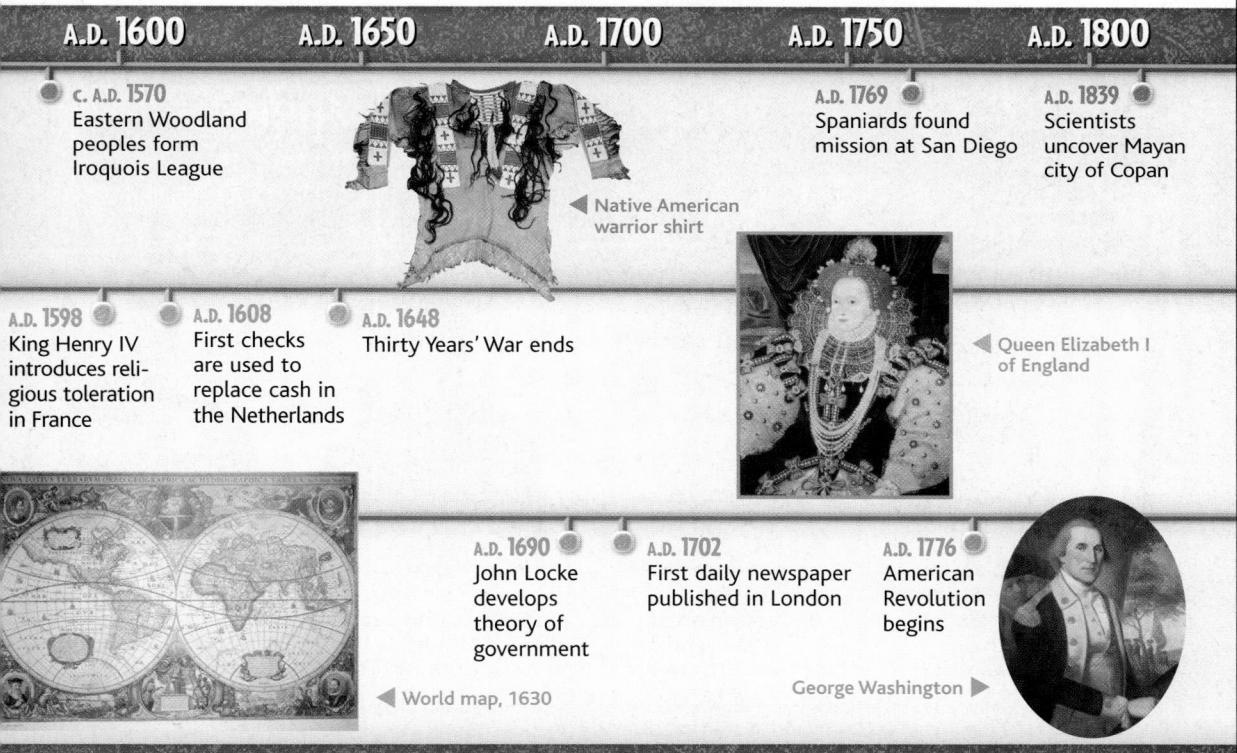

A.D. 1600   **A.D. 1650**   **A.D. 1700**   **A.D. 1750**   **A.D. 1800**

C. A.D. 1570
Eastern Woodland peoples form Iroquois League

Native American warrior shirt ◀

A.D. 1769
Spaniards found mission at San Diego

A.D. 1839
Scientists uncover Mayan city of Copan

A.D. 1598
King Henry IV introduces religious toleration in France

A.D. 1608
First checks are used to replace cash in the Netherlands

A.D. 1648
Thirty Years' War ends

Queen Elizabeth I of England ▶

A.D. 1690
John Locke develops theory of government

A.D. 1702
First daily newspaper published in London

A.D. 1776
American Revolution begins

World map, 1630 ◀

George Washington ▶

DIFFERENTIATED INSTRUCTION

This time period is characterized by a yearning among many people for better government; more effective economies; and safer, freer, and more equal nations. Different countries sought these goals in different ways.

English Learners: Have students point out events on the time line that they believe represent this trend toward a more effective organization of society.

Kinesthetic: Have students create a time line on a poster that incorporates this information from the unit time line. Instruct them to leave room to add to it as they read the chapters in the unit.

Intrapersonal: Have students consider a time when they have desired some sort of change in their own lives. Ask them to write a paragraph describing how their feelings mirror the efforts of these nations.

FOCUS

The unit preview provides a general layout of the regions and significant figures in the unit.

PREVIEWING GEOGRAPHY

Ask students to answer the following questions using the map.

1. **What continents appear to be the main focus of this unit?** (*North America, South America, Europe*)

2. **What ocean separates these continents?** (*Atlantic Ocean*)

PREVIEWING
People to Meet

Ask students the following questions using the biographies.

1. **Which two were queens?** (*Catherine de' Medici and Elizabeth I*)

2. **Which person lived between A.D. 1483 and 1546?** (*Martin Luther*) **What was significant about this person?** (*He was a German Protestant leader.*)

3. **Think about the descriptive facts for each person. What thematic categories do they fall into?** (*rulers and leaders, as well as scientists, mathematicians, and thinkers*)

Unit 5

Places to Locate

1 Machu Picchu
See The Americas
Chapter 16

2 Tikal
See The Americas
Chapter 16

NORTH AMERICA

Atlantic Ocean

Pacific Ocean

SOUTH AMERICA

People to Meet

Pachacuti
Ruled A.D. 1438–1471
Inca ruler
Chapter 16, page 589

Leonardo da Vinci
A.D. 1452–1519
Italian artist and scientist
Chapter 17, page 622

Martin Luther
A.D. 1483–1546
German Protestant leader
Chapter 17, page 638

Hernán Cortés
A.D. 1485–1547
Spanish conqueror
Chapter 16, page 598

566

PREVIEWING Places to Locate

Use the following descriptions to explain the images on the map.

1 Built by the Inca high in the Andes, Machu Picchu is one of the largest pre-Columbian sites still intact.

2 The Maya were impressive builders. Their city of Tikal covered 500 acres and included nine groups of courts and plazas built above swampy land and connected by bridges and causeways.

ASIA

EUROPE

AFRICA

Indian
Ocean

3 Sistine Chapel

See Renaissance and
Reformation Chapter 17

4 Wittenberg

See Enlightenment and
Revolution Chapter 18

5 Versailles

See Enlightenment and
Revolution Chapter 18

**Catherine
de' Medici**
A.D. 1519–1589
French queen
Chapter 17, page 647

Elizabeth I
Ruled A.D. 1558–1603
English queen
Chapter 18, page 665

John Locke
A.D. 1632–1704
English political
thinker
Chapter 18, page 683

**Isaac
Newton**
A.D. 1642–1727
English
mathematician
Chapter 18, page 677

567

TEACH

Organizing Information Have students create graphic organizers like the one below to organize data about the historical figures in the unit preview. *(Answers are provided.)* **L1/ EL**

Historical Figure	Prominent Accomplishment
Pachacuti	Incan ruler
Leonardi da Vinci	Italian artist and scientist
Martin Luther	German Protestant leader
Hernán Cortés	Spanish conquerer
Catherine de' Medici	French queen
Elizabeth I	English queen
John Locke	English political thinker
Isaac Newton	English mathematician

Writing Activity

Once students have completed their graphic organizers, organize students into groups of four. Have each person in each group research in an encyclopedia or on the Internet two of the people in the **People to Meet** feature, and write a one paragraph biography on each person. After students have completed their research, have them share their biographies with the other people in their group. **L2**

PREVIEWING Places to Locate

Michelangelo painted nine scenes from Genesis across the ceiling of the Sistine Chapel, located in Vatican City, Rome.

The great palace at Versailles represents the height of French classical building and the power of Louis XIV.

Martin Luther began the Protestant Reformation in Wittenberg.

Note: The following materials may be used when teaching Chapter 16.
Section level support materials are shown at point of use in the margins of the Teacher Wraparound Edition.

TEACHING TRANSPARENCIES

- Graphic Organizer Transparencies with Teaching Strategy and Student Activity **L2**
- Cause-and-Effect Transparencies with Teaching Strategy and Student Activity **L2**
- Then and Now Transparencies with Teaching Strategy and Student Activity **L2**
- In-text Map Transparency with Teaching Strategy and Student Activity **L1**
- Map Transparencies with Overlay, Teaching Strategy, and Student Activity **L2**

DIFFERENTIATED INSTRUCTION

- Differentiated Instruction Activity 16
- Time Line Activity 16
- Primary Source Reading 16 (with Document-Based Questions)
- Inclusion Strategies for the Middle School Social Studies Classroom
- StudentWorks Plus™ CD-ROM (with Audio Program)

READING SUPPORT

- Take-Home Review Activity 16 **L2**
- World Literature Reading 16 **L2**
- Workbook Activity 16 **L1**
- Reading Strategies for the Social Studies Classroom **L1/ EL**

ASSESSMENT

ASSESSMENT

- Authentic Assessment Activity 16 **L1/ EL**
- Chapter 16 Test Form A **L2**
- Chapter 16 Test Form B **L2**
- ExamView® Pro Testmaker CD-ROM

INTERDISCIPLINARY CONNECTIONS

- Geography and History Activity 16 **L2**
- People to Meet Activity 16 **L2**
- Economics Activity 16 **L2**
- Citizenship and Service Learning Activity 16 **L2**

SPANISH RESOURCES

- Spanish Reading Essentials and Study Guide
- Spanish Guided Reading Activities
- Spanish Quizzes, Tests, and Authentic Assessment (with Rubrics)
- Spanish Take-Home Review Activities

MULTIMEDIA

- ExamView® Pro Testmaker CD-ROM
- Glencoe Skillbuilder Interactive Workbook CD-ROM, Level 1
- Interactive Tutor Self-Assessment CD-ROM
- MindJogger Videoquiz
- Presentation Plus! CD-ROM
- StudentWorks Plus™ CD-ROM (with Audio Program)
- TeacherWorks CD-ROM
- Vocabulary PuzzleMaker CD-ROM
- *World History: Journey Across Time* Video Program
- World History Primary Source Document Library CD-ROM

STANDARDIZED ASSESSMENT SKILLS

- Standardized Test Skills Practice Workbook Activity 16 **L2**
- Critical Thinking Skills Activity 16 **L2**

Teaching strategies have been coded with suggested ability levels. However, most are suitable for all levels.

L1 BASIC activities for all students
L2 AVERAGE activities for average to above-average students
L3 CHALLENGING activities for above-average students
EL ENGLISH LANGUAGE activities

TIME MANAGEMENT

Unit Introduction	Chapter Introduction	Section 1	Section 2	Section 3	Chapter Wrap-Up
1 Day	1 Day	2 Days	2 Days	1 Day	1 Day

Block Scheduling Activities that are suited to use within the block scheduling framework are identified by: 📦

0:00 OUT OF TIME? Assign the Chapter 16 *Reading Essentials and Study Guide.* * 📁

SECTION RESOURCES

DAILY OBJECTIVES	REPRODUCIBLE RESOURCES	MULTIMEDIA RESOURCES
Section 1 **The First Americans** 1. It is thought that the first Americans came from Asia during the Ice Age. 2. The invention of farming led to civilizations and cultures based on agriculture and trade in the northern part of the Americas.	📁 Reproducible Lesson Plan 16–1 📁 Daily Lecture and Discussion Notes 16–1 📁 Vocabulary Activity 16–1 📁 Active Reading Note-Taking Guide 16–1 📁 Guided Reading Activity 16–1* 📁 Section Quiz 16–1* 📁 Reading Essentials and Study Guide 16–1*	🖊 Daily Focus Skills Transparency 16–1 💿 Interactive Tutor Self-Assessment CD-ROM 💿 ExamView® Pro Testmaker CD-ROM 💿 Presentation Plus! CD-ROM
Section 2 **Life in the Americas** 1. The Maya moved into the Yucatán while the Aztec of Mexico and the Inca of Peru built empires. 2. Diverse cultures arose in the lands north of Mexico.	📁 Reproducible Lesson Plan 16–2 📁 Daily Lecture and Discussion Notes 16–2 📁 Vocabulary Activity 16–2 📁 Active Reading Note-Taking Guide 16–2 📁 Guided Reading Activity 16–2* 📁 Section Quiz 16–2* 📁 Reading Essentials and Study Guide 16–2*	🖊 Daily Focus Skills Transparency 16–2 💿 Interactive Tutor Self-Assessment CD-ROM 💿 ExamView® Pro Testmaker CD-ROM 💿 Presentation Plus! CD-ROM 💿 Glencoe BookLink CD-ROM
Section 3 **The Fall of the Aztec and Inca Empires** 1. Christopher Columbus landed in the Americas while looking for a route to Asia. 2. Horses, guns, and European diseases helped Spanish conquerors defeat the Aztec and Inca.	📁 Reproducible Lesson Plan 16–3 📁 Daily Lecture and Discussion Notes 16–3 📁 Vocabulary Activity 16–3 📁 Active Reading Note-Taking Guide 16–3 📁 Guided Reading Activity 16–3* 📁 Section Quiz 16–3* 📁 Reading Essentials and Study Guide 16–3*	🖊 Daily Focus Skills Transparency 16–3 💿 Interactive Tutor Self-Assessment CD-ROM 💿 ExamView® Pro Testmaker CD-ROM 💿 Presentation Plus! CD-ROM 💿 Vocabulary PuzzleMaker CD-ROM 💿 Glencoe BookLink CD-ROM

*Also available in Spanish

History Online

Use our Web site for additional resources. All essential content is covered in the Student Edition.

You and your students can visit jat.glencoe.com, the Web site companion to *World History: Journey Across Time*. This innovative integration of electronic and print media offers your students a wealth of opportunities. The student text directs students to the Web site for the following options:

- Chapter Overviews
- Student Web Activities
- Self-Check Quizzes
- Multi-Language Glossaries
- Study Central™

Answers to the student Web activities are provided for you in the **Web Activity Lesson Plans.** Additional Web resources and ePuzzles and games are also available.

THE HISTORY CHANNEL.

The following videotape programs are available from Glencoe as supplements to Chapter 16:

Machu Picchu: City in the Sky
(ISBN 0-7670-0143-5)

The Maya
(ISBN 0-7670-0697-6)

Mexico: A Story of Conquest (4-Video Set)
(ISBN 0-7670-1622-X)

To order, call Glencoe at 1-800-334-7344. To find classroom resources to accompany many of these videos, check the following home pages:

A&E Television: www.aande.com
The History Channel: www.historychannel.com

MEETING SPECIAL NEEDS

In addition to the Differentiated Instruction strategies, the following resources are suitable for students with special needs:

- *ExamView® Pro Testmaker CD-ROM* allows teachers to tailor tests by reducing answer choices.
- *StudentWorks Plus™ CD-ROM (with Audio Program)* includes the entire narrative of the student edition so that less-proficient readers can listen to the words as they read them.
- The *Reading Essentials and Study Guide* provides the same content as the student edition but is written two grade levels below the textbook.

NATIONAL GEOGRAPHIC — TEACHER'S CORNER

Index to National Geographic Magazine:

The following articles relate to this chapter:

- "Mystery Mountain of the Inca," by Peter Frost, February 2004.
- "Yucatan's Mysterious Hill Cities," by George Stewart, April 2002.
- "Empires Across the Andes," by Virginia Morell, June 2002.

National Geographic Society Products:

To order the following, call National Geographic at 1–800–368–2728

- *Peru's Treasure Tomb* (Video)
- *PictureShow: Ancient Civilizations: Middle and South America* (CD-ROM)

NGS ONLINE

Access National Geographic's new dynamic MapMachine Web site and other geography resources at:

www.nationalgeographic.com
www.nationalgeographic.com/maps

Meeting NCSS Standards

World History: Journey Across Time

The following standards are highlighted in Chapter 16:

Section 1
- **II** Time, Continuity, and Change: C, E, G
- **VII** Production, Distribution, and Consumption: E
- **VIII** Science, Technology, and Society: E

Section 2
- **I** Culture: A, D, H
- **III** People, Places, and Environments: B, E, G, H
- **IV** Individual Development and Identity: B
- **V** Individuals, Groups, and Institutions: A, B

Section 3
- **I** Culture: A, B, F
- **VI** Power, Authority, and Governance: B, F, G
- **IX** Global Connections: B, I

State and Local Objectives

_____

_____

Timesaving Tools

TeacherWorks
All-In-One Planner and Resource Center

- **Interactive Teacher Edition** Access your Teacher Wraparound Edition and your classroom resources with a few easy clicks.
- **Interactive Lesson Planner** Organize your week, month, semester, or year with all the lesson helps you need to make teaching creative and relevant.

Use Glencoe's **Presentation Plus!** multimedia teacher tool to easily present dynamic lessons that visually excite your students. Using Microsoft PowerPoint® you can customize the presentations to create your own personalized lessons.

FOLDABLES™
Study Organizer
Dinah Zike's Foldables

Foldables are three-dimensional, interactive graphic organizers that help students practice basic writing skills, review key vocabulary terms, and identify main ideas. Every chapter contains a foldable activity, with additional chapter activities found in the *Reading and Study Skills Foldables* booklet. You can use the foldables as they are presented, or modify them to suit the needs of your individual class.

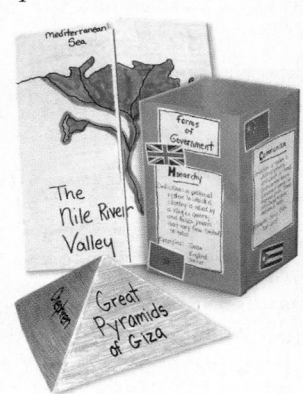

Planning Ahead

CHAPTER CULMINATING ACTIVITY

The Chapter Culminating Activity will help students organize and learn the important information from the chapter. Begin the chapter with this activity, and have students complete it as a culminating activity.

USING A MATRIX DIAGRAM

Purpose Matrix diagrams provide assistance in organizing information. Students will automatically organize information if they record their notes on such a grid. Because these diagrams organize information into categories, they can help students make comparisons and form generalizations. This matrix uses the six question words that reporters ask—*who, what, where, when, why,* and *how.* Students can use these questions to investigate any purpose for reading or research.

Introduction to Modeling

1. Explain that this chapter describes many early peoples who lived in the Americas—from the Arctic to the tip of South America.

2. Ask volunteers to make a wall-sized diagram by taping sheets of paper together or by using large pieces of poster board. Write the question words at the top of the columns. Students may then take turns recording entries.

3. Before reading each section, list the relevant indigenous people on the diagram. Next, ask students to form questions about them, using the six question words. Record the questions on the board. After the class selects one to three questions to investigate in the section, write them on the diagram.

4. While discussing the section, ask volunteers to record relevant answers on the diagram.

5. Encourage students to illustrate answers too. For example, locator maps might be used to answer "Where?" questions.

Ancient Americans	Who?	What?	Where?	When?	Why?	How?
First Americans						
Olmec						

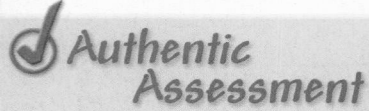

Authentic Assessment

Refer to Activity 16 in the Authentic Assessment section of the *Quizzes, Tests, and Authentic Assessment (with Rubrics)* booklet.

When & Where?

Refer students to the time line. Tell or remind them that the letter *c.* stands for *circa,* meaning "about." Ask students to suggest reasons why scientists do not know the precise dates for some entries. *(Possible answers: Some people did not have systems of writing so there are no records; dates are based on available artifacts.)* **L1/** **EL**

GLENCOE TECHNOLOGY

World History: Journey Across Time Video Program

To learn more about the Americas, students can view the Chapter 16 video in the *World History: Journey Across Time* Video Program.

MindJogger Videoquiz

Use the **MindJogger Videoquiz** to preview Chapter 16 content.

Available in DVD and VHS

Chapter 16

The Americas

▼ The ruins of Machu Picchu near Cuzco, Peru

NATIONAL GEOGRAPHIC When & Where?

c. 1500 B.C.	A.D. 500	A.D. 1000	A.D. 1500
c. 1200 B.C. Olmec build an empire in Mexico	**A.D. 500** Mayan cities flourish in Mesoamerica	**c. A.D. 1250** Aztec arrive in central Mexico	**A.D. 1492** Columbus reaches the Americas

---

Reading Strategy — PURPOSE FOR READING

Using a Graphic Organizer Write the term "Native American" in a circle on the board. Then draw several separate lines extending out around the circle from its edge. Think out loud by saying, "Native Americans lived in the Americas long before the arrival of Europeans. What do we know about these groups?" Write students' responses on the lines around the circle. Allow the class a few minutes to look through the chapter. Call on volunteers to name one new thing they noticed while skimming through the text. **L1/** **EL**

Chapter Preview

During Europe's medieval age, many different peoples were building civilizations in the Americas. Read about how these early Americans grew corn, beans, and other food products that are familiar to you today.

 View the Chapter 16 video in the *World History: Journey Across Time* Video Program.

Chapter Overview Visit jat.glencoe.com for a preview of Chapter 16.

Section 1 — The First Americans

The first people in the Americas arrived thousands of years ago. Farming led to the growth of civilizations in what is now Mexico, Central America, and Peru.

Section 2 — Life in the Americas

The Maya, Aztec, and many other Native American cultures developed in North and South America.

Section 3 — The Fall of the Aztec and Inca Empires

Spanish explorers and soldiers were drawn to the riches of Native American civilizations. Using horses and guns, they defeated the Aztec and Inca Empires in the early A.D. 1500s.

Organizing Information *Make this foldable to help you organize information about the history and culture of the Americas.*

Step 1 *Collect two sheets of paper and place them about 1 inch apart.*

Keep the edges straight.

Step 2 *Fold up the bottom edges of the paper to form four tabs.*

This makes all the tabs the same size.

Step 3 *When all the tabs are the same size, crease the paper to hold the tabs in place and staple the sheets together. Label each tab as shown.*

The Americas
The First Americans
Life in the Americas
The Aztec and Inca

Staple along the fold.

Reading and Writing *As you read the chapter, write the main ideas presented in each of the three sections under the tabs of your foldable. Note details that support the main ideas.*

569

MORE ABOUT THE PHOTO

Machu Picchu The ruins of the Incan city of Machu Picchu (meaning "manly peak") lie at an altitude of 8,000 feet (2,438 m) in the Andes mountain ranges of Peru. Built between A.D. 1460 and A.D. 1470 by the Incan ruler Pachacuti, Machu Picchu was most likely a royal estate and religious center. Its 200 buildings, mostly residences, were built of granite blocks cut with bronze or stone tools and smoothed with sand. Few people outside the ruler's court were actually aware of Machu Picchu. In the A.D. 1520s, a smallpox epidemic killed nearly 50 percent of the people living in the area. So by the time the Spanish arrived in Cuzco in A.D. 1532, Machu Picchu was already forgotten. In A.D. 1911, Hiram Bingham, a Yale professor, rediscovered Machu Picchu on an Andean expedition.

1 Learn It!

Having students summarize what they are reading is a valuable skill not only for comprehension but also as a way of reinforcing the major points of the text.

Read the following practice passage from page 583 aloud and ask students to work in pairs. Have one student provide a summary statement while another makes sure all the details are covered.

> In A.D. 1839 an American lawyer named John Lloyd Stevens and an English artist named Frederick Catherwood slashed their way into the tangled Yucatán rain forest. There they made an amazing discovery. They found the vine-covered ruins of an ancient city.

Ask students to continue reading silently. In groups of four, have them summarize what they read. The first student will tell only the major points about the Mayan city. The second person will add details the first student left out. The third and fourth students must read the text again carefully to add any omitted details. The original summarizer then will finish the exercise by "creatively summarizing," that is, adding details from his or her imagination that are not a part of the text. **L2**

Reading Skill
Summarizing

1 Learn It!

Summarizing Information

Summarizing what you have read, either orally or in writing, is a good way to increase your understanding of the text. Read the information about Christopher Columbus on pages 594–595, **Columbus Arrives in America** and **Columbus Returns.** With a partner, summarize the main points. One person should summarize what he or she read while the other listens. Then the second person should resummarize, adding details that the partner may have left out.

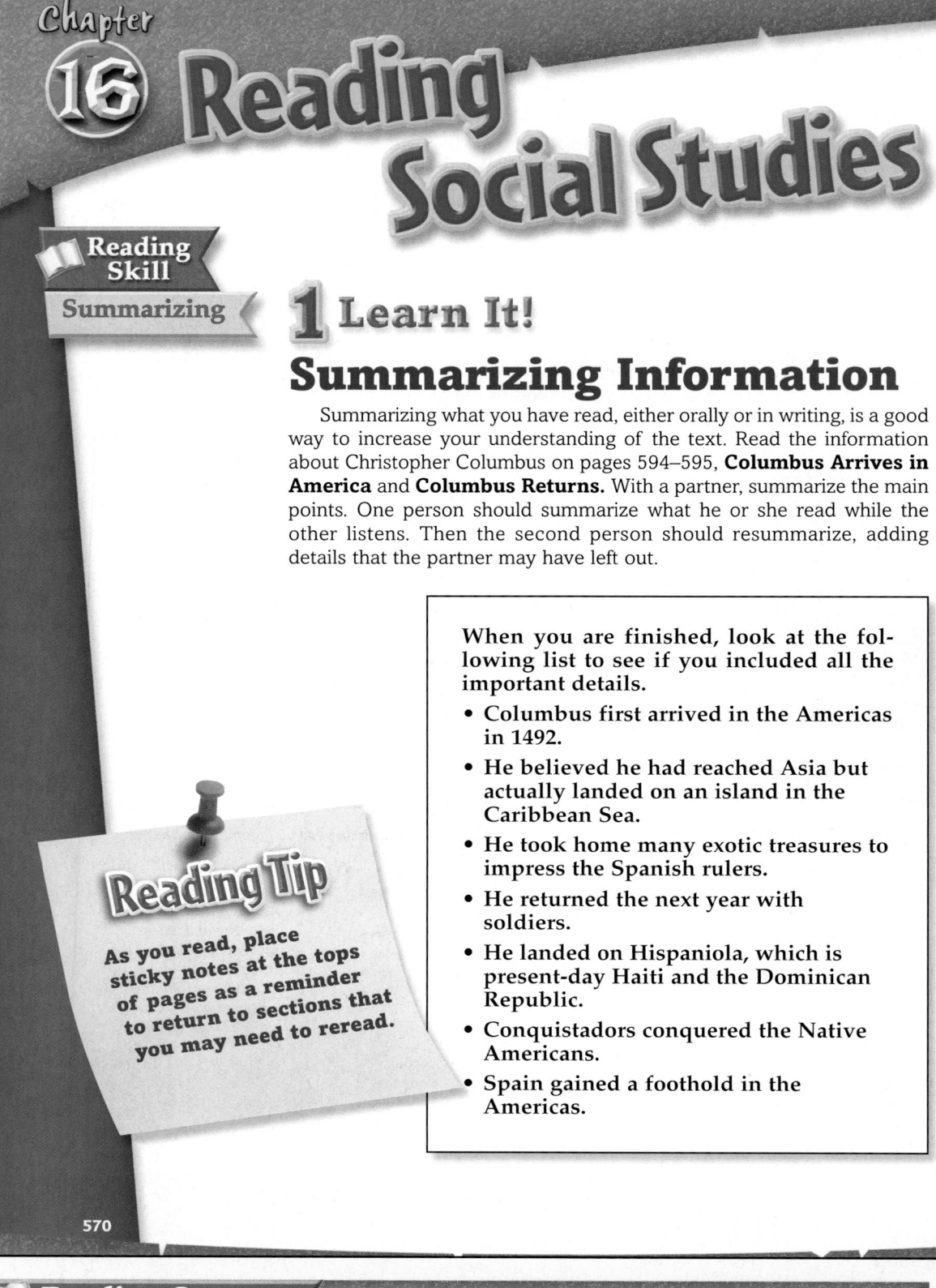

Reading Tip

As you read, place sticky notes at the tops of pages as a reminder to return to sections that you may need to reread.

When you are finished, look at the following list to see if you included all the important details.

- **Columbus first arrived in the Americas in 1492.**
- **He believed he had reached Asia but actually landed on an island in the Caribbean Sea.**
- **He took home many exotic treasures to impress the Spanish rulers.**
- **He returned the next year with soldiers.**
- **He landed on Hispaniola, which is present-day Haiti and the Dominican Republic.**
- **Conquistadors conquered the Native Americans.**
- **Spain gained a foothold in the Americas.**

570

Reading Strategy **COMPARING AND CONTRASTING**

Students are much more likely to become engaged in the text when the purpose is not only authentic but also relevant to their everyday lives or future goals. Look for such connections throughout the text. For example, ask students to read to find out why people in 3000 B.C. valued blubber. Readers may be surprised to learn that it added valuable calories to their bodies. Contrast the ancient value of "fat" with America's disdain of it today. Ask students who are especially good in mathematics to find the section that describes how the Maya invented the concept of zero, or encourage students who like animals to find in the text how much woolly mammoths weighed.

2 Practice It!

Retelling

Read the description of how **Spain Conquers Mexico** on pages 595–596. Before you begin, read the first paragraph about Cortés aloud:

> The voyages of Christopher Columbus, who sailed to the Americas four times, inspired many poor nobles to go to America to seek their fortunes. Many came from the part of Spain known as the Extremadura. Its poor soil, blistering hot summers, and icy winters held little chance for wealth. One of these nobles was 19-year-old Hernán Cortés.
>
> *—from pages 595–596*

With a partner, summarize the story of Cortés and how he destroyed the Aztec capital. As you are retelling, you may want to refer back to the text, reading aloud words in quotation marks or italics to provide an authentic voice to your story. Listen carefully so that you can add details that your partner may have left out.

Read to Write
Choose one of the historical figures from Chapter 16 and expand his or her story with details from your own imagination. Add quotes, descriptions, and events that you think might have happened to create a richer, although fictionalized, narrative.

3 Apply It!

As you read this chapter, practice summarizing. Stop after each section and write a brief summary of the major points in that section.

571

READING SOCIAL STUDIES

2 Practice It!

Analyzing Supporting Details As students are summarizing, this is an appropriate time to discuss the role details play in text. Ask them which details could be left out and which ones are essential to the meaning of the summary. Have students perfect their summarizing skills by purposely leaving out details of the text they are summarizing and having other student insert the details. This works especially well with narrative text, such as that in Section 2. A student may retell how hunters hunch over a seal's breathing hole in the ice, chopping a bigger hole with an ax and dragging the harpooned prey from the water. Another student may add the important detail that soft feathers are hung on a wooden frame over the hole that moves when the seal approaches.

3 Apply It!

To tap into various learning modalities, some students may prefer to draw their summaries, using frames to show the events. Others may be better able to summarize by acting out the events in the text. Students who write as a way of understanding may want to summarize in list or narrative forms.

Reading Strategy — READ TO WRITE

Historical novels focusing on a specific figure in history can make the character come to life while providing students with a realistic context for the period. Set the stage for writing by reading aloud a passage from one of the many adolescent historical fiction offerings, such as *I Sailed with Columbus* by Susan Martin. Ask students to close their eyes and imagine the character as you read a description from the book. Then have them choose one character from the textbook to describe in the same way. Encourage them to use a variety of techniques to make the character come alive, such as adding quotes, describing a character's specific actions, or showing the character through the eyes of other characters, such as fellow sailors describing Columbus.

① FOCUS

SECTION OVERVIEW

This section presents a theory on how the first people traveled to the Americas and describes how the development of farming shaped cultures in the Americas.

BELLRINGER
SKILLBUILDER ACTIVITY

Project **Daily Focus Skills Transparency 16–1** and have students answer questions. Discuss their responses.

Get Ready to Read!

Preteaching Vocabulary: Read aloud the first paragraph on page 573, which contains the definition of the term *glacier*. Then tell students to close their eyes and visualize a glacier. On the board, list the words and phrases that students use to describe glaciers.

Answers to Graphic: Olmec: near present-day Vera Cruz, Mexico; 1200–400 B.C.; farmers and traders; Moche: dry coastal desert in present-day Peru; c. A.D. 100–700; farmers, hunters, fishers, traders, built pyramids

Section ① The First Americans

Get Ready to Read!

What's the Connection?
While Western Europe rebuilt itself after the fall of Rome, diverse cultures thrived in the Americas.

Focusing on the Main Ideas
- It is believed that the first people in the Americas came from Asia during the Ice Age. *(page 573)*
- The invention of farming led to the rise of civilizations in the Americas. *(page 574)*
- Early people in the northern part of the Americas built complex cultures based on farming and trade. *(page 578)*

Locating Places
Mesoamerica (MEH•zoh•uh•MEHR•ih•kuh)
Teotihuacán (TAY•oh•TEE•wuh•KAHN)
Cuzco (KOOS•koh)
Cahokia (kuh•HOH•kee•uh)

Meeting People
Olmec (OHL•mehk)
Maya (MY•uh)
Toltec (TOHL•TEHK)
Moche (MOH•cheh)
Inca (IHNG•kuh)
Hohokam (HOH•hoh•KAHM)
Anasazi (AH•nuh•SAH•zee)

Building Your Vocabulary
glacier (GLAY•shuhr)
monopoly (muh•NAH•puh•lee)

Reading Strategy
Summarizing Information Create a chart to show the characteristics of the Olmec and Moche.

	Location	Dates	Lifestyle
Olmec			
Moche			

NATIONAL GEOGRAPHIC When & Where?

2000 B.C.	500 B.C.	A.D. 1000

c. 1200 B.C.
Olmec build an empire in Mexico

c. A.D. 500
Mayan cities flourish in Mesoamerica

A.D. 1100
Inca found city of Cuzco

Cahokia
Teotihuacán
Cuzco

SECTION RESOURCES

📂 **Reproducible Masters**
- Reproducible Lesson Plan 16–1
- Daily Lecture and Discussion Notes 16–1
- Vocabulary Activity 16–1
- Active Reading Note-Taking Guide 16–1
- Guided Reading Activity 16–1
- Section Quiz 16–1
- Reading Essentials and Study Guide 16–1

Transparencies
- Daily Focus Skills Transparency 16–1

Multimedia
- Interactive Tutor Self-Assessment CD-ROM
- ExamView® Pro Testmaker CD-ROM
- Presentation Plus! CD-ROM

Pathway to the Americas

Main Idea It is believed that the first people in the Americas came from Asia during the Ice Age.

Reading Focus When and how did the first people travel to the Americas? Nobody knows for sure. The story of their arrival remains one of history's mysteries.

We know people came to America a long time ago, but how did they get here? Today, America is not connected by land to the rest of the world, but in the past it was. Scientists have studied the earth's geography during the Ice Age—a period when temperatures dropped sharply. At that time, much of the earth's water froze into huge sheets of ice, or **glaciers** (GLAY•shuhrz).

As the ice froze and the seas fell, an area of dry land was exposed between Asia and Alaska. Scientists call this land bridge Beringia (buh•RIHN•jee•uh), after Vitus Bering, a famous European explorer. They think that people in Asia followed the animals they were hunting across this land bridge into the Americas. By testing the age of bones and tools at ancient campsites, scientists estimate that the first people arrived between 15,000 to 40,000 years ago.

When the Ice Age ended about 10,000 years ago, the glaciers melted and released water back into the seas. The land bridge to America disappeared beneath the waves.

Hunting and Gathering Hunters in the Americas were constantly on the move in search of food. They fished and gathered nuts, fruits, or roots. They also hunted massive prey, such as the woolly mammoth, antelope, caribou, and bison.

It took several hunters to kill a woolly mammoth, which could weigh as much as 9 tons. These big animals provided meat, hides for clothing, and bones for tools.

As the Ice Age ended, some animals became extinct, or disappeared from the earth. The warm weather, however, opened new opportunities to early Americans.

✓ **Reading Check** **Explain** Why is there no longer a land bridge between Asia and America?

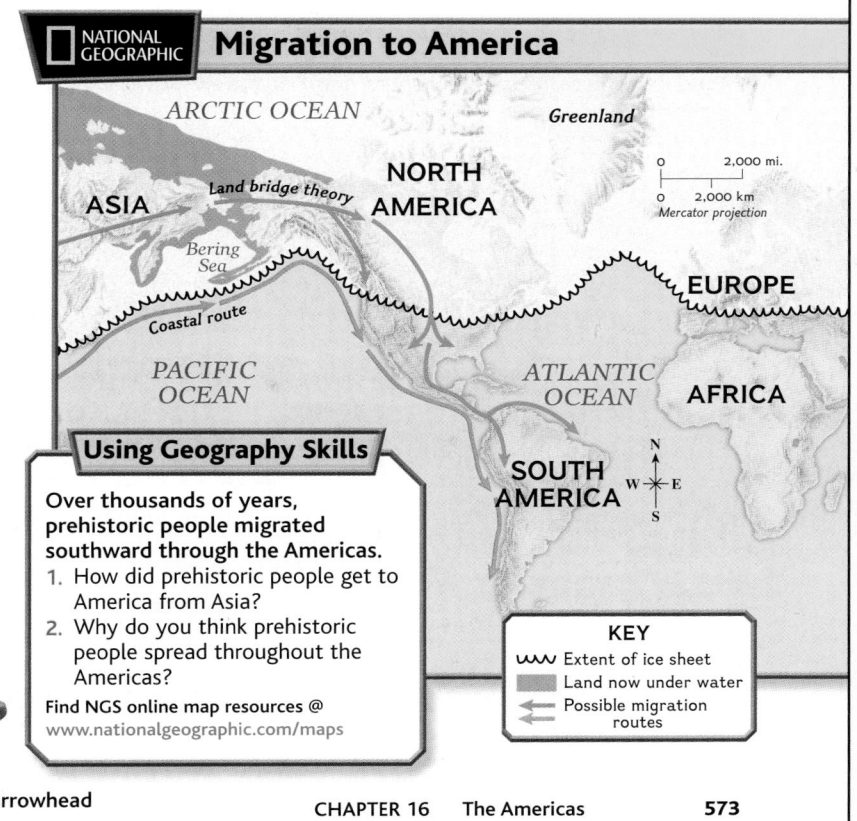

NATIONAL GEOGRAPHIC

Migration to America

ARCTIC OCEAN

Greenland

NORTH AMERICA

ASIA

Land bridge theory

Bering Sea

Coastal route

PACIFIC OCEAN

ATLANTIC OCEAN

EUROPE

AFRICA

SOUTH AMERICA

0   2,000 mi.
0   2,000 km
Mercator projection

N W E S

Using Geography Skills

Over thousands of years, prehistoric people migrated southward through the Americas.
1. How did prehistoric people get to America from Asia?
2. Why do you think prehistoric people spread throughout the Americas?

Find NGS online map resources @ www.nationalgeographic.com/maps

KEY

〰〰 Extent of ice sheet

▨ Land now under water

← Possible migration routes

◀ Stone arrowhead

CHAPTER 16   The Americas   573

② TEACH

Comparing a Geographic Area Direct students to the **Reference Atlas.** Have a volunteer describe the area between Asia and Alaska today. **Ask: What is the body of water between Asia and Alaska?** *(Bering Strait)* Tell students that the names *Beringia* and *Bering Strait* are related to Vitus Bering. **L1/ EL**

Daily Lecture and Discussion Notes 16–1

Use **Daily Lecture and Discussion Notes 16–1** for an outline of key concepts found in the section.

✓ **Reading Check**

Answer: The land bridge was covered by water when the glaciers melted.

Using Geography Skills

Answers:
1. Sea levels dropped; People walked across dry land between Asia and Alaska.
2. Possible answer: They were searching for better hunting grounds.

▮▮ Reading Strategy ⟩ READING THE TEXT

Sequencing Information Explain that this section discusses many early peoples who lived in the Americas. Point out that it would be helpful to construct a time line showing when these groups lived, to preview the peoples described in the section and to organize information about them. First, have students create a time line based on the time line at the beginning of the chapter, leaving space between each entry for additional ones. Have students scan the **Get Ready to Read!** feature at the beginning of each section and the **Main Ideas** in each section, then compile a list of important names and events. As students read the section, have them add the information from their lists to the time line. **L2**

Reading Strategy

Comparing Food Sources and Diet
Have students compare how the change from hunting/gathering to farming affected what early peoples ate. Compile student responses in a chart on the board. Also note losses of food sources, such as the woolly mammoth becoming extinct, on the chart. Suggest that students point out similarities in the foods that different peoples ate. Note these commonalities on the chart. Then have students use the chart data to decide which foods were most important to early peoples. **L2**

More About the Art

Modern scientists have found well-preserved remains of woolly mammoths in Siberia and Alaska.

Caption Answer:
Answers may include that larger animals supplied more food.

First American Civilizations

Main Idea The invention of farming led to the rise of civilizations in the Americas.

Reading Focus What would our lives be like if people had never learned to farm? Read to learn how farming made civilization possible in Mexico, Central America, and South America.

The first Americans were hunter-gatherers, but as the Ice Age ended and the climate warmed, people in America made an amazing discovery. They learned that seeds could be planted and they would grow into crops that people could eat.

Farming began in **Mesoamerica** (MEH•zoh•uh•MEHR•ih•kuh) 9,000 to 10,000 years ago. *Meso* comes from the Greek word for "middle." This region includes lands stretching from the Valley of Mexico to Costa Rica in Central America.

The region's geography was ideal for farming. Much of the area had a rich, volcanic soil and a mild climate. Rains fell in the spring, helping seeds to sprout. They decreased in the summer, allowing crops to ripen for harvest. Then, in the autumn, the rains returned, soaking the soil for the next year's crop.

The first crops grown in the Americas included pumpkins, peppers, squash, gourds, and beans. It took longer to develop corn, which grew as a wild grass. Early plants produced a single, one-inch cob. After hundreds of years, the early Americans finally learned how to cross corn

Hunting the Woolly Mammoth

Working in groups, hunters could bring down large prey, such as a woolly mammoth. *Why do you think early hunters preferred to hunt large animals such as mammoths instead of smaller animals?*

DIFFERENTIATED INSTRUCTION

Visual/Spatial: Have students make a poster-sized drawing of the map of Mesoamerica. Tell them to label the general areas where various cultures lived and to add illustrations showing features of those cultures.

English Learners: Assign students to write captions for the map and for any illustrations.

Gifted and Talented: Ask students to select a particular facet of one of the cultures and research more information about it. Have students add the results to the map.

Refer to ***Inclusion Strategies for the Middle School Social Studies Classroom*** in the TCR.

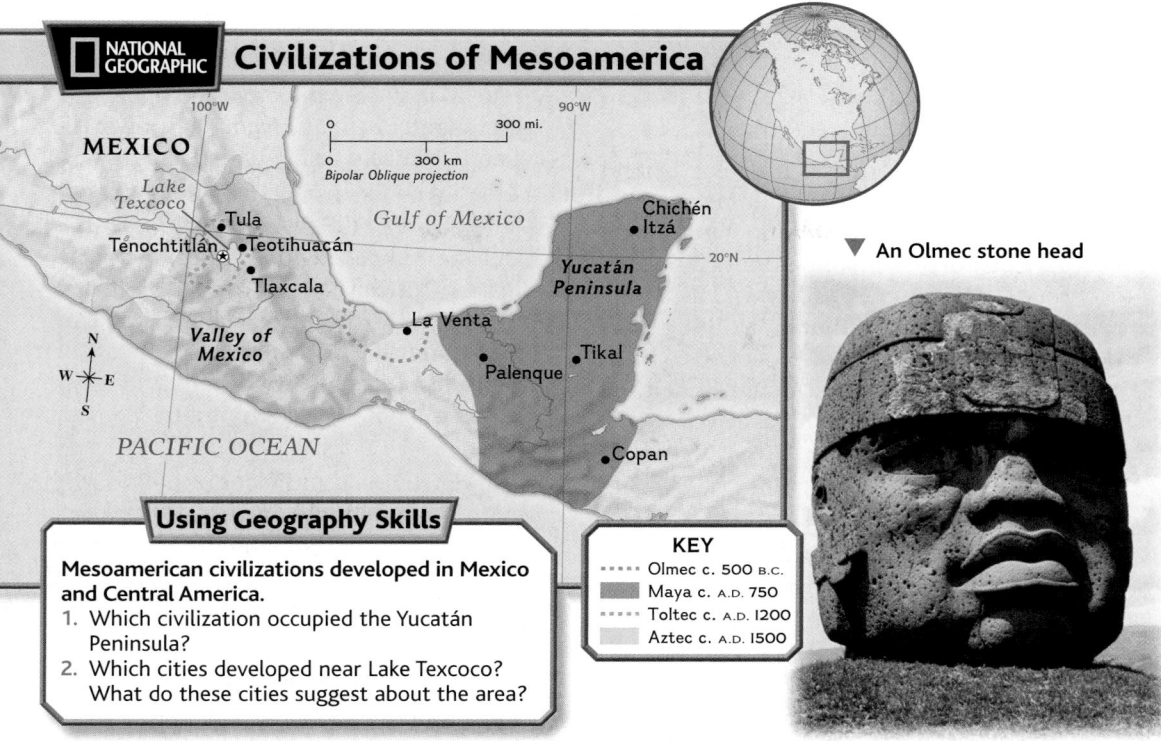

NATIONAL GEOGRAPHIC
Civilizations of Mesoamerica

MEXICO
Lake Texcoco
Tula
Tenochtitlán • Teotihuacán
Tlaxcala
Valley of Mexico
La Venta
Palenque
Gulf of Mexico
Chichén Itzá
Yucatán Peninsula
Tikal
Copan
20°N
PACIFIC OCEAN
100°W
90°W
0 / 300 mi.
0 / 300 km
Bipolar Oblique projection

▼ An Olmec stone head

KEY
..... Olmec c. 500 B.C.
Maya c. A.D. 750
..... Toltec c. A.D. 1200
Aztec c. A.D. 1500

Using Geography Skills

Mesoamerican civilizations developed in Mexico and Central America.
1. Which civilization occupied the Yucatán Peninsula?
2. Which cities developed near Lake Texcoco? What do these cities suggest about the area?

CONNECTING ACROSS TIME

The Mesoamericans put together a well-balanced diet. Beans and squash offered vegetable protein, corn supplied carbohydrates, and avocados added oils and fats. Mesoamericans got calcium by soaking their corn in limewater, while chiles supplied other vitamins. Call on students to name the Mesoamerican foods that people still consume today. **L2**

Using Geography Skills

Answers:
1. the Maya
2. Teotihuacán and Tenochtitlán; that the land was fertile because it could support a large population

in a word . . .

Archaeologists do not know what the **"Olmec"** called themselves, but they do know that these early Mesoamericans lived in a rubber-producing region. The name Olmec comes from an Aztec word meaning "rubber people."

with other grasses to get bigger cobs and more cobs per plant. With this discovery, corn, also known as maize, became the most important food in the Americas.

Mesoamerican Civilizations
Growing corn and other crops allowed the Mesoamericans to stop wandering in search of food. As a result, they formed more complex societies. Starting around 1500 B.C., the first of several ancient civilizations appeared.

Near present-day Vera Cruz, Mexico, a people called the **Olmec** (OHL•mehk) built a far-reaching trading empire. It started around 1200 B.C. and lasted about 800 years.

The Olmec enjoyed rich farming resources, but they lacked other raw materials. They traded salt and beans with inland peoples to get jade for jewelry and obsidian, or volcanic glass, to make sharp-edged knives. They used other trade goods, such as hematite, a shiny volcanic stone, to

make polished mirrors and basalt for carving gigantic stone heads.

The Olmec used the region's many rivers as highways for trade, but eventually, the inland peoples seized control of the trade. One of these groups built the first planned city in the Americas. It became known as **Teotihuacán** (TAY•oh•TEE•wuh•KAHN), or "Place of the Gods." The city reached its height around A.D. 400. It had a population of between 120,000 to 200,000 people.

As Teotihuacán's power spread, a people called the **Maya** (MY•uh) built another civilization in the steamy rain forests of the Yucatán Peninsula (YOO•kuh•TAN). They, too, traded throughout Mesoamerica. The Maya used their central location to reach into what is now southern Mexico and Central America. Mayan traders in sea-going canoes paddled along the coast, perhaps reaching as far as the present-day United States.

CHAPTER 16   The Americas   575

CRITICAL THINKING ACTIVITY

Drawing Conclusions Explain that stories handed down from generation to generation among a people may or may not be accurate descriptions of events that actually happened. If such a story is not completely true, it may still contain details about a real event or person. A group of Native Americans called the Paiute tell old stories that involve two animal characters, Raven and Coyote. One story recounts a time when the Paiute were trying to cross some ice, but the ice was so huge that it seemed to reach the sky. Raven struck the ice and it cracked, but people still could not cross it. Coyote twice encouraged Raven to attack the ice and he did. Finally, Raven broke the ice and the people ran across it.
Ask: How does this story show that Paiute ancestors may have entered the Americas during the Ice Age? *(Answers may include that the ice was very high and might have been a glacier.)* **L2**

More About the Photo

Tikal sprawls over approximately 50 square miles (about 130 sq. km). It includes about 3,000 large buildings at the heart of the city. The ruins at Tikal have revealed much information about the Maya. Some of it comes from the decorated ceramics that archaeologists have found in tombs and from monuments that have dates on them.

Caption Answer: No one knows for sure. There may have been a problem with overpopulation, a drought, or a revolution.

What Happened to the Maya? Teotihuacán and Mayan cities hit their peaks in the A.D. 400s and A.D. 500s. Then, around A.D. 600, Teotihuacán started to decline. No one is sure why this happened. Some experts say overpopulation drained the city of food and resources. Others blame a long drought, or period without rain. Still others say that the poor people rebelled against their rich rulers. Whatever the reason, by A.D. 750, the city had been destroyed.

◀ Figure of Mayan leader

The Mayan civilization lasted about 200 years longer. But it also came to a mysterious end. The Maya abandoned their cities, and by the A.D. 900s, the cities lay deserted, hidden in a thick tangle of vines.

As the Maya left their cities, a people called the **Toltec** (TOHL•TEHK) seized what is now northern Mexico. These warrior nomads built the city of Tula northwest of present-day Mexico City. From Tula, they conquered lands all the way to the Yucatán Peninsula.

Toltec rulers tightly controlled trade. They held a **monopoly** (muh•NAH•puh•lee), or sole right, to the trade in obsidian. As a result, the Toltec kept other people from making weapons to challenge them.

▼ This pyramid was in the Mayan city of Tikal, which was located in present-day Guatemala. *What caused the downfall of the Mayan civilization?*

INTERDISCIPLINARY CONNECTIONS ACTIVITY

Science Have a volunteer summarize how warmer weather at the end of the Ice Age affected glaciers and nearby land. Explain to students that some scientists believe that Earth is once again getting warmer. They call this process global warming. Ask a small group of students to prepare a special news report on this topic. The report should include information on the suggested causes of global warming and its effects on the polar ice caps. In addition, the report should explain the possible effects of global warming on the Americas. Other students should research arguments that global warming may not actually be occurring. Ask one group member to be the news anchor, and have other group members be reporters who present particular segments of the report. **L3**

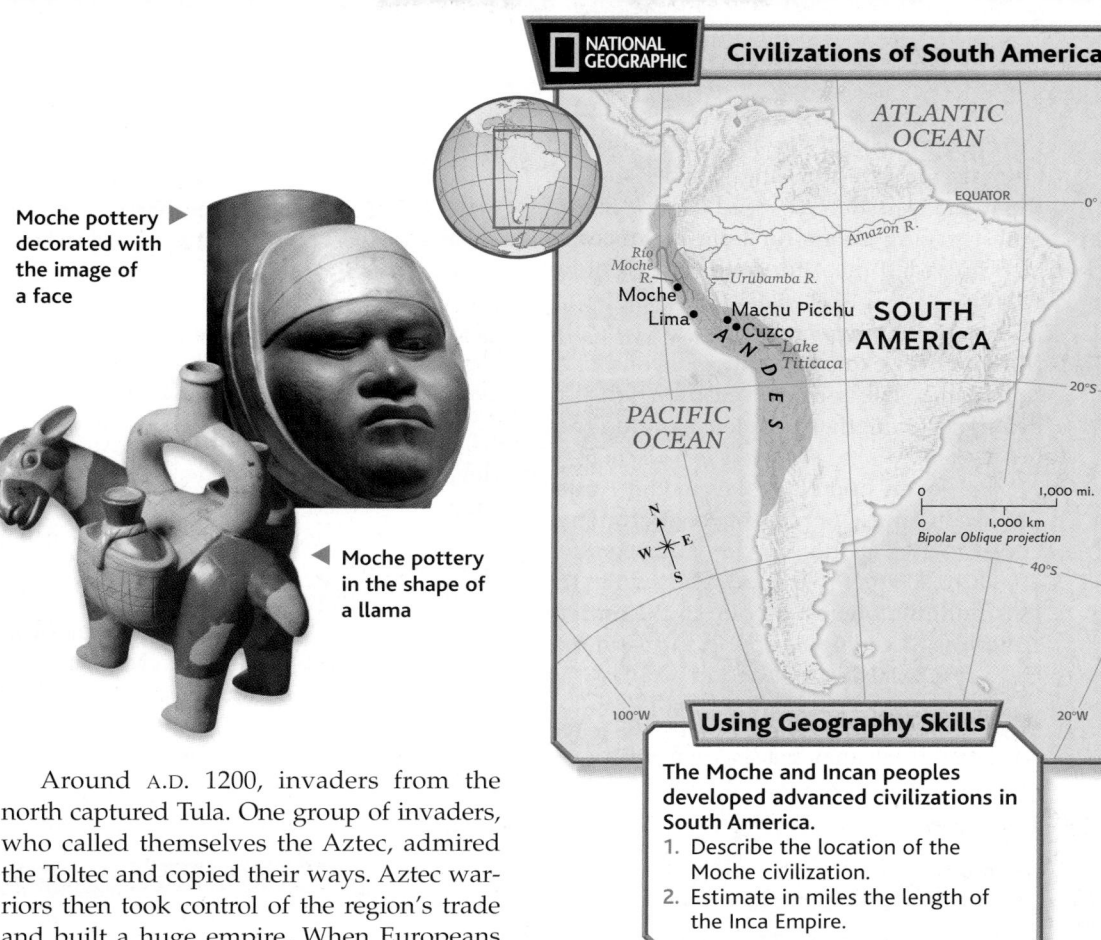

Moche pottery ▶
decorated with
the image of
a face

◀ Moche pottery
in the shape of
a llama

Using Geography Skills

Answers:

1. along the northwestern coast of South America

2. about 2,800 miles

Skills Practice

Ask: What city is Machu Picchu closest to? (*Cuzco*)

Writing Activity

Pair students and have them write a poem or a song with two voices about the Moche or another early American civilization. Have one student write one line and then pass it to the other student to write the next line. Students continue the process back and forth until they have jointly written at least 10 lines. Encourage pairs to read or perform their work. **L2**

Around A.D. 1200, invaders from the north captured Tula. One group of invaders, who called themselves the Aztec, admired the Toltec and copied their ways. Aztec warriors then took control of the region's trade and built a huge empire. When Europeans arrived in the A.D. 1500s, the Aztec ruled about five million people.

The Moche and Inca South of Mesoamerica, other civilizations developed along the west coast of South America. The **Moche** (MOH•cheh) people were located in the dry coastal desert of what is now Peru.

The Moche ruled from about A.D. 100 to A.D. 700. They dug canals that carried water from rivers in the Andes mountain ranges to their desert homeland. Because of this irrigation, the desert bloomed with crops.

The Moche suffered no shortage of food. They ate corn, squash, beans, and peanuts. They also hunted llamas and guinea pigs and fished in the nearby Pacific Ocean.

Using Geography Skills

The Moche and Incan peoples developed advanced civilizations in South America.

1. Describe the location of the Moche civilization.
2. Estimate in miles the length of the Inca Empire.

This wealth of food freed the Moche to do other things. Moche engineers designed huge pyramids, such as the Pyramid of the Sun. Moche traders exchanged goods with people as far away as the rain forests of the Amazon River valley. These goods included pottery, cloth, and jewelry.

The Moche did not have a written language. Instead, their culture's story is told

Web Activity Visit jat.glencoe.com and click on *Chapter 16—Student Web Activity* to learn more about civilizations in the Americas.

Objectives and answers to the student activity can be found in the **Web Activity Lesson Plan** feature at jat.glencoe.com

---

EXTENDING THE CONTENT

What Was Incan Music Like? The Inca produced a rich body of music, of which only fragments survive. Incan music often accompanied religious dance rituals. Musicians used repetitive rhythms and dissonant tones to create an almost hypnotic state in the dancers. Incan musicians did not have any stringed instruments before the arrival of Europeans. Instead they played wind instruments, such as the *quena*, or Andean flute, and percussion instruments—drums, bells, and small cymbals. They also played a type of bundled pipe made of bamboo or ceramic.

HISTORY Mystery

How Do We Know About People in Ancient Peru?

Two thousand years ago, the Nazca people of southern Peru etched into the ground more than 70 figures that can be clearly seen only from the air. Altogether covering almost 190 square miles (500 sq. km), the figures include trees, flowers, geometric shapes, animals, and birds. The lines may have been an outdoor temple, sacred walkways, an astronomical calendar, or copies of constellations, but their purpose remains a mystery.

in a word ...

"Mesa Verde" is Spanish in origin. *Mesa* means "table," and *verde* means "green." In 1776 the explorer Pedro Escalante saw this area from a distance. He named it Mesa Verde because the high, flat area was covered with junipers and evergreen piñons.

✓ Reading Check

Answer: They controlled the trade in obsidian, which was used to make weapons.

---

through artwork. Pottery often showed animals important to the Moche, such as the llama. The llama served as a pack animal, carrying goods for long distances. It also provided meat for food and wool for weaving.

For all their achievements, however, the Moche never expanded much beyond their homeland. The work of empire building belonged to another people called the **Inca** (IHNG•kuh).

The Incan homeland lay in the Andes mountain ranges of present-day Peru. They chose to live in high river valleys, often above 10,000 feet (3,048 m). Over time, the Inca built the biggest empire in the ancient Americas. It centered around the capital of **Cuzco** (KOOS•koh), founded in A.D. 1100.

✓ Reading Check **Explain** How did the Toltec keep other people from challenging them?

Civilizations in North America

Main Idea Early people in the northern part of the Americas built complex cultures based on farming and trade.

Reading Focus Would you be surprised to learn that early North Americans built large cities? Read to learn about the complex civilizations that developed in the American Southwest, then in the Mississippi River valley.

North of Mesoamerica, Native Americans developed their own ways of living. Still, they had learned something important from their Mesoamerican neighbors. They learned how to farm.

Farming in what would someday be the United States began in the American Southwest. It also spread from Mesoamerica along the coast and up the Mississippi, Missouri, and Ohio Rivers. As farming developed, so did new civilizations.

NATIONAL GEOGRAPHIC The Way It Was

Focus on Everyday Life

Anasazi Cliff Dwellings From far away they look like sand castles tightly stacked into the side of a canyon wall. Up close they are life-sized, ancient cliff homes. The two cowboys who discovered them in A.D. 1888 called them the "magnificent city." They found them while crossing a snowy flat-topped mountain in southwestern Colorado. The men had stumbled upon the homes of the Anasazi—an ancient people who once lived in the Southwest.

The Anasazi built nearly 600 cliff dwellings in the area now protected within Mesa Verde National Park. They began building villages under overhanging

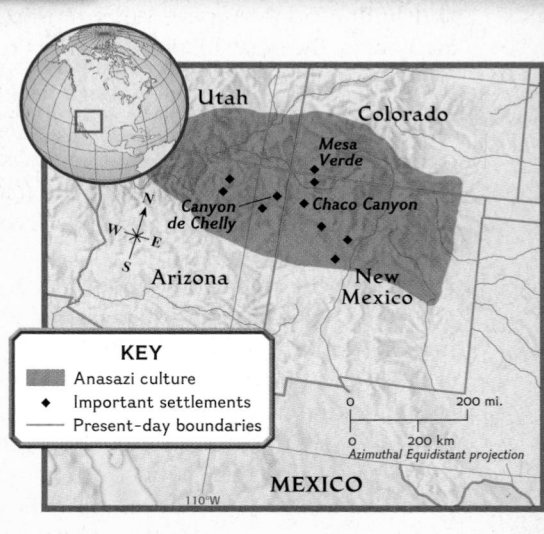

KEY
- Anasazi culture
- ◆ Important settlements
- — Present-day boundaries

0   200 mi.

0   200 km
Azimuthal Equidistant projection

CITIZENSHIP AND YOU

Comparing Responsibilities Remind students that Native Americans may have once occupied the lands where their community is now located. Ask small groups to research who these people were and how they governed themselves. As a class, discuss the responsibilities that members had toward their tribe(s). Compare these responsibilities with those that Americans have toward their government and country today. **L2**

The Hohokam and Anasazi News of farming traveled north along with Mesoamerican traders. But it took a long time for nomads in the scorching deserts of the Southwest to try farming.

Finally, around A.D. 300, a people called the **Hohokam** (HOH•hoh•KAHM) planted gardens on lands between the Salt and Gila Rivers. They dug more than 500 miles (805 km) of canals to carry river waters to their fields. They grew corn, cotton, beans, and squash. They also made pottery, turquoise pendants, and the world's first etchings by using cactus juice to eat through the surface of shells.

The Hohokam thrived for about 1,000 years. In the mid-A.D. 1300s, they mysteriously fled. Perhaps a long drought drove them away, or floods from heavy rains destroyed their canals. No one is sure.

Around A.D. 600, as the Hohokam planted fields near rivers, the **Anasazi** (AH•nuh•SAH•zee) moved into the region's canyons and cliffs. They also took up farming. However, they did not rely only on rivers for irrigation. They collected water that ran off cliffs during heavy rains and channeled it to their fields.

Anasazi culture reached its height at Chaco Canyon, an area in present-day New Mexico. The people there controlled the trade in turquoise. They used it like money, to buy goods from many different regions including Mesoamerica.

The Anasazi lived in huge apartment-like houses carved into cliffs. The cliff houses had hundreds of rooms and held thousands of people. Spanish explorers later called these buildings *pueblos*—the Spanish word for "village." The Anasazi

► The Cliff Palace at Mesa Verde National Park

cliffs around A.D. 1200. Many scholars believe they settled in the cliffs for protection from the weather and from other groups. Villages were not constructed according to any plan. Each home was built to fill the space available. Some homes are several stories tall. Sandstone and mud mortar still hold them together.

The Anasazi probably did much of their daily work in open courtyards. Artifacts have revealed their skill at making baskets, sandals, and pottery. By A.D.1300, the Anasazi had left Mesa Verde. A severe drought during that time may have forced them to leave the area.

► Anasazi pottery

◄ Anasazi jewelry

Connecting to the Past
1. Why do you think villages were not constructed according to a plan?
2. The Anasazi lived at Mesa Verde for only about 100 years. What—besides the drought—might have made them leave?

579

COOPERATIVE LEARNING ACTIVITY

Discovering the Hopewell Explain that the Hopewell people are known for their crafts and mounds. Then organize the class into small groups. Ask some groups to find photos of Hopewell metalwork and stonework, make copies of the pictures, and arrange them in a bulletin board display. Captions should provide background for each item. Other groups should investigate the mounds that the Hopewell built. Have each group make a labeled drawing or three-dimensional representation of one of the mounds. The labels should contain important information about the mound, such as its size, location, and, if possible, its use. Provide space in which groups may display their representations. **L2**

Refer to the **Quizzes, Tests, and Authentic Assessment (with Rubrics)** booklet for rubrics.

③ ASSESS

Assign Section 1 Review as homework or as an in-class activity.

◉ Have students use the **Interactive Tutor Self-Assessment CD-ROM** to review the section.

Assessment L2

Assign **Section 1 Quiz** to assess mastery of the material found in the section.

Reading Support L1/ EL

Assign **Reading Essentials and Study Guide 16–1** to help students review section material.

More About the Art

The Great Serpent Mound extends for nearly one-quarter of a mile. The mound looks like a snake trying to swallow a giant egg. Its builders did not intend for the Great Serpent Mound to be a tomb. Native American graves are nearby, not inside the mound.

Caption Answer: the Hopewell

prospered until a 50-year drought occurred in the early A.D. 1000s. Like the Hohokam, they also drifted away.

Who Were the Mound Builders?

Far to the east, across the Mississippi River, another civilization was taking shape. It started around 1000 B.C. and lasted until about A.D. 400. Its founders built huge mounds made of earth, some in the shape of animals. Such earthworks gave these people their name—"Mound Builders."

Two groups formed the mound-building culture—first the Adena, then the Hopewell. Together they settled on lands stretching from the Great Lakes to the Gulf of Mexico.

Although the Mound Builders lived mostly as hunters and gatherers, they experimented with farming. Scientists think they tamed many wild plants, including sunflowers, gourds, and barley. It is likely that women planted the first seeds. Women probably knew the most about plants because they gathered wild foods while the men hunted.

Corn was first brought to the region around A.D. 100, probably carried there by traders. These traders traveled near and far to find raw materials for weapons, jewelry, and fine carvings. Many of these objects were placed in huge burial mounds to honor the dead.

The Mississippians

The mound-building culture changed when the Hopewell mysteriously declined and a new people known as the Mississippians emerged. The Mississippians were named for their location in the Mississippi River valley. Their lands reached from present-day Ohio, Indiana, and Illinois, south to the Gulf of Mexico.

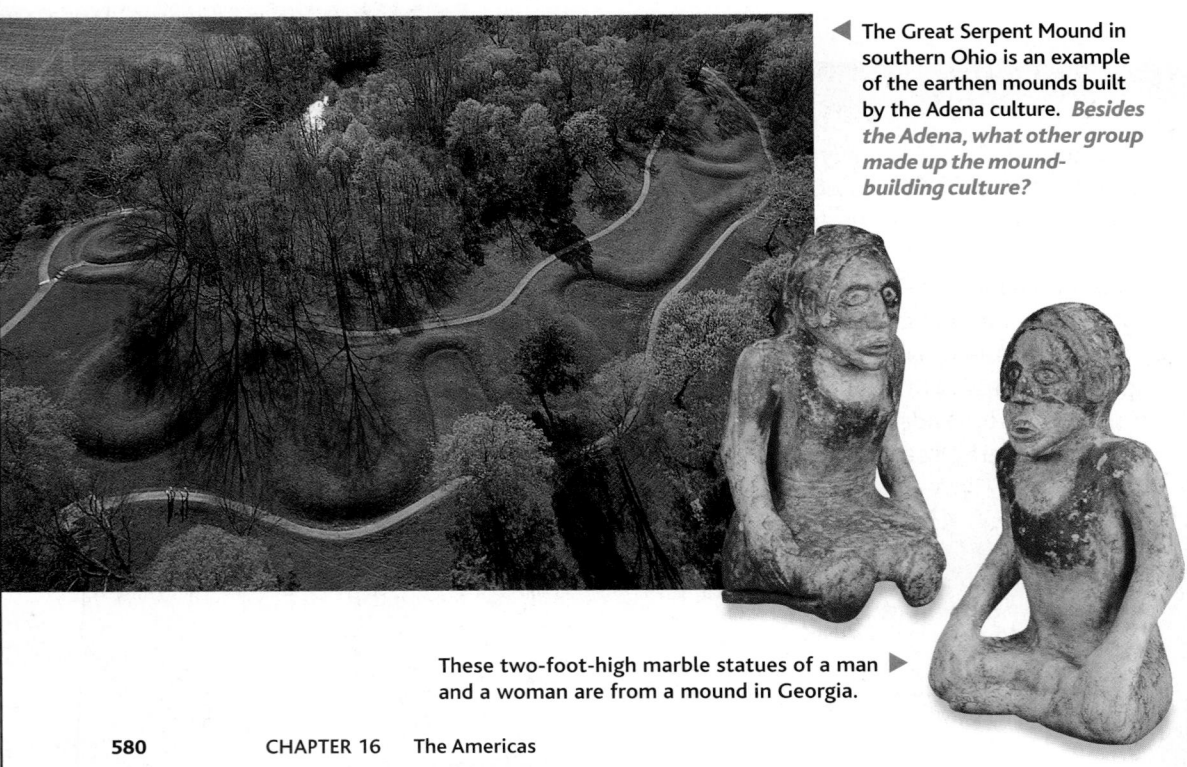

◀ The Great Serpent Mound in southern Ohio is an example of the earthen mounds built by the Adena culture. *Besides the Adena, what other group made up the mound-building culture?*

These two-foot-high marble statues of a man and a woman are from a mound in Georgia. ▶

CRITICAL THINKING ACTIVITY

Making Inferences Have a volunteer point out on a wall map the approximate area where the Mound Builders settled. Discuss how people probably traveled from place to place. *(on foot, by boat)* Ask students to speculate on the geographic features that facilitated travel in the eastern half of the present-day United States. *(inland waterways—rivers and lakes)* Have students pick out some connecting waterways, such as the Mississippi and Ohio Rivers, which exemplify the point. **L2**

◄ A Cahokia mound in Illinois ►

The Mississippians found that plants grew well in the rich floodplains along the river. They harvested enough crops to become full-time farmers. The most common crops included corn, squash, and beans.

As in Mesoamerica, large-scale farming led to the rise of cities. Some contained 10,000 or more people. The largest city, **Cahokia** (kuh•HOH•kee•uh), may have had 30,000 people. The remains of this city can still be seen in southwestern Illinois.

The Mississippians built a different kind of mound. Their mounds were pyramid shaped but with flat tops. The base of the biggest one covered 16 acres (6.5 ha), more than the base of the Great Pyramid of Egypt.

The finished mound, known today as Monks Mound, rose more than 100 feet (30 m) high. From the mound's summit, rulers gazed down at dozens of smaller mounds. The flat tops of the mounds held temples, homes for the rich, and burial places.

In the early A.D. 1300s, the Mississippian civilization collapsed, and the cities were abandoned. Perhaps other Native Americans attacked them, or the city may have become too big to feed itself.

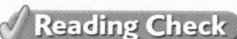 **Identify** How was turquoise used by the Anasazi of Chaco Canyon?

Study Central™ Need help with the material in this section? Visit jat.glencoe.com

Section 1 Review

Reading Summary

Review the Main Ideas

- The first Americans were most likely hunter-gatherers who came from Asia across a land bridge.

- A number of civilizations developed in the Americas, including the Olmec, Maya, and Toltec in Central America and Mexico, and the Moche and Inca in South America. All were dependent on farming.

- In North America, farming civilizations arose in the Southwest and then in the Ohio and Mississippi River valleys.

What Did You Learn?

1. Why was Mesoamerica's geography ideal for farming?

2. How did the first Americans develop corn?

Critical Thinking

3. **Summarizing Information** Draw a chart like the one below. Add details about the early peoples of North America.

Native Americans
Southwest
East/Mississippi River Valley

4. **Summarize** How and when did the first people come to the Americas, and how did they live once they were here?

5. **Geography** How did geography shape the development of the Anasazi civilization?

6. **Expository Writing** Write a short essay comparing the civilizations that developed in Mesoamerica to those that developed in South America.

7. **Reading** Summarizing Information Write a paragraph that summarizes how farming led to the development of civilizations.

ENRICH

Tell students that the Mississippians invented a heavy flint hoe that helped revolutionize farming. Ask students to suggest reasons why this tool helped make the Mississippians successful farmers. (*Answers may include that this durable hoe helped them break up the ground for planting crops.*) **L2**

Answer: as money

History Online

To help students understand section material, have them visit Study Central™ **at jat.glencoe.com**

RETEACH

Ask students to brainstorm what took place in the lives of hunter-gatherers after they began farming. **L1/ EL**

④ CLOSE

Ask students to summarize in four or five sentences the various early civilizations discussed in this section. **L2**

SECTION 1 REVIEW ANSWERS

1. It had rich, volcanic soil; a mild climate; and rainfall in spring and fall.

2. crossed corn with other grasses to get bigger cobs and more cobs per plant

3. Charts should be based on the text and include all the peoples in the section.

4. They may have come across a land bridge from Asia 15,000 to 40,000 years ago. They lived as hunter-gatherers.

5. lived in hot, dry area; Anasazi collected rain that ran off cliffs; lived in homes carved into cliffs

6. Essays will vary but may include the importance of agriculture, other economic activities, sources of power, and reason(s) for decline.

7. Answers will vary but should be based on facts from this section.

① FOCUS

SECTION OVERVIEW

This section explores how the Maya, Aztec, Inca, and the various peoples north of Mexico adapted to the environments in which they lived and established unique cultures.

BELLRINGER
SKILLBUILDER ACTIVITY

🖐 Project **Daily Focus Skills Transparency 16–2** and have students answer questions. Discuss their responses.

Get Ready to Read!

Preteaching Vocabulary: Explain that the textbook often uses punctuation, such as commas and dashes, to alert students that a definition is coming. Demonstrate the use of commas with the term *quipu* in this section. Then have volunteers explain their use for *igloo* and *confederation*.

Answers to Graphic: From highest to lowest: rulers and Coyas; head priest and commander of armies; regional army leaders; temple priests, army commanders, skilled workers (musicians, artisans, accountants); farmers, herders, soldiers

Section 2

Life in the Americas

Get Ready to Read!

What's the Connection?
In Section 1, you read about the rise of the first civilizations in the Americas. The first Americans had to use whatever natural resources the land had to offer. As a result, they developed many different cultures suited to where they lived.

Focusing on the Main Ideas
• The Maya adjusted to life in the tropical rain forest and built a culture based on their religious beliefs. *(page 583)*

• The Aztec moved into the Valley of Mexico, where they created an empire based on conquest and war. *(page 585)*

• To unite their huge empire, Incan rulers set up a highly organized government and society. *(page 588)*

• The geography in lands north of present-day Mexico shaped the developement of many different Native American cultures. *(page 590)*

Locating Places
Petén (peh•TEHN)
Tenochtitlán
(tay•NAWCH•teet•LAHN)

Meeting People
Pachacuti (PAH•chah•KOO•tee)
Iroquois (IHR•uh•KWOY)

Building Your Vocabulary
quipu (KEE•poo)
igloo
adobe (uh•DOH•bee)
confederation
(kuhn•FEH•duh•RAY•shuhn)

Reading Strategy
Organizing Information Use a pyramid to show the Inca's social classes.

NATIONAL GEOGRAPHIC When & Where?

A.D. 1300   A.D. 1400   A.D. 1500

C. A.D. 1250
Aztec arrive in central Mexico

A.D. 1325
Aztec build Tenochtitlán

C. A.D. 1438
Pachacuti starts to build Inca Empire

Tenochtitlán•
Cuzco•

582   CHAPTER 16   The Americas

SECTION RESOURCES

Reproducible Masters
• Reproducible Lesson Plan 16–2
• Daily Lecture and Discussion Notes 16–2
• Vocabulary Activity 16–2
• Active Reading Note-Taking Guide 16–2
• Guided Reading Activity 16–2
• Section Quiz 16–2
• Reading Essentials and Study Guide 16–2

Transparencies
• Daily Focus Skills Transparency 16–2

Multimedia
⊙ Interactive Tutor Self-Assessment CD-ROM
⊙ ExamView® Pro Testmaker CD-ROM
⊙ Presentation Plus! CD-ROM
⊙ Glencoe BookLink CD-ROM

The Mayan People

Main Idea The Maya adjusted to life in the tropical rain forest and built a culture based on their religious beliefs.

Reading Focus What would it be like to live in a jungle? What resources would be easy to find? Read to learn how the Maya adapted to life in the jungles of Mesoamerica.

In A.D. 1839 an American lawyer named John Lloyd Stevens and an English artist named Frederick Catherwood slashed their way into the tangled Yucatán rain forest. There they made an amazing discovery. They found the vine-covered ruins of an ancient city.

Stevens and Catherwood soon learned that the people who had built the city were called the Maya, and that they were the ancestors of the millions of Maya who still live in present-day Mexico, Guatemala, Honduras, El Salvador, and Belize.

Mayan City-States At first glance, it looked like the Maya had settled in one of the worst spots on Earth. They picked the **Petén** (peh•TEHN), the Mayan word for "flat region." Located in present-day Guatemala, the Petén's dense forests nearly blocked out the sun. Stinging insects filled the air. Poisonous snakes slithered on the ground, and monkeys and parrots screeched in the treetops. Even so, the ancient Maya thrived.

The Maya saw what others missed. Swamps and sinkholes gave them a year-round source of water. The sinkholes—areas where the earth has collapsed—connected the Maya with a huge system of underground rivers and streams. They served as Mayan wells.

Even with a ready water supply, only an organized culture could have succeeded in building cities and fields in the Petén. The effort required cooperation among many people, which could only be accomplished by having an organized government.

▲ This Mayan wall painting shows musicians celebrating a royal birth.
Where did the Maya first settle?

CHAPTER 16   The Americas   **583**

② TEACH

Reading Strategy

Forming Questions Read aloud the opening paragraph of this section. **Ask: If you had been Stevens or Catherwood, what would have been your first questions when you saw the vine-covered ancient city?** Record student questions and use them as a guide for reading about the Maya. **L1**

Daily Lecture and Discussion Notes 16–2

Use **Daily Lecture and Discussion Notes 16–2** for an outline of key concepts found in the section.

Reading Support L1/ EL

Use **Vocabulary Activity 16–2** to review important terms in the section.

More About the Art

The Maya honored their deities and kings in elaborate wall murals.

Caption Answer: in the Petén, or flat region, of present-day Guatemala

Reading Strategy ◄ READING THE TEXT

Making Predictions Ask: What types of information do you usually learn about a civilization? *(government, social classes, characteristics that people valued, important accomplishments, economy, contributions in the arts, and so on)* Then have the class skim pages 582–588 to learn which civilizations will be discussed. Write "Maya," "Aztec," and "Inca " as column headings on the board. Next, review what the class already knows about these civilizations and list the information under the headings. Remind or point out to students that the Maya had cities, the Aztec were a warlike people, and both the Aztec and the Inca built empires. Tell small groups of students to use what they know about civilizations in general and these peoples in particular to list three or four predictions about them. Have groups check their predictions after reading the section. **L2**

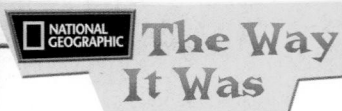

The Way It Was

Answers:

1. by using his hips to drive a hard rubber ball through a stone ring 27 feet (8 m) above the playing field
2. The losing team was sacrificed to the gods in a ceremony at the end of the game.

Reading Strategy

Writing Activity

Ask students to react to the Mayan ball game in a journal entry. Have them consider the following questions:

- Does the description of the game itself make it sound interesting or exciting to watch? Why or why not?
- Why might players have been willing to risk their lives to play in the game?
- How do you feel about the penalty for losing?
- Do you see any similarities between the importance of this game and sports today? Why or why not?

Encourage volunteers to share their entries with the class.
L1/ EL

NATIONAL GEOGRAPHIC The Way It Was

Sports & Contests

Mayan Ball Game Mayan cities had many ball courts. In a Mayan ball game, teams of two or three players tried to drive a hard rubber ball through a decorated stone ring. Players wore helmets, gloves, and knee and hip guards made of animal hide to protect themselves against the hard rubber balls. They were not allowed to use their hands or feet to throw or bat the ball. They had to use their hips to drive the ball through the stone rings.

Because the stone rings were placed 27 feet (8 m) above the ground on a large rectangular field, players had to have incredible skill to score a goal. Making a goal was so rare that when a player scored, crowds rewarded the hero with clothing and jewelry.

Scholars think that a Mayan ball game was more than a sport or contest. It had a religious and symbolic meaning—as well as deadly results. The losing team was sacrificed to the gods in a ceremony after the game.

▲ Mayan ballplayer

Connecting to the Past
1. How did a player score in a Mayan ball game?
2. Why was losing especially painful for a team?

The Maya set up city-states. Within each city-state, rulers supplied the leadership—and military force—for great building projects. Leadership passed from one king to the next, and the city-states often fought with each other.

Life in the Mayan Cities The rulers of Mayan city-states said they were descended from the sun. They claimed the right to rule as god-kings and expected every person to serve them. Service included building huge monuments to honor them.

As god-kings, Mayan rulers taught their subjects how to please the gods. One way was human sacrifice. The Maya believed that the gods gave their life-giving fluid, rain, to keep humans strong. So humans kept the gods strong by giving their own life-giving fluid, blood.

When the Maya marched into battle, they wanted captives more than they wanted land. During times of drought, Mayan priests offered the captives to Chac, the god of rain and sunlight. The Maya believed Chac lived in the waters below the sinkholes. Captives were often thrown into these watery pits to earn the god's favor.

The Maya believed that the gods controlled everything that happened on Earth. As a result, religion was at the core of Mayan life. A huge pyramid with a temple at the top towered over every city. Priests, who claimed to know what the gods wanted, set up a strict class system in which everyone had a place.

Royal Mayan women often married into royal families in distant Mayan city-states. This practice strengthened trade. It also helped form alliances—political agreements between people or states to work together.

DIFFERENTIATED INSTRUCTION

Visual/Spatial: Refer students to the **Aztec Daily Life** feature. Have them create a similar visual feature for the Maya, Inca, or one of the North American groups in this section.

English Learners: Have these students help make the display. As English learners encounter new vocabulary, they should make illustrated lists of the words and expressions and their meanings. Have these students help write the labels and make illustrations for the display.

Gifted and Talented: Ask students to serve as researchers for the display group. The researchers should help find information and pictures for the feature designers.

☞ Refer to *Inclusion Strategies for the Middle School Social Studies Classroom* in the TCR.

▲ Statue of a Mayan god

Women played a large role in the Mayan city-states. In one Mayan carving, a woman wears a war headdress and rides atop a platform carried by soldiers. In the city-state of Calakmul, at least two women served as all-powerful queens. One of them may have helped to found the city.

Mayan Science and Writing Both queens and kings turned to Mayan priests for advice. The priests thought gods revealed their plans through movements of the sun, moon, and stars, so they studied the heavens closely.

The Maya also needed to know when to plant their crops. By watching the sky, the priests learned about astronomy. They developed a 365-day calendar to keep track of heavenly movements. They used it to predict eclipses and to schedule religious festivals, plantings, and harvests. To chart the passage of time, the Maya developed a system of mathematics. They invented a method of counting based on 20.

The Maya also invented a written language to record numbers and dates. Like the Egyptians, the Maya used a system of hieroglyphics. Symbols represented sounds, words, or ideas. Only nobles could read them, however. After the collapse of the Mayan civilization, nobody could read them at all. Only in recent times have scholars begun to unlock the stories told by the hieroglyphics.

Reading Check **Identify** What was the main advantage of living in a tropical rain forest?

The Aztec

Main Idea The Aztec moved into the Valley of Mexico, where they created an empire based on conquest and war.

Reading Focus Why do you think some countries try to conquer other countries? Read to learn why the Aztec people conquered their neighbors and built an empire.

The warlike Aztec nomads who arrived in the Valley of Mexico about A.D. 1250 were anything but welcome. One king was sure he knew a way to get rid of them. He granted the Aztec a patch of snake-filled land. He expected the deadly serpents to destroy them. Instead, the Aztec feasted on roasted snakes and eventually built their own kingdom.

The Aztec Government The Aztec clearly knew how to survive. They had wandered for hundreds of years in search of a home that

An Aztec Warrior

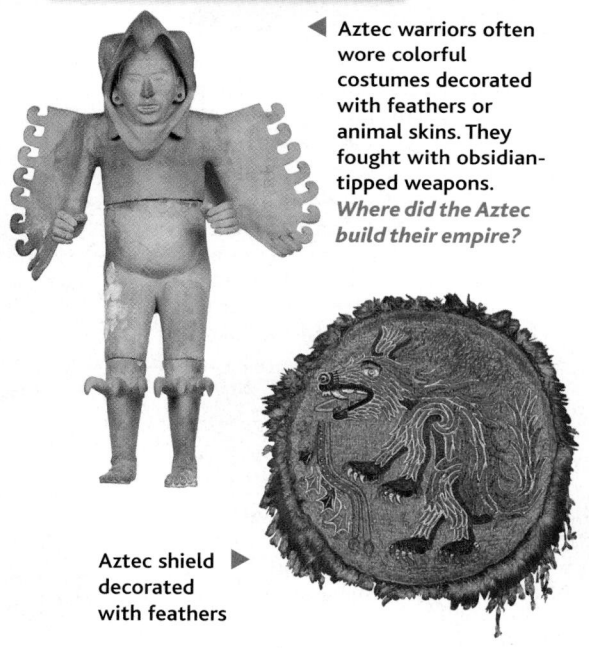

◀ Aztec warriors often wore colorful costumes decorated with feathers or animal skins. They fought with obsidian-tipped weapons. *Where did the Aztec build their empire?*

Aztec shield ▶ decorated with feathers

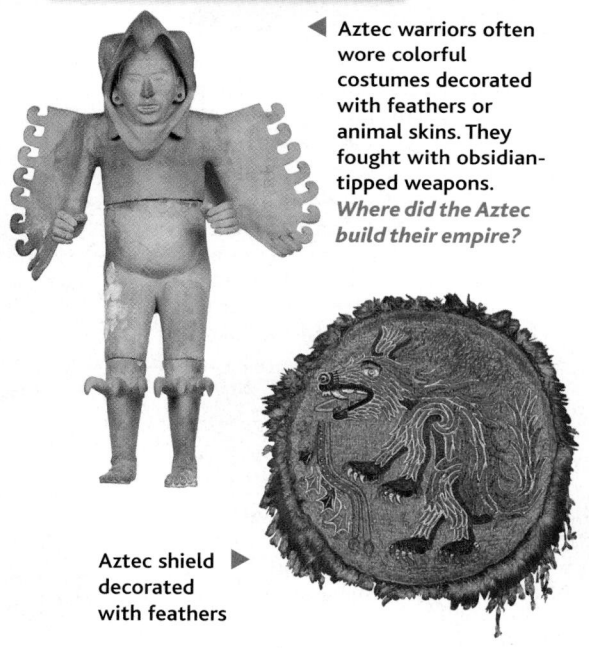

585

TIME TRAVELER

Chocolate was popular among the Maya. From common people to royalty, they drank it at nearly every meal. They poured it from spouted vessels known as chocolate pots. The Maya served a very thick chocolate with foam on the top. The recipe included such ingredients as honey, chili, maize, or water. In keeping with Mayan respect for chocolate, botanists gave the cacao tree the name *Theobroma cacao*—"food of the gods."

Reading Check

Answer: Swamps and sink-holes offered a year-round source of water.

More About the Art

The Aztec valued the bright feathers of parrots and the prized green quetzal. The Aztec not only used them for shields, but in headdresses and cloaks.

Caption Answer: in Mexico

CRITICAL THINKING ACTIVITY

Drawing Conclusions Elicit from students Aztec beliefs about how a person could have an afterlife. Explain that afterlife for the Aztec consisted of resting in the presence of the sun. **Ask:** Why would the Aztec consider being with the sun good or important? *(Answers may include that the sun symbolized the most important Aztec god and, therefore, being in his presence was the highest honor possible.)* Then discuss where other people went when they died and what opinion the Aztec might have of the Land of the Dead. *(Answers may include that it was inferior to being in the presence of the sun god.)* Point out that if ordinary people did not die in the service of the gods, they had no way of having an afterlife with the sun god. **Ask:** How would these religious beliefs probably have affected the Aztec? *(Answers may include that they would have been more willing to die for their gods.)* **L2**

Connecting Values and Actions
Ask students how the Aztec leader was selected. Then elicit the characteristics that the council looked for in a leader.
Ask: What do these choices show about the Aztec? (*They were a warlike people.*) L1/ EL

CONNECTING ACROSS TIME

The floating gardens are called *chinampas,* after an area in the Valley of Mexico. This area was called Xochimilco at the time of the Aztec and still is. *Xochimilco* means "where the flowers grow." The floating gardens method of agriculture was developed there. Ask a volunteer to describe how the Aztec made these floating gardens. L1/ EL

More About the Art

At its height in the A.D. 1400s, Tenochtitlán had about 200,000 people.

Caption Answer: Victims were sacrificed to the gods.

---

they believed their sun god—the feathered serpent Quetzalcoatl (KWEHT•suhl•kuh•WAH•tuhl)—had promised them. According to legend, the Aztec would know they had found this place when an eagle "screams and spreads its wings, and eats . . . the serpent."

According to Aztec legend, they found their homeland after they sacrificed a local princess to one of their gods. The princess's father vowed to wipe out the Aztec, who only numbered several hundred. The Aztec went on the run. In A.D. 1325, they took shelter on a soggy, swampy island in Lake Texcoco (tehs•KOH•koh). There an eagle greeted them from its perch on a prickly pear cactus. It tore apart a snake dangling from its beak. Then it spread its wings and screamed in triumph. Filled with wonder at this sight, the Aztec believed that they had reached the end of their journey.

Priests, speaking for the gods, told the Aztec what to do next: build a great city. Workers toiled day and night. They dug soil from the lake bottom to build bridges to the mainland. They built floating gardens, piling soil on rafts anchored to the lake bottom.

The Aztec called their new city **Tenochtitlán** (tay•NAWCH•teet•LAHN), which means "place of the prickly pear cactus." As the city rose from the marshes, the Aztec dreamed of conquest and wealth. They wanted to collect tribute, or payment for protection, from conquered peoples.

To fulfill their goal, the Aztec turned to strong kings who claimed descent from the gods. A council of warriors, priests, and nobles picked each king from the royal family. Council members usually chose the last king's son, but not always. They looked for a king who would bring glory to the Aztec. They expected a king to prove himself by leading troops into battle.

Tenochtitlán

At the center of Tenochtitlán was a walled ceremonial area. It contained temples, schools and the priests' houses. *What ceremonial act took place at the top of the Great Temple?*

The founding of ▶
Tenochtitlán

The Great Temple
Atop the Great Temple were two shrines dedicated to the rain god Tlaloc and the sun and war god Huitzilopochtli.

Round Temple
The round temple was dedicated to the Aztec god Quetzalcoatl.

Ball Court
Aztecs played a ritual ball game on courts that were often richly decorated.

INTERDISCIPLINARY CONNECTIONS ACTIVITY

Art Have several students research the present-day flag of Mexico. Ask them to reproduce the flag on poster board. Ask students if they can determine the meaning of the three colors on the flag. (*green: independence; white: the Catholic religion; red: union*) Have the class examine the design on the flag and explain its connection to the Aztec. (*According to tradition, the Aztec believed in a prophecy that stated that they would find their new home when they found an eagle sitting on a prickly pear cactus and eating a snake. The event took place when they were on an island, and the water stands for the lake.*) **Ask:** How do Mexicans probably think of the Aztec? (*Answers may include that Mexicans are proud of their Aztec heritage.*) L2

Aztec Daily Life

Aztec homes were simple and built for usefulness rather than beauty. **How do you think the Aztec used each of the household items shown here?**

▲ Aztec bowl and loom

Aztec ▶ grinding stone

▲ Painting of Aztec home

More About the Art

Aztec paintings were done on walls and amatl (paper made of pounded bark).

Caption Answer: loom: for weaving cloth; grinding stone: for grinding corn; painting: for decoration; bowl: for eating

Comparing Spartans and Aztec
Draw a chart on the board with the headings "Comparisons," "Spartans," and "Aztec." Then ask students to suggest the categories for comparison. The completed chart should include information about the role of women and girls, the role of boys and men, social values, and the accomplishments of the civilizations. **L2**

Childbirth carried special meaning for the Aztec. Parents consulted soothsayers who studied the birth date and predicted their infant's fortunes.

Answer: by an act of bravery in war

Life in the Aztec Empire

The king, or emperor, was at the top of Aztec society. The rest of the population fell into four classes: nobles, commoners, unskilled laborers, and enslaved people. Commoners formed the largest group, working as farmers, artisans, or traders. They could join the noble class by performing one act of bravery in war. They, or their children if the soldier died, received land and the rank of noble.

In serving their gods, the Aztec saw death as honorable. Those worthy of an afterlife included soldiers who died in battle, captives who gave their lives in sacrifice, and women who died in childbirth. Others went to the "Land of the Dead," the lowest level in the underworld.

From an early age, children learned about the glories of war and their duties as an Aztec. When a baby boy came into the world, the midwife, or woman who helped with the birth, cried: "You must understand that your home is not here where you have been born, for you are a warrior!"

A baby girl heard different words. As she drew her first breath, the midwife declared: "As the heart stays in the body, so you must stay in the house." Although women stayed at home, those who gave birth were honored as heroes by Aztec society.

Nearly everything the Aztec did grew out of a promise. Speaking through priests, the god Huitzilopochtli (wee•tsee•loh•POHKT•lee) vowed: "We shall conquer all the people in the universe."

This promise inspired the Aztec to honor the god with a huge pyramid in the center of Tenochtitlán. Known as the Great Temple, it rose 135 feet (41 m) high and had more than 100 steps. Thousands of victims were taken to the top, where they were sacrificed to the gods.

✓ **Reading Check** **Describe** How could commoners move into the noble class?

EXTENDING THE CONTENT

What Is Known About Mayan Literature? The *Popol Vuh* was found in a Dominican monastery in the A.D. 1500s. It contains the first written account of Mayan myths. The *Popol Vuh* describes the universe before Earth was created: "There is not yet one person, one animal, bird, fish, crab, tree, rock, hollow, canyon, meadow, forest. Only the sky alone is there; the face of the earth is not clear. Only the sea alone is pooled under all the sky; there is nothing whatever gathered together. It is at rest; not a single thing stirs."

Reading Strategy

Connecting Cause and Effect
Divide the class into three small groups—one each for the Maya, the Aztec, and the Inca. Ask each group to list the religious beliefs of their people. Where possible, groups should also record how their people acted as the result of a particular belief. Tell groups to organize their information under the following headings:

Belief → Action(s)

On the board, draw a pair of columns for each civilization and record group findings. Then examine the results in two ways. First, compare ways that religious beliefs affected actions. Did beliefs lead to the same or different actions across civilizations? Second, judge the importance of religion in these civilizations by discussing how it affected decisions. **L3**

Uniting an Empire Elicit from students why geography posed problems to establishing a centralized Incan government. Then discuss the relationship between good roads and maintaining central control. Make parallels with the Roman and Persian Empires. **L2**

Reading Check

Answer: took their sons to Cuzco for training

Life in the Inca Empire

Main Idea To unite their huge empire, Incan rulers set up a highly organized government and society.

Reading Focus Have you ever tried to organize a large number of people? It is not easy to get everyone to work together. Read how the Inca organized their society and developed ways to hold their empire together.

The ancient Inca blamed earthquakes on the god Pachacamac, "Lord of the earth." Whenever Pachacamac lost his temper, the earth shook. Pachacamac was the highest Incan god. It is not surprising that the greatest Incan leader took the name **Pachacuti** (PAH•chah•KOO•tee), which means "Earthshaker."

Pachacuti lived up to his name. Starting around A.D. 1438, Pachacuti and his son, Topa Inca, built the largest ancient empire in the Americas. It stretched north to south about 2,500 miles (4,023 km)—about the distance between present-day Los Angeles and New York.

▲ Incan gold mask

Pachacuti created a plan to hold his empire together. He set up a strong central government but let local rulers stay in power. To ensure their loyalty, he took their sons to Cuzco for training.

Pachacuti united the empire in other ways too. He required people to learn Quechua (KEH•chuh•wuh), the language spoken by the Inca. He also designed a system of roads, which covered about 25,000 miles (40,234 km) when finished.

An Organized Society The Inca believed the sun god Inti protected Cuzco, the Incan capital. The rulers who lived there called themselves "sons of the sun." As such,

rulers and their wives, known as Coyas, were at the top of society.

The head priest and commander of the armies were just below the royal couple. Next came regional army leaders. Below them were temple priests, army commanders, and skilled workers—musicians, artisans, and accountants. The bottom level consisted of farmers, herders, and ordinary soldiers.

The Inca further divided society into 12 job categories. Within these, every man, woman, and child over age five had work to do. Young girls, for example, were babysitters, while young boys chased birds from gardens.

What Was Incan Culture Like? The Inca rarely honored their gods with human sacrifice. They turned to sacrifice only in times of trouble, such as during earthquakes, or on special occasions. Priests most often sacrificed children, whom they thought were more pure than adults. The Inca worshiped the sacrificed children as gods.

To please their gods, the Inca built large works of stone. They had no system of writing, no wheels, and no iron tools. Yet they built places like Machu Picchu (MAH•choo PEE•choo), a retreat for Incan kings.

Building large structures required the Inca to develop a way to do mathematical calculations. The Inca used a **quipu** (KEE•poo), a rope with knotted cords of different lengths and colors. Each knot represented a number or item, which was also a way of keeping records.

The Inca were skilled engineers. Workers fit stones so tightly together that a knife could not slip between them. Because the Inca used no mortar, the stone blocks could slide up and down without collapsing whenever an earthquake rocked the earth.

Reading Check **Explain** How did Pachacuti make sure local leaders would be loyal to him?

COOPERATIVE LEARNING ACTIVITY

Presenting Machu Picchu Have students work in small groups to do an in-depth study of this royal retreat. Assign each of the following tasks to a different group:

- A labeled model or map of the present-day city or of the mountainous terrain around the city
- A report on the mummies that have been found there, on the importance of the city during the last days of the Inca Empire, or on the search for and discovery of Machu Picchu
- Labeled illustrations of items from everyday life, such as clothing, utensils, jewelry, and art objects

Ask a volunteer from each group to give a brief presentation about the most interesting information that members found. Allow groups time to display their projects and view other students' work. **L2**

Biography

PACHACUTI
Ruled 1438–1471

Pachacuti was the son of the eighth Inca king, Viracocha. In 1438 an enemy from the north attacked the capital city, Cuzco. Viracocha fled, but Pachacuti stayed behind to defend the city and defeat the enemy. Because of his victory, Pachacuti became king.

At first, Pachacuti concentrated on expanding the Inca Empire. When he wanted to conquer a kingdom, he first sent messengers to tell the local rulers all the benefits of being part of the Inca Empire and then asked them to join willingly. If they accepted, they were treated with respect and given some rights. If they refused, the Incas attacked with brutal force.

Pachacuti next turned his attention to rebuilding Cuzco. He was the first to use white granite as a building material. No mortar was needed to hold the granite stones together because the sides of each piece were cut accurately and fit closely together.

Pachacuti built an estate for himself called Machu Picchu. It was made of white granite and was located thousands of feet high in the Andes. Recent research suggests that Machu Picchu was used not only as a home for the royal family, but also as a center for celebrations and ceremonial gatherings.

According to legend translated from a sacred text, Pachacuti became very sick when he was an elderly man. He called all of his relatives to his bedside. He divided his possessions among them and then made a speech with instructions for his burial.

▲ Pachacuti

> **"I was born as a flower of the field . . . "**
> —Pachacuti, as quoted in
> *History of the Incas*

▲ Machu Picchu

Then and Now

How can a nation today get another nation to do something without threatening war?

589

Biography

TEACH

Pachacuti did more than wage expansionist wars. He sponsored a huge agricultural project that increased the amount of arable land in the Cuzco Valley. He had the valley floor leveled and terraces dug into the hillsides. In addition, Pachacuti set up a state religion and supported the idea that the Inca were duty-bound to propagate it. Rebuilding Cuzco, the capital, was another of his priorities.

Ask students what people believe are the most important issues for their local or state government to address. **Ask:** Are elected officials showing that these are important issues because they are working to solve these problems? *(Answers will vary, but they may include education and housing; students should support their opinions.)* **L2**

Then and Now

Answers may include refusing to buy goods from the other nation or offering the other nation needed goods or loans.

Reading List Generator CD-ROM

GLENCOE BOOKLINK

RECOMMENDED READING

Use the **Glencoe BookLink CD-ROM** to create customized reading lists based on your students' interests and reading levels. Below is an example based on content in this chapter. Also, see the Suggested Readings on pages 944–946 of the Appendix.

- Beck, Barbara L. *The Incas.* The Inca people were highlanders living in the Andes. Their capital was in Cuzco, where the ruler's palace had walls covered with gold.
- Buell, Janet. *Ice Maiden of the Andes.* In 1995, two scientists climbing in the Andes discover the frozen body of a young girl who died 500 years before, a sacrificial victim of the Inca.
- Burland, C.A. *Finding Out About the Incas.* Around 500 years ago, the Inca ruled a vast South American empire. Their capital city of Cuzco had great stone palaces and a temple to the sun god.

Life in North America

Main Idea The geography in lands north of present-day Mexico shaped the development of many different Native American cultures.

Reading Focus What would your life have in common with people living in a different place but with the same geography? Read to learn how the geography of North America shaped the life of Native Americans living here.

By A.D. 1500, about two million people lived north of Mesoamerica. They spoke around 300 languages and called themselves by thousands of different names.

These Native Americans had inherited the cultures of their ancestors. As early Americans spread out across North America, they adjusted to the varied environments where they settled. They not only survived—they lived well.

The People of the Far North Scientists think the early people who settled the Arctic regions of present-day Canada and Alaska arrived by boat, perhaps around 3000 B.C. This was long after the Ice Age had ended. These people called themselves the Inuit, which means "the people."

The Inuit, like other early Americans, found ways to live in their harsh environment. They built **igloos,** dome-shaped homes, from blocks of ice and snow. They used dogsleds to travel on land and sealskin kayaks to travel by sea.

Most peoples of the Far North hunted. They ate seals, walruses, and land animals like caribou and polar bears. They especially prized strips of blubber, or fat, from seals and whales. The fat provided oil for lamps, and it also gave the Inuit valuable calories.

NATIONAL GEOGRAPHIC **People and Cultures of North America** c. 1300–1500

KEY
Regions of North America
- Arctic (Tundra)
- California/Great Basin/Plateau
- Eastern Woodlands /Southeast
- Great Plains
- Northwest Coast
- Southwest
- Subarctic

KEY
- Farming
- Fishing
- Hunting
- Gathering

Using Geography Skills

North Americans found food in different ways, depending on the geography of their region.
1. In what regions was fishing a major method for getting food?
2. What was the most common method for obtaining food on the Great Plains?

CRITICAL THINKING ACTIVITY

Analyzing Elicit from students that the Pueblo were farmers who lived in a desert area. Then read aloud the following Pueblo song about the weather and seasons:

Hasten clouds from the four world quarters;
Come snow in plenty, that water may be abundant when summer comes;
Come ice, cover the fields, that the planting may yield abundance.
Let all hearts be glad.

Discuss the meaning of the poem. **Ask:** Why do the Pueblo want the snow and ice to come? *(They provide the water the Pueblo need for their crops in the summer.)* **L2**

The carved wooden totem (far right) was made by Native Americans from the Pacific Northwest. The kachina doll (right) was made by the Hopi people of the Southwest. *Why was the Pacific Northwest region heavily populated?*

Life on the West Coast

The groups that settled along North America's Pacific coast enjoyed a milder climate than the Inuit. In the Pacific Northwest, peoples such as the Tlingit (TLIHNG•kuht), Haida, and Chinook used towering cedar trees to build wooden houses and huge oceangoing canoes. They fished the seas for otters, seals, and whales. Each spring, saltwater salmon clogged the rivers as they swam upstream to lay eggs.

Because of rich food resources, the Pacific Northwest was one of the most heavily populated regions north of Mesoamerica. Only the area that is today California supported more people.

Scientists think California was home to about 500 early American cultures. Each culture specialized in using the natural resources found in California's many environments.

Along the northern coast, people like the Chumash fished. In the southern desert, the Cahuilla harvested dates from palm trees and gathered seeds, roots, and pods. In the central valley, the Pomo gathered acorns and pounded them into flour.

Life in the Southwest

People who settled in the dry deserts of the Southwest lacked the abundant resources of the California peoples. However, early Americans like the Hohokam and Anasazi had taught their descendants important lessons. The Hopi, Acoma, Pueblo, and Zuni knew how to farm the dry land. Like their ancestors, they dug irrigation canals. They built apartment-like homes, using a type of sun-dried mud brick called **adobe** (uh•DOH•bee).

In the A.D. 1500s, two groups of hunters—the Apache and the Navajo—moved into the area. The Apache remained hunters, but over time the Navajo started to farm like their neighbors.

Life on the Great Plains

People on the Great Plains farmed, but it was not easy. Seas of grass covered the lands stretching from the Rocky Mountains to the Mississippi River. The dense grass roots made farming difficult, especially without iron tools. Peoples like the Mandan, Hidatsa, and Pawnee grew gardens in the fertile land along the Missouri, Arkansas, and Red Rivers.

While the women tended gardens, the men hunted the huge herds of buffalo that grazed on the grasslands. They hunted on

CHAPTER 16   The Americas   591

EXTENDING THE CONTENT

The Importance of Fish The most important fish to Native Americans in the Pacific Northwest were rockfish, smelt, salmon, halibut, and eulachon. Beginning in the spring and continuing through the fall, huge runs of salmon returned upstream. Native Americans depended on storing large quantities of salmon for their winter food. Therefore, they planned their lives around being at their favorite fishing stations when the salmon were running. Once the salmon were caught, the women butchered them and the entire family became involved in drying them. Halibut also dried well and was used for winter food. The eulachon was small, but it was rich in oil. This fish was boiled and its oil was skimmed off the water. When cooled, the oil became a grease that was an important part of people's food. It was so valued that tribes traded for it.

ENRICH

Tell students that the English language has many borrowed words, such as *chipmunk*, *pow-wow*, and *skunk*, from Native American languages. Ask students what else Europeans have learned or borrowed from Native Americans. (*Answers may include foods, place names, and games.*) **L2**

Reading Check

Answer: It affected the types of homes they lived in, the food they ate, and how they got food.

To help students understand section material, have them visit **Study Central**™ at jat.glencoe.com

RETEACH

Describe the geography and/or climate of each region in North America. Help students connect the lifestyle of Native Americans in each area to those factors. **L1/ EL**

④ CLOSE

Ask volunteers to name similarities among the Maya, Aztec, and Inca. **L2**

foot, because at that time there were no horses in America. The buffalo gave them meat for food, bones for tools, and skins for clothing and shelter.

Life in the Eastern Woodlands Unlike the Plains, dense forests covered lands east of the Mississippi River. Here people combined farming with hunting and fishing. Farming was more widespread in the Southeast Woodlands, where a mild climate led to a long growing season. In the cooler Northeast Woodlands, people relied more on hunting.

All over the Woodlands, groups formed governments. Some, such as the Natchez in present-day Mississippi, set up strict social classes. Others, like the Cherokee in Georgia and North Carolina, had formal codes of law.

In a few cases, Native Americans in the Woodlands set up **confederations** (kuhn•FEH•duh•RAY•shuhnz), or governments that link several groups. The most famous was the league formed by the **Iroquois** (IHR•uh•KWOY). The Iroquois League included five groups: Onondaga, Seneca, Mohawk, Oneida, and Cayuga.

The Iroquois formed the league to end the fighting among themselves. A code of laws, known as the Great Peace, governed the league. Women, who controlled Iroquois land, selected male members to sit on a Grand Council. Together council members worked out their differences and made decisions in complete agreement. The Council helped members unite against other Woodland peoples, such as the powerful Algonquian (al•GAHN•kwee•uhn).

✓ Reading Check ▶ Describe How did geography shape the lives of the people north of present-day Mexcio?

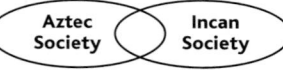

Section ② Review

Study Central™ Need help with the material in this section? Visit jat.glencoe.com

Reading Summary
Review the Main Ideas

- In the rain forests of Central America, the Maya developed a civilization divided into city-states.
- A fierce warrior people, the Aztec created a strong empire in central Mexico.
- In the Andes, the Inca created the largest empire in the Americas.
- North America's varied geography led to the development of many diverse Native American groups.

What Did You Learn?

1. How did the Incan leader Pachacuti maintain the great empire he built?
2. Who were the people of the Far North, and what sorts of food did they eat?

Critical Thinking

3. **Compare and Contrast** Draw a Venn diagram like the one shown. Add details to compare Aztec and Incan society.

   Aztec Society ⟷ Incan Society

4. **Science Link** How and why did the Maya study astronomy?

5. **Summarize** How did the Aztec find and build their capital city?

6. **Drawing Conclusions** Why do you think the Inca required everyone in their society to do a specific job? Do you think this is a good idea for a society? Explain.

7. **Descriptive Writing** Imagine you are an early European explorer in North America. Write a journal entry describing your encounter with a Native American people in one of the regions described in the section.

SECTION 2 REVIEW ANSWERS

1. set up strong central government while allowing local rulers to stay in control; took sons of local leaders to Cuzco; required use of Quechua; built a road system
2. Inuit; seal, walrus, whale, caribou, and polar bear
3. Venn diagrams should be based on information in the text.
4. by studying the skies; believed gods revealed their plans in the heavens and needed to know when to plant crops
5. Students should summarize the Aztec legend in the text and include descriptions of methods used to turn a swamp into a city.
6. Answers will vary, but students should support their opinions with logical examples.
7. Entries will vary but should describe the lifestyle of the people chosen.

Section 3

The Fall of the Aztec and Inca Empires

Get Ready to Read!

What's the Connection?

As the 1400s drew to a close, people in the Americas and Europe knew nothing of each other. This changed when Europeans began exploring the world and searching for trade routes to Asia.

Focusing on the Main Ideas

- Christopher Columbus found the Americas while trying to find a sea route to Asia. *(page 594)*
- Spanish conquerors defeated the Aztec with the help of horses, guns, and European disease. *(page 595)*
- The riches of the Aztec Empire led other Spanish conquerors to seek their fortunes in South America. *(page 599)*

Locating Places

Hispaniola (HIHS•puh•NYOH•luh)
Extremadura
(EHK•struh•muh•DUR•uh)

Meeting People

Christopher Columbus
Hernán Cortés
(ehr•NAHN kawr•TEHZ)
Montezuma II (MAHN•tuh•ZOO•muh)
Malintzin (mah•LIHNT•suhn)
Francisco Pizarro
(fran•SIHS•koh puh•ZAHR•oh)
Atahualpa (AH•tuh•WAHL•puh)

Building Your Vocabulary

conquistador
(kahn•KEES•tuh•DAWR)
treason (TREE•zuhn)

Reading Strategy

Cause and Effect Create a diagram to show the reasons Cortés was able to conquer the Aztec.

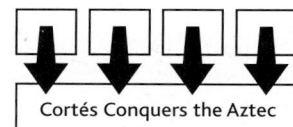

Cortés Conquers the Aztec

When & Where?

1450   1500   1550

1492
Christopher Columbus reaches the Americas

1521
Cortés defeats Aztec

1533
Francisco Pizarro conquers the Inca

Tenochtitlán
Cuzco

CHAPTER 16   The Americas   593

① FOCUS

SECTION OVERVIEW

This section describes how the Spanish conquerors who followed in the wake of Columbus managed to defeat the Aztec and Inca Empires.

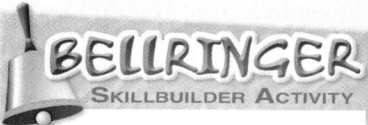

BELLRINGER

SKILLBUILDER ACTIVITY

Project **Daily Focus Skills Transparency 16–3** and have students answer questions. Discuss their responses.

Get Ready to Read!

Preteaching Vocabulary: Remind students that antonyms are words or phrases that have opposite or nearly opposite meanings. Provide the text definition for *treason* (disloyalty to government). Have students suggest an antonym for treason. *(loyalty)*

Answers to Graphic: horses, guns, help from Malintzin, European disease

---

SECTION RESOURCES

Reproducible Masters

- Reproducible Lesson Plan 16–3
- Daily Lecture and Discussion Notes 16–3
- Vocabulary Activity 16–3
- Active Reading Note-Taking Guide 16–3
- Guided Reading Activity 16–3
- Section Quiz 16–3
- Reading Essentials and Study Guide 16–3

Transparencies

- Daily Focus Skills Transparency 16–3

Multimedia

- Interactive Tutor Self-Assessment CD-ROM
- ExamView® Pro Testmaker CD-ROM
- Presentation Plus! CD-ROM
- Vocabulary PuzzleMaker CD-ROM
- Glencoe BookLink CD-ROM

② TEACH

Analyzing Decisions Use a wall map of the world as the class discusses paragraphs 1–3 under "Columbus Arrives in America." Help students understand that Columbus did not realize how big Earth is nor did he suspect that other continents and another ocean lay between Europe and Asia. **L2**

More About the Art

San Salvador means "Holy Savior" in Spanish. The resident Lucayan people, however, called it *Guanahani*. Today, the island is part of the Bahamas.

Caption Answer: He was hoping to reach Asia.

Daily Lecture and Discussion Notes 16–3

Use **Daily Lecture and Discussion Notes 16–3** for an outline of key concepts found in the section.

Reading Support L1/ EL

Use **Vocabulary Activity 16–3** to review important terms in the section.

The Spanish Arrive in America

Main Idea Christopher Columbus found the Americas while trying to find a sea route to Asia.

Reading Focus What is the most vivid memory you have of a place you have visited? Read to learn what the Spanish found when they set out to explore the world.

In 1492 the Aztec appeared unbeatable. Around 250,000 people lived in Tenochtitlán, making it the largest city in the Americas—if not the world. In just a few short years, however, people from Europe would destroy their empire.

Columbus Arrives in America As you learned previously, by the 1400s several strong European kingdoms had developed in Western Europe. Those kingdoms knew that money could be made if they could find a way to trade with the countries of East Asia without having to deal with the Muslim kingdoms in between.

One by one, the people of Western Europe took to the sea to find a route to Asia. The first were the Portuguese, who began mapping Africa's eastern coast, hoping to find a way around Africa.

Next were the Spaniards, who decided to finance a trip by an Italian sea captain named **Christopher Columbus.** Columbus convinced Spain's rulers that he could reach Asia by sailing west across the Atlantic Ocean. He had no idea that two continents blocked his way.

Columbus set sail with three ships in August 1492. In October, he landed on an island in the Caribbean Sea. Columbus believed he had arrived in Asia. He traveled farther into the Caribbean and landed on the island of **Hispaniola** (HIHS•puh•NYOH•luh), which is today Haiti and the Dominican Republic. He then returned home carrying colorful parrots, some gold and spices, and several Native American captives. His success astonished and pleased Spain's rulers and convinced them to pay for another trip.

Columbus Returns Columbus set out again in 1493. This time, he came to conquer, bringing soldiers to help him. In the spring of 1494, the Spanish landed on Hispaniola.

▲ In the painting above, Christopher Columbus is depicted landing on the island of San Salvador. *Why did Columbus sail west across the Atlantic?*

594   CHAPTER 16   The Americas

Visualizing Point out that visualizing, or picturing events in one's mind, can help students better remember the events and the order in which they happened. Compare visualizing to the process of watching a movie. Then have volunteers suggest several key scenes that would be in a movie about Columbus's discovery and exploration of the Americas. List them on the board. Lead a discussion about what each scene would show. Make sure that students include details from the text and the paintings in their descriptions. Conclude the movie with a scene of the Spanish claiming Hispaniola for Spain. To show the effectiveness of visualizing, have a volunteer describe how Spain gained a foothold in the Americas. **L1/ EL**

The Taino who lived there got their first look at the **conquistadors** (kahn•KEES•tuh•DAWRZ), the soldier-explorers sent to the Americas by Spain. What they saw frightened them. Armor-clad men rode on armor-clad horses. Snarling dogs ran by their sides. In a show of power, the soldiers fired guns that spit out flames and lead balls.

Soldiers claimed the island for Spain. Then they enslaved the Taino and forced them to work for the Spanish. Spain now had a foothold in the Americas.

✓ **Reading Check** **Identify** Who were the conquistadors?

Spain Conquers Mexico

Main Idea Spanish conquerors defeated the Aztec with the help of horses, guns, and European disease.

Reading Focus Think of decisions that you have already made today. Read to learn how the decisions made by two people—a Spanish conqueror and an Aztec king—changed the course of history.

The voyages of Christopher Columbus, who sailed to the Americas four times, inspired many poor nobles to go to America to seek their fortunes. Many came from the part of Spain known as the

Linking Past & Present
Chocolate

THEN The Aztec ruler Montezuma found chocolate more desirable than gold! He offered the bitter tasting drink made from the cacao bean to Spanish explorer Hernán Cortés. The explorer took the bean back to Europe after conquering the Aztec. After Europeans mixed it with milk and sugar, it became very popular among the rich.

▼ **Modern chocolate factory**

▲ **Native Americans making chocolate**

NOW In the United States, people eat an average of 12 pounds of chocolate each year. Hawaii is the only state that grows cacao beans, but the United States has more than 1,000 companies that produce chocolate and cocoa products. *Why do you think only the rich in Europe enjoyed chocolate in the 1500s?*

CHAPTER 16   The Americas   595

CHAPTER 16
SECTION 3, 593–600

Writing Activity ✏

After students have read the reaction of the Taino to the arrival of the Spanish, organize students into two groups. Students in Group A will role-play Taino, and students in Group B will role-play conquistadors. Tell the "Taino" and "conquistadors" to write monologues that describe the events from their points of view. Emphasize that the monologues should describe the participants' feelings. Have Taino and conquistadors take turns presenting their monologues to the class. **L2**

✓ **Reading Check**

Answer: soldier-explorers that Spain sent to the Americas

Linking Past & Present

Answer: Answers may include that chocolate was scarce and, therefore, very expensive, so only the rich could afford it.

DIFFERENTIATED INSTRUCTION

Visual/Spatial: Call on students to describe what is happening in the beach scene on page 594. **Ask:** Who is in the central lighted area and, therefore, most important? *(the Spanish)* How are the Native Americans reacting to Columbus's arrival? Point out that this scene was painted after the event. **Ask:** How does the artist feel about what is happening here?

English Learners: Have students reenact the beach scene from two viewpoints—that of the Spanish and the Native Americans. Make sure students know vocabulary for meeting new people (anger, rejection, surprise) to make the presentations interesting.

Gifted and Talented: To show a different point of view, ask students to research the Mexican painter Diego Rivera. Ask them to share his paintings with the class.

Extremadura (EHK•struh•muh•DUR•uh). Its poor soil, blistering hot summers, and icy winters held little chance for wealth. One of these nobles was 19-year-old **Hernán Cortés** (ehr•NAHN kawr•TEHZ).

As a teenager, Cortés had a choice of three jobs: priest, lawyer, or soldier. His parents picked lawyer, but Cortés picked soldier. In 1504 he set out for Hispaniola. In 1511 he took part in the Spanish invasion of Cuba. His courage impressed the Spanish commander, who gave Cortés control over several Native American villages and the goods they produced.

Six years later, smallpox swept across Cuba, killing thousands of Native Americans. The Spanish commander asked Cortés to find new people who could be forced to work for the Spanish. Cortés knew just where to look.

That same year, a ship sent to explore the coast of the Yucatán returned to Cuba. Unlike earlier search parties, the soldiers did not fight with the Maya who lived there. Instead a group of Maya paddled out to greet them. As one soldier recalled:

> 66 They brought gold cast in bars . . . a beautiful gold mask, a figurine [statue] of a man with a half mask of gold, and a crown of gold beads. 99
>
> —Juan Díaz, as quoted in "Conquest and Aftermath"

Cortés needed to hear no more. He made plans to sail. On February 18, 1519, Cortés set sail for Mexico.

Cortés Invades Mexico When Cortés arrived, the Aztec emperor was **Montezuma II** (MAHN•tuh•ZOO•muh), also called Moctezuma. Montezuma expected the invaders. In a dream, he looked into a mirror and saw a huge army headed over the mountains. "What shall I do?" cried the emperor. "Where shall I hide?"

The dreaded invasion began in April 1519 when Cortés stepped onto a beach near present-day Veracruz. He came with 550 soldiers, 16 horses, 14 cannons, and a few dogs. How could such a small force conquer a huge warrior empire?

▲ Spanish armor

▲ Spanish sword

▲ Aztec war club

◄ The Aztec's simple weapons were no match for the guns and cannons of the Spanish. *Besides weapons and horses, what else did the Spanish bring that would help them defeat the Aztec?*

596

First, Cortés knew how to use Spanish horses and guns to shock Native Americans. In a display of power, he forced thousands of Tabascans (tuh•BAS•kuhnz), a people living in Mesoamerica, to surrender. Second, the Tabascans gave Cortés another weapon—a Mayan woman named **Malintzin** (mah•LIHNT•suhn). She spoke both Mayan and Nahuatl (NAH•WAH•tuhl), the language of the Aztec.

Speaking through a Spaniard who knew Mayan, Malintzin described the Aztec Empire to Cortés. She also told Cortés how subjects of the Aztec resented their rulers and would join with him to fight Montezuma. Acting as a translator, she helped Cortés form alliances.

Finally, Cortés had the help of invisible allies—germs that carried diseases, such as measles and smallpox. These diseases would eventually kill more Aztec than the Spanish swords.

Cortés Defeats the Aztec

The Spaniards traveled 400 miles (644 km) to reach Tenochtitlán, the Aztec capital. Messengers reported their every move to Montezuma. The Aztec believed in a light-skinned god named Quetzalcoatl. This god, who opposed sacrifice, had sailed away long ago, promising to return someday to reclaim his land. Montezuma was afraid Cortés was the god returning home. As a result, he did not want to attack the Spaniards right away.

As Cortés marched closer, Montezuma decided to ambush the Spanish troops. Cortés learned of the plan and attacked first, killing 6,000 people. In November 1519, the Spaniards marched into Tenochtitlán and took control of the city. To prevent the Aztec from rebelling, Cortés took Montezuma hostage. He then ordered the Aztec to stop sacrificing people.

Primary Source
The Aztec Defeat

This excerpt describes the aftermath of Cortés's victory.

"Broken spears lie in the roads; we have torn our hair in our grief. The houses are roofless now, and their walls are red with blood. . . . We have pounded our hands in despair against the adobe walls, for our inheritance, our city, is lost and dead. The shields of our warriors were its defense, but they could not save it."

—author unknown, from *The Broken Spears*, edited by Miguel Leon-Portilla

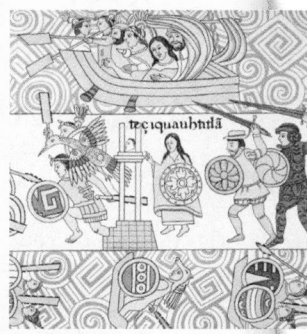

▲ Battle scene between Aztec and Spanish soldiers

DBQ Document-Based Question

The Aztec felt that their lost city was their inheritance. What does that mean?

Cortés's orders angered the Aztec, who planned a rebellion. Fighting erupted, and the Spanish killed thousands of Aztec. Montezuma tried to stop the fighting, but he too was killed. Outnumbered, the Spanish fought their way out of the city and took refuge in the nearby hills with their allies.

While Cortés prepared a second attack, smallpox broke out in Tenochtitlán. Greatly weakened, the Aztec were no match for the Spanish and their allies. In June 1521, the Spanish destroyed the Aztec capital.

Reading Check Explain Why did the Aztec think they should welcome Cortés?

CHAPTER 16   The Americas   597

Primary Source

Aztec intellectuals who survived the empire's defeat wrote about the Spanish conquest. Their accounts are in Nahuatl, the language of the Aztec, but they were written in Latin script.

Answer:
Answers may include that the Aztec felt that they had inherited the city from their ancestors, and they expected to hand it on to future generations who would enjoy and protect it.

Reading Check

Answer: Legend promised the return of a light-skinned Aztec god named Quetzalcoatl, and the Aztec thought Cortés might be him.

Reading Support L1/EL

Assign **Guided Reading Activity 16–3** to help students organize the information in the section.

INTERDISCIPLINARY CONNECTIONS ACTIVITY

Art An Aztec poet carved the following words into a wall:
   Will I leave only this:
   Like the flowers that wither?
   Will nothing last in my name? . . .
Ask: What did the poet mean by the word *this*? (that the poet's work did not last, only the inscription on the wall did) Why did the poet compare him- or herself to flowers? (because they do not last) Have volunteers prepare a multimedia presentation of Aztec artwork. **L3**

TEACH

A leader's beliefs and attitudes influence his or her actions. Cortés, for example, turned a possible trap to his advantage by seizing Montezuma, because he was willing to risk everything to defeat the Aztec. On the other hand, Montezuma believed in fate and tried to buy the Spanish off rather than call on his people to fight. **Ask: What are some of the most important issues facing world leaders today?** *(Answers will vary but may include stopping terrorism, promoting trade, and supporting better education and health care for citizens.)* **What seems to be the attitude of world leaders toward solving these problems?** *(Answers will vary, but students should support their opinions.)* **L3**

Then and Now

Possible answers include presidents of the United States and leaders of other countries who have shaped world politics *(Example: George W. Bush/Saddam Hussein).* Encourage students to give thoughtful reasons to support their suggestions.

Biography

MONTEZUMA II
1480–1520
HERNÁN CORTÉS
1485–1547

Montezuma ▶

Although Montezuma II became known as the emperor who let the Spanish capture the Aztec Empire, most of his years as a ruler had been very successful. Montezuma Xocoyotl was the youngest son of Emperor Axacayatl. Aztec leadership was not hereditary, so after Axacayatl's death a man named Ahuitzotl was selected emperor. Montezuma was in his early twenties when he was chosen emperor. He became a popular leader. He led his armies in battle and won over 40 battles against kingdoms south of the Aztec Empire. His one major mistake was in his dealings with the Spanish conquistadors.

Leading the Spanish march into the Aztec Empire in 1519 was a 34-year-old Spaniard named Hernán Cortés. Cortés was born in the province of Extremadura, Spain. At age 19, Cortés left the university and boarded a ship for the Spanish lands in America. He was determined to make his fortune.

In 1511, Spanish troops led by Diego Velázquez conquered Cuba. Cortés took part in the invasion, and his courage impressed Velázquez. He rewarded Cortés by giving him control of several Native American villages. Six years later, smallpox swept across Cuba, killing thousands of Native Americans. Without Native American workers, the farms and mines the Spanish had built in Cuba could not function. Velázquez asked Cortés to lead an expedition to the Yucatán Peninsula to find new peoples who could be forced to work for the Spanish. He was also asked to investigate reports of a wealthy civilization there. On February 18, 1519, Cortés set sail for Mexico.

▲ Hernán Cortés

Several years later, after conquering the Aztec, Cortés took part in one more expedition to Honduras and then served as Governor General of New Spain. He returned to Spain a very wealthy man and died near the city of Seville in 1547.

Then and Now

Because of their encounter in war, the names of Montezuma and Cortés often appear together in history books. What two leaders today do you think will be paired in future history books? Why?

Reading List Generator CD-ROM

GLENCOE **BOOKLINK**   **RECOMMENDED READING**

Use the **Glencoe BookLink CD-ROM** to create customized reading lists based on your students' interests and reading levels. Below is an example based on content in this chapter. Also, see the Suggested Readings on pages 944–946 of the Appendix.

- **Hughes, Jill.** *Aztecs.* The Aztec Indians lived in Mexico. Visit the Aztec capital city, Tenochtitlán.
- **Macdonald, Fiona.** *Step Into the Aztec and Maya Worlds.* Find out about the mysterious worlds of the Aztec and Maya.
- **Maestro, Betsy.** *Exploration and Conquest: The Americas After Columbus: 1500–1620.* Learn about the clash of Native American and European cultures in the Americas.

Pizarro Conquers the Inca

Main Idea The riches of the Aztec Empire led other Spanish conquerors to seek their fortunes in South America.

Reading Focus Have you ever done anything because you have seen other people do it and succeed? Read to learn how another conquistador followed the example of Cortés and conquered the Inca.

In 1513 Vasco Núñez de Balboa (VAHS·koh NOON·yays day bal·BOH·uh) led a band of soldiers across the jungle-covered mountains of present-day Panama. Native Americans said that if Balboa traveled south along a western sea, he would find a great empire filled with gold.

Balboa found the sea, known today as the Pacific Ocean. However, he never found the golden empire. A jealous Spanish official in Panama falsely charged him with **treason** (TREE·zuhn), or disloyalty to the government, and ordered him beheaded.

Francisco Pizarro (fran·SIHS·koh puh·ZAHR·oh), who marched with Balboa, took up the search. Pizarro could not write his name, but he knew how to fight. Like Balboa and Cortés, Pizarro came from the harsh Extremadura. Unlike his neighbors, however, he was not of noble birth.

At age 16, Pizarro fled a job herding pigs to fight in Italy. In 1502 he arrived in the Americas. Helping explore Panama, he became a wealthy landowner. But Pizarro longed to find the golden empire.

Pizarro and the Inca By the 1530s, the Inca thought they ruled most of the world. Two threats from the north soon proved they did not. The Inca could do nothing to stop the southward spread of smallpox. They also failed to scare away Pizarro, who led 160 adventurers up the mountains to the Incan homeland.

The Inca tried to ignore him, but Pizarro, now in his 50s, would not leave. He raided Incan storehouses and fired guns at villagers. The Incan emperor, **Atahualpa** (AH·tuh·WAHL·puh), thought Pizarro was crazy or a fool. How could this man stand up to an army of 80,000 Incan warriors?

Atahualpa misjudged Pizarro. The Spaniard had an advantage. The Inca knew little about the Europeans, but Pizarro knew a lot about Native Americans. He had spent more than 30 years fighting Native

Primary Source

Incan Record Keeping

A Spanish conquistador wrote about aspects of Incan culture.

"At the beginning of the new year the rulers of each village came to Cuzco, bringing their quipus, which told how many births there had been during the year, and how many deaths. In this way the Inca and the governors knew which of the Indians were poor, the women who had been widowed, whether they were able to pay their taxes, and how many men they could count on in the event of war, and many other things they considered highly important."

—Pedro de Cieza de Léon, *The Second Part of the Chronicle of Peru*

▲ Quipu

DBQ Document-Based Question

Quipus were used to calculate records and building plans. How else do you think the Inca might have used quipus?

3 ASSESS

Assign Section 3 Review as homework or as an in-class activity.

◉ Have students use the **Interactive Tutor Self-Assessment CD-ROM** to review the section.

Assessment L2

Assign **Section 3 Quiz** to assess mastery of the material found in the section.

Reading Support L1/ EL

Assign **Reading Essentials and Study Guide 16–3** to help students review section material.

Primary Source

The color of the yarn and the type of knot on a quipu conveyed different information. Only quipu-keepers knew what all the knots meant and could read the colored strings.

Answer:
Answers may include record keeping or calculations.

EXTENDING THE CONTENT

Was Pizarro Ever Afraid? Pizarro traveled with only a small force of Spaniards. However, he had help from dissatisfied people that the Inca ruled. At times, he feared that his Native American allies might overwhelm his own small force. While going to a meeting with Atahualpa at an Incan encampment, one soldier wrote: "So many were the tents that we were filled with fright. . . . But we dared not show it, much less turn back, for if they sensed the least weakness in us, the very Indians we brought with us would have killed us. So with a show of good spirits, after having thoroughly surveyed the town and tents, . . . we descended into the valley below."

ENRICH

Point out that Peru still has a large Quechua-speaking population. **Ask:** **How might geography and history explain this fact?** *(Geography: Mountains enabled people to preserve their Incan culture. History: The Inca spread the Quechua language.)* **L2**

 Reading Check

Answer: Pizarro did not free Atahualpa after receiving gold and silver from him.

History Online

To help students understand the section material, have them visit **Study Central**™ at jat.glencoe.com

RETEACH

Have students compare the Spanish conquests of the Aztec and the Inca. Ask them to use categories, such as "leaders," "weapons," or "geography" to explain how each conquest was carried out, how Native Americans resisted, and the duration of each conquest. **L2**

 CLOSE

Have students consider the main topic of the section. Then have them summarize the section in two to four sentences. **L2**

Americans. Also, his good friend Hernán Cortés gave Pizarro an inside look at the conquest of the Aztec. In late 1532, Pizarro decided on a plan so bold that even Cortés might not have risked it.

Pizarro Defeats the Inca Spanish messengers invited Atahualpa to a meeting. Atahualpa agreed but made the mistake of leaving most of his huge army behind. He believed that his 5,000 bodyguards were enough protection. He also decided, based on Pizarro's small force, that the Inca needed no weapons.

When they met, Pizarro wasted no time in asking the emperor to give up his gods. When Atahualpa laughed at his request, Pizarro ordered an attack. Cannons roared, trumpets blared, and sword-swinging soldiers shrieked battle cries. Pizarro then seized Atahualpa and dragged him off the battlefield.

Atahualpa tried to buy his freedom. He offered to fill his jail cell with gold and a nearby room with silver. Pizarro jumped at the deal. Atahualpa kept his part of the bargain. Pizarro did not. He charged the emperor with many crimes: plotting a rebellion, worshiping false gods, having too many wives, and more. In 1533 a military court found the emperor guilty and sentenced him to death.

To reward Pizarro, the Spanish king made him governor of Peru. Pizarro then chose a new emperor for the Inca, but the emperor had to follow Pizarro's orders. Pizarro's conquest of Peru opened most of South America to Spanish rule. Spain controlled a vast territory covering 375,000 square miles (975,000 sq km) with almost 7 million inhabitants. It was on its way to building the world's first global empire.

✔ **Reading Check** **Explain** How did Pizarro fail to keep his promise to Atahualpa?

History Online

Study Central™ Need help with the material in this section? Visit jat.glencoe.com

Section 3 Review

Reading Summary
Review the Main Ideas
- Searching for a sea route to Asia, Christopher Columbus arrived in the Americas and claimed lands there for Spain.
- With a small army, Spanish conquistador Hernán Cortés conquered Montezuma and the Aztec capital of Tenochtitlán.
- In Peru, a small Spanish force led by Francisco Pizarro captured the Inca Empire.

What Did You Learn?
1. How did Christopher Columbus convince Spanish rulers to pay for a second trip?
2. Why did Cortés sail from Cuba to Mexico in search of the Aztec?

Critical Thinking
3. **Sequencing Information** Draw a time line like the one shown. Fill in events related to Cortés's capture of Tenochtitlán.

1517:
Spanish ship brings back gold from Yucatán

4. **Predict** How might the history of the Aztec people be different without the legend of the Aztec god Quetzalcoatl?
5. **Analyze** Why were the Aztec and the Inca so easily defeated by smaller Spanish forces?
6. **Expository Writing** Imagine you are an Aztec or an Inca seeing a Spanish conquistador for the first time. Write a newspaper article describing what you have observed.

600   CHAPTER 16   The Americas

SECTION 3 REVIEW ANSWERS

1. His success pleased Spain's rulers.
2. He had heard of gold in the area.
3. February 1519: Cortés sets sail for Mexico; April 1519: Cortés lands in Mexico; November 1519: Cortés marches into Tenochtitlán and takes control of it; June 1521: Tenochtitlán falls
4. Answers may include that the Aztec might have immediately attacked and defeated Cortés.
5. Aztec: Spanish had guns, cannons, horses; European diseases killed many; Inca: same reasons as Aztec, plus Pizarro's trickery
6. Letters will vary but should reflect the Aztec or Inca experiences described in the text.

Section 1 The First Americans

Vocabulary
glacier
monopoly

Focusing on the Main Ideas
- It is believed that the first people in the Americas came from Asia during the Ice Age. *(page 573)*
- The invention of farming led to the rise of civilizations in the Americas. *(page 574)*
- Early people in the northern part of the Americas built complex cultures based on farming and trade. *(page 578)*

Section 2 Life in the Americas

Vocabulary
quipu
igloo
adobe
confederation

Focusing on the Main Ideas
- The Maya adjusted to life in the tropical rain forest and built a culture based on their religious beliefs. *(page 583)*
- The Aztec moved into the Valley of Mexico, where they created an empire based on conquest and war. *(page 585)*
- To unite their huge empire, Incan rulers set up a highly organized government and society. *(page 588)*
- The geography in lands north of present-day Mexico shaped the development of many different Native American cultures. *(page 590)*

▲ Mayan ballplayer

Section 3 The Fall of the Aztec and Inca Empires

Vocabulary
conquistador
treason

Focusing on the Main Ideas
- Christopher Columbus found the Americas while trying to find a sea route to Asia. *(page 594)*
- Spanish conquerors defeated the Aztec with the help of horses, guns, and European disease. *(page 595)*
- The riches of the Aztec Empire led other Spanish conquerors to seek their fortunes in South America. *(page 599)*

CHAPTER 16 The Americas **601**

PREVIEW/REVIEW

Vocabulary Activity Have students write a series of sentences in which they use each term correctly or incorrectly. Call on volunteers to read their sentences aloud. After each sentence, the rest of the class should answer "true" or "false." Students who respond "false" should be prepared to explain why they did so.

🌐 **Vocabulary PuzzleMaker CD-ROM**

🌐 **Interactive Tutor Self-Assessment CD-ROM**

CONDENSE

📁 Chapter 16 **Guided Reading Activities**

🎧 **StudentWorks Plus™ CD-ROM** (with Audio Program)

RETEACH

📁 **Differentiated Instruction Activity 16**

📁 Chapter 16 *Reading Essentials and Study Guide*

CHAPTER CULMINATING ACTIVITY

Have students finish the Chapter Culminating Activity from page 568D.

📁 Suggestions for rubrics may be found in the *Quizzes, Tests, and Authentic Assessment (with Rubrics)* booklet.

📖 **Reading Strategy** ▸ **READ TO WRITE**

Sequencing Events Have students review and expand the chapter time line on a separate piece of paper. Tell students to circle events that they consider turning points in history based on what they have read. Ask students to write a one-paragraph summary of why they picked these dates. Use the following rubric for assessment.

- **L1** students should have at least two dates with sentences explaining their choices.
- **L2** students should have two or more dates and include some cause-and-effect relationships.
- **L3** students should have two or more dates and exhibit mastery of cause-and-effect relationships.

CHAPTER 16
ASSESSMENT AND ACTIVITIES

GLENCOE TECHNOLOGY

MindJogger Videoquiz

Use the **MindJogger Videoquiz** to review Chapter 16 content.

 Available in DVD and VHS

Review Vocabulary

1. b
2. d
3. c
4. e
5. a

Review Main Ideas

6. 15,000 to 40,000 years ago; Asia

7. Farming allowed people to stop wandering in search of food and form more complex societies.

8. Maya: adjusted to life in tropical rain forest, built culture based on religious beliefs; Aztec: created empire based on conquest and war

9. It affected the kinds of homes they had, what they ate, and how they got their food.

10. to sail west across the Atlantic Ocean and reach Asia

11. horses, guns, and European diseases

Critical Thinking

12. used available resources to build igloos (Far North), wooden homes (Northwest), adobe (Southwest), buffalo hide shelters (Great Plains)

Review Vocabulary

Match the word in the first column with its definition in the second column.

___ 1. conquistador   **a.** disloyalty to the government

___ 2. glacier   **b.** Spanish soldier-explorer

___ 3. adobe   **c.** sun-dried mud bricks

___ 4. confederation   **d.** huge sheet of ice

___ 5. treason   **e.** form of government that links several different groups

Review Main Ideas

Section 1 • The First Americans

6. When did the first people arrive in the Americas? On which continent did they live originally?

7. How did farming lead to the rise and development of civilizations in present-day Mexico, Central America, and Peru?

Reading Skill — Summarizing

Summarizing Information

Read the paragraph below, then choose the statement that best summarizes its content.

The region's geography was ideal for farming. Much of the area had a rich, volcanic soil and a mild climate. Rains fell in the spring, helping seeds to sprout. They decreased in the summer, allowing crops to ripen for harvest.

15. **a.** The Ice Age ended as the climate warmed.
   b. Rain fell in the spring.
   c. Climate and soil made the region ideal for farming.
   d. Seeds that are planted grow into crops.

To review this skill, see pages 570–571.

Section 2 • Life in the Americas

8. Explain the differences between the Maya and Aztec civilizations.

9. How did geography shape the development of the Native American cultures north of present-day Mexico?

Section 3 • The Fall of the Aztec and Inca Empires

10. What was the goal of Christopher Columbus's voyage in 1492?

11. What three factors made it possible for the Spanish to conquer the Aztec and the Inca?

Critical Thinking

12. **Analyze** How do the houses of North American peoples reflect the geography of their regions?

13. **Infer** Why do you think the Mayan civilization came to an end?

14. **Predict** What do you think would have happened if the Inca had taken Pizarro's raids more seriously?

---

13. Answers will vary but may include overpopulation, bad weather, or war.

14. Answers will vary but many may include the defeat of Pizarro based on the overwhelming number of Inca.

Reading Skill

15. c

Geography Skills

16. to protect and defend the city

17. ridges

18. There was a lot of contact because roads head out in all directions.

Geography Skills

Study the map below and answer the following questions.

16. **Human/Environment Interaction** Why do you think the Inca built stone walls in parts of Cuzco?

17. **Location** What natural defenses existed around Cuzco?

18. **Movement** What do the roads leading out of Cuzco reveal about the contact between the capital city and the rest of the empire?

NATIONAL GEOGRAPHIC
Cuzco, Peru c. 1450

Fortress

0   0.25 mi.
0   0.25 km
Lambert Azimuthal
Equal-Area projection

Plaza

Plaza

Temple of the Sun

KEY

Cuzco	■ Assembly hall
— Road	● Palace
Surviving stone wall	■ Temple
	⌇⌇⌇ Ridge

Read to Write

19. **Persuasive Writing** Suppose you are a Native American during the Spanish conquests. Write a letter to the conquistadors to persuade them to trade with your culture rather than conquer it. Your letter should state the ways Europeans and Native Americans can learn from each other.

20. **Using Your FOLDABLES** Create an outline map of the Americas on poster board. It should be big enough for the entire class to work together. Label each country and the location of each civilization from your chapter. Then use your foldables to write facts about each civilization on the map.

History Online
Self-Check Quiz To help you prepare for the Chapter Test, visit jat.glencoe.com

Using Technology

21. **Preparing a Report** Use the Internet and your library to gather information about the Mound Builders. Note their reasons for mound building and the shapes of mounds. Then prepare an illustrated report on the computer to compare the mounds to other structures of early civilizations.

Linking Past and Present

22. **Evaluating Information** What impact have Native American ways of the past had on present-day life in the Americas?

23. **Building Citizenship Skills** The Iroquois League was an important confederation of the early Americas. Do confederations exist today? Do they serve the same purpose as the Iroquois League?

Primary Source **Analyze**

Some Europeans, including this Dominican friar, worked to protect the Native Americans by writing about their cultures.

"They [Native American leaders] issued public edicts and personal commands to all nobles and provincial governors, of whom there were many, that all poor, widows and orphans in each province should be provided for from their own royal rents and riches."

—Bartolomé de las Casas, "Apologetic History of the Indies"

DBQ Document-Based Questions

24. What does this tell you about Native American leaders' attitude toward those in need?

25. Do you think the nobles and provincial governors supported this edict? Why or why not?

History Online

Have students visit the Web site at jat.glencoe.com to review Chapter 16 and take the **Self-Check Quiz**.

Linking Past and Present

22. Possible answers: have affected language (*raccoon*), sports and recreation (*lacrosse*), and foods (*chocolate, popcorn*)

23. Answers may include unions, professional associations, and international bodies, such as the United Nations. Most agree to rules for the common good as did the Iroquois Confederacy.

Primary Source

24. They cared about and tried to help those in need.

25. Answers may include that their response depended upon their character and their wealth.

Bonus Question

Ask: Suppose the Inca had the choice of keeping Pachacuti as their leader or electing a new one. Which choice do you think they would have taken? Why? (*Possible answers: Some people would replace him with a less demanding leader. Others may want to keep him since he provided well for the Inca.*)

Read to Write

19. Letters will vary but should reflect the cultures described in this chapter.

20. **FOLDABLES** Outline maps should be accurately labeled with facts about each civilization. If there is not enough space to put the facts on the map, you may want to use yarn or string leaders to attach fact boxes to the correct civilization.

Using Technology

21. Reports will vary but should be supported by research. Comparisons may include the pyramids of Egypt, Kush, and Mesoamerica.

Note: The following materials may be used when teaching Chapter 17.
Section level support materials are shown at point of use in the margins of the Teacher Wraparound Edition.

TEACHING TRANSPARENCIES

- Graphic Organizer Transparencies with Teaching Strategy and Student Activity **L2**
- Cause-and-Effect Transparencies with Teaching Strategy and Student Activity **L2**
- Then and Now Transparencies with Teaching Strategy and Student Activity **L2**
- In-text Map Transparency with Teaching Strategy and Student Activity **L1**
- Map Transparencies with Overlay, Teaching Strategy, and Student Activity **L2**

DIFFERENTIATED INSTRUCTION

- Differentiated Instruction Activity 17
- Time Line Activity 17
- Primary Source Reading 17 (with Document-Based Questions)
- Inclusion Strategies for the Middle School Social Studies Classroom
- StudentWorks Plus™ CD-ROM (with Audio Program)

READING SUPPORT

- Take-Home Review Activity 17 **L2**
- World Literature Reading 17 **L2**
- Workbook Activity 17 **L1**
- Reading Strategies for the Social Studies Classroom **L1/ EL**

ASSESSMENT

- Authentic Assessment Activity 17 **L1/ EL**
- Chapter 17 Test Form A **L2**
- Chapter 17 Test Form B **L2**
- Exam*View*® Pro Testmaker CD-ROM

INTERDISCIPLINARY CONNECTIONS

- Geography and History Activity 17 **L2**
- People to Meet Activity 17 **L2**
- Economics Activity 17 **L2**
- Citizenship and Service Learning Activity 17 **L2**

SPANISH RESOURCES

- Spanish Reading Essentials and Study Guide
- Spanish Guided Reading Activities
- Spanish Quizzes, Tests, and Authentic Assessment (with Rubrics)
- Spanish Take-Home Review Activities

MULTIMEDIA

- Exam*View*® Pro Testmaker CD-ROM
- Glencoe Skillbuilder Interactive Workbook CD-ROM, Level 1
- Interactive Tutor Self-Assessment CD-ROM
- MindJogger Videoquiz
- Presentation Plus! CD-ROM
- StudentWorks Plus™ CD-ROM (with Audio Program)
- TeacherWorks CD-ROM
- Vocabulary PuzzleMaker CD-ROM
- *World History: Journey Across Time* Video Program
- World History Primary Source Document Library CD-ROM

STANDARDIZED ASSESSMENT SKILLS

- Standardized Test Skills Practice Workbook Activity 17 **L2**
- Critical Thinking Skills Activity 17 **L2**

Teaching strategies have been coded with suggested ability levels. However, most are suitable for all levels.

L1 BASIC activities for all students

L2 AVERAGE activities for average to above-average students

L3 CHALLENGING activities for above-average students

EL ENGLISH LANGUAGE activities

TIME MANAGEMENT

Chapter Introduction	Section 1	Section 2	Section 3	Section 4	Chapter Wrap-Up
1 Day	1 Day	2 Days	2 Days	2 Days	1 Day

Block Scheduling Activities that are suited to use within the block scheduling framework are identified by:

0:00 OUT OF TIME? Assign the Chapter 17 *Reading Essentials and Study Guide.* *

SECTION RESOURCES

DAILY OBJECTIVES	REPRODUCIBLE RESOURCES	MULTIMEDIA RESOURCES
Section 1 **The Renaissance Begins** 1. Italian city-states began a rebirth of learning and art in Europe. 2. Italy's location helped it grow wealthy from trade and banking.	Reproducible Lesson Plan 17–1 Vocabulary Activity 17–1 Guided Reading Activity 17–1* Section Quiz 17–1* Reading Essentials and Study Guide 17–1*	Daily Focus Skills Transparency 17–1 Interactive Tutor Self-Assessment CD-ROM ExamView® Pro Testmaker CD-ROM Presentation Plus! CD-ROM
Section 2 **New Ideas and Art** 1. Humanists studied the Greeks and Romans, and the printing press spread humanist ideas. 2. Renaissance art and ideas spread from Italy to northern Europe.	Reproducible Lesson Plan 17–2 Vocabulary Activity 17–2 Guided Reading Activity 17–2* Section Quiz 17–2* Reading Essentials and Study Guide 17–2*	Daily Focus Skills Transparency 17–2 Interactive Tutor Self-Assessment CD-ROM ExamView® Pro Testmaker CD-ROM Presentation Plus! CD-ROM Glencoe BookLink CD-ROM
Section 3 **The Reformation Begins** 1. Martin Luther broke with the pope and started Protestantism, which political leaders often supported. 2. John Calvin's ideas spread across Europe to North America.	Reproducible Lesson Plan 17–3 Vocabulary Activity 17–3 Guided Reading Activity 17–3* Section Quiz 17–3* Reading Essentials and Study Guide 17–3*	Daily Focus Skills Transparency 17–3 Interactive Tutor Self-Assessment CD-ROM ExamView® Pro Testmaker CD-ROM Presentation Plus! CD-ROM Glencoe BookLink CD-ROM
Section 4 **Catholics and Protestants** 1. Catholics and Protestants fought each other, and Henry VIII created a Protestant church in England. 2. Catholic kingdoms began sending missionaries overseas.	Reproducible Lesson Plan 17–4 Vocabulary Activity 17–4 Guided Reading Activity 17–4* Section Quiz 17–4* Reading Essentials and Study Guide 17–4*	Daily Focus Skills Transparency 17–4 Interactive Tutor Self-Assessment CD-ROM ExamView® Pro Testmaker CD-ROM Presentation Plus! CD-ROM Vocabulary PuzzleMaker CD-ROM Glencoe BookLink CD-ROM

*Also available in Spanish

History Online

Use our Web site for additional resources. All essential content is covered in the Student Edition.

You and your students can visit jat.glencoe.com, the Web site companion to *World History: Journey Across Time*. This innovative integration of electronic and print media offers your students a wealth of opportunities. The student text directs students to the Web site for the following options:

- Chapter Overviews
- Self-Check Quizzes
- Study Central™
- Student Web Activities
- Multi-Language Glossaries

Answers to the student Web activities are provided for you in the **Web Activity Lesson Plans.** Additional Web resources and ePuzzles and games are also available.

The following videotape programs are available from Glencoe as supplements to Chapter 17:

Michelangelo
(ISBN 1-56501-425-1)

Elizabeth I: The Virgin Queen
(ISBN 0-7670-0209-1)

Henry VIII
(ISBN 1-56501-917-2)

To order, call Glencoe at 1-800-334-7344. To find classroom resources to accompany many of these videos, check the following home pages:

A&E Television: www.aande.com
The History Channel: www.historychannel.com

MEETING SPECIAL NEEDS

In addition to the Differentiated Instruction strategies, the following resources are suitable for students with special needs:

- *ExamView® Pro Testmaker CD-ROM* allows teachers to tailor tests by reducing answer choices.
- *StudentWorks Plus™ CD-ROM (with Audio Program)* includes the entire narrative of the student edition so that less-proficient readers can listen to the words as they read them.
- The *Reading Essentials and Study Guide* provides the same content as the student edition but is written two grade levels below the textbook.

NATIONAL GEOGRAPHIC TEACHER'S CORNER

Index to National Geographic Magazine:

The following articles relate to this chapter:

- "The Danube: Europe's River of Harmony and Discord," by Cliff Tarpy, March 2002.
- "Po: River of Pain and Plenty," by Erla Zwingle, May 2002.
- "Italy's Endangered Art," by Erla Zwingle, August 1999.

National Geographic Society Products:

To order the following, call National Geographic at 1–800–368–2728

- *Renaissance Restoration* (Videocassette)
- *National Geographic Atlas of the World* (Book)

NGS ONLINE

Access National Geographic's new dynamic MapMachine Web site and other geography resources at:

www.nationalgeographic.com
www.nationalgeographic.com/maps

Meeting NCSS Standards

World History: Journey Across Time

The following standards are highlighted in Chapter 17:

Section 1 **II** Time, Continuity, and Change: B, C, D
VII Production, Distribution, and Consumption: D, E, I

Section 2 **I** Culture: A, B, C, D, E, F, G
IV Individual Development and Identity: A, C, D
VIII Science, Technology, and Society: A, B

Section 3 **V** Individuals, Groups, and Institutions: B, D, E, H
VI Power, Authority, and Governance: B, E

Section 4 **V** Individuals, Groups, and Institutions: C, D, F, G
IX Global Connections: A, H

State and Local Objectives

_____

_____

Timesaving Tools

TeacherWorks
All-In-One Planner and Resource Center

● **Interactive Teacher Edition** Access your Teacher Wraparound Edition and your classroom resources with a few easy clicks.

● **Interactive Lesson Planner** Organize your week, month, semester, or year with all the lesson helps you need to make teaching creative and relevant.

Use Glencoe's **Presentation Plus!** multimedia teacher tool to easily present dynamic lessons that visually excite your students. Using Microsoft PowerPoint® you can customize the presentations to create your own personalized lessons.

FOLDABLES™
Study Organizer

Dinah Zike's Foldables

Foldables are three-dimensional, interactive graphic organizers that help students practice basic writing skills, review key vocabulary terms, and identify main ideas. Every chapter contains a foldable activity, with additional chapter activities found in the *Reading and Study Skills Foldables* booklet. You can use the foldables as they are presented, or modify them to suit the needs of your individual class.

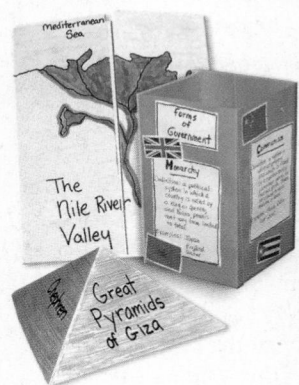

Planning Ahead

CHAPTER CULMINATING ACTIVITY

The Chapter Culminating Activity will help students organize and learn the important information from the chapter. Begin the chapter with this activity, and have students complete it as a culminating activity.

CREATING A CONCEPT MAP FOR THE CHAPTER

Purpose Concept mapping creates a concrete representation of the relationship among ideas. This organizational strategy is useful before, during, and after reading and as a procedure for organizing information for reports. Mapping works particularly well with materials that lack a cohesive structure and when ideas on a topic are scattered throughout the chapter.

Introduction to Modeling

1. Open the discussion with a brainstorming session in which students discuss all the information they know or think they know about the Renaissance and Reformation. Write the information on an overhead transparency.

The prereading map might look something like this:

2. As students read the chapter, they can add additional topics to the prereading map.

3. The arms of the map can become topics on note cards. As shown on the example, students would have four different note cards with the topics of *Economy, Culture, Government,* and *Geography.* Have students consolidate their information, keeping topical information separated on different cards. Finally, have students select one topic and write a summary of the information on the appropriate card.

604D

When & Where?

As students read the chapter, have them review the time line on this page. Ask them to explain why the Renaissance began in Italy. (*Italians became interested in their ancient Roman heritage; Italy's city-states could afford to pay talented artists to produce outstanding works.*) **L1**

GLENCOE TECHNOLOGY

World History: Journey Across Time Video Program

To learn more about the Renaissance and Reformation, students can view the Chapter 17 video in the *World History: Journey Across Time* Video Program.

MindJogger Videoquiz

Use the **MindJogger Videoquiz** to preview Chapter 17 content.

 Available in DVD and VHS

Chapter 17

The Renaissance and Reformation

▼ The Duomo, or Cathedral of Santa Maria del Fiore, in Florence, Italy

NATIONAL GEOGRAPHIC When & Where?

1350	1450	1550	1650
c. 1350 Renaissance begins in Italy	1434 Medici family begins rule of Florence	1517 Martin Luther writes Ninety-Five Theses	1648 Thirty Years' War ends

Reading Strategy   PURPOSE FOR READING

Predicting Have students fold a sheet of paper in half. Then tell them to skim the chapter for the Reading Check questions and to choose any five of them. For example, "Why did the Renaissance start in Italy?" is the first Reading Check question in the chapter. Tell students to write their selected questions in the left column of their paper. Instruct students to skip two spaces between questions. Next, ask students to predict the answers to the questions and to write their predictions in the right column. Suggest that students make their predictions brief and write them in pencil. Then tell them to look for answers to the questions as they read and to write the answers in ink below their predictions. **L1**

Chapter Preview

New ideas brought the Middle Ages to an end. Read this chapter to find out how advances in the arts and learning and dramatic changes to Christianity led to the beginning of modern times in Europe.

 View the Chapter 17 video in the *World History: Journey Across Time* Video Program.

 Chapter Overview Visit jat.glencoe.com for a preview of Chapter 17.

 ## The Renaissance Begins

During the Renaissance, new values and new art developed in wealthy Italian city-states.

 ## New Ideas and Art

Wealthy leaders in Italian city-states supported talented artists and writers, and Renaissance art and ideas spread from Italy to northern Europe.

 ## The Reformation Begins

Martin Luther and other reformers, such as John Calvin, broke from the Catholic Church and began a new Christian movement that came to be called Protestantism.

 ## Catholics and Protestants

While the Catholic Church attempted to carry out reforms, Catholics and Protestants fought bloody religious wars across Europe.

Study Organizer

Compare-Contrast *Make this foldable to help you compare and contrast what you learn about the Renaissance and Reformation.*

Step 1 *Fold a sheet of paper in half from side to side.*

Step 2 *Turn the paper and fold it into thirds.*

Step 3 *Unfold and cut the top layer only along both folds.*

This will make three tabs.

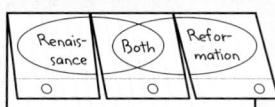

Fold it so the left edge lies about ½ inch from the right edge.

Step 4 *Label as shown.*

Renais-sance   Both   Refor-mation

Reading and Writing *As you read the sections on the Renaissance and Reformation, record important concepts and events under the appropriate tabs. Then record ideas similar to both under the middle tab.*

605

MORE ABOUT THE PHOTO

Il Duomo The cathedral of Santa Maria del Fiore (Holy Mary of the Flower) dominates Florence's skyline. It was started in 1296. The cathedral acquired its name *Il Duomo*, meaning "The Dome," because of the eight-sided dome that Filippo Brunelleschi designed and built (1420–1436). The dome was unique for its time because no wooden structures were used for support during construction. The dome is 128 feet (42 m) across—almost as large as that of the Parthenon. Brunelleschi used a series of stone half arches that taper from 7 feet (2.1 m) wide at the base to 5 feet (1.5 m) at the top, plus other materials, to support the dome. The dome actually consists of two domes, one inside the other, so that the outside could have a more appealing appearance.

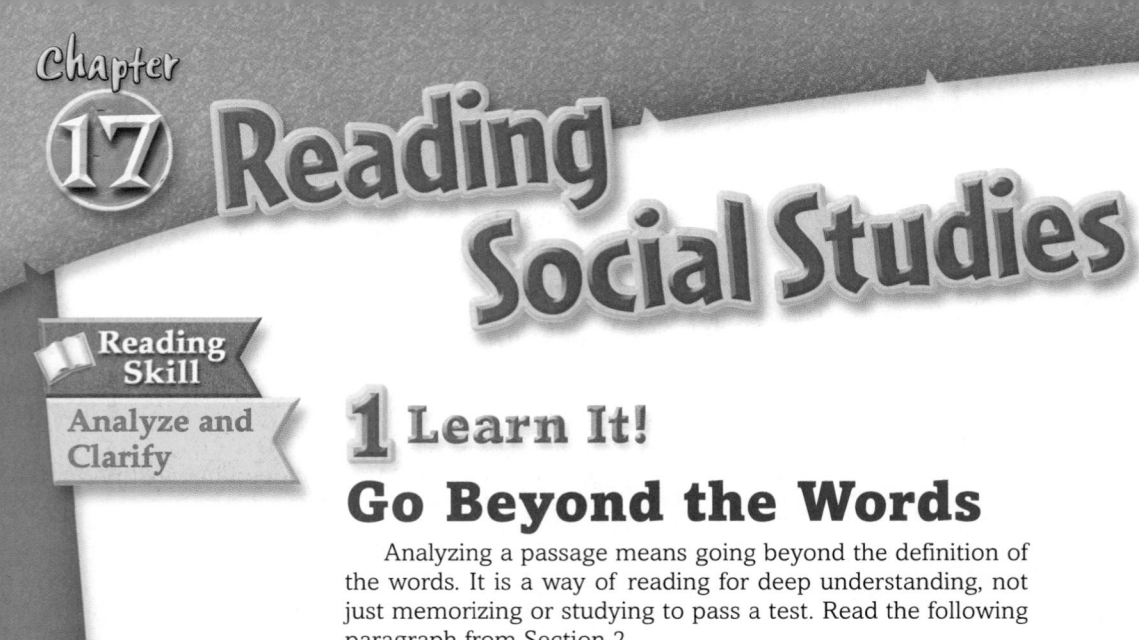

1 Learn It!

When students analyze and clarify while reading, they become adept at tackling and making sense of unfamiliar text. When readers encounter unfamiliar words or information, they often ask themselves questions about the text or make mental notes about it. Readers can do this with one paragraph or a series of them. Model this process by reading the paragraph from page 623 that begin with the sentence "Renaissance painters also used new techniques." Pause after each sentence and read the explanations that show how a careful reader might engage the text.

After Sentence 1: Reader—The paragraph is about techniques in painting. What are they?

After Sentence 2: Reader— Perspective is one technique. Why is being three-dimensional important?

After Sentence 3: Reader—This sentence does not tell me anything more about what perspective is.

After Sentence 4: Reader— Okay, perspective makes things look like they are at different distances. Is that important?

After Sentence 5: Reader— Having things look as though they are at different distances makes the picture look more realistic, and that is what makes perspective important.
L1/ **EL**

Chapter 17

Reading Social Studies

Reading Skill

Analyze and Clarify

1 Learn It!
Go Beyond the Words

Analyzing a passage means going beyond the definition of the words. It is a way of reading for deep understanding, not just memorizing or studying to pass a test. Read the following paragraph from Section 2.

> **Renaissance painters also used new techniques. The most important was perspective, a method that makes a drawing or painting look three-dimensional. Artists had tried to use perspective before, but Renaissance artists perfected it. Using perspective, objects in a scene appear to be at different distances from the viewer. The result is a more realistic image.**
>
> *—from page 623*

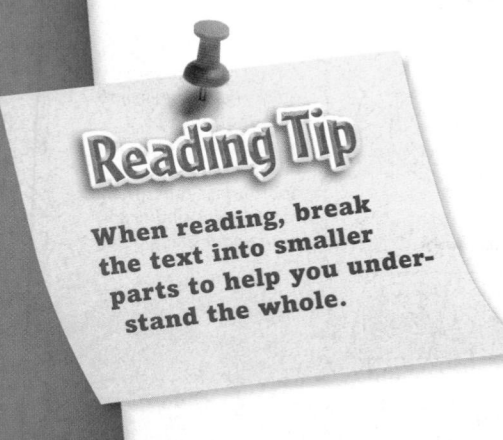

Reading Tip

When reading, break the text into smaller parts to help you understand the whole.

How can you analyze this passage? Here are some suggestions:
1. Look at the drawing on page 626. Is the drawing realistic as described by the paragraph?
2. Look at another painting or drawing in this book. Compare the perspective to the drawing on page 626. Which is more realistic? Why?
3. With a partner, sketch a view of your classroom. Exchange sketches and see if you can tell where your partner was standing when he or she made the sketch. Based on your experience, what are some difficulties an artist might encounter in trying to draw a large area realistically?

606

Reading Strategy **RECIPROCAL TEACHING**

Using Summarizing, Questioning, and Clarifying Use the following steps with students or have small groups of students use them to analyze and clarify the text under the subsection "Italy's City-States Grow Wealthy" from Section 1.

- **Summarize:** Readers summarize a portion of the text by identifying the most important information and then restating it in their own words.
- **Question:** Readers ask themselves or others about text they do not understand.
- **Clarify:** Readers reread, read ahead, or seek outside help in finding answers to their questions.
L1/ **EL**

2 Practice It!

Analyze as You Read

Read this paragraph from Section 2.

Read to Write ....
: Choose any painting or
: drawing in this book
: and analyze, in writing,
: what is taking place.
: Use the questions *who,*
: *what, when,* or *how* to
: help you get started.

> To make their paintings more realistic, Renaissance artists also used a technique called chiaroscuro. Chiaroscuro softened edges by using light and shadows instead of stiff outlines to separate objects. In Italian, *chiaro* means "clear or light," and *oscuro* means "dark." Chiaroscuro created more drama and emotion in a painting.
>
> —*from page 623*

▲ The *Mona Lisa*

Analyze the above paragraph by doing the following:

1. Look at the painting of Mona Lisa from page 622. Do you see the use of chiaroscuro? If so, in what way does it create drama or emotion?

2. Choose another painting in this or a different text. Look at it carefully to see if the technique of chiaroscuro was used. Describe to a partner the light and dark areas that you see.

3. Try your hand at drawing an object or scene using the technique of chiaroscuro.

3 Apply It!

As you read this chapter, choose at least one section to study and analyze for deeper meaning. Exchange your analysis with a classmate who has analyzed a different passage.

607

2 Practice It!

Remind students that visuals often clarify information in the text. Tell students to read the first two paragraphs under "Politics and Lutheranism" in Section 3. Have volunteers summarize each paragraph. Then ask students to write a brief description of Charles V's lands. Next, have the class locate these lands on the map on the same page. Ask volunteers to read what they first wrote about the extent of Charles's kingdom and what they could add after looking at the map. Discuss with the class how looking at a map clarified the size and location of his lands. **L1**

3 Apply It!

Suggest the following to students as possible ways to analyze and demonstrate a deeper meaning for their selected sections:

- Use an object that will help explain the text.
- Research a person, place, or thing in the text and present the findings to the class.
- Draw a map to show locations or relationships.
- Draw an illustration of an object referenced in the text.
- Create a series of questions to generate deeper understanding. **L2**

📖 Reading Strategy ⟨ READ TO WRITE

As part of brainstorming for their analyses, have students fold a sheet of paper in half vertically. Next, ask them to write the questions *Who?, What?, When?,* and *How?* in a column on the left side of the page, leaving space between each question word. Then tell students to review the information under "What Was New About Renaissance Art?" in Section 2 and list the main goals and techniques below the questions. Have students first answer the questions about their selected piece of art and put them in the right column. As the next step, ask students to notate how their piece of art meets the goals of Renaissance art or uses any of the new techniques, if indeed it does. Students should record these observations in the right column and note any other points they wish to add in their analyses. At this point, have students write their compositions.

❶ FOCUS

SECTION OVERVIEW

This section describes how Italian city-states grew wealthy and used their riches to bring a rebirth of art and ideas to Europe.

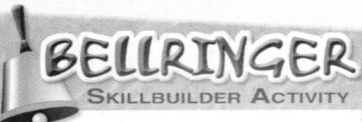

🖝 Project **Daily Focus Skills Transparency 17–1** and have students answer questions. Discuss their responses.

Get Ready to Read!

Preteaching Vocabulary: Explain that the Black Death made Italians more secular. Their interest in the world increased because they wanted to make it a better place.

Answers to Graphic: The long coastline with ports was an ideal location for trade; the Crusades brought Italian merchants into contact with Arab merchants; the rise of the Mongol Empire united almost all of Asia into one trade network.

Section ❶

The Renaissance Begins

Get Ready to Read!

What's the Connection?
Previously, you learned about life in medieval Europe. In this section, you will see how Europeans began to look to the ideals of the ancient Greeks and Romans as they left the Middle Ages behind.

Focusing on the Main Ideas
- The wealthy urban society of the Italian city-states brought a rebirth of learning and art to Europe. *(page 609)*
- Italy's location helped its city-states grow wealthy from trade and banking, but many of the cities fell under the control of strong rulers. *(page 611)*
- Unlike medieval nobles, the nobles of the Italian city-states lived in cities and were active in trade, banking, and public life. *(page 614)*

Locating Places
Florence (FLAWR•uhns)
Venice (VEH•nuhs)

Meeting People
Marco Polo (MAHR•koh   POH•loh)
Medici (MEH•duh•chee)
Niccolò Machiavelli (NEE•koh•LOH MA•kee•uh•VEH•lee)

Building Your Vocabulary
Renaissance (REH•nuh•SAHNS)
secular (SEH•kyuh•luhr)
diplomacy (duh•PLOH•muh•see)

Reading Strategy
Summarizing Information Complete a chart like the one below showing the reasons Italian city-states grew wealthy.

[ ] → [ ] → [ ]
↓
Wealth Grows in City-States

	1350	1450	1550
	c. 1350 Renaissance begins in Italy	**1434** Medici family begins rule of Florence	**1513** Machiavelli writes *The Prince*

Genoa • Venice • Florence • Rome

SECTION RESOURCES

📂 **Reproducible Masters**
- Reproducible Lesson Plan 17–1
- Daily Lecture and Discussion Notes 17–1
- Vocabulary Activity 17–1
- Active Reading Note-Taking Guide 17–1
- Guided Reading Activity 17–1
- Section Quiz 17–1
- Reading Essentials and Study Guide 17–1

🖝 **Transparencies**
- Daily Focus Skills Transparency 17–1

Multimedia
- Interactive Tutor Self-Assessment CD-ROM
- ExamView® Pro Testmaker CD-ROM
- Presentation Plus! CD-ROM

The Italian Renaissance

Main Idea The wealthy urban society of the Italian city-states brought a rebirth of learning and art to Europe.

Reading Focus Hollywood makes many of the world's movies. Why is it the center of the movie industry? Read to learn why the city-states of Italy became the center of art during the Renaissance.

Renaissance (REH•nuh•SAHNS) means "rebirth." The years from about 1350 to 1550 in European history are called the Renaissance because there was a rebirth of interest in art and learning.

In some ways the Renaissance was a rebirth of interest in the same subjects the Greeks and Romans had studied. After the horrible years of the Black Death, Europeans began looking to the past when times seemed better. They wanted to learn how to make their own society better.

During the Renaissance, Europeans also began to stress the importance of the individual. They began to believe that people could make a difference and change the world for the better.

People were still very religious during the Renaissance, but they also began to celebrate human achievements. People became more **secular** (SEH•kyuh•luhr). This means they were more interested in this world than in religion and getting to heaven.

② TEACH

Reading Strategy

Changing Viewpoints During the Middle Ages, religion and life after death, not life in this world, were the focal points of Christians' lives. Ask students to explain what the Black Death was and how it affected Europe. Then, discuss how this sickness changed people's viewpoints about what was important in life. **L2**

Daily Lecture and Discussion Notes 17–1

Use **Daily Lecture and Discussion Notes 17–1** for an outline of key concepts found in the section.

Reading Support L1/ EL

Use **Vocabulary Activity 17–1** to review important terms in the section.

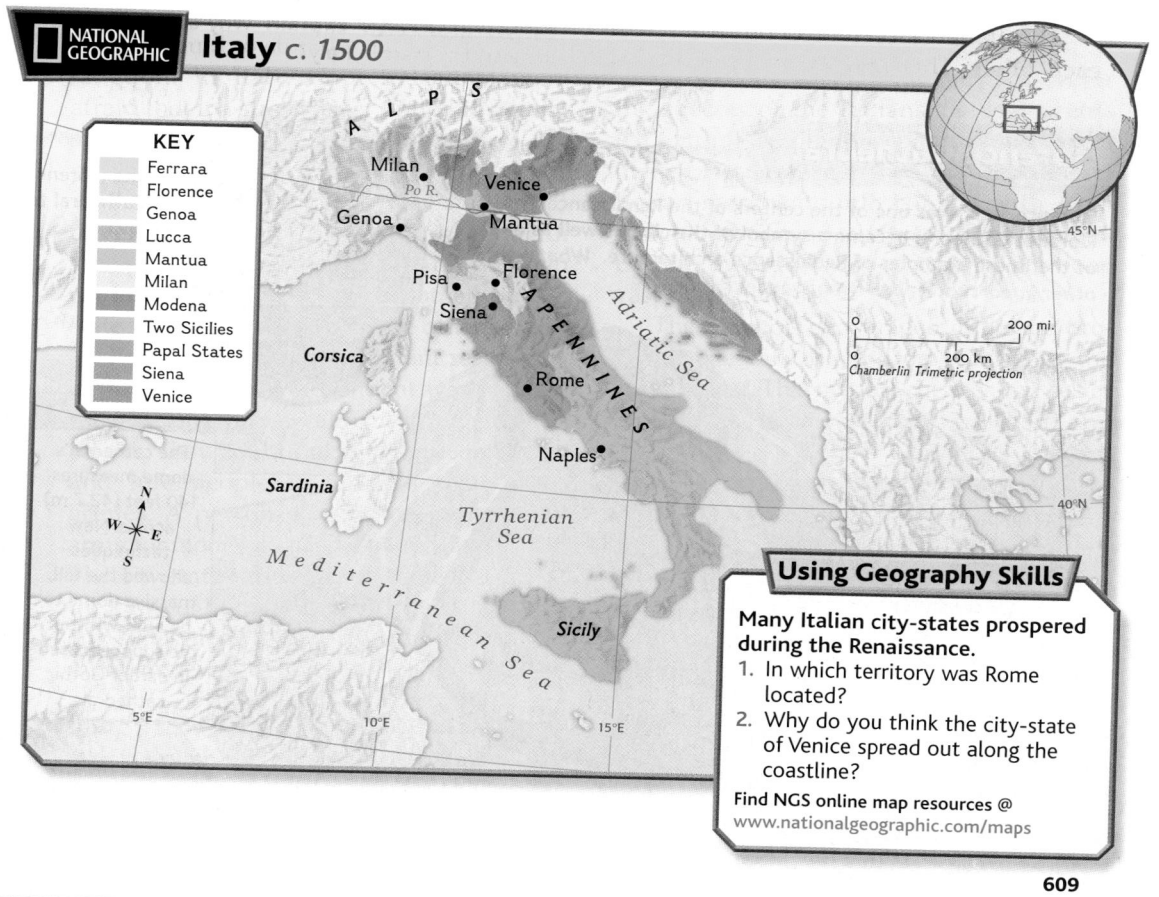

NATIONAL GEOGRAPHIC

Italy c. 1500

KEY
- Ferrara
- Florence
- Genoa
- Lucca
- Mantua
- Milan
- Modena
- Two Sicilies
- Papal States
- Siena
- Venice

Milan · Po R. · Venice · Genoa · Mantua · Pisa · Florence · Siena · Corsica · Rome · Naples · Sardinia · Sicily

ALPS · APENNINES · Adriatic Sea · Tyrrhenian Sea · Mediterranean Sea

45°N · 40°N · 5°E · 10°E · 15°E

0   200 mi.
0   200 km
Chamberlin Trimetric projection

Using Geography Skills

Many Italian city-states prospered during the Renaissance.
1. In which territory was Rome located?
2. Why do you think the city-state of Venice spread out along the coastline?

Find NGS online map resources @ www.nationalgeographic.com/maps

609

Using Geography Skills

Answers:
1. Papal States
2. to have more ports for trade

Reading Strategy   READING THE TEXT

Monitoring Comprehension Model the way students should monitor their comprehension. Read aloud the **Reading Focus** for the subsection "The Italian Renaissance." Comment to the class, "This section will tell us why Italy became the center of art during the Renaissance." Then read the next two paragraphs aloud. **Ask:** *What is the Renaissance? (rebirth of interest in Roman and Greek art and learning)* Comment again to the class, "So the Renaissance happened after the Black Death in part because the Black Death helped increase interest in the past." Then read the next two paragraphs aloud. Use the preceding process to ask about and discuss the change in thinking that occurred. Finally, instruct students to read the next six paragraphs to find three reasons why the Renaissance began in Italy. **L2**

additional effects. "The prices of these goods fell" is one such effect. Help students label each effects *and* causes. Ask students to complete the chain by predicting what the last event on the chain might cause. **L3**

Marco Polo became a commander three years after his return to Venice, and served in a sea battle between Venice and Genoa. The Genoese captured 7,000 Venetians, including Polo. While Polo was in a Genoese prison, he met another prisoner, Rustichello, who was known for his retelling of the stories of King Arthur. Together they produced "A Description of the World," Marco Polo's now-famous account of Asia and its riches as told to Rustichello.

More About the Art

The financial institutions of Florence were the forerunners of present-day banks.

Caption Answer:
Merchants needed to know the value of coins from different places, and Florentine bankers became the experts in this; they also lent money.

Why did the Renaissance begin in Italy? First of all, Italy had been the center of the

India to Muslim and Byzantine cities. As more and more silk and spices were shipped from Asia, the price of these goods fell. More Europeans could afford the luxuries, and demand for the items greatly increased. In turn, business for Italian merchants continued to grow.

Who Was Marco Polo?
Europeans were fascinated with Asia and its goods after reading a book written by **Marco Polo** (MAHR•koh POH•loh), a merchant from the city of Venice. In the 1270s, Marco Polo went on an amazing journey with his father and uncle to China. They set off to meet Kublai Khan, the ruler of the Mongol Empire.

When the Polo family finally made it to the khan's court, the great emperor was impressed with Marco Polo. He sent Marco Polo on business all over China. Marco Polo asked many questions and learned more about Asia than any other European. When he returned to Europe, he published a book about his travels. His stories helped increase interest in China and made many people want to buy China's goods.

Renaissance. Wealthy nobles and merchants wanted artists to produce works that

The Wealth of Florence
No city was more famous in the Renaissance than Florence. It was the first to grow wealthy, and it produced many famous artists. It sat on the banks of the Arno River surrounded by beautiful hills. It was walled and had many tall towers for defense. Its people were known for their love of elegant clothing.

At first, Florence's wealth came from trading cloth, especially wool. The city's merchants sailed to England to get sheep's wool. Artisans in Florence then wove it into fine fabrics. Florentines also found another way to make money—banking.

With goods pouring into Italy from around the world, merchants needed to know the value of coins from different countries. Florentine bankers became the experts. They used the florin, the gold coin of Florence, to measure the value of other money. Bankers also began lending money and charging interest. Florence's richest

▼ Lorenzo de' Medici

▲ This painting shows bankers in Florence doing business at a counter topped with brightly embroidered cloth. *Why did banking become so important in Florence?*

612   CHAPTER 17   The Renaissance and Reformation

INTERDISCIPLINARY CONNECTIONS ACTIVITY

Economics Point out that just as Florentine bankers measured the value of other money against the florin, bankers today often measure the value of other countries' money against the U.S. dollar. Then have students convert different amounts of U.S. dollars into foreign currencies assuming the following information. **L2**

• 1 U.S. dollar equals 1.33 Canadian dollars.
• 1 Canadian dollar equals 0.76 U.S. dollars.
• 1 U.S. dollar equals 0.79 euros.
• 1 euro equals 1.27 U.S. dollars.

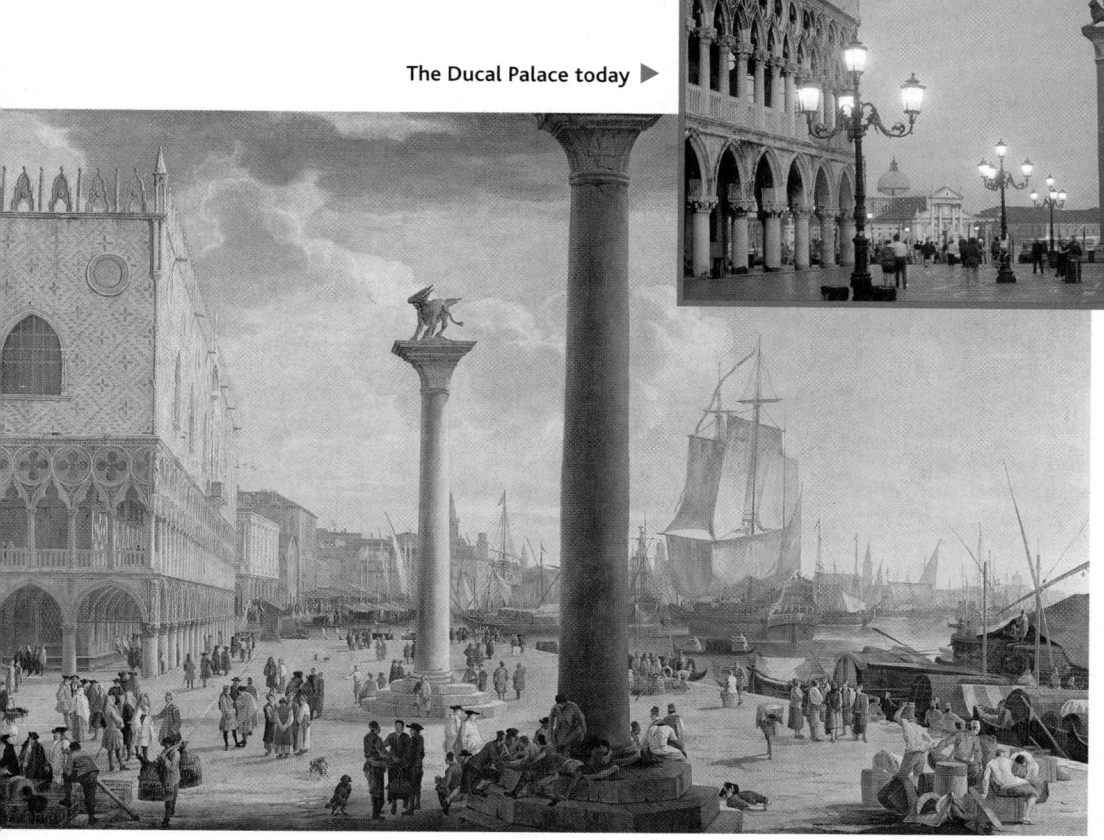
The Ducal Palace today ▶

▲ This painting from Renaissance Italy shows the busy pier and the Ducal Palace in Venice. *What industry provided some of Venice's wealth?*

family, the **Medici** (MEH•duh•chee), were bankers. They had branch banks as far away as London.

The Rise of Venice The wealthiest city-state of all was Venice, where Marco Polo was born. Venice is at the northern end of the Adriatic Sea. The Venetians were great sailors and shipbuilders. They built their city on many small, swampy islands just off the coast. Early Venetians learned how to drive long wooden poles into mud to support their buildings.

Instead of paving roads, the Venetians cut canals through their swampy islands and used boats to move about. Even today, many of the streets in the older parts of Venice are canals and waterways. Gondolas—a type of long, narrow boat—still carry people along these canals.

Some of Venice's wealth came from building ships. Artisans worked on ships at a shipyard known as the Arsenal. Teams of workers cut the wood, shaped it into hulls, caulked (or sealed) the wood, and made sails and oars. Sometimes Venetians needed ships quickly. When the Turks tried to take a Venetian colony in the Mediterranean, the Arsenal built 100 ships in only two months to prepare for battle.

✓Reading Check **Describe** How did Florence and the Medici family become so wealthy?

CHAPTER 17   The Renaissance and Reformation   **613**

EXTENDING THE CONTENT

Marco Polo's Return to Venice In 1292 Kublai Khan asked Marco Polo, his father Niccolò, and his uncle Maffeo to accompany a Tartar princess on a sea voyage to Persia. The Khan sent them off with 14 ships and 600 people. Out of the 600, only 18 survived the tumultuous voyage, but the Polos and the princess were among the survivors. After delivering the princess, the three Venetians traveled across northern Persia to Constantinople and from there to Venice. They reached Venice in 1295, which was 24 years after their original departure. According to tradition, their family had assumed they were dead and did not recognize the shabby strangers. However, when the three ripped open the seams of their clothing, rubies, diamonds, and emeralds spilled out. Then their relatives embraced them and treated them to a feast.

Caption Answer:
shipbuilding

Reading Support L1/ EL

Assign **Guided Reading Activity 17–1** to help students organize the information in the section.

③ ASSESS

Assign Section 1 Review as homework or as an in-class activity.

⊙ Have students use the **Interactive Tutor Self-Assessment CD-ROM** to review the section.

Assessment L2

Assign **Section 1 Quiz** to assess mastery of the material found in the section.

Reading Support L1/ EL

Assign **Reading Essentials and Study Guide 17–1** to help students review section material.

✓**Reading Check**

Answer: The city became wealthy by trading woolen cloth and by banking; the Medici family gained its wealth by banking.

Reading Strategy

Comparing Governments As students read the subsection "How Were Italian City-States Run?", have them consider how government works in their own state. Have them research their state government and write a short paragraph comparing it to that of the Italian city-states. **L3**

Primary Source

Machiavelli based *The Prince* on what he had seen happening in government and on historical events. The ruler in *The Prince* became the model for absolute power in Europe for the next two centuries.

Answer:
The first way does not always work.

ENRICH

Amerigo Vespucci went to Spain for Lorenzo de Medici. Eventually, Vespucci sailed to the New World and became America's namesake. Have students research Vespucci's trip and the reasons his name was used for America. **L2**

The Urban Noble

Main Idea Unlike medieval nobles, the nobles of the Italian city-states lived in cities and were active in trade, banking, and public life.

Reading Focus How does our society measure wealth? Before the Renaissance, wealth was based on the amount of land a person owned. Read to learn how that changed during the Renaissance.

The wealthy men of the Italian city-states were a new type of leader—the urban noble. Before this time, European nobles got their wealth from land, not trade. In fact,

Primary Source
The Prince

In Machiavelli's masterpiece, he explains his theories about human nature.

"You should consider then, that there are two ways of fighting, one with laws and the other with force. The first is properly a human method, the second belongs to beasts. But as the first method does not always suffice [meet your needs], you sometimes have to turn to the second. Thus a prince must know how to make good use of both the beast and the man."

—Niccolò Machiavelli, *The Prince*

▲ Niccolò Machiavelli

DBQ Document-Based Question

Why must a good leader know more than one way to fight?

they looked down on trade and believed themselves to be above the town merchants.

In the Italian city-states, old noble families moved to the cities. They mixed with wealthy merchants and decided that money from trade was just as good as money from land.

Meanwhile, wealthy merchants copied the manners and lifestyle of noble families. Soon, the sons and daughters of nobles and rich merchants were marrying each other. Eventually, the old nobles and wealthy merchant families blended together to become the upper class of the city-states.

How Were Italian City-States Run? At first, many of the city-states were republics. A republic is a government controlled by its citizens. Not everyone was a citizen, however, only the artisans and merchants who had membership in the city's guilds.

From your study of the ancient Romans, you might recall that when their cities faced war or rebellion, they gave power to a dictator. The Italian city-states did something similar. In many cases, the cities were ruled by one powerful man who ran the government.

In Venice, the head of state was the duke, or doge (DOHJ). At first, the doge had great power over his council of nobles. Later, he lost power to a small group of nobles.

In Florence, the powerful Medici family gained control of the government in 1434. The Medici ran Florence for many decades. Lorenzo de' Medici ruled the city from 1469 to 1492. Known as "the Magnificent," Lorenzo used his wealth to support artists, architects, and writers. Many of Italy's Renaissance artists owed their success to his support.

Politics in Italy was complicated. Within each city, the rulers had to keep the poor from

COOPERATIVE LEARNING ACTIVITY

Performing a Skit Present the following scenario to the class: The doge of Venice is concerned because poor Venetians are planning to rebel, and a group of wealthy Venetians are plotting to take power. To make matters worse, an army from Florence is advancing on the city. The doge consults his advisers, including Machiavelli, about what he should do. Organize the class into the following groups: poor Venetians, wealthy plotters, invaders from Florence, and the doge and his advisers. Ask each group to write and perform a three-minute skit that explains what they are going to do and why they are doing it. Tell students to base their skits on information from the section. **L2**

📁 Refer to the **Quizzes, Tests, and Authentic Assessment (with Rubrics)** booklet for rubrics.

rebelling and prevent other wealthy people from seizing power. They had to make deals with merchants, bankers, landlords, church leaders, and mercenaries. At the same time, they had to deal with the leaders of the other city-states.

To deal with the other states around them, the Italians developed **diplomacy** (duh•PLOH•muh•see). Diplomacy is the art of negotiating, or making deals, with other countries. Each city-state sent ambassadors to live in the other city-states and act as representatives for their city. Many of the ideas of modern diplomacy first began in Italy's city-states.

How could a ruler maintain power in the Italian city-states? **Niccolò Machiavelli** (NEE•koh•LOH MA•kee•uh•VEH•lee), a diplomat in Florence, tried to answer this question when he wrote *The Prince* in 1513. Machiavelli claimed that people were

▲ This palace served as a government building in Rome for hundreds of years. *What form of government did many of the city-states have at first?*

greedy and self-centered. Rulers should not try to be good, he argued. Rather, they should do whatever is necessary to keep power and protect their city, including killing and lying. Today when we say someone is being Machiavellian, we mean they are being tricky and not thinking about being good.

✓ **Reading Check** **Compare** How were medieval and Renaissance nobles different?

Section 1 Review

Reading Summary
Review the Main Ideas

- A rebirth of learning called the Renaissance began in wealthy Italian city-states in the 1300s.

- Italian city-states, including Florence and Venice, grew wealthy through trade, manufacturing, and banking.

- In the Italian city-states, a noble's wealth was based on trade, rather than the amount of land owned.

What Did You Learn?

1. Why is the era from 1350 to 1550 in Europe called the Renaissance?

2. Why did the Renaissance begin in Italy?

Critical Thinking

3. **Organizing Information** Draw a diagram like the one below. Add details about the characteristics of the Italian Renaissance.

```
        ( )   ( )
          \   /
   ( )—( Italian Renaissance )
          /   \
        ( )   ( )
```

4. **Economics Link** How did Renaissance cities gain their wealth? Give several examples.

5. **Summarize** Describe the governments of Italian city-states during the Renaissance.

6. **Analyze** Who were the Medicis and why were they important?

7. **Persuasive Writing** Write a letter to the editor of a Renaissance newspaper telling whether you agree or disagree with Machiavelli's beliefs about rulers and power during the Renaissance.

CHAPTER 17 The Renaissance and Reformation **615**

Caption Answer:
republics

✓ **Reading Check**

Answer: medieval: got their wealth from land; Renaissance: got their wealth from trade

To help students understand section material, have them visit Study Central™ at jat.glencoe.com

RETEACH

Ask students to compare Venice and Florence. **L2**

 CLOSE

Assign Venice to half of the class and Florence to the other half. Then allow students two minutes to write nouns associated with their city. Have volunteers share their lists. **L1**

SECTION 1 REVIEW ANSWERS

1. because of a rebirth in art and learning

2. Italy had been the center of the Roman Empire, the city-states were wealthy and competed with one another, and urban society promoted new ideas and art.

3. "rebirth," interest in Greeks and Romans, human achievements, more secular, importance of the individual

4. Florence: trade in wool and cloth and banking; Venice: trade and shipbuilding

5. Answers should be based on

information in the text.

6. The Medicis were the richest family in Florence. They ran the city for decades and supported many artists.

7. Letters will vary but should demonstrate a thoughtful response.

You Decide...

The Value of City-States

❶ FOCUS

Life in a city-state was neither all good nor all bad. Ask students to think about whether there were more advantages or disadvantages to living under a city-state form of government.

❷ TEACH

DEFINING TERMS

Ask pairs of students to make a list of synonyms for *advantage* and *disadvantage*. Next, have the class analyze the first two paragraphs to determine who was for and who was against the city-state form of government and why. Then tell students to read the lists of advantages and disadvantages and make their own decision about the city-state. **L2**

COMPARISON

Have students make a graphic organizer like the one below. Tell them that as they read, they should write the most important advantages and disadvantages on it. **L2** (Answers are provided.)

City-State Form of Government	
Advantages	Disadvantages
supported art and science	*common people mistreated*
preserved ancient knowledge	*weak were invaded*
generous rulers helped poor	*many poor, high taxes*
ended feudalism	*wealthy fight each other*

During the Renaissance, Italy was divided into more than 20 city-states. Some people think that the city-state form of government was a good idea. The leaders and wealthy nobles of the city-states encouraged the arts and sciences. This produced masterpieces by Michelangelo, Raphael, Leonardo, and others. Would this rebirth of arts and sciences have happened if Italy's independent city-states had not existed?

Other people, such as Girolamo Savonarola, were against the city-state form of government. After the fall of the Medici family in Florence, Savonarola spoke out in favor of a new type of leadership:

▲ A detail from the ceiling of the Sistine Chapel painted by Michelangelo

616

"I tell you that you must select a good form for your new government, and above all no one must think of making himself head if you wish to live in liberty."
—Girolamo Savonarola,
"This Will Be Your Final Destruction"

Examine the advantages and disadvantages of the city-state form of government. Then decide whether you think this system is primarily beneficial or primarily harmful.

Advantages:
- Because of their independent governments, each territory on the Italian peninsula was able to have its own culture.
- Some city-states were led by wealthy families, but most were led by a single leader. Almost all supported cultural and scientific advancement. The competition among city-states also encouraged the development of art and science.
- City-state rulers helped preserve the values and teachings of the ancient Greeks and Romans. They gave their own artists, architects, scholars, and writers opportunities to study classical works and interpret them in their own ways.

Extending the Content

Fiery Preacher Girolamo Savonarola (1452–1498) was an Italian religious and political reformer. He became a Dominican friar and lived in Florence, where he became known for his sermons attacking corrupt clergy and tyrannical rulers. After the overthrow of the Medici family in 1494, Savonarola set up a democratic republic in Florence. He tried to stamp out lax morals by having people give up their cosmetics, fine clothes, and questionable books and paintings to be burned in large bonfires. Savonarola's attacks on church and government officials earned him many enemies, including Pope Alexander VI. In 1497, the pope excommunicated Savonarola for heresy. A year later, Savonarola was hanged and burned in Florence's main square.

▲ Renaissance nobles

Disadvantages:

- Many city-states were led by one man. The common people were often mistreated until they revolted and threw out their leaders. This happened to Florence's Medici family in 1527.
- The divided city-states were weaker than a united Italy would have been, so they were often invaded by foreign groups.
- Smaller territories did not always have enough soldiers to defend their cities and land. They hired mercenaries—generals and armies from outside their city—to help them fight. Sometimes mercenaries took over the city-states that had hired them.
- Because many Italians were poor, there were noticeable class differences in the city-states. These differences often led to bloody conflicts between the social classes.
- Wealthy families often battled with each other for control of the city-states.
- Some city-state rulers became even wealthier by overseeing banking and trade. These leaders lived in luxury, while many citizens were very poor.

- Many citizens liked their city-state and wanted to help it. This encouraged patriotism.
- Some rulers were generous to the citizens of their city-states. For example, Duke Federigo da Montefeltro (1422–1482), a popular ruler in Urbino, built schools, hospitals, churches, and a library with his own money. He was known for talking to the commoners and helping the poor.
- The city-states helped bring an end to feudalism by making merchants, as well as landowners, wealthy and ending the relationship between lords and vassals.

You Be the Historian

Checking for Understanding
1. Do you think that the art of the Renaissance would have been created if Italy had not been divided into individual city-states? Why or why not?
2. Do you think Italian artists had more artistic freedom under this form of government? Why or why not?
3. Would you have enjoyed living during the Renaissance? Would you have wanted to be a ruler, noble, artist, or commoner? Why?

617

① FOCUS

SECTION OVERVIEW

This section describes how humanists spread ideas and Renaissance artists created great paintings and sculptures.

BELLRINGER
SKILLBUILDER ACTIVITY

✎ Project **Daily Focus Skills Transparency 17–2** and have students answer questions. Discuss their responses.

Get Ready to Read!

Preteaching Vocabulary: Point out that ideas written in the vernacular spread farther and faster than those in Latin because many more people could read about them. In addition, the invention of a printing press with movable type in 1450 meant that there were also more copies of books for people to read.

Answers to Graphic: shows people as they are in real life, shows people's emotions, uses perspective to make more realistic images, uses chiaroscuro to create more drama and emotion

Section 2
New Ideas and Art

Get Ready to Read!

What's the Connection?

In Section 1, you learned about the growth of Italian city-states. In this section, you will learn how the wealth of the city-states led to an age of artistic achievements.

Focusing on the Main Ideas

• Humanists studied the Greeks and Romans, and the development of the printing press helped spread their ideas. *(page 619)*

• Renaissance artists used new techniques to produce paintings that showed people in an emotional and realistic way. *(page 623)*

• Renaissance ideas and art spread from Italy to northern Europe. *(page 625)*

Locating Places
Flanders (FLAN•duhrz)

Meeting People
Dante Alighieri (DAHN•tay A•luh•GYEHR•ee)
Johannes Gutenberg (yoh•HAHN•uhs   GOO•tuhn•BUHRG)
Leonardo da Vinci (LEE•uh•NAHR•doh   duh   VIHN•chee)
Michelangelo Buonarroti (MY•kuh•LAN•juh•LOH   BWAW•nahr•RAW•tee)
William Shakespeare (SHAYK•SPIHR)

Building Your Vocabulary
humanism (HYOO•muh•NIH•zuhm)
vernacular (vuhr•NA•kyuh•luhr)

Reading Strategy
Organizing Information Create a diagram to show features of Renaissance art.

```
( ) — ( Art ) — ( )
          |
         ( )
```

| 1400 | | | 1500 | | | | 1600 |

c. 1455 Johannes Gutenberg uses printing press to print the Bible

1494 Leonardo begins painting *The Last Supper*

1512 Michelangelo finishes painting Sistine Chapel's ceiling

1601 Shakespeare writes *Hamlet*

SECTION RESOURCES

📂 **Reproducible Masters**
• Reproducible Lesson Plan 17–2
• Daily Lecture and Discussion Notes 17–2
• Vocabulary Activity 17–2
• Active Reading Note-Taking Guide 17–2
• Guided Reading Activity 17–2
• Section Quiz 17–2
• Reading Essentials and Study Guide 17–2

✎ **Transparencies**
• Daily Focus Skills Transparency 17–2

Multimedia
💿 Interactive Tutor Self-Assessment CD-ROM
💿 ExamView® Pro Testmaker CD-ROM
💿 Presentation Plus! CD-ROM
💿 Glencoe BookLink CD-ROM

Renaissance Humanism

Main Idea Humanists studied the Greeks and Romans, and the development of the printing press helped spread their ideas.

Reading Focus Have you ever tried to draw a copy of a painting you like? Is it harder to copy what other people have done or to come up with new ideas for your own pictures? Read to learn how Renaissance writers borrowed ideas from the past but tried to be original too.

In the 1300s, a new way of understanding the world developed in medieval Europe. This new approach was called **humanism** (HYOO•muh•NIH•zuhm). It was based on the values of the ancient Greeks and Romans. Humanists believed that the individual and human society were important. Humanists did not turn away from religious faith, but they wanted a balance between faith and reason. Their new ideas encouraged men to be active in their cities and achieve great things.

Ancient Works Become Popular

In the 1300s, Italians began to study early Roman and Greek works. For most of the Middle Ages, Western Europeans knew little about ancient Greek and Roman writings. When they went on the Crusades, however, they opened trade with the Middle East and began to get information from the Arabs. Arab scholars knew classic Greek and

Ancient Greek manuscript on Archimedes ▼

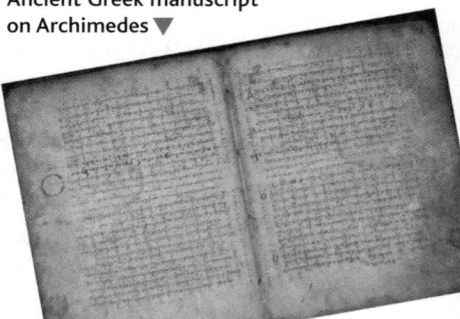

Roman works very well. In addition, when the Turks conquered Constantinople in 1453, many Byzantine scholars left and moved to Venice or Florence.

One famous scholar of the ancient works was Petrarch (PEH•TRAHRK). Francesco Petrarch was a poet and scholar who lived in the 1300s. He studied Roman writers like Cicero and wrote biographies of famous Romans.

Petrarch encouraged Europeans to search for Latin manuscripts in monasteries all over Europe. In time, his efforts paid off and new libraries were built to keep the manuscripts. The largest was the Vatican Library in Rome.

Italians studied more than ancient books. They studied the old buildings and statues all around them. All over Rome, one could see workers cleaning the dirt and rubble from broken columns and statues. Italian artists eagerly studied the proportions of the ancient works. If they knew how long a statue's arms were compared to its height, they would be able to understand why it looked so perfect.

◀ Francesco Petrarch has been called the father of Italian Renaissance humanism. *How did Petrarch contribute to the preservation of Roman knowledge?*

619

② TEACH

Reading Strategy

Tracking Information Have students work in pairs to make a two-column chart labeled "Challenge" on the left and "Solution" on the right. Ask them to list challenges that people of the Renaissance faced and the solutions that they used to meet the challenges. Use the following example as a model: Challenge: Petrarch wanted Roman manuscripts. Solution: Europeans searched monasteries for Latin manuscripts and built libraries to keep them. **L2**

Daily Lecture and Discussion Notes 17–2

Use **Daily Lecture and Discussion Notes 17–2** for an outline of key concepts found in the section.

More About the Art

As a poet, Petrarch is best known for the hundreds of love poems he wrote to an unknown, but beautiful, woman named Laura.

Caption Answer: He encouraged Europeans to look for Latin manuscripts in monasteries all over Europe.

Reading Strategy ◀ **READING THE TEXT**

Categorizing Information On the board, copy the following names from the section: *Petrarch, Dante Alighieri, Geoffrey Chaucer, Johannes Gutenberg, Leonardo da Vinci, Raphael Sanzio, Michelangelo Buonarroti, Jan van Eyck, Albrecht Dürer,* and *William Shakespeare*. As students read, tell them to write categories on a sheet of paper and list each name under the correct category. **Ask:** Which Renaissance person do you think is best known today? Explain your answer. *(Answers may include Leonardo da Vinci because copies of his* Mona Lisa *are highly utilized.)* **L1**

Reading Support L1/ EL

Use **Vocabulary Activity 17–2** to review important terms in the section.

HISTORY MAKERS

Gutenberg invented a new kind of ink for his printing press. It had to adhere evenly to metal type, so it needed to be more like oil paint than the ink that scribes used for their pens. Gutenberg drew on the expertise of Flemish painters who made their own paints with linseed oil.

Writing Activity

In *The Divine Comedy*, Dante meets Virgil, Homer, and Ovid, who are denied entrance into heaven because they were not Christians. Virgil explains: "For such defects are we lost, though spared the fire and suffering Hell in one affliction only: that without hope we live on in desire." Ask students to restate the quote in their own words. **L2**

NATIONAL GEOGRAPHIC

HISTORY MAKERS

Movable Type c. 1450

Johannes Gutenberg, a German goldsmith, built a printing press modeled after a winepress. Once the press was completed, Gutenberg spent two years printing his first book. For each page, he set metal letters in a frame, rolled ink over the frame, and pressed the frame against paper. Around 1455, he completed printing what is now known as the Gutenberg Bible, or the 42 Line Bible. This was the first book printed using movable metal type, sparking a revolution in publishing and reading.

▼ **Gutenberg Bible**

Changes in Literature During the Renaissance, educated people wrote in "pure" Latin, the Latin used in ancient Rome. Petrarch thought classical Latin was the best way to write, but when he wanted to write poems to the woman he loved, he wrote in the **vernacular** (vuhr•NA•kyuh•luhr). The vernacular is the everyday language people speak in a region—Italian, French, or German, for example. When authors began writing in the vernacular, many more people could read their work.

In the early 1300s, **Dante Alighieri** (DAHN•tay A•luh•GYEHR•ee), a poet of Florence, wrote one of the world's greatest poems in the vernacular. It is called *The Divine Comedy*. As a young man, Dante was active in politics, but when noble families began fighting over power, he had to leave Florence. That was when he wrote his long poem—more than 14,000 lines. *The Divine Comedy* tells the gripping tale of the main character's journey from hell to heaven. The horrible punishments for different sins were vividly described.

Another important writer who used the vernacular was Chaucer. Chaucer wrote in English. In his famous book, *The Canterbury Tales*, he describes 29 pilgrims on their journey to the city of Canterbury. *The Canterbury Tales* describes the levels of English society, from the nobles at the top to the poor at the bottom. The English Chaucer used in his writing is the ancestor of the English we speak today.

The Printing Press Spreads Ideas

The printing press was a key to the spread of humanist ideas throughout Europe. In the early 1450s, **Johannes Gutenberg** (yoh•HAHN•uhs GOO•tuhn•BUHRG) developed a printing press that used movable metal type. This type of printing press made it possible to print many books much more quickly. With more books available, more people learned to read. Scholars could read one another's works and debate their ideas in letters.

DIFFERENTIATED INSTRUCTION

Verbal/Linguistic: On the board, write the following from *The Parliament of the Fowls*, which is about courting: "The lyf so short, the craft so long to lerne, / Th' assay so hard, so sharp the conquering . . ." Ask a volunteer to read the lines. Then substitute the following words for the underlined ones: *life, learn, The, attempt, keen, victory.* Have students discuss how spelling and words have changed in English.

English Learners: Write the first line of the above poem and *life* and *learn* on the board. Ask students to rewrite the line, substituting the new words. Discuss how spelling has changed in English.

Gifted and Talented: Ask pairs of students to rewrite the prologue from an Old English version of *The Canterbury Tales* in modern English. Have volunteers share their version with the class.

Ideas grew and spread more quickly than ever before in Europe.

The Chinese had already invented movable type, but it did not work well with their large alphabet of characters. For Europeans, the printing press was a big improvement. It was easy to use with linen paper, another Chinese invention.

Gutenberg's Bible, printed in the 1450s, was the first European book produced on the new press. Soon books flooded Europe. About 40,000 books were published by 1500. Half of these were religious works like the Bible or prayer books.

How Did Humanism Affect Society?
Humanist scholars studied the Greeks and Romans to increase their knowledge of many different topics. They were curious about everything, including plants and animals, human anatomy and medicine, and the stars and planets. Their study of mathematics helped them in many subjects.

One of the best Renaissance scientists was also a great artist, **Leonardo da Vinci** (LEE•uh•NAHR•doh duh VIHN•chee). Leonardo dissected corpses to learn anatomy and studied fossils to understand the world's history. He was also an inventor and an engineer.

Most of what we know about Leonardo comes from his notebooks. Leonardo filled their pages with sketches of his scientific and artistic ideas. Centuries before the airplane was invented, Leonardo drew sketches of a glider, a helicopter, and a parachute. Other sketches show a version of a military tank and a scuba diving suit.

✓ **Reading Check** **Explain** What was the benefit of writing in the vernacular?

CONNECTING ACROSS TIME
During the Renaissance, cartographers used information from sailors and explorers, ink, paper, and math skills to create maps. Modern mapmakers use satellite imagery and software programs to make maps. Have students compare maps, such as those in Chapter 16 that show lands that would have been newly discovered, with present-day maps. Discuss the accuracy of the earlier maps. **L3**

✓ **Reading Check**

Answer: Many more people could read works written in their regional language.

Primary Source

Leonardo's Inventions

Leonardo da Vinci's notebooks contained sketches of inventions that would not be produced for hundreds of years.

DBQ Document-Based Question
Compare Leonardo's sketches of a helicopter and subway to their modern counterparts. How accurate was Leonardo?

◄ A multibarreled artillery piece

▲ A helicopter-like flying machine

Cross section of a palace ► with subways for carriages

Primary Source

Leonardo's notes about potential inventions mention a "camera obscura," or dark room where an image is projected through a small hole onto a wall, foreshadowing the development of cameras and movies.

Answer:
Answers may vary but should include the fact that he used two sets of blades, which is similar to modern helicopters.

CHAPTER 17   The Renaissance and Reformation   621

CRITICAL THINKING ACTIVITY

Predicting Consequences Tell small groups of students to read the subsection "The Printing Press Spreads Ideas." Have them imagine industries and jobs that could have grown and developed out of this new technology and the new abundance of printed works. Ask groups to list their ideas under the heading "Brand New Industries and Jobs." Finally, have small groups share their lists with one another. **L3**

Biography

TEACH

While Leonardo was in Verrocchio's studio, he learned how to paint and to sculpt. In addition, his sketches from this period, such as those of military weapons and pumps, show that he also learned about technical and mechanical subjects. When Leonardo moved to Milan in 1482, this diverse background served him well. As the duke's painter and engineer, Leonardo painted and sculpted, but he also designed court festivals. In addition, his advice was sought in the areas of fortifications, engineering related to water matters, and architecture.

When Leonardo was a boy, he was not interested in Latin, which was the key to most learning. He also did not study higher mathematics, such as advanced geometry. As an adult, Leonardo taught himself Latin. He began studying mathematics when he was 30 years old. **Ask:** Why do you think Leonardo became interested in Latin and mathematics? **L1/ EL**

Then and Now

Answers may include items such as the airplane, which Leonardo investigated himself, or inventions such as the space station, which were beyond even his imagination.

Biography

LEONARDO DA VINCI
1452–1519

Leonardo was born in Vinci, Italy, to a peasant woman named Caterina. Shortly after Leonardo's birth, she left the boy in the care of his father. By the time Leonardo was 15 years old, his father knew his son had artistic talent. He arranged for Leonardo to become an apprentice to the famous painter Andrea del Verrocchio.

By 1472, Leonardo had become a master in the painters' guild of Florence. He worked in Florence until 1481, and then he went to the city of Milan. There he kept a large workshop and employed many apprentices. During this time, Leonardo began keeping small pads of paper tucked in his belt for sketching. Later he organized the drawings by theme and assembled the pages into notebooks.

Seventeen years later, Leonardo returned to Florence, where he was welcomed with great honor. During this time, Leonardo painted some of his masterpieces. He also made scientific studies, including dissections, observations of the flight of birds, and research on the movement of water currents.

In 1516 Leonardo accepted an invitation to live in France. The king admired Leonardo and gave him freedom to pursue his interests. During the last three years of his life, Leonardo lived in a small house near the king's summer palace. He spent most of his time sketching and working on his scientific studies.

▲ Leonardo da Vinci

> "Nothing can be loved or hated unless it is first known."
>
> —Leonardo da Vinci

▲ The *Mona Lisa* by Leonardo da Vinci

Then and Now

Leonardo's curiosity fueled his creativity and interest in science. What invention created in the last 100 years do you think would impress Leonardo the most? Why?

Reading List Generator CD-ROM

GLENCOE BOOKLINK **RECOMMENDED READING**

Use the **Glencoe BookLink CD-ROM** to create customized reading lists based on your students' interests and reading levels. Below is an example based on content in this chapter. Also, see the Suggested Readings on pages 944–946 of the Appendix.

- McLanathan, Richard. *Leonardo da Vinci.* Leonardo da Vinci's notebooks held sketches and designs for an airplane, a parachute, and a submarine.
- Stanley, Diane. *Leonardo da Vinci.* An illustrated biography of the Italian Renaissance genius who painted the *Mona Lisa,* invented a submarine, and tried to build a flying machine.
- Wroble, Lisa A. *Kids During the Renaissance.* The Renaissance lasted from the 1300s to the early 1600s. It was an exciting time, when many things were changing.

Artists in Renaissance Italy

Main Idea Renaissance artists used new techniques to produce paintings that showed people in an emotional and realistic way.

Reading Focus Have you ever had trouble making your drawings look real and three-dimensional? Read to learn how Renaissance artists learned to make their art look natural and real.

During the Renaissance, wealthy Italian families and church leaders paid artists to create paintings, sculptures, and buildings for display throughout their cities. The pope himself funded many works of art to decorate the Vatican. Renaissance artists followed the models of the ancient Romans and Greeks but expressed humanist ideas.

What Was New About Renaissance Art?

If you compare medieval and Renaissance paintings, you will see major differences in their styles. Renaissance art tries to show people as they would appear in real life. It also tries to show people's emotions. When a medieval artist depicted the birth of Jesus, he wanted to remind Christians about their belief that Jesus was born to save the world. A Renaissance artist painting the same scene might try to show how tender Mary looked with her tiny baby.

Renaissance painters also used new techniques. The most important was perspective (puhr•SPEHK•tihv), a method that makes a drawing or painting look three-dimensional. Artists had tried to use perspective before, but Renaissance artists perfected it. Using perspective, objects in a scene appear to be at different distances from the viewer. The result is a more realistic image.

To make their paintings more realistic, Renaissance artists also used a technique called chiaroscuro (kee•AHR•uh•SKYUR•oh).

▲ The sculpture, *La Pieta*, by Michelangelo shows Mary holding the body of Jesus after his death. *What did Renaissance artists try to portray in their works?*

Chiaroscuro softened edges by using light and shadows instead of stiff outlines to separate objects. In Italian, *chiaro* means "clear or light," and *oscuro* means "dark." Chiaroscuro created more drama and emotion in a painting.

The Peak of the Renaissance
The artistic Renaissance lasted from about 1350 to 1550, but it hit its peak between 1490 and 1520. At that time, three great artists were producing their masterpieces—Leonardo da Vinci, Raphael Sanzio, and **Michelangelo Buonarroti** (MY•kuh•LAN•juh•LOH BWAW•nahr•RAW•tee).

Although Leonardo also became a great scientist and inventor, he trained as an artist. Born in 1452, he began his training in Florence at a young age. Training in workshops was an old tradition, but during the Renaissance, individual artists began to do something no medieval artist had done—they signed their own work.

One of Leonardo's most famous works is *The Last Supper,* which he began painting in 1494 on a wall behind a church altar. He painted on wet plaster with watercolor paint. A painting done this way is called a

The Way It Was

Answers:

1. to prepare materials for the master artist and his assistants

2. Yes; answers may include the building trades, medicine, and teaching.

✓ **Reading Check**

Answer: medieval: artists wanted to emphasize connection of the work with religion; did not use perspective; Renaissance: artists wanted to show real people and their emotions; used perspective and chiaroscuro to make pictures more realistic

Reading Support L1/ EL

Assign **Guided Reading Activity 17–2** to help students organize the information in the section.

NATIONAL GEOGRAPHIC The Way It Was

Focus on Everyday Life

The Life of a Renaissance Artist If a young boy in Renaissance Italy wanted to be an artist, he would become an apprentice at a workshop run by an established artist. The main job of apprentices was preparing materials for the master artist and his assistants. Apprentices used minerals, spices, egg yolk, and other everyday materials to mix paints. They readied wax and clay for sculpture modeling. Eventually, apprentices became assistants. Talented assistants could become masters of their own workshops.

Master artists could afford to have workshops because of the patronage system in Italy. Patrons—people who pay to support someone else's work— would commission, or hire, an artist to complete a project. That artist was usually helped by his assistants and apprentices. Patrons were usually political and church leaders, organizations, and wealthy bankers and merchants.

▲ Renaissance painter and apprentice

Connecting to the Past

1. What was the main job of apprentices?

2. Does the patronage system or the apprentice system exist today? If so, in what fields?

fresco (FREHS•koh), which in Italian means "fresh." Frescoes were painted in churches all over Italy.

One of Leonardo's great artistic skills is visible in *The Last Supper*. In this painting of Jesus and his disciples, Leonardo was able to show human emotions through small differences in how each apostle held his head or the apostle's position in relation to Jesus. Leonardo showed this skill again in the *Mona Lisa*. People still argue about what the woman in the portrait is thinking—what is the mystery behind her smile?

Although Raphael worked at the same time as Leonardo, he was much younger. Even as a young man, Raphael worked with ease and grace and became known as one of Italy's best painters. Italians especially loved the gentle Madonnas he painted. He also painted many frescoes in the Vatican Palace. Perhaps his best-known painting is the *School of Athens*, which depicts a number of Greek philosophers.

The third great Renaissance artist was Michelangelo. Like many other artists of the time, Michelangelo painted, sculpted, and designed buildings. He painted one of the best-known Renaissance works—the ceiling of the Sistine Chapel in Rome.

Although he painted many outstanding works, Michelangelo was a sculptor at heart. He believed his talents were inspired by God. He carved his statues to show perfect versions of human beings as a symbol of God's beauty and perfection. Michelangelo's best-known sculpture is the 13-foot-tall statue *David*. The sculptor made David seem calm, yet ready for action. Also impressive is Michelangelo's statue of the biblical Moses. The huge figure appears both wise and powerful.

✓ **Reading Check** **Compare and Contrast** What were some of the differences between medieval and Renaissance artists?

EXTENDING THE CONTENT

Rivalry Between Raphael and Michelangelo In 1505 Pope Julius II hired Michelangelo to create a magnificent marble tomb for him. The sculptor spent eight months at a quarry in Carrara, Italy, selecting blocks for the more than 40 figures that the pope wanted on his tomb. Meanwhile, a relative of Raphael, the architect Bramante, persuaded the pope to use the money allotted for the tomb to rebuild St. Peter's Basilica. Raphael, who did not want Michelangelo as a rival for projects, suggested that the pope use Michelangelo to paint the Sistine Chapel's ceiling. Because Michelangelo had never before painted a fresco, Raphael hoped that his rival's painting would compare badly to his own. Contrary to Raphael's plan, Michelangelo's completed ceiling was a masterpiece.

The Renaissance Spreads

Main Idea Renaissance ideas and art spread from Italy to northern Europe.

Reading Focus If you were a Canadian artist, would your painting look different than if you lived in Arizona? Read to learn how the Renaissance changed as it moved into northern Europe.

In the late 1400s, the Renaissance spread to northern Europe and later to England. The printing press helped humanist ideas to spread, as did people who traveled.

What Is the Northern Renaissance? The Northern Renaissance refers to the culture in places we know today as Belgium, Luxembourg, Germany, and the Netherlands. Like Italian artists, northern artists wanted their works to have greater realism, but they used different methods. One important method they developed was oil painting. First developed in **Flanders** (FLAN•duhrz)—

a region that is in northern Belgium today—oils let artists paint intricate details and surface textures, like the gold braid on a gown.

Jan van Eyck was a master of oil painting. In one of his best-known paintings, a newly married couple stands side by side in a formal bedroom. Van Eyck showed every fold in their rich gowns and every detail of the chandelier above their heads.

Albrecht Dürer (AHL•brehkt DUR•uhr) is perhaps one of the greatest artists of the Northern Renaissance. Dürer was able to master both perspective and fine detail. He is best known for his engravings. An engraving is made from an image carved on metal, wood, or stone. Ink is applied to the surface, and then the image is printed on paper.

Dürer's *Four Horsemen of the Apocalypse* is an outstanding example of a woodcut, a print made from carved wood. In it, four fierce horsemen ride to announce the end of the world.

③ ASSESS

Assign Section 2 Review as homework or as an in-class activity.

⊙ Have students use the **Interactive Tutor Self-Assessment CD-ROM** to review the section.

Assessment L2

Assign **Section 2 Quiz** to assess mastery of the material found in the section.

Reading Support L1/ EL

Assign **Reading Essentials and Study Guide 17–2** to help students review section material.

Globe Theater

William Shakespeare's plays were performed at the Globe Theater in London. It could hold about 3,000 people. Plays were performed every day of the week except Sunday. Performances occurred during the day, since the theater had no lights. *When did the Renaissance spread to northern Europe and England?*

Flags announced the type of play. White flags meant comedies, black flags meant tragedies, and red flags stood for history plays.

Wealthy and important people sat beneath the covered section.

Poor commoners, called groundlings, stood on the ground for the show. They often brought fruit and vegetables to throw at actors they did not like.

625

More About the Art

The Globe was built about 1599 from timbers that came from a previous theater. In 1613, the theater burned down and was rebuilt. The Puritans closed all theaters in 1642, and the Globe was torn down a few years later. It was rebuilt in the 1900s, using mostly traditional methods and materials.

Caption Answer: in the late 1400s

COOPERATIVE LEARNING ACTIVITY

Giving a Presentation About the Renaissance Allow small groups of students to choose the type of presentation they would like to give. Some options might be interviewing a famous artist, author, or politician; researching and sharing music and dance from the period; doing a skit based on an event, book, or play of the period; or setting up a gallery of the works of other artists. To prepare for the presentation, groups should put together an outline of what the presentation will entail and each group member's responsibilities. Give students time to prepare for and give their presentations. **L2**

📩 Refer to the **Quizzes, Tests, and Authentic Assessment (with Rubrics)** booklet for rubrics.

Reading Check

Answer: The Northern Renaissance took place in northern Europe, in Belgium, Luxembourg, Germany, and the Netherlands. Artists of the Northern Renaissance used different methods than Italian artists, including oil painting and prints made from engravings.

Who Was William Shakespeare? In England, the Renaissance took place in writing and theater more than in art. The Renaissance began in England in the later 1500s, during the rule of Elizabeth I.

Theater was popular in England in the 1500s. Admission was only one or two cents, so even the poor could attend. English playwrights, or writers who create plays, wrote about people's strengths, weaknesses, and emotions.

The greatest English writer of that era was **William Shakespeare** (SHAYK•SPIHR). He wrote tragedies, comedies, and historical plays. Some of his great tragedies include *Hamlet, Macbeth,* and *Romeo and Juliet.* In each tragedy, the characters' flaws cause their downfall. Among his most famous comedies are *A Midsummer Night's Dream, Twelfth Night,* and *Much Ado About Nothing.* His best-known historical plays include

▲ Dürer's *Four Horsemen of the Apocalypse*

Henry V and *Richard III.* Shakespeare's plays are still performed today and remain very popular.

Reading Check **Compare** How did the northern Renaissance differ from the Italian Renaissance?

Section 2 Review

Reading Summary
Review the Main Ideas

- During the Renaissance, scholars examined the ancient works of the Greeks and Romans, began to write in the vernacular, and explored many scientific fields.

- Italian Renaissance artists employed new techniques and created masterpieces of painting and sculpture.

- As the Renaissance spread to northern Europe and England, artists and writers, such as Dürer and Shakespeare, created great works.

What Did You Learn?

1. Explain the beliefs of humanists during the Renaissance.

2. Explain the artistic technique of perspective.

Critical Thinking

3. **Summarizing Information** Draw a chart like the one below. Use it to describe the artistic work and techniques of each artist listed.

Leonardo da Vinci	
Michelangelo	
Jan van Eyck	
Shakespeare	

4. **Evaluate** What was the importance of the printing press on Renaissance society?

5. **Science Link** Describe the scientific efforts and contributions of Leonardo da Vinci.

6. **Explain** How were the ideals of the Renaissance expressed in England? Provide examples in your answer.

7. **Expository Writing** Choose a painting or sculpture shown in this section. In a short essay, describe the work and explain how it demonstrates Renaissance techniques or characteristics.

626   CHAPTER 17   The Renaissance and Reformation

SECTION 2 REVIEW ANSWERS

1. believed the individual and human society were important; wanted a balance between faith and reason
2. By showing objects at different distances, artists create a scene that is more realistic.
3. Leonardo: painted frescoes such as *The Last Supper*;

Michelangelo: painted ceiling of the Sistine Chapel and sculpted *David* and *Moses*; van Eyck: used oil paints; Shakespeare: wrote tragedies, comedies, and historical plays
4. helped ideas grow and spread across Europe

5. Answers should be based on the text.
6. in writing and in plays, such as *Hamlet*
7. Answers will vary but should use information from the text.

A MIDSUMMER NIGHT'S DREAM

By William Shakespeare,
Adapted by E. Nesbit

Before You Read

The Scene: This story takes place in Athens, Greece, in a legendary time when magical creatures lived among humans.

The Characters: Hermia and Lysander are in love. Demetrius loves Hermia, and Helena loves Demetrius. Oberon and Titania are the King and Queen of the Fairies.

The Plot: Hermia and Lysander run away to be married. Demetrius follows them because he loves Hermia. Helena follows Demetrius because she loves him. The fairies they encounter try to use magic to help the four humans.

Vocabulary Preview

betrayed: gave to an enemy
mortal: human
quarrel: argument
glade: grassy open space in a forest

suitor: one who wants to marry another
bade: asked
scheme: plan

Have you ever tried to help someone but made the situation worse? In this story, fairies attempt to help four young people traveling through the woods, but their efforts do not go as planned.

WORLD LITERATURE

SUMMARY

Unable to marry, Hermia and Lysander flee to the woods. Demetrius, who is supposed to marry Hermia, follows her. Helena, in love with Demetrius, follows him. In the woods, Oberon, king of the fairies, tells his favorite fairy, Puck, to enchant Demetrius, but because of a misapplied potion, both Lysander and Demetrius fall in love with Helena. Meanwhile, Oberon enchants Titania, and she falls in love with a donkey-headed clown. In the end, Demetrius falls for Helena, Oberon and Titania are reconciled, and Lysander rediscovers Hermia.

Vocabulary Preview Before students begin reading, have them read **Before You Read** and the **Vocabulary Preview.** Point out that difficult words are footnoted throughout the text.

① FOCUS

Laughing at Follies The purpose of comedy is to entertain and to show follies that society will hopefully correct. This story is a comedy of errors, mistakes that cause silly situations and therefore laughter, often because the situations could have been avoided.

Reading Strategy | READING REINFORCEMENT

Plotting Conflict Help students understand the rising action that leads to the climax in the story by showing it visually. Begin by writing "Hermia must marry Demetrius" on the board. To the right, write "Hermia and Lysander decide to flee," and to the right of that "Demetrius follows Hermia." Have students suggest additional important events and keep adding them farther to the right. The placement of the notes on the board should also slowly climb, making a slope to show the rising action. The highest point would be "Lysander and Demetrius decide to duel" with a slightly lower point for "Puck puts potion on their eyes." The last events related to the two human couples are much lower. Show the subplot for the King and Queen separately, below the main plot. Discuss with students how the visual shows the rising tension until the climax is reached. **L1**

② TEACH

Ⓐ ACTIVE READING STRATEGIES

CONNECT Have students suggest possible options that Hermia and Lysander have and what the consequence of each might be.

Ⓑ CRITICAL THINKING

LOGICAL REASONING Ask students to explain why Helena's decision to follow Demetrius may cause her more pain than pleasure. *(Answers may include that Helena will feel hurt when Demetrius ignores her to pursue Hermia.)*

Ⓒ AUTHOR'S CRAFT

FORESHADOWING Ask students what the description of fairies being foolish may foreshadow. *(Answers may include that the fairies may do something foolish that involves humans because they are all in the same woods.)*

Ⓓ LITERARY ELEMENTS

MOOD Ask students how the author establishes a mood of anger or unhappiness between the king and queen. *(by contrasting what fairies usually do—dance all night as one happy court—with the fact that the king and queen are wandering through different parts of the woods)*

As You Read

Keep in mind that William Shakespeare wrote this story as a play. E. Nesbit rewrote the story in paragraph form to make it shorter and easier to read.

Hermia and Lysander were [in love]; but Hermia's father wished her to marry another man, named Demetrius.

Ⓐ Now in Athens, where they lived, there was a wicked law, by which any girl who refused to marry according to her father's wishes, might be put to death. . . .

Lysander of course was nearly mad with grief, and the best thing to do seemed to him for Hermia to run away to his aunt's house at a place beyond the reach of that cruel law; and there he would come to her and marry her. But before she started, she told her friend, Helena, what she was going to do.

628

Ⓑ Helena had been Demetrius' sweetheart long before his marriage with Hermia had been thought of, and being very silly, like all jealous people, she could not see that it was not poor Hermia's fault that Demetrius wished to marry her instead of his own lady, Helena. She knew that if she told Demetrius that Hermia was going, as she was, to the wood outside Athens, he would follow her, "and I can follow him, and at least I shall see him," she said to herself. So she went to him, and betrayed her friend's secret.

Ⓒ Now this wood where Lysander was to meet Hermia, and where the other two had decided to follow them, was full of fairies,[1] as most woods are, if one only had the eyes to see them, and in this wood on this night were the King and Queen of the fairies, Oberon and Titania. Now fairies are very wise people, but now and then they can be quite as foolish as mortal folk. Oberon and Titania, who might have been as happy as the days were long, had thrown away all their joy in a foolish quarrel. . . .

Ⓓ So, instead of keeping one happy Court and dancing all night through in the moonlight, as is fairies' use, the King with his attendants wandered through one part of the wood, while the Queen with hers kept state in another. And the cause of all

---

[1]**fairies:** imaginary beings, usually having small human form and magic powers

---

▌▌Reading Strategy ⟩ VOCABULARY READING TIP

Compound Words A compound word is made up of two or more words. Explain that knowing the meanings of the components of a compound word will help students of all English language abilities know the meaning of the compound word. For example, because most students know the meanings of *moon* and *light,* they are able to figure out the meaning of *moonlight.* Have students write the definitions of the following compound words by considering the meanings of their components. If necessary, help students look up meanings in the dictionary. **L1/ EL**

sandpaper *(paper that feels like sand)*
salesperson *(a person who sells something)*
skateboard *(a board used for skating)*

D this trouble was a little Indian boy whom Titania had taken to be one of her followers. Oberon wanted the child to follow him and be one of his fairy knights; but the Queen would not give him up.

On this night, in a glossy moonlight glade, the King and Queen of the fairies met.

"Ill[2] met by moonlight, proud Titania," said the King.

"What! jealous, Oberon?" answered the Queen. "You spoil everything with your quarreling. Come, fairies, let us leave him. I am not friends with him now."

E "It rests with you to make up the quarrel," said the King. "Give me that little Indian boy, and I will again be your humble servant and suitor."

"Set your mind at rest," said the Queen. "Your whole fairy kingdom buys not that boy from me. Come fairies."

And she and her train rode off down the moonbeams.[3]

"Well, go your ways," said Oberon. "But I'll be even with you before you leave this wood." **E**

Then Oberon called his favorite fairy, Puck. Puck was the spirit of mischief. . . .

"Now," said Oberon to this little sprite,[4] "fetch me the flower called Love-in-idleness. The juice of that little purple flower laid on the eyes of those who sleep will make them when they wake to love the first thing they see. I will put some of the juice of that flower on my Titania's eyes, and when she wakes, she will love the first thing she sees, were it lion, bear, or wolf, or bull, or meddling monkey, or a busy ape." **F**

---

[2]**ill:** causing suffering or distress
[3]**moonbeams:** rays of light from the moon
[4]**sprite:** fairy

E CRITICAL THINKING

CAUSE AND EFFECT Ask students what happens when Titania refuses to give the little Indian boy to Oberon. *(Oberon swears he will get even with her.)*

F ACTIVE READING STRATEGIES

PREDICT Have students predict the possible results of using this juice. *(Answers may include that Titania will fall in love with someone very strange.)*

GLENCOE BOOKLINK

Use **Glencoe BookLink** to create customized reading lists for your students' reading levels, interests, and abilities.

DIFFERENTIATED INSTRUCTION

Auditory/Musical: Have small groups of students write a song that one of the characters in the story might sing about him- or herself. The song should tell what happened to the character during the story and how he or she feels about those events. Instruct students to use the melody from a known song.

Verbal/Linguistic: Ask students to choose a character, such as Helena or the King, and write a short speech. The speech should express the character's point of view and justify his or her actions during the story. Have volunteers present their speeches to the class.

Less-proficient Readers: Make seven columns, each labeled with a different character's name. After reading each part of the story, discuss the characters' actions and what they show about the characters. List the actions and the character traits under the appropriate character's name.

🄶 ACTIVE READING STRATEGIES

EVALUATE Ask students how they think Oberon might have prevented the mix-up between Demetrius and Lysander. *(Answers may include that Oberon should have given Puck a detailed description of Demetrius.)*

🄷 CRITICAL THINKING

INFERRING Have students describe how Hermia may have felt as she pursued Lysander. *(Answers may include that Hermia was confused about why Lysander was ignoring her.)*

Glencoe Literature Library

As students study the unit, have them read *I, Juan de Pareja* by Elizabeth Borton de Treviño from the **Glencoe Literature Library.** In this story, the enslaved Juan must hide his artistic talent because he lives in seventeenth-century Spain where laws prohibit slaves from being artists. As the assistant to the painter Diego Velázquez, Juan searches for artistic and personal freedom.

While Puck was gone, Demetrius passed through the glade followed by poor Helena, and still she told him how she loved him and reminded him of all his promises, and still he told her that he did not and could not love her, and that his promises were nothing. Oberon was sorry for poor Helena, and when Puck returned with the flower, he bade him follow Demetrius and put some of the juice on his eyes, so that he might love Helena when he woke and looked on her, as much as she loved him. So Puck set off, and wandering through the wood found, not Demetrius, but Lysander, on whose eyes he put the juice; but when Lysander woke, he saw not his own Hermia, but Helena, who was walking through the wood looking for the cruel Demetrius; and directly he saw her he loved her and left his own lady, under the spell of the crimson flower.

When Hermia woke she found Lysander gone, and wandered about the wood trying to find him. Puck went back and told Oberon what he had done, and Oberon soon found that he had made a mistake, and set about looking for Demetrius, and having found him, put some of the juice on his eyes. And the first thing Demetrius saw when he woke was also Helena. So now Demetrius and Lysander were both following her through the wood, and it was Hermia's turn to follow her lover as Helena had done before. The end of it was that Helena and Hermia began to quarrel, and Demetrius and Lysander went off to fight. Oberon was

CRITICAL THINKING ACTIVITY

Making Critical Judgments Explain that a comedy is a type of drama that is humorous and has a happy ending. Add that humor is the quality that makes the characters and their situations seem funny, amusing, or ludicrous. Ask students if they think Shakespeare's *A Midsummer Night's Dream* is a successful comedy based on what they have read. Then tell them to explain their answer in two or three paragraphs. Students should use examples from the story to support their judgment. **L2**

enameled[5] skin of a snake. Oberon stooped over her and laid the juice on her eyes. . . .

    Now, it happened that when Titania woke the first thing she saw was a stupid clown, one of a party of players who had come out into the wood to rehearse their play. This clown had met with Puck, who had clapped[6] [a donkey's] head on his shoulders so that it looked as if it grew there. Directly Titania woke and saw this dreadful monster, she said, "What angel is this? Are you as wise as you are beautiful?"

    "If I am wise enough to find my way out of this wood, that's enough for me," said the foolish clown.

    "Do not desire to go out of the wood," said Titania. The spell of the love-juice was on her, and to her the clown seemed the most beautiful and delightful creature on all the earth. "I love you," she went on. "Come with me, and I will give you fairies to attend on you."

    So she called four fairies, whose names were Peaseblossom, Cobweb, Moth, and Mustardseed.

    "You must attend this gentleman," said the Queen. "Feed him with apricots, and dewberries, purple grapes, green figs, and mulberries. Steal honey-bags for him from the humble-bees, and with the wings of painted butterflies fan the moonbeams from his sleeping eyes." . . .

    "Would you like anything to eat?" said the fairy Queen.

---

[5]**enameled:** coated with a glassy substance
[6]**clapped:** forcefully put

631

very sorry to see his kind scheme to help these lovers turn out so badly. So he said to Puck:

    "These two young men are going to fight. You must overhang the night with drooping fog, and lead them so astray, that one will never find the other. When they are tired out, they will fall asleep. Then drop this other herb on Lysander's eyes. That will give him his old sight and his old love. Then each man will have the lady who loves him, and they will all think that this has been only a Midsummer Night's Dream. Then when this is done all will be well with them."

    So Puck went and did as he was told, and when the two had fallen asleep without meeting each other, Puck poured the juice on Lysander's eyes. . . .

    Meanwhile Oberon found Titania asleep on a bank. . . .There Titania always slept a part of the night, wrapped in the

▮ LITERARY ELEMENTS

IMAGERY Ask students to describe the fog. (*It is hanging over the night and drooping.*) Have students comment on the effectiveness of this description. (*Students may note that the words "overhang" and "drooping" help the reader visualize a thick, heavy fog settling in the woods.*)

▮ ACTIVE READING STRATEGIES

VISUALIZE Have students imagine Titania wrapped in a snake-skin. Ask them why they think she sleeps like this. (*Answers may include that the skin keeps her safe from passersby because they assume she is a snake.*)

▮ LITERARY ELEMENTS

CHARACTERIZATION Ask students how Titania shows she is under the spell of the love-juice. (*She calls the donkey-clown beautiful, tells it that she is in love with it, offers it fairies to wait on it, and kisses it.*)

▮ AUTHOR'S CRAFT

FIGURATIVE LANGUAGE Ask students what they think the author means by "fan the moonbeams from his sleeping eyes." (*Answers may include shield his eyes from the light of the moon.*)

EXTENDING THE CONTENT

Who and What Are Fairies? According to myth, fairies are creatures who live on Earth near human beings. They can be as tall as a human or as small as three inches (7.5 cm). They can appear as dwarfs or tiny, winged women. The term *fairy* has been used in Europe only since the Middle Ages, but these creatures are comparable to the nymphs of Greek mythology. Similar beings also exist in Arabic and Indian literature and folktales. In the British Isles, fairies appear particularly in the oral traditions of Cornwall, Wales, and Scotland. In British stories, they are usually handsome or beautiful. Fairies can and do carry people off to fairyland. To keep fairies away, people use herbs, such as yarrow and St. John's wort. Fairies are very fond of foxglove and hawthorn trees.

DIFFERENTIATED INSTRUCTION

EL Students Suggest dialogue for an incident in the story and write it on the board. Then demonstrate how the speaker is indicated in a play—with the character's name and a colon. Next, show students how to use quotation marks with speech, and have them use quotation marks with the dialogue.

Average Students Assign small groups of students different incidents in the story and ask them to write dialogue for their parts. When groups are finished, ask volunteers to perform the skits using their dialogue.

Gifted Students Give students copies of the play *A Midsummer Night's Dream*. Have them read one or more scenes and then discuss how the scenes in the story and the play compare. Ask students which version they prefer and why.

ASSESS

Assign the **Responding to the Reading** questions as an in-class activity or as homework.

CLOSE

Ask students to write a paragraph explaining why they liked or disliked the story.

L1/ EL

"I should like some good dry oats," said the clown—for his donkey's head made him desire donkey's food—"and some hay to follow."

"Shall some of my fairies fetch you new nuts from the squirrel's house?" asked the Queen.

"I'd rather have a handful or two of good dried peas," said the clown. "But please don't let any of your people disturb me, I am going to sleep."

Then said the Queen, "And I will wind thee in my arms."

And so when Oberon came along he found his beautiful Queen lavishing kisses and endearments on a clown with a donkey's head. And before he released her from the enchantment, he persuaded her to give him the little Indian boy he so much desired to have. Then he took pity on her, and threw some juice of the disenchanting flower on her pretty eyes; and then in a moment she saw plainly the donkey-headed clown she had been loving, and knew how foolish she had been.

Oberon took off the [donkey's] head from the clown, and left him to finish his sleep with his own silly head lying on the thyme and violets.

Thus all was made plain and straight again. Oberon and Titania loved each other more than ever. Demetrius thought of no one but Helena, and Helena had never had any thought of anyone but Demetrius. As for Hermia and Lysander, they were as loving a couple as you could meet in a day's march, even through a fairy-wood. So the four [mortals] went back to Athens and were married; and the fairy King and Queen live happily together in that very wood at this very day.

Responding to the Reading

1. How did Demetrius and Lysander fall in love with Helena?
2. How did the story get its title, *A Midsummer Night's Dream?*
3. **Cause and Effect** Why were Lysander and Demetrius preparing to fight?
4. **Predict** What do you think might have happened if Oberon had not interfered with the conflict among the four young people?
5. **Reading** **Read to Write** Reread the last paragraph in the story, then write another ending to the story that could replace that paragraph.

632

Responding to the Reading Answers

1. Oberon and Puck put a potion on the sleeping men's eyes. It made them fall in love with Helena—the first person they saw upon awakening.
2. Oberon says that when Lysander and Demetrius each have the lady who loves him, they will think the whole experience "has been a Midsummer Night's Dream."
3. They both loved Helena and planned to fight for her.
4. Answers may include that Demetrius or Lysander might have been killed.
5. Endings will vary, but they should include the main characters and flow logically from the events in the story.

The Reformation Begins

Get Ready to Read!

What's the Connection?
During the Middle Ages, all of Western Europe's Christians were Catholic. The movement called the Reformation, however, questioned Catholic beliefs and power.

Focusing on the Main Ideas
- The reforms of Martin Luther led to the creation of new Christian churches. *(page 634)*
- Political leaders often supported Protestantism because they wanted more power. *(page 639)*
- John Calvin's Protestant teachings spread across Europe and into North America. *(page 640)*

Locating Places
Wittenberg (WIH•tuhn•BUHRG)
Geneva (juh•NEE•vuh)

Meeting People
Martin Luther
Desiderius Erasmus (DEHS•ih•DIHR• ee•uhs   ih•RAZ•muhs)
John Calvin

Building Your Vocabulary
Reformation (REH•fuhr•MAY•shuhn)
indulgence (ihn•DUHL•juhns)
denomination (dih•NAH•muh•NAY•shuhn)
theology (thee•AH•luh•jee)
predestination (pree•DEHS•tuh•NAY•shuhn)

Reading Strategy
Cause and Effect Create a diagram to show some of the reasons for the Reformation.

Reasons for the Reformation

NATIONAL GEOGRAPHIC **When & Where?**

1500	1530	1560
1517 Martin Luther writes Ninety-Five Theses	1519 Charles V becomes Holy Roman Emperor	1555 Peace of Augsburg signed

London
Paris
Geneva
Wittenberg
Rome

CHAPTER 17   The Renaissance and Reformation   **633**

SECTION OVERVIEW

This section describes how Martin Luther's movement to reform the Roman Catholic Church resulted in new forms of Christianity.

BELLRINGER
SKILLBUILDER ACTIVITY

Project **Daily Focus Skills Transparency 17–3** and have students answer questions. Discuss their responses.

Get Ready to Read!

Preteaching Vocabulary: In opposing indulgences, Luther objected to the idea that money could buy pardons for sin.

Answers to Graphic: the idea that the Church needed to improve; Luther's 95 arguments against indulgences; the Church's focus on money, especially the sale of indulgences; Luther's excommunication

---

SECTION RESOURCES

 Reproducible Masters
- Reproducible Lesson Plan 17–3
- Daily Lecture and Discussion Notes 17–3
- Vocabulary Activity 17–3
- Active Reading Note-Taking Guide 17–3
- Guided Reading Activity 17–3
- Section Quiz 17–3
- Reading Essentials and Study Guide 17–3

 Transparencies
- Daily Focus Skills Transparency 17–3

Multimedia
- Interactive Tutor Self-Assessment CD-ROM
- ExamView® Pro Testmaker CD-ROM
- Presentation Plus! CD-ROM
- Glencoe BookLink CD-ROM

② TEACH

Previewing the Section Tell students to fold a sheet of paper in half along the width and then again along the length, creating eight boxes—four on the front and four on the back. Ask students to write a different heading from the section in each box. Next, have them write each highlighted vocabulary word and name below the appropriate heading. As students are reading the section, they should explain briefly in the boxes how each term or name relates to the appropriate heading. **L1**

Daily Lecture and Discussion Notes 17–3

Use **Daily Lecture and Discussion Notes 17–3** for an outline of key concepts found in the section.

Reading Support L1/ EL

Use **Vocabulary Activity 17–3** to review important terms in the section.

Caption Answer: to translate the Bible into the vernacular

Calls for Church Reform

Main Idea The reforms of Martin Luther led to the creation of new Christian churches.

Reading Focus Can you think of any reformers in the United States? Read to learn how some Europeans set out to reform the Catholic Church and ended up starting a new church instead.

In 1517 a young monk named **Martin Luther** challenged the Roman Catholic Church. He publicly argued that the pope could not decide what a person had to do to get into heaven. Eventually, his challenge to the pope's authority led to the creation of new churches in Western Europe.

At first, Luther only wanted to reform the Catholic Church. This is why we call these events the **Reformation** (REH•fuhr•MAY•shuhn). The Reformation, however, became the beginning of a movement in

▲ Desiderius Erasmus, the most famous Christian humanist, criticized the wealth and power of Catholic leaders. *What change did Erasmus want to make to the Bible?*

Christianity known as Protestantism. By the end of the Reformation, many new Christian churches had appeared in Europe. The religious unity the Catholic Church had created in Western Europe, and which had lasted for hundreds of years, had been broken.

What Ideas Led to the Reformation? In the last section, you read about humanism. When humanism spread to northern Europe, it led to a new movement in Christianity called Christian humanism. Its best-known leader was a scholar and clergyman named **Desiderius Erasmus** (DEHS•ih•DIHR•ee•uhs ih•RAZ•muhs).

Erasmus wrote that human beings could use their reason to become better Christians and thereby improve the Church. He studied ancient Christian works for inspiration.

One of Erasmus's goals was to translate the Bible into the vernacular. He wanted a farmer working in the fields to be able to stop and read the Bible. Erasmus also wrote that what mattered was that people be good in their everyday lives. It was not enough to participate in religious activities, like going to church on Sunday.

The Church Upsets Reformers By the 1300s, many people believed that the Church had problems. It taxed people heavily, and some bishops behaved like they were kings. They built palaces, spent money on fine art, and made sure that their relatives had good jobs. In many villages, priests could barely read or give a good sermon.

Many Catholics became angry at the Church's focus on money. One Church practice that especially angered them was the selling of indulgences. An **indulgence** (ihn•DUHL•juhns) was a pardon from the Church for a person's sins. The Church had given out indulgences before, but it did not usually sell them. In the 1500s, however, the

Understanding Prefixes Ask students to define the words *holy, conscious,* and *just. (Answers may include "related to God," "awake," and "fair.")* Point out to students that a prefix is a word part that comes before a base word or a root and changes the meaning of the word. For example, the prefix *un-* means "not." Then ask students to define *unholy, unconscious,* and *unjust. (Answers may include "not related to God," "not awake," and "not fair.")* Tell students to look for *unholy* (p. 635), *unconscious* (p. 636), and *unjust* (p. 637) and the thing or person each word describes as they read the section. *(unholy indulgence, unconscious Luther, unjust pope)* **L1**

pope needed money to repair the church of St. Peter's in Rome. To get that money, he decided to sell indulgences in northern Germany.

The sale of indulgences outraged Martin Luther. Luther had looked in the Bible and found nothing that said an indulgence could pardon sin. The whole idea of selling God's forgiveness seemed unholy to him.

Martin Luther was not the first person to question the pope's power. As early as the 1370s, an English priest named John Wycliffe (WIH•KLIHF) had opposed Church policies. He preached that Christians needed only to recognize Jesus Christ as a power above them, not the pope.

Wycliffe and Luther both challenged the pope's power, but they had something else in common—their respect for the Bible. Wycliffe wanted everyone to read the Bible. After Wycliffe died, his followers translated the Bible into English for the first time.

Who Was Martin Luther?
Martin Luther became one of the most famous men in history. His break with the Catholic Church led to a revolution in Christianity. Why would a religious man disagree with his faith? First of all, Luther was angered by the behavior of Church leaders. Secondly, he was worried about his own soul.

Luther was born in 1483 in a small German village. A bright and sensitive boy, he grew up in a disciplined family. His father wanted him to study law, but Luther often thought about serving the Church. One day, he was out riding when a bolt of

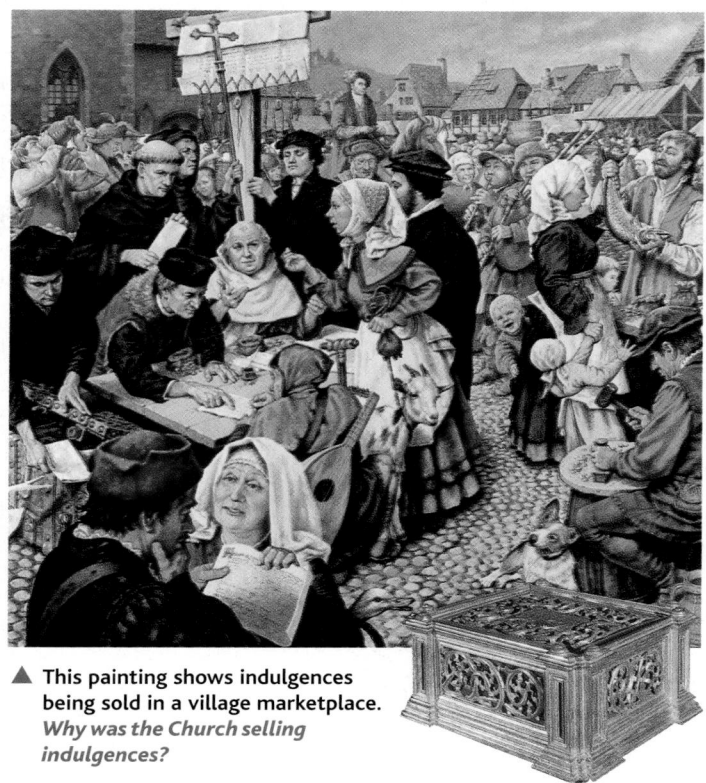

▲ This painting shows indulgences being sold in a village marketplace. *Why was the Church selling indulgences?*

▲ Indulgence box

lightning knocked him to the ground. According to legend, Luther made up his mind to be a monk at that moment.

When Luther went to Rome on a pilgrimage, he was shocked at the behavior of the Roman clergy. Back home in Germany, he taught at a university in the town of **Wittenberg** (WIH•tuhn•BUHRG). He worried about the Church's problems and also about his own soul. With the plague killing people all around him, it is not surprising that Luther worried about whether he would go to heaven when he died.

The Church said that Luther would be saved and would go to heaven if he performed good works and received the sacraments. Still Luther worried that this was not true. He prayed and fasted long hours as he searched for answers to his

CHAPTER 17　The Renaissance and Reformation　**635**

More About the Art

The Dominican preacher Johann Tetzel traveled throughout Germany, urging people to buy indulgences.

Caption Answer: because the pope needed money to repair the church of St. Peter in Rome

Reading Strategy

Writing Activity

Refer students to the material under the following headings:

- "The Church Upsets Reformers"
- "Who Was Martin Luther?"
- "Revolt Leads to New Churches"
- "Peasant Revolts"

Ask students to imagine Luther's life as a four-part made-for-television miniseries. Next, have students decide where each part begins and ends. Then tell them to write brief summaries for each part to go in a television program guide. Provide sample summaries for students to use as models. **L2**

DIFFERENTIATED INSTRUCTION

Visual/Spatial: Tell students that Erasmus lived in what is now the Netherlands, England, France, and Switzerland. Have students locate on a map of Europe where Erasmus, Luther, and Wycliffe lived. **Ask:** Do you think the ideas of Erasmus and Wycliffe may have influenced Luther even though they were from different countries? Why or why not? (*Answers may include that the printing press could have helped spread their ideas.*)

English Learners: Have students locate places on a map as they read about them in the section.

Gifted and Talented: Ask students to compare a map of present-day Western Europe with the map of the Holy Roman Empire on page 639. Elicit that most changes occurred in central Europe.

CONNECTING ACROSS TIME

Have students find references in the section that show that Erasmus, Wycliffe, and Luther thought knowledge of the Bible was important. Point out that politicians and the clergy often refer to or use passages from the Bible. Ask students to discuss whether or not they think this is an effective strategy today. Why, or why not? **L2**

Objectives and answers to the student activity can be found in the **Web Activity Lesson Plan** feature at jat.glencoe.com

▲ **Martin Luther began the Reformation when he made public his Ninety-Five Theses.** *How did the Catholic Church react to Luther's actions?*

questions. He prayed so long that sometimes he fell unconscious on the cold church floor.

Luther found his answers by studying the Bible. He concluded that only faith, not good works, brought salvation. He believed that salvation was a gift from God, not something earned by doing good works.

In 1517, when the Church began selling indulgences, Luther was astonished. How could the Church tell peasants that buying an indulgence would save them? He angrily prepared a list of 95 arguments against indulgences and sent them to his bishop. Some accounts say that Luther also nailed them to the door of Wittenberg

History Online

Web Activity Visit jat.glencoe.com and click on *Chapter 17—Student Web Activity* to learn more about the Reformation.

Cathedral for everyone to read. The list became known as the Ninety-Five Theses. Thousands of copies were printed and read all across the German kingdoms.

Revolt Leads to New Churches At first the Church did not take Luther very seriously. Soon, though, Church leaders saw that Luther was dangerous. If people believed Luther, they would rely on the Bible, not priests. Who would need priests if the sacraments were not needed to get to heaven?

The pope and Luther argued for several years, but Luther refused to change his position. Finally, the pope excommunicated Luther. This meant Luther was no longer a member of the Church and could no longer receive the sacraments. He was also no longer considered a monk.

In the following years, Luther's ideas led to the creation of a new **denomination** (dih•NAH•muh•NAY•shuhn), or organized branch of Christianity. It was known as Lutheranism and was the first Protestant denomination.

Lutheranism has three main ideas. The first is that faith in Jesus, not good works, brings salvation. The second is that the Bible is the final source for truth about God, not a church or its ministers. Finally, Lutheranism said that the church was made up of all its believers, not just the clergy.

Peasant Revolts Luther's debate with the pope was so famous that even peasants in the countryside had heard about it. They liked what they heard about Luther.

The life of a peasant had always been hard, but in the 1520s, it was terrible. The crops had been poor for several years. On top of that, noble landowners increased the taxes that peasants had to pay.

Because of their suffering, Luther's ideas stirred the peasants to revolt. If

CRITICAL THINKING ACTIVITY

Drawing Conclusions Tell students that many Christians at that time refused to read Roman and Greek classics because they were written by pagans. Add that Erasmus countered their arguments by writing "You tell me that we should not read Virgil because he is in hell. Do you think that many Christians are not in hell whose works we read? . . . If you want to give up everything pagan you will have to give up the alphabet and the Latin language, and all the arts and crafts." **Ask:** What conclusions can you draw about Erasmus based on this quote? *(Answers may include that he was thoughtful, logical, and witty.)* **L2**

Luther had a right to rebel against an unjust pope, then the peasants must have a right to stand up to greedy nobles.

The peasants began by listing their demands. Like Luther, they based their ideas on the Bible. One leader said the peasants would no longer work for the nobles, "unless it should be shown us from the Gospel that we are serfs."

When the nobles did not give in, huge revolts broke out. It was not long, however, before the peasants were defeated. The nobles had better weapons and horses and won easily, killing thousands of peasants.

At first Luther sympathized with the peasants, but he soon changed his mind. He was afraid of what might happen without a strong government. Luther used his powerful sermons to tell peasants that God had set the government above them and they must obey it.

✔ **Reading Check** **Cause and Effect** What was the result of the Church's decision to sell indulgences in 1517?

in a word ...

"**Protestant**" is based on the word *protest*, meaning "to object." *Protestant* describes the Christians who broke away from the Catholic Church and founded churches in protest of Catholic practices. Protestants also disagreed among themselves, as is evident from the fact that there are many Protestant denominations today.

✔ **Reading Check**

Answer: Martin Luther was so outraged that he wrote a list of 95 arguments against indulgences and sent them to his bishop, creating a conflict that led to the beginning of Protestantism.

Linking Past & Present

The Anabaptists, Amish, and Mennonites

THEN One Protestant group that formed during the Reformation was called the Brethren. Others called them Anabaptists, which means "to baptize again." They believed that adults should be baptized. The Mennonites and the Amish, many of whom came to the United States, developed from the Anabaptists.

▼ The Amish today

▲ A Mennonite couple in the 1600s

NOW Today most Amish and Mennonite groups are located in Pennsylvania, Ohio, and a few other states. They emphasize the value of community. Old Order Amish reject modern technology, such as electricity, cars, and television. *What, if anything, might prompt you to give up a modern lifestyle?*

Linking Past & Present

Answer: Answers will vary, but they should be realistic and demonstrate a thoughtful response.

CHAPTER 17   The Renaissance and Reformation   637

INTERDISCIPLINARY CONNECTIONS ACTIVITY

Daily Life Tell students that before and during the Reformation, the issue of how to attain salvation was important in people's lives. Have students make individual charts with the headings "Questions," "Very Important," "Important," and "Not Important." Then ask them to brainstorm what things are important to people today. List their responses on the board in the form of questions that begin, "How important is . . ." Have students copy them under the heading "Questions." Then tell students to have a friend or family member complete the questionnaire. Students should put the responses in a slotted box on your desk without showing them to classmates. Tally the responses and list them on the board. Finally, have the class compare the results of their questionnaire with the concerns of people in the 1500s. **L2**

Biography

Luther's demands did not end with his Ninety-Five Theses. In 1520 Luther also published "To the Christian Nobility of the German Nation Concerning the Reformation of the Christian Commonwealth." He called for a national German Church and the reform of schools and universities. Soon, 4,000 copies were sold.

Luther completed his translation of the New Testament into German in 1522. He then went on to translate the Old Testament, which he published in 1524. **Ask: Why did Luther think the Bible was important?** *(He thought the Bible contained God's instructions and teachings.)* **Why was translating the Bible into German important to Luther?** *(because more people would be able to read it in German than could when it was only in Latin)* **L1/ EL**

Then and Now

Students may name nationally known or local figures. They should include supporting details for their choices.

Biography

MARTIN LUTHER
1483–1546

▲ Martin Luther

Long before Martin Luther struggled with the Catholic Church, he faced difficult issues. Luther was born in Eisleben, Germany, in 1483 to a family of miners. Both his parents beat Luther as a child. Martin Luther and his father had terrible tempers. Luther later said his father's beatings caused him to feel bitter and hateful toward his family.

To avoid his abusive home life, Luther focused on his education. He was a student at the Latin School in Mansfield in 1488. As a teenager he went to two other schools away from home. At his father's urging, he considered studying law but instead earned a bachelor's degree in philosophy in 1502.

Later, Luther entered a monastery to separate himself from his abusive past. In 1505 he traveled to Erfurt and became a monk. He then went to Wittenberg in 1508 and stayed with a group of Augustinian hermits. There he continued his study of theology.

Luther was a determined young man. Although he was a priest, he began to question the practices of the Catholic Church. His reforms resulted in a break with the Church. In 1525 he married a former nun named Katharine von Bora. They had six children and lived in a former monastery.

> "He who gives to a poor man, or lends to a needy man, does better than if he bought pardons."
>
> –Martin Luther,
> "The Ninety-five Theses (1517)"

Although known for his hot temper—which cost him many friendships—Luther and his wife cared for as many as 20 orphans whose parents died from the plague. In his later years, Luther enjoyed gardening and music, and continued his lifelong love of writing. He died in 1546, probably of a heart attack.

▲ Wittenberg today

Then and Now

Martin Luther was willing to stand up for his beliefs, even if that meant offending people. Can you think of anyone in the news who has shown that same willingness?

Reading List Generator CD-ROM

GLENCOE **BOOKLINK** **RECOMMENDED READING**

Use the **Glencoe BookLink CD-ROM** to create customized reading lists based on your students' interests and reading levels. Below is an example based on content in this chapter. Also, see the Suggested Readings on pages 944–946 of the Appendix.

- Gail, Marzieh. *Life in the Renaissance.* Describes the daily life of Renaissance Europe.
- Stanley Diane. *Michelangelo.* The artist's life from his early training as a stonecutter to his painting of the Sistine Chapel in Rome.
- Stanley, Diane, and Peter Vennema. *Bard of Avon: The Story of William Shakespeare.* With only a grammar-school education, Shakespeare went to London and became a famous playwright.

Politics and Lutheranism

Main Idea Political leaders often supported Protestantism because they wanted more power.

Reading Focus Under the United States Constitution, the government cannot favor any one religion. Read to learn what happened in Europe during the Reformation when kings decided what faith people had to follow.

In the past, there had been thinkers who challenged Catholic beliefs, but the Church had always remained in control. What had changed in the 1500s that allowed Protestantism to take hold? One reason Protestantism succeeded is that some of Europe's kings realized they could increase their power by supporting Lutheranism against the Catholic Church.

You read earlier about the Holy Roman Empire, which covered much of central Europe. The heart of the empire was made up of about 300 small German kingdoms. In 1519 Charles V became the Holy Roman Emperor. His empire included the lands of the Holy Roman Empire, as well as all of Spain, the Netherlands, parts of Italy, and territories in the Americas.

The local rulers and nobles of the Holy Roman Empire were concerned about Charles V's power. They did not want a strong central ruler. They wanted to keep ruling their own little kingdoms.

Many German rulers decided to become Lutherans for religious and political reasons. By doing so, their kingdom also became Lutheran. After breaking with the Catholic Church, these rulers seized lands owned by Catholic monasteries in their kingdoms. Now they, and not the Church, would earn income from those lands.

At the same time, when the Catholic Church left a kingdom, it meant that church taxes no longer flowed out of the kingdom.

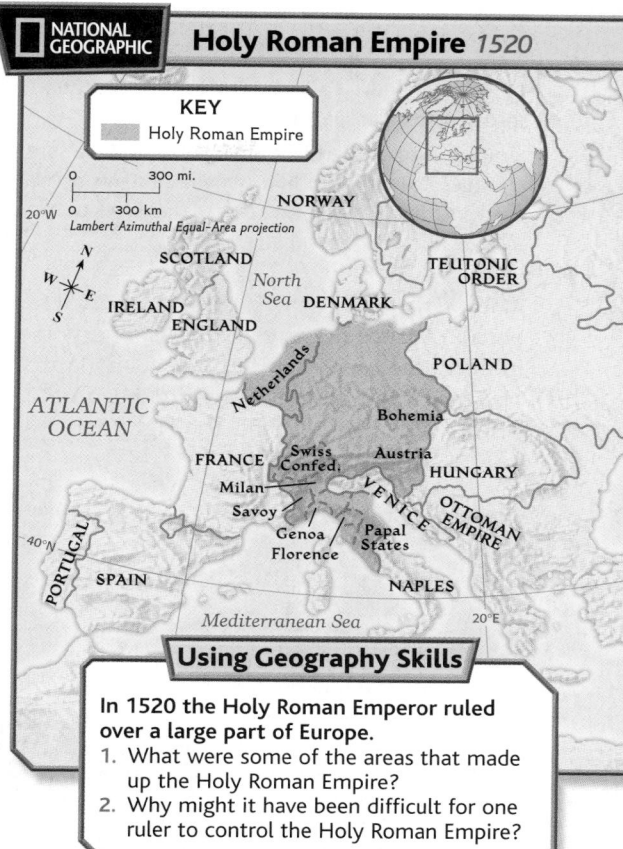

NATIONAL GEOGRAPHIC

Holy Roman Empire 1520

KEY
Holy Roman Empire

Lambert Azimuthal Equal-Area projection

Using Geography Skills

In 1520 the Holy Roman Emperor ruled over a large part of Europe.
1. What were some of the areas that made up the Holy Roman Empire?
2. Why might it have been difficult for one ruler to control the Holy Roman Empire?

Rulers could impose their own church taxes and keep the money for themselves. This made rulers who became Protestants stronger and the Church weaker.

Charles V eventually went to war with the German rulers who converted to Lutheranism, but he was unable to defeat them. In 1555 the fighting ended with the Peace of Augsburg. This agreement let each German ruler decide whether his kingdom would be Lutheran or Catholic. As a result most of northern Germany became Protestant, while the south stayed Catholic.

Reading Check **Explain** Why did many German princes support Martin Luther's ideas?

Using Geography Skills

Answers:
1. Austria, Bohemia, Netherlands, Swiss Confederation, states in northern Italy
2. It was very large and contained many different ethnic groups.

Reading Support L1/ EL

Assign **Guided Reading Activity 17–3** to help students organize the information in the section.

③ ASSESS

Assign Section 3 Review as homework or as an in-class activity.

⊚ Have students use the **Interactive Tutor Self-Assessment CD-ROM** to review the section.

✔ Reading Check

Answer: They wanted to weaken the Holy Roman Emperor, Charles V.

EXTENDING THE CONTENT

What Happened at the Diet of Worms? After Leo X excommunicated Luther, Luther could have been executed, but Prince Frederick the Wise refused to act against him without a hearing. Instead Frederick persuaded Charles V to give Luther safe-conduct and a hearing at the Diet, the assembly of the Holy Roman Empire, which was meeting at Worms in Germany. At the Diet, Luther acknowledged the books he had written, but he asked for time to think when he was asked to repudiate them. The next day Luther refused to do so. Instead he said, "Unless I am convicted by Scripture and plain reason, . . . I cannot and I will not recant anything for to go against conscience is neither right nor safe. God help me. Amen." The Diet eventually issued an edict that declared Luther a heretic and an outlaw who should be captured and turned over to Charles V.

Assessment L2

Assign **Section 3 Quiz** to assess mastery of the material found in the section.

Reading Support L1/ EL

Assign **Reading Essentials and Study Guide 17–3** to help students review section material.

Primary Source

John Calvin was born in Noyon, France. His father, who was the local bishop's secretary, had a falling out with the bishop and was excommunicated. When he died in 1531, the young Calvin tried unsuccessfully to give him a Christian burial. The struggle left Calvin bitter toward the Catholic Church.

Answer:
They must acknowledge that God is the source of life and every good.

Calvin and Calvinism

Main Idea John Calvin's Protestant teachings spread across Europe and into North America.

Reading Focus Are there some things you are sure are true? Read to learn how some Protestants developed a faith where everyone agreed that some people were going to heaven and others were not.

Who Was John Calvin? John Calvin was born in France in the early 1500s. Everyone in his hometown expected that such a dutiful and intelligent boy would become a priest. When he reached the right age, he went off to Paris to study **theology** (thee•AH•luh•jee). Theology is the study of questions about God.

Calvin was very interested in religion. He got up early to read books on theology. During the day, he debated ideas with other students and then went home to read late into the night.

Although Calvin lived in France, he began to hear about the ideas of Martin Luther. Secretly, Calvin began to read about Luther at his college. He and the other students were careful to whisper when they discussed Luther's ideas. The more Calvin read, the more he was convinced by Luther's new ideas.

Eventually, Calvin had to leave Paris because it became too dangerous to talk about Lutheranism. Sometimes he hid out at friends' houses. Once he dared to return to his hometown, but he was arrested and spent months in a damp jail. Calvin finally found safety in **Geneva** (juh•NEE•vuh), Switzerland, a Protestant city. There his powerful preaching convinced many people to follow him.

What Is Calvinism? Calvin agreed with Luther that faith was more important than good works, but he added other ideas too. Calvinism became the basis of many Protestant churches, including the churches of Puritans and Presbyterians in England and Scotland.

Calvin's main idea was that God's will is absolute and decides everything in the world in advance. God has decided who will go to heaven and who will not. This belief is called **predestination** (pree•DEHS•tuh•NAY•shuhn), meaning that no matter what people do, the outcome of their life is already planned.

Primary Source — Knowledge of God

John Calvin's writings helped Europeans accept Protestantism.

"What help is it . . . to know a God with whom we have nothing to do? Rather, our knowledge should serve first to teach us fear and reverence [respect]; secondly, with it as our guide and teacher, we should learn to seek every good from him, and having received it, to credit it to his account. . . . Again, you cannot behold him clearly unless you acknowledge him to be the fountainhead [source of life] and source of every good."

—John Calvin, *Institutes of the Christian Religion*

▲ John Calvin

DBQ Document-Based Question

According to Calvin, what is needed for believers to understand God clearly?

CITIZENSHIP AND YOU

Conflict Resolution The Reformation created quite a stir in Europe. Powerful forces were pitted against each other both politically and militarily, often with deadly results through war and other means. The United States is an increasingly diverse country. Unfortunately, this sometimes leads to violence and other disruptive conflicts. Lead students in a discussion to consider the rights and privileges enjoyed by people in the United States and how these apply in the matter of conflict. **Ask:** How might people during the Reformation have found alternative methods of conflict resolution to war? How might we do the same regarding issues in the United States today? What is our civic responsibility regarding the resolution of problems that affect society? **L3**

Some people could say that if their life's outcome were already determined, then why would it matter if they were good or bad? However, most people decided that they were probably among the saved. To prove it, they worked hard, behaved well, and obeyed the laws of their towns. In this way, Calvinism became a powerful tool in society. It encouraged people to work hard at their business and to behave themselves.

Another important idea of Calvinism is that neither kings nor bishops should control the Church. Calvinists believed that congregations should choose their own elders and ministers to run the church for them.

This idea had a strong impact on England and on many of the English settlers in America. The idea that a congregation should be allowed to choose its own

▲ In this picture, John Calvin is shown speaking before leaders in Geneva. *Which Protestant churches were based on Calvinism?*

leaders helped support the idea that the people should also be allowed to elect their own political leaders.

 Compare How did Calvin's ideas differ from those of Luther?

History Online
Study Central™ Need help with the material in this section? Visit jat.glencoe.com

Section 3 Review

Reading Summary

Review the Main Ideas

- Many Christians, including Martin Luther, believed the Catholic Church was becoming corrupt. This led people to leave the Church and create new Christian churches.

- Many European rulers and nobles supported Luther's reforms for political as well as religious reasons.

- John Calvin's Protestant teachings inspired his followers to work hard and live good lives.

What Did You Learn?

1. What were indulgences, and why did they become controversial?

2. What were John Calvin's basic beliefs about God's will?

Critical Thinking

3. **Organizing Information** Draw a diagram to list the three main ideas of Lutheranism.

Lutheranism

4. **Explain** What were the Ninety-Five Theses?

5. **Cause and Effect** Who was Erasmus, and how were his ideas about Christianity affected by humanism?

6. **Analyze** How did Germany's peasants react to Luther's teachings, and what was Luther's response?

7. **Creative Writing** Write a script for a play about an imaginary meeting between Martin Luther and John Calvin. Think about what the two men may have discussed concerning their beliefs and how they differed.

SECTION 3 REVIEW ANSWERS

1. An indulgence was a pardon for sin from the Church. Luther believed the sale of indulgences was unholy.

2. Calvin believed in predestination and that God's will was absolute.

3. Faith, not good works, brings salvation; the Bible is the final spiritual authority; and all believers, not just clergy, make up the Church.

4. Luther's arguments against the sale of indulgences

5. a scholar and a clergyman; believed reason could make people better Christians and improve the Church

6. They used Luther's teachings to legitimize their right to rebel; he told them God had put the government above them and they must obey it.

7. Scripts will vary but should be based on the text.

Caption Answer: the Puritan and Presbyterian churches

ENRICH

Organize students into groups. Assign a different form of Protestantism to each group for research. Ask the groups to sum up their findings in 10 major points on a poster. Display the groups' posters in the classroom. **L3**

 Reading Check

Answer: Calvin believed in predestination and that congregations should choose their own elders and ministers.

To help students understand section material, have them visit **Study Central**™ at jat.glencoe.com

RETEACH

Have students list the differences and similarities between Lutheranism and Calvinism. **L1**

④ CLOSE

Ask students to explain how the sale of indulgences and Luther's interpretation of the Bible led to his break with the Catholic Church. **L2**

641

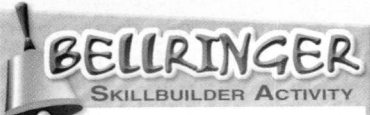

① FOCUS

SECTION OVERVIEW

This section describes religious clashes in Europe and the spread of Catholicism and Protestantism overseas.

BELLRINGER
SKILLBUILDER ACTIVITY

✏ Project **Daily Focus Skills Transparency 17–4** and have students answer questions. Discuss their responses.

Get Ready to Read!

Preteaching Vocabulary: Explain that the Church did not allow divorce. Only the pope could annul, or declare invalid, a marriage.

Answers to Graphic: Council of Trent: made Catholic beliefs clear, set strict rules for behavior of bishops and priests, set up seminaries to train and educate priests; Jesuits Formed: fought heresy, taught, preached

Section 4

Catholics and Protestants

Get Ready to Read!

What's the Connection?

In the last section, you learned about the rise of Protestantism. In this section, you will read about the Catholic Church's attempts at reform and the struggle between Europe's Protestants and Catholics.

Focusing on the Main Ideas

• Catholics and Protestants fought religious wars across Europe. **(page 643)**

• Henry VIII created the Anglican Church in England. **(page 648)**

• As part of the Counter-Reformation, Catholic kingdoms began sending missionaries overseas to convert people to Christianity. **(page 650)**

Locating Places
Trent
Navarre (nuh•VAHR)
Paris
London

Meeting People
Ignatius of Loyola (ihg•NAY•shuhs uhv loy•OH•luh)
Henry of Navarre
Henry VIII
Mary I
Elizabeth I

Building Your Vocabulary
seminary (SEH•muh•NEHR•ee)
heresy (HEHR•uh•see)
annul (uh•NUHL)

Reading Strategy
Cause and Effect Create a diagram to show the results of the Catholic Church's attempts at reform.

Reform

Results	Results

When & Where?

1550	1600	1650

1545 Pope Paul III opens the Council of Trent

1593 Henry of Navarre becomes Catholic to win French throne

1648 The Thirty Years' War ends

London • Paris • Trent • Rome

SECTION RESOURCES

📁 **Reproducible Masters**
• Reproducible Lesson Plan 17–4
• Daily Lecture and Discussion Notes 17–4
• Vocabulary Activity 17–4
• Active Reading Note-Taking Guide 17–4
• Guided Reading Activity 17–4
• Section Quiz 17–4
• Reading Essentials and Study Guide 17–4

✏ **Transparencies**
• Daily Focus Skills Transparency 17–4

Multimedia
⊕ Interactive Tutor Self-Assessment CD-ROM
⊕ ExamView® Pro Testmaker CD-ROM
⊕ Presentation Plus! CD-ROM
⊕ Vocabulary PuzzleMaker CD-ROM
⊕ Glencoe BookLink CD-ROM

Counter-Reformation

Main Idea **Catholics and Protestants fought religious wars across Europe.**

Reading Focus Have you visited Protestant and Catholic churches? Could you see any differences? Read to learn the reasons for those differences.

In the 1500s and 1600s, the Catholic Church set out to defeat Protestantism and convince people to return to the Church. This effort came to be called the Counter-Reformation. As you learned earlier, the Reformation also triggered a series of bloody wars in Europe between Catholic and Protestant rulers. When the last wars ended in 1648, Europe was divided into Catholic and Protestant areas.

The Church Tries to Reform Itself The
Catholic Church waged a war against Protestantism, but it knew it needed to reform itself. Pope Paul III understood this need. After becoming pope, Paul called a church council at **Trent**, near Rome. The council held meetings for 20 years, from the 1540s to the 1560s.

The Council of Trent made Catholic beliefs clear. It also set up strict rules for how bishops and priests should behave. The Catholic clergy were told to work even harder at instructing people in the faith. To train new priests, seminaries were set up. A **seminary** (SEH•muh•NEHR•ee) is a special school for training and educating priests.

In 1540 Pope Paul III took another important step. He recognized a new order of priests, the Society of Jesus, known as the Jesuits. Jesuits were the pope's agents in Europe. They taught, preached, and fought **heresy** (HEHR•uh•see). A heresy is a religious belief that contradicts what the Church says is true.

▲ The Council of Trent is believed to be the basis for the Catholic Counter-Reformation. *What did the Council of Trent accomplish?*

② TEACH

Identifying Text Structure Explain that authors use different structures to organize text. Two structures are chronological—arranging events in the order in which they occur—and compare-contrast—showing likenesses and differences. Certain words help readers determine the structure of a passage. For example, *on, during, after, first,* and dates often signal chronological text structure. *On the other hand* and *like* are signal words in a compare-contrast text structure. Tell students to read the subsection "The Church Tries to Reform Itself." Then discuss which text structure the author used. **L1**

Daily Lecture and Discussion Notes 17–4

Use **Daily Lecture and Discussion Notes 17–4** for an outline of key concepts found in the section.

More About the Art

The Council was made up of the pope and bishops from most of Catholic Europe.

Caption Answer: made Catholic beliefs clear; set up strict rules for the clergy; established seminaries

Reading Strategy ⟩ READING THE TEXT

Using Context Clues Explain that denotation is the dictionary meaning of a word and that connotation is the emotional value associated with a word. Next, direct students' attention to the last paragraph in the subsection "The Church Tries to Reform Itself." **Ask:** What is the dictionary meaning of *soldier? (someone serving in the army)* What kind of soldier does the author say Ignatius of Loyola is? *(daring)* Explain that this is an emotional value people often associate with *soldier.* Then ask a volunteer to look up the dictionary meaning of *saint* and share it with the class. **Ask:** What emotional values do you associate with the term *saint? (Answers may include holy, gentle, patient, or forgiving.)* What words does the author use to give *saint* a soldierlike connotation? *(brave, defend)* **L2**

After Ignatius of Loyola decided to imitate the saints, he spent three days confessing his sins. He renounced his life as a soldier by hanging his sword and dagger at a shrine to the Virgin Mary in Montserrat, Spain. For almost a year, Ignatius lived as a beggar and prayed seven hours a day. This period of his life ended with a pilgrimage to Palestine, where Ignatius visited landmarks in the life of Jesus.

Answer:
At first, he simply enjoyed reading and needed a way to pass the time. Later, he was interested in the topics.

Reading Support L1/ EL

Use **Vocabulary Activity 17–4** to review important terms in the section.

Primary Source Ignatius and Christianity

Ignatius of Loyola became devoted to the Christian religion while recovering from an injury.

"In everything else he was healthy except that he could not stand easily on his leg and had to stay in bed. As he was much given to reading . . . when he felt better he asked to be given some of them [books] to pass the time. But in that house none of those that he usually read could be found, so they gave him a Life of Christ and a book of the lives of the saints in Spanish. As he read them over many times, he became rather fond of what he found written there."

▲ Ignatius of Loyola

—*The Autobiography of St. Ignatius Loyola,*
Joseph F. O'Callaghan, trans.

DBQ Document-Based Question

Why do you think Ignatius read the religious books even though they were not the type of book he usually read?

The man who founded the Jesuits was a Spaniard, **Ignatius of Loyola** (ihg•NAY•shuhs uhv loy•OH•luh). He was a daring soldier, but his life changed when he was wounded in battle. While recuperating, he read about Christian saints who performed brave deeds to defend their faith. Ignatius decided he would be a soldier for Jesus Christ.

The Religious Wars in France John Calvin was originally from France, and many French people became interested in his ideas. As Calvinism spread in France, French Protestants became known as Huguenots.

Only about seven percent of the French people became Protestants, but almost half of France's nobles did, including the Bourbon family. The Bourbons were the second most powerful family in France. They ruled a kingdom in southern France called **Navarre** (nuh•VAHR) and were also in line for the throne of France.

Many French nobles wanted to weaken the king. The Huguenot nobles especially wanted the king weak so they could practice their religion freely. At the same time, France's king, Henry II, wanted to build a strong central government.

Henry II died in 1559, and his son Francis II died the following year. This meant that Francis's brother Charles, a 10-year-old boy, was now king. Since Charles was too young to rule, his mother ran the government for him. His mother was Catherine de' Medici—the daughter of Lorenzo de' Medici, the powerful Italian leader of Florence.

Catherine was determined to keep the French kingdom strong for her son. She believed the Huguenots were a threat to the king's power and refused to compromise with them. In 1562 a civil war that would last more than 30 years began in France between Protestants and Catholics.

In 1589 **Henry of Navarre,** the leader of Huguenot forces and head of the Bourbon family, became King Henry IV of France. For the next few years, the war continued because Catholic nobles would not accept a Protestant as king. Henry won most of his battles but was unable to capture **Paris.**

Henry IV then made a famous deal. He knew most French people were Catholic and that they demanded a Catholic king. Henry agreed to become a Catholic so the French people would accept him as king.

DIFFERENTIATED INSTRUCTION

Intrapersonal: Have each student rank the importance of the following values according to his or her beliefs: power, wealth, fame, religion, loyalty, peace. Then ask students how Henry IV might have ranked them. Record the results on the board. Discuss how students' priorities compare with Henry's.

English Learners: Explain that *compromise* means "to give up something to reach an agreement." Point out that heads of government often compromise. **Ask:** What did Henry IV give up to become king? *(his religion)* Then have students describe the other side of the compromise—with whom Henry made an agreement and what this person gave in return.

Gifted and Talented: Tell students to write a paragraph describing how they might feel if a friend treated them the way Henry IV treated his Huguenot followers.

In 1593 Henry went to Paris and put on white satin for the Catholic ceremony. As he passed through the church doors, he smiled and, according to tradition, said that Paris was "worth a mass." He meant it was worth becoming a Catholic to rule all of France.

Henry IV did not forget his Huguenot followers, however. He issued an edict, or order, while visiting the city of Nantes in 1598. The Edict of Nantes said Catholicism was France's official religion, but it also gave Huguenots the right to worship freely.

What Was the Thirty Years' War? The worst religious war of the Reformation era was fought in the Holy Roman Empire in the 1600s. The war began in Bohemia—today known as the Czech Republic. Protestant nobles in Bohemia rebelled against their Catholic king. Other Protestant kings in Germany decided to help the rebels, and the war expanded throughout the empire.

The war lasted 30 years, from 1618 to 1648, and quickly became a war of kingdoms. France, Sweden, Denmark, England, and the Netherlands sent troops to help the

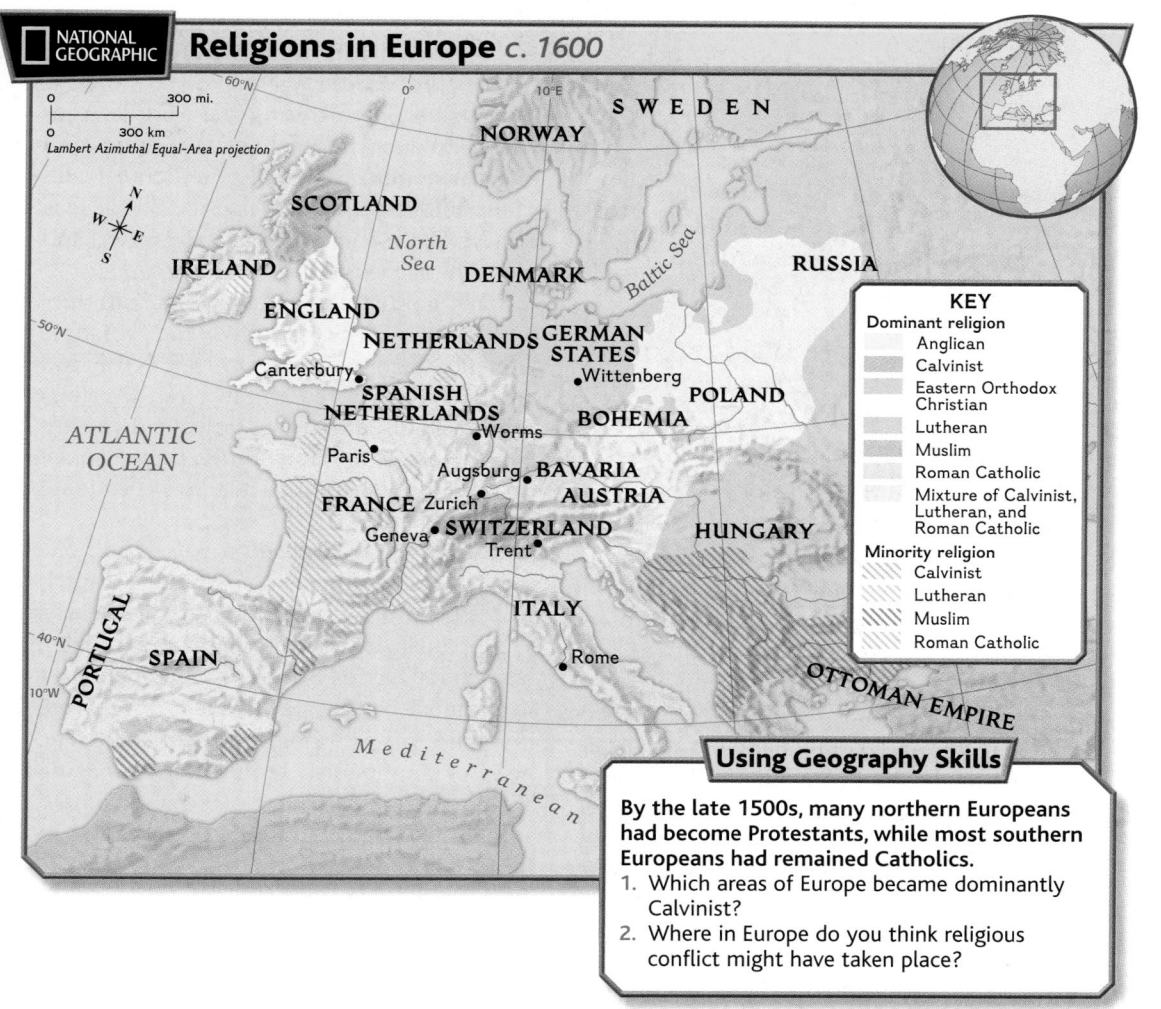

NATIONAL GEOGRAPHIC

Religions in Europe c. 1600

KEY
Dominant religion
- Anglican
- Calvinist
- Eastern Orthodox Christian
- Lutheran
- Muslim
- Roman Catholic
- Mixture of Calvinist, Lutheran, and Roman Catholic

Minority religion
- Calvinist
- Lutheran
- Muslim
- Roman Catholic

Using Geography Skills

By the late 1500s, many northern Europeans had become Protestants, while most southern Europeans had remained Catholics.
1. Which areas of Europe became dominantly Calvinist?
2. Where in Europe do you think religious conflict might have taken place?

CRITICAL THINKING ACTIVITY

Analyzing Information Read the following quotes from writers who lived during the Thirty Years' War:

• The condition of man ... is a condition of war of everyone against everyone.
—Englishman Thomas Hobbes (1588–1679)

• The good effect of Fortune may be short-lived. To build on it is to build on sand.
—Frenchman Honorat de Bueil (1589–1679)

Ask: How would you describe the tone of the writers' quotes? *(Answers may include pessimistic and cynical.)* How do you think the Thirty Years' War may have affected the writers' view of life? *(Answers may include that the war made peace and stability seem unattainable.)* **L3**

Solving a Problem On the board write "Problem—How to keep Spain loyal and united." Then write "Solutions" under "Problem." Tell students to read the subsection "The Reformation in Spain" and look for ways that Ferdinand and Isabella tried to solve the problem. Finally, discuss what students find. **L2**

✓ Reading Check

Answer: He agreed to become Catholic if he could be king.

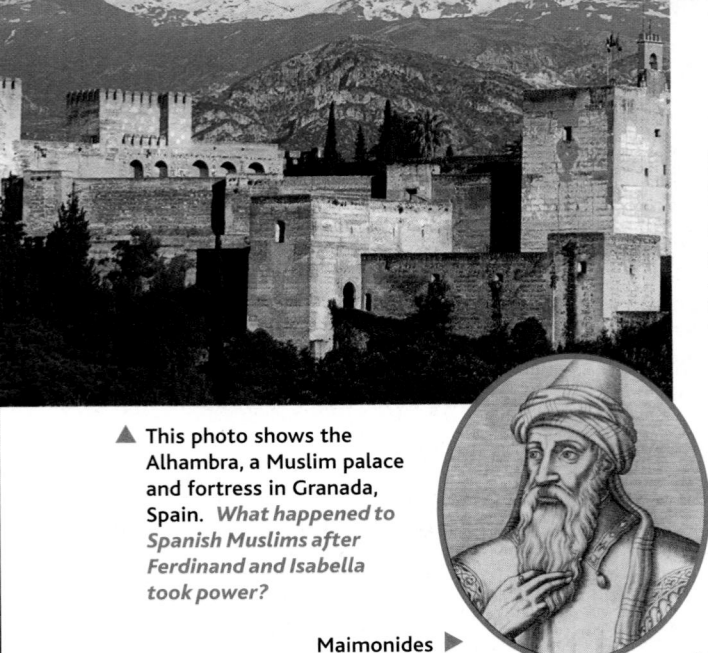

▲ This photo shows the Alhambra, a Muslim palace and fortress in Granada, Spain. *What happened to Spanish Muslims after Ferdinand and Isabella took power?*

Maimonides ▶

Protestants, while Spain and the Holy Roman Empire backed the Catholics.

Town fought against town, and roving troops murdered peasants on the roads. When it was over, only wolves were found wandering where some towns used to be. The war weakened Spain and helped make France one of Europe's most powerful countries.

The Reformation in Spain The ideas of Luther and Calvin never became very popular in Spain. Still, when Protestants began fighting in Europe, it affected Spain. Spanish rulers became suspicious of Protestant countries and of anyone in Spain who was not Catholic.

When the Reformation began in the 1500s, Spain was a young nation. It had been founded in 1469 when King Ferdinand and Queen Isabella married and joined their two kingdoms. These monarchs wanted a strong nation. They felt that all their subjects should be Catholic, because that would keep Spain's citizens loyal and united.

When Ferdinand and Isabella began to rule, many Muslims still lived in Spain. As you read in earlier chapters, Muslims ruled Spain from about A.D. 700 to 1200. During those years, people of different religions lived together in relative harmony.

The Muslims made non-Muslims pay special taxes and limited their rights, but they did not seek to kill or expel nonbelievers. Jews, for example, found life in Muslim Spain better than other places in Europe. As you read in earlier chapters, Jews were persecuted throughout Europe during the Middle Ages.

Muslim Spain during the Middle Ages was a golden age for Jewish thinkers and poets. The most famous Jewish scholar was Maimonides (my•MAH•nuh•DEEZ). He was born in Spain and his books on religion and medicine earned him great respect.

This golden age ended when Catholics took control of Spain. Jews and Muslims were no longer welcome. In 1492 Ferdinand and Isabella ordered all Jews and Muslims to convert to Catholicism or leave the country. To ensure religious unity, they also set up the Spanish Inquisition to investigate people's beliefs.

The Spanish Inquisition was a Catholic court, similar to the one the Catholic Church had set up in Europe to investigate heresy. The Spanish Inquisition was much crueler, however. Charges of heresy were made just to eliminate enemies. Horrible tortures were invented to force confessions of guilt. The head of the Spanish Inquisition, Tomás de Torquemada (TAWR•kuh•MAH•duh), executed some 2,000 Spaniards. Even the pope in Rome could not stop him.

✓ **Reading Check** **Identify** What deal earned Henry of Navarre the French throne?

INTERDISCIPLINARY CONNECTIONS ACTIVITY

Civics Tell students that in 1252, Pope Innocent IV authorized the use of torture in obtaining confessions for the Inquisition. Penalties for prisoners who confessed ranged from simple prayers to lifetime imprisonment. Those who were convicted but refused to confess could be put to death. The Spanish Inquisition used torture and punished heretics by burning them at the stake. Have students review the U.S. Constitution's Bill of Rights. **Ask:** Which amendments would make a Spanish-style Inquisition illegal in the United States? Why? *(The First Amendment protects freedom of religion. The Fifth Amendment says a person cannot be forced to testify against himself or herself. The Sixth Amendment guarantees the accused a speedy trial, witnesses, and legal assistance. The Seventh Amendment guarantees trial by jury. The Eighth Amendment forbids cruel or unusual punishment.)* **L3**

Biography

CATHERINE DE' MEDICI
1519–1589

Catherine de' Medici was an Italian woman who played an important role in French history. She was born in Florence to Lorenzo de' Medici and Madeleine de la Tour d' Auvergne. Catherine was orphaned as a baby and was raised by relatives. At age 14, Catherine was married to Henry, a French prince. Catherine took Italian artists, musicians, writers, and dancers with her to the French court. She was never fully accepted in France, however, because she was Italian and was not from a royal family.

In 1547 Catherine's husband became King Henry II. After he died in a jousting accident in 1559, their three oldest sons—Francis II, Charles IX, and Henry III—succeeded each other as king. Although Catherine was no longer queen, she still had much influence over her sons.

Catherine is blamed for many of the conflicts between French Catholics and French Protestants, called Huguenots. In 1568 she outlawed freedom of worship. In 1572 Catherine arranged the murder of a Huguenot adviser. His death sparked the Saint Bartholomew's Massacre, which resulted in the deaths of about 6,000 Huguenots. Catherine was not always opposed to Huguenots. In fact, she arranged the marriage of her daughter Margaret to Henry of Navarre, a former Protestant Huguenot who became King Henry IV of France.

Views on Catherine's accomplishments are mixed. Some blame her entirely for the French religious wars. Others remember her efforts to protect her sons. Still others remember her as a Renaissance woman because she supported the arts, added to the royal library, and sponsored a dance and theater pageant that is considered to be the first ballet. Catherine died in 1589 of pneumonia.

▲ Catherine de' Medici

> "God and the world will have reason to be satisfied with me."
>
> —Catherine de' Medici, *Biography of a Family*

◄ Catherine de' Medici meets with foreign ambassadors

Then and Now

If Catherine de' Medici were running for political office today, do you think she would be a popular candidate? Why or why not?

647

Biography

TEACH

For a while, the orphaned Catherine lived with her uncle, Pope Clement VII. He arranged the marriage between her and Henry, the second-oldest son of the French king Francis I. Tradition tells us that Catherine wanted to make a grand entrance at her first ball in the French court, so she consulted a Florentine shoemaker. He invented the first modern ladies' high-heeled shoes for Catherine to help compensate for her short height. They gave her stature and grace at the ball and caused a stir in French fashion circles.

Have students use information from the feature to diagram three generations in Catherine de' Medici's family tree. Then discuss with students what Catherine's experiences demonstrate about the monarchical form of government. *(the need for male heirs, preferably multiple ones, to keep the family in power; queens who can rule if necessary; political needs dominate when arranging marriages)* **L2**

Then and Now

Answers will vary but should take into account her actions that were designed to keep France strong.

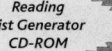
Reading List Generator CD-ROM

GLENCOE BOOKLINK **RECOMMENDED READING**

Use the **Glencoe BookLink CD-ROM** to create customized reading lists based on your students' interests and reading levels. Below is an example based on content in this chapter. Also, see the Suggested Readings on pages 944–946 of the Appendix.

- King, David C. *Dropping in on Italy*. Tour sunny Italy, a boot-shaped country the size of Arizona. First stop is Milan with its famous glass-domed Galleria. From there, visit Venice, Florence, Rome, and the ancient city of Pompeii, which was buried by a volcanic eruption.
- Meyer, Carolyn. *Isabel: Jewel of Castilla*. The early life of Spain's queen Isabella.

The English Reformation

Main Idea Henry VIII created the Anglican Church in England.

Reading Focus You have probably heard about the Pilgrims. Do you know why the Pilgrims left England to come here? Read to learn how the Reformation came to England and why some Protestants decided to leave England and go to America.

Because England is an island, ideas from Europe sometimes took longer to get there. Surprisingly, though, England broke away from the Catholic Church earlier than the rest of Europe. That change was based on a political decision by the English king. Later, however, the English people strongly debated Reformation ideas.

Henry VIII Starts His Own Church In the history of England, no king is more famous than **Henry VIII.** He ruled England from 1509 to 1547. He was stubborn, impatient, and cruel. Henry married six queens, divorced two, and beheaded two more. He imprisoned bishops and nobles in the Tower of **London** (LUHN•duhn) for disagreeing with him. They also were eventually beheaded.

◀ In his attempt to divorce his wife and marry another woman, Henry VIII broke away from the Catholic Church and created the Church of England. *Why did the pope refuse to annul Henry VIII's marriage?*

Henry and his father were members of the Tudor family. In the 1400s, before the Tudors came to the throne, England's nobles had been at war with each other. Henry was determined to keep the peace and to keep the Tudors on the throne.

To do this he needed a son to succeed him, but Henry had no son. His wife Catherine had given birth only to one surviving daughter. Henry asked the pope to **annul** (uh•NUHL), or cancel, his marriage to Catherine.

An annulment is not the same as a divorce. If the pope annulled the marriage, it would be as if the marriage had never happened. It would mean that Henry could find a new wife to give birth to sons. Those sons would be heirs to the throne, not the daughter Catherine had given him.

Popes had annulled marriages before, but this time the pope refused. Catherine was the daughter of Ferdinand and Isabella of Spain. Her nephew was the Holy Roman Emperor. Spain was the strongest Catholic kingdom at that time, and the pope did not want to make Catherine's family angry.

Henry had the archbishop of Canterbury—the highest bishop in England—annul the marriage. In response, the pope excommunicated Henry from the Church. Henry then declared that the king, not the pope, was the head of the Church in England.

Henry ordered all the priests and bishops in England to accept him as the new head of their church. Some refused and were killed. The most famous was Sir Thomas More, who was executed in 1535. Henry then seized the Catholic Church's land in England and gave some of it to his nobles. This kept the nobles loyal to the king and to the Church of England. If they ever let the Catholic Church regain power in England, they would have to give up their land.

EXTENDING THE CONTENT

What Was Sir Thomas More Like? More was a talented lawyer and writer. He was also a very pious Catholic who prayed regularly and fasted on holidays. His book *Utopia* was published in 1516. It described an ideal society in which no one owned anything, but everyone was rich and worked for the common good. In 1529 King Henry VIII appointed More Lord Chancellor. However, More refused to attend the coronation of Henry's second wife, Anne Boleyn. More also refused to acknowledge Henry as head of the Church in England. As a result, he was convicted of treason and beheaded. More stated that he was dying not for treason but "in the faith and for the faith of the Catholic Church, the king's good servant and God's first" (meaning he would serve God before the king).

Mary I (above) attempted to restore the Catholic religion in England, and she married Philip II (right), the Catholic king of Spain. *Why was Mary I known as "Bloody Mary"?*

Who Was Bloody Mary? The Church of England came to be known as the Anglican Church. It kept most of the rituals and sacraments of the Catholic Church. However, many English Catholics were not satisfied. They wanted to stay Catholic. They backed Henry and Catherine's daughter Mary when she became Queen **Mary I** in 1553. Mary had been raised Catholic and wanted to make England a Catholic kingdom again.

Mary restored the Catholic Church in England and arrested Protestants who opposed her. In her struggle to make England Catholic again, Mary burned 300 people at the stake. The English were horrified and called her "Bloody Mary."

Mary ruled about five years, then died. Her half-sister Elizabeth took over the throne, becoming Queen **Elizabeth I.** Elizabeth was a Protestant. She restored the Anglican Church and went on to become one of the greatest rulers in English history.

How Did Calvinism Affect England?

Although the Catholics were defeated, the religious battles were not over. A new fight began to make the Anglican Church more Protestant in its beliefs and rituals.

By the late 1500s, the ideas of John Calvin had reached England. Many educated people read Calvin's works and became convinced that he was right. They began to demand that the Anglican Church give up its Catholic ways of doing things. These reformers became known as Puritans because they wanted to purify the Anglican Church of Catholic ideas.

Puritans began to form their own congregations. These congregations were independent. They made their own decisions about what their congregations should and should not do. They did not report to a bishop of the Anglican Church, and they chose their own ministers.

Queen Elizabeth I tolerated the Puritans, but when James I became king in 1603, the Puritans faced harder times. James refused to allow anyone to disagree with the Anglican Church. The king headed the Anglican Church and appointed its leaders. The leaders, in turn, chose the priests for the congregations. James believed that by choosing their own ministers, the Puritans were challenging the king's power.

James I and the king who came after him, Charles I, persecuted the Puritans. They shut down Puritan churches and jailed Puritan leaders. Many Puritans decided to move to America to practice their religion freely. There they founded colonies that eventually became the states of Massachusetts, Connecticut, New Hampshire, and Rhode Island.

✓ **Reading Check** **Cause and Effect** Why did Henry VIII create the Anglican Church?

CHAPTER 17   The Renaissance and Reformation   **649**

Caption Answer: Mary killed many Protestants in trying to return England to Catholic ways.

③ ASSESS

Assign Section 4 Review as homework or as an in-class activity.

◉ Have students use the **Interactive Tutor Self-Assessment CD-ROM** to review the section.

Assessment L2

Assign **Section 4 Quiz** to assess mastery of the material found in the section.

Reading Support L1/ EL

Assign **Reading Essentials and Study Guide 17–4** to help students review section material.

✓ Reading Check

Answer: Henry wanted a male heir, but the pope refused to annul Henry's marriage. The leading English bishop then annulled Henry's marriage. The pope excommunicated Henry. Henry then declared that the king, not the pope, was head of the Church in England.

COOPERATIVE LEARNING ACTIVITY

Comparing Rulers Organize students into pairs, and assign each pair one of these rulers: Catherine de' Medici, Henry IV, Ferdinand, Henry VIII, or Queen Mary. Have partners create a summary of their assigned ruler. Then have students form new groups, with one person in each group representing each ruler. Have them share and discuss their summaries to determine which ruler they think was the most effective. Have students report their results to the class. **L2**

ENRICH

Read the following to students: Early in his reign, the pious Henry VIII wrote a pamphlet arguing against some of Luther's teachings. In 1521 the pope gave him the title "Defender of the Faith" as a reward. Ask students to explain how this same Henry could then break with the Church in 1532. **L2**

✓ **Reading Check**

Answer: in the Americas, Japan, and the Philippines

To help students understand section material, have them visit **Study Central**™ at jat.glencoe.com

RETEACH

Help students complete the following sentence for France, Spain, and England: During the Reformation, [name of country] [stayed Catholic/became Protestant] because [name of ruler(s)] [ruler's action]. **L1**

④ CLOSE

Ask students to explain how Henry VIII was similar to Ferdinand and Isabella. **L2**

Missionaries Go Overseas

Main Idea As part of the Counter-Reformation, Catholic kingdoms began sending missionaries overseas to convert people to Christianity.

Reading Focus Do you think spreading democracy is important? Read to learn how Catholic missionaries tried to spread their religion to other people in the world.

When the Counter-Reformation began, many Catholics became committed to spreading their faith. As part of this new energy and determination, Catholic kingdoms began sending missionaries overseas to America and Asia.

The Jesuits were active missionaries in the 1500s and 1600s. French and Spanish Jesuits headed to America and Asia. In America, the Native Americans called them the "Black Robes."

The first Jesuit missionary to Japan, Francis Xavier, arrived in 1549. The Japanese at first welcomed the Jesuits. By 1600, the Jesuits had converted thousands of Japanese to Christianity.

Eventually the Jesuits clashed with people who believed in Buddhism and Shintoism. The Japanese Shogun, or military ruler, banned Christianity in Japan and expelled all missionaries.

Spanish missionaries had much greater success in the Philippine Islands. Most of the people there eventually became Catholic. Today the Philippines are the only Asian country with a Catholic majority. French missionaries tried to convert the people of Vietnam but were expelled by Vietnam's emperor.

✓ **Reading Check** **Identify** In what parts of the world did Catholic missionaries teach?

Section ④ Review

History Online
Study Central™ Need help with the material in this section? Visit jat.glencoe.com

Reading Summary

Review the Main Ideas

- Across Europe, religious wars between Catholics and Protestants were fought in the 1500s and 1600s, while the Spanish monarchs tried to make Spain an exclusively Catholic country.

- In England, Henry VIII broke with the Catholic Church and created the Anglican Church. Puritans later tried to reform the Anglican Church and then fled to America.

- Catholic missionaries tried to spread their religion to Asia and America.

What Did You Learn?

1. What was the Council of Trent, and what did it accomplish?

2. Why was the Edict of Nantes important?

Critical Thinking

3. **Organizing Information** Draw a chart like the one below. Fill in details about the steps the Catholic Church took to counter the Reformation.

Church's Efforts to Stop Protestantism

4. **Analyze** Why did Henry VIII form the Anglican Church?

5. **Explain** Who were the Puritans, and what were their beliefs and practices?

6. **Predict** How do you think conflicts over religion affected the world outside of Europe?

7. **Expository Writing** Write a short essay summarizing the history of Catholicism in Spain in the 1400s and 1500s.

SECTION 4 REVIEW ANSWERS

1. a Church council that lasted 20 years; clarified Catholic beliefs and set up rules for the behavior of clergy

2. It made Catholicism the official religion but allowed Huguenots freedom of worship.

3. called the Council of Trent, created the Jesuits; sent missionaries abroad

4. because the pope refused to annul Henry's marriage

5. wanted to make the Anglican Church more Protestant; believed in predestination;

named their own ministers

6. Answers will vary but should note overseas settlements and missionaries.

7. Essays will vary but should be based on the text.

Section 1 The Renaissance Begins

Vocabulary
Renaissance
secular
diplomacy

Focusing on the Main Ideas
- The wealthy urban society of the Italian city-states brought a rebirth of learning and art to Europe. *(page 609)*
- Italy's location helped its city-states grow wealthy from trade and banking, but many of the cities fell under the control of strong rulers. *(page 611)*
- Unlike medieval nobles, the nobles of the Italian city-states lived in cities and were active in trade, banking, and public life. *(page 614)*

Section 2 New Ideas and Art

Vocabulary
humanism
vernacular

Focusing on the Main Ideas
- Humanists studied the Greeks and Romans, and the development of the printing press helped spread their ideas. *(page 619)*
- Renaissance artists used new techniques to produce paintings that showed people in an emotional and realistic way. *(page 623)*
- Renaissance ideas and art spread from Italy to northern Europe. *(page 625)*

Section 3 The Reformation Begins

Vocabulary
Reformation
indulgence
denomination
theology
predestination

Focusing on the Main Ideas
- The reforms of Martin Luther led to the creation of new Christian churches. *(page 634)*
- Political leaders often supported Protestantism because they wanted more power. *(page 639)*
- John Calvin's Protestant teachings spread across Europe and into North America. *(page 640)*

▲ Gutenberg Bible

Section 4 Catholics and Protestants

Vocabulary
seminary
heresy
annul

Focusing on the Main Ideas
- Catholics and Protestants fought religious wars across Europe. *(page 643)*
- Henry VIII created the Anglican Church in England. *(page 648)*
- As part of the Counter-Reformation, Catholic kingdoms began sending missionaries overseas to convert people to Christianity. *(page 650)*

CHAPTER 17   The Renaissance and Reformation   **651**

PREVIEW/REVIEW

Vocabulary Activity Have students use each vocabulary word in a separate sentence.

◉ **Vocabulary PuzzleMaker CD-ROM**

◉ **Interactive Tutor Self-Assessment CD-ROM**

CONDENSE

📁 Chapter 17 **Guided Reading Activities**

◉ **StudentWorks Plus™ CD-ROM (with Audio Program)**

RETEACH

📁 **Differentiated Instruction Activity 17**

📁 Chapter 17 *Reading Essentials and Study Guide*

CHAPTER CULMINATING ACTIVITY

Have students finish the Chapter Culminating Activity from page 604D.

📁 Suggestions for rubrics may be found in the *Quizzes, Tests, and Authentic Assessment (with Rubrics)* booklet.

▌Reading Strategy ◀ READ TO WRITE

Summarizing Have students write two to four paragraphs summarizing Renaissance and Reformation events that occurred in one of these countries: England, Italy, or Germany. Tell students to skim the chapter for facts and to use headings to help them separate one country's facts from another country's. Use the following rubric for assessment:

- **L1** students should write at least two paragraphs—one each on the Renaissance and the Reformation.
- **L2** students should include all the main ideas pertaining to their country and attempt grammar mastery.
- **L3** students should have logical, detailed, well-considered paragraphs.

Review Vocabulary

1. True
2. True
3. humanism
4. seminary
5. True
6. vernacular

Review Main Ideas

7. Roman antiquities surrounded Italians; Italian merchants and nobles were rich; Italy was made up of competing city-states; it had an urban society.

8. They lived in cities and their wealth came from trade and banking rather than from land.

9. that the individual and human society were important

10. used new techniques that showed people in an emotional and realistic way

11. His actions led to the creation of new Christian churches.

12. He believed that God's will is absolute and in predestination.

13. in Bohemia; Protestant nobles rebelled against their Catholic king

14. Henry VIII's desire for a divorce led him to declare himself the head of the Church in England.

Review Vocabulary

Write **True** beside each true statement. Replace the word in italics to make false statements true.

____ 1. *Diplomacy* is the art of negotiating.

____ 2. When the pope needed money in the 1500s, he sold *indulgences.*

____ 3. The Renaissance belief that the individual and human society were important was known as *theology.*

____ 4. A *heresy* is a special school for training and educating priests.

____ 5. *Predestination* encouraged Calvinists to prove they were among the saved.

____ 6. Writers began to write in the *secular,* the everyday language of a region.

Review Main Ideas

Section 1 • The Renaissance Begins

7. What set the stage for the Renaissance in Italy?

8. What made nobles of the Renaissance different from nobles of previous times?

Section 2 • New Ideas and Art

9. What did the humanists believe?

10. How did Renaissance art differ from the art of the Middle Ages?

Section 3 • The Reformation Begins

11. What happened when Martin Luther tried to reform the Catholic Church?

12. Describe John Calvin's teachings.

Section 4 • Catholics and Protestants

13. Where and why did the Thirty Years' War begin?

14. What changed England from a Catholic to a Protestant country?

Critical Thinking

15. **Analyze** Do you think banking played a role in the wealth and art of the Italian city-states? Explain.

16. **Conclude** Some Puritans moved to North America to practice their religion without interference from European leaders. How was that desire for religious freedom reflected in the U.S. Constitution?

Review
Reading Skill — Analyze and Clarify

Go Beyond the Words

17. Read this passage about the importance of the printing press. Then answer the questions at the right to help you analyze and clarify how the printing press affected Europe.

In the early 1450s, Johannes Gutenberg developed a printing press that used movable metal type. This type of printing press made it possible to print many books much more quickly. With more books available, more people learned to read. Scholars could read one another's work and debate their ideas in letters. Ideas grew and spread more quickly than ever before in Europe.

Who? _____   Where? _____
What? _____   Why? _____
When? _____

To review this skill, see pages 606–607.

Critical Thinking

15. Yes; Florentine bankers were the experts in the exchange of coins from different countries; the Medicis, Florence's richest family, were bankers.

16. The U.S. Constitution guarantees freedom of religion.

Reading Skill

17. Who: Johannes Gutenberg
What: developed a printing press that used movable type
When: 1450s
Where: in Europe
Why: to print books more quickly

Geography Skills

Study the map below and answer the following questions.

18. **Location** What geographical advantage does Venice have over Milan?

19. **Human/Environment Interaction** Why might Mantua have been at a disadvantage in terms of trade?

20. **Movement** If you traveled from the city of Florence to the city of Venice, in what direction would you be going?

NATIONAL GEOGRAPHIC Italy c. 1500

Read to Write

21. **Expository Writing** Research the life of Renaissance nobles, merchants, shopkeepers, or peasants. Then write an essay describing the lifestyle and position of the group you chose.

22. **Using Your FOLDABLES** Use information in your completed foldable to create a poster about one of the changes that occurred during the Renaissance and Reformation. Draw pictures, write captions, create titles, and so on. Present your poster to the class.

Self-Check Quiz To help you prepare for the Chapter Test, visit jat.glencoe.com

Using Technology

23. **Researching** The Renaissance revived the Greek idea that a well-rounded person took part in a variety of activities, including sports. Use the Internet and your local library to research one of the following sports of the Renaissance: javelin hurling, tennis, archery, fencing, boxing, or hunting. Present your findings to your classmates. Discuss who participated and any resemblances to modern-day sports.

Linking Past and Present

24. **Inferring** Renaissance artists, architects, and writers were greatly influenced by ancient Greek and Roman culture. Do you think people in those professions today are equally influenced by artists and writers of the past? Why or why not?

Primary Source Analyze

These are two of Luther's Ninety-Five Theses.

"37. Every true Christian, whether living or dead, has a share in all the benefits of Christ and of the Church, . . . even without letters of pardon. . . .

45. Christians should be taught that he who sees any one in need, and, passing him by, gives money for pardons, is not purchasing for himself the indulgences of the Pope but the anger of God. . . ."

—Martin Luther, "Ninety-five Theses"

DBQ Document-Based Questions

25. According to Luther, is the buying of indulgences necessary?

26. What does Luther say is a use for money that will please God?

History Online

Have students visit the Web site at jat.glencoe.com to review Chapter 17 and take the **Self-Check Quiz.**

Using Technology

23. Answers will vary but should be based on students' research.

Linking Past and Present

24. Possible answer: Yes; Western art, architecture, and literature are founded on styles developed by the Greeks and Romans and often reflect that directly.

Primary Source

25. no
26. giving it to people in need

Bonus Question

Ask: The expression *Renaissance person* means someone who is interested in many kinds of learning and is involved in many kinds of activities. In your opinion, which individual in this chapter is the best example of a Renaissance person? (*Students should include supporting details for their choice.*)

Geography Skills

18. borders the Adriatic Sea

19. It was one of the smaller city-states, was near the powerful city-states of Milan and Venice, and did not border water.

20. north

Read to Write

21. Essays will vary but should be based on the chapter and students' research.

22. **FOLDABLES** Students' posters should be creative as well as based on the text.

Chapter 18 Resources

Note: The following materials may be used when teaching Chapter 18.
Section level support materials are shown at point of use in the margins of the Teacher Wraparound Edition.

TEACHING TRANSPARENCIES

- Graphic Organizer Transparencies with Teaching Strategy and Student Activity **L2**
- Cause-and-Effect Transparencies with Teaching Strategy and Student Activity **L2**
- Then and Now Transparencies with Teaching Strategy and Student Activity **L2**
- In-text Map Transparency with Teaching Strategy and Student Activity **L1**
- Map Transparencies with Overlay, Teaching Strategy, and Student Activity **L2**

DIFFERENTIATED INSTRUCTION

- Differentiated Instruction Activity 18
- Time Line Activity 18
- Primary Source Reading 18 (with Document-Based Questions)
- Inclusion Strategies for the Middle School Social Studies Classroom
- StudentWorks Plus™ CD-ROM (with Audio Program)

READING SUPPORT

- Take-Home Review Activity 18 **L2**
- World Literature Reading 18 **L2**
- Workbook Activity 18 **L1**
- Reading Strategies for the Social Studies Classroom **L1/ EL**

ASSESSMENT

- Authentic Assessment Activity 18 **L1/ EL**
- Chapter 18 Test Form A **L2**
- Chapter 18 Test Form B **L2**
- ExamView® Pro Testmaker CD-ROM

INTERDISCIPLINARY CONNECTIONS

- Geography and History Activity 18 **L2**
- People to Meet Activity 18 **L2**
- Economics Activity 18 **L2**
- Citizenship and Service Learning Activity 18 **L2**

SPANISH RESOURCES

- Spanish Reading Essentials and Study Guide
- Spanish Guided Reading Activities
- Spanish Quizzes, Tests, and Authentic Assessment (with Rubrics)
- Spanish Take-Home Review Activities

MULTIMEDIA

- ExamView® Pro Testmaker CD-ROM
- Glencoe Skillbuilder Interactive Workbook CD-ROM, Level 1
- Interactive Tutor Self-Assessment CD-ROM
- MindJogger Videoquiz
- Presentation Plus! CD-ROM
- StudentWorks Plus™ CD-ROM (with Audio Program)
- TeacherWorks CD-ROM
- Vocabulary PuzzleMaker CD-ROM
- *World History: Journey Across Time* Video Program
- World History Primary Source Document Library CD-ROM

STANDARDIZED ASSESSMENT SKILLS

- Standardized Test Skills Practice Workbook Activity 18 **L2**
- Critical Thinking Skills Activity 18 **L2**

Teaching strategies have been coded with suggested ability levels. However, most are suitable for all levels.

L1 BASIC activities for all students

L2 AVERAGE activities for average to above-average students

L3 CHALLENGING activities for above-average students

EL ENGLISH LANGUAGE activities

Chapter 18 Resources

TIME MANAGEMENT

Chapter Introduction	Section 1	Section 2	Section 3	Section 4	Chapter Wrap-Up	Unit Wrap-Up
1 Day	2 Days	2 Days	2 Days	2 Days	1 Day	1 Day

Block Scheduling Activities that are suited to use within the block scheduling framework are identified by:

0:00 OUT OF TIME? Assign the Chapter 18 *Reading Essentials and Study Guide.**

SECTION RESOURCES

DAILY OBJECTIVES	REPRODUCIBLE RESOURCES	MULTIMEDIA RESOURCES
Section 1 **The Age of Exploration** 1. Social, political, and economic changes in the 1400s led to exploration and worldwide trade. 2. European explorers sailed to Asia, Africa, and the Americas.	Reproducible Lesson Plan 18–1 Vocabulary Activity 18–1 Guided Reading Activity 18–1* Section Quiz 18–1* Reading Essentials and Study Guide 18–1*	Daily Focus Skills Transparency 18–1 Interactive Tutor Self-Assessment CD-ROM Exam*View*® Pro Testmaker CD-ROM Presentation Plus! CD-ROM Glencoe BookLink CD-ROM
Section 2 **The Scientific Revolution** 1. The ancient world developed early forms of science. 2. European interest in science led to new discoveries.	Reproducible Lesson Plan 18–2 Vocabulary Activity 18–2 Guided Reading Activity 18–2* Section Quiz 18–2* Reading Essentials and Study Guide 18–2*	Daily Focus Skills Transparency 18–2 Interactive Tutor Self-Assessment CD-ROM Exam*View*® Pro Testmaker CD-ROM Presentation Plus! CD-ROM Glencoe BookLink CD-ROM
Section 3 **The Enlightenment** 1. Many Europeans believed that reason could improve government and society. 2. The Enlightenment was centered in France.	Reproducible Lesson Plan 18–3 Vocabulary Activity 18–3 Guided Reading Activity 18–3* Section Quiz 18–3* Reading Essentials and Study Guide 18–3*	Daily Focus Skills Transparency 18–3 Interactive Tutor Self-Assessment CD-ROM Exam*View*® Pro Testmaker CD-ROM Presentation Plus! CD-ROM Glencoe BookLink CD-ROM
Section 4 **The American Revolution** 1. British and French colonies in North America developed differently from each other. 2. The British colonies formed a new nation, the United States.	Reproducible Lesson Plan 18–4 Vocabulary Activity 18–4 Guided Reading Activity 18–4* Section Quiz 18–4* Reading Essentials and Study Guide 18–4*	Daily Focus Skills Transparency 18–4 Interactive Tutor Self-Assessment CD-ROM Exam*View*® Pro Testmaker CD-ROM Presentation Plus! CD-ROM Vocabulary PuzzleMaker CD-ROM

*Also available in Spanish

Use our Web site for additional resources. All essential content is covered in the Student Edition.

You and your students can visit jat.glencoe.com, the Web site companion to *World History: Journey Across Time*. This innovative integration of electronic and print media offers your students a wealth of opportunities. The student text directs students to the Web site for the following options:

- Chapter Overviews
- Self-Check Quizzes
- Study Central™
- Student Web Activities
- Multi-Language Glossaries

Answers to the student Web activities are provided for you in the **Web Activity Lesson Plans.** Additional Web resources and ePuzzles and games are also available.

The following videotape programs are available from Glencoe as supplements to Chapter 18:

Elizabeth I: The Virgin Queen
(ISBN 0-7670-0209-1)

Sir Isaac Newton: The Gravity of Genius
(ISBN 1-56501-982-2)

The American Revolution
(ISBN 1-56501-436-7)

To order, call Glencoe at 1-800-334-7344. To find classroom resources to accompany many of these videos, check the following home pages:

A&E Television: www.aande.com
The History Channel: www.historychannel.com

MEETING SPECIAL NEEDS

In addition to the Differentiated Instruction strategies, the following resources are suitable for students with special needs:

- *ExamView® Pro Testmaker CD-ROM* allows teachers to tailor tests by reducing answer choices.
- *StudentWorks Plus™ CD-ROM (with Audio Program)* includes the entire narrative of the student edition so that less-proficient readers can listen to the words as they read them.
- The *Reading Essentials and Study Guide* provides the same content as the student edition but is written two grade levels below the textbook.

Index to National Geographic Magazine:

The following articles relate to this chapter:

- "Last Voyage of the Slave Ship *Henrietta Marie*," by Jennifer Steinberg, August 2002.
- "Phips's Fleet," by R. James Ringer, August 2000.
- "Catherine the Great," by Erla Zwingle, September 1998.

National Geographic Society Products:

To order the following, call National Geographic at 1–800–368–2728

- *PicturePack: Geography of Europe* (Transparencies)
- *National Geographic Atlas of the World* (Book)

NGS ONLINE

Access National Geographic's new dynamic MapMachine Web site and other geography resources at:

www.nationalgeographic.com
www.nationalgeographic.com/maps

Meeting NCSS Standards

World History: Journey Across Time

The following standards are highlighted in Chapter 18:

Section 1	IV	**Individual Development and Identity: A, H, I**
	VII	**Production, Distribution, and Consumption: A, B, H, I**
	IX	**Global Connections: B, C, D, H**
Section 2	VIII	**Science, Technology, and Society: A, B, C, E**
Section 3	I	**Culture: D**
	II	**Time, Continuity, and Change: B, E**
	V	**Individuals, Groups, and Institutions: A, B, C, E, G, H**
	VI	**Power, Authority, and Governance: A, B, D, H, I**
Section 4	III	**People, Places, and Environments: B, H**
	X	**Civic Ideals and Practices: A, B, E**

State and Local Objectives

_____

_____

Timesaving Tools

All-In-One Planner and Resource Center

- **Interactive Teacher Edition** Access your Teacher Wraparound Edition and your classroom resources with a few easy clicks.

- **Interactive Lesson Planner** Organize your week, month, semester, or year with all the lesson helps you need to make teaching creative and relevant.

Use Glencoe's **Presentation Plus!** multimedia teacher tool to easily present dynamic lessons that visually excite your students. Using Microsoft PowerPoint® you can customize the presentations to create your own personalized lessons.

FOLDABLES™
Study Organizer
Dinah Zike's Foldables

Foldables are three-dimensional, interactive graphic organizers that help students practice basic writing skills, review key vocabulary terms, and identify main ideas. Every chapter contains a foldable activity, with additional chapter activities found in the *Reading and Study Skills Foldables* booklet. You can use the foldables as they are presented, or modify them to suit the needs of your individual class.

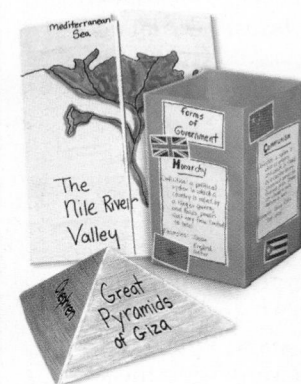

Planning Ahead

CHAPTER CULMINATING ACTIVITY

The Chapter Culminating Activity will help students organize and learn the important information from the chapter. Begin teaching the chapter with this activity, and have students complete it as a culminating activity.

CREATING A SEQUENCE CHART

Purpose Identifying and sequencing the events discussed in the chapter will help students see the general social, political, and economic trends that shaped the period of the Age of Exploration, the Enlightenment, the Scientific Revolution, and the European colonization of North America. Analyzing the events, with the goal of placing them in correct sequence, can also help students see causal relationships that cross national boundaries, as well as give them practice in logical and systematic thinking. In addition, this type of chart can be used to organize information for reports and as a study aid.

Introduction to Modeling

1. Begin the discussion with a brainstorming session. Ask students to list what they know or believe they know about the Age of Exploration, the Enlightenment, the Scientific Revolution, and the European colonization of North America. Write the information on an overhead transparency. Because of the large amount of information students may generate, you might want to split the activity into four parts, one focusing on each section of Chapter 18.

2. Ask students to copy this chart into their notebooks:

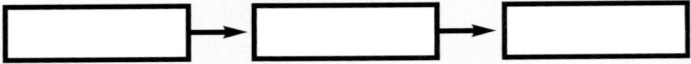

As students read the chapter, ask them to list important events. When they have finished reading the chapter, have them complete the boxes by writing in the events in the correct sequence. For example, students may want to begin with the Portuguese exploration of the coast of Africa. Remind students that they may have to collect events from the four sections before they can sequence them. Encourage them to add more boxes if necessary. Also, you might want to have students make four different sequence charts, one for each historical development.

3. As part of your chapter review, have students share their sequence charts. Encourage them to use their charts as study aids.

Refer to Activity 18 in the Authentic Assessment section of the *Quizzes, Tests, and Authentic Assessment (with Rubrics)* booklet.

When & Where?

As students read the chapter, have them review the time line on this page. Ask students to speculate about which event may have influenced the writing of the Declaration of Independence. *(John Locke writes about government)* **L1**

GLENCOE TECHNOLOGY

World History: Journey Across Time Video Program

To learn more about the important changes in the age of Enlightenment and Revolution, students can view the Chapter 18 video in the *World History: Journey Across Time* Video Program.

MindJogger Videoquiz

Use the **MindJogger Videoquiz** to preview Chapter 18 content.

 Available in DVD and VHS

Chapter 18

Enlightenment and Revolution

◀ A statue of Louis XIV on horseback outside of the palace of Versailles in France

NATIONAL GEOGRAPHIC When & Where?

1500	1600	1700	1800
1492 Columbus reaches the Americas	**1543** Copernicus supports idea of sun-centered universe	**1690** John Locke writes about government	**1776** Declaration of Independence is signed

---

▌ Reading Strategy PURPOSE FOR READING

Outlining Outlining may be used as a help for reading. Before students read the text, have them skim the chapter and write down the chapter section headings. Ask them to hypothesize about the purpose of these headings. *(to state main ideas)* Then ask students to label these headings with Roman numerals (I, I, III, and so on). Next, have students write down the subsection headings under each section heading and label them with capital letters. Explain that subsection headings represent the subtopics under each section heading, or main idea. As students read the chapter, they should write supporting details under each subtopic and label them with Arabic numerals. Each level should have at least two entries and should be indented from the level above. **L2**

Chapter Preview

By the end of the Renaissance, Europe and the rest of the world were entering a time of rapid change. Read this chapter to find out how voyages of exploration and scientific discoveries affected people in different parts of the world.

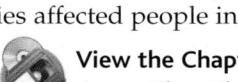 View the Chapter 18 video in the *World History: Journey Across Time* Video Program.

Chapter Overview Visit jat.glencoe.com for a preview of Chapter 18.

 Section 1

The Age of Exploration

In the 1400s, Europeans began to explore overseas and build empires. Trade increased and goods, technology, and ideas were exchanged around the world.

 Section 2

The Scientific Revolution

Scientific ideas and discoveries gave Europeans a new way to understand the universe.

 Section 3

The Enlightenment

During the 1700s, many Europeans believed that reason could be used to make government and society better.

 Section 4

The American Revolution

Britain and France established colonies in North America. Britain's American colonies eventually rebelled against Britain and formed a new nation, the United States.

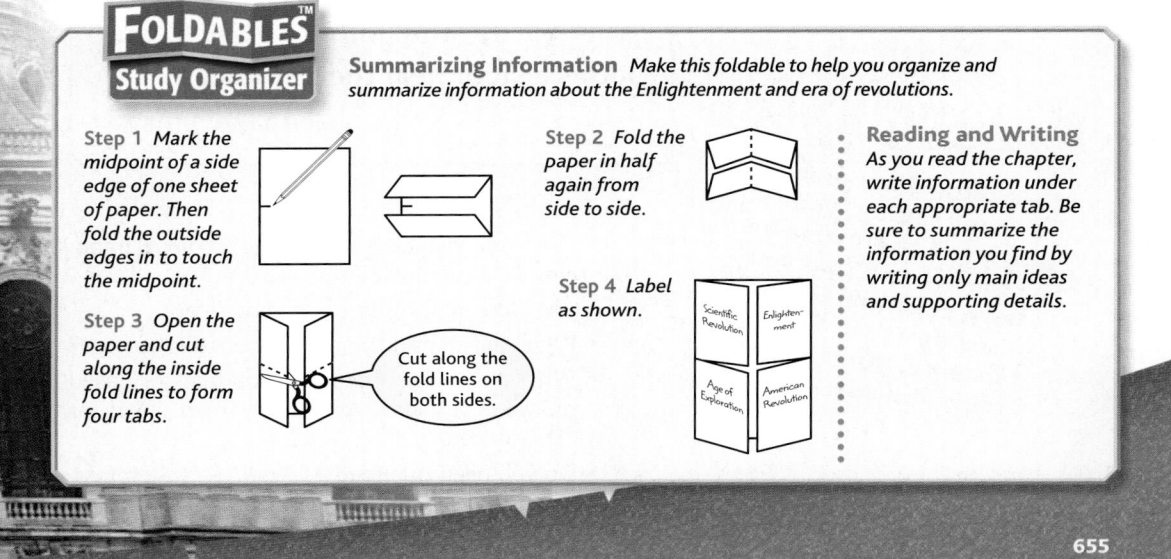

FOLDABLES™ Study Organizer

Summarizing Information *Make this foldable to help you organize and summarize information about the Enlightenment and era of revolutions.*

Step 1 *Mark the midpoint of a side edge of one sheet of paper. Then fold the outside edges in to touch the midpoint.*

Step 2 *Fold the paper in half again from side to side.*

Step 3 *Open the paper and cut along the inside fold lines to form four tabs.*

Cut along the fold lines on both sides.

Step 4 *Label as shown.*

Scientific Revolution | Enlightenment
Age of Exploration | American Revolution

Reading and Writing *As you read the chapter, write information under each appropriate tab. Be sure to summarize the information you find by writing only main ideas and supporting details.*

655

INTRODUCING CHAPTER 18

Introduce students to chapter content and key terms by having them access **Chapter Overview 18** at jat.glencoe.com

CHAPTER PREVIEW

After reading Chapter 18, students will be able to

1. summarize the causes and effects of the Age of Exploration;
2. discuss how science gave Europeans a new way to understand the universe;
3. describe how many Europeans came to believe that reason could improve government and society;
4. explain the events that led to the American Revolution and the formation of the United States.

FOLDABLES™ Study Organizer Dinah Zike's Foldables

Purpose Students use this foldable to organize information about notable dates and events. At the end of the chapter, students will use their foldables to make a question-and-answer game.

▱ Have students complete *Reading and Study Skills Foldables* Activity 18.

MORE ABOUT THE PHOTO

Palace of Versailles Versailles was the royal residence of French monarchs (except for one brief period) from 1682 until 1789 when the French Revolution began. Located outside of Paris, the palace was meant to be a home for King Louis XIV, France's most famous and powerful absolute monarch. During the time when royalty occupied Versailles, it was one of the most costly and extravagant buildings in the world. The land surrounding the palace was cleared for tree-lined terraces, decorative gardens, 1,400 fountains, and 400 pieces of sculpture. Today the Palace of Versailles is one of France's national monuments. The building is so large that only a small part of it is open to the public. Many of the rooms are government offices.

1 Learn It!

Tell students that some texts require a slow pace with sustained concentration, while others can be scanned quickly. Show students how to monitor and adjust their reading by modeling the following passage from page 676:

> In a book called *Principia*, published in 1687, Newton stated his laws, or well-tested theories, about the motion of objects in space and on Earth. The most important was the universal law of gravitation. It explains that the force of gravity holds the entire solar system together by keeping the sun and planets in their orbits.

1. Ask students to raise their hands when they do not understand something in the passage that you are going to read to them. Then read the passage to the class.

2. Stop reading when you see a hand raised. Ask the student to explain the comprehension problem.

3. Reread the sentence and ask if the problem is cleared up. If the student responds negatively, ask other questions to identify the problem.

4. Explain the word, sentence, or concept that the student does not understand. Use drawings or other aids as needed to help comprehension. **L1**

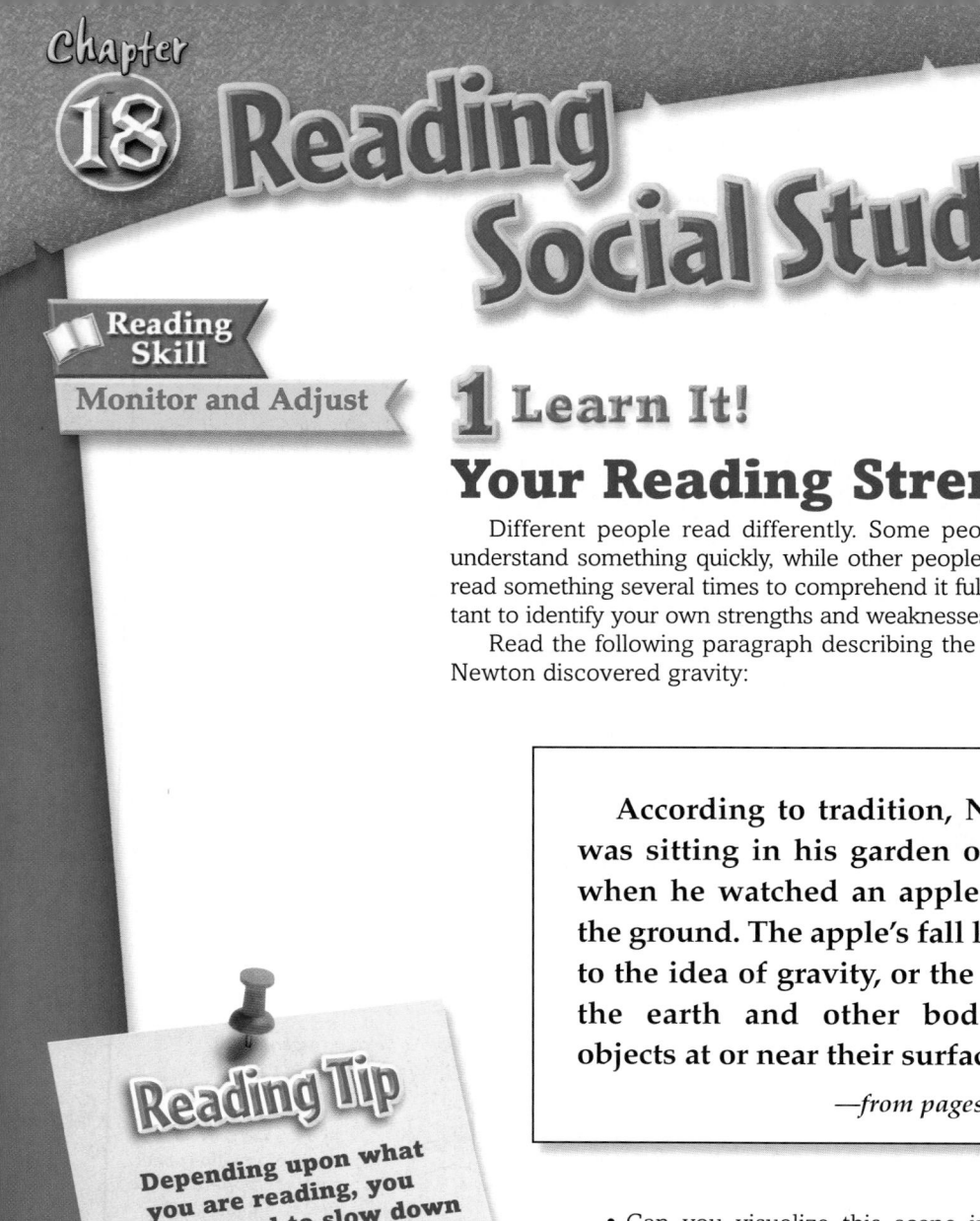

Chapter 18

Reading Social Studies

Reading Skill
Monitor and Adjust

1 Learn It!

Your Reading Strengths

Different people read differently. Some people read and understand something quickly, while other people may need to read something several times to comprehend it fully. It is important to identify your own strengths and weaknesses as a reader.

Read the following paragraph describing the story of how Newton discovered gravity:

> **According to tradition, Newton was sitting in his garden one day when he watched an apple fall to the ground. The apple's fall led him to the idea of gravity, or the pull of the earth and other bodies on objects at or near their surfaces.**
>
> —*from pages 675–676*

Reading Tip

Depending upon what you are reading, you may need to slow down or speed up. When you study, read more slowly. When you read for pleasure, you can read more quickly.

- Can you visualize this scene in your mind, almost like a movie?
- Are there any words you do not know?
- What questions do you have about this passage?
- What does this scene make you think of based on what you have previously read, seen, or experienced?
- Do you need to reread it?

656

Reading Strategy **THE METACOGNITIVE PROCESS**

Because the reading process is complex, help students learn to think about *how* they are reading. In this way, they can adapt to the skills needed for specific learning tasks. Help students recognize patterns, such as comparison/contrast and cause/effect, and keep graphic organizers on hand for students to use as they are making sense of new information. In addition, have students write often in order to understand more deeply. Above all, model prereading, during reading, and after reading strategies for students. **L1**

2 Practice It!

Improve Your Reading

The paragraph below appears in Section 3. Read the passage and answer the questions that follow.

> During the 1600s and 1700s, many European thinkers favored limits on government power. However, powerful kings and queens ruled most of Europe. This system was known as **absolutism.** In this system, monarchs held absolute, or total, power. They claimed to rule by divine right, or by the will of God. This meant that rulers did not answer to their people, but rather to God alone.
>
> —*from page 686*

- What words or sentences made you slow down as you read?
- Did you have to reread any parts?
- What questions do you still have after reading this passage?

Read to Write ·······

Choose one explorer, philosopher, or scientist that you were introduced to in this chapter. Write a list of questions that a modern talk-show host might ask if he or she interviewed this person.

▼ Catherine the Great

◄ Peter the Great

3 Apply It!

As you read the chapter, identify one paragraph in each section that is difficult to understand. Discuss each paragraph with a partner to improve your understanding.

657

2 Practice It!

Show students that identifying a reading problem when it first appears is a valuable tool for comprehension. First, post the following list on the board. It suggests actions that students can take to monitor and adjust comprehension.

- Stop and reread.
- Identify what you do not understand.
- Read slowly, paying attention to punctuation.
- Look at text graphics.
- Read for context clues.
- Ask someone else to read, and listen carefully.
- Ask for help.

Then ask volunteers to model how to apply one or more of these methods to the paragraph from page 686 or to other paragraphs.

3 Apply It!

At the end of the chapter, place students in groups of four. Have each group choose a facilitator and recorder. Tell students to identify problems they had with the text, as well as areas they found easy to comprehend. Ask the recorder to note the similarities and differences. Then allow time for group members to share ways to better understand difficult parts of the text. **L2**

Reading Strategy ❯ READ TO WRITE

Another way to monitor comprehension is to have students interact with the text. Having them write questions for an interview with a person they have read about will bring a human dimension to the text. Ask students to create at least five questions that they, as reporters, would ask one of the historical figures discussed in this chapter. Emphasize that students should choose someone about whom there is considerable information, so that they can base their questions on these facts. In addition, point out that as reporters they should act as though they have only heard the barest information about the selected individuals. For example, they might know that Magellan's ship has arrived in port or that Newton has developed some startling new theories. Then have students list their questions and possibly share their personal ones with the class. **L2**

① FOCUS

SECTION OVERVIEW

This section describes the factors that helped Europeans embark on an era of exploration, the nations that became involved in this exploration, and the methods they used to develop these new resources.

BELLRINGER
SKILLBUILDER ACTIVITY

✎ Project **Daily Focus Skills Transparency 18–1** and have students answer questions. Discuss their responses.

Get Ready to Read!

Preteaching Vocabulary: The words *import* and *export* are related. They both concern the movement of goods. The prefixes *in-* and *im-* mean "in" or "into," so to import something means to bring it into a country. The prefix *ex-* means "out of," so to export something means to send it out of a country. Remembering the word *exit* may help students recall the meaning of these two words.

Answers to Graphic: collapse of Mongol Empire; fall of Byzantine Empire; rising prices of Asian goods; new sailing technology; rise of strong kingdoms; new maps

---

Section 1

The Age of Exploration

Get Ready to Read!

What's the Connection?
You have learned how Italy's cities grew rich from trade. In the 1400s, other European states began exploring the world in search of wealth.

Focusing on the Main Ideas
• In the 1400s, trade, technology, and the rise of strong kingdoms led to a new era of exploration. *(page 659)*

• While the Portuguese explored Africa, the Spanish, English, and French explored America. *(page 661)*

• To increase trade, Europeans set up colonies and created joint-stock companies. *(page 666)*

• Exploration and trade led to a worldwide exchange of products, people, and ideas. *(page 668)*

Locating Places
Strait of Magellan (muh•JEH•luhn)
Netherlands (NEH•thuhr•luhnz)
Moluccas (muh•LUH•kuhz)

Meeting People
Vasco da Gama
Christopher Columbus
Magellan (muh•JEH•luhn)
John Cabot (KA•buht)
Jacques Cartier
(ZHAHK kahr•TYAY)

Building Your Vocabulary
mercantilism
(MUHR•kuhn•TUH•LIH•zuhm)
export (EHK•SPOHRT)
import (IHM•POHRT)
colony (KAH•luh•nee)
commerce (KAH•muhrs)
invest (ihn•VEHST)

Reading Strategy
Cause and Effect Complete a diagram like the one below showing why Europeans began to explore.

☐ ➤ ☐ ➤ ☐

NATIONAL GEOGRAPHIC When & Where?

1400	1500	1600

1420 Portugal begins mapping Africa's coast

1492 Columbus reaches the Americas

1520 Magellan's crew sails around the world

1588 England defeats the Armada

NORTH AMERICA • EUROPE • CHINA • AFRICA • INDIA • SOUTH AMERICA

SECTION RESOURCES

📁 **Reproducible Masters**
• Reproducible Lesson Plan 18–1
• Daily Lecture and Discussion Notes 18–1
• Vocabulary Activity 18–1
• Active Reading Note-Taking Guide 18–1
• Guided Reading Activity 18–1
• Section Quiz 18–1
• Reading Essentials and Study Guide 18–1

✎ **Transparencies**
• Daily Focus Skills Transparency 18–1

Multimedia
⊙ Interactive Tutor Self-Assessment CD-ROM
⊙ ExamView® Pro Testmaker CD-ROM
⊙ Presentation Plus! CD-ROM
⊙ Glencoe BookLink CD-ROM

Europe Gets Ready to Explore

Main Idea In the 1400s, trade, technology, and the rise of strong kingdoms led to a new era of exploration.

Reading Focus Do you like traveling to places that you have never been? Read to see why Western Europeans set off to explore the world.

In the 1400s and 1500s, nations in Western Europe began exploring the world. They soon gained control of the Americas and parts of India and Southeast Asia as well. Why did they begin exploring in the 1400s? Many events came together to create just the right conditions for exploration.

Trade With Asia As you have read, in the Middle Ages, Europeans began buying vast amounts of spices, silks, and other goods from Asia. In the 1400s, however, it became harder to get those goods.

First of all, the Mongol Empire had collapsed. The Mongols had kept the Silk Road running smoothly. When their empire collapsed, local rulers along the Silk Road imposed new taxes on merchants. This made Asian goods more expensive.

Next, the Ottoman Turks conquered the Byzantine Empire and blocked Italian merchants from entering the Black Sea. The Italians had trading posts on the coast of the Black Sea where they bought goods from Asia. Now, they could no longer reach them. They had to trade with the Turks instead, and this drove prices even higher.

Europeans still wanted the spices and silks of East Asia. Anyone who could find a way to get them cheaply would make a lot of money. Merchants began looking for a route to East Asia that bypassed the Middle East. If they could not get there by land, maybe they could get there by sea.

◀ Early compass

▲ European explorers and traders began to use smaller, faster ships called caravels in the 1400s. *What advantage did triangular sails offer a ship?*

Astrolabe ▲

New Technology Even though the Europeans wanted to go exploring, they could not do it without the right technology. The Atlantic Ocean was too dangerous and difficult to navigate.

By the 1400s, they had the technology they needed. From the Arabs, Europeans learned about the astrolabe and the compass. The astrolabe was an ancient Greek device that could be used to find latitude. The compass, invented by the Chinese, helped navigators find magnetic north.

Even with these new tools, the Europeans needed better ships. In the 1400s, they began using triangular sails developed by the Arabs. These sails let a ship zigzag into the wind.

CHAPTER 18 Enlightenment and Revolution **659**

② TEACH

Comparing and Contrasting New technologies helped spur an era of exploration in Europe in the 1400s. Ask students to think of modern technologies that have helped spur the exploration of different frontiers in our time. *(Possible answers: rocket technology for outer space; mountaineering equipment for mountainous regions)* **L2**

More About the Art

A typical caravel of the late 1400s was about 75 feet (23 m) long.

Caption Answer: allowed a ship to zigzag into the wind

Daily Lecture and Discussion Notes 18–1

Use **Daily Lecture and Discussion Notes 18–1** for an outline of key concepts found in the section.

Reading Support L1/ EL

Use **Vocabulary Activity 18–1** to review important terms in the section.

Reading Strategy **READING THE TEXT**

Previewing Review the strategy of previewing with students. **Ask:** How can previewing this section help you understand its contents? *(Previewing activates what students already know about the covered topics and helps them see what they will need to focus on in the section.)* Before students read this section, have them look over the title, headings, illustrations, maps, and other graphics. To develop a purpose for reading the section, ask students what they already know about topics highlighted in these elements and what they predict they will learn. **L2**

Using Word Parts Point out to students that the word *cartography* includes a Latin root (*carta* meaning "paper" or "map") and a Greek one (*graph* meaning "writing"). Ask students to think of other words using these roots. *(cartoon, autograph, photograph, phonograph)* Have students look up the words in a dictionary and report on how the root adds meaning to our word. **L2**

More About the Art

Prince Henry and his navigators were principally responsible for the great interest in exploring Africa during the 1400s.

Caption Answer: sailors, cartographers, and shipbuilders

✓ Reading Check

Answer: The cost of goods from Asia had risen due to the collapse of the Mongol and Byzantine Empires; new technology such as improved maps, an improved rudder, astrolabes, compasses, and triangular sails, were available; and strong kingdoms that could afford exploration arose.

▲ Prince Henry's school for navigation helped make possible the discovery of new water routes and new lands. Here, Prince Henry is shown watching for the return of his ships. *What types of professionals did Prince Henry invite to his research center?*

They also began building ships with many masts and smaller sails to make their ships go faster. A new type of rudder made steering easier. In the 1400s, these inventions came together in a Portuguese ship called the caravel. With ships like the caravel, Europeans could begin exploring the world.

The Rise of Strong Nations

Even with new technology, exploration was still expensive and dangerous. For most of the Middle Ages, Europe's kingdoms were weak and could not afford to explore. This situation began to change in the 1400s.

The rise of towns and trade helped make governments stronger. Kings and queens could tax the trade in their kingdom and then use the money to build armies and navies. Using their new power, they were able to build strong central governments.

By the end of the 1400s, four strong kingdoms—Portugal, Spain, France, and England—had developed in Europe. They had harbors on the Atlantic Ocean and were anxious to find a sea route to Asia. The question was where to go.

Did Maps Encourage Exploration?

By the 1400s, most educated people in Europe knew the world was round, but they only had maps of Europe and the Mediterranean. When the Renaissance began, however, people began to study ancient maps as well as books written by Arab scholars.

Twelve hundred years earlier, a Greek-educated Egyptian geographer named Claudius Ptolemy had drawn maps of the world. His book *Geography* was discovered by Europeans in 1406 and printed in 1475.

With the invention of the printing press, books like Ptolemy's could be printed and sold all over Europe. Ptolemy's ideas about cartography, or the science of mapmaking, were very influential. His basic system of longitude and latitude is still used today.

European cartographers also began reading a book written by al-Idrisi, an Arab geographer. Al-Idrisi had published a book in 1154 showing the parts of the world known to Muslims. By studying the works of al-Idrisi and Ptolemy, Europeans learned the geography of East Africa and the Indian Ocean. If they could find a way around Africa, they could get to Asia.

✓ **Reading Check** **Summarize** What were the main reasons the Europeans began exploring the world in the 1400s?

DIFFERENTIATED INSTRUCTION

Logical/Mathematical: Have students research and explain how a compass and an astrolabe work. Ask them to supplement their discussions with charts, diagrams, models, or any other visual aids that will make their explanations clearer.

English Learners: Ask students to make a list of terms related to navigation, directions, and travel. Have them write the words and definitions on index cards.

Gifted and Talented: Have students research and present information on contemporary technologies that have replaced and/or surpassed the compass and the astrolabe.

📁 Refer to *Inclusion Strategies for the Middle School Social Studies Classroom* in the TCR.

Exploring the World

Main Idea While the Portuguese explored Africa, the Spanish, English, and French explored America.

Reading Focus Have you ever done something daring or tried something new not knowing how it would turn out? Read to learn how European explorers took chances and went places no Europeans had ever been before.

By the early 1400s, Europeans were ready to explore. England and France were still fighting each other, however, and Spain was still fighting the Muslims. This gave Portugal the chance to explore first.

Who Was Henry the Navigator? In 1419 Prince Henry of Portugal, known as "Henry the Navigator," set up a research center in southern Portugal. He invited sailors, cartographers, and shipbuilders to come and help him explore the world.

In 1420 Portugal began mapping Africa's coastline and trading with Africa's kingdoms. It also seized the Azores (AY•ZOHRZ), Madeira (muh•DIHR•uh), and Cape Verde islands. Soon after, the Portuguese discovered sugarcane would grow on the islands.

Sugar was very valuable in Europe. To work their sugarcane fields, the Portuguese began bringing enslaved Africans to the islands. This was the beginning of a slave trade that would eventually bring millions of enslaved people to the Americas as well.

In 1488 the Portuguese explorer Bartolomeu Dias reached the southern tip of Africa. Nine years later, **Vasco da Gama** (VAS•koh dah GA•muh) rounded the tip of Africa, raced across the Indian Ocean, and landed on India's coast. A water route to East Asia had at last been found.

Santa María

The *Santa María*, Columbus's flagship, was larger and slower than the other two ships on the voyage. *What islands might Columbus have explored on his first voyage to the Americas?*

Crow's Nest
The crow's nest served as a platform for a lookout.

Captain's Cabin
This room served as Columbus's dining room, bedroom, and study.

Upper Deck
Sailors slept and cooked their meals on the upper deck.

Hold
Food, fresh water, and supplies for the voyage filled the ship's hold.

CRITICAL THINKING ACTIVITY

Drawing Conclusions Have students arrange a debate about this statement: Christopher Columbus was a hero. Students should choose teams to support both an affirmative and a negative position on the statement and to research their position. Leave time after the debate for a discussion of the issues that are raised. You may also want to have the audience vote on which team better presented its position. **L2**

Reading Primary/Secondary Sources Have students research the life and achievements of Portugal's Prince Henry. Ask them to share their findings with the class. Then have the class suggest modern-day counterparts of Henry the Navigator in different fields. **L3**

Mental Mapping The Portuguese mapped the west coast of Africa. Ask students why this task might have been difficult in the 1400s. *(lack of aerial photography, modern surveying equipment, and computers)* Then ask students to draw a map of the outer borders of your town or city. Have students discuss what they found difficult about the task. **L1**

More About the Art

When he was 26, Henry was made head of a special religious organization, sponsored by the pope. This organization, the Order of Christ, had the goal of converting non-Christians to Christianity. Because the order paid for much of Henry's exploration activities, his ships always had a red cross on their sails.

Caption Answer: Cuba, Hispaniola

TIME TRAVELER

Columbus died a disappointed man, in spite of his accomplishments. He lost his job as governor of Hispaniola in 1499. His patron Isabella died in 1504, and Ferdinand did not have the same high opinion of him. Columbus's last years were spent trying to regain his command. He died in 1506.

GLENCOE BOOKLINK

Use **Glencoe BookLink** to create customized reading lists for your students' reading levels, interests, and abilities.

NATIONAL GEOGRAPHIC | **European Exploration of the World**

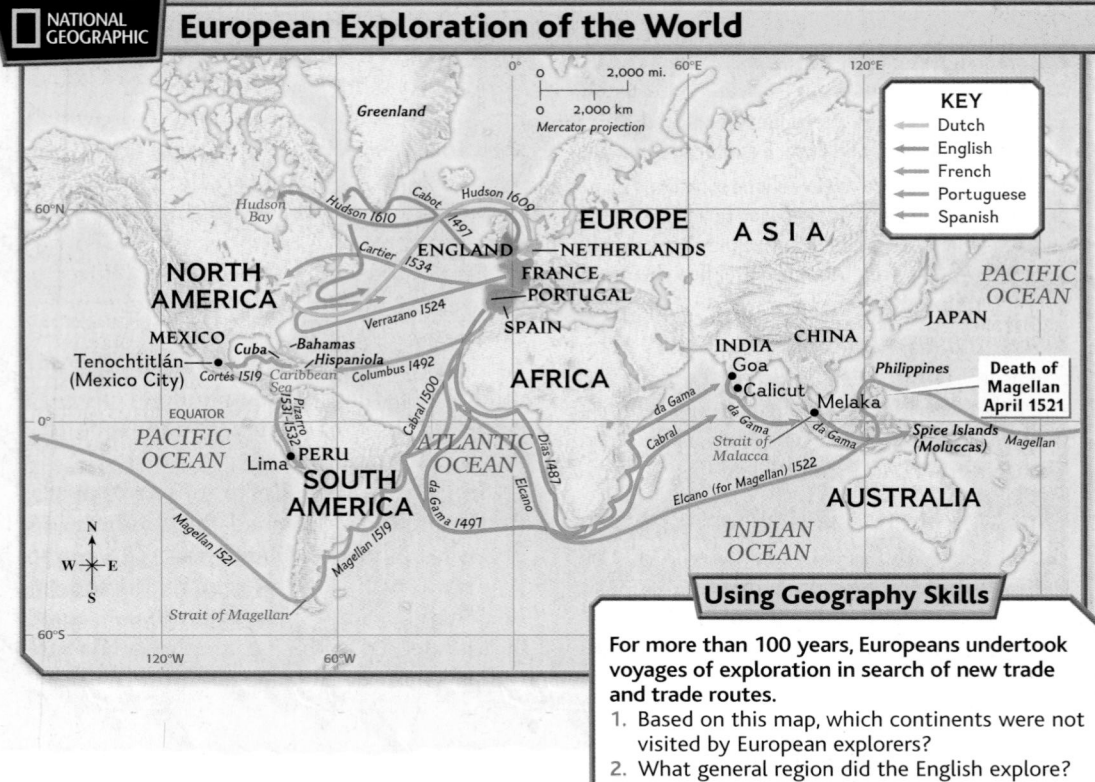

Using Geography Skills

For more than 100 years, Europeans undertook voyages of exploration in search of new trade and trade routes.

1. Based on this map, which continents were not visited by European explorers?
2. What general region did the English explore?

Find NGS online map resources @ www.nationalgeographic.com/maps

---

Christopher Columbus While the Portuguese explored Africa, an Italian navigator named **Christopher Columbus** came up with a daring plan to get to Asia. He would sail across the Atlantic Ocean.

Columbus needed money to make the trip. The rulers of Portugal, England, and France all turned him down. Finally in 1492 Ferdinand and Isabella of Spain said yes. Earlier that year, they had finally driven the Muslims out of Spain. They could now afford to pay for exploration.

Columbus outfitted three ships: the *Santa María*, the *Niña*, and the *Pinta*. In 1492 they left Spain and headed west. As the weeks passed, the crew grew desperate. Finally they sighted land, probably the island of San Salvador. Columbus claimed the land for Spain and then explored the nearby islands of Cuba and Hispaniola.

Columbus thought he was in Asia. He made three more voyages to the region but never realized he had arrived in the Americas. Eventually, Europeans realized they had reached two huge continents.

Who Was Magellan? Many Spaniards explored the Americas in the 1500s, but only Ferdinand **Magellan** (muh•JEH•luhn) tried to finish what Columbus had set out to do. In 1520 he left Spain and headed west to sail around the Americas and then all the way to Asia.

Magellan sailed south along South America. Finally, he found a way around the continent. The passage he found is named the **Strait of Magellan** (muh•JEH•luhn).

662   CHAPTER 18   Enlightenment and Revolution

INTERDISCIPLINARY CONNECTIONS ACTIVITY

Economics Point out to students that entrepreneurship, investment, and business ventures similar to the joint-stock company still form the basis of the economic system in the United States today. Have students find articles on the Internet or in books, newspapers, and magazines that explain how stocks are bought and sold and how entrepreneurs make profits from investments. **L2**

Analyzing Maps Have students consider the maps on this page. **Ask:** Which explorer traveled the western coast of North America? When? (*Cabrillo; 1542–1543*) L1/ EL

Important European Explorers

Christopher Columbus	Vasco da Gama	Ferdinand Magellan	Jacques Cartier	Henry Hudson
Voyages: 1492, 1493, 1498, 1502	Voyage: 1497–1499	Voyage: 1519–1522	Voyages: 1534, 1535, 1541	Voyages: 1607, 1608, 1609, 1610
First European to sail west searching for a water route to Asia	First European to sail around the south of Africa and reach India	Led the first expedition to sail completely around the world	Explored the St. Lawrence River	Explored the Hudson River and Hudson Bay

After passing through the stormy strait, his ship entered a vast sea. It was so peaceful, or pacific, that he named the sea the Pacific Ocean.

Magellan then headed west. His sailors nearly starved and had to eat leather, sawdust, and rats. Finally, after four months at sea, they reached the Philippines. After local people killed Magellan, his crew continued west across the Indian Ocean, around Africa, and back to Spain. They became the first known people to circumnavigate (suhr•kuhm•NA•vuh•GAYT), or sail around, the world.

The First English and French Explorers

As the news spread about Columbus's journey, England decided to search for a northern route to Asia. In 1497 an English ship commanded by **John Cabot** (KA•buht) headed across the Atlantic.

Cabot arrived at a large island he named Newfoundland. He then traveled south

CHAPTER 18 Enlightenment and Revolution 663

Writing Activity

Have students write a short dialogue between a European explorer of the Age of Exploration and a space scientist or astronaut of our own time. L3

CURRICULUM CONNECTION

Geography
The names of European explorers live on in names of geographic features in the places they visited. Have students use the index of an atlas to compile a list of places that are named after explorers discussed in this section. (*Strait of Magellan, Verrazano Narrows, Cabot Strait, Jacques Cartier Passage*)

EXTENDING THE CONTENT

The Northwest Passage For centuries, explorers hoped they would find an easy sea route to Asia by traveling northwest through or beyond North America. They called this route the Northwest Passage. In 1497 Henry VII of England sent John Cabot to search for it. The search for the Northwest Passage claimed many lives, including those of Henry Hudson and his young son. The deadliest expedition was the 1845 voyage of Sir John Franklin. The Englishman, along with 128 members of his crew, perished in the ice floes near King William Island, halfway between the Pacific and Atlantic Oceans.

▲ To defeat the Spanish Armada, the English sent ships that had been set on fire toward the Spanish warships. *Why was the defeat of the Spanish Armada important?*

along the coast of present-day Canada but did not find a path through to Asia. Cabot disappeared on his second trip and was never heard from again.

In 1524 France sent Giovanni da Verrazano to map America's coast and find a route through to Asia. Verrazano mapped from what is today North Carolina north to Newfoundland but found no path to Asia.

Ten years later, the French tried again. This time they sent **Jacques Cartier** (ZHAHK kahr•TYAY). Cartier sailed past Newfoundland and entered the St. Lawrence River. Hoping he had found a passage to Asia, Cartier made two more trips to map the St. Lawrence River. After these trips, France stopped exploring. By the mid-1500s, French Protestants and Catholics were fighting a civil war. There was no more exploring until it was settled.

Spain Fights England After Columbus, the Spanish went on to build a vast empire in America. They forced enslaved Native Americans to grow sugarcane and mine gold and silver. Later they brought enslaved Africans to the region to work on their farms.

Spanish nobles called conquistadors traveled to America in the hopes of becoming rich. Hernán Cortés conquered the Aztec, and Francisco Pizarro conquered the Inca. Soon after their victories, vast amounts of gold and silver began to flow to Europe from Spain's empire in America.

Meanwhile, England had become Spain's enemy. As you have read, in 1534 King Henry VIII of England broke from the Catholic Church and made his kingdom Protestant. By the 1560s, the Dutch had become Protestant, too, even though they were part of Spain's empire at that time. Spain was strongly Catholic and tried to stop Protestantism in the **Netherlands** (NEH•thuhr•luhnz). When the Dutch people rebelled against Spain, England came to their aid.

To help the Dutch, Queen Elizabeth I of England let English privateers attack Spanish ships. Privateers are privately owned ships that have a license from the government to attack ships of other countries. People nicknamed the English privateers "sea dogs." They raided the Spanish treasure ships that were bringing gold back from America.

England's raids frustrated Philip II, the king of Spain. In 1588 he sent a huge fleet known as the Spanish Armada to invade England. In July 1588, the Armada headed into the English Channel—the narrow body of water between England and Europe. The Spanish ships were large and had many guns, but they were hard to steer. The smaller English ships moved much more quickly. Their attacks forced the Armada to retreat north. There a great storm arose and broke up the Armada.

The defeat of the Spanish Armada was an important event. The Spanish were still strong, but England now had the power to stand up to them. This encouraged the English and Dutch to begin exploring both North America and Asia.

☑ **Reading Check** **Identify** Who was the first European to sail to India? Whose crew was first to sail around the world?

COOPERATIVE LEARNING ACTIVITY

Calling All Entrepreneurs Have students review the material on the creation of joint-stock companies and the role they played in the Age of Exploration. Then ask a group of students to write a charter (plan) for a joint-stock company. In it they should describe the nature of the trading business; the investments, responsibilities, risks, and rewards of the various members; and other relevant information. **L3**

Biography

ELIZABETH I
1533–1603

Elizabeth I is one of the most popular British rulers—but she was more loved by the people of England than by her father, King Henry VIII. Elizabeth's young life was filled with change and sadness. She was born to Henry VIII and his second wife, Anne Boleyn. The king was upset when Elizabeth was born, because he wanted a boy to inherit the throne.

When Elizabeth became queen, she surrounded herself with intelligent advisers. Together they turned England into a strong, prosperous country. Elizabeth supported Protestantism in England and in the rest of Europe. She sent aid to the French Huguenots and Protestants in Scotland and the Netherlands. She worked well with Parliament but called few sessions during her reign. She was a skilled writer and speaker and won the love and support of the English people.

Elizabeth never married, which was unusual at that time. Many men were interested in marrying her, but she turned down their proposals. One reason Elizabeth probably remained single was to maintain control of the government at a time when most rulers were men. She also used her status to the advantage of England. Many prominent men wanted to marry her, and she sometimes threatened to marry someone's enemy in order to get him to do what she wanted.

Elizabeth's personality also influenced England's society. She loved horse riding, dances, parties, and plays. Her support of the arts resulted in the development of new English literature and music. Elizabeth was so popular by the time of her death that the date she became queen was celebrated as a national holiday for 200 years.

▲ Queen Elizabeth I

> "I have the heart and stomach of a king and of a king of England, too."
>
> –Elizabeth I, "Armada Speech"

Then and Now

Even though Queen Elizabeth I had an unhappy childhood, she overcame it to become one of England's most popular leaders. Today England's Queen Elizabeth II has also faced sad situations. Research her life and write a short essay comparing her life to the life of Elizabeth I.

665

TEACH

Elizabeth might never have come to the throne of England. Her younger brother, Edward, was only nine when he became king after Henry's death in 1547. Edward lived barely six years and was followed by Elizabeth's older sister, Mary. Known as "Bloody Mary" for her persecutions of Protestants, the Catholic Mary was opposed by many of her subjects. When Mary died in 1558, the 25-year-old Elizabeth became queen.

Ask students to consider how the way she came to the throne might have affected Elizabeth's ideas about governing. (*She might have viewed the instability and religious conflict of the 1550s as something to avoid during her own reign.*) **L2**

Then and Now

Answers may include the tragic death of Princess Diana, the deaths of her mother and sister in her Golden Jubilee year, public criticism, and a fire in Windsor Castle. She was also a princess during World War II, when her country was bombed by the Germans.

RECOMMENDED READING

Use the **Glencoe BookLink CD-ROM** to create customized reading lists based on your students' interests and reading levels. Below is an example based on content in this chapter. Also, see the Suggested Readings on pages 944–946 of the Appendix.

- Alper, Ann Fitzpatrick. *Forgotten Voyager: The Story of Amerigo Vespucci.* Biography of the explorer whose name was given to two continents.
- Goodman, Joan Elizabeth. *Beyond the Sea of Ice: The Voyages of Henry Hudson.* Account of the explorer's four voyages.
- Stanley, Diane, and Peter Vennema. *Good Queen Bess: The Story of Elizabeth I of England.* A biography of one of England's greatest monarchs.

The Commercial Revolution

Main Idea To increase trade, Europeans set up colonies and created joint-stock companies.

Reading Focus Do you know anyone who works at home? Read to learn how merchants in the 1600s gave people jobs at home and changed the world trade system.

While Spain built its empire in America, Portugal began building a trading empire in Asia. In 1500, shortly after Vasco da Gama's trip, the Portuguese sent 13 ships back to India. Led by Pedro Alvares Cabral (PAY•throo AHL•vahr•ihs kuh•BRAHL), the Portuguese fought a war against the Muslim merchants in the Indian Ocean.

After defeating the Arab fleet, the Portuguese built trading posts in India, China, Japan, the Persian Gulf, and in the **Moluccas** (muh•LUH•kuhz), or Spice Islands of Southeast Asia. From these bases, they controlled most of southern Asia's sea trade.

What Is Mercantilism? As Europeans watched Spain and Portugal grow wealthy from their empires, they tried to figure out how they had become rich. They came up with the idea of **mercantilism** (MUHR•kuhn•TUH•LIH•zuhm). Mercantilism is the idea that a country gains power by building up its supply of gold and silver. Mercantilists believe the best way to do this is to **export** (EHK•SPOHRT), or sell to other countries, more goods than you **import** (IHM•POHRT), or buy from them. If you export more than you import, more gold and silver flows in from other countries than goes out.

Mercantilists also thought countries should set up colonies. A **colony** (KAH•luh•nee) is a settlement of people living in a new territory controlled by their home country. Colonists are supposed to produce goods their country does not have at home. That

▲ These ships sailed for the Dutch East India Company, which carried out trade in Asia. *Which European nation did the Dutch replace in the spice trade?*

way, the home country will not have to import those goods from other countries.

Trade Empires in Asia Mercantilism encouraged Europeans to set up trading posts and colonies in Asia and North America. By the end of the 1500s, Spain had set up a colony in the Philippines. The Spanish shipped silver to the Philippines from America and then used it to buy Asian spices and silk for sale in Europe.

In the 1600s, English and French merchants landed in India and began trading with the people there. In 1619 the Dutch built a fort on the island of Java, in what is now Indonesia. They slowly pushed the Portuguese out of the spice trade.

What Are Joint-Stock Companies? Trading overseas was very expensive. In the 1600s, however, new ways of doing business developed in Europe. Historians call this the "commercial revolution." **Commerce** (KAH•muhrs) is the buying and selling of goods in large amounts over long distances.

EXTENDING THE CONTENT

Top Dog The most famous English privateer, or sea dog, was Sir Francis Drake. Drake (1543–1590), who as a child lived in a rotting boat hull, went to sea at age 13 and learned to sail. Early in his career, Drake formed a hatred of Spain, and he later played an important role in the defeat of the Spanish Armada. He became a privateer in 1572 and plundered gold and silver from Spanish colonies and ships. In the years 1577–1580, he became the first man to sail his own ship around the world. The feat is even more amazing because his famous ship, the *Golden Hind,* was overloaded with plunder. When he returned to England, Queen Elizabeth I paid him the great honor of coming aboard the *Golden Hind* and knighting him.

To trade goods long distance, merchants needed a lot of money. They had to buy many goods, store them in warehouses, and ship them over land and sea. They had to know what people in distant lands wanted to buy and what prices were like there.

This new business created a new type of businessperson called an entrepreneur. Entrepreneurs **invest** (ihn•VEHST), or put money into a project. Their goal is to make even more money when the project is done.

Many projects were so large that a group of entrepreneurs had to come together and form a joint-stock company. A joint-stock company is a business that people can invest in by buying a share of the company. These shares are called stocks.

What Is the Cottage Industry?
To trade over a long distance, merchants need a large supply of goods. They also have to buy goods at low prices so they can make money selling them at higher prices elsewhere.

By the 1600s, merchants had become frustrated by artisans and guilds. They charged too much and could not make goods fast enough. So merchants began asking peasants to make goods for them. In particular, they asked the peasants to make wool cloth. The peasants were happy to make extra money and glad to find work they could do in their homes.

This system was called the "putting out" system. Merchants would buy wool and put it out to the peasants. This system is also sometimes called the "cottage industry," because the small houses where peasants lived were called cottages.

✓ **Reading Check** **Explain** How did merchants raise the money for overseas trade?

CONNECTING ACROSS TIME

Tell students that cottage industries still exist, even in the developed world. Explain that a famous kind of heavy wool cloth, Harris tweed, is woven by cottage weavers on the island of Harris in the Scottish Hebrides. Have students find information about Harris tweed and other products made by cottage industries today. **L2**

Writing Activity

Have students interview someone who works at home. Tell them to ask about its advantages and disadvantages. Then ask students to write a report and share it with the class. **L2**

✓ **Reading Check**

Answer: They created joint-stock companies.

Using Geography Skills

Answers:
1. England, France, Portugal, and the Netherlands
2. the Netherlands

Skills Practice

Ask: Why do you think that almost all the trading colonies were on coastlines? *(It was easier and more efficient to build colonies near water for ease of transportation.)*

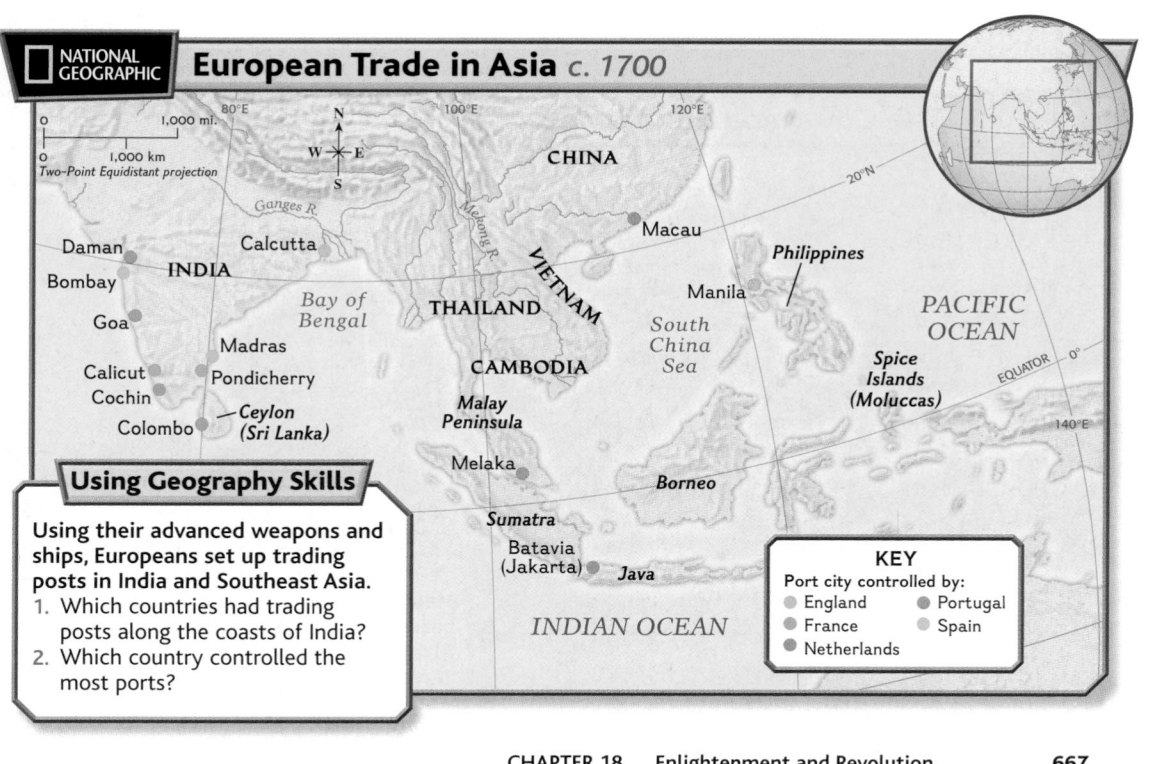

NATIONAL GEOGRAPHIC
European Trade in Asia c. 1700

Using Geography Skills

Using their advanced weapons and ships, Europeans set up trading posts in India and Southeast Asia.
1. Which countries had trading posts along the coasts of India?
2. Which country controlled the most ports?

KEY
Port city controlled by:
- England
- France
- Netherlands
- Portugal
- Spain

CHAPTER 18   Enlightenment and Revolution   667

DIFFERENTIATED INSTRUCTION

Visual/Spatial: Ask students to make cause-and-effect graphics to show how the Columbian Exchange affected people's ways of life. For example, the introduction of tomatoes into Italy led to the use of tomato sauces in cooking.

Naturalist: Tell students to investigate one or more of the plants that were part of the Columbian Exchange and share the results of their research in a display. For example, students could write questions on a poster and show the answers. Some possibilities are an illustration of a peanut plant or an explanation of how quinine is obtained.

📁 Refer to *Inclusion Strategies for the Middle School Social Studies Classroom* in the TCR.

A Global Exchange

Main Idea Exploration and trade led to a world-wide exchange of products, people, and ideas.

Reading Focus Have you heard about insects from other countries that hurt American crops? Read to learn how the movement of goods and people between America and the rest of the world caused great changes.

After the Age of Exploration, the economies of Europe, Africa, Asia, and America changed. As Europe traded with the world, a global exchange of people, goods, technology, ideas, and even diseases began. We call this transfer the Columbian Exchange, after Christopher Columbus.

Two important foods—corn and potatoes—were taken to Europe from North America. Corn was used to feed animals. Larger, healthier animals resulted in more meat, leather, and wool. The potato was also important. Europeans discovered that if they planted potatoes instead of grain, about four times as many people could live off the same amount of land.

Other American foods, such as squash, beans, and tomatoes, also made their way to Europe. Tomatoes greatly changed cooking in Italy, where tomato sauces became very popular. Chocolate was a popular food from Central America. By mixing it with milk and sugar, Europeans created a sweet that is still popular today.

Some American foods, such as chili peppers and peanuts, were taken to Europe, but they also made their way to Asia and Africa where they became popular. Both Europeans and Asians also began smoking tobacco, an American plant.

Many European and Asian grains, such as wheat, oats, barley, rye, and rice, were planted in the Americas. Coffee and tropical fruits, such as bananas, were brought to America as well. Eventually, coffee and

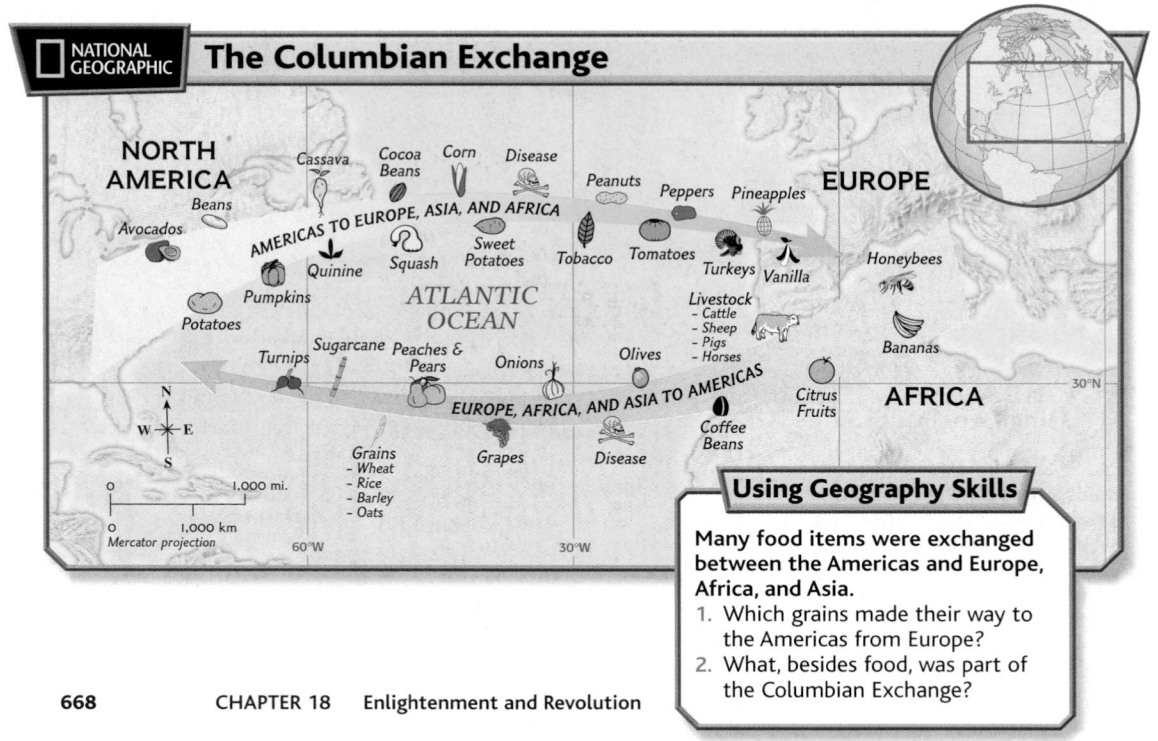

NATIONAL GEOGRAPHIC

The Columbian Exchange

NORTH AMERICA — Cassava — Cocoa Beans — Corn — Disease — Beans — Avocados — Quinine — Squash — Sweet Potatoes — Tobacco — Tomatoes — Turkeys — Vanilla — Peanuts — Peppers — Pineapples — EUROPE — Honeybees — Pumpkins — Potatoes — Turnips — Sugarcane — Peaches & Pears — Onions — Olives — Livestock - Cattle - Sheep - Pigs - Horses — Bananas

AMERICAS TO EUROPE, ASIA, AND AFRICA

ATLANTIC OCEAN

EUROPE, AFRICA, AND ASIA TO AMERICAS

Grains - Wheat - Rice - Barley - Oats — Grapes — Disease — Coffee Beans — Citrus Fruits — AFRICA

0 1,000 mi.
0 1,000 km
Mercator projection
60°W   30°W   30°N

Using Geography Skills

Many food items were exchanged between the Americas and Europe, Africa, and Asia.

1. Which grains made their way to the Americas from Europe?
2. What, besides food, was part of the Columbian Exchange?

CRITICAL THINKING ACTIVITY

Please, Your Majesty Have students place themselves in this scenario: They are explorers during the Age of Exploration. Their task is to convince a king or queen to pay for their voyage of exploration. Have them write a speech they could give to the monarch to convince him or her to underwrite the voyage. Remind them to include a description of the potential benefits as well as a reasonable assessment of the risks. Have students read their speeches to the class. Let the class decide which explorers to finance. **L2**

banana farms employed thousands of workers in Central and South America.

New animals such as pigs, sheep, cattle, chickens, and horses were also brought to America. Chickens changed the diet of many people in Central and South America, while horses changed the lives of Native Americans on the Great Plains. Horses provided a faster way to move from place to place. As a result, Native Americans began hunting buffalo as their main food source.

A huge movement of people also took place after Europeans obtained sugarcane from Asia and began growing it in the Caribbean. To plant and harvest the sugarcane, they enslaved millions of Africans and moved them to the Americas.

Europeans also changed Asian society. With their guns and powerful ships, the Europeans easily defeated Arab fleets and Indian princes. Across Asia, the Europeans forced local rulers to let them set up trading posts. Within a short time, the East India Company of England had built an empire in India, and the Dutch East India Company had built an empire in Indonesia.

The arrival of the Europeans in Japan also changed that society. Using guns and cannons imported from Europe, a new shogun was finally able to defeat the feudal lords, the daimyo, and reunite Japan.

Not everything exchanged between Europe and America was good. When Europeans arrived in America, they were carrying germs that could kill Native Americans. Many diseases, including smallpox, measles, and malaria, swept across the Americas killing millions of people.

✓ **Reading Check** **Describe** Describe the Columbian Exchange.

History Online
Study Central™ Need help with the material in this section? Visit jat.glencoe.com

Section ❶ Review

Reading Summary
Review the Main Ideas

- Rising prices of Asian goods, strong central governments, and new sailing technology led to European exploration of the world.
- Portugal found a route to India while Spain, England, and France explored America.
- Europeans used joint-stock companies to build colonies and trading posts in Asia following the ideas of mercantilism.
- European exploration and trade brought about a global exchange of goods, technology, and disease.

What Did You Learn?

1. What was a caravel, and why was it important?

2. Describe the accomplishments of Ferdinand Magellan.

Critical Thinking

3. **Organize Information** Draw a chart like the one below. Use it to name the explorers discussed in this section, the country they sailed for, and the places they explored.

Explorer	Country Sailed for	Area Explored

4. **Summarize** Describe the development of the African slave trade.

5. **Understand Cause and Effect** Why did merchants create joint-stock companies and use cottage industries?

6. **Analyze** How did foods imported from the Americas benefit Europe? Identify some of those foods.

7. **Reading** **Monitor and Adjust** Write a 10-question multiple choice test to help you review the important information in this section. Exchange tests with a classmate.

CHAPTER 18   Enlightenment and Revolution   669

ENRICH

Have students research and report to the class on the voyages of an explorer discussed in this section. **L3**

Answer: trading links between the Americas, Europe, and Africa; the Americas received plants and animals from Europe and Africa, while Europe received plants and animals from the Americas

To help students understand section material, have them visit **Study Central**™ at jat.glencoe.com

RETEACH

Help students create a graphic that summarizes the subsection "Europe Gets Ready to Explore." **L1**

❹ CLOSE

Write on the board the words *gold, glory,* and *God.* Have students discuss how each word applies to the explorers' motives. **L2**

SECTION 1 REVIEW ANSWERS

1. a small ship that used triangular sails; could zigzag into the wind

2. traveled around the tip of South America; his crew was the first to sail around the world

3. Answers should include explorers for Portugal, Spain, England, and France and be based on the text.

4. Europeans brought enslaved persons from Africa to work on sugarcane plantations in the Americas.

5. to raise money for long-distance trade; to produce cheap goods in large quantities

6. Corn was used to feed animals; potatoes became part of European diet; population became better fed.

7. Tests will vary but should be based on the text.

1 FOCUS

SECTION OVERVIEW

In this section, students will learn about the great advances that contributed to the Scientific Revolution.

BELLRINGER
SKILLBUILDER ACTIVITY

✎ Project **Daily Focus Skills Transparency 18–2** and have students answer questions. Discuss their responses.

Get Ready to Read!

Preteaching Vocabulary: Explain that the way that students carry out experiments in science class is based on the scientific method first developed in the 1500s and 1600s.

Answers to Graphic: Ptolemy: Earth is at the center of the universe; Copernicus: Sun is at the center of the universe; Both: explained how the universe worked.

Section 2
The Scientific Revolution

Get Ready to Read!

What's the Connection?

One result of the Renaissance was a new interest in science. During the 1600s, people began to observe, experiment, and reason to find new knowledge.

Focusing on the Main Ideas

* The thinkers of the ancient world developed early forms of science and passed this knowledge to later civilizations. *(page 671)*

* European interest in astronomy led to new discoveries and ideas about the universe and Earth's place in it. *(page 673)*

* The Scientific Revolution led to new discoveries in physics, medicine, and chemistry. *(page 675)*

* Using the scientific method, Europeans of the 1600s and 1700s developed new ideas about society based on reason. *(page 678)*

Meeting People
Ptolemy (TAH•luh•mee)
Copernicus (koh•PUHR•nih•kuhs)
Kepler (KEH•pluhr)
Galileo (GA•luh•LEE•oh)
Newton (NOO•tuhn)
Descartes (day•KAHRT)

Building Your Vocabulary
theory (THEE•uh•ree)
rationalism (RASH•nuh•LIH•zuhm)
scientific method
hypothesis (hy•PAH•thuh•suhs)

Reading Strategy
Compare and Contrast Use a diagram like the one below to show the similarities and differences in the views of Ptolemy and Copernicus.

Ptolemy   Copernicus

NATIONAL GEOGRAPHIC **When & Where?**

1500   1600   1700

London
Paris
Florence
Rome

1543 Copernicus supports sun-centered solar system

1632 Galileo publishes work supporting Copernicus's ideas

1687 Isaac Newton states laws about motion and gravity

SECTION RESOURCES

📁 **Reproducible Masters**
* Reproducible Lesson Plan 18–2
* Daily Lecture and Discussion Notes 18–2
* Vocabulary Activity 18–2
* Active Reading Note-Taking Guide 18–2
* Guided Reading Activity 18–2
* Section Quiz 18–2
* Reading Essentials and Study Guide 18–2

📖 **Transparencies**
* Daily Focus Skills Transparency 18–2

Multimedia
💿 Interactive Tutor Self-Assessment CD-ROM
💿 ExamView® Pro Testmaker CD-ROM
💿 Presentation Plus! CD-ROM
💿 Glencoe BookLink CD-ROM

The Scientific Revolution

Main Idea The thinkers of the ancient world developed early forms of science and passed this knowledge to later civilizations.

Reading Focus Have you ever taught a skill or passed on an idea to a younger brother or sister? Read in this chapter how the scientific ideas of early thinkers were passed on to later generations.

From earliest times, people have been curious about the world around them. Thousands of years ago, people began to use numbers, study the stars and planets, and watch the growth of plants and animals. These activities were the beginnings of science. Science is any organized study of the natural world and how it works.

Early Scientists

Early civilizations developed different kinds of science to solve practical problems. Among the first sciences were mathematics, astronomy, and medicine. Mathematics was used for record keeping and building projects. Astronomy helped people keep time and figure out when to plant and harvest crops. Early civilizations also developed medical practices, such as surgery, acupuncture, and the use of herbs, for treating illnesses.

The ancient Greeks left behind a large amount of scientific knowledge. They believed that reason was the only way to understand nature. As they studied the world, they developed theories. A **theory** (THEE•uh•ree) is an explanation of how or why something happens. A theory is based on what you can observe about something. It may not be correct, but it seems to fit the facts.

In Ancient Greece, the Greek philosopher Aristotle observed nature and collected vast amounts of information about plants and animals. He then took the facts

▲ This model shows the universe according to the ideas of the Polish astronomer Nicolaus Copernicus, with the sun at the universe's center. *What did Ptolemy's geocentric theory state?*

he gathered and classified, or arranged them into groups, based on their similarities and differences.

The Greeks made many important scientific advances, but their approach to science had some problems. For example, they did not experiment, or test, new ideas to see if they were true. Many of their conclusions were false because they were based on "common sense" instead of experiments.

For example, in the A.D. 100s, the Egyptian-born astronomer **Ptolemy** (TAH•luh•mee) stated that the sun and the planets moved around the earth in circular paths. After all, it did seem like the earth was the center of the universe. Astronomers in Europe accepted Ptolemy's geocentric, or earth-centered, theory for more than 1,400 years.

Science During the Middle Ages

Under Roman rule, most thinkers continued to accept the scientific knowledge of the Greeks. After the fall of Rome, during the Middle Ages, most people were more

CHAPTER 18   Enlightenment and Revolution   671

2 TEACH

Evaluating Have students choose which of the three branches of science—mathematics, astronomy, or medicine—was the most critical for ancient people and why. Then ask students to decide the same question for people today. Have them support their choices with reasons. **L3**

Predicting Review the definition of *theory*. Then ask students to predict how scientists determine the truth of different theories. **L1/ EL**

> **Caption Answer:** Sun and planets move around Earth in circular paths; Earth was the center of the universe.

Daily Lecture and Discussion Notes 18–2

Use **Daily Lecture and Discussion Notes 18–2** for an outline of key concepts found in the section.

Reading Support L1/ EL

Use **Vocabulary Activity 18–2** to review important terms in the section.

Reading Strategy   READING THE TEXT

Questioning Have students work with a partner to scan the section, paying attention to the headings, chart and map titles, and illustration captions. Have students make a list of five questions, based on their scanning of the text, that they hope to have answered. Possible questions might include:

• How did people react to the new ideas?
• Who were some important scientists, and what did they do?
• How did life change because of the Scientific Revolution?

Have students keep copies of their questions and answer them when they are finished reading the section. If any questions are not answered, have students brainstorm how to find answers. **L2**

CONNECTING ACROSS TIME

In our own day, many "facts" that have appeared to be supported by common sense have been proven untrue. Ask students to suggest some issues that appeared to earlier generations to be common sense but later were found to be mistaken. (*Possible suggestions might include racial inferiority, that smoking does not cause cancer, that disease is not caused by germs, and the division of society into strict and unchanging layers.*) **L2**

Understanding Charts

Both Ptolemy and Copernicus were limited by the complexity of their observations. **Ask: What things that exist in our solar system are missing from one or both charts? Why do you think these men did not include these objects in their schemes?** (*Uranus, Neptune, Pluto, the asteroids, other planets' moons, comets; they probably could not see them accurately with the tools they had*)

Answer:

five planets

interested in theology, the study of God, than in the study of nature. For scientific knowledge, they relied on Greek and Roman writings and saw no need to check their facts or to make their own observations. Many of these ancient works, however, were either lost or poorly preserved. In the writings that survived, errors were added as copies were made.

Meanwhile, Arabs and Jews in the Islamic Empire preserved much of the science of the Greeks and Romans. They carefully copied many Greek and Roman works into the Arabic language. They also came into contact with the science of the Persians and the Indian system of mathematics.

Arabic and Jewish scientists made advances of their own in areas such as mathematics, astronomy, and medicine. However, in spite of these achievements, scientists in the Islamic world did not experiment or develop the instruments necessary to advance their scientific knowledge.

During the 1100s, European thinkers became interested in science again as a result of their contacts with the Islamic world. Major Islamic scientific works were brought to Europe and translated into Latin. The Hindu-Arabic system of numbers also spread to Europe, where it eventually replaced Roman numerals. Christian thinkers, such as Thomas Aquinas, tried to show that Christianity and reason could go together. During the 1100s, Europeans began building new universities. They

A New View of the Universe

Ptolemaic Universe

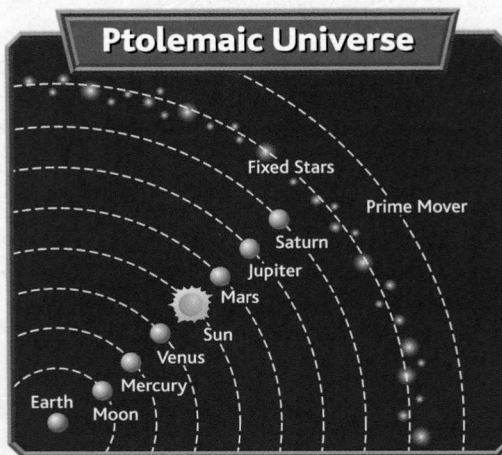

Fixed Stars
Prime Mover
Saturn
Jupiter
Mars
Sun
Venus
Mercury
Earth
Moon

The astronomical theory of Ptolemy (left) placed Earth at the center of the universe (above). His theory was accepted for more than a thousand years. *According to the diagram, how many planets besides Earth were known at the time of Ptolemy?*

DIFFERENTIATED INSTRUCTION

Kinesthetic: Have students construct models of the Ptolemaic and Copernican solar systems. Ask them to study the charts in the section as well as other sources. Give them a choice of materials and techniques. Display the models in the classroom.

English Learners: Ask students to explain to a partner the movement of the bodies in the solar system diagrams in the text. Have them begin with a list of prepositions and other useful words that will help them clarify the movements.

Gifted and Talented: Have students interview a local scientist about his or her early experiences in learning about the achievements of some of the figures discussed in this section. Ask students to write a short report summarizing the interview.

would play an important role in the growth of science.

Beginning in the 1400s, voyages of exploration further added to Europe's scientific knowledge. Better charts, maps, and navigational instruments helped voyagers reach different parts of the world. Through exploration, the size of oceans and continents became better known. Scientists gathered and classified new knowledge about plants, animals, and diseases in different parts of the world.

As scientific knowledge grew, the stage was set for a new understanding of the natural world that would shake Europe to its foundations.

✓ Reading Check **Describe** Describe scientific knowledge during the Middle Ages.

A Revolution in Astronomy

Main Idea European interest in astronomy led to new discoveries and ideas about the universe and Earth's place in it.

Reading Focus What would people on Earth think if life were discovered on other planets? Read to see how Europeans reacted to new discoveries about the universe.

During the 1500s, European thinkers began to break with the old scientific ideas. They increasingly understood that advances in science could only come through mathematics and experimentation. This new way of thinking led to a revolution, or sweeping change, in the way Europeans understood science and the search for knowledge. Astronomy was the first science affected by

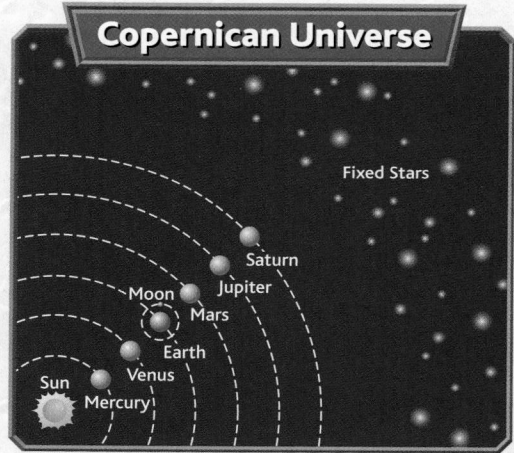

Copernican Universe

Fixed Stars
Saturn
Jupiter
Moon
Mars
Earth
Venus
Sun
Mercury

NICOLAS COPERNICUS

Nicolaus Copernicus (right), a Polish mathematician, believed that the sun was at the center of the universe. His model (above) placed Earth and the other planets in orbits around the sun. *Why did Europeans again become interested in science in the 1100s?*

CHAPTER 18   Enlightenment and Revolution   **673**

✓ Reading Check

Answer: largely based on Greek and Roman writings until contact with Muslims opened new possibilities

CURRICULUM CONNECTION

Language Arts
Make sure students understand the distinction between *astronomy*, the scientific study of bodies in space, and *astrology*, the non-scientific study of the motions of celestial bodies in the belief that they influence human affairs. Explain that while astrology and horoscopes can be fun, they are not based in science.

More About the Art

Although known for his astronomical theories, Copernicus also served as a Church official and practiced medicine. His theory of planetary movement is called "heliocentric" because the Greek word *helio* means "sun." Thus, the Sun was the center of the solar system.

Caption Answer:
Europeans came into contact with Islamic scientific works.

CRITICAL THINKING ACTIVITY

Evaluating Many of the scientific theories students have read about created tensions between Church officials and scientists. Have students name and then research scientific theories that have caused similar tensions in our own time or in the recent past. *(Possible events and developments might include evolution and the* Scopes *trial, cloning, organ donations and transplantation, and psychoanalysis.)* Ask students to present these issues and lead class discussions on the controversies the developments created. **L3**

TIME TRAVELER

Johannes Kepler also made the first modern discoveries in another important field. He was the pioneer in the study of how the human eye works. He explained the function of the pupil, which lets light into the eye, and how light is focused on the retina. His understanding of the optical characteristics of the eye also explained for the first time how eyeglasses, already in use for three centuries, helped people see better. The glass lens refocused the light image correctly on the retina.

Linking Past & Present

Answer: Answers will vary but may focus on current space-related developments.

---

the Scientific Revolution. New discoveries brought changes in the way Europeans saw the universe. They challenged traditional thinking that God had made the earth as the center of the universe.

Who Was Copernicus? Leading the Scientific Revolution was a Polish mathematician named Nicolaus **Copernicus** (koh•PUHR•nih•kuhs). In 1543 Copernicus wrote a book called *On the Revolutions of the Heavenly Spheres.* He disagreed with Ptolemy's view that the earth was the center of the universe. Copernicus believed that Ptolemy's theory was too complicated. Instead, he developed a simpler heliocentric, or sun-centered, theory of the universe. Copernicus's theory stated that the Sun, not Earth, was the center of the universe. The planets moved in circular paths around the Sun.

Kepler's Revolution The next step in the march of science was taken by a German astronomer named Johannes **Kepler** (KEH•pluhr). He supported Copernicus's theory but also made corrections to it. Kepler added the idea that the planets move in ellipses (ih•LIHP•SEEZ), or oval paths, rather than circular

Linking Past & Present
Telescopes

THEN Galileo's first telescope was made of two lenses inside a tube. Kepler improved the telescope by including an outward curving eyepiece, which increased the magnification and field of view. In 1663 James Gregory published a description of a reflecting telescope that would use a mirror to gather and focus light. It was not built until 1668.

▼ The Hubble Space Telescope

NOW Today, telescopes are large, complex, and powerful. The Hubble Space Telescope has been in orbit 380 miles above the earth's surface since 1990. It can see great distances because it is outside the atmosphere. *Why is astronomy important today?*

▲ Galileo's telescope

INTERDISCIPLINARY CONNECTIONS ACTIVITY

Technology In this section, students read about a number of important inventions and advances in existing technology: the clock, telescope, water thermometer, and barometer. Have students choose one of these inventions, or another that dates from the same period, and prepare a report on it. Have students include information on how the invention affected science and who helped develop it. Tell them to add more recent developments in this instrument's technology or its uses. **L2**

ones. His theory made it easier to explain the movements of the planets. It also marked the beginning of modern astronomy.

Who Was Galileo? An Italian scientist named Galileo Galilei made the third great breakthrough in the Scientific Revolution. **Galileo** (GA•luh•LEE•oh) believed that new knowledge could come through experiments that were carefully carried out. For example, Galileo challenged Aristotle's idea that the heavier the object is, the faster it falls to the ground. Galileo's experiments proved that Aristotle was wrong. Objects fall at the same speed regardless of their weight.

Galileo also realized that scientific instruments could help humans better explore the natural world. He improved instruments, such as the clock and telescope. With the telescope, Galileo found clear evidence supporting Copernicus's view that Earth revolves around the Sun.

Galileo also played an important role in the development of new scientific instruments. In 1593 he invented a water thermometer that, for the first time, allowed temperature changes to be measured. Galileo's assistant, Evangelista Torricelli, then used the element called mercury to build the first barometer, an instrument that measures air pressure.

When Galileo published his ideas in 1632, his work was condemned by the Roman Catholic Church. The Catholic Church held to the geocentric, or earth-centered, view of the universe, believing that it was taught in the Bible. The pope ordered Galileo to come to Rome to be tried for heresy. Church threats finally forced Galileo to withdraw many of his statements. Even so, Galileo's ideas spread throughout Europe and changed people's views about the universe.

✓ **Reading Check** **Explain** How did Galileo prove Copernicus's theory?

New Scientific Discoveries

Main Idea The Scientific Revolution led to new discoveries in physics, medicine, and chemistry.

Reading Focus Think about all the facts you know about medicine. For example, you know your heart pumps blood, your lungs breathe air, and your body is made of cells. Read to learn how scientists of the 1600s and 1700s made discoveries we often take for granted today.

Throughout the 1600s and 1700s, the Scientific Revolution continued to spread. Many new discoveries were made in physics, medicine, and chemistry.

Who Is Isaac Newton? Despite continuing scientific breakthroughs, the ideas of Copernicus, Kepler, and Galileo needed to be brought together as one system. This feat was accomplished by an English mathematician named Isaac **Newton** (NOO•tuhn).

According to tradition, Newton was sitting in his garden one day when he watched an apple fall to the ground. The

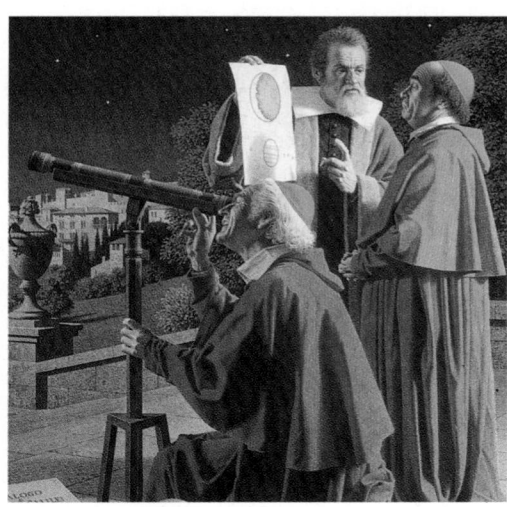

▲ In this painting, Galileo presents his astronomical findings to the Catholic clergy. *How did Galileo respond to the Church's condemnation of his work in astronomy?*

Writing Activity

Ask students to research and write a short biography of Copernicus or Kepler. Post the biographies in the classroom as you study this chapter. **L2**

in a word...

"Gravity" comes from a Latin root meaning "heavy" or "weighty." Other common English words from the same root include *grave* (meaning "serious"), *grief,* and *aggravate.*

More About the Art

When Galileo used a telescope to study the heavens, he made some startling discoveries. The Moon's surface was rough and uneven, not smooth. He also saw four moons around Jupiter. In addition, there were more stars in the sky than people could see without a telescope.

Caption Answer: Galileo was forced to withdraw many of his statements.

✓ **Reading Check**

Answer: With the telescope, Galileo found clear evidence that the Earth revolves around the Sun.

EXTENDING THE CONTENT

How Small Is Small? Antonie van Leeuwenhoek's microscope, the first of its kind, was a single-lens instrument. Its maximum magnification power was only about 300 times. However, it enabled him to see bacteria that were 2 to 3 millionths of a meter long. Subsequent microscopes employed electron beams, which allowed a magnification of 250,000 times. Even more recent microscopes use high-frequency sound waves. The latest microscope, called a scanning tunneling microscope, measures variations in an electric current. It is so powerful that it allows scientists to see the movement of individual atoms.

Objectives and answers to the student activity can be found in the **Web Activity Lesson Plan** feature at jat.glencoe.com

Predicting Ask students if they have any predictions about why Newton's conception of the universe as a well-ordered machine began to change in the early 1900s. Who might have brought about this change? *(Students may know about Einstein's theories on relativity.)* **L1/ EL**

Understanding Charts

Some of these scientists studied the physical universe while others examined humankind.
Ask: Which scientist in the chart do you think has made the most valuable contribution? Why?

Answers:

1. that the heart pumps blood
2. Boyle, Lavoisier

Reading Check

Answer: gravity

---

apple's fall led him to the idea of gravity, or the pull of the earth and other bodies on objects at or near their surfaces.

In a book called *Principia*, published in 1687, Newton stated his laws, or well-tested theories, about the motion of objects in space and on Earth. The most important was the universal law of gravitation. It explains that the force of gravity holds the entire solar system together by keeping the sun and the planets in their orbits. Newton's ideas led to the rise of modern physics, or the study of physical properties such as matter and energy.

Medicine and Chemistry Sweeping changes were made in medicine in the 1500s and 1600s. Since Roman times, European doctors had relied on the teachings of the Greek

The Scientific Revolution

Scientist	Nation	Discoveries
Nicolaus Copernicus (1473–1543)	Poland	Earth orbits the Sun; Earth rotates on its axis
Galileo Galilei (1564–1642)	Italy	other planets have moons
Johannes Kepler (1571–1630)	Germany	planets have elliptical orbits
William Harvey (1578–1657)	England	heart pumps blood
Robert Hooke (1635–1703)	England	cells
Robert Boyle (1627–1691)	Ireland	air is made of gases
Isaac Newton (1642–1727)	England	gravity; laws of motion; calculus
Antoine Lavoisier (1743–1794)	France	how materials burn

Understanding Charts

During the Scientific Revolution, scientists made discoveries in many fields, such as astronomy and medicine.
1. What did William Harvey discover?
2. **Identify** Which scientists' discoveries dealt with chemistry?

Web Activity Visit jat.glencoe.com and click on *Chapter 18—Student Web Activity* to learn more about early scientific discoveries.

physician Galen. Galen wanted to study the human body, but he was only allowed to dissect, or cut open, animals.

In the 1500s, however, a Flemish doctor named Andreas Vesalius began dissecting dead human bodies for research. In 1543 Vesalius published *On the Structure of the Human Body.* In this work, Vesalius presented a detailed account of the human body that replaced many of Galen's ideas.

Other breakthroughs in medicine took place. In the early 1600s, William Harvey, an English doctor, proved that blood flowed through the human body. In the mid-1600s, an English scientist named Robert Hooke began using a microscope, and he soon discovered cells, the smallest structures of living material.

Beginning in the 1600s, European scientists developed new ideas in chemistry. Chemistry is the study of natural substances and how they change. In the mid-1600s, Robert Boyle, an Irish scientist, proved that all substances are made up of basic elements that cannot be broken down.

European scientists of the 1700s also developed ways to study gases. They discovered hydrogen, carbon dioxide, and oxygen. By 1777, Antoine Lavoisier (AN•twahn luhv•WAH•zee•AY) of France had proven that materials need oxygen to burn. Marie Lavoisier, also a scientist, contributed to her husband's work.

Reading Check **Identify** According to Newton, what force held the planets in orbit?

DIFFERENTIATED INSTRUCTION

Intrapersonal: How did Galileo feel when he was forced by the Church to recant his life's work on the solar system? Did he take back his statements sincerely, or did he act that way in order to save his life? Have students write a journal entry explaining either point of view.

English Learners: Help students make a list of adjectives that describe the kinds of emotions that people involved in the heresy trial might have felt.

Gifted and Talented: Have students research Galileo's trial for heresy and write a scene from a play about it.

Refer to *Inclusion Strategies for the Middle School Social Studies Classroom* in the TCR.

Biography

SIR ISAAC NEWTON
1642–1727

Isaac Newton was born into a farming family on December 25, 1642, in Woolsthorpe, England. His father died before Newton was born. His mother remarried when he was three years old. His new stepfather did not want the boy to live with them, so Newton was raised by his grandmother.

Newton earned a degree from Trinity College, part of Cambridge University, in 1664. He planned to work for the university, but from 1664 to 1666, it closed because of the plague. Newton spent the next two years in his hometown. While there, he made some of his most important discoveries. He developed his theory of gravity, invented a new kind of mathematics called calculus, and discovered that white light is made up of all of the different colors of light.

Newton returned to Cambridge, earned a master's degree, and was appointed to several positions there. His life was very stressful because many scientists questioned his calculations. These criticisms made Newton reluctant to publish his discoveries, but eventually he did. His book *Principia* is considered one of the greatest scientific books ever written. In it Newton describes his three laws of motion and his ideas about gravity.

▲ Newton analyzing light rays

> "If I have seen farther, it is by standing upon the shoulders of giants."
> –Isaac Newton, in a letter to Robert Hooke

During his life, Newton won many awards for his discoveries. In 1705 he became the first scientist ever to be knighted by the English king.

▲ Trinity College today

Then and Now

Newton's findings were criticized by some scientists of his time. Do research to find a scientific discovery made in the last 50 years that others have questioned or criticized. Describe your findings to the class.

Biography

TEACH

When Isaac Newton arrived at the University of Cambridge in 1661, he found that outmoded ideas of science held sway. The new ideas of Copernicus, Kepler, and Galileo had made no impression on the faculty. Aristotle was considered the most important source, even though he had been dead for more than 17 centuries. Even as a student, however, Newton believed in searching further than ancient sources for understanding. On the first page of his notebook, he wrote in Latin, "Plato is my friend, Aristotle is my friend, but my best friend is truth."

Ask students to speculate on what kind of truth Newton wanted to "make friends with." *(understanding the truth about how the universe works)*
L1/ EL

Then and Now

Answers will vary, but the selected scientific discoveries should be supported with examples of the criticisms leveled against them.

Reading List Generator CD-ROM

GLENCOE BOOKLINK

RECOMMENDED READING

Use the **Glencoe BookLink CD-ROM** to create customized reading lists based on your students' interests and reading levels. Below is an example based on content in this chapter. Also, see the Suggested Readings on pages 944–946 of the Appendix.

- Cobb, Vicki. *Truth on Trial: The Story of Galileo Galilei.* Account of Galileo's heresy trial.
- Christianson, Gale E. *Isaac Newton and the Scientific Revolution.* Biography of Newton and his achievements.
- Veglahn, Nancy. *Dance of the Planets: The Universe of Nicolaus Copernicus.* An introduction to the career and theories of Copernicus.

The Triumph of Reason

Main Idea Using the scientific method, Europeans of the 1600s and 1700s developed new ideas about society based on reason.

Reading Focus What do modern scientists do in their laboratories? Read to understand how methods of scientific research changed Europeans' understanding of human society in the 1600s and 1700s.

As scientists made new discoveries, European thinkers began to apply science to society. For these thinkers, science had proven that the physical universe followed natural laws. By using their reason, people could learn how the universe worked. Using this knowledge, people also could solve existing human problems and make life better.

Descartes and Reason One of the most important scientific thinkers was the Frenchman René **Descartes** (day•KAHRT). In 1637 he wrote a book called *Discourse on Method*. In this book, Descartes began with the problem of knowing what is true. To find truth, he decided to put aside everything that he had learned and make a fresh start. To Descartes, one fact seemed to be beyond doubt—his own existence. Descartes summarized this idea by the phrase, "I think, therefore I am."

In his work, Descartes claimed that mathematics was the source of all scientific truth. In mathematics, he said, the answers were always true. This was because mathematics began with simple, obvious principles and then used logic to move gradually to other truths. Today, Descartes is viewed as the founder of modern **rationalism** (RASH•nuh•LIH•zuhm). This is the belief that reason is the chief source of knowledge.

What Is the Scientific Method?

Scientific thought was also influenced by English thinker Francis Bacon, who lived from 1561 to 1626. Bacon believed that

The Microscope

Although Robert Hooke did not invent the microscope, his improvements were important. Hooke's book *Micrographia* used detailed drawings to show a microscopic world that few people had even imagined. *What did Hooke discover about the structure of living material?*

Eyepiece

Lenses

Light source

Focusing screw

Specimen holder

COOPERATIVE LEARNING ACTIVITY

Talking About Rationalism Was Descartes correct when he stated that reason is the chief source of knowledge? What might other people have said about Descartes' idea? Ask a group of students to script, rehearse, and present a TV talk show featuring Descartes and some other individuals as guests. Have each student playing a figure research what that person might have said about rationalism and other ways of arriving at truth. Choose one student to play the host, and ask the players to leave time for "audience" questions. **L3**

ideas based on tradition should be put aside. He developed the **scientific method,** an orderly way of collecting and analyzing evidence. It is still the process used in scientific research today.

The scientific method is made up of several steps. First a scientist begins with careful observation of facts and then tries to find a **hypothesis** (hy•PAH•thuh•suhs), or explanation of the facts. Through experiments, the scientist tests the hypothesis under all possible conditions to see if it is true. Finally, if repeated, experiments show that the hypothesis is true, and then it is considered a scientific law.

Francis Bacon ▲

☑ **Reading Check** **Explain** What is the scientific method?

The Scientific Method

Observe some aspect of the universe.

↓

Hypothesize about what you observed.

↓

Predict something based on your hypothesis.

↓

Test your predictions through experiments and observation.

↓

Modify hypothesis in light of results.

Understanding Charts

The scientific method is still important today.
1. What is the next step after predictions are tested through experiments and observation?
2. **Conclude** Why is the scientific method necessary to create scientific law?

Section 2 Review

History Online
Study Central™ Need help with the material in this section? Visit jat.glencoe.com

Reading Summary
Review the Main Ideas
- The thinkers of the ancient world developed early forms of science and passed this knowledge to later generations.
- European interest in science led to new discoveries and ideas about the universe and Earth's place in it.
- The Scientific Revolution led to new discoveries in physics, medicine, and chemistry.
- Descartes invented rationalism, and Bacon developed the scientific method.

What Did You Learn?
1. Who was Copernicus, and what was the heliocentric theory?
2. Describe Francis Bacon's beliefs about scientific reasoning.

Critical Thinking
3. **Summarize** Draw a diagram like the one below. Add details to show some of the new ideas developed during the Scientific Revolution.

Ideas From Scientific Revolution

4. **Drawing Conclusions** What do you think Descartes meant when he said, "I think, therefore I am"?
5. **Science Link** Explain Kepler's view of the solar system.
6. **Analyze** Why did the Church condemn Galileo's astronomical findings?
7. **Writing Questions** Imagine that you could interview Galileo about his work and his life. Write five questions you would like to ask him. Include possible answers with your questions.

CHAPTER 18   Enlightenment and Revolution   **679**

Understanding Charts

Bacon believed in inductive reasoning, moving from the particular to the general.

Answers:
1. modify hypothesis
2. Hypotheses are rigorously checked for accuracy.

ENRICH

Have students prepare a one-person show about a scientist discussed in this section. **L3**

☑ **Reading Check**

Answer: a system of collecting/analyzing evidence

History Online

To help students understand section material, have them visit **Study Central™** at jat.glencoe.com

RETEACH

Ask students to describe one idea from each scientist. **L1**

④ CLOSE

Have the class discuss the effects of the Scientific Revolution. **L2**

SECTION 2 REVIEW ANSWERS

1. Polish astronomer; stated that the Sun was the center of the universe
2. A scientist should observe facts and form a hypothesis about them; predict something about facts; test predictions; modify hypothesis based on results.
3. sun-centered solar system; elliptical orbits; universal law of gravitation; blood flows through body; cells make up living material; materials need oxygen for fire
4. He knew that he was thinking and that proved his existence.
5. Planets move in oval orbits.
6. The Church leaders held that the earth-centered theory was taught in the Bible.
7. Questions and answers will vary but should reflect accurate information about Galileo.

① FOCUS

SECTION OVERVIEW

This section describes how European thinkers applied reason and science to the improvement of society and government.

SKILLBUILDER ACTIVITY

📖 Project **Daily Focus Skills Transparency 18–3** and have students answer questions. Discuss their responses.

Get Ready to Read!

Preteaching Vocabulary: Explain that separation of powers is a very important concept for understanding how the government of the United States works. It refers to a system in which the three separate branches, or parts, of government balance and control each other. The idea dates from the Enlightenment.

Answers to Graphic: Voltaire: religious toleration; freedom of speech; Montesquieu: separation of powers

---

Section

3

The Enlightenment

Get Ready to Read!

What's the Connection?
As you have read, the Scientific Revolution led to new discoveries. At the same time, it also led to many new ideas about government and society.

Focusing on the Main Ideas
• During the 1700s, many Europeans believed that reason could be used to make government and society better. *(page 681)*

• The Enlightenment was centered in France, where thinkers wrote about changing their society and met to discuss their ideas. *(page 684)*

• Many of Europe's monarchs, who claimed to rule by the will of God, tried to model their countries on Enlightenment ideas. *(page 686)*

Locating Places
Prussia (PRUH•shuh)
Austria (AWS•tree•uh)
St. Petersburg (PEE•tuhrz•BUHRG)

Meeting People
Thomas Hobbes (HAHBZ)
John Locke
Montesquieu (MAHN•tuhs•KYOO)
Voltaire (vohl•TAR)

Building Your Vocabulary
natural law
social contract
separation of powers
deism (DEE•IH•zuhm)
absolutism (AB•suh•LOO•TIH•zuhm)

Reading Strategy
Summarizing Information Complete a table like the one below showing the major ideas of Enlightenment thinkers.

Thinkers	Ideas

NATIONAL GEOGRAPHIC When & Where?

1600	1700	1800

1643
Louis XIV becomes king of France

1690
John Locke writes about government

1792
Mary Wollstonecraft calls for women's rights

St. Petersburg
Moscow
London
Paris
Berlin
Vienna

680 CHAPTER 18 Enlightenment and Revolution

SECTION RESOURCES

Reproducible Masters
• Reproducible Lesson Plan 18–3
• Daily Lecture and Discussion Notes 18–3
• Vocabulary Activity 18–3
• Active Reading Note-Taking Guide 18–3
• Guided Reading Activity 18–3
• Section Quiz 18–3
• Reading Essentials and Study Guide 18–3

Transparencies
• Daily Focus Skills Transparency 18–3

Multimedia
⊙ Interactive Tutor Self-Assessment CD-ROM
⊙ ExamView® Pro Testmaker CD-ROM
⊙ Presentation Plus! CD-ROM
⊙ Glencoe BookLink CD-ROM

New Ideas About Politics

Main Idea During the 1700s, many Europeans believed that reason could be used to make government and society better.

Reading Focus What makes people get along with each other? Do they need rules, a strong leader, or to learn to work together? Read to learn how thinkers in Europe answered these questions.

During the 1700s, European thinkers were impressed by scientific discoveries in the natural world. They believed that reason could also uncover the scientific laws that governed human life. Once these laws were known, thinkers said, people could use the laws to make society better.

As the Scientific Revolution advanced, many educated Europeans came to believe that reason was a much better guide than faith or tradition. To them, reason was a "light" that revealed error and showed the way to truth. As result, the 1700s became known as the Age of Enlightenment.

During the Enlightenment, political thinkers tried to apply reason and scientific ideas to government. They claimed that there was a **natural law,** or a law that applied to everyone and could be understood by reason. This law was the key to understanding government. As early as the 1600s, two English thinkers—Thomas Hobbes and John Locke—used natural law to develop very different ideas about how government should work.

Who Was Thomas Hobbes?

Thomas Hobbes (HAHBZ) wrote about English government and society. During his life, England was torn apart by civil war. Supporters of King Charles I fought those who backed Parliament. Charles I wanted to have absolute, or total, power as king. Parliament claimed to represent the people

▲ This illustration is from the title page of Hobbes's *Leviathan*. *What sort of government did Hobbes support in* Leviathan?

and demanded a greater voice in running England. The fighting finally led to Charles's execution. This event shocked Thomas Hobbes, who was a strong supporter of the monarchy.

In 1651 Hobbes wrote a book called *Leviathan*. In this work, Hobbes argued that natural law made absolute monarchy the best form of government.

According to Hobbes, humans were naturally selfish and violent. They could not be trusted to make decisions on their own. Left to themselves, people would make life "nasty, brutish, and short." Therefore, Hobbes said, they needed to obey a government that had the power of a leviathan, or sea monster. To Hobbes, this meant the rule of a king, because only a strong ruler could give people direction.

Why Is John Locke Important?

Another English thinker **John Locke** thought differently. He used natural law to affirm citizens' rights and to make government answerable to the people.

② TEACH

Drawing Conclusions Ask students if they agree with the idea that scientific laws can be applied to human society. Why or why not? **L3**

Daily Lecture and Discussion Notes 18–3

Use **Daily Lecture and Discussion Notes 18–3** for an outline of key concepts found in the section.

Caption Answer: absolute monarchy

Writing Activity

Ask students to discuss with a partner some ideas and principles that might be considered natural laws that apply to all people. Then have pairs make a list of five natural laws. Chart and discuss students' suggestions. **L2**

Reading Support L1/ EL

Use **Vocabulary Activity 18–3** to review important terms in the section.

Reading Strategy   READING THE TEXT

Reflecting and Responding Students who connect what they read to events, emotions, and ideas in their own lives are often better able to construct meaning in texts. They are also able to increase their enjoyment, comprehension, and recall of the text. Encourage students to connect what they are reading about the Enlightenment figures and their ideas about society to what they know about present-day civilization. Ask them to keep a list of things they believe have a connection to something in our society. Have students share their lists and discuss them as part of the section wrap-up. **L2**

Primary Source

Montesquieu's views on government seem modern to many people. He was also ahead of his time in his ideas about the role of women in society. He admired his wife's business sense so much that he left her in charge of his estates while he traveled in Europe and eventually moved to Paris.

Answer:
so they have freedom to make judgments without control and pressure from other government officials

Reading Strategy

Comparing and Contrasting Ask students to compare and contrast the ideas of Locke and Hobbes. (*Answers should reflect basic disagreements over preferred type of government, interpretation of natural law, and belief in human rights.*) **L3**

✓ Reading Check

Answer: Power should be separated, or divided, among legislative, executive, and judicial branches.

Primary Source — The Law of Nations

Montesquieu's beliefs about government are still influential today.

▲ Montesquieu

"Again, there is no liberty, if the judiciary power be not separated from the legislative and executive. Were it joined with the legislative, the life and liberty of the subject would be exposed to arbitrary control; for the judge would be then the legislator. Were it joined to the executive power, the judge might behave with violence and oppression."

—Montesquieu,
The Spirit of Laws

DBQ Document-Based Question

According to Montesquieu, why should judges be independent?

During Locke's life, another English king, James II, wanted to set up an absolute monarchy against Parliament's wishes. In 1688 war threatened, and James fled the country. Parliament then asked Mary, James's daughter, and her husband, William, to take the throne. This event came to be called the "Glorious Revolution."

In return for the English throne, William and Mary agreed to a Bill of Rights. In this document, they agreed to obey Parliament's laws. The document also guaranteed all English people basic rights, like those the Magna Carta had given to the nobles. For example, people had the right to a fair trial by jury and to freedom from cruel punishment for a crime.

In 1690 John Locke explained many of the ideas of the Glorious Revolution in a book called *Two Treatises of Government.* Locke stated that government should be based on natural law. This law, said Locke, gave all people from their birth certain natural rights. Among them were the right to life, the right to liberty, and the right to own property.

Locke believed that the purpose of government is to protect these rights. All governments, he said, were based on a **social contract,** or an agreement between rulers and the people. If a ruler took away people's natural rights, the people had a right to revolt and set up a new government.

Who Was Montesquieu? England's government after the Glorious Revolution was admired by thinkers in France. They liked it better than their own absolute monarchy. In 1748 Baron **Montesquieu** (MAHN•tuhs•KYOO), a French thinker, published a book called *The Spirit of Laws.*

In this book, Montesquieu said that England's government was the best because it had a separation of powers. **Separation of powers** means that power should be equally divided among the branches of government: executive, legislative, and judicial. The legislative branch would make the laws while the executive branch would enforce them. The judicial branch would interpret the laws and judge when they were broken. By separating these powers, government could not become too powerful and threaten people's rights.

✓ Reading Check **Explain** According to Montesquieu, how should government be organized?

DIFFERENTIATED INSTRUCTION

Gifted and Talented: Have students prepare a program of readings from the works of the Enlightenment authors discussed in this section, such as Locke, Hobbes, Voltaire, and Wollstonecraft.

English Learners: Ask students to supplement the readings with music from some of the composers discussed in **The Way It Was.**

Kinesthetic: Have students prepare costumes and sets for the readings, researching appropriate designs.

📁 Refer to *Inclusion Strategies for the Middle School Social Studies Classroom* in the TCR.

Biography

JOHN LOCKE
1632–1704

John Locke was born in Somerset, England. His father was a lawyer but also served as a cavalry soldier. Using his military connections, he arranged for his son John to get a good education. Locke studied classical languages, grammar, philosophy, and geometry at Oxford University. To Locke, the courses were not exciting, so he turned to his true interests—science and medicine.

After graduating, Locke went to work for governments in Europe. He continued to study science and philosophy. He particularly liked the work of Descartes. In 1671 Locke began recording his own ideas about how people know things. Nineteen years later, he published his ideas in *An Essay Concerning Human Understanding*. In this book, Locke argued that people's minds are blank when they are born and that society shapes what people think and believe. This idea meant that if people could make society better, it would also make people better.

▲ John Locke

> **"Law is not to abolish or restrain, but to preserve and enlarge freedom."**
> —John Locke, *Two Treatises of Government*

In 1683 Locke fled to Holland after the English government began to think his political ideas were dangerous. During that time, he was declared a traitor and was not able to return until after the Glorious Revolution of 1688. It was at that time that he wrote his famous *Two Treatises of Government*. Soon afterward, Locke retired to Essex. There he enjoyed frequent visits from Sir Isaac Newton and other friends until his death in 1704.

▲ William and Mary being crowned following the Glorious Revolution

Then and Now

Give examples of how Locke's ideas have influenced our lives and ideas.

Biography

TEACH

Locke's ideas about education, like his ideas about government and human nature, have also proven to be influential. In his 1693 book *Some Thoughts Concerning Education* and in other works, Locke describes his ideal education. It makes the learning of virtue more important than the acquiring of knowledge. As in his other works, Locke made experience the greatest teacher.

Ask students to discuss Locke's ranking of virtue over knowledge. Is learning to do the right thing more important in education than knowledge? **L3**

Then and Now

Answers will vary. Students may credit Locke with supporting individual freedoms and rights and with being a key influence on U.S. founding documents, such as the Declaration of Independence and the U.S. Constitution.

Reading List Generator CD-ROM

GLENCOE BOOKLINK

RECOMMENDED READING

Use the **Glencoe BookLink CD-ROM** to create customized reading lists based on your students' interests and reading levels. Below is an example based on content in this chapter. Also, see the Suggested Readings on pages 944–946 of the Appendix.

- Friedman, Estelle. *Ben Franklin.* Biography of the American political leader and inventor.
- Pickney, Andrea Davis. *Dear Benjamin Banneker.* Account of a free African American mathematician who protested slavery.
- Schleifer, Jay. *Our Declaration of Independence.* Summary of people and events behind the Declaration of Independence.

CONNECTING ACROSS TIME

Voltaire visited and wrote to many of the monarchs and leaders of Europe, including Frederick the Great of Prussia, Catherine the Great of Russia, and the English parliamentary leaders Bolingbroke and Walpole. Ask students what they think these leaders might have gained from their contact with Voltaire. Also ask if students think that today's politicians can learn from philosophers and writers. Why or why not? **L3**

Religion Voltaire and the other philosophes believed that governments should not support one religion over others. Ask students to research and report on one of the following countries and its religious policies: Great Britain, India, Saudi Arabia, Italy, Bhutan, or Japan. **L2**

More About the Art

Madame de Geoffrin's salon was one of the most popular in Paris in the 1700s. Painters met there on Mondays, while writers visited it on Wednesdays. Ask students to name eight people they would like to invite to a salon of their own.

Caption Answer: They used their skills as writers.

The French Philosophes

Main Idea The Enlightenment was centered in France, where thinkers wrote about changing their society and met to discuss their ideas.

Reading Focus What role do writers play in the United States today? Read on to find out what effect writers had on Europe during the Enlightenment.

During the 1700s, France became the major center of the Enlightenment. As the Enlightenment spread, thinkers in France and elsewhere became known by the French name *philosophe* (FEE•luh•ZAWF), which means "philosopher." Most philosophes were writers, teachers, journalists, and observers of society.

◄ Voltaire

▲ During the Enlightenment, upper-class nobles held gatherings of writers, artists, government officials, and other nobles in their homes to discuss and debate new ideas. *How did the philosophes spread their ideas?*

684   CHAPTER 18   Enlightenment and Revolution

The philosophes wanted to use reason to change society. They attacked superstition, or unreasoned beliefs. They also disagreed with Church leaders who opposed new scientific discoveries. The philosophes believed in both freedom of speech and the individual's right to liberty. They used their skills as writers to spread their ideas across Europe.

Who Was Voltaire? The greatest thinker of the Enlightenment was François-Marie Arouet, known simply as **Voltaire** (vohl•TAR). Born in a middle-class family, Voltaire wrote many novels, plays, letters, and essays that brought him fame and wealth.

Voltaire became known for his strong dislike of the Roman Catholic Church. He blamed Church leaders for keeping

CRITICAL THINKING ACTIVITY

Drawing Conclusions Tell students that John Locke believed that when people were born, their minds were a "blank slate," or in Latin, *tabula rasa*. He believed that this blank slate was filled in by their experiences. Ask students to evaluate this claim. Be sure that the discussion includes the effects of *nature*, or genetic background, and those of *nurture*, or life experiences that shape us. **Ask:** Do you agree with Locke that nurture is more important? Do you believe that some of what we are is affected by our nature? *(Answers will vary but should include supporting proof.)* **L3**

knowledge from people in order to maintain the Church's power. Voltaire also opposed the government supporting one religion and forbidding others. He thought people should be free to choose their own beliefs.

Throughout his life, Voltaire was a supporter of **deism** (DEE• ɪʜ•zuhm), a religious belief based on reason. According to the followers of deism, God created the world and set it in motion. He then allowed it to run itself by natural law.

Who Was Diderot? Denis Diderot was the French philosophe who did the most to spread Enlightenment ideas. With the help of friends, Diderot published a large, 28-volume encyclopedia. His project, which began in the 1750s, took about 20 years to complete.

The *Encyclopedia* included a wide range of topics, such as science, religion, government, and the arts. It became an important weapon in the philosophes' fight against traditional ways. Many articles attacked superstition and supported freedom of religion. Others called for changes that would make society more just and caring.

The Enlightenment and Women The Enlightenment raised questions about the role of women in society. Previously, many male thinkers claimed that women were less important than men and had to be controlled and protected. By the 1700s, however, women thinkers began calling for women's rights. The most powerful supporter of women's rights was the English writer Mary Wollstonecraft. Many people today see her as the founder of the modern movement for women's rights.

Primary Source · Natural Rights of Women

Mary Wollstonecraft argued that the natural rights of the Enlightenment should extend to women as well as men.

▲ Mary Wollstonecraft

"In short, in whatever light I view the subject, reason and experience convince me that the only method of leading women to fulfill their peculiar [specific] duties is to free them from all restraint by allowing them to participate in the inherent rights of mankind. Make them free, and they will quickly become wise and virtuous, as men become more so, for the improvement must be mutual."

—Mary Wollstonecraft,
A Vindication of the Rights of Woman: With Strictures on Political and Moral Subjects

DBQ Document-Based Question

What did Wollstonecraft believe would happen if women were allowed rights?

In 1792 Mary Wollstonecraft wrote a book called *A Vindication of the Rights of Woman*. In this work, she claimed that all humans have reason. Because women have reason, they should have the same rights as men. Women, Wollstonecraft said, should have equal rights in education, the workplace, and in political life.

Rousseau's Social Contract By the late 1700s, some European thinkers were starting to criticize Enlightenment ideas. One of these thinkers was Jean-Jacques Rousseau (zhahn zhahk ru•SOH).

Primary Source

Mary Wollstonecraft was at the center of liberal and radical thought in the late 1700s. Her friends included Tom Paine, author of *Common Sense*, and the writer William Godwin, whom she married. Their daughter also became famous. Mary Wollstonecraft Shelley was the author of *Frankenstein*.

Answer:
They would be better able to fulfill their duties; women and men would become wise and virtuous.

Reading Strategy

Comparing and Contrasting
Ask students how Diderot's *Encyclopedia* differs from and is similar to a modern one. *(Different: Diderot's encyclopedia had a point of view and "message"; Similar: it covers a wide range of topics.)* **L2**

CONNECTING ACROSS TIME

Mary Wollstonecraft believed that men and women should have equal rights. Have students discuss whether her dream is now a reality in the United States. **L2**

INTERDISCIPLINARY CONNECTIONS ACTIVITY

Music The four composers featured in **The Way It Was** are among the greatest who have ever lived. Ask a group of students to research and prepare a "listener's guide" that focuses on the works of these men. Encourage students to find out about their lives, as well as how their music reflected the events and ideas of their time. Have the group present segments from their guide and play representative selections by the composers. **L2**

Rousseau claimed that supporters of the Enlightenment relied too much on reason. Instead, people should pay more attention to their feelings. According to Rousseau, human beings were naturally good, but civilized life corrupted them. To improve themselves, he thought people should live simpler lives closer to nature.

In 1762 Rousseau published a book called *The Social Contract*. In this work, Rousseau presented his political ideas. A workable government, he said, should be based on a social contract. This is an agreement in which everyone in a society agrees to be governed by the general will, or what society as a whole wants.

Reading Check **Describe** Who were the philosophes?

The Age of Absolutism

Main Idea Many of Europe's monarchs, who claimed to rule by the will of God, tried to model their countries on Enlightenment ideas.

Reading Focus If you were given the chance to be a leader, how would you treat the people you ruled? As you read, think about the power of Europe's kings and queens during the 1600s and 1700s.

During the 1600s and 1700s, many European thinkers favored limits on government power. However, powerful kings and queens ruled most of Europe. This system was known as **absolutism** (AB•suh•LOO•TIH•zuhm). In this system, monarchs held absolute, or total, power. They claimed to rule by divine right, or by the will of God. This meant that rulers did not answer to their people, but rather to God alone.

NATIONAL GEOGRAPHIC — The Way It Was

Focus on Everyday Life

Music of the Enlightenment The 1700s was one of the greatest musical periods in history. Before this time, almost all music was religious in nature and was limited to church performances. During the Enlightenment, music was played in theaters for the first time, and some of the new pieces were not religious.

▲ A string quartet

Many types of music existed in the 1700s. Sonatas were performed with one instrument and a piano, and string quartets were played with four instruments. Concertos and symphonies were longer and involved an orchestra. Operas were full-scale theatrical performances using vocal and instrumental music.

Baroque music emphasized drama and emotion. Johann Sebastian Bach and George Frederick Handel composed baroque music. Bach composed

686

EXTENDING THE CONTENT

A Watershed Event The Glorious Revolution of 1688 marked the beginning of England's constitutional monarchy. James II, who had gained the throne in 1685, immediately alienated most of the English people by his absolutism and favoring of Catholicism. When his wife gave birth to a son, who was a Catholic and the heir to the throne, English parliamentary leaders feared a continuation of pro-Catholic and absolutist policies. They asked William and his wife, Mary, to take the throne, as long as they accepted the parliamentary checks on royal power. As a result, the king could no longer suspend laws nor could a Catholic become king.

However, as the Enlightenment spread, many of Europe's absolute rulers turned to philosophes for help in making their governments work better. At the same time, however, they did not want to lose any of their power. Historians used to call these rulers enlightened despots. Despots are rulers who hold total power.

Louis XIV: France's Sun King

During the 1600s, France was one of Europe's strongest nations. In 1643 Louis XIV came to the throne. As king, Louis XIV was the most celebrated absolute monarch. His reign of 72 years—the longest in European history—set the style for Europe's kings and queens. Louis was known as the Sun King, the source of light for his people and for Europe's nobles and rulers.

Louis relied on a bureaucracy, but he was the source of all political authority in France. He is said to have boasted, "I am the State."

Louis's army fought and won wars to expand France's territory, but these conflicts were costly in money and soldiers to France. The king's constant wars and excessive spending weakened France and the monarchy.

Frederick the Great

During the 1600s and 1700s, Germany was a collection of over 300 separate states. Of these states, two—**Prussia** (PRUH•shuh) and **Austria** (AWS•tree•uh)—became great European powers.

The most famous Prussian ruler was Frederick II, also called Frederick the Great. He ruled from 1740 to 1786. As Prussia's king, Frederick strengthened the army and fought wars to gain new territory for Prussia. He also tried to be an "enlightened ruler." He supported the arts and learning and tried to carry out enlightened reforms. He permitted his people to speak and publish more freely. He also allowed greater religious toleration.

many pieces of music that are still popular today. Handel wrote many operas, but he is best known for *Messiah*, an oratorio, or religious composition that mixes voices, orchestra, and organ.

Classical music emerged in the mid-1700s. Classical composers, inspired by the ancient Greeks and Romans, emphasized balance, harmony, and stability. Franz Joseph Haydn and Wolfgang Amadeus Mozart wrote classical music. Haydn's use of instruments made the symphony more popular. Mozart composed a large number of musical pieces that remain popular today.

Wolfgang Amadeus Mozart ▼

▲ Johann Sebastian Bach

Connecting to the Past
1. What is the difference in tone between baroque and classical music?
2. What factors allowed music to thrive during the 1700s?

687

Writing Activity

Ask students to write a paragraph describing what they think would happen if an American president, echoing Louis XIV, announced "I am the state." Encourage them to use humor in their descriptions. **L2**

Reading Support L1/ EL

Assign **Guided Reading Activity 18–3** to help students organize the information in the section.

NATIONAL GEOGRAPHIC **The Way It Was**

Answers:
1. Baroque emphasizes drama and emotion; classical emphasizes balance, harmony, and stability.
2. Nonreligious music was played in theaters for the first time; leaders supported music; very talented composers emerged.

COOPERATIVE LEARNING ACTIVITY

Natural Law Ask a group of students to research and prepare a panel discussion on the subject of natural law. Have them address questions, such as:

- What is natural law?
- Where does it come from?
- How is the idea used today?
- How do we know what natural laws are?
- How do we use natural law?

Remind the panel members to leave time for questions after the discussion. **L2**

Using Geography Skills

Answers:

1. West Pomerania

2. 1526–1699

Skills Practice

Ask: Look at the location of the Pomeranias. What new advantage did they give Prussia? (*Prussia acquired a coastline on the Baltic Sea and ports for trading.*)

3 ASSESS

Assign Section 3 Review as homework or as an in-class activity.

● Have students use the **Interactive Tutor Self-Assessment CD-ROM** to review the section.

Assessment L2

Assign **Section 3 Quiz** to assess mastery of the material found in the section.

Reading Support L1/ EL

Assign **Reading Essentials and Study Guide 18–3** to help students review section material.

NATIONAL GEOGRAPHIC

Growth of Prussia and Austria *c. 1525–1720*

KEY
East Prussia and possessions, 1618
Land added, 1619–1699
Land added, 1700–1720

KEY
Austrian Hapsburg lands, 1525
Land added, 1526–1699
Land added, 1700–1720

◀ Frederick the Great

▲ Joseph II

Using Geography Skills

By the 1700s, Prussia and Austria had emerged as the most powerful German states.

1. Which state did Prussia acquire between 1700 and 1720?
2. During which of the periods shown on the map did Austria expand its territory the most?

Austria's Hapsburg Rulers By the 1700s, the other powerful German state—Austria—ruled a large empire of many different peoples, languages, and cultures. This vast Austrian empire spread over much of central and southeastern Europe. It was ruled by a family known as the Hapsburgs.

In 1740 a young Hapsburg princess named Maria Theresa became Austria's ruler. Clever and talented, Maria Theresa worked hard to improve the lot of Austria's serfs, who worked for the nobles. She also tried to make government work better.

After Maria Theresa died in 1780, her son, Joseph II, became ruler. Joseph II admired Enlightenment ideas. He freed the serfs, made land taxes equal for nobles and

farmers, and allowed books to be published freely. Most of Joseph's reforms failed, however. The nobles opposed Joseph's changes, and he was forced to back down. However, the former serfs, now farmers, were allowed to keep their freedom.

Russia's Peter I and Catherine II To the east of Austria stretched the vast empire of Russia. As you read previously, Russia was ruled by all-powerful rulers known as czars. One of the most powerful czars was Peter I, also known as Peter the Great. During his reign from 1689 to 1725, Peter tried to make Russia into a strong and up-to-date European power. He began reforms to make the government work more smoothly.

688 CHAPTER 18 Enlightenment and Revolution

EXTENDING THE CONTENT

A Great Traveler When he was a young ruler, Peter the Great realized that his knowledge of the Western world, like that of most Russians, was very limited. In order to correct his ignorance, Peter undertook a grand tour of Western Europe. Traveling under a false name, Peter spent much of his time studying shipbuilding. He worked for several months in Dutch and English shipyards. He hoped that his knowledge would help Russia create a great navy. While in England, Peter also went to weapons arsenals, museums, factories, schools, and even to Parliament. He returned to Russia a year and a half later, better prepared to transform the huge, backward country into a modern nation.

Peter also improved Russia's military and expanded Russia's territory westward to the Baltic Sea. In 1703 he founded a city called **St. Petersburg** (PEE•tuhrz•BUHRG) in this area. A few years later, Russia's capital was moved to St. Petersburg from Moscow.

After Peter died, conflict erupted among Russia's nobles. Then, in 1762 a German princess named Catherine came to the throne of Russia. Early in her reign, Catherine was devoted to Enlightenment ideas. She studied about and wrote letters to the philosophes. She even thought about freeing the serfs, but a serf uprising changed her mind. In the end, she allowed the nobles to treat the serfs as they pleased.

Under Catherine, Russia gained even more land and increased its power in Europe. As a result, Catherine became known as "the Great." However, by 1796,

Russia grew more powerful ▶ during the reigns of Peter the Great (above) and Catherine the Great (right). *How did Peter try to make Russia a European power?*

the year Catherine died, the ideas of liberty and equality had spread across Europe. These ideas seriously threatened the rule of powerful kings and queens.

✓ **Reading Check** **Explain** How did the ideas of absolute monarchs conflict with the ideas of Enlightenment thinkers?

Study Central™ Need help with the material in this section? Visit jat.glencoe.com

Section 3 Review

Reading Summary

Review the Main Ideas

- In the 1700s, many Europeans thought reason could make government and society better. Hobbes, Locke, and Montesquieu developed ideas about how to improve government.

- Enlightenment thinkers, such as Voltaire, Diderot, and Rousseau, described ways to make society better.

- By the 1700s, most of Europe's rulers were absolute monarchs. Some, however, tried to create governments based on Enlightenment ideas.

What Did You Learn?

1. Who were the French philosophes?

2. What was the *Encyclopedia*, and what message did it attempt to deliver to its readers?

Critical Thinking

3. **Organizing Information** Draw a chart to list the rulers of the Enlightenment, their countries, and their accomplishments.

Ruler	Country	Accomplishments

4. **Cause and Effect** How did civil war in England affect Hobbes?

5. **Explain** Do you think enlightened despots were really enlightened?

6. **Conclude** Which of the Enlightenment thinkers discussed in this section do you think had the most impact on modern society? Explain your answer.

7. **Civics Link** Describe how beliefs about people and government during the Enlightenment are reflected in our government today.

ENRICH

Have students discuss whether the Enlightenment undermined Europe's monarchies. **L3**

✓ **Reading Check**

Answer: Monarchs: did not want to lose any of their power; Enlightenment thinkers: wanted government's power limited.

To help students understand section material, have them visit **Study Central**™ at jat.glencoe.com

RETEACH

Have students compare and contrast France, Prussia, Austria, and Russia. **L1**

④ CLOSE

Have students discuss how successful Europe's rulers were in applying Enlightenment principles. **L2**

SECTION 3 REVIEW ANSWERS

1. writers, journalists, and teachers

2. a reference work of 28 volumes; called for changes to make society more just and caring

3. Answers should include the rulers Frederick the Great, Maria Theresa, Joseph I, Peter I, and Catherine II; their countries; and their accomplishments.

4. led him to defend absolute monarchy

5. Answers will vary but should be supported by the text.

6. Answers will vary but should demonstrate a thoughtful response.

7. Answers will vary. Students should provide valid reasons based on the text for their choice.

689

① FOCUS

SECTION OVERVIEW

In this section, students will learn how Europeans set up colonies in North America and why the British colonies formed the United States.

BELLRINGER
SKILLBUILDER ACTIVITY

🖐 Project **Daily Focus Skills Transparency 18–4** and have students answer questions. Discuss their responses.

Get Ready to Read!

Preteaching Vocabulary: Explain that popular sovereignty means that people in a country have the right and responsibility to govern themselves.

Answers to Graphic: Examples include: Cause: Stamp Act; Effect: colonists boycott British goods; Cause: taxes on glass, lead, paper, paint, tea; Effect: Boston Massacre; Cause: Tea Act; Effect: Boston Tea Party; Cause: Intolerable Acts; Effect: First Continental Congress; Cause: battles of Lexington and Concord; Effect: Second Continental Congress; Cause: Paine's *Common Sense*; Effect: Declaration of Independence

Section 4
The American Revolution

Get Ready to Read!

What's the Connection?

Between the 1500s and 1700s, Europeans set up colonies in North America. In the British colonies, English traditions and the Enlightenment gave colonists a strong sense of their rights.

Focusing on the Main Ideas

• European colonies in North America developed differently from each other and from Europe. *(page 691)*

• Great Britain faced problems in North America, because the American colonists objected to new British laws. *(page 695)*

• The American colonies formed a new nation, the United States of America. *(page 698)*

Locating Places
Quebec (kwih•BEHK)
Jamestown
Boston
Philadelphia

Meeting People
Pilgrim
George Washington
Tom Paine
Thomas Jefferson

Building Your Vocabulary
representative government
constitution
popular sovereignty
  (SAH•vuh•ruhn•tee)
limited government

Reading Strategy
Cause and Effect Complete a cause-and-effect diagram showing why the British colonies declared independence.

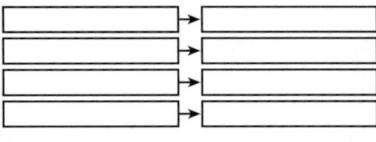

NATIONAL GEOGRAPHIC When & Where?

1600	
1620 Pilgrims found colony in Massachusetts	
1700	
1800	
1776 Declaration of Independence is signed	**1789** U.S. Constitution is adopted

Saratoga • Boston
• New York
Philadelphia
• Yorktown
• Charles Town

SECTION RESOURCES

📁 Reproducible Masters
• Reproducible Lesson Plan 18–4
• Daily Lecture and Discussion Notes 18–4
• Vocabulary Activity 18–4
• Active Reading Note-Taking Guide 18–4
• Guided Reading Activity 18–4
• Section Quiz 18–4
• Reading Essentials and Study Guide 18–4

🖐 Transparencies
• Daily Focus Skills Transparency 18–4

Multimedia
⊙ Interactive Tutor Self-Assessment CD-ROM
⊙ ExamView® Pro Testmaker CD-ROM
⊙ Presentation Plus! CD-ROM
⊙ Vocabulary PuzzleMaker CD-ROM

Settling North America

Main Idea European colonies in North America developed differently from each other and from Europe.

Reading Focus What would make you want to move to a new place? In this chapter, you will learn why Europeans settled in North America from the 1500s to the 1700s.

Previously, you learned that Spain and Portugal built colonies in the Americas in the 1500s. Beginning in the 1600s, the French, English, and other Europeans began setting up their own colonies in the Americas. While most of Spain's colonies were in the Caribbean, Mexico, and South America, most of France and England's colonies were in North America.

The Spanish in North America The Spanish did not ignore the lands north of Mexico and the Caribbean. In the 1500s, Spanish conquistadors explored the southeastern corner of North America and the lands north of Mexico. They had hoped to find wealthy empires like those of the Aztec and Inca. Instead, they found only small villages of Native Americans. As a result, Spain remained much more interested in its colonies in Mexico, Peru, and the Caribbean, because they provided large amounts of silver and gold.

The Spanish did not completely ignore the rest of North America. They built settlements and forts along the northern edge of their territory. These settlements, such as St. Augustine in Florida and Santa Fe in New Mexico, were intended to keep other Europeans out of Spanish territory.

2 TEACH

Activating Prior Knowledge Ask students to review what they learned about the Jesuits in Chapter 17. Then have them explain why the Jesuits became missionaries in French North America. *(Their order was especially devoted to missionary work and converting non-Christians.)* **L2**

Daily Lecture and Discussion Notes 18–4

Use **Daily Lecture and Discussion Notes 18–4** for an outline of key concepts found in the section.

Reading Support L1/ EL

Use **Vocabulary Activity 18–4** to review important terms in the section.

Using Geography Skills

Answers:
1. France
2. mountains

Skills Practice

Ask: Was most of New France located on the coast of North America or in the interior? *(in the interior)*

NATIONAL GEOGRAPHIC
Europeans in North America 1750

KEY
- British
- French
- Spanish
- Disputed

Using Geography Skills

By the 1700s, Britain, France, and Spain claimed much of the territory of North America.
1. Which country controlled the area of the Mississippi River?
2. What physical feature may have prevented expansion farther to the west?

Reading Strategy — **READING THE TEXT**

Visualizing Visualizing, or creating mental pictures of what is read, is a valuable technique that helps students develop active reading skills and increase comprehension. Forming a mental picture can also aid recall. As students read this section, ask them to visualize a mental picture based on the text. For example, have them visualize some of the important events, such as the settlement of Jamestown, the battles of Lexington and Concord, the Boston Tea Party, and the writing of the U.S. Constitution. **L2**

More About the Art

Jamestown was located in a bug-infested, swampy area. Many colonists died from diseases bugs carried.

Caption Answer: growing of tobacco for export

CURRICULUM CONNECTION

Economics

Cash crops are still an important part of the world economy, especially in developing countries. Have students research the importance of cash crops, such as tobacco, coffee, chocolate, tea, cotton, and linen.

Indigo was a plant that yielded a deep blue dye. The growing of indigo was critical in the Southern colonies, especially South Carolina. The first person to cultivate indigo plants successfully was Eliza Pinckney (1722–1793). Within ten years of her accomplishment, the colony was exporting a million pounds of indigo.

▲ This painting shows what the original settlement at Jamestown may have looked like in 1607. *What prevented the Jamestown settlement from collapsing?*

Spanish priests also headed north. They set up missions, or religious communities, to teach Christianity and European ways to the Native Americans. Missions were set up in California, New Mexico, Florida, and other areas of North America.

France Settles North America The French came to North America to make money from fur trading. By the 1600s, beaver fur had become very popular in Europe. In 1608 French merchants hired explorer Samuel de Champlain (sham•PLAYN) to help them. Champlain set up a trading post named **Quebec** (kwih•BEHK) in what is now Canada. Quebec became the capital of the colony of New France.

From Quebec, French fur trappers, explorers, and missionaries moved into other parts of North America. In 1673 the explorers Louis Joliet and Jacques Marquette found the Mississippi River. Then in 1682 a French explorer named La Salle followed the Mississippi all the way to the Gulf of Mexico. He named the region Louisiana in honor of King Louis XIV. The French settlers in southern Louisiana also began bringing in enslaved Africans to grow sugarcane, rice, and tobacco.

The English Settle in America
English settlers came to North America for many reasons. While merchants set up some English colonies to make money, others were set up by people who wanted religious freedom. England's colonies grew rapidly because of economic problems in England. Many people in England wanted to move to America because their landlords had evicted them from their farms. In America, they had a chance to own land for themselves. Still others came because they were unemployed and needed work.

By 1600, England's rulers had accepted the ideas of mercantilism. Colonies and trading posts in Asia and America were making Europe's kingdoms wealthy. The English government believed colonies were needed to keep England strong.

In 1607 the Virginia Company, an English joint-stock company, set up the first permanent English settlement in North America. The settlers named it **Jamestown** after King James I. Jamestown was the first town of a new colony called Virginia.

Life in Virginia was very hard. The colonists could barely find enough to eat. Many settlers died from starvation and the cold winters, and others were killed in clashes with Native Americans.

During those first years, the colony made no money for the merchants who had invested in it. It might have collapsed had not one of the settlers, John Rolfe, discovered that tobacco could grow in Virginia's soil.

DIFFERENTIATED INSTRUCTION

Intrapersonal: Have students consider what it was like to take part in the settlement of North America or the American Revolution. Ask students to write a diary entry from the perspective of a person their age about an event of their choosing in the section. Tell them to answer these questions: What feelings might you have? What would you hope for? What might you fear? Ask volunteers to read their diary entries to the class.

English Learners: Ask students to write diary entries after first making a list of ten new adjectives that describe people's feelings, such as *uneasy, overjoyed,* or *fearful*.

Gifted and Talented: Have students write a poem or short story about an event in the section.

Tobacco was popular in Europe in the 1600s. Soon the colonists in Virginia were growing it in large amounts and selling it for a lot of money. Tobacco became the first cash crop of the English colonies. A cash crop is grown in large quantities to sell for profit.

Eventually, tobacco was grown on large farms called plantations. Because plantations need many workers, the English began bringing in enslaved Africans to work the land. The success of Virginia encouraged the English government to set up more colonies in America to grow cash crops. The colony of South Carolina, for example, began growing rice and indigo. The English also began setting up colonies in the Caribbean to grow sugarcane.

Not all English settlers came to North America in search of wealth. Some came to find religious freedom. As you read in the last chapter, many Protestants in England were Puritans. Puritans wanted to rid the Anglican Church of Catholic rituals and allow each congregation to choose its own leaders. King James I and his son King Charles I both believed Puritans were a threat to their authority and persecuted them.

In 1620 a group of Puritans known as the **Pilgrims** decided to go to America so that they could worship freely. In 1620 they boarded a ship called the *Mayflower* and set out for North America. They landed just north of Cape Cod in what is today the state of Massachusetts. They named their settlement Plymouth.

The success of the Pilgrims encouraged other Puritans to begin leaving England for America. Led by John Winthrop, a group of Puritans landed in America and founded the colony of Massachusetts. Others soon followed. By 1643, more than 20,000 Puritans had moved to America. They founded Rhode Island, Connecticut, and New Hampshire.

Primary Source

The Mayflower Compact

The Pilgrims governed themselves according to this document.

"Having undertaken for the Glory of God, and Advancement of the Christian Faith, and the Honour of our King and Country, a Voyage to plant the first colony in the northern Parts of Virginia; Do . . . covenant [agree] and combine ourselves together into a civil Body Politick [political group], for our better Ordering and Preservation. . . . And by Virtue hereof do enact, constitute, and frame, such just and equal Laws, . . . and Offices, from time to time, as shall be thought most meet and convenient for the general Good of the Colony; unto which we promise all due Submission and Obedience."

—Mayflower Compact, November 21, 1620

▲ The Pilgrims sign the Mayflower Compact.

DBQ Document-Based Question

To what do the Pilgrims promise submission and obedience?

CRITICAL THINKING ACTIVITY

Analyzing Primary Sources Direct students to the two primary source documents in this section—the Mayflower Compact and the Declaration of Independence. Have students analyze each document to find the underlying assumptions of the writers of each document. Have students make a list of the assumptions that the documents share as well as any that differ. *(Both assume that people have the right to make decisions for themselves and choose their own form of government, and both assume that God is the source of these and other rights. The Declaration of Independence also seems to assume that people have the obligation to explain their actions to other nations.)* **L3**

Researching History Ask students to research the Seven Years' War involving France, Britain, and other European countries. In a class discussion, point out that the North American phase of this war is sometimes called the French and Indian War. Ask students to give their views about whether the war could be seen as a "world war." **L3**

CONNECTING ACROSS TIME

Have students review the ways American colonists worked together to make laws and influence policies. *(through representative assemblies, constitutions)* Then ask students to speculate on why laws and respect for the law are important in any society. Finally, ask volunteers to compare the ways colonists influenced policies with the ways they—and citizens in general—influence policies today in school, government, and society. **L3**

Using Geography Skills

Answers:

1. north of New York City
2. tobacco

✓ Reading Check

Answer: Jamestown was settled as part of a business venture while Plymouth was settled by people looking for religious freedom.

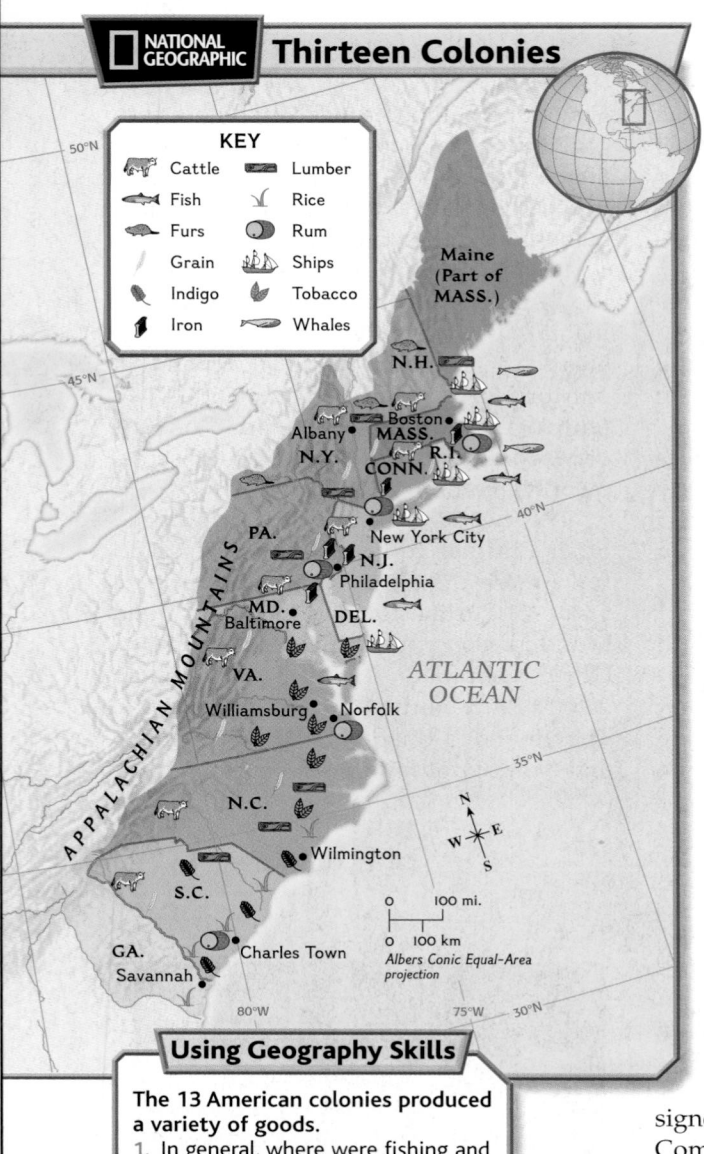

NATIONAL GEOGRAPHIC Thirteen Colonies

KEY
- Cattle
- Fish
- Furs
- Grain
- Indigo
- Iron
- Lumber
- Rice
- Rum
- Ships
- Tobacco
- Whales

Maine (Part of MASS.)

N.H.
Boston
Albany • MASS.
N.Y. R.I.
CONN.
New York City
PA.
N.J.
Philadelphia
MD.
Baltimore DEL.
ATLANTIC OCEAN
VA.
Williamsburg Norfolk
APPALACHIAN MOUNTAINS
N.C.
Wilmington
S.C.
GA.
Savannah Charles Town

0   100 mi.
0   100 km
Albers Conic Equal-Area projection

Using Geography Skills

The 13 American colonies produced a variety of goods.
1. In general, where were fishing and whaling industries located?
2. What was a major crop in Virginia and Maryland?

Other people seeking religious freedom set up colonies as well. English Catholics founded Maryland in 1634. The Quakers, another religious group that had been persecuted in England, founded Pennsylvania in 1680.

By the early 1700s, the English had created 13 colonies along the coast of North America. These colonies had different economies and societies, but they had one thing in common: they wanted to govern themselves.

Self-Government in America
The tradition of self-government began early in the English colonies. To attract more settlers, the head of the Virginia Company gave the colonists in Virginia the right to elect burgesses, or representatives, from among the men who owned land. The first House of Burgesses met in 1619. It was patterned after the English Parliament and voted on laws for the Virginia colony.

The House of Burgesses set an example for **representative government,** or a government in which people elect representatives to make laws and conduct government. It was not long before other colonies set up their own legislatures as well.

A year after the Virginia House of Burgesses met, the Pilgrims arrived in North America and began their own tradition of self-government. Before going ashore, the Pilgrims signed an agreement called the Mayflower Compact. They agreed to rule themselves by choosing their own leaders and making their own laws.

Over the years, most of the English colonies began drawing up **constitutions,** or written plans of government. These documents let the colonists elect assemblies and protected their rights.

✓ Reading Check **Compare and Contrast**
How was the founding of Jamestown different from the founding of Plymouth?

INTERDISCIPLINARY CONNECTIONS ACTIVITY

Language Arts Have students read and review books about America's colonial and revolutionary history. If the book is a novel, have students address plot, setting, characterization, themes, and the author's ability to make the period come to life. If the book is nonfiction or a biography, ask them to evaluate the author's point of view, the illustrations or photos, and their judgment about the book's accuracy. Possible novels include *Johnny Tremain* by Esther Forbes, *The Fighting Ground* by Avi, *Jump Ship to Freedom* by James and Christopher Collier, and *Amos Fortune, Free Man* by Elizabeth Yates. Nonfiction works include any of Jean Fritz's or Milton Meltzer's books about colonial and revolutionary figures, as well as *Constance: A Story of Early Plymouth* and *I'm Deborah Sampson* by Patricia Clapp. **L2**

Trouble in the Colonies

Main Idea Great Britain faced problems in North America, because the American colonists objected to new British laws.

Reading Focus Do you like to make your own decisions, without someone else telling you what to do? Read to find out why the American colonies wanted to make decisions without British interference.

During the early 1700s, there were many changes in England and its overseas colonies. In 1707 England united with Scotland and became the United Kingdom of Great Britain. The term *British* came to mean both the English and the Scots.

By 1750, Great Britain had become the world's most powerful trading empire. It had 13 prosperous colonies along the Atlantic coast of America and others in India and the Caribbean. For years, Britain and its American colonies seemed to get along well. This relationship changed, however, when the British tried to control trade and impose taxes on the colonies. These efforts angered colonists.

HISTORY Mystery

How Do We Know About Life in Early Virginia?
Since 1994, a program called Jamestown Rediscovery has been excavating the ruins of the first permanent British settlement in North America. Historians have explored the ruins of the first fort and have uncovered more than 150,000 artifacts. The artifacts include rings and jewelry, ceramics, tools, coins, weapons and armor, and household furnishings.

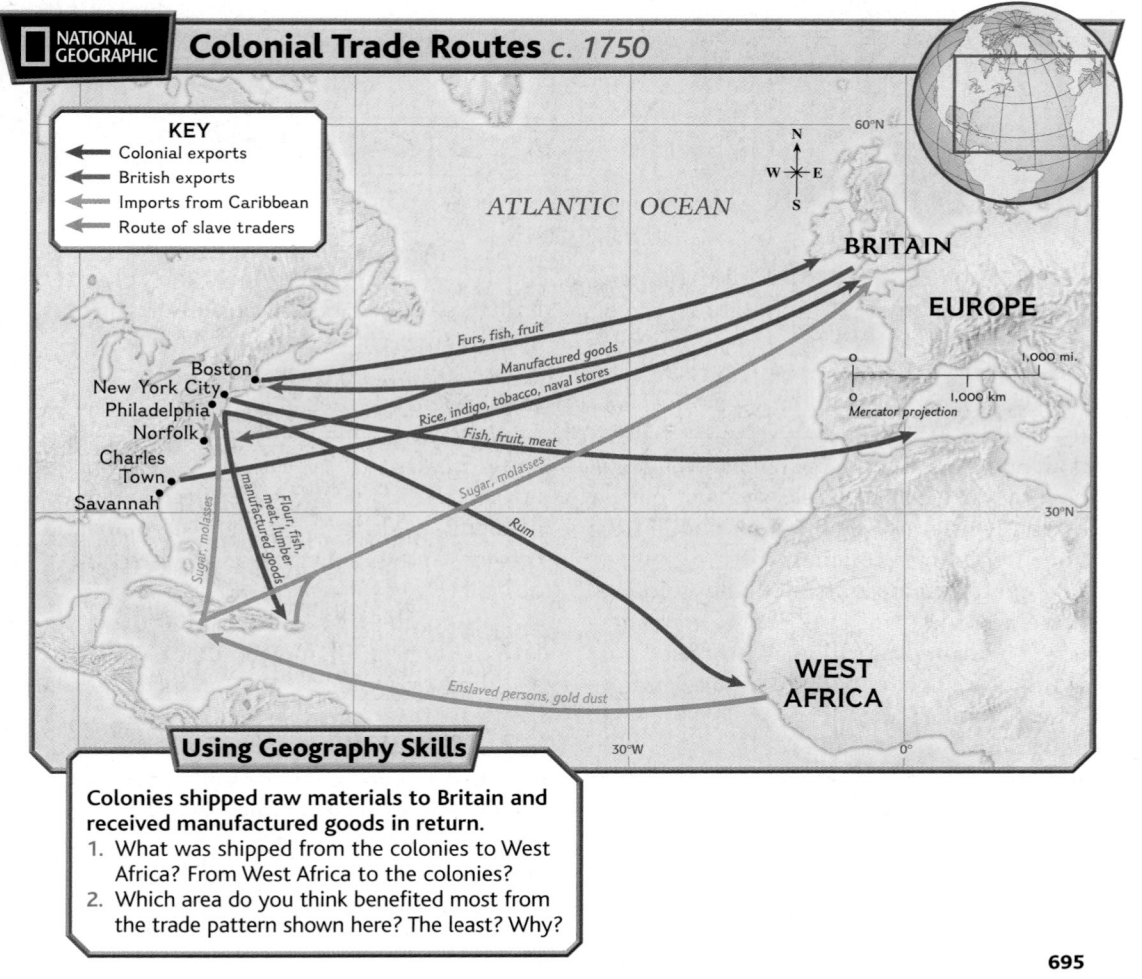

NATIONAL GEOGRAPHIC
Colonial Trade Routes *c. 1750*

KEY
- Colonial exports
- British exports
- Imports from Caribbean
- Route of slave traders

ATLANTIC OCEAN

Furs, fish, fruit
Manufactured goods
Rice, indigo, tobacco, naval stores
Fish, fruit, meat
Sugar, molasses
Rum
Flour, fish, meat, lumber manufactured goods
Sugar, molasses
Enslaved persons, gold dust

Boston
New York City
Philadelphia
Norfolk
Charles Town
Savannah

BRITAIN
EUROPE
WEST AFRICA

60°N
30°N
30°W
0°

0   1,000 mi.
0   1,000 km
Mercator projection

Using Geography Skills

Colonies shipped raw materials to Britain and received manufactured goods in return.
1. What was shipped from the colonies to West Africa? From West Africa to the colonies?
2. Which area do you think benefited most from the trade pattern shown here? The least? Why?

Using Geography Skills

Answers:
1. rum; enslaved persons, gold dust
2. Europe and the colonies; Africa; loss of many people to slavery

695

EXTENDING THE CONTENT

Origin of the Song "Amazing Grace" The composer of "Amazing Grace" was Englishman John Newton (1725–1807), the captain of a slave ship that carried captive Africans from Sierra Leone to the New World. Although he was not a religious man, during a terrible storm Newton prayed that his ship might not sink. After the ship survived the storm, Newton had a religious conversion. He left the slave trade, convinced of its immorality, and returned to England. There he eventually became a minister in the Anglican Church and preached strongly against slavery and the trade in Africans. He always honored the anniversary of the storm, May 10, 1748, when, he believed, "amazing grace" led him home.

More About the Art

The first Bostonian shot on that March day was Crispus Attucks, an African American sailor. He became one of the first Americans to lose his life in the struggle for independence. Today, a monument to him stands in Boston Common. A pro-independence leader named Sam Adams skillfully used the massacre to intensify emotions against the British.

Caption Answer: They resented being taxed by Britain.

Writing Activity

Have students write a paragraph describing the role of natural rights in the growing tensions that led to the Revolution. **L3**

Reading Strategy

Sequencing Information Have students review the events leading to the Revolution and make their own time line of events that contributed to increased tensions between the colonists and the British. *(Time lines should include most of the events discussed in the subsection "Trouble in the Colonies" and the beginning of "The War of Independence" and any others students know about.)* **L2**

▼ Riots against the Stamp Act broke out in many American cities. *Why was the Stamp Act unpopular in the colonies?*

◄ King George III

The Boston Massacre ▶

Colonial Government and Trade For many years, Great Britain had allowed the American colonies the freedom to run their local affairs. In each colony, men who owned property elected representatives to a legislature. Colonial legislatures passed laws and could tax the people. However, the governor of a colony could veto laws passed by the legislature. The king appointed the governor in most colonies.

Great Britain controlled the colonies' trade according to the ideas of mercantilism. The American colonies produced raw materials, such as tobacco, rice, indigo, wheat, lumber, fur, deerskin leather, fish, and whale products. These were then shipped to Great Britain and traded for manufactured goods such as clothing, furniture, and goods from Asia, such as tea or spices.

To control this trade, Britain passed a series of laws called the Navigation Acts in the 1600s. Under these laws the colonists had to sell their raw materials to Britain even if they could get a better price elsewhere. Any goods bought by the colonies from other countries in Europe had to go to England first and be taxed before they could be sent to the Americas. The trade laws also said that all trade goods had to be carried on ships built in Britain or the colonies and that the crews had to be British as well.

The colonists at first accepted the trade laws because it guaranteed them a place to sell their raw materials. Later, the colonists came to resent British restrictions. With population in the colonies growing, the colonists wanted to make their own manufactured goods. They also wanted to sell their products elsewhere if they could get higher prices. Many colonial merchants began smuggling, or shipping goods in and

696   CHAPTER 18   Enlightenment and Revolution

CITIZENSHIP AND YOU

Public Service Display the following quotation from Tom Paine's *The American Crisis*:

"These are the times that try men's souls. The summer soldier and the sunshine patriot may, in this crisis, shrink from the service of his country; but he that stands it now deserves the love and thanks of man and woman."

Have students discuss any parts of the quotation that they do not understand. Next, ask them to form groups and discuss how this statement can be applied to life and society in the United States today. Have volunteers report group discussions to the rest of the class. Then hold a class discussion about what it meant to be a good citizen in 1776 and what it means today. **L3**

▲ During the Boston Tea Party, a group of colonists, some dressed as Native Americans, dumped chests of tea into Boston Harbor. Many more colonists cheered them on from shore. *What was Britain's response to this event?*

More About the Art

Among the 50 to 60 Bostonians who boarded the three British tea ships in 1773 was a local silversmith and engraver. His name was Paul Revere. Just a few years earlier, his famous engraving of the Boston Massacre had stirred up public opinion against the British.

Caption Answer: passed laws closing down Boston Harbor and put Massachusetts under military rule

CURRICULUM CONNECTION

Literature
Ask a volunteer to rehearse and perform a dramatic reading of "Concord Hymn," Ralph Waldo Emerson's poem commemorating the Battle of Concord.

Predicting Ask students what specific steps, if any, Britain and the colonies might have taken to resolve their differences without conflict. **L3**

out of the country without paying taxes or getting government permission.

Why Did the British Tax the Colonies?
Between 1756 and 1763, the French and British fought for control of North America. The British won, gaining nearly all of France's North American empire. The war was very costly, however, and left the British government deep in debt. Desperate for money, the British made plans to tax the colonists and tighten trade rules.

In 1765 Parliament passed the Stamp Act, which taxed newspapers and other printed material. All of these items had to bear a stamp showing that the tax was paid. The colonists were outraged. They responded by boycotting, or refusing to buy, British goods.

Finally, delegates from nine colonies met in New York to discuss the Stamp Act. They sent a letter to the British government stating that the colonies could not be taxed except by their own assemblies. The British backed down for a while, but they still needed money. In 1767 Parliament placed taxes on glass, lead, paper, paint, and tea.

Tax Protests Lead to Revolt The American colonists grumbled about the new taxes. They bullied the tax collectors, and journalists drew ugly cartoons of King George III. Worried, the British sent more troops to **Boston,** Massachusetts, where the largest protests had taken place.

In March 1770, violence broke out. A crowd of colonists began insulting British soldiers and throwing snowballs at them. The soldiers fired into the crowd. Five people were killed. This event came to be called the Boston Massacre. Shortly thereafter, all of the taxes were repealed, or canceled, except the one on tea.

In 1773 Parliament passed the Tea Act. It allowed a British trading company to ship tea to the colonies without paying the taxes colonial tea merchants had to pay. This allowed the company to sell its tea very cheaply and threatened to drive the colonial tea merchants out of business.

In Massachusetts, angry colonists decided to take action. A group of protesters dressed as Native Americans boarded several British ships in Boston Harbor and dumped their cargoes of tea into the water. This event is known as the Boston Tea Party.

To punish the colonists, Parliament in 1774 passed laws that closed down Boston Harbor and put the government of Massachusetts under military rule. It also said that British troops should be quartered, or given a place to live, in colonists' homes. The colonists called these laws the Intolerable Acts, or laws they could not bear.

The Intolerable Acts made the colonists more determined to fight for their liberties.

COOPERATIVE LEARNING ACTIVITY

Focusing on the 13 Colonies Ask students to work in small groups to prepare a fact sheet on one of the 13 British colonies in North America. Have them include information such as when the colony was founded and by whom; what kind of government it had; what type of colony it was; its leading citizens; its economy; and its cultural, religious, and political life. Have each group contribute its fact sheet to a class binder. Make the binder available as you study this chapter. **L2**

698

Activating Prior Knowledge Have students brainstorm what they know about John Locke. List their ideas on the board. Then have partners discuss how Locke's ideas influenced Jefferson in writing the Declaration of Independence. *(Discussions should focus on natural law as the basis for human rights and on the social contract between the governed and the government.)* **L1/ EL**

✓ Reading Check

Answer: Protestors against the Tea Act dressed as Native Americans, boarded ships, and dumped tea into Boston Harbor.

Primary Source

Although Thomas Jefferson wrote much of the Declaration of Independence, he had the help of a specially appointed committee. The committee included John Adams and Benjamin Franklin. The members made minor changes in Jefferson's draft, as did the Continental Congress.

Answer:
They wanted the reasons for their decision for independence to be clearly understood.

In September 1774, delegates from 12 colonies met in Philadelphia. They called themselves the First Continental Congress. The Congress spoke out against the Intolerable Acts and called for their repeal.

Colonial leaders, however, were divided about what to do. Some, like George Washington of Virginia, hoped to settle the differences with Great Britain. Others, like Samuel Adams of Massachusetts and Patrick Henry of Virginia, wanted the colonies to become independent.

✓ Reading Check **Identify** What was the Boston Tea Party?

Primary Source
The Declaration of Independence

On July 4, 1776, Congress approved the Declaration of Independence. The preamble—the first part of the document—explains Congress's reason for issuing the declaration:

"When in the Course of human events, it becomes necessary for one people to dissolve the political bands which have connected them with another.... they should declare the causes which impel them to the separation."

The document also explained that people have certain basic rights:

"We hold these truths to be self-evident, that all men are created equal, that they are endowed by their Creator with certain unalienable Rights, that among these are Life, Liberty and the pursuit of Happiness."

—Declaration of Independence, July 4, 1776

DBQ **Document-Based Question**

Why do you think the Congress thought they had to issue a written declaration of independence?

▲ Benjamin Franklin, John Adams, and Thomas Jefferson, shown left to right, worked together to write the Declaration of Independence.

The War of Independence

Main Idea The American colonies formed a new nation, the United States of America.

Reading Focus What causes people to go to war? Read to find out how the war between Great Britain and the Americans shaped the course of world history.

Before the colonists could decide what to do, fighting broke out in Massachusetts. The British set out to destroy a store of weapons at Concord. On April 19, 1775, they met colonial troops at Lexington and fought the first battle of the American Revolution.

698   CHAPTER 18   Enlightenment and Revolution

CRITICAL THINKING ACTIVITY

Analyzing Information Point out to students that the text skips over much of the time period between the founding of the first colonies in Jamestown and Massachusetts and the coming of the American Revolution. Have students research and create an annotated time line of important political, economic, cultural, and scientific events during these years. Have them place their time line on a sheet of paper and display it for the class as you read this section. **L2**

▲ The American leaders who met in Philadelphia in 1787 and wrote the United States Constitution were some of the nation's greatest political minds. *What sort of system of government did the Constitution create?*

Caption Answer: a federal republic

Reading Support L1/ EL

Assign **Guided Reading Activity 18–4** to help students organize the information in the section.

③ ASSESS

Assign Section 4 Review as homework or as an in-class activity.

◉ Have students use the **Interactive Tutor Self-Assessment CD-ROM** to review the section.

Assessment L2

Assign **Section 4 Quiz** to assess mastery of the material found in the section.

Reading Support L1/ EL

Assign **Reading Essentials and Study Guide 18–4** to help students review section material.

In May 1775, the Second Continental Congress met in **Philadelphia. George Washington** was named head of a new colonial army. The Congress then tried again to settle their differences with Great Britain. They appealed to King George III, who refused to listen.

More and more Americans began to think that independence was the only answer. In January 1776, a writer named **Tom Paine** made up many minds when he wrote a pamphlet called *Common Sense.* Paine used strong words to condemn the king and urged the colonists to separate from Great Britain.

The Declaration of Independence On July 4, 1776, the Congress issued the Declaration of Independence. Written by **Thomas Jefferson** of Virginia, the Declaration stated that the colonies were separating from Great Britain and forming a new nation, the United States of America.

In the Declaration, Jefferson explained why the colonists were founding a new nation. To do this, Jefferson borrowed the ideas of John Locke. In Section 3, you learned about Locke's idea that people have the right to overthrow governments that violate their rights. The Declaration stated that "all men are created equal" and have certain God-given rights. It said that King

George III had violated colonists' rights, and so they had the right to rebel.

The Declaration also drew from earlier English documents, such as the Magna Carta and the English Bill of Rights. Both documents established the idea that governments are not all-powerful and that rulers had to obey the laws and treat citizens fairly.

How Did the Americans Win the War?

After the Declaration was made, the war between the British and Americans dragged on. The first important American victory came in 1777 at the Battle of Saratoga in New York. This battle marked a turning point in the war. France, Great Britain's old enemy, realized that the United States might actually win. In 1778 France agreed to help the Americans.

The French were very important in the final victory. This came in 1781 at the Battle of Yorktown on the coast of Virginia. The French navy blocked the British from escaping by sea, while American and French forces surrounded and trapped the British inside Yorktown. Realizing they could not win, the British laid down their weapons. Peace negotiations began, and two years later, the Treaty of Paris ended the war.

The United States Constitution In 1783 Great Britain recognized American

CHAPTER 18   Enlightenment and Revolution   **699**

COOPERATIVE LEARNING ACTIVITY

Service Learning: Honoring America's Past Ask a group of students to create a short presentation on the American Revolution for elementary students, residents of a retirement center, or another group of people. Have the group incorporate information from this section as well as from other sources. Encourage students to include music, art, and other elements to make a multimedia presentation. Help them make arrangements to give their multimedia presentation to an audience of their choosing. After the presentation, have the group members report back to the class about their experiences. **L3**

ENRICH

Have students compare freedoms as stated in the Bill of Rights in the United States with freedoms in other countries. **L3**

 Reading Check

Answer: King George III had violated colonists' natural rights.

 History Online

To help students understand section material, have them visit **Study Central™** at jat.glencoe.com

RETEACH

Have pairs of students work together to make an outline of the subsection "The War of Independence." **L1**

 CLOSE

Ask students how the slogan "No taxation without representation" applied to the American Revolution. **L2**

---

independence. At first the United States was a confederation, or a loose union of independent states. Its plan of government was a document called the Articles of Confederation. The Articles created a national government, but the states held most powers. It soon became clear that the Articles were too weak to deal with the new nation's problems.

In 1787, 55 delegates met in Philadelphia to change the Articles. Instead, they decided to write a constitution for an entirely new national government. The new United States Constitution set up a federal system, in which powers were divided between the national government and the states. Following the ideas of Montesquieu, power in the national government was divided between executive, legislative, and judicial branches. A system called checks and balances enabled each branch to limit the powers of the other branches.

Under the Constitution, the United States was a republic with an elected president instead of a king. Elections held in 1789 made George Washington the first president of the United States. That same year, a Bill of Rights was added to the U.S. Constitution. The Bill of Rights set out certain rights the government could not violate. These rights included freedom of religion, speech, and press, and the right to trial by jury.

The U.S. Constitution was also shaped by Enlightenment principles. One of these is **popular sovereignty** (SAH•vuh•ruhn•tee), or the idea that government receives its powers from the people. Another is **limited government,** or the idea that a government may use only those powers given to it by the people.

✓ **Reading Check** **Explain** Why did the colonists decide to separate from Great Britain and create a new nation?

History Online

Study Central™ Need help with the material in this section? Visit jat.glencoe.com

Section 4 Review

Reading Summary

Review the Main Ideas

- In North America, the French settled in Canada and along the Mississippi River, while the British settled along the Atlantic coast.
- Americans protested when the British government attempted to impose more control and more taxes on the colonies.
- The Americans defeated the British in the American Revolution and set up a republican form of government with powers divided among three branches.

What Did You Learn?

1. When and where was the first battle of the American Revolution fought?
2. What is the Bill of Rights?

Critical Thinking

3. **Sequence Information** Draw a time line like the one below. Fill in events related to the American Revolution.

4. **Analyze** Why did England's colonies in America grow quickly?

5. **Civics Link** Which of John Locke's ideas appeared in the Declaration of Independence?

6. **Explain** How did the search for religious freedom affect the founding of colonies in America?

7. **Persuasive Writing** Write two letters to the editor at a colonial newspaper. One should support British involvement in its American colonies. The other should support the colonists' arguments for independence.

SECTION 4 REVIEW ANSWERS

1. in 1775; at Lexington
2. the part of the Constitution that protects the rights of freedom of speech, religion, and press and the right to trial by jury
3. Events should begin with the Second Continental Congress and continue through the Battle of Yorktown.
4. The colonies prospered from agriculture and trade.
5. natural rights, right to life and liberty; people's right to revolt
6. Pilgrims, Puritans, Catholics, and Quakers seeking religious freedom left England and founded colonies.
7. Letters will vary. Students should correctly identify and support the political ideas on both sides.

Chapter 18 Reading Review

Section ① The Age of Exploration

Vocabulary
mercantilism
export
import
colony
commerce
invest

Focusing on the **Main Ideas**
- In the 1400s, trade, technology, and the rise of strong kingdoms led to a new era of exploration. *(page 659)*
- While the Portuguese explored Africa, the Spanish, English, and French explored America. *(page 661)*
- To increase trade, Europeans set up colonies and created joint-stock companies. *(page 666)*
- Exploration and trade led to a worldwide exchange of products, people, and ideas. *(page 668)*

Early astrolabe ▼

Section ② The Scientific Revolution

Vocabulary
theory
rationalism
scientific method
hypothesis

Focusing on the Main Ideas
- The thinkers of the ancient world developed early forms of science and passed this knowledge to later civilizations. *(page 671)*
- European interest in astronomy led to new discoveries and ideas about the universe and Earth's place in it. *(page 673)*
- The Scientific Revolution led to new discoveries in physics, medicine, and chemistry. *(page 675)*
- Using the scientific method, Europeans of the 1600s and 1700s developed new ideas about society based on reason. *(page 678)*

Section ③ The Enlightenment

Vocabulary
natural law
social contract
separation of powers
deism
absolutism

Focusing on the Main Ideas
- During the 1700s, many Europeans believed that reason could be used to make government and society better. *(page 681)*
- The Enlightenment was centered in France, where thinkers wrote about changing their society and met to discuss their ideas. *(page 684)*
- Many of Europe's monarchs, who claimed to rule by the will of God, tried to model their countries on Enlightenment ideas. *(page 686)*

Section ④ The American Revolution

Vocabulary
representative government
constitution
popular sovereignty
limited government

Focusing on the Main Ideas
- European colonies in North America developed differently from each other and from Europe. *(page 691)*
- Great Britain faced problems in North America, because the American colonists objected to new British laws. *(page 695)*
- The American colonies formed a new nation, the United States of America. *(page 698)*

PREVIEW/REVIEW

Vocabulary Activity Have students make a quiz using 10 of the terms and exchange quizzes with a partner. Have them review their quizzes together.

🌐 **Vocabulary PuzzleMaker CD-ROM**

🌐 **Interactive Tutor Self-Assessment CD-ROM**

CONDENSE

📁 Chapter 18 **Guided Reading Activities**

🌐 **StudentWorks Plus™ CD-ROM (with Audio Program)**

RETEACH

📁 **Differentiated Instruction Activity 18**

📁 Chapter 18 *Reading Essentials and Study Guide*

CHAPTER CULMINATING ACTIVITY

Have students finish the Chapter Culminating Activity from page 654D.

Suggestions for rubrics may be found in the *Quizzes, Tests, and Authentic Assessment (with Rubrics)* booklet.

📖 Reading Strategy ❯ READ TO WRITE

Persuasive Essay A persuasive essay tries to convince a reader through sound reasoning and supporting evidence. Ask students to take a position on the following statement and then support it in a persuasive essay: Revolution was the only way the colonies could have become independent.
- **L1** students should include one or two supporting details in their essays.
- **L2** students should include several appropriate supporting details in their essays, which should be adequately organized, reasonably creative, and soundly argued.
- **L3** students should include many supporting details in their essays, which should be well-organized, creative, soundly argued, and grammatically correct.

Chapter
18 Assessment and Activities

GLENCOE TECHNOLOGY

MindJogger Videoquiz

Use the **MindJogger Videoquiz** to review Chapter 18 content.

Available in DVD and VHS

Review Vocabulary

1. d

2. a

3. b

4. f

5. c

6. e

Review Main Ideas

7. trade, technology, and rise of strong nations

8. To increase trade, Europeans set up colonies and created joint-stock companies.

9. Newton: force of gravity holds the solar system together; Galileo: objects fall at the same rate regardless of their weight, and the Sun is at the center of the universe.

10. It provided an orderly way, based on reason, to acquire new knowledge.

11. They tried to model their countries on Enlightenment ideas.

12. Hobbes believed in absolute monarchy to keep order; Locke believed in a social contract and rights.

13. They believed that George III had violated their rights, and therefore, they had the right to rebel.

14. limited government, popular sovereignty, checks and balances

Review Vocabulary

Write the key term that completes each sentence.

   a. constitution
   b. scientific method
   c. separation of powers
   d. mercantilism
   e. commerce
   f. absolutism

1. According to the idea of ___, a country gains power by gathering gold and setting up colonies.

2. A(n) ___ is a written plan for government.

3. Francis Bacon developed the ___.

4. The system in which monarchs held total power was called ___.

5. Montesquieu believed that a(n) ___ was needed for good government.

6. The buying and selling of goods in large amounts over long distances is called ___.

Review Main Ideas

Section 1 • The Age of Exploration

7. What led to the European era of exploration?

8. How were joint-stock companies related to overseas trade?

Section 2 • The Scientific Revolution

9. Describe the scientific discoveries of Newton and Galileo.

10. What was the importance of the scientific method?

Section 3 • The Enlightenment

11. How did the Enlightenment affect Europe's rulers?

12. How did the ideas of Thomas Hobbes and John Locke about government differ?

Section 4 • The American Revolution

13. Why did the American colonists want independence from Britain?

14. How did the new government of America reflect ideas developed during the Enlightenment?

Critical Thinking

15. Economics Link How are the ideas of mercantilism reflected in our economy today?

Review Reading Skill — Monitor and Adjust

Your Reading Strengths

16. Write five questions you would ask to help you better understand the information in the following paragraph.

> To help the Dutch, Queen Elizabeth I of England let English privateers attack Spanish ships. Privateers are privately owned ships that have a license from the government to attack ships of other countries. People nicknamed the English privateers "sea dogs." They raided the Spanish treasure ships bringing gold back from America.

To review this skill, see pages 656–657.

Critical Thinking

15. Students' answers will vary but might mention tariffs to protect market and government subsidies to farmers and other economic groups.

Reading Skill

16. Students' five questions should answer who, what, how, where, and why.

Geography Skills

Study the map below and answer the following questions.

17. **Place** Which city in Europe was the first to receive the potato as part of the Columbian Exchange?

18. **Movement** Why do you think so much time passed before the potato was introduced in Sweden and Finland?

19. **Movement** Does it appear from the map that trade between nations followed a strict pattern?

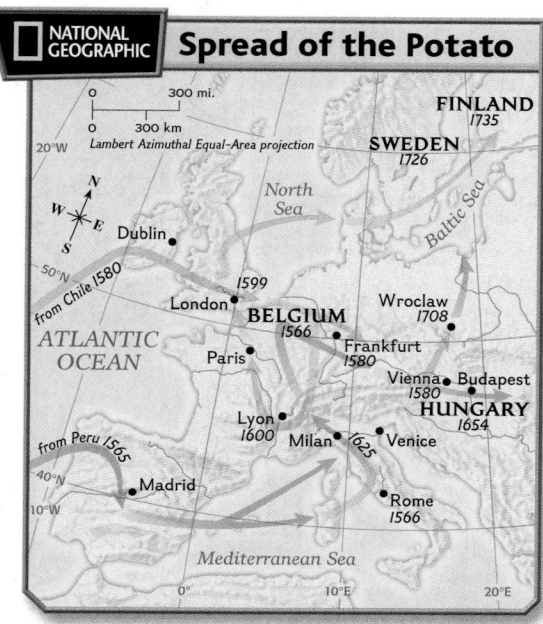

NATIONAL GEOGRAPHIC **Spread of the Potato**

Read to Write

20. **Descriptive Writing** Write a brief essay describing Montesquieu's beliefs about government and explaining how they are reflected in the U.S. Constitution.

21. **Using Your** 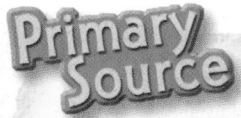 Work with a few classmates to create a question and answer game using the information in your foldables. Questions should cover the Scientific Revolution, Enlightenment, Age of Exploration, and American Revolution. Switch groups to play the games.

Using Technology

22. **Researching** Use the Internet and your local library to research present-day exploration in space and in the depths of the ocean. Find out about the technologies used, how these explorations are funded, and their impact on our knowledge of the universe. Write a report on how present-day explorers and their voyages are similar to and different from those of Europe in the Age of Exploration.

Linking Past and Present

23. **Analyzing** The music, art, and literature of the Enlightenment reflected people's views during that time. Write a description of how present-day music, art, and literature reflect how people currently feel about society. Give examples to support your opinion.

Primary Source Analyze

Portuguese official Duarte Barbosa described the way his country dealt with African kingdoms.

"The king of this city [Mombasa] refused to obey the commands of the King our Lord, and through this arrogance he lost it, and our Portuguese took it from him by force. He fled away, and they slew [killed] many of his people and also took captive many, both men and women, in such sort that it was left ruined and plundered and burned."

—Duarte Barbosa, "The East Coast of Africa"

DBQ Document-Based Questions

24. What did the king of Mombasa do that angered the Portuguese?

25. How did the Portuguese handle the conflict?

Have students visit the Web site at jat.glencoe.com to review Chapter 18 and take the **Self-Check Quiz**.

Using Technology

22. Answers will vary but should be supported by research.

Linking Past and Present

23. Answers will vary but should be supported by examples.

Primary Source

24. refused to obey Portuguese king

25. They took the city by force.

Bonus Question

Ask: Do you think the Enlightenment and the Scientific Revolution still have a powerful influence on our society today? Why or why not? If yes, what are some examples? *(Students' answers should reflect understanding of both movements as well as show knowledge of current society.)*

Geography Skills

17. Madrid

18. Students should note that those nations are isolated from the rest of Europe in terms of geography.

19. Most students will say no, since the arrows showing trade circle back on themselves and crisscross each other.

Read to Write

20. Essays will vary but should accurately explain separation of powers.

21. **FOLDABLES** Questions for the games should be accurate and based on the text.

REVIEWING UNIT OBJECTIVES

Having studied this unit, students should now be able to

1. describe the major civilizations of the Americas and the impact of European exploration on them;

2. identify the major events of the Renaissance and Reformation and explain the important effects of these two developments on Western civilization;

3. describe the major thinkers and ideas of the Enlightenment and Scientific Revolution, and discuss their influences on the Age of Exploration and the American Revolution.

UNIT REVIEW ACTIVITY

Analyzing Imports Have students use the chart to review the unit objectives. Ask them to contribute to a class list of 10 key ways the Renaissance and Reformation and the Enlightenment and Scientific Revolution helped shape today's world. Then ask them to choose the three most influential and explain the reasons for their choices. **L2**

Unit 5 Review

Comparing Early Modern Civilizations

Compare early modern civilizations by reviewing the information below. Can you see how the people of these civilizations had lives that were very much like yours?

Where in the World?

NATIONAL GEOGRAPHIC

- Chapter 16
- Chapter 17
- Chapter 18

	The Americas — Chapter 16	Renaissance and Reformation — Chapter 17	Enlightenment and Revolution — Chapter 18
Where did these civilizations develop?	• North America • Central America • Caribbean islands • South America	• Europe	• Western Europe • North America • Africa • South Asia • Southeast Asia
Who were some important people in these civilizations?	• Pachacuti, ruled A.D. 1438–1471 • Montezuma II, ruled A.D. 1502–1520 • Atahualpa, ruled A.D. 1525–1533	• Leonardo da Vinci A.D. 1452–1519 • Martin Luther A.D. 1483–1546 • Queen Isabella (Spain), ruled A.D. 1474–1504	• Christopher Columbus A.D. 1451–1506 • Queen Elizabeth I (England), ruled A.D. 1558–1603 • Galileo Galilei A.D. 1564–1642
Where did most of the people live?	• Hunter-gatherers • Farming villages • Cities (Tenochtitlán and Cuzco)	• City-states (Italy) • Commercial cities (London, Paris) • Farming villages	• Port cities (Lisbon, Amsterdam) • Overseas settlements and plantations
What were these people's beliefs?	• Traditional Native American religions	• Northern Europe: Protestant • Southern Europe: Roman Catholic • Jewish communities	• Europeans spread Christianity overseas • Rise of Deism in Europe and America

704

 Reproducible Masters
- Unit 5 Test Form A
- Unit 5 Test Form B
- Step Into World History Activity 5

Transparencies
- Unit 5 Map Overlay Transparencies

Multimedia
- Interactive Tutor Self-Assessment CD-ROM
- ExamView® Pro Testmaker CD-ROM
- Presentation Plus! CD-ROM

	The Americas Chapter 16	Renaissance and Reformation Chapter 17	Enlightenment and Revolution Chapter 18
What was their government like?	• Local groups ruled by chiefs and councils • Powerful emperors or kings (Maya, Aztec, and Inca)	• Italian city-states ruled by wealthy families • Most European areas ruled by kings, princes, and nobles	• English king's powers are limited, representative government spreads • United States founded as a republic
What was their language and writing like?	• Native Americans spoke hundreds of languages • Mayan and Aztec languages written in hieroglyphics • Inca had no written language	• Printed books helped spread knowledge • Vernacular used in Protestant worship • Latin remains language of Catholic Church	• Meeting of cultures meant spread of knowledge about languages • European languages brought by settlers to overseas colonies
What contributions did they make?	• Developed trade networks and methods of farming and building	• Furthered education • Created lifelike art • Different religions existed side by side	• Reason seen as a way to truth • General rules developed for scientific study • Beginning of modern democracy
How do these changes affect me? *Can you add any?*	• Native Americans passed on foods (corn, chocolate, potatoes) • Many place names in the Americas are based on Native American words (Chicago, Mississippi)	• Renaissance and Reformation Europeans passed on practice of printing books • School subjects (history, language) are rooted in Renaissance learning	• Supported rights (free speech, religion, press) that we enjoy today • Scientific tools (microscope, telescope) and vaccines for disease developed

UNIT WRAP-UP ACTIVITY

Causes and Effects The time period covered by this unit is good for helping students see the relationships of events to other events, especially the way some events help bring about other events. Have students work in discussion groups for this activity. Ask them to use the chart, along with the text material, to discuss causes and effects during the years covered in the unit. You may need to help them narrow their focus to a specific row on the chart or with specific questions.

For example, one discussion question might be "How did the development of new seafaring technology in Portugal lead to the spread of Christian ideas?" Students should understand that the new technology, such as the caravel and better navigation tools and cartography, allowed the missionary activities of the Jesuits and other groups to spread Christianity to the New World.

Have students consider broader questions as necessary. Leave time at the end of the activity to discuss groups' conclusions. **L3**

705

PROFESSIONAL DEVELOPMENT: USING LITERATURE

• Cochran, Judith, and Jan Keeling. *Using Literature to Learn about the First Americans: A Thematic Approach to Cultural Awareness.* Incentive Publications, 1993.
• Singleton, Laurel. *H Is for History: Using Children's Literature to Develop Historical Understandings.* Social Science Education Consortium, 1995.
• Steffey, Stephanie, and Wendy Hood. *If This Is Social Studies, Why Isn't It Boring?* Stenhouse, 1994.
• Van Middendorp, Judy, and Sharon Lee. "Literature for Children and Young Adults in a History Classroom." *The Social Studies,* May/June 1994.

Unit Resources

Note: The following materials may be used when teaching Unit 6.
Chapter and section level support materials can be found on the chapter and section resource pages.

TEACHING TRANSPARENCIES

 Writing Process Transparencies **L1**

DIFFERENTIATED INSTRUCTION

Step Into World History Activity 6 **L1**

ASSESSMENT

Unit 6 Test Form A **L2**
Unit 6 Test Form B **L2**

ADDITIONAL RESOURCES

- Glencoe Skillbuilder Interactive Workbook CD-ROM, Level 1
- Glencoe World History Primary Source Document Library CD-ROM
- Focus on World Art Prints
- Outline Map Resource Book
- World Desk Map
- World Art and Architecture Transparencies
- World Music: Cultural Traditions
- World Music: A Cultural Legacy
- Glencoe World Literature Library
- Reading in the Content Area
- Teaching Strategies for the World History Classroom (Including Block Scheduling Pacing Guides)
- Inclusion Strategies for the Middle School Social Studies Classroom

Blackline Master	CD-ROM
Poster	Audio Program
Transparency	DVD
Music Program	Videocassette

READING SUPPORT FROM
JAMESTOWN EDUCATION

- *Timed Readings Plus in Social Studies* help students increase their reading rate and fluency while maintaining comprehension. The 400-word passages are similar to those found on state and national assessments.
- *Reading in the Content Area: Social Studies* concentrates on six essential reading skills that help students better comprehend what they read. The book includes 75 high-interest nonfiction passages written at increasing levels of difficulty.
- *Reading Fluency* helps students read smoothly, accurately, and expressively.
- *Jamestown's Reading Improvement,* by renowned reading expert Edward Fry, focuses on helping build your students' comprehension, vocabulary, and skimming and scanning skills.
- *Critical Reading Series* provides high-interest books, each written at three reading levels.

To order these products, call Glencoe at 1-800-334-7344.

Reading List Generator CD-ROM

GLENCOE BOOKLINK

The Glencoe BookLink CD-ROM is a database that allows you to search more than 15,000 titles to create a customized reading list for your students.

- Reading lists can be organized by students' reading level, author, genre, theme, or area of interest.
- The database provides Degrees of Reading Power™ (DRP) and Lexile™ readability scores for all selections.
- A brief summary of each selection is included.

Leveled reading suggestions for this unit:

For students at a Grade 5 reading level:
- *Edith's Story*, by Edith Velmans

For students at a Grade 6 reading level:
- *Napoleon and the Napoleonic Wars*, by Albert Marrin

For students at a Grade 7 reading level:
- *China: Study of an Economically Developing Country*, by Julia Waterlow

To order this CD-ROM, call Glencoe at 1-800-334-7344.

Unit Reading Strategies

Each chapter in this unit contains special reading strategies. The following preview will help you teach these reading skills to your students.

Chapter 19: Reading for Meaning

Conceptual understanding requires that students synthesize background knowledge, make connections to other texts, and explore ideas instead of single definitions. Developing conceptual knowledge is a process that requires multiple exposures to text and reinforcement in the form of written and oral communication. Asking students to create and answer higher-level questions allows them to think more deeply about a concept, broadening and deepening their base of understanding.

Chapter 20: What's Important?

Determining importance means that students are able to distinguish between what is essential to know and supporting or less relevant details. While finding the main idea is a step in the right direction, the broader skill of determining importance leads to superior academic habits as well as an inherent ease with all types of text. Mastering other reading skills, such as activating background knowledge, analyzing text structure, and understanding the author's purpose, contributes to students' ability to determine importance in text. Students will practice determining relative value of different pieces of information.

Chapter 21: Building Discussion Skills

Discussion skills involve much more than stating an opinion about a certain topic. As the reader interacts with the text, he or she employs a myriad of reading skills, such as predicting, questioning, utilizing prior knowledge, analyzing, and synthesizing—the very skills necessary for an effective discussion. Students will practice formulating discussion questions and sharing and discussing them with classmates.

Chapter 22: Reading Beyond the Text

Motivation is a key factor in reading comprehension, and tapping student interest in the text is a good way to increase motivation. As students become independent readers, they may explore outside the text to satisfy their own curiosity. Such activity creates lifelong learners who see reading as a way of finding out what they need and want to know. Students will choose topics of their own interests as a basis for researching and learning more.

Use the **SkillBuilder Handbook** on pages 902–919 to help students practice important skills.

UNIT OVERVIEW

Unit 6 examines the forces, events, and figures of the last 200 years that helped create the world we live in today.

UNIT OBJECTIVES

After studying this unit, students should be able to

1. describe how revolution, industrialism, and nationalism have shaped the modern world;

2. explain how imperialistic ideas among powerful nations led to a shattering conflict, World War I;

3. describe the results of World War II and the Cold War;

4. discuss how numerous historical events and trends have helped create the world of today.

Why It's Important

Explain to students that this unit examines the forces that have shaped today's world. As they read, have them look for forces that are still active today.
L1

Unit
6
Modern Times

Why It's Important

Each civilization that you will study in this unit made important contributions to history.

- Western countries built new societies based on industry.
- Western rivalries over land and resources sparked World War I, the first global conflict.
- World War II made the United States and the Soviet Union world leaders.
- By 2000, advances in technology brought peoples of the world closer together. Conflicts, however, developed among different groups.

A.D. 1800 **A.D. 1825** **A.D. 1850** **A.D. 1875**

Industry and Nationalism
Chapter 19

A.D. 1804 Napoleon becomes French emperor

◄ Napoleon

A.D. 1848 Revolutions sweep Europe

A.D. 1861 U.S. Civil War begins

A.D. 1877 Edison invents the phonograph

Imperialism and World War I
Chapter 20

◄ African carving of European missionary

C. A.D. 1885 European powers divide Africa

World War II and the Cold War
Chapter 21

Building Today's World
Chapter 22

706

TIME LINE ACTIVITY

Direct students' attention to the multiple-tier time line on these pages. During the time period this unit covers, two powerful trends have dominated world political and economic relationships. One is the desire for independence and greater freedom. The other is the desire of powerful nations to gain influence over less-powerful ones. Have students list those events that describe either of these two contrasting desires. *(Possible suggestions include: revolutions sweep Europe, European powers divide Africa, African independence begins, and communism ends in Eastern Europe.)* **L2**

NATIONAL GEOGRAPHIC Where in the World?

Chapter 19
Chapter 20
Chapter 21
Chapter 22

0 2,000 mi.
0 2,000 km
Mercator projection

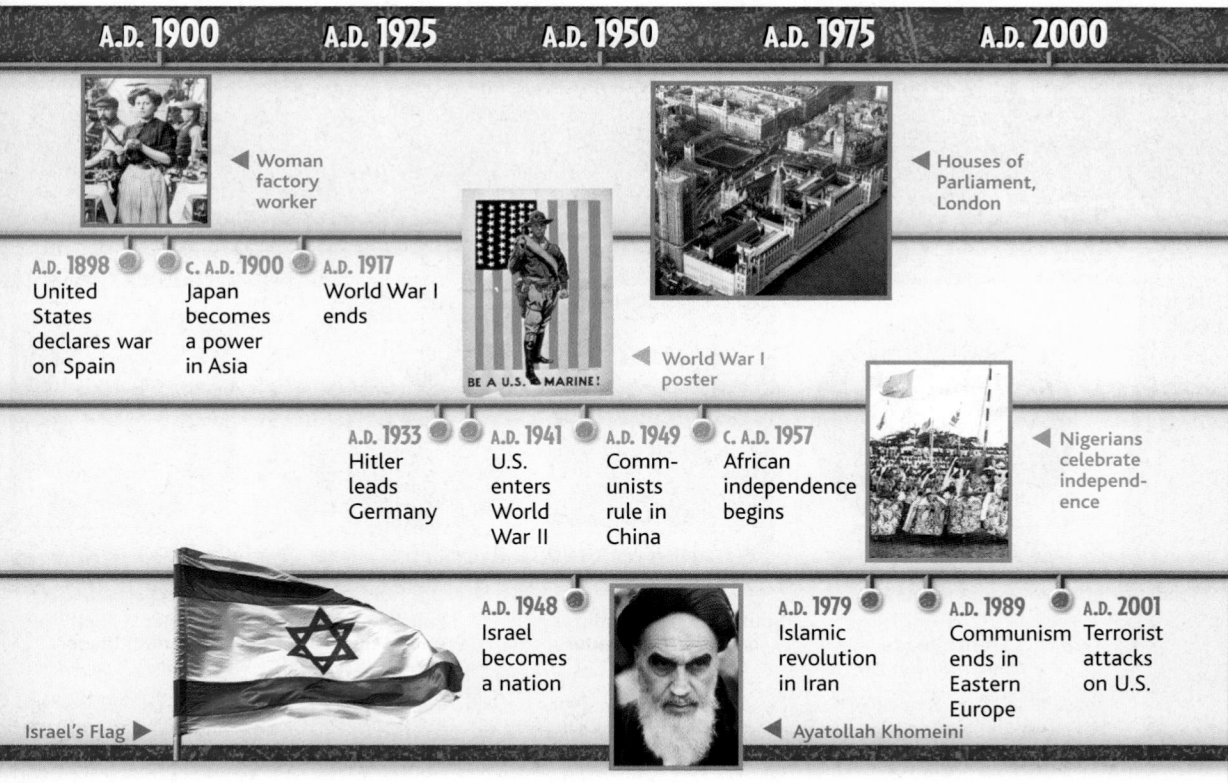

A.D. 1900　　A.D. 1925　　A.D. 1950　　A.D. 1975　　A.D. 2000

◀ Woman factory worker

◀ Houses of Parliament, London

A.D. 1898
United States declares war on Spain

C. A.D. 1900
Japan becomes a power in Asia

A.D. 1917
World War I ends

BE A U.S. MARINE!

◀ World War I poster

A.D. 1933
Hitler leads Germany

A.D. 1941
U.S. enters World War II

A.D. 1949
Communists rule in China

C. A.D. 1957
African independence begins

◀ Nigerians celebrate independence

A.D. 1948
Israel becomes a nation

A.D. 1979
Islamic revolution in Iran

A.D. 1989
Communism ends in Eastern Europe

A.D. 2001
Terrorist attacks on U.S.

Israel's Flag ▶

◀ Ayatollah Khomeini

NCLB NO CHILD LEFT BEHIND

Teaching Tip The goals of the NCLB Act include an emphasis on science and mathematics, in hopes of building better science and math skills among Americans. To help students sharpen science and math skills, try to focus on scientific advances. This unit is especially appropriate. For example, have students do special research projects on scientists, their discoveries and inventions, and how they have influenced civilization. To sharpen math skills, take every opportunity to have students use math as a tool for historical analysis. For example, ask students to graph world and regional population growth.

DIFFERENTIATED INSTRUCTION

English Learners: Have students choose one of the conflicts from the time line and read an encyclopedia article about it. Have them report their findings.

Visual/Spatial: Have students use their prior knowledge about an event or place named and draw a picture that represents it.

Kinesthetic: Ask students to research one of the inventions named and describe to the class how it works and its significance.

FOCUS

The unit preview provides a general layout of the regions and significant figures in the unit.

PREVIEWING GEOGRAPHY

Have students compare this map with the **Reference Atlas,** then answer the following questions.

1. **What part of the world is represented by this map?** *(almost the entire world)* **Why?** *(The unit covers events that impact almost everyone.)*

2. **In what country is the Arc de Triomphe located?** *(France)*

PREVIEWING People to Meet

Ask students the following questions using the biographies.

1. Which person was an Indian political and spiritual leader? *(Mohandas K. Gandhi)* **L1**

2. What was Marie Curie's field? *(science)* **L1**

3. Why do you think so many of the people on the list are political leaders? *(Possible answer: The time period included strong currents of nationalism and imperialism, and also spanned two world wars and several periods of political revolution.)* **L2**

▭ Refer to **People to Meet Activities** in the Unit Resource Books.

Unit 6 — Places to Locate

① **Arc de Triomphe**
See Industry and Nationalism Chapter 19

② **British Parliament**
See Imperialism and World War I Chapter 20

NORTH AMERICA

Atlantic Ocean

Pacific Ocean

SOUTH AMERICA

People to Meet

Napoleon Bonaparte
1769–1821
French leader
Chapter 19, page 721

Simón Bolívar
1783–1830
South American military and political leader
Chapter 19, page 750

Marie Curie
1867–1934
Polish-born French scientist
Chapter 19, page 740

Mohandas Gandhi
1869–1948
Indian leader
Chapter 21, page 844

708

PREVIEWING Places to Locate

Use the following descriptions to explain the images on the map.

 ① The colossal Arc de Triomphe in Paris, France, commemorates the victories under Napoleon Bonaparte.

 ② The grandeur of the Houses of Parliament in London, England, where the British parliament meets, reflects England's opulent rise to imperialism in the 1800s.

EUROPE

Mediterranean Sea

Red Sea

Persian Gulf

AFRICA

ASIA

Indian Ocean

3 Berlin Wall

See World War II and the Cold War
Chapter 21

4 Sarajevo, Bosnia

See Building Today's World
Chapter 22

5 Cape Town, South Africa

See Building Today's World
Chapter 22

Vladimir Lenin
1870–1924
Communist leader
Chapter 20, page 795

Franklin Roosevelt
1882–1945
U.S. president
Chapter 21, page 817

Golda Meir
1898–1978
Israeli prime minister
Chapter 22, page 877

Nelson Mandela
1918–present
South African president
Chapter 22, page 873

709

PREVIEWING Places to Locate

3 A symbol of the divisiveness of the Cold War, the Berlin Wall divided the city for nearly 30 years.

4 The city of Sarajevo, in the former Yugoslavia, was the scene of terrible war and bloodshed in the 1990s.

5 Rows and rows of small shacks line the tiny streets in the shantytowns outside of Cape Town, South Africa.

TEACH

Organizing Information Have students complete a table like the one below to organize information about the people discussed on these pages. *(Answers are provided.)* **L1/ EL**

Historical Figure	Prominent Accomplishment
Napoleon Bonaparte	French military and political leader
Simón Bolívar	South American military and political leader
Marie Curie	Polish-born French scientist
Vladimir Ilyich Lenin	Russian Communist leader
Franklin D. Roosevelt	U.S. President
Mohandas K. Ghandi	Indian political and spiritual leader
Golda Meir	Israeli prime minister
Nelson Mandela	South African president

Using a Map Ask students to refer to the maps in the **Reference Atlas.** Have them find the part of the world where each person on the time line lived. Then ask them to make a generalization based on the fact that many different regions of the world are represented. *(Sample generalization: The forces discussed in this unit influenced people all over the world.)* **L2**

Chapter 19 Resources

Note: The following materials may be used when teaching Chapter 19.
Section level support materials are shown at point of use in the margins of the Teacher Wraparound Edition.

TEACHING TRANSPARENCIES

- Graphic Organizer Transparencies with Teaching Strategy and Student Activity **L2**
- Cause-and-Effect Transparencies with Teaching Strategy and Student Activity **L2**
- Then and Now Transparencies with Teaching Strategy and Student Activity **L2**
- In-text Map Transparencies with Teaching Strategy and Student Activity **L1**
- Map Transparencies with Overlay, Teaching Strategy, and Student Activity **L2**

DIFFERENTIATED INSTRUCTION

- Differentiated Instruction Activity 19
- Time Line Activity 19
- Primary Source Reading 19 (with Document-Based Questions)
- Inclusion Strategies for the Middle School Social Studies Classroom
- StudentWorks Plus™ CD-ROM (with Audio Program)

READING SUPPORT

- Take-Home Review Activity 19 **L2**
- World Literature Reading 19 **L2**
- Workbook Activity 19 **L1**
- Reading Strategies for the Social Studies Classroom **L1/ EL**

ASSESSMENT

- Authentic Assessment Activity 19 **L1/ EL**
- Chapter 19 Test Form A **L2**
- Chapter 19 Test Form B **L2**
- Exam*View*® Pro Testmaker CD-ROM

INTERDISCIPLINARY CONNECTIONS

- Geography and History Activity 19 **L2**
- People to Meet Activity 19 **L2**
- Economics Activity 19 **L2**
- Citizenship and Service Learning Activity 19 **L2**

SPANISH RESOURCES

- Spanish Reading Essentials and Study Guide
- Spanish Guided Reading Activities
- Spanish Quizzes, Tests, and Authentic Assessment (with Rubrics)
- Spanish Take-Home Review Activities

MULTIMEDIA

- Exam*View*® Pro Testmaker CD-ROM
- Glencoe Skillbuilder Interactive Workbook CD-ROM, Level 1
- Interactive Tutor Self-Assessment CD-ROM
- MindJogger Videoquiz
- Presentation Plus! CD-ROM
- StudentWorks Plus™ CD-ROM (with Audio Program)
- TeacherWorks CD-ROM
- Vocabulary PuzzleMaker CD-ROM
- *World History: Journey Across Time* Video Program
- World History Primary Source Document Library CD-ROM

STANDARDIZED ASSESSMENT SKILLS

- Standardized Test Skills Practice Workbook Activity 19 **L2**
- Critical Thinking Skills Activity 19 **L2**

Teaching strategies have been coded with suggested ability levels. However, most are suitable for all levels.

L1 BASIC activities for all students

L2 AVERAGE activities for average to above-average students

L3 CHALLENGING activities for above-average students

EL ENGLISH LANGUAGE activities

Chapter ⑲ Resources

TIME MANAGEMENT

Unit Introduction	Chapter Introduction	Section 1	Section 2	Section 3	Section 4	Chapter Wrap-Up
1 Day	1 Day	1 Day	2 Days	2 Days	2 Days	1 Day

Block Scheduling Activities that are suited to use within the block scheduling framework are identified by:

0:00 OUT OF TIME? Assign the Chapter 19 *Reading Essentials and Study Guide.* *

SECTION RESOURCES

DAILY OBJECTIVES	REPRODUCIBLE LESSON PLANS	MULTIMEDIA RESOURCES
Section 1 **The French Revolution and Napoleon** 1. Terrible conditions and a desire for freedom and democracy led to the revolution. 2. Napoleon Bonaparte used military success to take control of the government.	▱ Reproducible Lesson Plan 19–1 ▱ Vocabulary Activity 19–1 ▱ Guided Reading Activity 19–1* ▱ Section Quiz 19–1* ▱ Reading Essentials and Study Guide 19–1*	⚙ Daily Focus Skills Transparency 19–1 ⊚ Interactive Tutor Self-Assessment CD-ROM ⊚ Exam*View*® Pro Testmaker CD-ROM ⊚ Presentation Plus! CD-ROM ⊚ Glencoe BookLink CD-ROM
Section 2 **The Industrial Revolution** 1. The Industrial Revolution began in Great Britain. 2. It brought great change as it spread to Europe and the United States.	▱ Reproducible Lesson Plan 19–2 ▱ Vocabulary Activity 19–2 ▱ Guided Reading Activity 19–2* ▱ Section Quiz 19–2* ▱ Reading Essentials and Study Guide 19–2*	⚙ Daily Focus Skills Transparency 19–2 ⊚ Interactive Tutor Self-Assessment CD-ROM ⊚ Exam*View*® Pro Testmaker CD-ROM ⊚ Presentation Plus! CD-ROM
Section 3 **Society and Industry** 1. Industrialism changed the way people lived in the 1800s. 2. New political, social, and economic ideas developed in response to industrialization.	▱ Reproducible Lesson Plan 19–3 ▱ Vocabulary Activity 19–3 ▱ Guided Reading Activity 19–3* ▱ Section Quiz 19–3* ▱ Reading Essentials and Study Guide 19–3*	⚙ Daily Focus Skills Transparency 19–3 ⊚ Interactive Tutor Self-Assessment CD-ROM ⊚ Exam*View*® Pro Testmaker CD-ROM ⊚ Presentation Plus! CD-ROM ⊚ Glencoe BookLink CD-ROM
Section 4 **Nationalism and Nation-States** 1. Nationalism and reform reshaped Europe politically during the mid-1800s. 2. Latin America gained independence, while the United States expanded its borders.	▱ Reproducible Lesson Plan 19–4 ▱ Vocabulary Activity 19–4 ▱ Guided Reading Activity 19–4* ▱ Section Quiz 19–4* ▱ Reading Essentials and Study Guide 19–4*	⚙ Daily Focus Skills Transparency 19–4 ⊚ Interactive Tutor Self-Assessment CD-ROM ⊚ Exam*View*® Pro Testmaker CD-ROM ⊚ Presentation Plus! CD-ROM ⊚ Vocabulary PuzzleMaker CD-ROM ⊚ Glencoe BookLink CD-ROM

*Also available in Spanish

Chapter 19 Resources

Use our Web site for additional resources. All essential content is covered in the Student Edition.

You and your students can visit jat.glencoe.com, the Web site companion to *World History: Journey Across Time*. This innovative integration of electronic and print media offers your students a wealth of opportunities. The student text directs students to the Web site for the following options:

- Chapter Overviews
- Self-Check Quizzes
- Study Central™
- Student Web Activities
- Multi-Language Glossaries

Answers to the student Web activities are provided for you in the **Web Activity Lesson Plans.** Additional Web resources and ePuzzles and games are also available.

The following videotape programs are available from Glencoe as supplements to Chapter 19:

Marconi: Whisper in the Air
(ISBN 1-56501-551-7)

Napoleon Bonaparte: The Glory of France
(ISBN 1-7670-1211-9)

Alexander Graham Bell: Voice of Invention
(ISBN 1-56501-946-6)

To order, call Glencoe at 1-800-334-7344. To find classroom resources to accompany many of these videos, check the following home pages:

A&E Television: www.aande.com
The History Channel: www.historychannel.com

MEETING SPECIAL NEEDS

In addition to the Differentiated Instruction strategies, the following resources are suitable for students with special needs:

- *ExamView® Pro Testmaker CD-ROM* allows teachers to tailor tests by reducing answer choices.
- *StudentWorks Plus™ CD-ROM (with Audio Program)* includes the entire narrative of the student edition so that less-proficient readers can listen to the words as they read them.
- The *Reading Essentials and Study Guide* provides the same content as the student edition but is written two grade levels below the textbook.

NATIONAL GEOGRAPHIC   TEACHER'S CORNER

Index to National Geographic Magazine:
The following articles relate to this chapter:

- "The Way West," by John G. Mitchell, September 2000.
- "Information Revolution," by Joel Swerdlow, October 1995.
- "Simón Bolívar: El Libertador," by Bryan Hodgson, March 1994.

National Geographic Society Products:
To order the following, call National Geographic at 1–800–368–2728

- *Inventors and Inventions* (Video)
- *National Geographic Atlas of the World* (Book)

NGS ONLINE

Access National Geographic's new dynamic MapMachine Web site and other geography resources at:

www.nationalgeographic.com
www.nationalgeographic.com/maps

 ## Meeting NCSS Standards

World History: Journey Across Time
The following standards are highlighted in Chapter 19:

Section 1   **V** Individuals, Groups, and Institutions: A
            VI Power, Authority, and Governance: A, F, I

Section 2   **VII** Production, Distribution, and Consumption: A
            VIII Science, Technology, and Society: A, B

Section 3   **I** Culture: A
            V Individuals, Groups, and Institutions: A, E, G
            VIII Science, Technology, and Society: B, D

Section 4   **VI** Power, Authority, and Governance: D, F
            VII Production, Distribution, and Consumption: A, E, F, H

State and Local Objectives

_____

_____

Timesaving Tools

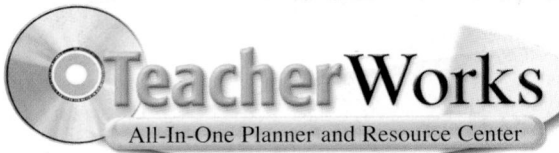

TeacherWorks
All-In-One Planner and Resource Center

- **Interactive Teacher Edition** Access your Teacher Wraparound Edition and your classroom resources with a few easy clicks.
- **Interactive Lesson Planner** Organize your week, month, semester, or year with all the lesson helps you need to make teaching creative and relevant.

Use Glencoe's **Presentation Plus!** multimedia teacher tool to easily present dynamic lessons that visually excite your students. Using Microsoft PowerPoint® you can customize the presentations to create your own personalized lessons.

FOLDABLES™
Study Organizer
Dinah Zike's Foldables

Foldables are three-dimensional, interactive graphic organizers that help students practice basic writing skills, review key vocabulary terms, and identify main ideas. Every chapter contains a foldable activity, with additional chapter activities found in the *Reading and Study Skills Foldables* booklet. You can use the foldables as they are presented, or modify them to suit the needs of your individual class.

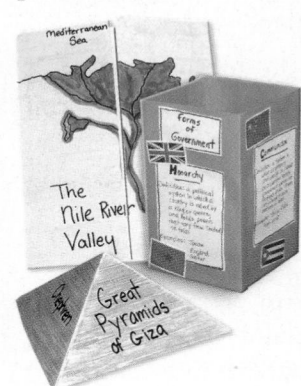

Planning Ahead

CHAPTER CULMINATING ACTIVITY

The Chapter Culminating Activity will help students organize and learn the important information from the chapter. Begin teaching the chapter with this activity, and have students complete it as a culminating activity.

CREATING A WHO-WHAT-WHEN-WHERE-WHY CHART

Purpose This type of organizer helps students organize and analyze information by identifying important figures and organizing information about them. It will focus students' attention on the most important people of the chapter, as well as help them understand these people's achievements, their role in history, and their place in the chapter chronology. It can also be used to organize information for reports and as a study aid.

Introduction to Modeling

1. Begin the discussion with a brainstorming session. Ask students to list what they know or believe they know about Napoleon and Karl Marx. Write the information on an overhead transparency.

2. Ask students to copy this chart into their notebooks:

Who	What	When	Where	Why
Napoleon				
Karl Marx				
Louis Pasteur				
William Gladstone				
Otto von Bismarck				
Símon Bolívar				

As students read the chapter, ask them to complete the boxes with the appropriate information about each important person. In the "Why" column, have them write notes that help explain why the person is significant. Have students add other important people to the chart as they read.

3. As part of your chapter review, have students share their Who-What-When-Where-Why charts. Encourage them to use their charts as study aids.

Use the **SkillBuilder Handbook** on pages 902–919 to help students learn the skill of summarizing.

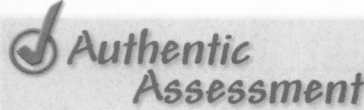

Authentic Assessment

Refer to Activity 19 in the Authentic Assessment section of the *Quizzes, Tests, and Authentic Assessment (with Rubrics)* booklet.

When & Where?

As students read the chapter, have them review the time line on page 710. Have them create their own time line by adding important dates from each section. **L1**

GLENCOE TECHNOLOGY

World History: Journey Across Time Video Program

To learn more about the Industrial Revolution and nationalism, students can view the Chapter 19 video in the *World History: Journey Across Time* Video Program.

MindJogger Videoquiz

Use the **MindJogger Videoquiz** to preview Chapter 19 content.

 Available in DVD and VHS

Chapter 19

Industry and Nationalism

Steel plant on the Tees River in Middlebough, England ▶

NATIONAL GEOGRAPHIC When & Where?

1750		1800	1850		1900
1769 Watt improves steam engine		**1799** Napoleon comes to power	**1848** Karl Marx writes *Communist Manifesto*		**1871** Germany is united

Reading Strategy PURPOSE FOR READING

Comparing and Contrasting Tell students that they will read how different countries addressed the powerful forces of industrialization, nationalism, and reform during the 1800s. **Ask:** How did the different countries and regions deal with major changes in the way people lived, worked, and thought? As they read, have students watch for ways that different countries were influenced by these three forces. **L2**

Chapter Preview

In the late 1700s, the French Revolution and the Industrial Revolution brought great changes to Europe and the United States. Read this chapter to find out how the rise of factories and the spread of nationalism changed how people lived their lives.

 View the Chapter 19 video in the *World History: Journey Across Time* Video Program.

Chapter Overview Visit jat.glencoe.com for a preview of Chapter 19.

 Section 1
The French Revolution and Napoleon

In 1789 the French overthrew their king and tried to build a republic. A few years later, however, Napoleon seized power and built a new French empire.

 Section 2
The Industrial Revolution

During the 1800s, Europe and North America began using machines to produce large quantities of goods. During this time, new inventions improved life for many people.

 Section 3
Society and Industry

The growth of industry led to the growth of cities and new social groups, as well as many new problems and new ideas.

 Section 4
Nationalism and Nation-States

Nationalism and liberalism led to new nations and the emergence of democracy in Europe and the Americas.

 FOLDABLES Study Organizer

Organizing Information *Make this foldable to help you organize and analyze information by asking yourself questions about industry and nationalism.*

Step 1 *Fold four sheets of paper in half from top to bottom.*

Step 2 *On each folded paper, make a cut 1 inch from the side on the top flap.*

Cut 1 inch from the edge through the top flap only.

Step 3 *Place the folded papers one on top of the other. Staple the four sections together and label the top four tabs: The French Revolution and Napoleon, The Industrial Revolution, Society and Industry, Nationalism and Nation-States.*

Staple here.

The French Revolution and Napoleon

Reading and Writing *As you read the chapter, write the main ideas for each section under the appropriate tabs of your foldable. Then write one statement for each tab that summarizes all of the main ideas in that tab.*

711

MORE ABOUT THE PHOTO

Industrial Plants This steel plant is one of many different companies and industries that came into existence as a result of industrialization. Though England and France had maintained something of an equilibrium in industrial development up to the early 1700s, England began to pull rapidly away later in that century. With the ability to refine steel and the advent of steam-powered ships and new canals, factories and towns sprang up throughout England. One region in particular, the Black Country in west central England, developed numerous industrial towns. The main industries in the Black Country were iron smelting and the manufacture of iron products. The region gained its name from the many factories pumping black smoke into the air.

Introduce students to chapter content and key terms by having them access Chapter Overview 19 at jat.glencoe.com

CHAPTER PREVIEW

After reading Chapter 19, students will be able to

1. summarize the causes and events of the French Revolution and the rise of Napoleon's empire;

2. explain how the Industrial Revolution began in Britain and spread to other countries;

3. describe new scientific, political, economic, and social ideas;

4. discuss the influences of nationalism and reform.

 FOLDABLES Study Organizer — Dinah Zike's Foldables

Purpose Students use this foldable to organize information about notable developments that took place during the late 1700s and 1800s in Europe and the Americas. Completed foldables will be a guide to those important developments.

📁 Have students complete *Reading and Study Skills Foldables* Activity 19.

1 Learn It!

Spending time thinking about all aspects of a word or asking oneself questions about a word may help students to make abstract concepts more concrete.

Read aloud the following passage from the subhead "Napoleon Fights Britain" in Section 1:

> Two forces helped to bring Napoleon's empire to an end. One was nationalism, or the desire of a people for self-rule. The nations of Europe rejected Napoleon's rule and the French customs he forced on them.

Explain that the paragraph makes it clear that the word *nationalism* means "the desire of a people for self-rule." However, students may not quite understand what that definition means.

Students should ask themselves probing questions to broaden their understanding of the word. Here are some good examples:

- How is nationalism different from patriotism?

- How does nationalism manifest itself in the United States? Among your friends?

- Is there such a thing as regional nationalism in a country, such as "southern-ism"?

- What color or music comes to mind when you think of nationalism? Why?

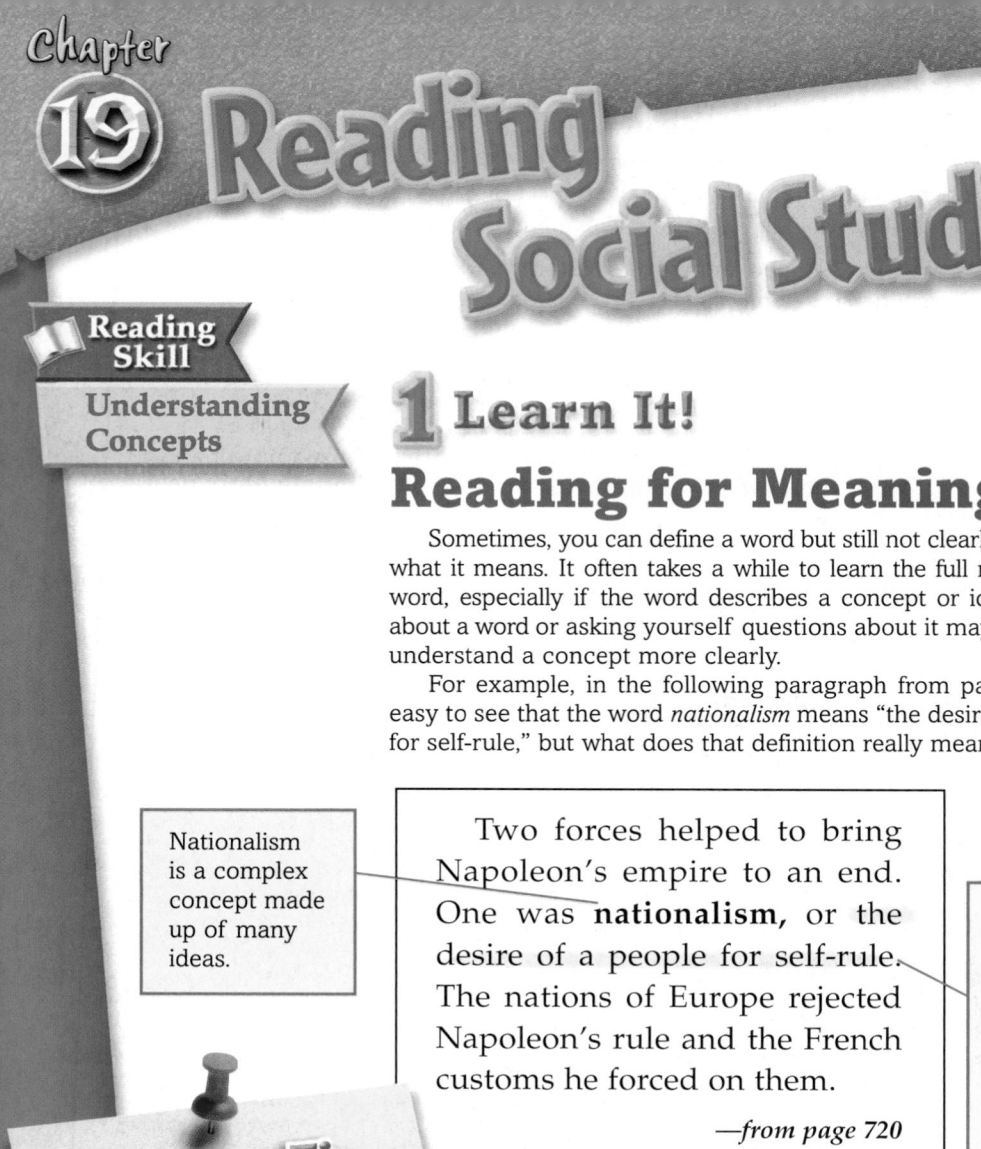

Chapter 19 Reading Social Studies

Reading Skill
Understanding Concepts

1 Learn It!

Reading for Meaning

Sometimes, you can define a word but still not clearly understand what it means. It often takes a while to learn the full meaning of a word, especially if the word describes a concept or idea. Thinking about a word or asking yourself questions about it may help you to understand a concept more clearly.

For example, in the following paragraph from page 720, it is easy to see that the word *nationalism* means "the desire of a people for self-rule," but what does that definition really mean?

> Nationalism is a complex concept made up of many ideas.

> Two forces helped to bring Napoleon's empire to an end. One was **nationalism,** or the desire of a people for self-rule. The nations of Europe rejected Napoleon's rule and the French customs he forced on them.
>
> —*from page 720*

> Definitions help you understand a word, but they do not always fully explain concepts.

Reading Tip

When you discover a new word in your reading, watch for multiple meanings of the word in books, movies, television, and conversations.

Ask yourself questions to increase your understanding of the word *nationalism*. Here are some questions you might ask:

- How is nationalism different from patriotism?
- How do we show nationalism in the United States?
- Is there such as thing as regional nationalism in a country, such as "southern-ism"?
- What color or music comes to mind when you think of nationalism? Why?

712

Reading Strategy **RECALLING WORDS**

Ask: Have you ever heard a word for the first time and then it seems as though you hear it again and again for days afterwards? When you discover a new word in your reading, be on the lookout for multiple meanings of the word in books, movies, television and conversations. Have students keep a list of new words they learn and the definitions that accompany them. Then have students use these new words in various sentences to help them understand the different nuances of the words and to improve their ability to utilize them. **L1/ EL**

2 Practice It!

Ask Questions

Choose one word that you do not understand fully from each section of Chapter 19. For each word, try to understand the meaning by asking the following questions:

1) **Who might use the word? When would he or she use it?**

2) **What else do you want to know about this word?**

3) **How would you illustrate the word?**

4) **What actions go along with this word?**

3 Apply It!

Choose a word from the chapter that is familiar to most people. Ask five people how they define the word. How did their answers help you to understand the word?

713

READING SOCIAL STUDIES

2 Practice It!

Conceptualizing One good method of helping students define terms is to try to conceptualize the meaning by thinking deeply about all aspects of the word. They do this by asking specific questions about the term, such as:

- Who might use the word? In what context?
- What more do you want to know about this word?
- How would you illustrate the word?
- What action would be associated with this word?
- How might the words that occur in the sentence near this word help give clues to its meaning?

Have students use these questions with several vocabulary terms from Section 1. Have them share their answers with a partner. **L2**

3 Apply It!

Have students look at the words under "Building Your Vocabulary" for Sections 2 through 4. Ask them to choose a word, and then have students ask 10 different people how they would define the word. They should record the answers and then compare them to the dictionary definition of the word. **L2**

Reading Strategy ⟩ READ TO WRITE

As students write about the term they have chosen, remind them to note anything that comes to mind when they read the word—associations, memories, or ideas that they may have about the word's meaning. Then ask them to search the word online or in a dictionary to broaden their written interpretation of the word.

① FOCUS

SECTION OVERVIEW

This section focuses on the causes and events of the French Revolution and how these causes eventually gave rise to the empire and dictatorship of Napoleon Bonaparte.

BELLRINGER
SKILLBUILDER ACTIVITY

📖 Project **Daily Focus Skills Transparency 19–1** and have students answer questions. Discuss their responses.

Get Ready to Read!

Preteaching Vocabulary:
Introduce the term *bourgeoisie* to students by saying it is a French word that corresponds to our term *middle class*. Ask students to watch for the role of the middle class, or bourgeoisie, in the events they are about to encounter.

Answers to Graphic: Causes: Members of the Third Estate resented the privileges of the nobles and clergy; food shortages caused discontent; people were worried about economic problems.

Section ① The French Revolution and Napoleon

Get Ready to Read!

What's the Connection?
Many ideas of the American Revolution also affected Europe. In France, the people started a revolution and overthrew the king. The French Revolution then led to the rise of Napoleon.

Focusing on the Main Ideas
- The French Revolution began because the people were treated unfairly and because their country had serious economic problems. *(page 715)*
- French radicals used terror to enforce their reforms. *(page 717)*
- Napoleon Bonaparte used his military success to take control of the French government. *(page 719)*
- Through military conquests, Napoleon built a huge, but short-lived, empire in Europe. *(page 720)*

Locating Places
Versailles (VUHR•SY)
Waterloo (WAW•tuhr•LOO)

Meeting People
King Louis XVI (LOO•ee)
Maximilien Robespierre (mak•see•meel•ya ROHBZ•PYEHR)
Napoleon Bonaparte (nuh•POH•lee•uhn BOH•nuh•PAHRT)

Building Your Vocabulary
estates
bourgeoisie (BURZH•WAH•ZEE)
coup d'etat (KOO day•TAH)

Reading Strategy
Cause and Effect Use a diagram like the one below to explain the causes of the French Revolution.

Cause:	→	The French Revolution
Cause:		

NATIONAL GEOGRAPHIC When & Where?

London • Paris • Madrid • Rome • Moscow • Vienna

1780		1800		1820
	1789 The Bastille falls	**1799** Napoleon comes to power	**1812** Napoleon invades Russia	**1814** Congress of Vienna meets

---

SECTION RESOURCES

📁 **Reproducible Masters**
- Reproducible Lesson Plan 19–1
- Daily Lecture and Discussion Notes 19–1
- Vocabulary Activity 19–1
- Active Reading Note-Taking Guide 19–1
- Guided Reading Activity 19–1
- Section Quiz 19–1
- Reading Essentials and Study Guide 19–1

📖 **Transparencies**
- Daily Focus Skills Transparency 19–1

Multimedia
 Interactive Tutor Self-Assessment CD-ROM
Ⓔ ExamView® Pro Testmaker CD-ROM
Ⓔ Presentation Plus! CD-ROM
Ⓔ Glencoe BookLink CD-ROM

The French Revolution Begins

Main Idea The French Revolution began because the people were treated unfairly and because their country had serious economic problems.

Reading Focus During the French Revolution, people tried to create a new society and government. If you could change our society today, what changes would you make?

Previously you learned about the American Revolution. The example of the American Revolution influenced many people in France. They, too, wanted political change based on the ideas of freedom and equality. The French Revolution, which began in 1789, changed France and all of Europe.

What Caused the French Revolution?

In the 1700s, France was one of Europe's most powerful countries. French kings ruled it with absolute power. Nobles had many privileges and lived in great wealth. Most people, however, were poor, had little education, and struggled to make a living.

The French people were divided into three **estates**, or classes. The First Estate was the Catholic clergy, or church officials. They did not pay taxes, and they received money from church lands. The Second Estate was the nobles. They filled the highest posts in government and the military. Like the clergy, the nobles were free from taxes. They lived in luxury at the king's court or in their country houses surrounded by large areas of land.

Everyone else in France belonged to the Third Estate. At the top of this group was the **bourgeoisie** (BURZH•WAH•ZEE), or the middle classes. They included merchants, bankers, doctors, lawyers, and teachers. Next were the city workers—artisans, day laborers, and servants. At the bottom were the peasants, who made up more than 80 percent of the French people.

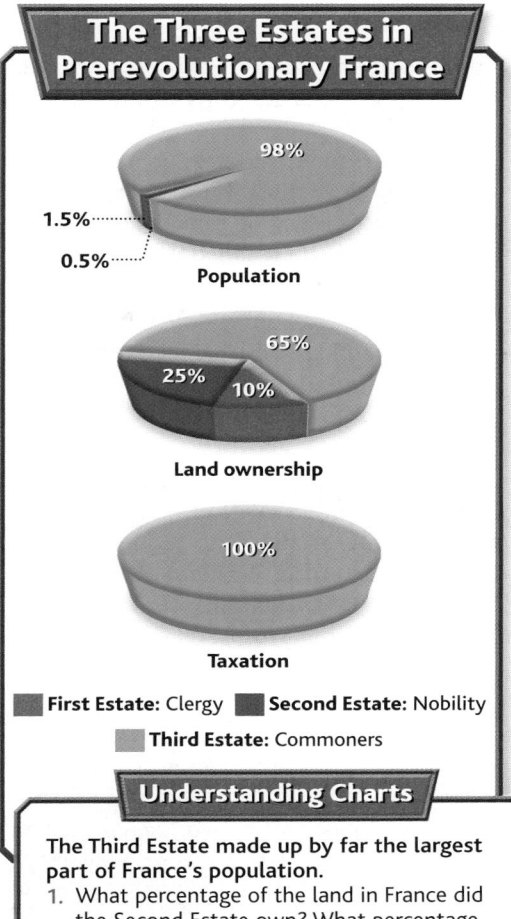

The Three Estates in Prerevolutionary France

98%
1.5%
0.5%
Population

65%
25%
10%
Land ownership

100%
Taxation

■ **First Estate:** Clergy   ■ **Second Estate:** Nobility
■ **Third Estate:** Commoners

Understanding Charts

The Third Estate made up by far the largest part of France's population.
1. What percentage of the land in France did the Second Estate own? What percentage of the population did they make up?
2. **Infer** From looking at these circle graphs, what inferences can you draw about why a revolution occurred in France?

Members of the Third Estate had no voice in the government, but they paid the country's taxes. As Enlightenment ideas about freedom and equality spread, the middle class came to resent more and more the privileges of the nobles and clergy.

The French King Is Overthrown

In 1788 food shortages and rising prices caused great discontent throughout the country. At the same time, the French government was

CHAPTER 19   Industry and Nationalism   **715**

② TEACH

▶ **Reading Strategy** ◀

Outlining Ask students to outline the subsection "The French Revolution Begins." Remind them to use the headings as guides when making their outlines. **L1**

Daily Lecture and Discussion Notes 19–1

Use **Daily Lecture and Discussion Notes 19–1** for an outline of key concepts found in the section.

Understanding Charts

1. 25%; 1.5%
2. The Third Estate was the only class that had to pay taxes.

Reading Support L1/ EL

Use **Vocabulary Activity 19–1** to review important terms in the section.

▶ **Reading Strategy** ◀   **READING THE TEXT**

Previewing Students who look over a section before they read it can benefit in two ways: they activate what they already know about the various topics covered, and they can see what they will need to know to be able to comprehend the text. Before they read this section, have students look over the title, headings, illustrations, maps, and other graphics. To develop a purpose for reading the section, ask students what they already know about topics highlighted in these elements and what students predict they will learn. **L2**

Writing Activity

Ask students to work in pairs. One student, writing as a Parisian, should write a letter to a rural relative about conditions in the capital in 1792. Have the other student respond with a description of life in the country. **L2**

Comparing Explain that Bastille Day is celebrated as France's national holiday. Ask students to compare and contrast the events commemorated on Bastille Day with those of our Independence Day national holiday. *(Both holidays celebrate a significant break with the past; Independence Day celebrates independence from a foreign power, and Bastille Day commemorates the overthrow of a tyrannical government.)* **L2**

Primary Source

Answer:
the right of being considered innocent until found guilty by process; the freedom of speech; equal taxation among all citizens

Reading Check

Answer: First Estate: the Catholic clergy; Second Estate: the nobles; the Third Estate: everyone else in France

---

almost bankrupt because of costly wars and increasing expenses for the king's court. After French banks decided they could no longer afford to loan the government money, **King Louis XVI** (LOO•ee) asked the nobles and clergy to pay taxes, but they refused. Louis then called a meeting of the country's legislative body, the Estates-General, at his palace at **Versailles** (VUHR•SY). It was the only way he could impose new taxes. The Estates-General was made up of representatives from all three estates.

In the Estates-General, the nobles and clergy refused to give up their privileges. Frustrated, the delegates of the Third Estate decided to meet separately. They declared themselves to be the National Assembly and began work on a new constitution for France.

The people celebrated this victory, but they began to worry. News came that the king was gathering troops at Versailles. The people of Paris got ready to fight. Early on July 14, 1789, a large crowd stormed a hated royal fortress and prison called the Bastille (ba•STEEL).

News of the Bastille's fall spread to the countryside, where the peasants rose against the nobles. To calm the people, the National Assembly passed new laws that ended the privileges of the clergy and nobles. It also issued the Declaration of the Rights of Man and the Citizen. The Declaration said that the powers of government came from the people, not the king.

In 1791 the National Assembly made France a constitutional monarchy. France was to be ruled by an elected assembly, and the king's power was limited. Louis, however, would not accept these changes. In June 1791, he and his wife Marie Antoinette tried to flee to Austria. They did not get far. At a town east of Paris, soldiers arrested the king and queen and returned them to Paris.

Worried that Austria's ruler would send troops to aid Louis, the National Assembly declared war on Austria in 1792. Soon after, Prussia joined Austria in fighting France. The war did not go well for France. Angry about France's defeats, radicals—or people wanting far-reaching changes—took over Paris and helped set up a new government called the National Convention.

Primary Source
Declaration of the Rights of Man and the Citizen

On August 26, 1789, the French National Assembly approved 17 articles that stated their basic freedoms. Four of the articles are listed below.

2. The aim of every political association is the preservation of the natural . . . rights of man. These rights are liberty, property, security, and resistance to oppression [hardship].

9. Every man being presumed innocent until he has been proven guilty, . . .

11. The free communication of ideas and opinions is one of the most precious of the rights of man; every citizen can then freely speak, write, and print. . . .

—Declaration of the Rights of Man and the Citizen (August 1789)

▲ Declaration of the Rights of Man and the Citizen

DBQ Document-Based Question

Which freedoms do Articles 2, 9, and 11 protect?

Reading Check **Identify** Who belonged to the three estates in France?

DIFFERENTIATED INSTRUCTION

Auditory/Musical: Pair students and have them take turns reading aloud paragraphs in "Napoleon's Empire." After each paragraph, have partners identify the main idea in the paragraph and record it. Pairs should also discuss and record the meanings of vocabulary words.

English Learners: Group English-speaking students with one or more English learners. Have English speakers read the section aloud. As the English learners encounter unfamiliar words, tell the English speakers to stop and explain the meaning of the words.

Gifted and Talented: Have students debate if Napoleon furthered or hindered the beliefs and values of the French Revolution.

📂 Refer to *Inclusion Strategies for the Middle School Social Studies Classroom* in the TCR.

The Reign of Terror

Main Idea French radicals used terror to enforce their reforms.

Reading Focus Have you ever heard the phrase "The end justifies the means"? In other words, if your goal is right, is it okay to do anything, even break the law or hurt people, to reach that goal? What do you think?

Many of the radicals who formed the National Convention—France's new government—belonged to the Jacobin club. This was a large network of political groups in France. They were called Jacobins (JA•kuh•buhnz) because they held meetings at the Jacobin monastery in Paris. Once in power, the Jacobins divided into two groups.

The Struggle for Power In the Convention, delegates argued about the revolution's future. One group of the Jacobins was the Girondists (juh•RAHN•dihsts), who came from the Gironde, a region in southwest France. The Girondists believed that the revolution had gone far enough. They wanted to protect the interests of the middle class.

Across the aisle was the group of Jacobins that favored still more changes. Its members were known as the Mountain, because they sat on high benches at the rear of the hall. Leaders of this group, such as Georges-Jacques Danton and Jean-Paul Marat, saw themselves as the voice of the people and defenders of the revolution.

More About the Art

Begun in 1370, the Bastille was used as a fort and prison. Ironically, at the time it was stormed, the Bastille held only seven prisoners. In defending the fortress, government soldiers killed 98 attackers. When they were finally successful, the attackers took apart the hated prison brick by brick.

Caption Answer: News came that the king was going to send troops against the National Assembly.

▲ When the Bastille was attacked on July 14, 1789, it was defended by a little more than 100 soldiers, and it held only 7 prisoners. *Why did the people of Paris storm the Bastille?*

CHAPTER 19 Industry and Nationalism 717

CRITICAL THINKING ACTIVITY

Drawing Conclusions Have students review the description of the struggle for supremacy among the different factions during the French Revolution. Then have them write several paragraphs taking a position on one of these statements: *Robespierre and his followers went too far in their pursuit of revolutionary goals* or *Napoleon was correct to assume complete power.* Remind them to give reasons to support their position. Ask volunteers to read their paragraphs to the class. Discuss issues that arise from the readings. **L2**

CURRICULUM CONNECTION

Music

Like many in Europe, the German composer Ludwig van Beethoven admired Napoleon. When Beethoven heard in 1804 that Napoleon had crowned himself emperor, Beethoven was outraged. Instead of dedicating his Third Symphony to Napoleon, he dedicated it "for the memory of a great man."

Reading Strategy

Comparing and Contrasting Have students list similarities and differences between the French and American Revolutions. **L2**

✓ Reading Check

Answer: He reorganized the government with new positions, reorganized the tax and legal system, and made peace with the Catholic Church.

▲ The Arc de Triomphe in Paris, a monument to French military victories, was begun by Napoleon in 1806 and finally finished in 1836. *What territories were included in Napoleon's empire?*

After his successes in Italy, Napoleon attacked the British in Egypt in 1799. While in Egypt, he heard of the worsening political troubles back home. He immediately returned to France. There, he took part in a **coup d'etat** (koo day•TAH). This is when the top government leaders are suddenly replaced by force by a new group of leaders. Napoleon became the most powerful man in the country, with the title of First Consul. France had the strong leader many believed it needed.

Napoleon moved quickly to strengthen his control. He reorganized the government, created many new schools, and appointed local officials. He reorganized the country's finances and tax system. He created a new legal system. Known as the Napoleonic Code, it was based on Enlightenment ideas. Napoleon also made peace with the Catholic Church, which had opposed the revolution.

Napoleon did not remain true to all of the ideas of the French Revolution. People were equal under the law, but freedom of speech and the press was limited. A new group of nobles, based on ability rather than wealth or family ties, was created. Then, in 1804, Napoleon crowned himself emperor, and France became an empire.

✓ **Reading Check** **Explain** After becoming consul, how did Napoleon strengthen his control?

Napoleon's Empire

Main Idea Through military conquests, Napoleon built a huge, but short-lived, empire in Europe.

Reading Focus Many talented people use their abilities to rise high. Some, however, try to do too much and fall. Read to learn how Napoleon finally lost his power and his empire.

Being emperor of France was not enough for Napoleon. He wanted to build a great empire. Beginning in 1803, Napoleon won a number of victories that helped him reach his goal. By 1807, Napoleon had an empire that stretched across Europe from the Atlantic Ocean to Russia.

Napoleon's empire included many different territories. Napoleon directly ruled France and parts of Germany and Italy. His relatives, however, governed other lands, such as Spain and the Netherlands. Outside the empire, independent countries, such as Prussia, Austria, and Sweden, were forced to become France's allies.

Napoleon Fights Britain Two forces helped to bring Napoleon's empire to an end. One was nationalism, or the desire of a people for self-rule. The nations of Europe rejected Napoleon's rule and the French customs he forced on them. The other force was the combined might of Britain and Russia.

Only Britain and Russia remained undefeated by Napoleon. The French emperor hoped to invade Britain. However, in 1805, the British admiral Lord Horatio Nelson destroyed the French fleet at the Battle of Trafalgar off Spain's coast. After that, Napoleon tried to obtain victory in a different way. He forbade the countries in his empire to trade with Britain. His plan, called the Continental System, was hard to enforce, and it proved unsuccessful.

CITIZENSHIP AND YOU

The Role of the Military Like many earlier rulers, Napoleon used the army to take control of the government in France. Point out that in the United States and most modern democracies, the military does not play a role in the political life of the country. Ask students to discuss the advantages of a nonpolitical military and the dangers of a tradition in which military leaders influence or control the government. **L3**

Biography

NAPOLEON BONAPARTE
1769–1821

Even though Napoleon Bonaparte's first battle was a snowball fight, he took the game seriously. At the time, Napoleon was a young cadet at the Brienne military academy in northeastern France. A surprise snowfall had given the boys a break from their schoolwork. Instead of throwing random snowballs at his classmates, Napoleon showed his leadership skills by forming a full-scale attack. He gave the boys on his team duties and places to stand. They easily beat the other team because of his warlike strategies.

Before the other cadets realized his abilities, Napoleon was picked on by his classmates because of his short height, unusual name, and Italian-sounding accent. Napoleon did not care for his fellow cadets because they were from wealthy families and were French. Napoleon's father was a lawyer, but Napoleon was one of eight children and the family was not wealthy. In fact, Napoleon often sent money home. Napoleon resented the French in general because they invaded his homeland, the Mediterranean island of Corsica, in 1768. Historians say that one year later—on the day he was born—Napoleon's homeland was forced to celebrate the anniversary of the French takeover.

Napoleon's teachers found him to be smart and capable, especially in mathematics, but a poor speller. He earned a scholarship to a Paris military academy and tested well enough to become a second lieutenant in the army at age 16. Little did anyone know that someday he would become a military leader and emperor of France.

▲ Napoleon Bonaparte

> **"I have sacrificed all of my interests to those of the country."**
> –Napoleon Bonaparte, "Farewell to the Old Guard"

Then and Now
What skills would prepare someone to be a good military leader today?

721

Biography

TEACH

Napoleon is considered one of the greatest military commanders in history. His tactics included quickness, trickery, and surprise. He had studied artillery at military school and learned to use cannons effectively in battle. However, he was also a great speaker and was able to rally his men with his inspirational speeches. He possessed tremendous energy and could make fast decisions. Perhaps most importantly, Napoleon had great self-confidence. He was able to transfer this confidence to the ordinary soldiers of his army.

Ask students how the qualities and knowledge Napoleon possessed that made him a great commander compare with those of a modern-day political leader. (*Students will probably say that most of Napoleon's qualities would be important and helpful for a modern political leader. Other qualities they may name include ability to delegate responsibility, knowledge of technology and communications, and humility.*) **L2**

Then and Now
Students' answers will vary. Have them think about current leaders they admire as a reference point.

RECOMMENDED READING

Use the **Glencoe BookLink CD-ROM** to create customized reading lists based on your students' interests and reading levels. Below is an example based on content in this chapter. Also, see the Suggested Readings on pages 944–946 of the Appendix.

- **Dickens, Charles.** *A Tale of Two Cities.* The tumultuous and bloody years leading up to the French Revolution of 1789 provide the setting for this classic novel.
- **Hugo, Victor.** *Russia 1812: from* The Expiation. In this vivid excerpt, the poet describes the retreat from Moscow of Napoleon's once-proud army.
- **Lasky, Kathryn.** *Marie Antoinette: Princess of Versailles.* Introduces students to Marie Antoinette as a 13-year-old princess in 1769. Discusses what life was like for a young girl in the Austrian court.

③ ASSESS

Assign Section 1 Review as homework or as an in-class activity.

● Have students use the **Interactive Tutor Self-Assessment CD-ROM** to review the section.

Assessment L2

Assign **Section 1 Quiz** to assess mastery of the material found in the section.

Using Geography Skills

Answers:

1. Trafalgar, Leipzig, Waterloo

2. Britain, Portugal, Sweden, and Russia; Britain was an island separated from France. Russia was a huge country, which would make it difficult to conquer.

Napoleon Invades Russia Napoleon next decided to take on Russia. He organized a large force of about 600,000 soldiers called the Grand Army. In the summer of 1812, the Grand Army invaded Russia. Except for one battle, the Russians refused to fight. Instead, they drew Napoleon's army deeper into Russia. When Russia's harsh winter arrived, Napoleon's forces were unprepared and helpless. Their retreat was a disaster. Fewer than 100,000 men returned alive.

France's enemies then captured Napoleon and exiled him to the Mediterranean island of Elba. He escaped to the French mainland in the spring of 1815. His troops flocked to their old commander. Napoleon returned to Paris in triumph. At **Waterloo** (WAW•tuhr•LOO) in Belgium, an international force led by Britain's Duke of Wellington finally defeated Napoleon. This time, Napoleon was sent to the island of St. Helena in the southern Atlantic Ocean, where he died in 1821.

NATIONAL GEOGRAPHIC

Napoleon's Empire

KEY
- France, 1799
- French Empire, 1812
- Dependent states, 1812
- States allied with Napoleon, 1812
- States allied against Napoleon, 1812
- ✹ French victory
- ✸ French defeat
- → Napoleon's invasion of Russia, June–December 1812

Using Geography Skills

From 1807 to 1812, Napoleon controlled a large part of Europe.
1. Which battles shown were French defeats?
2. Which countries were allied against Napoleon in 1812? What geographic factors might have allowed these states to remain free from French control?

Find NGS online map resources @ www.nationalgeographic.com/maps

722

COOPERATIVE LEARNING ACTIVITY

Creating a Talk Show Have a student group create a television talk show featuring guests from the three estates of prerevolutionary France. Have a student portray the role of the host and others in the studio audience. Have players research their roles and answer questions, interact, and so on in character. The host should prepare discussion questions for the guests. Encourage groups to use creativity and even humor to highlight important issues and sources of tension among the estates. **L3**

The Congress of Vienna In September 1814, European leaders met in the Austrian capital of Vienna. Their goal was to return Europe to the way it was before the French Revolution. The leader of the conference, known as the Congress of Vienna, was Austria's foreign minister Klemens von Metternich (MEH•tuhr•nihk). Like the other leaders, Metternich was a conservative. Conservatives at that time believed in traditional values, orderly ways, and a strong role for religion. They rejected calls for individual rights and self-rule. American conservatives today believe in traditional values, but they also support individual political rights and self-rule.

At the Congress of Vienna, Metternich and the other leaders wanted to create a balance of power, or equal strength among countries. They hoped that a balance of

◄ Klemens von Metternich

power would prevent any single nation, such as France, from controlling Europe.

The European leaders at Vienna were against individual rights and nationalism. Hoping to crush revolutionary ideas, they brought back to power the royal families who had ruled in Europe before Napoleon. To keep the peace, the leaders also agreed to meet from time to time at conferences. These meetings were called the Concert of Europe.

 Reading Check **Analyze** How did nationalism help defeat Napoleon?

Study Central™ Need help with the material in this section? Visit jat.glencoe.com

Section 1 Review

Reading Summary
Review the Main Ideas

- Rising prices, food shortages, and unemployment in France led the Third Estate to rebel, creating a new elected assembly.
- French radicals known as Jacobins gained control of the government and executed thousands of people who opposed their reforms.
- As political troubles in France worsened, Napoleon Bonaparte took control of the country.
- After creating a large empire, Napoleon was finally defeated. European leaders attempted to restore a balance of power.

What Did You Learn?

1. What was the main idea of the Declaration of the Rights of Man and the Citizen?

2. What were the goals of the Congress of Vienna?

Critical Thinking

3. **Organize Information** Draw a chart like the one below. Use it to describe the divisions in French society.

First Estate	
Second Estate	
Third Estate	

4. **Summarize** What were some of the achievements of the Committee of Public Safety?

5. **Compare and Contrast** Compare the goals of the French and American Revolutions.

6. **Sequence Information** What events led to Napoleon's defeat and the fall of the French Empire?

7. **Reading** **Understanding Concepts** Make a recruiting poster for the French army, either in the revolutionary period or under Napoleon. Use language and illustrations that convey the ideals, emotions, and events of the time.

CHAPTER 19   Industry and Nationalism   **723**

ENRICH

Have students discuss this question: *Could the French Revolution have been prevented? How?* **L3**

 Reading Check

Answer: The nations of Europe rejected Napoleon's rule in favor of self-rule.

To help students understand section material, have them visit Study Central™ **at jat.glencoe.com**

RETEACH

Ask students to create a 10-question quiz, with answers, on the content of this section. Have students exchange quizzes and take them. **L1**

④ CLOSE

Write on the board this statement: *The end justifies the means.* Have students discuss its relevance to the French Revolution. **L2**

SECTION 1 REVIEW ANSWERS

1. the powers of government come from the people
2. return Europe to way it was before French Revolution, create balance of power
3. First Estate: clergy, 1 percent of population, paid no taxes, owned 10 percent of land; Second Estate: nobility, 2 percent of population, paid no taxes, owned 25 percent of the land; Third Estate: mostly poor peasants, 80 percent of the population, paid all taxes
4. expanded education to all, set price controls, created a citizen army
5. Students' answers should be based on content from the section.
6. the failed invasion of Russia, defeat of the French army and Napoleon's exile to Elba, Napoleon's defeat at Waterloo
7. Posters will vary.

① FOCUS

SECTION OVERVIEW

In this section, students will learn about how the Industrial Revolution began in Britain in the 1700s and gradually spread to northern Europe and the United States.

BELLRINGER
SKILLBUILDER ACTIVITY

📖 Project **Daily Focus Skills Transparency 19–2** and have students answer questions. Discuss their responses.

Get Ready to Read!

Preteaching Vocabulary: Explain to students that *capital* is a word that means "money invested in business or industry." The availability of capital helped spur the growth of industries.

Answers to Graphic: Possible answers: James Hargreaves—the spinning jenny; Richard Arkwright—water-powered spinning machine; Edmund Cartwright—powered loom; James Watt—steam engine; Henry Cort—iron smelting; Henry Bessemer—steel process; Robert Fulton—steam engine in boat

---

Section 2
The Industrial Revolution

Get Ready to Read!

What's the Connection?
While France and other nations were undergoing political changes, the Industrial Revolution was changing the way people worked and lived.

Focusing on the Main Ideas
- The Industrial Revolution began in Great Britain because of the enclosure movement, Britain's natural resources, and new British inventions. *(page 725)*
- The Industrial Revolution spread beyond Great Britain's shores to Europe and the United States. *(page 729)*

Meeting People
James Hargreaves (HAHR•GREEVZ)
Richard Arkwright (AHRK•RYT)
Edmund Cartwright (KAHRT•RYT)
James Watt
Robert Fulton

Michael Faraday (FAR•uh•DAY)
Thomas Edison

Building Your Vocabulary
industrialism (ihn•DUHS•tree•uh•LIH•zuhm)
textile (TEHK•STYL)
capital
partnership
corporation (KAWR•puh•RAY•shuhn)

Reading Strategy
Organizing Information Use a diagram like the one below to show four of the major inventions and their inventors that helped start the Industrial Revolution.

The Industrial Revolution

NATIONAL GEOGRAPHIC **When & Where?**

NORTH AMERICA London • • Paris EUROPE
• New York

1750   1800   1850   1900

1769 Watt improves steam engine

1807 Robert Fulton builds steamboat

1876 Alexander Graham Bell invents telephone

1903 Wright brothers make first airplane flight

SECTION RESOURCES

📁 **Reproducible Masters**
- Reproducible Lesson Plan 19–2
- Daily Lecture and Discussion Notes 19–2
- Vocabulary Activity 19–2
- Active Reading Note-Taking Guide 19–2
- Guided Reading Activity 19–2
- Section Quiz 19–2
- Reading Essentials and Study Guide 19–2

📖 **Transparencies**
- Daily Focus Skills Transparency 19–2

Multimedia
- Interactive Tutor Self-Assessment CD-ROM
- ExamView® Pro Testmaker CD-ROM
- Presentation Plus! CD-ROM

Industrialism Begins

Main Idea The Industrial Revolution began in Britain because of the enclosure movement, Britain's natural resources, and new British inventions.

Reading Focus How would your life be different if you did not have cars, telephones, or electricity? All of these things came from the Industrial Revolution. Read to learn how industry began.

While political revolution swept through Europe, a new economic system known as **industrialism** (ihn•DUHS•tree•uh•LIH•zuhm) began in Britain. There, people began to rely on the use of machinery, rather than on animal or human power. Over the next 200 years, industrialism would spread from Britain to dramatically change life in other parts of the world. Industry changed life so much that historians call these changes the Industrial Revolution.

Before the rise of industrialism, most people lived in small farming villages. They raised their own food and made their own goods. In Britain during the early 1700s, cloth was made in villages. As you read previously, this system was known as cottage industry. Under this system, most

Reading Strategy

Comparing and Contrasting Have students make a simple chart that shows characteristics of the domestic and factory systems. (*Domestic depended on network of local workers, most work done in homes, small scale; factory used large machinery, workers came to central location, worked regular hours, work directed by managers.*) **L1**

Daily Lecture and Discussion Notes 19–2

Use **Daily Lecture and Discussion Notes 19–2** for an outline of key concepts found in the section.

Using Geography Skills

Answers:

1. coal mining and textile production

2. There are more industries and railroads in the northern part of Western Europe. This is probably due to the fact that the region is not as mountainous as other regions of Europe.

Reading Support L1/ EL

Use **Vocabulary Activity 19–2** to review important terms in the section.

NATIONAL GEOGRAPHIC

The Industrial Revolution 1870

FINLAND
NORWAY
Oslo
St. Petersburg
Stockholm
SWEDEN
Glasgow • Edinburgh
UNITED KINGDOM
Bradford
North Sea
Copenhagen
DENMARK
Liverpool • Leeds
Manchester
Birmingham • Sheffield
Bristol • London
Amsterdam NETH.
Hamburg
Moscow
Brussels
Berlin
BELGIUM
Cologne
POLAND
Breslau • Warsaw
RUSSIA
Paris
GERMANY
Prague
ATLANTIC OCEAN
Munich
Vienna • Budapest
FRANCE
SWITZ.
AUSTRIA-HUNGARY
Bordeaux
Turin • Milan Venice
Genoa
Florence
Black Sea
Marseille
SERBIA
Danube R.
Madrid
Mediterranean Sea
ITALY
Rome
SPAIN
Constantinople

400 mi.
400 km
Chamberlain Trimetric projection

KEY
Manufacturing and industrial area
• Major industrial center
+++++ Major railways by 1870

Industry:
🛒 Coal mining
Ironworking
Textile production

Using Geography Skills

The Industrial Revolution spread throughout Europe in the 1800s.
1. What were the major industries in the United Kingdom?
2. What patterns do you see in the distribution of industries, and what geographical factors might account for these patterns?

Reading Strategy READING THE TEXT

Understanding Text Structure Write the following questions on the board: *To where did the Industrial Revolution spread first? What two kinds of people invested in factories? What were the two largest industries in Britain before the Industrial Revolution? What happened in 1793 to change the British textile industry?*

Tell students they have two assignments. First, they should write the questions in the correct order, according to the content of Section 2. Then, as they read the section, they should write answers to the questions. Help students conclude that they can use the headings in the section to order the questions. **L2**

Name Origins Many common English family names come from different steps in the cloth-making industry. *Shepherds* looked after sheep, while *shearers* sheared them. *Fullers* and *walkers* helped process wool cloth. *Webbers* set up looms so *weavers* could make cloth. *Dyers* colored the cloth, then *tailors* (or *taylors*) made clothing. Have students use the Internet or other resources to find the origin of their own last name. **L2**

CURRICULUM CONNECTION

Science

One of the advances that made British agriculture more productive in the 1700s was crop rotation. A British politician with an interest in farming named Charles Townshend introduced the idea. He found that instead of letting a field lie fallow, or unused, for a year, planting crops like alfalfa or clover restored an important element, nitrogen, to the soil. Replacing the nitrogen made the soil more fertile. He was known as "Turnip" Townshend because he also encouraged farmers to plant root crops.

Focus on Everyday Life

Traveling by Early Railroad In the 1700s and early 1800s, the best way to travel in England was on horseback or by stagecoach. By the late 1840s, however, stagecoach companies were being forced out of business with a new invention: the steam locomotive. The locomotive was invented in England in the early 1800s. It was first used to move coal and iron ore from mines to factories. Then passengers started riding the trains.

Boarding and riding a grand locomotive, nicknamed the "iron horse," was an exciting trip. The wealthy bought tickets for first-class seats in fancy, enclosed passenger cars. These customers sat on plush cloth and leather benches with wood and brass handrails. The seats were located behind the locomotive

▲ Early English train from the 1840s

work was done in workers' cottages, where families worked together.

Merchants went from cottage to cottage, bringing the workers raw wool and cotton. Using hand-powered spinning wheels and looms, the workers would spin the thread and weave it into wool and cotton cloth. The merchants then picked up the finished cloth to sell. The Industrial Revolution began in the woven cloth, or **textile** (TEHK•STYL), industry. Merchants could make so much money from textiles that they began to look for ways to make cloth better and faster. By the 1700s, changes in Britain made this possible.

What Caused the Industrial Revolution?

The Industrial Revolution began in Britain for many reasons. One important cause of Britain's Industrial Revolution was a change in how Britain's landowners used their land. In the 1700s the enclosure movement began. Britain's Parliament passed new laws that allowed landowners to fence off their land. For hundreds of years, local villagers had rented the land from landowners and divided it into small strips, each worked by a family. Now the villagers were told they could not use the land the way they wanted.

Enclosure allowed landowners to make more money. Whole areas could grow the same crop, which meant larger harvests and greater profits. Often the land was turned into pasture for sheep whose wool was used by the textile industry.

Successful farming provided landowners with extra money. Many chose to invest, or put money, into new businesses. Money invested in businesses is called **capital.** A growing middle class joined wealthy landowners and merchants in investing capital in new industries.

726   CHAPTER 19   Industry and Nationalism

DIFFERENTIATED INSTRUCTION

Kinesthetic: Have pairs of students construct models or draw detailed diagrams explaining one of the important inventions of the early Industrial Revolution.

English Learners: Ask students to read about one of the inventions in the text and take turns explaining in their own words how these machines might have worked. Have students make lists of important verbs used in their explanations.

Gifted and Talented: Have students research the life of an important inventor of the period and present a short play to the class about the inventor and invention.

➤ Refer to *Inclusion Strategies for the Middle School Social Studies Classroom* in the TCR.

where the smoke would rise above the train's front section and not bother the riders.

People who bought cheaper tickets sat in the second-class section. Second-class railway cars were open to the air, and passengers had to wait their turn for a bench seat to become available. Third-class passengers could buy very cheap tickets and stand in train cars with open sides. Some had benches. The smoke from the coal-powered steam engines often dirtied the riders' clothes. They ignored this discomfort because riding a train was faster and cheaper than traveling in uncomfortable stagecoaches.

Connecting to the Past

1. What accommodations were provided for first-class passengers?
2. Why did third-class passengers prefer to travel by train than by stagecoach?

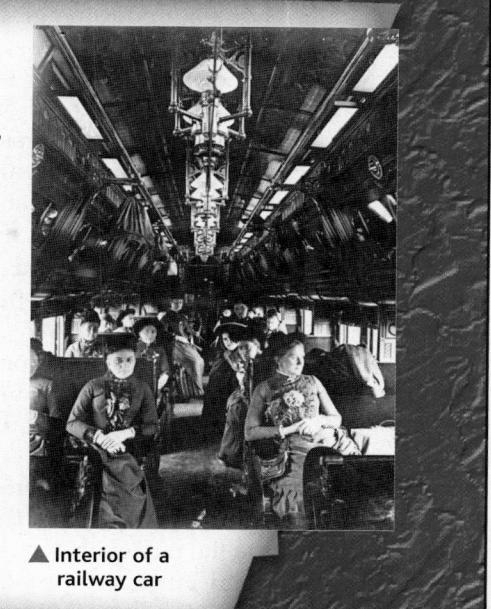

▲ Interior of a railway car

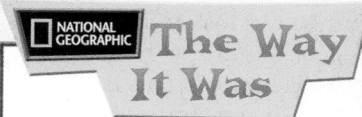

CONNECTING ACROSS TIME

Ask students to interview parents or grandparents about important technological advances that have occurred during their lifetimes. How have the changes affected their lives? Have students report their findings to the class. **L2**

NATIONAL GEOGRAPHIC The Way It Was

Answers:

1. First class had fancy cars and seats. Their seats were located in such a way that the smoke would not bother them.
2. Trains were faster and cheaper.

Still another cause was the large number of people available to work in industry. The enclosure movement forced many peasants off the land. They then moved to the cities and became workers in new industries.

In the 1700s, Britain's population grew rapidly. More and better food meant that people were healthier, lived longer, and had larger families. This increase in population also provided workers for the new factories.

Finally, Britain's natural resources and geography also helped in the rise of industry. The British had large supplies of coal and iron. Coal replaced wood as the fuel for running machines. Iron was used in building and in making machines. The country had many fine harbors and rivers for transporting goods. Rivers also provided power for the earliest cotton mills.

New Inventions Britain also had a number of talented inventors. Their inventions made the Industrial Revolution possible. Many of these first inventions were developed in the late 1700s for the textile industry. **James Hargreaves** (HAHR•GREEVZ) invented a spinning jenny that could spin cotton into thread very quickly. **Richard Arkwright** (AHRK•RYT) developed a way to power a spinning machine with water, and **Edmund Cartwright** (KAHRT•RYT) created a new powered loom. This machine could weave the thread into cloth as fast as the new spinning machines produced it.

In 1769 **James Watt** designed a steam engine that could power the new machines. Steam soon replaced water as the major source of power.

As the need for machines grew, iron was needed to make machine parts. In 1753 Henry Cort found a way to use coal to turn

Effects of Industrialization Ask students if they think the arrival of the Industrial Revolution made life better for most people in Great Britain. Have them explain the reasons for their judgment, using evidence from the text and their own conclusions. **L2**

Writing Activity ✏️

Point out that the textile industry gave rise to many of the early important technological advances of the Industrial Revolution. Ask students to decide which industry or business holds a comparable primary place in today's U.S. economy. Have them write a paragraph explaining the reasons for their selection. **L2**

CRITICAL THINKING ACTIVITY

Identifying Cause and Effect Draw a simple graphic organizer on the board to help students identify reasons why the Industrial Revolution began in Great Britain. Write "Industrial Revolution Begins in Britain" and circle the phrase. Then have students search the text to find reasons for this fact. Record each answer in a circle and connect it to the central circle with an arrow. Continue until students have named all the reasons in the text. (*Answers should include enclosure system and loss of farm jobs, improved agriculture, capital investment in new industries, increased number of workers in cities, improved food, better health, larger families, longer lives, abundant coal and iron, and availability of harbors and rivers.*) **L3**

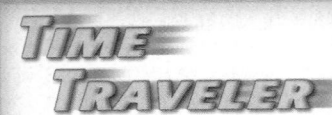

A key element of a corporation is the idea of limited liability. The owners, or stockholders, of the corporation invest a certain amount of money. This amount is the maximum they can lose if the business goes bankrupt. Their liability is limited. This is why British corporations include the word *Limited* (abbreviated Ltd.) in their names.

✓ Reading Check

Answer: The enclosure movement allowed landowners to make more money, which they could invest into new industries for profit. The enclosure movement also forced peasants off of the landowners' land, causing an increase in the labor force.

Caption Answer: They provided a faster and cheaper way to transport people and goods.

Reading Support L1 / EL

Assign **Guided Reading Activity 19–2** to help students organize the information in the section.

iron ore into pure iron. As a result, iron became cheaper, production grew, and coal mining became a major industry. In 1856 Henry Bessemer invented an inexpensive way to make large amounts of iron into steel, which was harder and stronger than iron. Soon mining towns and steel centers grew in areas with supplies of iron ore and coal.

The Rise of Factories and Railroads

Factories were the major centers of the Industrial Revolution. Why did they develop? Machines became too large and expensive for home use. Factories brought workers and machines together in one place under managers.

As the Industrial Revolution began, business owners reorganized their companies to raise the money they needed to buy machines and build factories. One way to do this was to form a **partnership** where two or more people owned the business and pooled their own money. Another way was to create a **corporation** (KAWR•puh•RAY•shuhn). A corporation raises money by selling shares in the company to investors. Creating a corporation allowed business leaders to build large factories with hundreds of workers.

New forms of transportation also led to industrial growth. In 1807 **Robert Fulton,** an American inventor, developed a boat powered by a steam engine. The biggest improvement in land transportation was the railroad. By the mid-1800s, steam-powered locomotives carried raw materials, finished goods, and people faster and cheaper than any other kind of transportation.

✓ Reading Check **Explain** How did enclosure help to bring about the Industrial Revolution?

Steam Engine

In a locomotive, coal is burned in the engine's firebox. The hot gases from the fire travel through tubes and empty into the smokebox, after heating water in the boiler and creating steam. The throttle releases steam into the steam chest, where a valve controls the movement of the steam into the cylinder. In the cylinder, the steam pushes the piston, which is connected to a drive rod that turns the locomotive's wheels. *How did railroads affect industry?*

Key

① Water compartment	④ Throttle Lever	⑦ Smokebox	⑩ Cylinder
② Coal bunker	⑤ Firebox	⑧ Blast pipe	⑪ Piston
③ Coal conveyer	⑥ Boiler tubes	⑨ Steam chest	

INTERDISCIPLINARY CONNECTIONS ACTIVITY

Literature One of the most important depictions of English industrial life during the 1800s is in the novels of Charles Dickens. *Hard Times* is set in Coketown, Dickens's name for the industrial center Manchester. It bitterly attacks materialism, industrial capitalism, and the educational ideas of the day. The theme of *Little Dorrit* is prisons, both real and symbolic. *Bleak House* examines the tangled web of the Victorian legal system. *Our Mutual Friend*, Dickens's last completed novel, exposes the corrupting influence of money on all of society. Have students research the life of Dickens and how his own youthful experiences affected his attitudes toward industrialism. **L2**

The Spread of Industry

Main Idea The Industrial Revolution spread beyond Great Britain's shores to Europe and the United States.

Reading Focus Important inventions fueled the spread of the Industrial Revolution. What inventions of your lifetime do you feel have had the greatest impact on your life today?

Britain's advances in industrial technology gave it an advantage over other countries. To protect that advantage, Britain's Parliament passed laws keeping ideas, inventions, and skilled workers from leaving the country. In spite of these laws, however, the Industrial Revolution soon spread to other areas.

Industry in Europe and America From Britain the Industrial Revolution spread to France, Belgium, Germany, and the United States. European governments encouraged the rise of industries. They helped build factories, railroads, canals, and roads. By the 1820s, British business owners and investors had made so much money from industry that they began to invest in factories and railroads in Europe. Their investments helped the Industrial Revolution get started in other countries.

The Industrial Revolution also took hold in the United States. British investors and American engineers built factories for making textiles and shoes. Workers, including women and children, left rural areas to work in cities.

Like Britain, the United States had many natural resources. Americans quickly built roads and canals to move goods and people across the vast nation. Fulton's steamboat improved transportation on inland waterways, and railroads soon crisscrossed the country.

HISTORY MAKERS

Edison's Lightbulb 1879

Edison once said, "The electric light has caused me the greatest amount of study and has required the most elaborate experiments." For these experiments, Edison carefully made the glass bulbs in his own glassblowing shed. Inside each bulb was a filament, or thin strip of material. The bulbs were incandescent, which means that electricity heats the filament, which becomes hot enough to glow and make light. For Edison, the trickiest part was finding the best material for the filaments. Eventually, he found that a carbonized cotton thread filament provided the best quality of light.

▲ Thomas Edison in his workshop

Edison gave the first public demonstration of his incandescent lightbulb on December 31, 1879, at his laboratory in Menlo Park, New Jersey. Edison's lightbulb made it possible for people to use small electric lamps in their homes and led to other uses for electricity.

HISTORY MAKERS

Edison's reputation as a clever and hardworking inventor was good enough to impress wealthy investors like J.P. Morgan and the Vanderbilt family. In 1878, they advanced Edison $30,000 for his work on the lightbulb. In less than two years, Edison and his staff had created a workable prototype. Over the next several years, electric lighting systems, using Edison's lightbulb, were installed in a steamship, a printing factory, hotels, theaters, and stores.

❸ ASSESS

Assign Section 2 Review as homework or as an in-class activity.

◉ Have students use the **Interactive Tutor Self-Assessment CD-ROM** to review the section.

Assessment L2

Assign **Section 2 Quiz** to assess mastery of the material found in the section.

Reading Support L1/ EL

Assign **Reading Essentials and Study Guide 19–2** to help students review section material.

EXTENDING THE CONTENT

The Pottery Man Another important British industry that was transformed by the Industrial Revolution was the making of pottery. The pioneer was Josiah Wedgwood (1730–1795). Born into a family of potters, Wedgwood applied scientific principles to the making of pottery. His new products, particularly a type of pottery called creamware, proved enormously popular with the growing middle classes in Britain and Europe. Wedgwood invented new glazes and a special high-temperature thermometer, and was the first to use steam engines in the production of pottery. He was also the grandfather of another scientific giant, Charles Darwin.

New Scientific Discoveries As the 1800s continued, many scientific discoveries helped to keep the Industrial Revolution going. Iron was replaced by steel. Starting in the 1870s, steel became the leading industrial metal. Other inventions made use of electricity. Electricity could be converted easily to heat, light, or motion, and could be sent through wires.

One important invention that used electricity was the telegraph, invented by Samuel Morse in the 1830s. The telegraph made communication possible across great distances by sending coded messages through wires. Other communications advances were the telephone, invented by Alexander Graham Bell in 1876, and the radio, developed by Guglielmo Marconi in 1895.

In 1831 **Michael Faraday** (FAR•uh•DAY) discovered that a magnet moving through a coil of copper wire produced an electric current. Within 40 years, this discovery led to the invention of electric generators. **Thomas Edison** developed the lightbulb, which used electricity to create light. As demand for electricity rose, investors in Europe and the United States funded the first power plants. These were powered by coal or oil.

Major breakthroughs also took place in transportation. In the 1880s Germany's Rudolf Diesel and Gottlieb Daimler invented internal combustion engines that produced a lot of power by burning oil-based fuels. Within a few decades, internal combustion engines powered boats. They also made possible two other new kinds of transportation: the car and the airplane. In 1903 two American inventors, Orville and Wilbur Wright, successfully tested the world's first powered airplane.

Reading Check **Cause and Effect** Which key inventions resulted from the development of electricity?

Section 2 Review

History Online
Study Central™ Need help with the material in this section? Visit jat.glencoe.com

Reading Summary

Review the Main Ideas

- Changes in agriculture and plentiful deposits of iron and coal helped Great Britain lead the way in the Industrial Revolution.

- France, Belgium, northern German states, and the United States soon followed Great Britain into the Industrial Age.

What Did You Learn?

1. What natural resources and features helped industries develop in Great Britain?

2. What important inventions were created following the development of electricity?

Critical Thinking

3. **Organize Information** Create a table like the one below. Fill in inventors' names and inventions.

Inventor	Invention

4. **Economics Link** Describe the difference between a partnership and a corporation.

5. **Describe** Describe the inventions that changed how people communicate.

6. **Analyze** What did Rudolf Diesel and Gottlieb Daimler invent, and why was it important?

7. **Expository Writing** Choose the invention or development from the chapter that you believe has had the greatest impact on the world. Write an essay explaining your choice.

730   CHAPTER 19   Industry and Nationalism

SECTION 2 REVIEW ANSWERS

1. supplies of coal and iron; waterways for transporting goods and powering mills
2. telegraph, telephone, radio, electric generator, lightbulb
3. Possible answers include: Hargreaves: spinning jenny; Cartwright: powered loom; Cort: iron smelting
4. A partnership involves two or more people working together. In a corporation, shares of the company are owned by many people who work together to make decisions and raise money.
5. The telegraph made possible communication over great distances by sending codes over wires; the telephone and the radio also helped communication.
6. the internal combustion engine; made the automobile and airplane possible
7. Answers will vary.

Section 3

Society and Industry

Get Ready to Read!

What's the Connection?
In the last section, you read about the causes of the Industrial Revolution. In this section, you will learn how industry changed society.

Focusing on the Main Ideas
- The Industrial Revolution caused cities to grow bigger and changed how people lived and worked. *(page 732)*

- The Industrial Revolution led to new ideas about politics, society, and the economy. *(page 734)*

- Artists, writers, and composers reflected the changes that industrialism brought to society. *(page 736)*

- Important scientific discoveries during the Industrial Revolution changed the way people lived and how they understood the world. *(page 738)*

Meeting People
Adam Smith
Karl Marx
Louis Pasteur (LOO•ee pas•TUHR)
Albert Einstein (EYEN•STYN)
Charles Darwin (DAHR•wuhn)

Building Your Vocabulary
urbanization (UHR•buh•nuh•ZAY•shuhn)
liberalism (LIH•buh•ruh•LIH•zuhm)
socialism (SOH•shuh•LIH•zuhm)
labor union

Reading Strategy
Contrasting Use a table like the one below to compare major ideas of the industrial era.

	Main Ideas
liberalism	
socialism	

When & Where?

NATIONAL GEOGRAPHIC

1800 — 1850 — 1900

c. 1780 Romanticism begins in the arts

1848 Karl Marx writes *Communist Manifesto*

1859 Charles Darwin presents theory of evolution

c. 1870 Impressionism begins in France

NORTH AMERICA — London, Paris, New York — EUROPE

CHAPTER 19 Industry and Nationalism 731

SECTION RESOURCES

Reproducible Masters
- Reproducible Lesson Plan 19–3
- Daily Lecture and Discussion Notes 19–3
- Vocabulary Activity 19–3
- Active Reading Note-Taking Guide 19–3
- Guided Reading Activity 19–3
- Section Quiz 19–3
- Reading Essentials and Study Guide 19–3

Transparencies
- Daily Focus Skills Transparency 19–3

Multimedia
- Interactive Tutor Self-Assessment CD-ROM
- *ExamView®* Pro Testmaker CD-ROM
- Presentation Plus! CD-ROM
- Glencoe BookLink CD-ROM

CHAPTER 19
SECTION 3, 731–741

1 FOCUS

SECTION OVERVIEW
This section discusses the new scientific, political, economic, and social ideas that arose in response to industrialization.

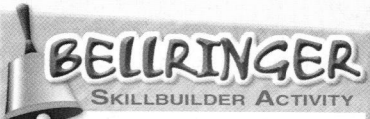
BELLRINGER
SKILLBUILDER ACTIVITY

Project **Daily Focus Skills Transparency 19–3** and have students answer questions. Discuss their responses.

Get Ready to Read!

Preteaching Vocabulary: A *labor union* is a group of workers who have formed an organization for the purpose of helping them to negotiate their employment conditions more effectively. There are still many labor unions today.

Answers to Graphic: liberalism: believed all people have basic rights, and endorsed voting rights only for men; socialism: believed all means of production should be owned and controlled by society; realism: writers and artists trying to show life how it truly was; romanticism: writers and artists valuing feelings and imagination as the best way to find truth.

② TEACH

Daily Lecture and Discussion Notes 19–3

Use **Daily Lecture and Discussion Notes 19–3** for an outline of key concepts found in the section.

Reading Support L1/ EL

Use **Vocabulary Activity 19–3** to review important terms in the section.

Caption Answer:
Machines replaced many rural workers, so many of them went to nearby cities looking for jobs.

Industry Changes Society

Main Idea The Industrial Revolution caused cities to grow bigger and changed how people lived and worked.

Reading Focus How is life in the country different from life in the city today? How is it similar? Read to learn about the new way of life rural people faced when they moved to the city during the Industrial Revolution.

The Industrial Revolution brought changes in many areas of life. These changes took place in Europe, North America, and elsewhere by the 1860s. Industrial growth still changes the way people live today.

Cities Grow in Size One important change was the rapid growth in the size of cities. **Urbanization** (UHR•buh•nuh•ZAY•shuhn) is the movement of people from rural areas to cities. A nation is urbanized when most of its people live in cities. Britain was the first country to become urbanized. City popula-tions also grew in the other parts of Europe and in the United States.

Why did cities grow so quickly? As farms used more machines, fewer workers were needed. To find jobs, many rural workers headed to nearby cities hoping to find work in the new factories.

What Was Industrial Life Like? Before the rise of industry, a person's place in society was set by birth. Few were able to rise to higher positions. The growth of industry, however, brought new opportunities.

In Europe, wealthy factory owners were able to live like nobles. They had several homes and many servants to wait on them. Less wealthy people such as managers, lawyers, doctors, and engineers formed the industrial middle class. Some of them also could afford servants and fine homes.

The growth of industry and cities also created a large working class. The working class was made up of people who toiled in the factories and mines. Their lives were

▼ This photograph from the late 1800s shows housing conditions in England. *Why did cities grow so rapidly during the Industrial Revolution?*

▲ This scene shows workers in a steel mill in France.

732   CHAPTER 19   Industry and Nationalism

much harder than those of the upper or middle classes.

Entire working-class families—children as well as adults—had to work to make enough money to live. Working conditions varied from barely acceptable to dreadful. Hours were long—up to 16 hours a day, 6 days a week. Injuries were common in hot, dirty, and unhealthy factories and mines. Many children lost fingers or limbs. Death and injury occurred often.

Living conditions in the cities were often wretched. However, workers still flocked to cities to fill factory jobs because they could not find work on the farms. Despite the low pay and long hours, most workers had better lives and more money than when they lived in the country. They found that city life had many benefits. Cities offered many leisure-time opportunities. These included parks, education for adults and children, concerts, libraries, museums, and sports. Women discovered a new independence.

As time passed, working conditions did improve. Some reformers, including many religious people, were able to better the lives of workers. Hours were reduced for female and young workers. Living conditions in the cities remained very unhealthy, but some improvements did occur. New laws were passed that made factories safer and reduced pollution and unclean food and water in the cities.

Life Changes for Women The Industrial Revolution greatly changed women's lives. At first, it was believed that a woman's place was in the home. Her job was to raise children and do household tasks. Women had fewer legal rights than men. During the 1800s, women worked to change their position and find new roles.

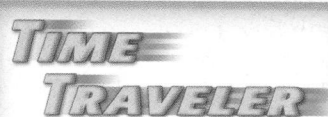

The Way It Was

Young People In...

Working Conditions in Mills For children working in mills and factories, the workday began early, often before dawn. A regular shift began at 5 in the morning. Children who arrived late for work usually did so in tears. They knew that their wages would be cut and that they would be severely punished.

Children arrived for work hungry, but breakfast was not allowed until 8 or 9 o'clock in the morning. Breakfast usually consisted of an oatcake and cans of boiled milk and water. Children ate their breakfast standing up, still working at their stations. Once a year, they were served cheese and brown bread for a special dinner. Because the children were tired and hungry, they often became drowsy while working. When this happened, the overseer woke them up by dunking them headfirst into a vat of cold water.

Many children developed breathing problems and became sick with an illness known as "mill fever." The air that children breathed was contaminated with dust, grease, oil, and gas.

▲ Child coal miners in England

Connecting to the Past
1. Why were children afraid to arrive late for work?
2. What was the cause of "mill fever"?

CONNECTING ACROSS TIME

Industrial workers in the early industrial age had none of the protections that workers today enjoy. Ask students to make a list of protections and benefits modern workers enjoy. **L2**

TIME TRAVELER

Working conditions at textile mills were very difficult. A woman who worked at the textile mill in Lowell, Massachusetts, wrote this in 1841: "I am going home, where I shall not be obliged to rise so early in the morning... Up before the day, at the clang of the bell—and out of the mill by the clang of the bell—into the mill, and at work in obedience to that ding-dong of a bell—just as though we were so many living machines."

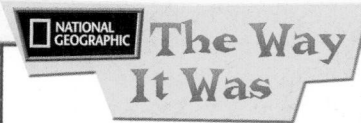

The Way It Was

Answers:
1. Their wages would be cut, and they would be punished.
2. breathing air contaminated by dust, grease, oil, and gas

DIFFERENTIATED INSTRUCTION

Visual/Spatial: Have students create a painting, drawing, poster, or other visual artwork about the changes caused by industrialization.

English Learners: Have students make a list of words that relate to the changes brought about by industrialization. Then have them use the words in a story about one of the events covered in this section.

Gifted and Talented: Have students write a poem or story about the life of a working-class person during the 1800s.

▱ Refer to *Inclusion Strategies for the Middle School Social Studies Classroom* in the TCR.

CONNECTING ACROSS TIME

Ask students to use the Internet and other resources to assemble a collection of early photographs of working-class life and working conditions in the 1800s. Have them examine the photographs for details about how people lived and worked, and point out differences with how we live and work today. **L3**

✓ Reading Check

Answer: People had time for leisure activities, and cities offered leisure-time opportunities.

Writing Activity ✏️

Have students write a letter from the perspective of a young person living in the early 1800s who has recently moved to an industrial city to take a factory job. Students should address their letter to a sibling still living at home in the country. Have them include details from the text. **L2**

Linking Past & Present

Answer: There are many career opportunities and chances at education for women in industrialized nations, though they often make less money than their male counterparts.

The workplace played a major role in changing the position of women. Women found jobs in both industry and government service. There were also more opportunities for education. A drop in family size during the 1800s helped to change the lives of women as well.

During the 1800s, women began to demand equal rights with men. In the United States, Britain, and other countries, women challenged long-standing ideas. They especially demanded the right to vote.

✓ Reading Check Identify What developed in cities as people began to work fewer hours?

Linking Past & Present

Women in the Workforce

THEN The Industrial Revolution brought jobs to women in Great Britain and the United States—but at a cost for some. Even though women gained independence through employment, many were forced to work long hours in bad conditions and for little pay. Safety issues were often overlooked and pollutants and dangerous machines caused health problems.

▼ Modern-day businesswomen

▲ Woman worker in an English cotton mill

NOW More women than men are entering colleges and universities in Great Britain and the United States. Women can build successful careers in most industries. However, in some countries, many women still work in factories under poor working conditions. *How did the rise of industry change job opportunities for women?*

New Political Ideas

Main Idea The Industrial Revolution led to new ideas about politics, society, and the economy.

Reading Focus What does the word *liberal* mean to you? Read to find out how a new philosophy with this name affected society in the 1800s.

The Industrial Revolution brought many changes, both good and bad. Starting in the early 1800s, people looked for ways to understand issues and solve the problems that industry had created. A number of different ideas developed to address these concerns.

CRITICAL THINKING ACTIVITY

Analyzing Information Have students take a position on this statement: *Factory owners in the 1800s were right to pay children less than adults because they could not do as much work as adults.* Ask students to support their position with evidence from the text and from their prior knowledge. In a class discussion, list supporting points for each position on the board. Encourage them to think critically, not just respond based on emotion. **L2**

What Is Liberalism?

One of these new ideas was **liberalism** (LIH•buh•ruh•LIH•zuhm). Liberalism is a political philosophy based on the ideas of the Enlightenment. The word *liberal* had a different meaning in the 1800s than it does today in the United States. Liberals today agree with liberals of the 1800s about some ideas but disagree on others. Earlier, you read about conservatives in the 1800s and how they too believed different things than conservatives do today.

Liberals in the 1800s believed that all people have basic rights. These include equality before the law and freedom of speech and the press. Many liberals wanted freedom of religion. Liberals also believed that the power of governments should be limited by written constitutions and that elected assemblies should make laws. Liberals did not believe that everyone should be allowed to vote. Most thought that this right should be restricted to men who owned property.

Liberalism was popular among the new middle class. Middle-class businesspeople believed that government should not interfere with business or society. British economist **Adam Smith** defended this idea. He argued that if government stayed out of the economy and let businesses compete, it would lead to more prosperity and a better society. This idea became known as "laissez-faire," a French word meaning "to let be."

Two British thinkers, however, wanted to use government to help make society better. Jeremy Bentham (BEHN•thuhm) and

History Online
Web Activity Visit jat.glencoe.com and click on *Chapter 19—Student Web Activity* to learn more about the rise of industry.

Primary Source
The Communist Manifesto

In outlining their plan for society, Karl Marx and his friend Friedrich Engels urged the working class to unite.

"In short, the Communists everywhere support every revolutionary movement against the existing social and political order of things. . . .

The Communists disdain [refuse] to conceal their views and aims. They openly declare that their ends can be attained only by the forcible overthrow of all existing social conditions. Let the ruling class tremble at a communist revolution. The proletarians have nothing to lose but their chains. They have a world to win.

Working men of all countries, unite!"

—Karl Marx and Friedrich Engels, *The Communist Manifesto*

▲ Karl Marx

DBQ Document-Based Question

What do Marx and Engels mean when they say that there is nothing to lose but chains?

John Stuart Mill were utilitarians. They believed society should promote the greatest happiness for the most people. Utilitarianism (yoo•TIH•luh•TEHR•ee•uh•NIH•zuhm) endorsed ideas like full rights for women, better education, and improved health services.

What Is Marxism?

Another new idea of the 1800s was **socialism** (SOH•shuh•LIH•zuhm). Socialists believe that factories, land, capital, and raw materials—what they called the means of production—should be

CHAPTER 19   Industry and Nationalism   **735**

Primary Source

Answer:
They are referring to the "chains" that hold the working class back from ending social classes and creating a classless society.

CURRICULUM CONNECTION

Language Arts
The word *liberalism*, like *liberate*, *liberty*, and *liberation*, comes from the Latin word for "free." The word *communism*, along with such words as *community* and *commonwealth*, is based on the Latin word for "common." Ask students to suggest ways that each word retains its original Latin meaning.

History Online

Objectives and answers to the student activity can be found in the **Web Activity Lesson Plan** feature at jat.glencoe.com

---

INTERDISCIPLINARY CONNECTIONS ACTIVITY

Music The differences among classicism, romanticism, and modernism are perhaps most evident in music. Music of the late 1700s classical period, as exemplified by Mozart and Haydn, emphasized balance, harmony, and stability. Romantic music, such as that of the later Beethoven, Schubert, Liszt, and Chopin, is dramatic and emotional. Modern music is less dependent on traditional ideas of melody, form, and harmony. The music of composers like Debussy, Stravinsky, and Ravel may strike some students as unpleasant or dissonant. Ask students to put together a panel discussion of music styles with background information and examples of works by these and other composers. **L3**

CONNECTING ACROSS TIME

Ask students to find out about the success of socialist political parties in one of these countries: Great Britain, France, Sweden, or Germany. Have them report to the class on how the party differed from Marx's ideas, as well as its success in governing. **L2**

Categorizing Have students review the characteristics of romanticism and realism. Then ask them to give examples of current books, movies, music, art, or other elements that they feel represent either romanticism or realism. Have them explain their categorizations. **L2**

✓ Reading Check

Answer: Society should promote the greatest happiness for the most people.

▲ This painting shows men, women, and children working in an early factory. *Why did labor unions develop?*

owned and controlled by society, through the government. Many people developed the ideas of socialism, but the most important person was a German writer named **Karl Marx.**

Marx was a German thinker who lived during the 1800s. Marx believed that competition among social classes harmed society. He predicted that, over time, the working class, which he called the proletariat (PROH•luh•TEHR•ee•uht), would rise up and create a communist society. Under communism, social classes would end and people would live in a classless society.

Marx's ideas, later called Marxism, were very influential. His ideas were the basic ideas of socialist political parties in Germany, Britain, Scandinavia, and other countries. These socialist parties favored government control of industry.

Another response to the horrors of factory life was the growth of labor unions. A **labor union** is an association of workers who unite to improve wages and working conditions. Strikes, or work stoppages, often forced owners to bargain with union leaders. In many European countries, unions supported socialist political parties.

✓ Reading Check **Describe** What did Jeremy Bentham and John Stuart Mill believe?

New Art and Literature

Main Idea Artists, writers, and composers reflected the changes that industrialism brought to society.

Reading Focus Art, music, and literature are often shaped by the society in which they are created. How do today's music, books, and movies reflect today's society?

The rise of industry changed how people lived and worked. It also led to new movements in art, literature, and music. The often ugly face of the new industrialized world caused some artists to turn away from it. Others, however, chose to portray it.

Romanticism and Realism In the late 1700s, artists and writers known as the romantics began to react against the Enlightenment. Instead of reason, their movement called romanticism valued feelings and the imagination as the best way to find the truth.

Poets, such as Britain's William Wordsworth and Germany's Johann von Goethe (yoh•HAHN fawn GUH•tuh), looked to nature, the past, and the unusual as their subjects. In their works, these writers tried to express their inner feelings about life. Romantic painters, such as Eugène Delacroix (yoo•JEEN DEH•luh•KWAH) of France, also chose strange and unusual subjects. The first great romantic musician was Ludwig van Beethoven (LOOD•wihg vahn BAY•TOH•vuhn). This German composer's music expressed strong emotion and intense drama.

By the mid-1800s, another movement—realism—took hold. Some artists turned away from the romantic emphasis on feelings. These writers and painters, known as realists, tried to show life as it truly was.

EXTENDING THE CONTENT

Robert Owen, Utopian One of the most interesting figures of the 1800s was Welsh industrialist and reformer Robert Owen. Having been born in the working class, Owen rose to a management position in an English textile mill. Owen believed that success in industry did not need to be based on the exploitation of workers. He put his reforming ideals into practice in the town and factory of New Lanark, Scotland. There he built workers' homes, stores, and schools that were much better than the standard. Owen later tried unsuccessfully to re-create his system in New Harmony, Indiana. His model influenced American reformers like Francis Cabot Lowell of Massachusetts.

Novelists like Charles Dickens of Great Britain, Honoré de Balzac (AHN•uh•RAY day BAWL•zak) of France, and Leo Tolstoy (tohl•stoy) of Russia focused on ordinary people in ordinary settings. They used details to create a picture of everyday life. Painters like France's Gustave Courbet (GUS•TAHV kur•BAY) also showed figures and scenes from ordinary life. While romantics tried to escape from industrialized society, realists chose to examine it closely.

Modernism and Impressionism

Two other movements appeared later in the 1800s. One was modernism. An important part of modernism was the study of social problems. Novelists such as Émile Zola of France, and Theodore Dreiser of the United States, and dramatist Henrik Ibsen of Norway explored social issues of the day. Subjects included crime, alcoholism, and women's rights. Other modernists took a different approach. Symbolist poets believed that the outer world was only a reflection of an individual's inner reality. They studied dreams and symbols for meaning and used them in their works.

A modernist movement in painting was called impressionism. Beginning in the 1870s, impressionists were especially interested in the effect of light on different outdoor objects and surfaces. The most famous impressionists were French. They included Claude Monet (moh•NAY), Pierre-Auguste Renoir, and Edgar Degas (duh•gah). Mary Cassatt of the United States was also a famous impressionist painter. Composers, led by France's Claude Debussy (DEH•byu•SEE), even translated impressionist ideas into dreamy, shimmering music.

✔ **Reading Check** **Describe** What element was most important to modernists?

▼ *The Stonebreakers* by Gustave Courbet, 1849

▲ *Nympheas* by Claude Monet, 1907

Courbet painted scenes from everyday life, while Monet focused on the beauty of nature. *Which artist rejected the artistic movement of romanticism?*

Writing Activity

Ask students to research the life of one of the artists, musicians, or authors described in the text. Have them write a short biography of the person. **L1**

CURRICULUM CONNECTION

Literature
Ask groups of students to put together dramatic readings about life in the industrial age from the writers mentioned in the text and others they may research. Have groups present their readings using appropriate props, scenery, or musical accompaniment.

✔ **Reading Check**

Answer: the study of social problems

Reading Support L1/ EL

Assign **Guided Reading Activity 19–3** to help students organize the information in the section.

Caption Answer:
Courbet went against romantic ideas by portraying more realistic things in his art.

COOPERATIVE LEARNING ACTIVITY

Class Presentations Have students brainstorm a list of different categories that were influenced by the Industrial Revolution. Suggestions might include Daily Life, Work, Art, Literature, Technology, Women's Lives, and Medicine and Health Care. Have students work in groups to prepare panel discussions on a topic. Encourage groups to include visual and other aids in their panel discussions. **L3**

☞ Refer to *Quizzes, Tests, and Authentic Assessment (with Rubrics)* booklet for rubrics.

in a word . . .

"Pasteurization" is the term we use for the heat treatment that destroys bacteria in food. It was named for Louis Pasteur, who showed that heating foods could destroy harmful microorganisms.

Evaluating The discoveries of Curie and Einstein, along with others, convinced many people that they lived in a world where everything could change and nothing was certain. Have students discuss the impact of such discoveries on people's religious beliefs. Have such discoveries weakened or strengthened people's belief in a higher power? How? **L3**

More About the Art

Louis Pasteur could have been an artist—he certainly had the talent for it. His portraits of his school friends won him much praise, but he later turned his attention to chemistry and other sciences. Pasteur became known for his discoveries in the treatment of anthrax, chicken cholera, and silkworm diseases.

Caption Answer: He showed that killing bacteria would prevent many diseases.

Science and Medicine

Main Idea Important scientific discoveries during the Industrial Revolution changed the way people lived and how they understood the world.

Reading Focus Do you know why children often look like their birth parents? Read to find out who discovered how characteristics are passed from one generation to another.

During the 1800s, scientists took many important steps forward. Their work brought many practical benefits to society in the fields of medicine and health. It also enabled people to better understand the world.

Why Was Pasteur Important? One of the first important medical advances was the discovery of vaccines to ward off disease. In 1796 the English doctor Edward Jenner noticed that dairy workers who caught cowpox did not get the deadly smallpox. Jenner believed that vaccinating or injecting people with cowpox would make them immune to smallpox. Jenner's theory proved correct.

It took a while, however, before the vaccination process could be explained. Finally, in 1868, French chemist **Louis Pasteur** (LOO•ee pas•TUHR) discovered bacteria, or germs. He also proved that they cause disease. Pasteur showed that killing bacteria would prevent many diseases.

Early surgery was a gruesome process. The discovery of anesthesia, or pain-deadening drugs such as ether, was a great step forward. So were the methods developed by Englishman Joseph Lister to sterilize medical equipment. Before Lister, many patients died after surgery due to infection.

An Austrian monk named Gregor Mendel was responsible for a key scientific breakthrough. In the 1860s his work with pea plants finally solved an ancient mystery: to predict which characteristics or traits get passed to the next generation. Based on his observations, Mendel developed a system of rules that could predict whether a living organism would inherit traits from its parents. Mendel's ideas became very influential, and he is known today as the father of the science called genetics.

Einstein and Physics By the end of the 1800s, new ideas in the physical sciences, or physics, changed the way people understand the world. Atomic theory is the idea that everything is made up of tiny particles called atoms. Scientists gradually learned more about atoms, including the composition of different elements and the qualities of X rays and electricity. They learned

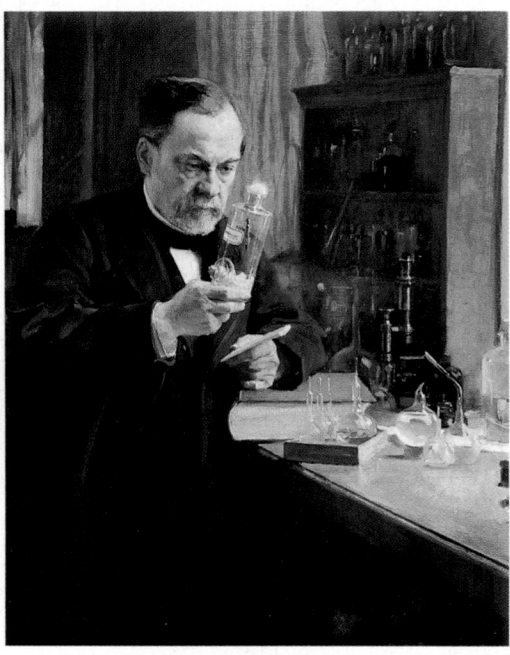

▲ Among his discoveries, Louis Pasteur developed a vaccine against rabies. *How did Pasteur's discovery of bacteria lead to the prevention of disease?*

EXTENDING THE CONTENT

Precocious Child James Mill had ideas about how to educate children, and he put them into practice with his son, the Utilitarian philosopher John Stuart Mill. By the time John was 8, he could read classical Greek authors in the original. Two years later, he had mastered Latin, geometry, and algebra and had begun teaching the younger children in his family. By 13, he was studying politics and economics, as well as Aristotle. Over the next few years, Mill traveled and studied chemistry, botany, psychology, Roman law, and French. By the time he was 20, however, John Stuart Mill had suffered what we would probably call a nervous breakdown. He emerged from his gloominess with a more expansive ideal of human happiness.

Major Scientific Discoveries

Year	Scientist	Discovery	Impact
1803	John Dalton	elements are composed of atoms	provided proof to support the atomic theory
1820s	Mary Anning	fossils of dinosaurs, including the plesiosaur	helped scientists learn more about the Jurassic period of history
1850s	Louis Pasteur	disease-causing bacteria	allowed for doctors to fight disease more easily
1859	Charles Darwin	all living things evolve as their environment changes	questioned whether mankind originated from God or nature
1890s	Wilhelm K. Roentgen	X rays	allowed doctors to see a person's bones from the inside
1890s	Ivan Pavlov	actions are unconscious reactions	determined that, through training, any action could be learned
1898	Marie and Pierre Curie	the element radium within atoms	proved that atoms were active
1900	Max Planck	energy is not continuous	influenced the study of the atom
1905	Albert Einstein	theory of relativity	led to the development of the atomic bomb
1905	Nettie Stevens	X and Y chromosomes determine gender	led to the advanced study of human genetic material

Understanding Charts

In the late 1800s and early 1900s, scientists and inventors made tremendous advances that would affect the world for years to come.
1. During what years did important advancements in the understanding of atoms take place?
2. Which two scientists had the greatest impact on medicine?

that atoms are composed of even smaller individual particles. A Polish scientist, Marie Sklodowska Curie (kyu•REE), and her French husband, Pierre Curie, discovered the element radium in 1898. Radium is radioactive, which means it gives off energy.

Within a few years, a German scientist named **Albert Einstein** (AL•buhrt EYEN•STYN) caused a revolution in people's thinking about the universe. Previously, you learned that people during the 1600s came to believe that the universe was a well-run machine that obeyed natural laws. In 1905, however, Albert Einstein overturned these long-held ideas about time, space, mass, and motion. His theory of relativity stated that space and time were relative and

changing, rather than permanent and unchanging. As a result of Einstein's theory, people were able to imagine a more fluid, unstructured view of reality.

Einstein also developed a famous equation—$E=Mc^2$—where E is energy, M is mass, and c is the speed of light. The equation shows that all physical things contain vast amounts of energy. Using this idea, scientists eventually created the atomic bomb and nuclear reactors.

③ ASSESS

Assign Section 3 Review as homework or as an in-class activity.

● Have students use the **Interactive Tutor Self-Assessment CD-ROM** to review the section.

Assessment L2

Assign **Section 3 Quiz** to assess mastery of the material found in the section.

Reading Support L1/ EL

Assign **Reading Essentials and Study Guide 19–3** to help students review section material.

Understanding Charts

1. 1803, 1898, 1900, and 1905
2. Louis Pasteur and Wilhelm K. Roentgen

CRITICAL THINKING ACTIVITY

Comparing and Contrasting Have students study the material under the heading "Science and Medicine." Tell them to keep in mind that the inventions in science and medicine in many ways brought profound changes to society. Once they have studied this material, have them consider how life changed for people where these inventions took place. Then ask them to write a three-paragraph essay that compares and contrasts life before and after these inventions came into play. L2

Biography

Biography

TEACH

Both Curie and Einstein helped disprove the old idea that the universe was composed of unchanging matter and forces that affected it. The Curies' discovery of radium showed that atoms were not small, solid, unchanging objects, like pellets. Instead they found that these tiny bodies gave off energy and were more like tiny, active systems than like pellets.

Einstein went even further, stating that matter is nothing but another form of energy. This discovery led finally to the understanding of the atom and the incredible amount of energy that it contained. The fateful result of this understanding was the development of nuclear power and weapons. **Ask:** Do you think scientists should be held responsible for the uses to which their discoveries are put? Why or why not? *(Some may say that scientists should know the possible dangers of their work, but most will probably say that scientists have no way of knowing all the ramifications of their work.)* **L2**

Then and Now

Answers will vary but could include medical research, public health, and many others. Answers should make clear how the study would improve people's lives.

ALBERT EINSTEIN
1879–1955
MARIE SKLODOWSKA CURIE
1867–1934

In the late 1800s and early 1900s, both Albert Einstein and Marie Curie helped to advance science.

Albert Einstein was born on March 14, 1879, in Württemberg, Germany. He grew up in Munich in a Jewish family. Einstein became a teacher and then worked in a patent office in Switzerland. Einstein earned many awards for his scientific theories, including the Nobel Prize in physics. Einstein fled Nazi Germany and moved to the United States in 1933. Although his famous equation $E=Mc^2$ helped to advance scientific knowledge, he was bothered by the fact that it also made the atomic bomb possible. Late in his life, he began urging nations to give up nuclear weapons. He died on April 18, 1955, in Princeton, New Jersey.

Marie Curie was born Maria Sklodowska in Warsaw, Poland, in 1867. She graduated from high school at age 15, then attended classes at the Floating University, an illegal night school forbidden by Poland's Russian rulers. When Maria enrolled at the Sorbonne University in Paris in 1891, she became known as Marie. There she met Pierre Curie. They were married in 1895 and had two daughters. She earned her doctorate in 1903, and when Pierre died in an accident in 1906, Marie took his position teaching and researching at the Sorbonne. During World War I, she used X-ray units to help doctors treat wounds. She also helped create the Curie Foundation in 1920 to advance science and medicine. Twice she was awarded the Nobel Prize in physics. Marie died on July 4, 1934, in France.

▲ Albert Einstein

> "Imagination is more important than knowledge."
> —Albert Einstein

▲ Marie Curie

Then and Now

Both Einstein and Curie wanted their discoveries to better society. Identify and describe a topic or subject you would like to study because you think advances in that area could help people live better lives.

RECOMMENDED READING

Reading List Generator CD-ROM

GLENCOE BOOKLINK

Use the **Glencoe BookLink CD-ROM** to create customized reading lists based on your students' interests and reading levels. Below is an example based on content in this chapter. Also, see the Suggested Readings on pages 944–946 of the Appendix.

- Blashfield, Jean F. *Women Inventors 3.* Caty Greene helped Eli Whitney invent the cotton gin. Madame C.J. Walker invented hair care products. Harriet Hosmer invented artificial marble.
- Linder, Greg. *Alexander Graham Bell.* Alexander Graham Bell's most famous invention was the telephone. But he did other important things too. He taught deaf people how to speak, made giant kites, and built a superfast boat that traveled above the water.
- Wells, H.G. *The Time Machine.* A scientist travels almost a million years into the future.

Who Was Charles Darwin? Like many others, **Charles Darwin** (DAHR•wuhn) wondered why there were so many different kinds of life in the world. His research led him to a conclusion: plants and animals change very slowly over time. The ones that survive do so because they are better adapted to their environment. They win the "battle" for survival and produce offspring. The offspring have the same characteristics that helped their parents adapt.

Darwin also believed that humans developed from animal species. His ideas were—and remain—controversial. Some religious people believed that his

▲ Charles Darwin

theories contradicted the biblical story of creation. Others believed it opened the door to a world without morals. Many people, however, came to accept Darwin's theory.

Some people believed that Darwin's ideas about competition between species applied to society as well. This idea, called Social Darwinism, was popular with those who supported laissez-faire economics. Why? They believed that different individuals, companies, and countries engaged in economic competition, just like species. Weaker ones would fail, while stronger ones would prosper.

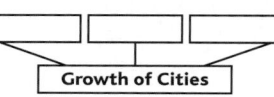 **Compare** How was the work of Edward Jenner similar to that of Louis Pasteur?

History Online
Study Central™ Need help with the material in this section? Visit jat.glencoe.com

Section 3 Review

Reading Summary
Review the Main Ideas

- The Industrial Revolution led to the growth of cities and the creation of the industrial working class.

- New political and economic philosophies, such as liberalism and socialism, developed during the Industrial Revolution.

- A number of different artistic movements arose during the Industrial Age, including romanticism, realism, modernism, and impressionism.

- Important scientific advances took place in the fields of medicine, biology, and physics during the 1800s.

What Did You Learn?

1. Describe the working conditions in Industrial Age factories.

2. How did the artistic movement known as realism approach life in the Industrial Age?

Critical Thinking

3. **Cause and Effect** Draw a diagram like the one below. Fill in causes that led to the growth of cities during the Industrial Age.

```
[   ]   [   ]   [   ]
      ↓   ↓   ↓
   [ Growth of Cities ]
```

4. **Economics Link** Describe the economic philosophy of Adam Smith. Which members of British society agreed with his ideas?

5. **Summarize** What is a labor union, why did they become popular, and how did they force businesses to negotiate?

6. **Analyze** How were Darwin's scientific theories applied to society?

7. **Writing Questions** Imagine you are a newspaper writer interviewing Karl Marx. Write three or four questions you might ask him about his beliefs. Include possible answers.

ENRICH

Have students discuss this statement: *The computer revolution of the late 1900s has had an impact as great as the Industrial Revolution.* **L3**

✔ **Reading Check**

Answer: Jenner believed that vaccinating people with cowpox could prevent smallpox. Pasteur was able to explain why Jenner's theory worked through the discovery of bacteria and germs.

To help students understand section material, have them visit **Study Central**™ at jat.glencoe.com

RETEACH

Ask students to work in pairs to summarize each of the four subsections in this section. **L1**

 CLOSE

Have students decide which invention, development, or idea discussed in this section has had the greatest impact on our lives today. Have them discuss their choices. **L2**

SECTION 3 REVIEW ANSWERS

1. long working hours; factories were hot, dirty, cramped, and dangerous

2. Realism focused on ordinary people and everyday life.

3. Farms used fewer workers; workers moved to cities to find jobs; factories used steam power and could be located away from rivers.

4. Smith believed that government should not interfere with business or society. Middle-class businesspeople agreed with him.

5. An association of workers who unite to improve wages and working conditions; the threat of strikes forced factory owners to negotiate.

6. Social Darwinism: individuals, companies, and countries engaged in economic competition, and the stronger would prosper

7. Students' questions will vary.

741

❶ FOCUS

Different people often have different values. What seems to be a benefit to one person can be a problem for another. Ask students to name situations that could be seen as creating either a benefit or a problem, depending on one's values.

❷ TEACH

DEFINING TERMS

Have students make a list of synonyms for the words *benefit* and *problem*. Then have them use each word in a sentence about your own community.

COMPARISON

Have students create a two-column graphic organizer like the one below. Ask them to use the table to list the problems and benefits of the Industrial Revolution. (Answers are provided.) **L1**

Industrial Revolution	
Benefits	**Problems**
• new inventions	• accidents and deaths
• many goods at low cost	• bad working conditions
• new forms of transportation and communication	• long working hours
• growth of middle class	• low pay
• growth of cities	• unhealthy living conditions
• job opportunities	• pollution
• independence for women	• loss of village communities
• education for children	• more time traveling
	• working in separate jobs

You Decide . . .

The Industrial Revolution: Benefits vs. Problems

Benefits

Many people, particularly factory owners, landowners, and financial investors, believed that the changes brought about by the Industrial Revolution benefited people of all classes. Lower-class men, women, and children worked in factories. Men of the middle class often served as managers. Men of the upper class were often factory owners.

Many debated the issue of child labor. One journalist published the following report:

"[T]he industry of the young not only contributes to the increase of our national wealth, but also to their own advantage. In many factories they are not only usefully employed, but, at the same time, are trained up in those habits of morality and good feeling which are most likely to ensure their own lasting happiness and to make them valuable members of society."

—*from* The Penny Magazine, *November 16, 1833*

Benefits of the Industrial Revolution included the following:

- new inventions and technology, such as lightbulbs, refrigerators, electric ovens, and medicine
- factories made goods at low cost, which made food and goods affordable for more people
- development of new forms of transportation and communication, such as railroads, steamships, automobiles, airplanes, and telephones
- growth of the middle class
- rapid growth of cities
- greater job opportunities
- greater independence for women
- greater opportunities for education

▲ Rolls Royce Silver Ghost, an early automobile from 1906

742

Extending the Content

Industrial Era Living Conditions Charles Dickens's feelings about the Industrial Revolution's effects on the environment and on working people's lives are clear from this description of Coketown, the setting of *Hard Times*. "In the hardest working part of Coketown; in the innermost fortifications of that ugly citadel, where Nature was as strongly bricked out as killing airs and gases were bricked in . . . [lived] the multitude of Coketown, generally called 'the Hands'—a race who would have found more favour with some people if Providence had seen fit to make them only hands . . ."

advised me to work no more in the factories; but I was not my own master. During the day, I frequently counted the clock, and calculated how many hours I had still to remain at work; my evenings were spent in preparing for the following day—in rubbing my knees, ankles, elbows, and wrists with oil, etc. I went to bed, to cry myself to sleep, and pray that the Lord would take me to himself before morning."

Problems created by the Industrial Revolution included the following:

- dangerous factory machinery caused serious accidents and deaths
- people worked in cramped, hot, and dimly lit factories
- long working hours—up to 16 hours a day, 6 days a week
- low pay
- unhealthy living conditions in crowded cities
- pollution from factories dirtied the air and rivers
- rise of cities broke up traditional small village communities
- people had to spend much more time traveling to and from work
- families did not work together all day on a farm; instead each family member had to go to separate jobs

▲ Workers at a mine in England

Problems

Other people, such as social reformers, doctors, and the lower-class factory workers themselves, believed that the Industrial Revolution not only created many problems, but that it seriously harmed those who worked in factories day after day. A young boy who started working in a textile factory at the age of six wrote this account:

"I have frequently worked at the frame till I could scarcely get home, and in this state have been stopped by people in the streets who noticed me shuffling along, and

You Be the Historian

Checking for Understanding
1. What were two benefits of the Industrial Revolution? What were two problems?
2. What problems caused by the Industrial Revolution are still problems today?
3. Do you think the benefits created by the Industrial Revolution outweighed the problems? Write a brief essay that explains your view. Be sure to use facts to support your position.

743

③ ASSESS

Reading Strategy

DEBATE THE ISSUE

Organize students into two teams and explain that the teams are going to prepare for and present a debate. One team should take the position that the Industrial Revolution delivered more benefits than problems. The other team should take the point of view that it created more problems than benefits. Tell teams to practice defending their position, using the points made in the feature and others they think of. Suggest that they use the library or Internet to find more information to support their position. When they are ready, have them debate. When both sides have presented their case, ask students to decide which side seemed to have the stronger argument. **L2**

You Be the Historian Answers

1. Answers will vary. Sample answer: Two benefits were new inventions and cheap goods. Two problems were dangerous factory machinery and unhealthy living conditions.

2. pollution, long times to commute to work
3. Essays will vary but should be supported by facts and logical arguments.

① FOCUS

SECTION OVERVIEW

In this section, students read about the influences of nationalism and reform on Europe and on North and South America during the 1800s.

BELLRINGER
SKILLBUILDER ACTIVITY

✎ Project **Daily Focus Skills Transparency 19-4** and have students answer questions. Discuss their responses.

Get Ready to Read!

Preteaching Vocabulary: Introduce the term *kaiser* by saying it is the German word for "emperor." Tell students that it comes from the name of the Roman emperor, Caesar, as does the Russian name for its emperor, *czar*.

Answers to Graphic: Possible answers: Simón Bolívar—won independence for Venezuela, Columbia, Panama, Ecuador, Bolivia, and Peru; José de San Martín—fought for independence of Argentina, Chile, and Peru

Section 4

Nationalism and Nation-States

Get Ready to Read!

What's the Connection?
The French Revolution and the Industrial Revolution led to increased feelings of nationalism. That desire for self-rule led to reforms and revolutions in many parts of the world.

Focusing on the Main Ideas
- Two powerful ideas, nationalism and reform, helped reshape Europe politically during the mid-1800s. **(page 745)**

- In the mid-1800s, two new countries, Italy and Germany, were created. **(page 747)**

- In the early 1800s, the people of Latin America rebelled and gained their independence. **(page 749)**

- Nationalism in the United States led the country to expand its borders, but differences between the North and South led to a bloody civil war. **(page 751)**

Meeting People
William Gladstone
Giuseppe Garibaldi (joo•ZEHP•pay GAR•uh•BAWL•dee)
Otto von Bismarck (AHT•oh fawn BIHZ•MAHRK)
Simón Bolívar (see•MAWN boh•LEE•VAHR)

Building Your Vocabulary
kaiser (KY•zuhr)
caudillo (kow•THEE•yoh)
abolitionism (A•buh•LIH•shuhn•IH•zuhm)

Reading Strategy
Organizing Information Use a table like the one below to list Latin American leaders and their achievements.

Leader	Achievements

NATIONAL GEOGRAPHIC When & Where?

| 1800 | 1835 | 1870 |

1803
U.S. buys Louisiana Territory

1821
Mexico gains independence

1832
British middle-class men gain the vote

1871
Germany is united

NORTH AMERICA
EUROPE
• Berlin
• Rome
Washington, D.C. •
SOUTH AMERICA

SECTION RESOURCES

 Reproducible Masters
- Reproducible Lesson Plan 19-4
- Daily Lecture and Discussion Notes 19-4
- Vocabulary Activity 19-4
- Active Reading Note-Taking Guide 19-4
- Guided Reading Activity 19-4
- Section Quiz 19-4
- Reading Essentials and Study Guide 19-4

✎ **Transparencies**
- Daily Focus Skills Transparency 19-4

Multimedia
- Interactive Tutor Self-Assessment CD-ROM
- ExamView® Pro Testmaker CD-ROM
- Presentation Plus! CD-ROM
- Vocabulary PuzzleMaker CD-ROM
- Glencoe BookLink CD-ROM

Nationalism and Reform

Main Idea Two powerful ideas, nationalism and reform, helped reshape Europe politically during the mid-1800s.

Reading Focus What does the term *self-rule* mean to you? What does it include? Who should have it?

Nationalism is the desire of people with the same history, language, and customs for self-rule. During the 1800s, nationalism, along with demands for political reform, led to dramatic and important changes in Europe and the Americas.

Democracy in Great Britain
While war and revolt raged in most of Europe, change came peacefully to Britain. In the early 1800s, nobles ran Britain's government, and the middle and working classes could not vote. This situation soon changed. In 1832 a liberal British government passed a law that gave voting rights to most middle-class men. New industrial cities gained more seats in Parliament. Industrial workers, however, still did not have the vote. In the 1840s their supporters, known as Chartists, demanded the vote for all men and the use of secret ballots.

The Chartists failed to get the government to agree to their demands. Britain's political parties continued to make reforms, however, especially after **William Gladstone** became prime minister in 1868. Gladstone

The British Parliament

Speaker's Chair
The speaker is a member of Parliament who is chosen to oversee the activities of the House.

Government Benches
The prime minister and other members of the ruling party sit here.

Table of the House
Bills that are being debated are placed here.

Opposition Benches
Members who are not in the ruling party sit here.

◀ The British Parliament is divided into two main bodies: the House of Lords and the House of Commons (left). The House of Commons is made up of officials elected by the public, and the House of Lords is made up of people appointed by members of the nobility. The two houses meet in separate rooms within the great Palace of Westminster.

The Palace of Westminster, which includes ▶ the giant clock tower Big Ben, was originally built in 1050. Two fires, in 1529 and 1834, destroyed much of the building, but it was fully restored by 1870 when the Parliament moved its headquarters into the building.
Who presides over the debate in the House of Commons?

---

2 TEACH

Writing Activity

During the period of revolution in Europe, nationalism and liberalism often went together. Have students write an essay examining whether this pairing is usually true today or not. Have them support their conclusions with evidence from current events. *(Students may point to events in the former Yugoslavia and other ethnic hotbeds as evidence that nationalism and liberalism do not necessarily go together.)* **L3**

Daily Lecture and Discussion Notes 19–4

Use **Daily Lecture and Discussion Notes 19–4** for an outline of key concepts found in the section.

Caption Answer: the Speaker

Reading Strategy READING THE TEXT

Setting a Purpose Encourage students to set their own purpose for reading. Write on the board the six question words—*who, what, when, where, why,* and *how*—that reporters use to search for information on a topic. Then organize the class into small groups and have them write questions about the section using these words. Get students started with this example: What groups made up the Austro-Hungarian Empire? **L1/EL**

CURRICULUM CONNECTION

Health

The Crimean War saw the birth of the profession of nursing. Under the direction of Florence Nightingale, British soldiers received care at her hospital in Turkey. In addition to disease; filthy conditions; rats and fleas; and lack of food, water, and supplies, she had to battle opposition from male doctors and military commanders. She succeeded, however, in vastly improving conditions and care. On her return to London after the war, she founded the world's first nursing school.

Reading Support L1/ EL

Use **Vocabulary Activity 19–4** to review important terms in the section.

✓ Reading Check

Answer: While bitter war erupted elsewhere, reform came peacefully in Britain.

---

led the Liberal Party, which was backed by many middle-class voters. He served four terms as British prime minister, or political leader. Gladstone's reforms allowed voters to cast their ballots in secret and reorganized electoral districts to give more equal representation.

Gladstone's great political rival was Benjamin Disraeli, leader of the Conservative Party. Disraeli served two terms as prime minister. In 1867 his government gave the vote to many workers. In 1900 a new political party was created. Claiming to represent the working class, this party was known as the Labour Party. It eventually replaced the Liberals as the main rival of the Conservatives.

In the early 1900s, British women known as suffragettes pushed for women to have the right to vote. They staged demonstrations and hunger strikes. In 1918 Parliament gave all women over 30 the right to vote.

The Revolutions of 1848 In 1848 revolutions swept across Europe. Their starting point was France. Protests in support of political reforms erupted in Paris. The French king Louis-Philippe was driven from his throne, and France became a republic.

Events in France sparked revolts in other parts of Europe. Seeking self-rule, Hungarians, Italians, and Germans all rebelled against their monarchs. These revolts failed, but the ideas of nationalism and political reform remained strong among Europe's middle and working classes.

In France, Napoleon's nephew, Louis Napoleon, was elected president and later emperor. Under Napoleon III, France enjoyed economic advances, but the government was not democratic.

In 1870 Napoleon III declared war on Prussia. The powerful German state won an easy victory, and Napoleon III's government fell. The defeat stirred unrest in France. Workers seized control of Paris and set up a socialist government known as the Commune. A bloody civil war broke out. Troops supported by the upper-class government crushed the workers. In 1875 France became a republic once again. Distrust between its upper and working classes remained strong, however.

Reform in Austria and Russia During the late 1800s, rulers in Austria and Russia tried to prevent political reform and weaken nationalist movements. Humiliating defeats in war, however, forced both Austria and Russia to make some changes.

In Austria, the government made a deal with the Hungarians, who wanted their freedom. In 1867 Hungary became a separate kingdom linked to Austria. Together they ruled the Austro-Hungarian Empire. The Hungarians were now satisfied, but other groups in Austria-Hungary were not. Their demands for self-rule continued throughout the rest of the 1800s.

In Russia, military defeat made the government realize that the country was far behind industrialized Europe. Czar Alexander II decided to create new industries and improve farming. In 1861 he freed the serfs—peasants who had to stay on the land where they were born and farm it for their landlords. Not enough land was given to the newly freed peasants, however, and they remained dissatisfied. Many writers and philosophers opposed to the czar's rule began calling for revolution.

✓ Reading Check Explain How did political change in Britain differ from political change in other parts of Europe?

746   CHAPTER 19   Industry and Nationalism

DIFFERENTIATED INSTRUCTION

Intrapersonal: Have students choose one situation described in this section. Have them make up diary entries for a person involved in the event. Ask them to write about what the person experienced, felt, and thought as he or she lived through the event.

English Learners: Have students exchange diary entries with another student and discuss vocabulary, grammar, and usage issues the entries raise.

Gifted and Talented: Have students turn their diary entries into a multimedia documentary using audio or videotape, visual arts, or other media.

📁 Refer to *Inclusion Strategies for the Middle School Social Studies Classroom* in the TCR.

The Rise of Italy and Germany

Main Idea In the mid-1800s, two new countries, Italy and Germany, were created.

Reading Focus Which do you think is more important for a nation: democracy or a strong economy where everyone has a job? Why? Read to find out about how two newly united countries answered this question.

In the early 1800s, the countries we know today as Italy and Germany did not yet exist. Instead, these areas were divided into many small, independent states. By the 1850s, the rise of nationalism in Europe strengthened the desire of many Italians and Germans to create united countries.

How Did Italy Become a Country? In 1848 most of Italy's states were dominated by Austria. Piedmont, in northern Italy, was independent, and it was ruled by King Victor Emmanuel and the prime minister, Camillo di Cavour (kah•MEEL•loh dee kuh•VUR).

Both of these men wanted to unite Italy. After Piedmont helped Britain and France in a war with Russia, France agreed to help Piedmont drive Austria out of Italy. In 1859, with France's help, Piedmont won a war against Austria. This victory was the first step toward uniting Italy. Soon, people in other northern Italian states revolted against their rulers and united with Piedmont.

CURRICULUM CONNECTION

Music
During the struggle for Italian unification, the Italian opera composer Giuseppe Verdi (VEHR•dee) became a musical spokesman for independence and freedom. His first great success, the opera *Nabucco*, contained a chorus of Hebrew slaves singing of their homeland from their captivity in Babylon. This stirring song became an unofficial anthem of the movement. Even Verdi's name was considered an acronym for the Italian words for "Victor Emmanuel, King of Italy."

Using Geography Skills

Answers:
1. Piedmont expanded to control Lombardy in 1859; Parma Modena, Tuscany, part of the Papal States, Naples, and the Kingdom of the Two Sicilies by 1860; Venetia by 1866, and the rest of Italy by 1870.
2. 1866–1867

NATIONAL GEOGRAPHIC
The Rise of Italy and Germany *1859–1871*

KEY
- Piedmont before 1859
- Added to Piedmont, 1859
- Added to Piedmont, 1860
- Added to Italy, 1866
- Added to Italy, 1870

KEY
- Prussia before 1866
- Added 1866–1867 as the North German Confederation
- Added in 1871
- Annexed in 1871 after the Franco-Prussian War

Using Geography Skills

Growing nationalism helped lead to the unification of both Italy and Germany.
1. Looking at the map, explain the sequence of events in Italy.
2. When was Schleswig Holstein added to the German state?

CRITICAL THINKING ACTIVITY

Identifying Central Issues Nationalists affirm the ideal of the nation-state and believe that national or ethnic groups deserve their own countries. Have students arrange a debate on this proposition: Every national or ethnic group that desires one should have its own country. Have each side research its case and present its evidence. After the debate, have the audience vote on a winner. **L2**

EVALUATING

Ask students to speculate on the role of a strong personality, such as Bismarck, Garibaldi, and Cavour, on historical events. **Ask: Do influential people shape events, or do important events encourage people to step forward and lead?** *(Answers will vary, but most students will agree that great people to some extent do shape events.)* **L2**

> **Caption Answer:** He planned to use military power to unite the country.

CONNECTING ACROSS TIME

The roots of German economic strength are found in Bismarck's development policies of the late 1800s. These resources helped Germany play a leading role in both World Wars. Even after the devastation of World War II, Germany was able, with help from the United States, to regain its economic power. Today, a newly united Germany is one of the world's wealthiest countries, as well as the largest and richest of Europe. Have students write a paragraph describing how Germany became united in the 1800s. **L2**

✓ Reading Check

Answer: He was the ruler of Piedmont, and he would become the leader of the constitutional monarchy established in 1861.

▲ King Victor Emmanuel (left) ruled a united Kingdom of Italy. Otto von Bismarck (right) served as prime minister under William I of Prussia and helped unite the German states. *What did Bismarck mean when he said he would unite Germany by "blood and iron"?*

At the same time, nationalists led revolts in southern Italy. Their leader was **Giuseppe Garibaldi** (joo•ZEHP•pay   GAR•uh•BAWL•dee). This revolutionary leader gained control of the island of Sicily in 1860. Garibaldi was a master of guerrilla warfare (guh•RIH•luh   WAWR•FEHR), a form of war in which soldiers make surprise attacks on the enemy and then go back into hiding. Garibaldi's army landed on Italy's mainland and gained control over more territory. People in the south then voted to join a united Italy.

In 1861 the Kingdom of Italy was set up as a constitutional monarchy under Victor Emmanuel. Two areas remained outside Italy. One was Rome, which was under the pope's control. The other was an area of northeast Italy, which remained Austrian. By 1870, wars had brought both areas into the new Italian kingdom, and the unity of the country was complete.

Bismarck Unites Germany Nationalism was also strong in the German states. Many of these states' rulers were not willing to give up their political power though. Nationalists, however, had strong support from the northern German state of Prussia, which had grown powerful and prosperous. Prussia was ruled by William I, who dreamed of uniting all German states under his leadership. In 1862 he appointed **Otto von Bismarck** (AHT•oh fawn BIHZ•MAHRK) as his prime minister.

Bismarck was a deeply conservative Junker (YUNG•kuhr), or wealthy landowner. He vowed to govern Prussia by "blood and iron" rather than by votes and speeches. Bismarck quickly raised money and strengthened the army. He used the army to easily defeat neighboring Denmark and Austria in two short wars.

As Bismarck hoped, these successes helped him unite all of northern Germany in Prussia's new empire. The mostly Catholic southern German states feared the power of Protestant Prussia. They feared France more, however. In 1870 Bismarck fought a war with France, known as the Franco-Prussian War.

This conflict was a great success for Prussia and a disaster for France. Prussia gained two of France's border territories. More importantly, the southern German states agreed to unite with Prussia. On January 18, 1871, William was proclaimed **kaiser** (KY•zuhr), or emperor, of a united Germany.

✓ **Reading Check** **Explain** What role did King Victor Emmanuel play in the unification of Italy?

INTERDISCIPLINARY CONNECTIONS ACTIVITY

Art/Literature/Music The period of revolution and nationalism in Europe inspired some of the world's greatest works of art, literature, and music. Have students choose one field and research how artists, writers, and composers were influenced by the events and beliefs of the period. For example, students could focus on novelists like Twain, Dickens, Tolstoy, and Dostoyevsky; poets like Whitman or Pushkin; composers like Tchaikovsky, Wagner, and Verdi; or artists like Delacroix. Have students share their findings with the class in a presentation. **L2**

Nationalism in Latin America

Main Idea In the early 1800s, the people of Latin America rebelled and gained their independence.

Reading Focus Do you want to be independent? What does that word mean to you? Read to learn what happened when people in Latin America fought for their independence.

While nationalism advanced in Europe, the European-ruled colonies of Latin America were moving toward independence. The American and French Revolutions stirred the people of Latin America to action. Everywhere, colonists tried to take charge of their own affairs.

New Nations in Latin America

The first successful revolt against European rule took place in Haiti, an island territory in the Caribbean Sea. There, François-Dominique Toussaint-Louverture led enslaved Africans in a revolt that eventually threw off French rule in 1804.

In Spanish and Portuguese Latin America, the fight for freedom increased in the next decade. In Mexico, two Catholic priests, Miguel Hidalgo and José María Morelos, urged poorer Mexicans to fight for freedom. Both men were defeated and executed.

Despite many battles, Mexicans did not gain their independence until 1821. After a short period of rule under an emperor, Mexico became a republic in 1823. Soon after, many people in Central America broke free from Mexican rule and began to form their own countries.

In the northern part of South America, **Simón Bolívar** (see•MAWN boh•LEE•VAHR), a wealthy military leader, led the fight for freedom. Between 1819 and 1825, forces under Bolívar's command defeated the Spanish and won independence for the present-day countries of Venezuela, Colombia, Panama, Ecuador, and Bolivia.

While Bolívar fought for freedom in the north, a soldier named José de San Martín (hoh•SAY day SAN•mahr•TEEN) was fighting for freedom in the south. In 1817 San Martín led his army from Argentina across the Andes mountain ranges and into Chile, taking the Spanish forces by surprise. A few years later, San Martín and Bolívar jointly defeated the Spanish in the Pacific coastal country of Peru.

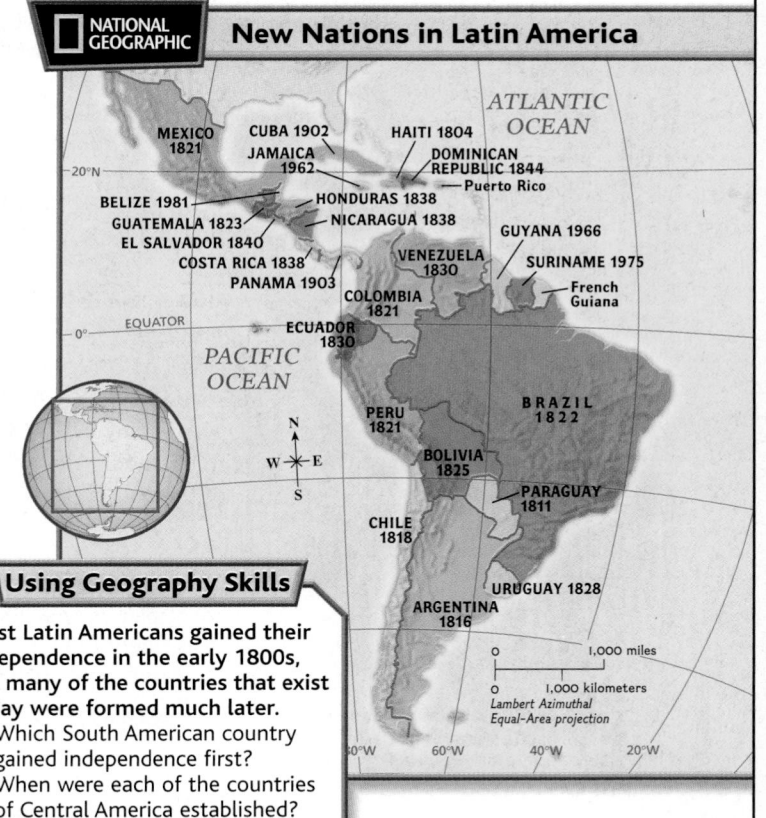

NATIONAL GEOGRAPHIC

New Nations in Latin America

MEXICO 1821 · CUBA 1902 · JAMAICA 1962 · HAITI 1804 · DOMINICAN REPUBLIC 1844 · Puerto Rico · BELIZE 1981 · HONDURAS 1838 · GUATEMALA 1823 · NICARAGUA 1838 · EL SALVADOR 1840 · COSTA RICA 1838 · GUYANA 1966 · PANAMA 1903 · VENEZUELA 1830 · SURINAME 1975 · French Guiana · COLOMBIA 1821 · ECUADOR 1830 · BRAZIL 1822 · PERU 1821 · BOLIVIA 1825 · PARAGUAY 1811 · CHILE 1818 · URUGUAY 1828 · ARGENTINA 1816

ATLANTIC OCEAN · PACIFIC OCEAN · EQUATOR

1,000 miles / 1,000 kilometers · Lambert Azimuthal Equal-Area projection

Using Geography Skills

Most Latin Americans gained their independence in the early 1800s, but many of the countries that exist today were formed much later.
1. Which South American country gained independence first?
2. When were each of the countries of Central America established?

EXTENDING THE CONTENT

Latin America's First Liberator Although François-Dominique Toussaint-Louverture was the grandson of an African king, he was born enslaved in Haiti in 1743. In 1791 he led a revolt of enslaved Africans against Haiti's French colonial rulers. Like many other revolutionary leaders, he was inspired by the French Revolution. In 10 years, Toussaint-Louverture had taken control of the island and freed all enslaved workers. Napoleon, however, refused to accept Toussaint-Louverture's control of Haiti. In 1802, Toussaint-Louverture was tricked into giving himself up. He was captured and taken to France, where he died in 1803. Toussaint-Louverture's dream of an independent Haiti came true a year later when French forces were driven out.

Biography

TEACH

While known as "The Liberator," Bolívar was not a true democrat. His inspiration for the liberation of South America was the French emperor Napoleon. He also admired the aristocratic government of Great Britain. Based on the British Parliament, Bolívar proposed for the new nations of South America a hereditary upper house, an elected lower house, and severely limited suffrage.

Bolívar's ideas about government were made clear when he set up the government of Bolivia in 1825. Bolívar installed an authoritarian government. During a period of civil war a few years later, he became dictator of Gran Colombia. However, liberals objected, and Bolívar narrowly escaped assassination.

Ask students to compare Bolívar's political ideas with those of George Washington. *(Washington refused offers to become king and chaired the constitutional convention that created America's republican form of government, while Bolívar was not a true democrat and supported authoritarian rule and limited voting rights.)* **L2**

Then and Now

Answers should examine the person's motivation. For example, Nelson Mandela became involved in the anti-apartheid struggle because he wanted to create a South Africa in which everyone enjoyed the same rights.

Biography

SIMÓN BOLÍVAR
1783–1830

▲ Simón Bolívar

Simón Bolívar was born July 24, 1783, in Venezuela. Although many people who lived in the area were poor, the Bolívars were rich and owned land. By age nine Simón's parents had died. His uncle hired tutors for him, but the young boy became bored and began to misbehave. When Bolívar was 11 years old, a man named Simón Rodríguez became his teacher and lifelong friend. Rodríguez introduced Bolívar to the ideas of European thinkers who believed in equality and freedom.

The two Simóns stayed together for many years, until Rodríguez left Venezuela in 1797. When Bolívar was 16, he visited his teacher and the two traveled across Europe. When he was 18, Bolívar married a young Spanish woman named María Teresa, and they moved back to Venezuela. She died eight months later, and Bolívar never married again.

Bolívar went to Paris and watched as Napoleon Bonaparte was crowned emperor. As Bolívar saw thousands cheering Napoleon, he realized he could earn the respect of the Venezuelan people if he freed them from Spain's harsh government. Bolívar traveled to Rome and on top of Monte Sacro, he pledged:

> "We have already seen the light, and it is not our desire to be thrust back into darkness."
> —Simón Bolívar, The Jamaica Letter

"I swear before you, I swear before the god of my fathers . . . that I shall not rest until I have broken the chains that oppress us [keep us down]."

He led many battles throughout South America before his goal to liberate his homeland came true. He became known among them as "El Libertador," which means "The Liberator."

▲ Statue of Simón Bolívar in Caracas, Venezuela

Then and Now

Identify other leaders who freed a territory or group of people. Why did they get involved?

Reading List Generator CD-ROM

GLENCOE BOOKLINK **RECOMMENDED READING**

Use the **Glencoe BookLink CD-ROM** to create customized reading lists based on your students' interests and reading levels. Below is an example based on content in this chapter. Also, see the Suggested Readings on pages 944–946 of the Appendix.

- Gleiter, Jan and Kathleen Thompson. *Simón Bolívar.* In the early 1800s, Simón Bolívar led the wars of independence that freed Peru, Bolivia, Colombia, Venezuela, and Ecuador from domination by Spain. He became known as "El Libertador." In English and Spanish.
- Wepman, Dennis. *Benito Juarez.* Born to poor Indian parents in Oaxaca, Benito Juarez ran away from home to seek an education. He eventually became Mexico's most revered president.

What Problems Did Latin America Face?

By the end of the 1820s, most of Spain's colonies in Latin America had won their independence. During the 1820s, Brazil also broke away from Portugal without bloodshed. Brazil was a monarchy before becoming a republic in 1889.

After Latin America won its independence, the United States made it known that it would protect the region. In 1823, United States president James Monroe warned the European powers not to interfere in the countries of Latin America. His statement, called the Monroe Doctrine, guided U.S. actions toward Latin America in the years ahead.

After gaining independence, most Latin Americans hoped their countries would become democratic and prosperous. These goals, however, were difficult to reach.

One major problem was frequent political conflict. Latin Americans quarreled over the role of religion in their society. Individual countries fought over boundary lines. Tensions developed between the rich and the poor.

At the same time, a series of strong leaders made it difficult for democracy and prosperity to develop. These were known as **caudillos** (kow • THEE • yohs). Caudillos were usually rich men, supported by the upper class. They often ruled as dictators. Some built roads, schools, and new cities. Many, however, favored the wealthy over the poor. Wealthy Latin Americans owned almost all of the land. The caudillos did nothing to help workers in the countryside, who remained landless and struggled to make a living. The wide divide between rich and poor is still a major problem in parts of Latin America today.

✓ **Reading Check** **Identify** Who were the caudillos?

Nationalism in the U.S.

Main Idea Nationalism in the United States led the country to expand its borders, but differences between the North and South led to a bloody civil war.

Reading Focus Do you feel a spirit of nationalism? How do you express it? Find out how Americans of an earlier time expressed their nationalism.

Nationalism also helped shape the United States during the 1800s and led to a steady growth in the size of the country. Many Americans believed expansion would make the young country richer and more powerful. However, nationalism also led to conflicting ideas about the nation's future.

The United States Expands West During the 1800s, the United States gradually expanded its borders westward. In 1803 the country doubled in size by buying the Louisiana Territory from France. During the first 50 years of the 1800s, the United States also gained Florida from Spain and the Oregon Territory from Britain. Many

▲ During the mid-1800s, many American settlers headed west to lands in the Oregon Territory. *What was Manifest Destiny?*

in a word …

"**Junta**" (HOON•tuh), the word we use for a group of military rulers who seize power after a coup, comes from Spanish. Juntas were especially common in Latin America. The term originally meant "conference."

Writing Activity

Ask students to write a short summary of the problems that Latin American countries faced in the 1800s. (*Problems should include the colonial legacy, political conflict, rule of caudillos, extreme poverty, border disputes, the role of the Church, and landlessness among peasants.*) **L1**

✓ **Reading Check**

Answer: They were rich men in Latin America who often ruled as dictators.

More About the Art

Conestoga wagons were one of the main modes of transportation by American settlers to the Oregon Territory. The wagons were custom built, so no two were ever completely alike. The heavy wagons often required four to six horses to pull them.

Caption Answer: the idea that the United States should stretch from the Atlantic Ocean to the Pacific Ocean.

COOPERATIVE LEARNING ACTIVITY

Group Portraits Have groups work together to present a "portrait" of a major country or region during the time of the rise of nationalism. Have groups choose among Great Britain, France, Italy, Germany, Austria, Russia, Mexico, and South America. Ask them to research and present their findings about their country or region. Have groups focus on such themes as industrialization, economy, population, political problems, culture, foreign policy, and leaders. **L2**

Americans came to believe in the "Manifest Destiny" of the United States, or the idea that the United States should stretch from the Atlantic Ocean to the Pacific Ocean.

In 1845, the United States annexed Texas, which had previously declared independence from Mexico. This greatly angered Mexico. A dispute over the Texas-Mexico border caused more trouble. By the following year, Mexico and the United States were at war. The United States defeated Mexico. In 1848 the peace treaty ending the war gave the United States the area that today includes California and several other western states.

Westward expansion brought new opportunities to settlers. They set up communities and built states in the new lands. The expansion also brought suffering—loss of land, culture, and often life—to Native Americans who had lived in the American West for centuries.

The American Civil War As the United States expanded westward, different ways of life developed in the Northern and Southern states. By the mid-1800s, these differences had begun to threaten national unity. The South was rural. Its agricultural economy depended on raising cotton.

Growth of the United States

◀ African American soldiers prepare for battle during the Civil War

▲ In the United States, slavery in the South helped cause the American Civil War. *What crop in the South depended on the use of enslaved workers?*

▲ Female suffragists marching for the right to vote

◀ Immigrants arriving in the United States at Ellis Island

COOPERATIVE LEARNING ACTIVITY

Interviewing The discussion of major wars in which the United States has fought creates an excellent opportunity for students to learn about the sacrifices others have made on their behalf. This can be accomplished by interviewing veterans, especially veterans of foreign wars. Have students work in groups of two or three and ask friends, family members, neighbors, or other people in their community to find someone who has served in the military. Have groups initiate contact with this person to set up an interview. Students should create a list of questions beforehand so that they are prepared for the interview. After asking the veteran's approval, students may wish to tape the interview to use as a record. They should then make a presentation on what they learned to the class. Students should also think of a creative way to thank the person they interview. **L2**

Cotton growing, in turn, depended on millions of enslaved African American workers. On the other hand, the North was building more and more industries. People, including new immigrants, or arrivals from overseas, were flocking to the growing cities. Some Northerners believed in **abolitionism** (A•buh•LIH•shuhn•IH•zuhm), a movement to end slavery.

The disagreement over slavery grew more and more heated. By 1860, the United States consisted of both free, or non-slave, states and slave states. That year, Abraham Lincoln, an opponent of slavery, was elected president. Fearing that Lincoln would try to end slavery, 11 states by early 1861 had seceded, or left, the United States. They formed a new nation: the Confederate States of America. Fighting erupted in April, and the American Civil War began.

The North had a much larger population and more factories and railroads than the South. In spite of this huge advantage, the Confederate States won most of the early battles. Gradually, however, the North's many resources gave it the upper hand. The war ended after four years of bloody fighting. More than 600,000 Americans died.

The war had other effects as well. The North's victory united the country. Millions

Reading Support L1/ EL

Assign **Guided Reading Activity 19–4** to help students organize the information in the section.

3 ASSESS

Assign Section 4 Review as homework or as an in-class activity.

Have students use the **Interactive Tutor Self-Assessment CD-ROM** to review the section.

Assessment L2

Assign **Section 4 Quiz** to assess mastery of the material found in the section.

Reading Support L1/ EL

Assign **Reading Essentials and Study Guide 19–4** to help students review section material.

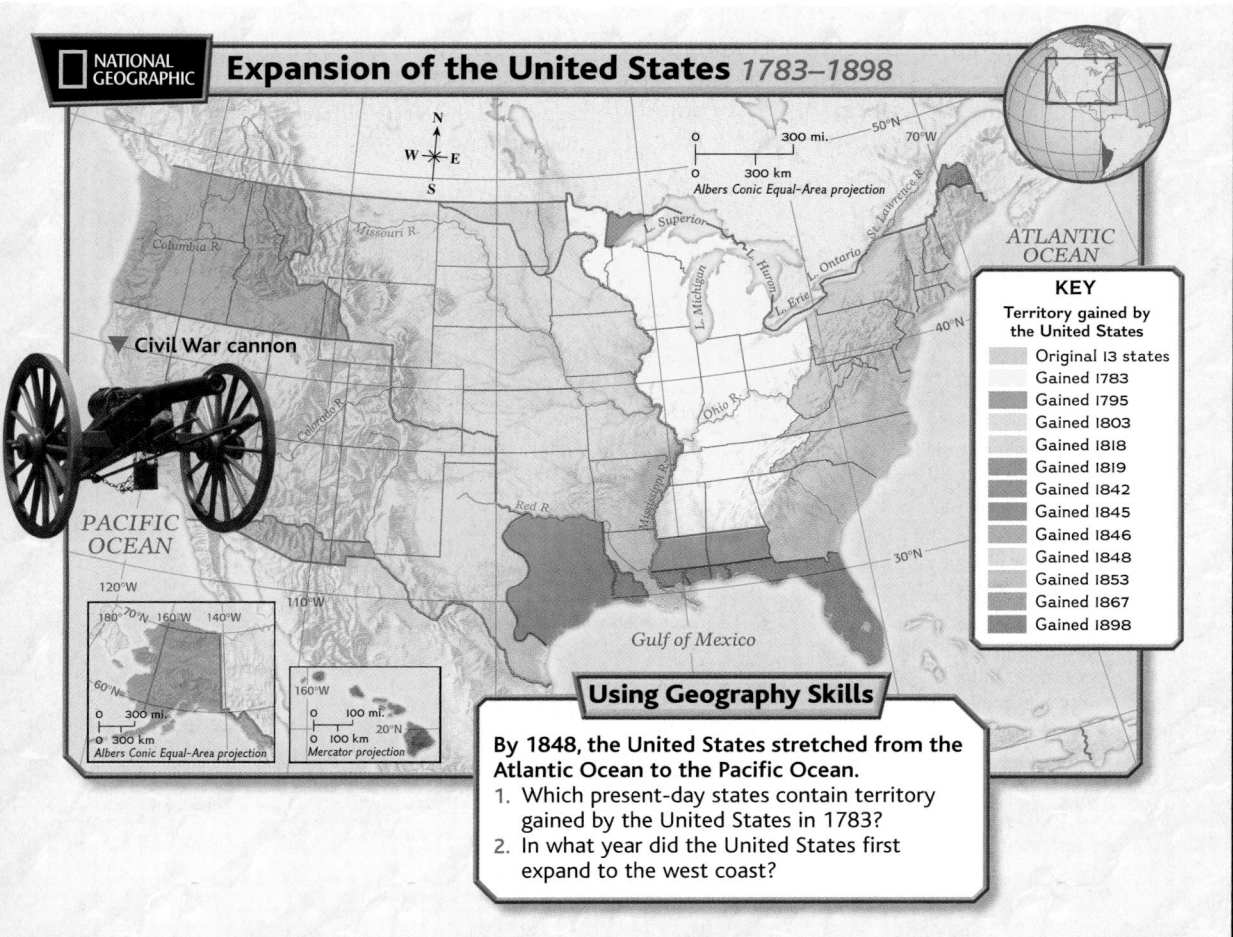

NATIONAL GEOGRAPHIC

Expansion of the United States *1783–1898*

Albers Conic Equal-Area projection

Columbia R.
Missouri R.
ATLANTIC OCEAN

Civil War cannon

KEY
Territory gained by the United States
- Original 13 states
- Gained 1783
- Gained 1795
- Gained 1803
- Gained 1818
- Gained 1819
- Gained 1842
- Gained 1845
- Gained 1846
- Gained 1848
- Gained 1853
- Gained 1867
- Gained 1898

Ohio R.
PACIFIC OCEAN
120°W
Red R.
Gulf of Mexico

Albers Conic Equal-Area projection
Mercator projection

Using Geography Skills

By 1848, the United States stretched from the Atlantic Ocean to the Pacific Ocean.
1. Which present-day states contain territory gained by the United States in 1783?
2. In what year did the United States first expand to the west coast?

Using Geography Skills

Answers:
1. Ohio, Michigan, Indiana, Illinois, Minnesota, Kentucky, Tennessee, Mississippi, Alabama, Georgia
2. 1846

EXTENDING THE CONTENT

Remember the Alamo The most famous battle preceding the war with Mexico took place at the Alamo, a Spanish mission in San Antonio. Its name means "cottonwood" in Spanish. In February 1836, Mexican troops laid siege to the band of fewer than 190 Texans, who had occupied the old mission in December. Their numbers include Davy Crockett, Jim Bowie, and William Travis. For 13 days, the Mexicans, commanded by Antonio López de Santa Anna, attacked the stronghold. Finally, the vastly larger Mexican force stormed the Alamo. All the defenders were killed, with only women and children spared. The defense and fall of the fort became an inspiration to Texans. Their battle cry "Remember the Alamo!" helped carry Texans to victory and independence.

ENRICH

Ask students to make up a list of five questions for one of the important figures discussed in the section. Then have them exchange lists with a partner and provide characteristic answers. **L3**

Reading Check

Answer: The South was rural and used enslaved labor. The North was more industrialized, and many there wanted to end slavery.

To help students understand section material, have them visit **Study Central**™ at jat.glencoe.com

RETEACH

Ask students to write four new Reading Checks and answers for this section. **L1**

4 CLOSE

Ask students to discuss this question: Which country that you read about in this section best succeeded in dealing with the rise of nationalism? Why? **L2**

of African Americans were freed from slavery. The federal government was strengthened. Also, new factories, railroads, and cities were built at an ever-increasing speed.

A New Society As industry grew, so did the United States's population. Between 1870 and 1900, the number of Americans doubled.

Immigrants contributed greatly to this growth. Before the Civil War, most immigrants came from northern Europe, mainly the British Isles, Germany, and Scandinavia. Then, during the late 1800s, immigration from southern and eastern Europe increased. After landing at Ellis Island in New York, most of these immigrants headed to the cities to find work.

Communities of Asian immigrants thrived along the west coast by the late 1800s as well. Chinese immigrants first came to California in the late 1840s to find gold and stayed to work in the mines and build railroads. By 1900, immigrants from Japan also arrived in the country.

Political Rights During the 1800s, the United States, like countries in Europe, became more democratic. The election of Andrew Jackson as U.S. president in 1828 was seen as a victory for the "common people." Jackson's election was made possible by the spread of voting rights to almost all adult white males.

As the 1800s moved forward, women also began to demand political equality. Women suffragists fought hard for women's right to vote. Finally, in 1920, the Nineteenth Amendment to the Constitution was ratified, or approved. This guaranteed women in all states the right to vote.

Reading Check **Contrast** How were the South and the North different during the period leading up to the American Civil War?

Study Central™ Need help with the material in this section? Visit jat.glencoe.com

Section 4 Review

Review the Main Ideas

- The idea of nationalism and the need for reform led to uprisings, wars, and political changes in Europe in the mid-1800s.
- Leaders like Garibaldi in Italy and Bismarck in Germany helped unite their respective countries.
- Colonies in Central and South America became independent countries following revolts against Spanish rule.
- The United States expanded to the Pacific coast, and then fought a terrible civil war over the issue of slavery.

What Did You Learn?

1. How did Bismarck unite the German states?

2. What were caudillos and how did they affect society in Latin America?

Critical Thinking

3. **Summarize** Draw a diagram like the one below. Fill in the outer ovals with territories gained by the United States during the 1800s.

United States Expansion

4. **Describe** Describe the reform attempted in Russia in the 1800s, why it occurred, and whether it was a success.

5. **Citizenship** Which of the countries discussed in the chapter became more democratic in the 1800s?

6. **Compare and Contrast** Compare the Northern and Southern states before the Civil War.

7. **Expository Writing** In a short essay, define *nationalism* and tell whether you think it is still a powerful idea in the world today.

SECTION 4 REVIEW ANSWERS

1. He defeated Denmark, Austria, and France, and convinced the states to join Germany.
2. Caudillos were leaders of Latin American countries. Most did nothing to fix the economic inequality that existed in Latin America.

3. Louisiana Purchase, Florida, Maine, Minnesota, North Dakota, Oregon, Texas, California
4. In 1861 Czar Alexander freed the serfs to catch up with Europe. It failed because serfs remained in poverty.
5. France and Great Britain

6. The Southern states were rural, and depended on growing cotton. The Northern states were industrial with many immigrants in large cities.
7. Students should correctly define *nationalism* and provide examples.

Section 1 The French Revolution and Napoleon

Vocabulary
estates
bourgeoisie
coup d'etat

Focusing on the Main Ideas
- The French Revolution began because the people were treated unfairly and because their country had serious economic problems. *(page 715)*
- French radicals used terror to enforce their reforms. *(page 717)*
- Napoleon Bonaparte used his military success to take control of the French government. *(page 719)*
- Through military conquests, Napoleon built a huge, but short-lived, empire in Europe. *(page 720)*

Section 2 The Industrial Revolution

Vocabulary
industrialism
textile
capital
partnership
corporation

Focusing on the Main Ideas
- The Industrial Revolution began in Great Britain because of the enclosure movement, Britain's natural resources, and new British inventions. *(page 725)*
- The Industrial Revolution spread beyond Great Britain's shores to Europe and the United States. *(page 729)*

Section 3 Society and Industry

Vocabulary
urbanization
liberalism
socialism
labor union

Focusing on the Main Ideas
- The Industrial Revolution caused cities to grow bigger and changed how people lived and worked. *(page 732)*
- The Industrial Revolution led to new ideas about politics, society, and the economy. *(page 734)*
- Artists, writers, and composers reflected the changes that industrialism brought to society. *(page 736)*
- Important scientific discoveries during the Industrial Revolution changed the way people lived and how they understood the world. *(page 738)*

Section 4 Nationalism and Nation-States

Vocabulary
kaiser
caudillo
abolitionism

Focusing on the Main Ideas
- Two powerful ideas, nationalism and reform, helped reshape Europe politically during the mid-1800s. *(page 745)*
- In the mid-1800s, two new countries, Italy and Germany, were created. *(page 747)*
- In the early 1800s, the people of Latin America rebelled and gained their independence. *(page 749)*
- Nationalism in the United States led the country to expand its borders, but differences between the North and South led to a bloody civil war. *(page 751)*

CHAPTER 19   Industry and Nationalism   755

PREVIEW/REVIEW

Vocabulary Activity Have students create a quiz using 10 of the terms and then exchange quizzes with a partner. Have them review their quizzes together.

◉ **Vocabulary PuzzleMaker CD-ROM**

◉ **Interactive Tutor Self-Assessment CD-ROM**

CONDENSE

📁 Chapter 19 **Guided Reading Activities**

◉ StudentWorks Plus™ **CD-ROM (with Audio Program)**

RETEACH

📁 **Differentiated Instruction Activity 19**

📁 Chapter 19 *Reading Essentials and Study Guide*

CHAPTER CULMINATING ACTIVITY

Have students finish the Chapter Culminating Activity from page 710D.

📁 Suggestions for rubrics may be found in the *Quizzes, Tests, and Authentic Assessments (with Rubrics)* booklet.

Reading Strategy   READ TO WRITE

Taking a Position Ask students to take a position on this statement and support it with reasoning and details from the chapter: Force sometimes is necessary to bring about greater freedom and democracy. Use the following rubric to assess students' work:

- **L1** students should include one or two reasons in their position statement.
- **L2** students should include several appropriate details and reasons in their position statement and attempt grammar mastery.
- **L3** students should write logical, detailed, well-considered position statements that provide strong support for their opinion.

Chapter 19 Assessment and Activities

GLENCOE TECHNOLOGY

MindJogger Videoquiz

Use the **MindJogger Videoquiz** to review Chapter 19 content.

Available in DVD and VHS

Review Vocabulary

1. b   5. d
2. c   6. g
3. e   7. a
4. f

Review Main Ideas

8. worsening economic and social conditions

9. He took control of the French government and built a huge but short-lived empire.

10. Great Britain

11. Europe and the United States

12. Some chose to escape from industrialism; some chose to depict it realistically.

13. The way people lived and understood the world changed.

14. nationalism and reform

15. In each country, the many small states united to form single nations.

Critical Thinking

16. Robespierre was largely responsible for the Reign of Terror, which he said was necessary because of the threat of foreign invasion. Once that threat lessened, the French were disgusted by the continued killings and believed the way to stop Robespierre was to execute him.

Review Vocabulary

Match the word in the first column with its definition in the second column.

____ 1. capital
____ 2. labor union
____ 3. coup d'etat
____ 4. bourgeoisie
____ 5. kaiser
____ 6. urbanization
____ 7. industrialism

a. way of life based on machinery and factories
b. money invested in businesses
c. association of united workers
d. German emperor
e. sudden government takeover
f. French middle class
g. movement from rural areas to cities

Review Main Ideas

Section 1 • The French Revolution and Napoleon

8. What caused the unrest among the French people that led to revolution?

9. What was the result of Napoleon Bonaparte's military successes?

Section 2 • The Industrial Revolution

10. In which country did the Industrial Revolution begin?

11. Which other areas were affected by the Industrial Revolution?

Section 3 • Society and Industry

12. How was industrialism reflected by artists, writers, and composers?

13. What was the result of important scientific discoveries during this time period?

Section 4 • Nationalism and Nation-States

14. Identify two ideas that reshaped Europe during the mid-1800s.

15. How did nationalism affect Italy and Germany?

Critical Thinking

16. **Explain** Why did French leaders decide to execute Robespierre?

17. **Cause and Effect** What new ideas resulted from the factory system?

18. **Contrast** How were the ideas of romanticism different from those of the Enlightenment?

Review Reading Skill Understanding Concepts

Reading for Meaning

19. Read the following sentences from pages 718–719. Based on the information, write a paragraph defining what Robespierre might have meant when he called for a "Republic of Virtue."

> During this time, Robespierre tried to create a "Republic of Virtue." He thought the revolution should inspire people to be good citizens. Under Robespierre's lead, the Committee opened new schools, had new farming skills taught to the peasants, and worked to keep prices under control.

To review this skill, see pages 712–713.

---

17. the financial organization of businesses into partnerships and corporations; the rise of railroads

18. Romanticism emphasized feelings, emotions, and the imagination, while the Enlightenment emphasized reason and order.

Reading Skill

19. Robespierre encouraged activities he thought would make good citizens. He wanted a society that was well educated and that advanced in new techniques of farming.

Geography Skills

Study the map below and answer the following questions.

20. **Region** What resources gave England an advantage in developing industries?
21. **Location** Which two industrial centers are located near both coal and iron ore fields?
22. **Analyze** Why do you think there were no railroads in northern Scotland and Ireland?

NATIONAL GEOGRAPHIC

Industrialization in Britain

15°W 10°W 5°W

KEY
- Iron ore fields
- Coal fields
- Railways, 1850
- Industrial centers

SCOTLAND

55°N

Glasgow

North Sea

0°

Belfast

IRELAND

Dublin

Liverpool   Leeds
Manchester

WALES

Birmingham

0   100 mi.
0   100 km
Chamberlain Trimetric projection

50°N

ENGLAND   London

ATLANTIC OCEAN

Read to Write

23. **Expository Writing** Write an essay comparing the events and results of the rules of Bismarck and Napoleon III (Louis Napoleon). What personal characteristics did each man have that contributed to his accomplishments?

History Online
Self-Check Quiz To help you prepare for the Chapter Test, visit jat.glencoe.com

24. **Using Your FOLDABLES** Work in a small group to create a poster or other visual aid using the information written on one of your foldable tabs. For example, your group may choose to reflect Society and Industry by showing pieces of art and literature that resulted from each social movement.

Using Technology

25. **Research** Unity is still a goal of many Europeans. Use the Internet and your local library to research efforts to unify Europe. Share your findings with the class.

Linking Past and Present

26. **Compare** How are the Declaration of the Rights of Man and the Citizen and the U.S. Constitution similar?

Primary Source Analyze

Captain Kincaid was a member of the Duke of Wellington's Rifle Brigade. He described this moment near the end of the battle at Waterloo.

"Presently a cheer which we knew to be British commenced far to the right, and made everyone prick up his ears; it was Lord Wellington's long-wished-for orders to advance.... Lord Wellington galloped up to us at the instant, and our men began to cheer him; but he called out, 'No cheering, my lads, but forward, and complete our victory!'"

—Captain J. Kincaid, "Waterloo, 18 June 1815: The Finale"

DBQ Document-Based Questions

27. Why did Wellington tell the soldiers not to cheer for him?
28. Why do you think the soldiers were eagerly waiting for the orders to advance?

Geography Skills

20. iron ore and coal
21. Glasgow and Birmingham
22. Those areas do not have iron ore or coal fields.

Read to Write

23. Essays will vary but should reflect information in the chapter.
24. **FOLDABLES** Posters will vary but should reflect information in the chapter.

History Online

Have students visit the Web site at jat.glencoe.com to review Chapter 19 and take the **Self-Check Quiz**.

Using Technology

25. Answers will vary. Students may mention the European Union, the unification of East and West Germany, and so on.

Linking Past and Present

26. Both are governing documents that endorse equal rights, freedom of speech and the press, and democratic government.

Primary Source

27. He wanted them to complete the task first—to win the battle before celebrating it.
28. Answers will vary, but most students will say that the soldiers were eager to advance in order to win the battle.

Bonus Question

Ask students to write a paragraph contrasting the positive and negative aspects of nationalism. *(Positive aspects may include building of national pride and strengthening of national culture, while negative aspects might include racism, war, and exploitation of other groups.)*

Chapter 20 Resources

Note: The following materials may be used when teaching Chapter 20.
Section level support materials are shown at point of use in the margins of the Teacher Wraparound Edition.

TEACHING TRANSPARENCIES

- Graphic Organizer Transparencies with Teaching Strategy and Student Activity **L2**
- Cause-and-Effect Transparencies with Teaching Strategy and Student Activity **L2**
- Then and Now Transparencies with Teaching Strategy and Student Activity **L2**
- Chapter 20 In-text Map Transparencies with Teaching Strategy and Student Activity **L1**
- Map Transparencies with Overlay, Teaching Strategy, and Student Activity **L2**

DIFFERENTIATED INSTRUCTION

- Differentiated Instruction Activity 20
- Time Line Activity 20
- Primary Source Reading 20 (with Document-Based Questions)
- Inclusion Strategies for the Middle School Social Studies Classroom
- StudentWorks Plus™ CD-ROM (with Audio Program)

READING SUPPORT

- Take-Home Review Activity 20 **L2**
- World Literature Reading 20 **L2**
- Workbook Activity 20 **L1**
- Reading Strategies for the Social Studies Classroom **L1/ EL**

ASSESSMENT

- Authentic Assessment Activity 20 **L1/ EL**
- Chapter 20 Test Form A **L2**
- Chapter 20 Test Form B **L2**
- ExamView® Pro Testmaker CD-ROM

INTERDISCIPLINARY CONNECTIONS

- Geography and History Activity 20 **L2**
- People to Meet Activity 20 **L2**
- Economics Activity 20 **L2**
- Citizenship and Service Learning Activity 20 **L2**

SPANISH RESOURCES

- Spanish Reading Essentials and Study Guide
- Spanish Guided Reading Activities
- Spanish Quizzes, Tests, and Authentic Assessment (with Rubrics)
- Spanish Take-Home Review Activities

MULTIMEDIA

- ExamView® Pro Testmaker CD-ROM
- Glencoe Skillbuilder Interactive Workbook CD-ROM, Level 1
- Interactive Tutor Self-Assessment CD-ROM
- MindJogger Videoquiz
- Presentation Plus! CD-ROM
- StudentWorks Plus™ CD-ROM (with Audio Program)
- TeacherWorks CD-ROM
- Vocabulary PuzzleMaker CD-ROM
- *World History: Journey Across Time* Video Program
- World History Primary Source Document Library CD-ROM

STANDARDIZED ASSESSMENT SKILLS

- Standardized Test Skills Practice Workbook Activity 20 **L2**
- Critical Thinking Skills Activity 20 **L2**

Teaching strategies have been coded with suggested ability levels. However, most are suitable for all levels.

L1 BASIC activities for all students

L2 AVERAGE activities for average to above-average students

L3 CHALLENGING activities for above-average students

EL ENGLISH LANGUAGE activities

758A

TIME MANAGEMENT

Chapter Introduction	Section 1	Section 2	Section 3	Section 4	Chapter Wrap-Up
1 Day	2 Days	2 Days	2 Days	1 Day	1 Day

Block Scheduling Activities that are suited to use within the block scheduling framework are identified by: 📦

0:00 OUT OF TIME? Assign the Chapter 20 *Reading Essentials and Study Guide.** 📁

SECTION RESOURCES

DAILY OBJECTIVES	REPRODUCIBLE LESSON PLANS	MULTIMEDIA RESOURCES
Section 1 **The New Imperialism** 1. Western European nations established empires in Southeast Asia and India. 2. European nations ruled almost all of Africa by the time the United States entered the race to build an empire.	📁 Reproducible Lesson Plan 20–1 📁 Vocabulary Activity 20–1 📁 Guided Reading Activity 20–1* 📁 Section Quiz 20–1* 📁 Reading Essentials and Study Guide 20–1*	📖 Daily Focus Skills Transparency 20–1 💿 Interactive Tutor Self-Assessment CD-ROM 💿 ExamView® Pro Testmaker CD-ROM 💿 Presentation Plus! CD-ROM
Section 2 **Nationalism in China and Japan** 1. Europeans undermined the Manchu government and society of China. 2. The Qing dynasty in China collapsed, and the nation of Japan created a vast empire.	📁 Reproducible Lesson Plan 20–2 📁 Vocabulary Activity 20–2 📁 Guided Reading Activity 20–2* 📁 Section Quiz 20–2* 📁 Reading Essentials and Study Guide 20–2*	📖 Daily Focus Skills Transparency 20–2 💿 Interactive Tutor Self-Assessment CD-ROM 💿 ExamView® Pro Testmaker CD-ROM 💿 Presentation Plus! CD-ROM 💿 Glencoe BookLink CD-ROM
Section 3 **World War I Begins** 1. Alliances, militarism, and trouble in the Balkans led to World War I. 2. After World War I began, most Americans supported the Allies.	📁 Reproducible Lesson Plan 20–3 📁 Vocabulary Activity 20–3 📁 Section Quiz 20–3* 📁 Guided Reading Activity 20–3* 📁 Reading Essentials and Study Guide 20–3*	📖 Daily Focus Skills Transparency 20–3 💿 Interactive Tutor Self-Assessment CD-ROM 💿 ExamView® Pro Testmaker CD-ROM 💿 Presentation Plus! CD-ROM
Section 4 **World War I Changes the World** 1. With American help, the Allies stopped the German advance. 2. The Bolsheviks rose to power in Russia.	📁 Reproducible Lesson Plan 20–4 📁 Vocabulary Activity 20–4 📁 Section Quiz 20–4* 📁 Guided Reading Activity 20–4* 📁 Reading Essentials and Study Guide 20–4*	📖 Daily Focus Skills Transparency 20–4 💿 Interactive Tutor Self-Assessment CD-ROM 💿 ExamView® Pro Testmaker CD-ROM 💿 Presentation Plus! CD-ROM 💿 Vocabulary PuzzleMaker CD-ROM 💿 Glencoe BookLink CD-ROM

*Also available in Spanish

Chapter 20 Resources

Use our Web site for additional resources. All essential content is covered in the Student Edition.

You and your students can visit jat.glencoe.com, the Web site companion to *World History: Journey Across Time*. This innovative integration of electronic and print media offers your students a wealth of opportunities. The student text directs students to the Web site for the following options:

- Chapter Overviews
- Self-Check Quizzes
- Study Central™
- Student Web Activities
- Multi-Language Glossaries

Answers to the student Web activities are provided for you in the **Web Activity Lesson Plans.** Additional Web resources and ePuzzles and games are also available.

The following videotape programs are available from Glencoe as supplements to Chapter 20:

China's Boxer Rebellion
(ISBN 0-7670-0617-8)

Woodrow Wilson: Reluctant Warrior
(ISBN 1-7670-0101-X)

Nicholas and Alexandra
(ISBN 0-56501-514-2)

To order, call Glencoe at 1-800-334-7344. To find classroom resources to accompany many of these videos, check the following home pages:

A&E Television: www.aande.com
The History Channel: www.historychannel.com

MEETING SPECIAL NEEDS

In addition to the Differentiated Instruction strategies, the following resources are suitable for students with special needs:

- *ExamView® Pro Testmaker CD-ROM* allows teachers to tailor tests by reducing answer choices.
- *StudentWorks Plus™ CD-ROM (with Audio Program)* includes the entire narrative of the student edition so that less-proficient readers can listen to the words as they read them.
- The *Reading Essentials and Study Guide* provides the same content as the student edition but is written two grade levels below the textbook.

Index to National Geographic Magazine:
The following articles relate to this chapter:

- "The Philippines," by Priit J. Vesiland, July 2002
- "Hawaii: Preserving the Breath," by Paul Theroux, December 2002.
- "Cuba's Golden Past," by Thomas B. Allen, July 2001

Additional National Geographic Society Products:
To order the following, call National Geographic at 1–800–368–2728

- *NGS PictureShow: World War I Era* (CD-ROM)
- *National Geographic Atlas of the World* (Book)

NGS ONLINE

Access National Geographic's new dynamic MapMachine Web site and other geography resources at:

www.nationalgeographic.com
www.nationalgeographic.com/maps

 ## Meeting NCSS Standards

World History: Journey Across Time
The following standards are highlighted in Chapter 20:

Section 1 — V Individuals, Groups, and Institutions: B, E
VII Production, Distribution, and Consumption: A, C, F, I
IX Global Connections: B, E, H

Section 2 — II Time, Continuity, and Change: B, C
IV Individual Development and Identity: E
VI Power, Authority, and Governance: C, D, F

Section 3 — I Culture: E, G
VIII Science, Technology, and Society: A

Section 4 — III People, Places, and Environments: B
X Civic Ideals and Practices: A

State and Local Objectives

_____

_____

Chapter 20 Resources

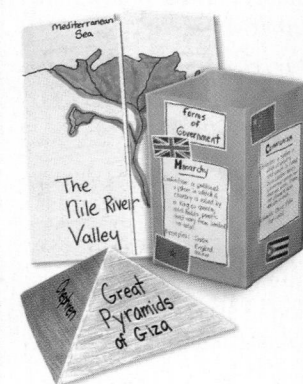
Planning Ahead

CHAPTER CULMINATING ACTIVITY

The Chapter Culminating Activity will help students organize and learn the important information from the chapter. Begin the chapter with this activity and have students complete it as a culminating activity.

CREATING VERTICAL TIME LINES

Purpose Identifying events happening in different places at the same time can help students analyze worldwide relationships. Vertical time lines can be especially helpful when studying a chapter that covers a concept such as imperialism, which takes the reader from one part of the globe to another.

Introduction to Modeling

1. Begin by determining student knowledge of events between 1800 and 1920. **Ask: What do you consider the most important event that happened in North America between 1800 and 1920? What was happening in the rest of the world at the same time?** Have students write down their responses.

2. Explain to students that they are going to create vertical time lines to organize events that happened in North

America, South America, Europe, Africa, and Asia. Tell them that each vertical time line will show events that happened around the world during a specific period of time. Students can also see a sequence of events on one continent by reading across the time lines.

3. Have students copy this time line graphic organizer:

	1800–1840	1841–1880	1881–1920
North America			
South America			
Europe			
Africa			
Asia			

As students read each section, ask them to find events that happened on each continent for as many time periods as possible. Have them fill in the chart as they complete the chapter.

4. As part of your chapter review, have students share their time lines. Consider asking them to combine their time lines into one large organizer. Encourage them to use their time lines as study aids.

Chapter 20

Imperialism and World War I

The Palace of Westminster in London, England, home to Big Ben and the Houses of Parliament ▼

 NATIONAL GEOGRAPHIC When & Where?

1860	1880	1900		1920
1869 Suez Canal opens	1884 France sets up protectorate in Vietnam	1900 Boxer Rebellion sweeps China	1914 World War I begins	1917 Lenin seizes power in Russia

Reading Strategy — PURPOSE FOR READING

Questioning Explain that the imperialism of the 1800s and 1900s had lasting consequences that are evident today. **Ask:** What are the official languages in Cuba, India, and South Africa? If students do not know the answers, have them refer to an encyclopedia. Point out that people in these countries still speak the language of their one-time colonial rulers. As they read, have students ask themselves which colonial policies probably had lasting effects on Asian, African, and Latin American nations. Instruct them to write their answers in their notebook and to check them by reading about the former colonies today. **L1**

Chapter Preview

The early 1900s was a period of conflict in much of the world. Read this chapter to find out how a war in Europe became a world war that affected millions of people.

 View the Chapter 20 video in the *World History: Journey Across Time* Video Program.

Chapter Overview Visit jat.glencoe.com for a preview of Chapter 20.

 ## The New Imperialism

By 1900, many industrial nations, including Britain, France, Germany, Spain, and the United States, had expanded their trade and built empires in different parts of the world.

 ## Nationalism in China and Japan

During the 1800s, Chinese and Japanese societies were influenced by Europeans and Americans.

 ## World War I Begins

Growing tension between European powers eventually led to World War I.

 ## World War I Changes the World

World War I led to the fall of empires, a revolution in Russia, and the creation of new nations and governments.

Identifying *Make this foldable to help you identify and learn key terms.*

Step 1 *Stack four sheets of paper, one on top of the other. On the top sheet of paper, draw a large circle.*

Step 2 *With the papers still stacked, cut out all four circles at the same time.*

Step 3 *Staple the paper circles together at one point around the edge.*

Staple here. → This makes a circular booklet.

Step 4 *Label the front circle as shown and take notes on the pages that open to the right.*

Chapter 20 Key Terms

Reading and Writing *As you read the chapter, write the terms from Locating Places, Meeting People, and Building Your Vocabulary in your foldable. Write a definition for each term. Then turn your foldable over (upside down) to write a short sentence using each term.*

759

INTRODUCING CHAPTER 20

History Online

Introduce students to chapter content and key terms by having them access **Chapter Overview 20** at jat.glencoe.com

CHAPTER PREVIEW

After reading Chapter 20, students will be able to

1. describe how Western powers built worldwide empires;
2. analyze the effects of nationalism on China and Japan;
3. summarize the events that led to World War I;
4. explain how World War I changed the world.

FOLDABLES Study Organizer — Dinah Zike's Foldables

Purpose Students use this foldable to identify important terms and people relating to the age of imperialism and World War I. Completed foldables will help students learn these terms.

☞ Have students complete *Reading and Study Skills Foldables* Activity 20.

MORE ABOUT THE PHOTO

Houses of Parliament and Big Ben The Houses of Parliament, also known as the Palace of Westminster, located in Westminster, London, was built between 1840 and 1860 by Sir Charles Barry, an English architect. It replaced several buildings that were destroyed by fire in 1834. The old palace served as the residence to British royalty until 1512. After Edward VI turned the palace over to the House of Commons and House of Lords in 1547, it became the main assembly for the British Parliament. The new palace is a massive complex based on neo-Gothic design and spans about eight acres of land along the Thames River. It has approximately 1,000 rooms, 100 staircases, and two miles of passageways. However, the most famous element of the new palace is the clock tower, affectionately known as Big Ben.

1 Learn It!

Have students read the following paragraph silently from Section 3 under the subhead "United States Declares War," and ask them to write any word or fact that they think is important.

> In January 1917, a German official named Arthur Zimmermann cabled the German ambassador in Mexico. In the cable, Zimmermann proposed that Mexico ally itself with Germany if war broke out between Germany and the United States. In return, Mexico would regain "lost territory in Texas, New Mexico, and Arizona" after the war. The British intercepted the Zimmermann telegram and gave it to American newspapers. Outraged Americans began demanding war with Germany.

Put students in small groups and ask them to complete a four-column chart using the words or facts they noted during their silent reading. Have them use the following heads: Very Important, Important, Somewhat Important, Not Very Important. Encourage them to discuss why they place the words in the categories. **L1**

Reading Skill
Prioritizing

1 Learn It!
What's Important?

As you study history, it may seem impossible to keep all the facts in your head. Once you understand that the author does not expect you to remember every word of the text, you can begin to focus on what is truly important or prioritize. Prioritize means "to list in order of importance." Prioritizing will help you read more critically and do better on tests.

Read the sentences below.

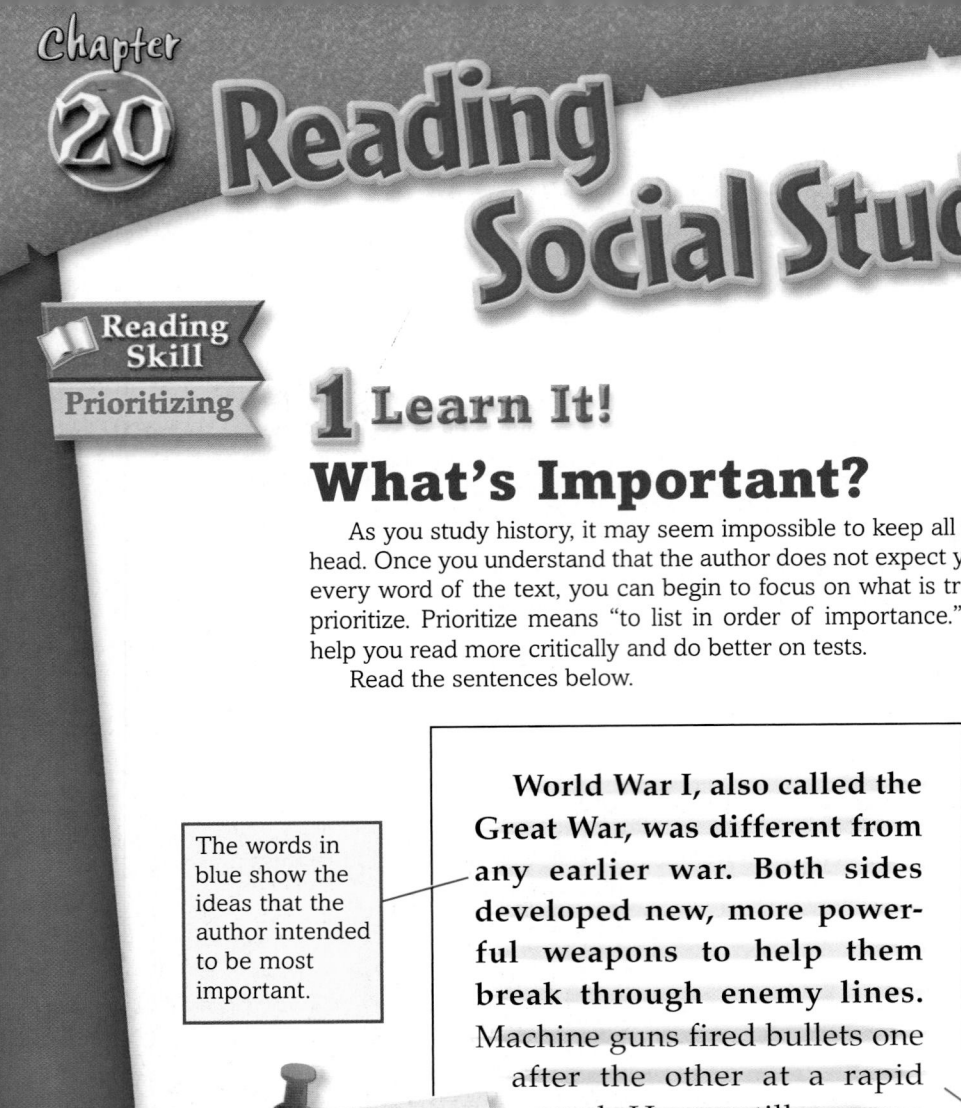

The words in blue show the ideas that the author intended to be most important.

> **World War I, also called the Great War, was different from any earlier war. Both sides developed new, more powerful weapons to help them break through enemy lines.** Machine guns fired bullets one after the other at a rapid speed. Huge artillery guns fired shells more than 75 miles (120 km). Poison gases were used for the first time, and tanks and flamethrowers were introduced.

The other sentences act as supporting details.

Reading Tip

Use the two-column note-taking method when you read. Record the most important points in one column and the supporting ideas in the other column.

Reading Strategy — **IDENTIFYING IMPORTANT IDEAS**

Learning to identify an important idea is the foundation for higher-level thinking skills such as analyzing, defending, or evaluating. Once students identify the most important ideas in a section of text, ask them to assume the role of author and defend to a partner why they, as the author, feel those are important ideas. The role playing could include questions such as "How did you show the reader that this part was most important?" or "Why did you choose these particular words?" **L1**

2 Practice It!

Read this paragraph from Section 4, page 791. Discuss the questions that follow with a learning partner to practice prioritizing.

> In January 1919, peace talks began at Versailles (vuhr•SY) outside Paris. The principal figures at the talks were U.S. president Woodrow Wilson, British prime minister David Lloyd George, French premier Georges Clemenceau, and Italian prime minister Vittorio Orlando.

Read to Write ⋯⋯⋯
Choose any three topics from Chapter 20 with interesting headings. Write a "study sheet" for each topic, noting the most important fact, sentence, or concept. Then explain why your statement reflects the most important part of the topic.

1. Is it important to remember the date of the peace talks?
2. Is it important to remember where the peace talks occurred?
3. Is it important to remember the principal figures at the talks?
4. If you had to remember only one of the principal figures, who would it be?
5. Is it important to read further to find out more about the peace talks?

3 Apply It!

Read the first page of Section 2 on page 772. What do you think is the most important idea on that page? Support your answer.

2 Practice It!

Summarizing Working in pairs, have students read silently or orally "The Causes of World War I" from Section 3. Each student should write the major headings, such as "Nationalism," on his or her paper. When students finish each section, have them write the most important idea from that section in their own words. Then have students compare what they wrote. Encourage them to defend their choices. Facilitate a whole-class discussion of important ideas in each section.

3 Apply It!

Students should be able to support their ideas with details from their reading. If they have trouble, ask them to consider why they think the author included this information. **Ask:** What purpose does this information serve? How can this information help you better understand interactions between China and the West?

761

Reading Strategy ⟩ READ TO WRITE

As students complete this assignment, they will have distilled the most important information from the section. However, this can still be a daunting challenge for some. One method that can help students see the relative importance of information they have gathered is to explain why they have chosen it. Writing a short paragraph can sometimes help them more effectively make such an argument better than simply discussing it. After students have finished their study sheets, have them write a short paragraph for each of the concepts they have chosen as the most important. Then have them compare their ideas with those of other students so that they can compare how others arrived at their conclusions.

SECTION OVERVIEW

This section explains why Western powers established empires in the 1800s and 1900s.

BELLRINGER
SKILLBUILDER ACTIVITY

✎ Project **Daily Focus Skills Transparency 20–1** and have students answer questions. Discuss their responses.

Get Ready to Read!

Preteaching Vocabulary: Explain that *imperialism* is a policy of one nation directly or indirectly controlling the political or economic life of other areas or nations. It can occur in different forms.

Answers to Graphic: Great Britain: Singapore, India, Egypt, Nigeria; France: Vietnam, Algeria, Tunisia, Morocco; Italy: Libya; Germany: Togo and Cameroon; Belgium: Congo; Portugal: Mozambique; United States: Puerto Rico and Guam

Section ①

The New Imperialism

Get Ready to Read!

What's the Connection?
In past chapters, you learned how the Industrial Revolution changed the lives of Europeans. By the 1800s, industry had also changed Europe's relationship with the world.

Focusing on the Main Ideas
- European nations built empires to help their economy and to spread their ideas. *(page 763)*
- Control of India passed from the East India Company to the British. *(page 764)*
- European nations ruled almost all of Africa by 1914. *(page 766)*
- The United States became an imperial nation after defeating Spain and taking control of the Philippines and Puerto Rico. *(page 769)*

Locating Places
Singapore (SIHNG•uh•POHR)
Cuba (KYOO•buh)
Philippines (FIH•luh•PEENZ)
Panama (PA•nuh•MAH)

Meeting People
Robert Clive
Leopold II
William McKinley

Building Your Vocabulary
imperialism (ihm•PIHR•ee•uh•LIH•zuhm)
colony
protectorate (pruh•TEHK•tuh•ruht)
sphere of influence
sepoy (SEE•POY)

Reading Strategy
Organizing Information Use a chart like the one below to show the colonies that each imperialist nation controlled.

Imperialist Nation	Colonies

NATIONAL GEOGRAPHIC When & Where?

NORTH AMERICA · EUROPE · SOUTH AMERICA · AFRICA · CHINA · INDIA · AUSTRALIA

1850 — **1875** — **1900**

- **1857** Revolt against British in India
- **1869** Suez Canal opens
- **1884** France sets up protectorate in Vietnam
- **1914** Panama Canal opens

SECTION RESOURCES

📁 **Reproducible Masters**
- Reproducible Lesson Plan 20–1
- Daily Lecture and Discussion Notes 20–1
- Vocabulary Activity 20–1
- Active Reading Note-Taking Guide 20–1
- Guided Reading Activity 20–1
- Section Quiz 20–1
- Reading Essentials and Study Guide 20–1

✎ **Transparencies**
- Daily Focus Skills Transparency 20–1

Multimedia
- Interactive Tutor Self-Assessment CD-ROM
- Exam*View*® Pro Testmaker CD-ROM
- Presentation Plus! CD-ROM

The Rise of Imperialism

Main Idea European nations built empires to help their economy and to spread their ideas.

Reading Focus A store owner with too many goods on the shelves must find new customers or he or she will lose money. Read on to find out how Europeans solved a similar problem on a grander scale.

As nationalism spread, the industrial countries of Europe looked abroad for raw materials and new markets. In the 1800s, they rushed to take over lands in Asia and Africa where these markets and goods were found. As a result, the world entered the Age of Imperialism. **Imperialism** (ihm•PIHR•ee•uh•LIH•zuhm) is a type of relationship between countries in which one nation directly or indirectly controls the government or the economy of another nation.

Building Empires
Europeans wanted new lands for more than just trade and profit. They believed that ruling foreign peoples would add to a country's power. They also believed that imposing their ideas and practices on others would improve the lives of foreign peoples.

Imperial nations ruled other people in many different ways. Sometimes they created a **colony,** which they ruled directly. Sometimes they set up a **protectorate** (pruh•TEHK•tuh•ruht). There the local people had their own government, but the imperial government controlled the military and could tell the local rulers what to do. In other cases they set up a **sphere of influence,** a region where only one imperial power had the right to invest or to trade.

The First Empires: Southeast Asia
As early as the 1500s, Europeans were drawn to Southeast Asia for its spices. They took control of many island groups, including the

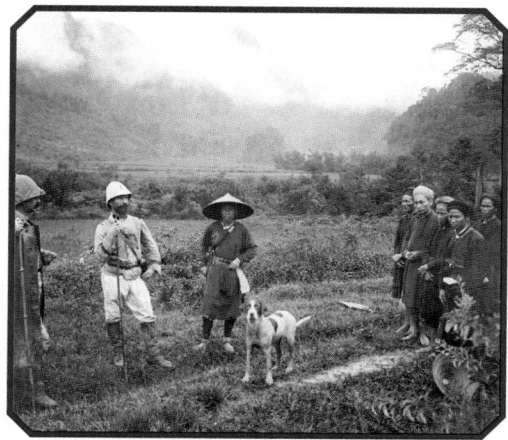

▲ French military officers with peasants in the Tonkin region of Vietnam

Philippines and the East Indies. During the 1800s, Europeans began taking over Southeast Asia's mainland. There they grew crops, such as coffee and tea. They also began to use the area's raw materials, such as petroleum, rubber, and tin.

In 1819 a British official named Thomas Stamford Raffles founded a colony on a small island at the tip of the Malay Peninsula. Known as **Singapore** (SIHNG•uh•POHR), or "the city of the lion," it became an important port for ships going to and from China.

The French followed the British to mainland Southeast Asia. Both countries soon competed for territory. The British took control of the rest of the Malay Peninsula and Burma to the north. Meanwhile, French Catholic missionaries entered nearby Vietnam. Fearing the British would move into Vietnam, the French sent in troops, and in 1884 Vietnam became a French protectorate. In all of Southeast Asia, only Siam—today known as Thailand—kept its freedom.

Reading Check **Contrast** What is the difference between a colony and a protectorate?

---

② TEACH

Reading Strategy

Interpreting Events As they read, have students create a list of the reasons for building empires. Then ask them what names they would use to describe individuals who take people's possessions. Discuss whether students would use the same names to describe imperialistic nations. **L1**

Daily Lecture and Discussion Notes 20–1

Use **Daily Lecture and Discussion Notes 20–1** for an outline of key concepts found in the section.

Reading Support L1/ EL

Use **Vocabulary Activity 20–1** to review important terms in the section.

Reading Check

Answer: A colony is ruled directly by an imperial power, whereas a protectorate has its own government, but the imperial government controls the military and can tell the protectorate what to do.

Reading Strategy   READING THE TEXT

Predicting Have students read the "Rise of Imperialism." Explain that predictions are educated guesses about what will happen. Tell them to use what they already know about occupied countries in today's news to predict what took place when Europeans took over Asian and African countries. **Ask:** How do you think Europeans gained control of a country? Do you think Africans and Asians welcomed or resisted their new rulers? Allow students to brainstorm answers to these questions and to write the ones they consider most likely in their notebook. Instruct them to continue reading to find out what really happened. **L1**

Writing Activity 📝

Tell students that Myanmar, once called Burma, covers an area as large as Texas, produces four-fifths of the world's teak, and grows about 30,000 varieties of rice. Then have them write an ad designed to attract British investors and settlers to Burma during the 1800s. **L2**

GLENCOE
BOOKLINK

Use **Glencoe BookLink** to create customized reading lists for your students' reading levels, interests, and abilities.

More About the Art

The woman and older girl in the picture of the upper-class Indian family are dressed in saris. These garments include several yards of material that are draped so that one end serves as a skirt and the other end falls over the shoulder or head.

Caption Answer: 1600

Britain's Empire in India

Main Idea Control of India passed from the East India Company to the British.

Reading Focus Has a new business ever moved into your neighborhood? What things did it make better or worse? As you read, ask how Britain made things better and worse in India.

Earlier you learned that the Moguls ruled India in the early 1600s. As time went on, their power weakened. Rulers spent too much money on wars and palaces, and Indian people began to resent this waste. At the same time, Hindus did not like the Moguls trying to make them Muslims. Rising discontent made it easy for Europeans to take over India.

What Was the East India Company? In 1600 British traders from the East India Company arrived in India. Over the next 50 years, they built a string of trading forts along India's coasts. The East India Company set up an army and supported local Indian rulers who agreed to work with them. The company's army also fought the French, Britain's main rival in India.

One of the most energetic East India Company officials was **Robert Clive.** He led British and Indian soldiers against French forts. By 1757, Clive and his army had pushed the French out of most of India. The French were left with only one fort and a few coastal holdings.

During the next 100 years, Britain's East India Company took over much of India and

Imperialism in Asia

▲ Troops traveling through India

▲ This photo shows an upper-class Indian family during the time of British rule.

These native workers are shown on a plantation in Ceylon. ▶

What year did British traders arrive in India?

764   CHAPTER 20   Imperialism and World War I

DIFFERENTIATED INSTRUCTION

Visual/Spatial: Assign different Asian countries to students, and project a map of Asia from the 1800s on the classroom wall. Have students trace the boundaries of their assigned country, research the country's resources, and draw symbols to represent the resources on their map.

Gifted and Talented: Have students create rules for a game using the resource map of Asia as a playing board. Suggest that players represent European nations that try to occupy countries with the raw materials their industries need.

📁 Refer to *Inclusion Strategies for the Middle School Social Studies Classroom* in the TCR.

grew wealthy. It brought many European ideas and practices to the Indian people. Many Indians, however, felt that the British were trying to change their culture.

In 1857 **sepoys** (SEE•POYZ), or Indian soldiers in the company's army, rebelled against their British officers. The revolt then spread rapidly across northern India. Britain quickly sent more soldiers to India and put down the rebellion. Afterward, there were bitter feelings between the British and the Indians.

British Rule in India Soon after the uprising, Britain took direct control of India from the company. A viceroy, an official standing in for Britain's Queen Victoria, arrived to head the Raj (RAHJ), as British India's government was now called. The viceroy's government both helped and hurt the Indian people.

The British brought order to India. The government was run well, and schools were founded. In addition, the British introduced railroads, the telegraph, and a postal service throughout India.

British rule, however, brought great hardships as well. Cheap British textiles flooded India and destroyed the local textile industry. The British also forced many farmers to grow cotton instead of food. Soon India did not produce enough food to feed its people. In the 1800s, millions of Indians died from starvation.

✓ **Reading Check** **Cause and Effect** Why did the Indians rebel against the British?

CURRICULUM CONNECTION

Language Arts
Assign some of Rudyard Kipling's short stories that are set in India and Burma to different students. As they read, have the students list plants, animals, and customs described in the stories.

CONNECTING ACROSS TIME

Khaki means "dust-colored" in Hindi, but in 1845 British soldiers began referring to their uniforms as "khakis." Originally, the uniforms of British soldiers in India were white. They soaked them in mud, coffee, and curry powder so they would blend in with the Indian landscape. Have students research the color of the uniforms worn by British soldiers today. **L1/EL**

✓ **Reading Check**

Answer: Many Indians felt that the British were trying to take away their culture.

Using Geography Skills

Answers:
1. Britain and the Netherlands
2. Thailand

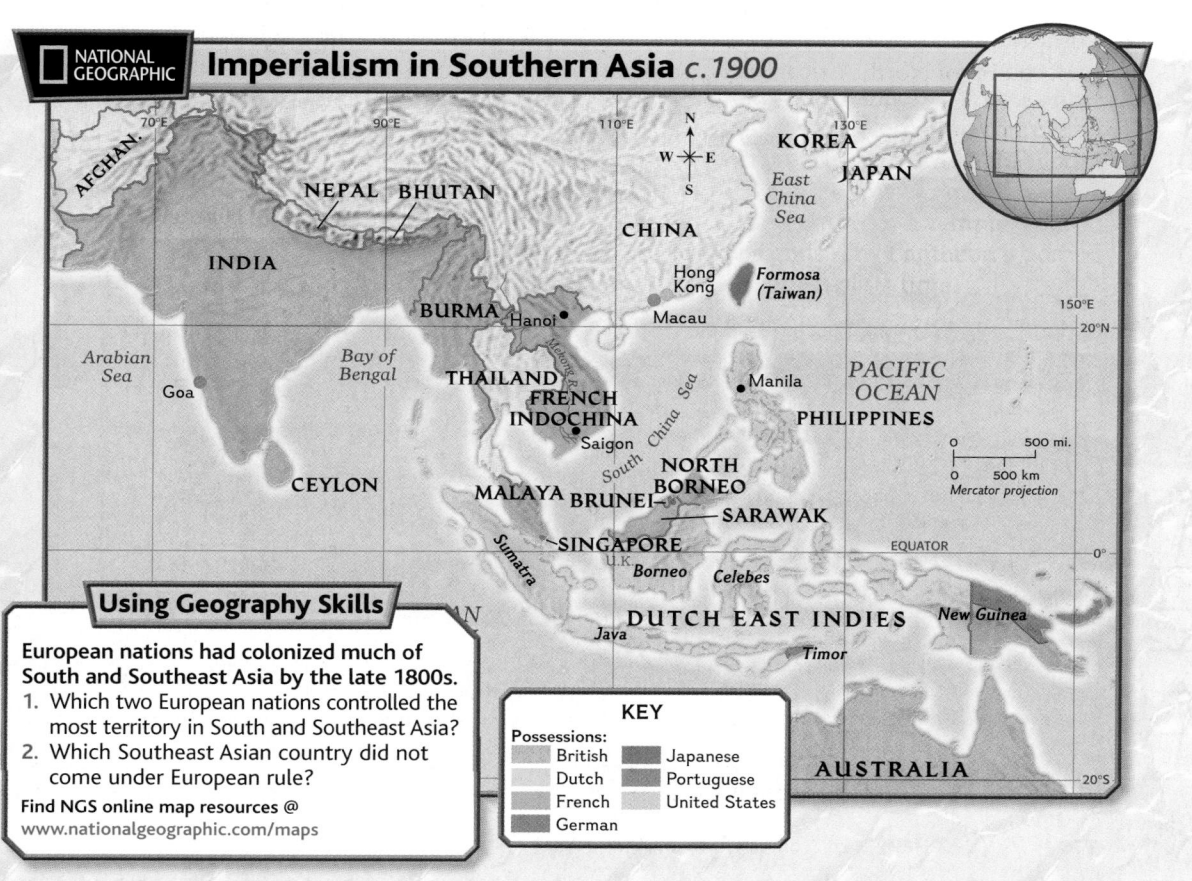

NATIONAL GEOGRAPHIC

Imperialism in Southern Asia c.1900

Using Geography Skills

European nations had colonized much of South and Southeast Asia by the late 1800s.
1. Which two European nations controlled the most territory in South and Southeast Asia?
2. Which Southeast Asian country did not come under European rule?

Find NGS online map resources @ www.nationalgeographic.com/maps

KEY
Possessions:
- British
- Dutch
- French
- German
- Japanese
- Portuguese
- United States

CRITICAL THINKING ACTIVITY

Sequencing Events On the board, write the events that led to the sepoy uprising in the following order: 1. At first, Hindus grumbled because they considered cows sacred, and Muslims protested because they considered pigs taboo. 2. The British arrested the rebellious sepoys. 3. The sepoys at an army post near Delhi refused to load their rifles. 4. In 1857 a rumor started that the British greased their bullets with cow and pig fat. 5. In response, other sepoys killed 50 Europeans. **Ask:** What do you think is the correct sequence of these events? *(Correct sequential order. 4, 1, 3, 2, 5)* **L2**

Primary Source

Because the British created Nigeria from the lands of many groups, Nigeria's culture is very diverse. For example, each ethnic group has its own variety of dance. Ishan dancers twist around on stilts, pairs of Tiv men dance the traditional *ajo*, teams of Tiv women do the *icough* as they sing about current events, and the Ubakala use dance to express values and to solve problems.

Answer:
They will pay landowners a reasonable amount and will protect the Africans from attack.

☞ See the **Primary Source Reading (with Document-Based Questions)** in the Unit Resource Books.

Europe Divides Africa

Main Idea European nations ruled almost all of Africa by 1914.

Reading Focus Have you ever bought something just because everyone else had it? Read to learn why Europeans competed to take over Africa.

Africa was the last populated continent to be colonized by Europeans. In previous chapters, you learned that Europeans in the 1500s built trading stations along Africa's west coast. In the 1800s, European missionaries and explorers finally opened up Africa's inland areas to European control.

The Struggle for North Africa The first part of Africa to be conquered by Europe was also the closest. In the early 1800s, Europeans crossed the Mediterranean and took control of North Africa. French soldiers seized control of the territories that are today the countries of Algeria and Tunisia. The last territory France claimed in North Africa was Morocco, which it divided with Spain in 1904.

At the eastern end of North Africa, European businesses began operating in Egypt. In 1869 they opened the Suez Canal. Built by Egyptian workers and paid for with French funds, it linked the Mediterranean and Red Seas. The Suez Canal provided a shorter water route to India and East Asia. In 1875 the British took control of the Suez Canal. After Egyptians rebelled, the British made Egypt a protectorate.

By 1900, only Tripoli, today known as Libya, remained free from European control. Then, in 1911, Italy defeated the Ottoman empire in a brief war and was given control of Tripoli.

Primary Source

"Standard Treaty"

The British Royal Niger Company presented this fill-in-the-blank treaty to many African leaders.

"We, the undersigned Chiefs of _____, with the view to the bettering of the condition of our country and people, do this day cede [give] to the Royal Niger Company, for ever, the whole of our territory extending from _____. . . .

The said Royal Niger Company agree to pay native owners of land a reasonable amount for any portion they may require.

The said Royal Niger Company bind themselves to protect the said Chiefs from the attacks of any neighboring aggressive tribes."

—Royal Niger Company, "Standard Treaty"

▼ British colonists in Nigeria

DBQ Document-Based Questions

What does the Royal Niger Company offer to the Africans in exchange for their land?

INTERDISCIPLINARY CONNECTIONS ACTIVITY

Geography Distribute large outline maps of the Eastern Hemisphere. Have students label the Suez Canal and the countries that they think would benefit from the canal. Next, tell them to select two pairs of countries. Each pair should include a European imperial power and one of its colonies or two colonies under the same imperial power. Instruct students to draw two lines between the countries in each pair. The first line should represent the shortest possible water route before the Suez Canal was built, and the second should represent the shortest water route after the canal was built. Tell them to use a different color for each pair of countries and solid and broken lines for each pair of routes. Finally, tell students to measure the routes in centimeters and record their results on a bar graph. Suggest that they use the same colors they used for their routes in their bar graph. **L1/EL**

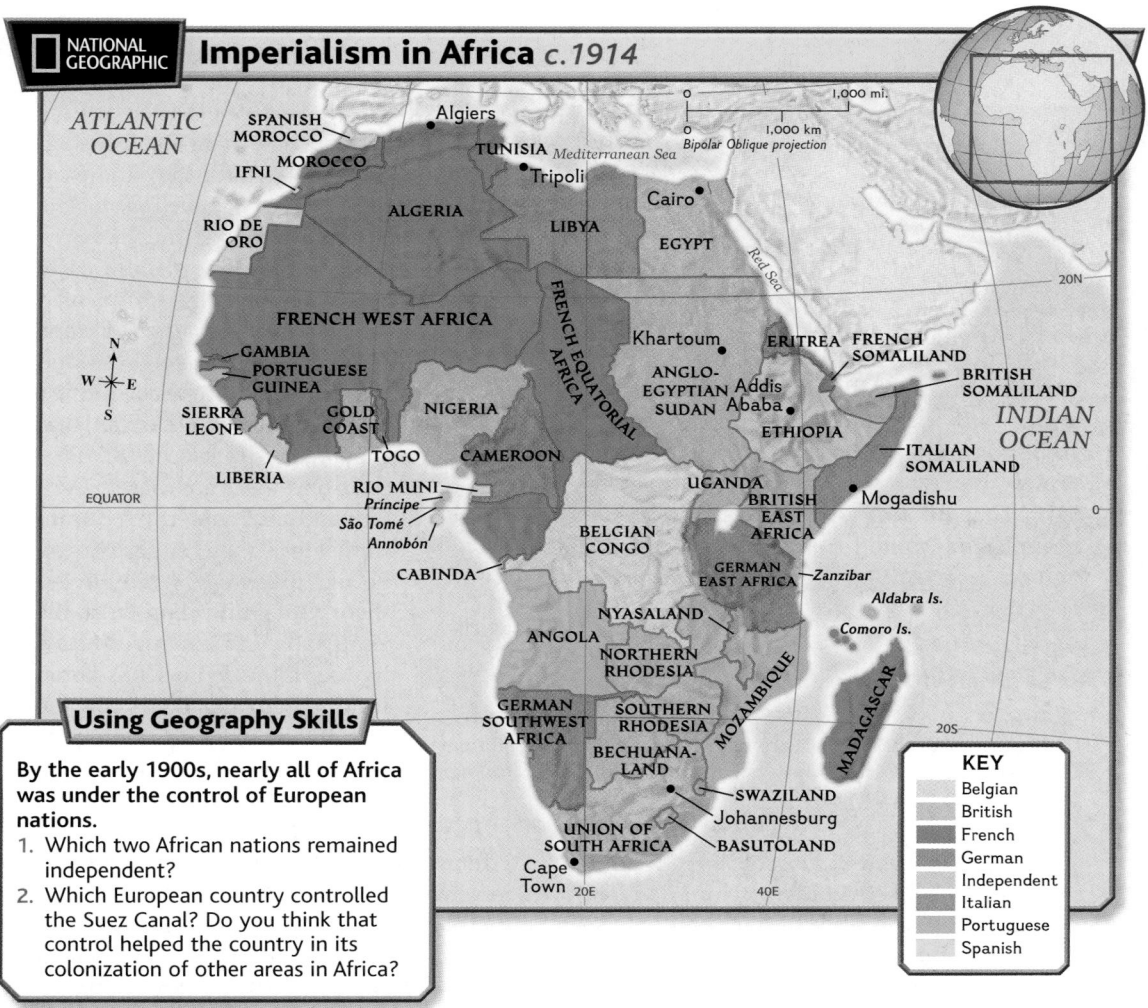

NATIONAL GEOGRAPHIC

Imperialism in Africa c.1914

ATLANTIC OCEAN

SPANISH MOROCCO
Algiers
MOROCCO
IFNI
TUNISIA *Mediterranean Sea*
Tripoli
RIO DE ORO
ALGERIA
LIBYA
Cairo
EGYPT

0   1,000 mi.
0   1,000 km
Bipolar Oblique projection

FRENCH WEST AFRICA

FRENCH EQUATORIAL AFRICA

Khartoum
ERITREA FRENCH SOMALILAND
ANGLO-EGYPTIAN SUDAN Addis Ababa
BRITISH SOMALILAND

GAMBIA
PORTUGUESE GUINEA
SIERRA LEONE
GOLD COAST
NIGERIA
ETHIOPIA
ITALIAN SOMALILAND

INDIAN OCEAN

20N

Red Sea

TOGO
CAMEROON
LIBERIA
RIO MUNI
Príncipe
São Tomé
Annobón
CABINDA

UGANDA
BRITISH EAST AFRICA
Mogadishu

EQUATOR

BELGIAN CONGO

GERMAN EAST AFRICA   Zanzibar

Aldabra Is.
Comoro Is.

0

NYASALAND
ANGOLA
NORTHERN RHODESIA

MOZAMBIQUE

MADAGASCAR

GERMAN SOUTHWEST AFRICA
SOUTHERN RHODESIA

20S

BECHUANA-LAND

SWAZILAND
Johannesburg
BASUTOLAND
UNION OF SOUTH AFRICA
Cape Town

20E   40E

KEY
- Belgian
- British
- French
- German
- Independent
- Italian
- Portuguese
- Spanish

Using Geography Skills

By the early 1900s, nearly all of Africa was under the control of European nations.

1. Which two African nations remained independent?
2. Which European country controlled the Suez Canal? Do you think that control helped the country in its colonization of other areas in Africa?

HISTORY Mystery

How Did We Find the Source of the Nile?

During the 1800s, a steady stream of British adventurers set out from Cairo to discover the source of the Nile. However, even seasoned explorers were thwarted by malaria, bandits, monsoons, and dense jungles. Some died looking for the source. It was not until more than a century later that satellite photographs showed that the Nile starts in the mountains of Burundi, halfway between Lake Tanganyika and Lake Victoria.

Using Geography Skills

Answers:

1. Liberia, Ethiopia
2. Britain; Students may note that Britain controlled many areas in Africa, and having easy access by sea probably aided that control.

West and Central Africa During the 1800s, most of West and Central Africa also came under European rule. For hundreds of years, Europeans had been involved in trading enslaved West Africans. By the early 1800s, however, many Europeans had decided slavery was wrong and should be stopped. When Britain declared the slave trade illegal, other European nations soon followed its lead.

Europeans then sought out West Africa's gold, timber, hides, and palm oil. To control this trade, Britain, France, and Germany took over areas along Africa's Atlantic coast. Eventually, they moved inland. Meanwhile, the only place in West Africa where non-Europeans ruled was Liberia. There, African Americans freed from slavery had founded the republic of Liberia in 1847.

In Central Africa, European control began when King **Leopold II** of Belgium decided to conquer the region. The king spoke often about improving the lives of Central Africa's people. His main concern, however, was making money by selling rubber grown on plantations in the Congo.

EXTENDING THE CONTENT

What Happened in King Leopold's Congo? King Leopold hired African mercenaries to create his own army called the Force Publique. The principal job of Leopold's army was making villagers harvest wild rubber. The soldiers did this by taking women and children from a village hostage and not releasing them until the men returned with the required amount of rubber. Villagers in the rubber-rich area along the Kasai River resisted the army's demands. A chief in the region allied himself with the Force Publique and had his followers burn a dozen villages. Afterward, the chief showed a missionary 81 severed hands and said: "I always have to cut off the right hands of those we kill to show the State. . . ." This was not an isolated incident. A European official noted in a report that to gather rubber in his part of the Congo, "one must cut off hands, noses and ears."

More About the Photo

Rubber is still produced in Africa. However, today most rubber is synthetically produced, lessening the need for African rubber.

Caption Answer: Belgium

TIME TRAVELER

The Zulu army numbered only 1,500 when a warrior-chieftain named Shaka took over in 1816. His first act was to reorganize the army. He forced the warriors to fight at close range by replacing their throwing spears with long-bladed knives. Then he divided his army into regiments, each with its own distinctive shield, headgear, and ornaments. Officers directed their regiment with hand signals to hide their intentions from the enemy. Within two years, Shaka's army had decimated its main rivals. By the 1870s, the Zulu army comprised 40,000 highly disciplined warriors.

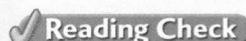
Reading Check

Answer: Congo, French Equatorial Africa

▲ These African workers are shown on a rubber plantation in French Equatorial Africa. The pails are full of liquid rubber tapped from rubber trees. *Which European country was the first to conquer territory in Central Africa?*

Leopold ordered his soldiers to force Africans to collect rubber for him. Anyone who resisted was shot. After missionaries and other Europeans protested, however, the king turned over the Congo to Belgium's government. The government did away with forced labor.

Leopold's move into the Congo spurred other European powers into action. Over the next few years, they divided the rest of the African continent among themselves. By 1914, Liberia and Ethiopia were the only independent African countries.

What Was the Boer War?
The European race for the African continent led to a war in South Africa. This conflict became known as the Boer War. It was fought between the British and the Boers. How did this war begin?

In the 1600s, Dutch settlers arrived on Africa's southwestern coast. There they founded the port of Cape Town. The Dutch settlers became known as Afrikaners or Boers. In the early 1800s, Britain seized the Dutch territory and renamed it Cape Colony. The Boers resented British rule. So they moved inland and settled areas that they named the Orange Free State and the Transvaal.

As the Boers moved into these areas, they fought African groups that were already living there. One group known as the Zulu had created a large empire in the 1800s. The Zulu often fought with the Boers. By the late 1800s, the Zulu were also fighting the British, who eventually destroyed the Zulu Empire.

Tensions grew between the British and Boers when British settlers discovered gold and diamonds in the Transvaal. Britain's Cecil Rhodes—Cape Colony's prime minister and the owner of several gold and diamond companies—decided to take the Transvaal from the Boers. War erupted in 1899 and ended with the Boers' defeat three years later.

In 1910 Britain united the Boer republics, the Cape Colony, and one other British colony into the Union of South Africa. This new country became self-governing within the British Empire. The Boers and British ran the government, keeping out South Africa's much larger nonwhite population.

Reading Check **Identify** What territories in Africa had rubber plantations?

CITIZENSHIP AND YOU

Conflict of Interest Read aloud the passage that explains how Cecil Rhodes planned to overthrow the Boers after British settlers unearthed gold and diamonds in Boer-held Transvaal. Point out that Rhodes had a conflict of interest—a conflict between his private interests and his public responsibilities as a person in a position of trust. In other words, Rhodes's desire to make a profit, rather than the welfare of the people of Cape Colony, might have been the reason he planned to overthrow the Boers.
Ask: What kinds of hardships did Rhodes's war probably cause for Boers and British? What kinds of harm can leaders cause if they make decisions based on their private interests rather than the general welfare? What might citizens do to prevent the abuse of power due to a conflict of interest? **L3**

The War of 1898

Main Idea The United States became an imperial nation after defeating Spain and taking control of the Philippines and Puerto Rico.

Reading Focus Did you know Puerto Rico is part of the United States? Read to learn how the United States built its early empire.

In the late 1800s, the United States joined European powers in the race for colonies. By that time, the United States had become an industrial nation. As its economic power rose, many Americans in business and government came to believe that their country needed raw materials and new markets overseas to keep the economy growing.

America Defeats Spain In its search for markets and raw materials, the United States looked to Latin America and islands in the Pacific. In the late 1800s, Spain still ruled the Caribbean islands of **Cuba** (KYOO•buh) and Puerto Rico. However, in 1895 Cuba rebelled against Spain.

American newspapers printed vivid stories of killing and cruelty in Cuba. As a result, U.S. president **William McKinley** sent the U.S. battleship *Maine* to protect Americans who lived and worked there. While anchored in the harbor of Havana, Cuba's capital, the ship exploded.

American newspapers blamed Spain and pressured the president to take action. In April 1898, McKinley asked Congress to declare war. Four months later, the United States had won the war. Spain lost much of its remaining empire. Cuba became a republic under American protection. Puerto Rico and the Pacific islands of Guam and the **Philippines** (FIH•luh•PEENZ) became American territories.

Panama Canal

The Panama Canal, completed in 1914, enables ships to pass from the Atlantic to the Pacific Ocean without traveling all the way around South America. The canal is made up of three main locks. These locks raise and lower ships from oceans to lakes and back again. The Gatun Lock, the largest in the canal, is pictured here. It contains three gates that hold ships in the water before they are raised or lowered to the next gate. Going through the Gatun Lock, a ship will be raised or lowered by over 85 feet. Passage through the 50 mile long canal takes 8 days! *How did the building of the canal affect trade in North and South America?*

CHAPTER 20
SECTION 1, 762-770

Reading Support L1/ EL

Assign **Guided Reading Activity 20–1** to help students organize the information in the section.

❸ ASSESS

Assign Section 1 Review as homework or as an in-class activity.

● Have students use the **Interactive Tutor Self-Assessment CD-ROM** to review the section.

Assessment L2

Assign **Section 1 Quiz** to assess mastery of the material found in the section.

Reading Support L1/ EL

Assign **Reading Essentials and Study Guide 20–1** to help students review section material.

Caption Answer: It opened up a faster route to the Pacific Ocean, allowing ships to travel there in far less time.

COOPERATIVE LEARNING ACTIVITY

A Research Report Tell students that many Americans supported the Spanish-American War because they believed the U.S. was helping Cubans win independence. On the other hand, American business people had $50 million invested in plantations and other Cuban enterprises. Have them explain why they think the United States became involved in these countries. Have small groups research and compile reports on American business interests in the following hot spots: Hawaii, the Philippines, Nicaragua, and the Dominican Republic. **L3**

ENRICH

Tell students that when it was finished, the Panama Canal saved American companies $1.5 billion a year in shipping costs and earned the U.S. $150 million a year in tolls, of which only $2.3 million went to the government of Panama. Discuss how students might react if Panamanians had a similar arrangement in the U.S., on a Great Lake, for example. **L2**

✓ Reading Check

Answer: U.S. steamships carrying goods to China could use the Philippines as safe fueling stations. These made trade easier, which helped the U.S. economy.

To help students understand section material, have them visit **Study Central**™ at **jat.glencoe.com**

RETEACH

Have students match the names of colonies from the section with the names of the powers that ruled them. **L2**

④ CLOSE

Challenge students to name a person, group, or place from the section for every letter in "imperialism." **L1**

The Philippines, however, rejected American rule. Led by Emilio Aguinaldo (ah•MEEL•yoh AH•gee•NAHL•doh), the Filipinos rebelled against the U.S. and attacked American troops. By 1903, the Americans had crushed their uprising.

In 1898 Hawaii also came under American control. American settlers in Hawaii had overthrown the Hawaiian queen Liliuokalani (lih•LEE•uh•woh•kuh•LAH•nee) in 1893. However, it was not until after the War of 1898 that Congress approved American control of Hawaii.

Imperialism in Latin America The War of 1898 had shown how important it was for the United States to be able to move its navy quickly between the east and west coasts. The trip around South America took a long time. It also slowed down trade between the coasts. As a result, U.S. president Theodore Roosevelt decided to build a canal across **Panama** (PA•nuh•MAH) to connect the Atlantic and Pacific Oceans. At that time, Panama was part of the country of Colombia.

Because Colombia was unwilling to give up its land, in 1903 Americans helped Panamanians rebel against Colombia. After winning independence, Panama signed a treaty allowing the United States to build the canal. The Panama Canal opened in 1914, greatly shortening the route between the Atlantic and Pacific Oceans.

✓ Reading Check **Analyze** How did control of the Philippines help the U.S. economy?

Study Central™ Need help with the material in this section? Visit jat.glencoe.com

Section ① Review

Reading Summary
Review the Main Ideas

- Following the Industrial Revolution, European nations began building empires in Asia and Africa.

- The East India Company built Britain's empire in India.

- Nearly all of Africa came under foreign rule as the Europeans sought resources.

- After the War of 1898, the United States took control of Puerto Rico, Guam, the Philippines, and Hawaii.

What Did You Learn?

1. Besides economics, what reasons did European countries have for building empires?

2. What was the Boer War and why was it fought?

Critical Thinking

3. **Summarizing Information** Draw a diagram like the one below. Fill in the ovals with the names of areas under British control in the 1800s.

British Possessions

4. **Explain** Why were European nations interested in the countries of Southeast Asia?

5. **Compare and Contrast** How did British rule both help and hurt India?

6. **Analyze** Describe the actions taken by the United States in Panama in the early 1900s. Why was the United States interested in Panama?

7. **Descriptive Writing** Imagine you are a native of India in the late 1800s. Write a letter to a friend describing how you feel about British rule.

8. **Reading** **Prioritizing** Look back on the rise of imperialism. Determine what the most important reasons were for countries to take control of other nations.

SECTION 1 REVIEW ANSWERS

1. to add to their country's power and to spread Western ways
2. Boers fought to keep the British out of South Africa.
3. Malay, Burma, India, Egypt, Sudan, Nigeria, South Africa, parts of West and East Africa
4. The British wanted Singapore for a trading stop. France took over Indochina to keep out the British.
5. The British set up efficient government, schools, and railroads but destroyed India's textile industry and caused starvation.
6. The U.S. encouraged a rebellion in Panama. They wanted to build a canal to speed up trade.
7. Answers should use facts from the section.
8. Answers may vary, but should be based on logical reasons and conclusions.

Section 2

Nationalism in China and Japan

Get Ready to Read!

What's the Connection?
European imperialism changed the shape of the world in the late 1800s. However, Chinese nationalism and Japanese imperialism also made their mark on global affairs.

Focusing on the **Main Ideas**
- The arrival of Europeans greatly changed Chinese society. *(page 772)*
- Sun Yat-sen introduced ideas that helped cause the collapse of the Qing dynasty. *(page 774)*
- After Americans visited Japan, the Japanese reorganized their society and economy and began building an empire. *(page 777)*

Locating Places
Hong Kong (HAHNG   KAHNG)
Edo (EH•doh)
Port Arthur

Meeting People
Sun Yat-sen (SUN   YAHT•SEHN)
Yuan Shigai (yu•AHN   SHIHR•KY)
Oda Nobunaga (ohd•ah   noh•bun•ah•gah)
Tokugawa Ieyasu (toh•kug•ah•wah ee•eh•yahs•u)
Matthew Perry
Mutsuhito (MOOT•suh•HEE•toh)

Building Your Vocabulary
extraterritoriality (EHK•struh•TEHR• uh•TOHR•ee•A•luh•tee)
daimyo (DY•mee•OH)

Reading Strategy
Summarizing Information Use a chart like the one below to summarize the work of three Asian leaders.

Leader	Accomplishments

NATIONAL GEOGRAPHIC **When & Where?**

1850	1875	1900
1842 The Opium War ends	**1868** Meiji era begins in Japan	**1900** Boxer Rebellion erupts in China — **1905** Japan defeats Russia

Beijing
Tokyo (Edo)
Shanghai
Hong Kong

CHAPTER 20   Imperialism and World War I   771

---

1 FOCUS

SECTION OVERVIEW

This section describes Chinese nationalism and Japanese imperialism in the 1800s and 1900s.

BELLRINGER
SKILLBUILDER ACTIVITY

✎ Project **Daily Focus Skills Transparency 20–2** and have students answer questions. Discuss their responses.

Get Ready to Read!

Preteaching Vocabulary: The heads of noble families who were also powerful leaders in Japan were called *daimyo*.

Answers to Graphic: Nobunaga: seized Kyoto and placed the ruling shogun under his control, established rule over Japan's central plains; Hideyoshi: banned Christian activities, expelled missionaries and most European merchants; Iesayu: began the "Great Peace"

SECTION RESOURCES

Reproducible Masters
- Reproducible Lesson Plan 20–2
- Daily Lecture and Discussion Notes 20–2
- Vocabulary Activity 20–2
- Active Reading Note-Taking Guide 20–2
- Guided Reading Activity 20–2
- Section Quiz 20–2
- Reading Essentials and Study Guide 20–2

Transparencies
- Daily Focus Skills Transparency 20–2

Multimedia
- Interactive Tutor Self-Assessment CD-ROM
- ExamView® Pro Testmaker CD-ROM
- Presentation Plus! CD-ROM
- Glencoe BookLink CD-ROM

② TEACH

Reading Strategy

Visualizing Instruct students to adopt a Chinese or British viewpoint as they read "What Was the Opium War?" Next, have them choose a fact from the reading, such as the British paying silver for Chinese goods or the Chinese emperor demanding an end to the opium trade. Then, tell them to draw a cartoon about the fact that expresses their viewpoint. **L1**

Daily Lecture and Discussion Notes 20–2

Use **Daily Lecture and Discussion Notes 20–2** for an outline of key concepts found in the section.

Reading Support L1/ EL

Use **Vocabulary Activity 20–2** to review important terms in the section.

Caption Answer: The Chinese opened five ports to British goods, limited taxes on British imports, paid for the costs of the war, and gave Hong Kong to the British.

China and the West

Main Idea The arrival of Europeans greatly changed Chinese society.

Reading Focus Have you ever played sports where everyone on the team gets a chance to play? Read to learn how the Open Door policy applied the same idea to China.

During the Age of Imperialism, China was ruled by the Qing dynasty. The Qing came to power in 1644. Qin rulers were descended from the Manchus, warriors who lived to the northeast of China. The Qing dynasty ruled China until 1911.

Under Qing rule, the Chinese followed their traditional way of life until the 1800s. Then came the Industrial Revolution in Europe. European businesses and merchants wanted to increase their trade with China.

What Was the Opium War? By 1800, the Chinese already were trading with many Europeans, including the British. Chinese demand for British goods, however, was low. On the other hand, British demand for Chinese goods, especially tea, was high. As a result, the British had to trade more valuable goods, such as silver, for Chinese products.

The British then tried to get the Chinese to buy more cotton from India. When that failed, the British started selling opium to the Chinese. Opium is an addictive drug, so demand shot up in southern China. Silver began flowing into, rather than out of, British pockets.

The Chinese emperor warned the British to stop trading opium. When the British refused, war broke out in 1839. Chinese troops surrounded the port at Guangzhou. They demanded that traders surrender their opium. British warships responded by destroying forts on China's coasts and rivers. The Chinese emperor surrendered, and the Opium War ended in 1842.

After the war, the Chinese agreed to open five ports to British ships, limit taxes on British goods, and pay for the costs of the war. They also gave the British the island of **Hong Kong** (HAHNG KAHNG), which in time became one of the world's busiest ports. Europeans who lived in China were subject to their own laws but not Chinese laws. This legal practice is called **extraterritoriality** (EHK•struh•TEHR•uh•TOHR•ee•A•luh•tee).

▼ Britain's navy was important to the spread of British power around the world. Here a British warship attacks Chinese naval forces. *What did the British gain by their victory in the Opium War?*

Reading Strategy   READING THE TEXT

Analyzing Problems and Solutions After students read "What Was the Opium War?" have them identify the problem that the British faced. *(Chinese demand for British goods was low while British demand for Chinese goods was high.)* **Ask:** How did the British first try to solve the problem? *(They tried to get the Chinese to buy more cotton from India.)* When that failed, what did the British try? *(to sell opium to the Chinese)* Why did the second solution work? *(Opium is an addictive drug, so demand shot up.)* What new problem did their solution cause? *(opposition from the Chinese emperor)* Point out that the British solution became the emperor's problem. Have students discuss what distinguishes a bad solution from a good solution. **L1**

NATIONAL GEOGRAPHIC

Spheres of Influence in China 1911

Lambert Azimuthal Equal-Area projection

0 — 600 mi.
0 — 600 km

60E

RUSSIA

SIBERIA

MONGOLIA

MANCHURIA

Vladivostok

AFGHANISTAN

Beijing

KOREA
Port Arthur
Weihai (U.K.)
Qingdao

Sea of Japan (East Sea)

JAPAN

Tokyo (Edo)

50N
30N

INDIA (U.K.)

TIBET

CHINA
Wuhan

Nanjing

Yellow Sea

Shanghai

East China Sea

PACIFIC OCEAN

140E

BURMA (U.K.)

GUANGDONG
Guangzhou
Macao (Port.)
Zhanjiang

Taiping
Hong Kong (U.K.)

TAIWAN

THAILAND
FRENCH INDOCHINA

PHILIPPINES (U.S.)

South China Sea

KEY

Qing Empire, 1911

Spheres of influence:
British
French
German
Italian
Japanese
Russian

Using Geography Skills

In the late 1800s, many European countries established spheres of influence in China.
1. Which country had the largest sphere of influence in China?
2. Which country do you think had the best-placed sphere of influence in China? Explain.

China Tries to Reform

During the 1850s, Chinese peasants were subject to high taxes and suffered from harsh weather. Crops failed, and many Chinese starved to death. As a result, peasant unrest spread across China.

In 1851 a religious leader named Hong Xiuquan (HAHNG ZHOO•GWAHN) organized a huge rebellion. He convinced many Chinese peasants that the time had come to overthrow the emperor and build a "Heavenly Kingdom" in China where life would be much better. The words Tai Ping mean "Heavenly Kingdom," so this rebellion became known as the Tai Ping Rebellion. It lasted for 13 years. The rebels captured many cities and controlled much of southern China. Eventually, Europeans helped the Chinese government destroy the rebel army. About 20 million people lost their lives in the Tai Ping Rebellion.

Reform-minded Chinese officials convinced the emperor that Western technology could help stop uprisings and foreign takeovers. As a result, the Chinese built railroads, weapons factories, and shipyards. Despite these changes, Europeans continued to chip away at the emperor's power.

European Spheres of Influence

After the Tai Ping Rebellion, powerful leaders arose in China's heartland. They sold the right to

CHAPTER 20 Imperialism and World War I **773**

trade, build, and mine in their area to European nations. In this way, different parts of China became spheres of influence under the control of Russia, Britain, France, and Germany. Even Japan, now a rising power, took part of China—the offshore island of Taiwan.

The United States did not claim a sphere of influence in China. Instead, it called for an Open Door policy under which China was open to trade with all countries. In 1899 the other nations agreed to this policy.

Many Chinese hated the foreigners in their country and began to organize secret societies to drive them out. Some members of China's government, including the Empress Tzu Hsi (TSOO SHEE), supported these secret societies. Europeans and Americans called them Boxers, because the name of their secret society meant "righteous and harmonious fists."

In 1900 the Boxers attacked foreigners and Chinese Christians in Beijing. Britain, France, Germany, Russia, Japan, and the U.S. sent in troops and crushed the Boxer Rebellion.

✓ **Reading Check** **Describe** What did Great Britain gain from winning the Opium War?

▲ Members of the secret society known as the Boxers are rounded up after the failed rebellion. *Why did the Boxer Rebellion fail?*

774   CHAPTER 20   Imperialism and World War I

The Revolution of 1911

Main Idea Sun Yat-sen introduced ideas that helped cause the collapse of the Qing dynasty.

Reading Focus If you could, how would you change the government? Read to find out what Chinese rebels did when they had the chance to make changes.

Chinese leaders tried to hold on to their power by making more changes. For example, they replaced China's civil service examination system with a European-style educational system. They also set up regional assemblies and a national assembly.

Middle-class Chinese considered these changes to be too little too late. They grew angry when they learned that the assemblies could not pass laws but only give advice to the emperor. Furthermore, peasants, artisans, and miners continued to resent the high taxes the government had imposed to pay its debts to foreign nations.

In 1905 a young medical doctor named **Sun Yat-sen** (SUN YAHT • SEHN) founded a movement of revolutionaries that later became known as the Nationalist Party. Its members believed the Qing dynasty could no longer rule the country. Unless China was united under a strong government, it would be at the mercy of other countries. Sun developed a three-stage plan to change China: (1) take over the government, (2) prepare the people for self-rule, and (3) establish a constitution and a democracy.

In 1911 Sun's followers staged an uprising, and the Qing dynasty fell. Sun's Nationalists did not have the military or political backing to set up a government, however. As a result, they turned to the head of the Chinese army, General **Yuan Shigai** (yu•AHN SHIHR•KY).

Linking Past & Present

Hong Kong

THEN Hong Kong is made up of one large island, 235 small rocky islands, a peninsula, and some mountains on the mainland. When China gave the large island to Britain in 1842, the British named it Hong Kong, which means "fragrant harbor." At that time, only a few farmers and fishermen lived on the island. The British soon built it into a major trading center.

▼ Modern Hong Kong

▲ Hong Kong waterfront, 1879

NOW Hong Kong today is a center of finance, trade, and manufacturing. It is home to nearly 7 million people. In 1997 Britain returned Hong Kong to China. China agreed that Hong Kong could trade freely with the world and have a separate government for 50 more years.
What effect did British colonization have on Hong Kong's economy?

Reading Strategy

Drawing Conclusions Point out that Yuan ruled China in a traditional way but that traditionalists, or supporters of the Qing dynasty, hated him. **Ask: How do you think reformers felt about Yuan? Explain.** (*Students probably will say they hated Yuan because he did not understand or push for Western reform and because he did away with the new Parliament.*) **L1**

Linking Past & Present

Answer: Hong Kong became a major trading center.

Reading Check

Answer: 1) take over the government, 2) prepare the people for democratic rule, and 3) establish a constitutional democracy

General Yuan agreed to serve as president of a new Chinese republic. However, Yuan understood little about democracy and freedom. He ruled in a traditional way and refused to listen to those who called for democracy. When Yuan put an end to the new parliament, the Nationalist Party launched a revolt. The rebellion failed, and Sun Yat-sen fled to Japan.

Yuan died in 1916. One of his officers succeeded him, but the central government started to fall apart. Warlords, or local military leaders, seized power in the provinces and fought one another. Their soldiers caused widespread destruction.

Sun Yat-sen returned to China in 1917 and worked to rebuild the Nationalist Party. In the early 1920s, he decided to create a Nationalist army with the help of Chiang Kai-shek, a young Chinese officer. Sun died in 1925, but three years later Chiang led the army to victory and reunited China under a Nationalist government.

Reading Check **Identify** What was Sun Yat-sen's three-stage plan to change China?

CHAPTER 20   Imperialism and World War I   **775**

INTERDISCIPLINARY CONNECTIONS ACTIVITY

Civics Explain that Yuan Shigai's government was not the last to oppose people who called for democracy. Modern Chinese regimes have consistently kept a tight rein on the people. Today, China's leaders regulate Internet activists. For example, in 2003 Huang Di was sentenced to five years in prison for posting articles on human rights and political issues on his Web site. Liu Di, a university student, spent one year in prison without a trial for expressing political views online. Then five people who signed petitions calling for Liu Di's release were arrested. Review the first 10 amendments to the U.S. Constitution with students and have them identify the ones that prevent our government from treating Americans in a similar way. (*Amendment I guarantees freedom of speech and the right to petition. Amendment VI guarantees the right to a speedy trial.*) **L2**

Biography

TEACH

In 1894 Sun Yat-sen gave up his medical practice in Canton and moved north. He tried to interest the governor of the new province in ideas to strengthen China but had little success. Sun Yat-sen then took his ideas to Hawaii and started the Revive China Society. Most of the group's members were powerless clerks, peasants, artisans, and people from his home province of Kwangtung. The group's real importance was that it foreshadowed the revolutionary movement that would carry Sun Yat-sen to power in China.

In 1924 Sun Yat-sen wrote: "The Chinese have only family and clan solidarity; they do not have national spirit . . . they are just a heap of loose sand. . . . Other men are the carving knife and serving dish; we are the fish and the meat." **Ask: Why do you think the Chinese lacked national spirit in the early 1900s? Who are the "other men" Sun writes about? L2**

Then and Now

Answers will vary, but students should recognize that Sun's studies in American and European politics probably convinced him that China should adopt more Western ideas. He felt that China needed a strong government in order to not be controlled by foreign nations.

SUN YAT-SEN
1866–1925

▲ Sun Yat-sen

Sun Yat-sen was born in 1866 to a farming family from the small Chinese village known as Cuiheng. From a young age, he wanted a life different from what his society offered. He did not want to be a farmer, although he did help in the fields and raised chickens and ducks. Nor did he want to enter the Chinese civil service. He begged his parents to let him travel to other lands with his older brother, Sun Mei. At first they refused because of his young age, but once Sun Yat-sen turned 12, they agreed to let him go to Honolulu, Hawaii. There he attended an Anglican boys' school, where he was introduced to Christianity.

Because his brother became a wealthy and respected businessman in Hawaii, Sun Yat-sen did not have to become a laborer, as did most other Chinese who migrated to the West. Instead, Sun Yat-sen concentrated on his studies. He studied the English language and European and American political ideas. He became convinced that China needed a revolution. He attended Oahu College and announced that he wanted to become a Christian. This upset his brother, who sent him back to China.

In China, Sun Yat-sen and some of his friends purposely damaged a wooden statue of the Northern God, a patron god of Cuiheng. His rebellious behavior shocked his family and the villagers. He was sent to Hong Kong, where he earned a medical degree and became involved in politics.

> **"[N]ationalism does not mean discriminating against people of different nationality."**
> —Sun Yat-sen

▲ Pagoda at the tomb of Sun Yat-sen

Then and Now

How did Sun Yat-sen's education prepare him for his role as a Chinese leader? Do research to find how our current president's education prepared him for his leadership role.

Reading List Generator CD-ROM

GLENCOE
BOOKLINK   **RECOMMENDED READING**

Use the **Glencoe BookLink CD-ROM** to create customized reading lists based on your students' interests and reading levels. Below is an example based on content in this chapter. Also, see the Suggested Readings on pages 944–946 of the Appendix.

- Butterfield, Fox. *China, Alive in the Bitter Sea*. Fox Butterfield, a *New York Times* correspondent, lived and traveled in China in 1979. He reflects on the political turmoil and everyday life for the Chinese he met.
- Stanley, Diane, and Peter Vennema. *Shaka: King of the Zulus*. Outcast by his father, Shaka was a poor shepherd boy who grew up to become king of the Zulus in Africa in the 1800s. He created an army of the finest warriors in Africa and used it to conquer an empire.

The Rise of Imperial Japan

Main Idea After Americans visited Japan, the Japanese reorganized their society and economy and began building an empire.

Reading Focus Have you ever watched what someone else did and then changed how you did things to match what they did? Read to learn how the Japanese changed their society to be more like Europeans and Americans.

Like China, Japan felt pressures from Europe and the United States. Previously you learned that Japan was in chaos at the end of the 1400s. The shogun, or the country's military ruler, no longer controlled the country. **Daimyo** (DY•mee•oh), or heads of noble families, ruled their own lands and waged war on their neighbors.

During the 1500s, three powerful leaders restored strong central government to Japan. The first was **Oda Nobunaga** (ohd•ah noh•bun•ah•gah). He seized Kyoto, the capital, and placed the shogun under his control. Then, he spread his rule over Japan's central plains. After Nobunaga, another strong military leader named Toyotomi Hideyoshi (toh•yoh•toh•mee hee•dee•yoh•shee) ruled Japan. Hideyoshi was, in turn, followed by the powerful daimyo **Tokugawa Ieyasu** (toh•kug•ah•wah ee•eh•yahs•u), who became shogun in 1603. Ieyasu's descendants remained in power until 1868. The Tokugawa family's long rule was known as the "Great Peace."

Europeans in Japan Meanwhile, Europeans were starting to trade with Japan. In fact, Hideyoshi and Ieyasu used European firearms to help unify Japan. Jesuit missionaries arrived soon after the traders and converted thousands of Japanese to Christianity by the late 1500s.

The Jesuits angered Hideyoshi by destroying Japanese shrines. As a result, he

▲ This Japanese painting shows Commodore Perry's arrival in Edo Bay in 1853. *Before Perry arrived in Japan, who were the only Europeans allowed to trade there?*

banned Christian activities, expelled all missionaries, and persecuted Japanese Christians. European merchants were the next to go. Ieyasu allowed only the Dutch to remain in Japan at the port of Nagasaki.

Tokugawa rulers oversaw major changes in Japan. The samurai gradually ceased to be a warrior class. Many became managers on the lands of the daimyo. Trade and industry spread, especially in cities such as **Edo** (known today as Tokyo), Kyoto, and Osaka. The class system became rigid. It excluded *eta,* or outcasts, who worked in trades thought to be impure, such as killing animals and tanning hides. Laws stated where the *eta* lived, how they dressed, and even how they wore their hair. Women also led very restricted lives.

Perry Arrives in Japan In 1853 Commodore **Matthew Perry** and four American warships arrived in Edo Bay (now Tokyo Bay). Perry presented a letter from U.S. president Millard Fillmore to the shogun. The letter invited

More About the Art

Perry's first visit to Japan included two steam frigates, the *Mississippi* and the *Susquehanna,* both powerful ships. The Japanese ordered Perry to take his fleet and depart to a different Japanese port. Knowing the strength of his ships, Perry refused. Instead, he waited defiantly in the harbor for nearly a week before presenting the president's invitation.

Caption Answer: the Dutch at the port of Nagasaki

Predicting Consequences Tell students that in the 1800s, the Japanese were divided into four social classes—the samurai at the top, the farmers second, the artisans third, and the merchants at the bottom. Add that a person could not change his or her social class or perform tasks that belonged to another class. Give the example of the samurai father who withdrew his son from school because he was learning mathematics—a subject fit only for merchants. **Ask: Which class—samurai or merchants—do you think would become more powerful after Japan began trading with the West? Explain. L2**

EXTENDING THE CONTENT

How Did the Tokugawa Shoguns Control the Daimyo? To ensure daimyo loyalty, Ieyasu set up a system called *sankin-kotai,* or attendance by turn. Each daimyo had to travel to Edo every other year, bringing tribute and remaining in the shogun's service for a full year. Thus, half the daimyo were directly under the shogun's control at any one time. Even when the daimyo returned to their estates, they had to leave their families at Edo as hostages. The daimyo spent much of their income traveling to and from Edo and maintaining several households. They also had to get the shogun's permission to marry and to repair or build their castles. *Sankin-kotai* kept them weak, obedient to the shogun, and less able to rebel against the government. Much like Louis XIV of France, the shogun turned his aristocracy into courtiers who were carefully watched and controlled.

③ ASSESS

Assign Section 2 Review as homework or as an in-class activity.

⬤ Have students use the **Interactive Tutor Self-Assessment CD-ROM** to review the section.

Assessment L2

Assign **Section 2 Quiz** to assess mastery of the material found in the section.

Using Geography Skills

Answers:

1. South Sakhalin Island, Ryuku Islands, Kuril Islands, Korea, Taiwan
2. Japan was small, with no natural room for expansion, and it needed raw materials.

NATIONAL GEOGRAPHIC — The Japanese Empire

KEY
- Japanese Empire, 1870
- Japanese acquisitions by 1910
- Japanese spheres of influence, 1918

Using Geography Skills

In the late 1800s, Japan began to build an empire in Asia.
1. What areas had Japan acquired by 1910?
2. How might Japan's geography have influenced the nation to expand?

The Meiji Restoration

The Meiji Restoration At the time the shogun was overthrown, Emperor **Mutsuhito** (MOOT•suh•HEE•toh) was known as the Meiji, or "Enlightened," emperor. Thus, the late 1800s and early 1900s is known in Japan as the Meiji era. Just as shoguns controlled earlier emperors, Japan's new ruling samurai now controlled Mutsuhito.

The Meiji leaders were determined to make Japan a great power able to stand up to the Europeans and Americans. First, they did away with the old social system. The daimyo lost much of their land, power, and privileges. Then, in 1889, Japanese leaders wrote a new constitution to set up a constitutional monarchy. The people elected lawmakers to the legislature.

Power, however, was held by the Meiji leaders, who acted on behalf of the emperor. They chose the prime minister and his advisers.

Japan's new government set up a modern army and navy. All Japanese men were expected to serve for a certain amount of time in the armed forces. Meiji leaders also made major changes in Japan's society. They improved roads and opened public schools. Education was required for all, including women.

Above all, the Meiji pushed for Japan to industrialize. They helped build new factories and gave certain privileges to the rich and powerful families who ran them. Japan's new industrial society also had a dark side though. Mill workers often worked 20-hour days, and miners were shot when they refused to work in extreme heat.

Japan Builds an Empire

Japan Builds an Empire As they watched European nations and the United States rise in power and wealth, Japanese leaders came

Japan to have trade and diplomatic relations with the United States.

Within six months, Perry and an even larger fleet returned to Japan for an answer to the president's letter. Fearing an American attack, the Japanese agreed to open ports to U.S. trade and to exchange ambassadors. Japan soon made similar agreements with European nations.

Many Japanese were unhappy with the treaties and considered them unfair. They feared the treaties would keep Japan weak. In 1868 a group of samurai attacked the shogun's palace in Kyoto and took power in the emperor's name.

778   CHAPTER 20   Imperialism and World War I

COOPERATIVE LEARNING ACTIVITY

Kabuki Costumes Tell students that Kabuki became popular in Japan during the Tokugawa era. Describe Kabuki as musical theater that is full of action and dramatic gestures. Display pictures of Kabuki performances to show students the kinds of costumes used. Next, have students imagine a Kabuki performance about Admiral Perry coming to Japan. Then divide the class into groups and assign one of the following characters to each group: Millard Fillmore, Matthew Perry, the shogun, the shogun's wife, a samurai, and a Japanese merchant. Ask the groups to make Kabuki-style costumes for their character. Encourage them to recycle materials from home such as cardboard, aluminum foil, yarn scraps, and old clothing and sheets. **L1/EL**

to believe a nation needed an empire to be strong. Colonies would supply Japan with raw materials, cheap labor, and markets for manufactured goods.

As the first step toward building an empire, in 1876 the Japanese navy forced Korea to open its ports to Japanese trade. The Chinese had controlled Korea for a long time and resented Japan's presence there.

In 1894 China and Japan went to war. The Japanese destroyed China's fleet and captured the Manchurian city of **Port Arthur.** In the peace treaty that followed, China agreed to give Taiwan to Japan and independence to Korea.

Russia also wanted to trade with Korea. As a result, Japan and Russia competed for markets there. In 1904 Japan attacked a Russian naval base at Port Arthur, which Russia had seized from China in 1898. The Japanese army then marched into Manchuria. Russian troops in the area tried to stop them but were driven back.

▲ Japan's modern naval fleet easily defeated Russia's forces. *Why did Japan come into conflict with Russia?*

Meanwhile, Russia sent its main fleet all the way around the world to attack Japan. When it arrived, Japan's new modern navy quickly sank the Russian ships. In 1905 Russia agreed to give up Port Arthur and part of Sakhalin (SA•kuh•LEEN), an island north of Japan. The whole world now recognized Japan as a major power.

 Explain Why did the samurai attack and replace the shogun?

Study Central™ Need help with the material in this section? Visit jat.glencoe.com

Section 2 Review

Reading Summary

Review the Main Ideas

- In the 1800s, European powers created spheres of influence and controlled trade within China.

- A revolution overthrew the Qing dynasty in 1911 but failed to create a democratic government for China.

- The Meiji Restoration changed Japan's society and economy and made Japan into a major world power.

What Did You Learn?

1. What were the causes of the Boxer Rebellion?

2. Why did Admiral Perry sail to Japan? What was the result of his mission?

Critical Thinking

3. **Sequencing Information** Draw a time line like the one below. Fill in dates and events related to changes in China in the 1800s and 1900s.

1842 ———————— 1916

4. **Cause and Effect** How did trade between Britain and China lead to the Opium War?

5. **Compare and Contrast** What was the Open Door policy, and how was it different from European policies?

6. **Summarize** Describe Japan's rise to power in the in the late 1800s and early 1900s.

7. **Persuasive Writing** Write an editorial for a newspaper in China presenting your views on China's treatment by the European powers.

ENRICH

Tell students that the Japanese loved Western-style ballroom dancing and imported baseball from the United States. Have students compare the popularity of Western culture in Japan during the early 1900s with Americans' fascination with Japanese comics and cartoons today. **L1**

Answer: He made unfair treaties with the West that they feared would keep Japan weak.

History Online

To help students understand section material, have them visit **Study Central™** at jat.glencoe.com

RETEACH

Have students summarize changes made in China and Japan after 1900. **L2**

④ CLOSE

Ask students to complete the following sentence: *The best thing to happen in East Asia during the 1800s and 1900s was . . .* **L1**

SECTION 2 REVIEW ANSWERS

1. Resentment of foreigners in China led to a society called the Boxers to rebel.

2. to open relations between the U.S. and Japan; Japan agreed to trade with the West

3. 1842: China loses Opium War; 1851: Tai Ping Rebellion; 1900: Boxer Rebellion; 1905:
Nationalist Party forms; 1911: Qing dynasty falls; 1916: China's central government falls apart

4. Britain sold opium to China. British ships fired on Chinese ports when Chinese leaders tried to stop the opium trade.

5. Europeans established spheres of influence, whereas the Open Door Policy proposed that China trade with all countries.

6. Japan defeated China and then Russia in wars.

7. Answers will vary.

① FOCUS

SECTION OVERVIEW

This section explains the causes of World War I and describes the beginning stages of the war.

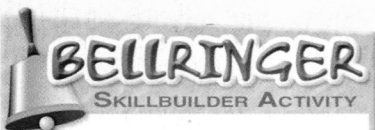

BELLRINGER
SKILLBUILDER ACTIVITY

🖉 Project **Daily Focus Skills Transparency 20–3** and have students answer questions. Discuss their responses.

Get Ready to Read!

Preteaching Vocabulary: Tell students that the military strength of Germany and Austria-Hungary made France, Russia, and Great Britain uneasy. The three countries decided to band together for safety, but Great Britain refused to sign a formal alliance with its rival France. Instead, the countries formed an *entente cordiale* or *entente*—a less binding understanding than an alliance.

Answers to Graphic: Allies: France, Russia, Great Britain, Italy, the United States; Central Powers: Austria-Hungary, Germany, the Ottoman Empire, Bulgaria

Section 3
World War I Begins

Get Ready to Read!

What's the Connection?
You have seen how imperialism contributed to tensions among Europeans. Eventually, these tensions led to a worldwide conflict.

Focusing on the Main Idea
- Alliances, militarism, and nationalism led to a crisis in Europe. *(page 781)*
- The assassination of Archduke Franz Ferdinand sparked World War I. *(page 784)*
- Americans supported the Allies because of pro-British feelings and business links. *(page 786)*

Locating Places
Balkans (BAWL•kuhnz)
Serbia (SUHR•bee•uh)

Meeting People
Franz Ferdinand
(FRANZ FUHR•duhn•AND)
Woodrow Wilson

Building Your Vocabulary
militarism
(MIH•luh•tuh•RIH•zuhm)
conscription (kuhn•SKRIHP•shuhn)
entente (ahn•TAHNT)
mobilization
(MOH•buh•luh•ZAY•shuhn)
rationing
propaganda (PRAH•puh•GAN•duh)
blockade

Reading Strategy
Contrasting Use a Venn diagram like the one below to show the major countries that made up the Allies and the Central Powers.

Allies — WWI Alliances — Central Powers

When & Where?
NATIONAL GEOGRAPHIC

BRITAIN
London • GERMANY RUSSIA
Paris •
• Berlin
FRANCE AUSTRIA-
HUNGARY
• Rome

1910   1915   1920

1908
Austria-Hungary takes over Bosnia

1914
World War I begins

1915
German submarine sinks the *Lusitania*

1917
U.S. enters World War I

SECTION RESOURCES

📁 **Reproducible Masters**
- Reproducible Lesson Plan 20–3
- Daily Lecture and Discussion Notes 20–3
- Vocabulary Activity 20–3
- Active Reading Note-Taking Guide 20–3
- Guided Reading Activity 20–3
- Section Quiz 20–3
- Reading Essentials and Study Guide 20–3

🖉 **Transparencies**
- Daily Focus Skills Transparency 20–3

Multimedia
- Interactive Tutor Self-Assessment CD-ROM
- ExamView® Pro Testmaker CD-ROM
- Presentation Plus! CD-ROM

The Causes of World War I

Main Idea Alliances, militarism, and nationalism led to a crisis in Europe.

Reading Focus Do you cheer for the American team during the Olympics and feel proud of your nation? Read to learn how national pride and feelings of independence led Europe to the brink of war.

After Napoleon was defeated, it would be almost 100 years before another major war erupted in Europe involving all the countries. In the early 1900s, however, tension was growing among the European powers.

Nationalism Nationalism, a feeling of intense loyalty to one's country, caused much of the tension in Europe. As you read in earlier chapters, nationalism led to the birth of new nations, such as Italy and Germany. The actions of Germany soon challenged the position of older nations such as Britain and France. At the same time, the spread of nationalism threatened to break apart other countries in Europe. Some groups of people, such as those in the Austro-Hungarian Empire, demanded independent nations of their own.

The Race for Empires Tensions in Europe also grew out of the desire of nations to enlarge their empires. As you read earlier, European nations competed for colonies in Africa, Asia, and other parts of the world. These not only created new markets and

NATIONAL GEOGRAPHIC

Europe Before World War I 1914

Using Geography Skills

Tensions in the part of southeast Europe known as the Balkans helped lead to World War I.

1. The area of Alsace and Lorraine was on the border of which countries?
2. Germany was a relatively new nation in the early 1900s. About how far across was Germany at its widest point?

CHAPTER 20   Imperialism and World War I   781

② TEACH

Reading Strategy

Predicting Before students begin the section, tell them to recall what they have read about rivalries between European nations. Next, have them list the causes of these rivalries. **Ask: Which of these causes do you think might lead to a major war?** Then instruct students to read "The Causes of World War I" to find out if their predictions are correct. **L1**

Daily Lecture and Discussion Notes 20–3

Use **Daily Lecture and Discussion Notes 20–3** for an outline of key concepts found in the section.

Reading Support L1/ EL

Use **Vocabulary Activity 20–3** to review important terms in the section.

Using Geography Skills

Answers:
1. Germany, France, Switzerland, and Luxembourg
2. almost 800 miles

Reading Strategy   **READING THE TEXT**

Reviewing Write the following skeleton outline on the board:

The Causes of World War I

I. Nationalism

   A.

   B.

After students read about nationalism, review the information by asking volunteers to write at least two facts to complete the outline section on the board. Repeat the process for other heads. Tell students to study the outline for the section review. **L1/ EL**

Writing Activity

Have students takes sides—the Triple Alliance or the Triple Entente. Then give students bumper-sticker-sized sheets of paper and tell them to write catchy slogans designed to rally the people behind their military. Offer examples such as "A Strong Navy for a Strong Nation" and "Your Emperor Needs You." Pair slogans from opposing nations and display them side by side. **L2**

Caption Answers:
Germany, France, Russia; Britain

TIME TRAVELER

In 1888 Otto von Bismarck, the German chancellor, wanted a German colony in the South Pacific. He sent ships to shell the islands into submission. Subsequently, they destroyed some American property on the island of Samoa. The United States responded by sending a fleet of its own. As the two sides prepared to fight, a hurricane struck and sunk the ships. German and American sailors ended up rescuing one another and forgetting the battle. If not for the hurricane, Germany and the United States might have gone to war right then.

▲ The competition for colonies led to a focus on military strength. This photo shows British troops on parade. *Which European countries used conscription to build large armies?*

▲ Prior to World War I, Germany built up its navy, including these battleships anchored in the harbor at Kiel, Germany. *Which country had the world's largest and strongest navy around 1900?*

supplied raw materials, they also added to a nation's prestige, or sense of greatness.

Britain and France already possessed large overseas empires and wanted to expand them even more. Germany, Italy, and Russia also wanted to increase their holdings. Because few areas were left to colonize, expansion by one nation often brought it into conflict with another.

Military Buildup

As nations competed for colonies, they strengthened their armies and navies to protect their interests. If one nation increased its military might, its rivals felt threatened and built up their own military in response. As a result of these buildups, Europeans were caught up in a spirit of **militarism** (MIH•luh•tuh•RIH•zuhm). This term refers to a fascination with war and the military.

In this atmosphere of militarism, Germany, France, and Russia developed huge armies. They used conscription to fill their armies with soldiers. **Conscription** (kuhn•SKRIHP•shuhn) requires citizens to serve in the military for a certain period of time. In the United States, people refer to conscription as "the draft."

Britain had the world's largest and strongest navy. In the early 1900s, Germany began to build up its navy. The British saw this action as a threat and began to build even more warships. A bitter rivalry soon grew between Britain and Germany.

Forming Alliances

As militarism grew, nations began to make alliances, or defense agreements to help each other if war breaks out. By 1914 two major alliances had been formed. Germany, Austria-Hungary, and Italy banded together in the Triple Alliance. Britain, France, and Russia joined in the Triple Entente. An **entente** (ahn•TAHNT) is an understanding among nations.

The alliances helped to keep peace by creating a balance of power. A balance of power keeps any one country from becoming too strong. Yet Europe's alliances actually created a great danger. An attack on one nation was all that was needed to trigger a war involving many countries. Europe was like a barrel of gunpowder. Only a spark

782   CHAPTER 20   Imperialism and World War I

DIFFERENTIATED INSTRUCTION

Interpersonal: On the board, write the following quote from the British writer H.G. Wells: "Our true nationality is mankind." Then have them write letters to Wells discussing what they think about the idea and its possible impact on the arms race in Europe.

English Learners: Ask students to explain what H.G. Wells meant in their own words.

Gifted and Talented: Have students research *The World Set Free*, the book that H.G. Wells wrote in 1914 in which he discusses the atomic bomb. Ask students to share their ideas about how Wells could predict the bomb's development more than 30 years before its creation.

📁 Refer to *Inclusion Strategies for the Middle School Social Studies Classroom* in the TCR.

was needed to set it off. It seemed likely that the spark would be lit in Europe's Balkan Peninsula.

The Balkan Crises In the early 1900s, the Balkan Peninsula in southeastern Europe was a hotbed of nationalist rivalries. For hundreds of years, the Ottoman and the Austro-Hungarian Empires had ruled the **Balkans** (BAWL•kuhnz). As nationalism spread, groups within these empires demanded independence.

Among these nationalist groups were the South Slavs. They included the Serbs, Bosnians, Croats, and Slovenes. The Serbs were the first to win their freedom. They formed a state called **Serbia** (SUHR•bee•uh) and believed their mission was to unite the South Slavs.

The Russians, who were Slavs as well, backed Serbia. Austria-Hungary, fearing the South Slavs in their empire would want to break away, tried to limit Serbia's growth. In 1908 Austria-Hungary took over Serbia's neighbor, Bosnia, from the Ottomans. The Serbs were furious. They wanted Bosnia to be part of their country.

With Russian support, the Serbs prepared for war. Then Emperor William II of Germany demanded that Russia accept Austria-Hungary's takeover of Bosnia or face war with Germany. Russia backed down. However, it was determined not to be humiliated by Germany again.

In 1912 the Balkan League—Bulgaria, Greece, Montenegro, and Serbia—declared war on the Ottoman empire. As a result, the Turks lost nearly all their European territory. However, the Balkan League soon fell apart.

Greeks and Serbs demanded land that Bulgaria had won in the war, so Bulgaria attacked the Greeks and Serbs. The Turks saw their chance to win back land and attacked Bulgaria. The Treaty of Bucharest ended the fighting, but Europeans expected the Balkan region to go to war again soon.

✓ **Reading Check** **Identify** What was the danger created by forming alliances?

NATIONAL GEOGRAPHIC
HISTORY MAKERS

Assassination of an Archduke *June 28, 1914*

Archduke Franz Ferdinand of Austria-Hungary visited Sarajevo in June of 1914 with his wife Sophie. Sarajevo was a city in the Austro-Hungarian Empire. Some people who lived in that part of the empire wanted to be free from Austria-Hungary. Those people were especially angry because the archduke and his wife arrived on the anniversary of a battle in which Serbia lost its independence. A terrorist organization made plans to kill the archduke and his wife during their visit. On June 28, a terrorist named Gavrilo Princip shot them while they were riding in a motorcade. A month later, Austria-Hungary declared war on Serbia. Each nation received help from its allies. The result was World War I.

Archduke Ferdinand and his wife in their car in Sarajevo ▶

✓ **Reading Check**

Answer: An attack on one nation could trigger a war among many countries.

CONNECTING ACROSS TIME

Have students compare the following maps: Europe in 1914 in this section, Europe After World War I in Section 4, and the map of present-day Europe on pages R16–R17. Then ask them to describe the boundary changes that have occurred in the Balkans over the last 90 years. **L1/EL**

NATIONAL GEOGRAPHIC
HISTORY MAKERS

As Franz Ferdinand's touring car sped to Sarajevo's city hall, Princip's co-conspirator threw a grenade at the archduke. The grenade bounced off his car and exploded, injuring about 20 people. To ensure a safe return, the general in charge of the archduke's security changed the planned route but forgot to tell the archduke's chauffeur. When he remembered, Princip was steps away from the archduke, and the driver could not back up fast enough to avoid the shooting.

CRITICAL THINKING ACTIVITY

Drawing Conclusions Tell students that because Gavril Princip was only 19, he was sentenced to 20 years of hard labor instead of hanging for the killing of the archduke and his wife. After the trial, Princip said, "As far as suggestions are concerned that somebody talked us into committing the assassination, that is not true. The idea for the assassination grew among us (his co-conspirators and himself), and we realized it. We loved our people." **Ask: If Princip was telling the truth, what can you conclude about Austria-Hungary's decision to declare war on Serbia?** *(The Serbian government was not directly to blame for the assassination.)* **L2**

Completing a Graphic On the board, draw the following graphic:

Have students read the first paragraph under "March to War." Then tell them to briefly describe the steps that led to the war using each arrow to represent a step in the progression. *(Austria-Hungary blames the Serbian government for the archduke's death and declares war on Serbia* ➜ *Russia mobilizes its troops* ➜ *Germany declares war on Russia* ➜ *France and Britain enter the war* ➜✳*).* **L1**

More About the Art

The British enlisted Jack Russell terriers to hunt and destroy rats, a major problem in the trenches. Europeans used thousands of other dogs to locate wounded and to pull them to safety in two-wheeled carts. The dogs made smaller targets than horses and could negotiate the bomb craters more easily than motor vehicles.

Caption Answer: keeping them covered and hidden and allowing for them to move about safely

The War Begins

Main Idea The assassination of Archduke Franz Ferdinand sparked World War I.

Reading Focus Remember how the terrorist attack on 9/11 led to a war? The same thing happened in 1914. A single terrorist helped set off World War I.

The spark that finally set off a major war was lit in Sarajevo (SAR•uh•YAY•voh), a small town in Bosnia. There, in June 1914, a man named Gavrilo Princip shot and killed Archduke **Franz Ferdinand** (FRANZ FUHR•duhn•AND), heir to the throne of Austria-Hungary. Princip was a member of a secret nationalist group called the Black Hand. This group wanted the Bosnian Serbs, ruled by Austria-Hungary, to be ruled by Serbia.

Austria-Hungary blamed the Serbian government for the archduke's death. It declared war on Serbia. Russia, Serbia's ally, began **mobilization** (MOH•buh•luh•ZAY•shuhn), or assembly and movement of troops. By mobilizing, Russia showed that it was ready to go to war to protect Serbia. Germany then showed its support of Austria-Hungary by declaring war on Russia. Shortly after, France entered the war on the side of Russia. Germany's plan for attacking France required German troops to go through Belgium. Britain had promised to help Belgium stay neutral, so when Germany invaded Belgium, Britain declared war on Germany too.

When the war broke out in 1914, France, Russia, and Great Britain became known as the Allies. Later, in 1915, Italy joined them. Austria-Hungary, Germany, the Ottoman empire, and Bulgaria were known as the Central Powers.

Trenches of World War I

The more powerful, longer-range weapons of World War I led to the development of complex systems of trenches. Frontline troops lived in the trenches between attacks. Soldiers stationed in forward listening posts gave advance warning of enemy offensives. Attacks were made in "no-man's land": the open ground between the trenches. Shell craters and barbed wire slowed down attackers, leading to their slaughter by machine guns and artillery. Communications trenches allowed reserves to be brought up to the front lines safely. *How did the trenches help protect soldiers during battle?*

Forward Listening Post

Communications Trench

No Man's Land and Barbed Wire

Front-line Dugout

784

INTERDISCIPLINARY CONNECTIONS ACTIVITY

Technology Have students read the material under "A New Kind of War." Tell them that according to studies, many new weapons—long-range artillery, bombers, submarines, poison gas, and tanks—made killing easier for the average soldier. The reason? They put distance between the soldiers and the people they killed. Studies also found that at close range, as many as one in five soldiers did not fire their weapons because their natural aversion to killing was so strong. However, pilots and artillery operators had few qualms about firing weapons that killed people from 75 miles away or 20,000 feet in the air. **Ask:** Do you think the development of even longer-range weapons is a desirable goal? Why or why not? **L3**

No Quick Victory Much of the fighting in World War I took place on the Western Front, the battle zone between France and Germany. There, the French and the British stopped the German advance in September 1914. However, the battle line barely moved for three years.

Troops on both sides dug themselves into the ground in trenches protected by barbed wire. This kind of fighting is called trench warfare. To get at the enemy, soldiers on each side had to climb out of trenches and cross open land while machine guns and artillery—modern versions of cannons—fired at them. In major battles, several hundred thousand soldiers were killed or wounded.

A New Kind of War World War I, also called the Great War, was different from any earlier war. Both sides developed new, more powerful weapons to help them break through enemy lines. Machine guns fired bullets one after the other at a rapid speed. Huge artillery guns fired shells more than 75 miles (120 km). Poison gases were used for the first time, and tanks and flamethrowers were introduced. Newly developed submarines attacked ships at sea, while early versions of airplanes battled in the sky.

World War I was also the first war in which civilians, or people who are not soldiers, were important to winning the war. As the war dragged on, it became a total war. This means governments made use of all their resources and people. Total war affected the lives of all citizens, not just soldiers.

Supplies had to be made and bought for millions of soldiers. To do this, governments decided what civilians could buy and sell.

Analyzing Propaganda Tell students that as the war progressed and morale sagged, governments were forced to use new techniques to motivate people. In one British recruiting poster, for example, a small daughter asked her father, "Daddy, what did you do in the Great War?" while her younger brother played with toy soldiers. Point out that Great Britain did not have conscription. **Ask: What do you think the poster was supposed to motivate men to do?** *(enlist)* **What emotions did the government try to evoke with the poster?** *(Answers may include guilt, patriotism, and shame.)* **L3**

CURRICULUM CONNECTION

Health
Tell students that psychiatric casualties were common during WWI. The British made it a policy to give soldiers 4 days of rest after every 12 days of combat. As a result, many British soldiers served for months without symptoms of psychological damage. Some of the symptoms people did suffer were crying fits, fainting spells, hypersensitivity to sound, and violent shaking.

◄ Soldiers in trenches during a battle in World War I

Machine Gun Bunker

Artillery

Headquarters Dugout

785

EXTENDING THE CONTENT

How Did Women Participate in the War? World War I created new roles for women. Because so many men left to fight at the front, women were asked to take over jobs that had not been available to them before. These included such occupations as chimney sweeps, truck drivers, farm laborers, and factory workers in heavy industries. For example, 38 percent of the workers in the Krupp Armaments works in Germany in 1918 were women. However, both men and women seemed to expect that the new jobs for women were only temporary. This was evident in the British poem "War Girls," written in 1916 by Jessie Pope: "Strong, sensible, and fit, / They're out to show their grit, / And tackle jobs with energy and knack. / No longer caged and penned up, / They're going to keep their end up/ Till the khaki soldier boys come marching back."

Making Inferences Tell students that the *Lusitania* was carrying 1,248 cases of artillery shells, 4,927 boxes of 1,000 bullets each, and 2,000 more cases of ammunition for small guns. Although the British and American officials knew about the shipment, they stated that the *Lusitania* was merely a passenger liner and did not carry armaments. **Ask: Why do you think the American and British officials said this about the *Lusitania*'s cargo?** (*The governments wanted Americans outraged about the sinking so that they would oppose Germany and support U.S. aid to the Allies.*) **L2**

✓ Reading Check

Answer: trench warfare, machine guns, artillery, poison gas

Using Geography Skills

Answers:

1. the Central Powers

2. Norway, Sweden, Denmark, the Netherlands, Switzerland, Spain, Albania

Reading Support L1/ EL

Assign **Guided Reading Activity 20–3** to help students organize the information in the section.

They used **rationing**, or a system of limiting the amount of foods and materials in use. They controlled trade and took over industries and railroads.

Total war also led to government control of public opinion. Wartime governments used **propaganda** (PRAH•puh•GAN•duh), or biased government-controlled information, to shape what people thought about the war. The government also controlled what was printed in newspapers and sometimes even stopped their publication.

✓ **Reading Check** **Describe** Why did so many soldiers die in World War I?

America Enters the War

Main Idea Americans supported the Allies because of pro-British feelings and business links.

Reading Focus Have you ever had to choose sides in an argument? How do you decide who to support? Read to learn why America chose sides in World War I.

When World War I began, U.S. president **Woodrow Wilson** declared that the United States was not supporting either side. "We must be impartial [not involved] in thought as well as in action." Despite the president's plea, many Americans took sides.

NATIONAL GEOGRAPHIC
World War I *1914–1918*

KEY

- Allied Powers
- Central Powers
- Neutral nations
- German unrestricted submarine warfare zone
- ← Allied offensives
- ← Central Powers' offensives
- ✱ Allied victory
- ✱ Central Powers' victory

❶ Tannenberg Aug. 1914
❷ Battle of the Marne Sept. 1914
❸ Gallipoli Apr. 1915–Jan. 1916
❹ *Lusitania* sunk May 7, 1915
❺ Battle of the Somme July–Nov. 1916
❻ Caporetto Oct.–Dec. 1917
❼ Battle of the Argonne Sept.–Nov. 1918

500 mi.
500 km
Lambert Azimuthal Equal-Area projection

Using Geography Skills

Fighting in World War I occurred from France to Russia to the Middle East.

1. Which side was victorious at the Battle of Gallipoli?

2. Which countries remained neutral in World War I?

COOPERATIVE LEARNING ACTIVITY

Making a Circle Graph Explain that Wilson campaigned as the "peace" candidate and used the campaign slogan "He kept us out of war" in his reelection bid. Add that his strategy was a success. On the board, write the following election results for the presidential race in 1916:

Democratic Party, Woodrow Wilson	9,129,606
Republican Party, Charles Evans Hughes	8,538,221
Socialist Party, Allan Louis Benson	585,113
Prohibition Party, James Franklin Handy	220,506
Socialist Labor Party, Arthur Elmer Reimer	13,403

Organize students into pairs, and have each pair convert the facts on the board into a circle graph. **L3**

Submarine Warfare Many of Wilson's advisers backed Britain. They believed that an Allied victory was the only way to keep a balance of power in the world. American loans to Germany were limited. In contrast, American loans to the Allies skyrocketed. By 1917, the Allies owed American banks more than $2 billion.

In addition to loans, the Allies received food, equipment, and other supplies from the United States. The British imposed a **blockade** on Germany. That is, they used their warships to stop goods from leaving or entering German ports. To fight back, the

History Online
Web Activity Visit jat.glencoe.com and click on *Chapter 20—Student Web Activity* to learn more about World War I.

Germans began using the world's first oceangoing submarines. The Germans called them U-boats. In February 1915, the Germans warned that U-boats would sink any ship sailing the waters around Britain.

Despite the warning, the British passenger liner *Lusitania* entered the war zone. A German submarine fired on the ship, killing nearly 1,200 passengers—including 128 Americans. Many Americans were

History Online

Objectives and answers to the student activity can be found in the **Web Activity Lesson Plan** feature at jat.glencoe.com

③ ASSESS

Assign Section 3 Review as homework or as an in-class activity.

● Have students use the **Interactive Tutor Self-Assessment CD-ROM** to review the section.

Assessment L3

Assign **Section 3 Quiz** to assess mastery of the material found in the section.

Reading Support L1/ EL

Assign **Reading Essentials and Study Guide 20–3** to help students review section material.

Using Geography Skills

Answers:
1. Bellar Wood
2. Central Powers, Allies

NATIONAL GEOGRAPHIC
The Western Front

World War I Military Deaths*

Allies:
- Italy 650,000
- British Empire 908,400
- France 1,385,000
- Russia 1,700,000
- Romania 335,700
- United States 107,000
- Others 74,200

Central Powers:
- Bulgaria 87,500
- Ottoman Empire 325,000
- Austria-Hungary 1,200,000
- Germany 1,773,000

* Figures are approximate

Map labels:
- 0 50 mi.
- 0 50 km
- Albers Conic Equal-Area projection
- 4°E
- 52°N
- NETHERLANDS
- English Channel
- Ypres Oct.–Nov. 1914 Apr.–May 1915 July 1917
- Antwerp Sept. 1914
- Neuve Chapelle Mar. 1915
- BELGIUM
- GERMANY
- Rhine R.
- Somme R.
- Somme Offensive 1918
- Somme July–Nov. 1916
- LUX.
- Seine R.
- Aisne Offensive 1918
- Belleau Wood June 1918
- Argonne Forest Sept.–Nov. 1918
- Paris
- FRANCE
- Château–Thierry May 1918
- Battle of the Marne Sept. 1914
- 48°N
- 8°E

KEY
- ▨ Allied Powers
- ▨ Central Powers
- ▨ Neutral nations
- ✹ Allied victory
- ✹ Central Powers' victory
- ← Allied offensives
- ← Central Powers' offensives
- — Farthest advance of Central Powers
- --- Line of trench warfare, 1915–1917

787

Using Geography Skills

On the Western Front, trench warfare meant that the battle lines moved relatively little over the course of the war.
1. Which of the battles shown was fought closest to Paris?
2. Based on the map, which side experienced the most success early in the war? Late in the war?

EXTENDING THE CONTENT

Who Opposed American Entry into WWI? Fifty-six members of Congress voted against the nation's entrance into World War I, including Jeanette Rankin, the first woman in Congress. She was a U.S. representative from Montana—one of the few states that allowed women to vote. As a legislator, she sponsored bills to grant federal voting rights to women and to provide women with health care. Today she is remembered mainly for her strong pacifism. Actually, during the first roll call vote on the declaration for war, Rankin abstained. During the second roll call, however, she stood up and said: "I want to stand by my country, but I cannot vote for war. I vote No." Rankin was reelected to Congress in 1940 as an isolationist. She was the only member of Congress to vote against declaring war on Japan and entering World War II.

▲ **American soldiers helped turn the tide of the war against Germany.** *Why did the United States decide to enter World War I?*

outraged, but the U-boats kept sinking ships. By 1916, however, German leaders had grown worried that the United States might enter the war. They promised to give ships warning before sinking them, so people could get off safely.

United States Declares War In January 1917, a German official named Arthur Zimmermann cabled the German ambassador in Mexico. In the cable, Zimmermann proposed that Mexico ally itself with Germany if war broke out between Germany and the United States. In return, Mexico would regain "lost territory in Texas, New Mexico, and Arizona" after the war. The British intercepted the Zimmermann telegram and gave it to American newspapers. Outraged Americans began demanding war with Germany.

In February, German submarines began sinking ships again without warning. German leaders knew the attacks might draw the United States into the war. However, they did not believe that Americans could mobilize quickly enough to save the Allies. Between February 3 and March 21, U-boats sank six American merchant ships without warning. On April 6, 1917, President Wilson asked Congress to declare war on Germany.

✓ **Reading Check** **Explain** Why did the United States favor Britain over Germany in World War I?

History Online
Study Central™ Need help with the material in this section? Visit jat.glencoe.com

Section 3 Review

Reading Summary
Review the Main Ideas
- In the early 1900s, nations of Europe formed alliances and built up their military forces.
- The assassination of an Austro-Hungarian archduke led to declarations of war across Europe.
- German submarine attacks against American ships eventually brought the United States into the war on the side of the Allies.

What Did You Learn?
1. What happened in Sarajevo in 1914, and why was it important?
2. Name three things that led to World War I.

Critical Thinking
3. **Organizing Information** Use a chart like the one below to list the countries that fought in World War I.

Allies	
Central Powers	

4. **Explain** What is militarism and what problems did it cause in Europe?

5. **Cause and Effect** Why did the soldiers decide to use trench warfare?
6. **Analyze** Why was World War I a "total war"?
7. **Expository Writing** Write a headline and a brief article about the U.S. entry into World War I. Discuss the reasons why the United States finally entered the war.

788   CHAPTER 20   Imperialism and World War I

Section 4

World War I Changes the World

Get Ready to Read!

What's the Connection?
As you read, by 1917 neither side was gaining ground in World War I. The arrival of American troops would mark a turning point in the war.

Focusing on the Main Ideas
- With American help, the Allies stopped the German advance. *(page 790)*
- The Bolsheviks rose to power as a result of the czar's poor leadership. *(page 793)*

Locating Places
Argonne Forest
Versailles (vuhr•SY)

Meeting People
David Lloyd George
Georges Clemenceau (zhawrzh KLEH•muhn•SOH)
Vittorio Orlando (veet•TAWR•yoh awr•LAN•doh)

Atatürk (AT•uh•TUHRK)
Vladimir Lenin (VLAD•uh•MIHR LEH•nuhn)

Building Your Vocabulary
armistice (AHR•muh•stuhs)
reparation (REH•puh•RAY•shuhn)
mandate (MAN•DAYT)
duma (DOO•muh)
soviet (SOH•vee•EHT)

Reading Strategy
Organizing Information Use a diagram like the one below to show the new territories created from the Ottoman empire.

Ottoman Empire

When & Where?

NATIONAL GEOGRAPHIC

BRITAIN
GERMANY
Berlin
FRANCE
ITALY
SOVIET UNION
TURKEY

| 1916 | 1920 | 1924 |

1917 Lenin seizes power in Russia

1918 World War I ends

1921 Communists win Russian Civil War

1923 Turkey becomes a republic

CHAPTER 20   Imperialism and World War I   789

SECTION RESOURCES

Reproducible Masters
- Reproducible Lesson Plan 20–4
- Daily Lecture and Discussion Notes 20–4
- Vocabulary Activity 20–4
- Active Reading Note-Taking Guide 20–4
- Guided Reading Activity 20–4
- Section Quiz 20–4
- Reading Essentials and Study Guide 20–4

Transparencies
- Daily Focus Skills Transparency 20–4

Multimedia
- Interactive Tutor Self-Assessment CD-ROM
- ExamView® Pro Testmaker CD-ROM
- Presentation Plus! CD-ROM
- Vocabulary PuzzleMaker CD-ROM
- Glencoe BookLink CD-ROM

① FOCUS

SECTION OVERVIEW
The section sums up the last years of the war, the results of the peace negotiations, and the events of the Russian Revolution.

BELLRINGER
SKILLBUILDER ACTIVITY

Project **Daily Focus Skills Transparency 20–4** and have students answer questions. Discuss their responses.

Get Ready to Read!

Preteaching Vocabulary: Tell students that the word *armistice* means "a cease-fire." The fact that an armistice ended the war suggests that neither side won a decisive victory. Germany signed an armistice because of chaos at home and only indirectly because of losses on the battlefield.

Answers to Graphic: Serbs, Croats, Slovenes

② TEACH

Reading Strategy

Questioning As students read "The War Ends," tell them to list events and ask themselves "How did this event help end the war?" Instruct them to write their answers next to the items on their list. After they finish reading, have pairs of students compare answers. **L1**

Daily Lecture and Discussion Notes 20–4

Use **Daily Lecture and Discussion Notes 20–4** for an outline of key concepts found in the section.

Reading Support L1/ EL

Use **Vocabulary Activity 20–4** to review important terms in the section.

Using Geography Skills

Answers:

1. Austria-Hungary, Montenegro, Serbia
2. Germany, Austria-Hungary

The War Ends

Main Idea With American help, the Allies stopped the German advance.

Reading Focus Have you ever heard the expression "the cavalry to the rescue"? As you read, decide which group represented the cavalry during World War I.

In late 1917, troopships carried wave after wave of American soldiers to Europe. Allied hopes soared. They would soon get the help they needed to win the war.

In November 1917, the Russians pulled out of the war. German troops on the Eastern Front were sent west. There, they strengthened Germany's army as it advanced toward Paris in 1918. On June 1, American and French troops blocked the advance at the town of Château-Thierry. Four months later, Americans launched their own massive attack in the Battle of the **Argonne Forest.** The Americans suffered major losses but shattered the German defenses.

Meanwhile, the Austro-Hungarian Empire was in chaos, and the Ottoman Turks surrendered. Faced with a mutiny in the navy and a popular revolt in Berlin, the German emperor stepped down. On November 11, 1918, Germany signed an **armistice** (AHR•muh•stuhs), or cease-fire, that ended the war.

NATIONAL GEOGRAPHIC **Europe After World War I**

Using Geography Skills

The treaties that ended World War I changed the map of Europe.

1. Use the map of Europe in 1914 on page 781 and name the countries that gave up territory to create the new country of Yugoslavia.
2. Which countries appear to have lost the most land following the war?

790

Reading Strategy ▶ READING THE TEXT

Synonyms Remind students that synonyms are words that have similar meanings. Point out to students that synonyms can be helpful when summarizing information. Organize the class into pairs, and have each pair of students divide the reading on the first page of the section between them. Instruct them to write all the common nouns in their half of the reading on a sheet of paper. Then tell them to exchange papers, to think of one or more synonyms for each noun, and to write their answers next to the original words from the reading. Have students exchange papers a second time. Then challenge them to add even more synonyms to the ones their partner wrote. Finally, have the pairs rewrite the page using synonyms from their papers. **L2**

The Treaty of Versailles In January 1919, peace talks began at **Versailles** (vuhr•SY) outside Paris. The principal figures at the talks were U.S. president Woodrow Wilson, British prime minister **David Lloyd George**, French premier **Georges Clemenceau** (zhawrzh KLEH•muhn•SOH), and Italian prime minister **Vittorio Orlando** (veet• TAWR•yoh awr•LAN•doh).

Wilson presented a plan called the Fourteen Points. The plan stated that national groups in Europe should form their own countries. It also called for a League of Nations, an organization in which member nations would cooperate to keep the peace.

The Treaty of Versailles stripped Germany of most of its armed forces and required the Germans to pay **reparations** (REH•puh•RAY•shuhnz), or war damages, of $33 billion to the Allies. The treaty also called for the creation of a League of Nations.

President Wilson returned to the United States to win approval for the treaty. Some senators argued that the League might force the United States to fight in more foreign wars. Twice the Senate voted on the treaty and twice rejected it. As a result, the League of Nations was formed without the United States.

New Nations in Europe The war and the treaties that followed redrew the map of Europe. Both the German and Russian empires lost territory in southeastern Europe. The Austro-Hungarian Empire disappeared completely.

The lands from these three empires became nation-states: Finland, Latvia, Estonia, Poland, Lithuania, Czechoslovakia, Austria, and Hungary. In addition, Romania gained territory from Russia, Hungary, and Bulgaria. Serbia became the center of a new state called Yugoslavia, which combined Serbs, Croats, and Slovenes.

▲ The four most important leaders at the Versailles conference were (left to right) Vittorio Orlando, David Lloyd George, Georges Clemenceau, and Woodrow Wilson. *How did the peace terms at Versailles affect Germany?*

The idea that peoples had a right to rule themselves shaped many of the decisions at the peace talks. However, different groups in Eastern Europe were mixed together. The treaties were not able to draw national borders neatly so that all people of a single ethnic group could be within one country. As a result, almost every new Eastern European country had a dominant group and many smaller groups. As time went on, friction between the different groups made these countries very unstable.

What Happened to the Ottoman Empire?

In making peace, the Allies also looked at the Middle East. Their major concern was what to do with the Ottoman empire, which had been defeated along with the other Central Powers.

The Allies decided to break up the Ottoman empire. The only area left to the Ottomans was the area of present-day Turkey. In 1919 Greece invaded Turkey and seized the western parts of the Anatolian Peninsula. In response, Turkish general Mustafa Kemal rallied forces to his country's defense. Turkish armies under Kemal finally drove out the Greeks. The Turkish victory led to the end of the Ottoman sultan's rule. In 1923 Turkey became a republic.

CHAPTER 20   Imperialism and World War I   791

Writing Activity

Distribute copies of the following passage from the Espionage Act passed by the U.S. Congress in June 1917: "Whoever, when the United States is at war, shall willfully cause or attempt to cause insubordination, disloyalty, mutiny, or refusal of duty in the military or naval forces of the United States, or shall willfully obstruct the recruiting or enlistment service of the U.S. . . ." will be subject to penalties of up to 20 years in prison. Tell students to rewrite the passage in their own words and to write their opinion of the Espionage Act. **L2**

Caption Answer:
Germany was stripped of its armed forces and forced to pay $3 billion in reparations.

 CURRICULUM CONNECTION

Music
Tell students that Americans produced rousing World War I songs, such as "Over There," "It's a Grand Old Flag," and "Johnny Get Your Gun," and at least one antiwar song, "I Didn't Raise My Boy to Be a Soldier." Ask volunteers to find the words and music to one or more of these songs and teach it to the class.

DIFFERENTIATED INSTRUCTION

Logical/Mathematical: On the board, list the number of war dead from the following countries: Germany, 1,773,000; Austria-Hungary, 1,200,000; Russia, 1,700,0000; France, 1,385,000; British Empire, 908,000; United States, 116,000. Have students convert the numbers into bar graphs that compare the countries' losses.

English Learners: Distribute bar graphs based on the figures on the board, but omit the labels. Tell students to label each bar with the correct country.

Gifted and Talented: Have students research the total number of casualties from the countries on the board and make two-color bar graphs that compare casualties to deaths.

📁 Refer to *Inclusion Strategies for the Middle School Social Studies Classroom* in the TCR.

Chapter 20 Section 4, 789–796

TIME TRAVELER

Atatürk was born in 1881 and named Mustafa. His father, Ali Riza, had served in the Russo-Turkish War of 1877–1878. He hung his sword over Mustafa's cradle as a sign that he was dedicating his son to military service. Against his mother's wishes, Mustafa followed his father's dream and chose to go to military school. There his classmates nicknamed him Kemal, which means "the perfect one."

CONNECTING ACROSS TIME

Ask volunteers to research Yugoslavia to make a time line showing major events in the region from 1918 to the present—after the country broke apart. **L2**

✓ Reading Check

Answer: Some senators feared the league might force the U.S. to fight in foreign wars.

NATIONAL GEOGRAPHIC

Middle East 1919–1935

KEY
🛢 Oil-producing areas

Using Geography Skills

Following World War I, the Ottoman empire was divided into a number of countries in the Middle East.

1. Where are the oil-producing areas in the Middle East generally found?
2. Which European nation ruled the largest area of mandated territory in the Middle East? Which countries did it rule?

These new territories were called **mandates** (MAN•DAYTZ). Under the mandate system, the League of Nations governed each territory but allowed a member nation to run it. Because these mandated territories were largely created by outsiders, most people in the Middle East did not feel loyal to them. The Arabs did, however, share a strong sense of Arab nationalism.

In the 1920s, a local leader named Ibn Saud united Arabs on the Arabian Peninsula. In 1932 he created the kingdom of Saudi Arabia. At first the new country was desperately poor. Then American businesses struck oil at Dhahran on the Persian Gulf and the kingdom grew wealthy.

Meanwhile, in Palestine—a mandate run by the British—nationalism caused new problems. In the late 1800s, nationalism began to affect Jews living in Europe. Jewish nationalists, known as Zionists, wanted to create a Jewish homeland in Palestine where the ancient Jewish city of Jerusalem was located. Zionist settlers began moving to the Middle East in the 1890s. During World War I Britain issued the Balfour Declaration promising Jews a nation in Palestine. Angry Arabs wondered how the Jews could establish a national home where the people were 80 percent Muslim. However, by 1939, more than 400,000 Jews lived in Palestine. To satisfy the Arabs, the British tried to limit the flow of Jewish settlers into the territory.

✓ Reading Check **Analyze** Why did the United States not join the League of Nations?

Kemal, whom the people called **Atatürk** (AT•uh•TUHRK), became president of Turkey. Atatürk introduced many social and political changes to modernize the country. Turkey began to consider itself European as well as Asian. For example, all Arabic features were erased from the Turkish language, and Turkish citizens had to adopt last names, like Europeans. Atatürk also tried to reduce the influence of Islamic religious leaders on the government.

New Countries in the Middle East
After the war, the Allies divided up the Arab regions of the Ottoman empire. France took control of Lebanon and Syria. Britain acquired Iraq, Jordan, and Palestine.

792 CHAPTER 20 Imperialism and World War I

CRITICAL THINKING ACTIVITY

Identifying Central Issues Explain that in the late 1800s and early 1900s, Jews in Germany, Austria-Hungary, and Eastern Europe received harsh treatment. For example, in Russia the government forced them to live in special regions and executed pogroms, or organized massacres of Jews. Hundreds of thousands of Jews emigrated from the region—some to the United States and other countries, and some to Palestine. For many Jews, Palestine, the land of ancient Israel, had long been the land of their dreams. **Ask:** What was a major challenge with making Palestine the new home of the Jews? *(Arab Palestinians already lived there.)* Lead students in a discussion of issues that Arabs might have worried about as increasing numbers of European Jews moved into their desert country. **L2**

The Russian Revolution

Main Idea The Bolsheviks rose to power as a result of the czar's poor leadership.

Reading Focus Have you ever seen a protest march? Do you think protest can change things? Read to learn how protests led to a revolution in Russia.

During World War I, Russia fought alongside Britain and France. However, the war only worsened Russia's problems at home. Russia's ruler, Czar Nicholas II, was unable to solve these problems. His rigid rule no longer fit the times. As a result, the Russian people turned against him when he failed to meet Russia's new challenges.

Problems in Russia During the early 1900s, most Russians were very discontent. Peasants paid high taxes. Groups that were not Russian were often mistreated, and middle-class reformers wanted a voice in the government. Urban workers were perhaps the most dissatisfied. They toiled long hours in dirty, airless factories and received little pay.

In 1904 a war between Russia and Japan made matters worse. The war cost Russia land and money. As a result, food prices went up and wages went down. Peasants, urban workers, and middle-class students blamed the czar for the poor economy.

In 1905 an uprising took place. It began when thousands of workers appeared in the square before the czar's palace in St. Petersburg. They carried petitions asking for a national assembly, freedom of speech and religion, and better conditions for workers and peasants. Government soldiers fired on the crowd, killing hundreds of unarmed people. Workers in the city responded by going on strike. Finally, Czar Nicholas II agreed to some of the workers' demands. A **duma** (DOO•muh), or national

▲ This 1913 photo shows Czar Nicholas II and his family, all of whom were killed during the revolution. *How did World War I help cause the Russian Revolution?*

assembly, was created, but it had only limited powers. The czar, however, closed down the duma when it tried to act independently.

The Czar Is Overthrown World War I brought still more hardships to the Russian people. The country did not have enough factories to produce weapons or enough railroads to carry supplies to the front. As a result, Russia suffered higher casualties than any other country. Nearly 8 million soldiers were killed or wounded in battle. Civilians suffered from a lack of food and fuel.

The Russian people could stand no more. In March 1917, they revolted. Striking workers, led by women textile workers, jammed the streets of St. Petersburg. They demanded bread and peace. The workers were soon joined by soldiers stationed in the city. Finally, the czar gave up his throne, and the 300-year-old Romanov dynasty came to an end.

CHAPTER 20   Imperialism and World War I   793

INTERDISCIPLINARY CONNECTIONS ACTIVITY

Literature Share the following summary about Alexis and Rasputin with your students: "The czar's son, Alexis, was born in 1904. He seemed healthy until at six weeks of age he started bleeding. His parents discovered that he had hemophilia—a deficiency in the ability of the blood to clot. In 1905 Czarina Alexandra met a monk named Grigori Rasputin who claimed to be a holy man. Rasputin turned out to be the only person who could stop Alexis's bleeding. By the time World War I started, Alexandra was consulting Rasputin on all of her important decisions, including decisions of state, which she made when Nicholas was at the battlefront. Unfortunately, Rasputin abused her trust to gain power and money." Have students find and read books, particularly fiction, written on the topic of the Romanovs and Rasputin. **L2**

Primary Source
Ten Days That Shook the World

John Reed was an American journalist who witnessed the Russian Revolution. The events described in this passage took place on November 8, 1917.

"It was just 8:40 when a thundering wave of cheers announced the entrance of the presidium [committee], with Lenin—great Lenin—among them. . . .

Now Lenin, . . . stood there waiting, apparently oblivious to the long-rolling ovation, which lasted several minutes. When it finished, he said simply, 'We shall now proceed to construct the Socialist order!' Again that overwhelming human roar. . . .

▲ John Reed

'The revolution of 6 and 7 November,' he ended, 'has opened the era of the Social Revolution. . . . The labour movement, in the name of peace and Socialism, shall win, and fulfil its destiny. . . .'"

—John Reed, *Ten Days That Shook the World*

DBQ Document-Based Question

Does John Reed agree or disagree with Lenin? How do you know?

Members of the duma then formed a provisional, or temporary, government. Alexander Kerensky served as its leader. Despite the suffering caused by the war, the provisional government did not withdraw Russian troops from the front. In fact, the provisional government became preoccupied with the war. As a result, it did not carry out reforms at home and lost the support of the people.

Who Is Lenin? Many workers, soldiers, and peasants believed that the provisional government was too middle class. They formed **soviets** (SOH • vee • EHTS), or committees, to represent their interests. Soon the soviets and the provisional government became locked in a bitter struggle for control of Russia.

Members of the soviets were workers and peasants from different socialist groups. As you read in earlier chapters, socialists wanted workers to overthrow capitalism and build a society in which all could share equally in the wealth. The most radical of these groups was the Bolsheviks. They believed that a small party of revolutionaries could use force to bring about this ideal society. Their leader was **Vladimir Lenin** (VLAD • uh • MIHR   LEH • nuhn).

Under Lenin, the Bolsheviks promised to take Russia out of the war and to give all land to the peasants. They vowed to give the factories to the workers and the government to the soviets. Three slogans summed up the Bolshevik program: "Peace, Land, Bread," "Worker Control of Production," and "All Power to the Soviets."

The Bolsheviks Seize Power In October 1917, Bolsheviks controlled the soviets in Russia's two largest cities: St. Petersburg and Moscow. As a result, the Bolsheviks were in a good position to take over Russia's government.

In November 1917, the Bolsheviks seized the Winter Palace in St. Petersburg. This was the location of the provisional government. The government collapsed with little bloodshed. Lenin became the head of the new government.

EXTENDING THE CONTENT

What Was the Great Flu Epidemic? In 1918 a flu epidemic struck that would prove disastrous to people around the world. Some observers believe that the epidemic began among American soldiers in Kansas. When they went to Europe to fight, they carried the virus with them. The disease spread quickly through Europe. Woodrow Wilson, Lloyd George, and Georges Clemenceau were all sick with the flu while negotiating the Versailles Treaty. Luckily, they survived their bouts. Others were not so lucky. In 1918 and 1919, the flu claimed 450,000 lives in Russia, 5 million lives in India, and 550,000 lives in the United States. All together about 22 million people worldwide died from the flu epidemic.

Biography

VLADIMIR LENIN
1870–1924

Vladimir Lenin ▶

Vladimir Lenin, the founder of the Bolshevik Party and the first leader of the Soviet Union, grew up as Vladimir Ilyich Ulyanov in a happy, close-knit family. Ulyanov developed a great passion for learning early in his childhood. Both of his parents were educated. His father was a teacher and school inspector. His mother was the daughter of a landowning physician.

In school, young Ulyanov excelled in his studies, particularly in Latin and Greek. He graduated first in his class from high school and seemed destined to become a scholar. However, two tragic events affected the direction of his life. First, in 1886, his father suddenly died from a brain hemorrhage. Then, the next year, his oldest brother, Alexander, was hanged for involvement with a revolutionary group. Because of his brother's revolutionary activities, Ulyanov was denied many academic opportunities. In response, he renounced religion and Russia's political system. In January 1889, he became a Marxist.

Ulyanov's high school principal helped him get into law school, and he graduated in 1891, once again first in his class. Two years later, he moved to St. Petersburg, where he worked as a lawyer and developed an underground Marxist movement. Ulyanov became more involved in revolutionary propaganda efforts, and in 1895 he was arrested and exiled to Siberia for three years.

After exile, Ulyanov and his wife moved to Munich, Germany, where they published a newspaper that attempted to unite Marxist groups throughout the world. In 1901 Ulyanov adopted the pseudonym "Lenin"—a reference to Russia's Lena River, which is longer than the mighty Volga and flows in the opposite direction.

> **"We shall now proceed to construct the Socialist order!"**
>
> –Vladimir Lenin, as quoted in *Ten Days That Shook the World*

◀ Parade in Moscow honoring Marx, Engels, and Lenin in 1988

Then and Now

Lenin was arrested and sent to Siberia for three years for his protests. Do research to find an example of a modern political or social leader who has been exiled for his or her political beliefs.

795

TEACH

After hearing the news of the revolution in 1917, Lenin wanted to return to Russia from Germany. Since Germany wanted Russia out of the war and knew that Lenin supported the withdrawal of troops, the Germans sent him to Russia on a special train. Upon reaching Russia, Lenin set out to organize the Bolsheviks and seize power from the provisional government.

Ask students to interpret the following quote by Lenin: "Every cook must learn to govern the state." (*Every single person should be interested in government and take part in its process. That way, everyone would be equal to the task of being in charge, if necessary. Also, everyone in his country, in theory, should have a role in how government works.*) **L3**

Then and Now

Student responses will vary, but research should include who the leader was, where he or she is from, and the beliefs that caused the exile.

Caption Answer: They were disorganized, outnumbered, and poorly equipped.

ENRICH

Quote Trotsky: "The dictatorship of the Communist Party is maintained by recourse to every form of violence." Then tell students to find passages in the section that support his statement. **L1**

✓ **Reading Check**

Answer: It became preoccupied with the war and failed to carry out domestic reforms.

History Online

To help students understand section material, have them visit **Study Central™** at jat.glencoe.com

RETEACH

Ask students to list the various conflicts discussed in the section. **L2**

④ CLOSE

Have each student name an interesting historical figure from the section and explain why that person is significant. **L2**

◀ Leon Trotsky used the draft to fill the Red Army and created a strong military force based on strict discipline. *Why did the Whites eventually lose the Civil War?*

The Russian Civil War Soon after, Lenin signed a peace treaty with Germany. A price was attached, however. In exchange for peace, the Bolsheviks had to give up large areas of land that had once been part of Russia's empire. Although the treaty ended Russia's involvement in World War I, it did not solve Russia's troubles at home.

Several groups—the czar's supporters, liberals, and moderate socialists—opposed Lenin's government. In 1918 these groups took up arms against the Bolsheviks—now known as Communists. In the war that followed, the Communists were called Reds because they flew a red revolutionary flag. Leon Trotsky organized the Red Army. He used force and education to make his soldiers loyal to the Communist cause.

The Communists' enemies became known as Whites. They promised to defeat the Reds quickly and get Russia back into World War I. As a result, the Allies and the United States sent them aid.

The Reds and Whites fought for three grim years. Both sides burned villages and killed civilians. Meanwhile, workers and peasants were starving. The Whites were disorganized, outnumbered, and poorly equipped. In 1921 they finally gave up. Lenin and the Communists now controlled the entire country.

✓ **Reading Check** **Identify** Why did the provisional government lose support?

History Online

Study Central™ Need help with the material in this section? Visit jat.glencoe.com

Section ④ Review

Reading Summary

Review the Main Ideas

- With American help, the Germans were defeated, ending the war. A number of new nations in Europe and the Middle East were created following the war.

- In Russia, the czar was overthrown, and the Bolsheviks, or Communists, took power.

What Did You Learn?

1. What were the Fourteen Points and why were they important?

2. What changes did Atatürk make after becoming president of Turkey?

Critical Thinking

3. **Organizing Information** Draw a diagram similar to the one below. In the outer ovals, fill in the names of new countries created after World War I.

New Nations

4. **Analyze** Were the attempts to create countries along ethnic lines following World War I successful? Why or why not?

5. **Sequencing Information** Describe the major events leading to the fall of the Russian czar.

6. **Analyze** How were Lenin and the Bolsheviks able to come to power in Russia?

7. **Writing Questions** Imagine you are a reporter in the era of World War I. Write a series of four or five questions that you would like to ask the leaders of Europe. Include possible answers to your questions.

SECTION 4 REVIEW ANSWERS

1. Wilson's plan for peace; to form a League of Nations

2. He erased Arabic features from the language, made Turks adopt last names, and rid government of Islamic influences.

3. Finland, Latvia, Estonia, Lithuania, Poland, Czechoslovakia, Austria, Hungary, Yugoslavia

4. The mix of peoples and Allied interests made countries of one ethnicity impossible.

5. Answers should be based on facts from the section.

6. Lenin and the Bolsheviks promised the people they would end the war and start reforms. They seized power from the provisional government.

7. Questions should reflect an understanding of the section.

Section 1 The New Imperialism

Vocabulary
imperialism
colony
protectorate
sphere of influence
sepoy

Focusing on the Main Ideas
- European nations built empires to help their economy and to spread their ideas. *(page 763)*
- Control of India passed from the East India Company to the British. *(page 764)*
- European nations ruled almost all of Africa by 1914. *(page 766)*
- The United States became an imperial nation after defeating Spain and taking control of the Philippines and Puerto Rico. *(page 769)*

Section 2 Nationalism in China and Japan

Vocabulary
extraterritoriality
daimyo

Focusing on the Main Ideas
- The arrival of Europeans greatly changed Chinese society. *(page 772)*
- Sun Yat-sen introduced ideas that helped cause the collapse of the Qing dynasty. *(page 774)*
- After Americans visited Japan, the Japanese reorganized their society and economy and began building an empire. *(page 777)*

Section 3 World War I Begins

Vocabulary
militarism
conscription
entente
mobilization
rationing
propaganda
blockade

Focusing on the Main Ideas
- Alliances, militarism, and nationalism led to a crisis in Europe. *(page 781)*
- The assassination of Archduke Franz Ferdinand sparked World War I. *(page 784)*
- Americans supported the Allies because of pro-British feelings and business links. *(page 786)*

Section 4 World War I Changes the World

Vocabulary
armistice
reparation
mandate
duma
soviet

Focusing on the Main Ideas
- With American help, the Allies stopped the German advance. *(page 790)*
- The Bolsheviks rose to power as a result of the czar's poor leadership. *(page 793)*

CHAPTER 20   Imperialism and World War I   797

PREVIEW/REVIEW

Vocabulary Activity Have students write synonyms or antonyms for as many vocabulary words as possible.

◉ **Vocabulary PuzzleMaker CD-ROM**

◉ **Interactive Tutor Self-Assessment CD-ROM**

CONDENSE

📁 Chapter 20 **Guided Reading Activities**

◉ **Student Works Plus™ CD-ROM** (with Audio Program)

RETEACH

📁 **Differentiated Instruction Activity 20**

📁 Chapter 20 *Reading Essentials and Study Guide*

CHAPTER CULMINATING ACTIVITY

Have students finish the Chapter Culminating Activity from page 758D.

Suggestions for rubrics may be found in the *Quizzes, Tests, and Authentic Assessments (with Rubrics)* booklet.

Reading Strategy   READ TO WRITE

Analyzing Cause-and-Effect Relationships Have students describe at least three cause-and-effect relationships that led to World War I. Tell them to skim the chapter for facts and to use a graphic with arrows to help separate the causes from the effects. Use the following rubric for assessment:

- **L1** students should describe at least three cause-and-effect relationships.
- **L2** students should answer the questions *What happened?* and *Why?*
- **L3** students should show logical and clear relationships.

GLENCOE TECHNOLOGY

MindJogger Videoquiz

Use the **MindJogger Videoquiz** to review Chapter 20 content.

Available in DVD and VHS

Review Vocabulary

1. g   **5.** b
2. a   **6.** f
3. d   **7.** e
4. c   **8.** h

Review Main Ideas

9. The nations wanted to control raw materials and markets, to add to their country's power, and to help Asians and Africans by imposing Western ways.

10. to spread Christianity and to improve and control trade

11. Europeans and other Westerners broke China up into spheres of influence for trade. The government began reforms to modernize China.

12. Sun wanted to form a strong government to get out from under foreign control. His followers staged an uprising, causing the Qing dynasty to fall.

13. alliances, militarism, and trouble in the Balkans

14. pro-British feelings and business links

15. The Allies stopped the advance with American help.

16. The Bolsheviks rose to power because they promised to get out of World War I and initiate domestic reforms in Russia.

Review Vocabulary

Write the vocabulary word that completes each sentence.

    a. soviets   e. reparations
    b. conscription   f. colony
    c. armistice   g. daimyo
    d. protectorate   h. entente

1. Heads of noble families in Japanese society were called ___.

2. Russian workers formed ___ to voice their concerns.

3. The government of a(n) ___ is guided by a foreign power.

4. A cease-fire is also called a(n) ___.

5. ___ requires citizens to join the military.

6. A(n) ___ was directly ruled by an imperial nation.

7. Germany paid war damages, or ___, to the Allies.

8. An understanding among nations is called a(n) ___.

Review Main Ideas

Section 1 • The New Imperialism

9. Why did European nations establish empires?

10. Why were European nations interested in Africa?

Section 2 • Nationalism in China and Japan

11. How did the arrival of the Europeans change Chinese society?

12. How did Sun Yat-sen's ideas lead to the collapse of the Qing dynasty?

Section 3 • World War I Begins

13. Explain the causes of World War I.

14. Why did Americans support the Allies?

Section 4 • World War I Changes the World

15. What resulted from the German advance on the Allies?

16. Why were the Bolsheviks able to rise to power in Russia?

Review
Reading Skill | **Prioritizing**

What's Important?

Read the passage below from page 784.

> The spark that finally set off a major war was lit in Sarajevo, a small town in Bosnia. There, in June 1914, a man named Gavrilo Princip shot and killed Archduke Franz Ferdinand, heir to the throne of Austria-Hungary.

17. If you had to answer the question "What event started World War I?", which information in this passage would be most important?

18. If you had to answer the question "When did the war begin?", which information would be most important?

To review this skill, see pages 760–761.

798   CHAPTER 20   Imperialism and World War I

Reading Skill

17. The assassination of Archduke Ferdinand

18. the sentence that includes the date of the assassination—1914

Critical Thinking

19. The Boer War began when the British started prospecting for gold and diamonds in the Boers' territory.

20. Answers will vary, but they should be supported by logical arguments.

21. Austria-Hungary blamed Serbia for the assassination and declared war on Serbia. Russia mobilized to defend Serbia, and Germany declared war on Russia. Germany also made plans to invade France, so Great Britain declared war on Germany.

Critical Thinking

19. **Cause and Effect** What caused the Boer War?

20. **Analyze** Instead of importing opium to China, what else might the British have done to restore the balance of trade?

21. **Explain** How did the assassination of Ferdinand lead to war?

22. **Analyze** Do you think the Treaty of Versailles asked too much of Germany? Why or why not?

Geography Skills

Study the map below and answer the following questions.

23. **Place** Which nation in the Middle East remained neutral during World War I?

24. **Movement** Why were Allied troops moving into the Ottoman empire?

25. **Analyze** Which group won most of the battles fought in the Ottoman empire?

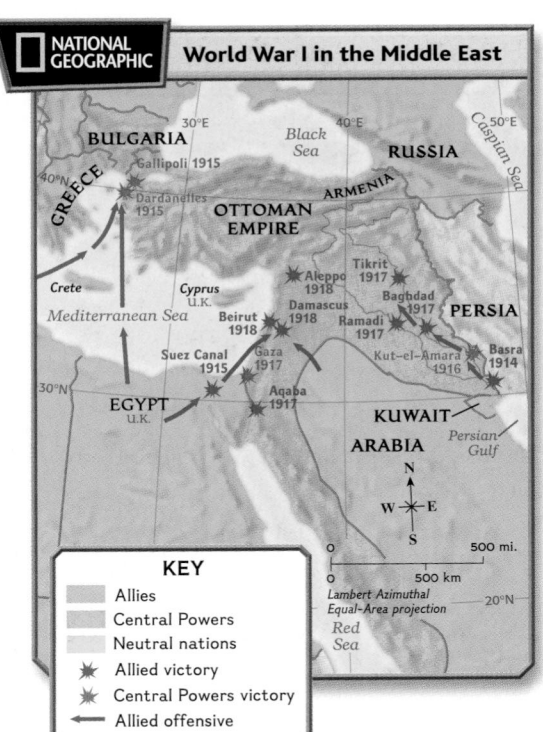

NATIONAL GEOGRAPHIC **World War I in the Middle East**

KEY
- Allies
- Central Powers
- Neutral nations
- ★ Allied victory
- ★ Central Powers victory
- → Allied offensive

Read to Write

26. **Expository Writing** Write a brief essay comparing and contrasting the causes of the revolutions in America, France, and Russia.

27. **Using Your FOLDABLES** Create a crossword puzzle using the terms on your foldable. Use the terms' definitions as the crossword clues. Be sure to provide an answer key.

Using Technology

28. **Researching** Use the Internet and your local library to research the total costs of World War I. On a computer, create a table or graph that shows the costs and number of deaths during the war.

Linking Past and Present

29. **Expository Writing** Choose one nation in Africa and research its history from the colonial era to the present. Write a short essay about your chosen country's history.

Primary Source Analyze

Journalist Henry Stanley located explorer and missionary David Livingstone in Africa in 1871:

"We have at last entered the town. There are hundreds of people around me. . . . It is a grand triumphal procession. . . .

. . . [A]s I come nearer I see the white face of an old man among them. . . . I am shaking hands with him. We raise our hats, and I say:

'Dr. Livingstone, I presume?'"

—H.M. Stanley, "Stanley Finds Livingstone, 10 November 1871"

DBQ Document-Based Question

Why do you think the Africans held a "grand triumphal procession" for Mr. Stanley?

CHAPTER 20   Imperialism and World War I   **799**

History Online
Have students visit the Web site at jat.glencoe.com to review Chapter 20 and take the Self-Check Quiz.

Using Technology

28. Tables should be based on students' research.

Linking Past and Present

29. Essays will vary but should be based on students' research.

Primary Source

30. Answers will vary. Students may say that the procession indicates that the Africans respect Dr. Livingstone and his acquaintances.

Bonus Question

Ask: Many well-intentioned persons tried to help others in the late 1800s and early 1900s. Which person discussed in the chapter do you think succeeded in making other people's lives better? Why do you think so? (Students should include supporting details for their choice.)

22. Answers will vary but should be supported by facts and logical arguments.

Geography Skills

23. Persia

24. The Ottoman Empire was part of the Central Powers.

25. Allies

Read to Write

26. Essays will vary but should include facts from the chapter.

27. **FOLDABLES** Students' foldables should be complete and focus on the accuracy of their definitions.

Note: The following materials may be used when teaching Chapter 21.
Section level support materials are shown at point of use in the margins of the Teacher Wraparound Edition.

TEACHING TRANSPARENCIES

- Graphic Organizer Transparencies with Teaching Strategy and Student Activity **L2**
- Cause-and-Effect Transparencies with Teaching Strategy and Student Activity **L2**
- Then and Now Transparencies with Teaching Strategy and Student Activity **L2**
- Chapter 21 In-text Map Transparency with Teaching Strategy and Student Activity **L1**
- Map Transparecies with Overlay, Teaching Strategy, and Student Activity **L2**

DIFFERENTIATED INSTRUCTION

- Differentiated Instruction Activity 21
- Time Line Activity 21
- Primary Source Reading 21 (with Document-Based Questions)
- Inclusion Strategies for the Middle School Social Studies Classroom
- StudentWorks Plus™ CD-ROM (with Audio Program)

READING SUPPORT

- Take-Home Review Activity 21 **L2**
- World Literature Reading 21 **L2**
- Workbook Activity 21 **L1**
- Reading Strategies for the Social Studies Classroom **L1/ EL**

ASSESSMENT

- Authentic Assessment Activity 21 **L1/ EL**
- Chapter 21 Test Form A **L2**
- Chapter 21 Test Form B **L2**
- ExamView® Pro Testmaker CD-ROM

INTERDISCIPLINARY CONNECTIONS

- Geography and History Activity 21 **L2**
- People to Meet Activity 21 **L2**
- Economics Activity 21 **L2**
- Citizenship and Service Learning Activity 21 **L2**

SPANISH RESOURCES

- Spanish Reading Essentials and Study Guide
- Spanish Guided Reading Activities
- Spanish Quizzes, Tests, and Authentic Assessment (with Rubrics)
- Spanish Take-Home Review Activities

MULTIMEDIA

- ExamView® Pro Testmaker CD-ROM
- Glencoe Skillbuilder Interactive Workbook CD-ROM, Level 1
- Interactive Tutor Self-Assessment CD-ROM
- MindJogger Videoquiz
- Presentation Plus! CD-ROM
- StudentWorks Plus™ CD-ROM (with Audio Program)
- TeacherWorks CD-ROM
- Vocabulary PuzzleMaker CD-ROM
- *World History: Journey Across Time* Video Program
- World History Primary Source Document Library CD-ROM

STANDARDIZED ASSESSMENT SKILLS

- Standardized Test Skills Practice Workbook Activity 21 **L2**
- Critical Thinking Skills Activity 21 **L2**

Teaching strategies have been coded with suggested ability levels. However, most are suitable for all levels.

L1 BASIC activities for all students

L2 AVERAGE activities for average to above-average students

L3 CHALLENGING activities for above-average students

EL ENGLISH LANGUAGE activities

Chapter 21 Resources

TIME MANAGEMENT

Chapter Introduction	Section 1	Section 2	Section 3	Section 4	Section 5	Chapter Wrap-Up
1 Day	2 Days	1 Day	1 Day	2 Days	2 Days	1 Day

Block Scheduling Activities that are suited to use within the block scheduling framework are identified by: 📦

0:00 OUT OF TIME? Assign the Chapter 21 *Reading Essentials and Study Guide.** 📁

SECTION RESOURCES

DAILY OBJECTIVES	REPRODUCIBLE LESSON PLANS	MULTIMEDIA RESOURCES
Section 1 **The Rise of Dictators** 1. Economic problems led to the rise of dictators. 2. Stalin ruled harshly in the USSR while militarism overran Japan.	📁 Reproducible Lesson Plan 21–1 📁 Vocabulary Activity 21–1 📁 Guided Reading Activity 21–1* 📁 Section Quiz 21–1* 📁 Reading Essentials and Study Guide 21–1*	📜 Daily Focus Skills Transparency 21–1 💿 Interactive Tutor Self-Assessment CD-ROM 💿 ExamView® Pro Testmaker CD-ROM 💿 Presentation Plus! CD-ROM
Section 2 **World War II Begins** 1. The rest of Europe allowed Germany to expand its territory. 2. France and Britain declared war on Germany in September 1939.	📁 Reproducible Lesson Plan 21–2 📁 Vocabulary Activity 21–2 📁 Guided Reading Activity 21–2* 📁 Section Quiz 21–2* 📁 Reading Essentials and Study Guide 21–2*	📜 Daily Focus Skills Transparency 21–2 💿 Interactive Tutor Self-Assessment CD-ROM 💿 ExamView® Pro Testmaker CD-ROM 💿 Presentation Plus! CD-ROM 💿 Glencoe BookLink CD-ROM
Section 3 **The Allies Win the War** 1. The war was fought in Europe and Asia 2. D-Day was the beginning of the end of the war.	📁 Reproducible Lesson Plan 21–3 📁 Vocabulary Activity 21–3 📁 Guided Reading Activity 21–3* 📁 Section Quiz 21–3* 📁 Reading Essentials and Study Guide 21–3*	📜 Daily Focus Skills Transparency 21–3 💿 Interactive Tutor Self-Assessment CD-ROM 💿 ExamView® Pro Testmaker CD-ROM 💿 Presentation Plus! CD-ROM
Section 4 **The Cold War** 1. The United States tried to stop the spread of communism. 2. The world experienced prosperity, change, and conflict.	📁 Reproducible Lesson Plan 21–4 📁 Vocabulary Activity 21–4 📁 Guided Reading Activity 21–4* 📁 Section Quiz 21–4* 📁 Reading Essentials and Study Guide 21–4*	📜 Daily Focus Skills Transparency 21–4 💿 Interactive Tutor Self-Assessment CD-ROM 💿 ExamView® Pro Testmaker CD-ROM 💿 Presentation Plus! CD-ROM
Section 5 **The End of Empire** 1. Nationalism led to the independence movement. 2. African colonies gained independence in the 1950s and 1960s.	📁 Reproducible Lesson Plan 21–5 📁 Vocabulary Activity 21–5 📁 Guided Reading Activity 21–5* 📁 Section Quiz 21–5* 📁 Reading Essentials and Study Guide 21–5*	📜 Daily Focus Skills Transparency 21–5 💿 Interactive Tutor Self-Assessment CD-ROM 💿 ExamView® Pro Testmaker CD-ROM 💿 Presentation Plus! CD-ROM 💿 Vocabulary Puzzle Maker CD-ROM 💿 Glencoe BookLink CD-ROM

*Also available in Spanish

Use our Web site for additional resources. All essential content is covered in the Student Edition.

You and your students can visit jat.glencoe.com, the Web site companion to *World History: Journey Across Time*. This innovative integration of electronic and print media offers your students a wealth of opportunities. The student text directs students to the Web site for the following options:

- Chapter Overviews
- Self-Check Quizzes
- Study Central™
- Student Web Activities
- Multi-Language Glossaries

Answers to the student Web activities are provided for you in the **Web Activity Lesson Plans.** Additional Web resources and ePuzzles and games are also available.

The following videotape programs are available from Glencoe as supplements to Chapter 21:

World War II: The War Chronicles
(ISBN 0-56501-484-7)

The Decision to Drop the Bomb
(ISBN 1-56501-600-9)

Anne Frank
(ISBN 0-7670-1409-X)

To order, call Glencoe at 1-800-334-7344. To find classroom resources to accompany many of these videos, check the following home pages:

A&E Television: www.aande.com
The History Channel: www.historychannel.com

MEETING SPECIAL NEEDS

In addition to the Differentiated Instruction strategies, the following resources are suitable for students with special needs:

- *ExamView® Pro Testmaker CD-ROM* allows teachers to tailor tests by reducing answer choices.
- *StudentWorks Plus™ CD-ROM (with Audio Program)* includes the entire narrative of the student edition so that less-proficient readers can listen to the words as they read them.
- The *Reading Essentials and Study Guide* provides the same content as the student edition but is written two grade levels below the textbook.

Index to National Geographic Magazine:

The following articles relate to this chapter:

- "Hanoi," by David Lamb, May 2004
- "Burma Road," by Donovan Webster, November 2003
- "Indonesia," by Tracy Dahlby, March 2001

Additional National Geographic Society Products:

To order the following, call National Geographic at 1–800–368–2728

- *Pearl Harbor* (Video)
- *National Geographic Atlas of the World* (Book)

NGS ONLINE

Access National Geographic's new dynamic MapMachine Web site and other geography resources at:

www.nationalgeographic.com
www.nationalgeographic.com/maps

Meeting NCSS Standards

World History: Journey Across Time

The following standards are highlighted in Chapter 21:

Section 1 — **VI** Power, Authority, and Governance: B, C, F, I

VII Production, Distribution, and Consumption: A, D, I

Section 2 — **II** Time, Continuity, and Change: B

IX Global Connections: B, C, E, F, G

Section 3 — **VIII** Science, Technology, and Society: B, C

X Civic Ideas and Practices: F, I

Section 4 — **I** Culture: A, B

Section 5 — **IV** Individual Development and Identity: A, B, C, F, G, H

V Individuals, Groups, and Institutions: A, B, C, D, F, G

State and Local Objectives

_____

_____

_____

Chapter ㉑ Resources

Timesaving Tools

TeacherWorks
All-In-One Planner and Resource Center

- **Interactive Teacher Edition** Access your Teacher Wraparound Edition and your classroom resources with a few easy clicks.
- **Interactive Lesson Planner** Organize your week, month, semester, or year with all the lesson helps you need to make teaching creative and relevant.

Use Glencoe's **Presentation Plus!** multimedia teacher tool to easily present dynamic lessons that visually excite your students. Using Microsoft PowerPoint® you can customize the presentations to create your own personalized lessons.

FOLDABLES™ Study Organizer

Dinah Zike's Foldables

Foldables are three-dimensional, interactive graphic organizers that help students practice basic writing skills, review key vocabulary terms, and identify main ideas. Every chapter contains a foldable activity, with additional chapter activities found in the *Reading and Study Skills Foldables* booklet. You can use the foldables as they are presented, or modify them to suit the needs of your individual class.

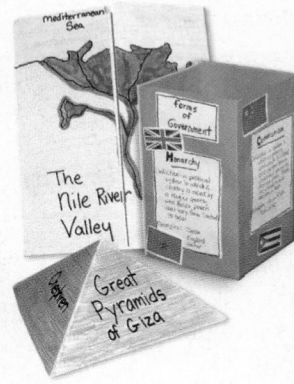

Planning Ahead

CHAPTER CULMINATING ACTIVITY

The Chapter Culminating Activity will help students organize and learn the important information from the chapter. Begin the chapter with this activity, and have students complete it as a culminating activity.

ANALYZING PROBLEM AND SOLUTION

Purpose A chart gives students a way to visualize problems, or conflicts, in and among nations and the steps that individuals and nations took to solve these problems. The graphic also serves as a tool for focusing on key ideas.

Introduction to Modeling

1. Draw this Problem-Solution Chart on the board. In the first box, write *Joblessness in America*. As students read Section 1, have them fill in the rest of the boxes. Answers have been provided.

2. Explain to students that they are going to make Problem-Solution Charts for major problems in each section. As they read, tell them to look for steps that individuals and nations took to solve a problem and record them in the "Action" boxes. Also, tell them to look for the results of the actions and record the results in the "Solution" box.

Problem
Joblessness in America

↓

Action
New Deal Agencies such as the Civilian Conservation Corps and the Works Progress Administration created jobs.

↓

Action
The Social Security Act set up pensions and provided insurance for people out of work.

↓

Solution
The New Deal helped the economy and gave Americans hope for the future.

3. When students have finished Chapter 21, have them review the chapter content by going over their charts. As students read each section, ask them to find events that happened on each continent for as many time periods as possible. Have them fill in the chart as they complete the chapter.

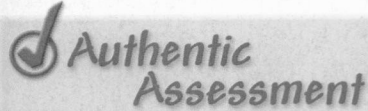

Authentic Assessment

Refer to Activity 21 in the Authentic Assessment section of the *Quizzes, Tests, and Authentic Assessment (with Rubrics)* booklet.

When &Where?

As students read the chapter, have them review the time line on page 800. Ask them to add events they think helped create the Cold War. **L1**

GLENCOE TECHNOLOGY

World History: Journey Across Time Video Program

To learn more about World War II and the Cold War, students can view the Chapter 21 video in the *World History: Journey Across Time* Video Program.

MindJogger Videoquiz

Use the **MindJogger Videoquiz** to preview Chapter 21 content.

Available in DVD and VHS

Chapter 21

World War II and the Cold War

World War II dive-bomber in flight ▼

NATIONAL GEOGRAPHIC When &Where?

1925	1935	1945	1955

1929
The Great Depression begins

1939
Germany invades Poland

1945
Atomic bombs are dropped on Japan

1950
The Korean War begins

1954
The French leave Vietnam

Reading Strategy — PURPOSE FOR READING

Visualizing Explain that visualizing can help students comprehend their reading. **Ask:** What pictures come to mind when you hear "World War II" and "Cold War"? Ask students to describe their mental pictures of these different kinds of wars, including details based on their personal lives and prior reading. Instruct them to draw details of their pictures in their notebooks and to refer back to the pictures as they read about the conflicts during the 1940s and after. **L1**

Chapter Preview

Chapter Overview Visit
jat.glencoe.com for a preview
of Chapter 21.

Read this chapter to learn about World War II and the Cold War, two very different conflicts that shaped the lives of your grandparents and parents.

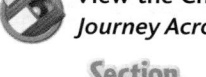 **View the Chapter 21 video in the** *World History: Journey Across Time* **Video Program.**

 ## The Rise of Dictators

The Great Depression led to the New Deal in the United States, but in Europe and Japan dictators and military leaders came to power.

 ## World War II Begins

Britain and France tried to appease Hitler in the 1930s, but in 1939 he invaded Poland and World War II began. Two years later, Japan attacked Pearl Harbor, and the United States entered the war as well.

 ## The Allies Win the War

From 1943 to 1945, the Allies pushed the Germans out of Italy, France, and Russia, and then invaded Germany. Meanwhile, American troops pushed back the Japanese in the Pacific, then dropped the atomic bomb on Japan.

 ## The Cold War

Soon after World War II, a conflict began between the United States and the Soviet Union. It was known as the Cold War.

 ## The End of Empire

In the decades following World War II, nations in Asia and Africa began to demand independence.

FOLDABLES™
Study Organizer

Sequencing Information *Make this foldable to help you sequence important events that occurred during World War II and the Cold War.*

Step 1 *Fold two sheets of paper in half from top to bottom. Cut each in half.*

Cut along the fold lines.

Step 2 *Turn and fold the four pieces in half from top to bottom.*

Reading and Writing *As you read the chapter, write the important events and dates that occurred during World War II and the Cold War on each section of your time line.*

Step 3 *Tape the ends of the pieces together (overlapping the edges slightly) to make an accordion time line.*

Pieces of tape

801

Introduce students to chapter content and key terms by having them access **Chapter Overview 21** at jat.glencoe.com

CHAPTER PREVIEW

After reading Chapter 21, students will be able to

1. explain how dictators rose to power in Europe;
2. describe the beginning of World War II;
3. summarize the events that ended World War II;
4. discuss the results of World War II and causes of the Cold War;
5. examine the end of empires around the world.

FOLDABLES™
Study Organizer Dinah Zike's Foldables

Purpose Students use this foldable to create a time line of important events during World War II and the Cold War. As students read this chapter, they should make notes about events and dates.

📁 Have students complete *Reading and Study Skills Foldables* Activity 21.

MORE ABOUT THE PHOTO

Helldiver The *Helldiver* was built by the U.S. Navy. In WWII, it destroyed more targets than any other U.S. aircraft. The *Helldiver* carried two pilots, weighed close to 17,000 pounds (with the bomb included), and reached a maximum speed of 281 miles per hour. To compete against its attacks, the Germans created the *Stuka*, an even more advanced dive bomber. *Stuka* became especially effective during blitzkrieg, or lightning war attacks. By the end of WWII, almost 6,000 *Stuka* dive bombers had been built. Piloting a dive bomber was an exciting but dangerous job. Dive bombers were aircraft that dove directly into the path of a target at full speed, released a bomb, then attempted to return to a safe flying speed and path. Many times pilots overestimated the distance and crashed.

1 Learn It!

Participating in a discussion after reading is an important part of relating to the text and thinking more deeply about the subject. Showing students how to use points from the text as a springboard for discussion will help them become critical readers and thinkers.

Have students read the following passage under the subhead "The Depression Spreads" in Section 1 and jot down any questions they have related to the text:

> The worst year of the depression was 1932. By that time, one out of four Americans and British and two out of five Germans were out of work. People who had been put out of their homes lived in shacks built out of cardboard or tin.

Facilitate a whole-class discussion by allowing students to ask their questions to the class. As students discuss their thoughts and questions, focus the discussion by asking questions such as:

- Do you agree with that view?
- Who thinks differently than the speaker?
- Can anyone answer the question?
- Does this question make you think of other questions you may have?

Modeling effective discussion skills shows students the importance of listening to each other, responding directly to classmates' comments, and respect differing views. **L1/EL**

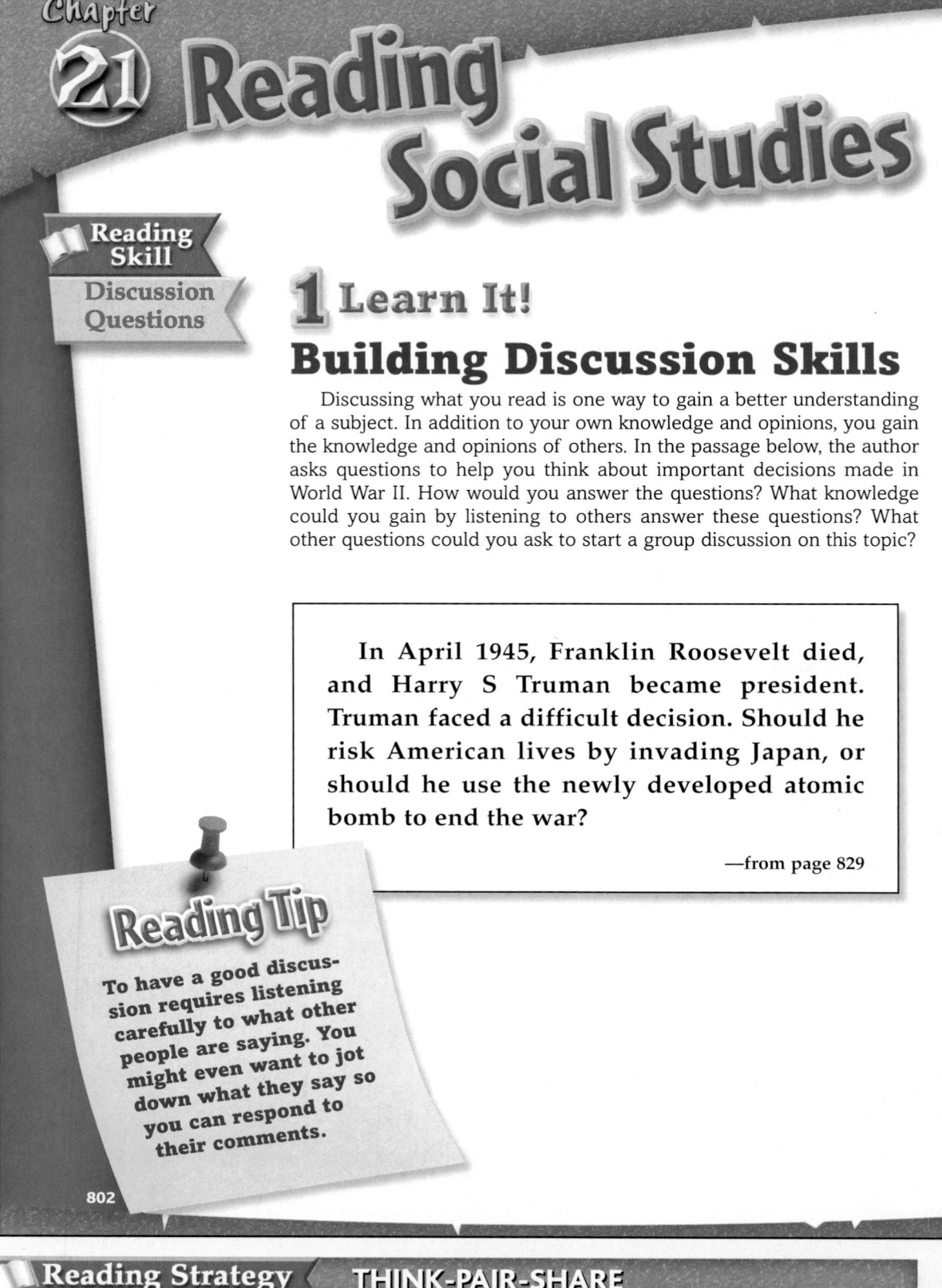

Chapter 21 Reading Social Studies

Reading Skill
Discussion Questions

1 Learn It!
Building Discussion Skills

Discussing what you read is one way to gain a better understanding of a subject. In addition to your own knowledge and opinions, you gain the knowledge and opinions of others. In the passage below, the author asks questions to help you think about important decisions made in World War II. How would you answer the questions? What knowledge could you gain by listening to others answer these questions? What other questions could you ask to start a group discussion on this topic?

> In April 1945, Franklin Roosevelt died, and Harry S Truman became president. Truman faced a difficult decision. Should he risk American lives by invading Japan, or should he use the newly developed atomic bomb to end the war?
>
> —from page 829

Reading Tip

To have a good discussion requires listening carefully to what other people are saying. You might even want to jot down what they say so you can respond to their comments.

802

Reading Strategy — **THINK-PAIR-SHARE**

Allowing students many opportunities to discuss in class will create strong listening and speaking skills. Often, during whole-class activities, ask students to sit quietly and think about what has been said. Then, ask them to turn to a partner and share their thoughts. Give them discussion starters, such as "What would you do in this situation..." or "What would have happened if..." to provide a purpose for dialogue and direct the discussion. This strategy helps to ensure that each student in the class is actively responding to the subject instead of passively listening to those for whom discussion comes more easily.

2 Practice It!

Read to Discuss

Read the passage below. As you read, write five questions that would help you launch a discussion with others and help you to gain a better understanding of the information in this passage. Share your questions in a discussion with a group of classmates.

Read to Write

During a class discussion, write down notes about things others say. After the discussion, do a quickwrite. Write everything you would like to say that you did not get a chance to say out loud.

> Reading the Bhagavad Gita proved to be one of the greatest influences on Gandhi's life. It returned him to the Hindu religion. It also exposed him to two ideas that he would come to live by in his life and work. One idea was that material goods kept a person from pursuing a spiritual life. The other idea was to be peaceful and even-tempered in all situations.
>
> —from page 844

3 Apply It!

As you read Chapter 21, keep a list of questions, comments, or statements from the text that you would like to talk about later.

803

2 Practice It!

Listening Ask students to read a portion of the text that may elicit strong reactions. Read aloud the following passage under the subhead "The Rise of Adolf Hitler" in Section 1:

> Nazis also tried to restrict women's rights. According to the Nazis, women were meant to be wives and mothers, not leaders. So the government discouraged women from becoming lawyers, doctors, or professors. Instead, posters urged women to "Get a hold of pots and pans…".

Give students a few minutes to think about the passage or write their thoughts. Then have students find a partner they have not talked with during the class period and discuss the passage with their partner for another few minutes. Finish by leading a whole-class discussion as a way of assimilating their talks. **L1**

3 Apply It!

Have students read an entire section and jot down at least five thoughts or questions they have while reading. Put students in groups of four, and assign a facilitator. One at a time, students will share their questions or comments related to the topic. The student facilitator then will call on other members of the group to respond to the statements. The activity continues until each person has had a chance to begin the discussion and each person has responded at least once. **L2**

Reading Strategy — READ TO WRITE

Ask students to assume the role of a talk show host who will interview one or more of the central figures in this chapter. Have them write a list of 10 key questions they will want to ask their guest and 10 follow-up questions. Encourage them to consider questions that begin with "Why," "How," or "What" for the purpose of eliciting thoughtful, complex answers that may lead to discussion. Extend this activity by having students role-play in small groups. Students may want to glance at all of the subheads before beginning to help them prepare. **L1**

① FOCUS

SECTION OVERVIEW

This section discusses how different countries dealt with the Great Depression and how this led to the rise of dictators.

BELLRINGER
SKILLBUILDER ACTIVITY

Project **Daily Focus Skills Transparency 21–1** and have students answer questions. Discuss their responses.

Get Ready to Read!

Preteaching Vocabulary: Ask students to visualize blowing up a balloon. Tell them that *inflation* in an economy means that prices increase rapidly like the size of the balloon when being inflated.

Answers to Graphic: Benito Mussolini: banned free speech, free press, and all political parties except his Fascist Party; Adolf Hitler: believed in German superiority, expansion of German territory, and anti-Semitism; Joseph Stalin: quick industrialization and collectivization of farms, brutally dealt with opposition

---

Section 1

The Rise of Dictators

Get Ready to Read!

What's the Connection?

The outcome of World War I and serious economic problems led to the rise of dictators in several countries.

Focusing on the Main Ideas

- New economic problems led to the Great Depression. *(page 805)*
- The Great Depression encouraged the rise of European dictators. *(page 808)*
- After Lenin's death, Stalin established a brutal regime in the USSR. *(page 810)*
- Economic problems led to militarism in Japan. *(page 811)*

Locating Places
Ruhr Valley (RUR   VA•lee)
Manchuria (man•CHUR•ee•uh)

Meeting People
Benito Mussolini (buh•NEE•toh MOO•suh•LEE•nee)
Adolf Hitler
Joseph Stalin

Building Your Vocabulary
inflation
depression
totalitarian state
   (toh•TA•luh•TEHR•ee•uhn)
collectivization
   (kuh•LEHK•tih•vuh•ZAY•shuhn)

Reading Strategy
Organizing Information Complete a diagram like the one below identifying the policies of three dictators.

Dictator	Policy

NATIONAL GEOGRAPHIC When & Where?

1921 — **1929** — **1937**

NORTH AMERICA   EUROPE   ASIA

1922 Mussolini becomes Italy's leader

1928 Stalin starts Five-Year Plans

1929 The Great Depression begins

1933 Hitler becomes dictator of Germany

SECTION RESOURCES

📁 **Reproducible Masters**
- Reproducible Lesson Plan 21–1
- Daily Lecture and Discussion Notes 21–1
- Vocabulary Activity 21–1
- Active Reading Note-Taking Guide 21–1
- Guided Reading Activity 21–1
- Section Quiz 21–1
- Reading Essentials and Study Guide 21–1

Transparencies
- Daily Focus Skills Transparency 21–1

Multimedia
- Interactive Tutor Self-Assessment CD-ROM
- ExamView® Pro Testmaker CD-ROM
- Presentation Plus! CD-ROM

Postwar Economic Problems

Main Idea New economic problems led to the Great Depression.

Reading Focus Have you ever wondered why people accept paper money? After all, it is just paper, not anything valuable. Read to learn what happened in Germany when paper money became worthless.

The end of World War I left many nations unhappy. Defeated peoples, such as the Germans, felt humiliated. They resented losing territory and making war payments. Even people in winning nations, such as Italy and Japan, felt that they did not get enough land for the sacrifices they had made. When economic troubles came, frustration and fear added to this anger.

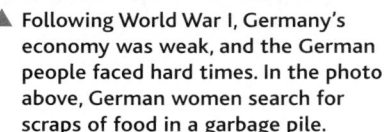

▲ Following World War I, Germany's economy was weak, and the German people faced hard times. In the photo above, German women search for scraps of food in a garbage pile.

At right, a woman uses worthless German paper money to start a fire in her kitchen stove. *What did France do when Germany could not pay the reparations it owed?* ▶

A Troubled Germany You read earlier that the Treaty of Versailles blamed Germany for causing the war. As a result, the Germans owed the Allies a huge sum in reparations, or payments for war damages. Germany's new democratic government made the first payment in 1921. The next year, however, it claimed that it could not afford to pay any more.

France had hoped to use its share of reparations to rebuild its economy after the war. When Germany could not pay, France sent troops into the **Ruhr Valley** (RUR VA• lee), a rich industrial area in western Germany. The French wanted to take the wealth from the valley's mines and factories to make up for the unpaid reparations.

Angry German workers resisted the French takeover by going on strike. To pay

CHAPTER 21   World War II and the Cold War   **805**

② TEACH

Reading Strategy

Monitoring Comprehension
Explain that the section includes details about the stock market that may be new to students. Point out that good readers have mental conversations with themselves when they encounter unfamiliar material. Also encourage students to read passages about events that led to the Great Depression more slowly than other passages and to reread passages they do not immediately understand. **L1**

Daily Lecture and Discussion Notes 21–1

Use **Daily Lecture and Discussion Notes 21–1** for an outline of key concepts found in the section.

More About the Photo

The German economy became so weak that about 6 million people were out of work.

Caption Answer: France sent troops into Germany's Ruhr Valley to take over the area's mines and factories.

Reading Strategy **READING THE TEXT**

Connecting Have students recall times in their lives when they believed they were treated unfairly. Help them brainstorm a list of emotions that they felt as a result of this treatment. *(The list may include sad, bitter, resigned, vengeful, hopeless, frustrated, and indignant, among others.)* Record students' answers on the board. Then have students read "A Troubled Germany." **Ask:** Why might Germans consider reparations unfair? *(Students may say that other countries shared the responsibility for World War I and yet paid no reparations.)* Encourage them to use words from the list on the board. **L1**

Reading Strategy

Writing Activity

Read aloud the following quotes about the Great Depression from Herbert Hoover, president from 1929–1933: "The crisis will be over in 60 days." (March 1930) "I am convinced we have now passed the worst." (May 1930) "We have hit the bottom and are on the upswing." (September 1930) Then have students write one or two paragraphs refuting Hoover's statements with facts from the lesson. **L2**

NATIONAL GEOGRAPHIC — The Way It Was

Answers:
1. They wandered around with their families looking for food and shelter.
2. They participated in hunger marches and voted for radical parties such as Communists and Fascists.

Reading Support L1/ EL

Use **Vocabulary Activity 21–1** to review important terms in the section.

NATIONAL GEOGRAPHIC — The Way It Was

Focus on Everyday Life

The Great Depression The Great Depression brought misery to millions of people. Begging for food on the streets became widespread.

More and more people became homeless. One person in Germany reported that: "An almost unbroken chain of homeless men extends the whole length of the great Hamburg-Berlin highway . . .— whole families had piled all their goods into baby carriages and wheelbarrows that they were pushing along as they plodded forward in dumb despair."

▲ Workers protest economic conditions.

Some of the unemployed staged hunger marches to get attention. In many countries, desperate people began to vote for political parties that offered extreme solutions. Across Europe, Fascist Parties and Communist Parties won more and more votes.

Connecting to the Past
1. What did some people in Europe do after they lost their jobs during the Great Depression?
2. How did people try to change their society during the Great Depression?

---

the strikers' wages, the German government began printing more and more paper money. When too much money is printed, it loses its value. As money loses value, businesses raise prices. This is called **inflation.** Germany's currency dropped in value so much it became almost worthless. People had to take wheelbarrows of money to the store just to buy a loaf of bread.

To help Germany recover, the United States and nations in Western Europe created the Dawes Plan in 1924. Developed by Charles Dawes, an American banker, the Dawes Plan reduced the amount Germany owed and set payments that its government could handle. The plan also arranged for American banks to loan $200 million to Germany. Good times followed, but they were short-lived.

What Caused the Great Depression?

During the 1930s, the world's industrialized countries were hit by an economic depression. A **depression** is a period of low economic activity when many people lose their jobs. The 1930s depression was so severe that it became known as the Great Depression. During this time, factories closed and millions of people lost their jobs.

One major cause of the Great Depression was the crash of the U.S. stock market. Before the depression struck, American companies were producing much of the world's manufactured goods. People saw their chance to make a fortune by investing in these companies. As a result, the U.S. stock market boomed.

Many investors bought stock on margin. In other words, they paid only a small amount of the stock price and borrowed the rest of the money. As long as stock

---

DIFFERENTIATED INSTRUCTION

Naturalist: Describe how grasses and trees had been cleared from the Great Plains to plant crops and how the crops had exhausted much of the soil. By the 1930s, Oklahoma and surrounding farmland were known as the Dust Bowl. Add that the CCC planted trees to hold soil in place with their roots. Have students create a display showing how root systems anchor and enrich the soil.

English Learners: Ask students to collect and identify a variety of roots to use in the display.

Gifted and Talented: Have students design and perform an experiment to demonstrate which of a variety of plants best help to conserve soil.

👉 Refer to *Inclusion Strategies for the Middle School Social Studies Classroom* in the TCR.

prices kept rising, buying on margin was safe. Investors would sell their stock when the price increased, repay their loan, and keep the difference as a profit.

Meanwhile, factories began having trouble selling everything they produced. Workers were not paid high enough wages to buy all the goods being made. This over-production forced factory owners to slow production. They then cut back the number of workers they employed.

In October 1929, fears about the economy grew. People were pressured to pay back their loans. When they failed to pay, panic struck. Stock prices tumbled and wiped out the fortunes of many investors. Banks collapsed, and when they did many people lost all of their savings.

The Depression Spreads Frightened American investors withdrew money from Germany and other European markets. These withdrawals caused the collapse of European banks as well. By 1931, trade was slow and jobs were scarce in both North America and Europe.

The worst year of the depression was 1932. By that time, one out of four Americans and British and two out of five Germans were out of work. People who had been put out of their homes lived in shacks built out of cardboard or tin.

FDR and the New Deal In the United States, President Franklin D. Roosevelt set up a program known as the New Deal. To provide people with money to buy food and housing and to put them back to work, the federal government set up several different agencies. One of these, the Civilian

▲ President Franklin D. Roosevelt often attempted to ease the concerns of the American public by addressing them over the radio. *What effect did Roosevelt's New Deal have?*

Conservation Corps (CCC), gave jobs mostly to young people. They planted trees and built facilities in the nation's parks. The Works Progress Administration (WPA) paid jobless workers to build dams, roads, bridges, and hospitals. It also gave work to artists and writers. Other new government agencies tried to help farmers, business leaders, and home owners.

The federal government also carried out reforms. In 1935 Roosevelt convinced Congress to pass the Social Security Act. This program gave pensions, or payments, to citizens after they turned 65 and retired. It also provided Americans with unemployment insurance. If someone lost their job, they received money from the government until they found a new one. Roosevelt's New Deal failed to restore the economy completely, but it did give Americans hope about the future.

✓ **Reading Check** **Describe** How did the Dawes Plan affect Germany?

CHAPTER 21   World War II and the Cold War   807

Civics Point out that Roosevelt's critics claimed that the U.S. Constitution did not permit the government to carry out policies like those in the New Deal. Then have students read the preamble to the Constitution and find words that Roosevelt could have used to answer his critics. (*We the people of the United States, in order to… promote the general welfare… do ordain and establish this Constitution*) **L2**

More About the Photo

Tell students that in 1921, Roosevelt contracted polio and lost his ability to walk. White House photographers made an unspoken pact never to photograph the president in his wheel-chair. He always appeared in public behind a podium, in a regular chair, or leaning on the arm of someone else.

Caption Answer: While it did not completely restore the economy, it gave Americans hope about the future.

✓ Reading Check

Answer: It helped the German economy by reducing the amount Germany owed, setting payments it could handle, and arranging for the U.S. to loan $200 million to Germany.

CRITICAL THINKING ACTIVITY

Analyzing Distribute copies of the following passage from an interview with former enslaved person Alice Alexander: "I was 88 years old 15th of last March. Born March 15, 1839 at Jackson Parish, La. My mother's name is Mary Marlow, an' father Henry Marlow. . . . We lived in a one room log hut, and slept on homemade rail bed steads wid cotton, an' sum times straw, mos'ly straw summers an' cotton winners." Then explain that the interview was one of a collection by authors in the WPA's Federal Writers Project. **Ask:** Do you think interviews with former enslaved persons in the 1930s and early 1940s were valuable? Why or why not? (*Students may answer that yes, the interviews were valuable because former enslaved people were historical resources who would not be around much longer.*) **L2**

Comparing Leaders Read aloud this quote from Benito Mussolini: "War alone keys up all human energies to their maximum tension and sets the seal of nobility on those people who have the courage to face it." Ask students to contrast this view with Franklin Roosevelt's: "War is a contagion." **Ask:** Do you subscribe to the philosophy of Mussolini or Roosevelt? Explain your choice. **L3**

in a word ...

"Dictator" comes from the Latin word for "to assert." In Roman times, the Senate appointed dictators to take over the government in emergencies. Modern dictators, however, answer to no one and usually rule oppressively.

More About the Photo

Many Italians bitterly opposed Mussolini, but the Fascists arrested, assaulted, and murdered those who spoke out.

Caption Answer: He banned all political parties except the Fascist Party and put an end to democratic rule in Italy. Personal freedoms and freedom of the press were done away with.

The Rise of Fascism and Nazism

Main Idea The Great Depression encouraged the rise of European dictators.

Reading Focus If you were penniless and homeless, would you vote for someone who promised to make your life better? Read to find out why Italians and Germans supported ruthless dictators.

The Great Depression brought fear to many people. Despite facing hard times, the people in the United States, Britain, and France held on to democracy. In many other countries, such as Italy and Germany, people had less loyalty to democratic values. They looked to strong leaders for help. These leaders became dictators—rulers who control their countries by force.

Under these dictators, a new form of government called totalitarianism developed. In a **totalitarian state** (toh•TA•luh•TEHR•ee•uhn), political leaders try to *totally* control the way citizens think and live. During the 1930s, totalitarian leaders used books, newspapers, the arts, and schools to influence their people. New technology, such as films and the radio, was also used to spread the government's point of view. People who disagreed or voiced other ideas were harshly punished.

Mussolini Takes Power The first country to become a totalitarian state was Italy. After World War I, Italy had a huge debt to pay off and many people did not have jobs. Workers went on strike for higher wages. Some hoped for a communist revolution similar to what was happening in Russia.

With the country in chaos, a man named **Benito Mussolini** (buh•NEE•toh MOO•suh•LEE•nee) created the Fascist Party and promised to restore order, fix Italy's economy, and make Italy a great nation. His followers wore black shirts and beat up people who

opposed them. In 1922 Mussolini's followers staged a huge march on Rome. To prevent violence, Italy's king agreed to appoint Mussolini as head of the government.

Mussolini was known as *Il Duce* (eel DOO•chay), or "The Leader." He quickly put an end to democratic rule in Italy. Within a few years, Mussolini had banned all political parties except his Fascist Party. Personal freedoms and a free press no longer existed. Boys and girls of all ages had to join groups that taught them loyalty to the Fascist government. Mussolini built up Italy's military and promised to regain the glory of the ancient Romans.

▲ To gain control of Italy, Benito Mussolini used violence and political pressure to destroy his opponents. *What political changes did Mussolini bring to Italy?*

INTERDISCIPLINARY CONNECTIONS ACTIVITY

Music As a young man, Hitler listened to the music of Richard Wagner for inspiration. From the 1830s to the 1880s, Wagner composed operas that dealt with epic struggles. His pieces swelled with emotion. In the 1930s, Wagner's pieces were used to provide dramatic background tracks for propaganda films featuring the German army. Ask volunteers to find and summarize the plots of Wagner operas such as *Das Rheingold* (The Rhine Gold) and *Götterdämmerung* (Twilight of the Gods). Distribute copies of the summaries to the class and play *Flight of the Valkyries* or another composition by Wagner as students read. **L3**

The Rise of Adolf Hitler

The Great Depression led to the rise of a totalitarian state in Germany. During the early 1930s, millions of Germans lost their jobs, and many businesses failed. Voters in large numbers supported a political leader named **Adolf Hitler.** In his speeches, Hitler appealed to people's fear about the economy and their bitterness about the Treaty of Versailles.

Hitler was leader of the National Socialist German Workers' Party, or the Nazi Party. Hitler and the Nazis portrayed the German people as better than all others. Germany, they believed, had a right to expand its territory. The Nazis were known for their anti-Semitism, or hatred of the Jews. They blamed the Jews for Germany's problems. Hitler presented these ideas in a book called *Mein Kampf,* or "My Struggle."

Many Germans, worried about the economy, began to vote for the Nazis. By 1932, the Nazi Party had become the largest party in the German parliament. A year later, Hitler was named Germany's chancellor, or prime minister. Next, the German parliament handed all power to Hitler while he dealt with the country's problems. In this way, Hitler became dictator of Germany.

Once in power, Hitler did away with all political parties except the Nazis. He had books about democracy burned. He took over the courts and set up a secret police.

▲ To gather support for the Nazi Party, Hitler often addressed the German people at large rallies and used other propaganda techniques. *What were some of the basic beliefs of the Nazi Party?*

He took over radio and newspapers and broke up unions. The Nazis also set up large prisons called concentration camps. There, they sent people who disagreed with Nazi ideas.

The Nazi government reflected Hitler's strong anti-Semitism. The Nazis took away the Jews' businesses and jobs. Jews could not go to school or get medical care.

Nazis also tried to restrict women's rights. According to the Nazis, women were meant to be wives and mothers, not leaders. So the government discouraged women from becoming lawyers, doctors, or professors. Instead, posters urged women to "Get a hold of pots and pans . . .".

✓ **Reading Check** **Analyze** Why do you think the king of Italy let Mussolini take control of Italy?

CHAPTER 21　World War II and the Cold War　**809**

TIME TRAVELER

Maksim Gorky was appointed by Stalin to take charge of Soviet culture. Gorky promoted a new literary style that soon became obligatory in the arts: socialist realism. Writers and artists created a "new reality" by glorifying Soviet heroes and achievements while denouncing the rumors about forced labor and terror. Artists who violated these dictates faced exile or imprisonment in labor camps.

Caption Answer: He wanted to industrialize the Soviet Union as quickly as possible.

Stalin and the Soviet Union

Main Idea After Lenin's death, Stalin established a brutal regime in the USSR.

Reading Focus If you ran the government, how would you fix the problems in your community? Do you think government ever causes problems by trying to fix things? Read to learn how Stalin's government caused great hardship when trying to change the USSR.

Harsh rule also came to Russia. Previously, you learned about Lenin, the Russian Revolution, and the civil war that followed. By 1922, Lenin's government was securely in power. In that year, Russia's Communist leaders formed the Union of Soviet Socialist Republics (USSR), or the Soviet Union. This vast territory included Russia and most of the conquered lands of the old Russian Empire.

Stalin Takes Power After a series of strokes, Lenin died in 1924. After Lenin died, a struggle for power took place in the Soviet Union. By the late 1920s, **Joseph Stalin** had become the ruler of the Soviet Union. Under Lenin, Stalin's job had been to appoint party officials. When the power struggle began, the thousands of officials Stalin had appointed supported him. Their support helped him seize power.

Government Plans the Economy Stalin wanted the Soviet Union to become an industrial power as soon as possible. Beginning in 1928, he introduced a series of Five-Year Plans. These were programs that set economic goals for a five-year period. Under the Five-Year Plans, steel mills, power plants, and oil refineries were built and kept under government control. Factory managers had to produce a certain amount of goods.

Under Stalin's orders, the government also took control of all farming. Stalin's plans called for **collectivization** (kuh•LEHK•tih•vuh•ZAY•shuhn). This meant combining small farms into large, factory-like farms run by the government.

Many peasants, however, wanted to keep working on their own farms. They resisted collectivization by destroying their houses, cows, and pigs. This resistance did not last long. Peasants who refused to cooperate with the government were either shot or sent to prison.

In Ukraine, a region south of Russia, Stalin caused a famine to control the people. He had officials seize the grain supplies. As a result, millions of peasants in Ukraine starved to death.

By 1939, the Soviet Union had become a major industrial power. The people, however, paid a high price for swift industrial growth. Workers labored long hours for low wages. Consumer goods, such as clothes and household goods, were poorly made

▲ Joseph Stalin (right) took power in the Soviet Union after the death of Vladimir Lenin (left). *Why did Stalin set up the Five-Year Plans?*

810   CHAPTER 21   World War II and the Cold War

CITIZENSHIP AND YOU

Priorities Read aloud the preamble of the U.S. Constitution, stressing the following passage: "to form a more perfect Union, establish Justice, insure domestic Tranquility, provide for the common defense, promote the general Welfare . . ." Point out that these are the generally accepted goals of government. Have students brainstorm a list of other purposes for government. Then tell students to reread the paragraphs about the Ukraine and the outcome of Stalin's Five-Year Plans, and to identify the hardships that Stalin's regime imposed. **Ask:** Which goal of government was high on Stalin's list of priorities? Which goals did Stalin fail to achieve or even address? How would you grade Stalin's government on a letter scale from A to F? **L3**

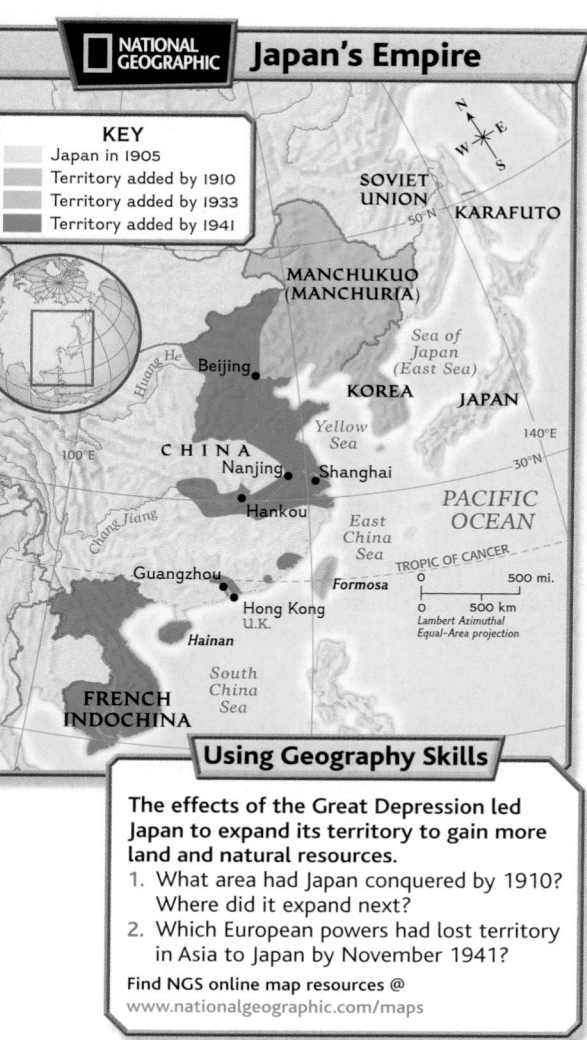

NATIONAL GEOGRAPHIC | Japan's Empire

KEY
- Japan in 1905
- Territory added by 1910
- Territory added by 1933
- Territory added by 1941

SOVIET UNION
KARAFUTO
50°N
MANCHUKUO (MANCHURIA)
Huang He
Beijing
Sea of Japan (East Sea)
KOREA
JAPAN
140°E
CHINA
Yellow Sea
Nanjing
Shanghai
Hankou
30°N
PACIFIC OCEAN
100°E
Chang Jiang
East China Sea
TROPIC OF CANCER
Guangzhou
Formosa
0   500 mi.
0   500 km
Lambert Azimuthal Equal-Area projection
Hong Kong U.K.
Hainan
South China Sea
FRENCH INDOCHINA

Using Geography Skills

The effects of the Great Depression led Japan to expand its territory to gain more land and natural resources.
1. What area had Japan conquered by 1910? Where did it expand next?
2. Which European powers had lost territory in Asia to Japan by November 1941?

Find NGS online map resources @ www.nationalgeographic.com/maps

and hard to find, and housing shortages were common.

Above all, millions of farmers, workers, and government officials suffered under Stalin. Those people who opposed Stalin's actions were killed or sent to remote prison camps deep in the vast forests of icy Siberia.

✓ Reading Check **Explain** What did Stalin's Five-Year Plans achieve? What problems did they cause?

The Military Rules Japan

Main Idea Economic problems led to militarism in Japan.

Reading Focus Is it ever okay for people to steal something if they need it? Read to learn how Japanese leaders used that argument to justify invading another country.

About the same time that the Soviet Union fell under Stalin's strict control, Japan's military gained control of Japan's government. As you read earlier, Japan had become an industrial power by the early 1900s. As Japan's economy grew, so too did its population. Between 1872 and 1925, the number of people in Japan rose from 35 million to 60 million.

What Problems Did Japan Face?

Japan's government hoped that new factories and new markets would create jobs for the larger population. So its leaders stressed manufacturing and foreign trade. Japan's industry grew rapidly, and Japanese factory-made goods were sold worldwide.

The Japanese government helped develop large private companies called *zaibatsu*. By the late 1930s, these companies controlled much of Japan's economy. While factory managers and rural landowners grew wealthy, factory workers and farmers were poorly paid and housed. Often there was not enough food to feed Japan's growing population. Food prices rose rapidly and often led to food riots. When the Great Depression reached Japan, workers and farmers suffered most.

Japan Invades Manchuria

The Great Depression caused a worldwide fall in prices. This brought disaster to Japan's factories. Millions of workers lost their jobs. Some began to starve.

CHAPTER 21   World War II and the Cold War   **811**

COOPERATIVE LEARNING ACTIVITY

A Bulletin Board Display Tell students that the four largest *zaibatsu* in 1937 were Mitsui, Mitsubishi, Sumitomo, and Yasuda. Organize the class into four groups and assign one of these companies to each group. Tell groups to research what has happened with their company since 1937. Is the company active today under another name? Does the company still manufacture the same kinds of products it produced in 1937, or has it expanded or changed its focus completely? Tell groups to use graphic organizers to illustrate how the companies have grown or withered and to display their trees on a bulletin board. Remind students to provide labels and a title for each tree. **L2**

ENRICH

Tell students that Japan passed a military draft in 1938, took strict control of economic resources, merged political parties into the Imperial Rule Assistance Association, and disbanded unions. **Ask: How do you think ordinary Japanese reacted to these developments? Explain. L1**

✓ Reading Check

Answer: Because *zaibatsu* controlled Japanese industries, wealth was concentrated among *zaibatsu* owners and managers, and the gap between the middle class and the working class widened.

To help students understand section material, have them visit **Study Central™** at jat.glencoe.com

RETEACH

Have students describe links between failing economies and the rise of totalitarian governments. **L2**

CLOSE

Announce place names such as *Italy* and *Manchuria* and have students relate at least one fact from the section about each place. **L1**

812

Starving workers and farmers blamed Japan's politicians for their problems. The leaders of Japan's military claimed that Japan's problems were caused by European and American ideas. They said that Japan should return to its old warrior traditions. Their ideas began to influence all areas of Japanese life.

As Japan's trade declined, Japan's military leaders argued that Japan needed more land and natural resources to make its economy stronger. Without government approval, army leaders in 1931 invaded **Manchuria** (man•CHUR•ee•uh), the northeast region of China. When Japan's prime minister tried to stop the war, the military killed him. From then on, Japan's government did what the military wanted. Over the next few years, several Japanese mili-

▲ In the 1930s, the Japanese military became more aggressive. This photo shows Japanese cavalry in China. *What area did Japan invade in 1931?*

tary officers were chosen to serve as prime minister. Under their leadership, Japan began making plans to build an empire in Asia even if it meant war with other countries.

✓ Reading Check **Explain** How did *zaibatsu* affect the social structure in Japan?

History Online
Study Central™ Need help with the material in this section? Visit jat.glencoe.com

Section 1 Review

Reading Summary
Review the Main Ideas

- The crash of the stock market led to the Great Depression. In the United States, Franklin Roosevelt introduced programs to help the economy.
- In Europe, Benito Mussolini became dictator of Italy and Adolf Hitler became dictator of Germany.
- In the Soviet Union, Joseph Stalin took power and placed all farms and factories under government control.
- Japan's economic problems enabled the military to take control of the government.

What Did You Learn?

1. What was the New Deal and why was it proposed?
2. What ideas did Adolf Hitler reveal in *Mein Kampf*?

Critical Thinking

3. **Compare and Contrast** Draw a chart like the one below. Fill in details about leaders and events in the 1920s and 1930s.

United States	Italy	Germany	Soviet Union	Japan

4. **Summarize** What was a totalitarian state, and how did totalitarian states gain the support of the country's citizens?

5. **Analyze** Were Stalin's economic plans for the Soviet Union, both industrial and agricultural, successful? Explain.

6. **Expository Writing** Imagine you are living in the U.S. in the 1930s. Write a letter to a pen pal in another country describing the actions the president is taking to help Americans during the Great Depression and whether or not you agree with those actions.

7. **Reading** Discussion Questions Write five questions that would help you launch a discussion about why Hitler and the Nazis were able to take power in Germany.

812   CHAPTER 21   World War II and the Cold War

SECTION 1 REVIEW ANSWERS

1. Roosevelt's policies to counteract the effects of the Great Depression

2. German nationalism, German superiority and right to land, and anti-Semitism

3. Charts should include details from the section.

4. a dictatorship in which the state had total control of citizens' lives; by using modern communications systems to spread propaganda

5. The Five-Year Plans spurred industrial growth, but collectivization led to the exile and death of many Soviets.

6. Students' letters should contain details about New Deal programs.

7. Questions should lead students to information in the text, such as disbanding trade unions and setting up concentration camps.

Section 2

World War II Begins

Get Ready to Read!

What's the Connection?
You have read how economic hard times paved the way for dictatorships in Europe. The goals of these dictators soon led to a new world war.

Focusing on the Main Ideas
• Other European nations stood by as Germany expanded its territory. **(page 814)**

• World War II began when Germany invaded Poland in September 1939, leading France and Britain to declare war. **(page 815)**

Locating Places
Rhineland
Sudetenland (soo•DAY•tuhn•LAND)
Munich (MYOO•nihk)
Nanjing (NAHN•JIHNG)
Pearl Harbor

Meeting People
Neville Chamberlain
(NEHV•uhl CHAYM•buhr•luhn)

Winston Churchill
(WIHN•stuhn CHUHRCH•HIHL)

Building Your Vocabulary
appeasement (uh•PEEZ•muhnt)

Reading Strategy
Sequencing Information Create a diagram like the one below to track the areas invaded by Germany.

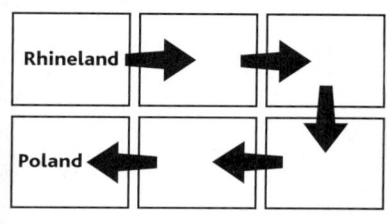

① FOCUS

SECTION OVERVIEW
This section describes German expansion and the beginning of World War II.

Project **Daily Focus Skills Transparency 21–2** and have students answer questions. Discuss their responses.

Get Ready to Read!

Preteaching Vocabulary:
Appeasement was the policy of giving in to German demands in order to avoid war. It comes from the Latin *a + pais* meaning "more at peace."

Answers to Graphic: Rhineland, Spain, Austria, Sudetenland, Czechoslovakia, Poland

NATIONAL GEOGRAPHIC When & Where?

NORTH AMERICA EUROPE ASIA

1934 — 1938 — 1942

1935 Hitler begins expanding Germany's army

1936 Spanish Civil War begins

1939 Germany invades Poland

1941 Japanese planes bomb Pearl Harbor

 ## SECTION RESOURCES

Reproducible Masters
• Reproducible Lesson Plan 21–2
• Daily Lecture and Discussion Notes 21–2
• Vocabulary Activity 21–2
• Active Reading Note-Taking Guide 21–2
• Guided Reading Activity 21–2
• Section Quiz 21–2
• Reading Essentials and Study Guide 21–2

Transparencies
• Daily Focus Skills Transparency 21–2

Multimedia
Interactive Tutor Self-Assessment CD-ROM
ExamView® Pro Testmaker CD-ROM
Presentation Plus! CD-ROM
Glencoe BookLink CD-ROM

② TEACH

Reading Strategy ▶

Analyzing As students read "Appeasement Fails," tell them to look for the reasons that the British and French adopted a policy of appeasement. Then ask students to write one or two paragraphs attacking or defending the policy. Remind them to support their opinions with facts from the reading. **L1/EL**

Daily Lecture and Discussion Notes 21–2

Use **Daily Lecture and Discussion Notes 21–2** for an outline of key concepts found in the section.

Reading Support L1/EL

Use **Vocabulary Activity 21–2** to review important terms in the section.

Using Geography Skills

Answers:
1. 1938
2. to appease him and avoid a war that they would certainly have to fight

Skills Practice

Ask: In what year did Hitler order troops into the Rhineland? *(1936)*

Appeasement Fails

Main Idea Other European nations stood by as Germany expanded its territory.

Reading Focus How do you deal with bullies? Is it better to stand up to them or give them what they want? Read on to find out how Europe's leaders dealt with Adolf Hitler's demands.

One reason Adolf Hitler was popular in Germany was because he criticized the Treaty of Versailles. Many Germans believed the treaty was unfair. Hitler promised in his speeches that he would no longer obey the treaty.

The Treaty of Versailles kept Germany's military forces small. Hitler, however, insisted that this was unfair. In March 1935, he stated that Germany would build a new air force and increase the size of its army. The Treaty of Versailles had also declared that no German troops could be in the **Rhineland**, a German territory west of the Rhine River along the French border. In 1936 Hitler ordered troops into the Rhineland.

France wanted to expel the German troops from the Rhineland, but the French government would not act without British help. Britain did not want to use force against Germany. Instead, British leaders chose a policy of **appeasement** (uh•PEEZ•muhnt). Appeasement is the idea that if you meet another government's demands, you can avoid war.

Hitler gained a close ally in Italy's Benito Mussolini. In 1935 Mussolini sent Italian forces to invade the African nation of Ethiopia. Britain and France opposed

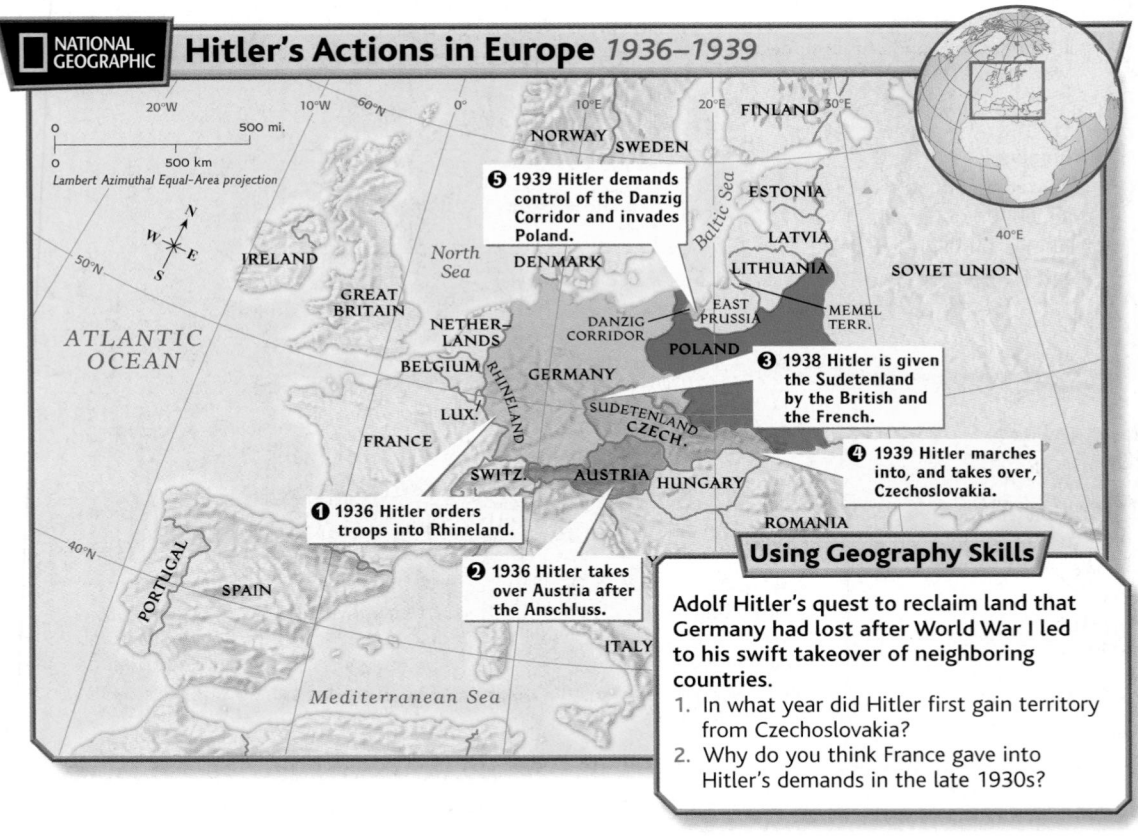

NATIONAL GEOGRAPHIC
Hitler's Actions in Europe *1936–1939*

500 mi.
500 km
Lambert Azimuthal Equal-Area projection

❺ 1939 Hitler demands control of the Danzig Corridor and invades Poland.

❸ 1938 Hitler is given the Sudetenland by the British and the French.

❹ 1939 Hitler marches into, and takes over, Czechoslovakia.

❶ 1936 Hitler orders troops into Rhineland.

❷ 1936 Hitler takes over Austria after the Anschluss.

Using Geography Skills

Adolf Hitler's quest to reclaim land that Germany had lost after World War I led to his swift takeover of neighboring countries.
1. In what year did Hitler first gain territory from Czechoslovakia?
2. Why do you think France gave into Hitler's demands in the late 1930s?

Reading Strategy ▶ READING THE TEXT

Responding Encourage students to note their reactions as they read the material under "Appeasement Fails." After students finish reading, distribute charts with the following column headings: *Passage/Strongly Agree/Agree Somewhat/Strongly Disagree/Not Sure*. Tell students to list numbers 1 through 5 under *Passage*. Next, read aloud this passage: "The Treaty of Versailles kept Germany's military forces small. Hitler, however, insisted that this was unfair." **Ask:** Do you agree with Hitler? Tell students to check one of the columns across from 1 in the first column. Repeat the process as you recite four more passages from the reading. Then have each student choose two more passages, copy the passages in the first column, and check the appropriate columns. Have students share their choices with the class. **L1/EL**

the invasion but took no military action to stop it. Hitler, however, threw his support to Mussolini.

Next, the two dictators intervened in Spain. From 1936 to 1939, a civil war divided that country. Germany and Italy helped a Spanish military leader, General Francisco Franco, overthrow Spain's new republic. Soon after, Italy and Germany formed an alliance.

Next, Hitler turned to Austria. He insisted that Austria, a German-speaking country, should be part of Germany. In March 1938, he sent troops into Austria and took it over.

Hitler then turned to Austria's neighbor, Czechoslovakia, and demanded that the Czechs give Germany the **Sudetenland** (soo•DAY•tuhn•LAND), an area in western Czechoslovakia where many Germans lived. Czechoslovakia was ready to fight to keep the Sudetenland, but Britain and France preferred to negotiate. In September 1938, European leaders met in the German city of **Munich** (MYOO•nihk).

At the Munich Conference, Britain and France agreed to give the Sudetenland to Germany. Hitler, in turn, promised not to expand Germany's territory further. The British prime minister, **Neville Chamberlain** (NEHV•uhl CHAYM•buhr•luhn), returned home and declared that there would be "peace in our time."

Hopes for peace were smashed the following year. In March 1939, German forces took over western Czechoslovakia and set up a Nazi-friendly state in the eastern part. Hitler then demanded control of Danzig, a German city inside Polish territory. In response, Britain promised to support Poland if the Germans invaded.

Reading Check **Analyze** Why did British and French leaders appease Hitler?

The War Begins

Main Idea World War II began when Germany invaded Poland in September 1939, leading France and Britain to declare war.

Reading Focus Have you ever had to do something really difficult? What helped you to do it? Read to learn how the British endured defeats and German bombings.

In the summer of 1939, Hitler prepared to invade Poland. He worried, however, that such an attack would anger Stalin because Poland bordered the Soviet Union. Though bitter enemies, Hitler and Stalin signed a treaty in August 1939 in which they promised not to attack each other. They also agreed to divide Poland between them. This agreement freed Hitler to attack Poland.

▲ This photo shows a Czech woman weeping as she salutes invading German troops. *What happened after Britain and France gave the Sudetenland to Germany?*

Writing Activity

Introduce students to the countries that the Germans took over in 1938 and 1939. Circulate travel folders and books showing pictures and describing customs in Austria and the present-day Czech Republic and Slovakia. Then have students choose a country, design a postcard from there, and describe an interesting building or event in a note on the postcard. Have students exchange postcards. **L2**

Literature Explain that *Homage to Catalonia* describes George Orwell's adventures serving with the rebels in the Spanish Civil War. Assign chapters of Orwell's book to different students and ask them to write summaries. Post the summaries in the order of the chapters and encourage students to take time to read them. **L3**

Reading Check

Answer: They wanted to avoid war.

Caption Answer:
Although Hitler promised he would not expand Germany's territory any farther, Germany took over the rest of Czechoslovakia the following year.

DIFFERENTIATED INSTRUCTION

Kinesthetic: Organize the class into pairs and have each pair draw a checkerboard and make paper checkers. Have them use the game to illustrate how Hitler took over Austria, Czechoslovakia, and Poland. Suggest that they label the checkers with names of countries and other elements of the conflict and arrange them on the board to show in a few moves how Germany took control.

English Learners: Pair each English Learner with a native speaker for the activity above.

Gifted and Talented: Challenge chess-playing students to use chess pieces and a chessboard to illustrate Hitler's strategy. Remind them to give appropriate labels to the pieces.

☞ Refer to *Inclusion Strategies for the Middle School Social Studies Classroom* in the TCR.

CONNECTING ACROSS TIME

Tell students that George Macbeth was growing up in London when the Germans were bombing the city. He recorded his memories in *A Child of War*. According to Macbeth, he and his friends collected shrapnel pieces as if they were toys. The greatest sacrifice he recalls is going without sweets. Licorice, sherbet, cream whirls, and Cadbury's Caramellos were unavailable, and tasteless Ration Chocolate replaced milk chocolate. **Ask:** Do you think George and his parents had similar memories of the war? Explain. **L2**

Caption Answer: Radar allowed Britain to detect incoming German airplanes.

To help students understand section material, have them visit **Homework Helper** at **jat.glencoe.com**

Reading Support L1/ EL

Assign **Guided Reading Activity 21–2** to help students organize the information in the section.

▲ During the Battle of Britain, German planes bombed British cities, hoping to break the will of the British people. *What advantage did the Royal Air Force have during the Battle of Britain?*

Poland and France Fall On September 1, 1939, Hitler sent his armies into Poland. Two days later, Britain and France declared war on Germany. The German attack on Poland was quick and fierce. In less than a month, the conquered country was split in half by Hitler and Stalin.

In April 1940, the Germans attacked Denmark and Norway. In May, they invaded the Netherlands and Belgium. German troops and tanks then smashed through French defenses and raced across northern

Web Activity Visit jat.glencoe.com and click on *Chapter 21—Student Web Activity* to learn more about World War II.

France. A few weeks later, on June 22, 1940, France surrendered to Germany. At this time, Italy joined the war on Germany's side.

What Was the Battle of Britain? Hitler expected the British to ask for peace. Instead, the new prime minister of Great Britain, **Winston Churchill** (WIHN•stuhn CHUHRCH•HIHL), declared, "We shall never surrender."

In August the German air force began an all-out effort to destroy Britain's Royal Air Force and clear the way for a German invasion of Britian. This air battle became known as the Battle of Britain.

The Royal Air Force also had a new technology called radar. Radar stations along the coast detected incoming German airplanes and directed British fighter planes to stop them. On October 12, 1940, Hitler cancelled his plans to invade Britain. Great Britain escaped invasion thanks to a few hundred pilots. Churchill told the British Parliament: "Never . . . was so much owed by so many to so few."

America Stays Neutral The United States remained neutral during the early years of the war. In the 1930s, Congress had passed several laws making it illegal to help other countries in a war if the U.S. was neutral. President Roosevelt, however, believed that Germany was a threat to the United States. He convinced Congress to approve a cash-and-carry policy. This law let Britain buy goods from American businesses as long as they paid cash and carried the goods to Britain in their own ships. A year later, he asked Congress to pass the Lend-Lease Act. This law allowed the U.S. to lend weapons to Britain. Roosevelt also ordered the American navy to protect the British ships from German submarines when they were close to the United States.

CRITICAL THINKING ACTIVITY

Determining Cause and Effect On the board, copy this chart, omitting the answers in cyan:

Problem	Effect
(Germans trapped Allied troops at Dunkirk.)	Warships and civilian boats rescued 300,000 troops.
(Churchill declared, "We will not surrender.")	German planes began to blitz London.
The Royal Air Force used radar.	(British fighters had a great advantage.)
British fighters stopped German warplanes.	(Hitler cancelled plans to invade Britain.)

Have students complete the chart with facts from the reading. Remind them that an effect can be a cause, too. **L2**

Biography

WINSTON CHURCHILL
1874–1965
FRANKLIN D. ROOSEVELT
1882–1945

Winston Churchill grew up in Blenheim Palace, England, raised by a beloved nanny. His father, Lord Randolph Churchill, was a member of the British Parliament. Churchill attended private schools where he struggled with his studies. When Churchill switched to the Royal Military Academy, he began doing well. He studied military tactics, mapmaking, and military law. Later he joined the cavalry and fought in India and Africa. Afterward, he became a journalist and found fame reporting on the Boer War.

Franklin Delano Roosevelt was born in Hyde Park, New York, to a wealthy family. Roosevelt was educated at home by a governess until he turned 14. Then he was sent to a school near Boston. Like Churchill, Roosevelt did not do well in school. Because President Theodore Roosevelt was his cousin, Roosevelt wanted to work in government. He went to Harvard University and Columbia Law School.

▲ Winston Churchill

At age 26, Churchill won election to the British Parliament. This was the beginning of his political career that led eventually to him becoming prime minister of England.

At age 28, Roosevelt won election to the New York State senate, but then came down with polio and lost much of the use of his legs. Refusing to allow his disability to end his career, he went on to become governor of New York and then president.

"Together we cannot fail."
–Franklin D. Roosevelt, *Fireside Chats*

▲ Franklin D. Roosevelt

Then and Now

Both Churchill and Roosevelt came from families already involved in politics. How do you think this affected their decision to pursue that type of career? Identify a few present-day families that are active in politics.

817

Biography

TEACH

Winston Churchill is renowned for the speeches he wrote during World War II and for the expressions he created for those speeches. Of special fame is the "blood, toil, tears, and sweat" phrase. Supposedly, Churchill also coined the term "iron curtain." In reality, however, phrases similar to "blood, toil, tears, and sweat" had been used by both John Donne and Lord Byron.

Roosevelt and Churchill became fast friends. Churchill spent the Christmas after Pearl Harbor in the White House. He brought his battle maps with him so he and Roosevelt could discuss strategy. Franklin's wife, Eleanor, observed: "They looked like two little boys playing soldier. They seemed to be having a wonderful time, too wonderful in fact. It made me a little sad somehow." **Ask:** Why do you think Churchill's and Roosevelt's enthusiasm about war strategy made Eleanor sad? L1/EL

Then and Now

Answers will vary. Students may mention the Bush and Kennedy families.

Reading List Generator CD-ROM

GLENCOE BOOKLINK **RECOMMENDED READING**

Use the **Glencoe BookLink CD-ROM** to create customized reading lists based on your students' interests and reading levels. Below is an example based on content in this chapter. Also, see the Suggested Readings on pages 944–946 of the Appendix.

- Marrin, Albert. *Secret Armies: Spies, Counterspies and Saboteurs in World War II.* During World War II, Hitler sent spies and saboteurs to England. British Military Intelligence caught them and turned many into double agents.

- Masters, Nancy Robinson. *Bombers of World War II.* Read about the Martin B-26 Marauder, the Lockheed P-38 Droop Snoot, and the Boeing B-17 Flying Fortress—some of the bombers used by the Allies in World War II.

③ ASSESS

Assign Section 2 Review as homework or as an in-class activity.

⊙ Have students use the **Interactive Tutor Self-Assessment CD-ROM** to review the section.

Assessment L2

Assign **Section 2 Quiz** to assess mastery of the material found in the section.

Reading Support L1/EL

Assign **Reading Essentials and Study Guide 21–2** to help students review section material.

More About the Art

One of the most devastating attacks in American history took place in less than two hours. At around 7:55 A.M. the first wave of Japanese attack planes swooped into Pearl Harbor. Fifteen minutes later, a second wave of attack planes flew in, and by 10 A.M. the raid was over. By 1 P.M. the Japanese carriers were headed back to Japan.

Caption Answer: The Japanese were angered at American actions.

Hitler Invades the Soviet Union Unable to defeat the British, Hitler decided that Germany needed the resources of the Soviet Union. He also believed that the Soviets' vast land area could provide "living space" for Germans in the future. In June 1941, German forces attacked the Soviet Union. They destroyed most of the Soviets' warplanes, disabled thousands of Soviet tanks, and captured half a million Soviet soldiers.

As the Germans advanced, Stalin ordered a scorched-earth policy. Soviet troops and civilians burned cities, destroyed their own crops, and blew up dams that produced electric power.

These actions made it harder for the Germans to supply their troops and keep moving forward. Then the rainy season began, turning the roads to mud and trapping German wagons and trucks. Soon afterward the harsh Russian winter set in, catching the German army unprepared.

Despite loss of soldiers and equipment, German troops reached the outskirts of Moscow on December 2, 1941. That was as far as they got. The Soviets refused to surrender, and the Germans were unable to break into the city.

Japan Attacks Pearl Harbor While Hitler and Mussolini waged war in Europe, the Japanese launched new attacks in East Asia. In Section 1, you learned about Japan's takeover of Manchuria in 1931. During the 1930s, the Japanese moved steadily southward into China. In December 1937, they

The Attack on Pearl Harbor

On December 7, 1941, Japan carried out its plan to attack the United States and bring them into World War II. Early that morning, a group of Japanese warplanes flew over the military base in Pearl Harbor, Hawaii. Without warning, they dropped bombs on the men and women below and destroyed countless ships as they sat in their docks unprotected. The attack cost many thousands of American lives and prompted the U.S. to enter the war. *Why do you think the Japanese chose to attack a base in Hawaii?*

COOPERATIVE LEARNING ACTIVITY

Daily Life Explain to students that daily life during World War II was a far cry from students' daily lives today, especially for German soldiers on the Soviet front. Then read the following diary passage by a German soldier who fought and died in the USSR: "December 26. The horses have already been eaten. I would eat a cat; they say its meat is also tasty. The soldiers look like corpses or lunatics, looking for something to put in their mouths. They no longer take cover from Russian shells; they haven't the strength to walk, run away and hide. A curse on this war!" Point out that the soldier was in Stalingrad on the day after Christmas. **Ask:** What other hardships besides hunger did the Germans face in the battle at Stalingrad? *(cold weather)* L2 seized **Nanjing** (NAHN • JIHNG), the Chinese capital. China's leader, Chiang Kai-shek, refused to surrender, and the government moved into China's interior.

Japan next moved into Southeast Asia. After the fall of France in 1940, Japanese forces sized the French colony of Indochina. Japan also planned to take the Dutch East Indies, British Malaya, and the American territory of the Philippines. The Japanese goal was to gain badly needed rubber, oil, and food supplies.

President Roosevelt wanted Britain to defeat Germany. He worried that Britain would also have to fight Japan if Japan attacked the British Empire in Asia. So Roosevelt tried to stop Japan by using economic pressure. When Japan invaded Indochina, President Roosevelt prevented the Japanese from withdrawing money they had in American banks. He also stopped the sale of oil, gasoline, and other natural resources that Japan lacked.

Angered by American actions, the Japanese decided to go to war against the United States. On December 7, 1941, Japanese warplanes carried out a surprise attack on the American fleet at **Pearl Harbor,** Hawaii. The attack destroyed many battleships and planes. More than 2,300 soldiers, sailors, and civilians were killed.

The next day, President Roosevelt asked Congress to declare war on Japan. He called December 7 "a date which will live in infamy [disgrace]." Congress quickly declared war on Japan. Three days later, Germany and Italy declared war on the United States.

Reading Check **Identify** What was the United States's cash-and-carry policy?

Section 2 Review

Study Central™ Need help with the material in this section? Visit jat.glencoe.com

Reading Summary

Review the Main Ideas

- In the mid-1930s, Germany began to rearm and seize surrounding territories, while Britain and France followed a policy of appeasement.

- The German invasion of Poland in 1939 began World War II. In 1941, Japan attacked Pearl Harbor, bringing the United States into the war.

What Did You Learn?

1. Describe what happened at the Battle of Britain.

2. Describe how the United States aided Britain before Pearl Harbor was attacked.

Critical Thinking

3. **Sequencing Information** Draw a time line like the one below. Fill in details about German aggressions in Europe beginning with the occupation of the Rhineland and ending with the invasion of Russia.

|———|———|———|———|———|———|———|
March **June**
1936 **1941**

4. **Analyze** Describe the British policy of appeasement. Why do you think such a policy did not work with Hitler?

5. **Evaluate** What was the importance of the Battle of Britain?

6. **Cause and Effect** What American actions caused Japan to carry out their attack on Pearl Harbor?

7. **Expository Writing** Choose an event from the section and write a newspaper article about it. Include a headline, details about the event, and why the event was important.

SECTION 2 REVIEW ANSWERS

1. The Germans bombed the British Air Force, but British fighters stopped them.

2. The U.S. sold goods and lent weapons to Britain.

3. 1938: Germans occupy Austria, Sudetenland, and Czechoslovakia; 1939: Germans sign pact with Soviets and invade Poland; 1940: Germans invade Denmark, Norway, the Netherlands, Belgium, France, and begin the Battle of Britain

4. If Germans met reasonable demands, other nations would be satisfied. However, only force could stop Hitler.

5. Because Germans failed to destroy the British air force, they canceled plans to invade Britain.

6. The United States froze Japanese assets and stopped selling them fuel.

7. Answers will vary.

ENRICH

Tell students that the U.S. military distrusted Japanese Americans and so interned about 100,000 in detention camps without accusing them of crimes or giving them trials. **Ask:** How did this violate the rights of Japanese Americans? *(Detention violated their right to freedom from unreasonable seizure, right to liberty, and right to a speedy trial guaranteed in the Bill of Rights.)* **L3**

Reading Check

Answer: The policy allowed the British to pay cash for American food and weapons and carry them to Britain in their own ships.

To help students understand section material, have them visit **Study Central**™ at jat.glencoe.com

RETEACH

Have students outline the main events in the section using boldfaced headings as main ideas and supporting details. **L2**

④ CLOSE

Ask students to identify the people and places listed under Get Ready to Read. **L1/EL**

SUMMARY

Eisik, a poor Jewish boy in Nazi-occupied Poland, has a series of dreams. In each dream, a man tells Eisik to look by the arch of a Krakow bridge to find a great treasure. When Eisik goes to the bridge, he meets a Nazi guard. The guard tells him that he, too, dreams. In his dreams, a man says that a treasure is hidden under the stove in the house of a boy named Eisik. However, the guard ignores his dreams and recommends that Eisik do the same. Eisik runs home, and there he and his father move the stove and uncover a box of gold and silver.

Vocabulary Preview Before students begin reading, have them read **Before You Read** and the **Vocabulary Preview.** Point out that difficult words are footnoted throughout the text.

① FOCUS

Reality Times Ten Authors sometimes take a relatively recent true story, like the one adapted by Gary Schmidt about Rabbi Eisik and his treasure, and add fanciful elements to turn fact into modern folklore. For many readers, folklore is often more entertaining and more inspiring than bare facts.

The Unexpected Treasure

Adapted by Gary Schmidt

Before You Read

The Scene: This story takes place in Kraków, Poland, shortly before World War II.

The Characters: Eisik is a poor Jewish boy living in Kraków with his family.

The Plot: Eisik's family is very poor. He has three dreams in which a man tells him to go to a particular place to find treasure. Eisik must decide whether or not to follow the dreams' directions.

Vocabulary Preview

embankment: raised structure that holds back water

slate: rock used as a construction material

flourished: waved boldly

sprinted: ran as fast as possible

Have you ever had a dream and wanted it to be true? In this story, a boy dreams about a solution to his family's problems and then tries to make the dream come true.

820

Reading Strategy READING REINFORCEMENT

Tracking Information Have each student draw a Venn diagram on a sheet of paper. Tell students to label the left part of their diagram "Eisik," the right part "Nazi guard," and the overlapping part "Both." As students read, ask them to write words and phrases that describe Eisik in the left part of the diagram, those that describe the Nazi guard in the right part, and a phrase that describes both in the overlapping section. Encourage students to use their prior knowledge and clues from the story to infer information about the two characters and add their inferences to the diagram. For example, the students might add "non-Jewish" or "unimaginative" under "Nazi guard." **L1**

As You Read

This story is a mixture of fact and fiction. It is based on a story about Rabbi Eisik, a man born in Kraków who found a great treasure and used it to build a House of Prayer in his neighborhood.

A

Eisik, the youngest boy in his family, believed that his must be one of the poorest families in all of Poland. Poorer than poor. When their Rabbi spoke of poverty, Eisik knew, he was speaking of Eisik's family. Even his hunger was hungry, and his jacket was more patch than jacket. He had seen plucked plump chickens hanging in the butcher's shop, but his mother had never, as far as Eisik knew, even been inside such a shop. He had never tasted a candy, and he wondered what one might taste like. He wondered if a house could ever be too warm. He knew that it could be too cold.

Eisik's family was very poor.

B

One night, Eisik dreamed that a man came to him and pointed to a bridge in Kraków.[1] "Look by the arch of the bridge,"[2] he said, "and you will find a great treasure." Eisik woke up that morning smiling, but he knew better than to believe in a silly dream, and he soon forgot about it.

The next night the dream came again. The same man pointed to the bridge. "Look by the arch of the bridge, and you will find a great treasure." Again, Eisik woke in the morning smiling, but he knew that it was just a silly dream. He soon forgot about it.

On the third night, the man came again into his dreams, and now he was angry. "Do I come all the way into the

[1]**Kraków:** a city in southern Poland
[2]**arch of the bridge:** curved pieces that connect the main structure to the banks on either side and support the weight of the bridge

---

② TEACH

A ACTIVE READING STRATEGIES

RESPOND Ask students what they feel for Eisik after reading this passage. (*Answers may include pity or compassion.*)

B CRITICAL THINKING

INFERRING Ask students to infer the reason Eisik wakes up smiling. (*A possible answer is that the mere thought of treasure makes Eisik smile because he is so poor.*)

GLENCOE
BOOKLINK

Use **Glencoe BookLink** to create customized reading lists for your students' reading levels, interests, and abilities.

Reading Strategy ‹ VOCABULARY READING TIP

Using Suffixes Remind students that the suffixes *-er* and *-est* create comparative and superlative adjectives when added to a simple adjective. Explain that a comparative is used when comparing two items, and a superlative is used when comparing three or more. Next, have students find an adjective, its comparative form, and its superlative form on the first page of the story (*poor, poorer, poorest*).
Ask: What does the use of *youngest* in the first sentence of the story imply? (*Eisik has more than one brother.*) As students read the rest of the story, tell them to look for a passage that supports their inference. (*Example: His father and mother and brothers and sisters were waiting for him.*) **L1**

C LITERARY ELEMENTS

IMAGERY Point out that *World of Confusion* is a metaphor for the characters' restricted and fearful life. **Ask: What image represents a way out of the World of Confusion?** *(the bridge)*

D ACTIVE READING STRATEGIES

CONNECT Have students recall times when they have looked for something in an unpleasant place like the damp, dark walk where Eisik was looking for treasure. Ask them to describe the way they felt as they searched. *(Answers may include that they felt unpleasant and frustrated.)*

E AUTHOR'S CRAFT

INDIRECT CHARACTERIZATION Ask students to explain how the author uses dialogue and a description of Eisik to show that the guard is a bully. *(Eisik feels scared and ashamed when the guard accuses him of "creeping about the bridge." Also, the guard laughs at Eisik for believing in "a silly dream.")*

F LITERARY ELEMENTS

CLIMAX Ask students to explain why this passage represents a major turning point in Eisik's story. *(Eisik realizes that his dreams are not silly and that the treasure actually exists.)*

World of Confusion[3] for nothing every night?" he demanded. "Now, boy, look by the arch of the bridge, and you will find a great treasure."

When Eisik woke, he was trembling. He went to his mother and asked if she believed that dreams can come true. She leaned down and kissed him on the forehead. "Of course they can come true. Weren't you born to us?"

Eisik packed some food and set off for Kraków.

It was a long walk, and the sun was well on its way to rest before Eisik reached the city and found the bridge. He scrambled down the embankment and onto a slate walk. It was slimy with the damp of the water, so he crept slowly, looking into all the shadows, testing the bricks to see if they might give and the treasure be hidden behind them. But there was nothing at all. Tired and wet, he climbed back up to the bridge.

"You there! What are you doing?" A swastikaed[4] guard. Eisik froze.

"What are you doing, creeping about the bridge like that?"

And Eisik, scared and ashamed, could only say, "It was a dream. A dream told me I should do it."

"A dream? A dream?" The guard laughed. "Don't you know better than to believe in a silly dream? Don't you know that dreams mean nothing? Why, these last three nights, I've had the same dream again and again: A man comes and tells me that there is a great treasure hidden under the stove in the house of a poor family with a boy named Eisik.

---

[3]**World of Confusion:** the characters' name for their way of life during a time of restrictions and fear
[4]**swastikaed:** wearing a swastika, a Nazi symbol

EXTENDING THE CONTENT

Kraków The Vistula River divides Kraków in two, so bridges, including the bridge in Eisik's story, are part of the city's world-famous architecture. The most famous structures, however, are the centuries-old buildings. Wawel Castle, where the medieval kings of Poland were crowned, and the Jangiellonian University, which was founded in 1364, still stand today. During the Nazi occupation, the German governor, who had offices in Wawel Castle, executed the teachers at the university and condemned 55,000 of the area's Jews to the nearby Birkenau death camp. Ironically, the venerable buildings and bridges that survived World War II are threatened today by pollution—a by-product of Kraków's success as an industrial center.

E "Do you see me running off, looking into every Jewish house with a boy named Eisik and digging under their stove? Do you?"

Eisik shook his head, but his heart stopped.

The guard flourished his rifle at him. "Off now, and don't trouble me with dreams."

F Eisik sprinted from the bridge and ran out of Kraków all the way home, where his father and mother and brothers and sisters were waiting for him. They threw their arms around him, and his mother wept, and even his father. "We thought . . ." they began, and could not go on. They feared to say aloud what they had thought in the World of Confusion where anything at all might happen.

And when they had all gone inside, Eisik and his father moved their iron stove. They pried up a layer of bricks, and beneath it they found a box filled with gold and silver coins. It was enough, said Papa, to get all of them, even Grandpapa and Tante,[5] out of Poland. Maybe even to America.

And Eisik hoped that that dream would come true as well.

_____
[5]**Tante:** French for _aunt_

Responding to the Reading

1. How does Eisik find treasure by looking by the arch of the bridge?

2. When Eisik talks with his mother about dreams, each of them is referring to a different type of dream. What are the two meanings of _dream_ used in that conversation?

3. **Analyze** Why do you think Eisik did not tell his family where he was going and that he would arrive home late?

4. **Compare** How do Eisik and the guard react differently to their dreams?

5. **Reading** **Read to Write** Eisik and his family had dreams of a future in which they were safe and had enough money for food and heat. What types of dreams do you have? Write a brief essay in which you identify three of your goals and explain what you need to do to make those dreams come true.

823

Responding to the Reading Answers

1. A Nazi guard catches Eisik and, without meaning to, tells him where the treasure is located.

2. Eisik refers to dreams that people have when they sleep. His mother refers to the goals people have for the future.

3. Answers will vary. Possible answers include that he did not want to get their hopes up or to have them worry about him all day.

4. Eisik follows the directions in his dreams while the guard ignores his dreams.

5. Essays will vary. Encourage students to think about what it may take to accomplish their dreams.

DIFFERENTIATED INSTRUCTION

EL Students Have students write each unfamiliar word from the story on one side of an index card and its dictionary meaning on the other side. Then organize the students into pairs, direct partners to exchange cards, and have them use the flash cards to test each other's recall of the words' meanings.

Average Students On the board, draw a graphic of six overlapping ovals. In the ovals, have students write descriptions of events from the story to create a "chain" of causes and effects.

Gifted Students Have students write essays that apply the lessons and imagery in Eisik's story to the situation of another people who experienced persecution during the 1800s and 1900s. Tell them to use facts from other parts of the unit in their essay. (_Lessons: dreams can be realized, hope conquers adversity; Imagery: bridges, hidden treasures_)

③ ASSESS

Assign the **Responding to the Reading** questions as an in-class activity or as homework.

④ CLOSE

Have students sum up in a sentence what they would do with the treasure if they were in Eisik's place. **L1/EL**

① FOCUS

SECTION OVERVIEW

American participation in World War II dragged on for four years while Nazis murdered more than 12 million Jews and other European civilians. Eventually the Allies won.

BELLRINGER
SKILLBUILDER ACTIVITY

✍ Project **Daily Focus Skills Transparency 21–3** and have students answer questions. Discuss their responses.

Get Ready to Read!

Preteaching Vocabulary: Explain that *gen* is derived from the Latin word for "race or kind," and *cide* comes from the Latin word that means "kill." So *genocide* means "the killing of a race." The word originated in 1944 with the Holocaust.

Answers to Graphic: Answers will vary. Sample answers: 1942: U.S. victory at Midway, British stopped Germans in Egypt; 1943: Allies landed in Italy, Tehran Conference; 1944: Allies took Rome, D-Day invasion; 1945: Germans surrendered, *Enola Gay* dropped the atomic bomb.

Section 3

The Allies Win the War

Get Ready to Read!

What's the Connection?
You have read about how dictators expanding their power and territory led to World War II. In this section, you will learn how the Allies defeated Germany, Japan, and Italy, and won World War II.

Focusing on the (Main Ideas)
• The Allies fought for four long years in Europe and in the Pacific. **(page 825)**

• The Nazis murdered millions of people in an attempt to destroy Jews and other European ethnic groups. **(page 827)**

• The successful invasion on D-Day was the beginning of the end of World War II. **(page 828)**

Locating Places
Auschwitz (OWSH•VIHTS)

Meeting People
Douglas MacArthur (muh•KAHR•thuhr)
Dwight D. Eisenhower (EYE•zuhn•HOWR)
Harry S Truman (TROO•muhn)

Building Your Vocabulary
genocide (JEH•nuh•SYD)
D-Day

Reading Strategy
Sequencing Complete a table like the one below showing two events that occurred in each year.

Year	Event	Event
1942		
1943		
1944		
1945		

NATIONAL GEOGRAPHIC **When & Where?**

1941   1943   1945

NORTH AMERICA   EUROPE   ASIA

1942 Battle of Midway stops Japanese advance

1943 Italy surrenders to Allies

1944 Allies land in France on D-Day

1945 Atomic bombs are dropped on Japan

SECTION RESOURCES

📁 **Reproducible Masters**
• Reproducible Lesson Plan 21–3
• Daily Lecture and Discussion Notes 21–3
• Vocabulary Activity 21–3
• Active Reading Note-Taking Guide 21–3
• Guided Reading Activity 21–3
• Section Quiz 21–3
• Reading Essentials and Study Guide 21–3

🖨 **Transparencies**
• Daily Focus Skills Transparency 21–3

Multimedia
🔘 Interactive Tutor Self-Assessment CD-ROM
🔘 ExamView® Pro Testmaker CD-ROM
🔘 Presentation Plus! CD-ROM

The Great Struggle

Main Idea The Allies fought for four long years in Europe and in the Pacific.

Reading Focus Have you ever had to follow a step-by-step plan to finish a project? Read to learn how step-by-step, the Allies pushed back the Axis powers.

World War II was a huge war. On one side were the Allies—the United States, Great Britain, the Soviet Union, and China. On the other side were the Axis powers—Germany, Italy, and Japan. It was fought on two fronts—in Europe and in the Pacific. Winning battles required outstanding leaders and hundreds of thousands of troops. At home, civilians worked hard to provide resources and goods for the war effort.

Stopping Japan's Advance By mid-1942, Japan had driven the Americans out of the Philippines and seized many islands in the Pacific. The United States set out to stop the Japanese advance. In June 1942,

The Pacific War 1941–1945

Using Geography Skills

To defeat Japan, the United States attacked some Japanese-held islands while bypassing others.
1. About how far did Japanese control extend from the home islands?
2. Where was the first Allied victory in the Pacific following the attack on Pearl Harbor?

KEY
- Japanese Empire and conquests
- Farthest extent of Japan's conquests, July 1942
- → Allied forces
- ✸ Allied victory
- ◎ Atomic bombing

② TEACH

Reading Strategy

Taking Notes Suggest students develop a form of shorthand when taking notes. As they read have them take notes by leaving out unimportant words, using abbreviations such as & and *WWII*, and assigning one letter to a word that will likely occur again and so it can be signified by that one letter. Tell students to use these techniques to make notes for the rest of the page. **L1/EL**

Daily Lecture and Discussion Notes 21–3

Use **Daily Lecture and Discussion Notes 21–3** for an outline of key concepts found in the section.

Using Geography Skills

Answers:
1. about 3,000–4,000 miles
2. Midway

Skills Practice

Ask: Where did the last Allied victory occur before the atomic bombings? (*Okinawa*)

Reading Strategy **READING THE TEXT**

Setting a Purpose Ask students to create a question based on each heading in the section. Give them the following example: What made the war a great struggle? Tell students to list one or two questions per page in their notebook. Then instruct them to look for the answers to the questions as they read the lesson and to write each answer under the appropriate question. (*Sample questions for the rest of the headings are: How was Japan's advance stopped? Who drove back the Germans? What was the Holocaust? How did the Allies win? When was D-Day? Why was the atomic bomb dropped? How was the world rebuilt?*) **L1/EL**

Reading Support L1/ EL

Use **Vocabulary Activity 21-3** to review important terms in the section.

Writing Activity

Ask students to choose one of the following persons: Douglas MacArthur, Chester Nimitz, Dwight D. Eisenhower, George Patton, or Bernard Montgomery. Tell them to research their chosen person and to write his résumé based on their research. Give students sample résumés to use as models. **L2**

More About the Photo

The Tehran Conference was held only two days after the Cairo Conference. Both conferences discussed how to win WWII. The Cairo Conference focused on defeating Japan, whereas the Tehran Conference focused on defeating Germany.

Caption Answer: divide Germany after the war, Soviet Union would help defeat Japan, they would join an international organization for keeping peace after the war

Reading Check

Answer: In the Pacific, the U.S. carried out a plan called island-hopping in which they attacked key islands and moved closer to Japan. In Europe, the Allies invaded by land and attacked Germany by air.

▲ The leaders of the three major Allied powers met at Tehran in 1943. Shown are (left to right) Joseph Stalin, Franklin D. Roosevelt, and Winston Churchill. *What did the Allies agree to at Tehran?*

the American forces won a major sea and air battle at Midway Island. This battle stopped Japan's advance and changed the course of the Pacific war in favor of the Allies.

During the next three years, U.S. commanders in the Pacific—General **Douglas MacArthur** (muh•KAHR•thuhr) and Admiral Chester Nimitz—carried out a plan called island-hopping. This called for attacking certain key islands. The United States then used these islands for jumping forward to others, moving closer and closer to Japan.

By 1945, the Americans had recaptured the Philippines and destroyed much of Japan's air force and navy. The Japanese, however, fought fiercely as American forces closed in on Japan itself.

Driving Back the Germans

Meanwhile, the war raged on in Africa, the Soviet Union, and Europe. After early German advances in North Africa, British forces in 1942 defeated the Germans in Egypt. Later that year, British and American forces landed in Morocco and Algeria. Moving swiftly eastward, they drove the Germans out of North Africa in May 1943.

Allied troops then moved into southern Europe. They took the island of Sicily in the summer of 1943 and landed on Italy's mainland in September. U.S. general **Dwight D. Eisenhower** (EYE•zuhn•HOWR) directed the overall invasion. Another American general, George Patton, and British general Bernard Montgomery actually led the troops.

As the Allies advanced, the Italians overthrew Mussolini and surrendered. German forces in Italy fought on but failed to stop the Allied move into central Italy. In June 1944, the Allies finally took Rome, Italy's capital.

Meanwhile, Allied leaders made plans for the world after the war was over. In late 1943 Roosevelt, Churchill, and Stalin met in the Middle East at Tehran, the capital of Iran. At this Tehran Conference, the leaders agreed to divide up Germany after defeating Hitler. Stalin also agreed to help the United States defeat Japan and to join an international organization for keeping peace after the war.

✓ **Reading Check** **Contrast** How was the war in the Pacific different from the war in Europe?

DIFFERENTIATED INSTRUCTION

Visual/Spatial: Distribute outline maps of the Mediterranean area. Have students try to label the countries in Europe and Africa from memory. As students read "Driving Back the Germans," tell them to write dates in the countries to which they relate and give the map an appropriate title.

English Learners: Refer students to the Reference Atlas maps for names of countries in the region.

Gifted and Talented: Have students use their prior knowledge to draw a freehand map of the Mediterranean area and label the approximate locations of countries mentioned in the lesson.

☞ Refer to *Inclusion Strategies for the Middle School Social Studies Classroom* in the TCR.

The Holocaust

Main Idea The Nazis murdered millions of people in an attempt to destroy Jews and other European ethnic groups.

Reading Focus Today many people use the word *Nazi* to mean "someone very evil." The main reason is the Holocaust. Read on to learn about this dark chapter in human history.

During World War II, the Nazis began a program of **genocide** (JEH•nuh•SYD), or the killing of an entire group of people. Hitler wanted to destroy all of Europe's Jews. As many as 6 million Jews were killed in what has become known as the Holocaust. Millions of others, including Slavs and Roma, or Gypsies, were also ruthlessly killed.

In Section 1, you learned that the Nazis passed laws against the Jews during the 1930s. These laws declared that Jews were no longer German citizens. By the end of the decade, Nazi actions became more violent.

On the night of November 9, 1938, the Nazis burned synagogues, destroyed Jewish shops, and killed many Jews. About 30,000 Jewish men were sent to concentration camps, large prison camps used to hold people for political reasons. This event became known as *Kristallnacht,* or the "night of shattered glass," because of the Jewish shop windows that were broken by Nazi mobs.

During World War II, the Nazis mistreated the Jews in the lands they conquered. They forced Jews to wear a yellow, six-pointed star on their clothing.

The Nazis began the mass killing of Jews when the German army invaded the Soviet Union in 1941. Special Nazi forces accompanied the army. They captured and shot any Jews they found and dumped them in mass graves.

In January 1942, German leaders agreed on what they called "the final solution." Nazis rounded up millions of Jews and hundreds of thousands of other innocent people in the areas they controlled. Then the prisoners traveled in trains and trucks to death camps, such as **Auschwitz** (OWSH•VIHTS) in Poland. At the camps, many people died in poison gas chambers. Others died of starvation. Still others were victims of cruel experiments carried out by Nazi doctors. Later, as Allied forces moved into Nazi-held areas, they saw firsthand the unspeakable horrors of the death camps. People around the world were stunned by this terrible result of Nazi brutality.

✓ **Reading Check** **Identify** What is genocide, and how did the Nazis attempt to carry it out?

▲ Toward the end of the war, Allied troops liberated a number of concentration camps. The survivors at the camps were often near starvation. *What was the "final solution"?*

CONNECTING ACROSS TIME

In 1982 Australian writer Thomas Keneally wrote *Schindler's List*, a novel based on the wartime experiences of Oskar Schindler. Schindler, a German manufacturer, saved his Jewish workers from the Holocaust. Steven Spielberg turned Keneally's book into an Oscar-winning movie in 1993. Have students research the Holocaust to write a short report on other people who helped save Jewish people. **L2**

✓ **Reading Check**

Answer: Genocide is the killing of an entire group of people. The Nazis sent Jews, Slavs, Gypsies, and other groups to death camps to kill them.

More About the Photo

The United States has tried to preserve the memory of those who suffered in the Holocaust by building the United States Holocaust Memorial Museum. It opened in Washington, D.C., in 1993 and shows exhibits, videos, and special lectures about those who died during the Holocaust.

Caption Answer: the Germans' plan to round up Jews and exterminate them in death camps

CRITICAL THINKING ACTIVITY

Evaluating Distribute copies of the following thoughts written by a young Jewish woman in 1942: "Of course, it is our complete destruction they want! But let us bear it with grace. . . . And a camp needs a poet, one who experiences life there, even there . . . and is able to sing about it. . . . At night as I lay in the camp on my plank bed . . . I was sometimes filled with an infinite tenderness, and lay awake for hours letting all the many, too many impressions of a much too long day wash over me, and I prayed, 'Let me be the thinking heart of these barracks.' And that is what I want to be again. The thinking heart of a whole concentration camp." **Ask:** How does the writer respond to the Nazis' attempts at genocide? *(with a call for grace)* Do you agree or disagree that a camp needs a poet? Give your reasons. **L3**

Understanding Cause and Effect
Tell students that according to an American woman who was in the USSR on D-Day, Soviets laughed and slapped each other on the back when they heard the radio broadcast about the Allied invasion of occupied France. **Ask: Why did the Allied invasion of France make Soviets happy?** (*D-Day opened up a second front, which would draw German soldiers from the Soviet front.*) **L2**

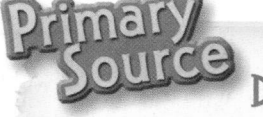

Primary Source

General Eisenhower assembled a force of 176,000 soldiers, 600 warships, and 10,000 aircraft for Operation Overlord, or the invasion of France. The troops on the ground received cover from English bombers that attacked German coastal defenses and from Allied troops who parachuted into France.

Answer:
gunfire, heavy tide, mines and obstacles

Reading Support L1/ EL

Assign **Guided Reading Activity 21–3** to help students organize the information in the section.

The Allies Win

Main Idea The successful invasion on D-Day was the beginning of the end of World War II.

Reading Focus Can you recall important days in your life? For Europeans who lived through World War II, June 6, 1944, stands out in their memory. Read on to find out why.

By 1944, the Germans and Japanese were falling back everywhere. No longer on the defensive, the Allies were preparing to invade Germany and Japan.

What Was D-Day? For months, Allied forces under General Eisenhower had been preparing for the invasion of occupied France. On June 6, 1944, or **D-Day**—the day of the invasions—ships carried troops and equipment across the English Channel to the French province of Normandy. As battleship guns pounded German positions, Allied soldiers moved onto the beaches.

From their Normandy foothold, the Allies launched an attack against the Germans. By early August, General Patton and his tanks were racing across northern France while General Montgomery and his British troops advanced along the coast into Belgium. At the same time, the people of Paris rose up against the Germans. On August 25, the Germans retreated, and Allied troops entered Paris.

On December 16, 1944, the Germans counterattacked. As their troops advanced, they pushed back the Allied lines, creating a bulge. The attack later became known as the Battle of the Bulge. After weeks of fighting, the Americans won the battle and then headed into Germany.

By late 1944, the Soviets had driven the Germans from Russia and back across Poland. By February 1945, Soviet troops were just outside Berlin. On April 30, 1945, Hitler committed suicide in Berlin. On May 7, 1945, the Germans surrendered.

Primary Source
D-Day

On D-Day, June 6, 1944, American troops landed in Normandy, France. Lieutenant John Bentz Carroll describes the invasion:

"Two hundred yards out, we took a direct hit....

... Somehow or other, the ramp door opened up ... Everyone started to jump off into the water. They were being hit as they jumped, the machine gun fire was so heavy.

... The tide was moving us so rapidly.... We would grab out at some of those underwater obstructions and mines built on telephone poles and girders, and hang on. We'd take cover, then make a dash through the surf....

The men would line up behind those poles. They'd say, 'You go—you go—you go,' and then it got so bad everyone just had to go anyway."

—quoted in *D-Day: Piercing the Atlantic Wall*

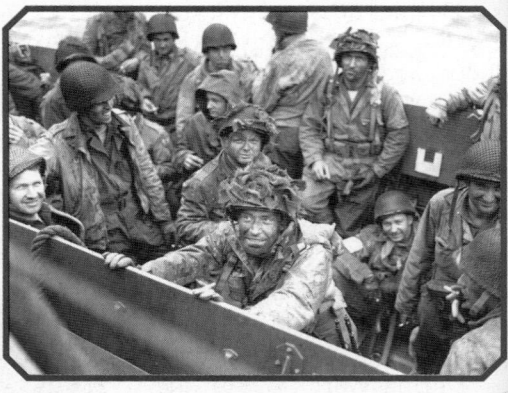

▲ **American soldiers in a landing craft on D-Day**

DBQ Document-Based Question

What made D-Day so dangerous for troops landing on the beaches?

INTERDISCIPLINARY CONNECTIONS ACTIVITY

Language Arts Tell students that American marines used radios to communicate on Pacific islands. Using radios, however, meant that the Japanese could intercept and translate the messages. So the marines recruited Navajo to serve as "code talkers." The Navajo language was a "hidden language" because it had no written alphabet and was known only to the Navajo and a few missionaries and anthropologists. The Navajo recruits developed a code using words from their own language for military terms. For example, the Navajo word *jay-sho*, or "buzzard," was code for bomber; *lotso*, or "whale," meant battleship; and *no-ma-si*, or "potatoes," stood for grenades. Organize the class into pairs. Tell each pair to devise their own code giving secret meanings to English nouns and verbs. Have them write a sentence in code on the board, and challenge the rest of the class to decipher it. **L2**

Dropping the Atomic Bomb
In October 1944, General McArthur invaded the Philippines with more than 160,000 troops and 700 ships. The Americans captured the islands about five months later. Meanwhile, other Americans continued island-hopping toward Japan. They finally came within reach of Japan in 1945.

On March 9, American bombers began dropping firebombs on Japan's cities. These bombs used jellied gasoline to start fires. During the firebombing of Tokyo, strong winds fanned the flames, creating an intense firestorm. The fire killed more than 80,000 Japanese and destroyed 250,000 buildings. Still, the Japanese would not surrender.

In April 1945, Franklin Roosevelt died, and **Harry S Truman** (TROO•muhn) became president. Truman faced a difficult decision. Should he risk American lives by invading Japan, or should he use the newly developed atomic bomb to end the war?

Since 1941, Americans had been building an atomic bomb. A team of engineers and scientists carried on their research at a secret laboratory in Los Alamos, New Mexico. Their program was called the Manhattan Project. On July 16, 1945, the first atomic bomb went off in a test near Alamogordo, New Mexico.

Truman's advisers disagreed about using the bomb. Admiral William Leahy opposed its use because it would kill thousands of civilians. He argued that an economic blockade and ordinary bombing would persuade the Japanese to surrender. Secretary of War Henry Stimson wanted to warn the Japanese about the bomb and at the same time offer to let them keep their emperor if they agreed to surrender.

Truman followed neither course. He threatened Japan with "prompt and utter destruction" if they did not surrender unconditionally. The Japanese failed to reply.

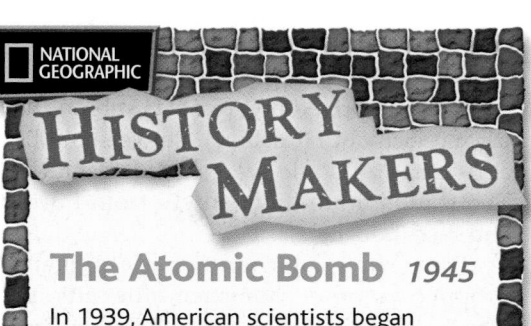

NATIONAL GEOGRAPHIC
HISTORY MAKERS

The Atomic Bomb 1945

In 1939, American scientists began racing to develop an atomic bomb before the Germans. By 1943, British, Canadian, and American scientists were working together on this project under the direction of J. Robert Oppenheimer. Most of the research was conducted in Los Alamos, New Mexico, and was code-named the "Manhattan Project."

On July 16, 1945, scientists in Alamogordo, New Mexico, tested the first atomic bomb. The explosion sent a great shock wave through the valley and was so hot that the desert sand turned into glass.

On August 6, 1945, one month after the first test, the United States dropped an atomic bomb on Hiroshima, Japan. The attack showed that war had changed. It was now possible to destroy an entire city with one bomb.

▲ Hiroshima after the atomic bomb hit

NATIONAL GEOGRAPHIC
HISTORY MAKERS

Historians today still debate whether or not using the atomic bomb was necessary. Some believe that it prevented an even longer and costlier war. Others assert that it was not necessary to drop the atomic bomb because the Japanese might have surrendered soon anyway. Either way, the death toll was catastrophic, and the Japanese soon gave in.

③ ASSESS

Assign Section 3 Review as homework or as an in-class activity.

● Have students use the **Interactive Tutor Self-Assessment CD-ROM** to review the section.

Assessment L2

Assign **Section 3 Quiz** to assess mastery of the material found in the section.

EXTENDING THE CONTENT

What Happened When the Bomb Fell on Hiroshima? Six years after the bomb fell on Hiroshima, a survivor described her experience this way: "[T]here was bright light in front of my eyes and an indescribable orange light surged in. . . . It must have been ten or fifteen minutes later when I recovered consciousness. . . . I looked over my shoulder and saw our house was a flattened wreck, and at the back waves of swirling flames were threatening to sweep down at any moment."

ENRICH

Admiral Nimitz later wrote that on Iwo Jima, "uncommon valor was a common virtue." Ask students to restate this quote in their own words. **L1/ EL**

Reading Check

Answer: Many thousands of people died instantly, but the Japanese surrendered.

To help students understand section material, have them visit **Study Central™** at jat.glencoe.com

RETEACH

Have students call out events that they remember from the section. Write the events on the board, and ask students to number the events in the order that they occurred. **L2**

④ CLOSE

Ask students to name persons whom they think showed outstanding bravery during World War II. **L1**

On August 6, 1945, a plane named the *Enola Gay* dropped an atomic bomb on the Japanese city of Hiroshima. Between 80,000 and 120,000 people were killed instantly. Thousands more died slowly from burns and radiation sickness.

Three days later, an American plane dropped another bomb on the city of Nagasaki. It killed between 35,000 and 74,000 people. On August 15, 1945, the Japanese surrendered.

Rebuilding the World About 55 million people died in World War II. These included 22 million Soviets, 8 million Germans, 2 million Japanese, and 300,000 Americans. Also included were millions killed in campaigns of genocide, or mass murders of ethnic groups.

Even before the war ended, the Allies had started an organization to keep the peace. In April 1945, representatives from 50 countries drew up a charter for the United Nations (UN). The UN General Assembly would vote on issues and choose members of the Security Council. The Security Council would investigate international problems and propose settlements. It had five permanent members—the United States, the USSR, Britain, France, and China—as well as other elected members.

After the war, the Allies tried Nazi leaders at Nuremberg, Germany, for "pursuing aggressive war" and for committing "crimes against humanity." Similar war trials took place in Japan. The war crimes trials punished many of the people responsible for World War II and the Holocaust. They also served notice that the world would not allow these crimes to be repeated.

Reading Check **Cause and Effect** What were the results of the atomic bombs dropped on Hiroshima and Nagasaki?

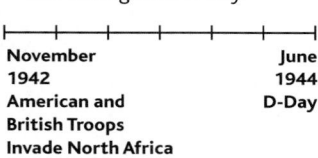

Study Central™ Need help with the material in this section? Visit jat.glencoe.com

Section 3 Review

Reading Summary
Review the Main Ideas
- In the Pacific, the Americans fought the Japanese island by island. In Europe, American and Allied troops invaded North Africa and Italy.
- During the Holocaust, the Germans murdered millions of people, including Jews and other minorities.
- The Allied invasion of France in June 1944, led to the fall of Germany. The United States's use of two atomic bombs on Japanese cities caused Japan to surrender.

What Did You Learn?
1. Describe the U.S. plan for defeating Japan in the war.
2. What was D-Day?

Critical Thinking
3. **Sequencing Information** Draw a time line like the one below. Fill in events related to the war against Germany beginning with the landings of Allied troops in North Africa and ending with D-Day.

November 1942	**June 1944**
American and British Troops Invade North Africa	**D-Day**

4. **Evaluate** Do you think it would have been more important to defeat the Germans or the Japanese first during the war? Explain your answer.
5. **Summarize** Describe the German persecution of Jews leading up to the Holocaust.
6. **Describe** Describe the organization and purpose of the United Nations.
7. **Creative Writing** Write the dialogue for a conversation that might have occurred between the Allied leaders—Roosevelt, Churchill, and Stalin—at the Tehran Conference in 1943.

830   CHAPTER 21   World War II and the Cold War

SECTION 3 REVIEW ANSWERS

1. The U.S. secured key islands and used them as bases to attack other islands.
2. the day Allied forces invaded occupied France
3. May 1943: Allies drove Germans from North Africa; summer 1943: Allies invaded Sicily; September 1943: Allies invaded Italy; June 1944: Allies captured Rome
4. Answers will vary. Sample answer: Defeating Germany first would free up troops to fight on Pacific islands.
5. Nazis restricted Jewish citizenship and marriage; killed Jews and burned homes, synagogues, and businesses; persecuted Jews in occupied lands; sent Jews to concentration camps; and shot Jews in the countryside.
6. Answers should include facts from the section.
7. Answers should include facts from the section.

Section 4 — The Cold War

Get Ready to Read!

What's the Connection?
In the last section, you learned that World War II devastated Europe and Asia. This section discusses a new international conflict that shaped the next 40 years.

Focusing on the Main Ideas
- Soviet efforts to spread communism led to conflict with the United States, which wanted to contain communism. *(page 832)*

- The Cold War spread to Asia after China's communist revolution and the outbreak of the Korean War. *(page 837)*

- People in the postwar world experienced prosperity, change, and conflict. *(page 839)*

Locating Places
Berlin
Taiwan (TY•WAHN)

Meeting People
Nikita Khrushchev
  (nuh•KEE•tuh   krush•CHAWF)
John F. Kennedy
Chiang Kai-shek
  (jee•AHNG   KY•SHEHK)
Mao Zedong (MOW   ZUH•DUNG)
Martin Luther King, Jr.

Building Your Vocabulary
containment
Truman Doctrine
Marshall Plan
racial segregation
  (SEH•grih•GAY•shuhn)

Reading Strategy
Organizing Information Complete a diagram like the one below to show the causes of the Cold War.

Cold War Begins

When & Where?

1945	1955	1965

1947 The Truman Doctrine is announced

1950 The Korean War begins

1955 The Soviets create the Warsaw Pact

1962 The Cuban missile crisis erupts

NORTH AMERICA
EUROPE •Berlin
ASIA
CUBA
KOREA

CHAPTER 21   World War II and the Cold War   831

---

1 FOCUS

SECTION OVERVIEW
Americans prospered during the postwar years. At the same time, the U.S. tried to curb the spread of communism during the Cold War.

BELLRINGER SKILLBUILDER ACTIVITY
Project **Daily Focus Skills Transparency 21–4** and have students answer questions. Discuss their responses.

Get Ready to Read!

Preteaching Vocabulary: Tell students that suffixes often change a verb into a noun. For example, adding -*ment* to the verb *contain* creates the noun *containment*, which means "the act of containing." Because *to contain* means "to hold back," *containment* means "the act of holding back."

Answers to Graphic: Possible answers: Americans wanted to spread democracy and free enterprise; Soviets wanted to spread communism; Potsdam Conference

---

SECTION RESOURCES

 Reproducible Masters
- Reproducible Lesson Plan 21–4
- Daily Lecture and Discussion Notes 21–4
- Vocabulary Activity 21–4
- Active Reading Note-Taking Guide 21–4
- Guided Reading Activity 21–4
- Section Quiz 21–4
- Reading Essentials and Study Guide 21–4

Transparencies
- Daily Focus Skills Transparency 21–4

Multimedia
- Interactive Tutor Self-Assessment CD-ROM
- ExamView® Pro Testmaker CD-ROM
- Presentation Plus! CD-ROM

② TEACH

📖 Reading Strategy

Predicting After students read the material under "The Cold War Begins," reread aloud the following passage: "the two enemies do not fight each other." **Ask: Do you think that means that the Cold War was bloodless?** After students answer, direct their attention to the subhead "War in Korea." Explain that although the Korean War was "hot," Americans were fighting an enemy supported by the Soviets but not the Soviets themselves. **L1/EL**

Daily Lecture and Discussion Notes 21–4

Use **Daily Lecture and Discussion Notes 21–4** for an outline of key concepts found in the section.

Reading Support L1/EL

Use **Vocabulary Activity 21–4** to review important terms in the section.

Using Geography Skills

Answers:

1. Spain, Ireland, Switzerland, Austria, Sweden, Finland
2. NATO

The Cold War Begins

Main Idea Soviet efforts to spread communism led to conflict with the United States, which wanted to contain communism.

Reading Focus Have you ever wanted to stop someone from doing something without having a fight? Read to learn how the United States tried to stop communism without going to war.

During World War II, the United States and the Soviet Union had set aside their differences. As they moved toward victory in 1945, these two powerful nations began to disagree about what the world was to be like after the war.

For Americans, economic growth was the key to world peace. They wanted to promote growth through world trade. They also wanted to spread democracy and free enterprise. Free enterprise, you remember, is the system in which businesses compete freely for profits with few government controls.

In contrast, Soviet leaders wanted to spread communism. As the war ended, Soviet armies had pushed back German armies in Eastern Europe and set up Communist governments in the region. The Soviets feared that one day Germany might try again to attack them. Having communist states in Eastern Europe would make a German invasion harder to do.

The deep differences between the Americans and the Soviets made them mistrust each other, and they began to compete for world leadership. This rivalry lasted from 1945 to 1990 and became known as the Cold War.

NATIONAL GEOGRAPHIC **Europe During the Cold War**

KEY
- Warsaw Pact member
- Communist nation outside Soviet bloc
- Neutral nation
- NATO member

Harry S Truman ▶

Using Geography Skills

After World War II, Europe was divided between Communist and non-Communist nations.

1. Which European nations remained neutral?
2. Which organization, NATO or the Warsaw Pact, had more member nations?

📖 Reading Strategy READING THE TEXT

Activating Prior Knowledge On the board, draw the chart below, omitting the answers in cyan:

FREE ENTERPRISE	COMMUNISM
competition for profits	(no competition)
few government controls	(total government control)

Have students recall what they have already learned about communism to complete the chart. **Ask: Do you think democracy is possible in a nation with a communist economy?** *(Students may answer no, because if the government controls the economy, people have little choice but to go along with the government.)* Have students consider this topic as they read. **L1/EL**

Yalta and Potsdam In February 1945, the "Big Three" Allied leaders—Roosevelt, Churchill, and Stalin—met at Yalta, a Soviet port on the Black Sea. They discussed, among other things, the fate of newly freed Europe. Their disagreements over Europe helped cause the Cold War.

Germany presented a special problem. The leaders finally agreed to divide Germany into four zones, or parts, until elections could be held to determine its future. The Soviet Union was to control the eastern part of Germany. The United States, Great Britain, and France were to divide the western part. The German capital of **Berlin** was also to be split among the four nations. At Yalta, the three leaders also agreed that other countries released from Nazi rule should have free elections.

In April 1945, U.S. president Roosevelt died. Vice President Harry S Truman then became president. The next month, American, Soviet, and British leaders met at Potsdam, Germany. At Potsdam, Stalin demanded that the Germans pay high reparations for damaging the Soviet Union. Truman firmly opposed this demand and angrily told the Soviets to keep their promises.

The Soviets soon broke their promises made at Yalta. Stalin did not hold free elections in Eastern Europe. Instead, the Soviets set up Communist governments there, and Soviet forces remained in the region.

What Was Containment? The British leader Winston Churchill was concerned about Soviet control in Eastern Europe. In 1946, in a speech in Fulton, Missouri, he warned that the Soviets might try to expand their control beyond Eastern Europe.

Like Churchill, President Truman and other U.S. government leaders worried

Primary Source
The Iron Curtain

In 1946, while visiting Fulton, Missouri, Winston Churchill gave a speech titled "The Sinews of Peace." In the speech, he tried to explain what was happening in Eastern Europe:

"From Stettin in the Baltic to Trieste in the Adriatic, an iron curtain has descended across the Continent [Europe]. Behind that line lie all the capitals of the ancient states of Central and Eastern Europe. Warsaw, Berlin, Prague, Vienna, Budapest, Belgrade, Bucharest and Sofia, all these famous cities and the populations around them lie in what I must call the Soviet sphere, . . . The Communist parties, which were very small in all these Eastern States of Europe, have been raised to preeminence and power far beyond their numbers and are seeking everywhere to obtain totalitarian control. Police governments are prevailing in nearly every case."

▲ Winston Churchill

—Winston Churchill,
The "Iron Curtain" Speech

DBQ Document-Based Question

What does the "iron curtain" divide?

about the growing Soviet threat. How were they to stop the Soviets?

For an answer, they turned to the ideas of George F. Kennan, an American diplomat and expert on Soviet affairs. Kennan claimed that the United States and the Soviet Union could not cooperate. He believed, however, that war could be avoided. He argued that the Soviet Union

Primary Source

Winston Churchill did not coin the phrase "iron curtain." In 1914 German-born Queen Elizabeth of Belgium responded to the German troops marching through her country by saying: "Between them [Germany] and me there is now a bloody iron curtain which has descended forever!" In 1918 author Vasili Rosanov used the phrase in reference to Russia: "With a rumble and a roar, an iron curtain is descending on Russian history."

Answer:
communist Europe from democratic Europe

Reading Strategy

Writing Activity

Explain that many Americans mourned the death of Franklin Delano Roosevelt. Ask students to write eulogies, or funeral speeches, highlighting Roosevelt's accomplishments. Have them review what they have read about Roosevelt and use facts from the chapter in their eulogy. **L2**

DIFFERENTIATED INSTRUCTION

Verbal/Linguistic: Have students peruse news magazines for information about an area of the world where human rights are being denied. Then tell them to use the information to create a brief speech against the injustices in that area. Tell them to use Churchill's speech as a model.

English Learners: Challenge students to memorize the passage from Churchill's speech and to give an impassioned delivery to the class.

Gifted and Talented: Have students locate the full text of Churchill's speech and identify techniques, such as parallels and lists, that make the speech effective.

📁 Refer to *Inclusion Strategies for the Middle School Social Studies Classroom* in the TCR.

834

had many internal economic problems, and he believed it would collapse if the United States could stop it from spreading communism. Kennan's ideas led to a new U.S. foreign policy known as **containment.** This policy held that the United States would try to "contain," or hold back the spread of communism.

Germany Divided

NATIONAL GEOGRAPHIC

KEY

- Allied occupation zone
- Soviet occupation zone
- Routes of the Berlin Airlift, 1948–1949
- Division of Allied zone

Lambert Azimuthal Equal-Area projection

Chamberlin Trimetric projection

DENMARK

EAST GERMANY

FRENCH SECTOR
BRITISH SECTOR
WEST BERLIN
EAST BERLIN
SOVIET SECTOR
AMERICAN SECTOR

EAST GERMANY

Hamburg

British Zone

Hannover

Braunschweig

POLAND

Berlin

WEST GERMANY (FEDERAL REPUBLIC OF GERMANY)

EAST GERMANY (GERMAN DEMOCRATIC REPUBLIC)

French Zone

Frankfurt

American Zone

FRANCE

Using Geography Skills

Following World War II, the Allied and Soviet sections of Germany formed two separate countries.

1. Which three nations occupied West Germany?
2. Which West German city on the route of the Berlin Airlift was closest to Berlin? How far away was it?

834   CHAPTER 21   World War II and the Cold War

The policy of containment soon went into effect. Civil war was raging in Greece. There, Communist rebels were trying to overthrow the Greek government. At the same time, the Soviets put enormous pressure on Turkey to give them naval bases on the Dardanelles straits leading to the Mediterranean Sea.

On March 12, 1947, Truman asked Congress for money to help Greece and Turkey. His speech outlined a plan that was later named the **Truman Doctrine.** Its immediate effects were to give aid to the Greeks and the Turks. In the long run, the doctrine pledged the United States to fight the spread of communism worldwide.

In June 1947, Secretary of State George C. Marshall proposed that the United States give aid to Western European countries as well. Their economies were in ruins, and the people were starving. The **Marshall Plan** pumped $13 billion worth of supplies, machinery, and food into Western Europe. The economic recovery that followed weakened the appeal of communism.

Germany Meanwhile, the western Allies and the Soviet Union disagreed on the future of Germany. President Truman believed that a reunited, prosperous Germany was important for Europe. Stalin, however, feared that a reunited Germany would attack the Soviet Union.

In June 1948, the United States, Britain, and France announced that they were uniting their zones to form a new West German republic. Each nation's section of Berlin would be included in the new republic as well, even though the city lay within Soviet-held eastern Germany.

In response, Soviet troops moved into position around West Berlin. They imposed a blockade, stopping all traffic on road, railroad, and water routes through eastern

CRITICAL THINKING ACTIVITY

Drawing Conclusions Tell students that Kennan advised Truman about the Soviets in a 5,540-word telegram from Moscow. Relate the following points in the telegram: Kennan explained that because Communists believed they were in a long-term struggle against capitalism, any permanent settlement with them was impossible. The Soviet system had several major economic and political weaknesses. If the United States could keep the Soviets from expanding their power, it was only a matter of time until the Soviet system would fall apart. **Ask:** Based on this information, which conclusion can you draw—the United States should declare war on the Soviet Union immediately or communism could be beaten without going to war? Explain your choice. *(Students may choose the second conclusion because Kennan implied that communism would wither naturally.)* **L2**

Germany to West Berlin. As a result, the city was cut off from needed supplies. The Soviets hoped this blockade would force the Americans, British, and French to reconsider their plan.

President Truman refused to give in to the Soviets. He ordered a massive airlift to save West Berlin. For almost a year, cargo planes carried food, medicine, fuel, and other supplies into the city. In May 1949, Stalin finally ended the blockade.

Despite the airlift's success, Berlin and Germany remained divided. By the end of 1949, there were two German states—West Germany, a democracy allied with the United States, and East Germany, a communist state tied to the Soviet Union.

To stop communism, the United States, Canada, and 10 West European countries formed the North Atlantic Treaty Organization (NATO) in 1949. Member nations agreed to aid any member who was attacked. Six years later, West Germany was allowed to form an army and to join NATO. In response, the Soviets in 1955 set up a military alliance with the Communist governments of Eastern Europe. It was known as the Warsaw Pact.

After Stalin died in 1953, **Nikita Khrushchev** (nuh•KEE•tuh krush•CHAWF) emerged as the new Soviet leader. In 1961 Khrushchev demanded that the Western powers withdraw from Berlin. U.S. president **John F. Kennedy** refused. Meanwhile, many East Germans fled to West Germany. The Soviets then built a wall that separated Communist East Berlin from the rest of the city. Guards on the wall shot anyone who tried to escape East Berlin. For nearly 30 years, the Berlin Wall was an important symbol of the Cold War struggle.

NATIONAL GEOGRAPHIC

The Way It Was

Focus on Everyday Life

Life in Divided Berlin When the Berlin Wall was first built, stretches of it consisted of only knee-high barbwire, so friends, neighbors, and families could still greet each other. Soon after, the barbwire was replaced with guard towers and cement blocks that divided the city.

If a person's home lay on one side of the Wall and his or her office on the other, that person could not go to work. West Berliners used raised platforms to see what was happening on the other side of the Wall. At night, the streets of West Berlin sparkled with lights, but in East Berlin, all was dark except for the guard towers. Anyone who tried to escape over the Wall to West Berlin was shot. West Berliners built a memorial of crosses dedicated to those who died trying to cross the Wall.

◄ Residents of West Berlin look over the Berlin Wall into East Berlin.

Connecting to the Past
1. Why do you think many East Germans risked their lives to cross over the Wall?
2. How would your life change if a wall were built in the center of your city?

Reading Strategy

Identifying Main Ideas As students read the material under "Germany," have them write the main idea of each paragraph in their notebook. **Ask: Which of the main ideas in your notebook do you think states the main idea of the entire reading?** (Possible answer: "For 30 years the Berlin Wall was the principal symbol of the Cold War.") **L3**

in a word ...

The word **"airlift"** is a recent term, originating in 1945. More mysterious is the date of origin of the related term, *airman*. The term means "pilot or aviator" but originated in 1873. Probably it was coined for those who flew hot-air balloons.

NATIONAL GEOGRAPHIC

The Way It Was

Answers:
1. They desperately wanted freedom.
2. Answers will vary. Most students will mention friends, family, favorite recreational activities, and so on, that are located on the other side of town.

INTERDISCIPLINARY CONNECTIONS ACTIVITY

Geography Have students use the Reference Atlas maps to locate the original 12 NATO countries— the United States, Canada, Great Britain, France, Italy, Belgium, Denmark, Portugal, the Netherlands, Norway, Luxembourg, and Iceland. **Ask: Why do you think the alliance was called the North Atlantic Treaty Organization?** (Many of the countries have a coast on the North Atlantic Ocean.) **Why did the Soviet Union set up the Warsaw Pact only after West Germany was admitted to NATO?** (German troops killed millions of Soviets in World Wars I and II, and the Soviet Union wanted to protect itself in case Germany became militarily strong again.) **L1/EL**

Nuclear Arms During the 1950s and 1960s, nuclear weapons played an important role in the Cold War. By the early 1950s, the Soviets had their own nuclear weapons. International tensions rose as the United States and the Soviet Union built up their missiles and bombers. By the 1960s, they were also using their rockets to send people into space. The Russians put the first man in space, but the Americans landed the first men on the moon.

The Cold War also spread to areas outside of Europe. In fact, the most dangerous Cold War dispute took place in Cuba, a small Caribbean island close to the United States—only 90 miles (144 km) south of Florida. There, in 1959, a new government came to power under a leader named Fidel Castro.

In October 1962, President Kennedy learned that the Soviets had placed long-range missiles in Cuba. Immediately, the president ordered the navy to blockade, or close off, Cuba until the Soviets removed the missiles. Kennedy also warned that the United States would launch a nuclear attack on the Soviets if they fired any of their Cuban missiles on the United States.

As the two superpowers neared the edge of nuclear war, people all over the world waited anxiously. After five difficult days, Soviet ships turned away from the blockade. Soviet leaders also agreed to withdraw their missiles from Cuba. The United States agreed not to invade Cuba. Nuclear war had been avoided.

✓ **Reading Check** **Explain** What was containment, and why was it used?

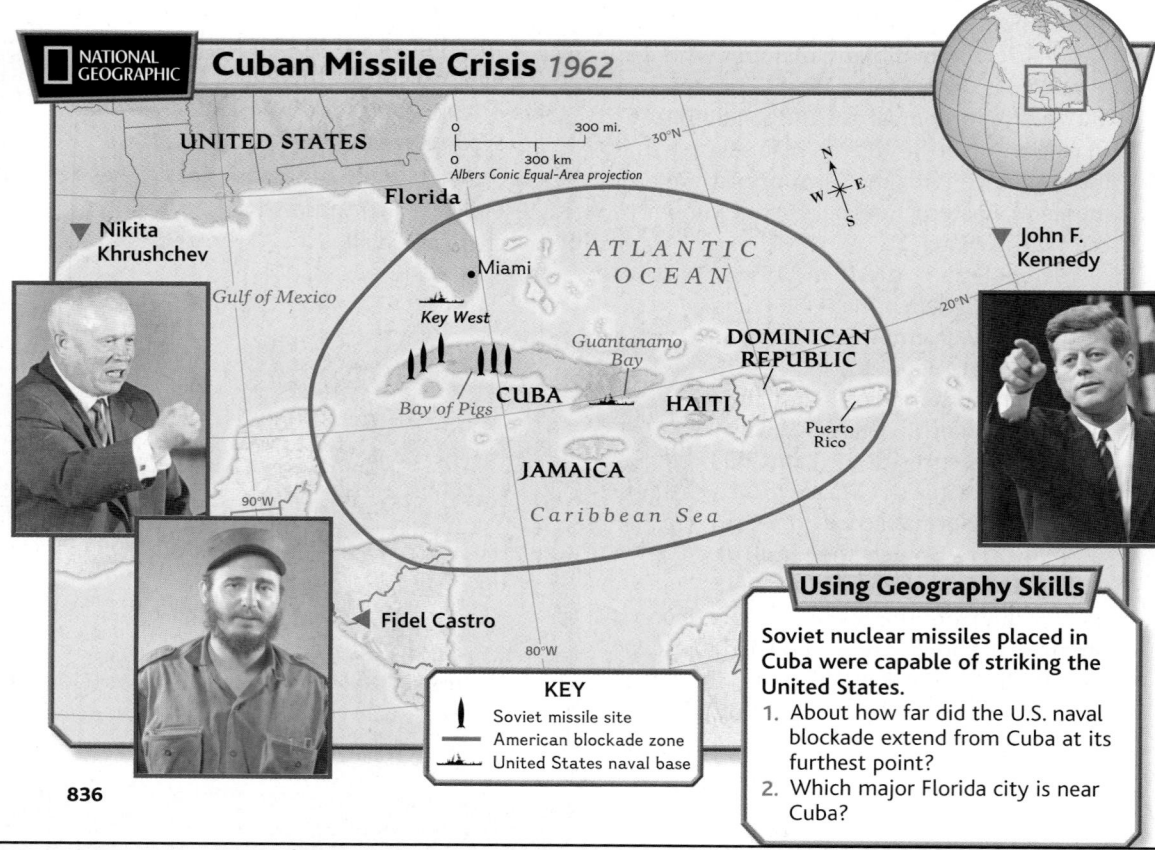

NATIONAL GEOGRAPHIC **Cuban Missile Crisis** *1962*

UNITED STATES

0   300 mi.
0   300 km
Albers Conic Equal-Area projection

Florida

▼ Nikita Khrushchev

Gulf of Mexico

• Miami

ATLANTIC OCEAN

Key West

Guantanamo Bay

DOMINICAN REPUBLIC

▼ John F. Kennedy

Bay of Pigs   **CUBA**   HAITI

Puerto Rico

JAMAICA

Caribbean Sea

90°W

80°W

30°N

20°N

▼ Fidel Castro

KEY
🔺 Soviet missile site
— American blockade zone
⚓ United States naval base

836

Using Geography Skills

Soviet nuclear missiles placed in Cuba were capable of striking the United States.
1. About how far did the U.S. naval blockade extend from Cuba at its furthest point?
2. Which major Florida city is near Cuba?

EXTENDING THE CONTENT

How Did Kennedy Plan to Stop Communism? Kennedy tried to reduce the threat of nuclear war and to stop the spread of communism with a range of programs. These included economic aid, the Peace Corps, and conventional weaponry programs, which Eisenhower had abandoned. In his Inaugural Address, Kennedy said: "Let the word go forth from this time and place . . . that the torch has been passed to a new generation of Americans—born in this century, tempered by war, disciplined by a hard and bitter peace, proud of our ancient heritage—and unwilling to witness or permit the slow undoing of those human rights to which this nation has always been committed. . . . Let every nation know, whether it wishes us well or ill, that we shall pay any price, bear any burden, meet any hardship, support any friend, oppose any foe, to assure the survival and the success of liberty."

The Cold War Spreads to Asia

Main Idea The Cold War spread to Asia after China's communist revolution and the outbreak of the Korean War.

Reading Focus Have you ever had a friend become your enemy or an enemy end up your friend? Read on to learn about the changing relationships among the United States and countries in Asia.

The Cold War also spread to Asia. In the late 1940s, Communist governments came to power in China and part of Korea. These Communist governments created challenges for the U.S. policy of containment.

Communist Revolution in China

Previously, you learned that **Chiang Kai-shek** (jee•AHNG KY•SHEHK) became leader of China in the mid-1920s. He tried to unite China and wipe out the Communists. However, in 1927, the Chinese Communists began a movement to gain control of the country. Their leader was **Mao Zedong** (MOW ZUH•DUNG).

During the 1930s, Chiang's Nationalist forces and Mao's Communist troops stopped fighting each other. They joined together to fight the Japanese, who had invaded China. After World War II, the struggle between the Nationalists and Communists continued. Despite American aid, Chiang Kai-shek lost the people's support.

In 1949 Mao's Communists forced the Nationalists to leave the Chinese mainland and go to the island of **Taiwan** (TY•WAHN). There, Chiang set up a Nationalist government, claiming it ruled all of China. The Communists set up their own government on mainland China headed by Mao Zedong. They called it the People's Republic of China.

Mao's main goal was to make China a strong, modern country. In the 1950s, Mao's

▲ Mao Zedong became the leader of China following the Communist defeat of Chiang Kai-shek's forces. *How did Mao attempt to make China into a strong, modern nation?*

government took over China's industries and businesses. It also created large, government-run farms from the small plots of land worked by peasants. Instead of food production increasing, it declined as a result of bad weather and the people's resistance. Famine soon struck, killing almost 15 million people. As result, the government was forced to back down from its more extreme policies.

War in Korea

At the end of World War II, the Americans and Soviets divided Korea at the 38th parallel. The Communists set up a government in the north, and an American-backed government took over the south. On June 25, 1950, North Korean troops invaded South Korea in an attempt to take over that country.

U.S. president Harry Truman saw the invasion as a test of the containment policy. He persuaded the United Nations to send troops. Most of these UN troops were

More About the Photo

Mao's sayings were collected in *Quotations From Chairman Mao Zedong*, which came to be known simply as *The Little Red Book*. He once wrote: "Every Communist must grasp the truth: Political power grows out of the barrel of a gun."

Caption Answer: The government took control of China's businesses and industries and created large, government-run farms from small peasant-owned plots.

CONNECTING ACROSS TIME

In theory, the Chinese Communists promoted equality. For example, women were made equal with men under the law and benefited from social reforms, such as state-run nurseries that provided child care. They were also expected to enter the workplace alongside men. However, few women were freed from household chores. Even fewer gained top positions in government and industry. **Ask: How did the situation for women in China under Mao compare with the situation for women in the United States today?** **L1/EL**

COOPERATIVE LEARNING ACTIVITY

Creating a Model Tell students that at one point in the struggle between Nationalists and Communists, the Nationalists nearly surrounded the Communists. Mao decided to retreat and took 100,000 followers to more friendly territory 6,000 miles away. Their journey, called the Long March, lasted a year. At times the line of marchers stretched for 50 miles. Have the class use poster board to create a model of the marchers traveling on their journey. Have them research as necessary to find additional details. **L1/EL**

Interpreting Share this saying of Truman: "If you can't stand the heat, stay out of the kitchen." Ask students to explain its meaning. **Ask: How might this saying apply to the Korean War?** (*A possible answer is that Truman meant this message for North Koreans when he persuaded the UN to send troops to Korea.*)

in a word . . .

"*Sputnik*," the name of the Soviet satellite, started its own language trend, as words gained a -*nik* ending for a for- eign-sounding effect. *Beatnik* described a person influenced by the style of the Beat writers such as Jack Kerouac and Allen Ginsberg, and *peacenik* was used to describe a peace activist.

Using Geography Skills

Answers:

1. Nov. 1950

2. 1950

Skills Practice

Ask: When did UN forces land? (*Sept. 15, 1950*) **When did UN forces reach their maximum advance?** (*Nov. 24, 1950*)

✓ Reading Check

Answer: The U.S. needed war supplies, so they poured $3.5 billion into Japanese facto- ries. Japanese shipbuilders, manufacturers, and electronics and pharmaceutical industries benefited. The result was an economic boom in Japan.

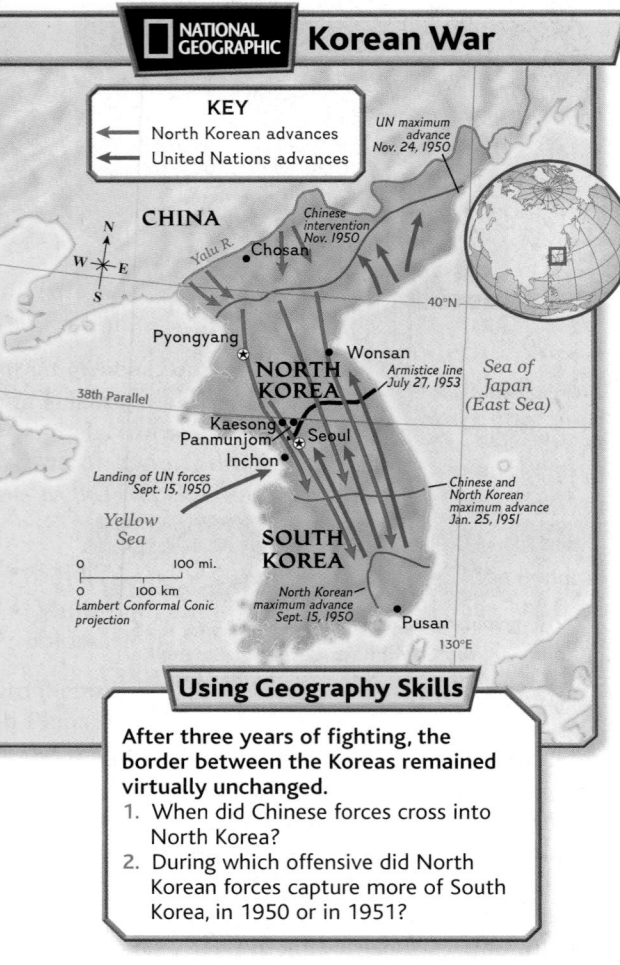

NATIONAL GEOGRAPHIC Korean War

KEY
⟵ North Korean advances
⟵ United Nations advances

UN maximum advance Nov. 24, 1950

CHINA

Chinese intervention Nov. 1950

Yalu R.

• Chosan

40°N

Pyongyang ✪

• Wonsan

NORTH KOREA

Armistice line July 27, 1953

Sea of Japan (East Sea)

38th Parallel

Kaesong • Panmunjom ✪ • Seoul
Inchon •

Landing of UN forces Sept. 15, 1950

Chinese and North Korean maximum advance Jan. 25, 1951

Yellow Sea

0   100 mi.
0 100 km
Lambert Conformal Conic projection

SOUTH KOREA

North Korean maximum advance Sept. 15, 1950

• Pusan

130°E

Using Geography Skills

After three years of fighting, the border between the Koreas remained virtually unchanged.

1. When did Chinese forces cross into North Korea?
2. During which offensive did North Korean forces capture more of South Korea, in 1950 or in 1951?

American and under the command of U.S. general Douglas MacArthur.

General MacArthur and the UN forces pushed the North Koreans back across the 38th parallel and then advanced toward the Chinese border. The Chinese Communists saw the advancing troops as a threat. Hundreds of thousands of Chinese crossed the border and drove the UN forces back to South Korea.

MacArthur suggested that dropping atomic bombs on Chinese bases and supply lines would gain a quick victory. President Truman, however, refused and fired MacArthur for disagreeing with him. He

did not want the Korean War to turn into a world war. By mid-1951, each army was dug in along a line near the 38th parallel. Both sides realized there was no chance for further gains. In 1953 North Korea and South Korea signed a truce. The two Koreas remain divided along a border near the 38th parallel.

Japan Recovers From 1945 to 1952, Japan was an occupied country. Allied military forces under General Douglas MacArthur controlled the country. This American-led government greatly reduced Japan's military so that Japan could no longer threaten its neighbors. It also introduced reforms. Japan received a democratic constitution. Japanese women and workers gained more rights. Small farmers also were given more land.

In 1952 Japan regained its independ- ence. The Korean War, however, kept Japan's ties to the United States very close. American troops needed all kinds of war supplies, from medicines to trucks. To have a source of supplies nearby, the United States poured $3.5 billion into Japan's facto- ries. Japanese shipbuilders, manufacturers, and electronics industries all benefited from American aid.

Help from the United States created an economic boom in Japan. The Japanese gov- ernment worked closely with business leaders to plan the country's industrial growth. For example, in the late 1950s, gov- ernment and industry agreed to invest heavily in the research and development of electronics products for the home. By the early 1970s, Japanese radios, televisions, stereos, and other items were competing with similar American products in the world market.

✓ Reading Check **Analyze** How did the Korean War help Japan's economy?

CRITICAL THINKING ACTIVITY

Comparing and Contrasting On the board, write the following percentages: United States 30.5%, Taiwan 6.6%, Hong Kong 6.5%, China 5.2%, and Germany 4.9%. Explain that the countries on the board are major export destinations for Japanese products and that the percentages represent the portions of Japan's total exports to each destination. **Ask: Who is Japan's best customer?** (*the United States*) The United States imports more from Japan than all four of its next best customers combined—true or false? (*true*) Have students use the figures to draw circle graphs entitled "Japan's Best Customers Today." Point out that the percentages on the board do not equal 100%, so a slice of the circle should be labeled "All Other Customers." **L2**

The Cold War Era

Main Idea People in the postwar world experienced prosperity, change, and conflict.

Reading Focus Can you recall hard times and good times in your life? Read on to learn which nations might consider the postwar years hard times and which might recall them as good times.

After World War II, the Soviet Union rebuilt its heavy industry and boosted its military might. In Soviet-controlled Eastern Europe, governments copied the Soviet system. Factories began producing more machinery and fewer consumer goods.

Life Behind the Iron Curtain Most Soviets and East Europeans fared poorly as a result of this push for heavy industry. Food, clothing, and housing were in short supply. The

average family lived in a one-room apartment. In addition, people feared being punished if they disagreed with the communist system.

East Europeans also disliked Soviet control of their countries. In October 1956, unrest swept Hungary. Students and workers staged street protests in Budapest, Hungary's capital, for changes in the government. Strikes and riots spread. A new government came to power and demanded an end to Soviet controls. In early November, Soviet tanks and troops poured into Hungary and crushed the revolt.

In January 1968, Czechoslovakia's leader Alexander Dubček also tried to make changes. He loosened controls on the press and travel abroad. Dubček's program was called "socialism with a human face." The program was short-lived, however. In

Categorizing Information After students finish reading "Life Behind the Iron Curtain," have them recall significant phrases and nouns from the lesson and write them on the board. *(Some possible answers are unrest, protests, Budapest, strikes, riots, controls, tanks, Soviet troops, revolt, Dubček, changes, press, and travel abroad.)* Next, tell them to fold a sheet of paper in half to form two columns. Ask them to write *Hungary* at the top of the first column and *Czechoslovakia* at the top of the second. Then, instruct them to write each phrase or noun on the board under the correct category. Point out that some nouns may fit in both categories. **L1/EL**

Caption Answer: The Cold War

Space Exploration

In the 1960s, the Soviet Union and the United States competed with one another to be the first to conquer space travel. This competition, called the Space Race, led to the advancement of technology and the further study of space. *During what period of history did the Space Race occur?*

▲ In 1961 Russia sent the spacecraft *Vostok* into orbit. Inside was Yuri Gagarin, the first human being ever to travel into space.

▲ The lunar module was used by NASA in 1969 to land two men safely on the moon. U.S. astronaut Neil Armstrong was the first human being ever to set foot on the moon.

CHAPTER 21 World War II and the Cold War **839**

EXTENDING THE CONTENT

What Happened to Alexander Dubček? About 500,000 troops from the Soviet Union and its allies in the Warsaw Pact invaded Czechoslovakia in 1968. They took control of Prague, the capital, and sent Dubček and other Czech leaders to Moscow. In April 1969, Dubček was replaced as party leader. In January 1970, he became ambassador to Turkey but later that year was expelled from the party entirely. He then became an inspector of the forestry ministry. In 1989 the Communist Party in Czechoslovakia lost total power, and Dubček returned as chairman of the Federal Assembly. In 1992 Dubček died at age 70 of injuries incurred in a traffic accident.

③ ASSESS

▲ To maintain control over its East European allies, the Soviet Union sometimes resorted to force. Here, Soviet tanks are shown on the streets of Czechoslovakia. *Why did the Soviets invade Czechoslovakia?*

August 1968, Soviet troops invaded Czechoslovakia and installed a strict Communist government.

Western Europe Rebuilds The Marshall Plan helped Europe rebuild quickly from the ruins of World War II. West Germany's recovery was called an "economic miracle." By the 1960s, West Germany had Europe's strongest economy.

In France, war hero General Charles de Gaulle was president for part of the 1950s and most of the 1960s. During his presidency, France enjoyed a stable government. It became a major producer of aircraft, weapons, and cars. As a result, the French economy grew at a fast rate—even faster than the American economy.

Meanwhile, in Great Britain the Labour Party defeated Churchill's Conservative Party. The new government worked to improve the lives of the British people. Insurance was provided for the aged, sick, and jobless. A national health care service gave medical care to everyone.

In 1957 France, West Germany, Belgium, the Netherlands, Luxembourg, and Italy set up the European Economic Community (EEC). EEC members agreed to end all trade barriers among them. This meant that businesses could sell their goods in other member nations without paying taxes to cross the border. The EEC was seen as the first step in building a united Europe.

Life in the United States During the 1950s, Americans earned higher wages and purchased more consumer goods than ever before. As a result, factory production soared. The postwar "baby boom," or increased birthrate, promised even more economic growth in the future.

A new civil rights movement also began in the 1950s. In 1954 the U.S. Supreme Court ruled against **racial segregation** (SEH•grih•GAY•shuhn), or separation of the races, in public schools. In the 1950s, President Dwight D. Eisenhower used federal agencies to make sure that states ended segregation in their schools. This was an important victory for African Americans, who had been working hard to gain civil rights throughout the 1940s and 1950s.

Led by Baptist minister **Martin Luther King, Jr.**, the civil rights movement next focused attention on discrimination, or unfair treatment, of African Americans in housing, voting, and public places. News coverage of King's speeches and marches convinced many Americans that discrimination against African Americans was wrong.

President John F. Kennedy expressed support for African Americans before he was assassinated in 1963. However, his successor, Lyndon Johnson, was the one who pushed a new Civil Rights Act and a Voting Rights Act through Congress. President Johnson also introduced many new

COOPERATIVE LEARNING ACTIVITY

programs designed to end poverty, improve education, and provide medical care to the poor and elderly. His programs came to be called the Great Society.

Meanwhile, women were demanding equality in the workplace. After World War II, more and more women became lawyers, doctors, and government leaders. Yet, women received lower pay than men for the same work.

In the early 1900s, the women's rights movement had been a strong force. The movement declined, however, after the passage of the Nineteenth Amendment giving women the right to vote. Concern over inequality in the workplace united women again in the 1960s. In 1963 supporters of women's rights won passage of the Equal

▲ President Lyndon Johnson (left) and Martin Luther King, Jr. (right) worked to end discrimination against African Americans. *What were Johnson's Great Society programs intended to do?*

Pay Act, which outlawed paying men more than women for the same job.

 Reading Check **Compare** How did the Soviets react to reforms in Hungary and in Czechoslovakia?

Caption Answer: end poverty, improve education, and provide medical care to the poor and elderly

ENRICH

Quote Dr. Martin Luther King, Jr.: "I have a dream that my four little children will one day . . . not be judged by the color of their skin, but by the content of their character." **Ask: Has King's dream been realized? Explain your answer. L2**

 Reading Check

Answer: The Soviets took control of both countries and replaced their leadership.

History Online

To help students understand section material, have them visit **Study Central™** at jat.glencoe.com

RETEACH

Have students list the names of countries from the section on a sheet of paper. Then tell them to rate each country's postwar years on a scale from 1 for "rotten" to 5 for "great." **L1**

 Section 4 Review

History Online
Study Central™ Need help with the material in this section? Visit jat.glencoe.com

Reading Summary
Review the Main Ideas

- During the Cold War, the United States and the Soviet Union competed for power in Europe, leading to the creation of NATO and the Warsaw Pact.
- In Asia, Communists took control of mainland China, and U.S. aid helped rebuild Japan.
- In the U.S. and Western Europe, economies grew strong. In Eastern Europe and the Soviet Union, people faced shortages, and some countries tried to overthrow Communist rule.

What Did You Learn?

1. What was the Marshall Plan, and why was it important?
2. Who were the original members of the EEC, and what was its purpose?

Critical Thinking

3. **Organizing Information** Draw a chart like the one below. Fill in details about issues facing the United States during the 1950s and 1960s.

Life in the United States During the 1950s and 1960s

4. **Summarize** How were the Truman Doctrine, the Marshall Plan, and the Berlin Airlift significant in the U.S. fight against communism?
5. **Cause and Effect** How did conflict in Asia following World War II affect Japan's economic recovery?
6. **Analyze** Why was life harsh for ordinary citizens in the Soviet Union and Eastern European nations in the 1950s?
7. **Persuasive Writing** Write a letter to the editor describing your views on a policy or event from the Cold War.

4 CLOSE

Ask students which country and year during the Cold War era would they choose to visit if they could travel back in time. **L1**

SECTION 4 REVIEW ANSWERS

1. U.S. aid for rebuilding European economies; it weakened communism's appeal and opened markets for trade.
2. France, West Germany, Italy, and the Benelux countries; to help the nations' economies
3. Answers will vary. Students may mention the baby boom, racial segregation, discrimination, and women's rights.
4. by pledging U.S. opposition to communism worldwide, weakening the appeal of communism, and preventing the soviet takeover of Berlin
5. The U.S. bought billions in war supplies from Japan, and the economy expanded as a result.
6. shortages of consumer goods, food, and housing and fear of punishment for disagreeing with the government
7. Students' answers should contain details about the Cold War.

Section 5

The End of Empire

① FOCUS

SECTION OVERVIEW

In the decades following World War II, India and countries in Southeast Asia and Africa gained their independence from European powers.

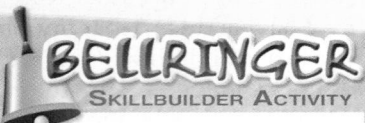

BELLRINGER
SKILLBUILDER ACTIVITY

✍ Project **Daily Focus Skills Transparency 21–5** and have students answer questions. Discuss their responses.

Get Ready to Read!

Preteaching Vocabulary: Point out that the prefix *dis-* can transform a word into its antonym, as in the case of *obedience* and *disobedience*. Add that *civil* refers to the law, and *civil disobedience* is about disobeying the law.

Answers to Graphic: war with Pakistan over Kashmir, civil war that resulted in the creation of Bangladesh, nuclear weapons race with Pakistan, multiple terrorist attacks

Get Ready to Read!

What's the Connection?
In past sections, you read about nationalism, communism, and the Cold War. This section explains how all three contributed to the collapse of European empires between 1945 and the present.

Focusing on the Main Ideas
- Led by Gandhi, India gained independence from Britain. *(page 843)*
- Nationalist movements led to independence for many Southeast Asian nations. *(page 846)*
- Most African colonies gained independence in the 1950s and 1960s. *(page 850)*

Locating Places
Pakistan (PA•kih•STAN)
Kashmir (KASH•MIHR)
Bangladesh (BAHNG•gluh•DEHSH)

Meeting People
Mohandas K. Gandhi (MOH•huhn•DAHS   GAHN•dee)
Jawaharlal Nehru (juh•WAH•huhr•LAHL   NEHR•oo)
Ho Chi Minh (HOH•CHEE•MIHN)
Nelson Mandela

Building Your Vocabulary
civil disobedience
Pan-Africanism
apartheid (uh•PAHR•TAYT)

Reading Strategy
Summarizing Information Complete a diagram like the one below to show the challenges India faced after becoming independent.

Challenges Since Independence

When & Where?

1930	1950	1970

1935 Britain passes the Government of India Act

1947 India and Pakistan become independent

1954 The French leave Vietnam

1963 Kenya becomes independent

MIDDLE EAST — ASIA — AFRICA — INDIA

SECTION RESOURCES

📁 **Reproducible Masters**
- Reproducible Lesson Plan 21–5
- Daily Lecture and Discussion Notes 21–5
- Vocabulary Activity 21–5
- Active Reading Note-Taking Guide 21–5
- Guided Reading Activity 21–5
- Section Quiz 21–5
- Reading Essentials and Study Guide 21–5

✍ **Transparencies**
- Daily Focus Skills Transparency 21–5

Multimedia
- Interactive Tutor Self-Assessment CD-ROM
- ExamView® Pro Testmaker CD-ROM
- Presentation Plus! CD-ROM
- Vocabulary PuzzleMaker CD-ROM
- Glencoe BookLink CD-ROM

India Becomes Independent

Main Idea Led by Gandhi, India gained independence from Britain.

Reading Focus Have you ever tried hard to win someone over to your point of view? Read to learn how Indians finally convinced the British to leave their country.

Previously, you learned that India came under British rule in the 1700s. The British built railroads, bridges, and ports in India. They did little, however, for India's people, who faced famine and other hardships. By the late 1800s, a movement for freedom began to take root and spread across the country.

The Indians who first called for independence were upper class and British-educated. Many lived in cities, such as Bombay (now Mumbai), Calcutta (now Kolkata), and Madras (now Chennai). Some were trained in British law and held government posts.

India's nationalists wanted reform and not revolution. The British, however, were slow in making changes. In 1885 a group of Indian leaders met in Mumbai to form the Indian National Congress (INC). The INC did not ask for independence right away. They did demand a role in ruling India.

Who Was Gandhi?
In 1919 a crowd of 10,000 Indians gathered for a political meeting at a walled garden in the city of Amritsar. Without warning, British troops blocked the exit from the garden and opened fire. They killed hundreds of people and wounded over a thousand. This Amritsar massacre made Indians more determined than ever to end British rule.

The most popular Indian leader was **Mohandas K. Gandhi** (MOH•huhn•DAHS GAHN•dee). He opposed violence in all

▲ Mohandas Gandhi (right) worked for an independent India along with Jahawarlal Nehru (left), who became India's first prime minister. *How did Gandhi protest British rule?*

forms. Instead, he protested British rule using nonviolent **civil disobedience**—the refusal to obey unjust laws.

In 1930 Gandhi led Indians in protesting the salt tax. The British taxed every grain of salt sold. They also made it illegal for Indians to collect salt on their own. Gandhi and his followers openly defied the British ban. The salt tax protests resulted in 60,000 arrests, including Gandhi's.

Pressured by protests, the British Parliament passed the Government of India Act in 1935. This law allowed Indians to run India's provinces, or regions. The British, however, kept control of India's national affairs.

Some Indians rejected the act. Others accepted it as a step toward full independence. The INC began running candidates for offices in regional governments. In 1937 candidates who were Hindu in religion won in 7 of the 11 provinces. As a result, India's Muslims began to worry how the much larger Hindu population might treat them in an independent India.

② TEACH

Reading Strategy

Summarizing Information Have students read the material under "India Becomes Independent " and "Who Was Gandhi?" Next, tell them to imagine they are Indian nationalists preparing for an interview by the international press. Then ask them to write a brief statement that sums up the nationalists' grievances against their British rulers. **L1/EL**

More About the Photo

Though he was not the best student, suffered from a slight speech impediment, and was afraid of the dark, Gandhi became one of the most admired and respected men in history.

Caption Answer: through nonviolent civil disobedience, the refusal to obey unjust laws

Reading Support L1/EL

Use **Vocabulary Activity 21–5** to review important terms in the section.

Daily Lecture and Discussion Notes 21–5

Use **Daily Lecture and Discussion Notes 21–5** for an outline of key concepts found in the section.

Reading Strategy | READING THE TEXT

Using Context Clues Remind students that context clues are words, phrases, and sentences that help them understand unfamiliar words. Then write the following questions on the board, and have students look for the answers under "India Becomes Independent" and "Who Was Gandhi?"

1. Which word tells you what Bombay [Mumbai], Calcutta [Kolkata], and Madras [Chennai] are? *(cities)*
2. Which sentence helps define *massacre*? *(They killed hundreds of people and wounded over a thousand.)*
3. Which kind of punctuation signals that a definition for *civil disobedience* follows? *(an em dash)*
4. Which word does the phrase "They also made it illegal" help define?" *(ban)*
5. Which small word signals that a definition for *provinces* follows? *(or)* **L1/EL**

TEACH

Gandhi's doctrine of moral nonviolent protest won him international attention. He believed that one could force an evil person or government to change by challenging it directly but without violence. Gandhi used the term *satyagraha* (suh•TYAH•gruh• huh), which means "truth force," to describe the nonviolent protests he led. One effective form of protest was the boycott, in which Indians refused to buy British cloth and other manufactured goods. As a step toward independence, Gandhi urged Indians to spin their own cloth.

On January 30, 1948, a Hindu militant shot Gandhi three times in the chest as Gandhi was going to morning prayer. **Ask: Why do you think a Hindu militant killed Gandhi?** (*A possible answer is that Gandhi's peaceful solutions may have frustrated the militant, who most likely wanted immediate but violent solutions.*)

Then and Now

Answers will vary. Students may mention that persecuted people need an alternative to terrorism and other forms of violence to resolve conflicts with oppressive governments.

Biography

MOHANDAS GANDHI

1869–1948

When Mohandas Gandhi was arrested in 1922 and charged with rebellion, he defended himself by saying, "Nonviolence is the first article of my faith." Gandhi's strong belief in nonviolence developed early in his childhood. His mother, Putlibai, who was a devout Hindu, taught the principles of peace and tolerance to Mohandas and his older siblings.

Gandhi grew up in Porbandar, the capital of a small territory in western India. He did not do well in school. In one school report, he was described as "good at English, fair in Arithmetic and weak in Geography; conduct very good, bad handwriting." At home, Gandhi helped his mother with chores and helped take care of his dying father. In his free time, he took long walks by himself.

Gandhi's family wanted him to follow in his father's footsteps and study law. So in 1888 Gandhi sailed to England and entered one of London's law colleges. While living in London, he read for the first time an English translation of the Bhagavad Gita. Reading the Bhagavad Gita proved to be one of the greatest influences on Gandhi's life. It returned him to the Hindu religion. It also exposed him to two ideas that he would come to live by in his life and work. One idea was that material goods kept a person from pursuing a spiritual life. The other idea was to be peaceful and even-tempered in all situations.

In his work as a lawyer, Gandhi found that his true calling was mediation, or helping opposing groups resolve conflicts. In his later role as a political and spiritual leader, his talent for mediation helped him tackle enormous conflicts involving colonialism, racism, and violence.

▲ Mohandas Gandhi

> "The force of love is the same as the force of the soul or truth."
>
> –Mohandas Gandhi, "Indian Home Rule"

Then and Now

Why do you think that Gandhi's approach to conflict resolution remains important and necessary in society today?

Reading List Generator CD-ROM

GLENCOE BOOKLINK   **RECOMMENDED READING**

Use the **Glencoe BookLink CD-ROM** to create customized reading lists based on your students' interests and reading levels. Below is an example based on content in this chapter. Also see the Suggested Readings on pages 944–946 of the Appendix.

- Eaton, Jeanette. *Gandhi: Fighter Without a Sword*. Mohandas Gandhi became a friend and champion of the poor and "Untouchables" in India. He also worked to free India from the British.

- Denny, Roz. *A Taste of India*. What do people eat in India? Learn about the exotic dishes of Bombay (Mumbai), Punjab, Delhi, and Rajasthan. Learn how to make everyday foods like *raita* and naan, as well as specialties like tandoori chicken.

British India Is Divided After World War II, India's Hindus and Muslims were bitterly divided. The British realized that India would have to be split into a Hindu country and a Muslim country. **Pakistan** (PA•kih•STAN)—the Muslim country—would be made up of two regions separated by India—the Hindu country. West Pakistan was northwest of India, and East Pakistan was to the northeast.

On August 15, 1947, India and Pakistan became independent. Many Hindus in Pakistan fled to India, while many Muslims in India fled to Pakistan. Fighting erupted during this mass movement, and more than 1 million people were killed.

Tensions With Pakistan When British India ended, local states ruled by princes had to decide their future. Most became part of India. Others went with Pakistan.

The state of Kashmir joined neither India nor Pakistan. Most people in **Kashmir** (KASH•MIHR) were Muslims, but the ruler was Hindu. Pakistan invaded Kashmir, and its ruler turned to India for help. The result was a war between Pakistan and India. In 1949 the war ended, with most of Kashmir controlled by India.

In addition to conflicts with India, Pakistan faced conflicts within. Military leaders took over the elected government and ruled from 1958 until 1971. Also in 1971, East Pakistan declared its independence. After a brief civil war, it became a new nation named **Bangladesh** (BAHNG•gluh•DEHSH).

India and Pakistan continued to clash. More wars were fought over Kashmir, and both nations built nuclear weapons. In December 2001, Kashmir terrorists killed

Writing Activity

Have students review information in the reading about the conflict between Hindus and Muslims. Then ask them to write editorials urging a peaceful transition from British India to India and Pakistan. Suggest that they cite Gandhi's principles to support their position. Distribute copies of a newspaper editorial for students to use as a model. **L2**

Geography Have students locate India, Pakistan, and Bangladesh in the Reference Atlas maps. Tell them to describe each place's relative location in relation to the other places. Then ask them to give the absolute location, or latitude and longitude, of each country's capital. (*New Delhi: about 29° N latitude and 77° E longitude, Islamabad: about 33° N latitude and 73° E longitude, Dhaka: about 24° N latitude and 90° E longitude*) **L2**

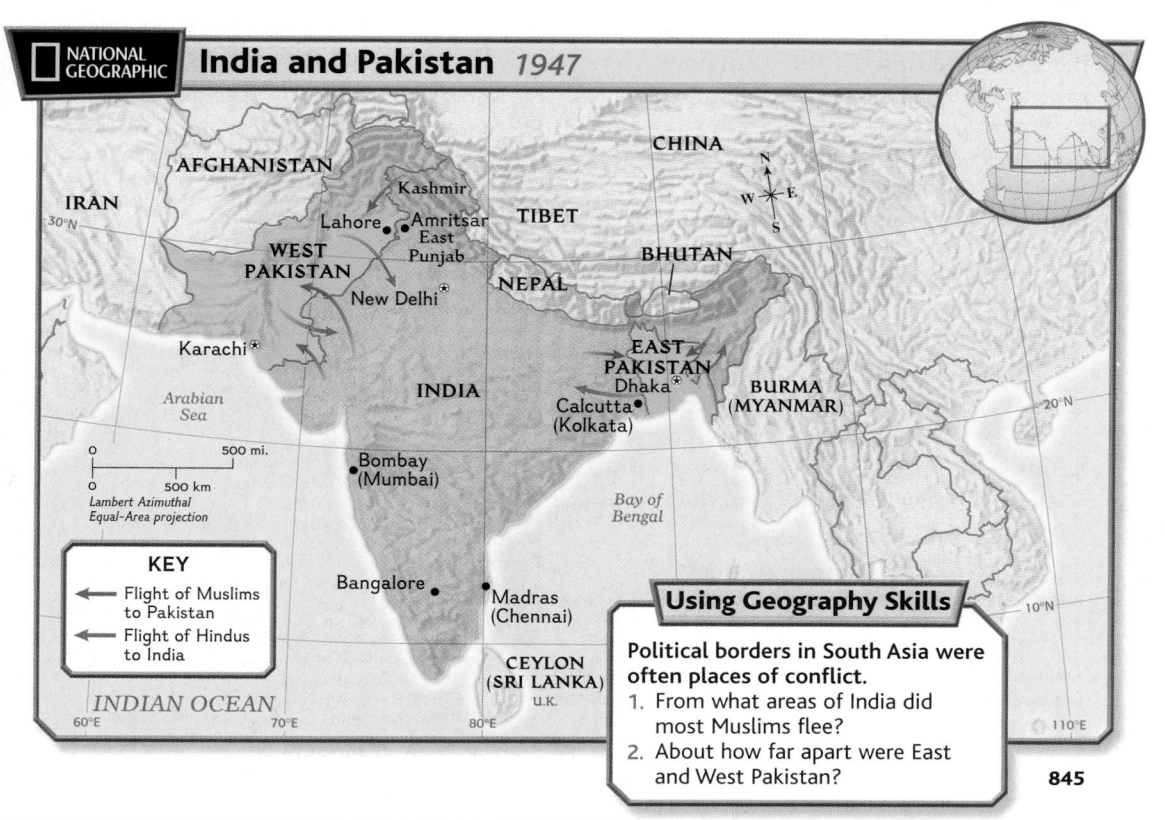

NATIONAL GEOGRAPHIC **India and Pakistan** *1947*

CHINA

AFGHANISTAN
Kashmir
IRAN
30°N
Lahore • Amritsar
East
Punjab
WEST
PAKISTAN
New Delhi ⊛
Karachi ⊛
TIBET
BHUTAN
NEPAL
EAST
PAKISTAN
Dhaka ⊛
Calcutta
(Kolkata)
BURMA
(MYANMAR)
20°N
Arabian Sea
INDIA
Bombay
(Mumbai)
Bay of Bengal
0   500 mi.
0   500 km
Lambert Azimuthal
Equal-Area projection

KEY
← Flight of Muslims to Pakistan
← Flight of Hindus to India

Bangalore •
• Madras
(Chennai)

CEYLON
(SRI LANKA)
U.K.
INDIAN OCEAN
60°E   70°E   80°E

10°N

110°E

Using Geography Skills

Political borders in South Asia were often places of conflict.
1. From what areas of India did most Muslims flee?
2. About how far apart were East and West Pakistan?

845

Using Geography Skills

Answers:
1. northwest and northeast
2. about 1,200 miles

Skills Practice

Ask: Which group fled to Pakistan? (*Muslims*)

DIFFERENTIATED INSTRUCTION

Auditory/Musical: Explain that extravagant musicals are very popular in Bollywood—the name for the Indian film industry. Play a soundtrack from a recent movie set in present-day India, and ask students to identify the Western and Indian elements in the music.

English Learners: Play the soundtrack from a recent made-in-India movie while students read the lesson.

Gifted and Talented: Tell a group of students to watch a Bollywood musical as homework and then to choreograph a dance to music from the video. Ask the group to perform its dance for the class.

📁 Refer to *Inclusion Strategies for the Middle School Social Studies Classroom* in the TCR.

846

Reading Strategy

Making a Time Line Draw a vertical line on the board with 1919 at the top and 2001 at the bottom. Divide the rest of the line into eight equal segments. Tell students to review the material from the beginning of "Who Was Gandhi?" to the end of "India Tries to Modernize." Then have them write years and events from the reading in the correct places along the time line. **L1/EL**

TIME TRAVELER

Indira Ghandi was swept from office in 1977 and did not return until 1980. At the time, some Sikhs in Punjab wanted their own state. Sikh separatists occupied the Golden Temple of Amritsar, Sikhism's holiest shrine. When talks failed, Gandhi used troops and tanks to drive out the separatists. Outraged at the shrine's violation, two of Gandhi's bodyguards, who were Sikhs, assassinated her.

✓ Reading Check

Answer: Indians became more determined to oust the British.

Caption Answer: They feared a Communist takeover.

---

nine people at India's Parliament building. The Indian government blamed Pakistan, but Pakistan denied responsibility. Five months later, terrorists attacked an Indian army base in Kashmir. This time, India and Pakistan almost went to war but pulled back after successful talks.

India Tries to Modernize After independence, the Indian National Congress, renamed the Congress Party, began to rule India. The party's leader and India's first prime minister was **Jawaharlal Nehru** (juh•WAH•huhr•LAHL NEHR•oo). A British-educated lawyer, Nehru had helped lead India's freedom movement. In 1948 Nehru lost a close ally when Gandhi was assassinated.

Nehru tried to raise the standard of living in India through Five-Year Plans. He placed industry under government control. He also expanded farmlands, which set the stage for India's Green Revolution, or rapid increase in crops. By 1979, Indians were raising enough crops to feed all of India.

Nehru died in 1964. Two years later, his daughter, Indira Gandhi, became prime minister. Gandhi continued her father's policies but was assassinated in 1984. Gandhi's son, Rajiv Gandhi, served as prime minister from 1984 to 1989. He, too, was killed while campaigning.

While India struggled politically, reforms in the 1990s helped shift the country toward a free enterprise economy. The government now encourages foreign investments. One of the fastest-growing industries in India today is the making of computer products.

✓ **Reading Check** **Cause and Effect** What was the result of the massacre at Amritsar?

Achmed Sukarno was Indonesia's first leader after ▶ the country gained independence. *Why did the Dutch give Indonesia independence?*

Empire Ends in Southeast Asia

Main Idea Nationalist movements led to independence for many Southeast Asian nations.

Reading Focus How old is the United States? Did you know that most countries in the world are less than 100 years old? Read to learn why so many new countries have appeared so recently.

Nationalism also erupted in Southeast Asia. After World War II, many Southeast Asian nations gained their freedom. Some countries reached this goal more easily than others did. For example, the United States granted independence to the Philippines in 1946, but the Netherlands was less willing to give up its control of the Dutch East Indies.

The Dutch Leave Indonesia After World War II, Achmed Sukarno and his nationalists declared the East Indies to be independent. They renamed their country Indonesia.

CRITICAL THINKING ACTIVITY

Identifying Tell students that after East Timor gained its independence, the Indonesian government announced a program of democratic reform. Then, in 2003, the government proclaimed a military emergency in regions of the country where its troops were fighting rebels. It imposed a ban on reporting and human rights monitoring. In addition, Indonesian courts sentenced 30 prisoners of conscience. Some were newspaper editors who criticized political leaders, and others were peace activists who protested government policies. In 2004 the government expelled workers in an international governmental organization that was monitoring human rights abuses in Indonesia. **Ask:** Which freedom did the Indonesian government suppress? *(freedom of speech)* Do you think the government wanted democratic reform? Explain your answer. **L2**

The Dutch at first opposed this move. Then, Indonesia's Communists revolted. Fearing a Communist takeover, the Dutch in 1949 accepted Sukarno's government.

In 1965 Indonesia's Communists tried again to seize power. Indonesia's army killed about 300,000 people believed to be Communist supporters. Then, the army's commander, General Suharto, replaced Sukarno as ruler.

In 1975 Suharto's troops seized the nearby Portuguese colony of East Timor. Suharto was a harsh leader, and East Timor's people fought his rule. Finally, in August 1999, Indonesia's government allowed East Timor to vote on independence. After the election, Indonesia's soldiers in East Timor staged attacks. The UN sent troops to stop the violence. With UN help, East Timor became independent in 2002.

The British Leave Myanmar and Malaysia

Burma, now Myanmar, had been under British rule for many years. In 1948 it became independent. Communists and ethnic groups within Burma soon rose up against the government. To restore order, military leaders seized control in 1962.

Burma's military leaders ran the economy and cracked down on opponents. The people of Burma protested. Finally, the military leaders agreed to hold elections in 1990. Before the voting took place, they arrested Aung San Suu Kyi (AWNG SAN SOO CHEE)—the key democratic leader. She won the election, but Burma's military leaders rejected the results. After her release in 1995, Aung San Suu Kyi continued to work for democracy.

Independence also came to British colonies on the Malay Peninsula and the island of Borneo. After defeating Communist guerrillas, the British granted freedom to these territories. In 1963 the territories united to form the independent Federation of Malaysia.

NATIONAL GEOGRAPHIC
Southeast Asia

Using Geography Skills

After many years of imperialism, the people of Southeast Asia finally gained their independence.
1. Which nation lies directly west of Thailand?
2. How far apart are the two main parts of Malaysia?

The French Fight in Vietnam During World War II, the Japanese seized Indochina from the French. A Communist named **Ho Chi Minh** (HOH • CHEE • MIHN) formed a group called the Vietminh to drive out the Japanese. Soon afterward, the United States began sending military aid to the Vietminh.

When Japan gave up control of Indochina, Ho Chi Minh declared Vietnam independent. France, however, wanted to get back Vietnam and the rest of Indochina. French troops returned to Vietnam in 1946 and drove the Vietminh into hiding.

The Vietminh fought the French and slowly won control of the countryside. Worried that Ho Chi Minh was a

CHAPTER 21   World War II and the Cold War   **847**

Reading Strategy

Predicting Have students read the heading "The British Leave Myanmar and Malaysia." Next, tell them to recall what happened after India and Israel won their independence from Britain. **Ask: What do you think happened after Burma, now Myanmar, became independent? Why?** Tell them to read the material under the heading to find out if their prediction is correct. **L1**

Using Geography Skills

Answers:
1. Burma
2. about 400 miles

CURRICULUM CONNECTION

Language Arts
Read aloud the following verse from *In the Quiet Land* by Aung San Suu Kyi about oppression in Myanmar: "In the Quiet Land, no one can hear /what is silenced by murder/ and covered by fear, / But, despite what is forced, freedom's a sound / that liars can't fake and no shouting can drown." **Ask: Where is the Quiet Land?** *(Myanmar)* **Who are the liars who can't fake freedom?** *(government officials)*

INTERDISCIPLINARY CONNECTIONS ACTIVITY

Civics Explain that Singapore's modern economic growth occurred under the authoritarian leadership of Lee Kuan Yew (lee kwahn yoo), who was prime minister from 1965 to 1990. Describe Lee Kuan Yew's administration this way: The government focused on encouraging high-technology industries and welcomed foreign investment. A prosperous economy and the high rate of savings by Singapore citizens helped finance quality housing, health care, and education. In spite of having these benefits, Singapore's people had limited rights and little freedom of speech. **Ask: Would you rather have quality housing, health care, and education, or personal freedom? Explain. Why did Lee Kuan Yew suppress freedom?** *(Answers will vary. A possible answer is that some leaders believe that total control is the only way to maintain economic growth.)***L2**

Communist and determined to stop communism's spread in Asia, the United States gave military aid to French forces in Vietnam.

Despite American help, the French could not beat the Vietminh. In 1954 the French decided to make peace and withdraw from Indochina.

An agreement called the Geneva Accords divided Vietnam at the 17th parallel. Ho Chi Minh controlled North Vietnam. A government supported by the United States ran South Vietnam. The Geneva Accords also accepted the independence of two other countries in Indochina—Cambodia and Laos.

Americans Fight in Vietnam The Geneva Accords called for elections to unite Vietnam, but South Vietnam's leader refused to hold them. He feared the elections in the Communist north would not be fair and worried that southern Vietnamese might vote for Ho Chi Minh. After South Vietnam refused to hold elections, Ho Chi Minh decided to unite Vietnam through force. He set up a guerrilla army in South Vietnam known as the Vietcong. To help South Vietnam's government fight the Vietcong, U.S. president Dwight D. Eisenhower sent aid and military advisers to South Vietnam.

The Vietnam War

◄ French soldiers wait in their trenches during a break in fighting in Dien Bien Phu, Vietnam. *In what year did the French troops withdraw from Vietnam?*

U.S. infantrymen leap from a military helicopter on their way to a mission in Vietnam. ▼

▲ Ho Chi Minh became the leader of North Vietnam following Japan's retreat from the country in World War II.

EXTENDING THE CONTENT

Why Did Ho Chi Minh Oppose French Rule? After Japan was defeated, Ho Chi Minh and one million other Vietnamese celebrated in Hanoi. He issued a Declaration of Independence that was modeled on the American Declaration of Independence. It began: "All men are created equal. They are endowed by their Creator with certain inalienable rights; among them are life, liberty, and the pursuit of happiness." Then the declaration listed grievances against the French: "They have built more prisons than schools. They have mercilessly slain our patriots, they have drowned uprisings in rivers of blood. They have fettered public opinion. . . . They have robbed us of our rice fields, our mines, our forests, and our raw materials."

During the 1960s, the United States was drawn deeper into the fight for Vietnam. In 1964 U.S. president Lyndon Johnson reported that North Vietnam had attacked American ships in the Gulf of Tonkin. In early August, Congress passed the Gulf of Tonkin Resolution giving Johnson permission to fight a war in Vietnam. In 1965 Johnson sent the first American combat troops to fight the Vietcong.

By the late 1960s, many Americans opposed the war. Finally, in 1973 U.S. president Richard Nixon withdrew American forces from Vietnam. At least 2 million people, including 58,000 Americans, died in the war.

About 10 million South Vietnamese became refugees. Many were called "boat people" because they fled the country in boats. Twenty years later, some boat people were still living in refugee camps far from home.

In 1975 North Vietnam's army reunited Vietnam and imposed a Communist government on the south. Faced with a failing economy, Vietnam's leaders began to allow privately owned businesses in the late 1980s. In 1995 Vietnam improved its relations and trade with the United States.

Reading Check **Explain** Why did the U.S. decide to help the French in Vietnam?

Robert McNamara, Johnson's Secretary of Defense, told Americans: "While on routine patrol in international waters, the U.S. destroyer *Maddox* underwent an unprovoked attack." This information was challenged by later findings that revealed that the *Maddox* was not on "routine patrol" but on a spying mission. In this case, an attack might have been justified. Also, the ship was in Vietnam's territorial waters, not international waters. There may not have been an actual attack on the *Maddox*. Nevertheless, McNamara's statement was used to persuade Congress to pass the Gulf of Tonkin Resolution.

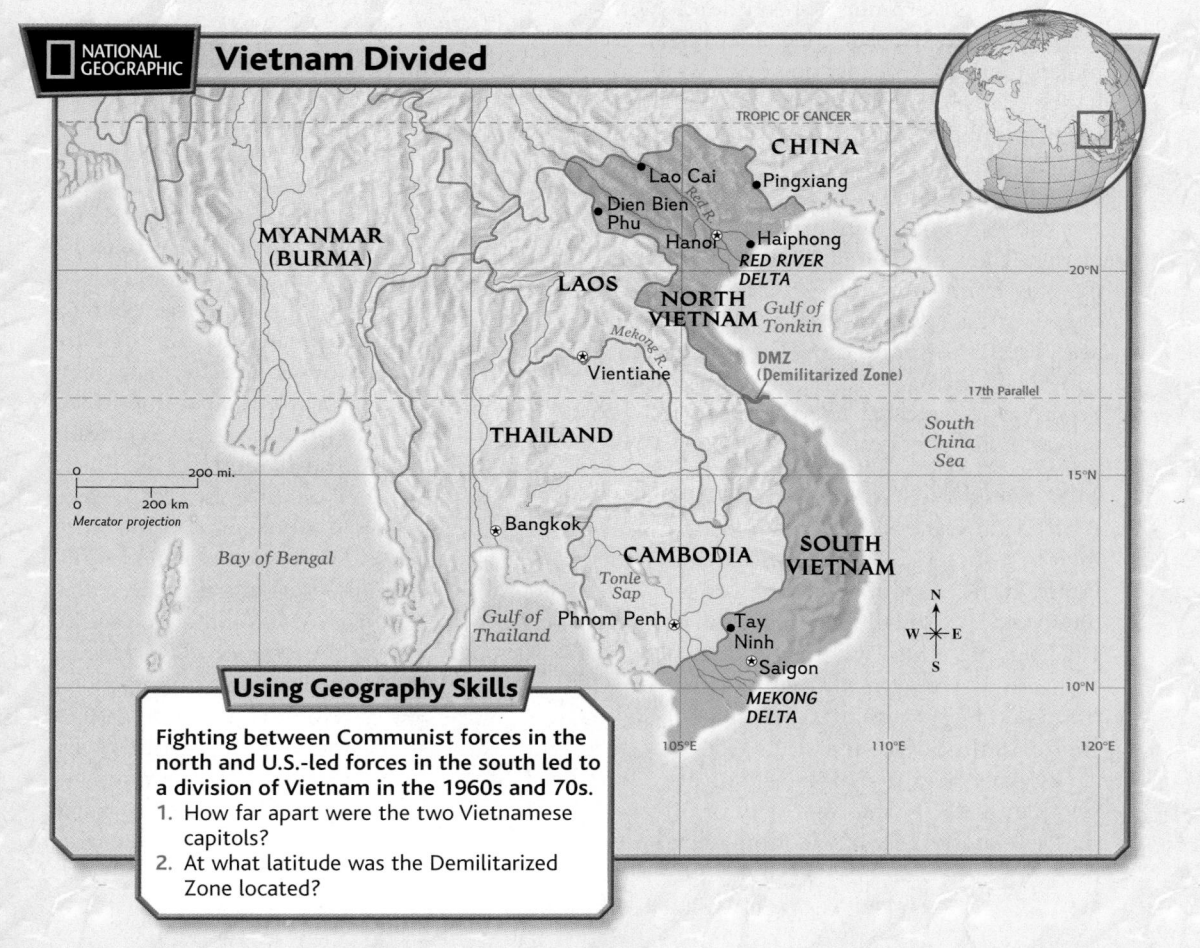

NATIONAL GEOGRAPHIC **Vietnam Divided**

Using Geography Skills

Fighting between Communist forces in the north and U.S.-led forces in the south led to a division of Vietnam in the 1960s and 70s.
1. How far apart were the two Vietnamese capitols?
2. At what latitude was the Demilitarized Zone located?

Using Geography Skills

Answers:
1. about 725 miles
2. 17th Parallel, or 17°N

Reading Check

Answer: Indonesian Communists challenged Sukarno's republican government. The United States preferred Sukarno's government to a Communist one.

COOPERATIVE LEARNING ACTIVITY

An Oral Presentation Tell students that in 1967 Martin Luther King, Jr., gave an eloquent antiwar speech at Riverside Church in New York. Then distribute copies of this excerpt: "Somehow this madness must cease. We must stop now. I speak as a child of God and brother to the suffering poor of Vietnam. I speak for those whose land is being laid waste, whose homes are being destroyed, whose culture is being subverted. I speak for the poor of America who are paying the double price of smashed hopes at home and death and corruption in Vietnam." Organize the class into groups. Have each group practice an oral presentation of the passage and perform it for the rest of the class.
L1/EL

TIME TRAVELER

Jomo Kenyatta was elected president of Kenya in 1964 and held office until 1978. He maintained a free-market economy and made Kenya a popular spot for tourists and international businesses.

Africa Becomes Independent

Main Idea Most African colonies gained independence in the 1950s and 1960s.

Reading Focus What do you do if you think you are not being treated fairly? Do you speak out? Read on to learn how Africans sought better treatment and independence from European rulers.

Black Africans fought in World War I with British and French forces. Many hoped they would be rewarded with independence. Instead, Britain and France further increased the size of their empires.

After the war, Africans became more politically active and staged protests. European governments responded with force and arrests. But they also began to make reforms. Africans, however, were not happy with these halfway steps. They wanted independence.

Nationalism was strong among European-educated Africans. Most of them worked in colonial government and businesses. They saw the striking gap between the way Europeans supported democracy at home yet denied it to colonial peoples overseas. From this group came the leaders who convinced Africans to demand their freedom. However, most of Africa would not gain independence until the 1960s.

New Arab States in North Africa

African movements for freedom had their first success in North Africa. After World War II, Egyptian nationalists set out to end British influence in Egypt. In 1952 Egypt's king, whom the British supported, was overthrown. British troops left Egypt, although Britain kept control of the Suez Canal until 1956.

Egypt's neighbor, Libya, won its freedom in 1951. The discovery of oil in 1959 made Libya's leaders very wealthy. The people of Libya, however, remained poor. In 1969 a military officer named Muammar al-Qaddafi overthrew Libya's king and set up a socialist government. Its goal was to spread Libya's oil revenue more equally among the people.

France began letting go of its North African empire in 1956. At this time, the French gave full independence to Morocco and Tunisia. Because many French people lived in Algeria, France decided to keep control there. Algerian Arabs, however, fought back to free their homeland. Algeria finally won independence in 1962.

Africa South of the Sahara

Freedom also came to African colonies south of the Sahara. Kwame Nkrumah (KWAHM•eh ehn•KROO•muh) led a nationalist movement in Britain's colony of the Gold Coast in West Africa. In 1950 Nkrumah led workers in a strike that put pressure on British officials. The British jailed Nkrumah but soon freed him as protests continued. In 1957 the Gold Coast, now renamed Ghana, became independent under Nkrumah.

Nigeria, Britain's largest African colony, won its freedom in 1960. Other British colonies in Africa followed. After a violent uprising in the 1950s, Kenya became independent in 1963 under the leadership of Jomo Kenyatta. The new nations of Zambia and Malawi arose in central Africa during the mid-1960s. Another colony in the region, Rhodesia, broke away from Britain. However, a small but powerful group of Europeans remained in control. This group refused to allow the

▲ Jomo Kenyatta

EXTENDING THE CONTENT

Fair Trade Chocolate From Ghana Originally from Central and South America, cacao trees traveled with the Dutch to islands off Africa's coast. From there cacao moved to Ghana. Today cacao makes up more than one-fourth of all Ghana's exports. In recent years the price of cacao has plummeted, devastating poor farmers and forcing their children to care for the trees instead of going to school. In response to the crisis, more than 35,000 cacao growers in Ghana have joined the Kuapa Kokoo Cocoa Fair Trade Cooperative. The Fair Trade System guarantees them a minimum price per pound and ensures that children go to school. Kuapa Kokoo is also part owner of the Day Chocolate Company and uses its profits from chocolate sales to pay for community projects.

▲ Ghana, led by Kwame Nkrumah, shown here speaking, was the first former British colony to gain independence in Africa. *What was Britain's largest African colony and when did it gain freedom?*

much larger black population to rule. After a long struggle, the African population finally won control. In 1980 Rhodesia became the independent nation of Zimbabwe.

France wanted to avoid conflicts in its colonies south of the Sahara. In 1958 the French gave their colonies a choice. They could have limited self-rule with French aid, or they could become totally independent with no help from France.

Guinea's nationalist leader, Ahmed Sékou Touré (ah•MEHD SEH•koo TOO•ray), chose full independence. France withdrew its officials from Guinea and vowed not to help the new nation. Then Guinea accepted aid from the Soviet Union. France did not want its other African colonies to

follow this same path, so it gave them both full independence and aid.

In the Belgian Congo, nationalist leaders demanded independence during the 1950s. Belgium reacted by arresting the leaders. As riots mounted, the Belgians finally gave the Congo its freedom in 1960. Ten years later, the country was renamed Zaire. Today it is known as the Democratic Republic of Congo.

Portugal ruled its colonies of Angola and Mozambique with an iron hand. During the 1960s, rebels attacked the Portuguese, but Portuguese troops kept the rebels in check until the 1970s. Then a revolution in Portugal unseated that country's dictator. Portugal's new democratic government freed Angola and Mozambique in 1975.

CHAPTER 21   World War II and the Cold War   **851**

Caption Answer: Nigeria, 1960

Reading Support L1/ EL

Assign **Guided Reading Activity 21–5** to help students organize the information in the section.

3 ASSESS

Assign Section 5 Review as homework or as an in-class activity.

⦿ Have students use the **Interactive Tutor Self-Assessment CD-ROM** to review the section.

Assessment L2

Assign **Section 5 Quiz** to assess mastery of the material found in the section.

Reading Support L1/ EL

Assign **Reading Essentials and Study Guide 21–5** to help students review section material.

CRITICAL THINKING ACTIVITY

Determining Cause and Effect Have students insert the effect of each cause. (Answers in cyan) **L2**

Cause France withheld help.	Cause Rulers of the Congo arrested nationalist leaders.	Cause Portugal ruled harshly in Mozambique and Angola.	Cause Europeans refused to allow the majority to rule.
↓	↓	↓	↓
Effect Africans struggle with Rhodesia.	Effect Guinea took Soviet aid.	Effect The people rioted.	Effect Rebels attacked the Portuguese.

ENRICH

Point out that many African nations took new names when they became independent. For example, Rhodesia became Zimbabwe, which referred to the 1,000-year-old city of Great Zimbabawe. **Ask: Why do you think newly independent African nations changed their names? L2**

 Reading Check

Answer: Guinea, a former French colony, received aid from the Soviet Union after gaining independence. France did not want their other colonies to do the same thing.

 History Online

To help students understand section material, have them visit **Study Central™** at jat.glencoe.com

RETEACH

Have students make generalizations about the independence movements in India, Southeast Asia, and Africa. **L1**

4 CLOSE

 Reading Strategy

Challenge students to write as many names from the section as they can in two minutes. **L1**

852

Some African leaders believed in **Pan-Africanism**—the unity of all black Africans. In 1963 thirty-two African states founded the Organization of African Unity (OAU). The OAU was the first step toward joining all the new countries in a broader community. Today, the OAU has been replaced by an even more closely united organization known as the African Union (AU).

Apartheid in South Africa Previously, you learned that Boer and British territories united in 1910 to form South Africa. Most of South Africa's people were black Africans, but the smaller European population ran the government. Black South Africans founded the African National Congress (ANC) in 1912 in hopes of gaining power.

In the 1940s, white South Africans strengthened their rule through a system known as apartheid, or "apartness."

Apartheid (uh•PAHR•tayt) was carried out through laws that separated racial and ethnic groups and limited the rights of blacks. For example, black South Africans had to live in separate areas called "homelands." People of non-European background were not even allowed to vote. Blacks protested the laws, and the white government responded by cracking down on the protesters.

In 1960 police opened fire on a peaceful march in the town of Sharpeville. They killed 69 people. Two thirds of them were shot in the back while running away. In 1962 police arrested **Nelson Mandela,** the leader of the ANC. The arrest did not end the protests against apartheid, but it would be nearly 30 years before South Africa abolished the apartheid system.

Reading Check **Explain** Why did France eventually give its African colonies aid and independence?

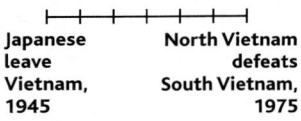 **History Online**
Study Central™ Need help with the material in this section? Visit jat.glencoe.com

Section 5 Review

Reading Summary
Review the Main Ideas
- India gained independence from Britain, struggled to modernize, then began building a free enterprise economy.
- Nationalist movements led many Southeast Asian colonies to independence. Communist and democratic nations fought to influence and control these new nations.
- Nationalist movements developed in Africa in the 1950s and 1960s. Many African colonies soon gained independence.

What Did You Learn?

1. What was the Gulf of Tonkin Resolution, and why was it important?

2. What was the INC, and what role did the INC play in India's independence movement?

Critical Thinking

3. **Sequencing Information** Draw a time line like the one shown. Fill in events related to the war in Vietnam.

Japanese leave Vietnam, 1945 — North Vietnam defeats South Vietnam, 1975

4. **Contrast** What were the differences between the independence movements in Algeria and Kenya?

5. **Cause and Effect** What was the result of Nehru's Five-Year Plans?

6. **Identify** Which groups were fighting for control of Indonesia after World War II?

7. **Creative Writing** Suppose you are the leader of a newly independent nation. Write five goals for your country and explain how the country will work toward those goals.

852   CHAPTER 21   World War II and the Cold War

SECTION 5 REVIEW ANSWERS

1. A resolution passed by Congress that gave the president power to make war; Johnson used that power to bomb North Vietnam.

2. an Indian nationalist organization; It used civil disobedience to pressure the British to grant independence.

3. French fight in Vietnam until 1954; U.S. fight in Vietnam until 1973; North Vietnam wins and imposes a Communist government

4. In Algeria, nationalists staged a civil war to win independence. In Kenya, Kenyatta went to London to negotiate, and Kenya eventually won independence peacefully.

5. It placed industry under government control and enabled Indian farmers to raise enough crops to feed India's people.

6. the Dutch, Indonesian Nationalists, and Communists

7. Goals should be logical.

Section The Rise of Dictators

Vocabulary
inflation
depression
totalitarian state
collectivization

Focusing on the Main Ideas
- New economic problems led to the Great Depression. *(page 805)*
- The Great Depression encouraged the rise of European dictators. *(page 808)*
- After Lenin's death, Stalin established a brutal regime in the USSR. *(page 810)*
- Economic problems led to militarism in Japan. *(page 811)*

Section World War II Begins

Vocabulary
appeasement

Focusing on the Main Ideas
- Other European nations stood by as Germany expanded its territory. *(page 814)*
- World War II began when Germany invaded Poland in September 1939, leading France and Britain to declare war. *(page 815)*

Section The Allies Win the War

Vocabulary
genocide
D-Day

Focusing on the Main Ideas
- The Allies fought for four long years in Europe and in the Pacific. *(page 825)*
- The Nazis murdered millions of people in an attempt to destroy Jews and other European ethnic groups. *(page 827)*
- The successful invasion on D-Day was the beginning of the end of World War II. *(page 828)*

Section The Cold War

Vocabulary
containment
Truman Doctrine
Marshall Plan
racial segregation

Focusing on the Main Ideas
- Soviet efforts to spread communism led to conflict with the United States, which wanted to contain communism. *(page 832)*
- The Cold War spread to Asia after China's communist revolution and the outbreak of the Korean War. *(page 837)*
- People in the postwar world experienced prosperity, change, and conflict. *(page 839)*

Section The End of Empire

Vocabulary
civil disobedience
Pan-Africanism
apartheid

Focusing on the Main Ideas
- Led by Gandhi, India gained independence from Britain. *(page 843)*
- Nationalist movements led to independence for many Southeast Asian nations. *(page 846)*
- Most African colonies gained independence in the 1950s and 1960s. *(page 850)*

CHAPTER 21 REVIEW

PREVIEW/REVIEW

Vocabulary Activity Have a student start a story by creating a sentence using a vocabulary word. Tell the next student to add a sentence to the story using another vocabulary word. Continue until each student has contributed a sentence to the story.

- **Vocabulary PuzzleMaker CD-ROM**
- **Interactive Tutor Self-Assessment CD-ROM**

CONDENSE

- Chapter 21 **Guided Reading Activities**
- **Student Works Plus™ CD-ROM** (with Audio Program)

RETEACH

- **Differentiated Instruction Activity 21**
- Chapter 21 *Reading Essentials and Study Guide*

CHAPTER CULMINATING ACTIVITY

Have students finish the Chapter Culminating Activity from page 800D.

Suggestions for rubrics may be found in the *Quizzes, Tests, and Authentic Assessment (with Rubrics)* booklet.

Reading Strategy   READ TO WRITE

Poem Have students write a poem about a grave injustice described in the chapter, such as the Amritsar massacre, the Holocaust, or apartheid. Urge them to address emotions that they feel and that the victims probably felt.

- **L1** students should write at least one stanza that includes one or two details from the chapter.
- **L2** students should write at least four stanzas that include several details and appropriate metaphors.
- **L3** students should write at least four stanzas that include many details and a recurring metaphor that provides a unifying theme.

Chapter 21 Assessment and Activities

GLENCOE TECHNOLOGY

MindJogger Videoquiz
Use the **MindJogger Videoquiz** to review Chapter 21 content.

Available in DVD and VHS

Review Vocabulary

1. inflation
2. true
3. racial segregation
4. genocide
5. true
6. collectivization

Review Main Ideas

7. The jobless and homeless supported dictators who promised to help them.
8. Stalin established a brutal regime.
9. They chose to avoid war by accepting Germany's demands.
10. when the French and British declared war on Germany in September 1939
11. to destroy Jews and other groups
12. the successful invasion on D-Day
13. the United States and the Soviet Union
14. Japan
15. nationalist movements
16. 1950s and 1960s

Review Vocabulary

Write **True** for each true statement. Replace the word in italics to make false statements true.

____ 1. Printing extra German money added to *depression* and caused prices to rise.
____ 2. Britain's *appeasement* policy led them to accept Germany's demands.
____ 3. The U.S. Supreme Court ruled against *Pan-Africanism*.
____ 4. The Nazis began a program of *apartheid* during World War II.
____ 5. Ghandi used *civil disobedience* to protest British rule.
____ 6. *Containment* means that a government takes over farmland.

Review Main Ideas

Section 1 • The Rise of Dictators
7. How did the Great Depression encourage the rise of European dictators?
8. What happened in the USSR after Lenin's death?

Section 2 • World War II Begins
9. Why did European nations stand by as Germany expanded its territory?
10. When did World War II begin?

Section 3 • The Allies Win the War
11. Why did the Nazis murder millions of people unconnected to their war with the Allies?
12. Which event is considered the beginning of the end of World War II?

Section 4 • The Cold War
13. Which two nations most shaped the postwar world?
14. Which nation became the chief American ally in Asia?

Section 5 • The End of Empire
15. What led to independence for many Southeast Asian countries?
16. During which decades did most African colonies gain independence?

Review Reading Skill — Discussion Questions

17. Read the excerpt below from page 809. Write five questions that you could ask about this topic to launch a discussion.

Once in power, Hitler did away with all political parties except the Nazis. He had books about democracy burned. He took over the courts and set up a secret police. He took over radio and newspapers and broke up unions.

To review this skill, see pages 802–803.

854   CHAPTER 21   World War II and the Cold War

Reading Skill

17. Student questions should be relevant to Hitler's actions as German chancellor.

Critical Thinking

18. Fascism is a political philosophy that stresses the need for a strong central government run by a dictator. It originated with Benito Mussolini in Italy.

19. Answers will vary. A possible answer is that Hitler believed his army would defeat the British.

20. The U.S. protected South Korea from communism and showed Communists that it would use force to contain communism.

Critical Thinking

18. **Identify** What is fascism and where did it originate?
19. **Analyze** Why do you think Hitler invaded Poland even though Britain had promised to support Poland?
20. **Explain** What was gained by U.S. involvement in the Korean War?

Geography Skills

Study the map below and answer the following questions.

21. **Place** Which nations had army headquarters in Berlin after World War II?
22. **Location** Which river ran through both East and West Berlin?
23. **Movement** Which nation controlled the largest area in Berlin?

NATIONAL GEOGRAPHIC

Berlin *1945–1949*

KEY
— Berlin Wall
· Army HQ 1945–1949
— Main roads

0 ____ 10 mi.
0 ____ 10 km
Lambert Azimuthal Equal-Area projection

French HQ
FRENCH
BRITISH
British HQ
SOVIET
Spree R.
Soviet HQ
American HQ
AMERICAN
EAST GERMANY

N W E S

Read to Write

24. **Creative Writing** Suppose you are living in West Berlin when the Wall is built and you can no longer even see your friends and family members in East Berlin. Write four diary entries explaining how the Wall is affecting your everyday life.

25. **Using Your** **FOLDABLES** Have students use posterboard to expand the dates and

events on their foldables into an illustrated time line. Students should use sketches and images from magazines or the Internet with each entry on the time line.

Using Technology

26. **Internet Research** Use the Internet and your local library to research the Holocaust and another, more recent, genocide in the African nation Rwanda. How are the two tragedies similar? How are they different? Discuss both genocides as a class and possible ways to prevent future genocides.

Linking Past and Present

27. **Analyzing** Is containment an important issue in U.S. foreign policy today? Explain your reasoning.

Primary Source

Analyze

A journalist with the Vietcong near Hanoi recorded the events of December 10, 1965.

"Then the sun goes down and everything starts to move.

. . . The engines are started and the convoys grind away through the darkness behind the pinpoints of masked headlamps. There are miles of them, heavy Russian-built trucks, anti-aircraft batteries, all deeply buried under piles of branches and leaves; processions of huge green haystacks. North Vietnam by day is abandoned; by night it thuds and grinds with movement."

—James Cameron, "The Vietnam War: A Reporter with the Vietcong, near Hanoi, 10 December 1965"

DBQ **Document-Based Questions**

28. When does all the movement of Vietcong supplies and machines take place?
29. What does "processions of huge green haystacks" refer to?

History Online

Have students visit the Web site at jat.glencoe.com to review Chapter 21 and take the **Self-Check Quiz**.

Using Technology

26. Discussions should include facts from students' research.

Linking Past and Present

27. Answers will vary. A possible answer is that because the Korean and Vietnam wars caused immeasurable suffering, permanently damaged the environment, and cost billions of dollars, the U.S. can no longer afford or justify making war to contain perceived threats.

Primary Source

28. at night
29. trucks, tanks, and other machinery that the Vietcong have hidden under branches and leaves

Bonus Question

Ask: Do you think ordinary Southeast Asians and Africans enjoy a better life today than under European rule? Why or why not? *(Answers should include supporting details from the chapter.)*

Geography Skills

21. France, Britain, the United States, and the Soviet Union
22. Spree River
23. Soviet Union

Read to Write

24. Diary entries will vary but should include facts from the chapter.
25. **FOLDABLES** Students' time lines should include all the dates on their foldables.

Chapter 22 Resources

Note: The following materials may be used when teaching Chapter 22.
Section level support materials are shown at point of use in the margins of the Teacher Wraparound Edition.

TEACHING TRANSPARENCIES

- Graphic Organizer Transparencies with Teaching Strategy and Student Activity **L2**
- Cause-and-Effect Transparencies with Teaching Strategy and Student Activity **L2**
- Then and Now Transparencies with Teaching Strategy and Student Activity **L2**
- Chapter In-text Map Transparency 22 **L1**
- Map Transparencies with Overlay, Teaching Strategy, and Student Activity **L2**

DIFFERENTIATED INSTRUCTION

- Differentiated Instruction Activity 22
- Time Line Activity 22
- Primary Source Reading 22 (with Document-Based Questions)
- Inclusion Strategies for the Middle School Social Studies Classroom
- StudentWorks Plus™ CD-ROM (with Audio Program)

READING SUPPORT

- Take-Home Review Activity 22 **L2**
- World Literature Reading 22 **L2**
- Workbook Activity 22 **L1**
- Reading Strategies for the Social Studies Classroom **L1/ EL**

ASSESSMENT

- Authentic Assessment Activity 22 **L1/ EL**
- Chapter 22 Test Form A **L2**
- Chapter 22 Test Form B **L2**
- ExamView® Pro Testmaker CD-ROM

INTERDISCIPLINARY CONNECTIONS

- Geography and History Activity 22 **L2**
- People to Meet Activity 22 **L2**
- Economics Activity 22 **L2**
- Citizenship and Service Learning Activity 22 **L2**

SPANISH RESOURCES

- Spanish Reading Essentials and Study Guide
- Spanish Guided Reading Activities
- Spanish Quizzes, Tests, and Authentic Assessment (with Rubrics)
- Spanish Take-Home Review Activities

MULTIMEDIA

- ExamView® Pro Testmaker CD-ROM
- Glencoe Skillbuilder Interactive Workbook CD-ROM, Level 1
- Interactive Tutor Self-Assessment CD-ROM
- MindJogger Videoquiz
- Presentation Plus! CD-ROM
- StudentWorks Plus™ CD-ROM (with Audio Program)
- TeacherWorks CD-ROM
- Vocabulary PuzzleMaker CD-ROM
- *World History: Journey Across Time* Video Program
- World History Primary Source Document Library CD-ROM

STANDARDIZED ASSESSMENT SKILLS

- Standardized Test Skills Practice Workbook Activity 22 **L2**
- Critical Thinking Skills Activity 22 **L2**

Teaching strategies have been coded with suggested ability levels. However, most are suitable for all levels.

L1 BASIC activities for all students

L2 AVERAGE activities for average to above-average students

L3 CHALLENGING activities for above-average students

EL ENGLISH LANGUAGE activities

Chapter 22 Resources

TIME MANAGEMENT

Chapter Introduction	Section 1	Section 2	Section 3	Section 4	Chapter Wrap-Up	Unit Wrap-up
1 Day	2 Days	2 Days	1 Day	2 Days	1 Day	1 Day

Block Scheduling Activities that are suited to use within the block scheduling framework are identified by: 🔲

0:00 OUT OF TIME? Assign the Chapter 22 *Reading Essentials and Study Guide.* * 📁

SECTION RESOURCES

DAILY OBJECTIVES	REPRODUCIBLE LESSON PLANS	MULTIMEDIA RESOURCES
Section 1 **Challenges in Latin America** 1. In Central America, social conflict prevented economic progress while Mexico faced a variety of problems as well. 2. South American countries have struggled to produce democracy and prosperity.	📁 Reproducible Lesson Plan 22–1 📁 Vocabulary Activity 22–1 📁 Guided Reading Activity 22–1* 📁 Section Quiz 22–1* 📁 Reading Essentials and Study Guide 22–1*	📁 Daily Focus Skills Transparency 22–1 💿 Interactive Tutor Self-Assessment CD-ROM 💿 ExamView® Pro Testmaker CD-ROM 💿 Presentation Plus! CD-ROM
Section 2 **Africa and the Middle East** 1. Africa south of the Sahara addressed monumental challenges in the late 1900s. 2. Conflicts throughout the Middle East made it one of the world's most dangerous regions.	📁 Reproducible Lesson Plan 22–2 📁 Vocabulary Activity 22–2 📁 Guided Reading Activity 22–2* 📁 Section Quiz 22–2* 📁 Reading Essentials and Study Guide 22–2*	📁 Daily Focus Skills Transparency 22–2 💿 Interactive Tutor Self-Assessment CD-ROM 💿 ExamView® Pro Testmaker CD-ROM 💿 Presentation Plus! CD-ROM 💿 Glencoe BookLink CD-ROM
Section 3 **The Cold War Ends** 1. The Soviet Union and its Eastern European empire fell apart. 2. The fall of communism unleashed deadly ethnic conflict in Yugoslavia.	📁 Reproducible Lesson Plan 22–3 📁 Vocabulary Activity 22–3 📁 Guided Reading Activity 22–3* 📁 Section Quiz 22–3* 📁 Reading Essentials and Study Guide 22–3*	📁 Daily Focus Skills Transparency 22–3 💿 Interactive Tutor Self-Assessment CD-ROM 💿 ExamView® Pro Testmaker CD-ROM 💿 Presentation Plus! CD-ROM
Section 4 **The World Enters a New Century** 1. Advances in technology have brought the world closer together. 2. The events of September 11, 2001, focused the world's attention on terrorism.	📁 Reproducible Lesson Plan 22–4 📁 Vocabulary Activity 22–4 📁 Guided Reading Activity 22–4* 📁 Section Quiz 22–4* 📁 Reading Essentials and Study Guide 22–4*	📁 Daily Focus Skills Transparency 22–4* 💿 Interactive Tutor Self-Assessment CD-ROM 💿 ExamView® Pro Testmaker CD-ROM 💿 Presentation Plus! CD-ROM 💿 Vocabulary PuzzleMaker CD-ROM

*Also available in Spanish

History Online

Use our Web site for additional resources. All essential content is covered in the Student Edition.

You and your students can visit jat.glencoe.com, the Web site companion to *World History: Journey Across Time.* This innovative integration of electronic and print media offers your students a wealth of opportunities. The student text directs students to the Web site for the following options:

- Chapter Overview
- Self-Check Quizzes
- Study Central™
- Student Web Activities
- Multi-Language Glossaries

Answers to the student Web activities are provided for you in the **Web Activity Lesson Plans.** Additional Web resources and ePuzzles and games are also available.

THE HISTORY CHANNEL.

The following videotape programs are available from Glencoe as supplements to Chapter 22:

Democracy Crushed: Tiananmen Square
(ISBN 0-7670-1622-X)

Nelson Mandela: Journey to Freedom
(ISBN 0-7670-0113-3)

Bay of Pigs/Cuban Missile Crisis (ISBN 1-7670-1199-6)

To order, call Glencoe at 1-800-334-7344. To find classroom resources to accompany many of these videos, check the following home pages:

A&E Television: www.aande.com
The History Channel: www.historychannel.com

SPECIAL NEEDS

In addition to the Differentiated Instruction strategies, the following resources are suitable for students with special needs:

- *ExamView® Pro Testmaker CD-ROM* allows teachers to tailor tests by reducing answer choices.
- *StudentWorks Plus™ CD-ROM (with Audio Program)* includes the entire narrative of the student edition so that less-proficient readers can listen to the words as they read them.
- The *Reading Essentials and Study Guide* provides the same content as the student edition but is written two grade levels below the textbook.
- *Guided Reading Activities* give less proficient readers point-by-point instructions to increase comprehension as they read each textbook section.

TEACHER'S CORNER

Index to National Geographic Magazine:
The following articles relate to this chapter:

- "City of Hope, City of Fear: Johannesburg," by Peter Godwin, April 2004.
- "Baghdad Before the Bombs," by Alexandra Boulat, June 2003.
- "Cities: Challenges for Humanity," by Erla Zwingle, November 2002.

Additional National Geographic Society Products:
To order the following, call National Geographic at 1–800–368–2728

- *PicturePack: World Geography PicturePack Library* (Transparencies)
- *National Geographic Atlas of the World* (Book)

NGS ONLINE

Access National Geographic's new dynamic MapMachine Web site and other geography resources at:

www.nationalgeographic.com
www.nationalgeographic.com/maps

Meeting NCSS Standards

World History: Journey Across Time
The following standards are highlighted in Chapter 22:

Section 1	**I**	**Culture: A, B, D, E**
	II	**Time, Continuity, Change: B**
	VII	**Production, Distribution, and Consumption: A, I, J**
Section 2	**I**	**Culture: A, C, D**
	III	**People, Places, and Environment: H, I, J**
Section 3	**VI**	**Power, Authority, and Governance: B, C, D**
	IX	**Global Connections: B, C, D**
	X	**Civic Ideals and Practices: D**
Section 4	**VIII**	**Science, Technology, and Society: C**
	IX	**Global Connections: C, D**

State and Local Objectives

_____

_____

_____

_____

Timesaving Tools

TeacherWorks
All-In-One Planner and Resource Center

● **Interactive Teacher Edition** Access your Teacher Wraparound Edition and your classroom resources with a few easy clicks.

● **Interactive Lesson Planner** Organize your week, month, semester, or year with all the lesson helps you need to make teaching creative and relevant.

Use Glencoe's **Presentation Plus!** multimedia teacher tool to easily present dynamic lessons that visually excite your students. Using Microsoft PowerPoint® you can customize the presentations to create your own personalized lessons.

FOLDABLES™
Study Organizer
Dinah Zike's Foldables

Foldables are three-dimensional, interactive graphic organizers that help students practice basic writing skills, review key vocabulary terms, and identify main ideas. Every chapter contains a foldable activity, with additional chapter activities found in the *Reading and Study Skills Foldables* booklet. You can use the foldables as they are presented, or modify them to suit the needs of your individual class.

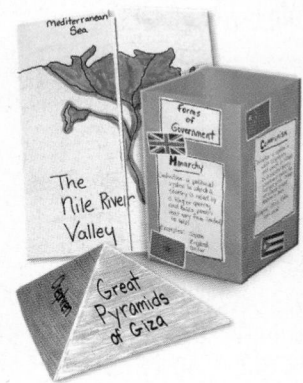

Planning Ahead

CHAPTER CULMINATING ACTIVITY

The Chapter Culminating Activity will help students organize and learn the important information from the chapter. Begin the chapter with this activity and have students complete it as a culminating activity.

CREATING VERTICAL TIME LINES

Purpose This type of organizer helps students organize and analyze information by identifying particular problems and their possible solutions. Because this chapter focuses on the serious challenges that the world and its regions faced and are facing, a problem and solution chart can be especially useful. Identifying and analyzing the problems discussed in the chapter will help students see the complexity of the issues. Suggesting possible solutions gives students practice in logical and systematic thinking. In addition, this type of chart can be used to organize information for reports and as a study aid.

Introduction to Modeling

1. Begin the discussion with a brainstorming session. Ask students to list what they know or believe they know about the problems faced from the mid-1900s to today in different parts of the world. Write the information on an overhead transparency.

2. Ask students to copy this chart into their notebooks:

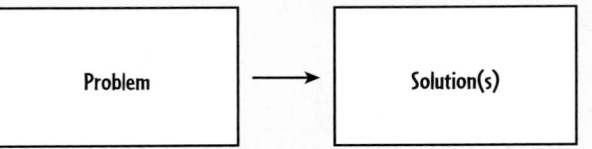

As students read the chapter, ask them to list important events. When they have finished reading the chapter, have them complete the boxes by writing in appropriate problems and solutions. For example, students may want to begin with "Poverty in Latin America." A solution might be "Nationalizing companies and industries," although there are other solutions as well. Encourage students to add more boxes if necessary. You might also want to have students make five different problem and solution charts, one each for Latin America, the Middle East, Africa south of the Sahara, Russia and Eastern Europe, and the world at large.

3. As part of your chapter review, have students share their problem and solution charts. Encourage them to use their charts as study aids.

Use the **Skillbuilder Handbook** on pages 902–919 to help students learn related skills.

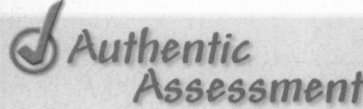

Authentic Assessment

Refer to Activity 22 in the Authentic Assessment section of the *Quizzes, Tests, and Performance Assessments (with Rubrics)* booklet.

When & Where?

As students read the chapter, have them review the time line on this page. **Ask:** Which event has had the greatest impact on our lives today? Why? **L1**

GLENCOE TECHNOLOGY

World History: Journey Across Time Video Program

To learn more about the world today, students can view the Chapter 22 video in the *World History: Journey Across Time* Video Program.

MindJogger Videoquiz

Use the **MindJogger Videoquiz** to preview Chapter 22 content.

 Available in DVD and VHS

Chapter 22

Building Today's World

A U.S. astronaut approaches ▶ the *Westar VI* satellite during a mission in space.

NATIONAL GEOGRAPHIC When & Where?

1960	1975	1990	2005
1959 Fidel Castro takes power in Cuba	1979 Revolution in Iran over-throws shah	1991 Soviet Union breaks up	2003 Iraq war begins

Reading Strategy ⟩ PURPOSE FOR READING

Using a Graphic Organizer Write the words "Struggle for democracy and prosperity" in a circle on the board. Then draw several separate lines extending out around the circle from its edge. Think out loud by saying, "People throughout the world are struggling to create democratic governments and economic prosperity. What do we know about this struggle?" Write students' responses on the lines around the circle. Allow the class a few minutes to look through the chapter. Call on volunteers to name one new thing they noticed while skimming through the text. As students read the chapter, have them add additional information to the graphic organizer. **L1/EL**

Chapter Preview

After the fall of communism, people looked forward to a new era of peace. Nations and ethnic groups, however, soon clashed around the world. Read this chapter to find out how the world community tries to solve these and other problems.

 View the Chapter 22 video in the *World History: Journey Across Time* Video Program.

History Online
Chapter Overview Visit jat.glencoe.com for a preview of Chapter 22.

 Section 1 Challenges in Latin America

Many countries in Latin America face economic problems, but they are making efforts to build stable democracies.

 Section 2 Africa and the Middle East

Apartheid in South Africa ends, but African nations still face many challenges. Conflict in the Middle East continues as Arab and Israeli leaders search for solutions.

 Section 3 The Cold War Ends

Revolutions in Eastern Europe and the collapse of the Soviet Union bring about the end of the Cold War in Europe.

 Section 4 The World Enters a New Century

As globalism and technology bring the world's people closer together, terrorism and war continue to be problems.

FOLDABLES™ Study Organizer

Organizing Information *Make the following foldable to help you organize information about today's world.*

Step 1 *Fold two sheets of paper in half from top to bottom.*

Fold both sheets to leave ½ inch tab on top.

Step 2 *Place glue or tape along both ½ inch tabs.*

Step 3 *Fit both sheets of paper together to make a cube as shown.*

Step 4 *Turn the cube and label the foldable as shown.*

The Cold War Ends
The World Enters a New Century
Challenges in Latin America
Africa and the Middle East

Reading and Writing *As you read the chapter, list the developments that impact our world today. Write the developments under the correct foldable category.*

857

INTRODUCING CHAPTER 22

 History Online

Introduce students to chapter content and key terms by having them access **Chapter Overview 22** at jat.glencoe.com

CHAPTER PREVIEW

After reading Chapter 22, students will be able to

1. summarize the challenges facing Latin America;
2. discuss the conflicts in Africa and the Middle East that threaten peace and prosperity;
3. explain the changes that led to the end of the Cold War;
4. describe the state of the world at the beginning of the 2000s.

FOLDABLES™ Study Organizer
Dinah Zike's Foldables

Purpose This foldable helps students identify the main ideas and supporting details in each section. As students read this chapter, have them write the main ideas and supporting details in each section of their foldables.

📁 Have students complete *Reading and Study Skills Foldables* Activity 22.

MORE ABOUT THE PHOTO

Satellites The space race contributed to a whole new era in communications. Over a thousand man-made satellites circle the earth, sending and receiving transmissions to places worldwide. Once placed in the proper orbit, satellites will remain in orbit indefinitely. This is because at sufficiently high altitudes, the satellite will escape the friction of the earth's atmosphere. Televisions, radio signals, and even the Internet are broadcast through satellites. However, satellites are also used for research, weather tracking, and navigation.

1 Learn It!

Students who learn to go beyond the textbook are more likely to become independent, lifelong learners.

After students complete a section of the chapter, ask them to complete a written interest inventory such as the following:

1. Which part most interested you? Why?

2. If you could talk to any one person in this section, who would it be?

3. If you could visit any one place in this section, where would you go?

4. If you could travel back in time, what time period would you choose to visit?

5. What one idea or concept puzzled you in some way?

Collect students' responses and read through them. Then place students in groups based on their common interests as the first step in having students complete research projects. **L1/ EL**

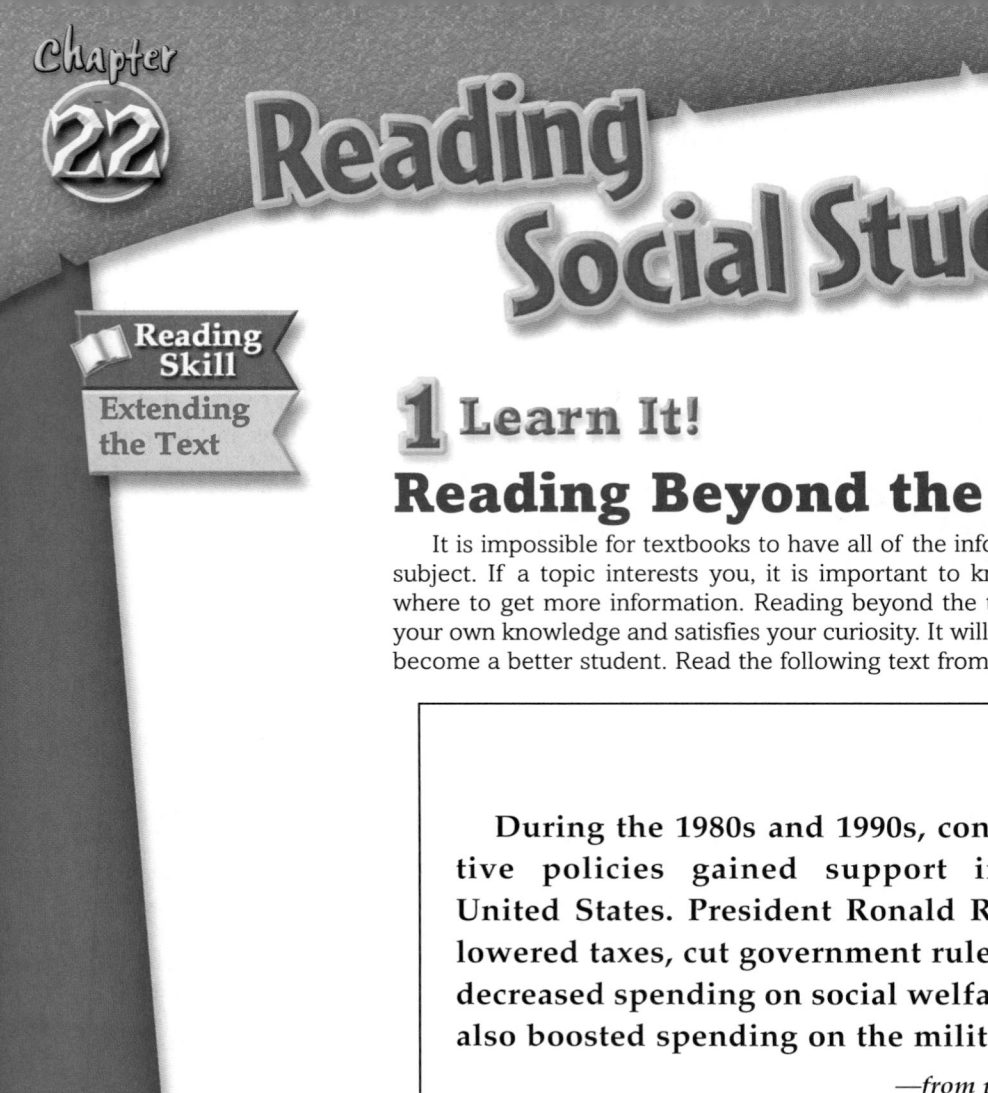

Chapter
22

Reading Social Studies

> **Reading Skill**
> Extending the Text

1 Learn It!
Reading Beyond the Text

It is impossible for textbooks to have all of the information on a subject. If a topic interests you, it is important to know how and where to get more information. Reading beyond the text increases your own knowledge and satisfies your curiosity. It will also help you become a better student. Read the following text from Section 4:

> During the 1980s and 1990s, conservative policies gained support in the United States. President Ronald Reagan lowered taxes, cut government rules, and decreased spending on social welfare. He also boosted spending on the military.
>
> —*from page 892*

Reading Tip

Keep your reading skills sharp by reading something every day!

If you were interested in learning more about President Reagan's policies or his life, you could:

• Do a Web search for Ronald Reagan.

• Check out a biography from a library.

• Ask adults what they remember about Reagan.

• Read news magazines, especially from June 2004 after Reagan died.

858

> **Reading Strategy** — **DIFFERENTIATED INSTRUCTION**

One way to provide instruction at each student's level is to assign individual or group projects based on areas of interest. Using the interest inventory, have students form groups to explore topics in greater depth. Allow for differences in process, product, and content based on the varying modalities and talents of students. Allow students to create rubrics for grading and give choices for evaluation, such as oral, written, or kinesthetic projects. **L1/ EL**

2 Practice It!

What Interests You?

The following paragraph refers to two other recent presidents, Bill Clinton and George W. Bush. Choose a topic from the paragraph that you would like to know more about, such as *Democrats, Republicans, welfare, Bill Clinton,* or *George W. Bush.* With a partner, think of three ways you could find out more about your chosen topic.

Read to Write

Writing a letter can help you to find out more about something that interests you. Write a letter to your state representative or senator asking him or her to answer questions you have about state politics.

> Clinton, a moderate Democrat, favored some conservative policies. Under Clinton, the budget was balanced, and the welfare system was changed. Then, in 2000, Republican George W. Bush was elected president. A conservative, Bush convinced Congress to pass large tax cuts and an education reform law.
>
> —*from page 892*

3 Apply It!

As you read about the **War on Terror** on pages 892–894, write down any word, phrase, or fact that interests you. Make a list of ways you could find more information.

859

2 Practice It!

Extending With Media Using the student interest inventory, choose several people, places, or things that you can enhance with the use of news magazines, guest speakers, maps, movie clips, music, or primary source documents that may not be included in the book.

After students have read the material under the subheading "The Technology Revolution" in Section 4, prompt them to learn more about the work of Bill Gates by reading one of many articles about him found in magazines such as *TIME* or *NEWSWEEK.* Then have them create a short, multimedia presentation using the computer and other resources to convey what they have learned. **L2**

3 Apply It!

Although students may tell teachers that they are not interested in learning more about topics presented in the text, the synergy of a class brainstorming session can motivate even the most disinterested student. Have each student name one topic he or she would like to know more about and list it on the board. Students must respond when it is their turn. To encourage student participation, accept all responses and assign no value to them. Record their ideas and have them research their chosen ideas. **L2**

Reading Strategy READ TO WRITE

As students complete their independent projects, ask them to write a summary or synopsis of what they have learned. Then publish their reports in a class booklet that can be shared with students in another class. These booklets can also be used to increase background knowledge of future students who will take this course. Assign class roles to further expand this project, such as small groups that will act as cover designers, fact finders, editors, or typists.

① FOCUS

SECTION OVERVIEW

This section examines the challenges Latin American countries faced in becoming democratic.

BELLRINGER
SKILLBUILDER ACTIVITY

✎ Project **Daily Focus Skills Transparency 22–1** and have students answer questions. Discuss their responses.

Get Ready to Read!

Preteaching Vocabulary: To *export* means "to sell things abroad." It uses the Latin prefix *ex*, which means "out of" or "away from." Thus, goods that are exported are taken out of one country and into another.

Answers to Graphic: Lázaro Cárdenas: nationalized foreign-owned oil wells; Getúlio Vargas: raised wages, allowed labor unions; Salvador Allende: nationalized industry, boosted wages, gave land to the poor

Section ① Challenges in Latin America

Get Ready to Read!

What's the Connection?
Nationalism in Asia and Africa led to independence for many colonies. Read how the already independent nations of Latin America struggled to become successful and democratic.

Focusing on the Main Ideas

- Latin America's economy has depended on exports and foreign investment. *(page 861)*

- In Central America, repressive governments, social conflict, and civil wars made progress difficult. *(page 863)*

- During the twentieth century, Mexico struggled to overcome economic, social, and political challenges. *(page 864)*

- Most South American countries have struggled to create fragile democracies and improve their economies. *(page 866)*

Locating Places
Mexico
Cuba
Argentina

Meeting People
Fidel Castro
Jean-Bertrand Aristide
Lázaro Cárdenas (KAHR•duhn•AHS)
Juan Perón (pay•ROHN)

Building Your Vocabulary
export
embargo (ihm•BAHR•goh)
nationalize (NASH•nuh•LYZ)

Reading Strategy
Summarizing Information Create a table to show the reforms put in place by Latin American leaders.

Leaders	Reforms

NATIONAL GEOGRAPHIC **When & Where?**

CUBA
MEXICO
BRAZIL
ARGENTINA

1920 — **1960** — **2000**

1933 Good Neighbor Policy begins

1959 Fidel Castro takes power in Cuba

1994 U.S., Mexico, and Canada sign NAFTA

860   CHAPTER 22   Building Today's World

SECTION RESOURCES

📁 **Reproducible Masters**
- Reproducible Lesson Plan 22–1
- Daily Lecture and Discussion Notes 22–1
- Vocabulary Activity 22–1
- Active Reading Note-Taking Guide 22–1
- Guided Reading Activity 22–1
- Section Quiz 22–1
- Reading Essentials and Study Guide 22–1

✎ **Transparencies**
- Daily Focus Skills Transparency 22–1

Multimedia
- Interactive Tutor Self-Assessment CD-ROM
- ExamView® Pro Testmaker CD-ROM
- Presentation Plus! CD-ROM

Latin America's Economy

Main Idea Latin America's economy has depended on exports and foreign investment.

Reading Focus What does it mean to be a good neighbor? Read to find out how a change in U.S. policy was aimed at building better relations with its neighbors.

Previously, you learned that countries in Latin America gained their independence in the 1800s. Latin Americans soon found out that it was easier to set up republics than to make them work. While the rich controlled social and political life, the poor had little, if any, power.

Exporting Raw Materials Latin America's economy depended on agriculture and mining. During the late 1800s, industrial countries demanded more of Latin America's food products and minerals. Businesspeople from these countries set up companies in Latin America. These companies **exported**, or sold abroad, Latin American products, such as bananas, sugar, coffee, copper, and oil.

As the number of exports rose, some Latin American countries grew only one or two key products. For example, Honduras raised bananas, and Colombia grew coffee. Prices and profits increased because of these exports, but any decline in demand had serious effects. Prices dropped, followed by severe losses in income and jobs.

Despite the problems it caused, Latin America's dependence on exports also brought benefits. Foreign investors built ports, roads, and railroads. Cities increased in size and population, and a middle class of lawyers, teachers, and businesspeople grew. Much, however, had not changed. The wealthy still held the power, and most Latin Americans struggled to make a living.

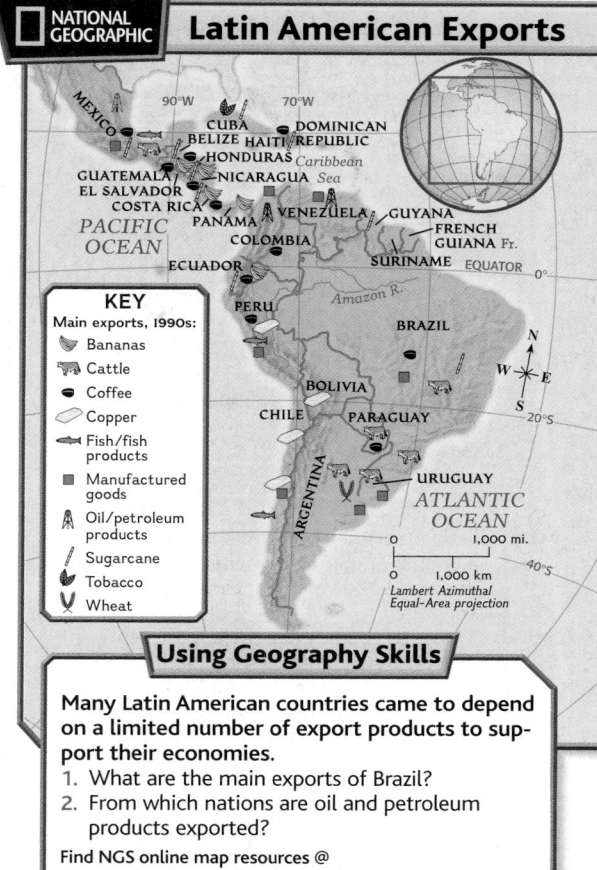

NATIONAL GEOGRAPHIC **Latin American Exports**

KEY
Main exports, 1990s:
- Bananas
- Cattle
- Coffee
- Copper
- Fish/fish products
- Manufactured goods
- Oil/petroleum products
- Sugarcane
- Tobacco
- Wheat

Using Geography Skills

Many Latin American countries came to depend on a limited number of export products to support their economies.
1. What are the main exports of Brazil?
2. From which nations are oil and petroleum products exported?

Find NGS online map resources @
www.nationalgeographic.com/maps

The United States and Latin America

During the 1900s, the United States increased its influence in Latin America. Previously, you learned about the American victory in the Spanish-American War of 1898. One result of the war was that the United States gained control of the Caribbean island of Puerto Rico.

Five years later, the United States helped Panama win its independence from Colombia. In return, Panama gave the United States control of the area where the

CHAPTER 22   Building Today's World   **861**

Art U.S. president Theodore Roosevelt cited an African saying as a guide for his foreign policy: "Speak softly and carry a big stick." Have students draw a political cartoon based on Roosevelt's famous saying as it applied to U.S. relationships with Latin America. **L2**

Understanding Charts

Answers:

1. Brazil; $236 million more

2. Prices go up, wages fall, and people lose their jobs.

Writing Activity

Ask students to write a short animal fable about the debt crisis of Latin America. Begin by having the class name characteristics of fables. Ask volunteers to read their fables aloud. **L3**

✓ Reading Check

Answer: Latin American economies weakened, prices rose, wages fell, and people lost their jobs.

CONNECTING ACROSS TIME

The United States supported anti-Communist guerrilla campaigns, often secretly, in Latin America in the 1950s through the 1980s. Ask students to discuss the morality of supporting guerrilla groups. Should the United States today try to overthrow dangerous foreign governments? Why or why not? **L2**

862

Debt in Latin America

Country	Total Amount Owed (in U.S. dollars)
Brazil	$242 billion
Mexico	$155 billion
Argentina	$140 billion
Chile	$42 billion
Venezuela	$37 billion
Colombia	$36 billion
Peru	$30 billion
Ecuador	$18 billion
Uruguay	$11 billion
Panama	$10 billion
El Salvador	$6 billion
Dominican Republic	$6 billion

Source: World Bank, 2002

Understanding Charts

Latin American countries borrowed large amounts of money to maintain their weak economies, but many of those economies still failed.

1. Which country has the largest debt? How much larger is that country's debt than that of the Dominican Republic?
2. **Conclude** Why does a high debt hurt a country's economy?

Panama Canal was built. Over the next 25 years, the United States sent troops to Haiti, Nicaragua, and the Dominican Republic to protect U.S. interests.

Meanwhile, American businesspeople increased their holdings in Latin America. One of the most powerful American firms in Latin America was the United Fruit Company. It owned land, railroads, and fruit-packing plants in many nations of Central America. American companies also controlled copper mines in Chile and Peru, as well as oil wells in **Mexico,** Peru, and Bolivia.

Many Latin Americans distrusted the United States because of its great wealth and power. To improve relations, U.S. president Franklin D. Roosevelt in 1933 announced the Good Neighbor Policy toward Latin America.

He promised that the United States would not intervene militarily in Latin America. He pledged a greater respect for the rights of the United States's southern neighbors.

Debt and Trade The Great Depression of the 1930s brought hardships to Latin America. Exports declined, and Latin Americans had less money to buy factory-made goods from abroad. They began to develop their own industries. Some of these industries were foreign-owned. Others were run by Latin American governments.

After World War II, agriculture was still important, but industries continued to grow in Latin America. Some of the money for new industries came from large, multinational corporations. Multinational corporations are companies that invest and do business in more than one country.

To encourage economic growth, Latin American leaders also borrowed heavily from banks in the United States and other countries. As a result, Latin America owed large sums of money to other parts of the world. This mounting debt seriously weakened Latin American economies. Prices rose, wages fell, and people lost jobs.

Difficult reforms in the 1980s helped strengthen many Latin American economies. The harshness of these changes, however, turned Latin Americans against their dictators. During the 1990s, democratic movements succeeded in several countries.

Today, Latin America's democratic governments face many challenges. Population is growing rapidly, but resources are limited. Differences between rich and poor still create social tensions. In addition, growing trade in drugs has increased crime and corruption in parts of Latin America.

✓ **Reading Check** **Cause and Effect** What was the result of Latin American debt to foreigners in the 1980s?

DIFFERENTIATED INSTRUCTION

Auditory/Musical: Pair students and have them take turns reading aloud the paragraphs in one subsection. After each paragraph, have partners identify the main idea in the paragraph and record it. Also, have pairs discuss any vocabulary terms they encounter.

English Learners: Record a reading of the subsection "Debt and Trade." Group an English-speaking student with one or more English learners. Have students play the tape and read along with the text. As English learners encounter unfamiliar words or grammar constructions, ask the English-speaking student to stop the tape and explain the words or constructions.

Gifted and Talented: Have students research the growth of one industry that grew up as a result of the Great Depression.

Problems in Central America

Main Idea In Central America, repressive governments, social conflict, and civil wars made progress difficult.

Reading Focus What would it be like to live in a country where a civil war was raging? What difficult choices might you have to make?

In the 1900s, a few people held most of the wealth and power in Central America and the Caribbean. Rebels fought for changes that they thought would better the lives of poorer Latin Americans.

The Cuban Revolution

Previously, you learned that **Cuba** won its freedom from Spain in 1898. During most of the 1900s, military dictators ruled Cuba. American companies controlled most of the country's wealth, which was based on sugar and mining. In 1959 a young lawyer named **Fidel Castro** led a revolution and took control of the government.

Castro promised democracy. Instead, he set up a communist state and accepted aid from the Soviet Union. When he seized American-owned property, relations with the United States became even worse. In 1961 the United States tried to overthrow Castro. A small force of Cubans who had fled the revolution were trained and armed by the American government. They were then sent to invade Cuba, but after landing at the Bay of Pigs in Cuba, they were quickly defeated by Castro's forces.

In 1962 the United States put in place an **embargo** (ihm•BAHR•goh), or ban on trade, against Cuba. Poor harvests, loss of trade, and bad government planning brought disaster to Cuba's economy. The country remained very poor, and Cubans continued to flee to the United States. Most of these Cubans settled in Florida.

▲ While fighting to overthrow Cuba's government, the guerrilla forces of Fidel Castro (standing, center) often hid in the island's jungles. *Why did Castro's new government come into conflict with the United States?*

Dictators and Rebels Castro wanted to spread communism in Latin America. The United States was just as determined to prevent it. The Cold War contributed to conflicts in many Central American nations in the 1970s and 1980s. In El Salvador, fighters supported by Castro battled government troops armed by the United States. Thousands of people died before a settlement ended the fighting in 1992.

In Nicaragua, rebels called Sandinistas overthrew the brutal dictator Anastasio Somoza in 1979. Nicaragua's new government turned to Cuba and the Soviet Union for aid.

People in Nicaragua who opposed the Sandinistas formed groups known as the contras, from the Spanish word meaning "against." With U.S. help, the contras fought Sandinista forces. This conflict finally ended in the early 1990s, when free elections were held and the Sandinistas lost power.

Another war took place in Guatemala. There, American-backed government forces

CHAPTER 22   Building Today's World   **863**

The Bay of Pigs invasion failed because of two miscalculations. The 1,500 or so Cuban exiles who landed on the island expected the Cuban people to join them. They did not. The exiles also hoped for direct U.S. military aid, but President Kennedy did not want to risk a confrontation with the Soviet Union. The failed invasion tarnished the international image of the United States and damaged the new president's prestige.

CURRICULUM CONNECTION

Music
The musical traditions of Cuba are rich and varied. Cuban music has both African and Spanish roots and has also been influenced by American jazz. Such popular dances as the cha-cha, rumba, bolero, and conga are Cuban, as are the characteristic melodies and rhythms of these dances. Afro-Cuban and Latin jazz enjoys a worldwide popularity through such musicians as Xavier Cugat, Tito Puente, Arturo Sandoval, and Mongo Santamaria.

CRITICAL THINKING ACTIVITY

Debating U.S. policy toward Cuba has been a focus of much disagreement since the 1950s. Some have counseled confrontation and endorsed tools like invasions and trade embargoes. Others have pushed for greater engagement in economic, political, and cultural spheres. Different approaches have been used with varied success. Have students debate this question: What is the best way for the United States to help create a free, democratic Cuba? You may wish to have them research for additional support. **L3**

Writing Activity

Have students research the life of one of the Latin American human rights activists and Nobel Peace Prize winners, Rigoberta Menchú of Guatemala or Oscar Romero of El Salvador, and write a short summary of his or her achievements. **L2**

 Reading Check

Answer: Conflict led to a U.S. embargo against Cuba. This crippled Cuba's economy.

More About the Photo

Despite opposition by industrialists and foreign investors, Cárdenas was a hero to the working class. After serving as president, he served as minister of national defense.

Caption Answer: Peasants and workers faced economic difficulties, which helped lead to his overthrow by liberal reformers.

 CURRICULUM CONNECTION

Film

Several movies have been made about the period of Latin American history described in this section. They include *Missing* (1981), about Allende's overthrow; *Salvador* (1986), about the Salvadoran civil war; *Under Fire* (1983), set in Nicaragua; and *Evita* (1996), the musical about Eva Perón.

---

fought rebel groups from 1960 to 1996. About 150,000 people died, and the civil war severely weakened the economy.

Because of income from the Panama Canal, Panama enjoyed some prosperity. In 1983 General Manuel Noriega, backed by the United States, took power. His harsh rule and drug dealing, however, soon cost him American support. In 1989 the United States invaded Panama and overthrew him.

In the Caribbean republic of Haiti, a family of cruel dictators called the Duvaliers (doo•VAL•yayz) ruled from 1957 to 1986. In 1990 a reformer named **Jean-Bertrand Aristide** (AR•ih•STEED) was elected president. Military officers forced Aristide out a year later. With U.S. help, he returned to power in 1994 but was overthrown again in 2004. Haiti's economy remains poor, and its people face many hardships.

Reading Check **Explain** How did the Cold War affect events in Cuba and Central America?

The Mexican Revolution

◄ As president of Mexico, Lázaro Cárdenas distributed 44 million acres of land to Mexican peasants.

Mexican dictator ► Porfirio Díaz ruled from 1877 to 1911.

864 CHAPTER 22 Building Today's World

Mexico Pushes to Modernize

Main Idea During the twentieth century, Mexico struggled to overcome economic, social, and political challenges.

Reading Focus What challenges in your life have forced you to make changes? Read to find out how Mexican leaders have made changes to improve their country.

Mexico is the United States's nearest southern neighbor. Since World War II, Mexico has developed many new industries and worked to better the lives of its people.

The Revolution of 1911 In the early 1900s, dictator Porfirio Díaz (pawr•FEER•yoh DEE•AHS) ruled Mexico. He encouraged foreigners to invest in Mexico's oil wells and other businesses. Wealthy Mexicans prospered, but peasants and workers faced increasing hardships.

▲ During the Mexican Revolution, armed bands of rebels fought government forces and seized the property of wealthy landowners. *Why was Porfirio Díaz overthrown?*

INTERDISCIPLINARY CONNECTIONS ACTIVITY

Geography Remind students of the importance of transportation to a prosperous economy. Ask them to name ways goods and people are transported in the United States *(automobiles and trucks, airplanes, trains, water transportation)*. Then have them analyze a physical/political map of Latin America. Ask them to find natural barriers to good transportation links, such as mountain ranges, rain forests, jungles, deserts, and other features. Have them make a list of suggestions for linking specific areas. For example, what might be the best way to link Santiago, Chile, and Montevideo, Uruguay? Have students explain their suggestions. **L2**

In 1911 liberal reformers overthrew Diaz. A dictator, however, seized power two years later. U.S. president Woodrow Wilson opposed the takeover. He ordered U.S. troops to take the Mexican port of Veracruz. This show of force ended the general's rule, and American troops withdrew.

Meanwhile, revolution swept Mexico. Regional leaders competed for power. Armies of farmers, workers, and ranchers fought each other. Fleeing the violence, many Mexicans moved to the United States.

By the early 1920s, Mexico had a stable government. However, only one political party ruled. It was called the Institutional Revolutionary Party. For the rest of the 1900s, most of Mexico's elected officials came from this party.

In the 1930s, Mexico entered a time of reform. President **Lázaro Cárdenas** (KAHR•duhn•AHS) gave land to landless peasants. He also worked to free Mexico's industries from foreign control. In 1938 he **nationalized** (NASH•nuh•LYZD), or had the government take over, foreign-owned oil wells. Owners of American and European oil companies were furious, but most Mexicans saw it as a positive change. Mexico later paid the oil companies for the takeover. A national company called PEMEX was set up to run the oil wells.

Slow but Steady Growth Thanks to its oil industry, Mexico made economic gains after World War II. The government, however, still had to borrow money from abroad to build new industries. When world oil prices fell in the 1980s, Mexico faced economic hardships.

To save money, the government cut services and jobs. It also sold off many government-owned businesses to private owners. Mexico's economic troubles made people turn away from the Institutional

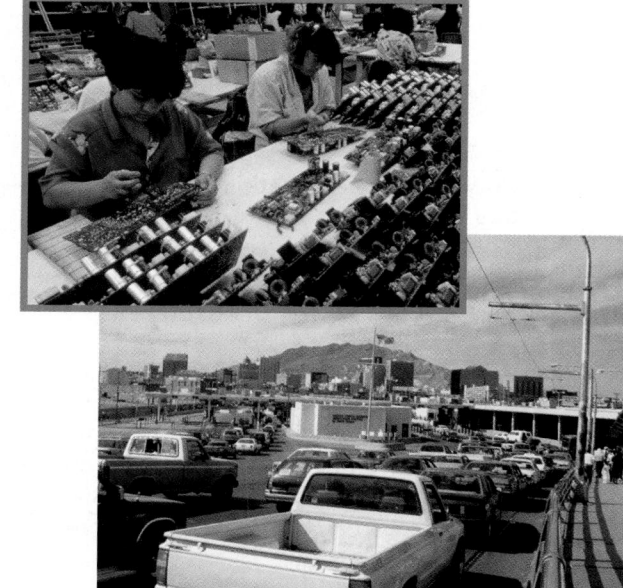

▲ The passage of NAFTA has led to even more traffic along the U.S.-Mexico border, as well as the creation of foreign-owned factories, or maquiladoras, near the border. *What three countries signed NAFTA?*

Revolutionary Party. In 2000 the newly elected president of Mexico, Vicente Fox, came from a different political party—for the first time in 70 years.

Meanwhile, Mexico moved to break down barriers to trade with other countries. In 1994 Mexico, the United States, and Canada signed the North American Free Trade Agreement (NAFTA). Mexico's leaders hoped that free trade would encourage companies to open factories and create more jobs.

As a result of NAFTA, Mexico has built new industries and boosted living standards. Along Mexico's border, many companies from the United States and elsewhere have built maquiladoras (muh•KEE•luh•DOHR•uhs), or factories that assemble parts made in other countries. These factories have given jobs to thousands of Mexican workers.

✔ **Reading Check** **Explain** How did government reforms help to improve Mexico's economy?

CHAPTER 22 Building Today's World **865**

Writing Activity 📝

Ask students to do an Internet search on the effects of NAFTA on your state. Have them write a summary of their findings and share them with the class. **L2**

More About the Photo

NAFTA eliminated a variety of taxes on most goods exchanged by the three signatories and has impacted many different areas of the economy, including agriculture, telecommunications, and financial services.

Caption Answer: Mexico, the United States, and Canada

in a word...

"*Maquiladora*" has an interesting derivation. It is Spanish for the place where farmers paid a miller to grind their grain. The old Spanish word, in turn, comes from Arabic, showing the ancient links between Spain and the Arab world. The Arabic root means "to measure."

✔ **Reading Check**

Answer: Mexico was able to get control of its oil industry, and NAFTA membership has encouraged new industries to come to Mexico.

EXTENDING THE CONTENT

Importance of Coffee One of the most important cash crops in Latin America is coffee, one of the world's most popular drinks. Coffee is an extremely valuable product, with a 2002 trade value estimated at $70 billion. Brazil and Colombia are the world's number one and two coffee producers, with Brazil alone producing as much as 42 percent of the world's coffee. Mexico, Costa Rica, Guatemala, and Nicaragua also grow high-quality coffee beans. The world's leading coffee-drinking nations are all in Scandinavia: Finland, Sweden, Denmark, and Norway. The coffee plant, ironically, is not native to Latin America. It is an African evergreen, first grown by Arabs in the A.D. 800s.

Reading Strategy

Identifying Similarities Have students list similarities of the governments of Argentina and Brazil under Perón and Vargas. *(Both were military dictatorships, appealed to workers, nationalized industries, seized power in a coup, and used authoritarian methods.)* **L1**

Primary Source

Neruda had a great impact on his country as the leader of the Chilean Communist Party. He also served as an ambassador to France.

Answer:
He wanted Cubans to focus on getting away from foreign interest and bettering their own situation.

EVALUATING

In 2000, Chilean dictator Augusto Pinochet was ordered to stand trial for human rights violations that occurred while he ruled Chile. A Chilean court eventually determined he was too old and sick to stand trial. **Ask: What are the advantages and disadvantages for a society to place former dictators on trial?** *(Advantages: learn the truth, obtain justice for victims; disadvantages: reopen old wounds, difficult to have a fair trial, looking back instead of toward future)* **L3**

Reform in South America

Main Idea Most South American countries have struggled to create fragile democracies and improve their economies.

Reading Focus Which is more important to people, democracy or prosperity? Read to find out how the desire for both affected the history of South America.

During most of the 1900s, South America was a region of great contrasts. Its cities grew rapidly, with both poor and wealthy neighborhoods. New industries developed, but old ways of farming were still practiced. Dictators ran governments

Primary Source
"Cuba Appears"

Pablo Neruda was a Chilean poet who won the Nobel Prize for Literature in 1971. Much of his poetry is about politics. This poem praises Fidel Castro's revolution in Cuba.

. . . .

"everything falls in the dust of the dead

when the people set their violins

and looking forward interrupt and sing,

interrupt the hatred of shadows and watchdogs,

sing and wake the stars with their song

▲ Pablo Neruda

and pierce the darkness with guns.

And so Fidel came forth cutting shadows

so that the jasmine tree could dawn."

—Pablo Neruda, "Cuba Appears"

DBQ **Document-Based Question**

What did Neruda mean by saying "interrupt the hatred"?

with the support of a small group of wealthy landowners and businesspeople. Despite some progress, many South Americans remained poor.

Argentina In the early 1900s, the economy of **Argentina** faltered, and military leaders took over. One of these military leaders, **Juan Perón** (pay•ROHN), came to power in the 1940s. With his popular wife Evita at his side, Perón tried to improve the economy and help workers. His crackdown on basic freedoms made people unhappy, however. In 1955 a revolt drove Perón from power, and democracy returned.

Military officers again took control of Argentina in the 1970s. They ruled harshly, and their use of force resulted in the deaths of many people. In 1982 Argentina lost a war with Britain over the Falkland Islands. The Falklands, also known as the Malvinas, lie in the Atlantic Ocean near Argentina. Argentina's loss weakened the military, and the country returned to democracy.

Brazil Like Argentina, Brazil had difficulty building a democracy. During the 1930s, dictator Getúlio Vargas (zhuh•TOOL•yoo VAHR•guhs) set up new government-run industries. He raised wages, cut working hours, and allowed labor unions. Vargas, however, used the army to stay in power until 1945.

During the mid-1960s, Brazil was a democracy. Fear of a Communist takeover, however, led the military to take power in 1964. The new leaders encouraged foreign investment to create industries. Progress was made, but workers gained few benefits.

In the 1980s, Brazil's people demanded change. The military gradually returned the country to democracy. In recent years, Brazil's government has tried to cut spending and improve its economy.

CITIZENSHIP AND YOU

Weakening the Bonds of Citizenship In this section, students have read how Latin American governments had many difficulties in gaining and holding the loyalty of all parts of society. Economic uncertainties, frequent coups, and authoritarian methods of rule have led to civil unrest and widespread suffering. Have students discuss how governments can gain the trust and loyalty of the people they rule. What kinds of policies and practices have the best chance of creating stable democracies? **L2**

Linking Past & Present

Coffee Cultivation in Brazil

THEN Coffee growing in Brazil began in the mid-1700s. The first coffee growers used large knives, called machetes, to clear land in the rain forest. As the demand for coffee grew, planters became wealthy owners of huge estates, or *fazendas*. Planters brought hundreds of thousands of enslaved Africans to Brazil to work on the plantations.

▼ Coffee workers toss beans to sift out debris.

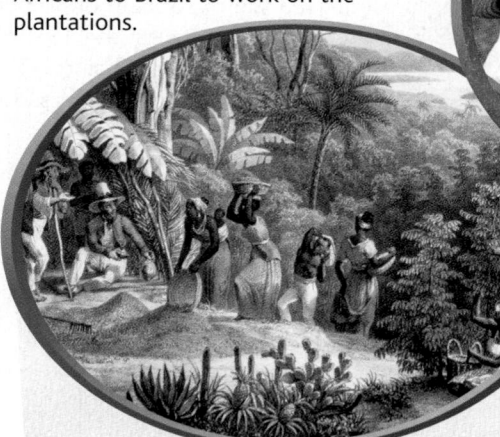

▲ Coffee harvest in Brazil in the early 1800s

NOW Today ripe, red coffee beans are often harvested by machine. Workers then rake up any coffee beans that fall to the ground. They toss the beans in the air in a large strainer to filter out twigs and leaves. *Why did the demand for coffee increase the demand for slaves in Brazil?*

Chile During most of the 1900s, Chile was South America's most stable democracy. Then, in 1970, Salvador Allende (ah•YAYN•day) was elected president. He was the first Marxist in the Americas to win office in a free election. Allende nationalized industries, boosted wages, and gave land to the poor.

Allende's reforms angered Chile's military and business groups. The military overthrew Allende in 1973. A general named Augusto Pinochet (PEE•noh•CHEHT) became Chile's new ruler.

Pinochet proved to be a ruthless dictator. He jailed Marxists and others opposed to his government and violated citizens' rights. Many people were tortured and killed. In 1990 public opposition and international pressure finally forced Pinochet to leave office. Chile returned to democracy. In 2004, Chile signed a free trade agreement with the United States that continued to boost the country's economic growth.

Venezuela Like much of Latin America, Venezuela went back and forth from democracy to military rule. Oil was its major source of wealth. As rising oil prices brought more money to the country, the middle class grew, and many people prospered.

CHAPTER 22   Building Today's World   **867**

Linking Past & Present

Answer: They needed more enslaved people to work on their plantations.

Reading Support L1/EL

Assign **Guided Reading Activity 22–1** to help students organize the information in the section.

③ ASSESS

Assign Section 1 Review as homework or as an in-class activity.

⊕ Have students use the **Interactive Tutor Self-Assessment CD-ROM** to review the section.

Assessment L2

Assign **Section 1 Quiz** to assess mastery of the material found in the section.

Reading Support L1/EL

Assign **Reading Essentials and Study Guide 22–1** to help students review section material.

COOPERATIVE LEARNING ACTIVITY

Service Learning Immigrants from Latin American countries, especially Mexico, have become much more numerous in the United States over the last few years. Ask students to research what programs are available in your community to ease the transition for immigrants from Latin America. Many towns, cities, and states offer programs, as do private, social, church, and other agencies. Have students choose one program and find out about volunteer opportunities for students. If your community does not have a significant number of Hispanic immigrants or a mixture of immigrants from different backgrounds, have students research programs for immigrants from other parts of the world.
L2

ENRICH

Have students research the life of one of the Latin American leaders described in this section. Have them share their findings with the class. **L2**

Reading Check

Answer: They were forced out by the people, as their harsh dictatorship made the public unhappy.

History Online

To help students understand section material, have them visit **Study Central**™ at jat.glencoe.com

RETEACH

Ask students to review with a partner the changes in government in Cuba, Mexico, Argentina, Brazil, Chile, and Venezuela from the 1930s to the present. **L1**

④ CLOSE

Reading Strategy

Have students discuss and decide on the five most important challenges facing Latin America today. **L2**

868

In the 1990s, oil prices fell, and Venezuela suffered. The government could no longer help the poor and jobless. In 1998 Venezuelans, angry at the government, elected a former military leader, Hugo Chavez, as president.

Chavez promised changes in the country's government and economy. His plans to increase his power, however, caused divisions among Venezuela's people. Chavez held on to power but faced much opposition to his rule.

Colombia Colombia, Venezuela's neighbor, was also marked by violence and civil war. From the late 1940s to the mid-1960s, fighting took place between rival political parties. About 300,000 people died. Then, in the mid-1960s, groups of rebels in the countryside began fighting the government. They demanded more land and rights for poor farmers.

By the 1980s, drug dealers had become a major force in Colombia. Dealers paid poor farmers more to grow coca leaves than the farmers could earn growing coffee. Coca leaves are used to make the drug cocaine. Drug dealers used their profits to build private armies. With help from the United States, Colombia's government has tried to break the power of the drug dealers but with little success.

Reading Check **Explain** Why did Argentina's and Chile's military dictators give up power?

History Online

Study Central™ Need help with the material in this section? Visit jat.glencoe.com

Section ① Review

Reading Summary
Review the Main Ideas

- Latin America's dependence on exports kept the region poor and made it difficult for democracy to succeed.

- Since the Mexican Revolution, Mexico has had a democratic government and has made economic progress.

- Poverty and social conflict have led to a number of violent revolutions and civil wars in the countries of Central America.

- For many years, dictators controlled the countries of South America. Recent attempts at democracy have not always been successful.

What Did You Learn?

1. How have multinational corporations affected Latin American countries?

2. How did Cárdenas change Mexico's economy?

Critical Thinking

3. **Summarizing Information** Draw a chart and list the changes that occurred in each South American country's government in the 1900s.

Country	Changes in Government

4. **Cause and Effect** What effects did the increased export of Latin American food products and raw materials in the late 1800s and early 1900s have on the region?

5. **Sequence** Describe the development of democracy in Mexico.

6. **Persuasive Writing** Create a poster encouraging citizens of a Latin American country to adopt a democratic system.

7. **Reading** **Extending the Text** Besides this textbook, list five places where you could find information about the challenges that Latin American countries face today.

868   CHAPTER 22   Building Today's World

SECTION 1 REVIEW ANSWERS

1. Many new industries have grown.

2. He gave land to peasants and nationalized foreign-owned oil wells.

3. Charts should reflect information from this section.

4. Foreign investors built city infrastructure, cities grew, a new middle class grew, but most Latin Americans were still very poor.

5. high population growth, limited resources, gap between the rich and poor, drugs

6. Students should show sequence of leaders starting with the dictator Díaz in the early 1900s, to President Fox in 2000.

7. Student posters should display the benefits of a democracy versus the current government in a Latin American country.

Section 2
Africa and the Middle East

Get Ready to Read!

What's the Connection?
While Latin American nations were struggling for stability, nations in Africa and the Middle East also faced challenges and conflicts.

Focusing on the Main Ideas
- The countries of Africa south of the Sahara faced many challenges in the late twentieth century. *(page 870)*
- Black South Africans won their freedom after years of hardship and struggle. *(page 872)*
- The creation of Israel in 1948 sparked a conflict that still exists today. *(page 874)*
- Political and social conflicts continue to keep the Middle East in turmoil. *(page 876)*

Locating Places
Israel (IHZ•ree•uhl)
Egypt (EE•jihpt)
Iran (ih•RAHN)
Iraq (ih•RAHK)

Meeting People
Nelson Mandela
Yasir Arafat (ahr•uh•FAHT)
Anwar el-Sadat
Ruhollah Khomeini
  (ru•HAWL•la koh•MAY•nee)
Saddam Hussein (hoo•SAYN)

Building Your Vocabulary
refugee (REH•fyu•JEE)
apartheid (uh•PAHR•TAYT)
intifada

Reading Strategy
Organizing Information Complete a diagram like the one below to show the challenges facing African nations.

Africa

NATIONAL GEOGRAPHIC
When & Where?

ISRAEL
IRAQ
SOUTH AFRICA

1950 .... 1975 2000

1956
Egypt takes over Suez Canal

1979
Revolution in Iran overthrows shah

1994
Nelson Mandela becomes South Africa's president

① FOCUS

SECTION OVERVIEW
This section describes the problems and successes in Africa and the Middle East.

SKILLBUILDER ACTIVITY

🔔 Project **Daily Focus Skills Transparency 22–2** and have students answer questions. Discuss their responses.

Get Ready to Read!

Preteaching Vocabulary: *Apartheid* was a policy enforced in the Republic of South Africa that separated Africans from those people of European descent. This discrimination was both political and economic. It comes from the Afrikaans *apart*, meaning "apart," and *heid*, meaning "hood."

Answers to Graphic: civil wars; uneven distribution of resources; drought and famine; urbanization and government difficulty in providing basic needs to new city dwellers; poor health care

---

SECTION RESOURCES

📁 **Reproducible Masters**
- Reproducible Lesson Plan 22–2
- Daily Lecture and Discussion Notes 22–2
- Vocabulary Activity 22–2
- Active Reading Note-Taking Guide 22–2
- Guided Reading Activity 22–2
- Section Quiz 22–2
- Reading Essentials and Study Guide 22–2

📀 **Transparencies**
- Daily Focus Skills Transparency 22–2

Multimedia
- Interactive Tutor Self-Assessment CD-ROM
- Exam*View*® Pro Testmaker CD-ROM
- Presentation Plus! CD-ROM
- Glencoe BookLink CD-ROM

② TEACH

Researching Have students prepare a bibliography for a report on the Hutu-Tutsi conflict in Rwanda or the United Nations intervention in Somalia, in which the United States took part. Suggest they consult the school or community library, Internet news sites, and other appropriate sources. **L1**

Daily Lecture and Discussion Notes 22-2

Use **Daily Lecture and Discussion Notes 22-2** for an outline of key concepts found in the section.

Using Geography Skills

Answers:

1. Sudan, Ethiopia, Mali, Somalia, Liberia, Eritrea, Angola, Mozambique
2. Morocco, Tunisia, and Libya

African Challenges

Main Idea The countries of Africa south of the Sahara faced many challenges in the late twentieth century.

Reading Focus What would it be like to be forced from your home? Read to find out how conflict has left many Africans homeless.

Africa south of the Sahara was politically unstable and was struggling with its economy during the late 1900s. War, drought, and famine blocked efforts to build modern societies.

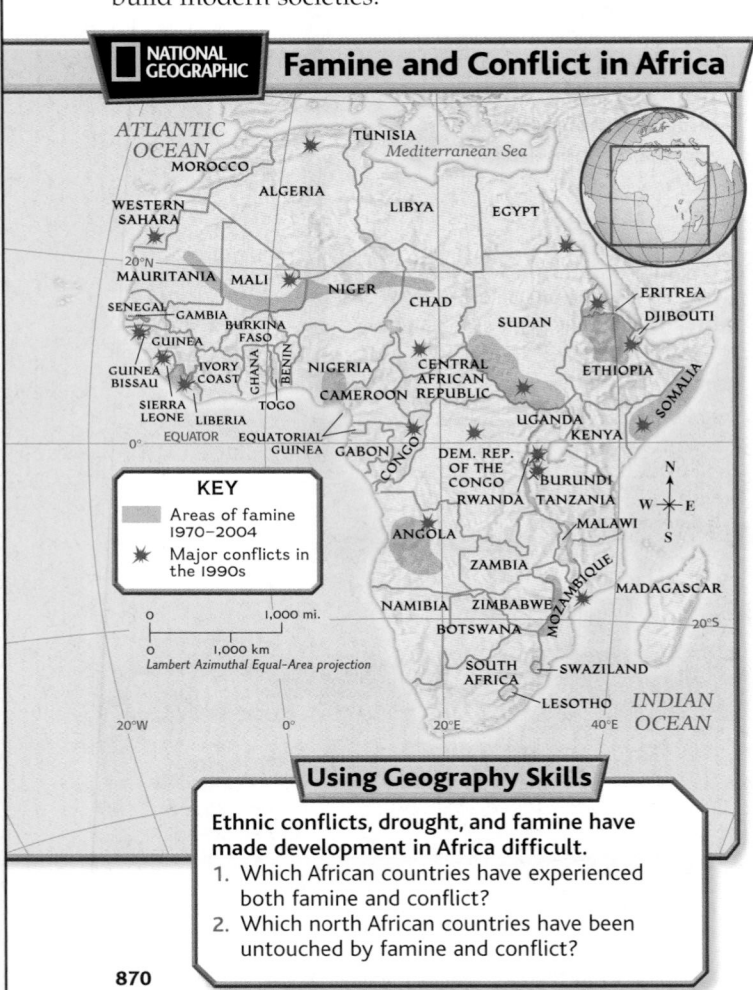

NATIONAL GEOGRAPHIC

Famine and Conflict in Africa

KEY

▨ Areas of famine 1970–2004

✴ Major conflicts in the 1990s

1,000 mi.

1,000 km

Lambert Azimuthal Equal-Area projection

Using Geography Skills

Ethnic conflicts, drought, and famine have made development in Africa difficult.

1. Which African countries have experienced both famine and conflict?
2. Which north African countries have been untouched by famine and conflict?

870

Civil Wars Since the 1960s, many African countries have suffered from civil war. Previously, you learned that European nations in the 1800s divided Africa into colonies. In doing so, they tore apart once-united regions and threw together ethnic and religious groups that did not get along.

After independence, many countries kept the old colonial boundaries. Within each new country, different groups began fighting each other. In recent years, ethnic conflicts have divided people in Nigeria, Ivory Coast, Liberia, Somalia, Sudan, Rwanda, Burundi, and the Democratic Republic of Congo.

In these wars, many people have died or have become **refugees** (REH•fyu•JEEZ), people who flee to another country to escape persecution or disaster. Unrest in one country often has spilled over into neighboring countries. In some cases, United Nations (UN) peacekeeping troops have been called in to maintain peace.

African Economies African nations have faced economic difficulties, too. Africa south of the Sahara is rich in mineral resources, such as oil, gold, and diamonds. These resources, however, are not evenly distributed. Some countries are rich, while others are poor.

Industry plays only a small role in Africa's economies. In the past, colonial rulers used Africa as a source of raw materials and left the continent largely undeveloped. Today

---

Reading Strategy ▸ READING THE TEXT

Analyzing The reading support strategy of analyzing involves looking critically at the different parts of a text. In this way, the reader is able to understand the entire selection. In this section, much of the text serves to describe the problems that an important area of the world faces. As students read this section, have them analyze the problems by identifying them and making notes. Then have them review their notes on the different problems and combine them into a comprehensive description. **L2**

African nations south of the Sahara are struggling to build factories and businesses.

Most people in Africa still depend on farming or livestock herding. They usually are able to grow only enough food to feed their families. Some farmers work on large, company-run farms that grow cash crops to send overseas. These crops include coffee, cacao, cotton, tea, peanuts, and bananas.

Like Latin America, many African economies rely on a single export crop to earn money. When prices for these crops drop, incomes fall and jobs are lost.

Drought and famine are constant problems for Africa. These disasters have led to many deaths in countries such as Ethiopia, Niger, Sudan, and Mali. Many African countries must buy food from other countries. Often this food is expensive and not plentiful. African governments are now teaching people better ways to farm, but much remains to be done to increase food production.

Ways of Life Independence has led to change in many African countries. Most Africans still live in villages, but cities have grown rapidly. In recent years, many Africans have left the countryside and moved to cities in search of jobs and better education. Governments find it difficult to

▲ As African populations continue to rise quickly, more and more people move to the cities, and shantytowns like this one in Cape Town, South Africa, continue to grow. *Why have many Africans left the countryside for cities?*

provide shelter, water, and electricity for so many new city dwellers.

Health care is also an issue in Africa. Millions of people have been infected with the virus that causes AIDS. People who have AIDS often cannot work to support their families, and many children have been orphaned by the disease. Governments are trying to deal with this emergency, but providing good health care is very expensive.

✓ **Reading Check** **Identify** List three things that contribute to economic difficulties in Africa.

CHAPTER 22   Building Today's World   871

Reading Support L1/ EL

Use **Vocabulary Activity 22–2** to review important terms in the section.

Writing Activity

UN peacekeepers have intervened in several African conflicts. Ask students to write a newspaper editorial either for or against the use of American soldiers in peacekeeping missions. Have them give reasons for their position. **L2**

Caption Answer: They are searching for better jobs and better education.

CONNECTING ACROSS TIME

Remind students about the Black Death that struck Europe in the 1300s. Ask them to compare that outbreak with the AIDS epidemic in Africa south of the Sahara today. How are the epidemics similar? How are they different? **L1**

✓ **Reading Check**

Answer: uneven distribution of resources; reliance on a single export crop; drought and famine lead to deaths and cause food to be expensive and scarce

---

DIFFERENTIATED INSTRUCTION

Auditory/Musical: Have students listen to a recorded speech of South African leader Nelson Mandela, Desmond Tutu, or Stephen Biko. Have them write a critique of the speaker's style and effectiveness as an orator.

English Learners: Ask students to read a part of a speech by one of the leaders and study the speaker's vocabulary and grammar. Then have them write a short summary of the speech.

Verbal/Linguistic: Have students learn and rehearse a speech by one of the leaders and present it to the class.

☞ Refer to *Inclusion Strategies for the Middle School Social Studies Classroom* in the TCR.

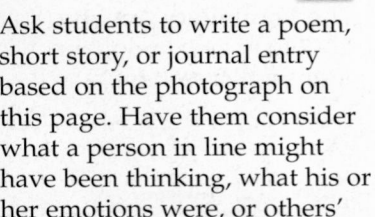

Writing Activity

Ask students to write a poem, short story, or journal entry based on the photograph on this page. Have them consider what a person in line might have been thinking, what his or her emotions were, or others' reactions to the historic vote. **L2**

More About the Photo

In the historic election, Mandela's party, the ANC, won 62.7 percent of the vote. De Klerk's party won 20.4 percent.

Answer: Many countries cut off trade with South Africa.

TIME TRAVELER

Following independence, many former European colonies took names from African history. The West African nations of Ghana and Mali were named after powerful ancient kingdoms. In southern Africa, the former Rhodesia became Zimbabwe, named after an ancient capital of Bantu culture.

✓ Reading Check

Answer: He was the leader of the ANC who was jailed for protesting apartheid. He eventually became the first black president of South Africa.

872

The End to Apartheid

Main Idea Black South Africans won their freedom after years of hardship and struggle.

Reading Focus What guarantees that you have the same rights as the person sitting next to you? Read to find how South Africans struggled to get the same guarantee.

Previously, you learned that South Africa was ruled by whites who denied basic rights to the much larger non-European population. This South African system of treating different groups separately and unequally was called **apartheid** (uh•PAHR•TAYT). From the 1950s to the 1980s, people inside and outside South Africa protested against apartheid.

Struggle for Freedom Within South Africa, blacks and other non-Europeans organized to bring about change. In the early 1960s, one of the largest groups, the African National Congress (ANC), called for an armed uprising. Soon South African government forces were battling guerrilla groups backed by the ANC.

Meanwhile, many black South Africans, such as ANC leader **Nelson Mandela,** were jailed for resisting apartheid. Others, such as church leader Desmond Tutu, worked for peaceful change. The United Nations condemned apartheid, and many countries cut off trade with South Africa.

A New South Africa Because of this pressure, the white-run government began to end apartheid in the late 1980s. Then, in 1990, the government released Nelson Mandela from prison. Over the next few years, talks led to the end of the remaining apartheid laws. All South Africans, regardless of race, were declared equal under the law.

In 1994 South Africa held its first democratic election that allowed people of different races to vote. South Africans elected Nelson Mandela to be their nation's first black president. He worked to unite and rebuild the country. Mandela served as president until 1999. His successor, Thabo Mbeki, carried on Mandela's policies.

✓ Reading Check **Identify**
Who is Nelson Mandela, and why is he important?

◄ These people are waiting in line to vote in South Africa's first democratic election in 1994. *Why did the white-run government in South Africa begin to end apartheid in the late 1980s?*

872 CHAPTER 22 Building Today's World

CRITICAL THINKING ACTIVITY

Making Generalizations Suggest that students think of generalizations as summaries. These draw together, or summarize, known facts in a broad statement. Have students review all the text information in the section about one event or country and make a generalization about the information. For example, a generalization students could make about the attainment of majority rule in South Africa is *Wise and patient leadership on all sides helped bring about the change.* Have students explain how the text information supports this generalization. Then ask them to do the same for other information in the text, such as the Arab-Israeli conflict, the Iranian Revolution, or the Palestinian *intifada.* **L2**

Biography

NELSON MANDELA
1918–

In 1990, a crowd of 50,000 people gathered at the city hall in Cape Town, South Africa, to welcome Nelson Mandela home from prison. While Mandela was imprisoned, his reputation had grown steadily. He had become a powerful symbol of the anti-apartheid movement. Free at last, Mandela immediately resumed his life's work to achieve a democratic, free, and equal society in South Africa.

Nelson Rolihlahla Mandela was born in the village of Qunu in Transkei, South Africa. Mandela's father, Henry Mgadia Mandela, served as the main adviser to the Paramount Chief of the Tembu Tribe. After his father's death, the Paramount Chief was young Mandela's guardian. Listening to cases that came before the Chief's court, Mandela decided that he wanted to become a lawyer. He was educated at University College of Fort Hare and the University of Witwatersrand. In 1952 Mandela and his longtime friend, Oliver Tambo, opened the first black law practice in South Africa. But not even their professional status as lawyers spared them from apartheid.

By the end of 1952, Mandela was deputy president of the African National Congress. The government responded to the ANC's strikes, boycotts, and civil disobedience—peaceful methods of resistance to apartheid—with force and violence. With Mandela as its commander-in-chief, a military wing of the ANC was formed to engage in violent forms of political struggle. In 1964 Mandela was sentenced to life imprisonment for plotting to overthrow the government.

While in prison, Mandela maintained a strict schedule of exercise and work and became a source of strength for other prisoners. The simple pleasure of sunlight was denied to him for nearly 30 years. Today, watching the sun set is one of Mandela's greatest pleasures.

▲ Nelson Mandela

"I greet you in the name of peace, democracy and freedom for all."
—Nelson Mandela, upon his release from prison as quoted in *Millennium Year by Year*

Then and Now

Nelson Mandela said, "The struggle is my life." In what way are these words significant not only to Mandela, but to the people of South Africa as well?

873

TEACH

In a speech he gave at the trial where he was sentenced to life in prison, Nelson Mandela defended his actions. He said,

"During my lifetime I have dedicated myself to this struggle of the African people. I have fought against white domination, and I have fought against black domination. I have cherished the ideal of a democratic and free society in which all persons live together in harmony and with equal opportunities. It is an ideal which I hope to live for and to achieve. But if needs be, it is an ideal for which I am prepared to die."

Ask students to discuss what Mandela meant by "equal opportunities." Then have them address whether equal opportunities for all exist in our country today. Why or why not? **L2**

Then and Now

Students' responses will vary. Sample response: Mandela sacrificed his youth and private life for the struggle to end apartheid and bring freedom, equality, and democracy to his people. His dedication to the struggle inspired people throughout the world to speak out against apartheid.

Reading List Generator CD-ROM

GLENCOE BOOKLINK   **FURTHER READING**

Use the **Glencoe BookLink CD-ROM** to create customized reading lists based on your students' interests and reading levels. Below is an example based on content in this chapter. Also, see the Suggested Reading on pages 944–946 of the Appendix.

- Roberts, Jack L. *Nelson Mandela: Determined to Be Free.* Nelson Mandela became the first black president of South Africa in 1994. Born the son of a tribal chief, he spent 27 years in prison for his protest activities in his fight for a free and democratic South Africa.
- Alcraft, Rob and Sean Sprague. *Mexico.* What is life like in Mexico today? Meet the Ugalde family, who live in the village of La Trinidad. Few families in La Trinidad can afford a car. Most walk to work in the fields or in the opal mines.

CONNECTING ACROSS TIME

Many Palestinians were expelled from their homes in Israel in 1948. The rights of these Palestinian refugees to return to their homes is one of the thorniest issues facing peace negotiators. Israelis and Palestinians have struggled to this day to reach a compromise agreeable to both sides. Ask students how they might try to resolve the issue. **L3**

Writing Activity

With the benefit of hindsight, ask students to write a memo to the United Nations about potential problems that the partition of Palestine might cause. Have them use information in this section to compose their memos. **L2**

More About the Art

The region of the Persian Gulf pumps more oil than any other region in the world—as many as 25 million barrels a day and sometimes more.

Answer: There are vast resources of oil in the Middle East that generate an enormous amount of wealth.

The Arab-Israeli Conflict

Main Idea The creation of Israel in 1948 sparked a conflict that still exists today.

Reading Focus Do you think that people of very different backgrounds can live together peacefully? Read to see how this issue affects the Middle East.

After World War II, many changes came to the Middle East. One was the founding of **Israel** (IHZ•ree•uhl). This new nation met the desire of many Jews for a homeland in Palestine. Israel also provided shelter for Jews who had survived the Holocaust. Its birth, however, sparked a bitter conflict with the Arabs that continues today.

Palestine Is Divided The horrors of the Holocaust brought the world's attention to the Jews. In 1947 the UN divided Palestine into a Jewish state and an Arab state. Arabs in Palestine and in neighboring countries opposed this decision. In 1948 the Jews set up Israel in their part of Palestine. David Ben-Gurion (BEHN•gur•YAWN) was Israel's first prime minister.

War soon broke out between Israel and its Arab neighbors. The war ended with Israel's victory and brought many changes. The fighting forced many Palestinian Arabs to flee to Arab countries. There, they settled in refugee camps, hoping to return home someday. Also, many Jews from Europe, Asia, and Africa began settling in Israel.

The Suez Crisis After Israel was formed, many Arabs united around President Gamal Abdel Nasser of **Egypt** (EE•jihpt). Nasser wanted to make Egypt strong and modern. He hoped that a new Egypt would lead the Arab world to greatness.

Oil in the Middle East

Many nations earn their wealth through oil, which is drawn from large fields. In order to get the natural oil reserves out of the ground, tall pumping towers are built. Before these towers can be put in place, however, a hole must first be drilled into the ground with an oil rig. The tall metal frame, or derrick, supports all of the equipment on the rig. A large and powerful drill is placed in the ground and digs its way to the oil beneath the surface. The drill bit is surrounded by a metal casing, which acts as a vacuum hose and removes mud, rock, and debris that the drill cuts through. The blades cut into the earth, leaving behind a hole from which the pumping towers can extract the oil. *Why are oil and oil products so important to the Middle East?*

Soil

Sediment

Rock

Air pocket

Oil

INTERDISCIPLINARY CONNECTIONS ACTIVITY

Economics/Mathematics Organize students into groups and have each group choose one of the following topics to research and create a suitable graph or chart: World output of petroleum by country and by world region *(circle graph, bar graph)*; Gross domestic products per capita (per capita GDP) of important countries in the Middle East and Africa south of the Sahara compared to the United States *(bar graph)*; numbers of people in Africa south of the Sahara who follow various religions *(bar graph, circle graph)*; population breakdown of Sunnis, Shiites, and Kurds in Iraq *(bar graph, circle graph)*; and population growth in Africa south of the Sahara and the Middle East from 1950 to the present *(line graph)*. **L3**

Nasser also set out to reduce Europe's influence in the Middle East. In 1956 he seized the Suez Canal from its European owners. Britain and France then joined Israel in invading Egypt. Britain and France hoped to get rid of Nasser and take back the canal. Israel wanted to end Egypt's military threat.

The United States and the Soviet Union both opposed the invasion. Worried that the invasion would make Egypt a Soviet ally, U.S. president Dwight Eisenhower pressured Britain, France, and Israel into withdrawing. Egypt kept the canal and began accepting Soviet aid. Nasser became even more popular in the Arab world.

The Six-Day War Tensions remained high between Israel and the Arabs. In 1967 another war broke out. Fearing an attack from Egypt, Israel bombed Egyptian airfields on June 5. Within six days, Israel had wiped out the air forces of its Arab neighbors. Israeli troops moved west into the Gaza Strip and Egypt's Sinai Peninsula and north into the Golan Heights, which were part of Syria. Israel also captured the old city of Jerusalem and the West Bank, the part of Jordan that was west of the Jordan River.

When the fighting ended, the UN asked Israel to leave the captured areas. It asked the Arab nations to accept Israel. Both sides refused. Israel's victory in 1967 has shaped events in the Middle East up to the present. About one million Palestinians came under Israeli rule. Israeli settlers also began building towns in the West Bank and Gaza Strip.

In 1964 **Yasir Arafat** (ahr•uh•FAHT) became the leader of the new Palestine Liberation Organization, or PLO. The PLO's goal was to destroy Israel and take its land for Palestinians. PLO members seized passenger planes and carried out

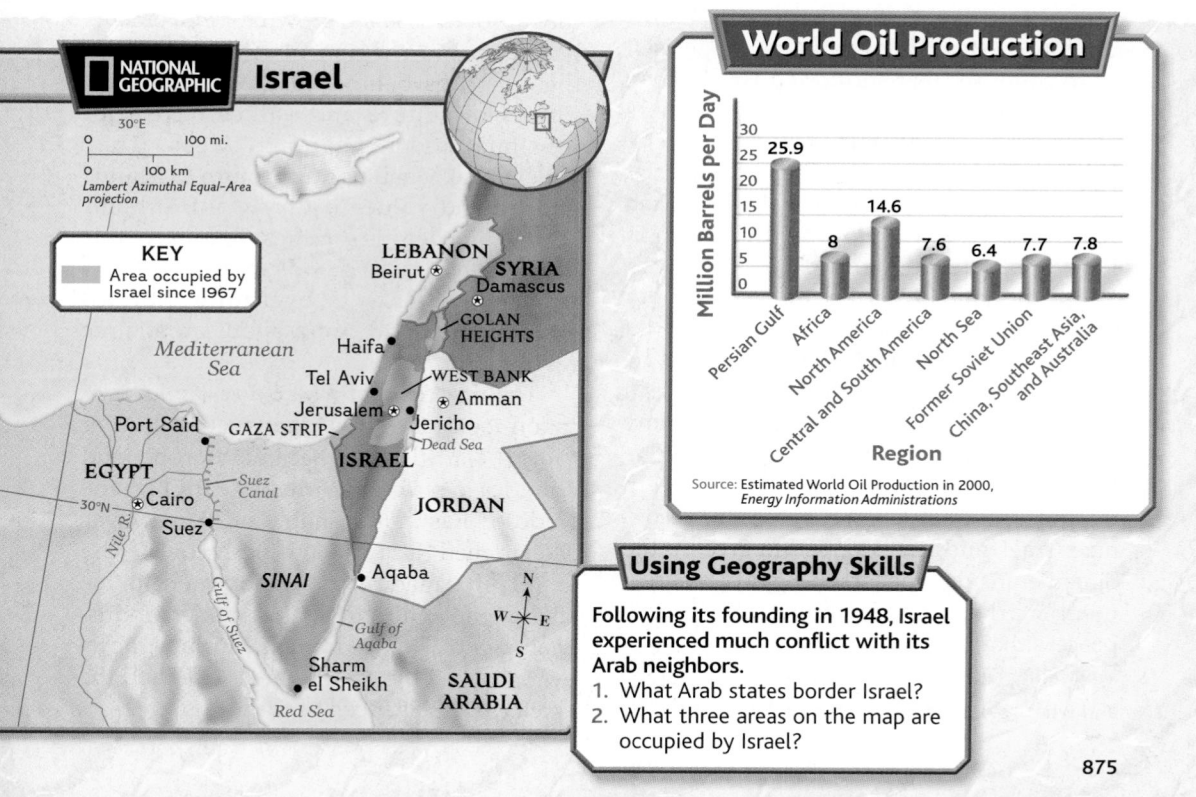

NATIONAL GEOGRAPHIC Israel

30°E

0   100 mi.
0   100 km
Lambert Azimuthal Equal-Area projection

KEY
Area occupied by Israel since 1967

LEBANON
Beirut ⊛
SYRIA
Damascus ⊛
GOLAN HEIGHTS
Haifa •
Mediterranean Sea
Tel Aviv •
WEST BANK
⊛ Amman
Jerusalem ⊛ • Jericho
Port Said •
GAZA STRIP
Dead Sea
EGYPT
ISRAEL
30°N • Cairo
Suez Canal
JORDAN
Suez •
Nile R.
SINAI
• Aqaba
Gulf of Suez
Gulf of Aqaba
Sharm el Sheikh •
SAUDI ARABIA
Red Sea

N
W—E
S

World Oil Production

Million Barrels per Day

- Persian Gulf — 25.9
- Africa — 8
- North America — 14.6
- Central and South America — 7.6
- North Sea — 6.4
- Former Soviet Union — 7.7
- China, Southeast Asia, and Australia — 7.8

Region

Source: Estimated World Oil Production in 2000, *Energy Information Administrations*

Using Geography Skills

Following its founding in 1948, Israel experienced much conflict with its Arab neighbors.
1. What Arab states border Israel?
2. What three areas on the map are occupied by Israel?

875

EXTENDING THE CONTENT

Jerusalem Holy city to three world religions, Jerusalem is at the center of today's Palestinian-Israeli standoff. Jews revere the city as the site of the Temple of Solomon and the ancient capital of the Jewish people. To Christians, the city has been the symbolic center of the world and site of the crucifixion and resurrection of Jesus. For Muslims, Jerusalem is the third-holiest site, after Makkah and Madinah, and the place where Muhammad rose to heaven.

Reading Strategy

Time Line Asks students to research and make an illustrated time line of important events of the Palestinian-Israeli conflict. Suggest they cut photos from magazines, download Internet photos, or make their own illustrations. **L2**

CURRICULUM CONNECTION

Religion

Both Iran and Iraq are majority Shiite countries, while most other Muslim countries have Sunni majorities. One key difference between the two religions is the Shiite belief in the *imam* as an authority over spiritual and sometimes even political matters. Shiite Muslims often follow charismatic religious leaders, sometimes called *imams*, like the Ayatollah Khomeini of Iran.

Reading Check

Answer: The Palestine Liberation Organization's goal is to destroy Israel and take its land for Palestine. They have used acts of terrorism against Israel's people.

---

acts of terrorism against Israel's people. Terrorism is the use of violence against civilians to achieve a political goal.

What Is OPEC? In 1973 Egypt's president, **Anwar el-Sadat,** ordered his military to attack Israel. Sadat hoped to recapture the Sinai Peninsula. Egypt's forces smashed through Israel's defenses, but eventually Israel, led by Prime Minister Golda Meir (meh•IHR), pushed them back. A cease-fire ended the fighting.

Many Arab countries belong to the Organization of Petroleum Exporting Countries, or OPEC. Formed in 1960, OPEC includes most of the world's major oil-producing countries. Its purpose is to control world oil prices by regulating how much oil OPEC members produce.

In the middle of the war between Egypt and Israel, the Arab members of OPEC announced that they would no longer sell oil to countries that supported Israel. They also convinced OPEC to make oil prices four times higher than they currently were. This caused an energy crisis and high inflation in the U.S. and Europe. Even after Arab states agreed to sell oil to the U.S. again in 1974, prices stayed high.

By the late 1970s, Egypt wanted both peace and American aid. President Sadat decided to reach out to Israel. In 1978 he and Israeli leader Menachem Begin (BAY•gihn) met with U.S. president Jimmy Carter at Camp David in Maryland. The talks led to the Camp David Accords. In this historic treaty, Egypt agreed to recognize Israel, and Israel agreed to give up the Sinai Peninsula. The Israeli-Egyptian agreement marked the beginning of a peace process that continues today.

Reading Check **Identify** What is the PLO, and what role did it play in the Middle East?

War in the Middle East

Main Idea Political and social conflicts continue to keep the Middle East in turmoil.

Reading Focus How do you keep yourself from getting discouraged after you fail at something? Read to find out how repeated failures affected the search for peace in the Middle East.

The conflict between Israel and the Palestinians is one of many challenges in the Middle East. As in other parts of the world, a few people are rich, while many are poor. Some countries prosper because of oil. Others lack resources. The number of people in the Middle East is growing rapidly, placing more demands on limited resources. One resource, water, is in short supply.

Iran's Islamic Revolution One response to these problems is the growth of movements based on the religion of Islam. Many of these groups believe that American and European culture and values have kept Muslim nations poor and weak. They believe that Muslims must return to Islamic culture and values if they want to build strong, prosperous societies. To achieve this goal, some of these groups try to use terrorism and violence to overthrow Muslim governments and bring about an Islamic revolution.

The first country where an Islamic revolution took place was **Iran** (ih•RAHN). After World War II, Iran became Europe and America's strongest Muslim ally in the Middle East. Its shah, or king, was Mohammed Reza Pahlavi (rih•ZAH PA•luh•vee). With American and European help, the shah began to turn Iran into a modern industrial country. Many Iranian Muslims, however, disliked the shah's harsh ways and the changes in their society.

COOPERATIVE LEARNING

"Town Meeting" in the Middle East Have two groups of students research and prepare a "town meeting" of Palestinians and Israelis to discuss the problems between them. Ask the two sides to research the history of the conflict. Have them also read about proposals for peace. Then have the two groups meet in front of the class to discuss the situation. Ask each side to prepare an agenda for the discussion. You may also want to allow questions from a "press corps" of students in the class audience. **L2**

Biography

GOLDA MEIR
1898–1978

Golda Meir overcame many hardships to help establish a Jewish homeland. She also became Israel's first female foreign minister and the first female prime minister of a Middle Eastern country. Meir accomplished goals that were unbelievable for a woman in the mid-1900s, but her journey was not easy.

During the early 1900s, Jewish families in Russia were persecuted. The Russian government passed hundreds of laws that restricted Russian Jews, including laws saying when they could marry and where they could live. Many Jews were forced to stay inside a fenced area called the Jewish Pale. Czar Nicholas blamed the Jews for economic problems. Many Jews were beaten to death.

Golda Meir lived in the Russian Ukraine with her parents Moshe and Blume Mabovits, and her siblings. Because her father was a carpenter, her family was allowed to leave the Jewish Pale and live in the city of Kiev, but many times Moshe did not get paid for his work because he was a Jew.

Meir and her family moved to the United States. She was a good student, loved politics, and was determined to help the Jewish people. She joined a Jewish movement in Colorado, collected money to help Jews in Poland and the Ukraine, and traveled to Palestine to see the new Jewish nation being built.

Meir later married Morris Meyerson and had children. But she remained active in politics. After World War II, she aided Jews rescued from German concentration camps. Once the Jewish state of Israel was created, Meir was active in its government. She served as prime minister from 1969 to 1974. Over time Golda Meir became one of the most influential leaders of Israel.

▲ Golda Meir

"Would it not be better for all to build a future for the Middle East based on cooperation?"
—Golda Meir, "Appeals for Reconciliation"

Then and Now
Read Meir's quote above. Give an example of how cooperation has been used to solve a problem in your own community.

877

Biography

TEACH

During her long career in Israeli politics, Meir was a strong supporter of peaceful relations with Israel's neighbors. She believed in diplomacy as the best way to peace. Meir personally tried to dissuade the king of Jordan from joining other Arab states in invading Israel following independence. She also supported programs aimed at winning Israel friends around the world, such as sending aid to developing African countries. As prime minister, she met with world leaders, including Pope Paul VI and German leader Willy Brandt. Her tireless pursuit of peace became even more impressive at her death, when it was revealed that she had suffered from leukemia for the last 12 years of her life.

Point out to students that in spite of the desires of leaders like Golda Meir, Israel has fought numerous wars with neighbors. Ask students to draw up a checklist that a nation's leaders might follow to determine if war is inevitable. Write the checklist items on the board and discuss the steps. **L3**

Then and Now
Answers will vary but might include Nelson Mandela, Napoleon, Bismarck, George Washington, Camillo di Cavour, Garibaldi, and Bolívar, as well as earlier figures from world history.

Reading List Generator CD-ROM

GLENCOE BOOKLINK   **FURTHER READING**

Use the **Glencoe BookLink CD-ROM** to create customized reading lists based on your students' interests and reading levels. Below is an example based on content in this chapter. Also, see the Suggested Reading on pages 944–946 of the Appendix.

- King, David C. *Dropping in on Israel.* Tour the small country of Israel, homeland of the Jewish people. You start at Haifa, Israel's largest seaport, then go on to visit a kibbutz near the Sea of Galilee, the Old City of Jerusalem, and ruins at the oasis of Jericho.
- Rosenberg, Tina. *The Haunted Land: Facing Europe's Ghosts After Communism.* Germany, Poland, the Czech Republic, and Slovakia broke with communism and cultivated democracy.

③ ASSESS

The Ayatollah Khomeini (left) brought back traditional Islamic ideas to Iranian society following the overthrow of Shah Mohammad Reza Pahlavi (above). *What is an Islamic republic?*

Revolution in Iran Angry with the shah, many Iranians looked to their religious leaders to guide them. The most powerful Iranian ayatollah, or clergyman, lived in exile in France. His name was **Ruhollah Khomeini** (ru•HAWL•la koh•MAY•nee). Khomeini organized protests against the shah's government. In 1979, as protests mounted, the shah fled the country. Khomeini then returned to Iran and became the nation's new ruler. He and the other religious leaders made Iran an Islamic republic and enforced the strict laws of a traditional Muslim society.

Many people in Iran hated the United States because it had supported the shah. In late 1979, student militants, or people with strong views, attacked the U.S. embassy and took 52 Americans as hostages, or captives, for more than a year.

Iran also clashed with **Iraq** (ih•RAHK). Iraq was led by a dictator named **Saddam Hussein** (hoo•SAYN). In the 1980s, Iran and Iraq fought a war that cost thousands of lives.

The Persian Gulf War Iraq was nearly broke after its long war with Iran. It decided to seize its oil-rich Persian Gulf neighbor, Kuwait. In 1990 Saddam Hussein sent his army to take over Kuwait.

In response, the United States joined other nations in a coalition, or a group united for action. In 1991 coalition forces pushed the Iraqis out of Kuwait. They also destroyed much of Iraq's army. Many wanted Saddam Hussein overthrown, but he stayed in power.

After this Persian Gulf War, the coalition wanted to keep Hussein from making chemical and biological weapons, such as poison gas and deadly germs. A UN team was sent to keep watch over Iraqi military programs.

A Fragile Peace During the 1980s, Palestinian Arabs in the West Bank and Gaza Strip grew increasingly angry at being under Israeli control. In 1987 their anger finally exploded in an *intifada,* or uprising. Workers went on strike, and street protesters hurled stones at Israeli soldiers.

Web Activity Visit jat.glencoe.com and click on *Chapter 22—Student Web Activity* to learn more about the Middle East.

CRITICAL THINKING ACTIVITY

Analyzing Many Muslims around the world distrust the United States, its allies, and modern civilization. A few even express their hatred and anger toward the West through acts of terrorism. Have students analyze this situation and make a step-by-step plan on how the United States and other industrialized countries can diffuse this hatred and anger. Ask them to consider economic, cultural, and political aspects of the problem. L3

In the early 1990s, the United States set up peace talks between Israel and the Palestinians. In 1993 Israel agreed to give the Palestinians self-rule in certain areas. In return, the Palestinians accepted Israel's right to exist. A government known as the Palestinian Authority was created to rule in the Palestinian areas. During the 1990s, Israel also signed a peace treaty with Jordan.

Many Israelis and Palestinians supported the peace efforts. Some, however, did not. In the late 1990s and early 2000s, Palestinian militants began setting off bombs in Israel.

In response, Israel seized or killed many Palestinian leaders. In 2002, Israel moved with force in the West Bank to crush militant groups. To keep out attackers, Israel also began building a wall along its border with the Palestinian areas.

◀ A long-time Palestinian leader, Yasir Arafat, became the head of the Palestinian Authority when it was created in the 1990s. *How did Israel respond to the wave of Palestinian attacks in the late 1990s?*

As a step toward freeing themselves of the Palestinian issue, the Israelis made plans in 2004 to pull out of the Gaza Strip. Meanwhile, Palestinians began to demand better government from the Palestinian Authority.

 Explain What happened when Iraqi troops invaded Kuwait in 1990?

ENRICH

Have students choose one ethnic conflict in the regions discussed and research it. Have them share their findings with the class. **L3**

Caption Answer: They seized or killed many Palestinian leaders.

Answer: The United States and other nations formed a coalition and went to war to push the Iraqis out of Kuwait.

To help students understand section material, have them visit Study Central™ at jat.glencoe.com

RETEACH

Ask students to make word webs for the following terms: *South Africa in the 1990s; Israel and Palestine; Islam at a Turning Point.* **L1**

④ CLOSE

Review with students the challenges and issues in Africa south of the Sahara and the Middle East. Make a list of class suggestions as you review them. **L2**

Section ② Review

History Online
Study Central™ Need help with the material in this section? Visit jat.glencoe.com

Reading Summary

Review the Main Ideas

• In the late 1900s, many countries in Africa south of the Sahara faced civil war, famine, disease, and political unrest as they attempted to modernize.

• The creation of an Israeli state in 1948 angered many Arabs and led to a number of wars and other conflicts in the region.

• The Israeli and Palestinian conflict, along with conflicts between Muslim groups and countries, has kept the Middle East in turmoil.

What Did You Learn?

1. What was apartheid, and what brought about its end?

2. What was the oil embargo of the early 1970s? Why was it put in place?

Critical Thinking

3. **Organizing Information** Draw a diagram like the one below. Use the outer ovals to list challenges faced by Africa south of the Sahara today.

Challenges

4. **Cause and Effect** What were the results of the Six-Day War? How did they affect Arab-Israeli relations at that time?

5. **Explain** How was Israel founded? Why did this cause problems?

6. **Analyze** What role has the United States played in the Middle East?

7. **Expository Writing** Write an essay discussing the problems facing the Middle East today and what might be done to ease tensions there in the future.

SECTION 2 REVIEW ANSWERS

1. the South African system of unequal treatment of different groups; the UN condemned apartheid, and many nations cut off trade

2. Oil-rich countries banned the sale of oil to the U.S. for supporting Israel over Egypt.

3. civil wars; drought and famine; poor health care

4. Israel captured Palestinian land; led to the creation of the PLO and the subsequent violence.

5. Israel was founded as a homeland for Jews after World War II. The UN divided Palestine into two states to form Israel.

6. The U.S. supported Israel against Egypt, aided Kuwait during the Persian Gulf War, and helped to set up peace talks between Israel and Palestine.

7. Essays will vary.

① FOCUS

SECTION OVERVIEW

In this section, students will read how changes in communist nations drastically reshaped the world.

BELLRINGER
SKILLBUILDER ACTIVITY

🔔 Project **Daily Focus Skills Transparency 22–3** and have students answer questions. Discuss their responses.

Get Ready to Read!

Preteaching Vocabulary: Tell students that *détente* is a French word meaning "loosening." In English, it refers to a policy of relaxing tensions between countries through increased diplomacy, and fostering economic and cultural ties. Ask students to look for ways détente helped bring about important changes in the world during the 1970s.

Answers to Graphic: Glasnost: "openness" policy where Soviet citizens were given freedoms of speech and the press; Perestroika: "rebuilding" policy to improve the Soviet economy; both: initiated by Gorbachev

---

Section ③ The Cold War Ends

Get Ready to Read!

What's the Connection?
In Chapter 21 you read about the Cold War. Read to find out how nations changed during the final decades of the Cold War.

Focusing on the Main Ideas
- After nearly 50 years of bitter rivalry with the United States, in the 1990s the Soviet Union and its Eastern European empire fell apart. *(page 881)*
- The fall of communism unleashed deadly ethnic hatreds in the Balkan nation of Yugoslavia. *(page 884)*
- China moved toward a free-market economy, but its leaders still opposed democratic reforms. *(page 885)*

Locating Places
Russia
Yugoslavia

Meeting People
Mikhail Gorbachev
    (GAWR•buh•CHAWF)
Boris Yeltsin
Josip Broz Tito
Slobodan Milosevic (SLOH•buh
    DAHN   muh•LOH•suh•VIHCH)
Deng Xiaoping
    (DUHNG   SYOW•PING)

Building Your Vocabulary
détente (day•TAHNT)
glasnost (GLAZ•nohst)
perestroika (PEHR•uh•STROY•kuh)
ethnic cleansing

Reading Strategy
Compare and Contrast Complete a Venn diagram to show the characteristics of glasnost and perestroika.

(Glasnost)(Perestroika)

NATIONAL GEOGRAPHIC **When & Where?**

1965   1985   2005

NORTH AMERICA   EUROPE   RUSSIA   CHINA

1966 Cultural Revolution begins in China

1991 Soviet Union breaks up

1995 Dayton talks settle Bosnian conflict

880   CHAPTER 22   Building Today's World

SECTION RESOURCES

Reproducible Masters
- Reproducible Lesson Plan 22–3
- Daily Lecture and Discussion Notes 22–3
- Vocabulary Activity 22–3
- Active Reading Note-Taking Guide 22–3
- Guided Reading Activity 22–3
- Section Quiz 22–3
- Reading Essentials and Study Guide 22–3

Transparencies
- Daily Focus Skills Transparency 22–3

Multimedia
- Interactive Tutor Self-Assessment CD-ROM
- ExamView® Pro Testmaker CD-ROM
- Presentation Plus! CD-ROM

The Fall of the Soviet Union

Main Idea After nearly 50 years of bitter rivalry with the United States, in the 1990s the Soviet Union and its Eastern European empire fell apart.

Reading Focus Why do things change in the world? Do you think people make a difference, or are big developments in economics and technology responsible? Read to learn why the Soviet Union collapsed.

Previously, you learned about the Cold War. In the 1970s, relations between the U.S. and the two Communist giants—the Soviet Union and China—began to improve.

What Was Détente?

In the 1970s, the United States introduced a new policy called détente. **Détente** (day•TAHNT) comes from a French word that means "a relaxation of tensions." How did détente begin?

In 1972 U.S. president Richard Nixon made a historic trip to China. There, Nixon and China's Communist leaders agreed to have diplomatic relations and to promote trade. Nixon's visit was carefully watched by the Soviets. The alliance between China and the Soviet Union had ended in the 1960s, and the Soviets no longer trusted China. The Soviets feared that closer U.S.-Chinese ties would be bad for them. So they began to reach out to the United States.

Later, in 1972, U.S. president Nixon and Soviet leader Leonid Brezhnev held talks and signed several agreements. One agreement was SALT, or the Strategic Arms Limitation Treaty. It put limits on the nuclear weapons of both superpowers.

Despite high hopes, détente did not last. In 1979 the Soviets invaded Afghanistan. There, Soviet forces fought to keep a Communist government in power. The United States opposed the invasion, and President Jimmy Carter reduced trade.

▲ The period of détente negotiated by Soviet leader Leonid Brezhnev (left) and President Richard Nixon (right) lasted seven years. *What ended the détente of the 1970s?*

Reagan Pressures the Soviets

In 1981 Ronald Reagan became president of the United States. Reagan was strongly anti-communist. Calling the Soviet Union an "evil empire," Reagan started a military buildup. In doing so, he challenged the Soviets to an arms race. The Soviet economy was already having problems, and the arms race weakened it further. The Soviet economic crisis helped bring to power Soviet leaders willing to reform their system.

Reagan also gave American support to groups trying to overthrow Communist governments. For example, the United States helped forces in Central America and Africa opposed to the spread of communism. It also backed Islamic groups fighting the Soviets in Afghanistan.

Who Was Gorbachev?

In 1985 **Mikhail Gorbachev** (GAWR•buh•CHAWF) became the Soviet leader. He swiftly began to transform the Soviet Union. Under the policy of

CHAPTER 22   Building Today's World   **881**

Reading Strategy   **READING THE TEXT**

Connecting Ask students to connect the information they read in this section to events in their daily lives and to current events they read about in other sources like newspapers, magazines, and the Internet. Making such connections increases their reading enjoyment and their understanding of the text. For example, ask students which current events might affect people today the way the fall of the Berlin Wall affected people in 1989. You might also ask them to describe situations from their own lives that have affected them the way the events in this section affected people in China, the Soviet Union, or Eastern Europe. **L2**

② TEACH

Interviews Have students interview an older relative about the period of the breakup of the Soviet Union and the end of the Cold War. Have students prepare a list of questions. After the interviews are complete, have students share some of their responses, either in written form or on audio- or videotape. **L1/EL**

More About the Photo

The tool that Nixon and Kissinger used to start détente was a most unusual one—a Ping-Pong paddle! In 1971, almost a year before Nixon himself visited China, the U.S. Ping-Pong team toured China playing exhibition matches. Team members were the first Americans to enter China since the Communist takeover in 1949.

Caption Answer: the Soviet invasion of Afghanistan

Daily Lecture and Discussion Notes 22-3

Use **Daily Lecture and Discussion Notes 22-3** for an outline of key concepts found in the section.

Reading Support L1/EL

Use **Vocabulary Activity 22-3** to review important terms in the section.

882

Primary Source

In his famous speech, Reagan echoed the words of an earlier U.S. president. On June 26, 1963, John F. Kennedy gave a speech in West Berlin. To emphasize that he stood with the people of West Berlin in their resistance to communism, he proclaimed, *"Ich bin ein Berliner."* (I am a Berliner.)

Answer:
He sees either the beginning of "profound changes," or "token gestures" that will not make positive changes.

Writing Activity

Ask students to research and write a short history of one of the Eastern European nations' overthrow of Communist rule. Assemble the histories into a class booklet. **L2**

Reading Strategy

Analyzing Ask students why they think many of the newly independent nations in the former Soviet Union and Eastern Europe have struggled to build strong economies and democratic systems of government. *(Possible answers include lack of practice; leftover corruption; outdated factories, banks, and other institutions; untrained leaders; and impatient citizens.)* **L2**

Primary Source "Tear Down This Wall"

On June 12, 1987, Ronald Reagan delivered a speech to the people of West Berlin while standing at a gate along the Berlin Wall.

"Behind me stands a wall that encircles the free sectors of this city. . . .

. . .We hear much from Moscow about a new policy of reform and openness. . . .

Are these the beginnings of profound changes in the Soviet state? Or are they token gestures, intended to raise false hopes in the West, or to strengthen the Soviet system without changing it? . . .

General Secretary Gorbachev, if you seek peace, if you seek prosperity for the Soviet Union and Eastern Europe, if you seek liberalization: Come here to this gate! Mr. Gorbachev, open this gate! Mr. Gorbachev, tear down this wall!"

—Ronald Reagan, "Remarks at the Brandenburg Gate"

▲ President Ronald Reagan speaking at the Berlin Wall

DBQ Document-Based Question

What two possibilities does Reagan see in the Soviet policies of reform and openness?

glasnost (GLAZ•nohst), or "openness," Soviet citizens could say and write what they thought without fear of being punished. Another policy, known as **perestroika** (PEHR•uh•STROY•kuh), or "rebuilding," aimed at boosting the Soviet economy. It gave factory managers more freedom and called for small, privately owned businesses. Gorbachev encouraged East European Communist leaders to follow his reforms.

The Berlin Wall Falls In 1987 U.S. president Ronald Reagan visited West Berlin. Standing at the Berlin Wall that divided the city, he said, "[I]f you seek peace, . . . Mr. Gorbachev, tear down this wall!"

Like the Soviet Union, the communist lands of Eastern Europe had weak economies. Their people began to push for democratic change. The first step was in Poland, where the labor union Solidarity called for reforms. East Europeans wondered if Gorbachev would act to stop reforms. Gorbachev, however, said he would not interfere.

Without Soviet support, the governments in Eastern Europe crumbled one by one. In 1989 revolutions took place in Poland, Hungary, Czechoslovakia, Romania, and Bulgaria. Free elections were held. East Europeans who opposed communism, such as Lech Walesa (lehk vah•LEHN•suh) in Poland and Vaclav Havel (VAHT•SLAHF HAH•vehl) in Czechoslovakia, were elected to lead the new governments.

Finally, it was Germany's turn. On November 9, 1989, East Germany's Communist leaders bowed to pressure. They threw open the main gate in the Berlin Wall. The next day, soldiers and civilians began knocking down the wall. Less than a year later, the two parts of Germany were reunited after more than 40 years of division.

DIFFERENTIATED INSTRUCTION

Visual/Spatial: Have students create a work of art on a theme they identify in this section. Examples include the fall of Communism, the opening of China, the tragedy of Yugoslavia, or the fall of the Berlin Wall.

English Learners: Ask students to view a history videotape of an event discussed in this section and describe scenes to each other.

Gifted and Talented: Have students research the life of one of the people identified in this section and share their findings in a talk.

▱ Refer to *Inclusion Stategies for the Middle School Social Studies Classroom* in the TCR.

NATIONAL GEOGRAPHIC — Breakup of the Soviet Union

KEY
— Border of the former Soviet Union
— National boundary
⊛ National capital

ARCTIC OCEAN

North Sea · *Baltic Sea* · *Barents Sea* · *Kara Sea* · *Laptev Sea* · *East Siberian Sea*

EUROPE
Riga · Tallinn · ⊛ **ESTONIA**
LITHUANIA · **LATVIA**
Minsk · Vilnius
BELARUS
Chişinău · Kiev · ⊛ Moscow
⊛ **UKRAINE**
MOLDOVA

RUSSIA

Ob R. · *Irtysh R.* · *Yenisey R.* · *Lena R.* · *Kolyma R.*

GEORGIA
T'bilisi · **ARMENIA** · Yerevan · Baku
AZERBAIJAN

Volga R. · *Kama R.* · *Ural R.* · *Caspian Sea* · *Black Sea*

ASIA

KAZAKHSTAN · ⊛ Astana

Aral Sea · *Lake Balkhash* · *Lake Baikal* · *Sea of Okhotsk* · *Sea of Japan*

UZBEKISTAN
Tashkent · ⊛ Bishkek
Ashgabat · Dushanbe · **KYRGYZSTAN**
TURKMENISTAN
TAJIKISTAN

0 ———— 1,000 mi.
0 ———— 1,000 km
Two-Point Equidistant projection

▲ Mikhail Gorbachev

◀ Boris Yeltsin

Using Geography Skills

The breakup of the Soviet Union led to the creation of 15 nations.
1. Which new nations separated the main part of Russia from the rest of Europe?
2. How do you think the breakup affected Russian trade?

884

Reading a Map Ask students to find the following places on a map: Serbia, Croatia, Bosnia-Herzegovina, Sarajevo, Kosovo, Slovenia, and Macedonia. **L1**

CONNECTING ACROSS TIME

Ask students to consider the history of Yugoslavia in the 1900s. Then ask why the countries of northern and western Europe were reluctant to become involved in the civil wars and repression during the breakup of Yugoslavia. *(World War I was set off by the assassination of the heir to the Austro-Hungarian throne in Sarajevo, Bosnia.)* **L1**

Reading Strategy

Solving a Problem Ask students what they would have done to prepare Yugoslavs for the breakup of their country and to help avoid the bloodshed that occurred because of ethnic hatreds. **L2**

> **Caption Answer:**
> Slovenia, Croatia, Bosnia-Herzegovina, and Macedonia

Reading Check

Answer: They wanted to use any means necessary to keep Yugoslavia together and to keep all Serbs within Yugoslavia.

The Breakup of Yugoslavia

Main Idea The fall of communism unleashed deadly ethnic hatreds in the Balkan nation of Yugoslavia.

Reading Focus What are some roles you think the United Nations can play? Read to find out one role the UN played in southeastern Europe.

In Eastern Europe, the fall of communism created a new wave of nationalism. Soon national and ethnic groups began opposing each other. These rivalries exploded, with horrifying results, in the country of **Yugoslavia.**

A Balkan Flashpoint Yugoslavia was a war-torn area located in Europe's Balkan Peninsula. Its problems began in 1980, the year Communist leader **Josip Broz Tito** died. Since World War II, Tito's strong dictatorship had held Yugoslavia's six republics

▲ A refugee walks past a war-damaged building in the city of Sarajevo, in what was formerly the country of Yugoslavia. *Which four republics of Yugoslavia declared their independence in the 1990s?*

together. When Tito died, however, different ethnic groups struggled for power.

In the early 1990s, four republics declared their independence. They were Slovenia, Croatia, Bosnia-Herzegovina, and Macedonia. The republic of Serbia, however, wanted to keep Yugoslavia together and to keep all Serbs within Yugoslavia. Its leader, **Slobodan Milosevic** (SLOH•buh•DAHN muh•LOH•suh•VIHCH), used force to keep some of the land in the other republics under Yugoslavia's control.

What Is Ethnic Cleansing? The heaviest fighting took place in Bosnia-Herzegovina. There, Serbs aided by Milosevic fought Croats and Muslims. The Bosnian Serbs carried out **ethnic cleansing**—using force to remove an entire ethnic group from an area. Many people died or became refugees.

The United States pushed for peace talks. In 1995 the leaders of Bosnia-Herzegovina, Serbia, and Croatia met in Dayton, Ohio. They signed a peace agreement that divided Bosnia into Croat-Muslim and Serb regions. NATO troops then entered Bosnia as peacekeepers.

Kosovo The Serbs next tried to remove Albanian Muslims from Kosovo. Kosovo had been a self-governing province of Yugoslavia. Albanians there wanted independence. As many refugees left Kosovo in 1999, NATO countries led by the United States bombed Serb military targets. The Serbs finally allowed a NATO peacekeeping force to enter Kosovo.

In 2000, Milosevic was overthrown, and a democratic government replaced him. Milosevic was arrested and brought to trial before an international court.

Reading Check **Explain** What was the goal of Serbia's foreign policy?

INTERDISCIPLINARY CONNECTIONS ACTIVITY

Art/Drama During Mao's Cultural Revolution, radicals used posters, music, plays, and other forms of art to criticize intellectuals, artists, and others they opposed. Ask students to discuss how art can be used to further political goals. Ask for examples from our own society of art that has supported a particular political goal or idea. *(Examples might include Uncle Sam army recruiting posters, and patriotic and antiwar popular songs.)* Ask students to explain the political messages of their art examples and discuss their effectiveness as political motivators. **L3**

Revolution and Reform in China

Main Idea China moved toward a free-market economy, but its leaders still opposed democratic reforms.

Reading Focus Do you think people who own their own businesses work harder than other people? Why or why not? Read to learn how private ownership of business changed China.

Previously, you learned that China became Communist in 1949. China's Communist leaders set out to make China a modern country. By the mid-1960s, China still had a long way to go. At this time, Chinese leaders tried new ways to move the country forward.

The Cultural Revolution Communist leader Mao Zedong feared China was losing its revolutionary spirit. In 1966 he began the Cultural Revolution. "Undesirables" were driven from the Communist Party, and thinkers who favored more freedom were arrested. Meanwhile, students called Red Guards attacked political leaders, teachers, and others and accused them of not supporting communism.

The Cultural Revolution disrupted daily life. People stopped working, and factory production slumped. Battles broke out between Red Guards and other citizens. The Chinese army finally was called out to stop the Cultural Revolution.

China Reforms Its Economy When Mao Zedong died in 1976, **Deng Xiaoping** (DUHNG SYOW•PING) became China's new leader. He cared more about economic growth than about revolutionary spirit. Deng supported a plan—the Four Modernizations—that called for changes in four areas: industry, culture, science and technology, and defense.

NATIONAL GEOGRAPHIC The Way It Was

Focus on Everyday Life

Cultural Revolution in China During the Cultural Revolution, millions of Red Guards embraced Mao Zedong's slogan: "It is right to rebel." Mao encouraged the Red Guards to rid China of all traces of its traditional values. During the Cultural Revolution, those values were called the Four Olds: old ideology, old culture, old customs, and old habits.

Relationships between people began to break down as individuals were encouraged to turn each other in for breaking even the most absurd rules. Students attacked their teachers. Children accused their parents. Brothers and sisters turned against one another. Husbands and wives suffered severe punishment, even torture and death, if they refused to inform on their spouses.

▲ Members of the Red Guard in front of a portrait of Mao Zedong

Connecting to the Past
1. What did Mao want to get rid of in China during the Cultural Revolution?
2. What impact did the Cultural Revolution have on relationships in society, such as ties among family members?

EXTENDING THE CONTENT

Russian Hotspot Chechens, who are mostly Muslims, have a long history of resistance to Russian, and later, Soviet rule. They fought against Czarist troops for most of the 1800s. When Bolsheviks gained power in 1918, anti-Communist Chechen guerrillas continued to battle Red Army soldiers. In 1944, Soviet dictator Josef Stalin lost patience and exiled the entire Chechen population to Siberia. The survivors of this exile were allowed to return in 1957. When the Soviet Union finally fell apart in 1991, Chechens declared their independence. However, the new Russian government disputed this declaration. The battle between the two countries continues into the present, with no resolution in sight.

Reading Support L1/ EL

Assign **Reading Essentials and Study Guide 22–3** to help students review section material.

ENRICH

Have students discuss why the Soviet Union's empire fell apart so quickly. **L2**

Reading Check

Answer: Students were protesting for China to become a democracy.

To help students understand section material, have them visit **Study Central™** at **jat.glencoe.com**

RETEACH

Ask students to complete the following sentence for each region discussed in this section: The major change in ___ during the 1980s and 1990s was ___. **L1**

Ask students to summarize section information regarding the former Soviet Union, the newly independent countries of Eastern Europe, and China. **L2**

Under Deng, the government relaxed its control over factories and farms. Factory managers could decide what goods to produce and what prices to charge. Farmers could keep some of the profits from the food they grew. Deng also encouraged foreigners to set up and run businesses in special areas of China known as economic zones.

Deng's reforms made China's economy grow. More goods were produced, and many Chinese enjoyed a better standard of living. For the first time, China's people were able to buy consumer goods, such as televisions and appliances.

Demands for Democracy Despite economic change, many Chinese were unhappy under Communist rule. They wanted to have free elections and basic rights, such as freedom of speech, religion, and the press.

In the spring of 1989, hundreds of thousands of people, mostly students, gathered in Tiananmen (TEE•EHN•AH•MEHN) Square in the heart of Beijing. They demanded that China become a democracy.

The protests were peaceful, but they frightened the government. So Deng sent soldiers and tanks into Tiananmen Square to break up the gatherings. Between 500 and 1,000 civilians were killed. Countries around the world protested China's harsh treatment of its citizens.

During the 1990s, China gained back territories lost in the 1800s to Europeans. China took control of Hong Kong from Britain in 1997. It gained the port of Macau from Portugal two years later. Both cities are centers of manufacturing, trade, and finance.

Reading Check **Explain** What was the purpose of the demonstration in Tiananmen Square in 1989?

Study Central™ Need help with the material in this section? Visit jat.glencoe.com

Section 3 Review

Reading Summary
Review the Main Ideas

- The Cold War between the United States and the Soviet Union came to an end in the 1990s. Communism fell in the USSR and in its Eastern European empire.

- When Communist governments fell, old ethnic hatreds arose in Yugoslavia and led to the breakup of that nation.

- Throughout the twentieth century, the Chinese people were denied democratic freedoms. However, leaders like Deng Xiaoping modernized the Chinese economy.

What Did You Learn?

1. Who were the Red Guards? What role did they play in the Cultural Revolution?

2. How did Ronald Reagan try to weaken the Soviet Union?

Critical Thinking

3. **Organizing Information** Complete a diagram like the one below to show the Four Modernizations of Deng Xiaoping.

```
          ┌────────────┐
      ○───│    Four     │───○
      ○───│Modernizations│───○
          └────────────┘
```

4. **Explain** What problems arose in Russia after the Soviet Union was dissolved?

5. **Analyze** Why do you think the people living in communist nations of Eastern Europe felt it was safe to rebel in 1989?

6. **Explain** Why did President Nixon go to China in 1972?

7. **Creative Writing** Do you think Mikhail Gorbachev was the most important leader in the 1900s? Write a brief essay giving your opinion and supporting it with historical facts.

886   CHAPTER 22   Building Today's World

SECTION 3 REVIEW ANSWERS

1. They were students who attacked political leaders, teachers, and others they accused of not supporting communism.

2. with an arms race and by giving support to groups trying to overthrow Communist governments

3. industry, culture, science and technology, and defense

4. The economy struggled, crime and violence spread, and a bloody war began in Chechnya.

5. They were not receiving Soviet support, as Gorbachev refused to intervene.

6. to establish diplomatic relations and to promote trade.

7. Essays should include facts to support opinions.

Section 4

The World Enters a New Century

Get Ready to Read!

What's the Connection?
Read to find out how the changes in the 1990s continued into the 2000s.

Focusing on the *Main Ideas*
- Advances in technology have brought the world closer together economically, politically, and culturally. *(page 888)*

- Political and economic changes continued to affect key regions of the world at the close of the twentieth century. *(page 890)*

- A devastating attack on September 11, 2001, focused the world's attention on terrorism. *(page 892)*

Locating Places
Iraq
Afghanistan (af•GA•nuh•STAN)

Meeting People
Bill Gates
Bill Clinton
George W. Bush
Osama bin Laden
(oh•SAHM•uh bihn LAHD•uhn)

Building Your Vocabulary
globalism (GLOH•buh•LIH•zuhm)
euro (YUR•oh)
deforestation
nuclear proliferation (NOO•klee•uhr pruh•LIH•fuh•RAY•shuhn)
terrorism
weapons of mass destruction

Reading Strategy
Identifying Information Complete a table like the one below to show the name and purpose of each regional trade organization.

Organization Name	Purpose

NATIONAL GEOGRAPHIC **When & Where?**

NORTH AMERICA   EUROPE   ASIA
AFRICA
SOUTH AMERICA   AUSTRALIA

1990 — 1998 — 2006

1993 European Union (EU) is formed

1995 WTO is created

2001 Terrorists attack the United States

2003 Iraq War begins

---

❶ FOCUS

SECTION OVERVIEW
This section describes key political, economic, and scientific changes that will continue to shape the world we live in for decades to come.

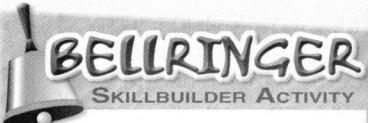

BELLRINGER
SKILLBUILDER ACTIVITY

🖋 Project **Daily Focus Skills Transparency 22–4** and have students answer questions. Discuss their responses.

Get Ready to Read!

Preteaching Vocabulary: Explain to students that *deforestation* means the large-scale cutting of forests. Ask students to define the prefix *de-* *(make the opposite of)*, and list and explain words that use it *(deactivate, debug, decertify, deform, decompose)*.

Answers to Graphic: World Bank and IMF: make it easier for businesses to invest in other countries; WTO: arranges trade agreements and settles trade disputes between countries; European Union: united Europe politically and economically; NAFTA: created free trade area for Canada, the U.S., and Mexico; APEC: created free trade among nations that border the Pacific Ocean

---

SECTION RESOURCES

📁 **Reproducible Masters**
- Reproducible Lesson Plan 22–4
- Daily Lecture and Discussion Notes 22–4
- Vocabulary Activity 22–4
- Active Reading Note-Taking Guide 22–4
- Guided Reading Activity 22–4
- Section Quiz 22–4
- Reading Essentials and Study Guide 22–4

🖋 **Transparencies**
- Daily Focus Skills Transparency 22–4

Multimedia
- Interactive Tutor Self-Assessment CD-ROM
- ExamView® Pro Testmaker CD-ROM
- Presentation Plus! CD-ROM
- Vocabulary PuzzleMaker CD-ROM

② TEACH

Identifying Text Structure Explain that authors use different structures to organize text. Two kinds of structure are chronological—arranging events in the order in which they occur—and cause and effect—showing how certain things cause and are caused by others. Clue words can help readers identify the structure in a passage. For example, words like *on, during, after, then,* and *first* often signal chronological structure. *Because, therefore,* and *as a result* usually show cause-and-effect structure. Ask students to identify each kind of structure as they read "The New Global Economy." **L1**

More About the Art

Early computers filled entire buildings. A new generation of computers fits the processor right inside the monitor, saving space and helping organize room!

Caption Answer: Through the Internet, people can write e-mail, conduct business negotiations, and research information others have produced.

The New Global Economy

Main Idea Advances in technology have brought the world closer together economically, politically, and culturally.

Reading Focus Describe something you know about the way people live in India, China, or South Africa. How do you know what you know? Read to find out why the world has become more connected during the last 30 years.

In recent years, the nations of the world have developed a global economy. This means that they depend on one another for raw materials, to make goods, and for markets in which to sell goods. Think of the many ways you use products from other countries. These are examples of how all the people on our planet are now closely linked together. What has made all of this possible?

The Technology Revolution One reason is the technology revolution. Today we take for granted computers, cell phones, cable television, and compact discs. Back in 1970, these things had either not been invented yet or were not widely available.

The invention that has driven the technology revolution is the computer. In the 1960s, scientists developed the integrated circuit, a small electronic device. A decade later, even more powerful circuits called microprocessors appeared. They made it possible to make smaller, much faster computers that could store a lot of information.

The Computer

The invention of the computer has opened up whole new avenues of communication across the world. Its conception, in the 1960s, helped make way for new technology. Computers are used by people every day to organize information, write documents, create images, and for countless other activities. The computer has become an essential tool for most of the world.
How do people use the computer for communication?

Power Supply · CD/DVD ROM Drive · Disk Drive · Fan · CPU (Central Processing Unit) · Monitor · Mouse · Video Card · Sound Card · Keyboard · Motherboard

Reading Strategy — READING THE TEXT

Visualizing Explain to students that visualizing, or picturing events in one's mind, can help them better remember the events and order in which these events happened. Compare visualizing to the process of watching a movie. Then have volunteers suggest key scenes that would be in a movie about the war on terror and the events of the early 2000s. List them on the board. Lead a discussion about what each scene would show. Make sure that students include details from the text and the illustrations in their descriptions. Ask students how they would conclude the "movie." **L2**

In 1976 Stephen Wozniak and Steven Jobs built the first small computer for personal use. In the 1980s, **Bill Gates** developed software that tells computers how to do specific tasks. Soon an affordable personal computer was available.

Through their personal computers, people are now able to go on the Internet. This is a huge web of linked computer networks. The Internet has made global communications almost instant.

What Is Globalism? The technology revolution has tied together people and nations more closely then before. It has contributed to the rise of **globalism** (GLOH•buh•LIH•zuhm). This is the idea that the world's economy and politics are all part of one big system. People and nations cannot stay separate from each other anymore.

Today, few nations can fully meet all the needs of their people without global trade. To encourage global trade, nations have created a number of organizations. After World War II, the United States and other nations set up the World Bank and the International Monetary Fund (IMF). These organizations made it easier for businesses to invest in other countries. Over the years, many nations also participated in talks to make trade between countries free and easy. These talks led to GATT treaties—General Agreement on Trade and Tariffs.

In 1995 the nations that had signed the GATT treaties over the years agreed to create the World Trade Organization (WTO). Made up of more than 140 member nations, the WTO arranges trade agreements and settles trade disputes.

In different world regions, nations have joined together to form trading groups. For example, nations in Europe formed the European Union (EU) in 1993. One of the EU's goals is to unite Europe politically and

NATIONAL GEOGRAPHIC

HISTORY MAKERS

The Internet

The Internet is a recent invention that has drastically changed the way people communicate. In 1965 Lawrence Roberts and his associates connected a computer in Massachusetts to one in California. Additional

▲ **Students using computers**

computers were added within a few years. In 1972 the network was demonstrated to the public for the first time. In that same year, electronic mail, or e-mail, was introduced. The system grew rapidly in the 1970s and 1980s. By the early 1990s, a new way of sending Internet information called hypertext transport protocol (http) had been devised. This combined with the invention of Web browsers to make it much easier for people to use the Internet. Today the Internet is widely used around the world and can be accessed from schools, homes, offices, libraries, and many other places.

economically. Toward this end, some EU members in 2002 began using a common currency called the **euro** (YUR•oh).

Elsewhere, the North American Free Trade Agreement (NAFTA) created a free-trade area for Canada, the United States, and Mexico. The Asia Pacific Economic

CHAPTER 22   Building Today's World   **889**

Reading Support L1/ EL

Use **Vocabulary Activity 22–4** to review important terms in the section.

NATIONAL GEOGRAPHIC

HISTORY MAKERS

One result of the development of the Internet was the "dot-com" economy of the 1990s. A variety of companies doing business over the Internet earned millions of dollars for stock investors, although few companies ever turned a profit from their business operations. When their stock prices plunged in 2000, serious doubts were raised about the potential for profitability of the dot-com business model.

CONNECTING ACROSS TIME

The computer revolution of the 1980s and 1990s has been compared to the first Industrial Revolution of the late 1700s and 1800s. Have students compare the impact of each on society. How did each event transform the way people lived, worked, and thought? **L2**

Interviews Ask students to interview a community member about how the technology revolution in communications, health care and medicine, agriculture, or transportation has affected him or her personally. **L1**

DIFFERENTIATED INSTRUCTION

Kinesthetic: Have students prepare a showcase, table, or other display about globalization. Have them include in the display objects that represent the global economy.

English Learners: Ask foreign students to share with the class the effects of globalism on their countries of origin.

Gifted and Talented: Have students write a play on the theme of globalism, addressing both benefits and disadvantages of a global economy.

👉 Refer to *Inclusion Strategies for the Middle School Social Studies Classroom* in the TCR.

Writing Activity

Have students compose letters to the editor of your local newspaper describing what community members can do about one of the world problems that impacts your own community. Begin by brainstorming some local approaches to the problems, such as educating residents about conserving resources or lowering dangerous emissions. **L2**

✓ **Reading Check**

Answer: They became smaller and much faster. The development of inexpensive personal computers led to a wide range of computer use among individuals, families, and schools.

Caption Answer: computers, radios, televisions, and telephones

---

Cooperation (APEC) agreement has tried to do the same among nations that border the Pacific Ocean.

Global Challenges Globalism has boosted trade and led to more prosperity in many parts of the world. It also has made people aware of issues that affect the world as a whole. Problems often cannot be solved by one nation alone. Therefore, nations must work together to find solutions.

In recent years, people have become aware of dangers to the world's environment. For example, many people fear that the earth's resources will soon be unable to support a rapidly rising world population. **Deforestation,** the clearing of forests, is one result of population growth. Water and food shortages also trouble many people.

Air and water pollution concern many scientists. Most experts believe nations have to work together to fix these problems. In 1987 twenty-three nations, including the U.S., agreed to ban chemicals suspected of harming the ozone layer—a part of the atmosphere that shields Earth from the Sun's radiation.

Many scientists also think that the earth is getting warmer and are worried that this may be caused by pollution. The idea of global warming is very controversial. In 1997 thirty-eight nations signed the Kyoto Protocol promising to reduce pollution that might be causing global warming. By early 2005, enough nations had ratified the treaty to put it into effect.

Another global problem is **nuclear proliferation** (NOO•klee•uhr pruh•LIH•fuh•RAY•shuhn), or the spread of nuclear weapons. Nuclear weapons programs in countries such as **Iraq,** North Korea, Libya, Iran, India, and Pakistan have been the focus of world concern.

✓ **Reading Check** **Describe** How did computers change between the 1940s and the 1980s?

890   CHAPTER 22   Building Today's World

A Changing World

Main Idea Political and economic changes continued to affect key regions of the world at the close of the twentieth century.

Reading Focus What are some things you own that were made in Asia? Read to find out how several East Asian countries became economic powers.

As a global economy has spread, many political changes have taken place. East Asia's countries now play a growing role in world affairs, and the nations of Europe are moving toward unity. In the United States, a conservative political movement has shaped the role of government.

The Rise of East Asia Today, a group of nations and territories in East Asia have been nicknamed the "Asian Tigers." They include South Korea, Taiwan, Singapore, and the Chinese port of Hong Kong. Why are they called this name? Following Japan's example, these four "Tigers" have built strong, modern economies.

While economically successful, some of the "Asian Tigers" are crowded and polluted. Many people, like those pictured below in Taipei, Taiwan, wear masks to protect themselves from pollution. *What are some products manufactured in Taiwan?* ▼

CRITICAL THINKING ACTIVITY

Evaluating Ask students to draw up a list for determining if the United States's war on terror is succeeding. Remind them to look at both short-term (e.g., number of recent terror attacks in the United States) and long-term (eliminating conditions that lead to terrorism) success. Have them give the country's policies a grade and suggest changes to the nation's policies that may lead to better success. **L2**

In the 1990s, South Korea moved from military rule to democracy. Its high technology and manufacturing industries have grown tremendously. South Korea now exports ships, cars, computers, and electronic appliances.

The island of Taiwan lies off China's coast. Taiwan is still a part of China, but it has a different government. Many Taiwanese would like Taiwan to be independent, but China's Communist leaders want Taiwan to be under their rule. Now a democracy, Taiwan has a booming economy that produces computers, radios, televisions, and telephones.

The port of Hong Kong is also part of China. Despite Communist rule, Hong Kong has been allowed to keep its strong, free-enterprise economy. Another prosperous port is Singapore at the tip of the Malay Peninsula. Although small in size, Singapore has a highly productive economy.

The European Union

Europe today ranks as one of the major economic and cultural centers of the world. In forming the European Union, some European countries want to make their continent an economic superpower like the United States.

Britain, once ruler of a global empire, has struggled with economic problems. During the 1980s, Conservative Party rule under Margaret Thatcher led to economic reforms. Since the 1990s, Britain's economy has done much better. Under the Labour Party, headed by Tony Blair, the government has given more power to regions such as Scotland and Wales.

France chose a Socialist, François Mitterand, as its president in 1981. Under Mitterand, the government ran some industries and passed laws to help workers. Since then, the French have twice voted for a

NATIONAL GEOGRAPHIC
Expansion of the European Union

KEY
Original members, 1957
Additional members:
by 1973
by 1986
by 1995
by 2004

500 mi.
500 km
Lambert Azimuthal Equal-Area projection

Using Geography Skills

The European Union was formed to improve trade and to build European economies.
1. Which countries were the original members of the European Union?
2. What does the growth of the European Union suggest about its value to European states? Explain.

conservative leader, Jacques Chirac, to deal with economic problems.

Germany enjoys a healthy economy, but has had difficulty in joining its western and eastern parts under one government. One challenge has been to close the gap between the prosperous west and less well-off east.

Europe's Mediterranean countries also have undergone many changes. In Italy, political power has changed hands many times. Also, rivalry between the wealthy north and the poorer south has caused

CHAPTER 22   Building Today's World   **891**

CONNECTING ACROSS TIME

Have students review information about the empire of Charlemagne (Chapter 15) in the early Middle Ages. Have them compare the problems he faced in unifying a large part of Europe with those faced by the organizers of the European Union today. How are the tasks similar? How do they differ? **L2**

Using Technology Ask students to search the Internet for an article about the economy of one of the five European nations discussed in the text. The article should come from a source from within the country itself. Then have students discuss how the article may differ from one written in the United States. **L2**

Evaluating Ask students to brainstorm ways the United States could make everyday life safer. Then have students critique each idea, weighing the advantage of increased safety versus the loss of individual civil liberties the idea might cause. **L2**

Reading Support L1/ EL

Assign **Guided Reading Activity 22–4** to help students organize information in the section.

✓ Reading Check

Answer: South Korea, Taiwan, Singapore, and Hong Kong

▲ New York City's World Trade Center soon after terrorists crashed airliners into the buildings

political tensions. Elsewhere, Spain, Portugal, and Greece are now democracies. Once isolated from Europe, they are taking active roles in European affairs.

The United States During the 1980s and 1990s, conservative policies gained support in the United States. President Ronald Reagan lowered taxes, cut government rules, and decreased spending on social welfare. He also boosted spending on the military.

To pay for the spending, the federal government had to borrow money, and as a result, the federal debt—or the money the government owed to banks—greatly increased. George Bush, who followed Reagan as president, faced an economic downturn. He was defeated by Democrat **Bill Clinton** in 1992.

Clinton, a moderate Democrat, favored some conservative policies. Under Clinton, the budget was balanced, and the welfare system was changed. Then, in 2000, Republican **George W. Bush** was elected president. A conservative, Bush convinced Congress to pass large tax cuts and an education reform law.

✓ Reading Check **Identify** What are the "Asian Tigers"?

The War on Terror

Main Idea A devastating attack on September 11, 2001, focused the world's attention on terrorism.

Reading Focus Where were you when you heard about the attacks of 9/11? What did you think and feel? Read to learn how these attacks caused change all over the world.

In recent years, the world has seen the growth of terrorism. **Terrorism** is the use of violence against civilians to reach a political goal. Terrorists—either as individuals or groups—act on their own and are usually not part of a government. Their goal includes changing governments, and their attacks are aimed at civilians as well as soldiers.

Since World War II, many terrorist groups have operated worldwide. For example, the Irish Republican Army (IRA) has used terrorism in an attempt to force Britain to give up control of Northern Ireland. Italy's Red Brigades killed political leaders whom they blamed for an unjust society. State-sponsored terrorism is terrorism that is led or aided by national governments. Governments in countries such as Iraq, Iran, Syria, Cuba, **Afghanistan** (af•GA•nuh•STAN), and North Korea have helped terrorist groups.

Today, most terrorist acts against Americans have been carried out by groups from the Middle East. Strong feelings against the United States are based in part on American support for Israel. Many Muslims also feel that American and European cultures undermine Islamic values.

What Happened on 9/11? On September 11, 2001, the world saw a horrifying act of terrorism. Terrorists seized four American passenger planes. Two planes were deliberately crashed into New York City's World Trade Center. A third plane was flown into the Pentagon, the U.S. military

EXTENDING THE CONTENT

Responding to 9/11 As soon as they had recovered from the initial shock of the attacks, Americans began responding to the needs of victims and rescue workers. More than $1 billion was donated, and food, blankets, and other supplies were collected all across the nation. People stranded at the busy Atlanta airport when air travel was suspended received food and lodging. A marching band from Alabama flew to New York to play music for rescue workers. An 11-year-old in Massachusetts baked 1,500 cookies for firefighters and police officers. More than 300 rescue dogs traveled to Ground Zero with their handlers to search for victims.

headquarters. A fourth plane was seized, but the passengers heroically fought back. This plane crashed in Pennsylvania. The attacks killed nearly 3,000 people.

The terrorists were later found to be part of al-Qaeda (al•KY•duh), a terrorist group created by a Saudi Arabian named **Osama bin Laden** (oh•SAHM•uh bihn LAHD•uhn).

Who Is Osama bin Laden?
Al-Qaeda grew out of the Muslim struggle against the Soviets in Afghanistan. Osama bin Laden was one of the fighters there. Using his family's wealth, bin Laden formed al-Qaeda to recruit new fighters.

When the Soviets left Afghanistan, bin Laden decided that all Americans and Europeans should be pushed out of the Muslim world. Bin Laden then turned al-Qaeda into a terrorist group. His followers set off bombs at U.S. embassies in Kenya and Tanzania in 1998. They also attacked a U.S. Navy ship in Yemen in 2000.

After the 9/11 attacks, the United States declared war on terrorism. It first focused at Afghanistan. There, bin Laden and al-Qaeda hid out with the help of the militant Muslim government called the Taliban. The Taliban was defeated, and the United States helped set up a new Afghan government.

in a word . . .

"*Taliban*" is an Arabic word meaning "students." The Taliban, who ruled Afghanistan from 1996 to 2001, were originally organized as regional groups of radical Islamic students.

Using Geography Skills

Answers:
1. Kenya and Tanzania
2. the general public; to effect greater fear and public response

3 ASSESS

Assign Section 4 Review as homework or as an in-class activity.

Have students use the **Interactive Tutor Self-Assessment CD-ROM** to review the section.

Assessment L2

Assign **Section 4 Quiz** to assess mastery of the material found in the section.

Reading Support L1/ EL

Assign **Reading Essentials and Study Guide 22–4** to help students review section material.

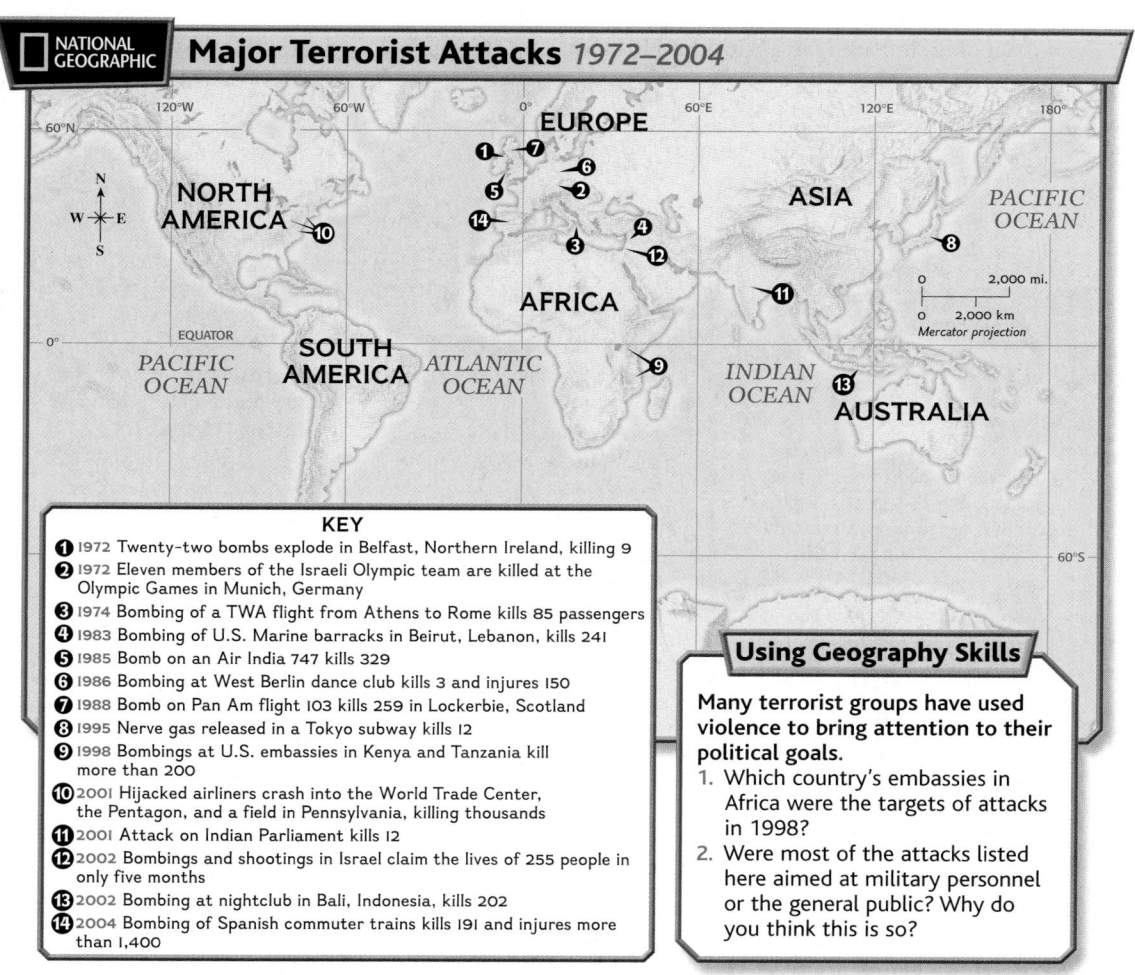

NATIONAL GEOGRAPHIC
Major Terrorist Attacks 1972–2004

KEY
1. 1972 Twenty-two bombs explode in Belfast, Northern Ireland, killing 9
2. 1972 Eleven members of the Israeli Olympic team are killed at the Olympic Games in Munich, Germany
3. 1974 Bombing of a TWA flight from Athens to Rome kills 85 passengers
4. 1983 Bombing of U.S. Marine barracks in Beirut, Lebanon, kills 241
5. 1985 Bomb on an Air India 747 kills 329
6. 1986 Bombing at West Berlin dance club kills 3 and injures 150
7. 1988 Bomb on Pan Am flight 103 kills 259 in Lockerbie, Scotland
8. 1995 Nerve gas released in a Tokyo subway kills 12
9. 1998 Bombings at U.S. embassies in Kenya and Tanzania kill more than 200
10. 2001 Hijacked airliners crash into the World Trade Center, the Pentagon, and a field in Pennsylvania, killing thousands
11. 2001 Attack on Indian Parliament kills 12
12. 2002 Bombings and shootings in Israel claim the lives of 255 people in only five months
13. 2002 Bombing at nightclub in Bali, Indonesia, kills 202
14. 2004 Bombing of Spanish commuter trains kills 191 and injures more than 1,400

Using Geography Skills

Many terrorist groups have used violence to bring attention to their political goals.
1. Which country's embassies in Africa were the targets of attacks in 1998?
2. Were most of the attacks listed here aimed at military personnel or the general public? Why do you think this is so?

COOPERATIVE LEARNING

Examining a Tiger Assign each of four groups of students one of the "Asian tigers" to research: Taiwan, South Korea, Singapore, and Hong Kong. Have each group determine the current economic situation and create a chart showing the different aspects of the economy. Suggest they include such elements as major companies, important products, import and export levels, rate of growth, and impact of development on citizens. Have them also address why their country has been successful, what setbacks it has overcome, and what challenges it may have to face in the future. **L3**

ENRICH

Have students read a primary and a secondary source about 9/11. Ask them to evaluate the strengths of each kind of source. **L3**

 Reading Check

Answer: Al-Qaeda grew out of the Muslim struggle against the Soviets in Afghanistan. The government of Afghansitan helped al-Qaeda hide in Afghanistan.

History Online

To help students understand section material, have them visit **Study Central**™ at jat.glencoe.com

RETEACH

Ask students to outline this section. Then have them exchange outlines and compare them. **L1**

④ CLOSE

 Reading Strategy

Ask students which of the challenges described in this section is the most important or urgent. Why? **L2**

The Invasion of Iraq In 2002, President George W. Bush turned his attention to countries that supported terrorism. He was also concerned about these countries producing **weapons of mass destruction** (WMD). These weapons include nuclear, chemical, and biological weapons that can kill tens of thousands of people at a time. The president feared these countries might give these weapons to terrorists.

Bush and some other world leaders believed that as long as Saddam Hussein stayed in power, Iraq would develop deadly weapons and support terrorists. In 2003, a coalition of countries led by the United States invaded Iraq. The Iraqi army was quickly defeated, and Saddam Hussein was captured.

For the United States and its partners, rebuilding Iraq was more difficult than defeating the Iraqi army. Saddam Hussein's supporters, foreign terrorists, and Islamic militants all battled coalition forces. These groups tried to defeat American efforts to rebuild Iraq's economy and create a democracy. In June 2004, the United States handed control of Iraq to a temporary Iraqi government. The new government began preparing Iraq for free elections.

To make it harder for terrorists to recruit followers, President Bush also announced plans to work for democracy in the Middle East. He also called for an independent Palestinian state in the region.

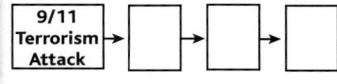 **Reading Check** **Explain** What was the connection between Afghanistan and al-Qaeda?

Section ④ Review

History Online

Study Central™ Need help with the material in this section? Visit jat.glencoe.com

Reading Summary

Review the Main Ideas

- The technology revolution has helped unite world economies, politics, and cultures. This globalism has led to new international organizations and problems.
- In the 1980s and 1990s, several Asian countries became economic powers, European nations created the EU, and the United States experienced changes in leadership and policy.
- A devastating act of terrorism occurred on September 11, 2001, in the United States and led to a worldwide war on terrorism.

What Did You Learn?

1. What are weapons of mass destruction?
2. Which nation did the "Asian Tigers" use as their economic model?

Critical Thinking

3. **Sequencing Information** Complete a diagram like the one below to show the events that occurred after the 9/11 terrorism attack.

9/11 Terrorism Attack → ☐ → ☐ → ☐

4. **Identify** What are some of the global problems nations are trying to address?
5. **Explain** What problems did the newly united Germany face?
6. **Analyze** Why is Taiwan's future uncertain?
7. **Expository Writing** Interview an adult to find out what technology was available when he or she was in school. Write an essay comparing technology back then to the technology available to your class today.

SECTION 4 REVIEW ANSWERS

1. nuclear, chemical, and biological weapons that can kill thousands of people at a time
2. Japan
3. U.S. declares war on terrorism; Taliban is defeated and a new Afghan government is set up; the U.S. goes to war with Iraq.
4. Possible answers include: deforestation, air and water pollution, global warming, nuclear proliferation.
5. closing the gap between the prosperous west and the less well-off east
6. They want to be independent, but China does not want to let them.
7. Interviews will vary.

Section 1 Challenges in Latin America

Vocabulary
export
embargo
nationalize

Focusing on the Main Ideas
• Latin America's economy has depended on exports and foreign investment. *(page 861)*
• In Central America, repressive governments, social conflict, and civil wars made progress difficult. *(page 863)*
• During the twentieth century, Mexico struggled to overcome economic, social, and political challenges. *(page 864)*
• Most South American countries have struggled to create fragile democracies and improve their economies. *(page 866)*

Section 2 Africa and the Middle East

Vocabulary
refugee
apartheid
intifada

Focusing on the Main Ideas
• The countries of Africa south of the Sahara faced many challenges in the late twentieth century. *(page 870)*
• Black South Africans won their freedom after years of hardship and struggle. *(page 872)*
• The creation of Israel in 1948 sparked a conflict that still exists today. *(page 874)*
• Political and social conflicts continue to keep the Middle East in turmoil. *(page 876)*

Section 3 The Cold War Ends

Vocabulary
détente
glasnost
perestroika
ethnic cleansing

Focusing on the Main Ideas
• After nearly 50 years of bitter rivalry with the United States, in the 1990s the Soviet Union and its Eastern European empire fell apart. *(page 881)*
• The fall of communism unleashed deadly ethnic hatreds in the Balkan nation of Yugoslavia. *(page 884)*
• China moved toward a free-market economy, but its leaders still opposed democratic reforms. *(page 885)*

Section 4 The World Enters a New Century

Vocabulary
globalism
euro
deforestation
nuclear proliferation
terrorism
weapons of mass destruction

Focusing on the Main Ideas
• Advances in technology have brought the world closer together economically, politically, and culturally. *(page 888)*
• Political and economic changes continued to affect key regions of the world at the close of the twentieth century. *(page 890)*
• A devastating attack on September 11, 2001, focused the world's attention on terrorism. *(page 892)*

PREVIEW/REVIEW

Vocabulary Activity Ask volunteers to use each of the vocabulary terms in a sentence. Challenge the students to use two terms in the same sentence.

🔘 **Vocabulary PuzzleMaker CD-ROM**

🔘 **Interactive Tutor Self-Assessment CD-ROM**

CONDENSE

📁 Chapter 22 **Guided Reading Activities**

💿 **StudentWorks Plus™ CD-ROM (with Audio Program)**

RETEACH

📁 **Differentiated Instruction Activity 22**

📁 Chapter 22 *Reading Essentials and Study Guide*

CHAPTER CULMINATING ACTIVITY

Have students finish the Chapter Culminating Activity from page 856D.

Suggestions for rubrics may be found in the *Quizzes, Tests, and Authentic Assessments (with Rubrics)* booklet.

Reading Strategy   READ TO WRITE

Taking a Position Ask students to agree or disagree with the following statement and support their position with reasoning and evidence: The trend of world events over the last 50 years has been in the direction of greater freedom and democracy.

• **L1** students should include one or two reasons and details in their position statement.
• **L2** students should include several valid reasons and details and attempt grammar mastery.
• **L3** students should write logical, detailed, well-considered position statements that provide support for their opinion.

Chapter 22 Assessment and Activities

Review Vocabulary

1. d   **4.** e

2. b   **5.** c

3. a

Review Main Ideas

6. the United States

7. There were repressive rulers and constant conflicts.

8. Civil war, drought, famine, and poor medical care were all challenges to Africa south of the Sahara.

9. Some countries are rich and have oil; others lack resources. As population grows, there are more and more demands on limited resources. Demand for water often leads to conflict as well.

10. In the 1990s, China gained back territories it lost to Europeans in the 1800s.

11. The fall of the Berlin Wall, the revolutions in Eastern Europe, and the failed military coup and subsequent fall of the Soviet Union in 1991 brought an end to the Cold War.

12. Through computers and the Internet, global communication has become almost instant.

13. the September 11, 2001, terrorist attacks against the United States

Review Vocabulary

Match the word in the first column with its definition in the second column.

___ 1. nationalize   **a.** forced removal of an ethnic group

___ 2. embargo   **b.** government prevention of trade

___ 3. ethnic cleansing **c.** violence against civilians to achieve a goal

___ 4. détente   **d.** to put under government control

___ 5. terrorism   **e.** relaxation of tensions

Review Main Ideas

Section 1 • Challenges in Latin America

6. Which nation influenced the development of Latin America in the 1900s?

7. What prevented economic progress in Central America?

Review Reading Skill — Extending the Text

Reading Beyond the Text

17. The Internet is a good source of information if you know how to narrow your search. List five guide words that you would use to search for more information about each of the topics listed below.

    a. the leader of China in 1950

    b. the role of apartheid in South African history

    c. the invention of the first computer

    d. the number of people who died in the Persian Gulf War compared to the number of people who died in the Vietnam War

To review this skill, see pages 858–859.

Section 2 • Africa and the Middle East

8. What challenged the countries of Africa south of the Sahara in the late 1900s?

9. Why is the Middle East one of the world's most dangerous regions?

Section 3 • The Cold War Ends

10. What was unique about China's progress in the late 1900s?

11. When and how did the Cold War end?

Section 4 • The World Enters a New Century

12. In what ways has technology brought the world closer together?

13. What event focused the world's attention on terrorism?

Critical Thinking

14. Identify How and when were West and East Germany reunited?

15. Contrast How were the policies of and support for Mexican leaders Porfirio Díaz and Lázaro Cárdenas different?

16. Explain What happened during the Six-Day War?

Critical Thinking

14. Western and Eastern Germany were reunited after the fall of the Berlin Wall in 1989.

15. Díaz was a dictator who encouraged foreign investment in Mexican businesses. Peasants and workers suffered under his rule. Cárdenas was the president of Mexico who gave land to peasants and nationalized Mexico's oil industry. Most Mexicans saw his reforms as positive changes.

16. Israel bombed Egypt and moved troops into the Gaza Strip, the Golan Heights, and the West Bank. These events led to the formation of the PLO and the subsequent fighting between the two groups.

Geography Skills

Study the map below and answer the following questions.

18. **Place** List the countries that formed after the breakup of Yugoslavia.

19. **Location** Which country has the most access to the Adriatic Sea?

20. **Movement** Why do you think that three of the capitals of former Yugoslavian countries are located on rivers?

NATIONAL GEOGRAPHIC
Breakup of Yugoslavia

AUSTRIA
HUNGARY
Ljubljana
SLOVENIA Zagreb
CROATIA
ROMANIA
Belgrade
BOSNIA &
HERZEGOVINA
Sarajevo
SERBIA &
MONTENEGRO
BULGARIA
Adriatic Sea
ITALY
Skopje
MACEDONIA
ALBANIA
GREECE

0 100 mi.
0 100 km
Lambert Azimuthal
Equal-Area projection

KEY
— Boundary of former Yugoslavia, 1991

Read to Write

21. **Descriptive Writing** Select three of the many challenges facing the world today. Write a brief essay about how these three challenges could affect your life and how you could help resolve these challenges.

22. **Using Your FOLDABLES** Work with a partner to create an outline map of the world on poster board. Indicate on your map the locations of each event and the development you recorded in your foldable.

Using Technology

23. **Create a Display** Use the Internet and other media to find information about the latest technological advances. Create a bulletin board using the information you found. Label and describe the new technology.

History Online
Self-Check Quiz To help you prepare for the Chapter Test, visit jat.glencoe.com

Linking Past and Present

24. **Evaluate** In 1994 power passed peacefully from the white minority government of South Africa to a multiracial government that includes black South Africans. How might that process serve as a model for solving problems in other countries?

Building Citizenship Skills

25. **Analyze** During the 1970s and 1980s, many Latin American nations were affected by civil war and internal conflicts. These wars were often in response to an unfair and unjust government. The United States supported many movements within these nations in order to overthrow dictators who had wrongfully taken power. It was necessary for the United States to aid those fighting against their governments in order to maintain or establish strong democratic values in the country. In what ways do people in the United States fight for what is right and protect democracy?

Primary Source Analyze

Czech leader Václav Havel spoke at the 1993 Council of Europe Summit about European unity.

"I think that all of us . . . can agree that the common basis of any effort to integrate Europe should be the wealth of values and ideals we share. Among them are respect for the uniqueness and the freedom of each human being, for a democratic . . . political system, for a market economy, and for the principles of civil society and the rule of law."

—Václav Havel, "The Council of Europe Summit: Vienna, October 8, 1993"

DBQ Document-Based Questions

26. What does Havel identify as the common basis for European unity?

27. What do you think Havel means by "principles of civil society"?

History Online

Have students visit the Web site at jat.glencoe.com to review Chapter 22 and take the Self-Check Quiz.

Read to Write

21. Essays will vary.

22. **FOLDABLES** Student maps should list events from the chapter.

Using Technology

23. Bulletin boards will vary.

Linking Past and Present

24. Student responses will vary but should note how South Africa passed power peacefully and what other countries would have to do to follow that model.

25. Answers will vary.

Primary Source

26. the wealth of values and ideals Europeans share

27. He is referring to the principles of European societies.

Bonus Question

Ask: Which world problem described in this chapter affects you personally the most? Why? (Students' answers should be supported by material in the section.)

Reading Skill

17. Possible answers include a.: Chinese leaders, China in 1950, Mao, Communist leaders, Communist countries; b.: apartheid, South Africa, Nelson Mandela, Thabo Mbeki, African National Congress; c.: the first computer, early computers, major technological advances, 20th century technology, history of computers; d.: the Persian Gulf War, deaths in the Persian Gulf War, military death numbers, battle dead in Persian Gulf War, number of American soldier deaths

Geography Skills

18. Slovenia, Croatia, Bosnia-Herzegovina, Macedonia

19. Croatia

20. For transportation and clean water

Unit 6 Review

REVIEWING UNIT OBJECTIVES

Having studied this unit, students should now be able to:

1. describe the rise of industry and the increase in nationalism around 1800;

2. describe how imperialistic competition between nations led to World War I;

3. explain the reasons for the outbreak of World War II and how it led to the Cold War;

4. identify the problems facing the world today.

UNIT REVIEW ACTIVITY

Analyzing World Changes Have students use the **Comparing Modern Civilizations** chart to review the unit objectives. Ask them to use the chart, as well as information from the text, to write short answers to these questions:

• In which period did the most important technological progress take place? Why?

• How did what people believed influence how they acted? What are some examples?

• In what ways did life for most people get better as time passed? How did it get worse?

• In which period were the greatest contributions made? Give reasons for your answers. **L2**

Comparing Modern Civilizations

Compare modern civilizations by reviewing the information below. Can you see how the people of these civilizations had lives that were very much like yours?

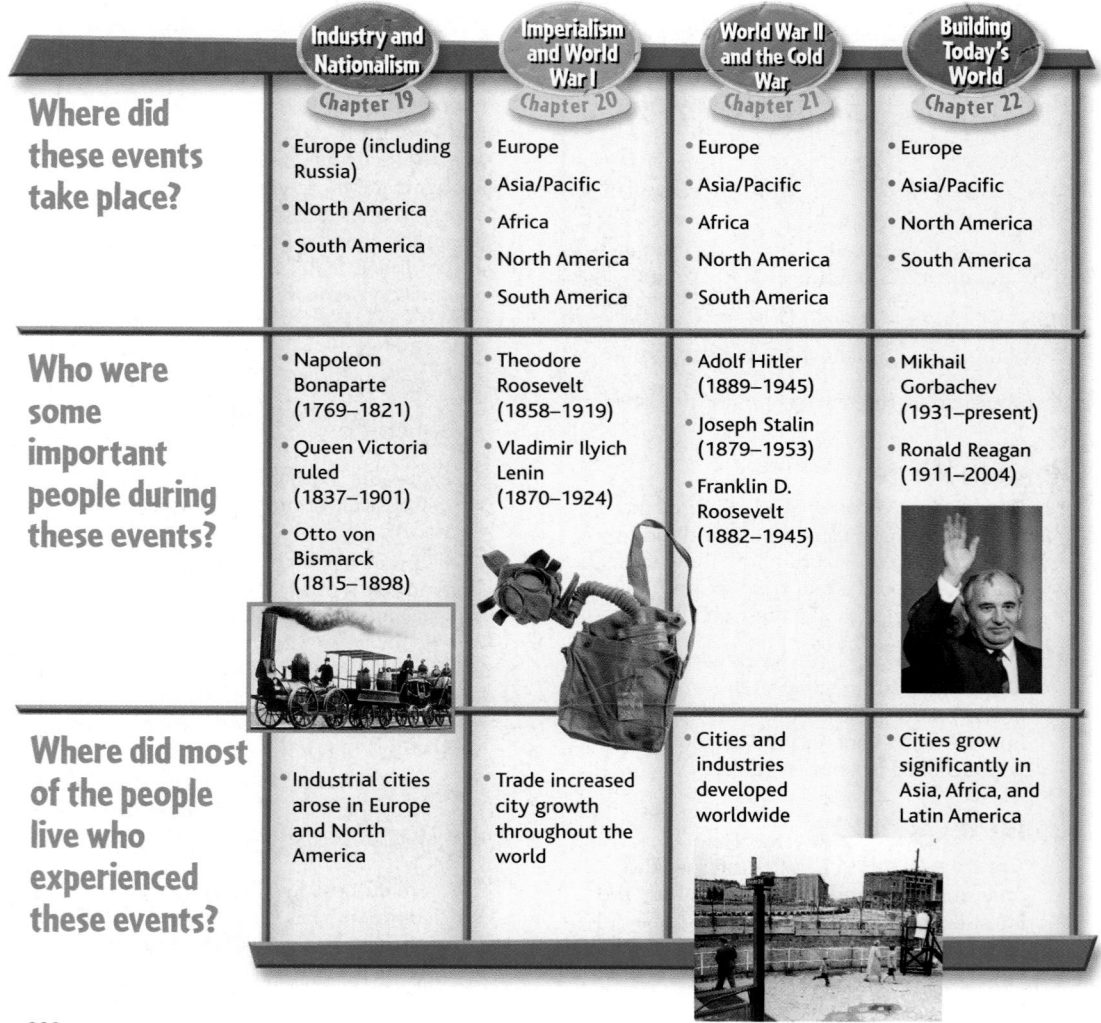

	Industry and Nationalism Chapter 19	Imperialism and World War I Chapter 20	World War II and the Cold War Chapter 21	Building Today's World Chapter 22
Where did these events take place?	• Europe (including Russia) • North America • South America	• Europe • Asia/Pacific • Africa • North America • South America	• Europe • Asia/Pacific • Africa • North America • South America	• Europe • Asia/Pacific • North America • South America
Who were some important people during these events?	• Napoleon Bonaparte (1769–1821) • Queen Victoria ruled (1837–1901) • Otto von Bismarck (1815–1898)	• Theodore Roosevelt (1858–1919) • Vladimir Ilyich Lenin (1870–1924)	• Adolf Hitler (1889–1945) • Joseph Stalin (1879–1953) • Franklin D. Roosevelt (1882–1945)	• Mikhail Gorbachev (1931–present) • Ronald Reagan (1911–2004)
Where did most of the people live who experienced these events?	• Industrial cities arose in Europe and North America	• Trade increased city growth throughout the world	• Cities and industries developed worldwide	• Cities grow significantly in Asia, Africa, and Latin America

END-OF-UNIT RESOURCES

Reproducible Masters
• Unit 6 Test Form A
• Unit 6 Test Form B
• Step Into World History Activity 6

Transparencies
• Unit 6 Map Overlay Transparencies

Multimedia
 Interactive Tutor Self-Assessment CD-ROM
ExamView® Pro Testmaker CD-ROM
Presentation Plus! CD-ROM

	Industry and Nationalism Chapter 19	Imperialism and World War I Chapter 20	World War II and the Cold War Chapter 21	Building Today's World Chapter 22
What were people's beliefs at this time?	• Scientific ideas challenged religious traditions	• Western missionaries spread Christianity	• Islam, Hinduism, and Buddhism influenced new nations	• Christianity remains strong in the Americas • Islam, Hinduism, and Buddhism influence the West
What were governments like at this time?	• Republics largely in the Americas • Monarchies in the rest of the world	• Western powers set up colonies in Africa and Asia • World War I: republics replaced monarchies	• World War II: democracies and Communist USSR fought Fascist dictators • Cold War: struggle between democracy and communism	• Communism ended in Europe • Democracy spreads, but dictators continue to rule in many places
What were world languages like during these events?	• Language was linked to pride in one's nation or group	• European languages spread to overseas colonies	• English became a major global language	• Global culture—different languages mix and borrow from each other
What changes took place during this time?	• Constitutional governments are formed • Variety of machine-made goods appeared	• Ideas, goods, and people moved from place to place	• Vote given to women and other groups	• Respect for human rights increases • Living standards improve
How do these changes affect me? *Can you add any?*	• Public-supported schools are founded • Organized sports developed • Automobiles and telephones are invented	• U.S. becomes active in world affairs • Airplane invented	• Radio, movies, and television introduced • U.S. highway network built	• Internet, personal computers, and cellular phones are widely used

899

UNIT WRAP-UP ACTIVITY

Predicting Consequences This unit ends with the world today. Students have seen how events in the past have led to consequences. They have studied wise decisions and dreadful miscalculations by important historical figures. In this activity, they will make predictions about recent events and decisions.

1. Organize the class into five groups. Each group will work together to come up with a list of predictions about a specific topic. Ask students to use the textbook and other resources to make their predictions. Remind them to base their predictions on evidence and analysis of past events.

2. Ask students to make predictions about: (a) the future of the war on terrorism and relations between nations in the Middle East and the West; (b) Latin America's hopes for greater democracy and prosperity; (c) how the former Soviet Union and its satellites will fare economically and socially in the 2000s; (d) China and East Asia as sleeping economic and political giants; and (e) Africa's future—full of hope or fear?

3. Have the groups prepare a report featuring their set of predictions. Discuss the issues raised by the presentations. **L2**

PROFESSIONAL DEVELOPMENT: NOTE TAKING

- Lim, Phyllis and William Smalzer. *Noteworthy: Listening and Notetaking Skills*. Stamford, 1996.
- Kesselman-Turkel, Judi and Franklynn Peterson. *Note-taking Made Easy.* University of Wisconsin, 2003.
- Fry, Ron. *Get Organized*. Delmar, 2000.
- Power, Brenda Miller. *Taking Note: Improving Your Observational Notetaking*. Stenhouse, 1996.

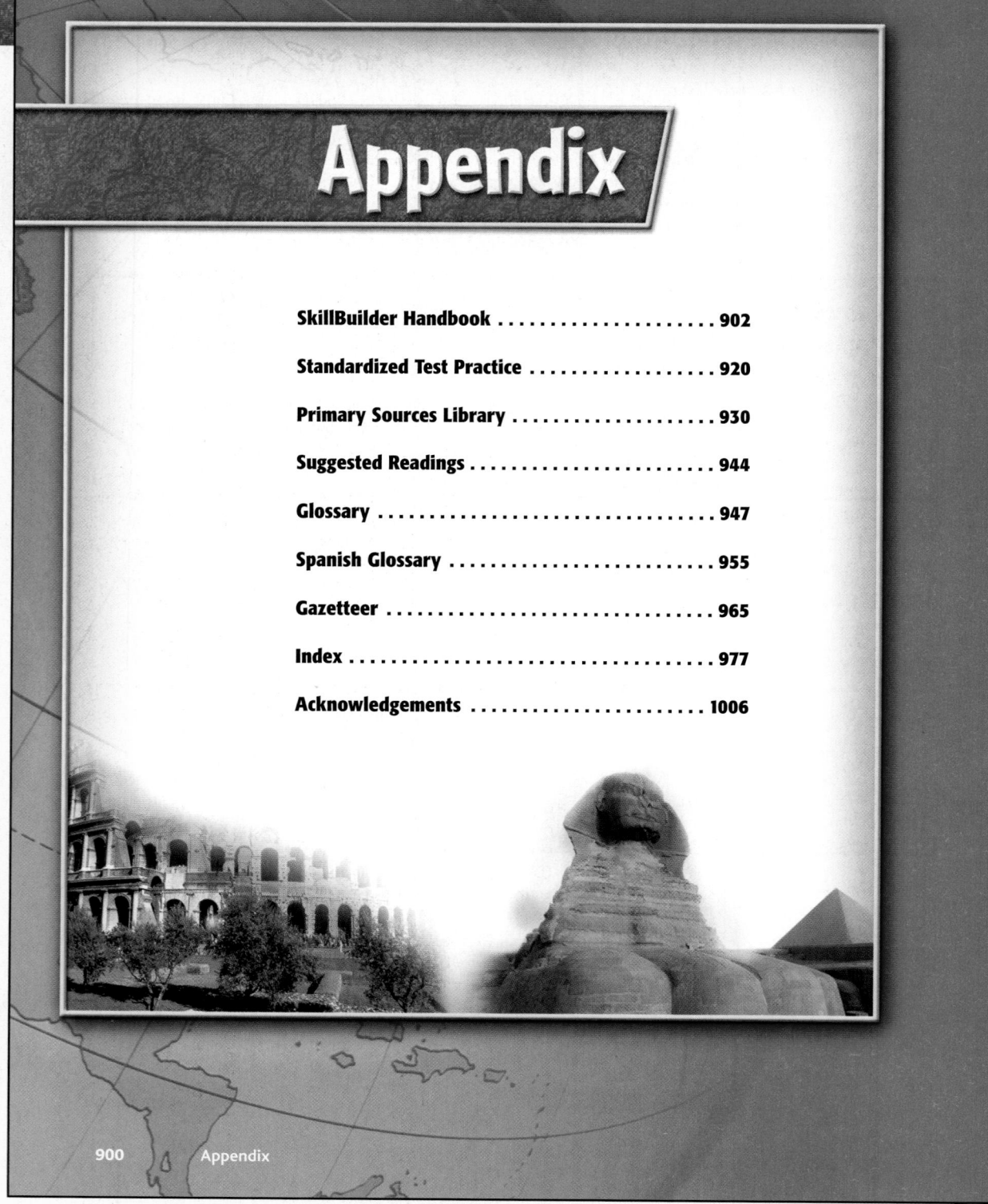

Appendix

What Is an Appendix?

An appendix is the additional material you often find at the end of books. The following information will help you learn how to use the Appendix in **Journey Across Time.**

SkillBuilder Handbook

The **SkillBuilder Handbook** offers you information and practice using critical thinking and social studies skills. Mastering these skills will help you in all your courses.

Standardized Test Preparation

The skills you need to do well on standardized tests are practiced in the **Standardized Test Practice** section of this Appendix.

Primary Sources Library

The **Primary Sources Library** provides additional first-person accounts of historical events. Primary sources are often narratives by a person who actually experienced what is being described.

Suggested Readings

The **Suggested Readings** list suggests the titles of fiction and non-fiction books you might be interested in reading. These books deal with the same topics that are covered in each chapter.

Glossary

The **Glossary** is a list of important or difficult terms found in a textbook. Since words sometimes have other meanings, you may wish to consult a dictionary to find other uses for the term. The glossary gives a definition of each term as it is used in the book. The glossary also includes page numbers telling you where in the textbook the term is used.

The Spanish Glossary

The **Spanish Glossary** contains everything that an English glossary does, but it is written in Spanish. A Spanish glossary is especially important to bilingual students, or those Spanish-speaking students who are learning the English language.

Gazetteer

The **Gazetteer** (GA•zuh•TIHR) is a geographical dictionary. It lists some of the world's largest countries, cities, and several important geographic features. Each entry also includes a page number telling where this place is talked about in your textbook.

Index

The **Index** is an alphabetical listing that includes the subjects of the book and the page numbers where those subjects can be found. The index in this book also lets you know that certain pages contain maps, graphs, photos, or paintings about the subject.

Acknowledgements and Photo Credits

This section lists photo credits and/or literary credits for the book. You can look at this section to find out where the publisher obtained the permission to use a photograph or to use excerpts from other books.

Test Yourself

Find the answers to these questions by using the Appendix on the following pages.

1. What does *dynasty* mean?
2. What is the topic of the first Unit 3 Primary Source reading?
3. On what page can I find out about Julius Caesar?
4. Where exactly is Rome located?
5. What is one of the Suggested Readings for Unit 3?

Have students complete the **Test Yourself** questions on page 901. As students answer the questions, have them identify where in the Appendix they found the answers.

Have students write on a sheet of paper five questions similar to those on page 901, with the answers written on the back of the paper. Have students exchange their questions with another student. Students should answer the questions using the Appendix and identify where they found each answer.

Have students review different books to see what other types of information can be placed in an Appendix. Have students use the Appendix throughout their study of the textbook.

TEST YOURSELF ANSWERS

1. A dynasty is a line of rulers from the same family
2. **A Woman on the Throne** is about how Emperor Alexius I turned the government of the Byzantine Empire over to his mother, Anna Dalassena.
3. Information on Julius Caesar can be found on pages 280–282, 284–285.
4. Rome, the capital of Italy, is located at 41°N 12°E.
5. Answers should match readings from the Suggested Readings list for Unit 3.

Introduction

The following **SkillBuilder Handbook** offers practice of individual critical thinking skills and research skills. Students can benefit in several ways from completing the lessons. First, being equipped with these skills makes students' reading more meaningful and supports the content of the text. Second, the lessons give students practice in using skills they will need to successfully complete the section and chapter assessments included in the text. Finally, the lessons help prepare students for standardized test taking since many of these skills are assessed on standardized tests.

The lessons are written to be used at any point in the text and in any order you choose. They also can be revisited as review lessons for students who need extra practice.

SkillBuilder Handbook

Contents

Finding the Main Idea

Why Learn This Skill?

Understanding the main idea allows you to grasp the whole picture and get an overall understanding of what you are reading. Historical details, such as names, dates, and events, are easier to remember when they are connected to a main idea.

1 Learning the Skill

Follow these steps when trying to find the main idea:

- Read the material and ask, "Why was this written? What is its purpose?"

- Read the first sentence of the first paragraph. The main idea of a paragraph is often found in the topic sentence. The main idea of a large section of text is often found in a topic paragraph.

- Identify details that support the main ideas.

- Keep the main idea clearly in your mind as you read.

2 Practicing the Skill

Read the paragraph at the top of the next column that describes how the culture of the world is changing. Answer the questions, and then complete the activity that follows. If you have trouble, use the graphic organizer to help you.

Cultural diffusion has increased as a result of technology. Cultural diffusion is the process by which a culture spreads its knowledge and skills from one area to another. Years ago, trade—the way people shared goods and ideas—resulted in cultural diffusion. Today communication technology, such as television and the Internet, links people throughout the world.

1. What is the main idea of this paragraph?
2. What are some details that support that main idea?
3. Do you agree or disagree with the main idea presented above? Explain.
4. Practice the skill by reading three paragraphs in your textbook and identifying their main ideas.

3 Applying the Skill

Bring a newspaper or magazine to class. With a partner, identify the main ideas in three different articles. Then describe how other sentences or paragraphs in the article support the main idea.

TEACH

Finding the Main Idea Help students to understand that the main idea of a paragraph is the single most important idea. Details are finer points that offer more information about the main idea. Have students look again at the paragraph under **Practicing the Skill.** **Ask: What are some other kinds of details the writer could have included that would provide more support for the main idea of the paragraph?** *(examples of ways these technologies have increased cultural diffusion, more types of technologies)* **L1**

GLENCOE TECHNOLOGY

Glencoe Skillbuilder Interactive Workbook CD-ROM, Level 1

This interactive CD-ROM reinforces student mastery of essential social studies skills.

PRACTICING THE SKILL ANSWERS

1. The process of cultural diffusion has increased because of changes in technology.

2. Technologies such as TV and the Internet link people throughout the world; to some extent, these new technologies have replaced trade as the main instrument of cultural diffusion.

3. Students should begin by identifying the topic sentence of each paragraph they chose, then look for details as a way of determining the main idea.

4. Most students will agree, citing the widespread influence of the new technologies in most parts of the world.

Applying the Skill Students' analyses of their articles should follow the basic process described on this page.

TEACH

Taking Notes and Outlining Before having students read the skill page, ask a student to present a short oral report on a topic discussed in Chapter 2, "Ancient Egypt." Ask students to write down the most important points of the oral presentation. Then have volunteers share what they have written.

Tell students that they should have noted the topic of the oral report. Under that, they should have listed important points. Remind them that the first sentence of an oral report, like the topic sentence of a paragraph, usually states the topic. Details that support the topic follow. Remind students that, when taking notes, only the most important details should be recorded. **L2**

Taking Notes and Outlining

Why Learn This Skill?

If you asked someone for his or her phone number or e-mail address, how would you best remember it? Most people would write it down. Making a note of it helps you remember. The same is true for remembering what you read in a textbook.

1 Learning the Skill

Taking notes as you read your textbook will help you remember the information. As you read, identify and summarize the main ideas and details and write them in your notes. Do not copy material directly from the text.

Using note cards—that you can reorder later—can also help. First write the main topic or main idea at the top of the note card. Then write the details that support or describe that topic. Number the cards to help you keep them in order.

```
Schools in the Middle Ages        ③
• Catholic church set up
cathedral schools.

• Only sons of nobles could go
to these schools.
```

You also may find it helpful to use an outline when writing notes. Outlining can help you organize your notes in a clear and orderly way.

First read the material to identify the main ideas. In this textbook, section headings and subheadings provide clues to the main ideas. Supporting details can then be placed under each heading. Each level of an outline must contain at least two items. The basic pattern for outlines is as follows:

Main Topic
  I. First idea or item
  II. Second idea or item
    A. first detail
    B. second detail
      1. subdetail
      2. subdetail
  III. Third idea or item
    A. first detail
    B. second detail

2 Practicing the Skill

Look back at Chapter 2, Section 1. Outline the main ideas of the section as shown above.

3 Applying the Skill

Use the outline that you created in step 2 to write a paragraph with a main idea and at least three supporting details.

PRACTICING THE SKILL ANSWER

Students' outlines should reflect the information highlighted by the section headings and subheadings in the text about the Nile Valley.

Applying the Skill Students' paragraphs should accurately use the information outlined from Chapter 2, Section 1.

Reading a Time Line

Why Learn This Skill?

Have you ever had to remember events and their dates in the order in which they happened? A time line is an easy way to make sense of the flow of dates and events. It is a simple diagram that shows how dates and events relate to one another. On most time lines, years are evenly spaced. Events on time lines are placed beside the date they occurred.

1 Learning the Skill

To read a time line, follow these steps:

- Find the dates on the opposite ends of the time line. They show the period of time that the time line covers.

- Note the equal spacing between dates on the time line.

- Study the order of events.

- Look to see how the events relate to each other.

2 Practicing the Skill

Examine the time line below. It shows major events in the history of early Egypt. Then answer the questions and complete the activity that follows.

1. When does the time line begin? When does it end?
2. What major event happened around 1550 B.C.?
3. How long did the Hyksos rule Egypt?
4. What happened to Egypt around 1670 B.C.?

3 Applying the Skill

List 10 key events found in Unit 1 and the dates on which these events took place. Write the events in the order in which they occurred on a time line.

Ancient Egypt

SkillBuilder Handbook

TEACH

Reading a Time Line To gain practice in placing dates on a time line, ask students to make a personal time line of events with which they are familiar. They might want to choose this school or calendar year, a sports team's current or past season, the events of a movie, or another defined chronological period. Review the characteristics of a time line discussed on this page. Remind students that the scale of the time line will need to be adjusted based on the time period they choose to represent. They may have to calibrate it by months or even days or hours. Ask volunteers to reproduce their time lines on the board. **L2**

GLENCOE TECHNOLOGY

Glencoe Skillbuilder Interactive Workbook CD-ROM, Level 1

This interactive CD-ROM reinforces student mastery of essential social studies skills.

PRACTICING THE SKILL ANSWERS

1. 3100 B.C.; A.D. 1500
2. The Hyksos are overthrown.
3. about 250 years
4. It became part of the Greek Empire.

Applying the Skill Events students choose should be accurately dated, placed in proper order, and focus on the topic *Early Civilizations*. The time line should also be correctly dated for the events chosen.

TEACH

Sequencing and Categorizing Information To show the importance of proper sequencing, write the following three steps on the board:

- Put two slices of bread together.
- Spread peanut butter on one slice.
- Spread jelly on the other slice.

Ask students to explain the problem with this sequence. *(The slices should not be put together until the peanut butter and jelly are spread on them.)*

To help explain categorizing, ask students to categorize their favorite musical groups and singers. Suggest that they include such categories as pop, rock, rap, jazz, country, and others. Point out that some performers may fit into more than one category and that the same is true when categorizing historical information. **L1**

Sequencing and Categorizing Information

Why Learn This Skill?

Sequencing means placing facts in the order in which they happened. *Categorizing* means organizing information into groups of related facts and ideas. Both actions help you deal with large quantities of information in an understandable way.

1 Learning the Skill

Follow these steps to learn sequencing and categorizing skills:

- Look for dates or clue words that provide you with a chronological order: *in 2004, the late 1990s, first, then, finally, after the Great Depression,* and so on.

- Sequencing can be seen in unit and chapter time lines or on graphs where information covers several years.

- If the sequence of events is not important, you may want to categorize the information instead. To categorize information, look for topics and facts that are grouped together or have similar characteristics. If the information is about farming, one category might be *tools of farming.*

- List these categories, or characteristics, as the headings on a chart.

- As you read, look for details. Fill in these details under the proper categories on the chart.

2 Practicing the Skill

Read the paragraph below and then answer the questions that follow.

Buddhism started in India about 500 B.C. but was mostly driven out by 300 B.C. The religion of Islam also influenced India's history. In the A.D. 700s, Muslims from southwest Asia brought Islam to India. In the 1500s, they founded the Mogul empire and ruled India for the next 200 years.

1. What information can be organized by sequencing?
2. What categories can you use to organize the information? What facts could be placed under each category?

3 Applying the Skill

Look at the Geographic Dictionary on pages GH14 and GH15. Record any terms that would fit into the category "bodies of water." Also, find two newspaper or magazine articles about an important local issue. Sequence or categorize the information on note cards or in a chart.

PRACTICING THE SKILL ANSWERS

1. the order in which the dated events happened
2. Information could be sorted by religion: *Buddhism* (started in India about 500 B.C.; was mostly driven out by 300 B.C.) and *Islam* (brought to India by Muslims from southwest Asia in A.D. 700s; Muslims founded the Mogul empire and ruled India from about A.D. 1500 to 1700).

Applying the Skill Bodies of water such as the following should be listed: ocean, sea, bay, gulf, river, sound, channel, mouth, strait, tributary, and lake; for the newspaper articles, sequencing and categorizing should be accurate and appropriate.

Recognizing Point of View

Why Learn This Skill?

If you say, "Cats make better pets than dogs," you are expressing a point of view. You are giving your personal opinion. Knowing when someone is giving his or her personal point of view can help you judge the truth of what is being said.

1 Learning the Skill

Most people have feelings and ideas that affect their point of view. A person's point of view is often influenced by his or her age, background, or position in a situation.

To recognize point of view, follow these steps:

- Identify the speaker or writer and examine his or her views on an issue. Think about his or her position in life and relationship to the issue.

- Look for language that shows an emotion or an opinion. Look for words such as *all, never, best, worst, might,* or *should.*

- Examine the speech or writing for imbalances. Does it have only one viewpoint? Does it fail to provide equal coverage of other viewpoints?

- Identify statements of fact. Factual statements usually answer the *Who? What? When?* and *Where?* questions.

- Determine how the person's point of view is reflected in his or her statements or writing.

2 Practicing the Skill

Read the following statement about wildlife in Africa, and answer the questions below.

> Mountain gorillas live in the misty mountain forests of East Africa. Logging and mining, however, are destroying the forests. Unless the forests are protected, all of the gorillas will lose their homes and disappear forever. As a concerned African naturalist, I must emphasize that this will be one of the worst events in Africa's history.

1. What problem is the speaker addressing?
2. What reasons does the speaker give for the loss of the forests?
3. What is the speaker's point of view about the problem facing the gorillas in East Africa?

3 Applying the Skill

Choose a "Letter to the Editor" from a newspaper. Summarize the issue being discussed and the writer's point of view about that issue. State what an opposing point of view to the issue might be. Describe who might hold this other viewpoint in terms of their age, occupation, and background.

SkillBuilder Handbook

TEACH

Recognizing Point of View
Distribute copies of two reviews of the same movie, book, television show, or music CD. After students have read both, ask them what the reviews reveal about the two critics' different points of view. Have them identify words and sentences that reveal the writers' points of view. Then have students read the skills lesson and complete the practice questions and activity. **L1**

GLENCOE TECHNOLOGY

 Glencoe Skillbuilder Interactive Workbook CD-ROM, Level 1

This interactive CD-ROM reinforces student mastery of essential social studies skills.

PRACTICING THE SKILL ANSWERS

1. the destruction of the gorillas' forest habitat
2. Logging and mining are destroying the forests.
3. He or she is very troubled by it.

Applying the Skill Summaries and analyses of point of view should accurately reflect the letters chosen.

TEACH

Distinguishing Fact From Opinion

Point out that students are confronted with facts and opinions every day in the media. Remind them to watch out for key clue words, as they will read about on this page. Ask where they would look for opinions. *(editorial pages of newspapers, signed columns in magazines, web logs on the Internet, movie and book reviews)* Where would they look for facts? Remind them that facts are things that can be measured or tied to specific data. *(news and sports stories, weather reports of the previous day, stock market reports)* Ask students to bring to class examples of both facts and opinions from media sources of their choosing. Have students check each other's samples to see if facts and opinions are correctly identified and key words underlined.
L2

Distinguishing Fact From Opinion

Why Learn This Skill?

Suppose a friend says, "Our school's basketball team is awesome. That's a fact." Actually, it is not a fact; it is an opinion. Knowing how to tell the difference between a fact and an opinion can help you analyze the accuracy of political claims, advertisements, and many other kinds of statements.

1 Learning the Skill

A **fact** answers a specific question such as: What happened? Who did it? When and where did it happen? Why did it happen? Statements of fact can be checked for accuracy and proven.

An **opinion,** on the other hand, expresses beliefs, feelings, and judgments. It may reflect someone's thoughts, but it cannot be proven. An opinion often begins with a phrase such as *I believe, I think, probably, it seems to me,* or *in my opinion.*

To distinguish between facts and opinions, ask yourself these questions:

- Does this statement give specific information about an event?
- Can I check the accuracy of this statement?
- Does this statement express someone's feelings, beliefs, or judgment?
- Does it include phrases such as *I believe,* superlatives, or judgment words?

2 Practicing the Skill

Read each statement below. Tell whether each is a fact or an opinion, and explain how you arrived at your answer.

(1) The Han dynasty ruled China from 202 B.C. to A.D. 220.

(2) The Han dynasty was a much better dynasty than the Qin dynasty.

(3) The Han divided the country into districts to be better able to manage such a large area.

(4) The government should not have encouraged support for arts and inventions.

(5) The Han kept very good records of everything they did, which helps historians today learn about them.

(6) Han rulers chose government officials on the basis of merit rather than birth.

(7) No other ruling family in the world can compare with the Han dynasty of China.

(8) Han rulers should have defended the poor farmers against the harsh actions of wealthy landowners.

3 Applying the Skill

Read one newspaper article that describes a political event. Find three statements of fact and three opinions expressed in the article.

PRACTICING THE SKILL ANSWERS

1. fact; dates
2. opinion; judgment words *much better*
3. fact; a recorded detail
4. opinion, judgment words *should not*
5. includes facts and opinions; *very good* is not measurable, but that they kept records that help historians today is a fact
6. fact; a recorded detail
7. opinion; cannot be measured
8. opinion; judgment words *should have, harsh*

Applying the Skill Remind students to refer to the methods listed on this page for distinguishing between facts and opinions, including the use of phrases such as *I believe* and superlatives.

Analyzing Library and Research Resources

Why Learn This Skill?

Imagine that your teacher has sent you to the library to write a report on the history of ancient Rome. Knowing how to choose good sources for your research will help you save time in the library and write a better report.

1 Learning the Skill

Not all sources will be useful for your report on Rome. Even some sources that involve topics about Rome will not always provide the information you want. In analyzing sources for your research project, choose items that are nonfiction and that contain the most information about your topic.

When choosing research resources ask these questions:

- Is the information up-to-date?
- Does the index have several pages listed for the topic?
- Is the resource written in a way that is easy to understand?
- Are there helpful illustrations and photos?

2 Practicing the Skill

Look at the following list of sources. Which would be most helpful in writing a report on the history of ancient Rome? Explain your choices.

(1) A travel guide to Italy today

(2) A guide to early Roman art and architecture

(3) A children's storybook about ancient Europe

(4) A history of ancient Greece

(5) A study of the rise and fall of the Roman Empire

(6) A book on modern republican ideas

(7) A biographical dictionary of ancient rulers of the world

(8) An atlas of the world

3 Applying the Skill

Go to your local library or use the Internet to create a bibliography of sources you might use to write a report on the history of ancient Rome. List at least five sources.

▲ Roman mosaic showing gladiators in battle

PRACTICING THE SKILL ANSWERS

The most helpful would probably be 5, followed by 2 and 7, because they deal specifically with ancient Rome. Others either deal with modern Rome or Italy or current ideas based on Roman ones (1, 6), might be written at too low a level (3), focus on another civilization (4), or are maps of today's world (8).

Applying the Skill You may have to define *bibliography* for students. Students might include reference works like encyclopedias and historical atlases, articles, excerpts from general history works, and others.

SkillBuilder Handbook

TEACH

Analyzing Primary Source Documents There are primary source quotes and excerpts throughout the textbook. Tell students that primary sources are a cornerstone of history, but that it is important to be able to analyze their reliability. Ask students to contribute to a class list of questions to ask about a written primary source document to help them determine its reliability. *(Questions might include who wrote it, when it was written, what was the relationship of the author to the event, what biases the author may have had, what the author's purpose was in writing the document, and so on.)* Then ask students if they can list items other than written documents that could be considered primary sources. *(Students should be able to name one of the following: photos, paintings, songs, cartoons, and others.)* **L2**

Analyzing Primary Source Documents

Why Learn This Skill?

Historians determine what happened in the past by combing through bits of evidence to reconstruct events. These types of evidence—both written and illustrated—are called primary sources. Examining primary sources can help you understand history.

1 Learning the Skill

Primary sources are sources that were created in the historical era being studied. They can include letters, diaries, photographs and pictures, news articles, legal documents, stories, literature, and artwork.

To analyze primary sources, ask yourself the following questions:

- What is the item?
- Who created it?
- Where did it come from?
- When was it created?
- What does it reveal about the topic I am studying?

2 Practicing the Skill

The primary source that follows comes from *Stories of Rome* by Livy. Livy was a Roman historian who lived from 59 B.C. to A.D. 17. Here he has written a story with a moral, or lesson to be learned. Read the story, and then answer the questions that follow.

Once upon a time, the different parts of the human body were not all in agreement. . . . And it seemed very unfair to the other parts of the body that they should worry and sweat away to look after the belly. After all, the belly just sat there . . . doing nothing, enjoying all the nice things that came along. So they hatched a plot. The hands weren't going to take food to the mouth; even if they did, the mouth wasn't going to accept it. . . . They went into a sulk and waited for the belly to cry for help. But while they waited, one by one all the parts of the body got weaker and weaker. The moral of this story? The belly too has its job to do. It has to be fed, but it also does feeding of its own.

Excerpt from *Stories of Rome*,
Livy, c. 20 B.C.

1. What is the main topic?
2. Who did the hands and mouth think was lazy?
3. What did the hands and mouth do about it?
4. What was the moral—or lesson—of the story?

3 Applying the Skill

Find a primary source from your past—a photo or newspaper clipping. Explain to the class what it shows about that time in your life.

PRACTICING THE SKILL ANSWERS

1. the way the parts of the human body work together for the common good
2. the belly
3. They decided not to allow food to reach the belly.
4. The belly needs to be fed, but it also feeds the other parts of the body. Everyone needs to do his or her share of the work.

Applying the Skill Make sure students know that they will share their primary source with the class on a voluntary basis. Students should be able to clearly explain the significance of the primary source to their lives.

Building a Database

Why Learn This Skill?

A database is a collection of information stored in a computer or on diskette files. It runs on software that organizes large amounts of information in a way that makes it easy to search and make any changes. It often takes the form of a chart or table. You might build databases to store information related to a class at school or your weekly schedule.

1 Learning the Skill

To create a database using word-processing software, follow these steps:

- Enter a title identifying the type of information in your document and file names.

- Determine the set of specific points of information you wish to include. As the database example on this page shows, you might want to record data on the imports and exports of specific countries.

- Enter the information categories along with country names as headings in a columned chart. Each column makes up a *field*, which is the basic unit for information stored in a database.

- Enter data you have collected into the *cells,* or individual spaces, on your chart.

- Use your computer's sorting feature to organize the data. For example, you might alphabetize by country name.

- Add, delete, or update information as needed. Database software automatically adjusts the cells in the chart.

2 Practicing the Skill

On a separate sheet of paper, answer the following questions referring to the database on this page.

1. What type of information does the database contain?

2. What related fields of information does it show?

3. The author learns that Canada also exports clothing, beverages, and art to the United States. Is it necessary to create a new database? Explain.

3 Applying the Skill

Build a database to help you keep track of your school assignments. Work with four fields: Subject, Assignment Description, Due Date, and Completed Assignments. Be sure to keep your database up-to-date.

U.S. International Commerce			
Country	Japan	United Kingdom	Canada
Exports to U.S.	Engines, rubber goods, cars, trucks, buses	Dairy products, beverages, petroleum products, art	Wheat, minerals, paper, mining machines
Value of Exports to U.S.	$128 billion	$35.2 billion	$232.6 billion
Imports from U.S.	Meat, fish, sugar, tobacco, coffee	Fruit, tobacco, electrical equipment	Fish, sugar, metals, clothing
Value of Imports from U.S.	$67.3 billion	$42.8 billion	$199.6 billion

TEACH

Building a Database Ask if any students have worked with database software. Have volunteers explain what kinds of information they were using, how it was organized, how they sorted or could sort the information, and whether they felt that using the software made working with the information easier.

Next, ask students to contribute to a class list of different fields, or major sortable categories, they might want to include in a database of their music collections. (*Possible fields are artist, title, type of music, date acquired, similar CDs, cross-references to other CDs, etc.*) **L2**

GLENCOE TECHNOLOGY

Glencoe Skillbuilder Interactive Workbook CD-ROM, Level 1

This interactive CD-ROM reinforces student mastery of essential social studies skills.

PRACTICING THE SKILL ANSWERS

1. types of products imported from and exported to the United States
2. country, major exports to the U.S., value of exports, major imports from the U.S., value of imports
3. No; this information can be added to the correct cell.

Applying the Skill To complete this activity, students will need equal access to a database software program. Students' databases should be correctly formatted and contain accurate information.

TEACH

Summarizing Remind students that when they prepare a report they summarize—condense—all the research information they uncovered. They cannot include every detail. Before students read the SkillBuilder activity, hand out copies of a newspaper editorial. Ask students which sentences best communicate the subject of the editorial. Ask them what this sentence is called. *(topic sentence)* Have them restate the idea expressed in the topic sentence in their own words. Then have them identify the sentences that give details that support the main idea. Ask students to list, in as few words as possible, these supporting points. **L3**

Summarizing

Why Learn This Skill?

Imagine you have been assigned a long chapter to read. How can you remember the important information? Summarizing information—reducing large amounts of information to a few key phrases—can help you remember the main ideas and important facts.

1 Learning the Skill

To summarize information, follow these guidelines when you read:

- Separate the main ideas from the supporting details. Use the main ideas in a summary.

- Use your own words to describe the main ideas. Do not copy the selection word for word.

- If the summary is almost as long as the reading selection, you are including too much information. The summary should be very short.

2 Practicing the Skill

To practice the skill, read the paragraph below. Then answer the questions that follow.

The Ming dynasty that followed the Mongols tried to rid the country of Mongol influence. The Ming leaders believed that China could become a great empire. They expanded Chinese control over parts of East Asia, including Korea, Vietnam, and Myanmar (Burma). To re-establish the importance of Chinese culture, they encouraged the practices of older Chinese traditions, especially in the arts. Chinese literature during the Ming era followed the styles of ancient Chinese writers. Some of the finest Chinese paintings and pottery were created during this period. Ming rulers also built the Forbidden City.

1. What are the main ideas of this paragraph?
2. What are the supporting details?
3. Write a brief summary of two or three sentences that will help you remember what the paragraph is about.

3 Applying the Skill

Read a newspaper or short magazine article. Summarize the article in one or two sentences.

PRACTICING THE SKILL ANSWERS

1. Ming leaders wanted to lessen Mongol influences. Ming leaders expanded China's empire over East Asia. They tried to reestablish older Chinese culture and traditions in the arts.

2. expanding into Korea, Vietnam, and Myanmar; following older models in literature, paintings, and pottery; building the Forbidden City

3. Ming leaders expanded China's empire into other parts of South Asia. They also reestablished Chinese culture by looking back at traditional models in the arts such as literature, painting, and pottery.

Applying the Skill Students' summaries should reflect understanding of the article and of the summarizing methods discussed and modeled in this activity.

Evaluating a Web Site

Why Learn This Skill?

The Internet has grown to become a necessary household and business tool as more people use it. With so many Web sites available, how do you know which one will be the most helpful to you? You must look at the details, so you do not waste valuable time in Web searches.

1 Learning the Skill

The Internet is a valuable research tool. It is easy to use, and it often provides fast, up-to-date information. The most common use of the Internet by students is in doing research. However, some Web site information is not really accurate or reliable.

When using the Internet to do research, you must evaluate the information very carefully. When evaluating the Web site, ask yourself the following questions:

- Do the facts on the site seem accurate?

- Who is the author or sponsor of the site, and what is that person's or organization's reason for maintaining it?

- Does the site information explore a subject in-depth?

- Does the site contain links to other useful resources?

- Is the information easy to read and access?

2 Practicing the Skill

To practice the skill, find three Web sites on the shoguns or samurai of Japan. Follow these steps and write your explanation.

1. Evaluate how useful these sites would be if you were writing a report on the topic.
2. Choose which one is the most helpful.
3. Explain why you chose that site.

3 Applying the Skill

If your school had a Web site, what kind of information would be on it? Write a paragraph describing this site.

A Japanese samurai warrior

TEACH

Evaluating a Web Site Before reading the SkillBuilder, ask students to discuss ways that researching on the Internet is different from using books or other printed material. *(Information on the Internet may be easier to find, but it is more difficult to evaluate its reliability.)* Then ask them to suggest ways that they could assess the trustworthiness of information they find on the Internet and in books. Create a class list of criteria that could be used to test a Web site that can be displayed and amended by students. *(Many students may recognize that information published in books undergoes fact checking and other editorial processing, while data in Web sites often do not.)* **L2**

GLENCOE TECHNOLOGY

Glencoe Skillbuilder Interactive Workbook CD-ROM, Level 1

This interactive CD-ROM reinforces student mastery of essential social studies skills.

PRACTICING THE SKILL ANSWERS

1. Evaluations should reflect understanding of the site content as well as the methods for evaluating Web sites discussed in this activity.
2. Answers will vary but should be supported by reasonable support details.
3. Answers should reflect understanding of the evaluation methods suggested in this activity.

Applying the Skill Possible answers include class and other academic news; profiles of students and faculty members; and information about sports teams, clubs, music performances, art shows, and volunteer activities.

TEACH

Understanding Cause and Effect

Explain the cause-and-effect relationship by asking students to write down an interesting or unexpected thing that happened to them recently. Then have them write a sentence explaining why the thing happened. Have volunteers share their sentences. Explain that the first event is the effect, while the reason it happened is the cause. Point out that causes and effects, in history as in everyday life, are not always clear-cut. In addition, remind students that causes can have many effects and that effects can have many different causes. **L1**

Understanding Cause and Effect

Why Learn This Skill?

You know if you watch television instead of completing your homework, you probably will not get a good grade. The cause—not doing homework—leads to the effect—not getting a good grade.

1 Learning the Skill

A *cause* is any person, event, or condition that makes something happen. What happens as a result is known as an *effect*.

These guidelines will help you identify cause and effect.

- Identify two or more events.
- Ask questions about why events occur.
- Look for "clue words" that alert you to cause and effect, such as *because, led to, brought about, produced,* and *therefore*.
- Identify the outcome of events.

2 Practicing the Skill

As you read the following passage, record cause-and-effect connections in a chart or graphic organizer.

Around 200 B.C., Mesopotamians were among the first in the world to blend copper and tin to make bronze.

Bronze brought many changes to life in Mesopotamia. For one thing, bronze was much harder than the copper products that were used until that time. Because it was harder, bronze made better tools and sharper weapons. This improvement in technology was a help to farmers, craftworkers, and soldiers alike.

Molten [melted] bronze was also easier to pour than the metals used earlier. Craftworkers were able to make finer arrows, ax-heads, statues, bowls, and other objects.

3 Applying the Skill

Look again at the chapter you are currently reading. Choose a major event that is described and list its causes.

◀ The Royal Banner of Ur

914   SkillBuilder Handbook

PRACTICING THE SKILL ANSWERS

Charts might highlight such causes and effects as:

- Making bronze led to changes for Mesopotamians.
- Bronze tools helped farmers.
- Bronze weapons helped soldiers.
- Molten bronze led to finer crafts.

Applying the Skill Lists should reflect understanding of the chapter content as well as of the cause-and-effect discussion in this SkillBuilder.

Making Comparisons

Why Learn This Skill?

Suppose you want to buy a portable CD player, and you must choose among three models. To make this decision, you would probably compare various features of the three models, such as price, sound quality, size, and so on. By making comparisons, you will figure out which model is best for you. In the study of world history, you often compare people or events from one time period with those from a different time period.

1 Learning the Skill

When making comparisons, you examine and identify two or more groups, situations, events, or documents. Then you identify any similarities (ways they are alike) and differences (ways they are different). For example, the chart on this page compares the characteristics of two ancient civilizations.

When making comparisons, apply the following steps:

• Decide what items will be compared. Clue words such as *also, as well as, like, same as,* and *similar to* can help you identify things that are being compared.

• Determine which characteristics you will use to compare them.

• Identify similarities and differences in these characteristics.

2 Practicing the Skill

To practice the skill, analyze the information on the chart at the bottom of this page. Then answer these questions.

1. What items are being compared?
2. What characteristics are being used to compare them?
3. In what ways were the Phoenicians and Israelites similar? In what ways were they different?
4. Suppose you wanted to compare the two peoples in more detail. What are some of the characteristics you might use?

3 Applying the Skill

Think about two sports that are played at your school. Make a chart comparing such things as: where the games are played, who plays them, what equipment is used, and other details.

Phoenician and Israelite Civilizations

Cultural Characteristic	Phoenicians	Israelites
Homeland	Canaan	Canaan
Political Organization	city-states	12 tribes; later, kingdom
Method of Rule	kings/merchant councils	kings/council of elders
Main Occupations	artisans, traders, shippers	herders, farmers, traders
Religion	belief in many gods and goddesses	belief in one, all-powerful god
Main Contribution	spread of an alphabet	principles of social justice

TEACH

Making Comparisons Begin this SkillBuilder by writing the words *cat* and *dog* on the board. Ask students to name ways the two animals are similar. (*Both are mammals, have fur and four legs, and are popular pets.*) Then have students identify differences. (*Cats meow, dogs bark; cats climb trees, dogs do not; cats are felines, dogs are canines; cats are often solitary, dogs like to live in packs or with people.*)

Point out that students have just practiced the important skill of making comparisons. This includes identifying how things are alike *and* different from one another. Ask them to brainstorm some things that historians might want to compare. (*nations, regions, leaders, important events, cultures, methods of government, and so on.*) Then have students read the skills lesson and answer the questions. **L2**

GLENCOE TECHNOLOGY

Glencoe Skillbuilder Interactive Workbook CD-ROM, Level 1

This interactive CD-ROM reinforces student mastery of essential social studies skills.

PRACTICING THE SKILL ANSWERS

1. the Phoenician and Israelite civilizations
2. homeland, political organization, method of rule, main occupations, religion, and main contribution
3. *similar:* homeland, rule by kings, trading; *different:* organized by city-states vs. tribes/kingdom, ruled by merchant council vs. council of elders, occupations of artisans and shippers vs. herders and farmers, belief in many gods vs. monotheism, contribution of an alphabet vs. principles of social justice
4. language, famous people, position of women, everyday life, architecture, art, literature

Applying the Skill Answers should show understanding of the dynamics of compare/contrast analysis and of the two chosen sports.

TEACH

Making Predictions Introduce the lesson by asking students what they think would probably happen if they watch a movie the evening before an important test instead of studying. Why do they think this outcome is likely? On what factors are they basing their predictions? *(prior experience, experiences of others, common sense)*

Point out that predicting consequences is an important element in making good decisions, and that people make predictions all the time based on these and other factors. In reading history, they can make predictions about what they read based on the same, and other, factors.

Ask when—in reading history—they think making predictions would naturally occur. *(Students might say predicting the outcome of a war, an exploration, or a migration.)* **L3**

Making Predictions

Why Learn This Skill?

In history you read about people making difficult decisions based on what they think *might* happen. By making predictions yourself, you can get a better understanding of the choices people make.

1 Learning the Skill

As you read a paragraph or section in your book, think about what might come next. What you think will happen is your *prediction*. A prediction does not have a correct or incorrect answer. Making predictions helps you to carefully consider what you are reading.

To make a prediction, ask yourself:

• What happened in this paragraph or section?

• What prior knowledge do I have about the events in the text?

• What similar situations do I know of?

• What do I think might happen next?

• Test your prediction: read further to see if you were correct.

◄ Aztec shield

2 Practicing the Skill

To practice the skill, read the following paragraph about the Aztec Empire. Then answer the questions.

The Aztec of ancient Mexico built the strongest empire of any Native American group. They mined gold, silver, and other goods for trade. In building their empire, they conquered many other Native American groups. The Aztec fought their enemies using wooden weapons with stone blades.

In the 1500s, a Spanish army seeking gold heard about the Aztec and their riches. Led by Hernán Cortés, the Spaniards were helped by enemies of the Aztec. Armed with steel swords, muskets, and cannons, the Spaniards moved towards the Aztec capital.

1. Choose the outcome below that is most likely to occur between the Aztec and Spaniards.
   a. The Spaniards will avoid the Aztec altogether.
   b. The two groups will become friends.
   c. The Spaniards will conquer the Aztec.
   d. The Aztec will conquer the Spaniards.
2. Explain why you chose the answer you did.

3 Applying the Skill

Watch a television show or a movie. Halfway through the show, write your prediction of how it will end on a piece of paper. At the end of the show, check your prediction.

PRACTICING THE SKILL ANSWERS

1. c
2. The Spanish are seeking gold, which the Aztec have; the Spanish were helped by enemies of the Aztec; the Spanish have much more powerful weapons than the Aztec.

Applying the Skill Answers will vary; students should be able to explain the basis for their predictions.

Drawing Inferences and Conclusions

Why Learn This Skill?

Suppose your teacher brought an artifact to class and a classmate exclaimed, "That came from Greece, didn't it?" You might infer that your classmate had an interest in Greece.

1 Learning the Skill

To *infer* means to evaluate information and arrive at a *conclusion*. Social studies writers do not always spell out everything in the text. When you make inferences you "read between the lines." You must then use the available facts and your own knowledge of social studies to draw a conclusion.

Use the following steps to help draw inferences and make conclusions:

• Read carefully for stated facts and ideas.

• Summarize the information and list the important facts.

• Apply related information that you may already know to make inferences.

• Use your knowledge and insight to develop some conclusions about these facts.

2 Practicing the Skill

Read the passage below and answer the questions.

> Many Greek temples were decorated with sculpture. Greek sculpture, like Greek architecture, was used to express Greek ideas. The favorite subject of Greek artists was the human body. Greek sculptors did not copy their subjects exactly, flaws and all. Instead, they tried to show their ideal version of perfection and beauty.

1. What topic is the writer describing?
2. What facts are given?
3. What can you infer about Greek cities from the information?
4. What conclusions can you draw about how the Greeks felt about sculptures?

3 Applying the Skill

Read one of the biographies in this text. What can you infer about the life of the person described? Draw a conclusion about whether or not you would like to meet this person.

 Ancient Greek sculptures of Socrates (far left), Plato (middle), and Aristotle (left)

TEACH

Drawing Inferences and Conclusions
Open the lesson by sharing this scenario with students: You walk into your home's living room late at night. The TV is on, and your sister is asleep on the couch. There is popcorn all over the floor. **Ask: What do you think happened?** *(The sister fell asleep watching TV, and the popcorn spilled onto the floor.)*

Explain that students have just drawn a conclusion, based on several inferences they made about the situation. The inferences are based on evidence in the room. Tell them that they will use the same skills when they read about events in history. **L1**

GLENCOE TECHNOLOGY

Glencoe Skillbuilder Interactive Workbook CD-ROM, Level 1

This interactive CD-ROM reinforces student mastery of essential social studies skills.

PRACTICING THE SKILL ANSWERS

1. Greek sculpture
2. Statues decorated temples, sculpture expressed Greek ideas, the human body was the favorite subject for statues, sculptors tried to capture ideal beauty, not reality.
3. They were probably beautiful, with many sculptures and buildings.
4. Sculptures were very important to them.

Applying the Skill Answers should reflect an understanding of the basic facts in the biography as well as of how to correctly make inferences and draw conclusions, as discussed in this SkillBuilder.

917

SkillBuilder Handbook

TEACH

Recognizing Economic Indicators
Have volunteers define *economic (having to do with the production, distribution, and consumption of goods or services)* and *indicator (a sign or number)* for the class. Post these definitions on the board for student reference. Economic indicators, along with all kinds of statistics, are useful and important tools of the historian and economist. Display the business section of a newspaper and point out to students some indicators listed there. Ask students to contribute to a class list of economic statistics they have heard or read about. In what context did they hear about them? Were the reports positive or negative? Why did the people citing the statistics think they were significant? **L3**

Recognizing Economic Indicators

Why Learn This Skill?

Every day, business and government leaders are faced with the challenge of trying to predict what will happen to the economy in the coming months and years. To help these leaders in making decisions, economists, or scientists who study the economy, have developed ways to measure an economy's performance. These ways are called economic indicators.

1 Learning the Skill

Economic indicators are statistics, or numbers, that tell how well the economy is doing and how well the economy is going to do in the future. They include the number of jobless, the rate at which prices rise over a period of time, and the amount of goods and services that are produced and sold. Each month, the U.S. Department of Commerce gathers data for 78 economic indicators covering all aspects of the state of the United States economy. The chart below lists some common terms for economic indicators that you may read about.

▲ Prices on the stock market often rise or fall based on changes in economic indicators.

2 Practicing the Skill

Start an Economics Handbook. Using a dictionary, look up each economic term listed on this chart. Write a definition for each term in your Economics Handbook.

3 Applying the Skill

Think about one of the countries you have read about in this text that has grown to be wealthy. Using the terms that you just defined, write a paragraph describing that country's wealth.

Economic Indicators

Term	Definition
Saving	
Income	
Expenditure	
Consumption	
Inflation	
Debt	
Gross Domestic Product (GDP)	
Interest Rates	
Credit	
Export	
Import	

PRACTICING THE SKILL ANSWERS

saving: money not spent; *income:* amount earned; *expenditure:* amount spent; *consumption:* use of goods and services by consumers; *inflation:* rise in prices over time; *debt:* amount owed; *GDP:* total value of goods and services produced in a country; *interest rates:* amount charged to borrow money; *credit:* borrowed money; *export:* send goods out of a country; *import:* bring goods into a country

Applying the Skill Paragraphs should show understanding of the historical information as well as of the terms discussed in this SkillBuilder.

Interpreting Political Cartoons

Why Learn This Skill?

Political cartoonists use art to express political opinions. Their work appears in newspapers, magazines, books, and on the Internet. Political cartoons are drawings that express an opinion. They usually focus on public figures, political events, or economic or social conditions. A political cartoon can give you a summary of an event or circumstance and the artist's opinion in a quick and entertaining manner.

1 Learning the Skill

To interpret a political cartoon, follow these steps:

- Read the title, caption, or conversation balloons. Most cartoons will carry at least one of these elements. They help you identify the subject of the cartoon.

- Identify the characters or people shown. They may be caricatures, or unrealistic drawings that exaggerate the characters' physical features.

- Identify any symbols shown. Symbols are things that stand for something else. An example is the American flag that is a symbol of our country. Commonly recognized symbols may not be labeled. Unusual symbolism will be labeled.

- Examine the actions in the cartoon—what is happening and why?

- Identify the cartoonist's purpose. What statement or idea is he or she trying to get across? Decide if the cartoonist wants to persuade, criticize, or just make people think.

2 Practicing the Skill

On a separate sheet of paper, answer these questions about the political cartoon below.

1. What is the subject of the cartoon?
2. What words give clues as to the meaning of the cartoon?
3. What item seems out of place?
4. What message do you think the cartoonist is trying to send?

3 Applying the Skill

Bring a news magazine to class. With a partner, analyze the message in each political cartoon that you find.

TEACH

Interpreting Political Cartoons
Bring several political cartoons to class. Good sources are weekly newsmagazines like *Newsweek* and *Time*. Before the class reads this SkillBuilder, distribute copies of the cartoons. Have pairs of students analyze the cartoons and decide their message. Also have them discuss how they determined the message. What techniques did the cartoonist use? You may also want to create a bulletin board with contributed political cartoons. Then have students complete the page. **L2**

GLENCOE TECHNOLOGY

Glencoe Skillbuilder Interactive Workbook CD-ROM, Level 1

This interactive CD-ROM reinforces student mastery of essential social studies skills.

PRACTICING THE SKILL ANSWERS

1. television violence
2. the name of the museum, the signs under the exhibits
3. the TV set
4. Television communicates violent messages and may even be as responsible for violence as the weapons shown in the other exhibits.

Applying the Skill Students should apply critical thinking and other skills to correctly interpret the message of the cartoon.

TEACH

Standardized Test Practice Have students write down everything they associate with the word *test*. Ask them to list helpful hints for taking tests. Lead a class discussion on successful test-taking strategies. For example, suggest that when taking tests, students look for clues in the question that support their answers, eliminate answers that do not make sense, and read the titles or keys of any graphics presented (graphs, charts, time lines, maps). L1/ EL

Standardized Test Practice

Standardized tests are one way educators measure what you have learned. This handbook is designed to help you prepare for standardized tests in social studies. On the pages that follow, you will find a review of the major social studies critical thinking skills that you will need to master to be successful when taking tests.

Contents

ADDITIONAL GLENCOE TEST PRACTICE RESOURCES

The following materials are available for further test practice:

- Glencoe Skillbuilder Interactive Workbook CD-ROM, Level 1
- Exam*View*® Pro Testmaker CD-ROM
- Reading Essentials and Study Guide
- Quizzes, Tests, and Authentic Assessment (with Rubrics)
- Critical Thinking Skills Activities
- Standardized Test Skills Practice Workbook
- Daily Focus Skills Transparencies
- MindJogger Videoquiz

Interpreting a Map

Before 1492, people living in Europe in the Eastern Hemisphere had no idea that the continents of North America and South America in the Western Hemisphere existed. That was the year Christopher Columbus first reached the Americas. His voyage of exploration paved the way for other European voyages to the Western Hemisphere. The voyages of the early explorers brought together two worlds. Previously these parts of the globe had no contact with each other. Trade between the hemispheres changed life for people on both sides of the Atlantic Ocean. The trade between the peoples of the Eastern Hemisphere and the Western Hemisphere is referred to as the Columbian Exchange.

Skills Practice

Although globes are the best, most accurate way to show places on the round earth, people can more easily use maps to represent places. A map is made by taking data from a round globe and placing it on a flat surface. To read a map, first read the title to determine the subject of the map. Then read the map key or the labels on the map to find out what the colors and symbols on the map mean. Use the compass rose to identify the four cardinal directions of north, south, east, and west. Study the map of the Columbian Exchange and answer the questions that follow on a separate sheet of paper.

1. What is the subject of the map?

2. What do the arrows represent?

3. What continents are shown on the map?

4. What foods did Europeans acquire from the Americas?

NATIONAL GEOGRAPHIC — The Columbian Exchange

Corn, Beans, Chocolate, Diseases
Cattle, Horses, Wheat, Diseases
Enslaved People
EUROPE
AFRICA
THE AMERICAS
ARCTIC CIRCLE
TROPIC OF CANCER
EQUATOR
30°N
90°W   60°W   30°W   0°

5. What did the Americas acquire from Europe?

6. What people were brought from Africa to the Americas?

7. In what direction is Europe from the Americas?

Standardized Test Practice

DIRECTIONS: Use the map and your knowledge of social studies to answer the following question on a separate sheet of paper.

1. Which of the following statements about the Columbian Exchange is true?

   A Food products were traded only between Africa and the Americas.

   B Europeans acquired cattle from the Americas.

   C Europeans introduced corn, tomatoes, and beans to Native Americans.

   D Enslaved Africans were brought to the Americas.

TEACH

Interpreting a Map Write the following on the board or on an overhead transparency: "In fourteen hundred and ninety-two, Columbus sailed the ocean blue." Ask students to analyze the verse. **Ask: What is the significance of 1492? What century is represented by that date? Who was Columbus? To which ocean does the verse refer?**

Review the steps of reading a map with students. *(1. Read all the map labels; 2. Identify each symbol and color shown in the map key and locate these on the map; 3. Use this information to look for similarities and differences in the regions shown on the map.)* **L1/ EL**

Skills Practice Answers:

1. the Columbian Exchange

2. trade routes between continents or hemispheres

3. North America, South America, Europe, Africa

4. corn, beans, chocolate

5. cattle, horses, wheat, diseases

6. enslaved people

7. east and northeast

STANDARDIZED TEST PRACTICE ANSWER

1. D
Test-Taking Strategy: Have students study the map carefully before answering the question.

They should then eliminate answers they know are incorrect or do not make sense.

TEACH

Interpreting a Political Map

Ask: Why did people come to live in the British colonies in North America? Have students discuss the many reasons why someone might want to go on a dangerous voyage to a new land. *(Students should be able to explain that the various colonies were founded and populated for religious freedom, for profit, for trade, for political freedom, and to escape debt.)*

Remind students to use the various parts of the map to help them interpret it. These map parts include the map key, labels, and compass rose. **L2**

Skills Practice Answers:

1. Massachusetts, Rhode Island, New Hampshire, Connecticut; Maine was part of Massachusetts

2. New Jersey, Pennsylvania, New York, Delaware

3. New York

4. Georgia

5. Atlantic Ocean

6. in the Southern Colonies; in South Carolina

Interpreting a Political Map

By 1750, or the middle of the eighteenth century, there were 13 British colonies in North America. A colony is a group of people living in one place who are governed by rulers in another place. The British colonists in America were ruled by the monarchy and Parliament of Great Britain. That meant that rulers living 3,000 miles away made laws for the American colonists.

Skills Practice

Political maps illustrate divisions between territories such as nations, states, colonies, or other political units. These divisions are called boundaries. Lines represent the boundaries between political areas. To interpret a political map, read the map title to determine what geographic area and time period it covers. Identify the colonies or other political units on the map. Look at the map key for additional information. Study the map on this page and answer the questions that follow on a separate sheet of paper.

1. List the New England Colonies.

2. Which were the Middle Colonies?

3. Which Middle Colony bordered Pennsylvania to the north?

4. Which was the southernmost early British colony?

5. Name the body of water that formed the eastern border of the colonies.

6. Where was Charles Town located?

NATIONAL GEOGRAPHIC

The Thirteen Colonies *1750*

Town or City
New England Colonies
Middle Colonies
Southern Colonies

Standardized Test Practice

DIRECTIONS: Use the map and your knowledge of social studies to answer the following questions on a separate sheet of paper.

1. The New England Colony that covered the largest land area was
   A Virginia.
   B Pennsylvania.
   C Massachusetts.
   D New Hampshire.

2. The northernmost Middle Colony is the present-day state of
   F Maryland.
   G New York.
   H Massachusetts.
   J Pennsylvania.

3. The settlement of Plymouth was located
   A near Jamestown.
   B in Massachusetts.
   C in the Southern Colonies.
   D in Virginia.

STANDARDIZED TEST PRACTICE ANSWERS

1. C
Test-Taking Strategy: Be sure students identify the New England Colonies before they choose their answer.

2. G
Test-Taking Strategy: Tell students to first locate the Middle Colonies. Then determine which Middle Colony is farthest north.

3. B
Test-Taking Strategy: Have students answer the question before reviewing the choices to see which choice matches their answer.

Interpreting Charts

Government is a necessary part of every nation. It gives citizens stability and provides services that many of us take for granted. However, governments can sometimes have too much power.

The United States was founded on the principle of limited government. Limited governments require all people to follow the laws. Even the rulers must obey rules set for the society. A democracy is a form of limited government. Not all forms of government have limits. In unlimited governments, power belongs to the ruler. No laws exist to limit what the ruler may do. A dictatorship is an example of an unlimited government.

Limited Governments

Representative Democracy	Constitutional Monarchy
People elect leaders to rule	King or queen's power is limited
Individual rights important	Individual rights important
More than one political party	More than one political party
People give consent to be governed	People elect governing body

Unlimited Governments

Dictatorship	Absolute Monarchy
One person or small group rules	King or queen inherits power
Few personal freedoms	Usually some freedoms
Rule by force, often military	Officials are appointed by king or queen
Ruler does not have to obey rules	Monarch has complete authority

Skills Practice

Charts are visual graphics that categorize information. When reading a chart, be sure to look at all the headings and labels. Study the charts on this page and answer the questions that follow on a separate sheet of paper.

1. What do the charts compare?

2. Which political systems are forms of limited government?

3. Which form of government often uses military rule?

4. In which political system does the king or queen have complete power?

Standardized Test Practice

DIRECTIONS: Use the charts and your knowledge of social studies to answer the following questions on a separate sheet of paper.

1. Information found in the charts shows that the most restrictive form of government is a
   A dictatorship.
   B representative democracy.
   C absolute monarchy.
   D constitutional monarchy.

2. Under which type of government do citizens have the most power?
   F unlimited government
   G limited government
   H absolute monarchy
   J dictatorship

3. An example of an unlimited government is
   A the United States in the 1960s.
   B Libya in the 1970s.
   C the United Kingdom in the 1980s.
   D Mexico in the 1990s.

TEACH

Making Comparisons Making comparisons is an important skill in all academic areas. Help students realize that making comparisons is also a life skill that we use every day by having volunteers give examples of recent situations in which they have had to make a comparison.

You may wish to create, as a class, a comparison chart of two professional sports teams, two entertainers, and so on. **L1/ EL**

Skills Practice Answers:

1. The chart compares the two houses of the United States Congress—the House of Representatives and the Senate.

2. To become a member of the U.S. Congress (in either house), a person must meet an age requirement, be a U.S. citizen, and live in the state he or she represents.

3. Senators are probably more experienced, because they serve longer terms.

Standardized Test Practice

Making Comparisons

The roots of representative democracy in the United States can be traced back to colonial times. In 1607 English settlers founded the colony of Jamestown in present-day Virginia. As the colony developed, problems arose. Later, colonists formed the House of Burgesses to deal with these problems. Citizens of Virginia were chosen as representatives to the House of Burgesses. This became the first legislature, or lawmaking body, in America.

Today citizens of the United States elect representatives to Congress. The major function of Congress is to make laws for the nation. There are two houses, or chambers, of the U.S. Congress. Legislative bodies with two houses are said to be bicameral. The bicameral Congress of the United States includes the Senate and the House of Representatives. Article I of the U.S. Constitution describes how each house will be organized and how its members will be chosen.

The U.S. Congress

House of Representatives	Senate
Qualifications: Must be 25 years old; Must be U.S. citizen for 7+ years; Must live in the state they represent	**Qualifications:** Must be 30 years old; Must be U.S. citizen for 9+ years; Must live in the state they represent
Number of Representatives: 435 total representatives; number of representatives per state is based on state population	**Number of Representatives:** 100 total senators; two senators elected from each state regardless of state population
Terms of Office: Two-year terms	**Terms of Office:** Six-year terms

Skills Practice

When you make a comparison, you identify and examine two or more groups, situations, events, or documents. Then you identify any similarities and differences between the items. Study the information presented on the chart on this page and answer the questions that follow on a separate sheet of paper.

1. What two things does the chart compare?

2. How are the qualifications for each house of the U.S. Congress similar?

3. The members of which house are probably more experienced? Why?

Standardized Test Practice

DIRECTIONS: Use the chart and your knowledge of social studies to answer the following questions on a separate sheet of paper.

1. Which of the following statements best reflects information shown in the chart?

   A The Senate has more members than the House of Representatives.

   B Representatives to the House are elected to two-year terms.

   C House members must be residents of their states for at least 9 years.

   D A state's population determines its number of senators.

2. One inference that can be made from information shown on the chart is that

   F Texas elects more senators than Rhode Island.

   G Texas elects more House members than Rhode Island.

   H Texas elects fewer senators than Rhode Island.

   J Texas elects fewer House members than Rhode Island.

STANDARDIZED TEST PRACTICE ANSWERS

1. B
Test-Taking Strategy: Tell students: Do not rely on your memory alone to answer the question. Check each answer choice with information presented in the chart.

2. G
Test-Taking Strategy: Ask: What do you know about the populations of Texas and Rhode Island? Which house uses population to determine the number of members?

Interpreting Primary Sources

When Thomas Jefferson wrote the Declaration of Independence, he used the term "unalienable rights." Jefferson was referring to the natural rights that belong to humans. He and the other Founders of our nation believed that government could not take away the rights of the people.

Skills Practice

Primary sources are records of events made by the people who witnessed them. A historical document such as the Declaration of Independence is an example of a primary source. Read the passage below and answer the questions that follow on a separate sheet of paper.

> "We hold these truths to be self-evident, that all men are created equal, that they are endowed by their Creator with certain unalienable Rights, that among these are Life, Liberty, and the pursuit of Happiness . . ."
>
> —Declaration of Independence, July 4, 1776

1. What does the document say about the equality of men?

2. List the three natural, or unalienable, rights to which the document refers.

After gaining independence, American leaders wrote the U.S. Constitution in 1787. The Bill of Rights includes the first 10 amendments, or additions, to the Constitution. The First Amendment protects five basic rights of all American citizens. Study the chart on this page and answer the questions that follow.

1. Which right allows Americans to express themselves without fear of punishment by the government?

2. Which right allows people to worship as they please?

3. Which right allows citizens to publish a pamphlet that is critical of the president?

4. What is the Bill of Rights?

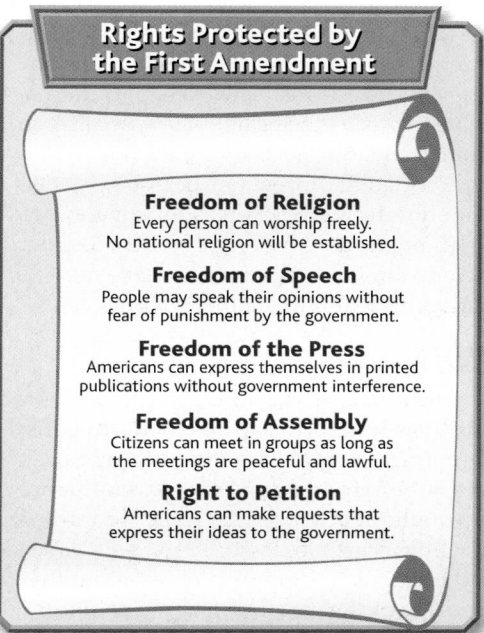

Rights Protected by the First Amendment

Freedom of Religion
Every person can worship freely. No national religion will be established.

Freedom of Speech
People may speak their opinions without fear of punishment by the government.

Freedom of the Press
Americans can express themselves in printed publications without government interference.

Freedom of Assembly
Citizens can meet in groups as long as the meetings are peaceful and lawful.

Right to Petition
Americans can make requests that express their ideas to the government.

Standardized Test Practice

DIRECTIONS: Use the chart and your knowledge of social studies to answer the following question on a separate sheet of paper.

1. Which First Amendment right protects citizens who are staging a protest outside a government building?

   A freedom of speech

   B freedom of the press

   C freedom of assembly

   D freedom of religion

TEACH

Interpreting Primary Sources
Have students explain the phrase "Founders of our nation." **Ask: What does the phrase mean? Who were the Founders of the United States? What did they do?** Have students speculate as to why the term *Founders* is capitalized.

Tell students that Thomas Jefferson was one of the most famous of the Founders of our nation because he wrote the Declaration of Independence. Ask students to recall the country from which Americans were declaring independence. Have students locate Great Britain on a map before they read this page. **L1/ EL**

Skills Practice Answers:

1. All men are created equal.

2. life, liberty, and the pursuit of happiness

----

1. freedom of speech

2. freedom of religion

3. freedom of the press

4. The Bill of Rights includes the first 10 amendments to the United States Constitution. These amendments protect basic liberties and rights.

STANDARDIZED TEST PRACTICE ANSWER

1. C
Test-Taking Strategy: Have students check each answer choice against the information presented in the chart.

Words in the question may not exactly match information in the chart. Encourage students to look for synonyms to support their answers.

Interpreting a Political Cartoon
Point out that the main purpose of political cartoons is to comment on a situation and, sometimes, to suggest a course of action. Help students understand that political cartoonists often use caricatures and symbols. A caricature is an unrealistic drawing of a real person. A symbol is a drawing that represents a concept. **L1/ EL**

Skills Practice Answers:

1. a man sitting at a desk writing about which freedoms to grant to Americans

2. freedom, liberty, rights, but not too much/many

3. a Founder of our nation, possibly a writer of the U.S. Constitution or Bill of Rights

4. writing the Bill of Rights

5. They suggest that the nation's Founders had to create a balance between freedoms and rights and the limits to them.

6. Americans' rights are restricted so that one person cannot interfere in the rights of another person. These limits are necessary to keep order in a society of so many people.

Interpreting a Political Cartoon

Just as the government of the United States is limited in its powers, freedoms extended to Americans also have limits. The First Amendment was not intended to allow Americans to do whatever they please without regard to others. Limits on freedoms are necessary to keep order in a society of so many people. The government can establish laws to limit certain rights to protect the health, safety, security, or moral standards of a community. Rights can be restricted to prevent one person's rights from interfering with the rights of another. For example, the freedom of speech does not include allowing a person to make false statements that hurt another's reputation.

Skills Practice

The artists who create political cartoons often use humor to express their opinions on political issues. Sometimes these cartoonists are trying to inform and influence the public about a certain topic. To interpret a political cartoon, look for symbols, labels, and captions that provide clues about the message of the cartoonist. Analyze these elements and draw some conclusions. Study the political cartoon on this page and answer the questions that follow on a separate sheet of paper.

1. What is the subject of the cartoon?

2. What words provide clues as to the meaning of the cartoon?

3. Whom does the person in the cartoon represent?

4. What is the person doing?

5. What do the subject's thoughts suggest about the task faced by those involved in planning the new nation's government?

6. What limits are placed on First Amendment rights? Why are these rights limited?

Standardized Test Practice

DIRECTIONS: Use the political cartoon and your knowledge of social studies to answer the following questions on a separate sheet of paper.

1. The most appropriate title for the cartoon is

   A Limits on Government.

   B Parliament at Work.

   C Limiting Rights.

   D Unlimited Government.

2. The sources of our rights as citizens of the United States come from which of the following?

   F the Declaration of Independence and the U.S. Constitution

   G the will of the president

   H unwritten customs and traditions

   J the United Nations charter

STANDARDIZED TEST PRACTICE ANSWERS

1. C
Test-Taking Strategy: Encourage students to look for clues. Words found in the cartoon show that the man is trying to grant rights with certain restrictions, or limited rights.

2. F
Test-Taking Strategy: This question requires students to understand the sources of our rights. Our government is a limited one, based on the Declaration of Independence and the U.S. Constitution.

Interpreting a Circle Graph

"E pluribus unum" is a Latin phrase found on United States coins. It means "Out of many, one." The United States is sometimes called a "nation of immigrants." Unless you are a Native American, your ancestors came to America within the last 500 years.

Groups of people who share a common culture, language, or history are referred to as ethnic groups. American neighborhoods include many different ethnic groups. The circle graph on this page shows the major ethnic groups in the United States.

Skills Practice

A circle graph shows percentages of a total quantity. Each part, or slice, of the graph represents a part of the total quantity. To read a circle graph, first read the title. Then study the labels to find out what each part represents. Compare the sizes of the circle slices. Study the circle graph and answer the questions that follow on a separate sheet of paper.

1. What information does this circle graph present?

2. Which ethnic group includes the largest percentage of Americans?

3. Which groups represent less than 1 percent of the people in the United States?

4. What percentage of the United States population is represented by African Americans?

5. The smallest ethnic group has lived in the United States the longest. What is this ethnic group?

NATIONAL GEOGRAPHIC

U.S. Ethnic Groups

African American 12.1%
Asian 3.6%
Native American/Inuit 0.7%
Other 1.9%
Hispanic 12.5%
White 69.2%

Source: U.S. Census Bureau, 2000.

Standardized Test Practice

DIRECTIONS: Use the graph and your knowledge of social studies to answer the following questions on a separate sheet of paper.

1. Which group's population is about three times greater than the number of Asians?

   A African American

   B White

   C Native American/Inuit

   D Other

2. How does the Hispanic population compare to the African American population of the United States?

   F It is greater than the African American population.

   G It is the smallest segment of the United States population.

   H It is less than half the size of the African American population.

   J It is slightly less than the African American population.

TEACH

Interpreting a Circle Graph Ask students to name a custom practiced in the United States that originated in another country. Examples include celebrations, types of food, music, dance, or other cultural practices. Lead a discussion focusing on the diverse cultural heritages of Americans. Explain to students that the practice of adopting the cultural traits of another group is called *cultural borrowing*.

Explain to students that a circle graph is like a sliced pie; often, it is even called a pie chart. Circle graphs show proportions rather than absolute amounts. They often are used when the information being compared totals 100 percent. **L1**

Skills Practice Answers:

1. ethnic groups in the United States

2. White

3. Native American/Inuit

4. 12.1 percent

5. Native American/Inuit

STANDARDIZED TEST PRACTICE ANSWERS

1. A

Test-Taking Strategy: Remind students to eliminate answers that do not make sense. Then students should multiply the percentage of Asians by three to find the correct answer, which will be the closest number.

2. F

Test-Taking Strategy: To answer this question, students must compare two slices of the total circle.

TEACH

Drawing Inferences and Conclusions
To help students become comfortable with making inferences and drawing conclusions, write the following sports page headline on the board: "Another Year of Futility—Hawks Fail to Make the Playoffs Again!" Ask students what information about the team they can draw from the headline. *(Most students will infer that it has been a long time since the Hawks had a successful season.)* Then have students suggest how the writer might feel about the situation. *(Students may suggest that the writer seems upset or frustrated.)* Then point out that students have just been drawing inferences and conclusions. **L1/ EL**

Skills Practice Answers:

1. immigration to the United States from 1820 to 1860
2. years (from 1820 to 1860)
3. number of immigrants
4. Students' answers will vary. Students may mention factors that pushed people out of their homelands to the U.S. and opportunities in the U.S. that pulled people to this country.

Drawing Inferences and Conclusions

During the mid-nineteenth century, immigration to the United States increased. People from European countries such as Germany and Ireland traveled to America seeking new opportunities. Life, however, was not easy for these immigrants.

Skills Practice

To infer means to evaluate information and arrive at a conclusion. When you make inferences, you "read between the lines." You must use the available facts and your own knowledge of social studies to form a judgment or opinion about the material.

Line graphs are a way of showing numbers visually. They are often used to compare changes over time. Sometimes a graph has more than one line. The lines show different quantities of a related topic. To analyze a line graph read the title and the information on the horizontal and vertical axes. Use this information to draw conclusions. Study the graph on this page and answer the questions that follow on a separate sheet of paper.

1. What is the subject of the line graph?
2. What information is shown on the horizontal axis?
3. What information is shown on the vertical axis?
4. Why do you think these immigrants came to the United States?

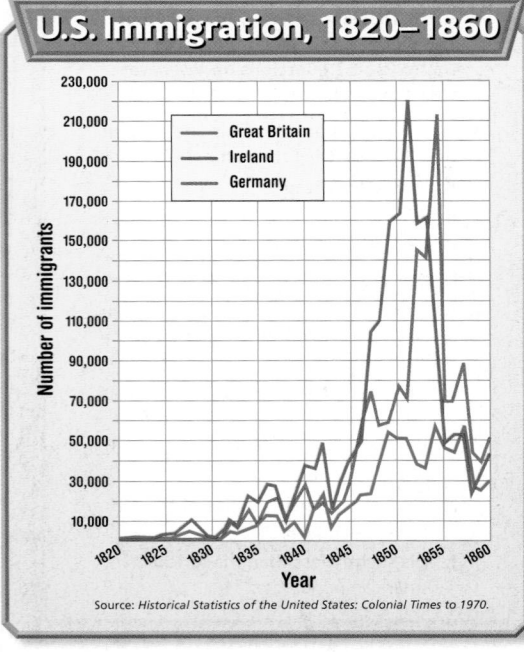

U.S. Immigration, 1820–1860

Legend: Great Britain, Ireland, Germany

Vertical axis: Number of immigrants (10,000 to 230,000)
Horizontal axis: Year (1820 to 1860)

Source: *Historical Statistics of the United States: Colonial Times to 1970.*

Standardized Test Practice

DIRECTIONS: Use the line graph and your knowledge of social studies to answer the following questions on a separate sheet of paper.

1. The country that provided the most immigrants to the United States between the years 1820 and 1860 was
   A Great Britain.
   B Ireland.
   C Germany.
   D France.

2. In about what year did the number of German immigrants to the United States reach a peak?
   F 1845
   G 1852
   H 1855
   J 1860

3. Irish migration to the United States increased in the mid-1800s because of
   A a terrible potato famine in Ireland.
   B the failure of a German revolution in 1848.
   C the nativist movement.
   D the availability of low-paying factory jobs.

STANDARDIZED TEST PRACTICE ANSWERS

1. B
Test-Taking Strategy: Remind students to check each answer choice against the graph to eliminate wrong answers.

2. H
Test-Taking Strategy: Students must first find the line that represents Germany and estimate the year of the peak.

3. A
Test-Taking Strategy: Students must make an inference. **Ask:** What would force people from Ireland to leave their country?

Comparing Data

The world's earliest civilizations developed more than 6,000 years ago. The discovery of farming led to the rise of ancient cities in Mesopotamia and the Nile River valley. These early cities shared one important characteristic—they each arose near waterways. Since water was the easiest way to transport goods, the settlements became centers of trade.

Since then cities have grown all over the world. Every 10 years, the United States Census Bureau collects data to determine the population of the United States. (A census is an official count of people living in an area.) The first census was conducted in 1790. At that time, there were 3.9 million people in the 13 original states. The most recent census occurred in 2000. The results of that census showed that more than 280 million people reside in the 50 states that make up our nation.

Skills Practice

The charts on this page show populations of the five most populous cities in the United States during different time periods. When comparing information on charts be sure to read the titles and headings to define the data being compared. Study the charts and answer the questions below on a separate sheet of paper.

1. Which U.S. city had the greatest population in 1790?

2. Which U.S. city had the greatest population in 2000?

3. What was the population of Philadelphia in 1790?

4. What was Philadelphia's population in 2000?

5. Which cities are on both lists?

Population of Five Largest U.S. Cities, 1790

City	Number of People
New York City	33,131
Philadelphia	28,522
Boston	18,320
Charleston	16,359
Baltimore	13,503

Population of Five Largest U.S. Cities, 2000*

City	Number of People
New York City	8,008,278
Los Angeles	3,694,820
Chicago	2,896,016
Houston	1,953,631
Philadelphia	1,517,550

*Numbers do not include metropolitan areas.

Standardized Test Practice

DIRECTIONS: Use the charts and your knowledge of social studies to answer the following questions on a separate sheet of paper.

1. One inference that can be made from the charts is that the most populous cities in the United States

   A have good weather.

   B were founded early in our nation's history.

   C are port cities.

   D are in the eastern United States.

2. In 1790 the major cities of the United States were all

   F larger than 20,000 people.

   G located in the East.

   H Northern cities.

   J founded for religious reasons.

TEACH

Comparing Data Tell students that determining populations is necessary for many reasons. For example, it is important to know the number of students in schools and school districts. The student population in each school helps officials decide how many teachers to hire. It also determines the amount of money districts receive.

Have the class find the total population of students in your school. What percentage of total students makes up each grade level? Have each student create a circle graph that shows this information. *(Students should find the number of students in each grade and convert those numbers into percentages before drawing slices of the circle graph. Check graphs for accuracy.)* **L2**

Skills Practice Answers:

1. New York City
2. New York City
3. 28,522
4. 1,517,550
5. New York City, Philadelphia

STANDARDIZED TEST PRACTICE ANSWERS

1. C

Test-Taking Strategy: To answer this question students must make an inference, or "read between the lines." Encourage students to read each answer choice, eliminating ones that do not make sense.

2. G

Test-Taking Strategy: To answer this question students must think of the location of each city and then eliminate incorrect answer choices.

INTRODUCTION

Have volunteers read and discuss the introduction to the **Primary Sources Library.** Have students complete the activities that follow to familiarize themselves with the types of primary sources.

PRINTED PUBLICATIONS

To help students analyze printed publications, instruct them to read the first two paragraphs of the Preamble to the Declaration of Independence. **Ask: What is the subject of these paragraphs? What do they tell you about the beliefs of the people who wrote and signed this document? L2**

SONGS AND POEMS

Ask students to write a poem about an important event in their lives. Suggest that the poem be in a standard form such as a limerick or other specific rhyme scheme. **L2**

ARTIFACTS AND VISUAL MATERIALS

To help students analyze artifacts and visual materials, provide the following instructions: Bring to class a primary source from your past—a photograph, piece of original art, and so on. Explain why you kept it and what it shows about the time from which the item comes. **L1**

Working With Primary Sources

Suppose that you have been asked to write a report on changes in your community over the past 25 years. Where would you get the information you need to begin writing? You would draw upon two types of information—primary sources and secondary sources.

Definitions

Primary sources are often first-person accounts by someone who actually saw or lived through what is being described. In other words, if you see a fire or live through a great storm and then write about your experiences, you are creating a primary source. Diaries, journals, photographs, and eyewitness reports are examples of primary sources. **Secondary sources** are second-hand accounts. For instance, if your friend experiences the fire or storm and tells you about it, or if you read about the fire or storm in the newspaper, and then you write about it, you are creating a secondary source. Textbooks, biographies, and histories are secondary sources.

Checking Your Sources

When you read primary or secondary sources, you should analyze them to figure out if they are dependable or reliable. Historians usually prefer primary sources to secondary sources, but both can be reliable or unreliable, depending on the following factors.

Time Span

With primary sources, it is important to consider how long after the event occurred the primary source was written. Chances are the longer the time span between the event and the account, the less reliable the account is. As time passes, people often forget details and fill in gaps with events that never took place. Although we like to think we remember things exactly as they happened, the fact is we often remember them as we wanted them to occur.

Reliability

Another factor to consider when evaluating a primary source is the writer's background and reliability. First, try to determine how this person knows about what he or she is writing. How much does he or she know? Is the writer being truthful? Is the account convincing?

Opinions

When evaluating a primary source, you should also decide whether the account has been influenced by emotion, opinion, or exaggeration. Writers can have reasons to distort the truth to

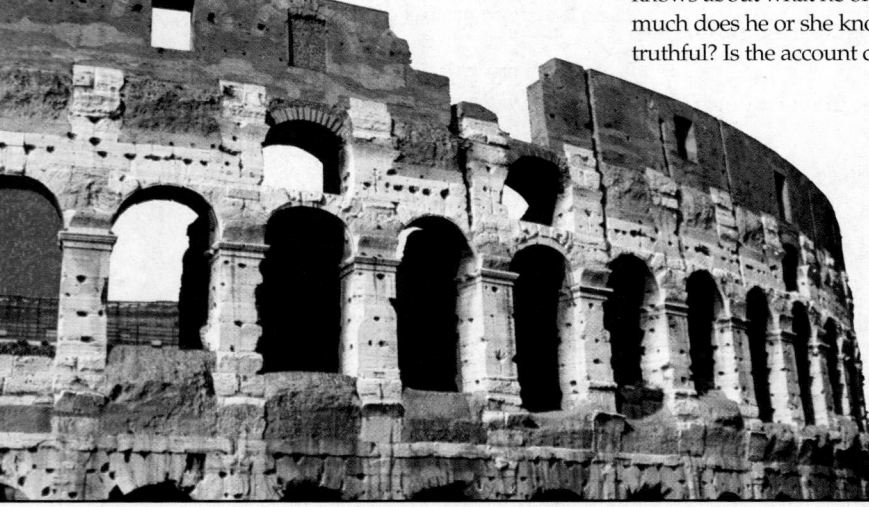
The Roman Colosseum

TEACHER NOTES

Through the study of the selections in the **Primary Sources Library** and their accompanying questions and activities, students should be able to:

• find the main idea in the selections.
• analyze information in a variety of writings in order to make inferences and generalizations.
• provide an interpretation of the material in their own words.

suit their personal purposes. Ask yourself: Why did the person write the account? Do any key words or expressions reveal the author's emotions or opinions? Compare the account with one written by another witness to the event. If they differ, ask yourself why they differ and which is more accurate.

Interpreting Primary Sources

To help you analyze a primary source, use the following steps:

• **Examine the origins of the document.**
You need to determine if it is a primary source.

• **Find the main ideas.**
Read the document and summarize the main ideas in your own words. These ideas may be fairly easy to identify in newspapers and journals, for example, but are much more difficult to find in poetry.

• **Reread the document.**
Difficult ideas are not always easily understood on the first reading.

• **Use a variety of resources.**
Form the habit of using the dictionary, the encyclopedia, and maps. These resources are tools to help you discover new ideas and knowledge and double-check other sources.

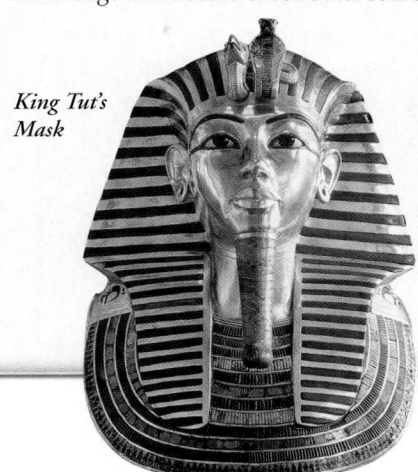

King Tut's Mask

Classifying Primary Sources

Primary sources fall into different categories:

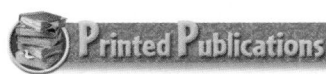

Printed publications include books such as autobiographies. Printed publications also include newspapers and magazines.

Songs and poems include works that express the personal thoughts and feelings or political or religious beliefs of the writer, often using rhyming and rhythmic language.

Visual materials include a wide range of forms: original paintings, drawings, sculptures, photographs, film, and maps.

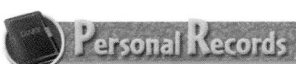

Oral histories are chronicles, memoirs, myths, and legends that are passed along from one generation to another by word of mouth. Interviews are another form of oral history.

Personal records are accounts of events kept by an individual who is a participant in, or witness to, these events. Personal records include diaries, journals, and letters.

 Artifacts

Artifacts are objects such as tools or ornaments. Artifacts present information about a particular culture or a stage of technological development.

Primary Sources Library

☺ ORAL HISTORIES

Work together with an English or language arts teacher to help students complete the following oral history activity. Provide the following guidelines to students: Interview a relative or friend who is much older than you. Your aim is to find out how much his or her life differed from yours. Devise a list of interview questions, such as: *What did you study in school? How did you and your friends spend your free time? What are some of the biggest changes you have seen in your lifetime? What was the most pressing world problem when you were my age?*

Ask students to provide a transcript, or written record, of the interview. If a tape recorder or video recorder is available, you may want to have students record the interview. Have students discuss their findings in class. **L2**

▣ PERSONAL RECORDS

Tell students that a journal is a daily record of events, thoughts, and feelings kept by an individual who is a participant or witness to these events. Ask students to keep a journal of interesting events they observe during a week's time. Encourage them to personalize the events by recording their own opinions or feelings about what they have witnessed. **L1**

TEACHER NOTES

After studying the introduction to the **Primary Sources Library,** students should be able to meet the following objectives:

• explain the difference between primary sources and secondary sources.
• identify the different types of primary sources.
• understand that primary sources offer a unique view of people and events in a particular era.

UNIT LINK

Use the primary source selections on pages 932–933 to accompany study of Unit 1, "Early Civilizations."

REINFORCING VOCABULARY

Review the **Reader's Dictionary** on page 932 with students to be sure they understand any unfamiliar terms before they begin reading the selections. Ask students to name places in the world that are steppes. (*Possible answers include the Great Plains of the United States, large areas of Russia and Ukraine, and the pampas of South America.*) **L2**

BACKGROUND INFORMATION

Printed Publications Although writing styles have changed immensely since the *Epic of Gilgamesh* was written, the subjects and themes of literature are quite similar. Ask students to list some themes of the reading. (*friendship, death, overcoming challenges, personal doubts and fears*) Then have them describe favorite novels, stories, and poems that address these same themes. Ask why these themes have proven to be of lasting importance to writers and readers over time. **L1**

For use with Unit 1

Early Civilizations

The people of early civilizations formed societies. These societies had a sense of justice and sets of values. As today, the family was the basic unit of society where values and justice were learned.

Reader's Dictionary

Bull of Heaven: mythical creature sent by the gods to kill Gilgamesh and Enkidu

Humbaba: evil spirit who guards the cedar forest through which Gilgamesh and Enkidu travel

steppe: wide, rolling, grassy plain

reproach: fault

Canaan: an ancient land that lay along the Syrian Desert

This Sumerian tablet is covered with cuneiform writing, the language in which the Epic of Gilgamesh *was written.*

The *Epic of Gilgamesh*

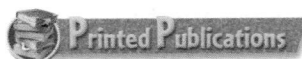
Printed Publications

The *Epic of Gilgamesh—written c. 2500 B.C.—* is one of the most well-known ancient tales. In this passage, Gilgamesh describes his adventures and journeys with his best friend, Enkidu.

We overcame everything: climbed the mountain,
captured the **Bull of Heaven** and killed him,
brought **Humbaba** to grief, who lives in the
   cedar forest;
entering the mountain gates we slew lions;
my friend whom I love dearly underwent with
   me all hardships.
The fate of mankind overtook him.
Six days and seven nights I wept over him
until a worm fell out of his nose.
Then I was afraid.
In fear of death I roam the wilderness. The case of
   my friend lies heavy in me.
On a remote path I roam the wilderness. The case
   of my friend Enkidu lies heavy in me.
On a long journey I wander the **steppe.**
How can I keep still? How can I be silent?
The friend I loved has turned to clay. Enkidu, the
   friend I love, has turned to clay.
Me, shall I not lie down like him,
never again to move?

EXTENDING THE CONTENT

A Real Superhero? Historians believe that the legendary hero of the *Epic of Gilgamesh* is based on a real king of the Sumerian city of Uruk. The ruins of the ancient city still stand today in southeastern Iraq. This person reigned sometime in the first half of the 2000s B.C. The sources for the tales of Gilgamesh come from several different civilizations speaking different languages. Some sources are in the Akkadian language, while others are in Sumerian.

An Egyptian Father's Advice to His Son

 Personal Records

U pper-class Egyptians enjoyed collecting wise sayings to provide guidance for leading an upright and successful life. This excerpt of instructions from Vizier Ptah-hotep dates from around 2450 B.C.

If you have, as leader, to decide on the conduct of a great number of men, seek the most perfect manner of doing so that your own conduct may be without **reproach.** Justice is great, invariable, and assured; it has not been disturbed since the age of Ptah. . . .

If you are a wise man, bring up a son who shall be pleasing to Ptah. If he conforms his conduct to your way and occupies himself with your affairs as is right, do to him all the good you can; he is your son, a person attached to you whom your own self has begotten. Separate not your heart from him. . . .

If you are powerful, respect knowledge and calmness of language. Command only to direct; to be absolute is to run into evil. Let not your heart be haughty, neither let it be mean. . . .

Ancient Israelites

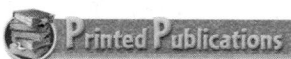 Printed Publications

M uch of the history of the ancient Israelites is recorded in the Bible. The Bible tells about a man named Abraham and his wife Sarah:

The Lord said to [Abraham], 'Leave your own country, your kin, and your father's house, and go to a country that I will show you. I shall make you into a great nation; I shall bless you. . . .'

[Abraham] . . . set out as the Lord had bidden him. . . . He took his wife [Sarah], his brother's son Lot, and all the possessions they had gathered . . . and they departed for **Canaan.**

When Abraham arrived in Canaan, the Bible says that God made a covenant, or special agreement, with him. It is considered by the Jewish people to be the beginning of their history.

When they arrived there, [Abraham] went on as far as the sanctuary. . . . When the Lord appeared to him and said, 'I am giving this land to your descendants,' [Abraham] built an altar there to the Lord who had appeared to him.

An ancient scroll from the Jewish Torah

Document Based Questions

1. What happened to the friend of Gilgamesh?
2. What is shown on the Sumerian tablet?
3. Does any part of the Egyptian father's advice have value today for sons or daughters? Be specific and support your answer.
4. According to the Bible, what did the Lord tell Abraham to do, and why?

 Primary Sources Library

Document Based Questions Answers

1. He died.
2. cuneiform writing
3. Yes, much of it does. For example, the advice to respect knowledge is timeless, and the suggestions to avoid haughtiness and meanness and to teach his son well are echoed in many other sources.
4. God told Abraham to leave his home and go to Canaan. If Abraham would do this, God would make Abraham and his descendants a great nation.

UNIT LINK

Use the primary source selections on pages 934–935 to accompany study of Unit 2, "The Ancient World."

REINFORCING VOCABULARY

Review the **Reader's Dictionary** on page 934 with students to be sure they understand any unfamiliar terms before they begin reading the selections. Have students list some regulations students at your school must follow. **L1/ EL**

BACKGROUND INFORMATION

Songs and Poems Songs and poems, like the selection from the *Rig Veda*, often use language to paint pictures. Ask students to point out an image created by the writer of the *Rig Veda*. (*For example, the stars are the many eyes of night.*) Then have them share examples of how language is used to create images in favorite songs or poems. **L1**

Primary Sources Library

For use with Unit 2

The Ancient World

Some of the greatest thoughts in modern civilization came from the ancient world. Important philosophers and religious leaders formed ideas we still express today. These ideas are timeless.

Reader's Dictionary

refinements: improvements

regulations: rules

nurture: upbringing

immortal: never dying

palpable: obvious

The *Analects* of Confucius

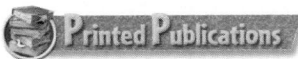 Printed Publications

An analect is a selected thought or saying. The sayings below were written by the Chinese philosopher Confucius in c. 400 B.C.

"If you make a mistake and do not correct it, this is called a mistake."

"Be dutiful at home, brotherly in public; be discreet and trustworthy, love all people, and draw near to humanity. If you have extra energy as you do that, then study literature."

"If leaders are courteous, their people will not dare to be disrespectful. If leaders are just, people will not dare to be [ungovernable]. If leaders are trustworthy, people will not dare to be dishonest."

A certain pupil asked Confucius about government: "What qualifies one to participate in government?"

Confucius said, "Honor five **refinements**. . . . Then you can participate in government."

The pupil asked, "What are the five refinements?"

Confucius said, "Good people are generous without being wasteful; they are hard working without being resentful; they desire without being greedy; they are at ease without being [proud]; they are dignified without being fierce."

Statue of Confucius

EXTENDING THE CONTENT

The *Vedas* The word *veda* means "knowledge." It comes from the Sanskrit language, which ancient Indians considered the most perfect of all languages. The *Vedas* are mostly hymns, songs, and poems that were used in the ancient religious rituals. Many are in praise of different gods and goddesses, who often represented natural forces like fire, the sun, winds, and rain. Although the ancient religion of the *Vedas* has evolved into modern Hinduism, the ancient scriptures are still honored and used in religious services today.

The Rights of Women

In the Republic, Plato presents his ideas on a just society in the form of dialogues, or imaginary conversations, between Socrates and his students. In this dialogue, Socrates has just finished questioning his student about the type of men who might make the best "watchdogs" of Athenian government. He surprises his student by turning to the subject of women.

Let us further suppose the birth and education of our women to be subject to similar or nearly similar **regulations** [as men]; . . .

What do you mean?

What I mean may be put into the form of a question, I said: Are dogs divided into hes and shes, or do they both share equally in hunting and in keeping watch and in the other duties of dogs? [O]r do we entrust to the males the entire and exclusive care of the flocks, while we leave the females at home, under the idea that the bearing and [feeding of] their puppies is labour enough for them?

No, he said, they share alike; the only difference between them is that the males are stronger and the females weaker.

But can you use different animals for the same purpose, unless they are [raised] in the same way?

You cannot.

Then, if women are to have the same duties as men, they must have the same **nurture** and education?

Yes.

The *Rig Veda*

The Vedas, written in ancient India, are the oldest writings of the Hindu religion. This song was written c. 1100 B.C.

The goddess Night has drawn near, looking about on many sides with her eyes. She has put on all her glories.

The **immortal** goddess has filled the wide space, the depths and the heights. She stems the tide of darkness with her light.

The goddess has drawn near, pushing aside her sister the twilight. Darkness, too, will give way.

As you came near to us today, we turned homeward to rest, as birds go to their home in a tree.

People who live in villages have gone home to rest, and animals with feet, and animals with wings, even the ever-searching hawks.

Ward off the she-wolf and the wolf; ward off the thief. O night full of waves, be easy for us to cross over.

Darkness—**palpable,** black, and painted—has come upon me. O Dawn, banish it like a debt.

A representation of the Hindu god Siva

Document Based Questions

1. What are the five refinements according to Confucius?
2. What does Plato think will help make men and women more equal?
3. Who is the sister to the goddess Night in the last reading?
4. What does the song say Dawn should do about Darkness?

Document Based Questions Answers

1. being generous without being wasteful; being hardworking without being resentful; desiring without being greedy; being at ease without being proud; and being dignified without being fierce

2. having the same kind of upbringing and education

3. the twilight

4. banish it

935

UNIT LINK

Use the primary source selections on pages 936–937 to accompany study of Unit 3, "New Empires and New Faiths."

REINFORCING VOCABULARY

Review the **Reader's Dictionary** on page 936 with students to be sure they understand any unfamiliar terms before they begin reading the selections. Ask them to use the word *trifling* in a sentence. **L1**

BACKGROUND INFORMATION

Personal Records Personal records can be among the most compelling accounts of important events. Pliny's letter about the death of his uncle is a good example. Ask students to make a class list of events from their lifetimes that most merit personal records, and then choose one to write about in the style of Pliny's letter. Have them also add to each event the kinds of people, and their relations to the event, who could provide the most interesting and important accounts of what happened. **L2**

For use with Unit 3

New Empires and New Faiths

With the growth of new empires came great change. Events occurred that gave people the chance to be great leaders and heroes. New faiths continued to form new ideas.

Reader's Dictionary

cognizant: aware

trifling: insignificant

posterity: future time

allay: calm

incurred: brought upon oneself

Incense burner from the Byzantine Empire in the shape of a church

A Woman on the Throne

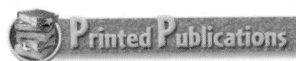 **Printed Publications**

In 1081 an able general named Alexius Commenus captured Constantinople. As Emperor Alexius I, he defended the Byzantine Empire against attacks from invaders. His daughter, Anna Comnena, retold the story of his reign in a book called The Alexiad *(uh•lehk•see•uhd). She begins her account by describing Alexius's decision to turn the government over to his mother Anna Dalassena.*

He really longed that his mother rather than himself should take the helm of the state, but so far he had concealed this design [plan] from her, fearing that if she became **cognizant** of it, she might actually leave the palace [for a convent]. . . . Therefore in all daily business he did nothing, not even a **trifling** thing, without her advice . . . and made her a partner in the administration of affairs, sometimes too he would say openly that without her brain and judgement the Empire would go to pieces.

. . . she was perhaps more devoted to her son than most women. And so she wished to help her son. . . . She ruled . . . with the Emperor, her son, and at times even took the reins alone and drove the chariot of Empire without harm or mishap. For besides being clever she had in very truth a kingly mind, capable of governing a kingdom.

EXTENDING THE CONTENT

Wearing Many Hats Pliny the Elder, who lived from A.D. 23 to A.D. 79, was a man of many talents. After gaining success as a cavalry commander, he also served Rome as a lawyer and district governor. In his spare time, he became one of the Roman Empire's greatest scientists. While serving as a naval commander south of Rome, with the charge to capture pirates, he noticed a strange cloud formation. Mount Vesuvius had erupted. He went ashore to reassure the frightened people—and there he died in the manner described by his nephew.

A Heroic Rescue Attempt

 Personal Records

Pliny the Elder—a Roman admiral and well-known author and scientist—died attempting to rescue people trapped at the foot of Mt. Vesuvius when it erupted. His nephew, Pliny the Younger, recorded his uncle's death in a letter written to a Roman historian named Tacitus. The letter forms an eyewitness account of the eruption and expresses Roman views of courage and duty.

Thank you for asking me to send you a description of my uncle's death so that you can leave an accurate account of it for **posterity**; . . .

As he was leaving the house he was handed a message from Rectina, . . . whose house was at the foot of the mountain, so that escape was impossible except by boat. She was terrified by the danger threatening her and implored him to rescue her. . . . Ashes were already falling, hotter and thicker as the ships drew near. . . . For a moment my uncle wondered whether to turn back, but when the helmsman advised this he refused, telling him that Fortune stood by the courageous. . . . This wind was . . . in my uncle's favour, and he was able to bring his ship in.

Meanwhile on Mount Vesuvius broad sheets of fire and leaping flames blazed at several points. . . . My uncle tried to **allay** the fears of his companions. . . . They debated whether to stay indoors or take their chance in the open,

for the buildings were now shaking with violent shocks, and seemed to be swaying. . . .

. . . A sheet was spread on the ground for him [uncle] to lie down, and he repeatedly asked for cold water to drink. Then the flames and smell of sulphur which gave warning of the approaching fire drove the others to take flight. . . . He stood . . . and then suddenly collapsed, I imagine because the dense fumes choked his breathing. . . . When daylight returned on the 26th—two days after the last day he had seen—his body was found. . . .

The Quran

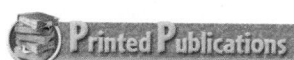 **Printed Publications**

The Quran is the holy book of Islam. The verses below come from Chapter 1, verses 2–7.

Praise be to Allah, the Lord of the Worlds,
The Compassionate, the Merciful,
Master of the Day of Judgement,
Only You do we worship, and only You
do we implore for help.
Lead us to the right path,
The path of those You have favoured
Not those who have **incurred** Your wrath or
have gone astray.

Document Based Questions

1. Why did Alexius conceal his plans to turn the government over to his mother?
2. Why did Pliny the Elder sail to Mt. Vesuvius?
3. Does Pliny the Younger consider his uncle a hero? Why or why not?
4. Who is the quote from the Quran praising?

Primary Sources Library

 ALTERNATIVE ASSESSMENT

Have students choose either the descriptive account by Anna Comnena or Pliny the Younger. Then have students plan and conduct a mock interview with one of the main figures in the account or with a fictional bystander. Have them write possible questions and provide answers in an interview format. **L3**

GLENCOE TECHNOLOGY

World History Primary Source Document Library CD-ROM

Use the CD-ROM to access primary source documents.

♫ **World Music: Cultural Traditions** and **World Music: A Cultural Legacy**

Use the world music programs to enhance the readings.

Document Based Questions Answers

1. He was afraid she might want to reject the responsibility and go live in a convent.
2. He wanted to rescue the people threatened by the volcano's eruption.
3. Probably; he writes the letter in order to preserve his uncle's memory for posterity, and he describes how, when offered the chance by the helmsman to escape to safety, his uncle refused.
4. Allah

UNIT LINK

Use the primary source selections on pages 938–939 to accompany study of Unit 4, "The Middle Ages."

REINFORCING VOCABULARY

Review the **Reader's Dictionary** on page 938 with students to be sure they understand any unfamiliar terms before they begin reading the selections. Ask them in what famous American speech they have heard the term *score*. *(the Gettysburg Address)* **L1**

BACKGROUND INFORMATION

Printed Publications Many documents have had a powerful and lasting effect on society. The Magna Carta is a good example. Ask students to read the statements and decide which ones have become important principles in our society, which was strongly influenced by England. Then have them point out any ways in which our nation's principles differ from the ideas expressed in the Magna Carta. *(Students may grasp that in most cases the Magna Carta's protections are extended only to free men.)* **L3**

For use with Unit 4

The Middle Ages

During the Middle Ages, civilizations began to develop to be more as we know them in modern times. There were still strong leaders—some good, some bad. But it became a time when the common people began to demand their rights. Women especially started to have a voice in their status and how they would live.

Reader's Dictionary

ebony: a hard, heavy wood

score: twenty

mitqal: an ancient unit of measure

heirs: descendants

abject: low

Drawing of Mansa Musa

The Sultan of Mali

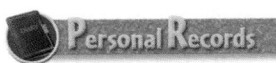
Personal Records

An Arab scholar named Ibn Fadl Allah al Omari describes the West African court and army of Mansa Musa in the 1330s. He refers to Mansa Musa as sultan, *the Arab word for "king."*

The sultan of this kingdom presides in his palace on a great balcony called *bembe* where he has a seat of **ebony** that is like a throne fit for a large and tall person: on either side it is flanked by elephant tusks turned towards each other. His arms stand near him, being all of gold, saber, lance, quiver, bow and arrows. He wears wide trousers made of about twenty pieces [of stuff] of a kind which he alone may wear. Behind him there stand about a **score** of Turkish or other pages which are bought for him in Cairo. . . . His officers are seated in a circle about him, in two rows, one to the right and one to the left; beyond them sit the chief commanders of his cavalry. . . . Others dance before their sovereign, who enjoys this, and make him laugh. Two banners are spread behind him. Before him they keep two saddled and bridled horses in case he should wish to ride.

Arab horses are brought for sale to the kings of this country, who spend considerable sums in this way. Their army numbers one hundred thousand men of whom there are about ten thousand horse-mounted cavalry: the others are infantry having neither horses nor any other mounts. . . .

The officers of this king, his soldiers and his guard receive gifts of land and presents. Some among the greatest of them receive as much as fifty thousand ***mitqals*** of gold a year, besides which the king provides them with horses and clothing. He is much concerned with giving them fine garments and making his cities into capitals.

EXTENDING THE CONTENT

The First Novel? *The Tale of Genji* is considered by some literary historians to be the first novel ever written. A novel is a long, invented prose narrative about human experiences that tells its story through a connected series of events and characters. Murasaki Shikibu's story of the young prince describes the delights of nature and court life. However, it grows more somber toward its end, a reflection of the Buddhist belief that everything in this world is vanity and illusion.

The Magna Carta

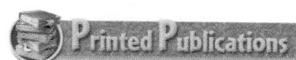
Printed Publications

The Magna Carta, signed in England in 1215, for the first time gave common people some freedoms and protections. It also limited the power of King John.

To all free men of our kingdom we have also granted, for us and our **heirs** for ever, all the liberties written out below. . . .

No widow shall be compelled [forced] to marry, so long as she wishes to remain without a husband. . . .

For a trivial offence, a free man shall be fined only in proportion to the degree of his offence. . . .

No sheriff, royal official, or other person shall take horses or carts for transport from any free man, without his consent. . . .

No free man shall be seized or imprisoned . . . or outlawed or exiled . . . except by the lawful judgement of his equals or by the law of the land.

To no one will we sell, to no one deny or delay right or justice.

All merchants may enter or leave England unharmed and without fear, and may stay or travel within it, by land or water, for purposes of trade. . . .

All these customs and liberties that we have granted shall be observed in our kingdom.

The Tale of Genji

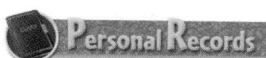
Personal Records

The Tale of Genji is the story of a young man searching for the meaning of life. It was written by Murasaki Shikibu in A.D. 1010. Genji's friend described three classes of women: those of high rank and birth whose weak points are concealed; those of the middle class; and those of the lower class. This is part of Genji's reply.

[Genji said] "It will not always be so easy to know into which of the three classes a woman ought to be put. For sometimes people of high rank sink to the most **abject** positions; while others of common birth rise to . . . think themselves as good as anyone. How are we to deal with such cases?"

Murasaki Shikibu

Document Based Questions

1. What conclusions can you draw about Mansa Musa's power?
2. Why do you think Mansa Musa treated his soldiers so well?
3. According to the Magna Carta, when can a man be imprisoned?
4. What does Genji seem to realize about the social classes that his friend does not?

Primary Sources Library

ALTERNATIVE ASSESSMENT

Ask students to choose one of the primary sources from pages 938–939, and have them create a drawing that represents some aspect of the selection. For example, they might illustrate one of the protections offered by the Magna Carta, Genji's conversation about the three types of women, or the fabulous court of Mansa Musa. Display the drawings as you study this unit. **L1/ EL**

GLENCOE TECHNOLOGY

World History Primary Source Document Library CD-ROM

Use the CD-ROM to access primary source documents.

♫ **World Music: Cultural Traditions** and **World Music: A Cultural Legacy**

Use the world music programs to enhance the readings.

Document Based Questions Answers

1. It was practically absolute, as well as backed by military force.
2. Students may point out that his power depended on military force; he may have feared what his soldiers might do to him if they became dissatisfied.
3. when he has been found guilty by his equals or by the law of the land
4. People's standing in society can be affected by their actions.

Primary Sources Library

UNIT LINK

Use the primary source selections on pages 940–941 to accompany study of Unit 5, "A Changing World."

REINFORCING VOCABULARY

Review the **Reader's Dictionary** on page 940 with students to be sure they understand any unfamiliar terms before they begin reading the selections. Ask them to name a more common English word that probably has the same origin as *stench*. *(stink)* **L1**

BACKGROUND INFORMATION

Oral Histories Throughout history, many people have handed down their culture, traditions, and other important information through the oral tradition. Famous speeches, such as Queen Elizabeth's, are one form. Another is family histories, which are passed from one generation to the next. Ask volunteers to share their family stories. Then have students discuss how stories help us understand the past. **L2**

For use with Unit 5

A Changing World

World exploration expanded as countries looked for new lands to conquer. There was great competition among European countries to claim undiscovered riches. This exploration did not always benefit the people already living in explored lands, however.

Reader's Dictionary

finery: fancier clothes and jewelry

installed: placed in

plunder: stolen goods, usually during war

stench: a very bad smell

scorn: anger

Aztec and Spanish soldiers in battle

Arrival of the Spaniards

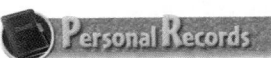

Aztec accounts of the Spanish conquest of Mexico in 1519 are recorded in The Broken Spears, *edited and translated by Miguel Leon-Portilla. This selection describes the meeting of Montezuma and Cortés.*

The Spaniards arrived . . . near the entrance to Tenochititlan. That was the end of their march, for they had reached their goal.

[Montezuma] now arrayed himself in his **finery**, preparing to go out to meet them. . . .

. . . Then he hung the gold necklaces around their necks and gave them presents of every sort as gifts of welcome.

When [Montezuma] had given necklaces to each one, Cortés asked him: "Are you [Montezuma]? Are you the king? . . ."

And the king said: "Yes, I am [Montezuma]." Then he stood up to welcome Cortés; he came forward, bowed his head low and addressed him in these words: "Our lord, you are weary. The journey has tired you, but now you have arrived on the earth. You have come to your city, Mexico. You have come here to sit on your throne. . . ."

When the Spaniards were **installed** in the palace, they asked [Montezuma] about the city's resources. . . . They questioned him closely and then demanded gold.

[Montezuma] guided them to it. . . .

. . . When they entered the hall of treasures, it was as if they had arrived in Paradise. . . . All of [Montezuma's] possessions were brought out: fine bracelets, necklaces with large stones, ankle rings with little gold bells, the royal crowns and all the royal finery—everything that belonged to the king. . . . They seized these treasures as if they were their own, as if this **plunder** were merely a stroke of good luck.

EXTENDING THE CONTENT

Journey of Horror The journey of the kidnapped Africans to the Americas was known as the Middle Passage. It marked the middle part of their journey from freedom to enslavement. The first was their kidnapping in Africa, while the last part of their journey was from the American port to their final home. The Middle Passage itself was terrible. People were packed like spoons so tightly in the holds of the ships that they could not turn over or stand up. The average space for each person was 16 inches (41 cm) wide. More than one in every ten prisoners died before reaching the Americas.

The Life of Olaudah Equiano

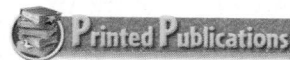
Printed Publications

Olaudah Equiano was kidnapped from West Africa and brought to America as a slave. In 1789 he wrote an account of this frightening journey. Here he describes the first part of that trip.

The first thing I saw was a vast ocean, and a ship, riding at anchor, waiting for its cargo. The ocean and the ship filled me with astonishment that soon turned to fear. I was taken to the ship and carried on board! . . .

The crew took me down below decks, into the ship's stinking hold. With the horribleness of the **stench** and my crying I was so sick and low that I couldn't eat. I wanted to die. . . .

That first day, among the poor chained men in the hold, I found some people of Benin.

"What are they going to do to us?" I asked.

"They are taking us away to work for them," a man from Benin explained.

"And do they only live here," I asked, "in this hollow place, the ship?"

"They have a white people's country," the man explained, "but it is far away."

"How can it be," I asked, "that in our whole country nobody ever heard of them?"

"They live *very* far away," another man explained.

Drawing of a slave ship

Queen Elizabeth's Speech To Her Troops

Oral Histories

In 1588, a Spanish fleet, known as the Spanish Armada, was sent to invade England. Queen Elizabeth I spoke to her troops before the battle.

Let tyrants fear: I have so behaved myself that under God I have placed my chiefest strength and safeguard in the loyal hearts and goodwill of my subjects. Wherefore I am come . . . to live and die amongst you all, to lay down for my God and for my kingdom and for my people mine honor and my blood even in the dust. I know I have the body but of a weak and feeble woman, but I have the heart and stomach of a king and a king of England too—and take foul **scorn** that . . . any prince of Europe should dare to invade the borders of my realm.

Queen Elizabeth I

Document Based Questions

1. What gifts did Montezuma give to Cortés?
2. Why do you think Montezuma took Cortés to see his personal treasury?
3. How did Equiano travel from Africa to the Americas?
4. In her speech, is Queen Elizabeth I encouraging or discouraging her troops? Explain.

Document Based Questions Answers

1. gold necklaces
2. The Spaniards demanded to see it. He might have hoped not to offend them by refusing.
3. in a ship with other enslaved Africans
4. She is encouraging them by saying that she is as brave and strong as a man and a king. She also says that she is prepared to die with the soldiers if necessary and that other kings invade her kingdom only at their great risk.

ALTERNATIVE ASSESSMENT

Ask students to write a story, poem, song, or other creative work about one of the selections from pages 940–941. They might choose to write from the perspective of an Aztec seeing the Spaniards for the first time, an African crossing the ocean on the ship, or one of Elizabeth's soldiers on the eve of the battle. Have volunteers share their creative work with the class. **L2**

GLENCOE TECHNOLOGY

World History Primary Source Document Library CD-ROM

Use the CD-ROM to access primary source documents.

♫ **World Music: Cultural Traditions** and **World Music: A Cultural Legacy**

Use the world music programs to enhance the readings.

Primary Sources Library

UNIT LINK

Use the primary source selections on pages 942–943 to accompany study of Unit 6, "Modern Times."

REINFORCING VOCABULARY

Review the **Reader's Dictionary** on page 942 with students to be sure they understand any unfamiliar terms. Ask students to name places in the world where they feel oppression occurs today. *(Possible answers include North Korea, Saudi Arabia, Iran, Cuba, Israel, and Sudan.)*

BACKGROUND INFORMATION

Visual Materials Although most people read speeches in printed form after they are given, the experience of hearing a live speech can be electrifying. Ask students to view a film of one of these speeches. Then ask them to compare the effects of reading the speech with those of experiencing it in a film. *(Reading: can go back and review parts, can pause and think about the ideas; "Live": can be affected by the speaker's rhetorical power, voice, and gestures, can be influenced by crowd reaction)* **L2**

For use with Unit 6

Modern Times

One of the major ideas of the world's modern times is the theme of justice and equality for all people. All over the world—in India, the United States, and Africa—this theme has been supported by great leaders.

Reader's Dictionary

doctrine: a principle or belief

Gentile: a person who is not Jewish

dichotomy: having two sides

oppression: cruel use of authority or power

Mohandas K. Gandhi

Peaceful Noncooperation

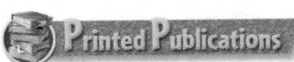
Printed Publications

Mohandas K. Gandhi, the great Indian nationalistic leader, spoke to over 500,000 people in 1920. He addressed them about his philosophy of peaceful rebellion against and noncooperation with the rule of Great Britain over India.

I have been told that non-cooperation is unconstitutional. I venture to deny that it is unconstitutional. On the contrary, I hold that non-cooperation is a just and religious **doctrine;** it is the inherent [natural] right of every human being and it is perfectly constitutional. . . . I do not claim any constitutionality for a rebellion successful or otherwise, so long as that rebellion means in the ordinary sense of the term, what it does mean, namely, wresting justice by violent means. On the contrary, I have said it repeatedly to my countrymen that violence, whatever end it may serve in Europe, will never serve us in India.

. . . I am asking India to follow this non-violent non-cooperation. . . . As soon as India adopts the doctrine of the sword, my life as an Indian is finished. It is because I believe in a mission special to India and it is because I believe the ancients of India after centuries of experience have found out that the one true thing for any human being on earth is not justice based on violence but justice based on sacrifice of self. . . . I cling to that doctrine and I shall cling to it forever. . . .

EXTENDING THE CONTENT

Historical Connections The connections between the three crusaders for justice are strong. When King was a seminary student in Pennsylvania, he studied the ideas and nonviolent philosophy of Mohandas Gandhi. Gandhi's influence also spread to other civil rights leaders and groups. Gandhi himself first met discrimination and racism while working in South Africa, and it was there he became a human rights activist. Finally, although he later modified his belief in nonviolence, Nelson Mandela early in his career supported nonviolence as the way to gain equality for South Africa's nonwhite population. After his release from prison, Mandela worked for the peaceful transition to majority rule.

I Have a Dream

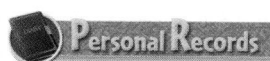 **Personal Records**

In 1963 civil rights leader Dr. Martin Luther King, Jr., spoke to more than 200,000 people in a peace march on Washington, D.C. He spoke about his dreams for the future of African Americans and the United States.

I say to you today, my friends, that in spite of the difficulties and frustrations of the moment I still have a dream. . . . I have a dream that one day this nation will rise up and live out the true meaning of its creed: "We hold these truths to be self-evident, that all men are created equal."

I have a dream that one day on the red hills of Georgia the sons of former slaves and the sons of former slaveowners will be able to sit down together at the table of brotherhood. . . .

I have a dream that my four little children will one day live in a nation where they will not be judged by the color of their skin but by the content of their character. . . .

. . . When we let freedom ring, when we let it ring from every village and every hamlet, from every state and every city, we will be able to speed up that day when all of God's children, black men and white men, Jews and **Gentiles,** Protestants and Catholics, will be able to join hands and sing the words of the old Negro spiritual: "Free at last! Free at last! Thank God Almighty, we are free at last!"

Dr. King speaking

Nobel Peace Prize Winner

 Printed Publications

In 1993 Nelson Mandela of South Africa accepted the Nobel Peace Prize for his efforts to end the unequal treatment of the black citizens of South Africa.

I extend my heartfelt thanks to the Norwegian Nobel Committee for elevating us to the status of a Nobel Peace Prize winner. . . .

We speak here of the challenge of the **dichotomies** of war and peace, violence and non-violence, racism and human dignity, oppression and repression and liberty and human rights, poverty and freedom from want.

We stand here today as nothing more than a representative of the millions of our people who dared to rise up against a social system whose very essence is war, violence, racism, **oppression,** repression and the impoverishment of an entire people.

I am also here today as a representative of the millions of people across the globe, the anti-apartheid movement, the governments and organizations that joined us, not to fight against South Africa . . . but to oppose an inhuman system. . . .

Because of their courage and persistence . . . we can, today, even set the dates when all humanity will join together to celebrate one of the outstanding human victories of our century.

Primary Sources Library

 ## Document Based Questions

1. What does Gandhi believe about violent rebellion in India?
2. What does Dr. King say is America's most important creed?
3. Nelson Mandela fought to end unequal treatment for what people in what country?
4. What is one belief each of these leaders seem to share? Explain.

Have students choose one of the speeches and research events, cultural elements, traditions, and important persons that influenced the speech. For example, Dr. King's speech grew out of African American slavery, the civil rights movement, the Christian religious tradition and Negro spirituals, and U.S. history. Have a group of students create a mural about the speech. In the mural, have them include elements that help define the milieu from which the speech was created. Have groups present and explain their murals and display them in the classroom. **L2**

GLENCOE TECHNOLOGY

World History Primary Source Document Library CD-ROM

Use the CD-ROM to access primary source documents.

♫ **World Music: Cultural Traditions** and **World Music: A Cultural Legacy.**

Use the world music programs to enhance the readings.

Document Based Questions Answers

1. It would be based on injustice and that it is not appropriate for India, regardless of how it is used in Europe.
2. that all people are created equal
3. blacks and other non whites in South Africa
4. Sample answer: people working together can overcome injustice, poverty, racism, and oppression

Suggested Readings

If you are interested in reading more about people and events in world history, the following list will help you. The book titles listed for each unit are fiction and nonfiction books you can read to learn more about that time period.

Unit 1:

Arnold, Caroline. *Stone Age Farmers Beside the Sea.* Clarion Books, 1997. A photo-essay describing the prehistoric village of Skara Brae.

Bunting, Eve. *I Am the Mummy Heb-Nefert.* Harcourt Brace, 1997. Fictional story of a mummy recalling her past life as the wife of the pharaoh's brother.

Courlander, Harold. *The King's Drum, and Other African Tales.* Harcourt, 1962. Folktales taken from Africa south of the Sahara.

Deem, James M. *Bodies from the Bog.* Houghton Mifflin, 1998. A photo-essay that looks at information from the well-preserved bodies found in a Danish bog.

Gregory, Kristiana. *Cleopatra VII: Daughter of the Nile.* Scholastic Inc., 1999. A fictional diary written by Cleopatra.

Herrmann, Siegfried. *A History of Israel in Old Testament Times.* Fortress Press, 1975. The Old Testament as a history of early Israel, with evidence from sources other than the Bible.

Lattimore, Deborah Nourse. *Winged Cat: A Tale of Ancient Egypt.* HarperCollins, 1995. A tale of a servant girl and a High Priest using the Book of the Dead to investigate the death of the girl's sacred cat.

Maltz, Fran. *Keeping Faith in the Dust.* Alef Design Group, 1998. Fictional account of a 16-year-old girl whose family is forced to flee their home near the Dead Sea to the fortress of Masada, where Roman forces are held off by the Jews for seven years.

Morley, Jacquelin. Mark Bergin, and John James. *An Egyptian Pyramid.* Peter Bedrick, 1991. Explains how the pyramids were built and their purpose.

Perl, Lila. *Mummies, Tombs, and Treasure: Secrets of Ancient Egypt.* Clarion Books, 1990. An account of what ancient Egyptians believed about death and the afterlife.

Travis, Lucille. *Tirzah.* Herald Press, 1991. Fictional story of a 12-year-old boy who flees from Egypt with Moses during the Exodus.

Trumble, Kelly. *Cat Mummies.* Clarion Books, 1996. Reasons and background examining why ancient Egyptians mummified thousands and thousands of cats.

Wetwood, Jennifer. *Gilgamesh, and Other Babylonian Tales.* Coward, McCann & Geoghegan, 1970. Retells ancient tales of Sumer and Babylon.

Unit 2:

Chang, Richard F. *Chinese Mythical Stories.* Yale Far Eastern Publications, 1990. Legends and myths of China.

Craft, Charlotte. *King Midas and the Golden Touch.* Morrow, 1999. The myth of King Midas and his greed for gold.

Evslin, Bernard. *Heroes and Monsters of Greek Myth.* Scholastic, 1988. A collection of Greek myths.

Fleischman, Paul. *Dateline: Troy.* Candlewick Press, 1996. Author uses modern wars (Persian Gulf, Vietnam) to better understand the Trojan War.

Ganeri, Anita. *Buddhism.* NTC Publishing Group, 1997. Overview of Buddhist history and beliefs.

Ganeri, Anita. *Hinduism.* NTC Publishing Group, 1996. Overview of Hindu history and beliefs.

Hamilton, Edith. *The Greek Way.* Norton, 1983. The story of the Greek spirit and mind told by great writers.

Harris, Nathaniel. *Alexander the Great and the Greeks.* Bookwright Press, 1986. Contributions Alexander made to the Greeks.

Homer and Geraldine McCaughrean. *The Odyssey.* Oxford, 1999. Illustrated retelling of *The Odyssey* using modern language.

Ross, Stewart. *The Original Olympic Games.* NTC Publishing Group, 1999. A history of the Olympics.

Theule, Frederic. *Alexander and His Times.* Henry Holt and Co., 1996. A pictorial and historic account of the life of Alexander the Great.

Unit 3:

Boyd, Anne. *Life in a 15th-Century Monastery (A Cambridge Topic Book).* Lerner Publications, 1979. An account of the daily life of monks in the monastery at Durham, England.

Browning, Robert. *The Byzantine Empire.* Charles Scribner's Sons, 1980. The Byzantine world from A.D. 500 to fall of Constantinople in 1453.

Burrell, Roy. *The Romans: Rebuilding the Past.* Oxford University Press, 1991. A historical outline of ancient Rome.

Comte, Fernand. *Sacred Writings of World Religions.* Chambers, 1992. The history, beliefs, and major figures of more than 20 religions, among them Judaism, Islam, and Christianity.

Dillon, Eilis. *Rome Under the Emperors.* Tomas Nelson, 1975. Views of Roman society and family life in the time of Trajan, as seen by young people of four different families and social classes.

Powell, Anton. *The Rise of Islam.* Warwick Press, 1980. An overview of Islamic culture.

Tingay, Graham. *Julius Caesar.* Cambridge University Press, 1991. An account of the life and achievements of Julius Caesar.

Unit 4:

Giles, Frances and Joseph. *Life in a Medieval Village.* Harper Perennial, 1990. An illustrated look at the way most medieval people passed their lives.

Haugaard, Erik Christian. *The Revenge of the Forty-Seven Samurai.* Houghton Mifflin, 1995. The tale of Jiro, a young boy who must aid 47 samurai who are attempting to avenge the unjust death of their lord. This historical novel provides a detailed look at Japanese feudal society.

Heer, Friedrich. *Charlemagne and His World.* Macmillan, 1975. Large, lavishly illustrated description of the period.

McKendrick, Meveena. *Ferdinand and Isabella.* American Heritage, 1968. Photographs and contemporary paintings help re-create the period.

Sanders, Tao Tao Liu. *Dragons, Gods, and Spirits from Chinese Mythology.* NTC, 1997. Collection of myths, legends, and folktales providing insight into the culture and historic development of China.

Scott, Sir Walter. *Ivanhoe.* Longmans, Green, and Co., 1897. A twelfth-century story of hidden identity, intrigue, and romance among the English nobility.

Wisniewski, David. *Sundiata: Lion King of Mali.* Houghton Mifflin, 1999. Story about the ancient king of Mali and how he defeated his enemies to become the ruler.

Unit 5:

Cowie, Leonard W. *Martin Luther: Leader of the Reformation (A Pathfinder Biography).* Frederick Praeger, 1969. A detailed biography of Luther.

Davis, Burke. *Black Heroes of the American Revolution.* Harcourt, Brace and Jovanovich, 1991. Highlights achievements of African Americans during the Revolution.

Hibbard, Howard. *Michelangelo.* Westview Press, 1985. Biography of Michelangelo told through his paintings, poems, and personal letters.

Hooks, William H. *The Legend of White Doe.* Macmillan, 1998. Tale about Virginia Dare, the first child of English settlers born in the Americas.

Lomask, Milton. *Exploration: Great Lives.* Scribners, 1988. Biographies of explorers.

Mee, Charles L. *Daily Life in the Renaissance.* American Heritage, 1975. Works of art showing people in their daily lives.

O'Dell, Scott. *The Hawk that Dare Not Hunt by Day.* Houghton Mifflin, 1975. Novel about a boy who helps the reformer Tyndale smuggle his translation of the Bible into England.

Stuart, Gene S. *America's Ancient Cities.* National Geographic Society, 1988. An illustrated collection of essays on cultures of North America and Mesoamerica.

Unit 6

Alvarez, Julia. *Before We Were Free.* Knopf Books for Young Readers, 2002. This story tells of a young girl and her family trying to flee the dictatorship of the Dominican Republic in the 1960s.

Ambrose, Stephen E. *The Good Fight: How World War II Was Won.* Atheneum Books for Young Readers, 2001. This book gives an account of World War II based on personal anecdotes from soldiers.

Blumberg, Rhoda. *What's the Deal? Jefferson, Napoleon, and the Louisiana Purchase.* National Geographic Society, 1998. This piece explores the Louisiana Purchase as something more than a simple business deal.

Chang, Jung. *Wild Swans: Three Daughters of China.* Doubleday, 1991. This fictional biography traces three generations of Chinese women as they live through Chinese warlords, Mao and Communism, and the Tiananmen Square massacre of 1989.

Connell, Kate. *They Shall Be Heard: Susan B. Anthony and Elizabeth Cady Stanton.* Steck-Vaughn, 1993. This book discusses the work of Anthony and Stanton during the early years of the struggle for woman suffrage.

Falstein, Mark. *Nelson Mandela.* Globe Fearon, 1994. This book tells the story of Mandela's life, from being in prison for 27 years to becoming president of South Africa in 1994.

Holliday, Laurel. *Children of Israel, Children of Palestine: Our Own True Stories.* Pocket Books, 1998. This book contains the stories of 36 men, women, and children of Israeli and Palestinian descent who reflect on their feelings on growing up during such a turbulent time.

Lewington, Anna. *Mexico: A Study of an Economically Developing Country.* Raintree Steck-Vaughn Publishers, 1996. This book explores the history, geography, economy, and people of Mexico in the modern world.

Marrin, Albert. *Napoleon and the Napoleonic Wars.* Viking Penguin, 1991. This is a biography of Napoleon Bonaparte, highlighting his military genius and goals for conquest.

Marrin, Albert. *Stalin: Russia's Man of Steel.* Viking Penguin, Inc., 1988. This book tells how Joseph Stalin used terror and an iron fist to transform Russia from a backward country into a major world superpower in the first half of the 1900s.

Moscow, Henry. *Russia Under the Czars.* American Heritage Publishing Co., Inc., 1962. This story tells how the Russian czars withstood external invasion, only to fall to the revolutionaries led by Lenin.

Murphy, Jim. *The Boys War: Confederate and Union Soldiers Talk About the Civil War.* Houghton Mifflin, 1993. This book uses primary sources to detail the role of juvenile soldiers in the Civil War, as well as the effects that their experiences had in shaping the rest of their lives.

Nordhoff, Charles and James N. Hall. *Falcons of France.* Little, Brown and Co., 1957. This novel tells of the Lafayette Flying Corps, an expert team of French fighter pilots in World War I.

Rosenberg, Tina. *The Haunted Land: Facing Europe's Ghosts After Communism.* Random House, 1995. This book tells of countries that broke from communism in the 1900s and built democracies.

Savage, Katharine. *The Story of the United Nations.* Henry Z. Walck, Inc., 1970. This book details the creation of the UN and its early history.

Severance, John B. *Gandhi: Great Soul.* Clarion Books, 1997. This book details the life of Mohandas Gandhi and highlights his nonviolent campaign for the independence of India.

Sommer, Robin Langley. *Nien Cheng: Prisoner in China.* Blackbirch Press, Inc., 1992. This book tells the story of Nien Cheng, a Chinese woman who spent six years in solitary confinement during the rule of Mao Zedong in China.

Stowe, Harriet Beecher. *Uncle Tom's Cabin.* Bantam Classics, 1983. This famous novel gives a fictional account of the evils of slavery in the United States in the mid-1800s.

Veciana-Suarez, Ana. *Flight to Freedom.* Scholastic, 2004. This fictional biography tells the story of thirteen-year-old Yara and how her life changes as she leaves Communist Cuba for a new life and new challenges in Florida.

Zeinert, Karen. *Those Incredible Women of World War II.* The Milbrook Press, 1994. This book focuses on the contributions of women during World War II.

Suggested Readings

Glossary

A

abolitionism movement to end slavery (p. 753)

absolutism system of rule in which monarchs held total power and claimed to rule by the will of God (p. 686)

acupuncture Chinese practice of easing pain by sticking thin needles into patients' skin (p. 246)

adobe sun-dried mud brick (p. 591)

agora in early Greek city-states, an open area that served as both a market and a meeting place (p. 122)

alphabet group of letters that stand for sounds (p. 85)

anatomy the study of body structure (p. 305)

animism belief that all natural things are alive and have their own spirits (p. 490)

annul to cancel (p. 648)

anthropologist scientist who studies the physical characteristics and cultures of humans and their ancestors (p. 9)

anti-Semitism hatred of Jews (p. 548)

apartheid policy of racial segregation in the Republic of South Africa from 1948–1991; Afrikaans for "apartness" or "separateness" (pp. 852, 872)

apostle early Christian leader who helped set up churches and spread the message of Jesus (p. 348)

appeasement idea that by meeting another government's demands, war can be avoided (p. 814)

aqueduct human-made channel built to carry water (p. 291)

archaeologist scientist who learns about past human life by studying fossils and artifacts (p. 9)

aristocrat noble whose wealth came from land ownership (p. 227)

armistice agreement to end fighting; cease-fire (p. 790)

artifact weapon, tool, or other item made by humans (p. 9)

artisan skilled craftsperson (p. 20)

astronomer person who studies stars, planets, and other heavenly bodies (pp. 30, 185)

B

barbarian uncivilized person (p. 435)

barter to exchange goods without using money (p. 319)

bazaar marketplace (p. 389)

blockade use of warships to stop goods and people from leaving or entering an area (p. 787)

bourgeoisie middle classes of society, including merchants, bankers, doctors, lawyers, teachers, and other professional people (p. 715)

Brahman in Hinduism, the universal spirit of which all gods and goddesses are different parts (p. 203)

Buddhism religion founded by Siddhartha Gautama, the Buddha; taught that the way to find truth was to give up all desires (p. 205)

bureaucracy a group of appointed officials who are responsible for different areas of government (p. 229)

C

caliph important Muslim political and religious leader (p. 380)

calligraphy beautiful handwriting (p. 421); the art of producing beautiful handwriting (p. 501)

capital money available for investment in business (p. 726)

caravan group of traveling merchants and animals (pp. 30, 373)

caste social group that a person is born into and cannot change (p. 199)

cataract steep rapids formed by cliffs and boulders in a river (p. 39)

caudillos strong leaders who mainly ruled by military force, usually with the support of the rich and upper class (p. 751)

census a count of the number of people (p. 432)

city-state independent state made up of a city and the surrounding land and villages (p. 19)

civil disobedience refusal to obey unjust laws of a government (p. 843)

Glossary

civilization complex society with cities, organized government, art, religion, class divisions, and a writing system (p. 17)

clan group of families related by blood or marriage (pp. 461, 487)

clergy religious officials, such as priests, given authority to conduct religious services (pp. 355, 538)

collectivization system of combining small farms into large, factory-like farms run by the government (p. 810)

colony settlement in a new territory that keeps close ties with its homeland (pp. 121, 666, 763)

comedy form of drama in which the story has a happy ending (p. 161)

commerce the buying and selling of goods in large amounts over long distances (p. 666)

concordat agreement between the pope and the ruler of a country (p. 521)

confederation a loose union of several groups or states (p. 592)

Confucianism system of beliefs introduced by the Chinese thinker Confucius; taught that people needed to have a sense of duty to their family and community in order to bring peace to society (p. 236)

conquistador Spanish conqueror or soldier in the Americas (p. 595)

conscription enrollment into military service by force; military draft (p. 782)

constitution written plan of government (pp. 488, 694)

consul one of the two top government officials in ancient Rome (p. 269)

containment U.S. policies that intended to prevent the spread of communism (p. 834)

corporation business organization that is allowed to own property and sell shares to investors in order to raise money (p. 728)

coup d'etat forced replacement of top government leaders by a new group of leaders (p. 720)

covenant agreement (p. 82)

crier announcer who calls Muslim believers to prayer five times a day (p. 394)

cuneiform Sumerian system of writing made up of wedge-shaped markings (p. 20)

currency system of money (p. 294)

D

daimyo powerful military lord in feudal Japan (pp. 496, 777)

Dao the proper way Chinese kings were expected to rule under the Mandate of Heaven (p. 230)

Daoism Chinese philosophy based on the teachings of Laozi; taught that people should turn to nature and give up their worldly concerns (p. 238)

D-Day June 6, 1944; the day in World War II when Allied forces invaded Normandy, France (p. 828)

deforestation clearing of forests (p. 890)

deism religious belief based on reason (p. 685)

deity god or goddess (p. 49)

delta area of fertile soil at the mouth of a river (p. 39)

democracy government in which all citizens share in running the government (p. 126)

denomination an organized branch of Christianity (p. 636)

depression a period of low economic activity when many people lose their jobs (p. 806)

détente policy promoting a relaxation of tensions between nations (p. 881)

dharma in Hinduism, the divine law that requires people to perform the duties of their caste (p. 204)

dhow an Arab sailboat (p. 452)

Diaspora refers to the scattering of communities of Jews outside their homeland after the Babylonian captivity (p. 96)

dictator in ancient Rome, a person who ruled with complete power temporarily during emergencies (p. 271)

diplomacy the art of negotiating with other countries (p. 615)

direct democracy system of government in which people gather at mass meetings to decide on government matters (p. 139)

disciple close follower of Jesus (p. 344)

doctrine official church teaching (p. 355)

domesticate to tame animals and plants for human use (p. 13)

drama story told by actors who pretend to be characters in the story (p. 160)

duma Russian national assembly of elected lawmakers (p. 793)

dynasty line of rulers from the same family (pp. 44, 210, 226)

economy organized way in which people produce, sell, and buy goods and services (p. 410)

embalming process developed by the ancient Egyptians of preserving a person's body after death (p. 49)

embargo order that bans or restricts trade with another country (p. 863)

empire group of territories or nations under a single ruler or government (pp. 23, 89)

entente understanding among nations that provides for a common course of action (p. 782)

epic long poem that tells about legendary or heroic deeds (p. 157)

Epicureanism philosophy founded by Epicurus in Hellenistic Athens; taught that happiness through the pursuit of pleasure was the goal of life (p. 184)

estates classes into which French people were divided before the French Revolution: the Catholic clergy (First Estate), the nobles (Second Estate), and the townspeople (Third Estate) (p. 715)

ethnic cleansing using force to remove an entire ethnic group from an area (p. 884)

euro common currency shared by countries of the European Union since 1999 (p. 889)

excommunicate to declare that a person or group no longer belongs to a church (pp. 361, 521)

exile period of forced absence from one's country or home (p. 94)

export to sell to another country (pp. 666, 861)

extended family family group including several generations as well as other relatives (p. 469)

extraterritoriality legal practice of foreigners living in a country but not subject to the host country's laws (p. 772)

fable short tale that teaches a lesson (p. 158)

feudalism political system based on bonds of loyalty between lords and vassals (pp. 497, 523)

fief under feudalism, the land a lord granted to a vassal in exchange for military service and loyalty (p. 524)

filial piety children's respect for their parents and older relatives, an important part of Confucian beliefs (p. 234)

fjord steep-sided valley that is an inlet of the sea (p. 518)

Forum open space in Rome that served as a marketplace and public square (p. 306)

fossil the trace or imprint of a plant or animal that has been preserved in rock (p. 9)

genocide the deliberate killing of a racial, political, or cultural group (p. 827)

glacier huge sheet of ice (p. 573)

gladiator in ancient Rome, person who fought animals and other people as public entertainment (p. 306)

glasnost Mikhail Gorbachev's Soviet policy that permitted open discussion of political and social ideas (p. 882)

globalism idea that every nation's economy and politics are part of one worldwide system (p. 889)

gospel ("good news") one of the four accounts of Jesus' life, teachings, and resurrection (p. 355)

grand jury group that decides whether there is enough evidence to accuse a person of a crime (p. 537)

griot storyteller (p. 449)

guild medieval business group formed by craftspeople and merchants (pp. 503, 530)

guru religious teacher and spiritual guide in Hinduism (p. 201)

Hellenistic Era period when the Greek language and Greek ideas spread to the non-Greek peoples of southwest Asia (p. 178)

helot person who was conquered and enslaved by the ancient Spartans (p. 126)

Glossary

Glossary

heresy belief that differs from or contradicts the accepted teachings of a religion (pp. 547, 643)

hierarchy organization with different levels of authority (p. 355)

hieroglyphics system of writing made up of thousands of picture symbols developed by the ancient Egyptians (p. 42)

Hinduism system of religion that grew out of the religion of the Aryans in ancient India (p. 203)

historian person who studies and writes about the human past (p. 9)

humanism Renaissance movement based on the values of the ancient Greeks and Romans, such as that individuals and human society were important (p. 619)

hypothesis proposed explanation of the facts (p. 679)

icon Christian religious image or picture (p. 359)

iconoclast person who opposed the use of icons in Byzantine churches, saying that icons encouraged the worship of idols (p. 360)

ideograph a character that joins two or more pictographs to represent an idea (p. 228)

igloo dome-shaped home built by the Inuit (p. 590)

imperialism a nation's direct or indirect control over the government or economy of other usually smaller or weaker nations (p. 763)

import to buy from another country (p. 666)

incense material burned for its pleasant smell (p. 62)

indulgence pardon from the Church for a person's sins (p. 634)

industrialism economic system in which people rely more on the use of machinery and technology than on animal or human power (p. 725)

inflation period of rapidly increasing prices (pp. 319, 806)

intifada armed uprising of Palestinians against Israeli occupation of the West Bank and Gaza Strip (p. 878)

invest to put money into a project (p. 667)

irrigation method of bringing water to a field from another place to water crops (p. 18)

kaiser German for "emperor" (p. 748)

karma in Hinduism, the good or bad energy a person builds up based upon whether he or she lives a good or bad life (p. 204)

knight in the Middle Ages, a noble warrior who fought on horseback (p. 524)

labor union association of workers who unite to improve worker rights, wages, benefits, and working conditions (p. 736)

laity church members who are not clergy (p. 355)

latifundia large farming estates in ancient Rome (p. 278)

legacy what a person leaves behind when he or she dies (p. 178)

Legalism Chinese philosophy developed by Hanfeizi; taught that humans are naturally evil and therefore need to be ruled by harsh laws (p. 239)

legion smaller unit of the Roman army made up of about 6,000 soldiers (p. 266)

liberalism political belief based on the ideas of the Enlightenment, which stress progress, the essential goodness of humankind, and individual freedom (p. 735)

limited government idea that a government may only use the powers given to it by the people (p. 700)

mandate formal order (pp. 230, 792)

Marshall Plan U.S.-sponsored program to provide economic aid to European countries after World War II, from 1948–51; named after U.S. Secretary of State George Marshall who proposed it to Congress (p. 834)

martial arts sports, such as judo and karate, that involve combat and self-defense (p. 499)

martyr person willing to die rather than give up his or her beliefs (p. 353)

mass Catholic worship service (p. 546)

matrilineal refers to a group that traces descent through mothers rather than fathers (p. 469)

meditation practice of quiet reflection to clear the mind and find inner peace (p. 499)

mercantilism the idea that a country gains power by building up its supply of gold and silver (p. 666)

messiah in Judaism, a deliverer sent by God (pp. 101, 344)

militarism fascination with war and the military (p. 782)

minaret tower of a mosque from which the crier calls believers to prayer five times a day (p. 394)

missionary person who travels to carry the ideas of a religion to others (pp. 363, 520)

mobilization assembly and movement of troops in order to prepare for action (p. 784)

monastery religious community where monks live and work (pp. 362, 413)

monopoly control of all (or almost all) trade or production of a certain good (p. 576)

monotheism the belief in one god (p. 81)

monsoon in South Asia, a strong wind that blows one direction in winter and the opposite direction in summer (p. 195)

mosaic picture made from many bits of colored glass, tile, or stone (p. 333)

mosque Muslim house of worship (p. 389)

mummy body that has been embalmed and wrapped in linen (p. 50)

myth traditional story describing gods or heroes or explaining natural events (p. 155)

nationalize remove from private ownership and place under government control (p. 865)

natural law law that applies to everyone and can be understood by reason (p. 681)

nirvana in Buddhism, a state of wisdom and freedom from the cycle of rebirth (p. 205)

nomad person who regularly moves from place to place (p. 10)

novel long fictional story (p. 432)

nuclear proliferation spread of nuclear weapons (p. 890)

oasis green area in a desert fed by underground water (p. 373)

ode poem that expresses strong emotions about life (p. 304)

oligarchy government in which a small group of people holds power (p. 126)

oracle sacred shrine where a priest or priestess spoke for a god or goddess (p. 156)

oral history the stories passed down from generation to generation (p. 470)

Pan-Africanism movement to unite black Africans throughout the world and to establish independence for African nations (p. 852)

papyrus reed plant of the Nile Valley, used to make a form of paper (p. 42)

parable story that used events from everyday life to express spiritual ideas (p. 345)

partnership business owned by two or more people who agree to share the profits and losses (p. 728)

paterfamilias ("father of the family") name for the father as head of the household in ancient Rome (p. 307)

patrician wealthy landowner and member of the ruling class in ancient Rome (p. 269)

Pax Romana ("Roman Peace") long era of peace and safety in the Roman Empire (p. 287)

peninsula body of land with water on three sides (p. 117)

perestroika Mikhail Gorbachev's plan to rebuild the Soviet Union's government and economy (p. 882)

persecute to mistreat a person because of his or her beliefs (p. 353)

pharaoh all-powerful king in ancient Egypt (p. 48)

philosopher thinker who seeks wisdom and ponders questions about life (pp. 140, 169)

philosophy study of the nature and meaning of life; comes from the Greek word for "love of wisdom" (p. 169)

pictograph a character that stands for an object (p. 228)

Glossary

Glossary

pilgrim person who travels to go to a religious shrine or site (p. 213)

plague disease that spreads quickly and kills many people (pp. 319, 554)

plane geometry branch of mathematics that shows how points, lines, angles, and surfaces relate to one another (p. 185)

plateau area of high flat land (p. 446)

plebeian member of the common people in ancient Rome (p. 269)

polis the early Greek city-state, made up of a city and the surrounding countryside and run like an independent country (p. 122)

pope the bishop of Rome, later the head of the Roman Catholic Church (p. 356)

popular sovereignty idea that a government receives its power from the people (p. 700)

porcelain type of ceramic ware that is made of fine clay and baked at high temperatures (p. 418)

praetor important government official in ancient Rome (p. 270)

predestination belief that no matter what a person does, the outcome of his or her life is already planned by God (p. 640)

propaganda controlled spread of biased information to influence what people think (p. 786)

prophet person who claims to be instructed by God to share God's words (p. 87)

protectorate small country ruled by and/or protected by a larger one (p. 763)

proverb wise saying (p. 89)

province political district (p. 28)

pyramid huge stone structure built by the ancient Egyptians to serve as a tomb (p. 50)

Q
---

quipu rope with knotted cords of different lengths and colors (p. 588)

Quran holy book of Islam (p. 377)

R
---

rabbi Jewish leader and teacher of the Torah (p. 101)

racial segregation separation or isolation of people to specific residential areas, organizations, or institutions based upon their race (p. 840)

raja prince who led an Aryan tribe in India (p. 199)

rationalism the belief that reason is the chief source of knowledge (p. 678)

rationing system of limiting the amounts of food and materials in use (p. 786)

Reconquista ("reconquest") Christian struggle to take back the Iberian Peninsula from the Muslims (p. 558)

reform change that tries to bring about an improvement (pp. 320, 411)

Reformation movement to reform the Catholic Church; led to the creation of Protestantism (p. 634)

refugee person who flees to another country to escape persecution or disaster (p. 870)

regent person who acts as a temporary ruler (p. 334)

reincarnation rebirth of the soul or spirit in different bodies over time (p. 204)

Renaissance ("rebirth") period of renewed interest in art and learning in Europe (p. 609)

reparation payments made to the winner of a war by a losing country to pay for damages; war damages (p. 791)

representative democracy system of government in which citizens choose a smaller group to make laws and governmental decisions on their behalf (p. 139)

representative government system of government in which people elect leaders to make laws (p. 694)

republic form of government in which the leader is not a king or queen but a person elected by citizens (p. 265)

resurrection the act of rising from the dead (p. 347)

rhetoric public speaking (p. 307)

 S

Sabbath weekly day of worship and rest for Jews (p. 94)

saint Christian holy person (p. 333)

salvation the act of being saved from sin and allowed to enter heaven (p. 350)

samurai class of warriors in feudal Japan who pledged loyalty to a noble in return for land (p. 494)

Sanskrit written language developed by the Aryans (p. 199)

satire work that pokes fun at human weaknesses (p. 304)

satrap official who ruled a state in the Persian Empire under Darius (p. 133)

satrapies the 20 states into which Darius divided the Persian Empire (p. 133)

savanna grassy plain (p. 69)

schism separation (p. 361)

scholasticism medieval way of thinking that tried to bring together reason and faith in studies of religion (p. 550)

scientific method orderly way of collecting and analyzing evidence (p. 679)

scribe record keeper (p. 20)

sect a smaller group with distinct beliefs within a larger religious group (p. 499)

secular interested in worldly rather than religious matters (p. 609)

seminary school for training and educating priests and ministers (p. 643)

separation of powers equal division of power among the branches of government (p. 682)

sepoy Indian soldier hired by the British East India Company to protect the company's interests in the region (p. 765)

serf peasant laborer bound by law to the lands of a noble (p. 524)

sheikh leader of an Arab tribe (p. 373)

Shiite Muslim group that accepts only the descendants of Muhammad's son-in-law Ali as rightful rulers of Muslims (p. 382)

shogun military ruler of feudal Japan (p. 495)

shrine holy place (p. 490)

social class group of people who share a similar position in society (p. 233)

social contract agreement between rulers and the people upon which a government is based (p. 682)

socialism social system based on shared or governmental ownership of businesses, factories, land, and raw materials (p. 735)

Socratic method way of teaching developed by Socrates that used a question-and-answer format to force students to use their reason to see things for themselves (p. 170)

solid geometry branch of mathematics that studies spheres and cylinders (p. 186)

Sophist professional teacher in ancient Greece; believed that people should use knowledge to improve themselves and developed the art of public speaking and debate (p. 169)

soviet Russian committee or council made up of representatives from the workers, soldiers, and peasants (p. 794)

specialization the development of different kinds of jobs (p. 15)

sphere of influence area in which an imperial or foreign power has exclusive rights and privileges (p. 763)

steppe wide, rolling, grassy plain (p. 424)

Stoicism philosophy founded by Zeno in Hellenistic Athens; taught that happiness came not from following emotions, but from following reason and doing one's duty (p. 184)

stupa Buddhist shrine that is shaped like a dome or mound (p. 211)

subcontinent large landmass that is part of a continent but distinct from it (p. 195)

sultan military and political leader with absolute authority over a Muslim country (pp. 383, 467)

Sunni Muslim group that accepts descendants of the Umayyads as rightful rulers of Muslims (p. 382)

Swahili refers to the culture and language of East Africa (p. 467)

synagogue Jewish house of worship (p. 94)

tanka Japan's oldest form of poetry; an unrhymed poem of five lines (p. 501)

technology tools and methods used to help humans perform tasks (p. 11)

terror violent actions that are meant to scare people into surrendering (p. 426)

terrorism use of violence against citizens to achieve political goals (p. 892)

textile woven or knit cloth (p. 726)

Glossary

theocracy government headed by religious leaders (p. 208)

theology the study of religion and God (pp. 550, 640)

theory an explanation of how or why something happens (p. 671)

Torah the laws that, according to the Bible, Moses received from God on Mount Sinai; these laws later became the first part of the Hebrew Bible (p. 82)

totalitarian state political state in which the government tries to totally control the way citizens think and live (p. 808)

tragedy form of drama in which a person struggles to overcome difficulties but meets an unhappy end (p. 160)

treason disloyalty to the government (pp. 431, 599)

trial jury group that decided whether an accused person was innocent or guilty (p. 537)

tribe group of related families (pp. 81, 424)

tribute payment made by one group or nation to another to show obedience or to obtain peace or protection (pp. 60, 89)

triumvirate in ancient Rome, a three-person ruling group (p. 280)

Truman Doctrine U.S. policy to provide economic aid to Greece and Turkey after World War II; named after U.S. President Harry S Truman who created the plan (p. 834)

tyrant person who takes power by force and rules with total authority (p. 125)

urbanization movement of people from rural areas to cities (p. 732)

vassal in feudalism, a noble who held land from and served a higher-ranking lord, and in return was given protection (pp. 496, 523)

vault curved structure of stone or concrete forming a ceiling or roof (p. 303)

vernacular everyday language used in a country or region (pp. 552, 620)

veto to reject (p. 270)

warlord military leader who runs a government (p. 409)

weapons of mass destruction nuclear, chemical, or biological weapons that can kill or destroy on a very large scale (p. 894)

Zoroastrianism Persian religion founded by Zoroaster; taught that humans had the freedom to choose between right and wrong, and that goodness would triumph in the end (p. 133)

Spanish Glossary

A

abolitionism / abolicionismo movimiento para terminar con la esclavitud (pág. 753)

absolutism / absolutismo sistema de gobierno en que los monarcas tiene poder absoluto y alegan gobernar según decreto divino (pág. 686)

acupuncture / acupuntura práctica china para aliviar el dolor clavando la piel de los pacientes con agujas delgadas (pág. 246)

adobe / adobe ladrillo de barro secado al sol (pág. 591)

agora / ágora en las primeras ciudades-estado griegas, un área abierta que servía tanto de mercado como de lugar de reunión (pág. 122)

alphabet / alfabeto grupo de letras que representan sonidos (pág. 85)

anatomy / anatomía estudio de la estructura corporal (pág. 305)

animism / animismo creencia de que todas las cosas naturales están vivas y tienen sus propios espíritus (pág. 490)

annul / anular el acto de invalidar (pág. 648)

anthropologist / antropólogo científico que estudia las características físicas y las culturas de los seres humanos y sus antepasados (pág. 9)

anti-Semitism / antisemitismo odio hacia los judíos (pág. 548)

apartheid / apartheid política de segregación racial establecida en Sudáfrica, que se aplicó de 1948 a 1991. Palabra en lengua afrikaans que significa separación (págs. 806, 872)

apostle / apóstol nombre dado a líderes cristianos que ayudaban a establecer iglesias y a difundir el mensaje de Jesucristo (pág. 348)

appeasement / conciliación evitar la guerra mediante la satisfacción de las demandas de un gobierno extranjero (pág. 814)

aqueduct / acueducto canal construido por el hombre para transportar agua (pág. 291)

archaeologist / arqueólogo científico que aprende acerca de la vida humana en el pasado estudiando fósiles y artefactos (pág. 9)

aristocrat / aristócrata noble cuya riqueza provenía de la propiedad de la tierra (pág. 227)

armistice / armisticio acuerdo para terminar las hostilidades; cese al fuego (pág. 790)

artifact / artefacto arma, herramienta u otro artículo hecho por humanos (pág. 9)

artisan / artesano persona hábil artísticamente (pág. 20)

astronomer / astrónomo persona que estudia las estrellas, a los planetas y a otros cuerpos celestiales (págs. 30, 185)

B

barbarian / bárbaro persona incivilizada (pág. 435)

barter / trueque intercambiar bienes sin utilizar dinero (pág. 319)

bazaar / bazar mercado (pág. 389)

blockade / bloqueo uso de embarcaciones de guerra para detener la entrada o salida de bienes y personas de un área (pág. 787)

bourgeoisie / burguesía clase media de la sociedad. Incluye comerciantes, banqueros, médicos, abogados, maestros y otros profesionales (pág. 715)

Brahman / Brahman en el hinduismo, el espíritu universal del que todos los dioses y diosas son partes diferentes (pág. 203)

Buddhism / budismo religión fundada por Siddhartha Gautama, Buda; enseñó que la manera de hallar la verdad era renunciar a todo deseo (pág. 205)

bureaucracy / burocracia grupo de funcionarios designados que son responsables de diferentes áreas del gobierno (pág. 229)

C

caliph / califa importante líder político y religioso musulmán (pág. 380)

calligraphy / caligrafía hermosa escritura a mano (pág. 421); el arte de producir tal hermosa escritura (pág. 501)

capital / capital dinero disponible para invertir en negocios (pág. 726)

Spanish Glossary

caravan / caravana grupo itinerante de mercaderes y animales (págs. 30, 373)

caste / casta grupo social en el que una persona nace y que no puede cambiar (pág. 199)

cataract / catarata rápidos empinados formados por precipicios y rocas erosionadas en un río (pág. 39)

caudillos / caudillos líderes fuertes que gobernaron mediante el uso de la fuerza militar. Generalmente contaban con el apoyo de los ricos y la clase alta (pág. 751)

census / censo conteo del número de personas (pág. 432)

city-state / ciudad-estado estado independiente compuesto por una ciudad y la tierra y aldeas circundantes (pág. 19)

civil disobedience / desobediencia civil rehusarse a obedecer leyes injustas de un gobierno (pág. 843)

civilization / civilización sociedad compleja, con ciudades, un gobierno organizado, arte, religión, divisiones de clase y un sistema de escritura (pág. 17)

clan / clan grupo de familias relacionadas por sangre o casamiento (págs. 461, 487)

clergy / clero funcionarios religiosos, como los sacerdotes, con autoridad concedida para llevar a cabo servicios religiosos (págs. 355, 538)

collectivization / colectivización sistema en el que se unen numerosas parcelas, para formar grandes campos agrícolas que funcionan como fábricas y son controladas por el estado (pág. 810)

colony / colonia asentamiento en un territorio nuevo que mantiene lazos cercanos con su tierra natal (págs. 121, 666, 763)

comedy / comedia forma de drama en el que la historia tiene un final feliz (pág. 161)

commerce / comercio compra y venta de bienes en cantidades grandes y a través de largas distancias (pág. 666)

concordat / concordato acuerdo entre el Papa y el gobernante de un país (pág. 521)

confederation / confederación unión libre de varios grupos o estados (pág. 592)

Confucianism / confucianismo sistema de creencias introducidas por el pensador chino Confucio; enseñó que las personas necesitaban tener un sentido del deber hacia su familia y la comunidad para llevar paz a la sociedad (pág. 236)

conquistador / conquistador soldado español en las Américas (pág. 595)

conscription / conscripción reclutamiento forzoso en el servicio militar; servicio militar (pág. 782)

constitution / constitución plan de gobierno (págs. 488, 694)

consul / cónsul uno de los dos altos funcionarios en la Roma antigua (pág. 269)

containment / contención políticas de los Estados Unidos diseñadas para evitar el avance del comunismo (pág. 834)

corporation / corporación organización empresarial, comercial o mercantil que puede poseer propiedades, así como obtener fondos mediante la venta de acciones a inversionistas (pág. 728)

coup d'etat / golpe de estado sustitución forzada de los dirigentes de gobierno por otros dirigentes (pág. 720)

covenant / pacto acuerdo (pág. 82)

crier / almuecín anunciador que llama a los creyentes musulmanes a orar cinco veces al día (pág. 394)

cuneiform / cuneiforme sistema sumerio de escritura compuesto de símbolos con forma de cuña (pág. 20)

currency / moneda sistema monetario (pág. 294)

daimyo / daimyo poderoso señor militar en el Japón feudal (págs. 496, 777)

Dao / Dao manera apropiada en que se esperaba que los reyes chinos gobernaran bajo el Mandato del Cielo (pág. 230)

Daoism / Daoism filosofía china basada en las enseñanzas de Laozi; enseñó que las personas debían volverse a la naturaleza y renunciar a sus preocupaciones terrenales (pág. 238)

D-day / Día D 6 de junio de 1944. Día en que las fuerzas aliadas invadieron Normandía, Francia, durante la Segunda Guerra Mundial (pág. 828)

deforestation / deforestación tala de los bosques (pág. 890)

deism / deísmo doctrina religiosa basada en la razón (pág. 685)

deity / deidad dios o diosa (pág. 49)

delta / delta área de tierra fértil en la boca de un río (pág. 39)

democracy / democracia forma de gobierno en la que todos los ciudadanos participan en la administración del gobierno (pág. 126)

denomination / denominación rama organizada del cristianismo (pág. 636)

depression / depresión periodo de baja actividad económica en el que muchas personas quedan desempleadas (pág. 806)

détente / detente política que promueve el aliviamiento de las tensiones entre países (pág. 881)

dharma / dharma en el hinduismo, la ley divina que llama a las personas a realizar los deberes de su casta (pág. 204)

dhow / dhow velero árabe (pág. 452)

Diaspora / diáspora se refiere al esparcimiento de las comunidades de judíos fuera de su tierra natal después del cautiverio babilónico (pág. 96)

dictator / dictador en la Roma antigua, una persona que gobernaba temporalmente con poder absoluto durante emergencias (pág. 271)

diplomacy / diplomacia el arte de negociar con otros países (pág. 615)

direct democracy / democracia directa sistema de gobierno en el que las personas se congregan en reuniones masivas para decidir sobre asuntos de gobierno (pág. 139)

disciple / discípulo seguidor de Jesucristo (pág. 344)

doctrine / doctrina enseñanza oficial de la iglesia (pág. 355)

domesticate / domesticar domar animales y plantas para uso humano (pág. 13)

drama / drama historia contada por actores que pretenden ser personajes en la misma (pág. 160)

duma / duma asamblea nacional rusa conformada por legisladores electos (pág. 793)

dynasty / dinastía línea de gobernantes de la misma familia (págs. 44, 210, 226)

economy / economía manera organizada en la que las personas producen, venden y compran bienes y servicios (pág. 410)

embalming / embalsamado proceso desarrollado por los antiguos egipcios para la conservación del cuerpo de una persona después de muerta (pág. 49)

embargo / embargo ley que prohibe o limita el intercambio comercial con otro país (pág. 863)

empire / imperio grupo de territorios o naciones bajo un mismo mandatario o gobierno (págs. 23, 89)

entente / pacto acuerdo entre naciones que permite realizar acciones comunes (pág. 782)

epic / epopeya poema largo que cuenta acerca de actos legendarios o heroicos (pág. 157)

Epicureanism / epicureísmo filosofía fundada por Epicuro en la Atenas helenista; enseñó que la felicidad a través de la persecución del placer era la meta de la vida (pág. 184)

estates / estados clases en las cuales se dividían los habitantes de Francia, antes de la Revolución: el clero católico (Primer estado), la nobleza (Segundo estado) y los ciudadanos (Tercer estado) (pág. 715)

ethnic cleansing / limpieza étnica uso de la fuerza para eliminar a un grupo étnico de una región determinada (pág. 884)

euro / euro moneda común de los países de la Unión Europea desde 1999 (pág. 889)

excommunicate / excomulgar declarar que una persona o grupo no pertenece más a la iglesia (págs. 361, 521)

exile / exilio período de ausencia forzada de una persona de su país u hogar (pág. 94)

export / exportar vender a otro país (págs. 666, 861)

extended family / familia extendida grupo familiar que incluye a varias generaciones así como a otros parientes (pág. 469)

extraterritoriality / extraterritorialidad práctica legal que se aplica a extranjeros que habitan en un país, pero no son sujetos de sus leyes (pág. 773)

fable / fábula cuento corto que enseña una lección (pág. 158)

Spanish Glossary

feudalism / feudalismo sistema político basado en lazos de lealtad entre señores y vasallos (págs. 497, 523)

fief / feudo bajo el feudalismo, la tierra que un señor otorgaba a un vasallo a cambio de su servicio militar y lealtad (pág. 524)

filial piety / piedad filial el respeto de los niños para sus padres y parientes mayores, una parte importante de las creencias confucianas (pág. 234)

fjord / fiordo valle de paredes abruptas que es una bahía del mar (pág. 518)

Forum / Foro espacio abierto en Roma que servía como mercado y plaza pública (pág. 306)

fossil / fósil huella o impresión de una planta o animal que se ha conservado en piedra (pág. 9)

genocide / genocidio asesinato deliberado de un grupo étnico, político o cultural (pág. 827)

glacier / glaciar masa inmensa de hielo (pág. 573)

gladiator / gladiador en la Roma antigua, persona que peleaba contra animales y otras personas como entretenimiento público (pág. 306)

glasnost / glasnost política establecida por Mikhail Gorbachev en la Unión Soviética, que permitió la discución abierta de ideas políticas y sociales (pág. 882)

globalism / globalismo noción de que la economía y las politicas de todos los países forman parte de un sistema mundial único (pág. 889)

gospel / evangelio ("buena nueva") uno de los cuatro relatos sobre la vida, enseñanzas y resurrección de Jesucristo (pág. 355)

grand jury / gran jurado grupo que decide si hay suficiente evidencia para acusar a una persona de un delito (pág. 537)

griot / griot narrador en poblados africanos (pág. 449)

guild / gremio grupo medieval de negocios formado por artesanos y mercaderes (págs. 503, 530)

guru / gurú maestro religioso y guía espiritual en el hinduismo (pág. 201)

Hellenistic Era / Era helenista período cuando el idioma y las ideas griegas se esparcieron a los habitantes no griegos del suroeste de Asia (pág. 178)

helot / ilota persona conquistada y esclavizada por los espartanos antiguos (pág. 126)

heresy / herejía creencia que difiere de las enseñanzas aceptadas de una religión o que las contradice (págs. 547, 643)

hierarchy / jerarquía organización con diferentes niveles de autoridad (pág. 355)

hieroglyphics / jeroglíficos sistema de escritura compuesto por miles de símbolos gráficos desarrollados por los antiguos egipcios (pág. 42)

Hinduism / hinduismo sistema religioso que se originó a partir de la religión de los arios en la antigua India (pág. 203)

historian / historiador persona que estudia y escribe acerca del pasado humano (pág. 9)

humanism / humanismo movimiento del renacimiento basado en las ideas y los valores de los antiguos romanos y griegos, de tal manera que los individuos y la sociedad humana eran importantes (pág. 619)

hypothesis / hipótesis explicación que se propone de los hechos (pág. 679)

icon / icono imagen o retrato religioso cristiano (pág. 359)

iconoclast / iconoclasta persona que se oponía al uso de ídolos en las iglesias bizantinas, aludiendo que los iconos alentaban el culto de ídolos (pág. 360)

ideograph / ideógrafo un carácter que une dos o más pictografías para representar una idea (pág. 228)

igloo / iglú casa con forma de domo construida por los inuitas (pág. 590)

imperialism / imperialismo ocurre cuando una nación controla el gobierno o la economía de otras naciones más pequeñas o más débiles (pág. 763)

import / importar comprar de otro país (pág. 666)

incense / incienso material que al quemarse despide un olor agradable (pág. 62)

indulgence / indulgencia perdonar la iglesia los pecados de una persona (pág. 634)

Industrialism / industrialismo sistema económico en el cual las personas dependen más del uso de maquinaria y tecnología, que del uso de fuerza animal o humana (pág. 725)

inflation / inflación período de incremento rápido de precios (págs. 319, 806)

intifada / intifada levantamiento armado de los palestinos contra la ocupación israelí de la Franja de Gaza y la Ribera Occidental (pág. 878)

invest / invertir poner dinero en un proyecto (pág. 667)

irrigation / irrigación método para llevar agua de otro lugar a un campo para regar las cosechas (pág. 18)

kaiser / káiser palabra alemana que significa emperador (pág. 748)

karma / karma en el hinduismo, la energía buena o mala que una persona desarrolla según si vive una vida buena o mala (pág. 204)

knight / caballero en la Edad Media, un guerrero noble que peleaba a caballo (pág. 524)

labor union / sindicato asociación de trabajadores que se unen para mejorar los derechos, los salarios, las prestaciones y las condiciones laborales de los trabajadores (pág. 736)

laity / laicado miembros de iglesia que no constituyen el clero (pág. 355)

latifundia / latifundios grandes propiedades agrícolas en la Roma antigua (pág. 278)

legacy / legado lo que una persona deja cuando muere (pág. 178)

Legalism / legalismo filosofía china desarrollada por Hanfeizi; enseñó que los humanos son naturalmente malos y por lo tanto necesitaban ser gobernados por leyes duras (pág. 239)

legion / legión unidad más pequeña del ejército romano, compuesta por aproximadamente 6,000 soldados (pág. 266)

liberalism / liberalismo corriente política basada en las ideas de la Ilustración, las cuales hacen énfasis en el progreso, la bondad intrínseca del ser humano y las libertades individuales (pág. 735)

limited government / gobierno limitado idea de que un gobierno sólo puede usar los poderes cedidos por los ciudadanos (pág. 700)

mandate / mandato orden formal (págs. 230, 792)

Marshall Plan / Plan Marshall programa patrocinado por los Estados Unidos para proporcionar ayuda a los países europeos después de la Segunda Guerra Mundial, de 1948 a 1951. Fue nombrada así en honor a George Marshall, entonces secretario de estado de los Estados Unidos, y quien la propuso al Congreso (pág. 834)

martial arts / artes marciales deportes, como el judo y el karate, que involucran combate y defensa personal (pág. 499)

martyr / mártir persona dispuesta a morir antes que renunciar a sus creencias (pág. 353)

mass / misa servicio de culto Católico (pág. 546)

matrilineal / matrilineal se refiere a un grupo de personas que busca su ascendencia a través de las madres más que de los padres (pág. 469)

meditation / meditación práctica de reflexión silenciosa para aclarar la mente y encontrar la paz interior (pág. 499)

mercantilism / mercantilismo doctrina según la cual un país obtiene poder al amasar un abastecimiento de oro y plata (pág. 666)

messiah / mesías en el judaísmo, un salvador mandado por Dios (págs. 101, 344)

militarism / militarismo fascinación con la guerra y los asuntos militares (pág. 782)

minaret / minarete torre de una mezquita desde donde el almuecín llama a los creyentes a la oración cinco veces al día (pág. 394)

missionary / misionero persona que viaja para llevar las ideas de una religión a otros (págs. 363, 520)

mobilization / movilización disposición y movimiento de tropas que se preparan para realizar acciones militares (pág. 784)

Spanish Glossary

monastery / monasterio comunidad religiosa donde los monjes viven y trabajan (págs. 362, 413)

monopoly / monopolio el control de todo (o casi todo) el comercio o la producción de ciertos bienes (pág. 576)

monotheism / monoteísmo la creencia en un solo dios (pág. 81)

monsoon / monzón en la Asia del sur, un viento fuerte que sopla en una dirección en el invierno y en la dirección opuesta en el verano (pág. 195)

mosaic / mosaico figura hecha con muchos trozos de vidrios de colores, azulejo o piedra (pág. 333)

mosque / mezquita casa de culto musulmana (pág. 389)

mummy / momia cuerpo que se ha embalsamado y envuelto en lino (pág. 50)

myth / mito cuento tradicional que describe dioses o a héroes o explica eventos naturales (pág. 155)

nationalize / nacionalizar eliminar la propiedad privada de bienes o de capital, para sustituirla por el control del gobierno (pág. 865)

natural law / ley natural ley que se aplica a todos y la cual puede entenderse por razonamiento (pág. 681)

nirvana / nirvana en el budismo, un estado de sabiduría y libertad del ciclo del renacimiento (pág. 205)

nomad / nómada persona que regularmente se mueve de un lugar a otro (pág. 10)

novel / novela historia ficticia larga (pág. 432)

nuclear proliferation / proliferación nuclear aumento del número de armas nucleares (pág. 890)

oasis / oasis área verde en un desierto, alimentada por agua subterránea (pág. 373)

ode / oda poema que expresa emociones fuertes acerca de la vida (pág. 304)

oligarchy / oligarquía gobierno en el que un grupo pequeño de personas mantiene el poder (pág. 126)

oracle / oráculo templo sagrado en donde un sacerdote o sacerdotisa hablaban a nombre de un dios o diosa (pág. 156)

oral history / historia oral historias transmitidas de generación en generación (pág. 470)

Pan-Africanism / Panafricanismo movimiento para unir a los africanos de piel negra de todo el mundo, con el fin de lograr la independencia de las naciones africanas (pág. 852)

papyrus / papiro planta de juncos del Valle de Nilo, empleada para hacer un tipo de papel (pág. 42)

parable / parábola historia que usa acontecimientos de la vida diaria para expresar ideas espirituales (pág. 345)

partnership / sociedad compañía que es propiedad de dos o más personas, quienes acuerdan compartir las ganancias y las pérdidas (pág. 728)

paterfamilias / paterfamilias ("padre de la familia") nombre dado al padre como cabeza de la casa en la Roma antigua (pág. 307)

patrician / patricio hacendado poderoso y miembro de la clase gobernante en la Roma antigua (pág. 269)

Pax Romana / Paz Romana era prolongada de paz y seguridad en el Imperio Romano (pág. 287)

peninsula / península extensión territorial rodeada de agua en tres lados (pág. 117)

perestroika / perestroika plan establecido por Mikhail Gorbachev para reconstruir el gobierno y la economía de la Unión Soviética (pág. 882)

persecute / perseguir maltratar una persona a causa de sus creencias (pág. 353)

pharaoh / faraón rey todopoderoso en el antiguo Egipto (pág. 48)

philosopher / filósofo pensador que busca la sabiduría y formula preguntas acerca de la vida (págs. 140, 169)

philosophy / filosofía estudio de la naturaleza y significando de la vida; viene de la palabra griega que significa "amor a la sabiduría" (pág. 169)

pictograph / pictógrafo carácter que representa a un objeto (pág. 228)

pilgrim / peregrino persona que viaja para ir a un relicario o sitio religioso (pág. 213)

plague / peste enfermedad que se esparce rápidamente y mata a muchas personas (págs. 319, 554)

plane geometry / geometría plana rama de las matemáticas que muestra cómo se relacionan los puntos, las líneas, los ángulos y las superficies (pág. 185)

plateau / meseta área de tierra alta y plana (pág. 446)

plebeian / plebeyo miembro de las personas comunes en la Roma antigua (pág. 269)

polis / polis antigua ciudad-estado griega, compuesta de una ciudad y las áreas circundantes y gobernada como un país independiente (pág. 122)

pope / Papa el obispo de Roma, posteriormente, la cabeza de la iglesia católica romana (pág. 356)

popular sovereignty / soberanía popular idea de que un gobierno recibe su poder de los ciudadanos (pág. 700)

porcelain / porcelana tipo de artículo de cerámica hecho de arcilla fina y horneado a altas temperaturas (pág. 418)

praetor / pretor importante funcionario de gobierno en la Roma antigua (pág. 270)

predestination / predestinación creencia de que sea lo que sea que haga una persona, el resultado de su vida ya ha sido planificado por Dios (pág. 640)

propaganda / propaganda diseminación controlada de información sesgada, para influir en las ideas de las personas sobre algún asunto determinado (pág. 786)

prophet / profeta persona que declara estar instruido por Dios para compartir Sus palabras (pág. 87)

protectorate / protectorado país pequeño que es protegido o que está bajo el dominio de un país más grande (pág. 763)

proverb / proverbio dicho sabio (pág. 89)

province / provincia distrito político (pág. 28)

pyramid / pirámide inmensa estructura de piedra construida por los antiguos egipcios para utilizarse como una tumba (pág. 50)

quipu / quipu lazo con cuerdas anudadas de longitudes y colores diferentes (pág. 588)

Quran / Corán libro sagrado del Islam (pág. 377)

rabbi / rabino líder judío y maestro del Torá (pág. 101)

racial segregation / segregación racial separación o aislamiento de personas en áreas habitacionales, organizaciones e instituciones específicas, según su etnicidad (pág. 840)

raja / rajá príncipe que dirigió a una tribu aria en la India (pág. 199)

rationalism / racionalismo la creencia de que la razón es la fuente principal del conocimiento (pág. 678)

rationing / racionamiento limitación de la cantidad de alimentos y materiales disponibles (pág. 785)

Reconquista* ("reconquest") / *reconquista lucha cristiana para recuperar la península Ibérica de los musulmanes (pág. 558)

reform / reforma cambio que intenta producir una mejora (págs. 320, 411)

Reformation / reforma movimiento para reformar la iglesia católica; condujo a la creación del protestantismo (pág. 634)

refugee / refugiado persona que huye hacia otro país para escapar de desastres o persecución (pág. 870)

regent / regente persona que opera como un gobernante temporal (pág. 334)

reincarnation / reencarnación renacimiento del alma o el espíritu en cuerpos diferentes a través del tiempo (pág. 204)

Renaissance / renacimiento ("nacer de nuevo") período en que se renovó el interés en las artes y el conocimiento en Europa (pág. 609)

reparation / gastos de reparación pagos que el país derrotado en una guerra se compromete a realizar, para resarcir al país victorioso de los daños sufridos; daños colaterales de la guerra (pág. 791)

Spanish Glossary

Spanish Glossary

representative democracy / democracia representativa
sistema de gobierno en el que los ciudadanos escogen a un grupo más pequeño para promulgar leyes y tomar decisiones gubernamentales en su nombre (pág. 139)

representative government / gobierno representativo
sistema de gobierno en que los ciudadanos eligen a sus líderes para promulgar leyes (pág. 694)

republic / república forma de gobierno en la que el líder no es un rey ni una reina sino una persona elegida por los ciudadanos (pág. 265)

resurrection / resurrección acto de volver a la vida (pág. 347)

rhetoric / retórica hablar en público (pág. 307)

Sabbath / sabbat día semanal de culto y descanso para los judíos (pág. 94)

saint / santo persona cristiana santificada (pág. 333)

salvation / salvación acto de ser salvado del pecado y aceptado para entrar al cielo (pág. 350)

samurai / samurai clase de guerreros en el Japón feudal que prometía lealtad a un noble a cambio de tierra (pág. 494)

Sanskrit / Sánscrito idioma escrito desarrollado por los arios (pág. 199)

satire / sátira obra que hace burla de las debilidades humanas (pág. 304)

satrap / sátrapa funcionario que gobernaba un estado en el Imperio pérsico durante la época de Darío (pág. 133)

satrapies / satrapies los 20 estados en los cuales Darío dividió al Imperio pérsico (pág. 133)

savanna / sabana llanura cubierta de hierba (pág. 69)

schism / cisma separación (pág. 361)

scholasticism / escolástica forma de pensamiento medieval que trató de unir a la razón y a la fe en estudios religiosos (pág. 550)

scientific method / método científico manera organizada de recoger y analizar pruebas (pág. 679)

scribe / escriba conservador de registros (pág. 20)

sect / secta un grupo más pequeño con creencias distintas dentro de un grupo religioso más grande (pág. 499)

secular / secular que se interesa en bienes materiales en lugar de asuntos religiosos (pág. 609)

seminary / seminario escuela en donde se entrenan y se educan a los sacerdotes y los ministros (pág. 643)

separation of powers / separación de poderes división equitativa de los poderes entre las ramas del gobierno (pág. 682)

sepoy / cipayo soldado indio contratado por la Compañía Británica del Oriente de la India (British East India Company) para proteger los intereses de la compañía en la región (pág. 765)

serf / siervo trabajador campesino atado por ley a las tierras de un noble (pág. 524)

sheikh / jeque líder de una tribu árabe (pág. 373)

Shiite / chiíta grupo musulmán que acepta sólo a los descendientes de Ali, el hijo político de Mahoma, como auténticos líderes de los musulmanes (pág. 382)

shogun / shogun gobernante militar del Japón feudal (pág. 495)

shrine / relicario lugar sagrado (pág. 490)

social class / clase social grupo de personas que comparten una posición semejante en la sociedad (pág. 233)

social contract / contrato social acuerdo entre mandatarios y ciudadanos sobre el cual se basa un gobierno (pág. 682)

socialism / socialismo sistema social basado en la propiedad compartida de empresas, fábricas, tierras y materias primas (pág. 735)

Socratic method / método socrático método de enseñanza desarrollado por Sócrates que emplea un formato de pregunta y respuesta para forzar a los estudiantes a utilizar su raciocinio para ver las cosas por sí mismos (pág. 170)

solid geometry / geometría sólida rama de las matemáticas que estudia a las esferas y los cilindros (pág. 186)

Sophist / Sofista maestro profesional en Grecia antigua; creían que las personas deben utilizar el conocimiento para mejorarse a sí mismas y desarrollaron el arte de hablar en público y el debate (pág. 169)

soviet / soviet consejo o comité ruso formado por representantes de los trabajadores, soldados y campesinos (pág. 794)

specialization / especialización desarrollo de diferentes tipos de trabajos (pág. 15)

sphere of influence / esfera de influencia área sobre la cual una potencia extranjera o imperial tiene derechos y privilegios exclusivos (pág. 763)

steppe / estepa ancha planicie ondeada cubierta de hierba (pág. 424)

Stoicism / estoicismo filosofía fundada por Zeno en la Atenas Helenista; enseñaba que la felicidad provenía no de seguir a las emociones, sino a la razón y de cumplir con nuestro deber (pág. 184)

stupa / estupa templo budista con forma de cúpula o montículo (pág. 211)

subcontinent / subcontinente gran masa de tierra que forma parte de un continente pero está separada de él (pág. 195)

sultan / sultán líder político y militar con autoridad absoluta sobre un país musulmán (págs. 383, 467)

Sunni / sunní grupo musulmán que sólo acepta a descendientes de los Omeyas como auténticos gobernantes de los musulmanes (pág. 382)

Swahili / suajili se refiere a la cultura e idioma de Africa del Este (pág. 467)

synagogue / sinagoga casa de culto judía (pág. 94)

tanka / tanka forma más antigua de poesía en Japón; poema sin rima de cinco líneas (pág. 501)

technology / tecnología instrumentos y métodos utilizados para ayudar a los humanos a realizar tareas (pág. 11)

terror / terror acciones violentas para atemorizar personas para que rendirse (pág. 426)

terrorism / terrorismo uso de la violencia contra los ciudadanos para lograr obejtivos políticos (pág. 892)

textile / textil ropa tejida o fabricada (pág. 726)

theocracy / teocracia gobierno dirigido por líderes religiosos (pág. 208)

theology / teología el estudio de la religión y de Dios (págs. 550, 640)

theory / teoría explicación de cómo o por qué ocurre algo (pág. 671)

Torah / Torá las leyes que, según la Biblia, Moisés recibió de Dios en el monte Sinaí; estas leyes se convirtieron después en la primera parte de la Biblia hebrea (pág. 82)

totalitarian state / estado totalitario estado en el que el gobierno trata de controlar por completo la manera en que las personas viven y piensan (pág. 808)

tragedy / tragedia forma de drama en la que una persona se esfuerza para vencer dificultades pero encuentra un final infeliz (pág. 160)

treason / traición deslealtad al gobierno (págs. 431, 599)

trial jury / jurado grupo que decide si una persona acusada es inocente o culpable (pág. 537)

tribe / tribu grupo de familias relacionadas (págs. 81, 424)

tribute / tributo pago realizado por un grupo o nación a otra para mostrar obediencia o para obtener paz o protección (págs. 60, 89)

triumvirate / triunvirato en la Roma antigua, un grupo gobernante de tres personas (pág. 280)

Truman Doctrine / Doctrina Truman política de los Estados Unidos diseñada para ayudar económicamente a Grecia y a Turquía, después de la Segunda Guerra Mundial. Recibió este nombre en honor a su creador, Harry S Truman, entonces presidente de los Estados Unidos (pág. 834)

tyrant / tirano persona que toma el poder por la fuerza y gobierna con autoridad total (pág. 125)

urbanization / urbanización migración de habitantes de áreas rurales hacia la ciudad (pág. 732)

vassal / vasallo en el feudalismo, un noble que ocupaba la tierra de un señor de más alto rango y lo servía, y a cambio le daba protección (págs. 496, 523)

Spanish Glossary

vault / cámara estructura curva de piedra o cemento que forma un techo (pág. 303)

vernacular / vernáculo idioma cotidiano empleado en un país o región (págs. 552, 620)

veto / veta rechazar (pág. 270)

warlord / caudillo líder militar que dirige un gobierno (pág. 409)

weapons of mass destruction / armas de destrucción masiva armas químicas, biológicas o nucleares que pueden matar a gran cantidad de gente o causar grave destrucción (pág. 894)

Zoroastrianism / zoroastrismo religión persa fundada por Zoroastro; enseñaba que los humanos tenían la libertad de escoger entre lo correcto y lo incorrecto, y que la bondad triunfaría al final (pág. 133)

Spanish Glossary

A Gazetteer (GA•zuh•TIHR) is a geographic index or dictionary. It shows latitude and longitude for cities and certain other places. Latitude and longitude are shown in this way: 48°N 2°E, or 48 degrees north latitude and two degrees east longitude. This Gazetteer lists most of the world's largest independent countries, their capitals, and several important geographic features. The page numbers tell where each entry can be found on a map in this book. As an aid to pronunciation, most entries are spelled phonetically.

Aachen [AH•kuhn] City in Germany near the Belgian and Dutch borders; capital of Charlemagne's Frankish empire. 50°N 6°E (pp. 512, 516)

Actium [AK•shee•uhm] Cape on the western coast of Greece. 37°N 23°E (p. 297)

Aden [ay•dehn] Port city of the Red Sea in southern Yemen. 12°N 45°E (p. 433)

Aden, Gulf of Western arm of the Arabian Sea, between Yemen, Somalia, and Djibouti. 11°N 45°E (p. 445)

Adrianople [AY•dree•uh•NOH•puhl] Ancient city in northwestern Turkey, now called Edirne. 41°N 26°E (p. 323)

Adriatic [AY•dree•A•tihk] **Sea** Arm of Mediterranean Sea between Italy and the Balkan Peninsula. 44°N 14°E (pp. 144, 263, 269, 274, 293, 516, 548, 609, 653, 688, 725, 747, 786, 832, 897)

Aegean [ih•JEE•uhn] **Sea** Gulf of the Mediterranean Sea between Greece and Asia Minor, north of Crete. 39°N 24°E (pp. 117, 134, 144, 149, 176, 548)

Afghanistan [af•GA•nuh•STAN] Central Asian country west of Pakistan. 33°N 63°E (pp. R3, R19, 176, 198, 765, 773, 845)

Africa [AF•rih•kah] Second-largest continent, south of Europe between the Atlantic and Indian Oceans. 10°N 22°E (pp. R2, R3, R4, R5, R20, R21, 33, 109, 262, 263, 269, 274, 293, 297, 352, 358, 361, 367, 380, 385, 433, 444, 446, 449, 460, 463, 468, 469, 473, 479, 518, 554, 565, 573, 658, 662, 668, 707, 709, 762, 767, 842, 870, 893)

Agincourt [A•juhn•KOHRT] Village in northern France. 52°N 6°E (pp. 557, 561)

Agra [AH•gruh] City in India, site of the Taj Mahal. 27°N 78°E (pp. 394, 845)

Ahaggar [uh•HAH•guhr] **Mountains** Arid, rocky, upland region in southern Algeria in the center of the Sahara. 25°N 6°E (p. 445)

Albania [al•BAY•nee•uh] Country on the Adriatic Sea, south of Yugoslavia. 42°N 20°E (pp. R3, 781, 786, 790, 832, 897)

Albany Capital city of New York. 42°N 73°W (p. 694)

Aleppo [uh•LEH•poh] City of northwest Syria near the Turkish border. 36°N 37°E (p. 799)

Alexandria [A•lihg•ZAN•dree•uh] City and major seaport in northern Egypt in the Nile River delta. 31°N 29°E (pp. 176, 179, 182, 189, 246, 293, 323, 329, 352, 361, 367, 374)

Algeria [al•JIHR•ee•uh] Country in North Africa. 29°N 1°E (pp. R2, R3, 767, 790, 870)

Algiers [al•JIHRZ] Capital city of Algeria, largest Mediterranean port of northwestern Africa. 36°N 2°E (pp. R3, 385, 767)

Alps [ALPS] Mountain system of south central Europe. 46°N 9°E (pp. 263, 269, 274, 513, 514, 609, 653)

Alsace [al•SAS] Region of France. 48°N 7°E (pp. 747, 781)

Altay Mountains Mountain range in Asia. 49°N 87°E (pp. R5, 225)

Altun Mountains Range of mountains that are a part of the Kunlun Shan in China. 35°N 83°E (p. 225)

Amazon [A•muh•ZAHN] **River** River in northern South America, second-longest river in the world. 2°S 53°W (pp. R2, R4, 473, 565, 577)

Amman [a•MAHN] Capital of Jordan. 32°N 36°E (pp. 792, 875)

Amsterdam [AHM•stuhr•dahm] Capital of the Netherlands. 52°N 4°E (pp. 548, 725)

Amur River River of northeast Asia flowing along the border between China and Russia. 52°N 141°E (pp. 773, 825)

Andes [AN•deez] Mountain range along the western edge of South America. 13°S 75°W (pp. R4, R15, 577)

Angola [ang•GOH•luh] Southern African country north of Namibia. 14°S 16°E (pp. R3, 767, 870)

Ankara [AHNG•kuh•ruh] Capital of Turkey. 40°N 33°E (p. 792)

Antioch [AN•tee•AHK] Ancient capital of Syria, now a city in southern Turkey. 36°N 36°E (pp. 246, 352, 361, 367, 542)

Antwerp [ANT•WUHRP] City in northern Belgium. 51°N 4°E (pp. 548, 787)

Anyang [AHN•YAHNG] City in northern China, was China's first capital. 36°N 114°E (pp. 224, 226, 251)

Apennines [A•puh•NYNZ] Mountain range that runs through Italy. 43°N 11°E (pp. 263, 269, 609, 653)

Appalachian Mountains Mountain system of eastern North America. 38°N 82°W (pp. R4, R11, 590, 694)

Aqaba [AH•kuh•buh] Port city in Jordan. 29°N 35°E (pp. 799, 875)

Arabia [uh•RAY•bee•uh] Desert peninsula of southwestern Asia across the Red Sea to Africa. 27°N 32°E (pp. R18, R19, 17, 70, 109, 246, 329, 380, 385, 425, 433, 554, 799)

Arabian [uh•RAY•bee•uhn] **Desert** Arid region in eastern Egypt; also called the Eastern Desert. 22°N 45°E (pp. R18, R19, 17, 28, 39, 75)

Arabian [uh•RAY•bee•uhn] **Peninsula** Great desert peninsula in extreme southwestern Asia. 28°N 40°E (pp. R5, R18, R19, 374, 445, 448, 452)

Arabian [uh•RAY•bee•uhn] **Sea** Portion of the Indian Ocean between the Arabian Peninsula and India. 16°N 65°E (pp. R3, R5, R19, 109, 176, 193, 195, 198, 210, 213, 219, 246, 374, 380, 409, 425, 433, 452, 554, 565, 765, 845)

Aragon Region and former kingdom in northeastern Spain. 42°N 1°W (p. 538)

Aral [AR•uhl] **Sea** Large inland sea in central Asia. 45°N 60°E (pp. R3, R5, 132, 198, 246, 380, 383, 397, 424, 425, 554)

Arctic Ocean Smallest of the four oceans. 85°N 170°E (pp. R2, R3, 573, 590)

Argentina [AHR•juhn•TEE•nuh] South American country east of Chile. 36°S 67°W (pp. R2, R14, 749, 860, 861)

Argonne [AHR•gawn] Wooded region of France. 49°N 5°E (pp. 786, 787)

Arkansas River River in the western United States. 38°N 100°W (pp. R11, 663)

Armenia [ahr•MEE•nee•uh] Southeastern European country between the Black and Caspian seas. 40°N 45°E (p. 883)

Asia Largest of the seven continents. 50°N 100°E (pp. R22, R23, 13, 17, 33, 409, 424, 439, 518, 565, 573, 662, 707, 709, 804, 813, 824, 831, 883, 893)

Asia Minor Region of the ancient world, roughly corresponding to present-day Turkey. 38°N 31°E (pp. R22, 17, 28, 117, 121, 132, 176, 179, 189, 269, 274, 277, 292, 293, 297, 323, 327, 329, 342, 352, 358, 361, 367, 374, 380, 385, 542)

Assyria [uh•SIHR•ee•uh] Ancient country in Asia that included the Tigris River valley in Mesopotamia. 35°N 42°E (p. 28)

Athens [A•thuhnz] Capital of Greece. 38°N 23°E (pp. 117, 121, 124, 125, 134, 138, 144, 149, 154, 176, 182, 293)

Atlantic Ocean Second-largest body of water in the world. 5°S 25°W (pp. R2–9, R11, R13–16, R20–22, 13, 121, 293, 329, 352, 361, 463, 473, 513, 516, 538, 555, 561, 573, 590, 645, 663, 691, 725, 769, 790, 832, 893)

Atlas [AT•luhs] **Mountains** Mountain range in northwestern Africa on the northern edge of the Sahara. 31°N 5°W (pp. R20, R21, 445)

Austerlitz Town in the southeast Czech Republic. 49°N 16°E (p. 722)

Australia [aw•STRAYL•yuh] Island continent southeast of Asia. 25°S 135°W (pp. R3, R5, 13, 33, 662, 707, 762, 825, 893)

Austria [AWS•tree•uh] Country in central Europe. 47°N 12°E (pp. R3, R16, 385, 548, 639, 688, 722, 747, 790, 814, 832, 891)

Austria-Hungary [AWS•tree•uh HUHNG•guh•ree] Nation in central Europe from 1867 to 1918 that included what are now Austria, Hungary, Slovakia, and the Czech Republic, as well as parts of present-day Poland, Romania, Italy, Slovenia, Croatia, Bosnia and Herzegovina, and Serbia and Montenegro. 20°E 47°N (pp. 780, 781, 786)

Axum [AHK•soom] Ancient kingdom in northeastern Africa. 14°N 38°E (p. 451)

Azerbaijan [A•zuhr•by•JAHN] European-Asian country on the Caspian Sea. 40°N 47°E (p. 883)

Azores [AY•zohrz] Group of nine islands in the North Atlantic Ocean. 37°N 29°W (pp. R2, R4, R20, R21)

Babylon [BA•buh•luhn] Ancient city, on the banks of the Euphrates River in northern Mesopotamia. 32°N 45°E (pp. 16, 17, 26, 28, 86, 93, 132, 174, 176)

Baghdad [BAG•DAD] Capital city of Iraq. 33°N 44°E (pp. R3, 374, 379, 380, 383, 385, 397, 423, 425, 452, 554, 792, 799)

Bahamas [buh•HAH•muhz] Country made up of many islands between Cuba and the United States. 23°N 74°W (pp. R2, R4, R13, 662)

Balkan [BAWL•kuhn] **Peninsula** Peninsula in southeastern Europe bounded by the Black, Aegean, Mediterranean, Adriatic and Ionian seas. 42°N 20°E (pp. 117, 327, 329)

Balkans [BAWL•kuhnz] Countries on the Balkan Peninsula, which include Slovenia, Croatia, Bosnia and Herzegovina, the Former Yugoslav Republic of Macedonia, Serbia and Montenegro, Albania, Greece, Romania, Bulgaria, and European Turkey. 23°E 44°N (pp. 781, 786)

Baltic [BAWL•tihk] **Sea** Sea in northern Europe connected to the North Sea. 55°N 17°E (pp. R3, R5, R16, R17, 513, 518, 538, 548, 555, 645, 688, 703, 722, 725, 781, 786, 790, 814, 832, 883)

Baltimore [BAWL•tuh•MOHR] City in northern Maryland in the United States. 39°N 77°W (p. 694)

Bangkok [BANG•KAHK] Capital of Thailand. 14°N 100°E (pp. R3, 433, 825, 849)

Bangladesh [BAHNG•gluh•DEHSH] South Asian country bounded by Myanmar and India. 24°N 90°E (pp. R3, 198, 845)

Barcelona [BAHR•suh•LOH•nuh] City in northeastern Spain. 41°N 2°E (p. 555)

Basutoland [buh•SOO•toh•luhnd] Country in southern Africa, now called Lesotho. 29°S 28°E (p. 767)

Bay of Bengal [BEHN•gawl] Arm of the Indian Ocean between India and the Malay Peninsula. 17°N 87°E (pp. R3, R5, R22, R23, 109, 193, 195, 210, 213, 246, 409, 411, 425, 433, 439, 565, 667, 765, 845)

Bay of Pigs Small inlet of the Caribbean Sea on the southern coast of western Cuba. 22°N 81°W (p. 836)

Bechuanaland [behch•WAH•nuh•luhnd] Region in south central Africa, now the nation of Botswana. 22°S 23°E (p. 767)

Beijing [BAY•JIHNG] Capital of China. 40°N 116°E (pp. R3, 409, 411, 423, 424, 425, 430, 431, 439, 554, 771, 773, 778, 811, 825)

Beirut [bay•ROOT] Capital of Lebanon. 34°N 36°E (pp. 792, 799, 875)

Belarus [BEH•luh•ROOS] Eastern European country west of Russia. 54°N 28°E (p. 883)

Belfast [BEHL•fast] Capital of Northern Ireland. 54°N 5°W (p. 757)

Belgium [BEHL•juhm] Country in northwestern Europe. 51°N 5°E (pp. R3, R16, 703, 725, 747, 781, 787, 790, 814, 832, 891)

Belgrade [BEHL•GRAYD] Capital of Yugoslavia. 45°N 21°E (pp. 548, 555, 688, 897)

Belize [buh•LEEZ] Central American country east of Guatemala. 18°N 89°W (pp. R2, R13, 583, 749, 861)

Benin [buh•NEEN] West African country west of Nigeria. 8°N 2°E (p. 870)

Bering Sea Part of the North Pacific Ocean between the Aleutian Islands and the Bering Strait. 55°N 175°E (pp. R2, R3, R4, R5, R23, 573, 825)

Berlin [behr•LIHN] Capital of Germany. 53°N 13°E (pp. 722, 725, 744, 747, 780, 781, 786, 789, 831, 834, 855)

Bhutan [boo•TAHN] South Asian country northeast of India. 27°N 91°E (pp. R3, R22, R23, 198, 765, 845)

Birmingham City in central England. 52°N 1°W (pp. 725, 757)

Black Sea Inland sea between southeastern Europe and Asia Minor. 43°N 32°E (pp. R3, R5, R17, R18, 109, 121, 132, 144, 176, 179, 189, 246, 255, 269, 274, 292, 293, 297, 323, 329, 352, 361, 367, 374, 380, 383, 385, 397, 425, 513, 518, 538, 542, 554, 565, 639, 722, 725, 781, 786, 790, 792, 832, 883)

Bohemia [boh•HEE•mee•uh] Historical region and former kingdom in what is now the Czech Republic. 49°N 13°E (pp. 639, 645, 688)

Bolivia [buh•LIHV•ee•uh] Country in South America. 17°S 64°W (pp. 749, 861)

Bombay City in western India, now called Mumbai. 18°N 72°E (pp. 667, 845)

Bordeaux [bawr•DOH] City in southwestern France. 44°N 0°W (pp. 557, 561, 725)

Borneo [BAWR•nee•oh] Island in the Malay Archipelago in southeastern Asia. 0°N 112°E (pp. R3, 246, 425, 433, 554, 667, 765, 825)

Bosnia-Herzegovina [BAHZ•nee•uh HEHRT•seh•GAW•vee•nuh] Country in southeastern Europe between Croatia and Serbia-Montenegro. 44°N 18°E (p. 897)

Boston [bahs•tuhn] Capital of Massachusetts. 42°N 71°W (pp. 691, 694, 695)

Botswana [bawt•SWAH•nah] Southern African country north of the Republic of South Africa. 22°S 23°E (p. 870)

Brazil [bruh•ZIHL] Largest country in South America. 9°S 53°W (pp. R2, 473, 749, 860, 861)

Breslau [BREHS•low] City in southwest Poland. 51°N 17°E (pp. 725, 747)

Bristol [BRIHS•tuhl] City in southwest England. 51°N 2°W (p. 725)

Britain Largest island in the British Isles. 54°N 4°W (pp. R2–3, R4–5, R16, 286, 293, 297, 302, 317, 323, 352, 358, 361, 695, 757, 780)

British East Africa Former group of British colonial possessions in East Africa, consisting of Kenya, Uganda, Zanzibar, and Tanganyika. 3°S 35°E (p. 767)

Bruges [BROOZH] City in northwestern Belgium. 51°N 3°E (p. 522)

Brunei [bru•NY] Southwest Asian country on the northern coast of the island of Borneo. 5°N 114°E (p. 765)

Brussels [BRUH•suhlz] Capital of Belgium. 51°N 4°E (pp. 722, 725, 747)

Buda [BOO•duh] Town in Hungary that combined with Pest and Óbuda to form Budapest. 47°N 19°E (p. 688)

Budapest [BOO•duh•PEHST] Capital of Hungary. 47°N 19°E (pp. 703, 725, 781, 786)

Bulgaria [BUHL•GAR•ee•uh] Country in southeastern Europe on the Balkan Peninsula. 42°N 24°E (pp. R3, R17, 176, 781, 786, 790, 799, 832, 897)

Burkina Faso [buhr•KEE•nuh FAH•soh] West African country. 12°N 3°E (p. 870)

Burma [BUHR•muh] Country in southeast Asia, now known as Myanmar. 16°N 96°E (pp. 765, 773, 825, 845, 847)

Burundi [bu•ROON•dee] Country in East Africa. 3°S 30°E (p. 870)

Byblos [BIH•bluhs] Ancient city of Phoenicia on the Mediterranean Sea, near present-day Beirut, Lebanon. 34°N 35°E (pp. 17, 90, 105, 132)

Byzantine [BIH•zuhn•TEEN] **Empire** Eastern part of the Roman Empire that survived after the breakup of the western part of the empire in the A.D. 400s; Constantinople was its capital. 41°N 29°E (pp. 383, 518, 538, 542)

Byzantium [buh•ZAN•tee•uhm] Ancient city that became the capital of the Eastern Roman Empire; was later renamed Constantinople and is now called Istanbul. 41°N 29°E (p. 293)

Cahokia [kuh•HOH•kee•uh] City in southwestern Illinois on the Mississippi River near St. Louis; largest city of the Mississippian Mound Builders. 38°N 90°W (p. 572)

Cairo [KY•roh] Capital of Egypt. 31°N 32°E (pp. R3, 380, 385, 452, 479, 767, 792, 875)

Calcutta [kal•KUHT•uh] City in eastern India, now known as Kolkata. 22°N 88°E (pp. R3, 845)

Calicut [KAL•ih•KUHT] Seaport in southwestern India, now called Kozhikode. 11°N 75°E (pp. 433, 662, 667)

California State in the western United States. 36°N 120°W (pp. R6, R8)

Cambodia [kam•BOH•dee•uh] Southeast Asian country south of Thailand and Laos. 12°N 104°E (p. 849)

Cameroon [ka•muh•ROON] Central African country. 6°N 11°E (p. 870)

Campania [kam•PAY•nyuh] Region in southern Italy on the Tyrrhenian Sea. 41°N 14°E (p. 263)

Canada [KA•nuh•duh] Country in North America north of the United States. 50°N 100°W (pp. R2, R6, R7)

Cannae [KA•nee] Ancient town in southern Italy. 41°N 16°E (p. 274)

Canterbury [KAN•tuhr•BEHR•ee] City in Kent in southeastern England. 51°N 1°E (p. 645)

Cape Town Legislative capital of the Republic of South Africa. 34°S 18°E (p. 767)

Caporetto Village in northwestern Slovenia. 46°N 13°E (p. 786)

Caribbean [KAR•uh•BEE•uhn] **Sea** Part of the Atlantic Ocean bordered by the West Indies, South America, and Central America. 15°N 76°W (pp. R2, R4, 473, 565, 590, 662, 663, 691, 836, 861)

Carpathian [kahr•PAY•thee•uhn] **Mountains** Mountain system in central and Eastern Europe. 49°N 20°E (p. 513)

Carthage [KAHR•thihj] Ancient city on the northern coast of Africa. 37°N 10°E (pp. 263, 268, 269, 274, 292, 293, 297, 329, 337, 367, 514)

Caspian [KAS•pee•uhn] **Sea** Saltwater lake in southeastern Europe and southwestern Asia, the largest inland body of water in the world. 40°N 52°E (pp. R3, R5, R17, 17, 109, 132, 176, 179, 198, 246, 255, 293, 297, 329, 361, 374, 380, 383, 385, 397, 424, 425, 513, 518, 542, 554, 565, 709, 786, 790, 792, 799, 883)

Castile [kas•TEEL] Former kingdom in Spain. 39°N 3°E (p. 538)

Çatal Hüyük [chah•TAHL hoo•YOOK] Early Neolithic community in present-day Turkey. 38°N 35°E (p. 8)

Caucasus [KAW•kuh•suhs] **Mountains** Range of mountains between the Caspian and Black seas. 43°N 42°E (pp. R17, 374)

Central African Republic African country south of Chad. 8°N 21°E (p. 870)

Central America Area of North America between Mexico and South America. 11°N 86°W (pp. 749, 861)

Ceylon [sih•LAHN] Country in the Indian Ocean, now called Sri Lanka. 8°N 82°E (pp. R22, 433, 667, 765, 845)

Chaco Canyon [CHAH•koh] Center of Anasazi civilization in present-day New Mexico. 36°N 108°W (p. 578)

Chad African country west of Sudan. 18°N 19°E (p. 870)

Chaeronea [KEHR•uh•NEE•uh] Ancient town in Greece near Thebes. 38°N 22°E (p. 176)

Changan [CHAHNG•AHN] Capital of China during the Tang dynasty, now called Xian. 34°N 108°E (pp. 240, 241, 246, 408, 409, 411, 416, 439)

Chang Jiang [CHAHNG JYAHNG] River in China, formerly called the Yangtze River. 30°N 117°E (pp. 225, 226, 230, 241, 246, 409, 411, 424, 425, 431, 439, 811)

Charles Town City in southeastern South Carolina, now called Charleston. 33°N 80°W (pp. 694, 695)

Chernigov [chehr•NEE•guhf] Principality in the Kievan Rus. 51°N 31°E (p. 548)

Chichén Itzá [chee•CHEHN eet•SAH] Most important city of the Mayans, located in the northern part of the Yucatán Peninsula. 20°N 88°W (p. 575)

Chile [CHEE•lay] Country in South America. 35°S 72°W (pp. 749, 861)

China [CHY•nuh] Country in East Asia, world's largest by population; now called the People's Republic of China. 37°N 93°E (pp. R3, R5, R22–23, 109, 198, 225, 226, 230, 241, 246, 409, 411, 416, 424, 425, 431, 433, 439, 554, 658, 662, 667, 762, 765, 773, 778, 811, 825, 838, 845, 847, 849)

Chittagong [CHIH•tuh•GAHNG] Port city in Bangladesh. 22°N 90°E (pp. 433, 554)

Chongqing [chung•CHING] City in south-central China on the Chang Jiang. 29°N 106°E (pp. 811, 825)

Clermont City in central France. 45°N 3°E (pp. 534, 542, 544)

Cologne [KUH•LOHN] City in west central Germany on the Rhine River. 50°N 6°E (pp. 542, 725, 747)

Colombia [kuh•LUHM•bee•uh] Country in South America west of Venezuela. 4°N 73°W (pp. 749, 861)

Congo [KAHNG•goh] Central African country. 3°S 14°E (p. 870)

Congo [KAHNG•goh] **River** River in Central Africa. 2°S 17°E (p. 469)

Connecticut A state in the northeastern United States. 41°N 73°W (p. 694)

Constantinople [KAHN•STAN•tuhn•OH•puhl] City built on the site of Byzantium, now known as Istanbul in present-day Turkey. 41°N 29°E (pp. 246, 302, 317, 323, 327, 329, 337, 351, 352, 358, 361, 367, 374, 379, 380, 425, 518, 542, 555, 725, 781, 786, 792)

Copan [koh•PAHN] Ancient city of the Mayan people, in northwestern Honduras. 14°N 89°W (p. 575)

Coral Sea Arm of the southwest Pacific Ocean bounded by Australia, Papua New Guinea, the Solomon Islands, and Vanuatu. 20°S 155°E (p. 825)

Cordoba [KAWR•duh•buh] City in southern Spain. 37°N 4°W (pp. 379, 380, 555)

Corinth City of ancient Greece, southwest of the modern city of Corinth. 37°N 22°E (pp. 117, 144, 269, 274)

Corsica [KOHR•sih•kuh] Island in the Mediterranean Sea. 42°N 8°E (pp. R5, R16, 121, 263, 269, 274, 293, 329, 337, 538, 555, 609, 653, 722, 832)

Costa Rica [KAWS•tah REE•kah] Central American country south of Nicaragua. 11°N 85°W (pp. R2, 749, 861)

Crécy [kray•SEE] Site in France of battle in which England defeated France in 1346. 50°N 48°E (pp. 557, 561)

Crete [KREET] Greek island southeast of mainland in the southern Aegean Sea. 35°N 24°E (pp. R17, 116, 117, 121, 132, 134, 149, 179, 189, 269, 274, 293, 329, 337, 385, 542, 548, 555, 799, 832)

Crimea [kry•MEE•uh] Peninsula in southeastern Ukraine. 45°N 33°E (p. 548)

Croatia [kroh•AY•shuh] Southeastern European country on the Adriatic Sea. 46°N 16°E (p. 897)

Cuba [KYOO•buh] Island country in the West Indies. 22°N 79°W (pp. R2, R4, 662, 749, 836, 860, 861)

Cuzco [KOOS•koh] City in southern Peru. 13°S 71°W (pp. 572, 577, 582, 593, 603)

Cyprus [SY•pruhs] Island country in the eastern Mediterranean Sea, south of Turkey. 35°N 31°E (pp. R3, R5, R17, 62, 90, 121, 132, 179, 189, 269, 274, 293, 329, 385, 542, 781, 792, 799, 832, 891)

Czechoslovakia [CHEHK•oh•sloh•VAH•kee•ah] Former country of central Europe; now called Czech Republic and Slovakia. 49°N 18°E (pp. 790, 814, 832, 891)

Damascus [duh•MAS•kuhs] Capital of Syria. 34°N 36°E (pp. 90, 105, 246, 352, 361, 374, 380, 383, 385, 397, 792, 799, 875)

Danube [DAN•yoob] **River** Second-longest river in Europe. 43°N 24°E (pp. R5, 176, 269, 274, 293, 297, 323, 329, 337, 383, 385, 397, 425, 513, 514, 516, 538, 555, 725)

Danzig City in northern Poland. 54°N 18°E (pp. 555, 814)

Dardanelles [dahr•dehn•EHLZ] Strait between the Aegean Sea and the Sea of Marmara that separates European Turkey from Asian Turkey. 40°N 26°E (p. 799)

Dead Sea Salt lake in southwestern Asia. 31°N 35°E (pp. R5, 17, 39, 75, 90, 105, 875)

Deccan [DEHK•uhn] **Plateau** Region in India. 19°N 76°E (pp. R5, 195, 198)

Delhi [DEH•lee] City in northern India. 28°N 76°E (pp. R3, 379)

Delos [DEE•LAHS] Greek island in the southern Aegean Sea. 37°N 25°E (pp. 138, 144)

Delphi [DEHL•FY] Ancient Greek town and site of Temple of Apollo. 38°N 22°E (p. 117)

Denmark [DEHN•MAHRK] Scandinavian country in northwestern Europe. 56°N 8°E (pp. R3, 639, 645, 688, 722, 725, 781, 786, 790, 814, 832, 834, 891)

Djibouti [jih•BOO•tee] East African country. 12°N 43°E (p. 870)

Dominican [duh•MIH•nih•kuhn] **Republic** Country in the West Indies. 19°N 71°W (pp. 749, 836, 861)

Dresden [DREHZ•duhn] A city of east-central Germany on the Elbe River. 51°N 13°E (p. 747)

Dublin [DUH•blihn] Capital of Ireland. 53°N 6°W (p. 757)

Dutch East Indies Islands of Southeast Asia now known as Indonesia. 40°S 118°E (p. 765)

E

East Africa Region in east Central Africa comprised of Burundi, Kenya, Rwanda, Somalia, Tanzania, and Uganda. 5°N 35°E (pp. R3, R5, R20, R21, 246)

East China Sea Arm of the Pacific Ocean between China and the Ryukyu Islands. 30°N 125°E (pp. R5, 225, 226, 230, 241, 251, 409, 411, 425, 765, 773, 778, 811)

Eastern Desert Arid region in eastern Egypt, also called the Arabian Desert. 22°N 45°E (pp. 39, 75)

East Germany Officially called the German Democratic Republic. 53°N 13°E (pp. 832, 834)

East Prussia [PRUH•shuh] Historical region and former province of Prussia on the Baltic Sea in present-day Poland and Russia. 54°N 20°E (p. 814)

East Sea Arm of the Pacific Ocean, lying between Japan and the Asian mainland; also called the Sea of Japan. 40°N 132°E (pp. R5, 225, 485, 778)

Ebro River River in northeastern Spain, emptying into the Mediterranean Sea. 42°N 2°W (pp. 516, 725)

Ecuador [EH•kwuh•DAWR] South American country southwest of Colombia. 1°S 79°W (pp. 749, 861)

Edinburgh Capital city of Scotland. 55°N 3°W (pp. 555, 725)

Edo [EH•doh] Village in Japan where the Sumida River joins Tokyo Bay, site of present-day Tokyo. 35°N 140°E (pp. 485, 507, 771, 773, 778)

Egypt [EE•jihpt] Country in North Africa on the Mediterranean Sea. 26°N 27°E

(pp. R3, 17, 28, 39, 62, 70, 75, 121, 132, 176, 246, 286, 293, 297, 302, 317, 327, 329, 352, 361, 367, 374, 380, 383, 385, 397, 448, 452, 479, 767, 792, 799, 870, 875)

Elba [EHL•buh] An island of Italy in the Tyrrhenian Sea. 42°N 10°E (p. 722)

El Salvador [ehl SAL•vuh•DAWR] Central American country southwest of Honduras. 14°N 89°W (pp. 749, 861)

England Part of the island of Great Britain lying east of Wales and south of Scotland. 51°N 1°W (pp. R2–3, R4–5, R16, 518, 522, 534, 538, 542, 544, 639, 645, 662, 757)

English Channel Narrow sea separating France and Great Britain. 49°N 3°W (pp. 557, 787)

Equator An imaginary circle that divides the earth into the Northern Hemisphere and the Southern Hemisphere. (pp. R2, R3, R4, R5, 33, 425, 433, 445, 452, 463, 469, 479, 554, 565, 577, 667, 707, 749, 765, 767, 769)

Equitorial Guinea [ee•kwuh•TOHR•ee•uhl GIH•nee] Central African country. 2°N 8°E (p. 870)

Eridu [EHR•ih•DOO] Ancient settlement in Mesopotamia. 31°N 46°E (p. 17)

Eritrea [EHR•uh•TREE•uh] East African country north of Ethiopia. (pp. 767, 870)

Estonia [eh•STOH•nee•uh] Republic in northeastern Europe, one of the Baltic states. 59°N 25°E (pp. 548, 790, 814, 883, 891)

Ethiopia [EE•thee•OH•pee•uh] East African country. 8°N 38°E (pp. 452, 479, 767, 870)

Etruria [ih•TRUR•ee•uh] Ancient region on the Italian peninsula that was home to the Etruscans; area is now called Tuscany. 30°N 46°E (p. 263)

Euphrates [yu•FRAY•TEEZ] **River** River in southwestern Asia that joins the Tigris River near the Persian Gulf. 36°N 40°E (pp. 17, 109, 121, 132, 176, 179, 189, 246, 255, 293, 297, 329, 374, 380, 383, 397)

Europe One of the world's seven continents, sharing a landmass with Asia. 50°N 15°E (pp. R3, R5, R16–17, 13, 28, 33, 109, 255, 473, 565, 573, 658, 662, 668, 695, 707, 724, 744, 762, 780, 781, 786, 790, 804, 813, 814, 824, 831, 832, 891, 893)

F

Federal Republic of Germany Formerly West Germany. 51°N 8°E (pp. 832, 834)

Fertile Crescent Region in the Middle East that reaches from Israel to the Persian Gulf, including the Tigris and Euphrates Rivers. 34°N 45°E (p. 17)

Finland [FIHN•luhnd] Northern European country east of Sweden. 63°N 26°E (pp. 790, 814, 832, 891)

Florence [FLOHR•uhnz] City in the Tuscany region of central Italy at the foot of the Apennines. 43°N 11°E (pp. 555, 608, 609, 639, 653, 670, 725, 747)

Florida State in the southeastern United States. 30°N 84°W (pp. 691, 836)

Formigny [FAWR•mee•NYUH] Site in northern France of a French victory during the Hundred Years' War. 49°N 0°W (pp. 557, 561)

Formosa [fawr•MOH•suh] An island in southeastern Asia off the coast of China, now known as Taiwan. 24°N 122°E (pp. 765, 811)

France [FRANS] Third-largest country in Europe, located south of Great Britain. 47°N 1°E (pp. R2–3, R4–5, R16, 380, 385, 518, 522, 534, 538, 542, 544, 548, 639, 645, 662, 722, 725, 747, 780, 781, 786, 787, 789, 790, 814, 832, 834, 891)

Frankfurt Port city in west central Germany on the Main River. 50°N 8°E (pp. 555, 688, 703, 747, 834)

French Equatorial Africa Former French colonial possession in western and central Africa, encompassing the present-day republics of Chad, the Central African Republic, the Republic of the Congo, and Gabon. 0°N 20°E (p. 767)

French Guiana [gee•A•nuh] French-owned territory in northern South America. 5°N 53°W (pp. 749, 861)

French Indochina [IHN•doh•CHY•nuh] Peninsula between India and China comprised of Cambodia, Laos, and Vietnam. 16°N 107°E (pp. 765, 773, 811, 825)

French West Africa Former French colonial unit comprised of the following eight modern countries: Senegal, Guinea, Côte d'Ivoire, Benin, Mauritania, Mali, Burkina Faso, and Niger. (p. 767)

Gabon [ga•BOHN] Central African country. 0° 12°E (p. 870)

Galilee [GA•luh•LEE] Region of ancient Palestine, now part of northern Israel, between the Jordan River and the Sea of Galilee. 32°N 35°E (pp. 352, 361, 367)

Gallipoli [guh•lih•PUH•lee] City and narrow peninsula of northwest Turkey. 40°N 26°E (pp. 786, 799)

Gambia [GAM•bee•uh] West African country along the Gambia River. 13°N 16°W (pp. 767, 870)

Ganges [GAN•JEEZ] **Plain** Flat, fertile area around the Ganges River. 24°N 89°E (pp. 195, 198)

Ganges [GAN•JEEZ] **River** River in India that flows from the Himalaya to the Bay of Bengal. 24°N 89°E (pp. R3, R5, R22, 193, 195, 198, 210, 213, 219, 246, 409, 424, 667)

Gaugamela [GAW•guh•MEE•luh] Area near Babylon and the Tigris River. 36°N 44°E (pp. 174, 176)

Gaul [GAWL] Ancient Roman name for the area now known as France. 45°N 3°E (pp. 274, 277, 286, 293, 297, 302, 317, 323, 352, 358, 361)

Gaza [GAH•zuh] **Strip** Coastal area along the Mediterranean Sea bordering Israel and Egypt. 31°N 34°E (p. 875)

Geneva [juh•NEE•vuh] City in western Switzerland. 46°N 6°E (p. 633)

Genoa [geh•NOH•uh] City in northwestern Italy. 44°N 9°E (pp. 542, 548, 555, 608, 609, 639, 653, 725, 747)

Georgia [JAWR•juh] Asian-European country bordering the Black Sea south of Russia. 42°N 43°E (p. 883)

German Democratic Republic Formerly East Germany. 53°N 13°E (pp. 832, 834)

Germany [JUHR•muh•nee] Western European country south of Denmark. 51°N 10°E (pp. R3, 518, 725, 747, 780, 781, 786, 787, 789, 790, 814, 834, 891)

Ghana [GAH•nuh] Country in West Africa on the Gulf of Guinea. 8°N 2°W (pp. R2, 448, 451, 870)

Giza [GEE•zuh] City in northern Egypt and site of the Great Pyramid. 29°N 31°E (pp. 17, 39, 47, 62, 75)

Glasgow [GLAHZ•goh] Largest city in Scotland. 55°N 4°W (pp. 725, 757)

Gobi [GOH•bee] Vast desert covering parts of Mongolia and China. 43°N 103°E (pp. R5, 109, 225, 246, 409, 411, 425, 431, 439)

Golan [GOH•lahn] **Heights** Region between northeast Israel and southwest Syria. 33°N 35°E (p. 875)

Gold Coast Former British colony, now the nation of Ghana in West Africa. 3°N 1°W (p. 767)

Gomel [GOH•muhl] Port city in southeastern Belarus. 52°N 31°E (p. 548)

Granada [gruh•NAH•duh] Province on the southern coast of Spain. 37°N 3°W (pp. 380, 394, 553)

Great Britain Island off the western coast of Europe comprising England, Scotland, and Wales. 54°N 2°W (pp. 814, 832)

Great Rift Valley Depression extending from Syria to Mozambique. 5°S 35°E (p. 445)

Great Wall Wall built in the 200s B.C. to protect China's northern border. 338°N 109°E (p. 431)

Greece [GREES] Country in southeastern Europe on the Balkan Peninsula. 39°N 21°E (pp. R3, R5, R17, 117, 121, 124, 132, 134, 138, 149, 154, 176, 263, 268, 269, 274, 277, 286, 292, 293, 297, 302, 317, 323, 351, 352, 358, 361, 367, 385, 781, 786, 790, 799, 832, 891, 897)

Guadalcanal [GWAHD•uhl•kuh•NAL] Largest of the Solomon Islands in the western Pacific Ocean. 9°S 160°E (p. 825)

Guam [GWAHM] U.S. possession in the Pacific Ocean. 14°N 143°E (p. 825)

Guangdong [GWAHNG•DUHNG] Province of southeast China on the South China Sea. 23°N 113°E (p. 773)

Guangzhou [GWAHNG•JOH] Port city in southern China on the Chang Jiang. 23°N 113°W (pp. R3, 246, 409, 411, 425, 431, 439, 773, 811)

Guantanamo [gwahn•TAH•nuh•MOH] **Bay** Inlet of the Caribbean Sea near Cuba. 20°N 75°W (p. 836)

Guatemala [GWAH•tay•MAH•lah] Central American country south of Mexico. 16°N 92°W (pp. 749, 861)

Guinea [GIH•nee] West African country. 11°N 12°W (p. 870)

Guinea-Bissau [GIH•nee bih•SOW] West African country. 12°N 20°W (p. 870)

Gulf of Mexico [MEHK•sih•KOH] Gulf on part of the southern coast of the United States. 25°N 94°W (pp. R2, R4, 565, 575, 590, 663, 691, 753)

Gulf of Tonkin [TAWN•kihn] Arm of the South China Sea off the coast of Vietnam. 20°N 108°E (p. 849)

Guyana [gy•AH•nuh] South American country between Venezuela and Suriname. 8°N 59°W (pp. 749, 861)

Hadrian's Wall Ancient Roman stone wall built to protect the northern boundary of Roman Britain. 55°N 3°W (pp. 293, 297)

Hainan [HY•NAHN] Province in southeastern China and island in the South China Sea. 32°N 120°E (pp. R5, 225, 811)

Haiphong [HY•FAWNG] City in northeast Vietnam on the Red River delta near

Gazetteer

the Gulf of Tonkin. 20°N 106°E (p. 849)

Haiti [HAY•tee] Country in the West Indies. 19°N 72°W (pp. 749, 836, 861)

Hamburg City in north central Germany. 53°N 10°E (pp. 548, 725, 747, 834)

Han [HAHN] Chinese state along Huang He and Chang Jiang. 33°N 112°E (p. 241)

Hangzhou [HAHNG•JOH] City in southeastern China. 30°N 120°E (pp. 246, 408, 409, 411, 416, 424, 425, 439, 554)

Hanoi [ha•NOY] Capital of Vietnam. 21°N 106°E (pp. 765, 849)

Hanover City in northwest Germany. 52°N 9°E (pp. 747, 834)

Harappa [huh•RA•puh] Ancient city in the Indus River valley in present-day Pakistan. (pp. 194, 198, 219)

Hawaii [huh•WY•ee] State of the United States in the central Pacific Ocean comprising the Hawaiian Islands. 20°N 157°W (p. 825)

Heian [HAY•ahn] Ancient capital city of Japan, now called Kyoto. 35°N 135°E (pp. 485, 491, 498, 507)

Himalaya [HIH•muh•LAY•uh] Mountain system forming a barrier between India and the rest of Asia. 29°N 85°E (pp. R5, R22–23, 193, 195, 198, 213, 219, 246, 409, 424, 425, 439)

Hindu Kush Major mountain system in central Asia. 35°N 68°E (pp. 109, 198, 213, 219)

Hiroshima [hee•roh•SHEE•mah] City in southern Japan. 34°N 132°E (p. 825)

Hispaniola [HIHS•puh•NYOH•luh] Island in the West Indies. 19°N 72°E (pp. R4, 662)

Hokkaido [hah•KY•doh] Second-largest island of Japan. 43°N 142°E (pp. R3, R5, 484, 485, 507)

Holstein [HOHL•steen] Region and former duchy of northern Germany. 54°N 10°E (p. 747)

Holy Roman Empire Lands in western and central Europe, empire founded by Charlemagne. 52°N 15°E (pp. 512, 522, 534, 538, 542, 544, 639)

Honduras [hahn•DUR•uhs] Central American country on the Caribbean Sea. 15°N 88°W (pp. 749, 861)

Hong Kong [HAWNG KAWNG] Port and industrial center in southern China. 22°N 115°E (pp. 765, 771, 773, 811, 825)

Honshu [HAHN•shoo] Largest island of Japan, called the mainland. 36°N 138°E (pp. R3, R5, 484, 485, 507)

Huang He [HWAHNG HUH] Second-longest river in China, formerly called the Yellow River. 35°N 113°E (pp. 225, 226, 230, 241, 246, 409, 411, 424, 425, 439, 811)

Hudson Bay Inland sea in Canada. 60°N 85°W (pp. R2, R4, 565, 590, 662, 691)

Hungary [HUHNG•guh•ree] Eastern European country south of Slovakia. 46°N 17°E (pp. R3, R16, 518, 538, 548, 639, 688, 703, 790, 814, 832, 891, 897)

Ifni [EEF•nee] Former Spanish possession, now part of Morocco. 29°N 8°W (p. 767)

India [IHN•dee•uh] South Asian country south of China and Nepal. 23°N 77°E (pp. R3, R5, R22, 109, 193, 194, 195, 198, 210, 213, 219, 246, 380, 383, 409, 425, 433, 435, 554, 662, 658, 667, 762, 765, 773, 825, 842, 845)

Indian Ocean Third-largest ocean. 10°S 70°E (pp. R3, R5, 13, 109, 195, 198, 210, 213, 425, 433, 452, 463, 469, 479, 554, 565, 662, 765, 767, 825, 845, 893)

Indonesia [IHN•duh•NEE•zhuh] Island republic in Southeast Asia, consisting of most of the Malay Archipelago. 40°S 118°E (pp. R3, R5, R23, 847)

Indus [IHN•duhs] **River** River in Asia that begins in Tibet and flows through Pakistan to the Arabian Sea. 27°N 68°E (pp. R3, R5, 109, 176, 193, 195, 198, 210, 213, 219, 246, 380, 383, 409, 424, 425, 565)

Ionian [eye•OH•nee•uhn] **Sea** Arm of the Mediterranean Sea. 38°N 18°E (pp. 117, 144, 149, 263)

Iran [EYE•ran] Southwest Asian country on the eastern shore of the Persian Gulf, formerly called Persia. 31°N 53°E (pp. R3, R19, 176, 198, 792)

Iraq [EYE•rak] Country in southwestern Asia near the Persian Gulf. 32°N 42°E (pp. R3, R18–19, R22, 176, 792, 869)

Ireland Island west of Great Britain occupied by the Republic of Ireland and Northern Ireland. 54°N 8°W (pp. R2, R4, R16, 518, 538, 645, 757, 790, 814, 832, 891)

Israel [IHZ•ree•uhl] Southwest Asian country south of Lebanon. 32°N 34°E (pp. R3, R18, 1, 90, 105, 176, 869, 875)

Issus [IHS•uhs] Ancient town of Asia Minor located north of the Syrian border. 37°N 36°E (p. 176)

Istanbul [ihs•tan•BUHL] Largest city in Turkey; formerly called Byzantium and Constantinople. 41°N 28°E (p. 792)

Italy Southern European country south of Switzerland and east of France. 43°N 11°E (pp. R3, R5, R16, 121, 262, 263, 268, 269, 274, 277, 286, 292, 293, 297, 302, 317, 323, 327, 329, 337, 342, 351, 352, 358, 361, 367, 385, 516, 518, 522, 542, 609, 645, 653, 688, 722, 725, 747, 781, 786, 789, 790, 814, 832, 891)

Ivory Coast Section of coastal western Africa. 7°N 6°W (p. 870)

Iwo Jima [EE•wuh JEE•muh] Largest of the Volcano Islands of Japan in the northwest Pacific Ocean east of Taiwan. 24°N 141°E (p. 825)

Jamaica [juh•MAY•kuh] Island country in the West Indies. 18°N 78°W (pp. 749, 836)

Jamestown Settlement in southeast Virginia. 37°N 77°W (p. 691)

Japan [juh•PAN] Chain of islands in the northern Pacific Ocean. 36°N 133°E (pp. R3, R5, R23, 225, 409, 425, 484, 485, 491, 498, 507, 662, 765, 773, 778, 811)

Java [JAH•vuh] Island in southern Indonesia. 8°S 111°E (pp. R3, R5, R23, R24, 425, 554, 765, 825)

Jeddah [JEHD•uh] City in western Saudi Arabia. 21°N 39°E (p. 433)

Jena [YAY•nuh] City in central Germany. 50°N 11°E (p. 722)

Jericho [JEHR•ih•KOH] Oldest Neolithic community, in the West Bank between Israel and Jordan. 25°N 27°E (pp. 8, 875)

Jerusalem [juh•ROO•suh•luhm] Capital of Israel and a holy city for Christians, Jews, and Muslims. 31°N 35°E (pp. 17, 28, 80, 86, 90, 93, 105, 132, 329, 342, 351, 352, 358, 361, 367, 374, 380, 383, 385, 397, 534, 542, 544, 792, 875)

Jordan [JAWRD•uhn] Southwest Asian country south of Syria. 30°N 38°E (p. 875)

Jordan [JAWRD•uhn] **River** River flowing from Lebanon and Syria to the Dead Sea. 30°N 38°E (pp. 17, 90, 105)

Judaea [ju•DEE•uh] Territory in southwest Asia and a region of historic Palestine. 31°N 35°E (pp. 342, 352, 361, 367)

Judah [JOO•duh] Southern kingdom of ancient Hebrews in Canaan, renamed Palestine. 25°N 49°E (pp. 90, 105)

Kamakura [kah•MAH•kuh•RAH] City in Japan, former location of the Shogun military government. 35°N 139°E (pp. 485, 491)

Karakorum [KAR•uh•KOHR•uhm] Capital of the Mongol Empire during most of the 1200s. 47°N 102°E (pp. 423, 424, 425)

Kashmir [KASH•mihr] Historical region of northwest India and northeast Pakistan. 33°N 77°E (p. 845)

Kathmandu [KAT•MAN•DOO] Capital of Nepal. 27°N 85°E (pp. 210, 845)

Kazakhstan [kuh•ZAHK•STAHN] Large Asian country south of Russia. 48°N 59°E (p. 883)

Kenya [KEHN•yuh] East African country. 1°N 37°E (p. 870)

Key West Island off the southern coast of Florida. 24°N 81°W (p. 836)

Khanbaliq [KAHN•buh•LEEK] Capital of Kublai Khan's Mongol Empire, now called Beijing. 40°N 116°E (pp. 423, 425)

Khartoum [kahr•TOOM] Capital of Sudan. 16°N 33°E (p. 767)

Khyber Pass Mountain pass in western Asia connecting Afghanistan and Pakistan. 34°N 71°E (p. 194)

Kiev [KEE•EHF] Capital of Ukraine, on the Dnieper River. 50°N 30°E (pp. R3, 425, 534, 548, 555, 722, 883)

Kievan Rus State made of small territories around Kiev, destroyed by Mongols in 1240. 50°N 30°E (p. 538)

Knossos [NAH•suhs] Ancient city on Crete. 35°N 24°E (pp. 116, 117, 149)

Korea Peninsula in eastern Asia, divided into the Democratic People's Republic of Korea (North Korea) and the Republic of Korea. 38°N 127°E (pp. R3, R5, R23, 225, 409, 411, 484, 491, 498, 765, 773, 778, 811, 831)

Kosovo [KOH•suh•voh] Province of southern Yugoslavia in the Serbian republic. 42°N 21°E. (p. 897)

Kunlun Shan [KOON•LOON shuhn] Major mountain system in western China. 35°N 83°E (p. 225)

Kush [KUHSH] Ancient region in present-day Sudan, formerly called Nubia. 21°N 33°E (p. 70)

Kut-el-Amara Town in southeastern Iraq on the Tigris River; also called Al Kut. 32°N 45°E (p. 799)

Kuwait [ku•WAYT] Country on the Persian Gulf between Saudi Arabia and Iraq. 29°N 48°E (pp. 792, 799)

Kyoto [kee•OH•toh] Ancient capital of Japan, formerly called Heian. 35°N 135°E (pp. 485, 491, 498, 507, 778)

Kyrgyzstan [KIHR•gih•STAN] Central Asian country on China's western border. 41°N 75°E (p. 883)

Kyushu [kee•OO•shoo] One of the four major islands of Japan. 33°N 131°E (pp. R3, 484, 485, 507)

Laos [LOWS] Southeast Asian country south of China and west of Vietnam. 20°N 102°E (pp. 847, 849)

Latin America [LA•tihn uh•MEHR•ee•kuh] Countries of the Western Hemisphere south of the United States, especially those countries that developed from the colonies of Spain, Portugal, and France. 5°S 65°W (p. 861)

Latium [LAY•shee•uhm] Region in west central Italy. 42°N 12°E (p. 263)

Latvia [LAT•vee•uh] Eastern European country west of Russia on the Baltic Sea. 57°N 25°E (pp. 790, 814, 883, 891)

Lebanon [LEH•buh•nuhn] Southwest Asian country on the eastern coast of the Mediterranean Sea. 34°N 34°E (pp. R3, 176, 792, 875)

Leeds City in north-central England. 53°N 1°W (pp. 725, 757)

Leipzig [LIHP•sihg] City in southeastern Germany. 51°N 12°E (pp. 722, 747)

Leon [lay•OHN] Historic region and former kingdom in Spain. 41°N 5°W (p. 538)

Lesotho [luh•SOH•TOH] Southern African country within the Republic of South Africa. 30°S 28°E (p. 870)

Liberia [ly•BIHR•ee•uh] West African country. 7°N 10°W (pp. 767, 870)

Libya [LIH•bee•uh] North African country west of Egypt. 28°N 15°E (pp. R3, 176, 767, 790, 870)

Lisbon [LIHZ•buhn] Capital of Portugal. 39°N 9°W (p. 555)

Lithuania [LIH•thuh•WAY•nee•uh] Eastern European country northwest of Belarus. 56°N 24°E (pp. 790, 814, 883, 891)

Liverpool City in northwestern England. 53°N 3°W (pp. 725, 757)

Lombardy [LAWM•buhr•dee] Region of northern Italy. 45°N 9°E (p. 747)

London [LUHN•duhn] Capital of the United Kingdom, on the Thames River. 52°N 0° (pp. R2, 518, 542, 553, 555, 557, 561, 633, 642, 670, 680, 703, 714, 722, 724, 725, 757, 780, 781, 786)

Lorraine [loh•RAYN] Historical region and former province of northeast France. 49°N 6°E (pp. 747, 781)

Luoyang [luh•WOH•YAHNG] City in northern China on the Huang He. 34°N 112°E (pp. 224, 230, 246, 251, 409, 439)

Luxembourg [LUHK•suhm•BUHRG] Small European country between France, Belgium, and Germany. 50°N 7°E (pp. 781, 786, 787, 790, 814, 832, 834, 891)

Macau [muh•KOW] Region on the southeastern coast of China. 22°N 113°E (pp. 430, 667, 765, 773)

Macedonia [MA•suh•DOH•nee•uh] Country in southeastern Europe on the Balkan Peninsula. 41°N 22°E (pp. 117, 174, 176, 269, 274, 897)

Machu Picchu [MAH•choo PEE•choo] Incan settlement in the Andes northwest of Cuzco, Peru. 13°S 72°W (p. 577)

Madagascar [MA•duh•GAS•kuhr] Island in the Indian Ocean off the southeastern coast of Africa. 18°S 43°E (pp. R3, R5, R21, 445, 479, 767, 870)

Madinah [mah•DEE•nuh] Holy Muslim city in western Saudi Arabia. 24°N 39°E (pp. 372, 380, 383, 385, 397, 792)

Madras [MAHD•ruhs] City in India, also called Chennai. 13°N 80°E (p. 845)

Madrid [muh•DRIHD] Capital of Spain. 41°N 4°W (pp. 714, 722, 725, 781)

Makkah [MAH•kuh] Holy city of Muslims, also known as Mecca, in western Saudi Arabia. 21°N 39°E (pp. 372, 374, 380, 383, 385, 397, 425, 433, 448, 452, 554, 792)

Malawi [mah•LAH•wee] Southern African country. 11°S 34°E (p. 870)

Malaya [muh•LAY•uh] Peninsula of Asia. 6°N 102°E (p. 765)

Malaysia [muh•LAY•zhuh] Southeast Asian country with land on the Malay Peninsula and on the island of Borneo. 4°N 101°E (p. 847)

Mali [MAH•lee] Republic in northwestern Africa. 15°N 0°W (pp. 451, 870)

Manchester City in northwest England. 53°N 2°W (pp. 725, 757)

Manchuria [man•choo•REE•uh] Region of northeast China comprising the provinces of Heilongjiang, Jilin, and Liaoning. 49°N 117°E (pp. 773, 778, 811, 825)

Manila [muh•NIH•luh] Capital of the Philippines. 15°N 121°E (pp. 765, 825)

Marathon [MAHR•uh•THAHN] Village of ancient Greece northeast of Athens. (p. 134)

Marne River in northeast France that flows into the Seine River. 49°N 3°E (p. 786)

Marseille [mahr•SAY] City in southern France. 43°N 5°E (pp. 542, 555, 725)

Massachusetts State in the northeastern United States. 42°N 72°W (p. 694)

Massalia [muh•SAH•lee•uh] Ancient Greek colony on the site of present-day Marseille. 44°N 3°E (p. 293)

Mauritania [mawr•uh•TAY•nee•uh] West African country. 20°N 14°W (p. 870)

Mediterranean [MEHD•ih•tuh•RAY•nee•uhn] **Sea** Inland sea of Europe, Asia, and Africa. 36°N 13°E (pp. R3, R5, 17, 28, 39, 62, 70, 75, 90, 105, 109, 117, 121, 132, 144, 149,

176, 179, 189, 263, 269, 274, 292, 293, 297, 323, 329, 337, 352, 361, 367, 374, 380, 383, 385, 397, 425, 445, 452, 463, 479, 513, 514, 518, 538, 542, 548, 555, 609, 639, 645, 653, 703, 709, 722, 725, 747, 767, 781, 786, 790, 832, 875)

Mekong [MAY•KAWNG] River River in southeastern Asia. 18°N 104°E (pp. 246, 409, 411, 424, 439, 667, 849)

Memel Territory [MAY•muhl] Former German territory, now part of Lithuania. 40°N 20°E (p. 814)

Memphis Ancient capital of Egypt. 29°N 31°E (pp. 38, 39, 47, 59, 62, 70, 75, 80)

Meroë [MEHR•oh•ee] Capital city of Kush. 7°N 93°E (pp. 68, 70, 452)

Mesa Verde National park in southwestern Colorado containing artifacts and cliff dwellings from the Anasazi. 37°N 108°W (p. 578)

Mesoamerica [MEH•zoh•uh•MEHR•ih•kuh] Ancient region including present-day Mexico and most of Central America. 10°N 92°W (p. 575)

Mesopotamia [MEH•suh•puh•TAY•mee•uh] Early center of civilization, in the area of modern Iraq and eastern Syria between the Tigris and Euphrates Rivers. 34°N 13°E (pp. 17, 28, 132, 380)

Mexico [MEHK•sih•KOH] North American country south of the United States. 24°N 104°W (pp. R2, 575, 662, 749 860, 861)

Mexico City Capital of Mexico. 19°N 99°W (pp. R2, 658, 662, 663)

Miami [my•AM•ee] City in southeast Florida. 25°N 80°W (p. 836)

Midway [MIHD•way] Islands Atoll in the North Pacific Ocean, about one-third of the way from Honolulu to Tokyo. 28°N 177°W (p. 825)

Milan [mih•LAHN] City in northern Italy. 45°N 9°E (pp. 548, 555, 609, 639, 653, 688, 703, 725)

Minsk [MIHNSK] Capital of Belarus. 54°N 28°E (p. 722)

Mississippi [MIHS•ih•SIHP•ee] River Large river system in the United States. 32°N 92°W (pp. R2, R4, 590, 663)

Modena [MOH•deh•nah] City in northern Italy. 44°N 10°E (p. 747)

Mogadishu [MAH•guh•DIH•shoo] Capital of Somalia. 2°N 45°E (pp. R3, 433, 452, 460, 479, 767)

Mohenjo-Daro [moh•HEHN•joh DAHR•oh] Ancient settlement in the Indus Valley. 27°N 68°E (pp. 198, 219)

Moldova [mawl•DAW•vuh] Small European country between Ukraine and Romania. 48°N 28°E (p. 883)

Moluccas [muh•LUH•kuhz] Group of islands in Indonesia, formerly called the Spice Islands. 2°S 128°E (pp. R5, 662, 667)

Mombasa [mawm•BAHS•uh] City and seaport of Kenya. 4°S 39°E (pp. 433, 452)

Mongolia [mahn•GOH•lee•uh] Country in Asia between Russia and China. 46°N 100°E (pp. R3, 225, 409, 425, 431, 439, 773, 825)

Monrovia [muhn•ROH•vee•uh] Capital of Liberia. 6°N 11°W (p. 767)

Montenegro [MAWN•tuh•NEHG•roh] Republic of Yugoslavia, in the southwest part of the country, bordering on the Adriatic Sea. 42°N 19°E (pp. 781, 786, 897)

Morocco [muh•RAH•koh] North African country. 32°N 7°W (pp. R20, R21, 380, 473, 479, 767, 786, 790, 870)

Moscow [MAHS•koh] Capital of Russia. 55°N 37°E (pp. R3, 425, 540, 714, 722, 725, 781, 883)

Mount Everest [EHV•ruhst] Highest mountain in the world, located in the Himalaya between Nepal and Tibet. 28°N 86°E (pp. 193, 195)

Mount Fuji [FOO•jee] Highest mountain in Japan. 35°N 138°E (pp. 485, 507)

Mount Olympus [uh•LIHM•puhs] Highest mountain in Greece on the border between Thessaly and Macedonia. 41°N 23°E (p. 117)

Mount Sinai [SY•NY] Part of a rocky mass on the Sinai Peninsula of northeastern Egypt. 29°N 33°E (p. 90)

Mozambique [moh•zahm•BEEK] Southern African country south of Tanzania. 20°S 34°E (pp. 767, 870)

Munich [MYOO•nihk] City in southeastern Germany. 48°N 11°E (p. 725)

Myanmar [MYAHN•MAHR] Southeast Asian country formerly called Burma. 21°N 95°E (p. 845)

Mycenae [MY•SEE•nee] Ancient city in Greece. 37°N 22°E (pp. 116, 117, 149)

Nagasaki [nah•gah•SAH•kee] City in Japan. 32°N 129°E (pp. 778, 825)

Namibia [nuh•MIH•bee•uh] Southern African country. 20°S 16°E (p. 870)

Nanjing [NAHN•JIHNG] City in eastern China, capital during the Ming dynasty. 32°N 118°E (pp. 430, 431, 433, 811, 825)

Napata [NA•puh•tuh] Ancient capital of Kush. 18°N 32°E (pp. 68, 70)

Naples [NAY•puhlz] City in Italy. 40°N 14°E (pp. 555, 609, 639, 653, 722, 747)

Nara [NAH•ruh] First permanent capital of Japan. 34°N 135°E (pp. 485, 491, 507)

Navarre [nuh•VAHR] Former kingdom in southern France and northern Spain. 42°N 1°W (p. 538)

Nazareth [NA•zuh•ruhth] Ancient town near Galilee, now in northern Israel. 32°N 35°E (pp. 352, 361, 367)

Nepal [nuh•PAWL] Mountain country between India and China. 28°N 83°E (pp. R3, 198, 202, 765, 845)

Netherlands [NEH•thuhr•luhnz] Country in northwestern Europe. 53°N 3°E (pp. R2–3, R4–5, R16, 639, 645, 662, 725, 747, 781, 786, 787, 790, 814, 832, 891)

New Carthage [KAHR•thihj] City in Spain, also called Cartagena. 38°N 1°W (pp. 269, 274)

New Delhi [NOO DEH•lee] Capital of India. 29°N 77°E (p. 845)

New Guinea [GIHN•ee] Island in the western Pacific Ocean, north of Australia. 5°S 140°E (pp. 765, 825)

New York State in northeastern United States. 43°N 78°W (p. 724)

New York City City in southeastern New York state at the mouth of the Hudson River. 41°N 74°W (p. 769)

Nicaragua [nih•kuh•RAH•gwuh] Central American country south of Honduras. 13°N 86°W (pp. 749, 861)

Niger [NY•juhr] West African country. 18°N 9°E (p. 870)

Nigeria [ny•JIHR•ee•uh] West African country. 9°N 7°E (pp. 767, 870)

Nile [nyl] River World's longest river flowing north from the heart of Africa to the Mediterranean Sea. 27°N 31°E (pp. R3, R5, R20, R21, 38, 39, 47, 59, 62, 68, 70, 75, 109, 121, 132, 176, 179, 189, 246, 269, 293, 297, 329, 374, 383, 385, 397, 425, 445, 452, 875)

Nineveh [NIH•nuh•vuh] Ancient capital of Assyria, on the Tigris River. 26°N 43°E (pp. 17, 26, 132)

Ningxia [NIHNG•shee•AH] Region in northwestern China. 37°N 106°E (p. 424)

Normandy [NAWR•muhn•dee] Region and former province of France. 49°N 2°E (p. 518)

North America Continent in the northern part of the Western Hemisphere between the Atlantic and Pacific Oceans. 45°N 100°W (pp. R2, R4, R6–11, 13, 565, 573, 590, 658, 662, 663, 668, 691, 707, 724, 744, 762, 813, 824, 831, 893)

North Korea [kuh•REE•uh] East Asian country in the northernmost part of the Korean Peninsula. 40°N 127°E (p. 838)

North Sea Arm of the Atlantic Ocean between Europe and Great Britain. 56°N 3°E (pp. R16, 293, 513, 514, 518, 538, 542, 548, 555, 639, 645, 722, 725, 757, 781, 786, 790, 814, 832)

Norway [NAWR•WAY] Northern European country on the Scandinavian peninsula. 63°N 11°E (pp. R3, R16, 538, 639, 645, 722, 725, 781, 786, 790, 814, 832)

Novgorod [NAHV•guh•RAHD] City in western Russia. 58°N 31°E (p. 540)

Nubia [NOO•bee•uh] Region in present-day Sudan on the Nile River, later known as Kush. 21°N 33°E (p. 39)

Nuremburg City in south central Germany. 49°N 11°E (pp. 555, 747)

Nyasaland [ny•ahs•uh•luhnd] Country in southeastern Africa, now called Malawi. 13°S 34°E (p. 767)

Oder River [OH•duhr] River in north central Europe, emptying into the Baltic Sea. 52°N 14°E (p. 513)

Okinawa [oh•keh•NAH•wuh] Island group of the central Ryukyu Islands in the western Pacific Ocean (p. 825)

Olympia [ohz•LIHM•pee•uh] Site of the ancient Olympic Games in Greece. 38°N 22°E (pp. 125, 154)

Oman [oh•MAHN] Country on the Arabian Sea and the Gulf of Oman. 20°N 57°E (pp. R3, R5, R19, 198)

Orléans [AWR•lay•AHN] City in north central France. 47°N 1°E (pp. 553, 557, 561)

Osaka [oh•SAH•kuh] City and port in Japan. 34°N 135°E (pp. R3, 507)

Oslo [AHZ•loh] Capital of Norway. 60°N 11°E (p. 725)

Ostia [AHS•tee•uh] Ancient city of Italy in Latium at the mouth of the Tiber River. 44°N 10°E (p. 293)

Ottoman Empire Turkish empire from the late 1200s in Asia Minor throughout the Middle East. 45°N 25°E (pp. 639, 645, 722, 781, 786, 799)

Pacific Ocean The largest and deepest of the world's four oceans, covering more than a third of the earth's surface. 0° 170°W (pp. R2–3, R4–5, R6–10, R12, R15, 13, 225, 409, 425, 426, 433, 485, 749, 765, 769, 773, 811, 825, 893)

Pakistan [PA•kih•STAN] Officially the Islamic Republic of Pakistan, a republic in South Asia, marking the area where South Asia converges with southwest Asia. 28°N 67°E (pp. R3, 176, 198, 845)

Palestine [PAL•ih•styn] Historic region, situated on the eastern coast of the Mediterranean Sea. 31°N 35°E (pp. 286, 293, 297, 302, 327, 383, 397, 534, 542, 792)

Panama [PA•nuh•MAH] Central American country on the Isthmus of Panama. 9°N 81°W (pp. 749, 861)

Panama [PA•nuh•MAH] **Canal** Ship canal crossing the Isthmus of Panama and connecting the Caribbean Sea with the Pacific Ocean. 9°N 79°W (p. 769)

Papal [PAY•puhl] **States** Territory in Italy formerly under direct temporal rule of the pope. 43°N 13°E (pp. 538, 639, 747)

Paraguay [PAR•uh•GWY] South American country northeast of Argentina. 24°S 57°W (pp. 749, 861)

Paris [PAR•uhs] Capital of France. 49°N 2°E (pp. 516, 518, 542, 555, 557, 633, 642, 714, 722, 724, 725, 780, 781, 786, 787)

Parma [PAHR-mah] City in north-central Italy. 44°N 10°E (p. 747)

Pataliputra [PAH•tuh•lih•POO•truh] Capital of Maurya. 24°N 86°E (pp. 209, 210, 246)

Pearl Harbor Inlet of the Pacific Ocean on the southern coast of Oahu, Hawaii. 21°N 157°W (p. 825)

Peloponnesus [PEH•luh•puh•NEE•suhs] A peninsula in southern Greece. 37°N 22°E (pp. 117, 124, 125, 144)

Pergamum [PUHR•guh•muhm] An ancient city of northwest Asia Minor in Mysia, now Turkey. 39°N 28°E (pp. 179, 189)

Persepolis [puhr•sei•puh•LEES] Ancient capital of Persian empire, now in ruins. 30°N 53°E (pp. 132, 176, 374)

Persia [PUHR•zhuh] The conventional European designation of the country now known as Iran. 32°N 55°E (pp. 132, 144, 176, 246, 374, 380, 383, 385, 397, 425, 554, 799)

Persian [PUHR•zhuhn] **Gulf** An arm of the Arabian Sea in southwestern Asia, between the Arabian Peninsula on the southwest and Iran on the northeast. 27°N 50°E (pp. R19, 17, 109, 132, 176, 374, 380, 383, 385, 397, 448, 452, 554, 565, 709, 792, 799)

Peru [puh•ROO] South American country south of Ecuador and Colombia. 10°S 75°W (pp. 749, 861)

Petrograd [PEH•troh•grad] City in Russia, now St. Petersburg. 59°N 30°E (p. 786)

Philadelphia [FIL•uh•DEHL•fee•uh] City in eastern Pennsylvania on the Delaware River. 40°N 75°W (pp. 690, 691, 694, 695)

Philippines [FIH•luh•PEENZ] Island country in the Pacific Ocean southeast of China. 14°N 125°E (pp. R3, R5, 662, 667, 765, 773, 825, 847)

Piedmont [PEED•mahnt] Region in northwest Italy bordering France and Switzerland. 45°N 8°E (p. 747)

Pisa [PEE•sah] City in central Italy. 43°N 10°E (pp. 542, 609, 653)

Plataea [pluh•TEE•uh] Ancient city of Greece. 39°N 22°E (p. 134)

Plateau of Tibet [tuh•BEHT] World's highest plateau region, bordered by the Himalaya, Pamirs, and Karakoram mountain ranges. (p. 225)

Plymouth [PLI•muhth] Town in eastern Massachusetts, first successful English colony in New England. 42°N 71°W (pp. 663, 691)

Poland [POH•luhnd] Country in central Europe. 52°N 17°E (pp. R3, R16–17, 538, 639, 645, 688, 725, 790, 814, 832, 834, 891)

Po River River in northern Italy, the longest in the country. 45°N 11°E (pp. 263, 274, 513, 514, 653, 688)

Port Arthur City in northeastern China, now called Lüshun. 38°N 121°E (pp. 773, 778)

Portugal [POHR•chih•guhl] A long narrow country on Atlantic Ocean, sharing the Iberian Peninsula with Spain. 38°N 8°W (pp. R2, 639, 645, 662, 722, 781, 786, 790, 814, 832, 891)

Portuguese Guinea [GIH•nee] Country in northwestern Africa, now called Guinea-Bissau. 11°N 14°W (p. 767)

Posen City in western Poland. 52°N 17°E (p. 548)

Prayagal City in central India, part of the Mauryan empire, 321 B.C. 26°N 81°E (p. 210)

Principe [prin•SEEP•e] Island of Africa in the Gulf of Guinea. 1°N 7°E (p. 767)

Prussia [PRUH•shuh] Former kingdom and state of Germany. (pp. 538, 722, 725, 747)

Puerto Rico [PWEHR•toh REE•koh] Island in the Caribbean Sea; U.S. Commonwealth. 19°N 67°W (pp. 749, 836)

Puteoli [pyu•TEE•uh•LY] Port city on the Bay of Naples. 42°N 14°E (p. 293)

Pyrenees [PIR•uh•nees] Mountain range in southwestern Europe, extending from the Bay of Biscay to the Mediterranean Sea. 43°N 0°E (pp. 269, 274, 513, 514, 516)

Qin [CHIHN] Chinese state along Huang He and Chang Jiang. 33°N 112°E (p. 241)

Gazetteer

Qingdao [CHING•DOW] City of eastern China on the Yellow Sea north of Shanghai. 36°N 120°E (p. 773)

Quanzhou [chuh•WAHN•JOH] City in south-eastern China. 25°N 111°E (pp. 431, 433)

Quebec [kih•BEHK] City in Canada. 47°N 71°W (pp. 663, 691)

Ramadi [ruh•MAH•dee] Town in central Iraq. 33°N 43°E (p. 799)

Red Sea Narrow, inland sea, separating the Arabian Peninsula, western Asia, from northeastern Africa. 23°N 37°E (pp. R3, R5, R18–19, R20, R21, 28, 70, 121, 132, 179, 246, 293, 329, 352, 361, 367, 374, 383, 385, 397, 425, 433, 445, 448, 554, 709, 792, 799, 875)

Rhineland [RYN•luhnd] Region along the Rhine River in western Germany. 38°N 91°W (p. 814)

Rhine [RYN] **River** One of the principal rivers of Europe. 50°N 7°E (pp. 293, 513, 514, 538, 542, 688, 722)

Rhodes [RODZ] Island in the Aegean Sea. 36°N 28°E (pp. 269, 274)

Rhodesia [roh•DEE•shuh] Region of south-central Africa south of Congo and comprising modern-day Zambia and Zimbabwe. 19°S 29°E (p. 767)

Rhone [RON] **River** River of southeastern France. 44°N 4°E (pp. 557, 561)

Rio de Oro [REE•o dai O•ro] Historical region in the southern section of the Western Sahara on the northwestern coast of Africa. 24°N 14°W (p. 767)

Rio Grande [REE•oh GRAND] River that forms part of the boundary between the United States and Mexico. 30°N 103°W (pp. R2, R4, 590, 663)

Rocky Mountains Mountain system in western North America. 50°N 114°W (pp. R4, 590)

Romania [ru•MAY•nee•uh] Eastern European country east of Hungary. 46°N 23°E (pp. 781, 786, 790, 814, 832, 897)

Rome [ROHM] Capital of Italy. 41°N 12°E (pp. R3, 262, 263, 268, 269, 274, 277, 286, 292, 293, 297, 302, 317, 323, 327, 329, 337, 342, 351, 352, 358, 361, 367, 514, 516, 518, 522, 534, 542, 548, 555, 608, 609, 633, 642, 645, 653, 670, 703, 714, 722, 725, 744, 747, 780, 781, 786)

Russia [RUH•shuh] Independent republic in Eastern Europe and northern Asia, the world's largest country by area. 61°N 60°E (pp. R3, R17, 645, 722, 725, 747, 773, 778, 781, 786, 883)

Rwanda [ruh•WAHN•duh] East African country. 2°S 30°E (p. 870)

Ryukyu [RYUK•yoo] **Islands** Island group of southwest Japan between Kyushu and Taiwan. 26°N 128°E (p. 778)

Sahara [suh•HAR•uh] Desert region in northern Africa that is the largest hot desert in the world. 23°N 1°W (pp. R5, R20, R21, 70, 374, 445, 448, 449, 479)

Saigon [sy•GAWN] City in Vietnam, now called Ho Chi Minh City. 10°N 106°E (pp. 765, 849)

St. Augustine [AW•gus•steen] City in north-eastern Florida on the Atlantic coast; oldest permanent existing European settlement in North America. 30°N 81°W (p. 663)

St. Petersburg Second-largest city and largest seaport in Russia, located in the northwestern part of the country. 59°N 30°E (pp. R3, 725, 786)

Sakhalin [sahk-HAH-lin] Island of southeast Russia in the Sea of Okhotsk; also called Karafuto. 51°N 143°E (p. 778)

Salamis [SA•luh•muhs] Island in eastern Greece in the Gulf of Saronikós. 37°N 23°E (p. 134)

Salonica City and port in northeastern Greece. 40°N 23°E (p. 548)

Samarkand [sah•mahr•KAHNT] City in southern Uzbekistan. 39°N 67°E (pp. 424, 425, 554)

Samaria [suh•MAHR•ee•uh] Ancient city and state in Palestine, located north of present-day Jerusalem east of the Mediterranean Sea. 32°N 35°E (pp. 86, 90, 105)

San Francisco City in northern California on the Pacific coast. 38°N 122°W (p. 769)

Santa Fe [SAN•tuh FAY] Capital of New Mexico located in the north central part of the state. 36°N 106°W (p. 663)

São Tomé [SAH•o TO•mai] Capital city and island in the Gulf of Guinea off western Africa. 1°N 7°E (p. 767)

Sarajevo [SAR•uh•YAY•voh] Capital of Bosnia and Herzegovina. 43°N 18°E (pp. 781, 786, 897)

Sardinia [sahr•DIN•ee•uh] Island off western Italy, in the Mediterranean Sea. 40°N 9°E (pp. R5, 263, 269, 274, 293, 329, 337, 538, 555, 609, 653, 722, 747, 832)

Sardis [SAWR•dihs] Ancient city of Asia Minor, now in Turkey. 38°N 28°E (pp. 132, 134)

Saudi Arabia [SOW•dee uh•RAY•bee•uh] Southwest Asian country, occupying most of the Arabian Peninsula. 22°N 46°E (pp. R3, R18–19, 176, 792, 875)

Savoy [sah•VO•yuh] Former duchy lying between Italy and France. 43°N 21°E (pp. 639, 747)

Saxony [SAHK•suh•nee] Historical region of northern Germany. 51°N 13°E (p. 747)

Scandinavia [SKAND•i•NAI•vee•ah] Region in northern Europe consisting of Norway, Sweden, and Denmark. 62°N 14°E (pp. 512, 544)

Schleswig [SHLEHS•wihg] Historical region and former duchy of northern Germany and southern Denmark. 54°N 9°E (p. 747)

Scotland One of the four countries that make up the United Kingdom in the northern part of Great Britain. 57°N 5°W (pp. R16, 518, 538, 639, 645, 757)

Sea of Japan Arm of the Pacific Ocean lying between Japan and the Asian mainland. 40°N 132°E (pp. R5, R23, 225, 485, 773, 778, 811, 825, 838)

Seine [SAYN] **River** River in northern France. 48°N 4°E (pp. 513, 514, 516, 518, 557, 561)

Seleucia [suh•LOO•shee•uh] Kingdom extending eastward from Asia Minor into what is now Pakistan. 36°N 36°E (pp. 179, 189)

Senegal [seh•nih•GAWL] West African country. 15°N 14°W (p. 870)

Seoul [SOHL] Capital of South Korea. 38°N 127°E (p. 838)

Serbia [SUHR•bee•uh] Republic in southeastern Europe. 44°N 21°E (pp. 725, 781, 786, 897)

Shanghai [SHANG•hy] City of eastern China at the mouth of the Chang Jiang. 31°N 121°E (pp. 771, 773, 778, 811, 825)

Sheffield City in north-central England. 53°N 1°W (p. 725)

Shikoku [shih•KOH•koo] One of the four largest islands of Japan. 33°N 133°E (pp. 484, 485, 507, 778)

Siam [sy•AM] Country of southeastern Asia, now called Thailand. 17°N 101°E (p. 825)

Siberia [sei•BIR•ree•yuh] Large region consisting of the Asian portion of Russia as well as northern Kazakhstan. 57°N 97°E (pp. R5, R23, 425)

Sichuan [SEHCH•WAHN] Province of south-central China. 30°N 103°E (p. 811)

Sicily [SIH•suh•lee] Largest island in the Mediterranean Sea off the coast of southern Italy. 37°N 13°E (pp. R5, 121, 262, 263, 269, 274, 293, 329, 337, 352, 361, 367, 538, 542, 553, 555, 609, 653, 722, 747)

Sidon [SEI•duhn] City in southwestern Lebanon on the Mediterranean Sea. 33°N 35°E (pp. 17, 90, 105, 293)

Sierra Leone [see•EHR•uh lee•OHN] West African country south of Guinea. 8°N 12°W (pp. 767, 870)

Silesia [sy•LEE•zhuh] Region of central Europe, once part of Prussia but now largely in Poland. 51°N 18°E (p. 747)

Silk Road Large network of trade routes stretching from western China to southwest Asia. 34°N 109°E (p. 246)

Sinai [SY•ny] **Peninsula** Land linking southwest Asia with northeast Africa. 29°N 34°E (p. 875)

Singapore [SIHNG•uh•POHR] Southeast Asian island country. 2°N 104°E (pp. 765, 825, 847)

Slovenia [sloh•VEE•nee•uh] Southeastern European country south of Austria. 46°N 15°E (pp. 891, 897)

Solomon Islands Island group of the western Pacific Ocean. 8°S 159°E (p. 825)

Somalia [soh•MAH•lee•uh] East African country. 3°N 45°E (p. 870)

Somaliland [soh•MAH•lee•luhnd] Region of eastern Africa comprising present-day Somalia, Djibouti, and southeast Ethiopia. 8°N 45°E (p. 767)

Somme [SOHM] River in northern France that flows west and northwest to the English Channel. 49°N 2°E (p. 786)

Songhai [SAWNG•HY] Empire located along the Niger River. 13°N 5°E (p. 451)

South Africa [A•frih•kuh] Country at the southern tip of Africa, officially the Republic of South Africa. 28°S 25°E (pp. 767, 869, 870)

South America Continent in the southern part of the Western Hemisphere. 15°S 60°W (pp. R2, R4, R14, R15, 13, 473, 565, 573, 577, 658, 662, 707, 744, 749, 762, 893)

South China Sea Arm of the Pacific Ocean off the eastern and southeastern coasts of Asia. 15°N 114°E (pp. R3, R5, 109, 225, 241, 246, 409, 425, 433, 439, 554, 565, 667, 765, 773, 811, 825, 847, 849)

South Korea [kuhx•REE•uh] East Asian country on the Korean Peninsula. 36°N 128°E (p. 838)

Soviet [SOH•vee•eht] **Union** Former communist country in eastern Europe and northern Asia that included Russia and 14 other soviet socialist republics. 55°N 37°E (pp. 790, 792, 811, 814, 825, 832, 883)

Spain [SPAYN] Country in southwestern Europe. 40°N 4°W (pp. R2–3, R16, 268, 269, 277, 286, 292, 293, 297, 302, 317, 323, 327, 329, 337, 352, 358, 361, 380, 385, 516, 518, 522, 534, 542, 544, 639, 645, 662, 722, 725, 781, 786, 790, 814, 832, 891)

Sparta [SPAHR•tah] City in ancient Greece and capital of Laconia. 37°N 23°E (pp. 117, 121, 124, 125, 134, 138, 144, 149)

Sri Lanka [sree•LAHNG•kuh] Country in the Indian Ocean south of India, formerly called Ceylon. 8°N 82°E (pp. R3, R5, R22, 198, 202, 433, 667, 845)

Stockholm [STAHK•HOHLM] Capital of Sweden. 59°N 18°E (pp. 555, 725)

Strait of Gibraltar [ji•BRAHL•tuhr] Narrow passage connecting the Mediterranean Sea with the Atlantic Ocean. 35°N 5°W (pp. R16, 380, 385)

Strait of Magellan [muh•JEHL•uhn] Channel between the Atlantic and Pacific Oceans on the southern tip of South America. 52°S 68°W (pp. R2, R4, R14, R15, 662, 769)

Strait of Messina [meh•SEE•nuh] Passage separating mainland Italy from the island of Sicily. 38°N 15°E (p. 263)

Strasbourg [STRAHS•boorg] City in eastern France. 48°N 7°E (pp. 548, 747)

Sudan [soo•DAN] East African country. 14°N 28°E (pp. 767, 870)

Sudetenland [soo•DAY•tuhn•LAND] Historical region of northern Czech Republic. 50°N 14°E (p. 814)

Suez Canal [SOO•ehz] Canal in Egypt connecting the Mediterranean and Red seas. 30°N 32°E (pp. 767, 799, 875)

Sumatra [soo•MAH•trah] Island in western Indonesia. 2°N 99°E (pp. R3, R5, R23, 425, 433, 554, 667, 765, 825)

Suriname [SUR•uh•NAH•muh] South American country between Guyana and French Guiana. 4°N 56°W (pp. 749, 861)

Susa [soo•SAH] Persian capital, in the region of southern Mesopotamia. 34°N 48°E (pp. 17, 132, 176)

Swaziland [SWAH•zee•LAND] Southern African country west of Mozambique, almost entirely within the Republic of South Africa. 27°S 32°E (pp. 767, 870)

Sweden [SWEED•uhn] Northern European country on the eastern side of the Scandinavian peninsula. 60°N 14°E (pp. R3, R16, R17, 538, 688, 703, 722, 725, 781, 786, 790, 814, 832, 891)

Switzerland [SWIHT•suhr•luhnd] European country south of Germany. 47°N 8°E (pp. 725, 747, 781, 786, 790, 814)

Syracuse [SIHR•uh•KYOOS] City in Sicily. 37°N 15°E (p. 182)

Syria [SIHR•ee•uh] Southwestern Asian country on the east side of the Mediterranean Sea. 35°N 37°E (pp. R3, R18–19, 62, 176, 177, 274, 286, 293, 329, 352, 374, 380, 383, 385, 792, 875)

Syrian [SIHR•ee•uhn] **Desert** Desert of the northern Arabian Peninsula, including northern Saudi Arabia, northeastern Jordan, southeastern Syria, and western Iraq. 32°N 40°E (pp. R18–19, 17, 90, 105)

Taiwan [TY•WAHN] Island country off the southeast coast of China; seat of the Chinese Nationalist government. 23°N 122°E (pp. R3, R5, R23, 225, 765, 773)

Tajikistan [tah•JIH•kih•STAN] Central Asian country. 39°N 70°E (p. 883)

Taklimakan [TAH•kluh•muh•KAHN] **Desert** Desert in northwestern China. 40°N 83°E (p. 225)

Tannenberg Village in northeast Poland. 53°N 20°E (p. 786)

Tanzania [TAN•zuh•NEE•uh] East African country. 7°S 34°E (p. 870)

Tarsus [TAHR•suhs] City in southern Turkey. 37°N 34°E (pp. 352, 361, 367)

Tenochtitlán [tay•NAWCH•teet•LAHN] Aztec city in the Valley of Mexico. 19°N 99°W (pp. 575, 582, 593, 662, 663)

Teotihuacán [TAY•oh•TEE•wuh•KAHN] Site in central Mexico that in ancient times was one of the largest cities in the world. 19°N 98°W (pp. 572, 575)

Turkmenistan [tuhrk•MEH•nuh•STAN] Central Asian country on the Caspian Sea. 41°N 56°E (p. 883)

Thailand [TY•LAND] Southeast Asian country east of Myanmar. 17°N 101°E (pp. 765, 773, 825, 849)

Thar [TAHR] **Desert** Desert in northwestern India. 25°W 72°E (p. 219)

Thebes [THEEBZ] Ancient city and former capital of Egypt. 25°N 32°E (pp. 28, 39, 59, 62, 70, 75, 132, 479)

Thermopylae [thuhr•MAH•puh•lee] Mountain pass in ancient Greece. 38°N 22°E (p. 134)

Tian [tee•AHN] **Shan** Mountain range in central Asia. 45°N 85°E (p. 225)

Tiber [TY•buhr] **River** River in north Italy. 42°N 12°E (pp. 263, 269, 274)

Tibet [tuh•BEHT] Country in central Asia. 32°N 83°E (pp. 246, 409, 424, 425, 439, 554, 773, 845)

Tigris [TY•gruhs] **River** River in southeastern Turkey and Iraq that merges with the Euphrates River. 34°N 44°E (pp. 17, 121, 132, 176, 179, 189, 246, 255, 293, 297, 329, 374, 380, 383, 397)

Gazetteer

Tikrit Town in Iraq. 34°N 43°E (p. 799)

Timbuktu [TIHM•BUHK•TOO] City of Muslim learning in West Africa. 16°N 3°W (pp. 444, 448, 451, 460, 468, 473, 479)

Timor [TEE•mor] Island of southeast Indonesia. 2°S 123°E (p. 765)

Tlaxcala [tlah•SKAH•luh] State in east central Mexico. 19°N 98°W (p. 575)

Togo [TOH•goh] West African country. 8°N 1°E (pp. 767, 870)

Tokyo [TOH•kee•OH] Capital of Japan. 34°N 131°E (pp. R3, 485, 507, 771, 773, 778, 825)

Toledo [to•LAI•do] Historic city in central Spain. 39°N 4°W (p. 555)

Tours [TOOR] City in west central France. 47°N 0°E (p. 516)

Trafalgar [truh•FAL•guhr] Cape off the southwest coast of Spain. 36°N 6°W (p. 722)

Transjordan Southwest Asian country, now called Jordan. 30°N 38°E (p. 792)

Tripoli [TRIH•puh•lee] Capital city of Libya. 32°N 13°E (pp. R3, 385, 448, 479, 767)

Tunis [TOO•nuhs] Capital city of Tunisia. 36°N 10°E (p. 385)

Tunisia [too•NEE•zhuh] North African country on the Mediterrean Sea. 35°N 10°E (pp. 767, 870)

Turkey [TUHR•kee] Country in southeastern Europe and western Asia. 38°N 32°E (pp. R3, R22, 176, 789, 790, 792)

Turkmenistan [tuhrk•MEH•nuh•STAN] Central Asian country on the Caspian Sea. 40°N 56°E (pp. R3, R22, 176)

Tuscany [TUS•kuh•nee] Region of northwest Italy. 43°N 11°E (p. 747)

Tyre [TYR] Town in southern Lebanon on the Mediterranean Sea. 33°N 35°E (pp. 17, 90, 121, 132, 176, 352, 542)

Tyrrhenian [tuh•REE•nee•uhn] **Sea** Arm of the Mediterranean Sea near Italy. 40°N 12°E (pp. 263, 609, 653)

Uganda [yoo•GAHN•dah] East African country. 2°N 32°E (pp. 767, 870)

Ukraine [yoo•KRAYN] Eastern European country west of Russia on the Black Sea. 49°N 30°E (pp. R3, R17, 548, 883)

Ulm City in southern Germany on the Danube River. 48°N 8°E (p. 722)

United Kingdom Western European island country made up of England, Scotland, Wales, and Northern Ireland. 57°N 2°W (pp. 722, 725, 781, 786, 790, 891, 832)

United States Country in North America made up of 50 states, mostly between Canada and Mexico. 38°N 110°W (pp. 753, 836)

Ur [OOR] Ancient city in Mesopotamia. 32°N 47°E (p. 17)

Ural [YUHR•uhl] **Mountains** Mountain range in Russia. 56°N 58°E (p. R5)

Uruguay [YUR•uh•GWAY] South American country south of Brazil. 33°S 56°W (pp. 749, 861)

Uruk Ancient settlement in Mesopotamia. 33°N 45°E (p. 17)

Uzbekistan [UZ•BEH•kih•STAN] Central Asian country south of Kazakhstan. 42°N 60°E (p. 883)

Venezuela [veh•nuh•ZWAY•luh] South American country on the Caribbean Sea between Colombia and Guyana. 8°N 65°W (pp. 749, 861)

Venice [VEHN•ihs] City in northeastern Italy. 45°N 12°E (pp. 522, 542, 548, 555, 608, 609, 653, 703, 725, 747)

Versailles [vuhr•SY] City in north-central France. 48°N 2°E (pp. 714, 716, 722)

Vienna [vee•EH•nuh] Capital of Austria. 48°N 16°E (pp. 714, 722, 725, 781, 786).

Vietnam [vee•EHT•NAHM] Southeast Asian country east of Laos and Cambodia. 18°N 107°E (pp. 847, 849)

Vistula [vis•TOO•lah] **River** Longest river in Poland. 52°N 20°E (p. 513)

Vladivostok [vluhd•yi•vah•STOK] City of extreme southeast Russia. 43°N 131°E (pp. 773, 778)

Volga [VOL•guh] **River** River in western Russia, longest in Europe. 47°N 46°E (pp. R3, R5, 424, 425, 513, 540)

Wales Principality of the United Kingdom on the western peninsula of the island of Great Britain. 52°N 4°W (p. 757)

Warsaw [WAWR•SAW] Capital of Poland. 52°N 21°E (pp. 725, 747)

Warsaw, Grand Duchy of Political unit created by Napoleon I in 1807 to restore Polish lands seized by Prussia. (p. 722)

Washington, D.C. Capital of the United States, in the District of Columbia. 39°N 77°W (p. 744)

Waterloo [WAW•tuhr•LOO] Town in central Belgium. 51°N 5°E (pp. 714, 722)

Wei He [WAY HUH] River in central China. 34°N 108°E (pp. 225, 226, 230, 241)

West Bank Disputed territory of southwest Asia between Israel and Jordan. 31°N 35°E (p. 875)

Western Sahara [suh•HAR•uh] Country in northwest Africa. 24°N 13°W (p. 870)

West Germany Officially called the Federal Republic of Germany. 51°N 8°E (pp. 832, 834)

West Indies Islands in the Caribbean Sea. 19°N 79°W (p. 473)

Wittenberg [WIH•tuhn•BUHRG] City in east central Germany on the Elbe River. 51°N 12°E (pp. 633, 645)

Xianyang [SHYEHN•YAHNG] City in northern China. 34°N 108°E (p. 241)

Xi Jiang [SHEE•JYAHNG] River in southern China. 24°N 110°E (p. 241)

Yathrib [YA•thruhb] Town in Saudi Arabia, now called Madinah. 24°N 39°E (p. 374)

Yellow Sea Arm of the Pacific Ocean bordered by China, North Korea, and South Korea. 35°N 122°E (pp. R5, R23, 225, 226, 230, 241, 424, 431, 485, 773, 778, 811, 838)

Yugoslavia [YOO•goh•SLAH•vee•uh] Eastern European country south of Hungary; includes Serbia and Montenegro. 44°N 21°E (pp. 790, 832, 897)

Zama [ZAY•muh] Town in northern Africa. 35°N 9°E (p. 274)

Zambia [ZAM•bee•uh] Southern African country. 14°S 24°E (p. 870)

Zanzibar [ZAHN•zuh•bawr] City of Tanzania on Zanzibar Island. 6°S 39°E (p. 767)

Zhanjiang [JAHN•JYAHNG] City of southeast China. 21°N 110°E (p. 773)

Zhou [JOH] Empire in what is now northern China. 34°N 110°E (p. 230)

Zimbabwe [zihm•BAH•bway] Southern African country. 18°S 30°E (p. 870)

Gazetteer

Italicized page numbers refer to illustrations. The following abbreviations are used in the index:
m = map, c = chart, p = photograph or picture, g = graph, crt = cartoon, ptg = painting, q = quote

Index

Index

Index

Index

Index

Index

Index

Index

J

Index

Index

Index

Q

Index

Index

Index

Index

Index

Index

Acknowledgements

Text

33 "The Mesopotamian View of Death" from *Poems of Heaven and Hell From Ancient Mesopotamia,* translated by N.K. Sandars (Penguin Classics, 1971), copyright © N.K. Sandars, 1971. Reprinted by permission of Penguin Group (UK). **53** From *The Prince Who Knew his Fate: an Ancient Egyptian Tale,* translated from hieroglyphs and illustrated by Lise Manniche, copyright © 1982 by Lise Manniche and IBIS. Used by permission of Philomel Books, A Division of Penguin Young Readers Group, A Member of Penguin Group (USA) Inc., 345 Hudson Street, New York, NY 10014. All rights reserved. **239** Excerpt from "Higher Good Is like Water" from *The Essential Tao,* translated and presented by Thomas Cleary. Copyright © 1991 by Thomas Cleary. Reprinted by permission of HarperCollins Inc. **264** Excerpt from *Virgil's Aeneid,* translated by Robert Fitzgerald. Translation copyright © 1981, 1982, 1982 by Robert Fitzgerald. Reprinted by permission of Random House, Inc. **311** "A Wild Goose Chase: The Story of Philemon and Baucis" reprinted with the permission of Margaret K. McElderry Books, an imprint of Simon & Schuster Children's Publishing Division from *Roman Myths* by Geraldine McCaughrean. Text copyright © 1999 by Geraldine McCaughrean. **420** "Seeing a Friend Off" and "Still Night Thoughts" by Li Bo, from *The Columbia Book of Chinese Poetry,* translated by Burton Watson. Copyright © 1984 by Columbia University Press. Reprinted by permission. **421** "Spring Landscape" by Tu Fu, translated by David Hinton, from *The Selected Poems of Tu Fu,* copyright © 1988, 1989 by David Hinton. Reprinted by permission of New Directions Publishing Corp. **454** "Mali-The Madinka Empire: Sundiata: The Hungering Lion" from *African Kingdoms of the Past,* copyright © 1996 by Kenny Mann. Reprinted by permission of the author. **470** "Dignity" by E.A. Babalola, from *Ants Will not Eat Your Fingers: A Selection of Traditional African Poems,* edited by Leonard W. Dobb. Copyright © 1966 by Leonard W. Dobb. Reprinted by permission of Walker and Company. **501** Tanka from the *Kokinshu,* from *From the Country of Eight Islands* by Hiroaki Sato and Burton Watson, copyright © 1981 by Hiroaki Sato and Burton Watson. Used by permission of Doubleday, a division of Random House, Inc. **627** "A Midsummer Night's Dream" from *The Children's Shakespeare* by E. Nesbit. Copyright © 1938 by Random House, Inc. Reprinted by permission. **820** "The Unexpected Treasure," adapted by Gary Schmidt from *Mara's Stories: Glimmers in the Darkness* by Gary Schmidt, © 2001 by Gary Schmidt. Reprinted by permission of Henry Holt and Company LLC. **932** Excerpt from *Gilgamesh* by John Gardner and John Maier, copyright © 1984 by the Estate of John Gardner and John Maier. Used by permission of Alfred A. Knopf, a division of Random House, Inc. **933** Excerpt from Genesis 12 from *The Revised English Bible,* copyright © 1989 Oxford University Press. Reprinted by permission. **934** Excerpts from *The Essential Confucius,* translated and presented by Thomas Cleary. Copyright © 1992 by Thomas Cleary. Reprinted by permission of HarperCollins Inc. **935** "Night" from *The Rig Veda,* translated by Wendy Diniger O'Flaherty (Penguin Classics, 1981), copyright © Wendy Doniger O'Flaherty, 1981. Reprinted by permission of Penguin Group (UK). **938** "Mali in the Fourteenth Century" from *The African Past: Chronicles from Antiquity to Modern Time,* by Basil Davidson. Copyright © 1964 by Basil Davidson. Reprinted by permission of Curtis Brown Ltd. **940** Excerpt from "Epic Description of the Beseiged City" from *The Broken Spears* by Miguel Leon-Portilla. Copyright © 1962, 1990 by Miguel Leon-Portilla. Expanded and updated Edition © 1992 by Miguel Leon-Portilla. Reprinted by permission of Beacon Press, Boston. **941** From *The Kidnapped Prince: The Life of Olaudah Equiano,* by Olaudah Equiano, adapted by Ann Cameron. Copyright © 1995 by Ann Cameron. Reprinted by permission of Alfred A. Knopf, a division of Random House, Inc.

943 From "I Have a Dream" by Dr. Martin Luther King, Jr. Reprinted by arrangement with the Estate of Martin Luther King, Jr., c/o Writers House as agent for the proprietor, New York, NY. Copyright 1963 Martin Luther King, Jr., copyright renewed 1991 Corretta Scott King. **943** From Nelson Mandela's Nobel Peace Prize acceptance speech. Reprinted by permission of The Nobel Institute.

Glencoe would like to acknowledge the artists and agencies who participated in illustrating this program: American Artists Rep., INC.; Mapping Specialists, Inc.; Studio Inklink; WildLife Art Ltd.

Photo Credits

COVER (bkgd)Christie's Images/CORBIS, (tl)Ric Ergenbright/ CORBIS, (tr)Paul Hardy/CORBIS, (b)Setboun/CORBIS; **GH1** (t)Dallas and John Heaton/CORBIS, (c)Jamie Harron CORBIS, (b)Owen Franken/CORBIS; **GH2** Getty Images; **GH3** Getty Images; **Tools 0** (t)Ron Sheridan/Ancient Art & Architecture Collection, (bl)AFP Worldwide, (br)James King-Holmes/Photo Researchers, (bkgd)Getty Images; **Tools 1** (t)Scala/ Art Resource, NY, (b)Nimatallah/Art Resource, NY; **Tools 2** (t)American Museum of Natural History, (tc)Scala/Art Resource, NY, (bc)Chester Beatty Library, Dublin/Bridgeman Art Library, (b)Reunion des Musees Nationaux/Art Resource, NY; **Tools 3** (t)National Museums of Scotland/Bridgeman Art Library, (c)Borromeo/Art Resource, NY, (b)Asian Art & Archaeology/ CORBIS; **Tools 4** (t)Richard T. Nowitz/CORBIS, (b)David Hiser/ Getty Images;**Tools 6** (t)Lawrence Manning/CORBIS, (b)Vanni Archive/CORBIS; **Tools 7** (c)Frans Lemmens Getty Images, (t)J. Bertrand/Photo Researchers, (br)Giraudon/Art Resource, NY; **Tools 10** Matthews/Network/CORBIS Saba; **Tools 11** (t)Dan Helms/NewSport/CORBIS, (tc)Tom Lovell/National Geographic Society Image Collection, (bc)Art Resource, NY, (b)CORBIS; **Tools 12** (t)The Art Archive/Bibliothèque Nationale Paris, (tc)Christopher Liu/ChinaStock, (bc)Jean-Leon Huens/National Geographic Society Image Collection, (b)NASA Media Resource Center; **Tools 13** (t)Ed Kashi/CORBIS, (b)Bettmann/CORBIS; **0** (t)Reunion des Musees Nationaux/Art Resource, NY, (c)John Heaton/CORBIS, (b)Tom Lovell/National Geographic Society Image Collection; **1** (tl)Brooklyn Museum of Art, New York/Charles Edwin Wilbour Fund/Bridgeman Art Library, (bl)Erich Lessing/Art Resource, NY, (others)SuperStock; **2–3** ©Worldsat International Inc. 2004, All Rights Reserved; **2** (t)S. Fiore SuperStock, (c)Scala/Art Resource, NY, (bl)Giansanti Gianni/CORBIS Sygma, (bc)Louvre Museum, Paris/Bridgeman Art Library, (br)Metropolitan Museum of Art, Rogers Fund and Edward S. Harkness Gift,1929 (29.3.3); **3** (t to b)Sylvain Grandadam/Getty Images, Timothy Kendall/Museum of Fine Arts, Boston, Gary Cralle/Getty Images, (l to r)O. Louis Mazzatenta/National Geographic Society Image Collection, SuperStock, Bettmann/CORBIS; **4–5** Georg Gerster/Photo Researchers; **10** Michael Holford; **11** American Museum of Natural History; **12** (tr)Giansanti Gianni/CORBIS Sygma, (bl)Kenneth Garrett; **14** (l)Michael Holford, (r)Ron Sheridan/Ancient Art & Architecture Collection; **17** Hirmer Verlag; **18** Scala/Art Resource, NY; **19** (l)Nik Wheeler CORBIS, (r)Michael Holford; **20** Scala/Art Resource, NY; **21** (l)Mesopotamian Iraq Museum, Baghdad, Iraq/Giraudon/Bridgeman Art Library, (r)Will Hart/PhotoEdit; **22** akg-images; **24** Reunion des Musees Nationaux/Art Resource, NY; **25** Louvre, Paris/Bridgeman Art Library; **28** Boltin Picture Library; **29** Gianni Dagli Orti/CORBIS; **30** S. Fiore/SuperStock; **31** Scala/Art Resource, NY; **34–35** Brian Lawrence/Image State; **37** Gianni Dagli Orti CORBIS; **40** John Lawrence/Getty Images; **41** Erich Lessing/Art Resource, NY; **42** (l)Giraudon/Art Resource, NY, (r)Gianni Dagli Orti/CORBIS; **43** (l)Caroline Penn/CORBIS, (r)Kenneth Garrett; **48** Sylvain Grandadam/Getty Images; **50** (t)The British Museum, (b)Musee du Louvre, Paris Explorer/SuperStock;

51 Musee du Louvre, Paris/Explorer SuperStock; 52 John Heaton/CORBIS; 60 Gianni Dagli Orti/CORBIS; 61 (l)Smithsonian Institution, (r)file photo; 63 Metropolitan Museum of Art, Rogers Fund and Edward S. Harkness Gift,1929 (29.3.3); 64 Erich Lessing/Art Resource, NY; 65 (t)Egyptian National Museum, Cairo/SuperStock, (b)Gavin Hellier/Getty Images; 66 (t)Michael Holford, (b)O. Louis Mazzatenta National Geographic Society Image Collection; 69 Egyptian Expedition of The Metropolitan Museum of Art, The Rogers Fund, 1930 (30.4.21)/The Metropolitan Museum of Art; 70 Timothy Kendall/Museum of Fine Arts, Boston; 71 Brooklyn Museum of Art, New York/Charles Edwin Wilbour Fund/Bridgeman Art Library; 72 SuperStock; 73 Egyptian National Museum, Cairo/SuperStock; 76–77 Anthony Pidgeon/Lonely Planet Images; 79 CORBIS; 81 Tom Lovell National Geographic Society Image Collection; 82 (l)North Wind Picture Archives, (r)Leland Bobbe/Getty Images; 83 (t)The Israel Museum, Jerusalem, (c)Stock Montage/SuperStock, (b)Laura Zito/Photo Researchers; 84 (l)Mary Evans Picture Library, (r)Charles & Josette Lenars/CORBIS; 87 Mary Evans Picture Library; 88 (t)Bettmann/CORBIS, (b)Private Collection/Bridgeman Art Library; 89 Stock Montage/SuperStock; 94 (l)Richard T. Nowitz/CORBIS, (c)Bill Aro/PhotoEdit, (r)SuperStock; 95 Walker Art Gallery, Liverpool, Merseyside, UK, National Museums Liverpool/Bridgeman Art Library; 96 CORBIS; 97 (l)Christie's Images Bridgeman Art Library, (r)Nathan Benn CORBIS; 98 Lawrence Migdale Getty Images; 99 SuperStock; 100 Richard T. Nowitz/CORBIS; 101 (t)Dave Bartruff/CORBIS, (c)Gary Cralle/Getty Images, (b)Paul Chesley/Getty Images; 102 Peter Turnley/CORBIS; 103 (t)Stock Montage/SuperStock, (b)SuperStock; 106 (t)Erich Lessing/Art Resource, NY, (b)Louvre Museum, Paris/Bridgeman Art Library; 107 (t)Boltin Picture Library, (tr)Stock Montage/SuperStock, (c)Smithsonian Institution, (b)CORBIS; 108 (t)National Museums of Scotland/Bridgeman Art Library, (c)Borromeo/Art Resource, NY, (b)file photo; 109 (t)Scala/Art Resource, NY, (c)Hugh Sitton/Getty Images, (b)Erich Lessing/Art Resource, NY; 110–111 ©Worldsat International Inc. 2004, All Rights Reserved; 110 (tl)Getty Images, (c)Archives Charmet/Bridgeman Art Library, (bl)Scala/Art Resource, NY, (bcl)Christie's, London/Bridgeman Art Library/SuperStock, (bcr)Vanni/Art Resource, NY, (br)Scala/Art Resource, NY; 111 (t to b)Robert Harding Picture Library, Victoria & Albert Museum, London/Art Resource, NY, Digital Vision, (l to r) Alinari/Art Resource, NY, Sandro Vannini/CORBIS, Hulton/Getty Images, National Geographic Society Image Collection; 112–113 Vanni Archive/CORBIS; 115 Foto Marburg/Art Resource, NY; 117 Steve Vidler SuperStock; 118 (t)Gianni Dagli Orti/CORBIS, (bl)Nimatallah/Art Resource, NY; 119 (t)Alberto Incrocci/Getty Images, (b)Nimatallah/Art Resource, NY; 122 The Art Archive/National Archaeological Museum Athens/Dagli Orti; 123 National Museums of Scotland/Bridgeman Art Library; 125 The Art Archive/E.T. Archive; 126 Foto Marburg/Art Resource, NY; 127 (l)Bettmann CORBIS, (r)Michael Holford; 128 (l)Tom Lovell/National Geographic Society Image Collection, (r)Dan Helms/NewSport/CORBIS; 129 (t)Nimatallah/Art Resource, NY, (b)The Brooklyn Museum, Charles Wilbour Fund; 130 Ronald Sheridan/Ancient Art & Architecture Collection; 131 (l)Mary Evans Picture Library, (c)Bettmann/CORBIS, (r)Roger Wood/CORBIS; 132 SEF/Art Resource, NY; 133 The Art Archive/Dagli Orti; 135 Bettmann/CORBIS; 136 Peter Connolly; 139 Steve Vidler/SuperStock; 141 (t)Scala/Art Resource, NY, (b)Vanni Archive/CORBIS; 142 Smithsonian Institution; 143 Nimatallah/Art Resource, NY; 144 Gianni Dagli Orti/CORBIS; 145 Scala/Art Resource, NY; 147 Nimatallah/Art Resource, NY; 150–151 Roger Wood/CORBIS; 153 Alinari/Art Resource, NY; 155 (cw from top)Bettman/CORBIS, The Art Archive/National Archaeological Museum Athens/Dagli Orti, The Art Archive/Achaeological Museum Tarquina/Dagli Orti, Lauros/Giraudon Bridgeman Art Library, Lauros/Giraudon/Bridgeman Art Library, The Art Archive/Archaeological Museum Venice/Dagli Orti, Fitzwilliam Museum, University of Cambridge, UK/Bridgeman Art Library, Giraudon/Bridgeman Art Library, Peter Willi/Bridgeman Art Library, Wolfgang Kaehler/CORBIS; 156 Mary Evans Picture Library; 157 James L. Stanfield/National Geographic Society Image Collection; 158 Alinari/Art Resource, NY; 159 Scala/Art Resource, NY; 160 (l)SuperStock, (r)Eric Robert/CORBIS; 161 (t)Erich Lessing/Art Resource, NY, (b)Mary Evans Picture Library; 162 (tl)Joel W. Rogers/CORBIS, (tc)Dave Bartruff/CORBIS, (tr)Vanni Archive/CORBIS, (b)Charles O'Rear/CORBIS; 168 Scala/Art Resource, NY; 169 Scala/Art Resource, NY; 170 (l)Mary Evans Picture Library, (cl)Scala/Art Resource, NY, (cr)Museo Capitolino, Rome/E.T. Archives, London/SuperStock, (r)Reunion des Musees Nationaux/Art Resource, NY; 172 (t)SEF/Art Resource, NY, (b)Scala/Art Resource, NY; 175 file photo; 177 Robert Harding Picture Library; 178 (l)Yan Arthus-Bertrand/CORBIS, (r)Archives Charmet/Bridgeman Art Library; 180 David Lees/CORBIS; 181 Sandro Vannini/CORBIS; 183 Araldo de Luca/CORBIS; 184 Erich Lessing/Art Resource, NY; 185 North Wind Picture Archives; 186 Scala/Art Resource, NY; 187 Sandro Vannini/CORBIS; 190–191 David Cumming/CORBIS; 196 (l)Robert Harding Picture Library, (c)National Museum of India, New Delhi, India/Bridgeman Art Library, (r)Borromeo/Art Resource, NY, (br)Harappan National Museum of Karachi, Karachi, Pakistan/Bridgeman Art Library; 200 (l)Carl Purcell/The Purcell Team, (r)AFP Worldwide; 203 (l)Robert Harding Picture Library, (r)Borromeo Art Resource, NY; 204 (t)SEF/Art Resource, NY, (b)Victoria & Albert Museum, London/Art Resource, NY; 205 Rajesh Bedi/National Geographic Image Collection; 206 Borromeo/Art Resource, NY; 207 (l)Archivo Iconografico, S.A./CORBIS, (r)Christie's Images, London Bridgeman Art Library SuperStock; 208 Sheldan Collins/CORBIS; 211 (l)Robert Harding Picture Library, (r)Hugh Sitton/Getty Images; 212 (l)Ancient Art & Architecture Collection, (r)Hulton Archive/Getty Images News Services; 214 The British Library, London/Bridgeman Art Library; 217 SEF/Art Resource, NY; 220–221 D.E. Cox/Getty Images; 223 file photo; 227 Asian Art & Archaeology CORBIS; 228 Bridgeman/Art Resource, NY; 229 (bl)file photo, (br)The Art Archive/ Musee Cernuschi Paris/Dagli Orti, (others)Asian Art & Archaeology/ CORBIS; 231 file photo; 232 (l)Robert Frerck/Odyssey Productions, (c)ChinaStock, (r)Dennis Cox; 234 Lawrence Manning/CORBIS; 235 (t)Seattle Museum of Art/Laurie Platt Winfrey, (b)Asian Art & Archaeology/CORBIS, (others)Christopher Liu/ChinaStock; 236 Chen Yixin ChinaStock; 237 Vanni/Art Resource, NY; 238 (tl)Robert Frerck/Odyssey Productions, (tc)ChinaStock, (tr)Dennis Cox, (b)Giraudon/Art Resource, NY; 243 (t)ChinaStock, (b)Robert Harding Picture Library; 244 Bibliotheque Nationale, Paris; 245 (l)Ontario Science Centre, (r)Dean Conger/CORBIS; 247 (l)The Art Archive/National Palace Museum Taiwan, (others)The Art Archive/British Library; 249 (t)file photo, (b)Giraudon/Art Resource, NY; 252 (l)Scala/Art Resource, NY, (c)Ancient Art & Architecture Collection, (r)Burstein Collection/CORBIS; 253 (tl)Erich Lessing/Art Resource, NY, (c)Victoria & Albert Museum, London/ Art Resource, NY, (bl)Ronald Sheridan/Ancient Art & Architecture Collection, (br)The British Museum, London/Bridgeman Art Library; 254 (l)Cott Nero DIV f.25v Portrait of St. Matthew/British Library, London/Bridgeman Art Library, (tr)Scala/Art Resource, NY, (br)Ancient Art & Architecture Collection; 255 (t)Pierre Belzeaux/Photo Researchers, (c)Brian Lawrence/SuperStock, (l)Nik Wheeler; 256–257 ©Worldsat International Inc. 2004, All Rights Reserved; 256 (t)Ric Ergenbright, (c)Sean Sexton Collection/CORBIS, (bl)Robert Emmett Bright Photo Researchers, (bcl)Scala/Art Resource, NY, (bcr)Danita Delimont

Ancient Art & Architecture Collection, (br)Werner Forman/Art Resource, NY; **257** (t to b)Brian Lawrence/SuperStock, Richard T. Nowitz CORBIS, Nabeel Turner/Getty Images, (l to r)Scala/Art Resource, NY, Scala/Art Resource, NY, Earl & Nazima Kowall/CORBIS, Bettmann CORBIS; **258–259** Roy Rainford Robert Harding/Getty Images; **261** Ronald Sheridan/ Ancient Art & Architecture Collection; **264** Francis Schroeder SuperStock; **265** (t)file photo, (b)Scala/Art Resource, NY; **266** Stock Montage; **267** Prenestino Museum, Rome/E.T. Archives, London/SuperStock; **269** Michael Holford; **270** Ronald Sheridan/Ancient Art & Architecture Collection; **271** The Art Archive Archeological Museum Beirut/Dagli Orti; **272** North Wind Picture Archives; **273** Alinari/Art Resource, NY; **278** The Art Archive/Archeological Museum Aquileia/Dagli Orti; **279** Scala/Art Resource, NY; **280** (tl)Archaeological Museum, Venice/E.T. Archives, London/SuperStock, (bl)Louvre, Paris Bridgeman Art Library, (c)Reunion des Musees Nationaux/ Art Resource, NY, (r)Ronald Sheridan/Ancient Art & Architecture Collection; **281** (l)SuperStock, (c)Museo e Gallerie Nazionali di Capodimonte, Naples, Italy/Bridgeman Art Library, (r)Mary Evans Picture Library; **282** Bettmann/CORBIS; **283** North Wind Picture Archive; **284** Nimatallah/Art Resource, NY; **285** Bridgeman Art Library; **287** Victoria & Albert Museum, London/ Bridgeman Art Library; **288** (t)C. Hellier/Ancient Art & Architecture Collection, (tc)Ronald Sheridan Ancient Art & Architecture Collection, (bc)The Art Archive/Museo Capitolino Rome/Dagli Orti, (b)The Art Archive/ Staatliche Glypothek Munich/Dagli Orti; **289** Robert Emmett Bright/Photo Researchers; **290** (l)Seamus Culligan ZUMA/CORBIS, (r)Jonathan Blair/CORBIS; **291** Ric Ergenbright; **292** (l)Roma, Museo Nazion/Art Resource, NY, (cr)Staatliche Glypothek, Munich, Germany/E.T. Archive, London/ SuperStock, (others)Archivo Iconografico, S.A./CORBIS; **294** (tl)B. Wilson/ Ancient Art & Architecture Collection, (tr)Erich Lessing/Art Resource, NY, (others)The Newark Museum/Art Resource, NY; **295** Michael Holford; **298–299** Picture Finders Ltd./eStock; **301** Erich Lessing/Art Resource, NY; **303** Nik Wheeler/CORBIS; **304** Bibliotheque Nationale, Paris, France, Giraudon/Bridgeman Art Library; **306** Pierre Belzeaux/Photo Researchers; **307** (t)Scala/Art Resource, NY, (b)Erich Lessing/Art Resource, NY; **308** Scala/ Art Resource, NY; **309** (l)Stanley Searberg, (r)Giraudon/Art Resource, NY; **310** Reunion des Musees Nationaux/Art Resource, NY; **318** CORBIS; **319** Scala/Art Resource, NY; **320** The Newark Museum/Art Resource, NY; **321** (t)Hagia Sophia, Istanbul, Turkey/E.T. Archives, London/SuperStock, (b)C. Boisvieux/Photo Researchers; **322** Scala/Art Resource, NY; **324** Mary Evans Picture Library; **325** (l)Sean Sexton Collection/CORBIS, (r)Donald Dietz/ Stock Boston PictureQuest; **328** Stapleton Collection, UK/Bridgeman Art Library; **330** Scala/Art Resource, NY; **331** Andre Durenceau/National Geographic Society Image Collection; **332** (l)Giraudon/Art Resource, NY, (c)Brian Lawrence SuperStock, (r)Ronald Sheridan/Ancient Art & Architecture Collection; **333** The Art Archive/Haghia Sophia Istanbul/Dagli Orti; **334** Ancient Art & Architecture Collection; **335** Giraudon/Art Resource, NY; **338–339** Richard T. Nowitz/CORBIS; **341** akg-images/Orsi Battaglini; **343** Nathan Benn CORBIS; **344** (l)Reunion des Musees Nationaux/Art Resource, NY, (r)Scala Art Resource, NY; **345** (l)Erich Lessing/Art Resource, NY, (r)Tate Gallery, London/Art Resource, NY; **346** (t)Elio Ciol/CORBIS, (b)Scala/Art Resource, NY; **347** Louvre, Paris/Bridgeman Art Library; **348** The New York Public Library/Art Resource, NY; **349** (t)Danita Delimont/Ancient Art & Architecture Collection, (b)Victoria & Albert Museum, London/Art Resouce, NY; **350** akg images/Orsi Battaglini; **353** Scala/Art Resource, NY; **356** Cott Nero DIV f.25v Portrait of St. Matthew/British Library, London/Bridgeman Art Library; **357** (t)Scala/Art Resource, NY, (b)Alinari/Art Resource, NY; **359** Scala/Art Resource, NY; **360** (t)Scala/Art Resource, NY, (b)Michael Holford; **362** (l)Galleria dell' Accademia, Florence, Italy/Bridgeman Art Library, (r)PRAT/CORBIS; **363** C.M. Dixon/Photo Resources; **364** Giraudon/Art Resource, NY; **365** Cott Nero DIV f.25v Portrait of St. Matthew/British Library, London/Bridgeman Art Library; **368–369** Nabeel Turner/Getty Images; **371** Paul Dupuy Museum, Toulouse, France/Lauros-Giraudon, Paris/SuperStock; **373** (l)DiMaggio/Kalish/CORBIS, (r)Kevin Fleming/CORBIS; **375** Bibliotheque Nationale, Paris/Bridgeman Art Library; **376** (t)C. Hellier Ancient Art & Architecture Collection, (b)George Chan/Photo Researchers; **377** (l)AFP/CORBIS, (r)ARAMCO; **380** The Art Archive/Hazem Palace Damascus/Dagli Orti; **381** Burstein Collection/CORBIS; **382** Alison Wright CORBIS; **383** Nik Wheeler; **384** James L. Stanfield/National Geographic Society Image Collection; **385** Bettmann/CORBIS; **386** Chester Beatty Library, Dublin/Bridgeman Art Library; **387** (l)Mary Evans Picture Library, (c)Bettmann/CORBIS; **388** Richard Bickel/CORBIS; **389** (t)Jeff Greenberg Photo Researchers, (b)The Art Archive/Harper Collins Publishers; **390** (l)Stapleton Collection, UK/Bridgeman Art Library, (r)David Turnley CORBIS; **391** (t)R & S Michaud/Woodfin Camp & Assoc., (b)Paul Dupuy Museum, Toulouse, France/Lauros-Giraudon, Paris/Super-Stock; **392** Bettmann/CORBIS; **394** Galen Rowell/CORBIS; **395** ARAMCO; **398** (t)Scala Art Resource, NY, (bl)Smithsonian Institution, (bc)Michael Holford, (br)Giraudon/Art Resource, NY; **399** (tl)Stock Montage, (tr)Michael Holford, (c)Scala/Art Resource, NY, (bl)Roy Rainford/Robert Harding/Getty Images, (br)Bibliotheque Nationale, Paris/Bridgeman Art Library; **400** (tl)The British Museum/Topham-HIP/The Image Works, (c)Angelo Hornak/CORBIS, (bl)Ronald Sheridan/Ancient Art & Architecture Collection, (br)Erich Lessing/Art Resource, NY; **401** (tl)Aldona Sabalis/Photo Researchers, (tc)National Museum of Taipei, (tr)Werner Forman/Art Resource, NY, (c)Ancient Art & Architecture Collection, (bl)Ron Dahlquist/SuperStock, (br)akg-images; **402–403** ©Worldsat International Inc. 2004, All Rights Reserved; **402** (t)Stock Boston, (c)Peter Adams/Getty Images, (bl)Art Resource, NY, (bcl)Ali Meyer/CORBIS, (bcr)Mary Evans Picture Library, (br)Kadokawa/Ancient Art & Architecture Collection; **403** (t to b)Tom Wagner/Odyssey Productions, Greg Gawlowski/Lonley Planet Images, Jim Zuckerman/CORBIS, (l to r)Museum of Fine Arts, Houston, Texas, USA, Robert Lee Memorial Collection, gift of Sarah C. Blaffer/Bridgeman Art Library, Courtesy Museum of Maritimo (Barcelona); Ramon Manent CORBIS, ChinaStock, Christie's Images/CORBIS; **404–405** CORBIS; **407** Kadokawa/Ancient Art & Architecture Collection; **410** (l)The Art Archive Bibliothèque Nationale Paris, (r)Christopher Liu/ChinaStock; **412** Ira Kirschenbaum/Stock Boston; **413** Bettmann/CORBIS; **414** Snark/Art Resource, NY; **415** Michael Freeman/CORBIS; **417** (l)Keren Su/CORBIS, (r)Philadelphia Free Library/ AKG, Berlin SuperStock; **419** Werner Forman Art Resource, NY; **420** The Art Archive/British Library; **421** (l)The Art Archive/National Palace Museum Taiwan, (c)Naomi Duguid/Asia Access, (r)Private Collection/Bridgeman Art Library; **422** (l)The British Museum Topham-HIP/The Image Works, (c)Laurie Platt Winfrey, (r)Seattle Art Museum/CORBIS; **424** (t)National Museum of Taipei, (b)J. Bertrand/Photo Researchers; **425** James L. Stanfield; **426** Werner Forman Archive; **427** (t)Kadokawa/Ancient Art & Architecture Collection, (b)Bibliotheque Nationale, Paris, France/Bridgeman Art Library; **428** The Bodleian Library, Oxford, Ms. Bodl. 264, fol.219R; **429** Hulton/Getty Images; **431** Christie's Images/CORBIS; **432** SEF/Art Resource, NY; **433** ChinaStock; **434** ChinaStock; **435** The Art Archive; **436** Bonhams, London, UK/Bridgeman Art Library; **437** Laurie Platt Winfrey; **440–441** Peter Adams/Getty Images; **443** Werner Forman/Art Resource, NY; **445** (t)Christine Osborne/Lonely Planet Images, (tc)Frans Lemmens/Getty Images, (bc)Brand X Pictures, (b)Michael Dwyer Stock Boston/PictureQuest; **449** Volkmar Kurt

(b)Michael Holford; **651** The Pierpont Morgan Library/Art Resource, NY; **654–655** Buddy Mays/CORBIS; **657** (t)Hermitage, St. Petersburg, Russia/Bridgeman Art Library, (b)Michael Holford; **659** (t)Peabody Essex Museum, Salem, MA, (c)SuperStock, (b)Michael Holford; **660** Bettmann/CORBIS; **663** (l)The Metropolitan Museum of Art, Gift of J. Pierpont Morgan, 1900(00.18.2), (cl)Stock Montage, (c)Collection of The New-York Historical Society, (cr)Reunion des Musees Nationaux/Art Resource, NY, (r)North Wind Picture Archives; **664** National Maritime Museum, London; **665** Reunion des Musees Gallery, London SuperStock; **666** Reunion des Musees Nationaux/Art Resource, NY; **671** Scala/Art Resource, NY; **672** Louvre, Paris/Bridgeman Art Library; **673** Bettmann/Nationaux/Art Resource, NY; **674** (l)Scala/Art Resource, NY, (r)Denis Scott/CORBIS; **675** Jean-Leon Huens/National Geographic Society Image Collection; **677** (t)North Wind Picture Archives, (b)Mike Southern; **679** Snark/Art Resource, NY; Eye Ubiquitous/CORBIS; **681** Bettmann/CORBIS; **682** Stefano Bianchetti CORBIS; **683** (t)National Portrait Gallery, London, (b)Bettmann/CORBIS; **684** (l)Giraudon/Art Resource, NY, (r)Erich Lessing/Art Resource, NY; **685** Tate Gallery, London/Art Resource, NY; **686** Mozart Museum, Prague, Czech Republic; Giraudon/ Bridgeman Art Library; **687** (t)The Art Archive/Society Of The Friends Of Music Vienna/Dagli Orti, (b)akg-images/SuperStock; **688** (l)Giraudon/Art Resource, NY, (r)Reunion des Musees Nationaux/Art Resource, NY; **689** (l)Michael Holford, (r)Giraudon/Art Resource, NY; **692** Association for the Preservation of Virginia Antiquities; **693** Private Collection/Picture Research Consultants; **696** (c)The Royal Collection, ©Her Majesty Queen Elizabeth II, (others)The Library of Congress; **697** North Wind Picture Archives; **698** ©Virginia Historical Society, All Rights Reserved; **699** Frances Tavern Museum, New York, NY; **701** Michael Holford; **704** (t)Vatican Museums & Galleries, Rome/Canali PhotoBank, (b)Boltin Picture Library; **705** (tl)Werner Forman/Art Resource, NY, (tr)Bettmann/CORBIS, (bl)Michel Zabe Art Resource, NY, (bc)The Pierpont Morgan Library/Art Resource, NY, (br)©Virginia Historical Society, All Rights Reserved; **706** (t)Reunion des Musees Nationaux/Art Resource, NY, (b)The Royal Pavilion Libraries and Museums, Brighton and Howe; **707** (tl)Mary Evans Picture Library, (tr)London Aerial Photo Library/CORBIS, (cl)Bridgeman Art Library, (cr)Archive Photo Library/CORBIS, (bl)CORBIS, (br)D.E.I, (b)CORBIS; **708–709** Worldsat International Inc. 2004, All Rights Reserved; **708** (t)Robert Holmes/CORBIS, (c)CORBIS, (bl)Erich Lessing/Art Resource, NY, (blc)Christie's Images, (brc)Hulton/ Archive by Getty Images, (br)Bettmann/CORBIS; **709** (t)Black Star, (c)Chris Rainier/CORBIS, (bl bcl bcr)Bettmann/ CORBIS, (br)Reuters/Mike Hutchings/Archive Photos; **710–711** PICIMPACT/CORBIS; **713** Erich Lessing/Art Resource, NY; **716** Giraudon/Art Resource, NY; **717** AKG, Berlin/ SuperStock; **718** (l)Stock Montage, (c)Giraudon/Art Resource, NY, (r)Photo Researchers; **719** Reunion des Musees Nationaux/Art Resource, NY; **720** Robert Holmes/CORBIS; **721** Erich Lessing/Art Resource, NY; **723** Austrian Information Service; **726** Archive Photos; **727** Bettmann/CORBIS; **729** The Library of Congress; **732** (l)Bettmann/CORBIS, (r)Mary Evans Picture Library; **733** Bettmann/CORBIS; **734** (l)Mary Evans Picture Library, (r)Jose Luis Pelaez/CORBIS; **735** Culver Pictures; **736** Explorer, Paris/ SuperStock; **737** (l)SuperStock, (r)Christie's Images/CORBIS; **738** Erich Lessing/Art Resource, NY; **740** (t)Art Resource, NY, (b)Hulton/Archive by Getty Images; **741** Bettmann/CORBIS; **742** Hulton-Deutsch Collection/CORBIS; **743** Hulton-Deutsch Collection/CORBIS; **745** London Aerial Photo Library/CORBIS; **748** (t)Hulton-Deutsch Collection/CORBIS, (b)Bettmann/CORBIS; **750** (t)Christie's Images/CORBIS, (b)Pablo Corral/CORBIS;

CORBIS; **751** Mongerson-Wunderlich Gallery, Chicago; **752** (t) b)Brown Brothers, (l r)Bettmann/CORBIS; **753** CORBIS; **758–759** CORBIS; **761** Bettmann/CORBIS; **763** Roger Viollet/Liaison/Getty Images; **764** (tl)Bridgeman Art Library, (tr)Laurie Platt Winfrey, Inc., (b)North Wind Picture Archives; **766** Hulton-Deutsch Collection/ CORBIS; **768** Hulton-Deutsch Collection/CORBIS; **772** Bridgeman/ Art Resource, NY; **774** Bettmann/CORBIS; **775** (l)Hulton-Deutsch Collection/CORBIS, (r)Derek M. Allan, Travel Ink/CORBIS; **776** (t)Keystone, Paris/Sygma, (b)Bettmann/CORBIS; **777** Courtesy of the United States Naval Academy Museum; **779** Culver Pictures; **782** (l)Bettmann/CORBIS, (r)CORBIS; **783** Bettmann/CORBIS; **785** Imperial War Museum; **788** Bettmann/CORBIS; **791** Bettmann/CORBIS; **793** Bettmann/CORBIS; **794** CORBIS; **795** (t)Bettmann/CORBIS, (b)Pete Turnley/CORBIS; **796** Bettmann/ CORBIS; **800–801** Bettmann/CORBIS; **803** J.A. Mills/ AP/Wide World Photos; **805** (l r)Bettmann/CORBIS; **806** Bettmann/ CORBIS; **807** Bettmann/CORBIS; **808** L'Illustration/Sygma/ CORBIS; **809** Hulton-Deutsch Collection/CORBIS; **810** Hulton-Deutsch Collection/CORBIS; **812** Bettmann/CORBIS; **815** Bettmann/ CORBIS; **816** The Library of Congress; **817** (t)Hulton Archive/ Getty Images, (b)Bettmann/CORBIS; **826** Bettmann/CORBIS; **827** CORBIS; **828** CORBIS; **829** National Geographic Society; **832** AP/Wide World Photos; **833** AP/Wide World Photos; **835** Black Star; **836** (tl tr)Bettmann/CORBIS, (b)Lester Cole/ CORBIS; **837** Bettmann/CORBIS; **840** Prache-Lewin/Sygma/ CORBIS; **841** CORBIS; **843** Bettmann/CORBIS; **844** J.A. Mills/ AP/Wide World Photos; **846** Bettmann/CORBIS; **848** (tl r)Bettmann/ CORBIS, (br)Charles Bonnay/TimePix; **850** Black Star; **851** CORBIS; **856–857** CORBIS; **859** Courtesy Ronald Reagan Library; **863** Bettmann/CORBIS; **864** (l)Bettmann/CORBIS, (r)CORBIS; **865** (t)Annie Griffiths Belt/CORBIS, (b)Pablo San Juan/CORBIS; **866** Bettmann/CORBIS; **867** (l)The Bridgeman Art Library, (r)Ricardo Azoury/CORBIS; **871** CORBIS; **872** Louis Gubb/ JB Pictures; **873** Reuters/Mike Hutchings/Archive Photos; **877** Bettmann/CORBIS; **878** (t)Leonard DeRaemy/Sygma/ CORBIS, (b)CORBIS; **879** UPPA/Photoreporters; **881** Wally McNamee/CORBIS; **882** Courtesy Ronald Reagan Library; **883** (l)Bernard Bisson & Thierry Orban/Sygma/CORBIS, (r)Reuters/CORBIS; **884** Chris Rainier/CORBIS; **885** Bettmann/ CORBIS; **888** Doug Martin; **889** Ed Kashi/CORBIS; **890** Bojan Brecelj/CORBIS; **892** Robert Clark/Aurora Quanta; **898** (l)Archive Photo, (lc)Collection of Stuart S. Corning, Photo: Rob Huntley/ Lightstream, (rc)Black Star, (r)Bernard Bisson & Thierry Orban/ Sygma/CORBIS; **899** (t)Hulton-Deutsch Collection/ Sygma/CORBIS; **900** (bkgd)CORBIS, (l)Picture Finders Ltd. eStock, (r)Sylvain (tc)Mongerson-Wunderlich Gallery, Chicago, (bc)NASA, (b)CORBIS; Grandadam/Getty Images; **901** CORBIS; **930** Getty Images; **931** Egyptian National Museum, Cairo/SuperStock; **932** Scala/ Art Resource, NY; **933** SuperStock; **934** Vanni/Art Resource, NY; **935** Victoria & Albert Museum, London/Art Resource, NY; **936** Scala/Art Resource, NY; **938** Giraudon/Art Resource, NY; **939** Mary Evans Picture Library; **940** Biblioteca Colombina, Sevilla, Spain; **941** (l)Art Resource, NY, (r)National Portrait Gallery, London/ SuperStock; **942** J.A. Mills/AP/Wide World Photos; **943** Bettmann/ CORBIS

One-Stop Internet Resources

This textbook contains one-stop Internet resources for teachers, students, and parents. Log on to jat.glencoe.com for more information.

Online study tools include Chapter Overviews, Self-Check Quizzes, ePuzzles and Games, and E-Flashcards. Online research tools include Student Web Activities, Beyond the Textbook Features, Current Events, Web Resources, and State Resources. The interactive online student edition includes the complete Interactive Student Edition along with textbook updates. Especially for teachers, Glencoe offers an online Teacher Forum, Web Activity Lesson Plans, and Literature Connections.